D1251864

APPLETON'S NEW CUYÁS

English-Spanish and Spanish-English

DICTIONARY

QUINTA EDICIÓN

NUEVO DICCIONARIO CUYÁS

Inglés-Español y Español-Inglés

de APPLETON

por ARTURO CUYÁS

corregido y aumentado por
LEWIS E. BRETT (Parte I)
y HELEN S. EATON (Parte II)
con la colaboración de Walter Beveraggi-Allende

Quinta edición, revisión editorial de CATHERINE B. AVERY

GROLIER INC.

FIFTH EDITION

APPLETON'S NEW CUYÁS

English-Spanish and Spanish-English

DICTIONARY

by ARTURO CUYÁS

revised and enlarged by
LEWIS E. BRETT (Part I)
and HELEN S. EATON (Part II)
with the assistance of Walter Beveraggi-Allende

Revision editor, Fifth Edition, CATHERINE B. AVERY

GROLIER INC.

Library of Congress
Card Number: 66–22193

686–2

IMPRESO EN LOS ESTADOS UNIDOS DE AMERICA

PARTE I

PART II

PART II

Spanish-English

PARTE II

Español-Inglés

PREFACE TO THE FIRST EDITION

In the compilation of this work the endeavor has been to produce in a compact volume that may be conveniently used by students, travelers, and business men a complete and accurate vocabulary of the Spanish language.

With this end in view, and for the purpose of including all the modern words with which the language has been enriched through a general advancement in human knowledge and activity, the thirteenth edition (1899) of the Dictionary of the Royal Spanish Academy—which is the latest and highest authority in Spanish lexicography—has been adopted as a groundwork, and every word, every acceptation, every idiom contained in that dictionary, with the exception of those that have become archaic, is defined in this volume.

Furthermore, many words and acceptations have been added which, while not purely Castilian, are in general use in Spanish-American countries and in the Philippine Islands, and also a great number of technical terms that are frequently used in commercial intercourse between Spanish- and English-speaking countries. Indeed, this rapidly increasing intercourse, and the ties that now bind to the United States several million people whose vernacular is the Spanish language, have been kept steadily in view during the preparation of the work, which is intended to be as helpful to the American or English student of Spanish as to the great number of Spaniards who are now studying English.

To accomplish this purpose, a radical departure has been made from the practice adopted in many dictionaries of giving long explanations in English of the meaning of a Spanish word, instead of supplying the student with the English equivalents. A bilingual dictionary, like a good rule, should work both ways, and to do this it should give equivalents rather than definitions.

Numberless examples might be cited here to show the laborious task implied in the search for correct equivalents, especially as regards technical terms, many of which are either omitted or erroneously translated in other dictionaries.

All the dictionaries of the Spanish and English languages, and especially those by Velázquez, Gray and Iribas, Lopes and Bensley, Ponce de León, Bustamente, Tolhausen, Wellesley and Gironés, have been frequently consulted and compared in the course of compilation, and acknowledgment is hereby made for valuable suggestions found in them.

Many new features, however, and thousands of words and acceptations not found in any similar work, have been introduced here, as any one may verify by careful comparison of a single page of this book with the corresponding page in any other dictionary. As illustrative examples of the exhaustiveness of this compilation, the reader is referred to such words as *a, de, con, por, que, le, se, nos, ese, uno; dar, hacer, coger, estar, correr, echar, ser, salir, seguir, poner, tirar, ver, venir; llave, medio, fuerza, ropa, tiro, título, viga, vida.*

One special feature will no doubt commend itself to students as a help toward the proper use of irregular verbs. The fundamental tenses of such verbs, from which other modes are formed, are given with each infinitive, as well as the literal mutations that some regular verbs undergo in some tenses.

ARTURO CUYÁS.

PREFACE TO THE FOURTH EDITION

The original English-Spanish, Spanish-English Dictionary compiled by Arturo Cuyás was based on the then latest edition of the Dictionary of the Royal Spanish Academy but also contained many words and meanings that, while not purely Castilian, were in general use in Latin-American countries. In the present edition the 1947 edition of the Dictionary of the Royal Spanish Academy was consulted.

The aim of the present revision is to bring the Cuyás Dictionary up to date. And, since the Dictionary is used extensively in the United States and the Spanish contacts in this country are increasingly with Latin America, the feature of including words peculiar to Latin-American countries mentioned by Cuyás has been appreciably expanded.

The difficulty of finding new material for a dictionary is obvious. Modern newspapers, periodicals, Bulletins of the United Nations, etc. in Spanish have been searched for new words, phrases, and meanings. Perhaps the largest number of these entered in the new edition of the Dictionary has been culled from consultations and discussions with native Latin-American speakers.

HELEN S. EATON.

PREFACE TO THE FIFTH EDITION

The vocabulary of the modern world grows by leaps and bounds. Developments in the fields of science and technology alone demand new terms that, in a matter of weeks, become a part of the living language. Because advances in such fields often have global implications, the special terms that arise from them assume worldwide circulation, passing, with modification, into many languages in a very short time. Although, in our age, developments in science and technology have been spectacular, advances, inventions and discoveries in other fields have kept pace, and produce new words at an equally rapid rate. And the language of the non-specialist is colored and augmented by the results and needs of the special technologies. At the same time, some old words adopt new meanings and others drop out of circulation entirely.

In recognition of these facts, in this revision of Cuyás we have added new words from all fields of interest; dropped those words that are no longer of frequent use; and modified those that have acquired new meanings or more precise equivalents in Spanish or in English. The Spanish-English vocabulary has been greatly expanded to include, as well as the new material, many terms formerly found only in the English-Spanish vocabulary.

It goes without saying that we have used the standard work on the Spanish language, the *Diccionario* of the Royal Academy (18th edition), as well as the *Nuevas normas de prosodia y ortografía* (1959) of the same institution, in the elaboration of this revision. These standard works, which as yet have not admitted many scientific terms of recent origin, have been supplemented by Spanish and English language newspapers, periodicals and United Nations Bulletins, as well as other recognized Spanish and English language dictionaries.

Changes in format in this edition—larger page size, more space between columns, larger type—make it easier to read and to locate desired information. The appearance and openness of the page itself tend to encourage frequent consultation.

We present this expanded edition of Cuyás, including an enlarged list of abbreviations of field categories, with the hope that the thousands of additions and changes made herein will maintain the approach and high level of usefulness of the original Cuyás.

Catherine B. Avery
Revision Editor

SPANISH PRONUNCIATION

The only way of learning the exact sounds in a foreign language is by hearing them spoken by a native speaker. English equivalents given below must, therefore, be looked on as only the nearest approximation possible in written letters.

Vowels

Vowels in Spanish are always pronounced (with one exception mentioned below under **u**). Accent marks over vowels are only to indicate stress or to distinguish between words spelled alike and make no difference in the pronunciation of the vowel.

The Spanish vowels are **a, e, i, o, u,** and **y** when it stands alone as the conjunction *and,* or is at the end of a word. In some parts of Spanish America, notably in Chile, **i** is used instead of **y** for the conjunction *and* or at the end of a word. The vowels *a, e, o,* are called strong vowels while *i* and *u* are called weak vowels.

The sound of **a** is full, open, as in *far, father, farm, alarm.*

The sound of **e** is between the English *a* in *mate* and the *e* in *met,* like the initial part of *e* in *they.* At the end of a word and not stressed, it becomes shorter. Before *n* or *r* at the end of a syllable, it is like the English *ai* in *fair:* see Spanish ard*e*r.

The sound of **i** is like the English *i* in *machine, ee* in *teeth.*

The sound of **o,** in open syllables, is like the English *o* in *note.* In closed syllables, as before *n* or *r* at the end of a syllable, it is like the English *o* in *nor:* see Spanish señ*o*r.

The sound of **u** is like the English *oo* in *moon, food.* It is silent in the syllables *que, qui;* also in the syllables *gue, gui,* unless marked with a dieresis (*güe, güi*).

The sound of **y** when a vowel is like the Spanish **i** (above).

Diphthongs

A diphthong in Spanish is a combination of a strong and a weak vowel or of two weak vowels in the same syllable.

When **a, e,** or **o,** is followed in the same syllable by an unstressed **i,** or **u,** the two vowels form a single syllable. The two vowels are both pronounced but the strong vowel is prolonged a bit more than the following weak one, as in b*ai*le, tr*ai*dor, p*ei*nar, *oi*go, c*au*sa, d*eu*da. At the end of a word such an **i** is written **y,** as in h*ay*, r*ey*, s*oy*.

When unstressed **i** or **u** precedes another vowel in the same syllable, the two vowels form a single syllable. In such cases the **i** is pronounced like English *y* in *y*es; and the **u** is like English *w.* In this situation the second vowel is the prolonged one, as in grac*ia*, d*ia*blo, b*ie*n, c*ie*lo, med*io*, atenc*ió*n, v*iu*da, c*ua*ndo, ig*ua*l, b*ue*no, p*ue*rta, l*ui*r (lweer), f*ui* (fwee), antig*uo*. At the end of a word such an **i** is written *y,* as in m*uy* (mwee).

Consonants

(Consonants that are pronounced approximately the same as in English are not listed.)

Contrary to the indication for vowels in Spanish, the consonants are pronounced much less emphatically than in English and in some cases are rather slurred.

B, b, has a softer sound than in English, produced by joining the lips, without pressure.

C, c, before *a, o, u,* or before another consonant, has the sound of the English *k,* as in *carro* (car), *costo* (cost), *cubo* (cube), *clase* (class), *crema* (cream), *acto* (act).

C, c, before *e, i,* has the sound of English *th* in *theft, thin,* as in **cinc,** which is pronounced *theenk.* However, in many parts of Spain and in Spanish America, **c** in these cases is pronounced like Spanish *s* (*seenk*).

Ch, ch, like English *ch* in *cheese, riches.* In Mexico it is often softened to a sound nearly like English *sh,* like *ch* in *machine.*

D, d, is softer than in English. It is sounded by touching the edge of the upper teeth with the tip of the tongue. In Spanish America *d* is always like this. Between two vowels (**todo,** *all*) and at the end of a word (**usted,** *you*) it has the sound of English *th* in *weather, with, although.*

G, g, before *a, o, u,* or another consonant, at the beginning of a syllable or after an *n,* has the sound of English *g* in *gas, go, gun, grand, ignorant.*

G, g, before *e* or *i* is like strongly aspirated English *h,* like *ch* in Scotch *loch.*

H, l , is *always* silent.

J, j, is like Spanish **g** before *e* or *i.*

Ll, ll, is a special letter, which sounds very much like English *lli* in *million, brilliant,* or, more exactly, like the combination *ll-y* in *all year.* In Spanish America it has only the English *y* sound.

Ñ, ñ, like *ny* in *canyon.*

R, r, at the beginning of a word or preceded by *l, n,* or *s,* is pronounced with a trill produced by vibrating the tip of the tongue with a strong expulsion of breath; elsewhere it is pronounced with a touch of the tongue against the roof of the mouth.

Rr, rr, is always trilled like the first indication of **r** above.

S, s, has the sound of English *s* in *sassafras,* and no other.

T, t, differs from English *t* in that it is sounded by placing the tip of the tongue between the teeth.

V, v, as in English, but in Spanish-American countries it is quite commonly pronounced like the Spanish *b.*

X, x, sounds like *ks* or *gs,* never like *sh.* In ***México, mexicano*** (written *Méjico, mejicano* in nearly all places outside of Mexico) and a few other words of Mexican origin, it is pronounced like Spanish *j.*

Y, y, when a consonant, between vowels, sounds like English *y* in *year, young.*

Z, z, has the sound of English *th* in *thick, thatch, thought.* However, in some parts of Spain and throughout Spanish America it is pronounced like Spanish *s* (English *s* in *less*).

Rules of Accentuation

1. Words that end in a consonant, except *n* or *s,* have the stress on the last syllable, *ciudad, animar, cruel.* If this rule is not to be followed, then an accent

mark (′) is written in over the vowel to be stressed, as in *capitán, interés, ángel.*

2. Words that end in a vowel or a diphthong have the stress on the next to the last syllable, *acto, arriba, casi, cuello, comedia, corte, edificio.* If this rule is not to be followed, then an accent mark (′) is written in over the vowel to be stressed, *médico, música, bahía, héroe, cámara, allí, acá, mamá.*

3. Final *y* as part of a diphthong is actually the vowel *i* but in accentuation is taken as a consonant, as in *Paraguay.*

4. With the exception of adverbs ending in *-mente,* no Spanish word has more than one emphatic vowel. In adverbs in *-mente,* the adjectives from which they are formed preserve their original emphatic syllable, and the first *e* of the ending is also emphasized. Thus, **tristemente** (from *triste*), **útilmente** (from *útil*), are accented thus: *tris'temen'te, u'tilmen'te.*

Bear in Mind—

1. That **ch, ll** and **ñ** are independent letters, coming after **c, l** and **n** respectively. Therefore, all words or syllables beginning with **ch** come after all words or syllables beginning with **c,** and similarly for words and syllables beginning with **ll** or **ñ.**

2. That in some parts of Latin-America, mainly in Chile, **i** is used instead of **y,** both as a conjunction (*and*) and at the end of words (**rei** for **rey, voi** for **voy**).

3. That in order to preserve the sound of the stem of certain words, the final consonant is necessarily changed in certain forms. Such forms, then, are in a different alphabetical position in the dictionary.

Examples of Consonant Changes:

nouns & adjs. ending in **-z**	change the **-z** to **-ces** in the plural	so **rapaces, voces,** etc. are to be found under **rapaz, voz,** etc.
regular verbs ending in **-car**	change the **-c-** to **-qu-** before **e**	so **saqué, saquemos,** etc. belong with the infinitive **sacar,** etc.
regular verbs ending in **-cer, -cir,** preceded by a consonant	change the **-c-** to **-z-** before **o** or **a**	so **venzo, esparzo,** etc. belong with the infinitives **vencer, esparcir,** etc.
most irregular verbs ending in **-cer, -cir,** preceded by a vowel	change the **-c-** to **-zc-** before **o** or **a**	so **conozco, luzca,** etc. belong with the infinitives **conocer, lucir,** etc.

(Some notable exceptions to this rule are: **cocer** and its compounds, and **mecer,** in which the **-c-** changes to **-z-**, and **hacer,** and **decir,** which are highly irregular.)

regular verbs ending in **-gar**	change the **-g-** to **-gu-** before **e**	so **pagué, paguen,** etc. belong with the infinitive **pagar,** etc.

regular verbs ending in **-ger, -gir**	change the **-g-** to **-j-** before **o** or **a**	so **cojo, dirijo,** etc. belong with the infinitives **coger, dirigir,** etc.
regular verbs ending in **-guar**	change the **-gu-** to **-gü-** before **e**	so **averigüé,** etc. belong with the infinitive **averiguar,** etc.
regular verbs ending in **-guir**	change **-gu-** to **-g-** before **o** or **a**	so **distingo,** etc. belong with the infinitive **distinguir,** etc.
regular verbs ending in **-zar**	change **-z-** to **-c-** before **e**	so **lancé, lancemos,** etc. belong with the infinitive **lanzar,** etc.

4. That in order to conform to Spanish rules of orthography, in some cases vowels are affected. Such affected forms are, then, in a different alphabetical position in the dictionary.

Examples of Vowel Changes:

regular verbs ending in **-eer**	change the **-i-** of diphthongal conjugational endings to **-y-**	so **creyó, leyendo,** etc. belong with the infinitives **creer, leer,** etc.

(This happens also to irregular verbs ending in **-uir,** as **atribuyo** from **atribuir,** etc.)

regular verbs ending in **-iar, -uar**	change the **-i-** to **-í-** and the **-u-** to **-ú-** when these vowels have the tonic accent	so **guío, continúo,** etc. belong with the infinitives **guiar, continuar,** etc.

5. That short **e** and **o** within a Latin stem taken into Spanish become diphthongized to **ie** and **ue** in Spanish when they receive the stress. Such forms are, then, in a different alphabetical position in the dictionary.

regular verbs having forms with **-e-** or **-o-** stressed	change **-e-** to **-ie-** and **-o-** to **-ue-** when these vowels have the stress	so **pienso, suenan,** etc. belong with the infinitives **pensar, sonar,** etc.

Irregular and Radical-Changing Verbs

The fundamental forms of irregular verbs are given both with their infinitives and, unless they are in the immediate vicinity of their infinitive, also in their proper alphabetical position in the dictionary. The same applies to the main forms of verbs changed in spelling to preserve the pronunciation of the radical or to conform to certain rules in Spanish (see 3, 4, and 5 above).

REGULAR

Infinitive, Present Participle, Past Participle	Present Indicative	Imperfect Indicative	Preterit	Compound Perfect Indicative	Future Indicative
1st Conjugation Regular verbs ending in **-ar**					
hablar	hablo	hablaba	hablé	he hablado	hablaré
	hablas	hablabas	hablaste	has hablado	hablarás
hablando	habla	hablaba	habló	ha hablado	hablará
	hablamos	hablábamos	hablamos	hemos hablado	hablaremos
hablado	habláis	hablabais	hablasteis	habéis hablado	hablaréis
	hablan	hablaban	hablaron	han hablado	hablarán
2nd Conjugation Regular verbs ending in **-er**					
vender	vendo	vendía	vendí	he vendido	venderé
	vendes	vendías	vendiste	has vendido	venderás
vendiendo	vende	vendía	vendió	ha vendido	venderá
	vendemos	vendíamos	vendimos	hemos vendido	venderemos
vendido	vendéis	vendíais	vendisteis	habéis vendido	venderéis
	venden	vendían	vendieron	han vendido	venderán
3rd Conjugation Regular verbs ending in **-ir**					
vivir	vivo	vivía	viví	he vivido	viviré
	vives	vivías	viviste	has vivido	vivirás
viviendo	vive	vivía	vivió	ha vivido	vivirá
	vivimos	vivíamos	vivimos	hemos vivido	viviremos
vivido	vivís	vivíais	vivisteis	habéis vivido	viviréis
	viven	vivían	vivieron	han vivido	vivirán

RADICAL-

Infinitive, Present Participle, Past Participle	Present Indicative	Imperfect Indicative	Preterit	Compound Perfect Indicative	Future Indicative
cerrar	cierro	regular	regular	regular	regular
	cierras				
cerrando	cierra				
	cerramos				
cerrado	cerráis				
	cierran				
dormir	duermo	regular	dormí	regular	regular
	duermes		dormiste		
durmiendo	duerme		durmió		
	dormimos		dormimos		
dormido	dormís		dormisteis		
	duermen		durmieron		
pedir	pido	regular	pedí	regular	regular
	pides		pediste		
pidiendo	pide		pidió		
	pedimos		pedimos		
pedido	pedís		pedisteis		
	piden		pidieron		
sentir	siento	regular	sentí	regular	regular
	sientes		sentiste		
sintiendo	siente		sintió		
	sentimos		sentimos		
sentido	sentís		sentisteis		
	sienten		sintieron		

VERBS

Conditional	Present Subjunctive	Imperfect Subjunctive	Future Subjunctive	Imperative
hablaría	hable	hablara, -se	hablare	
hablarías	hables	hablaras, -ses	hablares	habla
hablaría	hable	hablara, -se	hablare	
hablaríamos	hablemos	habláramos, -semos	habláremos	
hablaríais	habléis	hablarais, -seis	hablareis	hablad
hablarían	hablen	hablaran, -sen	hablaren	
vendería	venda	vendiera, -se	vendiere	
venderías	vendas	vendieras, -ses	vendieres	vende
vendería	venda	vendiera, -se	vendiere	
venderíamos	vendamos	vendiéramos, -semos	vendiéremos	
venderíais	vendáis	vendierais, -seis	vendiereis	vended
venderían	vendan	vendieran, -sen	vendieren	
viviría	viva	viviera, -se	viviere	
vivirías	vivas	vivieras, -ses	vivieres	vive
viviría	viva	viviera, -se	viviere	
viviríamos	vivamos	viviéramos, -semos	viviéremos	
viviríais	viváis	vivierais, -seis	viviereis	vivid
vivirían	vivan	vivieran, -sen	vivieren	

CHANGING VERBS

Conditional	Present Subjunctive	Imperfect Subjunctive	Future Subjunctive	Imperative
regular	cierre	regular	regular	
	cierres			cierra
	cierre			
	cerremos			
	cerréis			cerrad
	cierren			
regular	duerma	durmiera, -se	durmiere	
	duermas	durmieras, -ses	durmieres	duerme
	duerma	durmiera, -se	durmiere	
	durmamos	durmiéramos, -semos	durmiéremos	
	durmáis	durmierais, -seis	durmiereis	dormid
	duerman	durmieran, -sen	durmieren	
regular	pida	pidiera, -se	pidiere	
	pidas	pidieras, -ses	pidieres	pide
	pida	pidiera, -se	pidiere	
	pidamos	pidiéramos, -semos	pidiéremos	
	pidáis	pidierais, -seis	pidiereis	pedid
	pidan	pidieran, -sen	pidieren	
regular	sienta	sintiera, -se	sintiere	
	sientas	sintieras, -ses	sintieres	siente
	sienta	sintiera, -se	sintiere	
	sintamos	sintiéramos, -semos	sintiéremos	
	sintáis	sintierais, -seis	sintiereis	sentid
	sientan	sintieran, -sen	sintieren	

RADICAL-

Infinitive, Present Participle, Past Participle	Present Indicative	Imperfect Indicative	Preterit	Compound Perfect Indicative	Future Indicative
volver volviendo vuelto	vuelvo vuelves vuelve volvemos volvéis vuelven	regular	regular	regular	regular

ORTHOGRAPHIC-

Infinitive, Present Participle, Past Participle	Present Indicative	Imperfect Indicative	Preterit	Compound Perfect Indicative	Future Indicative
averiguar averiguando averiguado	regular	regular	averigüé averiguaste averiguó averiguamos averiguasteis averiguaron	regular	regular
conocer conociendo conocido	conozco conoces conoce conocemos conocéis conocen	regular	regular	regular	regular
continuar continuando continuado	continúo continúas continúa continuamos continuáis continúan	regular	regular	regular	regular
delinquir delinquiendo delinquido	delinco delinques delinque delinquimos delinquís delinquen	regular	regular	regular	regular
dirigir dirigiendo dirigido	dirijo diriges dirige dirigimos dirigís dirigen	regular	regular	regular	regular
enviar enviando enviado	envío envías envía enviamos enviáis envían	regular	regular	regular	regular
escoger escogiendo escogido	escojo escoges escoge escogemos escogéis escogen	regular	regular	regular	regular
esparcir esparciendo esparcido	esparzo esparces esparce esparcimos esparcís esparcen	regular	regular	regular	regular

CHANGING VERBS

Conditional	Present Subjunctive	Imperfect Subjunctive	Future Subjunctive	Imperative
regular	vuelva vuelvas vuelva volvamos volváis vuelvan	regular	regular	vuelve volved

CHANGING VERBS

Conditional	Present Subjunctive	Imperfect Subjunctive	Future Subjunctive	Imperative
regular	averigüe averigües averigüe averigüemos averigüéis averigüen	regular	regular	averigua averiguad
regular	conozca conozcas conozca conozcamos conozcáis conozcan	regular	regular	conoce conoced
regular	continúe continúes continúe continuemos continuéis continúen	regular	regular	continúa continuad
regular	delinca delincas delinca delincamos delincáis delincan	regular	regular	delinque delinquid
regular	dirija dirijas dirija dirijamos dirijáis dirijan	regular	regular	dirige dirigid
regular	envíe envíes envíe enviemos enviéis envíen	regular	regular	envía enviad
regular	escoja escojas escoja escojamos escojáis escojan	regular	regular	escoge escoged
regular	esparza esparzas esparza esparzamos esparzáis esparzan	regular	regular	esparce esparcid

ORTHOGRAPHIC-

Infinitive, Present Participle, Past Participle	Present Indicative	Imperfect Indicative	Preterit	Compound Perfect Indicative	Future Indicative
gozar gozando gozado	regular	regular	gocé gozaste gozó gozamos gozasteis gozaron	regular	regular
pagar pagando pagado	regular	regular	pagué pagaste pagó pagamos pagasteis pagaron	regular	regular
producir produciendo producido	produzco produces produce producimos producís producen	regular	produje produjiste produjo produjimos produjisteis produjeron	regular	regular
sacar sacando sacado	regular	regular	saqué sacaste sacó sacamos sacasteis sacaron	regular	regular
seguir siguiendo seguido	sigo sigues sigue seguimos seguís siguen	regular	seguí seguiste siguió seguimos seguisteis siguieron	regular	regular
vencer venciendo vencido	venzo vences vence vencemos vencéis vencen	regular	regular	regular	regular

IRREGULAR

Infinitive, Present Participle, Past Participle	Present Indicative	Imperfect Indicative	Preterit	Compound Perfect Indicative	Future Indicative
andar andando andado	regular	regular	anduve anduviste anduvo anduvimos anduvisteis anduvieron	regular	regular
argüir arguyendo argüido	arguyo arguyes arguye argüimos argüís arguyen	regular	argüí argüiste arguyó arguimos arguisteis arguyeron	regular	regular
asir asiendo asido	asgo ases ase asimos asís asen	regular	regular	regular	regular

CHANGING VERBS

Conditional	Present Subjunctive	Imperfect Subjunctive	Future Subjunctive	Imperative
regular	goce goces goce gocemos gocéis gocen	regular	regular	goza gozad
regular	pague pagues pague paguemos paguéis paguen	regular	regular	paga pagad
regular	produzca produzcas produzca produzcamos produzcáis produzcan	produjera, -se produjeras, -ses produjera, -se produjéramos, -semos produjerais, -seis produjeran, -ses	produjere produjeres produjere produjéremos produjereis produjeren	produce producid
regular	saque saques saque saquemos saquéis saquen	regular	regular	saca sacad
regular	siga sigas siga sigamos sigáis sigan	siguiera, -se siguieras, -ses siguiera, -se siguiéramos, -semos siguierais, -seis siguieran, -sen	siguiere siguieres siguiere siguiéremos siguiereis siguieren	sigue seguid
regular	venza venzas venza venzamos venzáis venzan	regular	regular	vence venced

VERBS

Conditional	Present Subjunctive	Imperfect Subjunctive	Future Subjunctive	Imperative
regular	regular	anduviera, -se anduvieras, -ses anduviera, -se anduviéramos, -semos anduvierais, -seis anduvieran, -sen	anduviere anduvieres anduviere anduviéremos anduviereis anduvieren	anda andad
regular	arguya arguyas arguya arguyamos arguyáis arguyan	arguyera, -se arguyeras, -ses arguyera, -se arguyéramos, -semos arguyerais, -seis arguyeran, -sen	arguyere arguyeres arguyere arguyéremos arguyereis arguyeren	arguye argüid
regular	asga asgas asga asgamos asgáis asgan	regular	regular	ase asid

IRREGULAR

Infinitive, Present Participle, Past Participle	Present Indicative	Imperfect Indicative	Preterit	Compound Perfect Indicative	Future Indicative
caber cabiendo cabido	quepo cabes cabe cabemos cabéis caben	regular	cupe cupiste cupo cupimos cupisteis cupieron	regular	cabré cabrás cabrá cabremos cabréis cabrán
caer cayendo caído	caigo caes cae caemos caéis caen	regular	caí caíste cayó caímos caísteis cayeron	regular	regular
cocer cociendo cocido	cuezo cueces cuece cocemos cocéis cuecen	regular	regular	regular	regular
conocer conociendo conocido	conozco conoces conoce conocemos conocéis conocen	regular	regular	regular	regular
creer creyendo creído	regular	regular	creí creíste creyó creímos creísteis creyeron	regular	regular
dar dando dado	doy das da damos dáis dan	regular	di diste dio dimos disteis dieron	regular	regular
decir diciendo dicho	digo dices dice decimos decís dicen	regular	dije dijiste dijo dijimos dijisteis dijeron	regular	diré dirás dirá diremos diréis dirán
erguir irguiendo erguido	yergo, irgo yergues, irgues yergue, irgue erguimos erguís yerguen, irguen	regular	erguí erguiste irguió erguimos erguisteis irguieron	regular	regular
estar estando estado	estoy estás está estamos estáis están	regular	estuve estuviste estuvo estuvimos estuvisteis estuvieron	regular	regular
haber habiendo habido	he has ha hemos habéis han	regular	hube hubiste hubo hubimos hubisteis hubieron	regular	habré habrás habrá habremos habréis habrán

VERBS

Conditional	Present Subjunctive	Imperfect Subjunctive	Future Subjunctive	Imperative
cabría	quepa	cupiera, -se	cupiere	
cabrías	quepas	cupieras, -ses	cupieres	cabe
cabría	quepa	cupiera, -se	cupiere	
cabríamos	quepamos	cupiéramos, -semos	cupiéremos	
cabríais	quepáis	cupierais, -seis	cupiereis	cabed
cabrían	quepan	cupieran, -sen	cupieren	
regular	caiga	cayera, -se	cayere	
	caigas	cayeras, -ses	cayeres	cae
	caiga	cayera, -se	cayere	
	caigamos	cayéramos, -semos	cayéremos	
	caigáis	cayerais, -seis	cayereis	caed
	caigan	cayeran, -sen	cayeren	
regular	cueza	regular	regular	
	cuezas			cuece
	cueza			
	cozamos			
	cozáis			coced
	cuezan			
regular	conozca	regular	regular	
	conozcas			conoce
	conozca			
	conozcamos			
	conozcáis			conoced
	conozcan			
regular	regular	creyera, -se	creyere	
		creyeras, -ses	creyeres	cree
		creyera, -se	creyere	
		creyéramos, -semos	creyéremos	
		creyerais, -seis	creyereis	creed
		creyeran, -sen	creyeren	
regular	dé	diera, -se	diere	
	des	dieras, -ses	dieres	da
	dé	diera, -se	diere	
	demos	diéramos, -semos	diéremos	
	deis	dierais, -seis	diereis	dad
	den	dieran, -sen	dieren	
diría	diga	dijera, -se	dijere	
dirías	digas	dijeras, -ses	dijeres	di
diría	diga	dijera, -se	dijere	
diríamos	digamos	dijéramos, -semos	dijéremos	
diríais	digáis	dijerais, -seis	dijereis	decid
dirían	digan	dijeran, -sen	dijeren	
regular	yerga, irga	irguiera, -se	irguiere	
	yergas, irgas	irguieras, -ses	irguieres	yergue, irgue
	yerga, irga	irguiera, -se	irguiere	
	irgamos	irguiéramos, -semos	irguiéremos	
	irgáis	irguierais, -seis	irguiereis	erguid
	yergan, irgan	irguieran, -sen	irguieren	
regular	esté	estuviera, -se	estuviere	
	estés	estuvieras, -ses	estuvieres	está
	esté	estuviera, -se	estuviere	
	estemos	estuviéramos, -semos	estuviéremos	
	estéis	estuvierais, -seis	estuviereis	estad
	estén	estuvieran, -sen	estuvieren	
habría	haya	hubiera, -se	hubiere	
habrías	hayas	hubieras, -ses	hubieres	he
habría	haya	hubiera, -se	hubiere	
habríamos	hayamos	hubiéramos, -semos	hubiéremos	
habríais	hayáis	hubierais, -seis	hubiereis	habed
habrían	hayan	hubieran, -sen	hubieren	

Infinitive, Present Participle, Past Participle	Present Indicative	Imperfect Indicative	Preterit	Compound Perfect Indicative	Future Indicative
hacer	hago	regular	hice	regular	haré
	haces		hiciste		harás
haciendo	hace		hizo		hará
	hacemos		hicimos		haremos
hecho	hacéis		hicisteis		haréis
	hacen		hicieron		harán
huir	huyo	regular	huí	regular	regular
	huyes		huiste		
huyendo	huye		huyó		
	huimos		huimos		
huído	huís		huisteis		
	huyen		huyeron		
ir	voy	iba	fui	regular	regular
	vas	ibas	fuiste		
yendo	va	iba	fue		
	vamos	íbamos	fuimos		
ido	vais	ibais	fuisteis		
	van	iban	fueron		
leer	regular	regular	leí	regular	regular
			leíste		
leyendo			leyó		
			leímos		
leído			leísteis		
			leyeron		
mecer	mezo	regular	regular	regular	regular
	meces				
meciendo	mece				
	mecemos				
mecido	mecéis				
	mecen				
oír	oigo	regular	oí	regular	regular
	oyes		oíste		
oyendo	oye		oyó		
	oímos		oímos		
oído	oís		oísteis		
	oyen		oyeron		
poder	puedo	regular	pude	regular	podré
	puedes		pudiste		podrás
pudiendo	puede		pudo		podrá
	podemos		pudimos		podremos
podido	podéis		pudisteis		podréis
	pueden		pudieron		podrán
poner	pongo	regular	puse	regular	pondré
	pones		pusiste		pondrás
poniendo	pone		puso		pondrá
	ponemos		pusimos		pondremos
puesto	ponéis		pusisteis		pondréis
	ponen		pusieron		pondrán
querer	quiero	regular	quise	regular	querré
	quieres		quisiste		querrás
queriendo	quiere		quiso		querrá
	queremos		quisimos		querremos
querido	queréis		quisisteis		querréis
	quieren		quisieron		querrán
raer	raigo, rayo	regular	raí	regular	regular
	raes		raíste		
rayendo	rae		rayó		
	raemos		raímos		
raído	raéis		raísteis		
	raen		rayeron		

Conditional	Present Subjunctive	Imperfect Subjunctive	Future Subjunctive	Imperative
haría	haga	hiciera, -se	hiciere	
harías	hagas	hicieras, -ses	hicieres	haz
haría	haga	hiciera, -se	hiciere	
haríamos	hagamos	hiciéramos, -semos	hiciéremos	
haríais	hagáis	hicierais, -seis	hiciereis	haced
harían	hagan	hicieran, -sen	hicieren	
regular	huya	huyera, -se	huyere	
	huyas	huyeras, -ses	huyeres	huye
	huya	huyera, -se	huyere	
	huyamos	huyéramos, -semos	huyéremos	
	huyáis	huyerais, -seis	huyereis	huid
	huyan	huyeran, -sen	huyeren	
regular	vaya	fuera, -se	fuere	
	vayas	fueras, -ses	fueres	ve
	vaya	fuera, -se	fuere	
	vayamos	fuéramos, -semos	fuéremos	
	vayáis	fuerais, -seis	fuereis	id
	vayan	fueran, -sen	fueren	
regular	regular	leyera, -se	leyere	
		leyeras, -ses	leyeres	lee
		leyera, -se	leyere	
		leyéramos, -semos	leyéremos	
		leyerais, -seis	leyereis	leed
		leyeran, -sen	leyeren	
regular	meza	regular	regular	
	mezas			mece
	meza			
	mezamos			
	mezáis			meced
	mezan			
regular	oiga	oyera, -se	oyere	
	oigas	oyeras, -ses	oyeres	oye
	oiga	oyera, -se	oyere	
	oigamos	oyéramos, -semos	oyéremos	
	oigáis	oyerais, -seis	oyereis	oíd
	oigan	oyeran, -sen	oyeren	
podría	pueda	pudiera, -se	pudiere	
podrías	puedas	pudieras, -ses	pudieres	———
podría	pueda	pudiera, -se	pudiere	
podríamos	podamos	pudiéramos, -semos	pudiéremos	
podríais	podáis	pudierais, -seis	pudiereis	———
podrían	puedan	pudieran, -sen	pudieren	
pondría	ponga	pusiera, -se	pusiere	
pondrías	pongas	pusieras, -ses	pusieres	pon
pondría	ponga	pusiera, -se	pusiere	
pondríamos	pongamos	pusiéramos, -semos	pusiéremos	
pondríais	pongáis	pusierais, -seis	pusiereis	poned
pondrían	pongan	pusieran, -sen	pusieren	
querría	quiera	quisiera, -se	quisiere	
querrías	quieras	quisieras, -ses	quisieres	quiere
querría	quiera	quisiera, -se	quisiere	
querríamos	queramos	quisiéramos, -semos	quisiéremos	
querríais	queráis	quisierais, -seis	quisiereis	quered
querrían	quieran	quisieran, -sen	quisieren	
regular	raiga, raya	rayera, -se	rayere	
	raigas	rayeras, -ses	rayeres	rae
	raiga	rayera, -se	rayere	
	raigamos	rayéramos, -semos	rayéremos	
	raigáis	rayerais, -seis	rayereis	raed
	raigan	rayeran, -sen	rayeren	

Infinitive, Present Participle, Past Participle	Present Indicative	Imperfect Indicative	Preterit	Compound Perfect Indicative	Future Indicative
reír	río	regular	reí	regular	regular
	ríes		reíste		
riendo	ríe		rió		
	reimos		reimos		
reído	reís		reísteis		
	ríen		rieron		
saber	sé	regular	supe	regular	sabré
	sabes		supiste		sabrás
sabiendo	sabe		supo		sabrá
	sabemos		supimos		sabremos
sabido	sabéis		supisteis		sabréis
	saben		supieron		sabrán
salir	salgo	regular	regular	regular	saldré
	sales				saldrás
saliendo	sale				saldrá
	salimos				saldremos
salido	salís				saldréis
	salen				saldrán
ser	soy	era	fui	regular	regular
	eres	eras	fuiste		
siendo	es	era	fue		
	somos	éramos	fuimos		
sido	sois	erais	fuisteis		
	son	eran	fueron		
tener	tengo	regular	tuve	regular	tendré
	tienes		tuviste		tendrás
teniendo	tiene		tuvo		tendrá
	tenemos		tuvimos		tendremos
tenido	tenéis		tuvisteis		tendréis
	tienen		tuvieron		tendrán
traer	traigo	regular	traje	regular	regular
	traes		trajiste		
trayendo	trae		trajo		
	traemos		trajimos		
traído	traéis		trajisteis		
	traen		trajeron		
valer	valgo	regular	regular	regular	valdré
	vales				valdrás
valiendo	vale				valdrá
	valemos				valdremos
valido	valéis				valdréis
	valen				valdrán
venir	vengo	regular	vine	regular	vendré
	vienes		viniste		vendrás
viniendo	viene		vino		vendrá
	venimos		vinimos		vendremos
venido	venís		vinisteis		vendréis
	vienen		vinieron		vendrán
ver	veo	veía	regular	regular	regular
	ves	veías			
viendo	ve	veía			
	vemos	veíamos			
visto	veis	veíais			
	ven	veían			

Conditional	Present Subjunctive	Imperfect Subjunctive	Future Subjunctive	Imperative
regular	ría	riera, -se	riere	
	rías	rieras, -ses	rieres	ríe
	ría	riera, -se	riere	
	riamos	riéramos, -semos	riéremos	
	riáis	rierais, -seis	riereis	reíd
	rían	rieran, -sen	rieren	
sabría	sepa	supiera, -se	supiere	
sabrías	sepas	supieras, -ses	supieres	sabe
sabría	sepa	supiera, -se	supiere	
sabríamos	sepamos	supiéramos, -semos	supiéremos	
sabríais	sepáis	supierais, -seis	supiereis	sabed
sabrían	sepan	supieran, -sen	supieren	
saldría	salga	regular	regular	
saldrías	salgas			sal
saldría	salga			
saldríamos	salgamos			
saldríais	salgáis			salid
saldrían	salgan			
regular	sea	fuera, -se	fuere	
	seas	fueras, -ses	fueres	sé
	sea	fuera, -se	fuere	
	seamos	fuéramos, -semos	fuéremos	
	seáis	fuerais, -seis	fuereis	sed
	sean	fueran, -sen	fueren	
tendría	tenga	tuviera, -se	tuviere	
tendrías	tengas	tuvieras, -ses	tuvieres	ten
tendría	tenga	tuviera, -se	tuviere	
tendríamos	tengamos	tuviéramos, -semos	tuviéremos	
tendríais	tengáis	tuvierais, -seis	tuviereis	tened
tendrían	tengan	tuvieran, -sen	tuvieren	
regular	traiga	trajera, -se	trajere	
	traigas	trajeras, -ses	trajeres	trae
	traiga	trajera, -se	trajere	
	traigamos	trajéramos, -semos	trajéremos	
	traigáis	trajerais, -seis	trajereis	traed
	traigan	trajeran, -sen	trajeren	
valdría	valga	regular	regular	
valdrías	valgas			val, vale
valdría	valga			
valdríamos	valgamos			
valdríais	valgáis			valed
valdrían	valgan			
vendría	venga	viniera, -se	viniere	
vendrías	vengas	vinieras, -ses	vinieres	ven
vendría	venga	viniera, -se	viniere	
vendríamos	vengamos	viniéramos, -semos	viniéremos	
vendríais	vengáis	vinierais, -seis	viniereis	venid
vendrían	vengan	vinieran, -sen	vinieren	
regular	vea	regular	regular	
	veas			ve
	vea			
	veamos			
	veáis			ved
	vean			

MONETARY UNITS OF THE AMERICAS AND THE IBERIAN PENINSULA

Argentina	100 centavos	=	1 peso
Bolivia	100 centavos	=	1 boliviano
Brasil	100 centavos	=	1 cruzeiro
Canadá	100 centavos	=	1 dollar
Colombia	100 centavos	=	1 peso
Costa Rica	100 centavos	=	1 peso
Cuba	100 centavos	=	1 peso
Chile	100 centavos	=	1 peso
Ecuador	100 centavos	=	1 peso
El Salvador	100 centavos	=	1 peso
España	100 centimos	=	1 peseta
Estados Unidos de América	100 centavos	=	1 dollar
Guatemala	100 centavos	=	1 quetzal
Haití	100 centimes	=	1 gourde
Honduras	100 centavos	=	1 lempira
México	100 centavos	=	1 peso
Nicaragua	100 centavos	=	1 cordoba
Panamá	100 centesimos	=	1 balboa
Paraguay	100 centimos	=	1 guarani
Perú	100 centavos	=	1 sol
Portugal	100 centavos	=	1 escudo
República Dominicana	100 centavos	=	1 peso
Uruguay	100 centavos	=	1 peso
Venezuela	100 centimos	=	1 bolivar

TABLES OF WEIGHTS AND MEASURES

Medidas de longitud

1 milímetro (mm.) = 0.039 inch (in.)
1 centímetro (cm.) = 0.393 inch (in.)
1 decímetro (dm.) = 3.937 inches (in.)
1 metro (m.) = 39.37 inches (in.)
1 decámetro (Dm.) = 32.81 feet (ft.)
1 hectómetro (Hm.) = 109.3 yards (yd.)
1 kilómetro (Km.) = 1,093 yards (yd.)(approx. 5/8 of a mile)

Medidas de superficie

1 centímetro cuadrado ($cm.^2$) = 0.155 square inch (sq. in.)
1 decímetro cuadrado ($dm.^2$) = 15.5 square inches (sq. in.)
1 metro cuadrado ($m.^2$) = 10.764 square feet (sq. ft.)
1 decámetro cuadrado ($Dm.^2$) = 1,076.4 square feet (sq. ft.)
1 hectómetro cuadrado ($Hm.^2$) = 2.471 acres (a.)
1 kilómetro cuadrado ($Km.^2$) = 247.1 acres (a.)

Medidas de capacidad para líquidos

1 centilitro (cl.) = 0.338 fluid ounces (fl. oz.)
1 decilitro (dl.) = 0.21 pints (pt.)
1 litro (l.) = 1.0567 quarts (qt.)
1 decalitro (Dl.) = 2.64 gallons (gal.)

Medidas de capacidad para áridos

1 decilitro (dl.) = 0.18 pints (pt.)
1 litro (l.) = 0.908 quarts (qt.)
1 decalitro (Dl.) = 1.14 pecks (pk.)
1 hectolitro (Hl.) = 2.84 bushels (bu.)

Unidades comunes de peso

1 miligramo (mg.) = 0.015 grains (gr.)
1 centigramo (cg.) = 0.154 grains (gr.)
1 decigramo (dg.) = 1.543 grains (gr.)
1 gramo (g.) = 0.035 ounces (oz.)
1 decagramo (Dg.) = 0.353 ounces (oz.)
1 hectogramo (Hg.) = 3.527 ounces (oz.)
1 kilogramo (Kg.) = 2.2046 pounds (lb.)
1 quintal (Q.) = 220.46 pounds (lb.)
1 tonelada (T.) = 1.1 tons (t.)

THERMOMETER

0° centígrado (freezing point) = 32° Fahrenheit
100° centígrados (boiling point) = 212° Fahrenheit

N. B. To convert Centigrade degrees into Fahrenheit, multiply by 9, divide by 5 and add 32.

ABBREVIATIONS

a.	adjective.
abbr.	abbreviation.
acc.	accusative.
adv.	adverb.
(aer.)	aeronautics.
(agr.)	agriculture.
(alg.)	algebra.
(Am.)	Spanish America(n).
(anat.)	anatomy.
(anc.)	ancient.
(Angl.)	Anglicism.
(app.)	applied.
(arch.)	architecture.
(archeol.)	archeology.
(Arg.)	Argentina(-ian).
(arith.)	arithmetic.
art.	article.
(artil.)	artillery.
(astr.)	astronomy.
(astrol.)	astrology.
(astronaut.)	astronautics.
(atom. ener.)	atomic energy.
aug.	augmentative.
(auto)	automobiles(-ism).
aux.	auxiliary verb.
(bacteriol.)	bacteriology.
(bib.)	Biblical.
(biochem.)	biochemistry.
(biol.)	biology.
(Bol.)	Bolivia(n).
(bot.)	botany.
(build.)	building.
(bus.)	business.
(C.A.)	Central America(n).
(Carib.)	Caribbean countries.
(carp.)	carpentry.
cf.	compare.
(chem.)	chemistry.
(chron.)	chronology(-ical).
(coll.)	colloquial.
(collect.)	collectively.
(Colomb.)	Colombia.
(com.)	commerce(-ial).
comp.	comparative.
conj.	conjunction.
(constr.)	construction.
(contempt.)	contemptuous.
contr.	contraction.
(cook.)	cooking.
(cryst.)	crystallography.
dat.	dative.
def.	definite.
defect.	defective.
(dent.)	dentistry.
(derog.)	derogative.
(diff.)	different.
dim.	diminutive.
(eccl.)	ecclesiastic.
(econ.)	economics, economy.
(Ecua.)	Ecuador(-ian).
(elec.)	electricity.
(electron.)	electronics.
(embryol.)	embryology.
(eng.)	engineering.
(Engl.)	English.
(entom.)	entomology.
(esp.)	especially.
(ethnol.)	ethnology.
(ext.)	extension.
f.	feminine.
(f. a.)	fine arts.
(fig.)	figurative(-ly).
(foll.)	followed.
(fort.)	fortifications.
fut.	future.
(Gal.)	Gallicism.
(gen.)	generally.
(genet.)	genetics.
(geog.)	geography.
(geol.)	geology.
(geom.)	geometry.
ger.	gerund.
(Gk.)	Greek.
(gram.)	grammar.
(Guat.)	Guatemala.
(her.)	heraldry.
(hist.)	history.
(Hond.)	Honduras.
(hort.)	horticulture.
(humor.)	humorous.
(hydraul.)	hydraulics.
(ichth.)	ichthyology, fish.
imp.	imperfect.
imper.	imperative.
impers.	impersonal.
ind.	indicative.
(Ind.)	Indian.
indef.	indefinite.
indir. obj.	indirect object.
inf.	infinitive.
(int. combust.)	internal-combustion.
(int.)	international.
interj.	interjection.
interrog.	interrogative.
(Ire.)	Ireland.
irreg.	irregular.
(jewel.)	jewelry.
(lang.)	language.
(Lat.)	Latin.
(ling.)	linguistics.
(lit.)	literally.
(lit., liter.)	literature.
(lith.)	lithography.
(log.)	logic.
m.	masculine.
(mason.)	masonry.
(math.)	mathematics.
(mech.)	mechanics.
(med.)	medical, pathological.
(metal.)	metallurgy, metal work.
(meteorol.)	meteorology.
(Mex.)	Mexico(-an).
(mil.)	military.
(min.)	mining, mineralogy.
(mov. pict.)	moving pictures.
(mus.)	music.
(mut.)	mutation(s).
(myth.)	mythology.
n.	noun.
(nat. hist.)	natural history.
(naut.)	nautical.
neut.	neuter.
nom.	nominative case.
(numis.)	numismatics.
obj.	object (gram.).
(obs.)	obsolete.
(opt.)	optics.
(ornith.)	ornithology, birds.
(paleontol.)	paleontology.
(parl.)	parliamentary.
(pathol.)	pathology.
pers.	person or personal.
(pert.)	pertaining.
(pharm.)	pharmaceutical.
(philol.)	philology.
(philos.)	philosophy.
(phon.)	phonetics; phonograph.
(photog.)	photography.
(phys.)	physics.
(physiol.)	physiology.
(P.I.)	Philippine Islands.
pl.	plural.
(poet.)	poetry.
(pol.)	politics(-al).

(Port.) . . . . . Portugal, Portuguese.
poss. . . . . . possessive.
pp. . . . . . . past participle.
(P.R.) . . . . . Puerto Rico.
pref. . . . . . prefix.
prep. . . . . . preposition.
pres.p. . . . . . present participle.
pret. . . . . . preterit.
(print.) . . . . . printing.
pron. . . . . . pronoun.
(pros.) . . . . . prosody.
(prov.) . . . . . provincial.
(psych.) . . . . . psychology.
(psychiat.) . . . . psychiatry.
(rad.) . . . . . radio.
(ref.) . . . . . referring to.
refl. . . . . . . reflexive (pronoun).
reg. . . . . . . regular.
(relig.) . . . . . religion.
(rhet.) . . . . . rhetoric.
(Rom. Cath.) . . . Roman Catholic.
(Rom. Hist.) . . . Roman History.
(Ry.) . . . . . railway, railroad.
(S.A.) . . . . . South America(-n).
(sew.) . . . . . sewing.
(Sp.) . . . . . Spain, Spanish.
(stat.) . . . . . statistics.
subj. . . . . . subject (gram.), subjunctive.
super. . . . . . superlative.
(surg.) . . . . . surgery.
(surv.) . . . . . surveying.
(tech.) . . . . . technology.
(tel.) . . . . . telegraph(y), telephone.
(text.) . . . . . textile.
(theat.) . . . . . theatre.
(theol.) . . . . . theology(-ical).
(topog.) . . . . . topography(-ical).
(TV) . . . . . television.
(Uru.) . . . . . Uruguay(-an).
(U. S.) . . . . . United States.
V. . . . . . . Vide, see.
v. . . . . . . verb.
va. . . . . . . active, transitive verb.
(Venez.) . . . . . Venezuela(-n).
(vet.) . . . . . veterinary.
vn. . . . . . . intransitive verb.
vr. . . . . . . reflexive verb.
(vulg.) . . . . . vulgar, low.
(W.I.) . . . . . West Indies(-ian).
(zool.) . . . . . zoölogy.

A NEW BILINGUAL DICTIONARY
OF THE
SPANISH AND ENGLISH LANGUAGES

SPANISH-ENGLISH PART

Abbreviations and proper names are given at the end.

A, a, *f.* a, first letter of the Spanish alphabet.—**a por a y be por be,** point by point, minutely.

a, *prep.* (1) to, to indicate (a) a noun indirect object, when it follows the direct object: *dí el libro a Juan,* I gave the book to John; (b) direction, purpose, destination, limit, in place, time, movement, or activity: *voy a Madrid,* I am going to Madrid; *él me enseñó a leer,* he taught me to read; *vine a verle,* I came to see him; *de once a doce,* from eleven to twelve; *con el agua a la cintura,* with water (up) to the waist; *echó a correr,* he started to run; (c) accord: *a mi gusto,* to my taste; *a mi pesar,* to my regret; (d) juxtaposition: *cara a cara,* face to face. (2) at, to indicate (a) location: *a la puerta,* at the door; *a la mesa,* at table; *a la derecha,* at the right; *a lo lejos,* at a (great) distance; *con el termómetro a 30°,* with the thermometer at 30°; *a dos millas de Lima,* (at) two miles from Lima; (b) rate, price: *a dos pesos por kilo,* at two dollars a kilo; *a la vez,* at a time; (c) time (when): *a mediodía,* at noon; *a las dos y media,* at half past two; *al fin* or *al cabo,* at last; *al principio* or *a los principios,* at the beginning, or, at first; *a la vista,* at sight; (d) accord: *a instancias de Vd.,* at your request; *a su disposición,* at your disposal; *a voluntad,* at will; *a lo menos* or *al menos,* at least. (3) by, to indicate (a) instrument, means: *a máquina,* by machine; *a mano,* by hand; *a fuerza bruta,* by brute force; (b) manner: *a pedazos,* by pieces; *a súplicas,* by entreaties; *paso a paso,* step by step; *poco a poco,* little by little; *al año,* by the year. (4) on, to indicate (a) simultaneity: *a mi llegada,* on my arrival; *al entrar,* on entering; (b) position in place or time: *a bordo,* on board; *al otro lado,* on the other side; *a la mañana siguiente,* on the next morning; (c) manner; *a caballo,* on horseback; *a pie,* on foot; (d) in many idioms such as: *al contrario,* on the contrary; *a causa de,* on account of; *a condición de que,* on condition that. (5) in, to indicate (a) style, manner: *a la francese,* in the French style, à la française; *a lo marinero,* in a seamanlike manner (or, like a seaman); *a lo caballero,* in a gentlemanly manner (or, like a gentleman); *a lo filósofo,* in the manner of philosophers (or, like a philosopher); *a lo bobo,* in the manner of a fool (or, like a fool); (b) time (within which): *a poco,* in a little while (or, presently); *a últimos de octubre,* in the latter part of October. (6) after, at the end of: *a la semana,* at the end of a week, a week after; *a los dos meses,* two months after; *a los pocos años,* a few years after (or, later). (7) not translated, to indicate (a) a direct object of a verb when denoting a specific and known person, or a thing when the subject also denotes a thing, or a geographical name not preceded by a definite article, etc.: *amo a mi madre,* I love my mother; *oigo a Juan,* I hear John; *esta línea encuentra a la otra,* this line meets the other; *veo a Nueva York,* I see New York; (b) a noun indirect object when it precedes the direct object: *dí el libro a Juan,* I gave John the book. (8) not translated, often to indicate the addition of, or treatment with, a material or substance, or a distinguishing ingredient (the corresponding English noun is used adjectively): *acero al carbono,* carbon steel; *papel al bromuro,* bromide paper, paper treated with bromide; *cuadro al óleo,* oil painting; *dibujo a lapiz,* pencil drawing.—This construction is commonly but improperly applied to denote the natural agent moving a machine, or some characteristic feature of an apparatus or another object: *máquina a* (properly, *de*) *vapor,* steam engine; *tubo al* (properly, *de*) *vacío,* vacuum tube; *motor a* (properly, *de*) *ocho cilindros,* eight-cylinder motor.—Followed by an infinitive, a forms implicitly negative phrases rendered by *if* and the subjunctive: *a estar él aquí,* if he were here, were he here. If, in such phrases, the infinitive is preceded by *no,* the translation may be made by using "but for": *a no venir Juan,* but for John's coming, had not John come; *a no ser por Vd.,* but for you; *a no ser que,* unless.—This preposition is used in many idioms such as: *a lo que,* from what; *a lo que veo,* from what I see; *a lo que parece,* as it seems; *a qué,* what for, what is the use; *a que,* I bet that. Most of the frequently used idioms will be found in the regular alphabetical position in the dictionary under the main word of a phrase.

aarónico, aaronita, *a.* Aaronic, pertaining to or descended from Aaron.

aba, *m.* aba, a coarse woolen fabric.

ababa, *f.* **ababol,** *m.* = AMAPOLA, *f.* poppy.

ab absurdo, *adv.* (math. & logic) ad absurdum.

abacá, *m.* (bot.) abaca; manila hemp; manila-hemp fabric.

abacería, *f.* grocery.

abacero, ra, *n.* grocer.

abacial, *a.* abbatial, pertaining to an abbot, abbess, or abbey.

abacista, *n.* abacist.

ábaco, *m.* abacus, calculating frame; (arch.) abacus; (min.) washing trough.
abactor, ra, *n.* (Arg.) horse thief.
abad, *m.* abbot.
abada, *f.* rhinoceros.
abadejo, *m.* = BACALAO, codfish; pollack. Spanish fly or blistering beetle; (ornith.) kinglet or golden-crested wren.
abadengo, ga, *a.* = ABACIAL.
abadernar, *va.* (naut.) to fasten with short ropes.
abadesa, *f.* abbess.
abadía, *f.* abbey.
abadiato, *m.* abbotship.
abajadero, *m.* slope, incline.
abajador, *m.* (min.) stable man; helper.
abajeño, ña, *a.* (Am.) lowlander.
abajo, *adv.* under, underneath, below, down.—**a. de,** *prep.* beneath.—**boca a.,** face down.—**de a.,** lower (*a.*).—**de arriba a.,** from top to bottom.—**por a.,** at the bottom; down there.—**venirse a.,** to fall.—**¡a. N.!** down with N.!
abalanzar. I. *va.* (*pret.* ABALANCÉ; *subj.* ABALANCE) to balance; to throw suddenly with force. **II.** *vr.* to rush impetuously; to venture.
abalaustrado, da, *a.* balustered.
abaleador, ra, *n.* grain cleaner or separator.
abalear, *va.* to clean or separate (grain) from chaff after winnowing.
abaleo, *m.* (agr.) cleaning or separating grain.
abalizar. I. *va.* (*pret.* ABALICÉ; *subj.* ABALICE) (naut.) to lay buoys in. **II.** *vr.* (naut.) to take bearings.
abalorio, *m.* glass bead; beadwork.
aballestar, *va.* (naut.) to haul a cable.
abanar, *va.* to ventilate with fans.
abanderado, *m.* standard-bearer.
abanderar, *va.* to register (a ship).
abanderlcé, abanderice, *v. V.* ABANDERIZAR.
abanderizador, ra, *n.* ringleader.
abanderizar. I. *va.* (*pret.* ABANDERICÉ; *subj.* ABANDERICE) to organize in bands. **II.** *vr.* to band together.
abandonado, da, *a.* negligent, shiftless; slovenly.
abandonamiento, *m.* forlornness; slovenliness; lewdness, debauchery.
abandonar. I. *va.* to leave; to forsake; to give up. **II.** *vr.* to despair; to give oneself up to.
abandono, *m.* = ABANDONAMIENTO.
abanicar, *va.* (*pret.* ABANIQUÉ; *subj.* ABANIQUE) to fan.
abanicazo, *m.* blow with a fan.
abanico, *m.* fan; anything fan-shaped; (coll.) sword; (naut.) derrick; crane.—**en a.,** fan-shaped.
abaniqué, abanique, *v. V.* ABANICAR.
abaniqueo, *m.* fanning; swinging motion; excessive gesturing in speaking.
abaniquería, *f.* fan factory or shop.
abaniquero, ra, *n.* fan maker or dealer.
abano, *m.* fan; hanging fan; ventilator.
abanto, *m.* (ornith.) African vulture.
abaratar. I. *va.* to cheapen; to abate. **II.** *vr.* to fall in price.
abarca, *f.* sandal worn by peasants and muleteers.
abarcado, da, *a.* sandaled; embraced, contained.
abarcador, ra, *n.* clasper; monopolist.
abarcadura, *f.*, **abarcamiento,** *m.* embracing, comprising.
abarcar, *va.* (*pret.* ABARQUÉ; *subj.* ABARQUE) to clasp, embrace, contain; to comprise; to monopolize; (com.) to corner, control (the market).—**quien mucho abarca poco aprieta,** one shouldn't bite off more than one can chew.
abarcón, *m.* a pole-ring in carriages; large iron clamp.
abarloar, *va.* (naut.) to bring alongside a ship or wharf.
abarqué, abarque, *v. V.* ABARCAR.
abarquero, ra, *n.* maker or seller of *abarcas.*
abarquillado, da, *a.* rolled up; curled up.
abarquillamiento, *m.* curling up into a roll.
abarquillar, *va.* to curl up; to form into a roll.
abarracarse, *vr.* to go into barracks.
abarraganarse, *vr.* to live in concubinage.
abarrancadero, *m.* heavy road; precipice; difficult business.
abarrancamiento, *m.* fall into a pit; embarrassment.
abarrancar. I. *va.* (*pret.* ABARRANQUÉ; *subj.* ABARRANQUE) to ditch; to form a ravine. **II.** *vr.* to fall into a pit; to become embarrassed.
abarredera, *f.* broom, carpet sweeper; anything that sweeps and cleans.
abarrotar, *va.* to bar; to strengthen with bars; (naut.) to stow; to overstock.
abarrote, *m.* (naut.) a small package for filling up; stop-gap; (Mex.) retail grocery.—*pl.* (Am.) goods; foodstuffs.
abarrotero, ra, *n.* (Mex.) retail grocer.
abastamiento, *m.* providing; supplying with provisions, stores, etc.
abastar, *va.* = ABASTECER.
abastardar, *va.* & *vn.* to bastardize.
abastecedor, ra, *n.* caterer, provider, purveyor.
abastecer, *va.* (*ind.* ABASTEZCO; *subj.* ABASTEZCA) to purvey; supply.—**abastecimiento,** *m.* providing; supply; provisions, supplies.—**el a. y la demanda,** supply and demand.
abastionar, *va.* (fort.) to protect or fortify with bastions.
abasto, *m.* supply of provisions; (fig.) anything abundant; (com.) supply.—**dar a. (a),** to be sufficient (for); to provide, furnish (to).
abatanar, *va.* to beat or full (cloth).
abate, *m.* abbe.
abatidamente, *adv.* dejectedly.
abatido, da, *a.* dejected; discouraged; crestfallen; abject, mean; (com.) depreciated, fallen in price or demand.
abatimiento, *m.* depression, low spirits; lowering, falling; taking apart; (naut., aer.) drift, leeway.—**a. de costado,** (aer.) side drift.
abatir. I. *va.* to throw down, overthrow, knock down; to bring down, shoot down; to fold down; to humble, debase; to discourage, dishearten; to lower, strike (a flag, etc.); to dismount, take apart. **II.** *vn.* to descend; stoop. **III.** *vr.* to be disheartened or depressed; (naut.) to have leeway; (aer.) to drift.
abayado, da, *a.* (bot.) baccate.
abazón, *m.* cheek pouch (of monkeys, etc.).
abdicación, *f.* abdication.
abdicante, *n.* & *a.* abdicant.
abdicar, *va.* (*pret.* ABDIQUÉ; *subj.* ABDIQUE) to abdicate.
abdicativo, va, *a.* abdicative.
abdomen, *m.* abdomen.
abdominal, *a.* abdominal.
abducción, *f.* (logic & math.) abduction.
abducir, *va.* (physiol.) to abduce, abduct.
abductor, *m.* (anat.) abducent muscle.
abecé, *m.* a-b-c, alphabet; rudiments.
abecedario, *m.* alphabet; primer.
abedul, *m.* (bot.) birch.
abeja, *f.* bee.—**a. machiega, maesa,** *or* **maestra,** queen bee.—**a. neutra,** *or* **obrera,** working bee, worker.—**a. reina,** queen bee.
abejar, *m.* place for beehives. Also COLMENAR.
abejarrón, abejorro, *m.* bumblebee.
abejaruco, abejeruco, *m.* (ornith.) bee eater.
abejera, *f.* ABEJAR; (bot.) balmmint or beewort.
abejero, *m.* beekeeper.
abejón, *m.* drone.
abejorro, *m.* bumblebee.
abejuno, na, *a.* pertaining to the bee.
abelmosco, *m.* (bot.) abelmosk.
abellacado, da, *a.* mean-spirited.
abellacarse, *vr.* to degrade oneself.
abellotado, da, *a.* acorn-shaped.
abencerraje, *n.* one of a famous Moorish family.
aberenjenado, da, *a.* eggplant-shaped or -colored.
aberración, *f.* aberration, error, mania; (phys., opt. & astr.) aberration.

aberrugado, da, *a.* warty.
abertal. **I.** *s.* crack; small opening. **II.** *a.* easily cracked or cleft.
abertura, *f.* aperture; opening; cleft, crevice, fissure; gap.
abestiado, da, *a.* beast-like.
abetal, *m.* fir wood or grove.
[1]**abete,** *m.* hook for holding cloth in shearing it.
[2]**abete,** *m.* (bot.) = ABETO.
abetinote, *m.* fir-tree rosin.
abeto, *m.* (bot.) silver tree; yew-leaved fir; spruce; hemlock.—**a. del norte, falso,** or **rojo,** spruce.
abetuna, *f.* fir-tree sprout.
abetunado, da, *a.* bitumen-like.
abetunar, *va.* = EMBETUNAR, to bituminize.
abey, *m.* (bot.) jacaranda; W. I. mahogany.
abiertamente, *adv.* frankly, openly.
abierto, ta. **I.** *pp. irreg.* of ABRIR. **II.** *a.* open, clear; candid, frank, outspoken; full-blown.
abigarrado, da, *a.* variegated, motley.
abigarrar, *va.* to paint with various ill-matched colors; to fleck.
abigeato, *m.* (law) cattle stealing.
abigeo, *m.* (law) cattle thief.
abigotado, da, *a.* having a heavy mustache.
ab intestato. **I.** *adv.* intestate. **II.** *a.* neglected, unprotected.—**abintestato,** *m.* legal adjudication of an intestate estate.
abiogénesis, *f.* abiogenesis.
abiología, *f.* abiology.
abiológico, ca, *a.* abiological.
abiosis, *f.* abiosis.
abiótico, ca, *a.* abiotic.
abirritar, *va.* (med.) to abirritate, relieve irritation.
abiselar, biselar, *va.* to bevel.
abisinio, a, *n.* & *a.* Abyssinian.
abismal. **I.** *a.* abysmal. **II.** *m.* clasp nail, shingle nail.
abismar. **I.** *va.* to depress, humble, destroy. **II.** *vr.* to think or feel deeply.
abismo, *m.* abyss; gulf; chasm; hell.
abitaque, *m.* joist.
abitar, *va.* (naut.) to bitt.
abitones, *m. pl.* (naut.) topsail sheet bitts.
abizcochado, da, *a.* biscuit-shaped.
abjuración, *f.* abjuration, recantation.
abjurar, *va.* to abjure, retract under oath.
ablación, *f.* ablation.
ablactación, *f.* weaning.
ablactar, *va.* to wean.
ablandabrevas, *m.* & *f.* (coll.) good-for-nothing.
ablandador, ra, *m.* & *f.* mollifier.
ablandahigos, *m.* & *f.* (coll.) good-for-nothing.
ablandamiento, *m.* softening, mollification.
ablandar, *va.* & *vn.* to soften, mellow, relent; to loosen; to assuage, mitigate, melt, soothe.
ablandativo, va, *a.* mollifying.
ablano, *m.* = AVELLANO, filbert.
ablativo, *m.* & *a.* (gram.) ablative.
ablegado, *m.* (eccl.) ablegate.
ablepsia, *f.* ablepsy, blindness; lack or loss of mental powers.
ablución, *f.* ablution.
abluente, *m.* & *a.* (med.) abluent.
abnegación, *f.* abnegation, self-denial.
abnegado, da, *a.* self-denying.
abnegar, *va.* (*ind.* ABNIEGO; *subj.* ABNIEGUE) to renounce; to deny oneself.
abobado, da, *a.* stultified, silly.
abobamiento, *m.* stupefaction, stupidity.
abobar. **I.** *va.* to stupefy. **II.** *vr.* to grow stupid.
abocado, *a.* (of wine) mild, agreeable.
abocamiento, *m.* approach; meeting, interview.
abocar (*pret.* ABOQUÉ; *subj.* ABOQUE). **I.** *va.* to bring near; to draw in place (as cannon); to open the mouth of (a bag); to decant; to seize with the mouth. **II.** *vr.* to meet by appointment. **III.** *vn.* (naut.) to occupy the mouth of, or enter, a channel, strait, etc.
abocardado, da, *a.* bell-mouthed (esp. of firearms).
abocardar, *va.* to widen or expand (the opening of a tube, hole, etc.); to ream.
abocardo, *m.* large drill.
abocinado, da, *a.* funnel- or trumpet-shaped; (of horses) with drooping head.
abocinar. **I.** *va.* to shape like a trumpet. **II.** *vn.* to fall on one's face.
abochornado, da, *a.* out of countenance, flushed, mortified.
abochornar. **I.** *va.* to overheat; to shame; to embarrass. **II.** *vr.* to blush; to become embarrassed; (agr.) to wilt from excessive heat.
abofeteador, ra, *m.* & *f.* buffeter; one who insults or slaps.
abofetear, *va.* to slap; to insult.
abogacía, *f.* law (as a subject or profession).
abogada, *f.* woman lawyer or mediator; lawyer's wife.
abogado, *m.* lawyer, barrister; mediator.—**a. de secano,** quack lawyer; charlatan.
abogar, *vn.* (*pret.* ABOGUÉ; *subj.* ABOGUE) to advocate, plead (as a lawyer); to intercede.
abolengo, *m.* ancestry, lineage; inheritance.
abolible, *a.* abolishable.
abolición, *f.* abolition, abrogation, extinction.
abolicionismo, *m.* abolitionism.
abolicionista, *m.* abolitionist.
abolir, *va. and defective* (*only those modes and persons are used having the letter i in their terminations*) to abolish; to revoke, repeal.
abolsado, da, *a.* puckered, purse-shaped; having or forming pockets.
abollado, *a.* & *m.* pleat(ed); fluted(-ing).
abolladura, *f.* unevenness, dent, embossment; bruise.
abollar, *va.* to emboss; to dent; to stun and confound; to bruise.
abollonar, *va.* to emboss.
abomaso, *m.* (anat.) abomasum.
abombar. **I.** *va.* to give a convex form to; to deafen; to confuse. **II.** *vr.* (Am.) (of meat, fluids, etc.) to begin to spoil.
abominable, *a.* abominable, execrable.
abominación, *f.* abomination, detestation, execration.
abominar, *va.* to abominate, abhor.
[1]**abonado, da.** **I.** *m.* & *f.* subscriber; commuter. **II.** *a.* reliable; apt, inclined.
[2]**abonado, da,** *a.* (of soil) rich.
abonador, ra, *m.* & *f.* (com.) surety or security for a principal, person responsible for one who himself acts as surety; barrel maker's augur.
abonamiento, *m.* = [1]ABONO; bail, security.
abonanzar, *vn.* (*impersonal verb*: *subj.* ABONANCE) to grow calm, clear up.
[1]**abonar.** **I.** *va.* to bail; to guarantee, indorse, answer for; to give credit; (com.) to credit with, put to the credit of. **II.** *vr.* to subscribe; to buy a season or commutation ticket.
[2]**abonar.** **I.** *va.* to improve; to enrich, manure (soil). **II.** *vn.* = ABONANZAR.
abonaré, *m.* promissory note; due-bill.
[1]**abono,** *m.* security, guarantee; subscription; allowance, discount; receipt, voucher.
[2]**abono,** *m.* manure, fertilizer.
aboqué, aboque, *v. V.* ABOCAR.
abordador, *m.* (naut.) boarder; intruder.
abordaje, *m.* (naut.) the act of boarding a ship.
abordar. **I.** *va.* (naut.) to board a ship; to run foul of a ship; to attack (a subject), enter upon (a matter). **II.** *vn.* to put into a port.
abordo, *m.* = ABORDAJE.
aborigen. **I.** *a.* aboriginal. **II.** *m. pl.* (**aborígenes**) aborigines.
aborrachado, da, *a.* bright red.
aborrascarse, *vr.* to become stormy.
aborrecedor, ra, *m.* & *f.* detester, hater.
aborrecer, *va.* (*ind.* ABORREZCO; *subj.* ABORREZCA) to hate, abhor; (of birds) to desert.—**aborreci-**

ble, *a.* hateful; abhorrent.—**aborrecimiento,** *m.* abhorrence, hate; dislike, grudge.
aborrezco, aborrezca, *v. V.* ABORRECER.
abortamiento, *m.* abortion.
abortar, *vn.* to miscarry, abort; to fail; (med.) to abort (a foetus or a disease).
aborticidio, *m.* aborticide.
abortifaciente, *m.* & *a.* abortifacient.
abortista, *n.* abortionist.
abortivo, va, *a.* abortive; producing abortion.
aborto, *m.* miscarriage, abortion; monstrosity.
abortón, *m.* the abortion of a quadruped; unborn lamb's skin.
aborujar, aburujar. I. *va.* to make lumps. **II.** *vr.* to muffle up, wrap oneself up.
abotagarse, *vr.* to become bloated.
abotinado, da, *a.* shaped like a gaiter.
abotonador, *m.* button-hook.
abotonar. I. *va.* to button. **II.** *vn.* (of plants) to bud.
abovedado, da, *a.* arched, vaulted.
abovedar, *va.* to arch, vault.
aboyado, da, *a.* (tilled) with oxen.
aboyar, *va.* (naut.) to lay buoys.
abozalar, *va.* to muzzle.
abra, *f.* bay, haven; cove, creek; dale, valley; fissure, gorge.
abracadabra, *m.* abracadabra.
abracé, abrace, *v. V.* ABRAZAR.
abracijo, *m. dim.* (coll.) an embrace, a hug.
abrahonar, *va.* (coll.) to hold one fast by the garment.
abrasador, ra, *a.* burning, exceedingly hot.
abrasamiento, *m.* taking fire, burning; excess of passion.
abrasar. I. *va.* to burn; to fire; to squander; to dry up; to provoke; to shame, humiliate. **II.** *vr.* (**en** or **de**) to burn (with); to boil (with) (any violent passion); to burn up, down.
abrasión, *f.* (geol. & med.) abrasion.
abrasivo, va, *m.* & *a.* abrasive.
abrazadera. I. *f.* clasp, clamp, band, cleat; (print.) brace or bracket {. **II.** *a.* **sierra a.,** lumberman's saw.
abrazador, ra, *n.* embracer; bolster used in P. I.
abrazamiento, *m.* embracing.
abrazar, *va.* (*pret.* ABRACÉ; *subj.* ABRACE) to embrace, hug; to clamp, cleat; to contain, comprise; to surround; to accept, follow; to embrace, adopt (a religion, etc.); to take charge of.
abrazo, *m.* hug, embrace.
ábrego, áfrico, *m.* southwest wind.
abrelata, abrelatas, *m.* (Am.) can opener.
abrenuncio, (Lat.) far be it from me; fie!
abrevadero, *m.* watering place for cattle; drinking trough.
abrevador, *m.* one who waters cattle; waterer.
abrevar, *va.* to water cattle; to irrigate; to soak skins.
abreviación, *f.* abbreviation; abridgment; shortening; contraction; reduction; acceleration; hastening.
abreviadamente, *adv.* briefly, summarily.
abreviador, ra. I. *m.* & *f.* one who abridges or shortens. **II.** *m.* (eccl.) abbreviator (Vatican officer).
abreviaduría, *f.* (eccl.) office of abbreviator.
abreviamiento, *m.* = ABREVIACIÓN.
abreviar, *va.* to abridge, abbreviate; to hasten.
abreviativo, va, *a.* abbreviatory.
abreviatura, *f.* abbreviation; contraction; shorthand.—**en a.,** in abbreviation; (coll.) hastily.
abreviaturía, *f.* = ABREVIADURÍA.
abribonarse, *vr.* to become lazy; to loaf; to become a rascal.
abridero. I. *m.* a variety of freestone peach. **II.** *a.* easily opened; freestone, freeshell.
abridor, *m.* (bot.) nectarine, peach tree; opener; grafting knife; eardrop or wire to keep the ears pierced. —**a. de guantes,** glove stretcher. —**a. de láminas,** engraver.—**a. de latas,** can opener.—**a. en hueco,** die sinker.
abrigadero, *m.* sheltered place, shelter.
abrigador, ra. (Am.) **I.** *a.* protecting; (of clothing) warm. **II** *n.* & *a.* concealer(-ing).
abrigaño, *m.* a place sheltered from the wind.
abrigar. I. *va.* (*pret.* ABRIGUÉ; *subj.* ABRIGUE) to shelter, protect; to cover; to warm; to lodge; to patronize; (fig.) to nourish; to cherish. **II.** *vr.* to take shelter; to cover oneself; to put on a wrap.
abrigo, *m.* shelter; protection; overcoat; wrap; aid, support; cover; (naut.) harbor, haven.—**al a. de,** sheltered from; under protection of, shielded by.
abrigué, abrigue, *v. V.* ABRIGAR.
abril, *m.* April.—*pl.* (fig.) (years of) youth.—**estar hecho,** or **parecer, un a.,** to be dressed up; to look very smart, or very smartly dressed. —**los dieciséis abriles,** sweet sixteen.
abrileño, ña, *a.* April (as *a.*), pert. to, or like, April.
abrillantar, *va.* to cut a diamond into facets; to make sparkle; to impart brilliance; to glaze, polish, brighten.
abrimiento, *m.* opening; cracking.
abrir. I. *va.* (*pp.* ABIERTO) to open, unlock, unfasten, uncover, unseal; to engrave; to expand, separate, distend; to cut open, cleave; to rend; to dig.—**a. los cimientos,** to dig the foundation trenches.—**a. paso,** to make way; to clear the way. **II.** *vn.* to open to unfold; to extend; to display; (Am.) to back out, withdraw. **III.** *vr.* to open, expand; to crack; to yawn; (fig.) to unbosom oneself; to burst open; to fall out, become estranged.
abrochador, *m.* buttoner; buttonhook.
abrochadura, *f.,* **abrochamiento,** *m.* lacing, fastening, buttoning.
abrochar, *va.* to clasp, buckle, button, fasten with hooks and eyes.
abrogación, *f.* abrogation, repeal.
abrogar, *va.* (*pret.* ABROGUÉ; *subj.* ABROGUE) to abrogate, annul, repeal.
abrojal, *m.* thistly ground.
abrojín, *m.* murex, a mollusk or its purple shell.
abrojo, *m.* (bot.) thistle, thorn, prickle; (mil.) caltrop; crowfoot; sharp metal ends of a lash. —*pl.* hidden rocks in the sea.
[1]**abromado, da,** *a.* (naut.) hazy, foggy.
[2]**abromado, da,** *a.* worm-eaten; barnacled.
abromarse, *vr.* (naut.) to be worm-eaten.
abroquelar. I. *va.* (naut.) to boxhaul. **II.** *vr.* to shield oneself.
abrótano, *m.* (bot.) southernwood.
abrumador, ra, *a.* overwhelming, crushing; wearisome.
abrumar. I. *va.* to crush, overwhelm, oppress; to weary, annoy. **II.** *vr.* to worry.
abrumarse, *vr.* to become foggy.
abrupción, *f.* (surg.) abruption.
abrupto, ta, *a.* abrupt; craggy, rugged.
abrutado, da, *a.* brutish, bestial.
absceso, *m.* abscess.
abscisa, *f.* abscissa.
abscisión, *f.* (med.) incision.
absenta, *f.* absinthe (liqueur).
absentismo, *m.* absenteeism.
absentista, *n.* & *a.* absentee.
ábside, *m.* or *f.* (arch.) presbytery.
absintina, *f.* (chem.) absinthin.
absintio, *m.* (bot.) absinthe, wormwood.
absintismo, *m.* (med.) absinthism.
absolución, *f.* absolution; pardon, acquittal.—**a. de la demanda,** finding for the defendant.—**a. libre,** verdict of not guilty, acquittal.
absoluta, *f.* dogmatic assertion, dictum.
absolutismo, *m.* despotism, absolutism.
absolutista, *n.* absolutist.
absoluto, ta, *a.* absolute, unconditional; imperious, despotic.—**en a.,** unqualifiedly, per-

emptorily; absolutely: (in negative sentences) at all.—**lo a.**, *n.* the absolute.
absolutorio, a, *a.* absolutory, absolving.
absolver, *va.* (*pp.* ABSUELTO; *ind.* ABSUELVO; *subj.* ABSUELVA) to absolve; to acquit.
absorbencia, *f.* absorbing, absorption; absorbency.
absorbente, *m.* & *a.* absorbent(-ing).
absorber, *va.* (*pp.* ABSORBIDO, ABSORTO) to absorb; to imbibe.
absorbibilidad, *f.* absorbability.
absorbible, *a.* absorbable.
absorbido, da, *a.* absorbed.
absorción, *f.* absorption.
absorto, ta. I. *pp. irreg.* of ABSORBER. **II.** *a.* amazed; absorbed in thought.
abstemio, mia, *a.* abstemious.
abstención, *f.* forbearance; abstention (as from voting).
abstencionista, *n.* abstainer.
abstenerse, *vr* (*ind. pres.* ME ABSTENGO, *pret.* ME ABSTUVE; *subj.* ME ABSTENGA) to abstain, forbear.—**a. de,** to abstain from, forbear.
abstergente, *a.* detergent; cleansing; abstergent.
absterger, *va.* to cleanse; to sterilize.
abstersión, *f.* abstersion, purification.
abstersivo, va, *a.* = ABSTERGENTE.
abstinencia, *f.* abstinence, temperance; fasting.
abstinente, *a.* abstinent, abstemious.
abstracción, *f.* abstraction; concentration.
abstraccionista, *n.* (f.a.) abstractionist.
abstracto, ta. I. *pp. irreg.* of ABSTRAER. **II.** *a.* abstract. **III.** *m.* abstract.—**en a.**, in the abstract.
abstraer. I. *va.* (*pp.* ABSTRAÍDO, ABSTRACTO; *ind. pres.* ABSTRAIGO, *pret.* ABSTRAJE; *subj.* ABSTRAIGA) to abstract. **II.** *vn.* **a. de,** to do without; to leave aside. **III.** *vr.* to be withdrawn mentally.
abstraído, da. I. *pp.* of ABSTRAER. **II.** *a.* retired; absent-minded.
abstraigo, abstraje, *v.* *V.* ABSTRAER.
abstruso, sa, *a.* abstruse, difficult.
abstuve, *pret. irreg.* of ABSTENERSE.
absuelto, ta. I. *pp. irreg.* of ABSOLVER. **II.** *a.* acquitted.
absuelvo, absuelva, *v.* *V.* ABSOLVER.
absurdidad, *f.* absurdity.
absurdo, da. I. *a.* absurd, nonsensical. **II.** *m.* absurdity, nonsense.—**reducción al a.**, reductio ad absurdum.
abubilla, *f.* (ornith.) hoopoe.
abuchear, *va.* & *vn.* to boo.
abucheo, *m.* boo, hooting.
abuela, *f.* grandmother.
abuelo, *m.* grandfather; elderly man; ancestor.
abuje, *m.* (zool.) (Cuba) a parasitic mite in plants and man, causing the itch.
abulia, *f.* (med.) abulia, a mental derangement.
abultado, da. I. *pp.* of ABULTAR. **II.** *a.* bulky, massive, big.
abultar. I. *va.* to augment; to enlarge. **II.** *vn.* to be bulky or large.
abundamiento, *m.* = ABUNDANCIA.—**a mayor a.**, furthermore; with greater reason.
abundancia, *f.* abundance.
abundante, *a.* abundant.—**abundantemente,** *adv.* abundantly.
abundar, *vn.* to abound.—**lo que abunda no daña,** better too much than too little; you can't have too much of a good thing.
abundosamente, *adv.* abundantly.
abundoso, sa, *a.* abundant.
abuñolado, da, abuñuelado, da, *a.* turned over (eggs); shaped like a fritter.
abuñuelar, *va.* to turn (eggs) over in frying; to shape like a fritter.
abur, *interj.* (coll.) = AGUR, good-bye.
aburar, *va.* to burn; scorch.
aburelado, da, *a.* dark red.
aburrición, *f.* = ABURRIMIENTO.
aburrido da. I. *pp.* of ABURRIR. **II.** *a.* weary; tiresome, boresome.
aburrimiento, *m.* tediousness, weariness, ennui; annoyance.
[1]**aburrir. I.** *va.* to vex, annoy; to tire, weary, bore. **II.** *vr.* to grow tired, weary; to be bored.
[2]**aburrir,** *va.* to risk, spend (money, time).
aburujar, aborujar, *va.* & *vr.* to form lumps; to clot.—**aburujarse,** *vr.* to wrap oneself up.
abusador, ra, *n.* abuser.
abusar, *vn.* to exceed, go too far; to take undue advantage.—**a. de,** to abuse, use wrongly; to betray (a confidence); to take undue advantage of; to impose upon.
abusión, *f.* abuse; superstition.
abusionero, ra, *a.* superstitious; fortune-telling.
abusivo, va, *a.* abusive.
abuso, *m.* misuse, abuse.—**a. de confianza,** betrayal of confidence.
abutilón, *m.* (bot.) abutilon.
abyección, *f.* abjection, abjectness.
abyecto, ta, *a.* abject, servile, slavish.
acá, *adv.* here; hither.—**a. y acullá,** or **a. y allá,** here and there.—**de ayer a.**, at present.—**¿de cuándo a.?** since when?—**desde entonces a.**, = DE AYER A.—**para a.**, hither, here.—**por a.**, here, hereabouts; this way.
acabable, *a.* that can be finished; achievable.
acabadamente, *adv.* completely, perfectly.
acabado, da. I. *pp.* of ACABAR. **II.** *a.* perfect, faultless; consummate; wasted, emaciated; worn out; dilapidated. **III.** *m.* (art) finish.
acabador, ra, *m.* & *f.* finisher.
acabalar, *va.* to complete, finish.
acaballadero, *m.* time and place at which horses cover mares.
acaballado, da. I. *pp.* of ACABALLAR. **II.** *a.* horselike.
acaballar, *va.* to cover (a mare).
acaballerado, da. I. *pp.* of ACABALLERAR. **II.** *a.* gentlemanlike.
acaballerar, *va.* to render genteel; to make a gentleman of.
acabamiento, *m.* completion, finishing; emaciation; death; end.
acabar. I. *va.* and *vn.* to finish; to complete; to end.—**a. con,** to finish, destroy; to use up, exhaust; to get rid of, extirpate.—**a. de** (foll. by *inf.*), to have just (foll. by *pp.*): *él acaba de llegar,* he has just arrived.—**a. por,** to end by, to . . . finally (*Juan acabó por decir,* John ended by saying, John finally said). **II.** *vr.* to be finished; to end, be over; to grow feeble or wasted; (foll. by *dat.*) to be or run out of, become exhausted (diff. constr : *se me acabó el pan,* I ran out of bread: *se me ha acabado la paciencia,* my patience is exhausted).
acabestrillar, *vn.* to go shooting (birds) with a stalking horse or ox.
acabildar, *va.* to unite persons by persuasion to do something.
acabóse, *m.* (coll.) end (usually disastrous).
acacia, *f.* (bot.) acacia.
acacina, *f.* acacin(e.
academia, *f.* academy; university; literary society or contest; (fine arts) academy figure.
académico, ca, *a.* & *n.* academic(-ian).
academista, *n.* academist.
acadiense, *n.* & *a.* Acadian.
acaecedero, ra, *a.* eventual, contingent.
acaecer, *vn. defect.* (*subj.* ACAEZCA) to happen, come to pass.
acaecimiento, *m.* event, incident.
acahual, *m.* (bot.) sunflower; (Mex.) weeds; stubble.
acal, *m.* (Mex.) canoe; craft, vessel.
acalabrotar, *va.* (naut.) to make a cable by intertwining three ropes of three strands each.
acalefo, fa, *n.* & *a.* (zool.) acalephan.—*m. pl.* Acalephæ, Acalepha.
acalenturarse, *vr.* to become feverish.

acalia, *f.* (bot.) marsh mallow.
acaloradamente, *adv.* heatedly, excitedly.
acalorado, da. I. *pp.* of ACALORAR. **II.** *a.* heated, fiery, excited, angry. **III.** *n.* (fig.) hothead.
acaloramiento, *m.* ardor, heat, excitement.
acalorar. I. *va.* to warm; to inflame, excite; to move, arouse enthusiasm in; to urge on; to further, promote. **II.** *vr.* to grow warm; to get overheated; to get excited.
acallar, *va.* to quiet, hush; to mitigate, assuage.
acamar, *va.* (of wind, rain) to beat down (plants).
acambrayado, da, *a.* cambric-like.
acamellado, da, *a.* camel-like.
acampamento, *m.* (mil.) encampment, camp.
acampanado, a, *a.* bell-shaped.
acampanar, *va.* to shape like a bell.
acampar, *va., vn.* & *vr.* to encamp.
acampo, *m.* common pasture.
ácana, *f.* a hard reddish Cuban wood.
acanalado, da. I. *pp.* of ACANALAR. **II.** *a.* striated, fluted, corrugated, grooved. **III.** *m. pl.* ridge of a horse's back.
acanalador, *m.* (mech.) grooving plane.
acanaladura, *f.* groove, stria, striation.
acanalar, *va.* to make a channel in; to flute, corrugate, groove.
acandilado, da, *a.* shaped like a three-cornered hat; dazzled.
acanelado, da, *a.* cinnamon-colored.
acanillado, da, *a.* ribbed, striped (cloth).
acantáceo, a, *a.* (bot.) acanthaceous.
acantalear, *vn.* to hail large hailstones.
acantilado, da. I. *a.* (of sea bottom) stepped; steep. **II.** *m.* scarp, escarpment.
acantino, na, *a.* acanthine.
acanto, *m.* (bot., arch.) acanthus.
acantocarpo, pa, *a.* (bot.) acanthocarpous.
acantocéfalo, la, *n.* & *a.* (zool.) acanthocephalan.
acantonamiento, *m.* cantonment.
acantonar, *va.* to quarter (troops).
acantopterigio, gia, *n.* & *a.* (zool.) acanthopterygian.
acañaverear, *va.* to wound with sharp-pointed canes.
acañonear, *va.* to cannonade.
acaparador, ra, *n.* monopolizer.
acaparar, *va.* to monopolize; to corner, control (the market).
acaparrarse, *vr.* to close a bargain.
acaparrosado, da, *a.* copperas-hued.
acapizarse, *vr.* (coll.) to grapple, clinch.
acaponado, da, *a.* capon-like.
acaracolado, da, *a.* spiral-shaped, winding.
acaramelado, da. I. *pp.* of ACARAMELAR. **II.** *a.* (coll.) overpolite, disgustingly attentive.
acaramelar, *va.* to cover with caramel.
acarar, *va.* to confront; to face; to brave.
acardenalar. I. *va.* to beat black and blue. **II.** *vr.* to be covered with welts.
acardia, *f.* (med.) acardia.
acareamiento, *m.* facing; confronting.
acarear, *va.* = ACARAR.
acariasis, *f.* (med.) acariasis.
acariciador, ra, *m.* & *f.* one who fondles and caresses.
acariciar, *va.* to fondle, caress; to cherish.
acarnerado, da, *a.* having a sheeplike head.
ácaro, *m.* (zool.) acarus.—**a. de queso,** cheese mite.
acarpo, pa, *a.* (bot.) acarpous.
acarralar, *va.* to skip a thread in weaving.
acarrarse, *vr.* to seek the shade (app. to sheep).
acarreadizo, za, *a.* portable.
acarreador, ra, *m.* & *f.* carrier· porter.
acarreamiento, *m.* carrying, transportation; cartage.—*pl.* supplies.
acarrear. I. *va.* to carry, cart, transport, convey; to occasion, cause. **II.** *vr.* to bring upon oneself.
acarreo, *m.* = ACARREAMIENTO.
acartonado, *a.* pasteboardlike.
acartonar. I. *va.* to give the appearance or consistence of pasteboard. **II.** *vr.* (coll.) to become dried up by age.
acasamatado, da, *a.* (fort.) having or resembling a casemate.
acaso. I. *m.* chance; accident. **II.** *adv.* by chance, by accident; maybe, perhaps.—**por si a.,** in case, if it should happen.
acastorado, da, *a.* like beaver skin.
acatable, *a.* worthy of respect.
acatadamente, *adv.* respectfully.
acataléctico, ca, *n.* & *a.* acatalectic.
acatalepsia, *f.* (med.) acatalepsia.
acataléptico, ca, *a.* acataleptic.
acatamiento, *m.* esteem, respect; obeisance.
acatante, *n.* & *a.* respecter(-ing).
acatar, *va.* to hold in high esteem; to respect, revere, do homage to; to treat with great deference or respect.
acatarrarse, *vr.* to catch cold.
acato, *m.* = ACATAMIENTO.
acatólico, ca, *n.* & *a.* noncatholic.
acaudalado, da. I. *pp.* of ACAUDALAR. **II.** *a.* rich, opulent, well-to-do.
acaudalar, *va.* to hoard up riches; (fig.) to acquire a reputation.
acáudeo, a, *a.* (zool.) acaudal, tailless.
acaudillador, *m.* commander of troops; leader.
acaudillamiento, *m.* leading, command.
acaudillar, *va.* to command, lead (esp. troops).
acaule, *a.* (bot.) short-stemmed.
acceder, *vn.* to accede, agree, consent.
accesibilidad, *f.* accessibility.
accesible, *a.* accessible, approachable; attainable.
accesión, *f.* accession; accessory; (med.) periodic attack of fever; (law) accession.
acceso, *m.* access; carnal intercourse; accession; (med.) access, attack.—**a. del sol,** (astr.) apparent motion of sun towards the equator
accesoria, *f.* outbuilding.
accesorio, ria, *n.* & *a.* accessory.
accessit, *m.* (Lat.) second prize or award.
accidentado, da. I. *pp.* of ACCIDENTARSE. **II.** *a.* troubled, agitated; undulating, rolling (ground).
accidental. I. *a.* accidental, contingent. **II.** *m.* (mus.) = ACCIDENTE.
accidentarse, *vr.* to be seized with a fit.
accidente, *m.* accident; chance; sudden fit; (mus.) accidental; (gram.) inflexion.—**a. del trabajo,** work accident, occupational accident. —**de,** or **por, a.,** accidentally, by chance.
acción, *f.* action; feat; lawsuit; gesticulation, gesture; battle; action in drama, plot; (art) posture; (com.) stock, share.—**a. de gracias,** thanksgiving.—**a. de guerra,** battle.—**a. de presencia,** (chem.) catalysis.—**en a.,** in action, at work.
accionamiento, *m.* action.
accionar. I. *va.* (mech.) to operate, move. **II.** *vn.* to gesticulate.
accionista, *n.* stockholder, shareholder.
accípitre, *m.* bird of prey.—**accipitrino, na,** *a.* like a bird of prey, accipitral.
acebadamiento, *m.* (vet.) disease of animals surfeited with barley.
acebadar, *va.* = ENCEBADAR, to overfeed.
acebal, *m.,* **acebeda,** *f.,* **acebedo,** *m.* plantation of holly trees.
acebo, *m.* (bot.) holly tree.
acebollado, da, *a.* damaged by *acebolladura.*
acebolladura, *f.* damage (to a tree) from separation of the woody layers.
acebuchal. I. *m.* grove or wood of wild olive trees. **II.** *a.* pertaining to wild olives.
acebuche, *m.* (bot.) wild olive tree.—**acebucheno, na,** *a.* = ACEBUCHAL, *a.*
acebuchina, *f.* wild olive.
acecé, acece. *v. V.* ACEZAR.
acecinado, da, *a.* corned.
acecinar. I. *va.* to salt and dry (meat.) **II.** *vr.* to grow old, dry, withered.
acechador, ra, *m.* & *f.* ambusher; observer, lookout; intruder, prier.
acechar, *va.* to lie in ambush for; to spy on.

acecho, *m.* waylaying, lying in ambush.—**al a.,** or **en a.,** *a.* in wait, in ambush.
acechón, na, *m.* & *f.* (coll.) = ACECHADOR.
acedamente, *adv.* sourly, bitterly.
acedar, *va.* to sour; to displease, vex.
acedera, *f.* (bot.) sorrel.
acederaque, *m.* (bot.) bead tree.
acederilla, *f.* (bot.) wood sorrel.
acederón, *m.* (bot.) a variety of sorrel.
acedía, *f.* acidity, heart-burn, sourness; roughness; asperity of address.
acedo, da, *a.* acid, sour; harsh, unpleasant.
acéfalo, la, *a.* acephalous.—*pl.* Acephali, members of a religious sect that recognized no head or hierarchy.
aceitada, *f.* spilled oil; cake kneaded with oil.
aceitar, *va.* to oil; to rub with oil.
aceitazo, *m. aug.* = ACEITÓN.
aceite, *m.* oil; essential oil.—**a. de ballena,** whale oil.—**a. de comer,** olive, sweet oil.—**a. de hígado de bacalao,** cod-liver oil.—**a. de palo,** balsam of copaiba.—a. **de ricino,** castor-oil.—a. **de vitriolo,** vitriol, oil of vitriol.—a. **lubricante,** lubricating oil.—**a. secante,** linseed oil.
aceitera, *f.* woman who sells oil; oil jar, oil cruet; oil can; (mech.) oil cup.—*pl.* **aceiteras,** casters (for oil, etc.).
aceitería, *f.* oil shop.
aceitero, ra, *m.* & *f.* oiler; oil seller.
aceitillo, *m.* (bot.) satinwood.
aceitón, *m.* lubricating oil.
aceitoso, sa, *a.* oily, greasy.
aceituna, *f.* olive.—**a. de la reina,** or **gordal,** queen olive.—**a. manzanilla,** manzanilla olive.—**a. picudilla** = A. ZORZALEÑA.—**a. zapatera,** stale olive.—**a. zofairón,** baby queen olive.—**a. zorzaleña,** crescent olive.
aceitunado, da, *a.* olive-colored.
aceitunero, ra, *n.* olive dealer.
aceituní, *m.* arabesque work.
aceitunil, *a.* olive-colored.
aceitunillo, *m.* (bot.) satinwood.
aceituno, *m.* (bot.) olive tree.
acelajado, da, *a.* showing clouds of various hues.
aceleración, *f.* acceleration; haste.
aceleración de gravedad, *f.* gravitational acceleration.
aceleración negativa, *f.* deceleration.
aceleradamente, *adv.* speedily, swiftly; hastily; at an accelerated speed.
acelerador, ra. I. *a.* accelerating. **II.** *m.* accelerator; (auto) accelerator; (med.) accelerator.
aceleramiento, *m.* = ACELERACIÓN.
acelerar. I. *va.* to accelerate; to hasten, hurry, rush. **II.** *vr.* to move fast; to make haste.
aceleratriz, *f. a.* (of force) accelerating.
acelerógrafo, *m.* (phys.) accelerograph.
acelerómetro, *m.* (aer.) accelerometer.
acelga, *f.* (bot.) salt-wort.
acémila, *f.* beast of burden; pack animal.—**acemilar,** *a.* pert. to mules and muleteers.
acemilería, *f.* mule stable.
acemilero, ra. I. *a.* pert. to ACEMILERÍA. **II.** *m.* muleteer.
acemita, *f.* bran bread, graham bread.
acemite, *m.* fine bran, middlings; pottage.
acendrado, da. I. *pp.* of ACENDRAR. **II.** *a.* purified, refined; unspotted, stainless.
acendrar, *va.* to purify or refine (metals); to free from stain or blemish.
acensuar, *va.* to tax (a property).
acento, *m.* accent, stress; accent, way of speaking.—**a. ortográfico,** written accent.—**a. prosódico** or **tónico,** tonic accent, emphasis.—**a. secundario,** secondary accent.
acéntrico, ca, *a.* (med.) acentric.
acentuación, *f.* accentuation.
acentuado, da, *a.* accented.
acentuar, *va.* to accentuate; to emphasize.
aceña, *f.* water mill.—**aceñero,** *m.* water-mill keeper.
acepar, *vn.* to take root. Also ENCEPAR.
acepción, *f.* acceptation, meaning.—**a. de personas,** unfair discrimination among persons.
acepilladura, *f.* planing; wood shavings.
acepillar, *va.* to plane; to brush; to polish.
aceptabilidad, *f.* acceptability.
aceptable, *a.* acceptable, admissible.—**aceptablemente,** *adv.* acceptably.
aceptación, *f.* acceptation; (formal) acceptance; approbation; (com.) acceptance.—**a. de personas** = ACEPCIÓN DE PERSONAS.
aceptado, da, *a.* admitted, accepted.
aceptador, ra, *m.* & *f.* acceptor.
aceptante, I. *m.* & *f.* accepter. **II.** *a.* accepting.
aceptar, *va.* to accept; (com.) to accept or honor.
acepto, ta. *a.* acceptable, agreeable.
aceptor, *m.* (phys.) acceptor.
acequia, *f.* trench; drain; channel; irrigation ditch.
acequiar, *va.* to construct ditches, channels, flumes in or for.
acequiero, *m.* canal or dike keeper.
ácer, *m.* (bot.) maple tree.
acera, *f.* sidewalk; row of houses on either side of a street; (arch.) face or facing stone (of a wall).
aceración, *f.* (metal.) acierage.
acerado, da. I. *pp.* of [1]ACERAR. **II.** *a.* made of steel; steel (as *a.*); strong; biting, acrimonious.
[1]**acerar,** *va.* to steel; to impregnate (liquids) with steel; to strengthen; to convert (iron) into steel; to cover with steel.
[2]**acerar,** *va.* (arch.) to lay the facing stones of (a wall).
acerbamente, *adv.* cruelly, severely, harshly.
acerbidad, *f.* acerbity, harshness; rigor, cruelty.
acerbo, ba, *a.* tart; harsh, severe, cruel.
acerca de, *prep.* about, with regard to.
acercamiento, *m.* approximation, approaching; rapprochement.
acercar. I. *va.* (*pret.* ACERQUÉ; *subj.* ACERQUE) to bring or place near, or nearer. **II.** *vr.* **(a)** to draw near (to), approach.
ácere, *m.* maple tree.
acerico, acerillo, *m.* pincushion; small pillow.
aceríneo, a. I. *a.* (bot.) aceraceous. **II.** *f.* *pl.* Aceraceæ.
acerino, na, *a.* (poet.) steel-like; of steel.
acero, *m.* steel; (fig.) cold steel (esp. sword); *pl.* (fig.) spirit, courage; (fig.) appetite.—a. **Bessemer,** Bessemer steel.—a. **carbono,** carbon steel.—a. **cementado,** blister steel.—a. **colado** or **fundido,** cast steel.—a. **cromo,** chrome steel.—a. **damasquino,** damask steel.—a. **dúctil,** mild or soft steel.—a. **eléctrico** or **de horno eléctrico,** electric steel.—a. **manganeso** or **mangánico,** manganese steel.—a. **níquel,** nickel steel.
acerola, *f.* haw, fruit of the hawthorn.
acerolo, *m.* (bot.) hawthorn.
acerqué, acerque, *v. V.* ACERCAR.
acérrimamente, *adv.* vigorously; strongly.
acérrimo, ma, *a. super.* very strong (taste, odor); very harsh; very vigorous; very stanch or stalwart.
acerrojar, *va.* to bolt; to lock.
acertadamente, *adv.* opportunely, fitly, wisely.
acertado, da. I. *pp.* of ACERTAR. **II.** *a.* fit, proper; wise.
acertador, ra, *m.* & *f.* good guesser.
acertar. I. *va.* (*ind.* ACIERTO; *subj.* ACIERTE) to hit the mark; to hit by chance; to succeed in; to guess (something). **II** *vn.* to guess right; to succeed; (agr.) to thrive.—**a. a,** to happen.—**a. con,** to find, come across.
acertijo, *m.* riddle, conundrum.
aceruelo, *m.* small packsaddle.
acervo, *m.* a heap; undivided estate; common property.
acescencia, *f.* acescence, slight sourness.
acescente, *a.* acescent, turning or slightly sour.
acetábulo, *m.* cruet; acetabulum (small cup); (anat.) acetabulum, socket (esp. for hip bone).
acetanilida, *f.* (chem.) acetanilide.

acetato, *m.* (chem.) acetate.
acetato de amilo, *m.* banana oil.
acético, ca, *a.* acetic.
acetificación, *f.* acetification.
acetificar, *va.* to acetify.
acetilcolina, *f.* (biochem.) acetylcholine.
acetilénico, ca, *a.* acetylene.
acetileno. *m.* acetylene.
acetilo, *m.* (chem.) acetyl.
acetimetría, *f.* acetimetry.
acetímetro, *m.* acetimeter.
acetín, *m.* (bot.) satinwood.
acetina, *f.* (chem.) acetin.
acetocelulosa, *f.* (chem.) cellulose acetate.
acetol, *m.* (chem.) acetol.
acetona, *f.* (chem.) acetone.
acetosa, *f.* (bot.) sorrel.
acetosidad, *f.* acetosity.
acetosilla, *f.* = ACEDERILLA, (bot.) wood sorrel.
acetoso, sa, *a.* acetous, containing acetic acid.
acetre, *m.* small bucket; holy-water font.
acezar, *vn.* (*pret.* ACECÉ; *subj.* ACECE) to pant.
acezo, *m.* pant, panting.—**acezoso, sa,** *a.* panting.
aciago, ga, *a.* unfortunate, sad, fateful.
acial, *m.* barnacle, twitch, (for horses).
aciano, *m.* (bot.) cornflower.
aciar, *m.* = ACIAL.
acíbar, *m.* aloes; aloe tree; bitterness; displeasure. —**acibarar,** *va.* to put aloes into; to embitter.
aciberar, *va.* to grind very fine, pulverize.
acicalado, *m.* act of polishing a weapon; polish.
acicalador, ra. I. *a.* polishing; embellishing; attiring. **II.** *m.* burnishing tool.
acicaladura, *f.*, **acicalamiento,** *m.* burnishing; polish, glossiness; adornment; dressing.
acicalar. I. *va.* to polish, burnish; to dress, adorn, embellish. **II.** *vr.* (fig.) to dress in style, make an elaborate toilet.
acicate, *m.* long-pointed Moorish spur; inducement; goad.
acíclico, ca, *a.* (elec.) acyclic, out of phase.
aciculado, da, *a.* (bot.) acerose.
acicular, *a.* aciculate; needle-shaped.
aciche, *m.* paving hammer; brick hammer.
acidez, *f.* acidity, tartness.
acidia, *f.* laziness; weakness.
acidificación, *f.* (chem.) acidification.
acidificar, *va.* to acidify.
acidimetría, *f.* acidimetry.
acidímetro, *m.* acidimeter.
acidioso, sa, *a.* lazy; weak; lax.
acidismo, *m.* (med.) acidosis.
ácido, da. I. *m.* (chem.) acid. **II.** *a.* acid; sour, tart.—**á. acético** or **piroleñoso,** (chem.) acetic acid.—**á. acrílico,** (chem.) acrylic acid.—**á. agállico,** (chem.) gallic acid.—**á. ascórbico,** (biochem.) ascorbic acid.—**á. barbitúrico,** (chem.) barbituric acid.—**á. benzoico,** (chem.) benzoic acid.—**á. bórico,** (chem.) boric acid.—**á. butírico,** (chem.) butyric acid.—**á. carbónico,** (chem.) carbonic acid.—**á. ciánico,** (chem.) cyanic acid.—**á. cítrico,** (chem.) citric acid.—**á. clórico,** (chem.) chloric acid.—**á. crómico,** (chem.) chromic acid.—**á. fénico,** (chem.) carbolic acid.—**á. fórmico,** (chem.) formic acid.—**á. fosfórico,** (chem.) phosphoric acid.—**á. fosforoso,** (chem.) phosphorous acid. —**á. graso,** (biochem.) fatty acid.—**á. hipofosfórico** or **hipofosforescente,** (chem.) hypophosphoric acid.—**á. hipofosforoso,** (chem.) hypophosphorous acid.—**á. hiposulfuroso,** (chem.) hyposulfurous acid.—**á. láctico,** (chem.) lactic acid.—**á. málico,** (chem.) malic acid.—**á. muriático** or **clorhídrico,** (chem.) muriatic acid.—**á. nicotínico,** (biochem.) nicotinic acid, niacin.—**á. nítrico,** (chem.) nitric acid.—**á. nitroso,** (chem.) nitrous acid.—**á. nucleico,** (chem.) nucleic acid.—**á. oleico,** (chem.) oleic acid.—**á. oxálico,** (chem.) oxalic acid.—**á. pícrico,** picric acid.—**á. prúsico** or **cianhídrico,** (chem.) prussic acid.—**á. sulfúreo,** (chem.) sulfurous acid.—**á. sulfúrico,** (chem.) sulfuric acid.—**á. tartárico** or **tártrico,** (chem.) tartaric acid.—**á. úrico,** (chem.) uric acid.
acidógeno, na, *a.* acid-forming.
acidular, *va.* to acidulate.
acídulo, la, *a.* (chem.) acidulous, tart.
[1]**acierto,** *m.* a good hit, good shot; ability; tact; knack; dexterity.
[2]**acierto, acierte,** *v.* *V.* ACERTAR.
aciforme, *a.* (bot.) aciform.
ácigo, ga, *a.* (anat.) azygous.
aciguatado, da. I. *pp.* of ACIGUATARSE. **II.** *a.* jaundiced.
aciguatarse, *vr.* to become ill with jaundice.
acijado, da, *a.* copper- or copperas-colored.
acije, *m.* copperas.—**acijoso, sa,** *a.* containing copperas; brownish.
acimboga, *f.* = AZAMBOA, citron (the fruit).
ácimo, ma, *a.* = ÁZIMO, unleavened.
acimut, *m.* azimuth.—**acimutal,** *a.* azimuthal, azimuth (as *a.*).
acinesia, *f.* (med.) akinesia, paralysis of the motor nerves.
aciniforme, *a.* (bot.) aciniform.
acino, *m.* (bot., anat.) acinus.
acinoso, sa, *a.* (bot.) acinose, acinous.
ación, *f.* stirrup strap.—**acionera,** *f.* piece of saddle from which stirrup strap hangs.—**acionero,** *m.* maker of stirrup straps.
acipado, da, *a.* well-milled (woolens).
acirate, *m.* landmark, boundary.
acitara, *f.* partition wall; rail of bridge; chair or saddle cover. Also CITARA.
acitrón, *m.* candied citron.
aclamación, *f.* acclamation.
aclamador, ra, *m.* & *f.* applauder.
aclamar, *va.* to shout, applaud, acclaim.
aclamatorio, ria, *a.* acclamatory.
aclaración, *f.* explanation.
aclarador, ra. I. *a.* explanatory. **II.** *m.* comb in looms.
aclarar. I. *va.* to make clear; to explain; to thin; to clarify; to rinse. **II.** *vn.* to clear up; to recover brightness; CLAREAR, to dawn.
aclaratorio, ria, *a.* explanatory.
aclasto, ta, *a.* (opt.) aclastic, not refracting.
acleido, da, *a.* (zool.) with no clavicles.
aclimatación, *f.* acclimatization, acclimatation.
aclimatado, da, *a.* acclimated.
aclimatar, *va.* & *vr.* to acclimatize, acclimate.
aclínico, ca. I. *a.* (phys.) aclinic. **II.** *m.* opera glasses.
aclocar I. *vn.* (*ind. pres.* ACLUECO, *pret.* ACLOQUÉ; *subj.* ACLUEQUE) (of hens) to brood, be broody. **II.** *vr.* to stretch out, lie down; (of hens) to become broody.
acmé, acme, *m.* (med.) acme.
acné, acne, *f.* (med.) acne.
acobardar, *va.* to daunt, intimidate, frighten.
acobijar, *va.* (agr.) to mulch.—**acobijo,** mulch.
acobrado, da, *a.* copper-hued.
acoceador, ra, *a.* that kicks, kicking.
acoceamiento, *m.* kicking.
acocear, *va.* to kick; to humiliate; to ill-trea
acocotar, *va.* = ACOGOTAR.
acocote, *m.* long gourd used in Mexico fo tracting the juice of the maguey.
acocharse, *vr.* to squat, stoop down.
acochinar, *va.* (coll.) to murder; to humble; (checkers game) to corner (a checker).
acodado, da, *a.* elbowed; cranked (axle); toggled.
acodadura, *f.* bending the elbow; (hort.) layering.
acodalamiento, *m.* (arch.) propping; staying.
acodalar, *va.* (arch.) to prop; to shore; to stay.
acodar, *va.* to lean the elbow upon; (hort.) to layer (cuttings); (arch.) = ACODALAR; (carp.) to square (timber).
acoderamiento, *m.* (naut.) bringing the broadside to bear.

acoderar, *va.* (naut.) to put a spring on a cable; to bring the broadside to bear.
acodiciar. I. *va.* to long for, covet. **II.** *vr.* to become covetous.
acodillar. I. *va.* to bend into an elbow or angle. **II.** *vr.* to sink down under a burden.
acodo, *m.* (agr.) shoot, scion.
acogedizo, za, *a.* collected promiscuously.
acogedor, ra, *m.* & *f.* harborer, protector.
acoger. I. *va.* (*ind.* ACOJO; *subj.* ACOJA) to receive; (fig.) to protect, shelter. **II.** *vr.* **(a)** to take refuge (in); to resort (to).
acogeta, *f.* shelter, cover, place of safety.
acogida, *f.* reception; place of meeting, confluence; asylum.—**dar a. a una letra,** (com.) to honor a draft.—**tener buena, mala a.,** to be well, unfavorably received.
acogido, *m.* collection of brood mares given to owner of principal steed, to keep them at a certain price; letting out of pasture for flocks.
acogimiento, *m.* = ACOGIDA.
[1]**acogollar,** *va.* to cover up (plants).
[2]**acogollar,** *vn.* to bud.
acogombradura, *f.* banking of plants.
acogombrar, *va.* = APORCAR, to cover (plants) with earth, to bank.
acogotar, *va.* to kill by a blow on the back of the neck.
acohombrar, *va.* (agr.) = ACOGOMBRAR.
acojinamiento, *m.* (mech.) cushioning.
acojinar, *va.* to quilt; (mech.) to cushion.
acojo, acoja, *v. V.* ACOGER.
acolada, *f.* accolade.
acolar, *va.* (her.) to unite (two coats of arms) under the same crown, shield, etc.
acolchado, *m.* (hydraul. eng.) mattress.
[1]**acholchar, acolchonar,** *va.* to quilt.
[2]**acolchar,** *va.* (naut.) to intertwine (cords).
acólito, *m.* acolyte, assistant.
acología, *f.* (med.) acology
acológico, ca, *a.* acologic.
acolladores, *m. pl.* (naut.) lanyards.
acollar, *va.* (*ind.* ACUELLO; *subj.* ACUELLE) (agr.) to cover with earth the base of a trunk; (naut.) to caulk.
acollarado, da, *a.* ring-necked.
acollarar, *va.* to yoke or harness (horses, oxen, etc.); to couple (hounds); to put a collar on.
acollonar, *va.* (coll.) = ACOBARDAR, to frighten.
acombar, *va.* to bend; to warp.
acomedirse, *vr.* to offer oneself, volunteer.
acometedor, ra, *n.* & *a.* aggressor(-ive); enterpriser(-ing).
acometer, *va.* to attack, rush on, (coll.) go for; to undertake; (of sleep, an illness) to overtake.
acometida, *f.*, **acometimiento,** *m.* attack, assault; branch or outlet (in a sewer).
acometividad, *f.* combativeness.
acomodable, *a.* easily arranged.
acomodación, *f.* accommodation.
acomodadamente, *adv.* commodiously, comfortably.
acomodadizo, za, *a.* accommodating.
acomodado, da. I. *pp.* of ACOMODAR. **II.** *a.* convenient, fit; well-to-do, wealthy; fond of comfort; moderate, reasonable.
acomodador, ra, *n.* one who accommodates; usher in a theatre.
acomodamiento, *m.* accommodation.
acomodar. I. *va.* to arrange; to accommodate; to set to rights; to place; to reconcile, compound, compromise; to furnish, supply; to take in, shelter, lodge. **II.** *vn.* to fit; to suit. **III.** *vr.* to condescend; to adapt oneself; to put up with; to settle, agree.
acomodaticio, cia, *a.* accommodating.
acomodo, *m.* employment, situation; lodgings.
acompañado, da. I. *pp.* of ACOMPAÑAR. **II.** *a.* frequented. **III.** *n.* assistant.
acompañador, ra. I. *n.* chaperon, attendant; companion; (mus.) accompanist. **II.** *a.* accompanying.
acompañamiento, *m.* attendance; retinue; (mus.) accompaniment; supernumeraries in a theatre; (her.) ornament around an escutcheon.
acompañante, ta, *n.* & *a.* = ACOMPAÑADOR.
acompañar. I. *va.* to accompany; to attend, escort; to enclose; (mus.) to accompany. **II.** *vr.* to hold a consultation.
acompasadamente, *adv.* rhythmically.
acompasado, da, *a.* measured, rhythmic; (coll.) monotonous and slow in speech or unhurried in gait; of fixed, regular habits.
acompasar, compasar, *va.* to measure with a compass; to arrange in order.
acomplexionado, da, *a.* of (good, bad) complexion.
acomunarse, *vr.* to unite, combine.
aconchabarse, conchabarse, *vr.* (coll.) to unite (esp. for evil purpose).
aconchar, *va.* to push to a place of shelter; (naut.) to run aground.
acondicionado, da. I. *pp.* of ACONDICIONAR. **II.** *a.* (of persons) of (good, bad) disposition; (of things) in (good, bad) condition; of (good, bad) quality.—**con aire a.,** air-conditioned.
acondicionador, ra. I. *a.* conditioning. **II.** *mf.* conditioner.—**a. de aire,** air conditioner.
acondicionamiento, *m.* conditioning, processing; drying (of silk, etc.).—**a. de aire,** air conditioning.
acondicionar. I. *va.* to prepare, arrange; to repair; to condition. **II.** *vr.* to acquire a quality or condition; to qualify (for a position).
acongojadamente, *adv.* sorrowfully, sadly.
acongojado, da, *a.* anguished, heartbroken.
acongojar. I. *va.* to afflict, grieve. **II.** *vr.* to become sad; to grieve.
aconítico, ca, *a.* (chem.) aconitic.
aconitina, *f.* (chem.) aconitine.
acónito, *m.* (bot.) aconite.
aconsejable, *a.* advisable.
aconsejado, da, *a.* advised.
aconsejador, ra. I. *n.* adviser, counselor. **II.** *a.* advisory.
aconsejar. I. *va.* to advise, counsel. **II.** *vr.* **(con)** to advise (with); to consult.
aconsonantar. I. *va.* to make (a word) rhyme with another; to use rhymes in prose. **II.** *vn.* to rhyme.
acontecedero, ra, *a.* possible, that may happen.
acontecer, *v. impers.* (*subj.* ACONTEZCA) to happen, come about.—**acontecido, a. I.** *pp.* of ACONTECER. **II.** *a.* sad, despondent.
acontecimiento, *m.* event, happening.
acontezca, *v. V.* ACONTECER.
acopado, da. I. *pp.* of ACOPAR. **II.** *a.* cuplike, cupped.
acopar, *vn.* to trim to shape; to cup, hollow.
acopetado, da, *a.* tufted.
acopiador, ra, *n.* one who stores or collects.
acopiamiento, *m.* gathering, collecting; collection; supply, stock.
acopiar, *va.* to gather, store, collect, garner.
acopio, *m.* gathering, storing; assortment; collection, quantity.
acoplado, da. I. *pp.* of ACOPLAR. **II.** *a.* fitted, adjusted; coupled; (carp.) scarfed.—**a. directamente,** (mech.) direct-connected.
acopladura, *f.* = ACOPLAMIENTO.
acoplamiento, *m.* coupling; joint; scarfing.
acoplar. I. *va.* to couple, join, connect; to hitch, yoke; to scarf (timber); to reconcile; to settle (differences); to pair, mate (animals). **II.** *vr.* to make up a difference; to settle, come to an agreement; (coll.) to become intimate.
acoquinamiento, *m.* intimidation.
acoquinar. I. *va.* to intimidate; frighten. **II.** *vr.* to be afraid.
acoracé, acorace, *v. V.* ACORAZAR.
acorar, *va.* to afflict; to cause grief.
acorazado, da. I. *a.* ironclad; shell (app. to transformers, as shell core). **II.** *m.* armored ship, ironclad.
acorazamiento, *m.* armoring; armor.

acorazar, *va.* (*pret.* ACORACÉ; *subj.* ACORACE) to armor.
acorazonado, da, *a.* heart-shaped.
acorchamiento, *m.* shrivelling.
acorcharse, *vr.* to shrivel; (of fruits) to get stale; to become torpid; (of arm, leg, etc.) to go to sleep.
acordada, *f.* (law) resolution, decision.
acordadamente, *adv.* by common consent, jointly; with mature deliberation.
acordado, da. I. *pp.* of ACORDAR. **II.** *a.* done with mature deliberation.
acordar. I. *va.* (*ind.* ACUERDO; *subj.* ACUERDE) to resolve; to agree; to remind; (mus.) (reg. conj. in this meaning) to tune; to dispose (figures) in a picture; to make flush, level, smooth. **II.** *vn.* to agree. **III.** *vr.* (de) to remember, recollect (*no me acuerdo de eso,* I do not remember that); to come to an agreement.—**si mal no me acuerdo,** if I remember rightly, if my memory does not fail me.
acorde. I. *a.* agreed; in tune; in accord. **II.** *m.* chord; harmony of sounds or colors.
acordelar, *va.* to measure with a cord.
acordemente, *adv.* by common consent; harmoniously; consistently.
acordeón, *m.* accordion.
acordeonista, *n.* accordionist.
acordonado, da. I. *pp.* of ACORDONAR. **II.** *a.* surrounded; in the form of a cord; accordion-pleated.
acordonamiento, *m.* act of lacing; milling (coins); cording; shirring.
acordonar, *va.* to lace; to mill (a coin); to cord, shirr, twine; to surround (with a cordon of troops, etc.).
acores, *m. pl.* (med.) achor, scald head.
acornar, *va.* (*ind.* ACUERNO; *subj.* ACUERNE) = ACORNEAR.
acorneador, ra, *n.* & *a.*; butter(-ing).
acornear, *va.* to butt (with the head).
ácoro, *m.* (bot.) sweet flag.
acorralamiento, *m.* corralling.
acorralar, *va.* to corral; to surround; to intimidate; to silence.
acorrucarse, accurrucarse, *vr.* to huddle up.
acortamiento, *m.* shortening; (astr.) difference between the distance from the sun or a planet to the earth and the projection of that distance on the plane of the ecliptic.
acortar. I. *va.* to shorten, lessen, reduce; to obstruct.—**a. la marcha,** to slow down.—**a. la vela,** (naut.) to shorten sail. **II.** *vr.* to shrivel, contract, shrink; to be bashful; to fall back.
acorullar, *va.* (naut.) to bridle (the oars).
acosador, ra, *n.* pursuer, persecutor.
acosamiento, *m.* relentless persecution.
acosar, *va.* to pursue relentlessly; to vex, harass.
acosmismo, *m.* (philos.) acosmism.
acostado, da. I. *pp.* of ACOSTAR. **II.** *a.* stretched out, lying down; laid down; in bed.
[1]**acostamiento,** *m.* stretching or laying down.
[2]**acostamiento,** *m.* stipend, emolument.
acostar. I. *va.* (*ind.* ACUESTO; *subj.* ACUESTE) to lay down; to put to bed; to bring (a vessel) alongside the shore. **II.** *vn.* to tilt, have a list. **III.** *vr.* to lie down; to go to bed.—**a. con las gallinas,** (coll.) to go to bed with the chickens.
acostumbrado, da, *a.* accustomed, used.
acostumbrar. I. *va.* to accustom. **II.** *vn.* to be accustomed, be in the habit (*acostumbro comer temprano,* I am in the habit of dining early). **III.** *vr.* to get used, or become accustomed.
acotación, *f.*, **acotamiento,** *m.* boundary mark or monument; directions (for a theatrical performance); marginal note; (surv.) elevation marked on a map.
[1]**acotar. I.** *va.* to set boundary marks on; to mark out. **II.** *vr.* to seek refuge outside the boundary line.
[2]**acotar,** *va.* to annotate; to accept; to select; to witness, vouch for; (surv.) to put the elevation figures on (a map).
[3]**acotar,** *va.* to prune (a tree).
acotiledón, *m.* (bot.) acotyledon.
acotiledóneo, ea. I. *a.* (bot.) acotyledonous. **II.** *f. pl.* (bot.) Acotyledons.
acotillo, *m.* sledgehammer.
acoyundar, *va.* to yoke (oxen).
[1]**acre,** *a.* sour; acrimonious; tart; mordant; keen.
[2]**acre,** *m.* acre.
acrecencia, *f.* increase; growth.
acrecentador, ra, *n.* & *a.* increaser(-ing).
acrecentamiento, *m.* = ACRECENCIA.
acrecentar (*ind.* ACRECIENTO; *subj.* ACRECIENTE), **acrecer** (*ind.* ACREZCO; *subj.* ACREZCA), *va.* to increase; to promote, advance.
acrecido, da, *a.* (bot.) accrete.
acreditado, da. I. *pp.* of ACREDITAR. **II.** *a.* well reputed, of good repute.
acreditar, *va.* to assure, affirm; to verify, prove; (com.) to recommend, answer for, guarantee; to accredit, authorize; to prove.
acreedor, ra. I. *a.* meritorious, deserving; creditor (as *a.*).—**a. a,** deserving or worthy of. **II.** *n.* creditor.—**a. hipotecario,** mortgagee.
acreencia, *f.* (Am.) debt claimed; balance in favor of creditor.
acremente, *adv.* sourly, bitterly.
acrescente, *a.* accrescent.
acrezca, acrezco, *v. V.* ACRECER.
acribador, ra, *n.* & *a.* one who sifts; sifting.
acribadura, *f.* sifting.—*pl.* siftings.
acribar, *va.* to sift; to perforate like a sieve.
acribillar, *va.* to pierce, perforate; to torment; to cover with wounds.
acriflavina, *f.* (pharm.) acriflavine.
acrilán, *m.* Acrilan (trademark).
acrílico, ca, *a.* (chem.) acrylic.
acriminación, *f.* crimination, accusation.
acriminador, ra, *n.* accuser, informer.
acriminar, *va.* to accuse, charge; to impeach; (law) to aggravate.
acrimonia, *f.* acrimony: tartness; sourness.
acrimonioso, sa, *a.* acrimonious.
acriollarse, *vr.* (Am.) (of Europeans, Anglo-Americans) to adopt native ways, get to be like a creole.
acrisoladamente, *adv.* honestly.
acrisolado, da, *a.* honest, virtuous, upright.
acrisolar, *va.* to assay; to refine; to purify, cleanse; to prove.
acristianar, *va.* (coll.) to baptize, christen.
acrítico, ca, *a.* (med.) acritical.
acritud, *f.* = ACRIMONIA.
acroamático, ca, *a.* acroamatic.
acrobacia, *f.* (aer.) fancy air maneuver, stunt.
acróbata, *n.* acrobat.
acrobático, ca, *a.* acrobatic.
acrobatismo, *m.* acrobatics.
acrocárpeo, pea, *a.* (bot.) acrocarpous.
acrocéfalo, la, *a.* (med.) acrocephalous.
acrógena, *f.* (bot.) acrogen.
acrol, *m.* (chem.) acrolein.
acroleína, *f.* (chem.) acrolein.
acrólito, *m.* (archeol.) acrolith.
acromático, ca, *a.* (opt.) achromatic, free from color.
acromatismo, *m.* achromatism.
acromatizar, *va.* (opt.) to make achromatic (lenses, etc.).
acromatopsia, *f.* color blindness.
acromegalia, *f.* (med.) acromegaly.
acromia, *f.* achroma, achromia.
acromial, acromiano, na, *a.* (anat.) acromial.
acromio, *m.* (anat.) acromion.
acrónico, ca, *a.* (astr.) acronical.
acrónimo, *m.* acronym.
acrópolis, *f.* acropolis.
acrósporo, ra, *a.* (bot.) acrosporous.
acróstico, ca, *a.* acrostic.
acrostolio, *m.* (naut.) acrostolium.
acrotera, *f.* (arch.) acroterium.
acta, *f.* act or record of proceedings; certificate

of election.—*pl.* acts or records of communities, chapters, councils; proceedings; transactions, minutes; papers, file, etc.—**a. notarial,** notarial certificate.—**tomar a.,** (Am.) to note, set down; to bear in mind.
actinia, *f.* (zool.) actinia, sea anemone.
actínico, ca, *a.* (chem.) actinic.
actínides, *m. pl.* (chem.) actinides.
actinio, *m.* actinium.
actinismo, *m.* actinism.
actinógrafo, *m.* (photog.) actinograph, actinometer, exposure meter.
actinometría, *f.* actinometry.
actinométrico, ca, *a.* (opt.) actinometric.
actinómetro, *m.* (opt.) actinometer.
actinomicina, *f.* (pharm.) actinomycin.
actinomicosis, *f.* (med., vet.) actinomycosis.
actinomorfo, fa, *a.* (bot.) actinomorphic, actinomorphous.
actinón, *m.* (chem.) actinon.
actinota, *f.* (miner.) actinolite.
actitud, *f.* attitude.
activación, *f.* activation.
activador, *m.* (chem.) activator.
activar, *va.* to make active; to expedite, hasten.
actividad, *f.* activity, energy.—**en a.,** in operation.
activista, *n.* activist.
activo, va. I. *a.* active. **II.** *m.* (com.) assets.
acto, *m.* act, action; public function; commencement in colleges, etc.; act (of a play); thesis defended in universities; carnal intercourse.—**a. continuo,** (*adv.*) immediately afterward.—**en el a.,** (*adv.*) at once.
actor, ra. I. *a.* acting, that acts.—**parte actora,** (law) prosecution; plaintiff. **II.** *m.* actor player; (law) plaintiff, claimant.
actriz, *f.* actress.
actuación, *f.* actuation; action.—*pl.* (law) proceedings.
actuado, da. I. *pp.* of ACTUAR. **II.** *a.* actuated; skilled, experienced.
actual, *a.* present, of the present time (not *actual*).—**actualidad,** *f.* present time (never *actuality*).—**en la a.,** at the present time, at present, nowadays.—**actualmente,** *adv.* at present, at the present time (never *actually*).
actuante, *a.* & *n.* defender of a thesis in colleges.
actuar. I. *vn.* to act; to perform judicial acts; to take the affirmative side in a university debate. **II.** *va.* to put in action, actuate.
actuario, ria. I. *a.* actuarial. **II.** *m.* clerk of a court of justice; *n.* actuary.—**a. de seguros,** actuary, expert on insurance.
acuadrillar. I. *va.* to form or head a gang. **II.** *vr.* to form a gang.
acuafortista, *n.* (f.a.) aquafortist, etcher.
acuantiar, *va.* to price, appraise, set a value upon.
acuaplano, *m.* (sport) aquaplane.
acuarela, *f.* water-color painting.
acuarelista, *m.* water-color painter.
acuario, *m.* Aquarius (in zodiac); aquarium.
acuartelado, da. I. *pp.* of ACUARTELAR. **II.** *a.* (her.) quartered, divided into quarters.
acuartelamiento, *m.* quartering or billeting (of troops); troops; quarters.
acuartelar, *va.* to quarter, billet.—**a. las velas,** (naut.) to flat in the sails.
acuartillar, *vn.* (of pack animals) to bend in the quarters under a heavy load.
acuático, ca, acuátil, *a.* aquatic, water (as *a.*).
acuatinta, *f.* aquatint.
acuatizaje, *m.* (aer.) alighting on the water; place for alighting on the water.
acuatizar, *vn.* (aer.) to alight on the water.
acubado, da, *a.* resembling a pail or bucket.
acucia, *f.* zeal, diligence; longing.
acuciamiento, *m.* urging, hastening.
acuciar, *va.* to urge, hasten; to covet.
acuciosamente, *adv.* actively, diligently; eagerly.
acucioso, sa, *a.* zealous, hasty, eager.
acuclillarse, *vr.* to crouch, squat.
acucharado, da, *a.* spoonlike.
acuchillado, da. I. *pp.* of ACUCHILLAR. **II.** *a.* schooled by experience; slashed (app. to garments).
acuchillador, ra, *n.* slasher; bully.
acuchillar. I. *va.* to cut, hack; to slash, cut open; to knife; to put to the sword. **II.** *vr.* to fight with knives or swords.
acudimiento, *m.* aid, assistance.
acudir, *vn.* to be present frequently; to attend; to go, come; to respond (to a call); to go or come to the rescue; to resort; to have recourse; to keep (an appointment).
acueducto, *m.* aqueduct; water-supply line, main.
acuello, acuelle, *v.* *V.* ACOLLAR.
ácueo, a, *a.* watery; aqueous.
acuerdado, da, *a.* aligned.
[1]**acuerdo,** *m.* resolution; determination; opinion; report, advice; remembrance, recollection; concurrence, accord; agreement, convention, pact; body of the members of a tribunal; harmony.—**de a.,** in agreement; unanimously; of the same opinion; complying, in accordance.—**de común a.,** unanimously; by mutual agreement.
[2]**acuerdo, acuerde,** *v.* *V.* ACORDAR.
acuerno, acuerne, *v.* *V.* ACORNAR.
acuesto, acueste, *v.* *V.* ACOSTAR.
acuidad, *f.* acuity.
acuitar. I. *va.* to afflict. **II.** *vr.* to grieve.
acular, *va.* (coll.) to make (a horse) back up.
aculeado, da, *m.* & *a.* (zool.) aculeate.
aculeata, *m.* (zool.) aculeate.
aculebrinado, da, *a.* in the form of a culverin.
aculeiforme, *a.* aculeiform.
acullá, *adv.* on the other side, opposite; yonder.
acumbente, *a.* (bot.) accumbent.
acumen, *m.* acumen, quick discernment.
acuminado, da, *a.* (bot.) acuminate.
acumulación, *f.* accumulation; gathering.
acumulado, da, *a.* accumulate, accumulative.
acumulador, ra, *n.* accumulator; (elec.) storage battery, accumulator.
acumular, *va.* to accumulate; to impute to, charge with; (law) to try or dispose of jointly.
acumulativamente, *adv.* cumulatively; (law) by way of prevention or precaution; jointly.
acumulativo, va, *a.* cumulative; joint.
acuñación, *f.* coining, minting; wedging.
acuñador, ra, *n.* coiner; wedge; (print.) shooting stick.
acuñar, *va.* to coin, mint; to wedge; (print.) to key, lock; to quoin.
acuosidad, *f.* wateriness.
acuoso, sa, aguoso, sa, *a.* watery, aqueous.
acupresión, *f.* (surg.) acupressure.
acupuntura, *f.* (surg.) acupuncture.
acure, *m.* (Venez.) Guinea pig.
acurrucarse, acorrucarse, *vr.* to huddle up.
acusación, *f.* accusation.
acusado, da, *n.* & *a.* defendant, accused.
acusador, ra, *n.* accuser; informer; prosecutor.
acusante, *a.* accusing, prosecuting.
acusar. I. *va.* to accuse; to prosecute; to indict; to acknowledge (receipt); at cards, to announce in due time that one holds certain cards that count so many points.—**a. las cuarenta,** to call out the forty honor points (at cards); (coll.) to give a piece of one's mind. **II.** *vr.* (**de**), to confess (to).
acusativo, *m.* & *a.* accusative.
acusatorio, ria, *a.* accusatory.
acuse, *m.* at cards, each of the cards duly announced in certain games.—**a. de recibo,** acknowledgment of receipt.
acusón, na, *a.* & *n.* (coll.) telltale, talebearer.
acústica, *f.* acoustics.

acústico, ca. I. *a.* acoustic; speaking (tube). II. *m.* acoustician; hearing aid.
acutángulo, *a.* (geom.) acute-angled.
acutí, *m.* (Arg.) agouti.
achacar, *va.* to impute.
achacosamente, *adv.* sickly.
achacoso, sa, *a.* sickly, ailing.
achaflanar, chaflanar, *va.* to chamfer, bevel.
achantarse, *vr.* (coll.) to hide during danger.
achaparrado, da, *a.* shrub-sized (tree).
achaparrarse, *vr.* (agr.) not to grow or thrive, to become stunted.
achaque, *m.* habitual indisposition; monthly courses; pregnancy; subject matter; excuse, pretext; frequent lapse or failing.—*pl.* matters.
achaquiento, ta, *a.* = ACHACOSO.
acharolado, da, *a.* japanned; japanlike.
acharolar, *va.* to japan; to enamel.
achatamiento, *m.* flattening.
achatar, *va.* to flatten.
achicado, da, *a.* childish.
achicador, ra, *m.* & *f.* diminisher; reducer; (naut.) scoop for bailing boats.
achicadura, *f.* diminution; (naut.) bailing.
achicamiento, *m.* = ACHICADURA.
achicar. I. *va.* to diminish, lessen; to humble, belittle; to bail, drain.—**a. el agua del navío,** to free the ship.—**a. un cabo,** to shorten a rope. II. *vr.* to humble oneself; to feel small.
achicoria, *f.* (bot.) chicory.
achicharrar, *va.* to fry too much; to overheat.
achichinque, *m.* (min.) scooper.
achilenado, da, *a.* (Peru) pro-Chilean.
achinado, da, *a.* (Arg.) plebeian; of dark reddish color.
achinar, *va.* (coll.) to intimidate, frighten.
achinelado, da, *a.* slipper-shaped.
achiote, *m.* (bot.) annatto tree; annatto (a dye).
achique, *m.* scooping, bailing, draining.
achispar. I. *va.* (coll.) to make tipsy. II. *vr.* to get tipsy.
achocadura, *f.* knock against an object.
achocar, *va.* to throw one against the wall; to knock asunder; (coll.) to hoard money.
achocolatado, da, *a.* chocolate-colored.
acholado, da, *a.* half Indian; half-breed.
achote, *m.* = ACHIOTE.
achubascarse, *vr.* (naut.) to become squally.
achucutarse, *vr.* (Am.) to become downhearted; to lose courage; to wither.
achuchar, achuchurrar, *va.* (coll.) to crush with a blow; to thrust; to push roughly, jostle.
achuchón, *m.* (coll.) push, squeeze.
achulado, da, *a.* (coll.) rough; tough.
achunchar, *va.* (Chile) to foil, frustrate.
achura, *f.* (Am.) gut (of cattle).
adáctilo, la, *a.* (zool.) adactylous.
adafina, *f.* stew eaten by the Jews in Spain.
[1]**adagio,** *m.* proverb, adage.
[2]**adagio,** *m.* (mus.) adagio.
adala, *f.* (naut.) pump dale.
adalid, *m.* chief, chieftain, leader.
adamado, da, *a.* effeminate, womanish.
adamantino, na, *a.* adamantine.
adamarse, *vr.* to become effeminate.
adamascado, da, *a.* damasklike.
adamascar, *va.* to damask.
adámico, ca, *a.* (geol.) (of sand or other deposit) accumulated by the tide.
adamita, *m.* Adamite, a nudist.
Adán, *m.* Adam; slovenly man.
adaptabilidad, *f.* adaptability, suitability.
adaptable, *a.* adaptable.
adaptación, *f.* adaptation.
adaptador, ra, *n.* & *a.* adapter(-ing).
adaptante, *a.* adapting.
adaptar. I. *va.* to adapt, fit. II. *vr.* to adapt oneself.
adaraja, *f.* (arch.) toothing.
adarce, *m.* dry sea froth.
adarga, *f.* oval leather shield.—**adargar,** *va.* to shield defend.—**adarguilla,** *f.* small shield.
adarme, *m.* half a drachm, 1/16 ounce (179 centigrams).—**por adarmes,** in driblets, stingily.
adarvar, *va.* to stun; to bewilder.
adarve, *m.* flat top of a wall.
adatar, *va.* to open an account; to credit.
adaza, *f.* (bot.) panic grass.
adecenamiento, *m.* formation with ten abreast.
adecenar, *va.* to form with ten abreast; to count by tens.
adecuación, *f.* fitness; adequateness.
adecuado, da. I. *pp.* of ADECUAR. II. *a.* adequate.
adecuar, *va.* to fit; to adapt.
adefagia, *f.* voracity.
adéfago, ga, *a.* voracious; (entom.) of the Adephaga, a beetle family.
adefesio, *m.* (coll.) nonsense, absurdity; blunder; queer person; ridiculous attire.
adefina, adafina, *f.* stew eaten by Spanish Jews.
adehala, *f.* gratuity, perquisite, tip.
adehesamiento, *m.* pasturage; turning into pasture.
adehesar, *va.* to convert land into pasture.
adelantadamente, *adv.* beforehand.
adelantado, da. I. *pp.* of ADELANTAR. II. *a.* anticipated; advanced; far ahead; proficient; precocious; bold, forward; (of a timepiece) fast; early (fruit, plants).—**por a.,** in advance. III. *m.* governor of a province.
adelantador, ra, *n.* one that advances, extends, or amplifies.
adelantamiento, *m.* progress; improvement, increase; furtherance; cultivation; anticipation; betterment, promotion.
adelantar. I. *va.* & *vn.* to progress, advance; to grow; to keep on; to anticipate; to pay beforehand; to improve; to go fast; (of a timepiece) to gain; to be fast; to set ahead. II. *vr.* to take the lead; to come forward;—**a. a,** to excel, outdo.
adelante, *adv.* ahead; farther on; forward, onward.—¡a! forward! go on! let's go! come in!—**de a.,** ahead, in the front; forward, head (as *a.*).—**de aquí en a., de hoy en a.,** or **en a.,** henceforth, from now on, in the future.—**llevar a.,** to go ahead with, carry on.—**más a.,** farther on.—**salir a.,** to come through, come out well or ahead.
adelanto, *m.* advance, progress; improvement; (com.) advanced payment.
adelfa, *f.* (bot.) rosebay.—**adelfal,** *m.* rosebay field.
adelgacé, adelgace, *v. V.* ADELGAZAR.
adelgazador, ra, *n.* one that makes thin or slender.
adelgazamiento, *m.* slenderness, thinness.
adelgazar. I. *va.* (*pret.* ADELGACÉ; *subj.* ADELGACE) to attenuate, make thin, slender; to lessen; to taper; to split hairs. II. *vr.* to become thin or slender.
adema, *f.* (min.) shore; strut; prop.
ademador, ra, *n.* (min.) one who props.
ademán, *m.* gesture, look, manner; attitude.—*pl.* manners.—**en a. de, as if getting ready, or going, to, showing an intention of.**
ademar, *va.* (min.) to shore.
además, *adv.* moreover, furthermore, besides; exceedingly, too.—**a. de,** besides, in addition to.
ademe, *m.* = ADEMA.
adenia, *f.* (med.) adenia.
adenitis, *f.* (med.) adenitis, gland inflammation.
adenografía, *f.* (anat.) adenography.
adenoidectomía, *f.* (surg.) adenoidectomy.
adenoideo, dea, *a.* adenoid.—**tumor a., vegetación a.,** adenoids.
adenología, *f.* (anat.) adenology.
adenoma, *m.* (med.) adenoma.
adenopatía, *f.* adenopathy.
adentellar, *va.* to bite, catch with the teeth.—**a. una pared,** to leave toothing stones or bricks in a wall to continue it.
adentro. I. *adv.* within, inside. II. *interj.* come

in!, let's go in! **III.** *m.* (in the *pl.*) the innermost thoughts.
adepto, ta, *a.* adept; initiated.
aderecé, aderece, *v.* *V.* ADEREZAR.
aderezamiento, *m.* embellishment; dressing.
aderezar, *va.* (*pret.* ADERECÉ; *subj.* ADERECE) to dress, embellish, adorn; to prepare; to cook, season; to clean; to repair; to mix (drinks); to blend (wines); to gum (silk); to size (goods).
aderezo, *m.* dressing; adorning; finery; gum, starch, used to stiffen cloth; set of jewelry; trappings of a saddle horse; furniture; hilt, hook, and other appendages of a sword.
aderra, *f.* rush rope.
adestrado, da. I. *pp.* of ADESTRAR. **II.** *a.* (her.) on the dexter side of the escutcheon.
adestrador, ra, *n.* teacher, trainer; censor, critic.
adestramiento, *m.* = ADIESTRAMIENTO.
adestrar. I. *va.* (*ind.* ADIESTRO; *subj.* ADIESTRE to guide, lead; to teach, train. **II.** *vr.* to practice, train.
adeudado, da. I. *pp.* of ADEUDAR **II.** *a.* indebted; in debt.
adeudar. I. *va.* to owe; to be dutiable; (com.) to charge, debit. **II.** *vr.* to run into debt.
adeudo, *m.* indebtedness; custom house duty; (com.) debit; charge.
adherencia, *f.* adhesion; adherence; relationship; bond.
adherente. I. *a.* adhesive, adhering; attached. **II.** *n.* follower, adherent. **III.** *m.* (gen. *pl.*) accessory; equipment.
adherir, *va.* & *vr.* (*ind.* ADHIERO; *subj.* ADHIERA) to adhere; to stick.
adhesión, *f.* adhesion; following, adherence.
adhesividad, *f.* concentration of mind; love o one's fellow beings.
adhesivo, va, *m.* & *a.* adhesive.
adhiero, adhiera, *v.* *V.* ADHERIR.
adiabático, ca, *a.* adiabatic.
adiafa, *f.* tip given to seamen at end of a voyage
adiaforesis, *f.* (med.) adiaphoresis.
adiamantado, da, *a.* adamantine.
adiamantar, *va.* to adorn with diamonds.
adianto, *m.* (bot.) adiantum, maidenhair fern.
adición, *f.* addition; remark or note put to accounts.—**a. de la herencia,** acceptance of an inheritance.—**adicional,** *a.* additional.
adicionar, *va.* to make additions in, add to; to extend, prolong.
adicto, ta, *n.* & *a.* addicted, devoted; follower, supporter.
adiestrador, ra, *a.* = ADESTRADOR.
adiestramiento, *m.* guiding; teaching, training; practice.
adiestrar, *va.* = ADESTRAR.
adiestro, adiestre, *v.* *V.* ADESTRAR.
adietar, *va.* to put on a diet.
adifés, *adv.* (Venez.) on purpose.
adinamia, *f.* adynamia, debility, prostration.
adinámico, ca, *a.* adynamic.
adinerado, da, *a.* rich, wealthy.
adinerar. I. *va.* to convert into cash, realize. **II.** *vr.* to get rich.
adintelado, da, *a.* (arch.) falling from an arch gradually into a straight line.
adiós, *interj.* good-bye, adieu.
adipocira, *f.* adipocere; waxy substance from buried animals.
adiposidad, *f.* adiposity.
adiposis, *f.* (med.) adiposis.
adiposo, sa, *a.* adipose.
adir, *va.* to accept (an inheritance).
aditamento, *m.* addition.—**por a.,** in addition, into the bargain.
aditivo, va, *m.* & *a.* additive.
adiva, *f.* **adive,** *m.* jackal.
adivas, *m. pl.* (vet.) vives, fives, the strangles.
adivinación, *f.* divination.—**a. del pensamiento,** mind reading, mental telepathy.
adivinador, ra, *n.* & *a.* diviner, soothsayer.
adivinaja, *f.* puzzle, conundrum.
adivinanza, *f.* prophecy; riddle; guess.
adivinar, *va.* to foretell; to divine, guess; to solve (a riddle).
adivino, na, *n.* soothsayer; fortune teller; wizard; guesser.
adjetivación, *f.* adjectival use or function; (gram.) agreement.
adjetivadamente, *adv.* adjectively.
adjetival, *a.* adjectival.
adjetivar, *va.* & *vr.* to use, or be used, adjectively; (gram.) to make agree.
adjetivo, va, *n.* & *a.* adjective.—**a. calificativo,** qualifying adjective.—**a. comparativo,** comparative adjective.—**a. determinativo,** limiting adjective.—**a. gentilicio,** proper adjective.
adjudicación, *f.* adjudgment, adjudication.
adjudicador, ra, *n.* & *a.* adjudicator(-ing).
adjudicar. I. *va.* to adjudge, adjudicate. **II.** *vr.* to appropriate.—**adjudicativo, va,** *a.* adjudicative.—**adjudicatario, ria,** *n.* grantee.
adjunción, *f.* (law) adjunction.
adjuntar, *va.* (Am.) to enclose, send enclosed or with something else.
adjunto, ta. I. *a.* joined, annexed, enclosed, attached, adjunct. **II.** *m.* adjective; addition.
adjutor, ra, *a.* & *n.* helper(-ing), assistant(-ing).
adminicular, *va.* to strengthen, reinforce, corroborate.
adminículo, *m.* auxiliary; helper.—*pl.* small things carried for emergencies.
administración, *f.* administration, management; office of an administrator.—**a. activa,** executive action.—**a. económica,** treasury department.—**a. militar,** commissariat.—**a. pública,** public administration.—**en a.,** in trust.—**por a.,** by the government; officially; by the management, company, firm, etc.
administrador, ra, *n.* administrator, manager; director, trustee.—**a. de aduanas,** collector of customs.—**a. de correos,** postmaster.—**a. municipal,** (U. S.) city manager.
administrar, *va.* to administer.
administrativamente, *adv.* administratively.
administrativo, va, *a.* administrative.
admirable, *a.* admirable, excellent.
admiración, *f.* admiration, wonder; exclamation point (! ¡).
admirado, da, *a.* admiring.
admirador, ra, *n.* admirer.
admirar. I. *va.* to admire. **II.** *vr.* to wonder; to be surprised, amazed.—**a. de,** to be surprised at; to regard with admiration, wonder at.
admirativo, va, *a.* admiring; admirable; filled with admiration.
admisibilidad, *f.* admissibility.
admisible, *a.* admissible.
admisión, *f.* admission, acceptance.
admitancia, *f.* (elec.) admittance.
admitir, *va.* to receive; to admit, grant; to accept; to permit.
admixtión, *f.* admixture.
admonición, *f.* admonition, warning, advice.
admonitor, *m.* monitor (esp. in some religious communities).
adnata, *f.* (anat.) conjunctiva, the external white membrane of the eye.
adnato, ta, *a.* adnate.
adobado, da. I. *pp.* of ADOBAR. **II.** *m.* pickled pork.
adobador, ra, *n.* dresser, preparer.
adobar, *va.* to dress, prepare or cook (food); to pickle (meat); to tan or dress (hides).
adobe, *m.* adobe, unburnt sun-dried brick.
adobera, *f.* mold for adobe; brick-shaped cheese, and mold for it.
adobería, *f.* brickyard; tannery.
adobo, *m.* repairing, mending; pickle sauce; dressing for seasoning; ingredients for dressing leather or cloth; pomade.

adocenado, da. I. *pp.* of ADOCENAR. II. *a.* common, ordinary, vulgar.
adocenar, *va.* to count or sell by dozens; to depreciate, underrate.
adoctrinamiento, *m.* indoctrination.
adoctrinar, *va.* to instruct, indoctrinate.
adolecer. I. *vn.* (*ind.* ADOLEZCO; *subj.* ADOLEZCA) to become ill.—**a. de,** to suffer from, be ill with; to be subject to. II. *vr.* to condole.
adolescencia, *f.* adolescence.
adolescente, *n.* & *a.* adolescent.
adolezco, adolezca, *v.* *V.* ADOLECER.
adolorido, da, dolorido, da, *a.* painful; doleful.
adonde (**adónde,** when *interr.*), *adv.* where, whither.
adondequiera, *adv.* wherever, anywhere, everywhere.
adónico, ca, *m.* & *a.* Adonic (verse).
adopción, *f.* adoption.—**adopcionismo,** *m.* adoptionism, an ancient Spanish sect.—**adopcionista,** *a.* adhering or pert. to adoptionism.
adoptable, *a.* adoptable.
adoptado, da, *a.* adopted.
adoptador, ra, *n.* adopter.
adoptante, *n.* & *a.* adopter(-ing).
adoptar, *va.* to adopt; to embrace (an opinion).
adoptivo, va, *a.* adoptive.
adoquín, *m.* paving stone or tile.—**adoquinado,** *m.* pavement.—**adoquinar,** *va.* to pave.
ador, *m.* time for watering land, where water is officially distributed.
adorable, *a.* adorable.
adoración, *f.* adoration, worship.
adorador, ra; adorante, *n.* adorer, worshipper.
adorar, *va.* to adore, worship.
adoratorio, *m.* Am. Indian temple for an idol.
adormecedor, ra, *a.* soporific, sleep-inducing.
adormecer. I. *va.* (*ind.* ADORMEZCO; *subj.* ADORMEZCA) to cause drowsiness or sleep; to lull to sleep; to calm, lull. II. *vr.* to fall asleep; to grow benumbed; to persist in vice.
adormecido, da. I. *pp.* of ADORMECER. II. *a.* langorous, sluggish; drowsy.
adormecimiento, *m.* drowsiness, sleepiness, numbness.
adormezco, adormezca, *v.* *V.* ADORMECER.
adormidera, *f.* (bot.) poppy.
adormir, *va.* & *vr.* (*ind. pres.* ADUERMO, *pret.* él ADURMIÓ; *subj.* ADUERMA) = ADORMECER.
adormitarse, *vr.* to doze, drowse.
adornado, da, *a.* ornamented, adorned.
adornador, ra, *n.* adorner, decorator.
adornamiento, *m.* embellishment, decoration.
adornar, *va.* to adorn, embellish, decorate, ornament, trim; to furnish, garnish; to be a gift or an accomplishment of.—**a. de,** to adorn with.
adornista, *m.* painter, decorator.
adorno, *m.* adornment; ornament; trimming; accomplishment.
adosar, *va.* to put on or near (something); to paste (as on a wall).
adquiero, adquiera, *v.* *V.* ADQUIRIR.
adquirente, adquiriente, *n.* acquirer.
adquirible, *a.* acquirable.
adquiridor, ra, *n.* acquirer.
adquirir, *va.* (*ind.* ADQUIERO; *subj.* ADQUIERA) to acquire, obtain, get.
adquisición, *f.* acquisition; attainment.
adquisidor, ra, *n.* = ADQUIRIDOR.
adquisitivo, va, *a.* that helps to acquire.
adquisividad, *f.* acquisitiveness.
adra, *f.* turn (in succession); portion of the population of a town.
adraganto, *m.* tragacanth, a gummy substance.
adrales, *m. pl.* hurdles, side boards (of a wagon).
adrede, adredemente, *adv.* purposely.
adrenalina, *f.* (chem.) adrenaline.
adresógrafo, *m.* Addressograph (trademark).
adrián, *m.* bunion; a magpie's nest.
adriático, ca, *a.* Adriatic.
adrizar, *va.* (naut.) to right.
adscribir, *va.* (*pp. irreg.* ADSCRIPTO, ADSCRITO) to inscribe; to add as an employee.
adscripción, *f.* inscription; appointment; adscription.
adscripto, ta, adscrito, ta. I. *irreg. pp.* of ADSCRIBIR. II. *a.* adscript, written after.
adsorbato, *m.* adsorbate.
adsorbente. I. *a.* adsorptive. II. *m.* adsorbent.
adsorber, *va.* to adsorb.
adsorción, *f.* adsorption.
aduana, *f.* custom house.
aduanar, *va.* to pass or put through (goods) at the custom house; to pay duty on.
aduanero, ra. I. *a.* custom house, customs (as *a.*). II. *m.* custom house officer; revenue officer.
aduanilla, *f.* food store.
aduar, *m.* Arab village or settlement; gipsy camp.
adúcar, *m.* coarse silk from outer part of cocoon; the stuff made from that silk.
aducción, *f.* adduction.
aducir, *va.* (*ind. pres.* ADUZCO, *pret.* ADUJE; *subj.* ADUZCA) to adduce, bring up in argument.
aductor, *m.* (anat.) adductor (muscle).
aduendado, da, *a.* fairylike.
adueñarse, *vr.* to take possession.
aduermo, aduerma, *v.* *V.* ADORMIR.
adufe, *m.* timbrel or tambourine.
adufero, ra, *n.* tambourine player.
adujadas, adujas, *f. pl.* (naut.) coil, coiled cable.
adujar, *va.* (naut.) to coil (a cable).
aduje, adujo, *v.* *V.* ADUCIR.
adula, dula, *f.* common pasture.
adulación, *f.* fawning, adulation.
adulador, ra, *n.* fawner, adulator, cringer.
adular, *va.* & *vn.* to adulate, flatter fawningly; to cringe to; to fawn, creep, crouch, grovel.
adulatorio, ria, *a.* flattering, honey-mouthed.
adulón, na, *n.* & *a.* toady, cringer(-ing).
adúltera, *f.* adulteress.
adulteración, *f.* adulteration.
adulterado, da, *a.* adulterate.
adulterador, ra, adulterante, *n.* & *a.* adulterator(-ing), adulterant; falsifier.
adulterar. I. *va.* to adulterate; to corrupt. II. *vn.* to commit adultery.
adulterino, na, *a.* adulterous; begotten in adultery; adulterated, falsified, forged.
adulterio, *m.* adultery.
adúltero, ra. I. *a.* adulterous. II. *n.* adulterer; *f.* adulteress.
adulto, ta, *n.* & *a.* adult.
adulzar, *va.* to render (metals) more ductile.
adumbración, *f.* adumbration, shade in a picture.
adunar, *va.* to unite, join; to unify.
adunco, ca, *a.* aduncous; curved; warped.
adunia, *adv.* abundantly.
adusto, ta, *a.* austere, stern, sullen.
aduzco, aduzca, *v.* *V.* ADUCIR.
advección, *f.* (meteorol.) advection.
advenedizo, za, *n.* & *a.* foreign(-er), newly arrived, immigrant; upstart, parvenu.
advenimiento, *m.* arrival; advent.
advenir, *vn.* to come; to arrive.
adventicio, cia, *a.* adventitious, accidental; (law) acquired by industry, (law) adventitious.
adveración, *f.* (law) averment.
adverbial, *a.* adverbial.—**adverbialmente,** *adv.* adverbially.
adverbio, *m.* adverb.
adversario, *m.* adversary, opponent; foe.
adversativo, va, *a.* (gram.) adversative.
adversidad, *f.* adversity, misfortune.
adverso, sa, *a.* adverse; calamitous; opposite, facing
advertencia, *f.* admonition, warning; remark, notice; foreword.
advertidamente, *adv.* advisedly, deliberately.
advertido, da. I. *pp.* of ADVERTIR. II. *a.* noticed; skilful; intelligent; expert; clever.

advertir, *va.* (*ind. pres.* ADVIERTO, *pret.* él ADVIRTIÓ; *subj.* ADVIERTA) to take notice of; to observe; to instruct, advise, give notice or warning; to acquaint; to mark, note.
adviento, *m.* Advent, the four weeks before Christmas.
advierto, advierta, advirtió, *v. V.* ADVERTIR.
advocación, *f.* appellation given to a church, chapel, or altar, dedicated to the Virgin or a saint.
adyacencia, *f.* adjacency, contiguity.
adyacente, *a.* adjacent.
aechadero, aechar, etc. = AHECHADERO, AHECHAR, etc.
aeración, *f.* aeration, charging with gas or with air; (med.) action of atmospheric air in the treatment of disease.
aéreo, rea, *a.* aerial; overhead; elevated; air (as *a.*, as in **fuerzas aéreas,** air forces); (fig.) airy, fantastic.—**por correo a.,** by airmail.
aerífero, ra, *a.* aeriferous, conveying air.
aerificar, *va.* to gasify; to aerify, aerate.
aeriforme, *a.* aeriform, gaseous.
aerobio. I. *a.* aerobic. **II.** *m.* aerobe.
aerobiosis, *f.* (biol.) aerobiosis.
aerobús, *m.* aerobus.
aerocisto, *m.* (bot.) aerocyst.
aerodinámica, *f.* aerodynamics.
aerodinámico, ca, *a.* streamline(d).
aeródromo, *m.* airdrome, aerodrome.
aeroembolismo, *m.* (med.) aeroembolism.
aeroespacial, *a.* aerospace.
aerofagia, *f.* (med.) aerophagia.
aerofobia, *f.* aerophobia morbid dread of air.
aeróforo, *m.* (med.) aerophore.
aerofoto, *m.* or *f.* aerophotograph.
aerofotografía, *f.* aerophotography, aerial photography; aerophotograph.
aerografía, *f.* aerography.
aerógrafo, *m.* aerographer; airbrush.
aerograma, *m.* wireless message, radiogram.
aerolito, *m.* aerolite, meteoric stone.
aerología, *f.* aerology.
aerólogo, *m.* aerologist.
aeromancia, *f.* aeromancy.
aeromántico, *m.* aeromancer.
aeromecánico, ca. I. *a.* aeromechanical. **II.** *f.* aeromechanics.
aeromedicina, *f.* aeromedicine.
aerometría, *f.* aerometry, pneumatics.
aerométrico, ca, *a.* aerometric.
aerómetro, *m.* aerometer.
aeromodelista, *n.* one who constructs model airplanes.
aeromoza, *f.* (aer.) stewardess.
aeronauta, *m.* aeronaut.
aeronáutica, *f.* aeronautics.
aeronáutico, ca, *a.* aeronautic.
aeronave, *f.* airship, dirigible.
aeronavegabilidad, *f.* airworthiness.
aeropausa, *f.* (meteorol.) aeropause.
aeroplano, *m.* aeroplane, airplane.
aeropostal, *a.* air-mail.
aeropuerto, *m.* airport.
aeroscopia, *f.* aerology.
aeroscopio, *m.* aeroscope.
aerosol, *m.* aerosol.
aerostación, *f.* aerostation, air navigation.
aerostática, *f.* aerostatics.
aerostático, ca, *a.* aerostatic.
aeróstato, *m.* aerostat, dirigible.
aerostero, ra, *a.* aviation (as *a.*), aeronautic.
aeroterapia, *f.* aerotherapeutics.
aerotransportado, da, *a.* air-borne.
aeta, *m.* mountain tribe in P. I.; their language.
afabilidad, *f.* affability.
afable, *a.* affable, pleasant.—**afablemente,** *adv.* affably.
áfaca, *f.* (bot.) yellow vetch.
afamado, da, *a.* celebrated, noted, famous.
afamar, *va.* to make famous, give fame to.
afán, *m.* anxiety, solicitude, eagerness.
afanadamente, *adv.* anxiously, laboriously, eagerly.
afanador, ra, *n.* & *a.* eager; painstaker(-ing); hustler(-ing); hurrier(-ying); laborious, toilsome.
afanar. I. *va.* to press, urge, hurry. **II.** *vn.* & *vr.* to act or work eagerly or anxiously; to toil.
afaníptero, ra. I. *a.* (entom.) aphanipterous. **II.** *m. pl.* Aphaniptera.
afanita, *f.* (min.) amphibolite, kind of rock.
afanosamente, *adv.* = AFANADAMENTE.
afanoso, sa, *a.* solicitous; laborious, painstaking; arduous, hard, difficult.
afarolarse, *vr.* (Am., coll.) to become unduly excited, (coll.) to make a fuss; to lose one's temper, (coll.) to get hot under the collar.
afarollonado, da, *a.* steep, cliffy.
afasia, *f.* aphasia.
afásico, ca, *a.* aphasic.
afeador, ra, *n.* & *a.* (something or someone) deforming, distorting or making ugly.
afeamiento, *m.* defacing; ugliness.
afear, *va.* to deform, deface; to make ugly or faulty; to impair; to decry; to condemn.
afeblecerse, *vr.* to grow feeble or delicate.
afección, *f.* affection, fondness; (med.) affection.
afección gastrointestinal, *f.* gastrointestinal disease.
afectación, *f.* affectation.
afectado, da. I. *pp.* of AFECTAR. **II.** *a.* affected.
afectador, ra, *n.* one who acts affectedly.
afectar. I. *va.* to affect, have an effect on; to affect, feign, put on; (law) to charge, impose, encumber. **II.** *vr.* to be moved; to be shocked.
afectividad, *f.* affection; (psych.) affectivity.
afectivo, va, *a.* affective.
afecto. I. *m.* affection, love, fondness. **II.** *a.* affectionate; (a) fond (of), inclined (to); (law) subject to charge or encumbrance.
afectuosidad, *f.* fondness, affection.
afectuoso, sa, *a.* affectionate.
afeitada, *f.* (Am.) shave, shaving.
afeitar. I. *va.* to shave; to beautify, embellish, make up; to trim (a tree, the tail, mane of a horse). **II.** *vr.* to shave (oneself); to make up.
afeite, *m.* paint, rouge, cosmetic; make-up.
afelio, *m.* (astr.) aphelion.
afelpado, da, *a.* plushlike or velvetlike.
afeminación, *f.* effeminacy; emasculation.
afeminado, da. I. *pp.* of AFEMINAR. **II.** *a.* effeminate.
afeminamiento, *m.* = AFEMINACIÓN.
afeminar, *va.* to make effeminate; to unman.
aferente, *a.* afferent.
aféresis, *f.* (gram.) aphæresis, omission of one or more initial letters of a word.
aferrado, da. I. *pp.* of AFERRAR. **II.** *a.* headstrong.
aferrador, ra, *n.* one that grapples or grasps.
aferramiento, *m.* grasping, grappling, seizing or binding; obstinacy.—**a. de las velas,** (naut.) furling of the sails.
aferrar. I. *va.* to grasp, seize; (naut.) to furl; to moor; to anchor. **II.** *vr.* to fasten to each other; to interlock; (**a** or **en**) to persist obstinately or persistently (in).
aferruzado, da. *a.* angry, irate.
afesis, *f.* (gram.) aphesis.
afestonado, da, *a.* festooned.
Afganistán, *m.* Afghanistan.
afgano, na, *n.* & *a.* Afghan.
afiancé, afiance, *v. V.* AFIANZAR.
afianzado, da, *n.* (law) warrantee.
afianzamiento, *m.* security, guarantee, bail; prop, support; fastening, securing.
afianzar, *va.* (*pret.* AFIANCÉ; *subj.* AFIANCE) to become bail or security for; to guarantee; to prop; to make fast, clinch.
afición, *f.* affection, fondness; taste, inclination; eagerness, enthusiasm.—**tomar a. a,** to take a liking to, become fond of.

aficionadamente, *adv.* fondly; amateurishly.
aficionado, da. I. *pp.* of AFICIONAR. **II.** (sport) *n.* & *a.* amateur; fan.—**a. a,** fond of, having a taste for.
aficionar. I. *va.* to cause or inspire affection fondness or liking. **II.** *vr.* (**a**) to fancy; to become fond of.
afidávit, *m.* affidavit.
áfido, afídido, *m.* (entom.) aphid.
afijo, ja. (gram.) **I.** *a.* affixal. **II.** *m.* affix.
afiladera, *f.* whetstone.
afilado. I. *pp.* of AFILAR. **II.** *a.* sharp, keen.
afiladura, *f.* sharpening, whetting.
afilamiento, *m.* slenderness of the face, nose, or fingers.
afilar. I. *va.* to whet, grind, sharpen; to render keen. **II.** *vr.* to grow thin.
afiliación, *f.* affiliation.
afiliado, da. I. *a.* affiliated; adopted. **II.** *n.* affiliate.
afiliar. I. *va.* (**a**) to affiliate (with). **II.** *vr.* (**a**) to join, affiliate oneself (with).
afiligranado, da, *a.* filigree, filigreed; slender, thin; delicate, neat; dainty.
afiligranar, *va.* to make filigree work; to polish, embellish.
áfilo, la, *a.* (bot.) leafless.
afilón, *m.* steel, knife sharpener; razor strop.
afilosofado, da, *a.* putting on airs of a philosopher.
afín. I. *a.* close by, contiguous; related. **II.** *m.* relation by affinity.
afinación, *f.* completion, finishing touch, refining; tuning.
afinadamente, *adv.* perfectly; delicately.
afinador, ra, *n.* finisher; piano tuner; tuning key.
afinadura, *m.* = AFINACIÓN.
afinamiento, *m.* AFINACIÓN; refinement.
afinar. I. *va.* to complete; to polish; to refine (metals); to trim (binding); to tune. **II.** *vr.* to become polished.
afincar, fincar, *vn.* & *vr.* to acquire real estate.
afine, *a.* = AFÍN.
afinidad, *f.* analogy, resemblance; relationship by marriage; (chem.) affinity.
afino, *m.* refinement (of metals).
afirmación, *f.* affirmation.
afirmadamente, *adv.* firmly.
afirmador, ra, afirmante, *n.* & *a.* afirmer(-ing).
afirmar. I. *va.* to make fast, secure, fasten; to affirm, assert, contend. **II.** *vr.* to hold fast; to steady oneself or make oneself firm; to maintain firmly.
afirmativo, va, *f.* & *a.* affirmative.
afistular, *va.* (med.) to render fistulous.
aflato, *m.* afflatus, inspiration.
aflechada, *a.* arrow-shaped (leaf).
aflicción, *f.* affliction, sorrow, grief.
aflictivo, va, *a.* afflictive, distressing.
aflicto, ta, *pp. irreg.* of AFLIGIR.
afligidamente, *adv.* sorrowfully, sadly.
afligido, da, *a.* anguished.
afligir. I. *va.* (*pp. irreg.* AFLICTO; *ind.* AFLIJO; *subj.* AFLIJA) to afflict, cause pain. **II.** *vr.* to grieve, languish, become despondent, lose heart.
aflijón, na, *a.* (Am., coll.) gloomy-tempered, ever-weeping.
aflojadura, *f.*, **aflojamiento,** *m.* relaxation; loosening, slackening.
aflojar. I. *va.* to loosen, slacken, relax, let loose; to relent; to debilitate.—**a. los obenques,** (naut.) to ease the shrouds. **II.** *vn.* to grow weak; to abate. **III.** *vr.* to grow cool in fervor or zeal; to lose courage.
aflorado, *a.* FLOREADO, (of bread) made of the finest flour; flowered, figured.
afloramiento, *m.* (min.) outcrop.
aflorar, *vn.* to crop out.
afluencia, *f.* plenty, abundance; fluency.
afluente. I. *a.* affluent, copious, abundant; loquacious. **II.** *m.* affluent, tributary.
afluir, *vn.* (*ind.* AFLUYO; *subj.* AFLUYA) (**a**) to congregate, assemble (in): to flow (into).
[1]**aflujo,** *m.* (med.) afflux, affluxion.
[2]**afluyo, afluya,** *v. V.* AFLUIR.
afofar, *va.* & *vr.* to make (become) spongy or light.
afogarar, *va.* = ASURAR, to burn, scorch.
afollar, *va.* (*ind.* AFUELLO; *subj.* AFUELLE) to blow with bellows.
afondar, *va., vn., vr.* to submerge; (naut.) to sink, founder.
afonía, *f.* (med.) aphonia.
afónico, ca, áfono, na, *a.* aphonic.
aforado. I. *pp.* of AFORAR. **II.** *a.* privileged, favored.
aforador, *m.* gauger; appraiser.
aforamiento, *m.* the giving of privileges.
aforar, *va.* to gauge, measure; to appraise; to give privileges (in this meaning: *ind.* AFUERO; *subj.* AFUERE).
aforestación, *f.* afforestation.
aforismo, *m.* aphorism, maxim.
aforístico, ca, *a.* aphoristical.
aforo, *m.* gauging; appraisal.
aforrador, ra, *n.* one who lines clothes.
aforrar. I. *va.* to line (clothes, vessels, tubes, etc.); (naut.) to sheathe.—**a. un cabo,** (naut.) to serve a cable. **II.** *vr.* to put on heavy underclothing; to gorge.—**aforro,** *m.* lining; (naut.) sheathing; (naut.) waist of a ship.
afortunado, da. I. *pp.* of AFORTUNAR. **II.** *a.* fortunate, lucky.
afortunar, *va.* to make happy.
afosarse, *vr.* (mil.) to entrench, "to dig in."
afoscarse, *vr.* to become hazy.
afrailar, *va.* (agr.) to prune (trees).
afrancesado, da. *a.* Frenchified, Frenchlike.
afrancesar. I. *va.* to Gallicize; to give a French termination to (words). **II.** *vr.* to be or become Frenchified; to be naturalized in France.
afrecho, *m.* bran.
afrenillar, *vn.* (naut.) to bridle (the oars).
afrenta, *f.* affront, outrage; disgrace.
afrentar. I. *va.* to affront; to insult. **II.** *vr.* to be ashamed; to blush.
afrentoso, sa, *a.* ignominious.
afretar, *va.* to scrub and clean.
Africa, *f.* Africa.
africado, da. I. *a.* affricative. **II.** *f.* (phon.) affricate.
africano, na, *n.* & *a.* African.
áfrico, ábrego, *m.* southwest wind.
afroamericano, na, *n.* & *a.* Afro-American.
afrobrasileño, ña, *n.* & *a.* Afro-Brazilian.
afrocubano, na, *n.* & *a.* Afro-Cuban.
afrodisia, *f.* (med.) aphrodisia.
afrodisíaco, ca, *n.* & *a.* aphrodisiac.
afrontar, *va.* to confront; to face.
afta, *f.* (med.) aphthæ, thrush.
aftoso, sa, *a.* (med.) aphthous.
afuello, afuelle, *v. V.* AFOLLAR.
afuera. I. *adv.* out; outside; in public.—**¡a.!** one side! clear the way! **II.** *f. pl.* suburbs, outskirts.
afuero, afuere, *v. V.* AFORAR.
afuetear, *va.* (Am.) to horsewhip.
afufa, *f.* (coll.) flight.—**afufar,** *vn.* & *vr.* (coll.) to run away; to escape.
afusión, *f.* affusion, shower bath.
afuste, *m.* (milit.) gun carriage.—**a. de mortero,** mortar bed.
agachadiza, *f.* (ornith.) snipe.—**hacer la a.,** (coll.) to hide (oneself).
agachar. I. *va.* to lower, bow down. **II.** *vr.* to stoop, squat, crouch, cower.—**a. las orejas,** (coll.) to humble oneself, bend the knee; to be dejected or crestfallen.
agalbanado, da, *a.* = GALBANOSO, indolent.
agalerar, *va.* (naut.) to tip (an awning).
agáloco, *m.* (bot.) aloes wood.
agalla, *f.* (bot.) gallnut; (anat.) tonsil; (vet.) windgalls of a horse; beaks of a shuttle; ear lobe (of a bird); gill (of a fish);—*pl.* (coll.)

courage; cheek, gall.—**a. de ciprés,** cypress gall.—**tener a.,** to have vim, be enterprising; (Am.) to be greedy; (Colomb. & Ecua.) to be stingy; (Peru) to be shrewd, cunning, wily.
agallado, da, *a.* steeped in an infusion of gall.
agallón, *m.* large gallnut.—**agallones,** *pl.* strings of hollow silver beads; wooden rosary beads.
agalludo, da, *a.* (Am.) stingy; cunning, foxy; brave.
agalluela, *f. dim.* of AGALLA.
ágama, *m.* (zool.) agama.
agamí, *m.* (Am.) (ornith.) trumpeter.
ágamo, ma, *a.* (biol.) agamic, asexual.
agamogénesis, *f.* (biol.) agamogenesis.
agamuzado, da, *a.* chamois-colored.
agangrenarse, gangrenarse, *vr.* to gangrene.
ágape, *m.* agape, love feast of early Christians; banquet.
agar-agar, *m.* or *f.* agar-agar.
agarbado, da, *a.* = GARBOSO, graceful, airy.
agarbarse, *vr.* to bend, stoop down, crouch.
agarbillar, *v.* = AGAVILLAR.
agareno, na, *a.* Mohammedan.
agárico, *m.* (bot.) agaric.
agarrada, *f.* (coll.) wrangle, scrap, scuffle.
agarradero, *m.* holder, handle; (coll.) protection, patronage; (naut.) anchorage.
agarrado, da. I. *pp.* of AGARRAR. **II.** *a.* stingy, close-fisted.
agarrador, ra, *n.* one that grasps or seizes; flatiron-holder; catch-pole; bailiff.
agarrafar, *va.* (coll.) to grab hard in a scuffle.
agarrar. I. *va.* to grasp, seize; (coll.) to obtain; to come upon. **II.** *vr.* to clinch, grapple, hold on.—**agarro,** *m.* grasp.
agarrochador, *m.* pricker, goader.
agarrochar, agarrochear, *va.* to prick with a pike or spear; to goad.
agarrón, *m.* fight, scrap, scuffle, encounter.
agarrotar, *va.* to compress with ropes; to garrote, execute with the garrote; to strangle.
agasajador, ra, *a.* kind, obliging.
agasajar, *va.* to receive and treat kindly; to fondle; to regale; to entertain.—**agasajo,** *m.* friendly treatment, kindness; consideration, regard; friendly present; afternoon refreshment.
ágata, *f.* agate.
agavanzo, *m.,* **agavanza,** *f.* (bot.) dog-rose.
agave, *m.* (bot.) agave; (commonly but erroneously) pita.
agavillar. I. *va.* to bind or tie in sheaves. **II.** *vr.* (coll.) to associate with a gang of sharpers.
agazapar. I. *va.* (coll.) to nab a person. **II.** *vr.* to hide oneself: to crouch.
agencia, *f.* agency; ministration, commission; agent's bureau, office; diligence.
agencia de colocación, *f.* employment agency.
agenciar, *va.* to solicit, promote, negotiate.
agencioso, sa, *a.* diligent, active.
agenda, *f.* notebook, memorandum book.
agenesia, *f.* (med.) impotence, agenesis.
agente, *m.* agent; solicitor, attorney.—**a. de bolsa, de cambio,** or **de cambio y bolsa,** exchange notary.—**a. de cambios,** bill broker. —**a. de negocios,** promoter.—**a. de policía,** policeman.—**a. fiscal,** assistant attorney.—**a. provocador,** (Gal.) agent provocateur.—**a. reductor,** (chem.) reducing agent.—**a. secreto,** secret agent.
agerasia, *f.* old age free from ailments.
agérato, *m.* (bot.) sweet milfoil or maudlin.
agestado, da (bien, mal), *a.* (well-, ill-) featured.
agibílibus, *m.* (coll.) cleverness, slickness; clever or slick person.
agible, *a.* feasible, practicable.
agigantado, da, *a.* gigantic; extraordinary.
ágil, *a.* nimble, fast, light.—**agilidad,** *f.* agility, nimbleness, sprightliness.—**agilitar,** *va.* to render nimble; to make active.—**ágilmente,** *adv.* nimbly, sprightly.
agio, agiotaje, *m.* (com.) exchange of paper money for coin, or coin for bills; premium: stockjobbing; usury; jobbing.
agiotador, ra; agiotista, *n.* money changer; bill broker; stockjobber; usurer.
agitable, *a.* agitable; that can be shaken.
agitación, *f.* agitation; excitement.
agitador, ra, *n.* & *a.* agitator(-ing), stirrer(-ing).
agitanado, da, *a.* gipsylike; bewitching.
agitar. I. *va.* to agitate; to stir, shake up; to ruffle. **II.** *vr.* to flutter; to become excited.
aglobar, *va.* to pile, put together.
aglomeración, *f.* agglomeration.
aglomerado, *m.* coal brick, made with coal dust and tar.
aglomerar, *va.* to agglomerate.
aglutinación, *f.* agglutination.
aglutinante. I. *a.* agglutinating, cementing. **II.** *m.* cementing material; (med.) sticking plaster.
aglutinar, *va,* to stick, cement, agglutinate.
agnación, *f.* (law) agnation.
agnado, da, *n.* & *a.* agnate.
agnaticio, cia, *a.* agnatic.
agnición, *f.* (rhet.) recognition of a person in a poem or drama.
agnocasto, *m.* = SAUZGATILLO, chaste-tree.
agnosticismo, *m.* agnosticism.
agnóstico, ca, *n.* & *a.* agnostic.
agnus, agnusdéi, *m.* Agnus Dei; ancient Spanish coin, of smallest value.
agobiante, *a.* backbreaking.
agobiar. I. *va.* to bend the body down; to overwhelm; to oppress. **II.** *vr.* to bow; to crouch.
agobio, *m.* bending down; oppression, burden.
agojía, *f.* water outlet in mines, drain.
agolpamiento, *m.* crowding, rush.
agolparse, *vr.* to crowd.
agonal, *a.* agonistic (esp. of the Janus games).
agonía, *f.* agony.
agónico, ca, *a.* agony (as *a.*), pertaining to the death struggle.
agonioso, sa, *a.* eager, persistent.
agonístico, ca. I. *a.* agonistic. **II.** *f.* agonistics, art of athletic contests.
agonizante. I. *a.* dying. **II.** *m.* a monk who assists a dying person; in some universities, one who assists students in their examinations.
agonizar. I. *va.* to assist (a dying person); to annoy, importune. **II.** *vn.* **estar agonizando,** to be dying.
ágono, na, *a.* (geom.) agonic.
ágora, *f.* (Gk. hist.) agora, marketplace.
agorafobia, *f.* (med.) agoraphobia.
agorar, *va.* (*ind.* AGÜERO; *subj.* AGÜERE) to divine, prognosticate.
agorero, ra, *n.* diviner, augur, fortune teller.
agorgojarse, *vr.* to be infested with grubs (app. to corn).
agostadero, *m.* summer pasture.
agostamiento, *m.* parching, drying up.
agostar. I. *va.* to parch. **II.** *vn.* to pasture cattle on stubbles in summer.
agostero, *m.* harvestman; religious mendicant who begs corn in August.
agostizo, za, *a.* born in August; (of animals) weak.
agosto, *m.* August; harvest time; harvest.—**hacer su a.,** to improve the opportunity, make hay while the sun shines.
agotable, *a.* exhaustible.
agotador, ra, *a.* draining; exhausting.
agotamiento, *m.* draining; exhaustion; depletion.—**a. del combustible,** (aer., rocketry) burnout.
agotar. I. *va.* to drain off (water); to beat out one's brains; to run through (a fortune); to exhaust. **II.** *vr.* to become exhausted; to give out; to wear oneself out; to be out of print.
[1]**agracejo,** *m.* unripened grape; unripe olive that falls.
[2]**agracejo,** *m.* (bot.) barberry.
agraceño, ña, *a.* as bitter as verjuice.

agracera. I. *f.* verjuice cruet. II. *a.* vine yielding unripening fruit.
agraciado, da. I. *pp.* of AGRACIAR. II. *a.* graceful, gracious. III. *m.* grantee.
agraciar, *va.* to adorn, embellish; to favor; to grace; to give employment to.
agracillo, agrecillo, *m.* = ²AGRACEJO.
agradable, *a.* agreeable, pleasing, pleasant.
agradar. I. *vn.* to be pleasing; to please, like (diff. const.: *esto le agrada,* this pleases him, he likes this. Here *le* is dative, not accusative.)
agradecer, *va.* (*ind.* AGRADEZCO; *subj.* AGRADEZCA) to thank for; to be grateful for.—**agradecido, da.** I. *pp.* of AGRADECER. II. *a.* grateful; thankful.
agradecimiento, *m.* gratefulness, gratitude.
agradezco, agradezca, *v.* *V.* AGRADECER.
agrado, *m.* affability, agreeableness; pleasure, liking.—**esto no es de mi a.,** this is not to my liking.—**ser del a. de uno,** to be to one's taste, have one's approval.
agrafia, *f.* (med.) agraphia.
agramadera, *f.* brake; scutch, instrument for dressing flax.
agramador, ra, *n.* flax or hemp breaker.
agramar, *va.* to dress (flax, hemp) with a brake.
agramilar, *va.* to point and color (a brick wall).
agramiza, *f.* the stalk of hemp; hemp, tow.
agrandamiento, *m.* enlargement.
agrandar, *va.* to enlarge, increase; let out (dress).
agranujado, da, *a.* grain-shaped; filled with grain.
agrario, ria, *a.* agrarian, rustic.
agrarismo, *m.* agrarianism.
agrarista, *n.* agrarian.
agravación, *f.* aggravation.
agravador, ra, *n.* aggravator; oppressor.
agravamiento, *m.* aggravating.
agravante, *a.* aggravating.
agravantemente, *adv.* aggravatingly; burdensomely.
agravar. I. *va.* to aggravate; to add to a burden; to oppress; to aggrieve; to exaggerate. II. *vr.* to become grave or worse.
agravatorio, ria, *a.* aggravating; (law) confirmatory and compulsory.
agraviadamente, *adv.* in an offended manner.
agraviador, ra, *n.* injurer, offender.
agraviamiento, *m.* wrong, offense, injury.
agraviante, *a.* offending.
agraviar. I. *va.* to wrong, offend, injure, harm. II. *vr.* to be piqued, take offense.
agravio, *m.* offense, insult, affront; injury, damage, harm.—**agravioso, sa,** *a.* offensive, insulting; injurious.
¹**agraz,** *m.* unripe grape; grape verjuice; (coll.) displeasure.—**en a.,** unseasonably.
²**agraz,** *m.* (bot.) red-berried mistletoe.
agrazada, *f.* verjuice water with sugar.
agrazar. I. *vn.* to taste sour. II. *va.* to vex.
agrazón, *m.* wild grape; (bot.) gooseberry bush; (coll.) displeasure, resentment.
agrecillo, *m.* = AGRACILLO, a kind of shrub.
agredir, *va.* (*defect.*) to attack, assault.
agregación, *f.* aggregation; aggregate, collection.
agregado, *m.* aggregate; congregation; assistant; attaché; farmhand living on another's farm or ranch; (eng.) aggregate (of concrete).
agregar, *va.* (*pret.* AGREGUÉ; *subj.* AGREGUE) to add; to collect, gather, heap; to nominate, appoint.
agremiar, *va.* & *vr.* **to form into a guild or union;** to unionize.
agresión, *f.* aggression; (law) battery.
agresivamente, *adv.* aggressively.
agresividad, *f.* aggressiveness.
agresivo, va, *a.* aggressive, offensive.
agresor, ra, *n.* aggressor, assaulter; (law) one who violates another's rights.
agreste, *a.* rustic, countrylike, wild; rude, uncultured, uncouth.
agrete, *a.* sourish, tartish.
agriamente, *adv.* sourly; harshly; tartly, bitterly, severely.
agriar. I. *va.* to make sour or tart; to irritate, exasperate. II. *vr.* to sour, turn acid.
agriaz, *m.* (bot.) bead tree.
agrícola, *a.* & *n.* agricultural; agriculturist.
agricultor, ra, *n.* husbandman, farmer, agriculturist.
agricultura, *f.* agriculture.
agridulce, *a.* bittersweet.
agrietamiento, *m.* cracking; crack, fissure.
agrietarse, *vr.* to crack.
agrifolio, *m.* (bot.) holly tree.
agrilla, *f.* (bot.) = ACEDERA, sorrel.
agrillarse, grillarse, *vr.* to sprout.
agrimensor, *m.* land surveyor.
agrimensura, *f.* land surveying.
agrimonia, *f.* (bot.) agrimony, liverwort.
agrio, ria. I. *a.* sour, acrid; rough (app. to a surface); rude, disagreeable; brittle, unmalleable. II. *m.* acidity.—*pl.* **agrios,** sour-fruit trees.
agrión, *m.* (vet.) callosity in a horse's knee.
agrisado, da, *a.* grayish.
agrisetado, da, *a.* flowered or small-figured (silk).
agrología, *f.* agrology.
agronometría, *f.* (agr.) science of soils.
agronomía, *f.* agronomy, science of agriculture.
agronómico, ca, *a.* agronomic.
agrónomo, ma. I. *a.* agricultural, agronomic. II. *m.* agronomist, agricultural scientist.
agropecuario, ria, *a.* agriculture and cattle (as *a.*).
agrupación, *f.* cluster; crowd; group; grouping; gathering.
agrupar, *va.* to group; to cluster.
agrura, *f.* acidity, acerbity; orchard of sour-fruit trees.
agua, *f.* water; (arch.) slope (of a roof); (naut.) leak; (naut.) route, course, direction.—**a. abajo,** downstream.—**a. amoniacal,** ammonia water, aqua ammoniæ.—**a. arriba,** upstream.—**a. bendita,** holy water.—**a. corriente,** running water.—**a. cruda,** hard water.—**a. de abono,** (agr.) liquid manure.—**a. de azahar,** orange-flower water.—**a. de cal,** limewater.—**a. de cepas,** (coll.) wine.—**a. de cerrajos,** worthless thing, truck, rubbish.—**a. de coco,** coconut milk.—**a. de Colonia,** Cologne water.—**a. de cristalización,** (chem.) water of crystallization.—**a. de lavanda,** (Am.) lavender water.—**a. del pantoque,** (naut.) bilge water.—**a. del timón,** wake of a ship.—**a. de manantial,** aqua fontana, spring water.—**a. de mar,** salt water.—**a. de nafa,** orange-flower water.—**a. de nieve,** ice water.—**a. de olor,** perfume.—**a. de pie,** running water.—**a. de pozo,** well water.—**a. de rosas,** rose water.—**a. de Seltz,** Seltzer.—**a. destilada,** distilled water, aqua pura.—**a. dulce,** fresh water.—**a. fuerte,** (chem., f. a.) aqua fortis; (chem.) nitric acid.—**a. gorda,** hard water.—**a. lluvia or llovediza,** rain water.—**a. manantial,** aqua fontana, spring water.—**a. mineral,** mineral water.—**a. mineral de Vichy,** Vichy water.—**a. muerta,** dead water, neap tide.—**a. nieve,** sleet.—**a. oxigenada,** (chem.) hydrogen peroxide.—**a. pesada,** (chem.) heavy water.—**a. potable,** drinking water.—**a. regia,** (chem.) aqua regia.—**a. rosada or de rosas,** rose water.—**a. salada,** salt water.—**aguas de albañal or fecales,** sewage.—**aguas jurisdiccionales,** (int. law) territorial waters.—**aguas gaseosas,** aerated waters.—**aguas madres,** (chem.) mother liquid or liquor.—**aguas mayores,** (coll.) stools, feces, excrement; equinoctial tide.—**aguas menores,** (coll.) urine.—**a. subterránea,** ground water.—**aguas vertientes,** drainage, drain water, flowoff; water shed, basin.—**aguas vivas,** spring tide.—**a. termal,** hot-spring water.—**a. tofana,** aqua tofana.—**a. viento,** wind-and-rain storm.—**a. viva,** running water.—**a. pasada no muele molino,**

that's water over the dam, let bygones be bygones.—**estar con el a. hasta la boca,** to be in a fix, be in deep water, be in trouble.—**estar entre dos aguas,** (coll.) to be in the middle of the road, be undecided.—**hacer a.,** (naut.) to leak.—**hacer aguas,** to make water, urinate.—**hacérsele a uno a. la boca,** to make one's mouth water.—**¡hombre al a.!** man overboard!—**nadie diga** or **no hay que decir de esta a. no beberé,** don't be too sure, you never can tell.—**tan claro como el a.,** clear, plain, obvious.
aguacatal, *m.* avocado plantation or grove.
aguacate, *m.* avocado, alligator pear; pear-shaped emerald.
aguacatillo, *m.* (bot.) a kind of avocado.
aguacero, *m.* heavy shower.
aguacibera, *f.* water used to irrigate ground sowed when dry.
aguachar. I. *va.* to load (a thing) with water; (Am.) to tame, break (a horse); to win the good will of with gifts. **II.** *vr.* to fatten in idleness (app. to horses). **III.** *m.* pool, puddle.
aguacharnar, *va.* = ENAGUAZAR, to flood.
aguachento, ta, *a.* (Am.) watery.
aguachinar, *va.* = AGUACHARNAR.
aguachirle, *f.* inferior wine; slipslop; any weak or stale liquor; trifle; frivolity.
aguada, *f.* watering station; flood in a mine; (naut.) ship's drinking-water supply; (art) water color.—**a la a.,** water color (picture).—**hacer a.,** (naut.) to take water.
aguaderas, *f. pl.* frames for jars of water carried by horses.
aguadero, m. watering place; water station.
aguadija, *f.* serum in pimples or sores.
aguado, da. I. *pp.* of AGUAR. **II.** *a.* watery; abstemious.—**manos aguadas,** butterfingers.
aguador, ra, *n.* water carrier; (mech.) sprocket.—**a. del real,** (mil.) sutler.
aguaducho, *m.* water course; stall for selling water.
aguadura, *f.* surfeit of water (in cattle).
aguafiestas, *n.* (coll.) wet blanket.
aguafuerte, *f.* etching; etched plate.
aguafuertista, *n.* (f.a.) aquafortist, etcher.
aguagoma, *f.* (painting) gum water.
aguaitamiento, *m.* watching, spying, lying for some one.
aguaitar, *va.* to spy, watch.
aguajaque, *m.* fennel gum.
aguajas, *f. pl.* (Chile) ulcers above the hoofs.
aguaje, *m.* tidal wave; (naut.) whirlpool or eddy at the rudder; sea current; wake of a ship.
agualluvia, *f.* = AGUA LLUVIA, rain water.
aguamanil, *m.* water jug; washstand.
aguamanos, *m.* water for washing the hands; washstand.
aguamarina, *f.* aquamarine.
aguamasa, *f.* (Am.) crushed-corn washings.
aguamelado, da, *a.* washed over with water and honey.
aguamiel, *f.* hydromel, honey and water, mead; unfermented juice of the maguey.
aguanieve, *f.* = AGUA NIEVE, sleet.
aguanieves, *f.* = AGUZANIEVES, *f.* magpie..
aguanosidad, *f.* aqueous substances.
aguanoso, sa, *a.* very wet; very watery.
aguantable, *a.* bearable, tolerable.
aguantar. I. *va.* to bear, endure; to resist; to maintain; (naut.) to carry a stiff sail. **II.** *vr.* to forbear.—**aguante,** *m.* strength, resistance; patience, tolerance.
aguañón, *m.* constructor of hydraulic works.
aguapié, *m.* weak, watered wine.
aguar. I. *va.* to dilute with water; to mar (pleasure). **II.** *vr.* to fill with water; to become thin (app. to liquids); (vet.) to become constipated from drinking water at the wrong time.
aguardar, *va.* to expect; to wait for; to grant time to.
aguardentado, da, *a.* containing aguardiente; tipsy, drunk.
aguardentera, *f.* liquor flask.
aguardentería, *f.* liquor shop; saloon.
aguardentero, ra, *n.* maker or seller of **aguardiente.**
aguardentoso, sa, *a.* mixed with aguardiente; harsh (app. to the voice).
aguardiente, *m.* aguardiente, brandy.—**a. de cabeza,** the first spirits drawn from the still.—**a. anisado,** anisette.—**a. de caña,** rum.
aguardo, *m.* hiding place for a hunter, blind.
aguarrás, *m.* oil of turpentine.
aguatero, ra. *n.* water carrier.
aguatinta, *f.* (f.a.) aquatint.
aguatocha, *f.* pump.
aguaturma, *f.* (bot.) Jerusalem artichoke.
aguavientos, *m.* (bot.) yellow sage tree.
aguaza, *f.* watery serum; sap from trees.
aguazal, *m.* marsh, fen.
aguazarse, *vr.* to become marshy.
aguazo, *m.* painting in gouache.
aguazoso, sa, *a.* = AGUANOSO.
agucé, aguce, *v.* *V.* AGUZAR.
agudeza, *f.* sharpness; fineness; witty saying; repartee; wit.
agudo, da, *a.* sharp; sharp-pointed; keen-edged; high-pitched; witty; clever(minded); brisk, ready, active or lively; (med., geom.) acute.
agüera, *f.* trench for irrigation.
[1]**agüero,** *m.* augury, prognostication; omen, sign, indication.
[2]**agüero, agüere,** *v.* *V.* AGORAR.
aguerrido, da. I. *pp.* of AGUERRIR. **II.** *a.* inured to war; veteran.
aguerrir. I. *va.* & *vr.* (*defect.*) to accustom to war.
aguijada, *f.* spur, goad.
aguijador, ra, *n.* one that goads, spurs, or urges.
aguijadura, *f.* spurring, urging, egging on.
aguijar. I. *va.* to prick, spur, goad; to incite, egg on. **II.** *m.* to march fast; to hurry.
aguijón, *m.* sting (of insect); prick; spur, goad.—**cocear,** or **dar coces, contra el a.,** to kick against the pricks.
aguijonazo, *m.* thrust with a goad.
aguijoneador, ra, *n.* one who pricks or goads.
aguijonear, *va.* to prick, goad; push, urge, egg on.
águila, *f.* eagle; eagle ray (fish).—**a. barbuda,** lammergeir, bearded vulture.—**a. blanca,** a variety of Andine vulture.—**a. cabdal,** or **caudal,** royal or golden, eagle—**a. de mar,** eagle ray.—**a. imperial,** imperial eagle.—**a. real** = A. CAUDAL.
aguileño, na, *a.* aquiline; hawknosed.
aguililla, *f.* *dim.*—**caballo a.,** (Am.) swift, pacing horse.
aguilón. I. *m.* boom of a crane. **II.** *n.* *aug.* of ÁGUILA.
aguilucho, *m.* young eagle, eaglet.
aguinaldo, *m.* New Year's or Christmas present; (Cuba) wild convolvulus that blossoms at Christmas.
aguja, *f.* needle; bodkin; hatpin; spire, steeple; obelisk; needlefish, hornfish; needle shell; hand of a watch; style of a dial; needle, magnetic compass; (Ry.) switch rail; (Ry., gen. *pl.*) switch; spindle; pin (in typography and artil.); brad; graft.—*pl.* ribs of an animal; (Ry.) switch, (Brit.) points.—**a. capotera,** darning needle.—**a. colchonera,** tufting needle.—**a. de arria, a. de enjalmar** or **espartera,** pack-needle.—**a. de mar,** (ichth.) sailfish.—**a. de marear,** binnacle, marine compass.
agujazo, *m.* prick with a needle.
agujerear, *va.* to pierce, perforate.
agujero, *m.* hole; needlemaker or seller; dugout.
agujeta, *f.* lace, string or latchet with metal tips.—*pl.* tip, gratuity; pains from overexercise.
agujetería, *f.* shop where *agujetas* are made or sold.
agujetero, ra, *n.* maker or seller of *agujetas*; ALFILETERO, (Am.) pin or needle case or cushion.
agujón, *m.* *aug.* large needle.
agujuela, *f.* brad.

aguosidad, *f.* lymph.
aguoso, sa, acuoso, sa, *a.* aqueous, watery.
agur, *adv.* (coll.) adieu, farewell, good-bye.
agusanarse, *vr.* to become infested with worms.
agustiniano, na; agustino, na, *n.* & *a.* Augustinian (monk, nun).
agutí, acutí, *m.* agouti.
agúzadera, *f.* whetstone.
aguzadero, *m.* haunt of wild boars.
aguzador, *n.* & *a.* sharpener(-ing).
aguzadura, *f.* whetting, sharpening.
aguzanieve, *f.* wagtail, a small bird.
aguzar, *va.* (*pret.* AGUCÉ; *subj.* AGUCE) to whet, sharpen; to urge, excite.—**a. el ingenio,** to sharpen the wits.—**a. las orejas,** to prick up the ears.—**a. la vista,** to sharpen the sight.
aguzonazo, *m.* blow with a poker.
¡ah!, *interj.* ah!
ahebrado, da, *a.* threadlike, fibrous.
ahechadero, *m.* place where grain is sifted.
ahechador, ra, *a.* & *n.* sifter(-ing).
ahechaduras, *f. pl.* refuse of grain, chaff.
ahechar, *va.* to sift (grain).—**ahecho,** *m.* sifting.
ahelear. I. *va.* to gall, embitter. **II.** *vn.* to taste bitter.
aherrojamiento, *m.* putting in irons, shackling.
aherrojar, *va.* to chain, put in irons, shackle.
aherrumbrar. I. *va.* to impart the taste and color of iron to. **II.** *vr.* to have the taste and color of iron (as water); to become ferruginous; to rust.
ahervorarse, *vr.* (of grain in a granary) to become heated.
ahí, *adv.* there; yonder.—**de a.,** hence.—**de por a.,** insignificant, nothing much.—**por a.,** somewhere around here; that way; over there.—**por a., por a.,** about, more or less.—**a. donde lo (la) ve,** although he (she) doesn't look it, although you wouldn't expect it.
ahidalgado, da, *a.* gentlemanly(-womanly).
ahijadero, *m.* breeding place for sheep.
ahijado, da, *n.* godchild; protegé.
ahijador, ra, *n.* shepherd in charge of a sheep breeding place.
ahijar. I. *va.* to adopt; to impute. **II.** *vn.* to bring forth young; to bud, shoot out.
ahilarse, *vr.* to become faint, weak; to grow sour; to grow thin.—**ahilo,** *m.* faintness, weakness.
ahinco, *m.* earnestness, eagerness, ardor.
ahitar, *va.* & *vr.* to surfeit, cloy, stuff.
ahitera, *f.* (coll.) violent or continued indigestion.
ahito, ta. I. *a.* gorged, surfeited; stuffed; full; disgusted, bored. **II.** *m.* indigestion; surfeit.
ahocicar, *vn.* (naut.) to pitch or plunge.
ahocinarse, *vr.* to run in deep and narrow ravines.
ahogadero, *m.* hangman's rope; stifling place; throatband, halter.
ahogadizo, za, *a.* easily drowned; (of fruit) harsh, rough; (of wood) heavier than water, non-floating.
ahogado, da. I. *pp.* of AHOGAR. **II.** *a.* close, unventilated.—**estar,** or **verse, a.,** to be overwhelmed or swamped. **III.** *n.* suffocated or drowned person.
ahogador, ra, *n.* hangman.
ahogamiento, *m.* suffocation; drowning.
ahogar. I. *va.* (*pret.* AHOGUÉ; *subj.* AHOGUE) to drown; to choke, throttle, smother; to oppress; to quench, extinguish; to water (plants) to excess. **II.** *vr.* to drown; to be suffocated; (naut.) to founder.—**ahogo,** *m.* oppression, tightness (of the chest, etc.); suffocation; pain; severe affliction; embarrassment.
ahogué, ahogue, *v. V.* AHOGAR.
ahoguijo, *m.* (vet.) quinsy, swollen throat.
ahoguío, *m.* oppression in the chest.
ahombrado, da, *a.* (coll.) mannish.
ahondar. I. *va.* to deepen; to dig; to go deep into. **II.** *vn.* to go deep, penetrate; to advance in knowledge; to investigate.
ahonde, *m.* act of sinking or digging; depth to which a mine should reach to acquire title.
ahora. I. *adv.* now.—**a. mismo,** just now; right now; at once.—**hasta a.,** hitherto, until now; so far.—**por a.,** for the present. **II.** *conj.* now; whether . . . or (*ahora hable, ahora escriba, lo hace bien,* whether he speaks or writes, he does it well).—**a. bien,** now, now then.
ahorcadura, *f.* (act of) hanging.
ahorcajarse, *vr.* to sit astride.
ahorcar. I. *va.* (*pret.* AHORQUE; *subj.* AHORQUE) to hang, kill by hanging. **II.** *vn.* to be hanged. **III.** *vr.* to hang, hang oneself.
ahorita, *adv.* (Am. coll.) just now.—**a. mismo,** just now, this very moment; right away, at once.
ahormar, *va.* to fit, shape, adjust; to break in (shoes); to bring to reason.
ahornagarse, *vr.* (of lands, plants, etc.) to become parched or burned.
ahornar. I. *va.* to put in an oven. **II.** *vr.* to be scorched in the oven without being baked.
ahorqué, ahorque, *v. V.* AHORCAR.
ahorquillado, da. I. *a.* forked.
ahorquillar. I. *va.* to stay, prop up with forks. **II.** *vr.* to become forked.
ahorrado, da. I. *pp.* of AHORRAR. **II.** *a.* unencumbered.
ahorrador, ra. I. *n.* emancipator; saver, economizer. **II.** *a.* saving.
ahorramiento, *m.* emancipation, enfranchisement; saving.
ahorrar, *va.* to save, economize; to spare; to enfranchise, emancipate.—**no ahorrarse,** or **no ahorrárselas, con nadie,** to be afraid of nobody, not to mince words with anybody.
ahorrativa, *f.* (coll.) = AHORRO.
ahorrativo, va, *a.* frugal, thrifty, saving.
ahorro, *m.* economy.—*pl.* savings.
ahoyadura, *f.* hole; digging.
ahoyar, *vn.* to dig holes.
ahuate, *m.* (Mex.) prickly hair (of sugar cane, etc.).
ahuchador, ra, *n.* hoarder, miser.
ahuchar, *va.* to hoard.
ahuecamiento, *m.* hollowing.
ahuecar. I. *va.* (*pret.* AHUEQUÉ; *subj.* AHUEQUE) to make hollow, scoop out; to loosen; to give (to the voice) a tone of solemnity. **II.** *vr.* to become hollow; to puff up, swell, put on airs.
ahuehué, ahuehuete, *m.* a Mexican coniferous tree like a cypress.
ahuequé, ahueque, *v. V.* AHUECAR.
ahumado, da. I. *a.* smoky; smoked. **II.** *f.* smoke signal from the coast.
ahumar. I. *va.* to smoke; to cure in smoke. **II.** *vn.* to fume; to emit smoke. **III.** *vr.* to be smoked; to look smoky.
ahusado, da. I. *pp.* of AHUSAR. **II.** *a.* spindle-shaped, tapered.
ahusar, *va.* & *vr.* to taper.
ahuyentador, ra, *n.* one that drives or scares away; scarecrow.
ahuyentar, *va.* to drive away, put to flight; to frighten away; to overcome (a passion), banish (care).
ai, *m.* or *f.* (zool.) three-toed sloth of S. America.
aijada, *f.* spur, goad.
ailanto, *m.* (bot.) ailanthus tree, tree of heaven.
aina, aínas, *adv.* soon; easily; almost.
aindiado, da, *a.* Indianlike.
airadamente, *adv.* angrily.
airado, da, *a.* angry, wrathful.
airamiento, *m.* wrath, anger.
airar. I. *va.* to anger; to irritate. **II.** *vr.* to grow angry.
aire, *m.* air; atmosphere; wind; pace (of a horse); air, carriage, gait; aspect, countenance, look; musical composition; frivolity.—**a. colado,** cold draught.—**al aire libre,** in the open air, outdoors.—(**con**) **a. acondicionado,** air-conditioned.—**en el a.,** in suspense, in the air.—**por a.,** by air.—**por el a.,** or **por los aires,** very rapidly, posthaste, like lightning.—**hablar al a.,** to make empty talk.—**¿qué aires lo**

traen a Vd. por acá? what good wind brings you here?—**tomar el a.,** to take a walk.
airear. I. *va.* to give air to, ventilate; to aerate; to charge with gas. II. *vr.* to take the air; to cool oneself.
[1]**airón,** *m. aug.* violent gale.
[2]**airón,** *m.* crested heron; egret; crest; ornament of plumes.
[3]**airón,** *m.* deep Moorish well.
airosamente, *adv.* gracefully, lightly.
airosidad, *f.* graceful deportment.
airoso, sa, *a.* airy, windy; graceful, gracious; lively; successful.
aislacionismo, *m.* isolationism.
aislacionista, *n.* & *a.* isolationist.
aisladamente, *adv.* in isolation, apart.
aislador, ra, *n.* & *a.* isolator(-ing); (elec., phys.) insulator(-ing).
aislamientismo, *m.* isolationism.
aislamientista, *n.* & *a.* isolationist.
aislamiento, *m.* isolation; (elec., phys.) insulation; insulating material.
aislamiento penal, *m.* solitary confinement.
aislar. I. *va.* to isolate; (elec., phys.) to insulate. II. *vr.* to become isolated; to seclude oneself.
¡aja! *interj.* aha! (denoting approval).
ajada, *f.* garlic sauce.
ajamiento, *m.* disfiguring; crumpling, rumpling.
ajaquecarse, *vr.* to have a headache.
[1]**ajar,** *m.* garlic field.
[2]**ajar,** *va.* to crumple, rumple.—**a. la vanidad a uno,** to pull down one's pride.
ajarafe, *m.* table-land; terrace; flat roof.
aje, *m.* chronic complaint.
ajea, *f.* brushwood for fuel.
ajear, *vn.* to cry (app. to a pursued partridge).
ajedrea, *f.* (bot.) winter savory.
ajedrecista, *n.* chess player.
ajedrez, *m.* chess; (naut.) netting, grating.
ajedrezado, da, *a.* checkered.
ajedrista, *n.* chess player.
ajenabe, ajenabo. *m.* (bot.) wild mustard.
ajengibre, jengibre, *m.* ginger.
ajenjo, *m.* (bot.) wormwood; absinth.
ajeno, na, *a.* another's; foreign; abhorrent, contrary; ignorant; improper; unsuited.—**a. a,** foreign to: free from.—**a. de,** devoid of, lacking; ignorant of; indifferent to.
ajenuz, *m.* (bot.) field fennel-flower.
ajeo, *m.*—**perro de a.,** setter.
ajero, ra, *n.* garlic dealer or vender.
ajesuitado, da, *a.* Jesuitical, Jesuit-like.
ajete, *m.* young garlic; leek; garlic sauce.
ajetrearse, *vr.* to tire; to fidget.—**ajetreo,** *m.* fatigue; agitation.
ají, *m.* chili, capsicum; chili sauce.
ajiaceite, *m.* mixture of garlic and oil.
ajiaco, *m.* dish made of boiled meat and vegetables; chili sauce.
ajicola, *f.* glue made of kidskin boiled with garlic.
ajilimoje, ajilimójili, *m.* pepper-and-garlic sauce.
ajillo, *m.* tender young garlic.
ajimez, *m.* arched window with pillar in centre.
ajipuerro, *m.* wild leek.
ajironar, *va.* to put colored pieces in (a dress, etc.).
[1]**ajo,** *m.* (bot.) garlic; garlic sauce; (coll.) rouge.
[2]**ajo,** *m.* (coll.) oath, swear word; shady business. —**echar ajos (y cebollas),** to swear, curse.
ajobar, *va.* to carry on the back.
ajobilla, *f.* common sea shell.
ajobo, *m.* a heavy load or burden.
ajofaina, aljofaina, *f.* wash bowl, basin.
ajolote, *m.* axolotl, a Mexican salamander.
ajomate, *m.* (bot.) a variety of seaweed.
ajonje, *m.* bird lime.
ajonjera, *f.*; **ajonjero,** *m.* (bot.) the low carline thistle.
ajonjolí, *m.* (bot.) benne, sesame.
ajoqueso, *m.* dish made of garlic and cheese.
ajorca, *f.* Moorish bracelet or anklet.
ajornalar, *va.* to hire by the day.
ajuagas, *f. pl.* (vet.) ulcers over the hoofs.
ajuanetado, da, *a.* bunionlike; having bunions.
ajuar, *m.* bridal apparel and furniture; trousseau; household furniture.
ajudiado, da, *a.* Jewish; Jewlike.
ajuiciado, da, *a.* wise, sensible
ajuiciar, *vn.* & *vr.* to become wise; to reform, mend one's ways.
ajustable, *a.* adjustable.
ajustadamente, *adv.* tightly; justly, rightly.
ajustado, da. I. *pp.* of AJUSTAR. II. *a.* exact, right; stingy; adapted; tight; fitted.
ajustador, ra. I. *n.* fitter, adjuster. II. *m.* close waistcoat, jacket; (print.), justifier; (mech.) adapter; adjusting tool.
ajustamiento, *m.* agreement; fitting; settling of accounts; receipts.
ajustar. I. *va.* to regulate; to adapt, adjust, fit; to justify (type); to agree about; to settle (an account, a controversy, etc.); to reconcile; to press close, oppress; to size, make true; to trim; to engage, hire. II. *vr.* to settle; to conform; to engage oneself; to be engaged or hired. III. *vn.* to fit.—**ajuste,** *m.* proportion of the constituent parts of a thing; adjustment, fitting; agreement, contract, covenant; engagement; settlement.—*pl.* couplings.
ajusticiar, *va.* to execute, put to death.
al (contraction of a and **el**) to the (foll. by a masc. noun); used also with the *inf.* of verbs to indicate coexistence or immediate anteriority, and often equivalent to "on" (foll. by *pres. p.*), "about," "on the point of": *al llegar,* on arriving; *al amanecer,* at daybreak; *estoy al partir,* I am about to leave; *Juan estuvo al perder su empleo,* John was on the point of losing (*or,* came very near losing) his position.
ala, *f.* wing; row, file; (mil., aer.) wing; wing (of a building); brim (of hat); (anat.) auricle; fin (of fish); leaf (of a door, table); (naut.) blade (of a propeller).—*pl.* **alas,** upper studding sails.—**a. de gavia,** maintop studding sail.—**a. de mesana,** (naut.) driver.—**a. de proa,** head of a ship.—**a. de sobremesana,** mizzentop studding sail.—**a. de velacho,** fore studding sail.—**cortar,** or **quebrantar, las alas a uno,** to discourage one or throw a wet blanket on one's plans; to deprive one of means or elements; to clip one's wings.
Alá, *m.* Allah, Arabic name of God.
alabado, *m.* hymn in praise of the sacrament.
alabador, ra, *n.* praiser.
alabamiento, *m.* praise.
alabamio, *m.* (chem.) alabamine.
alabancioso, sa, *a.* (coll.) boastful, ostentatious.
alabandina, *f.* manganese sulphide; alabandine, spinel ruby.
alabanza, *f.* praise, commendation.
alabar, *va.* & *vr.* to praise, commend.—**a. uno sus agujas,** (coll.) to blow one's own horn.
alabarda, *f.* halberd.—**alabardado, da,** *a.* halberd-shaped.—**alabardazo,** *m.* a blow with a halberd.—**alabardero,** *m.* halberdier; one of a theatre claque.
alabastrado, da, *a.* alabasterlike.
alabastrina, *f.* thin sheet of alabaster.
alabastrino, na, *a.* alabastrine.
alabastro, *m.* alabaster.
álabe, *m.* drooping branch of a tree; bucket (of a water wheel); mat used in carts; cam.
alabear, *va.* & *vr.* to warp.
alabega, *f.* (bot.) sweet basil.
alabeo, *m.* warping.
alabiado, da, *a.* lipped or ragged (coins).
alacena, *f.* cupboard; closet; (naut.) locker.
alacrán, *m.* scorpion; ring of the bit of a bridle; stop or hook in organ bellows; chain or link of a sleeve button; swivel.—**alacranado, da,** *a.* scorpion-bitten; vice- or disease-ridden.
alacranera, *f.* (bot.) scorpion grass.
alacridad, *f.* alacrity.
alacha, alache, *f.* anchovy.
alada, *f.* fluttering of the wings.

aladares, *m. pl.* forelocks over the temples.
aladica, *f.* (entom.) winged ant.
aladierna, alaterno, *m.* mock privet.
alado, da, *a.* winged.
aladroque, *m.* unsalted anchovy.
alafia, *f.*—**pedir a.,** (coll.) to beg pardon.
álaga, *f.* a species of yellow wheat.
alagar, *va.* to make ponds or lakes in.
alagartado, da, *a.* variegated, motley.
alajú, *m.* paste made of nuts and honey.
alamar, *m.* frog and braid trimming.
alambicadamente, *adv.* pedantically.
alambicado, da. I. *pp.* of ALAMBICAR. **II.** *a.* pedantic, euphuistic; given with a sparing hand.
alambicamiento, *m.* distillation; pedantry, affected language.
alambicar, *va.* to distil; to scrutinize; to use affected language.
alambique, *m.* still.—**por a.,** sparingly.
alambor, *m.* (arch.) face of a hewn stone; (fort.) inside slope.
alambrada, *f.* (mil.) wire entanglements.
alambrado, *m.* wire netting, wire screen; wire cover; electric wiring; wire fence; wire entanglements.
alambrar, *va.* to put a wire fence round.
alambre, *m.* wire; (anc.) copper, bronze, brass; sheep bells.—**a. cargado** or **activo,** (elec.) live wire.—**a. de púas,** barbed wire.—**a. de tierra,** (elec.) ground wire.
alambrera, *f.* wire netting; wire screen; wire cover; (agr.) wire trellis.
alameda, *f.* poplar grove; public walk.
alamín, *m.* clerk appointed to inspect weights and measures; surveyor of buildings; (prov.) farmer appointed to superintend irrigation.
álamo, *m.* (bot.) poplar.—**a. blanco,** white poplar.—**a. temblón,** aspen tree.
alampar, *va.* & *vr.* (**por**) (coll.) to long (for); to crave.
alamud, *m.* square bolt for a door.
alanceador, *m.* lancer.
alancear, *va.* to spear.
alandrearse, *vr.* (of silkworms) to become dry, stiff, and blanched.
alanés, *m.* a large Mexican deer.
alanina, *f.* (chem.) alanine.
alano, na. I. *a.* pert. to the Alani, barbarian invaders of Spain. **II.** *m.* large mastiff.
alantoides, *f.* (anat.) allantois.
alanzar, *va.* to spear.
alaqueca, *f.* bloodstone.
[1]**alar,** *m.* overhanging roof; (hunting) snare made with horsehair.
[2]**alar, halar,** *va.* (naut.) to haul.
alárabe, alarbe. I. *n.* & *a.* Arabian. **II.** *n.* unmannerly person.
alarde, *m.* review of soldiers, parade; ostentation, boasting, vanity.—**hacer a.,** to boast, brag; to show off.—**alardear,** *m.* to boast.
alardoso, sa, *a.* boastful, bragging; ostentatious.
alargadera, *f.* lengthening bar (of compasses, etc.); (chem.) adapter, lengthening tube.
alargador, ra, *n.* stretcher; one that lengthens or stretches.
alargamiento, *m.* lengthening; (eng.) elongation.
alargar. I. *va.* (*pret.* ALARGUÉ; *subj.* ALARGUE) to lengthen; to extend; to stretch; to protract, prolong; to increase; to hand (a thing to another).—**a. un cabo,** (naut.) to pay out a cable. **II.** *vr.* to be prolonged; to drag; to become longer; to go or move away; to deviate; to expatiate, enlarge.
alarguez, *m.* (bot.) dog-rose.
alaria, *f.* potters' finishing tool.
alarida, *f.* hue and cry.
alarido, *m.* howl, outcry, shout, scream.
alarije, arije, *f.* name of a large grape.
alarma, *f.* alarm.
alarmante, *a.* alarming.
alarmar. I. *va.* to alarm. **II.** *vr.* to become alarmed.
alarmista, *n.* alarmist.
alaskense, *n.* & *a.* Alaskan.
alastrar. I. *va.* (of animals) to throw back the ears; (of persons) to squint (to see better); (naut.) to ballast. **II.** *vr.* (of a bird in hiding) to lie flat.
alátere, *n.* (coll.) constant companion, shadow.
alaterno, *m.* (bot.) mock privet.
alatinado, da, *a.* (of language) Latinlike, puristic.
alatrón, *m.* froth of saltpetre.
alavanco, lavanco, *m.* a kind of wild duck.
alavense, alavés, *a.* Alavese, of Alava.
alazán, na, *a.* sorrel-colored.
alazo, *m.* a blow with the wings.
alazor, *m.* (bot.) bastard saffron.
alba, *f.* dawn of day; alb, white gown worn by priests.—**al a., al rayar del a.,** at daybreak.—**quebrar, rayar,** or **reír, el alba,** to dawn.
albacara, *f.* (fort.) round tower.
albacea, *m.* & *f.* (law) executor, executrix.
albaceazgo, *m.* (law) executorship.
albacora, *f.* fish resembling a tunny; a large fig.
albada, *f.* dawn; (Mex.) attack at daybreak.
albahaca, *f.* (bot.) sweet basil.
albahaquero, *m.* flowerpot; sweet-basil vender.
albahaquilla (de río), *f.* (bot.) pellitory.
albaida, *f.* (bot.) the shrubby gypsophila.
albalá, *m.* or *f.* (obs.) royal letter patent; a public instrument.
albanega, *f.* hair net; net for catching partridges or rabbits.
albanés, esa, *n.* & *a.* Albanian.
Albania, *f.* Albania.
albano, na, *n.* & *a.* Albanian.
albañal, albañar, *m.* common sewer; dirty water sink.
albañil, *m.* mason, builder.
albañilería, *f.* masonry (occupation or work).
albaquía, *f.* remnant.
albar, *a.* white.
albarán, *m.* "to-let" sign; royal grant or cedula; letter patent.
albarazada, *f.* marble-colored grape.
albarazado, da, *a.* affected with white leprosy; pale, whitish; (Mex.) cross between Chinese and half-breed parents.
albarazo, *m.* white leprosy.
albarca, abarca, *f.* peasant's sandal.
albarcoque, *m.* = ALBARICOQUE.
albarcoquero, *m.* apricot tree.
albarda, *f.* packsaddle.
albardado, da. I. *pp.* of ALBARDAR. **II.** *a.* (of animals) different-colored skin at the loins.
albardar, *va.* to put a packsaddle on; to lard (fowls).
albardela, *f.* small saddle.
albardería, *f.* packsaddle making or shop.
albardero, ra, *n.* packsaddle maker.
albardilla, *f.* small packsaddle; coping; border of a garden bed; wool tuft; bard.
albardín, *m.* (bot.) matweed.
albardón, *m.* large packsaddle.
albarejo, *m.* a variety of wheat.
albareque, *m.* fishing net.
albaricoque, *m.* apricot.—**albaricoquero,** *m.* apricot tree.
[1]**albarillo,** *m.* a tune on the guitar.
[2]**albarillo,** *m.* white apricot.
albarrada, *f.* dry wall; earth fence; wall for defense.
albarranilla, *f.* blue-flowered onion.
[1]**albarraz,** *m.* (bot.) lousewort.
[2]**albarraz,** *m.* = ALBARAZO.
albatita, *f.* (min.) albite.
albatros, *m.* albatross.
albayaldado, da, *a.* covered with white lead.
albayaldar, *va.* & *vr.* to cover with white lead.
albayalde, *m.* white lead, ceruse.
albazano, na, *a.* of dark chestnut color.
albear, *va.* to whiten. Also BLANQUEAR.
albedo, *m.* (phys.) albedo.

albedrío, *m.* will; free will; impulsiveness, wilfullness; (law) precedent; judgment.—**al a. de uno,** to, or according to, one's judgment or pleasure; as one likes.
albéitar, *m.* veterinarian.
albeitería, *f.* veterinary science.
albellón, *m.* = ALBAÑAL, sewer.
albenda, *f.* ornamented white-linen hangings.
albendera, *f.* woman who makes hangings; gadding woman.
albengala, *f.* gauze worn in turbans.
albéntola, *f.* fine fishing net.
alberca, *f.* pool; reservoir, tank; pond.—**a. natatoria, de natación,** swimming pool.—**en a.,** roofless.
albérchiga, *f.*, **albérchigo,** *m.* a variety of peach.
alberchiguero, *m.* variety of peach tree.
albergador, ra, *n.* one who shelters.
albergar. **I.** *va.* (*pret.* ALBERGUÉ; *subj.* ALBERGUE) to lodge, shelter, harbor; to take (lodgers). **II.** *vr.* to lodge; to find shelter or lodging.
albergue, *m.* lodging; shelter; (animal) den.
alberguería, *f.* inn; poorhouse.
albericoque, *m.* = ALBARICOQUE, apricot.
albero, *m.* whitish earth; dishcloth.
alberquero, *m.* tender of pools or tanks.
albicante, *a.* whitening, bleaching.
albigense, *n.* & *a.* Albigensian.
albihar, *m.* (bot.) oxeye.
albillo, lla. **I.** *a.*—**uva a.,** early white grape.—**vino a.,** white grape wine. **II.** *m.* = UVA A.
albín, *m.* bloodstone; carmine pigment.
albina, *f.* salt-water marsh.
albino, na, *a.* albino.—**albinismo,** *m.* albinism.
Albión, *f.* Albion (England).
albita, *f.* (min.) albite, white feldspar.
albitana, *f.* fence to inclose plants; (naut.) an apron.—**a. del codaste,** (naut.) inner post.
albo, ba, *a.* (poet.) snow-white.
alboaire, *m.* glazed tile work.
albogue, *m.* pastoral flute; martial music.
alboguero, ra, *n.* player of or composer for the *albogue*.
albohol, *m.* (bot.) red poppy.
albollón, *m.* gutter (on road), drain; sewer.
albóndiga, almóndiga, *f.* ball of forcemeat with eggs and spice.—**albondiguilla, almondiguilla,** *f. dim.* small ball of forcemeat.
albor, *m.* dawn; whiteness; beginning.—**a.,** or **albores, de la vida,** childhood, youth.
alborada, *f.* dawn; (mil.) battle at dawn; reveille; morning watch; musical piece celebrating dawn.
albórbola, *f.* shouting and yelling (gen. for joy).
alborear, *vn.* to dawn.
alborga, *f.* matweed sandal.
albornía, *f.* large glazed jug.
alborno, alburno, *m.* (bot.) alburnum.
albornoz, *m.* coarse woollen stuff; Moorish cloak; burnoose.
alborocé, alboroce, *v. V.* ALBOROZAR.
alboronía, almoronía, *f.* dish of eggplant, tomatoes, pumpkins, and pimento.
alboroque, *m.* treat to seal a bargain.
alborotadamente, *adv.* noisily, confusedly.
alborotadizo, za; alborotado, da, *a.* restive; excitable; turbulent.
alborotador, ra, *n.* agitator, rioter.
alborotapueblos, *m.* rioter, agitator; (coll.) good-natured person; promoter of gaieties.
alborotar. **I.** *va.* to disturb, agitate, excite; to make a noise; to start (the game). **II.** *vr.* to become excited; to fuss; to riot.
alboroto, *m.* disturbance, tumult; hubbub, fuss; (C. A.) (gen. *pl.*) pop corn.
alborozador, ra, *n.* promoter of mirth.
alborozar, *va.* (*pret.* ALBOROCÉ; *subj.* ALBOROCE) to exhilarate, gladden.
alborozo, *m.* merriment, gaiety, joy.
albotín, *m.* = TEREBINTO, turpentine tree.
albricias, *f. pl.* reward for good news; (Mex.) top holes in casting moulds.—**¡albricias!** joy! joy!
albudeca, *f.* (bot.) watermelon.
albufera, *f.* large lagoon by the sea.
albugíneo, a., *a.* entirely white; albuminous.
albugo, *m.* leucoma, a disease of the eye.
albuhera, *f.* lake or reservoir.
álbum, *m.* album.
albumen, *m.* albumen.—**albúmina,** *f.* albumin.
albuminar, *va.* to albumenize.
albuminato, *m.* albuminate.
albuminina, *f.* (chem.) albuminin.
albuminoide, *m.* & *a.* albuminoid.
albuminoideo, a, *adj.* albuminoid.
albuminoso, sa, *adj.* albuminous.
albuminuria, *f.* (med.) albuminuria.
albumosuria, *f.* (med.) albumosuria.
[1]**albur,** *m.* dace, river fish.
[2]**albur,** *m.* first draw at "monte"; risk, chance.—**correr un a.,** to venture, chance, risk.—*pl.* **albures,** a card game.
albura, *f.* whiteness; (bot.) = ALBURNO.
alburero, *m. albures* player.
alburno, *m.* (bot.) = ALBORNO, alburnum.
alca, *f.* (ornith.) auk, razorbill.
alcabala, *f.* sales tax.—**a. del viento,** duty paid by a visiting merchant.—**alcabalatorio,** *m.* book of alcabala rates; tax register.—**alcabalero,** *m.* taxgatherer, revenue officer.
alcacel, alcacer, *m.* green barley.
alcachofa, *f.* (bot.) artichoke; instrument to stop blood; fluted mallets.—**alcachofado, da.** **I.** *a.* artichokelike. **II.** *m.* artichoke dish.—**alcachofal,** *m.* artichoke bed.—**alcachofera,** *f.* artichoke plant.—**alcachofero, ra,** *a.* producing or selling artichokes.
alcahaz, *m.* large bird cage.—**alcahazada,** *f.* collection of birds in a cage.—**alcahazar,** *va.* to cage (birds).
alcahueto, ta, *n.* procurer; abettor; gossip.—**alcahuetear,** *va.* & *vn.* to aid, abet; to pander.
alcahuetería, *f.* pandering; (coll.) trick.
alcaicería, *f.* raw-silk exchange.
alcaico, *a.* (poet.) Alcaic verse in Latin.
alcaide, *m.* governor of a castle; jailer, warden.
alcaidesa, *f.* wife of an *alcaide*.
alcaidía, *f.* office of an *alcaide*; duty on cattle.
alcalaíno, na, *n.* & *a.* (one) from Alcalá.
alcaldada, *f.* abusive action of an *alcalde*.
alcalde, *m.* mayor; justice of the peace; leader; name of a card game.—**a. de barrio,** selectman to whom the mayor delegates his function in a section of a city.—**alcaldear,** *vn.* (coll.) to play the *alcalde*.—**alcaldesa,** *f.* wife of an *alcalde*; mayoress.—**alcaldía,** *f.* office and jurisdiction of an *alcalde*.
alcalescencia, *f.* (chem.) alkalescence.
alcalescente, *a.* (chem.) alkalescent.
álcali, *m.* (chem.) alkali.—**alcalificable,** *a.* alkalifiable.—**alcalígeno, na,** *a.* alkaligenous.—**alcalimetría,** alkalimetry.—**alcalimétrico,** alkalimetric.—**alcalímetro,** *m.* alkalimeter.—**alcalinidad,** *f.* alkalinity.—**alcalino, na; alcalizado, da,** *a.* alkaline.—**alcalización,** *f.* (chem.) alkalization.—**alcalizar,** *va.* (*pret.* ALCALICÉ; *subj.* ALCALICE) (chem.) to alkalize.—**alcaloide,** *m.* alkaloid.
alcaller, *m.* potter.
alcamonías. **I.** *f. pl.* various aromatic seeds for seasoning. **II.** *m.* (Venez.) go-between.
alcana, *f.* ALHEÑA, privet.
alcance, *m.* reach; overtaking; balance; arm's length; scope, extent; range (of fire arms, etc.); capacity, ability; fathom; compass; supplement, extra edition; postscript; (print.) copy; importance; last-minute news; (com.) deficit; *pl.* understanding, grasp, mental powers.—**al a. de,** within reach of.—**a largo a.,** long-term (as *a.*).—**dar a. a,** to overtake.—**irle a uno a, or en, los alcances,** to watch, or spy on, one.—**seguir los alcances a,** to pursue.
alcancé, alcance, *v. V.* ALCANZAR.
alcancía, *f.* bank, money box; earthen balls stuffed with flowers for missiles; (mil.) explosive bullet.

alcandía, *f.* (bot.) Turkey millet; sorghum.
alcandial, *m.* millet field.
alcandora, *f.* beacon; bonfire; white tunic.
alcanfor, *m.* camphor.
alcanforada, *f.* (bot.) shrub having a camphor-like odor.
alcanforado, da, *a.* camphorate.
alcanforar, *va.* to camphorate.
alcanforero, *m.* (bot.) camphor tree.
alcántara, *f.* cover for velvet in the loom.
alcantarilla, *f.* small bridge; culvert; drain; sewer.—**alcantarillado,** *m.* sewerage, sewerage system; providing with sewers.
alcantarillar, *va.* to make or install sewers.
alcanzadizo, za, *a.* easily reached or obtainable.
alcanzado, da. I. *pp.* of ALCANZAR. **II.** *a.* needy; short of money; in arrears; impecunious.
alcanzadura, *f.* (vet.) tumor in the pastern.
alcanzar. I. *va.* (*pret.* ALCANCÉ; *subj.* ALCANCE) to follow; to overtake, come up to; to reach; to acquire, obtain, attain; to comprehend; to be creditor of a balance; to be contemporaneous. **II.** *vn.* to share; to suffice, be enough; to reach. —**a.** a (*inf.*), to succeed in (*pres. p.*). **III.** *vr.* (of horses and cattle) to wound the pasterns with the feet.
alcaparra, *f.* **alcaparro,** *m.* (bot.) caper bush; caper.—**alcaparrado, da,** *a.* dressed with capers.—**alcaparral,** *m.* caper field.—**alcaparrón,** *m. aug.* large caper.
alcaparrosa, *f.* = CAPARROSA, copperas.
alcaraván, *m.* (ornith.) bittern.—**alcaravanero,** *m.* bittern hawk.
alcaravea, *f.* (bot.) caraway seed.
alcarceña, *f.* (bot.) bitter vetch.
alcarceñal, *m.* field sown with vetch.
alcarracero, ra, *n.* potter; shelf for earthenware
alcarraza, *f.* unglazed and porous jar.
alcartaz, *m.* = CUCURUCHO, cornucopia.
alcatifa, *f.* fine carpet or rug; layer of earth.
[1]**alcatraz,** *m.* (ornith.) pelican.
[2]**alcatraz,** *m.* = ALCARTAZ.
alcaucil, *m.* wild artichoke.
alcayata, *f.* spike.
alcázar, *m.* castle; fortress; (naut.) quarterdeck
alcazuz, *m.* licorice.
[1]**alce,** *m.* (zool.) elk; moose.
[2]**alce,** *m.* cut (at cards).
alcino, *m.* (bot.) wild basil.
alción, *m.* (ornith.) Chinese swallow; kingfisher.
alcista, *f.* bull (stock speculator).
alcoba, *f.* alcove; bedroom; case for the tongue of a balance; place for public weighing.
alcocarra, *f.* gesture, grimace.
alcohol, *m.* alcohol; galena; kohl.—**a. absoluto,** absolute alcohol.—**a. amílico,** amyl alcohol.—**a. butílico,** butyl alcohol.—**a. desnaturalizado,** denatured alcohol.—**a. etílico,** ethyl alcohol.—**a. metílico,** methyl alcohol, wood alcohol.—**a. puro,** absolute alcohol.
alcoholado, da. I. *pp.* of ALCOHOLAR. **II.** *a.* (of animals) of a darker color round the eyes. **III.** *m.* medication composed with alcohol.
alcoholador, ra, *n.* rectifier of spirits.
alcoholar, *va.* to paint or dye with antimony; to distil alcohol from; (pharm.) to pulverize.
alcoholato, *m.* alcoholate.
alcoholera, *f.* vessel for antimony or alcohol.
alcoholicé, alcoholice, *v. V.* ALCOHOLIZAR.
alcohólico, ca, *a.* alcoholic.
alcoholímetro, *m.* alcoholometer.
alcoholismo, *m.* alcoholism.
alcoholización, *f.* (chem.) alcoholization.
alcoholizado, da, *a.* affected by alcoholism.
alcoholizar, *va.* (*pret.* ALCOHOLICÉ; *subj.* ALCOHOLICE) to alcoholize.
alcor, *m.* hill.
Alcorán, *m.* Alcoran, Koran.
alcoránico, ca, *a.* Alcoranic, Koranic.
alcoranista, *m.* Koran expounder; Koran scholar.
alcornocal, *m.* plantation of cork trees.
alcornoque, *m.* (bot.) cork tree; blockhead.
alcornoqueño, ña, *a.* pertaining to the cork tree.
[1]**alcorque,** *m.* corkwood clogs or soles.
[2]**alcorque,** *m.* ditch for water round trees.
alcorza, *f.* sugar paste for frosting.
alcorzar, *va.* to frost with sugar.
alcotán, *m.* (ornith.) lanner, bird of prey.
alcotana, *f.* pickaxe.
alcrebite, *m.* sulphur. Also AZUFRE.
alcribis, *m.* (metal.) tuyere.
alcubilla, *f.* reservoir; basin, mill pond.
alcucero, ra. I. *n.* maker or seller of ALCUZAS. **II.** *a.* pertaining to an ALCUZA.
alcuña, alcurnia, *f.* ancestry, lineage.
alcuza, *f.* oil bottle or cruet; oil can, oiler.
alcuzada, *f.* cruetful of oil.
alcuzcuz, *m.* ball of flour, water, and honey.
aldaba, *f.* knocker (of a door); latch; sliding crossbar to secure doors and windows.—**tener buena a.,** or **buenas aldabas,** to be well protected, be pretty safe.—**aldabada,** *f.* rap with the knocker; sudden fear; pangs of conscience.—**aldabazo, aldabonazo,** *m.* knocking.—**aldabear,** *vn.* to rap or knock at the door.—**aldabía,** *f.* horizontal crossbeam.—**aldabilla,** *f. dim.* small knocker; latch.—**aldabón,** *m. aug.* large knocker; iron trunk handle.
aldea, *f.* village, hamlet.
aldeanamente, *adv.* in village style, countrylike.
aldeaniego, ga, *a.* pertaining to a hamlet.
aldeano, na. I. *n.* villager, peasant. **II.** *a.* rustic, uncultured.
Aldebarán, *m.* (astr.) Bull's Eye.
aldehido, *m.* (chem.) aldehyde.—**a. fórmico,** (chem.) formaldehyde.
aldehuela, aldeilla, *f. dim.* little village.
aldeorrio, *m.* small, insignificant village.
aldiza, *f.* small reed without knots.
aldrán, *m.* one who sells wine to shepherds.
ale, *f.* ale.
aleación, *f.* alloying; alloy.
[1]**alear,** *vn.* to flutter; to move the arms quickly up and down; to recover from sickness or fatigue.
[2]**alear,** *va.* to alloy.
aleatorio, ria, *a.* pertaining to games of chance; (law) aleatory; fortuitous.
alebrarse, *vr.* (*ind.* ALIEBRO; *subj.* ALIEBRE) to squat; to cower (from fear).
alebrastarse, alebrestarse, *vr.* to cut capers; to become frightened or excited; to get puffed up.
alebronarse, *vr.* to lose heart; to take fright.
aleccionamiento, *m.* instruction, coaching.
aleccionar, *va.* to teach, instruct, coach.
alece, *m.* ragout of fish liver.
alecrín, *m.* a Cuban fish of the shark family.
alechugar, *va.* to curl like lettuce; to flute.
aledaño, ña. I. *a.* bounding, bordering. **II.** *m.* boundary, border.
alefanginas, *f. pl.* purgative pills from spices.
alefricé, alefrice, *v. V.* ALEFRIZAR.
alefris, alefriz, *m.* mortise, rabbet.
alegación, *f.* allegation, argument.
alegado, da, *a.* alleged.
alegador, ra, *n.* alleger.
alegar, *va.* (*pret.* ALEGUÉ; *subj.* ALEGUE) to allege, affirm; to quote; to adduce.
alegato, *m.* allegation; (law) summing-up.
alegoría, *f.* allegory.
alegórico, ca, *a.* allegorical.
alegorización, *f.* allegorization.
alegorizar, *va.* (*pret.* ALEGORICÉ; *subj.* ALEGORICE) to turn into allegory.
[1]**alegrador, ra,** *n.* & *a.* (one) causing merriment.
[2]**alegrador,** *m.* paper spill; (mech.) reamer.
[1]**alegrar. I.** *va.* to make merry, gladden, comfort, exhilarate; to enliven; to beautify. **II.** *vr.* **(de),** to rejoice (at); to be glad (of, *foll. by noun*; to, *foll. by verb*); to exult (in, over); to get tipsy.
[2]**alegrar,** *va.* (mech.) to round, bore, ream, widen.
alegre, *a.* merry, joyful; light-hearted, full of gaiety, lively; cheerful; funny, comic, facetious; gay; showy, fine; brilliant, (of colors) bright; lucky, fortunate; (coll.) off-color (story); reck-

less, careless; optimistic; tipsy.—**a. de cascos,** featherbrained.—**alegremente,** *adv.* merrily, gaily; gladly, cheerfully; facetiously.
alegreto, *m. adv.* (mus.) allegretto.
alegría, *f.* mirth, merriment, gaiety; rejoicing, joy; (bot.) sesame; oily grain; sesame and honey paste.—*pl.* rejoicings, public festival.
alegro, *m.* (mus.) allegro, fast and brisk.
alegrón. I. *m.* (coll.) sudden, unexpected joy; a flash. **II. a., na,** *a.* tipsy; lively (from liquor).
alegué, alegue, *v. V.* ALEGAR.
alejamiento, *m.* removal to a distance; receding; retiring, withdrawal; estrangement.
[1]**alejandrino, na,** *n.* & *a.* Alexandrian (from Alexandria).
[2]**alejandrino,** *n.* & *a.* Alexandrine (verse).
alejar. I. *va.* to remove, to a distance; to separate; to withdraw; to estrange. **II.** *vr.* to recede; to draw or move away.
alejijas, *f. pl.* barley porridge.
alelarse, *vr.* to become stupified.
alelí, alhelí, *m.* (bot.) winter gilliflower
alelismo, *m.* (biol.) allelism.
alelo, *m.* (biol.) allele.
aleluya, *f.* hallelujah; joy, merriment; Easter time; (bot.) wood-sorrel.—*pl.* small prints thrown among the people on Easter eve; dull, poor verses, doggerel.
alema, *f.* allotted quantity of irrigation water.
alemán, mana. I. *n.* German; *f.* allemande (dance). **II.** *a.* German.
alemanda, *f.* allemande (dance).
Alemania, *f.* Germany.
alemanisco, ca, *a.* Germanic; cloth made in Germany; huckaback; damask table linen.
alentada, *f.* a long breath.
alentadamente, *adv.* bravely, gallantly.
alentado, da. I. *pp.* of ALENTAR. **II.** *a.* spirited, courageous; well, in good health.
alentador, ra. I. *n.* one who inspires courage. **II.** *a.* encouraging, cheering.
alentar. I. *vn.* (*ind.* ALIENTO; *subj.* ALIENTE) to breathe. **II.** *va.* to encourage, cheer; to inspire.
aleonado, leonado, da, *a.* lionlike; lion-colored.
alepín, *m.* a kind of bombazine.
alerce, *m.* (bot.) larch tree.
alergeno, *m.* allergen.
alergia, *f.* allergy.
alérgico, ca, *a.* allergic.
alergista, *n.* allergist.
alero, *m.* projecting part of a roof; eaves; gable end, corona; hood moulding; water table; splashboard of a carriage.—*pl.* snares for partridges.
alerón, *m.* (aer.) aileron.
alerta. I. *adv.* vigilantly, carefully.—**estar a.,** to be on the alert. **II.** *interj.* look out! watch out! **III.** *m.* (mil.) alarm, alert.
alertar, *va.* to render vigilant; to put on guard.
alerto, ta, *a.* vigilant, alert, guarded.
alesna, lesna, lezna, *f.* awl.—**alesnado, da,** *a.* awl-shaped, pointed.
aleta, *f. dim.* small wing; fin (of a fish); (arch.) alette; (mech.) leaf of a hinge; teeth of a pinion; blade (of a screw propeller).
aletada, *f.* motion of the wings.
aletargamiento, *m.* lethargy.
aletargarse, *vr.* to fall into a lethargy.
aletazo, *m.* blow with the wing; flapping.
aletear, *vn.* to flutter (wings or fins).
aleteo, *m.* fluttering (of wings or fins); palpitation (of heart).
aleto, halieto, *m.* (ornith.) sea eagle; (Peru) falcon.
aletría, *m.* vermicelli.
aleudarse, leudarse, *vr.* to become fermented.
aleurita, *f.* (bot.) tung tree, tung-oil tree.
aleurómetro, *m.* aleurometer.
aleurona, *f.* (bot., biochem.) aleurone.
aleve, *a.* treacherous, perfidious.
alevilla, *a.* (entom.) white moth resembling the silkworm's moth.
alevosa, *f.* (vet.) tumor under the tongue.
alevosamente, *adv.* treacherously.
alevosía, *f.* perfidy, treachery.
alevoso, sa, *a.* treacherous.
alexifármaco, ca, *a.* (med.) alexipharmic, antidotal, prophylactic.
alfa, *f.* alpha (Greek letter); beginning.
alfábega, *f.* = ALBAHACA, (bot.) sweet basil.
alfabético, ca, *a.* alphabetical.
alfabetismo, *m.* literacy.
alfabetización, *f.* literacy.
alfabetizar, *va.* to alphabetize; to teach reading and writing, make (a person) literate.
alfabeto, *m.* alphabet.
alfaguara, *f.* copious stream.
alfajía, *f.* wood frame for windows and doors.
alfajor, *m.* = ALAJÚ, nut and honey confection.
alfalfa, *f.* (bot.) lucern, alfalfa.—**alfalfal, alfalfar,** *m.* alfalfa field.—**alfalfe,** *m.* = ALFALFA.
alfana, *f.* strong and spirited horse.
alfandoque, *m.* candy made with molasses, cheese and ginger, or of thickened brown-sugar syrup.
alfaneque, *m.* white eagle; tent, booth.
alfanjado, da, *a.* cutlass-shaped.
alfanje, *m.* hanger, cutlass.—**alfanjete,** *m. dim.* small cutlass.—**alfanjazo,** *m.* wound with a cutlass.—**alfanjón,** *m. aug.* large hanger or cutlass.—**alfanjonazo,** *m.* cut with a large hanger.
alfaque, *m.* shoal or bar.
alfaquí, *m.* alfaqui, a Mussulman expounder and teacher of the Koran.
[1]**alfar,** *m.* pottery: ARCILLA, clay.
[2]**alfar,** *vn.* (of horses), to raise the head too much.
[3]**alfar,** *a.* (of a horse), that raises the head too much.
alfaraz, *m.* Moorish horse for light cavalry.
[1]**alfarda,** *f.* tax paid for land irrigation.
[2]**alfarda,** *f.* (arch.) light wooden beam.
[1]**alfardilla,** *f.* tax for cleaning water-supply ditches.
[2]**alfardilla,** *f.* galloon; gold or silver braid.
[1]**alfardón,** *m.* washer of a wheel.
[2]**alfardón,** *m.* = [1]ALFARDA.
alfarería, *f.* pottery; potter's art, workshop or store.
alfarero, ra, *n.* potter.
[1]**alfarje,** *m.* lower stone of an oil mill.
[2]**alfarje,** *m.* ceiling with carved wood; wainscot.
alfarjía, *f.* = ALFAJÍA.
alféizar, *m.* (arch.) splay of a door or window; embrasure.
alfeñicar, *va.* to frost with sugar.
alfeñicarse, *vr.* to become thin; (coll.) to affect delicateness.
alfeñique, *m.* sugar paste; (coll.) delicate person.
alferazgo, *m.* second lieutenancy.
alferecía, *f.* epilepsy.
alférez, *m.* ensign; second lieutenant.
alficoz, alpicoz, *m.* cucumber (plant & fruit).
alfil, *m.* bishop (in chess).
alfiler, *m.* pin; scarf-pin; brooch; tip, gift.—*pl.* alfileres, pin money.—**a. de París,** wire nail.—**a. de seguridad,** safety pin (more generally called IMPERDIBLE).—**con todos sus alfileres,** or, **de veinticinco alfileres,** dressed up in high style.—**no estar con sus alfileres,** not to be in a good mood.—**pedir para alfileres,** to ask for a tip.—**pegar,** or **prender, con alfileres,** to do in a slipshod way; (fig.) to build on sand.
alfilerazo, *m.* prick with a pin; large pin.
alfiletero, *m.* pin case, needlecase; pincushion.
alfitete, *m.* paste made of coarse wheat flour.
alfolí, *m.* granary; salt depot.—**alfoliero, alfolinero,** *m.* keeper of a granary or depot.
[1]**alfombra,** *f.* = [2]ALFOMBRILLA.
[2]**alfombra,** *f.* floor carpet.
alfombrar, *va.* to carpet.
alfombrero, ra, *n.* carpet maker.
[1]**alfombrilla,** *f.* small carpet, rug.

[2]**alfombrilla,** *f.* (med.) measles.
alfóncigo, *m.* pistachio; pistachio tree.
alfonsearse, *vr.* (coll.) to mock, banter.
alfónsigo, *m.* = ALFÓNCIGO.
alfonsina, *f.* solemn act held in the Alphonsine college of Alcalá.
alfonsino, na, *a.* pertaining to the Alphonsos (Spanish kings).
alforfón, *m.* buckwheat.
alforja, *f.* saddlebag; knapsack.
alforjero, *m.* maker or seller of saddlebags; lay brother who begs alms; one who carries the bag with provisions.—**perro a.,** watchdog.
alforjilla, ita, uela, *f. dim.* small saddlebag; small knapsack.
alforza, *f.* plait, tuck; (coll.) scar.
alfoz, *m.* & *f.* district, borough, neighboring district or dependency.
alga, *f.* (bot.) alga, seaweed.
[1]**algaida,** *f.* ridge of shifting sand; sand dune.
[2]**algaida,** *f.* jungle, brush.
algaído, da, *a.* (prov.) thatched.
[1]**algalia.** *f.* civet, substance used in perfume; *m.* civet cat.—**algaliar,** *va.* to perfume with civet.
[2]**algalia,** *f.* (surg.) catheter.
[1]**algara,** *f.* skin (of an egg, onion, etc.)
[2]**algara,** *f.* foraging party of cavalry.
algarabía, *f.* Arabic (language); (fig.) gabble, jargon; din, clamor; (bot.) centaury.
[1]**algarada,** *f.* loud cry, din; [2]ALGARA.
[2]**algarada,** *f.* (mil.) ancient catapult.
algarero, ra, *a.* prating, chattering, talkative.
[1]**algarrada,** *f.* driving bulls into the pen; bull baiting.
[2]**algarrada,** *f.* = [2]ALGARADA.
algarroba, *f.* (bot.) carob bean; honey mesquite.
algarrobal, *m.* carob tree plantation or grove.
algarrobera, *f.*, **algarrobo,** *m.* (bot.) carob tree.
algazara, *f.* huzza; din, clamor.
algazul, *m.* seaweed producing barilla.
álgebra, *f.* algebra; (anc. surg.) art of setting joints.
algebraico, ca; algébrico, ca, *a.* algebraic.
algebrista, *m.* algebraist; (anc. surg.) bonesetter.
algecireño, ña, *n.* & *a.* Algecirian, from, or pertaining to, Algeciras.
algidez, *f.* (med.) icy coldness.
álgido, da, *a.* algid, icy.
algo. I. *indef. pron.* some, something, aught; anything.—**a. de nuevo,** something new.—**a. es a.** or **más vale a. que nada,** something (anything) is better than nothing, every little bit counts. **II.** *adv.* somewhat, a little, rather.
algodón, *m.* cotton (substance, cloth, thread); cotton plant.—**a. en rama,** raw cotton.—**a. pólvora, pólvora de a.,** guncotton.—*pl.* CENDALES, cotton put in bottom of inkwells.
algodonal, *m.* cotton plantation.
algodonar, *va.* to cover or fill with cotton.
algodonería, *f.* cotton factory; cotton trade.
algodonero, ra. I. *a.* pertaining to cotton. **II.** *m.* cotton plant; cotton dealer; cottonwood poplar.
algodonoso, sa, *a.* cottony; covered with thick down; woolly; (of fruit) tasteless.
algología, *f.* algology.
algonquín, na, *n.* & *a.* Algonquin.
algorín, *m.* place in oil mills for receiving olives.
algoritmia, *f.* (math.) algorism.
algorítmico, ca, *a.* algorithmic.
algoritmo, *m.* algorithm; algorism; arithmetical or algebraic computation.
algoso, sa, *a.* full of algæ.
alguacil, *m.* constable, peace officer, bumbailiff; short-legged spider.
alguacilazgo, *m.* office of an *alguacil.*
alguarín, *m.* storeroom; flour-mill bucket.
alguaza, *f.* (prov.) hinge.
alguien, *indef. pron.* somebody, someone; anybody.
algún, *a. contr.* of ALGUNO, used before masculine nouns.—**a. tanto,** a little, somewhat.
alguno, na. I. *a.* some, any; (for emphasis, following a noun) not any (*no tengo dinero alguno,* I haven't any money at all).—**a. que otro,** a few, some.—**alguna que otra vez,** sometimes, once in a while.—**alguna vez,** sometime; sometimes, now and then. **II.** *indef. pron.* somebody, someone; anybody, anyone.—*pl.* some.
alhaja, *f.* jewel, gem; showy furniture; highly prized thing; an excellent person; (ironic) a bad one, a tough one (of persons, often in the form, **¡buena a.!**).
alhajar, *va.* to adorn; to furnish, fit up.
alhajuela, *f. dim.* little jewel.
alhamel, *m.* (prov.) beast of burden; porter; muleteer.
alhandal, *m.* (pharm.) colocynth, plant with purgative properties.
alharaca, *f.* clamor, fuss, ado.
alharaquiento, ta, *a.* fussy, grumbling.
alhárgama, alharma, *f.* (bot.) wild rue.
alhelí, alelí, *m.* (bot.) gilliflower.
alheña, *f.* (bot.) privet; powder from privet leaves used in dyeing; rust, mildew, blight (on corn).—**alheñar. I.** *va.* to dye with privet. **II.** *vr.* to become mildewed (app. to corn.)
alhoja, *f.* a bird resembling a lark.
alholva, *f.* (bot.) fenugreek, plant used for forage.
alhóndiga, *f.* public granary; wheat exchange.—**alhondiguero,** *m.* keeper of a public granary.
alhorma, *f.* Moorish camp or royal tent.
alhorre, *m.* (med.) meconium, first discharge from infant's bowels; skin eruption (on baby).
alhoz, *m.* = ALFOZ.
alhucema, *f.* (bot.) lavender.
alhumajo, *m.* pine needles.
aliabierto, ta, *a.* open-winged.
aliacán, *m.* (med.) jaundice.
aliacanado, da, *a.* jaundiced.
aliáceo, a, *a.* pertaining to or like garlic.
aliado, da. I. *pp.* of ALIARSE. **II.** *a.* & *n.* ally, allied.
aliaga, aulaga, *f.* (bot.) furze, whin.—**aliagar, aulagar,** *m.* furze field.
alianza, *f.* alliance; agreement, pact; (Bib.) covenant; alliance by marriage.
aliara, *f.* drinking horn.
aliaria, *f.* (bot.) garlic mustard.
aliarse, *vr.* to become allied; to form an alliance.
alias, *adv.* (Lat.) otherwise, alias.
alible, *a.* nutritive, nourishing.
álica, *f.* porridge of corn, wheat, and pulse.
alicaído, da, *a.* drooping, weak, extenuated; discouraged, depressed, downhearted.
alicántara, *f.*, **alicante,** *m.* a poisonous snake.
alicantina, *f.* (coll.) artifice, stratagem, trap.
alicantino, na, *n.* & *a.* (one) from Alicante.
alicatado, *m.* work inlaid with tiles in Arab style.
alicates, *m. pl.* pliers.
aliciente, *m.* attraction, inducement.
alicuanta, *a.* (math.) aliquant.
alícuota, *f. a.* (math.) aliquot; proportional.—**partes alícuotas,** (arith.) aliquot parts.
alidada, *f.* alidade, surveyor's telescope.
aliebro, aliebre, *v. V.* ALEBRARSE.
alienación, *f.* (law and med.) alienation.
alienado, da, *a.* insane.
alienar, *va.* (law) to alienate (property); to estrange; to numb.
alienista, *n.* alienist.
[1]**aliento,** *m.* breath; breathing; vigor; bravery; enterprise, activity.—**dar a.,** to encourage; to further; to cheer.—**de un a.,** in a single breath; without stopping.—**sin a.,** out of breath.
[2]**aliento, aliente,** *v. V.* ALENTAR
[1]**alifafe,** *m.* callous tumor on a horse's hock.
[2]**alifafe,** *m.* (coll.) chronic complaint.
alifar, *va.* (prov.) to polish, burnish.
alifara, *f.* (prov.) collation, luncheon.
alífero, ra, *a.* having wings, winged.
aliforme, *a.* aliform, wing-shaped.
aligación, *f.* binding together; (math.) alligation.
aligamiento, *m.* = ALIGACIÓN.
aligar, *va.* (*pret.* ALIGUÉ; *subj.* ALIGUE) = LIGAR, to bind, join.

aliger, *m.* cross guard (of a sword).
aligeramiento, *m.* alleviation, lightening.
aligerar, *va.* to lighten; to alleviate; to ease; to hasten, hurry (up); to shorten.
alígero, ra, *a.* (poet.) winged, fast, fleet.
aligué, aligue, *v. V.* ALIGAR.
alijador, ra, *n.* smuggler; (naut.) one who lightens (ship's cargo); (naut.) lighter; one who clears cotton of seeds.
[1]**alijar,** *va.* (naut.) to lighten (cargo); to clear (cotton) of seeds, to gin; to smuggle.
[2]**alijar,** *m.* waste, stony ground.—**alijarar,** *va.* to divide (waste lands) for cultivation.
alijarero, *m.* sharer of waste lands to till.
alijariego, ga, *a.* pertaining to waste lands.
alijo, *m.* (naut.) lightening of a ship's cargo; ginning (cotton); smuggling or smuggled goods.
alimaña, *f.* animal (gen. destructive ones).
alimentación, *f.* feeding; meals, board; nutrition.—**de a.,** feeding, feed (as *a.,* as in *agua de alimentación,* feed water).
alimentar, *va.* to feed, nourish; to feed (a machine); to support, supply with the necessaries of life; to nurture, fondle, encourage, further; to cherish, have (hope).
alimentario, ria, *n.* one who enjoys a maintenance.
alimenticio, cia, *a.* nourishing; feeding, food (as *a.*).
alimentista, *n.* = ALIMENTARIO.
alimento, *m.* nourishment, food, nutriment; anything furnished to keep something going, as a fire; encouragement, incentive.—*pl.* allowance, pension, alimony; meals, board.—**a. combustible,** (of foods) carbohydrate or fat.—**a. plástico,** protein, nitrogenous food.—**a. respiratorio** = A. COMBUSTIBLE.
alimentoso, sa, *a.* nourishing, nutritious.
alimo, *m.* (bot.) = ORZAGA, mountain spinach.
alimoche, *m.* a bird of prey, a kind of vulture.
alimonarse, *vr.* to turn yellowish from disease (said of tree leaves).
alindado, da, *a.* affectedly nice or elegant.
[1]**alindar,** *va.* to mark the limits of.
[2]**alindar,** *va.* to embellish, make beautiful.
alineación, *f.* alignment.
alineamiento, *m.* alignment.
alinear, *va.* & *vr.* to align, line, line up.
aliñador, ra, *n.* one who embellishes; one who seasons or dresses food.
aliñar, *va.* to adorn; to dress or season (food).
aliño, *m.* ornament, decoration; cleanliness; dressing or seasoning.—**aliñoso, sa,** *a.* dressed up, decked out; decorated.
alioli, *m.* (prov.) mixture of garlic and oil.
alionín, *m.* (ornith.) the blue-feathered duck.
alipata, *m.* a Philippine poison tree.
alípede, *a.* (poet.) winged, swift, nimble.
alípedo, da, *a.* (zool.) aliped, with toes connected by winglike skin.
aliquebrado, da, *a.* broken-winged; dejected.
alisador, ra, *n.* polisher, smoothing iron; silk stick; tool to shape wax candles.
alisadura, *f.* planing, smoothing, polishing.
alisaduras, *f. pl.* shavings, cuttings.
[1]**alisar,** *va.* to plane, smooth, polish, burnish.
[2]**alisar,** *m.* **aliseda,** *f.* alder-tree plantation.
alisios, *m. pl.* trade winds.
alisma, *f.* (bot.) water plantain.
aliso, *m.* (bot.) alder tree.
alisón, *f.* (bot.) alyssum.
alistado, da, listado, da, *a.* listed; enlisted.
alistador, ra, *n.* one who enrolls or lists.
alistamiento, *m.* enrollment; conscription, levy.
[1]**alistar,** *va.* & *vr.* to enlist, enroll.
[2]**alistar,** *va.* to get or make ready.
aliteración, *f.* alliteration.
aliterado, da, *a.* alliterative.
aliviador, ra, *n.* assistant; helper; spindle to raise or lower a running millstone.
aliviar, *va.* to lighten; to loosen; to alleviate, assuage, soothe, relieve; to hasten, speed up.
alivio, *m.* alleviation, easement; mitigation; relief; improvement, betterment.
alizar, *m.* dado or wainscotting of tiles.
alizarina, *f.* (chem.) alizarine.
aljaba, *f.* quiver (for arrows).
aljafana, *f.* = ALJOFAINA.
aljama, *f.* assembly of Moors or Jews; synagogue.
aljamía, *f.* (obs.) corrupted Arabic spoken by Moors; Moorish name of the Spanish language.
aljarafe, *m.* roof; terrace.
aljarfa, *f.,* **aljarfe,** *m.,* **aljerife,** *m.* tarred fishing net with small meshes.
aljévena, *f.* (prov.) = ALJOFAINA.
aljez, *m.* gypsum; plaster of Paris.—**aljezar,** *m.* gypsum pit.—**aljezón,** *m.* plaster rubbish; ALJEZ.
aljibe, *m.* cistern; reservoir, pool; (naut.) tank boat for supplying vessels with water.
aljibero, *m.* one who takes care of cisterns.
aljofaina, jofaina, *f.* washbowl, basin.
aljófar, *m.* misshapen pearl; (poet.) water or dewdrops.
aljofarar, *va.* to adorn with pearls.
aljofifa, *f.* mop.—**aljofifar,** *va.* to clean with a cloth; to mop.
aljonje, *m.* = AJONJE, bird lime.
aljonjera, *f.* **aljonjero,** *m.* = AJONJERA, (bot.) a kind of thistle.
aljonjolí, *m.* = AJONJOLÍ, (bot.) sesame.
aljor, *m.* crude gypsum.
aljorozar, *va.* to level, render smooth; to plaster.
aljorra, *m.* (Cuba) a very small insect which, carried by the wind, destroys plantations.
aljuba, *f.* a Moorish garment.
alma, *f.* soul; ghost; phantom; human being; vigor, strength; substance, main point; staff; (arch.) scaffolding pole; web (of a beam, rail, etc.) (gun) bore; core (of rope, of a casting); (naut.) body of a mast; sounding-post in a fiddle, etc.—**a. atravesada, de Caín,** or **de Judas,** devilish or heartless person.—**a. de cántaro,** fool.—**a. de Dios,** harmless, inoffensive person; simple, kind-hearted person.—**a. en pena,** soul in purgatory.—**a. mía, mi a.,** my dearest; my love.—**a., vida y corazón,** heart and soul.—**con toda el a.,** with all one's heart and soul.—**dar, entregar, exhaler,** or **rendir, el a.,** to give up the ghost, die.—**del a., de mi a.,** dearest.—**en el a.,** keenly, deeply; with all one's heart.—**tener el a. bien puesta,** to have courage and energy.
almacén, *m.* store, shop; warehouse; storage house, depot; (Arg. & Cuba) grocery store; naval arsenal, dockyard.—**a. de agua,** (naut.) water cask.—**a. de una bomba de agua,** (naut.) chamber of a pump.—**almacenado, da,** *a.* stored, bonded.—**almacenador,** *m.* warehouseman.—**almacenaje,** *m.* storage.—**almacenar,** *va.* to lay up, hoard; to store.—**almacenero,** *m.* shopkeeper.—**almacenista,** *m.* shop owner; salesman; (Cuba) wholesale grocer.
[1]**almáciga,** *f.* mastic; resin from certain trees.
[2]**almáciga,** *f.* tree nursery.
almacigado, da, *a.* perfumed with mastic.
almacigar, *va.* to perfume with mastic.
[1]**almácigo,** *m.* mastic tree.
[2]**almácigo,** *m.* = [2]ALMÁCIGA.
almaciguero, ra, *a.* pertaining to mastic.
almádana, almadaneta, *f.* sledge-hammer.
almádena, *f.* = ALMÁDANA.
almadía, *f.* canoe used in India; raft.
almadiero, *m.* a raft pilot.
almadraba, *f.* tunny fishing or fishery; tunny-fish net.—**almadrabero, ra,** *n.* tunny fisher.
almadreña, *f.* wooden shoe or sabot.
almagáneta, *f.* = ALMÁDANA.
almagesto, *m.* Almagest, anc. book on astronomy.
almagra, *f.* = ALMAGRE.
almagral, *m.* place abounding in ochre.
almagrar, *va.* to color with red ochre; (vulg.) to draw blood.
almagre, *m.* red ochre, red earth, Indian red.

almaizal, almaizar, *m.* gauze veil worn by Moors; sash worn by priests.
almajaneque, *m.* (mil.) battering ram.
almajara, *f.* (prov.) forcing bed, hotbed.
almajo, *m.* (bot.) plant yielding barilla.
almanac, almanaque, *m.* almanac, calendar.—**hacer almanaques,** (fig.) to muse, be pensive.
almanaquero, ra, *n.* maker or vender of almanacs.
almancebe, *m.* fishing net.
almandina, *f.* (min.) red garnet; almandine.
almanguena, *f.* = ALMAGRE.
almanta, *f.* space between rows of vines and olive trees; ridge between two furrows.
almarada, *f.* triangular poniard; needle for making rope sandals.
almarcha, *f.* town on marshy ground or lowland.
[1]**almarjal,** *m.* glasswort field.
[2]**almarjal, marjal,** *m.* marshy ground.
almarjo, *m.* (bot.) glasswort.
almaro, *m.* (bot.) common clary.
almarrá, *m.* cotton gin.
almarraja, almarraza, *f.* perforated glass bottle used for sprinkling or watering.
[1]**almártaga, almártega,** *f.* (chem.) massicot; litharge.
[2]**almártaga, almártiga,** *f.* halter; (Colomb.) sluggard; good-for-nothing.
almartigón, *m.* rough halter.
almástiga, *f.* mastic.—**almastigado, da,** *a.* containing mastic.
almatrero, *m.* one fishing with shad nets.
almatriche, *m.* irrigation canal.
almazara, *f.* (prov.) oil mill.—**almazarero,** *m.* oil miller.
almazarrón, *m.* = ALMAGRE.
[1]**almea,** *f.* Oriental poetess and dancer.
[2]**almea,** *f.* (bot.) dried bark of the storax tree.
almear, *m.* stack of hay, corn, or straw.
almeja, *f.* clam.—**almejar,** *m.* clam bed.
almejía, *f.* small cloak used by poor Moors.
almena, *f.* merlon of a battlement.
almenado, da. I. *pp.* of ALMENAR. **II.** *a.* having battlements. **III.** *m.* = ALMENAJE.
almenaje, *m.* series of merlons; battlement.
[1]**almenar,** *va.* to crown with merlons.
[2]**almenar,** *m.* cresset, cuplike metal torch.
[1]**almenara,** *f.* beacon; large candelabra.
[2]**almenara,** *f.* outlet channel for irrigation water.
almendra, *f.* almond; kernel; bean; almond-shaped diamond; cut glass drop; fine cocoon.—**a. confitada,** praline.—**a. de cacao,** cocoa bean; chocolate nut.—**a. garapiñada,** sugar almond, praline.
almendrada, *f.* almond milk.
almendrado, da. I. *a.* almondlike. **II.** *m.* macaroon.
almendral, *m.* almond-tree plantation.
almendrera, *f.* = ALMENDRO.
almendrero, *m.* dish for almonds; ALMENDRO.
almendrilla, *f.* almond-shaped file.—**almendrillas,** almond-shaped diamond earrings.
almendro, *m.* almond tree.
almendrón, *m.* Jamaican myrtle tree and its fruit.
almendruco, *m.* green almond.
almenilla, *f. dim.* small merlon; merlon-shaped fringe.
almete, *m.* helmet; soldier wearing a helmet.
almez, *m.* lotus tree.—**almeza,** *f.* fruit of the lotus tree.—**almezo,** *m.* = ALMEZ.
almiar, *m.* haystack.
almíbar, *m.* sugar sirup.—**almibares,** preserved fruit.
almibarado, da. I. *pp.* of ALMIBARAR. **II.** *a.* (fig.) honeyed (language); sweet (person); endearing.
almibarar, *va.* to preserve (fruit) in sugar; (fig.) to conciliate with soft words.
almicantarada, *f.*, **almicantarat,** *f.* (astr.) almucantar, small circle parallel to the horizon to determine the height of stars.
almidón, *m.* starch; fecula.
almidonado, da. I. *pp.* of ALMIDONAR. **II.** *a.* starched; (fig.) dressed with affected nicety; spruce; stiff.
almidonar, *va.* to starch.
almidonería, *f.* starch factory.
almilla, *f.* under waistcoat; short military jacket; (carp.) tenon; breast of pork.
almimbar, *m.* pulpit of a mosque.
alminar, *m.* minaret, turret of a mosque.
almiranta, *f.* (naut.) vice admiral's ship, flagship; admiral's wife.
almirantazgo, *m.* (naut.) board of admiralty; admiralty court; admiral's dues; admiralship.
almirante, *m.* admiral, commander of a fleet; head ornament for women; swimming master; a kind of shell.
almirez, *m.* brass mortar; wood engraver's tool.
almizclar, *va.* to perfume with musk.
almizcle, *m.* musk.—**almizcleña,** *f.* (bot.) musk, grape hyacinth.—**almizcleño, ña,** *a.* musky.
almizclero, ra. I. *a.* musky. **II.** *m.* muskdeer. **III.** *f.* muskrat.
almo, ma, *a.* (poet.) creating; animating, fostering (*cf.* alma mater); venerable.
almocadén, *m.* (anc.) infantry commander; cavalry officer commanding part of a platoon; delegated mayor of part of a city (in Morocco).
almocafre, *m.* gardener's hoe, dibble.
almocárabes, almocarbes, *m. pl.* (arch. and carp.) bow-shaped ornaments.
almocatracía, *f.* duty on broadcloths and woollens.
almocela, *f.* ancient hood.
almocrate, *m.* sal ammoniac.
almocri, *m.* reader of the Koran in a mosque.
almodí, *m.* = ALMUDÍ, a dry measure.
almodón, *m.* baking flour.
almodrote, *m.* sauce for eggplant; hodgepodge.
almófar, *m.* mail head cover under helmet.
almofía, *f.* = ALJOFAINA, washbowl, basin.
almofrej, almofrez, *m.* travelling bag for bedding.
almogama, *f.* (naut.) sternpost of a ship.
almogávar, *m.* soldier of raiding troops sent to enemy's territory; raider.—**almogavarear,** *va.* to raid.—**almogavaría, almogavería,** *f.* body of raiding troops.
almohada, *f.* pillow; bolster; pillowcase; (naut.) piece of timber on which the bowsprit rests.—**aconsejarse,** or **consultar, con la a.,** (coll.) to sleep on the matter, think it over carefully.—**dar a.,** to raise to the nobility (a ceremony in which the queen raises a lady to nobility by having her sit beside her on a cushion).
almohadilla, *f. dim.* small bolster or pillow; sewing cushion; pads of a harness; (arch.) projecting wall stone; (vet.) callous excrescence on the back of mules.
almohadillado, da, *a.* quilted; (arch.) with projecting wall stones.
almohadón, *m. aug.* large cushion or pillow.
almohatre, *m.* = ALMOCRATE, sal ammoniac.
almohaza, *f.* currycomb.
almohazador, *m.* groom.
almohazar, *va.* to curry with a currycomb.
almojábana, *f.* cake made of cheese and flour; cruller.
almojarifadgo, almojarifalgo, almojarifazgo, *m.* ancient duty on imports or exports.
almojarife, *m.* the king's taxgatherer; custom house officer.
almojaya, *f.* (build.) putlog.
almona, *f.* public stores; shad fishery; soap manufactory.
almóndiga, almondiguilla, *f.* = ALBÓNDIGA, etc., ball of forcemeat with eggs and spice.
almoneda, *f.* auction.—**almonedear,** *va.* to auction.
almoradux, *m.* (bot.) sweet marjoram.
almorávide, *n.* & *a.* Almoravide (name of an ancient Moorish tribe).
almorcé, *pret.* of ALMORZAR.

almorejo, *m.* (bot.) a species of grass.
almorí, almurí, *m.* sweetmeat or cake.
almoronía, *f.* = ALBORONÍA, eggplant, tomato dish.
almorranas, *f. pl.* (med.) piles, hemorrhoids.
almorraniento, ta, *a.* suffering from piles.
almorrefa, *f.* triangular tile.
almorta, *f.* (bot.) blue vetch.
[1]**almorzada,** *f.* as much as can be held in the hollow of both hands.
[2]**almorzada,** *f.* (Mex.) = [2]ALMUERZO.
almorzado, da. I. *pp.* of ALMORZAR. **II.** *a.* having already breakfasted.
almorzar. I. *vn.* (*ind. pres.* ALMUERZO, *pret.* ALMORCÉ; *subj.* ALMUERCE) to breakfast; (more often) to lunch. **II.** *va.* to eat (at or for breakfast or lunch).
almotacén, *m.* inspector of weights and measures; inspector's office or function.
almotacenazgo, *m.* office of ALMOTACÉN.
almotacenía, *f.* fee paid to ALMOTACÉN.
almozárabe, *m.* Christian subject to the Moors.
almud, *m.* a dry measure, about 0.8 of a liter.—**a. de tierra,** about ½ acre.—**almudada,** *f.* ground sufficient for one *almud* of seed.—**almudejo,** *m.* each of the weights kept by the *almudero*.—**almudero,** *m.* keeper of dry measures.
almudí, almudín, *m.* (prov.) measure containing six *cahíces*.
almuecín, almuédano, *m.* muezzin.
almuérdago, *m.* birdlime.
almuerza, *f.* = [1]ALMORZADA.
[1]**almuerzo, almuerce,** *v. V.* ALMORZAR.
[2]**almuerzo,** *m.* breakfast; (more often) lunch; breakfast cover.
almunia, *f.* orchard; vegetable garden.
alnado, da, *n.* = HIJASTRO, stepchild.
alo, *m.* (Mex.) a large cockatoo.
aloaria, *f.* (arch.) vault.
alobadado, da, *a.* bitten by a wolf; (vet.) laboring under morbid swellings.
alobaro, *m.* (meteorol.) allobar.
alobunado, da, *a.* wolf-colored.
alocadamente, *adv.* rashly, recklessly.
alocado, da, *a.* half-witted; wild, reckless.
alocución, *f.* allocution, address, speech.
alodial, *a.* (law) allodial.—**alodio,** *m.* alodium.
áloe, *m.* (bot.) aloe tree, aloes.—**aloético, ca,** *a.* aloetic.—**aloína,** *f.* aloin, active principle of aloes.
alófana, *f.* (min.) allophane.
alogamia, *f.* (bot.) allogamy.
aloína, *f.* (chem.) aloin.
aloja, *f.* mead, drink made with honey and spices.
alojamiento, *m.* lodging; quartering of soldiers; (naut.) steerage.—*pl.* (mil.) camp, quarters.
alojar. I. *va.* to lodge; to quarter (troops). **II.** *vr.* to take lodgings; to lodge; to dwell; to go (into), be contained or work (in).
alojería, *f.* mead shop.
alojero, ra, *n.* mead mixer and seller; *m.* (theat.) box near the pit.
alomado, da, *a.* (of animals) having a curved back.
alomar. I. *va.* to distribute equally (the load on a horse); to plow in furrows. **II.** *vr.* (of horses) to become strong and vigorous.
alón, *m.* plucked wing of any fowl.
alondra, *f.* (ornith.) lark.
alongamiento, *m.* delay; distance (separating points or things).
alongar, *va.* (*ind.* ALUENGO; *subj.* ALUENGUE) to enlarge; to extend; to prolong; to separate.
alópata, *m.* allopath.—**alopatía,** *f.* allopathy.—**alopático, ca,** *a.* allopathic.
alopecia, *f.* (med.) alopecia, baldness.
alopiado, da, *a.* opiate.
aloque, *a.* clear white or red and white (wine).
aloquín, *m.* stone inclosure in a wax bleachery.
alosa, *f.* (ichth.) = SÁBALO, shad.
alotar, *va.* (naut.) ARRIZAR, to reef, stow, lash.—**a. las anclas,** (naut.) to stow the anchors.
alotropia, *f.* (chem.) allotropy.
alotrópico, ca, *a.* (chem.) allotropic.
[1]**alpaca, alpaga,** *f.* alpaca (animal and fabric).
[2]**alpaca,** *f.* German silver.
alpañata, *f.* piece of chamois skin.
alpargata, *f.,* **alpargate,** *m.* fiber sandal.
alpargatado, da, *a.* wearing *alpargatas.*
alpargatar, *vn.* to make *alpargatas.*
alpargatería, *f. alpargata* shop or factory.
alpargatero, ra, *n.* maker or seller of *alpargatas.*
alpargatilla, *f. dim.* small *alpargata;* crafty, designing fellow.
alpechín, *m.* juice oozing from a heap of olives.
alpende, *m.* tool shed (esp. in mines).
alpestre, *a.* Alpine.
alpicoz, *m.* (prov.) = ALFICOZ, cucumber.
alpinismo, *m.* mountain climbing, Alpinism.
alpinista, *n.* mountain climber, Alpinist.
alpino, na, *a.* Alpine.
alpiste, *m.* birdseed.—**dejar a uno a.,** (coll.) to leave one out (of a business, etc.).—**quedarse a.,** (coll.) to be disappointed or to get left.—**alpistela, alpistera,** *f.* cake made of flour, eggs, sesame, and honey.—**alpistero,** *m.* sieve for canary seed.
alquequenje, *m.* Barbadoes winter cherry, used as a diuretic.
alquería, *f.* farmhouse.
alquermes, *m.* kermes, a cordial; (pharm.) medicinal sirup.
alquerque, *m.* place in oil mills for olives after the first pressing.
alquez, *m.* wine measure containing twelve *cántaras.*
alquibla, *f.* point toward which Mohammedans look when praying.
alquicel, alquicer, *m.* Moorish cloak; cover for benches, tables, etc.
alquifol, *m.* (min.) alquifou, potter's ore.
alquiladizo, za, *a.* that can be let or hired.
alquilador, ra, *n.* hirer.
alquilamiento, *m.* hiring or letting.
alquilar. I. *va.* to let, rent; to hire; to fee. **II.** *vr.* to serve for wages; to hire out.
alquilate, *m.* sales tax in Murcia.
alquiler, *m.* wages; rent, rental; the act of hiring or letting.—**de a.,** for hire, for rent; that may be hired or rented.
alquilón, na, *a.* (of person, disparaging) that can be hired.
alquilona, *f.* charwoman.
alquimia, *f.* alchemy.
alquímico, ca, *a.* alchemistic.
alquimila, *f.* (bot.) ladies' mantle.
alquimista, *m.* alchemist.
alquinal, *m.* veil or headdress for women.
alquitara, *f.* = ALAMBIQUE, a still.
alquitarar, *va.* to distil.
alquitira, *f.* (bot.) tragacanth.
alquitrán, *m.* tar, pitch; (naut.) stuff made of pitch, grease, etc.—**a. mineral,** coal tar.
alquitranado, *m.* (naut.) tarpaulin, tarred cloth.
alquitranar, *va.* to tar.
alrededor, *adv.* around.—**a. de,** about, around, (coll.) approximately.—**alrededores,** *m. pl.* environs.
alrota, arlota, *f.* coarse tow.
alsaciano, na, *n.* & *a.* Alsatian.
álsine, *m.* (bot.) scorpion grass.
alta, *f.* a kind of court dance; dancing exercise; fencing bout; certificate of discharge from a hospital, as being cured; (mil.) record or statement of the entrance of a man into active service; the man so entering.—**dar de a.,** to enroll (in the army); to discharge as cured, or declare fit.—**darse de a.,** to be admitted (in a profession, etc.), to join, become a member.
altabaque, tabaque, *m.* needlework basket.
altabaquillo, *m.* (bot.) small bindweed.
alta fidelidad, *f.* (rad.) high fidelity, (coll.) hi-fi.
altaico, ca, *n.* & *a.* Altaic.

altamente, *adv.* highly, exceedingly; (fig.) in a distinguished manner.
altanería, *f.* haughtiness, loftiness, insolence; hunting with hawks.
altanero, ra, *a.* soaring, towering; haughty, arrogant, insolent.
altar, *m.* altar; the church; bridge (in a furnace, etc.).—**a. mayor, high** altar.—**el A.,** (astr.) the Altar, Ara.
altarreina, *f.* (bot.) milfoil, yarrow.
altavoz, *m.* (radio) loudspeaker.
altea, *f.* (bot.) marsh mallow.
altearse, *vr.* (of land) to rise above the surrounding land.
alterabilidad, *f.* alterability.
alterable, *a.* changeable, alterable.
alteración, *f.* alteration; unevenness of the pulse; strong emotion; tumult, commotion.
alterado, da. I. *pp.* of ALTERAR. **II.** *a.* disturbed, agitated.
alterador, ra,] *n.* & *a.* alterer(-ing), disturber (-ing).
alterante, *a.* (med.) alterative.
alterar. I. *va.* to alter, change, transform; to disturb, stir up. **II.** *vr.* to become altered, disturbed, agitated; to become angry.
alterativo, va, *a.* alterative.
altercación, *f.*, **altercado,** *m.* altercation, controversy, quarrel, wrangle.
altercador, ra, *n.* arguer, wrangler, quarreler.
altercar, *va.* to dispute obstinately; to quarrel, bicker, wrangle.
álter ego, alter ego, second self.
alternación, *f.* alternation.
alternadamente, *adv.* = ALTERNATIVAMENTE.
alternador, *m.* (elec.) alternator.
alternante, *a.* alternant, alternate.
alternar, *va., vn.* & *vr.* to alternate.
alternativa, *f.* alternative; service by turn.
alternativo, va., *a.* alternate, alternating.
alterno, na, *a.* = ALTERNATIVO.—**corriente alterna,** (elec.) alternating current.
alteza, *f.* elevation, sublimity, highness, height; (A-) Highness (title).
altibajo, *m.* embossed velvet; downright blow in fencing.—*pl.* uneven ground; ups and downs.
altilocuencia, *f.* grandiloquence.
altilocuente (poet.), **altílocuo, cua,** *a.* grandiloquent.
altillo, lla. I. *a. dim.* rather high. **II.** *m.* hillock.
altimetría, *f.* altimetry; leveling.
altímetro, tra. I. *a.* pertaining to altimetry. **II.** *m.* altimeter, altitude indicator.
altiplanicie, *f.*, **altiplano,** *m.* plateau, tableland.
altiscopio, *m.* (opt.) altiscope.
altísimo, ma. I. *a. aug.* exceedingly high, most high. **II.** *m.* (A-), Most High.
altisonante, altísono, na, *a.* high-sounding.
altitonante, *a.* (poet.) thundering.
altitud, *f.* altitude, elevation.
altivamente, *adv.* loftily, haughtily.
altivarse, *vr.* to put on airs.
altivez, altiveza, *f.* haughtiness, arrogance, insolence; pride.
altivo, va, *a.* haughty, proud, lofty; high-handed; overbearing, arrogant.
[1]alto, ta. I. *a.* (of a building, hill, price, etc.) high; elevated; tall; arduous, difficult; eminent; enormous; deep.—**a. a bajo, (de)** downward; from the top down; from top to bottom.—**a. horno,** blast furnace.—**alta mar,** (naut.) high seas.—**a. relieve,** high relief.—**altas horas,** late hours.—**de a. bordo,** large seagoing (vessel).—**de lo a.,** from above.—**en a.,** up high. **II.** *m.* height, elevation; hill; top; story, floor; (naut.) depth or height of a ship; summit, mountain top, crest; top floor; heap, pile.—**pasar por a.,** to overlook, forget.—**altos y bajos,** ups and downs, vicissitudes. **III.** *adv.* (of tone of voice) loud, high.
[2]alto. I. *m.* (mil.) halt; place or time of rest.—**hacer a.,** to halt. **II.** (*interj.*) (mil. command) halt!—**¡a. ahí!** halt! stop there!—**¡a. de aquí!** move off!
altocúmulo, *m.* (meteorol.) alto-cumulus (cloud formation).
altoestrato, *m.* (meteorol.) alto-stratus (cloud formation).
altoparlante, *m*, (rad.) loudspeaker.
Alto Volta, *m.* Upper Volta.
altozano, *m.* hillock, knoll; height; paved terrace or platform in front of a building (gen. a church).
altramuz, *m.* (bot.) lupine *altramuces;* black voting balls.
altruísmo, *m.* altruism.
altruísta, *n.* & *a.* altruist(-ic).
altura, *f.* height, altitude; tallness, stature; summit, top; (naut.) the latitude; (geom.) altitude (of a plane figure), height (of a solid); (astr.) altitude.—**estar a la a. de (su) tarea,** to be equal to (his) task.—*pl.* **alturas,** the heavens, Heaven.
alúa, *f.* (Arg.) glowworm.
alubia, *f.* (bot.) French bean.
aluciar, *va.* to polish, burnish, brighten.
alucinación, *f.* hallucination.
alucinadamente, *adv.* erroneously.
alucinamiento, *m.* = ALUCINACIÓN.
alucinar, *va.* & *vr.* to dazzle, fascinate, delude.
alucón, *m.* barn owl.
alud, *m.* avalanche.
aluda, *f.* (entom.) winged ant or emmet.
aludel, *m.* (chem.) sublimating pots.
aludir, *vn.* to allude, refer.
aludo, da, *a.* winged, large-winged.
aluengo, aluengue, *v. V.* ALONGAR.
[1]alumbrado, da. I. *pp.* of ALUMBRAR. **II.** *a.* (coll.) flustered with wine, tipsy. **III.** *m.* lighting.—*pl.* illuminati.—**de a.,** illuminating (gas, etc.).
[2]alumbrado, da, *a.* aluminous, pert. to alum.
alumbrador, ra, *n.* lighter; linkboy.
alumbramiento, *m.* supplying with light; childbirth.
[1]alumbrar. I. *va.* to light, illuminate; to enlighten, instruct; to dig about the roots of (vines). **II.** *vn.* to give, or shed, light; to be delivered of, give birth to (a child). **III.** *vr.* to get tipsy; to become lively (from liquor).
[2]alumbrar, *va.* to dip (cloth) in alum water.
alumbre, *m.* alum.—**a. catino,** alkali from glasswort.—**a. de rasuras,** salt of tartar.—**a. sacarino,** alum medicinal mixture.
alumbrera, *f.* alum mine.—**a. artificial,** alum works.
alumbroso, sa, *a.* containing alum.
alúmina, *f.* (chem.) alumina.
aluminato, *m.* aluminate.
alumínico, ca, *a.*, **aluminífero, ra,** *a.* aluminous.
aluminio, *m.* aluminium, aluminum.
aluminita, *f.* aluminite.
aluminoso, sa, *a.* aluminous.
alumno, na, *n.* foster child; pupil, student.
alunado, da, *a.* lunatic; (of horses) jerky from constipation; long-tusked (boar); tainted (meat).
alunita, *f.* (min.) alunite.
alusión, *f.* allusion, reference, hint.
alusivo, va, *a.* allusive, hinting.
alustrar, lustrar, *va.* to give luster to.
alutrado, da, *a.* otter-colored.
aluvial, *a.* alluvial.
aluvión, *f.* alluvium.
alveario, *m.* (anat.) alveary, hollow of outer ear.
álveo, *m.* bed (of a river).
alveolado, da, *a.* alveolate.
alveolar, *a.* alveolar.
alvéolo, *m.* alveolus, alveole, small cavity.
alverja, alverjana, *f.* (bot.) common vetch; (Am.) (also ARVEJA), green pea.
alvino, na, *a.* (med.) alvine, intestinal.
alza, *f.* piece of leather put round the last to make the shoe wider; instrument used in rope-

walks; advance, rise (in price); (print.) overlay; (artil.) front sight (gen. app. to the notched-slide sight).
alzacuello, *m.* neck stock.
alzada, *f.* height, stature (of horses); appeal (to a higher governmental body).
alzadamente, *adv.* for a lump sum.
alzado, da. I. *pp.* of ALZAR. **II.** *a.* & *m.* (of) a lump sum; (of a) fraudulent bankrupt; *m.* (arch.) front elevation.
alzadura, *f.* elevation.
alzamiento, *m.* lifting, raising; higher bid (at an auction); rising (in arms), insurrection.
alzapaño, *m.* curtain holder.
alzapié, *m.* snare (for birds or animals).
alzaprima, *f.* lever; wedge; (naut.) heaver.—**dar a.,** to ruin or damage by treacherous cunning.—**alzaprimar,** *va.* to raise with a lever; (naut.) to move with handspikes; to incite, spur on.
alzapuertas, *m.* (theat.) supernumerary.
alzar. I. *va.* (*pret.* ALCÉ; *subj.* ALCE) to raise (a load, price, siege, building, penalty); to lift, heave; to pick up; to carry off; to hide, lock up; to cut (the cards); to gather up and arrange in order (printed sheets) for the binder; (eccl.) to elevate (the host); (naut.) to heave.—**a. cabeza,** to recover from a calamity or disease.—**a. el codo,** to be a toper.—**a. la casa,** to break up house.—**a. velas,** (naut.) to set the sails; to raise camp (fig.), to move. **II.** *vr.* to rise in rebellion; to rise; to make a fraudulent bankruptcy; to appeal (to a higher court).—**a. con,** to run away with; to embezzle; to steal; to usurp.—**a. con el santo y la limosna,** to carry away, or appropriate, everything.
allá, *adv.* there; thither, or to that place; (with a modifying *adv.*) far, beyond (*más allá,* farther; *muy allá,* much beyond, far beyond). Applied to time, it indicates remoteness, and either is not translated, or is rendered by "in the old times," "in times of old," "in the far-off time," etc.: *allá en mi niñez,* in the old times of my childhood; *allá en tiempo de Salomón,* in the far-off time of Solomon.—**a. por el año de 1900,** about 1900.—**a. arriba,** up there.—**a. veremos,** we shall see.—**a. voy,** I am coming.—**el más a.,** the beyond.—**por a.,** there, thereabouts, through there, that way.
allanador, *m.* leveller; gold-beater's book.
allanamiento, *m.* levelling; smoothing; acceptance of a judicial finding; affability, suavity.
allanar. I. *va.* to level, smooth; to flatten; to remove or overcome (difficulties); to pacify, subdue; to break into (a house). **II.** *vr.* to abide (by), acquiesce.
allegadizo, za, *a.* collected without selection.
allegado, da. I. *pp.* of ALLEGAR. **II.** *a.* near; related. **III.** *n.* relative; friend; ally.
allegador, ra, *n.* reaper; gatherer; board for gathering thrashed wheat; (fire) poker.
allegamiento, *m.* collecting; reaping, gathering; close friendship; union; relationship.
allegar. I. *va.* (*pret.* ALLEGUÉ; *subj.* ALLEGUE) to reap; to collect; to solicit, procure. **II.** *vr.* to come near, approach; to adhere (to a sect, etc.).
allende, *adv.* beyond, on the other side.—**a. el mar,** overseas.
allí, *adv.* there, in that place; thereto.—**¡a. fué Troya!** there the trouble began, then came the crash!—**de a.,** from there; thence.—**por a.,** that way; through there; there, thereabouts.
alloza, *f.* = ALMENDRUCO, green almond.
allozo, *m.* (bot.) wild almond tree.
alludel, *m.* earthen water pipe; ALUDEL.
ama, *f.* mistress of the house; landlady; (woman) owner; housekeeper; wet nurse; (anc.) governess.—**a. de cría** = A. DE LECHE.—**a. de gobierno** = A. DE LLAVES.—**a. de huéspedes,** boarding-house keeper.—**a. de leche,** wet nurse.—**a. de llaves,** housekeeper.
amabilidad, *f.* amiability, affability; kindness.
amable, *a.* amiable, affable; kind.—**amablemente,** *adv.* amiably; kindly; courteously.
amacayo, *m.* (Am.) fleur-de-lis, iris.
amaceno, na. I. *a.* Damascene. **II.** *f.* (bot.) damson plum.
amacollado, da, *a.* (bot.) grumous, bunchy.
amacollarse, *vr.* (of plants) to throw out shoots.
amachetear, *va.* to strike with a machete.
amador, ra, *n.* & *a.* lover (-ing).
amadrigar. I. *va.* (*pret.* AMADRIGUÉ; *subj.* AMADRIGUE) to receive well, esp. one not deserving. **II.** *vr.* to burrow; to seclude oneself.
amadrinar, *va.* to couple, yoke together; (naut.) to join (one thing to another for reinforcement); to act as godmother or bridesmaid to; to uphold.
amadroñado, da, *a.* resembling *madroños.*
amaestrado, da. I. *pp.* of AMAESTRAR. **II.** *a.* taught, schooled; trained, experienced.
amaestrar, *va.* to instruct, train, coach.
amagar. I. *va.* to threaten; to show signs of; to hint. **II.** *vn.* to threaten; to be impending; to feign. **III.** *vr.* (coll.) to hide.
amago, *m.* threatening; hint; empty promise; symptom of disease which does not develop.
ámago, *m.* bitter stuff found in some bee cells; nausea, loathing.
amainar. I. *va.* (naut.) to lower or shorten (sail); to relax. **II.** *vn.* to subside, lessen, moderate. **III.** *vr.* to give in, yield, desist.
amaitinar, *va.* to observe attentively.
amajadar. I. *va.* to keep (sheep) in a field to fertilize it. **II.** *vr.* (of sheep) to be in, or go to, the fold.
amalecita, *n.* & *a.* (Bible) Amalekite.
amalgama, *f.* amalgam.
amalgamación, *f.* amalgamation.
amalgamador, *m.* amalgamator.
amalgamar, *va.* to amalgamate.
amamantar, *va.* to nurse, suckle.
amán, *m.* amnesty.
amancebamiento, *m.* concubinage.
amancebarse, *vr.* to live in concubinage.
amancillar, *va.* to stain, pollute; to defame, tarnish one's reputation.
amanecer, *vn. defect.* (*ind.* AMANEZCO; *subj.* AMANEZCA) to dawn; to arrive, be or appear at daybreak or in the morning (often diff. constr.: *amanecimos en la costa,* we were on shore, we reached the shore at daybreak, it was daybreak when we arrived at the shore; *amaneció la noticia en los periódicos,* the news appeared in the papers in the morning). Often used with *Dios* as subject: *amaneció Dios,* it dawned (literally, God sent forth the dawn).—**amanecerá y veremos,** we shall see. **II.** *m.* dawn, daybreak.—**al a.,** at dawn, at daybreak.
amanecida, *f.* dawn, daybreak.
amanerado, da, *a.* full of mannerisms.
amaneramiento, *m.* mannerism.
amanerarse, *vr.* to adopt mannerisms; to become affected.
amanezco, amanezca, *v.* *V.* AMANECER.
amanita, *f.* (bot.) amanita.
amanojar, *va.* to gather by handfuls.
amansador, ra, *n.* tamer; horse breaker; soother, appeaser.
amansamiento, *m.* taming; breaking (horses).
amansar, *va.* to tame, domesticate; to break (a horse); to soften, pacify.
amantar, *va.* (coll.) to cloak.
[1]**amante,** *n.* & *a.* lover(-ing); sweetheart.
[2]**amante,** *m.* (naut.) rope, part of the running rigging.
amantillar, *va.* (naut.) to top the lifts.
amantillo, *m.* (naut.) lift.
amanuense, *m.* amanuensis, clerk.
amañar. I. *va.* to do cleverly. **II.** *vr.* to be handy; to adapt oneself.
amaño, *m.* cleverness, neatness.—*pl.* tools or implements; intrigue or machinations.

amapola, *f.* (bot.) poppy.
amar, *va.* to love.
amáraco, *m.* (bot.) = MEJORANA, marjoram.
amaraje, *m.* (aer.) landing, alighting (on water).
amarantáceo, a. I. *a.* (bot.) amaranthaceous. II. *f. pl.* (bot.) Amaranthaceæ.
amaranto, *m.* (bot.) amaranth.
amarar, *vn.* (aer.) to alight on the water.
amargado, da. I. *pp.* of AMARGAR. **II.** *a.* embittered.
amargaleja, *f.* bitter or wild plum.
amargar. I. *va.* (*pret.* AMARGUÉ; *subj.* AMARGUE) to make bitter; to exasperate, offend. **II.** *vn.* to be bitter. **III.** *vr.* to become bitter.
amargo, ga. I. *a.* bitter. **II.** *m.* bitterness; sweetmeat made of bitter almonds.—*pl.* bitters.
amargón, *m.* (bot.) dandelion.
amargor, *m.* bitterness.
amargoso, sa, *a.* bitter.
amargué, amargue, *v. V.* AMARGAR.
amarguillo, lla, *a. dim.* somewhat bitter.
amargura, *f.* bitterness.
amaricado, a, *a.* (coll.) effeminate.
amarilis, *f.* amaryllis.
amarilla, *f.* gold coin, especially the *onza;* (vet.) a liver disease of sheep.
amarillear, *vn.* to incline to yellow.
amarillejo, ja; amarillento, ta, *a.* yellowish.
amarillez, *f.* yellowness.
amarillo, lla. I. *a.* yellow. **II.** *m.* jaundice; a disease of silkworms.
amarinar, marinar, *va.* to salt (fish); (naut.) to man (a ship).
amariposado, da, *a.* (bot.) butterflylike.
amaro, *m.* (bot.) common clary.
amarra, *f.* cable; rope; martingale.
amarradero, *m.* hitching post; tying or fastening place or object; (naut.) mooring berth.
amarraje, *m.* moorage (charge for mooring).
amarrar, *va.* to tie, fasten; to lash, belay.
amarrazones, *pl.* (naut.) ground tackle.
amarre, *m.* tying; mooring; mooring line or cable. —**a. de retenida,** mooring guy (of a dirigible).
amartelar. I. *va.* to court, make love to; to love devotedly. **II.** *vr.* to fall in love.
amartillar, *va.* to hammer; to cock (gun, pistol).
amasadera, *f.* kneading bowl.
amasador, ra, *n.* kneader.
amasadura, *f.* kneading.
amasamiento, *m.* uniting; (med.) massage; AMASADURA.
amasar, *va.* to knead; to mold; to arrange for a purpose; (med.) to massage.
amasijo, *m.* dough; (act of) kneading; quantity of mortar or plaster; medley; plot; place where dough is made; (coll.) work, task.
amate, *m.* (Mex.) a fig tree the milky juice of which is used medically as a resolvent.
amatista, ametista, *f.* (min.) amethyst.
amatorio, ria, *a.* amatory.
amaurosis, *f.* (med.) amaurosis, loss of sight.
amayorazgar, *va.* (law) to entail.
amazacotado, da, *a.* heavy, thick; (of writings) jumbled, incoherent, clumsy.
amazona, *f.* Amazon; amazon; riding habit; horsewoman; (Am.) a large parrot of Brazil.
amazónico, ca, *a.* Amazonian.
amazonio, nia, *a.* Amazonian.
amazonita, *f.* (min.) Amazon stone, amazonite.
ambages, *m. pl.* maze; circumlocutions, beating about the bush.—**sin a.,** in plain language, without mincing words.
ambagioso, sa, *a.* ambiguous; circumlocutory.
ámbar, *m.* amber.—**a. gris,** ambergris.—**a. negro,** (min.) jet.—**a. prensado,** amberoid, ambroid.
ambarina, *f.* (bot.) scabious.
ambarino, na, *a.* pert. to amber; amberlike.
ambición, *f.* ambition; aspiration; covetousness.
ambicionar, *va.* to seek eagerly; to aspire to; to covet.
ambiciosamente, *adv.* ambitiously.
ambicioso, sa, *a.* ambitious, aspiring; covetous, greedy.
ambidextro, tra, *a.* ambidextrous.
ambiente. I. *a.* ambient. **II.** *m.* ambience, atmosphere, ambient air; environment, milieu.
ambigú, *m.* luncheon; collation.
ambigüedad, *f.* ambiguity.
ambiguo, gua, *a.* ambiguous.
ámbito, *m.* contour, boundary line; limit; compass, scope.
ambivalencia, *f.* ambivalence.
ambivalente, *a.* ambivalent.
ambladura, *f.* amble (gait).
amblar, *va.* to amble; (of quadrupeds) to pace.
ambleo, *m.* short, thick wax candle; candlestick for the same.
ambliopía, *f.* (med.) amblyopia, dimness of vision.
ambo, *m.* combination of two numbers in lotto.
ambón, *m.* pulpit on each side of the high altar.
ambos, bas, *a.* both.—**a. a dos,** both, or both together.
ambrosía, *f.* ambrosia; (fig.) any delicious viand or liquor.—**a. campestre,** (bot.) buckthorn.
ambrosíaco, ca, *a.* ambrosial.
ambrosiano, na, *a.* pertaining to St. Ambrose.
ambuesta, *f.* = ALMORZADA, a double handful.
ambulación, *f.* ambulation.
ambulacral, *a.* (zool.) ambulacral.—**a. pie,** (zool.) ambulacral foot.
ambulacro, *m.* (zool.) ambulacrum.
ambulancia, *f.* field hospital; ambulance.
ambulante, *a.* ambulant; shifting; roving.
ambular, *vn.* to ambulate, walk.
ambulativo, va, *a.* of a roving disposition; shifting; ambulatory.
ambulatorio, a, *a.* ambulatory, adapted for walking.
ameba, *f.* = AMIBA.
amebeo, *a.* & *m.* (pert. to) dialogue in verse.
amechar, *va.* to put a wick in; (cook.) (also **mechar**) to lard (meat).
amedrentado, da, *a.* afraid, frightened.
amedrentador, ra, *n.* & *a.* threatener(-ing); discourager(-ing); frightener(-ing).
amedrentar, *va.* to frighten, discourage, intimidate.
amelga, *f.* ridge between two furrows.
amelgado. I. *pp.* of AMELGAR. **II.** *m.* (prov.) boundary mound.
amelgar, *va.* to cut even furrows in for planting; to mark the boundaries of with mounds.
amelo, *m.* (bot.) golden starwort.
amelonado, da, *a.* melon-shaped.
[1]**amén,** *m.* amen, so be it.—**llevarle a uno el amén,** to agree to, or approve, everything one says, be one's echo.
[2]**amén,** *adv.* **a. de,** besides; aside from, except for.
amenacé, amenace, *v. V.* AMENAZAR.
amenaza, *f.* threat, menace.
amenazador, ra, *n.* & *a.* threatener(-ing).
amenazante, *a.* menacing, threatening.
amenazar, *va.* & *vn.* (*pret.* AMENACÉ; *subj.* AMENACE) to threaten, menace; be impending.
amenguamiento, *m.* diminution, lessening, abatement.
amenguar, *va.* to diminish; to defame.
amenice, amenice, *v. V.* AMENIZAR.
amenidad, *f.* amenity.
amenizar, *va.* (*pret.* AMENICÉ; *subj.* AMENICE) to render pleasant or agreeable.
ameno, na, *a.* pleasant, agreeable, pleasing.
amenorrea, *f.* (med.) amenorrhea.
amentáceo, cea, *a.* (bot.) amentaceous.
amentar, *va.* to lace (shoes).
amento, *m.* (bot.) ament; AMIENTO.
amerar, merar. I. *va.* to mix (wine or liquor) with water. **II.** *vr.* to percolate; to soak.
amerengado, da, *a.* like, or having, meringue; (coll.) prudish.
América del Norte, *f.* North America.

América del Sur, *f.* South America.
americanismo, *m.* Americanism (esp. app. to Lat. Am. Span.).
americanista. I. *a.* Americanistic. **II.** *n.* Americanist.
americanización, *f.* Americanization.
americanizar, *va.* & *vn.* to Americanize.
americano, na. I. *a.* American. **II.** *n.* American; *f.* sack coat.
americio, *m.* (chem.) americium.
amerind(i)o, d(i)a. I. *a.* Amerindian. **II.** *n.* Amerind, Amerindian.
amestizado, da, *a.* mestizolike.
ametalado, da, *a.* brass-colored.
ametista, *f.*, **ametisto,** *m.* = AMATISTA.
ametralladora, *f.* rapid-fire gun, machine gun.
ametrallar, *va.* to shoot with grapeshot; to shell; to machine-gun.
ametropía, *f.* (med.) ametropia.
amia, lamia, *f.* (ichth.) white shark.
amianto, *m.* (min.) amianthus; asbestos.
amiba, *f.*, **amibo,** *m.* (zool.) amœba.
amibiano, na, *a.* amœbic.
amiboideo, a, *a.* amœboid, amœbic.
amicísimo, ma, *a. super.* most friendly, being, or like, a very good friend.
amida, *f.* (chem.) amide.
amidina, amidinas, *f.* (chem.) amidine, soluble matter in starch.
amidógeno, *m.* (chem.) amidogen.
amidol, *m.* (chem.) amidol.
amiento, *m.* leather strap to secure helmet; shoe lace; leather string.
amiga, *f.* female friend; schoolmistress; kindergarten; concubine, mistress.
amigabilidad, *f.* amicability.
amigable, *a.* friendly; fit, suitable.
amigablemente, *adv.* amicably.
amígdala, *f.* tonsil.
amigdaláceo, a., *a.* (bot.) amygdalaceous.—*f. pl.* Amygdalaceæ.
amigdáleo, lea, *a.* amygdalate; almond-shaped.
amigdalina, *f.* (chem.) amygdalin.
amigdalitis, *f.* tonsilitis.
amigdaloide, *a.* (geol.) amygdaloid.
amigdalotomía, *f.* (med.) tonsilectomy.
amigo, ga. I. *n.* friend; *m.* boy friend; (coll.) lover, paramour; *f.* girl friend; (coll.) mistress, paramour.—**a. íntimo,** bosom friend.—**cara de pocos amigos,** mean-looking, unfriendly expression. **II.** *a.* friendly; fond.—**ser a. de,** to be a friend of; to like, be fond of.—**ser buenos amigos,** to be close friends.
amigote, *m. aug.* (coll.) dear old friend.
amiláceo, a, *a.* starchy.
amilanamiento, *m.* terror, abject fear; terrifying; cowing.
amilanar. I. *va.* to frighten, terrify; to stupefy; to cow. **II.** *vr.* to become terrified; to cower, quail; to flag.
amilasa, *f.* (biochem.) amylase.
amileno, *m.* (chem.) amylene.
amílico, ca, *a.* amylic, amyl.
amilo, *m.* (chem.) amyl.
amillaramiento, *m.* assessment of a tax.
amillarar, *va.* to assess a tax on.
amillonado, da, *a.* & *n.* very rich (person).
amimar, mimar, *va.* to fondle; to indulge.
amina, *f.* (chem.) amine.
amínico, ca, *a.* aminic.
aminoácido, *m.* (biochem.) amino acid.
aminorar, minorar, *va.* to lessen; to enfeeble.
amir, *m.* ameer.
amistad, *f.* friendship; concubinage.—**hacer amistad,** or **amistades,** to become acquainted; to make friends.—**hacer las amistades,** to make up, become reconciled.
amistar. I. *va.* to make (others) friends; to make acquainted. **II.** *vr.* to become acquainted; to become reconciled, make up.
amistoso, sa, *a.* friendly, amicable.
amito, *m.* amice, part of a priest's garment.

amitosis, *f.* (biol.) amitosis.
amitótico, ca, *a.* amitotic.
amnesia, *f.* amnesia, loss of memory.
amnios, *f.* (zool.) amnion, fœtal envelope.
amniótico, ca, *a.* (zool.) amniotic.
amnistía, *f.* amnesty.—**amnistiar. I.** *va.* to pardon, grant amnesty to. **II.** *vr.* to receive amnesty.
amo, *m.* master, head (of household or family); owner; foster father; overseer; (coll.) boss.
amoblar, *va.* (*ind.* AMUEBLO; *subj.* AMUEBLE) = AMUEBLAR, to furnish, provide with furniture.
amodita, *f.* = ALICANTE, a horned serpent.
amodorrado, da. I. *pp.* of AMODORRARSE. **II.** *a.* drowsy, sleepy.
amodorrarse, *vr.* to become drowsy.
amodorrido, da, *a.* = AMODORRADO.
amogotado, da, *a.* knoll-like.
amohecerse, *vr.* (*ind.* AMOHEZCO; *subj.* AMOHEZCA) to mold or rust.
amohinar, *va.* to irritate, annoy.
amojamar, *va.* to dry and smoke (tunny fish).
amojonador, *m.* one who sets landmarks.
amojonamiento, *m.* setting of landmarks.
amojonar, *va.* to set landmarks on (for marking boundaries).
amoladera, *f.* whetstone, grindstone.
amolador, *n.* & *a.* grinder(-ing); whetter(-ing); sharpener(-ing).
amoladura, *f.* whetting, grinding.
amolar, *va.* (*ind.* AMUELO; *subj.* AMUELE) to whet, grind, sharpen.
amoldar, *va.* to mold, fashion, figure; to adjust; to brand (cattle); to adapt.
amole, *m.* root of a plant used as soap.
amollador, ra, *n.* one who plays an inferior card, having a winning one.
amollar. I. *va.* (naut.) to slacken (a rope). **II.** *vn.* to play an inferior card, having a winning one.
amolletado, da, *a.* oblong, oval.
amomo, *m.* (bot.) plant producing seeds called grains of paradise, used medicinally.
amondongado, da, *a.* (coll.) coarse and fat.
amonedación, *f.* coining (money).
amonedar, *va.* to coin (money).
amonestación, *f.* admonition, warning; marriage banns.—**correr las amonestaciones,** to publish the banns.
amonestador, ra, *n.* & *a.* admonisher(-ing).
amonestar, *va.* to admonish, warn, advise; to publish (banns).
amoniacal, *a.* ammoniacal.
amoníaco, *m.* ammonia; ammoniac, gum resin.
amónico, ca, *a.* ammonic, ammonium (as *a.*).
amonio, *m.* ammonium.
[1]**amonita,** *f.* (zool.) ammonite, spiral fossil shell.
[2]**amonita,** *n.* & *a.* (pertaining to) Ammon (the people or their founder).
amontarse, *vr.* to flee to the mountains.
amontonador, ra, *n.* heaper, accumulator.
amontonamiento, *m.* heaping, accumulating; hoarding; gathering; crowding (of people).
amontonar. I. *va.* to heap, pile up; to accumulate indiscriminately; to hoard, lay up. **II.** *vr.* (coll.) to crowd; to pile up; to fly into a passion.
amor, *m.* love; the object of love.—*pl.* love affairs, amours.—**a. con a. se paga,** the punishment should fit the crime.—**a. patrio,** love of country, patriotism.—**a. propio,** self-esteem, amour propre.—**por a. de,** for the sake of; on account of.—**con** or **de mil amores,** with all one's heart, with the greatest pleasure.
amoral, *a.* amoral.—**amoralidad,** *f.* amorality.—**amoralismo,** *m.* amoralism.
amoratado, da, *a.* livid.
amorcillo, *m. dim.* slight love; (figure of) Cupid.
amordazar, *va.* (*pret.* AMORDACÉ; *subj.* AMORDACE) to gag, muzzle; (naut.) to fasten with bitts.
amorfía, *f.* amorphism; organic deformity.
amorfismo, *m.* amorphism.
amorfo, fa, *a.* amorphous.

amorgar, *va.* to stupefy (fish) with *morga* or *alpechín,* fetid olive juice.
amoricones, *m. pl.* (coll.) love looks, flirtations.
amorío, *m.* love making; love, amour.
amoriscado, da, *a.* Moorlike.
amorita, *n.* Amorite.
amormado, da, *a.* (vet.) having the glanders.
amoroso, sa, *a.* affectionate, loving; pleasing, gentle; mild.
amorrar. I. *vn.* (coll.) to be sullen; to muse; (naut.) (of a ship) to pitch. **II.** *vr.* to sulk.
amorreo, rrea, *a.* Amorite.
amortajar, *va.* to shroud (a corpse).
amortecer. I. *va.* (*ind.* AMORTEZCO; *subj.* AMORTEZCA) to deaden. **II.** *vr.* to faint, swoon.
amortecimiento, *m.* swoon, fainting.
amortezco, amortezca, *v. V.* AMORTECER.
amorticé, amortice, *v. V.* AMORTIZAR.
amortiguación, *f.,* **amortiguamiento,** *m.* softening, mitigation, lessening.
amortiguador, ra. I. *n.* & *a.* reducer(-ing). damper(-ing), softener(-ing). **II.** *m.* (mech.) dashpot; shock absorber.
amortiguar, *va.* to lessen, mitigate, deaden; to temper; to soften (colors); to absorb, take up (shocks); (radio) to damp (waves).
amortizable, *a.* amortizable.
amortización, *f.* amortization.
amortizar, *va.* (*pret.* AMORTICÉ; *subj.* AMORTICE) to amortize; to recoup, recover; to abolish (offices, etc.); to refund; to redeem (debt, etc.).
amoscar, *va.* & *vr.* (*pret.* AMOSQUÉ; *subj.* AMOSQUE) to shake off the flies; (coll.) to get peeved.
amostacé, amostace, *v. V.* AMOSTAZAR.
amostachado, *a.* having a mustache.
amostazar. I. *va.* (*pret.* AMOSTACÉ; *subj.* AMOSTACE) (coll.) to exasperate, provoke. **II.** *vr.* to be vexed, angry.
amotinado, da. I. *pp.* of AMOTINAR. **II.** *a.* mutinous. **III.** *n.* mutineer.
amotinador, ra, *n.* mutineer.
amotinamiento, *m.* mutiny.
amotinar. I. *va.* to excite to rebellion; to disorder (the mind). **II.** *vr.* to mutiny, rebel.
amover, *va.* (*ind.* AMUEVO; *subj.* AMUEVE) to discharge (from an employment).
amovible, *a.* removable.
amovilidad, *f.* quality of being removable.
amparador, ra, *n.* protector; shelterer.
amparar. I. *va.* to shelter; to protect, help, assist; to comply with the requirements for working (a mine). **II.** *vr.* to claim or enjoy protection; to defend oneself; to seek shelter.
amparo, *m.* favor, aid; protection; shelter, refuge, asylum.
ampelita, *f.* soft sandy slate.
ampelografía, *f.* viticulture, science of vine growing.
ampelográfico, ca, *a.* pert. to viticulture.
ampelógrafo, fa, *n.* one versed in viticulture.
amper, *m.* = AMPERIO.
amperaje, *m.* (elec.) amperage.
amperímetro, *m.* (elec.) amperometer, ammeter.
amperio, *m.* (elec.) ampere.—**a.-centímetro,** ampere centimeter.—**a.-hora,** ampere hour.—**a.-pie,** ampere foot.—**a.-vuelta,** ampere turn.
amperómetro, *m.* = AMPERÍMETRO.
amplexicaulo, la, *a.* (bot.) amplexicaul.
ampliación, *f.* enlargement (gen. & photog.).
ampliador, ra, *n.* & *a.* amplifier(-ying).
ampliar, *va.* to amplify, extend; (photog.) to enlarge.
ampliativo, va, *a.* amplifying, enlarging.
amplificación, *f.* enlargement; (rhet.) amplification.
amplificador, ra, *n.* & *a.* amplifier(-ying), enlarger(-ing).—*m.* (radio) amplifier.
amplificar, *va.* to amplify, enlarge, extend, expand; to dilate, expatiate.
amplificativo, va, *a.* amplificative, amplificatory.
amplio, lia, *a.* ample, roomy, extensive, large; full, bold (e.g. of a drawing).
amplitud, *f.* extent, largeness, fullness; (phys., astr.) amplitude.
ampo (de la nieve), *m.* pure, shining whiteness; snowflake.
ampolla, *f.* blister; decanter, cruet; water bubble; bulb (of a lamp).—[1]**ampollar. I.** *va.* to blister; to make hollow. **II.** *vr.* to bubble up.—[2]**ampollar,** *a.* blisterlike, bubblelike.—**ampolleta,** *f. dim.* small vial; cruet; sandglass or time taken for sand to run through; bulb; (naut.) watch glass.
ampulosidad, *f.* verbosity.
ampuloso, sa, *a.* pompous, bombastic.
amputación, *f.* amputation.
amputador, ra, *n.* amputator.
amputar, *va.* to amputate.
amuchachado, da, *a.* boyish, childish.
amueblar, *va.* to furnish (a house, etc.).
amueblo, amueble, *v. V.* AMOBLAR.
amuelo, amuele, etc. *v. V.* AMOLAR.
amuevo, amueve, *v. V.* AMOVER.
amugamiento, *m.* setting out boundary marks.
amugronador, ra, *a.* (of one) planting vines.
amugronar, *va.* to plant the shoot of a vine.
amujerado, da, *a.* effeminate.
amujeramiento, *m.* effeminacy.
amulatado, da, *a.* mulattolike.
amuleto, *m.* amulet.
amunicionar, *va.* to supply with ammunition.
amuñecado, da, *a.* puppetlike.
amura, *f.* (naut.) beam of a ship at one-eighth of its length from the bow; part on each side of the ship that corresponds to that section; tack (rope) of a sail.
amurada, *f.* (naut.) interior side of a ship.
amurallar, *va.* = MURAR, to wall.
amurar, *va.* (naut.) to haul (the tack) aboard.
amurcar, *va.* (of a bull) to gore with the horns.
amurco, *m.* (of a bull) blow with the horns.
amurillar, *va.* (agr.) to earth up.
amusco, ca, musco, ca, *a.* brown.
amusgar, *va.* (of an animal about to kick, bite, etc.) to throw back (the ears); to squint to see better.
ana, *f.* ell, a measure.
anabaptismo, *m.* Anabaptism.
anabaptista, *n.* & *a.* Anabaptist.
anabático, ca, *a.* (meteorol.) anabatic.
anabólico, ca, *a.* anabolic.
anabolismo, *m.* (biol.) anabolism.
anacant(in)o, *m.* (ichth.) anacanth.
anacarado, da, *a.* nacreous, pearly, resembling mother-of-pearl.
anacardiáceo, cea, *a.* (bot.) anacardiaceous.
anacardo, *m.* (bot.) cashew (tree or fruit).
anaco, *m.* (Peru, Bol.) Indian women's dress; (Ecua.) Indian women's hair-do, a single braid.
anacoluto, *m.* (gram.) anacoluthon.
anaconda, *f.* anaconda, a South-American boa.
anacoreta, *m.* anchorite, hermit.
anacorético, ca, *a.* anchoretic.
anacreóntico, ca, *a.* pertaining to or like the poet Anacreon or his poetry.
anacrónico, ca, *a.* anachronistic.
anacronismo, *m.* anachronism.
anacronístico, ca, *a.* anachronistic.
ánade, *m.* & *f.* (ornith.) duck; by extension, goose.—**anadear,** *vn.* to waddle.—**anadeja,** *f. dim.* duckling.—**anadino, na,** *n.* young duck.—**anadón,** *m.* mallard.
anadromo, ma, *a.* anadromous.
anaerobio, *n.* & *a.* (biol.) anaerobe (-ic).
anafase, *f.* (biol.) anaphase.
anafe, *m.* portable furnace.
anafilaxis, *f.* (med.) anaphylaxis.
anáfora, *f.* (rhet.) anaphora.
anafre, *m.* portable furnace.
anafrodisia, *f.* (med.) diminution of sexual desire.—**anafrodisíaco, ca,** *a.* anaphrodisiac.
anafrodita, *n.* abstainer from sexual intercourse.

anáglifo, *m.* anaglyph.
anagnórisis, *f.* (poet.) = AGNICIÓN.
anagoge, *m.* **anagogía,** *f.* anagoge.
anagógico, ca, *a.* anagogical.
anagrama, *f.* anagram.
anagramático, ca, *a.* anagrammatical.
anagramatista, *n.* anagrammatist.
anagramatizador, ra, *n.* anagrammatist.
anagramatizar, *va.* & *vn.* to anagrammatize.
anal, *a.* anal.
analectas, *f. pl.* analects.
analepsia, *f.* (med.) convalescence.
analéptico, ca, *a.* (med.) restorative.
anales, *m. pl.* annals.
analfabetismo, *m.* illiteracy.
analfabeto, ta, *a.* & *n.* illiterate (person).
analgesia, *f.* (med.) analgesia, insensibility to pain.—**analgésico, ca,** *n.* & *a.* analgesic.
analgesina, *f.* antipyrine.
analicé, analice, *v. V.* ANALIZAR.
análisis, *m.* or *f.* analysis; (gram.) parsing; (math.) analysis (gen. app. to infinitesimal calculus and the theory of functions).—**a. cualitativo,** qualitative analysis.—**a. cuantitativo,** quantitative analysis.—**a. espectral,** spectrum analysis.—**a. volumétrico,** volumetric analysis, titration (gen. in latter sense).
analista, *m.* annalist.
analítica, *f.* (philos.) analytics; (math.) analytic geometry.
analítico, ca, *a.* analytical.
analizable, *a.* capable of analysis.
analizador, *m.* analyzer.
analizar, *va.* (*pret.* ANALICÉ; *subj.* ANALICE) to analyze; (gram.) to parse.
análogamente, *adv.* analogously; in like manner, likewise.
analogía, *f.* analogy; resemblance; (biol., linguistics) analogy.
analógico, ca; análogo, ga, *a.* analogous.
anamnesia, *f.* anamnesis.
anamorfosis, *f.* anamorphosis.
ananá, ananás, *f.* (bot.) pineapple.
anandro, dra, *a.* (bot.) anandrous.
ananto, ta, *a.* (bot.) ananthous.
anapelo, *m.* (bot.) wolfsbane.
anapéstico, ca, *a.* anap(a)estic.
anapesto, *m.* anap(a)est.
anaplastia, *f.* (surg.) anaplasty.
anaplástico, ca, *a.* anaplastic.
anaquel, *m.* shelf.
anaquelería, *f.* shelving, case of shelves.
anaranjado, da. I. *a.* orange-colored. **II.** *n.* orange (color).—**a. de metilo,** methyl orange.
anarquía, *f.* anarchy.
anárquico, ca, *a.* anarchical.
anarquismo, *m.* anarchism.
anarquista, *n.* & *a.* anarchist(-ic).
anasarca, *f.* (med.) general dropsy.
anascote, *m.* woollen stuff like serge.
anastasia, *f.* = ARTEMISA, (bot.) mugwort.
anastigmático, ca, *a.* anastigmatic.
anastomosarse, anastomizarse, *vr.* (anat., bot.) to anastomose.
anastomosis, *f.* (anat., bot.) anastomosis.
anastomótico, ca, *a.* anastomotic.
anástrofe, *m.* (rhet.) anastrophe, inversion of the usual order of words.
anata, *f.* yearly income.—**media a.,** tax paid on assuming office (eccl. & secular).
anatema, *m.* or *f.* **anatematismo,** *m.* anathema.
anatematización, *f.* anathematization.
anatematizador, ra, *n.* anathematizer.
anatematizar, *va.* (*pret.* ANATEMATICÉ; *subj.* ANATEMATICE) to anathematize.
anatolio, lia, *n.* & *a.* Anatolian.
anatomía, *f.* anatomy; dissection.
anatomicé, anatomice, *v. V.* ANATOMIZAR.
anatómico, ca, *a.* anatomical; dissecting.
anatomista, *m.* anatomist.
anatomizar, *va.* (*pret.* ANATOMICÉ; *subj.* ANATOMICE) to anatomize or dissect; (art) to draw or carve the bones and muscles of.
anavajado, da, *a.* knife-scarred.
anca, *f.* croup (of animals); (coll.) buttock.
ancado, *m.* (vet.) contraction of muscles of the hind legs.
ancianidad, *f.* old age; antiquity.
anciano, na, *n.* & *a.* old (man, woman); ancient.
ancilario, ria, *a.* ancillary.
ancla, *f.* anchor.—**a. de la esperanza,** sheet anchor.—**a. flotante,** (aer.) drogue, sea anchor.—**al a.,** at anchor.—**el a. agarra,** the anchor bites.—**echar anclas,** to anchor.—**levar el a., levar anclas,** to weigh anchor.—**sobre el a., sobre las anclas,** at anchor, anchored.
ancladero, *m.* (naut.) anchorage, anchoring place.
anclado, da, *a.* anchored.
anclaje, *m.* casting anchor; anchoring ground.
anclar, *vn.* to anchor.
anclote, *m.* stream anchor, kedge.
anclotillo, *m.* kedge anchor.
ancón, *m.* corner; (arch.) bracket; cove, bay.
áncora, *f.* = ANCLA.
ancoraje, *m.* = ANCLAJE.
ancorar, *vn.* = ANCLAR.
ancorca, *f.* yellow ochre.
ancorel, *m.* large stone to secure fish-nets.
ancorería, *f.* anchor forge, workshop.
ancorero, *m.* anchorsmith.
ancusa, *f.* (bot.) alkanet, bugloss.
ancusina, *f.* (chem.) anchusin, alkanet.
anchamente, *adv.* widely, largely.
ancheta, *f.* small amount of goods ventured in trade; profit in a bargain.
anchicorto, ta, *a.* wider than long.
ancho, cha. I. *a.* broad, wide.—**ancha Castilla,** (coll.) as you please; without hindrance.—**a. de conciencia,** not overscrupulous, not too conscientious. **II.** *m.* width, breadth.—**a sus anchas,** with absolute freedom, unrestricted(ly), as one pleases; at ease.
anchoa, anchova, *f.* anchovy.
anchor, *m.* = ANCHURA.
anchuelo, la, *a. dim.* somewhat wide.
anchura, *f.* width, breadth; extent; laxity.
anchuroso, sa, *a.* large, spacious, extensive, vast, ample.
andada, *f.* track trail; "hike"; thin, crisp, waferlike cake.—*pl.* **andadas,** trail, tracks (esp. of birds or small animals).—**volver a las andadas,** to backslide; to go back to one's old tricks.
andaderas, *f. pl.* gocart (for learning to walk).
andadero, ra. I. *n.* runner. **II.** *m.* easy ground.
[1]**andado,** *m.* (coll.) (for *adnado*) stepchild.
[2]**andado, da. I.** *pp.* of ANDAR. **II.** *a.* beaten, trodden (path, etc.); busy, thronged (street); worse for wear, threadbare; common, ordinary; elapsed.
andador, ra. I. *a.* fast walking or running, swift; that walks. **II.** *m.* messenger of a court; (naut.) fine sailer; leading string; garden walk.
andadura, *f.* gait; amble.
andalón, *m.* (Am.) gadabout; wanderer.
andalucita, *f.* (min.) andalusite.
andaluz, za, *n.* & *a.* Andalusian.—**andaluzada,** *f.* boasting; exaggeration; (coll.) fish story, yarn.
andamiada, *f.*, **andamiaje,** *m.* scaffolding.
andamio, *m.* scaffold, platform, grandstand; (naut.) gangboard.
[1]**andana,** *f.* row, line, tier.
[2]**andana,** *f.*—**llamarse a.,** (coll.) not to fulfill a promise.
andanada, *f.* (naut.) broadside; grandstand for spectators; reproof, reprimand; tirade.
andaniño, *m.* gocart in which children learn to walk. Also ANDADERAS, POLLERA.
[1]**andante,** *a.* walking; (knight) errant.
[2]**andante,** *m.* (mus.) andante.
andantesco, ca, *a.* pert. to knights-errant.
andantino, *m.* (mus.) andantino.
andanza, *f.* (obs.) occurrence, event.—**buena** or

mala a., good or bad fortune.—*pl.* running about.
andar. I. *vn.* (*pret.* ANDUVE, *fut.* ANDUVIERE) (of a person) to walk, go; (of a watch, machine, etc.) to go, run, move; to act, behave; to elapse, pass; to be (esp. as *aux.* with *ger.* as *a. escribiendo,* to be writing); to get along, be going (*¿cómo anda el negocio?* how is the business going?).—**a. andando,** (Mex. C. A.) to roam about, "chase round."—**a. en,** to be attending to, or engaged in; to be going on, be near (*Juan anda en los veinte años,* John is going on twenty).—**a. en coche, automóvil,** etc., to go, ride in a carriage, automobile, etc.—**andarse por las ramas,** to beat about the bush.—**¡anda!** gracious! move on! get up! all right! go ahead! let it go! **II.** *m.* = ANDADURA, gait, pace.—**a largo a.,** in the long run.—**a más,** or **a todo, a.,** at full speed, quickly.—**a. un a.,** on the same level.
andaraje, *m.* wheel of a wheel and axle; frame of a garden roller.
andariego, ga, *a.* restless, roving; fast walker, runner.
andarín, *m.* professional walker, runner.
andarina, *f.* (ornith.) = GOLONDRINA, swallow.
andarivel, *m.* ferry cable; (naut.) safety ropes.
andarrío, *m.* (ornith.) white wagtail.
andas, *f. pl.* stretcher; litter; bier with shafts.
andén, *m.* bridle path; sidewalk by a road, wharf, or bridge; platform (of a railway station).
andero, ra, *n.* litter bearer; bier bearer.
andesita, *f.* (geol.) andesite, a volcanic rock.
andino, na, *a.* Andean.
ándito, *m.* gallery or path around a building.
andolina, *f.* (ornith.) = GOLONDRINA, swallow.
andón, na, *a.* roving, that walks a great deal; (of horses) ambling.—**andonear,** *vn.* to amble.
andorga, *f.* (coll.) belly.—**llenar la a.,** to gorge, stuff oneself.
andorina, *f.* = ANDOLINA.
andorra, *f.* street walker.
andorrear, *vn.* to gad about.
andorrero, ra. I. *a.* prone to walk or loiter about the streets. **II.** *m.* gadder, rover, tramp, *f.* street walker.
andosco, ca, *a.* two-year old (sheep).
andrajero, ra, *n.* ragpicker.
andrajo, *m.* rag, tatter; despicable person.
andrajoso, sa, *a.* ragged, in tatters.
andrina, endrina, *f.* (bot.) *f.* sloe.
andrino, *m.* (bot.) sloe tree, blackthorn.
androceo, *m.* (bot.) andrœcium.
androfobia, *f.* (med.) androphobia.
androgénesis, *f.* (biol.) androgenesis.
andrógeno, *m.* (biochem.) androgen.
androginia, *f.* androgyny.
andrógino, *m.* androgyne, being both male and female.
androide, *m.* automaton shaped like a man.
andrómina, *f.* (coll.) trick, fraud, fib.
androsemo, *m.* (bot.) parkleaves.
androsterona, *f.* (biochem.) androsterone.
andularios, *m. pl.* (coll.) long wide gown.
andullo, *m.* (naut.) canvas shield on harpings and blocks; plug tobacco.
andurriales, *m. pl.* byroads, lonely places.
anduve, anduviera, etc. *v. V.* ANDAR.
anea, *f.* (bot.) cattail; rush (used for chair seats).
aneaje, *m.* measuring by ells.
anear, *va.* to measure by ells.
aneblar. I. *va.* (*ind.* ANIEBLO; *subj.* ANIEBLE) to cloud, darken. **II.** *vr.* to become cloudy.
anécdota, *f.* anecdote.—**anecdótico, ca,** *a.* anecdotic.—**anecdotista,** *n.* anecdotist.
anegación, *f.* overflowing, inundation.
anegadizo, za, *a.* liable to be inundated.
anegamiento, *m.* = ANEGACIÓN.
anegar. I. *va.* to inundate, flood; to submerge; to flush; to drown. **II.** *vr.* to drown, sink; to become wet or soaked; to be flooded.
anegociado, da, *a.* full of business.
anejín, anejir, *m.* popular proverb which can be sung.
anejo. I. *m.* church depending on another. **II. a., ja, anexo, xa,** *a.* annexed, joined.
aneléctrico, ca, *a.* not susceptible to electrification.
anélido, da, *n.* & *a.* (zool.) annelid.—*m. pl.* Annelida.
anemia, *f.* (med.) anemia.—**a. perniciosa,** (med.) pernicious anemia.—**a. tropical,** uncinariasis, hookworm disease.
anémico, ca, *a.* anemic.
anemobiágrafo, *m.* (meteorol.) anemobiagraph.
anemografía, *f.* (meteorol.) anemography, science treating of winds.
anemográfico, ca, *a.* (meteorol.) anemographic.
anemógrafo, *m.* one who studies anemography; anemoscope.
anemometría, *f.* (meteorol.) anemometry.
anemómetro, *m.* anemometer, wind gauge.
anémona, anémone, *f.* (bot.) anemone, windflower.—**a. de mar,** sea anemone.
anemoscopio, *m.* (meteorol.) anemoscope.
anepigráfico, ca, *a.* without title or inscription.
anequín, *adv.*—**a,** or **de, a.,** at so much a head (in shearing of sheep).
aneroide, *a.* & *m.* aneroid (barometer).
aneroidógrafo, *m.* aneroidograph.
anestesia, *f.* anesthesia, anæsthesia.
anestesiador, ra, *n.* anesthetist, anæsthetist.
anestesiar, *va.* to anesthetize, anæsthetize.
anestésico, ca, *m.* & *a.* anesthetic, anæsthetic.
aneurisma, *m.* & *f.* (med.) aneurism.
aneurismal, *a.* aneurismal.
anexar, *va.* to annex.
anexidades, *f. pl.* annexes, appurtenances.
anexión, *f.* annexation.
anexionar, *va.* to annex.
anexionismo, *m.* annexationism.
anexionista, *n.* annexationist.
anexo, xa, *a.* = ANEJO, JA.
anfetamina, *f.* (pharm.) amphetamine.
anfibio, a, *n.* & *a.* (zool. & aer.) amphibian (-bious).
anfíbol, *m.* (min.) amphibole.—**anfibolita,** *f.* (min.) amphibolite.
anfibólico, ca, *a.* (min.) amphibolic, amphibological.
anfibología, *f.* amphibology.
anfibológico, ca, *a.* amphibological.
anfíbraco, *m.* (poet.) amphibrach, ⏑ — ⏑.
anfímacro, *m.* (poet.) amphimacer, — ⏑ —.
anfión, *m.* opium.
anfípodo, da, *n.* & *a.* amphipod.—*m. pl.* Amphipoda.
anfiprostilo, *m.* (arch.) amphiprostyle.
anfisbena, *f.* amphisbæna, a kind of lizard.
anfiscios, *m. pl.* inhabitants of the torrid zone.
anfisibena, *f.* amphisbæna.
anfiteatral, *a.* amphitheatric.
anfiteatro, *m.* amphitheatre.—**a. (anatómico),** dissecting room (of hospital or medical school).
anfitrión, *m.* host entertaining guests.
anfitrite, *f.* (poet. and zool.) amphitrite.
ánfora, *f.* amphora, two-handled narrow-necked jar; (Mex.) ballot box.—*pl.* cruets.
anfractuosidad, *f.* crookedness; anfractuosity.
anfractuoso, sa, *a.* anfractuous, winding.
angaria, *f.* ancient servitude; forced delay in sailing of ship (to use it for public service).
angarillas, *f. pl.* handbarrow; panniers; cruet stands; frames for things carried by horses.
angaripola, *f.* calico.—*pl.* gaudy ornaments.
ángaro, *m.* beacon.
angas, (Am.)—**por a. o por mangas,** in any case, some way or other, anyhow.
ángel, *m.* angel; a raylike fish.—**a. custodio,** or **de la guarda,** guardian angel.
angélica, *f.* (bot.) garden angelica.—**a. carlina,** (bot.) carline thistle.—**a. palustra,** wild angelica; (pharm.) purgative mixture.

angelical, *a.* angelic.
angélico, ca, *a.* angelic.
angelico, ito, *m. dim.* little angel.
angelón, angelonazo, angelote, *m. aug.* large figure of an angel placed on altars: fat child.
ángelus, *m.* Angelus.
angevino, na, *n.* & *a.* Angevin.
angina, *f.* angina.—**a. de pecho,** angina pectoris.
angiología, *f.* angiology, part of anatomy dealing with blood vessels and lymphatics.
angiospermo, ma, *n.* & *a.* (bot.) angiosperm (-ous).—*f. pl.* Angiospermæ.
angla, *f.* cape (of land).
anglesita, *f.* (min.) anglesite, a lead ore
anglicanismo, *m.* Anglicanism.
anglicano, na, *a.* Anglican.
anglicismo, *m.* Anglicism.
anglo, gla, *a.* Angle; English.
angloamericano, na, *n.* & *a.* Anglo-American.
anglófilo, la, *n.* & *a.* Anglophile.
anglofobia, *f.* Anglophobia.
anglófobo, ba, *n.* & *a.* Anglophobe.
anglomanía, *f.* Anglomania.
anglómano, na, *n.* Anglomaniac.
anglonormando, da, *n.* & *a.* Anglo-Norman.
anglosajón, jona, *n.* & *a.* Anglo-Saxon.
angora, *m.* or *f.* Angora.
angostar, *va.* & *vr.* to narrow; to contract.
angosto, ta, *a.* narrow, close; insufficient.
angostura, *f.* narrowness; strait; distress; narrows (in a river, etc.).
angra, *f.* small bay, cove.
angrelado, da, *a.* (her., arch.) serrated.
angstrom, *m.* (phys.) angstrom, angstrom unit.
anguarina, *f.* loose coat with long sleeves.
anguila, *f.* (zool.) eel.—**a. de cabo,** (naut.) rope to flog sailors.—**anguilas,** launching ways.
anguilazo, *m.* stroke with an ANGUILA DE CABO.
anguilero, *a.* (basket) for eels.
anguiliforme, *a.* anguiliform.
anguina, *f.* (vet.) the vein of the groins.
angula, *f.* the brood of eels.
angular, *a.* angular.
angulema, *f.* hemp stuff.—*pl.* (coll.) foolish flattery. Also ZALAMERÍA.
ángulo, *m.* angle; corner, nook.—**á. acimutal,** azimuth.—**á. agudo,** acute angle.—**á. de ataque,** (aer.) angle of attack.—**á. de avance,** angle of advance; (elec.) angle of lead.—**á. de balance,** (aer.) angle of bank or roll.—**á. de cabeceo,** (aer.) angle of pitch.—**á. de contacto,** (mech.) angle of contact.—**á. de contingencia,** (Ry.) angle of intersection.—**á. de depresión,** angle of depression.—**á. de deriva,** (aer.) drift angle.—**á. de derrape,** (aer.) angle of yaw.—**á. de deslizamiento,** (aer.) gliding angle.—**á. de desviación,** deflection angle.—**á. diedro,** (geom.) dihedral angle.—**á. de elevación,** angle of elevation; (artil.) angle of deflection.—**á. de entrada,** (hydraul.) angle of entrance.—**á. entrante,** reëntry angle.—**á. externo,** exterior angle.—**á. facial,** facial angle.—**á. de incidencia,** (phys.) angle of incidence.—**á. de planeo,** (aer.) gliding angle.—**á. de reflexión,** (phys.) angle of reflection.—**á. de refracción,** (phys.) angle of refraction—**á. de resistencia nula,** (aer.) angle of zero lift.—**á. de retraso,** (elec.) angle of lag.—**á. de rozamiento,** angle of friction.—**á. de subida,** (aer.) climbing angle.—**á. de torsión,** angle of torsion or twist.—**á. de tracción,** angle of traction.—**á. horario,** (astr.) hour angle.—**á. interno,** interior angle.—**á. oblicuo,** (geom.) oblique angle.—**á. plano,** (geom.) plane angle.—**á. poliedro,** (geom.) polyhedral angle.—**á. recto,** (geom.) right angle.—**ángulos adyacentes,** (geom.) adjacent angles.—**ángulos alternos,** (geom.) alternate angles.—**ángulos complementarios,** (geom.) complementary angles.—**ángulos correspondientes,** corresponding angles.—**ángulos opuestos por el vértice,** vertical angles.—**ángulos suplementarios,** (geom.) supplementary angles.—**en á.,** at an angle.—**en á. recto,** at right angles.
anguloso, sa, *a.* angular, angulate.
angustia, *f.* anguish, affliction, pang.
angustiadamente, *adv.* painfully.
angustiado, da. I. *pp.* of ANGUSTIAR. **II.** *a.* sorrowful; anxious; narrow-minded.
angustiar, *va.* to cause anguish to, afflict, worry.
angustioso, sa, *a.* full of, or causing, anguish.
anhelación, *f.* panting; longing.
anhelante, *a.* eager, deeply desirous, longing.
anhelar, *vn.* to breathe with difficulty; to desire anxiously, long for, covet.
anhélito, *m.* difficult respiration.
anhelo, *m.* strong desire; eagerness.—**anheloso, sa,** *a.* difficult (breathing); anxiously desirous.
anhídrido, *m.* (chem.) anhydride.—**a. carbónico,** carbon dioxide, carbonic-acid gas.—**a. sulfúrico,** sulphur trioxide.—**a. sulfuroso,** sulphur dioxide.
anhidrita, *f.* (min.) anhydrite.
anhidro, dra, *a.* anhydrous.
aní, *m.* (ornith.) (S. A.) a pretty creeping bird.
anidar, *vn.* to nest; to nestle; (fig.) to dwell, reside; to cherish; to shelter.
anieblar, *va.* to darken, obscure; to mystify.
anieblo, anieble, *v. V.* ANEBLAR.
anilina, *f.* (chem.) aniline.
anilla, *f.* ring; curtain ring; hoop.
anillado, da, *a.* in the form of a ring, annulated. —*m. pl.* (zool.) Annelida.
anillar, *va.* to form rings or hoops with; to fasten with rings.
anillejo, anillete, *m. dim.* small ring.
anillo, *m.* small hoop; finger ring; circlet: ring of a turbine; circular band; (naut.) hank or grommet; (arch.) astragal.—**a. de boda,** wedding ring.—**a. de matrimonio,** engagement ring.—**de a.,** honorary.—**venir como a. al dedo,** to fit like a glove; to come in the nick of time.
ánima, *f.* soul; (mech.) bore of a gun.—**ánimas,** ringing of church bells at sunset.
animación, *f.* animation, liveliness; bustle.
animado, da. I. *pp.* of ANIMAR. **II.** *a.* lively, animated; manful.
animador, ra, *n.* one who animates or enlivens.
animadversión, *f.* animadversion; enmity.
animal, *m.* & *a.* animal.
animálculo, *m.* animalcule.
animalejo, lico, lillo, *m. dim.* small or little animal.
animalidad, *f.* animality.
animalismo, *m.* animalism.
animalización, *f.* animalization.
animalizar, *va.* to animalize.
animalote, *m. aug.* big animal.
animalucho, *m.* ugly, hideous animal.
animante, *a.* animating; stimulating, exciting; animate, living, existing.
animar. I. *va.* to animate, enliven, comfort; to encourage; to revive; to incite, excite; to give power or vigor to. **II.** *vr.* to become lively; to feel encouraged, energetic; to cheer up.
anime, *f.* a myrrhlike resin.
animero, *m.* one who begs for souls in purgatory.
animismo, *m.* animism.
animista. I. *a.* animistic. **II.** *n.* animist.
ánimo, *m.* spirit, soul, mind; courage, valor, fortitude, manfulness; hardiness; mind, intention, will; thought; attention.—**hacer,** or **tener, a. de,** to intend to, make up one's mind to.
animosidad, *f.* animosity; courage.
animoso, sa, *a.* brave, spirited, courageous.
aniñado, da, *a.* childish.
aniñarse, *vr.* to become childish.
anión, *m.* (chem., phys.) anion.
aniquilación, *f.* annihilation.
aniquilador, ra, *n.* & *a.* annihilator(-ing).

aniquilamiento, *m.* destruction, annihilation; decay, wasting away.
aniquilar. I. *va.* to annihilate; to consume, waste away. II. *vr.* to decline; to decay; to waste away, become emaciated.
anís, *m.* (bot.) anise, aniseed; sugar-coated aniseed.
anisado, da. I. *a.* made of or flavored with anise. II. *m.* anisating; AGUARDIENTE ANISADO, a liquor flavored with anise.
[1]**anisar,** *va.* to tincture with anise.
[2]**anisar,** *m.* patch sowed with aniseed.
anisete, *m.* anisette.
anisilo, *m.* (chem.) anisyl.
anisófilo, la, *a.* (bot.) anisophyllous.
anisómero, ra, *a.* (bot.) anisomerous.
anisométrico, ca, *a.* anisometric.
anisotropía, *f.* (phys.) anisotropy.
anisotrópico, ca, *a.* (phys.) anisotropic.
aniversario, ria. I. *a.* annual, yearly. II. *m.* anniversary; holiday; annual memorial service.
anjeo, *m.* coarse linen.
ano, *m.* anus.
anobio, *m.* (entom.) deathwatch beetle.
anoche, *adv.* last night.
anochecedor, ra, *n.* person who retires late at night; (coll.) night hawk.
anochecer. I. *vn.* (*ind.* ANOCHEZCO; *subj.* ANOCHEZCA) to grow dark (at the approach of night); to be or reach (somewhere) at nightfall (*anochecimos en París,* we reached Paris at nightfall. The construction of this verb is similar to that of AMANECER). II. *vr.* to become dark (at nightfall). III. *m.* nightfall, dusk.—**al a.,** at nightfall, at dusk.
anochecida, *f.* nightfall, dusk.
anochezco, anochezca, *v. V.* ANOCHECER.
anódico, ca, *a.* anodal, anodic.
anodinia, *f.* (med.) anodynia, absence of pain.
anodino, na, *n.* & *a.* (med.) anodyne.
ánodo, *m.* (elec.) anode.
anofeles, *m.* (entom.) anopheles.
anomalía, *f.* anomaly; (astr.) anomaly.
anomalístico, ca, *a.* (astr.) anomalistic(al.
anómalo, la, *a.* anomalous.
anón, *m.* (bot.) custard apple tree.
[1]**anona,** *f.* annona or custard apple.
[2]**anona,** *f.* store of provisions.
anonáceo, a. I. *a.* (bot.) annonaceous. II. *m. pl.* Annonaceæ.
anonadación, *f.*; **anonadamiento,** *m.* annihilation; overwhelming, crushing.
anonadar. I. *va.* to annihilate; to diminish. II. *vr.* to humble oneself.
anónimo, ma, *a.* anonymous.
anormal, *a.* abnormal.
anormalidad, *f.* abnormality.
anormalmente, *adv.* abnormally.
anortita, *f.* (min.) anorthite.
anotación, *f.* annotation, note.
anotador, ra, *n.* commentator.
anotar, *va.* to make notes; to comment, annotate.
anqueta.—estar de media a., to be uncomfortably seated.
anquialmendrado, da, *a.* (of a horse) having a narrow croup.
anquiboyuno, na, *a.* having a croup like an ox.
anquilosar, *va.* & *vr.* to ankylose.
anquilosis, *f.* (med.) ankylosis.
anquilostomiasis, *f.* (med.) hookworm disease
anquilóstomo, *m.* (zool.) hookworm.
anquirredondo, da, *a.* having a rounded croup.
anquiseco, ca, *a.* lean-crouped.
ansa, hansa, *f.* commercial league among the free cities of Germany.
ánsar, *m.* goose.—**a. macho,** gander.
ansarería, *f.* goose farm.
ansarero, ra, *n.* gooseherd.
ansarino, na. I. *a.* (poet.) pert. to geese. II. *m.* gosling.
ansarón, *m.* = ÁNSAR.
anseático, ca, *a.* Hanseatic.
ansia, *f.* anxiety; eagerness, ardent desire; longing, hankering; greediness.
ansiadamente, *adv.* anxiously; earnestly.
ansiar, *va.* to desire anxiously; to long for; to hanker for; to covet.
ansiedad, *f.* anxiety; (med.) pain accompanying illness.
ansioso, sa, *a.* anxious; eager; greedy; hot.
[1]**anta,** *f.* elk.
[2]**anta,** *f.* obelisk, needle.—*pl.* (arch.) pillars of a building.
antagallas, *f. pl.* (naut.) spritsail reef bands.
antagónico, ca, *a.* antagonistic.
antagonismo, *m.* antagonism.
antagonista, *m.* antagonist; competitor.
antañazo, *adv.* (coll.) a long time ago.
antaño, *adv.* last year; long ago; yore.
antártico, ca, *a.* antarctic.
[1]**ante.** I. *prep.* before; in the presence of.—**representante, delgado, miembro, a.,** representative at, delegate to, member of, (an organization, as the U. N.).—**a. todo,** above all, first of all. II. *m.* first dinner course; (Peru) drink made of wine, sugar, cinnamon, nutmeg, etc.
[2]**ante,** *m.* elk; buffalo; buffalo skin.
anteado, da, *a.* buff-colored.
antealtar, *m.* chancel.
anteanoche, antenoche, *adv.* night before last.
anteayer, *adv.* day before yesterday.
antebrazo, *m.* forearm.
antecama, *f.* carpet laid in front of a bed.
antecámara, *f.* antechamber; lobby; hall.
antecapilla, *f.* anteroom to a chapel.
antecedencia, *f.* antecedence.
antecedente. I. *a.* antecedent, prior, previous. II. *m.* antecedent; *pl.* antecedents.
antecedentemente, *adv.* previously, beforehand.
anteceder, *va.* to precede, go before.
antecesor, ra, *n.* predecessor, forefather.—*pl.* ancestors.
antecoger, *va.* (*ind.* ANTECOJO; *subj.* ANTECOJA) to forereach; to gather in (thing), receive (person), too soon.
antecolumna, *f.* (arch.) column of a porch.
antecoro, *m.* entrance leading to the choir.
antecos, cas, *n.* & *a. pl.* (those) living on same meridian but on opposite sides of equator.
antedata, *f.* antedate.—**antedatar,** *va.* to antedate.
antedecir, *va.* (*ger.* ANTEDICIENDO; *pp.* ANTEDICHO; *ind. pres.* ANTEDIGO, *pret.* ANTEDIJE, *fut.* ANTEDIRÉ; *subj.* ANTEDIGA) to foretell.
antedicho, cha, *a.* aforesaid.
antediluviano, na, *a.* antediluvian.
antefirma, *f.* closing phrases (of a letter) or denomination of the signer, put before the signature.
anteiglesia, *f.* porch of a church; parochial church and district in Biscay.
antelación, *f.* precedence in order of time.
antemano.—de a., beforehand.
antemeridiano, na, *a.* of the forenoon (a. m.).
antemundano, na, *a.* antemundane.
antemural, *m.* **antemuralla,** *f.*, **antemuro,** *m.* fort, rock or mountain serving for the defense of a fortress; safeguard.
antena, *f.* (naut.) lateen yard; (zool., radio) antenna.—*pl.* antennæ.
antenatal, *a.* prenatal.
antenoche, anteanoche, *adv.* night before last.
antenombre, *m.* title before a proper name.
anténula, *f.* (zool.) antennule, small antenna.
antenupcial, *a.* before marriage, prenuptial.
anteojera, *f.* spectacle case; blinker (for horse).
anteojero, ra, *n.* spectacle maker or seller.
anteojo, *m.* spyglass; eyeglass; telescope (of a surveying instrument); opera glass; blinker (for horse),—*pl.* spectacles; goggles.—**a. de larga vista,** field glass.
antepagar, *va.* to pay beforehand.
antepasado, da. I. *a.* (of time) passed, elapsed. II. *n.* ancestor, predecessor.

antepascual, *a.* antepaschal.
antepecho, *m.* balcony, bridge rail; window sill railing; breastwork, parapet; footstep of a coach; poitrel (harness); breast roller of a loom.
antependio, *m.* (eccl.) antependium.
antepenúltimo, ma, *a.* antepenultimate.
anteponer, *va.* (*pp.* ANTEPUESTO; *ind. pres.* ANTEPONGO, *pret.* ANTEPUSE, *fut.* ANTEPONDRÉ; *subj.* ANTEPONGA) to prefer.—**a. a,** to prefer (one thing) to (another); to place before.
anteportada, *f.* front page (of a book) bearing the title only.
anteportal, antepórtico, *m.* vestibule, porch.
anteproyecto, *m.* preliminary plans, ground plan; draft, (fig.) blueprint.
antepuerta, *f.* portier; (fort.) inner gate.
antepuerto, *m.* (naut.) anteport.
antera, *f.* (bot.) anther.
anteridio, *m.* (bot.) antheridium.
anterior, *a.* anterior; former; above, preceding.
anterioridad, *f.* anteriority; priority; preference.—**con a.,** previously, beforehand.
anteriormente, *adv.* previously.
antero, *m.* worker in buckskin.
anteroversión, *f.* (med.) anteversion.
antes, *adv.* before; formerly; first; rather; on the contrary.—**a. bien,** on the contrary; rather.—**a. de,** before.—**a. de anoche** = ANTENOCHE.—**a. de ayer** = ANTEAYER.—**a. de que,** before.—**a. que,** before; rather than.
antesacristía, *f.* anteroom of a sacristy.
antesala, *f.* antechamber.—**hacer a.,** to be kept waiting, dance attendance.
antestatura, *f.* (mil.) improvised intrenchment of palisades and sandbags.
antetemplo, *m.* portico of a church.
antever, *va.* (*pp.* ANTEVISTO; *ger.* ANTEVIENDO; *ind.* ANTEVEO; *subj.* ANTEVEA) to foresee.
antevíspera, *f.* two days before.
antiácido, da, *m.* & *a.* antacid.
antiaéreo, a, *a.* anti-aircraft (as *a.*).
antiafrodisíaco, ca, *a.* anaphrodisiac.
antialcohólico, ca, *a.* (Am.) antialcoholic.
antiapopléctico, ca, *a.* antiapoplectic.
antiarina, *f.* (chem.) antiarin.
antiaro, *m.* upas tree.
antiartrítico, ca, *a.* (med.) antiarthritic.
antiasmático, ca, *a.* (med.) antiasthmatic.
antibactérico, ca, *a.* antibacterial.
antibaquio, *m.* antibacchius, foot in poetry.
antibilioso, sa, *a.* antibilious.
antibiótico, ca, *m.* & *a.* antibiotic.
anticátodo, *m.* anticathode.
anticiclon, *m.* (meteorol.) anticyclone.
anticipación, *f.* anticipation; foretaste.
anticipada, *f.* (fencing) unexpected thrust.
anticipadamente, *adv.* prematurely; in advance, beforehand.
anticipado, da, *a.* advanced (money); in advance (payment).
anticipador, ra, *n.* & *a.* anticipator(-ing).
anticipamiento, *m.* = ANTICIPACIÓN.
anticipante, *n.* & *a.* forestalling(-er).
anticipar. I. *va.* to anticipate (in the sense of to do, bring to happen, etc. before the regular time); to advance (money, payment); to lend. **II.** *vr.* (a) to anticipate, act ahead (of); to act or occur before the regular or expected time.
anticipo, *m.* advance; money lent; advance payment.
anticlerical, *a.* anticlerical.
anticlericalismo, *m.* anticlericalism.
anticlímax, *m.* or *f.* (rhet.) anticlimax.
anticlinal, *m.* (geol.) anticline.
anticohesor, *m.* (rad.) anticoherer.
anticoincidencia, *f.* (phys., elec.) anticoincidence.
anticomunista, *n.* & *a.* anticommunist.
anticoncepción, *f.* contraception.
anticonceptivo, va, *m.* & *a.* contraceptive.
anticongelante, *m.* & *a.* antifreeze.
anticresis, *f.* (law) antichresis.
anticristiano, na, *a.* antichristian.
anticristo, *m.* Antichrist.
anticrítico, *m.* opponent to a critic.
anticuado, da. I. *pp.* of ANTICUAR. **II.** *a.* antiquated.
anticuar. I. *va.* to antiquate, outdate. **II.** *vr.* to become antiquated.
anticuario, ria, *n.* antiquarian.
anticuerpo, *m.* antibody.
antideslizante, *a.* nonskidding (esp. auto tires).
antidetonante, *m.* & *a.* antiknock.
antidiftérico, ca, *m.* & *a.* (med.) antidiphtheritic.
antidoral, *a.* (law) remunerative.
antidotario, *m.* pharmacology: place in a pharmacy for antidotes.
antídoto, *m.* antidote.
antiemético, ca, *a.* (med.) antiemetic.
antiepiléptico, ca, *a.* (med.) antepileptic.
antier, *adv.* (coll.) day before yesterday.
antiesclavismo, *m.* antislavery.
antiesclavista, *a.* (Am.) antislavery.
antiescorbútico, ca, *a.* antiscorbutic.
antiescrofuloso, sa, *a.* antiscrofulous.
antiespasmódico, ca, *a.* antispasmodic.
antifaz, *m.* veil that covers the face; mask.
antifebril, *a.* (med.) antifebrile.
antifebrina, *f.* (chem.) acetanilide.
antiflogístico, ca, *a.* & *m.* (med.) antiphlogistic.
antífona, *f.* (eccl.) antiphony, responsive singing.
antifonal, antifonario, *m.* antiphonal.
antifonero, *m.* precentor.
antífrasis, *f.* (rhet.) antiphrasis.
antifricción, *m.* antifriction metal.
antígeno, *m.* (physiol.) antigen.
antigualla, *f.* object of remote antiquity; antique; out-of-date custom or object.
antiguamente, *adv.* formerly, in antiquity.
antiguar, *vn.* to attain seniority (in a position).
antigüedad, *f.* antiquity; ancient times; antique.
antiguo, gua. I. *a.* antique; ancient, old.—**A. Testamento,** Old Testament.—**a la antigua, a lo antiguo,** after the manner of the ancients, in an old-fashion manner.—**de antiguo,** from times of yore, since old times.—**lo antiguo,** ancient things; antiquity. **II.** *m.* aged member of a community; veteran (in an occupation); senior of a college.—**los antiguos,** the ancients.
antihelio, *m.* (meteorol.) anthelion.
antihelmíntico, ca, *a.* (med.) anthelmintic.
antiherpético, ca, *a.* (med.) antiherpetic.
antihigiénico, ca, *a.* unhygienic.
antihistamina, *f.* (pharm.) antihistamine.
antiimperialismo, *m.* anti-imperialism.
antiimperialista, *n.* & *a.* anti-imperialist.
antiinflacionista, *a.* anti-inflationary.
antilogaritmo, *m.* (math.) antilogarithm.
antilogía, *f.* antilogy, contradiction in terms.
antilógico, ca, *a.* illogical.
antílope, *m.* antelope.
antillano, na, *n.* & *a.* West-Indian.
Antillas, *f. pl.* Antilles, West Indies.
antimacasar, *m.* antimacassar.
antimateria, *f.* (phys.) antimatter.
antimesón, *m.* (phys.) antimeson.
antimilitarista, *n.* & *a.* antimilitarist.
antiministerial. I. *a.* opposed to the Administration. **II.** *n.* member of the opposition (to the government).
antimonárquico, ca, *a.* antimonarchical
antimonial, *a.* (chem.) antimonial.
antimoniato, *m.* antimonate.
antimónico, ca, *a.* antimonic.
antimonio, *m.* antimony.
antimonioso, sa, *a.* (chem.) antimonious.
antimonopolio, lia, *a.* antitrust.
antinefrítico, ca, *a.* (med.) antinephritic.
antineutrino, *m.* (phys.) antineutrino.
antineutrón, *m.* (phys.) antineutron.

antinomia, *f.* (law) antinomy.
antinómico, ca, *a.* self-contradictory.
antinucleón, *m.* (phys.) antinucleon.
antioqueno, *n.* & *a.* Antiochian.
antipalúdico, ca, *a.* antimalarial.
antipapa, *m.* antipope.
antipapado, *m.* antipapacy.
antipapal, *a.* antipapal.
antipapista, *n.* & *a.* antipapist.
antipara, *f.* screen; legging covering the front part of leg and foot.
antiparalelo, *m.* (phys.) antiparallel.
antiparras, *f. pl.* (coll.) spectacles.
antipartícula, *f.* (phys.) antiparticle.
antipatía, *f.* antipathy; dislike, aversion.
antipático, ca, *a.* uncongenial, disagreeable.
antipatizar, *vn.* not to be congenial.—**a. con,** to dislike, not to be congenial with.
antipatriótico, ca, *a.* unpatriotic.
antiperistáltico, ca, *a.* antiperistaltic.
antipirético, ca, *m.* & *a.* (med.) antipyretic.
antipirina, *f.* antipyrine.
antípoca, *f.* (law, prov.) agreement to lease.
antipocar, *va.* (law) to execute (a lease).
antípoda. I. *a.* antipodal. **II.** *m.* (in *pl.*) antipodes.
antiprotón, *m.* (phys.) antiproton.
antiproyectil, *a.* antimissile.
antipútrido, da, *a.* antiseptic.
antiquísimo, ma, *a. super.* very ancient.
antirrábico, ca, *a.* antirabic.
antirraquítico, ca, *m.* & *a.* antirachitic.
antirreglamentario, ria, *a.* against the rules.
antirreumático, ca, *m.* & *a.* antirheumatic.
antirrevolucionario, ria, *a.* antirevolutionary.
antirrino, *m.* (bot.) snapdragon.
antiscios, *m. pl.* (geog.) antiscians.
antisemita, *n.* & *a.* anti-Semite.
antisemítico, ca, *a.* anti-Semitic.
antisemitismo, *m.* anti-Semitism.
antisepsia, *f.* (med.) antisepsis.
antiséptico, ca, *n.* & *a.* antiseptic.
antisifilítico, ca, *a.* antisyphilitic.
antisocial, *a.* antisocial.
antispástico, ca, *a.* (med.) antispastic.
antistrofa, *f.* antistrophe.
antisuero, *m.* antiserum.
antitanque, *a.*—**cañon a.,** antitank gun.
antitérmico, ca, *a.* heat-resisting.
antítesis, *f.* antithesis.
antitétano, na, *a.* (med.) antitetanic.
antitético, ca, *a.* antithetical.
antitipo, *m.* antitype.
antitóxico, ca, *a.* antitoxic.
antitoxina, *f.* antitoxin.
antitrago, *m.* (anat.) antitragus.
antiveneno, *m.* antivenin.
antivenenoso, sa, *a.* antitoxic.
antivenéreo, rea, *a.* (med.) antivenereal.
antófago, ga; *a.* (zool.) anthophagous.
antojadizo, za; antojado, da, *a.* capriciously desirous, having whimsical desires for trifles; wishing, or taking a notion to, everything (gen. said of children and women).
antojarse, *vr.* to be desired capriciously or on the spur of the moment, to arouse a whimsical desire, or a fancy (diff. constr.: *se me antojó ese sombrero,* I took a fancy to (buy) that hat, (coll.) I fell in love with that hat and longed for it: *no hago eso porque no se me antoja,* I don't do that because it doesn't appeal to me, or, because I won't; *se nos antojó ir a Paris,* we took a notion to go to Paris); to occur (to the mind), seem probable (diff. constr.: *se me antojó que Juan no sabía,* it occurred to me, *or,* I suspected, that John did not know).—**a. de,** to take a fancy to, to desire capriciously.
antojo, *m.* whim, capricious desire, fancy; will.—**a su a.,** as one pleases; arbitrarily.
antojuelo, *m. dim.* slight desire.
antología, *f.* anthology.
antológico, ca, *a.* anthological.
antónimo, ma, *a.* & *m.* (pert. to) **antonym.**
antonomasia, *f.* (rhet.) antonomasia.
antonomástico, ca, *a.* antonomastic.
antorcha, *f.* torch, flambeau, taper; cresset.
antorchero, *m.* cresset.
antraceno, *m.* (chem.) anthracene.
antrácico, ca, *a.* (med.) anthracic.
antracita, *f.* anthracite coal.
antracnosis, *f.* (bot.) anthracnose.
ántrax, *m.* (med.) **anthrax.**
antro, *m.* cavern, grotto; (anat.) **antrum.**
antropocéntrico, ca, *a.* anthropocentric.
antropofagía, *f.* anthropophagy, cannibalism.
antropófago, ga, *n.* & *a.* cannibal.
antropogenia, *f.* anthropogeny.
antropografía, *f.* anthropography.
antropoide, *n.* & *a.* anthropoid.
antropología, *f.* anthropology.
antropológico, ca, *a.* anthropological.
antropólogo, *m.* anthropologist.
antropómetra, *n.* anthropometrist.—**antropometría,** *f.* anthropometry.—**antropométrico, ca,** *a.* anthropometric.
antropomórfico, ca, *a.* anthropomorphic.
antropomorfismo, *m.* anthropomorphism.
antropomorfita, *n.* anthropomorphite.
antropomorfo, fa, *a.* anthropomorphous.
antropozoico, ca, *a.* anthropozoic.
antruejo, *m.* the three days of carnival before Ash Wednesday.
antuviada, *f.* (coll.) unexpected blow or stroke.
antuviar, *va.* to forestall, anticipate; (coll.) to be first in striking.—**antuvión,** *m.* (coll.) sudden blow or attack.—**de a.,** unexpectedly.
anual, *a.* annual, yearly.—**anualidad,** *f.* annual recurrence; annuity.—**anualmente,** *adv.* annually, yearly.
anuario, *m.* yearbook; trade or professional directory.
anúbada, *f.* = ANÚTEBA, a call to war.
anubarrado, da, *a.* clouded.
anublado, da, *a.* overcast, clouded, cloudy.
anublar. I. *va.* to cloud, darken; to obscure. **II.** *vr.* to be blasted, withered, mildewed; to fail, fall through, fall off; to become cloudy.
anublo, *m.* = AÑUBLO, mildew (of grain).
anudar. I. *va.* to knot; to join, unite. **II.** *vn.* to wither, fade, pine away.—**anudarse la voz a uno,** (fig.) to become speechless.
anuencia, *f.* compliance, consent.
anuente, *a.* complying, consenting.
anulable, *a.* voidable.
anulación, *f.* abrogation, voiding, nullification.
anulador, ra, *n.* repealer.
[1]**anular,** *va.* to annul, make void; to frustrate.
[2]**anular,** *a.* ring-shaped.—**dedo a.,** ring finger.
anulativo, va, *a.* voiding.
anuloso, sa, *a.* annular, ring-shaped.
anunciación, *f.* announcement; Annunciation.
anunciador, ra. I. *n.* & *a.* announcer(-ing); advertiser(-ing). **II.** *m.* (elec.) annunciator; (radio) announcer (Arg. also SPEAKER).
anunciante, *n.* announcer; advertiser.
anunciar, *va.* to announce, proclaim; to foretell; to advertise.
anuncio, *m.* announcement, notice; omen, forerunner; advertisement; (com.) advice.
anuo, nua, *a.* = ANUAL, annual.
anuria, *f.* (med.) anuria.
anuro, *n.* (zool.) anuran.
anúteba, *f.* a call to war.
anverso, *m.* obverse (of coin, medal, etc.).
anzolero, *m.* fishhook maker or dealer.
anzuelo, *m.* fishhook; fritters.—**caer en el a., tragar el a.,** to be gullible, swallow the hook.
aña, *f.* (Peru) a kind of small fox.
añacal, *m.* wheat carrier to mills; baker's board to carry bread.
añada, *f.* good or bad season in a year; pasture or arable land lying fallow alternate years.
añadible, *a.* addible.

añadido, da. I. *a.* added, additional, adscititious. **II.** *m.* hair switch.
añadidura, *f.* addition, increase; extra, over.—**por a.,** in addition, into the bargain, (often in the sense of "to make matters worse"): over, to boot.
añadir, *va.* to add, join; to exaggerate.
añafil, *m.* a Moorish musical pipe.
añagaza, *f.* call, lure, or decoy; allurement, enticement.
añal. I. *a.* annual; yearling. **II.** *m.* offering in memory of a person one year after his death.
añalejo, *m.* ecclesiastical almanac.
añascar, *va.* (*pret.* AÑASQUÉ; *subj.* AÑASQUE) (coll.) to collect (small trinkets).
añejar. I. *va.* to make old. **II.** *vr.* to age (of things, either deteriorating or improving).
añejo, ja, *a.* old; aged (improved); stale, musty.
añicos, *n. pl.* fragments, "smithereens."—**hacer a.,** to break to smithereens.—**hacerse a.,** to take great pains, exert oneself to the utmost.
añil, *m.* (bot.) indigo; indigo blue.—**añilar,** *va.* to blue (clothes).—**añilería,** *f.* indigo farm.
añinero, *m.* dealer in lambskins.
añinos, *m. pl.* the fleecy skins of yearling lambs; lamb's wool.
año, *m.* year; cavalier; valentine drawn by lot on New Year's day; crop.—*pl.* birthday; long ago; old age.—**a. anomalístico,** anomalistic year.—**a. antepasado,** year before last.—**a. bisiesto,** leap-year.—**a. civil,** civil year.—**a. climatérico,** grand climacteric.—**a. de gracia,** year of grace.—**a. económico,** fiscal year.—**a. en curso,** current year.—**a. escolar,** school year.—**a. intercalar,** leap-year.—**a. nuevo,** New Year.—**a. platónico,** Platonic year.—**a. sideral,** sidereal year.—**a. sinódico,** synodic period of the earth and another planet.—**a. tras a.,** year after year.—**a. tropical,** tropical or solar year.—**al a.,** by the year.—**entrado en años,** of mature age, of uncertain age (not young).—**entre a.,** during the year.—**estar de buen a.,** to be in good health.—**por los años de . . . ,** about the year . . . —**tener . . . años,** to be . . . years old (*tengo 20 anos,* I am 20 years old; *¿cuántos años tiene Vd.?* how old are you?)
añojal, *m.* fallow land.
añojo, ja, *n.* yearling calf.
año-luz, *m.* light-year.
añoranza, *f.* nostalgia; loneliness (through bereavement).
añorar, *vn.* to suffer from nostalgia; to recall old times.
añoso, sa, *a.* old, aged, stricken in years.
añublado, da. I. *pp.* of AÑUBLAR. **II.** *a.* blindfolded.
añublar, añublarse, = ANUBLAR.
añublo, *m.* mildew (on grain). Also TIZÓN.
añusgar, *vn.* to choke; to become angry.
aojado, da, *a.* hoodooed.
aojador, ra, *n.* hoodoo, evil-eyed person.
aojadura, *f.* **aojamiento,** *m.* witchcraft, fascination, evil eye.
aojar, *va.* to charm, bewitch, hoodoo.
aojo, *m.* bewitching, fascination, evil eye.
aonio, nia, *a.* pertaining to the Muses.
aoristo, *m.* (gram.) aorist.
aorta, *f.* (anat.) aorta.—**aórtico ca,** *a.* aortic.
aovado, da, *a.* oviform, egg-shaped.
aovar, *vn.* to lay eggs.
aovillarse, *vr.* to crumple, shrink.
apabilar, *va.* to trim (a wick).
apabullar, *va.* (coll.) to flatten, crush.
apacentadero, *m.* grazing field, pasture.
apacentador, *m.* herdsman.
apacentamiento, *m.* grazing; pasturage.
apacentar, *va.* (*ind.* APACIENTO; *subj.* APACIENTE) to graze (cattle); to graze, feed on (grass, etc.); to teach, instruct spiritually; to incite.
apacibilidad, *f.* peaceableness, mildness.
apacible, *a.* peaceable, peaceful, gentle, placid, calm.—**apaciblemente,** *adv.* peacefully, gently.
apaciento, apaciente, *v. V.* APACENTAR.
apaciguador, ra, *n.* & *a.* pacifier(-fying).
apaciguamiento, *m.* pacification, appeasement.
apaciguar. I. *va.* to appease, pacify, calm. **II.** *vn.* (naut.) to abate. **III.** *vr.* to calm down.
apache, *m.* Apache, gangster, gunman.
apacheta, *f.* (Am.) devotional heap of stones on hills.
apachurrar, *va.* (Am.) to crush, flatten.
apadrinador, ra, *n.* patron, defender, protector; second (in a duel).
apadrinar, *va.* to act as second of, in a duel; to act as godfather to; to uphold, approve, favor.
apagable, *a.* extinguishable, quenchable.
apagadizo, za, *a.* poorly burning, of difficult combustion.
apagado, da, *a.* humble-minded, submissive, pusillanimous; dull (color).
apagador, *m.* one that extinguishes; damper, extinguisher; damper (in pianos).
apagaincendios, *m.* fire engine; fire extinguisher.
apagamiento, *m.* extinguishment.
apagapenoles, *m. pl.* (naut.) leech ropes, lines.
apagar. I. *va.* (*pret.* APAGUÉ; *subj.* APAGUE) to quench, put out, extinguish; to efface, destroy; (art) to soften (colors); (mech.) to deaden.—**a. cal,** to slake lime.—**a. la voz,** to put a mute on musical instruments.—**a. los fuegos,** or **el fuego, del enemigo,** to silence the enemy's guns. **II.** *vr.* to become extinguished, go out, die out.
apagón, *m.* blackout (as when electricity fails).
apainelado, da, *a.* elliptic (arch).
apaisado, da, *a.* of greater width than depth.
apalabrar, *va.* to make an engagement with; to speak about, discuss; to bespeak, engage.
apalache, *a.* Appalachian.
apalancar, *va.* (*pret.* APALANQUÉ; *subj.* APALANQUE) to move with a lever.
apaleador, ra, *n.* cudgeller.
apaleamiento, *m.* drubbing, beating.
apalear, *va.* to cane, cudgel; to horsewhip.
apaleo, *m.* moving or shovelling grain.
apanalado, da, *a.* honeycombed.
apancora, *f.* sea hedgehog.
apandar, *va.* (coll.) to pilfer, steal.
apandillar, *va.* & *vr.* to form a gang or faction.
apanojado, da, *a.* (bot.) paniculate.
apantanar, *va.* to flood; to inundate.
apantuflado, da, *a.* slipper-shaped.
[1]apañado, da, *a.* resembling woollen cloth in body.
[2]apañado, da, *a.* dexterous, skillful; (coll.) suitable.
apañador, ra, *n.* one that seizes; pilferer.
apañadura, *f.* act of seizing, snatching; trimming (on counterpanes).
apañar. I. *va.* to grasp, seize; to carry away; to pilfer; to dress, clothe; to fit close, wrap; to patch, mend. **II.** *vr.* (coll.) to be handy, to be skillful; to contrive, manage.—**apaño,** *m.* a seizing, grasping; knack; patch, repair.
apañuscar, *va.* (*pret.* APAÑUSQUÉ; *subj.* APAÑUSQUE) to rumple, crush, crumple.
apapagayado, da, *a.* parrotlike; aquiline (nose).
aparador, *m.* sideboard, cupboard; workshop of an artisan; show window.
aparadura, *f.* (naut.) garbel, garboard plank.
aparar, *va.* to stretch out the hands or skirts for catching; (agr.) to dress (plants); (shoemaking) to close (the uppers); to prepare, arrange; to dress with an adze, dub.—**a. un navío,** (naut.) to dub a ship.
aparasolado, da, *a.* (bot.) umbelliferous.
aparatado, da, *a.* prepared, disposed.
aparatero, ra, *a.* = APARATOSO.
aparato, *m.* apparatus; preparation; pomp, show; circumstance; signs, symptoms; elaborate scenic display; collection of surgical instruments; system, associated organs.—**a. de radio,** radio set.—**aparatoso, sa,** *a.* pompous, showy.
aparcería, *f.* partnership.
aparcero, ra, *n.* partner.
apareamiento, *m.* matching, mating, pairing.

aparear. **I.** *va.* to match, mate; to pair. **II.** *vr.* to be paired, matched, mated.
aparecer, *vn.* & *vr.* (*ind.* APAREZCO; *subj.* APAREZCA) to appear, show up, turn up.
aparecido, da. **I.** *pp.* of APARECER. **II.** *m.* ghost.
aparecimiento, *m.* apparition, appearing.
aparejado, da. **I.** *pp.* of APAREJAR. **II.** *a.* fit; ready.
aparejador, ra, *n.* one who prepares or gets ready; overseer of a building; (naut.) rigger.
aparejar. **I.** *va.* to get ready; to prepare; to saddle or harness; (naut.) to rig; to furnish; to size (work before painting or gilding). **II.** *vr.* to get ready; to equip oneself.
aparejo, *m.* preparation, disposition; harness, gear; packsaddle; (mech.) tackle; (art) sizing canvas or board; (mason.) bond; (naut.) tackle and rigging on a ship; furniture.—*pl.* equipment, trappings.—**a. real,** main tackle.
aparentar, *va.* to feign, pretend.
aparente, *a.* apparent, not real; fit, suited; evident, manifest.
aparezco, aparezca, *v.* *V.* APARECER.
aparición, *f.* apparition; appearance (coming in sight).
apariencia, *f.* appearance, aspect, looks; likeness, resemblance; vestige; outward show; pageant; probability, conjecture.—*pl.* scenic effects.
aparrado, da, *a.* shrubby, vinelike.
aparroquiado, da, *a.* established in a parish.
aparroquiar, *va.* to bring customers to.
apartadamente, *adv.* privately, apart.
apartadero, *m.* sidetrack, siding; free space (beside a road, etc.); sorting room.
apartadijo, *m.* small part, share, or portion.
apartadizo, *m.* recluse; small room; partition.
apartado, da. **I.** *pp.* of APARTAR. **II.** *a.* distant, retired; aloof; out-of-the-way, remote; distinct, different. **III.** *m.* room separated from others; smelting house; mail separated for early or special delivery; P. O. letter box; separation of cattle; board of cattle ranchers.
apartador, ra, *n.* one that divides or separates; sorter; separator.—**a. de metales,** smelter.
apartamiento, *m.* separation; retirement; secluded place; apartment, flat; waiver, relinquishment.
apartar. **I.** *va.* to part off; to separate, divide; to dissuade; to remove, dislodge; to sort. **II.** *vr.* to withdraw; to hold off; to desist; to retire.
aparte. **I.** *m.* paragraph; (theat.) aside. **II.** *adv.* separately; aside (on the stage); different, another, other (*ésta es cuestión aparte,* this is another matter).
aparvar, *va.* to heap (grain for thrashing).
apasionadamente, *adv.* passionately; unfairly, in a biassed way.
apasionado, da. **I.** *pp.* of APASIONAR. **II.** *a.* passionate; impassioned; intolerant; (of a part of the body) affected with pain; devoted, passionately fond. **III.** *m.* admirer.
apasionamiento, *m.* passion.
apasionar. **I.** *va.* to impassion; to afflict, torment. **II.** *vr.* to become passionately fond.
apatía, *f.* apathy.—**apático, ca,** *a.* apathetic.
apatita, *f.* (min.) apatite.
apátrida. **I.** *a.* stateless. **II.** *n.* stateless person.
apatusco, *m.* (coll.) ornament, dress.
apea, *f.* rope fetter for horses.
apeadero, *m.* landing, horseblock; Ry. station.
apeador, *m.* land surveyor.
apeamiento, *m.* = APEO.
apear. **I.** *va.* to dismount; to get out (of a carriage, etc.); to bring down; to survey; to set landmarks to; to fell; to block or scotch (a wheel); (arch.) to prop; (artil.) to dismount (a gun); to dissuade; to remove (difficulties); to shackle (a horse). **II.** *vr.* to alight.
apechugar, *va.* (*pret.* APECHUGUÉ; *subj.* APECHUGUE) to push with the breast; (fig.) to face with courage (something distasteful).
apedazar, *va.* (*pret.* APEDACÉ; *subj.* APEDACE) to patch, mend, repair.
apedernalado, da, *a.* (fig.) flinty.
apedreado, da. **I.** *pp.* of APEDREAR. **II.** *a.* variegated; pitted with the smallpox.
apedreador, ra, *n.* stoner, stone thrower.
apedreamiento, *m.* lapidation, stoning.
apedrear. **I.** *va.* to stone; to kill with stones. **II.** *vn.* to hail. **III.** *vr.* to be injured by hail.
apedreo, *m.* stoning.
apegadamente, *adv.* devotedly.
apegarse, *vr.* to become attached.—**apego,** *m.* attachment, fondness.
apelable, *a.* (law) appealable.
apelación, *f.* (law) appeal; (coll.) consultation (of doctors); (coll.) remedy, help.
[1]**apelado, da.** **I.** *a.* (law) successful in an appeal. **II.** *n.* (law) appellee.
[2]**apelado, da,** *a.* (of horses) of the same coat or color.
apelambrar, *va.* to steep (hides) in limewater.
apelante, *n.* & *a.* (law) appellant.
[1]**apelar,** *vn.* (law) to appeal; have recourse to.
[2]**apelar,** *vn.* (of horses) to be of the same color.
apelativo, va, *m.* & *a.* (gram.) appellative.
apeldar, *vn.* (coll.) to flee, run away.
apelde, *m.* (coll.) flight, escape.
apelmacé, apelmace, *v.* *V.* APELMAZAR.
apelmazado, da, *a.* compressed, compact.
apelmazamiento, *m.* compactness.
apelmazar, *va.* (*pret.* APELMACÉ; *subj.* APELMACE) to compress; to render less spongy.
apelotonar, *va.* & *vr.* to form into balls.
apellar, *va.* to dress (leather).
apellidamiento, *m.* naming.
apellidar. **I.** *va.* to name; to proclaim; to call to arms. **II.** *vr.* to be called (have the name).
apellido, *m.* surname, family name; nickname; forces called to arms.
apenar. **I.** *va.* to cause pain, sorrow. **II.** *vr.* to grieve.
apenas, *adv.* scarcely, hardly; only; with trouble; no sooner than, as soon as.
apencar, *vn.* (*pret.* APENQUÉ; *subj.* APENQUE) to accept with reluctance.
apendectomía, apendicectomía, *f.* (surg.) appendectomy.
apéndice, *m.* appendix.—**a. cecal, vermicular** or **vermiforme,** vermiform appendix.
apendicitis, *f.* appendicitis.
apendicitomía, *f.* (surg.) appendectomy.
apendiculado, da, *a.* appendiculate.
apendicular, *a.* appendicular.
apenqué, apenque, *v.* *V.* APENCAR.
apeo, *m.* survey; prop, propping.
apeonar, *va.* to walk or run swiftly (birds).
apepsia, *f.* (med.) apepsy, indigestion.
aperador, *m.* farmer; wheelwright; foreman.
aperar, *va.* to make, repair, equip.
apercepción, *f.* (psychiat.) apperception.
apercibimiento, *m.* preparation, preparedness order, advice, warning; summons.
apercibir, *va.* to provide; to get ready; to war advise; (law) to summon.
aperción, *f.* = ABERTURA, opening.
apercollar, *va.* (*ind.* APERCUELLO; *subj.* APERCUELLE) (coll.) to collar; to snatch.
aperdigar, *va.* to parboil, roast slightly.
apergaminado, da, *a.* parchmentlike.
aperiódico, ca, *a.* aperiodic.
aperitivo, va, *m.* & *a.* aperitive; (med.) aperien
apernador, *m.* dog that seizes game by the leg
apernar, *va.* (*ind.* APIERNO; *subj.* APIERNE) seize by the leg.
apero, *m.* farm implements; tools, outfit; shee fold; (often *pl.*) equipment (for an activity (Am.) luxurious riding equipment.
aperreador, ra, *n.* (coll.) importunate person nuisance; intruder.
aperrear. **I.** *va.* to throw to the dogs; to annoy bother. **II.** *vr.* to toil, overwork.
apersogar, *va.* (Mex.) to tether.
apersonarse, *vr.* (law) to appear (in court).

apertura, *f.* opening (of a convention, etc.); reading (of a will).
apesadumbrar, *va.* & *vr.* to grieve; to make (become) sad, grief-stricken.
apesaradamente, *adv.* mournfully, sadly.
apesarar, *va.* & *vr.* = APESADUMBRAR.
apesgamiento, *m.* sinking under a burden.
apesgar. I. *va.* (*pret.* APESGUÉ; *subj.* APESGUE) to overwhelm with a load. **II.** *vr.* to be aggrieved.
apestado, da. I. *pp.* of APESTAR. **II.** *a.* pestered, annoyed; satiated; full, overstocked.
apestar. I. *va.* to infect with the plague; to corrupt, turn putrid; to annoy, bother; to sicken, nauseate. **II.** *vn.* to stink.
apestoso, sa, *a.* foul-smelling, sickening, nauseating, offensive.
apétalo, la, *a.* (bot.) apetalous.
apetecedor, ra. I. *a.* longing; appetizing. **II.** *n.* one who longs or desires.
apetecer, *va.* (*ind.* APETEZCO; *subj.* APETEZCA); to like (a food or drink); to desire.—**apetecible,** *a.* appetizing; desirable.
apetencia, *f.* appetite, hunger; desire.
apetezco, apetezca, *v. V.* APETECER.
apetite, *m.* sauce, appetizer; inducement.
apetito, *m.* appetite; appetence.—**abrir el a.,** to stimulate appetite.
apetitoso, sa, *a.* appetizing, savory, palatable.
apezonado, da, *a.* nipple-shaped.
apezuñar, *vn.* to climb laboriously, sinking the edge of the hoof into the ground.
apiadarse. I. *va.* to inspire pity. **II.** *vr.* **(de)** to pity, take pity (on).
apiaradero, *m.* shepherd's account of the sheep.
apiario, ria. I. *a.* beelike. **II.** *m.* apiary.
apical, *a.* apical; (phon.) apical.
apicararse, *vr.* to become roguish.
ápice, *m.* apex, summit, top, pinnacle; trifle; whit, iota; written accent; most intricate and pointed part of a question.
apícola, *a.* apiarian.
apiculado, da, *a.* (bot.) apiculate.
apículo, *m.* (bot.) small, keen point.
apicultor, ra, *n.* apiculturist, beekeeper.
apicultura, *f.* apiculture, beekeeping.
apierno, apierne, *v. V.* APERNAR.
apilador, *m.* piler (esp. of wool).
apilamiento, *m.* piling up; crowding.
apilar, *va.* to heap, pile up.
apimpollarse, *vr.* to germinate, sprout.
apiñado, da. I. *pp.* of APIÑAR. **II.** *a.* pyramidal, pine-shaped; crowded, close together.
apiñadura, *f.*, **apiñamiento,** *m.* pressing together; crowd, jam, congestion.
apiñar, *va.* & *vr.* to press together, crowd.
apio, *m.* (bot.) celery.
apiolar, *va.* to gyve (a hawk); to tie by the legs; (coll.) to seize, apprehend; to kill, murder.
apiparse, *vr.* (coll.) to gorge.
apirético, ca, *a.* (med.) apyretic, free from fever.
apirexia, *f.* (med.) apyrexia.
apisonadora de vapor, *f.* steam roller.
apisonamiento, *m.* tamping.
apisonar, *va.* to tamp.
apitonamiento, *m.* (of deer, etc.) initial growing of horns; passion, anger.
apitonar. I. *vn.* (of deer, etc.) to begin to grow horns; to bud, germinate. **II.** *va.* to break with bill or horn; to shell. **III.** *vr.* to abuse each other.
apizarrado, da, *a.* slate-colored.
aplacabilidad, *f.* placability.
aplacable, *a.* placable.
aplacación, *f.* appeasement.
aplacador, ra, *n.* & *a.* appeaser(-ing).
aplacamiento, *m.* stay of execution.
aplacar, *va.* (*pret.* APLAQUÉ; *subj.* APLAQUE) to appease, pacify, calm.
aplacé, aplace, *v. V.* APLAZAR.
aplacer, *va.* to please.
aplacerado, da, *a.* (naut.) level and not very deep; (Am.) open, cleared of trees.
aplacible, *a.* pleasant.
aplacimiento, *m.* pleasure.
aplanadera, *f.* levelling board, float; rammer.
aplanador, *m.* leveller; (mech.) battledore, brusher, riveter; ingot hammer; cylinder roller; (print.) planer, planishing mallet.
aplanamiento, *m.* levelling, flattening.
aplanar. I. *va.* to smooth, make even; to flatten; to terrify or astonish. **II.** *vr.* to tumble down; to weaken; to dismay; to get depressed.
aplanchado, planchado, *m.* ironing (act or collection of clothes ironed or to be ironed).
aplanchador, planchador, ra, *n.* ironer.
aplanchar, *va.* to iron (clothes).
aplanético, ca, *a.* (optics) aplanatic.
aplantillar, *va.* to adjust or fit (stones).
aplaqué, aplaque, *v. V.* APLACAR.
aplastar. I. *va.* to flatten, crush, smash; to floor (an opponent). **II.** *vr.* to flatten; to collapse.
aplaudidor, ra, *n.* & *a.* applauder(-ing).
aplaudir, *va.* to applaud.
aplauso, *m.* applause; approbation, praise.
aplayar, *vr.* (of a river) to overflow the banks.
aplazamiento, *m.* convocation; summons; postponement.
aplazar, *va.* (*pret.* APLACÉ; *subj.* APLACE) to convene; to summon; to adjourn; to postpone.
aplebeyar. I. *va.* to make plebeian; to degrade. II. *vr.* to lower oneself; to become mean.
aplicabilidad, *f.* applicability.
aplicable, *a.* applicable.
aplicación, *f.* application.
aplicado, da. I. *pp.* of APLICAR. **II.** *a.* studious, industrious, assiduous.
aplicar. I. *va.* (*pret.* APLIQUÉ; *subj.* APLIQUE) to apply; to put on; to clap; to attribute or impute; (law) to adjudge. **II.** *vr.* to apply oneself.
aplicativo, va, *a.* applicative, applicatory.
aplomado, da. I. *pp.* of APLOMAR. **II.** *a.* lead-colored; calm, grave; heavy, dull, lazy.
aplomar. I. *va.* to overload, crush. **II.** *vn.* to plumb. **III.** *vr.* to tumble, fall to the ground.
aplomo. I. *m.* tact, prudence; self-possession, poise; (mus.) exactness in time; (art) due proportion. **II.** *a.* plumb, vertical.
apnea, *f.* (med.) apnea, suspension of respiration.
apocado, da. I. *pp.* of APOCAR. **II.** *a.* pusillanimous, cowardly; of low extraction.
Apocalipsis, *m.* Apocalypse, Revelation.
apocalíptico, ca, *a.* apocalyptical.
apocamiento, *m.* bashfulness; diffidence; pusillanimity, incapacity.
apocar. I. *va.* (*pret.* APOQUÉ; *subj.* APOQUE) to lessen; to cramp, contract. **II.** *vr.* to humble, belittle oneself.
apócema, apócima, *f.* (med.) apozem.
apocináceo, a. I. *a.* (bot.) apocynaceous, of the dogbane family. **II.** *f. pl.* Apocynaceæ.
apocopar, *va.* to apocopate.
apócope, *f.* (gram.) apocope; apocopation.
apócrifo, fa, *a.* apocryphal.—**Apócrifos,** (Bib.) Apocrypha.
apocrisiario, *m.* Byzantine envoy; (eccl.) apocrisiary, envoy of the pope.
apocromático, ca, *a.* (opt.) apochromatic.
apodador, *m.* wag, scoffer.
apodar, *va.* to give nicknames to, scoff at.
apoderado, da. I. *pp.* of APODERAR. **II.** *m.* proxy; attorney.
apoderar. I. *va.* to empower; to grant power of attorney to. **II.** *vr.* to take possession.
apodíctico, ca, *a.* apodictic; indisputable.
apodo, *m.* nickname.
ápodo, da, *a.* (zool.) apodal, without feet.
apódosis, *f.* (rhet.) apodosis.
apófige, *f.* (arch.) apophyge.
apófise, apófisis, *f.* (anat.) apophysis, process.
apogeo, *m.* apogee; height (of fame, etc.).
apógrafo, *m.* apograph, transcript.
apolillado, da. I. *pp.* of APOLILLAR. **II.** *a.* moth-eaten, worm-eaten.

apolilladura, *f.* moth hole.
apolillar. **I.** *va.* (of moths) to eat (clothes). **II.** *vr.* to become moth-eaten.
apoliticismo, *m.* lack of knowledge, interest or involvement in political matters.
apolítico, ca, *a.* apolitical.
apologético, ca. **I.** *a.* apologetic. **II.** *f.* (theol.) apologetics.
apología, *f.* apologia, defense, eulogy.
apológico, ca, *a.* pertaining to fables.
apologista, *n.* apologist.
apólogo, *m.* apologue, fable.
apoltronarse, *vr.* to grow lazy; to loiter.
apomazar, *va.* (*pret.* APOMACÉ; *subj.* APOMACE) to glaze; to burnish with pumice stone.
apomorfina, *f.* (pharm.) apomorphine.
aponeurosis, *f.* (anat.) aponeurosis.
aponeurótico, ca, *a.* (anat.) aponeurotic.
apoplejía, *f.* apoplexy.
apoplético, ca, *a.* apoplectic.
apoqué, apoque, *v.* *V.* APOCAR.
aporcadura, *f.* hilling around plants.
aporcar, *va.* (*ind. pres.* APUERCO, *pret.* APORQUÉ; *subj.* APUERQUE) to hill (plants).
aporisma, *m.* (med.) ecchymosis.
aporismarse, *vr.* to become an ecchymosis.
aporqué, aporque, *v.* *V.* APORCAR.
aporrar. **I.** *vn.* (coll.) to stand mute. **II.** *vr.* (coll.) to become importunate.
aporreado, da. **I.** *pp.* of APORREAR. **II.** *a.* cudgelled; miserable, dragged out. **III.** *m.* name of a Cuban dish made of highly seasoned beef.
aporreamiento, *m.* beating or pommelling.
aporrear. **I.** *va.* to beat, cudgel, knock, maul. **II.** *vr.* to study with intense application.
aporreo, *m.* beating, pommelling, cudgelling.
aportación, *f.* (law) contribution.
aportadera, *f.* pannier; large, long box for the side of a pack animal (used in pairs); wooden tub with handles to carry grapes from the vineyard.
aportadero, *m.* stopping place.
[1]aportar, *vn.* to make a port; to arrive; to reach an unexpected place.
[2]aportar, *va.* to cause, bring; (law) to contribute.
aporte, *m.* (Am.) contribution.
aportillar. **I.** *va.* to break down, break open. **II.** *vr.* to tumble down.
aposentador, ra, *n.* one that lets lodgings; usher.
aposentamiento, *m.* lodging.
aposentar. **I.** *va.* to lodge. **II.** *vr.* to take lodging.—**aposento,** *m.* room or apartment; temporary habitation; inn; (theat.) box.
aposesionar, posesionar. **I.** *va.* to give possession. **II.** *vr.* to take possession.
aposición, *f.* (gram.) apposition.
apositivo, va, *m.* & *a.* (gram.) appositive.
apósito, *m.* external medicinal application.
aposta, apostadamente, *adv.* designedly, on purpose.
apostadero, *m.* station for soldiers; (naut.) naval station.
apostador, ra, *n.* (Am.) better, one who bets.
apostal, *m.* good fishing place in a river.
apostar. **I.** *va.* (*ind.* APUESTO; *subj.* APUESTE) to bet; (reg. conj. in the next two meanings) to place (relays); to post (soldiers).—**apostar a que,** to bet that. **II.** *vr.* to station oneself.
apostasía, *f.* apostasy.
apóstata, *n.* apostate.
apostatar, *vn.* to apostatize.
apostático, ca, *a.* apostatical.
apostema, postema, *f.* abscess, tumor.
apostemación, *f.* (med.) formation of an abscess.
apostemar. **I.** *va.* to form an abscess in, fester. **II.** *vr.* to become abscessed.
apostilla, *f.* marginal note, annotation.
[1]apostillar, *va.* to annotate on the margin.
[2]apostillar, *vr.* to break out in pimples.
apóstol, *m.* apostle.—*pl.* (naut.) hawse pieces.
apostolado, *m.* apostleship; the twelve Apostles.
apostolicidad, *f.* apostolicity.
apostólico, ca, *a.* apostolic.
apostrofar, *va.* to apostrophize.
apóstrofe, *f.* (rhet.) apostrophe.
apóstrofo, *m.* apostrophe (written sign).
apostura, *f.* gentleness; neatness.
apotecia, *f.* (bot.) apothecium.
apotegma, *m.* apothegm, maxim.
apoteósico, ca, *a.* deifying, deific.
apoteosis, *f.* apotheosis, deification.
apotrerar, *va.* to take (horses) to pasture.
apoyadura, *f.* flow of milk in nursing.
apoyar. **I.** *va.* (**en**) to rest or lean (on); to favor, advocate, support; to back, defend; to aid; to abet; to bear out, confirm; (of horses) to droop (the head).—**a. la proposición,** to second the motion. **II.** *vn.* (**en** or **sobre**) to rest (on). **III.** *vr.* (**en**), to depend (on); to be based (on); to rest (on); to lean (on or against); to be supported (by).
apoyatura, *f.* (mus.) appoggiatura.
apoyo, *m.* prop, stay; support; fulcrum; protection, help, aid; approval, support, backing.
apreciable, *a.* appreciable, noticeable; worthy of esteem; (coll.) nice, fine; valuable; that can be priced; salable.
apreciación, *f.* estimation, valuation; appreciation; (tech.) least reading (of a vernier).
apreciadamente, *adv.* appreciatively.
apreciador, ra, *n.* estimator, appraiser.
apreciar, *va.* to appreciate; to appraise, estimate, price, value; to esteem.—**apreciativo, va,** *a.* appreciative.—**aprecio,** *m.* appraisement, valuation; esteem, regard, liking.
aprehender, *va.* to apprehend, seize; to conceive, think.—**aprehensión,** *f.* seizure, capture; apprehension, acuteness; fear.—**aprehensivo, va,** *a.* apprehensive.—**aprehensor, ra,** *n.* one that apprehends.
apremiador, ra, *n.* compeller.
apremiante, *a.* urgent, pressing.
apremiar, *va.* to press, urge; to compel, oblige.
apremio, *m.* pressure, constraint; (law) judicial compulsion.
aprendedor, ra, *n.* learner.
aprender, *va.* & *vn.* to learn.
aprendiz, za, *n.* apprentice.—**aprendizaje,** *m.* apprenticeship; (act of) learning.
aprensador, *m.* presser, calenderer.
aprensar, *va.* to dress, press, calender; to crush, oppress; (naut.) to stow.
aprensión, *f.* apprehension, scruple; fear; distrust, suspicion.
aprensivo, va, *a.* apprehensive, fearing.
apresador, ra, *n.* privateer; captor.
apresamiento, *m.* capture; clutch, hold.
apresar, *va.* to seize, grasp; to capture.
aprestar, *va.* to prepare, make ready; to size (cloth).—**apresto,** *m.* preparation; accoutrement; sizing (for cloth).
apresuración, *f.* haste.
apresuradamente, *adv.* hastily.
apresuramiento, *m.* hastiness, quickness.
apresurar. **I.** *va.* to hasten. **II.** *vr.* to make haste.
apretadamente, *adv.* tightly, closely, fast.
apretadera, *f.* strap or rope to tie with.—*pl.* pressing remonstrances.
apretadero, *m.* truss for ruptures.
apretadizo, za, *a.* easily compressible.
apretado, da. **I.** *pp.* of APRETAR. **II.** *a.* tight, compact; difficult, dangerous; stingy, tight.
apretador, *m.* one who presses; tightener; presser, rammer, quoin wedge; waistcoat; soft stays for children; broad bandage for infants; hair net.
apretadura, *f.* compression.
apretar. **I.** *va.* (*ind.* APRIETO; *subj.* APRIETE) to tighten; to press down, compress; to clench (teeth, fist); to grip (hand in greeting); to squeeze; to vex, distress; to urge, press, drive. **II.** *vn.* (of shoes, etc.) to pinch.—**a. a** (foll. by *inf.*) to start to, (foll. by *pres. p.*) to start, with

the implication of haste, effort, etc. (*apretamos a correr*, we started to run for all we were worth). —**¡aprieta!** gracious! nonsense!
apretazón, *f.* (Am.) crowd; congestion.
apretón, *m.* pressure (esp. strong and quick); struggle, conflict; short run, spurt.—**a. de manos,** handshake.
apretujar, *va.* (coll.) to squeeze, press hard.
apretujón, *m.* tight squeezing.
apretura, *f.* jamming, crush; narrowness; distress, anguish; straits, difficulties.
[1]**aprieto,** *m.* jamming, crush; stringency, scrape, difficulty; cramp, gripe.
[2]**aprieto, apriete,** *v. V.* APRETAR.
apriorismo, *m.* (philos.) apriorism.
apriorista, *n.* apriorist.
apriorístico, ca, *a.* aprioristic.
aprisa, *adv.* swiftly, promptly, fast.
apriscar, *va.* to gather (the sheep) in the fold.
aprisco, *m.* sheepfold.
aprisionar, *va.* to imprison.
aproar, *vn.* (naut.) to turn the prow.
aprobable, *a.* approvable.
aprobación, *f.* approval.
aprobador, ra, *n.* & *a.* approver(-ing).
aprobante, *n.* approver; examiner.
aprobar, *va.* (*ind.* APRUEBO; *subj.* APRUEBE) to approve; to pass (in an examination).
aprobatorio, ria, *a.* approbative, approving.
aproches, *m. pl.* (mil., eng.) approaches.
aprontar, *va.* to prepare quickly; to deliver at once; (P. R.) to advance (money).
apropiable, *a.* appropriable.
apropiación, *f.* appropriation, giving or taking possession; adaptation; (act of) fitting.
apropiadamente, *adv.* fitly, appropriately.
apropiado, da. I. *pp.* of APROPIAR. **II.** *a.* appropriate, fit.
apropiador, ra, *n.* appropriator.
apropiar. I. *va.* to give possession of; to apply, adapt, fit. **II.** *vr.* to appropriate, take possession of.
apropincuación, *f.* approach.
apropincuarse, *vr.* (coll.) to approach.
aprovechable, *a.* available; that can be used.
aprovechado, da. I. *pp.* of APROVECHAR. **II.** *a.* advanced, proficient; economical, saving.
aprovechamiento, *m.* utilization, use; exploitation, development; progress, proficiency.—**a. forestal,** forest products.
aprovechar. I. *vn.* to be useful, profitable or beneficial, to avail; to progress. **II.** *va.* to profit by, make use of. **III.** *vr.* to avail oneself.
aprovisionar, *va.* (Am.) to supply.
aproximación, *f.* approximation.
aproximado, da. I. *pp.* of APROXIMAR. **II.** *a.* approximate.—**a. hasta,** (arith.) approximate to.
aproximar, *va.* & *vr.* to approach, move near; to determine approximately; to be about.—**aproximarse a,** to move near to, approach.
aproximativo, va, *a.* approximate; approaching.
apruebo, apruebe, *v. V.* APROBAR.
ápside, *m.* (astr.) apsis.
ápterix, aptérix, *f.* (ornith.) apteryx, kiwi.
áptero, ra, *a.* (entom.) apterous, wingless.
aptitud, *f.* aptitude, fitness, ability.
apto, ta, *a.* apt, fit, competent.
apuerco, apuerque, *v. V.* APORCAR.
apuesta, *f.* bet, wager.
[1]**apuesto, ta,** *a.* elegant, stylish, spruce.
[2]**apuesto, apueste,** *v. V.* APOSTAR.
apulgarar, *vn.* to press, push with the thumb.
apulgararse, *vr.* (of white cloth) to mildew (from moisture).
apulso, *m.* (astr.) passing of the edge of a heavenly body over the vertical wire of the telescope; appulse, coming together of two heavenly bodies.
apunarse, *vr.* (Am.) to get ill from altitude.
apuntación, *f.* note; memorandum; musical notation.
apuntado, da. I. *pp.* of APUNTAR. **II.** *a.* pointed at both ends.
apuntador, ra, *n.* observer; one that takes or keeps notes; (theat.) prompter; (naut.) gunner.
apuntalamiento, *m.* propping.
apuntalar, *va.* to prop; to shore (a vessel).
apuntamiento, *m.* note, abstract, summary; judicial report.
apuntar. I. *va.* to aim, level; to point out, mark; to note, make a note of; to hint; to sketch; (sew.) to baste, tack; to sharpen; (theat.) to prompt. **II.** *vn.* to begin to appear; (of wine) to begin to turn.
apunte, *m.* APUNTAMIENTO; annotation, memorandum; rough sketch; prompt-book; stake (in games).
apuñadar, *va.* (prov.) to strike with the fist.
apuñalado, da, *a.* dagger-shaped.
apuñalar, *va.* to stab.
apuñar. I. *va.* to seize with the fist. **II.** *vn.* to tighten the fist.
apuñear, *va.* (coll.) to strike with the fist.
apuracabos, *m.* candle holder with a sharp point for the butt of the candle; catchall.
apuración, *f.* investigation; trouble, misfortune.
apuradamente, *adv.* punctually, exactly; with difficulty.
apurado, da. I. *pp.* of APURAR. **II.** *a.* needy; exhausted; difficult; conscientious.
apurador, *m.* refiner, purifier; APURACABOS.
apuramiento, *m.* research; exhaustion, consumption; pressing, urging; purification.
apurar. I. *va.* to purify; to clear up, verify, scrutinize; to consume, drain, exhaust; to push, hurry; to annoy. **II.** *vr.* to worry, fret, grieve; to exert oneself.
apuro, *m.* want, strait; scrape, tight spot, "jam."
aquejar, *va.* to grieve, sadden; to fatigue.
aquel (*f. sing.* **aquella;** *pl.* **aquellos, llas**). **I.** *a.* that, those, yonder. **II.** *pron. m.* & *f.* he, she (*pl.* they, those, such as) (*aquellos que deseen venir,* those who, or such as, wish to come); those (ones). **III. aquél, aquélla,** *n.* that one; the former, the first mentioned. **IV. aquello,** *pron. neut.* that; the former, the first-mentioned (fact, statement, etc.); that thing, that matter, the matter we spoke about, etc. (used with reference to something known to the listener or reader but that it is not desired to mention); attractiveness, appeal, "a certain something."—**a. de,** that matter of.—**a. de (que),** the common saying, notion, belief, rule (that) (*no creo en aquello de que el comercio es la base del progreso,* I do not believe in the common saying that commerce is the foundation of progress).
aquellare, *m.* witches' Sabbath.
aquende, *adv.* on this side of.
aqueo, a, *n.* & *a.* Achæan.
aquerenciarse, *vr.* (esp. of animals) to become attached to (a place).
aquí, *adv.* here; hither; then; now.—**de a.,** from here, from this place; hence.—**de a. en adelante,** from now on, hereafter.—**por a.,** here, hereabouts; this way, through here.
aquiescencia, *f.* (law) acquiescence, consent.
aquietar. I. *va.* to quiet, lull, pacify, hush, allay. **II.** *vr.* to become calm; to quiet down.
aquilatamiento, *m.* assay.
aquilatar, *va.* to assay; to examine closely.
aquilea, *f.* (bot.) milfoil, yarrow.
aquilino, na, *a.* (poet.) = AGUILEÑO, aquiline.
aquilón, *m.* north wind; north point.
aquilonal, aquilonar, *a.* northern, northerly.
aquillado, da, *a.* keel-shaped.
aquistar, *va.* to acquire.
ara, *f.* altar; communion table; altar slab, mensa.
árabe, *n.* & *a.* Arab, Arabian.
arabesco, ca. I. *a.* Arabian, Arab; (f. a.) arabesque. **II.** *m.* (f. a.) arabesque.
Arabia Saudita, *f.* Saudi Arabia.
arábico, ca, *a.* Arabic.
arábigo, ga. I. *a.* Arabian, Arab. **II.** *m.* (ling.)

Arabic.—**estar en a.**, to be illegible, be difficult to understand.—**goma a.**, gum arabic.—**número a.**, Arabic numeral.
arabismo, *m.* Arabism.
arabista, *n.* Arabist.
arácnido, da, *m.* & *a.* (zool.) arachnid.
aracnoide, *a.* (bot.) arachnoid.
aracnoideo, dea, *a.* (zool., anat.) arachnoid.
aracnoides, *f.* (anat.) arachnoid, arachnoid membrane.
aracnoiditis, *f.* (med.) arachnitis, arachnoiditis.
aracnología, *f.* arachnology.
arada, *f.* (agr.) plowed ground; land plowed in a day; husbandry.
arado, *m.* plow.
arador, *m.* plowman; (entom.) harvest mite.
aradura, *f.* plowing; land plowed in a day.
aragonés, esa, *n.* & *a.* Aragonese.
aragonita, *f.* **aragonito**, *m.* (min.) aragonite.
araguato, *m.* (zool.) ursine howler, howling monkey, howler.
arambel, *m.* rag, tatter.
arameo, a, *n.* & *a.* Aramean.
arana, *f.* imposition, trick; Cuban grass.
arancel, *m.* tariff.—**a. de aduanas**, customs, duty.
arancelario, ria, *a.* tariff, customs (as *a.*).
arandanedo, *m.* cranberry patch.
arándano, *m.* (bot.) cranberry.
arandela, *f.* the socket pan of a candlestick; (mech.) washer; axleguard; rivet plate, collar plate; guard around the staff of a lance; nave box of a gun carriage; (naut.) half-ports; glass candelabrum.
arandillo, *m.* a kind of bird; (prov.) hip pad.
aranero, ra, *a.* deceitful, tricky.
araña, *f.* (entom.) spider; chandelier; (zool.) common weaver; (bot.) crowfoot; (fig.) hustler, go-getter; disreputable woman, whore.—**a. de mar**, sea spider, spider crab.
arañador, ra, *n.* scratcher, scraper.
arañamiento, *m.* (act of) scratching.
arañar, *va.* to scratch; to scrape up (as money).
arañazo, *m. aug.* a scratch (on the skin).
araño, *m.* scratch, nipping.
arañuela, *f. dim.* small spider; a flower plant.
arañuelo, *m.* small spider; net (for bird-catching).
[1]**arar**, *va.* to plow, to work the soil.
[2]**arar**, *m.* an African coniferous tree.
araucano, na, *n.* & *a.* Araucanian.
araucaria, *f.* araucaria, a tall pine.
arauja, *f.* (Brazil) a creeping plant.
araza, *m.* a Uruguayan fruit tree.
arbalestrilla, *f.* an old surveying instrument.
arbellon, *m.* (prov.) gutter to drain roads.
arbitrable, *a.* arbitrable.
arbitración, *f.* arbitration.
arbitrador, ra, *n.* arbitrator; umpire, referee.
arbitraje, *m.* (com.) arbitrage; ARBITRAMENTO.
arbitral, *a.* arbitral.
arbitramento, arbitramiento, *m.* arbitration, arbitrament.
arbitrar, *va.* to arbitrate; to act unhampered; to contrive.
arbitrariedad, *f.* arbitrariness; arbitrary act.
arbitrario, ria; arbitrativo, va, *a.* arbitrary; (law) arbitral.
arbitratorio, ria; *a.* arbitral.
arbitrio, *m.* free will; means, expedient; arbitration; bond, compromise; discretion, judgment. —*pl.* excise taxes.
arbitrista, *m.* schemer, contriver.
árbitro, *m.* arbitrator, arbiter, umpire, referee.
árbol, *m.* (bot.) tree; (naut.) mast; in machines, upright post; (mech.) axle or shaft; arbor; spindle; drill; body of shirt; crown post of winding stairs.—**a. de Diana**, (chem.) arbor Dianæ.—**a. de la ciencia del bien y del mal**, (Bib.) tree of knowledge of good and evil.—**a. de la vida**, (Bib.) tree of life.—**a. del pan**, breadfruit tree.—**a. de María**, tolu-balsam tree.—**a. de pie**, seed-grown tree.—**a. de Saturno**, (chem.) arbor Saturni.—**a. de transmisión**, transmission shaft.—**a. genealógico**, family tree.—**a. motor**, driving shaft or axle.
arbolado, da. I. *pp.* of ARBOLAR. **II.** *a.* wooded; masted. **III.** *m.* woodland.
arboladura, *f.* (naut.) masts and spars.
arbolar. I. *va.* to hoist; to set upright.—**a. un navío**, (naut.) to mast a ship. **II.** *vr.* (of horses) to rear on the hind feet.
arbolario, *m.* = HERBOLARIO, madcap.
arboleda, *f.* grove.
arbolejo, *m. dim.* small tree.
arbolete, *m.* branch to fasten lime twigs on (for catching birds).
arbolillo, *m.* side of a blast furnace; small tree.
arbolista, *m.* arborist.
arbollón, albollón, *m.* floodgate, sluice, outlet.
arbóreo, rea, *a.* pertaining to trees.
arborescencia, *f.* arborescence.
arborescente, *a.* arborescent.
arboricultor, ra, *n.* arboriculturist.
arboricultura, *f.* arboriculture.
arboriforme, *a.* arboriform, tree-shaped.
arborista, *n.* arborist.
arborizado, *a.* foliagelike.
arbotante, *m.* vault-supporting arch.
arbusto, *m.* shrub.—**arbustillo**, *m. dim.* small shrub.
arca, *f.* chest, coffer; reservoir, tank; ark; tempering oven for blown glass.—**a. cerrada**, extremely reticent person.—**a. de la Alianza**, Ark of the Covenant.
arcabuco, *m.* (Am.) craggy spot.
arcabuz, *m.* harquebus, arquebus.
arcabuzazo, *m.* harquebus shot; wound inflicted by a harquebus.
arcacil, *m.* (bot.) a kind of wild artichoke.
arcada, *f.* retching; (arch.) row of arches.
árcade, *n.* & *a.*, **arcadio, dia**, *a.* Arcadian.
arcaduz, *m.* conduit; bucket; means, way.
arcaico, ca, *a.* archaic.
arcaísmo, *m.* archaism.
arcaísta, *n.* archaist.
arcaizante, *a.* archaistic.
arcaizar, *vr.* to use archaisms.
arcángel, *m.* archangel.
arcangélico, ca, *a.* archangelical.
arcano. I. *m.* arcanum. **II.** *a.* secret, recondite.
arce, *m.* (bot.) maple tree.
arcedianato, *m.* archdeaconship.
arcediano, *m.* archdeacon.
arcedo, *m.* maple grove.
arcén, *m.* border, brim, edge.
arcilla, argila, argilla, *f.* clay.—**arcilloso, sa**, *a.* clayey, argillaceous.
arciprestazgo, *m.* archpriesthood.
arcipreste, *m.* archpriest.
arco, *m.* arc; (arch.) arch; bow; fiddle bow; hoop (geom.) arc.—**a. apainelado**, three-center arch.—**a. de medio punto**, round, or semicircular, arch.—**a. iris**, rainbow.—**a. ojival**, equilateral arch.—**a. peraltado**, horseshoe arch.—**a. rebajado**, segmental arch.
arcón, *m. aug.* large chest; bin, bunker.
archicofradía, *f.* privileged brotherhood.
archidiácono, *m.* archdeacon.
archidiócesis, *f.* archdiocese.
archiducado, *m.* archdukedom, archduchy.
archiducal, *a.* archducal.
archiduque, *m.* archduke.—**archiduquesa**, *f.* archduchess.
archilaúd, *m.* large lute.
archimillonario, ria, *a.* multimillionaire.
archipámpano, *m.* very dignified person with imaginary authority.
archipiélago, *m.* archipelago.
archivar, *va.* to file; to deposit in archives; (fig.) to put on the shelf, pigeonhole, forget.
archivero, archivista, *m.* archivist.
archivo, *m.* archives; file, files.
archivolta, *f.* (arch.) archivolt.
arda, *f.* = ARDILLA, (zool.) squirrel.

ardalear, *vn.* (of vine roots) to grow sparse.
árdea, *f.* (ornith.) bittern.
ardentía, *f.* heat; phosphorescence; blink.
ardeola, *f.* (Am.) small kind of heron.
arder. **I.** *vn.* to burn; (of war, etc.) to rage. **II.** *vr.* (of fruit, grain, etc.) to spoil from heat.
ardero, ra, *a.* squirrel dog.
ardid, *m.* stratagem, artifice, cunning.
ardido, da. **I.** *pp.* of ARDER. **II.** *a.* heated; burning; (Am.) "burned up," angry.
ardiendo, *adv.* afire.
ardiente, *a.* ardent, burning; passionate, fervent; fiery.—**ardientemente,** *adv.* ardently, fervidly; fearlessly.
ardilla, *f.* (zool.) squirrel.
[1]**ardimiento,** *m.* conflagration.
[2]**ardimiento,** *m.* undaunted courage, hardihood.
ardita, *f.* (Colomb. & Venez.) squirrel.
ardite, *m.* ancient coin of little value; trifle; (fig.) straw, farthing.—**no importar un a.,** not to matter a particle.—**no se me da un a.,** I don't care a straw, or a rap.—**no valer un a.,** not to be worth a straw, not to amount to a hill of beans.
ardor, *m.* ardor; hotness, heat; dash, valor.
ardoroso, sa, *a.* fiery; ardent, vigorous.
arduidad, *f.* arduousness.
arduo, dua, *a.* arduous.
área, *f.* area; are, square decameter.
areca, *f.* palm tree of the Philippine Islands.
arefacción, *f.* drying out; emaciation.
arel, *m.* large sieve.—**arelar,** *va.* to sift.
arena, *f.* sand, grit; arena.—**arenáceo, ea,** *a.* arenaceous, sandy.—**arenal,** *m.* sandy ground, sand pit.—**arenalejo,** *m. dim.* small sandy place.—**arenar,** *va.* to sand; to rub with sand.
arencar, *va.* (*pret.* ARENQUÉ; *subj.* ARENQUE) to salt and dry (fish).
arenero, *m.* sand dealer; sand box.
arenga, *f.* harangue, speech.
arengador, ra, *n.* speech maker.
arengar, *vn.* (*pret.* ARENGUÉ; *subj.* ARENGUE) to harangue, deliver a speech.
arenilla, *f.* molding sand; sand to dry writing.—*pl.* granulated saltpeter.
arenisca, *f.* (min.) sandstone.
arenisco, ca; arenoso, sa, *a.* sandy, gravelly, gritty; sand (as *a.*).
arenque, *m.* herring.
arenqué, arenque, *v. V.* ARENCAR.
aréola, *f.* areola, circle around the nipple.
areolar, *a.* areolar.
areometría, *f.* hydrometry.
areómetro, *m.* hydrometer.
areópago, *m.* Areopagus.
areóstilo, *m.* (arch.) aræostyle.
arepa, *f.* corn griddle cake.
arequipa, *f.*, **arequipe, ariquipe,** *m.* (Am.) a kind of jelly made with rice, milk and sugar.
arestín, *m.* (vet.) frush.
arete, *m.* eardrop, earring.
arfada, *f.* (naut.) pitching of a ship.
arfar, *vn.* (naut.) (of a ship) to pitch.
argadijo, argadillo, *m.* reel, bobbin, winder; blustering, noisy, restless person; large wicker basket.
argado, *m.* prank, trick.
argal, *m.* argol, crude tartar.
argalia, *f.* = [2]ALGALIA, (surg.) catheter.
argallera, *f.* saw for cutting grooves; forkstaff plane, reed plane.
argamandel, *m.* rag, tatter.
argamandijo, *m.* collection of trifling implements.
argamasa, *f.* mortar.—**argamasar.** **I.** *vn.* to make mortar. **II.** *va.* to cement with mortar.
argamasón, *m.* large dry piece of mortar.
árgana, *f.* (mech.) crane.
árganas, *f. pl.* wicker baskets on a horse.
arganel, *m.* ring in an astrolabe.
arganeo, *m.* (naut.) anchor ring.
árgano, *m.* = ÁRGANA.
argel, *a.* (horse) whose right hind foot is white.
Argelia, *f.* Algeria.
argelino, na, *n.* & *a.* Algerian, Algerine.
argemone, *f.* (bot.) prickly or horned poppy.
argén, *m.* (her.) white or silver color, argent.
argentada, *f.* ladies' cosmetic.
argentado, da. **I.** *pp.* of ARGENTAR. **II.** *a.* silvered, silver-plated; silvery; slashed (shoes).
argentador, *n.* silversmith.
argentar, *va.* to plate or adorn with silver; to polish like silver.
argentario, *m.* silversmith; master of the mint.
argénteo, a, *a.* silvery; silver-plated.
argentería, *f.* embroidery in gold or silver.
argentero, *m.* = ARGENTARIO.
argentífero, ra, *a.* silver-bearing.
Argentina, *f.* Argentina; (a.) (bot.) silverweed.
argentinismo, *m.* word or expression peculiar to Argentina.
argentino, na. **I.** *a.* silvery, argentine; Argentine, Argentinean. **II.** *n.* Argentine, Argentinean; *m.* Argentine gold coin.
argento, *m.* (poet.) silver.
argentoso, sa, *a.* mixed with silver.
argila, argilla, *f.* clay.
argirosa, *f.* (min.) argentite.
argivo, va, *n.* & *a.* (person) of Argos.
argo, *m.* (chem.) argon.
argolla, *f.* ring; collar; staple; hoop; ring (in bowling); pillory.—**argolleta, ica, ita,** *f. dim.* small staple or ring.—**argollón,** *m. aug.* very large ring or staple.
árgoma, *f.* (bot.) furze.—**argomal,** *m.* furze plantation.—**argomón,** *m. aug.* large prickly furze, gorse.
argón, *m.* (chem.) argon.
argonauta, *m.* (myth.) Argonaut; (zool.) argonaut, paper nautilus.
argonáutico, ca, *a.* (myth.) Argonautic.
Argos, *m.* (myth.) Argus; very observant person.
argot, *m.* (Gal.) cant; French jargon.
argucia, *f.* subtilty, sophistry; trick, scheme.
argüe, *m.* windlass, capstan.
argüellarse, *vr.* (prov.) to become emaciated.
argüello, *m.* lack of health.
árguenas, árgueñas, *f. pl.* handbarrow.
argüir. **I.** *vn.* (*ind.* ARGUYO; *subj.* ARGUYA) to argue, dispute. **II.** *va.* to infer; to imply.
argumentación, *f.* argumentation.
argumentador, ra, *n.* arguer, reasoner.
argumentar, *vn.* to argue, dispute.
argumentativo, va, *a.* argumentative.
argumento, *m.* (logic, math.) argument; summary; plot (of a play, etc.); indication, sign.
arguyo, arguya, *v. V.* ARGÜIR.
aria, *f.* (mus.) aria, song for a single voice.
aricar, *va.* to plow across.
aridecer, *va.*, *vn.* & *vr.* (*ind.* ARIDEZCO; *subj.* ARIDEZCA) to render or become arid.
aridez, *f.* drought; barrenness, aridity.
árido, da. **I.** *a.* arid, dry, barren. **II.** *m. pl.* dry articles, esp. grains and vegetables, measured with dry measure.
Aries, *m.* Aries, sign of the zodiac.
arieta, *f. dim.* (mus.) arietta, short tune.
ariete, *m.* battering ram.—**a. hidráulico,** hydraulic ram.
arietino, na, *a.* like a ram's head.
arigue, *m.* Philippine timber.
arije, *f.* = ALARIJE, name of a large grape.
arijo, ja, *a.* (agr.) light, easily tilled.
arilado, da, *a.* arillate.
arilo, *m.* (bot.) aril.
arillo, *m. dim.* earring; neck-stock frame.
arimez, *m.* projection in a building.
ario, ia, *n.* & *a.* Aryan.
arisaro, *m.* (bot.) wake-robin.
arisblanco, ca, *a.* white-bearded (wheat).
arisco, ca, *a.* churlish, shy, cross, surly.

arisnegro, arisprieto, *a.* (of wheat) having blackish beard.
arista, *f.* beard or awn grains; (geom.) edge.—*pl.* (mil.) salient angles.
aristado, da, *a.* awned, bearded.
aristarco, ca, *n.* severe censurer.
aristocracia, *f.* aristocracy.
aristócrata, *m.* & *f.* aristocrat.
aristocrático, ca, *a.* aristocratic.
aristoloquia, *f.* (bot.) birthwort.
aristón, *m.* (arch.) edge, corner; groin rib.
aristoso, sa, *a.* having many beards or awns.
aristotélico, ca, *a.* Aristotelian.
aristotelismo, *m.* Aristotelianism
aritmética, *f.* arithmetic.
aritmético, ca. I. *a.* arithmetical. **II.** *m.* & *f.* arithmetician; accountant.
aritmo, *a.* (med.) arrhythmic.
aritmómetro, *m.* calculating machine.
arjorán, *m.* (bot.) an ornamental tree.
arlequín, *m.* harlequin, buffoon; mixed ice cream, Neapolitan.
arlequinada, *f.* harlequin's trick or joke.
arlo, *m.* (bot.) barberry.
arlota, alrota, *f.* tow of flax or hemp.
arma, *f.* weapon, arm; (mil.) technical division of military forces; (fig.) means, power, reason.—*pl.* troops, armies; armorial ensigns, coat of arms.—**a. arrojadiza,** missile weapon.—**a. blanca,** steel arm.—**a. de caballería,** cavalry.—**a. de fuego,** firearm.—**a. de infantería,** infantry.—**a. de puño,** hand steel arm (sword, etc.).—**a. falsa,** trial, or test, attack.—**armas de agua,** (Mex.) waterproof skins for riding.—**¡a las armas!** to arms!—**de armas tomar,** resolute; capable.—**sobre las armas,** under arms.
armada, *f.* navy; fleet; squadron; armada.—**a. naval,** royal navy, royal fleet.
armadera, *f.* (naut.) main timber of a ship.
armadía, *f.* raft, float.
armadijo, *m.* trap, snare for game.
armadillo, *m.* (zool.) armadillo.
armado, da. I. *pp.* of ARMAR. **II.** *a.* (mech.) mounted, assembled. **III.** *m.* man in armor in processions.
armador, *m.* outfitter, ship owner; privateer, cruiser; one who outfits whaleboats; (mech.) adjuster, fitter, assembler; jacket.
armadura, *f.* armor; framework, shell of a building; (mech.) setting, fitting; truss; (elec.) armature, yoke (of a magnet); framing, mounting; trestle; reinforcement (of concrete); armature (of a dynamo).
armajal, marjal, *m.* moor, bog.
armamentisto, ta, *a.* armaments (as *a.*).
armamento, *m.* armament, accoutrements.
armar. I. *va.* to arm; to man; (carp.) to bind; to assemble, mount; (mech.) to adjust, set, frame, piece, mount, make true, rig up; to reinforce (concrete, etc.); to form, prepare; to start, cause; (naut.) to équip, fit out, put in commission.—**a. caballero,** to knight.—**a. en corso,** to privateer.—**a. en guerra,** (naut.) to fit or equip (a ship) for war.—**a. un lío,** or, **líos,** to make a mess of something, or of things. **II.** *vr.* to prepare oneself; to arm oneself.—**armarse de,** to arm oneself with, put on; (Am.) to build up (a business).
armario, *m.* clothespress; cabinet; bookcase; wardrobe; closet.
armatoste, *m.* hulk; unwieldy machine; cumbersome piece of furniture; fat, clumsy fellow.
armazón, *f.* framework, skeleton, frame; hulk (of a ship)—*m.* skeleton of body.
armella, *f.* staple, box staple, screw eye.
armelluela, *f. dim.* small staple or ring.
armenio, nia, *n.* & *a.* Armenian.
armería, *f.* armory, arsenal; gunsmith trade or shop.
armero, *m.* armorer, gunsmith; keeper of arms; (mil.) rack or stand for firearms.
armífero, ra; armígero, ra, *a.* (poet.) warlike.
armilar, *a.* armillary.
armilla, *f.* (arch.) torus.
armiñado, da, *a.* trimmed or lined with ermine fur; ermine-white.
armiño, *m.* (zool.) ermine.
armipotente, *a.* (poet.) mighty in war.
armisticio, *m.* (mil.) armistice.
armón, *m.* (artil.) limber.
armonía, *f.* harmony.
armonicé, armonice, *v. V.* ARMONIZAR.
armónicamente, *adv.* harmonically, harmoniously.
armónico, ca. I. *a.* harmonic, harmonious; consonant. **II.** *m.* (mus.) harmonic; *f.* harmonica, harmonicon.
armonio, *m.* harmonium, reed organ.
armonioso, sa, *a.* harmonious.
armonista, *n.* harmonist; (mus.) harmonizer.
armonización, *f.* harmonization.
armonizar, *va.* (*pret.* ARMONICÉ; *subj.* ARMONICE) to harmonize.
armuelle, *m.* (bot.) orach.
arna, *f.* (prov.) beehive.
arnacho, *m.* (bot.) rest-harrow. Also GATUÑA.
arnés, *m.* harness; coat of mail, armor.—*pl.* harness, trappings; tools, outfit, equipment.
árnica, *f.* arnica.
[1]**aro,** *m.* hoop, rim; staple; hoop pole.—**entrar por el a.,** (coll.) to be forced to yield.
[2]**aro, yaro,** *m.* (bot.) arum.
aroma. I. *f.* flower of the aromatic myrrh tree. **II.** *m.* aroma; perfume, fragrance.
aromar, *va.* to give aroma to, perfume.
aromaticé, aromatice, *v. V.* AROMATIZAR.
aromaticidad, *f.* aromatic quality, perfume.
aromático, ca, *a.* aromatic, fragrant.
aromatización, *f.* aromatization.
aromatizador, *m.* (perfume) atomizer.
aromatizar, *va.* (*pret.* AROMATICÉ; *subj.* AROMATICE) to aromatize, perfume.
aromo, *m.* (bot.) aromatic myrrh tree.
aromoso, sa, *a.* aromatic, fragrant.
arpa, *f.* (mus.) harp.
[1]**arpado, da. I.** *pp.* of ARPAR. **II.** *a.* serrated, toothed.
[2]**arpado, da,** *a.* (poet.) (of a bird) singing.
arpadura, *f.* = ARAÑO, a scratch.
arpar, *va.* to tear to pieces, rend, claw.
arpegio, *m.* (mus.) arpeggio.
arpella, *f.* (ornith.) eagle; harpy.
arpeo, *m.* (naut.) grappling iron.
arpía, harpía, *f.* harpy; fiend; ugly shrew.
arpillador, *m.* (Mex.) packer.
arpilladura, *f.* packing with sackcloth.
arpillar, *va.* (Mex.) to pack with sackcloth.
arpillera, *f.* sackcloth, burlap.
arpista, *m.* (mus.) harper, harpist.
arpón, *m.* harpoon.—**arponado, da,** *a.* harpoonlike.—**arponear,** *va.* to harpoon.—**arponero,** *m.* harpooner; harpoon maker.
arqueada, *f.* drawing of bow across fiddle.
[1]**arqueador,** *m.* ship gauger.
[2]**arqueador,** *m.* wool beater.
arqueaje, *m.* gauging of a ship.
arqueamiento, *m.* = [2]ARQUEO.
arqueano, na, *a.* (geol.) Archean, Archæan.
[1]**arquear,** *va.* to arch; to beat (wool).
[2]**arquear,** *va.* to gauge (ships).
[1]**arqueo,** *m.* arching.
[2]**arqueo,** *m.* (naut.) tonnage.
[3]**arqueo,** *m.* (com.) checking of effects in a safe; balance (in accounting).
arqueología, *f.* archæology.
arqueológico, ca, *a.* archæological.
arqueólogo, *m.* archæologist.
arqueozoico, ca, *a.* (geol.) Archeozoic.
arquería, *f.* series of arches; (Mex.) aqueduct.
[1]**arquero, ra,** *n.* treasurer, cashier.
[2]**arquero, ra. I.** *a.* pert. to bows. **II.** *m.* archer; bow maker.
arqueta, *f. dim.* small chest.

arquetípico, ca, *a.* archetypal.
arquetipo, *m.* archetype.
arquibanco, *m.* bench with drawers.
arquidiócesis, *f.* archiepiscopal diocese.
arquiepiscopal, *a.* archiepiscopal.
arquimesa, *f.* (prov.) writing desk.
arquisinagogo, *m.* ruler of a synagogue.
arquitecto, *m.* architect.
arquitectónica, *f.* (philos.) architectonics.
arquitectónico, ca, *a.* architectural.
arquitectura, *f.* architecture.
arquitectural, *a.* architectural.
arquitrabe, *m.* (arch.) architrave.
arquivolta, *f.* (arch.) archivolt.
arrabal, *m.* suburb.—*pl.* environs, outskirts.
arrabalero, ra, *a.* suburban; ill-bred.
arrabio, *m.* cast iron melted for making steel.
arracachá, *f.* (bot.) arracacha.
arracada, *f.* earring with pendant.
arracimado, da. I. *pp.* of ARRACIMARSE. **II.** *a.* in clusters.
arracimarse, *vr.* to cluster.
arraclán, *m.* alder tree.
arráez, *m.* chief; captain or master of a ship.
arraigadamente, *adv.* fixedly, securely.
arraigadas, *f. pl.* (naut.) futtock shrouds.
arraigado, da. I. *pp.* of ARRAIGAR. **II.** *a.* owning real estate; fixed, inveterate.
arraigar. I. *vn.* to take root. **II.** *vr.* to settle, establish oneself; to take root.
arraigo, *m.* settling in a place; landed property.
arralar, *vn.* to become thin or sparse; (agr.) to give a poor yield.
arramblar, *va.* (of rushing rivers, etc.) to cover with sand and gravel; (fig.) to sweep away.
arrancaclavos, *m.* nail puller.
arrancada, *f.* (coll.) sudden departure; violent sally.
arrancadera, *f.* leading bell for cattle.
arrancadero, *m.* starting point; thickest part of a gun barrel.
arrancado, da. I. *pp.* of ARRANCAR. **II.** *a.* (coll.) "broke," poor, penniless.
arrancador, ra, *n.* extirpator; extractor, puller.
arrancadura, *f.,* **arrancamiento,** *m.* extirpation; pulling out.
arrancapinos, *n.* small person, (fig.) dwarf.
arrancar. I. *va.* (*pret.* ARRANQUÉ; *subj.* ARRANQUE) to root out, extirpate; to pull out, tear off. **II.** *vn.* (of train, etc.) to start, (ship) set sail.
arrancasiega, *f.* poor grain half mowed, half pulled up; quarrel, dispute.
arranciarse, *vr.* to grow or become rancid.
arrancharse, *vr.* to mess, take meals, together.
arranque, *m.* extirpation; impulse, fit (of passion, charity, love, etc.); sudden start, sudden impulse; (arch.) springer (of an arch); (mech.) start; starter.—**a. automático,** self-starter.
arranqué, arranque, *v. V.* ARRANCAR.
arrapar, *va.* (low) to snatch away, carry off.
arrapiezo, arrapo, *m.* tatter, rag; worthless youngster.
arras, *f. pl.* consideration of a contract; coins the bridegroom gives to the bride at the wedding; dowry; earnest money, pledge.—**a. de la bodega,** (naut.) wings of the hold.
arrasado, da. I. *pp.* of ARRASAR. **II.** *a.* like satin. **III.** *m.* satin-faced stuff.
arrasadura, rasadura, *f.* levelling.
arrasamiento, *m.* razing, demolition.
arrasar. I. *va.* to level, raze, demolish; to obliterate; to fill up to the brim. **II.** *vn., vr.* to clear up.
arrastradamente, *adv.* imperfectly; painfully, wretchedly.
arrastraderas, *f. pl.* (naut.) lower studding sails.
arrastradero, *m.* (naut.) careening place; log path, a path over which logs are dragged; (bullfighting) spot whence dead bulls are carried off.
arrastrado, da. I. *pp.* of ARRASTRAR. **II.** *a.* dragged along; (of life, etc.) dragging out; (coll.) knavish; destitute; (coll.) contemptible.
arrastramiento, *m.* dragging.
arrastrar. I. *va.* to drag; to drag down, degrade; to wash down, carry away (sand, stones, etc.); to haul; to attract; to prompt, move, urge.—**a. bayeta,** to perform the ceremonies required of applicants for a scholarship.—**a. el ala a,** (coll.) to make up to; to make love to. **II.** *vn.* (of one's coat, etc.) to drag, touch the floor or ground; (in cards) to play a trump. **III.** *vr.* to crawl, creep (literally and fig.).
arrastre, *m.* dragging; haulage; drayage; leading a trump; slope or grade in a mining shaft; applicant for a scholarship; (Mex.) mining mill.
arrate, *m.* pound of sixteen ounces.
arratonado, da, *a.* gnawed by mice.
arrayán, *m.* (bot.) myrtle.
arrayanal, *m.* myrtle field or plantation.
¡arre! *interj.* gee, get up!
arreador, *m.* muleteer; driving whip.
arrear, *va.* to drive (horses, mules, etc.).
arrebañador, ra, *n.* gleaner, gatherer.
arrebañadura, *f.* gleaning, picking up.
arrebañar, *va.* to glean, gather.
arrebatadamente, *adv.* precipitately, headlong, recklessly; violently.
arrebatado, da. I. *pp.* of ARREBATAR. **II.** *a.* rapid, violent; precipitate, rash, impetuous.
arrebatador, ra. I. *n.* one that snatches or carries away. **II.** *a.* that snatches or carries away; captivating, charming; violent; stirring.
arrebatamiento, *m.* carrying away by violence; fury, rage; rapture; ecstasy.
arrebatar. I. *va.* to carry off; to snatch; to attract, hold (the attention, etc.); to charm; to move, stir. **II.** *vr.* to be led away by passion.
arrebatiña, *f.* struggle, scramble, scuffle.
arrebato, *m.* surprise; sudden attack; fit, rage; rapture.
arrebocé, arreboce, *v. V.* ARREBOZAR.
arrebol, *m.* red sky or clouds; rouge.
arrebolar. I. *va.* to paint red. **II.** *vr.* to rouge.
arrebolera, *f.* rouge box; rouge seller; (bot.) four-o'clock or marvel of Peru.
arrebollarse, *vr.* to precipitate; to fall headlong.
arrebozar. I. *va.* (*pret.* ARREBOCÉ; *subj.* ARREBOCE) to overlay (meat) with jelly. **II.** *vr.* to wrap oneself up; (of insects) to swarm.
arrebujadamente, *adv.* confusedly.
arrebujar. I. *va.* to jumble together; to huddle. **II.** *vr.* to wrap oneself up.
arreciar. I. *vn.* to increase in strength or intensity. **II.** *vr.* to become stronger.
arrecife, *m.* stone-paved road; (naut.) reef.
arrecirse, *vr.* (*defect.*) to grow stiff with cold.
arrechucho, *m.* fit of anger; sudden and passing indisposition.
arredilar, *va.* to fold (sheep).
arredomado, redomado, da, *a.* artful, sly.
arredondar, redondear, *va.* to round off.
arredramiento, *m.* removing to a greater distance; backing out; fear.
arredrar. I. *va.* to remove, separate; to terrify, scare. **II.** *vr.* to be or become afraid; to fear.
arregacé, arregace, *v. V.* ARREGAZAR.
arregazado, da. I. *pp.* of ARREGAZAR. **II.** *a.* with the point turned up.
arregazar, *va.* (*pret.* ARREGACÉ; *subj.* ARREGACE) to tuck up (the skirts).
arreglable, *a.* adjustable.
arreglado, da. I. *pp.* of ARREGLAR. **II.** *a.* regular, moderate.
arreglar. I. *va.* to regulate, guide; to frame; to arrange; to settle, adjust; (Chile) to castrate. **II.** *vr.* to conform; to settle, come to an agreement; to compromise.
arreglo, *m.* rule; order; disposition, arrangement; adjustment; (com.) agreement; compromise, settlement.—**con a. a,** according to; in accordance with, pursuant to.
arregostarse, *vr.* to relish.
arrejacar, *va.* (*pret.* ARREJAQUÉ; *subj.* ARREJAQUE) to plow across for clearing weeds.
arrejaco, *m.* (ornith.) swift, martin.
arrejada, *f.* (agr.) paddle of a plow.

arrejaque, *m.* fishing fork with three prongs.
arrejaqué, arrejaque, *v. V.* ARREJACAR.
arrejerar, *va.* (naut.) to make (a ship) fast by casting two anchors fore and one aft.
arrel, arrelde, *m.* weight of four pounds.
arrellanarse, *vr.* to sit at ease; to be satisfied with one's situation.
arremangado, da. I. *pp.* of ARREMANGAR. **II.** *a.* turned upward.
arremangar. I. *va.* (*pret.* ARREMANGUÉ; *subj.* ARREMANGUE) to tuck up (the sleeves, etc.). **II.** *vr.* to be determined.
arremango, *m.* tucking up.
arremetedero, *m.* place through which a fortress can be attacked.
arremetedor, ra, *m.* assailant, aggressor.
arremeter. I. *va.* to assail, attack. **II.** *vn.* to launch forth; to attack.—**arremetida,** *f.* attack, assault; start of horses.
arremolinarse, *vr.* to form a crowd.
arrendable, *a.* rentable; farmable; tenantable.
arrendación, *f.* renting, lease.
arrendadero, *m.* ring to tie horses to.
[1]**arrendado, da,** *a.* obedient to the reins.
[2]**arrendado, da. I.** *pp.* of [2]ARRENDAR. **II.** *a.* rented, leased.
arrendador, *m.* landlord; lessor; hirer; tenant, lessee, holder; farmer.
arrendajo, *m.* mocking bird; (coll.) mimic.
arrendamiento, *m.* renting, letting; lease; rent.
[1]**arrendar,** *va.* (*ind.* ARRIENDO; *subj.* ARRIENDE) to bridle; to tie (a horse); to train (a horse).
[2]**arrendar,** *va.* (*ind.* ARRIENDO; *subj.* ARRIENDE) to rent, let, lease, hire.
[3]**arrendar,** *va.* to mimic.
arrendatario, ria, *n.* lessee, tenant.
[1]**arreo,** *m.* dress, ornament, decoration.—*pl.* appurtenances, accessories; harness, trappings.
[2]**arreo,** *adv.* successively, uninterruptedly.
arrepápalo, *m.* a kind of fritter.
arrepentido, da. I. *pp.* of ARREPENTIRSE. **II.** *a.* repentant. **III.** *n.* penitent.
arrepentimiento, *m.* repentance.
arrepentirse, *vr.* (*ind. pres.* me ARREPIENTO, *pret.* él se ARREPINTIÓ; *subj.* me ARREPIENTA) to repent.
arrepistar, *va.* to grind (rags) into pulp.
arrepisto, *m.* grinding or pounding (of rags).
arrepollado, da, *a.* cabbagelike.
arrepticio, cia, *a.* possessed by the devil.
arrequesonarse, *vr.* to curdle.
arrequife, *m.* singeing iron in cotton gins.
arrequives, *m. pl.* dress trimmings; ornaments; adornments; circumstances; requirements.
arrestado, da. I. *pp.* of ARRESTAR. **II.** *a.* bold, audacious.
arrestar. I. *va.* to arrest, imprison. **II.** *vr.* to be bold and enterprising; to dare.—**arresto,** *m.* imprisonment, arrest; spirit, enterprise.
arresto domiciliario, *m.* (law) house arrest.
arretín, *m.* = FILIPICHÍN, a kind of woolen cloth.
arretranca, *f.* (Am.) crupper of a packsaddle.
arrevesado, da, *a.* difficult, intricate.
arrezafe, *m.* place full of brambles.
arrezagar, *va.* to raise; to tuck up (sleeves, etc.).
arria, *f.* drove of beasts.—**aguja de a.,** packneedle.
arriada, riada, *f.* (prov.) flood, washout.
arrial, *m.* = ARRIAZ.
arrianismo, *m.* Arianism.
arriano, na, *n.* & *a.* Arian.
[1]**arriar,** *va.* (naut.) to lower, strike.—**a. la bandera,** to strike the colors.
[2]**arriar. I.** *va.* to flood. **II.** *vr.* to be flooded.
arriata, *f.* **arriate,** *m.* border, edge (in gardens); trellis; causeway.
arriaz, *m.* hilt-bar of a sword.
arriba, *adv.* above, high, on high, overhead; upstairs; (naut.) aloft.—**a. de,** above; higher up than; beyond (in an upward direction).—**de a. abajo,** from the top down; from top to bottom; from beginning to end; from head to foot.—**más a.,** higher up.—**para a.,** up, upwards (e.g. *de cuatro pesos para arriba,* from four pesos up).—**por a.,** at, or from, the top.—**por a. de,** above, over. **II.** *interj.* long live!
arribada, *f.* **arribaje,** *m.* (naut.) arrival.—**de arribada,** (naut.) putting into a port by stress.
arribar, *vn.* to arrive; (naut.) to put into a harbor in distress; (naut.) to fall off to leeward; to reach; to recover, convalesce.
arribeño, ña, *n.* (Mex.) highlander.
arribo, *m.* arrival.
arricé, arrice, *v. V.* ARRIZAR.
arricés, *m.* buckle of a stirrup strap.
arricete, *m.* shoal, sand bank.
[1]**arriendo,** *m.* renting; lease; rent.
[2]**arriendo, arriende,** *v. V.* ARRENDAR.
arrieraje, *m.* (Am.) (collect.) muleteers; ARRIERÍA.
arriería, *f.* driving of mules.
arriero, *m.* muleteer.
arriesgadamente, *adv.* dangerously, hazardously.
arriesgado, da, *a.* dangerous, risky; daring.
arriesgar. I. *va.* (*pret.* ARRIESGUÉ; *subj.* ARRIESGUE) to risk, hazard, jeopardize. **II.** *vr.* to expose oneself to danger; to dare.
arrimadero, *m.* support; stopping or landing place; shelter.
arrimadillo, *m.* mat, wainscot, dado.
arrimadizo, za, *a.* designed to be placed against or joined to a thing; parasitic, sycophantic, sponging.
arrimador, *m.* backlog in a fireplace.
arrimadura, *f.* act of ARRIMAR or ARRIMARSE.
arrimar. I. *va.* to place near; (naut.) to stow; to put beside or against; to put by; to give up, abandon; to lay down; to fling, dismiss; to discard.—**a. el hombro,** to work with a will; to lend a hand. **II.** *vr.* (a) to go near (to); to seek the protection (of); to seek shelter (in or under); to lean (on or against); to join.
arrime, *m.* proximity to the goal (in bowling).
arrimo, *m.* putting near, beside or against (some person or thing); abandonment, relinquishment, giving up; support, protection; staff, cane, crutch; (arch.) idle wall, wall bearing no load.—**al a. de,** protected or shielded by.
arrimón, *m.* loafer, idler.—**estar de a.,** to keep watch.
arrinconado, da. I. *pp.* of ARRINCONAR. **II.** *a.* distant, out of the way; neglected, put away, forgotten.
arrinconar. I. *va.* to lay aside, put away; to pigeonhole; to remove, dismiss; to neglect, forsake. **II.** *vr.* to live secluded.
arriñonado, da, *a.* kidney-shaped.
arriostrar, riostrar, *va.* to brace, stay.
arriscadamente, *adv.* boldly, audaciously.
arriscado, da. I. *pp.* of ARRISCARSE. **II.** *a.* forward, bold; brisk, easy, free; craggy.
arriscador, ra, *n.* (prov.) olive gleaner.
arriscar. I. *va.* (*pret.* ARRISQUÉ; *subj.* ARRISQUE) to risk. **II.** *vr.* to be vain, conceited; (of sheep, etc.) to plunge over a cliff.
arritmia, *f.* (med.) arrhythmia.
arrítmico, ca, *a.* arrhythmic.
arrizafa, *f.* = RUZAFA, garden, park.
arrizar, *va.* (*pret.* ARRICÉ; *subj.* ARRICE) (naut.) to reef, stow, lash.
arroba, *f.* weight of twenty-five pounds (about 11½ kg.); name of a variable liquid measure.
arrobadizo, za, *a.* (coll.) feigning ecstasy.
arrobador, ra, *a.* enchanting, entrancing.
arrobamiento, *m.* ecstatic rapture, bliss, trance.
arrobarse, *vr.* to be enraptured, entranced.
arrobero, ra. I. *a.* weighing an arroba. **II.** baker for a community.
arrobo, *m.* = ARROBAMIENTO.
arrocabe, *m.* wooden frieze.
arrocé, arroce, *v. V.* ARROZAR.
arrocero, ra, *n.* rice planter or dealer.
arrocinado, da. I. *pp.* of ARROCINARSE. **II.** *a.* jaded, worn-out (horse).

arrocinar. I. *va.* to brutalize. II. *vr.* to become foolishly enamored; to become stupid.
arrodajarse, *vr.* (Costa Rica) to sit on the ground with the legs crossed.
arrodelarse, *vr.* to be armed with a buckler.
arrodilladura, *f.*, **arrodillamiento,** *m.* kneeling.
arrodillar. I. *va.* to make kneel down. II. *vr.* to kneel down.
arrodrigar, arrodrigonar, *va.* to prop (vines).
arrogación, *f.* arrogation; child adoption.
arrogador, ra, *n.* one who claims arrogantly.
arrogancia, *a.* arrogance; haughtiness; bravery, courage; stately carriage.
arrogante, *a.* arrogant; haughty, proud.
arrogar. I. *va.* (*pret.* ARROGUÉ; *subj.* ARROGUE) to adopt; to arrogate. II. *vr.* to usurp.
arrojadamente, *adv.* audaciously, boldly.
arrojadizo, za, *a.* easily thrown or darted; missile that can be, or is intended to be, thrown.
arrojado, da. I. *pp.* of ARROJAR. II. *a.* rash, dashing, fearless.
arrojador, ra, *n.* thrower, flinger.
[1]**arrojar,** *va.* to make red-hot (a furnace, etc.).
[2]**arrojar.** I. *va.* to throw, fling, hurl; to cast out; to shed, emit; to bring forth (shoots, sprouts); (naut.) to drive or cast on rocks; to leave, show (a certain figure, as a balance, etc.); to turn away, dismiss. II. *vr.* to throw oneself (lit. from a height & fig.); to venture.
arroje, *m.* man who drops as counterweight to raise the curtain in a theater.
arrojo, *m.* fearlessness, dash, boldness.
arrollador, ra. I. *a.* (of waves, wind) violent, sweeping; winding, that winds or serves to wind. II. *n.* one that winds.
[1]**arrollamiento,** *m.* (elec.) winding.
[2]**arrollamiento,** *m.* = ARRULLO.
arrollar, *va.* to roll; to wrap; to twist; to carry off, sweep away; (Am.) to trample, run over; to defeat, rout, confound; to wind.
arromadizarse, *vr.* to catch cold.
arromar, *va.* to blunt; to dull.
arropamiento, *m.* wrapping, covering.
[1]**arropar,** *va.* to mix with boiled wine.—**arrope,** *m.* grape juice boiled to a syrup; boiled honey.
[2]**arropar,** *va.* to cover, wrap.
arropea, *f.* irons, fetters, shackles.
arropera, *f.* vessel for boiled must, etc.
arropía, *f.* taffy.—**arropiero, ra,** *n.* maker or seller of ARROPÍA.
arrostrar. I. *va.* to set about dauntlessly; to defy, face. II. *vr.* to fight face to face.
arroyada, *f.*, **arroyadero,** *m.* channel of a stream; gully; flood, freshet.
[1]**arroyar,** *vr.* to form, or run in, gullies.
[2]**arroyar,** *vr.* (agr.) to blight.
arroyo, *m.* rivulet, small stream, brook.
arroyuelo, *m. dim.* rill, brook.
arroz, *m.* rice.—**arrozal,** *m.* rice field.—**arrozar,** *va.* (*pret.* ARROCÉ; *subj.* ARROCE) to sow rice.
arruar, *vn.* to grunt like a wild boar.
arrufadura, *f.* (naut.) sheer of a ship.
arrufar. I. *va.* (naut.) to incurvate, to form the sheer. II. *vr.* (of dogs) to snarl.
arrufo, *m.* = ARRUFADURA.
arruga, *f.* wrinkle (in face, clothes, etc.).
arrugación, *f.*, **arrugamiento,** *m.* corrugation, wrinkling, wrinkle.
arrugar, *va.* (*pret.* ARRUGUÉ; *subj.* ARRUGUE) to wrinkle, corrugate; to crumple, rumple; to fold, gather, crease, pleat.—**a. el entrecejo,** to knit the brow.—**a. la frente,** to frown.
arrugia, *f.* (min.) gold mine.
arruinador, ra, *n.* & *a.* ruiner(-ing), demolisher (-ing), destroyer(-ing).
arruinamiento, *m.* destruction, ruin.
arruinar, *va.* to demolish, ruin, destroy.
arrullar, *va.* to lull; to court; to bill and coo.
arrullo, *m.* billing and cooing; lullaby.
arrumaco, *m.* caress, fondling.
arrumaje, *m.* (naut.) stowage.
arrumar, *va.* to stow.
arrumazón, *f.* (naut.) stowing; overcast horizon.
arrumbadas, *f. pl.* (naut.) wales of a row galley.
arrumbamiento, *m.* (naut.) bearing.
[1]**arrumbar,** *va.* to put away; to range (casks of wine) in a cellar; to silence; to remove from a trust.
[2]**arrumbar.** I. *va.* (naut.) to determine the direction of. II. *vn.*, *vr.* (naut.) to take bearings.
arrurruz, *m.* arrowroot.
arsáfraga, *f.* = BERRERA, (bot.) parsnip.
arsenal, *m.* shipyard, dockyard, navy yard; arsenal; (fig.) depository; collection of data.
arseniato, *m.* (chem.) arseniate.
arsenical, *a.* (chem.) arsenical.
arsénico. I. *m.* (chem.) arsenic; ratsbane. II. *a.* arsenic.
arsenioso, *a.* arsenious.
arsenito, *m.* arsenite.
arseniuro, *m.* arsenide.
arsenopirita, *f.* (min.) arsenopyrite.
arsfenamina, *f.* (pharm.) arsphenamine.
arsolla, arzolla, *f.* (bot.) milk thistle.
arta, *f.* (bot.) English plantain; ribwort.
artanica, artanita, *f.* (bot.) sow bread.
arte, *m.* or *f.* art; skill, craft, cunning; trade, profession; artifice, device; intrigue; fishing net.—**a. bella, liberal,** one of the fine, liberal arts.—**artes y oficios,** arts and crafts.—**no tener a. ni parte en,** to have nothing to do with.
artefacto, *m.* manufacture, handiwork, contrivance, appliance, device.
artejo, *m.* joint or knuckle of the fingers.
artemisa, artemisia, *f.* (bot.) mugwort.
artera, *f.* iron stamp (for marking bread).
arteramente, *adv.* craftily, cunningly, artfully.
artería, *f.* cunning, trick, artfulness.
arteria, *f.* (anat., fig.) artery; (elec.) feeder.
arterial, *a.* arterial.
arterialización, *f.* arterialization.
arterializar, *va.* to arterialize.
arteriografía, *f.* arteriography.
arteriola, *f.* (anat.) arteriole.
arteriología, *f.* arteriology.
arteriosclerosis, *f.* (med.) arteriosclerosis.
arterioso, sa, *a.* arterial.
arteriotomía, *f.* (surg.) arteriotomy.
arteritis, *f.* (med.) arteritis.
artero, ra, *a.* cunning, artful.
artesa, *f.* trough; bowl; canoe.
artesano, na, *n.* artisan, mechanic.
artesiano, *a.* Artesian
artesilla, *f.* trough.
artesón, *m.* kitchen tub; (arch.) carved panel on ceiling.—**artesonado, da,** *a.* panelled (ceiling).
artesuela, *f. dim.* small trough or bowl.
artético, ca, *a.* arthritic, gouty. Also ARTRÍTICO.
ártico, ca, *a.* arctic.
articulación, *f.* articulation, joint; pronunciation; (bot.) geniculation.
articulado, da. I. *pp.* of [1]ARTICULAR. II. *a.* jointed. III. *m.* (zool.) articulate.—*m. pl.* Articulata.
[1]**articular,** *va.* to unite, join; to articulate; (law) to question, interrogate.
[2]**articular; articulario, ria,** *a.* articular.
articulista, *n.* writer of articles.
artículo, *m.* article; (law) plea; (bot.) geniculation; (anat.) joint.—**a. de fondo,** leader, editorial.—*pl.* articles, things, goods, products.—**a. de consumo,** consumer goods.—**a. definido** or **determinado,** (gram.) definite article.—**a. de primera necesidad,** basic commodity.—**a. indefinido, genérico** or **indeterminado,** (gram.) indefinite article.
artífice, *n.* artificer, artisan, craftsman.
artificial, *a.* artificial.—**artificialmente,** *adv.* artificially.
artificio, *m.* workmanship, craft; artifice; cunning; trick, ruse; contrivance, device, appliance.
artificioso, sa, *a.* skilful, ingenious; artful, crafty, cunning.
artiga, *f.* land newly broken up.
artigar, *va.* to break and level (land).

artilugio, *m.* gadget, contrivance.
artillar, *va.* to mount (cannon).
artillería, *f.* gunnery, artillery; ordnance.—**a. de a lomo** = A. DE MONTAÑA.—**a. de avancarga,** muzzle-loading artillery.—**a. de campaña,** field artillery.—**a. de costa,** coast artillery.—**a. de montaña,** light mountain artillery.—**a. de plaza,** siege artillery.—**a. de retrocarga,** breech-loading artillery.
artillero, *m.* gunner, artilleryman.
artimaña, *f.* trap, snare, stratagem.
artimón, *m.* (naut.) mizzenmast.
artina, *f.* fruit of the boxthorn.
artiodáctilo, la, *m.* & *a.* (zool.) artiodactyl.
artista, *m.* artist.
artístico, ca, *a.* artistic.
artolas, *f. pl.* set of two back-to-back seats (put on a horse like saddle-bags).
artralgia, *f.* (med.) arthralgia, pain in a joint.
artrítico, ca, *a.* arthritic, gouty, rheumatic.
artritis, *m.* (med.) arthritis, gout.—**artritismo,** *m.* arthritism, disposition to joint affections.
artrografía, *f.* arthrography.
artrología, *f.* (anat.) arthrology.
artrópodo, da. I. *n.* & *a.* arthropod. **II.** *m. pl.* Arthropoda.
Arturo, *m.* (astr.) Arcturus.
arugas, *f.* (bot.) = MATRICARIA, feverfew.
árula, *f. dim.* small altar.
arundíneo, nea, *a.* (bot.) arundinaceous, arundineous.
aruñar, *va.,* **aruñazo,** *m.,* etc. (coll.) = ARAÑAR, to scratch, etc.
arúspice, *m.* augur, soothsayer.
aruspicina, *f.* art of divining from animals' entrails.
arveja, *f.* (bot.) carob tree and its fruit; (S. A.) green pea.—**arvejal, arvejar,** *m.* field of carob trees; (S. A.) greenpea garden.
arvejo, *m.* (bot.) bastard chickpea.
arvense, *a.* growing in sown fields.
arzobispado, *m.* archbishopric.
arzobispal, *a.* archiepiscopal.
arzobispo, *m.* archbishop.
arzolla, *f.* (bot.) lesser burdock; milk thistle.
arzón, *m.* saddletree.
as, *m.* (cards, dice, aer.) ace; Roman copper coin.
[1]**asa,** *f.* handle, haft.
[2]**asa,** *f.* juice of certain plants.—**a. dulce,** gum benzoin.
asación, *f.* (pharm.) decoction.
asadero, ra. I. *a.* fit for roasting. **II.** *m.* (Mex.), small flat cheese.
asado, da. I. *pp.* of ASAR. **II.** *m.* roast.
asador, *m.* spit, roasting jack.
asadura, *f.* entrails.—**a. de puerco,** haslet.
asaeteador, *m.* archer, bowman.
asaetear, *va.* to attack, kill with arrows.
asaetinado, da, *a.* satinlike.
asafétida, *f.* asafœtida, a resinous gum.
asainetado, da, *a.* farcical.
asalariado, da. I. *pp.* of ASALARIAR. **II.** *a.* working for a salary or wages; (contempt.) serving for hire. **III.** *n.* salaried person, wage earner; hireling.
asalariar, *va.* to fix a salary for; to hire.
asalmonado, da, *a.* tasting like salmon.
asaltador, *m.* assailant, assaulter; highwayman.
asaltante, *n.* & *a.* assailant.
asaltar, *va.* to assault, storm, assail; to surprise; to occur or come suddenly (to one).
asalto, *m.* assault; attack.—**a. de armas,** fencing bout.—**por a.,** by storm.
asamblea, *f.* assembly; legislature; meeting; junta; (mil.) assembly (bugle call).—**asambleísta,** *n.* assemblyman, member of an assembly.
asar. I. *va.* to roast. **II.** *vr.* (fig.) to be roasting, be very hot.
asarbácara, asáraca, *f.* (bot.) asarabacca.
asarero, *m.* (bot.) = ENDRINO, blackthorn, sloe.
asargado, da, *a.* sergelike, twilled.
ásaro, *m.* (bot.) asarum.
asativo, va, *a.* (pharm.) dressed or boiled in its own juice.
asaz, *adv.* enough, abundantly; greatly, very.
asbestino, na, *a.* pertaining to asbestos.
asbesto, *m.* asbestos.
ascalonia, *f.* (bot.) shallot.
áscar, *m.* army (in Morocco).—**áscari,** *m.* Moroccan infantryman.
ascárides, *f. pl.* ascarides, intestinal worms.
ascendencia, *f.* line of ancestors; origin.
ascendente, *a.* ascendant, ascending.
ascender, *vn.* (*ind.* ASCIENDO; *subj.* ASCIENDA) to ascend, mount, climb; to be promoted.—**a. a,** to amount to, add up to.
ascendiente, *n.* ancestor; influence, power.
ascensión, *f.* ascension; exaltation.—**a. recta,** (astr.) right ascension.
ascensional, *a.* (astr.) ascensional.
ascenso, *m.* promotion.
ascensor, *m.* lift, elevator.
asceta, *m.* ascetic, hermit.—**asceticismo, ascetismo,** *m.* asceticism.—**ascético, ca,** *n.* & *a.* ascetic.
ascidia, *f.* (bot.) ascidium; (zool.) Ascidium, ascidian.—*pl.* (zool.) Ascidian.—**ascidiáceo, a,** *a.* ascidiaceous.
asciendo, ascienda, *v. V.* ASCENDER.
ascios, *m. pl.* (geog.) Ascians.
asciro, *m.* (bot.) St. Andrew's cross.
ascitis, *f.* (med.) ascites, abdominal dropsy.—**ascítico, ca,** *a.* ascitic.
asclepiada, *f.* (bot.) swallowwort.
asco, *m.* nausea, loathing; despicable thing.—**estar hecho un a.,** to be very dirty.—**hacer ascos,** to turn up one's nose.
ascua, *f.* red-hot, or live, coal.—**¡ascuas!** how it hurts!—**en a.,** red hot.—**estar en ascuas,** to be greatly agitated.—**sacar el a. con la mano del gato,** or **con mano ajena,** (coll.) to get some one to pull one's chestnuts out of the fire.
aseado, da. I. *pp.* of ASEAR. **II.** *a.* clean, neat.
asear, *va.* to adorn, embellish, polish; to clean.
asechador, ra, *a.* ensnarer, waylayer.
asechamiento, *m.,* **asechanza,** *f.* waylaying, snare, trap, stratagem.
asechar, *va.* to waylay; to ambush.
asecho, *m.* ambuscade, trap.
asedado, da. I. *pp.* of ASEDAR. **II.** *a.* silky.
asedar, *va.* to work (esp. flax) soft as silk.
asediador, ra, *n.* besieger.
asediar, *va.* to besiege, blockade.—**asedio,** *m.* siege, blockade.
aseglararse, *vr.* (of a religious) to secularize oneself.
asegundar, *va.* to repeat.
asegurable, *a.* insurable.
aseguración, *f.* insurance.
asegurado, da. I. *pp.* of ASEGURAR. **II.** *n.* & *a.* insured (person).
asegurador, ra, *n.* & *a.* insurer(-ing), underwriter(-ing).
aseguramiento, *m.* securing; security; insurance.
asegurar. I. *va.* to secure, fasten, fix; to affirm, assert; (com.) to insure. **II.** *vr.* to make sure; hold fast; to get insured, take out insurance.
aseidad, *f.* self-existence (as of God).
asemejar. I. *va.* to make, or represent as, similar; to copy. **II.** *vr.* (a) to look like, resemble.
asendereado, da. I. *pp.* of ASENDEREAR. **II.** *a.* (of a road, path) beaten; frequented; worn out by trouble.
asenderear, *va.* to open a path in or through; to persecute.
asenso, *m.* assent, consent; credence.
asentada, *f.* session; sitting.
asentaderas, *f. pl.* (coll.) = NALGAS, buttocks.
asentadillas.—a a., *adv.* woman-fashion.
asentado, da. I. *pp.* of ASENTAR. **II.** *a.* seated; settled; permanent.
asentador, *m.* razor strop; turning chisel.
asentadura, *f.,* **asentamiento,** *m.* (law) posses-

sion of goods given by default; establishment, settlement.
asentar. **I.** *va.* (*ind.* ASIENTO; *subj.* ASIENTE) to place, fix, seat; to adjust; to stop at; to note down; to enter (an account, etc.); to strike; to found, establish; to hone; to estimate. **II.** *vn.* to fit; to sit down; to settle. **III.** *vr.* (arch.) to sink, settle.
asentimiento, *m.* assent.
asentir, *vn.* (*ind.* ASIENTO; *subj.* ASIENTA) to agree, to assent, acquiesce.
asentista, *m.* contractor.
aseo, *m.* cleanliness, neatness, tidiness.
asépalo, la, *a.* (bot.) without sepals.
asepsia, *f.* (med.) asepsis.
aséptico, ca, *a.* aseptic.
asequible, *a.* attainable, obtainable, available.
aserción, *f.* assertion, affirmation.
aserradero, *m.* sawmill; sawpit, sawhorse.
aserradizo, za, *a.* fit to be sawed.
aserrado, da. **I.** *pp.* of ASERRAR. **II.** *a.* serrate, serrated, dentate.
aserrador, *m.* sawer or sawyer.
aserradura, *f.* sawing, kerf.—*pl.* sawdust.
aserrar, *va.* (*ind.* ASIERRO; *subj.* ASIERRE) to saw.
aserrín, serrín, *m.* sawdust.
asertivamente, *adv.* affirmatively.
asertivo, va, *a.* assertive.
aserto, *m.* assertion, affirmation.
asesar, *vn.* to become wise.
asesinar, *va.* to assassinate.—**asesinato,** *m.* assassination.
asesino, na, *n.* assassin, murderer(-ess).
asesor, ra. **I.** *a.* advisory. **II.** *n.* adviser, consultant.
asesorar. **I.** *va.* to advise, give legal advice. **II.** *vr.* to take advice.
asesoría, *f.* office, pay and fees of a consultant or adviser.
asestadura, *f.* taking aim.
asestar, *va.* to aim, point; to deal (a blow); to discharge, fire.
aseveración, *f.* asseveration, assertion.
aseveradamente, *adv.* affirmatively.
aseverar, *va.* to asseverate, affirm, assert.
asexual, *a.* asexual.
asfaltado, *m.* asphalt pavement; asphalt paving, paving with asphalt.
asfaltar, *va.* to asphalt.
asfáltico, ca, *a.* asphaltic; asphalt (as *a.*): bituminous.
asfalto, *m.* asphalt, asphaltum.
asfíctico, ca, *a.* asphyxial.
asfixia, *f.* (med.) asphyxia.
asfixiante, *a.* asphyxiating.
asfixiar. **I.** *va.* to asphyxiate, suffocate. **II.** *vr.* to be asphyxiated.
asfódelo, *m.* asphodel, day lily.
asgo, asga, *v.* *V.* ASIR.
así, *adv.* so, thus, in this manner; therefore. Foll. by verb in *subj.*, it is translated by "would that."—**a., a.,** so so, middling.—**a. como,** as soon as, just as.—**a. como a.,** anyway, anyhow.—**a. (los fijos) como (las fijas),** both (sons) and daughters, (sons) as well as (daughters).—**a. es,** that, or it, is so.—**a. es (son),** such is (are).—**a. es que,** and so; (improper but common) that is the way to, that is how.—**a. no,** not that way, not so.—**a. que,** as soon as, after.—**a. y todo,** and yet; just the same.—**ponerse a.,** to take on so; to act like that.
Asia, *f.* Asia.
asiático, ca, *n.* & *a.* Asiatic.
asibilación, *f.* (phon.) assibilation.
asibilar, *va.* (phon.) to assibilate.
asidera, *f.* (S. A.) (harness) strap with rings.
asidero, *m.* handle; occasion, pretext.—**asideros,** (naut.) towropes.
asiduidad, *f.* assiduity.
asiduo, dua, *a.* assiduous.
[1]**asiento,** *m.* seat; site; solidity; settling; bottom; sediment, settlings; treaty; contract; entry; registry; judgment, wisdom; stability; permanence; mining district; list, roll; collar band; indigestion.—**a. de atrás,** back seat.—**a. de la válvula,** valve seat.—**a. de palco,** (theat.) box seat.
[2]**asiento, asienta,** *v.* *V.* ASENTIR.
[3]**asiento, asiente,** *v.* *V.* ASENTAR.
asierro, asierre, *v.* *V.* ASERRAR.
asignable, *a.* assignable.
asignación, *f.* assignment; distribution, partition; destination.
asignado, *m.* assignat.
asignante, *n.* assigner, assignor.
asignar, *va.* to assign.
asignatario, ria, *n.* (Am.) assign, assignee.
asignatura, *f.* subject (of study).
asilar, *va.* to shelter; to place in an asylum.
asilo, *m.* asylum; refuge; shelter.—**a. de huérfanos,** orphan asylum.—**a. de locos,** insane asylum.
[1]**asilla,** *f. dim.* small handle; slight pretext.
[2]**asilla,** *f.* (anat.) clavicle, collarbone.
asimetría, *f.* asymmetry; (stat.) skewness.
asimétrico, ca, *a.* asymmetric(al, unsymmetrical.
asimiento, *m.* grasp; attachment, affection.
asimilable, *a.* assimilable.
asimilación, *f.* assimilation.
asimilar. **I.** *vn.* to resemble. **II.** *va.* to assimilate.
asimilativo, va, *a.* assimilating.
asimismo, *adv.* likewise, so too, in like manner.
asimplado, da, *a.* like a simple, ingenuous person.
asincrónico, ca, *a.* asynchronous.
asincronismo, *m.* asynchronism.
asíndeton, *m.* (rhet.) asyndeton.
asinino, na, *a.* asinine; like a donkey.
asíntota, *f.* (geom.) asymptote.
asintótico, ca, *a.* asymptotic.
asir. **I.** *va.* & *vn.* (*ind.* ASGO; *subj.* ASGA) to grasp or seize; to hold; to take root. **II.** *vr.* **(de);** to avail oneself (of); to hold (to), to take hold (of); to take advantage (of); to dispute (with) each other.—**a. a las ramas,** to give foolish excuses.
asiriano, na; asirio, ria, *n.* & *a.* Assyrian.
asirio, ria, *n.* & *a.* Assyrian.
asiriología, *f.* Assyriology.
asiriólogo, *n.* Assyriologist.
asistencia, *f.* attendance, presence; assistance, aid; reward; board, meals.—*pl.* allowance; alimony.
asistenta, *f.* handmaid; waiting maid; attendant.
asistente, *m.* assistant, helper; chief officer of justice at Seville; orderly.
asistir. **I.** *vn.* (a) to attend, be present (at); to follow suit. **II.** *va.* to lend; to attend, take care of; to assist, help, serve; to accompany.
asma, *f.* asthma.—**asmático, ca,** *a.* asthmatic.
asna, *f.* female donkey.—*pl.* (carp.) rafters.
asnacho, *m.* (bot.) = GATUÑA, cammock.
asnada, *f.* foolish action.
asnado, *m.* side-wall timber in mines.
asnal, *a.* asinine, stupid, idiotic.
asnalmente, *adv.* foolishly, idiotically.
asnallo, *m.* (bot.) = ASNACHO.
asnería, *f.* collection of donkeys; idiotic action.
asnilla, *f.* stanchion or prop.
asnino, na, *a.* = ASININO.
asno, *m.* donkey, ass.
asobarcar, (coll. for) **sobarcar,** *va.* (*pret.* ASOBARQUÉ; *subj.* ASOBARQUE) to take under the arm; to lift up (the skirts).
asocarronado, da, *a.* crafty, cunning.
asociable, *a.* associable.
asociación, *f.*, **asociamiento,** *m.* association; fellowship; partnership, union.
asociacionismo, *m.* associationism.
asociado, *m.* associate, partner.
asociar. **I.** *va.* to associate. **II.** *vr.* to associate; to form a partnership; to join.
asociativo, va, *a.* associative.

asolación, *f.* desolation, devastation.
asolador, ra, *n.* & *a.* destroyer(-ing), ruiner(-ing).
asolamiento, *m.* destruction, havoc.
asolanar, *va.* (of the east wind) to damage (fruit, etc.).
[1]**asolar.** **I.** *va.* (*ind.* ASUELO; *subj.* ASUELE) to raze, devastate. **II.** *vr.* to settle, get clear (wine).
[2]**asolar.** **I.** *va.* (of the sun) to burn, parch. **II.** *vr.* (of soil) to become parched, dry up.
asoldar (*ind.* ASUELDO; *subj.* ASUELDE), **asoldadar,** *va.* to hire.
asolear. **I.** *va.* to sun; (Am.) to dry in the sun. **II.** *vr.* to be sunburnt; (Am.) to take a sun bath.
asomada, *f.* appearance; point from which something is first seen.
asomado, da. **I.** *pp.* of ASOMAR. **II.** *a.* fuddled.
asomar. **I.** *vn.* to begin to appear. **II.** *va.* to show, put out (as one's head out the window). **III.** *vr.* to become flustered with wine; to peep. —**a. a,** to look out of; to peep into.
asombradizo, za, *a.* timid, shy.
asombrado, da, *a.* astonished, amazed.
asombrador, ra, *a.* astonishing.
asombrar. **I.** *va.* to shade, darken; to frighten; to astonish, amaze. **II.** *vr.* (**de**) to wonder, be astonished (at).—**asombro,** *m.* dread, fear; amazement or astonishment.
asombroso, sa, *a.* wonderful, astonishing.
asomo, *m.* indication, sign; conjecture.
asonada, *f.* riotous crowd; mobbing, attack of a mob.
asonancia, *f.* consonance, harmony; (poet.) assonance.
asonantar, *va.* (poet.) to make assonant.
asonante, *n.* & *a.* assonant.
asonar, *vn.* (*ind.* ASUENO; *subj.* ASUENE) to be assonant; to accord.
asordar, *va.* to deafen.
asotanar, *va.* to excavate for a cellar.
aspa, *f.* cross; reel; wings of a windmill; cross stud.—**aspadera,** *f.* (mech.) reel.
aspado, da. **I.** *pp.* of ASPAR. **II.** *a.* having both arms extended.
aspador, ra. **I.** *n.* reeler; winder. **II.** *m.* reel.
aspalato, *m.* (bot.) rosewood.
aspalto, *m.* = ESPALTO, dark, clear paint.
aspar, *va.* to reel, wind; to crucify; to vex.
asparagina, aspargina, *f.* (chem.) asparagin(e.
aspaviento, *m.* exaggerated wonder or fear; fuss.
aspecto, *m.* aspect, look; (arch.) outlook; (astr.) aspect.
ásperamente, *adv.* rudely, harshly, gruffly.
asperear, *vn.* to taste acrid.
asperete, *m.* = [1]ASPERILLO.
aspereza, *f.* asperity; roughness; keenness; harshness, snappishness; rough place.
asperges, *m.* sprinkling.
asperiego, ga, *a.* sour (pippin).
[1]**asperillo,** *m.* sourish taste of unripe fruit.
[2]**asperillo, lla,** *a. dim.* tart, sourish.
asperjar, *va.* to sprinkle.
áspero, ra, *a.* rough; knotty; harsh, gruff.
asperón, *m.* grindstone; flagstone.
aspérrimo, ma, *a. super.* of ÁSPERO.
aspersión, *f.* aspersion; sprinkling.
aspersorio, *m.* water sprinkler.
áspid, áspide, *m.* asp.
aspidistra, *f.* (bot.) aspidistra.
aspillera, *f.* loophole, embrasure, crenel.
aspiración, *f.* aspiration; (mus.) short pause.
aspirado, da, *f.* & *a.* (phon.) aspirate.
aspirador, *m.* vacuum cleaner.
aspirante. **I.** *a.* **bomba a.,** suction pump. **II.** *m.* & *f.* aspirant, neophyte.
aspirar. **I.** *va.* to inhale; to aspire; to covet; to aspirate; to suck. **II.** *vn.* to aspire; to draw breath in, inhale.
aspiratorio, ria, *a.* aspiratory.
aspirina, *f* aspirin.
asquear. **I.** *va.* to loathe. **II.** *vn.* to be nauseated.
asquerosamente, *adv.* loathsomely; basely.
asquerosidad, *f.* filthiness, foulness; vileness, baseness.
asqueroso, sa, *a.* filthy, loathsome; vile, base.
asta, *f.* lance; staff, pole, flagstaff; horn, antler; shank; shaft, spindle.—**a media a.,** at half mast.
ástaco, *m.* crawfish.
astado, da, *a.* antlered.
astasia, *f.* (med.) astasia.
astático, ca, *a.* astatic.
astato, astatino, *m.* (chem.) astatine.
astenia, *f.* (med.) asthenia, debility.
asténico, ca, *a.* (med.) asthenic.
aster, *m.* (bot., biol.) aster.
asteria, *f.* (min.) starstone; (min.) cat's-eye.
asterisco, *m.* asterisk.
asterismo, *m.* (astron., min.) asterism.
asteroide, *m.* (astr.) asteroid.
asteroideo, dea, *m.* & *a.* (zool.) asteroidean.
astigmático, ca, *a.* astigmatic.
astigmatismo, *m.* (med.) astigmatism.
astigmómetro, *m.* astigmometer.
astil, handle; shaft; beam of a balance.
astilejos, *m. pl.* = ASTILLEJOS.
astilla, *f.* chip, splinter.—**astillar,** *va.* to chip.
astillazo, *m.* blow from a flying chip.
Astillejos, *m. pl.* (astr.) Castor and Pollux.
astillero, *m.* rack for lances, spears, pikes, etc.; shipyard, dockyard.
astilloso, sa, *a.* easily splintered.
astracán, *m.* astrakhan (cloth).
astrágalo, *m.* (arch.) astragal; (mil.) molding on a cannon; (bot.) milk vetch; (anat.) astragalus, anklebone; round molding; beads.
astral, *a.* astral.
astrancia, *f.* (bot.) masterwort.
astricción, *f.* astriction, binding.
astrictivo, va, *a.* astrictive, styptic.
astricto, ta, *a.* contracted; determined.
astrífero, ra, (poet.) starry.
astringencia, *f.* astringency.
astringente, *a.* astringent.
astringir, *va.* (*ind.* ASTRINJO; *subj.* ASTRINJA) to astringe, contract, compress.
astro, *m.* heavenly body.
astrobotánica, *f.* astrobotany.
astrofísico, ca. **I.** *a.* astrophysical. **II.** *n.* astrophysicist; *f.* astrophysics.
astrofotografía, *f.* astrophotography.
astrofotometría, *f.* astrophotometry.
astrogeología, *f.* astrogeology.
astrografía, *f.* astrography.
astroite, *m.* astroite, star-shaped fossil.
astrolabio, *m.* astrolabe.
astrología, *f.* astrology.
astrológico, ca, *a.* astrological.
astrólogo, *m.* astrologer.
astrometría, *f.* astrometry.
astronauta, *n.* astronaut.
astronáutico, ca. **I.** *a.* astronautic. **II.** *f.* astronautics.
astronave, *f.* space ship.
astronavegación, *f.* astronavigation, celestial navigation.
astronomía, *f.* astronomy.—**a. gravitacional,** celestial mechanics.
astronómico, ca, *a.* astronomical.
astrónomo, *m.* astronomer.
astroquímica, *f.* astrochemistry.
astrosamente, *adv.* meanly, basely.
astroso, sa, *a.* vile, loathsome.
astucia, *f.* cunning, slyness.
astur, ra, asturiano, na, *n.* & *a.* Asturian.
asturión, *m.* pony; (ichth.) sturgeon.
astuto, ta, *a.* astute, cunning, sly, crafty.
asueldo, asuelde, *v.* *V.* ASOLDAR.
asuelo, asuele, *v.* *V.* ASOLAR.
asueno, asuene, *v.* *V.* ASONAR.
asueto, *m.* school holiday, vacation.
asumir, *va.* to assume; to raise, elevate.
asunción, *f.* assumption; elevation, ascent.
asunto, *m.* subject, matter; affair, business.

asuramiento, *m.* (of cooking food) burning.
asurarse, *vr.* to burn; to become parched.
asurcano, na, *a.* (of land or those working it) neighboring.
asurcar, surcar, *va.* (*pret.* ASURQUÉ; *subj.* ASURQUE) to furrow; to plow.
asustadizo, za, *a.* easily frightened; shy.
asustado, da, *a.* affrighted, frightened.
asustar. I. *va.* to frighten, scare. **II.** *vr.* to be frightened.
atabacado, da, *a.* tobacco-colored.
atabal, *m.* kettledrum.—**atabalear,** *vn.* (of horses' hooves) to clatter; to drum (with the fingers).—**atabalero, ra,** *n.* kettledrummer.
atabanado, da, *a.* (of a horse) spotted white.
atabardillado, da, *a.* resembling spotted fever.
atabe, *m.* small vent in water pipes.
atabernado, da, *a.* (of wine) sold by the glass.
atabladera, *f.* roller.
atablar, *va.* to level, roll (ground already sown).
atacadera, *f.* blaster's rammer.
atacado, da. I. *pp.* of ATACAR. **II.** *a.* (fig.) irresolute, undecided; stingy, close.
atacador, *m.* aggressor; ramrod, rammer.
atacadura, *f.*, **atacamiento,** *m.* ramming.
atacamita, *f.* (min.) atacamite.
atacar, *va.* (*pret.* ATAQUÉ; *subj.* ATAQUE) to attack; to button; to fit; to ram; to corner.
atacir, *m.* (astrol.) division of the celestial arch into twelve parts.
ataderas, *f. pl.*, (Mex.) garters.
atadero, *m.* cord, rope; tying place or thing.
atadijo, ito, *m. dim.* (coll.) ill-shaped parcel.
atado, da. I. *pp.* of ATAR. **II.** *a.* pusillanimous, good-for-nothing. **III.** *m.* bundle, parcel.
atador, ra. I. *n.* tier, binder. **II.** *m.* bonnet-string.
atadura, *f.* fastening, binding; connection; knot.
atafagar, *va.* to stifle, stupefy; to tease, bother.
atafetanado, da, *a.* taffetalike.
ataguía, *f.* cofferdam.
ataharre, *m.* broad crupper of a packsaddle.
atahorma, *f.* (ornith.) osprey.
ataifor, *m.* deep dish; Moorish round table.
atairar, *va.* to mold (panels and frames of doors or windows).
ataire, *m.* molding in panels and frames.
atajadero, *m.* sluice gate.
atajadizo, *m.* partition.
atajador, *m.* one that stops or intercepts; (mil.) scout; (min.) boy who tends the horses.
atajar. I. *va.* to intercept, stop; to partition off. **II.** *vr.* to be confounded with shame or fear.
atajo, *m.* short cut; interception, stopping.—**echar por el a.,** (fig.) to escape through a loophole.
atalajar, *va.* to harness and hitch.
atalaje, *m.* breast harness; draft.
atalantar, = ATARANTAR.
atalaya. I. *f.* watchtower; height. **II.** *m.* guard; lookout.
atalayador, ra, *n.* sentry, lookout; prier.
atalayar, *va.* to watch, guard; to spy on, pry into.—**atalayero,** *m.* advance scout.
atalvina, talvina, *f.* porridge of almond meal.
atamiento, *m.* pusillanimity, meekness.
[1]**atanasia,** *f.* (bot.) costmary or alecost.
[2]**atanasia,** *f.* (print.) English type (14-point).
atanor, *m.* tile water pipe; tile (clay or concrete tube or pipe).
atanquía, *f.* depilatory; silk refuse.
atañer, *v. impers.* to belong appertain, concern.
ataque, *m.* attack; (mil.) offensive works; (med.) fit, seizure.—**a. aéreo,** air attack.—**a. simulado,** (mil.) feint.
ataqué, ataque, *v. V.* ATACAR.
ataquiza, *f.* laying (a vine).
ataquizar, *va.* to lay (a vine).
atar. I. *va.* to tie, bind; to lace; to deprive of motion, stop.—**a. cabos,** to put two and two together, draw one's own conclusions. **II.** *vr.* to become embarrassed.
ataracea, taracea, *f.* marquetry, inlaid work.
ataracear, taracear, *va.* to checker; to inlay.
atarantado, da, *a.* bitten by a tarantula; restless; wild; astonished, amazed; dizzy.
atarantar. I. *va.* to astound, dumbfound. **II.** *vr.* to be or become dumbfounded; to rush, dash.
atarazana, *f.* arsenal; spinner's shed.
atarazar, *va.* to bite.
atardecer. I. *m.* late afternoon. **II.** *vn.* to draw towards evening.
atareado, da. I. *pp.* of ATAREAR. **II.** *a.* busy.
atarear. I. *va.* to give or assign work to. **II.** *vr.* to be exceedingly busy.
atarjea, *f.* culvert; conduit; drain pipe.
atarquinar. I. *va.* to cover with mud. **II.** *vr.* to be covered with mud.
atarraga, *f.* (bot.) = OLIVARDA, elecampane.
atarrajar, *va.* = ATERRAJAR, to thread (a screw).
atarraya, *f.* casting net.
atarugamiento, *m.* wedging; stuffing.
atarugar, *va.* (*pret.* ATARUGUÉ; *subj.* ATARUGUE) to fasten; to wedge, plug, bung; to stuff, fill; (coll.) to silence.
atasajar, *va.* to jerk (beef).
atascadero, atascamiento, *m.* deep miry place; obstruction; impediment.
atascar. I. *va.* (*pret.* ATASQUÉ; *subj.* ATASQUE) to stop (a leak); to obstruct. **II.** *vr.* to stick in mire; to get stopped up; to be nonplussed. (coll.) to get stuck.—**atasco,** *m.* obstruction.
atasqué, atasque, *v. V.* ATASCAR.
ataúd, *m.* coffin, casket· anc. grain measure.
ataujía, *f.* damaskeening.
ataujiado, da, *a.* damaskeened.
ataurique, *m.* (arch.) ornamented plasterwork
ataviado, da, *a.* adorned, bedight.
ataviar, *va.* to deck out, trim, adorn.
atávico, ca, *a.* atavistic.
atavío, *m.* dress; finery, gear.
atavismo, *m.* atavism.
ataxia, *f.* (med.) ataxia.—**a. locomotriz,** locomotor ataxia.—**atáxico, ca,** *a.* ataxic.
atecé, atece, *v. V.* ATEZAR.
atediar. I. *va.* to bore, tire. **II.** *vr.* to be bored.
ateísmo, *m.* atheism.
ateísta. I. *a.* atheistic. **II.** *n.* atheist.
ateístico, ca, *a.* atheistic, atheistical.
ateje, *m.* a kind of hardwood tree (Cuba).
atelaje, *m.* harness; team.
atemorizado, da, *a.* afraid, frightened.
atemorizar, *va.* (*pret.* ATEMORICÉ; *subj.* ATEMORICE) to cause fear to, frighten.
atemperación, *f.* tempering, moderating.
atemperante, *a.* tempering, soothing, cooling.
atemperar, *va.* to temper, soften, assuage, cool; to accommodate (one thing to another).
atenacear, atenazar, *va.* to tear off the flesh of with nippers; to torture.
atención, *f.* attention; civility; kindness; deal in wool.—*pl.* affairs, business.—**en a. a,** considering, in view of.—*interj.* Attention! Look out!
atender. I. *vn.* (*pp.* ATENDIDO and ATENTO; *ind.* ATIENDO; *subj.* ATIENDA) to attend; to pay attention; to wait. **II.** *va.* to take care of (a person); to wait on; to show courtesy to; to treat.
atendible, *a.* worth noticing, considerable.
ateneo, *m.* athenæum.
atenerse (a), *vr.* (*ind. pres.* me ATENGO, *pret.* me ATUVE; *subj.* me ATENGA) to depend or rely (on); to abide (by), stick (to).
atengo, atenga, *v. V.* ATENERSE.
ateniense, *n.* & *a.* Athenian.
atenta, *f.*—**su a.,** (bus.) your favor (i.e. letter).
atentación, *f.* (law) illegal procedure.
atentadamente, *adv.* contrary to law.
[1]**atentado, da. I.** *pp.* of ATENTAR. **II.** *m.* (law) transgression, offense, violation; crime.
[2]**atentado, da,** *a.* discreet, moderate; noiseless.
atentamente, *adv.* attentively; politely.—**att^e^,** used abbrev. in ending to business letters.
atentar, *va.* (*ind.* ATIENTO; *subj.* ATIENTE) to attempt; to attempt (a crime) (reg. conj. in this meaning).

atentatorio, ria, *a.* tending to unlawful acts; leading to criminal act; with criminal or unlawful intent.
atento, ta. I. *pp. irr.* of ATENDER. **II.** *a.* attentive, heedful; polite, courteous.—**su a. seguro servidor,** (ending formal or business letter) very truly yours; (anc.) your obedient servant.
atenuación, *f.* extenuation, diminution; (rhet.) litotes.
atenuado, da, *a.* attenuate.
atenuante, *a.* attenuating; extenuating (circumstances).
atenuar, *va.* to attenuate, diminish, lessen; to tone down (as angry speaking).
ateo, a, *n.* & *a.* atheist (-ic).
atepocate, *m.* (Mex.) frog spawn.
aterclanado, da, *a.* afflicted with tertian fever.
aterciopelado, da, *a.* velvety.
aterimiento, *m.* stiffness from cold.
aterirse, *vr. defect.* (*ind.* me ATIERO; *subj.* me ATIERA) to become stiff with cold.
atermancia, *f.* (phys.) athermancy.
atérmano, na, *a.* (phys.) athermanous.
atérmico, ca, *a.* = ATÉRMANO.
ateroma, *f.* (med.) atheroma, a kind of tumor.
aterrador, ra, *a.* frightful, terrible, dreadful.
aterrajadora, *f.* (mech.) tapper.
aterrajar, *va.* to thread, tap (a screw).
aterramiento, *m.* terror; humiliation.
[1]**aterrar. I.** *va.* (*ind.* ATIERRO; *subj.* ATIERRE) to destroy, pull down, demolish. **II.** *vn.* (aer.) to land. **III.** *vr.* (naut.) to stand inshore.
[2]**aterrar. I.** *va.* (*this verb is regular*) to terrify; to awe; to appal. **II.** *vr.* to be filled with terror, to be awed or appalled.
aterrizaje, *m.* (aer.) landing, alighting.—**pista de a.,** runway; landing field.—**técnicos de a.,** landing experts.
aterrizar, *vn.* (aer.) to land.
aterronado, da, *a.* lumpy.
aterronar. I. *va.* to clot; to make bumpy. **II.** *vr.* to become lumpy; to cake.
aterrorizado, da, *a.* terrified, affrighted; frightened.
aterrorizar, *va.* to frighten, terrify.
atesador, *m.* (mech.) stretcher, tightener; brace pin.
atesar, *va.* (*ind.* ATIESO; *subj.* ATIESE) to pull tight, to tighten; (naut.) = TESAR, to haul taut.
atesorar, *va.* to treasure, hoard up.
atestación, *f.* attestation, testimony, affidavit.
atestado, da, *a.* attested, witnessed.
atestados, *m. pl.* certificates, testimonials.
atestadura, *f.* cramming or stuffing; must for soaking casks.
atestamiento, *m.* cramming, stuffing.
[1]**atestar,** *va.* (*ind.* ATIESTO; *subj.* ATIESTE) to cram, stuff, crowd; to fill up wine casks.
[2]**atestar,** *va.* (*reg. conj.*) to attest, witness.
atestiguación, *f.,* **atestiguamiento,** *m.* affidavit.
atestiguar, *va.* to depose, witness, attest; to give evidence; to prove.
atetado, da, *a.* mammilliform, teat-shaped.
atetar, *va.* to suckle.
atetillar, *va.* to trench around roots.
atezado, da. I. *pp.* of ATEZAR. **II.** *a.* black.
atezamiento, *m.* blackening.
atezar. I. *va.* (*pret.* ATECÉ; *subj.* ATECE) to blacken. **II.** *vr.* to become or get black.
atibar, *va.* (min.) to fill up (excavations).
atiborrar, *va.* to stuff with coarse wool.
aticé, atice, *v. V.* ATIZAR.
aticismo, *m.* Atticism; elegant, delicate diction.
ático, ca. I. *a.* Attic; elegant. **II.** *m.* Attic; (arch.) attic.
atiendo, atienda, *v. V.* ATENDER.
atiento, atiente, *v. V.* ATENTAR.
atiero, atiera, *v. V.* ATERIRSE.
atierre, *m.* deals; caving in; ruin; (mining) attle, heap of waste ore.
atierro, atierre, *v. V.* [1]ATERRAR.
atiesar, *va.* to stiffen.
atieso, atiese, *v. V.* ATESAR.
atiesto, atieste, *v. V.* [1]ATESTAR.
atifle, *m.* potter's trivet.
atigrado, da, *a.* marked like tiger skin.
atildadura, *f.,* **atildamiento,** *m.* punctuation; censure; tidiness, nicety.
atildar, *va.* to put a dash or TILDE over; to censure; to adorn.
atinadamente, *adv.* cautiously; wisely; judiciously.
atinar, *vn.* to hit the mark; to guess; to find out. —**a. a** (*inf.*), to succeed in (*pres. p.*).
atíncar, *m.* tincal, borax.
atinconar, *va.* (min.) to prop the side walls of.
atípico, ca, *a.* atypical.
atiplar. I. *va.* to raise the pitch of (a musical instrument). **II.** *vr.* to become sharp (in tone)
atirantar, *va.* (arch.) to stay, brace with ties.
atiriciarse, *vr.* (med.) to become jaundiced.
atisbadero, *m.* (Am.) peephole.
atisbador, ra, *n.* prier, observer.
atisbadura, *f.* prying, observing cautiously.
atisbar, *va.* to scrutinize; to pry, watch.
atisbo, *m.* = ATISBADURA.
atisuado, da, *a.* tissuelike.
atizadero, *m.,* **atizador, ra,** *n.* inciter; (fire) poker; (candle) snuffer; feeder.
atizar, *va.* (*pret.* ATICÉ; *subj.* ATICE) to poke (the fire); to snuff or trim (a candle, etc.); to rouse, stir.
atizonar. I. *va.* to bond (a wall) with headers; to embed (a beam in a wall). **II.** *vr.* (agr.) to become blighted.
atlantes, *m.* (arch.) atlantes.
atlántico, ca, *n.* & *a.* Atlantic.
atlas, *m.* atlas; (anat.) atlas; (com.) atlas (satin).
atleta, *m.* athlete.—**atlético, ca,** *a.* athletic.—**atletismo,** *m.* athletics.
atmómetro, *m.* (phys.) atmometer.
atmósfera, *f.* atmosphere; sphere of influence.
atmosférico, ca, *a.* atmospheric.
atoar, *va.* (naut.) to tow.
atocinado, da. I. *pp.* of ATOCINAR. **II.** *a.* fat, fleshy.
atocinar. I. *va.* to cut up (a pig); to convert into bacon; (coll.) to assassinate. **II.** *vr.* to swell with anger; to fall desperately in love.
atocha, *f.* tough feather grass, bassweed.
atochal, [1]**atochar,** *m.* bassweed field.
[2]**atochar,** *va.* to fill with bassweed.
atochón, *m.* panicle of tough feather grass.
atol, atole, *m.* non-alcoholic corn-flour drink.
atolería, *f.* place where ATOLE is sold.
atolero, ra, *n.* maker and vender of ATOLE.
atolón, *m.* atoll.
atolondrado, da. I. *pp.* of ATOLONDRAR. **II.** *a.* hare-brained, thoughtless, giddy, careless.
atolondramiento, *m.* confusion, perplexity, amazement; giddiness; recklessness.
atolondrar. I. *va.* to confound, amaze, perplex, rattle. **II.** *vr.* to become confused, rattled.
atolladero, *m.* deep miry place; difficulty, stumbling block.
atollar, *vn.* & *vr.* to fall into the mire; to stick in the mud; to be involved in difficulties, (coll.) to get stuck.
atomicidad, *f.* atomicity.
atómico, ca, *a.* atomic.—**bomba a.,** atom bomb. —**desintegración a.,** (phys.) atomic fission.—**energía a.,** (phys.) atomic energy.—**número a.,** (chem.) atomic number.—**peso a.,** atomic weight.—**pila a.,** atomic pile.—**reloj a.,** atomic clock.—**submarino a.,** atomic submarine.—**teoría a.,** atomic theory.
atomismo, *m.* atomism.
atomista, *m.* atomist.
atomístico, ca, *a.* atomistic.
atomización, *f.* atomization.
atomizar, *va.* to atomize.
átomo, *m.* atom.—**á. activo,** (nuclear phys.) hot atom.—**á. marcado,** (nuclear phys.) tagged atom.

átomo-gramo, *m.* (chem.) gram atom.
atonal, *a.* (mus.) atonal.
atonalidad, *f.* atonality.
atonalismo, *m.* (mus.) atonalism.
atondar, *va.* to spur (a horse).
atonía, *f.* (med.) atony; debility.
atónico, ca, *a.* (med., gram.) atonic.
atónito, ta, *a.* astonished, amazed, aghast.
átono, na, *a.* unaccented; atonic.
atontadamente, *adv.* foolishly, stupidly.
atontamiento, *m.* stupefaction, stunning.
atontar. **I.** *va.* to stun, stupefy; to confound, confuse. **II.** *vr.* to become stupid, dull, stunned.
[1]atorar. **I.** *va.* to obstruct; to jam, choke. **II.** *vr.* to stick in the mire; to fit the bore closely; to choke; to stuff oneself.
[2]atorar, *va.* to cut (wood) into logs.
atormentado, da, *a.* anguished, hagridden.
atormentador, ra, *n.* & *a.* tormentor(-ing).
atormentar, *va.* to torment, torture.
atornillar, *va.* to screw; to turn a screw.
atorozonarse, *vr.* (vet.) (of horses) to suffer colic.
atortolar. **I.** *va.* to confound; to intimidate. **II.** *vr.* to be intimidated.
atortorar, *va.* (naut.) to frap (a ship).
atortujar, *va.* to squeeze, make flat.
atosigador, ra, *n.* & *a.* poisoner(-ing).
atosigamiento, *m.* poisoning.
atosigar, *va.* (*pret.* ATOSIGUÉ; *subj.* ATOSIGUE) to poison; to harass, press.
atóxico, ca, *a.* nonpoisonous.
atrabancar, *va.* (*pret.* ATRABANQUÉ; *subj.* ATRABANQUE) to huddle; to perform in a hurry.
atrabanco, *m.* huddling, acting hurriedly.
atrabiliario, ria; atrabilioso, sa, *a.* atrabilious.
atrabilis, *f.* black bile.
atracadero, *m.* (naut.) landing place.
atracador, *m.* assaulter.
atracar. **I.** *va.* (*pret.* ATRAQUÉ; *subj.* ATRAQUE) (naut.) to overtake; to approach; to cram; to pamper; (Am.) (of robbers) to assault, attack, or hold up. **II.** *vn.* (naut.) to make the shore; to stop, moor. **III.** *vr.* to be pampered.
atracción, *f.* attraction.
atraco, *m.* assault.
atracón, *m.* overeating, gluttony; push.
atractivo, va. **I.** *a.* attractive. **II.** *m.* charm, grace; inducement.
atraer, *va.* (*ind. pres.* ATRAIGO, *pret.* ATRAJE; *subj.* ATRAIGA) to attract; to allure, charm.
atrafagar. **I.** *vn.* to toil, work hard. **II.** *vr.* to fidget, fuss.
atragantarse, *vr.* to choke; to become confused in conversation.
atraíble, *a.* attractable.
atraidorado, da, *a.* traitorlike, peculiar to traitors.
atraigo, atraje, atraiga, *v.* *V.* ATRAER.
atraillar, *va.* to leash; to follow (game) guided by a dog on a leash.
atramparse, *vr.* to be trapped; to be locked out; to be blocked up; to be involved in difficulties.
atramuz, *m.* (bot.) lupine.
atrancar, *va.* (*pret.* ATRANQUÉ; *subj.* ATRANQUE) to bar (a door); to obstruct; to stride; to read hurriedly.
atranque, *m.* difficulty, tight box, fix.
atrapamoscas, *f.* (bot.) Venus's flytrap.
atrapar, *va.* to overtake; to catch, grab; to trap, ensnare, deceive.
atraqué, atraque, *v.* *V.* ATRACAR.
atrás, *adv.* backward, behind, back; past.—**a. de,** behind, back of.—**dar marcha a.,** (auto) to back up, go into reverse.—**de a.,** back (as *a.*).—**hacerse a.,** to fall back.
atrasado, da. **I.** *pp.* of ATRASAR. **II.** *a.* short of funds, poor; backward; behind the times; late, tardy; (of timepiece) slow; back (number of a periodical).
atrasar, **I.** *va.* to retard, delay, detain; to set, put back (timepiece). **II.** *vn.* (of timepiece) to go or be slow. **III.** *vr.* to remain or be left behind; (of timepiece) to lose time; to be in arrears; to be late.
atraso, *m.* tardiness; backwardness.—*pl.* arrears.
atravesado, da. **I.** *pp.* of ATRAVESAR. **II.** *a.* squint-eyed; perverse; mestizo, crossbred, mongrel.
atravesaño, *m.* crosstimber; crosspiece.
atravesar. **I.** *va.* (*ind.* ATRAVIESO; *subj.* ATRAVIESE) to place across, lay athwart; to run through, pierce; to cross; to go through; to wager; (naut.) to lie to; to monopolize, corner (the market). **II.** *vr.* (**en**) to be, come or lie across or in the way (of); to break in, interrupt, (coll.) intrude (in); to meddle; to spring up, arise (as an obstacle); (**con**) to meet; to have an encounter or fight (with).
atravieso, *v.* *V.* ATRAVESAR.
atrayente, *a.* attractive.
atreguado, da, *a.* foolish; deranged; under truce.
atreguar. **I.** *va.* to give a truce to; to give an extension. **II.** *vr.* to agree to a truce.
atrenzo, *m.* conflict, difficulty.
atresia, *f.* (med.) atresia, occlusion of a channel.
atresnalar, *va.* to collect (grain) into shocks.
atreverse, *vr.* to dare; to venture.
atrevidamente, *adv.* daringly, boldly.
atrevido, da. **I.** *pp.* of ATREVERSE. **II.** *a.* bold, daring, fearless; forward, insolent.
atrevimiento, *m.* boldness, audacity; effrontery, impudence.
atribución, *f.* attribution; attribute.
atribuible, *a.* ascribable, attributable.
atribuir. **I.** *va.* (*ind. pres.* ATRIBUYO, *pret.* él ATRIBUYÓ; *subj.* ATRIBUYA) to attribute, ascribe, impute. **II.** *vr.* to assume, take to oneself.
atribular. **I.** *va.* to grieve, afflict. **II.** *vr.* to be or become sad or despondent; to lose heart.
atributivo, va, *a.* attributive.
atributo, *m.* attribute; (logic) predicate.
atribuyo, atribuya. *v.* *V.* ATRIBUIR.
atrición, *f.* contrition; (vet.) contraction.
atril, *m.* lectern; music stand; easel.
atrilera, *f.* ornamental cover for a lectern.
atrincheramiento, *m.* (mil.) entrenchment; trenches (collect.).
atrincherar, *va.* & *vr.* (mil.) to entrench.
atrio, *m.* atrium; paved terrace or raised platform in front of a building (gen. a church).
atrípedo, da, *a.* (zool.) black-footed.
atrirrostro, tra, *a.* (ornith.) black-beaked.
atrito, ta, *a.* contrite.
atrocidad, *f.* atrocity.
atrochar, *vn.* to go by cross-paths.
atrofia, *f.* atrophy.
atrofiado, da, *a.* atrophied.
atrofiar, *va.* & *vr.* to atrophy.
atrófico, ca, *a.* atrophic.
atrojarse, *vr.* (Mex., coll.) to be nonplussed.
atrompetado, da, *a.* trumpetlike.
atronado, da. **I.** *pp.* of ATRONAR. **II.** *a.* reckless, thoughtless.
atronador, ra, *n.* & *a.* thunderer(-ing).
atronadura, *f.* crack or split (in trees); (vet.) tumor in the pastern.
atronamiento, *m.* thundering; stupefaction; (vet.) crepance, wound or chap in the hoof.
atronar. **I.** *va.* (*ind.* ATRUENO: *subj.* ATRUENE) to deafen; to stun, stupefy; to stop (the ears of horses so they won't take fright); to kill (a bull). **II.** *vr.* to be thunderstruck.
atronerar, *va.* to make embrasures in.
atropar, *va.* to assemble in groups.
atropelladamente, *adv.* tumultuously, helter-skelter; unscrupulously.
atropellado, da. **I.** *pp.* of ATROPELLAR. **II.** *a.* hasty; precipitate.
atropellador, ra, *n.* trampler; transgressor, violator.
atropellamiento, *m.* trampling under foot; confusion.
atropellar. **I.** *va.* to trample under foot; to knock down; to run over, hit, injure; to push through;

to insult. **II.** *vr.* to move or act hastily or recklessly; to rush (through a job).
atropello, *m.* trampling, upsetting; running over, injuring (a pedestrian); abuse, insult, outrage.
atropina, *f.* atropine.
atroz, *a.* atrocious; (coll.) huge, vast, enormous.
atrozar, *va.* (naut.) to truss (a yard).
atrueno, atruene, *v. V.* ATRONAR.
atruhanado, da, *a.* scurrilous; rascally.
atufadamente, *adv.* peevishly.
atufar. I. *va.* to vex, irritate, plague. **II.** *vr.* to fret (liquors); to become angry.
atufo, *m.* vexation, annoyance.
atún, *m.* tunny fish.—**atunara,** *f.* place to catch tunny fish.—**atunera,** *f.* tunny-fish hook.
atunero, *m.* tunny fisherman or dealer.
[1]**aturar,** *va.* to close tight.
[2]**aturar,** *vn.* to act wisely, with good judgment.
aturdido, da. I. *pp.* of ATURDIR. **II.** *a.* harebrained, giddy, rattled.
aturdimiento, *m.* bewilderment; confusion.
aturdir. I. *va.* to bewilder, amaze; to rattle, perplex; to stun. **II.** *vr.* to become dazed, bewildered, rattled, stunned.
aturrullar, *va.* to confound, perplex, bewilder.
atusador, ra, *n.* hairdresser; plant trimmer.
atusar. I. *va.* to trim; to comb and smooth (the hair). **II.** *vr.* to overdress.
atutía, *f.* tutty.
atuve, *v. V.* ATENERSE.
auca, oca, *f.* goose.
audacia, *f.* audacity, boldness.
audaz, *a.* bold, fearless, audacious.
audibilidad, *f.* audibility.
audible, *a.* audible.
audición, *f.* hearing; audition.
audiencia, *f.* audience, hearing; audience chamber; court of oyer and terminer; audiencia (high court of justice).
audífono, *m.* audiphone; earphone; hearing aid.
audiófilo, la, *n.* audiophile.
audiofrecuencia, *f.* (radio) audio frequency.
audiómetro, *m.* audiometer.
audión, *m.* (radio) audion.
audiovisual, *a.* audiovisual.
auditivo, va, *a.* auditory.
auditor, *m.* judge; auditor.—**a. de guerra,** Judge Advocate (army).—**a. de la Rota,** member or auditor of the Rota.—**a. de marina,** Judge Advocate (navy).
auditoría, *f.* office of an AUDITOR.
auditorio, ria. I. *a.* auditory. **II.** *m.* audience, assembly of listeners.
auge, *m.* culmination, supreme height; (astr.) apogee.
augita, *f.* (min.) augite.
augur, *m.* augur, augurer.
auguración, *f.* augury.
augural, *a.* augurial.
augurar, *va.* to augur.
augurio, *m.* = AGÜERO, augury; omen.
augustal, *a.* Augustan.
augusto, ta, *a.* august, magnificent.
aula, *f.* lecture hall; class room; (poet.) palace.
aulaga, *f.* furze, whin, gorse.
áulico, ca, *a.* aulic, pertaining to a royal court.
aulladero, *m.* place where wolves congregate and howl.
aullador, ra, *n.* & *a.* howler(-ing); *n.* (zool.) howling monkey, howler.
aullar, *vn.* to howl, yell, cry.
aullido, aúllo, *m.* howl (of animals).
aumentación, *f.* increase; (rhet.) climax.
aumentado, da. I. *pp.* of AUMENTAR. **II.** *a.* increased, augmented; magnified.—**a. de,** or **en,** increased by.
aumentador, ra, *n.* & *a.* enlarger(-ing), amplifier(-ing).
aumentar, *va.* & *vr.* to augment, increase, enlarge, magnify.
aumentativo, va, *a.* increasing, enlarging; (gram.) augmentative.
aumento, *m.* augmentation, increase; enlargement; access, accession; growth.—*pl.* **aumentos,** promotion, advancement.
aun, *adv.* & *conj.* even; still; AÚN.—**a. cuando,** even if, even though, notwithstanding.
aún, *adv.* yet, still; as yet.—**a. no,** not yet, not as yet.—**más a.,** still more; nay; what is more; furthermore.
aunar. I. *va.* to unite, join; to combine, assemble; to unify. **II.** *vr.* to be united or confederated; to combine.
aunque, *conj.* though, although, notwithstanding, even if.
¡aúpa! ¡upa! *interj.* up, up! (to children).—**aupar,** *va.* to help (a person) get up.
[1]**aura,** *f.* gentle breeze; (med.) aura.—**a. popular,** popularity; popular acclamation.
[2]**aura,** *f.* (Am.) (zool.) turkey buzzard.
auranciáceo, *a.* aurantiaceous, orangelike.
aurato, *m.* (chem.) aurate.
áureo, rea. I. *a.* golden, gilt, gold.—**a. número,** golden number. **II.** *m.* ancient gold coin; weight of four scruples.
aureola, auréola, *f.* aureola; lunar corona.
aureomicina, *f.* (pharm.) aureomycin.
áurico, ca, *a.* (chem.) auric.
aurícula, *f.* (anat.) auricle; (bot.) primrose.
auricular. I. *a.* auricular. **II.** *m.* (tel.) receiver; (radio) earphone.
aurífero, ra, *a.* auriferous, gold-bearing.
auriga, *m.* coachman; (astr.) Auriga, Charioteer.
aurista, *m.* aurist, ear specialist.
aurora, *f.* dawn; first appearance; a beverage made from almonds and cinnamon; roseate hue; (naut.) morning watch gun.—**a. austral,** aurora australis.—**a. boreal,** aurora borealis.
aurragado, da, *a.* badly tilled and cultivated.
auscultación, *f.* (med.) auscultation.
auscultar, *va.* (med.) to auscultate.
ausencia, *f.* absence.
ausentarse, *vr.* to absent oneself.
ausente, *a.* absent.—**ausentismo,** *m.* = ABSENTISMO, absenteeism (app. to landlords).
auspiciar, *va.* (Am.) to sponsor, promote.—**auspiciado por,** under the auspices of, sponsored by.
auspicio, *m.* presage, prediction; protection, patronage; auspices.
austeridad, *f.* austerity.
austero, ra, *a.* austere; astringent, acrid.
austral, *a.* austral.
Australia, *f.* Australia.
australiano, na, *n.* & *a.* Australian.
Austria, *f.* Austria.
austríaco, ca, *n.* & *a.* Austrian.
austrino, na, *a.* austral.
austro, *m.* south wind; notus.
austrohúngaro, ra, *n.* & *a.* Austro-Hungarian.
autarquía, *f.* autarchy.
auténtica, *f.* certificate, attestation.
autenticación, *f.* authentication.
autenticar, *va.* (*pret.* AUTENTIQUÉ; *subj.* AUTENTIQUE) to authenticate; to attest.
autenticidad, *f.* authenticity.
auténtico, ca, *a.* authentic.
autentiqué, autentique, *v. V.* AUTENTICAR.
[1]**autillo,** *m.* a particular decree of the Inquisition.
[2]**autillo,** *m.* (ornith.) barn owl.
[1]**auto,** *m.* judicial decree or sentence; writ, warrant; edict, ordinance.—*pl.* proceedings.—**a. de fe,** auto-da-fé.—**a. sacramental,** allegorical or religious play.—**en autos,** informed.
[2]**auto,** *m.* (coll.) auto (automobile).
autoabsorción, *f.* self-absorption.
autoalimentador, ra. I. *a.* self-feeding. **II.** *m.* self-feeder.
autoamortizable, *a.* self-liquidating.
autobiografía, *f.* autobiography.
autobiográfico, ca, *a.* autobiographical.
autobiógrafo, fa, *n.* autobiographer.
autobombo, *m.* self-praise.
autobote, *m.* powerboat, motorboat.

autobús, *m.* autobus.
autocamión, *m.* autotruck.
autocar, *m.* autocar, bus.
autocargador, ra, *a.* self-loading.
autocatalítico, ca, *a.* (chem.) autocatalytic.
autocentrado, da, *a.* (mech.) self-centering.
autoclave, *f.* autoclave.
autocracia, *f.* autocracy.
autócrata, *m.* & *f.* autocrat.
autocrático, ca, *a.* autocratical.
autocrítica, *f.* self-examination.
autoctonía, *f.* autochthony.
autóctono, na. I. *a.* autochthonous, aboriginal. **II.** *n.* autochthon, aboriginal.
autodeterminación, *f.* (pol., philos.) self-determination.
autodeterminado, da, *a.* self-determined.
autodidacto, ta. I. *a.* autodidactic, self-educated, self-taught. **II.** *n.* autodidact, self-taught person.
autodino, *m.* (radio) autodyne.
autódromo, *m.* autodrome.
autoendurecible, *a.* self-hardening.
autoenvenenamiento, *m.* (med.) autointoxication.
autoexcitación, *f.* (elec.) self-excitation.
autofecundación, *f.* (bot.) autogamy, self-pollination.
autofecundado, da, *a.* (bot.) self-pollinated.
autofecundante, *a.* (bot.) autogamous.
autogamia, *f.* (bot., zool.) autogamy.
autógamo, ma, *a.* (bot.) autogamous.
autogenesis, *f.* autogenesis, spontaneous generation.
autógeno, na, *a.* autogenous.
autogiro, *m.* autogiro.
autografía, *f.* autography.
autografiar, *va.* to autograph.
autográfico, ca, *a.* autographical.
autógrafo, *m.* autograph.
autohipnosis, *f.* autohypnosis.
autoinducción, *f.* (elec.) self-induction.
autoinducido, da, *a.* (elec.) self-induced.
autoinfección, *f.* autoinfection.
autointoxicación, *f.* autointoxication, autotoxemia.
autolimitación, *f.* self-limitation.
automación, *f.* automation.
automantenido, da, *a.* self-sustaining.
autómata, *m.* automaton.
automático, ca, *a.* automatic.
automatismo, *m.* (physiol., philos., psych.) automatism.
automatización, *f.* automation.
automatizar, *va.* to automate, make automatic.
automotor, ra, triz, *n.* & *a.* automotor(-tive).
automóvil, *m.* automobile.—**automovilismo,** *m.* motoring as an amusement.—**automovilista. I.** *n.* devotee of motoring as an amusement; automobilist. **II.** *a.* automotive; automobile (as *a.*).
autonomía, *f.* autonomy; home rule; self-determination.
autonómico, ca, *a.* autonomic.
autonomista, *n.* autonomist.
autónomo, ma, *a.* autonomous, self-governing.
autoómnibus, *m.* autobus.
autopista, *f.* highway, superhighway, freeway.—**a. de peaje** or **portazgo,** turnpike, toll road.
autoplastia, *f.* (surg.) autoplasty.
autoplástico, ca, *a.* autoplastic.
autopolinación, *f.* (bot.) self-pollination.
autopolinado, da, *a.* (bot.) self-pollinated.
autopropagado, da, *a.* self-propagating.
autopropulsado, da, *a.* self-propelled.
autoprotección, *f.* fail-safe (automatic system of protection in the event of failure or error in the discharge of a nuclear device).
autopsia, *f.* autopsy.
autópsido, da, *a.* having a metallic lustre.
autor, ra, *n.* author, authoress; theatrical manager; (law) principal, perpetrator or abettor of a crime.—**autores clásicos** or **príncipes,** classical authors.
autorcillo, *m. dim.* writer of no account.
autoría, *f.* business management of a theater.
autoricé, autorice, *v. V.* AUTORIZAR.
autoridad, *f.* authority; ostentation, display.
autoritario, ria. I. *a.* authoritative; overbearing. **II.** *n.* & *a.* authoritarian.
autoritarismo, *m.* authoritarianism.
autoritarista, *n.* & *a.* authoritarian.
autoritativo, va, *a.* authoritative.
autorizable, *a.* that can be authorized.
autorización, *f.* authorization.
autorizadamente, *adv.* authoritatively, with authorization.
autorizado, da. I. *pp.* of AUTORIZAR. **II.** *a.* respectable, responsible.
autorizador, ra, *n.* & *a.* authorizer(-ing).
autorizamiento, *m.* = AUTORIZACIÓN.
autorizar, *va.* (*pret.* AUTORICÉ; *subj.* AUTORICE) to authorize, empower; to attest, legalize; to prove by quotation; to approve, exalt.
autorradiación, *f.* (phys.) self-radiation.
autorregistrador, ra, *a.* (teleg.) autographic, autographical; self-recording.
autorregulado, da, *a.* self-controlled.
autorregulador, ra, *a.* self-regulating.
autorrelleno, na, *a.* self-filling.
autorretrato, *m.* self-portrait.
autosoldable, *a.* self-sealing.
autosuficiencia, *f.* self-sufficiency.
autosuficiente, *a.* self-sufficient.
autosugestión, *f.* (psych.) autosuggestion.
autoterapia, *f.* (med.) autotherapy.
autotipia, *f.* (photog.) autotypy.
autotomía, *f.* (biol.) autotomy.
autotropismo, *m.* (bot.) autotropism.
autótropo, pa, *a.* autotrophic.
autumnal, otoñal, *a.* autumnal.
auxiliador, ra, *n.* & *a.* helper(-ing); abettor (-ing), saver(-ing).
auxiliante, *a.* helping, aiding.
[1]**auxiliar,** *va.* to aid, help, assist; to attend (a dying person).
[2]**auxiliar,** *a.* auxiliary; helping; (gram.) auxiliary.
auxiliatorio, ria, *a.* (law) auxiliary.
auxilio, *m.* aid, help, assistance.—*pl.* **primeros auxilios,** first aid.
avacado, da, *a.* (of a horse) cowlike.
avadarse, *vr.* to become fordable.
avahar. I. *va.* to warm with breath or vapor. **II.** *vn.* to fume, give out vapor.
aval, *m.* (com.) indorsement.
avalancha, *f.* avalanche.
avalentado, da, *a.* bragging, boasting.
avalentonado, da, *n.* & *a.* braggart(-ing).
avalo, *m.* slight movement; earthquake.
avalorar, *va.* to estimate, value, price; to inspirit, encourage.
avaluación, valuación, *f.* valuation, appraisal.
avaluador, ra, *n.* appraiser; appreciator.
avaluar, *va.* to value, appraise, estimate.
avalúo, *m.* valuation, appraisal.
avambrazo, *m.* armlet, armor for the arm.
avance, *m.* advance; attack, assault; (com.) payment in advance; balance sheet.
avancé, avance, *v. V.* AVANZAR.
avante, *adv.* ahead, forward.—**sacar a.,** to carry out, make a success of.—**salir a.,** to succeed.
avantrén, *m.* (mil.) limbers of a gun carriage.
avanzada, *f.* (mil.) outpost, advance guard.
avanzado, da, *a.* advanced (in age; in ideas).
avanzar. I. *vn.* (*pret.* AVANCÉ; *subj.* AVANCE) to advance; (Cuba) (vulg.) to vomit; (com.) to have a balance in one's favor. **II.** *va.* to advance, push forward.
avanzo, *m.* (com.) balance sheet.
avaramente, *adv.* avariciously.
avaricia, *f.* avarice.
avariciosamente, *adv.* greedily or covetously.
avaricioso. sa, *a.* = AVARIENTO.
avariento, ta, *a.* avaricious, miserly.
avaro, ra, *a.* = AVARIENTO.

avasallar. I. *va.* to subdue, subject, enslave. II. *vr.* to become a subject, vassal.
ave, *f.* bird; fowl.—**a. acuática,** water bird.—**aves de corral,** domestic fowl.—**a. del Paraíso,** bird of Paradise.—**a. de paso,** bird of passage, migratory bird.—**a. de rapiña,** bird of prey.—**a. lira,** lyre bird.—**a. pasajera** = A. DE PASO.—**a. rapaz** = A. DE RAPIÑA.
avecé, avece, *v. V.* AVEZAR.
avecica, illa, ita, *f. dim.* little bird.
avecinar, *va.* & *vr.* to get near, approach.
avecindamiento, *m.* citizenship.
avecindar. I. *va.* to admit as a citizen. II. *vr.* to establish a domicile.
avechucho, *m.* ugly bird; ragamuffin.
avejentado, da, *a.* old in appearance.
avejentar, *va.* & *vr.* to make (or become) old looking before one's time.
avejigar, *va.* to produce pimples; to blister.
avellana, *f.* filbert, hazelnut.
avellanado, da, *a.* nut-brown.
avellanador, *m.* countersink bit, rose bit; rimer.
avellanal, [1]avellanar, *m.* hazel plantation.
[2]avellanar. I. *va.* to countersink. II. *vr.* to shrivel.
avellaneda, *f.*, **avellanedo,** *m.* = AVELLANAL.
avellanera, *f.* = AVELLANO.
avellanero, ra, *n.* dealer in filberts.
avellano, *m.* hazelnut tree; filbert tree.
avemaría, *f.* Hail Mary; rosary bead.—**al a.,** at dusk.—**en un à.,** in the twinkling of an eye.
¡Ave María! *interj.* Good Heavens!
avena, *f.* oats; (poet.) pastoral pipe.
avenáceo, a, *a.* oatlike.
[1]avenado, da, *a.* pertaining to oats.
[2]avenado, da, *a.* lunatic.
avenal, *m.* oatfield.
avenamiento, *m.* draining, drainage.
avenar, *va.* to drain.
[1]avenate, *m.* oatmeal gruel.
[2]avenate, *m.* fit of madness.
avenencia, *f.* agreement; compact; bargain; conformity; compromise.
avengo, avenga, *v. V.* AVENIR.
aveníceo, cea, *a.* oaten.
avenida, *f.* flood, freshet; avenue; gathering; agreement; approach, way of access.
avenidor, ra, *n.* mediator.
avenimiento, *m.* convention; agreement.
avenir. I. *va.* (*ind. pres.* AVENGO, *pret.* AVINE; *subj.* AVENGA) to reconcile. II. *vr.* to settle differences; to compromise; to agree.
aventador, *m.* blowing fan; (arch.) scutcher; (gas) batwing; (agr.) winnower; pitchfork.
aventadura, *f.* (vet.) wind-gall.—**a. de estopa,** (naut.) leak.
aventajado, da, *a.* advantageous; superior, excelling.
aventajar. I. *va.* to advance, raise, better; to prefer; to be above or superior to. II. *vr.* (a) to be ahead (of); to advance, rise; to excel.
aventamiento, *m.* winnowing; fanning.
aventar. I. *va.* (*ind.* AVIENTO; *subj.* AVIENTE) to fan; to winnow, expel; to push away. II. *vn.* to breathe hard. III. *vr.* to be inflated or puffed up; to escape, run away; to be tainted (meat).
aventura, *f.* adventure; contingency, chance, event; risk.
aventurado, da, *a.* risky; uncertain.
aventurar, *va.* to venture, hazard, risk.
aventureramente, *adv.* adventurously.
aventurero, ra. I. *n.* (gen. *m.*) adventurer; knight-errant; free lance. II. *a.* adventurous; undisciplined.
avergoncé, *pret.* of AVERGONZAR.
avergonzado, da, *a.* ashamed.
avergonzar (*ind. pres.* AVERGÜENZO, *pret.* AVERGONCÉ; *subj.* AVERGÜENCE), **avergoñar.** I. *va.* to shame, abash, confound. II. *vr.* to be ashamed.
[1]avería, *f.* aviary; poultry yard; AVERÍO.
[2]avería, *f.* damage; (com.) average.—**a. gruesa,** (com.) general average.
averiarse, *vr.* to be damaged.
averiguable, *a.* investigable.
averiguación, *f.* investigation, inquiry, inquest.
averiguadamente, *adv.* certainly, surely.
averiguador, ra, *n.* & *a.* investigator(-ing), inquirer(-ing).
averiguar, *va.* to inquire, investigate, ascertain, find out.
averío, *m.* flock of birds.
averno, *m.* Avernus.
averroísmo, *m.* Averroism.
averroísta, *n.* & *a.* Averroist(-ic).
averrugado, da, *a.* having warts.
averrugarse, *vr.* to develop warts.
aversión, *f.* aversion, dislike, loathing.
avestruz, *m.* (ornith.) ostrich; (fig.) blockhead.
avetado, da, *a.* veined, streaked.
avetoro, *m.* (ornith.) bittern.
avezar, *va.* (*pret.* AVECÉ; *subj.* AVECE) to accustom, inure.
aviación, *f.* aviation.
[1]aviador, *m.* provider; calking auger; one who supplies money to work mines.
[2]aviador, ra, *n.* aviator, airman; aviatrix, airwoman.
aviar. I. *va.* to equip; to lend, advance money to; to supply; to prepare. II. *vr.* to prepare; to equip oneself; to go, get on the way.
avícola, *a.* avian.
avicultor, ra, *n.* aviculturist, bird keeper.
avicultura, *f.* aviculture, bird keeping.
avidez, *f.* covetousness, avidity.
ávido, da, (de), *a.* eager, anxious (for); covetous (of).
aviejarse, *vr.* to grow old.
[1]aviento, *m.* pitchfork; BIELDO, winnowing fork.
[2]aviento, aviente, *v. V.* AVENTAR.
aviesamente, *adv.* perversely.
avieso, sa, *a.* crooked, irregular; mischievous, perverse.
avigorar, *va.* to invigorate; to revive.
avilantez, avilanteza, *f.* forwardness, boldness, audacity; insolence.
avillanado, da, *a.* rustic; clownish; mean.
avillanar. I. *va.* to debase. II. *vr.* to become mean; to degenerate.
avinagradamente, *adv.* harshly.
avinagrado, da. I. *pp.* of AVINAGRAR. II. *a.* harsh, crabbed, peevish.
avinagrar. I. *va.* to sour, acidulate. II. *vr.* to become sour.
avine, *pret.* of AVENIR.
avío, *m.* preparation, provision; money advanced.—*pl.* equipment.—**avíos de pescar,** fishing tackle.—**¡al a.!** make ready! hurry up!
[1]avión, *m.* (aer.) airplane.—**a. de caza,** pursuit plane.—**a. de cubierta,** ship plane.—**a. de chorro,** jet plane.—**a. de turismo,** air coach.—**por a.,** by air mail.
[2]avión, *m.* (ornith.) martin, martlet.
avisadamente, *adv.* prudently.
avisado, da. I. *pp.* of AVISAR. II. *a.* cautious, sagacious, clear-sighted.—**mal a.,** ill-advised.
avisador, ra, *n.*, adviser, admonisher; announcer, informer.
avisar, *va.* to inform, announce, give notice of; to warn, advise, counsel, admonish.
aviso, *m.* information, notice, announcement; advertisement; advice, warning; prudence, care, attention; (naut.) advice boat.—**a. luminoso,** illuminated (advertising) sign; flashing signal.—**andar,** or **estar, sobre a.,** to be prepared; to be warned and take precautions.
avispa, *f.* wasp.
avispado, da, *a.* lively, brisk, clever.
avispar. I. *va.* to spur, incite, rouse. II. *vr.* to fret, worry.
avispero, *m.* wasp's nest; (med.) carbuncle.
avispón, *m.* hornet.
avistar. I. *va.* to descry at a distance. II. *vr.* to have an interview.
avitelado, da, *a.* vellumlike.

avituallamiento, *m.* (mil.) supply, supplying, provisioning.
avituallar, *va.* (mil.) to victual, provide food.
avivadamente, *adv.* lively, briskly.
avivador, ra. I. *n.* enlivener; hastener. **II.** *m.* rabbet plane; fluting plane; perforated paper for raising silkworms; (arch.) quirk.
avivamiento, *m.* enlivening, quickness.
avivar. I. *va.* to quicken, enliven; to encourage; (fig.) to heat, inflame; to revive; to make (fire, light) burn more brightly; to heighten (colors); to rabbet.—**a. el ojo,** to be watchful, look sharp. **II.** *vr.* to revive; cheer up.
avizor, *m.* one who watches.
avizorador, ra, *n.* & *a.* watcher(-ing).
avizorar, *va.* to watch; to keep a sharp lookout.
avocación, *f.*, **avocamiento,** *m.* (law) removing a lawsuit to a superior court.
avocar, *va.* (*pret.* AVOQUÉ; *subj.* AVOQUE) (law) to remove to a superior court.
avoceta, *f.* (ornith.) avocet, a wading bird.
avolcanado, da, *a.* volcanic.
avoqué, avoque, *v. V.* AVOCAR.
avora, *f.* (Cuba) oil palm.
avucasta, *f.* (ornith.) widgeon, wild duck.
avugo, *m.* very small early pear.
avuguero, *m.* a kind of pear tree.
avulsión, *f.* (surg.) extirpation.
avutarda, *f.* bustard, wild turkey.
avutardado, da, *a.* bustardlike.
axial, *a.* axial.
axil, *a.* axial.
axila, *f.* armpit; (bot.) axilla.
axilar, *a.* axillar; (bot., anat.) axillary.
axinita, *f.* (min.) axinite.
axioma, *m.* axiom; maxim.
axiomático, ca, *a.* axiomatic.
axis, *m.* (anat.) axis, second vertebra; (zool.) axis deer.
axo, *m.* a woolen garment of Peruvian Indians.
axoideo, a, *a.* (anat.) axoid, axoidean.
axon, *m.* (anat.) axon, nerve cell process.
axonometría, *f.* (math.) axonometry.
ay. I. *m.* moan, lament. **II.** *interj.* oh!, ouch!, alas!—**a. de,** woe to.—**¡a. de mí!** woe is me! wretched that I am! poor me!
aya, *f.* governess, instructress.
ayate, *m.* cloth made of maguey fiber or sisal.
aye-aye, *m.* (zool.) aye-aye, kind of lemur.
ayer, *adv.* yesterday.—**a. tarde,** yesterday afternoon.—**tarde a.,** late yesterday.
¡aymé! *interj.* = ¡AY DE MÍ!
ayo, *m.* tutor or guardian; teacher.
ayocote, (Mex.) kidney bean.
ayuda, *f.* help, aid, assistance, support; (med.) injection, enema, or clyster; syringe; (naut.) preventer rope.—**a. de cámara,** valet.—**a. de parroquia,** chapel for parishioners living far from the parish church.
ayudador, ra, *n.* & *a.* helper(-ing).
ayudante, *m.* assistant; (mil.) adjutant, aide-de-camp.
ayudantía, *f.* (mil.) adjutancy.
ayudar, *va.* to aid help, assist.
ayuga, *f.* (bot.) ground-pine.
ayunador, ra, ayunante, *n.* one who fasts.
ayunar, *vn.* to fast.
ayunas.—**en a.,** fasting before breakfast; on an empty stomach; without knowledge.—**quedarse en a.,** not to understand, (fig.) be left at sea, know nothing at all (about something).
[1]**ayuno,** *m.* fast, abstinence.
[2]**ayuno, na,** *a.* fasting, abstemious; uninformed; uncomprehending.
ayunque, yunque, *m.* anvil.
ayuntamiento, *m.* municipal government; sexual intercourse.
ayustar, *va.* (naut.) to splice.
ayuste, *m.* (naut.) splicing; scarf, scarfing.
azabachado, da, *a.* jetlike, jet-colored.
azabache, *m.* jet.—*pl.* jet trinkets.
azábara, *f.* (bot.) common aloe.
azacán, *m.* water carrier.
azacaya, *f.* (prov.) water pipe.
azache, *a.* inferior (silk), from the outside of the cocoon.
azada, *f.* (agr.) hoe; spade.—**azadica, illa, ita,** *f. dim.* small hoe.
azadón, *m.* hoe.—**a. de peto,** or **de pico,** pickaxe.—**azadonada,** *f.* blow with a hoe.—**azadonar,** *va.* to hoe, dig with a hoe.—**azadonazo,** *m.* blow with a hoe.—**azadoncillo,** *m. dim.* small hoe.—**azadonero,** *m.* hoer.
azafata, *f.* lady of the queen's wardrobe; (aer.) hostess.
azafate, *m.* low, flat basket; (Am.) tray.
azafrán, *m.* (bot.) saffron; (naut.) afterpiece (of the rudder).
azafranado, da. I. *a.* saffronlike.
azafranal, *m.* saffron plantation.
azafranar, *va.* to dye with saffron.
azafranero, *m.* saffron dealer.
azagador, *m.* path for cattle.
azagaya, *f.* javelin, spear.—**azagayada,** *f.* cast of a javelin.
azahar, *m.* orange or lemon blossom.
azainadamente, *adv.* perfidiously.
azalá, *m.* Mohammedan prayer.
azalea, *f.* (bot.) azalea.
azamboa, *f.* a kind of citron.
azamboero, azamboo, *m.* zamboa tree.
azanahoriate, *m.* preserved carrot.
azanca, *f.* subterranean spring.
azanoria, zanoria, *f.* carrot.
azar, *m.* unforeseen disaster; accident; disappointment; losing card or throw at dice; impediment; hazard, chance; cushion sides of a billiard pocket.—**al a.,** at random.—**correr (ese) a.,** to take (that) chance, run the risk.
azarar. I. *va.* to confuse, stagger, bewilder. **II.** *vr.* to get bewildered; to be frustrated, go wrong.
azarbe, *m.* irrigation ditch.
azarbeta, *f. dim.* small irrigation ditch.
azarcón, *m.* minium, red lead; orange (color).
azarja, *f.* instrument for winding raw silk.
azarolla, *f.* (bot.) fruit of the hawthorn.
azarollo, *m.* (bot.) true service tree.
azarosamente, *adv.* unfortunately.
azaroso, sa, *a.* unlucky, unfortunate.
azcón, *m.* **azcona,** *f.* dart, javelin.
azenoria, *f.* = AZANORIA.
azímico, ca, *a.* azymic.
ázimo, ma, ácimo, ma, *a.* unleavened.
azimut, acimut, *m.* (astr.) azimuth.
azimutal, acimutal, *a.* pert. to the azimuth.
aznacho, aznallo, *m.* Scotch fir; a species of rest harrow.
azoado, da, *a.* nitrogenous.
azoar. I. *va.* to treat with nitrogen, make nitrogenous. **II.** *vr.* to absorb nitrogen, become nitrogenous.
azoato, *m.* nitrate.
ázoe, *m.* (chem.) nitrogen.
azofaifa, *f.* = AZUFAIFA, jujube.
azófar, *m.* brass, latten.
azogado, da, *a.* restless; trembling.
azogamiento, *m.* overlaying with quicksilver; restlessness.
azogar. I. *va.* (*pret.* AZOGUÉ; *subj.* AZOGUE) to overlay, coat with quicksilver; to silver (a mirror, etc.); to slake (lime). **II.** *vr.* to be affected by mercury vapors; to get agitated.
[1]**azogue,** *m.* quicksilver; ship carrying quicksilver.
[2]**azogue,** *m.* market place.—**azoguejo,** *m.* small market place.
azoguería, *f.* amalgamation works.
azoguero, *m.* dealer in quicksilver; amalgamator.
[1]**azoico, ca,** *a.* (chem.) nitric.
[2]**azoico, ca,** *a.* (geol.) azoic, of time before life appeared.
azolar, *va.* (*ind.* AZUELO; *subj.* AZUELE) to dress or hew (timber).
azolvar, *va.* to obstruct.—**azolve,** *m.* (Mex.) obstruction.
azor, *m.* (ornith.) goshawk.

azoramiento, *m.* confusion.
azorar. I. *va.* to terrify; to confound; to excite; to prompt. **II.** *vr.* to become restless.
azorramiento, *m.* heaviness of the head.
azorrarse, *vr.* to be drowsy from heaviness.
azotacalles, *n.* street lounger, idler.
azotado. I. *pp.* of AZOTAR. **II.** *a.* variegated. **III.** *n.* criminal publicly whipped; penitent.
azotador, ra, *n.* & *a.* whipper(-ing).
azotaina, *f.* drubbing, flogging, spanking.
azotalengua, *f.* goose grass.
azotamiento, *m.* whipping, flogging.
azotar, *va.* to whip, horsewhip; to flagellate, strike repeatedly, scourge.
azotazo, *m. aug.* severe lashing or spanking.
azote, *m.* whip; lashing; spanking; scourge.—**el a. de Dios,** the Scourge of God (Attila).
azotea, *f.* flat roof.
azotera, *f.* multithonged whip; end of a long whip.
azotina, *f.* = AZOTAINA.
azteca, *n.* & *a.* Aztec.
azúcar, *m.* sugar.—**a. blanco,** refined sugar (app. to the highest quality).—**a. cande,** or **candi,** rock candy.—**a. de flor** = A. BLANCO.—**a. de leche,** sugar of milk.—**a. de pilón,** loaf sugar.—**a. de plomo,** calcined sugar of lead.—**a. de Saturno,** sal Saturni.—**a. moscobado,** muscovado.—**a. moreno,** brown sugar.—**a. negro,** or **prieto,** coarse brown sugar.—**a. quebrado,** brown sugar.—**a. refino** = A. BLANCO.—**a. terciado,** brown sugar.—**a. y canela,** sorrel gray.
azucarado, da. I. *pp.* of AZUCARAR. **II.** *a.* sugary; affable, pleasing. **III.** *m.* cosmetic.
azucarar, *va.* to sugar; to sweeten; to soften; to coat or ice with sugar.
azucarera, *f.* sugar bowl; sugar refinery.
azucarería, *f.* retail sugar shop.
azucarero. I. *m.* sugar master; sugar bowl; sugar producer or dealer; confectioner. **II.** *a.* pertaining to sugar; sugar (as *a.*).
azucarillo, *m.* fondant.
azucé, azuce, *v. V.* AZUZAR.
azucena, *f.* white lily.
azuche, *m.* pile shoe, pile ferrule.
azud, azuda, *f.* dam with a sluice; irrigation water wheel.
azuela, *f.* adze.—**a. curva,** hollow adze.—**a. de construcción,** shipwright's adze.
azuelo, azuele, *v. V.* AZOLAR.
azufaifa, *f.* jujube or jujubes.
azufaifo, azufeifo, *m.* jujube tree.
azufrado, da. I. *pp.* of AZUFRAR. **II.** *a.* fumigated with sulphur; sulphureous; sulphur-hued.
azufrador, *m.* machine for drying linen; instrument for sulphuring vines.
azufral, *m.* = AZUFRERA.
azufrar, *va.* to bleach; to sulphur.
azufre, *m.* sulphur; brimstone.—**azufrera,** *f.* sulphur mine.—**azufrón,** *m.* pyrites powder.—**azufroso, sa,** *a.* sulphureous.
azul, *n.* & *a.* blue.—**a. celeste,** sky-blue.—**a. de mar,** or **marino,** navy blue.—**a. de Prusia,** Prussian blue.—**a. de ultramar,** or **ultramarino,** ultramarine.—**a. turquí,** indigo.
azulado, da, *a.* azure, bluish.
azulaque, zulaque, *m.* (hydraul.) packing stuff.
azular, *va.* to dye or color blue.
azulear, *vn.* to have a bluish cast.
azulejo, *m.* little bluebird; glazed tile; (bot.) blue-bottle.
azulenco, ca, *a.* = AZULADO.
azulete, *m.* blue lining.
azulino, na, *a.* bluish.
azumar, *va.* to dye (the hair).
azumbrado, da, *a.* measured by AZUMBRES; (coll.) tipsy.
azumbre, *f.* a liquid measure (about 2 liters).
azur, *a.* (her.) azure.
azurina, *f.* (chem.) azurine.
azurita, *f.* (min.) azurite.
azuzar, *va.* (*pret.* AZUCÉ; *subj.* AZUCE) to urge, set (dogs) on; to incite.
azuzón, na, *n.* gossiping trouble maker.

B

B, b, *f.* b, second letter of the Spanish alphabet.
baalita, *n.* & *a.* Baalite.
baba, *f.* drivel, slaver, spittle; viscous substance.—**caérsela a uno la b., echar la b.,** to be a silly; to be delighted, tickled to death.
babada, *f.* = BABILLA.
babadero, babador, *m.* bib, chin cloth.
babaza, *f.* slime; BABOSA, slug.
babazorro, *m.* clown, ill-bred man.
babear, *vn.* to drivel; slaver; to court, woo with excessive demonstrations.
Babel, *f.* Babel, bedlam.
babeo, *m.* driveling, slavering.
babera, *f.* beaver of a helmet; bib.
babero, *m.* = BABADERO.
baberol, *m.* beaver of a helmet.
Babia, *f.*—**estar en B.,** to be absent-minded, or absorbed in other thoughts.
babieca, *m.* ignorant, stupid fellow; idiot.
Babilonia, *f.* crowd, uproar, confusion, bedlam.
babilónico, ca, *or* **onio, nia,** *a.* Babylonian.
babilla, *f.* muscles about the flank of a horse.
babirusa, *f.* (zool.) babiroussa, a wild hog.
babismo, *m.* Babism.
bable, *m.* Asturian dialect.
babor, *m.* (naut.) port, larboard.—**a b. todo,** hard a-port.—**de b. a estribor,** athwart ship.
babosa, *f.* (zool.), slug; young onion.
babosear, *va.* to drivel, slaver.
babosilla, *f. dim.* small slug.
baboso, sa, *a.* driveling, slavering, silly; spoony, over-affectionate.
babucha, *f.* slipper, babouche.
baca, *f.* top of a stagecoach; leather cover for a stagecoach.
bacalao, *or* **bacallao,** *m.* (ichth.) codfish.
bacanal. I. *a.* bacchanalian. **II.** *f.* bacchanal.
bacanales, *f. pl.* Bacchanalia.
bacante, *f.* bacchante.
bácara, bácaris, *f.* (bot.) great fleabane.
bacará, *m.* baccara(t.
bacelar, *m.* arbor with grapevines.
bacera, *f.* (vet.) swelling of the belly.
baceta, *f.* stock (card playing).
bacía, *f.* metal basin, washpot; shaving dish.
báciga, *f.* game played with three cards.
bacilar, *a.* (min.) of coarse fiber; (biol.) bacillar.
bacilo, *m.* bacillus.
bacillar, *m.* new vineyard.
bacín, *m.* high chamber pot; despicable man.
bacinada, *f.* filth thrown from a close-stool; despicable action.
bacinero, ra, *n.* person who carries about the poor box in a church.
bacineta, *f.* small poor box; pan (of a gun-lock).
bacinete, *m.* headpiece worn by warriors; cuirassier; (anat.) pelvis.
bacinica, *f.* small chamber pot.
bacinilla, *f.* chamber pot; alms basin.
baconiano, na, *a.* Baconian.
baconista, *n.* & *a.* Baconian.
bacteria, *f.* bacterium.—**bacteriano, na,** *a.* bacterial.
bactericida. I. *a.* bactericidal. II. *f.* bactericide.
bactérico, ca, *a.* bacterial.
bacteriófago, *m.* bacteriophage.
bacteriólisis, *f.* bacteriolysis.
bacteriología, *f.* bacteriology.
bacteriológico, ca, *a.* bacteriological.
bacteriólogo, ga, *n.* bacteriologist.
bacterioscopia, *f.* bacterioscopy.
bacteriostasis, *f.* bacteriostasis.
bacteriostático, ca, *a.* bacteriostatic.
bacterioterapia, *f.* bacteriotherapy.
bactriano, na, *n.* & *a.* Bactrian.
báculo, *m.* walking stick, staff; support, relief, aid.—**b. pastoral,** bishop's crosier.

bache, *m.* deep hole, rut; sweating place for sheep.
[1]**bachiller, ra,** *n.* bachelor (degree).
[2]**bachiller, ra,** *n.* babbler, prater.
bachilleramiento, *m.* conferring or obtaining the degree of bachelor.
bachillerar. I. *va.* to confer the degree of bachelor on. **II.** *vr.* to be graduated as a bachelor.
bachillerato, *m.* baccalaureate, B. A. degree.
bachillerear, *vn.* to babble, prattle.
bachillería, *f.* babble, prattle.
badajada, *f.* stroke of a clapper; idle talk.
badajazo, *m. aug.* large clapper.
badajear, *vn.* to talk nonsense.
badajo, *m.* clapper of a bell; idle talker.
[1]**badal,** *m.* muzzle (for dogs, etc.); (surg.) mouth opener.
[2]**badal,** *m.* shoulder and ribs of butcher's meat.
badán, *m.* trunk of a body.
badana, *f.* dressed sheepskin.
badazas, *f. pl.* (naut.) keys of the bonnets.
badea, *f.* watermelon; insipid muskmelon; dull, insipid fellow.
badén, *m.* channel made by rainfall; catchwater conduit.
badiana, *f.* (bot.) Indian aniseed, badian.
badil, *m.,* **badila,** *f.* fire shovel.
badomía, *f.* nonsense, absurdity.
badulacada, *f.* (Peru) foolishness.
badulaque, *m.* cosmetic; ragout of stewed livers; unreliable or good-for-nothing person.
[1]**baga,** *f.* rope to tie packs on the back of animals.
[2]**baga,** *f.* little head of flax.
bagaje, *m.* beast of burden; baggage of an army; horse appropriated by an army, or given to an officer.—**bagajero,** *m.* driver of military baggage.
bagar, *vn.* (of flax) to yield the seed.
bagasa, *f.* prostitute, harlot.
bagatela, *f.* bagatelle, trifle.
bagazo, *m.* bagasse; oil cake.
bagre, *m.* a Sp. Am. fish; (Am.) ugly low woman, baggage; (Am.) smart, alert person.
baguío, *m.* (P. I.) hurricane.
¡bah! *interj.* bah!
baharí, *m.* sparrow hawk.
bahía, *f.* bay, harbor.
bahorrina, *f.* slops; rabble.
bahuno, na, bajuno, na, *a.* base, vile.
baila, *f.* (ichth.) sea trout.
bailable. I. *a.* (of music) composed for dancing.—**té b.,** tea with dancing, tea dance. **II.** *m.* ballet.
bailadero, *m.* public dancing place.
bailador, ra, *n.* dancer.
bailar, *vn.* to dance, spin.—**b. como un trompo,** (S. A.) to dance well, be light on one's feet.
bailarín, na, *n.* dancer; caperer.
[1]**baile,** *m.* dance, ballet; ball, rout.—**b. casero,** family, informal dance.—**b. de figuras,** square dance.—**b. de máscaras,** masquerade.—**b. de San Vito,** St. Vitus' dance.—**b. de trajes,** fancy-dress ball.—**b. serio,** formal dance.
[2]**baile,** *m.* bailiff.
bailete, *m.* short ballet.
bailía, *f.,* **bailiazgo,** *m.* bailiwick.
bailiaje, *m.* commandery in the order of Malta.
bailío, *m.* knight commander of Malta.
bailotear, *vn.* (coll.) to dance frequently; to dance clumsily.—**bailoteo,** *m.* ungraceful dancing.
baivel, *m.* bevel with a curved leg.
bajá, *m.* pasha, bashaw.
baja, *f.* fall in price; (mil.) casualty; vacancy.—**dar de b.,** to drop (person from a list, etc.)—**darse de b.,** to drop out (as a member, etc.).
bajada, *f.* descent; slope; inclination of an arch.—**b. de aguas,** rainwater pipe, leader.
bajalato, *m.* office of a pasha.
bajamar, *f* low water, low tide.
bajamente, *adv.* basely, meanly.
bajar. I. *vn.* to descend, come or go down; to fall; to drop, lessen, diminish.—**b. de,** to be less than. **II.** *va.* to lower, reduce; to bring or take down, let down; to humble. **III.** *vr.* to bend over, stoop, to crouch, grovel; to alight, get out (of a vehicle); to get down, dismount.
bajel, *m.* (naut.) ship, boat, vessel.
bajelero, *m.* owner or master of a vessel.
bajero, ra, *a.* lower, under (as, *sábana bajera,* under sheet).
bajete, *m. dim.* (contempt.) short person; (mus.) baritone; (mus.) counterpoint exercise.
bajeza, *f.* meanness; lowliness; low action.
bajial, *m.* marsh.
bajío, *m.* shoal, sand bank, flat; obstacle.
bajista, *m.* (com.) bear (in stocks); (mus.) (Arg.) bassoon player.
bajo, ja. I. *a.* low, shallow; short; abject, despicable; common, humble; (of color) dull, faint; (of sound) low, soft, coarse, vulgar; downcast.—**b. relieve,** bas-relief.—**por lo b.,** on the sly, unobservedly; in an undertone. **II. bajo,** *adv.* underneath, below. **III.** *prep.* under.—**b. mano,** underhandedly, secretly. **IV.** *m.* (mus.) bass (voice, score, singer, player, instrument); ground floor; shoal; sand bank.—*pl.* underskirts; hoofs (of a horse).
bajoca, *f.* string bean; dead silkworm.
bajón, *m.* (mus.) bassoon; bassoon player.
bajoncillo, *m.* treble bassoon.
bajonista, *m.* bassoon player.
bajorrelieve, bajo relieve, *m.* bas-relief.
bajuno, na, *a.* vile, low, contemptible.
bala, *f.* ball, bullet, shot; bale; wax ball; printer's inking ball.—**b. de cadena,** or **encadenada,** chain shot.—**b. enramada,** bar shot.—**b. fría,** spent bullet.—**b. perdida,** stray bullet.—**b. rasa,** solid cannonball.—**b. roja,** red-hot incendiary ball.
balada, balata, *f.* ballad.
baladí, *a.* frivolous, trivial.
balador, ra, *n.* bleating animal.
baladrar, *vn.* to cry out, shout.
baladre, *m.* (bot.) rosebay.
baladrero, ra, *n.* shouter.
baladro, *m.* shout, outcry.
baladrón, na, *n.* boaster, bragger, bully.
baladronada, *f.* boast, bravado; rodomontade.
baladronear, *vn.* to boast, brag, bully.
balagar, *m.* haystack, hayrick.
bálago, *m.* grain stalk, straw; soap ball.—**balaguero,** *m.* rick of straw.
balaj, *m.* balas, spinel ruby.
balance, *m.* oscillation, rolling, rocking, swinging; (fig.) vacillation; (com.) balancing; balance; balance sheet; (Cuba) rocking chair; (aer.) rolling.
balancear. I. *va.* to balance; to put into equilibrium. **II.** *vn.* & *vr.* to roll, rock; to hesitate, waver.
balanceo, *m.* rocking, rolling; wobbling.
balancero, *m.* = BALANZARIO.
balancín, *m.* splinter bar, swing bar; whippletree, singletree, whiffletree; (mech.) walking beam, balancebeam; oscillating beam (as that of a beam engine); minting mill; tightrope-walker's pole.—**balancines,** (naut.) lifts.—**balancines de la brújula,** (naut.) brass rings of the compass.
balandra, *f.* (naut.) sloop.
balandrán, *m.* cassock.
balandro, *m.* (Cuba) fishing smack.
bálano, *m.* (anat.) balanus.
balante, *a.* (poet.) bleating.
balanza, *f.* scales; balance; tightrope-walker's pole; comparative estimate, judgment.—**b. de comercio,** balance of trade.—**en b.,** undecided; in danger, at stake.—**poner a uno en b.,** to cause one to doubt or hesitate.
balanzario, *m.* weighmaster (in the mint).
balanzón, *m.* (jewel.) cleaning pan.
balar, *vn.* to bleat.—**b. por,** to crave.
balastar, *va.* (Ry.) to ballast.
balasto, *m.* (Ry.) ballast.
balata, *f.* dancing song; ballad; (bot.) balata.
[1]**balate,** *m.* terrace; border of a trench.

[2]**balate,** *m.* (zool.) snail.
balausta, -tra, *f.* varieties of pomegranate.
balaustrada, *f.* balustrade.
balaustrado, da, balaustral, *a.* balustered.
balaústre, *m.* baluster.
balay, *m.* wicker basket.
balazo, *m.* shot; bullet wound.
balbucear, *vn.* to hesitate in speech, stammer.
balbucencia, *f.* stammering.
balbuceo, *m.* babble.
balbucir, *vn.* (*defect.*) = BALBUCEAR.
balcánico, ca, *n.* & *a.* Balkan.
balcón, *m.* balcony; porch.—**balconaje,** *m.*, range of balconies.—**balconcillo,** *m. dim.* small balcony.—**balconería,** *f.* = BALCONAJE.
balda, *f.* trifle.
baldadura, *f.*, **baldamiento,** *m.* a physical disability.
baldaquín, baldaquino, *m.* canopy, dais.
baldar, *va.* to cripple; (cards) to trump; obstruct.
[1]**balde,** *m.* bucket, pail.
[2]**balde.—de b.,** gratis; free; idle; in vain.—**en b.,** in vain, with no result.
baldear, *vn.* (naut.) to wash (the deck).
baldeo, *m.* (naut.) washing the decks.
baldés, *m.* soft dressed skin for gloves, etc.
baldíamente, *adv.* vainly, in vain; idly.
baldío, día, *a.* untilled, uncultivated; public (lands); idle, lazy; vagabond.—*m. pl.* public lands; common.
baldón, *m.* affront, insult.
baldonar, baldonear, *va.* to insult, affront.
[1]**baldosa,** *f.* ancient string instrument.
[2]**baldosa,** *f.* paving tile; flat paving stone, flag.—**baldosado,** *m.* tile pavement.—**baldosín,** *m.* small square tile; paving tile.
balduque, *m.* narrow red tape (used in offices to tie up packages of business papers).
balear, *va.* (Am.) to shoot (wound or kill).
baleárico, ca; balear̈io, ia, *a.* Balearic.
baleo, *m.* round mat.
balería, *f.* (artil.) pile of balls or shot.
balero, *m.* ball mold.
baleta, *f. dim.* small bale of goods.
balido, *m.* bleating, bleat.
balín, *m.* small bullet.—*pl.* mold shot, buckshot.
balista, *f.* ballista.
balístico, ca. I. *a.* ballistic. **II.** *f.* ballistics.
balitadera, *f.* call, a reed pipe for calling fawns.
baliza, *f.* buoy.
balneario, ria. I. *a.* pertaining to baths. **II.** *m.* bathing resort; watering place.
balneoterapia, *f.* (med.) balneotherapy.
balompié, *m.* football; soccer.
balón, *m.* football; game of football; large bale; bale of paper (24 reams); (auto) balloon tire.
baloncesto, *m.* basketball. Also BASKETBOL.
balota, *f.* ballot.
balotada. *f.* balotade, leap of a horse.
balotaje, *m.* (Am.) ballot, balloting.
balotar, *vn.* to ballot.
[1]**balsa,** *f.* pool; pond; half a butt of wine.
[2]**balsa,** *f.* (naut.) raft.
balsadera, *f.*, **balsadero,** *m.* ferry.
balsamera, *f.* flask for balsam.
balsamerita, *f.* small flask for balsam.
balsámico, ca, *a.* balsamic, balmy.
balsamífero, ra, *a.* balsamiferous.
balsamina, *f.* (bot.) balsam apple.
balsamita mayor, (bot.) = ATANASIA, costmary.—**b. menor,** (bot.) maudlin, tansy.
bálsamo, *m.* balsam, balm; (med. & fig.) balm.—**b. de copaiba,** balsam of copaiba.—**b. de calaba,** calaba balsam.—**b. de Judea,** or **de la Meca,** balsam of Mecca.—**b. del Canadá,** balsam of fir, Canada balsam.—**b. del Perú,** balsam of Peru.—**b. de María** = B. DE CALABA.—**b. de Tolú,** balsam of Tolu.
balsar, *m.* marshy ground with brambles.
balsear, *va.* to ferry on rafts.
balsero, ra, *n.* ferryman(-woman).
balso, *m.* rope with loops for raising men or goods on board ship; sling; a S.A. tree of very light wood used for rafts, balsa, corkwood.
balsopeto, *m.* large pouch carried near the breast; (fig. coll.) bosom.
bálteo, *m.* officer's belt.
báltico, ca, *a.* Baltic.
baluarte, *m.* bastion; bulwark; defense.
balumba, *f.* bundle of many miscellaneous things.
balumbo, balume, *m.* bulky thing.
ballena, *f.* whale; train oil; whalebone; (**B-,** astr.) Whale Cetus.—**b. blanca,** (zool.) beluga.
ballenato, *m.* young whale.
ballener, *m.* an ancient vessel.
ballenera, *f.* whaleboat.
ballenero, ra. I. *a.* whaling, whale (as *a.*). **II.** *n.* whaler, whale fisherman.
ballesta, *f.* crossbow; ballista; spring (of a carriage).—**ballestada,** *f.* shot from a crossbow.
ballestazo, *m.* blow with a crossbow.
ballestear, *va.* to shoot with a crossbow.
ballestera, *f.* loopholes for crossbows.
ballestería, *f.* archery; collection of crossbows or bowmen; armory for crossbows.
ballestero, *m.* archer, crossbowman; crossbow maker; king's armorer or porter; mace bearer.
ballestilla, *f.* crossbow; small whiffletree; fleam; cross-staff; (naut.) forestaff.
ballestrinque, *m.* (naut.) clove hitch.
ballico, *m.* (bot.) rye grass.
ballueca, *f.* wild oats.
bambalear, *vn.* = BAMBOLEAR.
bambalina, *f.* fly in theatrical scenery.
bambarria, *m.* lucky shot at billiards, fluke; fool, idiot.
bambochada, *f.* painting representing a spree.
bamboche, *n.* (coll.) plump, red-faced person.
bambolear, *vn.* & *vr.* to swing, sway.
bamboleo, *m.* swinging, swaying.
bambolla, *f.* (coll.) boast, humbug, sham.
bamboneo, *m.* = BAMBOLEO.
bambú, bambuc, *m.* bamboo.
bambuco, *m.* a Colombian popular air.
banana, *f.*, **banano,** *m.* banana. Also CAMBUR.
bananero, ra. I. *a.* of or pertaining to bananas. **II.** *m.* (bot.) banana tree.
bañas, *f. pl.* (Mex.) matrimonial banns.
banasta, *f.* large basket.—**banastero,** *m.* basket maker or dealer.—**banasto,** *m.* large round basket.
banca, *f.* bench; stand; washing box; Philippine canoe; name of a card game; (com.) banking.
bancada, *f.* bench; portion of masonry.
bancal, *m.* oblong orchard or garden plot; terrace; bench cover.
bancario, ria, *a.* banking; financial.
bancarrota, *f.* bankruptcy; failure.—**hacer b.,** (com.) to fail.
bancaza, *f.* (mech.) bedplate.
banco, *m.* form, bench; settee; pew; (mech.) bed, table, horse; planing bench; bench for rowers; cheeks (of the bit); pedestal; school of fish, shoal; (com.) bank.—**b. de ahorros,** savings bank.—**b. de emisión,** bank of issue.—**b. de hielo,** iceberg.—**b. de liquidación,** clearing-house.—**b. del tundidor,** shearing board.—**b. de nieve,** snowbank.
banda, *f.* sash; scarf; ribbon; band, strip (of material); band, gang; party; crew; brass band; covey; bank, border, edge; side of a ship; felloe (of wheel); cushion (of a billiard table).
bandada, *f.* covey; flock of birds.
bandaje, *m.* (Gal.) (auto) tire.
bandarria, *f.* (naut.) iron maul.
banda sonora, *f.* (cine.) sound track.
bandazo, *m.* (naut.) (of ship) violent roll to side.
bandeado, da, *a.* striped.
[1]**bandear. I.** *va.* to conduct. **II.** *vn.* to band.
[2]**bandear,** *vr.* to shift for oneself.
bandeja, *f.* tray.
bandera, *f.* flag, banner; colors; infantry.—**b.**

blanca, **b. de paz,** white flag, flag of truce.—**b. de popa,** (naut.) ensign.—**b. de proa,** (naut.) jack.—**a,** or **con, banderas desplegadas,** with flying colors; openly, in broad daylight (fig.); freely.—**bandereta,** *f. dim.* banneret, small flag.—*pl.* (mil.) camp colors.—**bandería,** *f.* band, faction.—**banderica, illa,** *dim.* banneret, small flag.

banderilla, *f.* banderilla, a small dart with a bannerol for baiting bulls.—**poner a uno una b.,** to taunt or provoke one.—**banderillear,** *va.* to thrust banderillas in (a bull).—**banderillero,** *m.* banderillero, banderilla man.

banderín, *m.* camp colors; flag; railway signal; recruiting post.

banderizar, *va.* to band together.

banderizo, za, *a.* partisan, party (as *a.*); fiery, agitating, strenuous.

banderola, *f.* bannerol; camp colors; streamer, pennant; signal flag.

bandidaje, *m.* brigandage, banditry; gang, ring of bandits.

bandido, da. I. *a.* fugitive from justice. **II.** *m.* bandit.

bandín, *m.* (naut.) seat in a row galley.

[1]**bando,** *m.* proclamation, edict.

[2]**bando,** *m.* faction, party.

bandola, *f.* mandolin; (naut.) jury mast.

[1]**bandolera,** *f.* bandoleer, shoulder belt.

[2]**bandolera,** *f.* bandit's wife; woman bandit.

bandolerismo, *m.* banditry, brigandage.

bandolero, *m.* highwayman, robber.

bandolín, *m.* = BANDOLA.

bandolina, *f.* bandoline.

bandolón, *m.* mandola, large mandolin.

bandullo, *m.* (vulg.) belly; the bowels.

bandurria, *f.* bandore, musical instrument like a guitar.

baniano, *m.* (bot.) banian.

banjo, *m.* banjo.

bánova, *f.* bedquilt, bedcover.

banquero, ra, *n.* (com. & gambling games) banker.

banqueta, *f.* three-legged stool; footstool; (mil.) banquette or footbank; (Mex.) sidewalk.—**b. de calafate,** (naut.) calking stool.—**b. de cureña,** (artil.) gun, carriage bed.

banquete, *m.* banquet.

banquetear, *vn.* to banquet, feast.

banquillo, *m. dim.* little stool; prisoner's or defendant's seat; (Am.) scaffold; gallows.

banzo, *m.* cheek of an embroidering frame.

bañadera, *f.* (Am.) bathtub.

bañadero, *m.* puddle; bathing place (for animals).

bañado, *m.* BACÍN, chamber pot.

bañador, ra, *n.* one who bathes; (*m.*) dipping tub for candle makers.

bañar. I. *va.* to bathe, wash, lave; to water; to dip; to coat, apply a coating or layer to. **II.** *vr.* to take a bath.

bañera, *f.* bathtub.

bañero, ra, *n.* bathhouse owner or keeper.

bañil, *m.* pool in which cattle bathe.

bañista, *m.* bather.

baño, *m.* bath; bathing; bathing place; bathtub; bathroom; foot tub; coat, coating (of paint, etc.); (chem.) bath.—**b. de María,** double boiler.—**b. de vapor,** (med.) vapor bath.—**b. revelador,** (photog.) developing bath.—*pl.* bathhouse; spa; watering place.

bao, *m.* (naut.) beam, cross timber.

baobab, *m.* (bot.) baobab.

baptisterio, bautisterio, *m.* baptistery.

baque, *m.* blow in falling; thud.

baquelita, *f.* bakelite.

baqueta, *f.* ramrod; switch used in breaking in young horses.—*pl.* drumsticks; (punishment) gantlet.—**a b., a la b.,** harshly, despotically, without consideration.

baquetazo, *m.* blow with a ramrod.

baqueteado, da. I. *pp.* of BAQUETEAR. **II.** *a.* inured (to hard work).

baquetear, *va.* to inflict the punishment of the gantlet on; to vex.

baquía, *f.* familiarity with a region (app. esp. to roads, forests, etc.); skill.

baquiano, na. I. *n.* guide. **II.** *a.* skilful, expert.

báquico, ca, *a.* Bacchic.

baquio, *m.* (poet.) a metrical foot.

bar, *m.* bar (for drinks).

baraja, *f.* pack of cards; game of cards.

barajadura, *f.* shuffling of cards; dispute.

barajar, *va.* to shuffle (the cards); to jumble together; to entangle; to stop; to trick out of.

baranda, *f.* railing; bannister; cushion (of a billiard table).—**barandado, barandaje,** *m.* balustrade.—**barandal,** *m.* upper and under piece of a balustrade; railing.—**barandilla,** *f. dim.* balustrade, railing.

barangay, *m.* (P. I.) a kind of rowboat; a native village.

barata, *f.* barter; reduction sale; bargain.

baratador, ra, *n.* barterer.

baratar, *va.* to barter, traffic.

baratear, *va.* to sell cheap; to sell under price.

baratería, *f.* barratry, fraud, deception.

baratero, ra, *n.* one who exacts money from winning gamblers; one who sells cheap; haggler.

baratijas, *f. pl.* trifles, trinkets, notions.

baratillero, ra, *n.* peddler; seller of second-hand goods or articles.

baratillo, *m.* second-hand shop; bargain counter; heap of trifling articles.

barato, ta. I. *a.* cheap.—**dar de b.,** to grant for the sake of argument.—**de b.,** gratis.—**echar,** or **meter, a b.,** to mix up or confuse things by too much fuss.—**lo b. es,** or **siempre es, caro,** cheap things are always dear. **II.** *m.* reduction sale; bargain sale; money given by winning gamblers to the bystanders. **III. barato,** *adv.* cheaply.

báratro, *m.* (poet.) hell; abyss.

baratura, *f.* cheapness.

baraúnda, *f.* noise, hurly-burly, confusion.

barba, *f.* chin; beard; whiskers; wattle; first swarm of bees; top of beehive; player who acts old men's parts.—*pl.* head of a comet; slender roots; fibers; rough edges of paper; (ornith.) vanes of a quill.—**b. a b.,** face to face.—**b. cabruna,** (bot.) yellow goat's beard.—**b. cerrada,** heavy, thick beard.—**b. de Aarón,** (bot.) Aaron's beard.—**b. de ballena,** whalebone.—**en sus barbas,** to his face.—**por b.,** a head, apiece.—**tener pocas barbas,** to be young or inexperienced.

barbacana, *f.* (mil.) barbican, outwork of fortified place; churchyard wall.

barbacoa, *f.* (Am.) barbecue; (Am.) stretcher; elevated board bed supported on sticks; rough sleeping or storage loft or attic, usually of boards or canes; trellis; greenwood broiler used by Indians, or the meat thus broiled.

barbada, *f.* jaw of a horse; bridle curb; dab, small flat fish.

barbado, da. I. *a.* bearded; barbed, barbated. **II.** *m.* full-grown man; vine or tree transplanted; shoot; sucker.

barbaja, *f.* (bot.) cut-leaved viper's grass.—*pl.* (agr.) first roots.

barbar, *vn.* to grow a beard; to rear bees; (of plants) to strike root.

bárbaramente, *adv.* barbarously, savagely; atrociously; rudely, coarsely.

barbáricamente, *adv.* like barbarians.

barbaricé, barbarice, *v. V.* BARBARIZAR.

barbárico, ca, *a.* barbarous, barbarian.

barbaridad, *f.* barbarity, barbarous deed, atrocity; cruelty; rashness; rudeness; (Am.) excess (in anything); wild statement or action; nonsense; blunder.

barbarie, *f.* fierceness; cruelty; barbarity; lack of culture, rusticity.

barbarismo, *m.* barbarism; barbarousness; barbarous deed; barbarians.

barbarizar. I. *va.* (*pret.* BARBARICÉ; *subj.* BARBARICE) to barbarize. II. *vn.* to make wild statements.
bárbaro, ra. I. *a.* barbarous; barbarian; rude, crude, unpolished. II. *n.* barbarian.
barbarote, *m. aug.* great barbarian.
barbear, *va.* to reach with the chin; to be almost as high as; to fell (cattle) by twisting the neck; to shave.
barbechar, *va.* to plough for seeding; to fallow.
barbechera, *f.* series of plowings; fallowing season; plowing.
barbecho, *m.* fallow.
barbera, *f.* barber's wife.
barbería, *f.* barber's shop or trade.
barberil, *a.* pertaining to a barber; barberlike.
barbero, *m.* barber; (ichth.) mutton fish.
barbeta, *f.* (naut.) racking, gasket; (artil.) barbette.—**a b.,** en barbette.
barbibermejo, ja, *a.* red-bearded.
barbiblanco, ca, *a.* gray- or white-bearded.
barbicacho, *m.* ribbon tied under the chin.
barbicano, na, *a.* gray-bearded.
barbiespeso, sa, *a.* having a thick beard.
barbihecho, cha, *a.* fresh-shaved.
barbilampiño, ña, *a.* smooth-faced, beardless.
barbilindo, barbilucio, *a.* small, good-looking (*rather*, pretty) and effeminate; dandy.
barbilla, *f.* point of the chin; (carp.) rabbet; (vet.) tumor under the tongue.
barbillera, *f.* tuft of tow; chin bandage.
barbinegro, gra, *a.* black-bearded.
barbiponiente, *a.* beginning to grow a beard; apprenticed.
barbiquejo, *m.* bonnet string; guard ribbon for a hat; curb chain; (naut.) bobstay.
barbirrubio, bia, *a.* blond-bearded.
barbirrucio, cia, *a.* having a black beard sprinkled with gray.
barbitaheño, ña, *a.* having a red beard.
barbital, *m.* (pharm.) barbital.
barbiteñido, da, *a.* having a dyed beard.
barbiturato, *m.* (chem.) barbiturate.
barbo, *m.* (ichth.) barbel, a river fish.
barbón, *m.* long-bearded man; Carthusian lay brother; buck.
barboquejo, *m.* chin strap; hat guard.
barbotar, *vn.* to mumble, mutter.
barbote, *m.* beaver of a helmet.
barbudo, da. I. *a.* having a long beard. II. *m.* vine transplanted with the roots.
barbulla, *f.* loud prattling noise.
barbullar, *vn.* to talk loud and fast.
barbullón, na, *a.* & *n.* loud, fast prattler.
barca, *f.* (naut.) boat, barge, bark.—**b. chata, b. de pasaje,** ferryboat.—**barcada,** *f.* passage in a ferryboat; boatload.—**barcaje,** *m.* ferriage. —**barcal,** *m.* wooden vessel.
barcarola, *f.* barcarole.
barcaza, *f.* barge, lighter; privilege of loading and unloading.
barcelonés, sa, *a.* from, or of, Barcelona.
barceno, na, *a.* = BARCINO.
barceo, *m.* dry bass or sedge for mats, ropes, etc.
barcia, *f.* chaff (from grain).
barcina, *f.* (Am.) grass net; large bundle of straw.
barcinar, *va.* (Am.) to load with sheaves.
barcino, na, *a.* (of animals) red-brown and white.
barco, *m.* boat, barge, vessel, ship; bottom.
barcolongo, barcoluengo, *m.* oblong boat with a round bow.
barcón, barcote, *m. aug.* large boat.
barchilón, *m.* (Am.) hospital nurse.
barda, *f.* bard, horse armor; thatch; reed.
bardado, da, *a.* barded, caparisoned.
bardaguera, *f.* (bot.) willow.
bardal, *m.* thatched wall or fence.
bardana, *f.* burdock.
bardar, *va.* to thatch (fences).
bardiota, *m.* Byzantine soldier.
bardo, *m.* bard, poet.
bardoma, *f.* (Am.) filth, mud.
bargueño, *m.* gilt and painted desk.
bario, *m.* (chem.) barium.
barita, *f.* (chem.) baryta or barytes.
baritel, *m.* = MALACATE, hoisting machine.
barítico, ca, *a.* (chem.) barytic.
baritina, *f.* barium sulphate.
barítono, *m.* (mus.) baritone.
barjuleta, *f.* knapsack, haversack; tool bag.
barloar, *va., vn.* & *vr.* (naut.) to grapple in order to board; ABARLOAR, to bring alongside.
barloas, *f. pl.* (naut.) relieving tackles.
barloventear, *vn.* (naut.) to ply to windward; to beat about.
barlovento, *m.* (naut.) windward.—**ganar el b.,** to get to windward.
barnacla, *m.* barnacle, sea goose.
barnicé, barnice, *v. V.* BARNIZAR.
barniz, *m.* varnish; cosmetic; printer's ink.—**b. del Japón,** japan.
barnizador, ra, *n.* & *a.* varnisher(-ing).
barnizar, *va.* (*pret.* BARNICÉ; *subj.* BARNICE) to varnish.
barógrafo, *m.* (meteorol.) barograph.
barometría, *f.* barometry.
barométrico, ca, *a.* barometric.
barómetro, *m.* barometer.—**b. aneroide,** aneroid barometer.—**b. metálico,** Bourdon gauge.
barometrógrafo, *m.* barometrograph.
barón, *m.* baron.—**barones del timón,** (naut.) rudder pendants and chains.—**baronesa,** *f.* baroness.—**baronía,** *f.* barony; baronage.
baroscopio, *m.* baroscope.
barotermógrafo, barotermómetro, *m.* instrument for measuring both atmospheric pressure and temperature.
barquear, *vn.* to go about in a boat; to cross (a river, lake) in a boat.
barquero, *m.* bargeman, boatman, ferryman.
barquilla, *f.* conical mold for wafers; little boat, wherry; (aer.) car, basket (of a dirigible).—**b. de la corredera,** (naut.) the log.
barquillero, ra. I. *n.* maker or seller of rolled wafers. II. *m.* wafer mold.
barquillo, *m.* cockboat; thin rolled wafer.
barquín, *m.,* **barquinera,** *f.* large bellows.
barquinazo, *m.* fall from a vehicle; tumble, fall.
barquino, *m.* wine skin. Also ODRE.
barra, *f.* (mech., eng.) bar, beam, rod; stripe; sandbar; gross-spun thread in cloth; mold for small candles; chase bar; shaft of a carriage; thill; (her.) third part of a shield; a country game in Spain; railing in a court room; visitors' gallery (in a parliamentary hall, etc.); (Am.) "fans" (at a game), supporters, (theat.) claque; (Arg.) "gang" (of boys); (naut.) spar.—*pl.* mining shares; stripes, bars (on a shield, etc.).—**b. colectora,** (elec.) busbar.—**b. de enganche,** (Ry.) drag link, dragbar.—**b. de tracción,** drawbar.—**en barra** or **en barras,** in bars, bar (as *a.*).
Barrabás, *m.* devil (fig.).—**barrabasada,** *f.* serious mischief; bold action.
barraca, *f.* barrack, cabin, hut; storage shed.
barracón, *m.* barracoon.
barracuda, *f.* (ichth.) barracuda.
barrado, da. I. *pp.* of BARRAR. II. *a.* corded; ribbed; striped: (her.) barred.
barragán, *m.* barracan, camlet; waterproof woollen stuff; waterproof overcoat.
barragana, *f.* concubine; morganatic wife.
barraganería, *f.* concubinage.
barraganete, *m.* (naut.) top-timber, futtock.
barral, *m.* (Am.) demijohn of about 25 pints.
barranca, *f.,* **barrancal,** *m.* deep hollow; gorge, ravine; cliff; precipice.
barranco, *m.* BARRANCA; great difficulty.
barrancoso, sa, *a.* uneven, rough.
barranquera, *f.* BARRANCA; obstruction, difficulty.
[1]**barrar,** *va.* to daub, smear.
[2]**barrar,** *va.* to bar, barricade.

barrear, I. *va.* to bar, barricade; to cancel, cross off. II. *vn.* to graze a knight's armor with a lance. III. *vr.* to intrench.
barredero, ra. I. *a.* that drags along; sweeping. II. *f.* sweeper (machine), cleaner (esp. for cleaning streets). III. *m.* baker's mop.
barredura, *f.* sweeping.—*pl.* sweepings, refuse, chaff.
barreminas, *m.* mine sweeper (ship).
barrena, *f.* drill; auger; gimlet; (aer.) spin; spinning dive.—**b. de diminución,** taper auger.—**b. de guía,** centerbit.—**b. de gusano,** wimble; rock drill.—**b. grande,** auger, borer.—**b. pequeña,** gimlet.
barrenado, da. I. *pp.* of BARRENAR. II. *a.* bored, drilled. III. *m.* boring, drilling.
barrenar, *va.* to bore, drill; to foil; to infringe (a law).—**b. un navío,** (naut.) to scuttle a ship.—**b. una roca,** or **mina,** to blast a rock, or a mine.
barrendero, ra, *n.* sweeper, dustman(-woman).
barrenero, *m.* maker or seller of augers and drills; blaster, driller.
barrenillo, *m.* insect that bores into trees.
barreno, *m.* large borer, drill or auger; bored hole, blast hole; vanity.—**dar b.** (naut.) to sink (a ship).
barreña, *f.*, **barreño,** *m.* earthen pan; tub.
barrer, *va.* to sweep; (naut.) to rake.—**al b.** (com.) on an average.
[1]**barrera,** *f.* barricade, barrier, parapet, fence; bar, tollgate, turnstile.—**b. de radar,** radar fence.—**b. sónica,** sonic or sound barrier.—**b. térmica,** thermic or heat barrier.
[2]**barrera,** *f.* clay pit; mound of earth; cupboard for crockery.
barrero, *m.* potter; marshy ground; salty soil.
barreta, *f.* small bar; shoe lining.
barretear, *va.* to fasten with bars; line (a shoe).
barriada, *f.* city ward, district, precinct, quarter.
barrial, *m.* mire.
barrica, *f.* cask containing about 60 gallons.
barricada, *f.* barricade.
barrido, *m.* sweeping.
barriga, *f.* belly; pregnancy.
barrigón, na, barrigudo, da, *a.* big-bellied.
barriguera, *f.* bellyband, cinch.
barril, *m.* barrel; (naut.) water cask.
barrilaje, *m.* (Mex.) barrels collectively; BARRILAME.
barrilame, barrilamen, *m.* stock of casks or barrels; barrel factory.
barrilejo, *m. dim.* rundlet, small barrel.
barrilería, *f.* = BARRILAME.
barrilero, ra, *n.* barrel maker, cooper.
barrilete, *m.* holdfast, dog, clamp; (naut.) mouse; (zool.) crab covered with prickles; keg; kite; upper joint of a clarinet.
barrilico, illo, ito, *m. dim.* keg, rundlet, small barrel, firkin.
barrilla, *f.* little bar; rod; (bot.) saltwort.
barrillar, *m.* barilla plantation; barilla pits.
barrio, *m.* city district, ward, precinct, quarter; suburb.—**el otro b.,** the other world; eternity.
barrizal, *m.* clay pit; mire.
[1]**barro,** *m.* clay; mud; earthenware; drinking vessel made of sugar clay.—**hacer un b.,** (Arg.) to make a break, put one's foot in it.
[2]**barro,** *m.* (gen. *pl.*) pimples on the face; (vet.) fleshy tumors.
barroco, ca, *a.* (f. a.) baroque.
barrocho, *m.* two-seat light wagon without top.
[1]**barroso, sa,** *a.* muddy, miry.
[2]**barroso, sa,** *a.* pimpled; reddish.
barrote, *m.* short and thick iron bar; round rung (of a ladder); (carp.) brace.—**barrotes,** (naut.) battens, scantlings.
barrueco, *m.* pearl of irregular form.
barrumbada, *f.* extravagant expense; boast.
barruntador, ra, *n.* conjecturer.
barruntamiento, *m.* conjecturing, guessing.
barruntar, *va.* to conjecture, guess.
barrunto, *m.* conjecture.
bartola, *f.*—**a la b.,** carelessly.
bartolillo, *m.* three-cornered little meat pie.
bártulos, *m. pl.* household goods; tools; means, measures, way (to do something).
baruca, *f.* cunning, deceit, trickery.
barullo, *m.* confusion, disorder, tumult.
barzón, *m.* idle walk; ring of a yoke.
barzonear, *vn.* to loiter, stroll about.
basa, *f.* pedestal, base; basis.
basada, *f.* stocks for ship building.
basal, *a.* basal, basic, fundamental.
basáltico, ca, *a.* basaltic.
basalto, *m.* basalt.
basamento, *m.* (arch.) base and pedestal.
basar. I. *va.* to support, give a base to; to base, found; (surv.) to refer (operation, etc.) to a base line. II. *vr.* **(en)** to base one's opinion (on).
basáride, *f.* (Mex.) bassaris, a species of racoon.
basca, *f.* squeamishness, nausea; swoon.
bascosidad, *f.* nastiness; filth.
báscula, *f.* platform scales.
base, *f.* base, basis; (mil., chem., alg., geom.) base; (surv.) base (line).—**b. naval,** naval base or station.
basicidad, *f.* (chem.) basicity.
básico, ca, *a.* basic.
báside, *m.* (bot.) basidium.
basificar, *va.* (chem.) to basify.
basilar, *a.* basilar, basilary.
basílica, *f.* royal palace; public hall; basilica, privileged church; (arch.) basilica; (anat.) basilic vein.
basilicón, *m.* (med.) basilicon, ointment.
basilio, lia, *n.* & *a.* Basilian (monk, nun).
basilisco, *m.* basilisk (animal, cannon).—**estar hecho un b.,** to be furious, (coll.) to be hot under the collar.
basketbol, *m.* basketball.—**basketbolista.** I. *n.* basketball player. II. *a.* basketball (as *a.*).—**basketbolero, ra,** *a.* basketball (as *a.*).
basketero, ra, *n.* basketball player.
basquear, *vn.* to be squeamish or nauseated.
basquetbol, etc. = BASKETBOL, etc.
basquilla, *f.* a disease of sheep.
basquiña, *f.* outer skirt.
basta, *f.* coarse stitch; basting.
bastaje, *m.* porter; carrier.
bastante. I. *a.* sufficient, enough. II. *adv.* enough; rather, fairly, pretty.—**bastantear,** *va.* (law) to acknowledge the validity of (a power of attorney).—**bastantemente,** *adv.* sufficiently.
bastanteo, *m.* acknowledging a power of attorney.
bastar, *vn.* to suffice; to be enough.—**¡basta!** that will do; stop!
bastarda, *f.* bastard file; piece of ordnance.
bastardear, *vn.* to degenerate; to bastardize.
bastardelo, *m.* notary's draft book; blotter, record book.
bastardía, *f.* bastardy; meanness.
bastardilla, *f.* a kind of flute; (print.) italic.
bastardo, da. I. *a.* bastard; (print.) bastard (type). II. *n.* bastard. III. *m.* boa (snake); a kind of saddle; (naut.) parrel rope.
[1]**baste,** *m.* = BASTA.
[2]**baste,** *m.* saddle pad.
bastear, *va.* (sewing) to baste.
bastero, *m.* maker or seller of packsaddles.
bastida, *f.* an ancient war engine.
bastidor, *m.* frame; easel; embroidery frame; stretcher for canvas; wing of stage scenery; window sash; frame of a screw propeller; (photog.) plate holder.—*pl.* (naut.) frames for canvas bulkheads.—**entre bastidores,** behind the scenes.
bastilla, *f.* (sew.) hem; bastille.
bastillar, *va.* (sew.) to hem.
bastimentar, *va.* to victual; to provision.
[1]**bastimento,** *m.* supply of provisions; building, structure; (naut.) vessel.

[2]**bastimento,** *m.* mattress tufting.
bastión, *m.* = BALUARTE, bastion.
[1]**basto,** *m.* packsaddle; pad; (cards) ace of clubs. —*pl.* clubs (cards).
[2]**basto, ta,** *a.* coarse; rude; gross; homespun.
bastón, *m.* walking cane; gad, truncheon; baton; roller of a silk frame.—**bastonada,** *f.*, **bastonazo,** *m.* bastinado.—**bastoncillo,** *m.* small cane or stick; narrow trimming lace.—**bastonear,** *va.* to cane.—**bastonero,** *m.* cane maker or seller; manager of a ball; cotillon leader; assistant jailer.
basura, *f.* sweepings, rubbish; garbage, refuse.
basurero, *m.* garbage collector, garbage man, (Engl.) dustman; wastebasket; dunghill.
basuriento, ta, *a.* (Am.) full of rubbish.
[1]**bata,** *f.* dressing gown, robe, wrapper.—**b. de baño,** bathrobe.
[2]**bata,** *n.* (P. I.) native child or half-breed minor.
batacazo, *m.* violent bump from a fall.
batahola, *f.* hurly-burly, bustle, hubbub.
batalla, *f.* battle; fencing bout; joust, tournament; (artil.) battle piece.—**b. campal,** pitched battle.
batallador, ra, *n.* & *a.* battler(-ing), fighter (-ing).
batallar, *vn.* to battle, fight, struggle; to fence.
batallola, *f.* (naut.) rail.
batallón, *m.* battalion.
batallona, *a.*—**cuestión b.,** vexed question, hard nut to crack.
batán, *m.* fulling mill.—*pl.* **batanes,** a boys' game.—**batanar,** *va.* to full (cloth).—**batanear,** *va.* to drub, thrash, beat.—**batanero,** *m.* fuller, clothier.
batanga, *f.* (P. I.) bamboo outrigger in boats.
batata, *f.* sweet potato.—**batatal, batatar,** *m.* sweet-potato field.
batatazo, *m.* (Am. coll.).—**dar b.,** (of horses) to win against all expectations.
bátavo, va, *a.* Batavian.
batayola, *f.* (naut.) rail.
bate, *m.* (Angl.) (Am.) baseball bat.
batea, *f.* painted tray; foot tub; flat-bottomed boat, punt; large wash tray or trough.
bateador, *m.* (baseball) batter.
batear, *va.* & *vn.* (in baseball) to bat.
batel, *m.* small vessel.
batería, *f.* (artil., elec., baseball) battery; (naut.) range of guns; (mus.) aggregate of percussion instruments; battering.—**b. de acumuladores,** (elec.) storage battery.—**b. de cocina,** kitchen utensils.—**b. seca,** (elec.) dry battery.
batero, ra, *n.* dressmaker; ladies' tailor.
batey, *m.* (Cuba) sugar mill town.
batiborrillo, *m.* = BATURRILLO, hodgepodge.
baticola, *f.* crupper.
batida, *f.* hunting party; battue.
batidera, *f.* beater (in masonry); stirrer (in glassmaking); batlet; batting arm; scutcher; nap of a churn; instrument for cutting honeycombs.
batidero, *m.* continuous striking or beating; collision; craggy ground; (naut.) washboard.
batido, da. I. *pp.* of BATIR. **II.** *a.* shot, chatoyant (silks); beaten, trodden, as roads. **III.** *m.* batter of flour, eggs, etc.
batidor, ra. I. *a.* that beats or shakes. **II.** *m.* beater; stirring rod; scout; comb (hair); *f.* churn.
batiente, *m.* jamb (of a door); leaf (of a door); port-sill; damper (of a piano); spot where the sea beats against the shore.—**b. de la bandera,** (naut.) fly of the ensign.—**b. de un dique,** apron of a dock.
batifulla, *m.*, **batihoja,** *m.* gold beater; sheet-metal worker; warp.
batimetría, *f.* bathymetry.
batimiento, *m.* beating.
batín, *m.* smoking jacket.
batintín, *m.* Chinese gong.
bationdeo, *m.* fluttering of a banner or curtain.
batiportar, *va.* (naut.) to house (a gun).
batiportes, *m. pl.* (naut.) port-sills.
batir. I. *va.* to beat, pound; to strike; to demolish; to flap; to stir; to comb; to adjust (reams of paper); to vanquish; to reconnoiter; to beat (a drum).—**b. banderas,** to salute with colors. —**b. el campo,** to reconnoiter the enemy's camp; to investigate.—**b. el record,** to beat the record.—**b. hoja,** to foliate.—**b. las olas,** to ply the seas.—**b. moneda,** to coin money. —**b. palmas,** to clap the hands.—**b. una catarata,** (med.) to couch a cataract. **II.** *vr.* to fight; to duel; to lose courage; to decline in health.
batiscafo, *m.* bathyscaphe.
batisfera, *f.* bathysphere.
batista, *f.* batiste, cambric.
batitermógrafo, *m.* bathythermograph.
bato, *m.* rustic, simpleton.
batojar, *va.* to gather (fruit from a tree) by knocking it down with a stick.
batología, *f.* battology, needless repetition.
batómetro, *m.* bathometer, bathymeter, an instrument used for determining depths at sea.
batracio, cia. (zool.) **I.** *n.* & *a.* batrachian. **II.** *m. pl.* Batrachia.
batuda, *f.* springboard jumping contest.
baturrillo, *m.* hodgepodge, mash, salmagundi; potpourri; medley.
batuta, *f.* conductor's wand; baton.—**llevar la b.,** to lead; to preside; to manage.
baúl, *m.* trunk, chest; belly.—**b. escaparate,** wardrobe trunk.—**b. mundo,** Saratoga trunk. —**b. ropero,** = B. ESCAPARATE.—**baulito,** *m. dim.* small trunk.
bauprés, *m.* (naut.) bowsprit.
bausán, na, *m.* manikin, effigy; fool, idiot.
bauticé, bautice, *v. V.* BAUTIZAR.
bautismal, *a.* baptismal.
bautismo, *m.* baptism, christening.
bautista, *n.* baptizer; Baptist.—**el B.,** the Baptist (John).
bautisterio, *m.* baptistery.
bautizante, *n.* baptizer, christener.
bautizar, *va.* (*pret.* BAUTICÉ: *subj.* BAUTICE) to baptize, christen; to name, call; to mix (wine) with water.
bautizo, *m.* baptism; christening party.
bauxita, *f.* (min.) bauxite.
bávaro, ra, *n.* & *a.* Bavarian.
baya, *f.* berry, any small globular fruit.
bayadera, *f.* Oriental dancer.
[1]**bayal,** *a.* long-stem autumn (flax).
[2]**bayal,** *m.* lever used in raising millstones.
bayeta, *f.* baize, thick flannel; (print.) blanket.
bayetón, *m.* coating, cloth for coats; (Am.) long baize poncho.
[1]**bayo, ya. I.** *a.* bay (color). **II.** *m.* bay horse; silkworm moth used as bait in fishing.—**uno piensa el b. y otro quien lo ensilla,** it is one thing to command and another to obey, it all depends on who is master and who servant.
[2]**bayo,** *m.* (Chile) poor man's bier.
[1]**bayoco,** *m.* Italian copper coin.
[2]**bayoco,** *m.* unripe or withered fig.
bayoneta, *f.* bayonet.—**bayonetazo,** *m.* bayonet thrust or wound.
bayoque, *m.* = [1]BAYOCO.
bayuca, *f.* tippling house, tavern.
baza, *f.* trick (at cards).—**no dejar meter b.,** not to let one put in a single word.
bazar, *m.* bazaar, market place; department store; fair.
bazo, za. I. *n.* & *a.* yellowish brown. **II.** *m.* (anat.) spleen.
bazofia, *f.* offal, waste meat, refuse, remnants.
bazucar, *va.* (*pret.* BAZUQUÉ: *subj.* BAZUQUE) to stir (liquids) by shaking; to dash.
bazuco, *m.* (mil.) bazooka.
bazuqueo, *m.* shaking (a liquid); jumble.
[1]**be,** *m.* baa, cry of sheep.
[2]**be,** *f.* b (the letter).—**b. por b.,** with all particulars, minutely.

beata, *f.* woman engaged in works of charity; overpious woman, one that devotes much of her time to praying and church going (gen. with the implication of prudery and bigotry).
beatería, *f.* affected piety; bigotry.
beaterío, *m.* pious women's house or institution.
beatificación, *f.* beatification.
beatíficamente, *adv.* beatifically.
beatificar, *va.* to beatify; to render respectable; to make happy.
beatífico, ca, *a.* (theol.) beatific.
beatilla, *f.* a kind of fine linen.
beatísimo, ma, *a. super.* of BEATO.—**b. padre,** Most Holy Father (the Pope).
beatitud, *f.* beatitude, blessedness, holiness.
beato, ta. I. *a.* happy, blessed; beatified; devout; overpious, prudish, bigoted. **II.** *n.* pious person; one who lives in pious retirement; overpious, prudish person.
beatón, na, *n.* hypocrite, bigot.
bebé, *m.* baby, babe.
bebedero, ra. I. *a.* drinkable. **II.** *m.* drinking place or trough; spout.—*pl.* strips for lining clothes; facing.
bebedizo, za. I. *a.* drinkable. **II.** *m.* medicinal potion; draught; philter or love potion; poisonous draught.
bebedo, da, bebido, da, *a.* drunk.
bebedor, ra, *n.* tippler, toper.
beber. I. *va.* & *vn.* to drink; to swallow; to pledge, toast.—**b. a la salud de alguno,** to drink some one's health.—**b. como una cuba,** to d ink like a fish.—**b. en,** to drink from, out of.—**b. los pensamientos a alguno,** to anticipate one's thoughts.—**b. los vientos,** to solicit with much eagerness. **II.** *m.* drinking; a drink.
bebible, *a.* pleasant to drink, drinkable.
bebida, *f.* drink, beverage; potion; time allowed to workmen for drinks.
bebido, da. I. *pp.* of BEBER. **II.** *a.* intoxicated.
bebirina, *f.* (chem.) bebeerine.
bebistrajo, *m.* mixture of drinks; a nasty drink.
beborrotear, *vn.* to sip often.
beca, *f.* scholarship, fellowship; pension; sash. —**b. de merced,** scholarship.
becabunga, *f.* (Am.) (bot.) brooklime; veronica.
becada, *f.* (ornith.) woodcock. Also CHOCHA.
becado, da, *n.* = BECARIO.
becafigo, *m.* (ornith.) figpecker.—**b. raro,** (ornith.) red-headed linnet.
becardón, *m.* (ornith.) snipe.
becario, ria, *n.* fellow, fellowship or scholarship holder.
becerra, *f.* (bot.) snapdragon.
becerril, *a.* bovine; calf (as *a.*).
becerro, rra, *n.* yearling calf; *m.* calfskin; (Sp.) register book (church, city hall, etc.).—**b. de oro,** (bib.) golden calf; (fig.) riches.—**b. descarriado,** (zool.) dogie, stray calf; (coll.) black sheep.—**b. marino,** (zool.) sea calf.
becoquín, *m.* cap tied under the chin.
becquerelita, *f.* (min.) becquerelite.
becuadrado, *m.* first property in plain song, or Gregorian mode.—**becuadro,** *m.* (mus.) the sign ♮, denoting a return to the natural tone.
bedel, *m.* beadle, warden.
bedelía, *f.* beadleship, wardenship.
bedelio, *m.* bdellium, an aromatic gum.
beduino, na, *a.* Bedouin; harsh, uncivil.
befa, *f.* jeer, scoff, mock, taunt.
befabemí, *m.* a musical sign.
befar. I. *va.* to mock, scoff, ridicule. **II.** *vn.* (of horses) to move the lips trying to catch the chain of the bit.
befo, fa. I. *a.* having a thick lower lip; knock-kneed. **II.** *m.* lip of an animal; a kind of monkey.
begonia, *f.* (bot.) begonia.—**begoniáceo, ea. I.** *a.* (bot.) begoniaceous. **II.** *f. pl.* Begoniaceæ.
behén, *m.* = BEN, a small, oil-bearing fruit.
behetría, *f.* free, independent town; confusion, disorder.
béisbol, *m.* (Am.) baseball (game).
beisbolero, ra; beisbolista. I. *a.* (Am.) of or pertaining to baseball. **II.** *n.* (Am.) baseball player.
bejel, *m.* (med.) yaws.
bejín, *m.* (bot.) common puffball, fuzzball; whining, peevish child.
bejucal, *m.* place where BEJUCOS grow.
bejuco, *m.* large creeping or climbing wild plant; rattan.
bejuquillo, *m.* gold chain made in China; (bot.) ipecacuanha; thin BEJUCO.
belcho, *m.* (bot.) horsetail tree.
beldad, *f.* beauty, belle.
belemnita, *f.* (paleontol.) belemnite.
Belén, *m.* Bethlehem; a Christmas crèche; confusion, bedlam.
beleño, *m.* (bot.) henbane, poison.
belérico, *m.* (bot.) a kind of myrobalan.
belez, *f.*, **belezo,** *m.* jar for oil or wine; furniture.
belfo, fa. I. *a.* having a thick lower lip. **II.** *m.* lip of an animal.
belga, *n.* & *a.* Belgian.
bélgico, ca. I. *a.* Belgian. **II.** *f.* (**B.**) Belgium.
bélico, ca, *a.* bellicose, warlike.
belicosidad, *f.* bellicosity.
belicoso, sa, *a.* warlike, bellicose; quarrelsome.
beligerancia, *f.* belligerency.
beligerante, *n.* & *a.* belligerent.
belígero, ra, *a.* (poet.) warlike, belligerent.
belísono, na, *a.* with martial, warlike sound.
belitre, *a.* low, mean, vile, vulgar; roguish.
bellacada, *f.* nest of rogues; knavish act.
bellacamente, *adv.* knavishly, roguishly.
bellaco, ca. I. *a.* artful, sly, cunning, roguish, deceitful. **II.** *m.* rogue, villain, knave.
bellacuelo, *m. dim.* tricky, cunning little fellow.
belladona, *f.* (bot.) belladonna.
bellamente, *adv.* prettily, gracefully, fairly.
bellaquear, *vn.* to cheat, swindle; to play knavish, roguish tricks; (Arg.) (of horse) to buck.
bellaquería, *f.* knavery, roguery, cunning; vile act or expression.
belleza, *f.* beauty.
bello, lla, *a.* beautiful, fair.—**bello sexo,** fair sex.—**bellas artes,** fine arts.—**las bellas,** the fair ones.
bellorio, ria, *a.* mouse-colored.
bellorita, *f.* (Am.) (bot.) primrose, cowslip.
bellota, *f.* acorn; carnation bud; perfume box.
bellote, *m.* large round-headed nail.
bellotear, *vn.* to feed on acorns.
bellotera, *f.* acorn season.
bellotero, ra. I. *n.* one who gathers or sells acorns. **II.** *m.* oak forest.
bembo, ba. I. *n.* & *a.* thick-lipped. **II.** *m.* thick lip, esp. Negro's lip.—**bembón, na,** *a.* (of persons) thick-lipped.
bemol, *m.* (mus.) flat.—**tener bemoles,** (coll.) to be very difficult, a tough job.
bemolado, *a.* flat(ted), lowered a semitone.
bemolar, *va.* (mus.) to flat.
ben, *m.* behen, a small oil-producing fruit.
benarriza, *f.* (ornith.) ortolan.
bencedrina, *f.* (pharm.) benzedrine.
bencénico, ca, *a.* pertaining to benzene.
benceno, *m.* (chem.) benzene.
bencílico, ca, *a.* benzilic.
bencilo, *m.* (chem.) benzil, benzyl.
bencina, *f.* benzine.
bendecidor, ra, *n.* & *a.* blesser(-ing).
bendecir, *va.* (*pp.* BENDITO and BENDECIDO; *ind. pres.* BENDIGO, *pret.* BENDIJE; *imper.* BENDICE; *subj.* BENDIGA) to bless; to consecrate.
bendición, *f.* benediction, blessing.—*pl.* or **bendiciones nupciales,** marriage ceremony.
bendigo, bendije, bendiga, *v. V.* BENDECIR.
bendito, ta. I. *pp. irreg.* of BENDECIR. **II.** *a.* sainted, blessed; simple, silly.—**es un b.,** he is a simpleton.

benedícite, *m.* (Lat.) permission solicited by ecclesiastics; grace before meals.
benedicta, *f.* (med.) benedict, electuary.
benedictino, na. I. *a.* Benedictine. **II.** *m.* benedictine.
benefactor, *m.* benefactor.
beneficencia, *f.* beneficence, charity; department of public welfare.
beneficiación, *f.* benefaction.
beneficiado, *m.* curate; beneficiary.
beneficiador, ra, *n.* benefactor; improver, developer, exploiter (of a mine, etc.).
beneficial, *a.* pertaining to benefices or ecclesiastical livings.
beneficiar. I. *va.* to benefit; to cultivate, develop, exploit; to confer a sinecure on; to purchase. **II.** *vr.* to profit.
beneficiario, ria, *n.* beneficiary.
beneficio, *m.* benefit; profits; favor, kindness, benefaction; benefit, ecclesiastical living; right belonging to one either by law or charter; working, development (of a mine); (com.) premium.—**b. bruto,** gross profit.—**b. neto,** clear profit.—**b. simple,** sinecure.—**beneficioso, sa,** *a.* beneficial, profitable.
benéfico, ca, *a.* beneficent, charitable; beneficial.
benemérito, ta, *a.* meritorious, worthy.
beneplácito, *m.* approval, consent.
benevolencia, *f.* benevolence, kindness
benévolo, la, *a.* benevolent, kind.
bengala, *f.* a kind of muslin; cane.
bengalí, *n.* & *a.* Bengalese.
bengalina, *f.* (text.) bengaline.
benignamente, *adv.* kindly, benevolently.
benignidad, *f.* benignity, kindness; mildness.
benigno, na, *a.* benign, kind; mild.
benito, ta, *n.* & *a.* Benedictine (friar or nun).
Benjamín, *m.* youngest son or daughter, "the baby."
benjamita, *a.* descending from, or pertaining to, Benjamin or the tribe of Benjamin.
benjuí, *m.* benzoin.
benzaldehido, *m.* (chem.) benzaldehyde.
benzamida, *f.* (chem.) benzamide.
benzoato, *m.* (chem.) benzoate.
benzoico, ca, *a.* benzoic.
benzoína, *f.* (chem.) benzoin.
benzol, *m.* (chem.) benzol.
beocio, cia, *n.* & *a.* Bœotian.
beodez, *f.* drunkenness.
beodo, da, *a.* drunk.
beorí, *m.* an American tapir.
beque, *m.* (naut.) head of the ship.
berberí, *n.* & *a.* Berber.
berberídeo, a. I. *a.* (bot.) berberidaceous. **II.** *m. pl.* Berberidaceæ.
berberina, *f.* (chem.) berberine.
berberís, *m.* (bot.) barberry, piperidge bush.
berberisco, ca, *n.* & *a.* Berber.
bérbero, *m.* barberry; a barberry confection.
berbí, *m.* a kind of woollen cloth.
berbiquí, *m.* drill brace, bitstock; wimble.
bereber = BERBERISCO.
berenjena, *f.* eggplant.—**berenjenado, da,** *a.* eggplant-colored.—**berenjenal,** *m.* bed of eggplants; difficulties, troubles.
bergamota, *m.* bergamot (fruit, essence, snuff).
bergamote, bergamoto, *m.* bergamot tree.
bergante, *m.* brazen-faced villain, ruffian, rascal.
bergantín, *m.* (naut.) brig, brigantine.
beriberi, *m.* beriberi.
berilato, *m.* (chem.) beryllate.
berilio, *m.* (chem.) beryllium.
berilo, *m.* (min.) beryl.
berkelio, *m.* (chem.) berkelium.
[1]**berlina,** *f.*—**en b.,** in a ridiculous position, exposed to ridicule; (diff. constr.) laughingstock.
[2]**berlina,** *f.* berlin (carriage); front compartment of a stagecoach or a railway carriage.
berlinés, sa, *a.* of or from Berlin.
berlinga, *f.* clothesline post; round timber.
berma, *f.* (mil.) berm, ground at the foot of a rampart.
bermejear, bermejecer, *vn.* to have a reddish color.
bermejizo, za. I. *a.* reddish. **II.** *m.* (zool.) red bat.
bermejo, ja, *a.* bright reddish.—**bermejón, na,** *a.* reddish.—**bermejuela,** *f.* (zool.) red gurnard; (bot.) heather.—**bermejuelo, la,** *a. dim.* somewhat reddish.—**bermejura,** *f.* reddishness, ruddy color.
bermellón, bermillón, *m.* vermilion.—**bermellonar,** *va.* to paint with vermilion.
bermudiana, *f.* (bot.) grassflower.
bernardina, *f.* fanfaronade; boast.
bernardo, da, *n.* & *a.* Bernardine (monk, nun).
bernegal, *m.* cup with scalloped edges.
bernés, sa, *n.* & *a.* Bernese.
bernia, *f.* rug; cloak made of rug.
berra, *f.* strong watercress plant.
berraza, *f.* water parsnip.
berrear, *vn.* to cry like a calf, low, bellow.
berrenchin, *m.* foaming, grunting of a wild boar; cry of wayward children.
berrendo, da, *a.* two-colored; spotted; (of silkworm) dark brown (from a disease).
berrera, *f.* (bot.) = BERRAZA.
berrido, *m.* bellowing.
berrín, *m.* child in a violent passion.
berrinche, *m.* anger, passion; sulkiness.
berrinchudo, *a.* (Am.) irritable, sulky.
berrizal, *m.* place full of watercress.
berro, *m.* (bot.) watercress.
berrocal, *m.* craggy or rocky place.
berrueco, *m.* rock; pin; a disease of the eye.
berza, *f.* (bot.) cabbage.—**b. común,** common cabbage.—**b. de perro,** dog's cabbage.—**b. lombarda,** red cabbage.—**berzaza,** *f. aug.* large cabbage.
besador, ra, *n.* & *a.* kisser(-ing).
besalamano, *m.* unsigned note in the third person beginning with the abbreviation B.L.M.
besamanos, *m.* reception at court; raising the hand to the lips in greeting.
besana, *f.* first furrow with a plow; series of parallel furrows.
besar. I. *va.* to kiss; (of inanimate things) to touch closely.—**b. la mano,** or **los pies,** expressions of courtesy and respect. **II.** *vr.* to strike heads or faces together accidentally.
besico, sillo, sito, *m. dim.* little kiss.—**besicos de monja,** (bot.) FAROLILLO, Indian heartseed.
beso, *m.* kiss; collision of persons or things; (among bakers) kissing crust.
bestezuela, *f. dim.* little beast.
bestia, *f.* beast, quadruped; (fig.) dunce, idiot; ill-bred fellow.—**b. de carga,** beast of burden.
bestiaje, bestiame, *m.* group of beasts of burden.
bestial, *a.* bestial, brutal.—**bestialidad,** *f.* brutality; stupid notion.—**bestialmente,** *adv.* bestially, brutally.
bestiaza, *m. aug.* great beast; big idiot.
bestión, *m. aug.* large beast.
béstola, bístola, *f.* paddle for cleaning the coulter of the plow.
besucador, ra, *n.* (coll.) kisser, spooner.
besucar. I. *va.* (*pret.* BESUQUÉ; *subj.* BESUQUE) to kiss repeatedly. **II.** *vn.* to spoon.
besucón, na, *n.* & *a.* spooner(-ing).
besugada, *f.* luncheon of sea breams.
besugo, *m.* (ichth.) sea bream, red gilthead.
besuguera, *f.* pan for dressing BESUGOS.
besuguero, ra. I. *n.* fishmonger who sells breams. **II.** *m.* fishing tackle for breams.
besuguete, *m.* (ichth.) red sea bream.
besuqué, besuque, *v. V.* BESUCAR.
besuqueador, ra, *n.* = BESUCADOR.
besuquear, *va.* & *vn.* = BESUCAR.—**besuqueo,** *m.*, (coll.) spooning.
[1]**beta,** *f.* bit or line of thread, tape.—**betas,** (naut.) pieces of cordage for all kinds of tackle.
[2]**beta,** *f.* beta (Greek letter).
betabel, *f.* (Mex.) = BETARRAGA.
betaína, *f.* (chem.) betaine.
betarraga, betarrata, *f.* (bot.) beet, beetroot.

betatrón, *m.* (phys.) betatron.
betel, *m.* betel, an Indian shrub.
bético, ca, *a.* Andalusian.
betlemita, *n.* & *a.* Bethlehemite.
betónica, *f.* (bot.) betony.
betuláceo, cea. I. *a.* (bot.) betulaceous. **II.** *f. pl.* Betulaceæ.
betulina, *f.* (chem.) betulin.
betún, *m.* bitumen, pitch; shoeblacking; coarse wax.—**b. judaico,** asphalt.—**betunar,** *va.* to pitch, tar.
bevatrón, *m.* (phys.) bevatron.
bey, *m.* bey, Turkish governor.
bezaar, bezar, *m.* = BEZOAR.
bezante, *m.* (her.) bezant.
bezo, *m.* thick underlip; (med.) proud flesh in a wound.
bezoar, *m.* bezoar.—**b. occidental, b. oriental,** Occidental, Oriental bezoar.—**bezoárico, ca,** *a.* bezoardic.
bezote, *m.* ring worn by Indians in under lip.
bezudo, da, *a.* thick lipped.
biangular, *a.* biangulated, biangulous.
biaxil, *a.* biaxial.
biazas, bizazas, *f. pl.* saddl
bibásico, ca, *a.* (chem.) bibasic.
biberón, *m.* nursing bottle.
Biblia, *f.* Bible.—**bíblico, ca,** *a.* Biblical.
bibliófilo, la, *n.* book lover, bibliophile.
bibliografía, *f.* bibliography.
bibliográfico, ca, *a.* bibliographical.
bibliógrafo, fa, *n.* bibliographer.
bibliomanía, *f.* bibliomania.
bibliómano, na, *n.* bibliomaniac.
biblioteca, *f.* library.
bibliotecario, ria, *n.* librarian.
bicameral, *a.* bicameral.
bicapsular, *a.* (bot.) having two carpels.
bicarbonato, *m.* (chem.) bicarbonate.—**b. de sosa** or **b. sódico,** (chem.) bicarbonate of soda.
bicéfalo, la, *a.* bicephalous.
bicéps, *m.* (anat.) biceps.
bicerra, *f.* wild or mountain goat.
bicicleta, *f.* bicycle.—**bicicletista,** *n.* cyclist.
biciclo, *m.* large bicycle.—**biciclista,** *n.* = BICICLETISTA.
bicípite, *a.* bicipital, two-headed.
bicloruro, *m.* (chem.) bichloride.—**b. de mercurio,** (chem.) bichloride of mercury.
bicoca, *f.* small fort; trifle, bagatelle.
bicolor, *a.* two-colored.
bicóncavo, va, *a.* biconcave, double-concave.
biconvexo, a, *a.* double-convex.
bicoquete, *m.* **bicoquín,** *m.* double-pointed skullcap.
bicorne, *a.* (poet.) bicorn, having two horns.
bicos, *m. pl.* gold trimmings on skullcaps.
bicromático, ca, *a.* two-color.
bicromato, *m.* bichromate.
bicromía, *f.* two-color print.
bicrón, *m.* (phys.) bicron.
bicuento, *m.* (arith.) billion.
bicúspide, *m.* & *a.* bicuspid.
bicha, *f.* snake; (arch.) fantastic caryatid.
bichero, *m.* (naut.) boat hook.
bicho, *m.* small grubs or insects; (coll.) beast (often app. to bulls); ridiculous fellow.
bidé, *m.* bidet, washtub.
bidentado, da, *a.* bidentate.
bidente. I. *a.* having two teeth or prongs. **II.** *m.* two-pronged spade.
biela, *f.* (mech.) connecting rod.
bielda, *f.* pitchfork with six or seven prongs, and a rack.—**bieldar,** *va.* to winnow corn with a BIELDO.—**bieldo, bielgo,** *m.* winnowing fork.
Bielorrusia, *f.* Byelorussia.
bielorruso, sa, *n.* & *a.* Byelorussian
bien. I. *m.* good; benefit; righteousness.—**mi b.,** my dearest, my darling.—**en,** or **por, b. de,** for the sake, good, or benefit of.—*pl.* property; possessions; estate.—**bienes de fortuna,** worldly possessions.—**bienes dotales,** dower.—**bienes forales,** leasehold estate.—**bienes gananciales,** property acquired during married life.—**bienes inmuebles** = BIENES RAÍCES.—**bienes monstrencos,** goods having no known owner.—**bienes muebles,** goods and chattels.—**bienes raíces,** real estate.—**bienes sedientes,** real estate.—**bienes semovientes,** cattle.—**de b.,** honest. **II.** *adv.* well; all right; right, uprightly; happily, prosperously; willingly, readily, heartily; very; perfectly, fully.—**b. a b.**; willingly.—**b. así como,** just as.—**b. que,** although.—**ahora b.,** now then.——**de b. en mejor,** better and better.—**encontrar,** or **hallar, b.,** to find satisfactory, approve.—**más b.,** rather; somewhat.—**no b.,** as soon as, just as.—**o b.,** or else; otherwise.—**por b.,** willingly.—**si b.,** while, though.—**y b.,** well, now then.—**¿y b.?** well? what of that?
bienal, *a.* biennial.
bienamado, da, *a.* dearly beloved.
bienandante, *a.* happy, prosperous.
bienandanza, *f.* happiness, welfare, prosperity.
bienaventuradamente, *adv.* luckily, happily.
bienaventurado, da, *a.* blessed; happy; fortunate; (ironic) simple, harmless.
bienaventuranza, *f.* beatitude; bliss; well-being.—*pl.* beatitudes.
bienestar, *m.* well-being, comfort.
bienfortunado, da, *a.* fortunate, successful.
biengranada, *f.* (bot.) curl-leaved goosefoot.
bienhablado, da, *a.* well and civilly spoken.
bienhadado, da, *a.* lucky, fortunate, happy.
bienhecho, cha, *a.* well-shaped; well-done.
bienhechor, ra, *n.* benefactor.
bienintencionado, da, *a.* well-meaning.
bienio, *m.* term or space of two years.
bienmandado, da, *a.* obedient, submissive.
bienmesabe, *m.* meringue batter.
bienquerencia, *f.* good will, affection, esteem.
bienquerer. I. *va.* (*ind. pres.* BIENQUIERO, *pret.* BIENQUISE, *fut.* BIENQUERRÉ; *subj.* BIENQUIERA) to esteem, to like. **II.** *m.* esteem, good will.
bienqueriente, *n.* well-wisher.
bienquistar, *va.* to reconcile.
bienquisto, ta. I. *pp. irreg. of* BIENQUERER. **II.** *a.* esteemed and respected.
bienteveo, *m.* = CANDELECHO, raised hut.
bienvenida, *f.* safe arrival; welcome.
bienvenido, da, *a.* welcome.
bienvivir, *vn.* to live in comfort; live uprightly.
bifásico, ca, *a.* (elec.) two-phase.
bife, *m.* (Arg.) beefsteak.
bífido, da, *a.* (bot.) bifid.
bifilar, *a.* bifilar; (elec.) two-wire.
bifloro, ra, *a.* (bot.) biflorous.
bifocal, *a.* bifocal.
biforme, *a.* biformed, biform.
bifronte, *a.* (poet.) double-fronted or -faced.
biftec, *m.* beefsteak. Also BISTEC.
biftequera, *f.* (Chile) beefsteak broiler.
bifurcación, *f.* branch railroad; junction; bifurcation or forking.
bifurcado, da, *a.* forked or branched, bifurcate.
bifurcarse, *vr.* to branch off; to divide in two.
biga, *f.* (poet.) team (of two horses).
bigamia, *f.* bigamy.
bígamo, ma, *a.* & *n.* bigamist.
bigardear, *vn.* to live licentiously; to gad.
bigardía, *f.* jest; fiction; dissimulation.
bigardo, *m.* licentious friar; lubber.
bígaro, bigarro, *m.* large sea snail.
bigarrado, da, *a.* = ABIGARRADO, variegated.
bignonia, *f.* (bot.) bignonia.
bigorneta, *f. dim.* small anvil.
bigornia, *f.* anvil.
bigotazo, *m. aug.* large mustache.
bigote, *m.* mustache; block; (print.) dash rule.
bigotera, *f.* leather cover for mustachios; ribbon ornament worn by women on the breast; folding seat in front of a chariot; bow compass.
bigotudo, *a.* having a large mustache.
bija, *f.* (bot.) arnotto tree; (com.) annatto dye.

bilabiado, da, *a.* (bot.) bilabiate.
bilabial, *a.* (phon.) bilabial.
bilateral, *a.* bilateral.
bilbaíno, na, *a.* of or from Bilbao.
biliar, *a.* biliary.
biliario, ria, *a.* (physiol.) biliary.
bilingüe, *a.* bilingual.
bilingüismo, *m.* bilingualism.
bilioso, sa, *a.* bilious.
bilis, *f.* bile.
bilítero, ra, *a.* biliteral.
bilobulado, da, *a.* bilobate.
bilocarse, *vr.* (*pret.* BILOQUÉ; *subj.* BILOQUE) to be simultaneously in two different places.
bilocular, *a.* (biol.) bilocular.
biltrotear, *vn.* (coll.) to gad.
biltrotera, *f.* (coll.) gadder, gossiping woman.
billa, *f.* (billiards) pocketing a ball after it has struck another.
billalda, billarda, *f.* a children's game.
billar, *m.* billiards, pool; billiard, pool, table.
billarista, *n.* billiard player.
billete, *m.* an order of the king; note, brief letter; love letter; ticket.—**b. de banco,** bank-note.—**b. de abonado,** commutation ticket.—**b. de ida y vuelta,** round-trip ticket.—**b. kilométrico,** mileage ticket.—**billetera,** *f.* (Am.) pocketbook, wallet.
billón, *m.* billion (gen. one million millions).
billonario, ria, *n.* billionaire.
billonésimo, ma, *n.* & *a.* billionth (gen. one millionth of one millionth).
bimano, na. I. *a.* (zool.) bimanous. **II.** *m.* bimane.—*pl.* Bimana.
bimembre, *a.* having two members.
bimensual, *a.* occurring twice a month.
bimestral, *a.* bimonthly.
bimestre. I. *a.* bimonthly. **II.** *n.* bimonthly rent, salary, subscription, pension, etc.
bimetálico, ca, *a.* bimetallic.
bimetalismo, *m.* bimetallism.
bimetalista. I. *a.* bimetallic. **II.** *n.* bimetallist.
bimotor, ra, *a.* two-motor.
bina, *f.* second plowing or digging.
binador, *m.* he who re-digs ground; weeding fork.
binar, *va.* to dig or plow the second time.
binario, ria, *a.* binary.
binazón, *f.* digging or plowing a second time.
binocular, *a.* binocular.
binóculo, *m.* binocle, dioptric telescope; marine or field glasses; opera glasses.
binomio, a. I. *a.* binomial. **II.** *m.* binomial.—**b. de Newton,** (alg.) binomial theorem.
binza, *f.* pellicle, lining of the shell of an egg; any thin membrane.
bioblasto, *m.* (biol.) bioblast.
bioclimatología, *f.* bioclimatology.
biodinámica, *f.* biodynamics.
biofísica, *f.* biophysics.
biogénesis, *f.* biogenesis.
biogenia, *f.* biogeny.
biógeno, na, *a.* (bot.) biogenous.
biografía, *f.* biography.
biográfico, ca, *a.* biographical.
biógrafo, fa, *n.* biographer.
biología, *f.* biology.
biológico, ca, *a.* biologic(al.
biólogo, ga, *n.* biologist.
biombo, *m.* folding screen.
biomecánica, *f.* biomechanics.
biometeorología, *f.* biometeorology.
bionomía, *f.* bionomy.
bioplasma, *f.* (biol.) bioplasm.
biopsia, *f.* (med.) biopsy.
bioquímico, ca. I. *a.* biochemical. **II.** *f.* biochemistry; *n.* biochemist.
biostática, *f.* biostatics.
biótico, ca, *a.* biotic.
biotita, *f.* (min) biotite.
bióxido, *m.* dioxide.
bipartido, da, *a.* (poet.) divided in two.
bípede, bipedo, da, *n.* & *a.* biped.
bipétalo, la, *a.* (bot.) bipetalous.
bipinado, da, *a.* (bot.) bipinnate.
biplano, *m.* (aer.) biplane.
bipolar, *a.* bipolar, two-pole.
biribís, *m.* = BISBÍS.
biricú, *m.* sword belt.
birimbao, *m.* (mus.) Jew's harp.
birla, *f.*, **birlo,** *m.* bowling pin.
birlador, ra, *n.* one who bowls a second time from the place where the ball stopped the first time.
birlar, *va.* to bowl a second time from the same place; to knock down at one blow; to kill with one shot; to snatch away; to rob, pilfer.
birlibirloque, *m.*—**por arte de b.,** (coll.) by occult and extraordinary means.
birlocha, *f.* paper kite.
birlocho, *m.* two-seat light wagon without top.
birlón, *m.* jack pin (in bowling).
birlonga, *f.* a card game.—**a la b.,** carelessly.
birmanés, nesa, *n.* & *a.* Burmese.
Birmania, *f.* Burma.
birmano, na, *n.* & *a.* Burman.
birrectángulo, la, *a.* (geom.) birectangular, having two right angles.
birrefringencia, *f.* double refraction of light rays.
birrefringente, *a.* producing double refraction.
birreme, *n.* & *a.* bireme.
birreta, *f.* biretta.
birrete, *m.* cap.—**birretina,** *f.* grenadier's and hussar's cap; small cap.
bis, *bis,* Latin word used in the sense of "twice," "repeated" or "second."
bisabuela, *f.* great-grandmother.
bisabuelo, *m.* great-grandfather.
bisagra, *f.* hinge; shoemaker's boxwood polisher.
bisanual, *a.* (bot.) biennial.
bisanuo, nua, *a.* (bot.) biennial.
bisayo, ya, *a.* native of or pertaining to the Bisayas Islands in the Philippines.
bisbís, *m.* a game resembling baccarat.
bisbisar, *va.* to mutter.—**bisbiseo,** *m.* muttering.
bisecar, *va.* to bisect.
bisección, *f.* bisection.
bisector, triz, *a.* & *n.* (geom.) bisector.
bisel, *m.* bevel, bevel edge, chamfer; (cooperage) sloping tool.
biselar, *va.* to bevel.
bisextil, *a.* bissextile.
bisexual, *a.* (bot.) bisexual.
bisiesto, *a.* leap (year).
bisílabo, ba, *a.* disyllabic.
bismuto, *m.* bismuth.
bisnieta, biznieta, *f.* great-granddaughter.
bisnieto, biznieto, *m.* great-grandson.
bisojo, ja, bizco, ca, *a.* squint-eyed, cross-eyed.
bisonte, *m.* bison.
bisoñada, bisoñería, *f.* act of a novice.
bisoño, ña, *n.* & *a.* novice, tyro, greenhorn; inexperienced, new.
bispón, *m.* roll of oilcloth.
bistec, *m.* beefsteak. Also BIFTEC.
bistorta, *f.* (bot.) great bistort, snakeweed.
bistre, *m.* bister, bistre.
bisturí, *m.* (surg.) bistoury, surgical knife.
bisulco, ca, *a.* bisulcous, cloven-footed.
bisulfato, *m.* bisulphate.
bisulfito, *m.* (chem.) bisulfite.
bisulfuro, *m.* disulphide.
bisunto, ta, *a.* dirty, greasy.
bisutería, *f.* bijouterie.
bitácora, *f.* (naut.) binnacle.
bitadura, *f.* (naut.) cable bitt; a turn of the cable.
bitas, *f. pl.* (naut.) bitts.
bitongo, ga, *a.* (of children) like an overgrown baby.
bitoque, *m.* bung, stopple.
bitor, *m.* (ornith.) bittern.
bituminizar, *va.* to bituminize.
bituminoso, sa, *a.* bituminous.
bivalencia, *f.* (chem.) bivalence, bivalency.
bivalente, *a.* (chem.) bivalent.
bivalvo, va, *a.* bivalve, bivalvular.

bivalvular, *a.* bivalvular.
biza, *f.* (ichth.) striped tunny.
bizantinismo, *m.* Byzantinism.
bizantino, na, *n.* & *a.* Byzantine.
bizarramente, *adv.* courageously, gallantly.
bizarrear, *vn.* to act spiritedly, gallantly.
bizarría, *f.* bravery, gallantry; generosity, magnanimity.
bizarro, rra, *a.* gallant, brave; generous, liberal.
bizaza, *f.* saddle-bag.
bizcar, *vn.* (*pret.* BIZQUÉ; *subj.* BIZQUE) to squint.
bizco, ca, *a.* = BISOJO, squint- or cross-eyed.
bizcochada, *f.* biscuit boiled in milk; French bread.
bizcochar, *va.* to bake a second time.
bizcochero, *m.* biscuit cask; one who makes or sells biscuits.
bizcocho, *m.* biscuit; hard-tack; sponge cake; whiting made of old plaster; bisque.
bizcochuelo, *m. dim.* sponge cake.
bizcorneto, ta, *a.* (Am.) = BIZCO.
bizcotela, *f.* light biscuit with sugar icing.
bizma, *f.* poultice.—**bizmar,** *va.* to poultice.
bizna, *f.* membrane dividing walnut kernel.
biznaga, *f.* (bot.) carrotlike ammi with sprigs used as toothpicks; useless, worthless thing.
biznieta, bisnieta, *f.* great-granddaughter.
biznieto, bisnieto, *m.* great-grandson.
bizqué, bizque, *v. V.* BIZCAR.
bizquear, *vn.* to squint.
blanca, *f.* old copper coin; mite; (coll.) money, funds; (mus.) half note.—**b. morfea,** (vet.) white scurf, ringworm.
blancazo, za, *a.* whitish.
blanco, ca. I. *a.* white; (of the complexion) fair; (coll.) cowardly; light-colored; blank (page). **II.** *n.* white person. **III.** *m.* white (color); white star or spot in horses; target; blank; gap left in writing; aim, goal; (print.) blank form; interlude, interval; white page; (her.) argent; sizing.—**b. de ballena,** spermaceti.—**b. de la uña,** half-moon of the nail.—**b. de París,** Paris white.—**b. de plomo,** white lead.—**dar en el b.,** to hit the mark.—**en b.,** blank.—**quedarse en b.,** to be frustrated, be disappointed.
blancor, *m.* whiteness; fairness (of skin).
blancote. I. *a.* cowardly. **II.** *n.* coward.
blancura, *f.* = BLANCOR.—**b. del ojo,** (vet.) white film on the eye.
blancuzco, ca, *a.* whitish.
blandamente, *adv.* softly, mildly, smoothly.
blandeador, ra, *n.* & *a.* softener(-ing).
[1]**blandear. I.** *va.* to soften, render mild; to persuade, convince. **II.** *vn.* to slacken; to yield, give in. **III.** *vr.* to soften, yield, change one's mind.
[2]**blandear,** *va.* = BLANDIR.
blandengue. I. *m.* Argentine lancer. **II.** *a.* exceedingly kind, bland.
blandiente, *a.* swaying, brandishing.
blandir, *va.* & *vr.* to brandish, flourish, swing.
blando, da. I. *a.* soft (to the touch); pliant; tender, kindly, mild, bland; delicate; pusillanimous, cowardly. **II.** *m. adv.* = BLANDAMENTE.
blandón, *m.* wax taper; large church candlestick.—**blandoncillo,** *m. dim.* small candlestick for wax tapers.
blandujo, ja, *a.* (coll.), rather soft.
blandura, *f.* softness; litheness, daintiness, delicacy; gentleness; emollient application; soft, endearing language; blandishing; white cosmetic; mild temperature.
blanduzco, ca, (Am.) = BLANDUJO.
blanqueación, *f.* blanching (metals); bleaching; whitewashing.
blanqueador, ra, *n.* blancher, whitener, whitewasher, kalsominer; bleacher.
blanqueadura, *f., or* **blanqueamiento,** *m.* = BLANQUEO.
blanquear. I. *va.* to whiten; to whitewash; to bleach; (of bees) to wax (the honeycomb) after winter to begin work; to give coarse wax to bees in winter. **II.** *vn.* to show white; to whiten.
blanquecedor, *m.* coin polisher (in the mint).
blanquecer, *va.* (*ind.* BLANQUEZCO; *subj.* BLANQUEZCA) to blanch (coin).
blanquecimiento, *m.* blanching.
blanquecino, na, *a.* whitish.
blanqueo, *m.* whitening, bleaching, whitewashing.
blanquería, *f.* bleaching place, bleach field.
blanquete, *m.* whitewash; white cosmetic.
blanquezco, blanquezca, *v. V.* BLANQUECER.
blanquición, *f.* blanching of metals.
blanquillo, lla. I. *a. dim.* whitish. **II.** *m.* a S.A. fish; (Peru, Chile) white peach; (Mex.) egg.
blanquimiento, *m.* bleaching solution.
blanquinoso, sa, *a.* = BLANQUECINO, whitish.
blanquizal, blanquizar, *m.* clay pit.
blanquizco, ca, *a.* whitish.
blao, *a.* (her.) azure.
blasfemador, ra, *n.* & *a.* blasphemer(-ing).
blasfemamente, *adv.* blasphemously.
blasfemante, *n.* & *a.* = BLASFEMADOR.
blasfemar, *vn.* to blaspheme; to curse.
blasfematorio, ria, *a.* blasphemous.
blasfemia, *f.* blasphemy; grave insult.
blasfemo, ma, *n.* & *a.* blasphemer(-ing).
blasón, *m.* heraldry, blazon, blazonry; armorial bearing; honor, glory.
blasonador, ra; blasonante, *n.* & *a.* boaster (-ing).
blasonar. I. *va.* to design or emblazon (a heraldic shield). **II.** *vn.* to boast, brag.
blasonería, *f.* boast, bravado.
blastema, *m.* (biol.) blastema.
blastocisto, *m.* (biol.) blastocyst.
blastodermo, *m.* (biol.) blastoderm.
blastogénesis, *f.* (biol.) blastogenesis.
blastómero, *m.* (biol.) blastomere.
blástula, *f.* (biol.) blastula.
blavo, va, *a.* yellowish gray and reddish.
bledo, *m.* (bot.) wild amaranth.—**no me importa un b.,** I don't care a straw.
blefaritis, *f.* (med.) blepharitis.
blenda, *f.* (min.) blende.
blenia, *f.* (ichth.) blenny, hake.
blenorragia, *f.* (med.) blennorrhea.
blenorrea, *f.* (med.) chronic blennorrhea.
blinda, *f.,* **blindas,** *pl.* (fort.) blindage.
blindado, da, *n.* & *a.* iron-clad.
blindaje, *m.* screening, shield; armor; (mil.) blindage.
blindar, *va.* to armor; to protect with blindage.
blocao, *m.* (mil.) portable blockhouse.
blonda, *f.* broad silk lace, blond lace.
blondina, *f.* narrow silk lace, narrow blond lace.
blondo, da, *a.* blond, fair; flaxen, light.
bloque, *m.* block (of stone, etc.).
bloqueador, ra, *n.* & *a.* blockader(-ing).
bloquear, *va.* to blockade.—**bloqueo,** *m.* blockade.—**b. efectivo,** (int. law) effective blockade.—**b. en el papel,** (int. law) paper blockade.
blusa, *f.* blouse.
boa, *f.* (zool.) boa; boa, neckpiece.
boardilla, buhardilla, *f.* garret; skylight.
boato, *m.* ostentation, pomp; acclamation.
bobada, *m.* = BOBERÍA.
bobalías, *n.* very stupid person, dolt.
bobalicón, ona; bobazo, za, *n.* blockhead; simpleton.
bobamente, *adv.* foolishly, stupidly; easily, without any trouble.
bobarrón, na; bobatel, *n.* simpleton.
bobático, ca, *a.* silly, foolish, stupid.
bobear, *vn.* to act or talk foolishly; to dally, fribble, fritter away (time).
bobería, *f.* foolish speech or action; trifle; folly, foolishness.—*pl.* idle conceits.
bóbilis.—**de b. b.,** easily, with no effort; for nothing.
[1]**bobillo, illa, ito, ita,** *n. dim.* little fool.
[2]**bobillo,** *m.* big-bellied jug with one handle; modesty piece, a frill or lace formerly worn by women around the tucker.

bobina, *f.* bobbin: (elec.) coil.—**b. apagachispas,** blow-out coil.—**b. de inducción,** induction coil.—**b. de reacción,** or **de reactançia,** choking, kicking, or reactance, coil.—**b. de sintonización,** tuning coil.
bobo, ba, *n.* dolt, fool, simpleton, ninny; ruff formerly worn by women; (ornith.) booby.—**b. de Coria,** great fool; fools in general.—**a bobas,** foolishly.—**bobón, na,** (Am.), **bobote, ta,** (coll.) *n. aug.* big dolt, great fool.
boca, *f.* mouth; entrance, opening; nozzle: muzzle; bunghole; pincers of crayfish; cutting part of edge tools; taste, flavor, relish; approach (to a tunnel, etc.).—**b. abajo,** flat on one's face, prone.—**b. a b.** = A B.—**b. arriba,** flat on one's back, supine.—**b. de agua,** hydrant.—**b. de dragón,** (bot.) snap dragon.—**b. de fuego,** firearm (esp. artillery).—**b. del estómago,** pit of the stomach.—**b. del metro,** subway entrance.—**b. de riego,** faucet (for a watering hose).—**a b.,** verbally, by word of mouth.—**a b. de,** at the beginning of.—**a b. de jarro,** drinking without measure; very near; at close range.—**a b. llena,** perspicuously, openly.—**andar de b. en b.,** to be the talk of the town.—**como b. de lobo,** pitch black.—**de b.,** A B.; boastingly.—**en b. cerrada no entra mosca,** (coll.) silence is golden, it pays to hold one's tongue.—**no decir esta b. es mía,** to keep a profound silence, not to say boo.
bocabarra, *f.* (naut.) barhole in a capstan.
bocacalle, *f.* opening of a street (into another); street intersection.
bocacaz, *m.* (hydraul.) spillway.
bocací, bocacín, *m.* fine glazed buckram.
bocadear, *va.* to divide into bits or morsels.
bocadico, illo, ito, *m. dim.* morsel, bit.
bocadillo, *m.* thin, middling sort of linen; narrow ribbon or tape, gimp; mid-morning luncheon given to laborers in the field; guava paste.
bocado, *m.* morsel, mouthful, bite, bit; modicum; bit of a bridle.—*pl.* preserved cut fruit.—**con el b. en la boca,** right after eating.—**no tener para un b.,** to be in absolute destitution.
[1]**bocal,** *m.* narrow-mouthed pitcher.
[2]**bocal,** *m.* (naut.) narrows (of a harbor); mouthpiece (of musical instrument).
bocamanga, *f.* part of a sleeve near the wrist.
bocamina, *f.* entrance to a mine.
bocanada, *f.* mouthful (of liquor); whiff, puff (of smoke).—**b. de gente,** crowd, rush, jam.—**b. de viento,** sudden gust of wind.
bocarte, *m.* ore crusher, stamp mill.
bocateja, *f.* front tile of each line of tiling.
bocatijera, *f.* socket for a carriage pole.
bocaza, *f. aug.* large wide mouth.
bocazo, *m.* fizzle (in blasting).
bocear, *va.* (vet.) = BOCEZAR.
bocel, *m.* (arch.) bowtel, solid cylindrical molding; tool for making bowtels.
bocelar, *va.* to make cylindrical moldings on.
bocelete, *m. dim.* small molding plane.
bocera, *f.* something sticking to the lip after eating or drinking.
boceto, *m.* sketch.
bocezar, *vn.* (vet.) (of horses) to move the lips from side to side.
bocín, *m.* round piece of bass mat put about the nave of a cart, as a cap of defense; feed pipe of an overshot wheel.
bocina, *f.* large trumpet, buglehorn, megaphone, foghorn, huntsman's horn; (Mex.) mouthpiece (of a telephone); horn (of a phonograph or of an automobile); shell used as a horn; speaking or hearing trumpet; blowgun; (**B-,** astr.) Ursa Minor; (mech.) bushing; wheel hoop.
bocinar, *vn.* to sound the trumpet or horn.
bocinero, *m.* trumpeter, hornblower.
bocio, *m.* (med.) goiter.
bocón, na, *n.* wide-mouthed person; braggart.
bocoy, *m.* hogshead, large barrel or cask.—**bocoyes abatidos,** shooks of hogsheads.
bocudo, da, *a.* large-mouthed.
bocha, *f.* bowl, ball for playing at bowls; fold or bag in ill-fitting clothes.—**bochar,** *va.* to dislodge (a ball).—**bochazo,** *m.* stroke of one bowl against another.
[1]**boche,** *m.* chuck hole (boys' game).
[2]**boche,** *m.* (Venez. coll.) disappointment; quarrel. row, riot; slight, contemptuous treatment —**dar b.,** or **un b.,** to slight, turn the cold shoulder on.
bochinche, *m.* (Am.) tumult, uproar, riot.
bochinchero, ra, *n.* (Am.) rioter; disturber.
bochista, *m.* good bowler.
bochorno, *m.* hot, sultry weather, scorching heat; rush of blood to the head; blush, flushing; humiliation, embarrassment.—**bochornoso, sa,** *a.* humiliating; embarrassing; sultry.
boda, *f.* nuptials, wedding.—**b. de negros,** (coll.) riotous carousal, orgy.—**bodas de diamante, de oro, de plata,** diamond, golden, silver wedding.
bode, *m.* (zool.) buck.
bodega, *f.* wine vault, cellar; abundant vintage; storeroom, warehouse; (Cuba, Mex.) retail grocery; (naut.) hold of a ship.
bodegaje, *m.* (Am.) storage (charges).
bodegón, *m.* low-class chophouse; alehouse; still life painting, esp. of edibles.—**bodegoncillo,** *m. dim.* low-class chophouse.—**bodegonear,** *vn.* to run from one alehouse to another.—**bodegonero, ra,** *n.* keeper of a BODEGÓN.
bodeguero, ra, *n.* butler, one in charge of a winecellar; (Cuba) retail grocer.
bodigo, *m.* small loaf of fine white bread presented as an offering in the church.
bodijo, *m.* mésalliance; marriage with little ceremony.
bodocal, *n.* a kind of black grape.
bodocazo, *m.* blow from a pellet shot from a crossbow.
bodoque, *m.* pellet, ball of clay shot from a crossbow; dunce, idiot.
bodoquera, *f.* blowgun; mold for clay pellets; cradle of a crossbow; pea-shooter.
bodorrio, *m.* (Am.) = BODIJO.
bodrio, *m.* soup formerly given to the poor; hodgepodge; mixture of hog's blood and onions for sausages.
bóer, *n.* & *a.* Boer.
boezuelo, *m.* stalking ox, or figure representing one, which serves to screen fowlers.
bofe, *m.* lung.—**echar los bofes,** to toil; (Am.) to pant, be out of breath.
bófeta, *f.* thin, stiff cotton stuff.
bofetada, *f.* slap in the face, buffet.
bofetón, *m.* slap in the face, buffet; (theat.) revolving-door trick.
[1]**boga. I.** *f.* vogue, popularity; rowing; rowing stroke. **II.** *m.* & *f.* rower.
[2]**boga,** *f.* small two-edged knife.
[3]**boga,** *f.* (ichth.) ox-eyed cackerel, mendole.
[1]**bogada,** *f.* space covered by a stroke of oars.
[2]**bogada,** *f.* bucking of clothes with lye.
bogador, *m.* rower (of a boat).
bogante, *n.* & *a.* rower(-ing) (a boat).
bogar, *vn.* (*pret.* BOGUÉ; *subj.* BOGUE) to row (a boat).
bogavante, *m.* (naut.) stroke oar; large lobster.
bogotano, na, *a.* of or from Bogotá.
bogué, bogue, *v. V.* BOGAR.
bohardilla, *f.* = BUHARDILLA, garret; skylight.
bohemiano, na, *n.* & *a.* Bohemian (person).
bohémico, ca, *a.* Bohemian (of Bohemia).
bohemio, mia. I. *n.* & *a.* Bohemian (of Bohemia); (pertaining to) a bohemian life or person; gypsy. **II.** *m.* short cloak formerly worn by the guard of archers; Czech (language).
bohemo, ma, *a.* of Bohemia.
bohena, boheña, *f.* pork sausage.
bohío, buhío, *m.* (Am.) Indian hut, hovel, cabin.
bohordo, *m.* short spear; dart; (bot.) scape.

boicot, *m.* boycott.—**b. de consumidores,** buyers' strike.
boicoteador, ra, *n.* & *a.* boycotter(-ing).
boicotear, *va.* & *vn.* to boycott.—**boicoteo,** *m.* boycott, boycotting.
boíl, *m.* ox stall.
boina, *f.* beret.
boj, *m.* box tree, boxwood; shoemaker's boxwood tool.
boja, *f.* southernwood. Also ABRÓTANO.
[1]**bojar, bojear. I.** *va.* (naut.) to sail round and measure (an island or cape). **II.** *vn.* to measure.
[2]**bojar,** *va.* to scrape off the stains from (leather).
bojedal, *m.* plantation of box trees.
bojeo, *m.* (naut.) sailing round and measuring an island or headland.
bojiganga, *f.* company of strolling players.
bojo, *m.* = BOJEO.
[1]**bol,** *m.* punch bowl.
[2]**bol,** *m.* Armenian bole, red earth.
bola, *f.* ball; marble; bolus; game of bowling; (coll.) lie, falsehood, humbug, hoax, fib; (Mex.) crowd; disturbance, tumult, riotous meeting; (naut.) truck, ball for signals; shoe blacking.—**b. de jabón,** wash ball.—**b. pampa, b. perdida,** (Arg.) a kind of Indian sling.—**dejar rodar la b.,** to let things run their natural course, keep hands off; to look on with indifference.
bolada, *f.* stroke (in billiards).
bolado, *m.* a sweetmeat; fondant.
bolandista, *n.* Bollandist.
bolazo, *m.* blow with a ball.—**de b.,** hurriedly.
bolchevique, *n.* & *a.* Bolshevik(-ist).
bolchevismo, *m.* Bolshevism.
bolchevista, *n.* & *a.* = BOLCHEVIQUE.
boleada, *f.* (Mex.) shoeshine.
boleador, *m.* (Mex.) bootblack.
boleadoras, *f. pl.* (Arg.) lariat with balls on one end, thrown so to twist round animal's legs.
[1]**bolear. I.** *vn.* to play billiards for pleasure; to bowl; to boast; to lie, fib. **II.** *va.* to throw; (Arg.) to throw BOLEADORAS at, or catch with them; (Arg.) to confuse.
[2]**bolear,** *va.* (Am.) to fail, not to pass (in an exam.); to reject, turn down (in an election).
boleo, *m.* bowling; bowling green, place where balls are thrown.
[1]**bolera,** *f.* bowling alley.
[2]**bolera,** *f.* woman dancer of the BOLERO.
[1]**bolero,** *m.* bolero, Andalusian dance; bolero dancer.
[2]**bolero, ra,** *a.* truant; fibbing, lying.
boleta, *f.* admission ticket; lodging billet; pay order; small package of tobacco; (Am.) ballot.—**b. de guardarropa,** (hat, baggage, etc.) check.
boletería, *f.* (Am.) box, or ticket, office.
boletero, ra, *n.* ticket agent.
boletín, *m.* bulletin; newsletter; (com.) price list; pay warrant.
boleto, *m.* (Am.) ticket; (Am.) ballot; (Am.) lottery ticket.
bolichada, *f.* casting (a fish net); fish caught in a net.—**de una b.,** at one throw, at the same time.
[1]**boliche,** *m.* jack; small bowling ball; a gambling game; furnace for lead smelting; cup and ball (toy).
[2]**boliche,** *m.* small dragnet; small fish caught in a dragnet near the shore.—*pl.* (naut.) foretop bowlines and top-gallant bowlines.
[1]**bolichero,** *m.* seller of BOLICHES, fish.
[2]**bolichero, ra,** *n.* one who runs a [1]BOLICHE, gambling table.
bólido, *m.* shooting star.
bolillo, *m.* bobbin for lace making; iron pin in the game of trucks; mold for stiffening lace cuffs; bone joined to skull of horses.—*pl.* paste nuts; starched lace cuffs.
bolín, *m.* jack; small bowl.—**de b., de bolán,** at random, carelessly.—**bolines,** (Am.) mold shot.
bolina, *f.* sounding line; punishment on shipboard; noise, turmoil; (naut.) bowline.—**echar de b.,** to boast.—**navegar de b.,** or **bolinear,** *vn.* to sail with bowlines hauled.
bolisa, *f.* embers, hot cinders.
bolita, *f. dim.* bead, drop; (Am.) ballot; (Am., coll.) illegal betting, numbers game.
bolitero, *m.* (Am., coll.) bookie.
Bolivia, *f.* Bolivia.
boliviano, na, *n.* & *a.* Bolivian.
[1]**bolo,** *m.* (bowling, etc.) a ninepin; game of ninepins; large pill; cushion for lacemaking; axis or core of winding staircase; dunce, blockhead.
[2]**bolo,** *m.* (P. I.) large knife like a machete.
[3]**bolo, la,** *a.* & *n.* (Am.) drunk (person).
bolométrico, ca, *a.* bolometric.
bolómetro, *m.* (elec.) bolometer.
bolonio, *n.* & *a.* ignorant (person).
boloñés, ñesa, *n.* & *a.* Bolognese.
bolsa, *f.* purse; pouch, bag; wrinkle, pucker (in cloth); (anat.) scrotum; (min.) pocket; (med.) sac; exchange center.—**b. de comercio,** stock exchange.—**b. de hielo,** ice pack.—**b. de pastor,** (bot.) shepherd's purse.—**b. de trabajo,** employment bureau or exchange.
bolsear, *vn.* to wrinkle, pucker.
bolsera, *f.* woman's hair bag or net.
bolsería, *f.* purse or bag shop or factory.
bolsero, ra, *n.* manufacturer or seller of purses.
bolsico, *m.* (Chile) poke, pocket.
bolsicón, *m.* (Am.) baize skirt of poor women.
bolsilibro, *m.* pocketbook; paperback (book).
bolsillo, *m.* pocket; (woman's) handbag, purse; money (belonging to a person).—**rascarse el b.,** to put one's hand in one's pocket (fig., in the sense of spending or paying), (slang) to come across.—**tener a una persona en el b.,** (coll.) to have a person in the palm of one's hand, or under one's thumb.
bolsín, *m.* gathering of brokers out of exchange hours.
bolsista, *m.* stockbroker; speculator.
bolso, *m.* purse of money, moneybag.
bolsón, *m. aug.* of BOLSO; large purse; large iron ring to hold braces of arches; board lining.
bolla, *f.* duty on woollens and silks formerly levied in Catalonia; tax on the manufacture of playing cards; in S. A., great richness of an ore.
bolladura, *f.* = ABOLLADURA, unevenness; dent.
[1]**bollar,** *va.* to mark (goods) with a lead seal.
[2]**bollar,** *va.* to emboss.
bollería, *f.* bakery, pastry shop.
bollero, ra, *n.* pastry cook; cake seller.
bollo, *m.* small loaf or roll, penny loaf; small biscuit or cake; puff in dress; tuft in upholstery; bruise made in metal; morbid swelling; lump; in Peru, bars of silver.—**bollos de relieve,** embossed or raised work.—**bollón,** *m.* brass-headed nail; bud on a plant; button earring.
bollonado, da, *a.* having brass-headed nails.
[1]**bomba,** *f.* pump; fire engine; lamp globe; high hat; slide (of a wind instrument).—**¡b.!** listen!—**b. alimenticia,** feed pump.—**b. al vacío,** vacuum pump.—**b. aspirante,** lift pump.—**b. aspirante-impelente,** lift-and-force pump.—**b. centrífuga,** centrifugal pump.—**b. de aire comprimido,** air lift.—**b. de alimentación** = B. ALIMENTICIA.—**b. de carena,** bilge pump.—**b. de doble efecto,** double-acting pump.—**b. de émbolo buzo,** plunger pump.—**b. de estribo,** stirrup pump.—**b. impelente,** force pump.—**b. marina,** waterspout.—**b. rotatoria,** rotary pump.—**dar a la b.,** to pump.
[2]**bomba,** *f.* bomb, shell.—**b. atómica,** atom(ic bomb.—**b. de cobalto,** cobalt bomb.—**b. de demolición,** demolition bomb.—**b. de fragmentación,** fragmentation bomb.—**b. de hidrógeno,** hydrogen bomb.—**b. de profundidad,** depth bomb or charge.—**b. de tiempo,** time bomb.—**b. incendiaria,** incendiary bomb.

—**b. lacrimógena**, tear gas bomb.—**b. plástica**, plastic bomb.
bombáceo, cea, *a.* (bot.) bombacaceous.
bombachas, *f. pl.* (Arg.) loose trousers fastened at the bottom.
bombacho, cha, *a.* (of trousers) loose, loos fitting.
[1]**bombarda**, *f.* bombard, ancient thick piece of ordnance; (naut.) bomb ketch or bomb vessel.
[2]**bombarda**, *f.* ancient wind instrument; stop of a pipe organ.
bombardear, *va.* to bombard, bomb.
bombardeo, *m.* bombardment, bombing.—**b. de precisión** or **saturación**, precision or saturation bombing.—**b. en picada**, dive bombing.
bombardero, *m.* (aer.) bomber; bombardier.
bombardón, *m.* (mus.) bombardon.
bombasí, *m.* bombazine, dimity.
bombástico, ca, *a.* bombastic, high-sounding.
bombazo, *m.* explosion or noise of a bursting bomb; throwing of a bomb; bomb hit; damage caused by a bomb.
bombé, *m.* light two-wheeled carriage open in front.
[1]**bombear**, *va.* (Am.) to pump; to praise, write up; (Am.) to watch, spy; (Peru, Arg.) to reconnoiter.
[2]**bombear**, *va.* to bomb, bombard; (Colomb.) to dismiss, "fire."
bombeo, *m.* pumping; curving, bulging.
[1]**bombero**, *m.* fireman; pumper.
[2]**bombero**, *m.* howitzer.
bómbice, *m.* (ent.) bombyx.
bombilla, *f.* (Am.) small tube for drinking MATE; (naut.) hand lantern; electric light bulb.
bombillo, *m.* lamp chimney; water-closet trap; small pump; sample or thief tube.
bombín, *m.* (Am.) bowler (hat).
bombista, *n.* pump maker; lamp-chimney maker; praiser, writer of write-ups.
bombo, ba. I. *a.* bewildered; astonished; (Am.) tepid. **II.** *m.* large drum; player on bass drum; (naut.) barge or lighter; leather pouch in billiards, for numbered balls.—**dar b.**, to praise excessively; to write up.
[1]**bombón**, *m.* bonbon, candy.
[2]**bombón**, *m.* (P. I.) vase made of cane; carboy.
bombonaje, *m.* screw pine.
bombonera, *f.* box for bonbons.
bonachón, na, *a.* good-natured, kind.
bonaerense. I. *a.* of or pertaining to Buenos Aires. **II.** *n.* native or inhabitant of Buenos Aires.
bonancible, *a.* moderate, calm, fair.
bonanza, *f.* fair weather; prosperity, success.—**ir en b.**, to be prosperous.
bonapartismo, *m.* Bonapartism.
bonapartista, *n.* & *a.* Bonapartist.
bonarense, *n.* & *a.* = BONAERENSE.
bonazo, za, *a.* good-natured, kind-hearted.
bondad, *f.* goodness, excellence; kindness, kindliness.—**tener la b. (de)**, please (*inf.*).
bondadosamente, *adv.* kindly.
bondadoso, sa, *a.* kind, good; (U. S., coll.) bighearted.
bonetada, *f.* salutation by taking off the hat.
bonetas, *f. pl.* (naut.) bonnets.
bonete, *m.* bonnet, college cap; secular clergyman; bonnet of a fortress; preserve jar; second stomach of ruminants.
bonetería, *f.* bonnet factory or shop.
bonetero, ra, *n.* bonnet maker or seller; (bot.) prickwood, gatheridge.
bonetillo, *m.* small bonnet; hair ornament.
bonga, *f.* a Philippine palm. Also ARECA.
bongo, *m.* (Am.) a large, rough canoe or boat.
bonhomía, *f.* honesty; naïvete, simplicity, ingenuousness.
boniato, buniato, *m.* sweet potato.
bonico, ca, *a. dim.* fairly good.
bonificación, *f.* allowance, discount; bonus.
bonificar, *va.* (*pret.* BONIFIQUÉ; *subj.* BONIFIQUE) to credit; to improve.
bonina, *f.* (bot.) oxeye chamomile.
bonísimo, ma, *a. super.* of BUENO: very good.
bonítalo, *m.* (ichth.) = [1]BONITO.
bonitamente, *adv.* prettily, neatly.
[1]**bonito**, *m.* (ichth.) striped tunny.
[2]**bonito, ta**, *a.* pretty.
bonizal, *m.* cornfield.
bonizo, *m.* corn grown wild in Asturias.
bono, *m.* (com.) bond; certificate; duebill.
bonote, *m.* cocoanut fiber; (naut.) coir.
bonzo, *m.* bonze, a priest of Buddha.
boñiga, *f.* cow dung; castings.
Bootes, *m.* Bootes, a northern constellation.
boqueada, *f.* gasp, gasping.
boquear. I. *vn.* to gape· to gasp; to breathe one's last; to end, terminate. **II.** *va.* to pronounce; to utter.
boquera, *f.* sluice in an irrigation canal; door; opening; cesspool; crack in the corner of the mouth; (vet.) ulcer in the mouth.—**boquerón**, *m.* wide opening, large hole; (ichth.) anchovy.
boquete, *m.* gap, narrow entrance.
boquiabierto, ta, *a.* open-mouthed; gaping.
boquiancho, cha, *a.* wide-mouthed.
boquiangosto, ta, *a.* narrow-mouthed.
boquiconejuno, na, *a.* rabbit-mouthed; (of horses) hare-lipped.
boquiduro, ra, *a.* (of horses, etc.) hard-mouthed.
boquifresco, ca, *a.* (of horses) tender-mouthed; frank, outspoken (esp. in disagreeable utterances).
boquifruncido, da, *a.* (of horses) pucker-mouthed.
boquihendido, da, *a.* (esp. of horses) large-mouthed.
boquihundido, da, *a.* (of horses) having a sunken mouth.
boquilla, *f. dim.* little mouth; opening of bottom of trouser leg; opening in an irrigation canal; chisel for mortising; mouthpiece of a wind instrument; cigar- or cigarette-holder; (mason.) verge, course; (mech.) nozzle; bushing, bush; gas burner; mouth of a scabbard.
boquimuelle, *a.* (of horses) sensitive-mouthed; unwary, easily imposed upon.
boquín, *m.* a kind of coarse baize.
boquinatural, *a.* (of horses) with a normally sensitive mouth.
boquinegro, gra. I. *a.* (of animals) black-mouthed. **II.** *m.* or *f.* a blackish snail.
boquirrasgado, da, *a.* deep-mouthed.
boquirroto, ta, *a.* loquacious, garrulous.
boquirrubio, bia, *a.* blabbing; simple, artless.
boquiseco, ca, *a.* dry-mouthed.
boquisumido, da, *a.* = BOQUIHUNDIDO.
boquitorcido, da; boquituerto, ta, *a.* wry-mouthed, having a crooked mouth.
boquiverde, *a.* plain-spoken about off-color matters.
borácico, ca, *a.* boracic.
boracita, *f.* (min.) boracite.
boratado, da, *a.* borated.
borato, *m.* borate.
bórax, *m.* borax. Also [2]BORRA, BORRAJ.
borbollar, *vn.* to bubble out, gush out.
borbollón, borbotón, *m.* bubbling, gushing up of water; flash.—**a borbollones**, impetuously.
borbollonear, *vn* = BORBOLLAR.
borbónico, ca, *a.* pertaining to the Bourbons.
borbonismo, *m.* Bourbonism.
borborigmo, *m.* rumbling in the bowels.
borbotar, *vn.* to gush out; to boil over.
borbotón, *m.* = BORBOLLÓN.—**a borbotones** = A BORBOLLONES.—**hablar a borbotones**, to speak in torrents.
borceguí, *m.* buskin, half-boot; lace shoe.
borceguinería, *f.* lace-shoe factory or shop.
borceguinero, ra, *n.* lace-shoe maker or retailer.
borcellar, *m.* brim of a vessel.
[1]**borda**, *f.* hut, cottage.
[2]**borda**, *f.* (naut.) gunwale.
bordada, *f.* (naut.) tack; pacing to and fro.—

dar una b., or, **dar bordadas,** (naut.) to tack; to promenade.
bordado, *m.* embroidery; embroidering.
bordador, ra, *n.* embroiderer.
bordadura, *f.* embroidery; (her.) border of an escutcheon.
bordaje, *m.* (naut.) side planks of a ship.
bordar, *va.* to embroider; to perform prettily and artistically.—**b. a tambor,** to tambour.
[1]**borde,** *m.* border, edge, verge, fringe, ledge; hem of a garment; brim of a vessel; (naut.) board, the side of a ship.—**b. de ataque,** (aer.) leading edge.—**b. de salida,** (aer.) trailing edge.—**a b.,** on the brink; on the eve.
[2]**borde,** *a.* (of plants, trees) wild, uncultivated; (of persons) bastard.
bordear, *vn.* (naut.) to ply to windward.
bordelés, sa, *a.* of or from Bordeaux.
bordo, *m.* board, the side of a ship; border, outer edge; tack.—**a b.,** on board, aboard.—**al b.,** alongside the ship.—**dar bordos,** (naut.) to tack.—**de alto b.,** (of ships) sea-going, major; (fig.) of importance, of heavy caliber, first rank; (of persons) high-up.
bordón, *m.* Jacob's staff, pilgrim's staff; bass-string; bass of an organ, iteration of words· refrain, burden of a song; staff, guide, or support of another.—*pl.* (naut.) shores, outriggers.
bordonear. I. *vn.* to try the ground with a stick; to rove about. **II.** *va.* to beat, cudgel.
bordonería, *f.* wandering idly about, on pretense of religious pilgrimage.
bordonero, ra, *n.* vagabond, roamer, tramp.
bordura, *f.* (her.) = BORDADURA.
boreal, *a.* boreal, northern.
bóreas, *m.* Boreas, the north wind.
Borgoña, *f.* Burgundy; *m.* Burgundy wine.
borgoñón, na, *a.* of or from Burgundy.—**a la borgoñona,** in Burgundy fashion.
borgoñota, *f.* a sort of ancient helmet.—**a la b.,** in the Burgundy fashion.
bórico, ca, *a.* boric.
boricua, *n.* & *a.* (Am.) Puerto Rican, Porto Rican.
borinqueño, ña, *n.* & *a.* Puerto Rican.
borla, *f.* tassel, tuft, lock, flaunt; in universities, doctor's hood; doctorship.—**tomar la b.,** to graduate.
borlilla, *f.* (bot.) anther.
borlón, *m. aug.* large tassel; napped stuff, made of thread and cotton yarn.
[1]**borne,** *m.* end of a lance; (elec.) binding post, binding screw; terminal.
[2]**borne,** *m.* (bot.) cytissus.
borneadero, *m.* (naut.) berth of a ship at anchor; swinging berth.
borneadizo, za, *a.* pliant, easily warped.
bornear. I. *va.* to bend, turn, twist; (arch.) to model and cut (pillars): to hoist and place (building stones, etc.). **II.** *vn.* (naut.) to swing around the anchor. **III.** *vr.* to warp, bulge.
borneo, *m.* turning or winding; swinging motion in dancing; (naut.) swinging round the anchor.
borneol, *m.* (chem.) borneol.
borní, *m.* (ornith.) lanner, a kind of falcon.
boro, *m.* (chem.) boron.
borona, *f.* Indian corn; cornbread; crumb
boronía, *f.* eggplant and tomato dish.
[1]**borra,** *f.* yearling ewe; thick wool; goat's hair; nap; floss, burl; tax on sheep; lees, sediment, waste, idle talk.—**b. de lana,** flock wool.—**b. de seda,** floss silk.
[2]**borra,** *f.* borax.
borracha, *f.* (coll.) a leather bottle for wine.
borrachear, *vn.* to get intoxicated often.
borrachera, borrachería, *f.* drunkenness; carousal, drunken feast, orgy; drunken condition, (coll.) drunk; (fig.) madness, great folly.
borrachero, *m.* a South American shrub, whose seed, when eaten, causes delirium.
borrachez, *f.* intoxication; perturbation of the judgment or reason.
borrachín, *m.* drunkard.
borracho, cha. I. *n.* drunkard. **II.** *a.* habitually drunk, violet-colored.—**borrachón, borrachonazo,** *m. aug.* great drunkard, toper.
borrachuela, *f.* (bot.) bearded darnel.
borrachuelo, la, *n. dim.* tippler.
borrador, *m.* rough draft; (com.) blotter.
borradura, *f.* erasure, scratching out.
borragíneo. I. *a.* (bot.) boraginaceous. **II.** *f. pl.* Boraginaceæ.
borraj, *m.* borax.
borraja, *f.* (bot.) borage.
borrajear, *vn.* to scribble, scrawl.
borrajo, *m.* = RESCOLDO, embers, hot ashes.
borrar, *va.* to cross out; to efface, erase, rub out, obliterate; (fig.) to cloud, darken, obscure.
borrasca, *f.* storm, tempest, squall; (Mex.) (min.) barren rock; (fig.) hazard, danger; obstruction.—**b. deshecha,** violent tempest.
borrascoso, sa, *a.* stormy, tempestuous.
borrasquero, ra, *n.* & *a.* reveller(-ing).
borregada, *f.* large flock of sheep or lambs.
borrego, ga, *n.* lamb not yet a year old; (fig.) simpleton.—**borreguero,** *m.* shepherd who tends lambs.—**borreguito,** *m. dim.* little lamb.
borrén, *m.* saddle-tree.
borrica, *f.* female donkey; ignorant woman.
borricada, *f.* drove of donkeys; cavalcade on donkeys; asinine word or action.
borrico, *m.* ass, donkey; (carp.) sawhorse.
borricón, borricote, *m. aug.* large jackass; plodder, laborious man; sawyer's horse.
borrilla, *f.* downy matter enveloping fruits.
borriqueño, ña, *a.* asinine.
borriquero, *m.* one who keeps or tends donkeys.
borriquete, *m.* (carp.) sawhorse.—**b. de proa,** (naut.) fore-topmast.
borriquillo, illa, ito, ita, *n. dim.* little donkey.
borriquillos, *m. pl.* crossbars of a table frame.
borro, *m.* male lamb not two years old; (coll.) dolt; duty on sheep.
borrón, *m.* blot; blur; rough draft; blemish, stigma, stain.—**borroncillo,** *m. dim.* small blot or stain.—**borronear,** *va.* to sketch; to waste (paper) by scribbling on it.
borroso, sa, *a.* full of dregs, thick, muddy; blurred, faded.
borrumbada, *f.* boast; extravagant expense.
boruca, *f.* noise, hubbub, uproar
borujo, *m.* pack, bundle; refuse of olive pits; oil cake.—**borujón,** *m.* = BURUJÓN. lump; badly wrapped parcel.
boruro, *m.* (chem.) boride.
borusca, *f.* withered leaf. Also SEROJA.
boscaje, *m.* cluster of trees, grove; (art) boscage, landscape.
boscoso, sa, *a.* bushy, bosky, wooded.
Bósforo, *m.* Bosporus.
bosnio, nia, *n.* & *a.* Bosnian.
bosque, *m.* wood, forest; grove.
bosquejar, *va.* to sketch, outline; to plan, design; to explain vaguely; to make a rough model of.
bosquejo, *m.* sketch; any unfinished work, writing or composition.—**en b.,** unfinished.
bosquete, *m.* wood; forest; artificial forest.
bosta, *f.* dung, manure.
bostecé, bostece, *v. V.* BOSTEZAR.
bostezar, *vn.* (*pret.* BOSTECÉ; *subj.* BOSTECE) to yawn, gape.—**bostezo,** *m.* yawn, yawning.
bota, *f.* boot; small leather wine bag; butt or pipe for liquids; liquid measure equal to about 125 gallons; (naut.) water cask.—**b. de montar,** riding boot.—**ponerse las botas,** to become rich or prosperous, (fig.) strike oil.
botado, da. I. *pp.* of BOTAR. **II.** *a.* (Am.) cheap, inexpensive; (Am.) (of person) lying down.
botador, *m.* thrower, pitcher; punch; instrument for pulling out nails; nail set; dentist's crow's bill or pelican; (naut.) starting pole, boat hook; (mech.) furnace bar, fire iron; bolt driver; (med.) refractor.
botafuego, *m.* (artil.) linstock, match staff; irritable, quick-tempered person.

botagueña, *f.* pig-haslets sausage.
botalón, *m.* (naut.) boom (of a crane or derrick).—**b. del foque,** jib-boom.
botamen, *m.* (naut.) collection of water casks on board a ship; collection of pots and jars in a drug store.
botana, *f.* plug; plaster on a wound; scar.
botánica, *f.* botany.
botánico, ca. I. *a.* botanical. **II.** *n.* botanist.
botanista, *n.* botanist.
botar. I. *va.* to cast, pitch, throw, fling; (Am.) to throw out (of a job), "fire"; (Am.) to squander, misspend; to throw away; (naut.) to shift (the helm).—**b. al agua,** (naut.) to launch. **II.** *vn.* to bound; rebound. **III.** *vn.* & *vr.* (of unbroken horse) to jump and kick, caper. *vr.* (Cuba) to carry to excess, overdo (something).
botaratada, *f.* rash, thoughtless action.
botarate, *m.* (coll.) madcap, thoughtless, blustering person; (Am.) spendthrift.
botarel, *m.* (arch.) buttress, abutment, spur, counter pillar.
botarga, *f.* loose breeches, galligaskins; motley dress; harlequin, buffoon; a kind of large sausage; DOMINGUILLO, tumbler (toy).
botasilla, *f.* (mil.) bugle signal for the cavalry to saddle.
botavante, *m.* (naut.) boarding pike.
botavara, *f.* (naut.) small boom or pole, gaff, sprit; boat hook.—**b. de cangreja,** gaffsail boom.
[1]**bote,** *m.* thrust with a weapon; rebound; frolicsome bound of a horse; chuck-farthing (boys' game).—**de b. y voleo,** instantly.
[2]**bote,** *m.* druggist's pot for medicine; can or jar.—**b. de tabaco,** snuff canister.
[3]**bote,** *m.* boat.—**b. de lastre,** ballast lighter.—**b. de salvamento,** (aer.) crash boat.—**b. salvavidas,** lifeboat.
[4]**bote,** *m.*—**de b. en b.,** crowded, jammed.
botella, *f.* bottle.—**b. de Leiden,** Leyden jar.
botellazo, *m.* blow with a bottle.
botellería, *f.* bottle factory; (Am.) BOTILLERÍA.
botellón, *m.* demijohn.
botequín, *m.* (naut.) cog, scull.
botería, *f.* (naut.) collection of casks of wine.
[1]**botero,** *m.* maker of wine bags and bottles.
[2]**botero, ra,** *n.* boatman, ferryman (-woman).
botica, *f.* apothecary's shop, drug store; medicines; (Arg.) shop, store.—**de todo, como en b.,** everything under the sun.
boticaria, *f.* apothecary's wife.
boticario, ria, *n.* apothecary.
botiga, *f.* (prov.) shop.—**botiguero,** *m.* shopkeeper.—**botiguilla,** *f. dim.* of BOTIGA.
botija, *f.* earthen round, short-necked jug; fat person.—**botijero,** *m.* one who makes or sells jars.—**botijilla, juela,** *f. dim.* small jar.
botijo, *m.* round earthen jar with a spout and handle; plump child.
botilla, *f. dim.* small wine bag; woman's shoe.
botiller, *m.* = BOTILLERO.
botillería, *f.* ice-cream parlor; (naut.) steward's room and stores.
botillero, ra, *n.* one who prepares or sells ice cream and refreshments.
botillo, *m. dim.* small leather wine bag.
[1]**botín,** *m.* buskin, half-boot; high shoe; leggings.
[2]**botín,** *m.* booty, spoils of war.
botina, *f.* modern gaiter; a woman's boot.
botinería, *f.* shoe shop or factory.
[1]**botinero, ra. I.** *a.* (of cattle) black-foot. **II.** *n.* shoemaker.
[2]**botinero,** *m.* soldier who took care of and sold the booty.
botinico, illo, ito, *m. dim.* little gaiter.
botiquín, *m.* medicine chest.
botito, *m.* man's gaiter with elastics or buttons.
botivoleo, *m.* recovering a ball on the rebound.
boto, ta. I. *a.* blunt; dull of understanding. **II.** *m.* wine skin; large gut filled with butter.
botón, *m.* button; sprout, bud; (fencing) tip of a foil; knob (of door or window); bead (in assaying); annulet of balusters, and of keys; piece of wood which fastens a fowling net; crankpin; dowel; handle.—**b. de fuego,** cautery in the form of a button.—**b. de oro,** (bot.) creeping double-flowered crowfoot.
botonadura, *f.* set of buttons.
botonazo, *m.* (fencing) thrust with a foil.
botonería, *f.* button maker's shop.
botonero, ra, *n.* button maker; button seller.
botones, *m. sing.* (*pl.* of BOTÓN) bellboy.
bototo, *m.* (Am.) gourd or calabash for water.
botriforme, *m.* (bot.) botryoidal.
botulismo, *m.* (med.) botulism.
botuto, *m.* stem of the papaw fruit; war trumpet of the Orinoco Indians.
bou, *m.* joint casting of a fish net by two boats.
bovaje, bovático, *m.* ancient duty on cattle.
bóveda, *f.* arch; vault; cave, cavern; vault for the dead.—**b. celeste,** firmament.—**b. craneal,** cranial cavity.—**b. palatina,** (anat.) palate.
bovedilla, *f.* (arch.) small vault, cove.—*pl.* (naut.) counters.
bóvido, da. I. *a.* (zool.) bovine. **II.** *m. pl.* Bovidæ.
bovino, na, *m.* & *a.* bovine.
boxeador, ra, *n.* (sports) boxer.
boxear, *vn.* to box.—**boxeo,** *m.* boxing.
bóxer, *m.* (zool.) boxer (dog); Boxer (Chinese).
boya, *f.* (naut.) beacon; buoy; net float.
boyada, *f.* drove of oxen.
boyal, *a.* pertaining to cattle.
boyante. I. *a.* buoyant, floating. **II.** *a.* (naut.) light, sailing well; prosperous, successful.
boyar, *vn.* (naut.) to buoy; to float.
boyazo, *m. aug.* large ox.
boyera, boyeriza, *f.* ox stall, cow house.
boyero, boyerizo, *m.* ox driver; cowherd.
boyezuelo, *m. dim.* young or small ox.
boyuno, na, *a.* bovine.
boza, *f.* (naut.) rope with one end fast in a bolt ring.—**bozas,** (naut.) stoppers.
bozal. I. *m.* muzzle (for dogs, etc.); bells on a harness. **II.** *a.* (of Negroes) pure, unmixed; (of Negroes) newly immigrating; novice, inexperienced, greenhorn; stupid, foolish; wild, not broken in, untamed.
bozalejo, *m.* small muzzle.
bozo, *m.* down that precedes the beard; mustache; mouth around the lips; headstall of a horse.
brabante, *m.* Brabant or Flemish linen.
braceada, *f.* violent stretching out of the arms.
[1]**braceaje,** *m.* coinage; beating metal for coining.
[2]**braceaje,** *m.* (naut.) bracing of yards; depth of water.
[1]**bracear,** *vn.* to move or swing the arms.
[2]**bracear,** *va.* (naut.) to brace; to fathom; (foundry) to tap (a furnace).
braceo, *m.* repeated swinging of the arms.
bracero. I. *m.* one who offers his arm to a lady; day laborer; strong-armed man.—**de b.,** arm in arm. **II.** *a.* (weapon) thrown with the hand.
bracete.—**de b.,** arm in arm.
bracillo, *m. dim.* branch of the bit of a horse's bridle; little arm
bracmán, *m.* Brahman; Brahmin.
bracmánico, ca, *a.* Brahmanic.
braco, ca, *a.* pug-nosed.
bráctea, *f.* (bot.) bract.
bractéola, *f.* (bot.) bractlet.
bradicardia, *f.* (med.) heart block.
brafonera, *f.* brassart, armor for the arm.
braga, *f.* breeches, knickerbockers; child's diaper; hoisting rope; (mil.) breeching, lashing rope.
bragada, *f.* flat of the thigh in animals.
bragado, da, *a.* with flanks of different color from the rest of the body; (fig.) ill-disposed, of depraved sentiments; energetic, firm.
bragadura, *f.* crotch (of the body, of trousers, etc.); flat of the thigh in beasts.

bragazas, *m.* & *a.* (coll.) (man) easily ruled or henpecked.
braguero, *m.* truss, bandage for a rupture, brace; (Peru) martingale.—**b. de cañón,** (artil.) breeching of a gun.
bragueta, *f.* fly (of trousers).
braguillas, *f. pl. dim.* little breeches; child wearing his first breeches; small, ugly child.
Brahma, *f.* Brahma, deity of the Hindus.
brahmán or **brahmín,** *m.* Brahman; Brahmin.
brahmánico, ca, or **brahmínico, ca,** *a.* Brahmanic(al, Brahminic(al.
brahmanismo, *m.* Brahmanism.
brahón, *m.* fold which, in ancient apparel, surrounded the upper part of the arm.
brama, *f.* rut, mating season.
bramadera, *f.* rattle; horn call.
bramadero, *m.* rutting place; (Am.) tethering post.
bramador, ra, *n.* & *a.* roarer(-ing).
[1]**bramante,** *m.* packthread, hempcord, twine; Brabant linen.
[2]**bramante,** *a.* roaring.
bramar, *vn.* to roar, bellow; to storm, bluster; to rage, cry.—**bramido,** *m.* cry uttered by wild beasts, howl; roaring of the elements.
branca, *f.* point of a horn.—**b. ursina** (bot.) = ACANTO, thistle.
brancada, *f.* dragnet or sweep net.
brancaursina, *f.* (bot.) bear's breech.
brandal, *m.* (naut.) backstay, ladder rope.
brandís, *m.* greatcoat formerly worn.
branquia, *f.* (ichth.) branchia, gill.
branquial, *a.* (ichth.) branchial, pert. to gills.
branquífero, ra, *a.* gill-bearing.
braña, *f.* summer pasture; brushwood.
braquial, *a.* brachial, pertaining to the arm.
braquicéfalo, la, *a.* (ethnol.) brachycephalous.
braquigrafía, *f.* brachygraphy.
braquiópodo, da, *m.* & *a.* (zool.) brachiopod.
brasa, *f.* live coal; red-hot coal or wood.—**estar en brasas**, to be on pins and needles.—**estar hecho unas brasas,** to be red in the face, flushed.
braserillo, *m. dim.* brazier, blazer.
brasero, *m.* brazier; fire pan; place where criminals were burnt; (Mex.) hearth, fireplace.
brasil, *m.* (bot.) braziletto; (bot.) brazilwood; (B.) Brazil.
brasilado, da, *a.* of a red color; ruddy.
brasileño, ña, *n.* & *a.* Brazilian.
brasilete, *m.* Jamaica wood, braziletto.
brasilina, *f.* brazilin, red coloring-matter of brazilwood.
brasmología, *f.* science of the tides.
bravamente, *adv.* bravely, gallantly; cruelly, barbarously; finely, extremely well; copiously.
bravata, *f.* bravado, boast, brag.
braveador, ra, *n.* bully, hector.
bravear, *vn.* to bully, hector, menace.
bravera, *f.* vent, chimney.
braveza, *f.* bravery; vigor; ferocity; fury (esp. of sea, wind, etc.).
bravío, vía. I. *a.* ferocious, wild, untamed; uncultivated; coarse, unpolished. **II.** *m.* fierceness (esp. of a bull).
bravo, va, *a.* brave, manly, fearless; angry; pungent, hot; bullying, hectoring; savage, wild, fierce; severe, untractable; rude, unpolished; rough (land); sumptuous, expensive; excellent, fine.—**¡bravo!** bravo!
bravonel, *m.* brave; hector, braggart.
bravosidad, *f.* = GALLARDÍA, bravery; gallantry.
bravucón, na, *n.* & *a.* boaster(-ing), braggart.
bravura, *f.* courage; ferocity; bravado; (mus.) bravura.
braza, *f.* fathom (measure).
brazada, *f.* uplifting of the arms; armful.
brazado, *m.* armful.
brazaje, braceaje, *m.* (naut.) depth of water.
brazal, *m.* bracer, brassart; bracelet; irrigation ditch from a river or canal; mourning band around the arm; (naut.) rail.—**brazalete,** *m.* armlet, bracelet.—*pl.* (naut.) brace pendants.
brazo, *m.* arm (of the body, a chair, a lever, the sea); upper half of the arm; foreleg; branch (of a tree, a chandelier); bravery, energy, enterprise. —*pl.* hands, laborers; assistance, protection, backing; protectors, backers.—**b. a b.,** hand to hand.—**b. de palanca,** lever arm.—**a b.,** by hand; swimming.—**a b. partido** = B. A B. —**con los brazos abiertos,** with open arms.— **con los brazos cruzados,** with folded arms. —**de b.,** arm in arm.—**hecho un b. de mar,** gorgeously attired.—**no dar el b. a torcer,** to be stubborn.—**ser el b. derecho de alguien,** to be somebody's righthand man.
brazolas, *f. pl.* (naut.) coamings of the hatchways.
brazuelo, *m. dim.* small arm; shoulder or fore thigh of beasts; branch of the bit of a bridle.
brea, *f.* pitch, tar; coarse canvas; sackcloth.
[1]**brear,** *va.* to pitch, tar.
[2]**brear,** *va.* to vex; thwart; (fig.) to play a joke on.
brebaje, *m.* beverage, potion; (naut.) grog.
breca, *f.* (ichth.) bleak or blay; dace.
brécol, bróculi, *m.,* **brecolera,** *f.* (bot.) broccoli.
brecha, *f.* breach, opening; (fig.) impression (on the mind).—**abrir b.,** to make a breach; to create an impression; to make progress.—**batir en b.,** (fort.) to batter, breach; to persecute.
brega, *f.* struggle; scrap, fight.—**andar a la b.,** to work hard.—**dar b.,** to be hard or laborious. —**dar b. (a),** to play a trick or joke (on).
bregar. I. *vn.* (*pret.* BREGUÉ; *subj.* BREGUE) to contend, struggle. **II.** *va.* to roll (dough).
bregma, *m.* (anat.) bregma.
bren, *m.* bran. Also SALVADO.
brenca, *f.* (bot.) maidenhair; sluice post.
breña, *f.,* **breñal, breñar,** *m.* craggy and brambled ground.
breñoso, sa, *a.* craggy and brambled.
breque, *m.* (ichth.) = BRECA.
bresca, *f.* honeycomb.—**brescar,** *va.* (*pret.* BRESQUÉ; *subj.* BRESQUE) to take combs from (a beehive).
bretaña, *f.* fine linen made in Brittany; (bot.) hyacinth.
[1]**brete,** *m.* fetters, shackles; perplexity, difficulties.—**estar en un b.,** to be in difficulties.
[2]**brete,** *m.* (P. I.) a food made of betel leaves.
bretón, na. I. *n.* & *a.* Breton. **II.** *m.* (bot.) borecole, kale.
breva, *f.* early fruit of a fig tree; early large acorn; choice cigar, rather flat; (coll.) any valuable thing obtained easily, (coll.) snap, cinch.
breval, *m.* (bot.) early fig tree.
breve. I. *a.* brief, short, concise; (phon.) short.— **en b.,** shortly, in a little while. **II.** *m.* apostolic brief. **III.** *f.* (mus.) breve, longest note.
brevedad, *f.* briefness, conciseness.
brevemente, *adv.* briefly, concisely.
brevete, *m.* = MEMBRETE, memorandum.
breviario, *m.* breviary; abridgement, epitome; (print.) brevier, small size of type.
brevipenne, *a.* (zool.) brevipennate.
brezal, *m.* heath, place planted with heaths.
brezo, *m.* (bot.) heath, heather.
briaga, *f.* bass-weed rope.
brial, *m.* rich silken skirt.
briba, *f.* truantship, idleness.
bribar, *vn.* to lead a vagabond life.
bribia, *f.* beggar's tale of woe.—**echar la b.,** to go a-begging.
bribón, na, *n.* vagrant; impostor; knave, scoundrel, rascal.—**bribonada,** *f.* knavery, petty villainy, mischief.—**bribonazo,** *m. aug.* great cheat, big rascal.—**briboncillo,** *m. dim.* little rascal.—**bribonear,** *vn.* to loiter about; to loaf.
bribonería, *f.* life of a vagabond; rascality.
bribonzuelo, *m. dim.* little rascal.
bricho, *m.* spangle, used in embroidery.
brida, *f.* bridle; rein; horsemanship, curb, re-

straint, check; rail coupling; fishplate; flange; clamp, staple (watchmaking).
bridecú, *m.* sword belt.
bridón, *m.* horseman riding a bur saddle; horse accoutred with a bur saddle; small bridle; (poet.) fine horse.
brigada, *f.* brigade; group of people doing a task together; beasts of burden for an army.—**brigadero,** *m.* man who tends beasts of burden in the army.
brigadier, *m.* (mil.) brigadier general; navy officer commanding a division of a fleet.
brigola, *f.* (mil.) battering ram.
Briján, *m.*—**saber más que B.,** to be very wise and cautious.
brillador, ra, *a.* sparkling, glittering.
brillante. I. *a.* brilliant, bright; shining, sparkling, glittering; glossy, lustrous; excellent, magnificent. **II.** *m.* brilliant, diamond.—**brillantemente,** *adv.* brilliantly; brightly, resplendently; splendidly.—**brillantez,** *f.* brilliance.—**brillantina,** *f.* brillantine; polishing powder (for metals).
brillar, *vn.* to shine, sparkle, glitter.
brillo, *m.* brilliance, brightness, lustre; splendor, magnificence.—**en b.,** (photog.) glossy.
brincador, ra, *n.* & *a.* leaper(-ing), jumper(-ing)
brincar. I. *vn.* (*pret.* BRINQUÉ; *subj.* BRINQUE) to leap, jump; to frisk, skip; to fly into a passion, become excited, (coll.) complain. **II.** *va.* to omit, skip; to throw (a child) up and down.
brinco, *m.* leap, jump; hop, bounce; small jewel worn in the hair.
brindar. I. *vn.*—**b. por,** to drink a person's health, toast. **II.** *va.* to offer, present, afford.
brindis, *m.* drinking the health of another; toast.
brinqué, brinque, *v. V.* BRINCAR.
brinquillo, brinquiño, *m.* gewgaw, small trinket; sweetmeat from Portugal.
brinza, *f.* blade, slip, sprig, shoot.
brío, *m.* vigor, enterprise, courage.
brioche, *m.* brioche.
briofita, *f.* (bot.) bryophyte.
briol, *m.* (naut.) bunt line.
briología, *f.* bryology.
brionia, *f.* (bot.) bryony.—**brionina,** *f.* (chem.) bryonin.
briós.—**¡voto a b.!** *interj.* by the Almighty!
brioso, sa, *a.* vigorous, enterprising, courageous; lively, spirited.
briozoario, ria, *m.* & *a.* (zool.) bryozoan.
[1]**brisa,** *f.* breeze.
[2]**brisa,** *f.* residue of pressed grapes.
brisca, *f.* a card game.
briscado, da. I. *pp.* of BRISCAR. **II.** *a.* mixed with silk (app. to gold and silver twist).
briscar, *va.* to embroider with gold or silver twist.
brisera, *f.*, **brisero,** *m.* glass screen for a candle.
brístol, *m.* Bristol board, Bristol paper.
británica, *f.* (bot.) great water dock.
británico, ca, *a.* British.
britano, na., *n.* & *a.* Briton.
brizar, *va.* to rock (a cradle).
brizna, *f.* fragment; splinter or chip; string (of beans, etc.).
briznoso, sa, *a.* full of fragments or scraps.
brizo, *m.* cradle.
[1]**broa,** *f.* (P. I.) a kind of biscuit or cracker.
[2]**broa,** *f.* (naut.) shallow cove.
broca, *f.* reel for twist, silk, or thread; conical drill for boring in iron; shoemaker's tack.
brocadillo, *m.* brocade of inferior quality.
brocado, da. I. *a.* embroidered like brocade. **II.** *m.* gold or silver brocade.
brocal, *m.* curbstone of a well; metal ring of the scabbard of a sword.—**b. de bota,** mouthpiece of a leathern wine bottle.
brocamantón, *m.* diamond brooch.
brocatel, *m.* stuff made of hemp and silk; white-streaked Spanish marble.
bróculi, *m.* broccoli.
brocha, *f.* painter's or shaving brush; loaded dice.—**de b. gorda,** (art) poorly done; (painter) of doors and windows; crude, badly done or written.
brochada, *f.* stroke of the brush.
brochado, da, *a.* pertaining to brocade.
brochadura, *f.* set of hooks and eyes.
brochazo, *m.* = BROCHADA.
broche, *m.* clasp; hook and eye; locket; fastener; hasp; brooch.—*pl.* cuff buttons.
brocheta, broqueta, *f.* (cook.) skewer.
brochón, *m. aug.* large brush; whitewash brush.
brodio, *m.* hodge-podge (of food); mixture of hog's blood and onions for sausages.
[1]**broma,** *f.* gaiety, merriment; noisy gathering; jest, joke.—**dar b.,** or **bromas,** to jest; to tease.—**por b.,** in jest, for fun.
[2]**broma,** *f.* shipworm; teredo.
[3]**broma,** *f.* (mason.) riprap; (Am.) (fig.) oatmeal gruel.
bromal, *m.* (chem.) bromal.
bromar, *va.* (of insects) to bore.
bromato, *m.* (chem.) bromate.
bromatología, *f.* bromatology, science of foods.
bromear, *vn.* to joke, jest, make fun.
bromeliáceo, cea, *a.* (bot.) bromeliaceous.
bromhidrato, *m.* (chem.) hydrobromide.
bromhídrico, ca, *a.* (chem.) hydrobromic.
bromhidrosis, *f.* (med.) fetid sweating.
brómico, ca, *a.* (chem.) bromic.
bromismo, *m.* (med.) brominism, bromism.
bromista, *n.*, merry person; practical joker.
[1]**bromo,** *m.* (chem.) bromine.
[2]**bromo,** *m.* (bot.) brome grass.
bromoformo, *m.* (chem.) bromoform.
bromurado, da, *a.* containing bromine; bromine (as *a.*, as in *agua bromurada,* bromine water).
bromuro, *m.* (chem.) bromide.—**b. potásico,** (chem.) potassium bromide.
bronca, *f.* practical joke; wrangle, quarrel.
broncamente, *adv.* peevishly, morosely.
bronce, *m.* bronze; brass; (poet.) trumpet, bell, or cannon.—**b. de aluminio,** aluminum bronze.—**b. de campanas,** bell metal.—**b. de cañón,** gun metal.—**b. fosforado,** phosphor bronze.—**b. mangánico,** manganese bronze.—**b. Uchatius,** steel bronze.
bronceado, da. I. *pp.* of BRONCEAR. **II.** *a.* bronze-colored; tanned, sunburnt. **III.** *m.* bronze-color finish(-ing).
broncear, *va.* to bronze; to adorn with brass.
broncería, *f.* collection of bronzes.
broncíneo, a, *a.* bronzelike.
broncista, *n.* worker in bronze.
bronco, ca, *a.* rough, coarse, unpolished; crusty; sturdy; morose, crabbed; rude; hard; abrupt, harsh; hoarse.
bronconeumonía, *f.* broncho-pneumonia.
broncorrea, *f.* (med.) bronchorrhea.
broncoscopio, *m.* bronchoscope.
bronquedad, *f.* harshness, roughness, rudeness; brittleness.
bronquial, *a.* (anat.) bronchial.
bronquina, *f.* dispute, quarrel, scrap.
bronquio, *m.* (anat.) bronchus, bronchial tube.
bronquíolo, *m.* (anat.) bronchiole.
bronquitis, *f.* (med.) bronchitis.
brontómetro, *m.* brontometer.
broquel, *m.* shield, buckler; support, protection.—**broquelazo,** *m. aug.* blow with a shield or buckler; large shield or buckler.—**broquelero,** *m.* one who makes or wears shields or bucklers; wrangler, disputer.—**broquelete,** *m. dim.* small buckler.—**broquelillo,** *m. dim.* small shield; small earring.
broqueta, *f.* = BROCHETA, skewer.
brosquil, *m.* sheepfold, sheepcote.
brota, *f.* vine bud.
brotadura, *f.* budding.
brótano, *m.* (bot.) southernwood.
brotar. I. *vn.* to bud, germinate, put forth shoots;

to gush, rush out; to issue, appear. **II.** *va.* (of the earth & fig.) to bring forth, produce.
brote, *m.* germ of vines; bud of trees; outbreak (of a disease); fragment, crumb, bit.
broza, *f.* rotten branches, leaves, etc., on the ground; weeds, underbrush; chaff, rubbish; BRUZA, (print.) brush.
brozar, bruzar, *va.* (print.) to brush (type).
brozoso, sa, *a.* full of rubbish.
brucero, *m.* brush and broom maker or seller.
bruces.—a, or **de, b.,** forward, headlong; face downward; on one's stomach.
brucita, *f.* (min.) brucite.
brugo, *m.* vine grub, plant louse.
bruja, *f.* witch, hag; owl.—**brujear,** *vn.* to practice witchcraft.—**brujería,** *f.* witchcraft, sorcery.
brujidor, *m.* glaziers' nippers. Also GRUJIDOR.
brujidura, *f.* bewitching, casting spells.
brujir, *va.* (of glaziers) to trim. Also GRUJIR.
brujo, *m.* sorcerer, conjurer, wizard.
brújula, *f.* magnetic needle; compass; sight, small hole to point a gun, peephole.
brujulear, *va.* at cards, to examine (one's cards) by slowly uncovering the tops; to discover by guess.—**brujuleo,** *m.* examining one's cards by slowly uncovering the tops; close examination; guess.
brulote, *m.* fire ship; an ancient engine of war.
bruma, *f.* mist, fog.
brumador, ra, *a.* = ABRUMADOR, overwhelming.
brumal, *a.* misty, foggy.
brumar, *va.* = ABRUMAR, to crush; to weary.
brumario, *m.* Brumaire (month in calendar of early French republic).
brumazón, *m.* thick fog or mist.
brumo, *m.* refined wax, for polishing tapers.
brumoso, sa, *a.* foggy, hazy, misty.
[1]**bruno,** *m.* black plum; plum tree.
[2]**bruno, na,** *a.* dark brown, blackish.
bruñido, *m.* polish, burnish.
bruñidor, ra. I. *n.* & *a.* burnisher(-ing), polisher(-ing). **II.** *m.* burnisher.
bruñimiento, *m.* polishing, burnishing; polish.
bruñir, *va.* to burnish, polish; (coll.) to put on rouge.
brusca, *f.* (naut.) bevel, sweep, or rounding of masts; brushwood.
brusco, ca. I. *a.* rude, rough, crude. **II.** *m.* (bot.) kneeholly, butcher's broom; trifling remains; refuse shearings.
brusela, *f.* (bot.) lesser periwinkle.
Bruselas, *f.* Brussels.
bruselense, *a.* & *n.* (native) of Brussels.
brusquedad, *f.* rudeness; rude action or treatment.
brutal. I. *a.* brutal; brutish. **II.** *m.* animal (esp. quadruped).—**brutalidad,** *f.* brutality; brutishness; stupidity; brutal or stupid action.—**brutalizar. I.** *va.* to brutalize. **II.** *vr.* to become brutalized.—**brutalmente,** *adv.* brutally.
brutesco, ca, *a.* = GRUTESCO, grotesque.
bruteza, *f.* roughness, want of polish; brutality.
bruto, ta. I. *a.* beastly, brutish, brutal; crude (ore, oil, etc.); gross (profits, etc.); unpolished, rough.—**en b.,** in a rough state, in the rough. **II.** *m.* brute, beast; ignoramus; blockhead.
bruza, *f.* horse brush; stove brush; scrubbing brush; printer's brush.—**bruzar,** *va.* to brush.
bu, *m.* bugaboo, bugbear.—**hacer el b.,** to scare, frighten.
búa, *f.* = BUBA, pustule.
buaro, buarillo, *m.* (ornith.) buzzard.
buba, *f.* pustule, small tumor.—*pl.* buboes.
búbalo, *m.* African antelope.
bubón, *m.* bubo.—**bubónico, ca,** *a.* bubonic.
buboso, sa, *a.* having pustules or buboes.
bucal, *a.* pertaining to the mouth; buccal.
bucanero, *m.* buccaneer.
búcare, *m.* a South American shade tree.
búcaro, *m.* vessel made of a fragrant earth of the same name; (Colomb.) BÚCARE.
buccino, *m.* (zool.) whelk, a marine gastropod.
buceador, ra, *n.* diver.
bucear, *vn.* to dive.
bucéfalo, *m.* bucephalus; blockhead, jackass.
buceo, *m.* diving; searching under water.
bucero, ra, *a.* (of dogs) black-nosed.
bucle, *m.* ringlet, curl, lock of hair; loop.
[1]**buco,** *m.* opening, aperture, gap.
[2]**buco,** *m.* (zool.) buck.
[1]**bucólica,** *f.* (coll.) food; meal.
[2]**bucólica,** *f.* bucolic, pastoral poetry.
bucólico, ca, *a.* bucolic.
buchada, *f.* mouthful. Also BOCANADA.
[1]**buche,** *m.* craw or crop; maw; belly; (coll.) bosom; mouthful; bag, pucker in clothes.
[2]**buche,** *m.* young suckling donkey; foal.
buchete, *m.* cheek puffed with wind.
buchón, ona, *a.* of a pouter (pigeon).
Buda, *m.* Buddha.
budare, *m.* (Venez.) large baking pan.
búdico, ca, *a.* Buddhic, Buddhistic.
budín, *m.* (Angl.) pudding.
budión, *m.* (ichth.) peacock fish.
budismo, *m.* Buddhism.
budista, *n.* & *a.* Buddhist.
buega, *f.* landmark; boundary marker.
buen, *a. contr.* of **bueno,** good. Used only before a masculine substantive, as *buen hombre,* good man, and before an infinitive used as a substantive, as *el buen decir,* correct speaking.
buenaboya, *m.* volunteer galley seaman.
buenamente, *adv.* freely, spontaneously; conveniently, easily.
buenandanza, *f.* = BIENANDANZA, prosperity.
buenaventura, *f.* fortune, good luck; fortune (as told by a fortune teller).
bueno [buen (*v.* BUEN)**], na. I.** *a.* good; kind; suited, fit; appropriate; well, in good health (*estoy bueno,* I am well); in good condition; great; high (excitement, fever, etc.); advisable, desirable; strange (often with *lo* in the expression **lo bueno es,** the strange thing is); simple, too good, (coll.) easy, soft.—**¡buena es ésa!** (coll.) that's strange; that is a pretty how-de-do, a pretty fix.—**bueno está lo bueno,** let good enough alone.—**buenas noches,** good night.—**buenas tardes,** good afternoon.—**buenos días,** good day, good morning.—**a buenas,** willingly, without compulsion.—**¿a dónde bueno?** where are you going?—**de buenas,** in good luck, lucky.—**de buenas a primeras,** all of a sudden, without warning. —**¿de dónde bueno?** where do you come from?—**por buenas, por las buenas** = A BUENAS. **II.** *adv.* well, very well, all right; that is enough.
buenparecer, *m.* good looks or appearance.
buey, *m.* ox, bullock.—**b. de caza,** stalking ox.—**b. marino,** sea calf.—**bueyazo,** *m. aug.* big ox.—**bueyecillo, -zuelo,** *m. dim.* little ox.—**bueyuno, na,** *a.* bovine; oxlike.
bufalino, na, *a.* pertaining to buffaloes.
búfalo, *m.* buffalo.
bufanda, *f.* muffler (for the neck), scarf.
bufar, *vn.* to puff and blow with anger; to snort.
bufete, *m.* desk or writing table; lawyer's office or clientele; bureau; sideboard.
bufetillo, *m. dim.* small desk or writing table.
bufido, *m.* bellow, roar, snort.
bufo, fa, *a.* & *n.* comic (singer).
[1]**bufón,** *m.* peddler, street vender.
[2]**bufón, na. I.** *a.* funny, comical. **II.** *m.* buffoon, merry andrew; fool, clown, jester.
bufonada, *f.* buffoonery, jest.
bufonazo, *m. aug.* great buffoon.
bufoncillo, *m. dim.* little merry andrew.
bufonearse, *vr.* to jest.
bufonería, *f.* = BUFONADA.
bufonesco, ca, *a.* clownish.
bugalla, *f.* gallnut growing on oak leaves.
buglosa, *f.* (bot.) alkanet; bugloss.
buharda, *f.* dormer window, skylight; garret.
buhardilla, *f.* garret; skylight.
buharro, *m.* (ornith.) eagle owl.

buhedera, *f.* embrasure, loophole.
buhedo, *m.* temporarily dried-out marsh.
buhero, ra, *n.* owl keeper.
buhío, *m.* = BOHÍO, Indian hut, hovel, cabin.
buho, *m.* (U. S., ornith.) great horned owl; (fig.) unsociable person.
buhonería, *f.* peddler's box; peddlery.
buhonero, *m.* peddler, hawker.
buitre, *m.* vulture.—**buitrera,** *f.* place to catch vultures.—**buitrero, ra. I.** *a.* vulturine. **II.** *m.* vulture fowler.
buitrón, *m.* osier basket to catch fish; partridge net; furnace where silver ores are smelted; snare for game.
bujarasol, *m.* fig with reddish pulp.
buje, *m.* axle box, bush box; pillow of a shaft.
bujeda, *f.*, **bujedal, bujedo,** *m.* = BOJEDAL, plantation of box trees.
bujería, *f.* gewgaw, bauble, toy, knickknack.
bujeta, *f.* boxwood box; perfume box; case for smelling bottle.
bujía, *f.* candle; candlestick; (physics) candle, candlepower; (int. combust. eng.) spark plug (called also **b. del encendido**); (surg.) solid probe.—**b. normal,** standard candle.
bujiería, *f.* office where wax candles are kept.
bula, *f.* papal bull.
bulario, *m.* collection of papal bulls.
bulbar, *a.* bulbar.
bulbo, *m.* (bot.) bulb.
bulboso, sa, *a.* bulbous.
buldog, *m.* (zool.) bulldog.
buleto, *m.* brief granted by the Pope or by his legate.
bulevar, *m.* (Gal.) boulevard.
Bulgaria, *f.* Bulgaria.
búlgaro, ra, *n.* & *a.* Bulgarian.
bulí, burí, *m.* (P. I.) a palm tree.
bulimia, *f.* (med.) bulimia, excessive appetite.
bulímico, ca, *a.* bulimic.
bulo, *m.* false rumor, canard.
bulto, *m.* bulk, anything which appears bulky; form, object not clearly discerned; protuberance; tumor, swelling; massiness; bust; bundle, parcel, package; pillowcase.—**a b.,** wholesale; as a whole; broadly.—**de b.,** obvious, manifest, striking.—**escurrir, huir,** or **sacar, el b.,** to sneak out.
bululú, *m.* strolling player (actor).
bulla, *f.* noise, bustle, fuss; noisy stir, crowd, mob.—**armar b.,** to make a racket.—**bullaje,** *m.* noisy crowd.—**bullanga,** *f.* tumult, riot.—**bullanguero, ra,** *n.* rioter, turbulent person.
bullar, *va.* to mark (goods) with a seal.
bullebulle, *m.* busybody, bustler, hustler.
bullicio, *m.* bustle, noise, uproar; sedition; heat.
bulliciosamente, *adv.* noisily.
bullicioso, sa, noisy; lively, merry; (of the sea) turbulent, boisterous.
bullidor, ra, *a.* = BULLICIOSO.
bullir. I. *vn.* to boil, bubble up; to move about, bustle, hustle. **II.** *va.* to move, stir.
[1]**bullón,** *m.* dye bubbling up in a boiler.
[2]**bullón,** *m.* metallic ornament for large books; puff (in sewing).
bumerang, *m.* boomerang.
buna, *m.* (chem.) buna; Buna (rubber) (trademark).
bungo, *m.* a Nicaraguan flatboat.
buniato, *m.* = BONIATO, sweet potato.
bunio, *m.* sort of earthnut or pignut.
buñolería, *f.* bun shop.
buñolero, ra, *n.* maker or seller of crullers or waffles.
buñuelo, *m.* fritter, bun, cruller; anything poorly done or spoiled; failure.
buque, *m.* vessel, ship; steamer; bulk, capacity (of a ship); hull (of ship).—**b. de guerra,** man-of-war.—**b. de torres,** turreted man-of-war.—**b. de vapor,** steamer.—**b. de vela,** sailing vessel.—**b. mercante,** merchant vessel.
burato, *m.* Canton crêpe; cypress (fabric); transparent veil of light silk.
burbuja, *f.* bubble.
burbujeante, *a.* bubbling.
burbujear, *vn.* to bubble.—**burbujeo,** *m.* bubbling.
burchaca, *f.* = BURJACA.
burche, *m.* tower.
burda, *f.* (naut.) backstay.
burdégano, *m.* hinny, mule.
burdel. I. *m.* brothel. **II.** *a.* libidinous.
burdo, da, *a.* coarse; common, ordinary.
burel, *m.* (her.) bar, the ninth part of a shield; (naut.) marlinespike.
bureo, *m.* court of justice; entertainment, amusement, diversion, spree.
bureta, *f.* (chem.) burette, a glass tube.
burga, *f.* spa, hot springs.
burgalés, *m.* native of Burgos.
burgomaestre, *m.* burgomaster.
burgrave, *m.* burgrave.
burgraviato, *m.* burgraviate.
burgués, guesa. I. *a.* bourgeois. **II.** *n.* bourgeois; burgess.
burguesía, *f.* bourgeosie.
burí, *m.* (bot.) buri, talipot palm.
buriel. I. *a.* reddish, dark red. **II.** *m.* kersey, coarse cloth; ropewalk.
buril, *m.* burin, engraver's chisel; graver.
burilada, *f.* line or stroke of a burin; silver taken by an assayer for testing.
buriladura, *f.* engraving with a burin.
burilar, *va.* to engrave with a graver.
burjaca, *f.* pilgrim's leather bag.
burla, *f.* scoff, flout, mockery, sneer; jest, fun, trick; jeer, gibe; hoax, deceit, cheat.—**b. burlando,** in an easy way, without effort.—**b. pesada,** biting jest.—**burlas aparte,** joking aside.—**de burlas,** in jest.—**hacer b.,** to make fun of, or a fool of.
burladero, *m.* refuge or covert in a bull ring.
burlador, ra. I. *n.* wag, jester, scoffer, practical joker; seducer. **II.** *m.* seducer, Don Juan; conjurer's cup.
burlar. I. *va.* to ridicule, mock, scoff; to abuse; to deceive, frustrate, disappoint, evade. **II.** *vr.* **(de)** to mock, laugh (at), make fun (of); to gibe, banter.
burlería, *f.* fun, mockery, scoffing; drolling; fish story, yarn, fairy tale; deceit, illusion; derision, banter, ridicule.
burlescamente, *adv.* comically, ludicrously.
burlesco, ca, *a.* burlesque, ludicrous, comical.
burlete, *m.* weather strip.
burlón, na, *n.* & *a.* banterer(-ing), jester(-ing), scoffer(-ing).
buró, *m.* bureau; writing desk.
burocracia, *f.* bureaucracy.
burócrata, *m.* or *f.* bureaucrat, public servant, officeholder.
burocrático, ca, *a.* bureaucratic.
burra, *f.* female donkey; ignorant, unrefined woman; industrious, strong woman.
burrada, *f.* drove of donkeys; stupid or foolish action or expression; play contrary to rule in the game of BURRO.
burrajo, *m.* dry stable dung for fuel.
burrero, *m.* ass keeper who sells asses' milk.
burrillo, *m.* (coll.) = AÑALEJO, church almanac.
burro, *m.* ass, donkey; sawyer's jack or horse; wheel of a reel; a game at cards; windlass.—**burros de la mesana,** (naut.) mizzen-bowlines.
burrumbada, *f.* = BARRUMBADA, extravagant outlay of money; boast.
bursátil, *a.* (com.) pert. to the stock exchange.
bursitis, *f.* (med.) bursitis.
burujo, *m.* lump of pressed wool or other matter; parcel, package; bagasse.
burujón, *m.* lump, badly made parcel.
Burundi. I. *m.* Burundi. **II.** *n.* & *a.* **(b.)** (of) Burundi.
bus, *m.* motorbus, bus.
busaca, *f.* (Am.) pocket (of a pool table); bag.

busca, *f.* search, research; pursuit; terrier; hunting party.—*pl.* (Mex.) perquisites.
buscada, *f.* search, research.
buscador, ra. I. *n.* & *a.* searcher(-ing), investigator(-ing). **II.** *m.* finder (optical appliance).
buscaniguas, *m.* (Am.) (coll.) = BUSCAPIÉS.
buscapié, *m.* hint.
buscapiés, *m. sing.* squib cracker; serpent firecracker.
buscapleitos, *n.* (Am.) quarrelsome person, trouble maker.
buscar. I. *va.* (*pret.* BUSQUÉ; *subj.* BUSQUE) to seek, look for.—**b. tres pies al gato,** to pick a quarrel. **II.** *vr.* to bring upon oneself.
buscarruidos, *n.* (coll.) quarrelsome person.
buscavidas, *n.* busybody, gossip monger; hustler; thrifty person.
busco, *m.* base of a sluice gate.
buscón, na, *n.* & *a.* searcher(-ing); cheat; pilferer(-ing), filcher(-ing).
busilis, *m.* (coll.) difficulty, difficult point.—**dar en el b.,** to hit the bull's eye.
busqué, busque, *v. V.* BUSCAR.
búsqueda, *f.* search.
busto, *m.* bust (statue); torso.
bustrófedon, *m.* boustrophedon, writing lines alternately from left to right and right to left.
butaca, *f.* armchair; easy-chair; orchestra seat in a theater.
butadieno, *m.* (chem.) butadiene.
butano, *m.* (chem.) butane.
butifarra, *f.* a sort of sausage made in Catalonia; (fig.) wide or badly fitting stockings or trousers; (Peru) ham sandwich.—**butifarrero, ra,** *n.* maker and seller of BUTIFARRAS.
butileno, *m.* (chem.) butylene.
butilo, *m.* (chem.) butyl.
butiondo, *a.* fetid; goatish; lustful.
butiráceo, cea, *a.* butyraceous, butyrous.
butírico, ca, *a.* (chem.) butyric.
butirilo, *m.* butyryl.
butirina, *f.* butyrin.
butirómetro, *m.* (chem.) butyrometer.
butrino, butrón, *m.* fowling net.
butuco, ca, *a.* (Hond.) thick, stumpy.
buyador, *m.* brazier.
buyo, *m.* (P. I.) chewing paste of bonga fruit and leaves, and lime.
buz, *m.* kiss of respect and reverent regard.—**hacer el b.,** to do homage or pay respect.
buzamiento, *m.* (geol.) dip of a stratum.
búzano, *m.* diver; a kind of culverin.
buzar, *va.* (geol.) to dip downward.
buzardas, *f. pl.* (naut.) breasthooks, forehooks.
buzo, *m.* diver; a kind of ancient ship.
buzón, *m.* conduit, canal; letter drop, letter box, drop box; lid, cover; hook to take off the lids of melting pots; sluice of a mill.
buzonera, *f.* drain or gutter in a courtyard.
byroniano, na, *a.* Byronic.

C

C, c, *f.* c, third letter of the Spanish alphabet.
¡ca! *interj.* oh, no! no, indeed! Also ¡QUIÁ!
cabal, *a.* just, exact; perfect, complete, thorough; full; faultless, consummate.—**por sus cabales,** exactly, perfectly, according to rule and order.
cábala, *f.* cabala, superstitious divination; secret science of Hebrew rabbis; cabal, intrigue, plot.
cabalgada, *f.* cavalcade; booty.
cabalgador, ra. I. *n.* rider, horseman(-woman). **II.** *m.* horse block.
cabalgadura, *f.* beast of burden; riding horse or mule; stirrup strap.
cabalgar. I. *vn.* (*pret.* CABALGUÉ; *subj.* CABALGUE) to ride on horseback; to parade on horseback; to go in a cavalcade. **II.** *va.* (of a horse) to cover (a mare); to ride.
cabalgata, *f.* cavalcade.
cabalgué, cabalgue, *v. V.* CABALGAR.
cabalhuste, *m.* ancient saddle with high semicircular pommel and cantle.
cabalidad, *f.* used in the expression **a cabalidad,** sensibly, justly; exactly, completely, fully.
cabalismo, *m.* cabalism.
cabalista, *m.* cabalist.
cabalístico, ca, *a.* cabalistic.
cabalmente, *adv.* exactly, completely, perfeetly, fully, precisely.
caballa, *f.* horse mackerel.
caballar, *a.* pert. to or like horses, equine.
caballear, *vn.* to ride horseback frequently.
caballejo, *m. dim.* little horse, nag; (vet.) shoeing-frame.
caballerato, *m.* ecclesiastical benefice granted by the Pope to a married layman; privilege of gentleman or esquire, in Catalonia.
caballerear, *vn.* to set up for a gentleman.
caballerescamente, *adv.* knightly, cavalierly.
caballeresco, ca, *a.* knightly, chivalrous; gentlemanly.
caballerete, *m. dim.* (coll.) spruce young gentleman.
caballería, *f.* riding animal; cavalry; art of riding, horsemanship; knight-errantry; chivalry; order of knights; knighthood; share of spoils given to a knight; (W.I.) a land measure (about 33½ acres).—**c. andante,** knight-errantry.—**c. mayor,** saddle horse or mule.—**c. menor,** ass, donkey.
caballeriza, *f.* stable; number of horses, mules, etc., in a stable; stud of horses; staff of grooms, hostlers, etc.; wife of a CABALLERIZO.
caballerizo, *m.* head groom of a stable.—**c. del rey,** equerry to the king.—**c. mayor del rey,** master of the horse to the king.
caballero, ra. I. *a.* riding. **II.** *m.* knight; cavalier; gentleman; rider, horseman; a sort of fortification; old Spanish dance; (ornith.) red-legged horseman; gambet.—**c. andante,** knight-errant.—**c. de industria,** defrauder, knave, one who lives by his wits, sponger.—**c. del hábito de Santiago,** knight of the military order of St. James.
caballerosidad, *f.* condition, quality of a gentleman; nobleness, honorable behavior.
caballeroso, sa, *a.* noble, generous; gentlemanlike, gentlemanly.
caballerote, *m.* (coll.) uncouth or unpolished gentleman.
caballeta, *f.* (entom.) field cricket.
caballete, *m.* ridge of a roof; carpenter's horse, sawhorse; trestle; easel; horse (instrument of torture); brake, for dressing hemp and flax; ridge between furrows; cap of a chimney; bridge of the nose; gallows of a printing press.—**c. de aserrar,** sawbuck, sawhorse.—**c. de colchar cabos,** (naut.) rope-laying truss, stakehead.
caballico, ito, *m. dim.* little horse, pony; hobby- or rocking-horse.—**c. del diablo,** dragon fly.
caballista, *m.* horseman; good rider; horse connoisseur.
caballo, *m.* horse; (cards) the queen; (chess) knight; (med.) bubo.—*pl.* (mil.) horse, cavalry.—**c. aguililla,** (Am.), a very swift pacing horse.—**c. amaestrado,** horse completely broken in.—**c. blanco,** a person who finances a doubtful enterprise.—**c. castizo,** blood horse.—**c. de agua** = C. MARINO.—**c. de aldaba** = C. DE REGALO.—**c. de batalla,** battle horse, charger; hobby, favorite idea; specialty, forte; main or crucial point.—**c. de carga,** pack horse.—**c. de carrera,** or **corredor,** race horse.—**c. de caza,** hunter.—**c. de Frisia,** (mil.) chevaux-de-frise.—**c. de fuerza,** = C. DE VAPOR.—**c. de mar** = C. MARINO.—**c. de montar,** saddle horse.—**c. de palo,** any vessel fit for sea; rack for criminals; (tannery) tanner's beam.—**c. de posta,** post horse.—**c. de regalo,** gala horse, handsome horse kept for special occasions.—**c. de silla**

saddle horse.—**c. de tiro,** draught horse.—**c. de Troya,** Trojan horse, (fig.) fifth column.—**c. de vapor,** horsepower.—**c. entero,** stallion.—**c. marino,** sea horse; hippopotamus.—**c. negro,** (pol.) dark horse.—**c. padre,** stallion.—**c. rabón,** docked horse.—**a c.,** on horseback.—**a c. regalado no hay que mirarle el diente** or **no se le mira el colmillo,** don't look a gift horse in the mouth.—**a mata c.,** at breakneck speed.

caballón, *m. aug.* large clumsy horse; ridge between two furrows.

caballuno, na, *a.* pertaining to horses; horselike.

cabaña, *f.* hut, cottage, cabin; hovel, mean dwelling; flock of ewes or breeding sheep; drove of mules; balk line in billiards.

cabañal. I. *a.* sheep-and-cattle (roads). **II.** *m.* village or settlement of huts.

cabañería, *f.* a shepherd's rations for a week.

cabañero, ra. I. *a.* pertaining to a CABAÑA in any of its meanings. **II.** *n.* keeper of a CABAÑA (of sheep or mules).

cabañil. I. *a.* pertaining to a shepherd's hut. **II.** *m.* man in charge of a drove of mules.

cabañuela, *f. dim.* small hut or cottage.—*pl.* weather forecast made in August for the following year; festival of Jews in Toledo.

cabaret, *m.* (Am.) cabaret, night club (gen. low-class).

cabás, *m.* cabas, workbasket.

[1]**cabe,** *m.* stroke on a ball in game of ARGOLLA. —**dar un c. al bolsillo,** or **a la hacienda,** (fig.) to hurt one in one's business, fortune, etc.

[2]**cabe,** *prep.* (poet.) near, nigh, by.

cabeceamiento, *m.* = CABECEO.

cabecear. I. *vn.* to nod; to shake the head in disapproval; to raise or lower the head (app. to horses); to incline to one side, to hang over (app. to a load); (naut., aer.) to pitch; (of carriages) to lurch. **II.** *va.* in writing, to give (the letters) a thick loop; among bookbinders, to put (the head-band) to (a book); to bind (cloth or rugs); to close by cauterization; to head (wine).—**cabeceo,** *m.* nod of the head; (naut., aer.) pitching.

cabecera, *f.* beginning or principal part; upper end; head or head-board of a bed; seat of honor; headwaters; capital of a province, district, nation; fortified point of a bridge; head piece or vignette; each extremity of the back of a book; pillow or bolster.—**c. de puente,** bridgehead.

cabeciancho, cha, *a.* broad-headed.

cabecica, ita, *f. dim.* small head.

cabeciduro, ra, *a.* (Am.) stubborn.

cabecilla, *m.* wrong-headed person; leader, ringleader.

cabellar, *vn.* to put on false hair.

cabellejo, *m. dim.* little hair.

cabellera, *f.* hair (collect.), head of hair; switch of hair; tail (of a comet).

cabello, *m.* a hair; hair of the head (collect.), also *pl.*; large sinews (in mutton); corn silk.—**cabellos de ángel,** sweetmeat made with CIDRACAYOTE.—**asirse de un cabello,** to resort to trivial pretexts or flimsy arguments, catch at trifles.—**traer por los cabellos,** to drag in irrelevantly, resort to or introduce farfetched (arguments, facts, etc.).

cabelludo, da, *a.* hairy; fibrous.

cabelluelo, *m. dim.* thin and short hair.

caber, *vn.* (*ind. pres.* QUEPO, *pret.* CUPE, *fut.* CABRÉ; *subj.* QUEPA) to go in or into (*la clavija no cabe en el agujero,* the peg does not go in the hole, the peg is too large for the hole); to have enough room, to be able to go through (often diff. constr.: *yo no quepo aquí,* I have not enough room here, this place is too small for me; *el elefante cabe por esta puerta,* the elephant can go through this door, this door is large enough for the elephant); to fall (to one), to befall, to have (often diff. constr.: *me ha cabido buena suerte,* good luck has befallen me, I have been fortunate; *me ha cabido el honor de ser nombrado,* the honor of being appointed has fallen to me, I have had the honor to be appointed); to be possible or natural (*todo cabe en la naturaleza,* in nature everything is possible); to be pertinent, appropriate or applicable.—**no cabe duda (de que),** there is no doubt (that).—**no cabe más,** that is the worst (or the best), that is the limit.—**no c. de,** to overflow, or be filled, with.—**no c. en sí,** to be puffed up with conceit, (coll.) to have a swelled head.

cabero, *m.* maker of handles for tools.

cabestraje, *m.* halter; fee paid to a drover.

cabestrante, *m.* (naut.) capstan.

cabestrar, *va.* to put on or lead by the halter.

cabestrear, *vn.* to be led by a halter.

cabestrería, *f.* shop where halters and collars are made and sold.

cabestrero, ra. I. *a.* that can be led by a halter. **II.** *n.* maker or seller of horse collars and halters.

cabestrillo, *m.* sling (for injured arm, etc.); gold or silver chain, necklace.

cabestro, *m.* halter; leading ox.—**llevar,** or **traer, de c.,** to lead by the halter; (fig.) to lead by the nose.

cabeza, *f.* head; chief, leader; understanding, mind, judgment, brains; beginning; end; forward, front end; big end; top or upper part; capital, seat (of a province, district, etc. (also **c. de partido**); head of cattle.—**c. a c.** (horse racing) neck and neck.—**c. de biela,** big end of connecting rod.—**c. de chorlito,** harebrained.—**c. de guerra,** warhead.—**c. de hierro,** stubborn, stiff-necked person.—**c. de playa,** (mil.) beachhead.—**c. de puente,** bridgehead.—**c. de turco,** scapegoat, (U. S., coll.) fall guy.—**c. mayor,** head of cattle.—**c. menor,** head of sheep, goats, etc.—**c. redonda,** blockhead.—**a la c.,** at the head.—**alzar c.,** to get better; to get on one's feet.—**de c.,** headfirst, headlong; by heart; brainy, smart. —**de pies a c.,** from head to foot, all over.—**hacer c.,** to lead.—**levantar c.,** to be restored in health or fortune.—**no tener pies ni c.,** to have neither head nor tail, neither rhyme nor reason.—**poner las cosas pies con c.,** to mix things up; to put topsyturvy.

cabezada, *f.* headshake; blow or butt given with the head, or on it; nod; headgear (of harness); headstall of a bridle; (naut., aer.) pitch, pitching, plunge; headband of a book; instep of a boot.—**dar cabezadas,** to nod (when napping).

cabezal, *m.* small pillow; (med.) compress; long round bolster; post of a door; fore part of a carriage; narrow mattress used by laborers.

cabezalejo, ico, illo, ito, *m. dim.* little pillow or bolster; small compress.

cabezalero, ra, *n.* executor of a will.

cabezazo, *m.* blow with the head.

cabezo, *m.* summit; reef; collar band.

cabezón, na. I. *a.* big-headed; obstinate. **II.** *m.* tax register; collar band; head; opening of a garment; cavesson or nose band, used in breaking in a horse.

cabezorro, *m. aug.* large, disproportioned head.

cabezota, *m.* & *f. aug.* (coll.) big-headed or obstinate person.

cabezudo, da. I. *a.* large-headed; headstrong; (of wine) heady. **II.** *m.* (ichth.) chub, mullet.

cabezuela, *f. dim.* small head; coarse flour; rose bud from which rose water is distilled; harebrained fellow, simpleton; (bot.) eryngo, ragwort-leaved centaury.

cabezuelo, *m. dim.* of CABEZA: little head.

cabida, *f.* content, capacity; space, room; influence.—**tener c.,** to be appropriate; to apply, be applicable.

cabila, *f.* (in Morocco) tribe.

cabildada, *f.* hasty, ill-advised proceeding.

cabildante, *m.* councilman, member of CABILDO.
cabildear, *vn.* to lobby; to influence or win votes in a corporation.—**cabildeo,** *m.* lobbying.
cabildero, ra, *n.* lobbyist.
cabildo, *m.* chapter of a cathedral or collegiate church; meeting of a chapter or place where held; municipal council; (in some places) city hall.
cabilla, *f.* (naut.) dowel; treenail; belaying pin.
cabillo, *m.* (bot.) stalk; stem; small end of a rope.
cabio, *m.* joist; breastsummer of a chimney; top or bottom piece of window or door frame.
cabito, *m. dim.* small end; butt.
cabizbajo, ja, *a.* crestfallen; thoughtful, pensive; melancholy.
cable, *m.* cable; cable's length, measure of 120 fathoms.—**c. coaxial,** coaxial cable.—**c. de cizalla,** (aer.) shear wire (of a dirigible).—**c. de sustentación,** (aer.) light wire.
cablear, cablegrafiar, *va.* to cable.
cablegráfico, ca, *a.* pertaining to submarine telegraphy; cable (as *a.*).
cablegrama, *m.* cablegram.
cabo, *m.* extreme, extremity; tip; bit; stub, stump; cape, headland, foreland; handle, haft, holder; rope, cord; thread; chief, leader; (mil.) corporal; end, termination, finish; parcel or package smaller than a bale.—*pl.* tail and mane (of a horse); loose pieces of apparel, as stockings, shoes, hats, etc.; divisions, sections, headings.—**c. de año,** anniversary funeral. —**c. de desgarro,** (aer.) rip cord, ripline.—**c. de escuadra,** (mil.) corporal.—**c. de maestranza,** foreman of a workmen's brigade.—**c. de presa,** prizemaster.—**cabos negros,** black hair, eyes, and eye-brows.—**al c.,** at last.—**al c. de,** at the end of, after.—**dar c. a,** to finish, end—**de c. a c.,** or **de c. a rabo,** from head to tail, from beginning to end.—**estar al c. de,** to be conversant with, or informed about.—**llevar a c.,** to carry out; to accomplish.—**llevar hasta el c.,** to carry to the end, see (something) through.
cabotaje, *m.* (naut.) coasting trade; pilotage.
cabra, *f.* goat; engine formerly used to throw stones.—*pl.* (Am.) little clouds; (Arg.) wavelets.
cabrahigadura, *f.* a fig-ripening process.
cabrahigal, [1]cabrahigar, *m.* wild-fig field.
[2]cabrahigar, *va.* to ripen figs artificially.
cabrahigo, *m.* wild fig tree; its fruit.
cabrería, *f.* herd of goats; goat's milk dairy.
cabreriza, *f.* goatherds' hut; woman goat tender.
cabrerizo, za. I. *a.* goatish, hircine. **II.** *n.* goatherd.
cabrero, ra, *n.* goatherd.
cabrestante, *m.* (naut.) capstan, winch.
cabria, *f.* crane; wheel and axle: winch; windlass; hoist; axletree: (naut.) sheers.
cabrilla, *f. dim.* little goat; (ichth.) a kind of fish; sawhorse; sawbuck.—*pl.* (astr.) Pleiades; marks on the legs, produced by being continually too near the fire; (naut.) whitecaps.
cabrillear, *vn.* to form whitecaps.
cabrilleo, *m.* the forming of whitecaps.
cabrio, *m.* (carp.) joist.
cabrío. I. *a.* goatish, hircine. **II.** *m.* herd of goats.
cabriola, *f.* caper; gambol, skip; nimble leap.
cabriolar, *vn.* to caper or cut capers; to jump, curvet, frisk.
cabriolé, *m.* a kind of sleeveless cloak; cabriolet.
cabriolear, *vn.* = CABRIOLAR.
cabritero, *m.* dealer in kids.
cabritilla, *f.* kid, dressed kidskin.
cabritillo, cabrito, *m. dim.* kid.
cabrón, *m.* buck, he-goat; (fig.) acquiescing cuckold.
cabronada, *f.* (low) infamous action which a man permits against his own honor; great annoyance or nuisance.
cabruno, na, *a.* goatish, goatlike.
cabujón, *m.* rough, unpolished ruby.
cábula, *f.* (Am.) trick, cunning scheme to get or accomplish something.
cabuya, *f.* (bot.) common American agave; sisal; sisal or hemp cord.—**dar c.,** (Am.) to tie, or bind.—**ponerse en la c.,** (Am.) to catch the drift; to become informed.
cabuyería, *f.* (Am.) ship chandlery.
cabuyero, *m.* (Am.) ship chandler.
cacahual, *m.* cacao plantation.
cacahuate, cacahué, cacahuete, cacahuey, *m.* (bot.) peanut.
cacalote, *m.* (Mex.) raven; (Am.) cracked corn and syrup; mistake, blunder.
[1]cacao, *m.* (bot.) cacao; cacao tree; cacao seed; chocolate.
[2]cacao, *m.*—**pedir c.,** (coll.) to beg for quarter, throw up the sponge.—(Am.) **tener c.,** to have vim, energy, courage.
cacaotal, *m.* cacao plantation.
cacaraña, *f.* pit caused by the smallpox.
cacarañado, da, *a.* pitted.
cacareador, ra, *n.* cackler; boaster, braggart.
cacarear, *vn.* to cackle; (coll.) to brag, boast.
cacareo, *m.,* cackling; boast, brag.
cacarizo, za, *a.* (Mex.) pock-marked.
cacatúa, *f.* (ornith.) cockatoo.
cacaxtle, *m.* (Mex.) crate to carry fruit.
cacé, cace, *v. V.* CAZAR.
cacear, *va.* to stir with a dipper or ladle.
cacera, *f.* irrigating canal; channel, conduit.
cacería, *f.* hunt, hunting.
cacerina, *f.* cartridge box or pouch.
cacerola, *f.* casserole.
caceta, *f. dim.* small pan.
cacica, *f.* wife or daughter of a cacique.
cacicato, cacicazgo, *m.* dignity and territory of a cacique.
cacillo, ito, *m. dim.* small dipper or ladle.
cacimba, *f.* hole dug on the sea shore for drinking water.
cacique, *m.* cacique, Indian chief; (coll.) boss; (ornith. Mex.) cacique.
caciquil, *a.* pert. to or like caciques; boss (as *a.*).
caciquismo, *m.* caciquism, bossism.
cacle, *m.* (Mex.) leather sandal.
caco, *m.* pickpocket; thief; coward.
cacodilato, *m.* (chem.) cacodylate.
cacodílico, ca, *a.* (chem.) cacodylic.
cacodilo, *m.* (chem.) cacodyl.
cacofonía, *f.* cacophony, harsh sound.
cacofónico, ca, *a.* cacophonous, ill-sounding.
cacografía, *f.* defective orthography.
cacomite, *m.* a Mexican flower plant.
cacomixtle, *m.* (Mex.) (zool.) cacomistle.
cácteo, a, *a.* (bot.) cactaceous.
cacto, (Am.) **cactus,** *m.* (bot.) cactus.
cacumen, *m.* top, height; head, acumen.
cacha, *f.* each of the two leaves of a razor or knife handle; (Am., coll.) handle.—**hasta las cachas,** (coll.) up to the hilt, as much as one can manage.—**hacer la c.,** to try, do what one can; (a), to make fun (of).
cachaco, *m.* (Am.) dandy, fop.
cachada, *f.* thrust or wound with the horns.
cachalote, *m.* sperm whale.
cachamarín, *n.* coasting lugger.
cachapa, *f.* (Venez.) corn bread with sugar.
cachar, *va.* to break in pieces; to split.
cacharpari, *m.* (Peru) farewell supper.
cacharrería, *f.* crockery store; collection or stock of earthen pots.
cacharrero, ra, *n.* maker or seller of crockery; (Am.) notion dealer; peddler.
cacharro, *m.* coarse earthen pot, or a piece of it; useless, worthless thing, truck; (Am.) notion, trinket.
cachava, *f.* children's sport resembling hockey or golf; stick for driving the ball.
cachavazo, *m.* stroke with the CACHAVA.
cachaza, *f.* slowness, tardiness; forbearance; (Am.) rum; first froth on cane juice when boiled.
cachazudo, da. I. *a.* slow, calm, phlegmatic. **II.** *m.* sluggard; (Am.) tobacco worm.
cache, *a.* (Arg.) uncouth.
cachemarín, *m.* = CACHAMARÍN.

cachemir, *m.*, **cachemira,** *f.* cashmere.
cacheo, *m.* search for hidden arms.
cachera, *f.* coarse shagged cloth or baize.
cachería, *f.* (Am.), small business; uncouthness.
cachetas, *f. pl.* teeth or wards in a lock.
cachete, *m.* punch in the face or head; cheek.
cachetero, *m.* short poniard; bullfighter who kills the bull with the poniard.
cachetina, *f.* hand-to-hand fight.
cachetudo, da, *a.* plump-cheeked, fleshy.
cachicamo, *m.* (Am.) armadillo.
cachicán, *m.* overseer of a farm; cunning, clever man.
cachidiablo, *m.* hobgoblin; one disguised in a devil's mask.
cachifo, fa, *n.* (Colomb., coll.) boy, girl.
cachifollar, *va.* (coll.) to disappoint; to vex, humble, banter, sit upon.
cachigordete, eta, ito, ita, *a.* squat, plump.
cachillada, *f.* litter (of animals).
cachimba, *f.* low well; (water) spring; (Cuba) disreputable woman; CACHIMBO.
cachimbo, *m.* (Am.) smoking pipe.—**chupar c.,** (Venez.) to smoke a pipe; to suck one's thumb.
cachipolla, *f.* (entom.) dayfly or May fly.
cachiporra, *f.* stick with a big knob; bludgeon, billy.
cachiporrazo, *m.* blow with a bludgeon.
cachirulo, *m.* earthen, glass, or tin pot for preserving liquor; head ornament formerly worn by women; (Mex.) reinforcing chamois skin patches on riding breeches; small three-masted vessel.
cachivache, *m.* pot, utensil; stuff, trash; broken crockery; trumpery; worthless fellow; (Am.) notion, trinket.
cachizo, *a.*—**madero c.,** thick, heavy log.
[1]cacho, *m.* slice, piece; a card game; bunch; (C. A.) joke, fun; (Chile, com.) left-over, goods unsold.
[2]cacho, *m.* (ichth.) surmullet.
[3]cacho, cha. I. *a.* bent, crooked. **II.** *m.* (Am.) horn.—**echar c.,** (Colomb.) to excel, get ahead.—**empinar el c.,** = EMPINAR EL CODO, to drink to excess, be a toper.
cacholas, *f. pl.* (naut.) cheeks of the masts.
cachón, *m.* breaker; small waterfall, cascade.
cachondez, *f.* sexual appetite.
cachondo, da, *a.* in heat, rutting.
cachones, *m. pl.* breakers (waves).
cachopo, *m.* (naut.) gulf; dry trunk, stump.
cachorrillo, ito. I. *n.* little cub or whelp. **II.** *m.* pocket pistol.
cachorro, rra. I. *n.* whelp, puppy, cub. **II.** *m.* pocket pistol.
cachú, *m.* catechu, astringent from plants.
cachúa, *f.* Indian dance in Peru, Bolivia, etc.
cachucha, *f.* rowboat; man's cloth or fur cap; Andalusian dance in three-quarter time with castanets.
cachuchero, ra, *n.* maker or seller of caps; maker or seller of pin or needle cases.
cachucho, *m.* oil measure, containing the sixth part of a pound; pin or needle case; clumsy earthen pot.
cachuela, *f.* fricassee of rabbits' livers and lights; gizzard.
cachuelo, *m.* (ichth.) small river fish like anchovy.
cachumbo, *m.* hard shell of cocoanut and other fruit.
cachunde, *f.* aromatic paste munched to sweeten the breath; cachou.
cachupín, *m.* Spaniard who settles in Spanish America.
cada, *a.* every, each.—**c. cual,** each; every one, everybody.—**c. que** = C. VEZ QUE.—**c. uno** = C. CUAL.—**c. vez que, c. y cuando,** every time, whenever; as soon as.
cadahalso, *m.* shed, cabin, shanty.
cadalecho, *m.* bed made of branches of trees.
cadalso, *m.* platform, stage, stand; scaffold for capital punishment.
cadañal, ñego, ga, *a.* annual, yearly.
cadañero, ra, *a.* lasting a year; CADAÑAL.—**mujer c.,** woman who bears a child every year.
cadarzo, *m.* coarse, entangled silk which can not be spun; cover of the cocoon; narrow silk ribbon.
cádava, *f.* burnt stump of furze.—**cadaval,** *m.* place where many CÁDAVAS remain standing.
cadáver, *m.* corpse, cadaver.
cadavérico, ca, *a.* cadaverous.
cadejo, *m.* tangled hair; small skein; threads put together to make tassels.
cadena, *f.* chain; bond, tie; series; range (of mountains); malefactors chained together to be led to the galleys; imprisonment for life; (arch.) buttress.—**c. de agrimensor,** surveyor's chain, Gunter's chain.—**c. de ancla,** (mar.) chain cable.—**c. de cangilones,** bucket chain. —**c. de montañas,** mountain chain.—**c. de rocas,** ledge or ridge of rocks.—**c. radial,** radio network, broadcasting system.—**c. sin fin,** endless chain.—**c. transportadora,** chain conveyor.
cadencia, *f.* cadence; fall of the voice; rhythm; measure; flow of verses or periods; in dancing, harmony of motion and music; (mus.) cadenza.
cadencioso, sa, *a.* rhythmical.
cadenear, *va.* & *vn.* (surv.) to chain.
cadenero, *m.* (surv.) chainman.
cadeneta, *f.* lace or needlework worked in form of a chain; chain stitch; work put upon the heads of books to reinforce the sewing.
cadenilla, ita, *f. dim.* small chain; pearls of a certain size.
cadente, *a.* decaying, declining; going to ruin; rhythmical.
cadera, *f.* hip, the joint of the thigh.
caderillas, *f. pl.* bustle (garment).
cadetada, *f.* injudicious, thoughtless action.
cadete, *m.* (mil.) cadet.
cadí, *m.* cadi, magistrate among Mohammedans.
cadillar, *m.* place where bur parsley grows.
cadillo, *m.* (bot.) great bur parsley; prickly bur weed; common burdock.
cadillos, *m. pl.* thrum; warp ends.
cadmía, *f.* (min.) calamine; tutty.
cadmio, *m.* (chem.) cadmium.
cado, *m.* ferret hole.
cadoso, cadozo, *m.* deep place in a river.
caducamente, *adv.* weakly, feebly.
caducante, *n.* & *a.* dotard, in one's dotage.
caducar, *vn.* (*pret.* CADUQUÉ; *subj.* CADUQUE) to dote (from old age); to be worn out by service; to fall into disuse; to become superannuated or extinct; (law, com.) to lapse.
caduceo, *m.* caduceus, Mercury's staff.
caducidad, *f.* (law) caducity; decrepitude.
caduco, ca. I. *a.* caducous; senile, decrepit; perishable, frail; (bot.) caducous, deciduous; (zool.) deciduous. **II.** *f.* (anat.) decidua.
caduquez, *f.* caducity; senility.
caedizo, za, *a.* ready to fall; (bot.) deciduous.
caedura, *f.* loose threads dropping from the loom.
caer. I. *vn.* (*ind. pres.* CAIGO, *pret.* él CAYÓ; *subj.* CAIGA) to fall, drop, tumble down; lighten; fall off; hang down, droop; fit; be becoming; deviate from the right path; fall due; decrease, decline, drop, fall; fall to one's lot; befall, happen to; come to pass; to understand, see; (of color) to become faint; to be included, fall (within certain limits, etc.).—**c. a,** to be (located) on (this or that side, etc.); to look out on, overlook (*la ventana cae a la playa,* the window overlooks the beach).—**c. bien (mal),** to create a good (bad) impression, to be well (unfavorably) received; to fit (not to fit); to be (not to be) becoming.—**c. de,** to fall on (*caer de espaldas,* to fall on one's back, or backwards).—**c. de plano,** to fall flat (stretched). —**c. en cama,** or **enfermo,** to be taken ill. —**c. en la cuenta,** to understand the situa-

tion; to realize.—**c. en la cuenta de,** to think, or take note, of—**c. en gracia,** to arouse liking, to become a subject of affection or esteem, to please.—**c. redondo,** to drop unconscious. —**al c. de la noche,** at nightfall.—**dejar c.,** to drop, let fall. **II.** *vr.* **caerse,** to fall; to lose heart, to become downcast.—**c. de su peso,** or **c. de suyo,** to be self-evident, to be obvious; to fall, or fail, by itself.—**c. redondo** = CAER REDONDO.—**caércele a uno la cara de vergüenza,** to be deeply ashamed, to feel like hiding one's face.

café, *m.* coffee; café, coffee-house; (bot.) coffee tree.—**c. cantante,** night club, cabaret, (U. S., coll.) night spot.—**c. con leche,** café au lait.—**c. expreso,** espresso (coffee).—**c. retinto,** very strong black coffee.—**c. tinto,** strong black coffee.

cafeína, *f.* (chem., pharm.) caffeine.

cafetal, *m.* coffee plantation.

cafetalista, *n.* (Am.) coffee grower; coffee planter; coffee worker.

cafetería, *f.* (Mex.) retail coffee shop; (Am.) cafeteria.

cafetero, ra. I. *a.* of or pertaining to coffee. **II.** *n.* (Am.) coffee grower; coffee planter; coffee worker; coffee seller; *f.* coffeepot.

cafetín, *m. dim.* small café or coffee shop.

cafeto, *m.* (bot.) coffee tree.

cafetucho, *m.* (derog.) small and untidy café or coffee shop.

cáfila, *f.* crowd, mob; caravan.

cafre, *n.* & *a.* Kafir, Kaffir.

cagachín, *m.* small reddish mosquito.

cagafierro, *m.* scoria, dross of iron.

cagajón, *m.* horse dung; dung of mules or asses.

cagalaolla, *m.* masquerader who dances in processions.

cagarrache, *m.* one who washes the olive pits in an oil mill.

cagarria, *f.* St. George's-mushroom.

cagarropa, *m.* = CAGACHÍN, small mosquito.

cagarruta, *f.* dung of sheep, goats, mice, etc.

cagatinta, *m.* (contempt.) minor office workers.

cahiz, *m.* nominal measure of twelve bushels.

cahizada, *f.* land sufficient for one CAHIZ of seed.

caída, *f.* fall; falling; tumble; downfall; lapse; drop; falling off; droop; diminution, drop; descent; (geol.) dip; landslip; interior gallery in houses of Manila, with views upon the courtyard.—*pl.* coarse wool cut off the skirts of a fleece; witty remarks, repartee; (sew.) reverse. —**c. de una vela,** depth or drop of a sail.—**a la c. de la tarde,** at the close of the afternoon. —**a la c. del sol,** at sunset.

caído, da. I. *pp.* of CAER. **II.** *a.* languid; downfallen. **III.** *m. pl.* arrears of taxes or rents; slanting lines to show the proper slant in writing.

caigo, caiga, *v. V.* CAER.

caimacán, *m.* kaimakam, assistant grand vizier; (coll.) big gun, person of importance.

caimán, *m.* cayman, alligator; sharp, exploiter.

caimiento, *m.* fall, drop; droop, languidness.

caimito, caimo, *m.* star apple.

caique, *m.* (naut.) skiff, small boat.

cairel, *m.* false hair or switch worn by women to embellish their head dress; fringe trimming; silk threads to which the hair of wigs is fastened.

cairelar, *va.* to trim with fringe.

caja, *f.* box; case; coffin; chest; cash box or safe; sheath; body (of a carriage, truck, etc.); stock (of firearm); cavity, hole; distributing or central post office; (com.) cash, funds; cashier's office; socket; frame; drum; printer's case; portable writing desk; well or cavity in which a staircase is raised; wooden case of an organ; (mil.) drum; drum case, or frame; (mech.) shell, block (of a pulley); (Chile) bed (of a river); (min.) barren rock.—**c. alta,** (print.) upper case.—**c. armónica,** (mus.) sounding board.—**c. baja,** (print.) lower case.—**c. chica,** (com.) petty cash.—**c. de ahorros,** savings bank.—**c. de amortización,** Department of Public Debts (an old branch of the Spanish administration); sinking fund.—**c. de caudales,** safe, strong box.—**c. de colores,** paint box. —**c. de conexiones,** (elec.) junction box.—**c. de embalar,** packing box or case.—**c. de engranajes,** gear box or case.—**c. de fuegos,** firebox.—**c. de grasa,** (mach.) grease box or cup.—**c. de hierro,** (Am.) strongbox, safe.—**c. de humos,** smoke box.—**c. de ingletes,** miter box or block.—**c. de las muelas,** (coll.) gums (of the mouth).—**c. del cuerpo,** (anat.) thorax, thoracic cavity.—**c. de música,** music box.—**c. de reclutamiento,** (mil.) recruiting branch.—**c. de reloj,** watch case.—**c. de sebo,** (Ry.) journal box or bearing.—**c. de seguridad,** safe-deposit box.—**c. de sorpresa,** jack-in-the-box.—**c. de válvula,** valve box or chest. —**c. de vapor,** steam chest.—**c. de velocidad,** (auto.) gear box, gear case, transmission.—**c. de volteo,** dump body (truck).—**c. fuerte,** safe, strong box.—**c. postal de ahorros,** post-office savings bank.—**c. registradora,** cash register.—**con cajas destempladas,** roughly, without ceremony; coldly, slightingly.—**en c.,** cash, cash on hand (kept in the safe); (fig.) in good condition.

cajero, ra. I. *n.* box maker; cashier. **II.** *m.* reservoir.

cajeta, *f.* little box; poor-box; (Mex.) box of jelly; (Cuba) tobacco box; cigar case; (Am.) puffed up townsman (so called by farmers).

cajete, *m.* (Mex.) flat earthen pulque bowl.

cajetilla, *f.* package (of cigarettes).

cajetín, *m. dim.* very small box; (print.) fount case, letter case.

cajiga, *f.* = QUEJIGO, *m.* a kind of oak.

cajigal, *m.* = QUEJIGAL, plantation of CAJIGAS.

cajista, *n.* compositor (in printing).

cajo, *m.* bookbinder's groove.

cajón, *m.* box, case, chest, (Am.) coffin; drawer, till, locker, mold for casting; space between the shelves of a bookcase; wooden stand or shed for selling provisions; (Mex.) dry-goods store; crib, caisson.—**c. de sastre,** confused mass; odds and ends.—**ser de c.,** to be a matter of course, go without saying.—**cajonada,** *f.* (naut.) lockers.—**cajoncito,** *m. dim.* small box or drawer.—**cajonera,** *f.* chest of drawers in a vestry.—**cajonería,** *f.* set of drawers; tallboy or chiffonier.

cajuela, *f. dim.* small box.

cal, *f.* lime.—**c. hidráulica,** hydraulic lime.—**c. muerta,** slaked lime.—**c. viva,** quicklime, unslaked lime.—**c. y canto** = CALICANTO, stone masonry.—**de c. y canto,** (fig.) firm, solid.

[1]**cala,** *f.* cove, small bay; fishing ground.

[2]**cala,** *f.* sample slice cut out of a fruit to try its flavor; hole made in a wall to try its thickness; (med.) suppository; (naut.) hold.

[3]**cala,** *f.* (bot.) calla lily.

calaba, *m.* calaba tree. Also CALAMBUCO.

calabacear, *va.* = DAR CALABAZAS.

calabacera, *f.* (bot.) pumpkin, gourd or squash plant. Also CALABAZA.

calabacero, ra. I. *n.* retailer of pumpkins. **II.** *m.* calabash tree.

calabacilla, *f.* core of gourd-shaped tassel; earring made of pearls in the shape of a gourd.

calabacín, *m.* small, young, tender pumpkin; silly person.—**calabacinate,** *m.* fried pumpkins.

calabacino, *m.* dry gourd, calabash bottle.

calabaza, *f.* (bot.) pumpkin; squash; gourd; (fig.) stupid, ignorant person.—**c. confitera,** or **totanera,** pumpkin.—**c. vinatera,** bottle gourd.—**dar calabazas,** to fail in examination; to refuse (a lover), give the mitten.—**calabazada,** *f.* knock with the head against something.—**darse de calabazadas,** (fig.) to labor in vain.—**calabazar,** *m.* pumpkin or-

chard.—**calabazate,** *m.* preserved pumpkin candied; piece of pumpkin steeped in honey.
calabazo, *m.* gourd.
calabobos, *m.* drizzle; mizzle.
calabocero, *m.* jailer; warden.
calabozaje, *m.* fee paid by prisoners to the jailer.
[1]**calabozo,** *m.* dungeon; cell; calaboose; jail.
[2]**calabozo,** *m.* curved pruning and weed-cutting knife.
calabrés, sa, *a.* Calabrian.
calabriada, *f.* mixture of different things; mixture of white and red wine; balderdash.
calabrote, *m.* (naut.) stream cable.
calacuerda, *f.* (mil.) drum call to attack.
calada, *f.* soaking; wetting through; rapid flight of birds of prey; reprimand.
caladio, *m.* (bot.) caladium.
calado, da. I. *pp.* of CALAR. **II.** *m.* open work in metal, stone, wood, or linen; fretwork; (naut.) draught of a vessel.—*pl.* **calados,** lace.
calador, *m.* perforator; borer; one who makes open work; (naut.) calking iron; surgeon's probe.
caladre, *f.* (ornith.) a bird of the lark family.
calafate, calafateador, *m.* calker.
calafateadura, *f.* calking.
calafatear, *va.* to calk.
calafateo, *m.*, **calafatería,** *f.* calking.
calafatín, *m.* calker's boy or mate.
calafraga, *f.* (bot.) saxifrage.
calagozo, *m.* bill or hedging hook.
calagraña, *f.* table grape, not fit for wine.
calaguala, *f.* (Peru, bot.) calaguala.
calahorra, *f.* public office where bread is distributed in times of scarcity.
calaíta, *f.* turquoise.
calaje, *m.* chest, trunk, coffer.
calamaco, *m.* calamanco, a woolen fabric.
calamar, *m.* (zool.) calamary, squid.
calambac, *m.* (bot.) calamba; eaglewood.
calambre, *m.* cramp (of muscles).
calambuco. I. *m.* (bot.) calaba tree. **II.** *a.* (Am.) pious, devout; (Cuba) pharisaical, hypocritical.
calamento, *m.* (bot.) mountain balm or calamint.
calamidad, *f.* calamity.
calamillera, caramillera, *f.* pothook of a crane.
calamina, *f.* calamine.
calaminta, *f.* = CALAMENTO.
calamita, *f.* loadstone; magnetic needle.
calamitoso, sa, *a.* calamitous, unfortunate.
cálamo, *m.* (bot.) sweet flag; (poet.) pen; ancient flute.
calamocano, *a.* fuddled; tipsy; unsteady.
calamoco, *m.* icicle.
calamón, *m.* (ornith.) purple water hen or gallinule; round-headed nail; stay supporting the beam of an oil mill.
calamorra, *f.* (coll.) head, (vulg.) block.
calamorrada, *f.* butt of horned cattle.
calamorrar, *va.* to butt.
calandraca, *f.* (naut.) mess of hard-tack.
calandrajo, *m.* rag hanging from a garment; ragamuffin.
calandrar, *va.* to calender.
[1]**calandria,** *f.* (ornith.) bunting, calendar lark.
[2]**calandria,** *f.* mangle; clothier's press; beetle mill; rolling press.
cálanis, *m.* (bot.) sweet flag.
calaña, *f.* pattern; sample; model, form; character; quality, kind, sort.
calañés, *a.* native of Calañas.—**sombrero c.,** Andalusian hat.
cálao, *m.* a large P.I. bird with serrated bill.
calapatillo, *m.* (zool.) weevil, or its grub.
calapé, *m.* turtle roasted in its shell.
[1]**calar. I.** *va.* to penetrate, soak through, permeate, drench; to go through, pierce, perforate; to make open work in (metal, wood, linen, or paper); (mech.) to wedge; to let down (a drawbridge); to fix (the bayonet); to pull down (the hat); to pick (a pocket); to see through (a person), understand; to sample, take or cut out a sample of. **II.** *vn.* (naut.) (of ships) to draw. **III.** *vr.* to put on; to get drenched; (of birds of prey) to rush, dart down, descend; to get in, squeeze in; to sneak in, enter clandestinely.
[2]**calar,** *a.* calcareous.
calato, ta, *a.* (Peru) nude, naked.
calavera, *f.* skull; (Am.) tail light; *m.* (coll.) madcap, wild fellow, daredevil.
calaverada, *f.* foolishness, tomfoolery.
calaverear, *vn.* to act foolishly and recklessly.
calaverilla, ita. I. *f. dim.* little skull. **II.** *m.* youth who sows his wild oats.
calaverón, *m. aug.* rake, debauchee.
calcado, *m.* tracing.
calcamar, *m.* a Brazilian sea bird.
calcáneo, *m.* (anat.) calcaneum.
calcañal, calcañar, *m.* heel, heel bone.
calcañuelo, *m.* a disease of bees.
calcar, *va.* (*pret.* CALQUÉ; *subj.* CALQUE) to trace; to trample on.
calcáreo, rea, *a.* calcareous.
calce, *m.* tire of a wheel; piece of iron or steel added to the coulter of a plow when it is worn; wedge; wheel shoe, a form of brake; (Am.) bottom (of a writing); (naut.) top.
calcé, calce, *v.* *V.* CALZAR.
calcedonia, *f.* chalcedony.
calcés, *m.* (naut.) masthead.
calceta, *f.* hose, stocking; fetters worn by criminals.—**hacer c.,** to knit.
calcetería, *f.* hosier's shop and trade; hosiery.
calcetero, ra, *n.* one who makes, mends, or sells thread stockings; hosier.
calcetín, *m.* sock.
calcetón, *m. aug.* cloth stocking worn under boots.
cálcico, ca, *a.* (chem.) calcic.
calcificación, *f.* calcification.
calcificar, *va.* to calcify.
calcímetro, *m.* lime meter, an instrument to determine the lime in soils.
calcina, *f.* mortar.
calcinable, *a.* calcinable.
calcinación, *f.* (chem.) calcination.
calcinar, *va.* & *vr.* to calcine.
calcinatorio, *m.* calcinatory, calcining vessel.
calcio, *m.* calcium.
calcita, *f.* (min.) calcite.
calco, *m.* tracing.
calcografía, *f.* chalcography, engraving on copper; place where engravings are made.
calcógrafo, *m.* engraver.
calcomanía, *f.* decalcomania.
calcopirita, *f.* (min.) chalcopyrite.
calcosina, calcocita, *f.* (min.) chalcocite.
calculable, *a.* calculable.
calculador, ra. I. *n.* calculator, computer. **II.** *m.* calculating machine.
calculadora digital, *f.* digital computer.
calcular, *va.* to calculate, compute; to estimate.
calculista, *n.* calculator, computer; designer.
cálculo, *m.* calculation, computation; estimate; conjecture; (math., med.) calculus.—**c. biliario,** (med.) gallstone.—**c. diferencial,** (math.) differential calculus.—**c. infinitesimal,** (math.) infinitesimal calculus.—**c. integral,** (math.) integral calculus.—**c. prudencial,** approximation, (coll.) educated guess.
calculoso, sa, *a.* (med.) calculous.
calcha, *f.* (Chile) workman's clothing and bedding.
calchona, *f.* (Am.) bogey, goblin.
calda, *f.* warming or heating.—*pl.* **caldas,** hot mineral-water baths.—**dar calda a,** to heat, reheat.
caldaico, ca, *a.* = [1]CALDEO.
caldear, *va.* to warm, heat; to weld.
[1]**caldeo, a,** *n.* & *a.* Chaldean, Chaldaic.
[2]**caldeo,** *m.* heating.
caldera, *f.* caldron; sugar kettle, boiling pan;

teakettle; (Am.) coffeepot; teapot; shell of kettle drum; (steam eng.) boiler.—**c. acuatubular,** water-tube boiler.—**c. de hogar interior,** flue boiler.—**c. de tubos de humos,** fire-tube boiler.—**c. de vapor,** steam boiler. —**c. fija,** stationary boiler.—**c. locomóvil,** portable boiler.—**c. marina,** or **marítima,** marine boiler.—**c. tubular,** tubular boiler.

calderada, *f.* caldronful.

calderería, *f.* brazier's or boiler maker's shop and trade.

calderero, *m.* brazier; coppersmith; boiler maker.

caldereta, *f. dim.* small caldron, kettle, pot; holy-water pot; fish stew; lamb stew; (Mex.) chocolate pot; (C. A.) thunderstorm.

calderilla, *f.* holy-water pot; any copper coin.

caldero, *m.* semispherical caldron or boiler; a copper; caldronful; ladle.

calderón, *m.* large caldron or kettle; mark for a thousand (Ə); (print.) paragraph (¶); (mus.) sign (𝄐) denoting a pause; hold.

calderoniano, na, *a.* Calderonian, pertaining to, or like, Calderón or his style.

calderuela, *f. dim.* small kettle; dark lantern used to drive partridges into the net.

caldillo, caldito, *m.* sauce of a ragout or fricassee; light broth.

caldo, *m.* broth; beef tea; bouillon; salad dressing; sauce; gravy.—*pl.* (com.) wine, oil and liquors.—**c. alterado,** medicinal broth.—**c. de carne,** consommé; beef tea.

caldoso, sa, *a.* having plenty of broth.

calducho, *m.* badly seasoned broth; hog wash.

calecer, *va.* to become heated.

caledonio, nia, *n.* & *a.* Caledonian.

calefacción, *f.* heating; heating system.—**c. central,** central heating.

calefaciente, *a.* (med.) heating.

calefactorio, *m.* calefactory, heated sitting-room (in convents).

caleidoscopio, *m.* (Am.) = CALIDOSCOPIO.

calenda, *f.* part of the martyrology which treats of the acts of the saints of the day.—*pl.* **calendas,** calends.—**calendas griegas,** Greek calends (a time that will never come, as there were no Greek calends).

calendario, *m.* almanac; calendar.—**hacer calendarios,** (fig.) to muse; to make hasty prophecies.—**calendarista,** *n.* calendar maker.

caléndula, *f.* (bot.) marigold.

calentador, *m.* heater; warming pan; (coll.) large, clumsy watch.

calentamiento, *m.* warming, heating; a horse disease.

calentano, na, *n.* (Am.) lowlander, native of a hot climate.

calentar. I. *va.* (*ind.* CALIENTO; *subj.* CALIENTE) to heat, warm; to roll and heat (a ball) in one's hand before it is played; to urge; press forward; despatch speedily. **II.** *vr.* to be in heat, rut; to get hot; become excited or angry.

calentón, *m.*—**darse un c.,** to take a bit of a warming.

calentura, *f.* fever.—**calenturiento, ta,** *a.* feverish.—**calenturilla,** *f. dim.* slight fever.—**calenturón,** *m. aug.* high fever.—**calenturoso, sa,** *a.* feverish.

calepino, *m.* (coll.) Latin dictionary.

[1]**calera,** *f.* lime kiln; lime pit.

[2]**calera,** *f.* fishing smack.

calería, *f.* place where lime is burnt and sold.

calero, ra. I. *a.* calcareous. **II.** *m.* lime burner, lime maker or seller.

calesa, *f.* two-wheeled calash, chaise.

calesera, *f.* bolero jacket.

calesero, *m.* driver of a calash.

calesín, *m.* light chaise.—**calesinero,** *m.* owner or driver of a light chaise.

caleta, *f.* (naut.) cove, creek, small bay; (Venez.) trade of carriers.—**caletero,** *m.* (Venez.) carrier.

caletre, *m.* (coll.) judgment, acumen.

calibeado, da, *a.* (med.) chalybean; chalybeate.

cálibes, *n. pl.* Chalybes.

calibración, *f.* calibration; gaging.

calibrador, *m.* gage (instrument); calipers.

calibrar, *va.* to calibrate (a ball, a firearm); to gage, measure.

calibre, *m.* caliber; diameter, bore (of a cylinder, pipe, etc.); gage (instrument); calipers; gage, diameter (of wire).

[1]**calicanto,** *m.* stone masonry.—**de c.,** (fig.) strong, firm, solid.

[2]**calicanto,** *m.* (Am.) (bot.) allspice.

calicata, *f.* (min.) trial pit.

caliciforme, *a.* (bot.) chaliced, chalice-shaped.

calicó, *m.* calico.

calicular, *a.* (bot.) calycular.

calículo, *m.* (bot.) calycle.

caliche, *m.* pebble burnt in a brick; crust of lime which flakes from a wall; (Peru and Chile) native saltpetre.

calidad, *f.* quality; grade; nobility; rank.—*pl.* conditions, terms, stipulations; personal qualifications; gifts, parts.—**en c. de,** as; in one's capacity as.

[1]**cálido, da,** *a.* warm; hot; piquant.

[2]**cálido, da,** *a.* crafty, artful.

calidoscópico, ca, *a.* kaleidoscopic.

calidoscopio, *m.* kaleidoscope.

calientapiés, *m.* foot warmer.

calientaplatos, *m.* plate warmer.

caliente, *a.* warm, hot; fiery.—**en c.,** while hot; at once.—**estar c.,** to be in heat, rut.

caliento, caliente, *v. V.* CALENTAR.

califa, *m.* caliph.—**califato,** *m.* caliphate.

calificable, *a.* qualifiable.

calificación, *f.* qualification; judgment, censure; proof; mark (in an examination).

calificado, da. I. *pp.* of CALIFICAR. **II.** *a.* qualified, authorized, competent.

calificador, ra, *n.* qualifier; censor.

calificar. I. *va.* (*pret.* CALIFIQUÉ; *subj.* CALIFIQUE) to qualify; rate, class; to pass on, judge; to authorize; to certify, attest; ennoble.—**c. de,** to call, declare. **II.** *vr.* to prove one's noble birth and descent according to law.

calificativo, va, *a.* (gram.) qualifying.

californiano, na, *n.* & *a.* Californian.

califórnico, ca, *a.* Californian.

californio, nia. I. *a.* Californian. **II.** *n.* Californian; *m.* (chem.) californium.

cáliga, *f.* caliga, a Roman soldier's sandal.

calígine, *f.* mist, obscurity, darkness.

caliginoso, sa, *a.* caliginous, dark, dim.

caligrafía, *f.* calligraphy, penmanship.

caligráfico, ca, *a.* calligraphic.

calígrafo, *m.* expert penman.

calilla, *f. dim.* a small suppository.

calima, calina, *f.* thick vapor; light mist, haze.

calimba, *f.* (Am.) branding iron.

calimbar, *va.* (Am.) to brand (cattle).

calinda, *f.* (Cuba) a popular creole dance.

calinoso, sa, *a.* vapory, misty, hazy.

calípedes, *m.* (zool.) a kind of sloth.

calipso, *m.* (mus.) calypso.

calisaya, *f.* (bot.) calisaya.

calistenia, *f.* calisthenics.—**calisténico, ca,** *a.* calisthenic.

cáliz, *m.* (eccl., poet.) chalice; bitter cup of grief and affliction; (bot.) calyx.

caliza, *f.* limestone (called also **piedra c.**).

calizo, za, *a.* calcareous; limy; calc (spar).

calma, *f.* calm; calmness, tranquillity; slowness; suspension of business; cessation of pain.—**c. chicha, c. muerta,** (naut.) dead calm.—**con c.,** calmly, quietly.—**en c.,** (of the sea) calm, smooth.

calmante. I. *a.* mitigating; quieting, soothing. **II.** *m.* & *a.* (med.) narcotic, anodyne, sedative.

calmar. I. *va.* to calm, quiet, pacify; to allay, mitigate, soothe. **II.** *vn.* to abate; to be be-

calmed. **III.** *vr.* to quiet down, abate; to calm oneself, be pacified.
calmo, ma, *a.* uncultivated, untilled; treeless; barren.
calmoso, sa, *a.* (of the sea) calm; slow, tardy.
calmuco, ca, *n.* & *a.* Kalmuck.
caló, *m.* cant; slang of gipsies and ruffians.
calofriarse, *vr.* to have a chill.
calofrío, *m.* chill, shiver. Also ESCALOFRÍO.
calomel, *m.*, **calomelanos,** *m. pl.* calomel.
calor, *m.* heat; glow; warmth, ardor; brunt of a battle; favor, kind reception.—**hacer c.,** (of weather) to be warm.—**tener c.,** (of person) to be, feel, warm.
caloría, *f.* calorie.
caloricidad, *f.* (physiol.) caloricity.
calórico, ca, *m.* & *a.* (chem.) caloric.
calorífero, ra. I. *a.* giving out heat. **II.** *m.* heater, radiator.—**c. de aire,** hot-air register. —**c. de vapor,** steam radiator.
calorificación, *f.* (physiol.) calorification.
calorífico, ca, *a.* calorific.
calorífugo, ga, *a.* non-conductor of heat; fireproof, non-combustible.
calorimetría, *f.* calorimetry.
calorimétrico, ca, *a.* calorimetric.
calorímetro, *m.* (chem.) calorimeter.
caloroso, sa, *a.* = CALUROSO.
calostro, *m.* colostrum, first milk secreted after childbirth.
caloyo, *m.* new-born lamb or kid.
calpamulo, la, *a.* (Mex.) half-breed, mestizo.
calpisque, calpixque, calpizque, *m.* (Mex.) tax collector, steward.
calpul, *m.* (Guat.) gathering, meeting; (Hond.) Indian mound.
calqué, calque, *v. V.* CALCAR.
calseco, ca, *a.* cured with lime.
calta, *f.* caltha, marsh marigold.
calumet, *m.* calumet (ceremonial pipe of N. American Indians).
calumnia, *f.* calumny, slander.
calumniador, ra, *n.* & *a.* slanderer(-ing).
calumniar, *va.* to slander.
calumnioso, sa, *a.* calumnious, slanderous.
calurosamente, *adv.* warmly; ardently; hotly; passionately.
caluroso, sa, *a.* warm, hot; heating; excited; vehement, enthusiastic.
calutrón, *m.* (phys.) calutron.
calva, *f.* bald head; bald pate; clearing, open space.—**c. de almete,** crest of a helmet.
calvar. I. *va.* to cheat, deceive. **II.** *vn.* to become bald.
calvario, *m.* Calvary; debts; tally; score.
calvatrueno, *m.* baldness of the whole head; a wild person.
calvero, *m.* barren spot; clearing, open space.
calvete, *m. dim.* little bald pate, when only part of the head is bald.
calvez, calvicie, *f.* baldness.
calvijar, *m.* = CALVERO.
calvinismo, *m.* Calvinism.
calvinista, *n.* & *a.* Calvinist(-ic).
calvo, va, *a.* bald; bare; barren.
calza, *f.* loose breeches; trousers; hose, stockings; garter or ribbon tied on some animals; wedge.—*pl.* fetters.—**c. de arena,** sandbag.—**calzas acuchilladas,** slashed trousers.—**echarle una c. a,** to size up (a person).—**en calzas prietas,** in an embarrassing or difficult position, in a tight fix.—**medias calzas,** stockings reaching to the knees.—**tomar las calzas de Villadiego,** to make a precipitate flight or escape, to bolt.
calzacalzón, *m.* galligaskins, loose breeches.
calzada, *f.* paved highway; (Am.) sidewalk.
calzadera, *f.* hempen cord; net twine.
calzado, da. I. *a.* (of monks, etc. who are not barefoot) shod; (of a horse) with white feet; (of birds) having feathers on the legs and feet. **II.** *m.* footwear.
calzador, *m.* shoeing leather; shoehorn.
calzadura, *f.* act of putting on the shoes; tip for this service; felloe, outer rim of a wheel.
calzar. I. *va.* (*pret.* CALCÉ; *subj.* CALCE) to put on (shoes, gloves, spurs, etc.); to scot or scotch (a wheel); (of firearms) to carry (a ball) of a certain size; to wedge, chock, key; (Am.) to fill (teeth); (Am.) to hill (plants); (print.) to overlay, raise, underlay; to shoe (an anchor); to put a steel edge on (an iron tool); to block (a wheel, carriage, to place something under the wheels to prevent sliding); to have (aptitudes, skill, ability, etc.).—**c. muchos (pocos) puntos en,** to be well (poorly) posted on, have a good (poor) knowledge of. **II.** *vr.* to put on; to control, dominate; to get, obtain.
calzo, *m.* (print.) frisket sheet, overlay; (Ry.) block, brake shoe; (mech.) wedge, quoin; shoe of a felloe; (naut.) skid, chock, bed, shoe.
calzón, *m.* ombre, a card game; (Mex.) a disease of the sugar cane from lack of irrigation.—*pl.* breeches; trousers; (naut.) goosewing.—**c. corto,** knee breeches.—**calzonarias,** *f. pl.* (Colomb.) suspenders (for trousers).—**calzonazos,** *m. aug.*—**ser un calzonazos,** to be a weak, soft fellow.—**calzoncillos,** *m. pl.* drawers, underdrawers.—**calzoneras,** *f. pl.* (Mex.) trousers buttoned down both sides.
calzorras, *m.* = CALZONAZOS.
[1]**callada,** *f.* a dish of tripe.
[2]**callada,** *f.* silence (only in certain phrases).—**a las calladas,** or **de callada,** privately, on the quiet.—**dar la c. por respuesta,** to answer by silence.
callado, da. I. *pp.* of CALLAR. **II.** *a.* silent; quiet; reticent.
callana, *f.* (Am.) an almost flat earthen bowl used as a baking griddle.
callandico, ito, *adv.* in a low voice; silently, without noise, slyly, softly.
callar, *vn.*, *va.* & *vr.* to keep silent; to stop talking (playing, singing, etc.); to shut up; to hush, conceal, keep from being known; to dissemble; (poet.) to abate, moderate, grow calm.—**c. su pico,** to hold one's tongue.—**¡calla!** or **¡calle!** you don't mean it! is it possible?—**quien calla, otorga,** silence gives consent.
calle. I. *f.* street; walk in a garden; passage, way. —**c. abajo,** down the street.—**c. de árboles,** path or space between two rows of trees; the rows themselves.—**c. hita,** from house to house.—**c. mayor,** main street.—**c. traviesa,** cross street.—**abrir c.,** to clear the way.—**azotar calles,** to loiter about, loaf.—**dejar en la c.,** to leave penniless, leave in destitution.—**echar a la c.,** to put on the street, to put out of the house; to make public.—**hacer c.** = ABRIR C. —**llevar,** or **llevarse, de c.,** to sweep away; to overmaster; to confound, silence. **II.** *interj.* make way! move aside!
callear, *va.* to clear (walks) in a vineyard.
calleja, *f.* bystreet, byway; (C.) used in the expression **ya se verá** or **ya verán quién es C.,** you shall see what I can do.
callejear, *vn.* to wander, roam, mosey, ramble, gad.
callejero, ra, *n.* loiterer, gadder.
callejo, *m.* trap, snare, pitfall.
callejón, *m. aug.* lane, alley.—**c. sin salida,** blind alley, dead end.
callejoncillo, *m. dim.*, **callejuca,** *f. dim.* alley, small narrow street.
callejuela, *f. dim.* bystreet, byway, alley; (fig.) shift, subterfuge, evasion.
callialto, ta, *a.* pert. to horseshoe with thick borders.
callicida, *m.* corn eradicator.
callista, *n.* corn doctor, chiropodist.
callo, *m.* corn, callous on foot; wen; (surg.) callus; extremity of a horseshoe.—*pl.* tripe.
callosidad, *f.* callosity, callousness.
calloso, sa, *a.* callous; corneous, horny.

[1]**cama,** *f.* bed; couch; bed hangings and furniture; seat or couch of wild animals; floor or body of a cart; part of a melon resting on the ground; straw laid under animals or on plants; slice of meat put upon another when cooking; garden bed; (mech.) bedplate; base; (geol.) layer, stratum.—**c. camera** or **ancha,** double bed.—**c. de dos pisos,** bunk bed, doubledecker bed.—**c. de tijera,** folding bed, cot.—**c. doble** or **melliza,** twin bed.—**c. plegadiza,** folding bed.—**caer en** or **en la c.,** to be bedridden.—**guardar** or **hacer c.,** to be confined to one's bed.—**hacer la c.,** to make the bed.—**hacerle la c. a uno,** (coll.) to fix one's wagon.

[2]**cama,** *f.* part of a plow that connects the share with the beam, the sheathe; felloe of a wheel; check of a bridle; V-shaped piece in a cloak; (mech.) cam, cog, catch, tooth.

camada, *f.* brood of young animals, litter; band of thieves.

camafeo, *m.* cameo.

camal, *m.* hempen halter; camail.

camaleón, *m.* chameleon; person who changes his opinions to suit his interest.

Camaleopardo, *m.* (astr.) Camelopard.

camalote, *m.* a South Am. river plant resembling a floating island.

camama, *f.* (coll.) sham, humbug.

camamila, camomilla, *f.* (bot.) common camomile.

camándula, *f.* chaplet or rosary of one or three decades.—**tener muchas camándulas,** to be very tricky.

camandulense, *n.* & *a.* Camaldolite, order of Camandula or reformed Benedictines.

camandulería, *f.* prudery; hypocrisy.

camandulero, ra, *a.* & *n.* hypocrite(-ic), dissembler(-ing).

cámara, *f.* hall; parlor; chamber; each of the two houses of a legislative body; chamber (of a firearm, a mine); cabin of a ship; (aer.) cockpit; granary; mow; (physiol.) stool; evacuation by stool; laxity; (photog.) camera.—**c. alta,** senate; House of Lords, upper house.—**c. ardiente,** = C. MORTUORIA.—**c. baja,** House of Commons, lower house, chamber of deputies.—**c. cinematográfica,** movie camera.—**c. clara,** (opt.) camera lucida.—**c. de aire,** (auto) inner tube; (hydraul.) air chamber.—**c. de comercio,** chamber of commerce.—**c. de combustión,** (astr.) combustion chamber.—**C. de Diputados,** Chamber of Deputies; House of Representatives.—**C. de los Comunes,** (Eng.) House of Commons.—**C. de los Lores,** (Eng.) House of Lords.—**c. de niebla,** (phys.) cloud chamber.—**C. de Representantes,** (U. S.) House of Representatives.—**c. fotográfica,** camera.—**c. lúcida,** (opt.) camera lucida.—**c. mortuoria,** funeral chamber.—**c. o(b)scura,** camera obscura; (photog.) dark room.—**c. plegadiza,** folding camera.

camarada, *n.* comrade, companion, crony, pal, or chum.—**camaradería,** *f.* (Gal.) comradeship, camaraderie.

camaraje, *m.* rent for a granary.

camaranchón, *m.* garret; attic.

camarera, *f.* head waiting maid; keeper of the queen's wardrobe; chambermaid; waitress.

camarero, *m.* chamberlain; steward or keeper of stores; waiter; valet.

camareta, *f. dim.* (naut.) small cabin; deck cabin; midshipman's cabin.

camariento, ta, *a.* having diarrhœa.

camarilla, *f. dim.* small room; coterie of private advisers of the king; coterie or ring of influential persons; clique.

camarín, *m.* place behind an altar where the images are dressed and the ornaments kept; closet; car (of elevator); (theat.) dressing room.

camarista. I. *m.* member of the supreme council; (Mex.) valet. **II.** *f.* maid of honor to the queen and princesses.

camarlengo, *m.* lord of the bedchamber of the kings of Aragon; camerlengo.

cámaro, camarón, *m.* (zool.) shrimp.

camarógrafo, *m.* cameraman.

camaronero, ra, *n.* shrimp seller.

camarote, *m.* (naut.) stateroom, cabin.

camasquince, *n.* meddlesome person.

camastra, *n.* (Chile) cunning, trickery.

camastrear, *vn.* (Chile) to dissemble, act cunningly.

camastro, *m.* poor, miserable bed.

camastrón, na, *n.* sly, artful, cunning person.

camastronazo, *m. aug.* great impostor, humbug.

camastronería, *f.* cunning, humbug, trickery.

camba, *f.* check of a bridle; felloe, outer rim of a wheel; a V-shaped piece in garments.

cambalache, *m.* (coll.) barter, swap; swapping.—**cambalachear,** *va.* to barter, to swap.—**cambalachero, ra,** *n.* barterer.

cámbaro, *m.* crawfish.

cambiable, *a.* exchangeable; changeable; changing.

cambiador, ra, *n.* barterer; money changer; (Chile, Mex.) (Ry.) switchman.

cambial, *m.* bill of exchange.

cambiamiento, *m.* change, alteration.

cambiante. I. *a.* bartering, exchanging; changing. **II.** *m.* banker, exchanger; iridescence; iridescent fabric.

cambiar. I. *va.* to change; to barter; to exchange. **II.** *vn.* to change, shift.—**c. de opinión,** to change one's mind.—**c. de traje,** to change (one's) clothes.

cambiavía, *m.* (Am.) (Ry.) switch; switch tender.

cambija, *f.* reservoir.

cambio, *m.* change; barter; exchange; premium paid or received for negotiating bills; rate of exchange (of money); rise and fall of the course of exchange; public or private bank; return of a favor; recompense.—**c. de destino,** reassignment.—**c. de tribunal,** (law) change of venue.—**c. de velocidad** or **de marcha,** gearshift; gear changing or shifting.—**c. extranjero,** foreign exchange.—**c. minuto,** small change.—**a c. de,** in exchange for.—**aguja de c.,** (Ry.) switch rail.—**en c.,** in return; on the other hand.—**en c. de,** in lieu of, instead of; in return for.—**libre c.,** (com.) free trade.

cambista, *n.* money broker, money changer, exchanger; banker; (Ry., Arg.) switchman.

Camboya, *f.* Cambodia.

camboyano, na, *n.* & *a.* Cambodian.

cambray, *m.* (text.) chambray, cambric.

cambrayado, da, *a.* cambric-like.

cambrayón, *m.* cambric (cotton fabric resembling chambray).

cambriano, na; cámbrico, ca. I. *a.* Cambrian; (geol.) Cambrian. **II.** *n.* Cambrian; *m.* (geol.) Cambrian.

cambrón, *m.* (bot.) buckthorn; bramble.

cambronal, *m.* brambled ground or place.

cambronera, *f.* (bot.) boxthorn.

cambuj, *m.* child's cap tied close to keep its head straight; mask.

cambujo, ja, *n.* & *a.* Indian mestizo; half-breed.

cambullón, *m.* (Peru) imposition, swindle.

cambur, *m.* a kind of plantain or banana.—**c. amarillo,** or **criollo,** yellow or Johnson banana.—**c. higo,** or **titiaro,** very small and fine variety of banana.—**c. manzano,** small banana with apple flavor.—**c. morado,** red banana.

camedrio, camedris, *m.* (bot.) wall germander.

camelar, *va.* to flirt; court, woo; seduce, deceive.

camelia, *f.* (bot.) camellia.

camelo, *m.* flirtation; courtship; joke, jest; false rumor, canard.

camelopardal, *m.* (zool.) camelopard.

[1]**camelote,** *m.* camlet, a waterproof garment.

[2]**camelote,** *m.* (bot.) a tropical weed.

[1]**camella,** [1]**gamella,** *f.* curve in each end of yoke (for animals).

[2]camella, [2]gamella, *f.* pail for feeding animals; milk pail.
[3]camella, *f.* she-camel; ridge in plowed land.
camellería, *f.* stable or stand for camels; employment of a camel driver.
camellero, *m.* keeper or driver of camels.
camello, *m.* camel; an ancient gun; engine for setting ships afloat in shoal water.—**c. pardal,** giraffe.
[1]camellón, *m.* ridge turned up by plow or spade; bed of flowers; camlet; (Am.) avenue, boulevard; cultivated lands in the islets of the Valley of Mexico.
[2]camellón, *m.* drinking trough; carpenter's horse.
camero, ra. I. *n.* upholsterer; one who lets beds. **II.** *a.* pertaining to beds.
Camerún, *m.* Cameroon, Cameroun.
camerunés, nesa, *n.* & *a.* Cameroonian.
camilla, *f. dim.* small bed, pallet, cot; litter, stretcher; clothes horse; shearer's frame.
caminador, ra, *n.* good walker.
caminante, *m.* traveler, walker.
caminar, *vn.* to walk, travel, go, move along.—**c. con pies de plomo,** to act cautiously, go slowly.—**c. derecho,** to act uprightly.
caminata, *f.* long walk for exercise; "hike"; promenade; excursion, jaunt, outing.
caminero, ra, *a.* road, highway (as *a.*).
camino, *m.* road; highway; path, pass; passage, trip, journey; profession, station, calling; way; manner, method; (min.) drift, gait; (naut.) ship's way, rate of sailing.—**c. carretero,** vehicle road, drive.—**c. cubierto,** (mil.) covert way.—**c. de herradura,** bridle road.—**c. de hierro,** railroad.—**c. de ruedas** = C. CARRETERO.—**c. de sirga,** tow path.—**c. real,** highway.—**c. trillado,** thoroughfare; routine; commonplace.—**c. vecinal,** municipal road, cared for by a municipality.—**abrir c.,** to open the way, find the means.—**de c.,** stopping on the way; traveling (as *a.*).—**de un c. dos mandados,** to kill two birds with one stone.—**en c. (de),** on the way (to), on one's way (to).—**fuera de c.,** off the road; unreasonable; astray.—**no llevar c.,** to be wrong, not to be cogent, not to lead anywhere.—**partir el c. con,** to meet half way.—**ponerse en c.,** to set out, start.—**traer a buen c.,** to disabuse, open the eyes of (one who is in error).
camión, *m.* dray, truck; (Mex.) bus.—**c. de mudanzas,** moving van.—**c. tanque,** tank truck.
camionaje, *m.* truckage.
camioneta, *f.* station wagon.
camisa, *f.* shirt; chemise; thin skin (of fruit); coat of whitewash; slough of a serpent; (mil.) chemise; (obs.) catamenia; jacket, case, casing; lining (of a furnace).—**c. alquitranada, embreada,** or **de fuego,** (naut.) fire chemise.—**c. de fuerza,** strait jacket.—**c. de una vela,** (naut.) body of a sail.—**c. de vapor,** steam jacket.—**meterse en c. de once varas,** to interfere in other people's affairs.—**no llegarle a uno la c. al cuerpo,** to be frightened; to be anxious.
camisería, *f.* shirt store, haberdashery.
camisero, ra, *n.* shirt maker, haberdasher.
camiseta, *f.* undershirt; short shirt with wide sleeves; chemisette.
camisola, *f.* ruffled shirt; dicky.
camisolín, *m.* shirt front; tucker; wimple.
camisón, *m. aug.* long and wide shirt; nightshirt; (Am.) (woman's) gown; (Cuba) chemise.
camisote, *m.* hauberk, long coat of mail.
camita, *n.* & *a.* Hamite(-tic).—**camítico, ca,** *a.* Hamitic.
camomila, *f.* chamomile.
[1]camón, *m. aug.* large bed; portable throne; glass partition; oriel window.
[2]camón, *m. aug.* each one of the round pieces forming the frame of a water wheel; oak tires of cart wheels; lath frame of an arch.
camoncillo, *m.* seat in a drawing-room.
camorra, *f.* quarrel.—**camorrear,** *vn.* to quarrel.
camorrista, *n.* noisy, quarrelsome person.
camote, *m.* (Am.) sweet potato; infatuation, love; lie, fib; lover; fool.—**tragar c.,** to hesitate in speaking, become confused, get rattled.
campal, *a.* field, camp (as *a.*).
campamento, *m.* encampment; camp.
campana, *f.* bell; anything bell-shaped; (fig.) parish church, parish; bell-shaped bottom of a well; (arch.) drum, corbel.—**c. de chimenea,** mantel of a chimney.—**c. de buzo,** diving bell.—**c. de rebato,** alarm bell.—**oír campanas y no saber dónde,** to have heard of a fact, but not to be well informed of its true nature.—**campanada,** *f.* stroke of a bell; scandal; sensational report.—**campanario,** *m.* belfry; noddle, head; rack (in looms).
campanear. I. *vn.* to ring the bells frequently. **II.** *va.* to divulge; to noise about.
campanela, *f.* a fancy step in dancing.
campaneo, *m.* bell ringing; chime; affected sway in walking.
campanero, *m.* bell founder; bellman; (ornith.) bellbird.
campaneta, *f. dim.* small bell.
campanil, *m.* small belfry.
campanilla, *f. dim.* small bell; hand bell; small bubble; (anat.) uvula; little tassel for ladies' gowns; (naut.) cabin bell; (bot.) bellflower.
campanillazo, *m.* violent ringing of a bell; signal given with a bell.
campanillear, *vn.* to keep ringing a small bell.
campanillero, *m.* bellman; public crier.
campanología, *f.* campanology.
campanólogo, ga, *n.* campanologist.
campante, *a.* surpassing; buoyant, cheerful.
campanudo, da, *a.* puffed up; bell-shaped; (bot.) campanulate; pompous, high-sounding.
campánula, *f.* (bot.) bellflower.
campanuláceo, a. I. *a.* (bot.) campanulaceous. **II.** *f. pl.* Campanulaceæ.
campaña, *f.* campaign; level country.—**c. naval,** (naut.) cruise.—**batir,** or **correr, la c.,** to reconnoiter.
campañol, *m.* water rat.
campar, *vn.* to excel; ACAMPAR, to encamp
campeador, ra, *a.* surpassing in bravery.
campear, *vn.* to be in the field; to pasture; frisk about; crop out; grow; be prominent, excel.
campecico, illo, ito, *m. dim.* small field.
campechana, *f.* (Cuba & Mex.) a kind of cocktail or mixed drink; (Venez.) hammock.
[1]campechano, na, *a.* frank; hearty; cheerful; generous.
[2]campechano, na, *n.* & *a.* native of or pert. to Campeche.
campeche, *m.* campeche wood, logwood.
campeón, *m.* champion; combatant; defender.
campeonato, *m.* championship.
campero, ra. I. *a.* exposed to the weather in the open field; unsheltered, unhoused; good at farming; (Mex.) having a gait like gentle trotting; pacing. **II.** *m.* friar who superintends a farm; field guard.
campesino, na; campestre. I. *a.* rural; country (as *a.*), rustic. **II.** *n.* countryman(-woman).
campilán, *m.* long, straight sabre used in P. I.
campillo, *m. dim.* small field.
campiña, *f.* flat tract of arable land; field; country; landscape.
campo, *m.* country; field, meadow, cattle range; camp; (mil.) camp; (her., agr., phys., sports) field; (fig.) field (of activity), scope; ground (of a painting).—**c. de acción de una fuerza,** (phys.) field of force.—**c. de Agramonte,** bedlam.—**c. de aplicación,** (stat.) coverage.—**c. de aviación,** airfield, flying field.—**c. de aterrizaje,** (aer.) landing field.—**c. de batalla,** battle field.—**c. de concentración,** concentration camp.—**c. de fútbol,** football field.—**c. de golf,** golf course or links.—**c. de labor,** cultivated ground; farm.—**c. del honor,** field of honor.—**c. de minas,** (naut., mil.) mine field.

—**c. de puna,** (Arg.) desolate region unsuitable for cattle raising.—**c. de recreo,** playground.—**c. de tiro,** shooting range, (mil.) rifle range; (mil.) field of fire.—**c. magnético,** (phys.) magnetic field.—**c. raso,** open field, outfield.—**c. santo,** cemetery.—**campos elíseos,** Elysian fields.—**c. visual,** field of vision.—**casa de c.,** country house.—**mariscal de c.,** field marshal.—**trabajo de c.,** (topog.) field work.—**a c. raso,** in the open field.—**a c. traviesa** or **travieso,** crosscountry.—**dar c. a,** (fig.) to give ground to.—**dar c. a la fantasía,** to give wings to one's fancy.—**quedar en el c.,** (mil.) to be killed in action.—**salir al c.,** to go out to fight a duel.
camposanto, *m.* cemetery.
camuatí, *m.* (Am.) hut, rough cabin.
camuesa, *f.* (bot.) pippin (apple).
camueso, *m.* (bot.) pippin tree; dunce, fool.
camuflage, *f.* (mil.) camouflage.
camuflar, *va.* (mil.) to camouflage.
camuñas, *f. pl.* all seeds, except wheat, barley, and rye.
can, *m.* dog; (arch.) bracket; shoulder; modillion; corbel; trigger; an ancient piece of ordnance.—**C. Mayor,** (astr.) Canis Major.—**C. Menor,** (astr.) Canis Minor.—**el C.,** the Dog Star.
[1]**cana,** *f.* gray hair.—**echar una c. al aire,** to go on a lark.
[2]**cana,** *f.* long measure, about two ells.
canabíneo, a. I. *a.* (bot.) pertaining to the hemp family. **II.** *f. pl.* the hemp family.
canáceo, a. I. *a.* (bot.) cannaceous. **II.** *f. pl.* Cannaceæ.
Canadá, *m.* Canada.
canadense, canadiense, *n.* & *a.* Canadian.
canal. I. *m.* channel; strait; canal; duct.—**abrir en c.,** to cut from top to bottom. **II.** *f.* natural underground waterway; long and narrow dell; any open conduit; groove; gutter; carcass, body of an animal killed and dressed for food; comb of the loom; hemp once hackled; front edge of a book; drinking trough; crease, slot in metalwork; bed of a hot press; (tel.) copper pole; well (of the rim of a wheel).—**c. maestra,** (arch.) main valley drain, or gutter (of a tiled roof).—**sombrero de c.,** priest's hat.
canalado, da, *a.* = ACANALADO, fluted; grooved.
canaladura, *f.* (arch.) hollow molding; groove.
canaleja, *f. dim.* small drinking trough; mill spout; SOMBRERO DE CANAL, priest's hat.
canalera, *f.* roof gutter.
canalete, *m.* bladed paddle for canoeing.
canalización, *f.* canalization; (elec.) wiring.
canalizar, *va.* to construct channels or canals in or for; to improve the channel of (a river, etc.); to canalize; (elec.) to wire.
canalizo, *m.* (naut.) narrow channel.
canalón, *m. aug.* gutter, leader, spout; gargoyle.
canalla. I. *f.* rabble, canaille. **II.** *m.* mean, despicable fellow, cur.—**canallada,** *f.* base, despicable act.—**canallesco, ca,** *a.* base, currish.
canana, *f.* cartridge belt.
cananeo, a, *n.* & *a.* Canaanite (-ish).
canapé, *m.* settee (sofa); couch; lounge; canapé (appetizer).
canard, *m.* (Am., Gal.) canard, a false report.
canaria, *f.* female canary bird.
canariense, *n.* & *a.* (person) of the Canary Islands.
canario, ria. I. *a.* CANARIENSE. **II.** *m.* canary bird; a dance introduced into Spain by natives of the Canaries; (naut.) a barge used in the Canary Islands; (Chile) generous patron (of hotel or restaurant), good tipper. **III.** *interj.* zounds!
canasta, *f.* hamper, crate; canasta (card game).
canastero, ra, *n.* basket maker.
canastilla, *f. dim.* small basket; gift to ladies of the court; an infant's basket; layette.
canastillo, *m.* small tray; pannier; small basket.
canasto, canastro, *m.* large basket.—**¡canastos!** *interj.* gracious! confound it!
[1]**cáncamo,** *m.* a rare gum resembling myrrh.
[2]**cáncamo,** *m.* (naut.) ringbolt.—**c. de argolla,** ringbolt.—**c. de ojo,** eyebolt.
cancamurria, *f.* (coll.) sadness, melancholy.
cancamusa, *f.* (coll.) trick to deceive.
cancán, *m.* cancan (dance).
[1]**cáncana,** *f.* cricket, stool for punishing children.
[2]**cáncana,** *f.* a kind of spider.
cancanear, *vn.* to loiter about, loaf; (Am.) to stammer.
cancaneo, *m.* (Am.) stammering.
cáncano, *m.* (coll.) louse.
cancel, *m.* wooden screen; glass partition in chapel for the king incognito.
cancela, *f.* front door grating or screen.
cancelación, canceladura, *f.* cancellation, expunging, obliteration.
cancelar, *va.* to annul; to dispel.
cancelaría, cancelería, *f.* papal chancery.
cancelario, *m.* chancellor in universities who grants degrees.
cáncer, *m.* (med.) cancer; (**C-,** astr.) Cancer.
cancerarse, *vr.* to develop a cancer; to become cancerous.
Cancerbero, *m.* (myth.) Cerberus; strict and incorruptible guard.
cancerismo, *m.* (med.) cancerism, cancerousness.
canceroso, sa, *a.* cancerous.
cancilla, *f.* wicker door or gate.
canciller, *m.* chancellor.
cancillerato, *m.* chancellorship.
cancilleresco, ca, *a.* pert. to or like a chancery.
cancillería, *f.* chancery, chancellery.
canción, *f.* song, lay, ballad.—**c. vernácula,** folk song.—**cancioncica, illa, ita,** *f. dim.* canzonet.—**cancionero,** *m.* song book; song writer.—**cancioneta,** *f. dim.* little song, canzonet.—**cancionista,** *n.* author or singer of songs, songster, ballad singer.
cancriforme, *a.* cancriform.
cancrinita, *f.* (min.) cancrinite.
cancro, *m.* (bot.) canker; (med.) cancer.
cancroide, *m.* (med.) cancroid tumor.
cancroideo, ea, *a.* cancroid, cancriform.
cancha, *f.* roasted corn or beans; (Am.) popcorn; cockpit; game grounds; (tennis) court.
canchal, *m.* ground full of boulders.
canchalagua, canchelagua, canchilagua, *f.* (Peru) a medicinal herb.
canchear, *vn.* (S. A.) to shirk, evade doing one's duty.
canchero, ra, *n.* (Am.) owner or keeper of game grounds; (S. A.) shirker; (Peru) (of some priests) extortioner, bleeder.
cancho, *m.* big boulder or rock.
candado, *m.* padlock; pendant; earring.—*pl.* cavities around the frog of a horse's feet.
candamo, *m.* an old rustic dance.
candar, *va.* to lock, shut.
candela, *f.* fire; light; candle, taper; flower or blossom of the chestnut tree; inclination of the balance needle towards the thing weighed.—**en c.,** (of a mast) vertical.
candelabro, *m.* candelabrum; bracket.
candelada, *f.* = HOGUERA, bonfire; blaze.
candelaria, *f.* Candlemas; (bot.) mullen.
candelecho, *m.* hut built on piles for watching a vineyard.
candelerazo, *m.* blow with a candlestick.
candelero, *m.* candlestick; student's lamp; fishing torch.—*pl.* (naut.) stanchions or crotches.—**estar en c.,** (fig.) to be high in office; to hold an exalted station.
candelilla, *f.* (surg.) bougie, catheter; blossom; will-o'-the-wisp; firefly; catkin, ament.—**le hacen candelillas los ojos,** (coll.) his eyes sparkle with the fumes of wine.
candelizas, *f. pl.* (naut.) brails.
candelizo, *m.* (coll.) = CARÁMBANO, icicle.
candencia, *f.* incandescence.
candente, *a.* incandescent, red-hot.

candidato, *m.* candidate.
candidatura, *f.* candidacy; list of candidates; (U. S. pol.) slate.
candidez, *f.* ingenuousness; whiteness.
cándido, da, *a.* simple, guileless; white, snowy.
candiel, *m.* sweetmeat of white wine, egg yolks, sugar, etc.
candil, *m.* kitchen or stable oil lamp; Greek lamp; (coll.) cock of a hat; (coll.) long irregular fold in petticoats; (Mex.) chandelier; top of a stag's horn.—**candilada,** *f.* (coll.) oil spilt from a lamp.—**candileja,** *f.* oil receptacle of a lamp.—*pl.* footlights of a theater; (bot.) willow-herb.—**candilejo,** *m. dim.* small kitchen lamp; (bot.) lucern.—**candilera,** *f.* (bot.) campion; lamp wick made from campion leaves. —**candilón,** *m. aug.* large open lamp.
candiota. I. *n.* & *a.* of the island of Candía. **II.** *f.* barrel; cask; large earthen jar for wine.—**candiotera,** *f.* wine cellar; storage place for casks.—**candiotero,** *m.* CANDIOTA maker.
candonga, *f.* (coll.) cunning; (coll.) merry, playful trick; practical joke; (coll.) draught mule.
candongo, ga, *a.* (coll.) cunning, artful.—**candonguear,** *va.* (coll.) to joke with; play a joke on; (coll.) to shirk.—**candonguero, ra,** *n.* (coll.) joker.
candor, *m.* pure whiteness; candor.
candoroso, sa, *a.* candid, ingenuous.
cané, *m.* a card game of chance.
caneca, *f.* glazed stone bottle for liquor and cordials.
canecillo, *m.* (arch.) corbel, modillion; truss; cantilever; console.
canéfora, *f.* (arch., Gk. hist.) canephoros.
canela, *f.* (bot.) cinnamon; (coll.) anything exquisitely fine; (Colomb.) vim, energy.
canelado, da, acanelado, da, *a.* = CANELO, *a.*
canelo, la. I. *a.* cinnamon-colored. **II.** *m.* cinnamon tree.
canelón, *m.* gargoyle; CANALÓN, gutter, spout; icicle; tubular fringe; cinnamon candy.—*pl.* end of a cat-o'-nine-tails.
canequí, caniquí, *m.* fine muslin.
canesú, *m.* corset cover; yoke of a shirt.
caney, *m.* (Venez.) log cabin; (Cuba) bend of a river; bight.
canfeno, *m.* (chem.) camphene.
canfor, alcanfor, *m.* camphor.
canforato, *m.* (chem.) camphorate.
canfórico, ca, *a.* (chem.) camphoric.
cangilón, *m.* earthen jar or pitcher; metal tankard for wine; bucket (of a water wheel); fold of a frilled collar; (Am.) hole, pit; ditch; (Peru) wrinkle (in a poorly made garment).
cangrejal, *m.* place frequented by crabs
cangrejero, ra, *n.* crab seller.
cangrejo, *m.* (zool.) crab; crawfish.
cangrejuelo, *m. dim.* small crab.
cangrena, gangrena, *f.* gangrene.—**cangrenarse, gangrenarse,** *vr.* to get gangrenous. —**cangrenoso, sa, gangrenoso, sa,** *a.* gangrenous.
canguelo, *m.* (coll.) fear.—**tener c.,** to show the white feather.
canguro, *m.* (zool.) kangaroo.
cania, *f.* (bot.) small nettle.
caníbal, *m.* cannibal, man-eater.
canibalismo, *m.* cannibalism.
canica, *f.* marble (game); marble, taw, mig; (bot.) kind of wild cinnamon.
canicie, *f.* whiteness of the hair.
canícula, *f.* dog days; (**C-,** astr.) Dog Star.
canicular, I. *a.* canicular, pert. to CANÍCULA. **II.** *m. pl.* dog days.—**canicularlo,** *m.* beadle who keeps dogs out of church.
cánidos, *m. pl.* (zool.) Canidæ, the dog family.
canijo, ja, *a.* (coll.) weak, infirm, sickly.
canil, *m.* coarse bread, dogs' bread.
canilla, *f.* long bone of leg or arm; any of the principal bones of the wing of a fowl; stopcock, faucet; reel, bobbin, spool; unevenness of the woof in thickness or color.—**c. de la pierna,** tibia, shin bone.—**c. del brazo,** ulna, arm bone.
canillado, da, *a.* ribbed, striped (cloth).
canillera, *f.* ancient leg armor; (Am.) fear.
canillero, ra. I. *n.* one who makes reels. **II.** *m.* small tap in a cask or vat; weaver's quill winder.
canime, *m.* (bot.) a Colombian tree producing a medicinal oil.
caninez, *f.* inordinate appetite.
canino, na, *a.* canine.
caniquí, *m.* cannequin, Indian fine muslin.
canje, *m.* (mil., dipl., com., journ.) exchange.
canjeable, *a.* that can be exchanged.
canjear, *va.* to exchange (prisoners, treaties, credentials, newspapers).
cano, na, *a.* gray-haired; hoary, hoar; frosty; ancient; (poet.) white.
canoa, *f.* canoe; (Am.) conduit; (Am.) trough (esp. for feeding animals).—**canoero,** *m.* canoeman.
canon, *m.* canon, rule, precept; catalogue of the books composing the Bible; catalogue, list; part of the mass; (law) fee paid in acknowledgment of superiority in a higher lord; (mus.) canon; (print.) canon type.—*pl.* canons canonical law.
canonesa, *f.* canoness.
canónica, *f.* canonic life in a convent.
canonical, *a.* canonical, pertaining to canons.
canonicato, *m.* = CANONJÍA.
canónico, ca, *a.* canonical, canonic.
canóniga, *f.* (coll.) nap taken before dinner.
canónigo, *m.* canon, prebendary.
canonista, *m.* canonist.
canonizable, *a.* worthy of canonization.
canonización, *f.* canonization.
canonizar, *va.* to canonize; consecrate; (fig.) to applaud or praise.
canonjía, *f.* canonship, canonicate; sinecure.
canoro, ra, *a.* canorous, musical, melodious.
canoso, sa, *a.* gray-haired, hoary, hoar, frosty.
canquén, *m.* (zool.) Chilean wild goose.
cansadamente, *adv.* botheringly, importunely.
cansado, da. I. *pp.* of CANSAR. **II.** *a.* tired; weary; tedious, tiresome, dry. **III.** *m.* bore.
cansancio, *m.* tiredness, weariness, fatigue.
cansar. I. *va.* to weary, tire, fatigue; to tease, harass; to bore; (agr.) to exhaust (the soil.) **II.** *vr.* to become tired or weary. **III.** *vn.* to be tiring or tiresome.
cansera, *f.* (coll.) fatigue; boredom.
cansino, na, *a.* (of animals) worn out by work.
cantable. I. *a.* that can be sung; (mus.) to be sung slowly. **II.** *m.* (mus.) passage in a simple, even tempo.
cantábrico, ca; cántabro, bra, *n.* & *a.* Cantabrian, of or from Cantabria.
cantada, *f.* = CANTATA.
cantador, *n.* singer (gen. of popular songs).
cantal, *m.* stone block.
cantaleta, *f.* charivari; tin-pan serenade.—**dar c.,** (coll.) to deride; laugh at; turn into ridicule; sermonize.—**estar con la misma c.,** to harp on the same string.—**cantaletear,** *va.* (Am.) to lecture, scold; to keep repeating ad nauseam.
cantante, *n.* & *a.* singer(-ing).
[1]**cantar,** *m.* song set to music.—**C. de los Cantares,** Song of Songs.—**cantares de gesta,** old legendary romances.—**ése, or eso, es otro c.,** (coll.) that is another story, that is a horse of another color.
[2]**cantar. I.** *va.* to sing.—**cantarlas claras,** to speak in plain language, to make no bones about, to call a spade a spade. **II.** *vn.* to sing; to speak out; (coll.) to creak, make a harsh, grinding noise; (coll.) to divulge or give away a secret; at cards, to call out the trump.—**c. de piano,** to make a full confession.
cántara, *f.* large, narrow-mouthed pitcher; a liquid measure (32 pints).
cantarera, *f.* shelf for jars, pitchers, etc.
cantarería, *f.* earthenware shop.

cantarero, ra, *n.* dealer in earthenware.
cantárida, *f.* Spanish fly; cantharides, Spanish fly blistering plaster; blister raised by the blistering plaster.
cantarillo, *m. dim.* small jar or pitcher.
cantarín, ina, *m.* & *f.* (coll.) songster(-tress); professional singer.
cántaro, *m.* large, narrow-mouthed pitcher, and the liquid contained in it; a wine measure; vessel into which votes are put.—**llover a cántaros,** to rain pitchforks, to pour.
cantata, *f.* (mus.) cantata, choral composition.
cantatriz, *f.* (woman) singer.
cantera, *f.* (stone) quarry; talent, genius.
cantería, *f.* art of hewing stone; building made of hewn stone; parcel of hewn stone.
cantero, *m.* stonecutter; extremity of a hard substance that can be easily separated from the rest.—**c. de heredad,** piece of ground.—**c. de pan,** crust of bread.
canticio, *m.* (coll.) constant or frequent singing.
cántico, *m.* canticle.
cantidad, *f.* quantity; amount; (phonet.) quantity.—**c. de movimiento,** (mech.) momentum.—**c. irracional,** (math.) surd.
cantiga, *f.* poetical composition to be put to music.
cantil, *m.* steep rock.
cantilena, *f.* = CANTINELA.
cantimplora, *f.* siphon; water cooler; (Chile, Mex.) canteen, water bottle; (Colomb.) powder flask; (Guat.) mumps.
cantina, *f.* wine cellar; (Am.) bar room, saloon, public house; canteen; restaurant (esp. in Ry. station); case used to cool wine on a journey.
cantinela, *f.* ballad; irksome repetition of a subject.
cantinera, *f.* vivandière.
cantinero, *m.* one in charge of drinks; saloon keeper, bartender.
cantiña, *f.* (coll.) a popular song.
cantizal, *m.* stony ground.
[1]**canto,** *m.* singing; short heroic poem; canto, division of a long poem; chant or canticle.—**c. tradicional,** folk song.—**al c. del gallo,** at cock's crow, at dawn.—**con un c. a los pechos,** with pleasure, alacrity.
[2]**canto,** *m.* end, edge, border; crust (of a loaf); thickness; back of a knife; front edge of a book; stone, pebble; game of throwing the stone (duck on a rock); quarry stone, block; ashlar stone.—**c. rodado,** boulder.—**a c.,** very near.—**al c.,** by the side of.—**de c.,** on edge.
cantón, *m.* corner; canton, region.—**cantonada,** *f.* corner.—**dar c.,** to disappoint or evade.
cantonal, *a.* cantonal.
cantonalismo, *m.* (pol.) a cantonal system.
cantonar, *va.* to quarter (troops).
cantonearse, *vr.* = CONTONEARSE, (coll.) to strut.
cantonera, *f.* plate nailed to the corners of a chest, etc.; corner plate, clip; angle iron; corner bracket; wench; street walker.
cantonero, ra, *n.* loafer.
cantor, ra. I. *n.* singer; minstrel; one who composes hymns or psalms; small singing bird. **II.** *a.* that sings.—**ave cantora,** song bird.
cantorral, *m.* = CANTIZAL, stony ground.
cantoso, sa, *a.* stony.
cantuariense, *a.* of or pert. to Canterbury.
cantueso, *m.* (bot.) French lavender, spike.
canturía, *f.* vocal music; musical composition; monotonous singing; method of performing musical compositions.
canturrear, canturriar, *va.* & *vn.* to hum, sing in a low voice.
cánula, *f.* canula, short tube used in surgery.
canutero, *m.* = CAÑUTERO.
canutillo, *m.* = CAÑUTILLO.
canuto, *m.* = CAÑUTO.
caña, *f.* cane; reed; reed spear; stem, stalk; walking stick; bone of arm or leg; leg, upper part of boot or stocking; chase (of a gun); groove (for the barrel of a firearm); subterranean passage in mines; shaft of a column; marrow; (naut.) helm, tiller; drill; ratchet drill; a long and narrow wine tumbler; an Andalusian song; crack in a sword's blade; glass blower's pipe; (carp.) shank; reed of wind instruments.—**c. brava,** (Am.) bamboo.—**c. de azúcar,** sugar cane.—**c. de Bengala,** rattan.—**c. de cuentas,** (bot.) Indian shot, Indian reed.—**c. de Indias,** rattan.—**c. de la India** = C. DE CUENTAS.—**c. del pulmón,** (anat.) trachea.—**c. de pescar,** fishing pole or rod.—**c. de vaca,** bone of a cow's leg.—**c. dulce,** sugar cane.—**correr cañas,** to engage in equestrian exercises with reed spears.
cañacoro, *m.* (bot.) Indian shot, Indian reed.
cañada, *f.* dell, ravine; cattle path.
cañadilla, *f.* a kind of murex, an edible mollusk.
cañaduzal, *m.* = CAÑAMELAR.
cañafístola, cañafístula, *f.* (bot.) a tropical tree with long pods, Cassia fistula; the pods.
cañaheja, cañaherla, *f.* (bot.) fennel-giant.
cañahuate, *m.* (bot.) a species of lignum-vitæ.
cañal, *m.* cane or reed plantation or field; reed weir for fishing; small channel for catching fish.
cañamar, *m.* hemp field.
cañamazo, *m.* coarse canvas; canvas for embroidery; embroidered canvas; burlap.
cañamelar, *m.* sugar-cane plantation.
cañameño, ña, *a.* hempen, made of hemp.
cañamiel, *f.* (bot.) sugar cane.
cañamiza, *f.* hemp bagasse; bun.
cáñamo, *m.* (bot.) hemp; cloth made of hemp.—**c. en rama,** undressed hemp.—**cañamón,** *m.* hemp seed.
cañar, *m.* = CAÑAL.
cañareja, *f.* = CAÑAHEJA.
cañariego, ga, *a.*—**pellejos cañariegos,** skins of sheep that die on the road.
cañarroya, *f.* (bot.) pellitory, wallwort.
cañavera, *f.* (bot.) reed grass.—**cañaveral,** *m.* cane or reed field; (Colomb.) bamboo field.
cañaverear, *va.* to wound with sharp-pointed canes.
cañedo, *m.* = CAÑAVERAL.
cañería, *f.* conduit; water or gas pipe line.
[1]**cañero, ra.** *n.* conduit maker; pipe layer.
[2]**cañero, ra. I.** *n.* (Am.) sugar-cane dealer; owner or manager of sugar-cane plantation. **II.** *m.* (Mex.) store room in a sugar mill.
cañete, *m. dim.* small tube.
cañilavado, da, *a.* (of horses, mules) small-limbed.
cañiza, *f.* coarse linen.
cañizal, cañizar, *m.* = CAÑAVERAL.
cañizo, *m.* hurdle, frame for rearing silkworms; hurdle used by hatters for shearing hats; (naut.) flake.
caño, *m.* tube, pipe; open sewer, ditch; gutter; spout; conduit; cellar or other place for cooling water; organ tube or pipe; (naut.) channel at the entrance to seaports.
cañón, *m.* any cylindrical tube or pipe; tube or pipe for blowing glass; quill; down, soft feathers; leg or sleeve of a garment; part of the beard next to the root; (Colomb.) trunk (of tree); cannon, gun; (min.) gallery; (mech.) socket; (Mex., P. R., Peru) gorge, ravine, canyon; bit of a bridle; flue (of a chimney); well (of a staircase).—**c. antiaéreo,** anti-aircraft gun.—**c. antitanque,** antitank gun.—**c. de electrones,** electrogun.—**c. obús,** howitzer.—**c. rayado,** rifled gun.
cañonazo, *m.* cannon shot; report of a gun.
cañoncico, illo, ito, *m. dim.* small cannon; small tube or pipe.
cañonear. I. *va.* to cannonade, bombard. **II.** *vr.* to cannonade each other.—**cañoneo,** *m.* cannonade; bombardment.—**cañonera,** *f.* embrasure for cannon; large tent; holster; gunboat.—**cañonería,** *f.* set of organ pipes; (mil.) number of cannons collectively.—**cañonero, ra. I.** *a.* (naut.) carrying guns. **II.** *f.* gunboat.
cañota, *f.* (bot.) paniculate sorghum.

cañucela, *f.* slender cane or reed.
cañuela, *f. dim.* small reed; (bot.) fescue grass.
cañutazo, *m.* (coll.) information, gossip, tale.
cañutería, *f.* set of organ pipes.
cañutero, *m.* pin or needle case.
cañutillo, *m. dim.* small tube or pipe; bugle for fringes, tassels, etc.; quill of gold or silver twist for embroidery.
cañuto, *m.* internode of a cane; small pipe or tube; informer, talebearer.—**cañutos helados,** (Mex.) small ice-cream cylinders.
caoba, caobana, *f.* (bot.) mahogany.
caobo, *m.* (bot.) mahogany (tree).
caolín, *m.* fine white clay used in pottery making.
caos, *m.* chaos.—**caótico, ca,** *a.* chaotic.
capa, *f.* cloak, mantle, cape; layer; coat, coating; lamina; cover; (fig.) cloak, mask, cover; color of an animal; hider, harborer; property; fortune; (com.) primage; an American rodent; the spotted cavy; third mold used in casting bells; coat of paint; bed, stratum, vein, seam; (mas.) bed, course; wrapper for tobacco.—**c. de Heaviside,** Heaviside layer.—**c. del cielo,** canopy of heaven.—**c. del timón,** rudder coat.—**c. magna,** bishop's cope.—**c. pluvial,** pluvial or choir cope.—**c. rota,** secret emissary.—**a c. y espada,** at any cost; through thick and thin.—**andar,** or **ir, de c. caída,** to be down in the mouth, seedy, crestfallen.—**de c. y gorra,** informal, informally.—**echar la c. al toro,** to risk all on a last effort, to play one's last trump.—**estar,** or **estarse, a la c.,** (naut.) to lie to.—**hacer de su c. un sayo,** to go one's way, to follow one's own judgment.
capá, *m.* capa, W. I. tree used for shipbuilding.
capacete, *m.* helmet, casque.
capacidad, *f.* capacity; contents; ability, capability; talent.
capacidad mental, *f.* brain power.
capacitación, *f.* training.
capacitancia, *f.* (elec.) capacitance.
capacitar, *va.* & *vr.* to enable, qualify, prepare; to commission, empower, delegate.
capacha, *f.* fruit basket, hamper.
capachero, *m.* one who carries things in baskets.
capacho, *m.* fruit basket; hamper, large-basket; hempen pressing bag; leaf wrapper (for salt, etc.); bundle (of salt) done up in leaves; (Peru) bag, pocket; (Bol.) old hat; (ornith.) common barn owl.—**c. de albañil,** bricklayer's hod.
capada, *f.* (coll.) anything carried in a person's cloak; cloakful.
capadocio, cia, *n.* & *a.* Cappadocian.
capador, *m.* gelder, castrator; gelder's whistle.
capadura, *f.* castration; scar from castration; leaf of second cut tobacco, used for filling or wrappers.
capar, *va* to geld, castrate; (coll.) to curtail, cut down, reduce.
caparazón, *m.* caparison; saddle cover; oil-cloth carriage cover; piano cover; hempen feed bag, nose bag; carcass of a fowl; shell of insects and crustaceans.
caparra, *f.* sheep louse.
caparrilla, *f. dim.* small tick that infests bees.
caparrós, *m.*, **caparrosa,** *f.* copperas.—**c. azul,** blue vitriol.—**c. blanca,** white vitriol.—**c. verde,** green vitriol.
capataz, *m.* overseer, foreman, steward, warden, conductor; leader.—**c. de cultivo,** practical agriculturist or forester.
capaz, *a.* capacious, ample, roomy, large; capable, able, competent.
[1]**capazo,** *m.* large basket; hamper; esparto mat
[2]**capazo,** *m.* blow with a cloak.
capazón, *m. aug.* very large esparto basket.
capciosidad, *f.* captiousness.
capcioso, sa, *a.* captious, insidious, artful.
capeador, *m.* bull fighter who challenges the bull with his cloak; cloak stealer.
capear, *va.* to strip or rob (one) of one's cloak; to challenge (a bull) with the cloak; (naut.) to lay to; (fig.) to evade (in discussion).
capeja, *f. dim.* small shabby cloak or cape.
capelina, *f.* (surg.) capeline, caplike bandage.
capelo, *m.* dues to bishops from their clergy; cardinal's hat or office; (Am.) glass bell.
capellada, *f.* toe piece of a shoe.
capellán, *m.* chaplain; clergyman.—**c. castrense,** army chaplain.—**c. de altar,** priest who assists at the mass.—**c. de honor,** the king's private chaplain.—**c. de navío,** navy chaplain.—**c. mayor de los ejércitos,** vicar-general of the army.
capellanía, *f.* chaplaincy.
capellina, *f.* headpiece of a helmet or casque; hood worn by country people; trooper wearing a helmet; (surg.) = CAPELINA.
capeo, *m.* challenging a bull with a cloak.
capeón, *m.* young bull challenged with a cloak.
capero, *m.* priest who carries the cope, or pluvial, in churches; cloak rack.
caperuceta, illa, ita, *f. dim.* small hood.—**Caperucita Roja,** or **Encarnada,** Little Red Ridinghood.
caperuza, *f.* pointed hood or cap; ulster cap.—**c. de chimenea,** chimney cap.—**dar en c.,** (coll.) to frustrate one's views and designs.
caperuzón, *m. aug.* large hood.
capeta, *f.* short cape.
capialzado, *a.* (arch.) arched cap piece; back (arch).
capibara, *m.* (Am.) capybara, a large S. A. rodent.
capichola, *f.* ribbed silk stuff.
capigorrista; capigorrón, na, *n.* (coll.) vagabond; slovenly person; student who never takes a high degree.
capilar, *n.* & *a.* capillary.
capilaridad, *f.* capillarity; capillary attraction.
capiliforme, *a.* (bot.) capilliform.
capilla, *f.* hood; cowl; chapel; small church; priests and others employed in chapel service; choir (musicians and singers) of a church; chapter or assembly of collegians; (print.) author's proof sheet; (mil.) portable chapel; death house.—**c. ardiente,** chapelle ardente, a hall or chamber where a dead body lies in state.—**estar en c.,** to be in the death house, to be sentenced to death and awaiting execution; (coll.) to be on pins and needles.
capillada, *f.* hoodful; blow with a hood.
capillejo, *m. dim.* small hood; skein of sewing silk.
capiller, capillero, *m.* sexton; churchwarden.
capilleta, ita, *f. dim.* small chapel; shrine.
capillo, *m.* child's cap; christening fee; baptismal cap; ancient hood for women; bud of a rose; toe-piece lining; cap of a distaff; net for catching rabbits; colander for wax; silk cocoon; cloth that covered church offering; (anat.) foreskin.
capilludo, da, *a.* resembling a hood or cowl.
capincho, carpincho, *m.* (zool.) = CAPIBARA.
capirotada, *f.* a batter made of herbs, eggs, etc.
capirotazo, *m.* fillip on the nose.
capirote. I. *a.* (of cattle) having the head of a different color from that of the body. **II.** *m.* hood; half-gown worn by collegians; sharp-pointed cap worn in processions; hood of a hawk.—**c. de colmena,** cover of a beehive.
capirucho, *m.* (coll.) = CAPIROTE.
capisayo, *m.* cloaklike garment; bishop's vestment.
capiscol, *m.* precentor, leader of church choir.
capiscolía, *f.* office and dignity of a precentor.
capita, *f. dim.* small cloak.
capitación, *f.* capitation, head or poll tax.
capitado, da, *a.* (bot.) capitate.
capital. I. *m.* capital; estate of a husband at his marriage; principal (money placed at interest, invested, etc.); (com.) capital, capital stock; (mil.) capital of a bastion. **II.** *f.* capital city. **III.** *a.* capital, pertaining to the head· main,

principal; leading; essential; great; excellent, unsurpassed.
capitalicé, capitalice, *v. V.* CAPITALIZAR.
capitalino, na, *a.* & *n.* (Am.) from or pertaining to the capital (city).
capitalismo, *m.* capitalism.
capitalista, *n.* & *a.* capitalist(-ic).
capitalización, *f.* capitalization.
capitalizar, *va.* (*pret.* CAPITALICÉ; *subj.* CAPITALICE) to capitalize, add interest to principal.
capitalmente, *adv.* fatally; seriously.
capitán, *m.* captain; ringleader; leader, commander.—**c. de bandera,** (naut.) flagship's commander.—**c. de corbeta,** (naut.) lieutenant commander.—**c. de fragata,** (naut.) commander.—**c. del puerto,** (naut.) port captain; harbor master.—**c. de navío,** (naut.) captain. —**c. general,** captain general.—**c. general de ejército,** field marshal.—**c. general de provincia,** commander-in-chief (of a military district).
capitana, *f.* flagship; captain's wife.
capitanear, *va.* to captain; to command; to lead, head.
capitanía, *f.* captainship; captaincy; company commanded by a captain; tax paid to the port captain by ships anchored in the harbor.—**c. del puerto,** harbor master's position.—**c. general,** captaincy general.
capitel, *m.* (arch.) capital of a column or pilaster; spire over the dome of a church.
capitolino, na, *a.* pertaining to the capitol; Capitoline.
capitolio, *m.* capitol; any lofty or majestic public building.
capitón, *m.* (zool.) pollard, chub.
capítula, *f.* lesson, Bible passage read at divine service.
capitulación, *f.* capitulation; stipulation, agreement.—**c. de matrimonio,** articles of marriage.
capitulante, *n.* & *a.* capitulator(-ing).
[1]**capitular. I.** *m.* capitular, member of a chapter. **II.** *a.* capitulary, pertaining to a chapter.
[2]**capitular. I.** *vn.* to enter into agreement; draw up the articles of a contract; to compound; to sing prayers at divine service; to capitulate. **II.** *va.* (law) to impeach.
capitulario, *m.* prayer book for divine service.
capitulear, *vn.* (Am.) to lobby.—**capituleo,** *m.* lobbying.
capítulo, *m.* chapter; meeting of the prelates of religious orders, and place where they meet; meeting; charge, reproof, reprimand.—**capítulos matrimoniales,** articles of marriage.—**llamar a c.,** to call to account, to take to task.
capnomancia, *f.* divination by smoke.
capoc, *m.* **capoca,** *f.* kapok.
capolar, *va.* to hash, mince, or chop; to behead.
[1]**capón. I.** *a.* castrated, gelded. **II.** *m.* eunuch; capon; fagot, bundle of brushwood; (naut.) anchor stopper at the cathead.
[2]**capón,** *m.* (coll.) fillip on the head.
capona, *f.* epaulet without fringe.
caponar, *va.* to tie up (the branches of vines).
caponera, *f.* coop, inclosure to fatten poultry; (coll.) place where one lives well at other people's expense; (coll.) jail; (mil.) caponier.
capoquero, *m.* (bot.) kapok tree.
caporal, *m.* chief, ringleader; (Mex.) keeper of horned cattle.
[1]**capota,** *f.* head of the teasel or fuller's thistle; light bonnet; leather top of some vehicles.
[2]**capota,** *f.* cape without a hood.
capote, *m.* raglan or cloak with sleeves to keep off rain; short cloak of bright color, used by bullfighters; browbeating; (coll.) thick cloud or mist.—**dar c.,** to leave a guest without dinner, for coming late; to win all the tricks at cards. —**dije para mi c.,** I said to myself.
capotear, *va.* to trick (a bull) with a CAPOTE; to wheedle, bamboozle; to evade cleverly.
capotera, *f.* (Am.) hat, or clothes, rack.
capotero, ra, *n.* cloak maker or dealer.
capotillo, *m.* cape, mantelet.—**c. de dos faldas,** a loose jacket.
capotudo, da, *a.* frowning.
caprario, ria, *a.* pertaining to the goat.
Capricornio, *m.* (astr.) Capricorn.
capricho, *m.* caprice, whim, fancy; great desire; (mus.) caprice, capriccio; (art) original work that ignores accepted rules.
caprichoso, sa, *a.* capricious; stubborn.
caprichudo, da, *a.* stubborn; whimsical.
caprificación, *f.* (agr.) caprification.
caprifoliáceo, a. I. (bot.) caprifoliaceous. **II.** *f. pl.* Caprifoliaceæ.
caprino, na, *a.* caprine, goatlike.
caprípedo, da, *a.* (zool.) capriped, goat-footed.
cápsula, *f.* metal cap on bottles; cartridge shell; (bot., anat., chem., pharm.) capsule.
capsuladora, *f.* bottle capper.
cápsula espacial, *f.* (astronaut.) space capsule.
capsular, *a.* capsular, capsulary.
captar, *va.* to captivate, attract, win.
captura, *f.* (law) capture, seizure.
capturar, *va.* (law) to apprehend; to arrest.
capuana, *f.* (coll.) spanking.
capucha, *f.* hood; cowl; capuche; (print.) circumflex accent.
capuchina, *f.* (bot.) nasturtium; small lamp with extinguisher; confection of egg yolks.—*pl.* (naut.) crotches and knees.
capuchino, na, *n.* & *a.* Capuchin (monk, nun).
capucho, *m.* cowl, hood.—**capuchón,** *m. aug.* of CAPUCHO; lady's cloak with hood; short domino.
capulí, capulín, *m.* capulin, a kind of cherry.
capullo, *m.* cocoon; flax knotted at the end; (com.) bunch of boiled flax; flower bud; coarse stuff of spun silk; acorn cup; chestnut bur; (anat.) foreskin.
capuz, *m.* ancient hooded cloak; CHAPUZ, ducking (a person).
capuzar, *va.* (naut.) to sink (a ship) by the head.
caquéctico, ca, *a.* (med.) cachectic.
caquexia, *f.* (med.) cachexia, emaciation and failing health.
caqui. I. *a.* khaki. **II.** *n.* khaki; *m.* (bot.) Japanese persimmon.
car, *m.* (naut.) larger end of the mizzenyard.
cara, *f.* face; visage, mien, countenance; base of a sugar loaf; façade, front, surface, facing.—**c. a c.,** face to face.—**c. apedreada** = C. EMPEDRADA.—**c. de acelga,** pale, sallow face.—**c. de ajo,** (fig., coll.) sour face.—**c. de aleluya,** (fig., coll.) smiling or cheerful face.—**c. de bronce,** (fig., coll.) brazen-faced.—**c. de cartón,** (fig.) wrinkled face.—**c. de corcho,** (coll.) bold-faced; poker face.—**c. de hereje,** (fig., coll.) ugly face, fright.—**c. de pascua,** (fig., coll.) smiling or cheerful face.—**c. de perro,** (fig., coll.) bearish face; unfriendly looking.—**c. de pocos amigos,** unfriendly looking.—**c. de vaqueta,** (fig., coll.) brazen-faced.—**c. de viernes,** (coll.) long face, glum looking.—**c. de vinagre,** (fig., coll.) vinegar face, sour puss.—**c. empedrada,** (coll.) face pitted by smallpox.—**c. sin expresión,** (coll.) dead pan.—**c. o cruz,** heads or tails.—**a c. descubierta,** (coll.) openly.—**buena c.,** (coll.) good mien.—**dar a uno con las puertas en la c.,** (coll.) to slam the door in one's face.—**dar el sol de c.,** (coll.) to have the sun in one's face.—**dar en c.,** (coll.) to call to task, throw in one's face.—**dar la c.,** (coll.) to face the music.—**dar la c. por otro,** (coll.) to fight someone else's battle; to answer for someone else.—**de c.,** opposite, facing.—**decírselo en su c.,** (coll.) to tell one to one's face.—**de dos caras,** (coll.) two-faced, false.—**guardar la c.,** to hide, conceal.—**lavar la c. a,** (fig., coll.) to bootlick.—**mala c.,** (coll.) bad expression or mien.—**no saber donde tiene la c.,** (coll.) to not know what is what (in one's

profession).—**no volver la c. atrás,** (coll.) not to flinch.—**saltar a la c.,** (coll.) to be as clear as water.—**tener c. de,** (coll.) to look like; to seem.—**tener c. de beato y uñas de gato,** (coll.) to be two-faced, be hypocritical.—**tener c. para,** (coll.) to have the nerve to.
carabao, *m.* (zool.) carabao.
cárabe, *m.* amber. Also ÁMBAR.
carabela, *f.* (naut.) caravel; large provision basket.—**carabelón,** *m.* (naut.) brig, brigantine.
carabina, *f.* fowling piece; carbine.—**c. rayada,** rifle carbine.—**la c. de Ambrosio,** a harmless weapon; a worthless thing; bluff.—**carabinazo,** *m.* report or firing of a carbine; carbine wound.—**carabinero, ra,** *n.* carabineer; internal-revenue guard.
[1]**cárabo,** *m.* a small Moorish vessel; (zool.) a kind of crab or cockle.
[2]**cárabo,** *m.* (ornith.) a large horned owl.
caracal, *m.* (zool.) a kind of lynx.
caracará, *m.* (ornith.) caracara, a kind of hawk.
caracoa, *f.* (P. I.) small oared barge.
caracol, *m.* (zool.) snail; winding staircase (also ESCALERA DE C.); prancing of a horse; nightdress used by women in Mexico; cochlea of the ear.—**c. marino,** periwinkle.—**caracola,** *f.* small snail with a whitish shell; shell used as a horn.—**caracolear,** *vn.* (of horses) to caracole, wheel.—**caracolejo,** *m. dim.* small snail or snail shell.—**¡caracoles!** *interj.* = ¡CARAMBA!
caracoleo, *m.* caracoling.
caracolero, ra, *n.* snail gatherer or dealer.
caracolillo, *m. dim.* small snail; (bot.) snail-flowered kidney bean; veined mahogany.—*pl.* trimmings, fringes.—**café c.,** pea-bean coffee.
caracolito, *m. dim.* small snail.
carácter, *m.* character; brand on cattle; temper, nature, disposition; loftiness of soul, firmness, energy; style of speaking or writing.—**caracteres de imprenta,** printing types.
caractericé, caracterice, *v. V.* CARACTERIZAR.
característica, *f.* characteristic; feature, fundamental property; (math.) characteristic.
característico, ca. I. *a.* characteristic, typical, distinctive, distinguishing. **II.** *m.* & *f.* actor or actress who plays the part of an old person.
caracterización, *f.* characterization.
caracterizado, da, *a.* characterized, distinguished; apt, competent; reliable, responsible.
caracterizar, *va.* (*pret.* CARACTERICÉ; *subj.* CARACTERICE) to characterize, distinguish by peculiar qualities; to confer a distinguished employment, dignity, or office on; to mark, point out; to act (a part) properly.
caracul, *m.* caracul, karacul (fur).
caracha, *f.,* **carache,** *m.* itch, mange (esp. of llamas).
caracho, cha, *a.* violet-colored.
caradura, *f.* brassiness, brazenness.
caramanchel, *m.* fixed or movable shed over the hatchways of ships.
caramanchón, *m.* = CAMARANCHÓN, garret.
[1]**caramba,** *interj.* (coll.) gracious! confound it!
[2]**caramba,** *f.* ancient headgear for women.
carámbano, *m.* icicle, a shoot of ice.
carambanado, da, *a.* forming icicles.
carambillo, *m.* (bot.) saltwort.
[1]**carambola,** *f.* carom, in billiards; a method of playing the card game called *revesino;* (coll.) device or trick to deceive.—**por c.,** (coll.) indirectly.
[2]**carambola,** *f.* (bot.) fruit of the carambola tree.
carambolear, *va.* (billiards) to carom.
carambolero, *m.* carom player; *revesino* player.
carambolo, *m.* (bot.) carambola tree.
caramel, *m.* (ichth.) a kind of pilchard or sardine.
caramelización, *f.* caramelization.
caramelizar, *va.* to caramelize.
caramelo, *m.* caramel; (P. I.) fondant.
caramente, *adv.* dearly; exceedingly, highly; rigorously; solemnly (swear, entrust, etc.).
caramillar, *m.* saltwort field.
caramilleras, *f. pl.* pothook.
caramillo, *m.* flageolet; small flute; (bot.) saltwort; confused heap of things; deceit; trick; gossip; tale-carrying.
caranga, *f.* (Am.), **carángano,** *m.* (Colomb., C. R., Cuba), louse.
carantamaula, *f.* (coll.) hideous mask or visor; ugly, hard-featured person.
carantoña, *f.* (coll.) ugly old woman who makes up and dresses stylishly.—*pl.* caresses, soft words and acts of endearment.—**carantoñera,** *f.* coquette.—**carantoñero,** *m.* flatterer, cajoler.
caraña, *f.* a kind of resinous American gum.
caráota, *f.* (Venez.) bean.
carapa, *f.* (bot.) carapa, carap.
carapacho, *m.* shell (cover of certain animals).
carapato, *m.* castor oil.
caraqueño, ña, *a.* of Caracas.
carasol, *m.* sun parlor, solarium.
carate, *m.* brown spots on the skin, similar to "liver spots"—common in the lowlands of S. A.
carátula, *f.* pasteboard or wire mask; (Am.) title page of a book; (fig.) the histrionic art.
caratulero, ra, *n.* mask maker or dealer.
carava, *f.* holiday meeting of country people.
caravana, *f.* caravan; company of traders, pilgrims, etc.
caravanero, ra, *n.* caravaneer; *f.* caravansary.
caravanseray, caravasar, *m.* caravansary.
[1]**caray, carey,** *m.* tortoise; tortoise shell.
[2]**caray,** *interj.* (Am.) = [1]¡CARAMBA!
carbamida, *f.* (chem.) carbamide, urea.
cárbaso, *m.* a kind of fine flax; (poet.) sail of a ship; an ancient tunic.
carbinol, *m.* (chem.) carbinol.
carbol, *m.* carbolic acid.
carbólico, ca, *a.* carbolic.
carbolíneo, *m.* (chem.) carbolineum.
carbón, *m.* coal; charcoal; carbon (of an arc lamp).—**c. animal,** bone black, animal charcoal.—**c. de arranque,** root charcoal (made from roots).—**c. de leña,** charcoal.—**c. de piedra,** or **mineral,** coal.—**c. vegetal** = C. DE LEÑA.
carbonada, *f.* coal charge of a furnace; broiled chop or steak; grillade: a kind of pancake.
carbonado, *m.* carbonado, carbon diamond.
carbonario, *m.* Carbonaro, member of a secret pol. party.—**carbonarismo,** *m.* Carbonarism.
carbonatado, da, *a.* (chem.) carbonated.
carbonatar, *va.* (chem.) to carbonate.
carbonato, *m.* (chem.) carbonate.—**c. de calcio,** (chem.) calcium carbonate.—**c. sódico** or **de sodio,** (chem.) sodium carbonate, sal soda.
carboncillo, *m. dim.* small coal; black crayon; carbon pencil.
carbonear, *vn.* & *va.* to make charcoal (of).
carboneo, *m.* carbonization; charring.
carbonera, *f.* wood prepared for burning into charcoal; place where charcoal is made; coal-house, coal hole, coal cellar, coal bin; coal pit, colliery, coal mine; woman who sells charcoal.
carbonería, *f.* coal yard, coal shed; coal mine.
carbonero, ra. I. *a.* pert. to coal or charcoal. **II.** *m.* & *f.* coal or charcoal seller. **III.** *m.* charcoal maker; collier, coal miner; coal merchant; (naut.) coal ship, collier.
carbonicé, carbonice, *v. V.* CARBONIZAR.
carbónico, ca, *a.* (chem.) carbonic.
carbónidos, *m. pl.* (chem.) carbon and its compounds.
carbonífero, ra, *a.* carboniferous.
carbonilo, *m.* (chem.) carbonyl.
carbonita, *f.* carbonite.
carbonización, *f.* carbonization.
carbonizar, *va.* (*pret.* CARBONICÉ; *subj.* CARBONICE) to carbonize; to char.
carbono, *m.* (chem.) carbon.
carbonoso, sa, *a.* carbonaceous, coaly, charry.
carborundo, *m.* carborundum.

carboxilo, *m.* (chem.) carboxyl.
carbuncal, *a.* carbuncular.
carbunclo, *m.* carbuncle, garnet; sometimes used for ruby (also CARBÚNCULO); CARBUNCO.
carbunco, *m.* gangrenous tumor.
carbuncoso, sa, *a.* = CARBUNCAL.
carbúnculo, *m.* *V.* CARBUNCLO.
carburación, *f.* carburation.
carburador, *m.* (auto, etc.) carburetor.
carburante, *n.* & *a.* containing hydrocarbons.
carburar, carburizar, *va.* to carburize, carburet.
carburo, *m.* (chem.) carbide.
carcaj, *m.* = [1]CARCAX.
carcajada, *f.* outburst of laughter.
carcamal, *n.* (coll.) old, decrepit person.
carcamán, *m.* tub; heavy, unseaworthy vessel.
carcañal, calcañal, *m.* heel bone, calcaneum.
cárcava, *f.* gully; (mil.) inclosure; mound; hedge; ditch; grave.
carcavina, *f.* = CÁRCAVA.
cárcavo, *m.* hollow in which a water wheel turns.
carcavón, *m.* large and deep ditch.
carcavuezo, *m.* deep pit.
[1]**carcax,** *m.*, **carcaza,** *f.* quiver; sash with a case in which the cross is borne in a procession; (Am.) leathern case for a rifle at the saddle bow.
[2]**carcax,** *m.* Moorish anklet.
carcayú, *m.* (zool.) carcajou, wolverine, glutton.
carcel, *m.* (elec.) carcel.—**lámpara c.,** carcel lamp.
cárcel, *f.* jail; prison; groove of a sluice gate; (carp.) clamp, clasp, cramp; (mech.) holder; cheek; collar; (print.) cheek of a printing press; (weaving) reed of a loom.
carcelaje, *m.* jailer's fees.
carcelario, ria, *a.* of or pertaining to a jail.
carcelería, *f.* imprisonment; bail given for the appearance of a prisoner.
carcelero, ra. I. *a.* = CARCELARIO. **II.** *m.* jailer, warden.
carcinogénesis, *f.* carcinogenesis.
carcinogénico, ca, *a.* carcinogenic.
carcinógeno, *m.* (med.) carcinogen.
carcinoma, *m.* (med.) carcinoma, cancer.
carcinomatoso, sa, *a.* (med.) carcinomatous.
cárcola, *f.* treadle of a loom.
carcoma, *f.* wood borer; woodlouse; wood tick; gribble; dust made by the wood borer; grief, anxiety; spendthrift.
carcomer. I. *va.* to gnaw; (of wood borers) to destroy; to consume or impair by degrees, to undermine. **II.** *vr.* to decay, decline; become worm- or insect-eaten.—**carcomido, da,** *a.* worm-eaten; consumed; decayed; impaired.
carda, *f.* act of carding; teasel; card; hatter's jack; severe reprimand or censure; (naut.) a small vessel like a galley.
cardador, ra, *n.* carder, comber; (entom.) myriapod.
cardadura, *f.* carding, combing (wool).
carda mecánica, *f.* carding machine.
cardamina, *f.* (bot.) lady's-smock.
cardamomo, *m.* (bot.) cardamom.
cardán, *m.* (mech.) Cardan joint, universal joint or coupling.
cardar, *va.* to card or comb (wool); to raise (the nap on cloth) with a teasel.
cardelina, *f.* (ornith.) goldfinch, thistle finch.
[1]**cardenal,** *m.* wale, welt.
[2]**cardenal,** *m.* (eccl.) cardinal; (ornith.) Virginian nightingale; cardinal bird.
cardenalato, *m.* cardinalate, cardinalship.
cardenalicio, cia, *a.* pert. to a cardinal.
cardencha, *f.* (bot.) teasel; card, comb.—**c. cardadora,** fuller's teasel.—**c. silvestre,** wild teasel.
cardenchal, *m.* place where teasels grow.
cardenillo, *m.* verdigris; (art) verditer, Paris green.
cárdeno, na, *a.* livid.
cardería, *f.* place where wool is carded.
cardero, ra, *n.* maker of cards (for wool).
cardíaca, *f.* (bot.) common motherwort.
cardiáceo, a, *a.* heart-shaped.
cardíaco, ca, *a.* (med.) cardiac.
cardialgia, *f.* (med.) cardialgia, heartburn.
cardiálgico, ca, *a.* pert. to cardialgia.
cardias, *m.* cardiac orifice of the stomach.
cardico, illo, ito, *m. dim.* small thistle.
cardillo, *m.* (bot.) golden thistle.
cardinal, *a.* cardinal (point); main, fundamental.
cardiografía, *f.* cardiography.
cardiógrafo, *m.* cardiograph.
cardiología, *f.* cardiology.
cardiópata, *n.* (med.) person with heart disease.
cardiopatía, *f.* (med.) cardiopathy.
cardioscopio, *m.* (med.) cardioscope.
carditis, *f.* (med.) carditis.
cardizal, *m.* land full of thistles and weeds.
cardo, *m.* (bot.) thistle.—**c. alcachofero,** garden artichoke.—**c. aljonjero,** stemless, carline thistle.—**c. arrocife,** cardoon artichoke.—**c. bendito,** blessed thistle, centaury, holy thistle.—**c. borriqueño,** (bot.) spear-plume thistle.—**c. corredor,** sea holly, field eringo.—**c. de comer, c. hortense** = C. ARROCIFE.—**c. huso,** wooly carthamus.—**c. lechero,** or **mariano,** milk thistle.—**c. santo** = C. BENDITO.—**c. setero** = C. CORREDOR.—**c. silvestre** = C. BORRIQUEÑO.
cardón, *m.* act and effect of carding; (bot.) CARDENCHA, teasel.
Cardona, *m.*—**más listo que C.,** very smart, clever fellow, sharp as a needle.
cardoncillo, *m.* (bot.) mountain carthamus.
carducé, carduce, *v. V.* CARDUZAR.
carducha, *f.* large iron comb for wool.
cardume, cardumen, *m.* school of fish; (Chile) multitude of things.
carduzador, *m.* carder.
carduzal, *m.* = CARDIZAL.
carduzar, *va.* (*pret.* CARDUCÉ; *subj.* CARDUCE) to card or comb (wool).
carear, *va.* (law) to confront (criminals); (coll.) to compare; to tend (cattle, sheep).—*vr.* to assemble or meet; to meet face to face.
carecer, *vn.* (*ind.* CAREZCO; *subj.* CAREZCA) (**de**) to lack, not to have.
carena, *f.* (naut.) careening, repairing; (poet.) ship.—**dar c.,** (coll.) to reprimand in a jocular way; to banter.—**carenar,** *va.* (naut.) to careen, repair.
carencia, *f.* lack; scarcity, deficiency.
carenero, *m.* careening place.
carente, *pres.p. irreg.* of CARECER.—**c. de,** in need of.
careo, *m.* (law) confrontation of criminals or witnesses; comparison; act of placing or meeting face to face; (fort.) front of a bastion or fortress.
carero, ra, *a.* (coll.) selling things dear.
carestía, *f.* scarcity, dearth; lack; famine; dearness, high price.
careta, *f.* mask.—**quitar la c.,** to tear off the mask, to unmask.
careto, ta, *a.* (of horses) having the forehead marked with a white spot or stripe.
carey, *m.* (zool.) tortoise; tortoise shell.
carezco, carezca, *v. V.* CARECER.
carga, *f.* load; burden; freight, cargo; loading; charge (of a cannon, furnace, etc.); nozzle of the flask which measures the powder for a charge; corn measure containing 4 FANEGAS; a preparation to cure sprains and inflammation in horses and mules: impost, duty, tax; (hydraul.) head; (mil.) charge, attack.—**c. alar** or **de ala,** wing loading.—**c. comercial, útil** or **de pago,** payload.—**c. concejil,** municipal obligatory service.—**c. de profundidad,** depth bomb or charge.—**c. de rotura** or **de fractura,** breaking load.—**c. fija,** (eng.) dead load.—**c. hidrostática,** (hydraul.) head.—**c. móvil,** (eng.) live load.—**c. nuclear,** (phys.) nuclear charge.—**c. onerosa,** dead weight.—**c. personal,** obligatory personal service.—**a cargas,**

abundantly, (coll.) heaps.—**volver a la c.,** to insist; to keep at it; to harp on the subject.
cargadas, *f. pl.* a card game.
cargadera, *f.* (naut.) downhauls, brails.—*pl.* (Colomb.) (trousers) suspenders.
cargadero, *m.* place where goods are loaded or unloaded; freight station.
cargadilla, *f.* (coll.) increase of a debt through the accumulation of interest.
cargado, da. I. *pp.* of CARGAR. **II.** *a.* full; fraught. —**c. de espaldas,** round-shouldered, stooping. —**c. de vino,** full, tipsy. **III.** *m.* Spanish step in dancing.
cargador, *m.* shipper; freighter; expressman, carrier; porter; rammer, ramrod; large pitchfork for straw; (arch.) post put in a doorway or window; (naut.) tackle; plate used in gilding.
cargamento, *m.* (naut.) cargo; shipment.
cargar. I. *va.* & *vn.* (*pret.* CARGUÉ; *subj.* CARGUE) to load; burden; to carry (a load); to charge (a furnace, battery, etc.); to attack; to ship; to overload, overburden; to clog; to lay in, collect; to charge on account; to book; to impose or lay (taxes); to impute, charge (one) with; to crowd; (coll.) to vex, annoy, pester; in cards, to take (a card with a higher one); (gram.) to put more stress or inflection on one letter or syllable.—**c. la mano,** to pursue with eagerness; to reproach with severity; to overcharge; to be too exacting. **II.** *vn.* to incline, tip; (**en** or **sobre**) to rest (on), be supported (by), lean (against); (of trees) to bear abundantly; (**con**) to assume (responsibility); bear (the blame); carry away; (**sobre**) to urge, press. **III.** *vr.* (**sobre**) to rest (on); (**contra**) to lean (against, on); (of clouds or sky) to gather, become denser, heavier or darker; (**de**) to have or obtain a large number or quantity (of); to load oneself (with); to become tired, peeved or vexed (about); to trouble oneself (with).—**c. de razón,** to strengthen one's position, find greater justification.
cargareme, *m.* receipt, voucher.
cargazón, *f.* cargo; abundance; clumsy, badly made thing.—**c. de cabeza,** heaviness of the head.—**c. de tiempo,** cloudy, thick weather.
cargo, *m.* act of loading; burden, load, weight; load of stones weighing 40 *arrobas* (1000 lb.); number of baskets piled one on the other and put in the oil press; load of pressed grapes to be re-pressed; total amount of what has been received, in a general account; post, dignity, office, ministry; charge, keeping, care; duty, obligation; command or management; fault or inefficiency in the performance of duty; charge, accusation; (law) count.—**c. concejil,** compulsory public office or function.—**c. de conciencia,** remorse, sense of guilt.—**c. y data,** (com.) creditor and debtor (Cr. and Dr.) —**a c. de,** in charge of, under the direction of —**hacer c. a uno de,** to charge one with.— **hacerse c. de,** to take charge of, be responsible for; to take into consideration; to make oneself acquainted with; to understand.
cargoso, sa, *a.* burdensome, onerous.
cargué, cargue, *v. V.* CARGAR.
carguera, *f.* (Colomb.) nursemaid.
carguero, ra. I. *a.* of burden (beast); freight-carrying. **II.** *m.* beast of burden; freighter.
carguío, *m.* cargo, freight; load.
cariacontecido, da, *a.* sad, mournful.
cariacuchillado, da, *a.* scar-faced.
cariado, da, *a.* (of bone, teeth) carious, decayed
cariadura, *f.* (med.) caries, bone ulcer.
cariaguileño, ña, *a.* (coll.) aquiline-nosed and pointed-faced.
carialegre, *a.* smiling, cheerful.
cariampollado, da, *or* **cariampollar,** *a.* round-faced, plump-cheeked.
cariancho, cha, *a.* broad-faced, chubby, chub-faced, bull-faced.
cariarse, *vr.* (med.) to become carious.
cariátide, *f.* (arch.) caryatides.
caribe, *m.* cannibal, man-eater, savage; Carib. Antilles Indian; (Venez.) a man-eating fish.
caribú, *m.* (zool.) caribou.
carica, *f.* a kind of spotted kidney bean.
caricatura, *f.* caricature; cartoon.
caricatural, *a.* caricatural.
caricaturar, caricaturizar, *va.* to caricature.
caricaturesco, ca, *a.* caricatural.
caricaturista, *n.* caricaturist.
caricia, *f.* caress; petting; endearing expression.
cariciosamente, *adv.* fondlingly, caressingly.
caricioso, sa, *a.* fondling, endearing, caressing.
caricuerdo, da, *a.* wise-looking.
caridad, *f.* charity, charitableness; refreshment given to travelers at the church door.—**la c. empieza por uno mismo, charity begins at** home.
caridelantero, ra, *a.* (coll.) brazen-faced, bold-looking.
caridoliente, *a.* mournful-looking.
caries, *f.* (med., bot.) caries.
carifruncido, da, *a.* (coll.) wrinkle-faced; frowning, cross-looking.
carigordo, da, *a.* (coll.) full-faced.
cariharto, ta, *a.* round-faced.
carilampiño, ña, *a.* (Am.) smooth-faced, beardless.
carilargo, ga, *a.* long-visaged.
carilucio, cia, *a.* (coll.) having a shining face.
carilla, *f. dim.* little or small face; face guard; silver coin in Aragon worth eighteen CINEROS, or deniers; page (of a book).
carilleno, na, *a.* (coll.) plump-faced.
carillón, *m.* carillon.
carimba, *f.* (Peru) brand on slaves.
carincho, *m.* a dish resembling chile con carne.
carinegro, gra, *a.* of a swarthy complexion; black-faced.
cariñana, *f.* ancient headdress like a nun's veil.
cariño, *m.* love, fondness, affection; endearing expression.—**tener c.** (*indir. obj.*), to be fond of.
cariñosamente, *adv.* fondly, kindly.
cariñoso, sa, *a.* affectionate, loving; affable.
cariocinesis, *f.* (biol.) mitosis.
cariofileo, lea, *a.* (bot.) caryophyllaceous.
cariofilina, *f.* (chem.) caryophyllin.
cariópside, *f.* (bot.) caryopsis.
carioquinesis, *f.* (incorrect for) CARIOCINESIS.
cariparejo, ja, *a.* (coll.) having an impassive countenance, "poker face."
carirraído, da, *a.* (coll.) brazen-faced, impudent.
carirredondo, da, *a.* round-faced.
carisma, *m.* divine gift or favor, charism.
carita, *f. dim.* little or small face.
caritán, *m.* (P. I.) gatherer of tuba (liquor from certain plants).
caritativamente, *adv.* charitably.
caritativo, va, *a.* charitable.
cariucho, *m.* (Ecua.) dish of meat, potatoes and garlic.
cariz, *m.* aspect.
carlanca, *f.* mastiff's collar.—**tener muchas carlancas,** to be very cunning or crafty.
carlancón, *m.* (coll.) very sharp or crafty person.
carlear, *vn.* to pant.
carlín, *m.* an ancient silver coin.
carlina, *f.* (bot.) carline thistle.
carlinga, *f.* (naut.) step of a mast.
carlismo, *m.* Carlism.—**carlista,** *n., a.* Carlist.
carlita, *f.* reading eyeglasses.
carlota, *f.* charlotte.—**c. rusa,** (cook.) charlotte russe.
carlovingio, gia, *a.* Carlovingian.
carmañola, *f.* carmagnole.
carmelita. I. *n.* & *a. f.* Carmelite. **II.** *f.* flower of Ind. cress.—**carmelitano, na,** *a.* Carmelite.
[1]**carmen,** *m.* country house and garden; villa.
[2]**carmen,** *m.* Carmelite religious order.
[3]**carmen,** *m.* verse; poem.
carmenador, *m.* teasler (man or machine).
carmenadura, *f.* teaseling (woolen cloth, etc.)

carmenar, *va.* to teasel; to disentangle, unravel; to comb (the hair); (coll.) to pull (the hair); to cheat.
carmes, *m.* kermes, the cochineal insect.
carmesí. I. *m.* cochineal powder. **II.** *n.* & *a.* crimson, bright red.
carmín, *m.* coloring matter of cochineal; carmine color; (bot.) pokeweed, phytolacca.—**c. bajo,** pale rose color.
carminativo, *m.* (med.) carminative.
carmínico, ca, *a.* carminic.
carminita, *f.* (min.) carminite.
carnada, *f.* bait.
carnadura, *f.* muscularity; flesh, fleshiness.
carnaje, *m.* salt beef.
carnal. I. *a.* carnal, sensual; related by blood; full (as in *hermano carnal,* full brother). **II.** *m.* time of the year when meat may be eaten (opposed to Lent and other fast days).
carnalidad, *f.* carnality, lustfulness.
carnaval, *m.* carnival.—**carnavalesco, ca,** *a.* pertaining to or resembling a carnival.
carnaza, *f.* fleshy side of a hide or skin; (coll.) abundance of meat; bait.
carne, *f.* flesh; meat; pulp (of fruit); flesh, one of the evil temptations; kin; name of a children's game with a hollow bone.—**c. ahogadiza,** meat from a drowned animal.—**c. asada en horno,** baked meat.—**c. asada en parrillas,** broiled meat.—**c. bien cocida,** well-done meat.—**c. cediza,** tainted meat.—**c. de cañón,** cannon fodder; inferior person or people.—**c. de carnero,** mutton.—**c. de gallina,** (fig.) goose flesh.—**c. de membrillo,** preserved quinces.—**c. de pelo,** meat of small quadrupeds (hare, rabbit, etc.).—**c. de pluma,** flesh of fowls.—**c. de puerco,** pork meat, pork.—**c. de res,** (Am.) beef.—**c.de ternera,** veal.—**c.de vaca,** beef.—**c. de vaca asada,** roast beef.—**c.de venado,** venison.—**c. fiambre,** cold meat.—**c. magra, c. mollar,** lean meat.—**c. nomia,** (coll.) choice meat without bones.—**c. sin hueso,** (fig.) much profit and little trouble.—**c. viva,** quick or raw flesh in a wound.—**c. y hueso,** flesh and blood.—**c. y sangre,** flesh and blood, near kindred.—**cobrar carnes,** to recover one's flesh or weight, to pick up.—**echar carnes,** (coll.) to grow fat, put on flesh.—**en carnes,** naked.—**en c. viva,** raw, with the flesh exposed.—**envuelto en carnes,** fleshy, fat.—**ni c. ni pescado,** neither flesh nor fish; nondescript; insipid.—**ser c. y hueso de,** to be flesh and blood of, to be part and parcel of.—**ser uña y carne,** (fig.) to be hand and glove, to be one, to be intimate.—**tener c. de perro,** to have an iron constitution.
carnecilla, *f.* small excrescence on the body.
carnerada, *f.* flock of sheep.
carneraje, *m.* tax or duty on sheep.
carnereamiento, *m.* poundage, penalty for the trespass of sheep.
carnerear, *va.* to fine for damage done by sheep.
carnerero, ra, *n.* shepherd(-ess).
carneril, *m.* sheepwalk; pasture for sheep.
[1]**carnero,** *m.* family vault, burying place; charnel house.
[2]**carnero,** *m.* sheep; mutton; sheepskin.—**c. ahogado,** stewed mutton.—**c. ciclán,** ridgil or ridgeling.—**c. de simiente,** ram kept for breeding.—**c. manso para guía,** bellwether.—**c. marino,** seal.—**no hay tales carneros,** (coll.) there is no such a thing.
carneruno, na, *a.* pert. to, or like, sheep.
carnestolendas, *f. pl.* carnival (the three carnival days before Ash Wednesday).
carnet, *m.* (Gal.) bank book; memorandum book.
carnicería, *f.* meat market, butcher's shop; slaughter house; carnage, slaughter.
carnicero, ra. I. *a.* (zool.) carnivorous; bloodthirsty, sanguinary; (of pasture) fattening; (coll.) meat fiend, (one) eating much meat; pertaining to shambles. **II.** *n.* butcher, one who sells meat. **III.** *m. pl.* (zool.) Carnivora.
cárnicol, *m.* hoof of cloven-footed animals.
carnificación, *f.* carnification.
carnificarse, *vr.* to carnify, convert into flesh.
carnina, *f.* (chem.) carnine.
carniola, *f.* (min.) carnelian.
carnívoro, ra. I. *a.* carnivorous. **II.** *m.* (zool.) carnivore.
carniza, *f.* (coll.) refuse of meat; cat or dog meat; decayed flesh.
carnosidad, *f.* (med.) proud flesh; fatness, fleshiness.
carnoso, sa, *a.* fleshy; full of marrow; meaty; (of fruit) pulpy.
carnotita, *f.* (min.) carnotite.
carnudo, da, *a.* = CARNOSO.
carnuza, *f.* disgusting coarse or heaped meat.
caro, ra. I. *a.* dear, costly; dear, beloved.—**c. mitad,** better half. **II.** *adv. m.* dearly, **at a** high price or cost.
caroca, *f.* decoration in public festivities; farcical piece; (coll.) caress, endearing action or expression made with a selfish purpose.
carocha, carrocha, *f.* insect eggs.—**carochar, carrochar,** *va.* (of insects) to lay eggs.
carolingio, a, *n.* & *a.* Carolingian, Carlovingian.
cárolus, *m.* an anc. Flemish coin used in Spain.
caromomia, *f.* the dry flesh of a mummy.
carona, *f.* padding of saddle next to animal's back; part of animal's back on which saddle lies.—**caroñoso, sa,** *a.* (of horses) old, galled.
caroquero, ra. I. *n.* wheedler, flatterer. **II.** *a.* honey-worded, fondling.
carosis, *f.* (med.) complete stupor.
carótida, *f.* & *a.* (anat.) carotid.
carozo, *m.* core of an apple, pear, etc.; corn cob.
[1]**carpa,** *f.* (ichth.) carp.
[2]**carpa,** *f.* part of bunch of grapes torn off.
[3]**carpa,** *f.* (Peru) canvas tent.
carpanel, *m.* (arch.) basket-handle arch.
carpanta, *f.* (coll.) keen appetite, hunger.
carpe, *m.* common hornbeam tree; witch-hazel.
carpedal, *m.* hornbeam plantation.
carpelar, *a.* (bot.) carpellary.
carpelo, *m.* (bot.) carpel.
carpeta, *f.* table cover; portfolio; (Am.) briefcase; letter file; folder; docket; writing desk; small curtain or screen before tavern door.
carpetazo, *m.*—**dar c.,** to lay aside; to table; to pigeonhole.
carpiano, na, *a.* (anat.) carpal.
carpincho, *m.* (zool.) carpincho, web-footed rodent (largest extant) of South America.
carpintear, *vn.* to do carpenter's work.
carpintería, *f.* carpentry; carpenter's shop.
carpintero, *m.* carpenter, joiner; (ornith.) woodpecker.—**c. de blanco,** joiner.—**c. de carretas,** cartwright.—**c. de navío,** shipwright.—**c. de obras de afuera,** carpenter who timbers or roofs houses.—**c. de prieto** = C. DE CARRETAS.—**c. de ribera** = C. DE NAVÍO.—**c. real.** (ornith.) ivory-billed woodpecker.
carpir, *vn.* to quarrel, wrangle; (Am.) to scratch (ground for clearing).
carpo, *m.* (anat.) carpus, wrist.
carpobálsamo, *m.* (bot.) balm of Gilead.
carpóforo, *m.* (bot.) carpophore.
carpología, *f.* (bot.) carpology.
carquesa, *f.* in glassworks, annealing furnace.
carquexia, *f.* (bot.) a species of broom plant.
[1]**carraca,** *f.* carack, large and slow-sailing ship; the Cadiz navy yard.
[2]**carraca,** *f.* rattle; ratchet brace.
carraco, ca, *a.* old, withered, decrepit.
carral, *m.* barrel, vat.
carraleja, *f.* black beetle with yellow stripes; oil beetle; Spanish blistering beetle.
carralero, *m.* cooper.
carramplón, *m.* (Colomb.) flintlock musket.
carranque, *m.* a Peruvian cranelike bird.
carraón, *m.* short-stemmed wheat.
carrasca, *f.*, **carrasco,** *m.* (bot.) pin oak, swamp

oak.—**carrascal, carrascalejo,** *m.* pin-oak field.—**carrascón,** *m. aug.* large pin oak.
carraspada, *f.* negus (beverage).
carraspera, *f.* (coll.) hoarseness; frog-in-the-throat; sore throat.
carraspique, *m.* (bot.) candytuft.
carrasposo, sa, *a.* suffering from chronic hoarseness or sore throat; (Colomb., Venez.) rough (to the touch).
carrasqueño, ña, *a.* pertaining to the pin oak; (coll.) harsh, sharp.
carrera, *f.* run; race; course; racetrack; highroad; avenue, broad street; row; stroke (of a piston); travel (of a valve); range of iron teeth in combing cards; line, parting of the hair; girder, joist; broken stitch in a stocking; course and duration of life; career; course, method of life; conduct, mode of action; route of a line of steamers; coach or stage line; Spanish step in dancing.—**c. armamentista,** armaments race.—**c. de baquetas,** gantlet, a military punishment.—**c. de equipos,** (sports) relay race.—**c. de obstáculo,** obstacle race; steeplechase.—**c. de relevos,** (sports) relay race.—**carreras de caballos,** horse racing.—**a c. abierta,** at full speed.—**de** or **a la c.,** hastily, in a hurry.—**no poder hacer c. con,** to not be able to bring (one) to reason.—**partir de c.,** to act in a rash and inconsiderate manner.—**poner en c.,** to give employment to; to procure employment for.
carrerilla, *f. dim.* rapid motion (in a Spanish dance); (mus.) run (of an octave).
carrerista, *n.* race fan; bicycle racer; *m.* outrider.
carrero, *m.* = CARRETERO, carter, driver.
carreta, *f.* long narrow cart, wagon.
carretada, *f.* cartful, cart load; (Mex.) measure for lime, = 3,000 pounds.—*pl.* great quantity.—**a carretadas,** (coll.) copiously, in abundance, in heaps.
carretaje, *m.* cartage; trade with carts.
carretal, *m.* rough, ragged building stone.
carrete, *m.* spool, bobbin, reel; reel of a fishing rod; (elec.) bobbin, coil.
carretear. I. *va.* to cart, to convey in a cart or wagon; to drive (a cart). **II.** *vr.* (of oxen or mules) to draw unevenly.
carretel, *m.* spool, reel, bobbin; fishing reel, line reel; (naut.) log reel; spunyarn winch; ropewalk reel.—**c. de carpintero,** carpenter's marking line.
carretela, *f.* calèche, calash.
carretera, *f.* wide, public road, highway; drive.
carretería, *f.* number of carts; trade of a carman; cartwright's yard; wheelwright's shop.
carretero, ra. I. *a.* vehicle, for vehicles.—**camino c.,** vehicle road. **II.** *m.* cartwright; carter, driver, truckman; *f.* highway, road.—**c. de portazgo,** toll road.—**c. de velocidad,** thruway.
carretil, *a.* pertaining to a cart or truck.
carretilla, *f. dim.* small cart; wheelbarrow, pushcart, trolley cart, handcart; (Ry.) truck; gocart; squib, firecracker; small wheel.—**c. de equipaje,** baggage truck or car.—**de c.,** mechanically, unconsciously, by rote.
carretón, *m.* cart; truck; go-cart.—**c. de lámpara,** pulley for raising or lowering lamps.
carretonada, *f.* wagonload, truckload.
carretonero, *m.* truckman, truck driver.
carricoche, *m.* ancient cart with a coachlike body; wagonette; muck cart, dung cart.
carricuba, *m.* watering or sprinkling cart.
carriego, *m.* osier fishing basket; rough basket for bleaching flax yarn.
carriel, *m.* (C. A.) traveling bag for papers and money; (Colomb.) GUARNIEL, pouch carried by strapping across shoulders and chest.
carril, *m.* rut, cartway; narrow road; furrow; (Ry.) rail.—**carrilera,** *f.* rut (in road); (Am. Ry.) siding; track.
carrillada, *f.* oily or medullar substance of a hog.
carrillera, *f.* jaw; chin strap (of helmet).
carrillo, *m. dim.* cheek; (naut.) hoisting tackle.
carrilludo, da, *a.* plump or round-cheeked.
carriola, *f.* trundle bed; small chariot, curricle.
carrizal, *m.* (bot.) reed-grass, -field.
carrizo, *m.* (bot.) common reed-grass.
carro, *m.* cart; car; (Am.) automobile; running gear of a carriage without the body; **(C-, astr.)** Great Bear, Dipper; (naut.) manufactory for cables and other ship cordage; measure for wood; cartload; bed of a printing press.—**c. de colchar,** rope maker's sledge.—**c. de riego,** sprinkling car.—**c. de volteo,** tip car, tilt car, dump car.—**C. Mayor,** Great Bear.—**C. Menor,** Little Bear, Ursa Minor.—**c. tranvía,** or **urbano,** street car.—**untar el c., (fig.) to** grease the palm, to bribe.
carrocería, *f.* shop where carriages are made, repaired, or sold; (auto) body.
carrocín, *m.* chaise, curricle.
carrocha, *f.* insect eggs.
carrochar, *vn.* (of insects) to lay eggs.
carromatero, *m.* carter; charioteer; carman.
carromato, *m.* long, narrow cart with two wheels and tilt.
carronada, *f.* (artil.) short gun of large calibre.
carroña, *f.* carrion, putrid flesh.
carroñar, *va.* to infect (sheep) with the scab.
carroño, ña. I. *a.* putrefied, putrid, rotten. **II.** *n.* & *a.* (Am.) coward(ly).—**carroñoso, sa,** *a.* rotting; ill-smelling.
carroza, *f.* large coach; superb state coach; caroche; (naut.) awning.
carruaje, *m.* vehicle; carriage; car.
carruajero, *m.* carter, wagon or coach driver.
carruco, *m.* small cart used in mountains.
carrucha, *f.* = GARRUCHA, pulley.
carrujado, da, *a.* corrugated, wrinkled.
carrusel, *m.* carrousel, merry-go-round.
carta, *f.* letter, epistle; royal ordinance; map, chart; playing card; written constitution, charter.—**c. abierta,** open letter.—**c. aérea,** airmail letter.—**c. amorosa,** billet doux.—**c. blanca,** carte blanche, full powers.—**c. certificada,** registered letter.—**c. credencial,** credentials.—**c. cuenta,** bill or account of sale.—**c. de amparo,** safe-conduct.—**c. de aviso,** letter of advice.—**c. de contramarca,** letter of reprisal.—**c. de crédito,** letter of credit.—**c. de creencia,** credentials.—**c. de dotes,** articles of marriage.—**c. de encomienda,** letter of safe-conduct.—**c. de espera,** (law) moratory permit, moratorium.—**c. de examen,** license to practice a trade or profession.—**c. de fletamento,** (com.) charter party.—**c. de guía,** safe-conduct, passport.—**c. de horro,** letter of enfranchisement.—**c. de libre,** (law) guardian's discharge.—**c. de marca,** letter of marque.—**c. de marear,** sea chart.—**c. de moratoria,** (law) moratory permit, moratorium.—**c. de naturaleza,** naturalization paper.—**c. de pago,** acquittance, receipt, discharge in full.—**c. de presentación** or **de recomendación,** letter of introduction.—**c. de sanidad,** bill of health.—**c. de seguridad,** safe-conduct.—**c. de Urías,** (coll.) trap, snare, traitorous scheme.—**c. de vecindad,** burgher brief.—**c. de venta,** bill of sale.—**c. de vuelta,** dead letter.—**c. en lista,** letter in poste restante; general-delivery letter.—**c. general,** (com.) form letter.—C. **Magna,** Magna Charta.—**c. orden,** mandatory letter.—**c. receptoria,** warrant, voucher.—**c. viva,** messenger who delivers his messages verbally.—**a c. cabal,** thorough, in every respect, every inch.—**a la c.,** (Am.) à la carte.—**enseñar las cartas,** to show one's hand.—**pecar por c. de más o de menos,** to have either too much or too little.—**tomar cartas en el asunto,** to take part; to be (in something); to take sides; to look into the matter.
cartabón, *m.* carpenter's square; drawing triangle; rule; shoemaker's slide, size stick; quadrant, gunner's square.
cartagenero, ra, *a.* of or from Cartagena.

cartaginense; cartaginés, esa, *n.* & *a.* Carthaginian.
cártama, *f.*, **cártamo,** *m.* (bot.) saffron.
cartapacio, *m.* memorandum book; student's notebook; book satchel; batch or pile of papers.
cartapel, *m.* memorandum filled with useless matter.
cartear. I. *vn.* to play low cards as feelers; to falsecard. **II.** *va.* & *vn.* (naut.) to steer by the chart. **III.** *vr.* to write to each other, correspond.
cartel, *m.* placard, handbill, poster; cartel.
cartela, *f.* slip of paper, piece of wood, or other materials on which a memorandum is made; (arch.) modillion, console, bracket; iron stay supporting a balcony.
cartelera, *f.* billboard.
cartelón, *m. aug.* long edict; show bill.
carteo, *m.* intercourse by letters.
cárter, *m.* (auto.) oil pan.
cartera, *f.* portfolio; writing case; briefcase; pocketbook; wallet; notebook; letter case, letter box; portfolio, office of a cabinet minister; pocket flap; (com.) securities forming part of the assets.
cartería, *f.* employment of letter carrier; sorting room in a post office.
carterista, *m.* pickpocket.
cartero, *m.* letter carrier, postman.
cartesianismo, *m.* Cartesianism.
cartesiano, na, *n.* & *a.* Cartesian.
carteta, *f.* a card game.
cartilagíneo, a; cartilaginoso, sa, *a.* (zool.) cartilaginous.
cartílago, *m.* (anat.) cartilage.
cartilla, *f. dim.* short letter, note; primer; certificate of a clergyman duly ordained.—**leerle a uno la c.** (fig.) to give one a lecture.—**no saber la c.,** to be extremely ignorant, know nothing.
cartografía, *f.* cartography.
cartográfico, ca, *a.* cartographic.
cartógrafo, *m.* cartographer.
cartomancía, *f.* cartomancy, fortune telling by playing cards.
cartómetro, *m.* curvometer.
cartón, *m.* pasteboard; cardboard; binders' board; metal ornament imitating the leaves of plants; cartoon, painting, or drawing on strong paper.—**c. piedra,** (art) staff; papier-maché.
cartonero, ra, *n.* pasteboard maker.
cartuchera, *f.* cartridge box or pouch.
cartucho, *m.* cartouch; cartridge; metallic cartridge; roll of coins; (Am.) paper cornet.
cartujano, na, *m.* & *a.* Carthusian.
cartujo, ja. I. *a.* Carthusian. **II.** *m.* Carthusian monk; (coll.) taciturn man; recluse; *f.* Carthusian order or monastery.
cartulario, *m.* archives or registry; archivist; coucher, register book in monasteries.
cartulina, *f.* bristol board, cardboard.—**c. común,** millboard.—**c. de porcelana,** enamelled card.—**c. en hojas,** sheet card.
carúncula, *f.* (zool.) caruncle.—**c. lagrimal,** lachrymal caruncle.
carunculado, da, *a.* carunculate.
caruncular, *a.* caruncular.
caruto, *m.* (bot.) caruto, genipap.
carvajal, carvallar, carvalledo, *m.* oak field.
carvajo, carvallo, *m.* (bot.) common British oak.
carvi, *m.* (bot.) common caraway; caraway seed.
casa, *f.* house; dwelling, home; household; firm, business establishment; square (of a chess or draught board).—**C. Blanca,** White House.—**c. consistorial,** city hall, town hall.—**c. cuna,** nursery (in a hospital); foundling home.—**c. de apartamentos,** apartment house.—**c. de ayuntamiento,** city hall, town hall.—**c. de banca,** banking house.—**c. de baños,** bathhouse.—**c. de beneficencia,** asylum, poorhouse.—**c. de campo,** country house.—**c. de caridad,** poorhouse.—**c. de comercio,** firm, business establishment.—**c. de correo,** post office.—**c. de departamentos,** apartment house.—**c. de Dios,** House of God, church.—**c. de empeño,** pawnshop.—**c. de expósitos,** foundling home.—**c. de fieras,** menagerie.—**c. de huéspedes,** boarding house.—**c. de juego,** casino, gambling house.—**c. de locos,** madhouse; (fig.) madhouse, bedlam.—**c. de maternidad,** lying-in hospital, maternity hospital.—**c. de moneda,** mint.—**c. de orates,** madhouse.—**c. de placer,** country house.—**c. de posada,** boarding house, inn.—**c. de postas,** post house.—**c. de pupilos,** boarding house.—**c. de sanidad,** health office.—**c. de socorro,** emergency hospital, first-aid station.—**c. de tía,** (coll.) jail.—**c. de tócame Roque,** (coll.) unruly household.—**c. de vacas,** dairy farm.—**c. de vecindad,** tenement house.—**c. de vicio,** disorderly house.—**c. exportadora,** export house.—**c. mortuoria,** funeral home; house where a death has recently occurred.—**c. pública,** brothel.—**c. real,** royal palace.—**c. solar** or **solariega,** manor, manor house, homestead.—**a** or **en c.,** at home.—**en c. de,** at the home of.—**los de c.,** the family.—**no tener c. ni hogar,** to have neither house nor home.
casabe, *m.* cassava.
casaca, *f.* dress coat; (coll.) marriage, wedding.—**volver c.,** to become a turncoat.
casación, *f.* (law) cassation, abrogation, repeal.
casacón, *m.* greatcoat; cassock.
casadero, ra, *a.* marriageable.
casado, da. I. *pp.* of CASAR. **II.** *a.* married. **III.** *m.* (print.) imposition.
casalicio, *m.* house, edifice.
casamata, *f.* (mil.) casemate.
casamentero, ra, *n.* match or marriage maker; marriage broker.
casamiento, *m.* marriage, matrimony; wedding.
casapuerta, *f.* vestibule, entrance hall.
casaquilla, *f.* short jacket.
[1]**casar. I.** *vn.* & *vr.* to marry, get married.—**c. con,** to marry, be married to (Shakespeare says "to marry *with*," as in Spanish).—**antes que te cases, mira lo que haces,** look before you leap. **II.** *va.* to marry, join in wedlock; to couple, pair; to match; to suit; (painting) to blend; (print.) to impose.
[2]**casar,** *va.* (law) to repeal, annul.
[3]**casar,** *m.* hamlet, small village.
casarón, *m. aug.* large old house.
casatienda, *f.* tradesman's shop and dwelling combined.
casca, *f.* grape skins; tanning bark; a kind of fruit cake.
cascabel, *m.* bell, jingle; rattle; cascabel, knob at the end of the breech of a cannon.—**poner el c. al gato,** to bell the cat, undertake a risky thing.—**ser un c.,** to be a rattlebrain.
cascabelada, *f.* jingling with small bells; (coll.) thoughtless or indiscreet speech or action, break.
cascabelear. I. *va.* to feed with vain hopes; to bamboozle. **II.** *vn.* to act with levity or recklessly.—**cascabeleo,** *m.* jingling of bells.
cascabelero, ra, *a.* light-witted.
cascabelillo, *m. dim.* small black plum.
cascabillo, *m.* hawk's bell; glume of cereals, chaff, husk; cup of an acorn.
cascaciruelas, *n.* (coll.) mean, base person.
cascada, *f.* waterfall, cataract, cascade.
cascado, da. I. *pp.* of CASCAR. **II.** *a.* broken, burst; decayed; infirm; crazy.
cascadura, *f.* bursting or breaking asunder.
cascajal, cascajar, *m.* gravel pit; gravelly place; place where grape husks are thrown.
cascajero, *m.* (Colomb.) CASCAJAL; old mine still containing some ore.
cascajo, *m.* gravel; fragments; rubbish; (coll.) old and useless furniture, junk; dry fruit.—**estar hecho un c.,** to be old and infirm, to be a total wreck.—**cascajoso, sa,** *a.* gravelly.
cascamajar, *va.* to break, crush slightly.
cascamiento, *m.* breaking, bruising.

cascanueces, *m.* nutcracker.
cascapiñones, *m.* one who shells hot pine nuts and cleans the seed; pine-nut cracker.
cascar. **I.** *va.* (*pret.* CASQUÉ; *subj.* CASQUE) to crack, burst, break into pieces; to crunch; (coll.) to lick, beat, strike. **II.** *vn.* (coll.) to talk too much. **III.** *vr.* to break open.
cáscara, *f.* rind, peel, shell, hull, husk; shell; bark (of trees); lansquenet, a card game.—**c. sagrada,** (med.) cascara sagrada, bark of the Californian buckthorn.—**de la c. amarga,** mischievous; rash; sporty; ultraradical, extremist.—*pl. interj.* by Jove!
cascarela, *f.* a card game.
cascarilla, *f. dim.* small thin shell, skin or bark; Peruvian bark; thin metal shell; powdered egg shell for cosmetic.
cascarillero, ra, *n.* gatherer of Peruvian bark.
cascarillo, *m.* (bot.) cascarilla.
cascarón, *m. aug.* eggshell; (arch.) arch, vault; calotte; niche for the sacrament; a trick in CASCARELA; (Mex.) eggshell filled with confetti.
cascarrabias, *m.* & *f.* (coll.) testy, irritable person.
cascarrón, na, *a.* (coll.) rough, harsh, rude.
cascarudo, da, *a.* with a thick rind or shell.
cascaruleta, *f.* (coll.) noise made by the teeth when chucked under the chin.
casco, *m.* skull, cranium; potsherd; fragments of an earthen vessel; quarter of a fruit; coat or tegument (of an onion); crown (of a hat); helmet; hull (of a ship); head (of a barrel); casque, headpiece; tree of a saddle; (com.) cask, pipe, vat, tank; printers' inking ball; sheepskin stripped of the wool; hoof.—*pl.* heads of sheep or bullocks without the tongues and brains.—**c. y quilla,** (naut.) bottomry, borrowing money for a trip with ship as security.
cascol, *m.* resin of a Guayaquil tree.
cascolote, *m.* (Mex.) thick bark of a tree.
cascote, *m.* rubbish, debris.
cascudo, da, *a.* large-hoofed.
caseación, *f.* coagulation of milk to make cheese.
caseato, *m.* (chem.) caseate.
caseico, ca, *a.* (chem.) lactic.
caseificación, *f.* (chem., med.) caseation.
caseificar, *va.* (chem.) to change into casein; to separate the casein from (milk).
caseína, *f.* casein.
caseoso, sa, *a.* caseous, cheesy.
casera, *f.* housekeeper.
caseramente, *adv.* informally.
casería, *f.* manor's lodge; outbuilding for farm hands.
caserío, *m.* group of houses; small village, settlement.
caserna, *f.* (mil.) casern; barracks.
casero, ra. **I.** *a.* domestic; homemade; house (as *a.*); familiar; housekeeping. **II.** *n.* landlord (-lady); tenant; house agent; caretaker.
caserón, *m. aug.* big house.
caseta, *f. dim.* small house, cottage, hut.—**c. de baños,** bathhouse (at seaside or spa).
casi, *adv.* almost, nearly.—**c. que, or c. c.,** very nearly.
casia, *f.* (bot.) bastard cinnamon, cassia.
casica, illa, ita, *f. dim.* small house, cabin.
casicontrato, cuasicontrato, *m.* (law) quasi contract.
casilla, *f.* ticket office; hut of a railway guard or flagman; cabin; booth; keeper's lodge; pigeonhole; square (of chessboard); (Cuba) bird trap; (Ecua.) privy; watercloset.—*pl.* ruled columns in accounts; points of a backgammon table.—**sacar a uno de sus casillas,** (coll.) to make one change one's habits; to vex one beyond patience.—**salir de sus casillas,** to lose self-control (esp. from anger, etc.).
casillero, *m.* desk or board with pigeonholes.
casimbas, *f. pl.* (naut.) buckets for baling.
casimir, *m.,* **casimira,** *f.,* cashmere.
casino, *m.* casino, dancing hall, public resort, clubhouse; social or political club.
Casiopea, *f.* (astr.) Cassiopeia.
casiterita, *f.* (min.) cassiterite.
caso, *m.* case; occurrence, event; (law, med., gram.) case.—**c. de conciencia, de honra,** a question of conscience, of honor.—**c. fortuito,** unexpected circumstances; (law) force majeure.—**c. que,** in case.—**dado c., or demos c.,** supposing that.—**de c. pensado,** deliberately.—**el c. es que,** the fact is that.—**en c. de que** = C. QUE.—**en c. necesario,** in case of necessity.—**en tal c.,** in such a case.—**en todo c.,** at all events anyway.—**hacer c.,** to mind, obey.—**hacer c. de,** to take notice of; to mind; to take into account; to esteem.—**hacer c. omiso de,** to ignore, pay no attention to.—**no hacer** or **no venir al c.,** to be irrelevant, to have nothing to do with the case.—**poner por c.,** to assume, suppose.—**vamos al c.,** let us come to the point.—**verse en el c. de,** to be obliged to, have to, must.
casón, *m. aug.* large house.
casorio, *m.* (coll.) hasty or unwise marriage; informal wedding.
caspa, *f.* dandruff, scurf.
caspera, *f.* fine comb for dandruff.
caspio, ia, *a.* Caspian.
caspiroleta, *f.* (Am.) eggnog.
¡cáspita! *interj.* gracious! confound it! by Jove!
casposo, sa, *a.* full of dandruff; lentiginous.
casqué, casque, *v.* *V.* CASCAR.
casquetazo, *m.* blow with the head.
casquete, *m.* helmet, skullcap, cap; skull; wig, periwig; (mech.) cap; (arch.) calotte; helmet shell; plaster to remove the scurf.—**c. esférico,** (geom.) spherical sector.
casquiacopado, da, *a.* cup-hoofed (horse).
casquiblando, da, *a.* soft-hoofed.
casquiderramado, da, *a.* wide-hoofed.
casquijo, *m.* gravel; ballasting material.
casquilla, *f.* cell of the queen bee.
casquillo, *m. dim.* little helm; tip, cap; ferrule; socket; iron arrowhead; (Am.) horseshoe.
casquimuleño, ña, *a.* (of horses) having narrow hoofs like a mule.
casquivano, na, *a.* feather-brained; ridiculously conceited.
casta, *f.* caste, race, breed; clan; offspring; kind or quality.—**hacer c.,** to get a particular breed.
Castálidas, *f. pl.* the Muses.
castaña, *f.* (bot.) chestnut; bottle, jug, jar; knot of hair, chignon; abandoned mine; (Mex.) valise, satchel.—**c. apilada,** or **pilonga,** dried chestnut.—**c. regoldana,** wild or horse-chestnut.—**dar a uno la c.,** to play a trick on one.
castañal, *m.,* **castañar,** *m.,* **castañeda,** *f.,* **castañedo,** *m.* chestnut grove or plantation.
castañero, ra, *n.* chestnut dealer or seller.
castañeta, *f.* castanet; snapping of the fingers.
castañetazo, *m.* blow with a castanet; cracking a chestnut in the fire; cracking of the joints.
castañeteado, *m.* sound of castanets.
castañetear. **I.** *va.* to rattle the castanets. **II.** *vn.* (of teeth) to chatter; (of knees) to creak; (of partridges) to cry.
castañeteo, *m.* sound of castanets; rattling the castanets; clattering; rattling noise.
castaño, ña. **I.** *a.* hazel, brown. **II.** *m.* (bot.) common chestnut tree; chestnut wood.—**c. de Indias,** horse-chestnut tree.—**c. regoldano,** wild chestnut tree.—**pasar de c. oscuro,** (coll.) to be beyond reason or endurance.
castañola, *f.* a large Mediterranean sea fish.
castañuela, *f.* castanet; (bot.) round tuberous-rooted cyperus.—*pl.* (naut.) cleats fastened to the yardarms.—**estar como unas castañuelas,** (coll.) to be very gay.
castañuelo, la, *a. dim.* of a light chestnut color.
castellán, *m.* castellan, governor of a castle.
castellana, *f.* mistress of a castle; wife of a CASTELLÁN; stanza in old Spanish poetry.
castellanía, *f.* independent district.
castellanizar, *va.* to make (a word) Spanish.
castellano, na. **I.** *a.* Castilian; Spanish (lang.,

gram., etc.). **II.** *m.* Sp. language; anc. Sp. coin, fiftieth part of gold mark; CASTELLÁN.
castellar, *m.* (bot.) St. John's-wort, tutsan.
casticidad, *f.* correctness, quality of being good Spanish.
castidad, *f.* chastity.
castigación, *f.* castigation, punishment; revision and correction.
castigadera, *f.* strap or rope for tying the clapper of a wether's bell; small cord with which the ring of a stirrup is tied to the girth.
castigador, ra, *n.* & *a.* punisher(-ing), chastiser (-ing), castigator(-ing).
castigar, *va.* (*pret.* CASTIGUÉ; *subj.* CASTIGUE) to chastise, punish, castigate; to afflict, put to pain, grieve; to revise and correct (proof sheets or writings).—**castigo,** *m.* chastisement, punishment; penalty; penance; censure, animadversion, reproach; alteration or correction.
castigué, castigue, *v. V.* CASTIGAR.
castillaje, *m.* = CASTILLERÍA.
castillejo, *m.* small castle; go-cart; scaffolding.
castillería, *f.* transit toll over castle property.
castillo, *m.* castle; wooden tower on the back of an elephant; mounting of a velvet loom; cell of the queen bee.—**c. de fuego,** fireworks.—**c. de naipes,** house of cards, flimsy structure; air castles.—**c. de proa,** (naut.) forecastle.—**c. roquero,** castle built on a rock.—**hacer castillos en el aire,** to build air castles.
castilluelo, *m. dim.* castlet, small castle.
castina, *f.* (chem. and metal.) flux.
castizo, za, *a.* of noble descent; of good breed; pure-blooded; pure, correct (language).
casto, ta, *a.* chaste.
castor, *m.* (zool.) beaver; beaver cloth; (Mex.) fine red baize.
Cástor, *m.* (astr.) Castor (a star).—**C. y Pólux,** (naut.) corposant, St. Elmo's fire.
castorcillo, *m.* a kind of rough sergelike cloth.
castoreño, ña, *a.* made of beaver.
castóreo, *m.* (med.) castoreum.
castorina, *f.* a kind of cloth similar to castor cloth; (chem.) castorin.
castra, *f.* pruning; pruning season.
castración, *f.* castration, gelding.
castradera, *f.* iron instrument with which honey is taken from a hive.
castrado, *m.* eunuch.
castrador, ra, *n.* gelder, castrator.
castradura, *f.* castration; scar from castration.
castrametación, *f.* (mil.) castrametation, laying out of camps.
castrapuercas, *m.* gelder's whistle.
castrar, *va.* to geld, castrate; (surg.) to cut away the proud flesh of (a wound); to prune; to cut the honeycombs from (beehives).
castrazón, *f.* act of cutting honeycombs out of hives; season when it is done.
castrense, *a.* military.
[1]**castro,** *m.* game played by boys; headland; hilltop with castle in ruins.
[2]**castro,** *m.* = CASTRAZÓN.
castrón, *m.* castrated goat.
casual, *a.* accidental, occasional, chance (as *a.*).
casualidad, *f.* chance; chance event; hazard; accident; coincidence.—**por c.,** by chance.
casualismo, *m.* casualism.
casualista, *n.* casualist.
casuario, *m.* (zool.) cassowary.
casuca, casucha, *f.*; **casucho,** *m.* (coll.) miserable hut or cottage; crib.
casuismo, *m.* casuistry.
casuista, *n.* casuist.
casuístico, ca. I. *a.* casuistical. **II.** *f.* casuistry.
casulla, *f.* chasuble, vestment worn by priests.
casullero, ra, *n.* one who makes chasubles and other vestments for priests.
cata, *f.* act of trying a thing by the taste; sample, trial; plummet for measuring heights; (Am.) buried treasure; trial excavation (of prospective mine); hidden thing (esp. if valuable).
catabólico, ca, *a.* catabolic.
catabolismo, *m.* catabolism.
catabre, *m.* (naut.) sheep-shank.
catacaldos, *m.* taster of wine, soup, etc.; sampler.
cataclismo, *m.* cataclysm; catastrophe.
catacresis, *f.* (rhet.) catachresis.
catacumbas, *f. pl.* catacombs.
catacústica, *f.* (phys.) catacoustics.
catadióptrica, *f.* (phys.) catadioptrics.
catadióptrico, ca, *a.* (phys.) catadioptric.
catador, *m.* taster, sampler.
catadura, *f.* act of tasting; (coll.) gesture, face.
catafalco, *m.* catafalque.
cataforesis, *f.* (chem.) cataphoresis.
catalán, lana, *n.* & *a.* Catalan, Catalonian.
catalanismo, *m.* Catalanism.
catalanista, *n.* Catalanist.
cataléctico, ca; catalecto, ta, *a.* (poet.) catalectic.
catalejo, *m.* telescope.
catalepsia, *f.* (med.) catalepsis.
cataléptico, ca, *a.* cataleptic.
catalicón, catolicón, *m.* (pharm.), a purgative.
catalina, *f.*—**rueda c.,** Catherine wheel.
catálisis, *f.* (chem.) catalysis.
catalítico, ca, *a.* catalytic.
catalizador, *m.* catalyser; catalytic.
catalizar, *va.* (chem.) to catalyze.
catalogación, *f.* cataloguing.
catalogador, ra. I. *a.* cataloguing. **II.** *n.* cataloguer, cataloguist.
catalogar, *va.* to catalogue, list.
catálogo, *m.* catalogue, table, list.
catalpa, *f.* (bot.) catalpa.
catalufa, *f.* a kind of floor carpet.
catán, *m.* Indian sabre or cutlass.
cataplasma, *f.* poultice; (Am. fig.) nuisance, vexer.
cataplexia, *f.* catalepy; apoplexy.
catapulta, *f.* catapult.
catar, *va.* to sample, try by tasting; to investigate; to judge, pass on; to esteem; to bear in mind; to cut the combs out of (beehives).
cataraña, *f.* (ornith.) sheldrake.
catarata, *f.* cataract, waterfall, cascade; cataract of the eye.—**abrirse las cataratas del cielo,** to rain heavily, to pour.—**tener cataratas,** (coll.) not to understand clearly.
catarral, *a.* catarrhal.
catarro, *m.* catarrh; head cold.
catarroso, sa, *a.* catarrhal; subject to colds.
catarsis, *f.* (med., psychiat.) catharsis.
catártico, ca, *a.* (med., psychiat.) cathartic.
catástasis, *f.* (rhet.) catastasis.
catastral, *a.* pertaining to the census.
catastro, *m.* former royal tax on real estate; census or list of real property of a county or state.
catástrofe, *f.* catastrophe; dénouement, winding up (esp. when sad or tragic).
catastrófico, ca, *a.* catastrophic, cataclysmal.
cataviento, *m.* (naut.) dogvane; weathercock.
catavino, *m.* small jug or cup for tasting wine; small hole at top of wine vessels for tasting wine.
catavinos, *m.* winetaster, expert sampler; (fig.) one going the rounds of taverns; drunkard.
cate, *m.* (P. I.) a weight, equal to 0.633 kg.
cateador, ra, *n.* (Am.) mine prospector; tester.
catear, *va.* (S. A.) to prospect (for minerals); (Am.) to raze.
catecismo, *m.* catechism.
catecú, *m.* = CATO, astringent from plants.
catecuménico, ca, *a.* catechumenical.
catecúmeno, na, *n.* catechumen.
cátedra, *f.* seat or chair of a professor; professorship; subject; lecture room; (eccl.) cathedra.—**c. del Espíritu Santo,** pulpit.—**c. de San Pedro,** Holy See.
catedral, *f.* & *a.* cathedral.
catedralicio, cia, *a.* cathedral.
catedralidad, *f.* dignity of a cathedral church.

catedrático, *m.* professor; contribution paid to bishops and prelates.
categorema, *f.* (logic) quality of being assignable to a category.
categoremático, ca, *a.* (log.) categorematic.
categoría, *f.* (philos.) category; class, condition; rank; level; character, quality.—**de c.,** of importance; of high rank, prominent.
categóricamente, *adv.* categorically.
categórico, ca, *a.* categorical, categoric.
catenaria, *n.* & *a.* catenary.
catenular, *a.* catenulate.
cateo, *m.* (Am.) testing, sampling; (Am.) prospecting.
catequesis, *f.* catechesis.
catequicé, catequice, *v.* *V.* CATEQUIZAR.
catequismo, *m.* catechesis, religious instruction; art of teaching by questions and answers.
catequista, *m.* catechist.
catequístico, ca, *a.* catechetical, catechetic.
catequizante, *n.* & *a.* catechiser(-ing).
catequizar, *va.* (*pret.* CATEQUICÉ; *subj.* CATEQUICE) to catechise; to instruct in the Christian faith; to persuade, induce.
caterético, ca, *a.* (med.) corrosive, catheretic.
caterva, *f.* multitude; throng, crowd.
catéter, *m.* (surg.) catheter.—**cateterismo,** *m.* catheterization.—**cateterizar,** *va.* to catheterize.
cateto, *m.* (arch.) cathetus; (geom.) leg (of a right-angled triangle).
catetómetro, *m.* cathetometer.
catilinaria, *f.* one of Cicero's orations against Catiline; severe criticism or denunciation.
catimarón, *m.* (naut.) catamaran.
catimbao, *m.* (Chile, Peru) clown; ridiculously dressed person; short and fat person.
catín, *m.* copper-refining crucible.
catinga, *f.* (Am.) bad smell (esp. that of sweating Negroes).—**catingoso, sa; catingudo, da,** *a.* (Am.) ill-smelling.
catión, *m.* (phys.) cation, kation.
catire, *n.* & *a.* (Am.) blond, light-haired.
catite, *m.* loaf of the best refined sugar.
cato, *m.* astringent from plants.
catoche, *m.* (Mex. coll.) bad humor.
catódico, ca, *a.* (elec.) cathodic.
cátodo, *m.* (elec.) cathode.
católicamente, *adv.* conforming to Catholicism.
catolicidad, *f.* catholicity.
catolicismo, *m.* Catholicism.
católico, ca. I. *a.* catholic, general or universal; true, infallible. **II.** *n.* & *a.* (Roman) Catholic. **no estar muy c.,** (coll.) to feel under the weather.
catolicón, *m.* (pharm.) a purgative.
catolizar, *va.* (*pret.* CATOLICÉ; *subj.* CATOLICE) to convert to Catholicism; to preach, propagate Catholicism.
catón, *m.* reading book for children.
catoniano, na, *a.* Catonian.
catóptrica, *f.* (opt.) catoptrics.
catóptrico, ca, *a.* catoptrical.
catorce, *n.* & *a.* fourteen; fourteenth.—**catorcena,** *f.* group of fourteen.—**catorceno, na,** *a.* fourteenth.
catorzavo, va, *n.* & *a.* fourteenth.
catre, *m.* small bedstead; cot.—**c. de mar,** hammock or cot.—**c. de tijera,** field bed.
catrecillo, *m.* camp canvas chair.
catricofre, *m.* folding bed, bed lounge.
catrín, catrina, *a.* (Mex.) dandyish, foppish.
caucáseo, a; caucásico, ca, *a.* Caucasian.
cauce, *m.* bed of a river; trench, ditch.
caución, *f.* caution, precaution; pledge, surety, guarantee.—**c. de indemnidad,** or **personal,** (law) bond given by another for person in custody.—**c. juratoria,** parole given by person in custody but not yet tried and sentenced.—**c. real,** bail.
caucionar, *va.* (law) to guard against an evil or loss; to bail.
cauchal, *m.* rubber plantation or patch.
cauchero, ra. I. *a.* (India) rubber (as *a.*). **II.** *n.* rubber man, one engaged in the rubber industry or trade.
cauchil, *m.* small basin or reservoir of water.
caucho, *m.* India rubber (material), gum elastic.
cauda, *f.* train or tail of a bishop's robe.
[1]**caudal,** *a.* (zool.) caudal, pert. to the tail.
[2]**caudal,** *m.* fortune, wealth, means; volume (of water); plenty, abundance.—**hacer c. de,** to value highly.—**caudalejo,** *m.* *dim.* middling fortune.
caudaloso, sa, *a.* of great volume, carrying much water; copious, abundant; rich, wealthy.
caudatario, *m.* clergyman who carries the train of an officiating bishop's robe.
caudato, ta, *a.* (astr. of a comet) having a tail.
caudatrémula, *f.* (ornith.) wagtail.
caudícula, *f.* (bot.) caudicle.
caudillaje, *m.* leadership; tyranny; bossism.
caudillismo, *m.* (Am.) = CAUDILLAJE.
caudillo, *m.* commander, chief, leader.
caudimano, na, *a.* (zool.) having a prehensile tail.
caudón, *m.* a bird of prey.
caulescente, *a.* (bot.) caulescent.
caulícolo, caulículo, *m.* (arch.) ornament of the capital of columns.
cauliforme, *a.* (bot.) cauliform.
cauro, *m.* northwest wind.
causa, *f.* cause; motive, reason; lawsuit, case; trial (at law).—**c. célebre,** famous (criminal) case, cause célèbre.—**c. final,** (philos.) final cause.—**c. impulsiva,** or **motiva,** prompting motive.—**c. primaria,** or **primera,** first cause.—**c. pública,** public welfare, commonweal.—**a,** or **por, c. de,** on account of, because, due to.—**formar c. a,** to sue, bring suit against.
causador, a, *n.* originator.
causahabiente, *m.* & *f.* (law) person holding a right from others.
causal, *a.* causal.—**causalidad,** *f.* causality.
causante. I. *a.* causing, originating, causative. **II.** *n.* originator; (law) the person from whom a right is derived; constituent, principal.
causar, *va.* to cause, occasion; to sue.
causativo, va, *a.* causative.
causeo, *m.* (Am.) light lunch between meals, snack.
causídico, ca. I. *n.* advocate, counsellor. **II.** *a.* (law) causidical, forensic.
causón, *m.* burning fever of short duration.
causticidad, *f.* causticity.
cáustico, ca. I. *a.* caustic, burning; biting, aggressive. **II.** *m.* (med.) caustic.
cautela, *f.* caution, prudence; craft, cunning.
cautelar, *va.* & *vr.* (de) to guard (against).
cauteloso, sa, *a.* cautious, wary.
cautericé, cauterice, *v.* *V.* CAUTERIZAR.
cauterio, *m.* (med.) cautery.—**c. actual,** actual cautery, burning with hot iron.—**c. potencial,** potential cautery, produced by chemicals.
cauterización, *f.* cauterization, cauterizing.
cauterizador, *m.* he who or that which cauterizes.
cauterizar, *va.* (*pret.* CAUTERICÉ; *subj.* CAUTERICE) to cauterize; to reproach with severity; to blame.
cautivador, ra, cautivante, *a.* captivating, charming.
cautivar, *va.* to take prisoner, carry into captivity; to captivate, charm.
cautiverio, *m.*, **cautividad,** *f.* captivity.
cautivo, va, *n.* & *a.* captive.
cauto, ta, *a.* cautious, wary, prudent.
cava, *f.* digging and earthing of vines; wine cellar in the royal palace.
cavacóte, *m.* mound made with the hoe.
cavadiza, *a.* dug out of a pit (as sand).
cavador, ra, *n.* digger.

cavadura, *f.* digging.
caván, *m.* (P. I.) a measure equivalent to seventy-five quarts.
cavar. I. *va.* to dig, excavate; (of horses) to paw. **II.** *vn.* to dig; to think carefully or intently; to go to the bottom (of a subject, etc.)
cavatina, *f.* (mus.) cavatina.
cavazón, *f.* digging.
cávea, *f.* (archeol.) cage or cave.
caverna, *f.* cavern, cave; (med.) hollow from a wound.
cavernícola. I. *a.* cave-dwelling; (coll.) reactionary. **II.** *n.* cave dweller, cave man; (coll.) reactionary.
cavernoso, sa, *a.* cavernous, caverned.
caveto, *m.* (arch.) cavetto.
caví, *m.* oca, a South-American tuber.
cavia, *f.* circular excavation at the foot of a tree to collect water.
cavial, caviar, *m.* caviar.
cavicornio, nia. I. *a.* (zool.) cavicorn. **II.** *m. pl.* Cavicornia.
cavidad, *f.* cavity.
cavilación, *f.* cavilling.
cavilar, *va.* to cavil; to criticize.
cavilosidad, *f.* captiousness, cavilling.
caviloso, sa, *a.* captious, overparticular; fault-finding.
cayada, *f.*, **cayado,** *m.* shepherd's hook, crook; crozier of a bishop; walking staff.
cayán, *m.* (P. I.) awning of matting in boats.
cayente, *a.* falling.
cayeputi, *m.* cajuput tree; cajuput oil.
cayo, *m.* rock, shoal, islet; key.
cayó, *v. V.* CAER.
cayote, *m.* (bot.) = CIDRACAYOTE, gourd.
cayuca, *f.* (Cuba, coll.) head (of person), "bean."
cayuco, *m.* (W. I., Venez., Mex.) dugout canoe.
caz, *m.* trench, ditch; mill race, flume.
caza, *f.* hunt, chase, hunting; game; *m.* (aer., mil.) pursuit plane.—**c. mayor,** big game.—**c. menor,** small game.—**andar a c. de,** to be or to go hunting for, be or go in search of.—**dar c.,** to pursue.—**de c.,** hunting, pursuit (plane, boat, etc.).
cazabe, *m.* (bot.) manioc, cassava; flour of the cassava plant; bread made with it.
cazadero, *m.* chase; hunting grounds.
cazador, ra. I. *a.* hunting. **II.** *n.* hunter.—**c. de alforja,** one who sports with dogs, snares, and other devices. **III.** *f.* huntress; hunting jacket.
cazamoscas, *m.* (ornith.) flycatcher.
cazar, *va.* (*pret.* CACÉ; *subj.* CACE) to chase, hunt; (coll.) to attain by skill; (coll.) to charm and captivate by caresses and deceitful tricks; to chase, pursue.—**c. una vela,** (naut.) to tally a sail; haul the sheet aft.
cazasubmarino, *m.* submarine chaser.
cazatorpedero, *m.* torpedo-boat destroyer.
cazcalear, *vn.* (coll.) to fidget and fuss.
cazcarria, *f.* mud splashings on clothes; (Am.) sheep dung.—**cazcarriento, ta,** *a.* (coll.) splashed.
cazo, *m.* dipper, ladle; founders' scoop; size kettle; glue pot; melting pan.
cazolero, *m.* (coll.) man who does women's work in the kitchen.
cazoleta, *f.* pan of a musket lock; boss or defence of a shield; hand guard or languet of a sword; a kind of perfume.
cazolón, *m. aug.* large earthen pot or stewpan.
cazón, *m.* (ichth.) dogfish or small shark.
cazonal, *m.* tackle for shark fishing.
cazonete, *m.* (naut.) toggle.
cazudo, da, *a.* (of knives) with a thick back.
cazuela, *f.* earthen cooking pan; stewing pan, crock; meat dressed in an earthen pan; (theat.) gallery reserved for women; (theat.) top gallery.
cazumbrar, *va.* to join (staves) with hempen cords.
cazumbre, *m.* hempen cord used to join staves.
cazumbrón, *m.* cooper.
cazurro, ra, *a.* (coll.) taciturn, sulky, sullen.
cazuz, *m.* (bot.) ivy.
[1]**ce,** *f.* cee, name of the letter *c*.—**c. por be, or c. por c.,** minutely, circumstantially.—**por c. o por be,** somehow or other.
[2]**¡ce!,** *interj.* hark! listen! come here! see here!
cea, cía, *f.* thigh bone.
ceanoto, *m.* (bot.) New Jersey tea, redroot.
ceba, *f.* fattening of domestic animals.
cebada, *f.* barley.—**c. perlada,** pearl barley.
cebadal, *m.* barley field.
cebadazo, za, *a.* pertaining to barley.
[1]**cebadera,** *f.* nose bag; barley bin.
[2]**cebadera,** *f.* (naut.) spritsail; (metal.) furnace charger.
cebadería, *f.* barley market.
[1]**cebadero,** *m.* place where game or fowls are fed; breeder and feeder of hawks; (metal.) mouth for feeding a furnace.
[2]**cebadero,** *m.* barley dealer; mule carrying the feed; bell mule.
cebadilla, *f.* (bot.) Indian caustic barley; (bot.) sneeze-wort; (bot., prov.) prickly oxeye; hellebore snuff.
cebador, *m.* one who fattens animals; priming horn, powder horn; (int. combust. eng.) primer.
cebadura, *f.* fattening of domestic animals.
cebar. I. *va.* & *vn.* to fatten (animals); to stuff, cram; to feed (a furnace, fire, lamp); to prime (a firearm); to start (a machine or apparatus); to light (a rocket or pyrotechnic piece); to re-magnetize; to excite and cherish (a passion); to bait (a fishhook). **II.** *vn.* to penetrate; to take hold of; to stick fast. **III.** *vr.* to be firmly bent upon a thing; to prey upon; to gloat over (a victim).
cebellina, *f.* (zool.) sable; sable fur.
[1]**cebo,** *m.* food given to animals, fodder; fattening of animals; bait; incentive; (artil.) priming of guns.—**c. fulminante,** percussion cap.
[2]**cebo,** *m.* a kind of monkey.
cebolla, *f.* (bot.) onion; onion bulb; any bulbous root; oil receptacle of a lamp; spherical screen in a water pipe.—**c. albarrana,** (bot.) squill. —**c. ascalonia,** (bot.) shallot garlic.—**cebollana,** *f.* (bot.) three-toothed globularia; chives.—**cebollar,** *m.* onion patch.—**cebollero, ra,** *n.* onion seller.—**cebolleta,** *f. dim.* tender onion.—**cebollino,** *m.* young onion fit to be transplanted; onion seeds; (bot.) chive.—**cebollón,** *m. aug.* large onion.—**cebolludo, da,** *a.* bulbous, having a big bulb.
cebón, *m.* fattened bullock or hog.
ceboncillo, *m. dim.* fatling.
cebra, *f.* (zool.) zebra.—**cebrado, da,** *a.* having stripes like the zebra.
cebratana, *f.* = CERBATANA, blowgun; ear trumpet.
cebruno, cervuno, na, *a.* deer-colored.
cebú, *m.* (zool.) zebu; (Arg.) a variety of monkey.
ceca, *f.* mint (for coining).
Ceca, *m.* name of the mosque that the Arabs had in Cordova, the most venerated after Mecca. —**de C. en Meca,** or **de la C. a la Meca,** to and fro, hither and thither.
cecal, *a.* (anat.) cæcal.
cecear. I. *vn.* to lisp. **II.** *va.* to call, hail; to lisp. —**ceceo,** *m.* lisping, lisp; calling, hailing.
ceceoso, sa. I. *a.* lisping. **II.** *n.* lisper.
cecial, *m.* fish cured and dried.
cecina, *f.* corned, dried, jerked, or hung beef.
cecografía, *f.* writing of the blind.
cecógrafo, *m.* a writing apparatus for the blind.
ceda, zeda, *f.* zee, last letter of the alphabet.
cedacería, *f.* shop where sieves or cribs are made or sold.
cedacero, *m.* maker or seller of sieves, cribs, etc.
cedacillo, ito, *m. dim.* small sieve.
cedazo, *m.* sieve, screen, strainer.
cedazuelo, *m. dim.* small sieve or strainer.
cedente. I. *a.* ceding, granting. **II.** *n.* conveyer, assigner, transferrer.

ceder. I. *va.* to transfer, cede, convey, yield, deliver up. II. *vn.* to yield, submit, comply, give in; to give out, slacken, fail; to happen turn out ill or well; to abate, diminish.
cedilla, *f.* cedilla.
cedizo, za, *a.* (of food) tainted.
cedoaria, *f.* (pharm.) zedoary.
cedras, *f. pl.* skin saddlebags.
cedria, *f.* resin from the cedar.
cédride, *m.* fruit of the cedar tree.
cedrino, na, *a.* pertaining to the cedar.
cedro, *m.* (bot.) cedar; Spanish juniper.—**c. colorado,** red cedar.—**c. de la India,** deodar.—**c. de las Antillas,** Spanish cedar.—**c. del Líbano,** cedar of Lebanon.—**c. de Misiones,** an Argentine cedar, producing fine wood and a valuable febrifuge.—**c. dulce,** red cedar.
cédula, *f.* cedula, slip of parchment or paper written or to write upon; order, bill, decree; cedule, a scroll or writing.—**c. ante diem,** secretary's summons of meeting to the members of a society.—**c. de abono,** order to remit a task.—**c. de aduana,** permit.—**c. de cambio,** (com.) draft.—**c. personal,** or **de vecindad,** official document declaring the name, occupation, domicile, etc. of the bearer, and to serve for identification.—**c. real,** royal letter patent.—**echar cédulas,** (coll.) to draw or cast lots.—**cedulaje,** *m.* fees or dues paid for a cedula.—**cedulilla, ita,** *f. dim.* small slip of paper.—**cedulón,** *m. aug.* large bill; long edict; proclamation; public notice.
cefalalgia, *f.* (med.) cephalalgia, headache.
cefalea, *f.* violent headache, migraine.
cefálico, ca, *a.* cephalic.
cefalitis, *f.* (med.) encephalitis.
céfalo, *m.* (ichth.) mullet, a kind of perch.
cefalópodo, da, *m.* & *a.* (zool.) cephalopod.
cefalotórax, *m.* (anat.) cephalothorax.
Cefeo, *m.* (astr.) Cepheus, a constellation.
céfiro, *m.* zephyr.
cefo, *m.* (zool.) a large African monkey.
cegajo, *m.* two-year-old he-goat.
cegajoso, sa, *a.* blear-eyed.
cegar. I. *vn.* (*ind. pres.* CIEGO, *pret.* CEGUÉ; *subj.* CIEGUE) to grow blind. II. *va.* to blind; to wall up (a door or window); to close up (a well); to stop up, close (a channel, road).—**c. una via de agua,** (naut.) to fother a leak. III. *vr.* to become or be blinded (by passion, etc.).
cegarra, *a.* (coll.) CEGATO.—**cegarrita,** *n.* (coll.) one who contracts the eye to see at a distance.
cegato, ta, *a.* (coll.) short-sighted.
cegatoso, sa, *a.* = CEGAJOSO.
cegesimal, *a.* (phys.) C. G. S. (app. to the system of units in which the fundamental units are the centimeter, gram and second).
cegué, *pret.* of CEGAR.
ceguedad, *f.* blindness; ignorance, intellectual darkness; obfuscation.
ceguera, *f.* disorder in the eye; absolute blindness; obfuscation.
ceiba, *f.* (bot.) sea moss, alga; *also* **ceibo,** *m.* ceiba, God tree, W. I. silkcotton tree.
Ceilán, *m.* Ceylon.
ceilanés, nesa, *n.* & *a.* Ceylonese.
ceja, *f.* eyebrow; edging of clothes; projecting part, as in the binding of books; bridge of a string instrument; summit; circle of clouds round a hill; cloud cap; (arch.) weather molding; rim; (carp.) rabbet; (naut.) opening in the clouds.—**dar entre ceja y ceja,** to tell one unpleasant truths to one's face.—**hasta las cejas,** to the utmost, to the extreme.—**quemarse las cejas,** to burn the midnight oil.—**tener entre c. y c.,** to dislike, have a grudge against; to have on one's brain, to think constantly about.
cejadero, *m.* hold-back strap of a harness.
cejar, *vn.* to go backward; to hold back; to hesitate; to slacken, relax.
cejijunto, ta, *a.* having eyebrows that meet.
¹cejo, *m.* fog from rivers.
²cejo, *m.* esparto cord tied round a bundle of esparto grass.
cejudo, da, *a.* having heavy and long eyebrows.
cejuela, *f. dim.* small eyebrow.
¹celada, *f.* ambuscade, ambush; snare; lurch; artful trick.
²celada, *f.* sallet; helmet without visor; part of the key of the crossbow; horse soldier with helmet.—**c. borgoñota,** visorless helmet.
celador, ra, *n.* watchman(-woman), caretaker; curator; monitor in a school; warden.
celaje, *m.* aspect of the sky with clouds of varied hues; cloud scenery; cloud effect; painting representing the rays of the sun breaking through clouds; presage, prognostic; skylight; sky of a picture.—*pl.* light, swiftly moving clouds; scud.
celandés, sa, *n.* & *a.* New Zealander.
¹celar, *vn.* & *va.* to fulfil (duties) with care; to watch (any person's motions) from suspicion.
²celar, *va.* to cover, conceal.
³celar, *va.* to engrave; to carve.
celda, *f.* cell (in convent, beehive, prison); (aer.) cell.
celdica, illa, ita, *f. dim.* cellule.
celdilla, *f.* cell in beehives; (bot.) cell; capsule.
celebérrimo, ma, *a. super.* most (very) famous.
celebración, *f.* celebration; praise, applause.
celebrador, ra, *n.* applauder, praiser, approver; celebrator.
celebrante, *n.* & *a.* celebrator(-ing); celebrant (officiating).
celebrar, *va.* to celebrate; to praise, applaud, approve; to revere, respect, venerate; to be glad of, rejoice at; to say (mass); to hold (formal meeting).
célebre, *a.* famous, renowned; (coll.) facetious, witty, funny.—**célebremente,** *adv.* with pomp; facetiously, humorously.—**celebridad,** *f.* celebrity, renown, fame; pomp, magnificence; public demonstration, celebration, pageant.
celecanto, *m.* (ichth.) cœlacanth.
celemín, *m.* a dry measure (about a peck).
celeminada, *f.* quantity contained in a CELEMÍN.
celenterado, da, celenterio, ria, *m.* & *a.* (zool.) cœlenterate.
célere. I. *a.* quick, rapid. II. *m.* one of the select three hundred knights of ancient Roman nobility.—**celeridad,** *f.* celerity, quickness.—**celerífero, ra,** *a.* rapid-transit.—**celerímetro,** *m.* speedometer.
celeste, *a.* celestial, heavenly; sky-blue.
celestial, *a.* celestial, heavenly; agreeable, delightful, excellent; (ironic) silly, sottish.
celestialmente, *adv.* celestially, heavenly.
¹celestina, *f.* (min.) celestite.
²celestina, *f.* procuress.
celíaco, ca. I. *a.* (anat.) cœliac. II. *f.* (med.) cœliac flux.
celibato, *m.* celibacy; (coll.) bachelor.
célibe, *a.* & *n.* unmarried (person).
célico, ca, *a.* (poet.) celestial, heavenly.
celidonia, *f.* (bot.) celandine, swallow-wort.
celindrate, *m.* ragout made with coriander seed.
celo, *m.* zeal, ardor, fervor; piety, devotion; heat, rut.—*pl.* jealousy; suspicions.—**dar celos,** to excite suspicions.
celofán, celofano, *m.* cellophane.
celosamente, *adv.* with zeal; jealously.
celosía, *f.* lattice; Venetian blind; jealousy.
celoso, sa, *a.* zealous; jealous; suspicious; (naut.) light and swift-sailing.
celotipia, *f.* jealousy.
celsitud, *f.* celsitude, elevation, grandeur; (obs.) highness, a title, now expressed by **alteza.**
celta, *n.* & *a.* Celt(ic).
celtibérico, ca; celtiberio, ria; celtíbero, ra, *n.* & *a.* Celtiberian.
céltico, ca, *a.* Celtic.
celtismo, *m.* Celticism.

celtista, *n.* Celtist.
celtohispánico, ca; celtohispano, na, *a.* Celtic-Spanish, Celto-Spanish (remains of the old Celtic civilization in Spain).
célula, *f.* cell.—**c. embrionaria,** (biol.) germ cell.—**c. fotoeléctrica,** photoelectric cell, photocell, electric eye.
celulado, da, *a.* cellulate, cellulated.
celular, celulario, ria, *a.* cellular.
celuloide, *m.* celluloid.
celulosa, *f.* cellulose, woody fibre.
celuloso, sa, *a.* cellulose, containing cells.
cellenco, ca, *a.* (coll.) decrepit.
cellisca, *f.* fine rain, snow, or sleet driven by a heavy wind.—**cellisquear,** *vn.* to sleet; to be squally with fine snow or rain.
cello, *m.* hoop used in cooperage.
cementación, *f.* cementation.
cementar, *va.* (metal.) to cement; to convert (metals); to subject to the process of cementation.
cementerio, *m.* cemetery, graveyard.
cemento, *m.* cement; (metal., dent., anat., geol.) cement.—**c. armado,** reinforced concrete.—**c. hidráulico,** hydraulic cement.—**c. de Pórtland** or **c. pórtland,** Portland cement.
cementoso, sa, *a.* cement-like.
cena, *f.* supper; by extension, the Last Supper.
cenaaoscuras, *n.* recluse; miser.
cenáculo, *m.* cenacle, room where Last Supper was held.
cenacho, *m.* basket for fruit and greens.
cenadero, *m.* supper room; summerhouse.
cenador, *m.* one fond of suppers; summerhouse in a garden; arbor, bower; gallery around a courtyard.
cenaduría, *f.* (Mex.) supper room, supper inn.
cenagal, *m.* slough, quagmire; arduous, unpleasant affair.
cenagoso, sa, *a.* muddy, miry, marshy.
cenar. I. *vn.* to sup. **II.** *va.* to have for supper.
cenceño, ña, *a.* lean, thin, slender.
cencerra, *f.* = CENCERRO.
cencerrada, *f.* charivari; tin-pan serenade.
cencerrear, *vn.* to jingle continually; to play on an untuned guitar; to make a din or rattling noise.
cencerreo, *m.* noise made by mule or cow bells.
cencerro, *m.* bell worn by the leading wether or cow; ill-tuned guitar.—**c. zumbón,** bell borne by the leading horse or mule.—**a cencerros tapados,** on the sly, quietly, by stealth.
cencerrón, *m.* small bunch of grapes unpicked.
cencido, da, *a.* untilled, uncultivated.
cencro, *m.* a Brazilian serpent.
cendal, *m.* light thin stuff of silk or thread; gauze; scarf used by priests in consecrating the host; barbs of a feather.—*pl.* cotton for an inkstand.
cendra, cendrada, *f.* bone-dust paste used for cupels.—**ser una c.,** (fig.) to be lively as a cricket.
cenefa, *f.* border; band or stripe on the edge of a stuff; middle piece of a priest's chasuble; rim, hangings, flounce, trimming; (naut.) top rim; paddle-box rim; awning.
cení, *m.* fine brass or bronze.
cenia, *f.* water-raising machine; noria, well wheel and axle; garden watered from a noria.
cenicero, *m.* ash hole, ash pit, ash pan.
cenicienta, *f.* thing or person unjustly despised or ill treated.—**la C.,** Cinderella.
ceniciento, ta, *a.* ash-color red.
cenicilla, *f.* (bot.) oidium.
cenit, *m.* (astr.) zenith.—**cenital,** *a.* zenith (as *a.*).
ceniza, *f.* ashes, cinders.—**cenizas azules,** blue paint; lapis lazuli.—**cenizas de estaño,** putty.—**cenizas de vegetales,** potash.—**cenizas graveladas,** weed ashes.
cenizal, *m.* heap of ashes.
cenizo, za. I. *a.* ash-colored. **II.** *m.* (bot.) white goosefoot.
cenizoso, sa, *a.* ashy; covered with ashes.
cenobial, *a.* pert. to a convent or monastery.
cenobio, *m.* cenoby, convent or monastery.
cenobita, *m.* Cenobite, monk.
cenobítico, ca, *a.* cenobitic.
cenobitismo, *m.* cenobitism.
cenojil, *m.* garter.
cenopegias, *f. pl.* Jewish feast of tabernacles.
cenotafio, *m.* cenotaph.
cenote, *m.* cenote, a water reservoir in a cave.
cenozoico, ca, *a.* (geol.) Cenozoic.
censal, *a.* = CENSUAL. *n.* = CENSO.
censalista, *m.* = CENSUALISTA, lessor.
censatario, ria; censero, ra, *n.* one who pays an annuity out of his estate; lessee.
censo, *m.* census; agreement for settling an annuity on a person; annual rent; lease; rental; income; polltax among the Romans.—**c. al quitar,** or **redimible,** quit rent or annuity that can be paid at once by a certain sum.—**c. de agua,** water tax.—**c. de por vida,** life annuity.
censontli, censontle, *m.* (Mex.) mocking bird.
censor, *m.* censor, critic; censorious person.
censoría, *f.* censorship; censor's office.
censorio, ria, *a.* censorial.
censual, *a.* pertaining to a lease, annuity, or rent; rental; pertaining to lawful interest.
censualista, *m.* lessor; annuitant.
censura, *f.* censorship; office of a censor; act of censoring; review (of a book); censure, blame, reproach; gossiping; spiritual punishment.
censurable, *a.* reprehensible, blameworthy.
censurador, ra; censurante, *n.* & *a.* critic(-al); faultfinder(-ing), censor(-ing).
censurar, *va.* to review, criticize, judge; to censure, blame; to accuse; to find fault with.
centaura, centaurea, *f.* (bot.) centaury.—**c. mayor,** great centaury.—**c. menor,** common erythræa.
centauro, *m.* (myth.) centaur; (**C-,** astr.) Centaur.
centavo, *m.* hundredth (part); cent.
centella, *f.* lightning; thunderbolt; flash of a flint struck with steel; flake of fire; (fig.) remaining spark of passion, smoldering fire.
centellador, ra, *a.* brilliant, flashing.
centellante, centelleante, *a.* sparkling, flashing.
centellar, centellear, *vn.* to sparkle, twinkle, scintillate.
centelleo, *m.* sparkling, twinkling.
centellón, *m. aug.* large spark or flash.
centén, *m.* an old Spanish gold coin worth about 25 pesetas.
centena, *f.* a hundred (collect.).
centenadas.—**a c.,** by hundreds.
[1]**centenal,** [1]**centenar,** *m.* = CENTENA.—**a centenares,** by hundreds.
[2]**centenal,** [2]**centenar,** *m.* rye field.
centenario, ria. I. *a.* centenary; secular. **II.** *m.* centennial.
centenazo, za, *a.* pertaining to rye.
centenero, ra, *a.* (of land, soil) good for rye.
[1]**centeno, na,** *a.* hundredth.
[2]**centeno,** *m.* (bot.) rye.
centenoso, sa, *a.* mixed with rye.
centesimal, *a.* (of a number) between one and one hundred.
centésimo, ma, *n.* & *a.* hundredth.
centiárea, *f.* centiare (square meter).
centígrado, da, *a.* centigrade.
centigramo, *m.* centigram.
centil, *m.* (stat.) centile.
centilitro, *m.* centiliter.
centiloquio, *m.* a work divided into a hundred parts.
centímano, na, *a.* (poet.) hundred-handed, having a hundred hands.
centímetro, *m.* centimeter.
centímetro-gramo-segundo, *m.* (phys.) centimeter-gram-second (C.G.S.).
céntimo. I. *m.* centime; hundredth part of a monetary unit. **II.** *n.* & *a.* hundredth.

centinela, *m.* & *f.* (mil.) sentry, sentinel; person on watch.—**c. a caballo,** vidette, sentinel on horseback.—**c. avanzado,** advance guard.—**c. de vista,** prisoner's guard.—**c. perdida,** forlorn hope.—**estar de c.,** or **hacer c.,** to be on sentry duty.
centinodia, *f.* (bot.) knot grass, persicaria.
centípedo, *m.* centipede.
centiplicado, da, *a.* centuple, hundredfold.
centola, centolla, *f.* center fish, a marine crab with spotted scales.
centón, *m.* crazy quilt; coarse covering of war engine in old times; cento, a literary composition.
centrado, da, *a.* centered.
central. I. *a.* central.—**calefacción c.,** central heating. **II.** *f.* main office, central office; *m.* (Am.) sugar mill, refinery.—**c. de electricidad,** central station.—**c. telefónica** or **de teléfonos,** exchange, telephone exchange.
centralicé. centralice, *v. V.* CENTRALIZAR.
centralidad, *f.* centrality.
centralismo, *m.* centralism.
centralista, *n.* & *a.* centralist (-ic).
centralización, *f.* centralization.
centralizador, ra. I. *a.* centralizing. **II.** *n.* centralizer.
centralizar, *va.* (*pret.* CENTRALICÉ; *subj.* CENTRALICE) to centralize.
centralmente, *adv.* centrally.
centrar, *va.* to center.
céntrico, ca, *a.* central.
centrifugar, *va.* (Am.) to put (sugar) through a centrifuge.
centrífugo, ga. I. *a.* centrifugal. **II.** *f.* centrifugal machine.
centrípeto, ta, *a.* centripetal.
centrista, *n.* centrist.
centro, *m.* center; middle, midst; innermost part, core; (mil.) center of an army; height and depth of a thing; main office, headquarters; (pol.) center; principal object of desire and exertion; social circle in which a person moves; club, social meeting place; (bot.) disk of flowers; short flannel dress worn by Indian women in Ecuador.—**c. de curvatura,** (geom.) center of curvature.—**c. de figura,** (geom.) center of figure.—**c. de giro,** (mech.) center of gyration.—**c. de gravedad,** (mech.) center of gravity.—**c. de masa,** (mech.) center of mass.—**c. de mesa,** centerpiece.—**c. nervioso,** (anat.) nerve center.—**estar en su c.,** to be in one's element.
centroamericano, na, *n.* & *a.* Central-American.
centrobárico, ca, *a.* centrobaric.
centroide, *m.* centroid.
centrosoma, *m.* (biol.) centrosome.
centunviral, *a.* centumviral.
centunvirato, *m.* centumvirate.
centunviro, *m.* centumvir.
centuplicación, *f.* centuplication.
centuplicado, da, *a.* centuplicate.
centuplicar, *va.* to centuplicate.
céntuplo, pla, *a.* centuple.
centuria, *f.* century (period of time; division of Roman army).
centurión, *m.* centurion.
centurionazgo, *m.* office of a centurion.
cenzalino, na, *a.* pertaining to mosquitoes.
cénzalo, *m.* (entom.) mosquito.
ceñido, da. I. *pp.* of CEÑIR. **II.** *a.* moderate in pleasure or expense; (of insects) narrow-waisted; beelike-waisted.
ceñidor, *m.* belt, girdle, cestus, sash.
ceñidura, *f.* act of girding.
ceñiglo, *m.* (bot.) white goosefoot, summer cypress.
ceñir. I. *va.* (*ind.* CIÑO; *subj.* CIÑA) to gird, surround, girdle; to hem in; to fit tight; to condense, abbreviate.—**c. el viento,** (naut.) to haul the wind.—**c. espada,** to wear a sword. **II.** *vr.* to reduce one's expenses; to confine or limit oneself; (of auto) to hug (as the inside of a curve).
[1]**ceño,** *m.* ring, hoop, band; (vet.) circle round upper part of horse's hoof.
[2]**ceño,** *m.* frown; browbeating; supercilious look; (poet.) gloomy aspect.—**ceñoso, sa; ceñudo, da,** *a.* frowning; browbeating; supercilious; grim, gruff.
ceo, *m.* (ichth.) doree, dory.
cepa, *f.* underground butt end of a tree stem; stump, stub; vinestock; stock or origin of a family; bud or root of the horns and tails of animals; (Mex.) hole, pit (dug for planting); (Am.) group of banana plants with common root; (arch.) pier of an arch; (agr.) sole of a plow; (carriage) tongue of a pole.—**de buena c.,** of acknowledged good quality; on good authority.—**de c.** blue-blood; thoroughbred.
cepacaballo, *m.* (bot.) cardoon.
cepeda, *f.* land overgrown with heath.
cepejón, *m.* butt end of tree branch torn off.
cepellón, *m.* ball of earth left around the roots of a plant for transplanting.
cepera, *f.* inflammation of the hoofs; CEPEDA.
cepilladura, *f.* wood shavings.
cepillar, *va.* to plane; to brush; to polish.
cepillo, *m.* brush; (carp.) plane; charity box, poor-box corban.—**c. bocel,** fluting plane; modelling plane.—**c. de cabeza,** hairbrush.—**c. de dientes,** toothbrush.—**c. de ropa,** clothesbrush.—**c. para la cabeza,** hairbrush.—**c. para ropa,** clothesbrush.
[1]**cepo,** *m.* bough or branch off a tree; stock of an anvil; stocks, for punishment; (naut.) bilboes; stock (of an anchor); reel for winding silk; trap, snare; charity box; (mil.) stocks of a gun carriage; (mech.) block; socket; clasp, clamp; joining press; shoemaker's horse.—*pl.* notch cleats.—**c. colombiano,** or **c. de campaña,** (Am.) an old form of military punishment in which the thumbs were tied together, the knees put between the arms, and one or two rifles placed on the arms between these and the legs.—**c. de maniguetes,** (naut.) crosspiece of the kevel.—**c. de molinete,** (naut.) knighthead of the windlass.—**¡cepos quedos!** keep still! keep quiet! stop that!
[2]**cepo,** *m.* = CEFO, an African monkey.
cepón, *m. aug.* large stub of a tree or vinestock.
ceporro, *m.* old vine pulled up for fuel.
cequí, *m.* an ancient gold coin.
cequión, *m.* (Chile) large ditch or channel.
cera, *f.* wax; beeswax; wax tapers and candles.—*pl.* honeycomb.—**c. aleda,** propolis, bee glue.—**c. de dorar,** gold size.—**c. de higos,** drum of figs.—**c. de los oídos,** earwax, cerumen.—**c. virgen,** virgin wax.—**no hay más c. que la que arde,** there is nothing more than what you see.—**ser como una c., ser una c., estar hecho de c.,** to be very condescending, very docile, very "easy."
ceráceo, ea, *a.* ceraceous, waxy.
cerachates, *f. pl.* wax stones.
cerafolio, *m.* (bot.) common chervil.
cerambícido, da, *m.* & *a.* (zool.) cerambycid.
cerámica, *f.* ceramic art; ceramics.
cerámico, ca, *a.* ceramic, pertaining to pottery.
ceramista, *m.* ceramist.
ceramita, *f.* a precious stone; a kind of brick of exceedingly high strength.
cerapez, *f.* plaster of wax and pitch.
cerasta, *f.,* **ceraste, cerastes,** *m.* cerastes, a horned serpent.
ceratias, *m.* double-tailed comet.
cerato, *m.* (pharm.) ointment containing wax.
cerbatana, *f.* blowgun, popgun, pea-shooter; ear trumpet for the deaf; small culverin.
cerbero, *m.* = CANCERBERO, Cerberus.
[1]**cerca,** *f.* fence; hedge.
[2]**cerca,** *adv.* near, close by, nigh. (Before a noun, pron., or adv., it requires **de:** *cerca de Paris,* near Paris; *cerca de aquí,* near here; but *aquí cerca,* near here).—**c. de** (when not used as ex-

plained), nearly, about.—**de c.,** closely; close at hand.—**por aquí c.,** somewhere near here.
cercado, da. I. *pp.* of CERCAR. **II.** *a.* inclosed, fenced in, walled in. **III.** *m.* garden or field fenced in; inclosure; fence; lock; (Peru) territorial division comprising state-capital and towns within its jurisdiction.
cercador, *m.* hedger, fencer; iron graver; marking iron; blunt chisel for repoussé work.
cercanamente, *adv.* near, nearly.
cercanía, *f.* proximity; (gen. *pl.*) neighborhood, vicinity, surroundings.
cercano, na (de) *a.* near (to); neighboring.
cercar, *va.* (*pret.* CERQUÉ; *subj.* CERQUE) to hem, circle, compass, gird; to surround; to fence in, hedge in, wall in; to pale; (mil.) to invest, lay siege to; to crowd about.
cercén.—a c., all around.
cercenador, *m.* clipper.
cercenadura, *f.* clipping, retrenchment.—*pl.* cuttings.
cercenar, *va.* to pare, clip; to lop off the ends of; to lessen, reduce, curtail, cut down.
cercera, *f.* air tube of a vault.
cerceta, *f.* (ornith.) widgeon, garganey, a species of duck.—*pl.* first growth of a deer's antlers.
cercillo, *m.* tendril of a vine.
cerciorar. I. *va.* to assure, affirm. **II.** *vr.* to make sure.
cerco, *m.* fence; hoop, ring; encirclement; rim, border, edge; halo; (mil.) blockade, siege; circular motion; circle of people; frame or case of a door or window.—**alzar,** or **levantar, el c.,** to raise a blockade.—**poner c. a,** to lay siege to, to blockade.
cercopiteco, *m.* (zool.) cercopithecus, an African monkey.
cercha, *f.* flexible wooden rule for measuring curved objects; (arch.) form or center for building arches; (carp.) segment of a rim.
cerchar, *va.* = ACODAR, to plant cuttings.
cerchón, *m.* = CIMBRA, (carp.) form; center.
cerda, *f.* horse's hair; bristle; (zool.) sow; newmown cereals; bundle of flax broken but not yet hackled.—*pl.* snares for birds.—**c. de puerco,** hog's bristle.
cerdamen, *m.* bristles prepared for brushes.
cerdear, *vn.* (of animals, esp. bulls) to be weak in the fore quarter; to emit a harsh and inharmonious sound (on string instrument); (coll.) to decline a request or demand; to look for excuses.
cerdo, *m.* hog.—**c. de muerte,** pig old enough to be slaughtered.—**c. de vida,** pig not old enough to be slaughtered.—**chuleta de c.,** pork chop.
cerdoso, sa; cerdudo, da, *a.* bristly; hairy.
cereal, *n.* & *a.* cereal.
cerebelitis, *f.* (med.) inflammation of the cerebellum.
cerebelo, *m.* (anat.) cerebellum.
cerebeloso, sa, *a.* cerebellar.
cerebración, *f.* cerebration.
cerebral, *a.* cerebral.
cerebrina, *f.* (chem.) cerebrin.
cerebritis, *f.* (med.) inflammation of the cerebrum.
cerebro, *m.* cerebrum; brain; judgment.
cerebroespinal, *a.* cerebrospinal.
cereceda, *f.* = CEREZAL.
cerecilla, *f. dim.* = GUINDILLA, red pepper pod.
ceremonia, *f.* ceremony; pomp, display; formality; ceremoniousness; compliment.—**de c.,** with all due ceremony; formal; (of dress) full, evening.—**guardar c.,** to comply with the formalities; to be formal.—**por c.,** simply as a matter of form or of etiquette.
ceremonial. I. *m.* book of ceremonies for public occasions. **II.** *a.* ceremonial, ceremonious.
ceremonialmente, *adv.* with all ceremony.
ceremoniáticamente, *adv.* ceremoniously.
ceremoniático, ca, *a.* ceremonious.
ceremoniosamente, *adv.* ceremoniously.
ceremonioso, sa, *a.* ceremonious, formal.
céreo, rea, *a.* cereous, waxen, waxy.
cereolita, *f.* soft, waxlike lava.
cerería, *f.* wax chandler's shop; chandlery in the royal palace.
cerero, ra, *n.* wax chandler.—**c. mayor,** royal chandler.
cereza, *f.* cherry.—**c. garrafal,** large whiteheart cherry, bigaroon.
cerezal, *m.* cherry orchard.
cerezo, *m.* (bot.) cherry tree; cherry wood.—**c. silvestre,** dog-cherry tree.
cergazo, *m.* (bot.) rockrose, cistus.
cérico, ca, *a.* ceric, pertaining to cerium.
céridos, *m. pl.* (chem.) cerium metals.
cerífero, ra, *a.* wax-producing.
ceriflor, *f.* (bot.) honeywort, honeyflower.
cerilla, *f.* wax taper in rolls; wax match; a kind of cosmetic; cold cream; wax tablet; earwax.
cerillera, *f.* lamplighter with a taper.
cerillo, *m.* (Mex.) wax match.
cerina, *f.* a variety of wax or waxlike material extracted from the cork tree.
cerinto, *m.* (bot.) wax flower, honeywort.
cerio, *m.* (chem.) cerium.
cerita, *f.* (min.) cerite.
cermeña, *f.* small early pear; muscadine.
cermeño, *m.* (bot.) muscadine pear tree.
cernada, *f.* cinder; leached ashes; (art) size on canvas; (vet.) plaster of ashes and other ingredients.—**cernadero,** *m.* coarse linen strainer for lye; linen or silk-and-linen fabric for collars.
cernedero, *m.* apron worn in sifting flour; place for sifting flour.
cernedor, *m.* sifter.
cerneja, *f.* fetlock of a horse.
cernejudo, da, *a.* having large fetlocks.
cerner. I. *va.* (*ind.* CIERNO; *subj.* CIERNA) to sift; to bolt. **II.** *vn.* to bud and blossom; to drizzle. **III.** *vr.* to waggle, wiggle, waddle; to soar.
cernícalo, *m.* (ornith.) kestrel; sparrow-hawk; person of scanty abilities.—**coger,** or **pillar, un c.,** (coll.) to get drunk.
cernidillo, *m.* drizzle; short and waddling gait.
cernido, *n.* sifting; the flour sifted.
cernidura, *f.* sifting.
cernir, *va.* = CERNER.
cero, *m.* zero; cipher; naught.—**ser un c.,** or **un c. a la izquierda,** to be a mere cipher, to be insignificant or of no account, not to count.
ceroleína, *f.* cerolein, a constituent of beeswax.
cerollo, lla, *a.* reaped when green and soft.
ceroma, *f.* ointment used by Roman athletes.
ceromancia, ceromancía, *f.* ceromancy (divination from figures formed by melted wax in water).
cerón, *m.* dross of wax.
ceroplástica, *f.* ceroplastics, modelling in wax.
cerotato, *m.* (chem.) cerotate.
cerote, *m.* shoemaker's wax; shoeblacking; (coll.) panic; fear.
cerótico, ca, *a.* cerotic.
ceroto, *m.* (pharm.) soft cerate of oil and wax.
cerqué, cerque, *v. V.* CERCAR.
cerquillo, *m. dim.* small circle or hoop; seam or welt of a shoe; ring of hair or tonsure; hair bangs.
cerquita, *adv.* at a short distance; very near.—**aquí c.,** close by, very near here.
cerrada, *f.* hide or skin covering the backbone.
cerradera, *f.,* **cerradero,** *m.* bolt staple; catch of a lock; catch, clasp; purse strings.—**echar la cerradera,** to turn a deaf ear; to refuse pointblank.
cerradero, ra, *n.* & *a.* locked (place); locking (device).
cerradizo, za, *a.* that may be locked or fastened.
cerrado, da. I. *pp.* of CERRAR.—**c. por reformas,** closed for alterations. **II.** *a.* incomprehensible, obscure; close, reserved; dissembling; secreted, concealed; obstinate; inflexible; cloudy, overcast; stupid, thick; dense.—**a**

puerta c., closed (meeting, etc.). **III.** *m.* fenced in field or garden.
cerrador, *m.* shutter; locker; lock; any contrivance that shuts or locks.
cerradura, *f.* lock; closure; act of shutting or locking.—**c. de golpe,** or **de muelle,** spring lock.—**c. embutida,** mortise lock.
[1]**cerraja,** *f.* lock of a door; bolt.
[2]**cerraja,** *f.* (bot.) common sow-thistle.
cerrajear, *vn.* to work as, or to be, a locksmith.
cerrajería, *f.* trade of a locksmith; locksmith's shop or forge.
cerrajero, *m.* locksmith.
cerrajón, *m.* steep, craggy cliff.
cerramiento, *m.* closure, occlusion; act of shutting or locking; costiveness; inclosure; (arch.) roof; (mason.) partition wall.
cerrar. I. *va.* & *vn.* (*ind.* CIERRO; *subj.* CIERRE) to close, shut, fasten, lock; to close, conclude (as an interview); to stop up, obstruct, block up; to inclose, include, contain; fence in; to fold and seal (a letter).—**c. la boca,** to be silent, shut up.—**c. los oídos,** to turn a deaf ear.—**c. los ojos,** to close one's eyes; die; sleep; to be stubborn.—**al c. del día,** at the close of day, at nightfall. **II.** *vr.* to close; to remain firm in one's opinion; to become cloudy and overcast; to close up, get close to each other.—**cerrársele a uno todas las puertas,** to find all avenues closed.
cerrazón, *f.* dark and cloudy weather preceding a storm.
cerrejón, *m.* hillock.
cerrero, ra, *a.* wild; untamed; unbroken (horse).
cerreta, *f.* (naut.) spar; rough tree.
cerril, *a.* mountainous; rough, uneven; wild, untamed, unbroken; (coll.) unpolished, rough, boorish.
cerrilla, *f.* die for milling.—**cerrillar,** *va.* to mill (coined metal).
cerrillo, *m. dim.*—*pl.* milling dies.
cerrión, *m.* icicle.
cerro, *m.* hill; peak; neck of an animal; backbone; hackled and cleaned flax or hemp.—**c. enriscado,** steep, rugged hill.—**en c.,** bareback; nakedly, without the proper or usual trappings.—**por los cerros de Ubeda,** (coll.) foreign to the purpose, irrelevant, (coll.) off the track.
cerrojillo, *m.* (ornith.) wagtail, warbler.
cerrojo, *m.* bolt, latch.
cerrón, *m.* a kind of coarse fabric made in Galicia.
cerruma, *f.* weak or defective quarter in horses.
certamen, *m.* literary contest; disputation; competition; (obs.) duel, battle.
certero, ra, *a.* well-aimed; good shot (shooter); sure; well-informed; skillful.
certeza, *f.* certainty, assurance.
certidumbre, *f.* certainty, conviction.
certificable, *a.* certifiable.
certificación, *f.* certification, certificate, attestation.
certificado, da. I. *a.* certified, attested. **II.** *m.* certificate, certification, attestation, testimonial; registered mail.
certificador, ra, *n.* certifier.
certificar, *va.* (*pret.* CERTIFIQUÉ; *subj.* CERTIFIQUE) to certify, attest; to register (a letter); (law) to prove by a public instrument.
certificatorio, ria, *a.* that serves to certify.
certifiqué, certifique, *v. V.* CERTIFICAR.
certísimo, *a. super.* of CIERTO: most certain.
cerúleo, lea, *a.* cerulean, sky-blue.
ceruma, *f.* (vet.) = CERRUMA.
cerumen, *m.* earwax, cerumen.
cerusa, *f.* ceruse, white lead.
cerusita, *f.* (min.) cerussite.
cerval, *a.* pertaining to deer.
cervantesco, ca; cervántico, ca; cervantino, na, *a.* like, or in the style of, Cervantes; pertaining or peculiar to Cervantes.
cervantista, *n.* expert in matters relating to Cervantes; Cervantes scholar.
cervario, ria, *a.* = CERVAL.
cervatica, *f.* (ichth.) = LANGOSTÓN, crawfish.
cervatico, illo, *m. dim.* small deer.
cervato, *m.* fawn.
cervecería, *f.* brewery; alehouse, beer-saloon.
cervecero, ra. I. *a.* beery. **II.** *n.* brewer; beer seller; *m.* set of beer jugs (mugs, etc.).
cerveza, *f.* beer, ale.
cervicabra, *f.* gazelle.
cervical; cérvico, ca, *a.* (anat.) cervical.
cérvido, da. I. *a.* (zool.) cervine, pertaining to deer or cervids. **II.** *n.* cervid. **III.** *m. pl.* Cervidæ.
cervigudo, da, *a.* high- or thick-necked.
cerviguillo, *m.* thick nape of the neck.
cervillera, *f.* helmet.
cervino, na, *a.* deerlike.
cerviz, *f.* cervix, nape of the neck.—**bajar,** or **doblar, la c.,** to humble oneself.—**levantar la c.,** to be elated; to grow proud.—**ser de dura c.,** to be incorrigible or stubborn.
cervuno, na, *a.* resembling or pertaining to deer; deer-colored.
cesación, *f.,* **cesamiento,** *m.* cessation, discontinuance, stopping, breakup, pause.—**c. a divinis,** suspension from religious functions.—**c. de hostilidad,** (mil.) cease-fire.
cesante. I. *a.* ceasing. **II.** *n.* dismissed or retired public officer, in some cases with a pension.
cesantía, *f.* state or pension of a retired official.
cesar, *vn.* to cease, stop; to desist; to retire; to leave a post or employment.—**c. de** (*inf.*), to stop (*pres. p.*).
cesáreo, rea, *a.* Cæsarean, pert. to imperial matters; (surg.) Cæsarean.
cesariano, na, *a.* Cæsarean, pert. to Cæsar.
cesarismo, *m.* Cæsarism.
cesarista, *n.* & *a.* Cæsarist(-ic).
cese, *m.* cessation; stoppage of pension.
cesible, *a.* (law) transferable.
cesio, *m.* (chem.) cæsium.
cesión, *m.* cession.—**c. de bienes,** surrender of property.
cesionario, ria, *n.* cessionary, grantee, assignee, transferee.
cesionista, *n.* transferrer, assigner, grantor.
cesonario, ria, *n.* = CESIONARIO.
césped, céspede, *m.* turf, sod, clod, sward, grass; grass plot, lawn; rind of a vine where it has been pruned.—**cespedera,** *f.* field where turf is cut.
cespitar, *vn.* to hesitate, vacillate.
cespitoso, sa, *a.* cespitose, matted.
cesta, *f.* basket, pannier, hamper; scoop or racket fastened to the arm for playing ball.—**cestada,** *f.* basketful.—**cestería,** *f.* basket factory or shop.—**cestero, ra,** *n.* basket maker or seller.
cestiaro, *m.* Roman pugilist who fought with the cestus.
[1]**cesto,** *m.* hand basket, maund, hutch.—**coger agua en c.,** to labor in vain.—**estar hecho un c.,** (coll.) to be overcome by sleep or liquor.—**quien hace un c. hará ciento,** he that steals a penny will steal a pound.—**ser un c.,** (coll.) to be ignorant and rude.
[2]**cesto,** *m.* cestus used by Roman boxers.
cestodo, da, *m.* & *a.* (zool.) cestode.
cestón, *m. aug.* large pannier or basket; (mil.) gabion.—*pl.* (mil.) corbeils.
cestonada, *f.* range of gabions.
cesura, *f.* cæsura, pause in poetry.
cetáceo, cea. I. *a.* (zool.) cetaceous, cetacean. **II.** *m.* (zool.) cetacean.
cetilo, *m.* (chem.) cetyl.
cetina, *f.* whale oil, sperm oil.
cetrería, *f.* falconry, hawking; fowling with falcons.
[1]**cetrero,** *m.* verger.
[2]**cetrero,** *m.* falconer; sportsman.
cetrino, na, *a.* citrine, lemon-colored; jaundiced, melancholy; pertaining to citron.
cetro, *m.* sceptre; reign of a prince; verge borne

by canons on solemn occasions; wand or staff; perch or roost for birds.—**empuñar el c.,** to ascend the throne, to begin to reign.

ceugma, zeugma, *f.* (rhet.) zeugma.

ceutí. I. *n.* & *a.* of, from, or pertaining to Ceuta. **II.** *m.* a very fragrant lemon.

C. G. S., *m.* (phys.) C. G. S. (centimeter-gram-second system of units).

cía, *f.* hip bone, huckle bone.

ciaboga, *f.* (naut.) putting a row galley about with the oars.—**hacer c.,** to turn the back, to flee.

cianamido, *m.* (chem.) cyanamide.

cianato, *m.* (chem.) cyanate.

cianhídrico, ca, *a.* hydrocyanic.

ciánico, ca, *a.* cyanic (acid).

cianita, *f.* (min.) cyanite.

cianógeno, *m.* cyanogen.

cianosis, *f.* (med.) cyanosis.

cianuración, *f.* (metal.) cyaniding.

cianúrico, ca, *a.* cyanuric.

cianuro, *m.* (chem.) cyanide.—**c. de potasio,** (chem.) potassium cyanide.—**c. de sodio,** (chem.) sodium cyanide.

ciar, *vn.* to back up, retrograde; (naut.) to back water; to go astern; to slacken, slow down.

ciática, *f.* (med.) sciatica.

ciático, ca, *a.* sciatic, sciatical.

ciato, *m.* (bot.) a tropical tree fern.

cibera, *f.* quantity of wheat put at once in the hopper; all seeds or grains fit for food; bagasse of grain, fruit, husks, etc.; hopper in a corn-mill.

cibernética, *f.* cybernetics.

cibica, *f.* clout; hurter of a wooden axle tree; (naut.) staple, cramp.

cibicón, *m.* large clout (for axle tree).

cíbolo, la, *n.* bison.

cibuí, *m.* (Peru) a variety of cedar.

cicadáceo, a; cicádido, da. I. *n.* & *a.* (bot.) cycad. **II.** *f. pl.* Cycadaceæ.

cicatear, *vn.* (coll.) to be sordidly parsimonious.

cicatería, *f.* niggardliness, stinginess.

cicatero, ra, *a.* niggardly, stingy.

cicateruelo, la, *n. dim.* stingy little person; little miser; curmudgeon.

cicatricé, cicatrice, *v. V.* CICATRIZAR.

cicatrícula, *f.* (embryol.) cicatricle.

cicatriz, *f.* cicatrice, scar.

cicatrización, *f.* cicatrization.

cicatrizal, *a.* cicatricial.

cicatrizante, *n.* & *a.* cicatrizant.

cicatrizar, *va.* & *vn.* (*pret.* CICATRICÉ; *subj.* CICATRICE) to cicatrize; to heal.

cicatrizativo, va, *a.* cicatrisive.

cicércula, cicercha, *f.* (bot.) = ALMORTA, vetch.

cícero, *m.* (print.) pica; (print.) unit of measurement for type bodies, equivalent to 12 points.

cicerone, *n.* cicerone, guide.

ciceroniano, na, *a.* Ciceronian.

ciclamino, *m.* (bot.) cyclamen.

ciclamor, *m.* an ornamental tree.

ciclatón, *m.* tunic formerly worn by women.

cíclico, ca, *a.* cyclical.

ciclismo, *m.* bicycling as a sport.

ciclista, *n.* cyclist, rider on a bicycle.

ciclo, *m.* cycle.

cicloidal, *a.* cycloidal.

cicloide, *f.* (geom.) cycloid.

cicloideo, dea, *a.* cycloid, cycloidal.

ciclometría, *f.* cyclometry.

ciclométrico, ca, *a.* cyclometric.

ciclómetro, *m.* cyclometer.

ciclón, *m.* cyclone.—**ciclonal,** *a.* cyclonic.

Cíclope, *m.* Cyclops.—**ciclópeo, a,** *a.* Cyclopean.

ciclorama, *m.* cyclorama.

ciclostilo, ciclóstilo, *m.* cyclostyle.

ciclóstoma, *m.* (ichth.) cyclostome.

ciclotrón, *m.* (phys.) cyclotron.

cicuta (bot.) hemlock, cicuta; water hemlock; spotted cowbane.

cid, *m.* brave, valiant man; leader, chief.—**el C.,** or **el C. Campeador,** El Cid, a title of the Spanish hero Rodrigo Díaz de Vivar.

cidra, *f.* (bot.) citron.

cidracayote, *f.* (bot.) American gourd or calabash.

cidrada, *f.* preserve made with citrons.

cidral, *m.* plantation of citron trees.

cidria, *m.* = CEDRIA, resin from the cedar.

cidro, *m.* (bot.) citron tree.

cidronela, *f.* citronella, common balm.

ciegayernos, *m.* showy, worthless thing; humbug.

[1]**ciego, ga. I.** *a.* blind; choked or closed; blinded. —**c. de,** blind with, blinded by.—**a ciegas,** blindly, in the dark; thoughtlessly. **II.** *n.* blind person; (anat.) cæcum or blind gut; large black pudding; (Cuba) isolated farm, ranch; hilly woodland.

[2]**ciego, ciegue,** *v. V.* CEGAR.

cieguecico, ica; illo, illa; ito, ita; cieguezuelo, ela, *n. dim.* little blind person.

cielito, *m.* S. A. tune and dance; darling, dearest, dearie.

cielo, *m.* sky, firmament; heaven(s); atmosphere, climate; ceiling; glory, felicity; paradise; roof; cover; canopy (of a bed).—**c. raso,** flat ceiling; clear sky.—**c. de la boca,** roof of the mouth.—**a c. descubierto,** in the open air; in the open, openly.—**a c. raso,** in the open air.—**escupir al c.,** to do bad deeds that turn against the doer, to throw a boomerang (fig.).—**estar hecho un c.,** to be splendid, brilliant.—**llovido del c.,** godsend.—**poner en,** or **por, el c.,** to praise to the utmost, to lionize.—**tomar el c. con las manos,** to be carried away with joy, grief, etc.—**un c. alegre,** a clear, beautiful sky.—**venirse el c. abajo,** to pour, rain pitchforks.—**ver el c. abierto,** to find an unforeseen opportunity.—**ver el c. por embudo,** not to know the world.

ciempiés, *m.* CIENTOPIÉS, (zool.) centipede; mediocre literary work.

cien, *a.* one hundred (used before nouns instead of **ciento,** as, *cien hombres,* a hundred men; *cien mujeres,* a hundred women). *V.* CIENTO.

ciénaga, *f.* marsh, moor, miry place.

ciencia, *f.* science; knowledge; certainty.—**ciencias exactas,** exact sciences.—**ciencias naturales,** natural sciences.—**ciencias sociales,** social sciences.—**a c. cierta,** with certainty, knowingly.—**a c. y paciencia de,** with the knowledge and consent of.

cienmilésimo, ma, *n.* & *a.* hundred-thousandth.

cienmilmillonésimo, ma, *n.* & *a.* hundred-thousand millionth.

cienmillonésimo, ma, *n., a.* hundred-millionth.

cieno, *m.* mud, mire, slime; slough, bog.

científico, ca. I. *a.* scientific. **II.** *n.* scientist.

ciento. I. *a.* (*V.* CIEN) one hundred; one hundredth (*calle ciento,* One-hundredth Street). **II.** *m.* a hundred. (Gen. without the article: *tengo ciento,* I have a hundred; *somos ciento,* we are a hundred. When used with the article before a noun, it is followed by **de:** *un ciento de libros,* a hundred books).—*pl.* tax assessed at so much per cent; piquet, a card game.—**por c.,** per cent; by the hundred.—**por cientos,** by hundreds, by the hundred; in large number.

cientopiés, *m.* (zool.) centipede.

cierna, *f.* the staminate blossom of vines, corn, and some other plants.

cierne.—en c., in blossom; in its infancy.

cierno, cierne, *v. V.* CERNER.

¡cierra España! *interj.* war cry of the ancient Spaniards.

cierrapuertas, *m.* door closer.

cierre, *m.* act and mode of closing; shutting, locking, fastening; snap; clasp; plug of a valve.—**c. hidráulico,** hydraulic seal, water seal.

[1]**cierro,** *m.* inclosure.—**c. de cristales,** glass-covered balcony or veranda.

[2]**cierro, cierre,** *v. V.* CERRAR.

ciertamente, *adv.* certainly, surely.

cierto, ta. I. *a.* certain, doubtless; sure, positive; true. (Used indefinitely, gen. without an article: *cierto lugar*, a certain place).—**ciertas hierbas, ciertos lienzos,** (coll.) certain people. —**de c.,** certainly, surely; in earnest.—**lo c. es que,** the fact is that.—**no por c.,** certainly not. —**por c., sí por c.,** certainly, surely, yes indeed.—**por c. que,** indeed. **II.** *adv.* certainly.
cierva, *f.* hind, female stag.
ciervo, *m.* deer, stag.—**c. volante,** stag beetle.
cierzo, *m.* cold northerly wind.
cifosis, *f.* (med.) outward bending of the spine.
cifra, *f.* figure, number, numerical character; cipher, code, cryptogram; monogram, device, emblem; sum total; contraction, abbreviation; music written with numbers.—**en c.,** secretly, mysteriously; briefly, concisely.
cifrar, *va.* to write in cipher; to abridge.—**c. en,** to place (one's hopes, etc.) on; to make (a thing) depend on.
cigarra, *f.* (entom.) cicada, harvest fly.
cigarral, *m.* in Toledo, orchard or fruit garden.
cigarrera, *f.* cigar cabinet or showcase; pocket cigarcase; woman cigar maker or dealer.
cigarrería, *f.* cigar shop.
cigarrero, ra, *n.* cigar maker or dealer.
cigarrillo, *m.* cigarette.
cigarrista, *n.* heavy smoker.
cigarro, *m.* cigar; (in some places) cigarette.—**c. de papel,** cigarette.—**c. puro,** cigar.
cigarrón, *m. aug.* large cicada.
cigofiláceo, cea, cigofileo, lea, *a.* (bot.) zygophyllaceous.
cigoma, *m.* (anat.) zygoma.
cigomático, ca, *a.* (anat.) zygomatic.
cigomorfismo, *m.* zygomorphism.
cigomorfo, fa, *a.* (bot.) zygomorphic, zygomorphous.
cigoñal, *m.* well sweep.
cigoñino, *m.* (ornith.) young stork.
cigoñuela, *f.* (ornith.) small storklike bird.
cigoto, *m.* (biol., genet.) zygote, egg.
cigua, *f.* (bot.) a tropical tree.
ciguatarse, *vr.* to have jaundice.
ciguatera, *f.* (Mex.) a kind of jaundice, from eating diseased fish.
ciguato, ta, *a.* suffering from CIGUATERA.
cigüeña, *f.* (ornith.) white stork; crane; bell crank; (mech.) crank, winch.—**cigüeñal,** *m.* CIGOÑAL; (int. combust. eng.) crankshaft.
cigüeñuela, *f. dim.* small crank or winch.—**c. de la caña del timón,** (naut.) gooseneck of the tiller.
cigüete, *f.* a variety of white grape.
cija, *f.* building for sheltering sheep; dungeon; granary.
cilanco, *m.* pool left by a river on the bank.
cilantro, *m.* (bot.) coriander.
ciliado, da, *a.* (zool.) ciliated.
ciliar, *a.* pert. to eyebrows or eyelashes.
cilicio, *m.* haircloth; hair shirt.
cilindrado, *m.* rolling; calendering.
cilindrar, *va.* to roll; calendar; to bore; rebore.
cilindricidad, *f.* cylindricity.
cilíndrico, ca, *a.* cylindrical.
cilindro, *m.* cylinder; (print.) roller; press roll; (mech.) chamber.
cilindroeje, *m.* (anat.) axis cylinder, axon.
cilindroide, *m.* (geom.) cylindroid.
cilla, *f.* granary; tithe.
cillazgo, *m.* storehouse fees paid on tithes.
cillerero, *m.* cellarist or butler of a monastery.
cilleriza, *f.* nun who directs the domestic affairs of a convent.
cillerizo, za, *n.* keeper of a granary.
cillero, *m.* keeper of a granary or storehouse for tithes; granary; vault; cellar; storeroom.
cima, *f.* summit, peak; top; cap, head; finish, completion; heart and tender sprouts of cardoons.—**dar c.,** to conclude happily.—**por c.,** in the uppermost part, at the very top.
cimacio, *m.* (arch.) cymatium, gola, ogee
cimarrón, na. I. *a.* (Am.) wild, unruly. **II.** *n.* runaway slave; maroon; (Arg.) black maté; (naut.) lazy sailor.
cimarronear, *vn.* (Am.) to run away; (Arg.) to drink black maté.
cimbalaria, *f.* (bot.) ivywort.
cimbalero, ra, cimbalista, *n.* cymbalist.
cimbalillo, *m. dim.* small bell.
címbalo, *m.* small bell; cymbal.
cimbanillo, *m.* = CIMBALILLO.
címbara, *f.* large sickle.
cimbel, *m.* decoy pigeon; rope used to tie decoy pigeons.
cimborio, cimborrio, *m.* (arch.) dome.
cimbra, *f.* (carp.) form, center (for an arch, etc.); (naut.) curvature; bending of a board.
cimbrado, *m.* quick bending movement in a Spanish dance.
cimbrar. I. *va.* to brandish; to shake; to sway, to bend; (carp.) to place cradlings in; (arch.) to arch; (coll.) to give a drubbing to. **II.** *vr.* to bend; to vibrate; to shake, tremble.
cimbre, *m.* subterranean gallery or passage.
cimbreante, *a.* flexible, pliable, easily bent.
cimbrear, *va.* & *vr.* = CIMBRAR.
cimbreño, ña, *a.* pliant, flexible; agile, limber, light-footed.
cimbreo, *m.* act of bending, brandishing, swaying, vibrating.
címbrico, ca, *a.* Cimbrian.
cimbro, bra, *n.* & *a.* Cimbrian.
cimbronazo, *m.* blow with flat of sword (also CINTARAZO); (Am.) jerk, sudden shaking.
cimentación, *f.* foundation; laying of a foundation.
cimentado, *m.* refining of gold.
cimentador, *m.* one that lays the foundation.
cimentar, *va.* (*ind.* CIMIENTO; *subj.* CIMIENTE) to lay the foundation of; to found; to ground; to establish the fundamental principles of; to refine (metals).
cimenterio, *m.* = CEMENTERIO, cemetery.
cimento, *m.* = CEMENTO, cement.
cimera, *f.* crest of a helmet or coat of arms.
cimerio, ria, *a.* Cimmerian
cimero, ra, *a.* placed at the height of some elevated spot; apical.
[1]**cimiento,** *m.* foundation; groundwork, bed; base; root, origin.
[2]**cimiento, cimiente,** *v.* *V.* CIMENTAR.
cimillo, *m.* flexible twig on which a decoy pigeon is tied.
cimitarra, *f.* scimitar, falchion.
cimo, *m.* (biol.) zyme.
cimófana, *f.* (min.) cymofane, cat's-eye.
cimogénesis, *f.* (biochem.) zymogenesis.
cimógeno, na. I. *a.* (biochem.) zymogenic. **II.** *m.* (biochem.) zymogen.
cimógrafo, *m.* (med.) kymograph.
cimología, *f.* zymology.
cimorra, *f.* (vet.) glanders.
cimosis, *f.* zymosis.
cimótico, ca, *a.* zymotic.
cimurgia, *f.* zymurgy.
cinabrio, *m.* (min.) cinnabar; vermilion.
cinamato, *m.* (chem.) cinnamate.
cinámico, *a.* (chem.) cinnamic.
cinamomo, *m.* (bot.) bead tree; (P. I.) privet.
cinc, *m.* zinc.
cinca, *f.* infraction of the rules of the game of ninepins (tenpins).
cincato, *m.* (chem.) zincate.
cincel, *m.* chisel; engraver; scorper; burin; drove.
cincelador, *m.* engraver; sculptor; stonecutter.
cincelar, *va.* to chisel, engrave, carve.
cíncico, ca, *a.* zincic, zincous.
cincífero, ra, *a.* zinciferous.
cincita, *f.* (min.) zincite.
cinco, *n.* & *a.* five; fifth (app. specially to dates) five-spot card; (Venez.) five-string guitar.—**decir cuántas son c.,** to threaten with re proof or punishment; to tell (one) what i

what.—**no saber cuántas son c.**, (coll.) not to know beans.
cincoenrama, *f.* (bot.) common cinquefoil.
cincograbado, *m.* zinc etching.
cincografía, *f.* zincography.
cincolina, *f.* (chem.) quinidine, quinidin.
cincomesino, na, *a.* five-month old.
cincona, *f.* (bot.) cinchona.—**cinconina,** *f.* (chem.) cinchonine.
cincuenta, *n.* & *a.* fifty; fiftieth (*calle cincuenta*, Fiftieth Street).
cincuentavo, *n.* & *a.* fiftieth.
cincuentén, *m.* piece of timber fifty palms in length (50 x 3 x 2).
cincuentena, *f.* group of fifty.—**una c. de,** fifty.
cincuentenario, ria, *m.* & *a.* semicentennial.
cincuenteno, na, *a.* fiftieth.
cincuentón, na. I. *a.* fifty-year-old. **II.** *n.* fifty-year old person.
cincha, *f.* girth, cinch.—**a revienta cinchas,** at breakneck speed; (Am.) grudgingly, unwillingly.
cinchadura, *f.* cinching, girthing.
cinchar, *va.* to girt, cinch up.
cinchera, *f.* girth place; (vet.) sore from girth.
cincho, *m.* belt, girdle, sash or bellyband; iron hoop; tire of a wheel; cheese mold; (Mex.) cinch; (arch.) transverse rib; (vet.) growth in horse's hoof.
cinchuela, *f. dim.* small cinch or girth; narrow ribbon.
cine, *m.*, **cinema,** *m.* (coll.) moving picture, "movie"; movie theatre.—**estrella de cine,** movie star.
cinegética, *f.* cynegetics, hunting with dogs.
cinegético, ca, *a.* cynegetic.
cinemadrama, *m.* photoplay.
cinemática, *f.* kinematics.
cinemático, ca, *a.* kinematic.
cinematografía, *f.* cinematography.
cinematográfico, ca, *a.* cinematographic.
cinematografista, *n.* cinematographer, (cine.) director.
cinematógrafo, *m.* cinematograph; moving-picture; movie house.
cineración, = INCINERACÍON, incineration.
cinerario, ria. I. *a.* cinerary. **II.** *f.* (bot.) cineraria.
cinéreo, rea; cinericio, cia, *a.* ashy; ash-colored.
cinescopio, *m.* (television) Kinescope (trademark).
cinesia, cinesis, *f.* (med.) kinesitherapy, kinesiatrics.
cinesiología, *f.* kinesiology.
cinesiterapia, *f.* (med.) kinesitherapy.
cinestesia, *f.* kinesthesia, kinesthesis; (psych.) cœnesthesis.
cinético, ca. I. *a.* kinetic. **II.** *f.* kinetics.
cinetógrafo, *m.* kinetograph, (cine.) camera.
cinetoscopio, *m.* kinetoscope.
cingalés, sa, *n.* & *a.* Singhalese.
cíngaro, ra, *n.* gipsy.
cinglador, *m.* (metal.) shingler.
cinglar, *va.* (metal.) to shingle, expel impurities of (iron) by hammering.
cingleta, *f.* rope with a cork to buoy up a net.
cíngulo, *m.* priest's girdle; ancient military badge.
cínicamente, *adv.* cynically.
cínico, ca. I. *a.* cynic, cynical; satirical; impudent, barefaced. **II.** *n.* cynic.
cínife, *m.* mosquito.
cinismo, *m.* cynicism; shamelessness, barefacedness, impudence.
cinocéfalo, *m.* (zool.) dog-headed.
cinógeno, *m.* (auto) starter.
cinoglosa, *f.* (bot.) hound's-tongue.
Cinosura, *f.* (astr.) Cynosure, Little Bear.
cinquén, *m.* an ancient Spanish coin.
cinta, *f.* ribbon; tape, band, strip, sash; (surv.) tape; strong net for tunny fishing; lowest part of the pastern of a horse; (arch.) fillet, belt, scroll; sidewalk curb; first course of floor tiles; (cine.) film.—**c. adherente** or **adhesiva,** Scotch tape (trademark).—**c. aisladora adherente,** friction tape.—**c. cinematográfica,** film, movie, movies.—**c. de fricción,** friction band (of a brake).—**c. magnetofónica,** magnetic tape, recording tape.—**c. métrica,** tape measure.—**cintas de navío,** wales.—**cintas galimas,** bow wales or harpings.—**en c.,** under subjection.
cintagorda, *f.* coarse fishing net.
cintajos, *m. pl.* knot or bunch of tumbled ribbons; tawdry ornaments in female dress.
cintarazo, *m.* slap with a sword or something flat.
cintarear, *va.* (coll.) to slap with a sword.
cinteado, da, *a.* adorned with ribbons.
cintería, *f.* ribbon trade; ribbon shop; collection or heap of ribbons.
cintero, ra. I. *n.* ribbon weaver or dealer. **II.** *m.* belt, girdle; hoisting rope.
cintilla, *f. dim.* small ribbon, narrow tape.
cintillo, *m.* hatband; ring set with precious stones.
cinto, ta. I. *pp. irreg.* of CEÑIR. **II.** *m.* belt, girdle.
cintra, *f.* (arch.) curvature (of an arch).
cintrel, *m.* (arch.) guide rule or line for arching.
cintura, *f.* waist; (woman's) girdle, belt; (arch.) throat of a chimney.—**meter en c.,** (coll.) to discipline, restrain, control.
cinturica, illa, ita, *f. dim.* small girdle; small or delicate waist.
cinturón, *m. aug.* large waist; sword belt; belt, girdle; (fig.) girdle, circle.
ciño, ciña, ciñé, ciñera, *v. V* CEÑIR.
cipariso, *m.* (poet.) cypress.
cipayo, *m.* Sepoy.
ciperáceo, cea, *a.* (bot.) cyperaceous.
cipo, *m.* milestone; signpost; boundary, or memorial, monument; large piece or fragment.
cipolino, na, *a.* cipoline, a kind of marble.
cipote, *n.* fool, blockhead, idiot; little one, youngster; short and fat person.
ciprés, *m.* cypress.—**cipresal,** *m.* cypress grove.
cipresino, na, *a.* pert. to or like cypress.
ciprino, na; ciprio, ia, *n.* & *a.* Cyprian.
ciquiricata, *f.* (coll.) caress; flattery.
circasiano, na, *n.* & *a.* Circassian.
circe, *f.* Circe; artful, deceitful woman.
circense, *a.* Circensian, pert. to Roman Circus.
circo, *m.* circus; amphitheatre.
circón, *m.* (min.) zircon.
circona, *f.* (chem.) zirconium oxide.
circonio, *m.* (chem.) zirconium.
circuición, *f.* act of surrounding or encircling
circuir, *va.* (*ind.* CIRCUYO; *subj.* CIRCUYA) to surround, compass, encircle.
circuito, *m.* circuit; contour, periphery; enclosure, field; (elec.) circuit.—**c. abierto,** (elec.) open circuit.—**c. cerrado,** (elec.) closed-circuit.—**c. impreso,** (elec.) printed circuit.—**c. recortador,** (electron.) clipper.—**c. de corriente intermitente,** (elec.) open circuit.—**c. de la placa,** (rad.) plate circuit.—**corto c.,** short circuit.
circulación, *f.* circulation; currency; traffic; movement.
circulante, *a.* circulatory, circulating.
[1]**circular. I.** *vn.* to circulate; travel, move; (of vehicles, traffic, etc.) to run. **II.** *va.* to circulate, pass round.
[2]**circular. I.** *a.* circular; circulatory; circling. **II.** *f.* circular, letter.
circularidad, *f.* circularity.
circulatorio, ria, *a.* circulatory.
círculo, *m.* circle; circumference; ring; circuit, district; social circle, club, casino.—**c. acimutal,** (naut.) azimuth circle.—**c. horario,** (astr.) hour circle.—**c. mamario,** (anat.) areola of the nipple.—**c. máximo,** (geom.)

great circle.—**c. polar,** (astr.) polar circle.—**c. repetidor,** (surv., etc.) repeating circle.—**c. vicioso,** vicious circle, reasoning in a circle.
circumambiente, *a.* surrounding.
circumcirca, *adv.* about, thereabout; almost.
circumpolar, *a.* circumpolar.
circuncidante, *n.* & *a.* circumciser(-ing).
circuncidar, *va.* to circumcise; to diminish, curtail, clip.
circuncisión, *f.* circumcision.
circunsiso, sa, *a.* circumcised.
circundar, *va.* to surround, circle, compass.
circunferencia, *f.* circumference.
circunferencial, *a.* circumferential.
circunferente, *a.* circumscribing.
circunferir, *va.* to circumscribe.
circunflejo, ja. I. *a.* (anat., gram.) circumflex. **II.** *m.* (gram.) circumflex.
circunfluente, *a.* circumfluent, circumfluous.
circunlocución, *f.* circumlocution.
circunlocutorio, ria, *a.* circumlocutory.
circunloquio, *m.* circumlocution.
circunnavegable, *a.* circumnavigable.
circunnavegación, *f.* circumnavigation.
circunnavegante, *n.* circumnavigator.
circunnavegar, *va.* to circumnavigate.
circunscribible, *a.* circumscribable.
circunscribir, *va.* (*pp.* CIRCUNSCRIPTO and CIRCUNSCRITO) to circumscribe; enclose, encircle.
circunscripción, *f.* circumscription.
circunscriptible, *a.* circumscribable.
circunscriptivo, va, *a.* circumscribing, limiting.
circunscripto, ta; circunscrito, ta, *a.* circumscribed.
circunspeción, *f.* circumspection, prudence; decorum, dignity.
circunspecto, ta, *a.* circumspect, cautious.
circunstancia, *f.* circumstance, incident; condition, state; particular, detail.—**c. agravante,** aggravating circumstance.—**c. atenuante,** extenuating circumstance.—**en las circunstancias presentes,** in, or under, the circumstances.
circunstanciadamente, *adv.* circumstantially, minutely, in detail.
circunstanciado, da, *a.* with all particulars, in detail.
circunstancial, *a.* circumstantial.
circunstante. I. *a.* surrounding; present, attending. **II.** *m. pl.* bystanders, persons present; audience.
circunvalación, *f.* (mil.) circumvallation.
circunvalar, *va.* to surround, encircle; (mil.) to circumvallate, surround with trenches.
circunvecino, na, *a.* neighboring, adjacent, contiguous, surrounding.
circunvolar, *va.* to fly around, encircle (in flying).
circunvolución, *f.* circumvolution, circumrotation; (anat.) convolution.
circunyacente, *a.* circumjacent.
circuyo, circuya, *v. V.* CIRCUIR.
cirenaico, ca, cireneo, nea, *n.* & *a.* Cyrenaic.
cirial, *m.* (eccl.) processional candleholder.
cirigaña, *f.* flattery.
cirineo, *m.* (coll.) mate, assistant.
cirio, *m.* thick and long wax taper.—**c. pascual,** paschal, or Easter, candle.
cirolero, *m.* (bot.) = CIRUELO.
cirquero, ra, *n.* (Mex.) acrobat.
cirrípedo, da, *m.* & *a.* (zool.) cirriped.
[1]**cirro,** *m.* (med.) scirrhus, kind of tumor.
[2]**cirro,** *m.* (bot., meteorol., zool.) cirrus.
cirrocúmulo, *m.* (meteorol.) cirro-cumulus (cloud formation).
cirroestrato, *m.* (meteorol.) cirro-stratus (cloud formation).
cirrosis, *f.* (med.) cirrhosis.
cirroso, sa, *a.* (bot.) fibrous; (meteorol.) cirrose.
cirrótico, ca, *a.* (med.) cirrhotic.
cirtolita, *f.* (min.) cyrtolite.
ciruela, *f.* plum; prune.—**c. de fraile,** long green plum.—**c. de yema,** yellow plum.—**c. pasa,** dried plum, prune.—**c. verdal,** greengage.
ciruelar, *m.* plantation of plum trees.
ciruelica, illa, ita, *f. dim.* small plum.
ciruelico, illo, ito, *m. dim.* dwarf plum tree.
ciruelo, *m.* (bot.) plum tree.
cirugía, *f.* surgery.
cirujano, na, *n.* surgeon.
cisalpino, na, *a.* cisalpine, on Roman side of Alps.
cisandino, na, *a.* cisandine.
cisatlántico, ca, *a.* cisatlantic.
cisca, *f.* reed for roofing huts and cottages.
ciscar. I. *va.* (*pret.* CISQUÉ; *subj.* CISQUE) (coll.) to smear, dirty. **II.** *vr.* to evacuate (bowels).
cisco, *m.* coal dust, culm, slack; breeze; (coll.) noisy wrangle, hubbub, hue and cry.
cisión, *f.* incision.
cisípedo, da, *a.* finger-footed.
cislunar, *a.* cislunar.
cisma, *m.* schism; disturbance in a community; discord.
cismático, ca. I. *a.* schismatic; disturbing; (Am.) finicky, prudish. **II.** *n.* schismatic; disturber.
cismontano, na, *a.* from or on this side of the mountains.
cismoso, sa, *n.* & *a.* troublemaker(-making).
cisne, *m.* (ornith.) swan; (C-, astr.) Cygnus, Swan; good poet or musician.
cisoide, *f.* (geom.) cissoid.
cispadano, na, *a.* on Roman side of the Po.
cisqué, cisque, *v. V.* CISCAR.
cisquero, *m.* coal-dust seller; pounce bag.
cistectomía, *f.* (surg.) cystectomy.
cistel, cister, *m.* Cistercian order of St. Bernard.
cisterciense, *n.* & *a.* Cistercian.
cisterna, *f.* cistern; reservoir; water tank.
cístico, ca. I. *a.* (med., anat.) cystic. **II.** *m.* (anat.) bladder duct.
cistitis, *f.* (med.) cystitis.
cisto, *m.* (bot.) cistus, rockrose.
cistocarpo, *m.* (bot.) cystocarp.
cistocele, *f.* (med.) cystocele.
cistoma, *m.* (med.) cystoma.
cistoscopio, *m.* (med.) cystoscope.
cistotomía, *f.* (surg.) cystotomy.
cistótomo, *m.* (surg.) lithotrite.
cisura, *f.* incision.
cita, *f.* appointment, engagement; summons; citation, quotation; (Mex.) (also) assignation.
citable, *a.* worthy of being cited, quotable.
citación, *f.* citation, quotation; summons, judicial notice.—**c. con apercibimiento,** (law) subpœna.
Citano, na, *n.* = ZUTANO, (Mr.) So-and-So.
citar, *va.* to make an appointment with; to convoke, convene; to quote; to summon; to give judicial notice.—**c. a junta,** to call a meeting.
citara, *f.* (mason.) partition wall of the thickness of a brick.—**citarilla,** *f. dim.* (mason.) thin partition wall.
cítara, *f.* cithara, zither, musical instrument.
citarista, *n.* zither player.
citatorio, ria, *a.* (law) (of a summons) citatory.
citereo, rea, *a.* Cytherean.
citerior, *a.* hither, nearer, toward this part.—**España c.,** the higher or northeastern part of Spain.
cítiso, *m.* (bot.) shrub trefoil, cytisus.
citoblasto, *m.* (biol.) cytoblast.
cítola, *f.* in corn mills, clack or clapper.
citolegia, *f.* primer (for learning to read).
citología, *f.* (biol.) cytology.
citoplasma, *m.* (biol.) cytoplasm.
citote, *m.* (coll.) summons, citation.
citramontano, na, *a.* = CISMONTANO.
citrato, *m.* (chem.) citrate.
cítrico, ca, *a.* (chem.) citric.
citrina, *f.* lemon oil.
citrón, *m.* lemon; (P. R., bot.) lime.
ciudad, *f.* city; civic body.
ciudadanía, *f.* citizenship.

ciudadano, na. I. *a.* pertaining to a city; civil; citylike. **II.** *n.* citizen.
ciudadela, *f.* (mil.) citadel, fortress; (Am.) tenement house.
ciudad-estado, *f.* city-state.
civeta, *f.* civet cat.
civeto, *m.* civet, the perfume.
cívico, ca, *a.* civic; domestic.
civil, *a.* civil; polite, courteous; (law) civil, not criminal.—**derechos civiles,** civil rights.
civilicé, civilice, *v. V.* CIVILIZAR.
civilidad, *f.* civility, politeness, urbanity.
civilista, *n.* attorney skilled in the civil law, especially the Roman law; (Am.) partisan of civil government, opponent of militarism.
civilización, *f.* civilization.
civilizador, ra, *a.* civilizing.
civilizar, *va.* (*pret.* CIVILICÉ; *subj.* CIVILICE) to civilize.
civismo, *m.* civism; patriotism.
cizalla, *f.* shears, plateshears; fillings, metal clippings.—**cizallar,** *va.* to shear.
cizaña, *f.* (bot.) darnel; weed; corrupting vice; discord, disagreement; pollution.
cizañador, ra, *n.* one who sows discord or enmity, troublemaker.
cizañar, *vn.* to sow discord; to provoke enmity.
cizañero, ra, *n.* = CIZAÑADOR.
clac, *m.* collapsible hat, opera hat.
clamar, *vn.* to utter loud outcries; to whine; to clamor, vociferate.—**c. por,** to want, require, demand, cry out for.
clámide, *f.* short cape, the chlamys of the Greeks.
clamor, *m.* clamor, outcry; whine, plaint; toll of bells, knell.
clamoreada, *f.* outcry, clamor; whine, plaint.
clamorear, *vn.* to clamor; to implore assistance, appeal; to toll.
clamoreo, *m.* repeated or prolonged clamor; knell; (coll.) importunate appeal.
clamoroso, sa, *a.* clamorous, loud, noisy.
clan, *m.* clan.
clandestinidad, *f.* clandestineness, secrecy.
clandestinista, *m.* & *f.* (Am.) smuggler of liquor.
clandestino, na, *a.* clandestine, secret.
clanga, *f.* (ornith.) = PLANGA, a kind of eagle.
clangor, *m.* (poet.) sound of a trumpet.
claque, *f.* (theat.) claque.
clara, *f.* white of an egg; piece of ill-woven cloth; bald spot; (coll.) short interval of fair weather on a rainy day.
claraboya, *f.* skylight; bull's-eye; transom.
clarar, *va.* = ACLARAR, to clarify; to clear up.
clarea, *f.* mulled wine, mulse.
clarear. I. *va.* to give light to. **II.** *vn.* to dawn, to grow light, to clear up. **III.** *vr.* to be transparent, translucent; to give oneself away.
clarecer, *vn.* (*subj.* CLAREZCA) to dawn, to grow or become light.
clarete, *m.* claret.
claridad, *f.* brightness, splendor, light; clearness, distinctness; glory of the blessed; celebrity, fame.—*pl.* plain truths, plain language.
clarificación, *f.* clarification, refining.
clarificadora, *f.* clarifying pan, evaporator.
clarificar, *va.* (*pret.* CLARIFIQUÉ; *subj.* CLARIFIQUE) to brighten; to illuminate; to clarify, purify, refine.
clarificativo, va, *a.* purifying; lightening.
clarilla, *f.* lye of ashes.
clarimente, *m.* an ancient lotion used by women.
clarín, *m.* bugle, clarion; organ stop; bugler; fine cambric; (ornith.) an American song bird.
clarinada, *f.* (coll.) uncalled-for, tart remark.
clarinado, da, *a.* (her.) bell-bearing.
clarinero, *m.* bugler.
clarinete, *m.* clarinet; clarinet player.
clarión, *m.* white crayon, chalk.
clarisa, *f.* Clare, nun of the order of St. Clare.
clarísimo, ma, *a.* (*super.* of CLARO) very clear, perfectly clear; most illustrious.
clarividencia, *f.* clairvoyance; clear-sightedness.
clarividente, *a.* clairvoyant; clear-sighted, sagacious.
claro, ra, I. *a.* clear; bright, light, nitid; neat; thin, rare, sparse; cloudless, fair; light, not deeply tinged; plain, clear; obvious, evident, indisputable; open, frank, ingenuous; celebrated, illustrious; sagacious, quick of thought. —**c. está,** of course; evidently.—**c. intervalo,** remission of madness; lucid interval.—**c. oscuro,** chiaroscuro.—**c. que no,** of course not.—**a la clara, a las claras,** in the open, openly. **II.** *adv.* = CLARAMENTE, clearly. **III.** *m.* skylight; break in a discourse; gap, lacuna, interval; bald spot; glade; clearing; light spot; (arch.) space between columns; (naut.) clear spot in the sky.—**de c. en c.,** evidently, manifestly.—**pasar la noche de c., or en c.,** not to sleep a wink.—**poner en c.,** to make plain.—**por lo c.,** clearly, manifestly, conspicuously. —**sacar en c.** = PONER EN C.; to conclude, arrive at a conclusion.
claror, *m.* = RESPLANDOR, light; brilliance.
claroscuro, *m.* combination of fine and heavy strokes in penmanship; monochrome, painting in one color; chiaroscuro, light and shade.
clarucho, cha, *a.* (coll.) too watery, too thin.
clase, *f.* class; classroom.—**c. alta,** upper class.—**c. baja,** lower class.—**c. obrera,** working class. —**c. proletaria,** working class.—**c. turista,** tourist class.—**primera c.,** first class.—**segunda c.,** second class.—**tercera c.,** third class.—**de c.,** of distinction, of high standing.—**toda c. de,** all kinds of.
clásicamente, *adv.* classically.
clasicismo, *m.* classic style, classicism.
clasicista, *n.* classicist.
clásico, ca. I. *a.* classic, classical; remarkable; (coll.) typical, characteristic. **II.** *n.* classicist; classic author; *m.* classic book.
clasificable, *a.* classifiable.
clasificación, *f.* classification; sorting.
clasificar, *va.* (*pret.* CLASIFIQUÉ; *subj.* CLASIFIQUE) to classify, class; to sort.—**c. por orden de magnitud,** (stat.) to array.
clástico, ca, *a.* clastic.
claudicación, *f.* claudication, limp; crookedness.
claudicante, *a.* halting, limping.
claudicar, *vn.* (*pret.* CLAUDIQUÉ; *subj.* CLAUDIQUE) to halt, limp; (coll.) to bungle, falter.
claustral, *a.* claustral, cloistral.
claustro, *m.* cloister; piazza; gallery around a court; faculty of a university; monastic state.
claustrofobia, *f.* (med., psychiat.) claustrophobia.
cláusula, *f.* (gram.) period, sentence; clause of a discourse; (law) clause, article.
clausulado, da, I. *a.* (rhet.) written in short sentences. **II.** *m.* (collect.) clauses or articles of a writing.
clausular, *va.* to close (a period), terminate (a speech).
clausulilla, *f. dim.* short or little clause.
clausura, *f.* cloister; inner recess of a convent, sanctum; clausure, confinement, retirement; cloture, closure.—**vivir en c.,** to lead a monastic or retired life.—**clausurar,** *va.* to bring to a close, conclude (as a meeting).
clava, *f.* club, cudgel; (naut.) scupper.
clavadizo, za, *a.* adorned with nails.
clavado, da. I. *pp.* of CLAVAR. **II.** *a.* nailed, adorned with nails, hobnailed; exact, precise.—**venir c.,** to fit exactly.
clavador, *m.* nail driver.
clavadura, *f.* wound made by driving a nail to the quick in horseshoeing.
clavar, *va.* to nail, fasten with nails; to fasten in, drive in, stick in, force in; to stick, prick, gore, pin, pierce; to set in gold or silver; (coll.) to cheat, to deceive.—**c. a un caballo,** to prick a horse in shoeing.—**c. la artillería,** to spike, to nail up the guns.—**c. las armas,** to ground the arms.—**c. los ojos,** or **la vista, en,** to stare or look with fixed eyes at.

clavaria, *f.* = CLAVERA, nail mold; nail hole.
clavario, *m.* = [1]CLAVERO, keeper of the keys.
clavazón, *f.* set of nails.
clave. **I.** *m.* clavichord. **II.** *f.* key of a code; (arch.) keystone of an arch; (mus.) clef, key. —**c. de do,** (mus.) C clef.—**c. de fa,** (mus.) bass or F clef.—**c. de sol,** (mus.) treble clef, G clef.—**echar la c.,** (fig.) to close, settle, conclude (a business deal); to close, end (a speech, an affair, etc.).
clavel, *m.* (bot.) pink, carnation.—**c. reventón,** large carnation.—**clavelito,** *m. dim.* (bot.) a plant bearing a small variety of pink.—**clavelón,** *m. aug.* (bot.) marigold.—**clavellina,** *f.* (bot.) pink, carnation; (mil.) vent stopple.
claveque, *m.* rock crystal cut like a diamond.
clavera, *f.* nail mold; heading stamp; nail hole; nail bore; screw hole; boundary where landmarks are set up.
clavería, *f.* office and dignity of the keybearer in military orders; (Mex.) treasury of a cathedral.
[1]**clavero, ra,** *n.* keeper of the keys; treasurer, cashier; key bearer of some military orders.
[2]**clavero,** *m.* aromatic clove tree.
clavete, *m. dim.* tack, small nail.—**clavetear,** *va.* to nail; to garnish with nails; to point or tag (a lace); (fig.) to finish up, put in final form.
clavicordio, *m.* clavichord, harpsichord.
clavicornio, nia. **I.** *n.* & *a.* (zool.) clavicorn. **II.** *m. pl.* Clavicornia.
clavícula, *f.* (anat.) clavicle, collar bone.
clavicular, *a.* (anat.) clavicular.
clavija, *f.* pin, peg; treenail, pintle, peg of a string instrument.—**c. maestra,** fore-axletree pintle.—**apretar las clavijas,** to push home an argument; to put on the thumb screws.
clavijera, *f.* water hole in walls.
clavijero, *m.* bridge of a clavichord.
clavillo, ito, *m. dim.* small nail, spill, brad, tack, pin.—**c. de hebilla,** rivet of a buckle.—*pl.* cloves.
clavíórgano, *m.* clavichord, instrument having strings and pipes.
clavo, *m.* nail; spike; (naut.) rudder of a ship; severe grief or pain; (vet.) tumor between the hair and the hoof of a horse; (min.) bunch of rich ore; corn (on the feet); (surg.) lint; tent. —**c. de especia,** clove.—**c. de gota de sebo,** semispherical-headed nail.—**c. de herradura,** hobnail.—**c. de rosca,** screw nail.—**c. romano,** (Am.) curtain knob, picture nail.—**c. tachuela,** tack.—**c. trabadero,** keyed bolt. —**c. trabal,** clasp nail.—**dar en el c.,** to hit the nail on the head.—**de c. pasado,** self-evident, well-known; easy (a "cinch").—**sacarse el c.,** to get even.—**un c. saca otro c.,** one grief cures another.
clazol, *m.* (Mex.) residue of sugar cane, etc.
clemátide, *f.* (bot.) traveller's-joy, virgin's-bower, clematis.
clemencia, *f.* mercy, clemency, forbearance.
clemente, *a.* merciful.—**clementemente,** *adv.* mercifully.—**clementísimo, ma,** *a. super.* of CLEMENTE.
clépsidra, *f.* clepsydra, water clock.
cleptomanía, *f.* kleptomania.
cleptomaníaco, ca; cleptómano, na, *n.* & *a.* kleptomaniac.
clerecía, *f.* clergy.
clerical. **I.** *a.* clerical, pert. to the clergy. **II.** *n.* (pol.) Clerical, belonging to the Clerical party. —**clericalismo,** *m.* clericalism.—**clericalmente,** *adv.* in a clerical manner.
clericato, *m.* state and dignity of a clergyman.
clericatura, *f.* clergy, ecclesiastical state.
clerigalla, *f.* (collect.) (contempt.) priests.
clérigo, *m.* clergyman.—**c. de misa,** presbyter. —**c. de misa y olla,** ignorant priest.—**c. suelto,** one fighting with an army but not belonging to it and not subject to orders.
clериguillo, *m. dim.* petty clergyman (a term of contempt).
clerizón, *m.* chorister.
clerizonte, *m.* layman who wears a clerical dress; ill-dressed or ill-mannered clergyman.
clero, *m.* clergy.
clerofobia, *f.* hatred of priests.
clerófobo, ba, *n.* & *a.* priest hater(-ing).
cliente, *n.* client; customer.
clientela, *f.* clientele, following; customers; protection, patronage.
clima, *m.* climate, clime.
climatérico, ca, *a.* climacteric; (coll.) ill-humored; (Am.) wrongly used for CLIMÁTICO.
climático, ca, *a.* climatic, pert. to climate.
climatización, *f.* air conditioning.
climatología, *f.* climatology.
climatológico, ca, *a.* climatological.
climatoterapia, *f.* (med.) climatotherapy.
clímax, *m.* (rhet.) climax.
clin, *f.* = CRIN, mane.
clínica, *f.* clinic (instruction and place); private hospital.
clínico, ca. **I.** *a.* clinic, clinical. **II.** *m.* & *f.* (eccl.) one asking for baptism on his deathbed.
clinometría, *f.* clinometry.
clinométrico, ca, *a.* clinometric.
clinómetro, *m.* clinometer.
clinopodio, *m.* (bot.) calamint.
clíper, *m.* (naut.) clipper.
clisado, *m.* (print.) stereotyping.
clisar, *va.* (print.) to stereotype; to make a cliché or stereotype plate of.
clisé, *m.* (print.) stereotype plate; (print.) cut.
clistel, clister, *m.* (med.) clyster, enema.
clisterizar, *va.* (med.) to clysterize, give an enema to.
clitómetro, *m.* (surv.) clinometer.
clítoris, *m.* (anat.) clitoris.
clivoso, sa, *a.* (poet.) sloping.
clo, clo, *m.* cackle of a hen.
cloaca, *f.* sewer; (zool.) cloaca, large intestine of fowls.
clocar, *va.* to cluck.
clónico, ca, *a.* (med.) clonic.
cloque, *m.* (naut.) grapnel; grappling iron, harpoon.
[1]**cloquear,** *va.* to angle; to hook fish (gen. tunny).
[2]**cloquear,** *vn.* to cluck, cackle.
cloqueo, *m.* cluck, chuck, cackle.
cloquera, *f.* (of birds) broodiness.
cloquero, *m.* tunny harpooner.
cloración, *f.* (chem.) chlorination.
clorador, *m.* (chem.) chlorinator.
cloral, *m.* (chem.) chloral.
cloramina, *f.* (chem.) chloramine.
clorar, *va.* (chem.) to chlorinate.
clorato, *m.* (chem.) chlorate.—**c. de sodio,** (chem.) sodium chlorate.
clorhidrato, *m.* (chem.) hydrochlorate.
clorhídrico, *m.* (chem.) hydrochloric.
clórico, ca, *a.* chloric.
cloris, *f.* (ornith.) greenfinch.
clorita, *f.* (min.) chlorite.
clorito, *m.* (chem.) chlorite.
cloro, *m.* (chem.) chlorine.
clorofila, *f.* chlorophyll, green coloring-matter of plants.—**clorofílico, ca,** *a.* chlorophyllous.
clorofórmico, ca, *a.* pertaining to chloroform.
cloroformización, *f.* chloroforming.
cloroformizar, *va.* (*pret.* CLOROFORMICÉ; *subj.* CLOROFORMICE) to chloroform.
cloroformo, *m.* chloroform.
clorometría, *f.* chlorometry (measurement of chlorine).
clorómetro, *m.* (chem.) chlorometer (device for measuring chlorine).
cloromicetina, *f.* (pharm.) chloromycetin.
cloropicrina, *f.* (chem.) chloropicrin.
cloroplasto, *m.* (bot.) chloroplast.
cloropreno, *m.* (chem.) chloroprene.
cloroquina, *f.* (pharm.) chloroquine.
clorosis, *f.* (med.) chlorosis, greensickness.
cloroso, sa, *a.* chlorous.
clorotiacida, *f.* (pharm.) chlorothiazide.

clorótico, ca, *a.* chlorotic.
clorpromasina, *f.* (pharm.) chlorpromazine.
cloruración, *f.* chlorination.
clorurar, *va.* to chloridize, transform into chloride.
cloruro, *m.* (chem.) chloride.—**c. amónico,** (chem.) ammonium chloride.—**c. de cal,** (chem.) chloride of lime.—**c. de calcio,** (chem.) calcium chloride.—**c. sódico cristalino,** (min.) halite.
club, *m.* club, social or political association.—**clubista,** *m.* & *f.* clubman(-woman).
clueco, ca. I. *a.* (of birds) broody; (coll.) decrepit. **II.** *f.* brooding hen.
cluniacense, *m.* & *a.* Cluniac.
coa, *f.* sharp stick used by Indians to till the land; (Mex.) a kind of hoe.
coacción, *f.* coaction; compulsion, coercion.
coacervar, *va.* to heap together.
coactible, *a.* coercible.
coactivo, va, *a.* coactive, coercive, compulsory.
coacusado, da, *n.* (law) co-defendant.
coacusar, *va.* (law) to accuse jointly.
coadjutor, *m.* coadjutor, assistant, associate, co-worker.—**coadjutora,** *f.* coadjutrix.—**coadjutoría,** *f.* help, assistance; coadjutorship.
coadministrador, *m.* co-administrator.
coadunación, *f.*, **coadunamiento,** *m.* coadunation.
coadunar, *va.* to join closely together.
coadyutor, *m.* = COADJUTOR.
coadyutorio, ria, *a.* cooperative.
coadyuvador, *m.* fellow helper, assistant.
coadyuvante. I. *n.* helper, assistant. **II.** *a.* cooperative, auxiliary.
coadyuvar, *va.* to help, assist, aid.
coagente, *m.* co-agent, associate.
coagulable, *a.* coagulable.
coagulación, *f.* coagulation.
coagulado, da, *a.* coagulated, clotted, clotty.
coagulador, ra. I. *a.* coagulative, coagulating. **II.** *m.* coagulator, coagulant.
coagulante, *n.* & *a.* coagulant.
coagular. I. *va.* to coagulate, to curd. **II.** *vr.* to coagulate, condense, clod, curdle.
coagulativo, va, *a.* coagulative.
coagulina, *f.* (chem.) coagulin.
coágulo, *m.* coagulum, clot.
coairón, *m.* piece of timber.
coalbacea, *n.* coexecutor.
coalescencia, *f.* (med.) coalescence.
coalescente, *a.* coalescent.
coalición, *f.* coalition.
coalicionista, *n.* coalitionist.
coalla, *f.* (ornith.) woodcock.
coapóstol, *m.* co-apostle.
coaptación, *f.* (surg.) coaptation.
coarmador, *m.* part owner of a vessel.
coarrendador, *m.* joint lessor.
coarrendatario, ria, *n.* joint tenant.
coartación, *f.* limitation, restriction; obligation to be ordained within a certain time.
coartada, *f.* (law) alibi.—**probar la c.,** to prove an alibi.
coartado, da, *a.* (slave) who has paid his master a partial sum to obtain freedom.
coartar, *va.* to limit, restrain.
coartífice, *n.* comaker, collaborator.
coate, ta, *a.* (Mex.) = CUATE, twin.
coatí, *m.* (zool.) coati.
coautor, ra, *n.* coauthor, joint author.
coaxil, coaxial, *a.* coaxial.
coba, *f.* (coll.) trick, dodge, knack; (coll.) flattery, cajolery.
cobáltico, ca, *a.* (chem.) cobaltic.
cobaltífero, ra, *a.* cobalt-bearing, cobaltic.
cobaltina, *f.* (min.) cobaltite.
cobalto. *m.* cobalt.
cobaltoso, sa, *a.* (chem.) cobaltous.
cobarde. I. *a.* cowardly, coward; faint-hearted, (coll.) chicken, chicken-hearted. **II.** *n.* coward.
cobardear, *vn.* to cower, be intimidated.
cobardemente, *adv.* cowardly.
cobardía, *f.* cowardice.
cobayo, *m.* (zool.) guinea pig.
cobeligerante, *n.* & *a.* cobelligerent.
cobertera, *f.* cover, potlid; bawd; procuress; white water lily.—*pl.* the two middle feathers of a hawk's tail.
cobertizo, *m.* shed, hut.
cobertor, *m.* coverlet, bedspread, quilt.
cobertura, *f.* cover, wrapper, covering, coverlet; ceremony of a grandee of Spain keeping his hat on for the first time in the presence of the king.
cobija, *f.* imbrex tile; short mantilla; small feather (of bird); cover; (Am.) blanket; (Mex.) shawl.—*pl.* (Mex.) bedclothes.
cobijador, ra, *a.* covering, protective.
cobijamiento, *m.* act of covering; lodging.
cobijar, *va.* to cover; shelter, protect; to lodge.
cobijo, *m.* = COBIJAMIENTO.
[1]**cobra,** *f.* rope for yoking oxen; number of mares (not less than five) for treading out corn.
[2]**cobra,** *f.* (zool.) cobra.
cobrable, *a.* = COBRADERO.
cobracapelo, *f.* (zool.) cobra.
cobradero, ra, *a.* that may be recovered or collected.
cobrador, ra. I. *a.* collecting.—**perro c.,** retriever. **II.** *m.* collector, receiving teller; (Ry., bus, etc.) conductor.
cobranza, *f.* recovery or collection of money; retrieval of game.
cobrar. I. *va.* to collect, receive (what is due); to recover (something lost); (of dog) to retrieve (shot game); to recuperate, regain; to gain; to charge (price, fee); to cash (check); to pull, draw in; to win, obtain.—**c. ánimo,** or **corazón,** to take courage.—**c. carnes,** to become fat, put on flesh.—**c. fuerzas,** to gather strength. **II.** *vr.* to recover; to come to.
cobratorio, ia, *a.* pertaining to collection of money; collectible.
[1]**cobre,** *m.* or, **c. de cecial,** pair of dried hake or haddock.
[2]**cobre,** *m.* copper; kitchen brass utensils; (mus.) brass instruments of an orchestra.—**c. quemado,** copper sulphate.—**c. verde,** malachite.—**batir el c.,** to pursue with spirit and vigor, to hustle.
cobreño, ña, *a.* made of copper.
cobrizo, za, *a.* coppery, cupreous; copper-colored.
cobro, *m.* COBRANZA; receptacle; place of safety.
[1]**coca,** *f.* (bot.) coca; coca leaves; juice from coca leaves, coca tea.
[2]**coca,** *f.* (prov.) ugly woman; bugbear.
[3]**coca,** *f.* (naut.) a kind of small vessel; side hair of women put back from the face; (coll.) head; (coll.) rap with knuckles on head.
[4]**coca,** *f.* cake.
[5]**coca,** *f.* a small berry.—**c. de Levante,** moonseed yielding India fishberries.
cocada, *f.* coconut candy or preserve.
cocador, ra, *a.* wheedling, coaxing, flattering.
cocaína, *f.* cocaine.
cocal, *m.* coca; (Peru & Bol.) coca plantation; (Am.) coconut or coconut tree plantation.
cocán, *m.* (Peru) breast of a fowl.
cocar, *va.* (coll.) to coax; to gain by wheedling and flattering; to flirt with; to make faces at.
cocarar, *va.* to supply coca leaves to.
cocaví, *m.* (Am.) coca and other provisions for a journey.
coccígeo, gea, *a.* (anat.) coccygeal.
coccíneo, nea, *a.* purple, purplish (color).
cocción, *f.* cooking, baking, calcining.
cóccix, *m.* (anat.) coccyx.
coceador, ra, *n.* & *a.* (of animals) kicker(-ing).
coceadura, *f.*, **coceamiento,** *m.* kicking.
cocear, *va.* & *vn.* to kick.—**c. contra el aguijón,** to kick against the pricks.
cocedero, ra. I. *a.* easily boiled. **II.** *m.* place where anything is cooked or baked.
cocedizo, za, *a.* = COCEDERO.

cocedura, *f.* act of boiling; cooking.
cocer. I. *va.* (*ind.* CUEZO; *subj.* CUEZA) to boil; to bake; to cook; to burn, bake, calcine (brick, etc.); to digest. **II.** *vn.* to boil, cook, ferment; to seethe, ferment without fire, as wine. **III.** *vr.* to suffer intense and continued pain.
coces, *pl.* of coz, kick.—**dar c.,** to kick.
cocido, da. I. *pp.* of COCER. **II.** *a.* boiled, baked, cooked; skilled, experienced. **III.** *m.* a Spanish dish of boiled meat and vegetables.
cociente, *m.* (math.) quotient.
cocimiento, *m.* cooking, decoction; bath or mordant for dyeing.
cocina, *f.* kitchen; cuisine, cookery; pottage of greens.—**c. de hierro,** cooking range.—**c. de presión,** pressure cooker.—**c. económica,** cooking range.—**c. eléctrica,** cooker.—**c. sin fuego,** fireless cooker.
cocinar. I. *va.* to cook. **II.** *vn.* (coll.) to butt in, meddle.
cocinero, ra, *n.* cook; chef.
cocinilla, *f. dim.* kitchenette; alcohol stove; fireplace; *n.* meddler.
cocktail, *m.* (Angl.) cocktail. Also COTEL.
cóclea, *f.* ancient machine for raising water; endless screw.
coclear, *a.* cochlear.
coclearia, *f.* (bot.) common scurvy grass.
[1]**coco,** *m.* (bot.) coconut (tree, shell, fruit); vessel made of coconut shell.—**c. avellanado,** dry coconut.—**c. de embarque,** select coconut.—**c. nacido,** sprout.—**c. pequeño,** cull.—**c. vano,** dry.—**c. zarazo,** rot.
[2]**coco,** *m.* worm or grub of seeds and fruit; scale insect; coccus (bacterium).
[3]**coco,** *m.* bugbear; phantasm; gesture, grimace; flattering gesture.—**hacer cocos,** (coll.) to flatter, wheedle; to flirt.
[4]**coco,** *m.* India berries from which rosaries are made.
cocobacilo, *m.* bubonic-plague bacillus.
cocobálsamo, *m.* fruit of the balm of Gilead.
cocobolo, *m.* (bot.) a hardwood tree; cocobolo.
cocodrilo, *m.* (zool.) crocodile.
cocol, *m.* (Mex.) (bread) roll.—**cocolero, ra,** *n.* roll baker.
cocoliste, *m.* (Mex.) an epidemic fever.
cócora, *f.* annoying person, bore.
cocoso, sa, *a.* worm-eaten; gnawed by grubs.
cocotal, *m.* clump of coconut trees; coconut plantation or field.
cocote, cogote, *m.* (anat.) occiput.
cocotero, *m.* (bot.) coconut tree.
coctel, *m.* (Angl.) cocktail.—**coctelera,** *f.* (Am.) cocktail shaker.
cocuyo, *m.* glowworm.
cocha, *f.* (min.) small water reservoir.
cochambre, *m.* (coll.) greasy, dirty thing.
cochambrería, *f.* (coll.) heap of filthy things.
cochambrero, ra; cochambroso, sa, *a.* (coll.) nasty, filthy, stinking.
cocharro, *m.* wooden or stone dish, cup, platter.
cochastro, *m.* little, sucking wild boar.
coche, *m.* carriage, coach; car.—**c. cama,** sleeping-car, pullman.—**c. celular,** prison van, Black Maria.—**c. comedor,** dining car.—**c. de alquiler,** taxi, cab, hack, hackney coach.—**c. de plaza or de punto,** hack, cab, taxi.—**c. de tranvía,** street car.—**c. de turismo,** touring car.—**c. de viajeros,** passenger car.—**c. dormitorio,** sleeping car.—**c. fúnebre,** hearse.—**c. salón,** parlor car.—**c. simón,** hack, hackney coach.—**c. usado,** secondhand car.
cochear, *vn.* to drive a carriage.
cochera, *f.* carriage house; (Ry.) car house, roundhouse, barn; garage; coachman's wife.—**puerta c.,** carriage porch; porte-cochère.
cocheril, *a.* (coll.) pert. to coachmen.
[1]**cochero,** *m.* coachman; C. (astr.) Charioteer.
[2]**cochero, ra,** *a.* easily boiled.
cocherón, *m. aug.* large coach house; engine house; roundhouse.
cochevira, *f.* lard.
cochevís, *m.* (ornith.) crested shore lark.
cochifrito, *m.* fricassee of lamb, mutton, etc.
cochigato, *m.* a Mexican bird.
cochina, *f.* sow.
cochinada, *f.* herd of swine; (coll.) hoggishness; mean, dirty action, dirty trick.
cochinata, *f.* (naut.) rider.
cochinería, *f.* foulness, filthiness; meanness, niggardliness, baseness.
cochinero, ra, *a.* (of poor fruit) for hogs.
[1]**cochinilla,** *f.* woodlouse.
[2]**cochinilla,** *f.* cochineal.
cochinillo, illa, *n. dim.* pig.—**c. de Indias,** guinea pig.—**c. de leche,** sucking pig.
cochino, na, *n.* **I.** hog (sow). **II.** *a.* & *n.* dirty, filthy, vile (person).
cochiquera, *f.* (coll.) hogsty, pigpen; small and filthy room.
cochite hervite, (coll.) helter-skelter.
cochitril, *m.* (coll.) pigsty; filthy room.
cochura, *f.* cooking; dough for a batch of bread.
coda, *f.* = COLA, tail; (mus.) coda, ending, finale.
codadura, *f.* layer of an old vine.
codal, I. *a.* one cubit long. **II.** *m.* elbow piece of ancient armor; short and thick wax candle; shoot of vine; frame of a handsaw; carpenter's square; prop, shore, stay, strut; stay bolt.
codaste, *m.* (naut., aer.) sternpost.
codazo, *m.* blow with the elbow; (Mex.) hunch.
codear. I. *vn.* to elbow. **II.** *va.* to nudge.
codeína, *f.* codein.
codelincuencia, *f.* joint delinquency, complicity.
codelincuente, *n.* partner in crime, accomplice.
codera, *f.* itch or scabbiness on the elbow; piece reinforcing the elbows of jackets; elbow rail; (naut.) breastfast.
codesera, *f.* spot grown over with hairy Cytisus.
codeso, *m.* (bot.) hairy Cytisus.
codeudor, ra, *n.* joint debtor.
códice, *m.* old manuscript; codex.
codicia, *f.* covetousness, cupidity, greediness.—**la c. rompe el saco,** covetousness is self-defeating.
codiciable, *a.* covetable.
codiciador, ra, *n.* & *a.* coveter(-ing).
codiciante, *a.* coveting.
codiciar, *va.* & *vn.* to covet.
codicilar, *a.* pertaining to a codicil.
codicilo, *m.* codicil.
codiciosamente, *adv.* covetously, greedily.
codicioso, sa, *a.* greedy, covetous, grasping; ambitious; (coll.) diligent; laborious; thrifty.
codificación, *f.* codification.
codificador, ra, *n.* codifier.
codificar, *va.* (*pret.* CODIFIQUÉ; *subj.* CODIFIQUE) to codify.
código, *m.* code (of laws).—**c. del honor,** code of honor.—**c. de minas,** mining code.—**c. de señales,** signal code.—**C. Justinianeo,** Justinian Code.—**c. mercantil,** mercantile code.—**c. militar,** military law.—**c. naval,** naval law.—**c. penal,** penal code.
codillo, *m.* knee of quadrupeds; bend; elbow; knee; breech; angle; codille, a term at ombre; part of a branch of a tree which joins the trunk; foot rule; stirrup of a saddle.—**codillos,** file used by silversmiths.
codito, ta, *a.* (Mex.) stingy.
codo, *m.* elbow; cubit; (mech.) angle, elbow, knee (of quadruped); foot rule.—**c. real,** royal cubit.—**alzar el c.,** to drink too much.—**comerse los codos de hambre,** to be starving to death.—**hablar por los codos,** to chatter, to be a chatterbox.—**levantar el c.** = ALZAR EL CODO.
codón, *m.* leather dock of a horse's tail.
codorniz, *f.* (ornith.) quail.
coeducación, *f.* coeducation.
coeducacional, *a.* coeducational.
coeficiencia, *f.* coefficiency.
coeficiente. I. *a.* coefficient. **II.** *m.* (math.) co-

efficient; factor.—**c. de absorción,** (phys.) absorption coefficient.—**c. de dilatación,** (phys.) coefficient of expansion.—**c. de dispersión magnética,** coefficient of magnetic leakage.—**c. de rozamiento,** (mech.) coefficient of friction.—**c. de salida,** (hydraul.) coefficient of discharge.—**c. de seguridad,** coefficient of safety, safety factor.—**c. de sensibilidad,** (elec.) coefficient of sensitiveness.—**c. de trabajo,** working stress.—**c. indeterminado,** (math.) undetermined coefficient.

coepíscopo, *m.* contemporary bishop.

coercer, *va.* (*ind.* COERZO; *subj.* COERZA) to coerce, check, restrain.

coercibilidad, *f.* coercibility, liability to restraint.

coercible, *a.* coercible, subject to check; (phys.) compressible.

coerción, *f.* coercion, restraint, check.

coercitivo, va, *a.* coercive, restraining.

coerzo, coerza, *v. V.* COERCER.

coetáneo, nea, *a.* contemporary.

coeternidad, *f.* coeternity.

coeterno, na, *a.* coeternal.

coevo, va, *a.* coeval.

coexistencia, *f.* coexistence.

coexistente, *a.* coexistent.

coexistir, *vn.* to coexist.

coextenderse, *vr.* to coextend.

coextensión, *f.* coextension.

coextensivamente, *adv.* coextensively.

coextensivo, va, *a.* coextensive.

cofa, *f.* (naut.) top of the lower masts.

cofia, *f.* hair net, cowl, headdress, coif; die case in coining.—**cofiezuela,** *f. dim.* small hair net or coif.

cofín, *m.* small basket for fruit; fruit box.

cofosis, *f.* complete deafness.

cofrade, da, *n.* member (of a confraternity or brotherhood).—**cofradía,** *f.* confraternity, brotherhood, sisterhood; trades union; association.

cofre, *m.* trunk for clothes; coffer; box, case; (print.) coffin of the imposing stone.

cofrecico, illo, ito, *m. dim.* small trunk or box.

cofrero, ra, *n.* trunk maker or seller.

cofto, ta, *a.* = COPTO, Coptic.

cogedera, *f.* rod for gathering grass hemp; box for catching swarming bees; pole for gathering fruit; handle.

cogedero, ra. I. *a.* ready to be gathered. **II.** *n.* handle.

cogedizo, za, *a.* that can be easily collected or gathered.

cogedor, *m.* collector, gatherer; dust box or dust pan; coal or ash shovel; box for the woven velvet.

cogedura, *f.* act of gathering or collecting.

coger. I. *va.* (*ind.* COJO; *subj.* COJA) to catch; to seize, grasp, take hold of; to fetch; gather, pick (fruit, etc.); to collect, take; to imbibe, soak; to have room or capacity for; to occupy, take up; to find, procure; to surprise, catch; to attack unexpectedly; to intercept, obstruct.—**c. la delantera,** to get the start. **II.** *vn.* to fit, have room, reach.

cogida, *f.* (coll.) gathering or harvesting of fruits; (coll.) yield of fruits; (coll.) act of the bull's catching the bullfighter; (fish) catch.

cogido, da. I. *pp.* of COGER. **II.** *m.* gather, fold in clothing, curtains, etc.; pleat.

cogitabundo, da, *a.* pensive, thoughtful.

cogitación, *f.* (obs.) meditation, cogitation.

cogitativo, va, *a.* cogitative; given to meditation.

cognación, *f.* cognation; kindred, relationship.

cognado, da, *n.* & *a.* cognate.

cognaticio, ia, *a.* cognatic.

cognición, *f.* cognition.

cognomento, *m.* cognomen, surname.

cognoscible, conocible, *a.* cognoscible, knowable.

cognoscitivo, va, *a.* cognitive.

cogollico, ito, *m. aim.* small heart of garden plants.

cogollo, *m.* heart of garden plants; shoot of a plant; top, summit; (Cuba & Mex.) sugarcane top, used as forage.

cogombro, *m.* = COHOMBRO, cucumber.

cogón, *m.* (bot.) bamboo used in the Philippines for thatching.

cogonal, *m.* COGÓN plantation.

cogotazo, *m.* slap on the back of the neck.

cogote, *m.* occiput, back of the neck; crest at the back of the helmet.—**ser tieso de c.,** (coll.) to be haughty, conceited, airy, stiff.—**cogotera,** *f.* neckprotector put round ox's neck.—**cogotudo, da,** *a.* thicknecked.

cogucho, *m.* sugar of coarse quality.

cogujada, *f.* (ornith.) crested lark.

cogujón, *m.* corner of a mattress or bolster.

cogujonero, ra, *a.* pointed, as the corners of mattresses or bolsters.

cogulla, *f.* cowl, monk's habit.—**cogullada,** *f.* = PAPADA DEL PUERCO, hog's dewlap.

cohabitación, *f.* cohabitation.

cohabitar, *vn.* to cohabit.

cohecha, *f.* (agr.) last tillage before sowing the crop.

cohechador, *m.* briber, suborner.

[1]**cohechar,** *va.* to bribe, suborn.

[2]**cohechar,** *va.* (agr.) to plow the last time before sowing.

[1]**cohecho,** *m.* bribery.

[2]**cohecho,** *m.* (agr.) plowing season.

cohen, *n.* soothsayer; procurer, pimp.

coheredero, ra, *n.* coheir; *f.* coheiress.

coherencia, *f.* coherence; connection.

coherente, *a.* coherent; connected; consistent; cohesive.

cohesión, *f.* cohesion.

cohesivo, va, *a.* cohesive.

cohesor, *m.* (radio) coherer.

cohete, *m.* skyrocket; rocket (missile).—**c. con propulsor sólido,** solid propellant rocket.—**c. de alcance intermedio,** intermediate-range rocket.—**c. de refuerzo,** booster rocket.—**c. fotónico,** photon rocket.—**c. nuclear,** nuclear rocket.—**c. tripulado,** manned rocket.

cohetear, *va.* (Mex.) to blast.

cohetería, *f.* fireworks shop.

cohetero, *m.* maker or seller of fireworks.

cohibición, *f.* cohibition, prohibition.

cohibir, *va.* to cohibit, prohibit, restrain.

cohobación, *f.* (chem.) cohobation.

cohobar, *va.* to redistil, cohobate.

cohobo, *m.* stag skin; (Am.) stag, deer.

cohombral, *m.* cucumber bed.

cohombrillo, *m. dim.* gherkin.

cohombro, *m.* cucumber; fritter cut into pieces like a cucumber.

cohonestación, *f.* specious justification (of an action), "whitewashing."

cohonestar, *va.* to give an honest appearance to (an action).

cohorte, *f.* cohort.

coima, *f.* perquisite received by the keeper of a gaming table.

coime, coimero, *m.* keeper of a gaming table; scorer at billiards.

coincidencia, *f.* coincidence.

coincidente, *a.* coincident.

coincidir, *vn.* to coincide.

coinquilinato, *m.* cotenancy.

coinquilino, na, *n.* cotenant.

coinquinarse, *vr.* to become stained.

cointeresado, da. I. *a.* jointly interested. **II.** *n.* joint party in interest.

coipo, coipú, *m.* coypu, a S. A. amphibious mammal similar to the beaver.

coirón, *m.* (S. A.) a kind of thatching grass.

coironal, *m.* COIRÓN field.

coito, *m.* coition, carnal copulation.

coja, *f.* (coll.) lewd woman.

cojear, *vn.* to limp, hobble; (of an unsteady table, etc.) to tilt; to deviate from virtue.—**c. de,** to limp with; to have the defect of.

cojera, *f.* lameness, hobble, limp.
cojijo, *m.* complaint of some slight injury; grub or insect.
cojijoso, sa, *a.* peevish, irritable.
cojín, *m.* cushion, pillow; saddle pad.
cojinete, *m. dim.* cushionet, small cushion, small pillow, pad; rail chair; (mech.) journal bearing, shaft bearing; pillow block.
cojitranco, ca, *a.* an epithet applied to evil-disposed lame persons.
[1]**cojo, coja,** *v. V.* COGER.
[2]**cojo, ja,** *a.* (of table, etc.) unsteady, tilting; *n.* & *a.* lame, cripple, halt.
cojudo, da, *a.* entire, not gelt or castrated.
cojuelo, ela, *a. dim.* a small cripple.
cok, coque, *m.* coke.
col, *f.* cabbage (this name is given to several varieties).—**c. común,** Savoy cabbage.
[1]**cola,** *f.* tail; cue; tail end; hind portion of anything; extremity; appendage; line of people awaiting turn; end seat in a row; lowest place in a school class; (arch.) inside joint; train of a dress; (mus.) prolonged note at the end of a song.—**c. de caballo,** (bot.) horsetail.—**c. de golondrino,** (fort.) hornwork.—(a) **c. de milano,** tongue-and-groove, dovetailed.—**de c.,** rear, last.—**hacer c.,** to stand in line.—**tener,** or **traer, c.,** (coll.) to be followed by serious consequences.
[2]**cola,** *f.* glue.—**c. clara,** transparent glue.—**c. de boca,** glue on stamp, envelope flap, etc.—**c. de pescado,** isinglass.—**c. de retazo,** or **retal,** size used by painters.
[3]**cola,** *f.* (bot.) cola, Kola; (pharm.) kola.
colaboración, *f.* collaboration, working together; contribution (to a periodical, etc.).
colaboracionista, *n.* collaborationist.
colaborador, ra, *n.* collaborator, co-worker; contributor (to a periodical, etc.)
colaborar, *vn.* to collaborate; to contribute.
colación, *f.* collation, critical comparison; act of bestowing an ecclesiastical benefice, or conferring degrees in universities; conference on spiritual affairs; slight repast, luncheon; sweetmeats given to servants on Christmas eve; precinct or district of a parish.—**sacar a c.,** to make mention of.—**traer a c.,** (coll.) to produce proofs or reasons; to introduce something irrelevant in conversation; to bring up for discussion.
colacionar, *va.* to collate.
colactáneo, a, *n.* foster brother or sister.
[1]**colada,** *f.* wash, buck, bucking; common, an open ground; road for cattle over a common; tap (of a furnace).
[2]**colada,** *f.* (coll.) good sword.
coladera, *f.* strainer, colander; wax-chandler's sieve; (Mex.) perforated sink cover.
coladero, *m.* colander, strainer, filtering bag; narrow passage; (min.) hole for dumping ore.
colador, *m.* colander; (print.) leach tub.
coladora, *f.* woman who bucks clothes.
coladura, *f.* straining, filtering.—*pl.* wax dregs.
colágeno, *m.* (biochem.) collagen.
colagogo, ga, *a.* (med.) stimulating bile secretion.
colaire, *m.* place through which a current of air passes.
colambre, *f.* (tanning) = CORAMBRE, pelts.
colanilla, *f.* small sliding bolt; sash bolt.
colaña, *f.* low partition in stairs or granaries; joist about twenty palms long and six inches broad.
colapez, colapiscis, *f.* isinglass. Also COLA DE PESCADO.
colapso, *m.* (med.) collapse, prostration.
colar. I. *va.* & *vn.* (*ind.* CUELO; *subj.* CUELE) to strain, drain, pass through, percolate, filter; to bleach clothing after washing; (coll.) to spread false news; to pass counterfeit money; to pass through a narrow place; (coll.) to pass muster; (coll.) to drink wine. **II.** *vr.* to strain, be filtered; to steal or squeeze into a place; (coll.) to be displeased with a jest.
colateral, *a.* collateral.
colatitud, *f.* (astr., naut.) colatitude.
colativo, va, *a.* filtering.
colbac, *m.* calpack, Turkish cap.
colcótar, *m.* (chem.) colcothar; rouge; jewellers' red.
colcha, *f.* coverlet, quilt, bedspread.
[1]**colchadura,** *f.* quilting.
[2]**colchadura,** *f.* (naut.) laying or twisting ropes.
[1]**colchar,** *va.* = ACOLCHAR, to quilt.
[2]**colchar,** *va.*—**c. cabos,** (naut.) to lay or twist ropes.
colchero, ra, *n.* quilt maker.
cólchico, *m.* (bot.) colchicum, meadow saffron.
colchón, *n.* mattress.—**c. de muelles,** spring mattress.—**c. de pluma,** feather bed.—**c. de viento,** air cushion, air bed.
colchoncico, illo, ito, *m. dim.* small mattress.
colchonero, ra, *n.* mattress maker.
colchoneta, *f.* quilted covering for a lounge.
coleada, *f.* wag of the tail; (S. A.) act of felling a bull by a twist of the tail.
coleador, *m.* (S. A.) man who fells a bull by twisting its tail.
coleadura, *f.* wagging of the tail; wriggling.
colear. I. *vn.* to wag (the tail). **II.** *va.* (Mex.) in bullfights, to take (the bull) by the tail, while on horseback, and, by suddenly starting the horse, to overturn him; (Am.) to pull down (cattle) by the tail; (fig.) to refuse, turn down.
colección, *f.* collection, aggregation, accumulation; set; array; gathering.
coleccionador, ra, *n.* collector (of stamps, birds, etc.).
coleccionar, *va.* to collect, form a collection of.
coleccionista, *n.* = COLECCIONADOR.
colecta, *f.* assessment; collect, a prayer; collection for charity.
colectación, *f.* levy; collecting rents, taxes, etc.
colectar, *va.* to collect (taxes, etc.).
colecticio, cia, *a.* untrained; (of soldiers) raw; compilatory, of the nature of a compilation.
colectividad, *f.* collectivity; mass of people; community.
colectivismo, *m.* collectivism.
colectivista, *n.* & *a.* collectivist(-ic).
colectivización, *f.* collectivization.
colectivo, va. **I.** *a.* collective; (gram.) collective. **II.** *m.* (gram.) collective, collective noun.
colectomía, *f.* (surg.) colectomy.
colector, *m.* collector, gatherer; tax or rent collector; water conduit; (elec.) commutator.
colecturía, *f.* collectorship; office of the collector; tax office.
colega, *m.* colleague; contemporary (newspaper).
colegatario, ra, *n.* collegatary, co-legatee.
colegiado, da, *a.* collegiate.
colegial. I. *a.* collegiate; college (as *a.*). **II.** *m.* collegian.—**colegiala,** *f.* college woman.
colegialmente, *adv.* in a collegial manner.
colegiarse, *vr.* to form an association.
colegiata, *f.* collegiate church.
colegiatura, *f.* fellowship in a college.
colegio, *m.* college; school, academy, seminary; body of students, students collectively; association; college, body of dignitaries, electors, etc.
colegir, *va.* (*ind. pres.* COLIJO, *pret.* el COLIGIÓ; *subj.* COLIJA) to collect or gather; to deduce, infer, conclude.
colegislador, ra, *a.* co-legislative (body).
coleo, *m.* wagging (of the tail); wriggling; (bot.) coleus.
coleóptero, ra. I. *a.* coleopterous. **II.** *m. pl.* Coleoptera.
coleorriza, *f.* (bot.) coleorhiza.
colera, *f.* ornament for a horse's tail.
cólera, *f.* (physiol.) bile; (fig.) anger, rage, fury; *m.* (med.) cholera.—**c. asiático,** (med.) Asiatic cholera.—**c. infantil,** (med.) cholera infantum.—**c. morbo,** (med.) cholera morbus.

colérico, ca, *a.* angry, wrathful; irascible, irritable; (med.) choleraic.
coleriforme, *a.* (med.) resembling cholera.
colerina, *f.* cholerine, a mild diarrhoea.
colesterina, *f.* (chem.) cholesterol, cholesterin.
coleta, *f.* cue or queue of the hair; (coll.) short addition to a discourse or writing; postscript; (Am.) burlap.—**cortarse la c.,** to quit the (bull) ring.
coletero, ra, *n.* maker or seller of buff doublets and breeches.
coletilla, *f. dim.* small cue (hair); postscript.
coletillo, *m. dim.* small buff doublet.
coleto, *m.* buff doublet or jacket; (coll.) body of a man; interior of a person.—**decir para su c.,** to say to oneself.—**echarse al c.,** (coll.) to read through; to eat or drink.
colgadero, ra. I. *a.* fit to be hung up, taken care of. **II.** *m.* hook or peg to hang things on; hat or coat rack; hanger
colgadizo, za. I. *a.* hanging, suspended. **II.** *m.* shed roof; carport; (Cuba) shed.
colgado, da, *a.* suspended, hanging; (coll.) disappointed, left (as in **dejar c.,** to disappoint, to fail; **quedarse c.,** to be foiled, to get left).
colgador, *m.* (print.) peel hanger; Y-lintel.
colgadura, *f.* tapestry, hanging or drapery; bunting.—**c. de cama,** bed hangings.
colgajo, *m.* tatter or rag hanging from clothes; bunch of grapes or fruit hung up to be preserved.—*pl.* the fleshy tissues left in some amputations to cover the wound.
colgandejo, *m.* (Colomb.) = COLGAJO.
colgandero, ra, *a.* = COLGANTE.
colgante. I. *a.* hanging, pending, clinging. **II.** *m.* (arch.) drop, pendent; (mech.) hanger; (carp.) king-post.
colgar. I. *va.* (*ind. pres.* CUELGO, *pret.* COLGUÉ; *subj.* CUELGUE) to hang up, suspend; to adorn with hangings; to attribute, charge with, make responsible for; (coll.) to kill by hanging.—**c. los hábitos,** to doff the cassock. **II.** *vn.* to hang, be suspended; to dangle; to flag, droop.
colgué, *v. V.* COLGAR.
colibacilo, *m.* intestinal microbe.
coliblanca, *f.* (ornith.) white-tailed S. A. eagle.
coliblanco, ca, *a.* (ornith.) white-tailed.
colibre, colibrí, *m.* (ornith.) humming bird.
colicano, na, *a.* gray-tailed.
cólico, ca. I. *a.* of or pertaining to the colon; colic, colicky. **II.** *m.* & *f.* (med.) colic.—**c. hepático,** hepatic colic.—**c. miserere,** ileus.—**c. nefrítico** or **renal,** renal colic.
colicuación, *f.* colliquation.
colicuante, *a.* colliquant; colliquative.
colicuar. I. *va.* to colliquate, melt, dissolve. **II.** *vr.* to colliquate; to become liquid.—**colicuativo, va,** *a.* colliquative.
colicuecer, *va.* (*ind.* COLICUEZCO; *subj.* COLICUEZCA) to fuse or melt.
coliflor, *f.* (bot.) cauliflower.
coligación, *f.* colligation; binding of things together; connection, union; alliance.
coligado, da. I. *pp.* of COLIGARSE. **II.** *a.* allied, associate, associated. **III.** *n.* leaguer, covenanter.
coligadura, *f.* **coligamiento,** *m.* = COLIGACIÓN.
coligarse, *vr.* to colligate, confederate, unite, become allies.
coligió, colijo, colija, *v. V.* COLEGIR.
colilla, *f. dim.* stub of a cigar or cigarette.—**colillero, ra,** *n.* person who gathers cigar stubs as a trade.
colimación, *f.* (opt.) collimation.
colimador, *m.* (opt.) collimator.
colín, *a.* short-tailed (horse).
[1]**colina,** *f.* hill, hillock, knoll.
[2]**colina,** *f.* seed of cabbage.
[3]**colina,** *f.* (biochem.) choline.
colinabo, *m.* (bot.) turnip; young cabbage.
colindante, *a.* contiguous, adjacent, abutting.
colindar, *vn.* **(con)** to be contiguous, or adjacent (to), to abut (on).
colino, *m.* small cabbage not transplanted.
colirio, *m.* (med.) collyrium, eyewash.
colirrábano, *m.* (bot.) kohlrabi.
colisa, *f.* (artil.) swivel gun.
coliseo, *m.* theatre, opera house, playhouse; coliseum, colosseum.
colisión, *f.* collision, crush, clash; bruise, chafe, soreness from rubbing; opposition, clash of ideas.
colitigante, *m.* co-litigant, one who carries on a lawsuit with another.
colitis, *f.* (med.) colitis.
colmadamente, *adv.* abundantly, plentifully.
colmado, da. I. *pp.* of COLMAR. **II.** *a,* **(de)** abundant, copious; full (of), filled (with). **III.** *m.* specialty eating house (gen. for sea food).
colmar, *va.* **(de)** to heap up, fill to the brim (with); to fulfil, make up; to bestow liberally.
colmena, *f.* beehive.—**colmenar,** *f.* apiary.
colmenero, ra, *n.* beekeeper, beemaster.
colmenilla, *f.* (bot.) morel, an edible mushroom.
colmillada, *f.* attack, or wound, with tusks or fangs.
colmillar, *a.* pert. to eyetooth, fang or tusk.
colmillazo, *m. aug.* large eyetooth; COLMILLADA.
colmillejo, *m. dim.* small eyetooth, fang or tusk.
colmillo, *m.* eyetooth, canine tooth; fang; tusk.—**escupir por el c.,** (coll.) to brag, boast.—**mostrar los colmillos,** (coll.) to show spirit and resolution.—**tener colmillos,** (coll.) to be quick-sighted, not easily imposed upon.
colmilludo, da, *a.* having long eyeteeth, fangs, or tusks; sagacious, quick-sighted.
[1]**colmo,** *m.* heap; finishing, completion, crowning; overmeasure; fill; thatched roof; height (of folly, etc.); acme, extreme.—**a c.,** abundantly, plentifully.—**llegar a c.,** to reach perfection.—**ser el c.,** (coll.) to be the limit.
[2]**colmo, ma,** *a.* heaping full.
colocación, *f.* place, situation, position, employment, job; laying, putting in place; placement; distribution of parts.
colocar. I. *va.* (*pret.* COLOQUÉ; *subj.* COLOQUE) to arrange, put in due place or order; to place, provide with employment, take on (in a job). **II.** *vr.* to take (a job).
colocasia, *f.* (bot.) Egyptian bean.
colocolo, *m.* a handsome S. A. wild cat; (Chile) an imaginary monster hatched from a rotten egg.
colocutor, ra, *n.* one taking part in a conversation.
colodión, *m.* collodion.
colodra, *f.* milk pail; kit; pailful; wooden can for measuring wine; drinking can with a handle; drinking horn with a cork bottom; whetstone case.—**ser una c.,** (coll.) to be a toper.
colodrazgo, *m.* tax on wine sold at retail.
colodrillo, *m.* occiput, nape of the neck.
colofón, *m.* (print.) colophon.
colofonia, *f.* colophony; resin.—**colofonita,** *f.* garnet of a light green or rosy red color.
coloidal, *a.* (chem.) colloidal.
coloide, *m.* & *a.* (chem.) colloid.
coloideo, dea, *a.* colloidal.
Colombia, *f.* Colombia.
colombiano, na, *n.* & *a.* Colombian.
colombino, na, *a.* Columbian, pertaining to Columbus.
[1]**colon,** *m.* (gram.) principal part of a period.
[2]**colon,** *m.* (anat.) colon.
colonato, *m.* system of colonization.
colonche, *m.* (Mex.) an intoxicating drink from the sap of the cactus and sugar.
colonia, *f.* colony; plantation; silk ribbon two fingers wide; (Mex.) extension, development, new quarter (of a town).
coloniaje, *m.* (Am.) colonial period.
colonial, *a.* colonial.
colonialismo, *m.* colonialism.
colonicé, colonice, *v. V.* COLONIZAR.
colónico, ca, *a.* colonic.

colonización, *f.* colonization.
colonizador, ra, *n.* & *a.* colonizer(-ing).
colonizar, *va.* (*pret.* COLONICÉ; *subj.* COLONICE) to colonize, settle.
colono, *m.* colonist, settler; tenant farmer.
coloño, *m.* load of wood carried on the back.
coloqué, coloque, *v. V.* COLOCAR.
coloquíntida, *f.* (bot.) colocynth; bitter apple or gourd.
coloquio, *m.* colloquy, talk.
color, *m.* color; dye, paint; rouge; pretext, pretense, false show or appearance; coloring, tint; complexion; flush, blush; aspect.—**c. muerto,** or **quebrado,** wan or faded color.—**c. vivo,** bright color.—**de c.,** colored.—**sacarle los colores a uno,** to make one blush.—**so c.,** on pretense, under pretext.
coloración, *f.* coloring, coloration, painting.
colorado, da. I. *pp.* of COLORAR. **II.** *a.* ruddy; red; indelicate, smutty; colored; specious.—**poner a uno c.,** to put one to the blush.—**ponerse c.,** to blush.
colorante, *a.* coloring.
colorar, *va.* to dye; to paint, stain, tint, color.
colorativo, va, *a.* coloring, giving color to.
colorear. I. *va.* to make plausible, palliate, excuse. **II.** *vn.* to redden, grow red.
colorete, *m.* rouge.
colorido, da. I. *pp.* of COLORIR. **II.** *a.* colored. **III.** *m.* coloring or color; pretext, pretense.
coloridor, ra, *n.* = COLORISTA.
colorimetría, *f.* colorimetry.
colorimétrico, ca, colorimetric.
colorímetro, *m.* colorimeter.
colorín, *m.* (ornith.) linnet; bright, vivid, loud color.
colorir, *va.* to color artistically; make plausible.
colorista, *m.* (painting) colorist.
colosal, *a.* colossal, huge, gigantic.
colosense, *n.* & *a.* Colossian.
coloso, *m.* colossus.
colostomía, *f.* (surg.) colostomy.
colotipia, *f.* collotype; collotypy.
colpa, *f.* whitish sort of copperas.
colpotomía, *f.* (surg.) colpotomy, incision of the vagina.
colquicina, *f.* (chem.) colchicine.
cólquico, *m.* (bot.) colchicum, meadow saffron.
columbario, *m.* columbarium.
columbino, na, *a.* dovelike, innocent, candid.
columbio, *m.* (chem.) columbium, niobium.
columbrar, *va.* to espy, perceive, discern at a distance; to trace by conjectures.
columelar, *m.* incisor.
columna, *f.* (arch., eng., mil., print.) column, supporter, protector; pile of things; column of air or water.—**c. dorsal,** spine.—**c. miliaria,** milestone.—**c. salomónica,** (arch.) twisted column.—**c. vertebral,** spine.—**columnario, ria,** *a.* columnar (app. to money coined in Sp. Am., with the impressions of two columns).
columnata, *f.* colonnade.
columpiar. I. *va.* to swing. **II.** *vr.* to swing; (coll.) to waddle.
columpio, *m.* swing; seesaw.
coluna, *f.* = COLUMNA.
colunita, *f. dim.* small column.
colurión, *m.* (ornith.) butcher bird, flusher.
coluro, *m.* (astr.) colure.
colusión, *f.* collusion.
colusorio, ria, *a.* collusive.
colutorio, *m.* (pharm.) gargle.
coluvie, *f.* gang of rascals; sewer, sink.
colza, *f.* (bot.) colza, summer rape.
[1]**colla,** *f.* (P. I.) continuous squalls preceding the monsoons; last oakum placed in a seam.
[2]**colla,** *f.* collet, piece of ancient armor; channel of an auger.
collado, *m.* height, fell, hillock.
collar, *m.* necklace; chain or cord from which hang certain insignia of honor; collar, collet.
collareja, *f.* (C. A.) wild pigeon.
collarejo, *m. dim.* small collar or necklace.
collarín, *m.* black neck stock edged with white, worn by the Roman Catholic clergy; collar of a coat; (mech.) tube, sleeve.
collarino, *m.* (arch.) half round, torus.
collazo, *m.* plowman, farmhand, laborer.
colleja, *f.* (bot.) lamb's-lettuce or corn salad.
collejas, *f. pl.* slender nerves in sheep's neck.
collera, *f.* collar, breast harness for draught cattle; horse collar; (naut.) stay of the dead blocks. —*pl.* (Am.) cuff buttons.
collerón, *m.* harness collar, hame.
colleta, *f.* (bot.) a kind of small cabbage.
collón, *m.* (coll.) coward, poltroon, base fellow.
collonada, *f.*, **collonería,** *f.* (coll.) cowardice.
[1]**coma,** *f.* comma; decimal point.
[2]**coma,** *m.* (med.) coma, profound insensibility.
comadre, *f.* midwife; mother or godmother with respect to each other; (coll.) gossip; pal, intimate friend; go-between.
comadrear, *vn.* to gossip, tattle.
comadreja, *f.* weasel.
comadreo, *m.* **comadrería,** *f.* gossip, gossipping.
comadrero, ra, *n.* & *a.* gossip (person), gossipping (person).
comadrón, *m.* obstetrician, accoucheur.
comal, *m.* (Mex.) flat earthenware pan for cooking maize cake.
comalía, comalición, *f.* an epizoötic disease of sheep.
comandado, da, *a.* (mil.) officered.
comandancia, *f.* command; office of a commander; province or district of a commander.—**C. general de Marina,** High Court of Admiralty.
comandanta, *f.* commander's wife.
comandante, *n.* commander, commandant, leader; major, (Colomb.) lieutenant colonel.—**c. en jefe,** commanding officer.
comandar, *va.* (mil.) to command, govern.
comandita, *f.* (com.) silent partnership.
comanditario, a. I. *a.* (com.) pertaining to a silent partnership; silent (partner, partnership). **II.** *n.* (com.) silent partner.
comando, *m.* (mil.) command.—*pl.* controls (of an airplane).
comarca, *f.* territory, region; border, boundary, limit.
comarcano, na, *a.* neighboring, near, bordering.
comarcar. I. *va.* (*pret.* COMARQUÉ; *subj.* COMARQUE) to plant (trees) in a straight line, so as to form walks. **II.** *vn.* to border, to abut (on).
comatoso, sa, *a.* (med.) comatose.
comba, *f.* curvature, warp, bend, bulge; game of jumping or skipping rope; skipping rope.
combadura, *f.* bending, bend, bulging, belly; sag.
combar. I. *va.* to bend, to curve. **II.** *vr.* to warp, bulge, sag.
combate, *m.* combat, fight, battle; agitation of the mind; struggle.
combatible, *a.* combatable, conquerable.
combatidor, ra, *n.* combatant.
combatiente, *n.* & *a.* combatant, fighter(-ing).
combatir, *va.* & *vn.* to combat, fight; to contest, attack, oppose; to struggle.
combatividad, *f.* combativeness.
combeneficiado, *m.* prebendary of the same church as another.
combés, *m.* open space; (naut.) waist of a ship; upper deck.
combinable, *a.* combinable.
combinación, *f.* combination; aggregate of words beginning with the same syllable; concurrence; (chem.) compound; (woman's) slip.
combinador, ra. I. *n.* & *a.* combiner(-ing). **II.** *m.* (elec.) controller (of electric car).
combinar, *va.* & *vr.* to combine, join, unite.
combinatorio, ria, *a.* combining, uniting; combinative; (math.) combinatorial.
combleza, *f.* concubine of a married man.
comblezo, *m.* one who lives in concubinage with a married woman.

combo, ba. **I.** *a.* bent, crooked, warped. **II.** *m.* stand or frame for casks.
comburente, *a.* producing combustion.
combustibilidad, *f.* combustibility.
combustible. **I.** *a.* combustible. **II.** *m.* fuel.
combustible nuclear, *m.* nuclear fuel.
combustión, *f.* combustion.
combusto, ta, *a.* burnt.
comedero, ra. **I.** *a.* eatable, edible. **II.** *m.* feeding trough; dining room, eating place; (Am.) haunt, place frequented by a person.
comedia, *f.* comedy; play, drama; farce; theater. —**c. de capa y espada,** costume play of the seventeenth century.—**c. de costumbres,** drawing-room comedy.—**c. de enredo,** play with a complicated plot.—**c. togada,** ancient Latin play; Grecian or Roman costume play.
comedianta, *f.* comedienne.
comediante, *m.* player, actor, comedian.
comediar, *va.* to divide into equal shares or parts; to average.
comedido, da. **I.** *pp.* of COMEDIRSE. **II.** *a.* civil, polite, courteous; prudent, moderate.
comedimiento, *m.* civility, politeness, kindness; moderation, prudency.
comedio, *m.* center of a realm or place; intermediate time between epochs.
comedión, *m.* long and tedious comedy.
comedirse, *vr.* (*ind.* me COMIDO; *subj.* me COMIDA) to govern oneself; to be moderate, civil, obliging, kind.
comedón, *m.* (med.) comedo.
comedor, ra. **I.** *n.* & *a.* eater(-ing), feeder(-ing). **II.** *m.* dining room.
comején, *m.* (entom.) termite, white ant.
comejenera, *f.* nest of COMEJÉN; (Venez.) disreputable resort.
comencé, *pret.* of COMENZAR.
comendador, *m.* knight commander of a military order; prefect of religious houses.
comendadora, *f.* superior of a nunnery.
comendatario, *m.* (eccl.) one holding a benefice.
comendaticio, cia, *a.* commendatory (letter).
comendatorio, ria, *a.* pertaining to letters of introduction or recommendation.
comendero, *m.* beneficiary of the crown.
comensal, *n.* commensal; member of a household; table companion.
comensalía, *f.* fellowship of house and table.
comentador, ra, *n.* commenter, commentator.
comentar, *va.* to comment.
comentario, *m.* commentary.
comentarista, *n.* commentator.
comento, *m.* comment.
comenzante, *n.* & *a.* beginner(-ing).
comenzar, *va.* & *vn.* (*ind. pres.* COMIENZO, *pret.* COMENCÉ; *subj.* COMIENCE) to commence, begin.
comer. **I.** *vn.* to eat; to feed; to dine.—**c. a dos carrillos,** to enjoy two places or benefices at the same time.—**c. como un sabañón,** (coll.) to eat excessively, to stuff oneself.—**c. de mogollón,** to live at other people's expense; to sponge.—**c.,** or **comerse, vivo,** to devour(fig.); to scalp (fig.); to be very painful or troublesome.—**tener que c.,** to have a competence. **II.** *va.* to eat; to have (an income); to spend, waste, exhaust; to corrode, consume; (of sun) to fade (colors); to take (a piece or checker in a game). **III.** *vr.* to omit, skip; to eat up.—**comerse a uno con los ojos,** to look daggers at one.—**comerse los codos de hambre,** (coll.) to be starved to death.—**comerse unos a otros,** to live like cats and dogs. **IV.** *m.* eating.—**ganar de c.,** to earn a living.
comerciable, *a.* merchantable, marketable; sociable, social, affable.
comercial, *a.* commercial.
comercialización, *f.* commercialization.
comercializar, *va.* to commercialize.
comercialmente, *adv.* commercially.
comerciante, *n.* trader, merchant.—**c. comisionista,** commission merchant.
comerciar, *vn.* to trade, deal; to commerce, have intercourse.
comercio, *m.* trade, commerce, communication, intercourse; unlawful sexual intercourse; tradesmen, body of merchants; business section of a town; store, shop; a card game.—**c. exterior,** foreign trade.—**c. interior,** domestic trade.—**bolsa de c.,** stock exchange.
comestible. **I.** *a.* eatable, edible. **II.** *m. pl.* foodstuffs, provisions.
cometa. **I.** *m.* (astr.) comet.—**c. crinito,** long-bearded comet. **II.** *f.* kite; a card game.
cometario, ria, *a.* (astr.) cometary.
cometedor, ra, *n.* offender, perpetrator.
cometer, *va.* to commit, charge, intrust; to commit, perpetrate; (com.) to order.—**cometido,** *m.* commission; charge, trust; task, duty.
comezón, *f.* itch, itching; longing desire.
comible, *a.* (coll.) eatable, fit to eat.
comicastro, tra, *n.* mediocre or poor actor.
comicial, *a.* comitial.
comicidad, *f.* comicalness.
comicios, *m. pl.* (anc. Rome) comitia; (pol.) primaries, district assemblies.
cómico, ca. **I.** *a.* comic, dramatic, pertaining to the stage; comical, ludicrous, funny. **II.** *n.* player, actor(-tress); writer of comedies.—**c. de la legua,** small-town touring actor, strolling player.
comida, *f.* eating; food, dressed victuals; dinner; meal, fare; feed.—**c. corrida** (Am.) table d'hôte.
comidilla, *f. dim.* slight repast; peculiar fancy, fad, or favorite amusement; hobby.
[1]**comido, da,** *a.* fed; having eaten.—**c. de,** eaten by, -eaten (*comido de gusanos,* worm-eaten).—**c. por servido,** hand-to-mouth wages.
[2]**comido, comida,** *v. V.* COMEDIRSE.
[1]**comienzo,** *m.* beginning, initiation, start.—**dar c.,** to make a beginning, a start.
[2]**comienzo, comience,** *v. V.* COMENZAR.
comilitón, *m.* parasite; fellow soldier.
comilitona, comilona, *f.* (coll.) splendid and plentiful repast.
comilón, na, *n.* great eater, glutton.
comilla, *f. dim.* of [1]COMA.—*pl.* quotation marks (" ").
cominear, *vn.* (coll.) to indulge in trifles or occupations belonging to women.
cominero. **I.** *a.* meddlesome, officious. **II.** *n.* cotquean, man meddling with women's affairs.
cominillo, *m.* (bot.) darnel. Also JOYO.
comino, *m.* (bot.) cumin plant, cumin seed; a Colombian tree producing very valuable construction and cabinet wood.—**no valer un c.,** not to be worth a rush.
comisar, *va.* to confiscate, sequestrate, attach.
comisaría, *f.,* commissaryship, commissariat.
comisariato, *m.* COMISARÍA; (Am.) police station.
comisario, *m.* commissary; delegate, deputy; manager.—**c. de barrio,** or **cuartel,** justice of the peace of a ward.—**c. de entradas,** in hospitals, the person that keeps an account of the patients who enter.—**c. de guerra,** (mil.) reviewing officer.—**c. de policía,** (Mex., Cuba, Arg.) chief of police.—**c. ordenador,** (mil.) assistant quartermaster.
comisión, *f.* trust; commission, assignment; mandate, charge; precept, order; ministration, ministry; committee; commission, perpetration.
comisionado, da. **I.** *pp.* of COMISIONAR. **II.** *a.* commissional or commissionary; commissioned, deputed, empowered. **III.** *n.* commissioner; (com.) agent; proxy, attorney.
comisionar, *va.* to commission, depute, empower, appoint.
comisionista, *m.* commissioner; commission merchant; commission agent.
comiso, *m.* (law) confiscation of prohibited goods; the goods when confiscated; (law) seizure, attachment.

comisorio, ria. *a.* obligatory for a time or valid for a fixed day.
comistión, *f.* = CONMISTIÓN, commixture.
comistrajo, *m.* (coll.) hodge-podge, mess.
comisura, *f.* (anat.) commissure; suture.
comital, *a.* = CONDAL, of an earldom.
comité, *m.* committee; commission.—**c. de timón, de orientación** or **de iniciativas,** steering committee.
comitente, *n.* & *a.* constituent.
comitiva, *f.* suite, retinue; party, group.
cómitre, *m.* (naut.) boatswain on board a galley; sea captain under orders of the admiral of the fleet.
comiza, *f.* (ichth.) a kind of barbel.
como. I. *adv.* how; in what manner; to what degree; as; like; about, approximately, a sort of; if; as soon as; in the same manner as; so that; such as; that; inasmuch as.—**c. que,** apparently, it seems that.—**c. quien no quiere la cosa,** unconcernedly.—**c. quiera que,** although; since. **II.** *interrog.* **cómo,** what? how? why?—**¿cómo?** what is it? what did you say? —**¿cómo así?** how? how so?—**¿cómo no?** why not? of course, naturally.—**¿a c.,** how much?—**¿a c. estamos?** what is the date? **III.** *interj.* why, is it possible?
cómoda, *f.* chest of drawers; bureau.
comodable, *a.* (law) that can be lent or borrowed.
comodante, *n.* (law) one who lends gratuitously for a limited time.
comodatario, ria, *n.* (law) borrower; pawnbroker.
comodato, *m.* loan; (law) contract of loan and restitution.
comodidad, *f.* comfort, convenience; ease, freedom from want; leisure; opportunity; profit, interest, advantage.
comodín, *m.* (coll.) something of general utility; in cards, a card that has different values.
cómodo, da. I. *a.* convenient, handy, suitable; comfortable. **II.** *m.* utility, profit; convenience.
comodoro, *m.* (naut.) commodore.
compactibilidad, *f.* compactness.
compacto, ta, *a.* compact, close, dense.
compadecer. I. *va.* (*ind.* COMPADEZCO; *subj.* COMPADEZCA) to pity, sympathize with. **II.** *vr.* to agree with each other, accord, conform; **(de)** to pity, sympathize (with).
compadraje, *m.* confederacy or alliance for mutual protection and advancement (gen used in a bad sense); ring, clique.
compadrar, *vn.* to become a godfather or -mother; to contract a spiritual affinity.
compadrazgo, *m.* COMPADRAJE; state of being COMPADRES.
compadre, *m.* godfather and father of a child, each with respect to the other; protector, benefactor; (coll.) friend, old chap (an expression of familiarity).—**compadrear,** *vn.* (coll.) to be on familiar terms.—**compadrería,** *f.* friendship between COMPADRES, companions, pals.—**compadrito,** *m. dim.* of COMPADRE; (Am.) boaster.
compaginación, *f.* arrangement, connection.
compaginador, ra, *n.* arranger, adjuster.
compaginar, *va.* to arrange in proper order; to unite, join.
companage, compango, *m.* cold cuts or lunch.
compaña, *f.* (obs.) family; company.
compañerismo, *m.* good fellowship, comradeship.
compañero, ra, *n.* companion, friend, pal, comrade, chum; fellow member; partner or associate; mate.—**c. de fórmula,** running mate.
compañía, *f.* company; society; partnership; co-partnership; (mil.) company; theatrical company.—**c. anónima,** stock company.—**c. comanditaria** or **en comandita,** limited partnership.—**c. cooperativa,** coöperative.—**c. de Jesús,** Society of Jesus.—**c. de la legua,** strolling company of players.—**c. fiduciaria** or **fideicomisaria,** trust company.—**c. mutual,** mutual company.—**hacer c. a,** to keep (someone) company.
comparabilidad, *f.* comparability.
comparable, *a.* comparable.
comparación, *f.* comparison.
comparador, *m.* comparing rule; comparer.
comparar, *va.* to compare; to confront, collate.
comparativo, va, *a.* comparative.
comparecencia, *f.* (law) appearance (in court).
comparecer, *vn.* (*ind.* COMPAREZCO; *subj.* COMPAREZCA) (law) to appear (before a judge, etc.).
compareciente, *n.* & *a.* (law) (one) that appears (before a judge, etc.)
comparendo, *m.* summons, citation.
comparezco, comparezca, *v. V.* COMPARECER.
comparición, *f.* (law) appearance.
comparsa. I. *f.* (theat.) retinue of personages; masquerade in carnival. **II.** *m.* & *f.* (theat.) supernumerary.
comparte, *n.* (law) joint party; accomplice.
compartimiento, *m.* compartment; division of a whole into parts; inclosure, department; (aer.) curtain (of a dirigible).
compartir, *va.* to divide into equal parts; to share.
comparto, *m.* (Colomb.) tax, contribution.
compás, *m.* compasses; dividers; calipers; territory and district assigned to a monastery; (mus.) measure, time, motion of the baton of a conductor; space on the staff between two bars; size, compass; rule of life, standard, pattern; springs of a coach roof.—**c. de barra,** beam compass.—**c. de calibres,** calipers.—**c. de división,** dividers.—**c. de espesores,** or **de gruesos,** spring calipers; thickness gage.—**c. de mar,** or **de marear,** mariner's compass.—**c. de proporción,** proportional dividers.—**c. de puntas secas,** or **de punta fija,** dividers. —**c. de regla,** beam compass.—**c. ternario,** (mus.) triple time.—**a c.,** (mus.) in time.—**a c. con,** keeping time with; in line or harmony with.—**llevar el c.,** (mus.) to keep or beat time.
compasadamente, *adv.* by rule and measure.
compasar, *va.* to measure with a rule and compass; to arrange properly; (mus.) to divide (a score) into equal parts.—**c. la carta de marear,** (naut.) to prick the chart.
compasible, *a.* pitiful; compassionate.
compasillo, *m.* (mus.) quadruple, or $\frac{4}{4}$ time.
compasión, *f.* compassion, pity, sympathy.—**tener c. de,** to take pity on, show mercy to.
compasivo, va, *a.* compassionate, merciful, tender-hearted.
compaternidad, *f.* = COMPADRAZGO, relationship between father and godfather of a child.
compatibilidad, *f.* compatibility.
compatible, *a.* compatible, suitable, consistent.
compatiblemente, *adv.* compatibly.
compatricio, cia; compatriota, *n.* countryman (countrywoman), compatriot, fellow citizen.
compatrón, *m.* = COMPATRONO.
compatronato, *m.* common right of patronage.
compatrono, na, *n.* fellow patron or patroness, joint patron.
compeler, *va.* to compel, force, constrain.
compendiador, ra, *n.* epitomizer, abridger.
compendiar, *va.* to abridge, condense.
compendiariamente, *adv.* briefly.
compendio, *m.* compendium, epitome, abridgment, summary, abstract.
compendioso, sa, *a.* brief; abridged, concise; compact.
compendizar, *va.* = COMPENDIAR.
compenetración, *f.* compenetration.
compenetrarse, *vr.* to pervade, intermix; to harmonize, be in full agreement.—**c. de,** to be thoroughly informed about; to be fully convinced of.
compensable, *a.* compensable.

compensación, *f.* compensation; recompense, reward.—**de c.,** compensating.
compensador, ra. I. *a.* compensated; balanced. **II.** *m.* compensator; compensating pendulum.
compensar, *va.* & *vn.* to compensate, recompense; to counterbalance; to balance, equilibrate; to make amends for, indemnify.
compensativo, va. I. *a.* compensating. **II.** *m.* (chem.) compensation.
compensatorio, ria, *a.* compensating.
competencia, *f.* competition, rivalry; competence; cognizance.—**a c.,** competitively.
competente, *a.* competent, apt, able; consistent (with); applicable (to); adequate.
competer, *vn.* to be one's business or concern, to be incumbent on.
competición, *f.* competition.
competidor, ra. I. *n.* competitor, rival, opponent. **II.** *a.* competing.
competir, *vn.* (*ind.* COMPITO; *subj.* COMPITA) to vie, contest, contend, compete; to be on a level or par with another.
compilación, *f.* compilation; compilement.
compilador, ra, *n.* compiler; collector.
compilar, *va.* to compile.
compinche, *m.* (coll.) bosom friend, comrade, chum, crony, pal.
compito, compita, *v. V.* COMPETIR.
complacedero, ra, *a.* = COMPLACIENTE.
complacencia, *f.* pleasure, satisfaction; complacency, compliance, condescension.
complacer. I. *va.* (*ind.* COMPLAZCO; *subj.* COMPLAZCA) to please, humor, accommodate. **II.** *vr.* (**en**) to be pleased (with or to), to delight (in), to take pleasure (in).—**complaciente,** *a.* pleasing, accommodating, kind, agreeable.
complazco, complazca, *v. V.* COMPLACER.
complejidad, *f.* complexity.
complejo, ja. I. *a.* complex. **II.** *m.* complex; (psych.) complex.—**c. de Edipo,** Oedipus complex.—**c. de inferioridad,** inferiority complex. —**c. de superioridad,** superiority complex.
complementario, ia, *a.* complementary; completing, perfecting.
complemento, *m.* complement; perfection; completion; (gram.) complement, object.
completar, *va.* to complete, perfect, finish.
completas, *f. pl.* (eccl.) compline.
completivo, va, *a.* completive, completing, finishing.
completo, ta, *a.* complete, perfect; finished, completed; full; absolute.—**por c.,** completely.
complexión, *f.* constitution, nature, complexion.
complexionado, da, *a.* constituted.—**bien c.,** of strong constitution.—**mal c.,** of weak constitution.
complexional, *a.* constitutional, temperamental.
complexo, xa. I. *a.* complex. **II.** *m.* (anat.) complexus.
complicación, *f.* complication.
complicado, da, *a.* complicated.
complicar, *va.* (*pret.* COMPLIQUÉ; *subj.* COMPLIQUE) to complicate; to jumble together.
cómplice, *m.* & *f.* accomplice.
complicidad, *f.* complicity.
compliqué, complique, *v. V.* COMPLICAR.
complot, *m.* plot, conspiracy.
componedor, ra. I. *n.* compositor, typesetter; writer, author; composer; contriver; repairer; arbitrator. **II.** *m.* (print.) composing stick.
componenda, *f.* fees paid for documents and licenses; arbitration; compromise; settlement.
componente, *n.* & *a.* component.
componer. I. *va.* (*pp.* COMPUESTO; *ind. pres.* COMPONGO, *fut.* COMPONDRÉ, *pret.* COMPUSE; *subj.* COMPONGA) to compose; compound; construct; prepare; amount to; devise, invent; to mend, repair; heal, restore; to strengthen, brace, fortify; to trim, fit up, garnish; to compose (differences), reconcile, adjust, settle; to ward off; to compose (music); to write (poetry, etc.); (print.) to compose.—**c. el semblante,** to put on a calm appearance.—**c. tanto de renta,** to have so much a year. **II.** *vr.* to prink, "doll up"; to compose, calm, quiet oneself.—**componérselas,** to shift for oneself.
compongo, componga, *v. V.* COMPONER.
componible, *a.* mendable, capable of repair; adjustable, that may be settled or compounded.
comporta, *f.* large basket for grape gathering.
comportable, *a.* bearable, endurable.
comportamiento, *m.* behavior, deportment.
comportar. I. *va.* to suffer, tolerate. **II.** *vr.* to comport, behave oneself.—**comporte,** *m.* behaviour, conduct; air, manner, carriage.
comportería, *f.* trade and shop of a COMPORTERO.
comportero, ra, *n.* maker or seller of COMPORTAS.
comportilla, *f. dim.* small basket.
composición, *f.* composition; repair, mending; making up, compromise, adjustment; (print.) composition; (fig.) composure; calm, modest, or sedate appearance.
compositivo, va, *a.* compositive, synthetic.
compositor, ra, *n.* composer (of music).
compostura, *f.* composure; mending, repair, repairing; cleanliness, neatness of dress; adjustment, settlement, compromise; modesty, circumspection, sedateness; adulterating compound.
compota, *f.* compote, stewed fruit; preserves.
compotera, *f.* compotier.
compra, *f.* purchase; buying, shopping.—**hacer compras,** to shop.—**ir de compras,** to go shopping.
comprable; compradero, ra; compradizo, za, *a.* purchasable.
comprado, compradillo, *m.* play in the game of ombre.
comprador, ra; comprante, *n.* buyer; purchaser; shopper; caterer.
comprar, *va.* to buy, purchase; to shop.
compraventa.—contrato de c., contract of sale.
comprehensivo, va, *a.* comprehensive.
comprendedor, ra, *a.* including; understanding.
comprender, *va.* to embrace, comprise, include, cover; to understand, comprehend.
comprensibilidad, *f.* intelligibility, comprehensibility.
comprensible, *a.* comprehensible, understandable.
comprensión, *f.* comprehension, understanding; comprehensiveness; act of comprising or containing.
comprensividad, *f.* understandability, quality of being understandable; understanding.
comprensivo, va, *a.* comprehensive; capable of understanding; comprising, containing.
comprensor, ra, *a.* & *n.* (one) that understands, attains or embraces; (theol.) blessed (one).
compresa, *f.* (surg.) compress.
compresbítero, *m.* fellow presbyter or priest.
compresibilidad, *f.* compressibility.
compresible, *a.* compressible.
compresión, *f.* compression; (gram.) synizesis.
compresivo, va, *a.* compressive, compressing, reducing, compacting.
compreso, *pp. irreg.* of COMPRIMIR.
compresor, ra, *n.* & *a.* compressor(-ing).—**c. de aire,** air compressor.
comprimente, *a.* compressing; restraining.
comprimible, *a.* compressible; repressible.
comprimir. I. *va.* (*pp.* COMPRIMIDO, COMPRESO) to compress, condense; to repress, restrain. **II.** *vr.* to become compact; to control oneself.
comprobación, *f.* verification, checking; proof, substantiation; (print.) checking up of proof corrections.
comprobante. I. *a.* proving, evidential. **II.** *m.* proof, evidence; voucher.
comprobar, *va.* (*ind.* COMPRUEBO; *subj.* COMPRUEBE) to verify, confirm, check; to compare; to prove, substantiate, evidence.
comprofesor, *m.* colleague in a profession.
comprometedor, ra. I. *a.* compromising, jeopardizing. **II.** *n.* one that jeopardizes.

comprometer. **I.** *va.* to compromise, arbitrate; to engage, bind; to render accountable or answerable; to risk; to expose, jeopardize, endanger. **II.** *vr.* to commit oneself; to undertake; to become liable; to bind oneself; to expose oneself; to become engaged, betrothed; to become involved.
comprometimiento, *m.* pledge, promise; adjustment; jeopardy, embarrassment, predicament.
compromisario, ria, *n.* arbitrator, umpire, referee; presidential elector.
compromiso, *m.* compromise, arbitration; pledge, obligation; commitment; jeopardy, embarrassment, predicament; engagement, betrothal; engagement, appointment.
compromisorio, ria, *a.* pertaining to an agreement, promise, or pledge.
compropietario, ia, *n.* joint owner.
comprovincial, *a.* comprovincial, of the same metropolitan church.
comprovinciano, na, *a.* from the same province.
compruebo, compruebe, *v.* *V.* COMPROBAR.
compuerta, *f.* hatch or half-door; lock, sluice, floodgate; door curtain of an old-fashioned coach; piece of cloth bearing a knight's badge. —**c. de marea,** (naut.) tide gate, tiderace.
compuestamente, *adv.* regularly, orderly.
compuesto, a. **I.** *pp.* of COMPONER. **II.** *a.* compound; composed, consisting, made up; repaired; arranged. **III.** *m.* compound, preparation, mixture; (gram.) compound.
compulsa, *f.* (law) authentic or attested copy of an instrument or writing duly compared.
compulsar, *va.* (law) to make an authentic copy or transcript of; to compare, collate.
compulsión, *f.* compulsion.
compulsivo, va, *a.* compulsive.
compulsorio, ria, *n.* compulsory decree of a court, ordering an authentic copy to be made.
compunción, *f.* compunction, repentance.
compungido, da, *a.* compunctious, repentant.
compungirse, *vr.* (*ind.* COMPUNJO; *subj.* COMPUNJA) to feel compunction or remorse.
compungivo, va, *a.* pricking, stinging.
compurgación, *f.* (law) compurgation.
compurgador, ra, *n.* (law) compurgator.
compurgar, *va.* (law) to prove (one's veracity or innocence) by the oath of another.
compuse, *pret.* of COMPONER.
computación, *f.* computation, calculation.
computador, ra, *n.* computer.
computador analógico, *m.* analogue computer.
computar, *va.* to compute, calculate.
computista, *m.* computist, computer.
cómputo, *m.* computation, calculation.
comulación, *f.* cumulation.
comulgante, *n.* (eccl.) communicant.
comulgar. **I.** *va.* (*pret.* COMULGUÉ; *subj.* COMULGUE) to administer communion.—**c. con ruedas de molino,** to fool, bamboozle, humbug. **II.** *vn.* to commune, communicate; to take communion.
comulgatorio, *m.* communion altar.
común. **I.** *a.* common, public; common, usual customary, ordinary, generally or extensively used; current; vulgar, mean, low.—**c. de dos,** (gram.) that applies to both genders.—**c. de tres,** (gram.) that applies to masculine, feminine, and neuter.—**en c.,** in common.—**por lo c.,** in general, generally. **II.** *m.* community; toilet, water closet.—**c. de las gentes,** the general public, the average person, the man in the street.
comuna, *f.* main irrigation channel; Commune (of Paris); (Am.) municipality.
comunal. **I.** *m.* commonalty, common people. **II.** *a.* common, commonable.
comunero, ra. **I.** *a.* popular, common, pleasing to the people. **II.** *n.* commoner, one of the common people; joint holder of a tenure of lands; member of the party that upheld liberty against the encroachments of Charles V.; (Colomb.) member of the body of first patriots that rose against Spanish rule.
comunicabilidad, *f.* communicability.
comunicable, *a.* communicable; communicative.
comunicación, *f.* communication, intercourse; communiqué, official statement.—*pl.* means of communication.
comunicado, *m.* article of a personal nature sent to a periodical for publication.
comunicante, *n.* one who communicates (something).
comunicar. **I.** *va.* (*pret.* COMUNIQUÉ; *subj.* COMUNIQUE) to communicate, impart, make known; to announce; to transmit, send. **II.** *vr.* to communicate; to connect.—**c. entre sí,** to communicate with each other; to correspond, exchange correspondence; to be in mutual communication.
comunicativo, va, *a.* communicative; unreserved, informative.
comunicatorio, ria, *a.* communicatory.
comunidad, *f.* commonness; commonalty, the common people; community; corporation, guild, society.—*pl.* the cities of Castile which rose in support of Spanish liberty against the government of Charles V.—**de c.,** conjointly.
comunión, *f.* communion; fellowship; familiar intercourse; congregation; political party.
comuniqué, comunique, *v.* *V.* COMUNICAR.
comunismo, *m.* communism.
comunista, *n.* & *a.* communist(-ic).
comunizar, *va.* & *vn.* to teach communism to, or make a communist of; to become a communist.
comúnmente, *adv.* commonly, usually, generally; frequently, often.
comuña, *f.* mixed wheat and rye, maslin, or meslin.—**comuñas,** seeds.
con, *prep.* with; by (when followed by infinitive: *con confesar se salvó,* by confessing, he saved himself); in other infinitive phrases, it simply indicates action, and the phrase is translated by Eng. *pres.p.* or *inf.* used as a noun (*con escribir basta,* writing is enough); notwithstanding, despite (also in infinitive phrases: *con ser muy enérgico, nada pudo hacer,* notwithstanding his being very energetic, he could do nothing); in (*con dolor,* in pain). With the pronouns *mí, sí, ti,* it forms the single words **conmigo,** with me, **consigo,** with himself, **contigo,** with thee.—**c. tal que,** provided that.—**c. que,** and so, then, so then.—**c. todo,** nevertheless, notwithstanding.—**para c.,** towards, in (one's) relations with.
conato, *m.* endeavour, effort, exertion; (law) crime attempted but not committed, attempt.
concadenar, *va.* to concatenate; to chain or link together.
concambio, *m.* exchange.
concanónigo, *m.* fellow canon.
concatedralidad, *f.* union of two cathedral churches.
concatenación, *f.* concatenation.
concatenar, *va.* to concatenate.
concausa, *f.* concause, joint cause.
cóncava, *f.* a hollow, cavity.
concavidad, *f.* concavity, hollowness; CÓNCAVA.
cóncavo, va. **I.** *a.* concave. **II.** *m.* concavity.
cóncavo-cóncavo, va, *a.* concavo-concave.
cóncavo-convexo, xa, *a.* concavo-convex.
concebible, *a.* mentally conceivable.
concebir, *va.* & *vn.* (*ind.* CONCIBO; *subj.* CONCIBA) to conceive, become pregnant; to conceive, have an idea of; to comprehend, understand.
concedente, *n.*, *a.* granter(-ing), conceder(-ing).
conceder, *va.* to give, bestow, grant; to concede, admit.
concedido, da, *a.* conceded, granted.
concejal, *m.* councilman.
concejil, *a.* pertaining to the municipal council; common, public, belonging to the public.
concejo, *m.* civic body of a small town; board of aldermen; municipal council; town hall; in Asturias, a district composed of several parishes with one common jurisdiction; foundling.

concento, *m.* concert of voices, harmony.
concentración, *f.* concentration.
concentrado, da. I. *pp.* of CONCENTRAR. **II.** *a.* concentered, concentrate.
concentrador, ra, *n.* concentrator.
concentrar. I. *va.* to concentrate; to concenter. **II.** *vr.* to concentrate.
concentricidad, *f.* concentricity.
concéntrico, ca, *a.* concentric.
concepción, *f.* conception, act of conceiving; idea; immaculate conception of the Virgin; feast of the Immaculate Conception; Madonna, picture of the Virgin.
conceptáculo, *m.* (bot.) conceptacle.
concepteаr, *vn.* to give smart repartees.
conceptible, *a.* conceivable.
conceptismo, *m.* exaggerated witticism.
conceptista, *m.* one who overdoes witticism.
concepto, *m.* concept, thought, idea; pithy sentence, epigram, flash of wit; judgment, opinion; expression of opinion; (com.) item, article; account.—**por c. de,** resulting from.
conceptual, *a.* conceptual.
conceptualismo, *m.* conceptualism.
conceptualista, *a.* conceptualistic.
conceptuar, *va.* to conceive; to judge, think, form an opinion of.
conceptuoso, sa, *a.* witty, sententious, epigrammatic.
concernencia, *f.* respect, concernment, relation.
concerniente, *a.* (a) concerning, relating (to); applicable.—**en lo c. a,** with regard to, as for. —**lo c.,** what concerns the matter, the proper action, consideration, etc.
concernir, *v. defect.* (*ind.* ello CONCIERNE; *subj.* ello CONCIERNA) (a) to concern, belong, appertain, be the business (of).
concertadamente, *adv.* regularly, orderly, methodically, concertedly; by agreement or appointment.
concertado, da. I. *pp.* of CONCERTAR. **II.** *a.* concerted.—**mampostería c.,** (mason.) rubble work.
concertador, *m.* regulator, adjuster, expediter.
concertante, *a.* (mus.) concerted, arranged for two or more voices or instruments.
concertar. I. *va.* (*ind.* CONCIERTO; *subj.* CONCIERTE) to arrange by agreement, adjust, harmonize, to agree on; to bargain, covenant, conclude (an agreement); close (a deal); to put in tune (musical instruments); to compare, estimate the relative qualities of; (shooting) to start or rouse (the game). **II.** *vn.* to agree, accord, suit one another; (gram.) to agree. **III.** *vr.* to go hand in hand; to covenant; to contrive, design.
concertina, *f.* concertina, a musical instrument similar to the accordion.
concertino, *m.* (mus.) concertmaster.
concertista, *n.* person who manages or performs in concerts.
concesible, *a.* grantable.
concesión, *f.* concession, grant.
concesionario, *m.* (law) grantee, concessionary.
concesivo, va, *a.* that may be granted.
concia, *f.* prohibited part of a forest.
concibo, conciba, *v. V.* CONCEBIR.
conciencia, *f.* conscience; conscientiousness; scruples; consciousness.—**a c.,** conscientiously; painstakingly.—**en c.,** in good faith, in truth. —**libertad de c.,** freedom of worship.
concienzudo, da, *a.* conscientious, scrupulous, thorough.
concierne, concierna, *v. V.* CONCERNIR.
[1]**concierto,** *m.* good order and arrangement; concert; bargain; agreement; contract; act of beating the wood with hounds to start the game; musical concert; concerto, a musical composition.—**de c.,** by agreement.
[2]**concierto, concierte,** *v. V.* CONCERTAR.
conciliable, *a.* reconcilable, capable of conciliation.
conciliábulo, *m.* conventicle; unlawful assembly or meeting.
conciliación, *f.* conciliation; settlement (of disputes); affinity; winning (esteem, favor, etc.).
conciliador, ra, *n.* & *a.* conciliator(-ing), peacemaker(-ing), reconciler(-ing).
[1]**conciliar,** *va.* to conciliate, compose, reconcile; to gain, win (affection, esteem).—**c. el sueño,** to induce sleep.—**c. las amistades,** to make friends.
[2]**conciliar. I.** *a.* conciliar, pertaining to councils. **II.** *n.* member of a council.
conciliativo, va, *a.* conciliating.
conciliatorio, ria, *a.* conciliatory.
concilio, *m.* council; collection of decrees.
concisión, *f.* conciseness.
conciso, sa, *a.* concise.
concitación, *f.* instigation, stirring up.
concitador, ra, *n.* instigator, incitor, agitator.
concitar, *va.* to excite, stir up, agitate.
concitativo, va, *a.* inciting; stirring.
conciudadano, *m.* fellow citizen, countryman.
conclave, cónclave, *m.* conclave; place for a conclave; meeting, convention.—**conclavista,** *m.* conclavist; domestic of a cardinal.
concluir, *va.* (*ind.* CONCLUYO; *subj.* CONCLUYA) to conclude, end, finish, close; to convince with reason, make evident, silence by argument; to decide finally, determine; to infer, deduce; to close (judicial proceedings); to submit to a final decision; (fencing) to disarm (an adversary) by engaging the guard of his sword.
conclusión, *f.* conclusion, end; winding up, denouement; close or closure; date; issue; conclusion of the proceedings in a lawsuit; conclusion, inference, deduction, consequence; thesis in schools.—**en c.,** finally, in conclusion; in closing.
conclusivo, va, *a.* conclusive, final.
concluso, sa, *a.* concluded, closed, terminated.
concluyente, *a.* concluding, conclusive; unanswerable.—**concluyentemente,** *adv.* conclusively.
concluyo, conluya, *v. V.* CONCLUIR.
concofrade, *m.* fellow member, brother (of a brotherhood).
concoide, *f.* (geom.) conchoid.
concoideo, a, *a.* (min.) conchoidal, shell-like.
concolega, *m.* fellow collegian.
concomerse, *vr.* (coll.) to shrug the shoulders.
concomido, concomimiento, *m.* (coll.) shrugging of the shoulders.
concomitancia, *f.* concomitance.
concomitante, *a.* concomitant, accompanying.
concomitar, *va.* to accompany, be a concomitant of, go with.
concordable, *a.* concordant, conformable, agreeable, consistent.
concordación, *f.* coördination, conformity.
concordador, ra, *n.* conciliator, peacemaker, moderator.
concordancia, *f.* concordance, conformity; harmony, concord of sounds; concordance of text or words; (gram.) concord, agreement.—*pl.* concordance (of a book, an author).
concordante, *a.* concordant, agreeing.
concordar. I. *va.* (*ind.* CONCUERDO; *subj.* CONCUERDE) to accord, regulate; to make agree. **II.** *vn.* to accord, agree, tally; to be congenial; to be in accord; (gram.) to agree.
concordata, *f.*, **concordato,** *m.* concordat, covenant made by a government with the Pope.
concordatorio, ria, *a.* concordat (as *a.*); of a, or the, concordat.
concorde, *a.* concordant, agreeing, tallying, in agreement.—**concordemente,** *adv.* with one accord, in agreement, concordably.
concordia, *f.* concord, conformity, harmony; agreement, settlement out of court; peace, good will.—**de c.,** jointly, by common consent.
concorpóreo, rea, *a.* (eccl.) becoming (through the Eucharist) of the same body with Christ.
concreción, *f.* concretion.

concrecionar, *vn.* & *vr.* to form concretions.
concrescencia, *f.* concrescence.
concretar. I. *va.* to unite, harmonize, bring into conformity; to reduce to its simplest form; to express concretely. **II.** *vr.* to limit or confine oneself (to a subject).
concreto, ta. I. *a.* concrete, not abstract; definite.—**en c.,** concretely; in brief, in so many words. **II.** *m.* concretion; (erroneously but commonly) concrete (building material) (properly, HORMIGÓN).
concubina, *f.* concubine, mistress.
concubinario, *m.* one who keeps a mistress.
concubinato, *m.* concubinage.
concúbito, *m.* coition.
concuerdo, concuerde, *v. V.* CONCORDAR.
conculcación, *f.* violation (of rights).
conculcador, ra, *n.* violator (of rights), oppressor.
conculcar, *va.* (*pret.* CONCULQUÉ; *subj.* CONCULQUE) to trample underfoot; to violate, infringe.
concuñado, da, *n.* brother- or sister-in-law, term confined to persons who are married to two brothers or sisters.
concupiscencia, *f.* concupiscence, lust, cupidity.
concupiscente, *a.* concupiscent.
concupiscible, *a.* concupiscible, exciting desire.
concurrencia, *f.* audience; attendance; concurrence, coincidence; competition.
concurrente, *a.* concurrent; coincident.
concurrido, da. I. *pp.* of CONCURRIR. **II.** *a.* frequented; (of a meeting, etc.) attended.
concurrir, *vn.* to concur; to meet in one point, time, or place; to attend; to contribute; to coincide, agree; to compete (in an examination, etc.)
concursar, *va.* (law) to declare insolvent.
concurso, *m.* concourse, confluence of persons; conflux, crowd, congregation, assembly; aid, assistance; call for bids (on a piece of work, a service, etc.); competitive contest between candidates for a professorship, curacy, etc.—**c. de acreedores,** meeting of creditors.
concusión, *f.* concussion, shaking, shock; exaction, extortion.
concusionario, ia. I. *a.* concussive, shaking. **II.** *n.* extortioner.
concha, *f.* shell, case, carapace; mollusk, shellfish; tortoise shell; any object that has the shape of a shell; prompter's box; bay in the shape of a horseshoe; basin; fixed grindstone in mills; ancient copper coin, worth about three farthings; (arch.) volute; conch; the external ear; shell of a dagger or cutlass; shell-shaped covering of the spike of Indian corn.—**c. de cabrestante,** (naut.) socket of the capstan.—**c. de nácar,** mother-of-pearl shell.—**conchas de escobenes,** (naut.) navel woods or navel hoods.—**meterse en su c.,** to become a recluse; to shut up like a clam.—**tener muchas conchas,** to be very reserved, artful, cunning.
conchabanza, *f.* manner of making oneself easy and comfortable; (coll.) plotting, conspiracy.
conchabar. I. *va.* to join, unite; to mix (inferior wool with superior); (Am.) to employ (gen. in domestic service). **II.** *vr.* to unite for some evil purpose; to plot, conspire.—**conchabo,** *m.* (Am.) work, job (gen. in domestic service).
conchado, da, *a.* scaly, shelly.
conchal, *a.*—**seda c.,** finest silk from choice cocoons.
conchífero, ra, *a.* conchiferous, shell-bearing.
conchil, *m.* rock shell; murex.
conchilla, ita, *f. dim.* small shell.
conchudo, da, *a.* shelly, scaly; cunning, crafty, reserved; cautious.
conchuela, *f. dim.* = CONCHILLA.
condado, *m.* earldom, county; dignity of a count or earl.
condal, *a.* pert. to the dignity of an earl or count.
conde, *m.* earl, count; overseer; elected head or chief of the gipsies.
condecente, *a.* convenient, fit, proper.
condecoración, *f.* decoration, embellishing or decorating; jewelled insignia of knighthood; medal; badge.
condecorar, *va.* to decorate, adorn, embellish; to bestow honors on; to bestow a medal or insignia on; to knight.
condena, *f.* court clerk's attestation of sentence imposed; sentence, term of imprisonment.
condenación, *f.* condemnation; sentence to penalty; conviction (of a criminal); punishment; damnation.
condenado, da, *a.* damned, condemned to eternal punishment; condemned; convicted.
condenador, ra, *n.* & *a.* condemner(-ing), blamer(-ing), incriminator(-ing).
condenar. I. *va.* to prove, find or declare guilty, convict; to sentence; to damn; to condemn, censure, blame; to disapprove; to nail or wall up (a door, window, passage); to condemn as unsafe. **II.** *vr.* to condemn oneself, acknowledge one's fault; to be damned (to hell).
condenatorio, ria, *a.* condemnatory, damnatory.
condensabilidad, *f.* condensability.
condensación, *f.* condensation.
condensado, *m.* condensate.
condensador, ra. I. *a.* condensing. **II.** *m.* (steam eng., elec.) condenser.—**c. de chorro,** (steam eng.) jet condenser.—**c. de mezcla,** (steam eng.) mixing condenser.—**c. de placas,** (elec.) plate condenser.—**c. de superficie,** (steam eng.) surface condenser.
condensante, *a.* condensing.
condensar. I. *va.* to thicken, condense, compress. **II.** *vr.* to be condensed; to gather.
condensativo, va, *a.* condensative.
condesa, *f.* countess.
condescendencia, *f.* compliance.
condescender, *vn.* (*ind.* CONDESCIENDO; *subj.* CONDESCIENDA) to yield, submit, comply.
condescendiente, *a.* agreeable, complaisant.
condesciendo, condescienda. *v. V.* CONDESCENDER.
condesita, *f. dim.* little or young countess.
condesito, *m. dim.* little earl; little count.
condesil, *a.* (coll.) pert. to counts or countesses.
condestable, *m.* constable; lord high constable; (naut.) master gunner.
condestablía, *f.* constableship.
condición, *f.* condition, quality, state; footing; habit, disposition, temper; constitution; quality; rank, class; fashion; clause, stipulation, specification.—**c. callada,** tacit condition, condition understood.—**c. imposible de derecho,** provision or stipulation contrary to the law.—**c. imposible de hecho,** physically impossible provision, provision impossible per se, or de facto.—**c. sine qua non,** condition sine qua non, or absolutely indispensable.—**a c. de que,** or **con la c. de que,** on condition that.—**de c.,** of importance, of high rank.—**de c. que,** so as to.—**estar en condiciones de,** to be in condition to.—**tener c.,** to be rude or ill-tempered.
condicionado, da. I. *pp.* of CONDICIONAR. **II.** *a.* conditioned; conditional.
condicional, *a.* conditional.
condicionalmente, *adv.* conditionally.
condicionamiento, *m.* conditioning.
condicionar, *vn.* to agree, accord; to impose conditions.
condicioncilla, ita, *f. dim.* hasty temper; small clause or stipulation.
condignamente, *adv.* deservedly, duly.
condigno, na, *a.* condign, suitable, deserved, due, merited.
cóndilo, *m.* (anat.) condyle.
condimentar, *va.* to dress or season (foods).
condimento, *m.* condiment, seasoning.
condiscípulo, *m.* schoolmate, fellow student.
condolencia, *f.* condolence.
condolerse, *vr.* (*ind.* CONDUELO; *subj.* CONDUELA)

(de) to condole (with), to be sorry (for), to sympathize (with); to regret.
condominio, *m.* joint ownership.
condómino, *m.* joint owner.
condón, *m.* condom.
condonación, *f.* condonation, pardoning.
condonante, *a.* condoning, forgiving, remitting.
condonar, *va.* to pardon, forgive, remit.
cóndor, *m.* Chilean and Colombian gold coin worth ten dollars; (ornith.) condor.
condotiero, condottiere, *m.* condottiere. (English *pl.* condottieri, as in Italian).
condrila, *f.* (bot.) common gum succory.
condrín, *m.* (P. I.) weight for precious metals = 0.3768 gram.
condrografía, *f.* (zool.) description of cartilages.
condrográfico, ca, *a.* pert. to CONDROGRAFÍA.
condrología, *f.* treatise on cartilages.
condropterigio, gia. I. *n.* & *a.* (ichth.) chondropterygian. **II.** *m. pl.* Chondropterygii.
conducción, *f.*, **conducencia,** *f.* conveyance; carriage; cartage, transportation; act of conveying or conducting, leading, guiding; conduct; stipulated rate or charge for transportation; (auto) driving.
conducente, *a.* conducive, conducent; official.
conducir. I. *va.* & *vn.* (*ind. pres.* CONDUZCO, *pret.* CONDUJE; *subj.* CONDUZCA) to convey, carry; to take, accompany; to direct, lead; to direct, manage, conduct; (auto) to drive. **II.** *vn.* (a) to conduce, contribute (to); to be suitable (for); to lead, tend (to). **III.** *vr.* to behave, act, conduct oneself.
conducta, *f.* conduct, behavior; conveyance, convoy; property convoyed; conduct, government, command, direction, management; party of recruits conducted to the regiment; contract made by a town or village with a physician to attend its sick.
conductero, *m.* one in charge of a convoy.
conductibilidad, *f.* conductibility.
conductible, *a.* conveyable, conductible.
conductividad, *f.* conductivity.
conductivo, va, *a.* conductive, conducting.
conducto, *m.* duct, conduit; channel through which any business is conducted or managed; means; mediator; person through whom anything is accomplished.—**por c. de,** by means of; through.
conductor, ra. I. *a.* conducting. **II.** *m.* conductor; leader; usher; guide; conveyer; (phys. & elec.) conductor; (auto) driver; (Mex.) (Ry. & street car) conductor. **III.** *f.* woman conductor or director.
conduelo, conduela, *v. V.* CONDOLER.
condueño, *m.* (com.) joint owner.
conduje, *pret.* of CONDUCIR.
condumio, *m.* (coll.) meat dressed to be eaten with bread plenty of food.
conduplicación, *f.* (rhet.) reduplication.
condutal, *m.* (mason.) leader; gutter.
conduzco, conduzca, *v. V.* CONDUCIR.
conectador, *m.* (mech.) connector.
conectar, *va.* to connect.
conectivo, va, *a.* connective, connecting.
conector, *m.* connector.
coneja, *f.* female rabbit.
conejal, conejar, *m.* rabbit warren.
conejera, *f.* warren for breeding rabbits; burrow; brothel; (coll.) den or cavern inhabited by poor people or frequented by bad characters, joint.
conejero. I. *m.* warrener, keeper of a rabbit warren. **II.** *a.* rabbit (as *a.*), for rabbits.
conejillo, lla; conejito, ta, *n. dim.* little rabbit. —**conejillo de Indias,** guinea pig.
conejo, ja, *n.* (zool.) rabbit.—**conejuna,** *f.* rabbit down or fur.—**conejuno, na,** *a.* pertaining to rabbits, rabbit (as *a.*)
conexidades, *f. pl.* rights annexed to the principal.
conexión, *f.* connection, union, joint; (mech.) connection, coupling.—**c. de estrella,** (elec.) Y connection.—**c. en delta** or **en triángulo,** (elec.) delta connection.
conexionarse, *vr.* to get in touch, make connections.
conexivo, va, *a.* connective.
conexo, xa, *a.* connected, united, related.
confabulación, *f.* confabulation, easy conversation, chat; leaguing, conspiracy, plot, collusion.
confabulador, ra, *n.* gossip; schemer, plotter.
confabular. I. *vn.* to confabulate; to talk informally, chat. **II.** *vr.* to league, conspire.
confalón, *m.* gonfalon, standard, ensign.
confalonier, confaloniero, *m.* gonfalonier, chief standard-bearer.
confección, *f.* any handwork; workmanship; fancy work, ready made article; (pharm.) confection, compound remedy, concoction.
confeccionador, ra, *n.* one who makes articles of dress or any handwork.
confeccionar, *va.* to make, prepare; put together; to compound, put up (medicines, prescriptions).
confederación, *f.* confederacy, confederation; federation, coalition; international treaty or convention.
confederado, da. I. *pp.* of CONFEDERAR. **II.** *n.* & *a.* confederate, convenanter(-ing), associate.
confederar, *va.* & *vr.* to confederate, join, form a confederacy.
confederativo, va, *a.* confederative.
conferencia, *f.* conference, meeting, conversation, interview; congress; daily lecture in universities; public lecture.
conferenciante, *n.* lecturer.
conferenciar, *vn.* to confer, consult together, hold an interview; to lecture.
conferencista, *n.* (Am.) = CONFERENCIANTE.
conferir. I. *va.* (*ind.* CONFIERO; *subj.* CONFIERA) to confer; to give, bestow, award; to compare. **II.** *vn.* to confer; to lecture.
confesa, *f.* widow who has become a nun.
confesado, da, *n.* (coll.) penitent.
confesante, *n.* one who confesses before a judge.
confesar. I. *va.* (*ind.* CONFIESO; *subj.* CONFIESE) to confess, acknowledge, own, avow, grant; to confess, hear or receive confessions; to confess to a priest.—**c. de plano,** to confess plainly or openly. **II.** *vr.* to confess or make confession; to shrive.
confesión, *f.* confession, avowal, acknowledgment; (relig.) confession.—**c. auricular,** auricular confession.
confesional, *a.* confessional.
confesionario, *m.* confessional; treatise with rules for confessing.
confesionista, *n.* Lutheran.
confeso, sa. I. *a.* & *n.* (one) confessing a crime; converted Jew. **II.** *m.* lay-brother.
confesonario, *m.* confessional.
confesor, *m.* father confessor; title given to holy men by the Roman Catholic Church.
confetti, *m. pl.* confetti.
confiable, *a.* trusty, reliable.
confiadamente, *adv.* trustingly, with confidence.
confiado, da. I. *pp.* of CONFIAR. **II.** *a.* confident, unsuspicious, trusting; presumptuous, arrogant or forward.
confiador, *m.* (law) joint surety, fellow bondsman.
confianza, *f.* confidence, trust, reliance, faith; courage, firmness of opinion; presumptuousness, forwardness, assurance; familiarity, intimacy.—**de c.,** informal, unceremonious.—**en c.,** confidentially.—**confianzudo, da,** *a.* presumptuous, bold, "fresh."
confiar. I. *vn.* **(en)** to rely (on), to trust (in). **II.** *va.* to confide, intrust, credit; to commit to the care of another.
confidencia, *f.* trust, confidence; secret or confidential information.—**hacer confidencias a,** to confide in, tell secrets to.
confidencial, *a.* confidential.—**confidencialmente,** *adv.* confidentially.
confidente. I. *n.* confidant, intimate, counsellor; detective, secret agent, spy; settee for two persons, tête-à-tête. **II.** *a.* true, faithful, trusty.

confiero, confiera, *v. V.* CONFERIR.
confieso, confiese, *v. V.* CONFESAR.
configuración, *f.* configuration.
configurar, *va.* to form, shape.
confín. I. *a.* bordering, abutting, conterminous; limiting, boundary (as *a.*) II. *m.* limit, boundary, confine, border.
confinación, *f.* = CONFINAMIENTO.
confinado, da, *n.* one confined to a place or region under surveillance.
confinamiento, *m.* confinement; banishment to a definite place; (law) confinement within certain bounds under surveillance.
confinante, *a.* = CONFÍN, *a.*
confinar, *va.* & *vn.* to banish to a definite place; to confine, imprison; to border on, abut.—**c. con,** to abut on, be bounded by.
confingir, *va.* (*ind.* CONFINJO; *subj.* CONFINJA) (pharm.) to mix into one mass.
confirmación, *f.* confirmation, corroboration, attestation; (eccl.) confirmation.
confirmadamente, *adv.* firmly, assuredly.
confirmador, ra, *n.* attester, confirmer.
confirmante, *n.* & *a.* confirmer(-ing).
confirmar, *va.* to confirm, corroborate, verify; to strengthen, support, ratify; (eccl.) to confirm.
confirmativo, va, *a.* confirmative.
confirmatorio, ria, *a.* confirmatory, confirmative.
confiscación, *f.* confiscation, forfeiture.
confiscado, da, *a.* confiscate, confiscated.
confiscador, ra, *n.* confiscator.
confiscar, *va.* (*pret.* CONFISQUÉ; *subj.* CONFISQUE) to confiscate.
confitado, da, *a.* candied; confident, sure.
confitar, *va.* to confect, to candy with melted sugar; to make into sweetmeats or into preserves; to dulcify, to sweeten.
confite, *m.* (gen. *pl.*) bonbon; sweets.—**estar a partir de un c.,** or **morder en un c.,** to be hand and glove, to be intimate.
confitente, *a.* (one) confessing a crime.
confíteor, *m.* (Rom. Cath.) confiteor.
confitera, *f.* bonbon container; candy box.
confitería, *f.* confectionery; confectioner's shop.
confitero, ra, *n.* confectioner; tray for sweets.
confitico, illo, ito, *m. dim.* small cookie or cake; caraway cookie.—*pl.* ornaments in the shape of cookies wrought on coverlets.
confitura, *f.* confection, sweetmeat, preserve.
conflación, *f.* fusion, melting of metals, smelting.
conflagración, *f.* conflagration; sudden and violent perturbation of towns and nations.
conflátil, *a.* fusible.
conflictivo, va, *a.* conflicting.
conflicto, *m.* conflict, struggle, strife, combat; (fig.) agony, pang.
confluencia, *f.* confluence.
confluente, *a.* confluent.
confluir, *vn.* (*ind. pres.* él CONFLUYE, *pret.* CONFLUYÓ; *subj.* CONFLUYA) to join (app. to rivers and sea currents); to assemble in one place.
conformación, *f.* conformation.
conformador, *m.* shaper; hat block; boot crimper.
conformar. I. *va.* to conform, adjust, fit. II. *vn.* to suit, fit, conform; to cohere; to level. III. *vr.* to comply; to yield, submit; to resign oneself.
conforme. I. *a.* alike, corresponding, suitable, congruent, consonant, accordant; correct, acceptable, O. K.; consistent; agreed; as (as in *todo queda c. estaba,* everything remains as it was); compliant, resigned.—**c. a,** consistent with, agreeable to.—**c. con,** resigned to; in agreement with. II. *adv.* in due proportion; agreeably, accordingly.
conformemente, *adv.* conformably, unanimously; correctly; agreeably.
conformidad, *f.* resemblance, likeness; conformity; agreement, consistence, consonance, congruence; concord, concordance; symmetry; close attachment of one person to another; affinity; submission, patience, resignation.—**de c.,** by common consent; correctly.—**en c.,** agreeably, suitably, accordingly.
conformismo, *n.* conformism.
conformista, *m.* conformist.
confort, *m.* well-being, comfort.
confortable, *a.* that comforts, consoles; comfortable.
confortación, *f.* comfort, consolation; encouragement.
confortador, ra, *n.* & *a.* comforter(-ing), consoler(-ing), strengthener(-ing).
confortamiento, *m.* comfort, consolation; encouragement.
confortante. I. *a.* & *n.* comforting, soothing (thing or person). II. *m. pl.* mitts.
confortar, *va.* to comfort, strengthen, enliven, invigorate; to encourage, console, cheer, solace.
confortativo, va, *a.* comforting; encouraging, cheering, strengthening.
conforte, *m.* = CONFORTACIÓN.
confracción, *f.* fracture, breaking.
confraternidad, *f.* confraternity, brotherhood.
confricación, *f.* rubbing, friction.
confricar, *va.* to rub.
confrontación, *f.* confrontation, confronting; comparison, comparing; sympathy, natural congeniality (between persons).
confrontante, *n.* & *a.* confronter(-ing).
confrontar. I. *va.* to collate, confront; to compare. II. *vn.* to agree in sentiments and opinion.—**c. con,** to border on.
confucianismo, *m.* Confucianism.
confucianista, *n.* & *a.* Confucian.
confuciano, na, *n.* & *a.* = CONFUCIANISTA.
confundir. I. *va.* (*pp.* CONFUNDIDO and CONFUSO) to confound, jumble; to perplex, confuse, darken, throw into disorder; to convince by argument; to abase, humiliate.—**c. con,** to confuse with, mistake for. II. *vr.* to be bewildered, perplexed, confounded, rattled, mixed up; to be ashamed and humbled.
confusamente, *adv.* confusedly; helter-skelter.
confusión, *f.* confusion, disorder; perplexity; embarrassment, entanglement, confusedness; obscurity; humiliation, shame, ignominy.
confuso, sa. I. *pp. irreg.* of CONFUNDIR. II. *a.* confused, mixed, confounded, jumbled together; obscure, doubtful, unintelligible; blurred, indistinct; fearful, timorous, perplexed.—**en c.,** confusedly.
confutación, *f.* confutation, disproof.
confutador, ra, *n.* confuter.
confutar, *va.* to confute, disprove, refute.
congelación, *f.* solidification, freezing, congealing; congealment.
congelador, ra. I. *a.* freezing, refrigerating. II. *m.* freezer; deep-freeze.
congelamiento, *m.* = CONGELACIÓN.
congelar. I. *va.* to congeal, freeze; (com.) to freeze. II. *vr.* to congeal, freeze.
congelativo, va, *a.* refrigerating, cooling; freezing.
congénere, congenérico, ca, *a.* congeneric, of like kind.
congenial, *a.* congenial; analogous.
congenialidad, *f.* congeniality.
congeniar, *vn.* to be congenial.
congénito, *a.* congenital, connate.
congerie, *f.* congeries, heap, mass.
congestión, *f.* congestion; jam; (med.) congestion.
congestionado, da, *a.* congested; (med.) congested.
congestionar. I. *va.* to congest; to jam; (med.) to congest. II. *vr.* to congest, become congested.
congestivo, va, *a.* (med.) congestive.
congiario, *m.* (anc. Rome) congiary, gift to the people.
congio, *m.* congius, an ancient liquid measure.
conglobación, *f.* being made into a ball; mixture and union of immaterial things; (rhet.) accumulation of proofs.

conglobado, da, *a.* conglobate.
conglobar, *va.* to form into a ball; heap together.
conglomeración, *f.* conglomeration, heterogeneous mixture.
conglomerado, da, *n.* & *a.* conglomerate.
conglomerar, *va.* to conglomerate.
conglutinación, *f.* conglutination, glutination, cementing, sticking.
conglutinado, da, *a.* conglutinate.
conglutinar. I. *va.* to conglutinate, cement, unite. **II.** *vr.* to conglutinate, stick together.
conglutinativo, va; conglutinoso, sa, *a.* viscous, glutinous, cementing.
Congo, *m.* Congo.
congo, ga. I. *a.* Congolese. **II.** *n.* Congolese; *m.* (Am., zool.) congo monkey; (Mex., Cuba) pig's foot.
congoja, *f.* anguish, dismay, anxiety, grief, sorrow.—**congojar,** *va.* to afflict, grieve.
congojosamente, *adv.* anxiously, sorrowfully.
congojoso, sa, *a.* afflictive, distressing; afflicted.
congoleño, ña, *n.* & *a.* Congo(l)ese.
congolés, lesa, *n.* & *a.* Congo(l)ese.
congosto, *m.* narrow pass, defile.
congraciador, ra, *n.* flatterer, fawner, wheedler; congratulator.
congraciamiento, *m.* flattery, fawning.
congraciar. I. *va.* to adulate, flatter. **II.** *vr.* **(con)** to get into the good graces (of).
congratulación, *f.* congratulation.
congratulador, ra, *n.* congratulant, congratulator.
congratular. I. *va.* to congratulate, compliment. **II.** *vr.* to congratulate oneself, rejoice.
congratulatorio, ria, *a.* congratulatory, congratulating.
congratulorio, ria, *a.* congratulant, congratulating.
congregación, *f.* congregation; meeting, assembly; fraternity, brotherhood.
congregacionalismo, *m.* Congregationalism.
congregacionalista, *n.* & *a.* Congregationalist.
congregado, da, *a.* congregate, conglomerate.
congregante, ta, *n.* member of a congregation, fraternity, or brotherhood.
congregar, *va.* & *vr.* (*pret.* CONGREGUÉ; *subj.* CONGREGUE) to assemble, meet, congregate, gather.
congresista, *n.* congressman(-woman).
congreso, *m.* congress, consistory, convention, assembly; sexual intercourse.—**C. de los Diputados,** House of Representatives.
congrio, *m.* (zool.) conger eel, sea eel.
congrua, *f.* competent sustenance to one who is to be ordained a priest.
congruamente, *adv.* conveniently; becomingly.
congruencia, *f.* convenience; fitness; congruence.
congruente, *a.* congruent, corresponding.
congruentemente, *adv.* suitably, congruously.
congruo, grua, *a.* congruous, apt, fit, suitable.
cónica, *f.* (math.) conic, conic section.
conicidad, *f.* conicity.
conicina, *f.* (chem.) conine, coniine.
cónico, ca, *a.* conical, conic.
conidio, *m.* (bot.) conidium.
conífero, ra. I. *a.* (bot.) coniferous. **II.** *f. pl.* Coniferæ.
coniforme, *a.* coniform, cone-shaped.
conirrostro, tra, *a.* (ornith.) conirostral.
conivalvo, va, *a.* (zool.) having a conical shell.
coniza, *f.* (bot.) great fleabane.
conjetura, *f.* conjecture, surmise, guess.
conjeturador, ra, *n.* conjecturer, guesser.
conjetural, *a.* conjectural.
conjeturalmente, *adv.* conjecturally, by guess.
conjeturar, *va.* to conjecture, guess.
conjuez, *m.* cojudge.
conjugable, *a.* (gram.) conjugable.
conjugación, *f.* conjugation.
conjugado, da. I. *pp.* of CONJUGAR. **II.** *a.* (math.) conjugate.
conjugar, *va.* (*pret.* CONJUGUÉ; *subj.* CONJUGUE) (gram.) to conjugate.
conjunción, *f.* conjunction, union, association, league; conjugation; copulation; act of coupling or joining together; consolidation; (gram., astr.) conjunction.
conjuntamente, *adv.* in all, all together, jointly.
conjuntiva, *f.* (anat.) conjunctiva.
conjuntival, *a.* conjunctival.
conjuntivitis, *f.* (med.) conjunctivitis.
conjuntivo, va, *a.* conjunctive.
conjunto, ta. I. *a.* united, connected; contiguous; allied by kindred or friendship; mixed or incorporated with another thing. **II.** *m.* whole, aggregate, entirety; (sport) team; unit, system of parts (as *c. de cola,* tail unit of an airplane).—**en c.,** as a whole; in all, totally.
conjura, conjuración, *f.* conspiracy, conjuration, plot, machination.
conjurado, da. I. *pp.* of CONJURAR. **II.** *n.* conspirator.
conjurador, ra, *n.* conspirator; exorcist.
conjuramentar. I. *va.* to administer an oath to, swear in. **II.** *vr.* to bind oneself by oath, take an oath.
conjurante, *a.* conjuring; conspiring.
conjurar. I. *vn.* to conspire, plot; to join in a conspiracy. **II.** *va.* to exorcise; to entreat, implore; to avert, ward off.
conjuro, *m.* conjuration; exorcism; entreaty.
conllevador, ra, *n.* helper, assistant.
conllevar, *va.* to aid; to bear with patience.
conmemorable, *a.* commemorable.
conmemoración, *f.* commemoration, celebration.
conmemorar, *va.* to commemorate, celebrate.
conmemorativo, va, conmemoratorio, ria, *a.* commemorative, commemoratory; memorial.
conmensal, *m.* messmate, fellow boarder.
conmensalía, *f.* eating together.
conmensurabilidad, *f.* commensurability.
conmensurable, *a.* commensurable.
conmensuración, *f.* commensuration.
conmensurar, *va.* to make commensurate.
conmensurativo, va, *a.* that makes commensurate.
conmigo, with me, with myself. *V.* CON.
conmilitón, *m.* comrade, companion; fellow soldier.
conminación, *f.* commination, threat.
conminar, *va.* to threaten; (law) to denounce punishment.—**conminatorio, ria,** *a.* comminatory, denunciatory, threatening.
conminuta, *a.* (surg.).—**fractura c.,** comminuted.
conmiseración, *f.* commisseration, pity, sympathy.
conmistión, *f.* commixture.
conmisto, ta, *a.* mixed, mingled, incorporated.
conmistura, *f.* = CONMISTIÓN.
conmixto, ta, *a.* = CONMISTO.
conmoción, *f.* commotion, excitement, stirring up, flurry, disturbance.
conmoción cerebral, *f.* (med.) concussion of the brain.
conmonitorio, *m.* written narrative of an event; (law) reminder from a superior to an inferior judge.
conmovedor, ra. I. *a.* touching; sad, pathetic; exciting, stirring. **II.** *n.* disturber, agitator.
conmover, *va.* (*ind.* CONMUEVO; *subj.* CONMUEVA) to touch, appeal to; to disturb, agitate, stir up.
conmovido, da, *a.* moved, touched.
conmutabilidad, *f.* commutability.
conmutable, *a.* commutable.
conmutación, *f.* commutation, exchange.
conmutador, *m.* electric switch; telegraph key.
conmutar, *va.* to exchange, barter.
conmutativo, va, *a.* commutative.
connato, ta, *a.* (bot.) connate.
connatural, *a.* connatural, inborn.
connaturalización, *f.* naturalization, adaptation to new conditions, acclimatization.

connaturalizarse, *vr.* to accustom oneself; to become inured or acclimated.
connaturalmente, *adv.* connaturally.
connivencia, *f.* connivance; plotting.
connotación, *f.* connotation; distant kinship or relationship.
connotado, *n.* remote relationship.
connotante, *a.* connotative.
connotar, *va.* to connote, imply.
connotativo, va, *a.* (gram.) connotative.
connovicio, cia, *n.* fellow novice.
connubial, *a.* connubial, matrimonial, conjugal.
connubio, *m.* matrimony, marriage, wedlock.
connumerar, *va.* to enumerate, include in a number.
cono, *m.* (geom.) cone; (bot.) cone, fruit of the pine family.
conocedor, ra. I. *a.* **(de)** familiar (with), expert (in). **II.** *n.* connoisseur, expert; chief herdsman.
conocer. I. *va.* (*ind.* CONOZCO; *subj.* CONOZCA) to know; to experience, observe, perceive, comprehend; to be, or become, acquainted with; to know carnally. **II.** *vn.* to know.—**c. de una causa,** or **pleito,** (law) to try a case (app. to a judge). **III.** *vr.* to know each other; to meet, get acquainted; to know oneself.
conocible, *a.* cognoscible, knowable.
conocidamente, *adv.* in a known manner.
conocido, da. I. *pp.* of CONOCER. **II.** *a.* prominent, well known. **III.** *n.* acquaintance.
conocimiento, *m.* knowledge, understanding; consciousness; skill, ability; acquaintance, slight friendship; (com.) (or **c. de embarque**) bill of lading; note of identification, voucher; (Am.) check for baggage.—*pl.* learning, erudition.—**poner en c. de,** to inform, notify.—**venir en c. de,** to learn of.
conoidal, *a.* conoidal.
conoide, *m.* (geom.) conoid.
conopial, conopio, *m.* (arch.) ogee arch.
conozco, conozca, *v. V.* CONOCER.
conque. I. *conj.* so then; now then; and so; well then. **II.** *m.* (coll.) wherewithal.
conquiforme, *a.* conchiform, shell-shaped.
conquiliología, *f.* (zool.) conchology.
conquiliólogo, ga, *n.* conchologist.
conquista, *f.* conquest, subjugation; conquered territory or thing; winning another's affections.
conquistable, *a.* conquerable; attainable, accessible.
conquistador, ra. I. *a.* conquering, subduing. **II.** *n.* conqueror, subduer.
conquistar, *va.* to conquer, overcome, subdue; to win (another's affections).
conrear, *va.* to grease (wool); (agr.) to hoe.
conreinar, *vn.* to reign with another.
consabido, da, *a.* already known, alluded to, in question, before-mentioned, aforesaid.
consabidor, ra, *n.* one who possesses knowledge jointly with others.
consagración, *f.* consecration.
consagrado, da. I. *pp.* of CONSAGRAR. **II.** *a.* sacred; devoted, given (to study, sports, etc.).
consagrante, *n.* consecrator.
consagrar. I. *va.* to consecrate, hallow, make sacred; to deify; to consecrate, devote, dedicate; to erect (a monument). **II.** *vr.* to devote or give oneself (to study, work, etc.)
consanguíneo, nea, *a.* consanguineous, cognate, kindred.—**consanguinidad,** *f.* consanguinity.
consciente, *a.* conscious; aware; of sound mind, sane; (law) compos mentis.
conscientemente, *adv.* consciously.
conscripción, *f.* (mil.) conscription.
conscripto, ta. I. *a.* conscript.—**padres conscriptos,** conscript fathers, senators of ancient Rome. **II.** *m.* conscript, draftee.
consectario, ria. I. *a.* consequent; annexed. **II.** *m.* corollary.
consecución, *f.* attainment, obtaining, acquisition.
consecuencia, *f.* consequence, conclusion, inference; issue; consistence, firmness, coherence; consequence, importance, moment, concern.—**a c. de,** because of.—**en c.,** consequently, therefore.—**guardar c.,** to be consistent.—**por c.** = EN C.—**ser de c.,** to be important.—**traer a c.,** to adduce, bring to bear, or as corroborative evidence.
consecuente. I. *m.* effect, issue, consequence; (math.) consequent. **II.** *a.* consequent, following; consistent, logical.
consecutivo, va, *a.* consecutive.
conseguimiento, *m.* attainment, obtainment, acquisition.
conseguir, *va.* (*ind.* CONSIGO; *subj.* CONSIGA) to attain, get, obtain (*consigue que venga,* he gets him to come); to succeed in.
conseja, *f.* story, fairy tale, fable.
consejera, *f.* counsellor's wife; woman adviser.
consejero, *m.* counsellor, member of a council; adviser; anything that gives warning.—**c. de la corona,** crown minister.—**c. en eficiencia,** (U. S.) efficiency expert.
consejo, *m.* counsel, advice; council, court, assembly of magistrates, advisory board, consulting body; council house.—**c. de guerra,** court-martial; council of war.—**c. de ministros,** cabinet.—**C. de Seguridad,** Security Council.—**c. municipal,** board of aldermen.—**c. privado,** privy council.—**seguir c. de guerra a,** to court-martial.
consenciente, *a.* consenting; conniving.
consenso, *m.* general assent; agreement of opinion, consensus.
consensual, *a.* (law) consensual.
consentido, da. I. *pp.* of CONSENTIR. **II.** *a.* spoiled (child), coddled.
consentidor, ra, *n.* complier, conniver; coddler.
consentimiento, *m.* consent; coddling; compliance, acquiescence; (med.) consent.
consentir. I. *va.* (*ind.* CONSIENTO; *subj.* CONSIENTA) to allow, permit, tolerate, acquiesce in, condescend to; to believe; to accept, admit; to admit of; to coddle, spoil, overindulge. **II.** *vn.* (mech.) to flag, give way, weaken, become loose.—**c. en** (foll. by inf.), to consent to (inf.). **III.** *vr.* to spring, crack, begin to break.
conserje, *m.* keeper or warden of a royal palace, castle, or public building; janitor, concierge.
conserjería, *f.* wardenship of a royal palace or castle; warden's dwelling; janitor's office, conciergerie.
conserva, *f.* conserve, preserve, jam; pickles; fleet of merchantmen under convoy of a ship of war.—**c. trojezada,** preserve of minced fruit.—**conservas alimenticias,** canned goods.—**en c.,** canned, preserved.
conservación, *f.* conservation; preservation; maintenance, upkeep.—**c. de la energía,** (phys.) conservation of energy.—**c. de la masa,** (phys.) conservation of mass.
conservador, ra. I. *n.* conservator, preserver; curator. **II.** *n.* & *a.* conserver(-ing); (pol.) Conservative.—**juez c.** person appointed to guard the rights of a community.
conservaduría, *f.* dignity in the order of Malta.
conservadurismo, *m.* conservatism.
conservante, *n.* & *a.* conserver (-ing).
conservar. I. *va.* to conserve, maintain, preserve, keep; to guard; to preserve or pickle (fruit), to can. **II.** *vr.* to keep young, be well preserved.
conservatismo, *m.* conservatism.
conservativo, va, *a.* conservative, preservative.
conservatoría, *f.* place and office of a JUEZ CONSERVADOR; grant to communities to choose their own conservators.—*pl.* letters patent granted by conservators.
conservatorio, ria. I. *a.* conservatory; having a preservative quality. **II.** *m.* conservatory, place for instruction in the fine arts.
conservero, ra, *n.* preparer of conserves.
considerable, *a.* considerable, great, large.
consideración, *f.* consideration, regard; notice; sake, account; reflection, contemplation, meditation; importance; urbanity, respect.—**en c.,**

considering, in, or into, consideration, in proportion.—**guardar,** or **tener, consideraciones a,** to show consideration to.—**ser de c.,** to be of importance or moment.
considerado, da, *a.* prudent; considerate; thoughtful, tactful; esteemed, distinguished.
considerador, ra, *n.* one who considers or who shows consideration.
considerando. I. *ger.* of CONSIDERAR. **II.** *conj.* whereas (as used in enumerating reasons or circumstances in legal language). **III.** *m.* introductory clause, introduced with "whereas."
considerante, *a.* considering.
considerar, *va.* to consider, meditate, think over; to treat with respect, show consideration to.
consiento, consienta, *v. V.* CONSENTIR.
consiervo, *m.* fellow serf.
consigna, *f.* (mil.) watchword, countersign.
consignación, *f.* consignation, assignation, apportionment; (com.) consignment, shipment.
consignador, ra, *n.* (com.) consignor.
consignar, *va.* to consign, assign, make over; to set apart, devote; to yield, intrust; to state in writing; to lay by, to deposit; (com.) to consign (goods); (law) to deposit in trust.
consignatario, *m.* trustee; (law) mortgagee who enjoys the property mortgaged until the debt be paid out of the proceeds; (com.) consignee.
[1]**consigo,** with oneself, himself, herself, themselves, yourself, yourselves. *V.* CON.—**c. mismo, c. propio,** or **c. solo,** alone, by oneself.
[2]**consigo, consiga,** *v. V.* CONSEGUIR.
consiguiente. I. *m.* consequence, result, effect. —**de c., por c., por el c.,** consequently, therefore. **II.** *a.* consequent, resulting, following; consistent, logical.—**consiguientemente,** *adv.* consequently.
consiliario, *m.* counsellor; assistant to head of a corporation.
consintiente, *a.* consenting, agreeing.
consistencia, *f.* consistence, consistency; stability; duration; coherence; conformity; firmness, solidity.
consistente, *a.* consistent, firm, solid.
consistir, *vn.* to consist, subsist, continue fixed; to be comprised, contained.—**c. en,** to lie, to be a matter of, consist in (*never* to consist *of,* in the sense of "to be composed of").
consistorial, *a.* consistorial, belonging or relating to an ecclesiastical court.
consistorio, *m.* consistory, ecclesiastical court; pontifical senate; in some Spanish towns, the municipal council and the townhouse or town hall.—**c. divino,** tribunal of God.
consocio, *m.* partner, associate; companion, fellow, comrade.
consol, *m.* (Peru) = CONSOLA.
consola, *f.* console, pier table; bracket shelf.
consolación, *f.* consolation, comfort; (in some card games) forfeit.
consolado, da. I. *pp.* of CONSOLAR. **II.** *a.* consoled, comforted.
consolador, ra, *n.* & *a.* comforter(-ing), consoler(-ing), soother(-ing).
consolante, *a.* comforting, consoling, soothing.
consolar, *va.* (*ind.* CONSUELO; *subj.* CONSUELE) to console, comfort, cheer, soothe.
consolativo, va; consolatorio, ria, *a.* consolatory, consoling, comforting.
consólida, *f.* (bot.) = CONSUELDA.—**c. real,** larkspur.
consolidación, *f.* consolidation.
consolidado, da, *a.* consolidated; (of debts) funded.—*pl.* consolidated annuities, consols, government securities.
consolidar. I. *va.* to consolidate, compact; to harden, strengthen; to fund (debts). **II.** *vr.* to consolidate, grow firm, hard, or solid; (law) to unite.
consolidativo, va, *a.* consolidant, consolidative.
consonancia, *f.* consonance, harmony, rime; consistency, congruence; consent; conformity.
consonante. I. *m.* riming word, rime; (mus.) consonous or corresponding sound. **II.** *f.* & *a.* (gram.) consonant. **III.** *a.* consonant, consistent, concordant.
consonar, *vn.* (*ind.* CONSUENO; *subj.* CONSUENE) (mus.) to make harmonious sounds; (poet.) to rime; to agree, harmonize, become, fit.
cónsones, *m. pl.* (mus.) harmonious chord.
cónsono, na, *a.* consonous, harmonious, consonant.
consorcio, *m.* consortium, partnership, society; marital union; friendly intercourse; mutual affection.
consorte, *n.* consort; companion, partner, mate; one who enters or defends an action jointly with another.
conspicuo, cua, *a.* conspicuous; prominent, distinguished.
conspiración, *f.* conspiracy, plot.
conspirado, da; conspirador, ra; conspirante, *n.* & *a.* conspirator(-ing).
conspirar, *vn.* to conspire, plot; to agree together, coöperate, combine.
constancia, *f.* constancy, perseverance; (Am.) record, written evidence.
constante. I. *a.* constant; continual, uninterrupted; firm, unalterable, immutable; loyal, constant; manifest, apparent, clear; composed, consisting. **II.** *f.* & *a.* (math.) constant.
constantemente, *adv.* constantly; firmly, unalterably; evidently, undoubtedly.
constantinopolitano, na, *a.* of or pertaining to Constantinople.
constar, *v. impers.* to be clear, evident, certain (with diff. constr. as *le consta que,* he is certain that); to be recorded, registered; (**de**) to be composed (of), consist (of); (of verses) to have the proper measure and accent.
constatación, *f.* (Gal.) substantiation, verification.
constatar, *va.* (Gal.) to verify, confirm; to record.
constelación, *f.* constellation; climate, temperature; (with **correr**) epidemic.—**una c. corre,** an epidemic is raging.
consternación, *f.* consternation, distress; horror, panic.
consternar, *va.* to terrify, strike with horror or amazement; to cause a panic to or in; to distress, grieve.
constipación, *f.* constipation; cold in the head.
constipado, da. I. *pp.* of CONSTIPAR. **II.** *a.* suffering from a cold. **III.** *m.* head cold.
constipante, *a.* constipating, binding.
constipar. I. *va.* to constipate, bind; to cause a cold. **II.** *vr.* to become costive; to catch cold.
constipativo, va, *a.* = CONSTIPANTE.
constitución, *f.* constitution (in all its meanings); rules and by-laws.
constitucional. I. *m.* constitutionalist. **II.** *a.* constitutional.
constitucionalidad, *f.* constitutionality.
constitucionalismo, *m.* constitutionalism.
constituir. I. *va.* (*ind.* CONSTITUYO; *subj.* CONSTITUYA) to constitute; erect, establish, make, create; appoint, depute. **II.** *vr.* **constituirse en obligación de,** to bind oneself to perform.
constitutivo, va. I. *a.* constitutive, essential. **II.** *n.* constituent.
constituyente, *n.* & *a.* constituent.
constituyo, constituya, *v. V.* CONSTITUIR.
constreñidamente, *adv.* compulsively.
constreñimiento, *m.* constraint compulsion.
constreñir, *va.* (*ind.* CONSTRIÑO; *subj.* CONSTRIÑA) to constrain, compel, force; (med.) to bind or make costive; to contract.
constricción, *f.* contraction.
constrictivo, va, *a.* binding, constricting, astringent; compelling, forcing.
constrictor, ra, *a.* constrictor.
constringente, *a.* constringent.
constriño, constriña, *v. V.* CONSTREÑIR.
construcción, *f.* construction; act and art of

constructing; architecture; structure; building; (gram.) construction.—**de c.**, structural.
constructivo, va, *a.* constructive.
constructor, ra, *n.* builder; maker.—**c. de buques,** shipbuilder.
construir, *va.* (*ind. pres.* CONSTRUYO, *pret.* él CONSTRUYÓ; *subj.* CONSTRUYA) to form, build, construct; to translate literally; (gram.) to construct.
constuprador, *m.* debaucher, defiler, corrupter.
constuprar, *va.* to defile, debauch, corrupt.
consubstanciación, *f.* (theol.) consubstantiation.
consubstancial, *a.* (theol.) consubstantial.
consubstancialidad, *f.* consubstantiality.
consuegrar, *vn.* to become joint fathers- or mothers-in-law.
consuegro, gra, *n.* parent-in-law with respect to the parent of one's son- or daughter-in-law.
consuelda, *f.* (bot.) comfrey.
[1]**consuelo,** *m.* consolation, comfort; joy, merriment.—**sin c.**, (coll.) without stint, to excess.
[2]**consuelo, consuele,** *v. V.* CONSOLAR.
consueno, consuene, *v. V.* CONSONAR.
consueta, *n.* stage prompter; (prov.) directory for divine service.—*pl.* short prayers.
consuetudinario, ria, *a.* customary, generally practised; common (law); (theol.) in the habit of sinning.
cónsul, *n.* consul.—**c. general,** consul general.
consulado, *m.* consulate; consulship; tribunal or court of commerce.—**c. general,** consulate general.
consular, *a.* consular.
consulta, *f.* question proposed, or the answer given in writing; consultation, conference; office hours (of a doctor); report made and advice given to the king in council.
consultable, *a.* worthy or necessary to be deliberated upon.
consultación, *f.* consultation, conference, meeting.
consultante, *n.* & *a.* consulter(-ing).
consultar, *va.* to consult, ask advice of; to advise; to deliberate about, discuss.—**c. con la almohada,** (coll.) to sleep on, think over.
consultivo, va, *a.* consultative, conciliary, advisory.
consultor, ra, *n.* & *a.* consulter(-ing), adviser (-ing), counsel, counsellor.
consultorio, *m.* bureau of information; (med.) consulting institution, clinic.
consumación, *f.* consummation, end, completion; destruction, suppression, total extinction. —**c. de los siglos,** end of the world.
consumadamente, *adv.* perfectly, completely, consummately.
consumado, da. I. *pp.* of CONSUMAR. **II.** *a.* consummate, complete, perfect. **III.** *m.* jelly broth; consommé.
consumador, ra, *n.* finisher; one who consummates, perfects, or finishes.
consumar, *va.* to consummate, finish, perfect, complete; to commit (a crime).
consumativo, va, *a.* consummate; (of the sacrament) that consummates or completes.
consumible, *a.* consumable.
consumido, da, *a.* (coll.) thin, exhausted, emaciated, wasted away; easily afflicted.
consumidor, ra, *n.* & *a.* consumer(-ing); -eating (as **países consumidores de arroz,** rice-eating countries).
consumimiento, *m.* consumption.
consumir. I. *va.* (*pp.* CONSUMIDO and CONSUNTO) to consume; to waste away; to destroy, extirpate; to wear out, exhaust; to afflict, grieve; to take (the Eucharist) in the mass (used also as *vn.*). **II.** *vr.* to be spent, exhausted, run out; to fret; to be uneasy, vexed; to waste away, pine, languish.—**c. de,** to be consumed by, or with.
consumo, *m.* consumption (of provisions, fuel, merchandise).—*pl.* excise tax.
consunción, *f.* consumption, waste, decline; (med.) consumption, tuberculosis.
consuno, na.—**de c.**, jointly, together, in accord.
consuntivo, va, *a.* consuming.
consunto, ta, *pp. irreg.* of CONSUMIR.
consustanciación, *f.* = CONSUBSTANCIACIÓN.
consustancial, *a.* = CONSUBSTANCIAL.
contabescencia, *f.* (med.) contabescence.
contabilidad, *f.* bookkeeping, accounting; calculability.
contabilista, *n.* (Am.) bookkeeper, accountant.
contable, *a.* countable.
contacto, *m.* contact; (elec.) contact; terminal, binding post; (auto) ignition.
contadero, ra. I. *a.* countable, numerable. **II.** *m.* narrow passage where sheep or cattle are counted.—**entrar,** or **salir, por c.**, to go in or out through a narrow passage.
contado, da. I. *pp.* of CONTAR. **II.** *a.* scarce, rare, uncommon; few (as *son contadas las personas que,* there are very few people that).—**al c.**, (for) cash.—**de c.**, cash; instantly, immediately; in hand.—**por de c.**, of course, as a matter of course.
contador, ra, *n.* purser, paymaster, cashier; computer; accountant, bookkeeper; numberer, automatic counter; telltale; meter for gas, water, or electricity; cash register, counter; table or bench in a business office, desk; (law) auditor; receiver.—**c. de Geiger,** Geiger counter.
contaduría, *f.* accountant's or auditor's office at the exchequer; auditorship; office of a cashier, paymaster or treasurer; box office, in a theater.
contagiar. I. *va.* to infect, communicate, spread by contagion; to corrupt, pervert. **II.** *vr.* **(de)** to become infected (with), take by contagion.
contagio, *m.* contagion; contagious disease; corruption of morals.
contagión, *f.* progressive malignity of a disease, as cancer; propagation of vice and evil habits.
contagiosidad, *f.* contagiousness.
contagioso, sa, *a.* contagious; perverting.
contal, *m.* string of beads for counting.
contaminación, *f.* contamination, pollution; defilement; stain, blot.
contaminado, da. I. *pp.* of CONTAMINAR. **II.** *a.* contaminated, corrupted, polluted.
contaminante, *m.* contaminant.
contaminar, *va.* to contaminate, defile, pollute; pervert, corrupt; to infect by contagion; to corrupt, vitiate, or destroy the integrity of (a text or original); to profane.
contante.—**dinero c.**, or **dinero c. y sonante,** ready money, cash.
contar. I. *va.* (*ind.* CUENTO; *subj.* CUENTE) to count, reckon, number; to relate, tell; to book; to place to account; to class; to rate; to consider, look upon. **II.** *vn.* to compute, figure.—**c. con,** to depend on, rely on; to reckon with, take into account.
contemperar, *va.* to temper, moderate.
contemplación, *f.* contemplation, meditation; compliance, complaisance.
contemplador, ra, *n.* contemplator.
contemplar, *va.* to contemplate, examine, study; to view, behold, look upon; to meditate, muse over; to be lenient or complaisant with; to coddle, overindulge, spoil (a child).
contemplativamente, *adv.* attentively, thoughtfully, contemplatively.
contemplativo, va. I. *a.* contemplative; studious; lenient; complaisant. **II.** *m.* contemplator; pious devotee.
contemporaneidad, *f.* contemporaneousness.
contemporáneo, nea, *n.* & *a.* contemporary, coetaneous, coeval.
contemporicé, contemporice, *v. V.* CONTEMPORIZAR.
contemporización, *f.* temporizing, compliance.

contemporizador, ra, *n.* temporizer; complier.
contemporizar, *vn.* (*pret.* CONTEMPORICÉ; *subj.* CONTEMPORICE) to temporize; to comply; to adapt oneself.
contención, *f.* contention; emulation; contest, dispute, strife.
contencioso, sa, *a.* contentious; quarrelsome, disputatious; (law) being the object of strife or dispute; litigious.
contendedor, *m.* = CONTENDOR.
contender, *vn.* (*ind.* CONTIENDO; *subj.* CONTIENDA) to fight, combat; contend, debate; dispute; litigate; to argue, discuss, expostulate.—**contendiente,** *n.* & *a.* fighter(-ing), disputant, litigant.—**contendor,** *m.* fighter, contender, antagonist, opponent.
contenedor, ra, *n.* holder, tenant.
contenencia, *f.* suspension in the flight of birds; a peculiar movement in Spanish dancing; (law) demurrer.
contener. I. *va.* (*ind. pres.* CONTENGO, *pret.* CONTUVE; *subj.* CONTENGA) to contain, hold; to comprise, include, embrace; to check, curb, restrain, stop. **II.** *vr.* to control oneself, to refrain.
contenible, *a.* containable.
contenido, da. I. *pp.* of CONTENER. **II.** *a.* moderate, prudent, temperate, modest. **III.** *m.* contents; inclosure.
conteniente, *a.* containing, comprising.
contenta, *f.* (com.) indorsement (also ENDOSO); satisfactory treat or present; (mil.) certificate of good conduct; (law) acknowledgment of payment, release.
contentadizo, za, *a.* (sometimes preceded by **bien**) easily pleased.—**mal c.,** hard to please.
contentamiento, *m.* contentment, joy, satisfaction, content.
contentar. I. *va.* to satisfy, gratify, please; (com.) to indorse (also ENDORSAR).—**ser de buen (mal) c.,** to be easy (hard) to please. **II.** *vr.* to be contented, satisfied; (Am.) to become reconciled, make up.
contentible, *a.* contemptible.
contentivo, va, *a.* containing, comprising.
contento, ta. I. *a.* glad, pleased, contented, satisfied, content. **II.** *m.* contentment, joy, satisfaction, mirth; (law) release, discharge.—**a c.,** to one's satisfaction.
contera, *f.* shoe (of cane, umbrella, etc.); chape of a scabbard; button of the cascabel of a gun; refrain of a song.—**por c.,** at the end, as a finish.
contérmino, na, *a.* contiguous, abutting.
conterráneo, nea, *n.* countryman(-woman), fellow citizen.
contertuliano, na; contertulio, lia, *a.* belonging to the same social circle, of the same set.
contestable, *a.* contestable, disputable.
contestación, *f.* answer, reply; contestation, the act of contesting; debate, altercation, dispute.
contestar. I. *va.* to answer, reply; to confirm (the deposition of another); to prove; to attest. **II.** *vn.* to agree, to accord.
conteste, *a.* (law) confirming the evidence of another.
contexto, *m.* intertexture; context.
contextuar, *va.* to prove by quoting authorities.
contextura, *f.* contexture, texture; context; frame and structure of the human body.
conticinio, *m.* dead of night.
contienda, *f.* contest, dispute, debate; strife, fray, struggle.
contiendo, contienda, *v. V.* CONTENDER.
contignación, *f.* (arch.) contignation.
contigo, with thee, you (intimate). *V.* CON.
contiguidad, *f.* contiguity, closeness.
contiguo, gua, *a.* contiguous, close, adjacent.
continencia, *f.* continence, self-control; abstinence, moderation; graceful bow in a dance; act of containing.—**c. de la causa,** (law) unity which should exist in every judgment or sentence.
continental, *a.* continental.
continente. I. *m.* continent; container; countenance, mien. **II.** *a.* continent, abstemious, sober, moderate.—**continentemente,** *adv.* moderately, abstemiously, chastely.
contingencia, *f.* contingency, emergency, possibility, risk.
contingente. I. *a.* contingent, accidental. **II.** *m.* contingent, share.—**contingentemente,** *adv.* casually, accidentally, contingently.
contingible, *a.* that may happen, possible.
continuación, *f.* continuation; prolongation, lengthening; continuance, stay.—**a c.,** immediately (afterwards).
continuado, da, *a.* continued.
continuador, ra, *n.* continuer, continuator.
continuamente, *adv.* continually; continuously.
continuar, *va.* & *vn.* to continue, pursue, carry on; to remain, or still be, in the same state, hold; to last, endure; to prolong.
continuativo, va, *a.* continuative.
continuidad, *f.* continuity.
continuo, nua. I. *a.* continuous, uninterrupted; prolonged; continual, constant, lasting; assiduous, steady, persevering; (mech.) endless.—**a la continua,** or **de continuo,** continually, constantly.—**corriente c.,** (elec.) direct current. **II.** *m.* continuous whole; yeoman of the crown; (math., phil.) continuum.
contómetro, *m.* Comptometer (trademark).
contonearse, *vr.* to walk with an affected air or manner, to strut.—**contoneo,** *m.* affected gait or manner of walking, strut.
contorcerse, *vr.* (*ind.* CONTUERZO; *subj.* CONTUERZA) to distort, twist one's body, writhe.
contorción, *f.* contortion.
contornado, *a.* (her.) (of animals' heads) turned toward the left side of the shield.
contornar, contornear, *va.* to trace the contour or outline of.—**contorneo,** *m.* = RODEO, a turn (round a place).
contorno, *m.* environs of a place; neighborhood; contour, outline.—**en c.,** round about.
contorsión, *f.* contortion, twist, wry motion, grotesque gesture.
contorsionista, *n.* contortionist.
contra. I. *prep.* against, across, athwart, in opposition to, counter, contrary to, opposite to; (in composition, gen.) counter.—**c. viento y marea,** against all odds. **II.** *m.* opposite sense; opposite opinion; pedal of an organ.—*pl.* (mus.) organ pipes forming the lowest bass.—**el pro y el c.,** the pros and cons. **III.** *f.* difficulty, obstacle; counter, in fencing; (Am.) ÑAPA, extra, something thrown in.—**en c., en c. de,** against, in opposition to.—**hacer la c., llevar la c.,** to oppose, to contradict.
contraabertura, *f.* (surg.) contrafissure.
contraábside, *n.* western absis.
contraaletas, *f. pl.* (naut.) counter-fashion pieces.
contraalisio, *m.* antitrade (wind).
contraalmirante, *m.* rear admiral.
contraamantillos, *f. pl.* (naut.) preventer lifts, counterbraces.
contraamura, *f.* (naut.) preventer tack.
contraaproches, *m. pl.* (fort.) counterapproaches.
contraarmiños, *m. pl.* (her.) black field and white spots.
contraatacar, *va.* & *vn.* to counterattack.
contraataque, *m.* (mil.) counter attack.—*pl.* fortified lines of defense.
contraaviso, *m.* counterinformation, counterorder.
contrabajo, *m.* (mus.) contrabass; contrabass viol; contrabassist, contrabasso.
contrabalancear, *va.* to counterbalance, counterpoise.
contrabalanza, *f.* CONTRAPESO, counterweight; counterbalance; CONTRAPOSICIÓN, contrast.
contrabandear, *vn.* to smuggle.

contrabandista, *m.* smuggler, contrabandist.
contrabando, *m.* contraband; smuggling; unlawful action.—**c. de guerra,** contraband of war.—**ir,** or **venir, de c.,** to go, or come, by stealth; to sneak out, or in.
contrabarrado, da, *a.* (her.) counterbarred.
contrabarrera, *f.* inner barrier in a bull ring.
contrabasa, *f.* (arch.) = PEDESTAL, pedestal.
contrabatería, *f.* counterbattery.
contrabatir, *va.* to fire upon (the enemy's artillery).
contrabitas, *f. pl.* (naut.) standards of the bitts.
contrabolina, *f.* (naut.) preventer bowline.
contrabovedilla, *f.* (naut.) second counter, upper counter.
contrabracear, *va.* (naut.) to counterbrace.
contrabraceo, *m.* (naut.) counterbracing.
contrabranque, *m.* (naut.) stemson, apron.
contrabraza, *f.* (naut.) preventer brace.
contrabrazola, *f.* (naut.) headledge.
contracalcar, *va.* to trace from the back, so as to obtain a back view of the original drawing.
contracambiada, *f.* changing of the forefoot by a horse.
contracambio, *m.* (com.) re-exchange; (fig.) = EQUIVALENTE, equivalent; compensation.
contracanal, *m.* counterchannel.
contracandela, *f.* (Am.) back fire, fire made to create a gap between part of a burning field and the rest, in order to prevent the spread of the conflagration.
contracarril, *m.* check rail, guard rail, safety rail; wing rail.
contracción, *f.* contraction, shrinking, shriveling; corrugation; abbreviation; abridgment.
contracebadera, *f.* (naut.) sprit-topsail.
contracédula, *f.* counterdecree.
contracifra, *f.* countercipher.
contracircuito, *m.* (elec.) circuit breaker.
contraclave, *f.* (arch.) voussoir next to the keystone.
contracodaste interior, *m.* (naut.) inner sternpost.—**c. exterior,** (naut.) back of the sternpost.
contraconcepción, *f.* contraception.
contracorriente, *f.* countercurrent, reverse current; stopwater.
contracosta, *f.* coast, shore opposite another.
contráctil, *a.* contractile, contractible.
contractilidad, *f.* contractility, contractibility.
contractivo, va, *a.* contractive, contracting.
contracto, ta, *pp. irreg.* of CONTRAER.
contractual, *a.* contractual.
contractura, *f.* (med.) contracture.
contracuartelado, da, *a.* (her.) having the quarters opposed in metal or color.
contracuerdas, *f. pl.* (naut.) outward deck planks or platforms.
contracurva, *f.* (Ry.) reversed curve.
contradancista, *m.* leader of a cotillon.
contradanza, *f.* contredanse, quadrille, cotillon.
contradecir, *va.* (*pp.* CONTRADICHO; *ind. pres.* CONTRADIGO, *pret.* CONTRADIJE, *fut.* CONTRADIRÉ; *subj.* CONTRADIGA) to contradict, gainsay.
contradicción, *f.* contradiction; opposition; gainsaying.
contradictor, ra, *n.* contradictor, gainsayer.
contradictoría, *f.* (logic) contradictory.
contradictorio, ria, *a.* contradictory.
contradicho, cha, *pp. irreg.* of CONTRADECIR.
contradigo, contradije, contradiga, *v. V.* CONTRADECIR.
contradique, *m.* counterdock, counterdike.
contradriza, *f.* (naut.) second halliard.
contradurmente, contradurmiente, *m.* (naut.) clamp.
contraeje, *m.* countershaft.
contraelectromotriz, *a.* (elec.) counter electromotive.
contraemboscada, *f.* counterambuscade.
contraemergente, *a.* (her.) countersalient.
contraempuñadura, *f.* (naut.) preventer earring.
contraendosar, *va.* to reindorse, indorse back.
contraer. I. *va.* & *vn.* (*pp.* CONTRAÍDO and CONTRACTO; *ind. pres.* CONTRAIGO, *pret.* CONTRAJE; *subj.* CONTRAIGA) to contract (an obligation); to catch (a disease); to tighten, join, unite; to incur; to acquire; to reduce.—**c. matrimonio,** to marry (get married). **II.** *vr.* to contract, diminish; to shrink.
contraescarpa, *f.* (mil.) counterscarp.
contraescota, *f.* (naut.) preventer sheet.
contraescotín, *m.* (naut.) preventer topsail sheet.
contraescritura, *f.* counterdeed.
contraespionaje, *f.* counterespionage.
contraestay, *m.* (naut.) preventer stay.
contrafajado, da, *a.* (her.) (of shields) having faces opposed in metal or color.
contrafallar, *va.* at cards, to overtrump.
contrafallo, *m.* overtrump at cards.
contrafianza, *f.* indemnity bond.
contrafigura, *f.* person or dummy that imitates a personage in the theater.
contrafilo, *m.* (armor) back edge (near point).
contraflorado, da, *a.* (her.) having flowers opposed in color and metal.
contrafoque, *m.* (naut.) foretop staysail.
contrafoso, *m.* (fort.) avantfosse or outer ditch.
contrafuero, *m.* infringement or violation of a charter or privilege.
contrafuerte, *m.* strap of leather to secure the girths on a saddletree; spur, counterfort (of a mountain); stiffener of a shoe; (fort.) counterfort; (arch.) abutment, buttress, spur.
contragolpe, *m.* (med.) effect of a blow on a part not actually struck; (eng.) back or reverse stroke (of a piston).
contraguardia, *f.* (fort.) counterguard.
contraguía, *f.* in a team, the near or left-hand animal.
contrahacedor, ra, *n.* imitator, impersonator.
contrahacer, *va.* (*pp.* CONTRAHECHO; *ind. pres.* CONTRAHAGO, *pret.* CONTRAHICE; *subj.* CONTRAHAGA) to counterfeit, falsify, forge; to imitate, copy; to pirate (the works of an author); to mimic, impersonate.
contrahaz, *m.* wrong side (of cloth).
contrahecho, cha. I. *pp. irreg.* of CONTRAHACER. **II.** *a.* humpbacked; deformed; counterfeit; spurious.
contrahice, *pret.* of CONTRAHACER.
contrahierba, *f.* (bot.) contrayerva, a South American medicinal plant; antidote.
contrahilera, *f.* line of defense that defends another.
contrahilo, *m.*—**a c.,** across the grain.
contrahoradar, *va.* to bore on the opposite side.
contrahuella, *f.* (arch.) riser of a stair.
contraigo, contraje, etc., *v. V.* CONTRAER.
contraindicación, *f.* (med.) contraindication.
contraindicante, *m.* (med.) contraindicant.
contraindicar, *va.* (*pret.* CONTRAINDIQUÉ; *subj.* CONTRAINDIQUE) (med.) to contraindicate.
contrairritante, *m.* (med.) counterirritant.
contralecho, *m.*—**a c.,** (arch.) crossbond.
contralizo, *m.* (weaving) back leash.
contralmirante, *m.* rear admiral.
contralor, *m.* comptroller, inspector.
contraloría, *f.* comptrollership.
contralto, *m.* contralto (voice), *m.* & *f.* (person).
contraluz, *f.* view (of thing) seen against the light.
contramaestre, *m.* overseer, foreman; (naut.) boatswain.
contramalla, contramalladura, *f.* double net for catching fish.
contramallar, *va.* to make CONTRAMALLAS.
contramandar, *va.* to countermand.
contramandato, *m.* countermand, contrary order.
contramangas, *f. pl.* oversleeves.
contramaniobra, *f.* countermanœuvre.
contramanivela, *f.* (mech.) drag link.
contramarca, *f.* countermark; duty to be paid on goods which have no customhouse mark

contramarcar, *va.* (*pret.* CONTRAMARQUÉ; *subj.* CONTRAMARQUE) to countermark.
contramarco, *m.* (carp.) counterframe.
contramarcha, *f.* countermarch, retrocession; part of a weaver's loom; (mil. and naut.) evolution.—**de c.,** reverse (lever, etc.).
contramarchar, *vn.* to countermarch; to go backwards.
contramarea, *f.* (naut.) countertide.
contramarqué, contramarque, *v. V.* CONTRAMARCAR.
contramesana, *f.* (naut.) mizzenmast.
contramina, *f.* countermine; (min.) driftway, heading.
contraminar, *va.* to countermine.
contramolde, *m.* countermold.
contramotivo, *m.* (mus.) countersubject.
contramuelle, *m.* (mech.) duplicate spring.
contramuralla, *f.,* **contramuro,** *m.* (mil.) countermure, low rampart.
contranatural, *a.* contranatural, unnatural.
contraofensiva, *f.* (mil.) counteroffensive.
contraorden, *f.* countermand.
contrapalanquín, *m.* (naut.) preventer clew garnet.
contrapares, *m. pl.* (arch.) counterrafters.
contraparte, *f.* counterpart.
contrapartida, *f.* (in bookkeeping) emendatory or corrective entry.
contrapás, *m.* a step in dancing.
contrapasamiento, *m.* act and effect of passing to the opposite side or party.
contrapasar, *vn.* to join the opposite party.
contrapaso, *m.* back step; (mus.) second part.
contrapelo.—a c., *adv.* against the grain.
contrapesar, *va.* to counterbalance; to countervail, offset.
contrapeso, *m.* counterweight; counterpoise, counterbalance, countervail; plummet; balancing weight; ropedancer's pole; equipollence, equivalence of power; something thrown in to make up the weight of meat, fish, etc.
contrapeste, *m.* remedy against pestilence or epidemic.
contrapilastra, *f.* (arch.) counterpilaster; (carp.) weatherstrip.
contrapolicía, *f.* police that secretly watches the ordinary police.
contrapóliza, *f.* insurance policy that annuls a previous one.
contraponedor, ra, *n.* one who compares.
contraponer, *va.* (*pp.* CONTRAPUESTO; *ind. pres.* CONTRAPONGO, *pret.* CONTRAPUSE; *subj.* CONTRAPONGA) to oppose; to compare.
contraposición, *f.* contraposition; counterview; contrast.
contrapozo, *m.* (fort.) counterblast.
contrapresión, *f.* back pressure.
contraprincipio, *m.* opposite principle, statement contrary to a principle known as such.
contraproducente, contraproducéntem, *a.* self-defeating, producing the opposite of the desired effect.
contrapromesa, *f.* withdrawal of a promise; promise opposed to another.
contraproposición, *f.* counterproposition.
contrapropósito, *m.* change of purpose; purpose opposed to another.
contraprueba, *f.* (print.) second proof.
contrapuerta, *f.* inner large door after the street door.
contrapuesto, ta, *pp. irreg.* of CONTRAPONER; (a) compared, contrasted (with); opposed (to).
contrapuntante, *n.* counterpoint singer.
contrapuntear. I. *va.* (mus.) to sing in counterpoint; to taunt; to revile. **II.** *vr.* to abuse one another; to wrangle, dispute.
contrapuntista, *m.* (mus.) contrapuntist, one skilled in counterpoint.
contrapunto, *m.* (mus.) counterpoint, harmony.
contrapunzón, *m.* puncheon for driving in a nail; counterpunch; gunsmith's mark on guns.
contrapuse, *pret.* of CONTRAPONER.
contraquerella, *f.* cross-complaint.
contraquilla, *f.* (naut.) false keel.
contrariar, *va.* to contradict, oppose, counteract, thwart, run counter to; to disappoint; vex, upset, annoy.
contrariedad, *f.* contrariety, contrariness; opposition, contradiction; disappointment, impediment, obstacle; trouble, vexation.
contrario, ria. I. *a.* contrary, opposite, contradictory; opposed, adverse; abhorrent; unfavorable, antagonistic. **II.** *m.* opponent, antagonist, competitor, rival.—**al c.,** on the contrary.—**de lo c.,** otherwise, if not.—**en c.,** against, in opposition to.—**por el c.,** or **por lo c.,** on the contrary. **III.** *f.*—**llevar la c.,** to contradict; to oppose.
contrarreclamación, *f.* counterclaim.
contrarreforma, *f.* counterreformation.
contrarregistro, *m.* control register.
contrarreguera, *f.* lateral drain.
contrarréplica, *f.* rejoinder, reply to an answer; rebutter.
contrarrestar, *va.* to resist, oppose, check; to counteract, offset; to return (a ball).
contrarresto, *m.* check; opposition, contradiction; player who strikes back the ball.
contrarrevolución, *f.* counter-revolution.
contrarrevolucionario, ria, *n.* & *a.* counter-revolutionist, counter-revolutionary.
contrarriel, *m.* (Ry.) guard rail, wing rail.
contrarroda, *f.* (naut.) stemson.
contrarronda, *f.* (mil.) counterround.
contrarrotura, *f.* (vet.) plaster or poultice applied to fractures or wounds.
contrasalida, *f.* (mil.) countersally.
contrasalva, *f.* (mil.) countersalute.
contraseguro, *m.* a contract by which an underwriter agrees to return to the insured, under specified conditions, all premiums previously paid.
contrasellar, *va.* to counterseal.
contrasello, *m.* counterseal, small seal superimposed on another seal.
contrasentido, *m.* countersense, opposite sense; conclusion contrary to premises; (Gal.) nonsense.
contraseña, *f.* countersign, countermark; (Cuba) check (for hat, baggage, etc.); (mil.) watchword.—**c. de salida,** (theat.) check (to readmit one who goes out).
contrasol, *m.* sunshade.
contrastador, ra, *a.* contrasting.
contrastante, *a.* contrasting.
contrastar. I. *va.* to contrast, place in opposition, oppose; to resist; contradict; to assay and stamp (metals); to examine, inspect (weights and measures). **II.** *vn.* to contrast, be different.—**c. bien,** (of colors, etc.) to go well together.—**c. mal,** (of colors, etc.) to clash.
contraste, *m.* contrast; opposition; strife, contest; assayer of the mint; assayer's office; assay; mark of assay; inspector of weights and measures; public office where raw silk is weighed; (naut.) sudden change of the wind, by which it becomes foul or contrary.
contrata, *f.* contract.
contratación, *f.* trade, commerce; enterprise, undertaking; business transaction.
contratante, *n.* & *a.* contractor(-ing).
contratar, *va.* to enter into an agreement about; to contract for; to engage, hire; to make a deal or bargain about.
contratela, *f.* among hunters, second inclosure of canvas to shut up game.
contratiempo, *m.* disappointment; misfortune, mishap.
contratista, *m.* contractor; lessee; patentee; grantee; covenanter.
contrato, *m.* contract.—**c. a la gruesa,** or **a riesgo marítimo,** respondentia.—**c. aleatorio,** aleatory contract.—**c. consensual,** consensual contract.—**c. de compraventa,** or **de compra y venta,** contract of bargain and

sale.—**c. de locación y conducción,** agreement to let one enjoy the use of property for a price or service.—**c. de retrovendendo,** reversion clause of bargain and sale.—**c. enfitéutico,** emphyteusis.—**c. perfecto,** contract of record.

contratorpedero, *m.* torpedo-boat destroyer.

contratrancaniles, *m. pl.* (naut.) inner waterways.

contratreta, *f.* counterplot.

contratrinchera, *f.* (mil.) countertrench.

contratuerca, *f.* check nut, lock nut.

contravalación, *f.* (mil.) contravallation.

contravalar, *va.* to form a contravallation about.

contravalor, *m.* (com.) countervalue, equivalent.

contravapor, *m.* (steam eng.) back steam.

contravención, *f.* contravention, violation (of a law).

contraveneno, *m.* counterpoison, antidote; precaution taken to avoid some infamy or mischief.

contravenir, *va.* (*ind. pres.* CONTRAVENGO, *pret.* CONTRAVINE; *subj.* CONTRAVENGA) to contravene, transgress, violate; to oppose, obstruct, baffle, countermine.

contraventana, *f.* window shutter.

contraventor, ra, *n.* transgressor, offender.

contravidriera, *f.* storm window.

contravine, *pret.* of CONTRAVENIR.

contravisita, *f.* second visit, made to verify the results of a previous one.

contravoluta, *f.* (arch.) inner volute.

contray, *m.* a sort of fine cloth.

contrayente, *a.* engaged (to be married).

contrecho, cha, *a.* crippled, maimed.

contrete, *m.* (Am.) (naut.) breastshore; crochet; angle iron; stay; gusset, face wheel in watches.

contribución, *f.* contribution; tax, impost.—**c. de sangre,** military service.—**c. territorial,** land tax.

contribuidor, ra, *n.* & *a.* contributor(-ing).

contribuir, *va.* & *vn.* (*ind.* CONTRIBUYO; *subj.* CONTRIBUYA) to contribute; (fig.) to help.

contribulado, da, *a.* grieved, afflicted.

contributario, *m.* contributor, taxpayer.

contribuyente. **I.** *a.* contributing; contributory. **II.** *n.* contributor; taxpayer.

contribuyo, contribuya, *v.* *V.* CONTRIBUIR.

contrición, *f.* contrition, compunction, repentance.

contrín, *m.* (P.I.) weight of 0.39 gramme, or 6½ grains.

contrincante, *m.* competitor, rival, opponent.

contristar, *va.* to sadden, grieve.

contrito, ta, *a.* contrite, repentant, penitent.

control, *m.* (Gal.) control, checking, verifying.—**controlar,** *va.* (Gal.) to control, check, verify (esp. in technical lang.).

contróler, *m.* (elec.) controller, esp. on elec. car or locomotive (better COMBINADOR).

controversia, *f.* controversy, debate.

controversista, *m.* controversialist, debater.

controvertible, *a.* controvertible, disputable.

controvertir, *va.* (*ind.* CONTROVIERTO; *subj.* CONTROVIERTA) to controvert, dispute, argue against.

contubernio, *m.* cohabitation, concubinage; base or infamous alliance.

contuerzo, contuerza, *v.* *V.* CONTORCERSE.

contumacia, *f.* obstinacy, stubbornness; (law) contumacy, non-appearance, contempt of court; default.

contumaz, *a.* obstinate, stubborn; contumacious, disobedient; guilty of contempt of court.

contumelia, *f.* contumely, insult, abuse; contumeliousness.

contumelioso, sa, *a.* contumelious, insulting.

contundente, *a.* (of a weapon or an act) producing contusion; impressing the mind deeply, forceful.

contundir, *va.* to contuse, bruise, pound.

conturbación, *f.* perturbation, uneasiness, anxiety.

conturbado, da. **I.** *pp.* of CONTURBAR. **II.** *a.* turbulent, troublesome.

conturbador, *m.* perturber, disturber.

conturbar. **I.** *va.* to perturb, disturb, trouble. **II.** *vr.* to become uneasy, agitated, anxious.

conturbativo, va, *a.* disquieting, disturbing.

contusión, *f.* contusion, bruise.

contuso, sa, *a.* bruised.

contutor, *m.* assistant tutor, fellow tutor.

contuve, *pret.* of CONTENER.

conuco, conusco, *m.* (Am.) patch of ground given to slaves; maize field.

convalecencia, *f.* convalescence.

convalecer, *vn.* (*ind.* CONVALEZCO; *subj.* CONVALEZCA) to recover from sickness; to recover lost prosperity, influence, etc.; (coll.) to come back.—**convaleciente,** *n.* & *a.* convalescent.

convalidar, *va.* (law) to confirm.

convección, *f.* (phys.) convection.

convecino, na, *a.* neighboring.

convelerse, *vr.* (med.) to twitch; to be contracted.

convencedor, ra, *n.* & *a.* convincer(-ing).

convencer. **I.** *va.* (*pp.* CONVENCIDO and CONVICTO; *ind.* CONVENZO; *subj.* CONVENZA) to convince; to prove irrefutably to (a person). **II.** *vr.* to become convinced.

convencible, *a.* convincible.

convencimiento, *m.* conviction, belief; (act of) convincing.—**en el c. de que,** being convinced that, believing that.

convención, *f.* convention; contract, agreement, pact; conformity.—**convencional,** *a.* conventional.

convencionalismo, *m.* conventionalism, conventionality.

convengo, convenga, *v.* *V.* CONVENIR.

convenible, *a.* docile, tractable, compliant; (of prices) reasonable, moderate.

convenido, da. **I.** *pp.* of CONVENIR. **II.** *a.* settled by consent; agreed.

conveniencia, *f.* conformity, congruity, consistence; suitability, fitness; desirability, expedience, advantage; self-interest; agreement, adjustment; employ, service; servant's place in a house or family; convenience, ease.—*pl.* emoluments, perquisites; income, property.

conveniente, *a.* useful, advantageous, good; conformable; fit, suitable; desirable, advisable; expedient, opportune, timely; decent, discreet.—**convenientemente,** *adv.* fitly, appropriately, suitably; expediently.

convenio, *m.* convention, agreement, pact; consent; contrivance.

convenio postal, *m.* postal convention.

convenir. **I.** *vn.* (*ind. pres.* CONVENGO, *pret.* CONVINE; *subj.* CONVENGA) to agree; coincide, cohere; to fit, harmonize, comport, suit; to correspond, belong; to assemble, convene.—**c. en,** to agree to. **II.** *v. impers.* to be to the purpose; (foll. by inf.) to be a good thing to (inf.).—**conviene a saber,** namely, to wit.—**según convenga,** according to circumstances, according to what seems best. **III.** *vr.* to agree, make a deal; to suit one's interests.

conventazo, *m. aug.* large convent.

conventico, illo, ito, *m. dim.* (coll.) tenement inhabited by persons of ill repute.

conventícula, *f.*, **conventículo,** *m.* conventicle.

convento, *m.* convent; monastery; nunnery; community of religious men or women.

conventual. **I.** *a.* conventual, monastic. **II.** *m.* conventual, a monk; Conventual, a member of the Conventual Franciscan order.—**conventualidad,** *f.* state of living in a convent or monastery; assignment of a monk to a convent.—**conventualmente,** *adv.* monastically.

convenzo, convenza, *v.* *V.* CONVENCER.

convergencia, *f.* convergence.

convergente, *a.* convergent, converging.

converger, convergir, *vn.* to converge; to agree in opinion.

conversa, *f.* chat, talk.

conversable, *a.* sociable, tractable.
conversación, *f.* conversation, talk; conference; commerce, intercourse, society, company; illicit intercourse.
conversador, ra, *n.* & *a.* (Am.) talker(-ative); good conversationalist.
conversar, *vn.* to converse, talk; to chat; to live in the company of others; to have social intercourse; (mil.) to change front, wheel.
conversible, *m.* & *a.* = CONVERTIBLE.
conversión, *f.* conversion; change, transformation; (rhet.) apostrophe; (mil.) wheel, wheeling.
conversivo, va, *a.* having the power of converting or changing.
converso, sa. I. *pp. irreg.* of CONVERTIR. **II.** *m.* convert; lay brother.
conversón, na, *a.* (Colomb. coll.) garrulous, talkative.
convertibilidad, *f.* convertibility.
convertible. I. *a.* convertible; movable, transferable. **II.** *m.* (auto) convertible.
convertido, da. I. *pp.* of CONVERTIR. **II.** *n.* & *a.* (one) converted.
convertidor, *m.* (elec., metal.) converter.
convertir. I. *va.* (*pp.* CONVERTIDO and CONVERSO; *ind.* CONVIERTO; *subj.* CONVIERTA) to convert; reform; change; transform. **II.** *vr.* to be converted, reformed.
convexidad, *f.* convexity.
convexo, xa, *a.* convex.
convexocóncavo, va, *a.* convexo-concave.
convicción, *f.* conviction, certainty, certitude.
convicto, ta. I. *pp. irreg.* of CONVENCER. **II.** *a.* convinced, persuaded, induced; (law) convicted, guilty. **III.** *n.* convict.
convictor, *m.* (prov.) boarder; person living in a college without being a member or student.
convictorio, *m.* among the Jesuits, living quarters of students.
convidada, *f.* invitation to drink, treat.
convidado, da. I. *pp.* of CONVIDAR. **II.** *a.* & *n.* invited (guest).
convidador, ra, *n.* inviter.
convidante, *n.* inviter, one who invites; host.
convidar. I. *va.* to invite; to treat; to allure, entice, induce. **II.** *vr.* to offer one's services spontaneously; to invite oneself, come uninvited.
convierto, convierta, *v. V.* CONVERTIR.
convincente, *a.* convincing; convincible.
convine, *pret.* of CONVENIR.
convite, *m.* invitation; banquet; treat.
convival, *a.* convivial.
convivencia, *f.* act of living together.
conviviente, *a.* living together.
convivir, *vn.* to live together.
convocación, *f.* convocation, calling.
convocador, ra, *n.* convener, convoker.
convocar, *va.* (*pret.* CONVOQUÉ; *subj.* CONVOQUE) to convene, convoke, call together, summon; to acclaim.
convocatoria, *f.* letter of convocation, edict, summons; notice of meeting.
convocatorio, ria, *a.* that convokes.
convóluto, ta, *a.* convolute.
convolvuláceo, cea, *a.* convolvulaceous.
convólvulo, *m.* (zool.) vine inchworm; (bot.) convolvulus.
convoqué, convoque, *v. V.* CONVOCAR.
convoy, *m.* convoy, conduct, escort, guard; property under convoy; (coll.) retinue; railway train.
convoyante, *a.* convoying.
convoyar, *va.* to convoy, escort, guard.
convulsión, *f.* convulsion.
convulsionar, *va.* to convulse.
convulsionario, ria, *a.* convulsive.
convulsivo, va, *a.* convulsive.
convulso, sa, *a.* convulsed.
conyugal, *a.* conjugal, connubial.
cónyuge, *n.* spouse, husband or wife.
coñac, *m.* cognac, brandy.
cooperación, *f.* coöperation.
cooperador, ra; cooperante, *n.* & *a.* coöperator (-ing, -ive); contributor(-ing).
cooperar, *vn.* to coöperate.
cooperario, ria, *n.* = COOPERADOR.
cooperativa, *f.* coöperative (ass'n or soc'y).
cooperativo, va, *a.* coöperative, coöperating.
coopositor, *m.* one of two candidates for a professorship, etc., to be obtained by competition.
coordenado, a. I. *a.* coördinate. **II.** *f.* (math.) coördinate.—**c. cartesiana,** Cartesian coördinate.—**c. polar,** polar coördinate.
coordinación, *f.* coördination.
coordinador, ra. I. *a.* coördinating. **II.** *n.* coördinator.
coordinamiento, *m.* = COORDINACIÓN.
coordinar, *va.* to coördinate.
copa, *f.* goblet, wineglass, cup; liquid contained in a glass; drink (of liquor); treetop; bower; crown of a hat; brasier, fire pan; roof or vault of an oven or furnace; gill, liquid measure; teacupful; (in cards) a card of heart suit.—**sombrero de c.,** (coll.) top hat.—*pl.* (cards) hearts; bosses of a bridle.
copada, *f.* (ornith.) = COGUJADA, crested lark.
copado, da, *a.* tufted, abundant in foliage.
copaiba, *f.* (bot.) copaiba.
copal, *m.* copal, a transparent resin.
copaljocol, copaljocote, *m.* a Mexican tree resembling a cherry tree.
copanete, cópano, *m.* an ancient small boat.
copaquira, *f.* (Am.) copperas.
copar, *va.* in monte, to put on a card a sum equal to what there is in the bank; (coll.) to corner; (mil.) to surprise; cut off the retreat of; to corner; to grab.
coparticipación, *f.* copartnership.
copartícipe, *n.* partieipant, copartner.
copayero, *m.* copaiba tree.
copaza, *f. aug.* large cup or glass with a stem.
copazo, *m. aug.* large fleece of wool; large flake of snow.
copec, *m.* kopeck (Russian coin).
copela, *f.* (metal.) cupel.
copelación, *f.* (metal.) cupellation.
copelar, *va.* (metal.) to cupel.
copépodo, da, *m.* & *a.* (zool.) copepod.
copera, *f.* cupboard, sideboard; china closet.
coperillo, *m. dim.* little cupbearer.
copernicano, na, *a.* Copernican.
copero, *m.* cupbearer; sideboard, buffet; glass rack.
copeta, *f. dim.* small cup or drinking vessel.
copete, *m.* toupee, tuft, pompadour, aigret; forelock of a horse; crownwork of a piece of furniture; top of the shoe that rises over the buckle; top, summit; projecting top or cop of sherbet or ice cream.—**asir la ocasión por el c.,** to profit by, or improve, the opportunity.—**de c.,** or **de alto c.,** of (the) blood, of the nobility; aristocratic, high-rank.—**tener mucho c.,** to put on airs, to be haughty or stuck up.
copetudo, da, *a.* copped, tufted; rising to a top or head; high, lofty.
copey, *m.* an American tree of excellent wood for engraving; bitumen found in Ecuador.
copia, *f.* copiousness, plenty, abundance; fertility; copy (of a letter, picture, person, etc.); "living image" (of another person); imitation; taking up; rate or valuation of tithe; (gram.) list of nouns and verbs, and the cases they govern; (poet.) couple.—**c. verbal,** literal, verbatim copy.
copiador, *m.* copyist, copier, transcriber.—**c. de cartas,** (copying) letter book.
copiante, *n.* copyist; imitator.
copiar, *va.* to copy; to imitate; to mimic, take up; ape; (poet.) to describe, depict.—**c. del natural,** to copy from life.
copilador, *m.* = COMPILADOR, compiler, collector.
copilar, *va.* = COMPILAR, to compile, collect.
copilla, *f. dim.* of COPA; cigarlighter.

copín, *m.* in Asturias, a grain measure equal to half a CELEMÍN.
copina, *f.* (Mex.) skin taken off whole.
copinar, *va.* to remove (a skin) entire.
copiosidad, *f.* copiousness, abundance.
copioso, sa, *a.* copious, abundant.
copista. I. *m.* & *f.* copyist, transcriber. **II.** *m.* copying machine.
copita, *f. dim.* small glass or cup.
copito, *m. dim.* small fleece or flake.
copla, *f.* couplet; popular song, ballad; sarcastic hint or remark; lampoon.
coplear, *vn.* to compose or sing ballads.
copleja, *f. dim.* little ballad.
coplero, ra, *n.* ballad seller; poetaster.
coplica, illa, ita, *f. dim.* little ballad
coplista, *n.* = COPLERO, poetaster.
coplón, *m. aug.* low, vile poetry (gen. used in the plural, **coplones**).
[1]**copo,** *m.* small bundle of cotton, hemp, flax, or silk, put on the distaff to be spun; snowflake; soap flake; cornering, surprise; grab; (Colomb.) = COPA, treetop.
[2]**copo,** *m.* bottom of a purse seine; hauling with a purse seine.
copón, *m. aug.* large cup or drinking vessel; ciborium.
coposo, sa, *a.* = COPADO.
copra, *f.* copra, dried kernel of the coconut.
coprófago, ga, *a.* coprophagous, dung-eating (as a beetle).
coprolito, *m.* (paleontol.) coprolite; (med.) intestinal calculus.
copropiedad, *f.* joint ownership; property held in common.
copropietario, ia, *n.* joint owner, co-proprietor.
cóptico, ca, *a.* Coptic.
copto, ta. I. *a.* Coptic. **II.** *n.* Copt; *m.* Coptic (language).
copudo, da, *a.* tufted, bushy, thick-topped (tree).
[1]**cópula,** *f.* joining, coupling two things together; connection; copulation, carnal union; (logic) copula.
[2]**cópula,** *f.* = CÚPULA, (arch.) cupola
copularse, *vr.* to copulate.
copulativamente, *adv.* jointly.
copulativo, va, *a.* joining or uniting together; (gram.) copulative.
coque, *m.* coke.
coqueluche, *f.* (Gal. for TOS FERINA), whooping cough.
[1]**coquera,** *f.* head or handle of a top.
[2]**coquera,** *f.* small hollow in a stone.
[3]**coquera,** *f.* coke scuttle or box.
[4]**coquera,** *f.* (Am.) a place for coca.
coquero, *m.* (Am.) dealer in coconuts.
[1]**coqueta,** *f.* feruling (esp. of schoolchildren); small loaf or roll (of bread).
[2]**coqueta,** *f.* coquette, flirt.—**coquetamente,** *adv.* coquettishly, flirtatiously.
coquetear, *vn.* to flirt, coquet.
coqueteo, *m.* coquetting, flirting; flirtation.
coquetería, *f.* coquetry; flirtation; affectation.
coquetón, tona. I. *a.* coquettish. **II.** *m.* (coll.) lady-killer.
coquetonamente, *adv.* coquettishly, flirtatiously.
coquimbo, *m.* (Am.) burrowing owl.
coquina, *f.* cockle, an edible bivalve; cockle shell; soft shelly stone.—**coquinero, ra,** *n.* cockleseller.
[1]**coquito,** *m. dim.* grimace to amuse children.
[2]**coquito,** *m.* turtledove of Mexico.
[3]**coquito,** *m.* a tall Chilean palm tree.
coráceo, a, *a.* = CORIÁCEO, leathery.
coracero, *m.* cuirassier; (coll.) poor cigar.
coracilla, *f. dim.* small coat of mail.
coracina, *f.* small breastplate.
coracora, *f.* (P.I.) coasting vessel.
coracha, *f.* leather bag.
corachín, *m. dim.* small leather bag.
coraje, *m.* courage, bravery; fortitude, mettle; anger, passion.—**corajoso, sa,** *a.* brave, dashing.—**corajudo, da,** *a.* angry, ill-tempered.
[1]**coral,** *m.* coral; (Venez., Colomb.) a white-and-red poisonous snake.—*pl.* string of corals.
[2]**coral,** *a.* choral, pert. to choir.
coralero, ra, *n.* worker or dealer in corals.
coralífero, ra, *a.* coral-bearing.
coralillo, *m.* a venomous coral-color snake.
coralina, *f.* coral insect, sea coralline; any sea animal resembling coral.
coralino, na, *a.* coralline, of or resembling coral.
corambre, *f.* hides, skins, dressed or undressed; pelts.—**corambrero,** *m.* dealer in hides and skins.
Corán, *m.* Koran.—**coránico, ca,** *a.* Koranic.
coranvobis, *m.* (coll.) corpulent person strutting about with affected gravity.
coraza, *f.* cuirass, armor plating; shell or carapace of a turtle, etc.; armor (of a vessel, cable, etc.)
coraznada, *f.* pith of a pine tree; fricassee of the hearts of animals.
corazón, *m.* heart; core, pith; love, benevolence, affection; spirit, courage, will, mind; middle or centre of anything; in a loom, cam.—**c. de un cabo,** (naut.) heart strand.—**anunciar,** or **decir, el c.,** to have a presentiment.—**arrancársele a uno el c.,** to be heartbroken, to bleed at the heart (diff. constr.: *se me arranca el corazón al ver su desgracia,* my heart bleeds at his misfortune).—**de c.,** heartily, sincerely; courageous, enterprising.—**llevar,** or **traer, el c. en la mano,** to wear one's heart upon one's sleeve.—**corazonada,** *f.* impulse of the heart; presentiment, foreboding; (coll.) entrails.—**corazonazo,** *m. aug.* great heart.—**corazoncico, illo, ito,** *m. dim.* little heart; faint-hearted person.—**corazoncillo,** *m.* (bot.) perforated St.-John's-wort.
corbachada, *f.* lash with a CORBACHO.
corbacho, *m.* cowhide whip.
corbata. I. *f.* cravat, necktie; scarf, neckcloth; sash or ribbon badge tied to banners; ribbon, insignia of an order.—**c. de lazo,** or **de mariposa,** bow tie.—**c. de nudo,** four-in-hand tie. **II.** *m.* magistrate not trained in law, so without a vote in certain cases.
corbatería, *f.* necktie shop.
corbatero, ra, *n.* necktie maker or dealer.
corbatín, *m.* cravat, tie; stock.
corbato, *m.* cooler, worm tub of a still.
corbatón, *m.* small knee, bracket.
corbe, *m.* an ancient measure for baskets.
corbeta, *f.* (naut.) corvette.—**c. de guerra,** sloop of war.
corcel, *m.* steady horse, charger.
corcesca, *f.* ancient barbed spear.
corcino, *m.* small deer.
corcova, *f.* hump, crooked back; hunch, protuberance, curvature.
corcovado, da. I. *pp.* of CORCOVAR. **II.** *a.* humpbacked, gibbous; crooked.
corcovar, *va.* to crook.
corcovear, *vn.* (of horse) to cut capers; to buck.
corcoveta, *f. dim.* small hump; (coll.) crookbacked person.
corcovo, *m.* spring, curvet made by a horse on the point of leaping; (coll.) crookedness, wrong step, unfair proceeding.
corcusido, da. I. *pp.* of CORCUSIR. **II.** *a.* clumsily mended or sewed on.
corcusir, *va.* (coll.) to darn clumsily.
[1]**corcha,** *f.* cork bark; wine cooler.
[2]**corcha,** *f.* (naut.) laying of a rope.
corchar. I. *va.* (naut.) to lay (strands of ropes); to accept (a challenge). **II.** *vn.* (Colomb.) not to pass an examination, "flunk."
corche, *m.* cork-soled sandal or clog.
corchea, *f.* (mus.) quaver, an eighth note.
corchear, *va.* to grain (leather) with a cork.
corchera, *f.* wine cooler made of cork.
corcheta, *f.* eye of a hook or clasp; (carp.) rabbet in a door or window frame.
corchete, *m.* clasp, hook, hook and eye (*pl.* **corchetes,** hooks and eyes); crotch; snaplock,

catch; (coll.) constable; brace to connect lines in writing or printing (⁀⁀); (carp.) bench hook.
corcho, *m.* cork; bark of the cork tree; wine cooler; beehive; cork box for carrying eatables; cork mat; cork-soled sandal or clog; float of a fishing line; (mil.) tampion.
corchoso, sa, *a.* corklike.
corda, *f.*—**estar a la c.,** (naut.) to be close-hauled or lying to.
cordado, da, *m.* & *a.* (zool.) chordate.
cordaje, *m.* rigging; cordage.
[1]**cordal,** *m.* string bar at the bottom of stringed instruments.
[2]**cordal,** *a.* & *f.* = MUELA C., double tooth; wisdom tooth.—*pl.* grinders.
cordato, ta, *a.* prudent, discreet, judicious.
cordel, *m.* cord, thin rope; (naut.) line; length of five steps; land measure in Cuba equal to about 1 sq. ch.—**c. de corredera,** log line.—**a c.,** in a straight line.—**cordelado, da,** *a.* twisted silk for ribbons or garters.—**cordelazo,** *m.* stroke or lash with a rope.—**cordelejo,** *m. dim.* small rope; fun, jest.—**dar c.,** to banter.
cordelería, *f.* cordage; ropewalk; (naut.) rigging.
cordelero, ra, *n.* ropemaker, cordmaker.
cordelito, *m. dim.* small rope, cord, or line.
cordellate, *m.* grosgrain, a kind of ribbed fabric.
cordera, *f.* ewe lamb; meek, gentle woman.
cordería, *f.* cordage; place where cordage is kept.
corderica, illa, ita, *f. dim.* little ewe lamb.
corderico, illo, ito, *m. dim.* little lamb.
corderillo, *m.* lambskin dressed with the fleece.
corderina, *f.* lambskin.
corderino, na, *a.* pertaining to lambs.
cordero, *m.* lamb; dressed lambskin; meek, gentle, or mild man.—**c. añal,** yearling lamb.—**c. de Dios,** Lamb of God (Christ).—**c. pascual,** paschal lamb.—**c. recental,** suckling lamb.
corderuela, *f. dim.* little ewe lamb.
corderuelo, *m. dim.* little or young lamb.
corderuna, *f.* lambskin.
cordeta, *f.* small bassweed rope.
cordezuela, *f. dim.* small rope.
cordíaco, ca, *a.* (med.) = CARDÍACO, cardiac.
cordial. I. *a.* cordial, hearty; sincere; invigorating. **II.** *m.* cordial; tonic.
cordialidad, *f.* cordiality, heartiness, sincerity.
cordialmente, *adv.* cordially, sincerely, affectionately, heartily.
cordiforme, *a.* heart-shaped.
cordila, *f.* spawn of tunny fish.
cordilo, *m.* an amphibious animal resembling a crocodile.
cordilla, *f.* guts of sheep given to cats to eat.
cordillera, *f.* cordillera, mountain range.
cordita, *f.* cordite (explosive).
corditis, *f.* inflammation of the vocal cords.
cordobán, *m.* cordovan, Spanish leather; tanned goatskin.—**cordobana,** *f.* nakedness, nudity.—**andar a la c.,** (coll.) to go stark naked.
cordobanero, ra, *n.* cordovan tanner.
cordobés, besa, *n.* & *a.* Cordovan.
cordón, *m.* cord, round cord, twine; (shoe) lace; monk's rope belt; (mil.) cordon; strand of a cable or rope; (arch.) torus molding; string course; milled edge of a coin.—*pl.* (mil.) aglets or aiguillettes; harness cords of a velvet loom.—**c. umbilical,** umbilical cord.
cordonazo, *m. aug.* large cord; blow with a cord or rope.—**c. de San Francisco,** first equinoctial storm in the autumn.
cordoncico, illo, ito, *m. dim.* small cord.
cordoncillo, *m.* twisted cord; round lace, lacing, braid; milling on edge of a coin.
cordonería, *f.* work of twisters or lace makers; lace maker's shop.
cordonero, ra, *n.* lace maker; ropemaker.
cordula, *f.* = CORDILO.
cordura, *f.* prudence, practical wisdom, sanity.
corea, *f.* dance accompanied by a chorus; (med.) chorea, St. Vitus's dance.
Corea, *f.* Korea.
coreano, na, *n.* & *a.* Korean.
corear, *vn.* to compose chorus music.
corecico, illo, *m. dim.* of CUERO, pelt.
[1]**coreo,** *m.* foot in Latin verse; trochee.
[2]**coreo,** *m.* connected harmony of a chorus.
coreografía, *f.* art of dancing; choreography, writing dance music.
coreográfico, ca, *a.* choreographic.
coreógrafo, fa, *n.* choreographer.
coreopsis, *m.* (bot.) coreopsis.
corezuelo, *m. dim.* small hide; suckling pig; small roasted pig.
cori, *m.* (bot.) Montpellier coris, St.-John's-wort.
coriáceo, a, *a.* coriaceous, leathery.
coriámbico, ca, *n.* & *a.*; **coriambo,** *m.* (poet.) choriambic, foot of two short between two long syllables.
coriandro, *m.* (bot.) coriander.
coribante, *m.* Corybantes, priest of Cybele.
coribantismo, *m.* corybantiasm, a kind of frenzy accompanied by many contortions.
corifeo, *m.* coryphæus, leader of anc. dramatic chorus; leader or member of a sect or party.
corimbo, *m.* (bot.) corymb.
corindón, *m.* corundum.
coríntico, ca, *a.* Corinthian.
corintio, tia, *n.* & *a.* Corinthian.
corión, *m.* (zool.) chorion.
corista, *n.* chorister, chorus singer.
corito, ta. I. *a.* naked; timid, pusillanimous. **II.** *n.* person who treads grapes in the wine press.
[1]**coriza,** *f.* leather sandal worn by peasants in some parts of Spain.
[2]**coriza,** *f.* (med.) coryza, head-cold.
corladura, *f.* gold varnish.
corlar, corlear, *va.* to cover with gold varnish.
corma, *f.* (restraining) stocks; trouble, uneasiness.
cornac, cornaca, *m.* keeper of tame elephants.
cornáceo, cea, *a.* (bot.) cornaceous.
cornada, *f.* thrust with the horns; upward thrust with a foil, in fencing.
cornadillo, *m. dim.* small coin.
cornado, *m.* old copper coin mixed with silver.
cornadura, *f.* = CORNAMENTA.
cornal, *m.* strap or thong with which oxen are tied to the yoke by the horns.
cornalina, *f.* (min.) cornelian, carnelian.
cornamenta, *f.* the horns of any animal.
cornamusa, *f.* cornemuse, a bagpipe; (mus.) a sort of brass horn; (naut.) belaying cleat.
cornatillo, *m.* a kind of olive.
córnea, *f.* (anat.) cornea.—**c. opaca,** sclera.
corneador, ra, *n.* & *a.* butting (animal).
cornear, *va.* = ACORNEAR, to butt.
cornecico, illo, ito, *m. dim.* cornicle, small horn.
corneja, *f.* (ornith.) crow; fetlock; dow.
cornejal, *m.* dogwood field.
cornejalejo, *m.* (bot.) pod.
cornejo, *m.* (bot.) hound tree or cornel tree, dogwood.
cornelina, *f.* = CORNALINA.
córneo, nea, *a.* corneous, corny, horny, callous; (bot.) cornaceous.
cornerina, *f.* = CORNALINA.
cornero, *m.*—**c. de pan,** crust (of bread).
corneta. I. *f.* bugle; horn used by swineherds; cornet, ensign of horse; flag carried by horse troops; troop of horse; (naut.) broad pennant; rear admiral's flag.—**c. de llaves,** cornet.—**c. de monte,** huntsman's horn.—**c. de posta,** post's horn. **II.** *n.* bugler.
cornete, *m. dim.* small bugle horn.
cornetín, *m.* cornet; cornettist.
cornezuelo, *m.* ergot of rye; (vet.) instrument for bleeding horses; (bot.) CORNICABRA.
corniabierto, ta, *a.* having wide-spread horns.
cornial, *a.* horn-shaped.
corniapretado, da, *a.* having horns close-set.
cornicabra, *f.* (bot.) turpentine tree, pistachio tree, wild fig tree; a kind of crescent olive.
cornidelantero, ra, *a.* (Mex.) with horns turned forward.

corniforme, *a.* horn-shaped.
cornigacho, cha, *a.* having the horns turned slightly downward.
cornígero, ra, *a.* (poet.) horned, cornigerous.
cornija, *f.* (arch.) = CORNISA.
cornijal, *m.* angle or corner of a mattress, building, etc.
cornijamento, cornijamiento, *m.* (arch.) = CORNISAMENTO.
cornijón, *m.* (arch.) entablature; street corner of a building.
cornil, *m.* = CORNAL.
corniola, *f.* = CORNALINA.
cornisa, *f.* (arch.) cornice.—**cornisamento, cornisamiento,** *m.* (arch.) entablature.
cornisica, illa, ita, *f. dim.* small cornice.
cornisón, *m.* = CORNIJÓN.
corniveleto, ta, *a.* having horns turned strongly upward.
cornizo, corno, *m.* = CORNEJO.
cornucopia, *f.* cornucopia; sconce; pier glass.
cornudo, da. I. *a.* horned. **II.** *m.* cuckold.
cornúpeta, *a.* (poet.) attacking with the horns.
[1]**coro,** *m.* choir; chorus; singing chorus; assembly unanimous in sentiment; choir loft; choir of angels.—**hablar a coros,** to speak alternately.—**hacer c. a,** to follow, support; to play second fiddle to.
[2]**coro,** *m.* memory.—**de c.,** from memory, by rote.
[1]**corocha,** *f.* an ancient loose coat.
[2]**corocha,** *f.* vine fretter or vine grub.
corografía, *f.* chorography.
corográfico, ca, *a.* chorographical.
corógrafo, fa, *n.* chorographer.
coroideo, a, *a.* (anat.) choroid.
coroides, *f.* (anat.) choroid, choroid coat of the eye.
corojo, *m.* a tropical palm bearing an oily nut; the nut itself.
corola, *f.* (bot.) corolla.
corolario, *m.* corollary.
corolifloro, ra. I. *a.* (bot.) corollifloral. **II.** *f. pl.* Corollifloræ.
corología, *f.* chorology, science of the distribution of organisms on the earth's surface.
corona, *f.* crown; wreath, garland; halo, aureola; coronet; top of the head; clerical tonsure; an old Spanish gold-and-silver coin; crown, English silver coin; Portuguese coin; reward, distinction, honor; splendor, ornament, decoration; end or crowning of a work; glory, triumph; rosary of seven decades; (astr.) corona; (naut.) pendant; (bot.) corona, crown; (mil.) crownwork; (arch.) corona, crown; (vet.) pastern of horses.—**C. austral,** (astr.) Corona Australis.—**C. boreal,** Corona Borealis.—**c. circular,** (geom.) circular ring, space between two concentric circles.—**c. de casco,** skin surrounding the top of hoof.—**c. de fraile,** three-toothed globularia.—**c. de rey,** (bot.) melilot.—**c. mural,** mural crown.—**c. real,** (bot.) annual sunflower.
coronación, *f.* coronation; crowning, completion; (arch.) crown.
coronado, *m.* tonsured Catholic clergyman.
coronador, ra, *n.* crowner, finisher.
coronal. I. *m.* (anat.) frontal bone. **II.** *a.* frontal; pert. to frontal bone or forehead.
coronamiento, *m.* end of a work; (arch.) top ornament; capping; (naut.) taffrail.
coronar, *va.* to crown; to cap, to top; to complete, perfect; to decorate the top of; to crowd on a roof or on the top of a hill.
coronaria, *f.* crown wheel of a watch.
coronario, ria, *a.* (anat.) coronary; (bot.) coronary; extremely refined (gold).
corondel, *m.* (print.) column rule; reglet; watermark in paper.
[1]**coronel,** *m.* (arch.) top molding; (her.) crown.
[2]**coronel,** *m.* colonel.
coronela, *f.* colonel's wife.
coronelato, *m.* (Am.) colonelship.
coronelía, *f.* colonelship.
coroner, *m.* (law) coroner.
coronilla, *f. dim.* small crown; top of the head; cock's comb; cap; chaplet; ear of a bell; (bot.) coronilla.—**c. de fraile,** French daisy.—**c. de rey,** nine-leaved coronilla.—**c. juncal,** rush coronilla.
coronio, *m.* (chem., astr.) coronium.
corotos, *m. pl.* (Am.) belongings; outfit.
coroza, *f.* cone hood of pasteboard worn as a mark of infamy; straw cape or cloak worn by farmers.
corozal, *m.* field or plantation of COROZO.
corozo, *m.* = COROJO, tropical palm.
corpanchón, corpazo, *m. aug.* very big body or carcass.—**c. de ave,** carcass of a fowl.
corpecico, illo, ito; corpezuelo, *m. dim.* little or small body, or carcass; underdoublet; waist; corset cover.
corpiño, corpiñejo, *m. dim.* = CORPECICO.
corporación, *f.* corporation, guild; community; institution, organization.
corporal. I. *a.* corporal, bodily, pert. to the body. **II.** *m.* (eccl.) corporal cloth.—**corporalidad,** *f.* corporality; any corporeal substance.—**corporalmente,** *adv.* corporally, bodily.
corporativo, va, *a.* corporate.
corpóreo, rea, *a.* corporeal, corporeous.
corpudo, da, *a.* corpulent, bulky.
corpulencia, *f.* corpulence, corpulency.
corpulento, ta, *a.* corpulent, fleshy, fat.
Corpus, *m.* Corpus Christi, religious festival and procession.
corpuscular, *a.* corpuscular; (philos.) atomistic.
corpusculista, *n.* (philos.) atomist.
corpúsculo, *m.* corpuscle.
corral, *m.* corral; yard; poultry yard; fold, stockyard; fishpond; ancient playhouse; blank left by students in writing the lectures.—**c. de madera,** timber yard.—**c. de vacas,** mean hovel, (fig.) pigsty.—**c. de vecindad,** tenement house.—**aves de c.,** domestic fowl.
corralera, *f.* an Andalusian song and dance; brazen-faced, impudent woman.
corralero, *m.* keeper of a dung yard.
corralillo, ito, *m. dim.* small corral or yard.
corraliza, *f.* yard, corral, court.
corralón, *m. aug.* large corral or yard.
correa, *f.* leather strap; tether, leash; toughness, flexibility; (mech.) belt, belting; hand strap.—*pl.* duster made of straps.—**c. de zapatos,** shoe string, lace, latchet.—**besar la c.,** (coll.) to be obliged to humble oneself to another.—**tener c.,** to bear wit or raillery without irritation; to be strong and hardy.—**correaje,** *m.* heap of leather straps or thongs; belting.—**correal,** *m.* reddish dressed deerskin.—**correar,** *va.* to draw out (wool) and prepare for use.—**correazo,** *m.* blow with a strap.
correcalles, *n.* loiterer.
corrección, *f.* correction; adjustment (of an instrument); correctness; proper demeanor; decorum.
correccional, *a.* correctional, corrective.
correccionalismo, *m.* system of eliminating criminal tendencies by education and correctional treatment in adequate institutions.
correccionalista, *n.* follower of, or believer in, CORRECCIONALISMO.
correccionalmente, *adv.* correctively.
correctamente, *adv.* correctly.
correctivo, va. I. *a.* corrective. **II.** *m.* corrective, corrective agent or measure.
correcto, ta, *a.* correct; conformable to the rules; irreproachable.
corrector, *m.* corrector, amender; (print.) proofreader; superior, or abbot, in the convent of St. Francis of Paula.
corredentor, ra, *n.* one who redeems from captivity jointly with another.
corredera, *f.* race ground; small wicket or back door; runner or upper grinding stone in a corn mill; street; procuress; (naut.) log or log line;

roller, metal cylinder for rolling plate glass; cockroach; (steam eng.) slide valve; (print.) track, slide, rail; (mech.) tongue, rail, guide (of piston rod, etc.), runner; (mint) milling machine.—**c. de aire,** (aer.) air log.
corredizo, za, *a.* running; sliding; easy to be untied, like a running knot.
corredor, ra. I. *a.* running; (ornith.) ratite. **II.** *n.* runner; broker; (Am.) travelling salesman, (U. S., coll.) drummer; *m.* racer, race horse; corridor; gallery, porch; (fort.) covert way; (mil.) scout, forerunner; *f.* (ornith.) ratite bird. —**c. de aduana,** customhouse broker.—**c. de Bolsa,** broker.—**c. de cambios** or **de oreja,** exchange broker; (coll.) talebearer; procurer, procuress.
corredorcillo, *m. dim.* passageway, narrow corridor; petty broker.
corredura, *f.* overflow (of liquid).
correduría, *f.* broker's office; brokerage.
correería, *f.* trade and shop of a strap maker.
correero, ra, *n.* strap maker or seller.
corregibilidad, *f.* corrigibility.
corregible, *a.* corrigible.
corregidor, *m.* corrector; corregidor, Sp. magistrate; mayor.—**corregidora,** *f.* CORREGIDOR'S wife.
corregimiento, *m.* office or district of a CORREGIDOR.
corregir. I. *va.* (*ind.* CORRIJO; *subj.* CORRIJA) to correct; to adjust (an instrument); to remove, destroy; remedy; to reprehend, admonish; to punish; to temper, mitigate.—**c. el cuerpo,** (coll.) to go to stool.—**c. pruebas,** (print.) to read proofs. **II.** *vr.* to mend, reform.
corregüela, correhüela, *f. dim.* small strap; child's play with stick and strap; (bot.) bindweed.
correinante, *a.* reigning jointly with another.
correjel, *m.* sole leather.
correlación, correlation.—**correlacionar,** *va.* to correlate.
correlativo, va, *m.* & *a.* correlative, correlate.
correligionario, ia, *a.* & *n.* (person) of the same religion or political views.
correncia, *f.* (coll.) looseness, diarrhœa.
correndilla, *f.* (coll.) short run.
correntía, *f.* artificial irrigation of stubbly ground.
correntiar, *va.* to irrigate (stubble ground).
correntío, tía, *a.* current; (of liquids) running; (coll.) light, free, unembarrassed.
correntón, na. I. *n.* gadder, man about town. **II.** *a.* gay, pleasant, cheerful.
correntoso, sa, *a.* (Am.) (of streams) swift, rapid, having a strong current.
[1]**correo,** *m.* (law) accomplice.
[2]**correo,** *m.* post, mail; courier; letter carrier; post office.—**c. aéreo,** airmail.—**c. certificado,** registered mail.—**c. marítimo,** packet boat. —**echar al correo,** to post, mail.—**lista de correos,** general delivery.
correón, *m. aug.* large leather strap.
correoso, sa, *a.* flexible, easily bent; (of food) tough, leathery.
correr. I. *vn.* to run; to race; to flow; (of wind) to blow; to pass away; to take the proper course; to extend, expand; to arrive; become due; to go on, continue; to prevail, be current or common; to pass, be accepted or admitted, be current; to be said, be common talk; (followed by **con**) to charge oneself with a matter, take care of.—**c. a cargo de,** to be the concern of.—**c. a rienda suelta,** to ride full speed; to give loose rein to passion.—**c. a uno,** to be one's concern, to be incumbent on one.—**c. la voz,** to be reported, to be said or rumored. —**c. por cuenta de uno,** to be one's affair, be "up to" one.—**a más c., a todo c.,** at full speed; swiftly.—**el que menos corre, vuela,** artful unconcern succeeds quickest. **II.** *va.* to cause to run or move swiftly; to race (a horse); to pursue; to move, push, draw aside, draw, slide; to meet with; to go over, travel; to sell at auction; (coll.) to snatch away; to disconcert, rattle, make blush.—**c. baquetas,** to run the gantlet.—**c. el gallo,** (Mex.) to pass the night carousing in the streets.—**c. el pico,** (coll.) to shut up, close one's mouth.—**correrla,** to go on a spree.—**c. la cortina,** to draw the curtain; (fig.) to discover; to conceal, hide. —**c. monte,** to go hunting.—**c. mundo,** to travel.—**c. un velo,** to draw a veil. **III.** *vr.* to file right or left; to slide, go through easily; to slide, slip; to spread itself; to melt, run out, run over; (coll.) to be very generous; to become confused; to run away, to flee.
correría, *f.* hostile incursion, foray, raid; pleasure trip, excursion.—*pl.* youthful escapades.
correspondencia, *f.* correspondence, relation, fitness, agreement; commerce, intercourse; correspondence (mail, writing); friendship, interchange; consent.—**en justa c.,** in retaliation, to get even.
corresponder. I. *vn.* (**a**) to return (a favor, love); to match, correspond; respond (to); fit, suit; pertain (to); to regard, concern; to agree. **II.** *vr.* to correspond, keep up intercourse by mail; to respect or esteem each other.
correspondiente. I. *a.* corresponding, respective; conformable, agreeable, suitable. **II.** *m.* correspondent.
corresponsal, *m.* correspondent; agent; corresponding clerk.—**c. de prensa,** newspaper correspondent.
corretaje, *m.* brokerage.
corretear, *vn.* to walk the streets, rove, ramble.
corretora, *f.* nun who directs the choir.
correvedile, correveidile, *m.* (coll.) talebearer; mischief maker; procurer, go-between.
correverás, *m.* spring or mechanical toy.
corrida, *f.* course, run, sprint, race; career; row, series; (Am.) (min.) bearing or direction of a lode; (Am.) (min.) outcrop; (aer.) taxying.—**c. de toros,** bull baiting, bullfight.—**de c.,** at full speed, swiftly; in haste; fast, without stopping.
corridamente, *adv.* currently, plainly; easily.
corrido, da. I. *pp.* of CORRER. **II.** *a.* exceeding in weight or measure; expert, experienced; abashed, confused, ashamed; continuous, unbroken.—**comida c.,** (Am.) table d'hôte.—**de c.** = DE CORRIDA. **III.** *m.* shed along the walls of a corral.
corriente. I. *a.* current; running, flowing; present (month or year), instant; plain, easy; generally received, admitted; ordinary, common, general; regular, standard; fluent (app. to style); marketable, merchantable; correct, acceptable.—**al c.,** posted, informed; punctually. **II.** *f.* current (of a river, of electricity, etc.); tendency; course.—**c. alterna,** or **alternativa,** alternating current.—**c. avatia,** or **devatiada,** (elec.) wattless current.—**c. continua,** (elec.) direct current.—**c. de aire,** draught (of air).—**c. del Golfo,** Gulf Stream. —**c. y moliente,** commonplace.—**contra la c.,** against the tide (fig.).—**dejarse llevar de la c.,** to follow the current, follow the crowd. **III.** *adv.* all right.
corrientemente, *adv.* currently.
corrigendo, da, *n.* inmate of a reformatory.
corrijo, corrija, *v. V.* CORREGIR.
corrillero, *m.* idler, lounger, loafer.
corrillo, *m.* group of talkers (gen. app. to gossips or loungers).
corrimiento, *m.* act of running; melting; (med.) running sore; gumboil; landslide; shyness.
corrincho, *m.* meeting of low, vulgar people.
corrivación, *f.* impounding of brooks and streams.
corro, *m.* group of gossipers or spectators; circular space.—**hacer c.,** to clear the way.
corroboración, *f.* corroboration.
corroborante, *n.* & *a.* corroborator(-ing, -ive).
corroborar, *va.* to corroborate.

corroborativamente, *adv.* corroboratively.
corroborativo, va, *a.* corroborative.
corrobra, *f.* treat to close a bargain. Also ROBRA.
corroer, *va.* to corrode.
corrompedor, ra, *n.* & *a.* corrupter(-ing).
corromper. I. *va.* (*pp.* CORROMPIDO and CORRUPTO) to corrupt; vitiate, mar; seduce, debauch; to bribe. **II.** *vn.* to stink. **III.** *vr.* to rot, get putrid; to become corrupt(ed).
corrompido, da. I. *pp.* of CORROMPER. **II.** *a.* corrupt; spoiled, unsound; depraved, degenerate.
corrosible, *a.* corrosible.
corrosión, *f.* corrosion.
corrosivamente, *adv.* corrosively.
corrosividad, *f.* corrosiveness.
corrosivo, va, *a.* corrosive.
corroyente, *a.* corroding, corrosive; abrasive.
corroyera, *f.* a kind of sumac used in tanning.
corrugación, *f.* corrugation, contraction into wrinkles.
corrugado, da, *a.* corrugated.
corrugador, *m.* (anat.) corrugator.
corrulla, *f.* (naut.) room under deck in a row galley.
corrumpente, *a.* corrupting, vitiating; (coll.) teasing, vexatious, wayward.
corrupción, *f.* corruption, putrefaction; decay; pollution, filth; stench; corruptness; perversion, distortion (of a writing); depravity, immorality.
corruptela, *f.* corruption; depravation, corruptness; (law) bad habit or practice contrary to law; abuse.
corruptibilidad, *f.* corruptibility.
corruptible, *a.* corruptible.
corruptivo, va, *a.* corruptive.
corrupto, ta. I. *pp. irreg.* of CORROMPER. **II.** *a.* corrupt.
corruptor, ra, *n.* & *a.* corrupter(-ing).
corrusco, *m.* (coll.) broken or dried bread.
corsario, ria, *n.* & *a.* privateer; corsair, pirate.
corsé, *m.* corset.
corsear, *vn.* to cruise against the enemy.
corsetería, *f.* corset factory or shop.
corsetero, ra, *n.* corset maker or dealer.
[1]**corso,** *m.* privateering.—**a c.,** posthaste, with post horses.
[2]**corso, sa,** *n.* & *a.* Corsican.
corta, *f.* felling of wood; cutting.
cortabolsas, *n.* (coll.) pickpocket, filcher.
cortacallos, *m.* corn cutter.
cortacigarros, *m.* cigar cutter.
cortacircuitos, *m.* (elec.) circuit breaker.
cortada, *f.* (Am.) cut, slash, gash.
cortadera, *f.* chisel for cutting hot iron; knife used by beekeepers.
cortadero, ra, *a.* cutting readily; easily cut.
cortadillo, *m.* small drinking glass; a liquid measure, about a gill; clipped piece of money. —**echar cortadillos,** to speak in an affected manner; to drink wine.
cortado, da. I. *pp.* of CORTAR. **II.** *a.* adapted, proportioned, fit, exact; (of hands) chapped; (her.) parted in the middle; confused, abashed; written in short sentences; (Chile, Arg.) short of funds. **III.** *m.* (dance) caper, cabriole.
cortador, ra. I. *n.* (tailoring, boot-making, etc.) cutter; that which, or one who, cuts; splitter. **II.** *m.* butcher; slicing machine, cutter; (tel.) interrupter; (zool.) scissorbill.—*pl.* incisor teeth. **III.** *f.* cutting board in a velvet loom.
cortadura, *f.* cut; cutting, incision; slit, slash; (fort.) parapet with embrasures and merlons; work raised in narrow passes.—*pl.* shreds.
cortafrío, *m.* cold chisel; cutting iron.
cortafuego, *m.* (agr.) clear space to prevent fire from spreading; (arch.) fire wall.
cortalápices, cortalápiz, *m.* pencil sharpener.
cortamente, *adv.* sparingly, scantily; curtly.
cortante. I. *a.* cutting, sharp. **II.** *m.* butcher.
cortapapel, *m.* paper cutter, paper knife.
cortapiés, *m.* (coll.) thrust at the legs in fencing.
cortapisa, *f.* obstacle, hindrance; elegance and grace in speaking; restriction with which a thing is given, "strings."
cortaplumas, *m.* penknife, pocketknife.
cortapuros, *m.* cigar cutter.
cortar. I. *va.* to cut, cup up, cut off, cut out; curtail; to disjoin, separate, hew, cleave, chop, hack, carve, fell; whittle; to shut or cut off (steam, water, etc.); dock; pare, prune; interrupt, stop, cut short; to abridge; to take a short cut; to suspend, restrain, keep back; to pronounce or enunciate; to read; to arbitrate or decide; (Am.) to speak ill of, criticize.—**c. a uno,** (fig.) to put one to the blush.—**c. la corriente,** (elec.) to break the circuit, cut off the current. **II.** *vr.* to be daunted, ashamed, confused; to curdle; to chap; to fret; to fray; (geom.) to intersect, cut each other.
cortavapor, *m.* cut-off of a steam engine.
cortavidrios, *m.* glazier's diamond.
cortaviento, *m.* windshield.
[1]**corte,** *m.* cutting edge; cutting; cut; felling of trees; arbitration, compromise or settlement; measure, expedient, step; notch, hack, slot; in tailoring, cut, fit, also length (of material) necessary for a garment (*un corte de chaleco,* length for a vest; *un corte de pantalón,* length for a pair of trousers; *un corte de vestido,* a dress length); edge of a book; (min.) shaft; cross opening; (in drawing) section, sectional view.
[2]**corte,** *f.* (royal) court; city where the court resides (*la C.,* in Spain, Madrid); (Am.) (law) court; levee; retinue, suite; yard; courtship; civility, politeness; stable for cattle; sheepfold; ancient tribunal of chancery.—*pl.* Cortes, Spanish parliament.—**c. celestial,** heaven.— **c. suprema,** Supreme Court.
cortedad, *f.* smallness, littleness, minuteness; dulness, stupidity; pusillanimity; timidity, bashfulness.—**c. de medios,** poverty, indigence.
cortejador, *m.* suitor; wooer.
cortejante. I. *a.* courting. **II.** *m.* gallant, beau.
cortejar, *va.* to accompany, escort, attend; to court, woo, make love to.
cortejo, *m.* court; homage paid to another; courtship; gift, present; gallant, beau; lover, sweetheart; paramour.
cortés, *a.* courteous, civil, gracious, polite.
cortesanazo, za, *a. aug.* awkwardly or fulsomely polite.
cortesanía, *f.* courtesy, civility, politeness.
cortesano, na. I. *a.* courtlike; courteous, obliging; courtly. **II.** *n.* courtier.
cortesía, *f.* courtesy; civility or courteousness; compliment; attention; gift, present; days of grace for payment; mercy, favor.
[1]**corteza,** *f.* bark of a tree; peel, skin, rind; crust of bread, pies, etc.; outward appearance; rusticity, want of politeness, crustiness.
[2]**corteza,** *f.* wild fowl of widgeon family.
cortezón, *m. aug.* thick bark, rind, or crust.
cortezudo, da, *a.* corticose, barky; rustic, unmannerly, unpolished.
cortezuela, *f. dim.* thin bark, skin, or rind.
cortical, *a.* cortical.
cortijada, *f.* collection of houses about a grange.
cortijo, *m.* farmhouse, grange, manse.—**alborotar el c.,** (coll.) to stir up a hornets' nest.
cortil, *m.* = CORRAL, corral; yard.
cortina, *f.* curtain; shade; portière; (fort.) curtain.—**cortinaje,** *m.* curtains, hangings.
cortinal, *m.* fenced-in land near a village or farmhouse.
cortinilla, *f.* small screen, shade; carriage curtain.
cortinón, *m. aug.* large heavy curtain.
cortiña, *f.* garden plot.
cortisona, *f.* cortisone.
corto, ta, *a.* short; dull, stupid; pusillanimous; shy, bashful, backward; imperfect, defective.— **c. circuito,** (elec.) short circuit.—**c. de alcances,** stupid.—**c. de genio,** diffident.—**c. de**

oído, hard of hearing.—**c. de vista,** near-sighted.—**a la corta o a la larga,** sooner or later.
cortocircuito, *m.* = CORTO CIRCUITO.
cortón, *m.* (entom.) mantis, an orthopterous insect.
corulla, *f.* in galleys, place for the stoppers of cables.
corundo, *m.* corundum. Also CORINDÓN.
coruñés, sa, *a.* of or pertaining to Corunna.
coruscación, *f.* coruscation, brilliancy, flashing.
coruscante, *a.* coruscant, glittering, brilliant.
coruscar, *vn.* (poet.) to coruscate, shine, sparkle.
corusco, ca, *a.* = CORUSCANTE.
corva, *f.* back of the knee, ham, hock; CORVAZA.
corvadura, *f.* curvature, crookedness, bend; humped-back state; (arch.) bend of an arch or vault.
corvato, *m.* young crow or rook.
corvaza, *f.* (vet.) curb, tumor on the hock.
corvecito, *m. dim.* little crow or rook.
[1]**corvejón,** *m.* hock joint of a quadruped.
[2]**corvejón,** *m.* (zool.) cormorant.
corveta, *f.* curvet; leap or bound of a horse.
corvetear, *vn.* to curvet, bound, leap.
córvidos, *m. pl.* (zool.) Corvidæ.
corvillo, *m.* hooked bill; pruning knife; shoemaker's paring knife; small sickle in velvet looms.
corvina, *f.* a variety of conger eel in the Mediterranean; corvina, a Californian fish.
corvino, na, *a.* corvine, rooklike; pertaining to rooks, crows, ravens.
corvo, va. I. *a.* bent, crooked; arched; stingy, mean. **II.** *m.* (ichth.) a variety of mullet; pothook.
corzo, za, *n.* roe deer, fallow deer.
corzuelo, *m.* wheat left in the husks by the thrashers.
cosa, *f.* thing; matter, affair.—**c. así,** the like, something like it.—**c. de,** about, more or less. —**c. del otro jueves,** (coll.) a marvellous thing; something out of date.—**c. de oír,** a thing worth hearing.—**c. de risa,** laughable thing, a thing to laugh at.—**c. de ver,** a thing worth seeing.—**c. no vista,** or **nunca vista,** unheard-of thing.—**c. rara,** a strange thing; strange to say.—**a c. hecha,** surely, as good as done (diff. constr.).—**cada c. para su c.,** everything in its place, or where it belongs.—**como quien no quiere la c.,** unconcernedly, in a go-as-you-please way.—**como si tal c.,** as if nothing had happened.—**cosas de,** doi gs, or tricks of (diff. constr.: *esas son cosas de Juan,* that is one of John's tricks; that is just like John).—**cosas del otro jueves,** something very unusual.—**fuerte c.,** nuisance.—**ni c. parecida, ni c. que lo parezca,** nor anything like it.—**no es c.,** it is nothing, it is but a trifle; no matter.—**no hay tal c.,** no such thing.—**no ser,** or **no valer, c.,** not to be worth a cent, to be of little account.—**no ser gran c.,** not to amount to much.—**otra c.,** something else.—**poquita c.,** (coll.) a pusillanimous person.—**¿qué c.?** (coll.) how goes it? what's the news?
cosaco, ca, *n.* & *a.* Cossack.
cosario, ria. I. *a.* pert. to carriers; (of roads) frequented, having much traffic. **II.** *m.* carrier, expressman; huntsman, hunter.
coscarana, *f.* (prov.) cracknel, crisp cake.
coscarse, *vr.* (coll.) = CONCOMERSE, to shrug.
coscoja, *f.* (bot.) kermes, or scarlet, oak; dry leaves of the kermes oak; ring or knob on the bit of a bridle.
coscojal, coscojar, *m.* plantation or field of kermes.
coscojo, *m.* kermes berry.—*pl.* chain of a horse's bridle.
coscomate, *m.* (Mex.) corn barn.
coscón, na, *a.* crafty, sly.
coscoroba, *f.* a South-American variety of swan.
coscorrón, *m.* blow on the head.
cosecante, *f.* (geom.) cosecant.
cosecha, *f.* harvest, crop; yield; harvest time; harvesting; reaping; aggregate of immaterial things, as virtues, vices, etc.—**c. de vino,** vintage.—**de su c.,** of one's own invention.—**cosechar,** *va.* to reap, gather (the harvest).—**cosechero, ra,** *n.* owner or reaper of a crop, harvester.
coselete, *m.* corselet, ancient coat of armor; pikeman; (entom.) thorax of insects.
coseno, *m.* (math.) cosine.—**c. verso,** coversed sine.
coser, *va.* to sew; to join, unite; to rivet (as a boiler); (naut.) to lash, nail, fix, frap, seize.—**c. a puñaladas,** (coll.) to stab repeatedly.—**c. un motón,** (naut.) to lash a block.—**c. y cantar,** to offer no difficulties; to be very easy, child's play.—**coserse con la pared,** to stick close to a wall.—**coserse la boca,** not to speak a word, to shut up like a clam.
cosera, *f.* piece of land that can be irrigated at one time.
cosetada, *f.* race, quick run, sprint.
cosible, *a.* that can be sewed.
cosicosa, *f.* = QUISICOSA, (coll.) enigma, puzzle.
cosido, da. I. *pp.* of COSER. **II.** *a.* **(a)** devoted (to), wedded (to). **III.** *m.* sewing; needlework. —**c. de cama,** quilt and blankets stitched together.
cosiduras, *f. pl.* (naut.) lashings.
cosignatario, ria. I. *a.* cosignatory. **II.** *n.* cosigner, cosignatory.
cosita, *f. dim.* small thing, trifle; (Cuba) luncheon.
cosmético, ca, *m.* & *a.* cosmetic.
cósmico, ca, *a.* cosmic.
cosmogonía, *f.* cosmogony.
cosmogónico, ca, *a.* cosmogonic.
cosmografía, *f.* cosmography, descriptive astronomy.
cosmográfico, ca, *a.* cosmographic.
cosmógrafo, fa, *n.* cosmographer.
cosmología, *f.* cosmology.
cosmológico, ca, *a.* cosmological.
cosmólogo, ga, *n.* cosmologist.
cosmonauta, *n.* cosmonaut.
cosmonáutica, *f.* cosmonautics.
cosmonave, *f.* spaceship.
cosmopolita, *n.* & *a.* cosmopolite, cosmopolitan.
cosmopolitismo, *m.* cosmopolitanism.
cosmorama, *m.* cosmorama.
cosmos, *m.* cosmos.
cosmotrón, *m.* cosmotron.
[1]**coso,** *m.* place or enclosure for bullfights or other public spectacles; main street.
[2]**coso,** *m.* timber worm.
cospel, *m.* coin blank, in the mint.
cospillo, *m.* refuse of the olive.
cosquillar, cosquillear. I. *va.* to tickle; to arouse the curiosity of. **II.** *vr.* to become disturbed or upset.
cosquillas, *f. pl.* tickling; ticklishness.—**buscarle a uno las c.,** (coll.) to tease, pick on one. —**hacer c.,** to tickle; to excite, disturb; to incite.—**tener c.,** to be ticklish.—**tener malas c.,** (coll.) to be easily offended; to be ill-tempered; to be overparticular.—**cosquillejas,** *f. pl. dim.* little tickling.
cosquilleo, *m.* tickling sensation.
cosquilloso, sa, *a.* ticklish; susceptible, easily offended.
[1]**costa,** *f.* cost, price, charge; expense, expensiveness.—*pl.* costs of a lawsuit.—**a c. de,** at the expense of; by dint of.—**a mi c.,** at my expense.—**a poca c.,** with little effort.—**a toda c.,** at any price; at all hazards.—**condenar en c.,** (law) to sentence to pay the costs.
[2]**costa,** *f.* coast, shore; beach, seashore, seaboard; cobbler's tool for polishing edges of soles.—**c. de barlovento,** (naut.) weather shore.—**C. de Marfil,** Ivory Coast.—**dar a la c.,** (naut.) to be blown or driven to shore, be beached.
costado, *m.* side; (mil.) flank.—*pl.* race, lineage,

succession of ancestors.—**c. de barlovento,** (naut.) weather side.

costal. I. *m.* sack or large bag; brace of frame for making adobe walls. **II.** *a.* costal, pert. to the ribs.—**costalada,** *f.*, **costalazo,** *m.* bump one gets when falling flat on the ground.—**costalejo,** *m. dim.* small sack.—**costalero,** *m.* porter who carries goods.—**costalito,** *m. dim.* small sack.

costanera, *f.* slope.—*pl.* (carp.) rafters.

costanero, ra, *a.* pert. to a coast; declivous, sloping.—**buque c.,** coaster, coasting vessel.

costanilla, *f. dim.* gentle slope; steep street.

costar, *vn.* (*ind.* CUESTO; *subj.* CUESTE) to cost; to cause or occasion detriment or loss.—**c. la torta un pan,** (coll.) to pay dear for one's whistle.—**c. un ojo de la cara,** (fig., coll.) to cost dear, cost a fortune.—**cuesta trabajo creerlo,** it's hard to believe.—**cueste lo que cueste,** at all costs.

Costa Rica, *f.* Costa Rica.

costarricense, costarriqueño, ña, *n.* & *a.* Costa Rican.

coste, *m.* = [1]COSTA.—**a c. y costas,** at cost.

[1]**costear. I.** *va.* to pay the cost of. **II.** *vr.* to pay; to produce sufficient to repay its cost.

[2]**costear,** *vr.* (naut.) to sail along the coast.

costeño, ña, *a.* from, or pertaining to, the coast or seashore; coasting (vessel).

costera, *f.* side of a bale of goods; surmullet, fishing season; outside quire of a ream; slope of a hill.

costero, ra. I. *a.* pertaining to the coast; outward. **II.** *m.* first plank cut from a pine tree.

costezuela, *f. dim.* slight declivity or slope.

costilla, *f.* rib; chop; cutlet; (coll.) wife, better half; rung of a chair; stave of a barrel; (carp.) fur; (arch.) rib of a cupola; springer; (coll.) property, wealth; (bot.) rib of a leaf.—*pl.* (coll.) shoulders, back; (agr.) wooden strips to which horses are tied in plowing; (mech.) cramp-irons, chimney ties.—**c. falsa,** false rib.—**c. flotante,** floating rib.—**costillas de un navío,** (naut.) ribs of a ship.—**medirle a uno las costillas,** to cudgel one.

costillaje, costillar, *m.* (anat.) the ribs, or rib system; (naut.) frame of a ship.

costilludo, da, *a.* (coll.) broad-shouldered.

[1]**costino, na,** *a.* pertaining to the costus root.

[2]**costino, na,** *a.* (Chile, Arg.) = COSTEÑO.

[1]**costo,** *m.* (bot.) sweet and bitter costus; costus root.

[2]**costo,** *m.* cost, price; charges, expense; labor, fatigue.—**a c. y costas,** at cost.—**c. de la vida,** cost of living.—**c., seguro y flete,** cost insurance and freight (c.i.f.).

costoso, sa, *a.* costly, dear, expensive; difficult to be obtained; sad, grievous.

costra, *f.* crust, scab; broken biscuit; incrusted part of a wick; crust of casting.

costrada, *f.* candied seedcake.

costroso, sa, *a.* crusty, having crusts or scabs.

costumbre, *f.* custom; habit; catamenia, courses.—**de c.,** usual, customary.—**tener por c.,** to be in the habit of.—*pl.* customs, ways.

costumbrista, *n.* genre writer, one who portrays everyday life and prevailing customs.

costura, *f.* sewing, needlework; seam, stitching; (surg.) suture; (mech.) crease, ridge; joint; riveting; (naut.) splicing of a rope; (carp.) joint.—**c. sobrecargada,** felting.—**sin c.,** seamless (esp. app. to tubes).—**costurera,** *f.* seamstress.—**costurero,** *m.* sewing box, table, or room.—**costurón,** *m. aug.* big seam; coarse suture; large scar.

[1]**cota,** *f.* coat of mail (called also **c. de malla**); coat of arms, tabard coat; back and callous part of a boar's hide.

[2]**cota,** *f.* (topog.) number indicating elevation above sea level or some other fixed level; quota, share.

cotana, *f.* mortise, mortise hole.

cotangente, *f.* (geom.) cotangent.

cotanza, *f.* a kind of medium-fine linen.

cotarrera, *f.* (coll.) gadding woman.

cotarro, *m.* charity hut to shelter beggars; side of a pit.—**alborotar el c.,** to cause disturbance.—**andar de c. en c.,** to go sauntering about.

cotejar, *va.* to compare, confront.

cotejo, *m.* comparison, collation.

cotel, *m.* cocktail. Also COCKTAIL.

cotense, *m.* (Mex.) coarse brown linen wrapper.

coterráneo, *a.* fellow (citizen).

cotí, cutí, *m.* ticking for mattresses.

coticé, cotice, *v. V.* COTIZAR.

cotidianamente, *adv.* daily.

cotidiano, na, *a.* daily, everyday; quotidian.

cotiledón, *m.* (bot.) cotyledon.

cotiledóneo, ea, *a.* (bot.) cotyledonous.

cotilla, *f.* stays, corsets.

cotillero, ra, *n.* stay maker.

cotillo, *m.* face or flat surface of a hammer.

cotillón, *m.* cotillion.

cotín, *m.* back stroke given to a ball.

[1]**cotiza,** *f.* (her.) cotise.

[2]**cotiza,** *f.* (S. A.) an Indian sandal.

cotizable, *a.* quotable; valued (at).

cotización, *f.* (com.) quotation; price current, price list.

[1]**cotizado, da,** *a.* (com.) quoted, listed.

[2]**cotizado, da,** *a.* (her.) cotised.

cotizador, ra, *n.* (com.) quoter.

cotizar, *va.* (*pret.* COTICÉ; *subj.* COTICE) (com.) to quote (prices); to call out (current prices) in the stock exchange.

[1]**coto,** *m.* (com.) combination among merchants; rate or price limitation; measure of a handbreadth; billiard contest.

[2]**coto,** *m.* inclosure of pasture ground; landmark, boundary; (money) fine.—**poner c. a,** to put a stop to, check.

[3]**coto,** *m.* (ichth.) chub.

[4]**coto,** *m.* (Am.) (med.) goiter.

cotobelo, *m.* opening in the branch of a bridle.

cotón, *m.* printed cotton.

cotona, *f.* (Mex.) chamois jacket.

cotonada, *f.* print; printed linen or cotton.

cotoncillo, *m.* button of a painter's maulstick.

cotonía, *f.* dimity, fine fustian.

cotorra, *f.* a kind of parrot; magpie; (coll.) loquacious woman.

cotorrear, *vn.* to chatter; to gossip.

cotorreo, *m.* chattering; gossiping.

cotorrera, *f.* hen parrot; (coll.) prattling woman.

cotorrón, ona. I. *a.* (of old persons) affecting youth, or acting silly like young people. **II.** *m.* (Am.) bachelor.

cotral, cutral, *m.* old worn-out ox.

cotudo, da, *a.* hairy, cottony; (Am.) having a goiter.

cotufa, *f.* (bot.) Jerusalem artichoke; tidbits; delicate food.—**pedir cotufas en el golfo,** to expect impossibilities.

cotufero, ra, *a.* producing tidbits or delicate food.

cotunto, *m.* (Cuba) a kind of night bird.

coturno, *m.* cothurnus, buskin.

covacha, *f.* small cave or hollow underground; grotto.—**covachuela,** *f. dim.* small cave or grotto; (coll.) office of a crown minister, formerly in vaulted corridors of royal palace.

covachuelista *or* **covachuelo,** *m.* (coll.) clerk in one of the COVACHUELAS.

covadera, *f.* (Peru) guano bed.

covanilla, *f.*, **covanillo,** *m. dim.* basket for gathering grapes.

covariancia, *f.* (math., stat.) covariance.

covezuela, *f. dim.* small cave.

coxal, *a.* hip (as *a.*), pert. to hip or hip joint.

coxalgia, *f.* hip-joint disease, coxalgia.

coxcojilla, ita, *f.* children's game; hopscotch.—**a c.,** lamely, haltingly, hippety-hoppety.

coxígeo, gea, *a.* (anat.) coccygeal.

coxis, *m.* (anat.) coccyx.

coy, *m.* (naut.) hammock, cot, sailor's bed.—**afuera coys,** all hammocks up.
coya, *f.* (Peru) queen, wife and sister of the Inca.
coyabra *f.* (Am.) = CUYABRA, bowl made from a gourd.
coyote. I. *a.* (Am.) native, domestic. **II.** *m.* (Mex.) coyote; (Mex.) (coll.) curbstone broker.
coyunda, *f.* strap for yoking oxen; shoestring; dominion, tyranny; matrimonial union.
coyuntura, *f.* joint, articulation; occasion, juncture, opportunity; nick of time.
coz, *f.* kick; drawback; recoil of a gun; flowing back of a flood; butt of a pistol; (coll.) churlishness, unprovoked brusqueness.—**c. de mastelero,** (naut.) heel of a mast.—**dar coces,** to kick.—**dar coces contra el aguijón,** to kick against the pricks.—**soltar una c.,** to answer rudely.—**tirar coces,** to kick.
cozcojilla, *f.* = COXCOJILLA.
crabrón, *m.* hornet.
crac, *m.* failure, bankruptcy.
crameria, *f.* krameria, rhatany.
cran, *m.* (print.) nick of a type.
craneal; craneano, na, *a.* cranial.
cráneo, *m.* skull, cranium.
craneología, *f.* craniology.
craneológico, ca, *a.* craniological.
craneometría, *f.* craniometry.
craneómetro, *m.* craniometer.
craneoscopía, *f.* cranioscopy.
craneotomía, *f.* (surg.) craniotomy.
craniano, na, *a.* cranial.
crápula, *f.* intoxication; crapulence, debauchery.
crapuloso, sa, *a.* drunken; dissolute, dissipated.
craquear, *va.* to crack (petroleum).
craqueo, *m.* cracking (of petroleum).
crasamente, *adv.* crassly; grossly; rudely.
crascitar, *vn.* to crow; to croak.
crasiento, grasiento, ta, *a.* greasy.
crasitud, *f.* fatness, corpulency, obesity; ignorance, stupidity, dulness.
craso, sa, *a.* fat, greasy; thick, gross, crass.
crasuláceo, cea, *a.* (bot.) crasulaceous.
cráter, *m.* crater of a volcano.
crátera, *f.* (archeol.) crater.
cratícula, *f.* small wicket through which nuns receive the communion.
craza, *f.* crucible.
crea, *f.* a kind of linen stuff.
creable, *a.* creatable.
creación, *f.* creation.
creado, da. I. *pp.* of CREAR. **II.** *a.* created, begotten, made.
creador, ra. I. *n.* & *a.* creator(-ing, -ive); originator(-ing). **II. C.** *m.* Creator.
crear, *va.* to create; to institute, establish; to appoint, be made; to invent, design.
crébol, *m.* (bot.) holly tree.
crecedero, ra, *a.* able to grow; increasable.
crecer. I. *vn.* (*ind.* CREZCO; *subj.* CREZCA) to grow; to bud forth; to increase; to swell; to augment in extrinsic value (app. to money).—**c. como la mala hierba,** to grow like weeds. **II.** *vr.* to swell with pride or with authority.
creces, *f. pl.* augmentation, increase, excess; additional quantity of corn paid by a farmer to a public granary, besides what he borrowed from it.—**con c.,** amply.
crecida, *f.* freshet.
crecidamente, *adv.* plentifully, copiously, abundantly.
crecidito, ta, *a. dim.* somewhat grown.
crecido, da. I. *pp.* of CRECER. **II.** *a.* grown, increased; grave, important; large, swollen.
crecidos, *m. pl.* widening stitches in knitting.
creciente. I. *a.* growing, increasing; crescent; susceptible of increase. **II.** *m.* (her.) half-moon with points upward. **III.** *f.* swell, freshet of waters; leaven; crescent (of the moon).—**c. de la marea,** (naut.) flood tide, flow, flowing.
crecientemente, *adv.* increasingly.
crecimiento, *m.* growth; growing; increase, increment.—**c. de la marejada,** (naut.) swell of the sea.
credencia, *f.* sideboard of an altar.—**credencial,** *f.* credential, accreditation.—*pl.* credentials.
credibilidad, *f.* credibility.
crédito, *m.* credit; acquiescence, assent; belief, faith; reputation, character, name, standing; note, bill, order for payment.—**créditos activos,** assets.—**créditos pasivos,** liabilities.—**a c.,** on credit.—**dar c.,** to believe.
credo, *m.* creed; Credo, Apostles' Creed.—**c. político,** political creed, platform.—**en un c.,** in a trice.
credulidad, *f.* credulity.
crédulo, la, *a.* credulous.
creedero, ra, *a.* credible.—**tener buenas creederas,** to be easy of belief.
creedor, ra, *a.* credulous.
creencia, *f.* belief; creed, persuasion.
creer, *va.* (*pret.* él CREYÓ) to believe; to credit; to think, think it probable.—**creerse del aire,** to be credulous.—**ver y c.,** seeing is believing.—**¡ya lo creo!** (coll.) of course, undoubtedly.
crehuela, *f.* Osnaburg, a sort of linen.
creíble, *a.* credible, likely, believable.
[1]**crema,** *f.* cream of milk; custard; cream, select society; cold cream; cosmetic.
[2]**crema,** *f.* (gram.) diaeresis.
cremación, *f.* cremation, incineration.
cremallera, *f.* ratch, rack; toothed bar.
cremar, *va.* to cremate.
crematística, *f.* political economy.
crematología, *f.* political economy.
crematológico, ca, *a.* pert. to political economy.
crematólogo, ga, *n.* political economist.
crematorio, ria. I. *a.* burning, cremating. **II.** *m.* or **horno c.,** crematory, incinerator.
cremómetro, *m.* instrument to measure fat content of milk.
cremonés, sa, *a.* of or pert. to Cremona.
crémor, *m.*—**c. tártaro,** cream of tartar.
crencha, *f.* parting of the hair into two parts; each of these parts.
creosol, *m.* (chem.) creosol.
creosota, *f.*, **creosoto,** *m.* (chem.) creosote.
creosotar, *va.* to creosote.
crepitación, *f.* crepitation, crackling; (surg.) crepitation of fractures.
crepitante, *a.* crackling, crepitant.
crepitar, *vn.* to crackle, crepitate.
crepuscular; crepusculino, na, *a.* crepuscular.
crepúsculo, *m.* crepuscule, twilight; dawn; dusk.
cresa, *f.* egg or larva of the queen bee; flyblow, egg of a fly; maggot.
crescendo, *m.* (mus.) crescendo.
crespilla, *f.* (bot.) agaric, a fungus.
crespina, *f.* hair net.
crespo, pa. I. *a.* curly; crispy; (bot.) crisp-leaved; obscure and bombastic; (Am.); angry, displeased, vexed. **II.** *m.* (Am.) curl.
crespón, *m.* crape.
cresta, *f.* comb (of a bird); cock's comb, aigrette, tuft; crest of a helmet; wave crest; top, brow; crest or summit of a mountain; (min.) crop; (mil.) cramp iron.—**c. de la explanada,** (fort.) crest of the glacis.—**alzar,** or **levantar, la c.,** to be elated with pride.
crestado, da, *a.* crested.
crestería, *f.* (arch.) cresting; (fort.) battlement.
crestomatía, *f.* chrestomathy.
crestón, *m. aug.* large crest; crest of a helmet; (min.) outcrop.
creta, *f.* chalk.
cretáceo, cea, *a.* cretaceous; chalky.
cretense; crético, ca, *n.* & *a.* Cretan.
crético, *m.* verse of three syllables.
cretinismo, *m.* cretinism.
cretino, na, *n.* & *a.* cretin.
cretona, *f.* cretonne.
creyente, *n.* & *a.* believer(-ing).
creyó, *pret.* of CREER.
creyón, *m.* (Gal.) crayon; charcoal pencil.
crezco, crezca, *v. V.* CRECER.

crezneja, crizneja, *f.* braid of hair; streak of bleached bassweed.
cría, *f.* act of nursing; breeding; rearing, bringing up; keeping (as bees); litter of animals; suckling; (coll.) child reared by a nurse.
criada, *f.* female servant; maid, maid servant.—**c. de mano,** (Cuba) housemaid; bat for beating clothes in washing.
criadero, ra. I. *a.* fruitful, prolific. **II.** *m.* nursery, plantation of young trees; breeding place; fish hatchery; (min.) seam; cocoon bed; hotbed.
criadilla, *f.* testicle of an animal; lamb fry; mountain oyster; small loaf or roll; potato; (bot.) truffle.
criado, da. I. *pp.* of CRIAR. **II.** *a.* bred. **III.** *m.* servant, menial, groom, valet.
criador, ra. I. *a.* creating creative; fruitful, fecund. **II.** *n.* rearer, raiser, breeder, keeper (as of bees); creator. **III.** *f.* wet nurse.
criaduelo, la, *n. dim.* little or young servant.
criamiento, *m.* renovation and preservation.
criandera, *f.* (Am.) wet nurse.
crianza, *f.* nursing; lactation; breeding; manners, education; nursery.—**dar c.,** to breed; to rear, educate, bring up.
criar, *va.* to create; to breed, procreate; to raise, rear, bring up; to nurse, nourish; to fatten (animals).—**c. carnes,** to grow fat.—**c. molleja,** to grow lazy.
criatura, *f.* creature; fœtus; baby, infant; child; being, man.—**es una c.,** he is but an infant, or like an infant.
criba, *f.* cribble, sieve, crib, screen.
cribado, da, *a.* sifted, screened.
cribador, ra, *n.* sifter.
cribar, *va.* to sift, sieve, screen.
cribo, *m.* = CRIBA.
cric, *m.* jackscrew, lifting jack. Also GATO.
crica, *f.* trench, fissure; (anat.) female pudenda.
cricoides, *m.* & *a.* (anat.) cricoid.
cricquet, *m.* = CRIQUET.
crimen, *m.* (law) felony; (theol.) mortal sin.
criminación, *f.* incrimination.
criminal, *n.* & *a.* criminal.
criminalidad, *f.* criminality, guilt.
criminalista, *m.* criminalist.
criminar, *va.* to accuse, incriminate.
criminología, *f.* criminology.
criminólogo, ga, *n.* criminologist.
criminoso, sa. I. *n.* delinquent, criminal. **II.** *a.* criminal, guilty.
crimno, *m.* coarse flour meal.
crin, *f.* mane, horsehair.
crinado, da, *a.* (poet.) maned, having long hair.
crinífero, ra, *a.* mane-bearing.
crinito, ta, *a.* = CRINADO.
crinoideo, dea, *m.* & *a.* (zool.) crinoid.
crinolina, *f.* (Mex.) crinoline.
crío, *m.* nursing baby.
criolita, *f.* (min.) cryolite.
criollo, lla. I. *n.* creole. **II.** *a.* indigenous, domestic; (of negroes) native (to Am.); (of Europeans) naturalized (in Am.).
criómetro, *m.* cryometer (low temperature thermometer).
crioscopia, *f.* (phys.) cryoscopy.
cripta, *f.* crypt.
criptoanalítica, *f.* cryptanalysis.
criptógamo, ma. I. *a.* (bot.) cryptogamous. **II.** *f.* (bot.) cryptogam.
criptografía, *f.* cryptography.
criptograma, *m.* cryptogram, a writing in cipher.
criptón, *m.* (chem.) krypton.
criquet, *m.* (Angl.) (sport) cricket.
cris, *m.* creese or kris, a Malayan dagger.
crisálida, *f.* (entom.) pupa, chrysalis.
crisantema, *f.*, **crisantemo,** *m.* (bot.) chrysanthemum.
crisis, *f.* crisis; judgment passed after mature deliberation; criterion; decisive moment.—**c. ministerial,** resignation or dismissal of the cabinet.
crisma, *m.* & *f.* (eccl.) chrism; *f.* (coll.) noodle, pate, head.—**romperse la c. con,** (coll.) to come to blows with.
crismera, *f.* chrismatory.
crisneja, *f.* = CRIZNEJA.
crisoberilo, *m.* (min.) chrysoberyl.
crisocola, *f.* (min.) chrysocola.
crisol, *m.* crucible; croslet or crosslet; cruset; hearth of a furnace.
crisolada, *f.* charge of a crucible.
crisolito, *m.* (min.) chrysolite.—**c. oriental,** yellow topaz.
crisopacio, *m.* = CRISOPRASA.
crisopeya, *f.* alchemy.
crisopo, *m.* (entom.) lacewing.
crisoprasa, *f.* (min.) chrysoprase.
crispamiento, *m.* contraction, twitching.
crispar. I. *va.* to cause (muscles) to contract convulsively. **II.** *vn.* to twitch.
crispatura, *f.* spasmodic contraction, twitching.
crispir, *va.* to marble, marbleize.
crista, *f.* (her.) crest.
cristal, *m.* (min. and chem.) crystal; flint glass; (window) pane (also **c. de ventana**); (watch) crystal (also **c. de reloj**); looking-glass; a fine shiny woollen stuff.—**c. de roca,** rock crystal.—**c. tallado,** cut glass.—**c. tártaro,** cream of tartar.
cristalería, *f.* glassware; glass store.
cristalicé, cristalice, *v. V.* CRISTALIZAR.
cristalino, na. I. *a.* crystalline, clear. **II.** *m.* (anat.) crystalline of the eye.
cristalización, *f.* crystallization.
cristalizador, *m.* (chem.) vessel in which crystals are made.
cristalizar, *va.* & *vr.* (*pret.* CRISTALICÉ; *subj.* CRISTALICE) to crystallize.
cristalografía, *f.* crystallography.
cristalográfico, ca, *a.* crystallographical.
cristaloide, *m.* (chem.) crystalloid.
cristel, clister, *m.* (med.) clyster, enema.
cristianamente, *adv.* Christianly.
cristianar, *va.* (coll.) to baptize, to christen.
cristiandad, *f.* Christendom; observance of the law of Christ; missionary's flock.
cristianesco, ca, *a.* applied to Moorish forms which imitate the Christian manner.
cristianicé, cristianice, *v. V.* CRISTIANIZAR.
cristianillo, illa, *n.* contemptible Christian; (app. to Spaniards by the Moors).
cristianísimo, *a. super.* most Christian (app. to certain sovereigns as a title).
cristianismo, *m.* Christianity; the body of Christians; christening.
cristianizar, *va.* (*pret.* CRISTIANICÉ; *subj.* CRISTIANICE) to christianize.
cristiano, na. I. *a.* Christian. **II.** *n.* Christian; (coll.) the Spanish language, opposed to Arabic or other foreign tongues; (coll.) living soul, person; (coll.) watered wine.
cristino, na, *a.* supporting Queen Regent María Cristina against pretender Don Carlos.
Cristo, *m.* Christ; image of Christ crucified.—**estar sin c.,** to be penniless, "broke."—**haber la de Dios es C.,** to have a grand dispute or quarrel.—**ni por un c.,** by no means, not for the world.—**poner como un c.,** to abuse, ill-treat.—**¡voto a C.!,** by the Almighty!
cristofué, *m.* (ornith., Venez.) yellow-green bird resembling the lark.
cristus, *m.* christcross, a cross formerly printed at the beginning of the alphabet; the alphabet.—**estar en el c.,** to be in the rudiments, or learning the A B C.—**no saber el c.,** to be very ignorant, not to know one's A B C.
crisuela, *f.* dripping pan of a lamp.
criterio, *m.* criterion; judgment, discernment.
crítica, *f.* criticism, critique; censure.
criticable, *a.* that may be criticized; blameworthy.

criticador, ra, *n.* & *a.* critic(-izing).
criticalidad, *f.* (chem.) criticality.
críticamente, *adv.* critically.
criticar, *va.* (*pret.* CRITIQUÉ; *subj.* CRITIQUE) to criticize; to judge; to blame, find fault with.
criticismo, *m.* critical, or Kantian, philosophy.
crítico, ca. I. *a.* critical, decisive; hypercritical; (med.) critical. **II.** *n.* critic; (coll.) affected writer or speaker; censurer, faultfinder.
criticón, na, *n.* & *a.* faultfinder(-ing).
critiqué, critique, *v.* *V.* CRITICAR.
critiquizar, *va.* to overcriticize, criticize for the sake of criticizing.
crizneja, *f.* braid of hair; rope of osiers or rushes.
croar, *vn.* to croak like a frog.
croata, *n.* & *a.* Croatian.
crocante, *m.* almond or peanut brittle.
croceína, *f.* (chem.) crocein.
crocino, na, *a.* of crocus, saffron.
crocitar, *vn.* to crow.
croco, *m.* (bot.) crocus.
crocodilo, *m.* crocodile.
croché, crochet, *m.* (Gal.) crochet.
crol, *m.* crawl (swimming stroke).
cromar, *va.* to chromium-plate.
cromático, ca. I. *a.* (mus., opt.) chromatic. **II.** *f.* chromatics.
cromatida, *f.* (biol.) chromatid.
cromatina, *f.* (biol.) chromatin.
cromatismo, *m.* (opt.) chromatic aberration.
cromato, *m.* (chem.) chromate.
cromatología, *f.* chromatics, the science of colors.
crómico, ca, *a.* (chem.) chromic.
cromito, *m.* (min., chem.) chromite.
cromo, *m.* (chem.) chromium, chrome; chromo, chromolithograph.
cromofotografía, *f.* color photography.
cromógeno, na, *a.* chromogenic.
cromolitografía, *f.* chromolithograph, colored lithograph; chromolithography.
cromolitografiar, *va.* to chromolithograph.
cromolitográfico, ca, *a.* chromolithographic; lithographed in colors.
cromolitógrafo, fa, *n.* chromolithographer.
cromoscopio, *m.* chromoscope.
cromosfera, *f.* (astr.) chromosphere.
cromoso, sa, *a.* (chem.) chromous.
cromosoma, *m.* (biol.) chromosome.
cromotipia, *f.* color printing.
cromotipografía, *f.* art of color printing.
crónica, *f.* chronicle.
crónico, ca. I. *a.* chronic. **II.** *f.* chronicle.
cronicón, *m.* brief chronicle.
cronista, *m.* chronicler, annalist.
crónlech, *m.* (archeol.) cromlech.
cronografía, *f.* = CRONOLOGÍA.
cronógrafo, *m.* annalist; chronograph.
cronograma, *f.* chronogram.
cronología, *f.* chronology.
cronológico, ca, *a.* chronological, chronologic.
cronologista; cronólogo, ga, *n.* chronologist.
cronometría, *f.* chronometry.
cronométrico, ca, *a.* chronometric.
cronometrista, *n.* chronometer maker.
cronómetro, *m.* chronometer.
cronoscopio, *m.* chronoscope.
cronotrón, *m.* chronotron.
croquet, *m.* croquet (game).
croqueta, *f.* croquette, fritter.—**c. de bacalao,** codfish cake.
croquis, *m.* sketch, rough draft.
croscitar, *vn.* to crow.
crótalo, *m.* castanet; rattlesnake (crotalus).
crotón, crotontiglio, *m.* (bot.) croton.—**aceite de c.,** croton oil.
crotorar, *vn.* to cry like a crane or stork.
cruce, *m.* crossing; crossroads.
crucé, cruce, *v.* *V.* CRUZAR.
crucera, *f.* withers of a horse.—*pl.* bolting pins.
crucería, *f.* Gothic architecture.
crucero, *m.* crucifer, cross-bearer; crossing of two streets or roads; railway crossing; (arch.) transept; (print.) crossbar of a chase; (carp.) crosspiece; binding beam; (naut.) cruising station; cruiser; (S. A.) (pleasure) cruise; (astr.) Cross, a constellation; (min.) cleavage plane.
cruceta, *f.* crosspiece; headstick; crosshead (of connecting rod); crosstail; (naut.) crosstree; trelliswork.
crucial, *a.* cross-shaped, cruciform.
cruciata, *f.* (bot.) crosswort.
cruciferario, *m.* crucifer, cross-bearer.
crucífero, ra. I. *a.* cruciferous; cross-shaped; bearing a cross; (bot.) cruciate. **II.** *m.* crucifer, cross-bearer; crutched friar. **III.** *f. pl.* (bot.) Cruciferæ.
crucificado, da. I. *pp.* of CRUCIFICAR. **II.** *a.* crucified.—**el C.,** the Crucified, Jesus Christ.
crucificar, *va.* (*pret.* CRUCIFIQUÉ; *subj.* CRUCIFIQUE) to crucify; to vex, torment, torture; to sacrifice; to ruin.
crucifijo, *m.* crucifix.
crucifiqué, crucifique, *v.* *V.* CRUCIFICAR.
crucifixión, *f.* crucifixion.
cruciforme, *a.* cruciform.
crucigrama, *m.* crossword puzzle.
crucillo, *m.* pushpin, a game.
crudamente, *adv.* rudely, crudely.
crudelísimo, ma, *a.* *super.* most cruel.
crudeza, *f.* crudity, crudeness; unripeness; rawness; (of water) hardness; rudeness; severity, rigor; (coll.) vapor, vain boasting.—**crudezas del estómago,** undigested food.
crudo, da, *a.* raw; crude; green, unripe; rude; cruel, pitiless; rough, unfinished; immature; hard of digestion; blustering, hectoring person; (of water) hard; (med.) unripe, not mature.
cruel, *a.* cruel.—**crueldad,** *f.* cruelty; cruel action or treatment.
cruelmente, *adv.* cruelly, with cruelty.
cruentamente, *adv.* bloodily, with effusion of blood; cruelly.
cruento, ta, *a.* bloody; cruel, inhuman.
crujía, *f.* (naut.) midship gangway of a galley; large open hall, corridor or passage in a building, with rooms on either side; great hall of a hospital; aisle of a ward; in cathedrals, passage between rails from choir to altar.—**c. de piezas,** suite of rooms.—**pasar c.,** to run the gantlet; to suffer great troubles.
crujidero, ra, *a.* creaking, crackling, rustling.
crujido, *m.* crack, creak, crackling, creaking; rustle; (metal.) flaw in a blade.
crujidor, ra. I. *a.* cracking, creaking. **II.** *n.* glass trimmer.
crujiente, *a.* cracking, creaking; rustling.
crujir, *vn.* to crackle, creak; rustle.
crúor, *m.* cruor; (poet.) blood.
cruórico, ca, *a.* of or pertaining to cruor; (poet.) bloody.
crup, *m.* (med.) croup.
crupal, *a.* (med.) croupous, croupy.—**tos c.,** croupous cough.
crupié, *m.* (Gal.) croupier.
crural, *a.* (anat.) crural.
crustáceo, cea. I. *a.* crustaceous, crustacean. **II.** *m.* (zool.) crustacean.
crústula, *f.* thin bark or rind.
cruz, *f.* cross; tail (of a coin); upper end of a tree trunk, where the branches begin; (vet.) withers; (print.) dagger, obelisk.—*pl.* wings of a reel.—**c. ancorada, or de Jerusalén,** anchor cross.—**C. de las bitas,** (naut.) crosstree of the bitts.—**C. del Sur,** (astr.) Southern Cross.—**c. de Malta,** Maltese cross.—**c. de San Andrés,** St. Andrew's cross.—**c. gamada,** swastika.—**c. griega,** Greek cross.—**c. latina,** Latin cross.—**c. potenzada,** potent cross.—**c. trebolada,** trefoil cross.—**c. y raya,** no more of this.—**de la c. a la fecha,** from beginning to end.—**en c.,** crosswise, crossing each other; cross-shaped.
cruzada, *f.* crusade; tribunal of the crusade; crossroads.

cruzado, da. I. *a.* crossed; cross (breed, etc.); crosswise, transverse, twilled.—**estarse con los brazos cruzados,** to be idle. **II.** *m.* an old Spanish coin; Portuguese coin; crusader; knight of a military order; manner of playing on the guitar; figure in dancing.
cruzamen, *m.* (naut.) square or width (of a sail).
cruzamiento, *m.* crossing.
cruzar. I. *va.* (*pret.* CRUCÉ; *subj.* CRUCE) to cross; to lay, place, pass, or go across; to honor with a cross or medal; to cruise; to cross (the breed); to twill.—**c. los brazos,** to fold the arms. **II.** *vr.* to be knighted; (of affairs) to accumulate.—**c. (con),** to pass (as on the street).—**c. de brazos,** to fold the arms; to be indolent; to be unmoved.
[1]cu, *m.* name of the letter q.
[2]cu, *m.* ancient Mexican temple.
cuácara, *f.* (Chile) work blouse or coat; (Colomb. coll.) frock coat.
cuaderna, *f.* double fours, in backgammon; fourth part of anything; (naut.) frame.—**c. maestra,** (naut.) midship frame.
cuadernal, *m.* (naut.) block, tackle.
cuadernalete, *m.* (naut.) short double block.
cuadernillo, *m.* quire of paper; clerical directory.
cuaderno, *m.* writing book, memorandum book, composition book; (print.) four printed sheets placed within each other; an ancient form of punishment for students; (coll.) pack of cards.—**c. de bitácora,** (naut.) log book.
cuadra, *f.* large hall; stable; ward in hospital, barracks, or prison; quarter of a mile; (S. A.) unit of length, about 275 ft.; (Am.) block of houses; (naut.) quarter of a ship.
cuadradamente, *adv.* exactly, completely.
cuadradillo, *m. dim.* little cube; block of sugar; cross-section paper, plotting paper.
cuadrado, da. I. *pp.* of CUADRAR. **II.** *a.* square; perfect. **III.** *m.* square; square ruler; clock, in stockings; gusset of a shirt sleeve; die; (arith., alg.) square; (astr.) quadrate; (carp.) square; (print.) quadrat, quad.—**de c.,** face to face; perfectly.
cuadragenario, ria. *a.* forty-year old.
cuadragésima, *f.* Lent.
cuadragesimal, *a.* Lenten.
cuadragésimo, ma, *a.* fortieth.
cuadral, *m.* (carp.) angle brace, truss; shoulder tie.
cuadrangular, *a.* quadrangular.
cuadrángulo, la, *m.* & *a.* quadrangle(-gular).
cuadrantal, *a.* (math.) quadrantal.
cuadrante, *m.* (geom., astr.) quadrant; sundial; face of clock or watch; (law) fourth part of an inheritance; ancient copper coin.
cuadrar. I. *va.* & *vn.* to square; to form into or reduce to a square; (arith.) to square; (art) [1]CUADRICULAR; to square, fit, suit, adjust; to please. **II.** *vr.* (mil.) to stand at attention; (coll.) to assume a very serious attitude; (Am.) to acquit oneself well, do well; (Chile) to be or get ready.
cuadrático, ca, *a.* quadratic.
cuadratín, *m.* (print.) quadrant.
cuadratura, *f.* squaring, square; (math., astr.) quadrature.
cuadrete, *m. dim.* small square.
cuadricenal, *a.* done every forty years.
cuadrícula, *f.* (collect.) squares (as on squared paper).
cuadriculado, da, *a.* cross-section, squared (paper).
[1]cuadricular, *va.* (art) to divide (design) into squares.
[2]cuadricular, *a.* squared, in squares.
cuadrienal, *a.* quadrennial, comprising four years.
cuadrienio, *m.* time and space of four years.
cuadrifido, da, *a.* (bot.) quadrifid.
cuadrifoliado, da, *a.* (bot.) quadrifoliated.
cuadriforme, *a.* four-faced.
cuadriga, *f.* quadriga.
cuadril, *m.* haunch bone; haunch; hip.
cuadrilátero, ra. I. *a.* quadrilateral, four-sided **II.** *m.* (geom.) quadrilateral.
cuadriliteral, *a.* consisting of four letters.
cuadrilongo, ga. I. *a.* rectangular. **II.** *m.* rectangle; (mil.) rectangular formation.
cuadrilla, *f.* meeting of four or more persons; gang; party; crew; herd; troop; band of armed men; patrol of the Inquisition.
cuadrillero, *m.* chief of a band; patrolman of the Inquisition; (P. I.) rural guard.
cuadrillo, *m. dim.* small square; Moorish dart.
cuadrimestre, *m.* period of four months.
cuadringentésimo, ma, *a.* four-hundredth.
cuadrinieto, ta, *n.* great-grandchild.
cuadripartido, da, *a.* quadripartite.
cuadriplicado, da, *a.* quadrupled.
cuadrípolo, *m.* (phys.) quadrupole.
cuadrisílabo, ba, *a.* quadrisyllabic.
cuadrivio, *m.* a quadrivial place; quadrivium, in the Pythagorean system.
cuadrivista, *m.* expert in the quadrivium.
cuadríyugo, *m.* cart with four horses; quadriga.
cuadro, *m.* square; picture, painting; picture frame; window frame; flower bed; (sport) team; (Am.) blackboard; (Am.) slaughterhouse; (mil.) square body of troops; (print.) platen; scene, tableau, division of a play; impressive spectacle; vivid description.—**c. de café,** (Cuba) 10,000-tree coffee plantation.—**c. de distribución,** (elec., tel.) switchboard.—**c. de servicio,** (Ry.) train schedule.—**cuadros de costumbres,** genre writings, on everyday life.—**c. vivo,** living picture, tableau vivant.—**en c.,** on each side, square (*tres pies en cuadro,* three feet square).—**estar,** or **quedarse, en c.,** to be bereft of either relatives or means; (mil.) to be reduced to the officers (of a body of troops having lost its soldiers).—**un traje a cuadros,** a checked dress.
cuadrúmano, na. I. *a.* (zool.) quadrumanous, four-handed. **II.** *m.* (zool.) quadrumane.
cuadrupedal, *a.* quadruped.
cuadrupedante, *a.* (poet.) four-footed.
cuadrúpede, cuadrúpedo, da. I. *a.* (zool.) quadruped; (fig., coll.) dull, blockish. **II.** *m.* (zool.) quadruped; (fig., coll.) nitwit, blockhead, nincompoop.
cuádruple. I. *a.* quadruple, quadruplex, fourfold. **II.** *m.* quadruple.
cuadrúplex, *m.* (tel.) quadruplex.
cuadruplicación, *f.* quadruplication.
cuadruplicar. I. *va.* to quadruple, quadruplicate. **II.** *vn.* to quadruple.
cuádruplo, pla, *m.* & *a.* = CUÁDRUPLE.
cuaga, *m.* (zool.) quagga, a South-African wild ass, similar to the zebra.
cuaima, *f.* (Venez.) a very poisonous snake; wily, cruel person.
cuajada, *f.* curd of milk separated from whey.
cuajadillo, *m.* fine heavy flower embroidery on silk.
cuajado, da. I. *pp.* of CUAJAR.—**leche cuajada,** junket. **II.** *a.* (coll.) dumfounded. **III.** *m.* a sort of mince pie.
cuajaleche, *f.* (bot.) yellow bedstraw; cheese rennet.
cuajamiento, *m.* coagulation.
[1]cuajar. I. *va.* to coagulate, curd, curdle; to ornament or decorate with too many ornaments. **II.** *vn.* (coll.) to succeed, materialize; to please, be well received. **III.** *vr.* to coagulate; to curdle; (coll.) to fill, become full (of people).
[2]cuajar, *m.* rennet bag, maw; stomach of a sucking animal; crop of a fowl; the fourth stomach, or abomasum, of a ruminant.
cuajarón, *m.* clot (of blood or other liquid).
cuajo, *m.* rennet, runnet, maw; curdling, bonnyclabber; concretion, coagulation; (sugar manufact.) thickening of the cane juice; (Mex.) idle chat; (Mex.) recess (in school).—**arrancar de c.,** to eradicate, to tear up by the roots.—**tener buen c.,** to be too dull and patient.

cuakerismo, cuaquerismo, *m.* Quakerism.
cuákero, cuáquero, ra, *n.* & *a.* Quaker.
cual (*pl.* **cuales**). **I.** *rel. pron.* which, such as, as. —**cada c.** *V.* CADA.—**el c., la c., los cuales, las cuales,** which, who.—**lo c.,** which.—**por lo c.,** for which reason, for that reason, whence. **II.** *adv.* as, like.—**c. (el padre), tal (el hijo),** like, as (father), like, so (son).—**c. si,** as if. **III.** (**cuál**) *interr. pron.* which, what.—**a c. más,** vyingly. **IV.** (**cuál**) *interjectional pron.* how. **V.** (**cuál**) *distributive or disjunctive pron.* some (*cuál más, cuál menos,* more or less).
cualesquier, *pl.* of CUALQUIER.
cualesquiera, *pl.* of CUALQUIERA.
cualidad, *f.* quality.
cualitativo, va, *a.* qualitative.
cualquier, *a. contr.* of CUALQUIERA (before noun).
cualquiera. I. *a.* any. **II.** *indef. pron.* anyone, anybody; some one, either one or the other; whichsoever, whoever.—**ser un c.,** to be a nobody, be a person of no account.
cuan, *adv. contr.* of CUANTO, how, as: used only before adjectives and adverbs.
cuando (*interr.* **cuándo**), *adv.* when; at, or during, the time of (**cuando la guerra,** at the time of the war); in case that, if; though, although, even; sometimes.—**c. más,** or **c. mucho,** at most, at best.—**c. menos,** at least. —**c. quiera (que),** when you please; whenever. —**de c. en c.** or **de vez en c.,** once in a while, from time to time, now and then.—**¿hasta c.?** when shall I see you again?
cuantía, *f.* amount, quantity; rank, distinction, importance, degree.
cuantiar, *va.* to estimate; appraise.
cuantidad, *f.* quantity.
cuantificación, *f.* (phys.) quantization.
cuantil, *m.* (stat.) quantile, fractile.
cuantimás, (coll.) = CUANTO MÁS.
cuantiosamente, *adv.* copiously.
cuantioso, sa, *a.* numerous, copious, abundant.
cuantitativo, va. *a.* quantitative.
cuanto, ta. I. *a.* as much as, all the; *pl.* as many as, all the (*cuantos libros halle,* all the books you find, as many books as you find). **II.** *m. adv.* as (in this sense **cuanto** is used in correlation with **tanto,** V.G., *tan bueno cuanto,* as good as). —**c. antes,** as soon as possible, immediately; without delay.—**c. antes mejor,** the sooner the better.—**c. más,** the more (*cuanto más habla, menos dice,* the more he talks, the less he says; *cuanto más tiene, tanto más quiere,* the more he has, the more he wants); let alone, to say nothing of (*él no tiene una casa, cuanto más un auto,* he has no house, to say nothing of a car).—**c. más antes,** as soon as possible, immediately; without delay.—**c. más que,** all the more because.—**en c.,** as soon as.—**en c. a,** as for, as far as, with regard to (*en cuanto a mí mismo,* as for me, as far as I am concerned, with regard to me).—**por c.,** inasmuch as.—**unos cuantos,** a few. **III.** *rel. pron* all (that), everything that, as much as (*cuanto Vd. quiera,* all you wish); *pl.* all those who (*cuantos fueren jugar,* all those who are going to play). **IV.** *m.* (phys., mech.) quantum.
cuánto, ta. I. *interrog. a.* & *interrog. pron.* how much; how long (*¿cuánto tiempo?* how long?); what (as an interjection, V.G., *¡cuánto dolor!* what suffering!); *pl.* how many. **II.** *interrog. adv.* how, how much; how long.
cuaquerismo, *m.* Quakerism.
cuáquero, ra. I. *a.* Quaker. **II.** *n.* Quaker; *f.* Quakeress.
cuarango, *m.* Peruvian-bark tree.
cuarcífero, ra, *a.* quartziferous.
cuarcita, *f.,* (min.) quartzite.
cuarenta, *n.* & *a.* forty; fortieth.
cuarentavo, va, *n.* & *a.* fortieth.
cuarentena, *f.* quarantine; period of forty days, months, or years; fortieth part; Lent; suspension of assent to anything; the number 40 in general, two-score.—**hacer c.,** to be in quarantine.
cuarentón, na, *n.* & *a.* (person) forty years old.
cuaresma, *f.* Lent; collection of Lent sermons.—
cuaresmal, *a.* Lenten.—**cuaresmero, ra,** *n.* (Chile) one who fasts every day in Lent.
cuarta, *f.* fourth, fourth part, quarter; quadrant, fourth part of a circle; (naut.) quarter, point of the compass; quart, sequence of four cards in piquet; (fencing) carte; span (of the hand); a lineal measure (¼ vara); quart, liquid measure; (mil.) quarter of a company of soldiers; (mus.) fourth; (carp.) square timber; section; (prov.) guide mule; (Mex.) short whip, riding crop.
cuartago, *m.* nag, pony, hack.
cuartal, *m.* bread weighing one quarter of a loaf; quarter, dry measure, fourth part of a fanega.
cuartán, *m.* grain measure (18 liters 8 centiliters); oil measure (4 liters 15 centiliters).
cuartana, *f.* (med.) quartan, an ague recurring every four days.
cuartanal, *a.* quartan.
cuartanario, ria, *a.* afflicted with a quartan.
cuartar, *va.* to plow for the fourth time.
cuartazo, *m.* (Mex.) blow with a whip.
cuartazos, *m. pl. aug.* coarse, corpulent person.
cuartear. I. *va.* to quarter, divide into four equal parts; to bid a fourth more on, at public sales; to make a fourth person at (a game); to zigzag up steep places; (Mex.) to whip. **II.** *vr.* to split, crack, rift.
cuartel, *m.* quarter, fourth part; district; ward of a city; barracks; duty imposed on villages for the quartering of soldiers; (coll.) dwelling, habitation; quarter, remission of life granted by victorious troops; flower bed; (poet.) quatrain; (her.) quarter; (naut.) hatch.—**c. de la salud,** safe place, shelter.—**c. general,** general headquarters.—**c. maestre general,** (mil.) quartermaster-general.—**estar de c.,** to be off active service with reduced pay.
cuartelada, *f.* military coup d'état, sedition of soldiers to carry out a coup d'état.
cuartelar, *va.* (her.) to quarter.
cuartelero, ra. I. *a.* pertaining to soldiers. **II.** *m.* (mil.) soldier who keeps the ward clean.
cuartelesco, ca, *a.* (Am.) = CUARTELERO.
cuarteo, *m.* act of dodging; crack, rift, fissure.
cuartera, *f.* dry measure (about 70 liters); land measure (about 36 acres); square timber.
cuarterada, *f.* land measure (about 8 sq. yds.).
cuartero, ra, *n.* collector of grain taxes.
cuarterola, *f.* quarter cask.
cuarterón, na. I. *n.* & *a.* quadroon. **II.** *m.* quartern, quarter, fourth part; quarter of a pound; upper shutter of windows; (carp.) door or wainscot panel.
cuarteta, *f.* (poet.) quatrain.
cuartete, cuarteto, *m.* (poet.) quatrain; (mus.) quartet.
cuartil, *m.* (stat.) quartile.
cuartilla, *f.* fourth part of an ARROBA (about 6 lbs.); grain measure (about 1.38 liters); liquid measure (about 4 qts.); fourth part of a large sheet of paper; sheet of paper; (print.) sheet of copy; pastern of horses.
cuartillo, *m.* pint, in liquid or dry measure; fourth part of a REAL (about 1¢).
cuartilludo, da, *a.* (horse) having long pasterns.
cuartito, *m. dim.* small room, hall room.
cuarto, ta. I. *n.* & *a.* fourth, fourth part, quarter. **II.** *m.* room, chamber, hall; copper coin worth four MARAVEDÍS; series of paternal or maternal ancestors; crack in horses' hoofs; quarter of clothes; quarter of animals or of criminals whose body is quartered; quarter of an hour; (astr.) quarter (of the moon); service in the royal palace.—*pl.* cash, money; well-proportioned members of an animal's body.—**c. a c.,** in a mean, stingy manner.—**c. bocel,** astragal. —**c. de baño,** bathroom.—**c. de conversión,** quarter wheeling.—**c. de costura,** sewing

room.—c. **de dormir,** bedroom.—c. **delantero,** forequarter.—c. **de tocador,** dressing room.—**c. de tono,** (mus.) quarter tone.—**c. de vestir,** dressing room.—**c. viento,** (naut.) quarter point.—**c. y comida,** board and lodging.—**de tres al c.,** of little moment.—**en c.,** (print.) quarter.—**no tener un c.,** (fig.) to not be worth a cent.—**tener cuartos** or **cuatro cuartos,** to be well off, have money.

cuartogénito, ta, *a.* fourth-born.

cuartón, *m.* quarter; large joist or girder; beam sixteen feet long; oblong patch of farming land; a liquid measure.

cuarzo, *m.* quartz.—**c. citrino,** Occidental topaz.

cuarzoso, sa, *a.* quartziferous, containing quartz.

cuasi, *adv.* almost.

cuasia, *f.* (bot.) quassia.

cuasicontrato, *m.* (law) quasi contract.

cuasidelito, *m.* (law) unintentional wrong.

cuasimodo, *m.* Quasimodo, first Sunday after Easter.

cuasina, *f.* (chem., pharm.) quassin.

cuate, *m.* (Mex.) twin.—**eso no tiene c.,** (coll.) that has no match.

cuaterna, *f.* union of four things; four points in the game of lotto.

cuaternario, ria. I. *a.* quaternary. **II.** *m.* (geol.) Quaternary.

cuaternidad, *f.* quaternity, quaternary.

cuaternio, *m.* (math.) quaternion, set of 4.

cuaterno, na, *a.* consisting of four numbers.

cuatezón, na, *a.* (Mex.) hornless ox or sheep.

cuatí, *m.* a South-American monkey.

cuatralbo, ba. I. *a.* having four white feet. **II.** *m.* commander of four galleys.

cuatratuo, tua, *a.* quadroon.

cuatrero, *m.* horse thief, cattle thief.

cuatriduano, na, *a.* lasting four days.

cuatrienio, *m.* = CUADRIENIO, 4 yrs. time.

cuatrillo, *m.* a card game.

cuatrillón, *m.* quadrillion.

cuatrimestre. I. *a.* lasting four months. **II.** *m.* period of four months.

cuatrín, *m.* an ancient small coin.—*pl.* (coll.) cash in general.

cuatrinca, *f.* union of four persons or things; four cards of a kind.

cuatrisílabo, ba, *a.* = CUADRISÍLABO.

cuatro. I. *n.* & *a.* four; fourth.—**c. gatos,** (contempt.) just a few people.—**c. letras,** a few lines.—**más de c.,** (coll.) a great many. **II.** *m.* figure 4; one delegated to vote for four absent persons; (mus.) quatuor, quartet; four, four-spot card; small four-string guitar; (Mex.) blunder. **III.** *pl. f.* **las cuatro,** four o'clock.

cuatrocientos, tas, *n.* & *a.* four hundred.

cuatrodoblar, *va.* to quadruple.

cuatropea, *f.* sales tax on horses.

cuatropeado, *m.* step in dancing.

cuatrotanto, *m.* (coll.) quadruple.

cuba, *f.* cask; tub, vat; (coll.) big-bellied person, tub; (coll.) toper, drunkard.

Cuba, *f.* Cuba.

cubano, na, *n.* & *a.* Cuban.

cubeba, *f.* (bot.) cubeb.

cubería, *f.* cooperage, cooper's shop.

cubero, *m.* cooper.

cubertura, *f.* cover, covering.

cubeta, *f. dim.* of CUBA; small barrel or cask, keg; tub, pail, bucket; trough; basin, cup or cistern (of a barometer); (photog.) developing tray; (Mex.) high hat.

cubetilla, ita, *f. dim.* small bucket.

cubeto, *m. dim.* of ²CUBO; small pail, tub, etc.

cúbica, *f.* cubica, fine worsted fabric.

cubicación, *f.* measurement of solids; calculation of volumes; cubing.

cubicar, *va.* (math.) to cube; to determine the volume of.

cúbico, ca, *a.* cubical, cubic.

cubículo, *m.* cubicle, cubiculum.

cubichete, *m.* (naut.) waterboards or weather-boards; (mil.) gun apron.

cubierta, *f.* cover, covering; envelope; wrapping; book cover; casing; coat, facing; roof; top of a carriage; pretext, pretense; deck (of ship).—**c. del motor,** (auto) hood.

cubiertamente, *adv.* secretly, under cover.

cubierto, ta. I. *pp. irreg.* of CUBRIR. **II.** *m.* cover, place for one at the table; roof; shed; covert, coverture, cover; allowance of a soldier; plate dinner; refreshment tray or plate.

cubil, *m.* lair or couch of wild beasts.

cubilar, *vn.* to take shelter.

cubilete, *m.* copper pan or mold for kitchen use; pastry made in it; dicebox, juggler's goblet; tumbler, mug; (Colomb., coll.) high hat; (Am.) political intrigue, wirepulling; (Am.) clique.

cubiletero, *m.* juggler; paste mold.

cubilote, *m.* cupola smelting furnace or pot.

cubilla, *f.*, **cubillo,** *m.* Spanish fly, blister beetle; water cooler; (theat.) small box near the stage; (naut.) socket for flagpole; bucket or scoop of a water-raising wheel.

cubismo, *m.* (art) cubism.

cubista, *a.* & *n.* (art) cubist.

cubital, *a.* cubital.

cúbito, *m.* (anat.) ulna, larger bone of forearm.

¹cubo, *m.* (geom., alg.) cube; (arch.) dado, die.

²cubo, *m.* wooden pail, bucket; tub, vat; mill pond; barrel of a watch or clock; fort, small tower; nave or hub of a wheel; bayonet socket; (mason.) hodful of mixed mortar; (mech.) tongue way, socket, shaft case; (carp.) stock.

cuboide, *m.* (anat.) cuboid bone.

cubrecama, *f.* coverlet, counterpane, bedspread.

cubrecorsé, *m.* corset cover.

cubrepán, *m.* fire shovel used by shepherds.

cubreplatos, *m.* wire-net cover for food in dishes.

cubriente, *a.* covering, hiding.

cubrimiento, *m.* covering; roofing.

cubrir. I. *va.* (*pp.* CUBIERTO) to cover; spread over; face; coat; envelop; veil; shroud; screen, hide, palliate; disguise, mask, dissemble, cloak; hood, drape, clothe; box up; case, incase; (mil.) to cover or protect; (arch.) to roof; (of male animals) to cover; (com.) to meet (a draft); to cover (a shortage or expenses); to compensate; to include, comprise.—**c. la cuenta,** to balance an account.—**c. la mesa,** to lay the table.—**c. los gastos,** to pay expenses. **II.** *vr.* to cover oneself; to protect oneself against loss, damage or attack; to hedge; to be covered; to put on one's hat; in fencing, to be well guarded.—**cubrírsele a uno el corazón,** to feel deep grief.

cuca, *f.* root tubercle of a sedge; a Peruvian plant; coca; sort of caterpillar; (coll.) gambling woman.—**c. y matacán,** a card game.—**mala c.,** (coll.) wicked person.

cucamonas, *f. pl.* (coll.) caresses, soft words.

cucaña, *f.* greased pole to climb for a prize; the sport itself; anything acquired with little trouble at other people's expense; easy thing, "child's play."

cucañero, *m.* (coll.) parasite, hanger-on.

cucaracha, *f.* cockroach, croton bug; cochineal; snuff.—**cucarachera,** *f.* cockroach nest.

cucarda, *f.* = ESCARAPELA, cockade.

cucarrón, *m.* (Colomb.) beetle.

cuclillas.—**en c.,** in a crouching or squatting position.—**sentarse en c.,** to squat.

cuclillo, *m.* (ornith.) cuckoo.

cuco, ca. I. *a.* (coll.) prim, dainty; cunning, crafty, astute; alert for one's own advantage. **II.** *m.* a kind of caterpillar; cuckoo; a card game; (coll.) gambler.

cucú, *m.* cuckoo, call of the cuckoo.

cuculza, *f.* (Am.) thread of the agave.

cuculí, *m.* a handsome wild pigeon of S. A.

cuculla, *f.* cowl, old-fashioned hood.

cucuma, *f.* bread made in Colombia from a root like yucca.

cucúrbita, *f.* distilling retort.

cucurbitáceo, cea, *a.* (bot.) cucurbitaceous.

cucurucho, *m.* paper cone; cornucopia.

cucuy, cucuyo, *m.* = COCUYO, glow-worm.
cucha, *f.* (Peru) = LAGUNA, lagoon.
[1]**cuchar,** *va.* to fertilize with CUCHO.
[2]**cuchar,** *f.* spoon; old corn measure, twelfth part of a peck; tax or duty on grain.—**c. herrera,** iron spoon.
cuchara, *f.* spoon; ladle; (mason.) trowel; (naut.) pitch ladle; (mil.) gunner's ladle; (naut.) scoop for baling boats; bucket, scoop (of dredging machine, excavator, etc.); (Am.) pickpocket, thief.—**c. cafetera,** teaspoon.—**c. de aire,** (aer.) air scoop.—**meter c.,** or **su c.,** to meddle, intrude; to put in one's oar.
cucharada, *f.* spoonful; ladleful.—**meter c.,** or **su c.** = METER CUCHARA. *V.* CUCHARA.
cucharadita, *f.* teaspoonful.
cucharal, *m.* spoon bag used by shepherds.
cucharero, ra, *n.* spoon maker or dealer.
cuchareta, *f. dim.* small spoon; a variety of wheat; inflammation of the liver in sheep.
cucharetear, *vn.* (coll.) to stir with a spoon; to busy oneself with other people's affairs.
cucharetero, *m.* maker or retailer of wooden spoons; spoon rack; petticoat fringe.
cucharilla, *f. dim.* small spoon, teaspoon, coffee spoon; (vet.) liver disease in swine; (surg.) scoop.—**c. de barrenero,** (min.) scraper.
cucharón, *m. aug.* large spoon; soup ladle, kitchen ladle, dipper; scoop, bucket (of a dredge, excavator, etc.)
cucharro, *m.* (naut.) harping; watering vessel made from a gourd.
cuchi, cuchí, *m.* (Am.) hog.
cuchichear, *vn.* to whisper.
cuchicheo, *m.* whisper, whispering.
cuchichiar, *vn.* to call like a partridge.
cuchilla, *f.* large chopping knife; cleaver; any knife; blade of a knife or sword; razor blade; ancient poniard; (poet.) sword; mountain ridge; knife edge.
cuchillada, *f.* cut or slash with a knife; gash, deep wound.—**dar c.,** (of competing actors) to win the preference of the public.—*pl.* fight, row.—**andar a c.,** to come to blows.
cuchillar, *a.* pertaining to knives.
cuchilleja, *f.*, **cuchillejo,** *m. dim.* small knife; paring knife used by horseshoers.
cuchillera, *f.* knife case or scabbard.
cuchillería, *f.* cutler's shop; cutlery.
cuchillero, *m.* cutler.
cuchillo, *m.* knife; knife edge; gore, triangular piece in a garment; right of governing; any object or place ending in a point or acute angle; (arch.) gable frame; (naut.) cant piece; triangular sail; goring of a sail; (carp.) beam, girder.—*pl.* chief feathers in a hawk's wing.—**c. de monte,** hunter's cutlass.
cuchillón, *m. aug.* large knife.
cuchipanda, *f.* (coll.) cheerful dinner shared by several persons.
cuchitril, *m.* narrow hole or corner; very small room, "den"; hut.
cucho, *m.* fertilizer of manure and compost.
cuchuco, *m.* (Colomb.) pork-and-barley soup.
cuchuchear, *vn.* = CUCHICHEAR, to whisper.
cuchufleta, *f.* joke, jest, fun.
cuchufletero, ra, *n.* jester, tease.
cuchuvo, *m.* (S. A.) saddle bag.
cudria, *f.* flat woven bast rope.
cudú, *m.* koodoo, an African antelope.
cuébano, *m.* = CUÉVANO, basket, hamper.
cuélebre, *m.* = DRAGÓN, dragon.
cuelga, *f.* bunch of grapes or other fruit hung up for use during the winter; (coll.) birthday present.—**c. de cebollas,** bunch of onions.
cuelgacapas, *m.* cloak hanger, rack.
cuelgasombreros, *m.* hatrack.
cuelgo, cuelgue, *v. V.* COLGAR.
cuelmo, *m.* candlewood.
cuelo, cuele, *v. V.* COLAR.
cuellicorto, ta, *a.* short-necked.
cuellierguido, da, *a.* stiffnecked; swelled up with pride.
cuellilargo, ga, *a.* long-necked.
cuello, *m.* neck; throat; collar (of garments); neck of a bottle; neck stock; small end of a wax candle; thinnest part of a mast, pole, cane, etc.; collar of a beam in oil mills.—**c. duro,** stiff collar.—**levantar el c.,** to be prosperous.
cuenca, *f.* wooden bowl; socket of the eye; basin of a river; deep valley.
cuenco, *m.* earthen bowl; sifting basket.
cuenda, *f.* end of packthread; tie of a skein; end of a skein.
cuenta. I. *f.* computation, calculation, count, reckoning; account; bill; note; statement (of accounts); narrative, report; obligation, care, duty; bead (of a rosary, etc.); accountability; reason, satisfaction; consideration, merit, importance.—**c. corriente,** (com.) account current.—**c. de venta,** (com.) account sales.—**c. en participación,** joint account.—**c. pendiente,** unsettled account.—**c. simulada,** pro forma account.—**c. y mitad,** (com.) joint account.—**cuentas del Gran Capitán,** account overcharged.—**a c.,** or **a buena c.,** on account, in part payment.—**a esa c., at** that rate.—**a fin de cuentas,** in the end.—**caer en la c.,** (fig.) to see, make out, "catch on."—**dar c.,** to answer, report, give an account.—**dar c. de algo,** (coll., ironic) to use up, waste, destroy.—**darse c. de,** to realize; to notice.—**de c. y riesgo de,** for account and risk of.—**en resumidas cuentas,** (coll.) in short, in a word; after all.—**estemos a cuentas,** let us settle this, let us come to an understanding.—**hacer cuentas,** to figure, reckon.—**hacer cuentas alegres,** or **galanas,** to build air castles.—**hacer de c. (que),** to pretend, act (as if).—**hacer la c.,** to figure out.—**hacer,** or **hacerse, la c.,** to imagine, take for granted.—**la c. es c.,** business is business.—**llevar c.,** or **la c.,** to keep account; to count, reckon.—**por c. de,** to the account of.—**por c. y mitad,** joint account.—**por c. y riesgo de uno,** at one's expense and risk; on one's own responsibility.—**por la c.,** as far as one can judge, judging from the facts known, stated, etc.—**rendir cuentas,** (lit. & fig.) to give, render an account.—**tener c.,** to answer the purpose; to be profitable or advantageous; **(con)** to be concerned (with), have a part (in).—**tener en c.,** to take into account, remember, bear in mind.—**tomar en c.,** to take under advisement, consider.—**tomar por su c.,** to take upon oneself.—**vamos a cuentas** = ESTEMOS A CUENTAS. **II.** *interj.* take care, look out!
cuentacorrentista, *n.* depositor.
cuentadante, *m.* one who renders an account of moneys received.
cuentagotas, *m.* dropper (for counting or measuring drops).
cuentahilos, *m.* thread counter; linen prover; weaver's glass.
cuentakilómetros, *m.* (auto.) mileage indicator.
cuentapasos, *m.* odometer.
cuentero, ra, *n.* & *a.* = CUENTISTA.
cuentezuela, *f. dim.* small account.
cuentista, *m.* talebearer, informer.
[1]**cuento,** *m.* tale, story; narrative; fable, fairy tale; gossip; million; million of millions; account; number;—**c. del tío,** (Am.) (coll.) confidence game, trick.—**c. de viejas,** old women's stories, notion, superstition.—**andar en cuentos,** to be at loggerheads; to carry tales; to gossip.—**dejarse de cuentos,** to stop beating about the bush, to come to the point.—**estar en el c.,** to be informed, to be on the inside.—**sin c.,** numberless.—**traer a c.,** to bring to bear upon the subject; to drag into the subject.—**venir a c.,** to be pertinent, to be to the point.
[2]**cuento,** *m.* articulation of a wing; ferrule of a pike; cane, or tool; prop, shore, support.
[3]**cuento, cuente,** *v. V.* CONTAR.
cuentón, na, *n.* story-teller, talebearer.
cuera, *f.* leather jacket.
cuerda, *f.* cord, rope, string; (fishing) line; string

for musical instruments; compass of a voice; (geom.) chord; match for firing a gun; spring, mainspring of a watch or clock; a West-Indian land measure (3.93 centiares); number of galley slaves tied together.—*pl.* human nerves.—**c. floja,** or **tesa,** tight rope, ropedancing rope. —**c. freno,** (aer.) dragrope.—**cuerdas de las cubiertas,** (naut.) deck streaks or strakes.—**cuerdas vocales,** vocal chords.—**bajo c.,** or **por debajo de c.,** underhandedly, deceitfully. —**dar c. a,** to wind up (a watch, clock).

cuerdamente, *adv.* prudently, wisely.

cuerdecica, illa, ita, *or* **cuerdezuela,** *f. dim.* funicle, small cord.

cuerdo, da, *a.* prudent, discreet, sensible, wise, judicious; in his senses, not mad.

cuerecico, ito, *m. dim.* small hide or skin.

cuerezuelo, corezuelo, *m.* suckling pig.

cuerna, *f.* horn vessel; stag's or deer's horn; sportsman's horn.

cuernecico, illo, ito, *m.* cornicle, small horn.

cuernezuelo, *m. dim.* cornicle, small horn; farrier's paring knife.

cuernito, *m.* (Am., cook.) croissant.

cuerno, *m.* horn; feeler, antenna of insect; horn of the moon; button of a manuscript roll; huntsman's horn; (bot.) horn; (naut.) outrigger; (vet.) a disease of horses; callosity.—**c. de abundancia,** cornucopia, horn of plenty.—**c. inglés,** (mus.) English horn.

cuero, *m.* pelt, fell, rawhide; tanned skin, leather; goatskin dressed entire, which serves as a bag to carry wine or oil; toper, drinker.—*pl.* hangings or drapery of gilded or painted leather.—**c. cabelludo,** scalp.—**c. de suela,** sole leather.—**c. exterior,** cuticle.—**c. interior,** skin.—**cueros al pelo,** raw hides, undressed hides.—**de cuero,** leathern, leather (as *a.*).—**en cueros,** or **en cueros vivos,** stark naked.—**entre c. y carne,** between the skin and the flesh.

cuerpecico, illo, ito; cuerpezuelo, *m. dim.* small body; small carcass.

cuerpo, *m.* body; trunk, build; mass, bulk; volume (of a book); corpus; corps; corpse; brigade, department, company; (arch.) entire part of a building up to a cornice or an entablature; (geom., print.) body.—**c. a c.,** hand to hand.—**c. astral,** (theosophy) astral body.—**c. compuesto,** (chem.) compound.—**c. de aviación,** Air Corps.—**c. de baile,** corps de ballet.—**c. de bomba,** barrel of a pump.—**c. de bomberos,** fire brigade or company.—**c. de caldera,** boiler shell.—**c. de combate,** (mil.) combat team.—**c. de ejército,** army corps.—**c. de guardia,** guard; guarded place, post of guard. —**c. del cabrestante,** (naut.) barrel of the capstan.—**c. del delito,** (law) corpus delicti.—**c. diplomático,** diplomatic body or corps.—**c. de sanidad,** sanitary corps.—**c. sin alma,** dull person.—**c. tiroides,** (anat.) thyroid gland.—**c. volante** (mil.) flying column.—**a c. de rey,** royally, like a king.—**a c. descubierto,** without cover or shelter; manifestly.—**dar con el c. en tierra,** to fall down.—**de c. entero,** full-length (picture).—**echar el c. fuera,** (coll.) to duck out, get away.—**en c.,** without cloak or wrap.—**en c. de camisa,** in shirt sleeves.—**en c. y alma,** (coll.) body and soul, wholly.—**estar de c. presente,** to be actually present; to lie in state.—**falsear el c.,** to duck, dodge (to avoid a blow).—**hacer del c.,** to go to stool. —**tomar c.,** to take shape; to increase, enlarge, grow.

cuerria, *f.* circular space fenced in where chestnuts are thrown to ripen.

cuerva, *f.* (ornith.) crow, rook; jay.

cuervecico, illo, ito, *m. dim.* little rook.

cuervo, *m.* (ornith.) raven; crow; rook.—**c. marino,** cormorant; (C., astr.) Corvus, a southern constellation.

cuesco, *m.* stone (of fruit); millstone of an oil mill; (coll.) noise from breaking wind; fisticuff; (Chile) man in love.

cuesquillo, *m. dim.* small stone of fruit.

[1]**cuesta,** *f.* = CUESTACIÓN.

[2]**cuesta,** *v.*—**c. trabajo creerlo,** it's hard to believe. *V.* COSTAR.

[3]**cuesta,** *f.* slope, grade.—**c. abajo,** down hill.—**c. arriba,** up hill; painfully, with great trouble and difficulty.—**a cuestas,** on one's shoulders or back; to one's charge or care.

cuestación, *f.* petition, solicitation or collection for a charitable purpose.

cuestero, ra, *n.* alms collector.

cuestezuela, *f. dim.* easy slope, light grade.

cuestión, *f.* question, dispute, quarrel; matter, problem, affair, business.—**c. batallona,** much-debated, or vexed, question.—**c. candente,** burning question.—**c. de gabinete,** state affair that may cause a change in the cabinet; serious matter.—**c. de tormento,** torture.

cuestionable, *a.* questionable, doubtful.

cuestionar, *va.* to dispute, discuss, argue.

cuestionario, *m.* questionnaire.

cuesto, cueste, *v. V.* COSTAR.

cuestor, *m.* questor; solicitor of alms.

cuestuario, ria; cuestuoso, sa, *a.* lucrative, productive.

cuestura, *f.* questorship.

cuete, *m.* firecracker; skyrocket.

cueto, *m.* (fort.) rocky peak; defended tor.

cuetzale, *m.* (ornith.) quetzal, a large Mexican bird of golden green plumage.

cueva, *f.* cave, grotto; cellar.—**c. de fieras,** den of wild beasts.—**c. de ladrones,** den of thieves.

cuévano, *m.* basket, hamper; (min.) sump basket.

cuevero, *m.* maker of caves and grottoes.

cueza, *f.,* **cuezo,** *m.* mortar hod.

cuezo, cueza, *v. V.* COCER.

cugujada, *f.* (ornith.) common field lark, skylark.

cugulla, cogulla, *f.* cowl.

cuicacoche, *f.* a Mexican song bird.

cuico, ca, *m.* (Mex.) policeman; *m.* & *f.* (Am.) gossip.

cuida, *f.* in ladies' seminaries, young lady who takes care of a young girl.

cuidado. I. *m.* care, solicitude; attention, heed; keeping, custody, charge, trust; carefulness, caution; fear, apprehension, anxiety.—**estar con c.,** to be anxious or apprehensive.—**estar de c.,** to be seriously ill.—**no hay c. (de que),** there is no danger (that).—**no pasar c.,** or **perder c.,** not to worry.—**tener cuidado (de),** to be careful (to); to be worried or anxious. **II.** *interj.* look out! beware!—**¡c. con él!** look out for him!—**¡c. con perderlo!** take care not to lose it!

cuidadoso, sa, *a.* careful; solicitous; painstaking; curious, observing.

cuidante, *n.* caretaker.

cuidar. I. *va.* to care for, look after, keep; to execute with care, diligence, and attention; take care of. **II.** *vn.* **c. de,** to take care of. **III.** *vr.* to take care of oneself.—**c. de,** to look out for, to be on guard against; to avoid; to pay attention to.—**cuido,** *m.* caretaking.

cuita, *f.* care, grief, affliction, trouble.—**contar sus cuitas,** to tell one's troubles.

cuitadamente, *adv.* afflictedly, sorrowfully.

cuitado, da, *a.* unfortunate, wretched; timid.

cuitamiento, *m.* bashfulness, timidity.

cuja, *f.* lance bucket; bedstead.

cuje, *m.* withe; pole supported by two vertical ones for hanging tobacco.—*pl.* hop poles.

cují, *m.* (bot.) sponge tree.

cujisal, *m.* plantation of sponge trees.

culantrillo, *m.* (bot.) maidenhair fern.

culantro, *m.* (bot.) coriander.

culata, *f.* buttock, haunch; butt of a firearm: screw pin which fastens the breech of a gun to the stock; rear part; (int. combust. eng.) cylinder head; (elec.) yoke (of an electromagnet).

culatada, *f.*, **culatazo,** *m.* kick; recoil of a firearm; blow with the butt of a firearm.
culcusido, corcusido, *m.* botch work.
culebra, *f.* snake; trick, fun, joke; hazing; distil worm; cock of a firearm; sudden disorder in a peaceful assembly.—**c. de cascabel,** rattlesnake.—**saber más que las culebras,** (coll.) to be very crafty and cunning.—**culebrazo,** *m. aug.* big snake; whipping given by jail prisoners to newcomers; hazing.—**culebrear,** *vn.* to wriggle (as a snake); to wind (as a rivulet).—**culebrilla,** *f.* tetter, ringworm; a skin disease; rocking staff of a loom; fissure in a gun barrel.—**culebrina,** *f.* (mil.) culverin; undulated meteor.—**culebrino, na,** *a.* snaky.—**culebrón, na,** *n. aug.* big snake; crafty fellow, double-dealer; intriguing woman.
culera, *f.* stain of urine in swaddling clothes; patch on the seat of trousers.
culero, ra. I. *a.* slothful, lazy. **II.** *m.* baby's diaper.
culinario, ia, *a.* culinary.
culminación, *f.* culmination; high tide.
culminante, *a.* culminating.
culminar, *vn.* to culminate.
culo, *m.* breech, backside, rump, buttock; bottom; socket; anus; bottom of anything.
culombio, *m.* (elec.) coulomb.
culón, *m.* (coll.) retired soldier.
culpa, *f.* fault; guilt; sin.—**echar la c. a,** to blame.—**no por (su) c.,** through no fault of (his) own.—**tener la c. de,** to be to blame, or responsible, for.
culpabilidad, *f.* culpability, guilt.
culpabilísimo, ma, *a. super.* guilty or culpable in the highest degree.
culpable, *a.* culpable, guilty; blamable, blameworthy.—**culpablemente,** *adv.* culpably.
culpación, *f.* inculpation, blame.
culpadamente, *adv.* culpably.
culpado, da. I. *pp.* of CULPAR. **II.** *a.* guilty.
culpar, *va.* to blame, accuse; condemn.
cultamente, *adv.* neatly, politely, in a refined manner; affectedly, in a showy manner.
cultedad, *f.* (humor.) affected elegance and purity of style; fustian.
culteranismo, *m.* high-flown style; fustian.
culterano, na. I. *n.* purist with affectation; fustianist. **II.** *a.* pertaining to fustian.
cultero, ra, *a.* (humor.) using high-flown style.
cultiparlar, *vn.* to speak with affected elegance.
cultiparlista, *a.* speaking with affected elegance and correctness.
cultipicaño, ña, *a.* (humor.) speaking with affected elegance and in a jeering manner.
cultivable, *a.* cultivable, arable.
cultivación, *f.* cultivation, culture.
cultivado, da, *a.* cultivated.
cultivador, ra, *a.* & *n.* cultivator (person or machine).
cultivar, *va.* to cultivate; to farm, develop, husband, till; to dress (a garden); to nurse (a plant); to preserve.
cultivo, *m.* cultivation; farming, tillage; culture of the mind; elegance of manners; (bacteriol.) culture.—*pl.* crops.
culto, ta. I. *a.* improved, cultivated; nursed (plants); pure, elegant, correct (style and language); cultured, educated; enlightened, civilized.—**II.** *m.* worship; religion; cult; respect or veneration for superior men; homage to lofty ideals.—**c. de dulía,** worship of saints and angels.—**c. de hiperdulía,** adoration of the Virgin.—**c. de latría,** worship of God.—**c. divino,** public worship in churches.—**c. externo,** external religious ceremonies.
cultura, *f.* cultivation of the soil or of the mind; urbanity, politeness; culture.
cultural, *a.* cultural.
culturar, *va.* to cultivate.
cuma, *f.* (Am.) godmother; crony.
cumárico, ca, *a.* (chem.) coumaric.
cumarina, *f.* (chem.) coumarin.
cumarú, *m.* Tonka bean, coumaron.
cumbé, *m.* a negro dance.
cumbre, cumbrera, *f.* top, summit, crest; peak of a mountain; acme; greatest height of favor, fortune, science, etc.; (carp.) ridgepole, tie beam, rooftree.
cúmel, *m.* kümmel (liqueur).
cúmplase, *m.* be it carried out—a term used by the executive of Spanish-American republics over his signature in approving an act of Congress; also, as a confirmation of an appointment.
cumpleaños, *m.* birthday.
cumplidero, ra, *a.* that must be fulfilled or executed; convenient, fit, suitable; accomplishable.
cumplido, da. I. *pp.* of CUMPLIR. **II.** *a.* full, complete, thorough; accomplished, perfect; large; plentiful, ample; fulfilled, lapsed, passed; due; polished, courteous. **III.** *m.* compliment; attention, courtesy; present; ceremony, formality.
cumplidor, ra. I. *n.* one who executes a commission. **II.** *a.* true to one's word, reliable.
cumplimentar, *va.* to compliment, congratulate; to show courtesy to; to fulfil, carry out.
cumplimentero, ra, *a.* (coll.) giving fulsome compliments; excessively courteous or formal; officious; ceremonious.
cumplimiento, *m.* completion, performance, fulfilment; lapse, expiration; compliment; civility, courtesy; formality, ceremony; complement.—**con c., con cumplimientos,** formally, ceremoniously.—**de c.,** formal.
cumplir. I. *va.* to execute, discharge, perform, obey, fulfil; keep (a promise).—**c. años,** to reach one's birthday (*hoy cumplo veinte años,* I am twenty years old to-day). **II.** *vn.* to perform one's duty; to fulfil a social engagement; to perform a duty in the name of another; to have served the time required in the militia; to mature, expire, fall due; to behoove; to be fit.—**c. con,** to fulfil, do, perform.—**c. por otro,** to perform in another's name.—**por c.,** as a matter of form. **III.** *vr.* to be realized or fulfilled; to come true; (of a period of time) to expire, be up; (com.) to mature, fall due.
cumquibus, *m.* (coll.) money, wherewithal.
cumulador, *m.* = ACUMULADOR, accumulator.
cumular, acumular, *va.* to accumulate.
cumulativo, acumulativo, va, *a.* cumulative.
cúmulo, *m.* heap, pile; congeries; large quantity or number, lot; cumulus (clouds).
cumulocirro, *m.* (meteorol.) cumulo-cirrus (cloud formation).
cumulonimbo, *m.* (meteorol.) cumulo-nimbus (cloud formation).
cumulostrato, *m.* (meteorol.) cumulo-stratus (cloud formation).
cuna, *f.* cradle; foundling hospital; place of birth; family, lineage; origin, source.
cunasiri, *m.* a Peruvian aromatic tree.
cuncuna, *f.*, a Chilean caterpillar; (Colomb.) wild pigeon.
cunchos, *m. pl.* an indigenous independent race in Chile.
cundido, *m.* provision of oil, vinegar, and salt given to shepherds; honey or cheese given to boys.
cundir, *vn.* to spread (app. to liquids or news); to yield abundantly; to grow, expand, propagate.
cunear. I. *va.* to rock (a cradle). **II.** *vr.* to swing; to rock.
cuneiforme, *a.* cuneiform, wedge-shaped.
cúneo, *m.* (mil.) triangular formation of troops; space between the passages in ancient theatres.
cuneo, *m.* rocking motion; (naut.) rolling, pitching.
cunera, *f.* cradle rocker, woman appointed to rock the infantas in the royal palace.
cunero, ra, *n.* foundling.
cuneta, *f.* (mil.) small trench; side ditch; gutter, road drain.
cuña, *f.* wedge, quoin; paving stone.

cuñada, *f.* sister-in-law.
cuñadía, *f.* relationship by marriage.
cuñado, *m.* brother-in-law.
cuñar, *va.* = ACUÑAR, to coin, mint; to wedge.
cuñete, *m.* keg; firkin.
cuño, *m.* coin; die for stamping money; the device stamped; mark on silver; (mil.) triangular formation of troops.
cuociente, *m.* quotient.
cuodlibetal, cuodlibético, ca, *a.* pert. to CUODLIBETO.
cuodlibeto, *m.* argument; debatable point; thesis; subtilty; pungent saying; quodlibet.
cuota, *f.* quota, share.
cupano, *m.* (P. I.) a large tree, the bark yielding a dyestuff and the wood being used for building.
cupe, cupiera, *v. V.* CABER.
cupé, *m.* coupé, cab; banquette of a coach.
cupido, *m.* gallant, lover.
cupitel.—tirar de c., (in game of bowls) to throw a bowl with a curve.
cupo, *m.* quota; tax rate; (Mex.) contents, capacity.
cupón, *m.* (com.) coupon.
cupresino, na, *a.* (poet.) made of or pertaining to the cypress tree.
cúprico, ca, *a.* (chem.) cupric.
cuprífero, ra, *a.* (chem.) cupriferous.
cuprita, *f.* (min.) cuprite.
cuproaluminio, *m.* duralumin.
cupromanganeso, *m.* cupromanganese.
cuproníquel, *m.* cupronickel.
cuproso, sa, *a.* (chem.) cuprous.
cúpula, *f.* cupola, dome, vault; turret of a monitor; (bot.) cupule, cup.—**c. de distribución,** steam dome.
cupulífero, ra, *a.* (bot.) cupuliferous, cup-bearing.
cupulino, *m.* (arch.) sky lantern.
cuquillo, *m.* (ornith.) cuckoo.
cura. I. *m.* parish priest, rector, curate; any clergyman. **II.** *f.* CURACIÓN; curing, seasoning (of timber, etc.); parsonage.—**c. de almas,** cure, or care, of souls.—**c. de misa y olla,** ignorant priest.—**c. de urgencia,** PRIMEROS AUXILIOS, first aid; emergency measure.
curable, *a.* curable.
curaca, *m.* (Peru) governor, potentate; master, boss.
curación, *f.* cure, healing; (surg.) dressing, care (of a wound).
curadero, *m.* bleaching place.
curadillo, *m.* (ichth.) codfish, ling fish.
curado, da. I. *pp.* of CURAR. **II.** *a.* hardened; tanned.
curador, ra, *n.* overseer, caretaker; healer; (law) guardian, administrator(-trix).—**c. de bacalao,** cod salter.—**c. de lienzo,** bleacher of linen cloth.
curaduría, *f.* guardianship.
curandero, *m.* quack, medicaster.
curar. I. *vn.* to recover from sickness; **(de),** to take care (of). **II.** *va.* to cure, heal, restore to health; to administer (medicines), prescribe; (surg.) to dress (a wound); to salt, cure, preserve; to bleach (fabrics); to cure, season (timber); to soothe, subdue. **III.** *vr.* to recover from sickness.
curare, *m.* curare.—**curarina,** *f.* (chem.) curarine.
curasao, *m.* curaçao.
curatela, *f.* (law) = CURADURÍA.
curativo, va, *a.* curative.
curato, *m.* curacy, parish.
curazao, *m.* curaçao.
curbaril, *m.* (bot.) W.I. locust tree; courbaril.
curculio, *m.* (entom.) curculio.
cúrcuma, *f.* (bot.) curcuma, turmeric.
curcusilla, *f.* = RABADILLA, coccyx; rump.
curdo, da, *n.* & *a.* Kurd(-ish).
cureña, *f.* gun carriage; stay of a crossbow; gunstock in the rough.—**a c. rasa,** (mil.) without parapet or breastwork; (coll.) without shelter or defense.—**cureñaje,** *m.* (collect.) gun carriages.
curesca, *f.* shear wool from the cloth.
curetaje, *m.* (surg.) curettage.
curí, *m.* (bot.) a S. A. coniferous tree, whose cones are used as food.
curia, *f.* ecclesiastical tribunal; bar, the legal profession; care, skill, nice attention; (old Roman) curia.—**c. romana,** pontifical court, aggregate of tribunals and congregations forming the Pope's court.—**curial. I.** *a.* curial. **II.** *m.* curialistic agent; officer of a court; attorney; (Roman) curial, member of a curia.
curialesco, ca, *a.* clerical, priestlike.
curiana, *f.* = CUCARACHA, cockroach.
curiara, *f.* (Am.) a long canoe.
curie, *m.* (phys.) curie.
curiel, *m.* (Cuba) guinea pig.
curio, *m.* (chem.) curium.
curiosamente, *adv.* curiously; neatly, cleanly; in a diligent, careful manner.
curiosear, *vn.* to act from curiosity; to pry into others' affairs; (coll.) to be a busybody.
curiosidad, *f.* curiosity, inquisitiveness; neatness, cleanliness; curious thing; rare object or person; curio.
curioso, sa, *a.* curious, inquisitive, prying; neat, clean; careful, attentive, diligent; quaint, rare.
curita, *f.* (min.) curite.
curricán, *m.* spinning tackle.
curro, rra, *a.* (coll.) showy, tawdry, loud; (Mex., Cuba) (coll.) native of Cadiz.
curruca, *f.* (ornith.) linnet, babbling warbler.
currutaco, ca. I. *a.* ultra-fashionable, dudish, exquisite. **II.** *n.* dude, fop, dandy.
cursado, da. I. *pp.* of CURSAR. **II.** *a.* accustomed, habituated, inured.
cursante. I. *a.* frequenting; assiduous. **II.** *n.* student, pupil.
cursar, *va.* to frequent, to do repeatedly; to study; to take action on, attend to. **II.** *vn.* (incorrectly used for CORRER) to circulate, be current.
cursi, *a.* vulgar, shoddy, in bad taste; clumsy.
cursillo, *m. dim.* short course of lectures in a university.
cursivo, va, *a.* (print.) cursive, script.
curso, *m.* course, direction, career, progress; run, route, current; course of study; term of tuition in schools; collection of the principal treatises used in instruction in some branch; lapse; succession; (com.) current rate.—*pl.* laxity or looseness of the bowels.—**c. de la corriente,** (naut.) current's way.—**ser de c.,** or **tener c. forzoso,** to be legal tender.
cursor, *m.* (mech.) slider, slide.
curtación, *f.* (astr.) curtation.
curtido, da. I. *pp.* of CURTIR. **II.** *a.* tanned, curried; accustomed, experienced, expert; weather-beaten. **III.** *m.* leather; tanning. **IV.** *m. pl.* tanned leather.
curtidor, *m.* tanner, currier, leather dresser.
curtiduría, *f.* tanyard; tannery.
curtiente, *n.* tanning material or substance.
curtimiento, *m.* tanning.
curtir. I. *va.* to tan (hides, the complexion); to inure to hardships, to harden.—**estar curtido,** (coll.) to be used or inured. **II.** *vr.* to become tanned, sunburned, weather-beaten.
curto, corto, ta, *a.* short, dock-tailed.
curú, *m.* (Peru) a clothes moth.
curuca, *f.* (ornith.) eagle owl.
curucucú, *m.* a disease caused by the bite of a South American snake.
curuja, *f.* (ornith.) eagle owl.
curul, *a.* (anc. Rome) curule; edile.
curva, *f.* curve; curvature; bend; (naut.) knee.—**c. acampanada,** (stat.) bell-shaped curve.—**c. de bao,** (naut.) spur.—**c. de enlace,** (Ry.) connecting curve.—**c. de frecuencias acumuladas,** (stat.) frequency curve.—**c. de nivel,**

(surv.) contour line.—**c. sedástica,** (stat.) scedastic curve.
curvatón, *m.* (naut.) small knee, bracket.
curvatura, *f.* curvature; curving.
curvidad, *f.* curvation.
curvilíneo, a, *a.* (geom.) curvilinear.
curvímetro, *m.* instrument for measuring curves.
curvo, va. I. *a.* curve, curved; crooked, bent. **II.** *m.* inclosed pasture ground.
cusculia, *f.* (bot.) = COSCOJA, scarlet oak.
cuscurro, *m.* end piece of bread, heel.
cuscuta, *f.* (bot.) common dodder.
cusir, *va.* (coll.) = CORCUSIR, to sew clumsily.
cuspidado, da, *a.* cuspidate, cuspidated.
cúspide, *f.* cusp, apex, top, summit, peak.
cuspídeo, dea, *a.* (bot.) cuspidate.
custodia, *f.* custody, safe-keeping; monstrance; shrine; guardian, custodian; tabernacle.—**c. protectora,** protective custody.
custodiar, *va.* to guard; to convoy; take care of.
custodio, *m.* guard, watchman; custodian.
cutáneo, nea, *a.* cutaneous, of the skin.
cúter, *m.* (naut.) cutter.
cutí, *m.* bedticking, crash.
cutícula, *f.* pellicle, cuticle, epidermis.
cuticular, *a.* cuticular.
cutio, *m.* labor, work.
cutir, *va.* to knock, strike, pound, beat, hammer.
cutis, *m.* or *f.* skin of the human body (esp. that of the face); complexion.
cutó, *m.* (naut.) dirk.
cutral, *n.* old worn-out ox or cow.
cutre, *m.* miser.
cuyabra, coyabra, *f.* (Colomb.) bowl or receptacle formed by halving a gourd lengthwise.
cuyo, ya, (*pl.* **cuyos, cuyas**). **I.** *pron. poss.* of which, of whom, whose, whereof. **II.** *a.* which, this, that (*por cuya razón,* for which reason; *en cuyo caso,* in that case). **III.** *m.* (coll.) beau, lover, suitor.
cuzma, *f.* (Peru) sleeveless shirt.
czar, *m.*; **czarevitz,** *m.*; **czariano, na,** *a.*; **czarina,** *f.* = ZAR, ZAREVITZ, etc., czar, etc.

CH

Ch, ch, *f.* fourth letter of the Spanish alphabet.
cha, *f.* (P. I.) tea.
chabacanamente, *adv.* bunglingly, clumsily.
chabacanería, *f.* bungle, muddle; vulgar expression or action.
[1]**chabacano, na,** *a.* awkward, clumsy.
[2]**chabacano,** *m.* (Mex.) a variety of apricot.
chacal, *m.* jackal.
[1]**chácara,** *f.* = CHACRA.
[2]**chácara,** *f.* (Venez.) large leather bag strapped across the back and chest over one shoulder.
chacarero, ra, *n.* (Am.) field laborer.
chacarrachaca, *f.* loud wrangle.
chacina, *f.* spiced pork for sausages and balls.
chaco, *m.* (Am.) hunt, hunting.
chacó, *m.* shako, military cap.
chacolí, *m.* chacoli, a light red wine made in Vizcaya, Spain.
chacolotear, *vn.* (of loose horseshoe) to clatter.
chacoloteo, *m.* clatter of a loose horseshoe.
chacón, *m.* (P. I.) a large lizard.
chacona, *f.* chaconne, an old Spanish dance.
chaconada, *f.* jaconet, a fine cotton material.
chacota, *f.* noisy mirth.—**echar a ch.,** (coll.) to carry off with a joke.—**hacer ch. de,** (coll.) to turn into ridicule, make fun of.—**chacotear,** *vn.* to indulge in noisy mirth.—**chacotero, ra,** *a.* (coll.) waggish, acting the merry-andrew.
chacra, *f.* (Am.) a small isolated farm.
chacuaco. I. *m.* (Mex., min.) small smelting furnace. **II.** *a.* (coll.) rustic, boorish.
chachalaca. I. *f.* (Mex.) a gallinaceous bird that cries continually while flying; (coll.) chatterbox. **II.** *a.* chattering, talkative.
cháchara, *f.* (coll.) prate, chitchat, idle talk.
chacharear, *vn.* (coll.) to prate, chatter, prattle.
chacharero, ra; chacharón, na, *n.* & *a.* prater (-ing), prattler(-ing).
chacho, *m.* (coll.) little boy (short for MUCHACHO); stake at the game of ombre.
Chad, *m.* Chad.
chadiano, na, *n.* & *a.* Chad.
chafaldetes, *m.* (naut.) clew lines.
chafaldita, *f.* (coll.) chaff, raillery, banter.
chafalditero, ra, *n.* (coll.) chaffer, person given to banter.
chafalmejas, *n.* (coll.) (painting) dauber.
chafalonía, *f.* (Peru) old plate.
chafallar, *va.* to botch, to mend clumsily.
chafallo, *m.* coarse patch, clumsy mending.
chafallón, na, *n.* (coll.) botcher.
chafar, *va.* to flatten; to crease, rumple, crumple; (coll.) to cut short.
chafarote, *m.* cutlass; (coll.) broadsword; (fig.) sword, military force.
chafarrinada, *f.* blot, spot, stain.
chafarrinar, *va.* to blot, stain.
chafarrinón, *m.* blot, stain.—**echar un ch. a,** (coll.) to disgrace; to defame, throw mud at.
chaflán, *m.* bevel, chamfer.
chaflanado, da, *a.* (arch.) canted.
chaflanar, *va.* to bevel, chamfer; (carp.) to cant.
chagra, *m.* a rustic in Ecuador.
chagrín, *m.* (Am.) grained morocco.
chaguarama, *f.* a Central-American palm.
chair, *m.* (tanning) inner side of a skin.
chaira, *f.* steel for sharpening knives, etc.
chal, *m.* shawl.
chala, *f.* (Peru) green corn husk.
chalado, da, *a.* addle-pated, light-witted.
chalán, na, *n.* hawker, huckster; horsedealer; horse breaker.
chalana, *f.* scow, lighter, wherry.
chalanear. I. *va.* to buy or sell cleverly; (Am.) to break (horses). **II.** *vn.* to deal in horses.
chalanería, *f.* artifice and cunning used by dealers in buying and selling.
chalate, *m.* (Mex.) small, lean horse.
chaleco, *m.* waistcoat, vest.
chalequero, ra, *n.* vest maker.
chalet, *m.* chalet, hut; cottage like a Swiss chalet.
chalí, *m.* mohair; challis, shalli; delaine.
chalina, *f.* cravat, scarf.
chalón, *m.* (text.) shalloon.
chalote, *m.* (bot.) shallot.
chalupa, *f.* (naut.) sloop, launch, small light vessel; long boat; (Mex.) a small canoe; (Mex.) corn pancake.—**chalupero,** *m.* boatman, canoeman.
chama, *f.* (low) barter, trade.
chamaco, *m.* (Am. esp. Mex.) youngster.
chamada, *f.* chips, brushwood, brush fire.
chamagoso, sa, *a.* (Mex.) greasy, filthy; ill-performed; low, vulgar.
chamar, *va.* (vulg.) to barter, trade off.
chamarasca, *f.* brushwood, brush fire.
chamarillero, ra, *n.* gambler; dealer in second-hand goods.
chamarillón, *m.* bad player at cards.
chamariz, *m.* (ornith.) blue titmouse.
chamarón, *m.* (ornith.) long-tailed titmouse.
chamarra, *f.* a garment of very coarse frieze.
chamarreta, *f.* a short, loose jacket.
chamba, *f.* (coll., billiards) fluke, scratch; (coll.) lucky stroke, chance; (Colomb.) wide deep ditch; (Mex., coll.) job.
chambear, *vn.* (Mex., coll.) to work.
chambelán, *m.* chamberlain.
chamberga, *f.* long and wide cassock.
chambergo, ga. I. *a.* belonging or pert. to the Chamberga regiment, serving as a guard to Charles II of Spain. **II.** *m.* (Arg.) soft hat.
chambilla, *f.* stone wall topped by iron railing.
chambón, na. I. *a.* (coll.) awkward, unhandy; bungling. **II.** *n.* botcher, bungler, greenhorn.
chambonada, *f.* (coll.) blunder.
chambra, *f.* dressing sack or jacket.

chambrana, *f.* doorcase, jamb dressing.
chamelote, camelote, *m.* camlet, waterproof material or garment.—**ch. de aguas,** shiny camlet.
chamelotón, *m.* coarse camlet.
chamicera, *f.* half-burnt woodland.
chamicero, ra, *a.* pertaining to scorched wood.
chamiza, *f.* (bot.) chamiso; brush used as kindling wood.—**chamizal,** *m.* chamiso thicket.
chamizo, *m.* half-burnt stick of kindling wood.
chamorra, *f.* (coll.) a shorn head.
chamorro, ra, *a.* shorn, with hair cropped.
champaca, *f.* (bot.) champac, champak.
champán, *m.* (naut.) pink stern; sampan.
champaña, *m.* champagne.
champola, *f.* (Cuba) refreshment made from GUANÁBANA, custard apple.
champú, *m.* shampoo.
champurrado. I. *pp.* of CHAMPURRAR. **II.** *m.* mixture of liquors; (Mex.) chocolate made with ATOLE instead of water.
champurrar, *va.* (coll.) to mix (liquors).
chamuchina, *f.* (Peru) populace, rabble.
chamuscado, da. I. *pp.* of CHAMUSCAR. **II.** *a.* (coll.) tipsy; addicted to vice; singed, scorched.
chamuscar, *va.* (*pret.* CHAMUSQUÉ; *subj.* CHAMUSQUE) to singe or scorch; to sear.—**chamusco,** *m.* = CHAMUSQUINA.—**chamuscón,** *m. aug.* bad singe or scorch.
chamusqué, chamusque, *v. V.* CHAMUSCAR.
chamusquina, *f.* scorching or singeing; (coll.) scolding, wrangling, high words.—**oler a ch.,** to look like (show signs of) a fight.
chanada, *f.* (coll.) trick, joke; deceit.
chanate, *m.* (Mex.) blackbird.
chancaco, ca. I. *a.* brown. **II.** *f.* (Am.) raw brown sugar; molasses cake.
chancear, *vn.* & *vr.* to jest, joke, fool.
chancero, ra, *a.* jocose, sportful, merry.
chanciller, *m.* chancellor.
chancillería, *f.* chancery; right and fees of a chancellor.
chancla, *f.* old shoe with worn-down heel.
chancleta, *f.* slipper.—**en ch.,** (of shoes) having no back.—**chancletear,** *vn.* to go in slippers.
chancleteo, *m.* clatter of slippers.
chanclo, *m.* patten; rubber, galosh, overshoe.
chancro, *m.* chancre, syphilitic ulcer.
chancroide, *f.* (med.) chancroid.
chancroso, sa, *a.* chancrous.
chancha, *f.* (Arg.) pod; string bean.
chanchira, *f.* (Colomb.) rag, ragged clothes.
chanchiriento, ta, *a.* (Colomb.) ragged.
chancho, cha. I. *a.* (Am.) dirty, unclean; mean; stingy. **II.** *n.* dirty person; pig; hog.—**ch. de monte,** (Peru) agouti.
chanchullero, ra, *n.* trickster, sharper; smuggler.
chanchullo, *m.* unlawful conduct; sharp practice, vile trick; "racket"; (Am.) contraband.
chanfaina, *f.* ragout of livers and lights.
chanflón, na. I. *a.* awkward, coarse, gawky. **II.** *m.* ancient copper coin beaten out.
changa, *f.* (Cuba) jest.
changador, *m.* (Am.) porter, carrier.
changamé, *m.* (ornith.) thrush of Panama.
chango, a. *n.* (Am.) monkey.
changote, *m.* (metal.) bloom, billet.
changuear, *vn.* to be sporty or jesting.
changuí, *m.* (coll.) jest, trick (used with DAR); (Cuba) a country dance.
changuito, ta, *n. dim.* little monkey.
chantado, *m.* wall or fence of upright flags.
chantaje, *m.* blackmail; blackmailing.
chantajista, *n.* blackmailer.
chantar. I. *va.* to put on (as clothes); to tell to one's face; to give a piece of one's mind to (diff. constr.); to build (a fence) with upright flagstones; to pave with flagstones. **II.** *vr.* to put on (clothes).
chanto, *m.* flagstone.
chantre, *m.* precentor.
chantría, *f.* precentorship.
chanza, *f.* joke, jest, fun.—**ch. pesada,** offensive or serious joke.
[1]**chanzoneta,** *f.* (coll.) joke, jest.
[2]**chanzoneta,** *f.* ballad, chansonette.
chanzonetero, ra, *n.* ballad writer; petty poet.
chapa, *f.* veneer; plate, sheet (of metal); (Am.) doorlock; foil; cap (of compass); leather chape; (Ecua.) policeman; rosy spot on the cheek, flush; rouge; transom and trunnion plates in gun carriages; judgment, good sense.—*pl.* game of tossing up coins; (Am.) rosy cheeks.
chapado, da, *a.* having red cheeks.—**ch. a la antigua,** old-fashioned.
chapalear, *vn.* = CHAPOTEAR; CHACOLOTEAR.
chapaleo, *m.* splash, splatter.
chapaleta, *f.* flap valve, clack valve; cap; clapper.
chapaleteo, *m.* continuous splashing of the waters on the shore.
chapapote, *m.* (Cuba) mineral tar, variety of asphalt.
chaparra, *f.* a kind of oak; ancient low-roofed carriage; bramble bush.
chaparrada, *f.* shower (of rain).
chaparral, *m.* (Am.) chaparral; plantation of evergreen oaks.
chaparrear, *vn.* to shower, to pour.
chaparreras, *f. pl.* chaps, chaparejos.
chaparro, *m.* (bot.) evergreen oak.—**c., ra,** *a.* & *n.* (Am.) short, stocky (person).
chaparrón, *m.* violent shower, downpour.
chapatal, *m.* mire; muddy place.
chapear. I. *va.* to veneer; inlay; cover with metal plate. **II.** *vn.* to splash, splatter.
chapelete, *m.* an ancient cover for the head.
chapeo, *m.* hat.
chapera, *f.* inclined plane.
chapería, *f.* ornament of metal plates.
chaperón, *m.* chaperon (ancient hood or cap).
chapeta, *f.* small metal plate; red spot on the cheek.
[1]**chapetón, na. I.** *n.* & *a.* (Am.) Spaniard (recently arrived in Am.), Spanish. **II.** *m.* CHAPETONADA.
[2]**chapetón,** *m.* (Mex.) silver plate on a riding harness.
chapetonada, *f.* (Peru) illness of Europeans due to change of climate; act or conduct worthy of a [1]CHAPETÓN.
chapín. I. *m.* woman's clog with a cork sole. **II.** *n.* & *a.* (Am.) (one) having defective feet; (Am.) bowlegged (person).
chapinazo, *m.* blow with a clog or patten.
chapinería, *f.* shop where clogs and pattens are made and sold; art of making them.
chapinero, ra, *n.* clog maker or seller.
chápiro, *m.* a word used only in the phrases, *¡por vida del chápiro verde!* good gracious! *¡voto al chápiro!* by Jove! by thunder!
chapitel, *m.* (arch.) spire; capital of a column; (naut.) agate socket of the needle.
chaple, *m.* graver.
chapó, *m.* four-handed billiard game.
chapodar, *va.* to lop (branches of a tree).
chapodo, *m.* lopping; branch lopped off.
chapola, *f.* (Am.) butterfly; moth.
chapón, *m.* large blot of ink.
chapona, *f.* = CHAMBRA, dressing jacket, sack.
chapote, *m.* black wax for cleaning the teeth.
chapotear. I. *va.* to wet with a sponge or wet cloth. **II.** *vn.* to paddle in the water, to dabble.
chapoteo, *m.* splash, splatter.
chapucé, chapuce, *v. V.* CHAPUZAR.
chapuceador, ra, *n.* blunderer, blunderhead.
chapucear, *va.* to botch, bungle, cobble.
chapuceramente, *adv.* fumblingly, clumsily, bunglingly.
chapucería, *f.* bungle, botch; clumsy fib.
chapucero, ra. I. *a.* rough, unpolished; clumsy, bungling; rude. **II.** *m.* blacksmith who makes nails, trivets, shovels, etc.; nailer; junk dealer.
chapurrar, *va.* to jabber (a language); to speak brokenly; to mix (app. to liquors).

chapurrear, *va.* to jabber (a language).
[1]**chapuz,** *m.* ducking.
[2]**chapuz,** *m.* unimportant work; clumsy performance.—*pl.* **chapuces,** (naut.) mast spars.
chapuzar. I. *va.* (*pret.* CHAPUCÉ; *subj.* CHAPUCE) to duck. **II.** *vn.* & *vr.* to dive, draggle, duck.
chaqué, chaquet, *m.* cut-away coat.
chaqueta, *f.* jacket; sack coat; (mech.) case, casing, jacket.
chaquete, *m.* the game of checkers.
chaquetear, *va.* (coll.) to turn one's coat, change sides.
chaquetilla, *f.* vestee.
chaquetón, *m. aug.* pea-jacket; (Cuba) overcoat.
chaquira, *f.* (Peru) fine mock pearl or glass colored bead; (Colomb.) bead.
charabán, *m.* char-à-banc, charabanc.
charada, *f.* word charade.
charadrio, *m.* (ornith.) common roller.
charal, *m.* (Mex.) a lake fish.
charamusca, *f.* (Mex.) twisted candy; (Peru) brushwood.
charamusquero, ra, *n.* (Mex.) seller of twisted candy.
charanga, *f.* military brass band; fanfare.
charango, *m.* (Peru) a kind of bandore or small guitar.
charanguero, ra. I. *a.* clumsy, unpolished. **II.** *m.* bungler, botcher; peddler, hawker; small coast-trading ship.
charca, *f.* pool, basin, pond.
charco, *m.* pool, puddle.—**pasar el ch.,** (coll.) to cross the big pond (the sea).
charla, *f.* prattle, chat, talk; loquaciousness; (ornith.) Bohemian chatterer, silktail.
charlador, ra, *n.* & *a.* prater(-ing), talker(-ative), chatterbox.
charladuría, *f.* garrulity, gossip, prattle.
charlante, *n.* gabbler, chatterer.
charlantín, na, *n.* (coll.) mean prattler, gossip.
charlar, *vn.* to chat, prattle, prate.
charlatán, na, *n.* prater, babbler; charlatan, quack, humbug.
charlatanear, *vn.* = CHARLAR.
charlatanería, *f.* garrulity, verbosity; charlatanry, quackery, humbug.
charlatanismo, *m.* charlatanry, quackery; verbosity, loquaciousness.
charlotear, *vn.* = CHARLAR.
charneca, *f.* (bot.) mastic tree.
charnecal, *m.* plantation of mastic trees.
charnela, *f.* hinge, chape of a buckle, hinge joint, knuckle.
charneta, *f.* (coll.) hinge joint.
charol, *m.* varnish, japan; patent leather.—**darse ch.,** to blow one's own horn, to brag.
charolar, *va.* to varnish, polish, enamel; japan.
charolista, *n.* gilder, varnisher.
charpa, *f.* leather belt with compartments for pistols; sling for a broken arm; (naut.) sling.
charpar, *va.* to scarp; to lap.
charque, *m.* (Am.) jerked beef.
charquear, *va.* (Am.) to jerk or dry (beef).
charqueo, *m.* (min.) cleaning of the drains; cleaning holy-water fonts.
charqui, *m.* = CHARQUE.
charquillo, *m. dim.* small pool or puddle.
charrada, *f.* speech or action of a peasant; country dance; (coll.) tawdriness, tinsel, gaudiness.
charrán, *a.* rascally, knavish.—**charranada,** *f.* knavish, roguish action.—**charranear,** *vn.* to play the knave.—**charranería,** *f.* rascality, knavery.
charrasca, *f.* folding knife; (coll., humor.) dangling sword.
charrería, *f.* tawdriness, gaudiness.
charretera, *f.* strap on the bottom of trousers; the buckle of the strap; (mil.) the lower part of trousers to fasten them with a buckle; the buckle; epaulet.—**ch. mocha,** shoulder knot; (coll.) shoulder pad for carrying loads.
charro, ra. I. *n.* churl; coarse, ill-bred person; (Mex.) cowboy. **II.** *a.* tawdry, showy, flashy, loud.
chascar, *vn.* to crackle, crack, sputter.
chascarrillo, *m.* (coll.) spicy anecdote.
chasco, *m.* practical joke, jest, trick; failure, disappointment.—**dar ch.,** to disappoint.—**dar un ch.,** to play a joke, trick.—**llevarse ch.** (**con**), to be disappointed (in), to get left.
chasí, *m.* photographic plate holder.
chasis, *m.* (auto) chassis.
chasponazo, *m.* mark made by a spent bullet.
[1]**chasquear. I.** *va.* to crack or snap (a whip). **II.** *vn.* to crack, snap; crepitate.
[2]**chasquear,** *va.* to fool; to play a trick on; to disappoint, fail; to cheat.
chasqui, *m.* (Peru) postboy, foot messenger.
chasquido, *m.* crack of a whip or lash; crack, noise made by timber when it breaks or splits.
chata, *f.* bedpan; (naut.) flat-bottomed boat.—**ch. alijadora,** lighter.—**ch. de arbolar,** sheer-hulk.—**ch. de carenar,** careening hulk.
chatarra, *f.* junk, scrap iron or metal.
chatarrero, *m.* junkman.
chatedad, *f.* flatness.
chato, ta, *a.* flat; flat- or pug-nosed; flattened.
chatón, *m.* bezel holding a gem; large gem set in.
chatre, *a.* (Ecua.). richly decked out.
chaucha, *f.* (Arg.) pod; string bean.
chaúl, *m.* blue Chinese silk.
chauvinismo, *m.* chauvinism.
chauvinista, *n.* & *a.* chauvinist(-ic).
chaval, la, *n.* lad, lass.
chaveta, *f.* bolt, forelock, pin, key, wedge; cotter, cotter pin.—**perder la ch.,** to become rattled.
chaya, *f.* (Chile) amusement consisting in throwing water on passers-by during carnivals; confetti; spray of a watering pot.
chayote, *m.* (Mex.) pear-shaped fruit with a large stone.—**chayotera,** *f.* (Mex.) a climbing plant yielding the CHAYOTE.
chaza, *f.* point where the ball is driven back or where it stops, in the game of PELOTA; mark where the ball stops; (naut.) space between ports.—**hacer chazas,** (of horses) to walk on the hind feet.
chazador, *m.* (in PELOTA) person employed to stop the ball and mark the game.
chazar, *va.* (in PELOTA) to stop (the ball) before it reaches the winning point; to mark the point whence the ball was driven back.
checo, ca, *n.* & *a.* Czech.
checoslovaco, ca, *n.* & *a.* Czechoslovak, Czechoslovakian.
Checoslovaquia, *f.* Czechoslovakia.
chécheres, *m. pl.* (Colomb.) small things, notions.
cheira, *f.* = CHAIRA, steel for sharpening.
chelín, *m.* shilling.
chepa, *f.* (coll.) hump, hunch.
cheque, *m.* (com.) check, sight draft.
chequear, *va.* (Angl.) (Am.) to check, verify; to check (mark).
cherna, *f.* (ichth.) ruffle, a salmonlike fish.
cherva, *f.* (bot.) castor-oil plant.
cheurón, *m.* (her.) chevron.
cheviot, *m.* (text.) cheviot.
[1]**chía,** *f.* short black mantle, cowl.
[2]**chía,** *f.* white medicinal earth; (bot.) lime-leaved sage.
chibalete, *m.* (print.) cabinet, composing frame.
chibcha. I. *a.* pert. to the Chibchas. **II.** *m.* one of the aborigines of the Bogotá plateau.
chibuquí, *m.* Turkish chibouk, smoking pipe.
chica, *f.* girl. *V.* CHICO.
chicada, *f.* herd of sickly kids; childish action.
chicalote, *m.* (bot.) Mexican argemone.
chicana, *f.* (Am.) chicanery.
chicanero, ra, *a.* (Am.) tricky, cunning.
chicle, *m.* chicle; (Am.) chewing gum.—**ch. de balón,** bubble gum.
chico. ca. I. *a.* little, small. **II.** *n.* little boy, little chap; little girl or lass; dear boy, dear fellow; dear girl; (coll. familiar) boy, old chap.

chicolear, *va.* (coll.) to pay compliments to (a woman).
chicoleo, *m.* (coll.) flattering compliment.
chicoria, *f.* (bot.) = ACHICORIA, chicory.
chicorrotico, ca, llo, lla, to, ta, *a.* dim. (coll.) very little or small, tiny (child).
chicorrotín, *a.* (coll.) very small, tiny.
chicotazo, *m.* (Mex.) blow with a whip.
chicote, ta. I. *n.* (coll.) fat strong boy or girl. **II.** *m.* (naut.) end of a rope or cable; junk; (Mex.) whip; (coll.) cigar.
chicotear, *va.* (Mex.) to whip.
chicozapote, *m.* (bot.) sapodilla.
chicuelo, la, *n. dim.* little boy; little girl.
[1]**chicha,** *f.* chicha, a popular fermented beverage, variously made from maize, pineapple, etc.
[2]**chicha,** *f.* children's term for meat.
chícharo, *f.* (bot.) pea.
chicharra, *f.* harvest fly, jarfly, cicada; talkative woman; kazoo, a plaything.—**cantar la ch.,** (coll.) to be scorching hot.
chicharrar, *va.* = ACHICHARRAR, to overheat.
chicharrear, *vn.* to creak; to chirp (said of the cicada).
chicharrero, ra. I. *n.* maker or seller of kazoos. **II.** *m.* (coll.) very hot place or climate.
chicharro, *m.* young tunny fish; horse-mackerel.
chicharrón, *m.* crackling, fried scrap, cracknel; (Mex.) thick, crisp bacon; overroasted meat; (coll.) person sunburnt or tanned.
chiche, *m.* (Am.) potted and devilled fish.
chichear, *va.* to hiss as a sign of displeasure.
chicheo, *m.* act of hissing.
chichería, *f.* tavern where [1]CHICHA is sold.
chichero, ra, *n.* seller or drinker of [1]CHICHA.
chichigua, *f.* (Mex., vulg.) wet nurse.
chichimeco, ca, *n.* & *a.* Chichimec(-an).
chichisbeador, *m.* gallant, wooer.
chichisbear, *va.* to woo, court.
chichisbeo, *m.* court paid to a lady; **cicisbeo,** gallant who trails a married woman.
chichón, *m.* bump; bruise.
chichoncillo, cito, *m. dim.* small bump.
chichonera, *f.* tumbling cap; child's wadded hood.
chichota, *f.*—**sin faltar ch.,** without lacking one iota.
[1]**chifla,** *f.* whistling, hissing.
[2]**chifla,** *f.* paring knife.
chiflacayote, *m.* a large kind of pumpkin.
chifladera, *f.* whistle.
chiflado, da, *a.* (Am.) (fig.) crazy, crackbrained.
chifladura, *f.* hissing, whistling; (coll.) crankiness; eccentricity; whim, fad; hobby.
[1]**chiflar. I.** *vn.* to hiss, whistle; (coll.) to tipple. **II.** *vr.* (coll.) to become mentally unbalanced; to lose one's head.
[2]**chiflar,** *va.* to pare (leather).
chiflato, *m.* whistle.
chifle, *m.* whistle; call; instrument to decoy birds; (naut.) priming horn; powderflask.
chiflete, *m.* whistle.
chiflido, *m.* shrill whistling sound.
chiflo, *m.* whistling.
chiflón, *m.* (Am.) draught (of air); (Mex.) waterspout; (min.) caving of loose stone.
chilaba, *f.* Moorish hooded garment.
chilacayote, *m.* (bot.) bottle gourd.
chilanco, *m.* = CILANCO, pool (of water).
chilar, *m.* field planted with chillies.
chile, *f.* (bot.) chilli, red pepper.
Chile, *m.* Chile.
chileno, na; chileño, ña, *n.* & *a.* Chilean.
chilindrina, *f.* (coll.) trifle, thing of little value; (coll.) joke, fun, witticism, anecdote.
chilindrinero, ra, *n.* & *a.* (coll.) trifler(-ing).
chilindrón, *m.* a card game.
chilote, *m.* (Am.) = JILOTE, **ear of green corn;** (Mex.) liqueur-like drink.
chiltipiquín, *m.* (Mex.) small hot chilli.
[1]**chilla,** *f.* call for foxes, hares, or rabbits.
[2]**chilla,** *f.* (carp.) clapboard.—**chillado,** *m.* clapboard roof.
chillador, ra, *n.* & *a.* screamer(-ing); screecher (-ing); creaking.
chillante, *a.* shrieking, screeching.
chillar, *vn.* to screech, scream, shriek; to crackle, creak; to imitate the notes of birds; (of something frying) to hiss, sizzle.
chilleras, *f. pl.* (naut.) shot lockers for balls; rowlocks.
chillido, *m.* screech, scream, shriek, shrill sound; bawling of a woman or child.—**dar un ch.,** to utter a scream.
chillo, *m.* call.
[1]**chillón,** *m.* lath nail.—**ch. real,** spike.
[2]**chillón, na. I.** *n.* (coll.) screamer, bawler; whiner. **II.** *a.* whining; screechy, shrill, harsh; showy, tawdry, loud; (of colors) loud.
chimachima, chimango, *m.* (Chile, Peru), a species of caracara, a vulture-like bird.
chimenea, *f.* chimney, smokestack; hearth, fireplace; kitchen range, cooking stove.—**ch. francesa,** fireplace with mantelpiece.
chimpancé, *m.* chimpanzee.
[1]**china,** *f.* pebble, small stone; game of shutting the hands, and guessing which contains the pebble.
[2]**china,** *f.* (**Ch.**) China; (bot.) Chinaroot; china, porcelain; China silk or cotton stuff; (P. R., Cuba) sweet orange.
[3]**china,** *f.* (Am.) maid servant; (C. A.) children's nurse; (Colomb.) little or young girl.
chinampa, *f.* small garden tract in lakes near Mex.—**chinampero,** *m.* tiller of a CHINAMPA.
chinanta, *f.* (P. I.) a unit of weight (about 14 lbs.)
chinarro, *m.* large pebble.
chinateado, *m.* stratum or layer of pebbles.
chinazo, *m. aug.* blow with a pebble.
chincharrazo, *m.* (coll.) = CINTARAZO, **slap.**
chincharrero, *m.* place swarming with bedbugs; fishing smack.
chinche, *m.* or *f.* bedbug; thumb tack; (coll.) tedious person, bore.—**chinchero,** *m.* bug trap made of twigs; place full of bedbugs.
chinchilla, *f.* (zool.) chinchilla; its fur.
chinchín, *m.* (Cuba, Carib.) drizzling rain.
chinchorrería, *f.* (coll.) nuisance, vexation; (coll.) mischievous tale.
chinchorrero, ra, *n.* insidious and pestering taleteller.
chinchorro, *m.* small dragnet; smallest rowboat on board a ship.
chinchoso, sa, *a.* (coll.) querulous, tiresome.
chinela, *f.* slipper; pattens, chopines, or clogs worn by women in bad weather.
chinero, *m.* china closet, cupboard.
chinesco, ca, *a.* Chinese.—*m. pl.* (mus.) bells.
chingar. I. *va.* (Am.) to annoy, bother; (C. A.) to cut off the tail of, bob. **II.** *va.* & *vn.* to drink to excess. **III.** *vr.* to get drunk; (S. A.) to be fooled, "get left."
chinguirito, *m.* (Mex.) rum from lees of sugar.
chinito, ta, *n.* (Am.) dearie, dearest.
chino, na. I. *a.* & *n.* Chinese. **II.** *m.* Chinese (language); (Colomb.) boy (esp. a newsboy, gamin, etc.); (Am.) crossbred (app. to offspring of non-white parents).
chinófilo, la, *n.* Sinophile, Sinophil.
chipichipi, *m.* (Mex.) mist; drizzle.
chipirón, *m.* calamary, a kind of cuttle-fish.
Chipre, *f.* Cyprus.
chiprio, pria, chipriota, chipriote, *n.* & *a.* Cypriot.
chiqueadores, *m. pl.* disks of tortoise shell formerly used in Mexico as a feminine ornament; small plasters for headache.
chiquero, *m.* pigpen; hut for goats; place where bulls are shut up.
chiquichaque, *m.* (coll.) sawyer; noise of things rubbing against each other.
chiquigüite, chiquihuite, *m.* (Mex.) willow basket.
chiquilicuatro, *m.* (coll.) dabbler, meddler.
chiquilín, na, *n.* (Mex. & C. A.) = CHIQUILLO.

chiquillada, *f.* childish speech or action.
chiquillería, *f.* (coll.) a great number of small children.
chiquillo, illa, *n.* small child, little one.
chiquirritico, ica, illo, illa, ito, ita, *a. dim.* very small, tiny.
chiquirritín, na, *n.* (coll.) baby boy; baby girl; very little child.
chiquitico, ca; llo, lla, *a. dim.* very small, tiny.
chiquitín, na, *n.* = CHIQUIRRITÍN.
chiquito, ta. I. *a.* small, little; very small, very little, tiny.—**andarse en chiquitas,** to be lenient, condescending.—**hacerse chiquito,** to be modest, to conceal one's accomplishments. **II.** *n.* little boy (girl), little one.
chiribitas, *f. pl.* (coll.) particles that float in the eyes and obscure the sight.
chiribitil, *m.* crib, narrow and low hole or corner; small room, "den."
chirigaita, *f.* a kind of gourd.
chirigota, *f.* (coll.) jest, joke, fun.
chirimbolos, *m. pl.* (coll.) odds and ends; utensils, traps.
chirimía. I. *f.* (mus.) flageolet. **II.** *n.* flageolet player.
chirimoya, *f.* (bot.) cherimoya, a tropical fruit.
chirimoyo, *m.* cherimoya tree.
chirinola, *f.* bowling, boys' game; trifle.—**estar de ch.** (coll.) to be in good spirits.
chiripa, *f.* in billiards, fluke; (coll.) stroke of good luck; chance or unexpected event.—**de ch.,** by chance, unexpectedly.—**chiripear,** *vn.* to make flukes at bililards.—**chiripero, ra,** *n.* poor player who wins by fluke; lucky person.
chirivía, *f.* (bot.) parsnip; (ornith.) wagtail.
chirla, *f.* mussel.
chirlador, ra, *n.* (coll.) clamorous prattler.
chirlar, *vn.* to talk fast and loud.
chirle. I. *a.* (coll.) insipid, tasteless. **II.** *m.* = SIRLE, dung of sheep and goats.
chirlo, *m.* large wound in the face and its scar.
chirona, *f.* (coll.) prison.
chirriadero, ra; chirriador, ra, *a.* hissing; sizzling, when frying; creaking, as a hinge; chirping.
chirriar, *vn.* to hiss; sizzle; creak, squeak; (coll.) to sing out of tune or time.
chirrido, *m.* chirping of birds; chattering; creaking; any shrill sound.
chirrío, *m.* creaking noise made by carts.
chirrión, *m.* tumbrel, creaking muck or dung cart; (Am.) heavy horsewhip.
chirrionero, *m.* scavenger, dung-cart driver.
chirumen, *m.* (coll.) common sense.
¡chis! *interj.* sh! hush! silence!
chisgarabís, *n.* (coll.) meddler, dabbler; insignificant, noisy person.
chisguete, *m.* (coll.) small draft of wine; small spout of any liquid, squirt.—**echar un ch.,** to drink.
chisme, *m.* tale of a gossip monger; gossip; (coll.) jigger, any household gadget.—**chismear,** *va.* to tattle, gossip.—**chismero, ra,** *n. & a.* talebearer(-ing), gossip(-ing).
chismografía, *f.* (coll.) gossip, tattle.
chismoso, sa, *n. & a.* = CHISMERO, RA.
chispa, *f.* spark; ember; sparkle; flake; very small diamond; small particle; little bit; state of drunkenness; cleverness, wit; rumor.—**coger una ch.,** (coll.) to get drunk.—**de ch.,** flintlock.—**echar chispas,** (coll.) to rave, be in a passion.—**ser ch.,** to be very lively.
chisparse, *vr.* (Am.) to get tipsy.
¡chispas! *interj.* fire and tow! blazes!
chispazo, *m.* flying off of a spark; damage it does; (coll.) tale mischievously circulated.
chispeante, *a.* sparking, sparkling.
chispear, *vn.* to spark; sparkle; to scintillate; to rain gently.
chispero, ra. I. *a.* sparkling. **II.** *m.* blacksmith; spark catcher; (coll.) Madrilenian ruffian.
chispo. I. *a.* (coll.) tipsy. **II.** *m.* short drink.
chisporrotear, *vn.* (coll.) to sputter sparks.
chisporroteo, *m.* (coll.) sputtering sparks.
chisposo, sa, *a.* sputtering, sparkling.
chistar, *vn.* to mumble, mutter; answer back.—**sin ch. ni mistar,** without (saying) a word.
chiste, *m.* witty saying; joke, jest.—**ch. verde,** off-color, risqué joke.—**dar en el ch.,** to guess right.
chistera, *f.* hand fish basket; (coll.) silk hat.
chistosamente, *adv.* facetiously, humorously.
chistoso, sa, *a.* funny, witty.
chita, *f.* ankle bone in sheep and bullocks; a game with this bone.—**a la ch. callando,** on the quiet, by stealth.
chiticalla, *m.* (coll.) discreet person; secret.
chiticallando, *adv.* (coll.) quietly, on the quiet. —**a la ch.,** noiselessly, quietly.—**andar, or ir, ch.,** to go on tiptoes, to go very quietly.
[1]**chito,** *m.* piece of wood or bone on which money is put in the game of CHITA.—**irse a chitos,** (coll.) to lead a debauched life, to go to the dogs.
[2]**¡chito! ¡**[1]**chitón!** *interj.* hush! not a word!
[2]**chitón,** *m.* mollusk with coat-of-mail shell.
chiva, *f.* kid; female goat.
chivata, *f.* shepherd's staff.
chivato, *m.* kid between six and twelve months old; (Colomb.) rascal, knave.
chivero, *m.* (Am.) puma.
chivetero, chivital, chivitil, *m.* fold for kids.
[1]**chivo, va,** *n.* kid; goat.
[2]**chivo,** *m.* pit for the lees of oil; (Colomb.) anger, angry spell.
¡cho! *interj.* whoa!
[1]**choca,** *f.* part of the game given to a hawk.
[2]**choca,** *f.* soap-boiler's paddle.
chocador, ra. I. *n. & a.* provoker(-ing). **II.** *a.* repulsive, disagreeable.
chocante, *a.* (Mex.) provoking; disagreeable; strange, surprising.
chocar. I. *vn.* (*pret.* CHOQUÉ; *subj.* CHOQUE) to strike, collide, hit, clash; to meet, fight, combat. **II.** *va.* to provoke; to displease, be disliked: to surprise.
chocarrear, *vn.* to joke, act the buffoon.
chocarrería, *f.* buffoonery, coarse jest.
chocarrero, ra, *a.* scurrilous, vulgar.
chocilla, *f. dim.* hut, low cottage.
choclar, *vn.* in the game of ARGOLLA, to drive the ball through the rings.
[1]**choclo,** *m.* clog, galosh.
[2]**choclo, chócolo,** *m.* (Am.) green ear of corn.
choclón, *m.* in the game of ARGOLLA, the driving of a ball through the rings.
choco, *m.* small cuttlefish.
chocolate, *m.* chocolate.
chocolatear, *vn.* (Am.) to drink chocolate.
chocolatera, *f.* chocolate pot; woman who makes or sells chocolate.
chocolatería, *f.* shop where chocolate is sold.
chocolatero, ra. I. *a.* fond of chocolate. **II.** *n.* chocolate maker or dealer. **III.** *m.* (Mex.) stiff north wind.
chocha, chochaperdiz, *f.* (ornith.) woodcock.
chochear, *vn.* to dote.
chochera, chochez, *f.* dotage.
[1]**chocho, cha,** *n. & a.* dotard(-ing).
[2]**chocho,** *m.* (bot.) lupine; cinnamon candy stick. —*pl.* sweetmeats, dainties.
chofer, chófer, *n.* chauffeur.
chofes, *m. pl.* livers and lights; lungs.
chofeta, *f.* chafing dish; fire pan; foot stove.
chofista, *n.* one living on livers and lights.
cholo, la, *n.* (Am.) a term applied by whites to Indians and servants; half-breed.
cholla, *f.* (coll.) skull, head, noddle; faculty.
chonta, *f.* a hardwood palm tree.
[1]**chontal,** *m.* CHONTA field or grove.
[2]**chontal,** *m.* one of the Chontal tribe of Nicaragua; (coll.) uncivilized Indian; uncultured person.
[1]**chopa,** *f.* (ichth.) a kind of sea bream.
[2]**chopa,** *f.* (naut.) top-gallant poop.
chopera, *f.* black-poplar grove.

[1]**chopo,** *m.* (bot.) black-poplar tree.
[2]**chopo,** *m.* (coll.) musket, gun.
choqué, choque, *v. V.* CHOCAR.
choque, *m.* impact; collision; clash; (mil.) skirmish; (naut.) chock, fur, rush; (Angl.) (elec.) shock.
choquezuela, *f.* (anat.) kneecap.
chordón, churdón, *m.* raspberry jam.
choricera, *f.* woman who makes or sells sausages; (mech.) sausage stuffer.
choricería, *f.* = SALCHICHERÍA, sausage shop.
choricero, ra, *n.* sausage maker or seller.
chorillo, *m.* (Peru) mill for coarse fabrics.
chorizo. I. *m.* pork sausage; tightrope walker's pole. **II. chorizo, za,** *n.* & *a.* (Colomb., Ecua.) fool(-ish), (fig.) idiot(-ic).
chorlito, *m.* (ornith.) curlew or gray plover; (ornith.) red shank.
chorlo, *m.* (min.) schorl, tourmalin.
chorote, *m.* (Venez.) poor-quality chocolate; (Colomb.) chocolate pot; (Cuba) any thick beverage.
chorreado, da. I. *pp.* of CHORREAR. **II.** *a.* (of cows) striped.
chorreadura, *f.* dripping, welling; stain from drippings.
chorrear, *vn.* to spout; to drip; to be dripping wet; to come out little by little or one by one.
chorreo, *m.* spouting, dripping.
chorrera, *f.* spout or place whence liquids drip; mark left by dripping or running water; ornament formerly appended to badges; shirt frill; (Am.) (coll.) string (of things), stream (of things, people), lot (in the sense of great quantity or number).
chorretada, *f.* (coll.) squirt, spurt, jet.
chorrillo, *m. dim.* small spout; (coll.) continual coming in and outgoing of money, etc.
chorrito, *m. dim.* small spout.
chorro, *m.* jet, spurt; stream; anything issuing, entering, flowing, or passing.—**ch. de voz,** voice of large volume.—**a chorros,** (coll.) abundantly.
chorroborro, *m.* (coll.) flood, inundation.
chorrón, *m.* dressed hemp.
chortal, *m.* fountain or spring.
chota, *f.* suckling kid; heifer calf.
chotacabras, *f.* (ornith.) goat-sucker, churn owl.
chote, *m.* (Cuba) = CHAYOTE, a kind of fruit.
chotear, *va.* (Cuba, coll.) to banter, gibe.
choteo, *m.* (Cuba, coll.) chaffing, jeering.
chotis, *m.* schottische (music and dance).
choto, *m.* suckling kid, calf.
chotuno, na, *a.* suckling (young goats or kids); poor, starved (lambs); goatish.—**oler a ch.,** to smell like a goat.
chova, *f.* (ornith.) jay, chough; jackdaw, crow.
choz, *f.* stroke, blow; suddenness.
choza, *f.* hut, hovel, cabin, shanty.
chozno, na, *m., f.* great-grandson(-daughter).
chozo, *m.* small hut or cabin.
chozpar, *vn.* to gambol, caper.
chozpo, *m.* gambol, leap.—**chozpón, na,** *a.* frisky, capering.
chozuela, *f. dim.* small hut or shanty.
chual, *m.* (bot.) pigweed or goosefoot.
chualar, *m.* place abounding in pigweed.
chubarba, *f.* (bot.) stonecrop.
chubasco, *m.* squall, shower.—**ch. de nieve,** blizzard.
chubascoso, sa, *a.* squally, gusty.
chúcaro, ra, *a.* (Am.) (of horses) shy; (of cattle) wild.
chucero, *m.* (mil.) pikeman.
chucha, *f.* female dog; (Am.) opossum.
chuchear. I. *va.* to fowl with calls, gins, and nets. **II.** *vn.* to whisper.
[1]**chuchería,** *f.* gewgaw, trinket, notion, titbit.
[2]**chuchería,** *f.* fowling with calls, gins, and nets.
chuchero, ra, *n.* birdcatcher; (Cuba) (Ry.) switch tender.
chucho. I. *m.* (coll.) dog; (Cuba) whip; (Cuba) railway switch; (Chile, Arg.) chill; malaria. **II.** *interj.* used to curb or scare off a dog.
chuchumeco, *m.* contemptible little fellow.
chueca, *f.* head of a bone; hockey; small hockey ball; (coll.) joke, trick; soap maker's paddle.
chuecazo, *m.* stroke given to a ball at hockey.
chueco, ca, *a.* (Am.) crooked, bent, out of shape.
chufa, *f.* (bot.) chufa, edible tuber of a sedge.
chufar, *vn.* & *vr.* to mock, to scoff.
chufería, *f.* place where chufa orgeat and sherbet are made or served.
chufero, ra, *n.* seller of chufas.
[1]**chufeta, chofeta,** *f.* chafing dish; fire pan.
[2]**chufeta,** *f.* (coll.) jest.
chufleta, *f.* (coll.) taunt, scoff.
chufletear, *vn.* (coll.) to show contempt.
chufletero, ra, *a.* (coll.) taunting, sneering.
chulada, *f.* droll speech or action; pleasant conversation; breach of manners.
chulear, *va.* to jest with, to poke fun at; (Mex.) to court, make love to.
chulería, *f.* pleasing manner.
chuleta, *f.* chop; cutlet; (carp.) chips for filling joints; (coll.) slap, blow with the fist.
chulillo, illa, ito, ita, *m.* & *f. dim.* little wag.
[1]**chulo, la. I.** *n.* punster, jester; funny person; sly, deceitful person. **II.** *m.* rascal, knave; pimp, man kept by a woman; bullfighter's assistant; butcher's mate. **III.** *f.* woman of low class loud in dress and manners.
[2]**chulo, la,** *a.* (Am.) pretty, nice, graceful, attractive.
chulla, *f.* slice of bacon.
chumacera, *f.* (mech.) journal bearing; (naut.) rowlock.
chumbe, *m.* (Am.) band to hold dress at waist.
chumbera, *f.* (bot.) opuntia, prickly pear.
chumbo, ba, *a.* prickly (pear); Indian (fig).
chumpipe, *m.* (C. A.) turkey.
chuncaca, *f.* (C. A.) = CHANCACA, brown sugar.
[1]**chunga,** *f.* (coll.) jest, fun, banter.—**estar de ch.,** to be in good humor.
[2]**chunga, chuña,** *f.* (ornith.) S. A. wading bird.
chungón, ona, *n.* jester.
chunguearse, *vr.* (coll.) to chaff, gibe, jest.
chuña, *f.* CHUNGA; (Chile) scramble, scuffle.
[1]**chupa,** *f.* (P. I.) liquid measure (0.735 liter); dry measure (0.37 liter).
[2]**chupa,** *f.* waistcoat; undercoat with sleeves.—**poner a uno como ch. de dómine,** (coll.) to wipe the floor with one.
chupada, *f.* suck, suction.
chupaderito, *m. dim.*—**andarse con,** or **en, chupaderitos;** to use ineffective means for difficult tasks.
chupadero, ra, dor, ra. I. *a.* sucking, absorbent. **II.** *m.* baby's coral or teething ring; (mech.) suction tube; (Am.) tippler.
chupado, da, *a.* (coll.) lean, emaciated.
chupadorcito, *m. dim.* of CHUPADOR; CHUPADERITO.
chupadura, *f.* act and effect of sucking.
chupaflores, *m.* (ornith.) humming bird.
chupalandero, *m.* snail that lives on plants.
chupamiel, chupamirtos, *m.* humming bird.
chupar, *va.* to suck; to draw, sip; to absorb; to imbibe; (coll.) to hang upon (others) for subsistence; to fool.—**ch. la sangre** (coll.) to stick like a leech.—**chuparse los dedos,** to eat with pleasure; to be overjoyed.
chupativo, va, *a.* of a sucking nature.
[1]**chupeta,** *f.* (naut.) roundhouse.
[2]**chupeta, illa, ita,** *f. dim.* short waistcoat.
chupetear, *va.* to suck gently and by starts.
chupeteo, *m.* gentle sucking.
chupetín, *m.* man's inner garment.
chupetón, *m.* violent suction.
chupón, na. I. *n.* & *a.* (coll.) sponge, parasite. **II.** *m.* (bot.) sucker, shoot; (mech.) sucker, plunger piston, valve bucket.
churdón, *m.* raspberry jam.
churla, *f.,* **churlo,** *m.* seroon, spicebag.
churra, *f.* little pin-tailed grouse; heifer one year old.

churrasco, *m.* (Am.) piece of broiled meat.
churrascón, *m.* scorching.
churre, *m.* (coll.) thick, dirty, oozing or dripping grease; anything dirty and greasy.
churrea, *f.* Californian grouse.
churriburri, *m.* = ZURRIBURRI, ragamuffin.
churriento, ta, *a.* greasy.
churrigueresco, ca, *a.* (arch.) overloaded, tawdry, loud.
churriguerismo, *m.* (arch.) overornamentation, tawdriness.
[1]**churro, ra,** *a.* (of wool) coarse; (of sheep) having coarse wool.
[2]**churro,** *m.* a sort of fritter, cruller.
churrullero, ra, *n.* tattler, gossip.
churrupear, *vn.* to sip wine.
churruscarse, *vr.* to be scorched.
churrusco, *m.* bread toasted too much.
churumbela, *f.* reed instrument resembling a flageolet; (Am.) small cup for maté.
churumen, *m.* (coll.) = CHIRUMEN, common sense.
churumo, *m.* (coll.) juice or substance.
chus ni mus.—(coll.) **no decir chus ni mus,** not to say a word, not to open one's mouth.
chuscada, *f.* pleasantry, joke.
chuscamente, *adv.* in a droll manner.
chusco, ca, *a.* droll, merry, funny.
chusma, *f.* crew and slaves of a row galley; rabble, mob, crowd.
chuspa, *f.* (Am.) bag.
chute, *m.* (C. A.) prick.
chuza, *f.* (Mex.) (bowling) a strike.
chuzar, *va.* (Colomb.) to prick.
chuzazo, *m.* large pike; prick; thrust with a prick or pointed weapon.
chuzo, *m.* pike; prick; anything pointed; (naut.) boarding pike.—**a. chuzos,** abundantly, impetuously.—**echar chuzos,** (coll.) to brag.
[1]**chuzón, na,** *n.* crafty, artful person; wag, punster, jester.
[2]**chuzón,** *m. aug.* = CHUZAZO.

D

D, d, *f.* d, fifth letter of the Spanish alphabet.
da, *v. V.* DAR.—**¡lo mismo da!** it amounts to the same thing!—**da lástima,** it's a pity, pitiful.
dable, *a.* possible, practicable.
daca (word formed by the verb **da** and the adv. **acá**), give me, give it me.—**andar al d. y toma,** to dispute.—**toma y d.,** give-and-take.
da capo, (mus.) da capo.
[1]**dacio, cia,** *n.* & *a.* Dacian.
[2]**dacio,** *m.* tribute, tax.
dación, *f.* (law) ceding, yielding or giving up.
dacrón, *m.* Dacron (trademark).
dactílico, ca, *a.* dactylic.
dáctilo, *m.* (poet.) dactyl.
dactilografía, *f.* typewriting.
dactilografista, *n.* typist.
dactilógrafo, *m.* typewriter (machine); typist.
dactilología, *f.* dactylology, talking with fingers.
dactiloscopia, *f.* study of finger prints.
dactiloscópico, ca, *a.* pert. to finger prints.
dádiva, *f.* gift, gratification, grant, keepsake.
dadivosidad, *f.* liberality, bounty.
dadivoso, sa, *a.* bountiful, liberal.
[1]**dado,** *m.* die; block, bushing; pivot collar; coin; (arch.) dado.—*pl.* (naut.) case shot or grapeshot.—**d. falso,** false die.—**dados de las velas,** (naut.) tablings of the bowling cringles.—**correr el d.,** (coll.) to be in good luck.—**estar como un d.,** to fit exactly.
[2]**dado, da,** *pp.* of DAR.—**d. que,** provided; so long as; assuming that.
dador, ra, *n.* giver; (com.) drawer of a bill of exchange; bearer (of a letter).
[1]**daga,** *f.* dagger.—**llegar a las dagas,** (coll.) to reach the most difficult point.
[2]**daga,** *f.* line of bricks in a kiln.
dagón, *m. aug.* large dagger.
daguerrotipar, *va.* to daguerreotype.
daguerrotipia, *f.* the making of daguerreotypes.
daguerrotipo, *m.* daguerreotype.
daguilla, *f. dim.* small dagger.
Dahomey, *m.* Dahomey.
dahomeyano, na, *n.* & *a.* Dahomeyan.
daifa, *f.* mistress, concubine.
dala, *f.* (naut.) pump dale of a ship.
¡dale! or ¡dale que dale! *interj.* expressive of displeasure at obstinacy.
dalia, *f.* (bot.) dahlia.
dálmata; dalmático, ca, *n.* & *a.* Dalmatian.
dalmática, *f.* dalmatica, wide-sleeve tunic.
daltoniano, na, *a.* color-blind.
daltonismo, *m.* color blindness, daltonism.
dallador, *m.* grass mower.
dallar, *va.* to mow.
dalle, *m.* scythe, sickle.
[1]**dama,** *f.* lady, dame; noble or distinguished woman; lady courted by a gentleman; lady of honor at court; mistress or concubine; king in checkers; an old Spanish dance.—**d. cortesana,** courtesan.—**segunda d.,** (theat.) woman who has a walk-on part.—**soplar la d.,** to huff a king in the game of draughts; (coll.) to carry off and marry a woman who was courted by another man.
[2]**dama,** *f.* (metal.) dam of a blast furnace.
damajuana, *f.* demijohn.
damán, *m.* (zool.) daman.
damascado, da, *a.* damasklike.
damascena, *f.* damson, plum.
damasceno, na, *a.* Damascene.
damasco, *m.* damask, figured silk stuff; Brussels apricot; damson, plum.
damasina, *f.* silk stuff resembling damask.
damasquillo, *m.* silk or woollen stuff resembling damask; apricot.
damasquinado, da, *a.* damaskeened.
damasquino, na, *a.* damaskeened; Damascene.—**a la d.,** Damascus fashion.
damería, *f.* excessive nicety in conduct, prudery.
damisela, *f.* young woman; (coll.) courtesan.
damnificar, *va.* (*pret.* DAMNIFIQUÉ; *subj.* DAMNIFIQUE) to hurt, to damage, to injure.
dancé, dance, *v. V.* DANZAR.
danchado, da, *a.* (her.) dentate, indented.
dandismo, *m.* dandies (collect.); dandylike behavior or speech.
danés, sa. I. *a.* Danish. **II.** *n.* Dane. **III.** *m.* Danish (language).
dango, *m.* (ornith.) a species of eagle.
dánico, ca, *a.* Danish.
danta, *f.* (zool.) tapir.
dante. I. *a.* giving. **II.** *n.* giver.
dantellado, da, *a.* dentated, serrated.
dantesco, ca, *a.* Dantesque.
dantista, *n.* Dantean.
danubiano, na, *a.* Danubian.
danza, *f.* dance; set or number of dancers; entangled affair; (Cuba and P. Rico) a slow dance and its tune.—**d. de espadas,** (coll.) quarrel, fight.—**meter en la d.,** (coll.) to draw into the fray, to involve.
danzador, ra, *n.* dancer.
danzante, ta, *n.* dancer; (coll.) active person, hustler; (coll.) fickle, airy person.
danzar, *vn.* (*pret.* DANCÉ; *subj.* DANCE) to dance; to whirl; (coll.) to introduce oneself into any business.
danzarín, na, *n.* dancer; (coll.) giddy, meddling person.
danzón, *m.* (Cuba) slow dance and its tune.
dañable, *a.* prejudicial, condemnable.
dañado, da. I. *pp.* of DAÑAR. **II.** *a.* spoiled, tainted, bad, wicked; damned.
dañador, ra. I. *a.* injurious. **II.** *n.* one who harms.
dañar. I. *va.* to hurt, damage, impair; to harm, injure; to spoil; to weaken. **II.** *vr.* to spoil; to be damaged; to get hurt, hurt oneself.

dañino, na, *a.* mischievous, destructive; harmful, hurtful, injurious.
daño, *m.* damage, hurt, loss, nuisance, hindrance; (com.) discount.—**d. emergente,** (law) damage caused by non-payment.—**daños y perjuicios,** damages.—**en daño de,** with damage to, to the injury of, to the detriment of.—**hacerse d.,** to get hurt, hurt oneself.
dañoso, sa, *a.* harmful, noxious, injurious.
dar. I. *va.* (*ind. pres.* DOY, *pret.* DI; *subj.* DÉ) to give; to hand, to deliver; to confer, grant; to inspire, suggest; to represent (as a play); to emit (as heat, light); to return, to render (as thanks); to proffer, to extend (as the hand); to suppose, to assume, to consider; to allow, admit, concede (a proposition); yield (as fruit, crops, income, etc.); to surrender, submit; to excite, to cause (as pain, sorrow); to strike (the hour); to hold, maintain; to deal (cards); to manifest, show (as signals); to enable, to allow; to apply, put on (as paint, a coating). When joined to some nouns, it expresses the action implied by the noun, as *dar saltos,* to jump; *dar golpes,* to strike (blows).—**d. a conocer,** to make known.—**d. a entender,** to insinuate.—**d. a luz,** to be delivered of, give birth to; to issue, publish.—**d. cabezadas,** to nod.—**d. caza,** to give chase to, pursue.—**d. calle,** to clear the way.—**d. comienzo,** to make a start, beginning.—**d. cuenta de,** to account for; to report on.—**d. cuerda a,** to wind up (clock, watch).—**d. culadas,** (naut.) to strike repeatedly.—**d. de baja,** to dismiss (from a team), muster out (from the army).—**d. de barato,** to grant, take for granted.—**d. de mano,** to depreciate or despise.—**d. diente con diente,** to shiver with cold.—**d. el espíritu,** to give up the ghost.—**d. el nombre,** or **el santo,** (mil.) to give the watchword.—**d. el sí,** to grant; to consent to marry.—**d. en cara,** or **en rostro,** to reproach, upbraid, throw in one's face.—**d. fiado,** to give on credit.—**d. fiador,** or **fianza,** to find bail, give security.—**d. fin a,** to complete, finish.—**d. fin de,** to destroy.—**d. fondo,** (naut.) to cast anchor.—**d. frente a,** to face, be facing.—**d. fruto,** to yield, bear fruit.—**d. gana,** or **ganas, de,** to excite a desire to, make one feel like (doing something); to have a mind to.—**d. garrote,** to garrote, strangle.—**d. golpe,** to astonish; to create a sensation, make a "hit."—**d. golpes a,** to beat, thrash.—**d. grima,** to strike with despair, terror, pity.—**d. gritos,** to shout.—**d. guerra,** to wage war; to torment.—**d. higa,** to miss fire.—**d. la cara por,** to go to the defense of.—**d. la ley,** to lay down the law, dictate.—**d. la razón a,** to say (a person) is right, agree with.—**d. largas,** to prolong an affair.—**d. las dos, tres,** etc., to strike two, three, o'clock.—**d. las espaldas a,** to turn one's back on.—**d. las gracias,** to thank.—**d. los buenos días,** to pass the time of day.—**d. los días a uno,** to congratulate one on one's birthday.—**d. lugar a,** to give rise to.—**d. memorias,** to give regards.—**d. pábulo a,** to substantiate.—**d. parte (de),** to report (about), communicate; to announce.—**d. pasos,** to take steps.—**d. pena a,** to grieve.—**d. poder,** to empower, authorize; to give power of attorney.—**d. por** (foll. by *pp.*), to take for, consider as.—**d. prestado,** to lend.—**d. principio,** to begin.—**d. punto,** (com.) to become insolvent.—**d. que decir,** to give occasion for censure or criticism.—**d. que hacer,** to give trouble.—**d. que pensar,** to arouse suspicions.—**d. que sentir,** to hurt others' feelings; to give occasion for regret.—**d. razón de,** to give information about.—**d. saltos,** to jump.—**d. satisfacción,** to apologize.—**d. suspiros,** to sigh.—**d. un abrazo,** to embrace.—**d. un grito,** to scream.—**d. un paseo,** to take a walk.—**d. un paso,** to take a step.—**d. una vuelta,** to take a turn, a stroll.—**d. voces,** to call out or scream.—**d. zapatetas,** to leap with joy.—**darla de,** (coll.) to brag of being, to set up for.—**no d. pie con bola,** not to do a thing right, to make a mess of it. **II.** *vn.* to give; to yield, stretch; to set in, come on (diff. constr.: *me dió fiebre,* I was taken with fever; *me dió catarro,* I took cold, or was taken with a cold).—**d. a,** to overlook, open on (*mi ventana da al parque,* my window overlooks the park).—**d. a la bomba,** to pump.—**d. al traste** (often with **con**), to give up; to spoil, destroy; to set aside, ignore.—**d. con,** to meet, to find (*por fin di con él,* at last I found him); to apply, cover with (paint, stucco, etc.).—**d. contra,** to knock or hit against.—**d. de,** to fall down, to fall on (*dar de espaldas,* to fall on one's back); to deal (blows, etc.).—**d. de beber,** to give a drink, water (animals).—**d. de codo,** to elbow; to treat with contempt.—**d. de comer,** to serve food, give meals; to feed (animals).—**d. de sí,** to give, stretch, extend.—**d. en,** to persist in; to fall into (as an error); to land on; to take to (as a hobby); to contract, acquire (as a custom); to guess, find out (as a joke, puzzle); to hit, to strike.—**d. en el clavo,** to hit the nail on the head.—**d. en que pensar,** to arouse suspicion; to set one to thinking.—**d. en un bajío** (naut.) to strike ground, to get on shore.—**d. en vacío,** or **en vago,** to fail.—**darle a uno por,** to take it into one's head to; to take to.—**d. mal,** to have poor luck at cards.—**d. sobre,** to rush on, to attack.—**d. tras,** to pursue, follow with hostility.—**dé donde diere,** inconsiderately, heedlessly. **III.** *vr.* (**darse**) to yield, surrender, submit; to devote oneself.—**d. a la vela,** to set sail.—**d. a merced,** to surrender at discretion; (hunting) to halt exhausted.—**d. cuenta de,** to realize.—**d. la mano,** or **las manos,** to shake hands.—**d. maña,** to manage ably.—**d. por** (followed by *pp.*), to consider oneself as.—**d. por sentido,** to show resentment, to take offense.—**d. por vencido,** to acknowledge defeat; to surrender; to give up.—**d. priesa,** or **prisa,** to make haste, hurry.—**d. tono,** to put on airs.—**d. una panzada,** (coll.) to eat to satiety, to stuff oneself.—**no se me da nada,** I don't care.—**no se me da un bledo,** I don't care a straw.
dardabasí, *m.* (ornith.) hawk, kite.
dárdano, na, *a.* Trojan, Dardanian.
dardo, *m.* dart, arrow; light lance; fresh-water fish, dartfish, dace.—**d. de pescador,** harpoon.
dares y tomares, *m. pl.* (coll.) give and take; disputes.—**andar en dares y tomares,** to dispute.
dársena, *f.* inner harbor; dock.
dartros, *m. pl.* (med.) dartre, herpes.—**dartroso, sa,** *a.* dartrous.
darviniano, na; darwiniano, na, *n.* & *a.* Darwinian.
darvinismo, darwinismo, *m.* Darwinism.
darvinista, darwinista, *n.* & *a.* Darwinian.
dasiuro, *m.* (zool.) dasyure.
dasocracia, *f.* forestry.
dasocrático, ca, *a.* forest (as *a.*), pertaining to forestry.
dasonomía, *f.* = DASOCRACIA.
dasonómico, ca, *a.* = DASOCRÁTICO.
data, *f.* date, day of month and year; item in an account; outlet of a reservoir.—**estar de mala d.,** to be in bad humor.
datar. I. *va.* to date; (com.) to credit on account. **II.** *vn.* to take origin, date.
dataría, *f.* (Rom. Cath.) datary.
datario, *m.* datary, a papal officer.
dátil, *m.* (bot.) date; (zool.) date shell.—**datilado, da,** *a.* datelike.—**datilera,** *f.* common date palm.—**datilillo,** *m. dim.* small date.
datismo, *m.* (rhet.) use of redundant synonyms.
dativo, *m.* & *a.* (gram.) dative.
[1]**dato,** *m.* datum.—*pl.* data.
[2]**dato,** *m.* title of dignity in Oriental countries.
datura, *f.* (bot.) datura.

daturina, *f.* (chem., med.) daturine, atropine.
dauco, *m.* (bot.) wild carrot.
davalar, *vn.* (naut.) to drift.
davídico, ca, *a.* Davidic, of David.
daza, *f.* (bot.) lucern; (bot.) panic grass.
de, *prep.* of; from (*soy de Boston,* I am from Boston); from, because of, out of (*confesó de miedo,* he confessed from fear; sometimes foll. by adj. translated by corresponding noun in Eng. *lloré de alegre,* I wept from joy); for, to (*hora de partir,* time to leave; *tiempo de arar,* time for plowing); with (*la dama de las camelias,* the lady with the camellias; *el señor de los guantes,* the gentleman with the gloves; *casa de tres pisos,* three-story house); on, at (*la casa de la derecha,* the house on the right); in (*dos pies de diámetro,* two feet in diameter); by, on the part of (*temido de sus enemigos,* feared by his enemies; *abandonado de Dios,* forsaken by God, God-forsaken; by, as (*médico de profesión,* a physician by profession). Sign of possessive: *la ley de Dios,* the law of God; *la casa de mi padre,* my father's house. Denotes the manner in which a thing is done: *comer de pie,* to eat standing; *se vistió de prisa,* he dressed in haste; *se bebió el vino de un trago,* he drank the wine at a gulp. Denotes the object or purpose to which a thing is put: *escopeta de caza,* fowling gun; *cuarto de fumar,* smoking room; *máquina de coser,* sewing machine. Indicates the material of which a thing is made: *vaso de plata,* silver cup. Is used by women before their husbands' family name: *doña Isabel Pérez de González.* Mrs. Isabel Pérez-González (née Pérez.) Indicates the moving power of a machine; *máquina de vapor,* steam engine; *molino de viento,* windmill. Sometimes used as an emphatic expletive after an adjective: *el pícaro del muchacho,* the rogue of a boy.—**d. a,** foll. by numerical expression, translated in Eng. by qualifying phrase: *billete de a cinco pesos,* a five-peso bill. —**d. . . . en,** by, after, in serial order (*de día en día,* day by day; *de grano en grano,* grain by grain; *de calle en calle,* from street to street.
dé, *irreg. imper. & pres. subj.* of DAR.
dea, *f.* (poet.) goddess.
deán, *m.* dean.
deanato, deanazgo, *m.* deanship.
debajo, *adv.* beneath, underneath.—**d. de,** under, beneath.—**por d.,** from below; underneath.—**por d. de,** under; below.
debate, *m.* debate; altercation.
debatir, *va.* to argue, discuss, debate.
debe, *m.* (com.) debtor side of an account, debit (Dr. in bookkeeping).
debelación, *f.* conquering in war; conquest.
debelador, ra, *n.* conqueror, victor.
debelar, *va.* to conquer; subdue, put down.
deber. I. *va.* to owe; must, ought, have to.—**d. de,** must have, must be (indicating probability): *él debe de haber salido,* he must have (I think he has) gone out. **II.** *m.* duty, obligation.
debidamente, *adv.* justly, duly, exactly.
debido, da, *pp.* of DEBER.—**d. a,** owing to, on account of.
debiente. I. *a.* owing. **II.** *n.* debtor.
débil, *a.* weak; feeble.—**debilidad,** *f.* weakness.
debilitación, *f.* debilitation, weakness.
debilitante, *a.* weakening, debilitating.
debilitar. I. *va.* to weaken; to debilitate, enfeeble, enervate. **II.** *vr.* to become feeble.
débito, *m.* debt; (or **d. conyugal**), conjugal duty.
debitorio, *m.* contract of bargain and sale upon credit, by virtue of a partial payment.
debó, *m.* scraper (for skins).
debutante, *n.* (Gal.) debutant, debutante.
debutar. *vn.* (Gal.) to make one's debut.
década, *f.* decade, ten.
decadencia, *f.* decadence, decay, decline.—**ir en d.,** to be on the decline.
decadente, *a.* decaying, declining, decadent.
decaedro, *m.* (geom.) decahedron.
decaer, *vn.* (*ind.* DECAIGO; *subj.* DECAIGA) to decay, fail, languish, fade; to fall off, lessen; (naut.) to fall to leeward.
decágono, *m.* (geom.) decagon.
decagramo, *m.* decagram.
decaído, da, *a.* decayed; (coll.) discouraged.
decaigo, decaiga, *v.* *V. decaer.*
decaimiento, *m.* decay, decline; weakness.
decalaje, *m.* (aer.) stagger.
decalitro, *m.* decaliter.
decálogo, *m.* decalogue.
decámetro, *m.* decameter.
decampar, *vn.* to decamp.
decanato, *m.* deanship; deanery.
decano, *m.* senior, dean; oldest member of a community or corporation.
decantación, *f.* pouring off, decantation.
decantado, da, *a.* boasted, exalted.
[1]**decantar,** *va.* to cry up, to exaggerate, to puff.
[2]**decantar,** *va.* to decant, to draw off.
decapaje, *m.* (phys.) pickling.
decapitación, *f.* beheading.
decapitar, *va.* to behead, decapitate.
decápodo, da, *m. & a.* (zool.) decapod.
decárea, *f.* decare, ten ares.
decasílabo, ba. I. *a.* decasyllabic, ten-syllable. **II.** *m.* decasyllable.
decastéreo, *m.* decastere, ten cubic meters.
deceleración, *f.* deceleration.
decena, *f.* ten; (mus.) tenth; (arith.) ten (figure in second place from the right).
decenal, *a.* decennial, lasting ten years.
decenar, *m.* group of ten.
decenario, ria. I. *a.* decennary, decennial. **II.** *m.* ten-bead rosary; decennial.
decencia, *f.* decency, propriety; cleanliness, tidiness; honesty, modesty.
decenio, *m.* decade, ten years, decennial.
deceno, na, *a.* tenth.
decentar. I. *va.* (*ind.* DECIENTO; *subj.* DECIENTE) to cut off the first slice of; to begin to lose, as the health. **II.** *vr.* to have bedsores.
decente, *a.* decent; honest; kind, "nice"; tidy; well-behaved.
decentemente, *adv.* decently; honorably; modestly; excessively (used ironically).
decenviral, *a.* decemviral.
decenvirato, *m.* decemvirate.
decenviro, *m.* decemvir.
decepción, *f.* disappointment, disillusionment; humbug.—**decepcionar,** *va.* (Am.) to disappoint.
deciárea, *f.* deciare, one-tenth of an are.
decibel(io), *m.* (phys.) decibel.
decible, *a.* utterable, speakable; expressible.
decidero, ra, *a.* utterable, speakable; mentionable.
decidido, *a.* decided, determined; devoted.
decidir. I. *va.* to decide, determine, resolve. **II.** *vr.* to decide, make up one's mind; to be determined.
decidor, ra. I. *n.* one who speaks with fluency and elegance; a wit. **II.** *a.* of pleasant speech, being a good talker.
deciduo, dua, *a.* deciduous.
deciento, deciente, *v.* *V.* DECENTAR.
decigramo, *m.* decigram.
decil, *m.* (stat.) decile.
decilitro, *m.* deciliter.
décima, *f.* (poet.) ten-line stanza; tenth stanza.
decimal. I. *a.* decimal; pertaining to tithes. **II.** *n.* decimal.
decimalmente, *adv.* decimally.
décimanovena, *f.* a register of a pipe-organ.
decímetro, *m.* decimeter.
décimo, ma, *n. & a.* tenth.
décimoctavo, va, *a.* eighteenth.
décimocuarto, ta, *a.* fourteenth.
décimonono, na, *a.* nineteenth.
décimonoveno, na, *a.* nineteenth.
décimoquinto, ta, *a.* fifteenth.
décimoséptimo, ma, *a.* seventeenth.

décimosexto, ta, *a.* sixteenth.
décimotercero, ra, *a.* thirteenth.
décimotercio, cia, *a.* thirteenth.
deciocheno, na, *n.* & *a.* eighteenth.
decir. I. *va.* & *vn.* (*ger.* DICIENDO; *pp.* DICHO; *ind. pres.* DIGO, *pret.* DIJE, *fut.* DIRÉ; *imper.* DI; *subj.* DIGA) to say, tell; speak; to name, call; to denote, bespeak, indicate, show, be a sign of.—**d. a uno cuántas son cinco,** to tell one where to get off; to give a piece of one's mind to.—**d. bien,** to be right, to speak true.—**d. mal,** to misspeak; to be mistaken.—**d. para sí,** or **para su capote,** to say to oneself.—**d. por d.,** to talk for the sake of talking.—**bien d.,** to be right in saying.—**como quien dice,** as who should say, as if to say, as if meaning.—**como quien no dice nada,** unconcernedly; and this is, or which is, no small matter.—**¡digo!,** I say!, listen!—**el qué dirán,** what people will say, gossip.—**ello dirá,** we shall see, time will tell.—**es d.,** that is to say, that is.—**por decirlo así,** so to speak.—**por mejor d.,** more properly speaking; rather.—**querer d.,** to mean, signify.—**se dice,** they say, it is said. **II.** *m.* a saw, proverbial or familiar saying; witty remark; language.—**el bien d.,** elegant style of language.—**el d. de las gentes,** the opinion of the people.—**es un d.,** it is a mere saying.
decisión, *f.* decision, determination, resolution, issue; decision, judgment by court of justice; verdict by a jury.
decisivamente, *adv.* decisively.
decisivo, va, *a.* decisive, final, conclusive.
decistéreo, *m.* decistere, one-tenth of a cubic meter.
declamación, *f.* declamation, harangue, oration, speech; oratorical invective; reading, recitation; delivery in reciting.
declamador, ra, *n.* orator; reciter.
declamar, *vn.* to declaim; recite; harangue; rant.
declamatorio, ria, *a.* declamatory.
declarable, *a.* declarable.
declaración, *f.* declaration; statement; interpretation, exposition; avowal; manifestation; account; overture, proposal; (law) deposition.
declaradamente, *adv.* declaredly, avowedly.
declarado, da, *a.* declared; stanch; firm.
declarador, ra, *n.* & *a.* declarer(-ing); deponent.
declarante. I. *a.* declaring, expounding. **II.** *n.* declarer, deponent; witness.
declarar. I. *va.* to declare, manifest, make known, state; to expound, explain; (law) to determine and decide, to find; (law) to testify. **II.** *vr.* to declare one's opinion, to explain one's mind; (coll.) to make a declaration of love.
declarativo, va, *a.* declarative, assertive.
declaratorio, ria, *a.* declaratory, explanatory.
declinable, *a.* (gram.) declinable.
declinación, *f.* declination, descent, decay, fall, decline, falling; (gram.) declension, inflection; (astr.) declination; (arch.) deviation.—**d. de la aguja,** magnetic declination.
declinante, *a.* declining; bending down.
declinar. I. *vn.* to decline; to lean downward or to either side, to bend, slope; to descend; (of illness) abate, diminish; to approach the end; (naut.) to vary from the true magnetic meridian. **II.** *va.* (gram.) to decline; (law) to challenge (a judge); to transfer to another tribunal.
declinatoria, *f.* (law) plea that questions the competency of a judge.
declinatorio, *m.* declinator (instrument).
declinómetro, *m.* declinometer.
declive, *m.* declivity, dip; descent, slope, fall; (Ry.) gradient, grade.—**en d.,** slanting, sloping.—**declividad,** *f.* declivity.—**declivio,** *m.* = DECLIVE.
decocción, *f.* decoction.
decoloración, *f.* discoloration; decolorizing, bleaching; fading.
decolorar. I. *va.* to discolor; to decolorize, bleach; to cause to fade. **II.** *vn.* to discolor; to bleach, lose color, become colorless; to fade.
decomisar, *va.* to confiscate, seize, forfeit.
decomiso, *m.* confiscation, forfeiture, seizure.
[1]decoración, *f.* decoration; ornament; (theat.) setting, props.
[2]decoración, *f.* act of committing to memory.
[1]decorado, *m.* decoration, ornamentation.
[2]decorado, *m.* thing committed to memory.
decorador, ra. I. *a.* decorating. **II.** *n.* decorator.
[1]decorar, *va.* to decorate; to adorn, embellish.
[2]decorar, *va.* to learn by heart; to recite; to repeat.
decorativo, va, *a.* decorative.
decoro, *m.* honor, respect, reverence due to any person; circumspection, gravity; integrity, purity, honesty; decorum, decency, civility; fitness, propriety.
decoroso, sa, *a.* decorous, decent.
decrecer, *vn.* (*ind.* DECREZCO; *subj.* DECREZCA) to decrease, diminish.
decreciente, *a.* diminishing, decreasing.
decrecimiento, *m.* degression, decrease.
decremento, *m.* decrement, decrease.
decrepitación, *f.* (chem.) decrepitation.
decrepitante, *a.* (chem.) decrepitant.
decrepitar. I. *va.* to decrepitate, to expose to a high heat. **II.** *vn.* to decrepitate, to crackle.
decrépito, ta, *a.* decrepit.—**decrepitud,** *f.* decrepitude.
decretal, *f.* & *a.* decretal.
decretalista, *m.* interpreter of papal decrees.
decretar, *va.* to decree, resolve; decide.
decretero, *m.* list of the names and offenses of criminals; decretal, collection of decrees.
decretista, *m.* propounder of Decretals.
decreto, *m.* decree; judicial decree or decision.
decretorio, ria, *a.* (med.) critical.
decrezco, decrezca, *v. V.* DECRECER.
decúbito, *m.* (med.) decubitus.
decumbente, *a.* decumbent.
decuplar, decuplicar, *va.* to decuple, multiply by ten.
décuplo, pla, *m.* & *a.* decuple.
decuria, *f.* decury; class of ten students.
decuriato, *m.* student belonging to a class of ten.
decurión, *m.* decurion, commander of a decury; in schools, monitor having the care of ten pupils.—**decurionato,** *m.* decurionship.
decurrente, *a.* (bot.) decurrent.
decursas, *f. pl.* (law) arrears of rent.
decurso, *m.* course, lapse of time.
decusación, *f.* decussation.
decusado, da, decuso, sa, *a.* (bot.) decussate.
dechado, *m.* model; sample, pattern, standard; linen on which young girls learn needlework
dedada, *f.* pinch (of honey, salt, etc.).—**dar una d. de miel,** (fig.) to feed one's hopes.
dedal, *m.* thimble; leather finger stall used by calkers.
dedalera, *f.* (bot.) foxglove.
dédalo, *m.* labyrinth; entanglement.
dedicación, *f.* dedication; consecration; inscription.
dedicante, *n.* & *a.* dedicator(-ing).
dedicar. I. *va.* (*pret.* DEDIQUÉ; *subj.* DEDIQUE) to dedicate, devote; to inscribe, autograph (a literary work). **II.** *vr.* **(a)** to devote oneself (to), to make a specialty (of), to interest oneself (in).
dedicativo, va, *a.* = DEDICATORIO.
dedicatoria, *f.* dedication; dedicatory inscription of a book or work of art.
dedicatorio, ria, *a.* dedicatory.
dedición, *f.* unconditional surrender.
dedil, *m.* thumbstall of rubber, linen, or leather.
dedillo, ito, *m. dim.* little finger.—**saber al d.,** to have at one's finger tips, know perfectly.
dediqué, dedique, *v. V.* DEDICAR.
dedo, *m.* finger; toe; forty-eighth part of a Spanish vara; finger's breadth, small bit.—**d. anular,** ring, or fourth, finger.—**d. auricular** =

DEDO MEÑIQUE.—**d. del corazón, cordial,** or **de enmedio,** middle finger.—**dedos de manteca,** (Arg.) butterfingers.—**d. gordo, d. grande,** thumb; big toe.—**d. índice,** index finger, forefinger.—**d. meñique,** little finger; little toe.—**d. pulgar,** thumb; big toe.—**d. saludador** = D. ÍNDICE.—**a dos dedos,** within an inch (fig.).—**alzar el d.,** to raise one's hand (in taking an oath, etc.).
deducción, *f.* derivation, origin; deduction, inference, conclusion; (mus.) natural progression of sounds; (math.) derivation (of a formula).
deducible, *a.* deducible, inferable.
deduciente, *a.* deducing, inferring.
deducir, *va.* (*ind. pres.* DEDUZCO, *pret.* DEDUJE; *subj.* DEDUZCA) to deduce, infer; to fetch, to devise, to draw; (law) to allege in pleading, to offer as a plea; (com.) to subtract, deduct; (math.) to derive (a formula).
deductivo, va, *a.* deductive.
deduje, deduzco, deduzca, *v. V.* DEDUCIR.
defácile, *adv.* easily.
defalcar, *va.* to cut off; to embezzle.
defecación, *f.* purification; voiding of excrement.
defecadora, *f.* defecator (in sugar refining).
defecar. I. *va.* (*pret.* DEFEQUÉ; *subj.* DEFEQUE) to defecate, purify, clarify. **II.** *vn.* to defecate, void excrement; to remove impurities.
defección, *f.* defection, apostasy, desertion.
defectible, *a.* that may be faulty or lacking.
defectillo, *m. dim.* slight fault or defect.
defectivo, va, *a.* defective, imperfect; (gram.) defective.
defecto, *m.* defect, fault, blemish, imperfection. —*pl.* (print.) sheets lacking, after a day's work, to complete the full number.
defectuoso, sa, *a.* defective, imperfect, faulty.
defendedero, ra, *a.* defensible.
defendedor, ra, *a.* & *n.* = DEFENSOR.
defender, *va.* (*ind.* DEFIENDO; *subj.* DEFIENDA) to defend; protect; to prohibit, forbid; to prevent, retard, delay.—**defendible,** *a.* defensible.
defenecer, *va.* (*ind.* DEFENEZCO; *subj.* DEFENEZCA) (com.) to close (an account).
defenecimiento, *m.* (com.) settlement.
defensa, *f.* defense; protection; shelter; (aer.) bumping bag, bumper; (law) defense; *pl.* (fort.) defense, fortification; (naut., mach.) skids, fenders.—**de d.,** sheltering, guarding, guard, safety.—**legítima d.,** (law) self-defense.
defensión, *f.* safeguard, defense.
defensiva, *f.* defensive.—**estar, ponerse, a la d.,** to be or stand on the defensive.
defensivo, va. I. *a.* defensive, justificatory, protective. **II.** *m.* defense, safeguard, preservative; (med.) wet compress.
defensor, ra, *n.* defender; supporter; (law), counsel for the defense, defender.
defensoría, *f.* duty and office of a defender.
defensorio, *m.* plea, defense.
defequé, defeque, *v. V.* DEFECAR.
deferencia, *f.* deference.
deferente, *a.* assenting, deferring to the opinion of another, deferential.
deferir. I. *vn.* (*ind.* DEFIERO; *subj.* DEFIERA) to yield, submit. **II.** *va.* to communicate; to share in jurisdiction or power.
deficiencia, *f.* deficiency.
deficiente, *a.* deficient, faulty.
déficit, *m.* deficit, shortage.
defiendo, defienda, *v. V.* DEFENDER.
defiero, defiera, *v. V.* DEFERIR.
definible, *a.* definable.
definición, *f.* definition; decision, determination. —*pl.* statutes of military orders.
definido, da. I. *pp.* of DEFINIR. **II.** *a.* definite.
definidor, ra. I. *n.* & *a.* definer(-ing). **II.** *m.* in some religious orders, member of the governing committee.
definir, *va.* to define; to establish, determine.
definitivo, va, *a.* definitive.—**en definitiva,** in conclusion; in short.
definitorio, *m.* governing assembly of a religious order; place where it meets.
deflacionista, *a.* deflationary.
deflagración, *f.* deflagration, sudden burning.
deflagrador, *m.* deflagrator, ignitor.
deflagrar, *va.* to deflagrate, burn suddenly.
deflector, *m.* deflector.
deflegmar, *va.* (chem.) to dephlegmate.
deflexión, *f.* deflection.
defoliación, *f.* defoliation, shedding of leaves.
deformación, *f.* deformation; defacing.
deformado, da, *a.* deformed.
deformador, ra, *n.* & *a.* deformer(-ing); defacer (-ing).
deformar. I. *va.* to deform, disfigure, misshape. **II.** *vr.* to become deformed, change shape.
deformatorio, ria, *a.* deforming, disfiguring.
deforme, *a.* deformed, disfigured; hideous.
deformemente, *adv.* deformedly.
deformidad, *f.* deformity; hideousness, ugliness; gross error.
defraudación, *f.* defrauding; fraud, deceit.
defraudador, ra, *n.* defrauder, defaulter.
defraudar, *va.* to defraud; to rob of; to intercept (light); to disturb (sleep).
defuera, *adv.* externally, outwardly, on the outside.—**por d.,** outwardly.
defunción, *f.* death, demise.
degeneración, *f.* degeneration, degeneracy.
degenerado, da, *n.* & *a.* degenerate.
degenerar, *vn.* to degenerate.
degenerativo, va, *a.* degenerative.
deglución, *f.* (physiol.) deglutition, swallowing.
deglutir, *va.* to swallow.
degollación, *f.* decollation, beheading.
degolladero, *m.* throttle, windpipe; slaughterhouse; stand with block where people were beheaded; (anc. theat.) board partitioning the pit.
degollado, *m.* low neck cut in a blouse or dress.
degollador, *m.* headsman, executioner.
degolladura, *f.* cutting of the throat; (mason.) joint; (carp.) slender part of balusters; DEGOLLADO.
degollante, *n.* (coll.) bore, nuisance.
degollar, *va.* (*ind.* DEGÜELLO; *subj.* DEGÜELLE) to behead, decapitate; to cut (a garment) low in the neck; to destroy, ruin; (coll.) to importune.
degollina, *f.* (coll.) slaughter, butchery.
degradación, *f.* degradation, humiliation, debasement; depravity, baseness, degeneracy; (art.) degradation, diminution, blending.
degradante, *a.* degrading.
degradar. I. *va.* to degrade, debase; humiliate, revile. **II.** *vr.* to degrade or lower oneself.
degu, *m.* a ratlike Chilean rodent.
[1]**degüello, degüelle,** *v. V.* DEGOLLAR.
[2]**degüello,** *m.* decollation, act of beheading or cutting the throat; neck or narrow part of many things; destruction, ruin; putting to the sword; attack without quarter.—**tirar al d.,** to endeavor to harm or ruin a person.
degustación, *f.* act of tasting.
dehesa, *f.* pasture ground.
dehesar, *va.* to turn into pasture ground.
dehesero, *m.* keeper of a pasture ground.
dehiscencia, *f.* (bot.) dehiscence.
dehiscente, *a.* dehiscent.
deicida, *n.* deicide, killer of a god.
deicidio, *m.* deicide, killing of a god.
deidad, *f.* deity, divinity; god, goddess.
deificación, *f.* deification.
deificar, *va.* (*pret.* DEIFIQUÉ; *subj.* DEIFIQUE) to deify; to exalt or praise extravagantly, lionize.
deífico, ca, *a.* deific, deifical, divine.
deifiqué, deifique, *v. V.* DEIFICAR.
deiforme, *a.* deiform, godlike.
Deípara, *f.* Deipara, the Mother of God (app. to the Virgin Mary).
deísmo, *m.* deism.
deísta, *n.* & *a.* deist(-ic).

deja, *f.* prominence between two fissures or notches.
dejación, *f.* abandonment, relinquishment, giving up; (law) assignment.
dejada, *f.* relinquishment.
dejadez, *f.* slovenliness, neglect.
dejado, da. I. *pp.* of DEJAR. **II.** *a.* slovenly; indolent, negligent; dejected, low-spirited.
dejamiento, *m.* act of leaving, relinquishing, or giving up; indolence, carelessness; languor, depression of spirits; abdication, resignation; coolness, indifference, estrangement.
dejar. I. *va.* to leave; to let; let go, relinquish; to permit, consent, allow; to leave, abandon; forsake, desert; to yield, produce, bring (as income, profit); to commit, give in charge, intrust; to deliver, deposit (as money); to fling up, to give up; to lay away.—**¡deja!,** let it go, never mind!—**d. caer,** to drop, let fall.—**d. cargado,** to debit.—**d. dicho,** to leave word or orders.—**d. en cueros,** to strip (one) of one's money or property.—**d. escrito,** to leave in writing.—**d. fresco,** to frustrate, to baffle.—**d. mucho que desear,** to leave much to be desired. **II.** *vr.* not to take care of oneself; to let or allow oneself (to die, be robbed, etc.); to become languid; to abandon oneself.—**d. caer** (**con** before noun or phrase) to insinuate, bring up as if casually; to drop in, appear unexpectedly; to give up.—**d. de,** to stop, leave off.—**d. ver,** to be seen, to be easy to see; to show; to appear, in public, at friends' homes, etc. **III.** *vn.* (**de** and *inf.*) to cease, stop (followed by present participle); to fail to.—**d. de ser,** to cease to be, disappear, die, be no longer.—**no d. de,** not to fail to.—**no d. de ser a,** to be, to be rather.—**no d. de tener,** not to be without, not to lack.
dejativo, va, *a.* lazy, slovenly, indolent.
dejillo, *m. dim.* slight relish or taste which remains after eating or drinking.
dejo, *m.* abandonment, relinquishment; end, termination; negligence, slovenliness; relish or taste which remains after eating or drinking; effect; peculiar inflection or accent in speaking.
de jure, de jure.
del, *contraction of* DE *and* EL: of the.
delación, *f.* accusation, information.
delantal, *m.* apron; dashboard of a carriage.
delante, *adv.* before, ahead, in front.—**por d.,** in front.—**d. de, por d. de,** *prep.* before, in front of, in the presence of.
delantera, *f.* front, fore end, fore part; front seats in theaters, etc.; front part of garments; boundary line of a town, village, property; lead, advance, advantage.
delantero, ra. I. *a.* foremost, first; front (as *a.*) **II.** *m.* postilion; front part; (sport) forward.
delatable, *a.* accusable, blamable.
delatante, *n.* informer, accuser.
delatar, *va.* to inform against, accuse, denounce.
delator, ra, *n.* accuser, informer, denouncer.
dele, *m.* (print.) dele, mark of deletion, delete (ϑ).
deleble, *a.* delible, capable of being deleted; effaceable; erasable.
delectación, *f.* delectation, pleasure, delight.
delegación, *f.* delegation; power conferred; proxy; office of a delegate.
delegado, da, *n.* delegate, proxy.
delegante, *n.* constituent, one that delegates.
delegar, *va.* (*ind.* DELEGUÉ; *subj.* DELEGUE) to delegate.
delegatorio, ria, *a.* delegatory.
deleitabilísimo, ma, *a. super.* most delightful.
deleitable, *a.* delectable, delightful.
deleitablemente, *adv.* delightfully.
deleitación, *f.* **deleitamiento,** *m.* delectation, pleasure, delight.
deleitante, *a.* delighting, delightful.
deleitar. I. *va.* to delight, please. **II.** *vr.* to delight, take delight or pleasure.—**deleite,** *m.* pleasure, delight; lust, carnal appetite.
deleitosamente, *adv.* delightfully; cheerfully.
deleitoso, sa, *a.* delightful, pleasing.
deletéreo, ea, *a.* deleterious, poisonous.
deletreador, *m.* speller.
deletrear, *va.* to spell, to spell out; to decipher or interpret.
deletreo, *m.* spelling; reading by spelling.
deleznable, *a.* crumbly; fragile, frail, perishable; smooth, slippery.
délfico, ca, *a.* Delphian, of Delphi.
[1]**delfín,** *m.* (ichth.) dolphin; (astr.) Dolphin, a northern constellation.
[2]**delfín,** *m.* dauphin, formerly title of eldest son of King of France.—**delfina,** *f.* dauphiness, wife of the dauphin.
delgadamente, *adv.* thinly, delicately; acutely, sharply, finely.
delgadez, *f.* thinness, tenuity; acuteness, ingenuity; slenderness, leanness.
delgado, da. I. *a.* thin; lean; lank, slender, slim; light, delicate, tenuous; acute, fine, ingenious, sharp; (agr.) poor, exhausted. **II.** *m.* (naut.) dead rise; flank of an animal.
delgaducho, cha, *a.* thinnish, lanky.
deliberación, *f.* deliberation.
deliberadamente, *adv.* deliberately.
deliberante, *a.* deliberating, deliberative.
deliberar. I. *vn.* to deliberate, ponder; to consult or take counsel together. **II.** *va.* to determine after mature consideration.
deliberativo, va, *a.* deliberative.
delicadez, *f.* delicateness, weakness of constitution; prudery; overscrupulousness.
delicadeza, *f.* delicacy, fineness, refinement; sensitiveness; daintiness, tenderness, softness; scrupulousness, susceptibility; subtlety, dexterity; acuteness of understanding, refinement of wit; perspicacity.
delicado, da, *a.* delicate; gentle, refined; effeminate, finical, ladylike; sensitive, susceptible; dainty, exquisite, delicious; thin, slender; subtile; fastidious, prudish; scrupulous, honest, upright; arduous, difficult; captious, suspicious.
delicia, *f.* delight, satisfaction; sensual pleasure.
delicioso, sa, *a.* delicious; delightful.
delictivo, va, *a.* pertaining to crime or guilt.
delicuescencia, *f.* (chem.) deliquescence.
delicuescente, *a.* (chem.) deliquescent.
delimitación, *f.* delimitation, demarcation.
delimitar, *va.* = DEMARCAR, to delimit.
delinco, delinca. *v. V.* DELINQUIR.
delincuencia, *f.* delinquency, guilt.—**d. de menores,** (law) juvenile delinquency.—**d. habitual,** (law) recidivism.
delincuente. I. *n.* delinquent, offender. **II.** *a.* delinquent, guilty.
delineación, *f.* delineation, draft, sketch.
delineador, ra, *n.* delineator, draftsman, designer.
delineam(i)ento, *m.* = DELINEACIÓN.
delineante. I. *a.* designing. **II.** *n.* draftsman.
delinear, *va.* to delineate, draw, sketch, design.
delinquimiento, *m.* delinquency, guilt.
delinquir, *vn.* (*ind.* DELINCO; *subj.* DELINCA) to transgress, to offend, to be guilty.
delio, a, *a.* & *n.* Delian, from or of Delos.
deliquio, *m.* swoon, faint; ecstasy, rapture.
delirante, *a.* delirious.
delirar, *vn.* to be delirious; to rave; to rant, talk nonsense.
delirio, *m.* delirium; frenzied rapture; nonsense. —**d. de grandeza,** delusions of grandeur.
delírium tremens, *m.* delirium tremens.
delito, *m.* transgression, offense, delict; misdemeanor; crime.—**d. de incendio,** (law) arson.
delta. I. *f.* delta (Δ), fourth letter of the Greek alphabet. **II.** *m.* delta (of a river).
deltaico, ca, *a.* deltaic, deltic.
deltoideo, a, *a.* deltoid, triangular.
deltoides. I. *a.* deltoid. **II.** *m.* (anat.) deltoid.
deludir, *va.* to delude.
delusivo, va, *a.* delusive, fallacious.

delusor, ra. I. *a.* delusive, delusory. II. *n.* deluder.
delusorio, ria, *a.* deceitful, fallacious.
della, dellas, dello, dellos, *contr.* of DE ELLA, etc.
demacración, *f.* (med.) emaciation, marasmus.
demacrar. I. *va.* (of the body) to cause to waste away. II. *vr.* to waste away.
demagogia, *f.* demagogism; demagogy.
demagógico, ca, *a.* demagogical.
demagogo, ga, *n.* demagogue.
demanda, *f.* demand, claim, complaint; request; petition, the act of asking charity; gathering, charity-box; image carried about by beggars of alms; question, inquiry; enterprise, endeavor; (com.) demand, call; (law) claim; (naut.) look-out.—**la oferta y la d.,** (com.) supply and demand.
demandadero, ra, *n.* messènger to do errands in convents or prisons.
demandado, da, *n.* (law) defendant.
demandador, ra, *n.* one who claims, asks, or begs; one who solicits charity for pious uses; (law) complainant, plaintiff.
demandante. I. *a.* demanding. II. *n.* (law) complainant, plaintiff.
demandar, *va.* to demand, ask, solicit; to wish for, desire; (law) to enter an action against.
demarcación, *f.* demarcation.
demarcador, *m.* boundary surveyor.
demarcar, *va.* to demarcate, demark, delimit.
demás, *a.* other.—**los d., las d.,** others; the others.—**lo d.,** the rest.—**por lo d.,** aside from this; furthermore; as to the rest.—**todo lo d.,** everything else.—**y d.,** and other things, or persons; and so forth. II. *adv.* besides, moreover.—**estar d.,** to be useless or superfluous; to be unwelcome, not wanted.—**por d.,** uselessly, in vain; too much.
demasía, *f.* excess, surplus, superabundance; boldness, audacity, insolence; badness, iniquity; guilt; outrage; affront; (min.) space between two claims.—**en d.,** excessively.
demasiadamente, *adv.* excessively; too.
demasiado, da. I. *a.* too, excessive; too much, too many. II. *adv.* too, excessively; too much.
demediar. I. *va.* to dimidiate, halve. II. *vn.* to be halved, be divided in two.
demencia, *f.* dementia, insanity.—**d. precoz,** dementia præcox.
dementar. I. *va.* to render demented or insane. II. *vr.* to become demented.
demente, *a.* demented, mad, insane.
demérito, *m.* that which renders (something) without merit; being undeserving.
demeritorio, ria, *a.* without merit, undeserving.
demisión, *f.* submission, humility.
demiurgo, *m.* (philos.) Demiurge.
democracia, *f.* democracy.
demócrata. I. *a.* democratic, democratical. II. *n.* democrat.
democrático, ca, *a.* democratic.
democratización, *f.* democratization.
democratizar, *va.* & *vr.* to democratize.
demografía, *f.* demography, vital statistics.—**demográfico, ca,** *a.* demographic.
demógrafo, fa, *n.* demographist.
demoledor, ra, *n.* & *a.* demolisher(-ing).
demoler, *va.* (*ind.* DEMUELO; *subj.* DEMUELA) to demolish, tear down, dismantle.
demolición, *f.* demolition, destruction.
demonche, *m.* (coll.) little devil.
demoníaco, ca. I. *a.* demoniac, demoniacal. II. *n.* demoniac.
demonio. I. *m.* demon; evil spirit; (the) devil. II. *interj.* the deuce!
demonolatría, *f.* demonolatry (esp. worship of the devil).
demonología, *f.* demonology.
demonomancia, *f.* divination with the assistance of demons.
demontre. I. *m.* devil. II. *interj.* the deuce!
demoñejo, demoñuelo, *m. dim.* little devil, imp.
demora, *f.* delay, procrastination; (naut.) bearing; (com.) demurrage; (Am.) period of work required of Indians in lieu of taxes, esp. eight months' work in the mines.
demorar. I. *va.* to delay. II. *vn.* to delay, tarry; (naut.) to bear (*la costa demora norte,* the coast bears north). III. *vr.* to delay; to be delayed, tarry, stop (on the way).
demostrabilidad, *f.* demonstrability.
demostrable, *a.* demonstrable.
demostrablemente, *adv.* demonstrably.
demostración, *f.* demonstration; proof; (public) demonstration.
demostrador, ra. I. *a.* demonstrating. II. *n.* demonstrator.
demostrar, *va.* (*ind.* DEMUESTRO; *subj.* DEMUESTRE) to demonstrate, show; to prove; to teach.
demostrativo, va, *a.* demonstrative.
demótico, ca, *a.* (of Egyptian writing) demotic.
demudación, *f.* change, alteration.
demudar. I. *va.* to alter, change, vary; to cloak, disguise. II. *vr.* to be changed; to change color or the expression of countenance suddenly.
demuelo, demuela, *v.* *V.* DEMOLER.
demuestro, demuestre, *v.* *V.* DEMOSTRAR.
demulcente, *a.* & *m.* demulcent, emollient.
denario, ria. I. *a.* denary. II. *m.* denarius.
dende, *prep.* (obs. or prov.) since.
dendriforme, *a.* dendriform, tree-shaped.
dendrita, *f.* (geol.) dendrite.
dendrítico, ca, *a.* (geol.) dendritic.
dendrografía, *f.* (bot.) dendrology
dendroide, dendroideo, dea, *a.* dendroid, tree-like (in form).
dendrómetro, *m.* (bot.) dendrometer.
denegación, *f.* denial, refusal, denegation.
denegar, *va.* (*ind. pres.* DENIEGO, *pret.* DENEGUÉ; *subj.* DENIEGUE) to deny, refuse, denegate.
denegrecer, *va.* (*ind.* DENEGREZCO; *subj.* DENEGREZCA) to blacken, darken.
denegrir, *va.* = DENEGRECER.
denegué, *pret.* of DENEGAR.
dengoso, sa, *a.* finicky, fastidious, overnice.
[1]**dengue,** *m.* fastidiousness, prudery; affectation; woman's cape with long points; (med.) dengue, breakbone fever.
[2]**dengue,** *m.* boat used in sardine fishing.
denguero, ra, *a.* prudish, affected.
deniego, deniegue, *v.* *V.* DENEGAR.
denigración, *f.* denigration, defamation, slander.
denigrante. I. *a.* slandering. II. *n.* denigrator, slanderer.
denigrar, *va.* to denigrate, defame, slander.
denigrativo, va, *a.* reviling; soiling.
denodadamente, *adv.* bravely, resolutely.
denodado, da, *a.* brave, daring, intrepid.
denominación, *f.* denomination.
denominadamente, *adv.* distinctly, markedly.
denominado, da, *a.* denominate.
denominador, *m.* (arith.) denominator.—**quitar,** or **hacer desaparecer, los denominadores,** (math.) to clear of fractions.
denominar, *va.* to call, give a name to.
denominativo, va, *a.* denominative.
denostadamente, *adv.* ignominiously, insultingly.
denostador, ra, *n.* &. *a* vilifier(-ing) or reviler (-ing).
denostar, *va.* (*ind.* DENUESTO; *subj.* DENUESTE) to insult, to revile, abuse (with words).
denotación, *f.* designation, denotation.
denotar, *va.* to denote, express; to explain.
denotativo, va, *a.* denoting, denotative.
densidad, *f.* density; closeness, compactness; specific gravity; obscurity, darkness; confusion.—**d. de población,** density of population.
densímetro, *m.* densimeter.
densitómetro, *m.* (opt., phys.) densitometer.
denso, sa, *a.* dense, thick; close. compact.

dentado, da. I. *pp.* of DENTAR. II. *a.* having teeth; denticulated, dentated, serrated, toothed; crenated, indented; cogged, pronged.
dentadura, *f.* set of teeth, denture.—**d. postiza,** dental plate, false teeth.
[1]**dental,** *a.* dental, pertaining to the teeth or to dentistry; (phon.) dental.
[2]**dental,** *m.* bed to which the plowshare is fixed; (agr.) teeth of a rake; fork used to separate the straw from corn.
dentalización, *f.* (phon.) dentalization.
dentar. I. *va.* (*ind.* DIENTO; *subj.* DIENTE) to tooth, to furnish with teeth or prongs; to indent; to cut into teeth. II. *vn.* to teethe, cut teeth.
dentario, ria. I. *a.* dental. II. *f.* (bot.) toothwort.
dentejón, *m.* yoke for oxen.
dentellada, *f.* gnashing of teeth; bite, nip, seizure with the teeth; mark made by the teeth.—**a dentelladas,** with the teeth.
dentellado, da. I. *pp.* of DENTELLAR. II. *a.* having teeth; denticulate; serrated; wounded with the teeth.
dentellar, *vn.* (of the teeth) to chatter.
dentellear, *va.* to bite; to bite on or into.
dentellón, *m.* piece of a door lock; (arch.) dentil.
dentera, *f.* sensation of having the teeth on edge; (coll.) envy.—**dar d.,** to set the teeth on edge; to cause great desire, make one's mouth water.
dentezuelo, *m. dim.* little tooth.
dentición, *f.* dentition, teething.
denticulación, *f.* (anat., zool.) denticulation.
denticular, *a.* dentiform, toothlike.
dentículo, *m.* (arch.) denticle, dentil.
dentífrico, ca. I. *a.* dentifrice. II. *m.* dentifrice.
dentina, *f.* (anat.) dentine, dentin.
dentirrostro, tra, *a.* (ornith.) dentirostral.
dentista, *n.* dentist.
dentistería, *f.* dentistry.
dentivano, na, *a.* (of horses) having long and large teeth.
dentolabial, *a.* (phon.) dentilabial.
dentón, na. I. *a.* (coll.) having large uneven teeth. II. *m.* a sea fish of the Sparus genus.
dentrambos, contraction of DE ENTRAMBOS, of both, from both.
dentro, *adv.* inside, within.—**d. de,** inside of.—**d. del año,** in the course of the year.—**d. de poco,** shortly, presently, soon.—**d. en,** in the interior of.—**a d.,** inside.—**de d.,** from inside.—**hacia d.,** towards the interior, inwards.—**por d.,** inside, on the inside; inwardly.
dentudo, da, *a.* having large uneven teeth.
denudación, *f.* (geol.) denudation.
denudar, *va.* (geol.) to denude.
denuedo, *m.* daring, bravery, intrepidity.
[1]**denuesto,** *m.* affront, insult, abuse.
[2]**denuesto, denueste,** *v.* *V.* DENOSTAR.
denuncia, *f.* denunciation; (law) arraignment, accusation; announcement, proclamation; (min.) application for a concession.
denunciable, *a.* that may be denounced.
denunciación, *f.* denunciation, denouncement.
denunciador, ra, *n.* denunciator, accuser; announcer; denouncer.
denunciante, *n.* & *a.* denouncer(-ing); informer (-ing); accuser(-ing).
denunciar, *va.* to advise, give notice; to denounce; to prognosticate, foretell; to pronounce, proclaim solemnly; (min.) to apply for a concession (to own or work).
denunciatorio, ria, *a.* denunciatory.
denuncio, *m.* (min.) DENUNCIA; (Am.) = DENUNCIA, DENUNCIACIÓN.
Deo gracias, *m.* Deo gratias (thanks be to God), a greeting; submissive, humble attitude.
deontología, *f.* deontology, ethics.
deparar, *va.* to offer, afford, furnish, present.
departamental, *a.* departmental.
departamento, *m.* department; branch; section; compartment; (Am.) apartment (dwelling).—**d. de mercería,** notions counter (in a department store).
departidor, ra, *n.* converser, interlocutor.
departir, *vn.* to chat, talk, converse.
depauperación, *f.* impoverishment; (med.) weakness, exhaustion.
depauperar, *va.* to depauperate, impoverish; (med.) to weaken, exhaust.
dependencia, *f.* dependence, dependency; subordination; branch office; business, affair; trust, charge; dependence, relation; (arch.) outbuildings; relation by blood or marriage.—*pl.* accessories.
depender, *vn.* (de) to depend, rely (on).
dependiente. I. *a.* dependent, subordinate. II. *m.* clerk, salesman.
depilación, *f.* depilation.
depilar, *va.* to depilate.
depilatorio, ria, *m.* & *a.* depilatory.
deplazamiento, *m.* (stat.) lag.
depletivo, va, *a.* depletive.
deplorable, *a.* deplorable, lamentable, pitiful.
deplorablemente, *adv.* deplorably, sadly.
deplorar, *va.* to deplore, lament, regret.
depondré, *fut.* of DEPONER.
deponente, *n.* & *a.* deposer(-ing), deponent; (gram.) deponent.
deponer. I. *va.* (*pp.* DEPUESTO; *ind. pres.* DEPONGO, *pret.* DEPUSE, *fut.* DEPONDRÉ; *subj.* DEPONGA) to lay by, put aside; to depose, remove from office; (law) to attest, depose; to take down, remove. II. *vn.* to evacuate the bowels.
depongo, deponga, *v.* *V.* DEPONER.
depopulador, ra, *n.* & *a.* depopulator(-ing); devastator(-ing).
deportación, *f.* deportation, banishment.
deportado, da. I. *a.* banished. II. *n.* deportee, exile.
deportar, *va.* to deport, exile, banish.
deporte, *m.* sport; amusement, recreation.
deportismo, *m.* sports, sporting.
deportista, *n.* sportsman(-woman).
deportivo, va, *a.* athletic, sport (as *a.*).
deposición, *f.* assertion, affirmation; deposition from a position or station; (law) deposition, testimony; evacuation (of the bowels).
depositador, ra, *n.* depositor.
depositante, *n.* & *a.* depositor(-ing).
depositar. I. *va.* to deposit; to intrust, confide; to put (a person) in safety, to bring (a person) out of danger of violence or intimidation; to inclose; to place (a corpse) in a receiving vault; to lay aside, put away. II. *vr.* (chem.) to settle.
depositaría, *f.* depository; subtreasury; trust.
depositario, ria. I. *a.* pertaining to a depository. II. *n.* depositary, trustee, receiver.
depósito, *m.* deposit, trust, depository; (com.) store, warehouse, depot; (mech.) chamber; (chem.) deposit, precipitate, sediment; (geol.) deposition.—**d. de agua,** tank, reservoir.—**en d.,** deposited; on deposit; in bond.
depravación, *f.* depravation, depravity.
depravado, da, *a.* depraved, lewd.
depravador, ra, *n.* depraver, corrupter.
depravar, *va.* to deprave, corrupt.
deprecación, *f.* petition, prayer, entreaty.
deprecante. I. *a.* supplicating, pleading; deprecatory, deprecative. II. *n.* deprecator.
deprecar, *va.* (*pret.* DEPREQUÉ; *subj.* DEPREQUE) to entreat, implore; to deprecate.
deprecativo, va, deprecatorio, ria, *a.* supplicating, pleading; deprecatory, deprecative.
depreciación, *f.* depreciation.
depreciar. I. *va.* to depreciate, to reduce the price of; to undervalue. II. *vr.* to depreciate.
depredación, *f.* depredation, plundering; malversation committed by guardians or trustees.
depredador, ra, *n.* & *a.* depredator(-ing), marauder(-ing).
depredar, *va.* to depredate, maraude, pillage.

deprequé, depreque, *v. V.* DEPRECAR.
depresión, *f.* depression; pressing down; (astr., com., meteorol.) depression.—**d. de horizonte,** (naut.) dip of the horizon.
depresivo, va, *a.* depressive, depressing.
depresor, ra, *n.* & *a.* depressor(-ing); oppressor (-ing).
deprimente, *a.* depressive, depressing.
deprimido, da, *a.* depressed, disheartened; (bot.) depressed.
deprimir. I. *va.* to depress, compress; to humiliate; to belittle, make light of. **II.** *vr.* to become depressed or compressed; to be or seem lower.
de profundis, *m.* De Profundis, the 130th psalm, sung at funerals.
depuesto, *pp. irreg.* of DEPONER.
depurable, *a.* purifiable.
depuración, *f.* depuration, purification; screening; (atom. ener., mech.) scavenging.
depurador, ra, *m.* & *a.* depurative.
depurar, *va.* to depurate, purify.
depurativo, va, *m.* & *a.* depurative.
depuse, *pret.* of DEPONER.
deputar, *va.* = DIPUTAR, to depute.
deque, *adv.* (coll.) since.
derecera, *f.* = DERECHERA.
derechamente, *adv.* directly, straight; wisely; honestly, justly.
derechera, *f.* direct or straight road; short cut.
derechero, *m.* clerk who collects fees.
derechista, *m.* & *f.* (pol.) rightist; reactionary.
derechito, *dim. adv.* right straight (ahead, etc.)
derecho, cha. I. *a.* right, straight, direct; right-handed; right, just, lawful; proper, correct; upright, standing.—**d. la caña,** (naut.) right the helm.—**hecho y d.,** perfect, complete; in all respects; grown up; true, certain; without doubt.—**ponerse d.,** to stand up straight. **II.** *m.* law; right; exemption, grant, privilege; road, path; right side (of cloth, etc.); *pl.* fees, dues, taxes, duties; *f.* right; right side; right hand; (pol.) right, right wing.—**d. administrativo,** administrative law.—**d. canónico,** canon law. —**d. civil** or **común,** civil law.—**d. constitucional,** constitutional law.—**d. consuetudinario,** common law, customary law.—**d. de gentes,** international law, law of nations.—**d. de guerra,** law of war.—**d. de nacimiento,** birthright.—**d. de reunión,** right of assembly. —**d. de visita,** (naut.) right of search.—**d. diferencial de bandera,** differential duties.—**d. divino,** divine right.—**d. internacional,** international law, law of nations.—**d. marítimo,** admiralty or maritime law.—**d. mercantil,** commercial law.—**d. municipal,** municipal law.—**d. natural,** natural law.—**d. no escrito,** common law, unwritten law.—**d. penal,** criminal law.—**d. político,** right to vote, franchise. —**d. positivo,** positive law.—**d. romano,** Roman law.—**derechos civiles,** civil rights.—**derechos consulares,** consular fees.—**derechos de aduana,** customhouse duties.—**derechos de almacenaje,** storage.—**derechos de anclaje,** anchorage dues or fees.—**derechos de autor,** copyright; royalties (on printed works).—**derechos de depósitos,** storage.—**derechos de entrada,** import duties.—**derechos de inventor,** patent.—**derechos del hombre,** rights of man.—**derechos de matrícula y enseñanza,** tuition fees.—**derechos de muelle,** wharfage, pierage.—**derechos de puerto,** harbor dues, port dues.—**derechos de remolque,** towage.—**derechos diferenciales de entrada,** differential duties.—**derechos humanos,** human rights.—**derechos reales,** inheritance tax; duty on transfer of real estate. —**escuela de d.,** law school, faculty of law.—**a derechas** or **a las derechas,** right, well done; honestly, rightly, justly.—**a la d.,** to the right, on the right-hand side; (mil.) right about.—**a tuertas o derechas,** right or wrong; inconsiderately.—**de d.,** de jure.—**del d.,** right-side out.—**estar (uno) en su d.,** to be within one's rights.—**tener d.,** to have a right.—**usar (uno) de sus derechos,** to stick to one's rights, stand up for one's rights. **III.** *adv.* directly, straight; wisely; honestly, justly.—**(todo) d.,** straight ahead.
derechuelo, *m.* first sewing taught to little girls.
derechura, *f.* straightness.—**en d.,** by the most direct road; as the crow flies.
deriva, *f.* (naut.) ship's course; deviation, drift; (aer.) drift; drifting.
derivación, *f.* derivation, descent; deduction, inference; draining of water, turning of its course; (gram.) derivation; (elec.) branch, tap (of a wire, current, etc.); shunt.—**en d.,** (elec.) shunt (as *a.*); shunted.
derivado, da. I. *a.* derived, derivative; (elec.) derived. **II.** *m.* (gram., chem.) derivative; by-product; *f.* (math.) derivative.
derivar. I. *vn.* & *vr.* to derive, proceed, descend **II.** *vn.* (naut., aer.) to drift. **III.** *va.* to guide lead, conduct; to derive, trace to its origin (elec.) to tap; to shunt.
derivativo, va, *a.* & *n.* derivative.
derivómetro, *m.* (aer.) drift meter.
dermalgia, *f.* (med.) neuralgia of the skin.
dermatitis, *f.* (med.) dermatitis.
dermatología, *f.* dermatology.
dermatológico, ca, *a.* dermatological.
dermatólogo, ga, *n.* dermatologist.
dermatosis, *f.* (med.) dermatosis.
dermesto, *m.* (zool.) larder beetle.
dérmico, ca, *a.* dermal, dermic.
dermis, *f.* dermis, derma, skin.
dermitis, *f.* (med.) dermatitis.
derogación, *f.* derogation, repeal; deterioration, diminution.
derogar, *va.* (*pret.* DEROGUÉ; *subj.* DEROGUE) to derogate, annul, revoke, repeal; to reform; to remove.
derogatorio, ria, *a.* annulling, repealing.
derogué, derogue, *v. V.* DEROGAR.
derrabadura, *f.* wound made in docking the tail of an animal.
derrabar, *va.* to dock the tail of.
derrama, *f.* apportionment of an assessment, tax, or contribution.
derramadamente, *adv.* profusely, lavishly; disorderly, confusedly.
derramadero, ra, *a.* = VERTEDERO, sink, dump.
derramado, da; derramador, ra, *a.* prodigal, extravagant.
derramamiento, *m.* pouring out; spilling, shedding; overflow; dispersion, scattering; lavishing, wasting.—**d. de sangre,** bloodshed.
derramar. I. *va.* to pour out; to spill; shed; scatter; to apportion (taxes); to publish, spread; to lavish, give freely; to waste. **II.** *vr.* to overflow, run over; to be scattered or spread.
derrame, *m.* overflow, running over; spread, scattering; shedding; portion of liquor or seed lost in measuring; leakage; waste; (arch.) chamfering, splay; declivity, slope; (naut.) draft of a sail; outlet of a ravine, driftway; (med.) effusion, discharge.
derramo, *m.* (arch.) chamfering, splay, flare, bevel, flanging of a door or window.
derrape, *m.* (aer.) yawing.
derredor, *m.* circumference, circuit.—**al d.,** or **en d.,** round about.—**al d. de, en d. de,** about, around.
derrelicto, a. I. *pp. irreg.* of DERRELINQUIR. **II.** *a.* derelict. **III.** *m.* (naut.) derelict.
derrelinquir, *va.* (*pp.* DERRELICTO; *ind.* DERRELINCO; *subj.* DERRELINCA) to abandon, forsake.
derrenegar, *vn.* (*ind. pres.* DERRENIEGO, *pret.* DERRENEGUÉ; *subj.* DERRENIEGUE).—**d. de,** (coll.) to hate, detest, loathe, abhor.
derrengada, *f.* (prov.) a step in dancing.
derrengado, da. I. *pp.* of DERRENGAR. **II.** *a.* bent, crooked; lame, crippled.

derrengadura, *f.* dislocation of the hip; lameness.
derrengar, *va.* (*ind.* DERRIENGO; *subj.* DERRIENGUE) to sprain or dislocate the hip of; to break or injure the spine of; to cripple; to bend, make crooked; to knock (fruit) off a tree.—**derrengo,** *m.* stick with which fruit is knocked down.
[1]**derreniego,** *m.* (coll.) = RENIEGO, curse.
[2]**derreniego, derreniegue,** *v. V.* DERRENEGAR.
derretido, da. I. *pp.* of DERRETIR. **II.** *a.* enamored, deeply in love.
derretimiento, *m.* thaw, liquefaction, fusion, melting; consuming love or passion.
derretir. I. *va.* (*ind.* DERRITO; *subj.* DERRITA) to liquefy, melt, fuse; (coll.) to change (money); to consume, expend, waste, exhaust. **II.** *vr.* to fuse, melt, thaw; to be deeply in love; to fall in love very easily; to grow tender; to be impatient.
derribado, da. I. *pp.* of DERRIBAR. **II.** *a.* (of horses) having a round and low rump.
derribador, *m.* slaughterer (in slaughterhouse).
derribar. I. *va.* to throw down, knock down; overthrow; fell; to demolish, tear down; to strike down (a bull) with a pike on horseback; to subdue (a passion). **II.** *vr.* to tumble down, to throw oneself on the ground.—**derribo,** *m.* demolition, pulling down; debris, ruins.
derriengo, derriengue, *v. V.* DERRENGAR.
derrito, derrita, *v. V.* DERRETIR.
derrocadero, *m.* rocky precipice.
derrocamiento, *m.* throwing down, overthrow.
derrocar, *va.* (*ind.* DERRUECO; *subj.* DERRUEQUE) to precipitate or fling down from a rock; to pull down, demolish; to pull down (from office, position, etc.), put down; to oust; to dethrone, overthrow.
derrochador, ra, *n.* prodigal, spendthrift, squanderer.
derrochar, *va.* to waste, squander.
derroche, *m.* waste, squandering.
derrota, *f.* defeat, rout; overthrow; route, road, path, track; (naut.) ship's course.
derrotar, *va.* to defeat; to waste away, wear away; to ruin; (naut.) to cause to drift.
derrote, *m.* thrust of a bull's horn.
derrotero, *m.* (naut.) collection of seacharts; ship's course; navigation track or route; course, way or plan of life, conduct, or action.
derrotismo, *m.* defeatism.
derrotista, *m.* & *f.* defeatist.
derrubiar, *va.* to undermine or wash away.
derrubio, *m.* alluvion, alluvium.
derrueco, derrueque, *v. V.* DERROCAR.
derruir, *va.* (*ind.* DERRUYO; *subj.* DERRUYA) to demolish, tear down, raze, destroy.
derrumbadero, *m.* precipice; craggy, steep, and broken ground: arduous affair.
derrumbamiento, *m.* landslide; collapse; downfall.
derrumbar. I. *va.* to throw down headlong. **II.** *vr.* to throw oneself headlong; to sink down, crumble away, tumble down.—**derrumbe,** *m.* tumbling down, collapse; landslide.
derruyo, derruya, *v. V.* DERRUIR.
derviche, *m.* dervish.
desabarrancar, *va.* (*pret.* DESABARRANQUÉ; *subj.* DESABARRANQUE) to drag, draw, or pull out of a ditch; to disentangle, extricate.
desabastecer, *va.* (*ind.* DESABASTEZCO; *subj.* DESABASTEZCA) to neglect to supply with, or impede the supply of, provisions.
desabejar, *va.* to remove bees from.
desabillé, *m.* dishabille; house or morning gown.
desabollador, *m.* tinworker's instrument.
desabollar, *va.* to tinker.
desabonarse, *vr.* to discontinue a subscription.
[1]**desabono,** *m.* discontinuance of a subscription.
[2]**desabono,** *m.* prejudice, injury.
desabor, *m.* insipidity, tastelessness.
desabordarse, *vr.* (naut.) to get clear of a ship which has run foul of one's vessel.
desaborido, da, *a.* tasteless, insipid; without substance; (coll.) dull, witless.
desabotonar. I. *va.* to unbutton. **II.** *vn.* to blow, bloom, blossom.
desabrido, da, *a.* tasteless, insipid; rude, disagreeable, peevish; kicking (gun); bleak, sharp.
desabrigadamente, *adv.* without covering; without shelter.
desabrigado, da, *a.* uncovered; shelterless; harborless; without support.
desabrigar. I. *va.* (*pret.* DESABRIGUÉ; *subj.* DESABRIGUE) to uncover; to strip; to deprive of shelter or harbor. **II.** *va.* & *vr.* to take off outer clothing.
desabrigo, *m.* lack of covering, clothing, shelter or harbor; destitution.
desabrillantar, *va.* & *vr.* to (make) lose luster.
desabrimiento, *m.* insipidity, flatness; rudeness, disagreeableness; despondency, lowness of spirits; recoil of firearms.
desabrir, *va.* to impart a bad taste to; to vex, plague, torment, harass.
desabrochar. I. *va.* to unclasp, unbutton, unfasten; burst open. **II.** *vr.* to unbosom oneself, to open one's heart.
desacalorarse, *vr.* to cool off.
desacatado, da. I. *pp.* of DESACATAR. **II.** *a.* disrespectful.
desacatador, ra. I. *a.* irreverent, uncivil, disrespectful. **II.** *n.* disrespectful person.
desacatamiento, *m.* disrespect.
desacatar, *va.* to show disrespect, disregard, treat disrespectfully.
desacato, *m.* disrespect, irreverence, disregard; incivility; contempt.—**d. a la autoridad del tribunal,** (law) contempt of court.
desaceitado, da, *a.* lacking oil.
desaceitar, *va.* to take off oil or grease from.
desacerar, *va.* to unsteel.
desacertado, da, *a.* wrong, mistaken; unwise.
desacertar, *vn.* (*ind.* DESACIERTO; *subj.* DESACIERTE) to err, make a mistake; act unwisely.
desacidificar, *va.* to remove acidity from; to neutralize (an acid).
[1]**desacierto,** *m.* error, mistake, blunder.
[2]**desacierto, desacierte,** *v. V.* DESACERTAR.
desacobardar, *va.* to remove fear from; to encourage, reassure.
desacollar, *va.* (*ind.* DESACUELLO; *subj.* DESACUELLE) to dig up the ground about (vines).
desacomodadamente, *adv.* incommodiously, inconveniently.
desacomodado, da. I. *pp.* of DESACOMODAR. **II.** *a.* destitute of conveniences; out of service; troublesome.
desacomodamiento, *m.* inconvenience, trouble.
desacomodar. I. *va.* to inconvenience; to trouble, discommode; to discharge, dismiss. **II.** *vr.* (of servants) to lose one's place.
desacomodo, *m.* discharge; loss of a position.
desacompañamiento, *m.* lack of company or society.
desacompañar, *va.* to leave the company of.
desaconsejado, da. I. *pp.* of DESACONSEJAR. **II.** *a.* ill-advised, imprudent; capricious.
desaconsejar, *va.* to dissuade.
desacoplar, *va.* to unfasten, disconnect.
desacordadamente, *adv.* unwisely, unadvisedly.
desacordado, da; desacordante. *a.* discordant.
desacordar. I. *va.* (mus.) (*reg. conj.* in this meaning) to put out of tune. **II.** *vr.* (*ind.* DESACUERDO; *subj.* DESACUERDE) to be forgetful.
desacorde, *a.* discordant; inharmonious, incongruous.
desacorralar, *va.* to let out of the corral; to bring (a bull) into the ring or open field.
desacostumbrado, da. I. *pp.* of DESACOSTUMBRAR. **II.** *a.* unaccustomed; unusual.
desacostumbrar, *va.* to disaccustom, break of a habit.

[1]**desacotar,** *va.* to lay open (a pasture); to take down (fences).
[2]**desacotar,** *va.* to raise or withdraw (a prohibition); to withdraw from (an agreement); among boys, to play without conditions or rules; to reject, refuse.
desacoto, *m.* taking fences off a pasture-ground.
desacreditar, *va.* to discredit; bring discredit on, injure the credit or reputation of.
desactivación, *f.* deactivation.
desactivar, *va.* to deactivate.
desacuello, desacuelle, *v. V.* DESACOLLAR.
[1]**desacuerdo,** *m.* discordance, disagreement; error, mistake, blunder; forgetfulness; mental derangement.
[2]**desacuerdo, desacuerde,** *v. V.* DESACORDAR.
desacuñador, *m.* (print.) shooting stick.
desacuñar, *va.* (print.) to unwedge, loosen.
desadaptación, *f.* (biol.) maladjustment.
desadaptado, da, *a.* maladjusted.
desaderezar, *va.* to ruffle, disarrange.
desadeudar, *va.* & *vr.* to free from debt.
desadormecer, *va.* (*ind.* DESADORMEZCO; *subj.* DESADORMEZCA) to wake, to rouse.
desadornar, *va.* to divest of ornaments.—**desadorno,** *m.* want of embellishments and charms.
desadvertidamente, *adv.* inadvertently.
desadvertido, da. I. *pp.* of DESADVERTIR. **II.** *a.* unwise, imprudent; unnoticed.
desadvertimiento, *m.* unwisdom; lack of reflection, thoughtlessness.
desadvertir, *va.* (*ind.* DESADVIERTO; *subj.* DESADVIERTA) to give no heed to, not to notice.
desafear, *va.* to remove or lessen the blemishes of.
desafección, *f.* disaffection.
desafecto, ta. I. *a.* disaffected; opposed. **II.** *m.* disaffection, discontent.
desaferrar, *va.* (*ind.* DESAFIERRO; *subj.* DESAFIERRE) (naut.) to unmoor, weigh anchor; to convince, bring to a change of opinion.
desafiadero, *m.* private dwelling ground.
desafiador, ra, *n.* challenger, duellist; one who dares or defies.
desafianzar, *va.* (Am.) to withdraw security.
desafiar, *va.* to challenge, dare; to defy; to rival, oppose, compete with.
desafición, *f.* disaffection.
desaficionar, *va.* & *vr.* to destroy or lose the desire, wish, or affection of.
desafierro, desafierre, *v. V.* DESAFERRAR.
desafijar, *va.* to disown as a son.
desafilar, *va.* to blunt.
desafinación, *f.* discordance, being out of tune.
desafinadamente, *adv.* dissonantly or discordantly.
desafinar. I. *vn.* (mus.) to be out of tune; to speak irrelevantly. **II.** *vr.* to get out of tune.
desafío, *m.* challenge; duel; struggle, contest, rivalry, competition.
desaforado, da. I. *pp.* of DESAFORAR. **II.** *a.* disorderly, lawless; impudent, outrageous; huge, uncommonly large.
desaforar. I. *va.* (*ind.* DESAFUERO; *subj.* DESAFUERE) to encroach upon the rights of; (mil.) to cashier. **II.** *vr.* to be outrageous or disorderly.
desaforrar, *va.* to take out the lining of; (naut.) to unserve, unsheath.
desafortunado, da, *a.* unfortunate, unlucky.
[1]**desafuero,** *m.* excess, outrage, open violence.
[2]**desafuero, desafuere,** *v. V.* DESAFORAR.
desagarrar, *va.* (coll.) to unfasten, loosen.
desagraciado, da, *a.* ungraceful.
desagraciar, *va.* to disfigure, make ungraceful.
desagradable, *a.* disagreeable, unpleasant.
desagradar, *va.* to displease, offend.
desagradecer, *va.* (*ind.* DESAGRADEZCO; *subj.* DESAGRADEZCA) to be ungrateful.
desagradecido, da, *a.* ungrateful.
desagradecimiento, *m.* ingratitude.
desagradezco, desagradezca, *v. V.* DESAGRADECER.
desagrado, *m.* discontent, displeasure.
desagraviar, *va.* to right a wrong to, to apologize to; to indemnify.
desagravio, *m.* satisfaction for an injury; compensation for damages; vindication.
desagregación, *f.* separation, segregation.
desagregar, *va.* (*pret.* DESAGREGUÉ; *subj.* DESAGREGUE) to disjoin, separate, segregate.
desaguable, *a.* drainable.
desaguadero, *m.* drain, waste pipe, outlet; drain of money.
desaguador, *m.* small drain for irrigation.
desaguar. I. *va.* to drain (of liquid), empty; to squander, waste. **II.** *vn.* (of rivers) to empty. **III.** *vr.* to discharge by vomit or stools.
desaguazar, *va.* to drain.
desagüe, *m.* drainage; drain, outlet; waste.
desaguisado, da. I. *a.* lawless, illegal, unjust. **II.** *m.* offense, injury, wrong, outrage.
desaherrojar, *va.* to unchain, unshackle.
desahijar. I. *va.* to wean; to separate (the young) from the dams. **II.** *vr.* (of bees) to breed swarms.
desahitarse, *vr.* to relieve indigestion.
desahogadamente, *adv.* comfortably, easily; freely, unobstructedly; in a brazen-faced or unconcerned manner, brazenly.
desahogado, da. I. *pp.* of DESAHOGAR. **II.** *a.* petulant, impudent, brazen-faced; clear, free, unencumbered; in comfortable circumstances; (naut.) having sea room.
desahogar. I. *va.* (*pret.* DESAHOGUÉ; *subj.* DESAHOGUE) to ease the pain of, alleviate, relieve. **II.** *vr.* to recover from fatigue or disease; to unbosom oneself, to disclose one's grief; to give a piece of one's mind; to express one's feelings; to extricate oneself from debt.
desahogo, *m.* ease, relief from pain or affliction; rest or respite from work; unbosoming oneself or disclosing one's troubles or grief; laxity; comfort, ease; comfortable circumstances.
desahogué, desahogue, *v. V.* DESAHOGAR.
desahuciado, da. I. *pp.* of DESAHUCIAR. **II.** *a.* despaired of, hopeless.
desahuciar, *va.* to take away all hope from; to give over; to declare (a patient) past recovery; to dispossess or oust (a tenant).
desahucio, *m.* dispossession of a tenant.
desahumado, da. I. *pp.* of DESAHUMAR. **II.** *a.* (of liquor) weakened (from standing open).
desahumar, *va.* to free from smoke.
desainadura, *f.* a disease of horses caused by their fat being consumed through overwork.
desainar. I. *va.* to take off the fat of (an animal); to lessen or diminish the thickness or substance of. **II.** *vr.* to lose fat.
desairadamente, *adv.* unhandsomely, clumsily, gracelessly.
desairado, da. I. *pp.* of DESAIRAR. **II.** *a.* unhandsome, graceless; unrewarded, unsuccessful.
desairar, *va.* to disregard, to slight, to ignore; to scorn; to rebuff.—**desaire,** *m.* slight, rebuff, disdain, disrespect; awkwardness, clumsiness.
desaislarse, *vr.* to cease to be insulated or isolated; to leave one's seclusion.
desajustar. I. *va.* to disarrange, disadjust. **II.** *vr.* to disagree, to withdraw from an agreement; to get out of order or adjustment.
desajuste, *m.* disarrangement, lack of adjustment; disagreement; maladjustment.
desalabanza, *f.* vituperation, disparagement.
desalabar, *va.* to dispraise, belittle, disparage.
desalabear, *va.* (carp.) to straighten.
desalabeo, *m.* (carp.) straightening.
desaladamente, *adv.* anxiously, swiftly, eagerly; greedily; hurriedly.
desalado, da, *a.* hasty, impatient, disordinate.
desaladura, *f.* (chem.) = DESALAZÓN.
[1]**desalar. I.** *va.* to cut off the wings of. **II.** *vr.* to run or walk swiftly; to be in great haste; to long for, to crave.
[2]**desalar. I.** *va.* to remove the salt from. **II.** *vr.* (of fish, meat, etc.) to lose its salt.

desalazón, *f.* (chem.) removing the salt from a liquid.
desalbardar, *va.* to take off the packsaddle from.
desalentadamente, *adv.* faintly, feebly.
desalentar. I. *va.* (*ind.* DESALIENTO; *subj.* DESALIENTE) to put out of breath by labor; to discourage, to dismay. **II.** *vr.* to jade, become exhausted.
desalfombrar, *va.* to take up the carpets from.
desalforjar. I. *va.* to take out of a saddlebag. **II.** *vr.* (coll.) to loosen one's garments; to make oneself easy.
desalhajar, *va.* to strip of fine furniture.
[1]**desaliento,** *m.* dismay, depression of spirits, discouragement, dejection; faintness, languor.
[2]**desaliento, desaliente,** *v. V.* DESALENTAR.
desalineación, *f.* lack of alinement; getting or putting out of alinement.
desalinear, *va.* to throw out of alinement.
desaliñar, *va.* & *vr.* to disarrange, disorder, ruffle; to make slovenly or dirty.
desaliño, *m.* slovenliness, negligence of dress; disarray; neglect.—*pl.* very long earrings.
desalivar, *vn.* to salivate.
desalmadamente, *adv.* soullessly, inhumanly.
desalmado, da. I. *pp.* of DESALMAR. **II.** *a.* soulless, inhuman, merciless; impious, profligate.
desalmamiento, *m.* inhumanity; perversity.
desalmar, *va.* & *vr.* to long for eagerly, to crave.
desalmenado, da, *a.* stripped of battlements.
desalmidonar, *va.* to take the starch out of.
desalojado, da. I. *pp.* of DESALOJAR. **II.** *a.*—**personas desalojadas,** displaced persons.
desalojamiento, *m.* dislodging; displacing.
desalojar. I. *va.* to dislodge, dispossess, oust, evict, eject; to displace. **II.** *vn.* to quit one's lodgings; to move out.
desalquilado, da, *a.* unrented, vacant.
desalquilar, *va.* & *vr.* to leave or cause to leave (a rented room or house); to become vacant.
desalterar, *va.* to allay, assuage, calm down.
desalumbradamente, *adv.* blindly, erroneously.
desalumbrado, da, *a.* dazzled, rattled, dazed; groping in the dark.
desalumbramiento, *m.* blindness, want of judgment, foresight, or knowledge.
desamable, *a.* unlovable.
desamador, ra, *n.* one who has ceased loving; one who dislikes persons or things.
desamar, *va.* to love no more; to dislike, hate.
desamarrar. I. *va.* to untie, unbind, unlash; to separate; (naut.) to unmoor; to unbend (a rope). **II.** *vr.* to get loose; to part.
desamasado, da, *a.* dissolved, disunited.
desamigado, da, *a.* unfriendly; estranged.
desamistarse, *vr.* to fall out, to quarrel.
desamoblar, *va.* = DESAMUEBLAR.
desamoldar, *va.* to change the form, proportion, or symmetry of; to disfigure.
desamor, *m.* disaffection; lack of sentiment and love; enmity, hatred.
desamorado, da. I. *pp.* of DESAMORAR. **II.** *a.* unloving, cold-hearted.
desamorar. I. *va.* to kill the love of. **II.** *vr.* to cease loving.
desamoroso, sa, *a.* unloving.
desamorrar, *va.* (coll.) to make lively, make (a person) talk.
desamortajar, *va.* to disenshroud.
desamortización, *f.* disentail.
desamortizador, ra, *a.* disentailing.
desamortizar, *va.* (*pret.* DESAMORTICÉ; *subj.* DESAMORTICE) to disentail.
desamotinarse, *vr.* to withdraw from mutiny.
desamparadamente, *adv.* helplessly.
desamparado, da. I. *pp.* of DESAMPARAR. **II.** *a.* forsaken; needy, helpless.
desamparador, ra, *n.* & *a.* forsaker(-ing).
desamparar, *va.* to forsake, abandon, leave; to quit; (naut.) to dismantle, dismast.
desamparo, *m.* abandonment, desertion; want of protection, helplessness, neediness; dereliction.
desamueblado, da, *a.* unfurnished.
desamueblar, *va.* to strip of furniture.
desanclar, desancorar, *va.* (naut.) to weigh the anchor of.
desandadura, *f.* going back over the same road.
desandar, *va.* (*pret.* DESANDUVE) to retrace (steps).—**d. lo andado,** to undo what has been done.
desandrajado, da, *a.* ragged, in tatters.
desanduve, *pret.* of DESANDAR.
desangramiento, *m.* bleeding to excess.
desangrar. I. *va.* to bleed to excess; to drain (a lake, etc.); to exhaust the means of, to make poor. **II.** *vr.* to lose blood, to bleed.
desanidar. I. *vn.* (of birds) to leave the nest. **II.** *va.* to dislodge from a post.
desanimación, *f.* (Am.) lack of enthusiasm; dullness.
desanimadamente, *adv.* spiritlessly, faintly, with discouragement.
desanimado, da, *a.* dull, flat; discouraged; (Am.) (of a party, etc.) poorly attended.
desanimar. I. *va.* to dishearten, discourage. **II.** *vr.* to get discouraged; to jade.
desánimo, *m.* discouragement, downheartedness.
desanublar. I. *va.* & *vr.* to calm down, cool off. **II.** *va.* to elucidate, make clear.
desanudar, *va.* to untie, loosen; to extricate, disentangle.
desañudadura, *f.* untying; disentanglement.
desañudar, *va.* = DESANUDAR.
desaojadera, *f.* woman supposed to dispel charms.
desaojar, *va.* to cure of the effects of the evil eye.
desapacibilidad, *f.* disagreeableness.
desapacible, *a.* disagreeable, unpleasant.
desapadrinar, *va.* to disapprove, disavow.
desaparear, *va.* to separate (two of a pair).
desaparecer. I. *va.* (*ind.* DESAPAREZCO; *subj.* DESAPAREZCA) to cause to disappear. **II.** *vn.* & *vr.* to disappear.
desaparecimiento, *m.* disappearance.
desaparejar, *va.* to unharness, unhitch; (naut.) to unrig (a ship).
desaparezco, desaparezca, *v. V.* DESAPARECER.
desaparición, *f.* disappearance; (astr.) occultation.
desaparroquiar. I. *va.* to remove from a parish. **II.** *vr.* to remove from one parish to another; (com.) to cease to be a customer.
desapasionado, da, *a.* dispassionate, calm, passionless.
desapasionarse, *vr.* to root out love or fondness.
desapegarse, *vr.* to lose liking or love (for a person or thing).—**desapego,** *m.* loss of love, affection, or liking; coolness; impartiality, disinterestedness; indifference.
desapercibidamente, *adv.* inadvertently, unpreparedly.
desapercibido, da, *a.* unprovided; unprepared, unguarded.
desapercibimiento, *m.* unpreparedness.
desapestar, *va.* to disinfect.
desapiadado, da, *a.* merciless.
desaplicación, *f.* lack of application, indolence.
desaplicado, da, *a.* indolent, careless, neglectful.
desaplomar, *va.* to put out of plumb.
desapoderadamente, *adv.* hastily, impetuously.
desapoderado, da. I. *pp.* of DESAPODERAR. **II.** *a.* impetuous, unruly.
desapoderamiento, *m.* seizure of another's possessions; depriving of power or authority.
desapoderar, *va.* to dispossess; to rob; to repeal or revoke the power of attorney of.
desapolillar. I. *va.* to free and clear of moths. **II.** *vr.* (coll.) to take the air when it is cold or after a long confinement.
desaporcar, *va.* (*ind. pres.* DESAPUERCO, *pret.* DESAPORQUÉ; *subj.* DESAPUERCA) to take away (from plants) earth which had been heaped about them.
desaposentar, *va.* to dispossess, oust, evict; to drive out of one's mind.

desaposesionar, *va.* to deprive of holdings.
desapoyar, *va.* to withdraw support of or from.
desapreciar, *va.* to undervalue, belittle.
desaprecio, *m.* depreciation, belittling, undervaluation.
desaprender, *va.* to unlearn, forget.
desaprensar. I. *va.* to take away the gloss of (clothes). **II.** *vr.* to extricate oneself.
desaprensivo, va, *a.* not tense, easy.
desapretar, *va.* (*ind.* DESAPRIETO; *subj.* DESAPRIETE) to slacken, loosen, loose; to ease, free from anxiety.
desaprisionar. I. *va.* to release, to set at liberty. **II.** *vr.* to extricate oneself.
desaprobación, *f.* disapprobation, disapproval.
desaprobar, *va.* (*ind.* DESAPRUEBO; *subj.* DESAPRUEBE) to disapprove of, condemn.
desapropiamiento, *m.* = DESAPROPIO.
desapropiarse, *vr.* **(de)** to divest oneself (of), surrender, transfer (one's property).
desapropio, *m.* surrender or transfer of property.
desaprovechado, da, *a.* unprofitable; unimproved; backward.
desaprovechamiento, *m.* lack of improvement; backwardness.
desaprovechar. I. *va.* to waste, misspend, make no use of. **II.** *vn.* to be backward, make little or no progress.
desapruebo, desapruebe, *v. V.* DESAPROBAR.
desapuntalar, *va.* to take away the props or supports of or from.
desapuntar, *va.* to rip out the stitching of; to lose the aim of (a gun).
desaquellarse, *vr.* to become disheartened.
desarbolar, *va.* (naut.) to unmast; to clear of trees.
desarbolo, *m.* stripping (a ship) of masts.
desarenar, *va.* to clear of sand.
desareno, *m.* clearing of sand.
desarmable, *a.* demountable.
desarmado, da, *a.* unarmed, barehanded; disassembled.
desarmador, *m.* hammer of a gun.
desarmadura, *f.*, **desarmamiento,** *m.* disarming, disarmament.
desarmar, *va.* to disarm; to prohibit the carrying of arms to; to dismount, take apart; to disband; to make (a bull) butt in the air; (naut.) to lay up; to dissassemble.
desarme, *m.* disarming, disarmament; disassembly.
desarraigar, *va.* (*pret.* DESARRAIGUÉ; *subj.* DESARRAIGUE) to eradicate, root out; to dig up (a tree); to extirpate, exterminate; to expel.
desarraigo, *m.* eradication; expulsion.
desarrancarse, *vr.* to desert, to separate from a body or association.
desarrapado, desharrapado, da, *a.* ragged.
desarrebozadamente, *adv.* frankly, clearly.
desarrebozar, *va.* & *vr.* to unmuffle; to lay open, manifest, uncover.
desarrebujar, *va.* to disentangle; to unfold, spread out; to uncover; to explain, clear up.
desarreglado, da, *a.* immoderate, intemperate; extravagant, excessive; slovenly, disorderly; disarranged; lawless, unruly.
desarreglar, *va.* to disarrange, derange, disorder. **—desarreglo,** *m.* disarrangement, disorder, confusion.
[1]**desarrendar,** *va.* (*ind.* DESARRIENDO; *subj.* DESARRIENDE) to break the lease of.
[2]**desarrendar,** (*for mut. V.* [1]DESARRENDAR). **I.** *va.* to unbridle (a horse). **II.** *vr.* (of a horse) to shake off the bridle.
desarrimar, *va.* to remove, separate; to dissuade.
desarrimo, *m.* lack of props or support.
desarrollable, *a.* that can be developed.
desarrollado, da. I. *pp.* of DESARROLLAR. **II.** *a.* developed.**—países poco desarrollados,** underdeveloped countries.
desarrollar. I. *va.* to develop; to unroll, unfold, unwind, unfurl; to promote, improve; to explain, expound; to work out; (math.) to develop (a surface), to rectify (a curve), to develop or expand (a power, a function); (Ry.) to develop (a line) (*v.* DESARROLLO). **II.** *vr.* to develop; evolve; to unwind, unfold.
desarrollo, *m.* development; unfolding; unwinding; (math.) development (of a surface, a curve); rectification, calculation of the length (of a curve); expansion, development (of a power, a function); (Ry.) development, lengthening of the line by curves to obtain the appropriate grade.
desarropar, *va.* to uncover, to undress.
desarrugadura, *f.* taking out wrinkles.
desarrugar, *va.* (*pret.* DESARRUGUÉ; *subj.* DESARRUGUE) to take wrinkles out of, to smooth out.
desarrumar, *va.* (naut.) to break out (the hold).
desarticulación, *f.* disarticulation.
desarticulado, da, *a.* disjointed, unjointed.
desarticular, *va.* & *vr.* to disarticulate, take or come apart at the joints; (naut.) to loose, disconnect.
desartillar, *va.* to take the guns out of.
desarzonar, *va.* to throw from the saddle, unhorse.
desasado, da, *a.* without handles.
desaseado, da, *a.* slovenly, not clean.
desasear, *va.* to make dirty or unclean; to disarrange, to disorder.
desasegurar. I. *va.* to loosen, unbrace, make unsteady. **II.** *vr.* (Am.) to cancel an insurance.
desasentar. I. *va.* (*ind.* DESASIENTO; *subj.* DESASIENTE) to displace, move, remove. **II.** *vn.* to be unbecoming; to be disliked, to displease. **III.** *vr.* to stand up.
desaseo, *m.* uncleanliness, untidiness, slovenliness.
desasgo, desasga, *v. V.* DESASIR.
desasiento, desasiente, *v. V.* DESASENTAR.
desasimiento, *m.* loosening or letting loose; alienation of affection; lack of interest.
desasimilación, *f.* (physiol.) katabolism.
desasir. I. *va.* (*ind.* DESASGO; *subj.* DESASGA) to loosen, let go, give up. **II.** *vr.* **(de)** to disengage or rid oneself (of); to give away, give up.
desasistir, *va.* to abandon, forsake.
desasnar. I. *va.* (coll.) to polish (one's manners). **II.** *vr.* to grow clever; to become polite.
desasociable, *a.* unsociable.
desasosegadamente, *adv.* uneasily, anxiously.
desasosegar, *va.* (*ind. pres.* DESASOSIEGO, *pret.* DESASOSEGUÉ; *subj.* DESASOSIEGUE) to disquiet, disturb, make uneasy or anxious.
desasosiego, *m.* restlessness, uneasiness.
desastrado, da, *a.* wretched, unfortunate; shabby, ragged.
desastre, *m.* disaster, catastrophe.
desastroso, sa, *a.* unfortunate, disastrous.
desatacar. I. *va.* (*pret.* DESATAQUÉ; *subj.* DESATAQUE) to loosen, untie, unfasten; to draw (the ramrod from). **II.** *vr.* to unfasten one's trousers.
desatadamente, *adv.* loosely, freely.
desatado, da. I. *pp.* of DESATAR. **II.** *a.* loose, untied.
desatador, ra, *n.* one that unties or unfastens.
desatadura, *f.* untying, loosening.
desatalantado, da, *a.* unwise, injudicious.
desatancar, *va.* (*pret.* DESATANQUÉ; *subj.* DESATANQUE) to clear of obstructions.
desataqué, desataque, *v. V.* DESATACAR.
desatar. I. *va.* to untie, undo (a knot), unfasten, unhitch, loose, loosen, unbind; to separate, detach; to let loose; to liquefy, dissolve; to unriddle, solve, find out, unravel. **II.** *vr.* to give a loose rein to one's tongue; to lose all reserve, fear, or bashfulness; to break loose, break out (as a storm).**—d. en,** to break out into, to let out, to pour out (insult, etc.).
desatascar, *va.* (*pret.* DESATASQUÉ; *subj.* DESATASQUE) to pull or draw out of the mud; to remove an obstruction from; to extricate from difficulties.
desataviar, *va.* to strip of ornaments.
desatavío, *m.* uncleanliness, disarray.

desate, *m.* glibness, excessive talk; disorderly proceeding.—**d. de vientre,** looseness of the bowels.
desatención, *f.* inattention; absent-mindedness; disrespect, slight, discourtesy.
desatender, *va.* (*ind.* DESATIENDO; *subj.* DESATIENDA) to pay no attention to; to be unheedful or unmindful of; to disregard, slight, neglect; to take no notice of.
desatentado, da. I. *pp.* of DESATENTAR. **II.** *a.* unwise, injudicious; excessive, rigorous; disordered.
desatentar, *va.* (*ind.* DESATIENTO; *subj.* DESATIENTE) to perturb the mind of, to perplex, confuse, derange.
desatento, ta, *a.* inattentive, careless, heedless, thoughtless; unmannerly, discourteous.
desaterrar, *va.* (*ind.* DESATIERRO; *subj.* DESATIERRE) (Am.) to free (a mine) from rubbish and debris; to remove obstructive earth or mud from.
desatesorar, *va.* to spend the treasure of.
desatibar, *va.* (min.) = DESATORAR.
desatiendo, desatienda, *v. V.* DESATENDER.
[1]**desatiento,** *m.* lack of the sense of touch; restlessness, uneasiness, worry.
[2]**desatiento, desatiente,** *v. V.* DESATENTAR.
desatierre, *m.* (min.) dumping ground; cleaning-up, removal of debris, etc.
desatierro, desatierre, *v. V.* DESATERRAR.
desatinado, da. I. *pp.* of DESATINAR. **II.** *a.* unwise, ill-advised, foolish, wild. **III.** *n.* idiot, fool.
desatinar. I. *va.* to rattle, to confuse, bewilder. **II.** *vn.* to act or talk foolishly; to get rattled or bewildered; to lose one's bearings.
desatino, *m.* lack of tact, adroitness, or address; unwisdom; foolish act or expression; irrelevancy; nonsense, folly, blunder.
desatolondrar. I. *va.* to bring (a person) to his senses. **II.** *vr.* to recover one's senses (fig.) to wake up, open one's eyes.
desatollar, *va.* = DESATASCAR.
desatontarse, *vr.* to recover from stupefaction.
desatorar, *va.* (naut.) to break out (the hold); (min.) to clear from rubbish.
desatornillar, *va.* to unscrew.
desatracar, *va.* (*pret.* DESATRAQUÉ; *subj.* DESATRAQUE) (naut.) to sheer off, to bear away.
desatraer, *va.* (*ger.* DESATRAYENDO; *ind. pres.* DESATRAIGO, *pret.* DESATRAJE; *subj.* DESATRAIGA) to disjoin, separate.
desatraillar, *va.* to unleash (hounds).
desatrampar, *va.* to clear out (a drain, etc.).
desatrancar, *va.* (*pret.* DESATRANQUÉ; *subj.* DESATRANQUE) to unbar; to clear, remove the obstructions from.
desatraqué, desatraque, *v. V.* DESATRACAR.
desatrayendo, *ger.* of DESATRAER.
desatufarse, *vr.* to go out from a close room; to become calm, to calm down, cool off.
desaturdir, *va.* to rouse from dizziness or stupor.
desautoricé, desautorice, *v. V.* DESAUTORIZAR.
desautoridad, *f.* want of authority.
desautorización, *f.* withdrawal of authority.
desautorizado, da, *a.* unauthorized; discredited.
desautorizar, *va.* (*pret.* DESAUTORICÉ; *subj.* DESAUTORICE) to take authority from, to deprive of authority.
desavahado, da, *a.* clear (weather), free from vapor; bold.
desavahamiento, *m.* uncovering a hot thing to let it cool.
desavahar. I. *va.* to expose to the air, to let cool off; to air, ventilate. **II.** *vr.* to become, or get, lively or sprightly.
desavecindado, da. I. *pp.* of DESAVECINDARSE. **II.** *a.* deserted, unpeopled.
desavecindarse, *vr.* to change one's domicile.
desavendré, *fut.* of DESAVENIR.
desavenencia, *f.* discord, disagreement, misunderstanding; quarrel.
desavengo, desavenga, *v. V.* DESAVENIR.
desavenido, da. I. *pp.* of DESAVENIR. **II.** *a.* discordant, disagreeing.
desavenir. I. *va.* (*ger.* DESAVINIENDO; *ind. pres.* DESAVENGO, *pret.* DESAVINE, *fut.* DESAVENDRÉ; *subj.* DESAVENGA) to disturb, unsettle. **II.** *vr.* to disagree, to quarrel.
desaventajado, da, *a.* disadvantageous; inferior.
desaviar. I. *va.* to mislead, lead astray; to strip of necessaries or conveniences. **II.** *vr.* to go astray; to lose the means of acquiring necessaries.
desavine, desaviniendo, *v. V.* DESAVENIR.
desavío, *m.* leading or going astray; want of necessary means.
desavisado, da. I. *pp.* of DESAVISAR. **II.** *a.* ill-advised, unadvised, misguided.
desavisar, *va.* to contradict (previous advice, news or reports); to countermand.
desayudar, *va.* to prevent from being aided.
desayunado, da. I. *pp.* of DESAYUNAR. **II.** *a.* having breakfasted.
desayunarse, *vr.* to breakfast; to have first intelligence; to be aware of something.
desayuno, *m.* light breakfast, morning meal (usually coffee or chocolate and rolls or bread).
desazogar. I. *va.* (*pret.* DESAZOGUÉ; *subj.* DESAZOGUE) to take off the quicksilver from (a looking-glass). **II.** *vr.* (Peru) to become restless.
desazón, *f.* insipidity, want of taste or flavor; displeasure, vexation; uneasiness, restlessness; unfitness of a soil for agricultural purposes.
desazonado, da, *a.* (agr.) unfit for cultivation; peevish, ill-humored; indisposed.
desazonar. I. *va.* to render tasteless; to vex, ruffle. **II.** *vr.* to become indisposed.
desazufrar, *va.* (chem.) to desulfur, desulfurize.
desbabar, *vn.* to drivel, to slaver.
desbagar, *va.* (*pret.* DESBAGUÉ; *subj.* DESBAGUE) to extract (the flaxseed) from the capsule.
desbancar, *va.* (*pret.* DESBANQUÉ; *subj.* DESBANQUE) to clear (a room) of benches, etc.; to win the bank from, to break the bank; to cut out, supplant in the affection of another.
desbandada, *f.* disbandment.—**a la d.,** in great disorder, helter-skelter.
desbandarse, *vr.* to disband; to withdraw (from others); (mil.) to desert.
desbanqué, desbanque, *v. V.* DESBANCAR.
desbarahustar, desbarajustar. I. *va.* to disorder, confuse, disarrange. **II.** *vr.* to get out of order, break down.—**desbarahuste, desbarajuste,** *m.* disorder, confused medley.
desbaratadamente, *adv.* brokenly, dispersedly.
desbaratado, da. I. *pp.* of DESBARATAR. **II.** *a.* (coll.) debauched, corrupted.
desbaratador, ra, *n.* destroyer, confounder, disturber; debaucher.
desbaratamiento, *m.* perturbation, commotion, disarrangement, ruin, downfall.
desbaratar. I. *va.* to destroy, break to pieces, smash, ruin; to waste, misspend, squander; to cross, impede, prevent, thwart; (mil.) to disperse, rout, break up. **II.** *vn.* to talk nonsense. **III.** *vr.* to be unbalanced; to get out of order; to fall to pieces; to become, or get, undone.
desbarate, desbarato, *m.* smash, breakage, destruction; (mil.) rout, defeat; waste, squandering.—**d. de vientre,** loose bowels.
desbarbado, da, *a.* beardless.
desbarbar, *va.* to trim, to cut off filaments from; (coll.) to shave.
desbarbillar, *va.* (agr.) to cut out (from young vines) the roots which spring from the stems.
desbardar, *va.* to remove thatch from.
desbarnizar, *va.* to remove the varnish from.
desbarrancadero, *m.* (Am.) precipice.
desbarrar, *vn.* to throw an iron bar without taking aim; to sneak, steal away; to act foolishly; to talk nonsense.
desbarretar, *va.* to unbar, unbolt.
desbarrigado, da, *a.* small-bellied.

desbarrigar, *va.* (*pret.* DESBARRIGUÉ; *subj.* DESBARRIGUE) (coll.) to rip open the belly of.
desbarro, *m.* foolish action; nonsensical talk; aimless throw of the bar (sports).
desbastador, *m.* dressing chisel, paring tool, hewer.
desbastadura, *f.* planing, trimming, hewing.
desbastar, *va.* to hew, pare, dress, trim, plane, smooth; to waste, consume, weaken; to educate and polish.—**desbaste,** *m.* hewing, rough dressing, trimming.
desbastecido, da, *a.* without provisions.
desbautizarse, *vr.* (coll.) to lose one's temper, fly into a passion; (Am.) (coll.) to fracture one's skull.
desbazadero, *m.* humid, slippery place.
desbeber, *va.* (coll.) to urinate.
desbecerrar, *va.* to wean (young animals).
desbocadamente, *adv.* impudently, shamelessly, without restraint.
desbocado, da, *a.* (artil.) (of cannon) wide-mouthed; runaway (horse); broken-lipped or -mouthed (as a jar); broken-faced (as a tool); foul-mouthed, indecent.
desbocamiento, *m.* impertinence, impudence; (of a horse) act of running away.
desbocar. I. *va.* (*pret.* DESBOQUÉ; *subj.* DESBOQUE) to break the mouth or spout of. **II.** *vn.* to debouch. **III.** *vr.* to run away; (coll.) to use abusive language, unloosen one's tongue.
desbonetarse, *vr.* (coll.) to take off one's cap.
desboqué, desboque, *v. V.* DESBOCAR.
desboquillar, *va.* to break or remove the mouthpiece or stem of (a pipe, etc.); to break or remove the nozzle of.
desbordamiento, *m.* inundation, overflowing.
desbordar, *vn.* & *vr.* to overflow; to lose one's temper or self control; to give free rein to one's tongue or passions.
desbornizar, *va.* to strip cork from (tree).
desborrar, *va.* to burl; to lop off the shoots of.
desboscar, *va.* (Am.) to deforest.
desbragado, da, *a.* (coll.) shabby.
desbravador, *m.* mustang breaker.
desbravar, = DESBRAVECER.
desbravecer. I. *va.* (*ind.* DESBRAVEZCO; *subj.* DESBRAVEZCA) to tame, to break in (horses). **II.** *vn.* to become less fierce; to diminish in force, to moderate, abate.
desbrazarse, *vr.* to stretch out the arms violently.
desbrevarse, *vr.* (of wine) to lose body and strength.
desbridamiento, *m.* (surg.) separation of fibrous tissues with an instrument.
desbridar, *va.* (surg.) to open up, separate the tissues of.
desbriznar, *va.* to chop or mince (meat); to cut or divide into small parts; to pluck the stamens, the filaments of.
desbroce, *m.* clippings, cuttings from pruning trees; clearing of lands or trenches.
desbrozar, *va.* (*pret.* DESBROCÉ; *subj.* DESBROCE) to clear away rubbish from.—**desbrozo,** *m.* = DESBROCE.
desbruar, *va.* to clean (cloth) of grease; to put (cloth) in the fulling mill.
desbrujar, *va.* = DESMORONAR. to abrade.
desbuchar, *va.* to disclose (one's secrets); (of birds) to ease (the stomach).
desbulla, *f.* oyster shell.
desbullar, *va.* to take (oyster) out of shell.
descabal, *a.* imperfect, incomplete.
descabalamiento, *f.* diminution, impairment.
descabalar, *va.* to take away a part of; to chop off, impair, damage, maim, cripple; to pilfer.
descabalgadura, *f.* dismounting or alighting from a horse.
descabalgar. I. *vn.* (*pret.* DESCABALGUÉ; *subj.* DESCABALGUE) to dismount, to alight from a horse. **II.** *va.* to dismount (a gun).
descabecé, descabece, *v. V.* DESCABEZAR.
descabelladamente, *adv.* wildly, haphazard, thoughtlessly.
descabellado, da. I. *pp.* of DESCABELLAR. **II.** *a.* dishevelled, disordered, disarranged; out of all reason, illogical, preposterous, absurd.
descabellar. I. *va.* & *vr.* to disarrange (the hair). **II.** *va.* to kill (the bull) by pricking it in the back of the neck with the sword.
descabello, *m.* killing the bull properly.
descabestrar, *va.* to unhalter.
descabezado, da. I. *pp.* of DESCABEZAR. **II.** *a.* beheaded; light-headed, injudicious, wild, rash.
descabezamiento, *m.* act of beheading; quandary, puzzling predicament.
descabezar. I. *va.* (*pret.* DESCABECÉ; *subj.* DESCABECE) to behead; to revoke (an assessment); to cut the upper parts or points of; to head, to top; to poll; to lop off; to overcome; (naut.) to break (a mast) through its neck.—**d. el sueño,** to take a nap. **II.** *vn.* to abut. **III.** *vr.* (coll.) to cudgel one's brains; (of cereals) to shed the grain.
descabritar, *va.* to wean (goats).
descabullirse, *vr.* to sneak off, to steal away, to scamper; to elude the strength of an argument.
descachar. I. *va.* (Chile) to cut off the horns of. **II.** *vr.* (billiards) to miscue.
descachazar, *va.* (Am.) to skim (sugar-cane juice).
descaderar, *va.* to sprain or dislocate the hip of.
descadillar, *va.* to cut off the loose threads or fag-end of (the warp).
descaecer, *vn.* (*defect. subj.* DESCAEZCA) to decline, droop, languish; decrease; (naut.) to edge away.
descaecimiento, *m.* weakness, debility; despondency, dejection, languor.
descaezca, *v. V.* DESCAECER.
descaimiento, *m.* = DESCAECIMIENTO.
descalabazarse, *vr.* (coll.) to cudgel one's brains in vain.
descalabrado, da. I. *pp.* of DESCALABRAR. **II.** *a.* injured; wounded on the head.—**salir d.,** to be a loser, to fail, be worsted.
descalabradura, *f.* slight wound in the head; scar remaining after such wound.
descalabrar. I. *va.* to wound slightly in the head; to attack or impeach the character of; to hurt, to injure; (naut.) to cause (a ship) considerable damage; to occasion losses to. **II.** *vr.* to fracture one's skull; (Peru) to become ruined or be violently destroyed.
descalabro, *m.* calamity; setback; misfortune.
descalandrajar, *va.* to rend or tear into rags.
descalcador, *m.* (carp.) ripping iron, claw; (naut.) ravehook.
descalcar, *va.* (*pret.* DESCALQUÉ; *subj.* DESCALQUE) (naut.) to extract oakum from (seams).
descalce, *m.* undermining, unwedging.
descalcez, *f.* lack of shoes, barefootedness.
descalificación, *f.* disqualification, withdrawal of authority.
descalificado, da, *a.* disqualified.
descalificar, *va.* to disqualify, to take the power or authority from.
descalostrado, da, *a.* (of a baby) having passed the days of the first milk.
descalzar. I. *va.* (*pret.* DESCALCÉ; *subj.* DESCALCE) to pull off the shoes and stockings from; to take off wedges or chocks from; to undermine. **II.** *vr.* to take off one's shoes and stockings; (of horses) to lose a shoe.—**d. los guantes,** to take off one's gloves.
descalzo, za, *a.* barefoot, barefooted, shoeless; (relig.) discalced, discalceate.
descamación, *f.* (med.) desquamation, (of skin) peeling off in scales.
descambiar, *va.* to cancel an exchange or barter.
descaminadamente, *adv.* absurdly, unreasonably, foolishly.
descaminado, da. I. *pp.* of DESCAMINAR. **II.** *a.* ill-advised, misguided, mistaken.
descaminar. I. *va.* to misguide, mislead, lead astray; to seize as contraband; declare contra-

band; punish for smuggling. **II.** *vr.* to go astray, to lose one's way.
descamino, *m.* leading or going astray; seizure of smuggled goods; the goods thus seized; error, blindness; deviation from justice, truth, reason.
descamisado, da. I. *a.* shirtless, naked, ragged. **II.** *m.* (coll.) ragamuffin.
descampado, da, *a.* disengaged, free, open, clear.—**en d.,** in the open air.
descansadamente, *adv.* easily, without toil or fatigue, leisurely.
descansadero, *m.* resting place.
descansado, da. I. *pp.* of DESCANSAR. **II.** *a.* rested, refreshed.
descansar. I. *vn.* to rest, take repose; to be quiet; to rest, lean upon; to be satisfied; to trust or place confidence (in a person); to lie at rest (as lands which lie fallow); to sleep in death. **II.** *va.* to aid or alleviate; to place or set down on a support or base.
descansillo, *m.* landing of a stairway.
descanso, *m.* rest, repose; let-up; relief, aid, help; sleep; landing of stairs; (mech.) seat, bench, support; (mil.) parade rest.
descantar, *va.* to clear of stones.
descantear, *va.* to smooth angles or corners in; to splay, chamfer, edge.
descanterar, *vn.* to take off the corners or ends of.
descantillar, *va.* to pare off, to chip; to subtract from.
descantillón, *m.* = ESCANTILLÓN, pattern.
descantonar, *va.* = DESCANTILLAR.
descañonar, *va.* to pluck out the feathers of; to shave close; (coll.) to trick (one) out of his money.
descaperuzar, *va.* & *vr.* to unhood, uncowl.
descaperuzo, *m.* taking off the cowl, hood, cap.
descapillar, *va.* to take the hood off.
descarado, da. I. *pp.* of DESCARARSE. **II.** *a.* impudent, barefaced, saucy.
descaramiento, *m.* = DESCARO, impudence.
descararse, *vr.* to behave in an impudent or insolent manner, to be saucy.
descarbonatar, *va.* (chem.) to decarbonate.
descarbonizar, *va.* to decarbonize, decarburize.
descarburación, *f.* decarbonization.
descarburar, *va.* to decarbonize.
descarcañalar, *va.* & *vr.* (of the heel of a shoe) to run down.
descarga, *f.* unburdening, unloading; (mil.) volley, round, discharge; (mason.) easement of a wall; (elec.) discharge.—**d. en abanico,** (elec., phys.) brush discharge.
descargadero, *m.* wharf, unloading place.
descargador, *m.* unloader, lighterman; wad hook.
descargadura, *f.* bone that a butcher takes out of meat.
descargar. I. *va.* (*pret.* DESCARGUÉ; *subj.* DESCARGUE) to unload, disburden; to ease, lighten; to empty, dump; to free or relieve; to take off the flap and bones of (meat); (mil.) to fire, to discharge (firearms); to unload (firearms), to draw out the charge of powder and ball from; (naut.) to brace (a lee), to clear (the sails or yards); (elec.) to discharge; to deal, give, inflict (as blows); to acquit, clear from a charge, exonerate; to free or release from a charge, obligation, or debt. **II.** *vn.* to disembogue or disgorge; to vent fury, to burst, to strike with violence (as a storm). **III.** *vr.* **(de)** to resign (from) (a job); to shirk duty by transferring it to another; to shake off, rid oneself (of); (law) to clear or vindicate oneself (of).
descargo, *m.* unloading, unburdening; exoneration, discharge, acquittal; (com.) acquittance, receipt, release, discharge, voucher; (law) plea or answer to an impeachment or action.
descargue, *m.* unloading; license to unload vessels.
descariñarse, *vr.* to withdraw or lose love or affection; to become cool.
descariño, *m.* coolness, indifference.
descarnada, *f.*—**la d.,** death.
descarnadamente, *adv.* plainly, without trimmings; with effrontery.
descarnado, da, *a.* thin, lean; bare, unadorned.
descarnador, *m.* (dent.) scraper; (tanning) hide scraper.
descarnadura, *f.* divesting of flesh.
descarnar. I. *va.* to clear of flesh; to take or eat away; to corrode, wash away, abrade, denudate; (tanning) to flesh, to scrape; to remove from earthly things. **II.** *vr.* to lose flesh, become emaciated.
descaro, *m.* impudence, barefacedness, effrontery, sauciness, assurance, "nerve," "cheek."
descarriamiento, *m.* going or leading astray.
descarriar. I. *va.* to lead astray, misguide, mislead; to separate (cattle). **II.** *vr.* to be separated; to deviate from justice or reason; to go astray; to lead a dissipated life.
descarrilamiento, *m.* derailment.
descarrilar. I. *va.* to derail. **II.** *vn.* & *vr.* to run off the track, be derailed.
descarrilladura, *f.* act of breaking the jaws.
descarrillar, *va.* to break the jaws of.
descarrío, *m.* going astray, losing the way.
descartar. I. *va.* to discard, throw away; lay aside. **II.** *vr.* to discard (at cards); to excuse oneself; to shirk.
descarte, *m.* cards discarded; act of discarding; act of shirking; evasion, subterfuge.
descasamiento, *m.* annulling (of marriage).
descasar, *va.* to annul the marriage of; to separate, put asunder; (print.) to alter the position of (the pages of a sheet).
descascar. I. *va.* (*pret.* DESCASQUÉ; *subj.* DESCASQUE) to remove the bark, husk, etc. from; to boast; to bluster; to mumble. **II.** *vr.* to break into pieces.
descascarar. I. *va.* to peel, shell, hull, husk. **II.** *vr.* to peel off, shell off.
descascarillar, *va.* to peel, husk; to take off the powder from (the face).
descaspar, *va.* to take dandruff from; (tanning) to scrape (a half-dressed hide).
descasque, *m.* removing bark (esp. of the cork tree).
descastado, da, *a.* showing little natural affection to whom it is due.
descastar, *va.* to deprive of caste; to exterminate.
descatolizar, *va.* to cause to abandon Catholicism.
descaudalado, da, *a.* ruined, penniless.
descebar, *va.* to unprime (firearms).
descendencia, *f.* descent, origin; descendants.
descendente, *a.* descending.
descender. I. *vn.* (*pp.* DESCENDIDO; *ind.* DESCIENDO; *subj.* DESCIENDA) to descend; get, come or go down; to flow or run, as liquids; (of temperature) to drop; to descend, be descended, derive; to stoop, lower oneself. **II.** *va.* to let down, lower; to bring down.
descendiente. I. *a.* descending. **II.** *m.* descendant, offspring.
descendimiento, *m.* descent, lowering.
descensión, *f.* descension, descent.
descenso, *m.* descent; lowering; decrease; fall, degradation; (med.) hernia, rupture; prolapse of the womb.
descentrado, da, *a.* out of center; out of plumb.
descentralización, *f.* decentralization.
descentralizador, ra, *a.* descentralizing.
descentralizar, *va.* (*pret.* DESCENTRALICÉ; *subj.* DESCENTRALICE) to decentralize; to grant local autonomy to.
descentrar. I. *va.* to uncenter. **II.** *vr.* to get out of center or out of plumb.
desceñidura, *f.* ungirding or loosening a belt.
desceñir, *va.* (*ind.* DESCIÑO; *subj.* DESCIÑA) to ungird, to loosen or take off (as a belt, a crown).
[1]**descepar,** *va.* to eradicate, to pull up by the roots; to extirpate.

[2]descepar, *va.* (naut.) to remove the stocks from (an anchor).
descerar, *va.* to take the empty combs from (a beehive).
descercador, *m.* one who forces the enemy to raise a siege.
descercar, *va.* (*pret.* DESCERQUÉ; *subj.* DESCERQUE) to destroy or pull down a wall, a fence, etc. of; to raise the siege of; to oblige (the enemy) to raise a siege.
descerco, *m.* the act of raising a siege.
descerezar, *va.* to pulp (the coffee berry).
descerqué, descerque, *v. V.* DESCERCAR.
descerrajado, da, *a.* (coll.) corrupt, wicked, ill-disposed.
descerrajadura, *f.* taking off locks or bolts.
descerrajar, *va.* to take the lock off; to discharge (firearms).
descerrumarse, *vr.* (vet.) to be wrenched or distorted at the joints.
descervigar, *va.* to twist the neck of; humiliate.
desciendo, descienda, *v. V.* DESCENDER.
descifrable, *a.* decipherable.
descifrador, ra, *n.* decipherer.
descifrar, *va.* to decipher, make out.
descimbramiento, *m.* (arch.) removing the centers.
descimbrar, *va.* (arch.) to remove the centers of.
descimentar, *va.* to demolish the foundations of.
descinchar, *va.* to ungirt.
desciño, desciña, *v. V.* DESCEÑIR.
descivilizar. I. *va.* to uncivilize. **II.** *vr.* to become uncivilized.
desclasificar, *va.* to declassify.
desclavador, *m.* carpenter's chisel; nail puller, claw wrench.
desclavar, *va.* to draw out the nails from, unpeg.
descoagulable, *a.* that can be redissolved after coagulation.
descoagular, *va.* to liquefy, dissolve (a clot).
descobajar, *va.* to pull the stem from (a grape).
descobijar, *va.* to uncover.
descocado, da. I. *pp.* of DESCOCARSE. **II.** *a.* (coll.) bold, excessively free and forward.
descocar. I. *va.* (*pret.* DESCOQUÉ; *subj.* DESCOQUE) to clean insects from (trees).
descocarse, *vr.* (coll.) to be impudent, saucy, or petulant.
descocer, *va.* (*ind.* DESCUEZO; *subj.* DESCUEZA) to digest.
descoco, *m.* barefacedness, impudence, sauciness.
descodar, *va.* to rip, to unstitch.
descoger, *va.* (*ind.* DESCOJO; *subj.* DESCOJA) to unfold, extend, spread, expand.
descogollar, *va.* to strip (a tree) of shoots; to take out the heart of (vegetables).
descogotado, da, *a.* (coll.) low-necked.
descogotar, *va.* to cut off the horns of (a stag).
descohesión, *f.* decohesion.
descohesor, *m.* (elec.) decoherer.
descojo, descoja, *v. V.* DESCOGER.
descolada, *f.* (Mex.) slight, discourtesy.
descolar, *va.* (*ind.* DESCUELO; *subj.* DESCUELE) to dock or crop the tail of; to cut off the fag end of (a piece of cloth); (carp.) to unglue; (Mex.) to ignore, slight; (C. A.) to dismiss, "to fire."
descolchar, *va.* (naut.) to untwist (a cable).
descolgar. I. *va.* (*ind. pres.* DESCUELGO, *pret.* DESCOLGUÉ; *subj.* DESCUELGUE) to take down; to let down. **II.** *vr.* to come down gently, to slip down (by a rope, etc.); to descend; (**con**) to make an unexpected remark or sally; to come on suddenly (as a cold snap).
descoligado, da, *a.* not belonging to a league, non-union.
descolmar, *va.* to strike off, level off (the heaping corn in a measure); to diminish.
descolmillar, *va.* to pull out or break the fangs or eyeteeth of.
descolorado, da. I. *pp.* of DESCOLORAR. **II.** *a.* discolored; pale, colorless, faded.
descoloramiento, *m.* discoloration; decolorizing, bleaching; fading.
descolorante. I. *a.* discoloring. **II.** *m.* bleacher, bleach.
descolorar. I. *va.* to discolor; to decolorize, bleach; to cause to fade. **II.** *vr.* to discolor; to bleach, lose color, become colorless; to fade.
descolorido, da. I. *pp.* of DESCOLORIR. **II.** *a.* discolored; pale, colorless, faded.
descolorimiento, *m.* = DESCOLORAMIENTO.
descolorir, *va.* & *vr.* = DESCOLORAR.
descolladamente, *adv.* loftily, haughtily.
descollamiento, *m.* = DESCUELLO, excessive height; superiority; haughtiness.
descollante, *a.* outstanding, prominent, conspicuous; main, principal.
descollar, *vn.* & *vr.* (*ind.* DESCUELLO; *subj.* DESCUELLE) to tower, stand out, be prominent or conspicuous, excel.
descombrar, *va.* to disencumber, to clear of obstacles, débris, etc.
descombro, *m.* disencumbering.
descomedido, da. I. *pp.* of DESCOMEDIRSE. **II.** *a.* excessive, disproportionate, immoderate; rude, impolite, disobliging.
descomedimiento, *m.* rudeness, incivility.
descomedirse, *vr.* (*ger.* DESCOMIDIENDO; *ind. pres.* DESCOMIDO, *pret.* DESCOMIDIÓ; *subj.* DESCOMIDA) to forget oneself; to be rude or disrespectful.
descomer, *vn.* (coll.) to evacuate (bowels).
descomidió, descomido, etc., v. *V.* DESCOMEDIRSE.
descomodidad, *f.* inconvenience, discomfort.
descompadrar. I. *va.* (coll.) to cause estrangement of. **II.** *vn.* (coll.) to disagree, to fall out.
descompaginar, *va.* to disarrange, upset.
descompás, *m.* excess, redundancy, want of measure or proportion.
descompasado, da. I. *pp.* of DESCOMPASARSE. **II.** *a.* excessive, extravagant, disproportionate; out of tune or time.
descompasarse, *vr.* to exceed all rule and measure; to be out of tune or time; forget oneself.
descomponer. I. *va.* (*pp.* DESCOMPUESTO; *ind. pres.* DESCOMPONGO, *pret.* DESCOMPUSE; *subj.* DESCOMPONGA) to disarrange, upset, disturb; to disable; to put out of order; to destroy the harmony of, set at odds; (chem.) to decompose; (mech.) to resolve (forces). **II.** *vr.* to decompose, spoil, rot; to get out of order; (Am.) to dislocate (arm, etc.); to lose one's looks (through illness); to forget oneself, lose one's temper; to change for the worse.
descompongo, descomponga, *v. V.* DESCOMPONER.
descomposición, *f.* discomposure, disagreement; disarrangement; disorder, confusion; decomposition, putrefaction, rotting; (chem.) decomposition, separation of elements; (mech.) resolution (of forces).
descompostura, *f.* disarrangement; disadjustment; slovenliness, uncleanliness, untidiness; forwardness, want of modesty; disrespectful conduct, impudence.
descompresión, *f.* decompression.
descompuesto, ta. I. *pp. irreg.* of DESCOMPONER. **II.** *a.* impudent, insolent; out of temper; immodest; out of order.
descompuse, *pret.* of DESCOMPONER.
descomulgado, da. I. *pp.* of DESCOMULGAR. **II.** *a.* perverse, nefarious, wicked.
descomulgar, *va.* (*pret.* DESCOMULGUÉ; *subj.* DESCOMULGUE) to excommunicate.
descomunal, *a.* extraordinary, monstrous, enormous, huge, colossal.—**descomunalmente,** *asv.* immensely, enormously, extraordinarily.
desconceptuar, *va.* & *vr.* to discredit.
desconcertadamente, *adv.* disorderly, confusedly, disconcertedly.
desconcertado, da. I. *pp.* of DESCONCERTAR. **II.** *a.* disconcerted; disorderly, slovenly.

desconcertador, ra, *n.* disturber, disconcerter.
desconcertadura, *f.* disturbance; confusion.
desconcertante, *a.* disconcerting, baffling.
desconcertar. I. *va.* (*ind.* DESCONCIERTO; *subj.* DESCONCIERTE) to disarrange, disturb, confuse; to disconcert, thwart, baffle; to disjoint, dislocate. **II.** *vr.* to disagree; to act or speak thoughtlessly or recklessly; to become disarranged; (of bones) to be or to become dislocated.
[1]**desconcierto,** *m.* disconcert, disagreement; disorder, confusion; disarrangement (as of machinery); want of prudence and circumspection; maladministration, mismanagement; flux or looseness of the body.
[2]**desconcierto, desconcierte,** *v. V.* DESCONCERTAR.
desconcordia, *f.* discord, disarrangement, disunion.
desconchabar, *va.* (Am.) to disarrange, upset.
desconchar. I. *va.* to strip off a surface (varnish, stucco, plaster, etc.). **II.** *vr.* to peel off, scale off.
desconectación, *f.* disconnection.
desconectar. I. *va.* to disconnect. **II.** *vr.* to become disconnected.
desconexión, *f.* (elec.) disconnection.
desconfiado, da. I. *pp.* of DESCONFIAR. **II.** *a.* diffident, distrustful; mistrustful, jealous.
desconfianza, *f.* diffidence; distrust; jealousy, suspicious fear.
desconfiar, *vn.* (de) to mistrust, be distrustful (of); to have no confidence (in); to suspect, doubt; to have little hope (of).
desconformar. I. *vn.* to dissent, disagree, differ in opinion. **II.** *vr.* to disagree; not to fit or suit each other.
desconforme, *a.* discordant, disagreeing, contrary.
desconformidad, *f.* disagreement, opposition, nonconformity; inequality, disparity.
descongelación, *f.* thawing, melting.
descongelador, *m.* deicer; thawer, defroster.
descongelar, *va.* (aer.) to deice; to thaw, melt, defrost.
descongestión, *f.* relieving of congestion.
descongestionar, *va.* to relieve the congestion of.
desconocer, *va.* (*ind.* DESCONOZCO; *subj.* DESCONOZCA) to fail to recognise; to disregard, ignore; to forget; to deny, disown, disavow; to be unacquainted with; to be ungrateful for.
desconocidamente, *adv.* ignorantly, unknowingly; ungratefully.
desconocido, da. I. *pp.* of DESCONOCER. **II.** *a.* ungrateful, unthankful; unknown. **III.** *n.* unknown person, stranger.
desconocimiento, *m.* ungratefulness, ingratitude; ignorance; disregard.
desconozco, desconozca, *v. V.* DESCONOCER.
desconsentir, *va.* (*ind.* DESCONSIENTO; *subj.* DESCONSIENTA) not to acquiesce in, to disapprove.
desconsideración, *f.* inconsiderateness.
desconsiderado, da, *a.* inconsiderate; imprudent, thoughtless, rash.
desconsiento, desconsienta, *v. V.* DESCONSENTIR.
desconsolación, *f.* disconsolateness, grief.
desconsolado, da. I. *pp.* of DESCONSOLAR. **II.** *a.* disconsolate, grief-stricken, dejected, downhearted.
desconsolador, ra, *a.* discouraging; lamentable.
desconsolar. I. *va.* (*ind.* DESCONSUELO; *subj.* DESCONSUELE) to afflict; to treat rudely. **II.** *vr.* to lose one's cheerfulness; to become low-spirited or afflicted.
[1]**desconsuelo,** *m.* affliction, disconsolateness; disorder in the stomach.
[2]**desconsuelo, desconsuele,** *v. V.* DESCONSOLAR.
descontable, *a.* (com.) discountable.
descontagiar, *va.* to purify, disinfect.
descontaminación, *f.* decontamination.
descontaminar, *va.* to decontaminate.
descontar. I. *va.* (*ind.* DESCUENTO; *subj.* DESCUENTE) to discount, deduct, allow, take off; to abate, lessen, diminish; to detract from the merit of; to take for granted. **II.** *vr.* to miscount.
descontentadizo, za, *a.* fastidious, hard to please, overparticular; easily displeased, squeamish.
descontentamiento, *m.* discontentment, displeasure; grief.
descontentar, *va.* to dissatisfy, displease.
descontento, ta. I. *a.* discontented, dissatisfied, displeased; uneasy. **II.** *m.* discontent; uneasiness, dissatisfaction.
descontinuación, *f.* discontinuance, cessation.
descontinuar, *va.* to discontinue, leave off, cease.
descontinuo, nua, *a.* disjoined, discontinued; discontinuous.
desconvengo, desconvenga, *v. V.* DESCONVENIR.
desconvenible, *a.* discordant, disparate, opposed.
desconveniencia, *f.* inconvenience, disadvantage.
desconveniente, *a.* inconvenient; discordant, incongruous.
desconvenir, *vn.* (*ind. pres.* DESCONVENGO, *pret.* DESCONVINE; *subj.* DESCONVENGA) to disagree; to be unlike or dissimilar; not to suit, match, or mate.
desconversable, *a.* unsociable, retiring.
desconvidar, *va.* to recall, take back (as an invitation or a promise).
desconvine, *pret.* of DESCONVENIR.
descopar, *va.* to lop off the top of (a tree).
descoqué, descoque, *v. V.* DESCOCAR.
descorazonadamente, *adv.* dejectedly, spiritlessly, with dismay.
descorazonamiento, *m.* low spirits, depression, dejection.
descorazonar, *va.* to tear out the heart of; to dishearten, discourage.
descorchador, *m.* uncorker, cork drawer.
descorchar, *va.* to bark (a cork tree); to uncork; to break (a beehive) to steal the honey; to break open.
descordar, *va.* to unstring (an instrument).
descorderar, *va.* to wean (lambs).
descornar. I. *va.* (*ind.* DESCUERNO; *subj.* DESCUERNE) to dehorn, to knock off the horns of. **II.** *vr.* to break one's skull by a fall.
descorrear, *vn.* & *vr.* to loosen the skin that covers the new horns of a deer.
descorrer. I. *va.* to run back over (the same ground); to draw (as a curtain); to draw (a bolt, unbolt a door, etc.). **II.** *vn.* to flow.
descorrimiento, *m.* flow.
descortecé, descortece, *v. V.* DESCORTEZAR.
descortés, *a.* impolite, uncivil, discourteous.
descortesía, *f.* incivility, discourtesy.
descortezador, *m.* one who strips off the bark; decorticator.
descortezadura, *f.*, **descortezamiento,** *m.* decortication, excortication; bark taken off.
descortezar. I. *va.* (*pret.* DESCORTECÉ; *subj.* DESCORTECE) to bark, peel; take off the crust of; to hull, shell (as fruits); to rough-hew; to polish or civilize. **II.** *vr.* (coll.) (of a person) to become polished.
descortinar, *va.* (fort.) to demolish or destroy (a curtain).
descosedura, *f.* ripping, unseaming.
descoser. I. *va.* to rip, unstitch; to separate, disjoin; (naut.) to unlash.—**no d. los labios,** to keep a profound silence. **II.** *vr.* to loose one's tongue.
descosidamente, *adv.* immoderately.
descosido, da. I. *pp.* of DESCOSER. **II.** *a.* ripped, unstitched; disjointed, disconnected; deranged. **III.** *n.* babbler, teller of secrets.—**comer** or

beber como un d., to eat or drink immoderately.
descostarse, *vr.* to draw away from an object or a coast.
descostillar. I. *va.* to strike or hit in the ribs; to take out the ribs of; to break the ribs of. **II.** *vr.* to fall flat on the ground.
descostrar, *va.* to take off the crust of.
descotar, *va.* to remove a restriction from.
descotarse, *vr.* to wear a low-neck dress.
descote, *m.* being décolleté, wearing of a low-neck dress.
descoyuntamiento, *m.* dislocation (of a joint); pain or tiredness from overexertion.
descoyuntar. I. *va.* to dislocate or disjoint; to vex, displease; to upset, disarrange. **II.** *vr.* to become disjointed, get out of joint.—**d. de risa,** to split one's sides with laughter.
descoyunto, *m.* = DESCOYUNTAMIENTO.
descrecencia, *f.* decrement, decreasing.
descrecer, *va.* & *vn.* (*ind.* DESCREZCO; *subj.* DESCREZCA) to decrease, diminish; to fall, to subside (tides and rivers); to grow short (days).
descrecimiento, *m.* decrease, diminution.
descrédito, *m.* discredit, loss of reputation.
descreer, *va.* to disbelieve; to deny due credit to; to disown or abjure.
descreídamente, *adv.* incredulously.
descreído, da. I. *pp.* of DESCREER. **II.** *n.* & *a.* unbeliever(-ing); infidel.
descreimiento, *m.* unbelief, lack of faith.
descrestar, *va.* to take off the crest or comb of; (Am., coll.) to impose upon; to swindle.
descrezco, descrezca, *v.* *V.* DESCRECER.
descriarse, *vr.* to weaken; to pine with desire or anxiety.
describir, *va.* (*pp.* DESCRITO) to describe; to sketch, delineate; to relate minutely.
descripción, *f.* description; sketch, delineation; (law) inventory, schedule
descriptible, *a.* describable.
descriptivo, va, *a.* descriptive.
descriptor, ra, *n.* & *a.* describer(-ing).
descrismar. I. *va.* (eccl.) to remove the chrism from; (coll.) to hit on the head. **II.** *vr.* (coll.) to lose patience, to lose one's temper.
descristianar, *va.* = DESCRISMAR.
descristianizar, *va.* to dechristianize.
descrito, ta, *pp. irreg.* of DESCRIBIR; described.
descruzar, *va.* (*pret.* DESCRUCÉ; *subj.* DESCRUCE) to uncross.
descuadernar. I. *va.* to unbind (books); to disarrange, disconcert, disorder. **II.** *vr.* to get disjointed, loose.
descuadrillado, da. I. *pp.* of DESCUADRILLARSE. **II.** *a.* separated from the rank or lines. **III.** *m.* (vet.) sprain in the haunch.
descuadrillarse, *vr.* to sprain the haunches.
descuajar, *va.* to dissolve, liquefy; to eradicate, to grub; to extirpate, uproot; to dishearten.
descuajaringarse, *vr.* (coll.) to be broken down by excessive fatigue; to fall to pieces.
descuaje, descuajo, *m.* (agr.) grubbing up weeds; clearing ground of underbrush.
descuarticé, descuartice, *v.* *V.* DESCUARTIZAR.
descuartizamiento, *m.* quartering; breaking or cutting in pieces; carving.
descuartizar, *va.* (*pret.* DESCUARTICÉ; *subj.* DESCUARTICE) to quarter; to carve.
descubierta, *f.* pie without an upper crust; (mil.) reconnoitering; (naut.) scanning of the horizon at sunrise and sunset.—**a la d.,** openly, in the open.
descubiertamente, *adv.* manifestly, openly.
descubierto, ta. I. *pp.* of DESCUBRIR. **II.** *a.* patent, manifest, exposed, unveiled; bareheaded. **III.** *m.* solemn exposition of the sacrament; shortage, deficiency, overdraft.—**al d.,** openly, manifestly.—**en d.,** (com.) uncovered; overdrawn; owing a balance.—**estar, quedar, en d.,** (com.) to owe a balance; to have overdrawn a bank account. **IV.** *f.* DESTAPADA, open pie.
descubridero, *m.* eminence commanding an extensive view; lookout.
descubridor, ra, *n.* discoverer; finder, descrier; (mil.) scout, spy; vessel on a voyage of discovery.
descubrimiento, *m.* discovery; find; disclosure; country or thing discovered.
descubrir. I. *va.* (*pp.* DESCUBIERTO) to discover; disclose, show, bring to light; to uncover, make visible, expose to view, lay open; to reveal, communicate, make known; (eccl.) to expose (the sacrament); (mil.) to reconnoiter; to overlook.—**d. la tierra,** (naut.) to make the land.—**d. por la popa** or **por la proa,** (naut.) to descry astern or ahead. **II.** *vr.* to take off one's hat.
descuelgo, descuelgue, *v.* *V.* DESCOLGAR.
descuelo, descuele, *v.* *V.* DESCOLAR.
[1]**descuello, descuelle,** *v.* *V.* DESCOLLAR.
[2]**descuello,** *m.* excessive height or tallness; prominence, superiority; loftiness, haughtiness.
[1]**descuento,** *m.* discount; deduction, rebate, allowance; diminution, decrease.
[2]**descuento, descuente,** *v.* *V.* DESCONTAR.
descuernacabras, *m.* cold north wind.
[1]**descuerno,** *m.* (coll.) slight, affront.
[2]**descuerno, descuerne,** *v.* *V.* DESCORNAR.
descuezo, descueza, *v.* *V.* DESCOCER.
descuida, *imper.* of DESCUIDAR. don't worry.
descuidado, da. I. *pp.* of DESCUIDAR. **II.** *a.* careless, negligent or thoughtless; unprepared, unaware; slovenly, unclean.
descuidar. I. *va.* to neglect, forget, overlook; to relieve from care; to divert the attention of. **II.** *vn.* to lack attention or diligence; to be careless or neglectful; to take one's ease; not to trouble oneself. **III.** *vr.* to be forgetful of duty, to become negligent.—**descuido,** *m.* carelessness, indolence, negligence, forgetfulness, absentmindedness; oversight, slip; lack of attention; incivility, coldness; improper or disgraceful action; imprudence; immodesty.—**al d.,** unobserved, on the sly; carelessly; (Am.) when least expected.—**al d.,** or **al d. y con cuidado,** with studied carelessness or naturalness.
descuitado, da, *a.* living without trouble or care.
descular, *va.* to break the bottom of (as of a jar).
deschuponar, *va.* (agr.) to strip (a tree) of its shoots or suckers.
desde, *prep.* since, from, after.—**d. ahora,** from now on.—**d. el punto de vista de,** from the point of view of.—**d. entonces,** since then, ever since.—**d. luego,** immediately, whereupon; doubtless, of course.—**d. niño,** from a child, ever since one's childhood.—**d. que,** since, ever since.
desdecir. I. *vn.* (*ger.* DESDICIENDO; *pp.* DESDICHO; *ind. pres.* DESDIGO, *pret.* DESDIJE, *fut.* DESDIRÉ; *subj.* DESDIGA) **(de)** to degenerate; to differ (from), disagree (with); to be unworthy (of) or unbecoming (to); to detract (from), to impair. **II.** *vr.* to retract, recant.
desdén, *m.* disdain, slight, scorn, contempt.—**al d.,** affectedly careless.
desdentado, da. I. *pp.* of DESDENTAR. **II.** *a.* toothless. **III.** *m. pl.* (zool.) edentates.
desdentar, *va.* (*ind.* DESDIENTO; *subj.* DESDIENTE) to draw teeth from.
desdeñable, *a.* contemptible, despicable.
desdeñadamente, *adv.* disdainfully, scornfully.
desdeñador, ra, *n.* & *a.* scorner(-ing), disdainer (-ing, -ful).
desdeñar. I. *va.* to disdain, scorn. **II.** *vr.* **(de)** to be disdainful (of); to loathe.
desdeñoso, sa, *a.* disdainful, contemptuous.
desdevanar, *va.* to unwind or unravel (a clue).
desdi, *pret.* of DESDAR.
desdibujado, da, *a.* (art) badly drawn.
desdibujo, *m.* faulty drawing.
desdicha, *f.* misfortune, ill-luck, misery.
desdichadamente, *adv.* unfortunately, unhappily.

desdichado, da. **I.** *a.* unfortunate; unhappy, unlucky, wretched. **II.** *n.* wretch, unfortunate one; good-for-nothing, insignificant person.
desdicho, *pp. irreg.* of DESDECIR.
desdiento, desdiente, *v. V.* DESDENTAR.
desdigo, desdiga, desdije, etc. *v. V.* DESDECIR.
desdinerar, *va.* to impoverish.
desdoblar, *va.* to unfold, to spread open.
desdorar. **I.** *va.* to take the gilding from; (fig.) to tarnish, slur, smear (reputation, etc.). **II.** *vr.* to lose its gilding; (fig.) to become tarnished or smeared (reputation, etc.).
desdoro, *m.* dishonor, stigma, shame.
desdoroso, sa, *a.* disreputable.
desdoy, *1st pers. pres. ind.* of DESDAR.
deseable, *a.* desirable.
deseablemente, *adv.* desirably.
deseador, ra, *n.* desirer, wisher.
desear, *va.* to desire, wish.
desecación, *f.* desiccation, exsiccation.
desecado, da, *a.* dry, desiccated.
desecador, *m.* drying room; dryer.
desecamiento, *m.* desiccation.
desecante, *a.* & *n.* dryer(-ing), desiccant, desiccative.
desecar, *va.* (*pret.* DESEQUÉ; *subj.* DESEQUE) to dry; to desiccate; to drain, to draw.
desecativo, va. **I.** *a.* desiccative, exsiccant. **II.** *m.* healing plaster.
desechable, *a.* disposable (as *d. Kleenex*).
desechadamente, *adv.* vilely, despicably.
desechar, *va.* to reject; to exclude; to depreciate, undervalue; decline, refuse; to put or lay aside; dispose of, throw away; cast off; to vote down.
desecho, *m.* residue, surplus, remainder; débris, rubbish, refuse, offal; rejection; disregard, contempt.—**de d.,** cast off, discarded; scrap (iron, etc.).
desedificación, *f.* scandal, bad example.
desedificar, *va.* (*pret.* DESEDIFIQUÉ; *subj.* DESEDIFIQUE) to set a bad example to; to be an evil influence on.
desegregación, *f.* desegregation.
desegregar, *va.* to desegregate.
deselectrización, *f.* diselectrification.
deselectrizar, *va.* to diselectrify.
desellar, *va.* to unseal, to take off the seals of.
desembalaje, *m.* unpacking, opening of bales.
desembalar, *va.* to unpack, open.
desembaldosar, *va.* to untile, take the tiles from.
desembanastar. **I.** *va.* to take out of a basket; (coll.) to draw (the sword). **II.** *vn.* to talk much and without sense. **III.** *vr.* to break out or break loose; (coll.) to alight from a carriage.
desembaracé, desembarace, *v. V.* DESEMBARAZAR.
desembarazado, da, *a.* free, disengaged; clear, open; unrestrained, unencumbered.
desembarazar. **I.** *va.* (*pret.* DESEMBARACÉ; *subj.* DESEMBARACE) to disembarrass, free, ease; to remove an impediment or encumbrance from; to clear; to unburden, disencumber, expedite. **II.** *vr.* to rid oneself of difficulties or hindrances.
desembarazo, *m.* disembarrassment, disencumbrance; disengagement; freedom, lack of restraint or hindrances; ease, naturalness.
desembarcadero, *m.* landing place; wharf, pier.
desembarcar. **I.** *va.* (*pret.* DESEMBARQUÉ; *subj.* DESEMBARQUE) to unload, put ashore, debark. **II.** *vn.* to land, disembark, go ashore; (coll.) to alight (from a vehicle); (coll.) to be delivered of a child; to end (as a staircase).
desembarco, *m.* landing, disembarkation, unloading; landing place at the top of stairs.
desembargador, *m.* chief magistrate and privy councillor in Portugal.
desembargar, *va.* (*pret.* DESEMBARGUÉ; *subj.* DESEMBARGUE) to remove impediments from; (law) to disembargo, raise an embargo.
desembargo, *m.* (law) raising of an embargo.
desembarque, *m.* landing or debarkation; unloading.
desembarqué, desembarque, *v. V.* DESEMBARCAR.
desembarrancar, *va.* (*pret.* DESEMBARRANQUÉ; *subj.* DESEMBARRANQUE) to extricate.
desembarrar, *va.* to clear of mud.
desembaular, *va.* to take out of a trunk; to empty; (coll.) to speak (one's mind) freely; to disclose (one's thoughts).
desembebecerse, *vr.* (*ind.* DESEMBEBEZCO; *subj.* DESEMBEBEZCA) to recover one's senses, to come to.
desembelesarse, *vr.* to recover from amazement or abstraction.
desembocadero, *m.*, **desembocadura,** *f.* exit, outlet; mouth (of a river, canal, etc.).
desembocar, *vn.* (*pret.* DESEMBOQUÉ; *subj.* DESEMBOQUE) **(en)** to flow (into); to end (at), lead (to).
desembocé, desemboce, *v. V.* DESEMBOZAR.
desembojadera, *f.* woman who takes the cocoons of silkworms from the southern-wood.
desembojar, *va.* to remove (silk-cocoons) from the southern-wood.
desembolsable, *a.* disbursable.
desembolsar, *va.* to empty from a purse; to pay out, disburse.
desembolso, *m.* disbursement, expenditure.
desemboque, *m.* = DESEMBOCADERO.
desemboqué, desemboque, *v. V.* DESEMBOCAR.
desemborrachar. **I.** *va.* to sober, to make sober, to cure of intoxication. **II.** *vr.* to sober up, get over one's intoxication.
desemboscarse, *vr.* to get out of the woods; to get clear of an ambuscade.
desembotar, *va.* to remove dulness from (a cutting edge); to sharpen (as wits).
desembozar, *va.* & *vr.* (*pret.* DESEMBOCÉ; *subj.* DESEMBOCE) to unmuffle or uncover; to unmask, show oneself in one's true colors (or others in theirs).
desembozo, *m.* uncovering the face.
desembracé, desembrace, *v. V.* DESEMBRAZAR.
desembragar, *va.* (*pret.* DESEMBRAGUÉ; *subj.* DESEMBRAGUE) to unbind from the cable; (mech.) to ungear, disengage, disconnect.
desembravecer, *va.* (*ind.* DESEMBRAVEZCO; *subj.* DESEMBRAVEZCA) to tame, domesticate; to calm, pacify.
desembravecimiento, *m.* taming or reclaiming from wildness.
desembrazar, *va.* (*pret.* DESEMBRACÉ; *subj.* DESEMBRACE) to take (something) off the arms; to dart or throw (weapons); to throw from the arms.
desembriagar. **I.** *va.* (*pret.* DESEMBRIAGUÉ; *subj.* DESEMBRIAGUE) to sober, to cure from intoxication. **II.** *vr.* to become sober, recover from drunkenness.
desembridar, *va.* to unbridle.
desembrollar, *va.* to unravel, disentangle, clear, extricate.
desembrozar, *va.* to clear of rubbish.
desembuchar, *va.* to disgorge, to turn out of the maw (birds); (coll.) to tell all.
desemejante, *a.* dissimilar, unlike.
desemejanza, *f.* unlikeness, dissimilarity.
desemejar. **I.** *vn.* to be dissimilar or unlike. **II.** *va.* = DESFIGURAR, to disfigure.
desempacar. **I.** *va.* (*pret.* DESEMPAQUÉ; *subj.* DESEMPAQUE) to unpack. **II.** *vr.* (coll.) to calm down, cool off.
desempachar. **I.** *va.* to make (the stomach) discharge undigested food. **II.** *vr.* (coll.) to grow bold, lose all bashfulness.
desempacho, *m.* ease; forwardness, unconcern.
desempalagar. **I.** *va.* & *vr.* (*pret.* DESEMPALAGUÉ; *subj.* DESEMPALAGUE) to remove nausea or loathing (from); to restore the appetite (to). **II.** *va.* to clear (a mill) of stagnant water.
desempañar, *va.* to clean (a glass); to take off the swaddling clothes from (children).
desempapelar, *va.* to unwrap, take out of a pack-

age: to take (hangings) off a wall, to take off the paper from.
desempaque, *m.* act of unpacking.
desempaqué, desempaque, *v. V.* DESEMPACAR.
desempaquetar, *va.* to unpack.
desemparejar, *va.* to unmatch, make unequal or uneven.
desemparentado, da, *a.* without relatives.
desempastado, da, *a.* (Am.) (of books) unbound.
desempastar, *va.* (Am.) to take the cover off (a book); to take the filling out of (a tooth).
desempastelar, *va.* (Am.) (print.) to distribute (mixed letters).
desempatar, *va.* to disjoint, disunite; to make unequal or uneven; to decide (a tie vote); to run, play, or shoot off a tie.
desempedrar, *va.* (*ind.* DESEMPIEDRO; *subj.* DESEMPIEDRE) to remove paving.—**ir desempedrando la calle,** (coll.) to go very rapidly.
desempegar, *va.* (*pret.* DESEMPEGUÉ; *subj.* DESEMPEGUE) to unglue; to take the pitch off.
desempeñado, da. I. *pp.* of DESEMPEÑAR. II. *a.* free or clear of debt.
desempeñar. I. *va.* to redeem, to recover (what was pledged), to take out of pawn; to clear or extricate from debt; to perform, discharge (a duty); to play (a part); to fill (an office, a function); to transact; to accomplish, carry out (an undertaking); to act (a part in a play); to acquit, free from an obligation; to disengage from a difficulty. II. *vr.* to extricate oneself from debt; in bull fighting, to disengage oneself from the attack of a bull.—**desempeñarse de la tierra,** or **costa,** (naut.) to claw off, to stand off shore.
desempeño, *m.* the act of redeeming a pledge; performance of an obligation or promise; fulfilment, discharge; acting of a part.
desempeorarse, *vr.* to recover from sickness, to regain health.
desemperezar, *vn.* & *vr.* (*pret.* DESEMPERECÉ; *subj.* DESEMPERECE) to relinquish habits of laziness and indolence; to shake off laziness.
desempernar, *va.* to unbolt, take out bolts.
desempiedro, desempiedre, *v. V.* DESEMPEDRAR.
desempleado, da, *n.* & *a.* unemployed.
desempleo, *m.* unemployment.
desemplomar, *va.* to remove the leaden seal from.
desemplumar, *va.* to pluck (a bird).
desempobrecer. I. *va.* (*ind.* DESEMPOBREZCO; *subj.* DESEMPOBREZCA) to relieve from poverty. II. *vr.* to extricate oneself from poverty.
desempolvar, *va.* to remove dust or powder from, to dust.
desempolvoradura, *f.* dusting.
desempolvorar, *va.* to dust.
desemponzoñar, *va.* to heal from the effects of poison; to free from poison.
desempotrar, *va.* to remove the support of; to take out.
desenalbardar, *va.* to take a packsaddle off (an animal).
desenamorar. I. *va.* to destroy the love or affection of. II. *vr.* to lose love or affection.
desenastar, *va.* to remove the handle or haft from.
desencabalgar, *va.* (*pret.* DESENCABALGUÉ; *subj.* DESEMCABALGUE) (mil.) to dismount (cannon).
desencabestrar, *va.* to disentangle the feet (of an animal) from the halter.
desencadenamiento, *m.* unchaining.
desencadenar. I. *va.* to unchain; to free, liberate. II. *vr.* to break loose, free oneself from chains; to become infuriated, lose one's self-control; (of a storm) to break out with fury; (of rain) to come down in torrents.
desencajamiento, *m.* = DESENCAJE.
desencajar. I. *va.* to disjoint, unjoin, disconnect, throw out of gear; to disarticulate; to dislocate. II. *vr.* to become rickety; to get disjointed, disconnected, out of gear.
desencaje, *m.* disjointedness; broken-down appearance; rickety appearance.
desencajonar, *va.* to unpack, take out of a box.
desencalabrinar, *va.* to remove dizziness from; to free from stupidity; to remove wrong impressions from.
desencalcar, *va.* (*pret.* DESENCALQUÉ; *subj.* DESENCALQUE) to loosen or dissolve (what was caked or close pressed).
desencallar, *va.* (naut.) to set (a stranded ship) afloat again.
desencaminar, *va.* to mislead, lead astray.
desencantamiento, *m.* = DESENCANTO.
desencantar, *va* to disenchant; disillusion.
desencantaración, *f.* act and effect of drawing lots or of balloting.
desencantarar, *va.* to draw (lots) for candidates out of a CÁNTARO; to withdraw (a name).
desencanto, *m.* disenchantment, disillusion.
desencapillar, *va.* (naut.) to unrig, to take off the rigging of.
desencapotar. I. *va.* to strip (one) of his cloak or greatcoat; (coll.) to uncover, to make manifest; to raise and keep up the head of (a horse). II. *vr.* (of the sky) to clear up; to put away anger, to smooth one's brow, put on a pleasing countenance.
desencaprichar. I. *va.* to dissuade from error or prejudice; to disabuse, to cure of conceit. II. *vr.* to desist, yield, get over a whim, give up a hobby or mania.
desencarcelar, *va.* to set free (from prison).
desencarecer, *va.* (*ind.* DESENCAREZCO; *subj.* DESENCAREZCA) to reduce, to lower the price of.
desencarnar, *va.* to prevent (dogs) from eating game; to lose affection, liking for; to divert the mind from.
desencastillar, *va.* to expel or drive out of a castle; to manifest, make appear, reveal.
desencepar, *va.* (naut.) to clear (the anchor).
desencerrar, *va.* (*ind.* DESENCIERRO; *subj.* DESENCIERRE) to free from confinement; to open; to disclose, make known.
desencintar, *va.* to remove ribbons from (a person or thing); to remove the curb of (a sidewalk).
desenclavar, *va.* to draw out nails from; to put (one) violently out of one's place.
desenclavijar, *va.* to unpeg, take the pegs or pins from.
desencoger. I. *va.* (*ind.* DESENCOJO; *subj.* DESENCOJA) to unfold, to spread open. II. *vr.* to lay aside bashfulness or reserve, to grow bold.
desencogimiento, *m.* ease, naturalness.
desencojo, desencoja, *v. V.* DESENCOGER.
desencoladura, *f.* act or effect of ungluing.
desencolar, *va.* to unglue, to unsize.
desencolerizarse, *vr.* to grow calm, to cool off.
desenconar. I. *va.* to allay (an inflammation); to calm, appease; to make mild and benign. II. *vr.* to become milder; to be appeased, to quiet down, cool off.
desencono, *m.* mitigation of anger or passion.
desencordar, *va.* (*ind.* DESENCUERDO; *subj.* DESENCUERDE) to unstring (a musical instrument).
desencordelar, *va.* to loosen, untie or take off strings or cords from.
desencorvar, *va.* to straighten.
desencrespar, *va.* to uncurl, unfrizzle.
desencuadernar, *va.* to unbind, to take off the binding of (a book).
desencuerdo, desencuerde, *v. V.* DESENCORDAR.
desendemoniar, desendiablar, *va.* to drive an evil spirit out of.
desendiosar, *va.* to humble the vanity of.
desenfadadamente, *adv.* without embarrassment, boldly, unconcernedly.
desenfadaderas, *f. pl.*—**tener d.,** (coll.) to be resourceful.

desenfadado, da. I. *pp.* of DESENFADAR. **II.** *a.* unencumbered, free; ample, spacious; bold.
desenfadar. I. *va.* to appease, pacify. **II.** *vr.* to calm down, become calm, cool off.
desenfado, *m.* freedom, ease, naturalness; relaxation, diversion, entertainment.
desenfaldar, *va.* to let fall the train of (a gown).
desenfardar, desenfardelar, *va.* to unpack (bales of goods).
desenfilado, da. I. *a.* (mil.) under cover from fire. **II.** *f.* (fort.) defilading.
desenfilamiento, *m.* defilading.
desenfilar, *va.* to put under cover from flank fire; (fort.) to defilade.
desenfrailar, *vn.* to leave the monastic life, become secularized; (coll.) to come out from subjection; to rest from business for a time.
desenfrenado, da. I. *pp.* of DESENFRENAR. **II.** *a.* ungoverned, unbridled, wild, wanton.
desenfrenamiento, *m.* unruliness, rashness, wantonness, licentiousness, boundless liberty or license; libidinousness.
desenfrenar. I. *va.* to unbridle. **II.** *vr.* to give loose rein to one's passions and desires; to fly into a violent passion; to be mad or wild.
desenfreno, *m.* = DESENFRENAMIENTO.—**d. de vientre,** diarrhea.
desenfundar, *va.* to take out of a bag, bolster, pillowcase, sheath, etc.
desenfurecerse, *vr.* (*ind.* DESENFUREZCO; *subj.* DESENFUREZCA) to become calm or appeased.
desenganchar, *va.* to unhook, unclasp, unpin, unfasten; to uncouple; to disengage; to unhitch, unharness.
desengañadamente, *adv.* truly, clearly, ingenuously; awkwardly, carelessly, scurvily.
desengañado, da. I. *pp.* of DESENGAÑAR. **II.** *a.* disabused, disillusioned; schooled by experience; despicable; ill-executed.
desengañador, ra, *n.* undeceiver, disabuser.
desengañar. I. *va.* to undeceive, disabuse, set right. **II.** *vr.* to be disillusioned, not to fool oneself.
desengaño, *m.* detection or discovery of an error; undeceiving; disillusion, disappointment; censure, reproof, reproach, upbraiding.—*pl.* sad lessons of experience.
desengarrafar, *va.* to unfasten or disengage from claws or clenched fingers.
desengarzar, *va.* to take out of a setting; to loosen from clasps, links or hooks.
desengastar, *va.* to take out of its setting.
desengomar, *va.* to ungum; to unsize (silk).
desengoznar, *va.* to unhinge; to disjoint.
desengranar. I. *va.* to uncouple; to disengage. **II.** *vr.* to get out of gear.
desengrane, *m.* disengaging of gear.
desengrasar, *va.* to clean from grease; to scour.
desengrase, *m.* removal of grease; cleaning, scouring.
desengraso, *m.* (Chile) dessert.
desengrosar, *va.* (*ind.* DESENGRUESO; *subj.* DESENGRUESE) to extenuate, make lean, weaken; to make thin or fine.
desengrudar, *va.* to scrape or rub off paste from.
desengrueso, desengruese, *v. V.* DESENGROSAR.
desenhebrar, *va.* to unthread.
desenhornar, *va.* to take out of the oven.
desenjaezar, *va.* (*pret.* DESENJAECÉ; *subj.* DESENJAECE) to unharness; to unsaddle.
desenjalmar, *va.* to take off a packsaddle from.
desenjaular, *va.* to uncage; (coll.) to remove from or let out of jail.
desenlabonar, *va.* to unlink.
desenlace, *m.* denouement, winding up; conclusion, end.
desenlacé, desenlace, *v. V.* DESENLAZAR.
desenladrillar, *va.* to take off the tiles or bricks of.
desenlazar, *va.* (*pret.* DESENLACÉ; *subj.* DESENLACE) to unlace, untie, loose; to unravel (a dramatic plot).
desenlodar, *va.* to remove, clean off, mud from.
desenlosar, *va.* to take up the flagstones of; to remove paving from.
desenlutar, *va.* & *vr.* to take off mourning (from); to banish sorrow.
desenmallar, *va.* to take (fish) out of the net.
desenmarañar, *va.* to disentangle; to sleave (as a skein); straighten up; unravel, make clear.
desenmascarar, *va.* to unmask.
desenmohecer, *va.* (*ind.* DESENMOHEZCO; *subj.* DESENMOHEZCA) to clear of rust.
desenmudecer. I. *va.* (*ind.* DESENMUDEZCO; *subj.* DESENMUDEZCA) to remove an impediment of speech from. **II.** *vn.* & *vr.* to break a long silence.
desenojar. I. *va.* & *vr.* to appease, pacify, calm, allay the passion of. **II.** *vr.* to amuse oneself.
desenojo, *m.* appeasement, getting over anger.
desenredar. I. *va.* to disentangle; to unravel; to extricate, loose; to clear. **II.** *vr.* to extricate oneself from difficulties.
desenredo, *m.* disentanglement; denouement.
desenrollar, *va.* to unroll, unwind.
desenronar, *va.* to remove débris from.
desenroscar, *va.* (*pret.* DESENROSQUÉ; *subj.* DESENROSQUE) to untwine, untwist; to unscrew.
desensabanar, *va.* (coll.) to change or take off the sheets of.
desensamblar, *va.* to disjoint, separate.
desensañar, *va.* to appease, pacify.
desensartar, *va.* to unthread, unstring.
desensebar. I. *va.* to strip of fat. **II.** *vn.* to change occupation or exercise in order to render one's work more endurable; to draw breath; to take away the taste of fat (with an olive or sweets).
desenseñar, *va.* to correct faulty learning.
desensillar, *va.* to unsaddle.
desensoberbecer. I. *va.* (*ind.* DESENSOBERBEZCO; *subj.* DESENSOBERBEZCA) to humble. **II.** *vr.* to become humble, to control one's pride.
desensortijado, da, *a.* dislocated, displaced.
desentablar, *va.* to rip up or off planks or boards from; to disturb, disarrange, confuse; to embroil; to break off (a bargain); to estrange.
desentalingar, *va.* (naut.) to unbend (a cable).
desentarimar, *va.* to remove a platform or stand from.
desentenderse, *vr.* (*ind.* DESENTIENDO; *subj.* DESENTIENDA) (**de**) to feign not to understand; to ignore; to pay no attention (to); to shirk.
desentendido, da. I. *pp.* of DESENTENDERSE. **II.** *a.* unmindful, showing or feigning ignorance.—**hacerse el d.,** or **darse por d.,** (coll.) to wink at a thing; to pretend not to have noticed.
desenterrador, *m.* one that disinters or digs up.
desenterramiento, *m.* disinterment.
desenterrar, *va.* (*ind.* DESENTIERRO; *subj.* DESENTIERRE) to disinter, dig up, unearth; to recall (to the mind).
desentiendo, desentienda, *v. V.* DESENTENDERSE.
desentierramuertos, *m.* (coll.) calumniator or abuser of the dead.
desentierro, desentierre, *v. V.* DESENTERRAR.
desentoldar, *va.* to take off an awning from; to strip of ornaments.
desentonación, *f.* dissonance.
desentonadamente, *adv.* inharmoniously.
desentonado, da. I. *pp.* of DESENTONAR. **II.** *a.* out of tune; inharmonious, discordant.
desentonamiento, *m.* dissonance.
desentonar. I. *va.* to humble; to wound the pride of. **II.** *vn.* to be out of tune; to be inharmonious. **III.** *vr.* to be rude or uncouth; to raise the voice in disrespect.—**desentono,** *m.* harsh, rude tone of voice; musical discord; false note.
desentornillar, *va.* to unscrew.
desentorpecer. I. *va.* (*ind.* DESENTORPEZCO; *subj.* DESENTORPEZCA) to free from torpor; to restore motion to (torpid limbs). **II.** *vr.* to be freed from torpor; to be restored from numbness; to become lively, smart, or pert.
desentrampar, *va.* to free from debts.

desentrañamiento. *m.* giving away one's belongings as a proof of love.
desentrañar. I. *va.* to eviscerate, disembowel; to penetrate or dive into; to bring out, reveal, dig out; (naut.) to remove loops, twists, from (ropes). II. *vr.* to give away one's all out of love.
desentristecer, *va.* (*ind.* DESENTRISTEZCO; *subj.* DESENTRISTEZCA) to soothe the sadness of, to cheer, comfort.
desentronizar, *va.* (*pret.* DESENTRONICÉ; *subj.* DESENTRONICE) to dethrone; to deprive of power or authority.
desentumecer. I. *va.* (*ind.* DESENTUMEZCO; *subj.* DESENTUMEZCA) to free from torpor. II. *vr.* to be freed from numbness.
desentumir, *va.* & *vr.* = DESENTUMECER.
desenvainar, *va.* to unsheath (as a sword); (coll.) to expose, uncover; to show (the claws).
desenvelejar, *va.* (naut.) to strip of sails.
desenvendar, *va.* to take off fillets or bands from.
desenvenenar, *va.* to extract, remove poison from; to destroy the poison of, or in.
desenvergar, *va.* (*pret.* DESENVERGUÉ; *subj.* DESENVERGUE) (naut.) to unbend (a sail).
desenviolar, *va.* to bless or purify (a holy place which has been desecrated).
desenvoltura, *f.* sprightliness, ease; impudence, effrontery; lewd posture or gesture in women; graceful and easy delivery in conversation or acting.
desenvolvedor, ra, *n.* unfolder, investigator.
desenvolver. I. *va.* (*pp.* DESENVUELTO; *ind.* DESENVUELVO; *subj.* DESENVUELVA) to unfold, unroll; unwrap; to decipher, discover, unravel; to develop (as a theme); to evolve. II. *vr.* to be forward, to behave with too much assurance; to unfold, unroll.
desenvolvimiento, *m.* unfolding, development.
desenvueltamente, *adv.* in a free and easy manner; expeditiously.
desenvuelto, ta. I. *pp. irreg.* of DESENVOLVER. II. *a.* forward; free, easy.
desenvuelvo, desenvuelva, *v.* *V.* DESENVOLVER.
desenyesar. I. *va.* to remove plaster from. II. *vr.* (of a plastered surface) to scale off.
desenzarzar, *va.* & *vr.* to disentangle from brambles; to appease, reconcile.
deseo, *m.* desire, wish.—**tener d. de, venir en d. de,** to desire, be eager to.
deseoso, sa, *a.* desirous.
desequé, deseque, *v.* *V.* DESECAR.
desequido, da, *a.* dry.
desequilibrado, da. I. *pp.* of DESEQUILIBRAR. II. *a.* unbalanced, unpoised; of an unbalanced mind; reckless, thoughtless.
desequilibrar, *va.* to put out of balance.
desequilibrio, *m.* lack of equilibrium; an unbalanced condition; disorder, disturbance, confusion.
deserción, *f.* desertion; (law) abandonment of a suit by plaintiff.
deserrado, da, *a.* free from error.
desertar. I. *va.* to desert; to abandon. II. *vn.* (de) to desert (from).—**d. a,** to go over to.
desertor, ra, *n.* deserter; forsaker.
deservicio, *m.* disservice; fault committed against a person who has a claim to services.
deservir, *va.* (*ger.* DESIRVIENDO; *ind. pres.* DESIRVO, *pret.* él DESIRVIÓ; *subj.* DESIRVA) not to perform one's duty to; to disserve.
desescamar, *va.* to scale; to remove scales from.
desescombrar, *va.* to clear of rubbish.
deseslabonar, *va.* to cut the links of; to unlink.
desespaldar, *va.* to wound in the shoulder.
desesperación, *f.* despondency, despair, desperation; anger, passion, fury.—**es una d.,** (coll.) it is unbearable.
desesperado, da. I. *pp.* of DESESPERAR. II. *a.* desperate, hopeless; furious, raving mad.
desesperancé, desesperance, *v.* *V.* DESESPERANZAR.
desesperante, *a.* causing despair, maddening; hopeless.
desesperanza, *f.* despair, hopelessness.
desesperanzado, da, *a.* despairing, hopeless, despondent, desponding.
desesperanzar. I. *va.* (*pret.* DESESPERANCÉ; *subj.* DESESPERANCE) to deprive of hope, to discourage. II. *vr.* to lose hope, to despair, become discouraged.
desesperar. I. *vn.* to lose hope, to despair. II. *va.* to make (one) despair, to discourage hope; (coll.) (fig.) to drive crazy. III. *vr.* to despair, to despond; to fret, to be grievously vexed.—**desespero,** *m.* (Am.) despair; vexation.
desestancar, *va.* (*pret.* DESESTANQUÉ; *subj.* DESESTANQUE) to take away (a monopoly) from; to declare open to trade, raise the monopoly on.
desestañar, *va.* & *vr.* to unsolder.
desesterar, *va.* to take up the matting (from floors).
desestero, *m.* act and season of taking up mats.
desestima, desestimación, *f.* disesteem, disrespect; crying down, rejection.
desestimar, *va.* to disesteem, undervalue; to reject, deny.
desfacedor, *m.* (obs.) destroyer.—**d. de entuertos,** undoer of injuries, righter of wrongs.
desfacer, *va.* (*pp.* DESFECHO; *ind. pres.* DESFAGO, *pret.* YO DESFICE, él DESFIZO, *fut.* DESFARÉ; *subj.* DESFAGA) (obs.) = DESHACER.—**d. agravios,** or **d. entuertos,** to right wrongs.
desfachatado, da, *a.* (coll.) impudent, saucy, "nervy," "cheeky," brazen.
desfachatez, *f.* (coll.) impudence, assurance, effrontery, barefacedness, "nerve," "cheek."
desfago, desfaga, *v.* *V.* DESFACER.
desfajar, *va.* to ungird.
desfalcador, ra, *n.* embezzler, defaulter.
desfalcar, *va.* (*pret.* DESFALQUÉ; *subj.* DESFALQUE) to take away part of; to cut off, to lop; to defalcate, embezzle.
desfalco, *m.* diminution, diminishing, detracting; defalcation, embezzlement, peculation.
desfalqué, desfalque, *v.* *V.* DESFALCAR.
desfallecer. I. *vn.* (*ind.* DESFALLEZCO; *subj.* DESFALLEZCA) to pine, to fall away; to grow weak; to swoon, faint. II. *va.* to weaken, debilitate.
desfalleciente, *a.* pining, languishing.
desfallecimiento, *m.* languor; dejection; swoon, fainting fit.
desfallezco, desfallezca, *v.* *V.* DESFALLECER.
desfavorable, *a.* unfavorable, contrary.
desfavorecer, *va.* (*ind.* DESFAVOREZCO; *subj.* DESFAVOREZCA) to disfavor, to discountenance; to despise, contemn; to injure, hurt; to contradict, oppose.
desfecho, *pp.* of DESFACER.
desfibrar, *va.* to rid of fibers; to extract the fiber from.
desfice, *pret.* of DESFACER.
desfiguración, *f.*, **desfiguramiento,** *m.* deformation, disfigurement.
desfigurado, da. I. *pp.* of DESFIGURAR. II. *a.* disfigured, deformed.
desfigurar. I. *va.* to disfigure, deform; misshape; to disguise (as the voice); to misrepresent, misstate, distort; to cloud, to darken. II. *vr.* to become disfigured.
desfijar, *va.* to take off, pull off, remove.
desfilachar, *va.* to ravel; to uncord.
desfilada, *f.* (mil.) single file.
desfiladero, *m.* defile, narrow passage; road at the side of a precipice.
desfilar, *vn.* (mil.) to defile, to march off by files, file off; to march in review, parade.
desfile, *m.* defiling, marching by files; parade.
desfizo, *pret.* of DESFACER.
desflecar, *va.* (*pret.* DESFLEQUÉ; *subj.* DESFLEQUE) to remove the flakes of (wool) or frettings of (cloth).
desflocar, *va.* (*ind. pres.* DESFLUECO, *pret.* DESFLOQUÉ; *subj.* DESFLUEQUE) = DESFLECAR.
desfloración, *f.* defloration.
desfloramiento, *m.* violation, ravishment.

desflorar, *va.* to tarnish; to ruffle, discompose; to violate, deflower; to treat superficially, touch upon.
desflorecer, *vn.* & *vr.* to lose the flowers.
desflorecimiento, *m.* falling of flowers.
desflueco, desflueque, *v. V.* DESFLOCAR.
desfogar. I. *va.* (*pret.* DESFOGUÉ; *subj.* DESFOGUE) to vent, to make an opening in for fire; to give loose rein to (a horse). **II.** *vr.* to vent one's anger.
desfogonar, *va.* to widen or burst the vent of (a cannon).
desfogue, *m.* venting or foaming out of passion.
desfogué, desfogue, *v. V.* DESFOGAR.
desfollonar, *va.* to strip useless leaves off.
desfondar, *va.* to break or take off the bottom of; (naut.) to penetrate the bottom of (a ship); (agr.) to cultivate or dig (the soil) to a great depth.
desformar, *va.* to disfigure, deform.
desfortalecer, *va.* (*ind.* DESFORTALEZCO; *subj.* DESFORTALEZCA) (mil.) to dismantle, to demolish.
desfrenar, *va.* to unbridle.
desfrutar, *va.* to take the green fruit off (a tree).
desgaire, *m.* graceless mien or deportment; slovenliness; affected carelessness in dress; contemptuous gesture.—**al d.,** affectedly careless; disdainfully.
desgajadura, *f.* disruption, tearing off the branch of a tree.
desgajar. I. *va.* to tear off the branches of; to break or tear off. **II.** *vr.* to be separated or disjointed; to be torn off; to fall off.
desgaje, *m.* act of breaking or tearing off.
desgalgadero, *m.* rugged steep place.
desgalgar, *va.* & *vr.* (*pret.* DESGALGUÉ; *subj.* DESGALGUE) to precipitate, to throw headlong.
desgalichado, da, *a.* (coll.) ungainly, ungraceful.
desgana, *f.* lack of appetite; unwillingness, reluctance.—**desganado, da,** having no appetite.
desganar. I. *va.* to discourage. **II.** *vr.* to lose one's appetite; to lose interest; to become reluctant or unwilling.
desganchar, *va.* to lop off the branches of.
desgano, *m.* = DESGANA.
desgañifarse, desgañitarse, *vr.* to shriek, to scream at the top of one's voice.
desgarbado, da, *a.* ungraceful, uncouth, ungainly, gawky.
desgargantarse, *vr.* (coll.) to get hoarse from bawling or screaming, to shout oneself hoarse.
desgargolar, *va.* to ripple (as flax or hemp); to take (a board) out of a groove.
desgaritar. I. *vn.* (naut.) to lose the course. **II.** *vr.* (of sheep) to go astray from a fold; to give up a plan or undertaking.
desgarradamente, *adv.* impudently, barefacedly, shamelessly.
desgarrado, da, *a.* licentious, dissolute; impudent, shameless, bold.
desgarrador, ra. I. *n.* tearer. **II.** *a.* tearing; heart-breaking, heart-rending.
desgarradura, *f.* rent, laceration, break.
desgarrar. I. *va.* to rend, tear; to claw; (Cuba) to expectorate, cough up (phlegm). **II.** *vr.* to withdraw from another's company; to tear oneself away.
desgarro, *m.* laceration, rent, break, breach; impudence, effrontery; looseness, criminal levity; idle boast, brag.
desgarrón, *m. aug.* large rent or role; piece of cloth torn off.
desgasificador, *m.* (chem.) deaerator.
desgastado, da. I. *pp.* of DESGASTAR. **II.** *a.* (U. S., coll.) beat-up, worn-out.
desgastar. I. *va.* to wear away, abrade, consume, waste by degrees; to corrode, gnaw, eat away. **II.** *vr.* to lose strength and vigor; to debilitate oneself; to wear down or away.
desgaste, *m.* slow waste; attrition, abrasion; wear and tear; erosion, fray.
desgausamiento, *m.* degaussing (method of protecting a ship in a minefield).
desgaznatarse, *vr.* = DESGAÑITARSE.
desglosar, *va.* to blot out marginal notes from; to take off; to separate sheets from (a book).
desglose, *m.* act of blotting out a comment or gloss.
desgobernado, da. I. *pp.* of DESGOBERNAR. **II.** *a.* ill-governed or ungovernable person.
desgobernar. I. *va.* (*ind.* DESGOBIERNO; *subj.* DESGOBIERNE) to disturb or upset the government of; to misgovern; to dislocate or disjoint (as bones); (vet.) to bar (a vein) on a horse's leg; (naut.) to neglect, not handle right. **II.** *vr.* to affect ridiculous motions in dancing.
[1]**desgobierno,** *m.* mismanagement; misrule; maladministration; (vet.) barring a vein on a horse's leg.
[2]**desgobierno, desgobierne,** *v. V.* DESGOBERNAR.
desgolletar, *va.* to break off the neck of (a bottle or other vessel); to uncover the neck of.
desgomar, *va.* to ungum, to unsize (silk).
desgonzar, *va.* = DESGOZNAR.
desgoznar. I. *va.* to unhinge, disjoint. **II.** *vr.* to be dislocated or disjointed; to be torn in pieces; to distort the body with violent motions.
desgracia, *f.* misfortune, mishap; affliction, sorrow, grief, bereavement; enmity, unfriendly attitude; disgrace, state of being out of favor; lack of grace, ungracefulness; unpleasantness, rudeness of language and address.—**caer en d.,** to lose favor.—**correr d.,** to fail.—**por d.,** unfortunately.
desgraciadamente, *adv.* unfortunately.
desgraciado, da. I. *pp.* of DESGRACIAR. **II.** *a.* unfortunate, unhappy, unlucky; misadventured, luckless, hapless; out of work; disagreeable, ungrateful. **III.** *n.* wretch, unfortunate person.
desgraciar. I. *va.* to displease; maim; to spoil. **II.** *vr.* to disgrace, to lose favor; to fall out (with a person); to become a cripple; to lose the perfection formerly possessed; to degenerate; to die young; to fail, fall through (as a project).
desgramar, *va.* to pull up the grass from.
desgranadera, *f.* grape picker.
desgranador, ra, *n.* sheller, thrasher; flail.
desgranar. I. *va.* to beat or shake out the grain from (cereals); to thrash, flail; to shell (as peas). **II.** *vr.* to shed the grains; to scatter about (as beads); (mil.) to wear away (app. to the vent of firearms).—**desgrane,** *m.* shelling; (of grain) becoming loose; scattering of grain or beads.
desgranzar, *va.* to separate the husks or chaff from; (art) to give the first grinding to (colors).
desgrasar, *va.* to remove the grease from.
desgrase, *m.* removal of grease.
desgreñar. I. *va.* to dishevel. **II.** *vr.* to quarrel; to pull each other's hair.
desguace, *m.* rough dressing (of lumber).
desguarnecer, *va.* (*ind.* DESGUARNEZCO; *subj.* DESGUARNEZCA) to strip of trimmings and ornaments; to deprive of strength; to strip of all accessories; to disarm; to unharness.
desguazar, *va.* to rough-dress (timber) with ax; (naut.) to take (ship) to pieces; to break up.
desguince, *m.* knife that cuts rags in paper-mills; dodging, dodge.
desguindar. I. *va.* (naut.) to take and bring down. **II.** *vr.* to slide down a rope.
desguinzar, *va.* to cut (cloth or rags) in paper mills.
deshabitado, da. I. *pp.* of DESHABITAR. **II.** *a.* uninhabited, untenanted, deserted.
deshabitar, *va.* to move out of; to depopulate.
deshabituación, *f.* disuse, disusage, desuetude.
deshabituar, *va.* to disaccustom.
deshacedor, *m.*—**d. c. agravios,** undoer of injuries, righter of wrongs.
deshacer. I. *va.* (*pp.* DESHECHO; *ind. pres.* DESHAGO, *pret.* yo DESHICE, él DESHIZO, *fut.* DESHARÉ; *subj.* DESHAGA) to undo; to destroy; take apart; to unwrap, untie (as a parcel); to upset

(plans); to consume, to diminish; to cancel, blot or scratch out; to efface; to cut to pieces, destroy; to put to flight; to melt, dissolve, liquefy; to cut up, divide; to violate (a treaty or agreement); (mil.) to discharge from service. —**d. agravios,** to right wrongs. **II.** *vr.* to be consumed, destroyed; to wear oneself out; to grieve, mourn; to disappear, vanish; to outdo oneself; to grow feeble or meagre; to be crippled, grievously maltreated.—**deshacerse de,** to get rid, or rid oneself, of; to part with.—**deshacerse en lágrimas,** to burst into tears.
deshago, deshaga, *v. V.* DESHACER.
deshaldo, *m.* = MARCEO, trimming honeycombs.
deshambrido, da, *a.* exceedingly hungry, famished, starving.
desharé, *fut.* of DESHACER.
desharrapado, da. *a.* shabby, ragged, in tatters.
desharrapamiento, *m.* misery, meanness.
deshebillar, *va.* to unbuckle.
deshebrar, *va.* to unthread, to ravel into threads to separate into filaments.
deshecha, *f.* simulation, evasion, shift; polite farewell; a step in a Spanish dance.—**a la d.,** dissemblingly; deceitfully.—**hacer la d.,** to dissemble, feign, pretend.
deshechizar, *va.* to disenchant; break a spell in.
deshechizo, *m.* disenchantment, breaking of a magic spell.
deshecho, cha. I. *pp.* of DESHACER. **II.** *a.* undone; exhausted; perfectly mixed (app. to colors).
deshelar. I. *va.* & *vr.* (*ind.* DESHIELO; *subj.* DESHIELE) to thaw; to melt. **II.** *v. impers.* to thaw.
desherbar, *va.* (*ind.* DESHIERBO; *subj.* DESHIERBE) to pluck up or extirpate herbs from; to weed.
desheredación, *f.*, **desheredamiento,** *m.* disinheriting, disinheritance.
desheredar. I. *va.* to disinherit; to cut out from an hereditary right. **II.** *vr.* to degenerate.
deshermanar. I. *va.* to destroy the similarity of **II.** *vr.* to violate the love due to a brother.
desherradura, *f.* (vet.) surbating.
desherrar, *va.* (*ind.* DESHIERRO; *subj.* DESHIERRE to unchain; to rip off the shoes of (horses).
desherrumbrar, *va.* to clean of rust.
deshice, *pret.* of DESHACER.
deshidratación, *f.* dehydration.
deshidratador, *m.* dehydrator.
deshidratar, *va.* to dehydrate.
deshidrogenar, *va.* to dehydrogenize.
[1]**deshielo,** *m.* thaw, thawing.
[2]**deshielo, deshiele,** *v. V.* DESHELAR.
deshierbo, deshierbe, *v. V.* DESHERBAR.
deshierro, deshierre, *v. V.* DESHERRAR.
deshilachar. I. *va.* to ravel, to uncord. **II.** *vr.* to fuzz; to ravel.
deshilado, da. I. *pp.* of DESHILAR. **II.** *a.* marching in a file.—**a la d.,** in file, one after another; stealthily; deceitfully, dissemblingly. **III.** (embroidery) openwork, drawn work.
deshiladura, *f.* ripping, ravelling out.
deshilar. I. *va.* to ravel; to scrape (lint); to distract (bees); to carve (a fowl) in thin strips. **II.** *vr.* to grow thin; to fuzz.
deshilo, *m.* obstructing the communication of bees, to get them into a new hive.
deshilvanado, da. I. *pp.* of DESHILVANAR. **II.** *a.* disjointed, disconnected; without sequence.
deshilvanar, *va.* to remove basting threads from.
deshincadura, *f.* act of drawing out anytning nailed or fixed.
deshincar, *va.* to draw out, pull out, remove.
deshinchadura, *f.* act of reducing a swelling.
deshinchar. I. *va.* to reduce the swelling of, to deflate; to appease the anger or annoyance of. **II.** *vr.* (of anything swollen) to contract, decrease, shrink, shrivel; (coll.) to stop putting on airs.
deshizo, *pret.* of DESHACER.
deshojado, da. I. *pp.* of DESHOJAR. **II.** *a.* defoliate, leafless, stripped of leaves.
deshojador, *m.* stripper of leaves.
deshojadura, *f.* defoliation.
deshojar. I. *va.* to defoliate, strip of leaves. **II.** *vr.* to defoliate.
deshoje, *m.* falling of leaves.
deshollejar, *va.* to peel, pare, skin (as grapes); to shell (as beans).
deshollinadera, *f.* chimney-sweeping broom.
deshollinador, *m.* chimney sweeper; any device used for sweeping chimneys; (coll.) one that examines and inspects minutely and curiously.
deshollinar, *va.* to sweep or clean (chimneys); to clean (ceilings and walls) with a turk's head; (coll.) to view and examine minutely.
deshonestarse, *vr.* to be indecorous or lewd.
deshonestidad, *f.* immodesty; indecency; dishonesty; lewdness.
deshonesto, ta, *a.* immodest; lewd, unchaste, lustful; dishonest, dishonorable.
deshonor, *m.* dishonor, disgrace; insult, affront.
deshonorar, *va.* to dishonor, disgrace; to deprive of office or employ.
deshonra, *f.* dishonor, disgrace; seduction or violation (of a woman).—**tener a d.,** to consider dishonorable or disgraceful.
deshonrabuenos, *n.* calumniator; degenerate.
deshonradamente, *adv.* dishonorably, shamefully, disgracefully.
deshonrador, ra, *n.* dishonorer, disgracer.
deshonrar, *va.* to affront, insult, defame; to dishonor, disgrace; to scorn, to despise; to seduce or ruin (a woman).
deshonrible, *a.* (coll.) shameless, despicable.
deshonroso, sa, *a.* dishonorable, disgraceful.
deshora, *f.* unseasonable or inconvenient time.—**a d.,** or **a deshoras,** untimely, unseasonably; extemporary.
deshornar, *va.* to take out of the oven.
deshospedamiento, *m.* inhospitality, act of refusing strangers a lodging.
deshuesar, *va.* to bone (an animal); to take the pits out of (fruits). Also DESOSAR.
deshuevo, deshueve, *v. V.* DESOVAR.
deshumanar. I. *va.* to dehumanize. **II.** *vr.* to become dehumanized.
deshumanizar, *va.* to dehumanize.
deshumano, na, *a.* inhuman.
deshumedecer. I. *va.* (*ind.* DESHUMEDEZCO; *subj.* DESHUMEDEZCA) to dry out, to deprive of humidity. **II.** *vr.* to dry, become dry.
desiderable, *a.* desirable.
desiderativo, va, *a.* desirous.
desiderátum, *m.* desideratum.
desidia, *f.* laziness, indolence.
desidioso, sa, *a.* lazy, indolent.
desierto, ta. I. *a.* deserted, uninhabited, lonely. **II.** *m.* desert, waste, wilderness.
designable, *a.* designable.
designación, *f.* designation.
designado, da, *a.* appointive.
designar, *va.* to intend; to designate, name, appoint.
designio, *m.* design, purpose, intention.
desigual, *a.* unequal, unlike; uneven, unlevel, rough, broken, craggy; arduous, difficult; perilous; changeable; abrupt; excessive, extreme.
desigualar. I. *va.* to make unequal or dissimilar; to mismatch. **II.** *vr.* to excel, to surpass.
desigualdad, *f.* inequality, difference; changeableness, inconstancy; wrong, injury, injustice; knottiness; unevenness, roughness, cragginess.
desilusión, *f.* disillusion, disillusionment.
desilusionar. I. *va.* to disillusion, disenchant; to undeceive. **II.** *vr.* to lose an illusion; to be disabused, undeceived; to become disillusioned.
desimanación, *f.* demagnetization.
desimanar. I. *va.* to demagnetize. **II.** *vr.* to become demagnetized, lose its magnetism.
desimantación, *f.* = DESIMANACIÓN.
desimantar, *va.* & *vr.* = DESIMANAR.
desimpresionar, *va.* to undeceive.
desinclinar, *va.* to disincline.
desincorporar, *va.* & *vr.* to dissolve (a corporation).

desincrustante. I. *a.* scale-removing. II. *n.* disincrustant, boiler compound.
desincrustar, *va.* to remove incrustations from.
desinencia, *f.* (gram.) declension, inflection, desinence; (rhet.) ending of a sentence.
desinfección, *f.* disinfection; disinfecting.
desinfectante, *n.* & *a.* disinfectant(-ing)
desinfectar, *va.* to disinfect; to sterilize.
desinficionamiento, *m.* disinfection.
desinficionar, *va.* to disinfect.
desinflación, *f.* deflation.
desinflamar, *va.* to remove the inflammation of.
desinflar, *va.* to deflate.
desinsaculación, *f.* act of drawing lots.
desinsacular, *va.* to draw lots or names from an urn or balloting box.
desintegrable, *a.* fissionable.
desintegración, *f.* disintegration; (nuclear phys.) decay, decay product.—**d. atómica,** atomic fission.—**d. en cadena,** (nuclear phys.) decay chain.
desintegrar, *va.* & *vr.* to disintegrate.
desinterés, *m.* disinterestedness.
desinteresadamente, *adv.* disinterestedly.
desinteresado, da, *a.* disinterested, impartial.
desintonizar, *va.* to detune.
desinvernar, *vn.* (mil.) to leave winter quarters.
desirvo, etc. *v.* *V.* DESERVIR.
desistencia, *f.*, **desistimiento,** *m.* desisting, act of desisting.
desistir, *vn.* **(de)** to desist (from), cease, give up; to flinch (from); (law) to waive (a right).
desjarretadera, *f.* hooked knife for hocking or hamstringing cattle.
desjarretar, *va.* to hock, to hamstring; (coll.) to weaken, to debilitate (as by bleeding a patient).
desjarrete, *m.* act of hamstringing or hocking.
desjugar, *va.* (*ind.* DESJUGUÉ; *subj.* DESJUGUE) to extract the juice from.
desjuiciado, da, *a.* lacking sense or judgment.
desjuntamiento, *m.* separation, disjunction.
desjuntar, *va.* & *vr.* to disjoint, divide; to separate, to part.
deslabonar. I. *va.* to unlink, to disjoin; to destroy. II. *vr.* to withdraw, to retire.
desladrillar, *va.* to remove tiles or bricks from.
deslamar, *va.* to clear of mud.
deslastrar, *va.* (naut.) to unballast, remove the ballast from.
deslatar, *va.* to take off the laths from.
deslavado, da. I. *pp.* of DESLAVAR. II. *a.* (fig.) impudent, barefaced.
deslavadura, *f.* washing, rinsing.
deslavar, *va.* to wash or cleanse superficially, to rinse; to wet, spoil by wetting; to take away the color, force, or vigor of.
deslavazar, *va.* = DESLAVAR.
deslazar, *va.* to unlace, untie.
desleal, *a.* disloyal; perfidious, faithless.
deslealmente, *adv.* disloyally, treacherously.
deslealtad, *f.* disloyalty, treachery, faithlessness.
deslechugador, *m.* vinedresser, pruner.
deslechugar, deslechuguillar, *va.* (agr.) to cut and prune the branches of (vines).
desleidura, *f.*, **desleimiento,** *m.* dilution; making thin or weak.
desleír, *va.* (*ind. pres.* yo DESLÍO, *pret.* él DESLIÓ; *subj.* yo DESLÍA) to dilute; dissolve; to make thin or weak.
deslendrar, *va.* (*ind.* DESLIENDRO; *subj.* DESLIENDRE) to clear (hair) of nits, delouse.
deslenguado, da. I. *pp.* of DESLENGUAR. II. *a.* loquacious; impudent; foul-mouthed, scurrilous.
deslenguamiento, *m.* loquacity; impudence.
deslenguar. I. *va.* to cut out the tongue of. II. *vr.* to speak impudently or recklessly, to unloosen one's tongue.
desliar, *va.* to untie, loose, unpack.
deslicé, deslice, *v.* *V.* DESLIZAR.
desliendro, desliendre, *v.* *V.* DESLENDRAR.
desligadura, *f.*, **desligamiento,** *m.* disjunction, untying.
desligar. I. *va.* (*pret.* DESLIGUÉ; *subj.* DESLIGUE) to loosen, untie, unbind; to disentangle, extricate, unravel; to absolve from ecclesiastical censure; excuse from an obligation; to remove (from a ship) part of its knees or futtock-timbers, or the spikes holding them; (med.) to unfasten (bandages or ligatures); (mus.) to play or sing staccato. II. *vr.* to get loose, to give way.
deslindador, *m.* one who sets boundaries.
deslindamiento, *m.* demarcation, determination of boundaries.
deslindar, *va.* to mark the boundaries of; to clear up, to define, circumscribe.
deslinde, *m.* = DESLINDAMIENTO.
desliñar, *va.* to clean (fulled cloth) before sending to the press.
deslío, deslió, etc. *v.* *V.* DESLEÍR.
desliz, *m.* slip; act of slipping or sliding; false step; frailty, slight fault; (min.) mercury that escapes in smelting silver ore.
deslizable, *a.* that can slip or slide.
deslizadero, ra. I. *a.* slippery. II. *m.* slippery place.
deslizadizo, za, *a.* = DESLIZADERO.
deslizador, *m.* (aer.) glider.
deslizamiento, *m.* slip, slipping; skidding.
deslizante, *a.* gliding.
deslizar. I. *vn.* & *vr.* (*pret.* DESLICÉ; *subj.* DESLICE) to slip; to slide; to skid; to glide; to act or speak carelessly. II. *vr.* to shirk, to evade.
deslomadura, *f.* act of breaking the back; (vet.) a disease of the muscles of the loins.
deslomar, *va.* to break the back of; to distort or strain the loins of, to chine.
deslucidamente, *adv.* ungracefully, inelegantly; poorly, badly, unsuccessfully.
deslucido, da, *a.* unadorned; ungraceful, awkward; useless, fruitless.—**quedar,** or **salir, d.,** to fail, make or be a failure, to make or be a fizzle.
deslucimiento, *m.* failure, lack of success; awkwardness, uncouthness.
deslucir. I. *va.* (*ind.* DESLUZCO; *subj.* DESLUZCA) to tarnish or impair the lustre and splendor of; to discredit, impair the reputation of. II. *vr.* to do poorly, to be a failure; to tarnish one's reputation.
deslumbrador, ra, *a.* dazzling, glaring.
deslumbramiento, *m.* glare, overpowering lustre, dazzling; confusion of sight or mind, hallucination.
deslumbrante, *a.* dazzling.
deslumbrar, *va.* to dazzle; to puzzle, to leave in doubt and uncertainty.
deslustrado, da. I. *pp.* of DESLUSTRAR. II. *a.* unglazed.
deslustrador, ra, *n.* & *a.* tarnisher(-ing).
deslustrar, *va.* to tarnish, to take away the lustre of, to dim; to remove the glaze from; to sponge; to make less beautiful or illustrious; to soil, stain, (reputation, etc.).
deslustre, *m.* spot or stain; dimness, dulness; disgrace, ignominy, stigma.
deslustroso, sa, *a.* unbecoming, ugly.
desluzco, desluzca, *v.* *V.* DESLUCIR.
desmadejamiento, *m.* languishment, languidness.
desmadejar. I. *va.* to enervate, to produce languor in. II. *vr.* to languish, to be enervated and weak.
desmadrado, da, *a.* (of animals) separated from the mother.
desmadrar, *va.* to separate (an animal) from the mother.
desmagnetizar, *va.* to demagnetize.
desmajolar, *va.* to pull up (vines) by the roots; to loosen or untie.
desmalladura, *f.* act of ripping up or breaking meshes.
desmallar, *va.* to cut and destroy the meshes of.
desmamar, *va.* = DESTETAR, to wean.
desmamonar, *va.* to cut off the young shoots of.

desmán, *m.* misbehavior; excess in actions or words; misfortune, mishap, calamity; (zool.) desman.
desmanarse, *vr.* to stray from a flock or herd.
desmandado, da. I. *pp.* of DESMANDAR. **II.** *a.* impudent; unbridled, lawless, unruly; disobedient.
desmandar. I. *va.* to repeal (an order), to countermand; to revoke. **II.** *vr.* to transgress the bounds of justice and reason; to be impudent; to lose moderation or self-control; to stray from the flock; to go astray.
desmanear, *va.* to unfetter, to take off fetters or shackles from (horses, mules, etc.).
desmangar, *va.* to take off the handle of.
desmanotado, da, *a.* unhandy, awkward.
desmantecar, *va.* to take butter or lard out of.
desmantelado, da. I. *pp.* of DESMANTELAR. **II.** *a.* dismantled, dilapidated.
desmantelamiento, *m.* dismantling; dilapidation, ruined condition.
desmantelar, *va.* to dismantle; to abandon, desert, forsake; (naut.) to unmast.
desmaña, *f.* awkwardness, clumsiness; laziness.
desmañado, da. I. *a.* unhandy, clumsy, awkward; lazy, indolent. II. *n.* (coll.) butterfingers.
desmarojar, *va.* to take dry leaves or branches off (a tree).
desmarrido, da, *a.* sad, dejected; exhausted.
desmatar, *adv.* = DESCUAJAR, to uproot.
desmayadamente, *adv.* weakly, dejectedly.
desmayado, da. I. *pp.* of DESMAYAR. **II.** *a.* pale, wan, faint of lustre; dismayed, discouraged.
desmayar. I. *vn.* to be dispirited, faint-hearted, discouraged. **II.** *va.* to dismay, depress, discourage. **III.** *vr.* to faint, swoon.
desmayo, *m.* swoon, fainting fit; lowering of vigor or strength; dismay, discouragement.
desmazalado, da, *a.* weak, dejected, faint-hearted, spiritless.
desmechado, da, *a.* (Am.) disheveled.
desmedidamente, *adv.* disproportionately, excessively.
desmedido, da. I. *pp.* of DESMEDIRSE. **II.** *a.* excessive, unconscionable.
desmedirse, *vr.* (*ger.* DESMIDIENDO; *ind. pres.* me DESMIDO, *pret.* se DESMIDIÓ; *subj.* me DESMIDA) to forget oneself, to be impudent or saucy; to lose self-control.
desmedrado, da. I. *pp.* of DESMEDRAR. **II.** *a.* damaged, injured; worn out; wasted, emaciated.
desmedrar. I. *vn.* to decrease, decay. **II.** *va.* to impair.
desmedro. *m.* diminution, detriment.
desmejora, *f.* deterioration, depreciation, impairment; diminution, loss.
desmejorar. I. *va.* to debase, to make worse, impair. **II.** *vn.* & *vr.* to decline, become worse; to deteriorate.
desmelar, *va.* (*ind.* DESMIELO; *subj.* DESMIELE) to take the honey from (a hive).
desmelenar, *va.* to dishevel, to disarrange or muss the hair of.
desmembración, *f.* dismemberment, amputation, division.
desmembrar, *va.* (*ind.* DESMIEMBRO; *subj.* DESMIEMBRE) to dismember, to tear asunder; to curtail; (surg.) to amputate; to separate, divide.
desmemoria, *f.* forgetfulness; lack of memory.
desmemoriado, da. I. *pp.* of DESMEMORIARSE. **II.** *a.* forgetful; devoid of memory.
desmemoriarse, *vr.* to become forgetful, to forget; to lose the memory.
desmenguar, *va.* to lessen; to diminish.
desmentida, *f.* act of giving the lie.
desmentidor, ra. I. *a.* that gives the lie, disproving. **II.** *n.* one who gives the lie; disprover.
desmentir. I. *va.* (*ind.* DESMIENTO; *subj.* DESMIENTA) to give the lie to; to convince of a falsehood; to contradict, disprove; to counterfeit, conceal, dissemble; to do things unworthy of (one's birth, character, profession). **II.** *vn.* to deviate from the right line. **III.** *vr.* to recant, retract, take back.
desmenucé, desmenuce, *v.* *V.* DESMENUZAR.
desmenuzable, *a.* crisp, crumbly, crimp, easily crumbled.
desmenuzador, ra, *n.* one who crumbles; investigator; purifier.
desmenuzamiento, *m.* crumbling, breaking into small pieces.
desmenuzar. I. *va.* (*pret.* DESMENUCÉ: *subj.* DESMENUCE) to crumble, crumb; to shred; to break or tear into bits; to chip, mill, fritter; to sift, examine minutely. **II.** *vr.* to crumble, to fall into small pieces.
desmeollamiento, *m.* taking out the marrow.
desmeollar, *va.* to take the marrow or pith from.
desmerecedor, ra, *a.* unworthy, undeserving.
desmerecer. I. *va.* (*ind.* DESMEREZCO; *subj.* DESMEREZCA) to become unworthy or undeserving of. **II.** *vn.* to lose worth; to deteriorate; to be comparatively inferior, compare unfavorably.
desmerecimiento, *m.* demerit, unworthiness.
desmerezco, desmerezca, *v.* *V.* DESMERECER.
desmesura, *f.* excess, lack of measure.
desmesuradamente, *adv.* disproportionately, excessively.
desmesurado, da. I. *pp.* of DESMESURAR. **II.** *a.* disproportionate, excessive.
desmesurar. I. *va.* to disorder, disarrange, disturb. **II.** *vr.* to be forward, impudent, saucy.
desmido, desmida, etc. *v.* *V.* DESMEDIRSE.
desmielo, desmiele, *v.* *V.* DESMELAR.
desmiembro, desmiembre, *v.* *V.* DESMEMBRAR.
desmiento, desmienta, *v.* *V.* DESMENTIR.
desmigajar. I. *va.* & *vr.* to crumble; to comminute (as bread). **II.** *vr.* to crumble.
desmigar, *va.* (*pret.* DESMIGUÉ; *subj.* DESMIGUE) to crumble (bread).
desmilitarización, *f.* demilitarization.
desmilitarizar, *va.* to demilitarize.
desmineralización, *f.* (med.) abnormal loss of mineral substances.
desmirriado, da, *a.* (coll.) lean, emaciated, exhausted; melancholy.
desmocha, desmochadura, *f.* lopping or cutting off; diminution or destruction of part of a thing.
desmochar, *va.* to lop or cut off the top of (a tree, etc.); to dehorn.
desmoche, *m.* = DESMOCHA.
desmocho, *m.* heap of things lopped or cut off.
desmogar, *vn.* to cast the horns, as deer.
desmogue, *m.* act of casting the horns.
desmolado, da, *a.* having no molars or grinders.
desmoldamiento, *m.* removal of a casting from the mold.
desmoldar, *va.* to remove from the mold, to "strike the frame."
desmonetización, *f.* demonetization; conversion of coins into bullion.
desmonetizar. I. *va.* to convert (money) into bullion; to demonetize. **II.** *vr.* (of stocks) to depreciate, lose value.
desmontable, *a.* demountable.
desmontado, da. I. *pp.* of DESMONTAR. **II.** *a.* unmounted, dismounted; (mech.) knocked down.
desmontador, ra, *n.* one who fells wood; dismounter.
desmontadura, *f.* felling timber, clearing of shrubbery.
desmontar. I. *va.* to clear (a wood); to remove (dirt or rubbish); to grub, to fallow; to uncock (firearms); to take apart (as a machine); to dismount (a troop of horse); to dismount (cannon). —**d. el timón,** (naut.) to unhang the rudder. **II.** *vn., vr.* to dismount, to alight from a horse, mule, etc.
desmonte, *m.* grubbing or clearing of trees and undergrowth; timber remaining on the spot; (Ry.) cut; (min.) discarded ore or rock.
desmoñar, *va.* (coll.) to undo (the hair knot).
desmoralicé, desmoralice, *v.* *V.* DESMORALIZAR.

desmoralización, *f.* demoralization; corruption.
desmoralizador, ra, *a.* demoralizing.
desmoralizar. I. *va.* (*pret.* DESMORALICÉ; *subj.* DESMORALICE) to demoralize, corrupt, deprave. **II.** *vr.* to become demoralized; (mil.) to lose the morale, to flag in morale.
desmoronadizo, za, *a.* easily crumbled, crumbly; lacking solidity or permanence.
desmoronamiento, *m.* crumbling.
desmoronar. I. *va.* to abrade, to destroy little by little, to ruin by insensible degrees. **II.** *vr.* to fall, decay, crumble.
desmostar. I. *va.* to separate the must from (grapes). **II.** *vn.* to ferment.
desmotadera, *f.* woman who burls cloth; burling iron.
desmotador, ra. I. *n.* & *a.* burler(-ing). **II.** *f.* cotton opener; (Am.) cotton gin.
desmotar, *va.* to burl; to gin.
desmovilización, *f.* demobilization.
desmovilizar, *va.* (mil.) to demobilize.
desmullir, *va.* to disarrange or impair the softness of.
desmurador, *m.* mouser (cat).
desnacionalización, *f.* denationalization.
desnacionalizar, *va.* to denationalize.
desnarigado, da. I. *pp.* of DESNARIGAR. **II.** *a.* noseless; having a tiny nose.
desnarigar, *va.* to cut off the nose of.
desnatadora, *f.* separator (cream).
desnatar, *va.* to skim; to take off the flower or choicest part of.
desnaturalicé, desnaturalice, *v. V.* DESNATURALIZAR.
desnaturalización, *f.* expatriation, denaturalization, denationalization.
desnaturalizado, da. I. *pp.* of DESNATURALIZAR. **II.** *a.* denaturalized; denatured; unnatural.
desnaturalizar. I. *va.* (*pret.* DESNATURALICÉ; *subj.* DESNATURALICE) to denaturalize, denationalize; to banish, exile; to disfigure, pervert (as a fact); to denature. **II.** *vr.* to abandon one's country.
desnegamiento, *m.* denial; contradiction; retraction, retractation.
desnegar. I. *va.* (*ind. pres.* DESNIEGO, *pret.* DESNEGUÉ; *subj.* DESNIEGUE) to deny, gainsay, contradict. **II.** *vr.* to retract, recant.
desnervar, *va.* to enervate.
desnevado, da. I. *pp.* of DESNEVAR. **II.** *a.* free from snow.
desnevar, *va.* (*ind.* DESNIEVO; *subj.* DESNIEVE) to thaw, dissolve.
desniego, desniegue, *v. V.* DESNEGAR.
desnievo, desnieve, *v. V.* DESNEVAR.
desnitrificación, *f.* denitrification.
desnitrificar, *va.* to denitrify.
desnivel, *m.*, **desnivelación,** *f.* unevenness, difference of elevation, drop.
desnivelar. I. *va.* to unlevel, make uneven. **II.** *vr.* to lose its level.
desnucar. I. *va.* (*pret.* DESNUQUÉ: *subj.* DESNUQUE) to break the neck of; to kill by a blow on the nape. **II.** *vr.* to break one's neck.
desnudador, ra, *n.* one that denudes.
desnudamente, *adv.* nakedly; evidently.
desnudamiento, *m.* (coll.) strip tease.
desnudar. I. *va.* to strip, undress, denude, uncover; to fleece; (naut.) to unrig. **II.** *vr.* to undress, to strip, to deprive oneself of; to rid oneself of.
desnudez, *f.* nudity, nakedness.
desnudista, *f.* (coll.) stripteaser.
desnudo, da. I. *a.* nude, naked; bare, uncovered; ill-clothed; plain, evident; empty-handed; destitute of merit, interest, resources, etc. **II.** *m.* nude figure in art.
desnuqué, desnuque, *v. V.* DESNUCAR.
desnutrición, *f.* malnutrition, underfeeding.
desnutrido, da. **I.** *pp.* of DESNUTRIR. **II.** *a.* undernourished.
desnutrir, *va.* & *vr.* to undernourish.
desobedecer, *va.* & *vn.* (*ind.* DESOBEDEZCO; *subj.* DESOBEDEZCA) to disobey.
desobediencia, *f.* disobedience.
desobediente, *a.* disobedient.
desobligar, *va.* (*pret.* DESOBLIGUÉ; *subj.* DESOBLIGUE) to release from an obligation; to disoblige; to offend; to alienate the good will of.
desobstrucción, *f.* clearing, removal of obstructions or obstacles.
desobstruir, *va.* (*ind.* DESOBSTRUYO; *subj.* DESOBSTRUYA) to remove obstructions from, to clear; (med.) to deobstruct.
desocupación, *f.* leisure; unemployment.
desocupadamente, *adv.* deliberately, leisurely.
desocupado, da. I. *pp.* of DESOCUPAR. **II.** *a.* idle, without occupation; vacant, unoccupied. **III.** *n.* unemployed person; (Am.) idler.
desocupar. I. *va.* to vacate; to evacuate; to empty. **II.** *vr.* to disengage oneself from a business or occupation.
desodorante, *n.* & *a.* deodorant.
desoír, *va.* (*ger.* DESOYENDO; *ind. pres.* DESOIGO, *pret.* él DESOYÓ; *subj.* DESOIGA) to pretend not to hear; not to heed.
desojar. I. *va.* & *vr.* to break or burst the eye of (as of a needle). **II.** *vr.* to strain one's sight; to look intently.
desolación, *f.* desolation, destruction, havoc; fall; intense grief or affliction.
desolado, da. I. *pp.* of DESOLAR. **II.** *a.* desolate; disconsolate.
desolar. I. *va.* (*ind.* DESUELO; *subj.* DESUELE) to desolate, lay waste; to harass. **II.** *vr.* to suffer great grief.
desoldar. I. *va.* (*ind.* DESUELDO; *subj.* DESUELDE) to unsolder. **II.** *vr.* (of soldered pieces) to come unsoldered, break apart.
desolladero, *m.* abattoir, slaughterhouse.
desollado, da. I. *pp.* of DESOLLAR. **II.** *a.* (coll.) forward, impudent, insolent.
desollador, ra. I. *n.* flayer, extortioner. **II.** *m.* butcher bird.
desolladura, *f.* act and effect of flaying or skinning; excoriation; extortion.
desollar, *va.* (*ind.* DESUELLO; *subj.* DESUELLE) to flay, to skin; to excoriate; to fleece; to cause great harm or injury to.—**d. vivo,** (coll.) to extort an immoderate price from; to speak ill of.—**falta el rabo por d.,** the worst is yet to come.
desollón, *m.* = DESOLLADURA.
desonzar, *va.* to discount or deduct a certain number of ounces per pound of; to insult, to defame, revile.
desopilar, *va.* (med.) to clear obstructions from.
desopilativo, va, *m.* & *a.* (med.) deobstruent.
desopinado, da. I. *pp.* of DESOPINAR. **II.** *a.* having lost reputation.
desopinar, *va.* to defame.
desoprimir, *va.* to free from oppression.
desorden, *m.* disorder, confusion, mess; lawlessness, excess; turmoil, disturbance, riot.
desordenado, da. I. *pp.* of DESORDENAR. **II.** *a.* disorderly, irregular; lawless, licentious.
desordenar. I. *va.* to disorder, disarrange, upset. **II.** *vr.* to exceed or go beyond all rule; to be out of order, to be irregular; to get unruly, be unmanageable (as a horse).
desorejado, da, *a.* (coll.) licentious, dissolute, degraded.
desorejamiento, *m.* cropping off the ears.
desorejar, *va.* to crop off the ears of.
desorganicé, desorganice, *v. V.* DESORGANIZAR.
desorganización, *f.* disorganization.
desorganizador, ra, *n.* & *a.* disorganizer(-ing).
desorganizar. I. *va.* (*pret.* DESORGANICÉ; *subj.* DESORGANICE) to disorganize; to break up, disperse; (chem.) to decompose; (mil.) to disband. **II.** *vr.* to become disorganized; to disband, disperse; (med.) to be altered, disorganized.
desorientación, *f.* lack of orientation, loss of bearings; confusion, lack of system.
desorientar, *va.* & *vr.* to disorient; to lose or

cause to lose one's bearings; to lose the way; to confuse, to lead into error.
desorillar, *va.* to cut off the selvage of (cloth); to cut the border off.
desortijado, da. I. *pp.* of DESORTIJAR. **II.** *a.* (vet.) sprained.
desortijar, *va.* to hoe or weed the first time.
desosar, *va.* (*ind.* DESHUESO: *subj.* DESHUESE) = DESHUESAR, to bone (an animal); to pit (fruit).
desovar, *vn.* (*ind.* DESHUEVO; *subj.* DESHUEVE) to spawn.
desove, *m.* spawning; spawning season.
desovillar, *va.* to unwind; to unclew, unravel, disentangle.
desoxidable, *a.* deoxidizable.
desoxidación, *f.* deoxidation.
desoxidante, *n.* & *a.* deoxidizer(-ing).
desoxidar, *va.* & *vn.* to deoxidize.
desoxigenación, *f.* deoxidation.
desoxigenante, *n.* & *a.* = DESOXIDANTE.
desoxigenar, *va.* to deoxidize.
desoyendo, desoyó, *v. V.* DESOÍR.
despabiladeras, *f. pl.* snuffers (for candles).
despabilado, da. I. *pp.* of DESPABILAR. **II.** *a.* vigilant; wakeful; lively, smart.
despabilador, ra. I. *n.* & *a.* snuffer(-ing). **II.** *m.* candle snuffer.
despabiladura, *f.* end of candlewick snuffed or trimmed.
despabilar. I. *va.* to trim or snuff (a candle); to trim, cut off from; to finish briefly or quickly (as a dinner or a fortune); to rouse, to enliven; (coll.) to rob, to plunder; (coll.) to kill.—**d. el ingenio,** to sharpen the wits.—**d. los ojos,** to keep a sharp lookout. **II.** *vr.* to wake up.
despacio. I. *adv.* slowly; deliberately. **II.** *interj.* softly, gently. **III.** *m.* (Am.) slowness.—**con d.,** slowly; carefully.
despacioso, sa, *a.* slow, phlegmatic, sluggish.
despacito, *adv.* (coll.) very slowly, gently, softly.
despachaderas, *f. pl.* (coll.) surly rejoinder; quickness, resourcefulness.
despachado, da. I. *pp.* of DESPACHAR. **II.** *a.* (coll.) impudent, bold-faced, brazen.
despachador, ra, *n.* sender, one who despatches.
despachar. I. *va.* to despatch; to expedite, abridge, facilitate; to send; to ship, to express; to perform with despatch; to get out, write and send, attend to (correspondence); to wait on, serve (as in a shop); to dismiss, discharge.—**d. géneros,** or **mercaderías, en la aduana,** to clear or take out goods or merchandise at the customhouse.—**d. un barco,** (com.) to clear a vessel at the customhouse. **II.** *vr.* to make haste. **III.** *vn.* in offices, to carry papers drawn up for the signature of the principal; (com.) to expend, to let goods go for money or barter; (coll.) to wait on customers.
despacho, *m.* expedient, determination; despatch, expedition; shipping, shipment, sending; custom, application from buyers; cabinet, department; office, bureau; countinghouse; depot; sale of goods; trade; demand; commission, warrant, patent; official communication or despatch.—**d. de aduana,** customhouse clearance.—**d. de billetes,** or **boletos,** ticket office. —**d. de localidades,** box office.—**d. telegráfico,** cablegram, telegram.—**d. universal,** state department.—**tener buen d.,** to be quick, to be energetic and prompt.
despachurrado, da. I. *pp.* of DESPACHURRAR. **II.** *a.* smashed, squashed, crushed.—**dejar a uno d.,** (coll.) to leave one dumfounded.
despachurrar, *va.* (coll.) to squash, smash, crush; (coll.) to make a jumble of (an explanation).—**d. el cuento,** to interrupt a story and prevent its conclusion.
despajadura, *f.* winnowing.
despajar, *va.* to winnow or separate (grain from chaff).—**despajo,** *m.* winnowing or cleaning.
despaldar, *va.* & *vr.* to dislocate or break the shoulder of.
despaldilladura, *f.* breaking or dislocation of an animal's shoulder.
despalillar, *va.* to remove the stems from (raisins); to strip (tobacco, etc.).
despalmador, *m.* (naut.) careening place, dockyard; hoof-paring knife.
despalmadura, *f.* calking, paying the bottom.
despalmar, *va.* (naut.) to grave, to calk; to pare (a horse's hoof).—**despalme,** *m.* = DESPALMADURA.
despampanador, *m.* pruner of vines.
despampanadura, *f.* act of pruning vines.
despampanar. I. *va.* to prune (vines); (coll.) to astound by a piece of news. **II.** *vn.* (coll.) to unbosom oneself, to give vent to one's feelings. **III.** *vr.* (coll.) to be injured by a fall.
despamplonar. I. *va.* to separate the shoots of. **II.** *vr.* to sprain the hand.
despancijar, despanzurrar, *va.* (coll.) to burst the belly of.
despapar, *vn.* (of a horse) to carry the head too high.
desparecer, *vn.* (*ind.* DESPAREZCO; *subj.* DESPAREZCA) = DESAPARECER, to disappear.
desparedar, *va.* to take down the walls of.
desparejar, *va.* to break a pair of, to separate from a pair.
desparpajado, da. I. *pp.* of DESPARPAJAR. **II.** *a.* pert, petulant, garrulous.
desparpajar. I. *va.* to undo in a disorderly manner. **II.** *vn.* & *vr.* (coll.) to rant, to prattle.
desparpajo, *m.* (coll.) pertness of speech or of manner.
desparramado, da. I. *pp.* of DESPARRAMAR. **II.** *a.* wide open; spread, scattered.
desparramador, ra, *n.* disperser; dilapidator; prodigal, waster, spendthrift.
desparramamiento, *m.* spreading, scattering; squandering, extravagance, dissipation.
desparramar. I. *va.* & *vr.* to scatter, disseminate, spread; to squander, dissipate, lavish. **II.** *vr.* to amuse oneself; to be dissipated.
despartidor, *m.* one who separates or divides.
despartimiento, *m.* separation, or division.
despartir, *va.* to part, separate, divide; to reconcile, make peace between.
desparvar, *va.* to undo the sheaves and spread the stalks of (grain) on the floor.
despasar, *va.* (naut.) to unsling, unreeve, shift.
despatarrada, *f.* (coll.) spreading of the legs; a certain change or movement in a Spanish dance.—**hacer la d.,** (coll.) to pretend disease or pain; to feign death.
despatarrarse, *vr.* (coll.) to straddle; to fall with spread legs; to do the splits; to be stupefied or dumfounded; to remain motionless.
despatillar. I. *va.* to tenon; (naut.) to break off the arm of (an anchor). **II.** *vr.* (coll.) to shave off one's whiskers.
despavesaderas, *f. pl.* = DESPABILADERAS.
despavesadura, *f.* act of snuffing a candle.
despavesar, *va.* to snuff (a candle).
despavorido, da, *a.* terrified, aghast.
despavorir, *vn.* & *vr.* (*defect.*: *it has only the moods and persons having the letter* **i**) to be terrified, to be frightened, to be aghast.
despeadura, *f.,* **despeamiento,** *m.* bruising the feet with travel; (vet.) surbating.
despearse, *vr.* to bruise the feet (or hoofs) or make them sore by much walking.
despectivo, va, *a.* depreciatory; contemptuous.
despechadamente, *adv.* angrily, spitefully.
[1]**despechar. I.** *va.* to enrage, to excite indignation in. **II.** *vr.* to fret; to despair; to be spiteful.
[2]**despechar,** *va.* (coll.) to wean.
despecho, *m.* spite; despair; grudge.—**a d. de,** despite, in spite of, in defiance of.
despechugadura, *f.* cutting off the breast of a fowl; uncovering one's breast.
despechugar. I. *va.* (*pret.* DESPECHUGUÉ; *subj.* DESPECHUGUE) to cut off the breast of (a fowl). **II.** *vr.* (coll.) to uncover the breast; to walk with bare breast.
despedacé, despedace, *v. V.* DESPEDAZAR.

despedazador, ra, *n.* & *a.* dissector(-ing); tearer(-ing); lacerator(-ing), mangler(-ing).
despedazamiento, *m.* laceration, dissection, cutting to pieces; mangling.
despedazar. I. *va.* (*pret.* DESPEDACÉ; *subj.* DESPEDACE) to cut into bits, to tear into pieces; to cut asunder; to limb, to claw; to lacerate, mangle; to torment, to harrow (as the feelings). **II.** *vr.* to break or fall to pieces.—**d. de risa,** to hold one's sides with laughter.
despedida, *f.* leave-taking, farewell; send-off; seeing a person off; discharge, dismissal.
despedimiento, *m.* = DESPEDIDA.
despedir. I. *va.* (*ger.* DESPIDIENDO; *ind. pres.* DESPIDO, *pret.* él DESPIDIÓ; *subj.* DESPIDA) to emit, discharge; fling, throw off or out; to dismiss, discharge; to see (a person) off on a journey; to escort (a guest) to the door; to dismiss (as from the mind). **II.** *vr.* **(de)** to take leave (of), say good-bye (to); to quit; to renounce; to go out from service, to leave one's occupation.—**d. a la francesa,** to take French leave, sneak away.
despedregar, *va.* to clear of stones.
despegable, *a.* that may be unglued or disjoined.
despegadamente, *adv.* unconcernedly, unaffectionately.
despegado, da. I. *pp.* of DESPEGAR. **II.** *a.* unglued; (coll.) sour of temper; unpleasant, harsh; distant, indifferent; unaffectionate, unfeeling.
despegadura, *f.* ungluing, detaching, separating.
despegamiento, *m.* DESAPEGO, indifference.
despegar. I. *va.* (*pret.* DESPEGUÉ; *subj.* DESPEGUE) to unglue, detach, separate, disjoin.—**d. los labios, la boca,** to speak. **II.** *vr.* to come off; to withdraw one's affection; to become indifferent. **III.** *vn.* (aer.) to rise, to take off.—**despego,** *m.* asperity; aversion; coolness, indifference, lack of affection.
despegué, despegue, *v.* *V.* DESPEGAR.
despegue, *m.* (aer.) take-off.
despeinado, da, *a.* uncombed, unkempt.
despeinar, *va.* to disarrange the hair of.
despejadamente, *adv.* expeditiously, readily, smartly, neatly.
despejado, da. I. *pp.* of DESPEJAR. **II.** *a.* sprightly, smart, vivacious; clear, cloudless; unobstructed, clear.
despejar. I. *va.* to remove impediments from, clear; (math.) to solve for, find the value of. **II.** *vr.* to become bright and smart; to amuse oneself; (of an ill person) to be relieved of pain; (of the weather, sky, etc.) to clear up.
despejo, *m.* removal of obstacles, clearing; sprightliness, smartness, briskness; grace, ease.
despelotar, *va.* to dishevel.
despeluzamiento, *m.* entanglement or disarrangement of the hair; making the hair stand on end; goose flesh.
despeluzar, *va.* & *vr.* to make (the hair) stand on end; to be horrified.
despeluznante, *a.* horrifying, frightful.
despeluznar, *va.* & *vr.* = DESPELUZAR.
despellejadura, *f.* scratch, slight wound; skinning.
despellejar, *va.* to flay, to skin, to strip; (fig.) to speak ill of.
despenar, *va.* to relieve from pain; (coll.) to kill.
despendedor, ra, *n.* spendthrift, prodigal, lavisher, waster.
despender, *va.* to spend; to waste, squander.
despensa, *f.* pantry, larder; store of provisions for a journey; butlership; provisions for daily use; marketing; contract for a yearly supply of fodder; (naut.) steward's room.
despensería, *f.* office of steward.
despensero, ra, *n.* butler; caterer, dispenser, distributer; (naut.) steward.
despeñadamente, *adv.* precipitately.
despeñadero, ra. I. *a.* steep, precipitous, headlong. **II.** *m.* precipice, crag; dangerous undertaking.
despeñadizo, za, *a.* steep, precipitous; glib, slippery.
despeñamiento, *m.* = DESPEÑO.
despeñar. I. *va.* to precipitate, to fling down a precipice. **II.** *vr.* to throw oneself headlong; to lead a riotous life.—**despeño,** *m.* precipitate fall; loss of fortune and character; diarrhea.
despepitadora, *f.* stoner, corer; seed separator. —**d. de algodón,** cotton gin.
despepitar, *va.* to remove the seeds from; to gin.
despepitarse, *vr.* to loosen one's tongue; to vociferate; to speak or act rashly or heedlessly.—**d. por,** to long for, to be dying or itching to.
despercudir, *va.* to clean or wash.
desperdiciadamente, *adv.* profusely, wastefully.
desperdiciado, da. I. *pp.* of DESPERDICIAR. **II.** *a.* wasted, destroyed, squandered.
desperdiciador, ra, *n.* spendthrift, squanderer.
desperdiciar, *va.* to waste; to squander, misspend; not to avail oneself of, not to utilize, to lose, miss (an opportunity, etc.).
desperdicio, *m.* waste; prodigality, profusion; (gen. *pl.*) refuse, offal, remains, garbage.
desperdigamiento, *m.* spreading, scattering.
desperdigar, *va.* to separate, disjoin; to scatter.
desperecerse, *vr.* (*ind.* DESPEREZCO; *subj.* DESPEREZCA) to crave, to long, to desire eagerly.
desperezarse, *vr.* to stretch one's limbs; to shake off sloth.
desperezco, desperezca, *v.* *V.* DESPERECERSE.
desperezo, *m.* = ESPEREZO, stretching (limbs).
desperfecto, *m.* deterioration, wear and tear; slight injury or damage, blemish, imperfection, flaw.
desperfilar, *va.* (art) to soften the lines of.
despernado, da. I. *pp.* of DESPERNAR. **II.** *a.* weary, fatigued, tired.
despernar. I. *va.* (*ind.* DESPIERNO; *subj.* DESPIERNE) to injure or cut off the legs of. **II.** *vr.* to injure or lose one's legs.
despertador, ra. I. *n.* awakener. **II.** *m.* alarm bell in clocks; alarm clock; warning, admonition, hint that causes worriment.
despertamiento, *m.* awakening.
despertar. I. *va.* & *vr.* (*pp.* DESPERTADO, DESPIERTO: *ind.* DESPIERTO; *subj.* DESPIERTE) to wake up, awaken; to enliven; to remind, recall; to excite, sharpen (as the appetite, curiosity). **II.** *vn.* to awake, wake up; to revive.
despesar, *m.* displeasure, aversion, dislike.
despestañar. I. *va.* to pluck out the eyelashes of. **II.** *vr.* to look intently, to study hard.
despezar, *va.* to bevel; to taper.
despezo, *m.* taper; bevel.—*pl.* (arch.) beveled faces of a stone at the joints.
despezonar. I. *va.* to cut off the stem of; to divide, to separate. **II.** *vr.* to break off (as the stalk of fruit or the arm of an axletree).
despezuñar. I. *va.* to cut off the hoof of. **II.** *vr.* (Am.) to rush at breakneck speed.—**d. por,** to long for; to hustle for, set one's heart on.
despiadado, da, *a.* unmerciful, pitiless.
despicar. I. *va.* (*pret.* DESPIQUÉ; *subj.* DESPIQUE) to satisfy, to gratify. **II.** *vr.* **(de** or **con)** to take revenge (for), get square (with).
despichar. I. *va.* to expel or discharge; to pick; (Am.) to crush, smash. **II.** *vn.* (coll.) to die.
despidida, *f.* gutter, passage for water.
despidiente, *m.* board between a hanging scaffold and the wall.—**d. de agua,** (arch.) flashing.
[1]**despido,** etc., *v.* *V.* DESPEDIR.
[2]**despido,** *m.* discharge, dismissal, layoff.
despierno, despierne, *v.* *V.* DESPERNAR.
despiertamente, *adv.* ingeniously, cleverly.
[1]**despierto, ta. I.** *pp. irreg.* of DESPERTAR. **II.** *a.* awake; watchful; diligent; lively, smart; clear-sighted.
[2]**despierto, despierte,** *v.* *V.* DESPERTAR.
despiezo, *m.* (arch.) = DESPEZO, bevel.
despilfarrado, da. I. *pp.* of DESPILFARRAR. **II.** *a.* ragged, shabby, in tatters; prodigal, wasteful.
despilfarrador, ra, *a.* spendthrift, wasteful.

despilfarrar, *va.* to waste, squander.
despilfarro, *m.* slovenliness, uncleanliness; waste, lavishment, squandering, extravagance; misgovernment, maladministration.
despimpollar, *va.* to prune away the useless stems of.
despincé, despince, *v. V.* DESPINZAR.
despinces, *m. pl.* tweezers. Also DESPINZAS.
despintar. I. *va.* to blot or efface; to disfigure; to mislead. **II.** *vn.* to degenerate. **III.** *vr.* to fade, wash off, lose color; to forget.
despinte, *m.* (Am.) (min.) low-grade or poor ore.
despinzadera, *f.* woman that burls.—*pl.* burling iron.
despinzar, *va.* (*pret.* DESPINCÉ; *subj.* DESPINCE) to burl.
despinzas, *f. pl.* burling iron; DESPINCES.
despiojar, *va.* & *vr.* to delouse; (coll.) to relieve from misery.
despique, *m.* vengeance, revenge.
despiqué, despique, *v. V.* DESPICAR.
despistar, *va.* to turn from the trail or course.
despizcar. I. *va.* (*pret.* DESPIZQUÉ; *subj.* DESPIZQUE) to triturate, crush; break or cut into small bits. **II.** *vr.* to exert oneself to the utmost.
desplacer. I. *va.* (*ind.* DESPLAZCO; *subj.* DESPLAZCA) to displease. **II.** *m.* displeasure.
desplanchar, *va.* to wrinkle, rumple, muss.
desplantación, *f.* eradication, uprooting.
desplantador, ra. I. *n.* eradicator, one who pulls up plants. **II.** *m.* trowel, scoop trowel.
desplantar. I. *vr.* to lose one's erect posture in fencing or dancing. **II.** *va.* to uproot; to deviate from the vertical.—**desplante,** *m.* oblique posture in fencing; injudicious action or speech.
desplatar, *va.* to separate silver from.
desplate, *m.* act of separating silver from other metals.
desplayar, *vn.* to recede from the shore (as the tide).
desplazamiento, *m.* displacement.
desplazar, *va.* (naut.) to displace, have a displacement of.
desplazco, desplazca, *v. V.* DESPLACER.
desplegadura, *f.* unfolding, spreading out; elucidation, explanation.
desplegar. I. *va.* (*ind.* DESPLIEGO; *subj.* DESPLIEGUE) to unfold, display; to spread, lay out; to explain, elucidate; (naut.) to unfurl.—**d. la bandera,** to hoist the flag. **II.** *vr.* to open, unfold (as flowers); to spread out, deploy (as (troops).
despleguetear, *va.* (agr.) to remove the folds from the tendrils of (vines).
despliego, despliegue, *v. V.* DESPLEGAR.
despliegue, *m.* unfurling, unfolding; spreading out; (mil.) deployment.
desplomar. I. *va.* (of a wall, etc.) to put out of vertical, to cause to lean. **II.** *vr.* to get out of plumb, to lean over; to tumble down, collapse, topple over; (aer.) to pancake.
desplome, *m.* leaning; collapse, tumbling down, downfall; (aer.) pancaking.
desplomo, *m.* deviation from the vertical.
desplumado, da. I. *pp.* of DESPLUMAR. **II.** *a.* deplumate, featherless.
desplumadura, *f.* plucking (a bird).
desplumar. I. *va.* & *vr.* to deplume, to pluck (a bird); (coll.) to despoil or strip of property. **II.** *vr.* to moult.
despoblación, *f.* depopulation.
despoblado, *m.* uninhabited place; wilderness.
despoblador, ra, *n.* & *a.* depopulator(-ing).
despoblar. I. *va.* (*ind.* DESPUEBLO; *subj.* DESPUEBLE) to depopulate; to despoil or desolate. **II.** *vr.* to become depopulated.
despojador, ra, *n.* & *a.* despoiler(-ing).
despojar. I. *va.* to despoil, strip of property; to deprive of, to cut off from, judicially; to dismiss, turn out of a place or employment. **II.** *vr.* (**de**) to take off (as a coat); to undress, to strip; to relinquish; to forsake; to divest oneself (of).
despojo, *m.* spoliation; plunder, spoils; slough, cast-off skin of a serpent; head, pluck, and feet of slaughtered animals.—*pl.* leavings, scraps from the table; giblets of fowls; débris; remains; second-hand building materials.
despolaricé, despolarice, *v. V.* DESPOLARIZAR.
despolarización, *f.* depolarization.
despolarizador, ra. I. *a.* depolarizing. **II.** *m.* (elec.) depolarizer.
despolarizar, *va.* (*pret.* DESPOLARICÉ; *subj.* DESPOLARICE) to depolarize.
despolvar, *va.* to dust.
despolvorear, *va.* to dust; to cast away, scatter, dissipate; (coll.) to sprinkle.
despopularizar, *va.* & *vr.* (*pret.* DESPOPULARICÉ; *subj.* DESPOPULARICE) to make or become unpopular.
desportillar, *va.* to chip off the corners or edges of; break the neck of (a bottle, pot, etc.); (arch.) to splay.
desposado, da. I. *pp.* of DESPOSAR. **II.** *a.* newly married; handcuffed.
desposar. I. *va.* to marry (to perform the marriage ceremony for). **II.** *vr.* to be betrothed, engaged or married.
desposeedor, ra. I. *a.* dispossessing. **II.** *n.* dispossessor.
desposeer, *va.* to dispossess, oust.
desposeimiento, *m.* dispossession.
desposorio, *m.* betrothal; (gen. *pl.*) mutual promise to contract marriage, engagement.
déspota, *m.* despot, tyrant.
despótico, ca, *a.* despotic.
despotismo, *m.* despotism, tyranny.
despotizar, *va.* & *vn.* to tyrannize, to oppress.
despotricar, *vn.* & *vr.* (coll.) to talk without restraint.
despreciable, *a.* contemptible, despicable, lowdown; inappreciable, negligible.
despreciador, ra, *n.* & *a.* despiser(-ing), scorner (-ing), contemner(-ing).
despreciar, *va.* to despise, scorn, look down on; to reject, lay aside; to neglect.—**despreciativo, va,** *a.* depreciative, depreciatory; contemptuous.—**desprecio,** *m.* scorn, contempt; slight; neglect; dispraise.
desprender. I. *va.* to unfasten, loose, separate; to emit, give out. **II.** *vr.* (**de**) to give way, to fall down; to issue (from), come out (of), break, or fall, off (of); to extricate oneself (from); to dispossess oneself (of), give away; to follow, be a consequence (of); to part (with); to rid oneself (of).
desprendido, da. I. *pp.* of DESPRENDER. **II.** *a.* disinterested, generous; loose.
desprendimiento, *m.* act of loosening; disinterestedness; indifference; landslide, landslip.
despreocupación, *f.* freedom from bias, openmindedness; unconventionality.
despreocupado, da. I. *pp.* of DESPREOCUPAR. **II.** *a.* unprejudiced; unconventional; freethinking.
despreocupar. I. *va.* to unbias, free from prejudice. **II.** *vr.* to become unbiased, to shake off prejudice; (**de**) to ignore; to discard, set aside; to pay no attention (to).
desprestigiado, da. I. *pp.* of DESPRESTIGIAR. **II.** *a.* having lost one's reputation, in bad repute, unpopular.
desprestigiar. I. *va.* to bring into disrepute, to impair the reputation of. **II.** *vr.* to lose reputation or prestige.—**desprestigio,** *m.* loss of reputation or prestige, unpopularity.
desprevención, *f.* improvidence, want of caution.
desprevenido, da, *a.* unprovided; unprepared.
desproporción, *f.* disproportion; disparity.
desproporcionado, da. I. *pp.* of DESPROPORCIONAR. **II.** *a.* disproportionate; out of proportion; unsuitable, unbecoming.
desproporcionar, *va.* to disproportion, to mismatch, to misproportion.
despropositado, da, *a.* absurd.

despropósito, *m.* absurdity, nonsense.
desproveer, *va.* (*pp.* DESPROVEÍDO, DESPROVISTO) to deprive of provisions or the necessaries of life.
desproveído, da. I. *pp.* of DESPROVEER. **II.** *a.* unprovided; unprepared.
desprovisto, ta. I. *pp. irreg.* of DESPROVEER. **II.** *a.* unprovided, lacking, wanting.—**d. de,** destitute of, all out of.
despueble, [1]despueblo, *m.* depopulation.
[2]despueblo, despueble, *v. V.* DESPOBLAR.
después, *adv.* after, afterward, next, then, later. —**d. de,** after; next to.—**d. de que, d. que,** after.
despulir, *va.* to tarnish; to frost, grind (glass).
despulsarse, *vr.* to be violently affected with any passion; (**por**) to be eagerly desirous (of).
despumación, *f.* despumation, skimming.
despumadera, *f.* = ESPUMADERA, skimmer.
despumar, *va.* = ESPUMAR, to skim.
despuntador, *m.* (min.) ore separator; hammer for breaking ore.
despuntadura, *f.* blunting, taking off the point.
despuntar. I. *va.* to blunt, to crop, cut off, wear out the point of; to cut away the dry combs of (a beehive); (naut.) to double (a cape). **II.** *vn.* to advance in knowledge; to manifest wit and genius; to begin to sprout or bud; to be outstanding; to surpass, excel, morally.—**d. el día, d. el alba, d. la aurora,** to dawn.
desquejar, *va.* to pluck up a shoot near the root of (a plant).—**desqueje,** *m.* pulling up a shoot near the root of a plant.
desquerer, *va.* to lose affection or liking for, to cease to love or like.
desquiciador, ra, *n.* he who or that which unhinges, unsettles or overthrows.
desquiciamiento, *m.* unhinging, disjoining; downfall.
desquiciar. I. *va.* to unhinge, to disjoint; to unsettle, disorder; to deprive of favor or protection; to undermine; to overthrow. **II.** *vr.* to become unhinged; to lose support or backing; to fall down.
desquijaramiento, *m.* act of breaking the jaws.
desquijarar, *va.* to break the jaws of; (naut.) to break the cheek of (a block).
desquijerar, *va.* (carp.) to tenon.
desquilatar, *va.* to diminish the intrinsic value of (gold).
desquitar. I. *va.* to retrieve (a loss). **II.** *vr.* (**de**) to win one's money back; to retaliate, take revenge (for); to get even.
desquite, *m.* compensation, recovery of a loss; revenge, retaliation.
desrabotar, *va.* to cut off the tail of.
desramar, *va.* to strip of branches.
desramillar, *va.* (agr.) to prune (vines).
desrancharse, *vr.* to leave a mess (eating together).
desrastrojar, *va.* to remove the stubble from.
desrazonable, *a.* (coll.) unreasonable.
desregladamente, *adv.*, **desreglado, da,** *a.*; **desreglarse,** *vr.* = DESARREGLADAMENTE, etc.
desrelingar, *va.* (naut.) to take away the boltropes from (the sails).
desreputación, *f.* (coll.) dishonor, disrepute.
desrizar, *va.* (*pret.* DESRICÉ; *subj.* DESRICE) to uncurl.
desroblar, *va.* to take the rivets out of.
destacado, da, I. *pp.* of DESTACAR. **II.** *a.* prominent, outstanding.
destacamento, *m.* (mil.) detachment; station; post.
destacar. I. *va.* (*pret.* DESTAQUÉ; *subj.* DESTAQUE) to bring out, make conspicuous, emphasize; (mil.) to detach. **II.** *vr.* to stand out, be conspicuous; to be prominent, outstanding; to loom.
destaconar, *va.* to wear out the heels of.
destajador, *m.* smith's hammer.
destajar, *va.* to contract for (a job); to do as taskwork; to cut (the cards); to bring out, make stand out. **II.** *vr.* to stand out; to tower, be conspicuous; to project.
destajero, ra, destajista, *n.* person who does taskwork.
destajo, *m.* job, taskwork.—**a d.,** by the job, piece (work); by the lump; earnestly, diligently.
destalonar, *va.* to break or wear out the heels of; to take off coupons from; (vet.) to level the hoofs of.
destallar, *va.* to prune useless branches from.
destapada, *f.* pie without an upper crust.
destapar. I. *va.* to uncover, take off (cover, lid, cap). **II.** *vr.* to become or get uncovered.
destapiado, *m.* place where mud walls have been torn down.
destapiar, *va.* to pull down the mud walls of.
destaponar, *va.* to remove the stopper from.
destarar, *va.* (com.) to diminish the tare of.
destartalado, da, *a.* huddled, jumbled; scantily and poorly furnished.
destazador, ra, *n.* one who cuts up slaughtered animals.
destazar, *va.* to cut up (a carcass).
destechadura, *f.* unroofing.
destechar, *va.* to unroof.
destejar, *va.* to remove tiles; to leave defenseless.
destejer, *va.* to unweave, ravel, unbraid.
destellar. I. *vn.* to twinkle, beam, sparkle, flash. **II.** *va.* to give forth, emit.
destello, *m.* sparkle, beam, flash, scintillation.
destemplado, da. I. *pp.* of DESTEMPLAR. **II.** *a.* inharmonious; out of tune; intemperate; (art) inharmonious, incongruous.
destemplanza, *f.* unsteadiness of the weather; disorder, intemperance; excess, abuse; (med.) indisposition, distemper; want of moderation.
destemplar. I. *va.* to disorder, alter; disconcert; to put to confusion; to put out of tune (a musical instrument). **II.** *vr.* to be ruffled, discomposed; to be out of order; to be irregular or abnormal; to get out of tune; to act improperly or rashly; to lose moderation; (of metal) to lose its temper.
destemple, *m.* discordance, disharmony; being out of tune; discomposure, disorder; intemperance, lack of moderation; slight indisposition; (of metals) untempering, lack of temper.
destentar, *va.* (*ind.* DESTIENTO; *subj.* DESTIENTE) to lead out of temptation.
desteñir, *va.* & *vr.* (*pret.* DESTIÑÓ; *subj.* DESTIÑA) to discolor, to change from the natural hue.
desternillarse, *vr.* to break a cartilage.—**d. de risa,** (coll.) to split one's sides with laughter.
desterradero, *m.* retired part of the town.
desterrado, da. I. *pp.* of DESTFRRAR. **II.** *n.* exile, outcast.
desterrar, *va.* (*ind.* DESTIERRO; *subj.* DESTIERRE) to banish, exile; to lay or put aside; to take the earth off the roots of.
desterronador, ra, *n.* clod crusher, stubble plow.
desterronar, *va.* & *vr.* to break the clods of.
destetadera, *f.* pointed instrument placed on the teats of cows to prevent the calves from sucking.
destetar. I. *va.* to wean. **II.** *vr.* to wean oneself from an evil habit or custom.
destete, *m.* weaning.
desteto, *m.* number of weanlings; place where newly-weaned mules are kept.
destiempo, *adv.*—**a d.,** unseasonably, untimely.
[1]destiento, *m.* surprise; mental commotion.
[2]destiento, destiente, *v. V.* DESTENTAR.
destierre, *m.* removal of dirt from ore, cleaning.
[1]destierro, *m.* exile, banishment; place where exile lives; any remote and solitary place.
[2]destierro, destierre, *v. V.* DESTERRAR.
destilable, *a.* distillable.
destilación, *f.* distillation; filtration; flow of serum.—**d. seca,** destructive distillation.
destiladera, *f.* still, alembic, distilling vessel; filter.
destilador, ra. I. *n.* & *a.* distiller(-ing). **II.** *m.* filtering stone; alembic, still.

destilar. I. *va.* to distil; to filter through a stone. II. *vn.* to distil, to drop, to fall in drops.
destilatorio, ria. I. *a.* distilatory, distilling. II. *m.* distillery; still, alembic.
destilería, *f.* distillery.
destinación, *f.* destination; assignment.
destinado, da. I. *pp.* of DESTINAR.—**estar d. a,** to be bound to (e.g. fail). II. *a.* (**a**), (of a letter, etc.) addressed (to).
destinar, *va.* to destine; to appoint; to designate; to allot, assign; (naut.) to station (ships).
destinatario, ria, *n.* addressee; consignee.
destino, *m.* destiny, fate; destination; appointment, job, employment; (naut.) station.—**con d. a,** bound for, going to.
destiño, etc. *v. V.* DESTEÑIR.
destiranizado, da, *a.* freed from tyranny.
destitución, *f.* dismissal from an employment, office, or charge; destitution, dereliction, abandonment.
destituíble, *a.* dismissable, removable.
destituir, *va.* (*ger.* DESTITUYENDO; *ind. pres.* DESTITUYO, *pret.* él DESTITUYÓ; *subj.* DESTITUYA) to deprive; to make destitute; to dismiss from office.
destocar, *va.* (*pret.* DESTOQUÉ; *subj.* DESTOQUE) to uncoif, to pull off the cap or headdress from.
destorcedura, *f.* untwisting; uncurling.
destorcer. I. *va.* (*ind.* DESTUERZO; *subj.* DESTUERZA) to undo, untwist, uncurl; to rectify, to straighten out. II. *vr.* to become untwisted; to bend, warp; to feaze, to unlay; to deviate; to drift.
destornillado, da. I. *pp.* of DESTORNILLAR. II. *a.* reckless, heedless, rash.
destornillador, *m.* unscrewer; screwdriver.
destornillamiento, *m.* unscrewing; recklessness, rashness, wildness.
destornillar. I. *va.* to unscrew. II. *vr.* to act recklessly, or wildly.
destoserse, *vr.* to feign a cough.
destostarse, *vr.* (of the skin) to lose the suntan.
destrabar, *va.* to unfetter, unbind, to untie, loosen, separate; to break the barriers of.
destraillar, *va.* to unleash.
destral, *m.* small axe or hatchet.—**destraleja,** *f.* very small hatchet.—**destralero, ra,** *n.* axe maker.
destramar, *va.* to unweave, to undo the warp of.
destrejar, *vn.* to work or act with expertness.
destrenzar, *va.* (*pret.* DESTRENCÉ; *subj.* DESTRENCE) to unplait, unbraid, undo a tress of.
destreza, *f.* dexterity, skill; nimbleness.
destricé, destrice, *v. V.* DESTRIZAR.
destrincar, *va.* & *vr.* (naut.) to loose, to unlash.
destripacuentos, *n.* one who interrupts often the person who is talking, one "butting in."
destripamiento, *m.* disembowelment; crushing.
destripar, *va.* to disembowel, gut, eviscerate; to crush, smash; to draw out the inside of; (coll.) to interrupt and spoil (a story).
destripaterrones, *m.* (coll.) harrower, clodbeater; uncultured person.
destripular, *va.* to discharge the crew of.
destrísimo, ma, *a. super.* very dexterous or skillful.
destriunfar, *va.* (cards) to draw out the trumps from (the other players).
destrizar. I. *va.* (*pret.* DESTRICÉ; *subj.* DESTRICE) to mince, crumble, break in pieces; to tear in strips. II. *vr.* to be heartbroken, to languish with grief.
destrocar, *va.* (*ind.* DESTRUECO; *subj.* DESTRUEQUE) to return (a thing bartered).
destrocé, destroce, *v. V.* DESTROZAR.
destrogiro, ra, *a.* clockwise.
destrón, *m.* blind man's guide.
destronamiento, *m.* dethronement.
destronar, *va.* to dethrone. overthrow.
destroncamiento, *m.* detruncation, amputation, lopping of trees; ruination.
destroncar, *va.* (*pret.* DESTRONQUÉ; *subj.* DESTRONQUE) to detruncate, lop, cut short; to maim, dislocate; to cut in pieces; to ruin, destroy; to tire out; (of animals) to overwork.
destrorso, sa, *a.* clockwise.
destrozar, *va.* (*pret.* DESTROCÉ; *subj.* DESTROCE) to destroy, to shatter, to mangle, to break or cut to pieces; to annihilate; to waste, squander.
destrozo, *m.* destruction, havoc, ruin; rout, defeat; massacre.—**destrozón, na,** *a.* destructive of wearing apparel, shoes, etc.
destrucción, *f.* destruction.
destructibilidad, *f.* destructibility.
destructible, *a.* destructible.
destructivamente, *adv.* destructively.
destructividad, *f.* destructiveness.
destructivo, va, *a.* destructive.
destructor, ra, *n.* & *a.* destructor, destroyer (-ive, -ing).
[1]**destrueco, destrueque,** *m.* mutual restitution of things bartered.
[2]**destrueco, destrueque,** *v. V.* DESTROCAR.
destruíble, *a.* destructible.
destruidor, ra, *n.* & *a.* = DESTRUCTOR, RA.
destruir. I. *va.* (*ger.* DESTRUYENDO; *ind. pres.* DESTRUYO, *pret.* él DESTRUYÓ; *subj.* DESTRUYA) to destroy; to ruin; to demolish; to squander; to baffle, thwart; to prevent from earning a living. II. *vr.* to destroy one another; (math.) to cancel.
destruyente, *a.* destroying, destructive.
destuerzo, destuerza, *v. V.* DESTORCER.
desubstanciar, *va.* = DESUSTANCIAR.
desucación, *f.* act of extracting the juice.
desudar, *va.* to wipe off the sweat from.
desueldo, desuelde, *v. V.* DESOLDAR.
desuelo, desuele, *v. V.* DESOLAR.
desuellacaras, *m.* (coll.) bad barber; (coll.) impudent, shameless person.
[1]**desuello,** *m.* act of flaying, fleecing, or skinning; forwardness, impudence, insolence; (coll.) extortion.
[2]**desuello, desuelle,** *v. V.* DESOLLAR.
desulfuración, *f.* desulphurization.
desulfurar, *va.* to desulphurize.
desuncir, *va.* (*ind.* DESUNZO; *subj.* DESUNZA) to unyoke.
desunidamente, *adv.* separately, severally; disunitedly.
desunido, da. I. *pp.* of DESUNIR. II. *a.* disunited, disrupted, unjointed.
desunión, *f.* separation, disunion, disjunction; discord, disunion, feud.
desunir. I. *va.* to separate, take apart; to occasion discord between, to estrange. II. *vr.* to loosen, to fall or break apart; to become separated.
desunzo, desunza, *v. V.* DESUNCIR.
desuñar. I. *va.* to tear off the nails of; to pull out the roots of. II. *vr.* to plunge into vice and dissipation; to work one's fingers to the bone, work oneself to death.
desurcar, *va.* (*ind.* DESURQUÉ; *subj.* DESURQUE) to remove or undo furrows in.
desurdir, *va.* to unweave; to upset, nip in the bud, stop, frustrate.
desurqué, desurque, *v. V.* DESURCAR.
desusadamente, *adv.* unusually, contrary to custom.
desusado, da. I. *pp.* of DESUSAR. II. *a.* obsolete, out of date, archaic.
desusar. I. *va.* to discontinue the use of. II. *vr.* to become obsolete; to go out of date.
desuso, *m.* disuse, obsoleteness, desuetude.
desustanciar, *va.* to enervate, deprive of strength and substance.
desvahar, *va.* (agr.) to take away the dry or withered part of (a plant).
desvaído, da, *a.* tall and graceless, gaunt; (of colors) dull.
desvainar, *va.* to shell, to husk.
desvalido, da, *a.* helpless, destitute, unprotected.
desvalijador, *m.* highwayman.
desvalijamiento, *m.* act of robbing the contents of a valise; robbery.
desvalijar, *va.* to take out the contents of (a valise or gripsack); to rob.

desvalimiento, *m.* dereliction or abandonment; want of favor or protection; want, neediness.
desván, *m.* garret, loft, attic.—**d. gatero,** cockloft, room over the garret.
desvanecer. I. *va.* (*ind.* DESVANEZCO; *subj.* DESVANEZCA) to disintegrate, spread, or divide into minute parts; to cause to vanish or disappear; to take away from the sight; to undo, to remove. **II.** *vr.* to pall, to grow vapid, to become insipid; to vanish, disappear; to swell with presumption or pride; to faint, swoon.
desvanecidamente, *adv.* haughtily, proudly.
desvanecimiento, *m.* pride, haughtiness, loftiness; giddiness, dizziness.
desvanezco, desvanezca, *v. V.* DESVANECER.
desvarar, *va., vn.* & *vr.* to slip, skid; (naut.) to set afloat a ship that was aground.
desvariado, da. I. *pp.* of DESVARIAR. **II.** *a.* delirious, raving; disorderly, irregular; nonsensical; long, crooked (as branches of trees).
desvariar, *vn.* to rave, rant; to dote; to make extravagant demands.
desvarío, *m.* extravagant action or speech; delirium, raving; inconstancy; caprice, whim; monstrousness, extravagancy; derangement, disunion.
desvedar, *va.* to raise the prohibition of.
desvelado, da. I. *pp.* of DESVELAR. **II.** *a.* watchful, vigilant, careful.
desvelamiento, *m.* watchfulness.
desvelar. I. *va.* to keep awake. **II.** *vr.* to go without sleep; to pass a sleepless night; be watchful or vigilant; to take great pains.
desvelo, *m.* watching, want or privation of sleep; watchfulness, vigilance; anxiety, uneasiness.
desvenar, *va.* to separate or clear the veins of; to extract from the veins of (mines) or the filaments of (plants); to raise the bit of (a bridle) so as to form an arch.
desvencijado, da, *a.* rickety, loose-jointed.
desvencijar. I. *va.* to disunite, weaken, divide, break. **II.** *vr.* to be ruptured, disjointed, loose, relaxed; (coll.) to be exhausted.
desvendar, *va.* to take off a bandage from, to unbandage.
desveno, *m.* arch of a horse's bit.
desventaja, *f.* disadvantage.
desventajoso, sa, *a.* disadvantageous, unfavorable, unprofitable, detrimental.
desventar, *va.* (*ind.* DESVIENTO; *subj.* DESVIENTE) to vent; to let out the air of.
desventura, *f.* misfortune, mishap; misery.
desventuradamente, *adv.* unhappily, unfortunately.
desventurado, da, *a.* unfortunate, unlucky, wretched; chicken-hearted, pusillanimous.
desvergoncé, *v. V.* DESVERGONZAR.
desvergonzado, da, *a.* impudent; shameless.
desvergonzarse, *vr.* (*ind. pres.* DESVERGÜENZO, *pret.* DESVERGONCÉ; *subj.* DESVERGÜENCE) to speak or act in an impudent or insolent manner.
desvergüenza, *f.* impudence, effrontery, assurance; shamelessness; shame, disgrace.
desvergüenzo, *v. V.* DESVERGONZARSE.
desvestir, *va.* & *vr.* to undress.
desvezar, *va.* (agr.) to cut the young shoots of (vines) near the roots.
desviación, *f.* deviation, deflection; detour; oblique direction; (med.) deviation from natural position (as the bones); (med.) extravasation of fluids; (astr.) deviation from the meridian; variation of the magnetic needle.
desviadero, *m.* (Cuba) railway siding.
desviado, da. I. *pp.* of DESVIAR. **II.** *a.* devious, out of the common track, askew.
desviador, ra. I. *a.* deflective. **II.** *m.* (elec.) divertor.
desviar. I. *va.* to deflect; to sway; to dissuade; to put by; (fencing) to ward off; (Ry.) to switch.—**d. la mirada,** to avoid (someone's) eyes. **II.** *vr.* **(de)** to deviate (from), wander (away from); to turn off (from); to swerve; (aer.) to drift (away from).
desviento, desviente, *v. V.* DESVENTAR.
desvío, *m.* deviation, turning away; going astray; deflection; aversion, displeasure; coldness, indifference; (Ry.) siding, side track; (mason.) steadying board (of a suspended platform).
desvirar, *va.* to pare off the fore part of (a sole); (bookbinding) to trim (a book); (naut.) to reverse (the capstan).
desvirgar, *va.* (low) to deflower.
desvirtuar, *va.* to lessen the value, strength or merit of; to detract from.
desvitrificar, *va.* devitrify.
desvivirse, *vr.* **(por)** to have excessive love (for); to show great interest (in behalf of); to long (for), be dying (for, to).
desvolvedor, *m.* nut wrench.
desvolver, *va.* (*pp. irreg.* DESVUELTO; *ind.* DESVUELVO; *subj.* DESVUELVA) to alter the shape of; to plow, till.
desvuelto, ta, *pp. irreg.* of DESVOLVER.
desvuelvo, desvuelva, *v. V.* DESVOLVER.
desyemar, *va.* (agr.) to remove buds from; (Am.) to separate yolk from white of (an egg).
desyerbador, ra, *n.* grubber, weeder.
desyerbar, *va.* to weed, grub.
deszocar, *va.* to disable the foot of.
deszumar, *va.* to extract the juice or substance from.
detallar, *va.* to detail, relate minutely, particularize; to specify; to retail.
detalle, *m.* detail, particular; (com.) retail.
detallista, *n.* one addicted to details (esp. a painter); (com.) retailer.
detasa, *f.* (Ry.) rebate.
detección, *f.* detection.
detective; detectivo, va, *n.* detective.
detectivismo, *m.* detective force or service.
detector, *m.* (elec., radio) detector.
detención, *f.* delay, stop, stay, halt, standstill, deadlock; (naut.) demurrage, arrest, embargo (of a ship).
detenedor, ra, *n.* detainer, stopper; check, arrester, catch.
detener. I. *va.* (*ind. pres.* DETENGO, *pret.* DETUVE, *fut.* DETENDRÉ; *subj.* DETENGA) to stop, detain, check; arrest; (naut.) to capture, to embargo; to keep back; to retain, reserve. **II.** *vr.* to tarry, stay, stop over; to stop halt; to pause.
detengo, detenga, *v. V.* DETENER.
detenidamente, *adv.* dilatorily; carefully, painstakingly, thoroughly.
detenido, da. I. *pp.* of DETENER. **II.** *a.* sparing, niggardly, parsimonious; dilatory; careful thorough, conscientious; (law) under arrest (person). **II.** *n.* prisoner.
detenimiento, *m.* care, thoroughness.
detentación, *f.* (law) deforcement.
detentador, *m.* deforciant.
detentar, *va.* to deforce (law), to retain or keep unlawfully.
detergente, *a.* (med.) detergent, detersive.
deterger, *va.* (med.) to cleanse (a wound, etc.)
deterioración, *f.* = DETERIORO.
deteriorado, da. I. *pp.* of DETERIORAR. **II.** *a.* deteriorated; (U. S., coll.) worn-out, beat-up.
deteriorar, *va.* & *vr.* to deteriorate; (U. S., coll.) to wear out.
deterioro, *m.* deterioration, damage, wear and tear.
determinable, *a.* determinable, ascertainable.
determinación, *f.* determination, resolution; conclusion or final decision; firmness.
determinado, da. I. *pp.* of DETERMINAR. **II.** *a.* determinate, determined, decided; fixed, resolute; settled, definite; (math.) determinate.
determinante. I. *a.* determining, determinate, determinative. **II.** *m.* (gram.) determining verb. **III.** *m.* or *f.* (math.) determinant.
determinar. I. *va* to determine, fix; to limit; to specify; to distinguish, discern; to appoint, to assign (as time and place); to decide, resolve; to conclude (as a lawsuit). **II.** *vr.* to determine, resolve; to make up one's mind.

determinativo, va, *a.* determinative.
determinismo, *m.* (philos.) determinism.
determinista, *n.* & *a.* (philos.) determinist.
detersión, *f.* (med.) detersion; cleansing.
detersivo, va; detersorio, ria, *a.* detersive, cleansing, detergent.
detestable, *a.* detestable; hateful.
detestación, *f.* detestation, abhorrence, abomination.
detestar, *va.* to detest, abhor, abominate.
detienebuey, *m.* (bot.) common rest-harrow.
detonación, *f.* detonation, blast, fulmination.
detonante, *a.* detonating.
detonar, *vn.* to detonate; to flash, to explode.
detorsión, *f.* (med.) distortion.
detracción, *f.* detraction, defamation, obloquy; detraction, withdrawing, taking away.
detractar, *va.* to detract; to defame, slander.
detractor, ra, *n.* & *a.* detractor(-ing), slanderer (-ing, -ous).
detraer, *va.* (*ger.* DETRAYENDO; *pp.* DETRAÍDO; *ind. pres.* DETRAIGO, *pret.* DETRAJE; *subj.* DETRAIGA) to detract, remove, take away; to defame, slander, villify.
detrás, *adv.* behind, after; back; in the rear.—**d. de,** behind, in back of.—**d. del telón,** (theat.) backstage.—**por d.,** from the rear, from behind; behind one's back.
detrimento, *m.* detriment, damage, harm.—**con (sin) d. de,** with (without) detriment to.
detrítico, ca, *a.* (geol.) detrital, detritic.
detrito, detritus, *m.* detritus, debris; (geol., med.) detritus.
detuve, *pret.* of DETENER.
deuda, *f.* debt; fault, offence; indebtedness; public debt.—**d. consolidada,** funded debt.—**d. exterior,** foreign debt.—**d. flotante,** floating debt.—**d. nacional,** national debt.—**d. pendiente,** unpaid balance.—**deudas activas,** assets.—**deudas pasivas,** liabilities.—**estar en d. con,** to be indebted to.
deudo, da, *n.* relative, kin, kindred; *m.* kinship, relationship.
deudor, ra. I. *a.* indebted, beholden. **II.** *n.* debtor.
deuterio, *m.* (chem.) deuterium.
deuterión, *f.* (chem.) deuteron.
deuterogamia, *f.* deuterogamy.
deuterógamo, ma, *n.* deuterogamist.
Deuteronomio, *m.* (relig.) Deuteronomy.
deuteruro, *m.* (chem.) deuteride.
deutón, *m.* (phys.) deuton.
deutoplasma, *m.* (embryol.) deutoplasm.
deutóxido, *m.* (chem.) deutoxide, dioxide.
devalar, *vn.* (naut.) to deviate, to drift.
devanadera, *f.* reel, spool, bobbin, winding frame.—**d. de golpe,** clock reel, snap reel; (naut.) log reel.
devanador, ra, *n.* winder, spool, reel; anything on which another thing is wound.—**d. de lanzadera,** shuttle winder.
devanar. I. *va.* to reel, wind. **II.** *vr.* (Am.) to be convulsed (with laughter); to writhe (with pain).—**d. los sesos,** to rack one's brain.
devanear, *vn.* to rave, talk nonsense.
devaneo, *m.* delirium, alienation of mind, giddiness; frenzy; idle or mad pursuit; dissipation; love affair.
devastación, *f.* devastation, destruction, havoc.
devastador, ra, *n.* & *a.* desolator(-ing), devastator(-ing).
devastar, *va.* to devastate, lay waste, ruin.
devengar, *va.* (*pret.* DEVENGUÉ; *subj.* DEVENGUE) to earn, draw (as salary, interest, etc.).
devenir, *vn.* to happen; to become.
deviación, *f.* = DESVIACIÓN.
devisar, *va.* (Am.) to descry; to see vaguely.
devoción, *f.* piety, devoutness; prayer; devotion, strong affection, faithful attachment.
devocionario, *m.* prayer book.
devolución, *f.* (law) devolution, restitution.—**d. de derechos,** (com.) drawback; debenture.
devolutivo, *a.* (law) returnable, restorable.
devolver, *va.* (*pp.* DEVUELTO; *ind.* DEVUELVO; *subj.* DEVUELVA) to return; to restore; to refund, pay back.
devoniano, na; devónico, ca, *a.* Devonian.
devorador, ra. I. *n.* devourer. **II.** *a.* devouring, intense, ravenous.
devorante, *a.* = DEVORADOR.
devorar, *va.* to devour, swallow up, consume ravenously, gobble.
devotería, *f.* false devoutness, overreligiosity.
devoto, ta, *a.* devout, pious; strongly attached, devoted.
devuelto, ta, *pp. irreg.* of DEVOLVER.
devuelvo, devuelva, *v. V.* DEVOLVER.
dexiocardia, *f.* (med.) dexiocardia.
dextrina, *f.* (chem.) dextrine.
dextro, *m.* area around a church.
dextrógiro, *m.* (chem.) dextrorotatory.
dextrórsum, *adv.* towards the right.
dextrosa, *f.* (chem.) dextrose.
dey, *m.* dey (a Moslem ruler).
deyección, *f.* (geol.) débris; (med.) dejection.
dezmable, *a.* subject to tithes.
dezmatorio, *m.* place where tithes are collected; tithing.
dezmeño, ña; dezmero, ra. I. *a.* pertaining to tithes. **II.** *m.* tither.
dezmería, *f.* tithe land.
[1]di, *pret. irreg.* of DAR.
[2]di, *imper.* of DECIR.
día, *m.* day; daylight, sunshine.—**d. civil,** calendar day.—**d. de abstinencia,** fast day, fish day.—**d. de año nuevo,** New Year's day.—**d. de años,** birthday.—**d. de ayuno,** fast or fasting day.—**d. de besamanos,** court day.—**d. de carne,** meat day.—**d. de ceniza,** Ash Wednesday.—**d. de cumpleaños,** birthday.—**d. de cutio,** working day.—**d. de descanso,** day of rest, Sabbath.—**d. de engañabobos,** All Fools' Day; April Fools' Day.—**d. de fiesta,** holiday.—**d. de gala,** gala day.—**d. de guardar,** (eccl.) holy day.—**d. de huelga,** day off, day of rest.—**d. de joya,** court day.—**d. del ajuste de cuentas,** day of reckoning.—**d. de las madres,** Mother's Day.—**d. del juicio,** doomsday.—**d. de los difuntos,** All Souls' Day.—**d. de los inocentes,** Holy Innocents' Day.—**d. de los padres,** Father's Day.—**d. del trabajo,** (U. S.) Labor Day.—**d. de pagos** or **de paga,** payday.—**d. de pescado,** fast day, fish day.—**d. de precepto,** holy day.—**d. de Ramos,** Palm Sunday.—**d. de recibo,** reception day, at-home day.—**d. de Reyes,** Twelfthtide, Twelfth-day, Epiphany.—**d. de San Martín,** Martinmas.—**d. de San Valentín,** St. Valentine's Day.—**d. de todos los santos,** All Saints' Day, Allhallows.—**d. de trabajo,** working day, weekday.—**d. de viernes,** Meager Day.—**d. de vigilia,** fast day, fish day.—**d. diado,** appointed day.—**d. entre semana,** working day, weekday.—**d. feriado** or **festivo,** holiday.—**d. hábil,** (law) court day.—**d. intercalar,** intercalary day of February.—**d. laborable,** working day, weekday.—**d. lectivo,** school day.—**d. medio,** mean day.—**d. onomástico,** a person's saint's day.—**d. pesado,** gloomy day.—**d. por medio,** every other day.—**d. quebrado,** half holiday.—**días caniculares,** dog days.—**días de gracia,** (com.) days of grace.—**días ha,** it is a long time since.—**d. sidéreo,** sidereal day.—**d. útil,** working day, weekday.—**a días,** at times, once in a while.—**al d.,** up to date; per day; by the day.—**al d. siguiente,** on the next day.—**a los pocos días,** a few days later.—**al otro d.,** on the following day.—**buenos días,** good morning.—**cada tercer d.** = UN D. SÍ Y OTRO NO.—**dar los días,** to send birthday congratulations.—**de d.,** by day, in the daytime.—**de d. en d.,** or **de un d. para otro,** from day to day.—**de hoy en ocho días,** this day week, a week from today.—**el d. de ayer,** yesterday.—**el d. de hoy,** or **hoy en d.,** the present day, today.—**el d. menos pensado,** one of these days, when

one least expects.—**el mejor d.**, some fine day. —**el otro d.**, the other day.—**en días de Dios, en los días de la vida**, never.—**en días pasados**, some days ago.—**en estos**, or **los últimos, días**, recently.—**en mis días**, in my day, in my lifetime.—**en su d.**, at the proper time. —**entre d.**, in the daytime.—**hasta el d. de hoy**, (up) to this day.—**hoy (en) d.**, nowadays.—**los días de uno**, one's saint's day or birthday.—**medio d.**, or **mediodía**, noon.—**ocho días**, a week.—**quince días**, two weeks, a fortnight.—**ser persona de días**, or **tener días**, to be of advanced age.—**todos los días**, daily, every day.—**un día sí y otro no**, day about, every other day.
diabasa, *f.* diorite, diabase, a kind of rock.
diabetes, *f.* diabetes.
diabético, ca, *n.* & *a.* diabetic.
diabla, *f.* (coll.) she-devil.—**a la d.**, carelessly, roughly.—**cosido a la d.**, (bookbinding) bound in paper.
diablear, *vn.* (coll.) to commit deviltries, play pranks.
diablejo, *m.* little devil, imp.
diablesa, *f.* (coll.) she-devil.
diablillo, *m. dim.* deviling, devilkin, little devil, imp; (coll.) smart, clever, mischievous fellow.—**d. cartesiano**, or **de Descartes**, (phys.) Cartesian diver.
diablo, *m.* devil, Satan; devil, a perverse, cunning, subtle or hideous person.—**¡d.!** the devil! the deuce!—**d. cojuelo**, artful devil.—**¡cómo diablos!**—(coll.) how the deuce.—**como un d.**, (coll.) like the deuce, like the devil.—**eso es el d.**, (coll.) that is the trouble.—**haber la de todos los diablos**, there to be (that is, *there* followed by the appropriate tense of *to be*) a great row or commotion.—**llevarse el d.**, to be ruined, fall through, be a fizzle.—**no valer un d.**, (coll.) to be good for nothing.—**pobre d.**, poor devil.—**¡qué d.!** or **¡un d.!** (coll.) the devil!—**ser de la piel del d.**, to be a limb of the devil.
diablura, *f.* diabolical undertaking; deviltry, mischief, wild prank.
diabólico, ca, *a.* diabolical, devilish.
diábolo, *m.* diabolo, an old game.
diacatalicón, *m.* (med.) diacatholicon, a laxative.
diacáustico, ca, *a.* (phys.) diacaustic.
diacitrón, *m.* lemon peel preserved in sugar.
diaconado, *m.* deaconship.
diaconal, *a.* diaconal.
diaconato, *m.* deaconship.
diaconía, *f.* deaconry.
diaconisa, *f.* deaconess.
diácono, *m.* deacon.
diacrítico, ca, *a.* (gram.) diacritical; (med.) diagnostic.
diactínico, ca, *a.* (photog.) diactinic.
diacústica, *f.* diacoustics.
díada, *f.* (chem.) dyad.
diadelfo, fa, *a.* (bot.) diadelphous.
diadema, *f.* diadem, crown; glory, halo.
diademado, da, *a.* (her.) diademed.
diado, da, *a.* appointed (day).
diafanidad, *f.* diaphaneity, transparency.
diáfano, na, *a.* transparent, clear, diaphanous.
diáfisis, *f.* (anat.) diaphysis.
diaforesis, *f.* (med.) diaphoresis, perspiration.
diaforético, ca. I. *a.* diaphoretic, diaphoretical. II. *m.* diaphoretic.
diafragma, *m.* (anat., mech., etc.) diaphragm.
diafragmático, ca, *a.* diaphragmatic.
diagnosis, *f.* (med.) diagnostics.
diagnosta, *n.* diagnostician.
diagnosticar, *va.* (*pret.* DIAGNOSTIQUÉ; *subj.* DIAGNOSTIQUE) to diagnose.
diagnóstico, ca. I. *a.* (med.) diagnostic. II. *m.* diagnosis.
diagnostiqué, diagnostique, *v. V.* DIAGNOSTICAR.
diagonal. I. *a.* diagonal; oblique. II. *f.* (geom.) diagonal; guy wire; stay.
diágrafo, *m.* diagraph.
diagrama, *m.* diagram.
diálaga, *f.* (min.) diallage.
dialectal, *a.* dialect (as *a.*), pert. to dialects.
dialéctica, *f.* dialectics.
dialéctico, ca. I. *a.* dialectic, dialectical. II. *n.* dialectician, logician.
dialecto, *m.* dialect; derived language.
dialectología *f.* dialectology, science or study of dialects.
diálisis, *f.* (chem.) dialysis.
dialítico, ca, *a.* dialytic.
dializador, ra. I. *a.* dialytic. II. *m.* (chem.) dialyzer.
dializar, *va.* (chem.) to dialyze.
dialogal, *a.* colloquial, dialogistic.
dialogar, *vn.* to dialogize; to chat, converse.
dialogismo, *m.* (rhet.) dialogism.
dialogístico, ca, *a.* colloquial, dialogistic.
dialogizar, *vn.* = DIALOGAR.
diálogo, *m.* dialogue.—**dialoguista,** *m.* dialogist.
dialtea, *f.* marsh mallow ointment.
diamagnético, ca, *m.* & *a.* (phys.) diamagnetic.
diamagnetismo, *m.* diamagnetism.
diamantado, da, *a.* diamondlike.
diamante, *m.* diamond; adamant.—**d. en bruto**, rough or uncut diamond; (coll.) an uncultured person of sterling qualities, "a rough diamond."
diamantífero, ra, *a.* diamantiferous, containing diamonds.
diamantino, na, *a.* adamantine, diamantine.
diamantista, *m.* diamond cutter; jeweller.
diametral, *a.* diametrical.
diámetro, *m.* diameter.—**d. interior**, internal diameter.
diamida, *f.* (chem.) diamide.
diana, *f.* (mil.) reveille; (poet.) the moon.
dianche, *m.* & *interj.* (coll.) the deuce! the devil!
diandro, dra, *a.* (bot.) diandrous.
diantre, *m.* (coll.) = DIANCHE.
diapasón, *m.* (mus.) tuning fork; diapason; pitch, accord; regular octave.—**d. normal**, standard pitch.
diapédesis, *f.* (med.) diapedesis.
diapente, *m.* (mus.) perfect fifth.
diapófisis, *f.* (anat.) diapophysis.
diapositiva, *f.* (photog.) plate; lantern slide.
diaprea, *f.* a sort of round plum.
diaquilón, *m.* (pharm.) diachylon, diachylum.
diariamente, *adv.* daily.
diario, ria. I. *a.* daily. II. *m.* journal, diary; daily newspaper; daily household expense.—**a d.**, *adv.* daily, every day.—**d. de navegación**, log book.
diarismo, *m.* journalism.
diarista, *n.* journalist, diarist.
diarquía, *f.* diarchy.
diarrea, *f.* diarrhea.
diarreico, ca; diárrico, ca, *a.* diarrheic.
diartrosis, *f.* (anat.) diarthrosis.
diascordio, *m.* (pharm.) diascordium.
diáspero, *m.* jasper.
diásporo, *m.* (min.) diaspore.
diastasa, *f.* (chem.) diastase.
diastasis, *f.* (surg.) diastasis.
diástilo, *a.* (arch.) diastyle.
diástole, *m.* (anat. and rhet.) diastole.
diastólico, ca, *a.* (physiol.) diastolic.
diatermancia, *f.* (phys.) diathermancy.
diatérmano, na; diatérmico, ca, *f.* (phys.) diathermanous.
diatermia, *f.* diathermy.
diatesarón, *m.* (mus.) diatessaron.
diatésico, ca, *a.* (med.) diathetic.
diátesis, *f.* (med.) diathesis.
diatomea, *f.* (bot.) diatom.
diatómico, ca, *a.* (chem.) diatomic.
diatónicamente, *adv.* (mus.) diatonically.

diatónico, ca, *a.* (mus.) diatonic.
diatriba, *f.* diatribe.
dibásico, ca, *a.* (chem.) dibasic.
dibujador, ra, *n.* draftsman(-woman).
dibujante. I. *a.* sketching. **II.** *m.* draftsman.
dibujar. I. *va.* to draw, make a drawing of; to depict, describe vividly. **II.** *vr.* to throw a shadow upon a surface.
dibujo, *m.* drawing; sketch; portrayal, description.—**d. animado,** animated cartoon.—**d. a pulso,** freehand drawing.—**d. del natural,** drawing from life or from nature.—**d. especificado,** detail drawing.—**d. lineal,** instrumental drawing.
dicacidad, *f.* pertness, sauciness, banter.
dicaz, *a.* (of speech) keen, biting.
dicción, *f.* diction, style, language.
diccionario, *m.* dictionary.
diccionarista, *n.* lexicographer.
dicente, diciente, *a.* saying, talking.
diciembre, *m.* December.
diciendo, *ger.* of DECIR.
diclino, na, *a.* (bot.) diclinous.
dicotiledón; dicotiledóneo, a. I. *a.* (bot.) dicotyledonous. **II.** *n.* dicotyledon. **III.** *f. pl.* Dicotyledones.
dicotomía, *f.* dichotomy.
dicotómico, ca; dicótomo, ma, *a.* dichotomic, dichotomous.
dicroico, ca, *a.* (phys.) dichroic.
dicroísmo, *n.* (phys.) dichroism.
dicromático, ca, *a.* dichromic.
dicromatismo, *m.* dichromatism.
dicromato, *m.* (chem.) dichromate.
dictado, *m.* title of dignity or honor; dictation.—*pl.* dictates, promptings.
dictador, ra, *n.* dictator.
dictadura, *f.* dictatorship.
dictáfono, *m.* Dictaphone (trademark).
dictamen, *m.* opinion, judgment; suggestion, insinuation, advice.
dictaminar, *vn.* to express an opinion, pass judgment.
díctamo, *m.* (bot.) dittany.—**d. bastardo,** shrubby white horehound.—**d. blanco,** or **real,** white flaxinella.—**d. crético,** marjoram.
dictar, *va.* to dictate; to command, prescribe, direct; to inspire, suggest, prompt.
dictatorial, *a.* dictatorial.
dictatorio, ria, *a.* dictatorial.
dicterio, *m.* taunt, keen reproach; insult.
dictógrafo, *m.* Dictograph (trademark).
dicha, *f.* happiness, good, luck, good fortune.—**a d.,** or **por d.,** *adv.* by chance.
dicharachero, ra, *a.* (coll.) that uses slang.
dicharacho, *m.* (coll.) vulgar, low, or slang expression.
dichero, ra, *a.* witty.
dicho, cha. I. *pp. irreg.* of DECIR.—**d. se está,** it goes without saying.—**d. y hecho,** no sooner said than done. **II.** *a.* (the) said, mentioned; this.—**lo d., d.,** I mean what I say, I have said it; it's agreed. **III.** *m.* saying, saw, proverb; expression, sentence; statement; witty remark, repartee; declaration, deposition; promise of marriage.—**d. de las gentes,** gossip; rumor.—**del d. al hecho hay gran trecho,** it is a long way from saying to doing; it is one thing to say, and quite another thing to do.
dichoso, sa, *a.* happy; fortunate, lucky.
didáctica, *f.* didactics.
didáctico, ca; didascálico, ca, *a.* didactic, didactical.
didelfo, fa, *n.* & *a.* (zool.) didelphian (as the kangaroo or the opossum).
didimio, *m.* (chem.) didymium.
dídimo, ma, *a.* (bot.) didymous.
diecinueve, *n.* & *a.* nineteen; nineteenth.
diecinueveavo, va, *n.* & *a.* nineteenth.
dieciochavo, va, *n.* & *a.* eighteenth.
dieciocheno, na. I. *a.* eighteenth. **II.** *m.* a kind of cloth.
dieciocho, *n.* & *a.* eighteen; eighteenth.
dieciseis, *n.* & *a.* sixteen; sixteenth.
dieciseisavo, va, *n.* & *a.* sixteenth.
dieciseiseno, na, *a.* sixteenth.
diecisiete, *n.* & *a.* seventeen; seventeenth.
diecisieteavo, va, *n.* & *a.* seventeenth.
diedro, dra. I. *a.* (math.) dihedral. **II.** *m.* dihedral angle.
dieléctrico, ca, *a.* dielectric.
diente, *m.* tooth; fang or tusk of wild boars or elephants; tooth (of a saw, comb, rake, file); cog (of a wheel or pinion); tine or prong (of a fork); tongue (of a buckle); clove (of garlic).—*pl.* indented edges of tools or ornaments, indentations.—**d. de leche,** milk, first tooth.—**d. de león,** (bot.) dandelion or lion's tooth.—**d. de lobo,** burnisher, spike.—**d. de perro,** sculptor's dented chisel; (bot.) dog-tooth violet.—**d. incisivo,** incisor, cutting tooth, foretooth.—**d. mamón,** = D. DE LECHE.—**d. molar,** molar tooth, back tooth.—**dientes caninos,** eye teeth, canine teeth.—**dientes postizos,** false teeth.—**aguzar los dientes,** to whet the appetite.—**a regaña dientes,** *adv.* most unwillingly.—**dar d. con d.,** to shiver with cold or fear, to be with teeth chattering.—**decir,** or **hablar, entre dientes,** to mumble, to mutter.—**de dientes afuera,** without sincerity, as mere lip service.—**tener buen d.,** to be a hearty eater.
diento, diente, *v. V.* DENTAR.
diéresis, *f.* diæresis.
diesi, *f.* (mus.) diesis; a sharp.
diestra, *f.* right hand; favor, support.
diestro, tra. I. *a.* right; dexterous, able, skilful, handy; dexter; sagacious, wise; sly, artful, cunning; favorable, propitious.—**a d. y siniestro,** recklessly; right and left. **II.** *m.* skilful fencer; bullfighter; halter or bridle.
[1]**dieta,** *f.* diet, prescribed or regulated meals.—*pl.* (naut.) provisions for the sick and wounded.
[2]**dieta,** *f.* diet, legislative assembly; (law) one day's journey of ten leagues by land; daily salary of judges and other officers of the law; daily fees paid a physician.—*pl.* allowance to public functionary while serving away from his residence.
dietario, *m.* family account book; record book, book where notable events are registered.
dietética, *f.* (med.) dietetics.
dietético, ca, *a.* dietetic, dietetical.
dietista, *n.* dietician, nutritionist.
diez, *m.* & *a.* ten; tenth.—**d. de bolos,** pin standing alone in front of the ninepins.—*pl. f.* **las diez,** ten o'clock.
diezmal, *a.* decimal.
diezmar, *va.* (of war, disease, etc.) to decimate: to tithe; (mil.) to punish one in ten of.
diezmero, *m.* one who pays or receives tithes.
diezmesino, na, *a.* ten months old.
diezmilésimo, ma, *n.* & *a.* ten-thousandth.
diezmilímetro, *m.* ten-thousandth of a meter.
diezmillonésimo, ma, *n.* & *a.* ten-millionth.
diezmo, *m.* tithe; tenth part; duty of ten per cent; decimation.
difamación, *f.* defamation
difamador, ra, *n.* & *a.* defamer(-ing).
difamar, *va.* to defame, to discredit.—**difamatorio, ria,** *a.* defamatory.
diferencia, *f.* difference, dissimilarity; disagreement; (math.) difference.—**a d. de,** unlike; as distinguished from.
diferenciación, *f.* (biol., math., etc.) differentiation.
diferencial. I. *a.* differential. **II.** *m.* (auto) differential. **III.** *f.* (math.) differential.
diferenciar. I. *va.* to differentiate, distinguish between; to alter the use or destination of. **II.** *vn.* to differ, dissent, disagree. **III.** *vr.* to differ, to be different; to distinguish oneself.
diferente, *a.* different.
diferido, da. I. *pp.* of DIFERIR. **II.** *a.* deferred (cablegram).

diferir. **I.** *va.* (*ind.* DIFIERO; *subj.* DIFIERA) to defer, postpone, put off; to adjourn, suspend; to protract, prolong, extend. **II.** *vn.* to differ, be different; (naut.) to remove the gaskets of a sail.
difícil, *a.* difficult, hard.
difícilmente, *adv.* with difficulty.
dificultad, *f.* difficulty; objection.
dificultador, ra. **I.** *n.* one who raises difficulties. **II.** *a.* causing difficulties.
dificultar, *va.* to make difficult; to impede.
dificultosamente, *adv.* with difficulty.
dificultoso, sa, *a.* difficult, hard; (coll.) ugly, homely.
difidación, *f.* declaration of war.
difidencia, *f.* diffidence; distrust.
difidente, *a.* distrustful; diffident.
difiero, difiera, *v.* *V.* DIFERIR.
difilo, la, *a.* (bot.) two-leaf.
difluencia, *f.* diffluence.
difluente, *a.* diffluent.
difluir, *vn.* (*ger.* DIFLUYENDO; *ind. pres.* DIFLUYO, *pret.* él DIFLUYÓ; *subj.* DIFLUYA) to be diffused or spread out.
difracción, *f.* diffraction.
difractar, *va.* (phys.) to diffract.
difrangente, *a.* diffractive.
difteria, *f.* (med.) diphtheria.
diftérico, ca, *a.* diphtheritic.
difteritis, *f.* (med.) diphtheritic inflammation.
difundido, da. **I.** *pp.* of DIFUNDIR. **II.** *a.* diffuse, diffused, scattered.
difundidor, ra. **I.** *a.* diffusing. **II.** *m.* diffuser.
difundir, *va.* to diffuse, spread out; to spread (as news); to divulge, publish; (radio) to broadcast.
difunto, ta. **I.** *a.* defunct, deceased, dead; late; decayed, withered. **II.** *m.* & *f.* corpse.
difusible, *a.* diffusible.
difusión, *f.* diffusion; diffusiveness, dispersion; exuberance of style; (radio) broadcasting.
difusivo, va, *a.* diffusive.
difuso, sa, *a.* diffuse; wordy; wide-spread.
difusor, ra. **I.** *a.* difusing, defusive; (radio) broadcasting. **II.** *m.* (sugar manufact.) diffuser. **III.** *f.* broadcasting station.
diga, digo, *v.* *V.* DECIR.
digástrico, ca, *a.* (anat.) digastric.
digerible, *a.* digestible.
digerir, *va.* (*ind.* DIGIERO; *subj.* DIGIERA) to digest; to bear; to put up with; (chem.) to digest.
digestibilidad, *f.* digestibility.
digestible, *a.* digestible.
digestión, *f.* (physiol. and chem.) digestion.
digestivo, va. **I.** *a.* digestive. **II.** *m.* (surg.) suppurative.
digesto, *m.* (law) digest, systematic compilation of laws.
digestor, *m.* digester (apparatus).
digiero, digiera, *v.* *V.* DIGERIR.
digitación, *f.* fingering.
digitado, da, *a.* (bot. and zool.) digitate.
digital. **I.** *a.* digital, finger (as *a.* as in *impresión digital,* fingerprint). **II.** *f.* (bot.) digitalis, foxglove.
digitalina, *f.* (chem.) digitalin.
digitígrado, da, *a.* (zool.) digitigrade.
dígito, ta. **I.** *a.* digital. **II.** *m.* (astr., arith.) digit.
diglifo, *m.* (arch.) diglyph.
dignación, *f.* condescension, accommodation.
dignamente, *adv.* worthily; with dignity.
dignarse, *vr.* to condescend, deign, vouchsafe.
dignatario, *m.* dignitary.
dignidad, *f.* dignity, high rank, office or position; honor, greatness; dignified bearing; archbishop or bishop.
dignificar, *va.* to dignify.
digno, na, *a.* meritorious, worthy, deserving; worthwhile; suitable, fit, fitting, appropriate.
digo, diga, *v.* *V.* DECIR.—**¡digo!,** listen! say!—**digo,** I mean (clarifying or amending a previous statement).
digresión, *f.* digression; (astr.) digression.
digresivo, va, *a.* digressive.
dihueñe, dihueñi, *m.* (Chile) an edible fungus growing on trees.
dij, dije, *m.* amulet, charm; trinket; watchcharm; any small piece of jewellery; (coll.) person of sterling qualities; (coll.) one gorgeously attired; (coll.) handy person.
dije, dijo, *v.* *V.* DECIR.
dilaceración, *f.* dilaceration, tearing apart.
dilacerar, *va.* to dilacerate, tear asunder.
dilación, *f.* delay, procrastination.
dilapidación, *f.* dilapidation.
dilapidado, da, *a.* dilapidated; dilated.
dilapidador, ra, *n.* dilapidator.
dilapidar, *va.* to dilapidate.
dilatabilidad, *f.* expansibility.
dilatable, *a.* dilatable, expansible.
dilatación, *f.* dilatation, expansion, distention; prolongation; enlargement; diffuseness, prolixity; calmness, serenity in sorrow; (phys., etc.) expansion.—**d. lineal,** linear expansion.
dilatado, da. **I.** *pp.* of DILATAR. **II.** *a.* large, extended, extensive, vast; drawn out.
dilatador, ra. **I.** *a.* dilating, expanding; retarding, causing delay. **II.** *m.* (surg.) dilator.
dilatar. **I.** *va.* & *vr.* to dilate, widen, expand, enlarge, lengthen, prolong; to swell, spread out; to defer, retard, delay, put off, protract; (fig.) to comfort, to cheer up. **II.** *vr.* to be diffuse, expatiate; to expand; to delay, tarry.
dilatativo, va, *a.* dilative.
dilatoria, *f.* delay, waste of time.
dilatorio, ria, *a.* dilatory, delaying, long.
dilección, *f.* dilection, love, affection.
dilecto, ta, *a.* loved, beloved.
dilema, *m.* dilemma.
diletante, *n.* & *a.* dilettante.
diletantismo, *m.* dilettantism.
diligencia, *f.* diligence, assiduity, industriousness; action, measure (to carry out something); speediness, activity, briskness; diligence, stagecoach; (coll.) affair, business, errand; (law) judicial proceeding.—**hacer d.,** or **la d.,** to endeavor, try.—**hacer una d.,** to do an errand; to attend, or go on, some business.
diligenciar, *va.* to conduct, to carry out; to further.
diligenciero, *m.* agent, attorney.
diligente, *a.* diligent, assiduous; prompt, swift.
diligentemente, *adv.* diligently, assiduously.
dilogía, *f.* ambiguity, double sense.
dilucidación, *f.* elucidation, explanation.
dilucidador, ra, *n.* elucidator.
dilucidar, *va.* to elucidate, explain, discuss.
dilucidario, *m.* explanatory writing.
dilución, *f.* dilution.
diluente, *a.* diluent.
diluir, *va.* & *vr.* (*ger.* DILUYENDO; *ind. pres.* DILUYO, *pret.* él DILUYÓ; *subj.* DILUYA) to dilute; to weaken.
diluvial. **I.** *a.* diluvian, diluvial; (geol.) diluvial. **II.** *m.* (geol.) diluvium.
diluviano, na, *a.* diluvian, diluvial.
diluviar, *vn. impers.* to rain heavily.
diluvio, *m.* flood, deluge; overflow, inundation; (coll.) vast abundance, a lot, lots.
diluyendo, diluyó, etc. *v.* *V.* DILUIR.
diluyente, *n.* & *a.* diluent.
dimanación, *f.* springing or issuing.
dimanar, *vn.* (**de**) to spring or proceed (from); to originate (in); to be due (to); to follow (from).
dimensión, *f.* dimension; extent, capacity, magnitude, size.—**dimensional,** *a.* dimensional.
dimes, *m. pl.*—**andar en d. y diretes,** to haggle, chaffer, quibble, argue.
dimetilo, *m.* (chem.) dimethyl.
dimidiar. **I.** *va.* to dimidiate, halve. **II.** *vn.* to be halved, be divided in two.
diminución, *f.* diminution.—**ir en d.,** to taper (as a pole); to be diminishing or becoming less or lower.

diminuir, *va., vn. & vr.* = DISMINUIR, diminish.
diminutamente, *adv.* diminutively; minutely; by retail.
diminutivamente, *adv.* (gram.) diminutively.
diminutivo, va. I. *a.* diminishing; diminutive. **II.** *m.* (gram.) diminutive.
diminuto, ta, *a.* diminutive, very little or small.
dimisión, *f.* resignation (of membership, office).
dimisorio, ria. I. *a.* dimissory. **II.** *f. pl.* (eccl.) dimissory letters; (coll.) dismissal, discharge, firing.
dimitente. I. *a.* resigning. **II.** *n.* person resigning.
dimitir, *va.* to resign, give up, relinquish.
dimorfismo, *m.* (min.) dimorphism.
dimorfo, fa, *a.* (min.) dimorphous.
din, *m.* (coll. for DINERO) money, boodle.
dina, *f.* (phys.) dyne.
Dinamarca, *f.* Denmark.
dinamarqués, quesa. I. *a.* Danish. **II.** *n.* Dane; *m.* Danish (language).
dinámetro, *m.* (opt.) dynameter.
dinámica, *f.* dynamics.
dinámico, ca, *a.* dynamic.
dinamismo, *m.* dynamism.
dinamista, *n. & a.* dynamist(-ic).
dinamita, *f.* dynamite.
dinamitero, ra, *n.* dynamiter.
dínamo, *f.* (gen. *m.* in Am.) dynamo.
dinamoeléctrico, ca, *a.* dynamo-electric.
dinamogénesis, *m.* (psychiat.) dynamogenesis.
dinamométrico, ca, *a.* dynamometric.
dinamómetro, *m.* dynamometer.
dinamotor, *m.* (elec.) dynamotor.
dinasta, *m.* dynast, sovereign, monarch.
dinastía, *f.* dynasty.
dinástico, ca, *a.* dynastic, dynastical.
dinastismo, *m.* fealty to a dynasty.
dinerada, *f.* large sum of money.
dineral, *m.* large sum of money; formerly, a set of weights for gold and silver.
dinerillo, *m.* small copper coin; (coll.) small sum of money.
dinero, *m.* money; currency, coin; gold, coinage; ancient Spanish silver coin; standard of silver, 24 grains; Peruvian silver coin; wealth, fortune. —**d. contante, d. contante y sonante, d. efectivo,** or **d. en tabla,** ready money, cash.—**d. suelto,** small, change.—**persona de d.,** person of means, or well off.
dineroso, sa, *a.* moneyed, rich.
dineruelo, *m. dim.* small coin; a little money, some money.
dingo, *m.* dingo, Australian wild dog.
dinodo, *m.* (nuclear phys.) dynode.
dinornis, *m.* (paleontol.) dinornis, moa.
dinosauro, *m.* (paleontol.) dinosaur.—*pl.* Dinosauria.
dinoterio, *m.* (paleontol.) dinothere, dinotherium.
dintel, *m.* (arch.) lintel, doorhead.
dintelar, *va.* to provide with lintels.
dintorno, *m.* (art) within the contour.
diocesano, na. I. *a.* diocesan. **II.** *m.* diocesan, bishop.
diócesi, diócesis, *f.* diocese.
diodo, *m.* (electron.) diode.
dioico, ca, *a.* (bot.) diœcious, diecious.
dionea, *f.* (bot.) dionæa, Venus's flytrap.
dionisia, *f.* bloodstone; hematite.
dionisíaco, ca, *a.* Dionysiac, Bacchic.
dioptra, *f.* (opt.) diopter, alidade; sight (of the instrument).
dioptria, *f.* (opt.) diopter (unit of refractive power).
dióptrica, *f.* (opt.) dioptrics.
dióptrico, ca, *a.* (opt.) dioptric.
diorama, *m.* diorama.
diorámico, ca, *a.* dioramic.
diorita, *f.* diorite, a kind of rock.
dios, *m.* god; (D-) God.—**D. delante,** with God's help.—**D. es D.,** as sure as God lives; by Jupiter!—**D. es grande,** trust in God; all things are possible.—**D. le guarde,** God be with you. —**D. lo haga,** or **lo quiera,** God grant.—**D. los hace y ellos se juntan,** birds of a feather flock together.—**D. mediante,** God willing, with God's help.—**D. me (nos) libre,** God forbid, God protect or deliver me (us).—**¡D. mío!** my God! goodness me! oh my!—**anda con D.,** farewell, adieu.—**la,** or **las, de D. es Cristo,** turmoil, bedlam, row.—**mediante D.,** God willing.—**no lo quiera D.,** God forbid.—**plegue a D.,** or **quiera D.,** God grant.—**¡por D.!** for Heaven's sake! goodness!—**sabe D.,** goodness knows, only God knows.—**sea como D. quiera,** be it as God wishes.—**¡válgame D.!** bless me!—**¡válgate D.!** God preserve, or bless, you!—**vaya Vd. con D.,** good-bye; go on; off with you, begone.—**¡vive D.!** as sure as God lives; by God! by Heaven!
diosa, *f.* goddess.
diostedé, *m.* S. A. bird like the toucan.
dipétalo, la, *a.* (bot.) dipetalous, bipetalous.
diploide, *m. & a.* (biol.) diploid.
diploma, *m.* diploma; charter.
diplomacia, *f.* diplomacy.—**d. del dólar,** dollar diplomacy.
diplomáticamente, *adv.* diplomatically.
diplomático, ca. I. *a.* diplomatic. **II.** *n.* diplomat, diplomatist; *f.* diplomatics; diplomacy.—**d. de profesión,** career diplomat.
diplopía, *f.* (med.) diplopia, seeing double.
dipsáceo, cea, *a.* (bot.) dipsacaceous.
dipsomanía, *f.* dipsomania.
dipsomaníaco, ca, dipsómano, na. I. *a.* dipsomaniacal. **II.** *n.* dipsomaniac.
díptero, ra. I. *a.* (entom., bot.) dipterous; (arch.) dipteral. **II.** *m.* (entom.) dipteran; (arch.) dipteros, dipteral building.
dipterocárpeo, pea, *a.* (bot.) dipterocarpaceous.
dipterología, *f.* dipterology.
díptica, *f.*, **díptico,** *m.* diptych.
diptongación, *f.* (gram.) diphthongization.
diptongar, *va.* to diphthongize.
diptongo, *m.* diphthong.
diputación, *f.* deputation; object of a deputation.
diputado, da. I. *pp.* of DIPUTAR. **II.** *m.* deputy, representative, delegate; (com.) assignee.—**d. a Cortes,** congressman.—**d. cunero,** (coll.) congressman who owes his election to the influence of the government.
diputador, ra, *n. & a.* constituent.
diputar, *va.* to depute, delegate, commission; to constitute, empower.
dique, *m.* dike, dam, mole, jetty; (naut.) dry dock; check, bar, stop; (min.) crop.
dirección, *f.* direction, course, tendency, trend, turn; direction, management, administration; order, command, instruction; address (for letters, etc.); board of directors, executive board; editorship of a newspaper; managership of a theater; office of a director.
directivo, va. I. *a.* directive, managing. **II.** *f.* governing board, board of directors, management.
directo, ta, *a.* direct; straight.
director, ra. I. *n. & a.* director(-ing). **II.** *n.* director, manager; chief; editor (of a newspaper); principal (of a school).—**d. de escena,** stage manager.—**d. de orquesta,** conductor, leader of an orchestra.—**d. espiritual,** father confessor.—**directoral,** *a.* directorial.
directorio, ria. I. *a.* directive, directorial. **II.** *m.* directory; body of directors, directorate.
directriz, *f.* (math.) directrix.
dirigente. I. *a.* directing, leading; ruling. **II.** *m. & f.* leader.
dirigible. I. *a.* dirigible; manageable; (aer.) dirigible. **II.** *m.* (aer.) dirigible.
dirigir. I. *va.* (*ind.* DIRIJO; *subj.* DIRIJA) to direct; to dedicate (a work); to address (a letter, etc.); to command, lead, head; to govern, control, manage; (naut.) to steer.—**d. la palabra,** to speak (to), address. **II.** *vr.* **(a)** to address,

speak (to); to apply, resort (to); to go (to or toward).
dirimente, *a.* breaking off, dissolving.
dirimible, *a.* that may be broken off.
dirimir, *va.* to dissolve, disjoin, separate; to annul, to declare void; to adjust, reconcile.
disanto, *m.* holy day.
discantar, *va.* to chant, sing; to comment; to descant, discourse much about; (mus.) to sing in counterpoint.
discante, *m.* small guitar; descant, comment, talk at length; (mus.) descant.
discar, *va.* to dial (telephone).
disceptación, *f.* argument, controversy.
disceptar, *vn.* to dispute, argue.
discernidor, ra, *n.* & *a.* discerner(-ing).
discerniente, *a.* discerning.
discernimiento, *m.* discernment, judgment, discrimination; (law) appointment of a guardian.
discernir, *va.* (*ind.* DISCIERNO; *subj.* DISCIERNA) to discern, judge, discriminate; (law) to appoint (a guardian).
disciplina, *f.* discipline; education, instruction; systematic training; any art or science taught; rule of conduct, order.—*pl.* scourge, cat-of-nine-tails; flagellation.
disciplinable, *a.* disciplinable.
disciplinado, da. I. *pp.* of DISCIPLINAR. **II.** *a.* disciplined, trained; marbled, variegated (as flowers).
disciplinal, *a.* disciplinal, disciplinary.
disciplinante. I. *a.* disciplinary; Disciplinant. **II.** *n.* Disciplinant.
disciplinar. I. *va.* to discipline, educate, instruct, train; (mil.) to drill. **II.** *vr.* to scourge oneself as penance.
disciplinario, ria, *a.* disciplinary.
disciplinazo, *m.* lashing; whipping.
discipulado, *m.* discipleship; education, instruction; group of pupils.
discipular, *a.* pertaining to a disciple or pupil.
discípulo, la, *n.* disciple; follower; pupil, student.
disco, *m.* disk, disc; record, phonograph record, (U. S., coll.) platter; discus; quoit; (astr., bot., zool.) disk.—**d. de goma,** washer.—**d. de llamada,** dial (telephone).—**d. de señales,** (Ry.) semaphore.—**d. volador** or **volante,** flying saucer.
discóbolo, *m.* discobolus. discus thrower.
discoidal, discoide, discoideo, a, *a.* disk-like, flat and round.
díscolo, la, *a.* ungovernable; wayward, froward.
discoloro, ra, *a.* (bot.) colorless.
disconforme, -midad = DESCONFORME, etc.
discontinuación, *f.* discontinuation.
discontinuar, *va.* to discontinue, to stop.
discontinuidad, *f.* discontinuity.
discontinuo, a, *a.* discontinuous.
disconveniencia, -niente, -nir, = DESCONVENIENCIA, -NIENTE, -NIR.
discordancia, *f.* disagreement, discordance.
discordante, *a.* dissonant, discordant.
discordar, *vn.* (*ind.* DISCUERDO; *subj.* DISCUERDE) to be in discord, disagree.
discorde, *a.* discordant; (mus.) dissonant.
discordemente, *adv.* discordantly.
discordia, *f.* discord, disagreement, discordance, opposition, clash.
discrasia, *f.* (med.) cacochymy.
discreción, *f.* discretion, judgment; acuteness of mind, sagacity; liberty of action and decision. —**a d.,** optional; (mil.) unconditionally.
discrecional, *a.* optional, discretionary.
discrepancia, *f.* discrepancy.
discrepante, *a.* disagreeing, discrepant.
discrepar, *vn.* to differ, to disagree.
discretear, *vn.* to affect discretion.
discreteo, *m.* affected discretion.
discreto, ta, *a.* discreet, circumspect, prudent; fairly good, not bad; ingenious, sharp, witty; (math.) (of quantity) discrete; (med.) discrete (as smallpox pustules).
discrimen, *m.* hazard, risk, peril; difference.
discriminador, ra, *n.* & *a.* (Am.) discriminator (-ing, -ive).
discriminar, *va.* (Am.) to discriminate.
discuerdo, discuerde, *v. V.* DISCORDAR.
disculpa, *f.* apology, excuse; exculpation.
disculpabilidad, *f.* excusability; pardonableness.
disculpable, *a.* excusable; pardonable.
disculpar, *va.* & *vr.* to exculpate; to excuse; to apologize.
discurrir. I. *vn.* to roam, ramble about; to flow (as a river); to reflect, think; to reason; to discourse. **II.** *va.* to invent, plan, contrive; to conjecture, infer.
discursante, *n.* discourser, lecturer.
discursar, *vn.* (**sobre** or **acerca de**) to discourse (on); to treat (of); to lecture (on).
discursear, *vn.* (coll. and contempt.) to harangue, to make a speech.
discursista, *m.* speech maker.
discursivo, va, *a.* discursive; thoughtful, meditative, cogitative.
discurso, *m.* discourse; cogitation, ratiocination, reasoning; speech, lecture, oration; dissertation, treatise, tract; conversation, talk; space of time.
discusión, *f.* discussion.
discutible, *a.* controvertible, disputable.
discutidor, ra, *n.* & *a.* arguer(-ing).
discutir, *va.* & *vn.* to discuss; to argue about.
disecación, *f.* = DISECCIÓN.
disecador, ra, *n.* dissector; taxidermist.
disecar, *va.* (*pret.* DISEQUÉ; *subj.* DISEQUE) to dissect; to do an autopsy on; to stuff (dead animals).
disección, *f.* dissection, anatomy.
disector, ra, *n.* dissector.
diseminación, *f.* dissemination; scattering, spreading.
diseminador, ra, *n.* & *a.* disseminator(-ing); spreader(-ing).
diseminar, *va.* to disseminate; spread, scatter.
disensión, *f.* dissent; contest, strife.
disenso, *m.* dissent, disagreement.
disentería, *f.* (med.) dysentery.
disentérico, ca, *a.* dysenteric.
disentimiento, *m.* dissent, disagreement.
disentir, *vn.* (*ger.* DISINTIENDO; *ind. pres.* DISIENTO, *pret.* él DISINTIÓ; *subj.* DISIENTA) to dissent, to disagree, to differ.
diseñador, ra, *n.* designer, delineator.
diseñar, *va.* to draw; to sketch, outline.
diseño, *m.* sketch, plan, outline; portrayal, description.
disertación, *f.* dissertation, disquisition.
disertador, ra; disertante, *n.* & *a.* discourser (-ing), expounder(-ing).
disertar, *vn.* (**sobre** or **acerca de**) to discourse (on), treat (of), discuss.
diserto, ta, *a.* eloquent, fluent.
disfagia, *f.* (med.) dysphagia.
disfasia, *f.* (med.) dysphasia.
disfavor, *m.* disregard, disfavor.
disfonía, *f.* (med.) dysphonia.
disformar, *va.* & *vr.* = DEFORMAR.
disforme, *a.* deformed, hideous; huge, big.
disformidad, *f.* deformity; excessive bigness.
disfracé, disfrace, *v. V.* DISFRAZAR.
disfraz, *m.* mask, costume, disguise; dissimulation, dissembling.
disfrazar. I. *va.* (*pret.* DISFRACÉ; *subj.* DISFRACE) to disguise; to misrepresent. **II.** *vr.* to disguise oneself; to masquerade; to travesty.
disfrutar. I. *va.* to benefit by; to have the benefit of; to enjoy (good health, etc.). **II.** *vn.* **d. de,** to enjoy, to have.—**disfrute,** *m.* use, benefit.
disgregable, *a.* separable.
disgregación, *f.* separation, disjunction; disintegration, dissociation.
disgregar, *va.* (*pret.* DISGREGUÉ; *subj.* DISGREGUE) to separate, disjoin, disperse.

disgregativo, va, *a.* disjunctive.
disgregué, disgregue, *v. V.* DISGREGAR.
disgustadamente, *adv.* with displeasure.
disgustado, da, *a.* disgusted; annoyed, bothered; peevish; sad, glum, unhappy; tasteless, insipid.
disgustar. I. *va.* to displease; to dislike (diff. constr.: *esto me disgusta,* I dislike this); to offend; to anger. **II.** *vr.* to be (get) displeased, hurt or angry; to fall out (with each other).
disgusto, *m.* disgust, loathing; ill humor; displeasure; unpleasantness, quarrel; vexation, annoyance; grief sorrow.—**a d.,** against one's will.—**estar a d.,** to be ill at ease, uncomfortable.
disidencia, *f.* dissidence, nonconformity.
disidente, *a.* & *n.* dissident, dissenter(-ing), nonconformist.
disidir, *vn.* to dissent, disagree.
disiento, disienta, *v. V.* DISENTIR.
disílabo, ba. I. *a.* dissyllabic. **II.** *m.* (gram.) dissyllable.
disimetría, *f.* dissymmetry, lack of symmetry.
disimétrico, ca, *a.* dissymmetric, unsymmetric.
disímil, *a.* dissimilar.
disimilación, *f.* (phon.) dissimilation.
disimilar. I. *a.* dissimilar. **II.** *va.* & *vr.* (phon.) to dissimilate.
disimilitud, *f.* unlikeness.
disimulable, *a.* that may be dissembled; excusable.
disimulación, *f.* dissimulation, dissembling.
disimuladamente, *adv.* dissemblingly, on the sly, on the quiet.
disimulado, da. I. *pp.* of DISIMULAR. **II.** *a.* dissembling; reserved, sullen; sly, cunning.—**hacer la d.,** (coll.) to feign ignorance.
disimulador, ra, *n.* & *a.* dissembler(-ing).
disimular, *va.* to dissimulate, dissemble; to feign, pretend; to tolerate, overlook, let pass; to misrepresent.
disimulo, *m.* dissimulation; tolerance.
disintiendo, disintió, *v. V.* DISENTIR.
disipable, *a.* easily scattered; capable of being dissipated.
disipación, *f.* dissipation; dispersion, scattering; evanescence; extravagance, waste.
disipado, da. I. *pp.* of DISIPAR. **II.** *a.* dissipated; prodigal; dissolute.
disipador, ra, *n.* & *a.* squanderer(-ing); spendthrift.
disipar. I. *va.* & *vr.* to dissipate, to disperse, to scatter (as clouds). **II.** *va.* to squander, misspend, lavish; to drive away; to dispel.
dislate, *m.* nonsense, absurdity.
dislocación, dislocadura, *f.* dislocation; sprain; (min.) slide.
dislocar, *va.* & *vr.* (*pret.* DISLOQUÉ; *subj.* DISLOQUE); to dislocate, displace, sprain, disjoint.
dismenorrea, *f.* (med.) dysmenorrhœa.
disminución, *f.* DIMINUCIÓN, diminution; (vet.) a disease in horses' hoofs.
disminuir. I. *va.* (*ger.* DISMINUYENDO; *ind. pres.* DISMINUYO, *pret.* él DISMINUYÓ; *subj.* DISMINUYA) to diminish, lessen, lower, decrease; to detract from. **II.** *vr.* to diminish, decrease.
dismutación, *f.* (chem.) disproportionation.
disnea, *f.* (med.) dyspnea, dyspnœa.
disneico, ca, *a.* dyspneic, dyspneal.
disociación, *f.* dissociation, separation.
disociador, ra, *a.* dissociative.
disociar, *va.* to dissociate, separate.
disolubilidad, *f.* dissolubility; solubility.
disoluble, *a.* dissoluble.
disolución, *f.* dissolution, disintegration; (chem.) dissolution; solution; dissoluteness, dissipation.—**d. de sociedad,** dissolution of partnership.
disolutivo, va, *a.* solvent.
disoluto, ta, *a.* dissolute, loose, dissipated.
disolvente, *m.* dissolvent, dissolver.
disolver. I. *va.* (*pp. irreg.* DISUELTO; *ind.* DISUELVO; *subj.* DISUELVA) to loosen, untie; to dissolve, break up (as a meeting); to separate, disunite; (phys., chem.) to dissolve. **II.** *vr.* to dissolve.
disón, *m.* (mus.) discord.
disonancia, *f.* harsh sound; disagreement, discord; (mus.) dissonance.
disonante, *a.* dissonant, inharmonious; discordant, unsuitable.
disonar, *vn.* (*ind.* DISUENO; *subj.* DISUENE) to disagree in sound, to be inharmonious; to be discordant, to disagree.
dísono, na, *a.* dissonant, inharmonious.
dispar, *a.* unlike, unequal, unmatched.
disparada, *f.* (Am.) sudden and hasty start; flight.—**a la d.,** at full speed; hurriedly and recklessly.—**de una d.,** promptly; at once.
disparadamente, *adv.* hurriedly.
disparadero, *m.* trigger (on firearms).
disparador, *m.* shooter; trigger; ratchet or ratchet wheel, in clockwork; (naut.) anchor tripper.
disparar. I. *va.* & *vn.* to shoot, discharge, fire; let off; to cast or throw with violence. **II.** *vn.* (coll.) to talk nonsense, to blunder. **III.** *vr.* to run headlong, to rush; to run away (as a horse); (naut.) to turn violently (as the capstan); to go off (as a gun).
disparatadamente, *adv.* blunderingly; absurdly, nonsensically.
disparatado, da. I. *pp.* of DISPARATAR. **II.** *a.* absurd, foolish, nonsensical.
disparatador, ra, *n.* nonsensical talker.
disparatar, *vn.* to act absurdly; to talk nonsense; to blunder.
disparate, *m.* blunder, mistake, (U. S., coll.) blooper; absurdity, nonsense.
disparatero, ra, *n.* (Am.) bungler; one who "talks through his hat."
disparatorio, *m.* nonsensical or blundering act, speech or writing.
disparejo, ja, *a.* uneven.
disparidad, *f.* disparity, inequality.
disparo, *m.* discharge, explosion; nonsense, absurdity.
dispendio, *m.* excessive expense; excessive waste.
dispendioso, sa, *a.* costly, expensive.
dispensa, *f.* dispense, privilege, exemption, dispensation; document granting a dispensation.
dispensable, *a.* dispensable; excusable.
dispensación, *f.* dispensation, exemption.
dispensador, ra. I. *a.* dispensing, distributing; dispensatory. **II.** *n.* dispenser, distributer; dispensator.
dispensar, *va.* to dispense, deal out, distribute; to exempt; to acquit, absolve; to excuse, pardon.
dispensario, *m.* (incorrectly used for) pharmacopoeia; clinic.
¡dispense! ¡dispénseme!, (*subj.* of DISPENSAR) excuse me! (beg) pardon!
dispepsia, *f.* (med.) dyspepsia.
dispéptico, ca, *a.* dyspeptic.
dispersador, ra. I. *a.* dispersive. **II.** *n.* disperser.
dispersar, *va.* & *vr.* to disperse, scatter.
dispersión, *f.* dispersion, breakup.
dispersivo, va, *a.* dispersive.—**poder d.,** (opt.) dispersive power.
disperso, sa, *a.* dispersed, separated; scattered.
dispertador, ra, *a.* & *n.* = DESPERTADOR.
dispertar, *va.* & *vn.* = DESPERTAR.
displacer, *va.* & *vn.* = DESPLACER.
displicencia, *f.* disagreeableness; lukewarmness.
displicente, *a.* disagreeable, unpleasant; peevish.
disponedor, ra, *n.* & *a.* disposer(-ing), distributer(-ing).
disponer. I. *va.* & *vn.* (*pp.* DISPUESTO; *ind. pres.* DISPONGO, *pret.* DISPUSE, *fut.* DISPONDRÉ; *subj.* DISPONGA) to dispose; arrange, prepare, lay out; to resolve, direct, order, command.—**d. de,** to have at one's disposal. **II.** *vr.* (**para** or **a**) to prepare oneself, to get ready (to); to make one's will.
dispongo, disponga, *v. V.* DISPONER.

disponibilidad, *f.* availability.—**d. de mano de obra,** labor supply.
disponible, *a.* disposable, available.
disposición, *f.* disposition, arrangement; disposal; aptitude, natural fitness, capacity; inclination; state of health; condition, circumstances; elegance of carriage; temper; ability, expediency; proportion, symmetry, measure; resolution, order, command; specification, requirement; provision, proviso, prescription; power, authority; (naut.) trim of a ship.—**a la d. de usted,** I am (or it is) at your disposal.
dispositivamente, *adv.* dispositively.
dispositivo, va. I. *a.* dispositive. II. *m.* device, contrivance; mechanism; appliance.—**d. de lanzamiento,** launcher.—**dispositivos investigadores del espacio,** space probe.
disprosio, *m.* (chem.) dysprosium.
dispuesto, ta. I. *pp. irreg.* of DISPONER. II. *a.* disposed, ready; genteel, graceful.—**bien d.,** quite well; favorably disposed or inclined.—**mal d.,** indisposed, ill; unfavorably disposed.
dispuse, dispuso, *v.* V. DISPONER.
disputa, *f.* dispute, controversy; contest; debate.—**sin d.,** undoubtedly, indisputably.
disputable, *a.* disputable; contestable.
disputador, ra, *n.* disputant, disputer.
disputar, *va.* & *vn.* to dispute, controvert, contend, debate, contest; to question; to debate, argue; to fight for.
disquisición, *f.* disquisition.
distancia, *f.* distance, interval of time or place; range, difference, disparity.—**d. focal,** (opt.) focal distance or length; focus.—**a d.,** at a distance, far.—**a larga d.,** (Am., tel.) long-distance.
distanciar, *va.* to distance; to place at a distance, put farther apart.
distante, *a.* distant, far, remote; (naut.) off.
distantemente, *adv.* distantly.
distar, *vn.* to be distant; to be different.—**d. de,** to be far from; to be (a specified distance) from.
distender, *va.* (*ind.* DISTIENDO; *subj.* DISTIENDA) (med.) to distend, to swell.
distensible, *a.* (med.) distensible.
distensión, *f.* distention, expansion.
dístico, ca. I. *a.* (bot.) distichous. II. *m.* (poet.) distich, couplet.—**d. heroico,** (poet.) heroic couplet.
distiendo, distienda, *v.* V. DISTENDER.
distinción, *f.* distinction; difference; prerogative, privilege; superiority (in culture); honor, consideration; order, precision.—**a d. de,** in contradistinction to, as distinguished from; unlike.
[1]**distingo,** *m.* restriction, qualification; (logic) distinction.
[2]**distingo, distinga,** *v.* V. DISTINGUIR.
distinguible, *a.* distinguishable.
distinguido, da. I. *pp.* of DISTINGUIR. II. *a.* distinguished, conspicuous, prominent.
distinguir. I. *va.* (*ind.* DISTINGO; *subj.* DISTINGA) to distinguish, tell apart; to see clearly at a distance, make out; to esteem, show regard for; to clear up, explain. II. *vr.* to distinguish oneself, to excel; (de) to differ, be distinguished (from).
distintamente, *adv.* distinctly; differently.
distintivo, va. I. *a.* distinctive. II. *m.* distinctive mark; distinguishing or peculiar feature or fact.
distinto, ta, *a.* distinct; plain, clear; different (separate, individual).
distocia, *f.* (med.) dystocia, difficult parturition.
distócico, ca, *a.* dystocial.
dístomo, *m.* (zool.) distomatous.
distracción, *f.* heedlessness, absent-mindedness; oversight; diversion, amusement, pastime; licentiousness, want of constraint.—**por d.,** for amusement, as a diversion; through an oversight.
distraer. I. *va.* (*ger.* DISTRAYENDO; *ind. pres.* DISTRAIGO, *pret.* DISTRAJE; *subj.* DISTRAIGA) to distract, to harass the mind; to perplex, bewilder, confuse; to divert, amuse, entertain; to lead astray. II. *vr.* to be absent-minded; to be inattentive; to amuse or enjoy oneself.
distraídamente, *adv.* absent-mindedly, without thinking.
distraído, da. I. *pp.* of DISTRAER. II. *a.* inattentive, heedless; absent-minded; dissolute, licentious.
distraigo, distraiga, *v.* V. DISTRAER.
distraimiento, *m.* = DISTRACCIÓN.
distraje, distrajo, distrayendo, *v.* V. DISTRAER.
distribución, *f.* distribution; division, apportionment; (print.) distribution of type.—**d. de frecuencias,** (stat.) frequency distribution.
distribuidor, ra. I. *n.* & *a.* distributer(-ing). II. *m.* (hydraul.) guides, guide system (of a turbine); (steam eng.) slide valve; valve gear.
distribuir, *va.* (*ger.* DISTRIBUYENDO; *ind. pres.* DISTRIBUYO, *pret.* él DISTRIBUYÓ; *subj.* DISTRIBUYA) to distribute, divide, deal out; to sort (as mail matter); (print.) to distribute (type).
distributivamente, *adv.* distributively.
distributivo, va, *a.* distributive, dissuading.
distributor, ra; distribuyente, *n.* & *a.* distributer(-ing).
distribuyo, etc. *v.* V. DISTRIBUIR.
distrito, *m.* district, ward, precinct, region.
distrofia, *f.* (med.) dystrophy.—**d. muscular,** (med.) muscular dystrophy.
disturbar, *va.* to disturb.
disturbio, *m.* disturbance, outbreak.
disuadir, *va.* to dissuade, deter.
disuasión, *f.* dissuasion, determent.
disuasivo, va. I. *a.* dissuasive, dissuading. II. *m.* deterrent.
disuelto, ta, *pp. irreg.* of DISOLVER.
disuelvo, disuelva, *v.* V. DISOLVER.
disueno, disuene, *v.* V. DISONAR.
disuria, *f.* (med.) dysuria.
disyunción, *f.* disjunction, separation; (gram.) disjunctive particle.
disyunta, *f.* (mus.) change of the voice.
disyuntiva, *f.* alternative.
disyuntivo, va. I. *a.* disjunctive. II. *f.* disjunctive proposition; dilemma.
disyuntor, *m.* (elec.) circuit breaker.
dita, *f.* surety, bondsman; security, bond.
ditá, *m.* (bot.) dita, a P. I. tree that yields ditamine.
ditaína, *f.*, ditamine, a febrifuge extracted from dita bark.
diteísmo, *m.* ditheism.
diteísta. I. *a.* ditheistic. II. *n.* ditheist.
ditiónico, ca, *a.* (chem.) dithionic.
ditirámbico, ca, *a.* dithyrambical.
ditirambo, *m.* dithyramb.
dítono, *m.* (mus.) ditone.
diuresis, *f.* (med.) diuresis, excess of urine.
diurético, ca, *a.* & *m.* diuretic.
diurno, na. I. *a.* diurnal. II. *m.* diurnal, prayer-book.—*f. pl.* butterflies, Lepidoptera.—*m. pl.* dayflies.
diuturnidad, *f.* long duration.
diuturno, na, *a.* lasting, of long duration.
divagación, *f.* wandering, digression.
divagador, ra, *n.* & *a.* roamer(-ing), rambler (-ing); digressor(-ing).
divagar, *vn.* (*pret.* DIVAGUÉ, *subj.* DIVAGUE) to roam, to ramble; to digress.
diván, *m.* divan, supreme council among the Turks; place of its meetings; divan, low cushioned sofa; collection of Oriental poems.
divergencia, *f.* divergence, divergency.
divergente, *a.* divergent; dissenting.
divergir, *vn.* to diverge; to dissent.
diversidad, *f.* diversity, unlikeness; variety, abundance, plenty.
diversificación, *f.* diversification.
diversificar, *va.* to diversify, vary.
diversiforme, *a.* diversiform, of varied forms.

diversión, *f.* entertainment, amusement; (mil.) diversion.
diversivo, va, *a.* (med.) divertive.
diverso, sa, *a.* diverse, different; various, several.
divertido, da. I. *pp.* of DIVERTIR. **II.** *a.* amusing, entertaining; humorous, funny.
divertimiento, *m.* diversion, amusement.
divertir. I. *va.* (*ind. pres.* DIVIERTO, *pret.* él DIVIRTIÓ; *subj.* DIVIERTA) to turn aside, divert; to amuse, entertain; (mil.) to divert (the enemy). **II.** *vr.* to amuse oneself, to have a good time.
dividendo, *m.* (arith. & com.) dividend.
divididero, ra, *a.* divisible.
dividir. I. *va.* & *vn.* to divide. **II.** *vr.* to divide; to split; to be divided; (**de**) to separate (from), part company (with).
dividivi, *m.* (bot.) dividivi, a tropical-American tree yielding valuable dyeing and tanning products.
dividuo, dua, *a.* (law) divisible.
divierto, divierta, *v. V.* DIVERTIR.
divieso, *m.* (med.) furuncle, boil.
divinación, *f.* divination.
divinatorio, ria, *a.* divinatory.
divinicé, divinice, *v. V.* DIVINIZAR.
divinidad, *f.* divinity; god; woman of great beauty.—**la D.,** the Deity.
divinización, *f.* deification.
divinizar, *va.* (*pret.* DIVINICÉ; *subj.* DIVINICE) to deify; (fig.) to sanctify.
divino, na. I. *a.* divine; excellent, admirable; most beautiful. **II.** *n.* diviner.
divirtió, *pret.* of DIVERTIR.
divisa, *f.* badge, emblem, impress; (law) devise. —*pl.* (com.) holdings; (law) devisen.
divisar, *va.* to descry at a distance, to perceive indistinctly; (her.) to vary.
divisibilidad, *f.* divisibility.
divisible, *a.* divisible.
división, *f.* division; distribution; section, quarter, ward, compartment; disunity, discord; hyphen; (mil.) division; (math. etc.) division.
divisional, *a.* divisional.
divisivo, va, *a.* divisible, divisive.
divisor, ra. I. *n.* & *a.* divider(-ing). **II.** *m.* (math.) divisor.
divisorio, ria. I. *a.* dividing. **II.** *m.* (print.) copyholder. **III.** *f.* (geol.) divide.
divo, va. **I.** *a.* (poet.) divine, godlike. **II.** *m.* (poet.) god; *f.* (poet.) goddess; diva; *m.* & *f.* opera singer.
divorciador, ra, *n.* divorcer.
divorciar. I. *va.* to divorce; to separate, part, divide. **II.** *vr.* to get divorced.
divorcio, *m.* divorce; disunion; breach.
divulgable, *a.* that may be divulged.
divulgación, *f.* publication, spreading abroad.
divulgador, ra, *n.* & *a.* divulger(-ing).
divulgar. I. *va.* (*pret.* DIVULGUÉ; *subj.* DIVULGUE) to publish, divulge, spread, give out, reveal; to popularize. **II.** *vr.* to become widespread.
diz (contr. of DÍCESE), it is said.—**dizque. I.** = DIZ QUE. **II.** *m.* objection, muttering; rumor.
[1]**do,** *m.* (mus.) first note of a diatonic scale.
[2]**do, dó,** *adv.* (poet.) DONDE, DÓNDE.
dobla, *f.* an ancient Spanish gold coin.
dobladamente, *adv.* doubly; deceitfully, artfully.
dobladilla, *f.* an ancient game of cards.—**a la d.,** doubly, repeatedly.
dobladillo, *m.* (sewing) hem, border; strong knitting thread.
doblado, da. I. *pp.* of DOBLAR. **II.** *a.* strong, robust, thick-set; deceitful, dissembling. **III.** *m.* measure of the fold in cloth.
doblador, ra, *n.* doubler, bender, folder.
dobladura, *f.* fold, crease.
doblamiento, *m.* doubling, bending, folding.
doblar. I. *va.* to double, make double; to fold; to crease; to bend; to subdue; to induce or influence.—**d. la esquina,** to turn the corner.—**d. un cabo,** (naut.) to double or round a cape. **II.** *vn.* to toll the passing bell. **III.** *vr.* to bend; bow, stoop; submit, acquiesce, give in, yield.
doble. I. *a.* double, twofold, duplicate; thick, heavy (as cloth); thick-set, robust, strong; two-faced, deceitful; (chem.) binary.—**al d.,** doubly.—**d. personalidad,** split personality. **II.** *m.* fold, crease; toll of the passing bell; step in a Spanish dance.
doblegable, *a.* pliable, pliant; easily folded.
doblegadizo, za, *a.* easily bent or folded.
doblegar. I. *va.* (*pret.* DOBLEGUÉ; *subj.* DOBLEGUE) to fold; twist; bend; to gain by persuasion, to dissuade. **II.** *vr.* to bend; to yield, submit, acquiesce.
doblemente, *adv.* doubly; deceitfully, artfully.
doblero, *m.* (carp.) piece of timber.
doblete. I. *a.* of medium thickness. **II.** *m.* doublet (gem); a stroke in billiards.
doblez. I. *m.* crease, ply, fold; duplication. **II.** *f.* duplicity, double-dealing.
doblón, *m.* doubloon, old Sp. gold coin.—**doblonada,** *f.* heap of doubloons or money.—**echar doblonadas,** (coll.) to exaggerate one's income.
doce. I. *n.* & *a.* twelve; twelfth. **II.** *f. pl.* **las doce,** twelve o'clock.
doceañista, *n.* maker or follower of the 1812 Spanish Constitution.
docena, *f.* dozen.—**d. de fraile,** baker's dozen.—**a docenas,** abundantly, in great quantities.
docenal, *a.* sold by dozens.
docenario, ria, *a.* containing a dozen.
doceno, na. I. *a.* twelfth. **II.** *n.* & *a.* (cloth) of twelve hundred threads.
docente, *a.* educational; teaching.
docientos, *a.* = DOSCIENTOS, two-hundred(-th).
dócil, *a.* docile, yielding, tractable; obedient; pliable, flexible, soft.—**docilidad,** *f.* docility, meekness; flexibility; tractableness.—**dócilmente,** *adv.* mildly, meekly.
docimasia, docimástica, *f.* docimacy.
docimástico, ca, *a.* docimastic.
docto, ta, *a.* learned, expert, well posted or informed; qualified.
doctor, ra. I. *n.* (academic) doctor; teacher of any art or science; (coll.) physician. **II.** *f.* (coll.) a bluestocking; (coll.) wife of a doctor.
doctorado, *m.* doctorate, doctorship.
doctoral, *a.* doctoral.
doctoramiento, *m.* act of conferring or taking the degree of doctor.
doctorando, *m.* one about to graduate as a doctor.
doctorar, *va.* to confer the degree of doctor on.
doctrina, *f.* doctrine; preaching of the Gospel; Sunday school; catechism; (Am.) curacy.
doctrinador, ra, *n.* instructor, teacher.
doctrinal. I. *m.* catechism. **II.** *a.* doctrinal.
doctrinar, *va.* to teach, to instruct.
doctrinario, ria. I. *a.* doctrinarian; doctrinal; party (as *a.*); pert. to, or following, doctrinairism. **II.** *n.* doctrinaire.
doctrinarismo, *m.* doctrinairism.
doctrinero, *m.* teacher of Christian doctrine; (Am.) curate, parish priest.
doctrino, na, *n.* charity pupil.
documentación, *f.* documentation; documents.
documentado, da, *a.* having the necessary documents or vouchers.
documental, *a.* documentary.
documentalmente, *adv.* with proper documents.
documentar, *va.* to document.
documento, *m.* document; instruction, advice to avoid evil; (com.) collateral security.
dodecaedro, *m.* (geom.) dodecahedron.
dodecágono, na. I. *a.* (geom.) dodecagonal. **II.** *m.* (geom.) dodecagon.
dodecasílabo, ba, *a.* having twelve syllables.
dogal, *m.* halter, noose, slipknot; hangman's rope.
dogma, *m.* dogma.
dogmático, ca. I. *a.* dogmatical or dogmatic. **II.** *n.* dogmatist.
dogmatismo, *m.* dogmatism.

dogmatista, *n.* dogmatist.
dogmatizador, dogmatizante, *m.* dogmatizer, dogmatist.
dogmatizar, *va.* to dogmatize.
dogo, ga, *n.* bulldog.
dogre, *m.* dogger, Dutch boat.
doladera, *n.* cooper's adze.
dolador, *m.* joiner; stonecutter.
doladura, *f.* shavings, splinters, chips.
dolaje, *m.* wine absorbed by its container.
dolamas, *f. pl.*, **dolames,** *m. pl.*, (Am.) (vet.) hidden vices and defects (of horses).
dolar, *va.* to hew (wood or stone).
dólar, *m.* dollar (U. S. money).
dolce, *a.* (mus.) dolce.
dolencia, *f.* aching, ache; disease, ailment.
doler. I. *vn.* (*ind.* DUELO; *subj.* DUELA) to pain, ache; (as *me duele la cabeza,* my head aches); to hurt; to cause regret or grief. **II.** *vr.* **(de)** to repent (of); to regret; to be moved (by), take pity (on), condole (with), feel or express sympathy (for); to complain (of).
dolerita, *f.* (min.) dolerite.
dolicocéfalo, la, *a.* dolichocephalic, dolichocephalous, long-headed.
doliente. I. *a.* aching, suffering; sorrowful; sick. **II.** *m.* mourner; patient (sick person).
dolmán, *m.* dolman.
dolmen, *m.* (archeol.) dolmen.
dolo, *m.* fraud, deceit, guile.
dolobre, *m.* stone hammer.
dolomía, *f.* (min.) dolomite.
dolomítico, ca, *a.* dolomitic.
dolor, *m.* pain, aching, ache; sorrow, affliction, grief; regret, repentance, contrition.—*pl.* throes of childbirth.—**d. de cabeza,** headache.—**d. de corazón,** heartache; repentance.—**d. de costado,** pneumonia.—**d. latente,** dull pain, constant but not severe pain.—**dolores del parto,** labor pains.—**estar con dolores,** to be in labor.
dolora, *f.* a short sentimental and philosophic poem.
dolorido, da. I. *a.* doleful, afflicted; painful, aching; sore, tender; heartsick. **II.** *m.* chief mourner.
Dolorosa, *f.* (art) Mater Dolorosa, Sorrowing Mary.
doloroso, sa, *a.* painful; regrettable; pitiful.
doloso, sa, *a.* deceitful; fraudulent.
doma, *f.* breaking in of a horse.
domable, *a.* tamable; conquerable.
domador, ra, *n.* tamer; horsebreaker.
domadura, *f.* act of taming or subduing.
domar, *va.* to tame; to break in; to subdue, overcome, master, conquer.
dombo, *m.* dome, cupola.
domeñar, *va.* to reclaim, to make tractable; to tame, domesticate; to master, subdue.
domesticable, *a.* tamable, capable of domestication.
domesticación, *f.* domestication.
domesticar. I. *va.* (*pret.* DOMESTIQUÉ; *subj.* DOMESTIQUE) to domesticate. **II.** *vr.* to become tame.
domesticidad, *f.* domesticity; domestication.
doméstico, ca. I. *a.* domestic; domesticated, tamed. **II.** *n.* household servant.
domestiquez, *f.* tameness.
domiciliar. I. *va.* to lodge. **II.** *vr.* to dwell.
domiciliario, ria, *a.* domiciliary.
domicilio, *m.* domicile; home; residence.
dominación, *f.* dominion, domination, authority, rule, command, power; (mil.) commanding ground.—*pl.* dominations, angelic beings.
dominador, ra. I. *a.* dominating, controlling; overbearing. **II.** *n.* dominator.
dominante. I. *a.* domineering, dictatorial, overbearing; prevailing; excelling; commanding, towering. **II.** *f.* (mus.) dominant.
dominar. I. *va.* to dominate; to stand out above (as a hill); to master (a subject, language, etc.); to subdue, repress. **II.** *vr.* to control oneself.
dominativo, va, *a.* = DOMINANTE.
dómine, *m.* dominie, teacher; puffed-up fool, pompous, empty-headed fellow.
domingada, *f.* Sunday festival or function.
domingo, *m.* Sunday.—**D. de Cuasimodo,** Low Sunday.—**D. de Ramos,** Palm Sunday.—**D. de Resurrección,** Easter Sunday.
dominguero, ra, *a.* done on Sunday; Sunday (as *a.*), pertaining to Sunday.
dominguillo, *m.* tumbler (a toy).
domínica, *f.* the Sabbath.
dominical. I. *a.* dominical, Sunday (as *a.*). **II.** *f.* Sunday function in universities.
dominicano, na; *n.* & *a.* Dominican; DOMINICO.
dominico, *m.* Jacobin, Dominican friar.
dominio, *m.* dominion, control; domination, rule, authority; dominion, domain; (law) fee.—**d. absoluto,** (law) fee simple absolute.—**d. directo,** (law) dominium directum.—**d. eminente,** (law) eminent domain.—**d. público,** public or general knowledge; (law) public domain, government or state property.—**d. útil,** (law) dominium utile.
dómino, *m.* domino (game piece); the game.
dominó, *m.* domino (for masquerade); DÓMINO.
dompedro, *m.* (bot.) morning-glory.
¹don, *m.* Don, title for a gentleman, equivalent to Mr. or Esq. in English, but used only before Christian names, as *Don Juan, Don Alfonso.*
²don, *m.* gift, present, donation; ability, natural gift, faculty, knack.—**d. de acierto,** tact.—**d. de errar,** (coll.) knack for doing things wrong. —**d. de gentes,** winning manners.
¹dona, *f.* woman, dame.
²dona, *f.* (Chile) legacy.—*pl.* wedding presents given by the bridegroom to the bride.
donación, *f.* donation, gift, grant.—**d. piadosa,** donary, pious donation.
donadío, *m.* property derived from royal grants.
donado, da, *n.* lay brother (sister).
donador, ra, *n.* donor, bestower, giver.
donaire, *m.* gracefulness, gentility; witticism.
donairoso, sa, *a.* graceful, elegant; witty.
donante, *n.* & *a.* giver(-ing).
donar, *va.* to give, bestow, contribute.
donatario, ria, *n.* donee, grantee.
donatismo, *m.* Donatism.
donatista, *n.* & *a.* Donatist.
donativo, *m.* donative, donation, gift.
doncel. I. *m.* king's page; virgin man. **II.** *a.* mild, mellow in flavor (as wine).
doncella, *f.* maid, servant; virgin; maiden, girl; lady's maid, waiting maid; (ichth.) snakefish.
doncelleja, *f. dim.* little maid.
doncellez, *f.* maidenhood.
doncellica, ita, *f. dim.* young maid, girl.
doncellueca, *f.* (coll.) old maid.
donde (*interr.* **dónde**) *adv.* where; wherein; in which; wherever; (Am.) to, or at, the house, shop, etc. of (*voy donde Juan,* I am going to John's [house]; *esto se vende donde Macy,* this is sold at Macy's).—**d. no,** otherwise.—**a d.,** where, whereto.—**¿de dónde?** where from, whence?; (Am.) how?—**¿en dónde?** where?—**¿por dónde?** whereabouts? by what way or road? by what reason or cause?
dondequiera, *adv.* anywhere; wherever.—**por d.,** everywhere, in every place.
dondiego, dondiego de día, (bot.) morning-glory.—**dondiego de noche,** *m.* (bot.) jalap, marvel of Peru.
dongón, *m.* (P. I.) a tree of very hard wood used in shipbuilding.
donillero, *m.* roper-in, decoy.
donjuán, *m.* (bot.) = DONDIEGO.
donosidad, *f.* gracefulness; wittiness.
donoso, sa, *a.* gay, witty; graceful.
donosura, *f.* gracefulness, elegance; wittiness.
¹doña, *f.* title given to a lady, equivalent to the English Mrs. or Miss, but used only before Christian names, as *Doña Isabel;* formerly, a duenna or a nun.

²doña, *f. pl.* present made every year to the miners in the iron mines in Spain.
doñear, *vn.* (coll.) to converse much with women.
doñegal, doñigal, *a.* a variety of fig.
doquier, doquiera, *adv.* = DONDEQUIERA.
dorada, doradilla, *f.* (ichth.) gilthead, giltpoll.
doradilla, *f.* (bot.) common ceterach.
doradillo, *m.* fine brass wire; (ornith.) wagtail; (S. A.) satinwood.
dorado, da. I. *pp.* of DORAR. **II.** *a.* gilt. **III.** *m.* (act or operation of) gilding.
dorador, ra, *n.* gilder.
doradura, *f.* gilding.
doral, *m.* (ornith.) flycatcher.
dorar, *va.* to gild; to palliate, excuse; (poet.) to illume (as sunshine).
dórico, ca, *a.* Doric.
dorio, ria, *n.* & *a.* Dorian.
dormán, *m.* dolman, huzzar's jacket.
dormida, *f.* sleep of the silkworm; place where animals repose; (Am.) alcove; bed.
dormidera, *f.* (bot.) garden poppy.—*pl.* (coll.) readiness to sleep.
dormidero, ra. I. *a.* soporiferous, narcotic. **II.** *m.* place where cattle repose.
dormilón, na, *n.* (coll.) sleepy head.
dormilona, *f.* screw earring.
dormir. I. *vn.* (*ind. pres.* DUERMO, *pret.* él DURMIÓ; *subj.* DUERMA) to sleep; to rest; (naut.) to be calm or still.—**d. a pierna suelta,** (coll.) to be fast asleep; to sleep soundly and peacefully. **II.** *vr.* to go to sleep, fall asleep.
dormirlas, *m.* hide and seek.
dormitar, *vn.* to doze, nap.
dormitivo, va, *m.* & *a.* (med.) dormitive.
dormitorio, *m.* dormitory; bedroom.
dornajo, *m.* small trough; tray; pan.
dornillo, *m.* small trough, wooden bowl.
dorsal, *a.* dorsal, pertaining to the back.
dorso, *m.* spine, back; dorsum.
dos. I. *a.* two; second (of the month). **II.** *m.* two; deuce.—**d. a d.,** two to two; two by two.—**a d. por tres,** suddenly.—**de d. en d.,** two abreast; by twos, in pairs.—**en un d. por tres,** in a twinkling.—**las d.,** two o'clock.—**los d.,** both. —**para entre los d.,** between you and me.
dosalbo, ba, *a.* (of horse) having two white stockings.
dosañal, *a.* biennial, of two years.
doscientos, tas, *n.* & *a.* two hundred; two-hundredth.
dosel, *m.* canopy, dais; portière.
doselera, *f.* valance, drapery of a canopy.
dosificación, *f.* proportioning; determination of the quantity of a substance; (med.) dosage.
dosificar, *va.* to measure out the doses of (a medicine); to proportion (ingredients, etc.); to determine the quantity of; to analyse.
dosimetría, *f.* dosimetry.
dosimétrico, ca, *a.* dosimetric.
dosímetro, *m.* (atom. ener.) dosimeter.
dosis, *f.* dose (of medicine); quantity.
dotación, *f.* endowment, foundation; allotment; settlement, dowry; equipment; (naut.) complement of a crew; (mil.) munition and garrison of a fortress; (Cuba) workmen on a plantation.
dotado, da, *pp.* of DOTAR.—**d. de,** endowed with, gifted with.
dotador, ra, *n.* endower, donor.
dotal, *a.* dotal, pertaining to a dowry.
dotar, *va.* to portion; to endow; to give a dowry to; to gift, to endow with powers or talents.
dote, *m.* & *f.* dowery, dowry; stock of counters to play with.—*f. pl.* gifts, natural talents.
dovela, *f.* (arch.) voussoir, stone of an arch.
dovelaje, *m.* voussoirs of an arch.
dovelar, *va.* to hew (a stone) for an arch.
doy, *1st pers. sing. pres.* of DAR.
dozavado, da, *a.* twelve-sided.
dozavo, va, *n.* & *a.* twelfth.
dracma, *f.* (pharm.) drachm, dram; Greek coin.
draconiano, na, *a.* Draconian.
dracúnculo, *m.* (zool.) dracunculus, nematode parasite.
draga, *f.* dredge.
dragado, *m.* dredging.
dragaminas, *m.* mine sweeper.
dragar, *va.* (*pret.* DRAGUÉ; *subj.* DRAGUE) to dredge.
drago, *m.* (bot.) dragon tree.
dragomán, *m.* dragoman, interpreter.
dragón, *m.* dragon; (zool.) dragon; (bot.) dragon; (metal.) feeding opening of a furnace; (mil.) dragoon, a soldier; (vet.) white spots in the pupils of horses' eyes; a kind of exhalation or vapor; (**D-,** astr.) Dragon, Draco.—**dragona,** *f.* (mil.) shoulder knot; female dragon.—**dragoncillo,** *m.* drake, ancient gun; little dragon or dragoon.
dragonear, *vn.* (Am.) (de) to pass oneself off (for), to pretend to be, play the; to boast.
dragontea, dragontía, *f.* (bot.) common dragon.
dragontino, na, *a.* dragonish.
drama, *m.* drama; play.
dramamina, *f.* (pharm.) Dramamine (trademark).
dramática, *f.* dramatic art.
dramático, ca, *a.* dramatic.
dramatismo, *m.* quality of being dramatic.
dramatizable, *a.* dramatizable.
dramatización, *f.* dramatization.
dramatizar, *va.* & *vn.* to dramatize.
dramaturgia, *f.* dramatic art.
dramaturgo, ga, *n.* playwright.
drástico, ca, *a.* (med.) drastic.
drávida, *n.,* **dravidiano, na,** *n.* & *a.* Dravidian.
dravídico, ca, *a.* Dravidian.
drenaje, *m.* drainage.
dríada, dríade, *f.* dryad.
dril, *m.* drilling, strong cloth, drill.
drino, *m.* a kind of poisonous serpent.
driza, *f.* (naut.) halyard.
drizar, *va.* (naut.) to hoist up (the yards).
droga, *f.* drug; medicine; fib; stratagem, artifice, deceit; nuisance.
drogmán, *m.* = DRAGOMÁN.
droguería, *f.* drug store; drug trade.
droguero, ra, *n.* druggist.
droguete, *m.* drugget, East Indian rug.
droguista, *n.* druggist; cheat, humbug, impostor.
drolático, ca, *a.* droll.
dromedario, *m.* dromedary; unwieldy animal.
drope, *m.* (coll.) vile, despicable man.
drosófila, *f.* (entom.) drosophila.
druida, *m.* druid.
druidesa, *f.* druidess.
druídico, ca, *a.* druidic.
druidismo, *m.* druidism.
drupa, *f.* (bot.) drupe, stone fruit.
drupáceo, cea, *a.* (bot.) drupaceous.
drusa, *f.* (min.) geode, vug.
dúa, *f.* (min.) gang of workmen.
dual, *a.* (gram.) dual.
dualidad, *f.* duality.
dualismo, *m.* (philos.) dualism.
dualista, *n.* & *a.* dualist(-ic).
dubio, *m.* (law) doubt.
dubitable, *a.* doubtful, dubious.
dubitación, *f.* dubitation, doubt.
dubitativo, va, *a.* doubtful, dubious.
ducado, *m.* duchy, dukedom; ducat.
ducal, *a.* ducal.
ducentésimo, ma, *a.* two-hundredth.
dúctil, *a.* ductile; yielding.
ductilidad, *f.* ductility.
ductivo, va, *a.* conducive.
duchar, *va.* & *vn.* to douche.
ducho, cha. I. *a.* skilful, expert. **II.** *f.* douche, shower bath; stripe (in cloth).
duda, *f.* doubt.—**sin d.,** certainly; doubtless.
dudable, *a.* dubious, doubtful.
dudar, *vn.* & *va.* to doubt; to hesitate (before doing something).—**d. de,** to doubt, distrust, question.

dudoso, sa, *a.* doubtful, dubious; hazardous.
duela, *f.* (cooperage) stave.
duelaje, *m.* wine absorbed by its container.
duelista, *m.* duellist.
¹duelo, *m.* duel.
²duelo, *m.* sorrow, grief, affliction; mourning; mourners; condolement; bereavement.—**duelos y quebrantos,** giblets and haslets, formerly eaten on Saturday.—**sin d.,** abundantly.
³duelo, duela, *v. V.* DOLER.
duende, *m.* elf, hobgoblin, ghost.
duendo, da. *a.* tame (as doves).
dueña, *f.* owner, proprietress, mistress, landlady; duenna; married lady.
dueñesco, ca, *a.* duennalike.
dueño, ña, owner, proprietor, landlord(-lady); master (to a servant).—**d. de sí mismo,** self-controlled.—**hacerse dueño de,** to appropriate to oneself, take possession of; to become familiar with, to master (a subject, a theory, etc.).—**ser d. de,** to own, be master of; to be at liberty to (do, etc.).
duermevela, *m.* (coll.) dozing, light sleep.
duermo, duerma, *v. V.* DORMIR.
duerna, *f.*, **duerno,** *m.* trough; bowl.
düerno, *m.* (print.) double sheet.
düeto, *m.* duet.—**duetista,** *m.* & *f.* duettist.
dugongo, *m.* (zool.) dugong.
dula, *f.* common pasture ground.
dulcamara, *f.* (bot.) bittersweet; (pharm.) dulcamara; nightshade.
dulce. I. *a.* sweet; (of water) fresh; comfortable, pleasing, pleasant, agreeable; soft, ductile (as metals); (mus.) dolce. **II.** *m.* sweetmeat, confection, bonbon, piece of candy.—**d. de almíbar,** preserves.
dulcedumbre, *f.* sweetness.
dulcémele, *m.* (mus.) dulcimer.
dulcera, *f.* preserve dish, compotier.
dulcería, *f.* confectionery shop.
dulcero, ra. I. *a.* fond of sweets. **II.** *n.* confectioner.
dulcificación, *f.* dulcification.
dulcificante. I. *a.* dulcifying, sweetening. **II.** *m.* sweetening, sweetener.
dulcificar, *va.* to sweeten, dulcify.
Dulcinea, *f.* (coll.) Dulcinea, sweetheart, beloved one.
dulcísono, na, *a.* sweet-toned.
dulero, *m.* shepherd; guardian of common pasture.
dulía, *f.* (Rom. Cath.) dulia, saint worship.
dulimán, *m.* long Turkish robe.
¹dulzaina, *f.* (coll.) quantity of sweetmeats.
²dulzaina, *f.* (mus.) flageolet.
dulzainero, *m.* flageolet player.
dulzaino, na, *a.* (coll.) too sweet or rich.
dulzamara, *f.* (bot.) = DULCAMARA.
dulzarrón, na, *a.* (coll.) sickening, too sweet.
dulzura, *f.* sweetness; meekness; gentleness; comfort, pleasure; forbearance; pleasing manner, kindliness.
duma, *f.* duma, douma.
duna, *f.* (geol.) dune.
dunita, *f.* dunnite (explosive).
dúo, *m.* (mus.) duo, duet.
duodecimal, *a.* (arith.) duodecimal.
duodécimo, ma, *a.* twelfth.
duodécuplo, pla, *a.* duodecuple.
duodenal, *a.* duodenal.
duodenario, ria, *a.* lasting twelve days.
duodenitis, *f.* (med.) duodenitis.
duodeno, na. I. *a.* twelfth. **II.** *m.* (anat.) duodenum.
duomesino, na, *a.* of two months.
dupla, *f.* in colleges, extra dish.
duplex, dúplex, *a.* (tel.) duplex.
dúplica, *f.* (law) answer.
duplicación, *f.* duplication, doubling.
duplicadamente, *adv.* doubly.
duplicado, da, I. *pp.* of DUPLICAR. **II.** *m.* duplicate; counterpart.—**por d.,** in duplicate.
duplicador, *m.* duplicator.
duplicar, *va.* (*pret.* DUPLIQUÉ; *subj.* DUPLIQUE) to double, duplicate; to repeat.
duplicativo, va, *a.* duplicative.
duplicatura, *f.* fold, crease.
dúplice, *a.* double.
duplicidad, *f.* duplicity, deceit, foul dealing; doubleness.
dupliqué, duplique, *v. V.* DUPLICAR.
duplo, pla. I. *a.* double, duple, duplicate. **II.** *m.* double, twice as much.
duque, *m.* duke; fold in mantillas.
duquecito, *m. dim.* young or little duke.
duquesa, *f.* duchess.
dura, *f.* (coll.) duration, continuance.
durabilidad, *f.* durability, permanence.
durable, *a.* durable, lasting.
duración, *f.* duration; life.—**ser de d.,** to wear well, last.
duraderamente, *adv.* durably, lastingly.
duradero, ra, *a.* lasting, durable.
duraluminio, *m.* Duralumin (trademark).
duramadre, duramáter, *f.* (anat.) dura mater.
duramen, *m.* (bot.) duramen.
duramente, *adv.* rigorously, harshly.
durante, *prep.* during.
durar, *vn.* to last; to endure; (of clothes) to wear (well).
duraznero, *m.* (bot.) peach tree.
duraznilla, *f.* a variety of peach.
durazno, *m.* (bot.) peach; peach tree.
dureza, *f.* hardness, solidity, firmness; sharpness of temper, obduracy; harshness, hardness of heart, cruelty; steadiness, perseverance; obstinacy; (art) crudeness; (med.) tumor or callosity.—**d. de vientre,** costiveness.
durillo, lla. I. *a. dim.* rather hard. **II.** *m.* (bot.) common laurestine; (vet.) callosity.
durina, *f.* (vet.) dourine.
durmiente. I. *a.* sleeping, dormant. **II.** *m.* (arch.) dormer; girder, stringer; crosstie; (Ry.) (Am.) tie, sleeper; (naut.) clamp, shelf.
durmió, *pret.* of DORMIR.
duro, ra. I. *a.* hard; solid, firm; stiff (collar); vexatious, unbearable; unjust, unkind; oppressive, rigorous, cruel; stubborn, obstinate; avaricious, stingy; rude, harsh, rough; (naut.) carrying a stiff sail; (art) harsh, crude; (mus.) harsh, inharmonious.—**a duras penas,** with difficulty; hardly, scarcely. **II.** *m.* dollar, peso; (Am.) low, rough saddle. **III.** *adv.* hard, with exertion; forcibly, violently.
duunvir, duunviro, *m.* duumvir.—**duunviral,** *a.* duumviral.—**duunvirato,** *m.* duumvirate.
dux, *m.* doge.

E

E, e, *f.* e, sixth letter of the Spanish alphabet.
e, *conj.* and (used only before words that begin with *i* or *hi* not followed by *e*).
¡ea! *interj.* (used to attract attention or as an encouragement).
ebanista, *m.* cabinetmaker.—**ebanistería,** *f.* cabinetwork; cabinetmaker's shop.
ébano, *m.* (bot.) ebony.
ebenáceo, a. I. *a.* (bot.) ebenaceous. **II.** *f. pl.* Ebenaceæ.
ebionita, *n.* & *a.* Ebionite.
ebonita, *f.* ebonite, hard rubber.
ebriedad, *f.* drunkenness, intoxication.
ebrio, bria; ebrioso, sa, *a.* intoxicated, drunk.
ebulición, ebullición, *f.* ebullition; boiling.
ebúrneo, a, *a.* eburnean, ivorylike.
ecarté, *m.* a card game.
Eccehomo, *m.* Ecce Homo; wretched, pity-inspiring person.
eclampsia, *f.* (med.) eclampsia, convulsions.
eclecticismo, *m.* eclecticism.
ecléctico, ca, *n.* & *a.* eclectic.
Eclesiastés, *m.* Ecclesiastes (one of the books of the Old Testament).
eclesiástico, ca. I. *a.* ecclesiastical. **II.** *m.* cler-

gyman, ecclesiastic, priest, minister; Ecclesiasticus.
eclesiastizar, *va.* to spiritualize.
eclímetro, *m.* clinometer.
eclipsable, *a.* that may be eclipsed.
eclipsar. I. *va.* (astr.) to eclipse; to outshine. **II.** *vr.* (astr.) to be eclipsed.
eclipse, *m.* (astr.) eclipse.
eclipsis, *f.* (gram.) = ELIPSIS, ellipsis.
eclíptico, ca, *a.* & *f.* (astr.) ecliptic.
eclisa, *f.* (Ry.) fishplate, shin.
écloga, égloga, *f.* eclogue.
eco, *m.* echo; distant sound (as of a drum); repetition of words.—**hacer e.,** to fit, correspond; to become important or famous; to create an impression; to be noised about.
ecoico, ca, *a.* pertaining to echo.
ecología, *f.* ecology.
ecológico, ca, *a.* ecologic(al.
ecólogo, ga, *n.* ecologist.
economato, *m.* guardianship, trusteeship.
economía, *f.* economy.—**e. animal,** (zool.) organism.—**e. política,** political economy, economics.—*pl.* savings.
económico, ca, *a.* economical, economic; saving, thrifty; frugal; miserly, niggardly.
economista, *m.* economist.
economizar, *va.* to economize; to save.
ecónomo, *m.* curator or guardian; trustee; ecclesiastical administrator.
ectasia, *f.* (med.) ectasis.
éctasis, *f.* (poet.) ectasis, lengthening of a short syllable.
ectima, *m.* (med.) ecthyma.
ectoblasto, ectodermo, *m.* (biol.) ectoblast, ectoderm.
ectodérmico, ca, *a.* ectodermic, ectodermal.
ectógeno, na, *a.* (bacteriol.) ectogenous.
ectoparásito, *m.* ectoparasite.
ectopia, *f.* (med.) ectopia, displacement.
ectoplasma, *m.* (zool., biol., bot.) ectoplasm; (spiritualism) substance supposed to emanate from a medium's body during a trance.
ectropión, *m.* (med.) ectropion, eversion of eyelid.
ecuable, *a.* equitable; equable; uniform (motion).
ecuación, *f.* equation.—**e. de primer grado,** linear or simple equation.—**e. de segundo grado,** quadratic equation.—**e. de tercer grado,** cubic equation.—**e. de tiempo,** (astr.) equation of time.
ecuador, *m.* equator; (E.) Ecuador.
ecuánime, *a.* equable, calm, serene.
ecuanimidad, *f.* equanimity.
ecuatorial. I. *a.* equatorial. **II.** *f.* equatorial telescope.
ecuatoriano, na, *n.* & *a.* Ecuadorian.
ecuestre, *a.* equestrian.
ecuménico, ca, *a.* œcumenical.
ecuóreo, rea, *a.* (poet.) pertaining to the sea.
eczema, *f.* (med.) eczema.—**eczematoso, sa,** *a.* eczematous.
echacantos, *m.* (coll.) rattle-brained fellow.
echacorvear, *vn.* (coll.) to pimp; to procure.
echacorvería, *f.* (coll.) profession of a pimp or procurer.
echacuervos, *m.* (coll.) pimp; procurer; cheat, impostor; a nickname given to some preachers.
echada, *f.* cast, throw; (sport) man's length.
echadero, *m.* place of rest or repose.
echadillo, *m.* foundling.
echadizo, za, *a.* spying; (of propaganda) artfully spread; foundling; rejected, discarded.
echador, ra, *n.* thrower.
echadura, *f.* brooding, hatching; winnowing.
echamiento, *m.* cast, throw; casting or throwing; rejection; ejection, expulsion.
echapellas, *m.* wool soaker.
echar. I. *va.* to cast, throw, fling, hurl, pitch, toss, dart; to turn or drive away, eject, throw out, expel; to discharge, dismiss, (coll.) fire; to emit, give out (as sparks); to pour (as wine); to serve (as food); to put (in, into); to jet (as cargo); to put on (as a cloak); to turn (as a key); to begin to have or grow (as teeth, hair, etc.); to put forth, produce, bear (shoots, fruit); to put on, to apply; to lay on or impose (as a tax); to play (as a game); to lean toward; to move, push, to set (aside); to tell (a fortune); to couple, mate (male and female animals for procreating); to impute, to ascribe; to perform for a wager; to deal (cards), deal out, to distribute; to publish, give out, issue; (with the words **rayos, centellas, chispas, fuego,** etc.) to show much annoyance, to be very angry; (with the name of a punishment) to condemn to.—**e. a,** to start, begin, to.—**e. abajo,** to overthrow, throw down; to tear down, demolish.—**e. a fondo,** or **a pique,** (naut.) to sink: to ruin, spoil, wreck.—**e. a la cara** = E. EN CARA.—**e. al mundo,** to create; to bring forth.—**e. a pasear,** or **a paseo,** = E. CON CAJAS DESTEMPLADAS.—**e. a perder,** to spoil, ruin.—**e. a pique,** to sink (a ship).—**e. baladronadas,** to boast, brag.—**e. bando,** to publish something through a crier; (coll.) to sermonize, lecture.—**e. boca,** to sharpen; to even the tip of.—**e. bravatas** = E. BALADRONADAS.—**e. carnes,** to put on flesh, gain weight.—**e. carrillos,** to grow plump in the cheeks.—**e. con cajas destempladas** or **enhoramala,** to dismiss contemptuously; to turn away in a harsh manner.—**e. coche,** to set up a coach.—**e. chufas,** to act the bully.—**e. de menos,** to miss, notice the absence or loss of.—**e. de ver,** to notice, observe; to happen to see.—**e. el bofe,** to work very hard; to solicit anxiously.—**e. el cuerpo fuera,** to withdraw from an affair.—**e. el escandallo,** (naut.) to take soundings.—**e. el guante,** to arrest.—**e. en cara,** or **en la cara,** to throw in one's face.—**e. en tierra** = E. ABAJO.—**e. la cargo a otro,** to throw the blame or responsibility on another.—**e. la corredera,** (naut.) to heave the log.—**e. la cuenta,** to balance the account.—**e. los bofes** = E. EL BOFE.—**e. los hígados,** to be exhausted, dead tired.—**e. los hígados por,** (coll.) to desire anxiously, to itch for (or to).—**e. mano a,** to grab, seize.—**e. mano de,** to resort to.—**e. plantas** = E. BALADRONADAS.—**e. por el suelo,** or **por tierra** = E. ABAJO.—**e. por en medio, e. por la calle de en medio,** to rush recklessly; to take a final resolution.—**e. raíces,** to put down roots, take root.—**e. suertes,** to draw lots.—**e. tierra a,** (fig.) to bury; to hush up; to drop (a matter).—**e. todo a rodar,** to make a fizzle.—**e. un pie,** (coll.) to take it on the lam, run away.—**e. un remiendo a,** to put a patch on; (fig.) to patch up, make up.—**e. un remiendo a la vida,** (coll.) to take a little refreshment.—**echarla de,** to pretend or claim to be, to boast of being, to pass oneself off as. **II.** *vn.*—**e. a** (foll. by *inf.*), to begin to, to start (foll. by *pres. p.*: *echar a correr,* to start running).—**e. de baranda,** to exaggerate, boast.—**e. en tierra,** (naut.) to land, to disembark.—**e. por,** to go by, take to, take the way of. **III.** *vr.* to lie down; to stretch oneself at full length; to throw oneself down; to apply oneself; (of a hen) to sit (on her eggs).—**e. a morir,** to give up in despair; to worry oneself to death.—**e. a perder,** (of food or drink) to spoil; to become stale; to become ruined or destroyed; to go down (in prestige, virtue, etc.)—**echarselas de,** = ECHARLA DE.—**e. en brazos de,** to throw oneself into the arms of; to trust in; to resort to.—**e. sobre,** to rush at, fall upon.
echazón, *f.* (naut.) jettison or jetsam.
echona, *f.* (Am.) sickle.
edad, *f.* age; epoch, era, time.—**e. crítica,** menopause.—**e. madura,** mature age, maturity.—**e. media,** Middle Ages.—**e. provecta,** = E. MADURA.—**de cierta e.,** of uncertain age, of somewhat mature age.—**mayor de e.,** of (legal) age.—**menor de e.,** underage (legally), minor.

edecán, *m.* (mil.) aide-de-camp.
edema, *f.* œdema, edema.
edematoso, sa, *a.* œdematous, edematose.
Edén, *m.* Eden, paradise.—**edénico, ca,** *a.* paradisiacal.
edición, *f.* edition, issue; publication.—**e. príncipe,** first edition.
edicto, *m.* edict, proclamation, placard.
edificación, *f.* construction, building; edification.
edificador, ra, *n.* & *a.* edifier(-ying); constructor (-ing), builder(-ing).
edificante, *a.* edifying; erecting.
edificar, *va.* & *vn.* (*pret.* EDIFIQUÉ; *subj.* EDIFIQUE) to edify; to build, construct, erect.
edificativo, va, *a.* edifying.
edificatorio, ria, *a.* pert. to building or making.
edificio, *m.* edifice, building, structure.
edil, *m.* edile, a Roman magistrate.
edilidad, *f.* edileship.
editar, *va.* to publish.
editor, ra, *n.* & *a.* publisher(-ing).
editorial. I. *n.* & *a.* editorial. **II.** *a.* publishing.
editorialista, *m.* editorial writer.
edredón, *m.* eider down; feather pillow.
educable, *a.* educable.
educación, *f.* education; good breeding, politeness.—**e. física,** physical culture.
educacional, *a.* educational.
educador, ra, *n.* & *a.* educator(-ing).
educando, da, *n.* pupil, student.
educar, *va.* (*pret.* EDUQUÉ; *subj.* EDUQUE) to educate, instruct, raise, train.
educativo, va, *a.* educational.
educción, *f.* deduction; eduction; (steam eng.) exhaust.
educir, *va.* to educe, extract, bring out.
edulcoración, *f.* (pharm.) sweetening.
edulcorar, *va.* (pharm.) to sweeten (bad-tasting substance).
eduqué, eduque, *v. V.* EDUCAR.
efe, *f.* Spanish name of the letter *f.*
efebo, *m.* (Gk. hist.) ephebe.
efectismo, *m.* (art) striving after effect.
efectista, *a.* (art) sensational.
efectivamente, *adv.* effectually; really, actually.
efectividad, *f.* effectiveness.
efectivo, va. I. *a.* effective; real, actual.—**hacer e.,** to cash (a check, etc.). **II.** *m.* (com.) cash, specie.—**e. en caja,** cash on hand.—**en e.,** in cash, in coin.
efecto, *m.* effect; impression; end, purpose, meaning; general intent; (in billiards) English.—*pl.* assets; merchandise, chattels, goods, movables; (com.) drafts.—**e. Doppler,** Doppler effect.—**efectos a pagar,** bills payable.—**efectos a recibir,** bills receivable.—**e. secundario,** aftereffect.—**efectos en cartera,** securities in hand.—**efectos públicos,** public securities.—**efectos sonoros** or **de sonido,** sound effects.—**al e.** or **a ese, este,** or **tal, e.,** for that purpose, to that end.—**con,** or **en, e.,** in fact, as a matter of fact, actually; (math., logic) for (in introducing the proof of a proposition).—**tener e.,** to become effective.
efectuación, *f.* accomplishment.
efectuar, *va.* to effect, carry out, do, make.
efedrina, *f.* (pharm.) ephedrine.
efémera, *a.*—**fiebre e.,** (med.) a one-day fever.
efemérides, *f. pl.* diary; ephemeris.
efémero, *m.* (bot.) iris.
efendi, *m.* effendi (Turkish title).
eferente, *a.* efferent.
efervescencia, *f.* effervescence; ardor, fervor.
efervescente, *a.* effervescent.
efesio, sia, *n.* & *a.* Ephesian.
eficacia, *f.* efficacy, efficiency.
eficaz, *a.* efficacious, effective.
eficiencia, *f.* efficiency, effectiveness.
eficiente, *a.* efficient, effective.
efigie, *f.* effigy, image.
efímera, *f.* (med.) EFÉMERA; (entom.) dayfly.
efímero, ra, *a.* ephemeral.
eflorecerse, *vr.* to effloresce.
eflorescencia, *f.* efflorescence.
eflorescente, *a.* efflorescent.
efluente, *a.* effluent.
efluvio, *m.* effluvium or effluvia; exhalation, emanation.
efluxión, *f.* effluence.
efod, *m.* ephod (a Jewish garment).
éforo, *m.* ephor (a Greek magistrate).
efugio, *m.* subterfuge, evasion, shift.
efundir, *va.* to effuse, pour out, spill.
efusión, *f.* effusion, shedding; warmth of manner.—**e. de sangre,** bloodshed.
égida, egis; protection, defense.
egílope, *f.* (bot.) wild bastard oat.
egipcíaco, ca; egipciano, na; egipcio, cia; egiptano, na, *n.* & *a.* Egyptian.
egiptología, *f.* Egyptology.
egiptólogo, *m.* Egyptologist.
égira, *f.* hegira.
eglantina, *f.* (bot.) eglantine.
égloga, écloga, *f.* eclogue, pastoral poem.
egocéntrico, ca. I. *n.* egocentric. **II.** *a.* egocentric, self-centered.
egoísmo, *m.* selfishness, self-love, egoism.
egoísta. I. *a.* selfish, egoistic. **II.** *m.* egoist.
ególatra. I. *a.* egotistic. **II.** *n.* egotist.
egolatría, *f.* self-idolatry.
egotismo, *m.* egotism.
egotista, *n.* & *a.* egotist(-ic).
egregio, gia, *a.* egregious, eminent.
egrena, *f.* iron clamp.
egreso, *m.* expense, debit.—*pl.* discharge.
egrisador, *m.* box for diamond dust.
egrisar, *va.* to polish (diamonds).
¡eh! *interj.* eh! here!
eidero, *m.* (orn.) eider duck.
einsteinio, *m.* (chem.) einsteinium.
eje, *m.* axis; axletree, axle; shaft, spindle, arbor; (fig.) main point, crux.—**e. auxiliar,** countershaft.—**e. cerebroespinal,** cerebrospinal axis.—**e. conjugado,** minor axis (of an ellipse).—**e. coordenado,** coördinate axis.—**e. de balancín,** balance arbor.—**e. de las abscisas,** axis of abscissæ.—**e. delantero,** front axle (of a vehicle).—**e. de las x y de las y,** x-axis and y-axis.—**e. de levas,** camshaft.—**e. del tambor,** drum-axle.—**e. del timón,** (aer.) rudder post.—**e. de ordenadas,** axis of ordinates.—**e. propulsor,** propeller shaft.—**e. secundario,** countershaft.—**e. trasero,** rear axle (of a vehicle).
ejecución, *f.* execution, carrying out; execution, capital punishment; (law) attachment; (mus.) technique.
ejecutable, *a.* feasible, practicable.
ejecutado, da, *a.* executed.
ejecutante, *n.* performer; (law) one who compels another to pay a debt by legal execution.
ejecutar, *va.* to execute, perform, make, do, carry out; to execute (a criminal); to impel, urge, importune, incite; (law) to attach the property of.
ejecutivamente, *adv.* executively; promptly.
ejecutivo, va. I. *a.* executive; active; executory. **II.** *m.* (Am.) executive (power or person).
ejecutor, ra, *n.* executor; executer; (law) officer who attaches property.—**e. de la justicia,** executioner.
ejecutoría, *f.* office of executive or attacher.
ejecutoria, *f.* sentence, judgment; letters patent of nobility, pedigree; executorship.
ejecutorial, *a.* (law) applied to the execution of the sentence of an ecclesiastical tribunal.
ejecutoriar, *va.* to obtain (a judgment) in one's favor; to establish the truth of.
ejecutorio, ria, *a.* (law) executory.
ejemplar. I. *a.* exemplary. **II.** *m.* pattern, model; precedent, example; specimen, sample; copy of a work; example, warning.—**sin e.,** without precedent; exceptional and not a precedent.

ejemplaridad, *f.* exemplariness.
ejemplificación, *f.* exemplification, illustration.
ejemplificar, *va.* to exemplify, to illustrate.
ejemplo, *m.* example, instance; copy.—**dar e.,** to set an example.—**por e.,** for example.—**sin e.,** without precedent or parallel, unheard-of.
ejercer, *va.* (*ind.* EJERZO; *subj.* EJERZA) to exercise, practise; perform, ply; to exert.
ejercicio, *m.* exercise, exertion; employment, office, task; ministry; practice; fiscal year; military drill.—**e. espiritual,** spiritual retreat.—**hacer e.,** to exercise; (mil.) to drill.
ejercitación, *f.* exercise, practice.
ejercitante. I. *n.* one who is in a spiritual retreat; exerciser. II. *m.* exercising, training.
ejercitar. I. *va.* to exercise, to put into practice; to drill (troops); to train. II. *vr.* to practice.
ejército, *m.* army.
ejerzo, ejerza, *v.* *V.* EJERCER.
ejido, *m.* common, public land.
ejión, *m.* (arch.) corbel piece, purlin, bracket.
ejote, *m.* (Mex.) string bean.
el, *art. masc. sing.* (*pl.* **los**) the.
él, *pron. masc. sing.* (*pl.* **ellos**) he.
elaboración, *f.* elaboration, working up (of material).
elaborado, da. I. *pp.* of ELABORAR. II. *a.* elaborate; manufactured, wrought.
elaborador, ra, *n.* & *a.* elaborator(-ing); manufacturer(-ing).
elaborar, *va.* to elaborate; to manufacture
elaborativo, va, *a.* elaborative.
elación, *f.* elation, haughtiness, pride; magnanimity, generosity; inflation of style.
elamita, *n.* & *a.* Elamite(-ic).
elasmobranquio, quia, *a.* & *m.* (ichth.) elasmobranch.
elástica, *f.* undershirt.
elasticidad, *f.* elasticity.
elástico, ca. I. *a.* elastic. II. *m.* an elastic (webbing); wire spring.—*pl.* suspenders.
elaterina, *f.* (chem.) elaterin.
elaterio, *m.* (bot.) elaterium.
elche, *m.* apostate, renegade.
ele, *f.* Spanish name of the letter *l.*
eleagnáceo, a. I. *a.* (bot.) elæagnaceous. II. *f. pl.* Elæagnaceæ.
eleático, ca, *n.* & *a.* (philos.) Eleatic.
eleatismo, *m.* (philos.) Eleaticism.
elebor, eléboro, *m.* (bot.) hellebore.
elección, *f.* election; choice, selection.
electivo, va, *a.* elective.
electo, ta. I. *pp. irreg.* of ELEGIR. II. *a.* elect. chosen. III. *n.* elect, person chosen or appointed.
elector, ra. I. *n.* & *a.* elector(-ing). II. *m.* elector, German prince.—**electorado,** *m.* electorate.—**electoral,** *a.* electoral.
electricé, electrice, *v.* *V.* ELECTRIZAR.
electricidad, *f.* electricity.
electricista, *m.* electrician.
eléctrico, ca, *a.* electric, electrical.
electrificable, *a.* electrifiable.
electrificación, *f.* electrification.
electrificado, da, *a.* electrified.
electrificar, *va.* to electrify.
electriz, *f.* electress.
electrización, *f.* electrification, electrization.
electrizador, ra; electrizante, *n.* & *a.* electrifier (-ying).
electrizar. I. *va.* (*pret.* ELECTRICÉ; *subj.* ELECTRICE) to electrify. II. *vr.* to become electrified.
electro. I. *pref.* electro- (electricity). II. *m.* electrum; (min.) amber.
electroaccionado, da, *a.* electrically-driven.
electroafeitadora, *f.* electric shaver.
electroanálisis, *f.* electroanalysis.
electrobomba, *f.* electropump.
electrobús, *m.* electrobus.
electrocaldera, *f.* electric boiler.
electrocardiografía, *f.* electrocardiography.
electrocardiógrafo, *m.* electrocardiograph.
electrocardiograma, *m.* electrocardiogram.
electrocinemático, ca, electrocinético, ca. I. *a.* electrokinetic. II. *f.* electrokinetics.
electrocirugía, *f.* electrosurgery.
electrocución, *f.* electrocution.
electrocutar, *va.* to electrocute.
electrocutor, *m.* electrocutioner.
electrodeposición, *f.* electrodeposition.
electrodepósito, *m.* electrodeposit.
electrodinámica, *f.* electrodynamics.
electrodinámico, ca, *a.* electrodynamic.
electrodinamómetro, *m.* electrodynamometer.
electrodo, *m.* electrode.—**e. acicular,** (surg.) electric needle.—**e. positivo,** (phys.) anode.
electroencefalógrafo, *m.* electroencephalograph.
electroencefalograma, *f.* electroencephalogram.
electrofisiología, *f.* electrophysiology.
electrofono, *m.* electrophone.
electroforesis, *f.* electrophoresis.
electróforo, *m.* electrophorus.
electrograbado, *m.* electrogravure.
electrografía, *f.* electrography.
electrógrafo, *m.* electrograph.
electroimán, *m.* electromagnet.
electroimpulsado, da, *a.* electrically-driven.
electrólisis, *f.* electrolysis.
electrolítico, ca, *a.* electrolytic.
electrólito, *m.* electrolyte.
electrolizable, *a.* electrolyzable.
electrolización, *f.* electrolyzation.
electrolizador, *m.* electrolyzer.
electrolizar, *va.* to electrolyze.
electrología, *f.* electrology.
electromagnético, ca, *a.* electromagnetic.
electromagnetismo, *m.* electromagnetism.
electromagneto, *m.* electromagnet.
electromecánico, ca. I. *a.* electromechanical. II. *f.* electromechanics.
electrometalurgia, *f.* electrometallurgy.
electrometría, *f.* electrometry.
electrométrico, ca, *a.* electrometric.
electrómetro, *m.* electrometer.—**e. absoluto,** absolute electrometer.—**e. de balanza,** electric balance.
electromoción, *f.* electromotion.
electromotor, ra. I. *a.* electromotor. II. *m.* electric motor.
electromotriz, *a.* electromotive (force).
electrón, *m.* (phys., chem.) electron.
electronegativo, va, *a.* electronegative.
electrónico, ca. I. *a.* electronic. II. *f.* electronics. —**e. astronáutica,** astrionics.
electrón-voltio, *m.* electron-volt.
electroplatear, *va.* to electroplate.
electropositivo, va, electropositive.
electropuntura, *f.* (med.) electropuncturation.
electroquímica, *f.* electrochemistry.
electroquímico, ca, *a.* electrochemical.
electroscópico, ca, *a.* electroscopic.
electroscopio, *m.* electroscope.
electrosíntesis, *f.* electrosynthesis.
electrosoldadura, *f.* electric welding.
electrostático, ca. I. *a.* electrostatic. II. *f.* electrostatics.
electrotecnia, *f.* electrotechnics, electrical engineering.
electroterapéutico, ca. I. *a.* electrotherapeutic. II. *f.* electrotherapeutics.
electroterapia, *f.* electrotherapy, electropathy.
electroterápico, ca, *a.* electrotherapeutic.
electrotipar, *va.* to electrotype.
electrotipia, *f.* electrotypy.
electrotípico, ca, *a.* pert. to electrotypy.
electrotipo, *m.* electrotype.
electrovalencia, *f.* electrovalence.
electrovalente, *a.* electrovalent.
electuario, *m.* electuary.
elefancía, *f.* (med.) elephantiasis.
elefancíaco, ca, *a.* (med.) elephantiac.
elefante, ta, *n.* elephant.
elefantíasis, *f.* (med.) = ELEFANCÍA.
elefantino, na, *a.* elephantine.
elegancia, *f.* elegance, gracefulness; neatness.

elegante, *a.* elegant, stylish, tasteful, graceful.
elegía, *f.* elegy.
elegíaco, ca, *a.* elegiac, mournful.
elegibilidad, *f.* eligibility.
elegible, *a.* eligible.
elegido, da. I. *pp.* of ELEGIR. **II.** *a.* elect, chosen.
elegir, *va.* (*pp.* ELEGIDO, ELECTO; *ind.* ELIJO; *subj.* ELIJA) to elect; choose, select, prefer.
élego, ga, *a.* mournful, plaintive.
elemental, *a.* elementary; fundamental.
elementar, *a.* elementary.
elemento, *m.* element; constituent, ingredient; (elec.) element.—*pl.* elements, rudiments.—**e. inestable,** (atom. ener.) unstable element.
elemí, *m.* elemi, gum resin.
elenco, *m.* catalogue, list, table, index; (theat.) cast; (Am.) personnel, members (of governing body).
eleusino, na, *a.* Eleusinian.
elevación, *f.* elevation; height; rise, ascent; exaltation, dignity; advancement; exaltation of mind, ecstasy, rapture; haughtiness, pride.
elevado, da. I. *pp.* of ELEVAR. **II.** *a.* elevated; high; exalted, grand, lofty.
elevador, *m.* elevator, lift, hoist.—**e. de granos,** grain elevator.
elevamiento, *m.* elevation; ecstasy, rapture.
elevar. I. *va.* to raise, elevate, heave, lift, hoist; exalt. **II.** *vr.* to rise, ascend, soar; to be enraptured; to be elated.
elfo, *m.* elf.
elidir, *va.* to weaken; (gram.) to elide.
elijable, *a.* (pharm.) that can be steeped.
elijación, *f.* (pharm.) steeping.
elijar, *va.* (pharm.) to steep.
elijo, elija, *v. V.* ELEGIR.
eliminación, *f.* elimination.
eliminador, ra, *n.* & *a.* eliminator(-ing).
eliminar, *va.* to eliminate.
eliminatorio, ria, *a.* eliminatory.
elipse, *f.* (geom.) ellipse.
elipsis, *f.* (gram.) ellipsis.
elipsoidal, (geom.) ellipsoidal.
elipsoide, *m.* (geom.) ellipsoid.
elipticidad, *f.* ellipticity.
elíptico, ca, *a.* elliptic, elliptical.
Elíseos, Elisios (Campos), *m. pl.* Elysian (fields).
elisión, *f.* (gram.) elision.
élitro, *m.* (entom.) elytron.
elixir, elíxir, *m.* elixir.
elocución, *f.* elocution; effective diction, style.
elocuencia, *f.* eloquence.
elocuente, *a.* eloquent.—**elocuentemente,** *adv.* eloquently.
elogiador, ra, *n.* eulogist, encomiast.
elogiar, *va.* to praise, extol, eulogize, laud.
elogio, *m.* eulogy, praise.
elogioso, sa, *a.* (Am.) eulogistic.
elongación, *f.* (astr.) elongation.
elote, *m.* (Mex., C. A.) ear of green corn.
El Salvador, *m.* El Salvador.
elucidación, *f.* elucidation.
elucidar, *va.* to elucidate.
eludible, *a.* eludible, avoidable.
eludir, *va.* to elude, to evade, avoid.
elzeviriano, na, *a.* Elzevir.
ella, *pron. fem. sing.* (*pl.* **ellas**) she.
elle, *f.* name of the letter *ll.*
ello, *pron. neuter sing.* it.—**e. dirá,** the event will tell.—**e. es que,** the fact is that (often expletive).
ellos, ellas, *pron. m.* & *f. pl.* they.
emaciación, *f.* (med.) emaciation.
emanación, *f.* emanation; effluvium.
emanante, *a.* emanating, issuing.
emanantismo, *m.* (philos.) emanationism, theory of creation by emanation.
emanar, *vn.* to emanate, issue; to follow, arise (from).
emancipación, *f.* emancipation.
emancipador, ra, *n.* & *a.* emancipator(-ing).
emancipar. I. *va.* to emancipate. **II.** *vr.* to free oneself; to become free or independent.
embabiamiento, *m.* (coll.) open-mouthed wonder.
embacé, embace, *v. V.* EMBAZAR.
embachar, *va.* to pen (sheep to be shorn).
embadurnador, ra, *n.* & *a.* dauber(-ing).
embadurnar, *va.* to besmear, to bedaub.
embaidor, ra, *n.* & *a.* swindler(-ing).
embaimiento, *m.* delusion, illusion; deceit, imposition, imposture.
embair, *va. defect.* (*only in forms having* **i** *in the ending*) to impose upon, deceive, humbug.
embajada, *f.* embassy, legation; (coll.) message, errand.
embajador, *m.* ambassador.—**e. cerca de,** ambassador to.—**embajadora, embajatriz,** *f.* ambassadress; ambassador's wife.
embalador, *m.* packer.
embalaje, *m.* packing, baling.
embalar, *va.* to bale, pack.
embaldosado, *m.* tile floor; pavement.
embaldosar, *va.* to pave with tiles or flagstones.
embalsadero, *m.* morass, swamp, marsh.
embalsamador, ra, *m.* embalmer.
embalsamamiento, *m.* embalming.
embalsamar, *va.* to embalm; to perfume.
embalsar, *va.* to put on a raft; to impound, dam (water); (naut.) to sling or hoist.
embalse, *m.* act of putting into a pond or on a raft; (naut.) slinging; impounding (of water).
embalumar. I. *va.* to load unequally. **II.** *vr.* to embarrass oneself with business.
emballenador, ra, *n.* corset maker.
emballenar, *va.* to stiffen with whalebones.
emballestado, da. I. *pp.* of EMBALLESTARSE. **II.** *m.* (vet.) contraction of nerves in feet.
emballestarse, *vr.* to get set to discharge a crossbow.
embanastar, *va.* to put into a basket.
embancarse, *vr.* (metal.) to stick to the walls of the furnace.
embanderar, *va.* to decorate with banners.
embanquetar, *va.* (Mex.) to build sidewalks for (a street).
embaracé, embarace, *v. V.* EMBARAZAR.
embarazada, *a. f.* pregnant.
embarazadamente, *adv.* with embarrassment.
embarazador, ra, *n.* & *a.* embarrasser(-ing).
embarazar, *va.* (*pret.* EMBARACÉ; *subj.* EMBARACE) to embarrass; (coll.) to impregnate.
embarazo, *m.* impediment; embarrassment, confusion, awkwardness; perplexity; pregnancy.
embarazoso, sa, *a.* embarrassing, vexatious; difficult, entangled.
embarbascado, da. I. *pp.* of EMBARBASCAR. **II.** *a.* difficult, intricate, involved.
embarbascar. I. *a.* to stupefy (fish) by throwing hellebore, mullein, etc., into the water; to perplex, confound, embarrass. **II.** *vr.* (of a plow) to become entangled among roots.
embarbecer, *vn.* (*ind.* EMBARBEZCO; *subj.* EMBARBEZCA) to have a beard appearing.
embarbillar, *va.* (carp.) to join.
embarcación, *f.* vessel, ship, craft; embarkation; navigation.—**e. de alijo,** (naut.) lighter.—**e. menor,** small craft.
embarcadero, *m.* wharf, quay, pier, ferry; (Ry.) freight station.
embarcador, ra, *n.* shipper.
embarcar. I. *va.* (*pret.* EMBARQUÉ; *subj.* EMBARQUE) to put on board (ship or train); to ship; to embark on an enterprise.—**e. agua,** (naut.) to ship a sea. **II.** *vr.* to embark, to go on board (ship or train).
embarco, *m.* embarkation (of persons).
embardar, *va.* to thatch.
embargador, ra, *n.* one who lays an embargo.
embargante, *a.* arresting, impeding, restraining. —**no e.,** notwithstanding, nevertheless.
embargar, *va.* (*pret.* EMBARGUÉ; *subj.* EMBARGUE) to impede, restrain, suspend; (law) to embargo, to seize, to attach.

embargo, *m.* indigestion; (law) embargo, sequestration, seizure, attachment.—**sin e.,** notwithstanding, however, nevertheless.—**sin e. de (que),** notwithstanding (that), in spite of (the fact that.)
embarnizadura, *f.* varnishing.
embarnizar, *va.* to varnish.
embarque, *m.* shipment (of goods).
embarqué, embarque, *v. V.* EMBARCAR.
embarrador, ra, *n.* plasterer, dauber; fibber, mischief maker.
embarradura, *f.* smear, plastering; mud stain.
embarrancar. I. *vn.* & *vr.* to run aground. **II.** *vr.* to stick in the mud.
[1]**embarrar. I.** *va.* to plaster roughly; to stain or smear with mud; to bedaub.
[2]**embarrar.**—*vr.* to collect on trees (as partridges).
embarrilador, *m.* packer in barrels.
embarrilar, *va.* to barrel.
embarrotar, *va.* (naut.) = ABARROTAR, to stow.
embarrullador, ra, *n.* muddler, one who makes a mess of things.
embarullar, *va.* (coll.) to muddle, make a mess of; to do carelessly or disorderly.
embasamiento, *m.* (arch.) foundation.
embastar, *va.* (sewing) to baste, to stitch.
embaste, *m.* (sewing) basting.
embastecer. I. *vn.* (*ind.* EMBASTEZCO; *subj.* EMBASTEZCA) to grow fleshy. **II.** *vr.* to become gross or coarse.
embate, *m.* dashing of the waves; sudden impetuous attack.—**embates de la fortuna,** sudden reverses of fortune.
embaucador, *m.* sharper, impostor.
embaucamiento, *m.* deception, humbug.
embaucar, *va.* (*pret.* EMBAUQUÉ; *subj.* EMBAUQUE) to deceive, trick, humbug.
embaular, *va.* to pack in a trunk; (coll.) to cram with food.
embausamiento, *m.* amazement, astonishment.
embazador, *m.* one who or that which dyes a thing brown.
[1]**embazadura,** *f.* brown dye or tinge.
[2]**embazadura,** *f.* (fig.) amazement, astonishment.
[1]**embazar,** *va.* (*pret.* EMBACÉ; *subj.* EMBACE) to dye, tinge, or shade brown.
[2]**embazar. I.** *va.* to astonish; to embarrass. **II.** *vn.* to be dumfounded. **III.** *vr.* to become tired, disgusted, or satiated.
embebecer. I. *va.* (*ind.* EMBEBEZCO; *subj.* EMBEBEZCA) to entertain, amuse. **II.** *vr.* to be struck with amazement.
embebecimiento, *m.* amazement, astonishment.
embebedor, ra, *n.* & *a.* imbiber(-ing).
embeber. I. *va.* to imbibe, drink in, absorb; to soak, saturate; to contain, include; to sink in, introduce, insert; to incorporate; to shrink, shorten, reduce, squeeze. **II.** *vn.* to shrink, to contract. **III.** *vr.* to be enraptured or ravished; to be absorbed in thought; to learn thoroughly, to master.
embebezco, embebezca, *v. V.* EMBEBECER.
embecadura, *f.* (arch.) spandrel.
embelecador, ra, *n.* impostor, sharper.
embelecar, *va.* (*pret.* EMBELEQUÉ; *subj.* EMBELEQUE) to impose upon, deceive, humbug.
embeleco, *m.* fraud, imposition, humbug.
embeleñado, da. I. *pp.* of EMBELEÑAR. **II.** *a.* enraptured, ravished; stupefied, besotted.
embeleñar, *va.* to narcotize with henbane; to charm, fascinate.
embelesamiento, *m.* rapture, ecstasy.
embelesar. I. *va.* to charm, enchant, fascinate. **II.** *vr.* to be charmed, ravished, or delighted.
embeleso, *m.* rapture, ecstasy, fascination, ravishment; charm.
embellaquecerse, *vr.* to become a knave.
embellecer, *va.* (*ind.* EMBELLEZCO; *subj.* EMBELLEZCA) to beautify, embellish.—**embellecimiento,** *m.* embellishment or beautifying.
embermejar, *va.* = EMBERMEJECER.
embermejecer. I. *va.* (*ind.* EMBERMEJEZCO; *subj.* EMBERMEJEZCA) to dye red; to put to blush, to shame. **II.** *vn.* to blush; to turn red.
emberrenchinarse, emberrincharse, *vr.* (coll.) to fly into a violent passion (as children).
embestida, *f.* assault, violent attack, onset, drive; (coll.) importunate demand.
embestidor, ra. I. *n.* & *a.* rusher(-ing). **II.** *n.* importunate solicitor or beggar.
embestidura, *f.* attack, assault, onset.
embestir. I. *va.* (*ind.* EMBISTO; *subj.* EMBISTA) to assail, attack, rush against; (coll.) to importune with unreasonable demands; (mil.) to attack, make a drive on. **II.** *vn.* to attack, rush.
embetunar, *va.* to bituminate; to black.
embicar, *va.* (*pret.* EMBIQUÉ; *subj.* EMBIQUE) (naut.) to top (the yards).
embijar, *va.* to paint with minium.
embisto, embista, *v. V.* EMBESTIR.
embizcar. I. *va.* to make cross-eyed. **II.** *vn.* & *vr.* to become cross-eyed.
emblandecer. I. *va.* (*ind.* EMBLANDEZCO; *subj.* EMBLANDEZCA) to soften, to mollify. **II.** *vr.* to soften, become soft; to be moved to pity.
emblanquecer. I. *va.* (*ind.* EMBLANQUEZCO; *subj.* EMBLANQUEZCA) to bleach or whiten. **II.** *vr.* to become white.
emblanquecimiento, *m.* whitening, bleaching.
emblema, *m.* emblem, symbol.
emblemático, ca, *a.* emblematic.
embobamiento, *m.* astonishment, enchantment, open-mouthed wonder.
embobar. I. *va.* to amuse, entertain; to enchant, fascinate. **II.** *vr.* to be struck with astonishment, to stand aghast.
embobecer. I. *va.* (*ind.* EMBOBEZCO; *subj.* EMBOBEZCA) to stultify, make foolish, stupefy. **II.** *vr.* to become stupefied or foolish.
embobecimiento, *m.* stultification.
embocadero, *m.* mouth of a channel.
embocado, da, *a.* tasty (wine).
embocadura, *f.* entrance by a narrow passage; (mus.) embouchure, mouthpiece; mouthpiece of a bridle; taste (of wine); mouth (of a river); (arch.) proscenium arch.
embocar, *va.* (*pret.* EMBOQUÉ; *subj.* EMBOQUE) to put into the mouth; to put through a narrow passage; (coll.) to swallow in haste, to cram; to hoax.
embocé, emboce, *v. V.* EMBOZAR.
embocinado, da, *a.* trumpet-shaped.
embochinchar, *vn.* to raise a row or a riot.
embodegar, *va.* to store.
embojar, *va.* to prepare sheds for (silkworms).
embojo, *m.* shed for silkworms.
embolada, *f.* piston stroke.
embolador, ra, *n.* bootblack.
[1]**embolar,** *va.* to put balls on the tips of (bulls' horns).
[2]**embolar,** *va.* to apply the gilding size to; to shine, polish (shoes).
embolia, *f.* (med.) embolism.
embolismador, ra, *n.* & *a.* detractor(-ing).
embolismal, *a.* embolismic (year).
embolismar, *vn.* (coll.) to gossip, to carry tales.
embolismático, ca, *a.* confused, muddled.
embolismo, *m.* embolism, intercalation; confusion, disorder, maze; (coll.) falsehood.
émbolo, *m.* (mech.) piston; (med.) embolus.—**e. buzo,** plunger (of a pump).
embolsar, *va.* to put into a purse; to reimburse.
embolso, *m.* act of putting (money) into a purse.
embonar, *va.* to make good, improve, repair; (naut.) to sheathe.—**embono,** *m.* (naut.) doubling, lining, stiffening, sheathing.
emboñigar, *va.* to plaster with cow dung.
emboque, *m.* passage through the mouth or a narrow place (as a ring or a channel); (coll.) deception, cheat, fraud.
emboqué, emboque, *v. V.* EMBOCAR.
emboquillar, *va.* to put a tip on (a cigarette); (min.) to make the entrance of (a shaft); to prepare the mouth of (a drill) for blasting.
embornal, *m.* (naut.) scupper hole.

emborracé, emborrace, *v.* *V.* EMBORRAZAR.
emborrachador, ra, *a.* intoxicating.
emborrachamiento, *m.* (coll.) intoxication.
emborrachar. I. *va.* to intoxicate. **II.** *vr.* to become intoxicated, get drunk.
emborrar, *va.* to stuff, wad, pad; to card a second time; (coll.) to cram (food).
emborrazamiento, *m.* basting a roasting fowl.
emborrazar, *va.* (*pret.* EMBORRACÉ; *subj.* EMBORRACE) to lard (a fowl).
emborricarse, *vr.* (coll.) to make a fool of oneself.
emborrizar, *va.* (*pret.* EMBORRICÉ; *subj.* EMBORRICE) to give the first combing to (wool).
emborronar. I. *va.* to blot. **II.** *va.* & *vn.* to scribble.
emborrullarse, *vr.* (coll.) to dispute noisily.
emboscada, *f.,* **emboscadura,** *f.* ambush, ambuscade.
emboscar. I. *va.* (*pret.* EMBOSQUÉ; *subj.* EMBOSQUE) (mil.) to place in ambush. **II.** *vr.* to retire into a forest; to lie in ambush.
embosquecer, *vn.* & *vr.* to become wooded.
embotado, da, *a.* blunt, dull.
embotador, ra, *n.* one who blunts the points or edges of swords, etc.
embotadura, *f.* bluntness or dulness (app. to weapons).
embotamiento, *m.* blunting of weapons; bluntness, obtuseness, dulness.
¹embotar. I. *va.* to blunt, to dull (an edge or point); to enervate, debilitate; to dull, stupefy. **II.** *vr.* to become dull.
²embotar, *va.* to put (tobacco) in a jar.
embotarse, *vr.* (coll.) to put on one s boots.
embotellador, ra, *n.* & *a.* bottler(-ing).
embotellar, *va.* to bottle; to bottle up.
embotijar. I. *va.* to set jars under (a tile floor) for draining; to put into jars or bottles. **II.** *vr.* (coll.) to swell, to expand; to be in a passion.
embovedar, *va.* = ABOVEDAR, to arch, vault.
embozadamente, *adv.* dissemblingly.
embozado, da. I. *pp.* of EMBOZAR. **II.** *a.* muffled, with face covered or concealed (esp. with a cloak). **III.** *n.* one with muffled face.
embozar. I. *va.* (*pret.* EMBOCÉ; *subj.* EMBOCE) to muffle; to cloak, to dissemble; to muzzle. **II.** *vr.* to muffle oneself up.
embozo, *m.* muffler; fold in upper part of bedclothing; artful way of expressing one's thoughts.—**quitarse el e.,** to take off one's mask, to show one's real intention, lay one's cards on the table.
embrace, *m.* curtain clasp.
embracé, embrace, *v.* *V.* EMBRAZAR.
embracilado, da, *a.* (coll.) carried about in the arms, as children.
embragar, *va.* (*pret.* EMBRAGUÉ; *subj.* EMBRAGUE) to throw in the clutch; (naut.) to sling.
embrague, *m.* clutch; coupling.
embravecer. I. *va.* (*ind.* EMBRAVEZCO; *subj.* EMBRAVEZCA) to enrage, to irritate. **II.** *vn.* (of plants) to become strong. **III.** *vr.* to become angry, to be enraged; (of the sea) to swell.
embravecimiento, *m.* fury, rage, passion.
embravezco, embravezca, *v.* *V.* EMBRAVECER.
embrazadura, *f.* clasp of a shield or buckler; grasp, clasping, embracing.
embrazar. I. *va.* (*pret.* EMBRACÉ; *subj.* EMBRACE) to clasp (a shield); to grasp, buckle. **II** *vn.* to gear, engage.
embreado, *m.,* **embreadura,** *f.* (naut.) paying with pitch, tarring.
embrear, *va.* (naut.) to pay with pitch.
embregarse, *vr.* to quarrel, wrangle.
embreñarse, *vr.* to hide among brambles.
embriagado, da. I. *pp.* of EMBRIAGAR. **II.** *a.* intoxicated, drunk.
embriagador, ra, or **embriagante,** *a.* intoxicating, inebriant.
embriagar. I. *va.* (*pret.* EMBRIAGUÉ; *subj.* EMBRIAGUE) to intoxicate; to transport, enrapture. **II.** *vr.* to become or be inebriated, to get drunk.
embriaguez, *f.* inebriation, drunkenness, intoxication; rapture.
embridar, *va.* to bridle; to govern, check.
embriogenia, *f.* (biol.) embryogeny.
embriogénico, ca, *a.* (biol.) embryogenic.
embriología, *f.* embryology.
embriológico, ca, *a.* embryologic.
embriólogo, ga, *n.* embryologist.
embrión, *m.* embryo.
embrionario, ria, *a.* embryonal, embryonic.
embroca, embrocación, *f.* (med.) embrocation.
¹embrocar, *va.* (*pret.* EMBROQUÉ; *subj.* EMBROQUE) to pour out of one vessel into another by joining the mouths; to place upside down.
²embrocar, *va.* (*for mut.* *V.* ¹EMBROCAR) to wind on a bobbin or quill; (shoemaking) to tack to the last; to toss between the horns.
embrochado, da, *a.* embroidered.
embrochalar, *va.* (carp.) to support (a beam) by a crosspiece or a stay.
embrolla. *f.* (coll.) = EMBROLLO.
embrollador, ra, *n.* & *a.* entangler(-ing), troublemaker(-ing).
embrollar, *va.* to entangle, muddle, mess up; to insnare, embroil.—**e. la bandera,** (naut.) to wait the ensign.
embrollo, *m.* imbroglio; tangle, muddle; trickery, deception.
embrollón, na, *n.* liar, talebearer; mischief-maker; entangler.
embrolloso, sa, *a.* tangled.
embromado, da. I. *pp.* of EMBROMAR. **II.** *a.* vexed, annoyed; (naut.) misty, hazy, foggy.
embromador, ra, *n.* one who is tumultuously merry; banterer, chaffer; wheedler; trickster.
embromar, *va.* to cajole, to wheedle; to chaff, banter; play jokes on; to vex, annoy; to detain, delay; to injure, harm.
embroqué, embroque, *v.* *V.* ¹ ²EMBROCAR.
embroquelarse, *vr.* to shield oneself.
embroquetar, *va.* to skewer the legs of.
embrosquilar, *va.* to put (cattle) into a fold.
embrujar, *va.* to bewitch.
embrutecer. I. *va.* (*ind.* EMBRUTEZCO; *subj.* EMBRUTEZCA) to brutalize, make irrational. **II.** *vr.* to become brutalized or irrational.
embrutecimiento, *m.* brutalization.
embrutezco, embrutezca, *v.* *V.* EMBRUTECER.
embuchado, *m.* a kind of sausage.
embuchar, *va.* to stuff with minced meat; to cram the maw of (animals); (coll.) to swallow without chewing.
embudador, *m.* one who funnels.
embudar, *va.* to put a funnel into; to trick; to scheme, to insnare.
embudista, *m.* trickster, intriguer.
embudo, *m.* funnel; wax candle mold; water-closet basin; trick; fraud.
embullarse, *vr.* (Cuba) to get ready for a ball, sport, etc.; to revel, to be gay.
embullo, *m.* (Cuba) excitement, anticipation; gaiety, revelry.
emburujar, *va.* (coll.) to jumble, muddle.
embuste, *m.* fib, lie; trick, fraud.—*pl.* gew-gaws, baubles, trinkets.
embustear, *vn.* to fib, lie; impose upon, gab.
embustería, *f.* deceit, imposture, trick.
embustero, ra, *n.* liar; talebearer; trickster, cheat; hypocrite; (coll.) cajoler.
embutidera, *f.* rivet knob.
embutido, da. I. *pp.* of EMBUTIR. **II.** *m.* inlaid work, marquetry; sausage.
embutidor, *m.* rivet set, punch.
embutidura, *f.* (naut.) worming.
embutir, *va.* to inlay, to enchase; to insert; to stuff; to pack tight; to force; to imbed; (coll.) to cram, to eat much; (naut.) to worm.
eme, *f.* Spanish name of the letter *m.*
emenagogo, *m.* (med.) emmenagogue.
emendable, *a.* = ENMENDABLE, amendable.
emendación, *f.* = ENMENDACIÓN, emendation, amendment, correction; satisfaction, amends.
emendador, *m.* = ENMENDADOR, corrector.

emendar, *va.* = ENMENDAR, to amend; reform; indemnify.
emergencia, *f.* act of emerging; emergency, accident; (opt.) emergence.
emergente, *a.* emergent, resulting, issuing.
emerger, *vn.* to emerge, surface, come to the surface.
emérito, *a.* emeritus.
emersión, *f.* (astr.) emersion.
emético, ca. I. *n.* & *a.* emetic. **II.** *m.* tartar emetic.
emetina, *f.* (chem.) emetine.
emétrope, *a.* emmetropic.
emetropía, *f.* (med.) emmetropia, normal vision.
emienda, *f.* = ENMIENDA, correction; indemnity.
emigración, *f.* emigration; group of emigrants; periodical migration of animals.
emigrado, da, *n.* emigrant; émigré.
emigrante, *n.* & *a.* emigrant.
emigrar, *vn.* to emigrate.
emigratorio, ria, *a.* emigration (as *a.*).
eminencia, *f.* eminence, prominence; height, hill; eminence, title of cardinals; outstanding person.—**con e.,** eminently.
eminencial, *a.* (philos.) acting eminently
eminente, *a.* eminent, prominent; high, lofty.
eminentemente, *adv.* eminently.
eminentísimo, ma, *a. super.* most eminent.
emir, *m.* emir, ameer.
emisario, *m.* emissary; spy; outlet, discharge; (physiol.) emunctory.
emisión, *f.* emission, vent; issue (of paper money, bonds, etc.); (med.) emission; (phys.) radiation.—*pl.* **emisiones radiofónicas,** or **radiotelefónicas,** broadcasting.
emisividad, *f.* (nuclear phys.) emissivity.
emisivo, va, *a.* emitting; emission (as *a.*).
emisor, ra. I. *a.* emitting; (radio) broadcasting. **II.** *m.* (radio) transmitter; broadcasting instrument or apparatus. **III.** *f.* (radio) broadcast; broadcasting station.
emitir, *va.* to emit, send forth; to issue (as bonds, etc.); to utter, express; (radio) to broadcast.
emoción, *f.* emotion.
emocional, *a.* emotive; emotional.
emocionante, *a.* touching, causing emotion.
emocionar. I. *va.* to touch, move, shock, arouse emotion in. **II.** *vr.* to be moved.
emoliente, *m.* & *a.* emollient.
emolumento, *m.* emolument, fee, perquisite.
emotivo, va, *a.* emotive, pertaining to emotion.
empacar, *va.* (*pret.* EMPAQUÉ; *subj.* EMPAQUE) to pack, to bale.
empacarse, *vr.* to persist, act stubbornly; to become confused or rattled; to balk.
empacón, *a.* (Am.) obstinate, stubborn; balky.
empachado, da. I. *pp.* of EMPACHAR. **II.** *a.* awkward, timid, bashful; surfeited, glutted; (naut.) overloaded.
empachar. I. *va.* to impede, embarrass; to overload, cram, encumber; to cause indigestion; to disguise. **II.** *vr.* to be ashamed, embarrassed, bashful; to surfeit.
empacho, *m.* bashfulness, timidity; embarrassment; obstacle; surfeit, indigestion.—**sin e.,** without ceremony; without blushing; unconcernedly.
empachoso, sa, *a.* embarrassing; disgraceful.
empadronador, *m.* census taker.
empadronamiento, *m.* census; tax list.
empadronar, *va.* to take the census of; to register (taxpayers).
empajada, *f.* hay with bran for horses.
empajar, *va.* to cover or stuff with straw; thatch.
empalagamiento, *m.* surfeit, cloying; boring.
empalagar, *va.* (*pret.* EMPALAGUÉ; *subj.* EMPALAGUE) to pall, cloy; surfeit; to vex, bother.
empalago, *m.* = EMPALAGAMIENTO.
empalagoso, sa, *a.* cloying, too rich or sweet, sickening; wearisome, annoying, boresome.
empalagué, empalague, *v. V.* EMPALAGAR.
empalamiento, *m.* empalement, empaling.
empalar, *va.* to empale.
empaliada, *f.* hangings of bunting.
empaliar, *va.* to adorn with hangings.
empalizada, *f.* palisade, stockade, pale fence.
empalizar, *va.* to palisade, to stockade, fence.
empalmadura, *f.* joint; coupling; splicing.
empalmar. I. *va.* to couple, join; to splice. **II.** *vn.* (Ry.) to branch, to join.
empalme, *m.* scarf, joint, connection; splicing; (Ry.) junction.
empalomado, *m.* (hydraul.) loose-stone damming wall.
empalomar, *va.* (naut.) to sew (the boltrope).
empalletado, *m.* (naut.) mattress barricade.
empamparse, *vr.* (Am.) to get lost in a pampa.
empanada, *f.* meat pie; fraudulent muddle or concealment.—**empanadilla,** *f. dim.* small pie; movable footstep in carriages.
empanado, da. I. *pp.* of EMPANAR. **II.** *a.* & *n.* (room) receiving light only from another room.
empanar. I. *va.* (cook.) to bread; to sow (grain). **II.** *vr.* (agr.) to be choked by too much seed.
empandar, *va.* to bend, to sag; to warp.
empandillar, *va.* (coll.) to cheat at cards.
empanizar, *va.* (cook.) to bread.
empantanar, *va.* to submerge; to swamp; to bemire; to embarrass; to obstruct.
empañadura, *f.* swaddling clothes.
empañar, *va.* to swaddle; to dim, blur, tarnish; to soil, sully (reputation).
empañetar, *va.* (Am.) to plaster.
empañicar, *va.* (naut.) to hand or furl.
empapar. I. *va.* to imbibe, saturate, soak, drench. **II.** *vr.* (**en**) to imbibe; to be soaked (in); to absorb; to enter into the spirit (of); (coll.) to surfeit.
empapelado, *m.* papering, paper hanging; paper (on a wall); paper lining.
empapelador, ra, *n.* paperhanger.
empapelar, *va.* to wrap up in paper; to paper.
empapirotar, *va.* (coll.) to adorn, to deck.
empapujar, *va.* (coll.) to make (one) eat too much, to stuff.
[1]**empaque,** *m.* packing.
[2]**empaque,** *m.* mien, appearance, looks; affected seriousness; (Chile, Peru, P. R.) boldness, brazenness, impudence.
empaqué, empaque, *v. V.* EMPACAR; EMPACARSE.
empaquetador, ra, *n.* packer.
empaquetadura, *f.* packing, gasket.
empaquetar, *va.* to pack; to stuff.
emparamado, da. (Am.) **I.** *pp.* of EMPARAMARSE. **II.** *a.* shivering with cold; (fig.) frozen.
emparamarse, *vr.* (Am.) to freeze to death; to shiver with cold.
emparamentar, *va.* to adorn, to bedeck.
emparchar, *va.* to cover with plasters.
emparedado, da. I. *pp.* of EMPAREDAR. **II.** *n.* recluse. **III.** *m.* sandwich.
emparedamiento, *m.* confinement, religious retirement; cloister.
emparedar, *va.* to immure, to shut up.
emparejador, ra, *n.* smoother, matcher, fitter.
emparejadura, *f.*, **emparejamiento,** *m.* matching; smoothing; evening up.
emparejar, *va.* & *vn.* to level, make even, smooth; to match, to fit; to put abreast.
emparentado, da. I. *pp.* of EMPARENTAR. **II.** *a.* related by marriage.
emparentar, *vn.* & *vr.* (*ind.* EMPARIENTO; *subj.* EMPARIENTE) to become related by marriage.
emparrado, *m.* vine arbor or bower.
emparrar, *va.* to embower.
emparrillado, *m.* (eng.) grillage; grate.
emparrillar, *va.* to broil on the gridiron.
emparvar, *va.* to lay (grain) for thrashing.
empastado, da, *a.* (bookbinding) bound with a stiff cover (cloth, calf, etc.).
empastador, ra. I. *a.* (painter) who impastes. **II.** *m.* paste brush. **III.** *n.* bookbinder.
empastar, *va.* to fill (a tooth); to paste; (art) to impaste; (bookbinding) to bind with a stiff cover (cloth, leather, etc.).—**empaste,** *m.* filling (of a tooth); binding; (art) impasto.

empastelar, *va.* & *vr.* (coll.) to compound, compromise; (print.) to pie.
empatadera, *f.* (coll.) checking, impeding.
empatar, *va.* to equal; to be a tie (in voting or games); to hinder, obstruct; to join.
empate, *m.* tie (in voting or games); hindrance, stopping, checking; joint; joining.
empatía, *f.* empathy.
empavesada, *f.* (naut.) waistclothes; armings; hammock cloth; boat's cloth.—**empavesadas de las cofas,** top armor.
empavesado, da. I. *pp.* of EMPAVESAR. **II.** *a.* covered with a large shield. **III.** *m.* soldier with large shield; dressing of a ship.
empavesar, *va.* (naut.) to dress (ships); (naut.) to spread (waistclothes).
empavonar, *va.* to paint (iron) (to preserve it).
empecatado, da, *a.* very wily, evil-minded, incorrigible; ill-starred, unlucky.
empecé, *pret.* of EMPEZAR.
empecer. I. *va.* (*ind.* EMPEZO; *subj.* EMPEZA) to hurt, offend. **II.** *vn.* to prevent.
empecimiento, *m.* damage; obstacle.
[1]**empecinado,** *m.* maker or seller of pitch.
[2]**empecinado, da. I.** *pp.* of EMPECINARSE. **II.** *a.* (Am.) stubborn.
empecinarse, *vr.* (en) (Am.) to persist (in), be stubborn (about), or bound (to).
empechar, *va.* to prevent, hinder.
empedernido, da, *a.* hard-hearted.
empedernir. I. *va.* (*defect., used only in forms with* **i** *in their termination*) to indurate, to harden. **II.** *vr.* to be petrified; to become hard-hearted.
empedrado, da. I. *pp.* of EMPEDRAR. **II.** *a.* (of the sky) spotted with clouds; (of the face) pitted from smallpox. **III.** *m.* stone pavement.
empedrador, *m.* stone paver.
empedramiento, *m.* stone paving.
empedrar, *va.* (*ind.* EMPIEDRO; *subj.* EMPIEDRE) to pave with stones.
empega, *f.* pitch varnish; mark with pitch.
empegado, *m.* tarpaulin.
empegadura, *f.* coat of pitch.
empegar, *va.* (*pret.* EMPEGUÉ; *subj.* EMPEGUE) to pay with pitch; to mark (sheep) with pitch.
empego, *m.* marking sheep with pitch; (Am.) pitchy taste.
empegué, empegue, *v. V.* EMPEGAR.
empeguntar, *va.* to mark (sheep) with pitch.
[1]**empeine,** *m.* groin; instep; hoof.
[2]**empeine,** *m.* (med.) tetter, ringworm; (bot.) cotton flower.—**empeinoso, sa,** *a.* full of ringworms.
empelar, *vn.* to grow hair.
empelazgarse, *vr.* (coll.) to become involved.
empelechar, *va.* to cover or line with marble.
empelotarse, *vr.* to get into a wrangle; (Am.) to take off all one's clothes.
empeltre, *m.* small shoot or sapling.
empella, *f.* vamp of a shoe.
empellar, *va.* (*ind.* EMPIELLO; *subj.* EMPIELLE) to push, shove, jostle.
empellejar, *va.* to cover or line with skins.
empeller, *va.* = EMPELLAR.
empellón, *m.* push, shove.—**a empellones,** pushing, by pushing rudely.
empenachado, da, *a.* plumed.
empenachar, *va.* to adorn with plumes.
empenta, *f.* prop, stay, shore.
empeñado, da. I. *pp.* of EMPEÑAR. **II.** *a.* determined, persisting.
empeñaduría, *f.* (Am.) pawnshop.
empeñar. I. *va.* to pawn; to pledge; to engage, oblige. **II.** *vr.* (en) to bind oneself (to); to persist (in); to insist, be bent (on); to intercede, mediate; (mil.) (of a battle) to begin.
empeñero, ra, *n.* (Mex.) pawnbroker.
empeño, *m.* pledge, pawn; engagement, contract; earnest desire; determination; protection, recommendation; recommender; (Mex.) EMPEÑADURÍA.—**casa de empeños,** pawnshop.—**con e.,** eagerly, persistently.
empeoramiento, *m.* deterioration; making matters worse; becoming worse.
empeorar. I. *va.* to impair, to deteriorate; make worse. **II.** *vn.* & *vr.* to grow worse.
empequeñecer, *va.* (*ind.* EMPEQUEÑEZCO; *subj.* EMPEQUEÑEZCA) to make smaller, diminish; belittle.
emperador, *m.* emperor.
emperatriz, *f.* empress.
emperchado, *m.* fence formed with interwoven green trees.
emperchar, *va.* to hang on a perch.
emperdigar, *va.* to brown (meat); to prepare.
emperejilar, *va.* & *vr.* to dress up or elaborately.
emperezar. I. *vn.* & *vr.* to be lazy, indolent. **II.** *va.* to retard, delay, obstruct.
empergaminado, da, *a.* bound in parchment.
emperifollar, *va.* & *vr.* = EMPEREJILAR.
emperlar, *va.* to impearl.
empernar, *va.* to bolt, nail, spike, peg.
empero, *conj.* yet, however, notwithstanding.
emperrada, *f.* a card game.
emperramiento, *m.* obstinacy.
emperrarse, *vr.* (en) (coll.) to be obstinate or stubborn (about); to persist (in); (Colomb.) (a llorar), to burst out (crying).
empersonar, *va.* to register in the census.
empesador, *m.* warp evener.
empetro, *m.* (bot.) crowberry.
empezar, *va.* & *vn.* (*ind. pres.* EMPIEZO; *pret.* EMPECÉ; *subj.* EMPIECE) to begin.—**e. la casa por el tejado,** to put the cart before the horse. —**e. por,** (*inf.*) to begin by (*pres. p.*).
empicarse, *vr.* to become too fond or infatuated.
empicotadura, *f.* act of pillorying.
empicotar, *va.* to pillory; to picket.
empiedro, empiedre, *v. V.* EMPEDRAR.
empiello, empielle, *v. V.* EMPELLAR.
empiema, *f.* (med.) empyema.
empiezo, empiece, *v. V.* EMPEZAR.
empilonar, *va.* (Cuba) to pile up (tobacco leaves).
empinada, *f.* (aer.) zooming.
empinado, da, *a.* steep; high, lofty.
empinador, ra, *n.* (coll.) toper.
empinadura, *f.*, **empinamiento,** *m.* erection, elevation, rising.
empinar. I. *va.* to raise; to exalt; to tip, incline. —**e. el codo,** to be a toper, to drink much. **II.** *vr.* to stand on tiptoe; to stand on the hind legs; to tower, rise high; (aer.) to zoom.
empingorotado, da. I. *pp.* of EMPINGOROTAR. **II.** *a.* haughty, stuck-up.
empingorotar, *va.* (coll.) to raise with a wedge or support.
empino, *m.* (arch.) summit of a curve.
empiolar, *va.* to tie by the legs; to arrest.
empíreo, a. I. *a.* empyreal; celestial, divine. **II.** *m.* empyrean.
empireuma, *f.* (chem.) empyreuma.
empireumático, ca, *a.* (chem.) empyreumatic.
empírico, ca. I. *a.* empirical. **II.** *n.* empiricist; (coll.) quack.
empirismo, *m.* empiricism; quackery.
empizarrado, *m.* slate roof.
empizarrar, *va.* to roof with slate.
emplacé, emplace, *v. V.* EMPLAZAR.
emplastadura, *f.*, **emplastamiento,** *m.* plastering, putting plasters on; applying paint or cosmetics (to the face).
emplastar. I. *va.* to apply plasters to; to paint the face of; (coll.) to stop, check, obstruct. **II.** *vr.* to get smeared.
emplastecer, *va.* (*ind.* EMPLASTEZCO; *subj.* EMPLASTEZCA) (art) to smooth for painting.
emplástico, ca, *a.* glutinous, sticky.
emplasto, *m.* plaster, poultice.
emplástrico, ca, *a.* glutinous, sticky; (med.) suppurative, dissolving.
emplazador, ra, *n.* (law) summoner.
emplazamiento, *m.* (law) summons.
emplazar, *va.* (*pret.* EMPLACÉ; *subj.* EMPLACE)

(law) to summon; (sport) to set (the hunting party).
empleable, *a.* employable.
empleado, da. I. *pp.* of EMPLEAR. **II.** *n.* employee; officeholder.
empleador, ra, *n.* employer.
emplear. I. *va.* to employ; give occupation to; to engage, hire; to appoint; to invest, to spend (as money); to use. **II.** *vr.* to be employed, to be in business.
empleita, *f.* plaited length of bast.—**empleitero, ra,** *n.* one who plaits and sells bass-weed.
emplenta, *f.* section of mud wall made at once.
empleo, *m.* employ, employment, occupation, job; public office; calling, profession; use; aim or object of desire; investment.—**e. insuficiente** or **reducido,** underemployment.
empleomanía, *f.* (coll.) mania for public office.
emplomado, *m.* roof covered with lead.
emplomador, ra, *n.* one who leads (covers, lines, etc. with lead.)
emplomadura, *f.* leading (covering, filling, etc., with lead); lead covering, lining, etc.
emplomar, *va.* to lead; to line with sheet lead; to put lead seals on.
emplumar. I. *va.* to feather; to adorn with plumes; to tar and feather; (Hond.) to thrash. **II.** *vn.* = EMPLUMECER.
emplumecer, *vn.* (*ind.* EMPLUMEZCO; *subj.* EMPLUMEZCA) to fledge, grow feathers.
empobrecer. I. *va.* (*ind.* EMPOBREZCO; *subj.* EMPOBREZCA) to impoverish. **II.** *vn.* to become poor.
empobrecimiento, *m.* impoverishment.
empocé, empoce, *v. V.* EMPOZAR..
empolvar, *va., vr.* to cover with dust; to powder.
empolvoramiento, *m.* covering with dust or powder.
empolvorar, empolvorizar, *va.* = EMPOLVAR.
empollador, ra. I. *n.* hatcher. **II.** *m.* incubator.
empolladura, *f.* brood of bees.
empollar. I. *va.* to brood, to hatch. **II.** *vn.* (of bees) to breed.
emponchado, da, *a.* (Am.) covered with, or wearing, a poncho.
emponzoñador, ra, *n.* & *a.* poisoner(-ing, -ous).
emponzoñamiento, *m.* poisoning.
emponzoñar, *va.* to poison; to corrupt.
empopar, *va.* (naut.) to poop.
emporcar, *va.* (*ind. pres.* EMPUERCO, *pret.* EMPORQUÉ; *subj.* EMPUERQUE) to soil, dirty, foul.
emporio, *m.* emporium, mart.
empotramiento, *m.* (arch.) embedding.
empotrar, *va.* (arch.) to embed, to fix in a wall; to scarf, to splice; to put (beehives) in a pit; (naut.) to fasten (cannon).
empotrerar, *va.* (Am.) to convert into pasture; to put (cattle) in a pasture.
empozar. I. *va.* (*pret.* EMPOCÉ; *subj.* EMPOCE) to throw into a well; to soak (flax). **II.** *vr.* (coll.) to be pigeonholed; (Am.) (of water) to collect in puddles.
empradizar. I. *va.* to turn into a meadow; (Colomb.) to weed. **II.** *vr.* to become a meadow.
emprendedor, *n.* & *a.* enterpriser(-ing).
emprender, *va.* to undertake, to engage in.—**e. a,** or **con,** to address, accost.
empreñar, *va.* to impregnate; to beget.
empresa, *f.* enterprise, undertaking; company, firm; device, motto; intention, purpose; management of a theater.
empresario, *m.* promoter; contractor; theatrical manager; impresario.
empréstito, *m.* loan.—**e. público,** government loan.
emprima, *f.* = PRIMICIA, first fruits.
emprimado, *m.* last combing of wool.
emprimar, *va.* to give the last combing to (wool); (coll.) to deceive.
empringar, *va.* = PRINGAR.
empuchar, *va.* to buck (skeins of thread).
empuerco, empuerque, *v. V.* EMPORCAR.
empuesta.—de e., from the rear, from behind.
empujar, *va.* to push, impel, shove.
empuje, empujo, *m.* push, pressure; energy, enterprise; (eng.) thrust.
empujón, *m.* push, violent shove.—**a empujones,** pushing, jostling.
empulgadura, *f.* drawing the string of a crossbow.
empulgar, *va.* to draw the string of (a crossbow).
empulgueras, *f. pl.* wings of a crossbow; thumbscrews.
empuñador, ra, *n.* grasper.
empuñadura, *f.* hilt (of a sword); beginning (of a story).
empuñar, *va.* to clinch, clutch, grip, hold tightly with the fist.
empuñidura, *f.* (naut.) earing.
emulación, *f.* emulation; envy, jealousy.
emulador, ra. I. *a.* emulative. **II.** *m.* emulator, rival.
emular, *va.* to emulate, rival, compete with.
emulgente, *a.* (physiol.) emulgent.
émulo, la. I. *a.* emulous. **II.** *n.* competitor, rival, emulator.
emulsión, *f.* emulsion.—**emulsionar,** *va.* to emulsify.
emulsivo, va, *a.* emulsive, emulsifying.
emulsor, *m.* grease mixer.
emunción, *f.* (med.) excretion.
emuntorio, *m.* emunctory.—*pl.* emunctory glands in armpits, groins, and back of the ears.
en, *prep.* in; at; on, upon (*en la mesa,* on the table; *en domingo,* on Sunday; *en la pared,* on the wall; *en esa ocasión,* on that occasion); to; into (*convertir en gas,* to convert into a gas; *convertirse en polvo,* to turn to dust); (before gerund) on, upon, immediately after (*en llegando,* on arriving; *en acabando esta carta,* immediately, or right, after finishing this letter). Foll. by *adj.* makes an adverbial phrase (*en alto,* on high).
enaceitarse, *vr.* to become oily or rancid.
enagua, *f.* gen. in the *pl.,* **enaguas,** underskirt, petticoat; skirt.
enaguachar, *va.* to load with water.
enaguazar, *va.* to flood.
enagüillas, *f. pl.* short skirt or petticoat; kilt.
enajenable, *a.* alienable.
enajenación, *f.,* **enajenamiento,** *m.* alienation (of property); absence of mind; rapture, overjoy.—**e. mental,** mental derangement.
enajenar. I. *va.* to alienate, to transfer (property); to transport, enrapture. **II.** *vr.* to be enraptured, ravished.
enálage, *f.* (gram.) enallage.
enalbardar, *va.* to saddle (beasts of burden); to cover with a batter; to bread.
enalmagrado, da. I. *pp.* of ENALMAGRAR. **II.** *a.* colored with ochre; vile, despicable.
enalmagrar, *va.* to cover with ochre.
enalmenar, *va.* to provide with battlements.
enaltecer, *va.* (*ind.* ENALTEZCO; *subj.* ENALTEZCA), to extol.
enaltecimiento, *m.* exaltation, extolling.
enamarillecer, *va.* & *vr.* (*ind.* ENAMARILLEZCO; *subj.* ENAMARILLEZCA) to dye yellow.
enamoradamente, *adv.* lovingly, wooingly.
enamoradizo, za, *a.* inclined to fall in love.
enamorado, da. I. *pp.* of ENAMORAR. **II.** *a.* fond of love-making; in love, enamored, lovesick. **III.** *n.* lover; sweetheart.
enamorador, ra, *n.* & *a.* courter(-ing), wooer (-ing); love-maker(-ing).
enamoramiento, *m.* love, being in love; courting, love-making.
enamorar. I. *va.* to inspire love in; to make love to, woo. **II.** *vr.* **(de)** to fall in love (with).
enamoricarse, *vr.* (coll.) to be slightly in love.
enanchar, *va.* (coll.) to widen, enlarge.
enangostar, *va.* to narrow, contract.
enanito, ita. I. *a. dim.* little, minute. **II.** *n.* little dwarf; midget.

enano, na. I. *a.* dwarfish, small, little. **II.** *n.* dwarf.
enante, *m.* (bot.) water dropwort.
enarbolar. I. *va.* to hoist, raise high, hang out (a flag, etc.). **II.** *vr.* = ENCABRITARSE.
enarcar, *va.* to arch; to hoop (barrels).
enardecer. I. *va.* (*ind.* ENARDEZCO; *subj.* ENARDEZCA) to fire with passion, to inflame. **II.** *vr.* to be kindled, inflamed (with passion).
enardecimiento, *m.* act of inflaming or state of being inflamed with passion; being or becoming fiery or impassioned.
enardezco, enardezca, *v. V.* ENARDECER.
enarenación, *f.* plaster for a wall before painting.
enarenar. I. *va.* to sand; to gravel. **II.** *vr.* (naut.) to ground.
enarmonar. I. *va.* to raise, to rear. **II.** *vr.* (of quadrupeds) to rise up on the hind feet.
enarmónico, ca, *a.* (mus.) enharmonic.
enartrosis, *f.* (anat.) enarthrosis.
enastado, da, *a.* horned.
enastar, *va.* to put a haft or handle on.
encabador, *m.* (Colomb.) penholder.
encabalgamiento, *m.* gun carriage.
encabalgar. I. *vn.* (*pret.* ENCABALGUÉ; *subj.* ENCABALGUE) to rest upon (as a beam on a joist). **II.** *va.* to provide horses for.
encaballadura, *f.* (mason.) lapping over.
encaballar, *va.* to lap over, to imbricate (as tiles).
encabar, *va.* (S. A.) to put a handle on.
encabellecerse, *vr.* (*ind.* ENCABELLEZCO; *subj.* ENCABELLEZCA) to grow hair.
encabestrar. I. *va.* to halter; to force to obedience. **II.** *vr.* to become entangled in the halter.
encabezador, *m.* header, reaping machine.
encabezadura, *f.* scarfing, heading.
encabezamiento, *m.* headline, heading, title; census taking; tax roll; act of enrolling taxpayers; tax rate.—**e. de factura,** billhead.
encabezar. I. *va.* to draw up (a tax roll); to put a heading or title to; to head, lead; to strengthen (wine) with alcohol; (carp.) to scarf, to join. **II.** *vr.* to compound for taxes; to compromise.
encabillar, *va.* (naut.) to scotch, pin, bolt.
encabrahigar, *va.* to ripen figs artificially.
encabriar, *va.* (arch.) to place the rafters of.
encabritarse, *vr.* to rise up on the hind feet.
encabuyar, *va.* (Am.) to tie with hemp cord.
encachado, *m.* (hydraul.) concrete lining.
encachar, *va.* (hydraul.) to line with concrete.
encadenación, encadenadura, *f.*, **encadenamiento,** *m.* chaining, enchainment; concatenation, linking, connection.
encadenar, *va.* to chain, fetter, shackle; to enslave; to concatenate, connect, link together (as thoughts); to captivate; to paralyze.
encajador, *m.* one who chases or inserts; chasing tool.
encajadura, *f.* act of chasing, inserting or joining; socket, groove.
encajar. I. *va.* to chase, drive in, fit in, insert; to push or force in; (carp.) to rabbet, join; (mech.) to gear; to fit closely (as a lid); to put in (a remark); to tell (a story); to throw out (a hint); to fire off; to throw, hurl (as a missile); to administer (as a scolding); to pass off (as a spurious coin). **II.** *vn.* to fit, fit in. **III.** *vr.* to thrust oneself into some narrow place; to intrude.
encaje, *m.* act of adjusting or fitting; socket, cavity, groove; enchasing; joining; lace; inlaid work, mosaic; looks, appearance.
encajera, *f.* woman who makes lace.
encajetillar, *va.* to packet (cigarettes, tobacco).
encajonado, da. I. *pp.* of ENCAJONAR. **II.** *a.* (of rivers) narrow, flanked by steep inclines. **III.** *m.* (mason.) packed work; cofferdam.
encajonamiento, *m.* packing in boxes or cases; (of rivers) narrowing between steep banks.
encajonar, *va.* to box; to case; to narrow.
encalabozar, *va.* (coll.) to put into a dungeon.
encalabrinado, da. I. *pp.* of ENCALABRINAR. **II.** *a.* headstrong, stubborn, obstinate.
encalabrinar. I. *va.* to affect the head of with some unpleasant smell or vapor. **II.** *vr.* (coll.) to become stubborn.
encalada, *f.* metal piece of a harness.
encalador, *m.* lime pit or vat.
encaladura, *f.* whitewashing.
encalar, *va.* to whitewash; to lime.
encalmadura, *f.* (vet.) a disease of horses caused by overheating.
encalmarse, *vr.* (vet.) to be overheated; (naut.) to be becalmed.
encalostrarse, *vr.* to become sick by sucking the first milk.
encalvecer, *vn.* (*ind.* ENCALVEZCO; *subj.* ENCALVEZCA) to become bald.
encalladero, *m.* (naut.) shoal, sand bank.
encalladura, *f.* (naut.) grounding, stranding.
encallar, *vn.* (naut.) to run aground; to fail.
encallecer. I. *vn.* (*ind.* ENCALLEZCO; *subj.* ENCALLEZCA) to get corns or callosities. **II.** *vr.* to become hardened or callous.
encallecido, da. I. *pp.* of ENCALLECER. **II.** *a.* hardened; hard-hearted; callous.
encallejonar, *va.* to put in, force into, an alley.
encallezco, encallezca, *v. V.* ENCALLECER.
encamación, *f.* (min.) stull.
encamarar, *va.* to store (grain).
encamarse, *vr.* (coll.) to stay in bed; (of game birds) to lie hidden; (of corn, etc.) to be beaten down by rain, wind, etc.
encambijar, *va.* to conduct (water).
encambrar, *va.* = ENCAMARAR.
encambronar, *va.* to hedge with brambles; to strengthen with iron.
encaminadura, *f.*, **encaminamiento,** *m.* act of putting on the right road.
encaminar. I. *va.* to guide, to put on the right road; to direct, to manage; to forward; to aim at, intend. **II.** *vr.* (a) to take the road (to); to be on the way (to); to be intended (for, to).
encamisada, *f.* (mil.) camisado; an ancient night masquerade.
encamisar. I. *va.* to put a shirt or a cover on. **II.** *vr.* to put a shirt over one's clothes for a camisado.
encampanado, da, *a.* bell-shaped.
encanalar, encanalizar, *va.* to convey through pipes or conduits.
encanallamiento, *m.* degeneracy, becoming base and despicable.
encanallarse, *vr.* to become low, base, mean.
encanarse, *vr.* (of infants) to stiffen from rage.
encanastar, *va.* to put in baskets.
encancerarse, *vr.* to become cancerous.
encandecer, *va.* (*ind.* ENCANDEZCO; *subj.* ENCANDEZCA) to incandesce, to make incandescent.
encandelar, *vn.* (agr.) (of trees) to bud.
encandiladera, *f.* (coll.) procuress.
encandilado, da. I. *pp.* of ENCANDILAR. **II.** *a.* (of hats) cocked.
encandiladora, *f.* = ENCANDILADERA.
encandilar. I. *va.* to dazzle; to daze, bewilder; (coll.) to stir (the fire). **II.** *vr.* to have bloodshot eyes, as from drink; to be dazzled.
encanecer, *vn.* (*ind.* ENCANEZCO; *subj.* ENCANEZCA) to grow gray-haired; to mold; to grow old.
encanijamiento, *m.* weakness, emaciation.
encanijar. I. *va.* to weaken (a baby) by poor nursing. **II.** *vr.* to pine, be emaciated.
encanillar, *va.* to wind on a quill or spool.
encantación, *f.* incantation.
encantado, da. I. *pp.* of ENCANTAR. **II.** *a.* absent-minded; haunted; enchanted, charmed.
encantador, ra. I. *n.* enchanter, sorcerer; charmer. **II.** *a.* charming, delightful.
encantamiento, *m.* enchantment.
encantar, *va.* to enchant, charm; bewitch; to fascinate; to delight.
encantarar, *va.* to put into a jar or ballot box.
encante, *m.* auction, public sale.
encanto, *m.* enchantment, charm, spell; fascination; delight.

encantorio, *m.* (coll.) enchantment.
encantusar, *va.* (coll.) to coax, wheedle.
encañada, *f.* gorge, notch.
encañado, *m.* conduit for water, pipe line; hedge or trellis of reeds.
encañador, ra, *n.* spool winder.
¹encañar. I. *va.* to hedge with reeds; to wind (silk). **II.** *vn.* (of cereals) to form stalks.
²encañar, *va.* to convey (water) through pipes; to drain.
encañizada, *f.* (fish) weir.
encañonar. I. *va.* to put into pipes; to plait, to fold; to wind on quills. **II.** *vn.* to fledge out.
encañutar, *va.* to flute.
encapachadura, *f.* collection of baskets of olives to be pressed.
encapachar, *va.* to put into a fruit basket; (agr.) to protect (grapes) with the shoots.
encapazar, *va.* to collect into a basket.
encaperuzado, da, *a.* hooded.
encaperuzarse, *vr.* to put on a hood.
encapillado, *n.* (Am.) clothes on one's back.
encapilladura, *f.* (naut.) top rigging.
encapillar. I. *va.* (naut.) to rig (the yards); (min.) to start a new gallery in. **II.** *vr.* to put clothes on over the head.
encapotadura, *f.*, **encapotamiento,** *m.* frown.
encapotar. I. *va.* & *vr.* to cloak; to muffle; to frown. **II.** *vr.* to become cloudy; (of horses) to lower the head too much.
encapricharse, *vr.* to indulge in whims; to become stubborn; (coll.) to be infatuated.
encapuchado, da, *a.* hooded, cowled.
encapuchar, *va.* to cover with a hood.
encapuzar, *va.* to cover with a cowl.
encarado, da. I. *pp.* of ENCARAR. **II.** *a.*—**bien (mal) e.,** well- (ill-) favored (in looks).
encaramar, *va.* & *vr.* to raise; to elevate; to extol; to climb; to reach a high post.
encaramiento, *m.* act of facing or aiming.
encarar. I. *vn.* to face. **II.** *va.* to aim, to point. **III.** *vr.* **(con)** to face, be face to face (with).
encaratularse, *vr.* to mask.
encarcelación, *f.* incarceration, imprisonment.
encarcelamiento, *m.* (law) incarceration; (law) custody.
encarcelar, *va.* to imprison; (carp.) to clamp, to jam; (mason.) to embed with mortar; (naut.) to woold.
encarecedor, ra, *n.* & *a.* praiser(-ing), extoller (-ing).
encarecer, *va.*, *vn.* & *vr.* (*ind.* ENCAREZCO; *subj.* ENCAREZCA) to raise the price; to overrate; to extol; to enhance; to recommend.
encarecidamente, *adv.* exceedingly, highly; eagerly, earnestly.
encarecimiento, *m.* enhancement, exaggeration.—**con e.,** ardently, earnestly.
encarezco, encarezca, *v.* *V.* ENCARECER.
encargado, da. I. *pp.* of ENCARGAR. **II.** *a.* in charge. **III.** *n.* person in charge; agent, representative.—**e. de negocios,** chargé d'affaires; (Mex.) agent, attorney.
encargar. I. *va.* (*pret.* ENCARGUÉ; *subj.* ENCARGUE) to entrust, put under the care (of a person); to advise, warn; to order (goods, etc.); to ask, request; to urge. **II.** *vr.* to take charge.
encargo, *m.* charge, commission, request; errand; job, assignment; place, employ; (com.) order.
encargué, encargue, *v.* *V.* ENCARGAR.
encariñamiento, *m.* endearment.
encariñar. I. *va.* to inspire affection or love, endear. **II.** *vr.* **(con)** to become fond (of).
encarna, *f.* giving entrails of game to dogs.
encarnación, *f.* incarnation; personification; (art) flesh color.
encarnadino, na, *a.* incarnadine.
encarnado, da. I. *pp.* of ENCARNAR. **II.** *a.* incarnate; flesh-colored; red.
encarnadura, *f.* (surg.) ENCARNAMIENTO; flesh wound made by a sharp weapon.
encarnamiento, *m.* (surg.) natural healing of the flesh.
encarnar. I. *vn.* to incarnate; to penetrate, or lodge in, the flesh; (med.) to granulate (as a wound); to make a strong impression upon the mind. **II.** *va.* to incarnate; to embody; to flesh (hunting dogs); to bait (a fishhook); to paint or make flesh-colored; to cause or produce granulation in (a wound). **III.** *vr.* to unite, mix (with one another).
encarnativo, *m.* & *a.* (surg.) incarnative.
encarne, *m.* entrails given to dogs.
encarnecer, *vn.* (*ind.* ENCARNEZCO; *subj.* ENCARNEZCA) to grow fleshy, put on flesh.
encarnicé, encarnice, *v.* *V.* ENCARNIZAR.
encarnizado, da. I. *pp.* of ENCARNIZAR. **II.** *a.* blood-, or flesh-, colored; cruel, pitiless; bloody, hard-fought.
encarnizamiento, *m.* act of fleshing (dogs); cruelty, rage, fury.
encarnizar. I. *va.* (*pret.* ENCARNICÉ; *subj.* ENCARNICE) to flesh (dogs); to provoke, irritate. **II.** *vr.* (of dogs) to be or become fond of flesh; to be cruelly bent, to gloat over injuring a person.
encaro, *m.* stare; blunderbuss; aim; levelling a musket.
encarpetar, *va.* to keep in a file or portfolio; (Am.) to lay (a motion, bill, etc.) on the table.
encarrilar, *va.* to put on the right track; to set right.
encarrilarse, encarrillarse, *vr.* (naut.) to be fouled on the sheave.
encarroñar. I. *va.* to infect, corrupt. **II.** *vr.* to be infected or corrupted.
encarrujado, da. I. *a.* curled; corrugated; fluted. **II.** *m.* fluting, shirring, gathering.
encarrujarse, *va.* & *vr.* to twist, coil, kink.
encartación, *f.* enrolment under a charter; vassalage, tenure at will; village under vassalage.—*pl.* charter lands, especially those adjoining the province of Vizcaya.
encartamiento, *m.* outlawry, proscription; sentence on an absent defendant; charter.
encartar. I. *va.* to ban, proscribe; to summon; to enrol; to register in a tax list; (in card games) to force to follow suit (when disadvantageous). **II.** *vr.* to have to follow suit so be unable to discard (in card games).
encarte, *m.* fortuitous order in which the cards remain at the close of a hand.
encartonador, ra, *n.* (bookbinding) one who applies boards.
encartonar, *va.* to bind in, or cover with, boards.
encasar, *va.* (surg.) to set (a bone).
encasillado, *m.* set of pigeonholes.
encasillar, *va.* to put in pigeonholes; to distribute, assign; to make a list of (candidates).
encasquetar. I. *va.* & *vr.* to pull down (one's hat) tight. **II.** *va.* to convince. **III.** *vr.* to persist in, to be headstrong about; to get a notion.
encasquillador, *m.* (Am.) farrier.
encasquillar, *va.* to shoe (horses).
encastar. I. *va.* to improve (a race of) by crossbreeding. **II.** *vn.* to breed.
encastillado, da, *a.* lofty, haughty.
encastillador, ra, *n.* one who shuts himself up in a castle; headstrong person.
encastillamiento, *m.* act of shutting up in a castle or steadfastly adhering to an opinion.
encastillar. I. *va.* to fortify with castles. **II.** *vn.* to make the cell of the queen bee in beehives. **III.** *vr.* to shut oneself up in a castle; to be unyielding or headstrong.
encastrar, *va.* to chase, embed.
encastre, *m.* fitting in; groove; socket.
encatarrado, da, *a.* having a cold.
encatusar, engatusar, *va.* (coll.) to wheedle.
encauchado, *m.* India-rubber poncho.
encauchar, *va.* to cover with rubber.
encausar, *va.* to prosecute, indict, sue.
encauste, *m.* = ENCAUSTO.
encáustico, ca, *a.* encaustic.
encausto, *m.* (art) encaustic painting.
encauzamiento, *m.* channeling; direction.

encauzar, *va.* to channel; to conduct through channels; to guide, lead, direct.
encavarse, *vr.* to hide in a cave.
encebadamiento, *m.* (vet.) surfeit.
encebadar. I. *va.* (vet.) to surfeit. **II.** *vr.* (of horses) to be surfeited.
encebollado, *m.* beef stew with onions.
encefálico, ca, *a.* encephalic.
encefalitis, *f.* (med.) encephalitis.—**e. letárgica,** encephalitis lethargica, sleeping sickness.
encéfalo, *m.* (physiol.) encephalon, brain.
encefaloideo, dea, *a.* encephaloid.
encelamiento, *m.* jealousy.
encelar. I. *va.* to excite jealousy in, make jealous. **II.** *vr.* to become jealous.
encella, *f.* cheese basket or mold.
encellar, *va.* to mold (curds or cheese).
encenagado, da. I. *pp.* of ENCENAGARSE. **II.** *a.* mixed or filled with mud.
encenagamiento, *m.* wallowing in dirt or vice.
encenagar. I. *va.* (*pret.* ENCENAGUÉ; *subj.* ENCENAGUE) to mud, to mire. **II.** *vr.* to wallow in dirt, mire, or vice.
encencerrado, da, *a.* carrying a wetherbell.
encendedor, ra. I. *n.* & *a.* lighter(ing). **II.** *m.* (cigarette, etc.) lighter.
encender. I. *va.* (*ind.* ENCIENDO; *subj.* ENCIENDA) to kindle, light; to inflame, inspirit, incite. **II.** *vr.* to take fire; to light up; to burn.—**e. en,** to burn with (anger, etc.); to become excited with.
encendidamente, *adv.* ardently.
encendido, da. I. *pp.* of ENCENDER: **II.** *a.* inflamed; red. **III.** *m.* (int. combust. eng.) ignition.
encendimiento, *m.* kindling, lighting; incandescence, glow; ardor, eagerness.
encenizar, *va.* to cover with ashes.
encentador, *m.* one who begins to use a thing.
encentadura, *f.*, **encentamiento,** *m.* act of beginning the use of a thing.
encentar. I. *va.* (*ind.* ENCIENTO; *subj.* ENCIENTE) to begin the use of. **II.** *vr.* to develop bedsores.
encepador, *m.* stocker, gunstocker.
encepadura, *f.* (carp.) tie joint.
encepar. I. *va.* to put in the stocks; to stock (a gun); (naut.) to stock (the anchor); (carp.) to join with ties. **II.** *vr.* to take root; (naut.) (of the anchor) to foul.
encepe, *m.* (agr.) taking firm root.
encerado, da. I. *pp.* of ENCERAR. **II.** *a.* wax-colored; like wax; thick; hard (as a boiled egg). **III.** *m.* oilcloth, oilskin; (naut.) tarpaulin; sticking plaster; blackboard in schools.
enceramiento, *m.* act and effect of waxing.
encerar, *va.* to wax; to inspissate (lime).
encernadar, *va.* to cover with leached ashes.
encerotar, *va.* to wax (thread).
encerradero, *m.* sheepfold; pen.
encerrador, ra, *n.* one who locks up; driver of black cattle.
encerradura, *f.* act of locking up; cloister, retreat; prison, jail, dungeon.
encerramiento, *m.* encirclement; ENCERRADURA.
encerrar. I. *va.* (*ind.* ENCIERRO; *subj.* ENCIERRE) to lock or shut up; to confine; to include, contain, involve. **II.** *vr.* to live in seclusion; to be locked up; to be closeted.
encerrona, *f.* (coll.) voluntary retreat.
encespedar, *va.* to cover with sod.
encestar, *va.* to put in a basket.
encía, *f.* gum (of the mouth).
encíclico, ca. I. *a.* encyclic. **II.** *f.* encyclical.
enciclopedia, *f.* encyclopedia, cyclopedia.
enciclopédico, ca, *a.* encyclopedic.
enciclopedismo, *m.* Encyclopedism.
enciclopedista, *a.* & *n.* encyclopedist.
enciendo, encienda, *v.* *V.* ENCENDER.
enciento, enciente, *v.* *V.* ENCENTAR.
[1]**encierro,** *m.* act of closing or locking up; confinement; inclosure; cloister, religious retreat; prison, lockup; folding (of cattle).
[2]**encierro, encierre,** *v.* *V.* ENCERRAR.
encima, *adv.* above; at the top; overhead; over and above, besides; in addition, to boot.—**e. de,** on, upon.—**por e.,** superficially, hastily.—**por e. de,** over, above; regardless of.
encimar. I. *va.* to place on top; to raise high; to throw in (something) to boot. **II.** *vr.* to rise above.
encina, *f.* (bot.) evergreen oak, holm oak.
encinal, encinar, *m.* holm-oak grove.
encinta, *a.* pregnant.
encintado, *m.* curb (of a sidewalk, etc.).
encintar, *va.* to trim with ribbon; (eng.) to put a curb, or curbs, on.
encismar, *va.* (coll.) to sow discord among.
encisto, *m.* encysted tumor.
encizañar, *va.* = CIZAÑAR, to sow discord.
enclaustrado, da, *a.* cloistered.
enclaustrar, *va.* to cloister.
enclavación, *f.* nailing or fixing.
enclavado, da. I. *pp.* of ENCLAVAR. **II.** *a.* enclaved, encircled.
enclavadura, *f.* (carp.) groove; embedding.
enclavar, *va.* to nail; to embed; (vet.) to prick (horses) in shoeing; to pierce through.
enclavijar, *va.* to join, pin; to peg (a guitar).
enclenque, *a.* weak, feeble, sickly.
enclítico, ca, *n.* & *a.* (gram.) enclitic.
enclocar, *vn.* & *vr.* (of hens, etc.) to become broody.
encloquecer, *vn.* = ENCLOCAR.
encobar, *vn.* & *vr.* (of hens) to sit on eggs.
encobijar, *va.* = COBIJAR, to cover; to shelter.
encobrado, da. I. *pp.* of ENCOBRAR. **II.** *a.* containing copper; copper-colored.
encobrar, *va.* to coat or cover with copper.
encoclar = ENCLOCAR.
encocorar, *va.* (coll.) to vex, annoy.
encofrado, *m.* (min.) plank lining, timbering.
encofrar, *va.* (min.) to plank, to timber.
encoger. I. *va.* (*ind.* ENCOJO; *subj.* ENCOJA) to contract, shorten, shrink; to discourage. **II.** *vr.* to be low-spirited, dismayed, or bashful; to shrink, to shrivel.—**e. de hombros,** to shrug the shoulders.
encogido, da. I. *pp.* of ENCOGER. **II.** *a.* bashful, timid.
encogimiento, *m.* contraction, shrinkage; pusillanimity; bashfulness; awkwardness.
encojar. I. *va.* to cripple, to lame. **II.** *vr.* to become lame; (coll.) to feign sickness.
encojo, encoja, *v.* *V.* ENCOGER.
encolado, *m.*, **encoladura,** *f.*, **encolamiento,** *m.*, gluing; priming, sizing.
encolar, *va.* to glue; to stick.
encolerizar. I. *va.* (*pret.* ENCOLERICÉ; *subj.* ENCOLERICE) to anger. **II.** *vr.* to become angry.
encomendable, *a.* commendable.
encomendado. da. I. *pp.* of ENCOMENDAR. **II.** *n.* one under a knight commander.
encomendamiento, *m.* = ENCOMIENDA.
encomendar. I. *va.* (*ind.* ENCOMIENDO; *subj.* ENCOMIENDE) to recommend, commend; to entrust; to knight. **II.** *vn.* to hold a knight commandery. **III.** *vr.* to put oneself in the hands, under the protection, of another; to send compliments.
encomendero, *m.* agent; commissionaire.
encomiador, ra, *n.* & *a.* praiser(-ing).
encomiar, *va.* to praise, eulogize, extol.
encomiasta, *m.* eulogizer, panegyrist.
encomiástico, ca, *a.* encomiastic, complimentary.
encomienda, *f.* commission, charge; message, compliment sent; encomienda (certain estates assigned or granted by the Spanish kings); knight commandery; land or rent belonging to a commandery; badge of a knight commander; patronage, protection, recommendation; compliments, respects; (S. A.) parcel-post parcel.
encomiendo, encomiende, *v.* *V.* ENCOMENDAR.
encomio, *m.* praise, encomium, eulogy.
encompadrar, *vn.* (coll.) to become a COMPADRE; to be close friends.

enconamiento, *m.* inflammation, soreness; infection; animadversion, anger.
enconar. I. *va.* to inflame, irritate, provoke; to increase the inflammation or soreness of; to infect. **II.** *vr.* to rankle; to fester, get infected.
enconcharse, *vr.* (Am.) to withdraw oneself from society; to retire into one's shell.
encono, *m.* rancor, ill-will; soreness; sore spot.
enconoso, sa, *a.* easily festered or infected; rancorous, resentful; irritating, difficult to deal with.
enconrear, *va.* to oil (wool) before carding.
encontradamente, *adv.* contrarily.
encontradizo, za, *a.* met, run across.
encontrado, da. I. *pp.* of ENCONTRAR. **II.** *a.* opposite; in front; hostile, opposed.
encontrar (*ind.* ENCUENTRO; *subj.* ENCUENTRE). **I.** *va.* to find; to meet. **II.** *vn.* to meet; to collide. **III.** *vr.* to meet; to collide; to be, find oneself; to feel (app. to health); to oppose, or be opposed to, each other; to conflict; to find; **(con)** to meet, come across or upon.
encontrón, encontronazo, *m.* collision, bump.
encopetado, da. I. *pp.* of ENCOPETAR. **II.** *a.* presumptuous, haughty, stuck-up; of high social standing or noble descent.
encopetar, I. *va.* to brush the hair up from the forehead. **II.** *vr.* to get well-groomed.
encorachar, *va.* to put in a leather bag.
encorajar. I. *va.* to encourage; to inflame. **II.** *vr.* to be furious, in a rage.
encorar. I. *va.* (*ind.* ENCUERO; *subj.* ENCUERE) to cover with or wrap up in leather; to cause or help the formation of skin in (a wound). **II.** *vn.* & *vr.* (of a wound) to heal, develop skin.
encorazado, da, *a.* covered with a cuirass; covered with leather.
encorchar, *va.* to hive (bees); to cork (bottles).
encorchetar, *va.* to put on hooks or clasps; to hook, to clasp.
encordado, da, *a.* = ENCORDELADO.
encordar, *va.* (*ind.* ENCUERDO; *subj.* ENCUERDE) (mus.) to string (instruments); to lash or bind with ropes.
encordelado, da, *a.* corded, stringed.
encordelar, *va.* to string; to bind with strings.
encordonado, da. I. *pp.* of ENCORDONAR. **II.** *a.* corded; adorned with cords.
encordonador, ra, *n.* corder, stringer.
encordonar, *va.* to cord; to tie with cords.
encorecer. I. *va.* (*ind.* ENCOREZCO; *subj.* ENCOREZCA) to cause the formation of skin in (a wound). **II.** *vn.* & *vr.* = ENCORAR.
encoriación, *f.* healing a wound.
encornado, da, *a.* horned.
encornadura, *f.* (of bulls, etc.) set of the horns.
encornudar, *vn.* to begin to grow horns.
encorozar, *va.* to put a COROZA, a kind of hood, on the head of (a criminal).
encorralar, *va.* to corral.
encorrear, *va.* to strap (cattle).
encorsetar, *va.* & *vr.* to put a corset on.
encortinar, *va.* to put up curtains on or in.
encorvada, *f.* act of bending the body; grotesque manner of dancing; (bot.) hatchet vetch coronilla.—**hacer la e.,** to feign sickness.
encorvadura, *f.*, **encorvamiento,** *m.* bending; incurvation, curvature; crookedness.
encorvar, *va.* & *vr.* to incurvate, bend, curve.
encostillado, *m.* timbering; lathing.
encostradura, *f.* incrustation, crust.
encostrar. I. *va.* to crust, to incrust. **II.** *vr.* to become crusty; to develop a crust or a scab.
encovadura, *f.* act of placing in a cellar.
encovar. I. *va.* (*ind.* ENCUEVO; *subj.* ENCUEVE) to put in a cellar; to keep, lock up, conceal. **II.** *vr.* to hide oneself.
encrasación, *f.* incrassation, thickening.
encrasado, da, *a.* incrassate, thickened.
encrasar, *va.* to incrassate, thicken, fatten.
encrespador, *m.* crisping iron, curling tongs.
encrespadura, *f.* act of curling the hair.
encrespamiento, *m.* curling; (of hair) standing on end; fury, roughness (of the sea, the waves, etc.)
encrespar. I. *va.* to curl; to set (the hair) on end; to ruffle (the feathers). **II.** *vr.* (naut.) (of the sea) to become rough and boisterous; to be agitated (by passion); to wrangle; (of affairs) to become entangled.
encrestado, da, I. *pp.* of ENCRESTARSE. **II.** *a.* adorned with a crest or comb; haughty, lofty.
encrestarse, *vr.* to stiffen the crest or comb (as a cock); to be proud or haughty.
encrucijada, *f.* crossroads; street intersection; ambush, trap.
encrudecer. I. *va.* (*ind.* ENCRUDEZCO; *subj.* ENCRUDEZCA) to make (a wound) worse or raw; to exasperate, irritate. **II.** *vr.* to be enraged.
encruelecer. I. *va.* (*ind.* ENCRUELEZCO; *subj.* ENCRUELEZCA) to excite to cruelty. **II.** *vr.* to become cruel.
encuadernación, *f.* binding (books).
encuadernador, ra, *n.* bookbinder.
encuadernar, *va.* (of books) to bind; to reconcile.—**sin e.,** unbound.
encuadrar, *va.* to frame.
encuarte, *m.* extra horse to draw a coach uphill.
encubar, *va.* to cask (liquids); to put (a ciminal) into a butt.
encubertar. I. *va.* (*ind.* ENCUBIERTO; *subj.* ENCUBIERTA) to caparison, trap (as a horse) **II.** *vr.* to put on armor.
encubierta, *f.* fraud, deceit, imposition.
encubiertamente, *adv.* hiddenly, secretly; deceitfully, fraudulently.
[1]**encubierto, encubierta,** *v. V.* ENCUBERTAR.
[2]**encubierto, ta,** *pp. irreg.* of ENCUBRIR.
encubridor, ra. I. *a.* concealing. **II.** *n.* concealer; (law) accessory after the fact.
encubrimiento, *m.* concealment.
encubrir, *va.* (*pp. irreg.* ENCUBIERTO) to hide, conceal, cloak, mask, palliate.
[1]**encuentro,** *m.* encounter, meeting; collision, clash; find, finding; (mil.) encounter, fight; joint (in fowls); in quadrupeds, points of the shoulder blades; (arch.) angle, nook, corner.—*pl.* temples of a loom.—**salir al e. de,** to go to meet; to encounter.
[2]**encuentro, encuentre,** *v. V.* ENCONTRAR.
encuerdo, encuerde, *v. V.* ENCORDAR.
encuero, encuere, *v. V.* ENCORAR.
encuesta, *f.* inquiry, investigation, poll, survey.
encuevo, encueve, *v. V.* ENCOVAR.
encuitarse, *vr.* to grieve.
enculatar, *va.* to cover (a beehive).
encumbrado, da. I. *pp.* of ENCUMBRAR. **II.** *a.* high, elevated; lofty, stately.
encumbramiento, *m.* act of raising or elevating; height, eminence.
encumbrar. I. *va.* to raise, elevate. **II.** *vn.* to ascend. **III.** *vr.* to rise; to be proud, rate oneself high.
encunar, *va.* to put in the cradle; to catch between the horns.
encurtido, *m.* pickle.
encurtir, *va.* to pickle.
enchabetar, *va.* (naut.) to forelock.
enchancletar, *va.* to put slippers on.
enchapado, *m.* veneer; plates or sheets forming a cover or lining.
enchapar, *va.* to veneer; to cover with metal plates or sheets.
enchapinado, da, *a.* built upon a vault.
encharcada, *f.* pool of water, puddle.
encharcarse, *vr.* to form puddles.
enchicharse, *vr.* (Am.) to drink chicha to excess; to become angry, flare up.
enchilada, *f.* (Mex.) pancake of maize with chilli.
enchilar, *va.* (Am.) to put chilli on or in; to anger.
enchiquerar, *va.* to shut (the bull) in the CHIQUERO (bull pen); (coll.) to imprison.
enchivarse, *vr.* (Colomb.) to get angry.
enchuchar, *va.* (Cuba) (Ry.) to switch.

enchufar, *va.* & *vr.* to fit (a tube) into another; to telescope.
enchufe, *m.* socket joint; telescoping, sliding of one thing into another; (elec.) plug; (also incorrectly used for) (elec.) socket.
ende.—por e., therefore, consequently.
endeble, *a.* feeble, weak, frail; flimsy.
endeblez, *f.* feebleness; flimsiness.
endecasílabo, ba, *a.* & *n.* hendecasyllable(-ic).
endecha, *f.* dirge, doleful ditty.
endechadera, *f.* = PLAÑIDERA, hired mourner.
endechar. I. *va.* to sing funeral songs to. **II.** *vr.* to grieve, mourn.
endehesar, *va.* to put (cattle) in the pasture.
endemia, *f.* (med.) endemic.
endémico, ca, *a.* (med.) endemic.
endemoniado, da, I. *pp.* of ENDEMONIAR. **II.** *a.* devilish, fiendish, perverse.
endemoniar, *va.* to possess with a devil; (coll.) to irritate, provoke, enrage.
endentado, da, *a.* (her.) serrated.
endentar, *va.* & *vn.* (*ind.* ENDIENTA; *subj.* ENDIENTE) to gear, engage, mesh; to indent.
endentecer, *vn.* (*ind.* ENDENTEZCO; *subj.* ENDENTEZCA) to cut teeth, to teethe.
enderecé, enderece, *v.* *V.* ENDEREZAR.
enderezadamente, *adv.* rightly.
enderezado, da. I. *pp.* of ENDEREZAR. **II.** *a.* fit, appropriate.
enderezador, ra, *n.* good manager; righter; straightener.
enderezamiento, *m.* straightening; setting right.
enderezar. I. *va.* (*pret.* ENDERECÉ; *subj.* ENDERECE) to straighten; to right, set right; to address, dedicate; to manage well. **II.** *vn.* to take the direct road. **III.** *vr.* to straighten up; to set oneself, prepare for an undertaking.
endérmico, ca, *a.* endermic.
endeudarse, *vr.* to contract debts.
endevotado, da, *a.* pious; devoted, fond.
endiablada, *f.* boisterous masquerade.
endiabladamente, *adv.* devilishly; horribly.
endiablado, da. I. *pp.* of ENDIABLAR. **II.** *a.* devilish, diabolical; ugly, deformed; perverse, wicked.
endiablar. I. *va.* to pervert, corrupt. **II.** *vr.* to be furious.
endíadis, *f.* (rhet.) hendiadys.
endibia, *f.* (bot.) endive, succory.
endiento, endiente, *v.* *V.* ENDENTAR.
endilgador, ra, *n.* (coll.) pander.
endilgar, *va.* to direct, guide; to assist; to thrust (a weapon, an insult), to deal (a blow); to spring (something) on (a person).
endiosamiento, *m.* haughtiness, pride; ecstasy, abstraction; deification.
endiosar. I. *va.* to deify. **II.** *vr.* to be elated with pride; to be devoutly abstracted.
endoblástico, ca, *a.* endoblastic.
endoblasto, *m.* (biol.) endoblast, hypoblast.
endocardíaco, ca, *a.* endocardiac.
endocardio, *m.* (anat.) endocardium.
endocarditis, *f.* (med.) endocarditis.
endocarpio, *m.* (bot.) endocarp.
endocrino, na. I. *a.* (anat., physiol.) endocrine. **II.** *f.* endocrine (gland).
endocrinología, *f.* endocrinology.
endodermo, *m.* (biol.) endoderm, endoblast.
endoesqueleto, *m.* (anat.) endoskeleton.
endogamia, *f.* endogamy.
endogámico, ca, *a.* endogamous, inbred.
endogénesis, *f.* (biol.) endogeny.
endogenia, *f.* (biol.) endogeny.
endógeno, na. I. *a.* endogenous. **II.** *f.* (bot.) endogen.
endolinfa, *f.* (anat.) endolymph, liquid that fills the labyrinth of the ear.
endometritis, *f.* (med.) endometritis.
endomingado, da, *a.* dressed in Sunday best; chic, dapper, elegant.
endomingarse, *vr.* to be dressed in Sunday best.
endomorfia, *f.* (min., anat.) endomorph.
endomórfico, ca, *a.* endomorphic.
endomorfismo, *m.* (geol.) endomorphism.
endoparásito, *m.* endoparasite.
endoplasma, *m.* (biol.) endoplasm.
endo(r)sable, *a.* indorsable.
endorsar, *va.* to indorse (as a draft); to transfer.
endorso, *m.* (com.) indorsement.
endosador, endosante, *m.* indorser.
endosar, *va.* to indorse (a draft, etc.).
endosatario, ria, *n.* indorsee.
endoscopio, *m.* (med.) endoscope.
endose, *m.* indorsement (of a draft, check, etc.).
endoselado, da, *a.* canopied.
endoselar, *va.* to hang; to provide with a dais.
endósmosis, *f.* (phys.) endosmosis.
endosmótico, ca, *a.* endosmotic.
endoso, *m.* = ENDOSE.
endospermo, *m.* (bot.) endosperm.
endosporo, *m.* (bot.) endospore.
endosteo, *m.* (anat.) endosteum.
endotelio, *m.* (anat.) endothelium.
endotérmico, ca, *a.* (chem.) endothermic.
endovenoso, sa, *a.* intravenous.
endriago, *m.* fabulous monster.
endrina, *f.* sloe, fruit of the sloe tree.
endrino, na. I. *a.* sloe-colored. **II.** *m.* (bot.) blackthorn, sloe tree.
endrogarse, *vr.* (Am.) to become burdened with debts.
endulcé, endulce, *v.* *V.* ENDULZAR.
endulzadura, *f.* sweetening.
endulzar, *va.* (*pret.* ENDULCÉ; *subj.* ENDULCE) to sweeten; to soften; (art) to soften, tone down.
endurador, ra, *a.* parsimonious, niggardly.
endurar, *va.* to harden; to save; to endure, bear; to delay, put off.
endurecer, *va.* & *vr.* (*ind.* ENDUREZCO; *subj.* ENDUREZCA) to harden; to inure; to exasperate.
endurecido, da. I. *pp.* of ENDURECER. **II.** *a.* hard, hardy; obdurate.
endurecimiento, *m.* hardness; hardening; obstinacy; tenaciousness; hard-heartedness.
endurezco, endurezca, *v.* *V.* ENDURECER.
ene, *f.* Spanish name of the letter *n.*
enea, *f.* (bot.) cattail, reed mace, rush.
enebral, *m.* plantation of juniper trees.
enebrina, *f.* fruit of the juniper tree.
enebro, *m.* (bot.) common juniper.
enejar, *va.* to put an axle on.
eneldo, *m.* (bot.) common dill.
enema, *f.* enema, injection, clyster.
enemiga, *f.* enmity, hatred, ill-will.
enemigo, ga. I. *a.* (**de**) inimical, hostile (to); opposed (to), adverse. **II.** *n.* enemy, foe. **III.** *m.* (mil.) enemy; devil.—**e. capital,** mortal enemy.—**e. jurado,** sworn enemy.—**e. público,** public enemy.—**el e. malo,** the devil.
enemistad, *f.* enmity, hatred.
enemistar. I. *va.* to make enemies of. **II.** *vr.* (**con**) to become an enemy (of); to fall out (with).
éneo, ea, *a.* (poet.) brazen, brass (as *a.*).
energía, *f.* energy; (mechanical) power.—**e. atómica,** atomic energy.—**e. cinética,** kinetic energy.—**e. eléctrica,** electric power.—**e. nuclear,** nuclear energy.—**e. potencial,** potential energy.—**e. radiante,** radiant energy.—**e. solar,** solar energy.—**transmisión de e.,** power transmission.
enérgico, ca, *a.* energetic, lively.
energúmeno, na, *n.* person possessed with a devil; violent, impulsive person.
enero, *m.* January.
enervación, *f.* enervation.
enervado, da, *a.* enervate.
enervante, *a.* enervating.
enervar. I. *va.* to enervate, unnerve; to weaken. **II.** *vr.* to become weak.
enésimo, *m.* (math.) nth.—**elevado a la enésima potencia,** to the nth degree or power.
enfadadizo, za, *a.* irritable, irascible, peevish.

enfadar. I. *va.* to vex, anger. II. *vr.* to get angry.
enfado, *m.* vexation, anger; trouble, drudgery.
enfadoso, sa, *a.* vexatious, annoying.
enfaldar. I. *va.* (agr.) to lop off the lower branches of. II. *vr.* to tuck up (the skirts).
enfaldo, *m.* act of tucking up one's clothes.
enfangar. I. *va.* (*pret.* ENFANGUÉ; *subj.* ENFANGUE) to soil with mud. II. *vr.* (naut.) to ground in the mud; (coll.) to soil one's reputation; to sink (into vice, etc.)
enfardar, *va.* to pack, bale, fardel.
enfardelador, *m.* packer.
enfardeladura, *f.* packing, baling.
enfardelar, *va.* to bale, pack.
énfasis, *m.* emphasis.
enfático, ca, *a.* emphatic.
enfermar. I. *vn.* (Am. *vr.*) to fall ill, be taken ill. II. *va.* to make ill.
enfermedad, *f.* illness, sickness, disease.—**e. contagiosa,** contagious disease.—**e. infecciosa,** infectious disease.—**e. por carencia,** deficiency disease.—**e. profesional,** occupational disease.—**e. venérea,** venereal disease.
enfermera, *f.* nurse.—**e. práctica,** practical nurse.
enfermería, *f.* infirmary, sanitarium.
enfermero, *m.* male nurse.
enfermizo, za, *a.* infirm, sickly; unhealthful.
enfermo, ma. I. *a.* ill, sick; sickly. II. *n.* patient.
enfermoso, sa, *a.* (C. A.) = ENFERMIZO; indisposed, somewhat ailing.
enfervorizar. I. *va.* to heat, inflame, incite. II. *vr.* to become fervorous or heated.
enfeudación, *f.* infeudation, enfeoffment.
enfeudar, *va.* to feoff, to enfeoff.
enfielar, *va.* to put in a balance.
enfiestarse, *vr.* (Am.) to have a good time, go on a lark.
enfilar, *va.* to place in a row or line; to pierce or string in a line; (mil.) to enfilade.—**e. el curso,** (naut.) to direct the course, to bear.
enfisema, *m.* (med.) emphysema.
enfisematoso, sa, *a.* emphysematous.
enfistolarse, *vr.* to become a fistula.
enfiteusis, *m.* & *f.* (law) emphyteusis.
enfiteuta, *m.* (law) emphyteuta.
enfitéutico, ca, *a.* emphyteutic.
enflaquecer. I. *va.* (*ind.* ENFLAQUEZCO; *subj.* ENFLAQUEZCA) *va.* to make thin or lean; to extenuate, to fade. II. *vn.* & *vr.* to become thin, lose weight. III. *vn.* to weaken.
enflaquecimiento, *m.* loss of flesh, emaciation.
enflaquezco, enflaquezca, *v.* *V.* ENFLAQUECER.
enflautado, da, *a.* (coll.) inflated.
enflautador, ra, *n.* (coll.) procurer.
enflautar, *va.* (coll.) to procure; (coll.) to deceive, cheat, humbug.
enflechado, da, *a.* (of a bow) ready to discharge.
enfocar, *va.* to focus; focus on.
enfoque, *m.* focussing; approach (to a problem, etc.)
enfoscar. I. *va.* (*pret.* ENFOSQUE; *subj.* ENFOSQUE) (mason.) to fill up (holes). II. *vr.* to be ill-humored; to be deep in a business; to be cloudy.
enfrailar. I. *va.* to make (one) a monk or friar. II. *vr.* to become a friar.
enfranquecer, *va.* to frank, to free.
enfrascamiento, *m.* entanglement.
enfrascar, *va.* (*pret.* ENFRASQUÉ; *subj.* ENFRASQUE) to bottle.
enfrascarse, *vr.* to be entangled or involved; to be deeply engaged in work.
enfrenador, ra, *n.* & *a.* bridler(-ing), restrainer (-ing).
enfrenamiento, *m.* bridling; checking, curbing.
enfrenar, *va.* to bridle; to govern by the bridle; to curb, to restrain: to put the brake on.
enfrentar. I. *va.* to confront, put face to face; to face. II. *vn.* (**con**) to face; to oppose.
enfrente, *adv.* opposite, in front.—**e. de,** opposite, in front of.—**de e.,** opposite, across (the street, etc.) (as *la casa de enfrente,* the house opposite).
enfriadera, *f.* bottle cooler, refrigerator.
enfriadero, enfriador, *m.* cooling place; refrigerator; cold storage.
enfriamiento, *m.* refrigeration; cooling; cold, chill (illness).
enfriar. I. *va.* to cool. II. *vr.* to cool; to cool off or down; (of person) to get chilled.
enfullar, *va.* & *vn.* (coll.) to cheat at cards.
enfundadura, *f.* casing; putting into cases.
enfundar, *va.* to case, to put into a case (as a pillow); to fill up, to stuff.
enfurecer. I. *va.* (*ind.* ENFUREZCO; *subj.* ENFUREZCA) to enrage, make furious. II. *vr.* to rage, to become furious or stormy.
enfurruñarse, *vr.* (coll.) to get angry; sulk.
enfurtir, *va.* to full (cloth); to felt.
engabanado, da, *a.* wearing an overcoat.
engace, *m.* catenation, connection.
engafar, *va.* to bend (a crossbow); to hook; to set (a gun) at half cock.
engaitador, ra, *n.* (coll.) wheedler.
engaitar. *va.* (coll.) to coax, to wheedle.
engalanado, da. I. *pp.* of ENGALANAR. II. *a.* adorned, bedight.
engalanar, *va.* to adorn, deck; (naut.) to dress.
[1]**engalgar,** *va.* to pursue closely.
[2]**engalgar,** *va.* to scotch (a wheel); (naut.) to back (an anchor).
engallado, da, *a.* erect, upright; haughty.
engallador, *m.* martingale.
engalladura, *f.* protoplasmic disk (of egg).
engallarse, *vr.* to draw oneself up arrogantly; (of horses) to keep the head near the chest.
enganchador, *m.* hooker.
enganchamiento, *m.* hooking; enlisting in the army; decoying.
enganchar. I. *va.* to hook, hitch, couple, connect; to entrap; to decoy into military service. II. *vr.* to engage; to enlist in the army; to be caught on a hook.
enganche, *m.* = ENGANCHAMIENTO.
engañabobos, *m.* (coll.) trickster; fool trap.
engañadizo, za, *a.* easily deceived.
engañado, da. I. *pp.* of ENGAÑAR. II. *a.* mistaken; deceived.
engañador, ra, *n.* & *a.* deceiver(-ing).
engañapastor, *m.* (ornith.) wagtail.
engañar. I. *va.* to deceive; cheat; fool, hoax; to wile away (as time). II. *vr.* to deceive oneself; to make a mistake, be mistaken.
engañifa, *f.* (coll.) deceit, trick, catchpenny.
engaño, *m.* deceit, fraud; hoax, lure; mistake, misunderstanding, misapprehension.
engañoso, sa, *a.* deceitful, artful, false; deceiving, misleading.
engarabatar. I. *va.* (coll.) to hook. II. *vr.* to become crooked.
engarabitarse, *vr.* (coll.) to climb, ascend.
engarbarse, *vr.* to perch high on a tree.
engarbullar, *va.* (coll.) to entangle, involve; to make a mess of.
engarce, *m.* linking; setting (of precious stone).
engarcé, engarce, *v.* *V.* ENGARZAR.
engargantar. I. *va.* to put into the throat. II. *vn.* to thrust the foot into the stirrup; to gear, to mesh, to interlock.
engargolar, *va.* to join (pipes).
engaritar, *va.* to fortify or adorn with sentry boxes or turrets; (coll.) to trick, fool.
engarrafar, *va.* (coll.) to grapple.
engarrotar. I. *va.* to garrote; to make numb (with cold). II. *vr.* to become numb with cold; (fig.) to be very cold, frozen.
engarzador, ra, *n.* one who hooks or enchains; stringer of beads.
engarzar, *va.* (*pret.* ENGARCÉ; *subj.* ENGARCE) to link, to hook; to curl; to set (precious stone).
engastador, *m.* enchaser, setter.
engastar, *va.* to set (as diamonds); to enchase.
engaste, *m.* setting (of stones); enchasing; pearl flat on one side.
engatado, da. I. *pp.* of ENGATAR. II. *n.* petty robber, pilferer.

engatar, *va.* (coll.) to cheat; to wheedle.
engatillado, da. I. *pp.* of ENGATILLAR. **II.** *a.* thick, high-necked (horses and bulls).
engatillar, *va.* (arch.) to bind with a cramp iron.
engatusador, ra, *n.* & *a.* coaxer(-ing), wheedler (-ing).
engatusamiento, *m.* (coll.) wheedling, coaxing.
engatusar, *va.* (coll.) to inveigle, wheedle.
engavillar, *va.* to bind in sheaves.
engazador, ra, *n.* = ENGARZADOR.
engazamiento, *m.* = ENGARCE.
[1]**engazar,** *va.* = ENGARZAR, to link.
[2]**engazar,** *va.* (naut.) to strap (blocks); to dye in the cloth.
engendrable, *a.* that may be engendered.
engendrador, ra, *n.* & *a.* generator(-ing); engenderer(-ing).
engendramiento, *m.* begetting, generating.
engendrar, *va.* to beget, engender, generate; to produce, bear; to create; (math.) to generate.
engendro, *m.* fœtus, shapeless embryo; bungling, badly-made thing; poor work; (coll.) show.—**mal e.,** perverse youth.
englobar, *va.* to englobe, inclose, include.
engolado, da, *a.* collared.
engolfar. I. *vn.* (naut.) to enter a gulf or deep bay. **II.** *vr.* to be engrossed or absorbed.
engolillado, da, *a.* wearing the GOLILLA, ruff.
engolondrinarse, *vr.* (coll.) to be elated with pride; to fall in love.
engolosinar. I. *va.* to allure. **II.** *vr.* to become fond of.
engolletado, da. I. *pp.* of ENGOLLETARSE. **II.** *a.* (coll.) conceited haughty.
engolletarse, *vr.* (coll.) to be conceited.
engomadura, *f.* first gumming; coat which bees lay over their hives.
engomar, *va.* to gum, to size; to glue.
engorar, *va.* (*ind.* ENGUERO; *subj.* ENGUERE) to addle.
engorda, *f.* (Am.) ENGORDE; number of animals fattened together or at a time.
engordadero, *m.* sty to fatten hogs.
engordador, ra, *a.* fattening; pampering.
engordar. I. *va.* to pamper, fatten. **II.** *vn.* to get fat; to become rich.
engorde, *m.* fattening (hogs, etc.).
engorro, *m.* embarrassment, nuisance.
engorroso, sa, *a.* troublesome, annoying.
engoznar, *va.* to hinge; to put hinges on.
engranado, da. I. *pp.* of ENGRANAR. **II.** *a.* geared, in gear.
engranaje, *m.* (mech.) gear, gearing.—**e. de cremallera,** (mech.) rack and pinion gear.—**e. de marcha atrás,** reverse gear (in automobiles).—**e. diferencial,** (mech.) differential gear.
engranar. I. *va.* to gear; to put in gear (automobile). **II.** *vn.* to gear; to interlock.
engrandar, *va.* = AGRANDAR, to enlarge.
engrandecer, *va.* (*ind.* ENGRANDEZCO; *subj.* ENGRANDEZCA) to augment, aggrandize; to enlarge; to exalt, extol; to exaggerate, magnify.
engrandecimiento, *m.* increase, enlargement; aggrandizement, exaltation; exaggeration.
engrandezco, engrandezca, *v. V.* ENGRANDECER.
engranerar, *va.* to store (grain).
engranujarse, *vr.* to become covered with pimples; to become a knave.
engrapar, *va.* (mason. and carp.) to cramp.
engrasación, *f.* lubrication, oiling, greasing.
engrasador, *m.* oiler, lubricator.
engrasamiento, *m.* = ENGRASACIÓN.
engrasar, *va.* to grease, oil, lubricate; to stain with grease; to dress (cloth); to manure.
engrase, *m.* = ENGRASACIÓN.
engredar, *va.* to clay, to chalk; to full.
engreído, da. I. *pp.* of ENGREÍR; **II.** *a.* conceited.
engreimiento, *m.* conceit, presumption, vanity.
engreír. I. *va.* (*ind.* ENGRÍO; *subj.* ENGRÍA) to encourage the conceit of, to make vain; to elate. **II.** *vr.* to become vain or conceited; (Am.) (con or de) to be, or become, fond (of), take a liking (to).
engrescar, *va.* & *vr.* to pick a quarrel; to make (one) join in merriment.
engrifar, *va.* & *vr.* to curl, crisp, crimp; to make (the hair) stand on end (from fright).
engringarse, *vr.* (coll.) to follow foreign customs, to act like foreigners.
engrío, engría, *v. V.* ENGREÍR.
engrosar. I. *va.* (*ind.* ENGRUESO; *subj.* ENGRUESE) to swell, enlarge; increase; to thicken, broaden. **II.** *vn.* & *vr.* to become strong or corpulent; to increase.
engrudador, *m.* paster.
engrudamiento, *m.* pasting.
engrudar, *va.* to paste.—**engrudo,** *m.* paste.
engrueso, engruese, *v. V.* ENGROSAR.
engruesar, *va.* = ENGROSAR.
engrumecerse, *vr.* to clot, to curdle.
engualdrapar, *va.* to caparison.
enguantarse, *vr.* to put gloves on.
enguedejado, da, *a.* wearing long hair.
enguijarrar, *va.* to pave with pebbles.
enguillar, *va.* (naut.) to wind (a thin rope around a thicker one).
enguirnaldar, *va.* to garland.
enguizcar, *va.* to incite, prompt, stimulate.
engullidor, ra, *n.* devourer, gobbler, glutton.
engullir, *va.* to devour, gobble.
engurrio, *m.* sadness, melancholy.
engurruñarse, *vr.* (coll.) to become melancholy.
enharinar, *va.* to cover with flour.
enhastiar, *va.* to annoy, cloy, bore.
enhastillar, *va.* to put arrows in (a quiver).
enhatijar, *va.* to cover (hives) with basswood.
enhebrar, *va.* to thread; to string.
enhenar, *va.* to cover with hay.
enherbolar, *va.* to poison with herbs.
enhestador, ra, *n.* one who raises or hoists.
enhestadura, *f.* erection, raising, hoisting.
enhestar. I. *va.* (*pp. irreg.* ENHIESTO; *ind.* ENHIESTO; *subj.* ENHIESTE) to erect; to raise, to hoist; to set upright. **II.** *vr.* to rise upright.
enhielar, *va.* to mix with gall or bile.
[1]**enhiesto, ta. I.** *pp. irreg.* of ENHESTAR. **II.** *a.* erect, upright; lofty.
[2]**enhiesto, enhieste,** *v. V.* ENHESTAR.
enhilado, da. I. *pp.* of ENHILAR. **II.** *a.* well-arranged, in good order, in line.
enhilar, *va.* to thread; to direct; to line.
enhorabuena. I. *f.* congratulation, felicitation. **II.** *adv.* well and good; all right.
enhoramala, *adv.* denoting disapproval, etc.; (lit.) in an evil hour.—**vete e.,** (coll.) go to blazes!
enhornar, *va.* to put into an oven.
enhuecar, *va.* = AHUECAR, to make hollow.
enhuerar, *va., vn.* & *vr.* to addle.
enigma, *m.* enigma.
enigmático, ca, *a.* enigmatical.
enigmatista, *m.* one who speaks in enigmas.
enjabonadura, *f.* washing.
enjabonar, *va.* to soap; to wash with soap; (coll.) to soft-soap.
enjaezar, *va.* (*pret.* ENJAECÉ; *subj.* ENJAECE) to trap, harness.
enjaguar, *va.* = ENJUAGAR.—**enjagüe,** *m.* adjudication required by the creditors of a ship.
enjalbegador, ra, *n.* whitewasher.
enjalbegadura, *f.* whitewashing.
enjalbegar, *va.* to whitewash; to paint (the face).
enjalma, *f.* packsaddle.—**enjalmar. I.** *va.* to put on a packsaddle. **II.** *vn.* to make packsaddles.
enjalmero, *m.* packsaddle maker.
enjambradera, *f.* queen bee; cell of queen bee.
enjambradero, *m.* place where bees form hives.
enjambrar. I. *va.* to hive (bees). **II.** *vn.* to breed a new hive; to produce abundantly.
enjambrazón, *f.* swarming of bees.
enjambre, *m.* swarm; crowd.
enjarciar, *va.* to rig (a ship).

enjardinar, *va.* to trim and arrange (trees), as in gardens.
enjaretado, *m.* grating, lattice work.
enjaretar, *va.* to run a string through (a hem); (coll.) to speak or act hurriedly and thoughtlessly.
enjaular, *va.* to cage; to imprison, confine.
enjebar, *va.* to steep in lye, to buck.
enjebe, *m.* lye; (act of) bucking.
enjergar, *va.* (coll.) to start and direct.
enjertación, *f.* grafting; insertion; inoculation; budding.
enjertar, *va.* = INJERTAR, (hort.) to graft.
enjerto, *m.* grafted plant or tree; mixture.
enjorguinar. I. *va.* to smear with soot. **II.** *vr.* to be blackened with soot.
enjoyar, *va.* to adorn with jewels; to set with precious stones; to adorn, embellish.
enjoyelado, da, *a.* worked into jewels; covered with jewels, bejeweled.
enjoyelador, *m.* setter, jeweler.
enjuagadientes, *m.* (coll.) mouth wash.
enjuagadura, *f.* rinsing the mouth.
enjuagar, *va.* to rinse (mouth, cups, etc.)
enjuagatorio, *m.* act of rinsing; mouth wash; finger bowl.
enjuague, *m.* plot, scheme; ENJUAGATORIO.
enjugador, ra. I. *n.* drier. **II.** *m.* drum for the drying of linen.
enjugar. I. *va.* (*pp. irreg.* ENJUTO; *pret.* ENJUGUÉ; *subj.* ENJUGUE) to dry; to wipe off moisture from. **II.** *vr.* to become lean.
enjuiciamiento, *m.* (law) act of instituting and prosecuting a judicial proceeding; suit.
enjuiciar, *va.* (law) to bring a suit or action against; to try, carry on (a case); to indict; to pass judgment on.
enjulio, enjullo, *m.* cloth beam of a loom; warp rod.
enjundia, *f.* fat in the ovary of fowls; grease or fat of any animal; substance, force.
enjundioso, sa, *a.* fat, fatty; substantial.
enjunque, *m.* (naut.) heavy ballast or cargo; kentledge.
enjuta, *f.* (arch.) spandrel.
enjutar, *va.* (mason.) to dry (plaster, etc.).
enjutez, *f.* dryness, aridity.
enjuto, ta. I. *pp. irreg.* of ENJUGAR. **II.** *a.* lean, skinny; austere. **III.** *m. pl.* brushwood; tidbits that stimulate thirst.
enlabiador, ra, *n.* wheedler.
enlabiar, *va.* to wheedle, cajole, entice.
enlabio, *m.* enticement, alluring by soft words.
enlace, *m.* connection; interlocking; link; train connection; marriage; relationship.
enlacé, enlace, *v. V.* ENLAZAR.
enlaciar. I. *va.* to render lax or languid. **II.** *vr.* to wither, to decay.
enladrillado, *m.* brick pavement.
enladrillador, *m.* bricklayer.
enladrilladura, *f.* brickwork.
enladrillar, *va.* to pave with bricks.
enlagunar, *va.* to flood, to turn into a pond.
enlajar, *va.* (Venez.) to pave with tiles or flags.
enlamar, *va.* to cover with slime.
enlanado, da, *a.* covered with wool.
enlardar, *va.* to baste (meat). Also LARDAR.
enlatar, *va.* to cover (a roof) with tin; to can.
enlazable, *a.* that can be joined.
enlazador, ra, *n.* binder, uniter.
enlazadura, *f.*, **enlazamiento,** *m.* connection, binding, uniting, linking, coupling; lacing.
enlazar. I. *va.* (*pret.* ENLACÉ; *subj.* ENLACE) to lace, bind, join, unite, connect. **II.** *vr.* to become joined in wedlock; to become related by marriage; to interlock; to join or be linked.
enlegajar, *va.* to sort or arrange (papers) into a batch or parcel.
enlejiar, *va.* to buck (clothes); to make into lye.
enlenzar, *va.* (*ind.* ENLIENZO; *subj.* ENLIENZE) to strengthen with adhesive strips.
enligarse, *vr.* to be caught with birdlime.
enlistonado, *m.* (carp., mason.) lathing, lath work.
enlistonar, *va.* to lath, lay lath work on.
enlizar, *va.* to provide (a loom) with leashes.
enlodadura, *f.* act of soiling with mud.
enlodar. I. *va.* to bemire, to soil with mud; to throw mud at. **II.** *vr.* to get muddy.
enloquecedor, ra, *a.* maddening.
enloquecer. I. *va.* (*ind.* ENLOQUEZCO; *subj.* ENLOQUEZCA) to madden, drive insane; to distract. **II.** *vn.* & *vr.* to become insane; to be vexed, annoyed or in despair; (of trees) to become barren.
enloquecimiento, *m.* madness, insanity.
enloquezco, enloquezca, *v. V.* ENLOQUECER.
enlosado, *m.* pavement; tile floor; paving, tiling.
enlosador, ra, *n.* tile layer, paver.
enlosar, *va.* to pave with flags, tile or slabs.
enlozanarse, *vr.* to make a show of vigor and strength.
enlucido, *m.* (coat of) plaster; plastering.
enlucidor, *m.* (mason.) plasterer.
enlucimiento, *m.* polishing; (mason.) plastering.
enlucir, *va.* (*ind.* ENLUZCO; *subj.* ENLUZCA) to polish (plate); (mason.) to plaster.
enlustrecer, *va.* to clean, brighten, polish.
enlutar, *va.* to put in mourning, put crape or mourning on, to crape; to veil; to darken.
enluzco, enluzca, *v. V.* ENLUCIR.
enllantar, *va.* to rim, to shoe (a wheel).
enllentecer, *va.* (*ind.* ENLLENTEZCO; *subj.* ENLLENTEZCA) to soften, blandish.
enmaderación, *f.*, **enmaderamiento,** *m.* woodwork; wainscoting.
enmaderar, *va.* to plank, board; to roof with timber; to floor with boards.
enmagrecer, *vn.* (*ind.* ENMAGREZCO; *subj.* ENMAGREZCA) to become lean or skinny.
enmalezarse, *vr.* to become weedy.
enmallarse, *vr.* to be caught in the meshes.
enmangar, *va.* to put a handle on.
enmantar. I. *va.* to cover with a blanket. **II.** *vr.* to become melancholy.
enmarañamiento, *m.* entanglement, intricacy.
enmarañar, *va.* to tangle (as hair, etc.); to entangle, perplex, involve in difficulties; to puzzle.
enmararse, *vr.* (naut.) to take sea room.
enmaridar, *vn.* & *vr.* to get a husband, marry.
enmarillecerse, *vr.* to become yellow.
enmaromar, *va.* to tie with a rope.
enmascarar. I. *va.* to mask. **II.** *vr.* to masquerade, put on a mask.
enmasillar, *va.* to putty, cement.
enmatarse, *vr.* to hide among the plants.
enmelar, *va.* (*ind.* ENMIELO; *subj.* ENMIELE) to bedaub with honey; to sweeten.
enmendable, *a.* emendable.
enmendación, *f.* emendation, correction.
enmendadamente, *adv.* accurately, exactly.
enmendador, ra, *n.* corrector, reviser.
enmendadura, *f.* = ENMIENDA.
enmendar. I. *va.* (*ind.* ENMIENDO; *subj.* ENMIENDE) to amend, correct; to repair; to reform; to indemnify. **II.** *vr.* to mend, reform, lead a new life.
enmienda, *f.* emendation, correction; reward, premium; (law) satisfaction, indemnity.
enmiendo, enmiende, *v. V.* ENMENDAR.
enmohecer, *va.* & *vr.* (*ind.* ENMOHEZCO; *subj.* ENMOHEZCA) to mold, mildew; to rust.
enmohecido, da. I. *pp.* of ENMOHECER. **II.** *a.* rusty, moldy.
enmohecimiento, *m.* rusting; molding.
enmohezco, enmohezca, *v. V.* ENMOHECER.
enmollecer, *va.* (*ind.* ENMOLLEZCO; *subj.* ENMOLLEZCA) to soften, mollify.
enmondar, *va.* to clear (cloth) from knots.
enmontarse, *vr.* (Colomb.) to become overgrown with weeds and trees.
enmordazar, *va.* to gag, muzzle.
enmudecer. I. *va.* (*ind.* ENMUDEZCO; *subj.* ENMUDEZCA) to hush, to silence. **II.** *vn.* to become dumb; to be silent.

enmugrar, *va.* to soil, cover with dirt.
ennegrecer, *va.* (*ind.* ENNEGREZCO; *subj.* ENNEGREZCA) to blacken; to darken, to obscure.
ennegrecimiento, *m.* blackening.
ennegrezco, ennegrezca, *v. V.* ENNEGRECER.
ennoblecedor, ra, *a.* ennobling, noble.
ennoblecer, *va.* (*ind.* ENNOBLEZCO; *subj.* ENNOBLEZCA) to ennoble; to adorn, embellish.
ennoblecimiento, *m.* ennoblement.
ennoblezco, ennoblezca, *v. V.* ENNOBLECER.
ennudecer, *vn.* (of trees) to be arrested in growth.
enodio, *m.* fawn, young deer.
enojada, *f.* (coll.) (Mex., P. R.) anger; getting angry.
enojadizo, za, *a.* fretful, peevish, ill-tempered.
enojado, da, I. *pp.* of ENOJAR. **II.** *a.* angry, cross.
enojar. I. *va.* to make angry, vex, irritate; to annoy. **II.** *vr.* to become angry, to get cross; (of the elements) to become violent, furious.
enojo, *m.* anger; (gen. *pl.*) trouble, suffering; annoyance.
enojón, na, *a.* (Am.) = ENOJADIZO.
enojoso, sa, *a.* troublesome; irritating.
enojuelo, *m. dim.* slight peevishness.
enología, *f.* œnology, art of wine making.
enológico, ca, *a.* œnological.
enólogo, *m.* œnologist.
enometría, *f.* wine alcoholometry.
enómetro, *m.* wine alcoholometer.
enorgullecer. I. *va.* (*ind.* ENORGULLEZCO; *subj.* ENORGULLEZCA) to make proud. **II.** *vr.* to be proud; to swell with pride.—**enorgullecimiento,** *m.* pride; haughtiness.—**enorgullecido, da. I.** *pp.* of ENORGULLECER. **II.** *a.* haughty, proud.
enorgullezco, enorgullezca, *v. V.* ENORGULLECER.
enorme, *a.* enormous; horrible, wicked, heinous.
enormidad, *f.* enormousness, great quantity or size; horridness; enormity, atrocity, outrage.
enormísimo, ma, *a. super.* most horrid.
enostosis, *f.* (med.) enostosis, bony tumor.
enotecnia, *f.* art of wine making and marketing.
enotécnico, ca, *a.* pertaining to wine making.
enquiciar, *va.* to put (a door, window) in place; to put in order; to make firm or stable.
enquillotrarse, *vr.* to become conceited; (coll.) to fall in love.
enquiridión, *m.* enchiridion, handbook, manual.
enquistar, *va.* & *vn.* (biol., surg.) to encyst.
enrabiar, *va.* to anger, enrage.
enraizar, *vn.* to take root.
enramada, *f.* bower, arbor; grove.
enramar, *va.* to embower or decorate with tree branches.
enramblar, *va.* to tenter (cloth).
enrame, *m.* act of embowering.
enranciarse, *vr.* to become rancid or stale.
enrarecer. I. *va.* (*ind.* ENRAREZCO; *subj.* ENRAREZCA) to thin, rarefy. **II.** *vr.* to become thin or rarefied.—**enrarecimiento,** *m.* rarefaction.
enrasar, *va.* (mason.) to make even or level, to flush.—**enrase,** *m.* (mason.) levelling course.
enrayar, *va.* to put spokes on (a wheel).
enredadera. I. *a.* (of plants) climbing, twining. **II.** *f.* (bot.) climber; vine; bindweed.
enredado, da. I. *pp.* of ENREDAR. **II.** *a.* entangled, matted, involved, intricate.
enredador, ra, *n.* entangler; tattler, busybody, intermeddler.
enredar. I. *va.* to entangle, snarl; to confound, puzzle; to snarl, mess up, involve in difficulties; to catch in the net; to lay, set (snares, nets); to sow discord among or between. **II.** *vn.* to fumble; to be frisky (as boys). **III.** *vr.* to get entangled, snarled; to get involved; (naut.) (of anchor) to foul.
enredo, *m.* tangle, entanglement; perplexity, puzzle; intricacy; falsehood, mischievous lie; plot (of a play, etc.).—**enredoso, sa,** entangled, intricate; beset with difficulties.
enrehojar, *va.* to bleach (wax leaves).
enrejado, *m.* railing, grating; trellis, lattice; grillwork, openwork.
enrejalar, *va.* to range bricks in crisscross tiers.
[1]**enrejar,** *va.* to fence with railing or grating; to put a trellis or lattice on.
[2]**enrejar,** *va.* to attach the plowshare to (the plow); to wound (cattle's feet) with a plowshare.
enrevesado, da, *a.* frisky; difficult; nonsensical.
enriado, *m.* retting, soaking of flax or hemp.
enriador, ra, *n.* one who rets, soaks flax or hemp.
enriar, *va.* to ret, soak (hemp, flax).
enrielar, *va.* to make ingots or rails from; to put on the track; to guide, start in the right direction.
enripiar, *va.* (mason.) to fill with riprap.
enriquecedor, ra, *n.* & *a.* enricher(-ing), wealth producer(-ing).
enriquecer. I. *va.* (*ind.* ENRIQUEZCO; *subj.* ENRIQUEZCA) to enrich; to adorn. **II.** *vr.* to become rich.
enriquecimiento, *m.* enrichment.
enriscado, da. I. *pp.* of ENRISCAR. **II.** *a.* mountainous, craggy; full of cliffs.
enriscamiento, *m.* act of raising; taking refuge among rocks.
enriscar. I. *va.* to lift, to raise. **II.** *vr.* to take refuge among rocks.
[1]**enristrar,** *va.* to string (onions, etc.)
[2]**enristrar,** *va.* to couch (the lance); to go direct to (a place); to overcome (a difficulty).
enristre, *m.* act of couching a lance.
[1]**enrocar,** *va.* (chess) to castle.
[2]**enrocar,** *va.* to put (flax or wool) on the distaff.
enrodelado, da, *a.* armed with a shield.
enrodrigonar, *va.* to prop or train with stakes.
enrojar, *va.* & *vr.* = ENROJECER.
enrojecer. I. *va.* (*ind.* ENROJEZCO; *subj.* ENROJEZCA) to redden; to make red-hot; to make blush. **II.** *vr.* to blush; turn red.
enrolamiento, *m.* enlistment; enrollment.
enrolar, *va.* to enlist, enroll.
enrollar, *va.* to roll, coil, wind, wrap, up.
enromar, *va.* to blunt, dull.
enrona, *f.* rubbish, refuse, débris.
enronar, *va.* to throw rubbish in (a place).
enronquecer. I. *va.* (*ind.* ENRONQUEZCO; *subj.* ENRONQUEZCA) to make hoarse. **II.** *vn.* & *vr.* to get hoarse.
enronquecimiento, *m.* hoarseness.
enronquezco, enronquezca, *v. V.* ENRONQUECER.
enroñar, *va.* to fill with scabs or scurf.
enroscadamente, *adv.* curlingly.
enroscadura, *f.* act of twisting; convolution, sinuosity, twist, curlicue.
enroscar. I. *va.* (*pret.* ENROSQUÉ; *subj.* ENROSQUE) to twine, to twist. **II.** *vr.* to curl or twist itself; to coil.
enrubiador, ra, *a.* that turns the hair blond.
enrubiar, *va.* to dye (the hair) blond, bleach.
enrubio, *m.* dyeing blond; the dye used.
enrudecer. I. *va.* (*ind.* ENRUDEZCO; *subj.* ENRUDEZCA) to make dull. **II.** *vr.* to become dull.
enruinecer, *vn.* & *vr.* (*ind.* ENRUINEZCO; *subj.* ENRUINEZCA) to become vile.
ensabanar, *va.* to wrap up in sheets.
ensacador, ra, *n.* sacker, bagger.
ensacar, *va.* (*pret.* ENSAQUÉ; *subj.* ENSAQUE) to put in a sack, bag.
ensaimada, *f.* light coffee cake.
ensalada, *f.* salad; hodge podge, medley.
ensaladera, *f.* salad dish or bowl.
ensaladilla, *f.* assortment of dry sweetmeats; jewel made up of different precious stones.
ensalcé, ensalce, *v. V.* ENSALZAR.
ensalmador, ra, *n.* bonesetter; quack.
ensalmar, *va.* to set (bones); to cure by spells.
ensalmista, *n.* & *a.* medicine man, quack.
ensalmo, *m.* enchantment, spell, charm.—**como por e.,** or **por e.,** as if miraculously, suddenly and unexpectedly.
ensalobrarse, *vr.* to become salty.

ensalzador, ra, *n.* exalter, praiser, extoller.
ensalzamiento, *m.* exaltation, praise.
ensalzar, *va.* (*pret.* ENSALCÉ; *subj.* ENSALCE) to extol, exalt, praise.
ensamblador, *m.* joiner.
ensambladura, *f.* joinery; act of joining; joint.
ensamblaje, *m.* joining, coupling.
ensamblar, *va.* to join, couple; connect.
ensamble, *m.* = ENSAMBLAJE.
ensancha, *f.* extension, enlargement.
ensanchable, *a.* expanding (as a tool).
ensanchador, ra. I. *a.* stretching, expanding. **II.** *m.* stretcher, expander, reamer; glove stretcher.
ensanchamiento, *m.* widening, enlargement, dilation, expansion, stretch.
ensanchar. I. *va.* to widen, extend, enlarge; to stretch.—**e. el corazón,** to cheer up. **II.** *vr.* to assume an air of importance; to expand, enlarge.
ensanche, *m.* dilatation, enlargement, widening, extension, expansion, stretch; material turned in in seams of garments.
ensandecer, *vr.* (*ind.* ENSANDEZCO; *subj.* ENSANDEZCA) to become stupid; to turn mad.
ensangrentamiento, *m.* covering with blood.
ensangrentar. I. *va.* & *vr.* (*ind.* ENSANGRIENTO; *subj.* ENSANGRIENTE) to stain with blood. **II.** *vr.* to become heated or fiery; to cover oneself with blood.
ensañamiento, *m.* ferocity, cruelty.
ensañar. I. *va.* to irritate, enrage. **II.** *vr.* to gloat; to vent one's fury; to be merciless.
ensarnecerse, *vr.* to get the itch.
ensartar, *va.* to string (as beads); to thread; to link; to tell disconnectedly, to rattle off.
ensay, *m.* assay, trial, proof.
ensayador, ra, *n.* assayer; rehearcer.
ensayar. I. *va.* to try, practice, rehearse; to test; to assay. **II.** *vr.* to train oneself, practice.
ensaye, *m.* assay, test (of metals).
ensayista, *n.* essay writer; (Chile) assayer.
ensayo, *m.* test; essay; trial, examination, experiment; rehearsal; exercise, preparatory practice; (com.) sample, test, trial.
ensebar, *va.* to grease, tallow.
enselvado, da. I. *pp.* of ENSELVAR. **II.** *a.* wooded.
enselvar. I. *va.* to place in a wood. **II.** *vr.* to hide in, or retire to, the woods; to become wooded.
ensenada, *f.* cove, inlet, small bay.
ensenado, da. I. *pp.* of ENSENAR. **II.** *a.* having the form of a cove or inlet.
ensenar. I. *va.* to put in one's bosom. **II.** *vr.* (naut.) to put (a ship) into a bay.
enseña, *f.* standard, colors, ensign.
enseñable, *a.* teachable.
enseñado, da. I. *pp.* of ENSEÑAR. **II.** *a.* accustomed; trained.
enseñador, ra, *n.* teacher, instructor.
enseñamiento, *m.* teaching; education.
enseñanza, *f.* ENSEÑAMIENTO.—**e. primaria,** or **primera e.,** primary education.—**e. secundaria,** or **segunda e.,** secondary, high-school education.—**e. superior,** higher, or professional education.
enseñar. I. *va.* to teach; to train; to show, point out. **II.** *vr.* to school oneself; to become accustomed, inured.
enseño, *m.* (coll.) education.
enseñorear. I. *va.* to lord, to domineer. **II.** *vr.* to take possession (of a thing).
enserar, *va.* to cover with matting.
enseres, *m. pl.* chattels; fixtures, accessories; implements; household goods.
enseriarse, *vr.* (Am.) to become serious.
ensiforme, *a.* ensiform, sword-shaped.
ensilaje, *m.* ensilage.
ensilar, *va.* to ensile, preserve in a silo.
ensillado, da. I. *pp.* of ENSILLAR. **II.** *a.* saddle-backed (horses).
ensilladura, *f.* part of a horse on which the saddle is placed.
ensillar, *va.* to saddle (a horse, etc.).
ensimismado, da, *a.* self-absorbed.
ensimismamiento, *m.* self-absorption.
ensimismarse, *vr.* to become absorbed in thought.
ensoberbecer. I. *va.* (*ind.* ENSOBERBEZCO; *subj.* ENSOBERBEZCA) to make proud. **II.** *vr.* to become proud and haughty; (of the elements) to become boisterous.
ensoberbecimiento, *m.* excessive pride.
ensoberbezco, ensoberbezca, *v.* *V.* ENSOBERBECER.
ensogar, *va.* to fasten with a rope.
ensolerar, *va.* to fix stools to (beehives).
ensolver, *va.* (*pp.* ENSUELTO; *ind.* ENSUELVO; *subj.* ENSUELVA) to inclose, include; to condense, abridge; (med.) to resolve
ensombrecer. I. *va.* to darken, shade, dim. **II.** *vr.* to become sad, become sullen.
ensopar, *va.* to steep, soak; to drench.
ensordecedor, ra, *a.* deafening.
ensordecer. I. *va.* (*ind.* ENSORDEZCO; *subj.* ENSORDEZCA) to deafen. **II.** *vn.* & *vr.* to become deaf; to become silent.
ensordecimiento, *m.* deafness.
ensordezco, ensordezca, *v.* *V.* ENSORDECER.
ensortijamiento, *m.* curling, crimping, crisping; ringlet, curlicue, kink.
ensortijar, *va.* & *vr.* to curl, to form ringlets; to kink; to put rings in (an animal's nose).
ensotarse, *vr.* to go into a thicket.
ensuciador, ra, *n.* & *a.* stainer(-ing), soiler(-ing).
ensuciamiento, *m.* staining, soiling, polluting.
ensuciar. I. *va.* to stain, soil, smear; to defile, pollute. **II.** *vr.* to soil one's bed, clothes, etc.; (coll.) to be dishonest; to lower oneself.
ensuelto, ensuelvo, etc. *v.* *V.* ENSOLVER.
ensueño, *m.* dream; illusion, fantasy.
entablación, *f.* act of flooring or boarding up; register in churches.
entablado, da. I. *pp.* of ENTABLAR. **II.** *m.* boarded or parqueted floor.
entabladura, *f.* act of flooring or boarding up; planking, timbering.
entablamento, *m.* (arch.) entablature.
entablar. I. *va.* to cover with boards; to board up; to plank; to initiate, start, begin (as a negotiation); to bring (a suit or action); to place (the men) on a chessboard; (surg.) to splint. **II.** *vr.* to settle (as the wind); to establish oneself.
entable, *m.* position of men on a chessboard; position, employment; business, business position or circumstances.
entablillar, *va.* (surg.) to splint.
entalamadura, *f.* awning of a cart, etc.
entalamar, *va.* to cover with an awning.
entalegar, *va.* (com.) to put in a bag.
entalingar, *va.* (naut.) to clinch (the cable).
entallable, *a.* capable of being carved.
entallador, *m.* sculptor, cutter in wood or stone; engraver; carver.
entalladura, *f.,* **entallamiento,** *m.* sculpture, carving; (carp.) mortise, groove, notch.
[1]**entallar,** *va.* to notch; to make a cut in, to sculpture, to carve; to engrave.
[2]**entallar,** *vn.* (of a garment) to fit well.
entallecer, *vn.* (agr.) to shoot, to sprout.
entapizar, *va.* to hang tapestry on.
entarascar, *va.* (coll:) to overdress.
entarimado, da. I. *pp.* of ENTARIMAR. **II.** *m.* parquetry, inlaid floor.
entarimar, *va.* to floor with boards.
entarquinamiento, *m.* fertilizing with slime.
entarquinar, *va.* to manure with slime; to bemire; to reclaim (swamp lands).
éntasis, *m.* (arch.) entasis.
ente, *m.* entity, being; (coll.) guy.
entecado, da; enteco, ca, *a.* sickly, weak, thin.
entejar, *va.* to tile.
entelequia, *f.* (philos.) entelechy.
entelerido, da, *a.* numb or shivering with cold or fright; (Am.) sick-looking, thin, frail.
entena, *f.* (naut.) lateen yard.

entenado, da, *n.* stepson(-daughter).
entenallas, *f. pl.* (mech.) pincers; handvise.
entendederas, *f. pl.* (coll.) understanding, brain.
entendedor, ra, *n.* one who understands.
entender. I. *va.* & *vn.* (*ind.* ENTIENDO; *subj.* ENTIENDA) to understand.—**e. de,** to be familiar with, be a judge of, be good at, know.—**e. en,** to be in charge of, deal with, attend to; to have authority to pass on or enquire into.—**dar a e.,** to intimate, insinuate, hint. **II.** *vr.* to be understood; to be meant.—**e. con,** to belong with, be included in; to have to do with; to deal with. —**e. por,** to be understood to be; to mean: (*entiéndese por aritmética la ciencia de los números,* arithmetic means the science of numbers). **III.** *m.* understanding, opinion.—**a mi e., según mi e.,** in my opinion, according to my understanding.
entendidamente, *adv.* knowingly.
entendido, da. I. *pp.* of ENTENDER. **II.** *a.* able; posted; prudent.—**darse por e.,** to take notice, pay attention.—**no darse por e.,** not to notice, to ignore; to pretend not to understand.—**tener e.,** to understand.
entendimiento, *m.* intellect, mind; understanding; comprehension.
entenebrecer, *va.* (*ind.* ENTENEBREZCO; *subj.* ENTENEBREZCA) to obscure, darken.
enterado, da. I. *pp.* of ENTERAR. **II.** *a.* posted, informed.
enteralgia, *f.* (med.) enteralgia.
enteramente, *adv.* entirely, fully; quite.
enterar. I. *va.* to inform, acquaint, advise; (Am.) to pay, deliver (in a public office). **II.** *vn.* (Am.) to get better. **III.** *vr.* (Am.) to make up for a loss, recoup one's losses.—**e. de,** to learn, become informed about or familiar with, find out about.
entereza, *f.* entirety, completeness; integrity, uprightness; perfection; fortitude, firmness; presence of mind.—**e. virginal,** virginity.
entérico, ca, *a.* (med.) enteric.
enterísimo, ma, *a. super.* most complete.
enteritis, *f.* (med.) enteritis.
enterizo, za, *a.* of, or in, one piece; whole.
enternecedor, ra, *a.* pitiful, touching.
enternecer. I. *va.* (*ind.* ENTERNEZCO; *subj.* ENTERNEZCA) to soften; to touch, move to pity. **II.** *vr.* to be moved to pity, to be affected.
enternecidamente, *adv.* compassionately.
enternecido, da, *a.* moved, touched.
enternecimiento, *m.* compassion, pity.
enternezco, enternezca, *v. V.* ENTERNECER.
entero, ra. I. *a.* entire, whole; sound, perfect; honest, upright; pure, uncorrupted; strong, robust, vigorous; informed, instructed; uncastrated; strong, thick (dry goods); (arith.) whole, integral.—**por e.,** entirely, fully. **II.** *m.* (arith.) integer; (Am.) payment, delivery; balance.—**los enteros,** (arith.) the integral part (of a decimal).
enterocele, *m.* (med.) enterocele, intestinal hernial tumor.
enterocolitis, *f.* (med.) enterocolitis.
enterotomía, *f.* (surg.) enterotomy, intestinal incision.
enterrador, *m.* gravedigger; sexton.
enterramiento, *m.* interment, burial, funeral.
enterrar, *va.* (*ind.* ENTIERRO; *subj.* ENTIERRE) to inter, bury; to survive.
enterronar, *va.* to cover with clods.
entesamiento, *m.* stretching, making taut.
entesar, *va.* to stretch, make taut.
entestado, da, *a.* obstinate, stubborn.
entibación, *f.* (min.) timbering.
entibador, *m.* one who shores up mines.
entibar. I. *vn.* to rest, to lean upon. **II.** *va.* (min.) to prop, shore up.
entibiadero, *m.* cooling room or bath.
entibiar. I. *va.* to make lukewarm; to cool; to temper, moderate. **II.** *vr.* to cool down; to slacken.
entibo, *m.* stay, prop; foundation.
entidad, *f.* entity; value, consequence, moment, importance.
entiendo, entienda, *v. V.* ENTENDER.
[1]**entierro,** *m.* burial, interment, funeral; grave.
[2]**entierro, entierre,** *v. V.* ENTERRAR.
entigrecerse, *vr.* (*ind.* ENTIGREZCO; *subj.* ENTIGREZCA) (coll.) to become furious as a tiger.
entimema, *f.* (logic) enthymeme.
entinar, *va.* to put into the dyeing vat.
entintar, *va.* to ink, ink in (a drawing); to stain with ink; to tint or dye.
entiznar, *va.* to stain; to revile, defame.
entoldado, *m.* tent or group of tents; covering with tents or awnings.
entoldamiento, *m.* covering with tents or with awnings.
entoldar. I. *va.* to cover with an awning; to adorn with hangings. **II.** *vr.* to dress gorgeously; to swell with pride; (of sky) to get cloudy.
entomizar, *va.* to tie bass cords around (posts or laths), so the plaster will stick.
entomófago, ga, *a.* (zool.) entomophagous, insectivorous.
entomofilia, *f.* (bot.) entomophily, pollination by insects.
entomófilo, la, *a.* (bot.) entomophilous.
entomología, *f.* entomology.
entomológico, ca, *a.* entomological.
entomólogo, *m.* entomologist.
entonación, *f.* modulation; intonation; blowing the bellows of an organ.
entonadera, *f.* blow lever of an organ.
entonado, da. I. *pp.* of ENTONAR. **II.** *a.* haughty, "stuck-up." **III.** *m.* (photog.) process of toning.
entonador, ra. I. *n.* one who sings in tune; (photog.) one that tones. **II.** *m.* organ blower.
entonamiento, *m.* intonation.
entonar. I. *va.* to modulate, intone; to sing in tune; (art) to harmonize (colors); (photog.) to tone (prints); to blow (the bellows of an organ); (med.) to tone up. **II.** *vr.* to put on grand airs.
entonatorio, *m.* book of sacred music.
entonces, *adv.* then.—**¿e.?** (Am.) then what? and then?—**de e.,** of that time.—**desde e.,** from then on.—**hasta e.,** up to that time.—**por e.,** at the time.
entonelar, *va.* to put in casks or barrels.
entono, *m.* act of intoning; arrogance, haughtiness, airs.
entontecer. I. *va.* (*ind.* ENTONTEZCO; *subj.* ENTONTEZCA) to make foolish; to confuse. **II.** *vn.* & *vr.* to become foolish.—**entontecimiento,** *m.* act of becoming foolish; state of foolishness.
entorchado, *m.* bullion fringe; bullion embroidery on the uniform of generals; (mus.) strings.
entorchar, *va.* to make a torch by twisting (candles); (mus.) to cover (a string) with wire.
entorilar, *va.* to stall (the bull).
entornar, *va.* to half-close; to set ajar.
entornillar, *va.* to form a screw or spiral of.
entorpecer, *va.* (*ind.* ENTORPEZCO; *subj.* ENTORPEZCA) to benumb; to stupefy; to clog, obstruct, delay.
entorpecimiento, *m.* torpor, numbness, stupefaction; dulness, stupidity; obstruction, delay.
entorpezco, entorpezca, *v. V.* ENTORPECER.
entortadura, *f.* crookedness.
entortar, *va.* (*ind.* ENTUERTO; *subj.* ENTUERTE) to bend; to make crooked; to make blind in one eye.
entosigar, *va.* to poison.
entozoario, *m.* (zool.) entozoan, internal parasite.
entozoico, ca, *a.* entozoic.
entrada, *f.* entrance, door, gate; admission; admittance (right of entry); entry; arrival; number of people in a theater (*entrada llena,* full house); beginning (of a book, speech, season, etc.); familiar access, intimacy; good hand at cards; entrée (course at dinner); (com.) entry (in a book); cash receipts; uptake, intake; (elec.) input.—*pl.* temples (of the head); receding hair at temples; (com.) income.—**e. gene-**

ral, (theat.) gallery seat; (Am.) main entrance. —**e. gratuita,** free admission; (U. S., coll.) Annie Oakley.—**entradas y salidas,** (fig.) collusion.
entrado, da, *pp.* of ENTRAR.—**e. en años,** advanced in years.
entrador, ra, *a.* (Am.) energetic, hustling; (Chile) intruding, intrusive, fond of butting in.
entramado, *m.* (carp.) framework, studwork, baywork.
entramar, *va.* (carp.) to provide with studwork or framework.
entrambos, bas, *a.* & *pron. pl.* both.
entrampar. I. *va.* to entrap, insnare; to trick, deceive; to entangle; to encumber. **II.** *vr.* (coll.) to become indebted; to be involved in difficulties.
entrante, *a.* entering; coming, next (*el mes entrante,* next month).
entraña, *f.* entrail.—*pl.* entrails, bowels; humaneness, kindness; (fig.) heart; affection; disposition; idiosyncrasy; the inmost recess of anything.
entrañable, *a.* most affectionate; deep (affection).—**entrañablemente,** *adv.* dearly; deeply.
entrañar. I. *va.* to penetrate to the core; to contain, involve, carry within. **II.** *vr.* to become intimately attached.
entrapada, *f.* coarse crimson cloth.
entrapajar, *va.* to bandage with rags.
entrapar. I. *va.* to powder (the hair) for a dry shampoo; (agr.) to manure with rags. **II.** *vr.* to become as dirty as a rag.
entrar. I. *vn.* **(a, en, por)** (the English equivalent is often transitive) to go (in), come (in), enter; to go (into); to flow (into); to attack, fight; to be admitted or have free entrance (to); to join; to begin; to be one (of), be counted (with); to be believable or understandable (to one); to be taken (with) (fear, etc.); to enter or go (into) (an agreement, etc.); to attack; to influence, convince; (of shoes, garment) to fit. **II.** *va.* to introduce, put in; to enter, take by force. **III.** *vr.* to enter; to squeeze or sneak (in); to break (in).
entre, *prep.* between, among, amongst, amidst; within.—**e. bastidores,** backstage.—**e. la espada y la pared,** between the devil and the deep blue sea.—**e. la vida y la muerte,** between life and death.—**e. manos,** in hand.—**e. mí,** within myself.—**e. nosotros** or **usted y yo,** between you and me.—**e. tanto,** in the meantime, meanwhile.
entreabierto, ta. I. *pp. irreg.* of ENTREABRIR. **II.** *a.* half-opened, ajar.
entreabrir, *va.* to half-open, to set ajar.
entreacto, *m.* (theat., etc.) intermission; small cigar.
entreancho, cha, *a.* neither wide nor narrow.
entrecalle, *m.* (arch.) clear between two consecutive moldings.
entrecanal, *f.* (arch.) fillet between flutes.
entrecano, na, *a.* grayish (hair or beard).
entrecara, *f.* interface.
entrecasco, *m.* = ENTRECORTEZA.
entrecava, *f.* very shallow digging.
entrecavar, *va.* to dig shallow.
entrecejo, *m.* space between eyebrows; frowning.
entreclaro, ra, *a.* slightly clear.
entrecogedura, *f.* act of catching.
entrecoger, *va.* (*ind.* ENTRECOJO; *subj.* ENTRECOJA) to catch; to intercept; to compel by arguments or threats.
entrecoro, *m.* chancel.
entrecortado, da, *a.* confused, hesitating.
entrecortadura, *f.* cut that does not sever.
entrecortar, *va.* to cut without severing.
entrecorteza, *f.* imperfection in timbers.
entrecriarse, *vr.* to grow among other plants.
entrecruzar, *va.* (*subj.* ENTRECRUCE) to intercross; interlace, interweave.
entrecubiertas, *f. pl.* (naut.) between decks.
entrecuesto, *m.* backbone.
entrechocarse, *vr.* to collide, impinge on each other.
entredicho, *m.* interdiction, prohibition.
entredoble, *a.* of medium thickness.
entredós, *m.* insertion; (print.) long primer.
entrefino, na, *a.* middling fine.
entrega, *f.* delivery, conveyance; fascicle of a publication; surrender.—**e. contra reembolso,** cash on delivery (C. O. D.).
entregadero, ra, *a.* (com.) deliverable.
entregador, ra, *n.* deliverer; executor.
entregamiento, *m.* delivery.
entregar. I. *va.* (*pret.* ENTREGUÉ; *subj.* ENTREGUE) to deliver; to give up, surrender; to hand (over); (com.) to transfer, to pay; to insert, introduce, embed.—**a e.,** (com.) to be supplied or delivered. **II.** *vr.* to deliver oneself up, to surrender, give in, submit.—**e. a,** to abandon oneself to or devote oneself to.—**e. de,** to receive, to take charge or possession of.
entrehierro, *m.* (elec.) air gap.
entrejuntar, *va.* (carp.) to join (the panels of a door) to the frame.
entrelazar, *va.* (*pret.* ENTRELACÉ; *subj.* ENTRELACE) to interlace, interweave, braid, entwine.
entreliño, *m.* (agr.) space between rows of trees.
entrelistado, da, *a.* striped or variegated.
entrelucir, *vn.* & *vr.* (*ind.* ENTRELUZCO; *subj.* ENTRELUZCA) to show through.
entremedias, *adv.* in the meantime; halfway.—**e. de,** between; among.
entremés, *m.* (theat.) one-act farce; side dish.
entremesear, *va.* to act in a farce; to throw into one's talk, bring up.
entremesista, *a.* writer or player of farces.
entremeter. I. *va.* to place between; to insert. **II.** *vr.* to intrude, obtrude; intermeddle; meddle; interpose officiously.
entremetido, da. I. *pp.* of ENTREMETER. **II.** *a.* meddlesome; officious. **III.** *n.* meddler, intruder, intermeddler; busybody; go-between.
entremetimiento, *m.* intrusion, intermeddling, meddlesomeness; interposition.
entremezcladura, *f.* intermixture.
entremezclar, *va.* to intermingle, intermix.
entremiche, *m.* (naut.) capstan, chock.
entremorir, *vn.* (*ind. pres.* él ENTREMUERE, *pret.* él ENTREMURIÓ; *pp.* ENTREMUERTO) to flicker (as a flame).
entrenador, ra, *n.* trainer, coach.
entrenamiento, *m.* (Gal.) training, coaching.
entrenar, *va.* & *vn.* (Gal.) to train.
entrencar, *va.* to put rods in (a beehive).
entrenzar, *va.* (*pret.* ENTRENCÉ; *subj.* ENTRENCE) to plait (the hair).
entreoír, *va.* (*ind.* ENTREOIGO; *subj.* ENTREOIGA) to hear indistinctly, half-hear.
entreordinario, ria, *a.* middling.
entrepalmadura, *f.* (vet.) a hoof disease.
entrepanes, *m. pl.* pieces of unsown ground.
entrepañado, da, *a.* composed of panels.
entrepaño, *m.* (arch.) intercolumniation; pier; (carp.) panel; shelf.
entreparecerse, *vr.* to show through.
entrepaso, *m.* rack pace (of horses).
entrepeines, *m. pl.* comb wool.
entrepelado, da, *a.* pied; variegated.
entrepelar, *vn.* & *vr.* (of hair) to be of different colors.
entrepernar, *vn.* (*ind.* ENTREPIERNO; *subj.* ENTREPIERNE) to put the legs between those of others.
entrepiernas, *f. pl.* inner surface of the thighs; pieces put into the crotch of breeches.
entrepiso, *m.* (min.) space between galleries.
entreplano, (aer.) gap.
entrepretado, da, *a.* (vet.) weak in the breast or shoulder.
entrepuentes, *m. pl.* (naut.) between decks.
entrepunzadura, *f.* pricking pain.
entrepunzar, *va.* to prick slightly.
entrerrenglón, *m.* interline.
entrerrenglonadura, *f.* interlineation.

entrerrenglonar, *va.* to interline.
entresaca, entresacadura, *f.* thinning of wood; pruning of branches; sorting; picking out.
entresacar, *va.* (*pret.* ENTRESAQUÉ; *subj.* ENTRESAQUE) to pick out or choose; to sift, cull; to thin out.
entresijo, *m.* (anat.) mesentery; anything hidden.
entresuelo, *m.* entresol, mezzanine.
entresurco, *m.* space between furrows.
entretalla, entretalladura, *f.* bas-relief.
entretallar, *va.* to carve in bas-relief; to engrave; to make openwork on; to intercept.
entretanto, *adv.* meanwhile.
entretejedor, ra, *a.* interweaver.
entretejedura, *f.* intertexture, interweaving.
entretejer, *va.* to interweave, intermix, intertwine; to variegate; to insert, mix, mingle.
entretejimiento, *m.* intertexture, interweaving; variegation.
entretela, *f.* (sewing) interlining.
entretelar, *va.* to insert an interlining in.
entretención, *f.* (Am.) entertainment.
entretenedor, ra, *n.* & *a.* entertainer(-ing).
entretener (*ind. pres.* yo ENTRETENGO, él ENTRETIENE, *pret.* ENTRETUVE, *fut.* ENTRETENDRÉ; *subj.* ENTRETENGA). **I.** *va.* to amuse, entertain; to keep in hope or expectation; to allay (pain), make less troublesome; to delay, put off, postpone. **II.** *vr.* to amuse oneself; to be tied up, delayed.
entretenida, *f.*—**dar con la e.** or **dar la e.,** to give excuses (to); to get out of doing something by promises or evasions.
entretenido, da. I. *pp.* of ENTRETENER. **II.** *a.* entertaining, pleasant, amusing.
entretenimiento, *m.* amusement, entertainment, sport, pastime.
entretiempo, *m.* spring or autumn, between-season.
entretiene, entretuve, *v. V.* ENTRETENER.
entreuntar, *va.* to anoint or paint lightly.
entrevenarse, *vr.* to diffuse through the veins.
entreventana, *f.* (arch.) window pier.
entrever, *va.* (*ind. pres.* ENTREVEO, *pret.* yo ENTREVÍ, él ENTREVIÓ; *subj.* ENTREVEA; *pp.* ENTREVISTO) to see imperfectly.
entreverado, da. I. *pp.* of ENTREVERAR. **II.** *a.* intermingled, intermixed.
entreverar, *va.* to intermix, intermingle.
entrevía, *f.* (Ry.) gauge or gage.
entrevista, *f.* interview, meeting, conference.
entrevistar, *va.* to interview.
entripado, da. I. *a.* contained in the intestines; (of dead animal) not yet cleaned. **II.** *m.* (coll.) anger or displeasure.
entristecedor, ra, *a.* sad, saddening.
entristecer. I. *va.* (*ind.* ENTRISTEZCO; *subj.* ENTRISTEZCA) to sadden, grieve. **II.** *vr.* to grieve, to become sad.
entristecimiento, *m.* sadness; fretting.
entristezco, entristezca, *v. V.* ENTRISTECER.
entrojar, *va.* to garner (grain).
entrometer, *va.* & *vr.* = ENTREMETER.
entrometido, da. I. *pp.* of ENTROMETER. **II.** *a.* = ENTREMETIDO.
entrometimiento, *m.* intermeddling, intrusion.
entronar, *va.* to enthrone.
entroncar, *vn.* to be descended from the same stock; to be related; (also *vr.*) to be connected; (Ry.) (Am.) to form a junction.
entronerar, *va.* (billiards) to pocket (a ball).
entronicé, entronice, *v. V.* ENTRONIZAR.
entronización, *f.* enthronement.
entronizar. I. *va.* (*pret.* ENTRONICÉ; *subj.* ENTRONICE) to enthrone; to exalt. **II.** *vr.* to be elated or puffed up with pride.
entronque, *m.* cognation; connection, relationship; (Am.) railway junction.
entropía, *f.* (phys.) entropy.
entropión, *m.* (med.) entropion, introversion of the eyelids.
entruchada, *f.,* **entruchado,** *m.* (coll.) plot intrigue.
entruchar, *va.* (coll.) to decoy, lure, entice.
entruchón, na, *n.* decoyer, plotter.
entrujar, *va.* to store up; (coll.) to reimburse.
entubar, *va.* to provide with casing (oil well, etc.)
entuerto, *m.* wrong, injustice.—*pl.* afterpains.
entullecer. I. *va.* (*ind.* ENTULLEZCO; *subj.* ENTULLEZCA) to stop, check, obstruct. **II.** *vn.* to be crippled or maimed.
entumecer. I. *va.* (*ind.* ENTUMEZCO; *subj.* ENTUMEZCA) to benumb. **II.** *vr.* (of limbs) to become numb, go to sleep; (of sea, etc.) to swell, surge.
entumecimiento, *m.* torpor, deadness; numbness; swelling.
entumezco, entumezca, *v. V.* ENTUMECER.
entumirse, *vr.* to become numb.
entunarse, *vr.* (Am.) to be pricked by a thorn.
entunicar, *va.* to plaster for fresco painting.
entupir, *va.* to obstruct, block up; to compress.
enturbiar. I. *va.* to muddle; to make muddy or turbid; to obscure, dim, confuse. **II.** *vr.* to get muddy; to get disordered or disarranged.
entusiasmar. I. *va.* to make enthusiastic; to enrapture. **II.** *vr.* to become enthusiastic.
entusiasmo, *m.* enthusiasm.
entusiasta, *n.* enthusiast.
entusiástico, ca, *a.* enthusiastic.
énula campana, *f.* (bot.) elecampane, inula.
enumerable, *a.* (Am.) numerable.
enumeración, *f.* enumeration.
enumerar, *va.* to enumerate.
enumerativo, va, *a.* enumerative.
enunciación, *f.,* **enunciado,** *m.* statement.
enunciar, *va.* to state.
enunciativo, va, *a.* enunciative.
envainador, ra, *a.* sheathing.
envainar, *va.* to sheathe (as a sword).
envalentonamiento, *m.* encouragement.
envalentonar. I. *va.* to encourage, to inspirit; to make bold. **II.** *vr.* to become courageous.
envalijar, *va.* to pack or put in a valise.
envanecer. I. *va.* (*ind.* ENVANEZCO; *subj.* ENVANEZCA) to make vain. **II.** *vr.* to become vain. —**envanecimiento,** *m.* conceit.
envaramiento, *m.* stiffness, numbness.
envarar, *va.* to benumb, stiffen.
envasador, *m.* filler, packer; funnel.
envasar, *va.* to put into a container (barrel, bottle, etc.); to drink (liquor) to excess; to sack (grain); to run through the body with (as a sword).
envase, *m.* filling, bottling; container; packing.
envedijarse, *vr.* to get entangled; (coll.) to wrangle.
envejecer. I. *va.* (*ind.* ENVEJEZCO; *subj.* ENVEJEZCA) to make old; to make look old. **II.** *vn.* to become old. **III.** *vr.* to become old or old-fashioned; to hold out a long time.
envejecido, da. I. *pp.* of ENVEJECER. **II.** *a.* accustomed, habituated.
envejecimiento, *m.* oldness, age; aging.
envejezco, envejezca, *v. V.* ENVEJECER.
envenenador, ra, *n.* & *a.* poisoner(-ing).
envenenamiento, *m.* poisoning.
envenenar, *va.* to envenom, to poison.
enverar, *vn.* to look ripe.
enverdecer, *vn.* & *vr.* to become green.
envergadura, *f.* breadth of the sails; wing-spread of birds; (aer.) span.—**e. de alas,** wingspan.
envergar, *va.* (*pret.* ENVERGUÉ; *subj.* ENVERGUE) (naut.) to bend (the sails).
envergues, *m. pl.* (naut.) ropebands.
envero, *m.* color of ripe grape.
envés, *m.* back or wrong side; back, shoulders.
envesado, *m.* fleshy part of hides.
envestir, *va.* (*ind. pres.* ENVISTO, *pret.* él ENVISTIÓ; *subj.* ENVISTA) to invest (as with authority).
enviada, *f.* sending, shipment.
enviadizo, za, *a.* missive.
enviado, *m.* envoy; messenger.—**e. extraordinario,** envoy extraordinary.
enviajado, da, *a.* (arch.) oblique, sloped.

enviar, *va.* to send; to ship, dispatch.—**e. a uno a pasear,** (coll.) to send one about his business; to give one his walking ticket.—**e. enhoramala,** (coll.) to send to the devil.
enviciador, ra, *a.* habit-forming.
enviciar. I. *va.* to corrupt, teach bad habits to. **II.** *vn.* (of plants) to have luxuriant foliage and little fruit. **III.** *vr.* **(en)** to acquire bad habits; to acquire the habit (of); to take (to) (drinking, etc.).
envidador, *m.* challenger at cards.
envidar, *va.* to stake a sum against.
envidia, *f.* envy.
envidiable, *a.* enviable.
envidiar, *va.* to envy.
envidioso, sa, *a.* envious.
envilecedor, ra, *a.* degrading, debasing.
envilecer I. *va.* (*ind.* ENVILEZCO; *subj.* ENVILEZCA) to vilify, debase. **II.** *vr.* to degrade oneself.
envilecimiento, *m.* vilification, debasement.
envinagrar, *va.* to put vinegar into.
envinar, *va.* to add wine to (water).
envío, *m.* (com.) remittance; consignment of goods, shipment.
envión, *m.* push, shove.
envirotado, da, *a.* airy, stuck-up.
enviscamiento, *m.* daubing with birdlime.
[1]**enviscar. I.** *va.* (*pret.* ENVISQUÉ; *subj.* ENVISQUE) to daub with birdlime. **II.** *vr.* to be glued with birdlime.
[2]**enviscar,** *va.* to irritate, anger.
envite, *m.* stake at cards; invitation; offer; push, **al primer e.,** at once, right off; at the start.
enviudar, *vn.* to become a widower or widow.
envoltorio, *m.* bundle; defective woof.
envoltura, *f.* swaddling clothes; cover, wrapper, envelope, sheath; covering, wrapping.
envolvedero, envolvedor, *m.* wrapper, wrapping, envelope, cover.
envolver. I. *va.* (*pp.* ENVUELTO; *ind.* ENVUELVO; *subj.* ENVUELVA) to wrap, make up into a bundle; to swaddle; to floor (an opponent); to imply, mean; to contain, carry with it; (mil.) to surround. **II.** *vr.* to be implicated, involved; to be unlawfully connected (with women); to be mixed with a crowd.
envolvimiento, *m.* envelopment; wrapping.
envuelto, ta, *pp. irreg.* of ENVOLVER.
envuelvo, envuelva, *v. V.* ENVOLVER.
enyerbar. I. *va.* (Cuba) to sod. **II.** *vr.* to become covered or overgrown with grass.
enyesado, *m.* plasterwork; plaster; plastering.
enyesadura, *f.* plastering.
enyesar, *va.* to plaster; to chalk; to whitewash.
enyugar, *va.* to yoke.
enzainarse, *vr.* to look askance; (coll.) to become treacherous or deceitful.
enzamarrado, da, *a.* having on a shepherd's jacket of undressed sheepskin; wearing chaps.
[1]**enzarzar. I.** *va.* to throw among brambles; to sow discord among or between. **II.** *vr.* to be entangled among brambles; to become involved in difficulties; to squabble, to wrangle.
[2]**enzarzar,** *va.* to put hurdles for (silkworms).
enzima, *f.* (biochem.) enzyme.
enzootia, *f.* enzoöty.
enzoótico, ca, *a.* enzoötic.
enzunchar, *va.* to bind with iron bands or hoops.
enzurdecer, *vn.* & *vr.* (*ind.* ENZURDEZCO; *subj.* ENZURDEZCA) to become left-handed.
enzurronar, *va.* to bag; (coll.) to inclose.
eñe, *f.* name of the letter *ñ*.
eoceno, na, *n.* & *a.* Eocene.
eólico, ca; eolio, lia, *a.* Æolian, Æolic.
eolípila, *f.* (phys.) eolipile.
eolítico, ca, *a.* eolithic.
eolito, *m.* (archeol.) eolith.
eón, *m.* eon, æon, a long period of time.
eosina, *f.* (chem.) eosin.
eosinófilo, la, *a.* & *m.* (physiol.) eosinophile.
epacta, *f.* (astr.) epact.
epactilla, *f.* annual devotional calendar.
epéndimo, *m.* (anat.) ependyma.
epéntesis, *f.* (lang.) epenthesis.
epentético, ca, *a.* (gram.) epenthetic.
eperlano, *m.* (ichth.) smelt.
epiblasto, *m.* (biol.) epiblast.
épica, *f.* epic poetry.
epicáliz, *m.* (bot.) epicalyx.
epicanto, *m.* (anat.) epicanthus.
epicardio, *m.* (anat.) epicardium.
epicarpio, *m.* (bot.) epicarp.
epicedio, *m.* epicedium, elegy.
epiceno, na, *a.* (gram.) epicene.
epicéntrico, ca, *a.* epicentral.
epicentro, *m.* (geol.) epicenter, portion of the earth over the center of an earthquake.
epicíclico, ca, *a.* epicyclic.
epiciclo, *m.* epicycle.
epicicloide, *f.* epicycloid.
épico, ca, *a.* (poet.) epic, heroic.
epicóndilo, *m.* (anat.) epicondyle.
epicráneo, *m.* (anat.) epicranium, the scalp.
epicureísmo, *m.* epicurism; Epicureanism.
epicúreo, rea, *n.* & *a.* epicurean.
epidemia, *f.* (med.) epidemic.
epidemial; epidémico, ca, *a.* epidemic.
epidemiología, *f.* epidemiology.
epidemiólogo, ga, *n.* epidemiologist.
epidérmico, ca, *a.* epidermic.
epidermis, *f.* epidermis, outer skin.
epidermoide, *a.* epidermoid.
epidídimo, *m.* (anat.) epididymis.
epidota, epidoto, *m.* (min.) epidote.
epifanía, *f.* Epiphany; twelfth night.
epifenómeno, *m.* (med.) epiphenomenon, secondary symptom.
epífisis, *f.* (anat.) epiphysis.
epífito, ta. I. *a.* (bot.) epiphytic. **II.** *f.* (bot.) epiphyte, aerophyte.
epifonema, *f.* (rhet.) epiphonema.
epigástrico, ca, *a.* epigastric, pert. to abdomen.
epigastrio, *m.* epigastrium.
epigénesis, *f.* (biol.) epigenesis.
epiglotis, *f.* (anat.) epiglottis.
epígrafe, *m.* epigraph.—**epigrafía,** *f.* epigraphy.
epigráfico, ca, *a.* epigraphic.
epigrafista, *n.* epigrapher.
epigrama, *m.* epigram; witticism; inscription.
epigramatario, ria. I. *a.* = EPIGRAMÁTICO. **II.** *m.* epigrammatist; collection of epigrams.
epigramático, ca, *a.* epigrammatic.
epigramatista, epigramista, *n.* epigrammatist.
epilaje, *m.* epilation, depilation.
epilepsia, *f.* (med.) epilepsy.
epiléptico, ca, *n.* & *a.* epileptic.
epilogación, *f.* = EPÍLOGO.
epilogal, *a.* epilogistic, compendious.
epilogar, *va.* (*pret.* EPILOGUÉ; *subj.* EPILOGUE) to epilogize, recapitulate, sum up.
epilogismo, *m.* (astr.) epilogism, computation.
epílogo, *m.* epilogue; summing up.
epilogué, epilogue, *v. V.* EPILOGAR.
epinefrina, *f.* (chem.) epinephrine, adrenalin.
epineuro, *m.* (anat.) epineurium.
epinicio, *m.* epinicion, triumphal ode.
epiplon, epíploon, *m.* (anat.) omentum.
epiquerema, *m.* (logic) epicheirema.
epiqueya, *f.* mild interpretation of the law, taking circumstances into consideration.
episcopado, *m.* episcopacy; episcopate; bishopric, see.
episcopal. I. *a.* episcopal; Episcopal; Episcopalian. **II.** *n.* Episcopalian.
episcopalismo, *m.* episcopalism; Episcopalism.
episcopologio, *m.* chronological list of bishops.
episódico, ca, *a.* episodic, episodical.
episodio, *m.* episode; digression.
epispástico, ca, *a.* epispastic, blistering.
epistaxis, *f.* (med.) epistaxis, nosebleed.
epistemología, *f.* epistemology.
epistemológico, ca, *a.* epistemological.
epistilo, *m.* (arch.) epistyle, architrave.

epístola, *f.* epistle, letter; (eccl.) epistle.
epistolar, *a.* epistolary.
epistolario, *m.* epistolary; volume of letters.
epistolero, *m.* (eccl.) epistler.
epístrofe, *f.* (rhet.) epistrophe.
epitafio, *m.* epitaph.
epitalamio, *m.* epithalamium, nuptial song.
epítasis, *f.* (anc. drama) epitasis.
epitelial, *a.* epithelial.
epitelio, *m.* (zool.) epithelium.
epitelioma, *m.* (med.) epithelioma, a cancer.
epítema, *f.* (med.) epithem, a moist external application.
epíteto, *m.* (gram.) epithet.
epítima, *f.* = EPITEMA.
epitimar, *va.* to apply an epithem to.
epítimo, *m.* (bot.) lesser dodder.
epitomadamente, *adv.* concisely.
epitomador, ra. I. *a.* epitomizing. II. *n.* epitomist, epitomizer.
epitomar, *va.* to epitomize, abstract, summarize.
epítome, *m.* epitome, abstract, summary.
epizoario, a, *a.* (zool.) epizoic, epizoan.
epizootia, *f.* (vet.) epizoöty, epidemic influenza.
epizoótico, ca, *a.* epizoötic.
época, *f.* epoch, age, era; time.—**é. cenozoica**, (geol.) cenozoic age.—**é. mesozoica**, (geol.) mesozoic age.—**é. paleozoica**, (geol.) paleozoic age.—**é. victoriana**, Victorian age.—**hacer é.**, (coll.) to open a new era, to be a turning point.
epoda, *f.*, **epodo**, *m.* (poet.) epode.
epónimo, ma. I. *m.* eponym. II. *a.* eponymous, eponymic.
epopeya, *f.* epopee, epic poem.
épsilon, *f.* epsilon (Greek letter).
epsomita, *f.* Epsom salts.
epulón, *m.* gourmand, heavy eater.
equiángulo, la, *a.* (geom.) equiangular.
equidad, *f.* equity, equitableness; impartiality, justice.
equidiferencia, *f.* (math.) equidifference, arithmetical progression.
equidistancia, *f.* equidistance.
equidistante, *a.* equidistant.
equidistar, *vn.* to be equidistant.
equidna, *m.* (zool.) echidna, porcupine anteater.
equilátero, ra, *a.* (geom.) equilateral.
equilibración, *f.* equilibration, balance.
equilibrado, da, *a.* balanced.
equilibrador, *m.* equilibrator.
equilibrar, *va.* to equilibrate, balance; to counterpoise, counterbalance.
equilibre, *a.* balanced, equilibrious.
equilibrio, *m.* equilibrium, balance, equipoise.—**e. europeo**, European balance of power.
equilibrista, *n.* aerialist, equilibrist, balancer.
equimolecular, *a.* equimolecular.
equimosis, *m.* (med.) a bruise, black-and-blue.
[1]**equino, na**, *a.* equine.
[2]**equino**, *m.* (zool.) echinus; (arch.) echinus.
equinoccial, *a.* equinoctial.
equinoccio, *m.* equinox.
equinococo, *m.* (med.) echinococcus.
equinodermo, ma, *a.* & *m.* (zool.) echinoderm.
equinoideo, dea, *a.* & *m.* (zool.) echinoid.
equipado, da, *a.* equipped, furnished, provided.
equipaje, *m.* baggage or luggage; equipment; (naut.) crew; (mil.) baggage train.
equipar, *va.* to fit out, equip, furnish.
equiparación, *f.* comparison, collation.
equiparar, *va.* to compare, to match.
equipo, *m.* equipment; (mil.) fitting out; accoutrement, trappings; (sports) team.
equiponderancia, *f.* equiponderance, equiponderancy.
equiponderante, *a.* equiponderant.
equiponderar, *vn.* to counterbalance.
equipotencial, *a.* (phys.) equipotencial.
equis, *f.* name of the letter *x*.
equisetáceo, a, *a.* (bot.) equisetaceous.
equiseto, *m.* (bot.) equisetum.
equitación, *f.* horsemanship, riding.
equitativamente, *adv.* equitably.
equitativo, va, *a.* equitable, fair, just.
equivalencia, *f.* equivalence; equivalent.
equivalente, *a.* equivalent, tantamount; compensatory, compensative.
equivaler, *vn.* (*ind. pres.* EQUIVALGO, *fut.* EQUIVALDRÉ; *subj.* EQUIVALGA) to be equivalent.
equivocación, *f.* mistake, error; equivocation.
equivocadamente, *adv.* mistakenly, by mistake.
equivocado, da. I. *pp.* of EQUIVOCAR. II. *a.* mistaken.
equivocar. I. *va.* (*pret.* EQUIVOQUÉ; *subj.* EQUIVOQUE) to mistake; to confuse, mix up (things). II. *vr.* to be mistaken; to make a mistake.—**e. de**, to (verb) the wrong (noun) (as *me equivoqué de autobús*, I took the wrong bus; *me equivoqué de puerta*, I went to the wrong door.
equívoco, ca. I. *a.* equivocal, ambiguous. II. *m.* equivocation, quibble, pun.
equivoqué, equivoque, *v. V.* EQUIVOCAR.
equivoquista, *n. dim.* quibbler; punster.
[1]**era**, *f.* era, age.—**e. común, cristiana, or vulgar**, Christian era.
[2]**era**, *f.* thrashing floor; vegetable patch; garden bed.
[3]**era**, *imp.* of SER.
eradicativo, va, *a.* eradicative.
eral, *m.* two-year-old ox.
erar, *va.* to lay out (a garden).
erario, *m.* exchequer, public treasury.
erasmiano, na, *a.* & *n.* Erasmian.
erbio, *m.* (chem.) erbium.
ere, *f.* name of the letter *r*.
erección, *f.* erection, raising; erectness, elevation; foundation, establishment.
eréctil, *a.* erectile.—**erectilidad**, *f.* erectility.
erector, ra, *n.* erector, founder.
eremita, *m.* hermit, recluse, eremite.
eremítico, ca, *a.* eremitic, solitary.
eremitorio, *m.* place with hermitage(s).
eretismo, *m.* (med.) erethism.
erg, *m.* (phys.) = ERGIO.
ergástula, *f.*, **ergástulo**, *m.* slave prison.
ergio, *m.* (phys.) erg (a unit of energy).
ergosterina, *f.* (pharm.) ergosterin, ergosterol.
ergoterapeuta, *n.* occupational therapist.
ergoterapia, *f.* occupational therapy.
ergotina, *f.* (med.) ergotine.
ergotinina, *f.* (chem.) ergotinine.
[1]**ergotismo**, *m.* (med.) ergotism.
[2]**ergotismo**, *m.* sophistry.
ergotista, *m.* debater, sophist.
ergotizar, *vn.* to argue fallaciously.
erguido, da, *a.* erect.
erguimiento, *m.* straightening up.
erguir. I. *va.* (*ind. pres.* IRGO or YERGO, *pret.* él IRGUIÓ; *subj.* IRGA or YERGA; *ger.* IRGUIENDO) to erect, to set up straight. II. *vr.* to straighten up; to stand or sit erect; to swell with pride.
erial, eriazo, za. I. *a.* unplowed, untilled, uncultivated. II. *m.* unimproved land.
erica, *f.* (bot.) heath, heather.
ericáceo, cea, *a.* (bot.) ericaceous.
ericé, erice, *v. V.* ERIZAR.
Erídano, *m.* (astr.) Eridanus.
erigir, *va.* (*ind.* ERIJO; *subj.* ERIJA) to erect, raise, build; to found, establish.
eringe, *f.* (bot.) field eringo.
erío, ría, *a.* untilled, uncultivated.
erisipela, *f.* (med.) erysipelas.—**erisipelar**, *va.* to cause erysipelas to.—**erisipelatoso, sa**, *a.* (med.) erysipelatous.
erístico, ca, *a.* eristic, disputatious.
eritema, *f.* (med.) erythema, redness of skin.
eritrina, *f.* (chem.) erythrin.
eritroblasto, *m.* (physiol.) erythroblast.
eritrocito, *m.* (physiol.) erythrocyte.
eritromicina, *f.* (pharm.) erythromycin.
erizado, da. I. *pp.* of ERIZAR. II. *a.* covered with bristles.—**e. de.**, beset with (difficulties, etc.); covered with, abounding in; bristling with.

erizamiento, *m.* setting on end, as the hair; bristling up.
erizar. I. *va.* (*pret.* ERICÉ; *subj.* ERICE) to set on end, to bristle. **II.** *vr.* to bristle; (of the hair) to stand on end.
erizo, *m.* (zool.) hedgehog; prickly husk, as a chestnut bur; (mech.) urchin, carding roller; sprocket wheel, rag wheel, spar-toothed wheel. —**e. de mar,** or, **marino,** (zool.) sea urchin.
ermita, *f.* hermitage.—**ermitaño, ña,** *n.* hermit.
ermitorio, *m.* = EREMITORIO.
ermunio, *a.* exempt from tribute and service.
erogación, *f.* expense.
erogar, *va.* (*pret.* EROGUÉ; *subj.* EROGUE) to distribute property; (Mex.) to lay out, spend.
erogatorio, *m.* pipe through which liquor is drawn.
erogué, erogue, *v. V.* EROGAR.
erosión, *f.* erosion, wearing away.
erotema, *f.* (rhet.) interrogation.
eróticamente, *adv.* erotically.
erótico, ca, *a.* erotical, erotic.
erotismo, *m.* erotism, eroticism.
erotomanía, *f.* (med.) erotomania, love madness.
errabundo, da, *a.* wandering.
erradicación, *f.* eradication.
erradicar, *va.* to eradicate.
erradizo, za, *a.* wandering to and fro.
errado, da. I. *pp.* of ERRAR. **II.** *a.* mistaken, in error; erroneous.
erraj, *m.* fine coal made from the stones of olives.
errante, *a.* errant; roving, wandering, nomadic.
errar. I. *va.* (*ind.* YERRO; *subj.* YERRE) to miss (the target, blow, etc.); to fail in one's duty to; to offend. **II.** *vn.* to wander, roam, to err. **III.** *vn.* & *vr.* to be mistaken; to commit an error.
errata, *f.* erratum, typographical error.—**erratas,** or **fe de erratas,** errata, list of errata.
errático, ca, *a.* wandering, vagabond; erratic.
errátil, *a.* (coll.) wavering, not firm or steady.
erre, *f.* name of the double letter *rr*, and of *r* when it has the same sound.—**e. que e.,** pertinaciously, obstinately.
erróneo, nea, *a.* erroneous, mistaken.
erronía, *f.* opposition, dislike, grudge.
error, *m.* error, mistake; (coll.) bobble.—**e. craso,** crass error.—**e. de imprenta,** misprint.
erubescencia, *f.* erubescence, blush.
erubescente, *a.* blushing, erubescent, bashful.
eructación, *f.* eructation, belching.
eructar, *vn.* to belch, eructate.
eructo, *m.* belching, eructation.
erudición, *f.* erudition, learning.
erudito, ta, *a.* & *n.* erudite, learned (person).
eruginoso, sa, *a.* rusty, musty.
erupción, *f.* eruption, bursting forth; (med.) eruption, rash.
eruptivo, va, *a.* eruptive.
erutación, *f.*, **erutar,** *vn.*, **eruto,** *m.* = ERUCTACIÓN, etc., eructation, etc.
ervato, *m.* (bot.) sea sulphurwort.
ervilla, *f.* (bot.) bitter vetch seed.
es, *irreg. form of* SER.
esa, ésa, *a.* & *pron.*, *f. form of* ESE, ÉSE. Sometimes used colloquially in the sense of "one," "that," "that thing," "that story," "that situation," etc.: *ésa es buena*, that is a good one, that is a strange thing; *ésa no la creo*, I don't believe that, I can't go that one; *no venga con ésa*, don't come with that stuff; you don't say! don't tell me that.
esbatimentar. I. *va.* (art) to delineate (a shadow). **II.** *vn.* to cast a shadow.
esbatimento, *m.* shade (in a picture).
esbeltez, esbelteza, *f.* tall and elegant stature.
esbelto, ta, *a.* tall, slender and well built, svelte.
esbirro, *m.* bailiff, apparitor; myrmidon.
esbozar, *va.* to sketch.
esbozo, *m.* sketch, outline; rough draught.
escabechar, *va.* to souse, pickle; (coll.) to stab and kill.
escabeche, *m.* souse, pickle; pickled fish.
escabel, *m.* footstool; small seat; bench.
escabiosa, *f.* (bot.) field scabious.
escabioso, sa, *a.* (med.) scabious.
escabro, *m.* scab, itch, or mange in sheep; roughness on the bark of trees.
escabrosidad, *f.* inequality, unevenness, roughness; cragginess; hardness, asperity.
escabroso, sa, *a.* rough, uneven; craggy, rugged; rude, unpolished.
escabullimiento, *m.* evasion, slipping away.
escabullirse, *vr.* to escape, to evade; to slip or sneak away.
escacado, da, *a.* (her.) checkered.
escafandro, *m.* diving suit.
escafilar, *va.* to trim (a brick or tile).
escafoideo, dea, *a.* scaphoid.
escafoides, *m.* (anat.) scaphoid (bone).
escala, *f.* ladder, stepladder; scale; graduated rule or instrument; seaport stopping place; (mus.) scale; (mil.) military register.—**e. cromática,** (mus.) chromatic scale.—**e. franca,** free port.—**a e. vista,** openly.—**hacer e. en,** to touch or stop at (a port).
escalada, *f.* (mil.) escalade, scalado.
escalado, da. I. *pp.* of ESCALAR. **II.** *a.* (of fish or meat) cut open to be salted or cured.
escalador, ra, *n.* & *a.* climber(-ing), scaler(-ing).
escalafón, *m.* roster, roll, list; army register.
escalamera, *f.* (naut.) rowlock.
escalamiento, *m.* (mil.) scaling.
escálamo, *m.* (naut.) thole, tholepin; rowlock.
escalar. I. *a.* & *m.* (math.) scalar. **II.** *va.* to scale; to enter surreptitiously.
escaldado, da. I. *pp.* of ESCALDAR. **II.** *a.* cautious, suspicious, wary. **III.** *f.* loose and lewd woman.
escaldar, *va.* to burn, scald; to make red-hot.
escaleno, na, *a.* (anat., geom.) scalene.
escalentamiento, *m.* (vet.) foot inflammation.
escalera, *f.* staircase; stair; ladder; sloats of a cart.—**e. de caracol,** winding stair.—**e. de costado,** (naut.) quarter-deck ladder.—**e. de desahogo** = E. EXCUSADA.—**e. de mano,** ladder.—**e. de servicio,** service stairs.—**e. excusada,** or **falsa,** stairs leading to bedrooms or family apartments.—**e. real** = E. DE COSTADO.—**escalereja,** *f. dim.* small ladder; stepladder; (mech.) rack; drenching instrument.—**en escalereja,** in degrees; stepped.—**escalerilla,** *f.* = ESCALEREJA.—**escalerón,** *m. aug.* large staircase.
escaleta, *f.* frame for raising carriages.
escalfado, da. I. *pp.* of ESCALFAR. **II.** *a.* poached (eggs).
escalfador, *m.* barber's pan; water heater; chafing dish.
escalfar, *va.* to poach (eggs).
escalfarote, *m.* wide boot lined with hay.
escalfeta, *f.* small pan for live coals; chafing dish; dish warmer.
escalímetro, *m.* (nuclear phys.) scaler.
escalinata, *f.* (arch.) perron, high stoop.
escalio, *m.* land abandoned for tillage.
escalmo, *m.* barlock, rowlock.
escalofriado, da, *a.* shivering, chilled.
escalofrío, *m.* chill.
escalón, *m.* stair; step of a stairway; stepping stone; rank, degree of dignity; (mil.) echelon.
escalonado, da, *a.* stepped.
escalonar, *va.* (mil.) to form in echelon; to step.
escaloña, *f.* (bot.) eschalot, shalot, scallion.
escalpar, *va.* to scalp.
escalpelo, *m.* (surg.) scalpel, dissecting knife.
escalplo, *m.* currier's or tanner's knife.
escama, *f.* fish scale; small scaly piece in ancient armors; any scaly formation; resentment, grudge.
escamada, *f.* embroidery in the shape of scales.
escamado, *m.* work in the shape of scales.
escamadura, *f.* scaling (a fish); arousing suspicion.
escamar. I. *va.* to scale (fish); (coll.) to cause suspicion. **II.** *vn.* to embroider scale or shell

fashion. **III.** *vr.* to have learned by painful experience.
escamel, *m.* sword-maker's anvil.
escamocho, *m.* remnants of a meal; (of bees) after-swarm.
escamonda, *f.* (agr.) pruning.
escamondadura, *f.* pruned branches.
escamondar, *va.* to prune, lop; to trim.
escamondo, *m.* pruning or clearing of trees.
escamonea, *f.* (bot.) scammony.
escamoneado, da, *a.* pertaining to scammony.
escamonearse, *vr.* (coll.) to be suspicious.
escamosidad, *f.* scaliness.
escamoso, sa, *a.* scaly, squamous.
escamotar, *va.* in juggling, to palm; to rob by artful means, to "play for a sucker."
escamoteador, ra, *n.* juggler, prestidigitator, conjurer; sharp, swindler.
escamotear, *va.* = ESCAMOTAR.—**escamoteo,** *m.* juggling, sleight of hand; exploitation, getting money from others by artful means, swindling.
escampada, *f.* stampede.
escampado, da. I. *pp.* of ESCAMPAR. **II.** *a.* open, clear.
escampar. I. *vn.* to stop raining; (of the sky) to clear up; to leave off working. **II.** *va.* to clear out.
escampavía, *f.* (naut.) tender; revenue cutter.
escampo, *m.* clearing out; clearing up (of rain).
escamudo, da, *a.* full of scales.
escamujar, *va.* to prune.—**escamujo,** *m.* lopped-off olive branch; time of pruning olive trees.
escancia, *f.* pouring or serving wine.
escanciador, ra, *n.* cupbearer.
escanciar, *va.* to pour, serve, or drink (wine).
escanda, *f.* (bot.) spelt-wheat.
escandalar, *m.* (naut.) room for the compass.
escandalicé, escandalice, *v. V.* ESCANDALIZAR.
escandalizador, ra, *n.* & *a.* scandalizer(-ing).
escandalizar. I. *va.* (*pret.* ESCANDALICÉ; *subj.* ESCANDALICE) to scandalize, shock. **II.** *vr.* to be shocked, scandalized; to be irritated.
escandalizativo, va, *a.* scandalous.
escándalo, *m.* scandal; licentiousness; tumult, commotion; astonishment.
escandalosa. *f.* (naut.) gaff sail.
escandaloso, sa, *a.* scandalous; turbulent.
escandallar, *va.* (naut.) to sound.
escandallo, *m.* (naut.) deep-sea lead; proof, trial, experiment.
escandia, *f.* (bot.) Cienfuegos wheat.
escándico, ca, *a.* (chem.) scandic.
escandina, *f.* (min.) scandia, scandium oxide.
escandinavo, va, *n.* & *a.* Scandinavian.
escandio, *m.* (chem.) scandium, a rare metal.
escandir, *va.* (poet.) to scan.
escanilla, *f.* cradle.
escansión, *f.* (poet.) scansion.
escantillar, *va.* to gauge; to measure from a point or line; to measure off; to hew by patterns.—**escantillón,** *m.* pattern, templet; rule.
escaña, *f.* (bot.) St. Peter's corn.
escaño, *m.* bench with a back; (naut.) sheer-rail.
escañuelo, *m.* footstool.
escapado, da. I. *a.* escaped, loose. **II.** *n.* escapee; *f.* escapade, escape, flight.—**en una e.,** in a minute, in a jiffy.
escapamiento, *m.* = ESCAPADA.
escapar. I. *va.* to drive (a horse) at great speed. **II.** *vn.* & *vr.* to escape, to flee; to run away; to make one's escape; (of a regrettable remark, etc.) to slip out.—**e. en una tabla,** to have a narrow escape.
escaparate, *m.* press, glass case, cupboard, cabinet, wardrobe; show window.—**escaparatico,** *m. dim.* little cupboard, cabinet or wardrobe.
escaparatista, *n.* window dresser.
escapatoria, *f.* escape, fleeing, flight; excuse, evasion, subterfuge; loophole, way out (of difficulty, etc.).
escape, *m.* escape, flight; subterfuge, evasion; escapement (of a watch); exhaust (of steam eng., etc.).—**a e.,** or **a todo e.,** at full speed, in great haste.—**de e.,** (of steam eng.) exhaust (as *a.*).
escapismo, *m.* escapism.
escapista, *n.* escapist.
escapo, *m.* (arch.) shaft of a column.
escápula, *f.* (anat.) scapula, shoulder blade.
[1]**escapular,** *a.* scapular.
[2]**escapular,** *va.* (naut.) to clear (a cape).
escapulario, *m.* (eccl.) scapulary, a sort of cape.
escaque, *m.* any of the squares of a chessboard; (her.) any of the squares of a coat of arms.—*pl.* chess.—**escaqueado, da,** *a.* checkered.
escara, *f.* (surg.) eschar, scab, slough.
escarabajear. I. *vn.* to crawl to and fro like insects; to scrawl, scribble. **II.** *va.* (coll.) to worry, harass.
escarabajo, *m.* (entom.) beetle, dorbug; scarab, (anc. Egypt) scarabæus; (metal.) flaw.—*pl.* scrawl.—**e. bupréstido,** (entom.) buprestid beetle.—**e. pelotero,** (entom.) tumblebug.
escarabajuelo, *m. dim.* (entom.) small beetle; (entom.) vine beetle.
escarabídeo, dea, *a.* & *m.* scarabæid.
escaramucear, *vn.* to skirmish.
escaramujo, *m.* (bot.) dog-rose, hep tree; hep; (zool.) goose barnacle.
escaramuza, *f.* (mil.) skirmish; dispute, quarrel.
escaramuzador, ra, *n.* skirmisher; disputer.
escaramuzar, *vn.* to skirmish.
escarapela, *f.* cockade, badge; quarrel ending in blows.
escarapelar. I. *vn.* & *vr.* (esp. of women) to dispute, wrangle, quarrel. **II.** *vr.* (Am.) to have the hair stand on end, get goose flesh.
escarbadero, *m.* scratching place (for animals).
escarbadientes, *m.* toothpick.
escarbador, ra, *n.* scratcher, scraper.
escarbadura, *f.* scratching.
escarbaorejas, *m.* earpick.
escarbar, *va.* to scrape or scratch (as fowls); to dig, dibble; to poke (the fire); to dig into, to investigate.—**escarbo,** *m.* scraping, scratching.
escarcela, *f.* large pouch; game bag; cuish; kind of headdress for women.
escarceo, *m.* small broken waves occasioned by currents.—*pl.* bounds and windings of spirited horses.
escarcina, *f.* a kind of cutlass.
escarcuñar, *va.* = ESCUDRIÑAR, to scrutinize.
escarcha, *f.* white frost, rime; frostwork.
escarchada, *f.* (bot.) ice plant, fig marigold.
escarchado, *m.* gold or silver embroidery; frosting on cakes.
escarchador, *m.* freezing tool.
escarchar. I. *vn.* to freeze, frost. **II.** *va.* to put frosting on; to dilute (potter's clay) with water.
escarcho, *m.* (ichth.) red surmullet.
escarda, *f.* weedhook, rubbing hoe; weeding.
escardadera, *f.* woman weeder; gardener's hoe.
escardador, ra, *n.* & *a.* weeder(-ing).
escardadura, *f.,* **escardamiento,** *m.* weeding.
escardar, escardillar, *va.* to weed; to weed out, root out.
escardillo, lla, *n.* small weedhook; gardener's hoe; thistledown.
escariador, *m.* reamer.
escariar, *va.* to ream.
escarificación, *f.* (surg.) scarification.
escarificador, *m.* (agr.) scarifier, harrow, cultivator; (surg.) scarificator.—**e. de discos,** (agr.) disk harrow.
escarificar, *va.* (surg. and agr.) to scarify.
escarioso, sa, *a.* (bot.) scarious.
escarizar, *va.* (surg.) to clean by taking away the scurf or scab.
escarlador, *m.* comb polisher.
escarlata, *f.* scarlet, red; cloth of a scarlet color; (med.) scarlet fever.
escarlatina, *f.* (com.) red or crimson woollen fabric; (med.) scarlatina.
escarmenador, *m.* comb for wool, etc.

escarmenar, *va.* to comb (wool, silk, etc.); to disentangle; to cheat.
escarmentado, da, *a.* taught by punishment or painful experience.
escarmentar. I. *vn.* (*ind.* ESCARMIENTO; *subj.* ESCARMIENTE) to be taught by experience, to take warning. **II.** *va.* to correct severely, to inflict an exemplary punishment on.
[1]**escarmiento,** *m.* warning, lesson, punishment.
[2]**escarmiento, escarmiente,** *v. V.* ESCARMENTAR.
escarnecedor, ra, *n.* & *a.* scoffer(-ing), scorner (-ing).
escarnecer, *va.* (*ind.* ESCARNEZCO; *subj.* ESCARNEZCA) to scoff, mock, ridicule, jeer, gibe.
escarnecidamente, *adv.* scornfully.
escarnecimiento, *m.* scoffing, derision.
escarnezco, escarnezca, *v. V.* ESCARNECER.
escarnio, *m.* scoff, gibe, jeer, mock.
[1]**escaro,** *m.* (ichth.) a kind of mutton fish.
[2]**escaro, ra,** *a.* having crooked feet.
escarola, *f.* (bot.) endive; ruff, frill.
escarolado, da, *a.* curled, frilled.
escarolar, *va.* to frill, ruffle.
escarótico, ca, *a.* (surg.) escharotic, caustic.
escarpa, *f.* declivity, slope, bluff, cliff; (mil.) scarp.
escarpado, da. I. *pp.* of ESCARPAR. **II.** *a.* steep, craggy, rugged.
escarpadura, *f.* escarpment; bluff, cliff.
[1]**escarpar,** *va.* to rasp (works of sculpture).
[2]**escarpar,** *va.* (mil.) to escarp.—**escarpe,** *m.* escarpment; (arch.) scarf of a wall; scarf joint.
escarpelo, *m.* rasp; (surg.) scalpel.
escarpia, *f.* tenterhook, meat hook; spike.
escarpiador, *m.* clamp, fastener; ESCARPIDOR.
escarpidor, *m.* large-toothed comb.
escarpín, *m.* thin-soled shoe; dancing pumps; woollen slippers.
escarpión.—en e., in the form of a tenterhook.
escarza, *f.* (vet.) sore in the hoofs.
escarzano, *a.*—**arco e.,** (arch.) segment arch.
escarzar, *va.* (bee culture) to remove honeycombs from (a hive).
[1]**escarzo,** *n.* (bee culture) black comb without honey; operation and time of removing honey from a hive; floss silk.
[2]**escarzo, za,** *a.* (vet.) lame from hoof sores.
escasear. I. *va.* to give sparingly; to spare, to husband. **II.** *vn.* to be scarce; to diminish.
escasez, *f.* scarcity, shortage; poverty, want.
escaso, sa, *a.* small, limited; little; sparing, parsimonious, niggardly; scarce, scanty, short.
escatimado, da. I. *pp.* of ESCATIMAR. **II.** *a.* little, scanty.
escatimar, *va.* to curtail, lessen; to misinterpret.
escatimoso, sa, *a.* cunning, malicious.
escatófago, ga, *a.* (nat. hist.) scatophagous.
[1]**escatología,** *f.* scatology.
[2]**escatología,** *f.* eschatology, doctrine of ultimates.
[1]**escatológico, ca,** *a.* scatologic.
[2]**escatológico, ca,** *a.* eschatologic.
escaupil, *m.* (Mex.) ancient padded armor.
escavanar, *va.* (agr.) to loosen and weed (the ground) with a grub hoe.
escayola, *f.* stucco, plasterwork.
escena, *f.* stage; scenery; scene; sight, view; incident, episode.
escenario, *m.* (theat.) stage, "boards."
escénico, ca, *a.* scenic, pertaining to the stage.
escenificación, *f.* (theat., fig.) staging.
escenificar, *va.* (theat., fig.) to stage.
escenografía, *f.* scenography.
escenográficamente, *adv.* scenographically.
escenográfico, ca, *a.* scenographic.
escenógrafo, *m.* scenographer.
escepticismo, *m.* skepticism.
escéptico, ca, *n.* & *a.* skeptic.
esciagrafía, *f.* skiagraphy.
esciágrafo, *m.* skiagraph.
escila, *f.* (bot.) squill.
escinco, *m.* (zool.) skink, a lizard.
escintilación, *f.* (chem.) scintillation.
escirro, *m.* (med.) scirrhus, a tumor.
escirroso, sa, *a.* (med.) scirrhous.
escisión, *f.* division; schism; (surg.) excision; (chem., phys.) fission.
escita, *n.* & *a.*; **escítico, ca,** *a.* Scythian.
esclarecedor, ra, *n.* & *a.* enlightener(-ing).
esclarecer. I. *va.* (*ind.* ESCLAREZCO; *subj.* ESCLAREZCA) to lighten, illuminate; to enlighten; elucidate; to ennoble. **II.** *vn.* to dawn.
esclarecidamente, *adv.* illustriously.
esclarecido, da, *a.* illustrious, prominent.
esclarecimiento, *m.* enlightening; elucidation; dawn; ennoblement; merit, worth.
esclarezco, esclarezca, *v. V.* ESCLARECER.
esclavicé, esclavice, *v. V.* ESCLAVIZAR.
esclavina, *f.* pilgrim's cloak; collar worn by priests; tippet; cape.
esclavista, *a.* pro-slavery.
esclavitud, *f.* slavery.
esclavizar, *va.* (*pret.* ESCLAVICÉ; *subj.* ESCLAVICE) to enslave.
esclavo, va, *n.* slave.—**e. ladino,** formerly, one who had been a slave for more than a year.
escleroftalmia, *f.* (med.) sclerophthalmia.
escleroma, *m.* (med.) scleroma.
esclerosis, *f.* (med.) sclerosis.—**e. cerebroespinal,** (med.) insular sclerosis.—**e. múltiple,** (med.) multiple sclerosis.
escleroso, sa, *a.* sclerotic.
esclerótica, *f.* (anat.) sclera.
esclerotitis, *f.* (med.) sclerotitis.
esclerotomía, *f.* (surg.) sclerotomy.
esclusa, *f.* lock; sluice; floodgate; milldam.
escoa, *f.* (naut.) bend of a ship's rib.
escoba, *f.* broom; (bot.) Spanish broom.
escobada, *f.* sweep, sweeping.
escobadera, *f.* woman sweeper.
[1]**escobajo,** *m.* old broom.
[2]**escobajo,** *m.* stalk of a bunch of grapes.
[1]**escobar,** *va.* to sweep with a broom.
[2]**escobar,** *m.* (bot.) broom field.
escobazar, *va.* to sprinkle with a broom.
escobazo, *m.* blow with a broom.—**echar a escobazos,** to dismiss harshly or roughly, (fig.) to kick out.
escobén, *m.* (naut.) hawse hole.
escobera, *f.* (bot.) Spanish broom.
escobero, ra, *n.* broom maker or seller.
escobeta, *f.* small brush.
escobilla, *f.* brush; whisk, small broom; (bot.) bur of the teasel; gold or silver sweepings; (elec.) brush (of a dynamo).
escobillón, *m.* (mil.) merkin; swab.
escobina, *f.* chips cut in boring; filings.
escobo, *m.* brushwood, briers, brambles.
escobón, *m. aug.* large broom; (naut.) Turk's-head, a kind of knot; scrubbing brush; swab.
escocedura, *f.* burning pain.
escocer. I. *vn.* (*ind.* ESCUECE; *subj.* ESCUEZA) to feel a sharp, burning pain; to smart. **II.** *vr.* to smart; to chafe.
escocés, sa, *n.* & *a.* Scotch.
escocia, *f.* (arch.) scotia; (com.) codfish; (E.) Scotland.
escociante, *a.* tingling; atingle; itching.
escocimiento, *m.* smart, sharp pain.
escoda, *f.* stonecutter's hammer.
escodar, *va.* to hew or cut (stones).
escofieta, *f.* = ESCOFIA.
escofina, *f.* rasp, file; wood rasp.
escofinar, *va.* to rasp.
escogedor, ra, *n.* & *a.* chooser(-ing).
escoger, *va.* (*ind.* ESCOJO; *subj.* ESCOJA) to choose, select, pick out, sort; elect.
escogidamente, *adv.* choicely, selectly; nicely.
escogido, da, *pp.* & *a.* chosen, choice, select.
escogimiento, *m.* selection, choice, choosing; sorting, separation.
escojo, escoja, *v. V.* ESCOGER.
escolar. I. *n.* pupil, student. **II.** *a.* scholastic. school (as *a.*).

escolasticismo, *m.* scholasticism.
escolástico, ca. I. *a.* scholastic, scholastical; school (as *a.*). **II.** *n.* Scholastic, Schoolman.
escoliador, ra, *n.* scholiast, writer of comments.
escoliar, *va.* to gloss, explain, comment.
escoliasta, *n.* = ESCOLIADOR.
escolimado, da, *a.* (coll.) weak, delicate.
escolimoso, sa, *a.* (coll.) fastidious, hard to please, fussy.
escolio, *m.* scholium; gloss, commentary.
escoliosis, *f.* (med.) scoliosis, a spinal curvature.
escolopendra, *f.* (entom.) scolopendra, centipede; a marine worm; (bot.) spleenwort.
escolta, *f.* escort, convoy, guard.
escoltar, *va.* to escort, convoy, guard.
escollera, *f.* breakwater, jetty; cliff.
escollo, *m.* reef; difficulty, danger.
escombra, *f.* clearing, removal of obstacles.
escombrar, *va.* to clear of rubbish; to clean.
escombrera, *f.* (min.) refuse dump.
[1]**escombro,** *m.* rubbish, a small inferior raisin.
[2]**escombro,** *m.* (ichth.) mackerel.
escomerse, *vr.* to wear out.
esconce, *m.* corner, angle.
escondedero, *m.* hiding or lurking place.
esconder. I. *va.* to hide, conceal; to include, contain. **II.** *vr.* to hide; to skulk.
escondidamente, *adv.* secretly, hiddenly.
escondidas, escondidillas.—a e., on the sly, hiddenly.
escondimiento, *m.* concealment.
escondite, *m.*, **escondrijo,** *m.* lurking place; hiding place.—**jugar al e.,** to play hide and seek.
esconzado, da, *a.* angular, oblique.
escopeta, *f.* shotgun.—**e. de aire comprimido,** air rifle or gun.—**e. de dos cañones,** double-barrel gun.
escopetar, *va.* to dig out (gold mines).
escopetazo, *m.* gunshot; gunshot wound.
escopetear, *va.* to shoot at with a shotgun; to compliment, pay compliments to.
escopeteo, *m.* gunshot fire.
escopetería, *f.* infantry armed with guns; repeated gunshots.
escopetero, *m.* gunner, musketeer; gunsmith.
escopetilla, *f. dim.* small gun.
escopladura, escopleadura, *f.* mortise hole, chisel cut.
escoplear, *va.* to chisel, mortise, notch.
escoplillo, ito, *m. dim.* small chisel.
escoplo, *m.* chisel.
escopolamina, *f.* (pharm.) scopolamine, truth serum or drug.
escora, *f.* (naut.) stanchion, bilge head, prop, outrigger; (naut.) central line of a vessel; (naut.) tilt.—**e. lateral,** (aer.) rolling.
escorar. I. *va.* (naut.) to prop, to shore up. **II.** *vn.* (naut.) to list, to heel.
escorbútico, ca, *a.* scorbutic, scorbutical.
escorbuto, *m.* (med.) scurvy.
escorchapín, *m.* passage boat, ferry.
escorchar, *va.* to flay, to skin.
escordio, *m.* (bot.) water germander.
escoria, *f.* dross, slag, scoria; lee; mean or worthless thing.—*pl.* scoriæ, volcanic ashes.
escoriáceo, cea, *a.* scoriaceous.
escoriación, *f.* = EXCORIACIÓN, flaying.
escorial, *m.* dumping place for dross; slag heap.
escoriar, *va.* = EXCORIAR, to flay.
escorificación, *f.* (chem.) scorification.
escorificar, *va.* (chem.) to scorify, reduce to scoria or slag.
escoriforme, *a.* scoriform.
escorpena, escorpina, *f.* (ichth.) grouper.
escorpioide, *f.* (bot.) scorpion grass.
escorpión, *m.* (entom.) scorpion; (ichth.) fish resembling a grouper; ancient ballister; (E-, astr.) Scorpion; cat-o'-nine-tails with metal points.
escorpionídeo, dea, *a.* & *m.* (zool.) scorpionid.
escorrozo, *m.* (coll.) pleasure, enjoyment.
escorzado, *m.* (art) foreshortening.
escorzar, *va.* (art) to foreshorten.
escorzo, *m.* (art) foreshortening.
escorzón, *m.* toad.
escorzonera, *f.* (bot.) viper root or garden viper grass.
[1]**escota,** *f.* stonecutter's hammer.
[2]**escota,** *f.* (naut.) sheet.
escotado, *m.* = ESCOTADURA.
escotadura, *f.* low cut in the neck (of a dress); armhole in armor; large trapdoor of a stage.
[1]**escotar,** *va.* to cut (a dress) low in the neck; to draw (water) by a trench.
[2]**escotar,** *va.* to club together, contribute to a common cause.
[1]**escote,** *m.* low neck, décolleté; tucker.
[2]**escote,** *m.* share, quota.
escotera, *f.* (naut.) sheet hole.
escotero, ra, *a.* free, disengaged, unburdened.
escotilla, *f.* (naut.) hatchway.
escotillón, *m.* scuttle, trapdoor; stage trap.
escotín, *m.* (naut.) topsail sheet.
escotismo, *m.* Scotism (doctrines of Scotus).
escotista, *n.* Scotist.
escotoma, *m.* (med.) scotoma, blind or dark spot.
escotomía, *f.* (med.) scotomy.
escozor, *m.* smart, sharp pain, burning, smarting; grief, affliction.
escriba, *m.* scribe, among the Hebrews.
escribanía, *f.* office or employment of an actuary or scrivener; escritoire, scrutoire; portable writing case; ornamental inkstand.
escribano, *m.* actuary.—**e. de cámara,** clerk of a high court of justice.—**e. del agua,** (entom.) water skater.—**e. de número,** or **del número,** one of a certain number of notaries public.
escribido, *pp. reg.* of ESCRIBIR, used only in the idiom **leído y escribido,** (coll.) would-be learned, posing as learned.
escribidor, ra, *n.* would-be writer, scribbler.
escribiente, *m.* & *f.* amanuensis, clerk.
escribir. I. *va.* (*pp. irreg.* ESCRITO) to write.—**e. a máquina,** to type. **II.** *vr.* to enroll oneself; to carry on correspondence with each other.
escriño, *m.* straw hamper; jewel box, casket.
escrita, *f.* (ichth.) spotted skate fish.
escritillas, *f. pl.* lamb's fries.
escrito, ta. I. *pp. irreg.* of ESCRIBIR. **II.** *m.* writing; manuscript; literary composition; (law) writ; brief.—**por e.,** in writing.
escritor, ra, *n.* writer, author.—**escritorcillo, lla,** *n. dim.* petty writer, writer of no account.
escritorio, *m.* writing desk; countinghouse; office, study.
escritura, *f.* writing, handwriting, penmanship; deed, indenture, instrument; (E-) Scripture.—**e. de seguro,** insurance policy.
escriturar. I. *va.* (law) to bind by deed; to indenture; to engage (as an artist). **II.** *vr.* to sign articles.
escriturario, ria. I. *a.* (law) scriptory, scriptorian; scriptural. **II.** *n.* scripturist.
escrófula, *f.* (med.) scrofula.
escrofularia, *f.* (bot.) figwort.
escrofulariáceo, cea, *a.* (bot.) scrophulariaceous.
escrofulismo, *m.* (med.) scrofulism.
escrofuloso, sa, *a.* scrofulous.
escrotal, *a.* (anat.) scrotal.
escroto, *m.* scrotum.
escrupulillo, *m. dim.* slight scruple; jingle.
escrupulizar, *vn.* to scruple, doubt, hesitate.
escrúpulo, *m.* scruple, hesitation; scrupulosity, conscientiousness; (pharm.) scruple, a small weight (20 gr.).
escrupulosamente, *adv.* scrupulously; precisely, minutely, thoroughly.
escrupulosidad, *f.* scrupulosity, conscientiousness; exactness, nicety, thoroughness.
escrupuloso, sa, *a.* scrupulous, conscientious; nice, exact, thorough; hypercritical, squeamish.
escrutador, ra, *n.* examiner, inquirer, searcher; inspector of an election.
escrutar, *va.* to count (votes); to scrutinize.

escrutinio, *m.* scrutiny, investigation; election returns.
escrutiñador, *m.* scrutator, investigator.
escuadra, *f.* carpenter's square; drawing triangle; angle iron; knee, angle brace; (mil.) squad; (naut.) squadron, fleet.—**e. de agrimensor,** (surv.) cross-staff.—**e. sutil,** light coastguard fleet.—**a e.,** square, at right angles.—**falsa e.,** bevel square.—**fuera de e.,** out of square, at an oblique angle.
escuadración, *f.* squaring.
escuadrador, *m.* squaring tool; groover.
escuadrar, *va.* (carp.) to square.
escuadreo, *m.* squaring, quadrature.
escuadría, *f.* scantling of timber; square.
escuadrilla, *f.* (aer., naut.) escadrille.
escuadro, *m.* = ESCRITA, (ichth.) spotted skate.
escuadrón, *m.* (mil.) squadron, troop of horse.—**e. volante,** (mil.) flying column.
escuadronar, *va.* to form in squadrons.
escuadronista, *m.* (mil.) tactician.
escualidez, *f.* squalor, wretchedness.
escuálido, da, *a.* weak, languid; squalid, filthy.
escualo, *m.* (ichth.) spotted dogfish; shark.
escualor, *m.* squalor, filthiness.
escucha, *f.* (mil.) scout; vedette; sentinel, sentry; in convents, a chaperon; listening hole.
escuchador, ra; escuchante, *n.* listener.
escuchar. I. *va.* to listen to; to mind, heed. **II.** *vn.* to listen. **III.** *vr.* to speak with affected pauses.
escudar, *va.* to shield, protect, defend.
escuderaje, *m.* service of a page or footman.
escuderear, *va.* to serve as a page or squire to.
escudería, *f.* service of a page or squire.
escuderil, *a.* pertaining to a page or squire.
escudero, *m.* shield bearer, squire, page; gentleman of illustrious ancestry; shield maker.
escuderón, *m.* conceited squire.
escudete, *m.* escutcheon; gusset; rain stain on olives; (bot.) white water lily.
escudilla, *f.* bowl, large cup.
escudillar, *va.* to pour into bowls; to lord it over, domineer.
escudillo, ito, *m. dim.* small shield; a gold coin.
escudo, *m.* shield, buckler, escutcheon, coat of arms; escutcheon of a lock or knocker; shield, protection; monetary unit of Portugal; bandage used in bleeding; sideplate of a gun; (naut.) backboard of a boat.—**e. de armas,** arms (on a flag, etc.).—**e. de popa,** (naut.) stern escutcheon.
escudriñador, ra, *n.* & *a.* prier(-ying); scrutinizer(-ing), searcher(-ing); investigator(-ing).
escudriñamiento, *m.* investigation, scrutiny.
escudriñar, *va.* to scrutinize, search, pry into.
escuece, *v. V.* ESCOCER.
escuela, *f.* school; schoolhouse; (art) school, style; experience, training.—**e. de artes y oficios** or **práctica,** vocational school.—**e. de baile,** dancing school.—**e. de derecho,** law school.—**e. de internos,** boarding school.—**e. de medicina,** medical school.—**e. dominical,** Sunday school.—**e. normal,** normal school.—**e. parroquial,** parochial school.—**e. particular,** private school.—**e. politécnica,** politechnic institute or school.—**e. primaria,** primary and grammar school.—**e. pública,** (U. S.) public school.—**e. secundaria,** high school.—**e. superior,** institution of higher learning or of professional studies (college, university, etc.).
escuerzo, *m.* (zool.) toad; (coll.) flabby person.
escueto, ta, *n.* disengaged, free from encumbrances; solitary, uninhabited.
esculcar, *va.* to spy, to watch; to search; (Am.) to search the pockets of.
esculpidor, ra, *n.* engraver.
esculpir, *va.* & *vn.* to sculpture; to engrave.
escultor, *m.* sculptor.—**escultora,** *f.* sculptress.
escultórico, ca, *a.* sculptural.
escultura, *f.* sculpture; carved work.
escultural, *a.* sculptural.
escullador, *m.* dipper for oil.
escupidera, *f.* spittoon, cuspidor.
escupidero, *m.* spitting place; disgraceful situation.
escupido, da. I. *pp.* of ESCUPIR. **II.** *m.* spittle.
escupidor, ra, *n.* great spitter.
escupidura, *f.* spitting, spittle; fever sore.
escupir, *va.* & *vn.* to spit; to break out on the skin; to fling, cast away; to work out, throw off.
escupitajo, *m.,* **escupitina,** *f.,* **escupitinajo,** *m.* (coll.) spit.
escurar, *va.* to scout (cloth) before milling.
escurialense, *a.* belonging to, or like, the Escorial (a famous Spanish monastery).
escurreplatos, *m.* dish-draining rack.
escurribanda, *f.* (coll.) evasion, subterfuge; diarrhœa; scuffle, bustle.
escurrida, *a.* wearing tight-fitting skirts; having narrow hips.
escurridero, *m.* drain pipe or conduit (in mines); draining or wringing place.
escurridizo, za, *a.* slippery; difficult to hold.
escurridor, *m.* colander; ESCURREPLATOS.
escurriduras, escurrimbres, *f. pl.* rinsings (as of wine); lees, dregs.
escurrimiento, *m.* dripping, running off; sneaking out; trickle.
escurrir. I. *va.* to drain off (liquid) from; to wring (as clothes).—**e. el bulto,** to sneak away. **II.** *vr.* to drop, drip, ooze, leak, trickle; to slip, slide, glide; to escape, slip out, sneak away.
escutiforme, *a.* scutiform.
esdrújulo, la, *a.* (gram.) (word) accented on the antepenultimate syllable.
[1]**ese,** *f.* name of the letter *s*; link of a chain having the shape of an *s*.—*pl.* **eses,** reeling of a drunken man (gen. in the phrase **hacer eses,** to reel).
[2]**ese,** *m.,* **esa,** *f.* (*pl.* **esos, esas**), *a.* that (*pl.* those), as *ese hombre,* that man; *esas mujeres,* those women.
ése, *m.,* **ésa,** *f.* (*pl.* **ésos, ésas**), *dem. pron.* that (one) (*pl.,* those), as *tengo ése,* I have that one; *dame ésas,* give me those. *V.* ESA.
esecilla, *f. dim.* small link of a chain.
esencia, *f.* essence, being; (chem.) essence, perfume.—**esencial,** *a.* essential.
esfacelado, da, *a.* sphacelate.
esfacelar, *va.* & *vn.* (med.) to sphacelate, mortify.
esfacelo, *m.* (med.) sphacelus.
esfagníneo, nea. I. *a.* (bot.) sphagneous. **II.** *f.* (bot.) sphagnum.
esfalerita, *f.* (min.) sphalerite, zincblende.
esfenoidal, *a.* (anat.) sphenoidal.
esfenoides, *m.* (anat.) sphenoid bone.
esfera, *f.* sphere; clock dial; quality, condition, rank; (poet.) heaven.—**e. armilar,** armillary sphere.—**e. celeste,** celestial sphere.—**e. de actividad,** sphere of action.—**e. paralela,** (astr.) parallel sphere.—**e. recta,** (astr.) right sphere.
esferal, *a.* = ESFÉRICO.
esfericidad, *f.* sphericity.
esférico, ca, *a.* spherical.
esferoidal, *a.* spheroidal.
esferoide, *f.* spheroid.
esferómetro, *m.* spherometer.
esfígmico, ca, *a.* (physiol.) sphygmic.
esfigmógrafo, *m.* sphygmograph.
esfigmomanómetro, *m.* sphygmomanometer.
esfigmómetro, *m.* sphygmometer.
esfinge, *f.* sphinx.—**esfíngido, da,** *a.* sphinxlike.
esfínter, *m.* (anat.) sphincter.
esforcé, *pret.* of ESFORZAR.
esforrocinar, *va.* to remove the ESFORROCINOS from.
esforrocino, *m.* sprig shooting from the trunk of a vine.
esforzado, da. I. *pp.* of ESFORZAR. **II.** *a.* strong, vigorous; brave; enterprising.
esforzador, ra, *n.* & *a.* encourager(-ing).
esforzar. I. *va.* (*ind. pres.* ESFUERZO, *pret.* ESFORCÉ; *subj.* ESFUERCE) to strengthen, invigorate; to encourage. **II.** *vr.* to exert oneself, make efforts, try hard.

[1]**esfuerzo,** *m.* courage, spirit, vigor; effort, strong endeavor; (eng.) stress.—**e. cortante,** (eng.) shear, shearing stress.
[2]**esfuerzo,** *v. V.* ESFORZAR.
esfumado, da. I. *pp.* of ESFUMAR. **II.** *a.* (art) sfumato.
esfumar. I. *va.* (art) to stump. **II.** *vr.* to evanesce, vanish.
esfumino, *m.* (art) stump (for shading).
esgarrar, *va.* & *vn.* to raise phlegm; to clear one's throat.
esgrafiado, *m.* (art) graffito.
esgrafiar, *va.* to decorate with graffito; to scratch on with a graffito tool or graver.
esgrima, *f.* fencing (the art).
esgrimidor, *m.* fencer or fencing master.
esgrimidura, *f.* fencing (the act).
esgrimir, *va.* to wield (a weapon).
esgrimista, *n.* (Am.) fencer; (Chile) sponger.
esguazable, *a.* fordable.
esguazar, *va.* to ford (as a river).—**esguazo,** *m.* fording.
esgucio, *m.* (arch.) quarter-round molding.
esguín, *m.* young salmon before entering sea.
esguince, *m.* dodging, dodge; frown; twist or sprain of a joint.
esguízaro, ra, *n.* & *a.* Swiss.—**pobre e.,** ragamuffin.
eslabón, *m.* link of a chain; steel for striking fire with a flint; table steel; name of a very poisonous scorpion.
eslabonado, da, *a.* concatenate; chained.
eslabonador, *m.* chain maker.
eslabonamiento, *m.* linking, uniting; connection, sequence, concatenation.
eslabonar, *va.* to link, interlink; to join, unite, to connect, concatenate.
eslavismo, *m.* Slavism.
eslavo, va, *n.* & *a.* Slav.
eslinga, *f.* (naut.) sling, span.
eslingar, *va.* (naut.) to sling up, hoist.
eslora, *f.* (naut.) length of a ship.—*pl.* binding strakes of the deck.
eslovaco, ca, *n.* & *a.* Slovakian.
esloveno, na, *n.* & *a.* Slovene.
esmaltador, ra, *n.* enameller.
esmaltadura, *f.* enamelling; enamel work.
esmaltar, *va.* to enamel; to adorn, embellish.
esmalte, *m.* enamel; enamel work; smalt.
esmaltín, *m.* smalt, a dark blue pigment.
esmaltina, *f.* (min.) smaltite.
esmerado, da. I. *pp.* of ESMERAR. **II.** *a.* careful, painstaking, carefully done.
esmeralda, *f.* emerald.
esmeraldino, na, *a.* emeraldlike (gen. in color).
esmerar. I. *va.* to polish, to brighten. **II.** *vr.* (**con** or **en**) to do one's best, to take pains (with).
esmerejón, *m.* (ornith.) merlin; small-caliber gun.
[1]**esmeril,** *m.* small-caliber gun.
[2]**esmeril,** *m.* emery.
esmerilador, ra, *n.* & *a.* grinder(-ing). *f.* grinding machine.
esmerilar, *va.* to burnish, to polish with emery, to grind.
esmero, *m.* careful attention, painstaking.
esmiláceo, cea. I. *a.* (bot.) smilacaceous. **II.** *m.* (bot.) smilax.
esmoladera, *f.* whetstone.
esmuciarse. *vr.* to slip from the hands.
esnob. I. *a.* snobbish. **II.** *n.* snob.
esnobismo, *m.* snobbery, snobbishness, snobbism.
eso, *dem. pron. neut.* that (that thing, fact, etc.). —**e. de,** that matter of; AQUELLO DE.—**e. es,** that's it; that's right.—**e. mismo,** the very thing.—**a e. de,** toward, about.—**no es e.,** it isn't that.—**por e.,** for that; for that reason, on that account.—**por e. es por lo que** (or, incorrectly but commonly, **por e. es que**), that is the reason that, that is why.
esofágico, ca, *a.* esophageal.
esófago, *m.* (anat.) esophagus, gullet.
esotérico, ca, *a.* esoteric; confidential, secret.
espabiladeras, *f. pl.* (candle) snuffers.
espabilar, *va.* to snuff (a candle).
espaciador, *m.* spacer, space bar.
espacial, *a.* spatial.
espaciar. I. *va.* to space; diffuse, expand, dilate, spread; (print.) to lead; to space. **II.** *vr.* to walk to and fro; to amuse oneself; to cheer up; to expatiate.
espacio, *m.* space; room, capacity; slowness, delay; blank, (empty) space; (mus.) interval.—**e. aéreo,** air space.—**e. interestelar,** interstellar space.—**e. sideral,** sidereal space.—**e. ultraterrestre,** outer space.
espaciosidad, *f.* spaciousness, capacity.
espacioso, sa, *a.* spacious, roomy, ample; slow, deliberate.
espada, *f.* sword; blade, rapier; swordsman; (cards) spade; (ichth.) swordfish; matador, bullfighter who kills the bull.—**entre la e. y la pared,** between the devil and the deep sea.
espadachín, *m.* dexterous swordsman; bully, hackster.
espadador, *m.* hemp beater.
espadaña, *f.* (bot.) reed mace; belfry.
espadañada, *f.* regurgitation; spewing.
espadañal, *m.* place where reed mace grows.
espadañar, *va.* to spread out (the tail feathers).
espadar, *va.* to brake, scutch, swingle.
espadarte, *m.* (ichth.) swordfish.
espadería, *f.* sword cutler's shop.
espadero, *m.* sword cutler, bladesmith.
espadíceo, cea, *a.* (bot.) spadiceous.
espádice, *m.* (bot.) spadix.
espadilla, *f.* red insignia of the order of Santiago; swingle, hemp brake; (naut.) scull, oar used as helm; (cards) ace of spades; hair bodkin; (Am.) (bot.) corn flag.
espadillar, *va.* to brake, scutch, swingle.
espadillazo, *m.* bad luck at cards.
espadín, *m.* small gala sword; rapier.
[1]**espadón,** *m. aug.* spadone, large sword, broadsword.
[2]**espadón,** *m.* eunuch.
espadrapo, *m.* = ESPARADRAPO, court-plaster.
espagírica, *f.* metallurgy.
espagírico, ca, *a.* metallurgic.
espahí, *m.* (mil.) spahi.
espalación, *f.* (phys.) spallation.
espalda, *f.* (anat.) back, shoulders; (fort.) shoulder of a bastion.—*pl.* back or back part; (mil.) rearguard.—**a. espaldas,** or **a espaldas vueltas,** treacherously.—**de espaldas,** backwards, on one's (its) back; from behind.—**hablar por las espaldas de uno,** to talk behind one's back.—**por la e.,** from behind; in the back; behind one's back.
espaldar, *m.* backplate of a cuirass; back of a seat; espalier in gardens.—*pl.* tapestry hangings against which chairs lean.
espaldarazo, *m.* accolade; light blow on the back.
espaldarcete, *m.* palette in ancient armor.
espaldarón, *m.* backplate in armor.
espaldear, *va.* (naut.) to dash against the poop of.
espalder, *m.* stern rower in a galley.
espaldera, *f.* espalier, trelliswork.
espaldilla, *f.* scapula, shoulder blade; back of a waistcoat or jacket.
espalditendido, da, *a.* (coll.) stretched on one's back.
espaldón, *m.* (carp.) tenon; (fort.) intrenchment, barrier; (naut.) a hawse piece.
espaldudo, da, *a.* broad-shouldered.
espalera, *f.* espalier, trelliswork.
espalmadura, *f.* (vet.) parings of hoofs.
espalmar, *va.* = DESPALMAR, (vet.) to pare hoofs.
espalto, *m.* dark-colored paint; spalt.
espantable, *a.* frightful, horrid, terrible.
espantada, *f.* stampede, running away; giving up from fear, (coll.) cold feet.
espantadizo, za, *a.* timid, skittish, shy.
espantador, ra, *n.* bugbear, frightener.
espantajo, *m.* scarecrow; fright.

espantalobos, *m.* (bot.) bladder or bastard senna.
espantamoscas, *m.* fly net; flyflap.
espantapájaros, *m.* scarecrow.
espantar. **I.** *va.* to scare, frighten, daunt; to chase or drive away. **II.** *vr.* to be astonished, to marvel.
espantavillanos, *m.* gaudy stuff or trinket.
espanto, *m.* fright, dread; horror; threat; wonder; hideousness; (Am.) apparition, spook.
espantoso, sa, *a.* frightful, dreadful; fearful; wonderful.
España, *f.* Spain.
español, la. **I.** *n.* & *a.* Spanish. **II.** *n.* Spaniard (*f.* Spanish woman).
españolado, da. **I.** *a.* Spanishlike. **II.** *f.* Spanish action or behavior.
españolar, *va.* (coll.) = ESPAÑOLIZAR.
españoleta, *f.* ancient Spanish dance.
españolismo, *m.* love for, devotion to Spanish things; Hispanicism, a Spanish idiom.
españolizar. **I.** *va.* to make Spanishlike. **II.** *vr.* to adopt the customs and manners of Spain.
esparadrapo, *m.* court-plaster.
esparaván, *m.* (vet.) spavin; (ornith.) sparrow hawk.—**e. de garbanzuelo** = E. SECO.—**e. huesoso,** (vet.) bone spavin.—**e. seco,** (vet.) muscle spavin.
esparavel, *m.* casting net; (mason.) hod.
esparceta, *f.* (bot.) sainfoin.
esparciata, *a.* Spartan.
esparcidamente, *adv.* separately, scatteredly.
esparcido, da. **I.** *pp.* of ESPARCIR. **II.** *a.* scattered; merry, festive, gay.
esparcidor, ra, *n.* & *a.* scatterer(-ing), spreader (-ing).
esparcimiento, *m.* scattering, dissemination; amusement, recreation, diversion, relaxation; frankness, openness.
esparcir. **I.** *va.* (*ind.* ESPARZO; *subj.* ESPARZA) to scatter, spread; disseminate; divulge. **II.** *vr.* to amuse oneself; to make merry.
esparragado, *m.* dish of asparagus.
esparragador, ra, *n.* asparagus grower.
esparragamiento, *m.* cultivation of asparagus.
esparragar, *vn.* to grow asparagus.
espárrago, *m.* (bot.) asparagus; pole of an awning; (min.) peg ladder.
esparragón, *m.* corded silk stuff.
esparraguera, *f.* asparagus plant; asparagus bed.
esparraguero, ra, *n.* asparagus seller.
esparraguina, *f.* (min.) asparagin.
esparrancado, da. **I.** *pp.* of ESPARRANCARSE. **II.** *a.* spread apart (esp. the legs).
esparrancarse, *vr.* (coll.) to spread the legs apart.
espartal, *m.* matweed field.
espartano, na, *n.* & *a.* Spartan.
esparteína, *f.* (chem.) sparteine.
esparteña, *f.* rope-sole sandal.
espartería, *f.* mat-work factory or shop.
espartero, ra, *n.* maker and seller of mat-work.
espartilla, *f.* mop of esparto grass.
espartizal, *m.* esparto field.
esparto, *m.* (bot.) esparto grass, matweed.
esparzo, esparza, *v.* *V.* ESPARCIR.
espasmo, *m.* (med.) spasm.
espasmódico, ca, *a.* spasmodic, convulsive.
espasticidad, *f.* (med.) spasticity.
espástico, ca, *a.* (med.) spastic.
espata, *f.* (bot.) spathe.
espatarrada, *f.* spreading (of legs).
espatarrarse, *vr.* to straddle.
espático, ca, *a.* (min.) spathic.
espato, *m.* (min.) spar.—**e. calizo,** calcite, calcspar.—**e. de Islandia,** Iceland spar.—**e. flúor,** fluorspar.—**e. pesado,** barite, heavy spar.
espátula, *f.* spatula; (art) palette knife.
espatulado, da, *a.* spatulate.
espaviento, *m.* = ASPAVIENTO, fear; fuss.
espavorido, da, *a.* = DESPAVORIDO, terrified.
especería, *f.* = ESPECIERÍA.
especia, *f.* spice.—*pl.* medicinal drugs.
especiado, da, *a.* spicy.
especial, *a.* special, particular.—**en e.,** specially, in particular.
especialidad, *f.* specialty; major field of studies.
especialista, *a.* & *n.* specialist.
especialización, *f.* specialization; specializing.
especializado, da, *a.* & *n.* specialist.
especializar. **I.** *va.* to specialize; to limit, confine. **II.** *vr.* (en) to specialize (in).
especiar, *va.* to spice, season.
especie, *f.* species; kind, sort; event, incident; case, affair, business; piece of news; statement; pretext, show.—**en e.,** in kind.
especiería, *f.* grocery shop.
especiero, *m.* grocer.
especificación, *f.* specification.
especificadamente, *adv.* in a specified manner.
específicamente, *adv.* specifically.
especificar, *va.* (*pret.* ESPECIFIQUÉ; *subj.* ESPECIFIQUE) to specify, particularize, itemize.
especificativo, va, *a.* specific, specifying.
específico, ca. **I.** *a.* specific. **II.** *m.* (med.) specific.
especifiqué, especifique, *v.* *V.* ESPECIFICAR.
espécimen, *m.* specimen, sample.
especioso, sa, *a.* neat; beautiful; apparent, specious, deceiving.
especiota, *f.* (coll.) hoax, false news.
espectable, *a.* notable, eminent; conspicuous.
espectacular, *a.* spectacular.
espectáculo, *m.* spectacle, show, pageant.
espectador, ra, *n.* spectator.—*pl.* audience.
espectral, *a.* (phys.) spectral, spectrum (as *a.*).
espectro, *m.* spectre, specter, phantom, hobgoblin; (opt.) spectrum.
espectrógrafo, *m.* (phys.) spectrograph.—**e. de masa,** (phys.) mass spectrograph.
espectroheliógrafo, *m.* (phys.) spectroheliograph.
espectrómetro, *m.* spectrometer.
espectroscopia, *f.* (opt.) spectroscopy.
espectroscópico, ca, *a.* spectroscopic.
espectroscopio, *m.* (opt.) spectroscope.
especulación, *f.* speculation, contemplation; speculation, venture.
especulador, ra, *n.* & *a.* speculator(-ing).
especular. **I.** *va.* to behold, view, inspect; to speculate, meditate about. **II.** *vn.* to speculate; (com.) to speculate. **III.** *a.* (phys.) specular.
especulativa, *f.* understanding.
especulativamente, *adv.* speculatively.
especulativo, va, *a.* speculative; thoughtful.
espéculo, *m.* speculum.
espejado, da, *a.* mirrorlike.
espejear, *vn.* to shine.
espejeo, *m.* = ESPEJISMO.
espejería, *f.* mirror factory or shop.
espejero, ra, *n.* mirror maker or seller.
espejismo, *m.* mirage; illusion.
espejo, *m.* looking-glass, mirror; (naut.) stern; frame.—**e. de cuerpo entero,** full-length glass, pier glass.—**e. ustorio,** burning glass.
espejuela, *f.* curve of the bit.—**e. abierta,** snaffle.
espejuelo, *m.* *dim.* small looking-glass; specular stone, selenite; leaf of mica; device for catching larks; candied citron; (vet.) wart on pastern.—*pl.* eyeglass lenses; spectacles, eyeglasses.
espeleología, *f.* speleology.
espeleólogo, ga, *n.* speleologist.
espelta, *f.* (bot.) spelt, a cereal.
espélteo, a, *a.* pertaining to spelt.
espelunca, *f.* dark, gloomy cave.
espeluzar, *va.* = DESPELUZAR, to be horrified.
espeluznante, *a.* (coll.) setting the hair on end, dreadful, horrifying.
espeluznar, *va.* & *vr.* to dishevel the hair; to set the hair on end (from fright).
espeque, *m.* handspike; pump brake; strut, prop; lever.
espera, *f.* waiting; stay, pause; (mus.) stop, interval; restraint, prudence; (law) respite, adjourn-

ment; ancient piece of ordnance; (carp.) notch. —**en e.**, waiting.—**en e. de**, waiting for, awaiting; expecting.—**sala de e.**, waiting-room.
esperador, ra, *a.* expectant.
esperantista, *n.* Esperantist.
esperanto, *m.* Esperanto.
esperanza, *f.* hope; (often *pl.*) prospects.—**dar e.**, or **esperanzas**, to give encouragement; to promise, to bid fair.—**no hay e.**, there is no hope, or no chance, the case is hopeless.
esperanzado, da, *a.* hopeful, full of hope.
esperanzar, *va.* to give hope to.
esperar. I. *va.* to hope; to expect; to wait for, await, look for; to fear. **II.** *vn.* to wait; to hope. —**e. lo imposible**, to hope against hope.—**quien espera desespera**, long hoping ends in despair or in hopelessness. **III.** *vr.* to wait, stay.
esperezarse, *vr.* to stretch oneself.
esperezo, *m.* stretching one's arms and legs.
espérgula, *f.* (bot.) spurry.
esperma, *f.* sperm.—**e. de ballena**, spermaceti.
espermaceti, *m.* (com.) spermaceti.
espermático, ca, *a.* spermatic, seminal.
espermatocito, *m.* (biol.) spermatocyte.
espermatogénesis, *f.* (biol.) spermatogenesis.
espermatogenia, *f.* (biol.) spermatogenesis.
espermatología, *f.* (biol., bot.) spermatology, spermology.
espermatorrea, *f.* (med.) spermatorrhœa.
espermatozoario, espermatozoide, espermatozoo, *m.* spermatozoön.
espermiducto, *m.* spermatic duct.
espernada, *f.* split end link of a chain.
espernancarse, *vr.* = ESPARRANCARSE.
esperón, *m.* (naut.) = ESPOLÓN, fender beam.
esperpento, *m.* horrible or hideous thing or person; absurdity, nonsense.
espesamiento, *m.* thickening.
espesar. I. *va.* to thicken, inspissate, coagulate, curdle; to mass, assemble; to make closer (as knitting). **II.** *vr.* to condense; to thicken, become thicker.—**espesativo, va**, *a.* thickening.
espeso, sa, *a.* thick, dense; curdy; frequent, often repeated; slovenly, dirty; dull, heavy.
espesor, *m.* thickness.
espesura, *f.* thickness, density, closeness; thicket, close wood; abundant head of hair; slovenliness.
espetaperro, espetaperros.—**a e.**, at breakneck speed, precipitately.
espetar. I. *va.* to spit, to skewer; to pierce, run through; (coll.) to spring (something) on (one). **II.** *vr.* to be stiff with pride; (coll.) to thrust oneself into place.—**e. en**, to fit in, go into.
espetera, *f.* kitchen rack, scullery; kitchenware.
espetón, *m.* spit, poker, rake, iron prong, large pin; (zool.) sea-pike.
[1]**espía**, *n.* spy.—**e. doble**, treacherous spy who acts for both sides.
[2]**espía**, *f.* (naut.) warp, chest rope.
[1]**espiar**, *va.* to spy on; to lie in wait for.
[2]**espiar**, *vn.* (naut.) to warp.
espibia, *f.*, **espibio, espibión**, *m.* (vet.) dislocation in the nape of the neck.
espicanardi, *f.*, **espicanardo**, *m.* (bot.) spikenard.
espiciforme, *a.* (bot.) spicate.
espícula, *f.* (zool.) spicule.
espichar. I. *va.* to prick. **II.** *vn.* (coll.) to give up the ghost, to die.
espiche, *m.* sharp-pointed weapon; meatspit; spigot.
espichón, *m.* wound with a pointed weapon.
espiga, *f.* (bot.) tassel (as of corn); (carp.) tenon, dowel, peg; (mech.) pin, tongue, shank, treenail, stem; tang of a sword; brad, headless nail; (mil.) fuse of a bomb or shell; (naut.) masthead.
espigadera, *f.* gleaner.
espigado, da. I. *pp.* of ESPIGAR. **II.** *a.* tall, grown; (agr.) eared, ripe.
espigador, ra, *n.* gleaner.
espigar. I. *vn.* (*pret.* ESPIGUÉ; *subj.* ESPIGUE) to glean; to collect, cull; (carp.) to tenon. **II.** *vn.* (agr.) to tassel (as corn). **III.** *vr.* to grow tall; to go to seed.
espigón, *m.* sting (as of bees); point of a sharp tool or dart; bearded spike; ear of corn; peak; breakwater or pier.
espigué, espigue, *v.* *V.* ESPIGAR.
espigueo, *m.* gleaning; gleaning season.
espiguilla, ta, *f.* *dim.* spikelet; small edging of lace, tape, or inkle.
espina, *f.* thorn; fishbone; spine, backbone; splinter; scruple, doubt, suspicion.—**e. blanca**, (bot.) woolly-cotton thistle.—**e. dorsal**, vertebral or spinal column, spine.—**dar mala e.**, to cause suspicion or anxiety.—**estar en espinas**, to be anxious, to be on pins and needles. —**sacarse la e.**, to get even, to retrieve one's losses.
espinaca, *f.* (bot.) spinach.
espinadura, *f.* pricking with a thorn.
espinal, *a.* spinal, dorsal.
espinapez, *m.* herringbone (pattern).
[1]**espinar**, *va.* to prick with thorns; to surround (trees) with thorn bushes; to nettle, provoke.
[2]**espinar**, *m.* place full of thorn bushes; dangerous undertaking, arduous enterprise.
espinazo, *m.* spine, backbone.
espinel, *m.* trotline.
[1]**espinela**, *f.* (poet.) ten-line stanza.
[2]**espinela**, *f.* spinel ruby.
espíneo, ea, *a.* made or full of thorns.
espinera, *f.* (bot.) = ESPINO.
espineta, *f.* (mus.) spinet.
espingarda, *f.* a small cannon; Moorish gun.
espingardada, *f.* wound from an ESPINGARDA.
espinilla, *f.* shin bone; blackhead.
espinillera, *f.* (armor) greave, jambe.
espino, *m.* (bot.) hawthorn, buckthorn.
espinor, *m.* (math.) spinor.
espinosismo, *m.* Spinozism.
espinosista, *n.* & *a.* Spinozist(-ic).
espinoso, sa, *a.* thorny; arduous; dangerous.
espinzar, *va.* to burl. Also DESPINZAR.
espiocha, *f.* pickaxe.
espión, *m.* spy.
espionaje, *m.* espionage, spying.
espira, *f.* spiral line, helix; spire, steeple; turn (of a winding); (arch.) surbase of a column.
espiración, *f.* exhalation, respiration.
espiráculo, *m.* (zool.) spiracle.
espirador, ra, *n.* one who exhales or breathes.
espiral. I. *a.* spiral, winding. **II.** *f.* (math.) spiral.
espirante, *a.* exhaling, respiring.
espirar. I. *va.* to breathe, exhale; to move, animate; to infuse a divine spirit in. **II.** *vn.* to exhale, breathe.
espirativo, va, *a.* that infuses spirit.
espirea, *f.* (bot.) spiræa.
espirilo, *m.* (biol.) spirillum.
espiritado, da, *a.* (coll.) extremely thin.
espiritar. I. *va.* = ENDEMONIAR, to possess with a devil. **II.** *vr.* (coll.) to be agitated, to fret.
espiritismo, *m.* spiritism, spiritualism.
espiritista, *n.* & *a.* spiritist(-ic).
espiritoso, sa, *a.* spirituous; spirited, lively.
espíritu, *m.* spirit; soul; genius; ardor, courage; inclination, turn of mind; spirit, liquor.—*pl.* spirits, demons, hobgoblins; (chem.) spirits, ether.—**e. de contradicción**, contradictory temper, mania of contradicting.—**e. de sal**, spirit of salt (hydrochloric acid).—**e. de vino**, spirits of wine, rectified spirit.—**e. inmundo, e. maligno**, the devil.—**E. Santo**, Holy Ghost.
espiritual, *a.* spiritual; ghostly.
espiritualidad, *f.* spirituality; incorporality.
espiritualismo, *m.* (philos.) spiritualism, idealism (as opposed to materialism).
espiritualista, *a.* & *n.* spiritualist(-ic), idealist (-ic) [as opposed to materialist(-ic)].
espiritualización, *f.* spiritualization.
espiritualizar, *va.* to spiritualize.
espirituoso, sa, *a.* spirituous; ardent; spirited.
espirómetro, *m.* spirometer.

espiroqueta, *f.* (bacteriol.) spirochete.
espita, *f.* faucet, stopcock, spigot, spout; tap; (coll.) tippler, drunkard.
espitar, *va.* to put a faucet on; to tap.
espito, *m.* (print.) peel, hanger.
esplendente, *a.* (poet.) shining, resplendent.
esplender, *vn.* (poet.) to shine, glitter.
esplendidez, *f.* splendor, grandeur; abundance; liberality.
espléndido, da, *a.* splendid, magnificent, grand; generous, liberal; resplendent.
esplendor, *m.* splendor, magnificence, grandeur; fulgency, radiance; nobleness.
esplendoroso, sa, *a.* splendid, radiant.
esplenético, ca; esplénico, ca, *a.* splenic.
esplenio, *m.* (anat.) splenius.
esplenitis, *f.* (med.) splenitis.
esplenotomía, *f.* (surg.) splenotomy.
espliego, *m.* (bot.) lavender.
esplín, *m.* (coll.) spleen, melancholia, the blues.
esplique, *m.* bird snare.
espolada, *f.* prick with a spur.—**e. de vino,** (coll.) large draught of wine.
espolazo, *m.* violent prick with a spur.
espoleadura, *f.* wound made with a spur.
espolear, *va.* to spur; to instigate, incite.
[1]**espoleta,** *f.* fuse (of a bomb).
[2]**espoleta,** *f.* wishbone.
espolín, *m. dim.* small goad spur; shuttle for brocading or flowering; silk brocade.
espolinar, *va.* to brocade; to flower.
espolio, *m.* (eccl.) spolium.
espolique, *m.* running footman.
[1]**espolista,** *m.* running footman.
[2]**espolista,** *m.* one who farms a spolium.
espolón, *m.* cock's spur; ridge, crag of a mountain; (arch.) spur, buttress; (eng.) mole, breakwater, jetty, groin, starling; (naut.) ram of a man-of-war; (naut.) fender-beam.
espolonado, da. I. *a.* (ornith.) spical, spicate(d. **II.** *f.* sudden onset of horsemen.
espolvorear, espolvorizar, *va.* to sprinkle with powder; to dust (remove dust).
espondaico, ca, *a.* (poet.) spondaic.
espondeo, *m.* (poet.) spondee.
espondil, espóndilo, *m.* (anat.) spondyl, vertebra.
espondilitis, *f.* (med.) spondylitis.
esponja, *f.* sponge; (coll.) sponger.
esponjado, da. I. *pp.* of ESPONJAR. **II.** *a.* puffed up. **III.** *m.* = AZUCARILLO, a sweetmeat.
esponjadura, *f.*, **esponjamiento,** *m.* sponging; flaw in cast metal; puffing up.
esponjar. I. *va.* to sponge, soak, imbibe. **II.** *vr.* to swell; to puff up; (coll.) to glow with health.
esponjera, *f.* sponge holder.
esponjilla, ita, uela, *f. dim.* small sponge.
esponjosidad, *f.* sponginess.
esponjoso, sa, *a.* spongy, porous.
esponsales, *m. pl.* betrothal, engagement.
esponsalicio, cia, *a.* nuptial, spousal.
espontanearse, *vr.* to avow or declare spontaneously or of one's own accord.
espontaneidad, *f.* spontaneity, spontaneousness
espontáneo, nea, *a.* spontaneous; willing.
espontón, *m.* (mil.) spontoon, half-pike.
espontonada, *f.* salute or blow with a spontoon.
espora, *f.*, (bot.) spore.
esporádico, ca, *a.* sporadic, isolated.
esporangio, *m.* (bot.) sporangium.
esporidio, *m.* (bot.) sporidium.
esporífero, ra, *a.* (bot.) sporiferous.
esporo, *m.* (bot.) spore.
esporocarpio, *m.* (bot.) sporocarp.
esporofito, *m.* (bot.) sporophyte.
esporóforo, *m.* (bot.) sporophore.
esporogénesis, *f.* (bot.) sporogenesis.
esporogonio, *m.* (bot.) sporogonium.
esporozoario, esporozoo. I. *n.* & *a.* (zool. sporozoan. **II.** *m. pl.* Sporozoa.
esportada, *f.* fruit basket; basketful.
esportear, *va.* to carry in panniers or baskets.
esportilla, *f. dim.* small fruit basket.
esportillero, *m.* porter, carrier.
esportillo, *m.* pannier; fruit basket.
esportón, *m. aug.* large pannier or fruit basket.
espórulo, *m. dim.* (bot., biol.) sporule.
esposa, *f.* spouse, wife.—*pl.* manacles, handcuffs shackles.—**esposar,** *va.* to shackle, handcuff.
esposo, *m.* spouse, husband, consort.
espuela, *f.* spur, rowel; stimulus, incitement.—**e. de caballero,** (bot.) larkspur.
espuerta, *f.* two-handled fruit basket.—**a. espuertas,** abundantly.
espulgador, ra, *n.* one who cleans off lice or fleas.
espulgar, *va.* (*pret.* ESPULGUÉ; *subj.* ESPULGUE) to clean lice or fleas from; to examine closely.—**espulgo,** *m.* act of cleaning lice or fleas from.
espuma, *f.* froth; lather; foam; scum.—**e. de la sal,** sea froth.—**e. de mar,** meerschaum.—**e. de nitro,** aphronitrum.—**e. de plata,** litharge of silver.
espumadera, *f.* skimmer, colander.
espumador, ra, *n.* & *a.* skimmer(-ing).
espumajear, *vn.* to froth at the mouth.
espumajo, *m.* froth.—**espumajoso, sa,** *a.* foamy, frothy.
espumante, *a.* foaming, frothing, lathering; sparkling (wine).
espumar. I. *va.* to skim, to scum. **II.** *vn.* to froth, foam.
espumarajo, *m.* foam or froth from the mouth.
espumero, *m.* place where salt water crystallizes.
espumilla, *f.* gauzy fabric; (Am.) meringue.
espumillón, *m.* heavy silk crape.
espumosidad, *f.* frothiness, foaminess.
espumoso, sa, *a.* foamy, frothy; lathery; sparkling (wine).
espundia, *f.* (vet.) cancerous ulcer.
espurio, ria, *a.* spurious, adulterated; bastard.
espurrear, espurriar, *va.* to sprinkle with water or another liquid held in the mouth.
esputar, *va.* & *vn.* to expectorate, spit.
esputo, *m.* spittle, saliva; sputum.
esquebrajar, *va.* to crack, split.
esqueje, *m.* (agr.) cutting, slip.
esquela, *f.* billet, note.
esqueletado, da, *a.* very thin, emaciated.
esquelético, ca, *a.* skeletal; thin, wasted.
esqueleto, *m.* skeleton; very thin person; (naut.) carcass, framework of a ship; (auto) carcass (of a tire); (Am.) form, blank (as bill forms, application blanks, etc.); (Chile) outline, rough draft.—**en e.,** unfinished.
esquema, *m.* symbol; scheme, plan.
esquemáticamente, *adv.* schematically.
esquemático, ca, *a.* schematic.
esquematismo, *m.* schematism.
esquematizar, *va.* to sketch, outline.
esquena, *f.* spine of fishes.
esquero, *m.* leather bag or pouch.
esquí, *m.* ski.
esquiador, ra. I. *a.* of or pertaining to skiing. **II.** *n.* skier.
esquiagrafía, *f.* skiagraphy.
esquiar, *vn.* to ski.
esquiciar, *va.* to sketch, outline, delineate.
esquicio, *m.* sketch, outline.
esquifada, *f.* skiff or boat load; vault of a cistern.
esquifar, *va.* (naut.) to fit out (a ship).
esquifazón, *f.* (naut.) boat's crew.
esquife, *m.* skiff, small boat; (arch.) cylindrical vault.
[1]**esquila,** *f.* small bell; cattle bell.
[2]**esquila,** *f.* (ichth.) prawn; (entom.) waterspider; (bot.) squill.
[3]**esquila,** *f.* sheepshearing.
esquilador, *m.* sheepshearer, clipper.
esquilar, *va.* to shear, crop, clip.—**e. la carona,** to shear the back of a mule.—**sin e.,** unshorn.
esquileo, *m.* shearing (of sheep, dogs, etc.)
esquilimoso, sa, *a.* (coll.) fastidious, overnice.
esquilmar, *va.* to harvest; to impoverish; to cheat, to swindle, to exploit.

esquilmo, *m.* harvest; farm produce.
esquilón, *m.* large call or cattle bell.
esquimal, *n.* & *a.* Eskimo.
esquina, *f.* corner, angle (outside).
esquinado, da. I. *pp.* of ESQUINAR. **II.** *a.* intractable, unsociable.
esquinal, *m.* corner plate; angle iron; iron knee.
esquinante, to, *m.* (bot.) aromatic rush.
esquinar. I. *va.* to form a corner with, meet forming a corner; to square (timber, etc.); to estrange, cause to quarrel, set against. **II.** *vr.* to quarrel, to fall out.
esquinazo, *m.* corner; (Chile) serenade.—**dar e.,** to avoid, to evade, get out of the sight of (one that follows), shake off; to abandon, leave in the lurch.
esquinco, *m.* skink, lizard. Also ESTINCO.
esquinela, *f.* (armor) greave, jambe.
esquinzador, *m.* rag room in paper mills; rag engine.
esquinzar, *va.* to cut (rags) in paper mills.
esquirla, *f.* (surg.) splinter of a bone.
esquirol, *m.* (coll.) strike breaker, scab, blackleg; (prov.) squirrel.
esquisto, *m.* (min.) schist; slate.
esquistoso, sa, *a.* laminated; schistose, slaty.
esquitar, *va.* to pardon, to remit (a debt).
esquite, *m.* (Mex., C. A.) popped corn.
esquivar. I. *va.* to shun, elude, avoid, evade, escape; to hush up (a matter). **II.** *vr.* to disdain, withdraw.
esquivez, *f.* disdain, asperity, coldness.
esquivo, va, *a.* elusive, evading; shy, reserved, coy, cold.
esquizado, da, *a.* mottled (as marble).
esquizocarpo, *m.* (bot.) schizocarp.
esquizofrenia, *f.* (med.) schizophrenia.
esquizofrénico, ca, *a.* & *n.* schizophrenic.
estabilidad, *f.* stability.
estabilísimo, *adv. super.* very stable or firm.
estabilización, *f.* stabilization.
estabilizador, ra. I. *a.* stabilizing. **II.** *n.* stabilizer; *m.* (mech., aer.) stabilizer.
estabilizar. I. *va.* to stabilize. **II.** *vn.* to become stabilized.
estable, *a.* stable, steady, firm, fast.
establear, *va.* to tame, accustom to the stable.
establecedor, ra, *n.* founder.
establecer. I. *va.* (*ind.* ESTABLEZCO; *subj.* ESTABLEZCA) to establish, found; to decree, enact. **II.** *vr.* to establish or settle oneself.
establecimiento, *m.* establishment; statute, law, ordinance, decree; establishment, founding; institution.
establero, *m.* hostler, groom, horsekeeper.
establezco, establezca, *v.* *V.* ESTABLECER.
establo, *m.* stable; cattle barn.
estabulación, *f.* stabling.
estaca, *f.* stake, picket, pile, pole; stick, cudgel, bludgeon; (agr.) grafting twig; cutting; (carp.) clamp nail.
estacada, *f.* (mil.) palisade, stockade; paling, fence work; pile pier; place for a duel.—**dejar (a uno) en la e.,** to leave (one) in the lurch, "holding the bag."
estacar. I. *va.* (*pret.* ESTAQUÉ; *subj.* ESTAQUE) to stake; to fence with stakes; to tie to a stake. **II.** *vr.* to remain stiff as a pole.
estación, *f.* station; season; stay, stop; party of persons posted at some place; place, location.—*pl.* (eccl.) stations of the cross.—*pl.* seasons.—**e. meteorológica,** weather station.—**e. naval,** naval station or base.
estacional, *a.* seasonal; (astr.) stationary.
estacionamiento, *m.* stationing, settling; (auto) parking.
estacionar. I. *va.* to park (a car, etc.). **II.** *vr.* to park; to remain stationary.
estacionario, ria, *a.* stationary.
estacionero, ra, *n.* one who prays before stations in church.
estacte, *m.* oil of myrrh.
estacha, *f.* (naut.) towline, hawser; harpoon rope.
estada, *f.* stay, sojourn.
estadal, *m.* a linear measure of about 10 ft. 9 in.; blessed ribbon worn around the neck.
estadia, *f.* (surv.) stadia, stadia transit.
estadía, *f.* (com. and naut.) stay, detention; demurrage; cost of such stay.
estadígrafo, fa, *n.* statistician.
estadio, *m.* stadium; race course; stadium (road measure).
estadiómetro, *m.* stadiometer.
estadista, *m.* statesman.
estadístico, ca. I. *a.* statistical, statistic. **II.** *n.* statistician; *f.* statistics.—**estadísticas vitales,** biostatistics.
estadizo, za, *a.* stagnant (as water).
estado, *m.* state; condition (of persons or things) (as, *eso llego en mal estado,* that came in bad condition); estate, class, rank; profession; status (single, married, or widowed); state, nation, commonwealth; state, government; statement, account, report; a measure of length (1.85 yds.).—*pl.* States, legislature (*los Estados Generales,* the States-General).—**e. de guerra,** or **e. de sitio,** martial law (*declarar una ciudad en estado de guerra,* to declare a city in a state of martial law, to put it under martial law).—**e. general,** or **e. llano,** the commons, the common estate (as distinguished from the nobility, etc.).—**e. mayor,** (mil.) staff.—**e. mayor general,** (mil.) general staff.—**Estados Unidos de América,** United States of America.
estadounidense, estadunidense, *n.* & *a.* (citizen) of the U. S.
[1]estafa, *f.* stirrup.
[2]estafa, *f.* swindle, trick, deceit.
estafador, ra. I. *a.* that cheats or swindles. **II.** *n.* cheater, swindler.
estafar, *va.* to swindle, defraud.
estafermo, *m.* movable wooden figure of an armed man; idle fellow.
estafeta, *f.* courier, post, express; post office; general-delivery office or department (of post office); post-office branch.
estafetero, *m.* postmaster; post-office clerk.
estafetil, *a.* pertaining to a courier or post.
estafilocacia, *f.* (bacteriol.) infection due to staphylococci.
estafilococo, *m.* (bacteriol.) staphylococcus.
estafiloma, *m.* (med.) staphyloma.
estafisagria, *f.* (bot.) stavesacre, lousewort.
estagirita, *n.* & *a.* Stagirite.
estagnación, *f.* (Am.) stagnation; paralyzation, cessation (of business, etc.).
estala, *f.* seaport, stopping place.
estalación, *f.* class, rank, order.
estalactita, *f.* stalactite.
estalactítico, ca, *a.* stalactitic, stalactic.
estalagmita, *f.* stalagmite.
estalagmítico, ca, *a.* stalagmitic.
estallar, *vn.* to explode, burst; (of fire, etc.) to break out.
estallido, estallo, *m.* crack, crackling, crashing, crash, snap, outburst; report (as of firearms).
estambrar, *va.* to spin (worsted).
estambre, *m.* worsted, woollen yarn; (bot.) stamen.
estamenara, *f.* (naut.) futtock.
estamento, *m.* one of the estates composing the Cortes in Aragon (clergy, nobility, commons).
estameña, *f.* tammy cloth, serge.
estameñete, *m.* a kind of serge.
estamíneo, nea, *a.* made of worsted; (bot.) stamineous.
estaminífero, ra, *a.* (bot.) staminate.
estampa. I. *f.* print, stamp, cut; engraving; first sketch; printing, press; track, impression, footstep; (fig.) impression.—**estampas iluminadas,** colored plates.—**la e. de la herejía,** (coll.) a hideous face; (one) dressed in bad taste.
estampado, *m.* cotton print, calico; impression, stamping; cloth printing.

estampador, *m.* stamper; stamp, puncheon.
estampar, *va.* to print, stamp, emboss; to imprint (a kiss); to impress, fix (in the mind).
estampería, *f.* office for printing or selling prints.
estampero, ra, *n.* stamp or print maker or seller.
estampida, *f.* stampede.—**dar una e.,** (coll.) (Am.) to run away (often leaving debts).
estampido, *m.* report of a gun; crack, crash.
estampilla, *f. dim.* small print; rubber stamp; signet seal; (Am.) postage stamp.
estampillado, *m.* stamping, marking.
estampillar, *va.* to stamp, mark.
estampita, *f. dim.* small print or stamp.
estancación, *f.*, **estancamiento,** *m.* stagnation.
estancado, da, *a.* stagnant.
estancar. I. *va.* (*pret.* ESTANQUÉ; *subj.* ESTANQUE) to stanch, check, stem; (naut.) to fother (a leak); (com.) to corner, to monopolize; to interdict, suspend. **II.** *vr.* to stagnate, become stagnant.
[1]**estancia,** *f.* (poet.) stanza.
[2]**estancia,** *f.* stay, sojourn; dwelling, habitation; sitting room, living room; (Am.) small farm.
estanciero, ra, *n.* small farmer.
estanco, ca. I. *a.* leakproof, watertight. **II.** *m.* monopoly; government monopoly; state store; cigar store; repository, archives, files.
estandarte, *m.* standard, flag, banner, colors.
estangurria, *f.* (med.) strangury; catheter.
estannato, *m.* (chem.) stannate.
estánnico, ca, *a.* (chem.) stannic.
estannoso, sa, *a.* (chem.) stannous.
estanque, *m.* pond, reservoir, pool.
estanqué, estanque, *v. V.* ESTANCAR.
[1]**estanquero,** *m.* reservoir keeper.
[2]**estanquero, ra.** *n.* retailer of monopoly goods; tobacconist.
estanquillero, ra, *n.* tobacconist.
estanquillo, *m.* cigar store; shop where monopolized goods are sold; (Mex.) small shop; (Ecua.) liquor shop.
estanquito, *m. dim.* small pond, pool.
estantal, *m.* (arch.) buttress.
estantalar, *va.* to buttress, support.
estante. I. *a.* existing, extant; fixed, permanent. **II.** *m.* shelf; bookcase; (print.) cabinet.—*pl.* (naut.) props of the crossbeams.
estantería, *f.* shelfing, shelves (collect.).
estantigua, *f.* phantom, vision, hobgoblin; (coll.) tall, skinny, uncouth person.
estantío, tía, *a.* standing still, stationary; dull, slow.
estañador, *m.* tinner, tinman.
estañadura, *f.* tinning.
estañar, *va.* to tin, blanch; to solder.
estañero, *m.* tinner; seller of tinware.
estaño, *m.* (chem.) tin.
estaqué, estaque, *v. V.* ESTACAR.
estaquero, *m.* year-old buck or doe.
estaquilla, ita, *f.* (shoemaking) peg; wooden pin; spike, long nail.
estaquillador, *m.* (shoemaking) pegging awl.
estaquillar, *va.* to peg, to fasten with pegs.
estar. I. *vn.* (*ind. pres.* ESTOY, *pret.* ESTUVE; *subj.* ESTÉ) to be. When followed by the gerund of a reflexive verb, it sometimes takes the reflexive pronoun from that verb (*estarse vistiendo,* instead of *estar vistiéndose,* to be dressing). When preceded by a dative case, "for" is used in English before the corresponding objective case (*este sombrero me está demasiado grande,* this hat is too large for me; *eso no me es posible,* that is not possible for me).—**e. a,** to sell at (so much) apiece.—**e. al,** to be on the point of.—**e. bien,** to be well; to be all right, acceptable, suitable. **e. con,** to live in company with; to be engaged or talking with; to have (a disease), to be ill with; to be in a state of (anxiety, anger, hurry, etc.).—**e. de,** to be in the condition or doing the act indicated by the following noun (*estoy de mudanza,* I am moving; *estoy de prisa,* I am in haste; *estoy de vacaciones,* I am on my vacation; *Juan está de cónsul,* John is serving as consul).—**e. en,** to understand, comprehend (*estoy en lo que Vd. me dice,* I understand what you say); to be of opinion; to stand, to cost (*este sombrero me está en seis pesos,* this hat costs me six dollars); to depend (*en eso está,* it depends on that); to consist in.—**e. en grande,** to live in luxury.—**e. en sí,** to know what one is doing.—**e. para,** to be about to; to be in a mood or in condition to or for (*no estoy para eso,* I am in no mood for that).—**e. por,** to be for, in favor of; (followed by *infin.*) to remain to be, not to have been (followed by *pp.*); to have a mind to, to have a notion or a desire to.—**e. por ver,** to remain to be seen.—**e. sobre sí,** to be cautious or wary; to be puffed up with conceit.—**¿a cómo estamos? ¿a cuántos estamos?** what day (of the month) is it? what is the date?—**¡dónde estamos!** what have we come to! what a thing!—an expression of admiration or disgust at what is seen or heard.—**está escrito,** it is written.—**¿estamos?** is it agreed? do you understand?—**estamos a** (followed by the day, date), this is, it is (*estamos a lunes,* this is Monday; *estamos a cinco,* this is the fifth).—**¡está bien!** or, **bueno!,** all right! —**¿está Vd.?** do you understand? do you see the point? **II.** *vr.* to be, to keep; to stay, to remain (*Juan nunca se está callado,* John is never silent, or, never keeps silent; *debemos estarnos aquí,* we must remain here.)
estarcido, *m.* pounced drawing; stencil.
estarcir, *va.* to stencil.
estarna, *f.* (ornith.) small partridge.
estasis, *f.* (med.) stasis.
estatal, *a.* pert. to the state, state (as *a.*).
estática, *f.* (mech.) statics.
estático, ca, *a.* static, statical.
estatismo, *m.* (pol.) statism.
estator, *m.* (mech., elec.) stator.
estatorreactor, *m.* (aer.) athodyd, ramjet.
estatoscopio, *m.* (phys.) statoscope.
estatua, *f.* statue.—**quedarse hecho una e.,** to stand aghast, to be rooted to the ground.
estatuar, *va.* to adorn with statues.
estatuaria, *f.* (art) statuary, sculpture.
estatuario, ria. I. *a.* pert. to statuary. **II.** *m.* statuary; sculptor.
estatúder, *m.* stadtholder.
estatuderato, *m.* stadtholdership.
estatuído, da, *a.* statutory.
estatuir, *va.* (*ind.* ESTATUYO; *subj.* ESTATUYA) to establish, ordain, enact.
estatura, *f.* stature, height of a person.
estatutario, ria, *a.* statutory.
estatuto, *m.* statute, law, ordinance.
estatuyo, estatuya, *v. V.* ESTATUIR.
estay, *m.* (naut.) stay.
[1]**este,** *m.* east, orient.
[2]**este,** *m.*, **esta,** *f.*, *a.* this.—*pl.* **estos, estas,** these.
éste, *m.*, **ésta,** *f. pron. dem.* this, this one; the latter.—*pl.* **éstos,** *m.*, **éstas,** *f.*, these; the latter.
esté, *v. V.* ESTAR.
esteapsina, *f.* (biochem.) steapsin.
estearato, *m.* (chem.) stearate.
esteárico, ca, *a.* (chem.) stearic.
estearina, *f.* (chem.) stearin.
esteatita, *f.* (min.) steatite, soapstone.
[1]**esteba,** *f.* prickly plant growing in swamps.
[2]**esteba,** *f.* stevedore's pole.
estebar, *va.* to put (cloth) in the dye kettle.
estegosaurio, *m.* (paleontol.) stegosaurus.
[1]**estela,** *f.* (naut.) wake of a ship.—**e. de condensación,** (aer.) contrail.
[2]**estela,** *f.* (arch.) stele.
estelar, *a.* sidereal, stellar.
estelaria, *f.* (bot.) silvery lady's-mantle.
estelárido, da. I. *n.* & *a.* (zool.) asteroidean. **II.** *m. pl.* Asteroidea, starfishes.
estelífero, ra, *a.* (poet.) stelliferous, starry.
esteliforme, *a.* stelliform, star-shaped.
estelión, *m.* (zool.) stellion, a lizard; toadstone.

estelionato, *m.* (law) stellionate.
estelón, *m.* toadstone.
estemple, *m.* (min.) stemple.
estenia, *f.* (med.) sthenia.
esténico, ca, *a.* sthenic.
estenografía, *f.* stenography, shorthand.
estenografiar, *va.* to take down in shorthand.
estenográfico, ca, *a.* stenographic.
estenógrafo, fa, *n.* stenographer.
estenosis, *f.* (med.) stenosis, narrowing.
estenotipia, *f.* stenotypy.
Estentor, *m.* (myth.) Stentor.
estentóreo, a, *a.* stentorian.
[1]**estepa,** *f.* steppe, barren plain.
[2]**estepa,** *f.* (bot.) rockrose.
estepar, *m.* rockrose field.
estepilla, *f.* (bot.) white-leaved rockrose.
estequiometría, *f.* (chem., phys.) stoichiometry.
éster, *m.* (chem.) ester.
estera, *f.* mat, matting.
esterar. I. *va.* to cover with matting. **II.** *vn.* (coll.) to wear winter clothes before time.
estercoladura, *f.*, **estercolamiento,** *m.* manuring.
estercolar. I. *va.* to dung, muck, manure. **II.** *vn* to void the excrements.—**estercolero,** *m.* driver of a muck cart; dung hill, dung heap.
estercolizo, za; estercóreo, a, *a.* stercoraceous
estéreo, *m.* stere (one cubic metre).
estereobato, *m.* (arch.) stereobate.
estereocromía, *f.* stereochromy.
estereofonía, *f.* stereophony.
estereofónico, ca, *a.* stereophonic, (coll.) stereo.
estereografía, *f.* stereography.
estereográfico, ca, *a.* stereographic.
estereógrafo, *m.* stereographer.
estereograma, *m.* (stat.) stereogram.
estereometría, *f.* stereometry.
estereómetro, *m.* stereometer.
estereóptico, *m.* stereopticon.
estereoscópico, ca, *a.* stereoscopic.
estereoscopio, *m.* stereoscope.
estereotipa, *f.* = ESTEREOTIPIA.
estereotipador, *m.* stereotyper.
estereotipar, *va.* to stereotype; to print from stereotypes.
estereotipia, *f.* stereotypography, stereotyping; place where stereotypes are made.
estereotípico, ca, *a.* stereotypic.
estereotipo, *m.* stereotype.
estereotomía, *f.* stereotomy.
esterería, *f.* matting factory or shop.
esterero, ra, *n.*, matting maker or seller.
estéril, *a.* sterile, barren; unfruitful, fruitless.
esterilidad, *f.* sterility, barrenness, infertility; scarcity, failure of crops.
esterilización, *f.* sterilization.
esterilizador, ra, *n.* & *a.* sterilizer(-ing).
esterilizar, *va.* to sterilize.
esterilla, *f. dim.* small mat; straw plait; narrow gold or silver braid.
esterlín, *m.* = BOCACÍ, glazed buckram.
esterlina, *a.* (Eng. money) sterling (pound).
esternón, *m.* (anat.) sternum, breastbone.
[1]**estero,** *m.* inlet, estuary.
[2]**estero,** *m.* covering with matting; matting season.
esterquilinio, *m.* dunghill, dung heap.
estertor, *m.* rattle in the throat; stertor.
estertoroso, sa, *a.* stertorous.
estesia, *f.* esthesia.
esteta, *n.* æsthete; æsthetician.
estética, *f.* æsthetics.
estéticamente, *adv.* æsthetically.
estético, ca. I. *a.* æsthetic. **II.** *m.* æsthete.
estetógrafo, *m.* (med.) stethograph.
estetómetro, *m.* stethometer.
estetoscopia, *f.* (med.) stethoscopy.
estetoscópico, ca, *a.* stethoscopic.
estetoscopio, *m.* (med.) stethoscope.
esteva, *f.* plow handle; reach of a carriage.
estevado, da, *a.* bow-legged.
estevón, *m.* = ESTEVA.
estezado, *m.* = CORREAL, dressed deerskin.
estiaje, *m.* low-water mark.
estiba, *f.* rammer; place where wool is compressed; (naut.) stowage.
estibador, *m.* stevedore, longshoreman.
estibar, *va.* to compress (wool); (naut.) to stow.
estibia, *f.* (vet.) = ESPIBIA, neck dislocation.
estíbico, ca, *a.* stibial.
estibina, *f.* (min.) stibine.
estibio, *m.* antimony, stibium.
estiércol, *m.* dung, manure.
estigio, gia. I. *a.* Stygian. **II.** *f.* (E.) Styx.
estigma, *m.* birthmark; stigma, brand, mark of infamy; affront, disgrace; (bot.) stigma.
estigmatizador, ra, *n.* & *a.* stigmatizer(-ing).
estigmatizar, *va.* to stigmatize; to affront.
estilar. I. *va.* to use, be in the habit of using; to draw up (a document). **II.** *vr.* to be in style.
estilete, *m.* stiletto (dagger); small chisel or burin; (surg.) flexible probe.
estilicidio, *m.* (of liquid) issuing drop by drop.
estilista, *n.* stylist, master of style.
estilita, *a.* (eccl. hist.) stylite, pillarist; **(E-),** Stylites (St. Simeon).
estilizado, da, *a.* stylized.
estilizar, *va.* to stylize.
estilo, *m.* style (writing instrument); gnomon or style of a sun dial; (arch. and lit.) style; use, custom, fashion; (bot.) style.—**e. antiguo,** (chron.) old style.—**e. familiar,** colloquial style.—**e. nuevo,** (chron.) new style.—**al e. de,** in the style of.—**de e.,** usual, customary.—**por el e.,** or **por ese e.,** of that kind, like that.
estilóbato, *m.* (arch.) stylobate, pedestal.
estilográfico, ca. I. *a.* stylographic.—**pluma e.,** fountain pen. **II.** *f.* fountain pen.
estilógrafo, *m.* stylograph..
estiloideo, dea, *a.* (anat.) styloid.
estima, *f.* esteem, estimation; (naut.) dead reckoning.
estimabilidad, *f.* estimableness; worth.
estimabilísimo, ma, *a. super.* most estimable.
estimable, *a.* estimable, worthy; computable.
estimación, *f.* esteem, regard; estimate, valuation.—**e. propia,** self-respect.
estimador, ra, *n.* esteemer; estimator.
estimar, *va.* to estimate, value; to esteem, respect, honor; to judge, to think.
estimativa, *f.* power of judging; instinct.
estimulación, *f.* (med.) stimulation.
estimulante. I. *a.* stimulating, exciting. **II.** *m.* stimulant.
estimular, *va.* to stimulate; to goad, incite, encourage.
estímulo, *m.* stimulus; inducement; incitement; stimulation; encouragement.
estinco, *m.* skink, a kind of lizard.
estío, *m.* summer.
estiomenar, *va.* (med.) to mortify (flesh).
estiómeno, *m.* (med.) mortification, gangrene.
estipendiar, *va.* to give a stipend to.
estipendiario, ria, *a.* & *m.* stipendiary.
estipendio, *m.* stipend, salary, pay, fee.
estípite, *m.* (arch.) pilaster in the form of an inverted pyramid.
estipticar, *va.* (med.) to apply a styptic to.
estipticidad, *f.* (med.) stypticity.
estíptico, ca. I. *a.* styptic, astringent; costive; (fig.) miserly, stingy. **II.** *m.* styptic, astringent.
estiptiquez, *f.* (med.) (Am.) costiveness.
estípula, *f.* (bot.) stipule.
estipulación, *f.* stipulation, proviso, specification, requirement.
estipular, *va.* & *vn.* to stipulate, specify, covenant.
estira, *f.* knife used by curriers.
estiracáceo, cea, *a.* (bot.) styracaceous.
estiradamente, *adv.* scarcely; with difficulty; violently, forcibly.
estirado, da. I. *pp.* of ESTIRAR. **II.** *a.* stiff, stuck-

up; drawn.—**e. en frío,** (of metals) hard-drawn. **III.** *m.* stretching; drawing.
estirador, ra, *n.* stretcher; drawing frame.
estirajar, *va.* (coll.) = ESTIRAR.
estirajón, *m.* (coll.) = ESTIRÓN.
estiramiento, *m.* stretching, pulling; drawing (of metals).
estirar. I. *va.* to stretch, lengthen; to pull; to draw (metals).—**e. en frío,** to hard-draw. **II.** *vr.* to stretch; to put on airs.—**estirazar,** *va.* (coll.) = ESTIRAR.—**estirón,** *m.* strong pull; haul or hauling; rapid growth.
estirpe, *f.* stock, lineage, pedigree.
estítico, ca, *a.* = ESTÍPTICO.
estivada, *f.* burning of undergrowth.
estival, vo, va, *a.* summer (as *a.*).
esto, *pron. dem. neut.* this.—**e. es,** that is; that is to say.—**a e.,** hereto, hereunto.—**a todo e.,** meanwhile.—**con e.,** herewith.—**en e.,** at this juncture, point; at once, right away; herein, hereinto.—**por e.,** for this reason; on this account.—**por e. es por lo que,** (or, improperly but commonly, **por e. es que**), this is the reason, this is why.—**sobre e.,** hereon, hereupon.
estocada, *f.* stab, thrust, tilt, lunge.
estocafís, *m.* (com.) stockfish, dried cod.
estocástico, ca, *a.* (stat.) stochastic.
estofa, *f.* quilted silk stuff; quality, condition.
[1]**estofado, da. I.** *pp.* of [1]ESTOFAR. **II.** *a.* quilted; ornamented.
[2]**estofado,** *m.* stew.
estofador, *m.* quilter.
[1]**estofar,** *va.* to quilt; to paint on a gilt ground; to size before gilding.
[2]**estofar,** *va.* to stew.
estofo, *m.* quilting; painting on gilt; sizing.
estoicidad, *f.* imperturbability.
estoicismo, *m.* stoicism.
estoico, ca, *n.* & *a.* stoic(-al).
estola, *f.* stole, worn by priests.
estolidez, *f.* stupidity, incapacity.
estólido, da, *a.* stupid, foolish.
[1]**estolón,** *m. aug.* large stole.
[2]**estolón,** *m.* (bot.) stolon.
estoma, *m.* (bot.) stoma.
estomacal, *a.* stomachic.
estomagar, *vn.* & *va.* (*pret.* ESTOMAGUÉ; *subj.* ESTOMAGUE) to bore; to annoy, make angry.
estómago, *m.* stomach.—**tener buen e.,** or **mucho e.,** to ignore slights and offenses, to be thick-skinned; to have an elastic conscience.
estomagué, estomague, *v.* *V.* ESTOMAGAR.
estomaguero, *m.* baby's bellyband.
estomápodo, da, *a.* & *m.* (zool.) = ESTOMATÓPODO.
estomáquico, ca, *a.* stomachic, stomachichal.
estomatical, *a.* stomachic.
estomaticón, *m.* stomach plaster.
estomatitis, *f.* (med.) mouth inflammation, stomatitis.
estomatópodo, da, *a.* & *m.* (zool.) stomatopod.
estonio, nia; estoniano, na, *a.* & *n.* Est(h)onian.
estopa, *f.* tow; burlap; oakum.
estopada, *f.* quantity of tow for spinning.
estopear, *va.* to calk with oakum.
estopeño, ña, *a.* tow (as *a.*).
[1]**estoperol,** *m.* tow wick.
[2]**estoperol,** *m.* (naut.) scupper nail.
estopilla, *f.* finest part of hemp or flax; lawn, batiste, cheesecloth.
estopín, *m.* (artil.) priming tube; quick match.
estopón, *m.* coarse tow.
estopor, *m.* (naut.) stopper.
estoposo, sa, *a.* towlike, filaceous.
estoque, *m.* estoc, rapier; (bot.) corn flag; (bot.) gladiolus.
estoqueador, *m.* matador (bull fighter).
estoquear, *va.* to make a thrust at with a rapier.
estoqueo, *m.* thrusting or stabbing.
estor, *m.* shade, window shade.
estoraque, *m.* (bot.) officinal storax; gum of the storax tree.
estorbador, ra, *n.* & *a.* hinderer(-ing), obstructor(-ing).
estorbar, *va.* to hinder; obstruct; be in the way.
estorbo, *m.* hindrance, obstruction, nuisance.
estorboso, sa, *a.* hindering, in the way.
estornija, *f.* linchpin; washer; a boys' play.
estornino, *m.* (ornith.) starling.
estornudar, *vn.* to sneeze.—**estornudo,** *m.* sneeze.—**estornutatorio,** *m.* sneeze inducer.
estovar, *va.* to heat (meat) slowly.
estoy, *v* *V.* ESTAR.
estrábico, ca, *a.* strabismic.
estrabismo, *m.* (med.) strabismus, squint.
estrabotomía, *f.* (surg.) strabotomy.
estracilla, *f.* small rag; coarse brown paper blotting paper.
estrada, *f.* causeway, paved road.—**e. encubierta,** (mil.) covert way.
estradiota, *f.* a kind of lance.—**a la e.,** riding with long stirrups and stiff legs.
estradivario, *m.* (mus.) Stradivarius (violin).
estrado, *m.* drawing-room; drawing-room furniture; dais for a throne; baker's table; lecturing platform.—*pl.* court rooms.
estrafalariamente, *adv.* (coll.) carelessly, slovenly; wildly, queerly, strangely.
estrafalario, ria, *a.* queer, eccentric, odd; (coll.) slovenly.
estragador, ra, *a.* corrupting, destroying.
estragamiento, *m.* disorder, depravation.
estragar, *va.* (*pret.* ESTRAGUÉ; *subj.* ESTRAGUE) to deprave, vitiate, corrupt, spoil.
estrago, *m.* ravage, ruin, havoc; wickedness.
estragón, *m.* (bot.) tarragon wormwood.
estragué, estrague, *v.* *V.* ESTRAGAR.
estrambote, *m.* refrain of a song.
estrambóticamente, *adv.* oddly, queerly.
estrambótico, ca, *a.* odd, queer, eccentric.
estramonio, *m.* (bot.) fireweed, common thorn apple, stramonium.
estrangol, *m.* inflammation in a horse's tongue.
estrangul, *m.* (mus.) mouthpiece.
estrangulación, *f.* strangling; (surg.) strangulation; (steam eng.) throttling; (hydraul.) stoppage.
estrangulado, da, *a.* strangled, strangulated.
estrangulador, ra. I. *a.* strangling. **II.** *n.* strangler.
estrangular. I. *va.* to strangle, choke, throttle; (med.) to strangulate; (steam eng.) to throttle. **II.** *vr.* to strangle (oneself).
estraperlista, *n.* black marketeer.
estraperlo, *m.* black market.
estratagema, *f.* stratagem; trick, artful deception; craftiness; finesse; fetch.
estrategia, *f.* (mil.) strategy.
estratégico, ca. I. *a.* (mil.) strategic. **II.** *n.* Also **estratego, ga,** *n.* strategist.
estratificación, *f.* (geol.) stratification.
estratificar, *va.* & *vr.* (geol.) to stratify.
estratiforme, *a.* (geol.) stratiform.
estratigrafía, *f.* (geol.) stratigraphy.
estratigráfico, ca, *a.* (geol.) stratigraphical.
estrato, *m.* (geol.) stratum, layer; stratus (cloud).
estratosfera, *f.* (meteorol.) stratosphere.
estrave, *m.* (naut.) stem knee.
estraza, *f.* rag, fragment of cloth.
estrechamente, *adv.* narrowly; tightly, closely; intimately; nearly; hardly; exactly, punctually; strongly, forcibly; strictly; scantily, penuriously.
estrechamiento, *m.* tightening; narrowing; (econ.) bottleneck.
estrechar. I. *va.* to tighten; to narrow, reduce, contract; to take in (a coat, etc.); to constrain, compel; to press; to follow closely.—**e. la mano,** to shake hands; to greet; to send regards or good wishes. **II.** *vr.* to narrow; to bind oneself strictly; reduce one's expenses; to become related or intimate; to act in concert.
estrechez, *f.* narrowness; tightness; compactness, closeness; intimacy; austerity; penury, poverty; strait, pass, narrow passage.

estrecho, cha. I. *a.* narrow; tight; intimate, close; rigid, austere; exact, punctual; narrow-minded, illiberal, mean-spirited; poor, indigent, penurious; stingy, close.—**e. de conciencia,** overscrupulous, narrow-minded. II. *m.* Valentine; predicament, fix; (geog.) strait, channel.—**al e.,** by force, by compulsion.—**poner en e.,** to force.
estrechón, *m. aug.* (naut.) flapping, pitching, jerk.—**e. de manos,** handshake.
estrechura, *f.* narrowness, straitness; narrow passage, narrows; austerity; distress, predicament, straits; intimate familiarity.
estregadera, *f.* scrubbing brush, mop.
estregadero, *m.* object against which animals scratch themselves; place for washing clothes.
estregadura, *f.,* **estregamiento,** *m.* rubbing; scrubbing.
estregar, *va.* (*ind. pres.* ESTRIEGO, *pret.* ESTREGUÉ; *subj.* ESTRIEGUE) to rub; scour, scrub; scratch (as matches).
estregón, *m. aug.* rough rubbing.
estregué, *pret.* of ESTREGAR.
estrella, *f.* star; star wheel; (theat., etc.) star, lead; star (on a horse's forehead); (mil.) star fort.—**e. de mar,** starfish.—**e. de rabo,** comet.—**e. fija,** fixed star.—**e. fugaz,** shooting star.—**e. polar,** polestar, Polaris.—**con estrellas,** after nightfall, before sunrise.—**poner por las estrellas,** to lionize, to overpraise.—**ver. estrellas,** to feel racking pain; (fig.) to see stars.
estrellada, *f.* (bot.) lady's mantle.
estrelladera, *f.* (cook.) instrument for turning eggs, etc.
estrelladero, *m.* pan for candied yolks.
estrellado, da. I. *pp.* of ESTRELLAR. II. *a.* starry; (of horses) star-faced; fried (eggs).
estrellamar, *f.* (bot.) plantain; (ichth.) starfish.
[1]**estrellar.** I. *va.* (coll.) to dash to pieces, smash (up); to fry (eggs). II. *vr.* to fail; (**contra**) to crash or dash (against), be shattered (by) (with implication of failure, damage or destruction).
[2]**estrellar,** *a.* stellated, starry.
estrellero, ra, *a.* (of horses) tossing the head.
estrellica, ita, uela, *f. dim.* little star.
estrellón, *m aug.* large star; star-shaped piece in fireworks.
estremecedor, ra, *a.* frightful, terrifying.
estremecer. I. *va.* (*ind.* ESTREMEZCO; *subj.* ESTREMEZCA) to shake, to make tremble. II. *vr.* to shake, tremble, shudder.
estremecimiento, *m.* trembling, shaking; shudder, shuddering.
estremezco, estremezca, *v. V.* ESTREMECER.
estrena, *f.* gift; love offering, remembrance; first use of a thing; inauguration; début.
estrenar. I. *va.* to use or to do for the first time; to commence, inaugurate; (theat.) to open. II. *vr.* to begin to act in some capacity; (theat.) to make one's début; (of a play) to open.
estreno, *m.* commencement, good-luck gift, inauguration; (theat.) first performance; début.
estrenque, *m.* stout esparto rope.
estrenuidad, *f.* vigor, energy, enterprise.
estrenuo, nua, *a.* strong, vigorous; enterprising.
estreñido, da. I. *pp.* of ESTREÑIR. II. *a.* costive; stingy.
estreñimiento, *m.* costiveness.
estreñir. I. *va.* (*ind.* ESTRIÑO; *subj.* ESTRIÑA) to bind, constipate. II. *vr.* to become costive.
estrepada, *f.* (naut.) a pull in unison.
estrépito, *m.* crash, din, deafening noise.
estrepitoso, sa, *a.* noisy, deafening; boisterous, obstreperous.
estreptococia, *f.* (med.) infection by streptococci.
estreptococo, *m.* (bacteriol.) streptococcus.
estreptomicina, *f.* streptomycin.
estría, *f.* (arch.) fluting, stria, groove.
estriación, *f.* striation, striature.
estriado, da, *a.* striated.
estriadura, *f.* (arch.) fluting, grooving.
estriar. I. *va.* (arch.) to flute, to gutter. II. *vr.* to become grooved, striated.
estribación, *f.* (geog. and arch.) counterfort.
estribadero, *m.* prop, stay.
estribar, *vn.* (**en**) to rest (on); to be based (on) to lie (in).
estribera, *f.* stirrup (of a saddle or an arbalist).
estribería, *f.* stirrup factory or shop.
estriberón, *m.* stepping stone; (mil.) temporary road.
estribillo, *m.* burden or refrain of a song.
estribo, *m.* stirrup; step or footboard of a coach; (mech.) brace, stay, stirrup bolt; clasp of wheel rims; (arch.) buttress, abutment; (fig.) rest, support, basis; (carp.) cross prop, main brace; (geog.) counterfort.—**perder los estribos,** to talk nonsense; to lose one's head.
estribor, *m.* (naut.) starboard.
estricnina, *f.* (med.) strychnine.
estricote.—**al e.,** without rule or order.
estrictez, *f.* (Am.) strictness.
estricto, ta, *a.* strict.
estridencia, *f.* stridency.
estridente, *a.* obstreperous; strident.
estridor, *m.* noise, creak, screech.
estriduloso, sa, *a.* (med.) stridulous.
estriego, estriegue, *v. V.* ESTREGAR.
estrige, *f.* (ornith.) screech owl; vampire.
estrigilación, *f.* (med.) strigilation.
estriño, estriña, *v. V.* ESTREÑIR.
estro, *m.* (poet.) afflatus, inspiration.
estrobiliáceo, cea, *a.* (bot.) strobilaceous.
estróbilo, *m.* (bot.) strobile, cone.
estrobo, *m.* (naut.) loop formed with a short rope or cable; (aer.) grummet.
estrofa, *f.* (poet.) stanza.
estrógeno, *m.* (biochem.) estrogen.
estroma, *m.* (anat.) stroma.
estrombo, *m.* (zool.) strombus.
estromo, *m.* (bot.) stroma.
estrona, *f.* (biochem.) estrone.
estronciana, *f.* (chem.) strontia.
estroncianita, *f.* (min.) strontianite.
estroncio, *m.* (chem.) strontium.
estropajear, *va.* (mason.) to rub; to scrub.
estropajeo, *m.* (mason.) rubbing, scrubbing.
estropajo, *m.* mop; swab, dishcloth; esparto scrubbing broom; worthless thing.
estropajoso, sa, *a.* (coll.) ragged, slovenly; (coll.) tough (meat); (coll.) stammering.
estropear. I. *va.* to maim, cripple; to damage or spoil by rough usage; to spoil, ruin (a thing, plan, etc.); (mason.) to stir (mortar). II. *vr.* to be out of order, damaged.
estropeo, *m.* rough usage; injury or damage; fatigue, weariness.
estropicio, *m.* (coll.) breakage, crash (of tableware, etc.); needless turmoil.
estructura, *f.* structure; order, method.
estructural, *a.* structural.
estruendo, *m.* din, clangor, clamor, clatter; confusion, turmoil; pomp, ostentation.
estruendoso, sa, *a.* obstreperous, noisy, loud.
estrujadura, *f.,* **estrujamiento,** *m.* pressing, squeezing, crushing, rumpling.
estrujar, *va.* to press, squeeze, crush, rumple, mash, jam, bruise.—**estrujón,** *m.* last pressing of grapes; crush, squeeze, pressure, jam.
estruma, *f.* (med.) struma.
estrumoso, sa, *a.* strumous.
estuación, *f.* flow of the tide.
estuante, *a.* hot, boiling, glowing.
estuario, *m.* estuary, inlet.
estucador, *m.* stucco plasterer.
estucar, *va.* & *vn.* (mason.) to stucco.
estuco, *m.* stucco; plaster, scagliola.
estuche, *m.* case (as for jewelry, etc.); box, casket; étui, sheath (for scissors, etc.); cabinet; small comb; in card games, certain combination of cards; a clever, handy fellow.
estudiado, da, *a.* studied, elaborate; studious.
estudiador, ra, *a.* (coll.) very studious.

estudiantado, *m.* (Am.) students (collect.).
estudiante, *n.* student.
estudiantil, *a.* (coll.) of or pertaining to students.
estudiantino, na. I. *a.* (coll.) pertaining to or in the manner of students. **II.** *f.* strolling band of students.
estudiantón, *m. aug.* (coll.) grind.
estudiar, *va.* & *vn.* to study; (art) to copy.
estudio, *m.* study; investigation; discussion, paper (article, writing); college, school; library, reading room; studio.—*pl.* sciences, letters.—**estudios mayores,** higher studies.
estudiosidad, *f.* studiousness.
estudioso, sa, *a.* studious.
estufa, *f.* stove; heater; hothouse; drying chamber, dry bath; sweating room; small brasier.
estufador, *m.* stewpan.
estufero, estufista, *m.* stove maker.
estufilla, *f.* hand muff; foot stove; chafer.
estulticia, *f.* foolishness, silliness.
estulto, ta, *a.* foolish, silly.
estuosidad, *f.* burning, heat, glow.
estuoso, sa, *a.* hot, ardent, glowing.
estupefacción, *f.* stupefaction, numbness.
estupefaciente, *a.* & *m.* narcotic.
estupefactivo, va, *a.* stupefying.
estupefacto, ta, *a.* stupefied, motionless.
estupendo, da, *a.* stupendous, wonderful.
estúpidamente, *adv.* stupidly.
estupidez, *f.* stupidity.
estúpido, da, *a.* & *n.* stupid (person).
estupor, *m.* (med.) stupor; amazement.
estuprador, *m.* ravisher, violator.
estuprar, *va.* to ravish, violate.
estupro, *m.* ravishment, rape.
estuque, *m.* stucco.—**estuquería,** *f.* stuccoing; stucco work.—**estuquista,** *n.* stuccoer.
esturar, *va.* to dry by fire; overcook.
esturgar, *va.* to polish (delft ware).
esturión, *m.* (ichth.) sturgeon.
estuve, estuvo, *v. V.* ESTAR.
ésula, *f.* (bot.) leafy-branched spurge.
esviaje, *m.* (arch.) obliquity.
eta, *f.* eta (Greek letter).
etalaje, *m.* bosh (of a blast furnace).
etano, *m.* (chem.) ethane.
etapa, *f.* (mil.) ration given to troops in the field; stage; station, stop.
etcétera, etc., *f.* et cetera, etc., and so forth.
éter, *m.* (phys., chem.) ether; (poet.) the sky.
etéreo, rea, *a.* ethereal; (poet.) heavenly.
eterificación, *f.* (chem.) etherification.
eterificar, *va.* (chem.) to etherify, convert into ether.
eterismo, *m.* etherism, effect of excessive ether.
eterización, *f.* (med.) etherization.
eterizar, *va.* (med.) to etherize.
eternal, *a.* eternal.—**eternalmente,** *adv.* eternally; everlastingly.
eternicé, eternice, *v. V.* ETERNIZAR.
eternidad, *f.* eternity.
eternizar. I. *va.* (*pret.* ETERNICÉ; *subj.* ETERNICE) to eternize, perpetuate; to prolong indefinitely. **II.** *vr.* to be everlasting, (fig.) to be exceedingly slow, to stay forever.
eterno, na, *a.* eternal, everlasting.
etesio, *a.* (of winds) etesian, recurring yearly.
ética, *f.* ethics.
[1]**ético, ca. I.** *a.* ethical, moral. **II.** *n.* moralist.
[2]**ético, ca,** *a.* = HÉTICO, (med.) hectic, consumptive.
etileno, *m.* (chem.) ethylene.
etílico, ca, *a.* (chem.) ethylic.
etilo; *m.* (chem.) ethyl.
etimología, *f.* etymology.
etimológico, ca, *a.* etymological.
etimologista, *m.* etymologist.
etimologizar, *va.* to etymologize.
etimólogo, ga, *n.* etymologist.
etiología, *f.* (philos. and med.) etiology.
etíope, *a.* & *n.* Ethiopian, Ethiop.
Etiopía, *f.* Ethiopia.
etiópico, ca, *a.* Ethiopian, Ethiopic.
etiópide, *f.* (bot.) Ethiopian mullein, clary.
etiopio, pia, *a.* & *n.* Ethiopian.
etiqueta, *f.* etiquette, ceremony, formality; (com.) label.—**de e.,** ceremonious, formal.—**estar de e.,** to be distant, cool to each other.
etiquetero, ra, *a.* ceremonious, formal.
etiquez, *f.* = HETIQUEZ, (med.) consumption.
etites, *f.* (min.) eaglestone, ætites.
etmoides, *m.* (anat.) ethmoid.
étnico, ca, ethnic.
etnografía, *f.* ethnography.
etnográfico, ca, *a.* ethnographic.
etnógrafo, *m.* ethnographer.
etnología, *f.* ethnology.
etnológico, ca, *a.* ethnologic.
etnólogo, *m.* Ethnologist.
etología, *f.* ethology.
etrusco, ca, *n.* & *a.* Etruscan.
eubeo, a; euboico, ca, *n.* & *a.* **Eubœan, Euboic.**
eubolía, *f.* discretion in speech.
eucaína, *f.* (pharm.) eucaine.
eucalipto, *m.* (bot.) eucalyptus.
eucaliptol, *m.* eucalyptus oil.
eucaristía, *f.* Eucharist.
eucarístico, ca, *a.* Eucharistic.
euclídeo, a; euclidiano, na, *a.* **Euclidian.**
eucologio, *m.* (eccl.) euchologion.
eucósmido, *m.* (entom.) codling moth.
eucrasia, *f.* (med.) sound health.
eucrático, ca, *a.* (med.) in sound health.
eudemonismo, *m.* (philos.) eudemonism.
eudemonista, *n.* eudemonist.
eudiómetro, *m.* (chem.) eudiometer.
eufemismo, *m.* (rhet.) euphemism.
eufemístico, ca, *a.* euphemistic(al.
eufonía, *f.* euphony.
eufónico, ca, *a.* euphonic, euphonious.
eufonizar, *va.* to euphonize.
euforbiáceo, cea, *a.* (bot.) euphorbiaceous.
euforbio, *m.* (bot.) euphorbia, officinal spurge; (pharm.) euphorbium.
euforia, *f.* resistance to disease; (med.) euphoria, feeling well, sense of good health.
eufótida, *f.* (geol.) euphotide.
eufrasia, *f.* (bot.) eyebright.
eufuismo, *m.* euphuism.
eufuista, *n.* euphuist.
eugenesia, *f.* eugenics; eugenism.
eugenésico, ca, *a.* eugenic.
eugenol, *m.* (chem.) eugenol.
eunuco, *m.* eunuch.
eupatorio, *m.* (bot.) eupatorium.
eupepsia, *f.* eupepsy, good digestion.
eupéptico, ca, *n.* & *a.* digestive.
eurasio, sia, eurasiático, ca, *a.* & *n.* Eurasian.
eureka, *interj.* eureka! (I found it).
euritmia, *f.* (arch.) eurythmy.
eurítmico, ca, *a.* eurythmic.
euro, *m.* eurus, east wind.—**e. austro, or noto,** (poet.) southeast wind.
Europa, *f.* Europe.
europeizar, *va.* & *vn.* to Europeanize.
europeo, a, *n.* & *a.* European.
europio, *m.* (chem.) europium.
euscaro, ra; éusquero, ra, *n.* & *a.* **Basque;** Basque language.
éustilo, *m.* (arch.) eustyle.
eutanasia, *f.* euthanasia.
eutéctico, ca, *a.* (phys.) eutectic.
eutiquiano, na. *a.* Eutychian.
eutrapelia, eutropelia, *f.* moderation in pleasures; pastime, sport.
eutrapélico, ca; eutropélico, ca, *a.* moderate, temperate.
euxenita, *f.* (min.) euxenite.
evacuación, *f.* evacuation; exhaustion.
evacuado, da, *n.* evacuee.
evacuante, *a.* evacuant, evacuating.
evacuar, *va.* to empty, evacuate; to quit, vacate,

leave.—**e. un negocio,** or **una diligencia,** to transact a business; to do an errand.
evacuativo, va; evacuatorio, a, *a.* evacuative.
evadir. I. *va.* to evade, elude, avoid. **II.** *vr.* to escape, sneak away.
evaluación, *f.*, **evaluar,** *va.* = VALUACIÓN, etc.
evanescente, *a.* evanescent.
evangélico, ca, *a.* evangelical.
evangelio, *m.* gospel.—*pl.* gospel relic booklet worn by children around the neck.
evangelismo, *m.* evangelism.
evangelista, *m.* evangelist; gospel chanter.
evangelización, *f.* evangelization.
evangelizador, ra, *n.* & *a.* evangelizer(-ing).
evangelizar, *va.* to evangelize.
evaporable, *a.* evaporable.
evaporación, *f.* evaporation.
evaporador, ra, *a.* & *n.* evaporating(-or).
evaporar, *va.* & *vr.* to evaporate.
evaporatorio, ria, *a.* evaporative.
evaporizar, *va.* & *vr.* (*pret.* EVAPORICÉ; *subj.* EVAPORICE) to vaporize.
evasión, *f.*, **evasiva,** *f.* evasion; escape.
evasivamente, *adv.* evasively.
evasivo, va. I. *a.* evasive, elusive. **II.** *f.* evasion.
evección, *f.* (astr.) evection.
evento, *m.* event, contingency.
eventual, *a.* contingent; fortuitous.—**eventualidad,** *f.* contingency.—**eventualmente,** *adv.* by chance, fortuitously.
eversión, *f.* destruction, ruin.
evicción, *f.* eviction.
evidencia, *f.* evidence, proof; obviousness.
evidenciar, *va.* to prove, make evident.
evidente, *a.* evident.
evitable, *a.* avoidable, preventable.
evitación, *f.* avoidance.
evitar, *va.* to avoid; to shun; to spare; to prevent.
eviterno, na, *a.* imperishable, lasting.
evo, *m.* age, long time, æon; eternity.
evocación, *f.* evocation, evoking.
evocador, ra, *a.* evocative.
evocar, *va.* (*pret.* EVOQUÉ; *subj.* EVOQUE) to call out, evoke.
evolución, *f.* evolution; change (of conduct, policy, etc.); (mil., naut.) evolution, manœuvre.
evolucionar, *vn.* to change one's conduct, policy, etc., (mil., naut.) to perform evolutions or manœuvres; (biol., philos.) to evolve.
evolucionario, ria, *a.* evolutionary.
evolucionismo, *m.* evolutionism.
evolucionista. I. *a.* evolutionary, evolution (as *a.*). **II.** *n.* evolutionist.
evolutivo, va, *a.* evolutionary, evolution (as *a.*).
evolvente, *a.* (geom.) evolvent; (Cuba, coll.) of or pertaining to a person economically independent.
evoqué, evoque, *v. V.* EVOCAR.
evulsión, *f.* (surg.) evulsion.
ex, *prep. prefix,* ex, out, out of, off; formerly.
ex abrupto, *adv.* abruptly, violently.
exacción, *f.* exaction; impost, tax, levy.
exacerbación, *f.* exasperation; exacerbation.
exacerbar, *va.* to irritate, exasperate; exacerbate.
exactitud, *f.* exactness; punctuality; accuracy.
exacto, ta, *a.* exact; correct; accurate; precise; punctual; assiduous.
exactor, *m.* tax collector.
exaedro, *m.* (geom.) hexahedron.
exageración, *f.* exaggeration.
exagerador, ra, *n.* & *a.* exaggerator(-ing).
exagerante, *a.* exaggerating.
exagerar, *va.* to exaggerate.
exagerativo, va, *a.* exaggerating.
exagonal, *a.* hexagonal.
exágono, na. I. *a.* hexagonal. **II.** *m.* hexagon.
exaltación, *f.* exaltation, elevation; (chem.) sublimation.
exaltado, da, *a.* hot-headed; ultra-radical.
exaltamiento, *m.* exaltation; ultra-radicalism.
exaltar. I. *va.* to exalt, elevate, lift; to praise, extol. **II.** *vr.* to become excited.
examen, *m.* examination; inquiry; interrogatory; inspection, investigation, search; survey.—**e. de Rorschach,** (psych.) Rorschach test.—**e. final,** final examination.—**e. parcial,** midterm examination.
exámetro, *m.* = HEXÁMETRO, hexameter.
examinador, ra, *n.* & *a.* examiner(-ing).
examinando, *m.* one going up for examination.
examinante, *a.* examining.
examinar. I. *va.* to examine; to question; to investigate, inspect, search. **II.** *vr.* to take (an) examination(s).
exangüe, *a.* exsanguine, anæmic; weak.
exanimación, *f.* lifelessness.
exánime, *a.* spiritless, weak, lifeless.
exantema, *f.* (med.) exanthema, an eruptive disease.
exantemático, ca, *a.* exanthematic.
exasperación, *f.* exasperation.
exasperador, ra; exasperante, *a.* exasperating.
exasperar, *va.* to exasperate.
excandecencia, *f.* anger, passion.
excandecer. I. *va.* (*ind.* EXCANDEZCO; *subj.* EXCANDEZCA) to irritate, provoke, enrage. **II.** *vr.* to become angry.
excarcelación, *f.* (law) discharge (from custody).
excarcelar, *va.* to set (a prisoner) free.
ex cáthedra, *adv.* ex cathedra.
excava, *f.* (agr.) pit around the root of a plant.
excavación, *f.* excavation.
excavador, ra. I. *a.* excavating, digging. **II.** *n.* excavator, digger; *f.* excavator, power shovel.
excavar, *va.* to excavate, dig.
excedente. I. *a.* exceeding. **II.** *m.* (com.) surplus.
exceder. I. *va.* to exceed, surpass; to overstep. **II.** *vr.* to go too far; to forget oneself; to overstep one's authority.
excelencia, *f.* excellence, superiority; excellency (title).—**por e.,** par excellence.—**Su E.,** His Excellency.—**Vuestra E.,** Your Excellency.
excelente. I. *a.* excellent, first-rate.—*interj.* good! fine! **II.** *m.* Also **e. de la granada,** ancient Spanish gold coin.
excelentísimo, ma, *a. super.* most excellent.
excelsamente, *adv.* sublimely.
excelsitud, *f.* excelsitude, loftiness.
excelso, sa, *a.* elevated, sublime, lofty.—**el E.,** the Most High.
excentricidad, *f.* eccentricity.
excéntrico, ca. I. *a.* eccentric, eccentrical; odd, queer. **II.** *f.* (mech.) eccentric.
excepción, *f.* exception; (civil law) plea in defense, denying cause for action.
excepcional, *a.* exceptional, unusual.
excepcionar, *va.* (law) to deny the validity of or ground for (a legal action).
exceptivo, va, *a.* exceptive.
excepto, *adv.* excepting, except, with the exception of.
exceptuado, da, *a.* exclusive.
exceptuando, *prep.* excepting.
exceptuar, *va.* to except.
excerta, *f.* excerpt, extract, citation.
excesivo, va, *a.* excessive.
exceso, *m.* excess; (com.) surplus.—**e. de equipaje,** or **de peso,** baggage excess.—**en e.,** in excess; excessively, to excess.
excipiente, *m.* (pharm.) excipient.
excisión, *f.* (surg.) excision.
excitabilidad, *f.* excitability.
excitable, *a.* excitable.
excitación, *f.* excitation, exciting, excitement.—**e. impulsiva,** (rad.) impulse excitation.
excitado, da, *a.* excited.
excitador, *m.* (elec.) exciter.
excitante, *a.* exciting, excitant.
excitar. I. *va.* to excite, move, stir up, rouse; (elec.) to excite, energize. **II.** *vr.* to become excited, lose one's equanimity.
excitativo, va, *a.* exciting, excitative.
excitatriz, *f.* (elec.) exciter, exciting dynamo.
exclamación, *f.* exclamation.
exclamar, *vn.* to exclaim.

exclamativo, va; torio, ria, *a.* exclamatory.
exclaustración, *f.* secularization of monks.
exclaustrado, *m.* secularized monk.
exclaustrar, *va.* to secularize (monks).
excluir, *va.* (*pp.* EXCLUIDO, EXCLUSO; *ind.* EXCLUYO; *subj.* EXCLUYA) to exclude; to bar, debar.
exclusión, *f.* exclusion, shutting out, debarring.
exclusiva, *f.* refusal; rejection, exclusion; sole right or agency.
exclusivamente, *adv.* exclusively.
exclusive, *adv.* exclusively; exclusive, excluded.
exclusividad, *f.* exclusiveness; exclusivity.
exclusivismo, *m.* exclusivism.
exclusivista, *n.* & *a.* exclusivist(-ic), (of persons) exclusive.
exclusivo, va, *a.* exclusive.
excluso, *pp. irreg.* of EXCLUIR.
excluyo, excluya, *v. V.* EXCLUIR.
excogitable, *a.* imaginable, reasonable.
excogitar, *va.* to excogitate, meditate; find, invent, devise.
excomulgado, da. I. *pp.* of EXCOMULGAR. **II.** *a.* & *n.* excommunicated (person); wicked, perverse (person).
excomulgador, ra, *n.* excommunicator.
excomulgar, *va.* (*pret.* EXCOMULGUÉ; *subj.* EXCOMULGUE) to excommunicate; to anathematize, curse.
excomunión, *f.* excommunication.—**e. mayor,** anathema.
excoriación, *f.* excoriation, flaying.
excoriar, *va.* & *vr.* to excoriate, flay; skin.
excrecencia, *f.* excrescence, excrescency.
excreción, *f.* excretion.
excremental, *a.* = EXCREMENTICIO.
excrementar, *va.* to evacuate (the bowels).
excrementicio, cia, *a.* pertaining to excrement or excretion.
excremento, *m.* excrement; excretion.
excretar, *vn.* to excrete; eject the excrements.
excreto, ta, *a.* excreted, ejected.
excretorio, ria, *a.* excretory, excretive.
excrex, *m.* (*pl.* **excrez**) (law) increase of dower.
exculpación, *f.* exculpation; exoneration.
exculpador, ra, *a.* exculpatory.
exculpar, *va.* to exculpate; to exonerate.
excursión, *f.* excursion, trip, tour; (law) excussion, liquidation.
excursionista, *n.* excursionist.
excusa, *f.* excuse.
excusabaraja, *f.* basket with a cover.
excusable, *a.* excusable.
excusadamente, *adv.* unnecessarily.
excusado, da. I. *pp.* of EXCUSAR. **II.** *a.* exempted, privileged; unnecessary; reserved, set apart. **III.** *m.* ancient privilege of exemption from the payment of tithes; washroom; toilet.
excusador, ra. I. *a.* excusing. **II.** *n.* excuser; substitute, vicar.
excusalí, *m.* small apron.
excusar. I. *va.* to excuse; to exempt; to prevent, avoid, shun; to decline, refuse. **II.** *vr.* to excuse oneself; to apologize.
excusión, *f.* (law) excussion, attachment.
execrable, *a.* execrable.—**execrablemente,** *adv.* execrably.
execración, *f.* execration.
execrador, ra, *n.* & *a.* execrater(-ing).
execrando, da, *a.* execrable.
execrar, *va.* to execrate.—**execratorio, ria,** *a.* execratory.
exedra, *f.* (arch.) exedra.
exégesis, *f.* exegesis.
exégeta, *m.* exegete.
exegético, ca, *a.* exegetic, explanatory.
exención, *f.* exemption.
exentamente, *adv.* freely; frankly, clearly, simply, sincerely.
exentar. I. *va.* to exempt; to excuse. **II.** *vr.* to except oneself.
exento, ta. I. *pp. irreg.* of EXIMIR. **II.** *a.* exempt; free, freed, disengaged; clear, open, unobstructed. **III.** *m.* officer in the Spanish life-guards.
exequátur, *m.* exequatur.
exequias, *f. pl.* exequies, obsequies.
exequible, *a.* attainable.
exergo, *m.* (numis.) exergue.
exfoliación, *f.* exfoliation, scaling or peeling off.
exfoliar. I. *va.* to exfoliate. **II.** *vr.* to scale off.
exhalación, *f.* exhalation; bolt of lightning; shooting star; fume, vapor, emanation.
exhalador, ra, *n.* & *a.* exhaler(-ing).
exhalar. I. *va.* to exhale, breathe forth, emit. **II.** *vr.* to exhale, evaporate; to be exhausted by violent exercise.
exhaustivo, va, *a.* exhaustive.
exhausto, ta, *a.* exhausted.
exheredación, *f.* disinheritance.
exheredar, *va.* to disinherit.
exhibición, *f.* exhibition, exposition.
exhibicionismo, *m.* (psych.) exhibitionism.
exhibicionista, *n.* (psych.) exhibitionist.
exhibir. I. *va.* to exhibit, expose, display, show. **II.** *vr.* to exhibit oneself, call attention, show off.
exhilarante, *a.* exhilarating.
exhortación, *f.* exhortation, admonition.
exhortador, ra, *n.* & *a.* exhorter(-ing).
exhortar, *va.* to exhort, admonish.
exhortatorio, ria, *a.* exhortatory.
exhorto, *m.* (law) letters requisitorial.
exhumación, *f.* exhumation, disinterment.
exhumador, ra. I. *a.* of or pertaining to a burial. **II.** *n.* exhumer.
exhumar, *va.* to exhume, disinter, dig up.
exigencia, *f.* exigency; requirement; demand.
exigente, *a.* exacting.
exigible; exigidero, ra, *a.* exigible, requirable.
exigir, *va.* (*ind.* EXIJO; *subj.* EXIJA) to require; exact, demand; need; to urge.
exigüidad, *f.* exiguousness, scantiness, smallness.
exiguo, gua, *a.* exiguous, small, scanty.
exijo, exija, *v. V.* EXIGIR.
exilado, da, *a.* & *n.* = EXILIADO.
exilar, *va., vn.* & *vr.* = EXILIAR.
exiliado, da. I. *a.* exiled, banished. **II.** *n.* exile, expatriate.
exiliar. I. *va.* & *vn.* to exile, banish; to be exiled, be banished. **II.** *vr.* to go into exile.
exilio, *m.* exile.
eximente, *a.* exempting.
eximio, mia, *a.* famous, most excellent.
eximir, *va.* (*pp. irreg.* EXENTO) to exempt, excuse, except.
exinanición, *f.* inanition; debility.
exinanido, da, *a.* debilitated, very weak.
existencia, *f.* existence; life, being.—*pl.* (com.) stock in hand, goods.—**en e.,** (com.) in stock.
existencial, *a.* existential.
existencialismo, *m.* (philos.) existentialism.
existencialista, *a.* & *n.* existentialist.
existente, *a.* existing, extant, existent; (com.) on hand, in stock.
existimación, *f.* estimation, opinion.
existimar, *va.* to form an opinion of, to judge.
existir, *vn.* to exist, to be.
éxito, *m.* issue, result, end; (also **buen e.**) success.
exitoso, sa, *a.* successful, effective.
exodermo, *m.* (bot.) exoderm, ectoderm.
Éxodo, *m.* Exodus; (**é.**) exodus, emigration.
exoftalmia, *f.* (med.) exophthalmia.
exogamia, *f.* exogamy.
exógeno, na, *a.* exogenous.
exoneración, *f.* exoneration, exemption.
exonerar, *va.* to exonerate.
exonerativo, va, *a.* exonerative.
exorable, *a.* exorable, that can be persuaded.
exorar, *va.* to beg, entreat.
exorbitancia, *f.* exorbitance.
exorbitante, *a.* exorbitant, excessive.
exorcismo, *m.* exorcism.
exorcista, *n.* exorciser, exorcist.
exorcizante, *n.* & *a.* exorciser(-ing).
exorcizar, *va.* to exorcise.

exordio, *m.* exordium, beginning.
exornación, *f.* (rhet.) making flowery.
exornar, *va.* to adorn, embellish.
exosfera, *f.* (meteorol.) exosphere.
exosmosis, *f.* (phys., chem.) exosmosis.
exosmótico, ca, *a.* exosmotic.
exotérico, ca, *a.* exoteric, public, common.
exotérmico, ca, *a.* (chem.) exothermic, heat-evolving.
exoticidad, *f.* exoticism.
exoticismo, *m.* exoticism, exotism.
exótico, ca, *a.* exotic, foreign, extraneous.
exotiquez, *f.* exoticism.
expansibilidad, *f.* expansibility.
expansible, *a.* expansible.
expansión, *f.* expansion, extension.
expansivo, va, *a.* expansive; sociable, communicative.
expatriación, *f.* expatriation.
expatriado, da, *a.* & *n.* expatriate.
expatriar. I. *va.* to expatriate. **II.** *vr.* to emigrate, leave one's country.
expectable, *a.* conspicuous, eminent.
expectación, *f.* expectation, expectancy.
expectante, *a.* expectant.
expectativa, *f.* expectation, expectancy, hope; (law) expectancy, abeyance.
expectoración, expectoration; sputum.
expectorante, I. *a.* expectorating. **II.** *m.* (med.) expectorant.
expectorar, *va.* & *vn.* to expectorate.
expedición, *f.* expedition; despatch, speed, nimbleness, facility; (eccl.) pontifical brevet or bull; (mil.) expedition; excursion, jaunt, journey.
expedicionario, ria, *a.* expeditionary.
expedidor, ra, *n.* (com.) forwarding merchant, agent, shipper, sender, despatcher.
expediente, *m.* (law) action, proceedings; file of papers bearing on a case; despatch, course of business; expedient, measure, resource, means to an end; facility in the management of affairs; reason, motive, pretext; supply, provision.—**cubrir el e.,** to pretend, make believe to be doing something; to keep up appearances; save one's face.
expedienteo, *m.* (law) procedure, taking action on the papers or documents in the case; (coll.) entangling and confusing matters; red tape.
expedir, *va.* (*ind.* EXPIDO; *subj.* EXPIDA) to expedite, facilitate; to issue; to draw out; to ship, send.
expeditivo, va, *a.* expeditious, speedy, quick.
expedito, ta, *a.* prompt, expeditious, quick.
expeler, *va.* (*pp.* EXPELIDO, EXPULSO) to expel, eject, throw out.
expendedor, ra. I. *a.* spending. **II.** *n.* dealer, retailer, agent, seller; (law) distributor of counterfeit money.
expendeduría, *f.* shop where tobacco and other officially monopolized goods are sold.
expender, *va.* to expend, spend, lay out; to sell at retail, to deal in; (com.) to sell on commission; (law) to pass (counterfeit money or stolen goods).
expendición, *f.* retail selling; commission selling.
expendio, *m.* expense, outlay; consumption; (Am.) EXPENDICIÓN; (Am.) EXPENDEDURÍA.
expensar, *va.* (Am.) to defray the expense of.
expensas, *f. pl.* expenses, costs, charges.—**a e. de uno,** at one's own expense.
experiencia, *f.* experience; experiment, trial.
experimentación, *f.* experimentation.
experimentado, da. I. of EXPERIMENTAR. **II.** *a.* (of person) experienced.
experimentador, ra, *n.* experimenter.
experimental, *a.* experimental.
experimentar, *va.* to experience; to experiment, test, try.
experimento, *m.* experiment, test, trial.
experto, ta, *n.* & *a.* expert.
expiación, *f.* expiation, atonement; purification.
expiar, *va.* to expiate, atone for, make amends for; to purify.—**expiativo, va,** *a.* expiational.
expiatorio, ria, *a.* expiatory.
expido, expida, *v.* *V.* EXPEDIR.
expillo, *m.* (bot.) = MATRICARIA, feverfew.
expiración, *f.* expiration.
expirante, *a.* expiring.
expirar, *vn.* to expire, come to an end; to die.
explanación, *f.* explanation, elucidation; (Ry.) roadbed.
explanada, *f.* lawn; (fort.) esplanade, glacis; (artil.) platform.
explanar, *va.* to level, grade; explain, elucidate.
explayar. I. *va.* to extend, dilate, enlarge. **II.** *vr.* to dwell upon a subject; to be extended; to enjoy an outing.
expletivo, va, *n.* & *a.* expletive.
explicable, *a.* explicable, explainable.
explicación, *f.* explanation.
explicaderas, *f. pl.* (coll.) facility in explaining.
explicar. I. *va.* (*pret.* EXPLIQUÉ; *subj.* EXPLIQUE) to explain, expound, construe. **II.** *vr.* to explain oneself; to understand (the reason, cause).
explicativo, va, *a.* explicative, explanatory.
explícito, ta, *f.* explicit.
expliqué, explique, *v.* *V.* EXPLICAR.
explorable, *a.* explorable.
exploración, *f.* exploration; (phys.) scanning.
explorador, ra. I. *a.* exploring. **II.** *n.* explorer; *m.* Boy Scout; (Am.) frontiersman; (phys.) scanner; *f.* Girl Scout.
explorar, *va.* to explore; investigate, search into, examine; (mil.) to scout.
exploratorio, ria, *a.* exploratory, exploring.
explosión, *f.* explosion; outburst; (min.) blast.—**hacer e.,** (Am.) to explode.
explosivo, va, *n.* & *a.* explosive.
explosor, *m.* exploder; (radio) oscillator.
explotable, *a.* exploitable; (min.) workable.
explotación, *f.* exploitation; development, working (of a mine, etc.); plant, works; operation, running (of a factory, railroad,etc.).
explotador, ra, *n.* & *a.* exploiter(-ing).
explotar, *va.* to exploit; to work (a mine, etc.); to develop (mines, lands, etc.); to operate, run (a business, a railroad, etc.); to exploit (to one's own advantage); (Am.) to explode.
expoliación, *f.* spoliation.
expoliador, ra, *n.* & *a.* spoliator(-ing).
expoliar, *va.* to spoliate, despoil.
exponencial, *f.* & *a.* (math.) exponential.
exponente. I. *n.* & *a.* exponent. **II.** *m.* (math.) exponent.—**e. de un átomo,** atomic number.
exponer. I. *va.* (*pp.* EXPUESTO; *ind. pres.* EXPONGO, *pret.* EXPUSE, *fut.* EXPONDRÉ; *subj.* EXPONGA) to expose, show, lay bare; to expound, explain; to expose, put in danger, jeopardize; to expose, abandon (a child). **II.** *vr.* to run a risk, lay oneself open to.
exportable, *a.* exportable.
exportación, *f.* exportation, export.—**de e.,** export (as *a.*, as in *derechos de exportación*, export duties).
exportador, ra, *n.* & *a.* exporter(-ing).
exportar, *va.* to export.
exposición, *f.* exposition, statement; peril, risk, jeopardy; petition, claim; exposition, exhibition, fair; (drama) exposition; (arch.) situation, orientation.
exposímetro, *m.* (photog.) exposure meter.
expositivo, va, *a.* explanatory, expositive.
expósito, ta, *n.* & *a.* foundling.
expositor, ra, *n.* & *a.* expounder(-ing), exponent; exhibitor(-ing).
expremijo, *m.* cheese vat.
exprés. (Am. esp. Mex.) **I.** *n.* & *a.* express (train, etc.). **II.** *m.* transport company or office.
expresado, da, *a.* before-mentioned, aforesaid.
expresamente, *adv.* expressly; clearly.
expresar. I. *va.* (*pp.* EXPRESADO, EXPRESO) to express, state, tell; (art) to delineate, design. **II.** *vr.* to express oneself, to speak.

expresión, *f.* expression; declaration, statement; form; phrase, utterance; present, **gift**; expression, squeezing, pressing out (of oils, etc.).—*pl.* regards.
expresionismo, *m.* (f. a.) expressionism.
expresionista, *n.* & *a.* expressionist.
expresivamente, *adv.* expressively.
expresividad, *f.* expressivity.
expresivo, va, *a.* expressive; affectionate, kind.
expreso, sa. I. *pp. irreg.* of EXPRESAR. **II.** *a.* expressed; express, clear; express, fast (train, etc.). **III.** *m.* express (train).
exprimidera, *f.*, **exprimidero,** *m.*, squeezer.
exprimido, da, *pp.* & *a.* squeezed; dry.
exprimir, *va.* to squeeze, press out; to express (one's thoughts) vividly.
ex profeso, *adv.* on purpose, expressly.
expropiación, *f.* expropriation.
expropiar, *va.* to expropriate.
expuesto, ta. I. *pp. irreg.* of EXPONER. **II.** *a.* on display; exposed, liable; dangerous; in danger.
expugnable, *a.* (mil.) pregnable.
expugnación, *f.* (mil.) taking by storm.
expugnador, ra, *n.* & *a.* (mil.) (one) that takes by storm.
expugnar, *va.* (mil.) to take by storm.
expulsar, *va.* (*pp.* EXPULSADO, EXPULSO) (gen. of people) to expel, eject, drive out.
expulsión, *f.* expulsion, expelling, ejection.
expulsivo, va, *a.* expelling.
[1]**expulso, sa,** *pp. irreg.* of EXPELER.
[2]**expulso, sa,** *pp. irreg.* of EXPULSAR.
expulsor, ra, *n.* & *a.* expeller(-ing), ejector(-ing).
expurgación, *f.* expurgation; (coll.) purge (of people).
expurgador, ra, *n.* expurgator.
expurgar, *va.* (*pret.* EXPURGUÉ; *subj.* EXPURGUE) to expurgate, expunge, purge, purify.
expurgatorio, ria, *a.* expurgatory.—**índice e.,** (Rom. Cath.) Index Expurgatorius.
expurgo, *m.* expurgation, purification.
expuse, *pret.* of EXPONER.
exquisitez, *f.* exquisiteness.
exquisito, ta, *a.* exquisite, delicious.
éxtasi, éxtasis, *m.* ecstasy.
extasiado, da, *a.* enrapt.
extasiar, *va.* & *vr.* to delight; to enrapture.
extático, ca, *a.* ecstatic.
extemporal; extemporáneo, a, *a.* untimely, inopportune.—**extemporáneamente,** *adv.* untimely, inopportunely.
extender. I. *va.* & *vr.* (*pp.* EXTENDIDO, EXTENSO; *ind.* EXTIENDO; *subj.* EXTIENDA) to extend, enlarge, prolong, spread, expand, outstretch; to unfold, unfurl; to draw up or issue (a document); (com.) to extend, prolong. **II.** *vr.* to extend, reach; to stretch out; to enlarge upon, expatiate; to spread, become general or popular.
extendidamente, *adv.* extensively.
extendido, da, *a.* extended, elongated; extensive.
extensibilidad, *f.* extensibility.
extensible, *a.* extensible, extensile.
extensión, *f.* extension; extent, length; expanse; space, capacity; (logic, Mex. tel.) extension.
extensivo, va, *a.* ample.
extenso, sa. I. *pp. irreg.* of EXTENDER. **II.** *a.* extended, extensive, spacious; general, widely spread.—**por e.,** at length, with full particulars.
extensómetro, *m.* extensometer.
extensor, ra. I. *a.* extending. **II.** *m.* (anat.) extensor.
extenuación, *f.* attenuation; emaciation.
extenuado, da, *a.* emaciated, wasted.
extenuar. I. *va.* to emaciate, weaken. **II.** *vr.* to languish, waste away.
extenuativo, va, *a.* weakening, emaciating.
exterior. I. *a.* exterior; external, outside, outward; foreign (commerce, debt, etc.).—**lo e.,** the outside; outside things or matters; foreign affairs. **II.** *m.* outside; personal appearance; foreign (or overseas) countries.
exterioridad, *f.* exteriority; demeanor; show, pomp.
exteriorización, *f.* exteriorization, externalization.
exteriorizar. I. *va.* to externalize, make manifest. **II.** *vr.* to unbosom oneself.
exteriormente, *adv.* externally, outwardly.
exterminador, ra, *n.* & *a.* exterminator(-ing).
exterminar, *va.* to exterminate; to raze.
exterminio, *m.* extermination, ruin, destruction.
externado, *m.* day-student school or college.
externamente, *adv.* externally.
externo, na. I. *a.* external, outward; exterior (angle, etc.). **II.** *n.* day pupil.
extiendo, extienda, *v. V.* EXTENDER.
extinción, *f.* extinction; extinguishment; suppression, abolition; obliteration.
extingo, extinga, *v. V.* EXTINGUIR.
extinguible, *a.* extinguishable.
extinguido, da, *a.* extinguished; extinct.
extinguir, *va.* (*pp.* EXTINGUIDO, EXTINTO; *ind.* EXTINGO; *subj.* EXTINGA) to quench, extinguish, put out; to suppress, destroy.
extintivo, va, *a.* (law) extinguishing.
extinto, ta. I. *pp. irreg.* of EXTINGUIR. **II.** *a.* extinct; late, deceased.
extintor, *m.* fire extinguisher.
extirpación, *f.* extirpation, eradication.
extirpador, ra. I. *n.* & *a.* extirpator(-ing). **II.** *m.* (agr.) cultivator.
extirpar, *va.* to extirpate, root out, eradicate.
extorcionista, *n.* extortioner, extortionist.
extorsión, *f.* extortion, exaction; overcharge.
extorsionar, *va.* to extort.
extra, *n.* & *a.* (coll.) extra.—**e. de,** besides, in addition to.
extracción, *f.* extraction; lineage (gen. low, humble); drawing numbers in the lottery.
extracta, *f.* (law) true copy, extract.
extractador, ra, *n.* abstractor.
extractar, *va.* to abstract, epitomize, abridge.
extractivo, va, *a.* extractive.
extracto, *m.* abstract, summary; (pharm.) extract.—**e. de saturno,** white lead.
extractor, ra, *n.* & *a.* extractor(-ing).
extracurricular, *a.* extracurricular.
extradición, *f.* extradition.
extradós, *m.* (arch.) extrados.
extraente, *n.* & *a.* extractor(-ing).
extraer, *va.* (*ger.* EXTRAYENDO; *pp.* EXTRAÍDO; *ind. pres.* EXTRAIGO, *pret.* EXTRAJE; *subj.* EXTRAIGA) to extract, draw out, remove; (math.) to extract (a root); (law) to take a copy of; (chem.) to extract.
extraigo, extraje, etc., *v. V.* EXTRAER.
extrajudicial, *a.* extrajudicial.
extrajudicialmente, *adv.* extrajudicially.
extralimitarse, *vr.* to overstep one's authority; to take advantage of another's kindness.
extramundano, na, *a.* extramundane.
extramuros, *adv.* outside (a town), without.
extranjería, *f.* status of a foreigner.
extranjerismo, *m.* foreignism; (ling.) loan word.
extranjerizar. I. *vn.* to introduce foreign customs. **II.** *vr.* to act like a foreigner, adopt foreign ways.
extranjero, ra, *a.* & *n.* foreign(-er), alien.—**el e.,** foreign countries, abroad.—**estar en el e.,** to be abroad.—**irse al e.,** to go abroad.
extranjía, *f.* (coll.) = EXTRANJERÍA.
extranjis.—de e., (coll.) foreign; strange, unexpected.
extrañación, *f.*, **extrañamiento,** *m.* alienation; (law) banishment.
extrañar, *va.* to banish; to cut, ignore (a person); to estrange; to wonder at, find strange; to miss.
extrañeza, *f.* oddity, queerness; surprise, wonderment; estrangement.
extraño, ña. I. *a.* strange; foreign; extraneous. **II.** *n.* stranger; foreigner.
extraoficial, *a.* extraofficial, non-official.

extraordinario, a. I. *a.* extraordinary. **II.** *m.* extra dish at dinner; special courier.
extrasensorio, ria, *a.* extrasensory.
extraterritorial, *a.* extraterritorial.
extraterritorialidad, *f.* extraterritoriality.
extrauterino, na, *a.* extrauterine.
extravagancia, *f.* oddness; folly; freak.
extravagante. I. *a.* eccentric; unusual, queer, odd, grotesque. **II.** *f. pl.* (eccl.) extravagants.
extravasación, *f.* (med.) extravasation.
extravasarse, *vr.* to extravasate, exude.
extravenarse, *vr.* to exude through the veins.
extraviado, da. I. *pp.* of EXTRAVIAR. **II.** *a.* disorderly; (of places) unfrequented.
extraviar. I. *va.* to mislead, misguide; to misplace, mislay; to embezzle. **II.** *vr.* to go astray; to be off course; to miscarry (as a letter); to deviate, to err.
extravío, *m.* deviation; aberration; misconduct; misplacement.
extremadamente, *adv.* extremely.
extremadas, *f. pl.* time for making cheese.
extremado, da. I. *pp.* of EXTREMAR. **II.** *a.* extreme; consummate (in good or bad).
extremar. I. *va.* to carry to an extreme. **II.** *vr.* to exert oneself to the utmost, take special pains.
extremaunción, *f.* (eccl.) extreme unction.
extremeño, ña, *a.* Estremenian.
extremidad, *f.* extremity; end; edge, brink, border, brim; extreme or remotest part; (anat.) extremity.
extremismo, *m.* extremism, radicalism.
extremista, *n.* & *a.* extremist.
extremo, ma. I. *a.* extreme, last, terminal; furthest; greatest, of the highest degree, utmost. **II.** *m.* extreme, utmost point, highest degree; apex; furthest end, extremity; greatest care.—**con e.,** extremely, in the utmost degree.—**de e. a e.,** from one end to the other.—**en e.** = CON E.—**hacer extremos,** to express one's feelings with vehemence, to gush.—**por e.** or **por todo e.** = CON E.
extremoso, sa, *a.* extreme, vehement; very affectionate.
extrínsecamente, *adv.* extrinsically.
extrínseco, ca. *a.* extrinsic.
extroversión, *f.* (med., psych.) extroversion.
extrovertido, da, *a.* & *n.* extrovert.
extrusión, *f.* extrusion.
exuberancia, *f.* exuberance.
exuberante, *a.* exuberant.
exudación, *f.* exudation.
exudado, *m.* exudate.
exudar, *vn.* & *va.* to exude; to ooze out.
exulceración, *f.* (med.) exulceration.
exulcerar. I. *va.* (med.) to exulcerate, ulcerate. **II.** *vr.* to become ulcerated.
exultación, *f.* exultation, great joy.
exultar, *vn.* to exult, rejoice.
exutorio, *m.* (med.) exutory, issue.
exvoto, *m.* votive offering.
eyaculación, *f.* (physiol.) ejaculation, ejection.
eyacular, *va.* (physiol.) to ejaculate.
eyector, *m.* ejector (in fire arms).

F

F, f, *f.* f. seventh letter of the Spanish alphabet.
fa, *m.* (mus.) fa, F.
fabada, *f.* in Asturias, pork and beans.
fabianismo, *m.* Fabianism.
fabiano, na, *a.* & *n.* Fabian.
fábrica, *f.* fabric, fabrication; structure, building, pile; factory, works, mill, manufactory; stone or brick masonry; church funds (esp. for building repairs).—**f. piloto,** pilot plant.
fabricación, *f.* fabrication, fabric, make; construction, building; manufacture, manufacturing.—**f. en serie,** mass production.
fabricador, ra. I. *a.* fabricative, manufacturing. **II.** *n.* maker, manufacturer.
fabricante, *m.* maker, manufacturer.
fabricar, *va.* (*pret.* FABRIQUÉ; *subj.* FABRIQUE) to build, construct, frame; to manufacture, make; to fabricate, contrive, devise.
fabricoide, *m.* Fabrikoid (trademark), fabric resembling leather.
fabril, *a.* manufacturing.
fabriqué, fabrique, *v. V.* FABRICAR.
fabriquero, ra, *n.* manufacturer; church warden.
fabuco, *m.* (bot.) beech mast.
fábula, *f.* fable, fiction, legend, tale; rumor, report, common talk; story, falsehood.—**f. milesia,** Milesian tale.
fabulador, *m.* fabulist, author of fables.
fabulista, *n.* fabulist, writer of fables.
fabulosamente, *adv.* fabulously.
fabuloso, sa, *a.* fabulous; marvellous.
faca, *f.* jackknife used by seamen.
facción, *f.* faction, turbulent party; (mil.) battle; any act of military service.—*pl.* features, lineaments, physiognomy.—**f. de testamento,** (law) faculty of testating.
faccionario, ria, *a.* factional, partisan.
faccioso, sa. I. *a.* factious. **II.** *n.* rebel.
faceta, *f.* (jewel.) facet of a gem; (entom.) facet of an insect's eye.
facetada, *f.* (Mex.) flat or poor joke.
facial, *a.* facial; intuitive.—**ángulo f.,** facial angle.
facialmente, *adv.* intuitively.
facies, *f.* (med. & biol.) facies, characteristic appearance.
fácil, *a.* easy; facile; convenient, handy; probable, likely; docile; easily persuaded or seduced.—**f. de** (followed by *inf.*), easy to.
facilidad, *f.* ease, easiness, facility; ready compliance, convenience; opportunity.—*pl.*—**dar f.,** to facilitate.
facilitación, *f.* facilitation.
facilitar, *va.* to facilitate, expedite; to supply, deliver, afford.
facilitón, na, *n.* (coll.) one who assumes the position of making everything easy.
facineroso, sa. I. *a.* wicked, villainous. **II.** *n.* habitual criminal; villain, rascal.
facistol, *m.* faldstool; lectern, chorister's desk
facóquero, ra, *n.* wart hog.
facsímil, facsímile, *m.* facsimile.
factible, *a.* feasible, practicable.
facticio, cia, *a.* factitious, artificial.
factitivo, va, *a.* (gram.) factitive.
factor, *m.* factor, element, cause; (com.) factor, agent, commissioner; (mil.) victualler; (Ry.) baggagemaster; (math.) factor.—**f. de eficiencia,** (stat.) efficiency factor.—**f. Rh,** (biol.) Rh(esus) factor.
factoraje, *m.* agency; trading in a foreign country; entrepôt.
factoría, *f.* factory, plant; (com.) factorage.
factorial, *n.* (math.) factorial.
factótum, *m.* factotum, man of all work; busybody.
factura, *f.* (com.) invoice, bill; (art) handling.—**f. consular,** consular invoice.—**f. simulada, proforma,** invoice.
facturar, *va.* (com.) to invoice, to bill; (Ry.) to check (baggage).
fácula, *f.* (astr.) facula.
facultad, *f.* faculty; power, authority; science, art; (in a university) branch, school (as *facultad de derecho,* Law School); graduates (collect.); (med.) physiological power or ability; license, permission.—*pl.* fortune, wealth.—**facultades del alma,** mental faculties or powers.
facultar, *va.* to empower, authorize.
facultativo, va. I. *a.* facultative; optional; pertaining to a faculty. **II.** *n.* physician.
facundia, *f.* facundity, eloquence.
facundo, da, *a.* eloquent, fluent.
facha, *f.* (coll.) appearance, look, mien, face.—**f. a f.,** face to face.—**en f.** (naut.) lying to.

fachada, *f.* (arch.) façade; frontispiece of a book; (coll.) figure, build (of a person).—**hacer f. a,** to face, be in front of.
fachenda. I. *f.* (coll.) vanity, conceit. **II.** *n.* (coll.) vain, conceited person.
fachendear, *vn.* (coll.) to brag, boast.
fachendista, dón, na, doso, sa, *a.* conceited, vain, bluffing.
fachoso, sa, *a.* ill-favored, of ridiculous mien; (Mex.) conceited, bluffing.
fada, *f.* fairy, enchantress, witch; (bot.) small pippin apple.
faena, *f.* work, labor, task, toil; (Cuba, Guat., Mex.) extra or overtime work; (Chile) gang of workers; (Ecua.) morning work (in the country).—*pl.* business affairs.
faenero, ra, *n.* (Am.) farm hand.
faetón, *m.* phaeton.
fagocito, *m.* (biol.) phagocyte.
fagot, *m.* (mus.) bassoon, fagotto.
Fahrenheit, *a.* Fahrenheit (degrees temperature).—**escala F.,** Fahrenheit scale.
faisán, na, *n.* (ornith.) pheasant.
faja, *f.* band, bandage, roller, fillet; swathing band; sash; girdle; border; (geog.) zone; newspaper wrapper; (arch.) fascia, belt, fillet; (naut.) reef band.—**f. de desgarre,** (aer.) rip (-ping) panel, or strip.
fajadura, *f.* swathing, swaddling; (naut.) band round a rope.
fajamiento, *m.* rolling or swathing.
fajar, *va.* to swathe, swaddle; to band, belt, girdle.—**f. con,** (coll.) to fall on, to attack.
fajardo, *m.* meat pie, patty; vol-au-vent.
fajeado, da, *a.* banded, fasciated.
fajero, *m.* crochet swaddling band.
fajín, *m. dim.* small band or sash; general's sash.
fajina, *f.* toil, task, work; (agr.) shock, stook, rick of sheaves; fagot of brushwood; (mil.) bugle call; (fort.) fascine.
fajinada, *f.* (fort.) fascine work or revetment.
fajo, *m.* bundle; sheaf.—*pl.* swaddling clothes.
fajón, *m. aug.* large band, roller, or sash; plaster border.
falacia, *f.* deceit; perfidy; fallacy.
falange, *f.* (anat., mil.) phalanx; (pol.) (**F.**) Falange.
falangeta, *f.* (anat.) third phalanx.
falangia, *f.*, **falangio,** *m.* (entom.) phalangium, or daddy longlegs.
falangiano, na, *a.* (anat.) phalangeal.
falangio, *m.* *V.* FALANGIA.
falangista, *a.* & *n.* Falangist.
falansterio, *m.* phalanstery.
falárica, *f.* phalaric, fire dart.
fálaris, *f.* (ornith.) coot, scoter.
falaz, *a.* deceitful, perfidious; fallacious, deceptive.
falazmente, *adv.* deceitfully; fallaciously.
falbalá, *m.* flounce, furbelow; flap on the skirt of a coat.
falca, *f.* small wedge; (naut.) washboard.
falcado, da. I. *a.* hooked, falcated. **II.** *m.* scythed chariot.
falce, *f.* sickle, reaping hook; falchion.
falcidia, *f.* (law) Falcidian.
falcinelo, *m.* (ornith.) glossy ibis.
falcón, *m.* ancient small cannon; (ornith.) falcon.
falconete, *m.* falconet, small cannon.
falda, *f.* skirt, flap; the lap; incline, slope; loin (of beef, etc.); tasset, tuilles, in armor.—*pl.* (fig.) skirts, women.
faldamenta, faldamento, *m.* skirt.
faldar, *m.* tasset, tuille, in armor.
faldear, *va.* to skirt (a hill).
faldellín, *m.* overskirt; underskirt.
faldero, ra, *a.* pertaining to the lap; fond of women.
faldeta, *f. dim.* small skirt; covering cloth or canvas.
faldicorto, ta, *a.* having short skirts.
faldillas, *f. dim. pl.* skirts; coat tails.
faldistorio, *m.* bishop's stool.
faldón, *m. aug.* long flowing skirt, flap; coat tail; shirt tail; hanging drapery; flap of a saddle; top millstone; (arch.) gable; tympanum.
faldriquera, *f.* pocket.
falencia, *f.* misstatement, mistake.
falibilidad, *f.* fallibility.
falible, *a.* fallible.
fálico, ca, *a.* phallic.
falimiento, *m.* untruth, deceit, falsehood.
falismo, *m.* phallicism, phallism.
falo, *m.* (anat. & bot.) phallus.
falordía, *f.* story, fairy tale, fable.
falsa, *f.* garret; FALSILLA; (mus.) dissonance.
falsabraga, *f.* (fort.) low rampart.
falsada, *f.* irregular flight of birds.
falsamente, *adv.* falsely, untruly.
falsario, ria. I. *a.* falsifying, forging, counterfeiting. **II.** *n.* forger, counterfeiter, falsifier.
falsarregla, *f.* bevel square, bevel rule.
falseador, ra, *n.* forger, counterfeiter, falsifier.
falsear. I. *va.* to adulterate, counterfeit, falsify, forge; to pierce; (carp.) to bevel.—**f. la puerta,** (Am.) to open the door with a skeleton key or break the lock. **II.** *vn.* to slacken; (mus.) (of a string) to be false, out of tune.
falsedad, *f.* falsehood, lie; deceit, guile; perfidy, duplicity.
falseo, *m.* (mason. and carp.) bevelling.
falsete, *m.* spigot; small door; (mus.) falsetto voice.
falsía, *f.* = FALSEDAD.
falsificable, *a.* falsifiable.
falsificación, *f.* falsification, forgery.
falsificador, ra, *n.* falsifier, counterfeiter, forger.
falsificar, *va.* (*pret.* FALSIFIQUÉ; *subj.* FALSIFIQUE) to falsify, counterfeit, forge, adulterate.
falsilla, *f.* guide lines for writing.
falso, sa. I. *a.* false, untrue; incorrect; deceitful, dishonest; spurious, forged, counterfeit; sham, imitation, (coll.) phony; vicious (horses or mules); defective, false (weights or honeycombs); (mech.) temporary; unsubstantial.—**f. flete,** dead freight.—**f. posición,** (arith.) position (an old method of solution).—**f. testimonio,** false testimony; slander, libel; imposture.—**de f., en f.,** deceitfully, falsely; without proper safety or strength (in this sense, **sobre falso** also used). **II.** *m.* (sewing) facing, skirt binding.
falta, *f.* lack, want, absence, deficiency, shortage; fault, mistake; defect, flaw; fault, failing, shortcoming; offense, misdeed, misbehavior, misdemeanor; deficiency in the weight of coin; (law) default; (law) petty offense; (med.) absence of catamenia during pregnancy.—**f. de aceptación,** (com.) nonacceptance.—**f. de pago,** (com.) nonpayment.—**a f. de,** in want of, for lack of.—**hacer f.,** to be necessary; to be missing; to be missed; to be needed (diff. constr.: *Vd. me hace mucha falta,* I need you very much).—**¡no faltaba más!** of all things (people, etc.)!—**poner faltas a,** to find fault with.—**sin f.,** for sure; without fault.
faltante, *a.* wanting, lacking.
faltar, *vn.* to be wanting, lacking; to be needed; to fall short; to fail, falter, flinch; not to fulfil one's promise, not to perform one's engagement; to need, lack, be in want of (diff. constr.: *me faltan dos pesos,* I lack, *or* need, *or* am short, two dollars); to offend; to sin; to be absent or missing; to die; (naut.) to break, part, give way.—**f. a.,** to offend against, to break (an appointment, etc.); to be absent from; to be unfaithful to.—**f. a la verdad,** to speak untruthfully, to lie.—**f. al respeto a,** to treat disrespectfully.—**f. para** (used impersonally), to be lacking to (or for), to be . . . to (*falta un cuarto para las dos,* it is a quarter to two; *falta una semana para vencerse la letra,* it lacks a week for the draft to be due).—**f. poco para,** not to be long before; come near (diff. constr.: *falta poco para termi-*

nar, it will not be long before the end; *poco faltó para que la matasen*, she came near being killed). —**¡no faltaba más!** (coll.) that is the limit! that's the last straw! the idea! of course!
falto, ta, *a.* devoid; short; deficient, defective.
faltriquera, *f.* pocket.
falúa, *f.* (naut.) small boat, tender.
falucho, *m.* (naut.) felucca, lateener.
[1]**falla,** *f.* a sort of head covering.
[2]**falla,** *f.* fault, failure; (P. I.) fine paid by Indians for leaving work; (naut.) defect, deficiency; (geol.) fault, break, slide.
[1]**fallar,** *va.* (law) to pass sentence, render a verdict on.
[2]**fallar. I.** *va.* to ruff (at cards). **II.** *vn.* to fail, be deficient or wanting.
falleba, *f.* shutter bolt.
fallecer, *vn.* (*ind.* FALLEZCO; *subj.* FALLEZCA) to die; to fail, run out, expire.
fallecimiento, *m.* decease, death, demise.
fallezco, fallezca, *v. V.* FALLECER.
fallido, da. I. *a.* deceived, disappointed, frustrated. **II.** *a.* & *n.* (com.) bankrupt.
[1]**fallo,** *m.* (law) verdict, judgment, decision.
[2]**fallo, lla. I.** *a.* (at cards) lacking a card of the suit played. **II.** *m.* lack of a card of suit played.
fama, *f.* fame; report, rumor; reputation.—**es f.,** it is said.
famélico, ca, *a.* hungry, ravenous.
familia, *f.* family; household.
familiar. I. *a.* familiar; domestic; common, frequent; plain, homelike, unceremonious. **II.** *m.* domestic member of the household; servant, especially of the clergy; college servitor; bosom friend; relative; officer of the Inquisition; demon, familiar spirit.—*pl.* attendants, suite.
familiaricé, familiarice, *v. V.* FAMILIARIZAR.
familiaridad, *f.* familiarity.
familiarizar. I. *va.* (*pret.* FAMILIARICÉ; *subj.* FAMILIARICE) to make well known, to make popular; familiarize. **II.** *vr.* to accustom, habituate oneself; to become familiar.
famoso, sa, *a.* famous; (coll.) great, excellent.
fámula, *f.* (coll.) maidservant.
famular, *a.* domestic (servant).
famulato, famulicio, *m.* (servant's) occupation.
fámulo, *m.* famulus; (coll.) servant.
fanal, *m.* lighthouse; lantern; bell glass; candle screen.—**buque f.,** lightship.
fanáticamente, *adv.* fanatically.
fanático, ca, *n.* & *a.* fanatic; (sports) fan.
fanatismo, *m.* fanaticism.
fanatizador, ra, *n.* one who spreads fanaticism.
fanatizar, *va.* to make fanatical.
fandango, *m.* (dance) fandango; (coll.) brawl,
fandanguero, ra, *a.* frequenter of balls.
faneca, *f.* (ichth.) pout, whiting pout.
fanega, *f.* grain measure (about 1.60 bu.).—**f. de cacao,** 116 lbs. of cocoa.—**f. de sembradura,** ground necessary to sow a FANEGA of seed.—**f. de tierra,** a land measure (about 1.59 acres).
fanegada, *f.* = FANEGA DE TIERRA.—**a fanegadas,** in great plenty or abundance.
fanerógamo, ma, *a.* (bot.) phanerogamous, flowering.
fanfarrear, *vn.* to bully, brag, swagger.
fanfarria, *f.* (coll.) swagger, bluster; fanfare.
fanfarrón, rrona. I. *a.* (coll.) blustering, blustery, swaggering. **II.** *n.* blusterer, swaggerer, braggart; bully.
fanfarronada, *f.* fanfaronade, boast, brag, bluff.
fanfarronear, *vn.* to brag, boast.
fanfarronería, *f.* fanfaronade, bragging.
fanfurriña, *f.* (coll.) fit of the sulks.
fangal, fangar, *m.* slough, marsh, quagmire.
fango, *m.* mire, mud.—**fangoso, sa,** *a.* muddy, miry.
fantasear, *vn.* to fancy, to imagine.
fantasía, *f.* fantasy, fancy, imagination; caprice, whim, conceit; (coll.) vanity, conceit; (naut.) dead reckoning; (mus.) fantasia.—*pl.* string of pearls.
fantasioso, sa, *a.* (coll.) conceited, vain.
fantasma. I. *m.* phantom, ghost, apparition; vain, conceited person. **II.** *f.* scarecrow.
fantasmagoría, *f.* phantasmagoria.
fantasmagórico, ca, *a.* phantasmagoric.
fantasmón, na. I. *a. aug.* (coll.) enormously conceited. **II.** *m.* presumptuous coxcomb.
fantástico, ca, *a.* fantastic, fanciful; conceited.
fantoche, *m.* puppet; insignificant man.
fañado, da, *a.* one year old.
faquín, *m.* porter, carrier, laborer.
faquir, *m.* fakir.
fara, *f.* (zool.) an African serpent.
farachar, *va.* to beat (hemp).
farad, faradio, *m.* (elec.) farad.
farádico, ca, *a.* (elec.) faradic.
faradización, *f.* (med.) faradization.
faradizar, *va.* (med.) to faradize, treat with electricity.
faralá, *m.* flounce, ruffle, frill.
farallón, *m.* headland; cliff.
faramalla. I. *f.* (coll.) cajolery; (Chile) conceit, airs; trash, worthless thing. **II.** *n.* (coll.) cajoler. —**faramallero, ra, llón, na,** *n.* (coll.) cajoling tattler.
farandola, *f.* farandole (a dance).
farándula, *f.* profession of a low comedian; strolling troupe of players; (coll.) cajolement; show, conceit, ostentation.
farandulero, ra, *n.* comedian, player; (coll.) cajoler; boaster, vain person.
farandúlico, ca, *a.* pert. to strolling players.
Faraón, *m.* Pharoah: (**f-**), faro (card game).
faraónico, ca, *a.* Pharaonic.
faraute, *n.* trusted messenger; player who recites the prologue; (coll.) meddling person, busybody, butter-in.
[1]**farda,** *f.* ancient tax.
[2]**farda,** *f.* bundle of clothing.
[3]**farda,** *f.* (carp.) notch.
fardacho, *m.* (zool.) lizard.
fardaje, *m.* fardage, dunnage.
fardar, *va.* to furnish or supply with clothes.
fardel, *m.* bag, knapsack; parcel, bundle.
fardería, *f.* collection of packages, luggage.
fardo, *m.* bale, parcel, bundle; burden, load.
farellón, *m.* rocky headland, cliff.
farfalá, *f.* flounce, furbelow.
farfalloso, sa, *n.* & *a.* stutterer(-ing).
farfante; farfantón, na, *n.* (coll.) boasting babbler.
farfantonada, farfantonería, *f.* idle boast.
fárfara, *f.* (bot.) colt's-foot; shell membrane (of an egg).—**en f.,** immature, as an egg without a shell; unfinished, half done.
farfulla. I. *f.* (coll.) gibberish, gabble, jabber. **II.** *n.* (coll.) jabberer, gabbler.
farfulladamente, *adv.* hurriedly and recklessly.
farfullador, ra, *n.* & *a.* (coll.) jabberer(-ing).
farfullar, *vn.* (coll.) to gabble, to jabber, to gibber; (coll.) to act hurriedly.
farfullero, ra, *n.* gabbler, jabberer.
fargallón, na. I. *n.* (coll.) bungler, botcher. **II.** *a.* slovenly, untidy.
farillón, *m.* = FARALLÓN, headland, cliff.
farináceo, cea, *a.* farinaceous.
faringe, *f.* (anat.) pharynx.
faríngeo, gea, *a.* pharyngeal.
faringitis, *f.* (med.) pharyngitis.
faringoscopio, *m.* (med.) pharyngoscope.
farisaicamente, *adv.* pharisaically.
farisaico, ca, *a.* pharisaical, pharisaic.
farisaísmo, fariseísmo, *m.* pharisaism.
fariseo, *m.* Pharisee; hypocrite; (coll.) tall, lean, ugly person.
farmacéutico, ca. I. *a.* pharmaceutical. **II.** *m.* pharmacist, apothecary, druggist.
farmacia, *f.* pharmacy, drugstore, apothecary's; pharmaceutics (science).
farmacognosia, *f.* pharmacognosy.
farmacología, *f.* pharmacology.
farmacológico, ca, *a.* pharmacological.

farmacólogo, *m.* pharmacologist.
farmacopea, *f.* pharmacopœia.
farmacópola, *n.* apothecary, pharmacist, druggist, chemist.
farmacopólico, ca, *a.* pharmaceutical.
faro, *m.* lighthouse; beacon; (auto) light, headlight.—**f. aéreo,** air beacon.
farol, *m.* lantern, light; street lamp; conceited fellow; bluff, misleading.—**echar un f.,** to bluff.—**faroles de señales,** (naut.) signal lanterns.
farola, *f.* street light with several arms; big lantern; lighthouse.
farolear, *vn.* (coll.) to boast, brag.
faroleo, farolería, *f.* boast, bragging, show.
farolero, ra, *n.* lantern maker or seller; lamplighter; (coll.) strutting coxcomb.
farolillo de jardín, (bot.) Indian heartseed.
farolón, *n.* & *a.* boaster(-ing), braggart(-ing); (coll.) coxcomb, boaster; large lantern.
farota, *f.* brazen-faced woman.
farotón, na, *a.* (coll.) brazen-faced, cheeky.
farpa, *f.* pointed scallop on the edge of draperies.
farpado, da, *a.* scalloped, notched.
[1]**farra,** *f.* (ichth.) a kind of salmon.
[2]**farra,** *f.* (Arg., Bol., Chile) spree.
fárrago, farrago, *m.* farrago, medley.
farragoso, sa, *a.* full of confused ideas; full of confusion.
farraguista, *n.* person having the head full of confused ideas or half-digested knowledge.
farro, *m.* peeled barley; spelt wheat.
farsa, *f.* farce; company of players; a badly constructed play; sham, humbug.
farsanta, *f.* farce actress.
farsante, *m.* humbug, fraud; comedian.
farseto, *m.* quilted jacket.
farsista, *n.* writer of farces.
fas.—por f. o por nefas, justly or unjustly.
fascal, *m.* (agr.) shock, stook, rick.
fasces, *f. pl.* fasces.
fascial, *a.* (anat.) fascial.
fascicular, fasciculado, da, *a.* fascicular.
fascículo, *m.* (anat., print.) fascicle.
fascinación, *f.* fascination, enchantment.
fascinador, ra, *n.* & *a.* fascinator(-ing), charmer (-ing).
fascinante, *a.* fascinating, charming.
fascinar, *va.* to fascinate, bewitch, enchant; to deceive, allure.
fascismo, *m.* Fascism.
fascista, *a.* & *n.* Fascist.
fase, *f.* phase, aspect; (astr., elec.) phase.
fásoles, *m. pl.* (bot.) beans.
fastial, *m.* (arch.) crowning pyramid.
fastidiar. I. *va.* to sicken; to vex, annoy, bother, bore; to disappoint. **II.** *vr.* to weary; to become vexed, bored or displeased.
fastidio, *m.* squeamishness; dislike; weariness, ennui; nuisance, bother.
fastidiosamente, *adv.* squeamishly.
fastidioso, sa, *a.* squeamish, sickening; vexing, annoying; tedious, tiresome; displeased, annoyed.
fastigio, *m.* (arch.) fastigium; pinnacle, apex, top.
fasto, ta. I. *a.* happy (day or event). **II.** *m.* pomp, pageantry, show.—*pl.* fasti; annals.
fastoso, sa; fastuoso, sa, *a.* pompous, ostentatious.
fatal, *a.* fatal, unavoidable; unfortunate, fated.
fatalidad, *f.* (philos.) fatality, necessity; fate, destiny; fatality, calamity.
fatalismo, *n.* fatalism, determinism.
fatalista, *n.* & *a.* fatalist(-ic), determinist(-ic).
fatalmente, *adv.* fatedly, fatefully; necessarily, unavoidably; calamitously, unluckily; exceedingly bad, wretchedly.
fatídicamente, *adv.* prophetically.
fatídico, ca, *a.* fatidic, oracular, prophetic.
fatiga, *f.* fatigue, tiredness, weariness; hardship; anguish, anxiety; hard breathing.
fatigadamente, *adv.* with difficulty, with toil.
fatigador, ra, *a.* annoying; tiring.
fatigar. I. *va.* (*pret.* FATIGUÉ; *subj.* FATIGUE) to fatigue, tire; to annoy **II.** *vr.* to tire, get tired.
fatigosamente, *adv.* painfully, wearisomely.
fatigoso, sa, *a.* tiring; tiresome, boring; tired, fatigued.
fatigué, fatigue, *v. V.* FATIGAR.
fatimí, fatimita, *n.* Fatimite.
fatuidad, *f.* fatuity, foolishness; stupidity; conceit, vanity.
fatuo, tua, *a.* fatuous, stupid; pompous; vain.
fauces, *f. pl.* (anat.) fauces, gullet.
fauna, *f.* fauna.
fauno, *m.* faun.
fausto, ta. I. *a.* happy, fortunate. **II.** *m.* pomp, ostentation; great luxury.
faustoso, sa, *a.* = FASTUOSO, SA.
fautor, ra, *n.* abetter, helper, supporter.
fautoría, *f.* aid, assistance.
favo, *m.* (med.) favus, fungus disease of the skin; honeycomb.
favonio, *m.* westerly wind, zephyr.
favor, *m.* favor; help, aid, service; gift, grace; compliment; love token.—**a f. de,** in behalf of; in favor of; on account of; taking advantage of, aided by; under cover of.—**hacer el f. de,** (Am.) **f. de,** please (in a request).—**por f.,** please (in asking for something).
favorable, *a.* favorable.
favorecedor, ra, *a.* favorer; helper; client, customer.
favorecer, *va.* (*ind.* FAVOREZCO; *subj.* FAVOREZCA) to favor; to help, befriend; to abet; (of colors, clothes, etc.) to be becoming.
favoritismo, *m.* favoritism.
favorito, ta, *n.* & *a.* favorite.
faz, *f.* face; (arch.) front.—**f. a f.,** face to face.
fe, *f.* faith; faithfulness; testimony; credit, credence; promise given; certificate; testimonial; assertion, asseveration.—**f. de bautismo,** certificate of baptism.—**f. de casado,** certificate of marriage.—**f. de erratas,** (print.) errata, list or table of errors.—**f. de nacimiento,** birth certificate.—**f. de óbito,** death certificate.—**f. púnica,** Punic faith.—**a buena f.,** doubtless.—**a f.,** in truth, in good earnest.—**a f. mía,** by my faith.—**dar f.,** to give credit, to attest, to certify, to witness.—**de buena (mala) f.,** in good (bad) faith.—**en f.,** consequently.—**en f. de lo cual,** in witness whereof.—**por mi f.,** by my faith.—**tener f. a,** to have faith in.
fealdad, *f.* ugliness, homeliness; deformity; hideousness; turpitude, foulness.
feamente, *adv.* uglily, deformedly; unworthily, indecorously; brutally, inordinately.
febeo, bea, *a.* Phœbean.
feble. I. *a.* weak, feeble; (jewel) deficient in weight or quality. **II.** *m.* light coin.
feblemente, *adv.* feebly, weakly.
Febo, *m.* (poet.) Phœbus.
febrero, *m.* February.
febricitante, *a.* (med.) slightly feverish.
febrífugo, ga, *a.* & *m.* (med.) febrifuge.
febril, *a.* (med.) febrile, feverish.
febroniano, na, *a.* Febronian.
fecal, *a.* (med.) fæcal.
fécula, *f.* fecula; starch.
feculencia, *f.* feculence, dregs.
feculento, ta, *a.* containing fecula; feculent, foul.
feculoso, sa, *a.* starchy.
fecundable, *a.* capable of fecundation.
fecundación, *f.* fecundation, fertilization.
fecundar, *va.* to fertilize, fecundate, inseminate.
fecundativo, va, *a.* fecundating, fertilizing.
fecundidad, *f.* fecundity, fertility, fruitfulness.
fecundizar, *va.* to fecundate, fertilize.
fecundo, da, *a.* fecund, fruitful, fertile, prolific; abundant, copious.
fecha, *f.* date; standing.—**de la cruz a la f.,** from the beginning to the end.—**en próxima f.,** at an early date.—**hasta la f.,** to date.

fechador, *m.* dater; (Am.) post-office cancelling stamp.
fechar, *va.* to date (a letter, etc.).
fecho, cha, (obs.) *pp. irreg.* of FACER (= HACER): used only in official documents, meaning done, issued, or executed.
fechoría, *f.* misdeed, villainy.
federación, *f.* federation, confederation.
federal. I. *a.* federal. **II.** *m.* federalist.
federalismo, *m.* federalism
federal(ista), *a.* & *n.* federalist.
federalización, *f.* federalization.
federar, *va.* to federalize.
federativo, va, *a.* federative.
fehaciente, *a.* (law) authentic.
feldespático, ca, *a.* (min.) feldspathic.
feldespato, *m.* (min.) feldspar.
felice, *a.* (poet.) happy.
felicidad, *f.* felicity, happiness; good luck, good fortune.
felicitación, *f.* congratulations, felicitations.
felicitar, *va.* to congratulate, felicitate.
félido, da, *a.* & *m.* (zool.) feline.
feligrés, sa, *n.* parishioner.
feligresía, *f.* parish, parishioners.
felino, na, *n.* & *a.* feline.
feliz, *a.* happy, fortunate, felicitous.
felón, na, *n.* (law) felon, criminal.
felonía, *f.* treachery, disloyalty, felony.
felpa, *f.* plush; (coll.) reprimand, drubbing
felpado, da, *a.* plushy, shaggy, villous.
felpilla, *f.* chenille.
felposo, sa, *a.* felted; plush-covered.
felpudo, da. I. *a.* plushy. **II.** *m.* doormat.
femenil, *a.* feminine, womanish.
femenilmente, *adv.* effeminately, womanishly.
femenino, na, *a.* feminine; female.
fementidamente, *adv.* perfidiously.
fementido, da, *a.* false, unfaithful.
femineidad, *f.* femineity; (law) state of belonging to a woman (property).
feminismo, *m.* feminism, doctrine of the social and political equality of woman.
feminista, *n.* feminist, follower of feminism.
femoral, *a.* (anat.) femoral.
fémur, *m.* (anat.) femur.
fenacetina, *f.* (pharm.) phenacetin.
fenacina, *f.* (chem.) phenazine.
fenacita, *f.* (min.) phenacite.
fenaquistoscopio, *m.* (phys.) phenakistoscope.
fenda, *f.* crack in the bark of trees.
fendiente, *m.* gash, deep cut or wound.
fenecer. I. *va.* (*ind.* FENEZCO; *subj.* FENEZCA) to finish, conclude, close. **II.** *vn.* to die; to end.
fenecimiento, *m.* finish, termination, end; death.
feneco, *m.* (zool.) fennec.
fenestrado, da, *a.* fenestrate.
fenezco, fenezca, *v. V.* FENECER.
fenianismo, *m.* Fenianism.
feniano, na, *n.* & *a.* Fenian.
fenicar, *va.* to carbolize, put carbolic acid in or on.
fenicio, cia, *n.* & *a.* Phœnician.
fénico, ca, *a.* (chem.) phenylic, carbolic.
fenilacético, ca, *a.* phenylacetic.
fenilamina, *f.* (chem.) phenylamine.
fenileno, *m.* (chem.) phenylene.
fenilo, *m.* (chem.) phenyl.
fenix, *m.,* phœnix; model; king (in the sense of excellent or highest person).
fenobarbital, *m.* (pharm.) phenobarbital.
fenogreco, *m.* (bot.) fenugreek.
fenol, *n.* phenol.
fenolftaleína, *f.* phenolphthalein.
fenología, *f.* (biol.) phenology.
fenomenal, *a.* phenomenal, extraordinary.
fenomenalismo, *m.* (philos.) phenomenalism.
fenómeno, *m.* phenomenon; prodigy; (coll.) freak.
fenomenología, *f.* (philos.) phenomenology.
feo, ea. I. *a.* ugly homely; improper; heinous; serious, alarming.—**dejar,** or **hacer, f.,** to slight. **II.** *m.* slight, affront.
feote, ta; feotón, na, *a. aug.* exceedingly ugly.
feracidad, *f.* fruitfulness, fertility (of land).
feral, *a.* cruel, bloodthirsty.
feraz, *a.* fertile, fruitful; abundant, plentiful.
féretro, *m.* bier, coffin.
feria, *f.* market, fair, bazaar; gift bought at a fair; (eccl.) any week day (excepting Saturday or a feast day); holiday; rest, repose; (Mex.) small change (money).—**hacer f. de,** to display, boast.
feriado, da. I. *pp.* of FERIAR. **II.** *a.*—**día f.,** day when courts are not open; (Am.) holiday.
ferial. I. *a.* ferial. **II.** *m.* market, fair.
feriante, *n.* trader at fairs.
feriar. I. *va.* to trade, barter; to purchase at a fair; to give a gift bought at a fair. **II.** *vn.* to suspend work; to keep holidays.
ferino, na, *a.* wild, ferocious.—**tos f.,** whooping cough.
fermata, *f.* (mus.) pause or hold (𝄐).
fermentable, *a.* fermentable.
fermentación, *f.* fermentation.
fermentante, *a.* fermenting.
fermentar, *vn.* & *va.* to ferment.
fermentativo, va, *a.* fermentative.
fermento, *m.* ferment, leaven, leavening; (chem.) enzyme.
fermio, *m.* (chem.) fermium.
fernambuco, *m.* Pernambuco wood.
fernandina, *f.* a kind of linen stuff.
feroce, *a.* (poet.) ferocious.
ferocidad, *f.* ferocity.
feróstico, ca, *a.* (coll.) irritable, wayward.
feroz, *a.* ferocious, fell, fierce; ravenous.
ferozmente, *adv.* ferociously.
ferra, *f.* = [1]FARRA, (ichth.) a variety of salmon.
ferrada, *f.* iron-knobbed club.
ferrado, da. I. *a.* ferrate, iron-bound. **II.** *m.* a corn measure (between 13 and 16 liters); a land measure (between 4 and 6 acres).
ferrar, *va.* (*ind.* FIERRO; *subj.* FIERRE) to trim with iron.
ferrato, *m.* (chem.) ferrate.
férreo, rea, *a.* ferrous; iron (as *a.*), made of iron; harsh, stern, severe.—**vía férrea,** railroad.
ferrería, *f.* ironworks, foundry.
ferreruelo, *m.* short cloak without cape.
ferrete, *m.* sulphate of copper used to color glass; marking iron.
ferretear, *va.* to bind, mark, or work with iron.
ferretería, *f.* hardware; hardware shop.
ferretero, ra, *n.* hardware dealer.
ferricianhídrico, ca, *a.* ferricyanic.
ferriciánogeno, *m.* ferricyanogen.
ferricianuro, *m.* ferricyanide.
férrico, ca, *a.* containing iron; (chem.) ferric.
ferrífero, ra, *a.* ferriferous, iron-bearing.
ferrificarse, *vr.* to be converted into iron.
ferrizo, za, *a.* ferreous, iron (as *a.*), of iron.
ferro, *m.* (naut.) anchor.
ferrocalcita, *f.* (min.) ferrocalcite.
ferrocarril, *m.* railroad, railway.—**f. aéreo,** elevated railroad.—**f. de cable,** cable railway.—**f. de circunvalación,** belt, or girdle, railway.—**f. de cremallera,** rack railroad.—**f. de sangre,** animal-power railroad; horse tramway.—**f. de vapor,** steam railroad.—**f. eléctrico,** electric railroad.—**f. elevado,** elevated railroad.—**f. funicular,** cable railroad; ropeway.—**f. subterráneo,** underground railroad.—**f. urbano,** street railroad.
ferrocarrilero, ra, *a.* (Am.) = FERROVIARIO.
ferrociánogeno, *m.* ferrocyanogen.
ferrocianuro, *f.* ferrocyanide.
ferrocromo, *m.* (min.) ferrochrome, ferrochromium.
ferromagnético, ca, *a.* (phys.) ferromagnetic.
ferromanganeso, *m.* (min.) ferromanganese.
ferrón, *m.* ironworker.
ferroprusiato, *m.* (chem.) ferroprussiate.

ferrosilicio, *m.* (min.) ferrosilicon.
ferroso, sa, *a.* (chem.) ferrous.
ferrotipo, *m.* (photog.) ferrotype.
ferrovía, *f.* railway.—**ferrovial,** *a.* railroad (as *a.*); pert. to railroads.—**ferroviario, ria. I.** *a.* = FERROVIAL. **II.** *n.* railroad employee.
ferrugiento, ta, *a.* containing iron.
ferrugíneo, nea; ferruginoso, sa, *a.* ferruginous, iron-bearing.
fértil, *a.* fertile, fruitful; copious, plentiful.
fertilicé, fertilice, *v. V.* FERTILIZAR.
fertilidad, *f.* fertility; fruitfulness; abundance, plenty.
fertilización, *f.* (agr., biol.) fertilization.
fertilizador, ra, *a.* fertilizing.
fertilizante, *n.* & *a.* fertilizer(-ing).
fertilizar, *va.* (*pret.* FERTILICÉ; *subj.* FERTILICE) to fertilize, enrich, make fruitful.
fértilmente, *adv.* fruitfully.
férula, *f.* ferule; rule, yoke, authority; (surg.) splint; (bot.) ferula.
feruláceo, ea, *a.* ferulaceous.
ferventísimo, ma, *a. super.* very fervent or pious.
férvido, da, *a.* fervid, ardent.
ferviente, *a.* = FERVOROSO.
fervor, *m.* intense heat; fervor.
fervorcillo, *m. dim.* slight and brief fervor.
fervorizar, *va.* to heat, inflame, incite.
fervoroso, sa, *a.* fervent; active, efficient.
festejador, ra, *n.* & *a.* entertainer(-ing).
festejante, *a.* feasting, entertaining; wooing.
festejar, *va.* to entertain, to feast; to court, to woo, to make love to; to celebrate.
festejo, *m.* feast, entertainment; obsequiousness; courtship.
festero, ra, *n.* director of church music.
festín, *m.* feast, banquet.
festinación, *f.* speed, haste, hurry.
festinar, *va.* (Am.) to hasten.
festival, *m.* festival.
festividad, *f.* festivity; rejoicing, gaiety, merry-making; holiday; witticism.
festivo, va, *a.* festive, gay; humorous, witty; festival, festal.—**día f.,** holiday; (eccl.) holy day.
festón, *m.* garland, wreath, festoon.
festonar, festonear, *va.* to festoon.
fetación, *f.* fetation.
fetal, *a.* fetal, fœtal.
feticida. I. *n.* one committing feticide. **II.** *a.* feticidal.
feticidio, *m.* feticide.
fetiche, *m.* fetich, fetish.
fetichismo, *m.* (relig.) fetichism, fetishism.
fetichista. I. *a.* fetichistic. **II.** *n.* fetichist.
fetidez, *f.* fetidity.
fétido, da, *a.* fetid.
feto, *m.* fetus, fœtus.
fetor, *m.* = FETIDEZ.
feúco, ca, cho, cha, *a.* ugly, repulsive.
feudal, *a.* feudal.
feudalismo, *m.* feudalism.
feudatario, ria, *a.* & *n.* feudatory.
feudista, *m.* (law) feudist.
feudo, *m.* fief, feod, feoff.—**f. franco,** (law) freehold.
fez, *m.* fez, Turkish cap.
fiable, *a.* trustworthy, responsible.
fiado, da. I. *pp.* of FIAR. **II.** *m.*—**al f.,** on trust, on credit.—**en f.,** on bail.
fiador, ra. I. *n.* bondsman, guarantor, surety, bail.—**f. carcelero,** one who is bail or surety for a person.—**dar f.,** to give surety.—**salir f.,** to go surety. **II.** *m.* fastener; (mech.) stop, catch, pawl, click, trigger; tumbler of a lock; (falconry) creance.
fiambrar, *va.* to cook for cold cuts or lunch.
fiambre. I. *a.* served cold (as food). **II.** *m.* cold food, cold lunch; (coll.) old joke or piece of news, "chestnut."
fiambrera, *f.* lunch basket; dinner pail.
fianza, *f.* surety, bail, bond, caution, guarantee, security; suretyship.—**f. de aduana,** custom-house bond.—**f. juratoria,** parole.—**bajo f.,** on bail.
fiar. I. *va.* to answer or go surety for; to bail; to sell on trust, give credit for; to intrust, confide. **II.** *vn.* to confide; to sell on trust, give credit. —**ser de f.,** to be trustworthy. **III.** *vr.* **(de)** to have confidence (in), depend (on), trust.
fiasco, *m.* failure, fiasco.
fíat, *m.* consent; (law) fiat.
fibra, *f.* fibre, filament, staple; energy, stamina, vigor; (min.) vein of ore.—**f. acrílica** or **de vidrio,** Fiberglas.
fibrila, fibrilla, *f.* fibril.
fibriloso, sa, *a.* fibrillose.
fibrina, *f.* (biochem.) fibrin, fibrine.
fibrinógeno, *m.* (biochem.) fibrinogen.
fibrinoso, sa, *a.* fibrinous.
fibrocartílago, *m.* (anat.) fibrocartilage.
fibroideo, a, *a.* fibroid.
fibroma, *m.* (surg.) fibroma.
fibroso, sa, *a.* fibrous.
fíbula, *f.* (archeol.) fibula, pin.
ficción, *f.* fiction, invention; tale, story.
fice, *m.* (ichth.) whiting.
ficoideo, dea, *a.* & *f.* (bot.) ficoid.
ficología, *f.* (bot.) phycology.
ficticio, cia, *a.* fictitious.
ficto, ta. I. *pp. irreg.* of FINGIR. **II.** *a.* counterfeited, artificial.
ficha, *f.* (card games, etc.) chip, counter; domino; counter, marker; filing card.—**f. antropométrica,** anthropometric data, card or record.—**mala f.,** (of a person) bad character.—**fichar,** *va.* to take and record anthropometric data.
fichero, *m.* card index, file cabinet or case.
fidedigno, na, *a.* trustworthy; creditable.
fideero, ra, *n.* maker of FIDEOS.
fideicometido, da, *a.* trust (as *a.*).
fideicomisario, *m.* fideicommissioner.
fideicomiso, *m.* trust; feoffment to use.
fideísmo, *m.* (philos.) fideism, acceptance of faith as the foundation of truth.
fidelidad, *f.* fidelity, faithfulness; honor; fealty, loyalty.
fidelísimo, ma, *a. super.* of FIEL.
fideos, *m. pl.* vermicelli; spaghetti.
fiduciario, ria, *n.* & *a.* fiduciary; trusteeship.
fiebre, *f.* fever; intense excitement, heat of passion.—**f. aftosa,** foot and mouth disease.—**f. amarilla,** yellow fever; malaria.—**f. cerebral,** brain fever.—**f. de Malta** or **mediterránea,** Malta or Mediterranean fever. —**f. del oro,** gold fever.—**f. héctica,** hectic fever.—**f. intermitente,** intermittent fever.—**f. láctea,** milk fever, lacteal fever.—**f. miliar,** miliary fever.—**f. palúdica,** malaria. —**f. perniciosa,** pernicious intermittent fever. —**f. puerperal,** puerperal fever.—**f. remitente,** remittent fever.—**f. reumática,** rheumatic fever.—**f. tifoidea,** typhoid fever.
fiel. I. *a.* faithful, loyal, devoted; true, exact, accurate. **II.** *m.* public inspector, especially of weights and measures; pointer of a balance or steelyard; pin of the scissors.—**f. contraste,** official who weighs and stamps metals.—**f. de muelle,** wharfinger, owner or guardian of a wharf.—**f. de romana,** official inspector of meat weighing in slaughter houses.—**f. medidor,** inspector of measures.—**en f.,** equal weight, even balance.
fielato, fielazgo, *m.* office of the FIEL; octroi at a city's gates.
fieltro, *m.* felt; felt hat, overcoat or rug.
fiemo, *m.* (prov.) dung, manure.
fiera, *f.* wild beast; fierce; vicious animal or person; (bullfighting) bull; (coll.) exceedingly able, shrewd or cunning person; person strenuously or habitually given or devoted to something, "fiend."

fierabrás, *m.* (coll.) bully, blusterer; wayward, froward child.
fieramente, *adv.* fiercely, ferociously; haughtily.
fiereza, *f.* fierceness, ferocity; deformity.
fiero, ra. I. *a.* fierce, cruel; ferocious; ugly, deformed; rough, rude; haughty; huge, enormous; furious, terrible; wild, savage. **II.** *m. pl.* fierce threats and bravadoes.
[1]**fierro,** *m.* iron; brand.
[2]**fierro, fierre,** *v. V.* FERRAR.
fiesta, *f.* feast, entertainment, party; festivity, festival; holiday; (coll.) act of endearment or to attract attention.—**f. campestre,** country dance; (Am.) barn dance.—**f. de guardar** or **de precepto,** holy day, Mass day.—**f. fija** or **inmoble,** immovable feast.—**f. movible,** movable feast.—**aguar la f.,** (coll.) to mar one's pleasure.—**hacer f.,** to take a holiday.—**hacer fiestas,** to caress; to wheedle, to fawn to.—**por fin de f.,** to end, top off with. —**se acabó la f.,** (coll.) it's all over; drop it, let's drop it.
figle, *m.* (mus.) ophicleide, a wind instrument.
figón, *m.* eating house, chophouse.
figonero, ra, *n.* keeper of an eating house.
figulino, na, *a.* terra cotta (as *a.*).
figura. I. *f.* figure; shape; build; mien, looks; physique; face card or court card; silhouette; (law) form, mode; (mus.) musical note; (gram., rhet., geom.) figure.—**f. de bulto,** figure in sculpture; high relief.—**f. de retórica,** figure of speech. **II.** *m.* stiffly pompous person.
figurable, *a.* imaginable.
figuración, *f.* figuration.
figurado, da, *a.* figurative; rhetorical, ornate, florid.
figurante, ta. I. *m.* figurant. **II.** *f.* figurante.
figurar. I. *va.* to shape, fashion; to draw, sketch; to represent; to feign. **II.** *vn.* to figure, be conspicuous. **III.** *vr.* to fancy, imagine to occur, come to mind; to seem.
figurativo, va, *a.* figurative, typical; symbolical, emblematic.
figurería, *f.* grimace, affected gesture.
figurero, ra, *n.* (coll.) one who makes grimaces or affected gestures; maker of statuettes.
figurilla, ita, *f. dim.* (coll.) little insignificant person; (art) figurine, statuette.
figurín, *m.* fashion plate; lay figure.
figurón, *m. aug.* huge figure having a ridiculous appearance; (coll.) pretentious nobody.—**f. de proa,** (naut.) figurehead.
fija, *f.* door hinge; (mason.) trowel.
fijable, *a.* fixable.
fijación, *f.* stability, firmness; billposting; fixing; immobilizing; (psych.) fixation.
fijador, ra. I. *n.* & *a.* fixer(-ing); fastener(-ing). **II.** *m.* (mason.) pointer, workman that points the joints; (carp.) door and window setter; (photog. and art) fixing liquid; locking (plate, wire, pin, etc.).
fijamente, *adv.* firmly, assuredly; intensely, attentively; fixedly, steadfastly.
fijar. I. *va.* (*pp.* FIJADO, FIJO) to fix, fasten; to make fast, firm, or stable; to determine, settle, establish; clinch; to post (as bills); to fix (the eyes, the attention, etc.); (photog., art) to fix; to set (a date). **II.** *vr.* (**en**) to settle (in); to determine, resolve; to rivet one's attention (on); to take notice (of), pay attention (to).
fijativo, va, *a.* & *m.* fixative.
fijeza, *f.* firmness, stability; steadfastness.
fijo, ja. I. *pp. irreg.* of FIJAR. **II.** *a.* fixed; firm; settled; permanent; (mech.) stationary.—**a punto f.,** exactly; with certitude.—**de f.** certainly.—**hora f.,** time agreed on.
fil, *m.*—**f. derecho,** leapfrog.—**f. de roda,** (naut.) right ahead.—**estar en f.,** to be in line.
fila, *f.* tier, row, line, range; (mil.) rank.—**en f.,** in (a) line, in a row; (mil.) abreast.
filacteria, *f.* phylactery.
filadelfo, fa, *a.* & *n.* Philadelphian.
filadiz, *m.* floss silk.
filagrama, *f.* wire mold for a watermark.
filamento, *m.* filament, fibre, thread.
filamentoso, sa, *a.* filamentous, fibrous.
filandria, *f.* (zool.) filander, backworm.
filandro, *m.* (zool.) philander.
filantropía, *f.* philanthropy.
filantrópicamente, *adv.* philanthropically.
filantrópico, ca, *a.* philanthropic.
filántropo, pa, *n.* philanthropist.
filaria, *f.* (zool.) filaria, a parasitic worm.
filariasis, filariosis, *f.* (med.) filariasis, infection with filariæ.
filárico, ca, *a.* (med., zool.) filarial.
filarmonía, *f.* love of music.
filarmónico, ca, *a.* philharmonic.
filástica, *f.* (naut.) rope yarn.
filatelia, *f.* philately.
filatélico, ca, *a.* philatelic.
filatelista, *n.* philatelist.
filatería, *f.* verbosity, wordiness.
filatero, ra, *n.* verbose or wordy speaker.
filatura, *f.* spinning.
filderretor, *m.* superfine camlet, a rich fabric.
fileli, *m.* superfine flannel.
fileno, na, *a.* (coll.) delicate, small.
filete, *m.* (arch.) fillet, listel; (sewing) narrow hem; small spit for roasting; welt of a shoe; snaffle bit; (mech.) edge, border, rim; thread (of a screw); (print.) fillet, ornamental line; fillet (of meat or fish).
filetear, *va.* to fillet; to crease; to tool.
filetón, *m. aug.* (arch.) large fillet or listel; heavy bullion for embroidering.
filfa, *f.* (coll.) fib, hoax, fake.
filiación, *f.* filiation; connection, relationship; personal description; (mil.) regimental register.
filial, *a.* filial.—**filialmente,** *adv.* filially.
filiar. I. *va.* to register the pedigree and description of. **II.** *vr.* to enroll.
filibote, *m.* flyboat, light vessel.
filibusterismo, *m.* (Sp. hist,) filibusterism.
filibustero, *m.* (Sp. hist., not U. S. meaning) filibuster.
filicida, *n.* filicide, one who kills his child.
filicidio, *m.* filicide, killing a son or daughter.
filiforme, *a.* filiform.
filigrana, *f.* filigree, filigrane; spun work; watermark in paper; delicate, fanciful thing.
filillí, *m.* (coll.) fineness, neatness, delicacy.
filipéndula, *f.* (bot.) dropwort spiræa.
filipense, *n.* & *a.* Philippian.
filípica, *f.* Philippic; invective.
filipichín, *m.* moreen, woollen cloth.
Filipinas, *f. pl.* Philippines.
filipino, na, *n.* & *a.* Philippine.
filis, *m.* knack; trinket, charm.
filisteo, tea. I. *n.* & *a.* Philistine. **II.** *n.* (coll.) very tall and corpulent person.
filmación, *f.* (mov. pict.) filming, shooting.
filmar, *va.* to film, shoot (a moving picture).
filme, *m.* (movies, photog.) film.
filo, *m.* cutting edge, blade (of a knife); edge, ridge; line; (biol.) phyllum; (arch.) arris.
filocartista, *n.* collector of postal cards.
filodio, *m.* (bot.) phyllode.
filófago, ga, *a.* (entom.) phyllophagous.
filogenia, *f.* (biol.) phylogenesis, phylogeny.
filogénico, ca, *a.* phylogenetic, phylogenic.
filología, filológica, *f.* philology.
filológico, ca, *a.* philological.
filólogo, ga, *n.* philologist.
filomanía, *f.* (bot.) phyllomania.
filomela, filomena, *f.* nightingale, philomel.
filón, *m.* (geol.) vein, lode.
filópodo, da, *a.* & *m.* (zool.) phyllopod.
filoseda, *f.* vesting; silk and worsted or cotton cloth.
filosofador, ra, *n.* & *a.* philosophizer(-ing).
filosofar, *vn.* to philosophize.

filosofastro, *m.* philosophaster.
filosofía, *f.* philosophy.
filosófico, ca, *a.* philosophical, philosophic.
filosofismo, *m.* philosophism, spurious philosophy.
filosofista, *m.* philosophist.
filósofo, fa, *n.* philosopher.
filotaxia, *f.* (bot.) phyllotaxis.
filote, *m.* (Colomb.) silk (of ear of corn).
filoxera, *f.* phylloxera.
filtrable, *a.* filtrable, filterable.
filtración, *f.* filtration.
filtrador, ra. I. *n.* & *a.* filterer(-ing). **II.** *m.* filter.
filtrar. I. *va.* & *vn.* to filter. **II.** *vn.* to percolate, filter. **III.** *vr.* to leak out; disappear; to filter through.
[1]**filtro,** *m.* filter.—**f. de vacío,** vacuum filter.—**f. prensa,** filter press for refining sugar.
[2]**filtro,** *m.* philter, love potion.
fílum, *m.* (biol.) phyllum.
fillo, *m.* a sort of fritter.
fimbria, *f.* border of a skirt.
fimbriado, da, *a.* (bot., zool.) fimbri(c)ate(d.
fimo, *m.* dung, manure.
fimosis, *f.* (med.) phimosis.
fin, *m.* end, ending, conclusion; end, object, purpose.—**a f. de,** in order to, so as to.—**a f. de que,** so that, to the end that.—**a fines de,** towards or at the end of, late in (the week, etc.).—**al f.,** at last.—**al f. y a la postre,** or **al f. y al cabo,** at last; lastly; after all.—**en f.,** finally, lastly; in short; well (as expletive: *en fin, veremos,* well, we shall see).—**poner f. a,** to put an end to, stop, get rid of.—**por f.,** at last, finally.—**sin f.,** endless; numberless.
finado, da. I. *pp.* of FINAR. **II.** *a.* dead, deceased, late. **III.** *n.* deceased, dead person.
final. I. *a.* final; ultimate; conclusive. **II.** *m.* end, termination, conclusion.—*pl.* (sports) finals.
finalidad, *f.* finality; end pursued or attained.
finalista, *n.* follower of the doctrine of final causes; (sports) one playing in the finals.
finalizar. I. *va.* to finish, conclude; (law) to execute (a contract, deed). **II.** *vn.* to end, to be finished or concluded.
finamiento, *m.* death, decease, demise.
financiación, *f.,* **financiamiento,** *m.* (Am.) financing.
financiar, *va.* (Am.) to finance.
financiero, ra. I. *a.* financial. **II.** *m.* financier.
financista, *m.* & *f.,* (Am.) = FINANCIERO.
finanzas, *f. pl.* (Gal.) (Colomb.) public finances.
finar. I. *vn.* to die. **II.** *vr.* to long, yearn.
finca, *f.* real estate, land, house property; country estate, farm, ranch.
fincar, *vn.* & *vr.* (*pret.* FINQUÉ; *subj.* FINQUE) to buy or deal in real estate.—**f. la esperanza de,** to pin one's hopes on.
finchado, da, *a.* swelling with pride.
finés, sa, *a.* Finnic, Finnish.
fineza, *f.* fineness; goodness, purity; kindness, expression of regard, courtesy; friendly influence or assistance; keepsake, gift, favor.
fingido, da, *pp.* & *a.* feigned, dissembled.
fingidor, ra, *n.* & *a.* dissembler(-ing), feigner (-ing).
fingimiento, *m.* simulation, deceit, pretense.
fingir, *va.* & *vr.* (*pp.* FINGIDO, FICTO; *ind.* FINJO; *subj.* FINJA) to feign, dissemble, pretend, affect, sham; to fancy, imagine.
finible, *a.* capable of being finished.
finiquitar, *va.* to settle and close (an account).
finiquito, *m.* settlement of accounts; adjustment, release, quittance.
finítimo, ma, *a.* bordering, contiguous, near.
finito, ta, *a.* finite.
finjo, finja, *v. V.* FINGIR.
finlandés, desa, *a.* & *n.* Finnish, Finn.
Finlandia, *f.* Finland.
fino, na, *a.* fine; perfect, pure; thin, sheer; slender, subtle; delicate, nice; affectionate, true; sagacious, cunning, shrewd; sharp (as a point); courteous, polite; refined (as gold); (naut.) sharp.
finqué, finque, *v. V.* FINCAR.
[1]**finta,** *f.* an ancient tax.
[2]**finta,** *f.* (fencing) feint.
finura, *f.* fineness; purity; politeness; courtesy.
fiñana, *m.* black-bearded wheat.
fiordo, *m.* fiord.
fique, *m.* (Mex., Colomb., Venez.) = CABUYA, sisal (cord).
firma, *f.* signature; sign manual, hand (as hand and seal); subscription; act of signing; (com.) firm, house; firm name.—**f. en blanco,** blank endorsement; full powers.—**buena f.,** reliable firm or house.—**dar,** or **llevar, la f.,** to empower or be empowered to sign the firm name.
firmamento, *m.* firmament, sky.
firmán, *m.* firman, an edict.
firmante, *n.* signer, subscriber.
firmar, *va., vn.* & *vr.* to sign.—**f. en blanco,** to give a blank endorsement.
firme. I. *a.* firm, stable, solid; hard, compact; unswerving, stanch, unyielding.—**estar en lo f.,** to be certain or positive, in the right. **II.** *m.* groundwork, bed, foundation; ballast or gravel bed on a road; roadbed.—**de f.,** steadily; solidly; violently, strongly.—**en f.,** definitive, final, in final form. **III.** *adv.* firmly, strongly.
firmeza, *f.* firmness, stability; hardness, compactness.
firmón, na, *n.* one who signs another's work.
fiscal. I. *a.* fiscal. **II.** *m.* attorney-general; district attorney, public prosecutor; (coll.) intermeddler, prier.
fiscalía, *f.* office and business of a FISCAL.
fiscalicé, fiscalice, *v. V.* FISCALIZAR.
fiscalización, *f.* discharge of a FISCAL's duties.
fiscalizador, ra. I. *a.* acting as a FISCAL. **II.** *n.* prier, censurer, faultfinder.
fiscalizar, *va.* (*pret.* FISCALICÉ; *subj.* FISCALICE) to prosecute; to criticise, censure.
fisco, *m.* national treasury, exchequer.
[1]**fisga,** *f.* grain or bread of spelt wheat.
[2]**fisga,** *f.* harpoon; raillery, banter, chaff.
fisgador, ra, *n.* harpooner; banterer.
fisgar, *vn.* to chaff, banter; to fish with a harpoon; to peep, to pry.
fisgón, na, *n.* banterer, chaffer, jester; prier.
fisgonear, *vn.* to pry habitually.
fisgoneo, *m.* habitual or frequent prying.
físico, ca. I. *a.* physical. **II.** *n.* physicist; physician; military or naval surgeon; physique; (coll.) face; *f.* physics.—**f. nuclear,** nuclear physics.
fisicoquímico, ca. I. *a.* physicochemical. **II.** *f.* physical chemistry.
físil, *a.* fissile.
fisiocracia, *f.* physiocracy, a system of pol. econ.
fisiócrata, *n.* physiocrat.
fisiografía, *f.* physiography.
fisiográfico, ca, *a.* physiographic(al.
fisiógrafo, *m.* physiographer.
fisiologia, *f.* physiology.
fisiológicamente, *adv.* physiologically.
fisiológico, ca, *a.* physiological.
fisiologista, fisiólogo, *m.* physiologist.
fisión, *f.* (phys.) fission.—**f. nuclear,** nuclear fission.
fisionable, *a.* fissionable.
fisionar, *va.* & *vr.* to fission, split.
fisionomia, *f.* physiognomy, appearance, looks, features.
fisioterapia, *f.* (med.) physiotherapy.
fisiparidad, *f.* (biol.) fissiparity.
fisíparo, ra, *a.* (biol.) fissiparous.
fisípedo, da, *a.* (zool.) fissipedal.
fisirrostro, ra. I. *a.* (zool.) fissirostral. **II.** *m. pl.* Fissirostres.
fisonomía, *f.* = FISIONOMÍA.
fisonómico, ca, *a.* physiognomical.

fisonomista, fisónomo, *m.* physiognomist.
fistol, *m.* crafty person; shrewd gambler; (Mex.) scarf pin.
fístola, fístula, *f.* water pipe or conduit; (mus.) reed or pipe; (surg.) fistula.
fistular, *a.* (med.) fistular, fistulous.
fistuloso, sa, *a.* fistulous.
fisura, *f.* (geol.) fissure, cleft; (surg.) fissure of bone, or "green-stick" fracture; (surg.) fissure in the anus.—**fisurar,** *vn.* (Am.) to split.
fitófago, ga, *a.* phytophagous, herbivorous.
fitogeografía, *f.* phytogeography.
fitografía, *f.* (bot.) phytography, description of plants.
fitográfico, ca, *a.* pertaining to phytography.
fitógrafo, *m.* phytographer.
fitología, *f.* phytology, botany.
fitonomía, *f.* (bot.) phytonomy.
fitotecnia, *f.* applied botany (in industry, dietetics).
fitotomía, *f.* phytotomy, vegetable anatomy.
fitotoxina, *f.* (bot.) phytotoxin.
flabelífero, ra, *a.* fan-carrying (in ceremonies).
flabeliforme, *a.* flabelliform, fan-shaped.
flabelo, *m.* (eccl.) flabellum.
flaccidez, *f.* flaccidity, laxness, limberness.
fláccido, da, *a.* flaccid, limber, lax, soft; (auto) low pressure, balloon (tire); (aer.) nonrigid (airship).
flaco, ca. I. *a.* thin, lean; feeble, languid; frail, weak of resolution.—**f. de memoria,** short of memory. **II.** *m.* weak point, weakness.
flacucho, cha, *a.* rather thin or lank.
flacura, *f.* thinness, lack of flesh, leanness.
flagelación, *f.* flagellation, scourging.
flagelador, ra, *n.* flagellator.
flagelante, *n.* & *a.* flagellant(-ing).
flagelar, *va.* to scourge, flagellate, whip.
flageliforme, *a.* flagelliform.
flagelo, *m.* lash, scourge; flagellum.
flagrancia, *f.* flagrancy.
flagrante, *a.* resplendent; present.—**en f.,** flagrante delicto, in the very act.
flagrar, *vn.* (poet.) to burn, glow, shine.
flama, *f.* flame, excessive ardor.
flamante, *a.* flaming, bright, resplendent; brand-new, fresh, spick and span.
flamear, *vn.* to flame, blaze; (naut.) (of sails) to flutter.
flamen, *m.* (Rom. hist.) flamen, a priest.—**f. dial,** flamen Dialis.—**f. marcial,** flamen Martialis.—**f. quirinal,** flamen quirinalis.
flamenco, ca. I. *a.* & *n.* Flemish; Andalusian (dance, song, etc.). **II.** *m.* (ornith.) flamingo.
flamenquilla, *f.* small platter; (bot.) marigold.
flámeo, *m.* ancient bridal veil.
flamero, *m.* torch holder.
flamígero, ra, *a.* (poet.) flammiferous.
flámula, *f.* (naut.) streamer, pennon.
flan, *m.* flan, rich custard.
flanco, *m.* side; (mil. and fort.) flank.
flanear, *vn.* to stroll, amble.
flanquear, *va.* (mil. and fort.) to flank.
flanqueo, *m.* (mil.) flank attack, flanking.
flaquear, *vn.* to flag, weaken; to become weak; to threaten ruin or downfall.
flaqueza, *f.* leanness, thinness, emaciation; feebleness, weakness; frailty, foible; flagginess.
flato, *m.* (med.) flatus, windiness.
flatoso, sa, *a.* (med.) subject to flatus.
flatulencia, *f.* flatulence, windiness; (med.) pneumatosis.
flatulento, ta, *a.* flatulent, windy.
flatuoso, sa, *a.* = FLATOSO.
flauta, *f.* (mus.) flute.—**f. travesera,** German flute.
flautado, da. I. *a.* fluted, flutelike. **II.** *m.* flute stop in an organ.
flauteado, da, *a.* (of voice) flutelike, soft and sweet.
flautero, ra, *n.* flute maker.
flautillo, *m.* = CARAMILLO, flageolet.
flautín, *m.* (mus.) octave flute, piccolo.
flautista, *n.* flutist, flautist, flute player.
flavo, va, *a.* fallow.
flébil, *a.* deplorable, lamentable.
flebitis, *f.* phlebitis, inflammation of a vein.
flebotomía, *f.* phlebotomy, bloodletting.
flebotomiano, na, *n.* phlebotomist.
fleco, *m.* fringe, purl, flounce.
flecha, *f.* arrow, dart; (fort.) work of two faces and two sides; (naut.) front piece of the cut-water; (eng., arch.) maximum ordinate; deflection (as of a beam).
flechador, *m.* archer.
flechaduras, *f. pl.* (naut.) ratlines.
flechar. I. *va.* to dart, to shoot (an arrow or dart); to strike with an arrow; (coll.) to inspire sudden love; (Mex.) to point out, without fear, in gambling. **II.** *vn.* to make a bow ready to shoot.
flechaste, *m.* (naut.) ratline.
flechazo, *m.* stroke with a dart or arrow.
flechera, *f.* (Am.) long, sharp canoe.
flechería, *f.* shower of arrows.
flechero, ra, *n.* archer, bowman; arrow maker.
flegmasía, *f.* (med.) phlegmasia, inflammation.
fleje, *m.* iron hoop or strap.—**flejes para aros,** hoop poles.
flema, *f.* (physiol., fig.) phlegm.
flemático, ca, *a.* phlegmatic.
fleme, *f.* (vet.) fleam.
flemón, *m.* (med.) gumboil; phlegmasia, inflammation of cellular tissue.
flemonoso, sa, *a.* pertaining to gumboils or phlegmasia.
flemoso, sa, *a.* mucous, phlegmy.
flemudo, da, *a.* phlegmatic.
flequezuelo, *m. dim.* narrow fringe.
flequillo, *m. dim.* (of haircut) bang, fringe.
fletador, ra, *n.* (com.) freighter, charterer.
fletamento, *m.* (com.) charter, charterage, charter party.
fletar, *va.* to freight or charter (a ship).
flete, *m.* freight, freightage; freight (charges); cargo, load.
flexibilidad, *f.* flexibility.
flexible. I. *a.* flexible; lithe; supple; manageable, docile. **II.** *m.* electric cord; soft hat.
flexión, *f.* flexion, flexure.
flexional, *a.* (gram.) flectional, inflectional.
flexor, ra. I. *a.* bending. **II.** *m.* bender; (anat.) flexor.
flexuoso, sa, *a.* (bot.) flexuose.
flictena, *f.* (med.) phlyctena, small blister.
flin, *m.* (cutlery) polishing stone.
flirtear, *vn.* to flirt.
flirteo, *m.* flirt, flirting.
flocadura, *f.* (sewing) fringe trimming.
floculación, *f.* flocculation.
flogístico, ca, *a.* (chem.) phlogistic.
flogisto, *m.* (chem.) phlogiston.
flogosis, *f.* inflammation, phlegmasia.
flojamente, *adv.* slowly, carelessly, laxly.
flojear, *vn.* to slacken, to grow weak.
flojedad, *f.* weakness, feebleness, laxity; sloth, laziness, negligence.
flojel, *m.* wool shorn from cloth; down, soft feathers.
flojera, *f.* (coll.) = FLOJEDAD.
flojizo, za, *a.* flabby; flaccid, lax, loose; soft.
flojo, ja, *a.* loose, lax, slack; weak; flaccid; lazy; (Colomb.) timorous, cowardly.
floqueado, da, *a.* fringed.
flor, *f.* flower; blossom; down of fruits newly gathered; prime; film on the surface of liquors; (chem.) flower, powder; compliment; grain, outside of tanned leather; cheating trick of gamblers; (gen. *pl.*) flowers, menstruation.—**f. compuesta,** (bot.) compound flower.—**f. de amor,** (bot.) amaranth.—**f. de azufre,** (chem.) flowers of sulphur.—**f. de harina,** flour.—**f. de la edad,** youth; prime of life, bloom of youth.—**f. de la Trinidad,** (bot.) pansy.—**f. de la vida.**

prime of life, bloom of youth.—**f. de lis,** fleur-de-lis, iris.—**f. del sol,** (bot.) sunflower.—**f. de mano,** artificial flower.—**flores blancas,** leucorrhea.—**flores de cantueso,** trifle, small matter.—**f. silvestre,** (bot.) wildflower.—**f. y nata,** flower, élite.—**botón de f.,** flower bud.—**tienda de flores,** flower shop.—**a f. de,** flush with; (naut.) awash.—**decir** or **hechar flores,** to pay compliments, flatter.

flora, *f.* (bot.) flora.

floración, *f.* (bot.) flowering, florescence.

florada, *f.* season of flowers with beemasters.

floral, *a.* (bot.) floral.

florales, *a. pl.* Floralia, floral (feasts or games).

florar, *vn.* to flower, blossom, bloom.

flordelisado, da, *pp.* & *a.* (her.) fleurette.

flordelisar, *va.* (her.) to adorn with irises.

floreado, da. I. *pp.* of FLOREAR. **II.** *a.* flowered, figured (goods); made of the finest flour.

florear, *va.* to flower; to bolt (flour); to flourish, brandish; (mus.) to flourish on the guitar; to pay compliments to.

florecer. I. *vn.* (*ind.* FLOREZCO; *subj.* FLOREZCA) to flower, bloom, blossom; to flourish, thrive, prosper. **II.** *vr.* to mould, become mouldy.

floreciente, *a.* flourishing, flowering.

florecimiento, *m.* flowering; flourishing.

florentín, tino, tina, *n.* & *a.* Florentine.

florentísimo, ma, *a. super.* very prosperous.

floreo, *m.* witty but idle talk; compliment; (fencing, mus.) flourish; cross caper, in dancing.

florería, *f.* (Am.) flower shop, florist.

florero, ra. I. *a.* flattering. **II.** *n.* florist. **III.** *m.* flowerpot; flower vase; flower stand, jardinière; (art) flower piece. **IV.** *f.* flower girl.

florescencia, *f.* (bot.) florescence, flowering.

floresta, *f.* forest, woods.

florestero, *m.* forester, forest keeper or guard.

floreta, *f.* leather border on the edge of a girth.

florete. I. *a.* (com.) first quality, superfine. **II.** *m.* fencing foil.

floretear, *va.* to garnish with flowers.

floretista, *m.* fencer.

florezco, florezca, *v.* *V.* FLORECER.

floricultor, ra, *n.* floriculturist.

floricultura, *f.* floriculture.

florido, da, *a.* flowery; full of flowers, in bloom; choice, select.—**pascua f.,** Easter Sunday.

florífero, ra; florígero, ra, *a.* floriferous.

florilegio, *m.* florilegium, anthology.

florín, *m.* florin (coin).

floripondio, *m.* (bot.) floripondio.

florisar, *va.* = FLORDELISAR.

florista, *n.* maker of artificial flowers; florist.

floristería, *f.* (P. R.) flower shop, florist.

florón, *m. aug.* large flower; (arch.) fleuron, rosette.

flósculo, *m.* (bot.) floscule, floret.

flota, *f.* (naut.) fleet of merchant ships; (obs.) squadron.—**f. aérea,** air forces.

flotabilidad, *f.* buoyancy.

flotable, *a.* flotable; navigable.

flotación, *f.* flotation, flotage, floating.—**línea de f.,** waterline (of ship).

flotador, ra. I. *n.* & *a.* floater(-ing). **II.** *m.* float.

flotadura, *f.*, **flotamiento,** *m.* = FLOTACIÓN.

flotante, *a.* floating.

flotar, *vn.* to float (on a liquid or in the air).

flote, *m.* floating.—**a f.,** afloat.—**estar,** or **mantenerse, a f.,** (fig.) to have enough to live on.

flotilla, *f. dim.* flotilla; small fleet.

flox, *m.* (bot.) phlox.

fluctuación, *f.* fluctuation; wavering.

fluctuante, *a.* fluctuating.

fluctuar, *vn.* to fluctuate; waver, oscillate; to be in danger; to hesitate, vacillate.

fluctuoso, sa, *a.* fluctuant, wavering.

fluencia, *f.* fluency; flowing; spring, source of a stream; (elec.) creepage.

fluente, *a.* fluent, flowing.

fluidez, *f.* fluidity, fluidness; fluency.

fluidificar, *va.* to fluidize.

flúido, da. I. *a.* fluid; fluent (as speech). **II.** *m.* fluid.

fluir, *vn.* (*ger.* FLUYENDO; *ind. pres.* FLUYO, *pret.* FLUYÓ; *subj.* FLUYA) *vn.* to flow; to issue, ooze, run out.

flujo, *m.* flux, flow, flowage, flowing; influx; (med.) hemorrhage; (naut.) rising tide; (chem.) flux.—**f. blanco,** the whites.—**f. de palabras,** flow of words, volubility.—**f. de reír,** habit of laughing.—**f. de risa,** fit of laughter.—**f. de sangre,** hemorrhage.—**f. de vientre,** diarrhea.—**f. magnético,** magnetic flux.

fluminense, *a.* from Rio de Janeiro.

flúor, *m.* (chem.) fluorine; (chem.) flux.

fluorescencia, *f.* (phys.) fluorescence.

fluorescente, *a.* fluorescent.

fluorhidrato, *m.* hydrofluoride.

fluorhídrico, ca, *a.* hydrofluoric.

fluórico, ca, *a.* (chem.) fluoric.

fluorímetro, *m.* fluorimeter.

fluorina, fluorita, *f.* (min.) fluor spar, fluorite.

fluorización, *f.* fluoridation.

fluorizar, *va.* to fluoridate.

fluorografía, *f.* fluorography.

fluoroscopia, *f.* (med.) fluoroscopy.

fluoroscópico, ca, *a.* fluoroscopic.

fluoroscopio, *m.* fluoroscope.

fluoruro, *m.* (chem.) fluoride.

fluvial, *a.* fluvial, fluviatile.

fluviógrafo, fluviómetro, *m.* fluviograph, fluviometer.

flux, *m.* (Am.) suit (of clothes); flush, at cards.—**estar a f.,** (Mex., Arg.) to have nothing, be penniless.—**hacer f.,** (coll.) to spend one's whole fortune without paying a debt.—**tener f.,** (Am.) to be lucky.

fluxión, *f.* (med.) fluxion; cold in the head.

fluyo, fluya, etc., *v.* *V.* FLUIR.

fobia, *f.* (psych.) phobia.

foca, *f.* (zool.) fur-bearing seal.

focal, *a.* (geom. and phys.) focal.

foceifiza, *f.* a kind of Arabian mosaic.

focino, *m.* goad for elephants.

foco, *m.* focus; center, source; (med.) core or center of an abscess; (mil.) touchhole of a gun; (auto) headlight.—**f. de luz eléctrica,** (electric) light bulb.

fóculo, *m.* small fireplace.

fodolí, *a.* meddlesome, intrusive.

fofo, fa, *a.* spongy, soft; (of style) empty, trashy.

fogaje, *m.* hearth money, an ancient tax.

fogarada, *f.* blaze, bonfire.

fogaril, *m.* cresset, torch.

fogarizar, *va.* to build bonfires in.

fogata, *f.* bonfire, blaze; fougade.

fogón, *m.* hearth, fireside; cooking place, cooking stove, kitchen range; touchhole of a gun; (naut.) caboose, cuddy; firebox (of a boiler, locomotive, etc.); (Am.) fire.

fogonadura, *f.* (naut.) mast hole.

fogonazo, *m.* powder flash; flash in a pan.

fogonero, *m.* fireman, stoker.

fogosidad, *f.* fieriness, heat, vehemence.

fogoso, sa, *a.* fiery, vehement, impetuous; spirited (as a horse).

fogueación, *f.* numbering of hearths or fires.

foguear, *va.* to accustom to the discharge (noise) of firearms; (artil.) to scale (a gun).

foguezuelo, *m. dim.* small fire.

[1]**foja,** *f.* (law) leaf of a manuscript or folio.

[2]**foja,** *f.* (ornith.) coot, scoter.

folgo, *m.* foot muff or warming bag.

foliáceo, *a.* (bot.) foliaceous.

foliación, *f.* foliation, numbering the pages of a book; (bot.) foliation.

foliado, da, *a.* foliated.

foliar, *va.* to number the pages of a book, etc.

foliatura, *f.* paging (of a book).

folículo, *m.* (bot.) follicle, pericarp; (anat.) follicle, membranous sac.

folijones, *m. pl.* an ancient Castilian dance.

folio, *m.* folio, leaf of a book; size of a bookleaf.—**f. de Descartes,** (geom.) folium of Descartes.

—**f. índico,** (bot.) Indian leaf.—**al primer f.,** at first sight.—**de a f.,** (coll.) very great, monumental (truth, fact, etc.); egregious (blunder, etc.).
folíolo, *m.* (bot.) foliole of a compound flower.
folklore, *m.* folklore.—**folklórico, ca,** *a.* folkloric, pertaining to folklore.—**folklorista,** *n.* folklorist, one versed in folklore.
foluz, *f.* an ancient small copper coin.
folla, *f.* irregular conflict in a tournament; medley, variety show.
follada, *f.* puff-paste patty.
follaje, *m.* foliage; leafage; gaudy ornament; superabundance of figures of speech; fustian.
[1]**follar,** *va.* (*ind.* FUELLO; *subj.* FUELLE) to blow with bellows.
[2]**follar,** *va.* to form into leaves.
follero, folletero, *m.* bellows maker or seller.
folletín, *m.* feuilleton, serial story in a newspaper.
folletinista, *n.* writer of FOLLETINES.
folletista, *n.* pamphleteer.
folleto, *m.* pamphlet, booklet.
follón, na. I. *a.* lazy, indolent; cowardly. **II.** *m.* coward; rogue, knave; conceited fellow; noiseless rocket; disturbance, rumpus.
fomentación, *f.* (med.) fomentation.
fomentador, ra, *n.* & *a.* fomenter(-ing), promoter(-ing).
fomentar, *va.* to foment, to warm; to promote, further, encourage; to prompt; (med.) to foment; (agr.) to improve.
fomento, *m.* fomentation; warmth, fuel; fostering, furtherance, promotion; improvement, development; (med.) fomentation, lotion.
fomes, *m.* (med.) fomes; cause of excitement.
fonación, *f.* phonation, vocalization.
fonas, *f. pl.* (sewing) gores, gussets.
fonda, *f.* inn; eating house.
fondable, *a.* fit for anchoring.
fondado, da, *a.* (cooperage) with reinforced heads.
fondeadero, *m.* (naut.) anchoring ground; haven.
fondear. I. *va.* (naut.) to sound; to raise from the bottom of water; to search (a ship); to examine closely. **II.** *vn.* to cast anchor.
fondeo, *m.* (naut.) search; casting anchor.
fondillón, *m.* dregs and lees of a cask of liquor; old Alicante wine.
fondillos, *m. pl.* seat of trousers.
fondista, *n.* innkeeper, hotel keeper.
fondo, *m.* bottom; depth; rear part, back, furthest end; ground (of stuffs); head (of a boiler, cylinder, etc.); substance; (art) background; thickness of a diamond; extent of a man's capacity; disposition, nature (of a person); principal or essential part of a thing; stock, quantity, store (of virtues, vices, etc.); fund, capital; (mil.) space occupied by a rank; (mech.) bed, bottom plate, foundation; (cooperage) head; (naut.) bottom.—*pl.* funds, resources.—**f. de amortización,** sinking fund.—**f. de reserva,** reserve fund.—**f. doble,** false bottom.—**f. para imprevistos,** contingency fund.—**fondos disponibles,** uncommitted funds.—**fondos fiduciarios,** trust funds.—**fondos públicos** or **del Erario,** public funds.—**fondos vitalicios,** life annuities.—**a f.,** perfectly, thoroughly.—**andar mal de fondos,** to be short of money.—**dar f.,** to cast anchor.—**de f.,** abreast; editorial (article).—**echar a f.,** to sink.—**en f.,** abreast.—**en el f.,** at bottom, at heart, in substance.—**irse a f.,** to sink, founder; (fencing) to thrust.—**limpiar los fondos,** (naut.) to hog a ship's bottom.—**tocar f.,** to touch bottom.
fondón, *m.* FONDILLÓN; ground of silk or velvet; brocade; (min.) fondon.
fonema, *m.* (phon.) phoneme.
fonémico, ca. I. *a.* phonemic. **II.** *f.* phonemics.
fonendoscopio, *m.* (med.) phonendoscope.
fonética, *f.* phonetics.
fonético, ca, *a.* phonetic.
fonetismo, *m.* phonetism.
fonetista, *n.* phonetician.
fónico, ca. I. *a.* phonic. **II.** *f.* phonics.
fonil, *m.* (naut.) wooden funnel.
fonio, *m.* (phys.) phon (unit of sound).
fonje, *a.* bland, soft, spongy.
fonocaptor, *m.* pickup (of a record player).
fonografía, *f.* phonography.
fonográfico, ca, *a.* phonographic.
fonógrafo, *m.* phonograph.
fonograma, *m.* phonogram.
fonolita, *f.* (min.) clinkstone, phonolite.
fonología, *f.* phonology.
fonológico, ca, *a.* phonologic.
fonólogo, ga, *n.* phonologist.
fonometría, *f.* phonometry.
fonométrico, ca, *a.* phonometric.
fonómetro, *m.* phonometer.
fonón, *m.* (phys.) phonon.
fonoscopio, *m.* phonoscope.
fonotipia, *f.* phonotypy.
fonotípico, ca, *a.* phonotypic.
fonotipo, *m.* phonotype.
fonsadera, *f.* an ancient war tax.
fonsado, *m.* (fort.) foss or ditch.
fontal, *a.* fontal; original, main.
fontana, *f.* (poet.) fountain, spring, water jet.
fontanal. I. *a.* fontal, pertaining to fountains or springs. **II.** *m.* source or spring of water; place abounding in springs.
fontanar, *m.* water spring.
fontanela, *f.* (anat.) fontanel; (surg.) seton needle.
fontanería, *f.* pipe laying; water-pipe system, pipe line.
fontanero, ra, *n.* pipe layer.
fontegí, *m.* a variety of wheat.
fontezuela, *f. dim.* small fountain.
fontículo, *m.* (surg.) fonticulus, issue.
foque, *m.* (naut.) jib.—**f. de caza,** or **f. mayor,** standing jib.—**f. segundo,** forestay sail.
forajido, da, *n.* outlaw, fugitive from justice.
foral, *a.* (law) statutory.
foralmente, *adv.* judicially.
foramen, *m.* (anat., bot.) foramen; hole in the nether millstone.
foraminífero, ra. I. *a.* (zool.) foraminiferous. **II.** *m.* (zool.) foraminifer.
foráneo, nea, *a.* foreign.
forastero, ra. I. *a.* foreign; exotic. **II.** *n.* stranger.
forbante, *m.* freebooter.
forcé, *pret.* of FORZAR.
forcejar, forcejear, *vn.* to struggle, strive, labor; contest, contend.
forcejo, *m.* struggle, strife.
forcejón, *m.* violent effort or struggle.
forcejudo, da, *a.* strong, robust.
forceps, *m.* (surg.) forceps.
forchina, *f.* (mil.) forklike weapon.
forense, *a.* (law) forensic.
forero, ra. I. *a.* conformable to the statute law of a country. **II.** *m.* owner of leasehold estate; lessee.
forestación, *f.* (Chile) forestation.
forestal, *a.* forestal.
forillo, *m.* backing, in theatrical scenery.
forja, *f.* smelting furnace; chafery; bloomery, smithy; forge; forging; (mason.) mortar.
forjador, *m.* forger; ironmaster, smith, blacksmith; goldbeater.
forjadura, *f.* forging.
forjar, *va.* to forge, hammer or stamp into shape; to frame, form, fabricate; to counterfeit, falsify; to invent, concoct (as a falsehood).—**forjarse ilusiones,** to delude oneself; to build castles in the air.
forma, *f.* form, shape; frame, make; method, order; manner; hand, form or cast of writing; pattern, mold, matrix; (print.) form, format; block (for hats); (eccl.) host for the communion of the laity.—*pl.* (of persons) build, figure.—**dar f. a,** to give final form to, shape; to put in order, arrange.—**de f. que,** so as, so that.—

en debida f., or en f., in due form, properly.—en f., en toda f., in due form or manner; thoroughly, in a thorough and proper manner.—tomar f., to develop, to become realized, to materialize.
formación, *f.* formation, forming; form, shape; twisted cord for gold embroidery; (geol.) formation, system; (mil.) formation, array.
formador, ra, *n.* & *a.* former(-ing).
formaje, *m.* cheese vat; cheese; (Mex.) sugar mold.
formal, *a.* formal, regular, methodical; proper, genuine; serious, grave, steady, sedate; truthful, reliable; well-behaved.
formaldehido, *m.* formaldehyde.
formalicé, formalice, *v. V.* FORMALIZAR.
formalidad, *f.* formality; exactness, punctuality; gravity, seriousness, solemnity; requisite, requirement; "red tape"; established practice; legal precedent.—**con f.,** in earnest.
formalina, *f.* (chem.) formalin.
formalismo, *m.* formalism.
formalista, *n.* formalist.
formalizar. I. *va.* (*pret.* FORMALICÉ; *subj.* FORMALICE) to put in final form; to execute, legalize (a deed, etc.); to make explicit, formulate, formulize; to formalize. **II.** *vr.* to become serious or earnest.
formar. I. *va.* to form; shape, fashion; (mil.) to combine, arrange.—**f. parte de,** to be a member of (an organization, etc.). **II.** *vn.* to adjust the edges of embroidery work; (mil.) to draw up. **III.** *vr.* to form, take form, grow, develop.
formativo, va, *a.* formative.
formato, *m.* (Am.) format (of a book).
formatriz, *f. a.* = FORMADORA.
formejar, *va.* (naut.) to clear (the ship); to trim (the hold).
formeno, *m.* (chem.) formene.
formero, *m.* (arch.) side arch of a vault.
formiato, *m.* (chem.) formate.
formicante, *a.* (med.) weak, rapid (pulse).
fórmico, *m.* (chem.) formic (acid or ether).
formidable, *a.* formidable; immense, huge.
formidoloso, sa, *a.* timorous, timid; dreadful, frightful, horrible.
formilo, *m.* (chem.) formyl.
formillón, *m.* hat block or form.
formol, *m.* (chem.) formaldehyde.
formón, *m.* chisel; punching press for cutting wafers.
fórmula, *f.* formula; recipe, prescription; (eccl.) profession of faith.—**f. leucocitaria,** white blood count.—**f. sanguínea,** blood count.—**por f.,** as a matter of form.
formulación, *f.* formulation.
formular, *va.* to formulate, formulize.
formulario, *m.* formulary.
formulismo, *m.* formulism; red tape.
formulista, *n.* & *a.* formulist(-ic).
fornáceo, cea, *a.* (poet.) furnacelike.
fornelo, *m.* portable little oven or furnace.
fornicación, *f.* fornication.
fornicador, ra, *n.* & *a.* fornicator(-ing).
fornicar, *va.* to fornicate.
fornicario, ria, *a.* pertaining to or addicted to fornication.
fornicio, *m.* = FORNICACIÓN.
fornido, da, *a.* robust, lusty, stout.
fornitura, *f.* (mil.) furniture; (print.) types cast to complete sorts.
fórnix, *m.* (anat., bot.) fornix.
foro, *m.* forum; court of justice; bar, the legal profession; back, in stage scenery; leasehold; rental.—**llmar al f.,** (law) to call to the bar.—**por tal f.,** on such conditions.
forrado, da. I. *pp.* of FORRAR. **II.** *a.* doubled.
forraje, *m.* forage, fodder; foraging; (coll.) trifles.
forrajeador, ra, *n.* forager, fodderer.
forrajear, *vn.* to gather forage or fodder.
forrajera, *f.* (mil.) shako guard.
forrajero, ra, *a.* forage, fodder (as *a.*).
forrar. I. *va.* to line (as clothes); to cover (as a book or an umbrella); (anat.) to sheathe, to fur. **II.** *vr.* (**Mex.,** Guat.) to eat well, have a good meal.
forro, *m.* lining, doubling, inside, backing; (naut.) furring, planking, sheathing; cover of a book.—**f. de cabos,** (naut.) service, serving ropes.—**f. sobrepuesto de cable,** (naut.) keckling, rounding.
fortachón, na, *a.* (coll.) powerfully strong.
fortalecedor, ra, *n.* & *a.* fortifier(-fying).
fortalecer, *va.* (*ind.* FORTALEZCO; *subj.* FORTALEZCA) to fortify, strengthen, corroborate; to fortify (a place); to aid, encourage, support.
fortalecimiento, *m.* fortifying, strengthening; fortification, defenses.
fortaleza, *f.* fortitude; firmness; courage, strength, vigor; stronghold, fortress, fort.
fortalezco, fortalezca, *v. V.* FORTALECER.
forte. I. *interj.* (naut.) avast! **II.** *a.* (mus.) forte, loud.
fortepiano, *m.* (mus., obs.) pianoforte.
fortezuelo, la. I. *a. dim.* not very strong. **II.** *m.* small fort.
fortificable, *a.* fortifiable.
fortificación, *f.* fortification; fort; military architecture.—**f. de campaña,** field fortification.
fortificador, ra, *n.* & *a.* fortifier(-fying).
fortificante, *a.* fortifying.
fortificar, *va.* (*pret.* FORTIFIQUÉ; *subj.* FORTIFIQUE) to strengthen, invigorate; (mil.) to fortify.
fortín, *m. dim.* fortin, fortlet, small fort.
fortísimo, ma. I. *a. super.* of FUERTE; (mus.) fortissimo. **II.** *adv.* (mus.) fortissimo.
fortitud, *f.* fortitude.
fortuitamente, *adv.* fortuitously, accidentally.
fortuito, ta, *a.* fortuitous, accidental.
fortuna, *f.* fortune, chance, fate; good luck; wealth, resources; storm, tempest; accident of the sea.—**por f.,** fortunately, luckily.
fortunón, *m. aug.* great stroke of fortune; immense fortune (wealth).
forúnculo, furúnculo, *m.* (med.) furuncle, boil.
forzado, da. I. *pp.* of FORZAR. **II.** *a.* forced.—**trabajos f.,** hard labor (penal). **III.** *n.* criminal sentenced to the galleys.
forzador, *m.* ravisher; forcer.
forzal, *m.* solid part of a comb.
forzamiento, *m.* act of forcing or violating.
forzar, *va.* (*ind. pres.* FUERZO, *pret.* FORCÉ; *subj.* FUERCE) to force, break in (as a door); to compel, force; to subdue by force; to ravish.
forzoso, sa. I. *a.* forced, necessary, unavoidable; obligatory, compulsory.—**paro f.,** unemployment. **II.** *f.* decisive move at the game of draughts; compulsion.—**hacer la f. a uno,** (coll.) to compel one to act against one's will, put on the pressure.
forzudamente, *adv.* with great power and force.
forzudo, da, *a.* strong, vigorous, lusty.
fosa, *f.* grave; (anat.) fossa.
fosar, *va.* to dig a pit or trench around.
fosca, *f.* haze; thicket, jungle.
fosco, ca, *a.* frowning, cross.
fosfatado, da, *a.* containing phosphate.
fosfático, ca, *a.* (chem.) phosphatic.
fosfato, *m.* (chem.) phosphate.
fosfaturia, *f.* (med.) phosphaturia.
fosfeno, *m.* (physiol.) phosphene.
fosfina, *f.* (chem.) phosphine.
fosfito, *m.* (chem.) phosphite.
fosforado, da, *a.* containing phosphate.—**bronce f.,** phosphor bronze.
fosforar, *va.* to phosphorate.
fosforecer, *vn.* = FOSFORESCER.
fosforera, *f.* match box.
fosforero, ra, *n.* vender of matches.
fosforescencia, *f.* phosphorescence.
fosforescente, *a.* phosphorescent.
fosforescer, *vn.* (*ind.* FOSFOREZCO; *subj.* FOSFOREZCA) to phosphoresce.
fosfórico, ca, *a.* phosphoric.

fosforita, *f.* (min.) phosphorite.
fósforo, *m.* phosphorus; friction match; morning star.
fosforoscopio, *m.* (phys.) phosphoroscope.
fosforoso, sa, *a.* phosphorous.
fosfuro, *m.* phosphide, phosphuret.
fosgeno, *m.* (chem.) phosgene (gas).
fósil, *a.* & *m.* fossil.
fosilífero, ra, *a.* fossiliferous.
fosilización, *f.* fossilization.
fosilizado, da. I. *pp.* of FOSILIZARSE. **II.** *a.* fossilized.
fosilizarse, *vr.* to fossilize, become fossil.
foso, *m.* pit, hole in the ground; (theat.) cellar under the stage; (fort.) moat, ditch, foss.—**f. séptico,** septic tank.
fótico, ca, *a.* photic.
fotingo, *m.* (Am., coll.) flivver, cheap automobile.
fotinia, *f.* (bot.) Photinia.
fotio, *m.* (phys.) phot (unit of light).
foto. I. *pref.* photo- (light). **II.** *f.* (coll.) photo(graph), shot.
fotoactínico, ca, *a.* photoactinic.
fotoactivación, *f.* photoactivation.
fotoactivo, va, *a.* photoactive.
fotocátodo, *m.* (phys.) photocathode.
fotocélula, *f.* (elec.) photocell.
fotocincografía, *f.* photozincography.
fotocinético, ca, *a.* photokinetic.
fotocolografía, *f.* photocollography.
fotocomposición, *f.* (print.) photocomposition.
fotocopia, *f.* photocopy, photostat.
fotocromía, *f.* photochromy.
fotodesintegración, *f.* (phys.) photodisintegration.
fotodinámico, ca, *a.* photodynamic.
fotoeléctrico, ca, *a.* photoelectric.
fotoelectrón, *m.* (chem., phys.) photoelectron.
fotoemulsión, *f.* (phys.) photoemulsion.
fotofísico, ca. I. *a.* photophysic. **II.** *f.* photophysics.
fotofisión, *f.* (nuclear phys.) photofission.
fotofobia, *f.* (med.) photophobia.
fotófobo, ba, *a.* suffering from photophobia.
fotófono, *m.* (phys.) photophone.
fotogénico, ca, *a.* photogenic.
fotograbado, *m.* photoengraving, photogravure.
fotograbador, ra, *n.* photoengraver.
fotograbar, *va.* & *vn.* to photoengrave.
fotografía, *f.* photography; photograph.
fotografiar, *va.* to photograph.
fotográficamente, *adv.* photographically.
fotográfico, ca, *a.* photographic.
fotógrafo, *m.* photographer.
fotoionización, *f.* (phys.) photoionization.
fotólisis, *f.* photolysis.
fotolitografía, *f.* photolithography; photolithograph.
fotolitografiar, *va.* to photolithograph.
fotolitográfico, ca, *a.* photolithographic.
fotología, *f.* photology, optics.
fotomapa, *m.* photomap.
fotomecánico, ca, *a.* (print.) photomechanical.
fotomesón, *m.* (phys.) photomeson.
fotometría, *f.* photometry.
fotométrico, ca, *a.* photometric.
fotómetro, *m.* photometer.
fotomicrografía, *f.* photomicrography.
fotomontaje, *m.* (photog.) photomontage.
fotomultiplicador, *m.* (phys.) photomultiplier.
fotomural, *m.* photomural.
fotón, *m.* (phys.) photon.
fotopartícula, *f.* (phys.) photoparticle.
fotoplaca, *f.* photoplate.
fotoproducción, *f.* (phys.) photoproduction.
fotoprotón, *m.* (phys.) photoproton.
fotoquímico, ca. I. *a.* photochemical. **II.** *f.* photochemistry.
fotorrelieve, *m.* photorelief.
fotosensitivo, va, *a.* photosensitive.
fotosfera, *f.* (astr.) photosphere.
fotosíntesis, *f.* (bot.) photosynthesis.
fotospectroscopio, *m.* photospectroscope.
fotostático, ca, *a.* photostatic.
fotostato, *m.* photostat, photocopy.
fototactismo, *m.* (biol.) phototaxis.
fototelefonía, *f.* phototelephony.
fototelegrafía, *f.* phototelegraphy.
fototerapia, *f.* (med.) phototherapeutics.
fototerápico, ca, *a.* phototherapeutical.
fototipografía, *f.* phototypography.
fototipográfico, ca, *a.* phototypographic.
fototropismo, *m.* (bot.) phototropism.
fotuto, *m.* (Cuba) whistle; trumpet, horn.
foya, *f.* oven full of charcoal.
foyer, *m.* foyer.
frac, *m.* dress coat.
fracasar, *vn.* to fail, come to naught; (naut.) to crumble, to break in pieces.
fracaso, *m.* downfall, ruin; calamity; failure.
fracción, *f.* breaking into parts; fragment (broken off); (math.) fraction.—**f. continua,** continued fraction.—**f. decimal periódica,** repeating decimal.
fraccionado, da. I. *pp.* of FRACCIONAR. **II.** *a.* fractional.
fraccionamiento, *m.* division into fractions.
fraccionar, *va.* to fraction, fractionate.
fraccionario, ria, *a.* fractional.
fractura, *f.* fracture, breaking; (surg.) fracture.
fracturar, *va.* & *vr.* to fracture, break, rupture.
[1]**fraga,** *f.* a kind of raspberry.
[2]**fraga,** *f.* thicket of brambles.
fragancia, *f.* fragrance, scent; good name or reputation.
fragante, *a.* fragrant; flagrant, notorious.—**en f.** = EN FLAGRANTE, in the very act.
fragaria, *f.* (bot.) strawberry.
fragata, *f.* (naut.) frigate.—**f. de aviso,** packet boat.—**f. ligera,** light fast-sailing vessel.
frágil, *a.* brittle, breakable, fragile; frail, weak.
fragilidad, *f.* fragility, brittleness; frailty.
fragmentación, *f.* fragmentation.
fragmentario, ria, *a.* fragmentary.
fragmento, *m.* fragment.
fragor, *m.* noise, clamor, crash.
fragoroso, sa, *a.* (poet.) noisy, obstreperous, thundering, roaring.
fragosidad, *f.* roughness; impenetrability, thickness (of a forest); craggedness, cragginess.
fragoso, sa, *a.* craggy, rough, uneven; full of brambles and briers; noisy, roaring.
fragua, *f.* forge, as for iron; blacksmith's shop.
fraguado, *m.* setting, hardening.
fraguador, ra, *n.* schemer.
fraguar. I. *va.* to forge; to hammer out; to plan, plot, brew, scheme, concoct. **II.** *vn.* (mason) (of concrete, etc.) to set.
fragura, *f.* = FRAGOSIDAD.
frailada, *f.* (coll.) rude or unbecoming action of a monk.
fraile, *m.* friar, monk; fold turned up at bottom of a skirt; priest; (arch.) hood over a hearth; (print.) friar, badly inked spot; (bookbinding) fold in a leaf; upright post of a floodgate; (Cuba) residue from sugar making.
frailear, *va.* (agr.) to prune close to the trunk.
frailecillo, *m. dim.* little friar (ornith.) lap-wing; wedge securing the spindle of a silk reel.
frailengo, ga, leño, ña, *a.* = FRAILESCO.
frailería, *f.* (coll.) monks in general; priests in general; body of monks or priests.
frailesco, ca, *a.* monkish, friarlike; priestlike.
frailía, *f.* body of monks; regular clergy.
frailote, *m. aug.* big and coarse friar.
frailuco, *m.* despicable friar.
frailuno, na, *a.* (coll.) friarlike; priestlike.
frambesia, *f.* (med.) frambesia, yaws.
frambuesa, *f.* (bot.) raspberry.
frambueso, *m.* (bot.) raspberry bush.
frámea, *f.* javelin, dart.
francachela, *f.* (coll.) a gala meal.
francalete, *m.* leather strap with a buckle.
francés, cesa. I. *a.* French.—**a la francesa,** in the

French fashion.—**despedirse a la f.**, (coll.) to take French leave. **II.** *n.* Frenchman(-woman). **III.** *m.* French language.
francesada, *f.* anything characteristic of the French; French invasion (of Spain in 1808).
francesilla, *f.* (bot.) common yard crowfoot.
Francia, *f.* France.
francio, *m.* (chem.) francium.
franciscano, na, *a.* Franciscan; gray-colored.
francisco, ca, *a.* Franciscan.
francmasón, *m.* Freemason, Mason.
francmasonería, *f.* Freemasonry.
franco, ca. I. *a.* frank, open; free, clear, disengaged; exempt, privileged; Frankish; (com.) duty free; in compound words. French or Franco-, as *francoamericano,* Franco-American. —**f. a bordo,** free on board, f. o. b.—**f. de porte,** prepaid, duty-free. **II.** *m.* franc (monetary unit of France, Belgium and Switzerland); period or time (during a fair) when merchandise is duty-free.
francófilo, la, *a.* & *n.* Francophile, Gallophile.
francófobo, ba, *a.* & *n.* Francophobe, Gallophobe.
francolín, *m.* (ornith.) francolin.
francote, ta, *a. aug.* (coll.) frank, open-hearted.
franchipán, *m.* franchipane, a perfume.
franchipaniero, *m.* (Am., bot.) frangipani tree.
franchute, *a.* & *n.* (der.) Frenchy.
franela, *f.* flannel.
frange, *m.* (her.) division of the field of a shield.
frangente. I. *a.* frangent, fracturing. **II.** *m.* accident, disaster, mishap.
frangible, *a.* brittle, frangible, breakable.
frangir, *va.* to break into pieces.
frangollar, *va.* (coll.) to do hurriedly.
frangollo, *m.* porridge of wheat and milk; (Am.) poorly-made stew.
frangote, *m.* (com.) bale of goods.
frángula, *f.* (bot.) berry-bearing alder.
franja, *f.* (sewing) fringe, trimming, band, braid, border; stripe; strip (of land).
franjar, franjear, *va.* (sewing) to trim with braids, bands, or stripes; to border.
franqueamiento, *m.* = FRANQUEO.
franquear. I. *va.* to exempt, to grant immunity to; enfranchise; to prepay (postage); to make liberal grants or gifts; to open, clear; to free (a slave). **II.** *vr.* to yield easily to the desire of others; to unbosom oneself; (naut.) to be ready for sailing.
franqueo, *m.* postage; liberating a slave.
franqueza, *f.* frankness; freedom, liberty, exemption.—**con f.,** frankly.
franquía, *f.* (naut.) sea room, offing.—**en f.,** ready.
franquicia, *f.* exemption from taxes; franchise, privilege, grant.
frasca, *f.* small branches.
frasco, *m.* flask, vial, bottle; powder flask.
frase, *f.* phrase; idiom, epigram; style of a writer. —**f. hecha,** proverb, saying, saw.—**f. musical,** (mus.) phrase.—**f. sacramental,** standard form.—**hacer frases,** to speak much saying little.
frasear, *va.* to phrase; (mus.) to phrase.
fraseología, *f.* phraseology; style of a writer; verbosity, pomposity.
frasquera, *f.* bottle case, liquor case.—**f. de fuego,** (naut.) fire case or fire chest.
frasqueta, *f.* (print.) frisket.
frasquete, frasquillo, ito, *m. dim.* small flask.
fratás, *m.* plastering trowel.
fratasar, *va.* to smooth with the trowel.
fraterna, *f.* (coll.) severe reprimand, lecture.
fraternal, *a.* fraternal, brotherly.
fraternalmente, *adv.* fraternally.
fraternidad, *f.* fraternity, brotherhood.
fraternización, *f.* fraternization.
fraternizar, *vn.* to fraternize.
fraterno, na, *a.* fraternal, brotherly.
fratría, *f.* phratry.
fratricida, *n.* fratricide, murderer (of one's brother).
fratricidio, *m.* fratricide, murder (of one's brother).
fraude, *m.* fraud.
fraudulencia, *f.* fraudulence.
fraudulento, ta, *a.* fraudulent; deceitful, artful.
fray, *m. contr.* of FRAILE, used as a title before the names of clergymen belonging to certain religious orders, as *Fray Luis de Granada.*
frazada, *f.* blanket.
frecuencia, *f.* frequency.—**f. acústica** or **audible,** acoustic or audible frequency, audiofrequency; speech frequency.—**f. armónica,** harmonic frequency.—**f. de clase,** (stat.) class frequency.—**f. de señal,** signal frequency.—**f. modulada,** FM, modulated frequency (wave). —**f. musical,** musical frequency, audiofrequency.—**f. sonora,** sound or sonic frequency. —**f. ultrasónica,** ultrasonic frequency.—**f. visual,** video frequency.—**alta f.,** high frequency.—**baja f.,** low frequency.—**con f.,** frequently.
frecuentación, *f.* frequenting.
frecuentador, ra, *n.* & *a.* frequenter(-ing).
frecuentar, *va.* to frequent; to repeat.
frecuentativo, *a.* (gram.) frequentative.
frecuente, *a.* frequent.
fregadero, *m.* scullery; kitchen sink.
fregado, *m.* scouring or scrubbing; (coll.) complicated affair; fracas.
fregador, ra. I. *n.* & *a.* washer(-ing). **II.** *m.* scullery; dishcloth, mop, scrubbing brush.
fregadura, *f.* rubbing, scrubbing, scouring.
fregamiento, *m.* = FRICACIÓN, friction.
fregar, *va.* (*ind. pres.* FRIEGO, *pret.* FREGUÉ; *subj.* FRIEGUE) to rub; to scrub, mop, swab, scour; to wash (dishes); (Am.) to annoy, bother.
fregatriz, fregona, *f.* kitchenmaid; dishwasher.
fregonil, *a.* (coll.) wenchlike.
fregué, *pret.* of FREGAR.
freidura, *f.* frying or dressing in a pan.
freila, *f.* (eccl.) lay sister.
freile, *m.* knight or priest of a military order.
freír, *va.* (*pp.* FRITO; *ger.* FRIENDO; *ind. pres.* FRÍO, *pret.* él FRIÓ; *subj.* FRÍA) to fry or dress in a frying pan.—**freírse de calor,** to be excessively hot, to be baking.—**freírsela a uno,** (coll.) to deceive one premeditatedly.—**al f. será el reír,** he laughs best who laughs last.
fréjol, frejol, *m.* (bot.) kidney bean.
frémito, *m.* roar.
frenar, *va.* to bridle, to govern by the bridle; to brake, apply the brake to.
frenería, *f.* bridle making; harness shop.
frenero, *m.* bridle maker or seller; (Ry.) brakeman.
frenesí, *m.* frenzy, fury, madness; folly.
frenéticamente, *adv.* frantically, madly.
frenético, ca, *a.* mad, frantic, frenzied.
frénico, ca, *a.* phrenic.
frenillar, *va.* (naut.) to bridle (the oars).
frenillo, *m.* (anat.) frenum; (naut.) bridle, fox, ratline.—**no tener f. en la lengua,** to be outspoken, not to mince one's words.
freno, *m.* bridle or bit of the bridle; (carriage) brake (for wheel); (mech.) check, stop, brake; curb, restraint, control.—**f. de vacío,** vacuum brake.—**f. hidráulico,** hydraulic brake.—**f. neumático,** air brake.
frenología, *f.* phrenology.
frenológico, ca, *a.* phrenological.
frenólogo, *m.* phrenologist.
frenópata, *m.* alienist.
frentazo, *m.* (Mex.) rebuff, turning down.
frente. I. *f.* forehead; countenance, mien; intellect.—**no tener dos dedos de f.,** not to have any sense at all, a particle of brains. **II.** *adv.* in front, opposite, across the way. **III.** *m.* (mil.) front; (fort.) face of a bastion; front, fore part, face, façade; obverse (of coins, etc.).—**f. a,**

opposite, facing; (fig.) in the face or eyes of.—**f. a f.**, face to face.—**f. popular**, (pol.) popular front.—**f. por f.**, directly across or opposite.—**a f.**, straight ahead.—**al f.**, opposite; (com.) carried forward.—**al f. de**, in front of; in charge of.—**de f.**, from the front; front (as *a.*); (mil.) facing; abreast.—**del f.**, brought forward; opposite, across (the street, etc.).—**en f.**, = F. POR F.—**en f. de**, = AL F. DE.—**hacer f. a**, to face (a problem, etc.); to meet (a demand, etc.).

frentón, ona, *a.* having a large forehead.

freo, *m.* (naut.) narrow channel, strait, fretum.

fresa, *f.* (bot.) strawberry; (mech.) drill, bit, milling tool.

fresadora, *f.* (mech.) milling machine; (dent.) burr.

fresal, *m.* strawberry patch.

fresar, *va.* (mech.) to mill; to drill; to machine.

fresca, *f.* cool air, fresh air; piece of one's mind, biting remark.—**decir cuatro frescas a uno**, to rebuke one without mincing words.—**tomar la f.**, to take the air.

frescachón, na, *a.* robust and fresh-looking; (naut.) (of wind) brisk.

frescal, *a.* (fish) not entirely fresh, but preserved with little salt.

frescamente, *adv.* recently, lately, of late; coolly; bluntly.

fresco, ca. I. *a.* (of food) fresh; (of weather, etc.) cool; recent, newly come; just made, finished, or gathered; latest; fresh, buxom, ruddy; calm, cool; bold, forward, cheeky; unconcerned, unabashed, unmoved.—**estar, o quedar, f.**, to be disappointed, to fail.—**quedarse f.**, to act coolly, to show no scruple or concern. **II.** *m.* cool air, fresh air; (art) fresco; (Am.) cooling drink.—**al f.**, in the open air; in the night air; (art) fresco (painting).—**hacer f.**, (of atmosphere) to be cool.—**tomar el f.**, to get, go out for, some fresh air.

frescor, *m.* cool, refreshing air; freshness; (art) flesh-color.

frescote, ta, *a. aug.* (coll.) fresh, ruddy, youthful.

frescura, *f.* freshness; coolness; luxuriant verdure or foliage; frankness, openness; freedom of manner, ease; tranquillity, coolness, unconcern.

fresero, ra. I. *n.* strawberry vender. **II.** *f.* (bot.) strawberry plant.

fresnal, *m.* pertaining to the ash tree.

fresneda, *f.* plantation of ash trees.

fresnillo, *m.* (bot.) white fraxinella.

fresno, *m.* ash tree; (com.) ash wood.—**f. americano**, white ash.—**f. húngaro**, Hungarian ash.

fresón, *m.* (bot.) Chile strawberry.

fresquecito, ta. I. *a. dim.* (coll.) little cool; nice and fresh. **II.** *n.* cool breeze.

fresquera, *f.* meat safe.

fresquería, *f.* (Am.) ice-cream parlor.

fresquero, ra, *n.* vender of fresh fish.

fresquillo, lla, *a.* = FRESQUECITO, TA.

fresquista, *m.* fresco painter.

fresquito, ta. I. *a. dim.* cool, coolish; fresh, just made, gathered, etc. **II.** *m.* cool, fresh air. **III.** *adv.* freshly made, recent, latest.

freudiano, na, *a.* & *n.* (psych.) Freudian.

freudismo, *m.* Freudianism, Freud's theory.

frey, *m. contr.* of FREILE; used as a title before the name of a clergyman belonging to a military order.

frez, [1]**freza**, *f.* dung, excrement.

[2]**freza**, *f.* spawning; trail of fish in spawning; roe; time when silkworms eat; hole dug by an animal.

frezada, *f.* blanket.

[1]**frezar**, *vn.* (*pret.* FRECÉ; *subj.* FRECE) to eject excrement; to eject the droppings of grubs from hives.

[2]**frezar**, *va.* (of silkworms) to nibble (leaves); (of fish) to spawn; (of hogs) to root; (of dogs, etc.) to scratch (the ground).

friabilidad, *f.* friability, brittleness.

friable, *a.* friable, fragile, brittle.

frialdad, *f.* coldness; unconcern, coolness; nonsense; (med.) impotence.

friático, ca, *a.* foolish, graceless, silly.

fricación, *f.* friction, frication.

fricandó, *m.* (cook.) fricandeau.

fricar, *va.* to rub together.

fricasé, *m.* (cook.) fricassee.

fricativo, va, *a.* (ling.) fricative.

fricción, *f.* friction, rubbing.

friccionar, *va.* to rub.

friega, *f.* friction, rubbing.

friego, friegue, *v. V.* FREGAR.

friera, *f.* chilblain on the heel.

frigáneo, *m.* (entom.) caddis fly.—**larva del f.**, caddis worm.

frigidez, *f.* frigidity.

frígido, da, *a.* frigid.

frigio, gia, *n.* & *a.* Phrygian.

frigorífero, *m.* (Am.) = FRIGORÍFICO.

frigorífico, ca. I. *a.* refrigerating. **II.** *m.* cold-storage house or room; packing house.

friísimo, ma, *a. super.* extremely cold.

fríjol, frijol, *m.* kidney bean.

frimario, *m.* Frimaire, third month of the French-Revolution calendar.

fringilago, *m.* (ornith.) titmouse.

fringílido, da, *a.* & *m.* (ornith.) fringilline.

[1]**frío, ía. I.** *a.* cold; impotent; indifferent, unmoved, unemotional; dull, graceless, witless.—**hacer f.** (of weather) to be cold.—**tener f.**, (of person) to be, feel, cold. **II.** *m.* cold, coldness (of temperature).—*pl.* (Am.) malaria.

[2]**frío, frió, fría**, *v. V.* FREÍR.

friolento, ta, *a.* chilly; very sensitive to cold.

friolera, *f.* trifle, bauble, gewgaw.

friolero, ra, *a.* FRIOLENTO; (ironic) very important.

frisa, *f.* frieze; (fort.) palisade.

frisado, *m.* curly silk plush or shag.

frisador, ra, *n.* frizzler.

frisadura, *f.* frizzling, shagging.

frisar. I. *va.* to frizzle or frizz (cloth); **to rub**; (naut.) to line, to pack. **II.** *vn.* **(en)** to resemble; to approach, to be near (to).

friso, *m.* (arch.) frieze; wainscot, dado, mopboard.

frisol, frísol, *m.* (bot.) string bean.

frisón, na. I. *n.* & *a.* Frisian. **II.** *m.* large draught horse.

frisuelo, *m.* string bean.—*pl.* fritters.

frita, *f.* (ceramics) frit, ferretto.

fritada, *f.* fry; dish of anything fried.

fritar, *va.* to frit.

fritillas, *f. pl.* fritters, pancakes.

frito, ta. I. *pp. irreg.* of FREÍR, fried.—**estar f.**, (Mex., P. R.) to be annoyed; (Arg.) to be lost. **II.** *m.* fry.

fritura, *f.* fry, fritter.

frivolidad, *f.* frivolity; frivolousness.

frivolité, *f.* tatting, fancywork.

frívolo, la, *a.* frivolous.

[1]**fronda**, *f.* (bot.) leaf; frond.—*pl.* foliage, verdure.

[2]**fronda**, *f.* (surg.) a sling-shaped bandage.

fronde, *m.* (bot.) frond, fern leaf.

frondífero, ra, *a.* frondiferous, frondose, leafy.

frondosidad, *f.* frondage, leafy foliage.

frondoso, sa, *a.* frondose, leafy; luxuriant.

frontal. I. *a.* frontal, pertaining to the forehead. **II.** *m.* (eccl.) frontal, altar hanging; (anat.) frontal bone.

frontalera, *f.* brow band (of a bridle); brow pad under a yoke; (eccl.) trimmings of an altar frontal; place where church frontals are kept.

frontera, *f.* frontier, boundary, border; binder of a fruit basket; (arch.) façade; side of a soft-brick mold.

fronterizo, za, *a.* frontier (as *a.*); facing, opposite.

frontero, ra. I. *a.* opposite, facing; frontal. **II.** *m.* person in command of frontier forces. **III.** *adv.* in front.

frontil, *m.* yoke pad for draught oxen.
frontino, na, *a.* marked in the face.
frontis, *m.* (arch.) frontispiece, façade.
frontispicio, *m.* (of book, arch.) frontispiece; (coll.) face.
frontón, *m.* main wall of a handball court; fives court; (arch.) pediment.
frontudo, da, *a.* (of animals) having a large forehead.
frotación, *f.* rubbing.
frotador, ra, *n.* one who or that which rubs.
frotadura, *f.* rubbing.
frotamiento, *m.*, **frotante,** *a.* rubbing.
frotar, *va.* to rub.
frote, *m.* friction. rubbing; attrition.
frotis, *m.* (bact.) smear.—**f. sanguíneo,** (med.) blood smear.
fructífero, ra, *a.* fructiferous, fruit-bearing; fruitful.
fructificación, *f.* (bot.) fructification.
fructificador, ra, *n.* & *a.* fertilizer(-ing).
fructificar, *vn.* (*pret.* FRUCTIFIQUÉ; *subj.* FRUCTIFIQUE) to fructify, bear fruit; to yield profit.
fructosa, *f.* (chem.) fructose.
fructuario, ria, *a.* (law) usufructuary.
fructuosamente, *adv.* fruitfully, profitably.
fructuoso, sa, *a.* fruitful, profitable.
fruente, *a.* enjoying.
frufrú, *m.* (text.) froufrou.
frugal, *a.* frugal, parsimonious, thrifty.
frugalidad, *f.* frugality, thrift.
frugalmente, *adv.* frugally, thriftily.
frugívoro, ra, *a.* frugivorous, fruit-eating.
fruición, *f.* fruition, enjoyment, gratification.
fruir, *vn.* (*ger.* FRUYENDO; *ind. pres.* FRUYO, *pret.* él FRUYÓ; *subj.* FRUYA) to enjoy what has been hoped for.
fruitivo, va, *a.* enjoyable.
frumentario, ria; frumenticio, cia, *a.* (bot.) frumentaceous.
frunce, *m.* (sewing) shirr, shirring, gather.
fruncido, da. I. *pp.* of FRUNCIR. **II.** *a.* contracted.
fruncimiento, *m.* shirring, gathering; humbug, deceit, imposture.
fruncir. I. *va.* (*ind.* FRUNZO; *subj.* FRUNZA) (sewing) to gather, shirr; to pucker; to contract. reduce; to conceal or disguise (the truth).—**f. el ceño** or **entrecejo,** to frown.—**f. las cejas,** to knit the brows.—**f. los labios,** to curl or pucker the lips. **II.** *vr.* to affect modesty; to be shocked.
fruslera, *f.* brass turnings or clippings.
fruslería, *f.* trifle, bauble, tidbit.
fruslero, ra, *a.* trifling, frivolous, futile.
frustración, *f.* frustration, disappointment.
frustrado, da. I. *pp.* of FRUSTRAR. **II.** *a.* frustrated, disappointed.
frustraneo, nea, *a.* vain, useless, nugatory.
frustrar. I. *va.* to frustrate, defeat, thwart. **II.** *vr.* to miscarry, to fail, to fall through, to be a failure.
frustratorio, ria, *a.* frustrative, defeating.
fruta, *f.* a piece of fruit; fruitage.—*pl.* fruit (edible, esp. table, tree fruits).—**f. del tiempo,** fruit eaten in season; anything incidental or peculiar to a season.—**f. de sartén,** pancake, fritter.—**f. nueva,** something new, novelty.
frutaje, *m.* (art) painting of fruits and flowers.
frutal. I. *a.* (bot.) fruit-bearing, fruit (as *a.*). **II.** *m.* fruit tree.
frutar, *vn.* to bear or yield fruit.
frutería, *f.* fruitery, fruit store.
frutero, ra. I. *n.* fruiterer; fruit basket, fruit dish. **II.** *m.* napkin or doily over a fruit dish; (art) painting representing fruit; ornamental piece of artificial fruit.
frutescente, *a.* frutescent; shrublike, shrubby.
frútice, *m.* perennial shrub.
fruticoso, sa, *a.* (bot.) fruiticose.
frutilla, *f. dim.* small fruit; (Am.) strawberry; bead for rosaries.
frutillar, *m.* (Am.) strawberry bed.
fruto, *m.* fruit; any useful produce of the earth; any product of man's intellect or labor; benefice, profit.—*pl.* (com.) produce, commodities. —**f. de bendición,** child lawfully begotten.—**sacar f. de,** or **con,** to derive benefit from, succeed in.
fruyo, fruyó, etc. *v. V.* FRUIR.
ftaleína, *f.* (chem.) phthalein.—**ftálico, ca,** *a.* phthalic.—**ftatilo,** *m.* phthatyl.
fu, *interj.* of disgust; sound imitating the snarling of a cat.
fucáceo, cea, *a.* (bot.) fucaceous.
fúcar, *m.* rich, opulent man; nabob.
fucilar, *vn.* (poet.) to flash, to lighten.
fucilazo, *m.* heat lightning.
fuco, *m.* (bot.) fucus (seaweed).
fucsia, *f.* (bot.) fuchsia.
fucsina, *f.* (chem.) fuchsine.
fuego. I. *m.* fire; conflagration; beacon fire; bonfire, watch fire; skin eruption, rash; firing of firearms; hearth, fireplace; ardor, heat of an action; hearth, house; (vet.) cautery.—*pl.* lights, lighthouse; (mil.) fire, firing.—**f. de Santelmo,** (naut.) St. Elmo's fire; (naut.) Castor and Pollux.—**f. fatuo,** jack-o'-lantern, will-o-the-wisp, ignis fatuus.—**f. graneado,** (mil.) continued fire, drumfire.—**f. griego,** Greek or wild fire.—**f. nutrido,** (mil.) drumfire.—**f. sacro,** (med.) St. Anthony's fire, erysipelas.—**fuegos artificiales,** fireworks.—**fuegos en los labios,** (med.) fever blister or sore. —**a sangre y f.,** by fire and sword.—**dar f. a,** to give a light to (for a cigarette).—**dar f. a un navío,** (naut.) to bream a ship.—**donde f. se hace, humo sale,** where there is smoke, there is fire.—**echar f.,** (fig.) to spit fire, throw out sparks.—**echar f. por los ojos,** (fig.) to look or stare daggers, look angry.—**entre dos fuegos,** (fig.) between two fires, between the devil and the deep blue sea.—**hacer f.,** to fire (a weapon). —**jugar con f.,** (fig.) to play with fire.—**meter f.,** to get it started, push ahead, build a fire under something.—**pegar f.,** to set afire.—**romper el f.,** (mil.) to open fire, start shooting. **II.** *interj.* (mil.) fire!—**¡f.! ¡f. de Cristo!** or **¡f. de Dios!** blazes! confound it!
fueguino, na, *a.* & *n.* Fuegian.
fuellar, *m.* bright talcum ornament on wax tapers.
fuelle, *m.* bellows; blower; (carriage) hood, top; clouds over mountains; (sewing) puckers in clothes; (coll.) talebearer.
fuente, *f.* water spring; fountain; source; (often *pl.*) headwaters, source (of a river); dish platter; (surg.) seton, issue.—**beber en buenas fuentes,** to be well-informed.—**f. de información,** source of information, "contact."
fuer, *m. contr. of* FUERO.—**a f. de,** *adv.* as a, in the manner of (*a fuer de caballero,* as or like a gentleman).
[1]**fuera. I.** *adv.* out, without, outside.—**f. de,** out of; outside of; besides, in addition to.—**f. de lugar,** out of place; irrelevant.—**f. de orden,** (parl. law) out of order.—**f. de quicio,** unhinged; out of order, out of joint.—**f. de sí,** beside oneself; berserk; aghast.—**f. de tono,** off key.—**de f.,** from the outside, externally. —**hacia f.,** outward.—**por f.,** on the outside. **II.** (**¡fuera!**) *interj.* out! away! put him out! get out!
[2]**fuera,** etc. *v. V.* SER and IR.
fuerarropa.—**hacer f.,** a command used in the galleys for the rabble to undress.
fuero, *m.* statute law; jurisdiction, judicial power; privilege or exemption granted to a province; compilation of laws.—**f. de la conciencia,** tribunal of conscience; heart of hearts.—**f. exterior,** or **externo,** statute law; legal tribunals. —**f. interior,** or **interno,** = F. DE LA CONCIENCIA.—**a f.,** according to law or custom.—**de f.,** de jure; according to law.
fuerte. I. *a.* strong; powerful; intense, severe;

secure, fast, impregnable; firm, compact; efficacious; thick, heavy; proficient, surpassing; loud; manly, determined, unswerving; hard, not malleable; terrible; grave; excessive; having excess of weight.—**es f. cosa,** it is very hard. **II.** *m.* fort, fortress; strong point, forte; (mus.) forte, loud (marked *f*). **III.** *adv.* strongly, hard, copiously, abundantly, excessively.

fuertemente, *adv.* strongly, firmly, fast; powerfully; vehemently.

fuerza, *f.* force; strength; stress; violence; firmness, stanchness; efficacy; fortitude, courage; virtue, efficiency; mental power; (mech.) power; (mil., gen. *pl.*) force(s); (fort.) fortress, a strong place; strongest part of a thing; proneness, strong propensity; the third of a sword next the hilt; (sewing) stiffening piece in garments.—**f. aérea,** air force.—**f. animal,** animal power.—**f. bruta,** brute force.—**f. centrífuga,** centrifugal force.—**f. centrípeta,** centripetal force.—**f. contraelectromotriz,** counterelectromotive force.—**f. de agua,** water power.—**f. de atracción,** attractive force.—**f. de gravedad,** gravitational force.—**f. de sangre,** animal power.—**f. de trabajo,** labor force.—**f. de vapor,** steam power.—**f. electromotriz,** electromotive force.—**f. mayor,** (law & com.) superior force, force majeure.—**f. motriz,** motive power, moving force; power.—**f. nuclear,** nuclear force.—**f. paramilitar,** paramilitary forces.—**f. viva,** (mech.) vis viva (twice the kinetic energy).—**fuerzas conspirantes,** conspiring forces or powers.—**fuerzas de mar y de tierra,** naval and land forces.—**a f. de,** by dint of, by force of.—**a la f.** = DE POR F.—**a viva f.,** by main force; with the utmost effort.—**de por f.,** by force, forcibly; necessarily.—**en f. de,** on account of.—**hacer f. de remos,** (naut.) to pull hard at the oars.—**hacer f. de velas,** (naut.) to crowd sail, to carry a press of sail; to make a strenuous effort.—**por f., por la f.** = DE POR F.—**ser f.,** to be necessary.

fuerzo, fuerce, *v. V.* FORZAR.

fuetazo, *m.* (Am.) blow with a whip.—*pl.* horsewhipping.—**dar,** or **pegar, fuetazos,** *m.* (Am.) to horsewhip.

fuete, *m.* (Am.) horsewhip, riding whip.

fufú, *m.* (Am.) mashed yam, plantain, etc.

fuga, *f.* flight; escape; runaway; elopement; leak, leakage; (mus.) fugue.—**f. deshecha,** precipitate flight.—**f. precipitada,** stampede.—**poner en f.,** to put to flight, rout.

fugacidad, *f.* fugacity, brevity.

fugar, *vr.* (*pret.* me FUGUÉ; *subj.* me FUGUE) to flee, to run away; to escape, leak out.

fugaz, *a.* fugacious; fugitive, running away; brief, fleeting.—**estrella f.,** shooting star.

fugitivo, va. I. *n.* & *a.* fugitive, runaway. **II.** *a.* brief, perishable, unsteady, unstable.

fugué, fugue, *v. V.* FUGAR.

fuí, etc. *v. V.* SER and IR.

fuina, *f.* (zool.) = GARDUÑA, marten.

fulanito, ta; fulano, na, *n.* so-and-so.—**F. de tal,** John Doe, so-and-so.—**F., Zutano y Mengano,** Tom, Dick and Harry.

fular, *m.* (text.) foulard.

fulcro, *m.* (mech.) fulcrum.

fulgente, *a.* (poet.) refulgent, brilliant.

fúlgido, da, *a.* bright, resplendent.

fulgor, *m.* fulgency, brilliancy.

fulguración, *f.* flash; flashing; (med.) lightning stroke.

fulgurante, *a.* resplendent, shining.

fulgurar, *vn.* to flash, shine with brilliancy.

fulgurita, *f.* (geol.) fulgurite.

fulguroso, sa, *a.* fulgurous.

fúlica, *f.* (ornith.) fulica, coot.

fuliginoso, sa, *a.* fuliginous, dark, sooty.

fulminación, *f.* fulmination, thundering.

fulminador, ra, *n.* & *a.* thunderer(-ing); fulminator(-ing).

fulminante. I. *a.* fulminating, thundering; exploding, explosive; (of illness) serious; fatal. **II.** *m.* (artil.) cap, percussion cap.

fulminar. *va.* to fulminate; (of lightning) to flash; to cause to explode; to throw out as an object of terror; to thunder, utter wrathfully.

fulminato, *m.* (chem.) fulminate.—**f. de mercurio,** fulminating mercury.

fulminatriz, *f. a.* fulminating.

fulmíneo, nea, *a.* fulmineous.

fulmínico, *a.* (chem.) fulminic (acid).

fulminoso, sa, *a.* fulminatory.

fulleresco, ca, *a.* pert. to cheaters, sharpers.

fullería, *f.* cheating at games; guile, cunning.

fullero, ra. I. *a.* "shady," dishonest; (Am.) conceited, arrogant. **II.** *n.* cheat; sharper.

fullingue, *a.* (Chile) of bad quality; sickly, lifeless.

fullona, *f.* (coll.) dispute, quarrel, wrangle.

fumable, *a.* good to smoke.

fumada, *f.* puff, whiff (of smoke).

fumadero, *m.* smoking room.

fumador, ra. I. *n.* smoker. **II.** *a.* addicted to smoking.

fumar, *va.* & *vn.* to smoke (cigars, etc.).

fumarada, *f.* puff, whiff, or blast of smoke; pipeful of tobacco.

fumaria, *f.* (bot.) fumitory.

fumárico, ca, *a.* (chem.) fumaric.

fumarola, *f.* (geol.) fumarole.

fumífero, ra, *a.* (poet.) smoking.

fumífugo, ga, *a.* smoke-dispersing.

fumigación, *f.* fumigation.

fumigador, ra, *n.* & *a.* fumigator(-ing).

fumigar, *va.* (*pret.* FUMIGUÉ; *subj.* FUMIGUE) to fumigate.

fumigatorio, ria. I. *a.* fumigatory. **II.** *m.* perfuming pan.

fumista, *n.* stove worker or plumber.

fumistería, *f.* stove works or shop.

fumívoro, ra, *a.* smokeless.

fumorola, *f.* = FUMAROLA.

fumosidad, *f.* smokiness.

fumoso, sa, *a.* fumy, smoky.

funambulesco, ca, *a.* funambulatory.

funámbulo, la, *n.* funambulist, tightrope walker.

función, *f.* function; duty; functioning, operation, working; religious ceremony, public demonstration; (theat.) performance, play; (math., physiol.) function; (mil.) fight, engagement, battle.

funcional, *a.* (math., physiol.) functional.

funcionamiento, *m.* (mech.) functioning, working, running, performance.—**de f.,** operating.

funcionar, *vn.* to function; (of machines) to work, run.

funcionario, *m.* functionary, public official.

funda, *f.* case, sheath, cover, envelope, slip.—**f. de almohada,** pillowcase.

fundación, *f.* foundation; founding, establishing; erection, raising, building; basis; rise, beginning, origin; endowment, foundation, endowed institution; (arch.) foundation, base, groundwork.

fundadamente, *adv.* with good reason, with good evidence or proof.

fundador, ra, *n.* founder.

fundamental, *a.* fundamental.

fundamentalismo, *m.* (relig.) fundamentalism.

fundamentalista, *a.* & *n.* (relig.) fundamentalist.

fundamentar, *va.* to found; to establish on a basis; to ground; to base; to set firm.

fundamento, *m.* foundation, groundwork; basis; reason, fundamental principle; source, origin, root; (of children) good behavior, orderliness; (weaving) weft, woof.

fundar. I. *va.* to found; to raise, erect, build; to establish, institute; to base, ground. **II.** *vr.* **(en)** to base one's opinion (on).

fundente. I. *a.* (chem.) fusing, melting, smelting. **II.** *m.* (chem.) flux; (med.) dissolvent.

fundería, *f.* foundry; smelting work.

fundible, *a.* fusible.
fundibulario, *m.* Roman soldier armed with a sling.—**fundíbulo,** *m.* ancient war engine for throwing stones.
fundición, *f.* fusion, melting, casting; foundry, smeltery; cast; cast iron; (print.) font.
fundidor, *m.* melter, smelter.
fundir. I. *va.* to fuse or melt; to smelt; to cast. **II.** *vr.* to fuse, melt; to merge, blend, unite; (Am.) to be ruined.
fundo, *m.* (law) rural property.
fúnebre, *a.* funereal, mournful, sad; funeral; dark, lugubrious.
funeral, *n.* & *a.* funeral (as a *n.*, often *pl.*).
funerala.—**a la f.,** (mil.) inverted (arms).
funerario, ria, *a.* funeral.
funéreo, rea, *a.* mournful, sad, funereal.
funestar, *va.* to blot, tarnish, stain, profane.
funesto, ta, *a.* regrettable, untoward; mournful, sad, dismal.
fungible, *a.* consumable; (law) fungible.
fungicida, *m.* fungicide.
fungiforme, *a.* fungiform.
fungir, *vn.* (Am.) to act in some capacity.
fungo, *m.* (med.) fungus.
fungosidad, *f.* (med.) spongy morbid growth.
fungoso, sa, *a.* fungous, excrescent, spongy.
funicular, *a.* funicular.
funículo, *m.* (bot.) funicle or funiculus.
fuñique, *a.* awkward; timorous, pusillanimous.
furente, *a.* furious, raging, frantic.
fúrfura, *f.* (med.) furfur, dandruff, scurf.
furfuráceo, cea, *a.* furfuraceous.
furgón, *m.* wagon; car.
furia, *f.* fury; rage; fit of madness; ill-tempered person; hurry, hustling; zeal, ardor.—**a toda f.,** with utmost speed.
furibundo, da, *a.* furious, enraged, frantic.
furiente, *a.* = FURENTE.
furierismo, *m.* Fourierism.
furierista, *n.* & *a.* Fourierist(-ic).
furioso, sa, *a.* furious, frantic; excessive.
furlón, *m.* = FORLÓN, anc. two-seat chaise.
[1]**furo, ra,** *a.* shy, unsociable, reserved; untamed, wild.
[2]**furo,** *m.* (Cuba) opening of a sugar mold.
[3]**furo.**—**hacer f.,** to hide a thing with the intention of keeping it.
furor, *m.* furor, fury, madness, rage, anger; enthusiasm, exaltation of fancy; rage, fashion.—**f. uterino,** (med.) nymphomania.—**hacer f.,** to be the rage, "make a hit."
furriel, furrier, *m.* (mil.) quartermaster; clerk of the king's mews.
furriela, furriera, *f.* place of keeper of the keys of the king's palace.
furrusca, *f.* (Colomb.) row, brawl.
furtivamente, *adv.* by stealth, clandestinely.
furtivo, va, *a.* furtive, clandestine.
furúnculo, forúnculo, *m.* (med.) furuncle, boil.
furunculoso, sa, *a.* furunculose.
fusa, *f.* (mus.) demisemiquaver.
fusado, da, *a.* (her.) charged with fusils or spindles.
fusca, *f.* (ornith.) a dark-colored duck.
fusco, ca, *a.* fuscous, brown, dark.
fuselado, da, *a.* (aer.) streamlined.
fuselaje, *m.* (aer.) fuselage.
fuselar, *va.* (aer.) to streamline.
fusente, *a.* receding (tide).
fusibilidad, *f.* fusibility.
fusible. I. *a.* fusible. **II.** *m.* (elec.) fuse.
fusiforme, *a.* fusiform, spindle-shaped.
fusil, *m.* rifle, gun, musket.—**f. de aguja,** needle gun.—**f. de chispa,** flintlock musket.—**f. de percusión,** or **de pistón,** musket.—**f. de retrocarga,** breechloader.—**f. rayado,** rifle.
fusilamiento, *m.* execution by shooting.
fusilar, *va.* to shoot, execute by shooting.
fusilazo, *m.* musket shot, rifle shot.
fusilería, *f.* (mil.) musketry; body of fusileers or musketeers.
fusilero, *m.* fusileer, musketeer.
fusión, *f.* fusion; melting; union; (com.) merger.—**f. nuclear,** (phys.) nuclear fusion.
fusionar. I. *va.* to unite, bring together, merge. **II.** *vr.* (com.) to merge, form a merger.
fusionista, *n.* fusionist.
fusique, *m.* bottle-shaped snuffbox.
fusor, *m.* smelting ladle or vessel.
fusta, *f.* brushwood; woollen stuff; whiplash; (naut.) lateen-rigged lighter.
fustán, *m.* fustian (cloth); (Am.) petticoat.
fustanero, *m.* fustian manufacturer.
fuste, *m.* wood, timber; tree and bows of a saddle; (poet.) saddle; shaft of a lance; foundation of anything not material; substance, importance; (arch.) fust, shaft of a column.
fustero, ra. I. *a.* pertaining to a fust, foundation, etc. **II.** *m.* turner or carpenter.
fustete, *m.* (bot.) Venetian sumac; fustic, yellowwood.
fustigante, *a.* fustigating, beating.
fustigar, *va.* to lash, fustigate.
fustina, *f.* place for fusing metals.
fútbol, *m.* football.
futbolero, ra, futbolístico, ca, *a.* of or pertaining to football.
futbolista, *n.* football player.
futesa, *f.* trifle, bauble, bagatelle, gewgaw.
fútil, *a.* futile, feckless, trivial.
futilidad, *f.* futility, triviality.
futre, *m.* (Chile) dude, fop, coxcomb.
futura, *f.* acquired right to an office or employment before its vacancy; (coll.) betrothed, intended bride.
futurismo, *m.* (art) futurism.
futurista, *n.* & *a.* (art) futurist(-ic).
futuro, ra. I. *a.* future. **II.** *m.* betrothed, future husband; future, futurity; (gram.) future.—**en lo f.,** in future, hereafter.

G

G, g, *f.* g, eighth letter of the Spanish alphabet.
gabacho, cha. I. *a.* Pyrenean; (coll.) Frenchified, Gallicized, Frenchy. **II.** *n.* Pyrenean; Gallomaniac; *m.* (ling.) Gallicized Spanish.
gabán, *m.* greatcoat, overcoat.
gabaonita, *n.* & *a.* Gabaonite.
gabarda, *f.* (bot.) wild rose.
gabardina, *f.* gabardine.
gabarit, *m.* (Ry.) track gauge.
gabarra, *f.* (naut.) lighter, barge, gabbard.
gabarrero, *m.* (naut.) lighterman.
gabarro, *m.* flaw or defect in goods; error, mistake; drudgery, burdensome obligation; (mason. and art) badigeon, filling; (vet.) swelling on the pastern of horses; pip (disease of fowls).
gabazo, *m.* bagasse.
gabela, *f.* gabelle, tax; duty, burden.
gabinete, *m.* cabinet (ministers of state and privy councillors); private room where the cabinet meets; reception room, sitting room; private parlor; library, study; studio; ladies' boudoir or dressing room; laboratory.—**g. de lectura,** reading room.—**de g.,** theoretical, parlor (as *a.*, app. to one with purely theoretical knowledge).
gablete, *m.* (arch.) gable.
Gabón, *m.* Gabon.
gabonés, nesa, *n.* & *a.* Gabonese.
gabote, *m.* (prov.) shuttlecock.
gacel, *m.*, **gacela,** *f.* gazelle.
gaceta, *f.* gazette; record (a publication); newspaper.—**mentir mas que la g.,** to be an inveterate liar.
gacetera, *f.* woman who sells newspapers.
gacetero, *m.* news writer; seller of newspapers.
gacetilla, *f.* personal-news column; town talk, gossip; newspaper squib; newsmonger.
gacetillero, *m.* newspaper reporter; paragrapher; wretched writer, penny-a-liner.

gacetista, *n.* one who delights in reading newspapers; newsmonger, gossip.
gacha, *f.* very thin watery mass; (Cuba) unglazed crock.—*pl.* porridge; pap; caresses, pettings.—**hacerse unas gachas,** to be too soft or affectionate.
gaché, *m.* (prov.) fellow, guy.
[1]**gacheta,** *f.* spring lever, or tooth, of a latch.
[2]**gacheta,** *f.* sticking paste.
gacho, cha, *a.* turned or bent downward; (of cattle) with down-curved horns; (of hat) slouch. —**a gachas,** (coll.) on all-fours.
gachón, na. I. *a.* (coll.) graceful, sweet, attractive, bright. **II.** *n.* pampered, spoiled child.
gachonada, gachonería, *f.* (coll.) gracefulness, cunningness, brightness, piquancy.
gachumbo, *m.* (Am.) shell of various fruits, from which cups and other vessels are made.
gachupín, *m.* Spaniard settled in Lat. Am.
gádido, da. I. *n.* & *a.* (ichth.) gadid. **II.** *m. pl.* (ichth.) Gadidae.
gaditano, na, *a.* of or pertaining to Cadiz.
gadolinio, *m.* (chem.) gadolinium.
gaélico, ca. I. *a.* Gaelic. **II.** *n.* Gael; *m.* (ling.) Gaelic.
gafa, *f.* hook for bending a crossbow.—*pl.* (naut.) can hooks, grapple hooks; spectacles; spectacle bows.
gafar, *va.* to hook, to claw, to catch with a hook or with the nails.
gafedad, *f.* (med.) claw hand.
gafete, *m.* clasp, hook and eye.
gafo, fa, *a.* suffering from claw hand.
gago, ga, *n.* stammerer, stutterer.
gaguear, *vn.* (Am.) to stutter.
gaguera, *f.* (Am.) stuttering.
gaita, *f.* flageolet; hurdy-gurdy; (coll.) neck.—**g. gallega,** bagpipe.—**estar de g.,** (coll.) to be very merry.—**templarle la g. a uno,** to humor one.
gaitería, *f.* gay and gaudy dress.
gaitero, ra. I. *a.* (coll.) unbecomingly sportive and gay; (coll.) gaudy, showy, flamboyant. **II.** *n.* piper, one who plays the bagpipe.
gaje, *m.* salary, pay, wages.—*pl.* perquisites, fees.
gajo, *m.* branch (of a tree); part of a bunch of grapes torn off; pyramidal raceme of any fruit; (orange, pomegranate, etc.) section; prong or tine of pitchforks, etc.; spur of a mountain ridge.
gajoso, sa, *a.* composed of GAJOS.
gala, *f.* gala; full, or court, dress; graceful, pleasing address; parade, ostentation; choicest part; (Am.) prize.—*pl.* regalia, finery, trappings, paraphernalia.—**galas de novia,** bridal trousseau.—**de g.,** full-dress (suit, uniform).—**hacer g. de,** or **tener a g.,** to be proud of, glory in, boast of.
galabardera, *f.* (bot.) wild rose.
galáctico, ca, *a.* (astr.) galactic.
galactita, galactites, *f.* fuller's earth.
galactómetro, *m.* lactometer.
galactosa, *f.* (chem.) galactose.
galafate, *m.* artful thief, cunning rogue.
galaico, ca, *n.* & *a.* = GALLEGO, Galician.
galamero, ra, *a.* dainty, sweet-mouthed.
galán, *m.* spruce, well-made man; gallant, courtier; lover, wooer; ladies' man; (theat.) leading man or woman.—**g., g.,** easily, without effort. —**segundo g.,** (theat.) man who has a walk-on part.
galancete, *m. dim.* spruce little man or lad; (theat.) juvenile leading man.
galanga, *f.* (bot.) officinal galangal.
galano, na, *a.* smartly dressed; tasteful; (of literary style) elegant, pleasing; beautiful, fresh (as flowers); (Cuba) mottled, parti-colored.
galante, *a.* gallant, polished, attentive to ladies.
galanteador, *m.* wooer, lover; flatterer.
galantear, *va.* to court, woo, pay attention to.
galanteo, *m.* gallantry, courtship, wooing.
galantería, *f.* gallantry, courtesy, politeness; grace, elegance; compliment to a lady; liberality, generosity.
galantina, *f.* (cook.) galantine.
galanura, *f.* prettiness, gorgeousness, elegance.
galapagar, *m.* place where tortoises abound.
galápago, *m.* fresh-water tortoise; (agr.) bed of plowshare; frame for boring guns; mold for convex tiles; (foundry) pig, ingot; (mason.) small centering frame; (surg.) strip with ends forked or deeply notched; English saddle; (Am.) sidesaddle; (mil.) shed formed with shields joined together; mantelet, vinea, cat castle, sow; (vet.) scratch.
galapaguera, *f.* aquarium for tortoises.
galapo, *m.* (rope-making) laying top.
galardón, *m.* guerdon, reward, prize.
galardonador, ra, *n.* & *a.* rewarder(-ing).
galardonar, *va.* to reward, recompense, requite.
gálata, *n.* & *a.* Galatian.
galato, *m.* (chem.) gallate.
galaxia, *f.* soapstone, steatite; (astr.) Galaxy, Milky Way.
galayo, *m.* cliff.
galbana, *f.* sloth, laziness, indolence.
galbanado, da, *a.* yellowish-grey.
galbanero, ra, *a.* (coll.) lazy, indolent.
gálbano, *m.* (pharm.) galbanum.
galbanoso, sa, *a.* indolent, lazy, shiftless.
gálbulo, *m.* nut of the cypress tree.
galdrufa, *f.* spinning top.
gálea, *f.* galea, ancient helmet.
galeato, ta, *a.* preface in answer to actual or probable criticism.
galeaza, *f.* (naut.) galleas.
galega, *f.* (bot.) officinal goat's-rue.
galena, *f.* (min.) galena.
galénico, ca, *a.* Galenic.—**galenismo,** *m.* Galenism.—**galenista,** *n.* Galenist.
galeno, na, *a.* (naut.) moderate, soft (wind).
gáleo, *m.* (ichth.) swordfish.
galeón, *m.* (naut.) galleon.
galeota, *f.* (naut.) galliot.
galeote, *m.* galley slave.
galera, *f.* (naut.) galley; wagon, van; (Hond., Mex.) shed; house of correction for women; extra line of beds in a hospital ward; (print.) galley; (arith.) fraction line; (carp.) smooth plane, organ-builder's plane; furnace for distilling sulphur.
galerada, *f.* carload, van load; (print.) galley; galley proof.
galerero, *m.* wagoner, van driver.
galería, *f.* gallery, lobby, corridor; (theat.) gallery; art museum; collection of paintings; (fort.) narrow covered passage across a moat; (min.) gallery, driftway, heading.—**g. de pinturas,** picture gallery.—**g. de popa,** (naut.) stern gallery or balcony.—**g. principal,** (theat.) dress circle.
gallerín, *m. dim.* (print.) wooden galley.
galerita, *f.* (ornith.) crested lark.
galerna, *f.,* **galerno,** *m.* (naut.) stormy northwest wind.
galerón, *m.* (Mex.) large room serving as jail or prison; (Am.) a kind of popular air and dance.
galés, sa, *n.* & *a.* Welsh.
galfarro, *m.* rogue, loafer, idler; (ornith.) hawk.
[1]**galga,** *f.* rolling stone; (mill) stone wheel that grinds olives.
[2]**galga,** *f.* (med.) a kind of eruption or rash.
[3]**galga,** *f.* bier or stretcher on which poor people are taken to be buried; drag, Scotch brake for a wheel; (naut.) back of an anchor.
[4]**galga,** *f.*—*pl.* long ankle ties for women's slippers.
[5]**galga,** *f.* (zool.) greyhound bitch.
galgo, ga. I. *a.* (Am.) hungry; eager. **II.** *n.* greyhound.
galgueño, ña, *a.* resembling, or pertaining to, greyhounds.
gálgulo, *m.* (ornith.) roller.
galianos, *m. pl.* shepherd's meal.
galibar, *va.* (naut.) to trace, to mould.

gálibo, *m.* templet, pattern, mold; (Ry.) gauge for the width and height of an open freight car (to determine whether there will be enough clearance in tunnels, etc.).
galicado, da, *a.* (of words, style, etc.) French in construction or form.
galicano, na, *n.* & *a.* Gallican.
galicismo, *m.* Gallicism.
galicista, *n.* Gallicizer, user of Gallicisms.
gálico, *m.* venereal disease; syphilis.
galicoso, sa, *a.* (coll.) infected with syphilis.
galilea, *f.* (arch.) galilee porch or chapel.
galileo, a, *n.* & *a.* Galilean.
galillo, *m.* uvula, soft palate.
galimatías, *m.* gibberish.
[1]**galio,** *m.* (bot.) cheese-rennet bedstraw.
[2]**galio,** *m.* (chem.) gallium.
galiopsis, *f.* (bot.) common hedge-nettle.
galiparlista, *n.* = GALICISTA.
[1]**galipodio,** *m.* white frankincense.
[2]**galipodio,** *m.* galipot.
galizabra, *f.* lateen-rigged vessel.
galo, la, *n.* & *a.* Gaul; Gallic.
galocha, *f.* galosh, clog, patten.
galófilo, la, *n.* & *a.* Gallophile.
galofobia, *f.* Francophobia.
galófobo, ba, *n.* & *a.* Gallophobe.
galomanía, *f.* Gallomania.
[1]**galón,** *m.* galloon, tape, braid, binding lace; stripe, or gold or silver braid on uniforms.—*pl.* (naut.) sheer rails.
[2]**galón,** *m.* (Angl.) gallon. liquid measure.
galoneadura, *f.* (sewing) trimming.
galonear, *va.* (sewing) to bind, to trim with galloons.
galonero, ra, *n.* braid or galloon maker.
galonista, *m.* (coll.) pupil of a military college wearing corporal stripes as a reward.
galop, *m.* (dance) galop.
galopar, *vn.* to gallop.
galope, *m.* gallop; haste, speed.—**a g.,** or **de g.,** hurriedly, speedily.
galopeado, da. I. *pp.* of GALOPEAR. **II.** *a.* (coll.) hastily done. **III.** *m.* (coll.) whipping, flogging.
galopear, *vn.* = GALOPAR.
galopillo, *m. dim.* scullion, kitchen boy.
galopín, *m.* ragamuffin; rascal, rogue; shrewd fellow; clever knave; (naut.) swabber, cabin boy; scullion.
galopinada, *f.* roguish act, knavery.
galopo, *m.* rascal, rogue.
galpón, *m.* (Am.) old-time slaves' quarters; (W. I., S. A.) shed.
galtoniano, na, *a.* Galtonian, of or pertaining to Galton's theory of inheritance.
Galván, *m.*—**eso no lo entenderá G.,** (coll.) that is a puzzle, that is a hard nut to crack.
galvanicé, galvanice, *v. V.* GALVANIZAR.
galvánico, ca, *a.* galvanic.
galvanismo, *m.* (phys.) galvanism.
galvanización, *f.* (phys.) galvanization.
galvanizar, *va.* (*pret.* GALVANICÉ; *subj.* GALVANICE) to galvanize; to electroplate.
galvanocauterio, *m.* (med.) galvanocautery.
galvanometría, *f.* galvanometry.
galvanométrico, ca, *a.* galvanometric.
galvanómetro, *m.* galvanometer.
galvanoplastia, galvanoplástica, *f.* galvanoplasty, electrotypy.
galvanoplástico, ca, *a.* galvanoplastic.
galvanoscopio, *m.* galvanoscope.
galladura, *f.* cicatricle, plasma bit of an egg.
gallar, gallear, *va.* (of a cock) to copulate with.
gallarda, *f.* a Spanish dance and its music; (print.) type of a size between minion and brevier.
gallardear, *vn.* to act with grace or elegance.
gallardete, *m.* (naut.) pennant, streamer.
gallardetón, *m.* (naut.) broad pennant.
gallardía, *f.* gracefulness; fine bearing; gallantry, bravery, nobleness; activity, briskness.
gallardo, da, *a.* graceful, elegant; magnanimous, generous; lively; brave, gallant.
gallareta, *f.* (ornith.) widgeon.
gallarón, *m.* (ornith.) a kind of bustard.
gallaruza, *f.* hooded garment.
gallear. I. *va.* (of cocks) to copulate with. **II.** *vn.* to surpass, excel; to assume an air of importance; to raise the voice in anger; to crow; to bully; (foundry) to have flaws.
gallegada, *f.* a group of GALLEGOS; peculiar action or speech of a GALLEGO; a Galician dance and its tune.
gallego, ga. I. *n.* & *a.* Galician, from province of Galicia; (Am.) Spanish(-iard). **II.** *m.* northwest wind.
galleo, *m.* (foundry) flaw in casting.
gallera, *f.* cockpit.
[1]**galleta,** *f.* ship biscuit, hardtack; cookie; (Mex., C. A., W. I.) slap.
[2]**galleta,** *f.* small vessel or pan.
gallillo, *m.* = GALILLO, uvula, soft palate.
gallina. I. *f.* hen.—**g. de Guinea,** Guinea hen. **II.** *n.* coward, chicken-hearted person.—**g. ciega,** blindman's buff.
gallináceo, cea, *a.* (ornith.) gallinaceous.
gallinaza, *f.* hen dung; (ornith.) GALLINAZO.
gallinazo, *m.* (ornith.) gallinazo, turkey buzzard.
gallinería, *f.* poulterer's shop; hencoop or henhouse; cowardice, pusillanimity.
gallinero, ra. I. *a.* chicken-eating. **II.** *n.* poulterer, poultry dealer. **III.** *m.* poultry yard; hencoop, henroost, henhouse; basket for carrying poultry; ladies' club or bee; (coll., theat.) nigger heaven, top gallery.
gallineta, *f.* (ornith.) sandpiper; ruffed grouse.
gallipato, *m.* (ornith.) merganser.
gallipava, *f.* a large variety of hen.
gallipavo, *m.* (ornith.) turkey; (coll.) false, unpleasant note in singing.
gallipuente, *m.* bridge without rails.
gallístico, ca, *a.* of gamecocks or cockfights.
gallito, *m. dim.* small cock; beau, coxcomb: cock of the walk, bully.
gallo, *m.* (ornith.) cock, rooster; (ichth.) dory, sea fish; boss, chief, leader; cork float for fishing; (carp.) wall board of the roof; false note in singing.—**g. de pelea,** or **inglés,** gamecock.—**alzar el g.,** to speak loud and arrogantly.—**hacerse el g.,** to become the ruler in any meeting, body, etc.—**otro g. le cantara,** he would be better (or worse) off, he would have fared differently.—**salir con una pata de g.,** to give a foolish or irrelevant answer.—**ser el g.** = HACERSE EL G.—**tener mucho g.,** to be very arrogant and overbearing.
gallocresta, *f.* (bot.) annual clary sage.
gallofa, *f.* food given to pilgrims; greens for salad and pottage; idle tale; French roll; directory of divine service.
gallofar, gallofear, *vn.* to loaf about as a beggar.
gallofero, ra; gallofo, fa. I. *a.* idle, lazy, vagabond. **II.** *n.* tramp.
gallón, *m.* green sod, turf; (arch.) echinus.
[1]**gama,** *f.* (zool.) doe.
[2]**gama,** *f.* (mus.) gamut.
gamarra, *f.* (harness) martingale, check, strap.
gamarza, *f.* (bot.) wild Syrian rue.
gámbaro, *m.* = CÁMBARO, (ichth.) crawfish.
gambax, *m.* = GAMBAJ.
gamberra, *f.* prostitute, strumpet.
gambesina, *f.*, **gambesón,** *m.* = GAMBAJ.
gambeta, *f.* (dance) crosscaper; prance.
gambetear, *vn.* to caper like a horse.
gambeto, *m.* quilted greatcoat; cap for a newborn child.
gambir, *m.* (bot., pharm.) gambier.
gambito, *m.* (chess) gambit.
gamboa, *f.* (bot.) a variety of quince.
gambota, *m.* (naut.) counter timber, arched timber.
[1]**gamella,** *f.* bow (of yoke).
[2]**gamella,** *f.* large wooden trough or tub; washtub; boundary mound.

gamelleja, *f. dim.* small trough or tub.
gamellón, *m. aug.* large tub; trough in which grapes are trodden.
gameto, *m.* (biol.) gamete.
gametogénesis, *f.* (biol.) gametogenesis.
gamezno, *m. dim.* little young fallow deer.
gamma, *f.* gamma (third letter of the Greek alphabet).
gammagrafía, *f.* gammagraphy.
gamo, *m.* buck of the fallow deer.
gamogénesis, *f.* (biol.) gamogenesis.
gamón, *m.* (bot.) asphodel.
gamonal, *m.* asphodel field or patch; (Am.) boss.
gamonalismo, *m.* (Am.) bossism.
gamonito, *m.* shoot, tiller, sucker.
gamopétalo, la, *a.* (bot.) gamopetalous.
gamosépalo, la, *a.* (bot.) gamosepalous.
gamuno, na, *a.* chamois skin (as *a.*), shammy.
gamuza, *f.* (zool.) chamois; chamois skin.
gamuzado, da, *a.* chamois-colored.
gana, *f.* appetite, hunger; desire; mind.—**dar g.,** or **ganas, de** (foll. by *inf.*) to arouse desire to, to make (one) feel like (foll. by *pres. p.*); to feel like.—**de buena g.,** willingly.—**de g.** energetically, in earnest.—**de mala g.,** unwillingly.—**no me da la g.,** I don't want to, I won't.—**tener g.,** or **ganas, de,** to desire; to wish to; to have a mind to.—**tenerle g.,** or **ganas, a,** to desire; to wish to have a fight with.
ganable, *a.* that may be gained or won, gainable.
ganadería, *f.* cattle raising; cattle ranch; stock farm; live stock; cattle brand.
ganadero, ra. I. *a.* pertaining to cattle. **II.** *n.* grazier, owner of cattle; stock farmer; dealer in cattle; drover.
ganado, *m.* live stock; cattle; herd, flock, drove; (coll.) rabble.—**g. caballar,** horses.—**g. de cerda** = G. MORENO.—**g. de pata hendida,** oxen, cows, sheep, goats.—**g. lechero,** dairy cattle.—**g. mayor,** cattle (including horses, asses, mules).—**g. menor,** sheep.—**g. moreno,** swine, hogs.—**g. ovejuno,** sheep.—**g. vacuno,** bovine cattle.
ganador, ra. I. *a.* winning, conquering. **II.** *n.* winner, conqueror.
ganancia, *f.* gain, profit, advantage.—**g. bruta,** gross profit.—**g. líquida,** net profit.—**ganancias de capital,** capital gains.—**ganancias y pérdidas,** (com.) profit and loss.
ganancial, *a.* pertaining to earnings or profit.
ganancioso, sa, *a.* lucrative, profitable; gaining.
ganapán, *m.* drudge; common laborer; rude, coarse man.
ganapierde, *m.* give-away, losing game.
ganar, *va.* to gain; to win; to earn; to clear, to make (money); to attain, obtain, acquire; to surpass, be superior to; to draw (interest).—**g. de,** or **por, mano,** to get ahead of (in acquiring something), to "beat to it."—**g. el pan,** or **el sustento,** or **la vida,** to earn one's living, make a living.
ganchero, *m.* raftsman guiding logs down a river.
ganchillo, ito, *m. dim.* little hook or crotch.
gancho, *m.* hook; crook, crotch; hairpin; shepherd's crook; sheephook; (coll.) allurer, roper-in; pimp; procurer, pander; (coll.) attractiveness, especially of a woman.—**echar el g. a,** (fig.) to catch; to hook, land.
ganchoso, sa, *a.* hooked, curved.
ganchudo, da, *a.* hooky.
gándara, *f.* low jungle.
[1]**gandaya,** *f.* laziness, idleness.—**andar a la g.,** to gad, loaf, lounge.
[2]**gandaya,** *f.* a kind of cap.
gandido, da, *a.* (Am.) gluttonous.
gandinga, *f.* (min.) washed fine ore; (Cuba) liver stew.
gandir, *va.* to eat.
gandujado, *m.* accordion plaiting.
gandujar, *va.* (sewing) to plait, shirr, fold.
gandul, la, *n.* (coll.) idler, loafer, tramp.
gandulear, *vn.* to loaf, lounge, gad.
gandulería, *f.* idleness, laziness, lounging.
ganeta, *f.* (zool.) = GINETA, genet.
ganforro, ra, *n.* (coll.) rogue, rascal.
[1]**ganga,** *f.* (ornith.) little pin-tailed grouse.
[2]**ganga,** *f.* (min.) gangue; (coll.) child's play, "cinch"; bargain.
ganglio, *m.* (anat., med.) ganglion.—**g. linfático,** (anat.) lymph node.
ganglionar, *a.* (anat.) ganglionic.
gangoso, sa, *a.* speaking with a nasal twang.
gangrena, *f.* (med.) gangrene, blood poisoning.
gangrenar, *va.* & *vn.* to gangrene, canker, become gangrenous.
gangrenoso, sa, *a.* gangrenous.
ganguear, *vn.* to speak with a nasal twang.
gangueo, *m.* nasal twang.
ganguero, *a.* (coll.) running after easy jobs.
gánguil, *m.* (naut.) fishing barge; dump scow.
ganoideo, dea, *m.* & *a.* (ichth.) ganoid.
ganoso sa, *a.* desirous, wishing.
gansada, *f.* (coll.) stupidity.
gansarón, *m.* (ornith.) gosling; tall, thin, gawky man.
ganso, sa, *n.* (ornith.) gander, goose; slow, lazy person; silly person, ninny.—**g. bravo,** wild goose.
gante, *m.* linen manufactured in Ghent.
gantés, esa, *a.* from, or pertaining to, Ghent.
ganzúa, *f.* picklock, skeleton key; picklock, burglar; one skilled in drawing secrets out of others.
gañán, *m.* day laborer; farm hand; rustic.
gañanía, *f.* gang of laborers; lodge for the same.
gañido, *m.* yelping, howling.
gañiles, *m. pl.* cartilaginous larynx; gills of the tunny fish.
gañir, *va.* (*pret.* él GAÑÓ; *ger.* GAÑENDO) to yelp or howl (as a dog); to croak, cackle, crow; (coll.) to talk hoarsely.
gañón, gañote, *m.* (coll.) throat; a kind of fritter.
garabatada, *f.* (coll.) throwing a hook at (something).
garabatear. I. *vn.* to throw a hook at, or for, something; to scrawl, scribble; (coll.) to beat about the bush. **II.** *va.* to hook.
garabateo, *m.* hooking; scribbling, scrawling.
garabato, *m.* hook; pothook; grapple, grapnel, creeper, claw bar, hand bale hook; meathook or gambrel; (Am.) scrawl, scribble; muzzle; winsome ways.—*pl.* (Am.) scrawling; hand gestures.
garabatoso, sa, *a.* full of scrawls; charming, attractive.
garabito, *m.* market stall.
garaje, (improperly) **garage,** *m.* garage.
garambaina, *f.* gaudiness; (coll.) ridiculous affectation or mannerism; illegible scrawl.
garante. I. *a.* responsible. **II.** *n.* (com. and law) warranter, guarantor, surety; bondsman, bail.
garantía, *f.* guarantee; (com. and law) warranty, guaranty, security; indorsement; collateral; bail.
garanticé, garantice, *v. V.* GARANTIZAR.
garantir, *va. defect.* (*used only in forms having the letter* **i** *in their endings*) to guarantee.
garantizar, *va.* (*pret.* GARANTICÉ; *subj.* GARANTICE) to guarantee; to indorse, answer or vouch for.
garanón, *m.* stallion jackass; male breeding camel.
garapacho, *m.* tortoise.
garapiña, *f.* congealed particles of any liquid; scalloped galloon or lace; (Cuba) fermented pineapple juice.
garapiñado, da. I. *pp.* of GARAPIÑAR. **II.** *a.* candied, sugarcoated; (jewelry) frosted.
garapiñar, *va.* to ice, to freeze (cream, sirup, etc.); to candy.
garapiñera, *f.* ice-cream freezer; wine cooler.
garapita, *f.* net for small fish.
garapito, *m.* small insect, like a tick.
garapullo, *m.* paper dart; shuttlecock.
garatura, *f.* (tanning) scraper.
garatusa, *f.* a card game; (coll.) caress.

garbancero, ra, *n.* chickpea dealer; (Mex.) young servant (boy or girl).
garbanzal, *m.* ground sown with chickpeas.
garbanzo, *m.* (bot.) chickpea.
garbanzuelo, *m. dim.* small chickpea; (vet.) a disease in horses' feet; ESPARAVÁN, spawn.
garbar, *va.* (agr.) to sheaf or sheave.
garbear. I. *va.* (agr.) to sheaf. **II.** *vn.* to affect an air of dignity and grandeur.
garbera, *f.* (agr.) shock of sheaves.
garbías, *m. pl.* omelet of herbs, cheese and flour.
garbillador, ra, *n.* sifter; riddler; garbler.
garbillar, *va.* (agr.) to sift; (min.) to riddle; to garble.—**garbillo,** *m.* coarse sieve for grain; (min.) riddle; riddled ore.
garbino, *m.* southwest wind.
garbo, *m.* grace, gracefulness, gentility, elegant carriage; knack; frankness, nobleness, generosity.
garbón, *m.* (ornith.) male partridge.
garbosamente, *adv.* gracefully; nobly.
garboso, sa, *a.* natty, spruce, graceful, sprightly; noble, generous.
garbullo, *m.* noisy crowd, esp. of children.
garcero, ra, *a.* (ornith.) heron hawk.
garceta, *f.* (ornith.) little egret; side locks of hair. —*pl.* sprouting horns (on deer, etc.).
gardenia, *f.* (bot.) gardenia.
garduja, *f.* barren stone in quicksilver mines.
garduña, *f.* (zool.) marten.
garduño, ña, *a.* (coll.) filcher, petty thief.
garete, *m.*—**al g.,** (naut.) adrift.
garfa, *f.* claw of a beast or bird; hand (in contempt); ancient tax.—**echar la g.,** to claw or seize anything with the nails.
garfada, *f.* clawing or seizing with the nails.
garfear, *vn.* to hook, to seize with a hook.
garfio, *m.* hook, drag hook; gaff.
gargajeada, *f.* spitting out of phlegm.
gargajear, *vn.* to expectorate phlegm.—**gargajeo,** *m.* = GARGAJEADA.
gargajiento, ta, *a.* that expectorates phlegm.
gargajo, *m.* phlegm.—**gargajoso, sa,** *a.* = GARGAJIENTO.
garganchón, *m.* = GARGÜERO.
garganta, *f.* throat; gullet; instep; gorge, notch, (agr.) sheath of a plow; (arch.) shaft of a column or balustrade; (mech.) neck, throat, gullet, waist, groove of a sheave.—**tener buena g.,** to be a good singer.
gargantada, *f.* liquid or blood ejected from the throat.
gargantear, *vn.* to quaver, to warble; (naut.) to strap a deadeye.
garganteo, *m.* quavering, warbling.
gargantil, *m.* cutout in barbers' basins.
gargantilla, *f.* necklace; (P. I.) water jug.
gárgara, *f.* gargle, gargling.—**hacer gárgaras,** to gargle.
gargarismo, *m.* gargle; gargling.
gargarizar, *vn.* to gargle, gargarize.
[1]**gárgol,** *a.* empty, addle (eggs).
[2]**gárgol,** *m.* (mech.) groove, furrow, mortise.
[1]**gárgola,** *f.* (arch.) gargoyle.
[2]**gárgola,** *f.* linseed.
gargüero, garguero, *m.* gullet; windpipe.
garifalte, *m.* (ornith.) = GERIFALTE, gerfalcon.
garifo, fa, *a.* = JARIFO, showy; natty.
gariofilea, *f.* (bot.) common avens or herb bennet.
garita, *f.* sentry box; porter's lodge; watercloset, privy.
garitero, *m.* master of a gaming house; gamester, gambler.
garito, *m.* gaming house; watchman's house; gambling den; profits of gambling.
garla, *f.* (coll.) talk, chatter.
garlador, ra; garlente, *n.* & *a.* (coll.) babbler (-ing), prater(-ing).
garlar, *vn.* (coll.) to babble prattle, chatter.
garlito, *m.* fish trap; snare, trap, or gin.—**caer en el g.,** (coll.) to fall into a trap.—**coger en el g.,** to detect in wrong-doing.
garlocha, *f.* goad stick.
garlopa, *f.* (carp.) jack plane, long plane.
garma, *f.* steep slope.
[1]**garnacha,** *f.* judge's robe or gown; company of strolling players.
[2]**garnacha,** *f.* a kind of purple grape; wine made from it.
garniel, *m.* belt with hanging pouch; (Ecua., Mex.) leather pouch.
garra, *f.* claw; (fig.) hand; catch, claw, hook, fang, clutch.—**g. delantera,** forepaw.—**caer en las garras de,** to fall into the clutches of.—**echarle a uno la g.,** (coll.) to grasp, arrest, imprison one.—**sacar de las garras de,** to free from.
garrafa, *f.* carafe, decanter.
garrafal, *a.* (of cherries) specially large and sweet; great, huge.
garrafiñar, *va.* (coll.) to grapple, snatch away.
garrafón, *m. aug.* large carafe; demijohn, carboy.
garrama, *f.* tax paid by Mohammedans; imposition, fraud, robbery.
garramar, garranar, *va.* to rob, plunder, pillage.
garrancha, *f.* (coll.) sword.
garrancho, *m.* branch broken off a tree.
garranchuelo, *m.* (bot.) crab grass.
garrapata, *f.* sheep and cattle tick; (mil.) disabled horse.
garrapatear, *vn.* to scribble, to scrawl.
garrapato, *m.* pothook, scrawl.
garrar, *vn.* (naut.) to drag.
garrasí, *m.* side-buttoned breeches worn by Venezuelan plainsmen.
garrear, *vn.* = GARRAR.
garrido, da, *a.* handsome, graceful.
garroba, *f.* carob bean.—**garrobal,** *m.* plantation of carob trees.—**garrobilla,** *f.* (tanning) chips of carob trees for staining.
garrocha, *f.* a sort of alpenstock; goad stick.
garrochada, *f.*, **garrochazo,** *m.* prick or blow with a goad stick.
garrocheador, ra, *n.* goader, pricker.
garrochear, *va.* = AGARROCHAR, to goad.
garrochón, *m. aug.* spear or goad stick used by bullfighters on horseback.
garrofa, *f.* carob bean.—**garrofal,** *m.* = GARROBAL.
garrón, *m.* spur of cocks and birds; talon of a bird of prey; paw of rabbits, etc.
garrotal, *m.* plantation of olive trees, grown from cuttings taken from fully developed trees.
garrotazo, *m.* blow with a cudgel.
garrote, *m.* club, bludgeon, truncheon, cudgel; garrote (for capital punishment); hazel basket or panier; (naut.) turning fid.—**dar g.,** to garrote, execute with the garrote.
garrotear, *va.* (Am.) = APALEAR, to cudgel.
garrotillo, *m.* (med.) croup.
garrubia, *f.* = ALGARROBA, carob bean.
garrucha, *f.* pulley.—**g. combinada,** sheave, block.—**g. fija,** fast pulley.—**g. movible,** movable pulley.—**g. simple,** single pulley.
garrucho, *m.* (naut.) cringle, mast hoop.
garrudo, da, *a.* muscular, brawny, strong.
garrulador, ra, *a.* garrulous.
garrulería, *f.* prattle, chatter.
garrulidad, *f.* garrulity.
gárrulo, la, *a.* chirping, as birds; chattering, prattling; garrulous.
garúa, *f.* (Am.) drizzle.—**garuar,** *vn.* to drizzle.
garujo, *m.* = HORMIGÓN, concrete.
garulla, *f.* loose grapes; (coll.) rabble.
garullada, *f.* gang of rogues.
garvier, *m.* small pouch.
garza, *f.* (ornith.) heron; (Colomb.) stork.—**g. real,** purple heron.
garzo, za. I. *a.* blue; blue-eyed. **II.** *m.* agaric, fungus, mushroom.
garzón, *m.* lad, boy; waiter; adjutant in the life guards; (Am.) (ornith.) heronlike wading bird.
garzota, *f.* (ornith.) night heron; plumage, aigrette; crest of a helmet.
garzul, *m.* a kind of wheat.
gas, *m.* gas; vapor, emanation, fume; (coll.) gas

light.—**g. de agua**, water gas.—**g. de alumbrado**, illuminating gas.—**g. de hulla**, coal gas.—**g. de ipirita**, mustard gas.—**g. de los pantanos**, marsh gas.—**g. de petróleo**, oil gas.—**g. hilarante**, laughing gas.—**g. inerte**, inert gas.—**g. lacrimógeno**, tear gas.—**g. mostaza**, mustard gas.—**g. natural**, natural gas.—**g. neurotóxico**, (mil.) nerve gas.—**g. pobre**, producer gas.—**g. tóxico**, poison gas.—**llevar g.**, (coll.) to speed.
gasa, *f.* gauze.
gascón, na; nés nesa, *n.* & *a.* Gascon.
gasconada, *f.* gasconade, boast, bravado.
gaseiforme, *a.* gasiform, gaseous.
gaseosa, *f.* soda water.
gaseoso, sa, *a.* gaseous.
gasificable, *a.* gasifiable.
gasificación, *f.* gasification.
gasificar, *va.* to gasify.
gasiforme, *a.* gasiform.
gasista, *n.* gas fitter.
gasolina, *f.*, **gasoleno**, *m.*, gasoline.
gasometría, *f.* gasometry.
gasómetro, *m.* gasometer; gas meter.
gasón, *m.* YESÓN, plaster rubbish; large clods of unbroken earth; sod.
gastable, *a.* expendable.
gastadero, *m.* (coll.) place where anything is wasted or spent; wasting; spending.
gastado, da. I. *pp.* of GASTAR. **II.** *a.* worn-out, useless; blasé.
gastador, ra. I. *a.* lavish, prodigal, extravagant. **II.** *n.* spender, spendthrift; (mil.) pioneer, sapper; criminal sentenced to hard labor.
gastamiento, *m.* consumption; wearing out.
gastar. I. *va.* to spend, expend; to waste, use, consume, wear out, fret; to have or wear habitually; to own, keep (as carriages, etc.); to plunder, pillage, sack; to digest.—**g. frases y rodeos**, (coll.) to beat around the bush.—**gastarlas**, (coll.) to act, behave, conduct oneself.—**g. salud**, to enjoy good health. **II.** *vr.* to become old or useless; to waste away, wear out; to fray.
gasterópodo, da, *a.* (zool.) gasteropod.
gasterosteo, *m.* (ichth.) stickleback.
gasto, *m.* expenditure, expense; consumption; spending, consuming; waste, use, wear and tear; (hydraul.) discharge.—**gastos de escritorio**, stationery expenses (in an office).—**gastos de explotación**, operating, running or working expenses.—**gastos de representación**, incidental expenses (of a public functionary); allowance for incidental expenses.
gastoso, sa, *a.* = GASTADOR.
gastralgia, *f.* (med.) gastralgia, stomach pains.
gástrico, ca, *a.* gastric.
gastrina, *f.* (biochem.) gastrin.
gastritis, *f.* (med.) gastritis.
gastrocele, *m.* (med.) gastrocele.
gastrocolitis, *f.* (med.) gastrocolitis.
gastroenteritis, *f.* (med.) gastroenteritis.
gastrointestinal, *a.* gastrointestinal.
gastrología, *f.* science and art of cooking.
gastromanía, *f.* gluttony.
gastrómano, na, *n.* & *a.* glutton(-ous).
gastronomía, *f.* gastronomy, epicurism.
gastronómico, ca, *a.* gastronomic.
gastrónomo, *m.* epicure, gastronomer.
gastrorrafia, *f.* (surg.) gastrorraphy.
gastrorragia, *f.* gastrorrhagia.
gastroscopio, *m.* (med.) gastroscope.
gastrotomía, *f.* (surg.) gastrotomy.
gástrula, *f.* (biol.) gastrula.
gata, *f.* female cat; (coll.) woman born in Madrid; (bot.) GATUÑA; (mech.) jack, screw jack; (mil.) cat castle; (naut.) cathead.—**g. del ancla**, (naut.) cat tackle.—**g. parida**, wasted person, (fig.) skeleton.—**a gatas**, on all fours.
gatada, *f.* cat trick; clawing; turn of a hare when closely pursued; (coll.) artful dodge, scurvy trick.
gatallón, *m.* (coll.) rogue, cheat, scamp.
gatatumba, *f.* (coll.) affected civility or submission; dissembling, pretense.
gatazo, *m. aug.* large cat; (coll.) artful trick, cheat, deception.
gateado, da. I. *pp.* of GATEAR. **II.** *a.* feline, catlike. **III.** *m.* a very compact American striped wood.
gateamiento, *m.* scratching; clambering; going on all fours.
gatear. I. *vn.* (of children) to creep; to climb up, clamber; to go upon all fours. **II.** *va.* (coll.) to scratch or claw; to steal, to rob.
gatera, *f.* cat's hole; (bot.) common catmint; (naut.) cathole.
gatería, *f.* number of cats together; (coll.) gang of toughs or ill-bred boys; (coll.) simulated humility, cunning, trick.
gatero, ra, *a.* frequented by cats.
gatesco, ca, *a.* (coll.) feline, catlike.
gatillazo, *m.* noise made by a trigger at firing.
gatillo, *m. dim.* little cat; pelican, dentist's forceps; (artil.) trigger; nape of a bull or ox; (arch.) cramp iron; filcher, petty thief.
gato, *m.* cat, tomcat; moneybag and the money kept in it; (cooperage) hooping tong; (mech.) jack, lifting jack, screw jack; (artil.) gun searcher; (coll.) pickpocket, petty thief, filcher; (coll.) shrewd fellow; (coll.) native of Madrid.—**g. cornaquí**, (naut.) jackscrew.—**g. de algalia**, (zool.) civet cat.—**g. de angora**, Angora cat.—**g. encerrado**, (coll.) nigger in the woodpile; fishy business.—**g. hidráulico**, hydraulic jack.—**g. maltés**, Maltese cat.—**g. montés**, wildcat.—**cuatro gatos**, (contempt.) just a few people.—**dar, meter** or **vender g. por liebre**, (coll.) to sell gold bricks, give chalk for cheese.—**todos los gatos son pardos de noche**, all cats are gray at midnight.
gatuna, gatuña, *f.* (bot.) rest-harrow, cammock.
gatuno, na, *a.* catlike, feline.
gatuperio, *m.* hotchpotch; (coll.) fraud, snare.
gauchada, *f.* (Am.) artifice; act of a Gaucho.—**hacer una g.**, (Arg.) to do a favor.
gauchaje, *m.* meeting or body of Gauchos.
gauchesco, ca, *a.* pert. to or like Gauchos.
gaucho, cha. I. *n.* Gaucho; (Arg.) pampas man (woman); good horseman; (Am.) cowboy. **II.** *a.* GAUCHESCO; knavish; (Arg., Chile) tricky; (Arg.) rude, vulgar.
gaudeamus, *m.* (coll.) feast, entertainment or merrymaking.
gaulteria, *f.* (bot.) gaultheria.
gavanza, *f.* (bot.) flower of the dog-rose.
gavanzo, *m.* (bot.) dog-rose.
gaveta, *f.* drawer, till, locker.
[1]**gavia**, *f.* (naut.) main topsail; top (in galleys); mad man's cage; ditch;—*pl.* (naut.) topsails of the main and fore mast.
[2]**gavia**, *f.* (min.) gang of basket passers.
[3]**gavia**, *f.* (ornith.) = GAVIOTA.
gavial, *m.* gavial, an East-Indian crocodile.
gaviar, *vn.* (Am.) (of corn) to tassel.
gaviero, *m.* (naut.) topman, mastman.
gavieta, *f.* (naut.) scuttle, bowsprit bee.
gaviete, *m.* (naut.) davit in a longboat.
gavilán, *m.* (ornith.) sparrow hawk; fine hair stroke in penmanship; nib of a pen; (armor) quillon of a sword; brad or pin of a goad stick; (naut.) iron hook; (bot.) thistle flower; (naut.) tholes.
gavilancillo, *m. dim.* young hawk; incurvated point of an artichoke leaf.
gavilla, *f.* (agr.) gavel or sheaf of grain; bundle of vine shoots; gang of thugs.
gavillero, *m.* (agr.) place where gavels of grain are collected.
gavina, *f.* (ornith.) = GAVIOTA.
gavión, *m.* (mil.) gabion; (coll.) large hat.
gaviota, *f.* (ornith.) gull, sea gull.
gavota, *f.* gavotte, a French dance.
gaya, *f.* stripe on stuffs, etc.; badge given to victors in Roman games; (ornith.) magpie.

gayado, da. I. *pp.* of GAYAR. **II.** *a.* motley, striped.
gayadura, *f.* garniture, parti-colored trimming.
gayar, *va.* to streak, stripe; to trim with ribbons of various colors; to variegate.
gayata, *f.* crook, sheephook.
gayo, ya, *a.* gay, festive, merry; showy.—**gaya ciencia,** poesy, minstrelsy, art of poetry.
gayola, *f.* (naut.) cage; (coll.) jail; (prov.) raised hut for watching vineyards.
gayomba, *f.* (bot.) white single-seed broom.
gayuba, *f.* (bot.) red-berried arbutus.
gayubal, *m.* GAYUBA field.
gaza, *f.* loop of a bow; (naut.) strap, loop, collar, splice, noose.
gazafatón, *m.* nonsense, foolish talk, balderdash.
gazapa, *f.* lie, fib; falsehood.
gazapatón, *m.* = GAZAFATÓN.
gazapera, *f.* warren for rabbits; (coll.) den where suspicious characters meet; (coll.) brawl, row.
gazapina, *f.* assembly of ruffians; brawl, row.
gazapo, *m.* cony, young rabbit; shrewd, artful fellow; (coll.) great lie; blunder, mistake.
gazapón, *m.* gambling house or profits.
gazmiar. I. *va.* to steal and eat tidbits. **II.** *vr.* (coll.) to complain; to resent.
gazmol, *m.* a kind of growth on the tongue of birds of prey.
gazmoñada, gazmoñería, *f.* prudery.
gazmoñero, ra; gazmoño, ña, *a.* prudish, priggish.
gaznápiro, ra, *n.* churl, simpleton, booby.
gaznar, *vn.* = GRAZNAR, to croak, caw, cackle.
gaznatada, *f.* blow on the windpipe; (Am.) BOFETADA, slap in the face.
gaznate, *m.* throttle, windpipe; a kind of fritter.
gaznatón, *m.* GAZNATADA; pancake, fritter.
gazofia, *f.* = BAZOFIA, refuse; offal.
gazofilacio, *m.* gazophylacium, treasury of the temple of Jerusalem.
gazpachero, ra, *n.* maker of GAZPACHO.
gazpacho, *m.* Andalusian dish made of biscuit, oil, vinegar, onions, and garlic; crumbs of bread fried in a pan.
gazuza, *f.* (coll.) keen appetite, hunger.
ge, *f.* Spanish name of the letter *g*.
gea, *f.* mineral or inorganic constituents of a region, and the work describing it.
geato, *m.* (chem.) humate.
gehena, *m.* Gehenna, hell.
géiser, *m.* geyser.
gel, *m.* (chem.) gel.
gelatina, *f.* gelatine; jelly.
gelatiniforme, *a.* gelatinelike.
gelatinoso, sa, *a.* gelatinous.
gelatinudo, da, *a.* (Am.) gelatinous; (Am.) phlegmatic, lazy, slow.
gelfe, *m.* black slave.
gélido, da, *a.* (poet.) gelid, frigid.
gema, *f.* gem; (carp.) slab, flitch; (bot.) bud.
gemación, *f.* (bot.) gemmation.
gemela, *f.* (bot.) Arabian jasmine.
gemelífloro, ra. *a.* (bot.) geminiflorous.
gemelo, la. I. *a.* twin. **II.** *n.* twin; *m.* (anat.) gemellus; *pl.* twins; *pl.* cuff links; *pl.* binoculars; *pl.* **G.,** (astr.) Gemini; *f.* (bot.) Arabian jasmine.—**gemelos de campaña,** field glasses.—**gemelos de teatro,** opera glasses.
gemido, *m.* moan, groan; howl.
gemidor, ra. I. *a.* moaning, groaning; howling. **II.** *n.* moaner, groaner; howler.
geminación, *f.* gemination.
geminado, da. I. *pp.* of GEMINAR. **II.** *a.* geminate; semidetached.
geminar, *va.* to geminate.
geminífloro, ra, *a.* geminiflorous.
géminis, *m.* (pharm.) a kind of plaster; (G-astr.) Gemini.
gemir, *vn.* (*ind. pres.* GIMO, *pret.* él GIMIÓ; *subj.* GIMA; *ger.* GIMIENDO) to groan, moan; to grieve; to howl; (of sea or wind) to roar, whistle.
gen, *m.* (biol.) gene.
genciana, *f.* (bot.) gentian.
gencianáceo, a. I. *n.* & *a.* (bot.) gentian(-aceous). **II.** *f. pl.* Gentianaceæ.
gencianeo, ea, *a.* gentianaceous.
gendarme, *m.* gendarme.
gendarmería, *f.* (mil.) gendarmerie.
genealogía, *f.* genealogy.
genealógico, ca, *a.* genealogical.
genealogista, *n.* genealogist.
geneático, ca, *a.* pert. to astrology.
geneo, *m.* a Peruvian banana.
generable, *a.* that can be generated.
generación, *f.* generation; succession, lineage.
generador, ra. I. *n.* & *a.* generator(-ing). *a. f.* = GENERATRIZ. **II.** *m.* (mech. and elec.) generator.
general. I. *a.* general; common, usual.—**en g., por lo g.,** in general, generally. **II.** *m.* (mil.) general; (eccl.) superior of a religious order; lecture hall in a university; (prov.) custom house.—**g. de brigada,** brigadier general.—**g. de división,** major general.
generala, *f.* (mil.) the general (a roll of the drum); wife of a general.
generalato, *m.* (eccl. and mil.) generalship.
generalero, *m.* majority; customhouse officer.
generalicé, generalice, *v.* *V.* GENERALIZAR.
generalidad, *f.* generality; (prov.) community, corporation; (prov.) custom duties.
generalísimo, *m.* generalissimo.
generalización, *f.* generalization.
generalizador, ra, *n.* & *a.* generalizer(-ing).
generalizar. I. *va.* (*pret.* GENERALICÉ; *subj.* GENERALICE) to generalize. **II.** *vr.* to become general, usual, or popular; to spread.
generar, *va.* to generate, produce.
generativo, va, *a.* generative.
generatriz, *f.* (math.) generatrix.
genérico, ca, *a.* generic.
género, *m.* genus; class; kind; kin; manner, way, sort; cloth, stuff, material; (gram.) gender.—*pl.* dry goods; (com.) goods, merchandise, commodities.—**g. humano,** mankind.—**de g.,** (art) genre.
generosidad, *f.* generosity; hereditary nobility; bravery, fortitude.
generoso, sa, *a.* generous; noble, magnanimous; excellent, choice (said mainly of wine).
genesíaco, ca, *a.* pert. to genesis.
genésico, ca, *a.* pert. to generation.
génesis. I. *m.* (G-) Genesis. **II.** *f.* origin, beginning; cause; genesis.
geneticista, *n.* geneticist.
genético, ca. I. *a.* genetic. **II.** *f.* genetics.
gengibre, *m.* ginger.
genial, *a.* pert. to disposition; delightful; brilliant (person).
genialidad, *f.* temperament, disposition.
geniano, na, *a.* (anat., zool.) genial, of or pertaining to the chin.
geniazo, *m. aug.* strong temper.
geniculación, *f.* (biol.) geniculation, kneelike joint or bend.
geniculado, da, *a.* (biol.) geniculate, jointed, bent.
genio, *m.* genius; temperament, nature, disposition, temper; character, genius, peculiarities (as of a language); representative type, embodiment; angel, spirit.—**g. del mal,** evil spirit.—**buen g.,** good nature, equable temper.—**de buen (mal) g.,** good- (evil-) tempered.—**mal g.,** bad, or ill, temper.
genista, *f.* (bot.) = RETAMA, genista.
genital. I. *a.* genital. **II.** *m.* testicle.
genitivo, va. I. *a.* generative. **II.** *m.* (gram.) genitive or possessive case.
[1]**genízaro, ra,** *a.* (Mex.) half-breed.
[2]**genízaro,** *m.* Janizary, Turkish infantryman.
genocidio, *m.* genocide.
genol, *m.* (naut.) futtock.
genoma, *f.* (biol.) genome.
genovariación, *f.* (biol.) genovariation.
genovés, vesa, *n.* & *a.* Genoese.
gente, *f.* people, folk, crowd, any number of

persons; army, troops; gang; retinue; gens, clan, race, nation; (coll.), family, folks.—**g. baja,** lower classes; rabble, mob.—**g. bien,** (Am.) upper class.—**g. común,** common folk.—**g. de bien,** honest people.—**g. de capa parda,** villagers, countrymen, rustics.—**g. de color,** colored people.—**g. de la cuchilla,** butchers. —**g. de la garra,** thieves, pickpockets.—**g. de la vida airada,** the underworld, libertines.—**g. del bronce,** merry crowd.—**g. de paz,** a friend, or friends.—**g. de pelo, or de pelusa,** people of property.—**g. de trato,** tradesmen, dealers.—**g. de traza,** well-behaved people.—**g. fina,** cultured people.—**g. menuda,** children, "small fry."—**g. perdida,** vagrants, vagabonds.—**g. principal,** the nobility or gentry.—**g. vulgar** = G. COMÚN.—**de g. en g.,** from one to another, from generation to generation.—*pl.* Gentiles (as in *el Apóstol de las gentes,* the Apostle of the Gentiles, St. Paul)
gentecilla, *f.* low, contemptible people.
gentil. I. *a.* Gentile; genteel, graceful; gracious; excellent, exquisite. **II.** *n.* gentile, pagan, heathen.
gentileza, *f.* gentility, gracefulness; easiness, sprightliness, nattiness; ostentation, pageantry; courtesy, politeness.
gentilhombre, *m.* fine fellow; my good man; gentleman, the servant who waits about the person of a man of rank; person sent to the king with important despatches.—**g. de cámara,** lord of the bedchamber.—**g. de manga,** nobleman who attends the princes of Spain while children.
gentilicio, ia, *a.* national, tribal; hereditary.
gentílico, ca, *a.* heathen, gentile, pagan.
gentilidad, *f.* gentilism, heathenism, paganism; the body of heathens or gentiles.
gentilismo, *m.* = GENTILIDAD.
gentilizar, *vn.* to observe the rites of gentiles or heathens.
gentilmente, *adv.* gently, politely; heathenishly.
gentío, *m.* crowd, multitude.
gentualla, gentuza, *f.* rabble, mob; people of no account, small fry.
genuflexión, *f.* genuflexion.
genuino, na, *a.* genuine.
geocéntrico, ca, *a.* geocentric.
geoda, *f.* (geol.) geode.
geodesia, *f.* geodesy.
geodésico, ca, *a.* geodetical.
geodesta, *m.* geodesist.
geodinámica, *f.* geodynamics.
geófago, ga, *a.* geophagous, earth-eating.
geofísico, ca, *n.* geophysicist; *f.* geophysics.
geogenia, *f.* (geol.) geogeny.
geogénico, ca, *a.* geogenic.
geognosia, *f.* (geol.) geognosy.
geognosta, *m.* geognost, geologist.
geognóstico, ca, *a.* geognostic.
geogonía, *f.* = GEOGENIA.
geogónico, ca, *a.* geogonic.
geografía, *f.* geography.
geográficamente, *adv.* geographically.
geográfico, ca, *a.* geographical.
geógrafo, fa, *n.* geographer.
geoide, *m.* geoid.
geología, *f.* geology.
geológico, ca, *a.* geological.
geólogo, ga, *n.* geologist.
geomancía, *f.* geomancy.
geomántico, ca. I. *a.* geomantic, pert. to geomancy. **II.** *m.* geomancer, one divining by random throw of earth.
geómetra, *n.* geometer, geometrician.
geometría, *f.* geometry.—**g. analítica,** analytic geometry.—**g. del espacio,** solid geometry.—**g. descriptiva,** descriptive geometry.—**g. no euclidiana,** non-Euclidean geometry.—**g. plana,** plane geometry.
geométricamente, *adv.* geometrically.
geométrico, ca, *a.* geometrical, geometric.
geometrino, *m.* (entom.) geometrid, measuring worm, inchworm.
geomorfía, *f.* (geol.) geomorphology.
geonomía, *f.* (geol.) science treating of vegetable properties of the earth.
geonómico, ca, *a.* pertaining to GEONOMÍA.
geopolítico, ca. I. *a.* geopolitical. **II.** *f.* geopolitics.
geoponía, *f.* geoponics, agriculture.
geopónico, ca. I. *a.* geoponic, agricultural. **II.** *f.* geoponics.
geoquímico, ca. I. *a.* geochemical. **II.** *f.* geochemistry.
georama, *m.* georama.
georgiano, na, *n.* & *a.* Georgian.
geórgico, ca, *f.* & *a.* (poet.) georgic.
geoscopia, *f.* geoscopy.
geosinclinal, *m.* (geol.) geosyncline.
geotectónico, ca, *a.* (geol.) geotectonic.
geotérmico, ca, *a.* geothermic.
geotropismo, *m.* (bot.) geotropism.
geraniáceo, cea, *a.* (bot.) geraniaceous.
geranio, *m.* (bot.) crane's-bill; geranium.—**g. de rosa,** rose geranium.
gerbo, *m.* (zool.) jerboa, mouselike rodent.
gerencia, *f.* (com.) managership, management.
gerente, *m.* (com.) manager.
geriatría, *f.* geriatrics.
gericaya, *f.* (Mex., cooking) custard.
gerifalco, gerifalte, *m.* (ornith.) gerfalcon.
germanesco, ca, *a.* pertaining to the jargon of the gipsies.
germanía, *f.* jargon or cant of the gipsies, thieves, etc.; slang; concubinage; a faction in Valencia during the days of Charles V.
germánico, ca, *a.* Germanic, German.
germanio, *m.* (chem.) germanium.
germanismo, *m.* Germanism, German form employed in another language.
[1]germano, na, *n.* & *a.* German(-ic) (app. only to Germania, ancient Germany).
[2]germano, na. I. *a.* genuine. **II.** *a.* & *n.* german, full (brother, sister.)
germanófilo, la, *n.* & *a.* pro-German.
germen, *m.* germ; spring, source.—**g. plasma,** (biol.) germ plasm.
germicida. I. *a.* germicidal. **II.** *m.* germicide.
germinación, *f.* (bot.) germination.
germinal. I. *a.* germinal. **II.** *m.* Germinal, seventh month of the French revolutionists.
germinar, *vn.* to germinate.
germinativo, va, *a.* germinative.
gerundense, *a.* of or belonging to Gerona.
gerundiada, *f.* (coll.) pompous and unmeaning expression.
gerundiano, na, *a.* pompous, empty (style or phrase).
[1]gerundio, *m.* (gram.) gerund.
[2]gerundio, *m.* (coll.) pompous, bombastic speaker.
gesta, *f.* gest, a narrative of a person's deeds; romance.
gestación, *f.* (med.) gestation; exercise among the Romans for the health.
gestatorio, ria, *a.* portable, carrying (chair).
gestear, *vn.* to gesticulate, make grimaces.
gestero, ra, *n.* & *a.* (one) that makes grimaces or faces; making grimaces; gesticulator(-ing).
gesticulación, *f.* gesticulation, gesture.
[1]gesticular, *vn.* to gesticulate, make gestures or grimaces.
[2]gesticular, *a.* gesticulatory.
gestión, *f.* conduct; exertion, effort, action, measure, step; negotiation, management.
gestionar, *va.* to conduct, manage; to take steps to attain or carry out.
gesto, *m.* facial expression; grimace; gesture.—**estar de buen g.,** to be in good humor.—**hacer gestos,** to make a face; to gesticulate; to make signs.
gestor, *m.* (com.) superintendent, manager, agent, promotor, representative, attorney.
gestudo, da, *a.* (coll.) ill-humored, cross.

Ghana, *f.* Ghana.
ghanés, nesa, *n.* & *a.* Ghanaian.
ghetto, *m.* ghetto.
giba, *f.* hump, crooked back, hunch, gibbosity; (coll.) nuisance, annoyance.
gibado, da. I. *pp.* of GIBAR. **II.** *a.* hunchbacked.
gibar, *va.* to crook; (coll.) to molest, annoy, vex.
gibelino, na, *n.* & *a.* Ghibelline.
gibón, *m.* (zool.) gibbon.
giboso, sa, *a.* gibbous, humpbacked.
gibraltareño, ña, *a.* Gibraltar (as *a.*).
gícama, *f.* (Mex.) a root resembling yucca.
giganta, *f.* giantess; (bot.) sunflower.
gigante. I. *a.* gigantic. **II.** *m.* giant.
gigantea, *f.* (bot.) sunflower.
giganteo, a; gigantesco, ca, *a.* gigantic.
gigantez, *f.* gigantic stature or size.
gigantilla, *f.* large-headed figure.
gigantismo, *m.* (med.) giantism, gigantism.
gigantón, na, *n. aug.* giant of enormous size.—**gigantones,** gigantic figures of pasteboard.—**echar los gigantones a,** (coll.) to reprehend severely, to give a dressing down.
gijonense; gijonés, sa, *a.* of Gijon.
gilí, *a.* (coll.) foolish, stupid.
gilvo, va, *a.* honey-colored or pinkish.
gimnasia, *f.* = GIMNÁSTICA.
gimnasio, *m.* gymnasium; school, academy.
gimnasta, *m.* gymnast.
gimnástica, *f.* gymnastics, calisthenics.
gimnástico, ca, *a.* gymnastic, gymnastical.
gímnico, ca, *a.* pert. to athletic contests or acrobatic dancing.
gimnosofista, *m.* (anc. Hindu) gymnosophist.
gimnospermo, ma, *a.* (bot.) gymnospermous.
gimnoto, *m.* (zool.) gymnotus, electric eel.
gimo, gima, *v. V.* GEMIR.
gimotear, *vn.* (coll.) to whine.—**gimoteo,** *m.* whining.
[1]**ginebra,** *f.* Moorish rattle; confusion, bedlam; a card game.
[2]**ginebra,** *f.* gin (liquor).
ginebrada, *f.* a kind of puff-paste tart.
ginebrés, sa; ginebrino, na, *n.* & *a.* Genevan.
gineceo, *m.* (bot.) gynæceum; women's quarters in house.
ginecocracia, *f.* gynecocracy, government by women.
ginecología, *f.* (med.) gynecology.
ginecológico, ca, *a.* gynecological.
ginecólogo, ga, *n.* gynecologist.
ginesta, *f.* = HINIESTA, genista.
gineta, *f.* genet, a kind of weasel.
gingidio, *m.* (bot.) wild spinach.
gingival, *a.* (anat.) gingival, pertaining to the gums.—**gingivitis,** *f.* gingivitis, inflammation of the gums.
ginglimo, *m.* (anat.) ginglymus.
ginsén, ginseng, *m.* (bot., pharm.) ginseng.
gipsófila, *f.* (bot.) gypsophila.
girada, *f.* (dance) gyration; pirouette.
girado, *m.* (com.) drawee.
girador, girante, *m.* (com.) drawer.
giralda, *f.* vane or weathercock in the form of an animal or human figure (from that on the spire of the cathedral of Seville); **(G-)** name of this tower.
giraldete, *m.* surplice without sleeves.
giraldilla, *f. dim.* small vane or weathercock; a popular dance in Asturias.
girándula, *f.* (fireworks) girandole.
girar, *vn.* to revolve, rotate; to turn; (com.) to draw (a check, draft).—**g. contra,** or **a cargo de,** to draw on.
girasol, *m.* (bot.) sunflower.
giratorio, ria. *a.* revolving, rotary, turning.
girino, *m.* embryo of a frog.
giro, *m.* turn; revolution, rotation; gyration, course or turn of affairs; bend, tendency; bias, trend; turn of a sentence; threat, bravado; (com.) draft; circulation; bulk of business; line of business, specialty.—**g. postal,** money order.—**tomar otro g.,** to take another course; to change one's mind.
giroestabilizador, *m.* (aer., naut.) gyrostabilizer.
giroflé, *m.* (bot.) aromatic clove tree.
girofrecuencia, *f.* (phys.) gyrofrequency.
giromagnético, ca, *a.* (elec.) gyromagnetic.
girondino, na, *n.* & *a.* Girondist, Girondin.
giroscópico, ca, *a.* gyroscopic.
giroscopio, *m.* gyroscope.
girostático, ca. I. *a.* gyrostatic. **II.** *f.* (phys.) gyrostatics.
giróstato, *m.* gyrostat.
girovago, ga, *a.* = VAGABUNDO, vagabond.
gis, *m.* crayon.
gitana, *f.* gipsy woman, girl.
gitanada, *f.* mean, contemptible trick; blandishment, wheedling, caress, flattery.
gitanamente, *adv.* in a sly, winning manner.
gitanear, *va.* to flatter, wheedle, cajole.
gitanería, *f.* wheedling, flattery, cajolery.
gitanesco, ca, *a.* gipsylike, gipsy (as *a.*).
gitanismo, *m.* gipsy life, dress, ways.
gitano, na. I. *a.* gipsylike; gipsy; sly, artful, honey-mouthed. **II.** *n.* gipsy.
glabro, bra, *a.* bald; beardless.
glacial, *a.* glacial.
glaciar, *m.* glacier.
glaciario, ria, *a.* (geol.) glacial.
glaciarismo, *m.* glaciology.
glacis, *m.* (fort.) glacis.
gladiador, gladiator, *m.* gladiator.
gladiatorio, ria, *a.* gladiatorial, gladiatory.
gladio, gladiolo, *m.* (bot.) gladiolus.
glande, *m.* (anat.) glans, head of the penis.
glandífero, ra; glandígero, ra, *a.* acorn-bearing.
glándula, *f.* gland.—**g. de secreción interna,** (anat.) ductless gland.—**g. endocrina,** (anat.) endocrine gland.—**g. pineal,** (anat.) pineal gland.—**g. pituitaria,** (anat.) pituitary gland, hypophysis.—**g. prostática,** (anat.) prostate gland.—**g. salival,** (anat.) salivary gland.—**g. submaxilar,** submaxillary gland.—**g. sudorípara,** (anat.) sweat gland.—**g. suprarrenal,** (anat.) adrenal gland.—**g. tiróides,** (anat.) thyroid gland.
glandular, *a.* glandular.
glanduloso, sa, *a.* glandulous, glandular.
glasé, *m.* glacé or glacé silk.
glaseado, da, *a.* glossy, glacélike.
glasear, *va.* to calender (paper).
glasto, *m.* (bot.) woad or dyers' weed.
glauberita, *f.* glauberite.
glaucio, *m.* (bot.) celandine.
glauco, ca. I. *a.* (bot.) glaucous; light green. **II.** *m.* (zool.) a mollusk of the Glaucus genus.
glaucoma, *m.* (med.) glaucoma.
gleba, *f.* lump or clod turned up by the plow.
glera, *f.* = CASCAJAR, gravel pit.
glicerato, *m.* (chem.) glycerate.
glicérido, *m.* (chem.) glyceride.
glicerina, *f.* glycerine.
glicerito, *m.* (pharm.) glycerite.
glicerol, *m.* (chem.) glycerol.
glicocola, *f.* (chem.) glycocoll.
glicógeno, *m.* (biochem.) glycogen.
glicol, *m.* (chem.) glycol.
glicolato, *m.* (chem.) glycolate.
glicólico, ca, *a.* (chem.) glycolic.
glicosuria, *f.* (med.) glycosuria.
glifo, *m.* (arch.) glyph, groove.
glioma, *f.* (med.) glioma.
glíptica, *f.* glyptics, gem engraving (as an art).
gliptodonte, *m.* (paleontol.) glyptodon.
gliptografía, *f.* glyptography, gem or stone engraving (as an art).
global, *a.* global, overall.
globina, *f.* (chem.) globin.
globo, *m.* globe, sphere; the earth; balloon; globular lamp shade.—**g. aerostático,** air balloon.—**g. cautivo,** captive balloon.—**g. celeste,** (astr.) celestial globe.—**g. cometa,** (aer.) kite

balloon.—**g. dirigible,** dirigible balloon, airship.—**g. nodriza,** (aer.) nurse balloon.—**g. piloto,** (aer.) pilot balloon.—**g. sonda,** (aer.) sounding balloon, captive balloon with recording instruments.—**g. terráqueo,** or **terrestre,** (the) globe, (the) earth.—**en g.,** as a whole; without details; in bulk.
globoso, sa, *a.* globe-shaped.
globular, *a.* globular.
globulariáceo, a, *a.* (bot.) globulariaceous.
globulillo, *m. dim.* globulet, globule; homeopathic pill.
globulina, *f.* (chem.) globulin.—**g. gama,** (physiol.) gamma globulin.
glóbulo, *m. dim.* small globe; (biol.) corpuscle.
globuloso, sa, *a.* globulous, globulose.
glomérulo, *m.* (anat., bot.) glomerule.
glonoína, *f.* glonoin.
gloria. I. *f.* glory; heavenly state, bliss, blessedness; pride, boast; transparent gauze, gossamer, tissue; a kind of cream tart or cake; (art) opening in the sky representing angels, splendors, etc.—**saber a g.,** to taste delicious. **II.** *m.* (eccl.) gloria, doxology.—**G. Patri,** or **Gloriapatri,** (eccl.) Gloria Patri, the lesser doxology.
gloriarse, *vr.* (**de** or **en**) to boast (of), be proud (of), take delight (in).
glorieta, *f.* summerhouse, bower, arbor; circle or square at intersection of streets.
glorificación, *f.* glorification; praise.
glorificador, ra; glorificante, *n.* & *a.* glorifier (-fying).
glorificar. I. *va.* (*pret.* GLORIFIQUÉ; *subj.* GLORIFIQUE) to glorify, adore, worship; to exalt; to praise, honor, extol. **II.** *vr.* = GLORIARSE.
glorioso, sa, *a.* glorious; enjoying the bliss of heaven, blessed; boastful, ostentatious.
glosa, *f.* gloss, scholium; comment, commentary, note; (com. and law) explanatory annotation in accounts; (poet.) a kind of rondelet; (mus.) variation of a theme.
glosador, ra, *n.* commentator, glosser, glossarist; (com.) auditor.
glosar, *va.* to gloss, annotate, comment; (com.) to audit; (poet.) to compose (rondelets); (mus.) to vary (a theme).
glosario, *m.* glossary.
glose, *m.* glossing, commenting.
glosilla, *f. dim.* short gloss, comment, or note; (print.) minion type, 7-point.
glositis, *f.* (med.) glossitis, tongue inflammation.
glótico, ca, *a.* glottic, pertaining to the glottis.
glotis, *f.* (anat.) glottis.
glotón, tona. I. *a.* gluttonous, greedy. **II.** *n.* glutton; *m.* (zool.) glutton, wolverine, carcajou.
glotonear, *vn.* to be a glutton, gormandize.
glotonería, *f.* gluttony.
gloxínea, *f.* (bot., Am.) gloxinia.
glucina, *f.* (chem.) glucina.
glucinio, *m.* (chem.) glucinum, beryllium.
glucogenia, *f.* (physiol.) glycogeny (esp. of the liver).
glucómetro, *m.* glucometer, hydrometer for determining the quantity of sugar in a liquid.
glucosa, *f.* (chem.) glucose.
glucósido, *m.* (chem.) glucoside.
glucosuria, *f.* (med.) glucosuria.
gluma, *f.* (bot.) glume.
glumáceo, cea, *a.* (bot.) glumaceous.
gluten, *m.* gluten; glue.
glúteo, tea, *a.* gluteal, pert. to buttocks.
glutinosidad, *f.* glutinousness, viscosity.
glutinoso, sa, *a.* glutinous, viscous.
gneis, *m.* (geol.) gneiss, a kind of rock.
gnéisico, ca, *a.* (geol.) gneissic.
gnetáceo, a, *a.* (bot.) gnetaceous.
gnómico, ca, *a.* gnomic.
gnomo, *m.* gnome, fabulous being.
gnomon, *m.* gnomon, sundial; (mason.) square.—**g. movible,** bevel square.
gnomónica, *f.* science of making sundials.
gnomónico, ca, *a.* pert. to GNOMÓNICA.
gnosticismo, *m.* gnosticism.
gnóstico, ca, *n.* & *a.* gnostic.
gnu, *m.* (zool.) gnu, wildebeest.
goa, *f.* pig-iron bloom; (agr.) dibble.
goal, *m.* (Angl.) (football) goal.
gobernación, *f.* government; governor's office or official house.
gobernador, ra. I. *a.* governing. **II.** *n.* governor; *f.* governor's wife.—**g. general,** governor general.
gobernadorcillo, *m.* (P. I.) justice of the peace.
gobernalle, *m.* (naut.) rudder, helm.
gobernante. I. *n.* & *a.* ruler(-ing). **II.** *n.* (coll.) self-appointed manager or leader.
gobernar. I. *va.* & *vn.* (*ind.* GOBIERNO; *subj.* GOBIERNE) to govern, rule; to command, lead, direct; to manage, run; to control, steer, helm. **II.** *vn.* (naut.) to obey the helm. **III.** *vr.* to manage (as one's affairs), carry on.
gobernativo, va, *a.* governmental.
gobernoso, sa, *a.* (coll.) methodical, tidy.
gobierna, *f.* weather vane.
gobiernista. I. *a.* gubernatorial, government (as *a.*); that supports the government. **II.** *n.* supporter of the government.
[1]**gobierno,** *m.* government; ministers composing a cabinet; dignity, office, and term of a government; district or province under a governor; guidance, management, direction; control (of a business, an automobile, an airplane); (naut.) helm, rudder; steering, conning.—**g. de casa,** household.—**de g.,** controlling (lever, etc.), control (as *a.*); of the State.—**para su g.,** for your guidance.—**servir de g.,** to be a guide or norm; to be a warning or a lesson.
[2]**gobierno, gobierne,** *v. V.* GOBERNAR.
gobio, *m.* (ichth.) gudgeon.
goce, *m.* enjoyment; fruition; possession.
gocete, *m.* neck guards in ancient armor.
gociano, na, *a.* Gothic.
gocha, *f.* (coll.) sow.
gocho, *m.* (coll.) hog.
godesco, ca; godible, *a.* joyful, cheerful.
godo, da, *n.* & *a.* Goth(-ic); (Colomb., pol.) conservative.—**ser g.,** (Spain, coll.) to be of noble blood.
gofio, *m.* (Cuba) roasted corn meal or maize.
gofo, fa, *a.* stupid, ignorant; (art) dwarf figure.
gol, *m.* (Angl.) (football) (making a) goal.
gola, *f.* gullet, throat; gorget in ancient armor; (mil.) gorget, crescent-shaped insignia of duty; (fort.) gorge; (arch.) cyma, ogee.—**g. inversa,** or **reversa,** (arch.) cyma reversa.
goldre, *m.* quiver for shafts or arrows.
goleta, *f.* (naut.) schooner.
golf, *m.* golf.—**golfista,** *m.* & *f.* golfer.
golfán, *m.* (bot.) water lily.
golfillo, *m. dim.* small gulf; urchin.
golfín, *m.* (ichth.) dolphin.
[1]**golfo,** *m.* (geog.) gulf; sea, main; (poet.) gulf, abyss; faro (game).—**g. de Adén,** Gulf of Aden.—**g. de Bengala,** Bay of Bengal.—**g. de Corinto,** Gulf of Corinth.—**g. de México,** Gulf of Mexico.—**g. Pérsico,** Persian Gulf.
[2]**golfo,** *m.* (Madrid) ragamuffin.
golilla. I. *f.* (sewing) gorget, ruff; collar worn by some magistrates in Spain; (mason.) short joining pipe; flange of a pipe. **II.** *m.* (coll.) magistrate wearing a GOLILLA.
golillero, ra, *n.* collar maker.
golondrina, *f.* (ornith.) swallow; (ichth.) flying gurnard, swallow fish.—**g. de mar,** (ornith.) tern.
golondrinera, *f.* (bot.) swallowwort, celandine.
golondrino, *m.* (ornith.) male swallow; vagrant, deserter; (med.) large tumor in the armpit.
golondro, *m.* (coll.) desire, longing.—**andar en golondros,** (coll.) to feed on vain hopes.—**campar de g.,** (coll.) to live at another's expense, to sponge.
golosamente, *adv.* eagerly; inordinately.
golosear, *va.* = GOLOSINAR.

golosina, *f.* dainty, delicacy, sweet morsel, tidbit; daintiness, sweet tooth; inordinate desire or appetite; trifle.
golosinar, golosinear, golosmear, *vn.* to look for and eat tidbits, dainties, or sweetmeats; to taste and relish nice things.
goloso, sa, *a.* having a sweet tooth, fond of dainties, niceties, or sweetmeats.
golpazo, *m. aug.* heavy blow, stroke, or knock.
golpe, *m.* blow; stroke, hit, knock; wound, hurt; shock, clash; attack, spell; action, push, act; crowd, throng of people; abundance; heart beat; spring bolt of a lock; (sew.) passementerie trimming; pocket flap (of a coat); attack in fencing; astonishment, surprise; witty sally or remark; hole for planting; number of cuts planted in one hole; (mech.) stroke (of piston); travel (of a valve); (naut.) sweep; (mus.) touch, act of striking a key, etc.—**g. de arco,** bowing of a violin.—**g. de cuartel,** military coup.—**g. de estado,** coup d'état.—**g. de fortuna,** stroke of good fortune.—**g. de gracia,** finishing stroke, coup de grâce.—**g. del reloj,** tick of the watch or clock.—**g. de mar** (naut.) surge, heavy sea.—**g. de remo,** oar stroke.—**g. de vista,** glance; sight.—**g. seco,** sharp, quick blow or stroke.—**dar g.,** to cause surprise; to create a sensation.—**de g.,** suddenly, all at once. —**de g. y porrazo,** unexpectedly, unawares.—**de un g.,** at one blow; all at once.
golpeadero, *m.* place much beaten; repeated blows.
golpeador, ra, *n.* & *a.* striker(-ing), beater(-ing), hitter(-ing).
golpeadura, *f.* percussion; act of beating, hammering, or striking.
golpear. I. *va.* to strike, hit, hammer; to bruise. **II.** *vn.* to beat; to knock, pound (as a piston); to tick (as a watch).
golpeo, *m.* repeated striking, beating or knocking.
golpete, *m.* door catch (to keep it open).
golpetear, *va.* & *vn.* to strike or pound continually; to rattle.
golpeteo, *m.* continued striking; constant hammering; knocking, pounding; rattling.
gollería, gollería, *f.* dainty; delicious morsel; (coll.) delicacy, superfluity, excess.
gollete, *m.* throttle, upper part of the throat; neck of a bottle; neckband of some religious habits.—**estar hasta el g.,** (coll.) to be full (after eating); to be in difficulties; to have lost patience.
gollizo, *m.* narrow passage of mountains or rivers.
goma, *f.* gum; India rubber; rubber band; rubber eraser; (surg.) gumma, a kind of syphilitic tumor; (Am.) "hang-over" (after drinking).—*pl.* (Am.) overshoes, rubbers.—**g. adragante,** gum tragacanth.—**g. arábiga,** gum arabic.—**g. de borrar,** rubber eraser.—**g. de mascar,** chewing gum.—**g. elástica,** India rubber.—**g. laca,** lac.—**g. tragacanta** = G. ADRAGANTE.
gomaguta, *f.* gamboge.
gomecillo, *m.* blind person's guide.
gomero, ra. I. *a.* pert. to gums or to rubber. **II.** *m.* one engaged in the rubber business.
gomía, *f.* bugbear; (coll.) glutton.—**g. del caudal,** spendthrift.
gomífero, ra, *a.* gummiferous.
gomorresina, *f.* gum resin.
gomosidad, *f.* gumminess, viscosity.
gomoso, sa. I. *a.* gummy; gum-producing; full of viscous matter. **II.** *m.* dude, dandy.
gónada, *f.* (anat.) gonad.
gonce, *m.* hinge.
góndola, *f.* gondola; omnibus, stage, carry-all.
gondolero, ra, *n.* gondolier.
gonela, *f.* skirt formerly worn in Aragon.
gonfalón, *m.* banner, gonfalon, pennant.
gonfalonier, niero, *n.* chief standard-bearer.
gonfosis, *f.* (anat.) gomphosis.
gong, gongo, *m.* gong.
gongórico, ca; gongorino, na, *a.* euphuistic.
gongorismo, *m.* euphuism.
gongorista, *n.* (poet.) euphuist.
gongorizar, *vn.* to write euphuistically.
goniometría, *f.* goniometry.
goniométrico, ca, *a.* goniometric.
goniómetro, *m.* goniometer.
gonococo, *m.* (biol.) gonococcus.
gonóforo, *m.* (anat., bot.) gonophore.
gonórrea, *f.* (med.) gonorrhœa.
gonorreico, ca, *a.* gonorrhœal.
gorbión, gurbión, *m.* coarse twisted silk or cloth.
gordal, *a.* fat, big, fleshy.
gordana, *f.* oil extracted from oxen's testicles.
gordazo, za, *a. aug.* very fat and big.
gordiflón, na; gordinflón, na, *a.* (coll.) chubby, flabby, fat.
gordo, da. I. *a.* fat, corpulent, fleshy, stout; fat, rich, oily; great, large, big.—**agua g.,** hard water.—**hacer la vista g.,** to pretend not to see, wink at.—**llevarse un susto g.,** to get a bad scare. **II.** *m.* fat, suet.
gordolobo, *m.* (bot.) great mullein.
gordura, *f.* grease, fat; fatness, stoutness.
gorfe, *m.* a deep hole in a river forming a whirlpool or eddy.
gorga, *f.* hawk food; whirlpool.
gorgojarse, *vr.* (of corn) to be infested with grubs.
gorgojo, *m.* grub, weevil; (coll.) dwarfish person.
gorgojoso, sa, *a.* infested with grubs or weevils.
Gorgona, *f.* (myth.) Gorgon.
gorgóneo, nea, *a.* Gorgonian.
gorgonia, *f.* (zool.) gorgonia, sea fan.
gorgorán, *m.* a sort of silk grosgrain.
gorgorita, *f.* rain bubble.—*pl.* = GORGORITO.
gorgoritear, *vn.* (coll.) to warble, trill.
gorgorito, *m.* (coll.) (vocal) trill, shake.
gorgorotada, *f.* swallow (as of water).
gorgotear, *vn.* to gurgle.
gorgoteo, *m.* gurgle, gurgling sound.
gorgotero, ra, *n.* peddler, hawker.
gorguera, *f.* (sew.) gorgeret ruff; (armor) gorget.
gorguerín, *f. dim.* small neck ruff or frill.
gorguz, *m.* javelin, shaft.
gorigori, *m.* (coll.) chant at funerals.
gorila, *m.* (zool.) gorilla.
gorja, *f.* throat, throttle; rejoicing, merrymaking; (naut.) head of the keel.
gorjal, *m.* collar of a doublet; (armor) gorget.
gorjeador, ra, *n.* & *a.* warbler(-ing), modulator (-ing).
gorjear. I. *vn.* to warble, trill, quaver, sing. **II.** *vr.* to gabble (as a child).
gorjeo, *m.* warble, trilling; gabble of a child.
gormar, *va.* to vomit.
gorra. I. *f.* cap, bonnet; woman's hat; hunting cap; (mil.) bearskin cap; (coll.) intrusion at feasts without invitation; (coll.) sponging—**g. de señora,** lady's hat or bonnet.—**de g.,** (coll.) at other people's expense, sponging, as a sponge.—**ir, comer, andar,** etc. **de g.,** to "sponge." **II.** *m.* parasite, sponger.
gorrada, *f.* = GORRETADA.
gorrero, ra, *n.* cap maker; parasite, sponger, deadhead.
gorretada, *f.* raising the cap in greeting.
gorrete, *m. dim.*; **gorrica, illa, ita,** *f. dim.*; **gorrico, illo, ito,** *m. dim.* small cap.
gorrín, *m.* small pig, sucking pig.
gorrinada, *f.* (coll.) dirty, hoggish action.
gorrinera, *f.* pigsty, pigpen.
gorrino, na, *n.* small pig, sucking pig.
gorrión, *m.* (ornith.) sparrow.
gorrionera, *f.* (coll.) den of rogues.
gorrista, *n.* parasite, sponger.
gorro, *m.* cap, coif.—**g. de dormir,** nightcap.—**g. frigio,** Phyrgian cap, cap of liberty.
[1]**gorrón, na,** *n.* sponger, parasite; libertine.
[2]**gorrón,** *m.* round smooth pebble; (mech.) spindle; pivot or gudgeon of a gate or door; pillow, swing block; lazy, unhealthy silkworm.
gorronal, *m.* place full of pebbles or gravel.

gorronear, *vn.* to sponge, eat or drink at another's expense.
gorullo, *m.* lump or ball (as of wool).
gorupo, *m.* (naut.) granny's bend.
gosipino, na, *a.* having a cottony surface.
gota, *f.* drop of liquid; (med.) gout; (arch.) gutta.—**g. a g.,** drop by drop.—**g. caduca,** or **coral,** (med.) epilepsy, falling sickness.—**g. militar,** chronic gonorrhea.—**g. serena,** (med.) amaurosis.—**gotas amargas,** bitters.—**la g. que colmó el vaso,** the straw that broke the camel's back, the last straw.—**sudar la g. gorda,** to sweat blood.
goteado, da. I. *pp.* of GOTEAR. **II.** *a.* spotted, speckled.
gotear, *vn.* to drop, drip, dribble, leak; to sprinkle, begin to rain; to measure by drops; to give by dribblets.
goteo, *m.* trickle.
gotera, *f.* leak, leakage; drip, dripping; (arch.) gutter; valance of a canopy or tester; (agr.) disease of trees caused by infiltration; chronic ailing.
goterón, *m.* large raindrop; (arch.) throating.
gótico, ca, *a.* Gothic.—**gotón, na,** *n.* & *a.* Goth.
gotoso, sa, *a.* gouty.
goyesco, ca, *a.* pertaining to, or like, Goya, or his style, Goya (as *a.*).
gozador, ra, *n.* enjoyer.
gozante, *n.* & *a.* enjoyer(-ing).
gozar. I. *va.* to enjoy; to have possession or fruition of. **II.** *vn.* (**de**), to enjoy, have possession (of). **III.** *vr.* to rejoice.
gozne, *m.* hinge.
gozo, *m.* joy, pleasure, glee, mirth, gladness; sudden blaze of dry chips of wood.—*pl.* couplets with a burden, in praise of the Virgin.—**¡el g. a pozo!** all has come to naught!—**no caber de g.,** or **saltar de g.,** to be in high spirits, to be very happy.
gozoso, sa, *a.* joyful, cheerful, glad, merry.
gozque, *m.* a cur dog.
grabación, *f.* engraving, etching; recording, record, tape recording.
grabado. I. *pp.* of GRABAR. **II.** *a.* engraved, carved, cut. **III.** *m.* engraving; art of engraving; cut, picture, illustration.—**g. al agua fuerte,** etching.—**g. al agua tinta,** aquatint.—**g. al barniz blando,** soft-ground etching.—**g. al humo,** mezzotint.—**g. a media tinta** = G. AL AGUA TINTA.—**g. a puntos,** stipple engraving, stipple.—**g. en fondo,** or **en hueco,** punch or die sinking.—**g. en madera,** wood engraving, wood carving.—**g. en negro** = G. AL HUMO.—**g. punteado** = G. A PUNTOS.
grabador, ra, *n.* engraver, carver; cutter, sinker; *f.* tape recorder.
grabadura, *f.* act of engraving; sculpture.
grabar, *va.* to engrave; to cut, carve; to impress upon the mind.—**g. al agua fuerte,** to etch.—**g. en hueco, en blanco,** or **relieve,** to emboss.
grabazón, *f.* engraving, sculpture.
gracejada, *f.* (Mex., C. A.) joke (gen. in bad taste).
gracejar, *vn.* to write or speak wittily.
gracejo, *m.* graceful, winsome way.
gracia, *f.* grace; gracefulness; cleverness; free gift, benefaction, kindness; graciousness, condescension; benevolence, courtesy, pleasing manners; pardon, mercy; remission of a debt; witty saying or expression; joke, jest; humor, facetiousness; comicalness; brightness, cuteness of a child; (coll.) name (of a person).—*pl.* thanks; accomplishments; (myth., **G-**) (the Three) Graces.—**Ministerio de G. y Justicia,** Dep't of Justice & Eccl. Affairs.—**gracias,** thanks, thank you.—**gracias a,** thanks to.—**gracias a Dios,** thank God.—**caer de la gracia de,** to lose the favor or good will of.—**caer en g.,** to please, to be liked.—**dar gracias,** to thank, to give thanks.—**decir dos gracias,** to tell home truths.—**de g.,** gratis, for nothing.—**en g.,** in favor.—**en g. de,** for the sake of, out of regard for; in consideration of.—**hacer g.,** to please; to amuse, strike as funny.—**hacer g. de,** to excuse from; to free from.—**¡qué g.!,** (ironic) how fine! how funny!—**tener g.,** (ironic) to be surprising.
graciable, *a.* good-natured, affable, amiable; easily granted.
grácil, *a.* gracile, slender, small.
graciola, *f.* (bot.) hedge hyssop.
graciosamente, *adv.* gracefully; graciously or kindly, gratuitously; facetiously.
graciosidad, *f.* gracefulness, beauty, excellence.
gracioso, sa. I. *a.* graceful, pleasing, accomplished; facetious, witty, funny; liberal, gracious; gratuitous, free. **II.** *m.* (theat.) low comedian, fool. **III.** *f.* (theat.) soubrette, chambermaid.
[1]**grada,** *f.* step of a staircase; gradin (as of an amphitheatre); stand or gallery having gradins; superaltar; brake.—*pl.* (arch.) perron, gradatory; wide steps to a building entrance; bleachers (at ball park, etc.)—**g. de astillero,** (naut.) altar.—**g. de dique,** (naut.) altar.
[2]**grada,** *f.* (eccl.) locutory; (agr.) harrow.—**g. de cota,** brush-harrow.—**g. de dientes,** toothed harrow.
gradación, *f.* (mus.) gradation; (rhet.) climax; grading; graded series of things or events.
gradado, da, *a.* having gradins or steps.
gradar, *va.* (agr.) to harrow.
gradeo, *m.* (agr.) harrowing.
gradería, *f.* series of steps, gradins or superaltars.
gradiente, *m.* (math., meteorol.) gradient.
[1]**gradilla,** *f.* tile or brick mold.
[2]**gradilla,** *f.* small stepladder.
gradina, *f.* gradine.
gradinar, *va.* (art) to chisel with a gradine.
gradiolo, *m.* (bot.) = GLADIOLO, gladiolus.
[1]**grado,** *m.* step of a staircase; degree (of kindred); degree, academic title; (mil.) rank; (math., geog.) degree; (com.) grade, class, graduation of value or quality; (gram.) degree (of comparison); (law) state of proceedings.—*pl.* minor orders.—**de g. en g.,** gradually, by degrees.—**en g. superlativo,** or **en sumo g.,** in the highest degree.
[2]**grado,** *m.* will, willingness, pleasure.—**de g.** or **de buen g.,** willingly, with pleasure.—**de mal g.,** unwillingly.—**de su g.,** = DE G.—**mal de mi g.,** against my wishes, much to my regret, unwillingly.
graduable, *a.* that can be graduated; adjustable.
graduación, *f.* graduation; (mil.) rank.
graduado, da. I. *pp.* of GRADUAR. **II.** *a.* (mil.) brevet; graduated. **III.** *m.* graduate.
graduador, *m.* graduator, gauge.
gradual. I. *a.* gradual. **II.** *m.* (eccl.) response sung at mass.—**gradualmente,** *adv.* gradually.
graduando, *m.* one recently, or about to be graduated.
graduar. I. *va.* to compare, grade, classify; to graduate; to give military rank to; (com.) to gauge, to appraise; to adjust; to set (a fuse, etc.). **II.** *vr.* (**en**) to graduate (from), be graduated, take a degree.
gráfico, ca. I. *a.* graphic, graphical; clear, vivid. **II.** *m.* or *f.* graph, diagram.
gráfila, *f.* milled edge of coin.
grafio, *m.* graver for graffito or scratchwork.
grafioles, *m. pl.* biscuits in the form of an S.
grafítico, ca, *a.* graphitic.
grafitización, *f.* (metal.) graphitization.
grafito, *m.* (min.) graphite.
grafófono, *m.* graphophone.
grafolita, *f.* grapholite.
grafología, *f.* graphology.
grafomanía, *f.* graphomania, mania, for writing (books, articles) for publication.
grafómano, na, *n.* one who has GRAFOMANÍA.
grafómetro, *m.* (surv.) graphometer.
grafostática, *f.* graphic statics.
gragea, *f.* minute colored bonbons.
graja, *f.* (ornith.) female jackdaw; jay.

grajal, *a.* pert. to crows, ravens, or magpies.
grajear, *vn.* to caw, as crows; to chatter, as magpies.
grajero, ra, *a.* abounding in, or frequented by, jackdaws.
grajo, *m.* (ornith.) jackdaw.
grama, *f.* (bot.) creeping cynodon; couch, dog's, or grama grass; (Am.) lawn.
gramal, *m.* couch grass or dog's grass field.
gramalla, *f.* long scarlet gown formerly worn in Aragon; coat of mail.
gramallera, *f.* pothanger (in a fireplace).
gramar, *va.* to knead.
gramática, *f.* grammar; study of the Latin language.—**g. parda,** (coll.) horse sense, shrewdness.
gramatical, *a.* grammatical.
gramático, ca. I. *a.* grammatical. II. *n.* grammarian.—**gramatiquear,** *vn.* (contempt.) to grammatize, to talk grammar.
gramatiquería, *f.* (coll. & contempt.) things grammatical, grammatical stuff.
gramil, *m.* (carp.) joiner's marking gauge.
gramilla, *f.* bed of hemp brake; (Arg.) (grass) lawn.
gramíneo, ea, *a.* (bot.) gramineous.
graminívoro, ra, *a.* graminivorous.
gramo, *m.* gramme, gram (weight).
gramófono, *m.* gramophone; phonograph.
gramómetro, *m.* (print.) type gauge.
gramoso, sa, *a.* covered with couch grass; pertaining to couch grass.
grampa, *f.* staple, clamp, cramp.
gran, *a. contr.* of GRANDE (*used only in sing. and before m. or f. nouns*), large, big; grand, great.—**g. bestia,** tapir, elk.—**g. duque,** grand duke.—**g. mogol,** Grand Mogol, Great Mogol.
[1]**grana,** *f.* (agr.) act of seeding; seeding time; small seed of some plants.
[2]**grana,** *f.* (entom.) cochineal; kermes; kermes berry; scarlet grain; scarlet color; fine scarlet cloth; fresh red color of the lips and cheeks.—**g. del paraíso,** (bot.) cardamomum.
granada, *f.* (bot.) pomegranate; (mil.) grenade, shell.—**g. de mano,** hand grenade.
granadera, *f.* (mil.) grenadier's pouch.
granadero, *m.* (mil.) grenadier; (coll.) very tall person.
granadilla, *f.* (bot.) passion flower, granadilla.
granadillo, *m.* (bot.) West-India red ebony.
granadino, na. I. *a.* Granada, of or pertaining to Granada; pertaining to pomegranate. II. *n.* inhabitant of Granada; *m.* pomegranate flower; *f.* grenadine (drink); (text.) grenadine.
[1]**granado, da.** I. *pp.* of GRANAR. II. *a.* remarkable, noted, illustrious; mature; select, choice.
[2]**granado,** *m.* (bot.) pomegranate tree.
granador, *m.* (fireworks making) granulating sieve; spot destined for this operation.
granalla, *f.* (foundry) granulated metal.
granar, *vn.* (agr.) (of corn) to start forming kernels.
granate, *m.* garnet.
granazón, *f.* seeding, forming seeds or kernels.
grancé, *a.* madder-colored.
grande. I. *a.* large, big; great; grand; (Mex.) old.—**en g.,** on a large scale. II. *n.* grandee.—*pl.* grandees; great men.—**grandecico, ica, illo, illa, ito, ita,** *a.* pretty large.—**grandemente,** *adv.* greatly; very well; extremely; grandly.
grandevo, va, *a.* (poet.) of advanced age.
grandeza, *f.* greatness; grandeur, magnificence; grandeeship; grandees collectively; bigness; quantity; size, magnitude.
grandilocuencia, *f.* grandiloquence.
grandilocuente; grandílocuo, cua, *a.* grandiloquent.
grandillón, na, *a. aug.* excessively large or big.
grandiosidad, *f.* greatness; grandeur; abundance.
grandioso, sa, *a.* grandiose, grand, magnificent.
grandísono, na, *a.* (poet.) high-sounding.
grandor, *m.* size.
grandote, ta, *a. aug.* (coll.) very big.
grandullón, na, *a.* overgrown.
graneado, da. I. *pp.* of GRANEAR. II. *a.* grained, spotted, granulous; (Peru) select, choice.—**fuego, g.,** (mil.) drumfire.
graneador, *m.* (art) stipple graver.
granear, *va.* (agr.) to sow (grain); (art) to stipple: to grain (a lithographic stone); (Am.) GRANAR.
granel, *m.* heap of grain.—**a g.,** in a heap; (com.) in bulk.
granelar, *va.* (tanning) to grain (leather).
graneo, *m.* (agr.) act of shedding or sowing seed; (art) stippling.
granero, *m.* granary, barn; grange; cornloft; grain-producing country.
granete, *m.* (mech.) countersink, punch.
granévano, *m.* (bot.) goat's-thorn.
granguardia, *f.* (mil.) grand guard.
granilla, *f.* nap on wrong side of cloth.
granillo, *m. dim.* granule, small grain; gain or profit frequently obtained; pimple on the rump of canary birds and linnets.
granilloso, sa, *a.* granulous, granular.
granítico, ca, *a.* granitic.
granito, *m. dim.* small grain; pimple; (min.) granite; (pharm.) granule; small egg of a silkworm.
granívoro, ra, *a.* granivorous.
granizada, *f.* hailstorm; deluge (fig.), great number (of things, facts, etc.); water ice.
granizar, *vn.* to hail; to pour down with violence.
granizo, *m.* hail; hailstorm; film in the eyes.
granja, *f.* grange, farm, farmhouse.—**g. lechera,** dairy farm.—**g. modelo,** model farm.
granjear. I. *va.* to gain, earn, profit. II. *va.* & *vr.* to get, win (as the goodwill of another).
granjeo, *m.* act of getting or acquiring; gain, profit, advancement.
granjería, *f.* gain, profit, advantage.
granjero, ra, *n.* farmer, husbandman; dealer in profitable commodities.
grano, *m.* grain; cereal; each single seed; (pharm.) grain (20 make an English scruple, and 24 a Spanish scruple); (artil.) bushing (or bouching) of a cannon; pimple; (jewel.) unit of weight (.05 g.).—*pl.* (com.) cereals, corn, breadstuffs.—**granos del paraíso,** (bot.) grain of paradise.—**ir al g.,** (coll.) to come to the point, to get down to brass tacks.
granoso, sa, *a.* granulous, grainy, granular, granulated (as leather).
granuja. I. *f.* loose berries of grapes; grapestone; group of roving boys. II. *m.* (coll.) rogue, waif, gamin, urchin.
granujado, da, *a.* = AGRANUJADO, grainlike.
granujiento, ta, *a.* full of pimples.
granujo, *m.* (coll.) pimple or tumor in the flesh.
granujoso, sa, *a.* full of pimples.
granulación, *f.* (chem. and med.) granulation.
granulado, da, *a.* granulated.
granulador, ra, *m.* or *f.* granulating machine.
[1]**granular.** I. *va.* to granulate. II. *vr.* to become covered with granules or pimples.
[2]**granular,** *a.* granular; full of pimples.
gránulo, *m. dim.* granule; pellet.
granulocito, *m.* (biol.) granulocyte.
granulopenia, *f.* (med.) granulopenia.
granulosidad, *f.* granularity.
granuloso, sa, *a.* granulous, granular.
granza, *f.* (bot.) madder; garancine.
granzas, *f. pl.* siftings, chaff; dross of metals.
granzón, *m.* (min.) ore screenings.—*pl.* refuse of straw left by cattle.
granzoso, sa, *a.* full of chaff or screenings.
grañón, *m.* pap made of boiled wheat; boiled grain of wheat.
grao, *m.* strand, shore.
grapa, *f.* clamp, clasp, clutch, cramp iron; (carp.) holdfast; (vet.) mangy ulcers in the joints.
grapón, *m. aug.* (mech.) brace, hook, ram, iron dog.
grasa, *f.* grease; fat; suet; oil; gum of juniper

trees; GRASILLA; (naut.) slush; slag of metals; base of an ointment or pomade.—**g. de ballena,** whale oil, blubber.—**g. de pescado,** fish oil.—**grasera,** *f.* vessel for fat or grease; slush-tub; dripping pan.
grasería, *f.* tallow chandler's shop.
grasero, *m.* (min.) slag dumper.
graseza, *f.* quality of fat or grease.
grasiento, ta, *a.* greasy, oily; filthy.
grasilla, *f.* pounce, a fine powder formerly used to keep ink from spreading, etc.
graso, sa. I. *a.* fat, oily, unctuous, lardy. **II.** *m.* fat, grease.
grasones, *m. pl.* wheat porridge.
grasoso, sa, *a.* = GRASIENTO.
grasura, *f.* = GROSURA, fat, suet; meat diet.
grata, grataguja, *f.* burnisher, smoothing chisel; wire brush; rasp.
gratar, *va.* to brush or burnish.
gratificación, *f.* gratification; reward; gratuity, tip; fee.
gratificador, ra, *n.* & *a.* gratifier(-ing); rewarder (-ing); tipper(-ing).
gratificar, *va.* (*pret.* GRATIFIQUÉ; *subj.* GRATIFIQUE) to reward, recompense; to tip, fee; to gratify, please.
gratil, *m.* (naut.) edge of a sail; luff, leech.
gratis, *adv.* gratis, free, for nothing.
gratisdato, ta, *a.* gratuitous, given away.
gratitud, *f.* gratitude, gratefulness.
grato, ta, *a.* pleasing, pleasant; acceptable; grateful; gratuitous.—**su grata (carta),** (com.) your favor.
gratonada, *f.* chicken ragout or fricassee.
gratuito, ta, *a.* GRATIS; gratuitous, uncalled-for; unfounded.
gratulación, *f.* congratulation.
gratular. I. *vn.* to congratulate. **II.** *vr.* to rejoice.
gratulatorio, ria, *a.* congratulatory.
grava, *f.* gravel; broken stone.
gravable, *a.* (law) liable.
gravamen, *m.* tax; charge, obligation, hardship, burden, inconvenience, nuisance; encumbrance; (law) mortgage, lien.
gravar, *va.* to burden, oppress; to fatigue; to tax; (law) to encumber.
gravativo, va, *a.* injurious; burdensome.
grave, *a.* weighty, ponderous, heavy; grave, serious; circumspect; troublesome, vexatious; arduous, difficult; (mus.) grave (tone); deep (voice); (gram.) grave (accent); (word) having the stress on the penultimate syllable.
gravear, *vn.* to weigh, gravitate, sink.
gravedad, *f.* gravtiy, graveness, seriousness; (phys.) gravity.—**de g.,** serious; seriously, dangerously.
gravedoso, sa, *a.* haughty, self-important.
gravemente, *adv.* gravely; seriously, dangerously.
gravidez, *f.* pregnancy.
grávido, da, *a.* (poet.) gravid, pregnant.
gravimetría, *f.* gravimetry.
gravimétrico, ca, *a.* gravimetric.
gravímetro, *m.* (phys.) gravimeter.
gravitación, *f.* (phys.) gravitation.
gravitar, *vn.* to gravitate; to rest, press (on).
gravoso, sa, *a.* costly; onerous; vexatious.
graznador, ra, *a.* croaking; cawing; cackling.
graznar, *vn.* to croak, caw, cackle.
graznido, *m.* croak, caw, cackle; croaking.
greba, *f.* (armor) greave(s) or jambe(s).
greca, *f.* Grecian fret.
Grecia, *f.* Greece.
greciano, na; grecisco, ca, *a.* Grecian.
grecismo, *m.* Grecism, Hellenism.
grecizar, *va.* & *vn.* to Grecize, Hellenize.
greco, ca. I. *a.* Grecian. **II.** *n.* Greek.
grecolatino, na, *a.* Greco-Latin.
grecorromano, na, *a.* Greco-Roman.
greda, *f.* clay, chalk, marl, potter's clay.
gredal. I. *m.* clay pit, marl pit, loam pit. **II.** *a.* clayey, loamy.
gredoso, sa, *a.* clayey, marly.
grefier, *m.* registrar in the house of Burgundy.
[1]**gregal,** *m.* northeast wind in Mediterranean.
[2]**gregal,** *a.* gregarious, going in flocks.
gregario, ria, *a.* (one) of a crowd; dull, stupid.
gregoriano, na, *a.* Gregorian.
gregorito, *m.* (Mex.) disappointment; practical joke.
greguería, *f.* outcry, clamor, hubbub.
gregüescos, *m. pl.* Grecian wide breeches.
greguisco, ca, *a.* Grecian.
greguizar, *va.* to Grecize.
gremial. I. *a.* belonging to a guild or trade-union, union (as *a.*). **II.** *m.* member of a guild; union man; (eccl.) lapcloth used by bishops at divine service.
gremio, *m.* lap; body, society, company, guild, corporation; fraternity; trade-union.
grenchudo, da, *a.* having a long mane.
greña, *f.* long entangled or matted hair; anything entangled; (prov.) heap of grain to be thrashed; (prov.) first leaves of a vine shoot.—**andar a la g.,** (of women) to pull each other's hair; to argue excitedly.—**en g.,** (Mex.) (of silk, etc.) raw.
greñudo, da. I. *a.* dishevelled; shy (horse). **II.** *m.* shy horse.
gres, *m.* pottery material consisting of clay and quartzose sand.
gresca, *f.* carousal, revelling, clatter; wrangle, quarrel, row.
grey, *f.* flock, herd; congregation of the faithful; people, race, nation.
grial, *m.* grail, legendary holy chalice.
griego, ga. I. *a.* Greek, Grecian. **II.** *n.* Greek, Grecian; *m.* Greek (language); (coll.) cheating gambler; (fig.) Greek, unintelligible language.
grieta, *f.* crevice, crack, cleft; chink, fissure, cranny, flaw; split, vein, shake, rent; scratch in the skin.—**grietas en las manos,** chapping of the hands.
grietado, da, *a.* fissured, cracked, showing flaws.
grietarse, *vr.* to crack, split; to part in clefts or fissures; to become chapped.
grietoso, sa, *a.* cracked; crannied, having flaws.
grifa, *f.* (print.) script.
grifado, da, *a.* script (type).
grifalto, *m.* a kind of small culverin, firearm.
[1]**grifo, fa,** *a.* (print.) script.
[2]**grifo, fa. I.** *a.* (Am.) bristling (hair, fur); (of hair) kinky, tangled. **II.** *m.* griffin or griffon, a fabled animal; (Am.) child of a negro and an Indian; (mech.) faucet, cock.—*pl.* frizzled hair.
grifón, *m. aug.* fountain faucet.
grigallo, *m.* (ornith.) a variety of francolin.
grilla, *f.* female cricket.—**ésa es g.,** (coll.) that is a fake.
grillarse, *vr.* to shoot, to sprout.
grillera, *f.* cricket hole; cricket cage.
grillero, *m.* he who puts on and takes off the irons of prisoners.
grillete, *m. dim.* shackle, fetter.
[1]**grillo,** *m.* (entom.) cricket.—**andar a grillos,** to waste one's time in trifles.
[2]**grillo,** *m.* —(bot.) shoot, sprout.
[3]**grillo,** *m.* —*pl.* fetters, irons, gyves, shackles.
grillotalpa, *m.* (ent.) mole cricket.
grima, *f.* fright, horror; disgust.—**dar g.,** to disgust; to cause discouragement or fear.
grimoso, sa, *a.* horrible; repulsive, disgusting.
grímpola, *f.* (naut.) pennant, streamer.
gringo, ga, *n.* (Am.) foreigner (esp. app. to Englishmen and Americans).
[1]**griñón,** *m.* wimple worn by nuns.
[2]**griñón,** *m.* apricot grafted in peach tree.
gripa, *f.* (Am.) = GRIPE.
gripal, a. (med.) pertaining to la grippe.
gripe, *f.* (med.) grip, grippe, influenza.
gris. I. *a.* gray. **II.** *m.* (zool.) minever, Siberian squirrel and its fur; (coll.) cold, sharp air.
grisáceo, a; gríseo, a, *a.* grayish.
grisalla, *f.* (art) grisaille, camaieu.
[1]**griseta,** *f.* flowered silk stuff; (agr.) disease of trees caused by infiltration of water.

[2]**griseta,** *f.* (Gal.) French grisette.
grisón, *m.* (zool.) grison.
grisú, *m.* (min.) fire damp.
grita, *f.* clamor, outcry, uproar; screaming, halloo, shouting; hooting, catcall.—**g. foral,** (law) summons, citation.
gritador, ra, *n.* & *a.* clamorer(-ing), shouter (-ing), screamer(-ing).
gritar, *vn.* to shout, cry out, scream, shriek; to hoot, catcall.
gritería, *f.* outcry, uproar, shouting.
grito, *m.* cry, scream, howl, shriek, shout; hoot, whoop.—**a gritos, a g. en cuello, a g. herido, a g. pelado, a todo g.,** loudly; at the top of one's voice; vociferously, with loud cries, howling.—**alzar el g.,** to talk loud and haughtily. —**estar en un g.,** to be in continual pain.—**levantar el g.** = ALZAR EL G.—**poner el g. en el cielo,** to cry to heaven, to complain loudly, (coll.) to make a great fuss, to howl.
gritón, na, *a.* (coll.) vociferous, clamorous.
gro, *m.* grosgrain, twilled silk fabric.
groelandés, sa; groenlandés, sa, *n.* & *a.* Greenlander(-ish), Greenland (as *a.*).
groera, *f.* (naut.) rope hole.
grog, *m.* grog (drink).
gromo, *m.* (bot.) leafy bud, young shoot.
grosella, *f.* (bot.) berry of the red currant.—**g. blanca,** gooseberry.
grosellero, *m.* (bot.) currant bush.
groseramente, *adv.* grossly, coarsely, roughly; rudely, in an unmannerly way.
grosería, *f.* rudeness, ill-breeding; rusticity; discourtesy; coarseness, clumsiness; ignorance.
grosero, ra, *a.* coarse, rough; plain, homespun, not fine; thick, fat, bulky; rude, unpolished; discourteous, churlish, uncivil.
grosezuelo, la, *a. dim.* somewhat stout.
grosísimo, ma, *super. of* GRUESO: exceedingly stout; very bulky.
groso, *m.* coarse snuff, badly powdered.
grosor, *m.* thickness.
grosularia, *f.* (min.) grossularite.
grosularico, a, *a.* (bot.) grossulaceous.
grosulina, *f.* (chem.) grossulin.
grosura, *f.* fat, suet, tallow; meat diet, in contrast to fasting.
grotesco, ca, *a.* grotesque.
grúa. *f.* crane, derrick, hoisting machine; an ancient war engine; (naut.) bend.—**g. corredera,** traveling crane.—**g. de caballete,** gantry crane.—**g. de la cuaderna maestra,** midship bend.—**g. de puente,** gantry crane.—**g. de tijeras,** shears, device used in hoisting.—**g. fija,** stationary crane.—**g. flotante,** crane ship; floating crane.—**a la g.,** in and out.
gruesa, *f.* gross, twelve dozen; (eccl.) chief part of a prebend; (law) bottomry.
gruesamente, *adv.* grossly, coarsely.
grueso, sa. I. thick; bulky, corpulent; fleshy, stout; (coll.) pregnant; big; coarse, homespun, dense, thick, heavy; large around (as a post, etc.); (of type) heavy, black; heavy, dull, stupid, slow. **II.** *m.* thickness; bulk, corpulence; density, heaviness; main part, main body of an army; down stroke in penmanship.—**en g.,** (com.) in gross, in the gross, in bulk, by wholesale.
gruir, *vn.* (*ind. pres.* GRUYO, *pret.* él GRUYÓ; *subj.* GRUYA; *ger.* GRUYENDO) to cry like a crane.
grujidor, *m.* glazier's nippers.
grujir, *va.* to trim or pare with a GRUJIDOR.
grulla, *f.* (ornith.) crane.
grullada, *f.* (coll.) gang or crowd of idlers; (coll.) patrol of constables or police officers.
grullo, lla. I. *a.* (Am.) (of horses) dark grey. **II.** *m.* (Am.) peso, dollar; breeding horse.
grumete, *m.* (naut.) cabin boy, ship boy.
grumo, *m.* clot; cluster, bunch; (agr.) bud of trees; tip of a fowl's wing.—**g. de leche,** curd.
grumoso, sa, *a.* full of clots, clotted.
gruñido, *m.* grunt.
gruñidor, ra, *n.* & *a.* grunter(-ing), growler (-ing).
gruñimiento, *m.* grunting, growling, grumbling.
gruñir, *vn.* (*pret.* él GRUÑO; *ger.* GRUÑENDO) to grunt; to creak (as doors, hinges, etc.); to grumble, growl.
gruñón, na, *n.* & *a.* (coll.) cranky, irritable.
grupa, *f.* croup, rump of a horse.
grupada, *f.* squall, burst of wind and rain.
grupera, *f.* cushion at the back of a saddle for carrying a satchel, etc.; crupper (of saddle).
grupo, *m.* group; set; clump, cluster.—**g. sanguíneo,** blood group.
gruta, *f.* cavern, grotto, grot.—*pl.* crypts, vaults, subterranean galleries.
grutesco, ca, *m.* & *a.* (f. a.) grotesque.
gruyere, *m.* Gruyère (cheese).
gruyo, gruyó, gruya, etc. *v. V.* GRUIR.
¡gua! *interj.* (Am.) gracious! horrors!
guabina, *f.* (Colomb.) a popular peasant air.
guaca, *f.* Indian grave, esp. one containing treasure; (Am.) buried treasure; (Am.) hole in the ground where gathered fruit is put to ripen.
guacamaya, guacamayo, *m.* (ornith.) macao or macaw.
guacamole, *m.* (Cuba) salad of alligator pear.
guacia, *f.* (bot.) acacia; acacin, gum arabic.
guaco, *m.* (bot.) guaco, birthwort; (ornith.) curassow.
guachapear. I. *va.* (coll.) to splatter (water) with the feet; (coll.) to make a botch of. **II.** *vn.* to clap, as horses' shoes when loose; to clatter.
guachapelí, *m.* solid strong wood used for ships in Guayaquil.
guacharaca, *f.* (ornith.) a Mexican bird.
guácharo, ra. I. *a.* sickly; dropsical. **II.** *m.* birdling, especially of a sparrow; (ornith.) oilbird, guacharo.
guache, *m.* (Am.) low, despicable man, tough.
guachinango, ga, *a.* (Cuba) (contempt.) Mexican; (Mex.) artful, cunning.
guacho, cha. I. *a.* & *n.* (Am.) orphan, foundling; solitary, forlorn; (Chile) odd (only one of a pair). **II.** *m.* birdling of a sparrow.
guadafiones, *m. pl.* hopple, fetterlock.
guadalajareño, ña, *a.* of or pertaining to Guadalajara.
guadamací, cil, *m.* = GUADAMECÍ.
guadamacilería, *f.* embossed-leather factory.
guadamacilero, *m.* manufacturer of embossed leather.
guadamecí, guadamecil, *m.* embossed leather. —**g. brocado,** gilt or silvered embossed leather.
guadameco, *m.* ornament worn by women.
guadaña, *f.* (agr.) scythe.
guadañar, *va.* (agr.) to scythe, mow.
[1]**guadañero,** *m.* scytheman.
[2]**guadañero,** *m.* (Cuba) owner of a guadaño.
guadañil, *m.* mower of hay.
guadaño, *m.* (Cuba) small boat in the port of Havana; transport vessel.
[1]**guadapero,** *m.* (bot.) wild common pear.
[2]**guadapero,** *m.* boy who carries food to field workers.
guadarnés, *m.* harness room or locker; harness keeper; officer of the king's mews.
guadijeño, ña. I. *a.* native to, or, of Guadix; pert. to Guadix. **II.** *m.* poniard, stiletto, knife.
guadramaña, *f.* trick, deceit, imposition.
guadua, *f.* (Am.) a variety of large, thorny bamboo.—**guadual,** *m.* GUADUA field.
[1]**guagua,** *m.* & *f.* (S. A.) baby.
[2]**guagua,** *f.* (Am.) insect that destroys fruit; trivial thing.—**de g.,** free, gratis.
[3]**guagua,** *f.* (Cuba) omnibus; street car.
guagüero, ra, *n.* (Cuba) bus or street car driver; (Am.) sponger.
guaicán, *m.* (ichth.) = RÉMORA, remora.
guaina, *m.* (Arg., Chile) boy, youth.
guainambí, *m.* (Mex., C. A.) humming bird.
guaira, *f.* (Am.) smelting furnace; (naut.) leg-of-mutton sail.

guairo, *m.* (Am.) small two-masted coaster.
guaita, *f.* (mil.) night watch or sentinel.
guajada, *f.* (Mex.) nonsense, frivolity.
guajalote, *m.* (Mex.) turkey.
guajamón, na, *a.* (Cuba) orange-colored; bay.
guájar, *m.* & *f.*, **guájaras,** *f. pl.* fastnesses, roughest part of a mountain.
guaje, *m.* (Mex.) gourd used in learning to swim.
guájete por guájete, tit for tat.
guajira, *f.* a Cuban popular song.
guajiro, ra, *n.* & *a.* (Cuba) rustic, rural; rude, boorish.
guajolote, *m.* = GUAJALOTE.
¡gualá! *interj.* assuredly; by God!
gualatina, *f.* dish made of boiled apples, milk of almonds, and broth, beaten up with spice and rose water.
gualda, *f.* (bot.) weld, wild woad, dyer's weed, reseda.
gualdado, da, *a.* weld-colored; yellowish.
gualdera, *f.* (artil.) trail, bracket; (carp.) stringboard; (naut.) whelp, check.
gualdo, da, *a.* weld, yellow or gold-colored.
gualdrapa, *f.* horse trappings, housing; (coll.) tatter, rag hanging from clothes.
gualdrapazo, *m.* (naut.) flap of a sail; jerk.
gualdrapear. I. *va.* to put end to head, or in consecutive order (as pins with the point of each on the head of the next). **II.** *vn.* (naut.) to flap (as sails).
gualdrapeo, *m.* flapping of the sails.
gualdrapero, *m.* ragamuffin, ragged fellow.
gualdrín, *m.* weather strip.
guamá, *m.* guamá, a West-Indian tree much used for shade.
guama, *f.* fruit of the guamo.
guamo, *m.* guamo, a large fruit tree.
guanábana, *f.* bullock's-heart, custard apple.
guanábano, *m.* (bot.) custard apple (tree).
guanaco, *m.* guanaco, a kind of llama; (Guat., Hond.) boor, rustic; (Mex., C. R., Chile) (coll.) simpleton, idiot.
guanajo, *m.* (Cuba) turkey; *a.* & *n.* (Mex., W. I.) (coll.) fool.
guancoche, *m.* (Mex., C. A.) burlap.
guanche, *n.* ancient inhabitant of the Canaries.
guando, *m.* (Am.) stretcher, litter.
guanera, *f.* place abounding in guano.
guanina, *f.* (bot.) (Am.) a leguminous plant.
[1]**guano,** *m.* any palm tree; palm leaves used for thatching.
[2]**guano,** *m.* guano, seabirds' droppings used as fertilizer.
guantada, *f.*, **guantazo,** *m.* slap.
guante, *m.* glove; collection for charity.—*pl.* extra pay, fee, or tip.—**guantes de ante,** buff gloves.—**guantes de cabritilla,** kid gloves.—**echar el g. a,** to challenge; (coll.) to seize, grasp; to imprison.—**echar un g.,** to take a collection for charitable purposes.—**poner como un g.,** to render as pliable as a glove; (coll.) to abuse, dress down.—**salvo el g.,** (coll.) excuse my glove.
guantelete, *m.* gauntlet.
guantería, *f.* glove factory or shop; glove making.
guantero, ra, *n.* glover, glove maker.
guañín, *m.* (Am.) base gold.
guañir, *vn.* (*pret.* él GUAÑÓ) to grunt like pigs.
guao, *m.* (Mex., S. A.) a terebinthine tree whose seeds are used as hog feed and whose wood is used for charcoal; (West Indies) guao, a poisonous tree.
guapamente, *adv.* (coll.) bravely, courageously.
guapear, *vn.* (coll.) to boast of courage; (coll.) to take pride in fine dress.
guapetón, na, *a. aug.* brave, daring, bold.
guapeza, *f.* (coll.) bravery; ostentation in dress; good looks, handsomeness.
guapinal, *m.* (C. A.) a resin-yielding tree.
guapo, pa. I. *a.* (coll.) brave, daring; enterprising; good-looking or handsome; spruce, neat; ostentatious, vain; gay, sprightly. **II.** *m.* gallant, beau; brawler, quarrelsome person.
guapote, ta, *a.* (coll.) good-natured; good-looking, handsome.
guaquero, *m.* vessel for drinking chicha found in ancient Peruvian tombs.
guaracha, *f.* a Spanish clog dance; a Cuban song.
guarache, huarache, *m.* (Mex.) sandal.
guaraná, *f.* (bot.) a Brazilian shrub yielding astringent and nerve-stimulating substances.
guarango, ga. I. *a.* (Chile, Arg.) ill-bred, unmannerly. **II.** *m.* (bot.) (Peru, Ecua.) a species of wild acacia; (Venez.) (bot.) dividivi.
guaraní. I. *a.* Guaranian. **II.** *m.* Guarani.
guarapo, *m.* juice of the sugar cane; fermented cane liquor.
[1]**guarda. I.** *n.* guard; keeper; (Arg.) conductor (on street car, etc.).—**g. de cota,** gamekeeper.—**g. de la aduana,** officer of the custom house. **II.** *f.* custody; trust, wardship, safe-keeping; observance of a law or ordinance; nun who accompanies men through convents; outside rib or guard of a fan; (bookbinding) flyleaf, blank sheet; ward of a lock or of a key; (mech.) guard plate, shoe; sheath of a pruning knife.—**g. bauprés,** (naut.) knightheads, bollard timbers.
[2]**guarda,** (*imper.* of GUARDAR) *interj.* take care! beware! look out!
guardaaguas, *m.* (naut.) spurn water; (carp.) flashing board; (car) splash leather.
guardaagujas, *m.* (Ry.) switchman.
guardaalmacén, *m.* storekeeper.
guardabanderas, *m.* (naut.) yeoman of signals.
guardabarrera, *m.* (Ry.) gatekeeper.
guardabarro, *m.* (auto) mudguard.
guardabosque, *m.* forester; game warden.
guardabrazo, *m.* (armor) brassard.
guardabrisa, *m.* glass shade for candles; (auto) windshield.
guardacabras, *m.* goatherd.
guardacalada, *f.* opening in eaves.
guardacamisa, *f.* (Venez.) undershirt.
guardacantón, *m.* protective stone at corner of buildings.
guardacartuchos, *m.* (naut.) cartridge case.
guardacostas, *m.* (naut.) revenue cutter; Coast Guard.
guardacuños, *m.* keeper of the dies in the mint.
guardadamas, *m.* officer who escorted ladies of the court.
guardado, da. I. *pp.* of GUARDAR. **II.** *a.* guarded, reserved.
guardador, ra. I. *a.* very thrifty and provident; law-abiding; stingy, miserly. **II.** *m.* guardian; (mil.) keeper of the spoils.
guardaespaldas, *m.* bodyguard.
guardafango, *m.* (auto.) mudguard.
guardafaro, *m.* lighthouse keeper.
guardafrenos, *m.* (Ry.) brakeman.
guardafuego, *m.* (naut.) breaming board.
guardaguas, *m.* = GUARDAAGUAS.
guardagujas, *m.* = GUARDAAGUJAS.
guardainfante, *m.* farthingale, hoop (for skirt).—*pl.* (naut.) capstan whelp.
guardaja, *f.* = GUEDEJA, lock of hair; lion's mane.
guardajoyas, *m.* keeper of the crown jewels; place where the crown jewels are kept.
guardalado, *m.* battlement of a bridge.
guardalmacén, *n.* = GUARDAALMACÉN.
guardalobo, *m.* (bot.) poet's cassia.
guardamalleta, *f.* lambrequin.
guardamancebo, *m.* (naut.) manrope.
guardamano, *f.* guard of a sword.
guardamateriales, *m.* buyer of bullion and other necessaries for a mint.
guardameta, *m.* goalkeeper.
guardamonte, *m.* (artil.) guard of a gunlock; (Am.) forester, keeper of a forest.
guardamuebles, *m.* storeroom for furniture; person in charge of the furniture of a palace.
guardamujer, *f.* servant of the queen.

guardapapo, *m.* (armor) gusset.
guardapelo, *m.* locket.
guardapesca, *n.* boat that inspects and guards fisheries.
guardapiés, *m.* skirt.
guardapolvo, *m.* dust guard; dust wrapper; cover; inner lid of a watch; projection over a window or door to carry off the water.
guardapuerta, *f.* storm door.
guardar. I. *va.* to keep; to guard, protect, watch over; to lay up, store, lay by, reserve; to keep (one's word, the law, a secret, etc.); to fulfil (one's duty).—**g. la cara,** to hide, to dissemble. —**g. miramientos,** to show regard or consideration.—**guardársela a uno,** to bide one's time to take revenge on.—**g. silencio,** to keep silent, not to answer. **II.** *vr.* **(de)** to guard (against), avoid, beware (of), take care not (to).
guardarraya, *f.* (Cuba) path in cane or coffee plantations; (min.) boundary of a drill hole.
guardarriel, *m.* (Ry.) reinforcing plate on rail.
guardarrío, *m.* (ornith.) kingfisher.
guardarropa. I. *f.* wardroom, coat room. **II.** *m.* keeper of a wardrobe; wardrobe, clothes closet; (bot.) lavender cotton.
guardarropía, *f.* (theat.) wardrobe.
guardarruedas, *m.* = GUARDACANTÓN.
guardasellos, *m.* seal keeper.
guardasol, *m.* = QUITASOL, parasol, sunshade.
guardatimón, *m.* (naut.) stern chaser.
guardavajilla, *f.* room for keeping the (royal) plate or table service.
guardavalla, *m.* goalkeeper.
guardavía, *m.* (Ry.) signalman; lineman.
guardavientos, *m.* (agr.) windbreak.
guardera, *f.* female keeper.
guardería, *f.* keepership.
guardia. I. *f.* guard (body of armed men); defense, custody, protection; (naut.) watch; turn of persons on duty; (fencing) guard.—**g. civil,** body of rural police in Spain.—**g. de babor,** larboard watch.—**g. de corps,** lifeguard.—**g. de estribor,** starboard watch.—**g. del tope,** masthead lookout.—**g. municipal,** city police. —**g. valona,** Walloon guard.—**en g.,** on guard. —**estar de g.,** (mil.) to be on guard duty.—**montar la g.,** to mount guard.—**mudar la g.,** to relieve the guard.—**salir de g.,** to come off guard. **II.** *m.* soldier belonging to the guards, guardsman.—**g. civil,** a member of the rural police in Spain.—**g. marina,** midshipman.—**g. municipal,** policeman.
guardián, na. I. *n.* keeper, guardian, warden; watchman. **II.** *m.* local superior of convents of the order of St. Francis; (naut.) boatswain's mate; quarterman; gunner's yeoman; (naut.) strong hawser.
guardianía, *f.* guardianship of a convent and the district assigned to it.
guardilla, *f.* garret, attic; (sewing) guard, welt; each of the two end thick teeth of a comb.
guardín, *m.* (naut.) tiller rope, tiller chain; (naut.) port lanyard.
guardoso, sa, *a.* frugal, parsimonious; niggardly, stingy.
guarecer. I. *va.* (*ind.* GUAREZCO; *subj.* GUAREZCA) to shelter, protect, preserve; to cure. **II.** *vr.* to take refuge or shelter.
guarentigio, gia, *a.* (law) (contract) containing a warranty clause.
guarezco, guarezca, *v. V.* GUARECER.
guarida, *f.* den, cave, lair of a wild beast; shelter; lurking place, cover, haunt.
guarimán, *m.* (bot.) (Am.) tree of the magnolia family, with aromatic bark used as spice.
guarín, *m.* suckling pig.
guarismo, *m.* (arith.) figure, digit; number.
guarne, *m.* (naut.) turn (of a cable or tackle).
guarnecedor, ra, *n.* & *a.* garnisher(-ing), furbisher(-ing), trimmer(-ing).
guarnecer, *va.* (*ind.* GUARNEZCO; *subj.* GUARNEZCA) to garnish, adorn, embellish, decorate, furbish; (sewing) to trim, bind, edge, face, border, line, welt; (jewelry) to set in gold, silver, etc.; (mason.) to plaster; (armor) to put a guard on; to harness; (mil.) to garrison.
guarnecido, *m.* (mason.) plastering; stucco work.
guarnés, *m.* harness room.
guarnezco, guarnezca, *v. V.* GUARNECER.
guarnición, *f.* (sewing) trimming, binding, edging, welt, flounce, furbelow, garniture, garnish, any ornamental hem, lace, or border; (jewelry) setting; (mech.) packing; (armor) guard of a sword; (mil.) garrison.—*pl.* gears or traces of mules and horses; harness; fixtures, fittings (for gas, electric lamps, etc.); accessories.
guarnicionar, *va.* (mil.) to garrison.
guarnicionería, *f.* harness maker's shop.
guarnicionero, *m.* harness maker.
guarniel, *m.* leather pouch with divisions or pockets, strapped across the back and chest over one shoulder; (Mex.) powderflask.
guarnigón, *m.* (ornith.) young quail.
guarnir, *va.* GUARNECER; (naut.) to reeve; to rig.
[1]**guaro,** *m.* a very talkative small parrot.
[2]**guaro,** *m.* (C. A.) sugar-cane liquor.
guarra, *f.* sow.
guarro, *m.* hog.
¡guarte! *interj.* take care! beware! look out!
guaruba, *f.* (ornith.) a red-necked American parrot; howling monkey.
guasa, *f.* (coll.) jest, fun, joke; dulness; **(W. I.)** (ichth.) jewfish.—**de g.,** jokingly, in fun.
guasanga, *f.* (Cuba) noisy mirth.
guasanguero, ra, *a.* (Cuba) jolly, merry, noisy.
guasca, *f.* (Peru), piece of cord or rawhide; (Colomb.) strip of raw fiber, fibrous bark, etc., to tie with.—**dar g.,** to whip.
guaso, *m.* Gaucho; lasso.
guasón, na, *a.* (coll.) jocose, witty; dull, uninteresting.
guasquea , *va.* (Am.) to whip, to scourge.
guataca, *f.* (Cuba) spade; (Cuba) (coll.) large ear.
guataquear, *va.* (Cuba) to spade.
Guatemala, *f.* Guatemala.
guatemalteco, ca, *n.* & *a.* Guatemalan.
guateque, *m.* (Cuba) country dance.—**guatequear,** *va.* (Cuba) to dance (as in the country).
guatiní, *m.* (Cuba) = TOCORORO (ornith.) trogon.
guau, *m.* bowwow, the bark of a dog.
guavina, *f.* = GUABINA, (Colomb.) a peasant tune.
¡guay! *interj.* alas! alack!
guaya, *f.* grief, sorrow, affliction.
guayaba, *f.* fruit of the guava tree; guava jam or jelly; (Am.) lie, fib.
guayabal, *m.* guava-tree orchard or field.
guayabero, ra, *n.* (Am.) liar, fibber.
guayabo, *m.* (bot.) guava tree.
guayacán, *m.* (bot.) lignum-vitæ, guaiacum.
guayacana, *f.* (bot.) date-plum.
guayaco, *m.* = GUAYACÁN.
guayacol, *m.* (chem.) guaiacol.
guayaquileño, ña. I. *a.* Guayaquil, of or pertaining to the city of Guayaquil. **II.** *n.* inhabitant or native of the city of Guayaquil.
guayule, *m.* (bot.) guayule.
guazubirá, *m.* an Argentine deer.
gubán, *m.* (P. I.) a large canoe.
gubernamental, *a.* governmental.
gubernativo, va, *a.* administrative, governmental, gubernatorial.
gubia, *f.* (carp.) gouge, centering chisel; (artil.) vent searcher.
gubiadura, *f.* notch, channel.
guedeja, *f.* long lock of hair; forelock; lion's mane.—**guedejilla,** *f. dim.* small lock of hair.
guedejón, na, joso, sa, judo, da, *a.* long-haired.
güeldo, *m.* shrimps, clams, etc., used as bait.
güelfo, fa, *n.* & *a.* Guelph.
guelte, gueltre, *m.* money, cash; wealth.
güemul, *m.* guemul, an Andean variety of deer.
güepil, *m.* (Mex.) = HUIPIL, Aztec dress.

güermeces, *m.* morbid swelling in the throat of birds of prey.
guerra, *f.* war. warfare.—**g. a muerte,** war without quarter; war to the death.—**g. civil,** civil war.—**g. de guerrillas,** guerrilla warfare.—**g. de secesión,** (U. S.) War of Secession.—**g. fría,** cold war.—**g. mundial**, World War.—**g. preventiva,** preventive war.—**g. psicológica,** psychological warfare.—**corcel de g.,** war horse.—**dar g.,** to annoy, bother, trouble.—**en pie de g.,** on a war footing, up in arms.—**grito de g.,** war cry.—**impuesto de g.,** war tax.—**neurosis de g.,** shell shock.
guerreador, ra. I. *a.* warring. **II.** *n.* warrior.
guerreante, *a.* warring.
guerrear, *vn.* to war, wage war, fight.
guerreramente, *adv.* warlike.
guerrero, ra. I. *a.* martial, warlike. **II.** *m.* warrior, fighter, soldier, military man.
guerrilla, *f.* guerrillas, skirmishers, bushwhackers; guerrilla warfare.
guerrillear, *vn.* to engage in guerrilla warfare.
guerrillero, ra. I. *a.* guerrilla. **II.** *m.* guerrilla, bushwhacker; guerrilla leader.
guía. I. *n.* guide, cicerone; leader, director, adviser.—**g. de forasteros,** court guide. **II.** *m.* (mil.) guide. **III.** *f.* guide, guide sign; guidebook; directory; (mech.) guide, rule, guide bar, guide pin, guide screw, guide tube, etc.; (com.) custom house permit, cocket; driving shaft of a water wheel; (agr.) young shoot left on a vine or tree for training others; young shoot or sucker of a vine; (naut.) guy, leader, span, hauling-line, preventer-rope; (min.) leader; handlebar of a bicycle; guard of a fan; leader, foremost horse; (fireworks) fuse.—*pl.* guide lines, reins for controlling the leader horses.—**g. por inercia,** (aer.) inertial guidance.—**g. radial,** (printed) radio program.—**g. terminal,** terminal guidance.—**a guías,** driving four-in-hand.
guiadera, *f.* guide or conductor in mills; upright guide in oil mills, lifts, etc.
guiado, da. I. *pp.* of GUIAR. **II.** *a.* guided; having a guide or a permit.
guiador, ra, *n.* guide, director, leader.
guiar. I. *va.* to guide, lead; to drive (auto, etc.); to pilot; (agr.) to train (a plant.) **II.** *vr.* **(por)** to go or be governed (by), to follow.
guiguí, *m.* (P. I.) (zool.) flying squirrel.
guija, *f.* pebble; gravel; (bot.) ALMORTA, blue vetch.—*pl.* (coll.) strength, force, vigor.
guijarral, *m.* place abounding in pebbles.
guijarrazo, *m.* blow with a pebble or a cobble.
guijarreño, ña, *a.* pebbly, gravelly; hardy, strong.
guijarro, *m.* pebble, cobble.
guijarroso, sa, *a.* pebbly.
guijeño, ña, *a.* pertaining to or resembling pebbles; hard, relentless.
guijo, *m.* gravel.
guijón, *m.* = NEGUIJÓN, caries, tooth decay.
guijoso, sa, *a.* gravelly, pebbly.
guilalo, *m.* (P. I.) coasting vessel with sails of matting.
guilla, *f.* plentiful harvest.
guillame, *m.* joiner's rabbeting plane.
guillote, *m.* husbandman who enjoys the produce of a farm; (naut.) treenail or iron pin; vagrant; sponger; idle fellow; novice gambler.
guillotina, *f.* guillotine; cardboard-cutting machine.—**de g.,** (of windows, etc.) opening up and down.
guillotinar, *va.* to guillotine.
guimbalete, *m.* pump brake, pump handle.
guimbarda, *f.* an ancient dance; (carp.) grooving plane.
guinchar, *va.* to prick, goad.
guincho, *m.* goad, pike; (Cuba) sea gull.
[1]**guinda,** *f.* (bot.) berry of the mazard.—**echar guindas a la tarasca,** (coll.) to be very easy, child's play.
[2]**guinda,** *f.* (naut.) total height of the masts.
[1]**guindado, da. I.** *pp.* of GUINDAR. **II.** *a.* hoisted, set up.
[2]**guindado, da,** *a.* garnished with mazard berries.
guindajos, *m. pl.* (Cuba) hangings, fringe, tassels.
guindal, *m.* (bot.) mazard tree.
guindalera, *f.* plantation of mazard trees.
guindaleta, *f.* crank rope; fulcrum of a balance.
guindaleza, *f.* (naut.) hawser.
guindamaina, *f.* salute by dipping the flag.
guindar. I. *va.* to hang on high; (coll.) to obtain or procure in competition with others; (coll.) to hang (a person). **II.** *vn.* to be suspended, to hang.
guindaste, *m.* (mech.) horse, frame; (naut.) timber head jeer, knighthead of the jeers.
guindilla, *f. dim.* pod of the red pepper.
guindillo de Indias, *m.* (bot.) shrub of the capsicum family; red pepper.
guindo, *m.* (bot.) mazard tree.—**g. griego,** large mazard cherry tree.
guindola, *f.* (naut.) triangular hanging stage; life buoy
guineo, nea. I. *a.* Guinea, Guinean.—**gallina g.,** Guinea hen. **II.** *n.* Guinea, Guinean; *f.* **(G.,)** Guinea; guinea (former English gold coin equal to 21 shillings); *m.* a Negro dance; banana.
guinga, *f.* gingham.
guinja, *f.* **guinjo,** *m.* jujube.
guinjo, guínjolero, *m.* (bot.) jujube tree.
guiñada, *f.* wink; (naut.) yaw, lurch.
guiñador, ra, *n.* & *a.* winker(-ing).
guiñadura, *f.* = GUIÑADA.
guiñapiento, ta, *a.* ragged, tattered, torn.
guiñapo, *m.* tatter, rag; ragamuffin, tatterdemalion.—**guiñaposo, sa,** *a.* = GUIÑAPIENTO.
guiñar, *va.* to wink; (naut.) to yaw, to lurch.
guiño, *m.* = GUIÑADA.
guión, *m.* cross, standard carried before prelates and corporations; gonfalon in processions; royal standard; master of ceremonies; leader of a dance; hyphen; explanatory text or reference table; (theat., radio, TV) script; (mil.) guidon; (mus.) repeat; (naut.) loom of an oar.
guionaje, *m.* office of guide or conductor.
guipar, *va.* (coll. and vulgar) to see.
güipil, *m.* (Mex.) = HUIPIL, Aztec dress.
guipuzcoano, na. I. *n.* & *a.* native of or belonging to the province of Guipúzcoa. **II.** *m.* one of the Basque dialects.
guira, *f.* (bot.) calabash tree.
guirgüesco, ca, *a.* = GREGÜISCO, Grecian.
guiri, *n.* anti-Carlist; Liberal.
guirigay, *m.* (coll.) gibberish; jargon.
guirindola, *f.* frill of a shirt.
guirlache, *m.* roast almond caramel; brittle.
guirlanda, guirnalda, *f.* garland, wreath; (naut.) puddening; (mil.) light ball.
guirnaldeta, *f. dim.* small garland.
güiro, *m.* bottle gourd, fruit of the calabash tree; (Cuba) gourd used as an instrument to accompany dance music; (Arg., etc.) green corn stalk.
guirre, *m.* (prov. Canaries) vulture.
guisa, *f.* manner, fashion.—**a g. de,** like, in the manner of.
guisado, *m.* stew; ragout, fricassee.
guisador, ra; guisandero, ra, *n.* cook.
guisantal, *m.* pea patch.
guisante, *m.* (bot.) pea.—**g. de olor,** sweet pea.
guisar, *va.* to cook or dress (food); to arrange, prepare, adjust.
guiso, *m.* cooked dish; seasoning, condiment.
guisopillo, *m.* = HISOPILLO, (med.) mouth swab.
guisote, *m.* poorly cooked dish.
guita, *f.* packthread, twine; (coll.) money.
guitar, *va.* to sew with packthread.
guitarra, *f.* (mus.) guitar; (mason.) muller for pulverizing gypsum.—**guitarrazo,** *m.* blow with a guitar.—**guitarrear,** *vn.* to play the guitar.—**guitarrería,** *f.* factory or shop for guitars, mandolins, etc.—**guitarrero, ra,** *n.* guitar maker; guitar player.—**guitarresco,**

ca, *a.* (coll.) pertaining to the guitar.—**guitarrillo,** *m.*; **lla,** *f. dim.* small guitar.
guitarrista, *n.* guitar player.
guitarro, *m.* (mus.) small four-string guitar.
guitarrón, *m. aug.* large guitar; (coll.) cunning knave.
guitero, ra, *n.* twine maker.
guito, ta, *a.* treacherous, (of mules, etc.) vicious.
[1]**guitón,** *m.* an ancient coin.
[2]**guitón, na,** *n.* mendicant, vagrant, tramp.
guitonear, *vn.* to loiter, loaf, idle about.
guitonería, *f.* idleness; vagabond life.
guizazo, *m.* (Cuba) (bot.) a kind of weed.
guizgar, *va.* to excite, invite.
guizque, *m.* hook of a hanging lamp.
guja, *f.* (armor) vogue or voulge.
gula, *f.* gluttony, inordinate appetite.
gules, *m. pl.* (her.) gules, red.
guloso, sa, *a.* gluttonous; greedy.
gulusmear, *vn.* (coll.) to eat tidbits.
gullería, gollería, *f.* dainty; delicious tidbit.
gulloría, *f.* (ornith.) a kind of lark; GULLERÍA.
gúmena, *f.* (naut.) cable.—**gumeneta,** *f. dim.* (naut.) small cable.
gumía, *f.* a kind of dagger or poniard.
gumífero, ra, *a.* gum-producing, gummiferous.
gura, *f.* (ornith.) (P. I.) a crested wild pigeon.
[1]**gurbión,** *m.* coarse twisted silk; heavy silk cloth.
[2]**gurbión,** *m.* spurge gum resin.
gurdo, da, *a.* silly, simple, nonsensical.
gurriato, *m.* nestling sparrow.
gurrufero, *m.* (coll.) deformed and vicious nag.
gurrumina, *f.* (coll.) uxoriousness, excessive doting on one's wife; (Am.) trifle.
gurrumino, na. I. *a.* mean, contemptible. **II.** *n.* (C. A.) boy, girl, child. **III.** *m.* (coll.) henpecked husband.
gurullada, *f.* (coll.) = GRULLADA, gang of idlers; (coll.) patrol of policemen.
gurullo, *m.* lump or knot.
gurullón, *m.* a knot of wool in cloths.
gurvio, a, *a.* (of tools) curved.
gurvión, *m.* = [1]GURBIÓN.
gusanear, *vn.* HORMIGUEAR, to itch.
gusanera, *f.* place where worms or microbes are bred; (coll.) ruling passion.
gusaniento, ta, *a.* grubby, full of vermin, maggoty, worm-eaten.
gusanillo, *m. dim.* small worm or grub; (sewing) gold, silver, or silk twist; twist-stitch embroidery; (mech.) bit of a gimlet or auger.
gusano, *m* (zool.) worm, grub, caterpillar; threadworm, pinworm; meek, dejected person; distemper of sheep.—**g. de la conciencia,** worm of conscience, remorse.—**g. de luz** = LUCIÉRNAGA.—**g. de San Antón,** gray grub.—**g. de seda,** silkworm.—**g. revoltón,** vine inchworm.
gusarapiento, ta, *a.* wormy, grubby; filthy; rotten.
gusarapo, *m.* water worm; any annelid found in liquids, especially vinegar.
gustable, *a.* pert. to taste; (Am.) tasty.
gustadura, *f.* gustation, tasting.
gustar. I. *va.* to taste; to try. **II.** *vn.* to be pleasing, to cause pleasure; (diff. constr.) to like (as: *esto me gusta,* I like this; *¿le gusta a Vd. la música?* do you like music? *la comida nos gustó mucho,* we liked the dinner very much; *como Vd. guste,* as you like, as you will).—**g. de,** to like, to have a liking for; to enjoy.
gustativo, va, gustatorio, ria, *a.* gustatory.
gustazo, *m. aug.* (coll.) great pleasure.
gustillo, *m. dim.* peculiar flavor, or relish.
gusto, *m.* taste; tasting; pleasure; liking; will, determination; choice; discernment; caprice, fancy, whim; diversion.—**a g., at** will, to one's taste or judgment.—**con mucho g.,** with great pleasure.—**cosa de g.,** tasty, fancy article.—**dar g.,** to gratify, to please.—**darse g.,** to indulge in pleasure, to have a good time; to live well.—**de buen (mal) g.,** in good (bad) taste.—**de mi g.,** to my taste; to my liking.—**el g. del día,** prevailing taste or fashion.—**tener g. en,** to take pleasure in, to be glad to.—**tener g. por,** to have a taste for, to like.—**tengo mucho g. en conocerle,** (on being introduced) I'm very glad to meet you.
gustoso, sa, *a.* savory, palatable; tasty; cheerful, merry, joyful; pleasing, pleasant; willing, ready.
gutagamba, *m.* (bot.) tree producing gamboge; gamboge.
gutapercha, *f.* gutta-percha.
gutiámbar, *m.* gamboge.
gutífero, ra, *a.* guttiferous, gum-yielding.
gutural, *a.* guttural.
guzmán, *m.* nobleman who formerly served as midshipman or cadet.

H

H, h, *f.* h, ninth letter of the Spanish alphabet.
ha, *verbal form. V.* HABER.
¡ha!, *interj.* ah! alas!
haba, *f.* broad bean; lima bean; bean; kernel; ballot (ball); (vet.) tumor in the palate of horses; (min.) prill.—**h. común caballar,** (bot.) horse bean.—**h. de Egipto,** Egyptian bean.—**h. de las Indias,** sweet pea.—**h. de San Ignacio,** St. Ignatius' bean.—**h. marina,** navelwort, kidneywort.—**h. tonca,** Tonca bean.—**esas son habas contadas,** that is a sure thing; that is as clear as daylight.
habado, da, *a.* (vet.) having HABAS; dappled (as a horse).
habanera, *f.* (mus.) a Cuban air and dance tune.
habanero, ra, *a.* Havanese, of Havana.
habano. I. *a.* Havana (as *a.*). **II.** *m.* Havana cigar.
habar, *m.* bean field.
habascón, *m.* (S. A.) a parsniplike root.
hábeas corpus, *m.* habeas corpus.
háber, *m.* doctor of the law among the Jews.
haber. I. *va.* (*ind. pres.* HE, *pret.* HUBE, él HUBO, *fut.* HABRÉ; *subj.* HAYA) to have, own, possess; (gen. passive) to catch, lay hands on; to get (*el ladrón no pudo ser habido,* the thief could not be caught; *el niño lee cuantos libros puede haber,* the boy reads all the books he can get). **II.** *v. auxil.* to have (*haber hablado,* to have spoken; *habiendo hablado,* having spoken; *yo he hablado,* I have spoken). **III.** *vn.* **(de)** to have (to), must (*hemos de salir,* we have to, or must, go out; *ha de saber Vd.,* you must know). **IV.** *v. imp.* to be (in phrases, "there is," "there are"); to take place. In this sense, the third person of the indicative is **hay,** and only the third person singular is used in all modes and tenses, for the verb has no subject: the word or phrase which in English is the subject of the equivalent "to be" is in Spanish the accusative, not the subject, of "haber" (*hay peligro,* there is danger; *aquí hay un buen teatro,* there is a good theater here: *en Colombia hay muchas minas,* there are many mines in Colombia; *ayer hubo dos accidentes,* there were two accidents yesterday; *mañana no habrá escuela,* there will be no school tomorrow). The form **ha,** applied to time, has the adverbial value of "ago" (*dos años ha,* two years ago).—**hay para,** there is enough for.—**hay que,** must, to be necessary (*hay que ir,* it is necessary to go; *hay que hacerlo,* it's got to be done).—**lo que hay es,** what happens is; the fact is.—**no hay de qué,** (after being thanked) you're welcome.—**no hay más que,** there is nothing more to; there is nothing but; it's enough, it'll do.—**no hay para que,** there is no occasion for; it is better not to; there's no point in.—**no hay que,** one should not; it's not necessary to.—**no hay remedio,** it can't be helped.—**¿qué hay?** what's happening? what's the matter?—**¿qué hay de nuevo?** what's new? what's the news? **V.** *vr.* **habérselas con,** to deal with; to face, to cope with.—**VI.** *m.* in bookkeeping, credit, Cr.; (gen. *pl.* **haberes)** property, possessions, estate.—**h. monedado,** coin, specie.

haberío, *m.* beast of burden.
habichuela, *f.* (bot.) French bean or kidney bean.—**h. verde,** string bean.
habiente, *a.* (law) having, possessing.
hábil, *a.* capable, skillful.—**día, h.,** work day.
habilidad, *f.* ability, skill; talent.—*pl.* accomplishments.
habilidoso, sa, *a.* skillful, able.
habilitación, *f.* habilitation, qualification; outfit, equipment; (mil.) office and bureau of a paymaster.—**h. de bandera,** concession to a foreign vessel to engage in the coasting trade.
habilitado, da. I. *pp.* of HABILITAR. **II.** *a.* qualified; competent. **III.** *m.* paymaster.
habilitador, ra, *n.* qualifier; outfitter.
habilitar, *va.* to qualify, enable; to provide, supply with, fit out, equip.
habitabilidad, *f.* habitability, habitableness.
habitable, *a.* habitable.
habitación, *f.* dwelling, residence, habitation, abode, lodging; room, chamber, suite of rooms, apartment; (law) caretaking; habitat.
habitáculo, *m.* dwelling, residence, abode.
habitador, ra, *n.* inhabitant, resident, dweller.
habitante, *a.* & *n.* inhabiting(-ant).
habitar, *va.* to inhabit, live, dwell, reside.
hábito, *m.* dress, habit, habiliment, garment; habit, custom.—*pl.* dress of ecclesiastics; robes of the military orders.—**tomar el h.,** to become a monk or a nun.
habituación, *f.* habit, custom.
habitual, *a.* habitual, usual, customary.
habituar. I. *va.* to accustom, habituate, inure. **II.** *vr.* to become accustomed, accustom oneself, get used.
habitud, *f.* relation, connection.
habla, *f.* speech; language, tongue; dialect; conversation, talk.—**al h.** (naut.) within speaking distance.—**estar en h.,** to talk.—**estar sin h.,** or **perder el h.,** to be or become speechless.—**negar,** or **quitar, el h.,** to cease speaking to, to cut.—**ponerse al h.,** to communicate, get in touch, speak.
hablado, da, *a.*—**bien h.,** using choice language.—**mal h.,** using vile or vulgar language.
hablador, ra. I. *a.* talkative. **II.** *n.* talker, gabbler, prattler, chatterbox; gossip.
habladuría, *f.* impertinent speech; gossip, empty talk.
hablanchín, ina, *a.* & *n.* = HABLANTÍN.
hablante, *a.* speaking, talking.
hablantín, na, *a.* & *n.* (coll.) talkative person.
hablar. I. *vn.* to speak; to talk, converse.—**h. a,** to speak to; to hail (a ship).—**h. a chorros,** to speak fast.—**h. a destajo,** (coll.) to talk much and at random.—**h. a gritos,** to shout.—**h. al alma,** to speak things that touch the quick.—**h. alto,** to speak loud.—**h. a tontas y a locas,** to speak recklessly or disconnectedly.—**h. claro,** to speak in plain language, to call a spade a spade.—**h. con,** to speak with; to court, to woo.—**h. de,** to speak, or talk, of or about.—**h. de chanza,** to joke, to speak in jest.—**h. en griego,** or **en gringo,** to talk gibberish, to talk Greek (fig.).—**h. en plata** = H. CLARO.—**h. entre dientes,** to mutter, to mumble.—**h. gordo,** to bully, to bluff.—**h. por boca de ganso,** to speak from hearsay; to be a mouthpiece.—**h. por h.,** to talk for the sake of talking.—**h. por los codos,** to talk incessantly, to chatter.—**estar hablando,** to be perfect; to be manifest. **II.** *va.* to speak, utter, say.—**h. disparates,** to talk nonsense. **III.** *vr.* to speak to each other; to be on speaking terms.
hablilla, *f.* rumor, gossip, report, little tale.
hablista, *n.* scholar, scholarly writer.
hablistán, *n.* (coll.) prattler, chatterer.
habón, *m. aug.* wheat, whelk.
habré, *v. V.* HABER.
haca, *f.* pony, pad, small horse.
hacán, *m.* learned man among the Jews.
hacanea, *f.* nag, small horse.
hacecico, illo, ito, *m. dim.* small sheaf; fascicle.—**h. de rayos luminosos,** pencil of luminous rays.
hacedero, ra, *a.* feasible, practicable.
hacedor, *m.* maker; steward, manager of a farm.—**el H.,** the Creator, the Maker.
hacendado, da. I. *pp.* of HACENDAR. **II.** *a.* landed, owning real estate. **III.** *m.* landholder, farmer, planter, rancher.
hacendar. I. *va.* (*ind.* HACIENDO; *subj.* HACIENDE) to transfer or make over. **II.** *vr.* to purchase real estate.
hacendeja, *f. dim.* small farm or ranch.
hacendera, *f.* public work at which all the neighborhood assists.
hacendero, ra, *a.* industrious, sedulous.
hacendilla, duela, *f. dim.* small farm or ranch.
hacendista, *m.* (pol.) economist; financier.
hacendoso, sa, *a.* assiduous, industrious.
hacer. I. *va.* (*pp.* HECHO; *ind. pres.* yo HAGO, él HACE, *pret.* yo HICE, él HIZO, *fut.* HARÉ; *subj.* HAGA) to make; to produce, form; to prepare; conceive, devise, compose: deliver, utter (as a plan, a poem, a speech); to arrange, make (a bed), pack (a trunk, valise); to shed, cast, project (as a shadow); to raise, produce (as dust, smoke); to do; to gain, earn; to accustom, inure; to assemble, convoke; to act, perform (as a play, a part); to do, execute, carry out; to lead (a life); to take (a trip); to suppose, think (*yo hacía a Juan en Paris,* I thought John was in Paris; *le hacíamos muy rico,* we supposed he was very rich); to hold in, feel, have (*hacer estimación,* or *aprecio,* to hold in esteem, to have regard for); (followed by *inf.*), to order, have (followed by *pp.*: *Juan hizo construir la casa,* John had the house built; *Juan hizo nombar a Pedro,* John had Peter appointed); (followed by *inf.*) to make, compel (*la haremos confesar,* we shall make her confess; *lo hice firmar,* I made him sign).—**h. agua,** (naut.) to leak.—**h. alarde,** to boast.—**h. ánimo,** to mean, to intend.—**h. antesala,** to dance attendance, to be kept waiting.—**h. bancarrota,** to fail, to become bankrupt.—**h. boca,** to work up an appetite.—**h. bola,** to play hookey; to stay away.—**h. buen tercio,** to do a good turn.—**h. cara, h. cara a,** to face, resist, oppose.—**h. caso,** to mind, pay attention.—**h. caso de,** to take into account, pay attention to.—**h. con,** to supply, provide, furnish (*te haré con dinero,* I will provide you with money.—**h. corrales** = H. BOLA.—**h. cuentas,** to figure, reckon; to estimate.—**h. chacota (de)** to ridicule, to turn into ridicule.—**h. daño a,** to hurt, harm; (of an article of food) not to agree with.—**h. de** = H. CON.—**h. de cuenta (que),** to pretend, act (as if).—**h. de las suyas,** to be up to one's old tricks, to run true to type.—**h. de tripas corazón,** to pluck up courage or heart.—**h. diligencia,** to try, to endeavor, to take measures.—**h. el favor,** to do the favor (*hágame el favor,* do me the favor, please).—**h. falta,** to be lacking, missing (diff. constr. *le hace falta dinero,* he needs money).—**h. fiesta,** to take a holiday.—**h. fiestas a,** to fondle, caress; cajole; fawn to.—**h. frente** = H. CARA.—**h. frente a,** to meet (demands, etc.).—**h. fuego,** (mil.) to fire.—**h. fuerza,** to struggle; to exert force; to carry weight, exert influence, appeal.—**h. fuerza a,** to do violence to; to impress, convince.—**h. fuerza de vela,** (naut.) to crowd sail.—**h. furor,** to "make a hit."—**h. gasto,** to spend.—**h. h.,** to have made, cause to be made, order to be made.—**h. juego,** to be well matched.—**hacerla,** to act unworthily; to fall below expectations; to act (with modifying word indicating the character of the action—usually bad).—**h. la barba,** to shave; (Mex.) to flatter.—**h. la corte,** to court, to woo; to pay court in palace.—**h. la cuenta,** to figure out.—**h. la cuenta sin la huéspeda,** to reckon without the host.—**h. la guerra,** to war, to wage or make war.—**h. las amistades,** to become reconciled, make

up.—**h. la vista gorda,** to wink at, to connive at.—**h. limosna,** to give alms.—**hacerlo bien (mal),** to perform, or acquit oneself, well (badly).—**h. mal,** to do wrong, harm; to act wrongly; to be injurious.—**h. mal de ojo,** to fascinate.—**h. memoria de,** to remember.—**h. milagros,** to do wonders.—**h. mofa de,** to mock, scoff at.—**h. morisquetas,** to play pranks.—**h. papel,** to cut a figure; to play a part.—**h. pedazos,** to break or tear into pieces; to break (as the heart).—**h. presente,** to remind of, call attention to.—**h. que,** to pretend, feign; to have, order (diff. constr. *hace que escribe,* he pretends to be writing; *haga que lo traigan,* have it brought).—**h. saber,** to make known; to inform, notify.—**h. señas,** to motion.—**h. su agosto,** to make hay while the sun shines.—**h. su apacheta,** to have made a fortune; to make one's pile.—**h. un barro,** to make a break, put one's foot in it.—**h. un enfoque general,** to make a broad approach.—**h. una pregunta,** to ask a question, put a question.—**h. vela,** (naut.) to set sail.—**h. ver,** to show, demonstrate.—**¿qué hace?** (a form of greeting) how do you do? how are you? **II.** *vn.* to matter, signify; to be pertinent, or to the purpose (*¿que le hace?* what does it matter? *eso no hace al caso,* that has nothing to do with the case); to agree, accord, match (*esto no hace con eso,* this does not agree with (or match) that).—**h. como que, h. como si,** to act as if.—**h. de,** to act as (*hacer de notario,* to act as a notary; *hago de carpintero,* I am doing a carpenter's work).—**h. del** (*f.* **de la**) to pretend to be, to play the (*hacer del bobo,* to play the idiot).—**h. del cuerpo,** to go to stool.—**h. el** (*f.* **la**) = H. DEL.—**h. para, h. por,** to endeavor, to try, make an effort, do one's best to (*haré por venir,* I will endeavor to come; *hacer por,* or *para, salvarse,* to strive to save oneself.—**h. por h.,** to act to no purpose.—**h. por la vida,** to eat something.—**no le hace,** never mind, let it go. **III.** *v. impers.* (referring to the state of the weather and followed by a noun) to be (with "it" as subject: *hace mal tiempo,* it is bad weather; *hace buen día,* it is a good day), or to be (with "it" as subject and followed by the corresponding English adjective: *hace calor,* it is warm; *hace viento,* it is windy). Applied to a lapse of time, it is rendered by "to be." with "it" as subject, or by "ago" (*hace un año,* it is now one year, or, a year ago; *ayer hizo un mes,* a month ago yesterday, or it was a month yesterday; *hace años* (*días,* etc.), many years (days, etc.) ago; *hace una semana que está aquí,* he has been here a week; *hace una semana que le vi,* it is a week since I saw him; *hace mucho* (*poco*), a long (short) time ago; *hace tiempo,* a long time ago).—**¿cuánto (tiempo) hace?** how long ago?—**¿cuánto (tiempo) hace que?** since when? **IV.** *vr.* (**hacerse**) to become, to grow; to move shift, recede, draw aside; to inflict upon oneself (as a wound, a scratch): to pretend to be, pass oneself off for.—**h. a,** to become accustomed or inured to; to come by, acquire.—**h. a la vela,** (naut.) to set sail.—**h. añicos,** to break to smithereens.—**h. chiquito,** to pretend to be modest; to conceal one's knowledge.—**h. de miel,** to be sweet, lenient, or obliging.—**h. de rogar,** to like to be coaxed.—**h. el sueco,** to pretend not to understand.—**h. el tonto,** to "play dumb," play the fool.—**h. ilusiones,** to be under an illusion, fool oneself.—**hacérsele a uno,** to be . . . to one, to seem . . . to one (*eso se me hace misterioso,* that seems mysterious to me).—**h. pedazos,** to break into, or to, pieces.—**h. tarde,** to grow late.—**h. tortilla,** to fall down flat.

hacera, *f.* sidewalk.

hacezuelo, *m. dim.* of HAZ.

hacia, *prep.* toward, in the direction of; near, about.—**h. abajo,** downward; in the lower part, toward the bottom.—**h. acá,** hither, this way.—**h. adelante,** forward.—**h. allá,** thither, that way.—**h. arriba,** upward; in the upper part, toward the top.—**h. atrás,** backward.—**h. casa,** homeward.—**h. dónde,** whither, toward which (what) place, where.—**h. el cielo,** heavenward.—**h. el mar,** seaward.—**h. popa,** (naut.) abaft.—**h. proa,** (naut.) afore.—**partir h. (Europa),** to leave for (Europe).

hacienda, *f.* landed property; plantation; farm; ranch; estate, fortune, wealth; finance.—*pl.* domestic work, household duties.—**h. de beneficio** (Mex., min.) reduction works.—**h. pública,** public treasury; public funds; public finances.—**real h.,** public treasury, public funds (in a monarchy).

haciendo, haciende, *v. V.* HACENDAR.

hacina, *f.* (agr.) shock, stack; pile, heap.

hacinador, ra, *n.* (agr.) stack maker.

hacinamiento, *m.* accumulation; heaping or stacking.

hacinar, *va.* (agr.) to stack; to pile, heap; accumulate; to hoard.

[1]**hacha,** *f.* large taper with four wicks.—**h. de viento,** flambeau, torch.

[2]**hacha,** *f.* axe; ancient Sp. dance; (naut.) link.—**h. de armas,** battle axe.

hachazo, *m.* blow or stroke with an axe.

hache, *f.* name of the letter *h.*

hachear. I. *va.* to cut with an axe; to hew. **II.** *vn.* to strike with an axe.

[1]**hachero,** *m.* (mil.) axeman; woodsman, wood cutter.

[2]**hachero,** *m.* torch stand.

hachich, hachís, *m.* hashish, hasheesh.

hacho, *m.* torch or link; beacon hill.

hachón, *m.* large torch or link; cresset.

hachote, *m. aug.* large axe.

hachuela, *f. dim.* small hatchet or axe; hand axe, adze.

hada, *f.* fairy.

hadar, *va.* to divine, foretell; to enchant.

hado, *m.* fate, destiny, doom.

hafnio, *m.* (chem.) hafnium.

haga, *v. V.* HACER.

hagiografía, *f.* (eccl.) hagiography.

hagiógrafo, fa, *n.* hagiographer.

hagiología, *f.* hagiology.

hago, *v. V.* HACER.

Haití, *m.* Haiti.

haitiano, na, *n.* & *a.* Haitian.

¡hala! *interj.* (naut.) pull! haul!

halagador, ra. I. promising, rosy; flattering; coaxing. **II.** *n.* flatterer, cajoler, coaxer.

halagar, *va.* (*pret.* HALAGUÉ; *subj.* HALAGUE) to cajole, to flatter; to coax, allure, wheedle; to fondle, treat with tenderness.

halago, *m.* cajolery, flattery; caress, cooing.

halagué, halague, *v. V.* HALAGAR.

halagüeñamente, *adv.* endearingly, flatteringly; promisingly, alluringly.

halagüeño, ña, *a.* endearing; attractive, alluring; promising, bright; fawning, flattering.

halar, (coll.) **jalar. I.** *va.* (naut.) to haul, pull, tow. **II.** *vn.* to pull ahead.

halcón, *m.* (ornith.) falcon.—**halconado, da,** *a.* falconlike.—**halconcico, illo, ito,** *m. dim.* jashawk.—**halconear,** *va.* (coll.) to inveigle, allure.—**halconera,** *f.* place where falcons are kept.

halconería, *f.* falconry.

halconero, *m.* falconer, hawk trainer.

halda, *f.* FALDA, skirt; a lapful; packing bag.—**haldas en cinta,** (coll.) disposed and ready for anything.—**de haldas o de mangas,** (coll.) justly or unjustly, with good or ill will, in any way.—**haldada,** *f.* skirtful.—**haldear,** *vn.* to run along with billowing skirts.—**haldica, illa, ita,** *f. dim.* small skirt.—**haldudo, da,** *a.* full-skirted.

haleche, *m.* (ichth.) anchovy.

halieto, *m.* (ornith.) sea eagle.

haliéutico, ca, *f.* halieutic, pert. to fishing.

haliótide, haliotis, *m.* (zool.) abalone.
halita, *f.* (min.) halite.
hálito, *m.* breath; vapor, effluvium; breeze.
halitosis, *f.* halitosis.
halo, *m.* (astr.) halo.
halófilo, la, *a.* (bot.) halophilous.
halógeno, *m.* (chem.) halogen.
halografía, *f.* (chem.) halography.
haloideo, a, *a.* (chem.) haloid.
halón, *m.* (astr.) halo.
haloque, *m.* (naut.) an ancient small vessel.
haloza, *f.* wooden shoe.
hallado, da, *pp.* & *a.* found.—**bien h.,** welcome; easy, contented.—**mal h.,** uneasy, constrained.
hallador, ra, *n.* finder, discoverer.
hallar. I. *va.* to find; come across; to find out; to discover; to detect, catch; to understand, solve, interpret, decipher. **II.** *vr.* to be (in a place or condition); to reside; to feel (as to health), to fare.—**h. bien (con),** to be pleased (with), content (in).
hallazgo, *m.* act of finding; find, thing found; recovering anything lost; reward.
hallulla, *f.* **hallullo,** *m.* cake baked on or under hot stones or ashes.
hamaca, *f.* hammock; hammock litter.
hamadríada, *f.* (myth.) hamadryad.
hamaquero, *m.* hammock maker; hammock bearer; hammock hook.
hambre, *f.* hunger; appetite; famine; greediness; eagerness, longing, desire.—**h. canina,** canine appetite, inordinate hunger.—**h. y valentía,** pride and poverty.—**tener h.,** to be hungry.
hambrear. I. *va.* to hunger, starve, famish; to subdue by famine. **II.** *vn.* to hunger, to be hungry.
hambrientamente, *adv.* hungrily.
hambriento, ta, *a.* hungry; starved; greedy, covetous; longing; (Colomb., coll.) stingy.
hambrón, na, *n.* (coll.) hungry person.
hamburgués, sa, *a.* from or pertaining to Hamburg, Hamburg (as *a.*).
hamez, *f.* distemper in falcons that makes them lose their feathers.
hamo, *m.* fishhook.
hampa, *f.* life of a company of rogues and vagabonds formerly in Andalusia.
hampesco, ca, *a.* vagabond, villainous.
hampo, hampón, *m.* rowdy, bully, gangster.
hanega, *f.* = FANEGA, a dry measure.
hanegada, *f.* land sown with a FANEGA of corn.
hangar, *m.* hangar.
hannoveriano, na, *n.* & *a.* Hanoverian.
hansa, *f.* Hanse, Hanseatic League.
hanseático, ca, *a.* Hanseatic.
haploide, *m.* & *a.* (biol.) haploid.
haplología, *f.* (philol.) haplology.
hará, haré, etc., *v.* *V.* HACER.
haragán, na. I. *n.* idler, loiterer, loafer; idle, lazy person. **II.** *a.* idle, slothful, indolent.
haraganamente, *adv.* idly, lazily, slothfully.
haraganear, *vn.* to lead an idle life; to be lazy, to act the truant; to lounge, idle, loiter.
haraganería, *f.* idleness, laziness, sloth.
harakiri, *m.* hara-kiri.
harapiento, ta, haraposo, sa, *a.* ragged, tattered.
harapo, *m.* tatter, rag.
harca, *f.* military expedition; expeditionary forces.
harem, harén, *m.* harem.
harija, *f.* mill dust, stive.
harina, *f.* flour, meal; farina; breadstuffs; powder, dust.—**h. de otro costal,** another matter, a horse of a different color.
harinado, *m.* flour dissolved in water.
harinero, ra. I. *a.* made of or pertaining to flour. **II.** *m.* mealman, flour dealer; flour chest.
harinoso, sa, *a.* mealy; farinaceous; flourlike.
harmonía, harmonio, harmonioso, etc. = ARMONÍA, ARMONIO, etc.
harnerico, illo, ito, *m.* *dim.* small sieve.
harnero, *m.* sieve, sifter.—**estar hecho un h.,** to be covered with wounds.
harón, na, *a.* slow, sluggish; balky.—**haronear,** *vn.* to dawdle, move sluggishly; to be tardy or slow; to balk.—**haronía,** *f.* sluggishness, laziness.
harpa, *f.* = ARPA, harp.
[1]**harpado, da,** *a.* = [1]ARPADO, serrated, toothed.
[2]**harpado, da,** *a.* = [2]ARPADO, (poet.) singing (bird).
harpía, *f.* = ARPÍA, harpy.
harpillera, *f.* burlap; sackcloth.
hartada, *f.* = HARTAZGO.
hartar, *va.* & *vr.* (*pp.* HARTADO and HARTO) to glut, stuff, gorge; to sate, satiate, gratify desire; to satisfy, cloy, fill to excess.
hartazgo, hartazón, *m.* satiety, glut, fill.
harto, ta. I. *pp. irreg.* of HARTAR. **II.** *a.* sufficient, full, complete. **III.** *adv.* enough or sufficiently; (Mex.) abundantly, very much.
hartura, *f.* satiety, glut, fill; plethora, superabundance; full gratification.
hasta. I. *prep.* till, until; up to, down to; as far as; even (emphatic) (as: *allá hasta los niños fuman,* there even children smoke).—**h. ahora,** heretofore, hitherto.—**h. aquí,** heretofore; thus far, up to here.—**h. después,** or **h. luego,** good-bye, "so long."—**h. la vista,** (in parting) "so long," au revoir.—**h. mañana,** (in parting) see you tomorrow.—**h. no más,** to the utmost. **II.** *conj.* also even.—**h. que,** until.
hastial, *m.* (arch.) gable wall; coarse, rude man; (min.) side face of a gallery.
hastiar, *va.* to loathe, disgust; to cloy, sate.
hastío, *m.* loathing, disgust; wearisomeness.
hataca, *f.* large wooden ladle; rolling pin.
hatajar, *va.* to divide (cattle) into flocks or herds.
hatajo, *m.* small herd or flock; (coll.) lot, multitude, lots.
hatear, *vn.* to collect one's belongings when travelling; to supply shepherds with provisions.
hatería, *f.* allowance of provisions and clothes for shepherds.
hatero, ra. I. *a.* (animals) that carry a shepherd's baggage. **II.** *m.* carrier of provisions to shepherds; (Cuba) cowboy; cattle herder.
hatijo, *m.* covering of straw or feather grass over beehives.
hatillo, *m.* *dim.* small bundle; a few clothes; (Colomb.) a sort of telescoping rawhide hamper.—**coger el h.,** (coll.) to quit, to pack and go.—**echar el h. al mar,** (coll.) to lose one's temper.—**tomar su h.** = COGER EL H.
hato, *m.* herd of cattle; flock of sheep; (Am.) farm or cattle ranch; shepherds' lodge; provisions for shepherds; clothes, wearing apparel; heap, lot, cluster; gang, band or meeting of suspicious people.
hawaiano, na, hauaiano, na, *n.* & *a.* **Hawaiian.**
haxix, *m.* hasheesh.
hay, *impers. irreg. form* of HABER: there is, there are.
[1]**haya,** *v.* *V.* HABER.
[2]**haya,** *f.* (bot.) beech tree.
hayal, hayedo, *m.* beech forest or field.
hayo, *m.* (Am.) (bot.) coca; coca leaves prepared for chewing.
hayuco, *m.* beech mast, fruit of the beech.
[1]**haz,** *m.* fagot, fascine, bundle, bunch; (agr.) gavel, sheaf; (mil.) file of soldiers, also troops arranged in divisions; (phys.) beam, pencil; *f.* face, visage; surface: right side or outside of cloth; (arch.) facing, façade.—*pl.* fasces.—**h. atómico,** atomic beam.—**h. molecular,** molecular beam.—**a sobre h.,** apparently, at first sight.—**ser de dos haces,** to be doubled-faced.—**sobre la h. de la tierra,** upon the face of the earth.
[2]**haz,** *v. imper.* of HACER.
haza, *f.* piece of tillable land.
hazalefa, *f.* towel.
hazaña, *f.* feat, exploit, heroic deed.
hazañería, *f.* affected fear or admiration.

hazañero, ra, *a.* prudish, affectedly grave and scrupulous.
hazañosamente, *adv.* valorously, bravely.
hazañoso, sa, *a.* gallant, courageous, heroic.
hazmerreír, *m.* laughing stock
[1]**he,** *interj.* generally followed by the adverbs **aquí** or **allí,** or by a pronoun, to introduce or call attention to: *he aquí,* here is, here you have; lo! lo and behold! *heme aquí,* here I am: *helos allí,* there they are.
[2]**he,** *v. ind.* of HABER.
hebdómada, *f.* hebdomad, week; period of seven years.
hebdomadario, ria. I. *a.* weekly. **II.** *n.* (eccl.) hebdomadary.
hebefrenia, *f.* (path.) hebephrenia.
hebén. I. *n.* white grapes like muscatels. **II.** *a.* insignificant, of no account.
hebetado, da, *a.* (Am.) brutalized, sottish.
hebilla, *f.* buckle, clasp.—**hebillaje,** *m.* set of buckles.—**hebillero, ra,** *n.* buckle maker or seller.—**hebilleta, hebilluela,** *f. dim.* small buckle.—**no faltar hebilleta,** to be complete.—**hebillón,** *m. aug.* large buckle.
hebra, *f.* fibre, thread, filament; string; staple; grain (of wood); needleful of thread; pistil of the blossom of saffron; (min.) vein, layer, stratum.—*pl.* (poet.) hair.—**ser, or estar, de buena h.,** to be strong and robust.
hebraico, ca, *a.* Hebrew.
hebraísmo, *m.* Hebraism.
hebraísta, hebraizante, *n.* Hebraist.
hebreo, a, *n.* & *a.* Hebrew; (coll.) pawnbroker; (coll.) usurer(-ious).
hebrero, *m.* esophagus of ruminants.
hebrica, illa, ita, *f. dim.* small needleful of thread.
hebroso, sa, *a.* fibrous, stringy.
hecatombe, *f.* hecatomb.
hectárea, *f.* hectare (10,000 sq. meters).
héctico, ca, *a.* hectic.
hectiquez, *f.* (med.) phthisis.
hectógrafo, *m.* hectograph.
hectogramo, *m.* hectogram.
hectolitro, *m.* hectoliter.
hectómetro, *m.* hectometer.
hectóreo, ea, *a.* pertaining to Hector.
hectovatio, *m.* hectowatt, 100 watts.
hecha, *f.* (obs.) date; irrigation tax.—**de esta h.,** from this time.
hechicé, hechice, *v. V.* HECHIZAR.
hechiceresco, ca, *a.* relating to witchcraft.
hechicería, *f.* witchcraft, witchery, enchantment; charm, fascination; sorcery.
hechicero, ra. I. *n.* witch, wizard; hag; charmer, enchanter, bewitcher **II.** *a.* entrancing, charming, bewitching, fascinating.
hechizar, *va.* (*pret.* HECHICÉ; *subj.* HECHICE) to bewitch, enchant, entrance; to charm, to fascinate.
hechizo, za. I. *a.* artificial, feigned; made to order; (Chile, C. R., Colomb.) domestic, made in the (given) country; portable, easily mounted. **II.** *m.* charm (used to bewitch), enchantment.
hecho, cha. I. *pp. irreg.* of HACER. **II.** *a.* made; done; ready-made; finished; fully matured, ripe or developed; accustomed, inured, used.—**h. un león,** like a lion, furiously; angry.—**h. y derecho,** in every respect; true, real; perfect. complete.—**a lo h., pecho,** one must make the best of a bad bargain.—**bien h.,** well done or made; all right; right (in a moral sense).—**mal h.,** wrong, unrighteous; badly done or made. **III.** *m.* fact; event; act, action, deed; point at issue.—**análisis de hechos,** factual analysis.—**de h.,** in fact, as a matter of fact, actually; in earnest; de facto.—**de h. y de derecho,** de facto and de jure.—**en h. de verdad,** in truth.
hechura, *f.* making, make; workmanship; form; build (of a person); work done and price paid for it; creature, henchman.—**no tener h.,** to be impracticable or not feasible.
hedentina, *f.* stench, stink.
heder, *vn.* (*ind.* HIEDO; *subj.* HIEDA) to stink; to vex, annoy, bore.
hediondamente, *adv.* stinkingly.
hediondez, *f.* stench, stink.
hediondo, da, *a.* stinking, fetid; annoying, wearisome; dirty, repulsive; lewd, obscene.
hedonismo, *m.* hedonism.
hedonista, *n.* & *a.* hedonist(-ic).
hedor, *m.* stench, stink.
hegelianismo, *m.* Hegelianism.
hegeliano, na, *n.* & *a.* Hegelian.
hegemonía, *f.* (pol.) hegemony.
hégira, héjira, *f.* Hegira.
helable, *a.* congealable.
helada, *f.* frost; nip.—**h. blanca,** hoarfrost.
heladera, *f.* (Am. esp. Arg. & Chile) refrigerator; ice-cream dish.—**h. eléctrica,** (or **mecánica**) electric refrigerator.
heladería, *f.* (Am.) ice-cream parlor or shop.
heladero, ra, *n.* (Chile) ice-cream maker or seller.
heladizo, za, *a.* easily congealed.
helado, da. I. *pp.* of HELAR. **II.** *a.* frigid; frostbitten; cold, indifferent. **III.** *m.* ice cream; water ice, sherbet.
helador, ra. I. *a.* freezing. **II.** *f.* ice-cream freezer.
helamiento, *m.* congealing, freezing, frost.
helar. I. *va.* & *vn.* (*ind.* HIELO; *subj.* HIELE) to congeal, to freeze; astonish, amaze; dispirit, discourage, dissuade. **II.** *v. impers.* to freeze (*aquí hiela frecuentemente,* it freezes often here). **III.** *vr.* to freeze, to congeal, to be coagulated; to grow motionless; to be stupefied, dispirited.—**se me heló la sangre,** my blood curdled.
hele, hételo, aquí, *interj.* behold it! *V.* [1]HE.
helechal, *m.* fern field.
helecho, *m.* fern.
helena, *f.* (naut.) jack-with-a-lantern.
helénico, ca, *a.* Hellenic.
helenio, *m.* (bot.) sneezeweed.
helenismo, *m.* Hellenism; Greek idiom.
helenista, *m.* Hellenist.
helenizar, *va.* & *vr.* to Hellenize.
heleno, na, *a.* Hellenic.
helera, *f.* pip, disease of fowls.
helero, *m.* snowcap on mountains; (geol.) glacier.
helgado, da, *a.* jag-toothed.
helgadura, *f.* space between, or irregularity of, the teeth.
helíaco, ca, *a.* (astr.) heliacal, pert. to the sun.
heliantemo, *m.* (bot.) a helianthaceous plant.
heliantina, *f.* (chem.) methyl orange.
helianto, *m.* (bot.) helianthus, sunflower.
hélice, *f.* (H-, astr.) Ursa Major; (geom.) helix; (naut., aer.) screw propeller.
helicoidal, *a.* helicoidal.
helicoide, *m.* (geom.) helicoid.
Helicón, *m.* (myth.) Helicon; (**h.**) (mus.) helicon.
helicónides, *f. pl.* (myth.) the Muses.
heliconio, nia, *a.* (myth.) Heliconian.
helicóptero, *m.* (aer.) helicopter.
helio, *m.* (chem.) helium.
heliocéntrico, ca, *a.* heliocentric.
heliocromía, *f.* heliochromy, color photography.
heliograbado, *m.* heliogravure.
heliografía, *f.* blue print.
heliográfico, ca, *a.* heliographic.
heliógrafo, *m.* heliograph, signalling device.
heliómetro, *m.* heliometer.
helioscopio, *m.* helioscope.
helióstato, *m.* heliostat.
helioterapia, *f.* (med.) heliotherapy.
heliotropina, *f.* (chem.) piperonal.
heliotropio, *m.* (bot.) heliotrope; (min.) bloodstone; (astr.) heliostat.
heliotropismo, *m.* (bot.) heliotropism.
heliotropo, *m.* = HELIOTROPIO.
heliozoario, *m.* (zool.) heliozoan.
helipuerto, *m.* heliport.
hélix, *m.* (anat., zool.) helix.
helmintiasis, *f.* (med.) helminthiasis.
helminto, ta. I. *a.* helminthic. **II.** *m.* (zool.) helminth.

helmintología, *f.* (med.) helminthology.
helmintólogo, ga, *n.* helminthologist.
helvecio, cia; helvético, ca, *a.* Helvetic.
hemático, ca, *a.* hematic.
hematidrosis, *f.* (med.) hematidrosis.
hematíe, *m.* (physiol.) erythrocyte, red (blood) cell.
hematina, *f.* (physiol.) hematin.
hematita, *f.* (physiol.) red blood corpuscle.
hematites, *f.* (min.) hematite.
hematoblasto, *m.* (physiol.) hematoblast.
hematocele, *m.* (med.) hematocele.
hematoideo, dea, *a.* hematoid.
hematología, *f.* (med.) hematology.
hematoma, *m.* (med.) hematoma.
hematómetro, *m.* (med.) hæmatometer.
hematoscopio, *m.* hæmoscope.
hematosis, *f.* (physiol.) hæmatosis.
hematoxilina, *f.* (chem.) hematoxylin.
hematuria, *f.* (med.) hematuria.
hembra, *f.* female; (coll. or vulg.) woman; (sewing) eye (of hook and eye); (mech.) nut of a screw; bolt clasp, staple.—**h. del timón,** (naut.) gudgeon of the rudder.
hembraje, *m.* (S. A.) female cattle.
hembrear, *vn.* to be inclined to females; to produce females only, or chiefly.
hembrica, illa, ita, *f. dim.* little female.
hembrilla, *f.* (mech.) small piece into which another fits (as a nut, staple, etc.); ring or eyebolt.
hemialgia, *f.* (med.) hemialgia.
hemiciclo, *m.* semicircle; (Spain) central space of the House of Deputies.
hémico, ca, *a.* hemic.
hemicordio, dia, *m.* & *a.* (zool.) hemichordate.
hemicránea, *f.* (med.) hemicrania, megrim.
hemiedría, *f.* (min.) hemihedrism.
hemiédrico, ca, *a.* (min.) hemihedral.
hemiedro, dra. I. *a.* hemihedral. **II.** *m.* (min.) hemihedron.
hemina, *f.* a liquid and area measure.
hemíono, *m.* (zool.) hemionus, kiang, an Asiatic wild ass.
hemiplejía, *f.* (med.) hemiplegia.
hemipléjico, ca, *a.* hemiplegic.
hemíptero, ra, *a.* (entom.) hemipterous, hemipteral.
hemisférico, ca, *a.* hemispherical.
hemisferio, *m.* hemisphere.
hemisferoidal, *a.* hemispheroidal.
hemistiquio, *m.* (poet.) hemistich.
hemitropía, *f.* (min.) hemitropism, hemitropy.
hemodinamómetro, *m.* blood-pressure gauge.
hemofilia, *f.* (med.) hemophilia.
hemoglobina, *f.* (physiol.) hemoglobin.
hemograma, *m.* blood count.
hemopatía, *f.* (med.) blood diseases (collect.).
hemóptisis, *f.* (med.) hæmoptysis.
hemorragia, *f.* (med.) hemorrhage.
hemorrágico, ca, *a.* hemorrhagic.
hemorroidas, *f. pl.* = HEMORROIDES.
hemorroidal, *a.* hemorrhoidal.
hemorroides, *f. pl.* piles, hemorrhoids.
hemorroo, *m.* (zool.) serpent.
hemostático, ca, *a.* hemostatic.
henaje, *m.* haying.
henal, *m.* hayloft.
henar, *m.* hayfield.
henchidor, ra, *n.* filler.
henchidura, *f.* fill, filling.
henchimiento, *m.* filling, fill.—*pl.* (naut.) filling timbers.
henchir. I. *va.* (*gerund,* HINCHIENDO; *ind. pres.* HINCHO, *pret.* él HINCHIÓ; *subj.* HINCHA) to fill, to stuff. **II.** *vr.* to fill or stuff oneself.
hendedor, ra, *n.* divider, splitter, cleaver.
hendedura, *f.* fissure, crack, cleft, crevice, cut.
hender, *va.* (*ind.* HIENDO; *subj.* HIENDA) to chink, crack, cleave, split; to go through; to cut (as the water); to elbow or open (a passage) through a crowd.
hendible, *a.* cleavable; fissionable, fissile.
hendido, da. I. *pp.* of HENDIR. **II.** *a.* crannied, full of chinks.
hendidura, *f.* = HENDEDURA.
hendiente, *m.* down stroke of a sword.
hendimiento, *m.* splitting.—**h.** (or **ruptura**) **del núcleo atómico,** nuclear fission, splitting of the atom.
henequén, *m.* (bot.) sisal, henequen.
henificar, *va.* to cut and dry for forage.
henil, *m.* hayloft, barn.
heno, *m.* (bot.) hay.
henojil, *m.* garter.
henrio, *m.* (elec.) henry.
heñir, *va.* (*ger.* HIÑENDO; *ind. pres.* HIÑO, *pret.* él HIÑÓ; *subj.* HIÑA) to knead.—**hay mucho que h.,** (coll.) there is much to do.
heparina, *f.* (chem.) heparin.
hepática, *f.* (bot.) liverwort.
hepático, ca, *a.* (med.) hepatic, hepatical.
hepatisis, *f.* (med.) consumption of the liver.
hepatita, *f.* (min.) hepatite.
hepatitis, *f.* (med.) hepatitis.
hepatización, *f.* (med.) hepatization.
hepatizarse, *vr.* (med.) to undergo hepatization.
hepatología, *f.* hepatology.
heptacordo, *m.* (mus.) heptachord.
heptágono, na. I. *a.* heptagonal. **II.** *m.* (geom.) heptagon.
heptámetro, tra. I. *a.* (poet.) heptameter, heptametrical. **II.** *m.* (poet.) heptameter.
heptano, *m.* (chem.) heptane.
heptarca, *m.* heptarch.
heptarquía, *f.* heptarchy.
heptasílabo, ba, *a.* heptasyllabic.
Heptateuco, *m.* Heptateuch.
heráldica, *f.* heraldry.
heráldico, ca, *a.* heraldic.
heraldo, *m.* herald; harbinger.
herbáceo, cea, *a.* herbaceous.
herbajar. I. *va.* to put out to graze, to pasture. **II.** *vn.* to pasture, graze, browse.
herbaje, *m.* herbage, grass, pasture; pasturage fee; coarse cloth.
herbajear, *va.* & *vn.* = HERBAJAR.
herbajero, *m.* one who rents pastures.
herbar, *va.* (*ind.* HIERBO; *subj.* HIERBE) to dress (skins) with herbs.
herbario, ria. I. *a.* herbal. **II.** *m.* herbalist, herbarian; herbarium.
herbaza, *f. aug.* large weed.
herbazal, *m.* herbous place; pasture ground.
herbecer, *vn.* (of herbs or grass) to begin to grow.
herbero, *m.* esophagus of a ruminant.
herbífero, ra, *a.* herbiferous.
herbívoro, ra. I. *a.* (zool.) herbivorous. **II.** *m.* (zool.) herbivore.
herbolado, da, *a.* poisoned with juice of plants.
herbolar, *va.* to poison with herbs.
herbolario, ria, *n.* herbist, herbman, one who sells herbs; (coll.) nonsensical person.
herborización, *f.* herborization; botanizing.
herborizador, ra, herborizante, *n.* herbalist, herborist.
herborizar, *vn.* to herborize, botanize.
herboso, sa, *a.* herby, grassy.
herciano, na, *a.* (phys.) Hertzian.
hercúleo, ea, *a.* herculean.
heredad, *f.* improved piece of ground; country estate, farm.
heredado, da. I. *pp.* of HEREDAR. **II.** *a.* landed, owning real estate. **III.** *n.* heir to property.
heredamiento, *m.* landed property.
heredar, *va.* to inherit; to deed to another; to institute as heir.
heredero, ra, *m.* heir, inheritor; *f.* heiress.—**h. forzoso,** heir apparent.—**h. legal,** heir at law.—**h. presuntivo,** heir presumptive.—**h. universal,** residuary legatee.
heredípeta, *n.* legacy seeker.
hereditario, ria, *a.* hereditary.
hereje, *n.* heretic.
herejía, *f.* heresy; injurious expression.
herejote, ta, *n.* (coll.) great heretic.

herén, *m.* (bot.) vetch.
herencia, *f.* inheritance, heritage; heredity.
heresiarca, *m.* heresiarch, leader in heresy.
heretical; herético, ca, *a.* heretical.
heria, *f.* life of vagrancy. Also HAMPA.
herida, *f.* wound.
herido, da. I. *pp.* of HERIR. **II.** *a.* & *n.* wounded (person).—**mal h.,** dangerously wounded.
heridor, ra, *n.* & *a.* wounder(-ing).
herir, *va.* (*ger.* HIRIENDO; *ind. pres.* HIERO, *pret.* él HIRIÓ; *subj.* HIERA) to wound; to hurt, harm; to strike; to affect, touch, move; to offend (the senses); to pique, irritate.
herma, *m.* (art) herm, a pillar surmounted by a head.
hermafrodito, ta. I. *a.* hermaphrodite, hermaphroditic, hermaphroditical; (zool., bot.) hermaphrodite. **II.** *n.* hermaphrodite.
hermafroditismo, *m.* hermaphroditism.
hermana, *f.* sister; nun.—**h. de la caridad,** Sister of Charity. (For phrases *v.* HERMANO.)
hermanable, *a.* fraternal, brotherly; compatible.
hermanablemente, *adv.* fraternally.
hermanado, da, *pp.* & *a.* mated, matched.
hermanamiento, *m.* mating, matching.
hermanar. I. *va.* to mate, match, pair; to suit, harmonize; to own as a brother. **II.** *vn.* to fraternize, join, match, agree. **III.** *vr.* to love one another as brothers; to be compatible; to harmonize.
hermanastro, tra, *n.* stepbrother(-sister).
hermanazgo, *m.* fraternity, brotherhood.
hermandad, *f.* fraternity, brotherhood, confraternity; conformity, resemblance; amity, friendship.
hermanear, *va.* to treat as a brother.
hermanecer, *vn.* to have a little brother just born.
hermanito, ta, *n. dim.* little brother (sister).
hermano, na. I. *a.* brotherly, brother; sisterly, sister. **II.** *m.* brother; *f.* sister; *n.* twin, mate, companion.—**hermana de la caridad,** Sister of Charity.—**h. carnal,** blood brother.—**h. consanguíneo,** half brother by the same father (mother).—**h. de leche,** foster brother.—**h. de madre,** half brother by the same mother.—**h. de padre,** half brother by the same father.—**h. político,** brother-in-law.—**h. por mezcla de sangre,** blood brother.—**h. uterino,** half brother by the same mother.—**primo h.,** first cousin.
hermanuco, *m.* name given in contempt to lay brothers of some religious orders.
hermenéutica, *f.* hermeneutics.
hermenéutico, ca, *a.* hermeneutic.
hermético, ca, *a.* hermetic, air-proof, air-tight.
hermosamente, *adv.* beautifully, handsomely; perfectly, properly.
hermoseador, ra, *n.* & *a.* beautifier(-fying).
hermosear, *va.* to beautify, embellish, adorn.
hermoso, sa, *a.* beautiful, handsome.
hermosura, *f.* beauty, handsomeness; belle, beauty (pretty woman).
hernia, *f.* (med.) hernia.
herniario, ria, *a.* (med.) hernial.
hernioso, sa, *a.* (med.) having hernia.
hernista, *n.* specialist in herniotomy.
Herodes, *m.* Herod (proper noun).—**de H. a Pilatos,** from pillar to post.
herodiano, na, *a.* Herodian.
héroe, *m.* hero.
heroicamente, *adv.* heroically.
heroicidad, *f.* heroism; heroic deed.
heroico, ca, *a.* heroic.—**a la heroica,** in the manner of the heroic times.
[1]**heroína,** *f.* heroine.
[2]**heroína,** *f.* (chem.) heroin.
heroísmo, *m.* heroism.
herpe, *m.* or *f.* (med.) herpes, tetter.
herpético, ca, *a.* (med.) herpetic.
herpetismo, *m.* (med.) tendency to herpes.
herpetología, *f.* (zool.) herpetology, science dealing with reptiles.
herpil, *m.* bag of esparto netting with wide meshes, for carrying large fruit.
herrada. I. *a.* (water) in which red-hot iron has been cooled. **II.** *f.* pail, bucket.
herradero, *m.* branding of cattle; place where cattle are branded.
herrador, *m.* farrier, horseshoer.
herradora, *f.* (coll.) farrier's wife.
herradura, *f.* horseshoe.
herraj, *m.* = ERRAJ, coal made from stones of pressed olives.
herraje, *m.* ironwork, pieces of iron used for ornament and strength; iron or metal fittings or accessories, hardware (gen. *pl.*).
herramental, *m.* tool bag; tool chest.
herramienta, *f.* tool; implement; set of tools.—*pl.* horns; (coll.) teeth, grinders.
herrar, *va.* (*ind.* HIERRO; *subj.* HIERRE) to shoe (horses); to brand (cattle); to garnish or bind with iron.
herrén, *m.* meslin, mixed grain for horses.
herrenal, herreñal, *m.* meslin patch or field.
herrera, *f.* (coll.) blacksmith's wife.
herrería, *f.* iron works; blacksmith's shop, smithy; forge; blacksmith's trade, smithery; clamor, confused noise.
herrerico, herrerillo, *m.* name of a small bird.
herrero, *m.* or **h. de grueso,** blacksmith.
herrerón, *m.* clumsy smith.
herreruelo, *m.* (ornith.) wagtail.
herrete, *m.* tag, ferrule; branding-iron.
herretear, *va.* to tag.
herrezuelo, *m.* light piece of iron.
herrín, *m.* iron rust.
herrón, *m.* quoit; washer; iron prop for young trees; (Colomb.) point of a spinning top.
herronada, *f.* violent blow with a quoit; blow with a bird's beak.
herrumbre, *f.* rust; iron taste.
herrumbroso, sa, *a.* rusty, rusted.
hertziano, na, *a.* (phys.) Hertzian.
hérulo, la. I. *n.* & *a.* Herulian. **II.** *m. pl.* Heruli.
herventar, *va.* to boil by putting a hot body into a liquid.
hervidero, *m.* ebullition, boiling; small spring whence water bubbles out; rumbling in the throat or chest; multitude, crowd.
hervidor, *m.* vessel, tube, etc. for boiling.
herviente, *a.* boiling, seething.
hervir (*ger.* HIRVIENDO; *ind. pres.* HIERVO, *pret.* él HIRVIÓ; *subj.* HIERVA). **I.** *va.* & *vn.* to boil; to seethe. **II.** *vn.* (of the sea) to become choppy; to bubble, effervesce; to surge (as a crowd).—**h. en,** to teem with, be full of.
hervor, *m.* ebullition, boiling; fervor, heat; vigor; fret; noise and movement of waters.—**h. de sangre,** rash.
hervoroso, sa, *a.* fiery, ardent, impetuous.
hesitación, *f.* hesitation, hesitancy.
hespéride. I. *a.* (astr.) pert. to the Pleiades; (poet.) western. **II.** *f. pl.* (astr.) Pleiades.
hesperidio, *m.* (bot.) hesperidium.
hespérido, da, *a.* = HESPÉRIDE.
Héspero, *m.* (astr.) Hesperus, the evening star.
heteo, a, *n.* & *a.* Hittite.
hetera, *f.* hetæra, hetaira, Greek courtesan.
heterocigosidad, *f.* (genetics) heterozygosity.
heterocigótico, ca, *a.* (genetics) heterozygous.
heterocigoto, *m.* (genetics) heterozygote.
heteróclito, ta, *a.* (gram.) heteroclite; irregular, abnormal.
heterodino, na, *m.* & *a.* (rad.) heterodyne.
heterodoxia, *f.* heterodoxy.
heterodoxo, xa, *a.* heterodox.
heterogamia, *f.* heterogamy.
heterógamo, ma, *a.* (bot.) heterogamous.
heterogeneidad, *f.* heterogeneity.
heterogéneo, nea, *a.* heterogeneous.
heterogénesis, heterogenia, *f.* (biol.) heterogenesis.
heterogrado, da, *a.* (stat.) heterograde.

heteromancía, *f.* superstitious divination by the flight of birds.
heteromorfo, fa, *a.* heteromorphous.
heteromorfosis, *f.* heteromorphosis.
heterónomo, ma, *a.* heteronymous.
heteroplastia, *f.* (surg.) heteroplasty.
heterópsido, da, *a.* (of metals) lusterless.
heteroscios. *m. pl.* (geog.) heteroscians.
heterosis, *f.* (genetics) heterosis.
hético, ca, *a.* hectic, consumptive.
hetiquez, *f.* (med.) consumption.
heurístico, ca, *a.* heuristic.
hévea, *f.* (bot.) hevea, Para-rubber tree.
hexacordo, *m.* (mus.) hexachord.
hexaedro, *m.* (geom.) hexahedron.
hexagonal; hexágono, na, *a.* hexagonal.
hexágono, *m.* (geom.) hexagon.
hexámetro, tra. I. *a.* hexametric, hexametrical. **II.** *m.* (poet.) hexameter.
hexángulo, la, *a.* hexangular.
hexápeda, *f.* = TOESA, ancient linear measure.
hexapétalo, la, *a.* (bot.) hexapetalous.
hexápodo, da. I. *a.* (zool.) hexapod, hexapodous. **II.** *m.* (zool.) hexapod.
hexástilo, *m.* (arch.) hexastyle, portico with six columns.
Hexateuco, *m.* Hexateuch.
hez, *f.* lees, bottom, sediment, dregs of liquors; dross of metals; grains of malt.—*pl.* fæces, excrements.—**la h. del pueblo,** the scum of the people.
Híadas, Híades, *f. pl.* (astr.) Hyades.
hialino, na, *a.* hyaline, transparent; translucent.
hialita, *f.* (min.) hyalite.
hialitis, *f.* (med.) hyalitis.
hialografía, *f.* hyalography, engraving on glass.
hialógrafo, *m.* hyalograph.
hialoideo, dea, *a.* vitreous, glasslike.
hialoides, *f.* hyaloid membrane.
hialotecnia, *f.* hyalography.
hialurgia, *f.* glass-working art.
hiante, *a.* (verse) with a hiatus.
hiato, *m.* (gram., poet.) hiatus.
hibernación, *f.* hibernation.
hibernal, *a.* hibernal, wintry.
hibernés, sa, *a.* Hibernian, Irish.
hibernizo, za, *a.* = HIBERNAL.
hibisco, *m.* (bot.) hibiscus.
hibridación, *f.* hybridization.
hibridez, *f.*, **hibridismo,** *m.* hybridism.
híbrido, da, *n.* & *a.* hybrid.
hicaco, *m.* (bot.) icaco, coco plum.
hice, hiciera, *v. V.* HACER.
hicotea, *f.* (Am.) fresh-water turtle.
hicso, sa, *n.* & *a.* Hyksos.
hidalga, *f.* noblewoman; lady.
hidalgamente, *adv.* nobly, in a gentlemanly way.
hidalgo, ga. I. *a.* noble, illustrious, excellent, exalted. **II.** *n.* hidalgo, nobleman(-woman).—**h. de bragueta,** one entitled to nobility from being the father of seven successive sons.
hidalgón, na, gote, ta, *n. aug.* old ceremonious hidalgo.
hidalgüejo, ja, güelo, la, guete, ta, guillo, lla, *n. dim.* pretty hidalgo.
hidalguez, hidalguía, *f.* nobility; rights of an hidalgo, nobleness, liberality.
hidátide, *f.* (med. & zool.) hydatid.
hidatídico, ca, *a.* (med.) hydatidinous.
hidra, *f.* (zool.) a poisonous serpent; hydra, fresh-water polyp; (**H-,** myth., astr.) Hydra.
hidrácido, *m.* (chem.) hydracid.
hidracina, *f.* (chem.) hydrazine.
hidragogo, ga, *m.* & *a.* (med.) hydragogue.
hidrargírico, ca, *a.* hydrargiric.
hidrargirismo, *m.* (med.) hydrargyriasis, mercurialism, chronic mercurial poisoning.
hidrargirita, *f.* (min.) native oxide of mercury.
hidrargiro, *m.* (chem.) hydrargyrum.
hidratación, *f.* hydration, hydrating.
hidratado, da, *pp.* & *a.* hydrate(d).
hidratar, *va.* (chem.) to hydrate.
hidrato, *m.* (chem.) hydrate.—**h. amónico,** (chem.) ammonium hydroxide.—**h. de carbono,** (chem.) carbohydrate.
hidráulico, ca. I. *a.* hydraulic. **II.** *n.* hydraulician, one skilled in hydraulics; hydraulic engineer; *f.* hydraulics.—**h. fluvial,** flood control.
hidria, *f.* hydria (an ancient water jar).
hídrico, ca, *a.* (chem.) hydric.
hidroaeroplano, *m.* (aer.) hydroplane, seaplane.
hidroavión, *m.* (aer.) hydroplane, seaplane.—**h. de flotadores,** float seaplane.
hidrocarburo, *m.* (chem.) hydrocarbon.
hidrocefalía, *f.* (med.) hydrocephalus, dropsy of the brain.
hidrocéfalo, la, *a.* (med.) hydrocephalous.
hidrocele, *f.* (med.) hydrocele.
hidrocinético, ca. I. *a.* hydrokinetic. **II.** *f.* hydrokinetics.
hidroclorato, *m.* (chem.) hydrochlorate.
hidroclórico, ca, *a.* (chem.) hydrochloric.
hidrocortisona, *f.* (chem.) hydrocortisone.
hidrodinámica, *f.* hydrodynamics.
hidrodinámico, ca, *a.* hydrodynamic.
hidroeléctrico, ca, *a.* hydroelectric.
hidrófana, *f.* (min.) hydrophane.
hidrofilacio, *m.* hydrophylacium, water reservoir.
hidrófilo, la, *a.* water-loving; absorbent (cotton).
hidrófita, *f.* (bot.) hydrophyte.
hidrofobia, *f.* (med.) hydrophobia; rabies.
hidrofóbico, ca, *a.* (med.) hydrophobic; rabid.
hidrófobo, ba. I. *a.* hydrophobic, hydrophobous, suffering from hydrophobia; rabid. **II.** *n.* hydrophobe, one who suffers from hydrophobia.
hidrófono, *m.* (naut., hydraul.) hydrophone.
hidrófugo, ga, *a.* nonabsorbent, moistureproof.
hidrogala, *m.* mixture of milk and water.
hidrogenación, *f.* (chem.) hydrogenation.
hidrogenado, da, *a.* hydrogenous.
hidrogenar, *va.* to hydrogenize.
hidrógeno, *m.* (chem.) hydrogen.—**h. pesado,** heavy hydrogen.
hidrogeológico, ca, *a.* hydrogeological.
hidrogeólogo, ga, *n.* hydrogeologist.
hidrognosia, *f.* hydrognosy.
hidrogogía, *f.* science of canal making and the conveyance of water.
hidrografía, *f.* hydrography.
hidrográfico, ca, *a.* hydrographical.
hidrógrafo, *m.* hydrographer.
hidroide, *m.* (zool.) hydroid.
hidrólisis, *f.* (chem.) hydrolysis.
hidrolítico, ca, *a.* hydrolitic.
hidrolizar, *va.* & *vn.* to hydrolize.
hidrología, *f.* hydrology.
hidrológico, ca, *a.* hydrologic.
hidrólogo, ga, *n.* hydrologist.
hidromancía, *f.* hydromancy.
hidromántico, ca, *a.* hydromantic.
hidromecánica, *f.* hydromechanics.
hidromedusa, *f.* (zool.) hydromedusa; a large South American turtle.
hidromel, hidromiel, *m.* hydromel, mead.
hidrometalurgia, *f.* hydrometallurgy.
hidrometeoro, *m.* hydrometeor.
hidrómetra, *n.* one versed in hydraulic measurements.
hidrometría, *f.* science of hydraulic measurements (velocity, discharge, etc.).
hidrométrico, ca, *a.* hydrometric.—**péndulo h.,** hydrometric pendulum.
hidrómetro, *m.* instrument for measuring rate of flow, force, etc. of liquids.
hidrópata, *m.* (med.) hydropath.
hidropatía, *f.* (med.) water cure, hydrotherapy.
hidropático, ca, *a.* hydropathic.
hidropesía, *f.* (med.) dropsy.
hidrópico, ca, *a.* dropsical.
hidroplano, *m.* (aer.) hydroplane, seaplane.
hidroponía, *f.* (hort.) hydroponics.
hidroquinona, *f.* (chem.) hydroquinone.
hidroscopio, *m.* hydroscope.
hidrosfera, *f.* hydrosphere.
hidrostática, *f.* hydrostatics.

hidrostáticamente, *adv.* hydrostatically.
hidrostático, ca, *a.* hydrostatical.
hidrosulfúrico, ca, *a.* hydrosulphuric.
hidrosulfuro, *m.* (chem.) hydrosulfide.
hidrotecnia, *f.* hydraulic engineering.
hidroterapia, *f.* hydrotherapeutics.
hidroterápico, ca, *a.* hydrotherapeutic.
hidrotermal, *a.* hydrothermal.
hidrotórax, *m.* (med.) hydrothorax.
hidrotropismo, *m.* hydrotropism.
hidróxido, *m.* (chem.) hydroxide.—**h. sódico,** (chem.) sodium hydroxide.
hidruro, *m.* (chem.) hydride, hydrid.
hiedo, hieda, *v. V.* HEDER.
hiedra, *f.* (bot.) ivy.—**h. inglesa,** (bot.) English ivy.—**h. terrestre,** (bot.) ground ivy.
hiel, *f.* gall, bile; bitterness, malice.—**h. de la tierra,** (bot.) fumitory or earth smoke.—**echar la h.,** (coll.) to work very hard.—**no tener h.,** (coll.) to be meek and gentle.
[1]**hielo,** *m.* ice; frost, congelation; coolness, indifference; astonishment, stupefaction.
[2]**hielo, hiele,** *v. V.* HELAR.
hielo seco, *m.* dry ice.
hiemal, *a.* wintry, hibernal.
hiena, *f.* (zool.) hyena.
hienda, *f.* dung.
hiendo, hienda, *v. V.* HENDER.
hierático, ca, *a.* hieratic, sacerdotal.
hierba, *f.* (bot.) grass; weed; herb; food for cattle; herbage.—**mala h.,** weed; (fig.) bad character, evil person.—*pl.* poison given in food; among the clergy, greens, garden stuff.—**y otras hierbas,** (humor.) and so forth.
hierbabuena, *f.* (bot.) mint.
hierbatero, ra, *n.* herb doctor; maté gatherer; one who prepares maté; YERBATERO.
hiere, hiero, hiera, *v. V.* HERIR.
hierofanta, te, *m.* hierophant.
hieroglífico, ca, *m.* & *a.* = JEROGLÍFICO.
hierología, *f.* hierology.
hieros, *m. pl.* (bot.) = YEROS, tare, vetch.
hierosolimitano, na, *a.* pert. to Jerusalem.
hierrezuelo, *m. dim.* small piece of iron.
[1]**hierro,** *m.* iron; any iron tool, instrument or structural shape; brand stamped with a hot iron; iron head of a shaft, arrow, or dart; any pointed weapon, as a sword or goad; cutter, cutting edge or part of a cutting tool.—*pl.* fetters, shackles, handcuffs; (naut.) bilboes.—**h. albo, h. caliente,** red-hot iron.—**h. colado,** cast iron.—**h. cuadrillado.** square iron.—**h. de doble T,** I-beam.—**h. de marcar,** branding iron.—**h. dulce** or **de fragua,** wrought iron.—**h. en lingotes,** pig iron.—**h. en planchas,** sheet iron.—**h. especular,** specular iron.—**h. forjado,** wrought iron.—**h. fundido,** cast iron.—**h. galvanizado,** galvanized iron.—**h. laminado,** sheet iron.—**h. varilla,** round iron.—**h. viejo,** junk, scrap iron or metal.—**machacar en h. frío,** to labor in vain.
[2]**hierro, hierre,** *v. V.* HERRAR.
hierva, hiervo, *v. V.* HERVIR.
higa, *f.* amulet, charm hung about a baby's neck; method of pointing derisively at a person; ridicule, derision.—**dar h.,** (of firearms) to hang fire.—**dar higas,** to despise.—**no dar dos higas,** not to give a farthing; not to care a rap.
higadilla, *f.* **llo,** *m. dim.* small liver; liver of birds, fishes, and other small animals.
hígado, *m.* liver.—*pl.* (coll.) courage, bravery.—**hasta los hígados,** to the heart.—**malos hígados,** (coll.) ill will.
higate, *m.* pottage of figs, pork, etc.
higiene, *f.* hygiene; sanitation.—**h. pública,** public health.
higiénicamente, *adv.* hygienically.
higiénico, ca, *a.* hygienic, sanitary.
higienista, *m.* hygienist.
higienizar, *va.* to make sanitary.
higo, *m.* (bot.) fig.—**h. chumba,** or **de pala,** prickly pear.—**de higos a brevas,** in a long while.—**no se me da un h.,** I don't care a fig.
higrometría, *m.* hygrometry.
higrométrico, ca, *a.* hygrometric.
higrómetro, *m.* hygrometer.
higroscopia, *f.* hygroscopy, hygrometry.
higroscópico, ca, *a.* hygroscopic.
higroscopio, *m.* hygroscope.
higuera, *f.* (bot.) fig tree.—**h. chumba,** or **de Indias,** Indian fig tree, prickly-pear cactus.—**h. infernal,** castor-oil plant, castor bean.—**h. nopal** = H. CHUMBA.
higueral, *m.* plantation of fig trees.
higuereta, *f.* (bot.) = RICINO, castor-oil plant.
higuerón, *m.* a large American tree.
higuito, *m. dim.* small fig.
hija, *f.* daughter.—**h. política,** daughter-in-law. For phrases *V.* HIJO, JA.
hijadalga, *f.* = HIDALGA, noblewoman.
hijastro, tra, *n.* stepchild.
hijito, ita, *n. f. dim.* little child, little dear.
hijo, ja, *n.* son (daughter); young of an animal; son, native; (bot.) shoot; sucker; child, issue, offspring; fruit, result; junior (after a person's name: *Alejandro Dumas, hijo,* Alexander Dumas, Jr.).—**h. adoptivo,** adopted child.—**h. bastardo,** bastard, illegitimate child.—**h. de bendición,** legitimate child.—**h. de familia,** minor.—**h. de ganancia** = H. BASTARDO.—**h. de la cuna,** foundling.—**h. del agua,** good sailor; good swimmer.—**h. de la piedra,** foundling.—**h. de leche,** foster child.—**h. del hombre,** Son of Man (Jesus).—**h. de su madre** = H. BASTARDO.—**h. de su madre (padre),** his mother's (father's) son, very much like his mother (father).—**h. de vecino,** native (of a town); mother's son (in the colloquial sense of "person").—**h. natural,** illegitimate child.—**h. político,** son-in-law.
hijodalgo, *m.* = HIDALGO, nobleman.
hijuela, *f. dim.* little daughter; (sewing) gore or piece for widening a garment; small mattress put between others to make the bed even; (eccl.) pall, chalice cover; small drain; estate of a deceased person; (law) schedule given to an heir of his share in the partition of the estate; crossroad; postman of a rural mail route; palm seed; fascine of kindling wood; leader for fishhooks.
hijuelo, la, *n. dim.* young child; (bot.) shoot, sucker.
[1]**hila,** *f.* HILERA, row, line; thin gut.—**h. de agua,** small ditch for irrigation.—**a la h.,** in a row, single file.
[2]**hila,** *f.* spinning.—*pl.* (surg.) lint.—**hilas raspadas,** scraped lint.
hilacha, *f.,* **hilacho,** *m.* fraying, shred, filament or thread ravelled out of cloth.—*pl.* lint.
hilachoso, sa, *a.* shreddy, ragged; filamentous.
hilada, *f.* row or line; (mason.) course.
hiladillo, *m.* narrow ribbon or tape.
hilado, *m.* spinning; yarn.
hilador, ra. I. *n.* & *a.* spinner(-ing). **II.** *f.* spinning machine, spinning jenny.
hilandera, *f.* woman spinner.
hilandería, *f.* spinnery, spinning mill.
hilanderilla, *f. dim.* spinning girl.
hilandero, ra. I. *n.* & *a.* spinner(-ing). **II.** *m.* spinning room, spinnery.
hilanderuelo, la, *n. dim.* spinning boy (girl).
hilar, *va.* & *vn.* to spin; to reason; (of discourse) to connect.—**h. delgado,** to be exceedingly careful or particular; to act with great nicety; to split hairs.
hilaracha, *f.* = HILACHA.
hilarante, *a.* laughing (gas).
hilaridad, *f.* hilarity.
hilaza, *f.* yarn; fibre; uneven thread.—*pl.* lint.
hilera, *f.* row, line, tier, file; (metal.) wiredrawer; fine yarn; slit or catch of a spindle; (arch.) ridgepole; (mil.) file.
hilero, *m.* thread of a river or stream.
hilete, *m. dim.* small thread.
hililllo, *m.* trickle (of water).

hilo, *m.* thread; yarn; filament, fibre; string; linen; wire; edge of a sword or razor; slender thread formed by falling liquids; (min.) seam; continuation, series; cross wire, cross hair (of a telescope).—**h. bramante, h. de a carreto, h. de palomas,** packthread, twine.—**h. de velas,** or **volatín,** sailmaker's yarn.—**h. de una corriente,** (naut.) thread of a current.—**a h.,** successively, one after another; in line. —**al h.,** along the thread (of cloth), with the grain (in wood).—**de h.,** directly, instantly.
hilván, *m.* (sewing) tacking, basting.—**hablar de h.,** (coll.) to speak very fast.
hilvanar, *va.* (sewing) to tack, baste; to plan; to do or make in a hurry.
himen, *m.* (anat.) hymen.
himeneo, *m.* hymen, nuptials; epithalamium.
himenio, *m.* (bot.) hymenium.
himenóptero, ra. I. *a.* (entom.) hymenopterous, hymenopteran. **II.** *m.* (entom.) hymenopteran.
himnario, *m.* hymnal, hymn book.
himno, *m.* hymn, anthem.—**h. nacional,** national anthem.
himplar, *vn.* to roar, bellow.
hin, *m.* whinny, neigh.
hincadura, *f.* thrusting, driving; prick.
hincapié, *m.* stamping the foot (for emphasis).—**hacer h. en,** to emphasize, to dwell upon.
hincar. I. *va.* (*pret.* HINQUÉ; *subj.* HINQUE) to thrust; drive; to plant.—**h. el diente,** to bite; to calumniate.—**h. la rodilla,** to kneel down. **II.** *vr.* to kneel down.
hincón, *m.* ferry post, hitching post.
hincha, *f.* (coll.) hatred, enmity, grudge.
hinchadamente, *adv.* airily, pompously.
hinchado, da, *a.* & *pp.* swollen; airy, arrogant, presumptuous; inflated, high-flown (style).
hinchar. I. *va.* to swell. **II.** *vr.* to swell; to become arrogant, conceited or puffed up, (coll.) to get a swelled head.
hinchazón, *m.* swelling, tumefaction; ostentation, vanity, airs; inflation, euphuism.
hincho, hincha, hinchió, *v. V.* HENCHIR.
hindu, *n.* & *a.* Hindu; Hindustani.
hiniesta, *f.* (bot.) genista.
hinojal, *m.* (bot.) fennel bed.
[1]**hinojo,** *m.* (bot.) fennel.—**h. marino,** (bot.) samphire.
[2]**hinojo,** *m.* knee.—**de hinojos,** kneeling.
hinqué, hinque, *v. V.* HINCAR.
hintero, *m.* baker's kneading table.
hiño, hiña, *v. V.* HEÑIR.
hioideo, dea, *a.* hyoid.
hioides, *m.* & *a.* (anat.) hyoid.
hiosciamina, *f.* (chem.) hyoscyamine.
hioscina, *f.* (pharm.) hyoscine, truth serum or drug.
hipar, *vn.* to hiccough; to pant; desire eagerly, be anxious; be overfatigued.
hiperacidez, *f.* (med.) hyperacidity.
hipérbaton, *m.* (rhet.) hyperbaton.
hipérbola, *f.* (geom.) hyperbola.
hipérbole, *f.* (rhet.) hyperbole.
hiperbólico, ca, *a.* hyperbolic.
hiperbolizar, *vn.* to use hyperboles.
hiperboloide, *f.* (geom.) hyperboloid.
hiperbóreo, rea, *a.* hyperborean.
hipercrisis, *f.* (med.) violent crisis.
hipercrítica, *f.* hypercriticism, excessive or exaggerated criticism.
hipercrítico, ca, *a.* hypercritical.
hiperdulía, *f.* (eccl.) hyperdulia.
hiperemia, *f.* (med.) hyperæmia.
hiperémico, ca, *a.* hyperæmic, congested.
hiperestesia, *f.* (med.) hyperæsthesia, excessive sensitivity (to pain, heat, touch, etc.).
hipericíneo, a. I. *a.* & *n.* hypericaceous (plant). **II.** *m. pl.* Hypericaceæ.
hipérico, *m.* (bot.) hypericum.
hipermetría, *f.* (rhet.) hypermeter.
hipermétrope, *n.* hyperope, hypermetrope, abnormally far-sighted person.
hipermetropía, *f.* (med.) hyperopia, hypermetropia, condition of abnormal far-sightedness.
hiperón, *m.* (phys.) hyperon.
hipersensible, hipersensitivo, va, *a.* hypersensitive.
hipersónico, ca, *a.* hypersonic.
hipertensión, *f.* (med.) hypertension.
hipertenso, sa, *n.* & *a.* hypertensive.
hipertrofia, *f.* (med.) hypertrophy, abnormal increase in size (of an organ, tissue, etc.).
hipertrofiarse, *vr.* to hypertrophy.
hipertrófico, ca, *a.* hypertrophic.
hípico, ca, *a.* equine, pertaining to horses.
hipil, *m.* (Am.) loose garment worn by Indians.
hipnal, *m.* hypnale, a kind of serpent said to cause sleep.
hipnología, *f.* hypnology, science dealing with sleep.
hipnosis, *f.* hypnosis.
hipnótico, ca, *n.* & *a.* hypnotic.
hipnotismo, *m.* hypnotism.
hipnotización, *f.* hypnotization.
hipnotizador, a, *n.* & *a.* hypnotizer(-ing).
hipnotizar, *va.* to hypnotize.
hipo, *m.* hiccough; longing; anger.
hipoblasto, *m.* (biol.) hypoblast.
hipocampo, *m.* (myth., ichth., anat.) hippocampus.
hipocausto, *m.* (anc. Rome) hypocaust.
hipocentauro, *m.* hippocentaur.
hipocicloide, *f.* (geom.) hypocycloid.
hipoclorito, *m.* (chem.) hypochlorite.
hipocloroso, sa, *a.* (chem.) hypochlorous.
hipocondría, *f.* (med.) hypochondria.
hipocondríaco, ca; hipocóndrico, ca, *n.* & *a.* hypochondriac(-al).
hipocondrio, *m.* (anat.) hypochondrium.
hipocotíleo, *m.* (bot.) hypocotyl.
hipocrás, *m.* hippocras, medicinal wine.
hipocrático, ca, *a.* Hippocratic.
Hipocrénides, *f. pl.* (poet.) the Muses.
hipocresía, *f.* hypocrisy.
hipócrita, *n.* & *a.* hypocrite(-ical).
hipócritamente, *adv.* hypocritically.
hipocritón, na, *n. aug.* great hypocrite.
hipodérmico, ca, *a.* hypodermic.
hipódromo, *m.* hippodrome.
hipófisis, *f.* (anat.) hypophysis, pituitary gland.
hipofosfato, *m.* hypophosphate.
hipofosfito, *m.* hypophosphite.
hipogástrico, ca, *a.* hypogastric.
hipogastro, *m.* (anat.) hypogastrium.
hipogénico, ca, *a.* (geol.) hypogene.
hipogeo, *m.* (arch.) hypogeium.
hipógino, na, *a.* (bot.) hypogynous.
hipogloso, sa. I. *a.* (anat.) hypoglossal. **II.** *m.* (anat.) hypoglossal nerve; (ichth.) halibut.
hipogrifo, *m.* (myth.) hippogriff.
hipomanes, *m.* (vet.) vaginal discharge from the mare when in heat.
hiponitrato, *m.* (chem.) subnitrate.
hiponítrico, ca, *a.* hyponitrous.
hiponitroso, sa, *a.* (chem.) hyponitrous.
hipopótamo, *m.* (zool.) hippopotamus.
hiposo, sa, *a.* having hiccoughs.
hipóstasis, *f.* (theol.) hypostasis.
hipostático, ca, *a.* hypostatic.
hiposulfato, *m.* (chem.) hyposulphate.
hiposulfito, *m.* (chem.) hyposulfite.—**h. de sodio,** (chem.) sodium hyposulfite.
hiposulfuroso, sa, *a.* (chem.) hyposulfurous.
hipoteca, *f.* mortgage, pledge; (law) hypothecation, hypothec.
hipotecable, *a.* mortgageable.
hipotecar, *va.* (*pret.* HIPOTEQUÉ; *subj.* HIPOTEQUE) to hypothecate, pledge, mortgage.
hipotecario, ria, *a.* pertaining to a mortgage; hypothecary.
hipotequé, hipoteque, *v. V.* HIPOTECAR.
hipotenusa, *f.* (geom.) hypotenuse.

hipótesis, *f.* hypothesis.—**h. nebular** or **de Laplace,** (astr.) nebular hypothesis.
hipotético, ca, *a.* hypothetic.
hipsometría, *f.* hypsometry.
hipsométrico, ca, *a.* hypsometric.
hipsómetro, *m.* hypsometer.
hipurato, *m.* (chem.) hippurate.
hipuria, *f.* (med.) hippuria.
hipúrico, ca, *a.* (chem.) hippuric.
hircano, na, *n.* & *a.* Hircanian.
hircino, na, *a.* hircinous, goatlike.
hirco, *m.* (zool.) wild goat.
hiriente, *a.* hurting, cutting, offensive.
hiriera, hirió, *v. V.* HERIR.
hirma, *f.* selvage of cloth.
hirsuto, ta, *a.* hirsute, hairy, bristly.
hirundinaria, *f.* (bot.) swallow-wort.
hirviendo, *gerund* of HERVIR.
hirviente, *a.* boiling, seething.
hirviera, hirviese, hirvió, *v. V.* HERVIR.
hisca, *f.* birdlime.
hiscal, *m.* esparto rope of three strands.
hisopada, *f.* water sprinkled with an aspergill.
hisopear, *va.* to sprinkle with an aspergill.
hisopillo, *m. dim.* small aspergill; (med.) mouth swab; (bot.) winter savory.
[1]**hisopo,** *m.* (bot.) hyssop; (eccl.) aspergill, sprinkler.
[2]**hisopo,** *m.*—**h. húmedo,** (pharm.) grease collected in washing fleeces of wool.
hispalense, *a.* native of or pertaining to Seville.
hispánico, ca, *a.* Hispanic.
hispanismo, *m.* Hispanicism. Spanish idiom.
hispanista, *n.* Spanish scholar.
hispanizado, da. I. *pp.* of HISPANIZAR. **II.** *a.* Spanishlike.
hispanizar. I. *va.* to Hispanicize, Hispaniolize. **II.** *vr.* to become Hispanicized.
hispano, na. I. *a.* Hispanic, Spanish; Spanish-American. **II.** *n.* Spaniard; Spanish-American.
hispanoamericano, na, *n.* & *a.* Spanish-American.
hispanófilo, la, *n.* & *a.* Hispanophile.
híspido, da, *a.* bristly, hirsute.
hispir, *va.* & *vn.* to swell; make or become spongy.
histamina, *f.* (chem.) histamine.
histerectomía, *f.* (surg.) hysterectomy.
histéresis, *f.* (phys.) hysteresis.
histeria, *f.* (med.) hysteria, hysterics.
histérico, ca. I. *a.* (med.) hysterical, hysteric. **II.** *n.* (med.) hysteric, hysterical person; *m.* (med.) hysterics, hysteria.
histerismo, *m.* (med.) hysteria.
histerotomía, *m.* (surg.) hysterotomy.
histidina, *f.* (chem.) histidine.
histogenia, *f.* (biol.) histogenesis, histogeny.
histograma, *m.* (stat.) histogram.
histólisis, *f.* (biol.) histolysis.
histología, *f.* histology.
histológico, ca, *a.* histological.
histólogo, *m.* histologist.
historia, *f.* history; tale, story; fable; (art) history piece.—**h. antigua,** ancient history.—**h. medieval,** medieval history.—**h. moderna,** modern history.—**h. natural,** natural history.—**dejarse de historias,** to stop beating about the bush and come to the point; to cut out the nonsense, stop fooling.—**picar en h.,** to be more serious than it seems.—**ser de h.,** to have a history (bad antecedents).
historiado, da, *pp.* & *a.* (coll.) excessively adorned; (art) well-composed (figure, painting).
historiador, ra, *n.* historian.
historial, *a.* historical, historic.
historialmente, *adv.* historically.
historiar, *va.* to record, to chronicle, to narrate; (art) to represent, paint, depict.
históricamente, *adv.* historically.
histórico, ca, *a.* historical.
historieta, *f. dim.* short story; comics, comic strip.
historiografía, *f.* historiography.
historiógrafo, *m.* historiographer.
historión, *m.* tedious, long-winded story.
histrión, *m.* actor, player; buffoon, juggler.
histriónico, ca, *a.* histrionic.
histrionisa, *f.* actress or danseuse.
histrionismo, *m.* histrionism.
hita, *f.* headless nail, brad, wire nail; guide post.
hitita, *n.* & *a.* Hittite.
[1]**hito, ta,** *a.* black (horse).
[2]**hito, ta. I.** *a.* (of a house or street) adjoining; fixed, firm. **II.** *m.* landmark; guidepost; milestone; hob and quoits; (artil.) target.—**a h.,** fixedly, firmly.—**dar en el h.,** to hit the nail on the head; to see the point.—**mirar de h. en h.,** to stare at; to look at from head to foot.
hitón, *m.* large cut nail.
hizo, *pret.* of HACER.
hobachón, na, *a.* fat and lazy; (Colomb.) (of horses) shy.
hobachonería, *f.* laziness, sloth.
hocicada, *f.* blow with the snout.
hocicar. I. *va.* to root (as hogs). **II.** *vn.* to fall headlong with the face to the ground; to knock one's face against an object; (coll.) to get into difficulties; (naut.) to pitch.
hocico, *m.* snout, muzzle, nose (of animal); big-lipped mouth; pouting; (coll.) face.—**de hocicos,** by the nose; face downwards.—**estar con,** or **de, h.,** to be ill-humored, sulky.—**meter el h.,** to stick one's nose in other people's business.
hocicón, na, *or* **hocicudo, da,** *a.* long-snouted; blubber-lipped, flabby-mouthed.
[1]**hocino,** *m.* (agr.) bill, billhook.
[2]**hocino,** *m.* glen, dell; narrow gorge or canyon —*pl.* gardens in glens.
hociquillo, ito, *m. dim.* little snout.
hodómetro, *m.* = ODÓMETRO, cyclometer.
hogañazo, hogaño, *adv.* (coll.) this present year; in these days.
hogar, *m.* home (often called **h. doméstico**); hearth, fireplace; (steam eng.) furnace.
hogareño, ña, *a.* home-loving, domestic.
hogaza, *f.* large loaf of bread.
hoguera, *f.* bonfire; blaze.
hoja, *f.* leaf (of a plant, a book, a door); petal; leaf, foil, sheet or thin plate (of metal); blade (of a sword or knife); sword; sheet (of paper); veneer; half of each of the principal parts of a garment; window shutter; ground cultivated one year and lying at rest for another.—*pl.* (arch.) leaf ornaments, foliation.—**h. de estaño,** tinfoil.—**h. de lata,** tin plate.—**h. de servicios,** record; (mil.) certificate setting forth the rank and services of a military officer.—**h. de tocino,** side of a hog.—**h. suelta,** leaflet (not folder), handbill.—**h. toledana,** Toledo blade.—**h. volante,** fly sheet; handbill; supplement, extra.—**doblemos la h.,** no more of that, let's drop it.—**poner le a uno como h. de perejil,** to give one a tongue lashing.—**ser de h.,** or **de una sola h.,** (Arg.) (esp. of people) to be first rate, of highest order.—**volver la h.,** to turn the page; to change one's views; to fail to keep one's promise; to change the subject (of conversation).
hojalata, *f.* = HOJA DE LATA, tin plate.
hojalatería, *f.* tinware; tin shop.
hojalatero, *m.* tinsmith.
hojaldra, *f.* (Am.) = HOJALDRE.
hojaldrado, da. I. *pp.* of HOJALDRAR. **II.** *a.* resembling puff paste, lamellar, foliated.
hojaldrar, *va.* to make into puff paste.
hojaldre, *m.* or *f.* puff paste.—**quitar la h. al pastel,** (coll.) to detect a fraud, to discover a plot.
hojaldrista, *n.* puff paste baker.
hojarasca, *f.* dead leaves; excessive foliage; trash, rubbish.
hojarascoso, sa, *a.* trashy.
hojear. I. *va.* to turn the leaves of; to glance at (a book), look over hastily. **II.** *vn.* to scale off.
hojica, illa, ita, *f. dim.* small leaf.

hojilla de navaja (de afeitar), razor blade.
hojoso, sa; hojudo, da, *a.* leafy, fronded.
hojuela, *f. dim.* small leaf, leaflet; pancake; gold or silver flat thread for embroidery; skins of pressed olives.
¡hola! *interj.* hello! hi! (naut.) hoy! ahoy!
holán, holán batista, *m.* cambric; batiste.
Holanda, *f.* fine Dutch linen, cambric.
holandés, sa, *n.* & *a.* Dutch, Hollander(-ish).—**a la holandesa,** (bookbinding) in cloth.
holandeta, holandilla, *f.* brown holland.
holgachón, na, *a.* (coll.) used to an easy and comfortable life.
holgadamente, *adv.* amply, fully, loosely, easily; quietly, carelessly; comfortably.
holgado, da. I. *pp.* of HOLGAR. **II.** *a.* loose, lax, easy; large, spacious; disengaged, at leisure; comfortable; well-off.
holganza, *f.* leisure, ease; diversion, recreation.
holgar. I. *vn.* (*ind.* HUELGO; *subj.* HUELGUE) to rest; to quit work; to be idle; to be needless or useless; to take pleasure or satisfaction. **II.** *vr.* to sport, dally, trifle; to idle; to amuse oneself.
holgazán, na. I. *a.* idle, lazy, indolent. **II.** *n.* idler, loiterer, lounger.
holgazanear, *vn.* to idle, to loiter, to lounge.
holgazanería, *f.* idleness, laziness, indolence.
holgón, a, *a.* indolent and pleasure-loving.
holgorio, *m.* (coll.) boisterous frolic or spree.
holgueta, *f.* (coll.) feast, merrymaking.
holgura, *f.* frolic, merrymaking; width, breadth; ease, comfort; plenty of room or space; (mech.) play.
holmio, *m.* (chem.) holmium.
holocausto, *m.* holocaust, burnt sacrifice.
holocéfalo, la, *m.* & *a.* (zool.) holocephalan.
holoédrico, ca, *a.* (cryst.) holohedral.
holoedro, *m.* (cryst.) holohedron.
hológrafo, fa, *m.* & *a.* (law) holograph.
holómetro, *m.* holometer, pantometer.
holosérico, ca, *a.* all-silk.
holoturia, *f.* (zool.) holothurian, sea cucumber.
holotúrido, da; holoturioideo, a. I. *n.* & *a.* (zool.) holothurian. **II.** *m. pl.* Holothuroidea.
holladura, *f.* trampling; duty paid for the run of cattle.
hollar, *va.* (*ind.* HUELLO; *subj.* HUELLE) to tread upon, trample under foot; to humiliate.
hollejo, *m.* skin (of a fruit, etc.).
hollejuelo, *m. dim.* small piece of skin; thin skin.
hollín, *m.* soot, lampblack.
holliniento, ta, *a.* fuliginous, sooty.
homarrache, *m.* clown.
hombracho, hombrachón, *m. aug.* heavy-built man.
hombrada, *f.* manly action; impulse.
hombradía, *f.* manliness.
hombrazo, *m. aug.* big man.
hombre, *m.* man; (vulg.) husband; ombre, a card game; (coll., in addressing or speaking to a friend, often as a mere expletive) boy, old chap, dear fellow, man, my dear man.—**¡hombre!** an exclamation of surprise.—**h. achaparrado,** short and lusty man.—**¡h. al agua!** man overboard.—**h. bueno,** (law) arbiter, arbitrator, referee.—**h. de armas,** military man.—**h. de bien,** a reputable, reliable man.—**h. de estado,** statesman.—**h. de puños,** strong, valiant man.—**ser muy h.,** to be a real man, or quite a man.
hombrear. I. *vn.* to pretend to man's estate prematurely. **II.** *vn.* & *vr.* to vie with another.
hombrecico, cito, cillo, zuelo, *m. dim.* little man; youth.
hombrecillos, *m. pl.* (bot.) hops.
hombrera, *f.* (armor) shoulder armor.
hombría, *f.* (Am.) manliness, courage.—**h. de bien,** probity, honesty.
hombrillo, *m.* (sewing) yoke of a shirt.
hombro, *m.* shoulder.—**h. con h.,** cheek by jowl. —**a h.,** on the shoulders.—**arrimar el h.,** to lend a hand; to exert oneself.—**echar al h.,** to shoulder; to become responsible for.—**encogerse de hombros,** to shrug the shoulders. —**llevar en hombros,** to carry on the shoulders; to support, to protect.—**sobre los hombros** = A H.
hombrón, *m. aug.* big, lusty man.
hombronazo, *m. aug.* huge man.
hombruno, na, *a.* mannish.
homenaje, *m.* homage; obeisance; fealty, allegiance; respect.
homeópata, *n.* & *a.* homœopath(-ic).
homeopatía, *f.* homœopathy.
homeopático, ca, *a.* homœopathic.
homérico, ca, *a.* Homeric.
homicida. I. *a.* homicidal, murderous. **II.** *n.* murderer, homicide.
homicidio, *m.* homicide, assassination, murder. —**h. impremeditado,** (law) murder in the second degree.—**h. premeditado,** (law) murder in the first degree.
homilía, *f.* homily.
homiliario, *m.* homiliary, book of homilies.
homilista, *n.* homilist.
hominal, *a.* pertaining to man.
hominicaco, *m.* (coll.) insignificant fellow, whippersnapper.
homocéntrico, ca, *a.* concentric.
homocigosidad, *f.* (genetics) homozygosity.
homocigótico, ca, *a.* (genetics) homozygous.
homocigoto, *m.* (genetics) homozygote.
homodino, *m.* (rad.) homodyne.
homofonía, *f.* homophony.
homófono, na, *a.* homophonous.
homogeneidad, *f.* homogeneity.
homogeneizar, *va.* to homogenize.
homogéneo, a, *a.* homogeneous.
homógrafo, fa, *a.* homographic.
homologación, *f.* (law) homologation.
homologar, *va.* (law) to homologate, ratify.
homología, *f.* homology.
homólogo, ga, *a.* (geom.) homologous; proportional; (logic) synonymous.
homonimia, *f.* homonymy.
homónimo, ma, *a.* homonymous; namesake.
homóptero, ra, *m.* & *a.* (zool.) homopterous.
homosedástico, ca, *a.* (stat.) homoscedastic.
homosexual, *n.* & *a.* homosexual.
homosexualidad, *f.* homosexuality.
homósporo, ra, *a.* (bot.) homosporous.
homúnculo, *m.* homunculus, dwarf.
honda, *f.* sling (for hurling stones).—**h. y precinta,** (naut.) parbuckle.
hondable, *a.* (naut.) soundable.
hondamente, *adv.* deeply, profoundly.
hondarras, *f. pl.* dregs, lees, sediment.
hondazo, *m.* a shot with a sling.
hondear, *va.* (naut.) to sound; to unload (ship).
hondero, *m.* soldier armed with a sling.
hondijo, *m.* sling.
hondillo, *m.* any of the pieces which form the seats of breeches or drawers.
hondo, da. I. *a.* deep; low. **II.** *m.* depth, bottom. —**de h.,** in depth.
hondón, *m.* bottom; dell, glen; deep hole; footpiece of a stirrup; eye of a needle.
hondonada, *f.* dale, ravine, glen; depression.
hondura, *f.* depth; profundity.—**meterse en honduras,** (fig.) to go beyond one's depth.
Honduras, *f.* Honduras.
hondureño, ña, *n.* & *a.* Honduran, Honduras.
honestamente, *adv.* honestly; modestly; virtuously.
honestar, *va.* to honor; to excuse, palliate.
honestidad, *f.* modesty; purity; decorum.
honesto, ta, *a.* honest; decent, decorous; pure, chaste; reasonable, just.
hongo, *m.* (bot.) mushroom; derby, bowler; (med.) fungus, fungosity.
hongoso, sa, *a.* fungous.
honguillo, *m. dim.* small fungus.
honor, *m.* honor; fame.—*pl.* dignity, rank, office, honors, privileges, honorary title or position.

honorable, *a.* worthy, honorable; illustrious; reputable, reliable.
honorablemente, *adv.* honorably, creditably.
honorario, ria. I. *a.* honorary. **II.** *m.* honorarium, fee.
honoríficamente, *adv.* honorably; honorarily.
honorífico, ca, *a.* honorary; honorable.
honra, *f.* honor; reverence, respect; reputation, fame; purity, chastity.—**tener a h.,** to regard as an honor, be proud of.—*pl.* obsequies.
honradamente, *adv.* honorably, honestly.
honradez, *f.* honesty, probity, integrity.
honrado, da, *a.* honest, honorable.
honrador, ra, *n.* & *a.* honorer(-ing).
honramiento, *m.* honoring.
honrar. I. *va.* to honor, do honor to; to be an honor for; (com.) to honor. **II.** *vn.* to honor; to be an honor. **III.** *vr.* to deem it an honor; to be honored.
honrilla, *f. dim.* keen sense of honor or duty, punctiliousness (usually **la negra h.**).
honrosamente, *adv.* honorably; creditably.
honroso, sa, *a.* honorable, decorous; honoring, honor-giving.—**ser h.,** to be an honor.
hontanal, *m.* HONTANAR.—*pl.* feasts of the ancients held at fountains.
hontanar, *m.* place abounding in springs.
hopa, *f.* long cassock; sack for an executed criminal.
hopalanda, *f.* (anc.) gown worn by students.
hopear, *vn.* to wag the tail.
hoplita, *m.* hoplite.
hoploteca, *f.* = OPLOTECA, museum for weapons.
hopo, *m.* bushy tail (as of a fox).
hoque, *m.* treat to close a bargain.
hora. I. *f.* hour; time, season for doing anything; distance covered in an hour; league.—*pl.* (eccl.) prayerbook.—**horas canónicas,** (eccl.) canonical hours.—**h. de,** time to, or for (*hora de almuerzo,* time for breakfast, or breakfast time; *hora de tren,* time for the train, or train time).—**h. de comer,** meal time.—**h. del tropel,** rush hour.—**h. de verano,** daylight-saving time.—**h. legal,** standard time.—**h. menguada,** fatal or unhappy hour.—**horas de consulta,** office hours (doctor, etc.).—**horas de oficina,** office or business hours.—**horas extraordinarias de trabajo,** overtime.—**horas menores,** (eccl.) little hours.—**a buena h.,** opportunely, at the proper time.—**a la h.,** at once, right away; then.—**a la h. de ésta,** or **a la h. de ahora,** or **a estas horas,** (coll.) at this moment.—**a última h.,** at the last moment, at the eleventh hour.—**cuarenta horas,** (eccl.) forty hours.—**dar la h.,** to strike the hour; to adjourn (the meeting, etc.); to dismiss (the class, etc.).—**de última h.,** up-to-date.—**en h. buena, en buen,** or **buena h.,** well, happily; it is well; very well, all right.—**en h. mala, en mal,** or **mala h.,** = ENHORAMALA (used to indicate dissatisfaction, disapproval, etc.; rendered according to the situation).—**no ver la h. de,** to look forward to.—**por horas,** by instants.—**¿qué h. es?** (in some places, **¿qué horas son?**), what time is it?—**vete en h. mala,** (coll.) begone, get out of my sight. **II.** *adv.* now, at this time, at present.
horadable, *a.* capable of being pierced.
horadación, *f.* perforation; boring, piercing.
horadado, *m.* silkworm's cocoon bored through.
horadador, ra, *n.* & *a.* perforator(-ing); borer(-ing); burrower(-ing).
horadar, *va.* to perforate, bore; burrow.
horado, *m.* hole bored through; cavern, grotto.
horambre, *m.* hole in the cheeks of mills.
horario, ria. I. *a.* horary, horal, hour (as *a.*). **II.** *m.* hour hand of a clock or watch; (Ry.) timetable.
horca, *f.* gallows, gibbet; (agr.) hayfork, pitchfork; forked prop for trees or vines; yoke for dogs or hogs; rope or string of onions or garlic.
horcado, da, *a.* forked, forky.
horcadura, *f.* fork of a tree.
horcajadas, horcajadillas.—a h., astride or astraddle.
horcajadura, *f.* crotch (of human body).
horcajo, *m.* yoke or collar for mules; in oil mills, the Y-shaped division of the beam; fork or confluence of two streams.
horcate, *m.* hame (of a harness).
horco, *m.* rope or string of onions or garlic.
horcón, *m.* forked pole to support the branches of fruit trees.
horchata, *f.* orgeat, drink made from almonds.
horchatería, *f.* place where orgeat is sold.
horchatero, ra, *n.* orgeat maker or seller.
horda, *f.* horde.
hordiate, *m.* pearl barley; barley water.
horero, *m.* (S. A.) hour hand.
horizontal, *a.* & *f.* horizontal.
horizonte, *m.* horizon.—**h. artificial,** artificial horizon.—**h. racional,** celestial horizon, rational horizon.—**h. sensible,** sensible horizon, visible horizon (= horizon in the ordinary sense).
horma, *f.* mold, model; shoemaker's last; hatter's block; (mason.) dry wall.—**hallar la h. de su zapato,** (ironic) to meet with one's match.
hormadoras, *f. pl.* (Colomb.) underskirt.
hormaza, *f.* (mason.) dry wall.
hormazo, *m.* blow with a last or block; heap of stones; house and garden.
hormero, *m.* last maker.
hormiga, *f.* ant; (med.) itch or cutaneous pruritus.—**h. blanca,** (entom.) white ant.—**h. león,** (entom.) ant lion.—**h. melífera,** (entom.) honey ant.—**h. roja,** (entom.) horse ant.
hormigo, *m.* (min.) sifted ashes used in smelting quicksilver.—*pl.* sweetmeat of mashed almonds or filberts; coarse parts of flour or poorly-ground wheat.
[1]**hormigón,** *m.* (vet.) a disease of cattle; (bot.) a disease of some plants.
[2]**hormigón,** *m.* (eng.) concrete.—**h. armado,** reinforced concrete.—**h. hidráulico,** hydraulic-cement concrete; hydraulic-lime mortar.
hormigonera, *f.* concrete mixer.
hormigoso, sa, *a.* formicine; ant-eaten.
hormigueamiento, *m.* (med.) itching.
hormigueante, *a.* tingling, atingle; itching.
hormiguear, *vn.* to itch; to swarm.
hormigüela, *f. dim.* small ant.
hormigueo, *m.* (med.) itching.
hormiguero, *m.* formicary, ant hill, ants' nest; swarm, crowd, throng; pile of burned fertilizer; (ornith.) wryneck.
hormiguillar, *va.* (min.) to mix (grains of silver) with salt.
hormiguillo, *m.* (vet.) a disease of horses' hoofs; people ranged in a line, who pass materials or loads from hand to hand; (Mex.) a spicy sirup; almond sweatmeat; (min.) amalgamating mixture.
hormiguita, *f. dim.* small ant.
hormilla, *f. dim.* small last; buttonmold or core.
hormón, *m.,* **hormona,** *f.* (physiol.) hormone.
hormonal, *a.* hormonal.
hormónico, ca, *a.* hormonic.
hornabeque, *m.* (fort.) hornwork.
hornablenda, *f.* (min.) hornblende.
hornacero, *m.* (metal.) crucible man.
hornacina, *f.* (arch.) vaulted niche.
hornacho, *m.* shaft of a mine; furnace for casting statues.
hornachuela, *f.* cave or hut.
hornada, *f.* batch, bread baked at one time; melt (of a blast furnace).
hornaguear, *va.* to dig for coal.
hornaguera, *f.* pit coal, hard coal.
hornaguero, ra, *a.* wide, spacious; coal-bearing.
hornaje, *m.* fee for baking.
hornaza, *f.* jewellers' furnace; (art) light yellow color; yellow glazing.
hornazo, *m.* Easter cake ornamented with eggs; Easter present given to preacher.

hornear, *vn.* to carry on the trade of a baker.
hornería, *f.* trade of a baker.
hornero, ra, *n.* baker.
horniga, *f.* brushwood for an oven.
hornijero, ra, *n.* brushwood carrier.
hornilla, *f.* grated chamber in a masonry kitchen range; compartment in a pigeon cote for nesting; nest pan.
hornillo, *m. dim.* portable furnace or stove; (min.) blast hole; (mil.) fougade.—**h. de atanor,** self-feeding furnace.
hornito, *m.* (Mex.) mud volcano.
horno, *m.* oven; kiln; furnace; cavity in which bees lodge.—**h. boliche** = H. DE REVERBERO.—**h. de cal,** limekiln.—**h. de calcinación,** calcining furnace.—**h. de copela,** cupelling or cupellation furnace.—**h. de cuba,** blast furnace in general.—**h. de ladrillo,** brickkiln.—**h. de manga,** cupola furnace.—**h. de reverbero,** or **tostadillo,** Spanish furnace, or reverberatory furnace.—**h. eléctrico,** electric furnace.—**alto h.,** (high) blast furnace.
horología, *f.* horology.
horometría, *f.* horometry, measurement of time.
horón, *m.* large round hamper.
horópter, *m.* (opt.) horopter.
horoptérico, ca, *a.* (opt.) horopteric.
horóptero, *m.* (opt.) horopter.
horóscopo, *m.* horoscope.
horqueta, *f. dim.* forked pole or stake; crotch of a tree; (Arg.) sharp turn of a stream or of the adjacent land.
horquilla, *f.* forked pole, bar, pipe, etc.; pitchfork, croom; hairpin; double-pointed tack; a disease causing the hair to split; upper extremity of the sternum; wish-bone; (surg.) fourchette; (mil.) fork rest; (naut.) oarlock; (vet.) frog of a horse's foot.—*pl.* (naut.) crutches, curbs.—**horquillas de dar fuego,** breaming forks.
horrendamente, *adv.* horribly.
horrendo, da, *a.* hideous, horrible, awful.
hórreo, *m.* barn, mow; granary built on pillars.
horrero, *m.* keeper of a granary.
horribilidad, *f.* dreadfulness, hideousness.
horribilísimo, *a. super.* most horrible.
horrible, *a.* horrid, horrible; hideous, heinous.
horriblemente, *adv.* horribly; heinously.
horridez, *f.* horridness.
hórrido, da, *a.* horrible; hideous.
horrífico, ca, *a.* (poet.) horrific, awful, horrid.
horripilación, *f.* dread, fright; (med.) horripilation, goose flesh.
horripilante, *a.* horrifying, harrowing.
horripilar. I. *va.* & *vn.* to cause or feel horror. **II.** *vr.* to be horrified.
horripilativo, va, *a.* (med.) causing goose flesh.
horrísono, na, *a.* (poet.) of a terrifying noise.
horro, ra, *a.* enfranchised, freed; not pregnant.
horror, *m.* horror; enormity, hideousness, frightfulness.
horrorizado, da, *a.* horrified, horror-stricken.
horrorizar. I. *va.* to horrify, terrify. **II.** *vr.* to be terrified.
horrorosamente, *adv.* horribly.
horroroso, sa, *a.* horrible; hideous, frightful.
horrura, *f.* filth, dirt, scoria, dross.
hortaliza, *f.* garden produce, vegetables.
hortatorio, ria, *a.* = EXHORTATORIO, hortatory.
hortecillo, *m. dim.* small garden.
hortelana, *f.* gardener's wife.
hortelano, na. I. *a.* HORTENSE. **II.** *m.* horticulturist; (ornith.) ortolan.
hortense, *a.* pert. to kitchen garden or orchard.
hortensia, *f.* (bot.) hydrangea.
hortera. I. *f.* wooden bowl. **II.** *m.* in Madrid, drygoods clerk.
hortícola, *a.* horticultural.
horticultor, ra, *n.* horticulturist.
horticultura, *f.* horticulture.
horuelo, *m.* common; meeting place for young people.
hosanna, *m.* (eccl.) hosanna.
hosco, ca, *a.* dark-colored (as a mulatto); sullen, gloomy.
hoscoso, sa, *a.* crisp, rough.
hospedador, ra, *n.* one who gives lodging.
hospedaje, hospedamiento, *m.* lodging, board.
hospedar. I. *va.* to lodge, harbor. **II.** *vn.* & *vr.* **(en)** to lodge or take lodgings (at); to stop (at), live (in).
hospedería, *f.* hospice; hostel in universities; hostelry, inn; spare room, guest room; lodging.
hospedero, ra, *n.* host; innkeeper.
hospiciano, na, *n.* poor person who lives in a house of charity.
hospicio, *m.* hospice; poor house; orphan asylum.
hospital, *m.* hospital.—**h. de sangre,** (mil.) field hospital.
hospitalario, ria. I. *a.* hospitable. **II.** *m.* Hospitaler.
hospitalero, ra, *n.* hospital manager; hospitaler; hospitable person.
hospitalidad, *f.* hospitality; hospitalizing, stay in a hospital.
hospitalización, *f.* hospitalization.
hospitalizar, *va.* to hospitalize.
hospitalmente, *adv.* hospitably.
hostal, *m.* hostelry, inn.
hostalero, ra, *n.* inn or tavern keeper, host(-ess).
hostelero, ra, *n.* innkeeper, tavern keeper.
hostería, *f.* inn, tavern, hostelry.
hostia, *f.* sacrificial victim; (eccl.) host, wafer; sugar wafer.—**hostiario,** *m.* wafer box.—**hostiero,** *m.* person who prepares the host.
hostigador, ra, *a.* = HOSTIGOSO.
hostigamiento, *m.* chastisement; vexation.
hostigar, *va.* (*pret.* HOSTIGUÉ; *subj.* HOSTIGUE) to lash, scourge, chastise; to vex, trouble, harass; to gall, bore, tire; (Am.) to satiate, become distasteful to.
hostigo, *m.* lash; weather-beaten wall; beating of rain and wind against a wall.—**hostigoso, sa,** *a.* (Chile & Guat.) tiresome, boring; satiating.
hostigué, hostigue, *v. V.* HOSTIGAR.
hostil, *a.* hostile.—**hostilidad,** *f.* hostility.
hostilizar, *va.* (*pret.* HOSTILICÉ; *subj.* HOSTILICE) to commit hostilities against, be hostile to, antagonize.
hostilmente, *adv.* with hostility.
hotel, *m.* hotel; villa.—**hotelero, ra,** *n.* hotel manager.
hotentote, ta, *n.* & *a.* Hottentot.
hovero, ra, *a.* = OVERO, peach-colored (horse).
hoy, *adv.* to-day; now, at the present time, nowadays.—**h. día,** or **h. en día,** nowadays.—**h. mismo,** this very day.—**h. por h.,** at the present time; for the present; this very day.—**de h. a mañana,** before to-morrow; when you least expect it.—**de h. en adelante,** or **de h. más,** henceforward, in future.—**por h.,** for the present.
hoya, *f.* hole, pit; grave; valley, dale, glen; basin (of a river).
hoyada, *f.* low dale.
hoyanca, *f.* potter's field in cemeteries.
hoyito, *m. dim.* small hole.
hoyo, *m.* hole, pit, excavation; dent, indentation, hollow; pockmark; grave.
hoyoso, sa, *a.* full of holes.
hoyuela, *f. dim.* of HOYA; hollow in the neck below Adam's apple.
boyuelo, *m. dim.* small hole; dimple.
[1]**hoz,** *f.* sickle.—**meter la h. en mies ajena,** to meddle in others' affairs.
[2]**hoz,** *f.* defile, narrow pass; ravine.—**de h. y de coz,** (coll.) headlong.
hozadero, *m.* hogs' rooting place.
hozadura, *f.* rooting (of hogs).
hozar, *va.* to root (as hogs).
huaca, *f.* = GUACA, Indian burying ground.
huacal, *m.* crate; (Mex.) hurdle basket.
huaco, *m.* idol found in HUACAS.
huaico, *m.* (Peru) large mass of rock fallen into a river or stream.
huairuro, *m.* Peruvian variety of red bean.

huaquero, *m.* (Peru) pitcher found in HUACAS.
huarache, *m.* (Mex.) sandal.
huasca, *f.* (Peru) whip, lash.
hube, hubo, *v.* *V.* HABER.
hucha, *f.* large chest; money box, bank; savings.
huchear, *va.* to hoot, shout, cry out, call.
¡húchohó! *interj.* used to call birds.
huebra, *f.* ground plowed in one day by a yoke of oxen; pair of mules with a plowman hired for a day's work.—**huebrero,** *m.* laborer who plows with a pair of mules; one who lets out mules by the day.
hueca, *f.* spiral groove of a spindle.
hueco, ca. I. *a.* hollow; empty; vain, empty-headed; resonant; inflated; soft, spongy (as ground or wool). **II.** *m.* hole; hollow, gap, void, break; notch or nick of a wheel; interval of time or space; vacancy.
huecograbado, *m.* rotogravure.
huecú, *m.* (Chile) deep slough covered with grass.
huélfago, *m.* (of animals) difficulty in breathing.
huelga, *f.* rest, repose, leisure; strike (of workers); recreation, merrymaking; (agr.) lying fallow; (mech.) windage.—**h. de hambre,** hunger strike.—**h. de solidaridad,** sympathy strike.—**h. sentada,** sit-down strike.
[1]**huelgo,** *m.* breath, respiration; (mech.) windage; room, space, play.—**tomar h.,** to take breath.
[2]**huelgo, huelgue,** *v.* *V.* HOLGAR.
huelguista, *n.* striker.
huelguístico, ca, *a.* (workers') strike (as *a.*).
huelo, huela, etc., *v.* *V.* OLER.
huella, *f.* track, footstep, footprint; tread; trampling; stair tread, treadboard; impression; trace, vestige, trail.
[1]**huello,** *m.* treading; lower part of an animal's hoof.
[2]**huello, huelle,** *v.* *V.* HOLLAR.
huequecito, *m. dim.* small hole or space.
huérfago, *m.* (vet.) = HUÉLFAGO.
huerfanito, ita, *n. dim.* little orphan.
huérfano, na, *n.* & *a.* orphan(-ed).
huero, ra, *a.* empty, vain; (Mex.) fair, blonde.
huerta, *f.* large vegetable or kitchen garden; irrigated land.
huertezuela, *f. dim.* small kitchen garden.
huertezuelo, *m. dim.* small orchard.
huerto, *m.* orchard, fruit garden.
huesa, *f.* grave, tomb.
huesarrón, *m. aug.* large bone.
huesecico, illo, ito, *m. dim.* little bone.
hueso, *m.* bone; stone, core; part of a limestone which remains unburnt in the kiln; drudge, drudgery.—**h. duro de roer,** (coll.) a hard nut to crack, hard to deal with.—**h. innominado,** (anat.) innominate bone.—**h. malar,** (anat.) zygomatic bone.—**h. navicular,** (anat.) scaphoid or navicular bone.—**h. occipital,** (anat.) occipital bone.—**h. palomo,** (anat.) coccyx.—**h. sacro,** (anat.) sacrum.—**h. temporal,** (anat.) temporal, temporal bone.—**a h.,** (mason.) dry (without mortar).—**a otro perro con ese h.,** tell that to the marines.—**estar en los huesos,** to be a bag of bones, be nothing but skin and bones.—**la sin h.,** the tongue.—**no dejar h. sano a,** (fig.) to rake over the coals.—**no poder con sus huesos,** (coll.) to be dog tired.—**soltar la sin h.,** (coll.) to talk one's head off, talk too much.—**tener los huesos molidos,** (coll.) to be tired to death, be all in.
huesoso, sa, *a.* bony, osseous.
huésped, da, *n.* guest, lodger; host(-ess) innkeeper, tavern keeper.
hueste, *f.* host, army.
huesudo, da, *a.* bony, having large bones.
hueva, *f.* spawn of fishes, roe. Also OVAS, *pl.*
huevar, *vn.* (of poultry) to begin to lay.
huevecico, illo, ito, zuelo, *m. dim.* small egg.
huevera, *f.* ovary of birds; egg stand, egg cup.
huevería, *f.* egg shop.
huevero, ra, *n.* egg dealer.
huevo, *m.* egg; (shoe) hollow piece of wood for shaping the sole.—**h. de Colón,** or **de juanelo,** anything that seems difficult to do, but is easy after one learns how to do it.—**h. duro,** hard (boiled, fried) egg.—**huevos de faltriquera,** candied yolks of egg.—**huevos escalfados,** poached eggs.—**huevos estrellados,** fried eggs.—**huevos hilados,** threadlike sweetmeat made of eggs and sugar.—**huevos moles,** yolks of eggs made up with pounded almonds and sugar.—**huevos pasados por agua,** soft-boiled eggs.—**huevos revueltos,** scrambled eggs.—**huevos y torreznos,** bacon and eggs.—**sórbete,** or **chúpate, ese h.,** (coll.) put that in your pipe and smoke it.
hugonote, ta, *n.* & *a.* Huguenot.
huída, *f.* flight, escape; outlet.
huidero, *m.* cover, shelter; laborer in quick-silver mines.
huidizo, za, *a.* fugitive, fleeing.
huillín, *m.* a kind of Chilean otter.
huipil, *m.* (Am.) Aztec woman's garment.
huir. I. *vn.* & *vr.* (*ger.* HUYENDO; *ind. pres.* HUYO, *pret.* él HUYÓ; *subj.* HUYA) to flee, to escape; to run away, elope; to slip away, fly; (**de**) to keep away (from), shun, avoid. **II.** *va.* to avoid, shun.—**h. la cara de,** to avoid, keep away from.
hule, *m.* oilcloth, oilskin; (Am.) India rubber.
hulero, *m.* rubber gatherer.
hulla, *f.* mineral (gen. bituminous) coal.—**h. aglutinante,** coking coal.—**h. blanca,** white coal (water).—**h. conglutinante,** coking coal.—**h. grasa,** fat coal.—**h. magra,** non-coking coal.
hullero, ra. I. *a.* containing or pertaining to soft coal. **II.** *f.* colliery.
humada, *f.* = AHUMADA, smoke signal from coast.
humanamente, *adv.* humanely; humanly.
humanar. I. *va.* to humanize; to soften. **II.** *vr.* to become man; to become human.
humanidad, *f.* humanity; mankind; human weakness; humaneness; (coll.) corpulence, fleshiness.—*pl.* humanities.
humanista, *n.* humanist, scholar.
humanitario, ria, *a.* humanitarian.
humanitarismo, *m.* humanitarianism.
humanizar, *va.* & *vr.* = HUMANAR.
humano, na. I. *a.* human; humane. **II.** *m.* man, human being.
humarazo, *m.* = HUMAZO.
humareda, *f.* a great deal of smoke.
humazga, *f.* hearth money, fumage.
humazo, *m.* dense and abundant smoke.
humeante, *a.* smoking, fuming, fumant.
humear. I. *vn.* to smoke, emit smoke, fumes, or vapors. **II.** *va.* (Am.) to fumigate.
humectación, *f.* dampening.
humectante, *a.* (med.) moistening.
humectar, *va.* (med.) to moisten, wet.—**humectativo, va,** *a.* moistening.
humedad, *f.* humidity, moisture, dampness.
humedal, *m.* humid soil, marsh.
humedecedor, *m.* humidifier.
humedecer, *va.* (*ind.* HUMEDEZCO; *subj.* HUMEDEZCA) to moisten, dampen.
humedecimiento, *m.* humidification.
húmedo, da, *a.* humid, wet, moist, damp.
humera, *f.* (coll.) fit of drunkenness.
humeral, *a.* (anat.) humeral.
húmero, *m.* (anat.) humerus.
humero, *m.* smoke pipe; chimney flue; meat-smoking place; much smoke.
húmico, ca, *a.* humic; (chem.) humic.
húmido, da, *a.* = HÚMEDO.
humildad, *f.* humility; meekness; lowliness.
humilde, *a.* humble; meek; lowly.
humildemente, *adv.* humbly, modestly, meekly.
humillación, *f.* humiliation; humbling.
humilladero, *m.* road chapel or shrine.
humillador, ra, *n.* & *a.* humiliator(-ing).
humillante, *a.* humiliating.
humillar. I. *va.* to humiliate; humble; crush,

subdue. **II.** *vr.* to humble oneself; to lower oneself.
humillo, *m. dim.* (gen. *pl.*) vanity, petty pride; a disease of suckling pigs.
humita, *f.* (Peru) cake of maize and sugar.
humo, *m.* smoke; vapor, steam, fume.—*pl.* families or houses in a town or village; airs, conceit. —**echar humos,** to put on airs.
humor, *m.* humor, wit; disposition, temper; (physiol.) body fluid.—**h. acuoso,** (physiol.) aqueous humor.—**buen h.,** good nature, jovial disposition.—**estar de buen (mal) h.,** to be in good (bad) humor or spirits.—**mal h.,** ill temper.
humorada, *f.* pleasant joke, humorous saying.
humorado, da, *a.* full of humors.—**bien (mal) h.,** in good (bad) humor; having a good (bad) temper.
humoral, *a.* (physiol.) pert. to body fluid.
humorcico, illo, ito, *m. dim.* little temper.
humorismo, *m.* humor (esp. in literary style); (anc. med.) humorism.
humorista. I. *a.* humorous. **II.** *n.* humorist.
humorístico, ca, *a.* jolly, humorous, facetious.
humorosidad, *f.* abundance of humors.
humoroso, sa, *a.* watery, containing fluid.
humoso, sa, *a.* smoky, fumy.
humus, *m.* humus.
hundible, *a.* sinkable.
hundimiento, *m.* sinking; cave-in; downfall, collapse.
hundir. I. *va.* to submerge, sink; stave in, crush; destroy, ruin; to refute, confound. **II.** *vr.* to sink, be sinking; to cave in, fall down, crumble, collapse; (coll.) to hide, lie in hiding, disappear.
húngaro, ra, *n.* & *a.* Hungarian.
Hungría, *f.* Hungary.
huno, na, *n.* & *a.* Hun(-nish).
hupe, *f.* punk, touchwood, amadou.
hura, *f.* carbuncle on the head.
huracán, *m.* hurricane.—**huracanado, da,** *a.* of hurricane proportions.
hurañamente, *adv.* unsociably, shyly.
hurañería, hurañía, *f.* unsociability; shyness.
huraño, ña, *a.* unsociable, shy.
hurgar, *va.* (*pret.* HURGUÉ; *subj.* HURGUE) to stir, to poke; to stir up, excite.—**peor es hurgallo,** let well enough alone.
hurgón, *m.* poker, fire rake; (coll.) thrust with a sword.—**hurgonada,** *f.* poking (the fire); thrust.—**hurgonazo,** *m.* blow with a poker; thrust.—**hurgonear,** *va.* to poke (the fire); (coll.) to make a thrust at.—**hurgonero,** *m.* fire poker.
hurgué, hurgue, *v. V.* HURGAR.
hurí, *f.* houri.
hurón, na. I. *n.* (zool.) ferret; (coll.) ferreter, prier. **II.** *a.* unsociable, shy.—**huronear,** *va.* to hunt with a ferret; (coll.) to pry into; to ferret out.—**huronera,** *f.* ferret hole; (coll.) lurking-place; small dark room.—**huronero,** *m.* ferret keeper.
¡hurra! *interj.* hurrah!
hurraca, *f.* (ornith.) magpie.
hurtadillas.—a h., *adv.* by stealth, on the sly.
hurtadineros, *m.* money box, toy bank.
hurtador, ra, *n.* robber, thief.
hurtagua, *f.* watering pot.
hurtar. I. *va.* to steal, rob of, to cheat in weight or measure; to eat away (land, as the sea or a river); to alienate.—**h. el cuerpo,** to flee; to dodge, shy away. **II.** *vr.* to withdraw, move away; to hide.
hurto, *m.* theft, robbery, stealing; thing stolen; (min.) driftway, heading.—**a h.,** by stealth.
husada, *f.* spindleful of yarn.
húsar, *m.* (mil.) hussar.
husero, *m.* beam of an antler.
husillero, *m.* one who tends the spindle in oil mills.
[1]**husillo,** *m. dim.* small spindle; (mill) wheel spindle or shaft; screw pin.
[2]**husillo,** *m.* (dirty water) drain.
husita, *n.* Hussite.
husma.—andar a la h., (coll.) to explore in a prying manner, to nose about.
husmeador, ra, *n.* & *a.* scenter(-ing); prier(-ing), noser(-ing, -y).
husmear. I. *va.* to scent, smell, wind; (coll.) to pry, peep, nose into. **II.** *vn.* (of meat) to become tainted, gamey, or high.
husmeo, *m.* scenting, smelling; prying, nosing.
husmo, *m.* taint of meat.—**estar al h.,** (coll.) to be on the scent; to wait or watch for a favorable opportunity.
huso, *m.* spindle; cop tube; bobbin; drum of a windlass; (aer.) fuselage.
huta, *f.* hut, hunter's blind.
hutía, *f.* (zool.) hutia, a West-Indian rodent.
¡huy! *interj.* of surprise, astonishment, grief or alarm.
huyo, huya, huyó, etc. *v. V.* HUIR.
hyaluronidasa, *f.* (med.) hyaluronidase.

I

[1]**I, i,** *f.* i, tenth letter of the Spanish alphabet.
[2]**i,** *conj.* and (used in some parts of S. A.).
iba, *imperf.* of IR.
iberamericano, na, *a.* & *n.* (Am.) = IBEROAMERICANO.
ibérico, ca, *a.*; **iberio, ria,** *a.*; **ibero, ra,** *n.* & *a.* Iberian.
iberoamericano, na, *n.* & *a.* Latin-American.
íbice, *m.* ibex, a kind of goat.
ibídem, *adv.* ibidem, in the same place.
ibis, *f.* (ornith.) ibis, a wading bird.
ibiyaú, *m.* an Argentine night bird.
ibón, *m.* lake or basin on the slopes of the Pyrenees.
icaco, *m.* (bot.) coco plum.
icario, a, *a.* Icarian.
icástico, ca, *a.* natural, plain, unadorned.
iceberg, *m.* iceberg.
icneumón, *m.* (zool.) ichneumon.—**mosca i.,** (entom.) ichneumon, ichneumon fly.
icnografía, *f.* (arch.) ichnography.
icnográfico, ca, *a.* ichnographical.
icnología, *f.* ichnology.
icón, icono, *m.* icon.
iconoclasta. I. *a.* iconoclastic. **II.** *n.* iconoclast.
iconoclastia, *f.* iconoclasm.
iconografía, *f.* iconography.
iconográfico, ca, *a.* iconographical.
iconólatra, *m.* iconolater, worshipper of icons.
iconología, *f.* (art) iconology.
iconómaco, *a.* iconoclastic.
iconoscopio, *m.* Iconoscope (trademark).
iconostasio, *m.* (eccl.) iconostasis, altar screen.
icor, *m.* (med.) watery discharge (as from a wound).
icoroso, sa, *a.* ichorous, serous.
icosaedro, *m.* (geom.) icosahedron.
ictericia, *f.* (med.) icterus, jaundice.
ictericiado, da, ictérico, ca, *a.* icteric, icterical, jaundiced.
ictíneo, *m.* submarine vessel.
ictiofagia, *f.* ichthyophagy.
ictiófago, ga. I. *a.* ichthyophagous, fish-eating. **II.** *n.* ichthyophagous person.
ictioideo, dea, *m.* & *a.* ichthyoid.
ictiol, *m.* (chem.) ichthyol.
ictiología, *f.* ichthyology.
ictiológico, ca, *a.* ichthyologic.
ictiólogo, *m.* ichthyologist.
ictiornis, *m.* (paleontol.) ichthyornis.
ictiosauro, *m.* ichthyosaurus.
ictiosis, *f.* ichthyosis.
ida, *f.* departure; trip out; impetuosity; rash proceeding; sally; trail.—**i. del humo,** departure never to return.—**i. y vuelta,** out and back, round trip, excursion.—**idas,** frequent visits.—**idas y venidas,** comings and goings.—**de i. y vuelta,** return (ticket).—**en dos idas y venidas,** (coll.) in a jiffy.—**¡la i. del cuervo!** he's off, good riddance!

idea, *f.* idea.
ideación, *f.* (philos.) ideation.
ideal, *m.* & *a.* ideal.
idealidad, *f.* ideality.
idealismo, *m.* idealism.
idealista. **I.** *a.* idealistic, idealistical. **II.** *n.* idealist; ideologist.
idealización, *f.* idealization.
idealizar, *va.* to idealize.
idear, *va.* to conceive the idea of; to devise, contrive, plan, design.
ideario, *m.* philosophy, system of ideas and principles, ideology.
ideático, ca, *a.* (Am.) whimsical, capricious.
ídem, idem, ditto, the same.
idénticamente, *adv.* identically.
idéntico, ca, *a.* (a) identic, identical (with).
identidad, *f.* identity.—**de i.,** identification (as a.).
identificación, *f.* identification.
identificar, (*pret.* IDENTIFIQUÉ; *subj.* IDENTIFIQUE). **I.** *va.* to identify. **II.** *vr.* **(con)** to identify oneself (with).
ideo, ea, *a.* pertaining to Mount Ida.
ideografía, *f.* ideography.
ideográfico, ca, *a.* ideographic.
ideograma, *m.* ideogram.
ideología, *f.* ideology.
ideológico, ca, *a.* ideological.
ideólogo, *m.* ideologist.
idílico, ca, *a.* idyllic.
idilio, *m.* idyl.
idioelectricidad, *f.* idioelectricity.
idioeléctrico, ca, *a.* idioelectric.
idioma, *m.* language, tongue.
idiomático, ca, *a.* idiomatic.
idiomorfismo, *m.* (cryst.) idiomorphism.
idiomorfo, fa, *a.* (cryst.) idiomorphic.
idiopatía, *f.* idiopathy.
idiopático, ca, *a.* idiopathic.
idiosincrasia, *f.* idiosyncrasy.
idiosincrásico, ca, *a.* idiosyncratic.
idiota. **I.** *a.* idiotic. **II.** *n.* idiot.
idiotez, *f.* idiocy, idiotism.
idiotismo, *m.* idiocy; ignorance; idiom.
ido, *pp.* of IR.
idólatra. **I.** *a.* idolatrous; heathen. **II.** *n.* idolater; (coll.) ardent lover.
idolatradamente, *adv.* idolatrously.
idolatrar, *va.* to idolize, worship, adore.
idolatría, *f.* idolatry; idolization.
idolátrico, ca, *a.* idolatrous.
ídolo, *m.* idol.
idolología, *f.* science dealing with idols.
idoneidad, *f.* competence, fitness, capacity.
idóneo, nea, *a.* competent; fit, able.
idumeo, a, *n.* & *a.* Idumean.
idus, *m.* ides.
iglesia, *f.* church; ecclesiastical state; clergy; chapter; diocese; right of immunity enjoyed in churches.—**i. anglicana,** Church of England.—**i. colegial,** collegiate church.—**i. matriz,** metropolitan church.—**i. mayor,** main church; cathedral.—**i. militante,** church militant.—**i. oriental,** Greek Church.—**i. ortodoxa,** Orthodox Church.—**i. ritualista,** High Church.—**i. triunfante,** church triumphant.—**llevar a una mujer a la i.,** to take a woman to the altar, get married.
iglesiero, ra, *n.* & *a.* churchgoing.
iglú, *m.* igloo.
ignaro, ra, *a.* ignorant.
ignavia, *f.* idleness, laziness, carelessness.
ígneo, ea, *a.* igneous.
ignición, *f.* ignition.
ignícola. **I.** *a.* fire-worshiping. **II.** *n.* fire-worshiper.
ignífero, ra, *a.* igniferous, fire-bearing.
ignífugo, ga, *a.* fireproofing.
ignipotente, *a.* (poet.) ignipotent.
igniscencia, *f.* ignescence.
ignitibilidad, *f.* ignitibility, inflammability.
ignitible, *a.* ignitible, ignitable, inflammable.
ignito, ta, *a.* ignited, inflamed, red-hot.
ignitor, *m.* igniter.
ignitrón, *m.* (elec.) ignitron.
ignívomo, ma, *a.* (poet.) vomiting fire.
ignografía, *f.* = ICNOGRAFIA.
ignominia, *f.* ignominy, infamy, disgrace.
ignominiosamente, *adv.* ignominiously.
ignominioso, sa, *a.* ignominious.
ignorado, da. **I.** *pp.* of IGNORAR. **II.** *a.* unknown, hidden; fameless, obscure.
ignorancia, *f.* ignorance.—**i. crasa,** crass ignorance.—**i. no quita pecado,** ignorance of the law is no defense.—**i. supina,** ignorance from negligence.
ignorante. **I.** *a.* ignorant. **II.** *n.* ignoramus.
ignorantemente, *adv.* ignorantly.—**ignorantón, na.** **I.** *a. aug.* rather ignorant. **II.** *n.* ignoramus.
ignorar, *va.* to be ignorant of, not to know.
ignoto, ta, *a.* unknown, undiscovered.
igorrote, *m.* Igorrot, Luzon hunting tribesman; Igorrot language.
igual. **I.** *a.* equal; level, even, uniform; equable; constant, firm, unchangeable, consistent.—**i. que** (common but incorrect for *igual a*), equal to, the same as.—**(me) es i.,** it is all the same (to me), it makes no difference (to me). **II.** *m.* equal; (math.) equal sign (=).—**al i.,** equally.—**al i. que,** the same as, as well as.—**en i. de,** instead of, in lieu of.—**por i.,** or **por un i.,** equally; evenly.—**serle a uno i.,** to be all the same, a matter of indifference, to one.—**sin i.,** unrivaled, matchless; without parallel.
iguala, *f.* agreement, convention, stipulation; equalizing, equalization; (mason.) level; stipend or gratuity on agreement.—**a la i.,** equally.
igualación, *f.* equalizing, equalization; levelling, smoothing; matching; agreement, stipulation; (math.) equating; (carp.) countergauge.
igualado, da. **I.** *pp.* of IGUALAR. **II.** *a.* equalled (said of birds with even plumage).
igualador, ra. **I.** *a.* equalizing; smoothing; levelling. **II.** *n.* equalizer; smoother; leveller.—**i. de atenuación,** (rad.) attenuator equalizer.
igualamiento, *m.* = IGUALACIÓN.
igualar. **I.** *va.* to equalize; to match, mate, pair; to even, level, smooth; to size, face, adjust, fit; to hold in equal estimation; to adjust; (math.) to equate. **II.** *vn.* to be equal; (sports) to be tied (in score). **III.** *vr.* **(a, con)** to put oneself on the same plane (as), compare oneself (with).
igualdad, *f.* equality; evenness, smoothness, regularity, uniformity.—**i. de ánimo,** evenness of disposition; constancy, equability, equanimity.—**signo de la i.,** (math.) equal sign.
igualitario, ria, *a.* equalizing; equitable.
igualmente, *adv.* equally; likewise; constantly.
iguana, *f.* (zool.) iguana.
iguanodonte, *m.* (zool.) iguanodon.
igüedo, *m.* buck (goat).
ijada, *f.* flank (of an animal); pain in the side; colic—**tener su i.,** to have a weak side or point.
ijadear, *vn.* to pant; to palpitate.
ijar, *m.* flank (of an animal).
ilación, *f.* illation, inference; connectedness.
ilativo, va, *a.* illative, inferential.
ilegal, *a.* illegal, unlawful.
ilegalidad, *f.* illegality, unlawfulness.
ilegalmente, *adv.* illegally, unlawfully.
ilegibilidad, *f.* illegibility.
ilegible, *a.* illegible.
ilegítimamente, *adv.* illegitimately; foully.
ilegitimar, *va.* to make illegitimate.
ilegitimidad, *f.* illegitimacy.
ilegítimo, ma, *a.* illegal, unlawful; illegitimate.
íleo, *m.* (med.) ileus, colic.
[1]**íleon,** *m.* (anat.) ileum, part of intestine.
[2]**íleon,** *m.* (anat.) = ILION.
ileso, sa, *a.* unhurt, unscathed; harmless; sound.
iletrado, da, *a.* ignorant, uncultured.
[1]**ilíaco, ca,** *a.* iliac, pert. to the ilium.
[2]**ilíaco, ca,** *a.* pertaining to Ilium (Troy).

Ilíada, *f.* Iliad.
iliberal, *a.* illiberal.
iliberalidad, *f.* illiberality.
ilicíneo, a, *a.* (bot.) ilicineous.
ilícitamente, *adv.* illicitly, unlawfully.
ilícito, ta, *a.* illicit; unlawful; immoral.
ilicitud, *f.* illicitness, unlawfulness.
ilimitable, *a.* illimitable.
ilimitado, da, *a.* unlimited, boundless; unrestricted.
ilion, *m.* (anat.) ilium.
ilíquido, da, *a.* unliquidated.
ilírico, ca; ilirio, ria, *n.* & *a.* Illyrian.
iliterato, *a.* illiterate, unlearned.
ilógico, ca, *a.* illogical.
ilota, *m.* helot.
ilotismo, *m.* helotism.
iludir, *va.* to elude.
iluminación, *f.* illumination, lighting; (art) painting in distemper.
iluminado, da. I. *pp.* of ILUMINAR. **II.** *a.* illuminate, enlightened. **III.** *m. pl.* illuminati.
iluminador, ra. I. *a.* illuminating, illuminative. **II.** *n.* illuminator.
iluminante, *a.* illuminant, illuminating.
iluminar, *va.* to illumine, illuminate, light; to color, illumine (books); to enlighten.
iluminaria, *f.* = LUMINARIA, illumination.
iluminativo, va, *a.* illuminating.
iluminismo, *m.* Illuminism.
ilusión, *f.* illusion.—**hacerse ilusiones sobre,** to bank on.—**tener ilusiones de** (*inf.*), to have hopes of (*pres. p.*).
ilusionar. I. *va.* to cause illusion, fascinate. **II.** *vr.* **(con)** to have illusions; to get up hopes (of).
ilusionista, *n.* illusionist, visionary.
ilusivo, va, *a.* illusive, false, deceiving.
iluso, sa, *a.* deluded, deceived, beguiled.
ilusoriamente, *adv.* illusively, illusorily.
ilusorio, ria, *a.* illusory, deceptive; (law) null, void, nugatory.
ilustración, *f.* illustration; learning, erudition; elucidation, explanation; enlightment; learning; illustrated or pictorial publication.
ilustrado, da. I. *pp.* of ILUSTRAR. **II.** *a.* illustrated, picture (as *a.*); learned, well-informed.
ilustrador, ra. I. *a.* illustrative. **II.** *n.* illustrator.
ilustrar. I. *va.* to illustrate (a publication); to enlighten; to explain, elucidate; (theol.) to give divine light to, to inspire. **II.** *vr.* to educate oneself, to acquire knowledge, learn; to become illustrious.
ilustrativo, va, *a.* illustrative.
ilustre, *a.* illustrious, distinguished.
ilustremente, *adv.* illustriously.
ilustrísimo, ma, *a. super.* very illustrious, most illustrious (title given to bishops).
imadas, *f. pl.* (naut.) ways, sliding planks.
imagen, *f.* image.—**i. ampliada,** blown up image. —**i. confusa,** blurred image.—**i. de bulto,** image in sculpture; high relief.—**i. desenfocada,** out-of-focus image.—**i. fantasma,** (TV) ghost image, double image.—**i. nítida,** clear or sharp image.
imaginable, *a.* imaginable.
imaginación, *f.* imagination; imagining.
imaginar. I. *va.* to imagine; to think up, figure out; to think, suspect. **II.** *vr.* to imagine; to suspect; to picture to oneself, often used imperatively in a somewhat expletive or emphatic manner, in the sense of "just think," "just imagine," "why," etc. (*imagínese Vd. que no teníamos ni un centavo,* just think, we did not have a cent; *imagínese Vd. que allá hasta los niños fuman,* why, there even children smoke).
imaginariamente, *adv.* imaginatively.
imaginario, ria. I. *a.* imaginary, imaginative; (math.) imaginary. **II.** *f.* (mil.) reserve guard.
imaginativa, *f.* imagination, fancy.
imaginativo, va, *a.* imaginative, fanciful.
imaginería, *f.* imagery, fancy embroidery in colors; (art) statuary.
imaginero, *m.* painter or sculptor of religious images.
imago, *m.* (zool.) imago (adult form of an insect).
[1]**imán,** *m.* imam (Mohammedan priest).
[2]**imán,** *m.* magnet; (fig.) magnetism, loadstone.—**i. director,** (elec.) control or directing magnet. —**i. freno,** (elec.) braking magnet.—**i. móvil,** (elec.) moving magnet.
imanación, *f.* magnetization.
imanar, *va.* to magnetize.
imantación, *f.* = IMANACIÓN.
imantar, *va.* = IMANAR.
imbécil, *n.* & *a.* imbecile.
imbecilidad, *f.* imbecility, stupidity.
imbele, *a.* feeble, weak; unfit for war.
imberbe, *a.* beardless.
imbibición, *f.* imbibition, imbibing.
imbornal, *m.* (naut.) scupper hole.
imborrable, *a.* indelible, ineffaceable.
imbricación, *f.* imbrication, overlapping.
imbricado, da, *a.* imbricated, overlapped.
imbuir, *va.* (*ind.* IMBUYO; *subj.* IMBUYA) to imbue, infuse, persuade.
imbursación, *f.* putting into a sack.
imbursar, *va.* to put into a sack or bag.
imbuyo, imbuya, *v. V.* IMBUIR.
imitable, *a.* imitable.
imitación, *f.* imitation.
imitado, da. I. *pp.* of IMITAR. **II.** *a.* imitation (as *a.*), mock.
imitador, ra. I. *a.* imitative. **II.** *n.* imitator.
imitante, *a.* imitating, given to imitating.
imitar, *va.* to imitate; to mimic; to ape; to counterfeit.
imitativo, va, *a.* imitative (as arts).
imóscapo, *m.* (arch.) apophyge.
impacción, *f.* impact, collision.
impaciencia, *f.* impatience.
impacientar. I. *va.* to vex, irritate, make (one) lose patience. **II.** *vr.* to become impatient.
impaciente, *a.* impatient; anxious; peevish.
impacientemente, *adv.* impatiently, anxiously; peevishly.
impactado, da, *a.* (dent.) impacted.
impacto, *m.* impact.—**i. lunar,** lunar impact.
impagable, *a.* unpayable.
impalpabilidad, *f.* impalpability.
impalpable, *a.* impalpable.
impanación, *f.* (theol.) impanation.
impar, *a.* unmatched, odd; (arith.) odd.
imparcial, *a.* impartial.
imparcialidad, *f.* impartiality.
impartible, *a.* indivisible.
impartir, *va.* to impart; (law) to demand or require (assistance).
impasable, *a.* impassable.
impasibilidad, *f.* impassiveness.
impasible, *a.* impassive, unmoved.
impávidamente, *adv.* undauntedly, calmly.
impavidez, *f.* intrepidity, calm, composure.
impávido, da, *a.* dauntless, intrepid, calm.
impecabilidad, *f.* impeccability.
impecable, *a.* impeccable.
impedancia, *f.* (elec.) impedance.—**i. de entrada,** (elec.) input impedance.—**i. iterativa,** (elec.) iterative impedance.—**impedancias de imágenes,** (elec.) image impedances.
impedido, da. I. *pp.* of IMPEDIR. **II.** *a.* disabled, crippled.
impedidor, ra, *n.* obstructor.
impediente, *a.* hindering, obstructing.
impedimenta, *f.* (mil.) impedimenta.
impedimento, *m.* impediment; obstacle, hindrance, encumbrance.
impedir, *va.* (*ind.* IMPIDO; *subj.* IMPIDA) to impede, hinder, prevent; to block (the way); (poet.) to suspend.
impeditivo, va, *a.* impeding, hindering.
impelente, *a.* forcing, impelling, propelling.
impeler, *va.* to push, impel, drive; to spur, urge, incite, move.
impender, *va.* to spend, invest.
impenetrabilidad, *f.* impenetrability.

impenetrable, *a.* impenetrable, impervious; incomprehensible; fathomless.
impenitencia, *f.* impenitence.
impenitente, *a.* impenitent, obdurate.
impensa, *f.* (law) expense.
impensable, *a.* unthinkable.
impensadamente, *adv.* unexpectedly; inadvertently.
impensado, da, *a.* unexpected, unforeseen.
imperante, *a.* commanding; (astrol.) ruling.
imperar, *vn.* to command; to reign; to prevail.
imperativamente, *adv.* imperatively.
imperativo, va. I. *a.* imperative; domineering, "bossy." **II.** *n.* & *a.* (gram.) imperative.
imperatoria, *f.* (bot.) masterwort.
imperatorio, ria, *a.* imperial.
imperceptibilidad, *f.* imperceptibility, imperceptibleness.
imperceptible, *a.* imperceptible.
imperceptiblemente, *adv.* imperceptibly.
imperdible. I. *a.* that cannot be lost. **II.** *m.* safety pin.
imperdonable, *a.* unpardonable, unforgivable.
imperecedero, ra, *a.* imperishable, undying.
imperfección, *f.* imperfection, defect, fault, flaw.
imperfectamente, *adv.* imperfectly, inadequately.
imperfecto, ta. I. *a.* imperfect, defective, faulty. **II.** *n.* & *a.* (gram.) imperfect.
imperforación, *f.* (med.) imperforation.
imperforado, da, *a.* imperforate, imperforated.
imperial. I. *a.* imperial. **II.** *f.* coach top; top seats on a stage-coach; (naut.) poop royal.
imperialismo, *m.* imperialism.
imperialista. I. *a.* imperialistic, imperialist. **II.** *n.* imperialist.
impericia, *f.* unskilfulness, inexpertness.
imperio, *m.* empire; dominion, command, sway; dignity of an emperor.
imperiosamente, *adv.* imperiously, overbearingly.
imperiosidad, *f.* imperiousness.
imperioso, sa, *a.* imperious, overbearing.
imperitamente, *adv.* unskilfully.
imperito, ta, *a.* unskilled, inexpert.
impermeabilidad, *f.* impermeability, condition of being water-tight or waterproof.
impermeabilizar, *va.* to make waterproof.
impermeable. I. *a.* water-tight, impervious, waterproof. **II.** *m.* waterproof garment, mackintosh, raincoat.
impermutable, *a.* unexchangeable.
impersonal, *a.* impersonal.—**en,** or **por, i.,** impersonally.
impersonalizar, *va.* (gram.) to use impersonally.
impersonalmente, *adv.* impersonally.
impersuasible, *a.* not susceptible of persuasion.
impertérrito, ta, *a.* intrepid, dauntless, serene.
impertinencia, *f.* impertinence, folly, nonsense; peevishness; intrusion; minute accuracy.
impertinente. I. *a.* not pertinent; impertinent, importunate, meddlesome. **II.** *m. pl.* lorgnette.
impertinentemente, *adv.* impertinently.
imperturbabilidad, *f.* imperturbability.
imperturbable, *a.* imperturbable.
imperturbablemente, *adv.* imperturbably.
impesantez, *f.* weightlessness.
impétigo, *m.* (med.) impetigo.
impetra, *f.* diploma, license, permission; (eccl.) bull granting dubious benefices.
impetrable, *a.* (law) impetrable.
impetración, *f.* impetration; entreaty.
impetrado, da. I. *pp.* of IMPETRAR. **II.** *a.* impetrate, impetrated, granted.
impetrador, ra, *n.* one who entreats.
impetrante. I. *a.* entreating, beseeching. **II.** *m.* (law) grantee; impetrator.
impetrar, *va.* to entreat, impetrate, obtain by entreaty.
impetú, *m.* impetus, impulse; impetuosity.
impetuosamente, *adv.* impetuously.
impetuosidad, *f.* impetuosity.
impetuoso, sa, *a.* impetuous, impulsive, violent.
impíamente, *adv.* impiously.
impido, impida, *v.* *V.* IMPEDIR.
impiedad, *f.* impiety; irreligion, infidelity.
impiedoso, sa, *a.* impious, irreligious.
impiísimo, ma, *a. super.* very impious.
impío, pía. I. *a.* impious; irreligious, godless. **II.** *n.* impious person; infidel, enemy of religion.
impla, *f.* wimple; material for wimples.
implacabilidad, *f.* implacability.
implacable, *a.* implacable; inexorable.
implacablemente, *adv.* implacably.
implacentario, ria, *m.* & *a.* (zool.) implacental.
implantación, *f.* implantation, introduction (of new ideas, systems, etc.).
implantar, *va.* to implant, to introduce.
implantón, *m.* piece of timber.
implaticable, *a.* not fit to talk about, unmentionable.
implicación, *f.* contradiction.
implicante, *a.* contradictory; implicating.
implicar. I. *va.* to implicate, involve, entangle. **II.** *vn.* to imply contradiction.
implicatorio, ria, *a.* implying contradiction, contradictory.
implícitamente, *adv.* implicitly.
implícito, ta, *a.* implicit.
imploración, *f.* imploration.
implorante, *a.* imploring, entreating.
implorar, *va.* to implore, entreat, beg.
implosión, *f.* (phon.) implosion.
implosivo, va, *f.* & *a.* (phon.) implosive.
implotar, *vn.* to implode, burst inward.
implume, *a.* unfeathered, unfledged.
impolítica, *f.* incivility, discourtesy; indiscretion, tactlessness.
impolíticamente, *adv.* impolitically, unwisely.
impolítico, ca, *a.* impolitic, indiscreet, imprudent, unwise, untactful.
impoluto, ta, *a.* unpolluted, pure, untarnished.
imponderabilidad, *f.* imponderability.
imponderable, *a.* imponderable; beyond all praise, most excellent.
imponedor, ra, *n.* imposer, assessor.
imponente, *a.* imposing.
imponer. I. *va.* (*pp.* IMPUESTO; *ind. pres.* IMPONGO, *pret.* IMPUSE, *fut.* IMPONDRÉ; *subj.* IMPONGA) to impose or levy (as a tax, a penalty); to impute falsely; to advise, give notice, acquaint; to inspire, arouse, command (respect, fear); (print.) to impose. **II.** *vr.* **(a),** to assert oneself, impose one's authority (on), dominate, get one's way; to be imperative or necessary; to command respect.
imponible, *a.* taxable, dutiable.
impopular, *a.* unpopular.
impopularidad, *f.* unpopularity.
imporosidad, *f.* imporosity.
imporoso, sa, *a.* imporous.
importable, *a.* (com.) importable.
importación, *f.* (com.) importation, imports.
importador, ra, *n.* & *a.* importer(-ing).
importancia, *f.* importance.
importante, *a.* important.
importantemente, *adv.* importantly, materially.
importar. I. *vn.* to be important; to concern.—**eso no importa,** that doesn't matter.—**eso no le importa a Vd.,** that does not concern you; that is none of your business.—**eso no me importa,** I don't care (about that); that makes no difference to me.—**no importa,** no matter, never mind.—**¿qué importa?** what does it matter? what difference does it make? **II.** *va.* to import; to amount to; to be worth; to imply.
importe, *m.* (com.) amount; price, cost, value.—**i. medio,** average amount.
importunación, *f.* importunity.
importunadamente, *adv.* importunately.
importunador, ra, *n.* & *a.* importuner(-ing), pesterer(-ing).
importunamente, *adv.* inopportunely; importunately, persistently.
importunar, *va.* to importune, pester.

importunidad, *f.* importunity, importunacy.
importuno, na, *a.* inopportune; importunate, persistent, vexatious, annoying.
imposibilidad, *f.* impossibility.
imposibilitado. I. *pp.* of IMPOSIBILITAR. **II.** *a.* helpless, without means, poor; disabled, unfit for service.
imposibilitar, *va.* to disable, unfit for service.
imposible, *a.* impossible.—**i. de toda imposibilidad,** (coll.) altogether impossible.—**los imposibles,** a kind of Spanish dance.
imposiblemente, *adv.* impossibly.
imposición, *f.* imposition (of a duty, etc.); tax, duty, tribute, burden; (print.) imposition.—**i. de manos,** (eccl.) imposition, laying on of hands.
imposta, *f.* (arch.) impost; springer; fascia.
impostor, ra, *n.* impostor.
impostura, *f.* imputation; imposture.
impotable, *a.* unpotable, undrinkable.
impotencia, *f.* impotence.
impotente, *a.* impotent.
impotentemente, *adv.* impotently.
impracticabilidad, *f.* impracticability.
impracticable, *a.* impracticable; impassable.
imprecación, *f.* imprecation.
imprecar, *va.* to imprecate.
imprecatorio, ria, *a.* imprecatory.
impreciso, sa, *a.* imprecise, undefined.
impregnación, *f.* impregnation.
impregnado, da, *a.* impregnated.
impregnador, *m.* impregnator.
impregnar. I. *va.* to impregnate, saturate. **II.** *vr.* to become impregnated.
impremeditación, *f.* unpremeditation.
impremeditado, da, *a.* unpremeditated.
imprenta, *f.* printing; printing office or house; print; press.—**libertad de i.,** freedom of the press.
imprescindible, *a.* essential, imperative, indispensable.
imprescindiblemente, *adv.* necessarily, unavoidably; absolutely.
imprescriptible, *a.* imprescriptible.
impresión, *f.* impression; impress, stamping, stamp; print, printing, presswork; edition, issue; footprint; influence, moral or physical effect.—**i. digital,** fingerprint.
impresionabilidad, *f.* impressibility.
impresionable, *a.* impressionable, emotional.
impresionante, *a.* impressive.
impresionar. I. *va.* to impress, fix on the mind or memory; to affect, influence; (photog.) to effect chemical changes on (a plate) by exposure to light; to cut (phon. record). **II.** *vr.* to be moved.
impresionismo, *m.* (art) impressionism.
impresionista, *n.* & *a.* (art) impresionist(-ic).
impreso, sa. I. *pp. irreg.* of IMPRIMIR. **II.** *a.* printed; stamped. **III.** *m.* pamphlet; publication; printed matter, print.
impresor, ra. I. *n.* printer. **II.** *f.* printer's wife.
imprestable, *a.* that cannot be lent.
imprevisible, *a.* unforeseeable, unpredictable.
imprevisión, *f.* lack of foresight; improvidence; inadvertency, oversight, thoughtlessness.
imprevisto, ta. I. *a.* unforeseen, unexpected. **II.** *m. pl.* incidental or unforeseen expenses.
imprimación, *f.* (art) priming; stuff for priming.
imprimadera, *f.* (art) priming tool.
imprimador, ra, *n.* (art) one who primes.
imprimar, *va.* (art) to prime.
imprimátur, *m.* imprimatur.
imprimir, *va.* (*pp. irreg.* IMPRESO) to print, stamp, imprint, impress; fix in the mind.
improbabilidad, *f.* improbability.
improbable, *a.* improbable, unlikely.
improbablemente, *adv.* improbably.
improbar, *va.* (*ind.* IMPRUEBO; *subj.* IMPRUEBE) to disapprove.
improbidad, *f.* dishonesty; iniquity.
ímprobo, ba, *a.* dishonest, corrupt; laborious, painful, arduous.
improcedencia, *f.* unrighteousness.
improcedente, *a.* contrary to law, unrighteous.
improductivo, va, *a.* unproductive, unfruitful, barren, unprofitable.
impromptu, *m.* (mus.) impromptu.
impronta, *f.* (art) cast; stereotype plate.
impronunciable, *a.* unpronounceable.
improperar, *va.* to upbraid, gibe, taunt.
improperio, *m.* insult, indignity.—*pl.* (eccl.) improperia.
impropiamente, *adv.* improperly.
impropicio, cia, *a.* inauspicious, unfavorable, unpropitious.
impropiedad, *f.* impropriety; unfitness, inappropriateness.
impropio, pia, *a.* inappropriate, unfitting; improper, unbecoming; (arith.) improper (fraction).
improporción, *f.* disproportion.
improporcionado, da, *a.* disproportionate.
improrrogable, *a.* that cannot be prorogated or extended.
impróspero, ra, *a.* unprosperous.
impróvidamente, *adv.* improvidently.
improvidencia, *f.* improvidence.
impróvido, da, *a.* improvident, thoughtless.
improvisación, *f.* improvisation.
improvisado, da. I. *pp.* of IMPROVISAR. **II.** *a.* makeshift (as *a.*).
improvisador, ra, *n.* improviser.
improvisamente, *adv.* unexpectedly, suddenly.
improvisar, *va.* to improvise; extemporize.
improviso, sa; improvisto, ta, *a.* unexpected, unforeseen.—**al,** or **de, i.,** or **a la improvista,** unexpectedly, suddenly.
imprudencia, *f.* imprudence, indiscretion.
imprudente, *a.* imprudent, indiscreet, unwise.
imprudentemente, *adv.* imprudently.
impúber; impúbero, ra, *a.* immature, below the age of puberty.
impudencia, *f.* impudence, insolence.
impudente, *a.* impudent, shameless.
impúdicamente, *adv.* immodestly; impudently.
impudicia, *f. contr.* of IMPUDICICIA.
impudicicia, *f.* immodesty, impudicity.
impúdico, ca, *a.* immodest; impudent.
impuesto, ta. I. *pp. irreg.* of IMPONER. **II.** *a.* imposed; informed.—**estar,** or **quedar i. de,** to be informed about, to have received notice of or information about. **III.** *m.* tax, impost, duty.—**i. deducido en la fuente,** withholding tax.
impugnable, *a.* impugnable.
impugnación, *f.* opposition, impugnation.
impugnador, ra, *n.* impugner, objector.
impugnar, *va.* to impugn, oppose, criticize.
impugnativo, va, *a.* impugning.
impulsar, *va.* to impel, actuate, move, prompt; (mech.) to drive, force.
impulsión, *f.* impulsion, impulse, impetus; influence, motive.—**i. por engranaje reductor,** (mech.) backgear power.
impulsivamente, *adv.* impulsively.
impulsividad, *f.* impulsiveness.
impulsivo, va, *a.* impulsive.
impulso, *m.* impulsion; impulse.—**i. de contacto,** (elec.) contact impulse.—**dar i. a,** to set off; (coll.) to trigger.
impulsor, ra. I. *a.* impellent, propellent. **II.** *n.* impeller, propellant.—**i. de herramientas,** tool pusher.
impune, *a.* unpunished.
impunemente, *adv.* with impunity.
impunidad, *f.* impunity.
impuramente, *adv.* obscenely, impurely.
impureza, *f.* impurity; adulteration; unchastity; obscenity, foulness.
impurificación, *f.* defilement.
impurificar, *va.* to defile, to make impure; to adulterate.
impuro, ra, *a.* impure; defiled; adulterated.
impuse, *pret.* of IMPONER.
imputabilidad, *f.* imputability.

imputable, *a.* imputable.
imputación, *f.* imputation.
imputador, ra, *n.* & *a.* imputer(-ing).
imputar, *va.* to impute, attribute; (com.) to credit on account.
imputativo, va, *a.* imputative, imputing.
imputrescible, *a.* nonrotting.
inabordable, *a.* unapproachable.
inabrogable, *a.* irrepealable, irrevocable, inalterable.
inacabable, *a.* interminable; everlasting.
inaccesibilidad, *f.* inaccessibility.
inaccesible, *a.* inaccessible.
inaccesiblemente, *adv.* inaccessibly.
inacción, *f.* inaction, inactivity.
inaceptable, *a.* unacceptable.
inacidez, *f.* inacidity.
inactivamente, *adv.* inactively, idly.
inactividad, *f.* inactivity, idleness.
inactivo, va, *a.* inactive.
inadaptable, *a.* unadaptable.
inadecuado, da, *a.* inadequate.
inadmisible, *a.* inadmissible.
inadoptable, *a.* unadoptable.
inadvertencia, *f.* inadvertency, oversight.
inadvertidamente, *adv.* inadvertently.
inadvertido, da, *a.* inadvertent, careless; unseen, unnoticed.
inafectado, da, *a.* natural, unaffected.
inagotable, *a.* inexhaustible.
inaguantable, *a.* unbearable.
inajenable, *a.* inalienable.
inalámbrico, ca, *a.* wireless.
inalcanzable, *a.* unattainable.
inalienable, *a.* inalienable.
inalterabilidad, *f.* unalterability.
inalterable, *a.* unalterable, changeless.
inalterablemente, *adv.* unalterably.
inalterado, da, *a.* unchanged, unaltered.
inamisible, *a.* not liable to be lost.
inamovible, *a.* immovable.
inamovilidad, *f.* immovability.
inanalizable, *a.* incapable of being analyzed.
inane, *a.* empty, void, inane.
inania, *f.* inanity.
inanición, *f.* (med.) inanition, inanity.
inanidad, *f.* inanity.
inanimación, *f.* inanimation.
inanimado, da, *a.* inanimate, lifeless.
inapagable, *a.* inextinguishable, unquenchable.
inapeable, *a.* that cannot be lowered or levelled; inconceivable; obstinate, stubborn.
inapelable, *a.* unappealable.
inapetencia, *f.* inappetence, lack of appetite.
inapetente, *a.* having no appetite.
inaplazable, *a.* undeferable, that cannot be deferred.
inaplicable, *a.* inapplicable.
inaplicación, *f.* indolence; lack of application.
inaplicado, da, *a.* indolent, careless, inactive.
inapreciable, *a.* invaluable; inappreciable.
inaprensivo, *a.* inapprehensive.
inapropiado, da, *a.* inappropriate, malapropos.
inarmónico, ca, *a.* inharmonious.
inarticulado, da. I. *a.* inarticulate. **II.** *m. pl.* (zool.) Inarticulata.
in artículo mortis, in articulo mortis, at the point of death, in the moment of death.
inasequible, *a.* unattainable, not obtainable.
inasimilable, *a.* unassimilable.
inastillable, *a.* splinterproof.
inatacable, *a.* that cannot be attacked.
inaudibilidad, *f.* inaudibility.
inaudible, *a.* inaudible.
inaudito, ta, *a.* unheard-of, strange, unexpected, most extraordinary.
inauguración, *f.* inauguration; coronation; unveiling (of statue), (ceremony of) opening (of building, etc.).
inaugural, *a.* inaugural.
inaugurar, *va.* to inaugurate; to unveil (statue); to dedicate; to open (exhibition, etc.); to divine by the flight of birds.
inaveriguable, *a.* unascertainable.
inca, *n.* & *a.* Inca, Incan.
incaico, ca, incásico, ca, *a.* Incan, Inca.
incalculable, *a.* incalculable.
incalescencia, *f.* incalescence.
incalescente, *a.* incalescent.
incalificable, *a.* impossible to judge or characterize; unutterably bad, most reprehensible.
incalmable, *a.* that cannot be calmed or subdued.
incandescencia, *f.* incandescence.
incandescente, *a.* incandescent.
incandescer, *va.* & *vn.* to incandesce.
incansable, *a.* indefatigable, untiring.
incansablemente, *adv.* indefatigably, tirelessly.
incantable, *a.* that cannot be sung.
incapacidad, *f.* incapacity; incompetence.
incapacitar, *va.* to incapacitate, disable.
incapaz, *a.* incapable; unable; incompetent.
incasable, *a.* unmarriageable; opposed to marriage.
incasto, ta, *a.* unchaste.
incautación, *f.* (law) attachment of property.
incautamente, *adv.* unwarily, incautiously.
incautarse, *vr.* (law) to attach property.
incauto, ta, *a.* unwary; gullible, "easy."
incendiar, *va.* to set on fire.
incendiario, ria, *n.* & *a.* incendiary.
incendio, *m.* fire, conflagration; (fig.) stew.
incensación, *f.* perfuming with incense.
incensar, *va.* (*ind.* INCIENSO; *subj.* INCIENSE) (eccl.) to incense; to bestow fulsome praise or adulation.
incensario, *m.* incensory, thurible.
incensurable, *a.* unblamable, not culpable.
incentivo, *m.* incentive, inducement; encouragement.
incertidumbre, *f.* uncertainty.
incertísimo, ma, *a. super.* extremely uncertain.
incesable, *a.* incessant, unceasing.
incesablemente, *adv.* incessantly.
incesante, *a.* unceasing, continual.
incesantemente, *adv.* incessantly, continually.
incesto, *m.* incest.
incestuosamente, *adv.* incestuously.
incestuoso, sa, *a.* incestuous.
incidencia, *f.* incident; (geom., phys.) incidence.
incidental, *a.* incidental, dependent, subsidiary.
incidentalmente, *adv.* incidentally.
incidente. I. *a.* incidental. **II.** *m.* incident, occurrence.—*pl.* (com.) appurtenances.—**incidentes de comercio,** lease and good will.
incidentemente, *adv.* incidentally.
incidir, *vn.* (en) to fall (into) (as an error).
[1]**incienso,** *m.* incense; reverence; flattery.
[2]**incienso, inciense,** *v. V.* INCENSAR.
inciertamente, *adv.* uncertainly.
incierto, ta, *a.* uncertain; untrue; unknown.
incinerable, *a.* (of bank bills, burned when withdrawn) to be withdrawn from circulation.
incineración, *f.* incineration, cremation; (chem.) ignition.
incinerador, *m.* incinerator.
incinerar, *va.* to incinerate, cremate; (chem.) to ignite.
incipiente, *a.* incipient.
incircunciso, sa, *a.* uncircumcised.
incircunscripto, ta, *a.* uncircumscribed.
incisión, *f.* incision, cut.
incisivo, va. I. *a.* incisive; keen, sharp, cutting (as a remark). **II.** *m.* incisor, incisor tooth.
inciso, sa. I. *a.* incised, cut. **II.** *m.* sentence; clause; comma.
incisorio, ria, *a.* (surg.) incisory.
incitación, *f.* incitation, incitement.
incitador, ra. I. *a.* inciting, instigating. **II.** *n.* instigator, inciter.
incitamento, incitamiento, *m.* incitement, impulse, incentive.
incitante, *a.* inciting, exciting.
incitar, *va.* to incite, excite, spur, instigate.
incitativo, va. I. *a.* inciting; (law) AGUIJATORIO, re-mandatory. **II.** *m.* incitement. **III.** *f.* (law)

writ from a superior to a lower court urging that justice be administered.
incivil, *a.* uncivil.—**incivilidad,** *f.* incivility.
incivilmente, *adv.* uncivilly, rudely.
inclasificable, *a.* unclassifiable.
inclemencia, *f.* inclemency; severity, rigor, unmercifulness.—**a la i.,** unsheltered, at the mercy of the elements.
inclemente, *a.* inclement, severe; unmerciful.
inclinabilidad, *f.* inclinability.
inclinable, *a.* inclinable.
inclinación, *f.* inclination; propensity, tendency, bent; tilt, slant, pitch; declivity, slope; (Ry.) grade; (min.) dip, hade, underlay; (phys.) dip, inclination (of the needle).—**i. de la brújula,** (naut.) dip of a needle.
inclinado, da. I. *pp.* of INCLINAR. **II.** *a.* inclined; slanting, sloping; disposed, minded.
inclinador, ra, *m.* & *f.* one who inclines.
inclinante, *a.* inclining.
inclinar. I. *va.* to incline; to bow; to tilt; to influence. **II.** *vn.* to resemble. **III.** *vr.* to incline, slope; to lean; to incline, be favorably disposed; to stoop, bow; to yield; (naut.) to heel.
inclinómetro, *m.* (aer.) inclinometer.
ínclito, ta, *a.* distinguished, illustrious.
incluir, *va.* (*pp.* INCLUÍDO, INCLUSO; *ind. pres.* INCLUYO, *pret.* él INCLUYÓ; *subj.* INCLUYA) to include; to enclose.
inclusa, *f.* foundling asylum.
inclusero, ra, *n.* & *a.* foundling.
inclusión, *f.* inclusion; friendship.
inclusivamente, inclusive, *adv.* inclusive, including.
inclusivo, va, *a.* inclusive, including.
incluso, sa. I. *pp. irreg.* of INCLUIR. **II.** *a.* inclosed; including, included (in this sense it is gen. used as an *adv.*).
incluyente, *a.* including, inclosing.
incluyo, incluyó, *v. V.* INCLUIR.
incoación, *f.* inchoation, early stage.
incoado, da. I. *pp.* of INCOAR. **II.** *a.* inchoate, begun.
incoagulabilidad, *f.* incoagulability.
incoagulable, *a.* uncoagulable.
incoar, *va.* (*only the infinitive and pp. used*) (law) to commence, begin.
incoativo, va, *a.* inchoative, inceptive.
incobrable, *a.* irrecoverable, irretrievable; (com.) uncollectable.
incoercible, *a.* incoercible.
incógnito, ta. I. *a.* unknown.—**de i.,** incognito; hiddenly or clandestinely. **II.** *f.* (math.) unknown (quantity).
incognoscible, *a.* unknowable.
incoherencia, *f.* incoherence, disconnection.
incoherente, *a.* incoherent, disconnected.
íncola, *m.* inhabitant, resident.
incoloro, ra, *a.* colorless.
incólume, *a.* sound, safe, unharmed.
incolumidad, *f.* security, safety.
incombinable, *a.* uncombinable.
incombustibilidad, *f.* incombustibility.
incombustible, *a.* incombustible, fireproof.
incombusto, ta, *a.* not burned.
incomerciable, *a.* contraband, unlawful, prohibited; unsalable, unmarketable.
incomestible, incomible, *a.* inedible, indigestible.
incómodamente, *adv.* inconveniently; uncomfortably.
incomodar. I. *va.* to disturb, inconvenience, trouble. **II.** *vr.* to be or get vexed or angry; to trouble oneself.
incomodidad, *f.* inconvenience; uncomfortableness; nuisance, annoyance; vexation, anger.
incómodo, da, *a.* inconvenient; uncomfortable; troublesome, unhandy, cumbersome.
incomparable, *a.* incomparable, matchless.
incomparablemente, *adv.* incomparably.
incomparado, da, *a.* = INCOMPARABLE.
incompartible, *a.* indivisible.
incompasible, incompasivo, va, *a.* pitiless, unsympathetic.
incompatibilidad, *f.* incompatibility.
incompatible, *a.* incompatible; uncongenial.
incompensable, *a.* incapable of being compensated, unindemnifiable.
incompetencia, *f.* incompetence; unfitness.
incompetente, *a.* incompetent; (law) incompetent, unauthorized.
incomplejo, ja, *a.* incomplex; simple.
incompletamente, *adv.* incompletely.
incompleto, ta, *a.* incomplete.
incomplexo, xa, *a.* disunited, disconnected, disjointed.
incomponible, *a.* unmendable.
incomportable, *a.* intolerable, unbearable.
incomposibilidad, *f.* incompatibility.
incomposible, *a.* incompatible; inconsistent.
incomposición, *f.* want of proportion.
incomprehensibilidad, *f.* incomprehensibility.
incomprehensible, *a.* incomprehensible.
incomprensibilidad, *f.* incomprehensibility.
incomprensible, *a.* incomprehensible.
incomprensiblemente, *adv.* inconceivably, incomprehensibly.
incomprensión, *f.* misunderstanding; lack of understanding.
incompresibilidad, *f.* (phys.) incompressibility.
incompresible, *a.* (phys.) incompressible.
incomprimible, *a.* incompressible.
incomunicabilidad, *f.* incommunicability.
incomunicable, *a.* incommunicable.
incomunicado, da I. *a.* isolated. **II.** *m.* isolated prisoner, incommunicado.
incomunicar, *va.* (*pret.* INCOMUNIQUÉ; *subj.* INCOMUNIQUE) to deprive of intercourse or communication; to isolate, put in solitary confinement.
inconcebibilidad, *f.* inconceivableness, inconceivability.
inconcebible, *a.* inconceivable.
inconciliable, *a.* irreconcilable.
inconcino, na, *a.* disordered, disarranged.
inconcluso, sa, *a.* inconclusive, unfinished.
inconcluyente, *a.* inconclusive.
inconcusamente, *adv.* certainly, unquestionably.
inconcuso, sa, *a.* incontrovertible, unquestionable, indisputable.
incondicional, *a.* unconditional.
incondicionalmente, *adv.* unconditionally.
inconducente, *a.* nonconducive.
inconexión, *f.* incoherence, disconnection.
inconexo, xa, *a.* unconnected, not pertinent; incoherent.
inconfeso, sa, *a.* unconfessed.
inconfidencia, *f.* distrust, mistrust.
inconfundible, *a.* unmistakable.
incongruamente, *adv.* incongruously.
incongruencia, *f.* incongruence.
incongruente, *a.* incongruous, incongruent.
incongruentemente, *adv.* incongruously, incompatibly.
incongruo, grua, *a.* incongruous.
inconmensurabilidad, *f.* incommensurability.
inconmensurable, *a.* incommensurable.
inconmovible, *a.* immovable; unbending, inexorable, unyielding.
inconmutabilidad, *f.* immutability; incommutability.
inconmutable, *a.* immutable; incommutable.
inconquistable, *a.* unconquerable; unbending.
inconsciencia, *f.* unconsciousness.
inconsciente, *a.* unconscious.
inconscientemente, *adv.* unconsciously.
inconsecuencia, *f.* inconsistency.
inconsecuente, *a.* inconsistent.
inconservable, *a.* unpreservable.
inconsideración, *f.* lack of consideration; thoughtlessness, inadvertency.
inconsideradamente, *adv.* inconsiderately; thoughtlessly.

inconsiderado, da, *a.* inconsiderate; thoughtless.
inconsiguiente, *a.* inconsistent, not logical.
inconsistencia, *f.* incoherence; instability, lack of permanency.
inconsistente, *a.* unsubstantial, unstable.
inconsolable, *a.* inconsolable.
inconsolablemente, *adv.* inconsolably.
inconstancia, *f.* inconstancy, fickleness.
inconstante, *a.* inconstant, changeable, fickle.
inconstantemente, *adv.* inconstantly, fickly.
inconstitucional, *a.* unconstitutional.
inconstitucionalidad, *f.* unconstitutionality.
inconstruíble, *a.* that cannot be constructed.
inconsútil, *a.* seamless.
incontable, *a.* innumerable, uncountable.
incontaminado, da, *a.* undefiled, uncontaminated, pure.
incontestable, *a.* incontestable, unquestionable.
incontestablemente, *adv.* unquestionably.
incontinencia, *f.* incontinence; (med.) incontinence of urine.
[1]**incontinente,** *a.* incontinent.
[2]**incontinente, incontinenti,** *adv.* instantly, immediately, at once.
incontrastable, *a.* invincible, insuperable, unconquerable; unanswerable; unconvincible.
incontratable, *a.* = INTRATABLE, intractable.
incontrolable, *a.* uncontrollable.
incontrovertible, *a.* incontrovertible.
inconvencible, *a.* unconvincible.
inconvenible, *a.* uncompromising.
inconveniencia, *f.* inconvenience, trouble; disadvantage; uncomfortableness.
inconveniente. I. *a.* inconvenient, troublesome; uncomfortable; undesirable, inadvisable. **II.** *m.* difficulty, obstacle, objection; disadvantage.
inconversable, *a.* unsociable, uncommunicative, surly, intractable.
inconvertible, *a.* inconvertible.
incordio, *m.* (med.) bubo; (vulg.) nuisance.
incorporación, *f.* incorporation.
incorporador, ra, *n.* incorporator.
incorporal, *a.* incorporeal.
incorporalmente, *adv.* incorporeally.
incorporar. I. *va.* to incorporate, unite, embody; to mix; to raise or to make (a patient) sit up in bed. **II.** *vr.* to incorporate, mingle; to join (as a mil. unit); to form a corporation; to sit up in bed; (naut.) to sail in company.
incorporeidad, *f.* incorporeity, immateriality.
incorpóreo, rea, *a.* incorporeal.
incorporo, *m.* = INCORPORACIÓN.
incorrección, *f.* incorrectness; inaccuracy; impropriety.
incorrectamente, *adv.* incorrectly; improperly.
incorrecto, ta, *a.* incorrect; improper.
incorregibilidad, *f.* incorrigibleness.
incorregible, *a.* incorrigible.
incorrosible, *a.* noncorrosive, incorrodable, incorrodible.
incorrupción, *f.* integrity, honesty; incorrupt condition.
incorruptamente, *adv.* incorruptly.
incorruptibilidad, *f.* incorruptibility.
incorruptible, *a.* incorruptible.
incorrupto, ta, *a.* incorrupt or uncorrupted; chaste, pure.
incrasante, *a.* thickening.
incrasar, *va.* to thicken, incrassate.
increado, da, *a.* uncreated.
incredibilidad, *f.* incredibility, incredibleness.
incredulidad, *f.* incredulity.
incrédulo, la. I. *a.* incredulous. **II.** *n.* unbeliever.
increíble, *a.* incredible, unbelievable.
increíblemente, *adv.* incredibly.
incrementación, *f.* incrementation, increase.
incrementador, *m.* incrementer.
incrementar, *va.* to increase, intensify, augment.
incremento, *m.* increment, increase.
increpación, *f.* rebuke, chiding, reproach.
increpador, ra. I. *a.* chiding, rebuking. **II.** *n.* chider, rebuker.
increpante, *a.* chiding, scolding, rebuking.
increpar, *va.* to chide, reprehend, rebuke.
incriminación, *f.* incrimination.
incriminante, *a.* incriminating.
incriminar, *va.* to incriminate; to exaggerate.
incristalizable, *a.* uncrystallizable.
incruento, ta, *a.* bloodless.
incrustación, *f.* incrustation; scale (in boilers); (geol.) sinter; (art) inlaying.
incrustador, ra, *n.* inlayer.
incrustante, *a.* (of water) scale-forming.
incrustar, *va.* to incrust; encase; inlay.
incuartación, *f.* (chem.) quartation.
incubación, *f.* incubation; hatching.
incubador, ra. I. *n.* & *a.* incubator(-ing). **II.** *f.* incubator (apparatus).
incubar, *va.* to incubate; to hatch.
íncubo, *m.* incubus; (med.) nightmare.
incuestionable, *a.* unquestionable.
inculcación, *f.* inculcation; pressing (one thing against another); (print.) binding or wedging in a form.
inculcador, ra, *n.* inculcator.
inculcar. I. *va.* (*pret.* INCULQUÉ; *subj.* INCULQUE) to inculcate, impress, teach; to make (one thing) tight (against another); (print.) to lock up (types). **II.** *vr.* to be obstinate.
inculpabilidad, *f.* guiltlessness; blamelessness.
inculpable, *a.* guiltless, blameless.
inculpablemente, *adv.* blamelessly.
inculpación, *f.* inculpation.
inculpadamente, *adv.* faultlessly.
inculpado, da. I. *pp.* of INCULPAR. **II.** *n.* & *a.* accused.
inculpar, *va.* to accuse, inculpate, blame.
inculqué, inculque, *v.* *V.* INCULCAR.
incultamente, *adv.* rudely, unrefinedly.
incultivable, *a.* inarable, untillable.
inculto, ta, *a.* uncultivated, untilled, unimproved; uncivilized; unrefined, uncultured.
incultura, *f.* lack of culture.
incumbencia, *f.* incumbency; obligation, duty, concern.
incumbir, *vn.* to concern, pertain.
incumplido, da, *a.* unfulfilled; unpunctual.
incumplimiento, *m.* nonfulfilment.
incunable, *m.* & *a.* (print.) incunabula.
incurabilidad, *f.* incurability, incurableness.
incurable, *a.* incurable; hopeless.
incuria, *f.* negligence; shiftlessness.
incurioso, sa, *a.* negligent, careless.
incurrimiento, *m.* act of incurring.
incurrir, *vn.* (**en**) to incur, become liable (to); to bring on oneself; to commit (error or crime).
incursión, *f.* (mil.) incursion.
incusar, *va.* to accuse.
incuso, sa, *a.* incuse, stamped (as some coins).
indagación, *f.* investigation, search, inquiry, examination, inquest; (law) defendant's unsworn testimony.
indagador, ra, *n.* & *a.* investigator(-ing), inquirer(-ing), examiner(-ing).
indagar, *va.* (*pret.* INDAGUÉ; *subj.* INDAGUE) to investigate, inquire into or about.
indagatoria, *f.* (law) unsworn statement made by, or required of, an arraigned person.
indagatorio, ria, *a.* (law) investigatory.
indagué, indague, *v.* *V.* INDAGAR.
indebidamente, *adv.* unduly; improperly; illegally, unlawfully.
indebido, da, *a.* improper; illegal, unlawful.
indecencia, *f.* indecency; obscenity; nuisance; indecent or low act or conduct.
indecente, *a.* indecent, obscene; foul.
indecentemente, *adv.* indecently.
indecible, *a.* inexpressible, unutterable.
indeciblemente, *adv.* inexpressibly, unutterably; exceedingly.
indecisamente, *adv.* irresolutely.
indecisión, *f.* irresolution, indecision.
indeciso, sa, *a.* irresolute, hesitant; undecided.
indeclinable, *a.* unavoidable; (gram.) indeclinable; (law) unwaivable.

indecoro, *m.* indecorum, indecorousness.
indecorosamente, *adv.* indecorously, unbecomingly.
indecoroso, sa, *a.* indecorous, unbecoming.
indefectibilidad, *f.* indefectibility.
indefectible, *a.* indefectible, unfailing.
indefectiblemente, *adv.* unfailingly.
indefendible, *a.* indefensible.
indefensable, indefensible, *a.* = INDEFENDIBLE.
indefenso, sa, *a.* defenseless.
indeficiente, *a.* indefectible, unfailing.
indefinible, *a.* undefinable.
indefinidamente, *adv.* indefinitely.
indefinido, da, *a.* indefinite; undefined.
indehiscencia, *f.* (bot.) indehiscence.
indehiscente, *a.* (bot.) indehiscent.
indelebilidad, *f.* indelibility.
indeleble, *a.* indelible, ineffaceable.
indeleblemente, *adv.* indelibly.
indeliberación, *f.* lack of premeditation; irreflection.
indeliberadamente, *adv.* without premeditation or reflection.
indeliberado, da, *a.* unpremeditated; unconsidered.
indelicadeza, *f.* indelicacy, discourtesy.
indemne, *a.* undamaged, unhurt.
indemnicé, indemnice, *v. V.* INDEMNIZAR.
indemnidad, *f.* bond of indemnity.
indemnizable, *a.* that can be indemnified.
indemnización, *f.* indemnification, compensation; indemnity; reimbursement.
indemnizar, *va.* (*pret.* INDEMNICÉ; *subj.* INDEMNICE) to indemnify, compensate.
indemostrable, *a.* undemonstrable.
indentación, *f.* indentation.
indentador, *m.* indenting unity.
independencia, *f.* independence.
independiente, *a.* independent.
independientemente, *adv.* independently.
independizar. (Am.) **I.** *va.* to free, emancipate. **II.** *vr.* to become independent, win freedom.
indescifrable, *a.* undecipherable.
indescribible, *a.* = INDESCRIPTIBLE.
indescriptible, *a.* indescribable.
indeseable, *a.* undesirable (esp. app. to aliens).
indesignable, *a.* that cannot be designated.
indestructibilidad, *f.* indestructibility.
indestructible, *a.* indestructible.
indeterminable, *a.* underterminable, unascertainable; irresolute, undecided.
indeterminación, *f.* indetermination; irresolution, hesitancy.
indeterminadamente, *adv.* indeterminately.
indeterminado, da, *a.* indeterminate; undetermined, irresolute, hesitating; (gram.) indefinite (article); (math.) indeterminate (problem, equation); (math.) undetermined (coefficient).
indeterminismo, *m.* (philos.) indeterminism.
indeterminista, *n.* & *a.* (philos.) indeterminist (-ic).
indevoción, *f.* lack of devoutness, irreligiousness.
indevoto, ta, *a.* not devout, irreligious.
indezuelo, la, *n. dim.* little Indian.
India, *f.* India.
indiada, *f.* (Am.) crowd or multitude of Indians.
indiana, *f.* printed calico.
indianismo, *m.* (Am.) interest in, or study of, Am. Indian questions.
indianista, *n.* (Am.) student of, or expert in, Am. Indian culture; student of, or expert in, East Indian culture.
indiano, na. I. *a.* native or resident of America or West Indies; Indian, East Indian. **II.** *m.* nabob, one who returns rich from America.—**i. de hilo negro,** (coll.) skinflint, miser.
indicación, *f.* indication, sign; hint, suggestion; direction, instruction.
indicado, da. I. *pp.* of INDICAR. **II.** *a.* indicated, appropriate (to conditions, etc.).
indicador, *m.* indicator, pointer, recorder, gauge, detector, index; (elec.) annunciator disc; (steam eng.) indicator.—**i. acústico,** (rad.) ringing set.—**i. de calado y estiba,** (naut.) draft and trim indicator.—**i. de combustible,** (auto.) fuel gauge.—**i. de desviación,** drift indicator.—**i. de incendios,** fire alarm.—**i. de inclinación,** inclination gauge.—**i. del calor,** (auto.) temperature gauge.—**i. de luz fuerte,** (auto.) telltale lamp.—**i. de llamada,** (elec.) call signal.—**i. de nivel,** (steam eng.) water-level indicator, gauge glass.—**i. de peso,** weight indicator.—**i. de rumbo,** (naut.) path indicator.—**i. de vacío,** vacuum gauge.—**i. térmico,** (elec.) thermal indicator.
indicante. I. *a.* indicating. **II.** *m.* (med.) indicant.
indicar, *va.* (*pret.* INDIQUÉ; *subj.* INDIQUE) to indicate, suggest, hint, show, point out.
indicativo, va. I. *a.* indicative; (gram.) indicative. **II.** *m.* (gram.) indicative.
indicatorio, ria, *a.* indicatory, demonstrative.
indicción, *f.* convening of a synod, council, etc.; (Rom. Empire) indiction.
índice, *m.* index; hand of a watch, etc.; index, table of contents; forefinger.—**í. cefálico,** cephalic index.—**í. de refracción,** weight indicator.—**í. expurgatorio,** (eccl.) Index Expurgatorius.—**í. luminoso,** (elec.) spot.
indiciado, da. I. *pp.* of INDICIAR. **II.** *a.* suspected of a crime or vice. **III.** *n.* suspicious character.
indiciador, ra, *n.* one who suspects another; informer.
indiciar, *va.* (law) to give reasons to suspect or surmise; to report (offenders) to the magistrates.
indicio, *m.* indication, mark, sign, evidence, clue. —*pl.* (chem.) traces.—**indicios vehementes,** (law) circumstantial evidence.
índico, ca, *a.* East-Indian.
indiferencia, *f.* indifference.
indiferente, *a.* indifferent.—**eso es i.,** (coll.) that is immaterial, that makes no difference.
indiferentemente, *adv.* indifferently, without difference.
indiferentismo, *m.* indifferentism.
indígena. I. *a.* indigenous, native; (app. to Am.) Indian. **II.** *n.* indigene; native; (app. to Am.) Indian.
indigencia, *f.* indigence, destitution, need.
indigente, *a.* needy, indigent, destitute.
indigestarse, *vr.* to cause indigestion; (of persons) to cause aversion or dislike, to be unbearable.
indigestible, *a.* indigestible.
indigestión, *f.* indigestion.
indigesto, ta, *a.* indigestible; confused, disordered; surly, grouchy, harsh.
indignación, *f.* indignation.
indignado, da, *a.* & *pp.* indignant, angry.
indignamente, *adv.* unworthily, unbecomingly; harshly, rudely.
indignante, *a.* indignant; irritating.
indignar. I. *va.* to irritate, anger, make indignant. **II.** *vr.* to become indignant.
indignidad, *f.* indignity; unworthy act.
indigno, na, *a.* unworthy, undeserving; unbecoming, contemptible; despicable, low.
índigo, *m.* indigo.—**indigotina,** *f.* (chem.) indigotin, indigo blue.
indiligencia, *f.* negligence, carelessness.
indio, ia. I. *a.* Indian; Hindu; blue, azure. **II.** *n.* Hindu; Indian. **III.** *m.* (chem.) indium.
indiqué, indique, *v. V.* INDICAR.
indirecto, ta. I. *a.* indirect. **II.** *f.* hint, innuendo. —**i. del Padre Gobos,** broad hint.—**echar indirectas,** to make insinuations.
indirigible, *a.* indirigible, ungovernable, unmanageable.
indiscernible, *a.* indiscernible, imperceptible, inconspicuous.
indisciplina, *f.* lack of discipline or training.

indisciplinable, *a.* intractable; untrainable.
indisciplinado, da, *a.* undisciplined; untrained.
indiscreción, *f.* indiscretion, imprudence.
indiscretamente, *adv.* indiscreetly.
indiscreto, ta, *a.* indiscreet, imprudent, unwise.
indisculpable, *a.* inexcusable.
indiscutible, *a.* unquestionable, indisputable.
indisolubilidad, *f.* indissolubility.
indisoluble, *a.* indissoluble.
indisolublemente, *adv.* indissolubly.
indispensable, *a.* indispensable, essential; unfailing.
indispensablemente, *adv.* indispensably; necessarily; unfailingly.
indisponer. I. *va.* (*pp. irreg.* INDISPUESTO; *ind. pres.* INDISPONGO, *pret.* INDISPUSE, *fut.* INDISPONDRÉ; *subj.* INDISPONGA) to disable, indispose, render unfit; to make ill; (**con**) to prejudice, set (against). **II.** *vr.* to be indisposed, to become ill; to fall out (with a person).
indisposición, *f.* disinclination, dislike; indisposition, slight ailment.
indisposicioncilla, *f. dim.* slight indisposition.
indispuesto, ta. I. *pp. irreg. of* INDISPONER. **II.** *a.* indisposed; at variance.
indispuse, *pret.* of INDISPONER.
indisputabilidad, *f.* indisputability.
indisputable, *a.* indisputable, unquestionable.
indisputablemente, *adv.* indisputably.
indistinción, *f.* lack of distinction.
indistinguible, *a.* undistinguishable.
indistintamente, *adv.* indistinctly; indifferently, without distinction.
indistinto, ta, *a.* indistinct, vague, not clear.
individuación, *f.* individuation.
individual, *a.* individual; peculiar; personal.
individualidad, *f.* individuality.
individualismo, *m.* individualism.
individualista, *n.* & *a.* individualist(-ic).
individualizar, *va.* to individualize.
individualmente, *adv.* individually.
individuamente, *adv.* indivisibly.
individuar, *va.* to distinguish, particularize, individualize.
individuo, dua. I. *a.* individual; indivisible, inseparable. **II.** *n.* individual, person; member, fellow (of a society, etc.).
indivisamente, *adv.* indivisibly.
indivisibilidad, *f.* indivisibility.
indivisible, *a.* indivisible.
indivisiblemente, *adv.* indivisibly.
indivisión, *f.* undividedness, entirety.
indiviso, sa, *a.* undivided.
indo, da, *n.* & *a.* East-Indian, Hindu.
indócil, *a.* indocile, unteachable; headstrong, froward, unruly; inflexible, brittle.
indocilidad, *f.* indocility; inflexibility.
indoctamente, *adv.* ignorantly.
indocto, ta, *a.* ignorant, untaught.
indocumentado, da, *a.* lacking the documents for identification.
indochino, na, *n.* & *a.* Indo-Chinese.
indoeuropeo, a, *n.* & *a.* Indo-European.
indogermánico, ca, *n.* & *a.* Indo-Germanic.
indoísmo, *m.* Hinduism, Hindooism.
índole, *f.* disposition, nature; class, kind.
indolencia, *f.* indolence.
indolente, *a.* indolent.—**indolentemente,** *adv.* indolently.
indoloro, ra, *a.* painless.
indomable, *a.* untamable, indomitable; unmanageable; unconquerable.
indomado, da, *a.* untamed.
indomesticable, *a.* untamable, not susceptible of domestication.
indoméstico, ca, *a.* untamed, intractable.
indómito, ta, *a.* untamed; unruly.
Indonesia, *f.* Indonesia.
indonesio, sia, *n.* & *a.* Indonesian.
indostanés, nesa, indostano, na, *n.* & *a.* Hindu, Hindoo.
indostani, *m.* Hindustani (language).
indostánico, ca, *a.* Hindu, Hindoo.
indotación, *f.* (law) lack of a dowry.
indotado, da, *a.* unendowed; without a dowry.
indubitable, *a.* indubitable, unquestionable.
indubitablemente, *adv.* undoubtedly.
indubitado, da, *a.* undoubted, unquestionable.
inducción, *f.* inducement, persuasion; (logic) induction; (elec.) induction.
inducible, *a.* inducible.
inducido, *m.* (elec.) armature (of a dynamo).
inducidor, ra, *n.* inducer, persuader.
inducimiento, *m.* inducement.
inducir, *va.* (*ind. pres.* INDUZCO, *pret.* INDUJE; *subj.* INDUZCA) to induce; to persuade, influence; (elec.) to induce.
inductancia, *f.* (elec.) inductance.
indúctil, *a.* inductile.
inductividad, *f.* (elec.) inductivity.
inductivo, va, *a.* inductive.
inductor, ra. I. *a.* (elec.) inductive. **II.** *m.* (elec.) field (magnet) (of a dynamo).
indudable, *a.* indubitable, certain.
indudablemente, *adv.* undoubtedly.
induje, *pret.* of INDUCIR.
indulgencia, *f.* indulgence; forbearance, leniency.
indulgente, *a.* indulgent, lenient, forbearing.
indulgentemente, *adv.* indulgently.
indultar, *va.* to pardon; to free, exempt.
indultario, *m.* he who by virtue of a pontifical privilege can dispense ecclesiastical benefices.
indulto, *m.* pardon, forgiveness, amnesty; (legal) pardon or commutation or exemption.
indumentaria, *f.* study of ancient apparel.
indumentario, ria, *a.* pertaining to clothes.
indumento, *m.* garment, vestment.
induración, *f.* (med.) induration.
indurado, da, *a.* (med.) indurated.
indurar, *va.* (med.) to indurate.
industria, *f.* industry, manufacturing.—**de i.,** designedly, intentionally.—**ser caballero de i.,** to live by one's wits.
industrial. I. *a.* industrial, manufacturing. **II.** *n.* industrialist, manufacturer.
industrialismo, *m.* industrialism.
industrialista, *a.* favoring industrialism.
industrialización, *f.* industrialization.
industrializar. I. *va.* to industrialize. **II.** *vn.* to be or become industrialized.
industriar, *va.* & *vn.* to educate, teach, train, coach; to find means.
industriosamente, *adv.* industriously.
industrioso, sa, *a.* industrious.
induzco, induzca, *v. V.* INDUCIR.
inebriar, *va.* & *vr.* = EMBRIAGAR.
inecuación, *f.* (math.) inequality.
inedia, *f.* fast, abstinence from food.
inédito, ta, *a.* unpublished.
ineducación, *f.* unmannerliness, unrefinement.
ineducado, da, *a.* unmannerly, unpolished.
inefabilidad, *f.* ineffability, unspeakableness.
inefable, *a.* ineffable, unutterable.
inefablemente, *adv.* ineffably.
ineficacia, *f.* inefficacy, inefficiency.
ineficaz, *a.* inefficacious, ineffectual, ineffective.
ineficazmente, *adv.* inefficaciously.
inejecución, *f.* inexecution, nonperformance; nonfulfillment.
inejecutable, *a.* impracticable, not feasible.
inelástico, ca, *a.* inelastic.
inelegancia, *f.* inelegance, inelegancy.
inelegante, *a.* inelegant.
inelegibilidad, *f.* ineligibility.
inelegible, *a.* ineligible.
ineluctable, *a.* ineluctable; inevitable.
ineludible, *a.* inevitable, unavoidable.
inenarrable, *a.* inexplicable, inexpressible.
inepcia, *f.* ineptitude, inability.
ineptamente, *adv.* ineptly, incompetently.
ineptitud, *f.* ineptitude, incompetency.
inepto, ta, *a.* inept, incompetent; unfit; foolish.
inequívoco, ca, *a.* unequivocal, unmistakable.
inercia, *f.* inertia; inertness, inactivity.

inerme, *a.* unarmed, defenseless.
inerrable, *a.* inerrable, unmistakable.
inerrante, *a.* (astr.) fixed (star).
inerte, *a.* inert; dull, slow, sluggish; unskilful; paralyzed, senseless.
inervación, *f.* innervation.
inervar, *va.* (physiol.) to innervate, innerve.
inescrutabilidad, *f.* inscrutability.
inescrutable, *a.* inscrutable; unconfirmable.
inescudriñable, *a.* inscrutable.
inesperadamente, *adv.* unexpectedly.
inesperado, da, *a.* unexpected, unforeseen.
inestabilidad, *f.* instability.
inestable, *a.* unstable.
inestimabilidad, *f.* invaluableness.
inestimable, *a.* invaluable.
inestimablemente, *adv.* invaluably.
inestimado, da, *a.* (law) unestimated, not appraised, unvalued.
inevitabilidad, *f.* inevitability.
inevitable, *a.* inevitable, unavoidable.
inevitablemente, *adv.* inevitably.
inexactamente, *adv.* inexactly.
inexactitud, *f.* inexactness; inaccuracy.
inexacto, ta, *a.* inexact, inaccurate.
inexcusable, *a.* inexcusable; indispensable.
inexcusablemente, *adv.* inexcusably.
inexhausto, ta, *a.* unexhausted, unspent.
inexigible, *a.* inexigible, unrequirable; that cannot be demanded.
inexistencia, *f.* inexistence, nonexistence.
inexistente, *a.* inexistent, nonexistent.
inexorabilidad, *f.* inexorability, inexorableness.
inexorable, *a.* inexorable, relentless, unbending.
inexperiencia, *f.* inexperience.
inexperto, ta, *a.* unskilful, inexperienced.
inexpiable, *a.* inexpiable.
inexplicable, *a.* inexplicable, unexplainable.
inexplorado, da, *a.* unexplored.
inexplosible, *a.* unexplosive, nonexplosive.
inexplotable, *a.* unexploitable, unworkable.
inexpresable, *a.* inexpressible; unspeakable, unutterable.
inexpresivo, va, *a.* inexpressive.
inexpugnable, *a.* inexpugnable, impregnable; firm, obstinate, stubborn.
in extenso, in extenso, at full length.
inextenso, sa, *a.* unextended, extensionless.
inextinguible, *a.* inextinguishable, unquenchable; perpetual.
inextirpable, *a.* inexterminable, not capable of being eradicated.
in extremis, in extremis, on the point of death.
inextricable, *a.* inextricable.
infacundo, da, *a.* ineloquent.
infalibilidad, *f.* infallibility.
infalible, *a.* infallible.—**infaliblemente,** *adv.* infallibly.
infamación, *f.* slander, defamation.
infamador, ra, *n.* & *a.* defamer(-ing).
infamante, *a.* defaming; opprobrious.
infamar, *va.* to defame, dishonor, disgrace.
infamativo, va, *a.* defaming; disgracing.
infamatorio, ria, *a.* defamatory, libellous.
infame. I. *a.* infamous, dishonorable. **II.** *n.* infamous person.
infamemente, *adv.* infamously.
infamia, *f.* infamy; baseness; infamous act.
infancia, *f.* infancy; childhood.
infando, da, *a.* unmentionable, unspeakable.
infanta, *f.* female child under seven years of age; infanta, any daughter of the King of Spain; wife of a prince royal.
infantado, *m.* territory assigned to a prince of the royal blood of Spain.
infante, *m.* infant, male child under seven years of age; infante, any son of the King of Spain, except the heir apparent; infantry soldier.—*pl.* choristers, choir boys.
infantería, *f.* infantry.—**i. de la guardia real,** (Engl.) Foot Guard.—**i. de marina,** (U. S.) Marine Corps.—**i. ligera,** (mil.) light infantry.
infanticida, *n.* infanticide, child murderer.
infanticidio, *m.* infanticide, murder of a child.
infantil, *a.* infantile, childlike.
infantilismo, *m.* infantility; (med.) infantilism.
infanzón, *m.* ancient nobleman.—**infanzonado, da,** *a.* pertaining to an INFANZÓN.—**infanzonazgo,** *m.* territory of an INFANZÓN.—**infanzonía,** *f.* dignity or condition of INFANZÓN.
infartación, *f.* (med.) infarction.
infarto, *m.* (med.) infarct.
infatigable, *a.* indefatigable, untiring.
infatigablemente, *adv.* indefatigably.
infatuación, *f.* infatuation.
infatuado, da, *a.* infatuated, infatuate.
infatuar. I. *va.* to infatuate. **II.** *vr.* to become infatuated.
infaustamente, *adv.* unluckily.
infausto, ta, *a.* unlucky; unhappy, accursed.
infebril, *a.* fever-free.
infección, *f.* infection.—**i. focal,** (med., dent.) focal infection.
infeccionar, *va.* to infect.
infeccioso, sa, *a.* infectious, infective.
infectar. I. *va.* to infect; spread contagion; to corrupt, vitiate, pervert. **II.** *vr.* to become infected.
infectivo, va, *a.* infective, infectious.
infecto, ta, *a.* infected, tainted, corrupt.
infecundidad, *f.* infecundity, sterility.
infecundo, da, *a.* infecund, barren, sterile.
infelice, *a.* (poet.) unhappy, wretched.
infelicidad, *f.* unhappiness, infelicity.
infeliz. I. *a.* unhappy, wretched; unfortunate, luckless. **II.** *n.* poor devil.
infelizmente, *adv.* unhappily, unluckily.
inferencia, *f.* inference.
inferior. I. *a.* inferior; lower; under (part); elementary (school, math., etc.). **II.** *a.* & *n.* inferior.
inferioridad, *f.* inferiority.
inferir (*ind. pres.* INFIERO, *pret.* él INFIRIÓ; *subj.* INFIERA; *ger.* INFIRIENDO). **I.** *va.* to infer; to imply, lead to; to inflict (as a wound); to offer (as an insult). **II.** *vr.* to follow as a consequence.
infernáculo, *m.* a boys' game, hopscotch.
infernal, *a.* infernal, hellish.
infernalmente, *adv.* hellishly, infernally.
infernar, *va.* (*ind.* INFIERNO; *subj.* INFIERNE) to damn; to irritate, vex, provoke.
inferno, na, *a.* (poet.) infernal.
infestación, *f.* infestation.
infestar, *va.* to infest, overrun; to infect; to harass; to fill with stench.
infesto, ta, *a.* (poet.) prejudicial, dangerous.
infeudar, *va.*; **infeudación,** *f.* = ENFEUDAR, etc.
infibulación, *f.* (vet.) infibulation.
infibular, *va.* (vet.) to infibulate.
inficionar, *va.* to infect; to poison; corrupt, defile, pervert, vitiate.
infidelidad, *f.* infidelity; unfaithfulness, faithlessness; unbelief, want of faith; unbelievers as a class.
infidelísimo, ma, *a. super.* of INFIEL.
infidencia, *f.* unfaithfulness, faithlessness; treason; (law) misfeasance.
infidente, *a.* unfaithful.
infiel. I. *a.* unfaithful, faithless; infidel, pagan; inaccurate, inexact. **II.** *m.* unbeliever, infidel.
infielmente, *adv.* unfaithfully.
infiernillo, *m.* small alcohol stove.
[1]**infierno,** *m.* (often in the *pl.*) hell; refectory or eating room in some convents; (chem.) large retort; cave of a baking machine; tank in oil mills.—**el quinto i.,** or **los quintos infiernos,** the end of the world (fig., app. to a very remote place).
[2]**infierno, infierne,** *v. V.* INFERNAR.
infiero, infiera, *v. V.* INFERIR.
infigurable, *a.* incorporeal, that cannot be represented by any material figure.
infiltración, *f.* infiltration; percolation.—**i. afluente,** influent seepage.
infiltrar, *va.* & *vr.* to infiltrate, percolate, filter; to imbue, infuse.

ínfimo, ma, *a.* lowest, least; most abject, vilest; (com.) most inferior in quality.
infinidad, *f.* infinity; (fig.) infinite number, lot.
infinitamente, *adv.* infinitely.
infinitesimal, *a.* infinitesimal.
infinitésimo, *m.* (math.) infinitesimal.
infinitivo, *n.* & *a.* (gram.) infinitive.
infinito, ta. I. *a.* infinite. **II.** *adv.* infinitely, immensely. **III.** *m.* **(el i.)** infinity.
infinitud, *f.* = INFINIDAD.
infirió, infiriendo, *v. V.* INFERIR.
infirmar, *va.* (law) to invalidate.
inflable, *a.* inflatable.
inflación, *f.* inflation; conceit, vanity, airs.
inflacionista. I. *a.* inflationary. **II.** *n.* inflationist.
inflado, da. I. *pp.* of INFLAR. **II.** *a.* inflated, swollen.
inflamabilidad, *f.* inflammability.
inflamable, *a.* inflammable.
inflamación, *f.* inflammation; ignition.
inflamador, ra, inflamante, *a.* inflaming; inflammatory.
inflamar. I. *va.* to inflame, kindle, set on fire; to excite. **II.** *vr.* to take fire, ignite; to become fiery or excited; (med.) to become inflamed.
inflamatorio, ria, *a.* inflammatory.
inflar. I. *va.* to inflate; to elate, puff up with pride. **II.** *vr.* to swell; to strut.
inflativo, va, *a.* inflating.
inflectivo, va, *a.* (gram.) inflective, inflectional.
inflexibilidad, *f.* inflexibility; stiffness, rigidity; inexorability.
inflexible, *a.* inflexible, rigid; unbending, unyielding.
inflexiblemente, *adv.* inflexibly, inexorably.
inflexión, *f.* inflection, bending; (gram.) inflection; accent, modulation.
inflictivo, va, *a.* inflictive.
infligir, *va.* (*ind.* INFLIJO; *subj.* INFLIJA) to impose (a penalty), condemn to.
inflorescencia, *f.* (bot.) inflorescence.
influencia, *f.* influence; (theol.) divine grace.
influenciar, *va.* (Am.) to influence.
influente, *a.* influencing, influential.
influenza, *f.* (med.) influenza, grippe, (U. S., coll.) flu.—**i. asiática,** Asian or Asiatic flu.
influir. I. *va.* (*ind.* INFLUYO; *subj.* INFLUYA) to influence; to act on; (theol.) to grace with inspiration. **II.** *vn.* **(en)** to have influence (on), to affect; to contribute (to), have a part (in).
influjo, *m.* influence; influx; (naut.) rising tide.
influyente, *a.* influential.
influyentemente, *adv.* influentially.
influyo, influya, *v. V.* INFLUIR.
infolio, *m.* book in folio form.
Inforciado, *m.* Infortiate, second part of the Pandects of Justinian.
información, *f.* information; report; inquiry, investigation; judicial inquiry and process; (law) brief.—**i. preliminar,** briefing.—**fuente de i.,** source of information, contact.
informado, da. I. *pp.* of INFORMAR. **II.** *a.* informed.
informador, ra. I. *a.* informing, informative. **II.** *n.* informer.
informal, *a.* informal; unreliable; unconventional.
informalidad, *f.* informality, unconventionality; breach of etiquette; unreliability.
informante. I. *a.* informing, informative. **II.** *n.* informer.
informar. I. *va.* to inform, tell, advise, report to; to give form to, shape. **II.** *vn.* (law) to plead. **III.** *vr.* **(de)** to acquaint oneself (with), to inquire (into), to find out (about).
informativo, va, *a.* instructive, informative.
[1]informe, *a.* shapeless, formless.
[2]informe, *m.* information; report, account, statement; advice; reference; (law) plea, pleading.
informidad, *f.* shapelessness.
infortificable, *a.* that cannot be fortified.
infortuna, *f.* (astrol.) evil influence of the stars.
infortunado, da. I. *a.* unfortunate, unlucky. **II.** *n.* unfortunate.
infortunio, *m.* misfortune, ill luck; mishap; misery, suffering.
infosura, *f.* (vet.) a disease of horses.
infracción, *f.* infraction, breach, infringement, trespass.
infracto, ta, *a.* steady, not easily moved.
infractor, ra, *n.* infractor, breaker, violator, transgressor.
in fraganti, *adv.* = EN FLAGRANTE, in the act.
infrahumano, na, *a.* subhuman.
infraluminescencia, *f.* infraluminescence.
infraluminescente, *a.* infraluminescent.
inframaxilar, *a.* (anat.) inframaxillary.
infrangible, *a.* infrangible; inviolable.
infranqueable, *a.* unsurmountable.
infraorbitario, ria, *a.* (anat.) infraorbital.
infrarrojo, ja, *a.* infrared.
infrascripto, ta; infrascrito, ta, *a.* undersigned; hereinafter mentioned.
infrasónico, ca. I. *a.* infrasonic. **II.** *f.* infrasonics.
infrecuente, *a.* infrequent, unusual.
infrecuentemente, *adv.* infrequently, rarely, seldom.
infringir, *va.* (*ind.* INFRINJO; *subj.* INFRINJA) to infringe, violate, break.
infructífero, ra, *a.* unfruitful; unprofitable.
infructuosidad, *f.* unfruitfulness, unproductiveness, uselessness.
infructuosamente, *adv.* unfruitfully, uselessly.
infructuoso, sa, *a.* fruitless, unproductive; unprofitable, abortive, unsuccessful.
infrugífero, ra, *a.* = INFRUCTÍFERO.
ínfulas, *f. pl.* (eccl.) infulæ, headdress, mitre; conceit, airs.
infundadamente, *adv.* groundlessly, without cause or reason.
infundado, da, *a.* groundless, baseless.
infundible, *a.* infusible.
infundibuliforme, *a.* (bot.) funnel-shaped.
infundíbulo, *m.* (anat.) infundibulum.
infundio, *m.* (coll.) fib, story.
infundir, *va.* (*pp.* INFUNDIDO and INFUSO) to infuse, to inspire with; to imbue, to instil.
infurción, *f.* ancient ground lease.
infurcioniego, ga, *a.* subject to ground lease.
infurtir, *va.* = ENFURTIR, to full (cloth).
infusibilidad, *f.* infusibility.
infusible, *a.* infusible.
infusión, *f.* infusion; inspiration; (pharm.) infusion; (eccl.) baptism by sprinkling.
infuso, sa, *a.* infused (with the grace of God).
infusorio, ria, *m.* & *a.* (zool.) infusorian.
ingenerable, *a.* ingenerable, that cannot be produced or generated.
ingeniar. I. *va.* to conceive, contrive, devise, scheme. **II.** *vr.* to endeavor and manage skilfully; to find means to get or do a thing.
ingeniatura, *f.* (coll.) ingenuity, acuteness, skilful management; (Am.) engineering.
ingeniería, *f.* engineering.—**i. aerostera, civil,** etc. *V.* INGENIERO.
ingeniero, ra, *n.* engineer.—**i. aeróstata,** aeronautic engineer.—**i. aerostero,** aviation engineer.—**i. agrónomo,** agricultural engineer.—**i. civil,** civil engineer (gen. app. to all nonmilitary engineers).—**i. de caminos, canales y puertos,** civil engineer.—**i. de la armada,** or **de marina** = I. NAVAL.—**i. de minas,** mining engineer.—**i. de montes,** forestry engineer.—**i. electricista,** electrical engineer.—**i. en jefe,** chief engineer.—**i. forestal,** forestry engineer.—**i. industrial** = I. QUÍMICO.—**i. jefe,** chief engineer.—**i. naval,** marine engineer.—**i. químico,** chemical engineer.—**i. sanitario,** sanitary engineer, public health engineer.
ingenio, *m.* talent; mind, creative or inventive faculty; cleverness, skill, smartness; ingenuity,

wit(s); talented person (esp. author); engine, machine, mechanical apparatus; device, contrivance; (bookbinding) plowcutter, plowpress. —**i. de azúcar**, sugar mill, sugar plantation.—**i. de pólvora**, powdermill.
ingeniosamente, *adv.* ingeniously.
ingeniosidad, *f.* ingenuity, ingeniousness.
ingenioso, sa, *a.* ingenious.
ingénito, ta, *a.* unbegotten; innate, inborn.
ingente, *a.* very large, huge, prodigious.
ingenuamente, *adv.* candidly, ingenuously.
ingenuidad, *f.* ingenuousness, candor.
ingenuo, nua, *a.* ingenuous, open, candid; (law) ingenuous, freeborn.
ingerencia, *f.* interference, intermeddling.
ingeridor, *m.* grafting knife.
ingeridura, *f.* grafting.
ingerir. I. *va.* (*ind.* INGIERO; *subj.* INGIERA) to insert, introduce, inclose; (agr.) to graft. **II.** *vr.* to interfere, intermeddle.
ingestión, *f.* (med.) ingestion, introduction of food into the stomach.
ingiero, ingiera, *v. V.* INGERIR.
ingina, *f.* = QUIJADA, jaw, jawbone.
ingle, *f.* groin, part next the thigh.
inglés, sa. I. *a.* English.—**a la inglesa**, in the English fashion. **II.** *n.* Englishman(-woman). **III.** *m.* English (the language).
inglesar, *va.* & *vr.* to Anglicize.
inglesismo, *m.* Anglicism.
inglete, *m.* diagonal; angle of 45°.
inglosable, *a.* admitting no gloss or comment.
ingobernable, *a.* ungovernable, unmanageable, unruly.
ingobernablemente, *adv.* uncontrollably, ungovernably.
ingratamente, *adv.* ungratefully.
ingratitud, *f.* ingratitude, ungratefulness.
ingrato, ta. I. *a.* ungrateful; thankless; disagreeable. **II.** *n.* ingrate.
ingravidez, *f.* weightlessness.
ingrávido, da, *a.* light, weightless.
ingrediente, *m.* ingredient.
ingresar, *vn.* **(en)** to enter; (of money, profits, etc.) to come (in); to deposit (money); to join (a party, etc.); to enter (a university).
ingreso, *m.* entrance; entering; joining; (com.) entry, money received; (eccl.) surplice fees.—*pl.* (com.) revenue, receipts, earnings.
íngrimo, ma, *a.* (Mex.) (coll.) alone, solitary; deserted.
inguinal; inguinario, ria, *a.* (anat.) inguinal.
ingurgitación, *f.* (med.) ingurgitation.
ingurgitar, *va.* to ingurgitate, swallow.
ingustable, *a.* unsavory, unpalatable.
inhábil, *a.* unable; incompetent; unfit, unskilful; unqualified.
inhabilidad, *f.* inability; incompetence; unskilfulness.
inhabilitación, *f.* disqualification; disability; deprivation (of civil rights).
inhabilitar. I. *va.* to disqualify; to disable, render unfit. **II.** *vr.* to lose a right; to become disabled.
inhabitable, *a.* uninhabitable.
inhabitado, da, *a.* uninhabited.
inhabituado, da, *a.* unaccustomed.
inhacedero, ra, *a.* impracticable, unfeasible.
inhalador, ra, *n.* inhaler.
inhalación, *f.* (med.) inhalation.
inhalar, *va.* (med.) to inhale.
inherencia, *f.* inherence.
inherente, *a.* inherent.
inhestar, *va.* (*ind.* INHIESTO; *subj.* INHIESTE) = ENHESTAR, to erect; to raise.
inhibición, *f.* inhibition; prohibition.
inhibido, da, *a.* inhibited.
inhibidor, *m.* (chem.) inhibitor.
inhibir, *va.* (law) to inhibit (esp. an inferior court from proceeding further).
inhibitorio, ria, *a.* inhibitory.
[1]**inhiesto, inhieste**, *v. V.* INHESTAR.
[2]**inhiesto, ta**, *a.* = ENHIESTO, erect; steep.
inhomogeneidad, *f.* inhomogeneity, incompatibility, discordance.
inhomogéneo, nea, *a.* inhomogeneous, incompatible, discordant.
inhonestamente, *adv.* immodestly.
inhonestidad, *f.* immodesty, indecency.
inhonesto, ta, *a.* immodest, indecent.
inhospedable, *a.* = INHOSPITALARIO.
inhospitable, inhospital, *a.* = INHOSPITALARIO.
inhospitalario, ria, *a.* inhospitable, reluctant to entertain guests; unsheltering.
inhospitalidad, *f.* inhospitableness.
inhumación, *f.* interment, burying.
inhumanamente, *adv.* inhumanly, cruelly.
inhumanidad, *f.* inhumanity, cruelty.
inhumano, na, *a.* inhuman, cruel.
inhumar, *va.* to bury, inhume, inter.
iniciación, *f.* initiation, introduction.
iniciado, da, *n.* & *a.* initiate.
iniciador, ra. I. *a.* initiating, starting. **II.** *n.* initiator, starter.
inicial, *f.* & *a.* initial.
iniciar. I. *va.* to initiate; to begin, start. **II.** *vr.* to be initiated; (eccl.) to receive first orders.
iniciativo, va. I. *a.* initiating, initiatory. **II.** *f.* initiative; right to propose laws, etc.
inicuamente, *adv.* iniquitously.
inicuo, cua, *a.* iniquitous, wicked.
in illo tempore, *adv.* formerly, in times of yore.
inimaginable, *a.* unimaginable, inconceivable.
inimicísimo, ma, *a. super. irreg.* of ENEMIGO, most inimical.
inimitable, *a.* inimitable.
ininterrumpido, da, *a.* uninterrupted, unremitting, continuous.
inio, inión, *m.* (anat.) inion.
iniquidad, *f.* iniquity, unrighteousness.
iniquísimo, ma, *a. super.* of INICUO.
injerencia, injeridura, injerir = INGERENCIA, INGERIDURA, etc.
injertar, *va.* (*pp.* INJERTADO, INJERTO) (agr.) to ingraft, to graft.
injertera, *f.* orchard of grafted trees.
injerto, *m.* graft, grafting, ingrafted tree.
injuria, *f.* offense, wrong, insult, abuse, affront; injustice; damage, harm.
injuriado, da, *a.* & *pp.* injured, wronged.
injuriador, ra, *n.* aggressor, offender, abuser.
injuriante, *a.* injuring; offensive, insulting.
injuriar, *va.* to insult, offend, abuse; to annoy; to harm, hurt.
injuriosamente, *adv.* insultingly, offensively; injuriously, hurtfully.
injurioso, sa, *a.* injurious; insulting, offensive, abusive.
injustamente, *adv.* unjustly.
injusticia, *f.* injustice.
injustificable, *a.* unjustifiable.
injustificadamente, *adv.* unjustifiably.
injustificado, da, *a.* unjustified, unjustifiable.
injusto, ta, *a.* unjust.
inlegible, *a.* illegible.
inllevable, *a.* unbearable.
inmaculadamente, *adv.* immaculately.
inmaculado, da, *a.* immaculate.—**Inmaculada Concepción**, (eccl.) Immaculate Conception.
inmaduro, ra, *a.* = INMATURO.
inmaleable, *a.* immalleable, unmalleable.
inmanejable, *a.* unmanageable; unruly.
inmanente, *a.* immanent, inherent.
inmarcesible, *a.* unfading, unwithering.
inmaterial, *a.* immaterial, incorporeal.
inmaterialidad, *f.* immateriality.
inmaturo, ra, *a.* immature.
inmediación, *f.* contiguity, contact.—*pl.* environs, suburbs, outskirts; neighborhood.
inmediatamente, *adv.* contiguously; immediately, forthwith.
inmediato, ta, *a.* contiguous, close, adjoining, next, immediate.—**dar por las inmediatas**, (fig.) to force to the wall; to silence (in a discussion).—**llegar**, or **venir, a las inmediatas**,

to come to the thick, or hardest, part of a fight or dispute.
inmedicable, *a.* incurable, irremediable.
inmejorable, *a.* unimprovable, unsurpassable, most excellent.
inmemorable, *a.* immemorial.
inmemorablemente, *adv.* immemorably.
inmemorial, *a.* immemorial.
inmensamente, *adv.* immensely, infinitely.
inmensidad, *f.* immensity, vastness; infinity; immensity of space, boundless space; great multitude or number.
inmenso, sa, *a.* immense; unbounded, infinite; countless.
inmensurable, *a.* immeasurable.
inmerecidamente, *adv.* undeservedly.
inmerecido, da, *a.* unmerited, undeserved.
inmergir, *va.* to immerse.
inméritamente, *adv.* unmeritedly.
inmérito, ta, *a.* undeserved, unmerited.
inmeritorio, ria, *a.* undeserving.
inmersibilidad, *f.* immersibility.
inmersible, *a.* immersible.
inmersión, *f.* immersion.
inmetódico, ca, *a.* unmethodical.
inmigración, *f.* immigration.
inmigrado, da. I. *pp.* of INMIGRAR. **II.** *a.* & *n.* immigrant.
inmigrante, *n.* immigrant.
inmigrar, *vn.* to immigrate.
inmigratorio, ria, *a.* immigration (as *a.*).
inminencia, *f.* imminence, nearness.
inminente, *a.* imminent, impending, near.
inmiscibilidad, *f.* (chem., phys.) immiscibility.
inmiscible, *a.* (chem.) non-mixing.
inmiscuir. I. *va.* to mix. **II.** *vr.* to interfere, to intermeddle.
inmobiliario, ria, *a.* pertaining to real estate.
inmoble, *a.* unmovable, immovable, fixed; motionless; unshakable, constant.
inmoderación, *f.* immoderation, excess.
inmoderadamente, *adv.* immoderately.
inmoderado, da, *a.* immoderate, excessive.
inmodestamente, *adv.* immodestly.
inmodestia, *f.* immodesty, indelicacy.
inmodesto, ta, *a.* immodest, indelicate.
inmódico, ca, *a.* excessive.
inmolación, *f.* immolation, sacrifice.
inmolador, ra, *n.* & *a.* immolator(-ing).
inmolar. *va.* to immolate; to sacrifice.
inmoral, *a.* immoral.
inmoralidad, *f.* immorality.
inmoralmente, *adv.* immorally.
inmortal, *a.* immortal.
inmortalidad, *f.* immortality.
inmortalización, *f.* immortalization.
inmortalizar. I. *va.* to immortalize. **II.** *vr.* to become immortal.
inmortalmente, *adv.* immortally.
inmortificación, *f.* licentiousness.
inmortificado, da, *a.* unmortified.
inmotivado, da, *a.* without reason or cause.
inmoto, ta, *a.* unmoved.
inmovible, *a.* immovable.
inmóvil, *a.* motionless; fixed; unshaken.
inmovilidad, *f.* immovability, fixedness.
inmovilismo, *m.* inflexibility, rigidity; immutability.
inmovilizaoión, *f.* immobilization.
inmovilizar, *va.* to immobilize, fix.
inmudable, *a.* immutable.
inmueble. I. *a.* (law) immovable, real (property). **II.** *m.* (law) immovables.
inmundicia, *f.* filth, dirt; garbage; refuse; nastiness, filthiness; uncleanliness; impurity.
inmundo, da, *a.* unclean, filthy.
inmune, *a.* free, exempt; immune.
inmunidad, *f.* immunity; exemption, franchise, freedom.
inmunización, *f.* immunization.
inmunizar, *va.* to immunize, render immune.
inmunología, *f.* immunology.
inmutabilidad, *f.* immutability.
inmutable, *a.* immutable.
inmutación, *f.* change, alteration.
inmutar. I. *va.* to change, alter. **II.** *vr.* to change countenance from some emotion, to become disturbed, lose one's calm.
inmutativo, va, *a.* that changes or causes alterations.
innatismo, *m.* (philos.) innatism.
innato, ta, *a.* innate; inborn.
innatural, *a.* unnatural.
innavegable, *a.* unnavigable; unseaworthy.
innecesariamente, *adv.* unnecessarily.
innecesario, ria, *a.* unnecessary.
innegable, *a.* undeniable.
innegablemente, *adv.* undeniably.
innoble, *a.* ignoble.
innocuidad, *f.* innocuity.
innocuo, cua, *a.* innocuous, harmless.
innominable, *a.* unnamable.
innominado, da, *a.* nameless.
innovación, *f.* innovation.
innovador, ra. I. *a.* innovating. **II.** *n.* innovator.
innovamiento, *m.* innovation.
innovar, *va.* to innovate.
innumerabilidad, *f.* innumerability.
innumerable, *a.* innumerable, numberless.
innumerablemente, *adv.* innumerably.
innúmero, ra, *a.* numberless, countless.
inobediencia, *f.* disobedience.
inobediente, *a.* disobedient; unmanageable.
inobservable, *a.* unobservable, inobservable.
inobservancia, *f.* disregarding (of law, etc.); non-conforming.
inobservante, *a.* disregarding (law, etc.); nonconformist (in religion).
inocencia, *f.* innocence; harmlessness.
inocentada, *f.* (coll.) simple or silly speech or action; practical joke or trick.
inocente, *a.* innocent; harmless; simple, gullible, unsophisticated, easily duped, "easy."
inocentemente, *adv.* innocently; harmlessly.
inocentón, na. I. *a. aug.* very simple and credulous. **II.** *n.* simpleton.
inoculación, *f.* inoculation.
inoculador, ra, *n.* & *a.* inoculator(-ing).
inoculante. I. *a.* inoculating. **II.** *m.* (med.) inoculum, inoculant.
inocular, *va.* (med.) to inoculate; to contaminate.
inocuo, ca, *a.* = INNOCUO.
inodoro, ra. I. *a.* inodorous, odorless. **II.** *m.* water closet.
inofensivo, va, *a.* inoffensive, harmless.
inoficioso, sa, *a.* (law) inofficious (will).
inolvidable, *a.* unforgetable.
inope, *a.* poor, penniless, destitute.
inoperable, *a.* (med.) inoperable.
inoperación, *f.* inoperation.
inopia, *f.* indigence, poverty, penury.
inopinable, *a.* indisputable; inconceivable.
inopinadamente, *adv.* unexpectedly.
inopinado, da, *a.* unexpected, unforeseen.
inoportunamente, *adv.* inopportunely.
inoportunidad, *f.* inopportuneness, untimeliness.
inoportuno, na, *a.* inopportune, untimely.
inordenadamente, *adv.* inordinately.
inordenado, da; inordinado, da, *a.* inordinate, irregular, disorderly.
inorgánico, ca, *a.* inorganic.
inosculación, *f.* inosculation.
inoxidabilidad, *f.* inoxidability.
inoxidable, *a.* inoxidizable; nonrusting.
inoxidación, *f.* inoxidizing.
inoxidar, *va.* to inoxidize, prevent oxidation (in).
in pace (Lat.). **I.** *adv.* in peace. **II.** *m.* dungeon where scandalous persons were formerly confined.
in pártibus, (Lat.), *adv.* (coll.) having a nominal appointment.
in péctore (Lat.), *adv.* (coll.) (of resolutions, decrees, etc.) not yet made known.

in perpétuum (Lat.), *adv.* in perpetuum, in perpetuity, forever.
in promptu (Lat.), *adv.* offhand, impromptu, extempore.
in púribus (Lat.), *adv.* (coll.) stark naked.
inquebrantable, *a.* irrevocable.
inquiero, inquiera, *v. V.* INQUERIR.
inquietador, ra, *n.* disturber.
inquietamente, *adv.* restlessly.
inquietante, *a.* disquieting, disturbing.
inquietar. I. *va.* to disquiet, trouble, worry; to vex, tease, harass; to stir up or excite. **II.** *vr.* to become uneasy or restless, to fret, worry.
inquieto, ta, *a.* restless; anxious, solicitous, uneasy, worried.
inquietud, *f.* restlessness, uneasiness, anxiety.
inquilinato, *m.* (law) lease, leasehold.
inquilino, na, *n.* tenant, lodger; (law) lessee.
inquina, *f.* (coll.) aversion, hatred, grudge.
inquinamento, *m.* infection.
inquinar, *va.* to contaminate.
inquiridor, ra, *n.* inquirer, investigator.
inquirir, *va.* (*ind.* INQUIERO; *subj.* INQUIERA) to inquire, look into, search, investigate.
inquisición, *f.* inquest, examination, inquiry; (eccl.) Inquisition; Holy Office.
inquisidor, ra. I. *n.* inquirer, examiner. **II.** *m.* (eccl.) inquisitor.
inquisitivo, va, *a.* inquisitive, demanding.
inquisitorial, *a.* inquisitorial.
inri, *m.* I. N. R. I. (inscription on the cross); brand, stigma, stain.
insabible, *a.* unknowable.
insaciabilidad, *f.* insatiableness, greediness.
insaciable, *a.* insatiable; greedy.
insaciablemente, *adv.* insatiably.
insaculación, *f.* (law) balloting for names.
insaculador, *m.* (law) balloter.
insacular, *va.* to ballot, to vote by ballot.
insalivación, *f.* insalivation.
insalivar, *va.* to insalivate.
insalubre, *a.* insalubrious, unhealthful.
insalubridad, *f.* insalubrity, unhealthfulness.
insanable, *a.* incurable, irremediable.
insania, *f.* insanity.
insano, na, *a.* insane, mad, crazy.
insatisfecho, cha, *a.* unsatisfied.
insaturable, *a.* insaturable.
inscribible, *a.* inscribable.
inscribir. I. *va.* (*pp. irreg.* INSCRITO, INSCRIPTO) to inscribe, register, record, book; (geom.) to inscribe; (law) to record (deeds). **II.** *vr.* to register; to enroll.
inscripción, *f.* inscription; record, register, entry; registration; government bond.
inscriptible, *a.* (geom.) inscribable.
inscripto, ta, *pp. irreg.* of INSCRIBIR.
inscrito, ta, *pp. irreg.* of INSCRIBIR.
insculpido, da, *a.* insculped, engraved.
insculpir, *va.* to engrave, cut.
insecable, *a.* (coll.) that cannot be dried.
insecticida, *n.* & *a.* insecticide(-al).
insectil, *a.* insectile, insectean.
insectívoro, ra, *a.* insectivorous.
insecto, *m.* (entom.) insect.
inseguridad, *f.* insecurity, unsafety; uncertainty.
inseguro, ra, *a.* insecure, unsafe; uncertain.
inseminación, *f.* insemination.
inseminar, *va.* to inseminate, impregnate.
insenescencia, *f.* quality of not becoming old.
insensatamente, *adv.* insensately, madly, stupidly.
insensatez, *f.* stupidity, folly.
insensato, ta, *a.* insensate, stupid, mad.
insensibilidad, *f.* insensibility, unconsciousness; hard-heartedness.
insensibilizar, *va.* to make insensible or insensitive.
insensible, *a.* insensible, senseless, unconscious; imperceptible; unfeeling, heartless.
insensiblemente, *adv.* insensibly; imperceptibly.
inseparabilidad, *f.* inseparableness.
inseparable, *a.* inseparable; undetachable.
inseparablemente, *adv.* inseparably.
insepulto, ta, *a.* unburied, uninterred.
inserción, *f.* insertion; grafting.
inserir, *va.* (*pp. irreg.* INSERTO) to insert; to graft.
insertar. I. *va.* (*pp.* INSERTADO, INSERTO) to insert, to introduce. **II.** *vr.* (zool. and bot.) to become inserted or attached.
inserto, ta, *pp. irreg.* of INSERIR & INSERTAR.
inservible, *a.* unserviceable, useless.
insidia, *f.* ambush, snare.
insidiador, ra, *n.* plotter, waylayer.
insidiar, *va.* to plot against, waylay, ambush.
insidiosamente, *adv.* insidiously, guilefully.
insidioso, sa, *a.* insidious, sly, guileful.
insigne, *a.* noted, famous, renowned.
insignemente, *adv.* signally, famously.
insignia, *f.* decoration, device, medal, badge, standard; (naut.) pennant.—*pl.* insignia.
insignificancia, *f.* insignificance; insufficiency, uselessness; trifle.
insignificante, *a.* insignificant, unimportant.
insignificativo, va, *a.* insignificant.
insinceridad, *f.* insincerity.
insincero, ra, *a.* insincere, hypocritical.
insinuación, *f.* insinuation, innuendo; hint, suggestion; (law) exhibition of a public instrument before a judge.
insinuante, *a.* insinuative, crafty, artful, sleek.
insinuar. I. *va.* to insinuate, hint, suggest. **II.** *vr.* to ingratiate oneself; to creep in; to grow (on one, as a habit).
insinuativo, va, *a.* insinuating; insinuative; slick, smooth.
insípidamente, *adv.* insipidly.
insipidez, *f.* insipidity, insipidness.
insípido, da, *a.* insipid, tasteless; unsavory; spiritless, vapid, flat.
insipiencia, *f.* ignorance, lack of judgment.
insipiente, *a.* ignorant, uninformed.
insistencia, *f.* persistence, insistence, obstinacy.
insistente, *a.* insistent, persistent.
insistir, *vn.* **(en)** to insist (on), persist (in); to dwell (upon), emphasize.
ínsito, ta, *a.* inherent, inborn, connatural.
in situ (Lat.) *adv.* in situ, in its natural place.
insociabilidad, *f.* unsociability, unsociableness.
insociable, insocial, *a.* unsociable.
insolación, *f.* (med.) insolation, sunstroke.
insolar. I. *va.* to expose to the sun's rays. **II.** *vr.* (med.) to be sunstruck.
insoldable, *a.* that cannot be soldered or welded.
insolencia, *f.* insolence.
insolentar. I. *va.* to make bold. **II.** *vr.* to become insolent.
insolente, *a.* insolent.—**insolentemente,** *adv.* insolently.
in sólidum, *adv.* (law) insolidum, joint and several.
insólito, ta, *a.* unusual, unaccustomed.
insolubilidad, *f.* insolubility; unsolvability.
insolubilización, *f.* insolubilization, indissolubility.
insolubilizar, *va.* to insolubilize, render insoluble.
insoluble, *a.* insoluble; fast, strong; unsolvable.
insolvencia, *f.* insolvency.
insolvente, *a.* insolvent.
insomne, *a.* insomnious, sleepless.
insomnio, *m.* insomnia, sleeplessness.
insondable, *a.* unfathomable, fathomless; inscrutable, unsearchable; abysmal.
insonoro, ra, *a.* not sounding clear.
insoportable, *a.* unbearable, intolerable.
insostenible, *a.* indefensible.
inspección, *f.* inspection, survey; superintendence; inspector's office.—**i. subterránea,** underground survey.
inspeccionar, *va.* to inspect, examine, oversee.
inspector, ra, *n.* inspector, examiner; supervisor, superintendent, overseer.
inspectoría, *f.* (Am.) inspectorship, inspectorate.
inspiración, *f.* inspiration; (med.) inhalation.

inspirador, ra. I. *a.* inspiring; (anat.) inspiratory. II. *n.* inspirer.
inspirante, *a.* inspiring.
inspirar, *va.* to inspire; to inhale.
inspirativo, va, *a.* inspiring.
inspiratorio, ria, *a.* (anat.) inspiratory.
instabilidad, *f.* instability; inconstancy.
instable, *a.* unstable; inconstant, changeable.
instalación, *f.* installation, instalment; settling; plant, works, factory; system (as of gas pipes and fittings, etc.); induction (of an officer).—**i. de consumidor,** (elec.) consuming installation.
instalador, ra, *n.* installer; *m.* (eccl.) inductor.—**i. de cañerías,** plumber.
instalar. I. *va.* to install; to put in, lay, set up; to induct (into office). II. *vr.* to establish oneself, settle.
instancia, *f.* instance or instancy; memorial, petition; prosecution or process of a suit; pressing argument; entreaty, request.—**a instancia de,** at the request of.
instantáneamente, *adv.* instantly; instantaneously.
instantáneo, nea. I. *a.* instantaneous. II. *f.* (photog.) snapshot.
instante. I. *a.* instant, pressing, urgent. II. *m.* instant, moment.—**al i.,** immediately.—**por instantes,** incessantly, every moment.
instantemente, *adv.* instantly.
instar. I. *va.* to press, urge; in schools, to impugn the solution of a question. II. *vn.* to be urgent.
instauración, *f.* renovation, restoration.
instaurar, *va.* to renovate, restore.
instaurativo, va, *a.* restorative.
instigación, *f.* instigation, incitement.
instigador, ra, *n.* instigator, abetter.
instigar, *va.* (*pret.* INSTIGUÉ; *subj.* INSTIGUE) to instigate, incite, urge.
instilación, *f.* instillation.
instilar, *va.* to instil, infuse, insinuate.
instintivo, va, *a.* instinctive.
instintivamente, *adv.* instinctively.
instinto, *m.* instinct; divine inspiration.—**por i.,** instinctively.
institución, *f.* institution, establishment; education, instruction; (law) institution, instituting.—*pl.* institutes (of a science).
institucional, *a.* institutional.
instituente, *a.* instituting; founding.
instituidor, ra, *n.* institutor, founder.
instituir, *va.* (*ind.* INSTITUYO; *subj.* INSTITUYA) to institute, establish, found; to teach, instruct; to appoint, constitute, institute.
instituta, *f.* (law) institutes.
instituto, *m.* institute, established law; settled order; institute, institution (of learning); school.—**i. de segunda enseñanza,** or **general y técnico,** high school.
institutor, ra, *n.* institutor.
institutriz, *f.* governess, instructress.
instituyente, *n.* institutor; founder.
instituyo, instituya, *v. V.* INSTITUIR.
instrucción, *f.* instruction, teaching; education; lesson; knowledge, learning; (law) court proceedings.—*pl.* instructions, directions, orders.—**i. primaria,** primary education.—**i. pública,** public education.—**i. secundaria,** high-school education.—**i. superior,** higher, or college, education.
instructivamente, *adv.* instructively.
instructivo, va, *a.* instructive.
instructor, ra, *n.* instructor, teacher.
instruído, da. I. *pp.* of INSTRUIR. II. *a.* learned, well-educated, well-posted.
instruir, *va.* (*ind.* INSTRUYO; *subj.* INSTRUYA) to instruct, teach, train, coach; to inform, advise; (mil.) to drill, train; (law) to put in legal form, to formulate according to established rules.
instrumentación, *f.* (mus.) instrumentation, orchestration.
instrumental, *a.* (mus.) instrumental; (law) pertaining to legal instruments.
instrumentalmente, *adv.* instrumentally.
instrumentar, *va.* (mus.) to orchestrate.
instrumentista, *m.* instrument maker; (mus.) instrumentalist, player on a musical instrument.
instrumento, *m.* instrument, implement, appliance, engine, machine, apparatus; agent or means; (law) instrument, indenture, deed; (mus.) instrument.—**i. de boca,** wind instrument.—**i. de canto,** musical instrument.—**i. de cuerda,** stringed instrument.—**i. de percusión,** percussion instrument.—**i. de viento,** or **i. neumático,** wind instrument.
instruyo, instruya, *v. V.* INSTRUIR.
insuave, *a.* unpleasant, disagreeable.
insubordinación, *f.* insubordination.
insubordinado, da. I. *pp.* of INSUBORDINAR. II. *a.* insubordinate, rebellious.
insubordinar. I. *va.* to incite to insubordination. II. *vr.* to rebel, to mutiny.
insubsistencia, *f.* instability.
insubsistente, *a.* unable; groundless, baseless.
insubstancial, *a.* unsubstantial, inane, shallow, pointless.
insubstancialidad, *f.* inanity.
insubstancialmente, *adv.* inanely.
insudar, *vn.* to toil, drudge, work hard.
insuficiencia, *f.* insufficiency, inadequateness.
insuficiente, *a.* insufficient, inadequate.
insuficientemente, *adv.* insufficiently.
insuflación, *f.* (med.) insufflation.
insuflador, *m.* (med.) insufflator.
insuflar, *va.* (med.) to insufflate.
insufrible, *a.* intolerable, unbearable.
insufriblemente, *adv.* insufferably, unbearably.
ínsula, *f.* (archaic) isle, island.
insular; insulano, na, *a.* insular.
insulina, *f.* (biochem.) Insulin (trademark).
insulsamente, *adv.* insipidly.
insulsez, *f.* insipidity, flatness.
insulso, sa, *a.* insipid, tasteless; dull, heavy.
insultador, ra. I. *a.* insulting, abusing, abusive. II. *n.* insulter, abuser.
insultante, *a.* insulting.
insultar. I. *va.* to insult; to call names. II. *vr.* (coll.) to have a fit.
insulto, *m.* insult, affront; sudden fit of illness.
insume, *a.* costly, expensive.
insumergibilidad, *f.* insubmersibility.
insumergible, *a.* insubmergible.
insuperabilidad, *f.* insuperability.
insuperable, *a.* insuperable, insurmountable.
insupurable, *a.* that cannot suppurate.
insurgente, *n.* & *a.* insurgent.
insurrección, *f.* insurrection, rebellion.
insurreccional, *a.* insurrectional, insurrectionary, revolutionary.
insurreccionar. I. *va.* to cause to rebel, to raise in insurrection. II. *vr.* to rebel.
insurrecto, ta, *n.* & *a.* insurgent, rebel.
insustancial, *a.* = INSUBSTANCIAL.
intacto, ta, *a.* untouched, intact whole; pure.
intachable, *a.* unexceptionable, irreproachable.
intachablemente, *adv.* irreproachably.
intangibilidad, *f.* intangibility.
intangible, *a.* intangible; not to be touched.
integérrimo, ma, *a. super.* of ÍNTEGRO, most honorable, unspotted, irreproachable.
integrable, *a.* integrable.
integración, *f.* integration.
integracionista, *n.* integrationist.
integrado, da, *pp.* of INTEGRAR.—**i. por,** consisting of. formed by.
integrador, *m.* integrator (instrument).
integral. I. *a.* integral; whole. II. *f.* (math.) integral.
integralmente, *adv.* integrally, wholly.
íntegramente, *adv.* entirely, wholly.
integrante, *a.* integral; integrant; integrating.
integrar, *va.* to integrate; to compose, form, make up; (com.) to reimburse; (math.) to integrate.
integridad, *f.* wholeness, completeness; integrity, honesty, uprightness; virginity.

íntegro, gra, *a.* entire, complete, whole; upright, honest.
integumentario, ria, *a.* integumentary.
integumento, *m.* integument.
intelección, *f.* intellection, understanding.
intelectiva, *f.* intellect, intelligence.
intelectivo, va, *a.* intellective, intelligent.
intelecto, *m.* intellect, understanding.
intelectual, *a.* intellectual, mental.
intelectualidad, *f.* intellectuality.
intelectualismo, *m.* intellectualism.
intelectualista. I. *a.* intellectualistic. **II.** *n.* intellectual.
intelectualmente, *adv.* intellectually.
inteligencia, *f.* intellect, mind, understanding; intelligence; comprehension; knowledge; understanding (between persons); skill, ability, experience; sense, meaning.—**en la i.,** in the understanding.—**examen de i.,** intelligence test.
inteligenciado, da, *a.* (coll.) instructed, informed.
inteligente, *a.* intelligent; talented, smart, bright, clever; skilful, able.
inteligibilidad, *f.* intelligibility.
inteligible, *a.* intelligible.
inteligiblemente, *adv.* intelligibly.
intemperancia, *f.* intemperance, excess.
intemperante, *a.* intemperate.
intemperie, *f.* rough or bad weather.—**a la i.,** in the open air, outdoors, unsheltered.
intempestivamente, *adv.* unseasonably, inopportunely.
intempestivo, va, *a.* unseasonable, inopportune.
intención, *f.* intention, purpose; viciousness (of animals); caution, discretion.—**dar i.,** to give hope.—**de primera i.,** provisionally, tentatively; frankly, impulsively, without disguise; (surg.) by first intention.—**de segunda i.,** double-facedly, deceitfully.—**por primera i.,** (surg.) = DE PRIMERA I.
intencionadamente, *adv.* intentionally.
intencionado, da, *a.* inclined, disposed.
intencional, *a.* intentional.
intencionalmente, *adv.* intentionally.
intendencia, *f.* intendancy (province); administration, management; office or district of an intendant.
intendenta, *f.* wife of an INTENDENTE.
intendente, *m.* intendant; administrator; sub treasurer of the government.—**i. de ejército,** quartermaster general.—**i. de marina,** commandant of a navy yard.
intensamente, *adv.* intensely.
intensar, *va.* to intensify.
intensidad, *f.* intensity.—**i. de ionización,** ionization level.—**i. del campo,** (rad.) field strength or intensity.—**i. del campo radioeléctrico,** radio field intensity.—**i. luminosa,** (elec.) luminous intensity.—**i. nominal,** (elec.) rated current.
intensificación, *f.* intensification, augmentation.
intensificador, *m.* intensifier.—**i. de imágenes,** image intensifier.
intensificar, *va.* to intensify.
intensión, *f.* = INTENSIDAD.
intensivo, va; intenso, sa, *a.* intense, intensive, vehement, ardent, lively.
intentar, *va.* to try, attempt, endeavor; to intend, purpose, mean; (law) to enter (an action), to commence (a lawsuit).
intento, *m.* intent, purpose, design.—**de i.,** purposely, knowingly.
intentona, *f.* (coll.) rash attempt.
[1]**ínter,** *prep.* between.—**i. nos,** between ourselves, between you and me.
[2]**ínter,** *m.* interim; (Peru) substitute curate.
interacción, *f.* interaction.
interamericano, na, *a.* inter-American.
intercadencia, *f.* interruption, interposition; unevenness; inconstancy; (med.) intermission or inequality of the pulse.
intercadente, *a.* changeable, variable.
intercadentemente, *adv.* changeably.
intercalación, *f.* intercalation, interpolation, insertion.
[1]**intercalar,** *va.* to intercalate, interpolate.
[2]**intercalar,** *a.* intercalary.
intercambiable, *a.* interchangeable.
intercambiablemente, *adv.* interchangeably.
intercambialidad, *f.* interchangeability.
intercambio, *m.* interchange.—**i. comercial,** international trade.—**i. de monedas,** (com.) foreign exchange.
interceder, *vn.* to intercede.
intercelular, *a.* intercellular.
interceptación, *f.* interception, stoppage.
interceptador, *m.* interceptor.
interceptar, *va.* to intercept, cut off.
intercesión, *f.* intercession, mediation.
intercesor, ra, *n.* intercessor, interceder.
interciso, sa, *a.*—**día de i.,** half holiday.
interclusión, *f.* shutting in or up.
intercolegiado, da, *a.* intercollegiate.
intercolumnar, *a.* intercolumnar.
intercolumnio, intercolunio, *m.* (arch.) intercolumniation.
intercomunicación, *f.* intercommunication.
intercomunicador, *m.* intercommunicator.
intercomunicar, *vn.* to intercommunicate.
interconectado, da, *a.* interconnected.
interconectador, ra. I. *a.* interconnecting. **II.** *m.* interconnector.
interconectar, *va.* to interconnect.
interconexión, *f.* interconnection.
intercontinental, *a.* intercontinental.
intercostal, *a.* intercostal.
intercostero, ra, *a.* intercoastal.
intercurrencia, *f.* (med.) intercurrence.
intercurrente, *a.* intercurrent, intervening.
intercutáneo, nea, *a.* (med.) subcutaneous.
interdecir, *va.* to interdict, prohibit.
interdental, *a.* interdental; (phon.) interdental.
interdepartamental, *a.* interdepartmental.
interdicción, *f.* interdiction, prohibition.
interdicto, *m.* prohibition, interdiction; interdict; (law) judgment of summary possession.
interdigital, *a.* interdigital, between the fingers.
interés, *m.* interest; (com. often *pl.*: *los intereses se han pagado ya,* the interest has already been paid); attraction, inducement.—*pl.* interests; money matters, business affairs.—**i. compuesto,** compound interest.—**i. simple,** simple interest.—**intereses acumulados,** accrued interest.—**intereses creados,** vested interests.—**intereses exonerados de impuestos,** interest free of tax.—**intereses sobre depósitos,** interest on deposits.—**intereses sobre préstamos,** interest on loan.—**intereses vencidos,** interest due.
interesable, *a.* avaricious, mercenary.
interesado, da. I. *pp.* of INTERESAR. **II.** *a.* interested, concerned; selfish, mercenary. **III.** *n.* associate; person interested; (law) party in interest.
interesante, *a.* interesting.
interesar. I. *vn.* & *vr.* **(en, por, con)** to be concerned (with) or interested (in); to take an interest (in). **II.** *va.* to invest; to give an interest; to interest, attract.
interescapular, *a.* (anat., zool.) interscapular.
interescolar, *a.* interscholastic, intercollegiate.
interesencia, *f.* assistance, attendance.
interesente, *a.* present, concurring.
interesillo, *m. dim.* slight interest.
interestatal, *a.* interstate.
interestelar, *a.* interstellar.
interfecto, ta, *n.* (law) murdered person, victim.
interferencia, *f.* interference; (phys., rad.) interference.—**i. entre canales adyacentes,** (rad.) adjacent channel interference.—**i. heterodina,** (rad.) heterodyne interference.—**i. perjudicial,** (rad.) harmful interference.—**interferencias atmosféricas,** (rad.) atmospheric interference.

interferente, *a.* (phys., rad.) interferential.
interferómetro, *m.* interferometer.
interfoliar, *va.* to interleave (a book).
intergubernamental, *a.* inter-governmental.
ínterin. I. *m.* character of acting or pro tempore. **II.** *adv.* meanwhile, interim.—**en el í.,** in the interim.
interinamente, *adv.* in the interim, meantime, provisionally, pro tem.
interinidad, *f.* = ÍNTERIN.
interino, na, *a.* provisional, temporary; pro tempore, acting, interim (as *a.*).
interior. I. *a.* interior, internal, inner, inside; home (as *a.*), domestic (commerce, etc.).—**lo i.,** the inside; home or domestic (national) affairs; (pol.) the Interior. **II.** *m.* interior; inside; inner part; mind, soul; in coaches with three compartments, the middle one.—*pl.* entrails, intestines, (coll.) insides.
interioridades, *f. pl.* family secrets; inwardness.
interiormente, *adv.* internally; inwardly.
interjección, *f.* (gram.) interjection.
interlínea, *f.* (print.) lead, space line.
interlineación, *f.* interlineation; double space; (print.) leading.
interlineado, da, *a.* (print.) leaded.
interlineal, *a* interlineal.
interlinear, *va.* to write between lines; (print.) to lead, to space; to double-space.
interlocución, *f.* interlocution, dialogue.
interlocutor, ra, *n.* interlocutor.
interlocutoriamente, *adv.* (law) intermediately.
interlocutorio, ria, *a.* (law) interlocutory, intermediate.
intérlope, *a.* interloping.
interludio, *m.* (mus.) interlude.
interlunar, *a.* interlunar.
interlunio, *m.* interlunar period, interlunation.
intermaxilar, *a.* intermaxillary.
intermediar, *va.* to interpose, mediate.
intermediario, ria. I. *a.* intermediary. **II.** *n.* intermediary; mediator; (pol. econ.) intermediary, middleman.
intermedio, dia. I. *a.* intermediate, intervening, interposed. **II.** *m.* interval, interim; (theat.) interlude, intermission.—**por i. de,** (Am.) through, with the help of.
interminable, *a.* interminable, endless.
intermisión, *f.* intermission, interruption.
intermisor, ra, *n.* intermitter.
intermitencia, *f.* (med.) intermission.
intermitente, *a.* intermittent.
intermitir, *va.* to intermit, discontinue.
internación, *f.* going or taking inside or into.
internacional, *a.* international.
internacionalidad, *f.* internationality.
internacionalismo, *m.* international relations; internationalism (socialistic doctrine).
internacionalista, *n.* internationalist.
internacionalizar, *va.* to internationalize.
internado, da, *n.* (mil.) internee; *m.* boarding-school system; state of being a boarder; boarders, boarding students.
internamente, *adv.* internally.
internamiento, *m.* (mil.) internment.
internar. I. *va.* to send into the interior of a country; to place, or order placed, in an institution. **II.** *vn.* to enter. **III.** *vr.* (en) to go into the interior (of); to go deeply (into) (a subject); to worm oneself into another's confidence.
interno, na. I. *a.* interior, internal, inward; boarding (student). **II.** *n.* boarding student.
internodio, *m.* (bot.) internode.
internuclear, *a.* internuclear.
internuncio, *m.* interlocutor; (eccl.) internuncio.
interoceánico, ca, *a.* interoceanic.
interocular, *a.* interocular, between the eyes.
interóseo, a, *a.* interosseous, between bones.
interpaginar, *va.* (bookbinding) to interleave.
interpelación, *f.* interpellation; summons.
interpelar, *va.* to appeal to, to implore the aid of; to interpellate; (law) to summon.
interpenetración, *f.* interpenetration.
interpenetrar, *va.* to interpenetrate.
interplanetario, ria, *a.* interplanetary.
interpolación, *f.* interpolation.
interpoladamente, *adv.* in an interpolated way.
interpolar, *va.* to interpolate; to intermix; to stop or pause briefly in (an address, etc.).
interponer. I. *va.* (*pp. irreg.* INTERPUESTO; *ind. pres.* INTERPONGO, *pret.* INTERPUSE, *fut.* INTERPONDRÉ; *subj.* INTERPONGA) to interpose, place between; to appoint as a mediator; (law) to present (a petition) to a court. **II.** *vr.* to go between, to interpose.
interposición, *f.* interposition; mediation; meddling, interference.
interpósita persona, (Lat.) (law) intermediary, agent.
interprender, *va.* (mil.) to take by surprise.
interpresa, *f.* (mil.) taking by surprise.
interpretable, *a.* interpretable.
interpretación, *f.* interpretation.—**i. de lenguas,** Translation Bureau (in the State Department of Spain).
interpretador, ra, *n.* interpreter.
interpretante, *n.* & *a.* interpreter(-ing).
interpretar, *va.* to interpret.
interpretativamente, *adv.* interpretatively.
interpretativo, va, *a.* interpretative.
intérprete, *n.* interpreter; sign, mark.
interpuesto, ta. I. *pp. irreg.* of INTERPONER. **II.** *a.* interposed, intervening.
interregno, *m.* interregnum.—**i. parlamentario,** period during which the Spanish Cortes are not in session.
interrogación, *f.* interrogation, question; (print.) question mark.
interrogante. I. *a.* interrogative; interrogating; question (mark). **II.** *n.* interrogator, questioner. **III.** *m.* question mark.
interrogar, *va.* (*pret.* INTERROGUÉ; *subj.* INTERROGUE) to question, to interrogate.
interrogativamente, *adv.* interrogatively.
interrogativo, va, *a.* interrogative.
interrogatorio, *m.* interrogatory; (law) cross-examination.
interrogué, interrogue, *v. V.* INTERROGAR.
interrumpidamente, *adv.* interruptedly.
interrumpido, da. I. *pp.* of INTERRUMPIR. **II.** *a.* interrupted, broken, discontinued.
interrumpir, *va.* to interrupt.
interrupción, *f.* interruption.
interruptor, ra. I. *n.* interrupter. **II.** *m.* (elec.) switch; circuit-breaker.—**i. automático,** (elec.) automatic circuit-breaker.—**i. bipolar,** two-pole switch.—**i. de aceite,** oil-break switch.—**i. de arranque,** starting switch.—**i. de botón,** push-button switch.—**i. de concha,** (eng.) tumbler switch.—**i. de cuchilla,** knife switch.—**i. de dos direcciones,** two-way switch.—**i. de la lámpara trasera,** (auto.) stop light switch.—**i. del alumbrado,** (auto.) light switch.—**i. del encendido,** ignition switch.—**i. de mano,** hand switch.—**i. de parada,** (mech.) stopping switch.—**i. de retardo,** (elec.) delay breaker.—**i. de sección,** (elec.) section circuit-breaker.—**i. de seguridad,** safety switch.—**i. de techo,** ceiling or top switch.—**i. de tres direcciones,** three-way switch.—**i. horario,** time switch.—**i. trifásico,** three-phase switch.—**i. tripolar,** three-pole switch.—**i. unipolar,** single-pole switch.
intersecarse, *vr.* to intersect (as two lines).
intersección, *f.* intersection.
intersideral, *a.* (astr.) interstellar.
intersticial, *a.* interstitial.
intersticio, *m.* interstice; lapse of time, period, interval.
intertropical, *a.* intertropical.
interurbano, na, *a.* interurban.
interusurio, *m.* (law) interest for a delay.
intervalo, *m.* interval; (mus.) interval.
intervención, *f.* intervention; supervision, superintendence; mediation, interposition; auditing

of accounts; (law) intervention; (surg.) operation.
intervencionismo, *m.* interventionism.
intervencionista, *n.* & *a.* interventionist.
intervengo, intervenga, intervendré, *v. V.* INTERVENIR.
intervenir (*ger.* INTERVINIENDO; *ind. pres.* yo INTERVENGO, él INTERVIENE, *pret.* INTERVINE, *fut.* INTERVENDRÉ; *subj.* INTERVENGA). **I.** *vn.* to intervene, mediate, intermediate; to interfere. **II.** *va.* to supervise, superintend; to audit (accounts); to control, to regulate; to offer to pay (a draft). **III.** *v. impers.* to occur, happen.
interventor, ra, *n.* comptroller; supervisor, inspector, superintendent; auditor.
intervertebral, *a.* intervertebral.
intervine, interviniendo, *v. V.* INTERVENIR.
intervocálico, ca, *a.* (phon.) intervocalic.
interyacente, *a.* interjacent, intervening.
intestado, da, *a.* intestate.
intestinal, *a.* intestinal.
intestino, na. I. *a.* intestine, internal; civil, domestic. **II.** *m.* intestine.—**i. ciego,** blind gut, cæcum.—**i. delgado,** small intestine.—**i. grueso,** large intestine.
intima, intimación, *f.* intimation, hint.
íntimamente, *adv.* intimately.
intimar. I. *va.* to intimate, indicate, suggest, hint. **II.** *vr.* to pierce, penetrate; to become intimate.
intimatorio, ria, *a.* (law) intimating.
intimidación, *f.* intimidation.
intimidad, *f.* intimacy.
intimidar, *va.* to intimidate.
íntimo, ma, *a.* internal, innermost; intimate.
intitular. I. *va.* to entitle; to confer a title on. **II.** *vr.* to use a title; to call oneself (a name).
intocable, *a.* untouchable.
intolerabilidad, *f.* intolerableness.
intolerable, *a.* intolerable, unbearable.
intolerancia, *f.* intolerance.
intolerante, *a.* intolerant.
intonso, sa, *a.* (poet.) unshorn; unpolished; (bookbinding) bound with uncut leaves.
intorsión, *f.* (bot.) intortion.
intoxicación, *f.* (med.) intoxication, poisoning.
intoxicar, *va.* (*pret.* INTOXIQUÉ; *subj.* INTOXIQUE) (med.) to poison.
intradós, *m.* (arch.) intrados.
intraducible, *a.* untranslatable.
intramolecular, *a.* intramolecular.
intramural, *a.* (anat.) intramural.
intramuros, *adv.* within the city.
intranquilidad, *f.* restlessness, uneasiness.
intranquilizar, *va.* to worry, make uneasy.
intranquilo, la, *a.* uneasy, restless.
intransferible, *a.* not transferable.
intransigencia, *f.* intransigence, intransigency.
intransigente, *a.* intransigent, irreconcilable.
intransitable, *a.* impassable.
intransitivo, va, *a.* (gram.) intransitive.
intransmisible, *a.* untransmissible.
intransmutabilidad, *f.* immutability.
intransmutable, *a.* intransmutable.
intratabilidad, *f.* intractability.
intratable, *a.* intractable; unruly, unmanageable; unsociable; rude, grouchy; impassable.
intravenoso, sa, *a.* intravenous.
intrépidamente, *adv.* intrepidly, fearlessly.
intrepidez, *f.* intrepidity, courage, bravery.
intrépido, da, *a.* intrepid, daring, gallant.
intriga, *f.* intrigue; entanglement, embroilment; (complicated) plot of a play.
intrigante. I. *a.* intriguing. **II.** *n.* intriguer.
intrigar (*pret.* INTRIGUÉ; *subj.* INTRIGUE). **I.** *va.* to arouse (one's) interest or curiosity. **II.** *vn.* to intrigue, plot, scheme. **III.** *vr.* **(en),** to be interested (in) or curious (about).
intrincable, *a.* intricate; perplexed.
intrincación, *f.* intricacy, intricateness.
intrincadamente, *adv.* intricately.
intrincado, da, *a.* & *pp.* intricate.
intrincamiento, *m.* intricateness.
intrincar, *va.* (*pret.* INTRINQUÉ; *subj.* INTRINQUE) to entangle, complicate, confuse.
intríngulis, *m.* (coll.) crafty intention, hidden motive; mystery, enigma.
intrinqué, intrinque, *v. V.* INTRINCAR.
intrínsecamente, *adv.* intrinsically.
intrínseco, ca, *a.* intrinsic, intrinsical.
introducción, *f.* introduction.
introducir. I. *va.* (*ind. pres.* INTRODUZCO, *pret.* INTRODUJE; *subj.* INTRODUZCA) to introduce; to usher in, put in, insert; to present (a person). **II.** *vr.* **(en)** to gain access (to), to get in, to ingratiate oneself (with); to interfere (in).
introductivo, va, *a.* introductive, introductory.
introductor, ra, *n.* introducer.
introduje, introduzco, etc., *v. V.* INTRODUCIR.
introito, *m.* beginning of an oration; (eccl.) introit; (theat.) prologue.
intrometer, *va.* & *vr.* = ENTREMETER.
intromisión, *f.* intromission; intrusion.
intromitente, *a.* intromittent.
introrso, *m.* (bot.) introrse.
introspección, *f.* introspection.
introspectivo, va, *a.* introspective.
introversión, *f.* introversion.
introverso, sa, *a.* introverted; (psych.) introvert.
intrusamente, *adv.* intrusively.
intrusarse, *vr.* to obtrude, intrude.
intrusión, *f.* intrusion, obtrusion.
intrusivo, va, *a.* (geol.) intrusive, intruded.
intruso, sa. I. *a.* intruded, intrusive, obtrusive. **II.** *m.* intruder, obtruder, squatter.
intubación, *f.* (med.) intubation.
intubar, *va.* (med.) to intubate, insert a tube.
intuición, *f.* intuition.
intuir, *va.* to know or perceive by intuition.
intuitivamente, *adv.* intuitively.
intuitivo, va, *a.* intuitive, evident.
intuito, *m.* view, look, glance.—**por i.,** in consideration, by reason of.
intumescencia, *f.* intumescence, swelling.
intumescente, *a.* intumescent, swollen.
intumescer, *vn.* to intumesce, swell.
intususcepción, *f.* intussusception
ínula, *f.* (bot.) elecampane.
inulina, *f.* (bot., chem.) inulin.
inulto, ta, *a.* (poet.) unavenged, unpunished.
inundación, *f.* inundation, flood; confluence; multitude.
inundante, *a.* inundating; inundant.
inundar, *va.* to inundate, flood.
inurbanamente, *adv.* uncivilly, discourteously.
inurbanidad, *f.* incivility, discourtesy.
inurbano, na, *a.* uncivil, impolite, unmannerly.
inusitadamente, *adv.* unusually.
inusitado, da, *a.* unusual, not in use.
inútil, *a.* useless; fruitless; needless.
inutilicé, inutilice, *v. V.* INUTILIZAR.
inutilidad, *f.* uselessness; needlessness.
inutilizar. I. *va.* (*pret.* INUTILICÉ; *subj.* INUTILICE) to render useless; to disable; to spoil, ruin. **II.** *vr.* to become useless.
inútilmente, *adv.* uselessly, to no purpose.
invadeable, *a.* unfordable.
invadir, *va.* to invade; encroach upon.
invaginación, *f.* invagination.
invaginar, *va.* to invaginate.
invalidación, *f.* invalidation, invalidity.
inválidamente, *adv.* invalidly.
invalidar, *va.* to invalidate, nullify.
invalidez, *f.* invalidity; invalidness.
inválido, da. I. *a.* invalid; cripple; feeble, weak; null, void. **II.** *m.* invalid.
invariabilidad, *f.* invariability.
invariable, *a.* invariable, constant.—**invariablemente,** *adv.* invariably.
invariación, *f.* immutability, invariableness.
invariadamente, *adv.* unvariedly.
invariado, da, *a.* unvaried, constant.
invariancia, *f.* invariance.
invariante, *f.* (math.) invariant.

invasión, *f.* invasion; attack.
invasor, ra. I. *a.* invading. **II.** *n.* invader.
invectiva, *f.* invective, harsh censure.
invencible, *a.* invincible, unconquerable.
invenciblemente, *adv.* invincibly.
invención, *f.* invention.—**I. de la Santa Cruz,** (eccl.) Invention of the Cross.
invencionero, ra, *n.* inventor; plotter; trifler.
invendible, *a.* unsalable.
inventar, *va.* to invent; to fib.
inventariar, *va.* to inventory, take inventory of.
inventario, *m.* inventory.
inventiva, *f.* faculty of invention, inventiveness.
inventivo, va, *a.* inventive.
invento, *m.* invention.
inventor, ra, *n.* inventor; fibber, fabricator, romancer.
inverecundo, da, *a.* shameless, impudent.
inverisímil, *a.* unlikely, improbable.
inverisimilitud, *f.* improbability.
invernáculo, *m.* greenhouse, hothouse, conservatory.
invernada, *f.* winter season.
invernadero, *m.* winter quarters; hothouse, conservatory.
invernal. I. *a.* hibernal, winter (as *a.*). **II.** *m.* winter shed (for cattle and fodder).
invernar, *vn.* (*ind.* INVIERNO; *subj.* INVIERNE) to winter, pass the winter.
invernizo, za, *a.* winter (as *a.*); winterly, hibernal; winter-beaten.
inverosímil, *a.* = INVERISÍMIL.
inverosimilitud, *f.* = INVERISIMILITUD.
inversamente, *adv.* inversely; contrariwise.
inversión, *f.* inversion; (com.) investment.
inversionista, *n.* (com.) investor.
inverso, sa. I. *pp. irreg.* of INVERTIR. **II.** *a.* inverse, inverted.—**a,** or **por, la inversa,** on the contrary.
inversor, ra. I. *a.* inverting; (elec., mech.) reversing. **II.** *n.* reverser; reverse gear; reversing mechanism.—**i. del sentido,** (elec.) reverser.—**i. de polos,** (elec.) pole reverser.
invertasa, *f.* (chem.) invertase.
invertebrado, da, *m.* & *a.* invertebrate.
invertible, *a.* invertible.
invertido, da. I. *pp.* of INVERTIR. **II.** *a.* inverse, inverted; homosexual; (chem.) invert. **II.** *n.* (psych.) invert, homosexual.
invertina, *f.* (chem.) invertase.
invertir, *va.* (*pp.* INVERTIDO, INVERSO; *ger.* INVIRTIENDO; *ind. pres.* INVIERTO, *pret.* él INVIRTIÓ; *subj.* INVIERTA) to invert; to reverse, to spend (time); (com.) to invest.
investidura, *f.* investiture.
investigable, *a.* investigable.
investigación, *f.* investigation, research; inquest.
investigador, ra. I. *a.* investigating, investigative. **II.** *n.* investigator.
investigar, *va.* (*pret.* INVESTIGUÉ; *subj.* INVESTIGUE) to investigate, ascertain, inquire into; to do research work.
investir, *va.* (*ger.* INVISTIENDO; *ind. pres.* INVISTO, *pret.* él INVISTIÓ; *subj.* INVISTA) to invest, to confer upon.
inveteradamente, *adv.* inveterately.
inveterado, da. I. *pp.* of INVETERARSE. **II.** *a.* inveterate.
inveterarse, *vr.* to become antiquated, old, or chronic.
invictamente, *adv.* triumphantly, valiantly.
invicto, ta, *a.* invincible, unconquered.
[1]**invierno,** *m.* winter; rainy season (in countries having no astronomical seasons, as in the tropics).
[2]**invierno, invierne,** *v. V.* INVERNAR.
invierto, invierta, *v. V.* INVERTIR.
invigilar, *vn.* to watch carefully.
inviolabilidad, *f.* inviolability.
inviolable, *a.* inviolable; inviolate.
inviolablemente, *adv.* inviolably; infallibly.
inviolado, da, *a.* inviolate, unhurt, uninjured.
invirtió, invirtiendo, *v. V.* INVERTIR.
invisibilidad, *f.* invisibility.
invisible, *a.* invisible.—**en un i.,** (coll.) in less than no time.—**invisiblemente,** *adv.* invisibly.
invisto, invista, invistió, etc. *v. V.* INVESTIR.
invitación, *f.* invitation.
invitado, da, *n.* invited person; guest.
invitador, ra, *n.* inviter.
invitar, *va.* to invite; entice; treat.
invitatorio, *m.* (eccl.) invitatory.
invocación, *f.* invocation.
invocador, ra, *n.* & *a.* invoker(-ing).
invocar, *va.* (*pret.* INVOQUÉ; *subj.* INVOQUE) to invoke, implore.
invocatorio, ria, *a.* invocatory.
involucela, *f.* (bot.) involucel.
involución, *f.* (math., med.) involution.
involucrado, da, *a.* involucred.
involucral, *a.* (bot.) involucral.
involucrar, *va.* to introduce as a digression.
involucro, *m.* (bot.) involucre.
involuntariamente, *adv.* involuntarily.
involuntariedad, *f.* involuntariness.
involuntario, ria, *a.* involuntary.
involuta, *f.* (geom.) involute.
invoqué, invoque, *v. V.* INVOCAR.
invulnerabilidad, *f.* invulnerability.
invulnerable, *a.* invulnerable.
inyección, *f.* injection; (U.S., coll.) shot.—**i. de aire** or **de gas,** air flooding.
inyectabilidad, *f.* injectability.
inyectable, *a.* injectable.
inyectado, da. I. *pp.* of INYECTAR. **II.** *a.* (Am.) bloodshot (eyes).
inyectar, *va.* to inject.
inyector, *m.* (mech.) injector.
iodo, (chem.) = YODO, iodine.
ion, *m.* (chem.) ion.
iónico, *m.* (elec.) ionic.
ionio, *m.* (chem.) ionium.
ionizable, *a.* ionizable.
ionización, *f.* ionization.
ionizar, *va.* to ionize.
ionógeno, *m.* (chem.) ionogen.
ionosfera, *f.* (meteorol.) ionosphere.
ionosférico, ca, *a.* ionospheric.
iota, *f.* iota (Greek letter); jot, trifle, whit.
ipecacuana, *f.* (bot.) ipecacuanha, ipecac.—**i. de las Antillas,** wild ipecac.
[1]**ipil,** *m.* (P. I.) (bot.) a hardwood tree.
[2]**ipil, hipil,** *m.* (Am.) Indian loose outer garment.
ípsilon, *f.* upsilon (Greek letter).
ipso facto (Lat.) *adv.* ipso facto, by the fact itself, by the very fact.
ipso jure (Lat.) *adv.* ipso jure, by the law itself.
ir. I. *vn.* (*pp.* IDO; *ger.* YENDO; *ind. pres.* VOY, *imperf.* IBA, *pret.* FUÍ; *subj.* VAYA) to go, move, walk; to fit, be becoming, suit; to concern, interest, affect, involve (diff. constr.: *poco me va en eso,* that concerns me very little; *en eso me va la reputación,* that involves, or affects, my reputation); to get along, do (diff. constr. *me fué bien,* I got along, or did, well); to differ, to be different (diff. constr.: *¡lo que va de ayer a hoy!* how today differs from yesterday!); to lead (*todos los caminos van a Roma,* all roads lead to Rome); to be, find oneself, be doing (*el enfermo va bien,* the patient is doing well); to be, to elapse (*de hoy al lunes van tres días,* it is three days from today to Monday); (arith.) to be, to leave (diff. constr.: *de 3 a 5 van 2,* 3 from 5 leaves 2); (arith.) to carry (*4, y van 2,* 4, and 2 to carry); (followed by *pp.*) to be (*voy herido,* I am wounded; *va descarriado,* he is astray or off the way). Before a gerund, it implies the beginning of the action the gerund denotes, or its continued performance or occurrence (*va anocheciendo,* it is getting dark; *voy comprendiendo,* I begin to understand; *Juan va perdiendo la paciencia,* John is losing patience; *voy viendo los cuadros,* I am looking at the pictures; *va traba-*

jando, he is working).—**i. a**, to go to; to be going to, to purpose or intend to (*voy al teatro*, I am going to the theater; *voy a hablarle*, I am going, or intend, to speak to him; *¿adónde va Vd.?* where are you going?); to bet on (*voy al caballo negro*, I bet on the black horse).—**i. a buscar**, to go get, fetch.—**i. a caballo**, to ride, to be riding on horseback.—**i. adelante**, to go (march, ride, etc.) at the front; to be ahead; to go on; to go ahead.—**i. a esperar a**, to go to meet.—**i. a medias**, to go halves.—**i. de bracero**, or **de brazo**, to walk arm in arm.—**i. delante**, to go ahead.—**i. en alcance**, (print.) to divide the (original) copy among various compositors.—**i. en coche**, to drive, to ride in a carriage.—**i. en demanda de**, (naut.) to be on the lookout for.—**i. pasando**, to be so so, to be as usual, to be getting along.—**i. por delante** = I. DELANTE.—**i. por ojo** = IRSE A PIQUE.—**algo**, or **mucho**, **va de Pedro a Pedro**, all people aren't alike, there are people and people.—**¿cómo le va?** how are you?—**¿cómo vamos?** how are you? how goes it with you?—**no me va ni me viene**, does not concern, or affect, me in the least.—**no vaya (vayan) a** (foll. by *inf.*), don't, don't go and (*inf.*).—**¡qué va!** nonsense! you don't say! don't tell me!—**¿quién va?** or **¡quién va allá?** who's there? who goes there?—**¡vámonos!** let's go! (Ry.) all aboard!—**¡vamos!** let's go! come on! also as expletive: why! well!—**¡vamos a ver!** let's see! let me see! what is it?—**vamos claros**, let's be plain, let's get down to business.—**¡vaya!** what a (*¡vaya una idea!* what an idea!)—**¡vaya con (ella)!** good for (her)!—**vaya (que)**, all right, let it be; indeed.—**¡vaya si (es verdad)!** I should say so!—**vaya Vd. a paseo**, go on, get out.—**vaya Vd. con Dios**, farewell; God be with you. **II.** *vr.* to go, go away, depart, quit; to leak, to ooze; to exhale, evaporate; to break wind; to break to pieces; to grow old.—**i. abajo**, to topple down.—**i. a pique**, (naut.) to founder, to go to the bottom, to be wrecked.—**i. atrás**, to go back, to flinch.—**i. de boca**, to speak thoughtlessly or recklessly.—**i. los ojos tras de**, to gaze admiringly or longingly at.—**írsele a uno el alma por**, to long for.—**írsele a uno la mula**, to speak unadvisedly from carelessness or anger.—**irse** (foll. by *ger.*), to be gradually (*pres. p.*).—**allá se va**, it is all the same, it amounts to the same thing.

ira, *f.* ire, anger, wrath, rage.—**¡i. de Dios!** Lord deliver us!

iraca, *f.* (Am.) Panama-hat palm.

iracundia, *f.* irascibility, ire, irascibleness.

iracundo, da, *a.* wrathful; angry, enraged.

iradé, *m.* irade, Sultan's decree.

Irak, *m.* Iraq, Irak.

Irán, *m.* Iran.

iranio, nia, *n.* & *a.* Iranian.

iraqués, quesa, *n.* & *a.* Iraqi.

iraquiano, na, *n.* & *a.* Iraqi.

irascibilidad, *f.* irascibility.

irascible, *a.* irascible, irritable.

irenarca, *m.* (anc. Rome) irenarch, magistrate.

irgo, irga, irguió, etc., *v.* *V.* ERGUIR.

iribú, *m.* (Arg.) turkey buzzard.

iridáceo, cea, *a.* (bot.) iridaceous, irideous.

íride, *f.* (bot.) iris.

iridectomía, *f.* (surg.) iridectomy.

irídeo, dea, *a.* (bot.) irideous, iridaceous.

iridio, *m.* (chem.) iridium.

iridiscencia, *f.* iridescence.

iridiscente, *a.* iridescent.

iridiscer, *vn.* to iridesce.

iris, *m.* iris, rainbow; (anat.) iris; **(min.) opal.—i. de paz**, mediator, peacemaker.

irisación, *f.* irisation.

irisado, da, *a.* rainbow-hued.

irisar, *vn.* to be iridescent.

iritis, *f.* (med.) iritis, inflammation of the iris.

irlanda, *f.* cotton and woollen cloth; fine Irish linen; (**I.**) Ireland.

irlandés, esa. I. *a.* Irish. **II.** *m.* Irishman; Irish language. **III.** *f.* Irishwoman.

ironía, *f.* (rhet.) irony.

irónicamente, *adv.* ironically.

irónico, ca, *a.* ironical, sarcastic.

iroqués, sa, *n.* & *a.* Iroquois.

irracional. I. *a.* irrational, absurd; **(math.)** irrational. **II.** *m.* irrational (being).

irracionalidad, *f.* irrationality.

irracionalmente, *adv.* irrationally.

irradiación, *f.* radiation.

irradiar, *va.* to radiate.

irrazonable, *a.* unreasonable.

irrealidad, *f.* unreality.

irrealizable, *a.* unrealizable, unattainable.

irrebatible, *a.* indisputable.

irreconciliabilidad, *f.* irreconcilability.

irreconciliable, *a.* irreconcilable.

irreconciliablemente, *adv.* irreconcilably.

irrecuperable, *a.* irrecoverable, irretrievable.

irrecusable, *a.* unimpeachable.

irredentista, *n.* & *a.* (pol.) Irredentist.

irredento, ta, *a.* irredenta, unredeemed.

irredimible, *a.* irredeemable.

irreducible, irreductible, *a.* irreducible.

irreemplazable, *a.* irreplaceable.

irreflexión, *f.* rashness, indiscretion.

irreflexivo, va, *a.* thoughtless, impulsive.

irreformable, *a.* unreformable.

irrefragable, *a.* irrefutable.

irrefragablemente, *adv.* irrefutably.

irrefrangibilidad, *f.* irrefrangibility.

irrefrangible, *a.* (opt.) irrefrangible.

irrefrenable, *a.* unbridled, unruly, unmanageable, uncontrollable.

irrefutable, *a.* irrefutable, indisputable.

irregular, *a.* irregular.

irregularidad, *f.* irregularity.

irreligión, *f.* irreligion.

irreligiosamente, *adv.* irreligiously.

irreligiosidad, *f.* irreligiousness.

irreligioso, sa, *a.* irreligious.

irremediable, *a.* irremediable, incurable; hopeless.—**irremediablemente**, *adv.* irremediably, hopelessly.

irremisible, *a.* irremissible, unpardonable.

irremisiblemente, *adv.* unpardonably, irremissibly.

irremovible, *a.* irremovable.

irremunerado, da, *a.* unremunerated.

irreparable, *a.* irreparable, irretrievable.

irreparablemente, *adv.* irreparably, irretrievably, irrecoverably.

irreprensible, *a.* irreprehensible, irreproachable.

irreprensiblemente, *adv.* irreproachably.

irreprimible, *a.* irrepressible.

irreprochable, *a.* irreproachable.

irresistibilidad, *f.* irresistibility.

irresistible, *a.* irresistible.

irresistiblemente, *adv.* irresistibly.

irresoluble, *a.* indeterminable; unsolvable; irresolute.

irresolución, *f.* irresolution, hesitation.

irresolutamente, *adv.* irresolutely.

irresoluto, ta, *a.* irresolute, wavering.

irrespetuoso, sa, *a.* disrespectful.

irrespirable, *a.* irrespirable.

irresponsabilidad, *f.* irresponsibility.

irresponsable, *a.* irresponsible.

irresuelto, ta, *a.* = IRRESOLUTO.

irreverencia, *f.* irreverence.

irreverente, *a.* irreverent.

irreversibilidad, *f.* irreversibility.

irreversible, *a.* irreversible.

irrevocabilidad, *f.* irrevocability.

irrevocable, *a.* irrevocable.

irrevocablemente, *adv.* irrevocably.

irrigable, *a.* irrigable.

irrigación, *f.* irrigation; (med.) irrigation.

irrigador, *m.* irrigator.

irrigar, *va.* to irrigate; (med.) to irrigate.

irrisible, *a.* laughable.

irrisión, *f.* derision, ridicule.
irrisoriamente, *adv.* derisively.
irrisorio, ria, *a.* derisive.
irritabilidad, *f.* irritability.
[1]**irritable,** *a.* irritable.
[2]**irritable,** *a.* (law) voidable.
[1]**irritación,** *f.* irritation, commotion, agitation; (med.) irritation.
[2]**irritación,** *f.* (law) invalidation, abrogation.
irritador, ra, *n.* & *a.* irritator(-ing), stimulator (-ing), irritant.
írritamente, *adv.* (law) invalidly.
irritamiento, *m.* irritation, anger.
[1]**irritante. I.** *a.* irritant, stimulating. **II.** *m.* stimulant, irritant.
[2]**irritante,** *a.* (law) annulling, voiding.
[1]**irritar,** *va.* to irritate, exasperate, anger; (med.) to irritate.
[2]**irritar,** *va.* (law) to annul, void.
írrito, ta, *a.* (law) null, void.
irrogar, *va.* (*pret.* IRROGUÉ; *subj.* IRROGUE) to cause, to occasion (damage).
irrompible, *a.* unbreakable.
irrumpir, *vn.* to raid, invade; break into.
irrupción, *f.* irruption, inroad, invasion, raid.
irruptivo, va, irruptor, ra, *a.* irruptive.
isabelino, na, *a.* (coin) stamped with the bust of Isabella II.; partisan or defender of Queen Isabella; light bay (horse).
isagoge, *f.* introduction, exordium.
isagógico, ca, *a.* introductive, introductory.
isla, *f.* isle, island; city block.—**en i.,** insulated.
islam, *m.* Islam.—**islámico, ca,** *a.* Islamic.
islamismo, *m.* Islamism, Islam.
islamita, *n.* & *a.* Islamite(-itic).
islandés, desa, *n.* Icelander; *m.* Icelandic (language).
Islandia, *f.* Iceland.
islándico, ca, *a.* Icelandic.
isleño, ña, *n.* islander; (Cuba) native of the Canary Islands.
isleo, *m.* chain of small islands.
isleta, ita, illa, *f. dim.* small isle, islet, holm.
islilla, *f.* (anat.) collar bone.
islote, *m.* small barren island, key.
ismaelita, *a.* Ishmaelite, Arab.
isobárico, ca, *a.* isobaric.
isobaro, ra. I. *a.* (meteorol., chem.) isobaric. **II.** *m.* (chem.) isobar; *f.* (meteorol.) isobar.
isoclinal, isoclino, na, *a.* isoclinal, isoclinic.
isocre. *a* isochroous, of uniform color.
isocromático, ca, *a.* (opt.) isochromatic.
isocromatismo, *m.* isochromatism.
isocronismo, *m.* isochronism.
isócrono, *a.* isochronous, equal in time.
isodiáfero, *m.* (phys.) isodiaphere.
isodiamétrico, ca, *a.* isodiametric.
isodimorfismo, *m.* isodimorphism.
isodimorfo, fa, *a.* isodimorphic.
isodinámico, ca, *a.* isodynamic.
isoelectrónico, ca, *a.* (chem.) isoelectronic.
isogónico, ca, *a.* (geom.) isogonic, isogonal.—**línea i.,** isogonic line.
isógono, na, *a.* (geom.) isogonic, isogonal.
isohipsa, *f.* (meteorol.) contour.
isomagnético, ca, *a.* isomagnetic.
isomagnetismo, *m.* isomagnetism.
isomería, *f.* (chem.) isomerism.
isomérico, ca, *a.* (chem.) isomeric.
isómero, ra. I. *a.* isomeric. **II.** *m.* isomer.
isométrico, ca, *a.* isometric.
isometropía, *f.* isometropia.
isomorfismo, *m.* (min.) isomorphism.
isomorfo, fa, *a.* (biol., chem., min.) isomorphic.
isoniacida, *f.* (pharm.) isoniazid.
isoperímetro, tra, *a.* isoperimetrical.
isopiéstico, ca, *a.* isopiestic.
isoploide, *a.* (genet.) isoploid.
isópodo, da, *m.* & *a.* (zool.) isopod.
isoquímeno, na, *a.* (of climate) isocheimal.
isósceles, *a.* (geom.) isosceles.
isospóreo, a, *a.* (bot.) isosporous.
isosporo, *m.* (bot.) isospore.
isotermia, *f.* isothermy.
isotermo, ma, *a.* isothermal.
isótero, ra, *a.* isotheral.
isotonicidad, *f.* isotonicity.
isotónico, ca, *a.* isotonic.
isótono, *m.* (chem.) isotone.
isotopia, *f.* isotopy.
isotópico, ca, *a.* isotopic.
isótopo, *m.* (chem.) isotope.
isotropía, *f.* (phys.) isotropy.
isotrópico, ca, *a.* (phys.) = ISÓTROPO.
isotropismo, *m.* (phys.) isotropy.
isótropo, pa, *a.* (phys.) isotropous.
isquiático, ca, *a.* (anat.) ischiatic, sciatic, sciatical.
isquion, *m.* (anat.) ischium.
Israel, *m.* Israel.
israelí, *n.* & *a.* Israeli.
israelita, *n.* & *a.* Israelite.
israelítico, ca, *a.* Israelitish, Israelitic.
istle, ixtle, *m.* ixtle, ixtli; a Mexican fiber.
istmeño, ña, *n.* & *a.* isthmian.
ístmico, ca, *a.* isthmian.
istmo, *m.* (geo.) isthmus; (anat.) isthmus.
istriar, *va.* = ESTRIAR, (arch.) to flute.
istrio, tria, *n.* & *a.* Istrian.
Italia, *f.* Italy.
italianismo, *m.* Italianism.
italianizado, da, *a.* Italianate, Italianized.
italianizar, *va.* & *vn.* to Italianize.
italiano, na. I. *a.* Italian. **II.** *n.* Italian; *m.* (ling.) Italian.
itálico, ca. I. *a.* Italic; (print.) italic. **II.** *f.* (print.) italic, italics.
italiota, *n.* Italiot, Italiote.
ítem, *m.* section, clause, article; addition, additament.—**í.,** or **í. más,** also, likewise, furthermore.
iterable, *a.* iterable.
iteración, *f.* interation.
iterar, *va.* to iterate.—**iterativo, va,** *a.* iterative.
iterbia, *f.* (chem.) ytterbia.
iterbio, *m.* (chem.) ytterbium.
itinerario, ria. I. *a.* itinerary. **II.** *m.* itinerary, book of travels; railroad guide, time-table.
itria, *f.* (min.) yttria.
itrio, *m.* (chem.) yttrium.
izador, ra, *a.* hoisting.
izaga, *f.* place abounding in rushes and reeds.
izar, *va.* (naut.) to hoist, heave, haul up.
izquierda, *f.* left hand; (pol.) Left, Left wing.—**a la i.,** left-handed (screw, etc.).—**de la i.,** on the left.
izquierdista, *n.* & *a.* (pol.) leftist, radical.
izquierdo, da. I. *a.* left-handed; left; crooked. **II.** *f.* left hand; left, left-hand side; (pol.) Left (Liberal party).—**a la i.,** to the left; on the left.

J

J, j, *f.* j, eleventh letter of the Spanish alphabet.
jaba, *f.* (Am.) basket; crate.
jabalcón, *m.* (arch.) bracket, purlin, strut.
jabalconar, *va.* to build or support with struts.
jabalí, *m.* (zool.) wild boar.
[1]**jabalina,** *f.* sow of a wild boar.
[2]**jabalina,** *f.* javelin.
jabalón, *va.* = JABALCÓN.
jabalonar, *va.* = JABALCONAR.
jabardear, *vn.* (of bees) to swarm.
jabardillo, *m.* noisy swarm of insects or birds; (coll.) noisy crowd.
jabardo, *m.* small swarm of bees; (coll.) noisy crowd.
jabato, *m.* young wild boar.
jábeca, *f.* sweep net.
jábega, *f.* fishing smack; dragnet.
jabegote, *m.* man who drags the sweep net.
jabeguero, ra. I. *a.* pertaining to sweep-net fishing. **II.** *n.* sweep-net fisherman.
[1]**jabeque,** *m.* (naut.) xebec.

[2]jabeque, *m.* (coll.) knife wound in the face.
jabí, *m.* small wild apple; small kind of grapes; (C. A.) (bot.) breakax.
jabillo, *m.* (bot.) a Central-American tree of the spurge family.
jabirú, *m.* jabiru, a Brazilian wading bird.
jabladera, *f.* crozer, cooper's tool.
jable, *m.* (cooperage) croze.
jabón, *m.* soap; a piece of soap.—**j. blando,** soft soap.—**j. de olor,** toilet soap.—**j. de piedra,** hard soap.—**j. de sastre,** steatite, soapstone.—**j. detergente,** detergent soap.—**j. duro,** hard soap.—**j. en escamas,** soap flakes.—**j. en polvo,** soap powder.—**dar un j.,** (coll.) to reprimand severely, lecture, dress down.
jabonado, da, *m.* wash, washing.
jabonadura, *f.* washing.—*pl.* suds or soap suds; lather.—**dar, or echar, una j.,** to reprimand severely, lecture, call down.
jabonar, *va.* to soap; (coll.) to reprimand severely, lecture, dress down.
jaboncillo, *m.* soapstone, steatite; toilet soap; (bot.) soap tree.
jabonera, *f.* soap dish; woman who sells soap; (bot.) soapwort.
jabonería, *f.* soap manufactory or shop.
jabonero, ra, *n.* soap maker or seller.
jabonete, jabonete de olor, *m.* toilet soap.
jabonoso, sa, *a.* soapy, saponaceous.
jaborandi, *m.* (bot.) jaborandi.
jabuco, *m.* (Cuba) large straw basket.
jaca, *f.* nag, pony, jennet, cob, bidet, tit.
jacal, *m.* (Mex.) Indian hut, wigwam.
jacamar, *m.* (ornith.) jacamar.
jacana, *f.* (ornith.) jacana, a tropical wading bird.
jácara, *f.* merry ballad; a kind of dance and its music; group of night wanderers singing JÁCARAS; (coll.) vexation; idle talk or prattle; story, tale; fable, lie, vainglorious fiction.
jacaranda, *f.* (bot.) jacaranda.
jacarandana, jacarandina, *f.* slang; gang of ruffians and thieves.
jacarandoso, sa, (coll.) blithe, merry, gay.
jacarear, *vn.* to sing JÁCARAS; (coll.) to sing in the streets at night; to taunt with offensive remarks.
jacarero, *m.* ballad singer; wag or merry droll.
jacarilla, *f. dim.* of JÁCARA.
jácaro, ra. I. *a.* pert. to singers of JÁCARAS. **II.** *m.* boaster, bully.—**a lo j.,** boastfully, braggingly.
jácena, *f.* (arch.) girder.
jacerina, *f.* coat of mail.
jacilla, *f.* mark left on the ground.
jacinto, *m.* (bot.) hyacinth; harebell; (min.) hyacinth.—**j. de Ceilán,** zircon.—**j. de Compostela,** red crystalized quartz.—**j. occidental,** topaz.—**j. oriental,** ruby.
[1]**jaco**, *m.* sorry nag, jade.
[2]**jaco**, *m.* short jacket.
jacobínico, ca, *a.* Jacobinic, Jacobinical.
jacobinismo, *m.* Jacobinism.
jacobino, *m.* Jacobin; bloody revolutionist.
jacobita, *a.* & *n.* Jacobite.
jactancia, *f.* boasting.
jactanciosamente, *adv.* boastingly.
jactancioso, sa, *a.* boastful, vainglorious.
jactarse, *vr.* to vaunt, boast, brag.
jaculatoria, *f.* ejaculation, short prayer.
jaculatorio, ria, *a.* jaculatory.
jachalí, *m.* (bot.) custard apple.
jada, *f.* (agr.) hoe; spade.
jade, *m.* (min.) jade, axestone.
jadeante, *a.* panting, out of breath.
jadear, *vn.* to pant.—**jadeo,** *m.* pant, palpitation.
jadiar, *va.* to dig up with a spade, to hoe.
jaecero, ra, *n.* harness maker.
jaén, *m.* a kind of large white grape.
jaenés, sa, *a.* of or belonging to Jaen.
jaez, *m.* harness; trappings; (fig.) manner, kind, quality.—*pl.* trappings.
jafético, ca, *a.* Japhetic, Indo-Germanic.
jagua, *f.* (bot.) jagua or inaja palm and its fruit.
jaguar, jaguarete, *m.* (zool.) jaguar.
jaguarzo, *m.* (bot.) helianthemum.
jagüey, *m.* (S. A.) large pool or basin; (Cuba) (bot.) liana.
jaharrar, *va.* to plaster.
jaharro, *m.* (mason.) plaster; plastering.
jaiba, *f.* (Cuba) (ichth.) crab.
jaique, *m.* cape with a hood.
jaira, *f.* bezel of a plane bit.
jairar, *va.* (shoemaking) to bevel (leather).
jaire, *m.* (shoemaking) bevel cut.
¡ja, ja, ja! *interj.* ha, ha!
jalapa, *f.* (bot.) jalapa; jalap.
jalapina, *f.* (chem.) jalapin.
jalar, *va.* (coll.) = HALAR, to pull.
jalbegar, *va.* to whiten, whitewash.
jalbegue, *m.* whitewash; whitewashing.
jaldado, da; jalde; jaldo, da, *a.* bright yellow crocus-colored.
jaldre, *m.* yellow peculiar to birds.
jalea, *f.* jelly.—**j. de guayaba,** guava jelly.—**j. del agro,** conserve of citron.—**hacerse una j.,** to love with excessive fondness.
jaleador, ra, *n.* one who encourages hounds or dancers.
jalear, *va.* to encourage (hounds) to follow the chase; to animate dancers, by clapping hands; to quaver (the voice).
jaleco, *m.* Turkish jacket.
jaleo, *m.* clapping of hands to encourage dancers; Andalusian dance; (coll.) jest; (coll.) carousal.
jaletina, *f.* calf's foot jelly; gelatine.
jalma, *f.* kind of packsaddle.
jalmería, *f.* packsaddler's trade.
jalmero, *m.* packsaddle maker.
jalón, *m.* (surv.) pole, rod, flag pole.
jalonero, *m.* (surv.) rodman.
jaloque, *m.* = SIROCO, southeast wind.
jallullo, *m.* bread toasted in ashes.
Jamaica, *f.* Jamaica; (**j.**) (Mex.) charity fair.
jamaiquino, na, *a.* & *n.* Jamaican.
jamar, *va.* (prov.) to eat.
jamás, *adv.* never.—**nunca j.,** or **por j.,** never, nevermore.—**por siempre j.,** forever and ever.
jamba, *f.* (arch.) door jamb, window post.
jambaje, *m.* door or window case.
jámbico, ca, *a.* iambic.
jamelgo, *m.* (coll.) jade, sorry nag.
jamerdana, *f.* sewer of a slaughterhouse.
jamerdar, *va.* to clean the guts of; to wash hastily.
jamete, *m.* rich silk stuff.
jametería, *f.* = ZALAMERÍA, flattery.
jámila, *f.* = ALPECHÍN, oozing olive juice.
jamón, *m.* ham, salted haunch of a hog.
jamona, *n.* (coll.) big middle-aged woman.
jámparo, *m.* (Colomb.) small boat or canoe.
jamuga, jamugas, *f.* mule chair.
jándalo, la, *n.* & *a.* a term app. to Andalusians and those who give *h* a strong guttural sound.
jangada, *f.* (coll.) silly sally; (naut.) raft, float.
jangar, *m.* hangar.
jangua, *f.* small armed vessel.
jansenismo, *m.* Jansenism.
jansenista, *n.* & *a.* Jansenist(-ic).
jantato, *m.* (chem.) xanthate.
jántico, ca, *a.* (chem.) xanthic.
jantina, *f.* (chem.) xanthine.
jantofila, *f.* (biochem.) xanthophyll.
jantoxilo, *m.* (bot.) zanthoxylum, xanthoxylum.
japón, pona. I. *a.* & *n.* Japanese. **II.** *m.* (**J.**) Japan.
japonés, nesa. I. *a.* Japanese. **II.** *n.* Japanese; *m.* Japanese (language).
[1]**jaque**, *m.* (chess) check; braggart, boaster.—**j. mate,** (chess) checkmate.
[2]**jaque**, *m.* saddlebag; smooth hairdo.
jaquear, *va.* to check (at chess).
jaqueca, *f.* megrim; headache.
jaquecoso, sa, *a.* tiresome, annoying, bothersome.

jaquel, *m.* (her.) square.
jaquelado, da, *a.* checkered.
jaquero, *m.* fine-toothed comb.
jaqueta, *f.* jacket, short loose coat.
jaquetilla, *f. dim.* small JAQUETA.
[1]**jaquetón,** *m. aug.* large, wide coat.
[2]**jaquetón,** *m. aug.* great boaster, bully.
jáquima, *f.* headstall of a halter.
jaquimazo, *m.* blow with the headstall of a halter; (coll.) displeasure; disappointment.
jara, *f.* (bot.) cistus or rockrose; a kind of dart or arrow.
[1]**jarabe,** *m.* sirup; any sweet mixed drink.—**j. de pico,** empty talk; lip service.
[2]**jarabe,** *m.* (Am.) a popular dance in Lat. Am.
jarabear. I. *va.* to prescribe sirups very often. **II.** *vr.* to take sirups frequently.
jaraíz, *m.* pit for pressing grapes.
jaral, *m.* bramble, brake; intricate or puzzling point.
jaramago, *m.* (bot.) hedge mustard.
jarameño, ña, *a.* (cattle) from the Jarama.
jaramugo, *m.* small or young fish.
jarana, *f.* (coll.) carousal, revelry, romping; (coll.) scuffle, quarrel.
jaranear, *vn.* (coll.) to jest; to carouse.
jaranero, ra; jaranista, *a.* fond of jests or sprees; jolly.
jarano, *m.* Mexican sombrero.
jarapote, *m.* (prov.) = JAROPEO.
jarapotear, *va.* to stuff with drugs.
jarazo, *m.* blow or wound with a dart.
jarcia, *f.* accoutrements; heap of things; (naut.) tackle, rigging, and cordage; shrouds; fishing tackle.
jardín, *m.* garden; (baseball) field, outfield; flaw that disfigures an emerald; (naut.) privy.—**j. botánico,** botanical garden.—**j. zoológico,** zoölogical garden, zoo.
jardincito, *m. dim.* small garden.
jardinería, *f.* gardening.
jardinero, ra. I. *n.* gardener. **II.** *f.* flowerstand, jardinière; basket carriage.
jareta, *f.* (sewing) fold or tuck for gathering; (naut.) netting, harpings.
jaretera, *f.* garter. Also JARRETERA.
jarife, *m.* = JERIFE, sherif, shereef.
jarifo, fa, *a.* showy, spruce, nobby, natty.
jaripeo, *m.* (Mex.) bronco-busting; rodeo.
jaro, ra, *a.* resembling a wild boar.
jarocho, *m.* (Mex., coll.) rough countryman.
jaropar, *va.* to stuff with sirups or medicines.
jarope, *m.* sirup; nasty potion.
jaropear, *va.* = JAROPAR.—**jaropeo,** *m.* medicine habit.
jaroso, sa, *a.* full of brambles.
jarra, *f.* jar; pitcher; ancient order of chivalry.—**en j.** or **de jarras,** akimbo.
jarrear, *vn.* to take out water or wine with a jar or dipper.
jarrero, ra, *n.* jar maker or seller.
jarreta, *f. dim.* small jar.
jarrete, *m.* hock; gambrel.
jarretera, *f.* garter; Order of the Garter.
jarrito, *m. dim.* small jug or pitcher.
jarro, *m.* pitcher, jug, pot, ewer; chatterer.
jarrón, *m. aug.* large jar, urn, flower vase.
jaspe, *m.* (min.) jasper.
jaspeado, da, *a.* spotted, mottled, variegated.
jaspeadura, *f.* marbling.
jaspear, *va.* to marble, vein, speckle.
jastial, *m.* (arch.) façade of an edifice.
jateo, tea, *n.* (of dogs) fox hunter.
jato, ta, *n.* calf.
¡jau! *interj.* to incite animals, esp. bulls.
jaula, *f.* bird cage; cell for insane persons; (min.) miner's cage.
jaulón, *m. aug.* large bird cage; aviary.
jauría, *f.* pack of hounds.
jauto, ta, *a.* insipid, flat, tasteless.
javanés, nesa, *a.* & *n.* Javanese, Javan.
javo, va, *a.* & *n.* Javan, Javanese.
jayán, na, *n.* robust, burly person.
jayanazo, za, *n. aug.* huge, big person.
jazmín, *m.* (bot.) jessamine or jasmine.—**j. de la India,** (bot.) gardenia.
jazmíneo, a, *a.* (bot.) jasminaceous.
jea, *f.* ancient duty on Moorish goods.
jebe, *m.* rock alum; (S. A.) India-rubber.
jebuseo, a, *n.* & *a.* Jebusite(-ic).
jedive, *m.* khedive, Viceroy of Egypt.
jefatura, *f.* position or headquarters of a chief.
jefe, fa, *n.* chief, head, leader; "boss"; (mil.) commanding officer.—**j. de día,** (mil.) officer of the day.—**j. de despacho,** executive secretary.—**j. de escuadra,** (naut.) rear admiral.—**j. de estación,** stationmaster, station agent.—**j. de manzana,** air-raid warden.—**j. de policía,** police commissioner or chief.—**j. político,** political boss.—**j. de redacción,** editor in chief.—**en j.,** in chief.
Jehová, *m.* Jehovah.
jeja, *f.* white wheat.
jején, *m.* (Cuba) gnat, gall midge.
jema, *f.* badly squared part of a beam.
jemal, *a.* having the length of a JEME.
jeme, *m.* distance from the end of the thumb to the end of the forefinger (both extended); (coll.) woman's face.
jemoso, sa, *a.* badly squared beam.
jenabe, jenable, *m.* mustard.
jengibre, *m.* ginger.
jeniquén, *m.* (Cuba) henequen; sisal.
jenízaro. I. *a.* cross-bred; (Mex.) born of Chinese and Indian parents. **II.** *m.* Janizary.
jeque, *m.* Moorish chief.
[1]**jera,** *f.* ground that can be plowed in a day with a pair of oxen.
[2]**jera,** *f.* present, gift.
jerapellina, *f.* old ragged garment.
jerarca, *m.* hierarch.
jerarquía, *f.* hierarchy.
jerárquico, ca, *a.* hierarchical.
jerbo, *m.* (zool.) jerboa (mouse).
jeremiada, *f.* jeremiad, lamentation, whining.
Jerez, *m.* sherry wine.
jerezano, na, *a.* & *n.* (one) from, or of Jerez.
[1]**jerga,** *f.* coarse frieze; straw bed.
[2]**jerga,** *f.* jargon; gibberish.
[1]**jergón,** *m. aug.* straw bed; ill-fitting clothes; ill-shaped person.
[2]**jergón,** *m.* (jewelry) zircon.
jerguilla, *f.* silk or worsted serge.
jerife, *m.* shereef, sherif.
jerifiano, na, *a.* pertaining to the sherif.
jerigonza, *f.* (coll.) jargon, gibberish, slang; strange and ridiculous action.—**andar en jerigonzas,** to quibble.
jeringa, *f.* syringe, clyster; sausage stuffer.
jeringación, *f.* (coll.) syringing, injection; annoyance, botheration.
jeringador, ra, *a.* (coll.) bothersome, persevering, persistent.
jeringar, *va.* (*pret.* JERINGUÉ; *subj.* JERINGUE) to inject with a syringe; to vex, annoy, tease.
jeringazo, *m.* clyster, injection.
jeringué, jeringue, *v. V.* JERINGAR.
jeringuilla, *f.* (bot.) syringa, mock orange.
jeroglífico, ca. I. *a.* hieroglyphical. **II.** *m.* hieroglyph.
jerónimo, ma, *a.* & *m.* (eccl.) Hieronymite.
jerosolimitano, na, *a.* of or pert. to Jerusalem.
jerpa, *f.* sterile shoot of a vine.
jerricote, *m.* pottage of almonds, sugar, sage, and ginger.
jersey, *m.* (Angl.) sweater, jersey.
jervilla, *f.* a kind of short boot.
jesuato, ta, *a.* child dedicated to Jesus when born.
jesuíta, *m.* Jesuit; (coll.) hypocrite.
jesuíticamente, *adv.* Jesuitically; hypocritically.
jesuítico, ca, *a.* Jesuitical; hypocritical.
jesuitismo, *m.* Jesuitism.
Jesús, *m.* Jesus; often used by itself, or followed by other sacred names (José, María), and with no implication of profanity, as an exclamation

in the sense of "gracious!" "goodness!" "my!" etc.—¡ay J! alas! good gracious!—**en un decir J.,** in the twinkling of an eye.—**no saber ni el J.,** not to know even one's A B C.—**sin decir J.,** suddenly.

jesusear, *vn.* to repeat often the name of Jesus.

jeta, *f.* thick, heavy lips; hog's snout; (coll.) person's face.

jetar, *va.* to dilute, dissolve.

jeto, *m.* empty beehive rubbed with honey to attract bees.

jetón, na; jetudo, da, *a.* thick-lipped.

ji, *f.* chi (Greek letter).

jíbaro, ra. I. *a.* (Am.) rustic, rude, wild. **II.** *n.* countryman(-woman).

jibia, *f.* (zool.) cuttlefish.

jibión, *m.* cuttlefish bone.

jibraltareño, ña, *a.* of or from Gibraltar.

jícara, *f.* chocolate cup.

jicarazo, *m. aug.* blow with a chocolate cup.—**dar un j.,** (coll.) to give poison.

jicarón, *m. aug.* large chocolate cup.

jicotea, *f.* (Am.) tortoise.

jifa, *f.* refuse from slaughtered animals.

jifería, *f.* slaughtering.

jifero, ra. I. *a.* pertaining to the slaughterhouse. **II.** *m.* butcher's knife; butcher.

jifia, *f.* (ichth.) xiphias, swordfish.

jiga, *f.* jig (dance and tune).

jigote, *m.* (cooking) hash; minced meat.

jiguilete, *m.* indigo plant.

jijallar, *m.* bramble.

jijallo, *m.* (bot.) prickly broom.

jijene, *m.* (S. A.) sand fly.

¡ji, ji, ji! *interj.* ha, ha, ha!

jijona, *f.* variety of flinty wheat.—**turrón de J.,** sweet-almond paste.

jilguero, *m.* (ornith.) linnet; (ornith.) goldfinch.

jilote, *m.* (Mex.) ear of green corn.

jimagua, (Cuba) twin.

jimelga, *f.* (naut.) fish of a mast.

jimenzar, *va* to ripple (flax or hemp).

jinestada, *f.* sauce made with milk, dates, etc.

jineta, *f.* art of horsemanship; an ancient short lance; sergeant's shoulder knot; ancient tribute upon cattle.—**a la j.,** (riding) with high stirrups and bent knees.—**tener los cascos a la j.,** to be harebrained, wild, giddy.

jinete, *m.* trooper; cavalryman; horseman, rider, equestrian; fine, pure-breed horse.

jinetear. I. *va.* (Am.) to break in (a horse); to ride (a horse). **II.** *vn.* to ride around on horseback, mainly for show.

jinglar, *vn.* to swing, vibrate, oscillate.

jingoísmo, *m.* jingoism.

jingoísta, *n.* & *a.* jingoist(-ic).

jínjol, *m.* jujube. Also AZUFAIFA.

jip, *m.* jeep.

jipijapa, *f.* very fine woven straw; Panama-hat straw.

jiquilete, *m.* (bot.) indigo tree.

[1]**jira,** *f.* strip, piece of cloth.

[2]**jira,** *f.* picnic, outing; tour.

jirafa, *f.* (zool.) giraffe.

jirapliega, *f.* purgative confection.

jirasal, *f.* (bot.) fruit of the lac tree.

jirel, *m.* rich caparison for a horse.

jíride, *f.* (bot.) = LIRIO HEDIONDO, gladwin.

jirofina, *f.* a kind of sauce.

jiroflé, *m.* clove tree.

jirón, *m.* (sew.) facing of a skirt; shred, piece torn from clothing; pointed banner, pennant; small part (of anything); (Peru) avenue, long street.

jironado, da, *a.* torn into or garnished with strips or tatters.

jirpear, *va.* to dig about vines.

jiste, *m.* froth of beer.

jitar, *va.* (prov.) to emit, vomit; to throw out.

jitomate, *m.* (Mex.) tomato.

jiu-jitsu, *m.* jujitsu.

¡jo! *interj.* whoa!

jobo, *m.* (bot.) tree of the terebinth family.

jockey, *m.* jockey.

jocó, *m.* jocko, an ape.

jocosamente, *adv.* jocosely, humorously.

jocoserio, ria, *a.* tragic-comic.

jocosidad, *f.* jocularity, jocosity, waggery.

jocoso, sa, *a.* jocose, waggish, humorous.

jocoyote, *m.* (Am.) youngest child, pet.

jocundidad, *f.* joviality.

jocundo, da, *a.* jovial, jolly.

jofaina, *f.* washbasin, washbowl.

jojoto, *m.* (Venez.) maize in the milk.

jolgorio, *m.* = HOLGORIO, boisterous frolic.

jolito, *m.* rest, leisure; (naut.) calm.

joloano, na, *n.* & *a.* Joloano (from Sulu, P. I.).

jólote, *m.* (C. A.) turkey.

jónico, ca; jonio, nia, *n.* & *a.* Ionian.

¡jopo! *interj.* (coll.) out of here! be off!

jorcar, *va.* = AECHAR, to sift (grain).

jorco, *m.* licentious feast and dance.

jordán, *m.* anything that purifies, revives, or gives a fresh bloom.

Jordania, *f.* Jordan.

jordanio, nia, *a.* & *n.* Jordanian.

jorfe, *m.* dry stone wall; steep rock, cliff.

jorguín, *m.* wizard, or sorcerer.—**jorguina,** *f.* witch, or sorceress.—**jorguinería,** *f.* witchcraft, spell.

jornada, *f.* one-day march; working day; stage, journey, travel, trip; (mil.) expedition; king's stay in a royal country residence; opportunity, occasion, circumstance; span of life; transit from life to eternity; act of a play; (print.) number of sheets printed off in a day.—**j. de ocho horas,** 8-hour (working) day.—**a grandes,** or **a largas, jornadas,** by forced marches.—**al fin de la j.,** at the end.

jornal, *m.* daywork, journeywork; day wages.—**a j.,** by the day.—**jornalero,** *m.* day laborer.

joroba, *f.* hump; (coll.) importunity, annoyance, nuisance.

jorobado, da. I. *pp.* of JOROBAR. **II.** *a.* crooked, gibbous, humpbacked. **II.** *n.* hunchback.

jorobar, *va.* (coll.) to importune, bother, annoy.

jorrar, *va.* to haul.

jorro, *m.* (Cuba) bad tobacco.

josa, *f.* orchard of vines and fruit trees.

jostrado, da, *a.* round-headed (shaft or dart).

[1]**jota,** *f.* name of the letter *j*; iota, jot, tittle.—**no saber,** or **no entender, j.,** or **ni j.,** or **una j.,** not to know "beans", to be absolutely ignorant.—**sin faltar una j.,** not a dot missing, with not a whit left out.

[2]**jota,** *f.* an Aragonese dance and tune.

[3]**jota,** *f.* pottage of greens and spices.

jote, *m.* a Chilean vulture of the turkey-buzzard family.

joule, *m.* (elec.) joule. Also JULIO.

jovada, *f.* ground tilled by a pair of mules in one day.

joven. I. *a.* young. **II.** *n.* youth; young man; young woman; young person.

jovenado, *m.* (eccl.) juniorate.

jovencillo, illa, *n.* youngster, lad, lass.

jovenzuelo, la. I. *a.* youngish. **II.** *n.* youth.

jovial, *a.* Jovian; jovial, gay, merry, cheerful.

jovialidad, *f.* joviality, jollity, gaiety.

joya, *f.* jewel, gem; piece of jewellery; present, gift; (arch. and artil.) astragal.—*pl.* jewels, trinkets; wedding outfit.

joyante, *a.* extremely glossy (silk).

joyel, *m.* small jewel, valuable trinket.

joyelero, *m.* jewel case, jewel box.

joyera, *f.* woman jeweller.

joyería, *f.* jeweller's shop.

joyero, *m.* jeweller; jewel-casket.

joyita, *f. dim.* = JOYUELA.

joyo, *m.* (bot.) bearded darnel, darnel grass.

joyón, *m. aug.* large jewel.

joyuela, *f. dim.* jewel of small value.

juaguarzo, *m.* (bot.) Montpellier rockrose.

Juan, *m.* John.—**J. Lanas,** simpleton, poor devil, (a) nobody.—**buen J.,** poor, silly fellow.

juanas, *f. pl.* glove stretcher.
juanete, *m.* bunion; prominent cheek bone; (naut.) gallant sail.—**j. de sobremesana,** mizzen-topgallant sail.—**j. mayor,** main-topgallant sail.
juanetudo, da, *a.* having bunions.
juarda, *f.* stain in cloth.
juardoso, sa, *a.* stained, spotted (cloth).
jubete, *m.* doublet covered with mail.
jubilación, *f.* retirement; retirement pension.
jubilar. I. *va.* to pension off; to superannuate; to retire; (coll.) to lay aside as useless. **II.** *vr.* to become a pensioner; to be retired. **III.** *vn.* to jubilate, rejoice.
jubileo, *m.* jubilee, public festivity; (eccl.) concession of plenary indulgence.—**por j.,** rarely, once in a long while.
júbilo, *m.* glee, joy, merriment, rejoicing.
jubiloso, sa, *a.* joyful, merry, gay.
jubón, *m.* doublet, jacket; blouse, upper part (of dress).—**j. de azotes,** (coll.) public whipping.
juboncito, *m. dim.* small doublet or waist.
jubonero, *m.* maker of doublets or waists.
júcaro, *m.* a West-Indian hardwood tree.
judaico, ca, *a.* Judaical, Jewish.
judaísmo, *m.* Judaism.
judaizante, *n.* & *a.* Judaizer(-ing).
judaizar, *va.* & *vn.* to judaize.
Judas, *m.* Judas; traitor; silkworm that does not spin; effigy of Judas burnt in the streets during Lent.
Judea, *f.* Judea.
judería, *f.* Jewry; ghetto; tax on Jews.
[1]**judía,** *f.* (bot.) bean, string bean.—**j. de careta,** small spotted French bean.
[2]**judía,** *f.* Jewess.
judiada, *f.* inhuman action; usurious profit.
judiar, *m.* bean field or patch.
judicante, *m.* judge appointed to try impeachment cases.
judicativo, va, *a.* judicative.
judicatura, *f.* judicature; judgeship.
judicial, *a.* judicial, juridical.
judicialmente, *adv.* judicially.
judiciario, ria. I. *a.* astrological. **II.** *m.* astrologer. **III.** *f.* judicial astrology.
judiego, *f.* inferior kind of olives.
[1]**judihuela,** *f.* a small French bean.
[2]**judihuela, lo,** *n.* young Jewess or Jew.
judío, día. I. *a.* Jewish; usurious. **II.** *m.* Jew.—**j. de señal,** converted Jew, wearing a distinguishing badge.
judión, *m.* a large variety of French bean.
[1]**juego,** *m.* play, sport, game; gaming, gambling; set of good cards; movement, work, working (of a mechanism); set; suit, suite; ability, artfulness, cunning; running gear of a vehicle; (mech.) play, free space, clearance.—*pl.* public feasts, games.—**j. de azar,** game of chance.—**j. de bochas,** bowling alley.—**j. de boliche,** pigeonholes (an old game); trollmadam.—**j. de bolos,** ninepins.—**j. de café,** coffee set.—**j. de cajones,** nest of boxes or drawers.—**j. de cartas,** card game.—**j. de compadres,** collusion or conspiracy under pretense of rivalry or opposition among those concerned.—**j. de habitaciones,** suite of rooms.—**j. de manos,** juggling feat, legerdemain.—**j. de naipes** = J. DE CARTAS.—**j. de niños,** child's play.—**j. de palabras,** pun, quibble, play upon words.—**j. de pelota,** ball game (app. to several games in which a ball is thrown).—**j. de prendas,** forfeits.—**j. de suerte** = J. DE AZAR.—**j. de te,** tea set.—**j. de velas,** (naut.) set of sails. **j. de vocablos,** or **de voces** = J. DE PALABRAS. **j. limpio,** fair play.—**j. parásito,** (meteorol.) backlash.—**j. público,** public gambling house. —**juegos florales,** floral games.—**juegos malabares,** jugglery, juggling.—**juegos olímpicos,** Olympic games.—**j. sucio,** foul play.—**conocerle a uno el j.,** to know one's intentions.—**entrar en j.,** to come into action.—**hacer j.,** to match, to fit.—**mostrar el j.,** to show one's hand (fig.).—**poner en j.,** to bring into play, make use of.—**por j.,** or **por modo de j.,** in jest, for fun.—**tener j.,** (naut.) to have fetched way; not to be firm or steady.—**verle a uno el j.,** to see through (a person), read (his) thoughts.
[2]**juego, juegue,** *v. V.* JUGAR.
jueguecico, illo, ito, *m.* little game, bit of play.
juera, *f.* sieve made of esparto.
juerga, *f.* (coll.) spree, carousal.
juerguista, *n.* (coll.) reveler, carouser.
jueves, *m.* Thursday.—**j. santo,** holy Thursday.
juez, *m.* judge; justice; juror, juryman; *m.* & *f.* umpire; arbitrator.—**j. árbitro,** arbitrator, umpire.—**j. conservador,** person appointed to defend the rights of a community.—**j. de alzadas,** judge in appeal cases.—**j. de hecho,** lay judge.—**j. de paz,** justice of the peace.—**j. de primera instancia,** judge of the primary court of claims.
jugada, *f.* play, act of playing; a throw, move, stroke; ill turn, mean trick.
jugadera, *f.* shuttle for network.
jugador, ra, *n.* player; gamester, gambler.—**j. de manos,** juggler, prestidigitator.
jugar, *va.* & *vn.* (*ind. pres.* JUEGO, *pret.* JUGUÉ; *subj.* JUEGUE) to play; to sport, frolic; to game, gamble; to stake; to move in a game; to move (a part of the body); to wield, handle (a weapon); to move on joints or hinges; to intervene; to take an active part in an affair; to exercise; to mock, to make game of.—**j. a cara o cruz,** to bet on the toss of a coin.—**j. a la baja,** (com.) to bear the market.—**j. a la bolsa,** to dabble in stocks.—**j. al alza,** (com.) to bull the market.—**j. a los naipes,** to play cards.—**jugarle a uno una mala volada,** or **mala partida,** to play a mean trick on one.—**jugársela a uno de codillo,** (coll.) to trick or outwit one.
jugarreta, *f.* (coll.) bad play; bad turn, nasty trick.
juglándeo, dea. I. *a.* (bot.) juglandaceous. **II.** *f. pl.* Juglandaceæ, the walnut family of trees.
juglar, *m.* juggler, mountebank, buffoon.
juglara, juglaresa, *f.* woman buffoon.
juglaresco, ca, *a.* pertaining to jugglers.
juglaría, juglería, *f.* jugglery, buffoonery mimicry.
jugo, *m.* juice; fluid, liquid; sap; (fig.) substance. —**j. gástrico,** (physiol.) gastric juice.—**j. pancreático,** (physiol.) pancreatic juice.
jugosidad, *f.* succulence, juiciness.
jugoso, sa, *a.* juicy, succulent, full of sap.
jugué, *pret.* of JUGAR.
juguete, *m.* toy, plaything; jest, joke; carol; (theat.) comedietta.—**j. de movimiento,** mechanical toy.—**por j.,** jestingly.
juguetear, *vn.* to frolic, sport, gambol.
juguetería, *f.* toyshop, toy trade.
juguetero, *m.* toy dealer; etagère, whatnot.
juguetón, na, *a.* playful, frolicsome.
juicio, *m.* judgment; decision; prudence, wisdom; forecast of yearly events by astrologers; good behavior; (law) trial.—**j. de Dios,** ordeal (to determine guilt or innocence).—**j. ejecutivo,** levy, attachment.—**j. final,** final judgment.—**estar fuera de su j.,** to be crazy.—**formar j. de,** to judge, form an opinion about.—**no estar en su j.,** to be out of one's senses.—**no tener j.,** to be wild, to be a harum-scarum fellow.—**pedir en j.,** to sue at law.—**perder el j.,** to become insane; to go mad.—**tener j.,** to be wise; to be cautious; to be well-behaved.
juiciosamente, *adv.* judiciously, wisely.
juicioso, sa, *a.* judicious, wise; well-behaved.
julepe, *m.* (pharm.) julep; a card game; (coll.) reprimand, punishment; (Peru, Chile, Arg.) fear.
juliano, na, *a.* Julian.
[1]**julio,** *m.* July.

[2]julio, *m.* (elec.) joule.
julo, *m.* bell-mule, bell-cow.
juma, *f.* (Am.) drinking spree.
jumenta, *f.* female donkey, jenny.
jumental, jumentil, *a.* pert. to donkeys.
jumentillo, illa, ito, ita, *n. dim.* small donkey or beast of burden.
jumento, *m.* donkey, ass; stupid person.
juncada, *f.* (cook.) a kind of fritter; (vet.) medicine for the glanders.
juncago, *m.* (bot.) bastard rush.
juncal, juncar, *m.* ground full of rushes.
júnceo, a. I. *a.* rushlike; (bot.) juncaceous. **II.** *f. pl.* Juncaceæ.
juncia, *f.* (bot.) sedge.—**j. olorosa, galangal.**
junciana, *f.* (coll.) brag, boast.
junciera, *f.* earth vessel with perforated lid, for aromatic roots.
juncino, na, *a.* pert. to or made of rushes.
[1]**junco,** *m.* (bot.) rush.—**j. de Indias,** (bot.) rattan.—**j. florido,** (bot.) flowering rush.—**j. oloroso,** (bot.) camel grass.
[2]**junco,** *m.* (naut.) Chinese junk.
juncoso, sa, *a.* rushlike; producing rushes.
jungla, *f.* jungle.
junio, *m.* June, the sixth month.
júnior, *m.* (eccl.) junior.
junípero, *m.* (bot.) = ENEBRO, juniper.
junquera, *f.* (bot.) rush.
junqueral, *m.* = JUNCAL.
junquillo, *m.* (bot.) jonquil; reed, rattan; (arch.) boltel molding.
junta, *f.* junta, board, council; meeting, conference; session, sitting; whole, entirety; union, junction; fraternity; seam; joint; coupling.—**j. a inglete,** (mech.) miter joint.—**j. a tope,** (mech.) butt joint.—**j. cardánica,** (mech.) Cardan joint.—**j. central de planificación,** Central Planning Board.—**j. de accionistas,** stockholders' meeting.—**j. de acreedores,** (com.) meeting of creditors.—**j. de comercio,** board of trade.—**j. de dilatación,** expansion joint.—**j. de educación,** school board, board of education.—**j. de enchufe** = J. ENCHUFADA.—**j. de expansión,** expansion joint.—**j. de médicos,** (med.) consultation.—**j. de recubrimiento,** lap joint.—**j. de sanidad,** board of health.—**j. de solapa,** lap joint.—**j. de yuxtaposición,** butt joint.—**j. directiva,** managing board, executive board.—**j. enchufada,** bell-and-spigot joint.—**j. remachada,** riveted joint.—**j. universal,** universal joint, Cardan joint.
juntamente, *adv.* jointly, together.
juntar. I. *va.* to join, connect, unite; to assemble, congregate; to amass, collect, gather, lay up; to pool (resources). **II.** *vr.* to join, meet, assemble, gather; to be closely united; to copulate; **(con)** to associate (with).
juntera, *f.* (carp.) jointing plane.
junterilla, *f. dim.* (carp.) small joiner's plane.
[1]**junto,** *adv.* near, close at hand, near at hand; at the same time.—**j. a.,** next to, by, beside.—**j. con,** together with.—**de por j.,** wholesale.—**en j.,** together, in all.—**por j.** = DE POR J.
[2]**junto, ta,** *a.* united, joined; together.
juntorio, *m.* an ancient tax.
juntura, *f.* juncture, joining; (anat.) joint, articulation; seam; (naut.) scarf; (bot.) knuckle.
Júpiter, *m.* (astr.) Jupiter; (chem.) tin.
jura, *f.* oath; swearing.
jurado, *m.* jury; juror, juryman.
jurador, ra, *n.* swearer, profane swearer.
juraduría, *f.* office of a juror.
juramentado, da, *a.* jurant, swearing, taking an oath.
juramentar. I. *va.* to swear in. **II.** *vr.* to be sworn in, take the oath.
juramento, *m.* oath; act of swearing; curse, imprecation.—**j. asertorio,** declaratory oath.—**j. falso,** perjury.
jurar, *va.* & *vn.* to swear, to take an oath.—**j. en falso,** to commit perjury.—**jurársela,** or **jurárselas, a uno,** to threaten one with revenge, have it in for one.
jurásico, ca, *a.* Jurassic.
juratoria, *f.* Gospel tablet for administering the oath.
juratorio, a. I. *a.* juratory. **II.** *m.* instrument setting forth the oaths taken by Aragonese magistrates.
jurel, *m.* (ichth.) jurel, a carangoid sea fish.
jurguina, *f.* witch, sorceress.
jurídicamente, *adv.* legally, juridically.
jurídico, ca, *a.* legal, juridical.
jurisconsulto, *m.* jurisconsult, jurist; lawyer.
jurisdicción, *f.* jurisdiction; boundary, territory.
jurisdiccional, *a.* jurisdictional.
jurispericia, *f.* = JURISPRUDENCIA.
jurisperito, ta, *n.* jurisconsult.
jurisprudencia, *f.* jurisprudence, law; laws, legislation.
jurista, *m.* jurist; lawyer; pensioner.
juro, *m.* right of perpetual property; annuity, pension.—**de j.,** certainly.
jusbarba, *f.* (bot.) field myrtle.
jusello, *m.* pottage of broth, cheese, and eggs.
jusi, *m.* (P. I.) striped thin gauze.
justa, *f.* joust, tilt, tournament; contest.
justador, *m.* tilter, jouster.
justamente, *adv.* justly; just, exactly.
justar, *vn.* to joust, tilt, tourney.
justicia, *f.* justice; judge; court of justice; punishment; (coll.) execution (of a criminal).—**de j.,** justly, deservedly.—**la j.,** the police, the authorities, the officers of the law.
justiciable, *a.* justiciable, actionable (in law).
justiciazgo, *m.* justiceship, judgeship.
justiciero, ra, *a.* just, fair.
justificable, *a.* justifiable.
justificación, *f.* justification, defense; production of evidence; equity; sanctification by grace; (print.) adjustment, justifying.
justificadamente, *adv.* justly, justifiably.
justificado, da, *pp.* & *a.* justified.
justificador, ra. I. *n.* & *a.* justifier(-ing). **II.** *m.* (print.) dressing stick, justifier.
justificante, *n.* & *a.* justifier(-ing).
justificar. I. *va.* (*pret.* JUSTIFIQUÉ; *subj.* JUSTIFIQUE) to justify; to free from sin; to absolve, exculpate; (law) to prove or establish before a court; to rectify, adjust; (print.) to justify, adjust. **II.** *vr.* to vindicate one's character, to clear oneself; to justify one's conduct.
justificativo, va, *a.* justifying, justificatory.
justifiqué, justifique, *v. V.* JUSTIFICAR.
justillo, *m.* waistcoat, jerkin; corset cover.
justinianeo, a, *a.* Justinian.
justipreciador, ra, *n.* appraiser.
justipreciar, *va.* to appraise.
justiprecio, *m.* appraisal.
justo, ta. I. *a.* just; pious; correct, exact, strict; fit, tight, close. **II.** *m.* just and pious man.—**al j.,** fitly, duly; completely, punctually. **III.** *adv.* tightly.
juta, *f.* (S. A.) (ornith.) a kind of goose.
jutía, *f.* (Cuba) = HUTÍA, a W. I. rodent.
juvenil, *a.* juvenile, youthful.
juventud, *f.* youthfulness, youth; young people.
juvia, *f.* (bot.) Brazil-nut tree.
juzgado, *m.* court of justice; judicature.
juzgamundos, *n.* (coll.) faultfinder.
juzgante. I. *a.* judging. **II.** *n.* judge.
juzgar, *va.* & *vn.* (*pret.* JUZGUÉ; *subj.* JUZGUE) to judge; to pass or render judgment (on).

K

NOTE.—Many words that by some are begun with *k* are properly spelled with *qu* if the following letter is *e* or *i*, and with *c* in other cases.
K, k, *f.* k, twelfth letter of the Spanish alphabet.
ka, *f.* name of the letter *k.*

káiser, *m.* kaiser.
kaiserismo, *m.* kaiserdom.
kaki, *a.* & *m.* khaki.
kalmia, *f.* (Am., bot.) kalmia.
kan, *m.* khan, a Tartar chief.
kanato, *m.* Khanate.
kantiano, na, *a.* & *n.* Kantian.
kantismo, *m.* Kantianism.
kantista, *a.* & *n.* Kantian.
kapoc, *m.* kapok.
kappa, *f.* kappa (Greek letter).
kayak, *m.* kayak.
Kenia, *f.* Kenya.
keniano, na, *a.* & *n.* Kenyan.
kepis, *m.* (mil.) small shako, kepi, a military cap.
kermes, *m.* = QUERMES, (entom.) kermes.
kerosén, *m.*; **keroseno**, *m.*; **kerosina**, *f.* kerosene.
kiliárea, *f.* kiloare, one thousand ares.
kilo. I. (*as a prefix*) kilo (a thousand). **II.** *m.* kilo, kilogram.
kiloamperio, *m.* (elec.) kiloampere.
kilocaloría, *f.* (phys.) kilocalorie.
kilociclo, *m.* (rad.) kilocycle.
kiloergio, *m.* (phys.) kilerg.
kilográmetro, *m.* kilogrammeter, metric unit of work (about 7.25 ft.-lb.)
kilogramo, *m.* kilogram (about 2.2 lb.)
kilojulio, *m.* (elec.) kilojoule.
kilolitro, *m.* kiloliter.
kilométrico, ca, *a.* kilometric; mileage (ticket); (coll.) very long, interminably long.
kilómetro, *m.* kilometer (about 0.62 mile).
kilovatio, *m.* (elec.) kilowatt.—**k.-hora**, kilowatt-hour.
kilovoltamperio, *m.* (elec.) kilovolt-ampere.
kilovoltio, *m.* (elec.) kilovolt.
kimógrafo, *m.* (med.) kymograph.
kimono, *m.* kimono.
kindergarten, *m.* kindergarten.
kinesiterapia, *f.* kinesitherapy.
kiosco, *m.* kiosk, small pavilion; newsstand.
kirie, *m.* (eccl.) kyrie (eleison).
kirieleisón, *m.* = KIRIE; (coll.) funeral chant.—**cantar el k.**, to beg for quarter, to cry for mercy.
kirsch, *m.* kirschwasser.
kiwi, *m.* (ornith.) kiwi.
klistrón, *m.* (electron.) Klystron (trademark).
kodak, *m.* kodak.
krausismo, *m.* Krausism.
krausista, *a.* & *n.* Krausist.
Kremlín, *m.* Kremlin.
kumis, *m.* kumiss, koomiss.
kumquat, *m.* (bot.) kumquat.
Kuwait, *m.* Kuwait.
kuwaiti, *a.* & *n.* Kuwaiti.

L

L, l, *f.* l, thirteenth letter of the Spanish alphabet.
[1]**la. I.** *def. art. fem. sing.* the. Often used before the surname (not the first name) of a woman, especially actresses and singers, and is not translated, or is translated by Miss, Madame, etc.: *la Patti, la Pavlowa*, Patti, Pavlowa: *la Guerrero, la Farrar*, Miss Guerrero, Miss Farrar; *la Schumann-Heink*, Madame Schumann-Heink. **II.** *pron. pers. acc. f. sing.* her, it. Formerly, and still occasionally, used as a dative (*yo la dije*, I told her).
[2]**la**, *m.* (mus.) la, A, sixth note of the scale.
labanco, *m.* (Am., ornith.) a South American duck.
lábaro, *m.* labarum, a kind of standard, banner.
labe, *f.* stain, spot.
labelo, *m.* (bot.) labellum.
laberíntico, ca, *a.* labyrinthine.
laberinto, *m.* labyrinth, maze; intricate matter; (anat.) labyrinth of the ear.
labia, *f.* (coll.) eloquence, persuasive speech.
labiado, da, *a.* & *f.* (bot.) labiate.
labial, *a.* labial.
labializar, *va.* (phon.) to labialize.
labiérnago, *m.* (bot.) laburnum.
labihendido, da, *a.* hare-lipped.
lábil, *a.* labile.
labio, *m.* lip; (by ext.) mouth; edge, brim.—**l. leporino**, harelip.
labiodental, *a.* (phon.) labiodental.
labionasal, *a.* (phon.) labionasal.
labor, *f.* labor, task, toil, work; design, scrollwork; (sew.) needlework, embroidery, fancywork; trimming; a thousand tiles or bricks; cultivation; husbandry, tillage; egg of a silkworm; figures raised upon a ground; diaper; (min.) works, working.
laborable, *a.* tillable; workable; working, week (day).
laborador, ra, *n.* tiller, farmer: worker.
laboral, *a.* labor, working.
laborante. I. *a.* tilling, working. **II.** *m.* (Cuba) conspirator.
laborantismo, *m.* (Cuba) (pol.) movement for independence from Spain.
laborar, *va.* & *vn.* to till; to work.
laboratorio, *m.* laboratory.—**l. activo**, or **radiactivo**, hot laboratory.
laborcica, illa, ita, *f. dim.* pretty needlework.
laborear, *va.* to work; (naut.) to reeve, to run.
laboreo, *m.* (naut.) reeving, running; (min.) works; working, exploitation, development.
laborera, *f.* clever, skilful workwoman.
laboriosamente, *adv.* laboriously.
laboriosidad, *f.* laboriousness, assiduity.
laborioso, sa, *a.* assiduous, industrious; arduous, laborious.
laborismo, *m.* (Engl.) Labourism.
laborista, *n.* (Engl.) Labourite.
labra, *f.* stone cutting or carving; working, cutting (of metal, stone, etc.).—**de l. fácil**, free-cutting, free-turning (metal).
labrada, *f.* land plowed and fallowed.
labradero, ra; labradío, día, *a.* tillable, arable; workable.
labrado, da. I. *pp.* of LABRAR. **II.** *a.* wrought; figured, hewn. **III.** *m. pl.* cultivated lands.
labrador, ra. I. *n.* farmer, tiller, peasant. **II.** *a.* industrious.
labradoresco, ca, *a.* pertaining to farmers, rustic.
labradorita, *f.* (min.) labradorite.
labrandera, *f.* seamstress, embroiderer.
labrante, *m.* stonecutter; sculptor.
labrantín, *m.* petty farmer.
labrantío, tía, *a.* arable, tillable.
labranza, *f.* tillage, cultivation; farming; farm land.
labrar. I. *va.* to elaborate, work; to manufacture, make; to till, cultivate; to build, erect; to cut, dress, carve (stone); to embroider; to make designs in; to form; cause, bring about; to work out (a man's destiny, etc.). **II.** *vn.* to make a strong impression on the mind.
labrero, ra. I. *a.* (fishing nets) for sharks. **II.** *n.* (Chile) mine overseer or foreman.
lábrido, da, *a.* (ichth.) labroid.
labriego, ga, *n.* peasant, farmer.
labro, *m.* (entom., zool.) labrum.
labroideo, dea, *a.* (ichth.) labroid.
labrusca, *f.* wild grapevine.
laburno, *m.* (bot.) laburnum.
laca, *f.* lac, gum lac; red color; lake, a pigment; lacquer, a varnish.—**l. en grano**, seed-lac.—**l. en palillos**, stick lac.—**l. en tablillas**, shellac.
lacayesco, ca, *a.* = LACAYUNO.
lacayo, *m.* lackey, groom, footman; knot of ribbons worn by women.
lacayuelo, *m. dim.* foot-boy, groom.
lacayuno, na, *a.* pertaining to a lackey; lackey-like, servile.
lacear, *va.* to lace, trim, or tie with bows; to pin up (the game) or drive within shot.

lacedemón; lacedemonio, a, *n.* & *a.* Lacedemonian.
laceración, *f.* laceration, tearing.
lacerado, da. I. *pp.* of LACERAR. **II.** *a.* unfortunate, unhappy; leprous.
lacerar, *va.* to mangle, tear in pieces, lacerate; to hurt, damage.
laceria, *f.* misery, poverty wretchedness; drudgery, weariness.
lacería, *f.* set of bows.
lacerioso, sa, *a.* miserable, wretched.
lacero, *m.* lassoer, cowboy.
lacertoso, *a.* muscular, athletic.
lacinia, *f.* (bot.) lacinia, slender lobe.
laciniado, da, *a.* (bot.) laciniate, slashed.
lacio, cia, *a.* faded, withered; flaccid, lanquid; straight (as hair).
lacón, *m.* (Spain) picnic ham.
lacónicamente, *adv.* laconically.
lacónico, ca, *a.* laconic.
laconio, nia, *n.* & *a.* Laconian.
laconismo, *m.* laconism.
lacra, *f.* mark or trace left by illness; fault, defect; viciousness.
¹lacrar, *va.* to injure or impair (the health); to cause pecuniary damage or loss to.
²lacrar, *va.* to seal with sealing wax.
lacre, *m.* sealing wax.
lacrimal, *a.* lachrymal.
lacrimatorio, ria, *a.* & *m.* lachrymatory.
lacrimógeno, na, *a.* lachrymatory, tear-producing.—**bomba l.,** tear bomb.—**gas l.,** tear gas.
lacrimosamente, *adv.* tearfully.
lacrimoso, sa, *a.* tearful, lachrymose.
lactación, *f.* suckling.
lactancia, *f.* lactation, period of suckling.
lactante, *n.* & *a.* feeding on milk.
lactar. I. *va.* to nurse; to feed with milk. **II.** *vn.* to suckle; to feed on milk.
lactario, ria, *a.* lacteous.
lactasa, *f.* (chem.) lactase.
lactato, *m.* (chem.) lactate.
lácteo, tea, *a.* lacteous, milky, lacteal.
lactescencia, *f.* lactescence, milkiness.
lactescente, *a.* lactescent.
lacticíneo, a, *a.* = LÁCTEO.
lacticinio, *m.* any kind of milk food.
láctico, ca, *a.* (chem.) lactic.
lactífero, ra, *a.* lactiferous.
lactina, *f.* (chem.) lactose, lactin, milk sugar.
lactoflavina, *f.* (chem.) lactoflavin.
lactómetro, *m.* lactometer.
lactona, *f.* (chem.) lactona.
lactosa, *f.* = LACTINA.
lactoscopio, *m.* lactoscope.
lactucario, *m.* (pharm.) lactucarium.
lactumen, *m.* (med.) milk crust.
lacunario, *m.* (arch.) lacunar.
lacustre, *a.* lacustrine.
¹lacha, *f.* (ichth.) anchovy.
²lacha, *f.* shame.
lada, *f.* (bot.) cystus.
ládano, *m.* labdanum, gum labdanum.
ladeado, da, *a.* & *pp.* tilted, inclined to one side.
ladear. I. *va.* & *vr.* to tilt, tip, incline to one side. **II.** *vn.* to skirt; to deviate; to be even. **III.** *vr.* to incline to an opinion or party; to lean; to tilt, incline to one side; (Chile) to fall in love.
ladeo, *m.* inclination or motion to one side.
ladera, *f.* declivity, slope, hillside.—*pl.* rails or staves of a truck; cheeks of a gun carriage.
ladería, *f.* small dale on a mountainside.
ladero, ra, *a.* lateral.
ladierno, *m.* (bot.) buckthorn.
ladilla, *f.* crab louse; (bot.) common barley.
ladillo, *m.* shifting panel placed in the sides of coaches.
ladinamente, *adv.* artfully, sagaciously, cunningly.
ladino, na. I. *a.* sagacious, cunning, crafty. **II.** *n.* Spanish Jew; *m.* Sephardic dialect.
lado, *m.* side; border, margin, edge; (mil.) flank; party, faction; mat for the side of carts, etc.; course, bend, manner; mode of proceeding.—*pl.* patrons, advisers.—**l. a l.** side by side.—**l. flaco,** weak side, spot.—**al l.,** just by, near at hand; to one side; next door.—**a un l.,** aside.—**dejar a un l.,** to set aside.—**de l.,** incidentally; sideways; from or on the side.—**hacerse a un l.,** to move aside, to get out of the way.—**mirar de l.,** to look askance; to look out of the corner of the eye; to look at contemptuously, look down upon.—**por el l.,** around, in the general direction of.—**por otro l.,** on the other hand.—**por todos lados,** on all sides.—**por un l. . . . por otro,** on the one hand, . . . on the other; in a way . . . in a way.
ladón, *m.* (bot.) = LADA, cystus.
ladra, *f.* barking.
ladrador, ra; ladrante, *n.* & *a.* barker(-ing).
ladrar, *vn.* to bark.
ladrido, *m.* barking; outcry; (coll.) calumny, slander.
ladrillado, *m.* brick floor.
ladrillador, *m.* = ENLADRILLADOR, brick layer.
ladrillal, *m.* brick yard.
¹ladrillar, *m.* = LADRILLAL.
²ladrillar, *va.* to lay bricks on, pave with bricks.
ladrillazo, *m.* blow with a brickbat.
ladrillejo, *m. dim.* little brick; boys' amusement of knocking at doors with a brick.
ladrillera, *f.* (Am.) place for making bricks; (Ecua.) mold for making bricks.
ladrillero, *m.* brick maker.
ladrillo, *m.* brick, tile.—**l. de chocolate,** cake of chocolate.
ladrilloso, sa, *a.* bricky.
ladrón, na. I. *n.* thief; robber. **II.** *m.* lock, sluice gate; melted wax on sides of a candle.
ladronamente, *adv.* thievishly.
ladroncillo, *m. dim.* petty thief, filcher.
ladronear, *vn.* to go about robbing or stealing.
ladronera, *f.* nest of rogues, den of robbers; filching, extortion; sluice gate in a mill; money box.
ladronería, *f.* = LADRONICIO.
ladronesco, ca. I. *a.* (coll.) pert. to thieves, thievish. **II.** *f.* gang of thieves.
ladronicio, *m.* larceny, theft, robbery.
ladronzuelo, la, *n. dim.* petty thief.
lagaña, *f.* blearedness.
lagañoso, sa, *a.* = LEGAÑOSO, blear-eyed.
lagar, *m.* wine press.
lagarejo, *m.* small wine press.
lagarero, *m.* wine presser; olive presser.
lagareta, *f.* small wine press; puddle, pool.
lagarta, *f.* female lizard; (coll.) sly, cunning woman.
lagartado, da, *a.* = ALAGARTADO, variegated.
lagartera, *f.* lizard hole.
lagartija, *f.*, **lagartijo,** *m.*, **lagartillo,** *m. dim.* small lizard.
lagarto, *m.* lizard; (Am.) alligator; (anat.) biceps; (coll.) sly, artful person.—**l. de Indias,** cayman, alligator.
lago, *m.* lake.—**l. de leones,** den of lions.
lagostín *m.* (ichth.) = LANGOSTÍN, crayfish.
lagotear, *vn.* (coll.) to flatter, wheedle, cajole.
lagotería, *f.* (coll.) flattery.
lagotero, ra, *a.* (coll.) flattering, honey-mouthed.
lágrima, *f.* tear; drop of any liquid; drop-like exudation from a tree; wine that drips from the grape without pressure.—**l. de David,** or **de Jacob,** (bot.) Job's tears.—**lágrimas de Batavia,** or **de Holanda,** Prince Rupert's drops, glass globules.—**lágrimas de cocodrilo,** crocodile tears.—**lágrimas de San Pedro,** pebbles, stones thrown at a person.—**derramar** or **verter una l.,** to shed a tear.
lagrimable, *a.* deserving tears.
lagrimal. I. *a.* lachrymal. **II.** *m.* lachrymal caruncle.
lagrimar, lagrimear, *vn.* to shed tears.
lagrimeo, *m.* shedding tears.
lagrimón, *m. aug.* large tear.

lagrimoso, sa, *a.* tearful, lachrymose; (of eyes) watery; (bot.) exuding.
laguna, *f.* lagoon; hiatus, gap.
lagunajo, *m.* puddle, pool.
lagunar, *m.* (arch.) lacunar.
lagunero, ra, *a.* pertaining to lagoons.
lagunoso, sa, *a.* marshy, fenny, swampy.
laical, *a.* = LAICO.
laicidad, *f.* laity; secularism.
laicismo, *m.* secularism.
laicista, *n.* & *a.* secularist(-ic).
laicización, *f.* laicization.
laicizar, *va.* to laicize, make laic.
laico, ca, *a.* lay, laic.
laja, *f.* flagstone; slab; (naut.) rock at the entrance of a harbor.
[1]**lama,** *f.* mud, slime, ooze; seaweed; fine sand used for mortar; dust of ores in mines.
[2]**lama,** *f.* lamé, gold or silver cloth.
[3]**lama,** *n.* lama, Tibetan monk or nun.
lamaísmo, *m.* Lamaism.
lamaísta, *n.* & *a.* Lamaist(-ic).
lamarquiano, na, *a.* & *n.* Lamarckian.
lamarquismo, *m.* (biol.) Lamarckism.
lamarquista, *a.* & *n.* Lamarckian.
lambda, *f.* lambda (Greek letter).
lambel, *m.* (her.) lambel, label.
lambrequines, *m. pl.* (her.) mantelets.
lambrija, *f.* worm bred in the human body; (coll.) skinny, thin person.
lamedal, *m.* musty, miry place.
lamedero, *m.* saltlick.
lamedor, ra, *n.* licker; wheedling; (pharm.) syrup.—**dar lamedor,** to feign losing at play in order to insure greater success.
lamedura, *f.* act of licking.
lamela, *f.* lamella.
lamelibranquio, quia, *a.* & *m.* (zool.) lamellibranch.
lamelicornio, nia, *a.* & *m.* (entom.) lamellicorn.
lameliforme, *a.* lamelliform.
lamelirostro, tra, *a.* (zool.) lamellirostral.
lamentable, *a.* lamentable, deplorable.
lamentablemente, *adv.* lamentably.
lamentación, *f.* lamentation, wail.—**muro de las lamentaciones,** Wailing Wall (in Jerusalem).
lamentador, ra, *n.* & *a.* lamenter(-ing), mourner(-ing), complainer(-ing).
lamentar. I. *va.* to lament, mourn; to regret, be sorry for. **II.** *vn.* & *vr.* to lament, grieve, wail; to complain; to moan.
lamento, *m.* lamentation, lament, moan, wail.
lamentoso, sa, *a.* lamentable, mournful.
lameplatos, *m.* (coll.) glutton, gorger; one who feeds on leavings.
lamer, *va.* to lick; to lap; to touch slightly.
lamerón, na, *a.* (coll.) fond of dainties.
lamia, *f.* lamia, a fabulous monster; shark.
lamido, da. I. *pp.* of LAMER. **II.** *a.* (of persons) worn out.
lamiente, *n.* & *a.* lick, licker(-ing).
lamín, *m.* dainty tidbit.
lámina, *f.* plate, sheet; lamina; engraving, print, picture, illustration; engraving plate.
laminado, da, *a.* laminated; (of metals) rolled.
laminador, *m.* rolling mill; rolling press; plate roller.
laminagrafía, *f.* (med.) laminagraphy.
[1]**laminar,** *va.* to roll or beat (metal) into sheets.
[2]**laminar,** *va.* to lick; to guzzle (dainties).
[3]**laminar,** *a.* laminar, lamellar; in sheets.
laminera, *f.* bee advanced before its companions.
[1]**laminero, ra,** *n.* manufacturer of metal plates; maker of shrines for relics.
[2]**laminero, ra,** *a.* fond of sweets.
laminoso, sa, *a.* laminose, laminate.
lamiscar, *va.* (coll.) to lick greedily.
lamoso, sa, *a.* slimy, muddy.
lampa, *f.* (Am.) (agr.) shovel for grain.
lampacear, *va.* (naut.) to swab.
lampadéforo, lampadóforo, *m.* lampadephoria.
lampante, *a.* refined (olive oil).
lampar, *vn.* & *vr.* = ALAMPAR, to crave, long for.
lámpara, *f.* lamp; light, luminous body; (radio) tube; grease stain; bough placed at the door on festivals or rejoicings.—**l. Argand,** Argand lamp, student lamp.—**l. colgante,** portable lamp.—**l. de arco,** arc lamp.—**l. de seguridad,** safety lamp.—**l. de soldar,** blowtorch.—**l. de techo,** ceiling or top lamp.—**l. eléctrica,** electric lamp or bulb.—**l. fluorescente,** fluorescent lamp.—**l. incandescente,** incandescent lamp.—**l. indicadora,** pilot light.—**l. instantánea de relámpago,** photoflash lamp. —**l. neón,** neon lamp.—**l. normal,** standard lamp.—**l. piloto,** pilot lamp.—**l. termiónica,** (radio) thermionic tube or valve.—**l. ultravioleta,** ultraviolet lamp.—**atizar la l.,** (coll.) to refill the glasses.
lamparería, *f.* lamp factory; lamp store.
lamparero, ra, *n.* lamp maker or seller; lamplighter.
lamparilla, *f. dim.* small lamp; night taper; a sort of camlet; aspen or trembling poplar.
lamparín, *m.* lamp holder.
lamparista, *n.* = LAMPARERO.
lamparita, *f.* (S. A.) electric light bulb.
lamparón, *m. aug.* large grease spot; (med.) scrofula; (vet.) a disease of horses.
lampatán, *m.* a Chinese plant.
lampazo, *m.* (bot.) burdock; (naut.) swab, mop.
lampiño, ña, *a.* beardless.
lampión, *m.* large lantern.
lampo, *m.* flash of light; (poet.) refulgence.
lampote, *m.* (P. I.) domestic cotton cloth.
lamprea, *f.* (ichth.) sea lamprey.
lamprear, *va.* to dress or season with wine and sour gravy.
lampreazo, *m.* (coll.) slashing, whipping.
lamprehuela, lampreílla, *f.* river lamprey.
lámpsana, *f.* (bot.) common nipple wort.
lampuga, *f.* (ichth.) yellow mackerel.
lana, *f.* wool, fleece; any woollen fabric.—**l. de roca,** rock wool.
lanada, *f.* (artil.) sponge.
lanado, da, *a.* (bot.) lanate.
lanar, *a.* wool (as *a.*).
lanaria, *f.* (bot.) cudweed.
lancán, *m.* (P. I.) barge.
lance, *m.* cast, throw; casting of a fish net; catch in a net; critical moment; incident, episode; event, occurrence; transaction; quarrel, dispute; move or turn in a game.—**l. de honor,** duel.—**de l.,** cheap, at a bargain; at second hand.—**tener pocos lances,** to be uninteresting.
lancé, lance, *v. V.* LANZAR.
lanceado, da, *a.* (bot.) lanceolate.
lancear, *va.* to wound with a lance.
lancéola, *f.* (bot.) rib-grass plantain.
lanceolado, da, *a.* (bot.) lanceolate.
lancera, *f.* lance rack in an armory.
lancería, *f.* aggregate of lances; body of lancers.
lancero, *m.* pikeman; lancer; maker of pikes.
lanceta, *f.* (surg.) lancet; (vet.) fleam.
lancetada, *f.,* **lancetazo,** *m.* opening or wounding with a lancet.
lancetero, *m.* case for carrying lancets.
lancinante, *a.* stabbing, piercing.
lancinar, *va.* to lancinate.
lancita, *f. dim.* small lance.
lancurdia, *f.* small trout.
lancha, *f.* flagstone, slab; (naut.) boat, gig; lighter, launch; snare for partridges.—**l. cañonera,** gunboat.—**l. de pescar,** fishing smack. —**l. de socorro,** life-saving boat.
lanchada, *f.* lighter load.
lanchaje, *m.* (com.) ferriage; lighterage.
lanchar, *m.* flagstone quarry.
lanchero, *m.* bargeman, boatman, oarsman.
lanchón, *m. aug.* (naut.) lighter, barge, scow.—**l. alijador,** lighter.
lanchonero, *m.* lighterman, bargeman.

landa, *f.* wasteland; pasture.
landgrave, *m.* landgrave.
landgraviato, *m.* landgraviate.
landó, *m.* landau, carriage with folding top.
landre, *f.* small tumor on the glands; concealed pocket in the clothes.
landrecilla, *f.* small round body in some glandular tissues.
landrero, ra, *a.* hoarder of money in a concealed pocket.
landrilla, *f.* (vet.) tongue worm.
lanería, *f.* shop where wool is sold.
lanero, ra. I. *a.* woollen. **II.** *n.* dealer in wool. **III.** *m.* warehouse for wool.
langa, *f.* small dry codfish.
langarucho, cha, *a.* (coll.) longish, tallish.
langaruto, ta, *a.* (coll.) tall and skinny; thin.
langosta, *f.* (entom.) locust; (ichth.) lobster.
langostero, a. I. *n.* lobster fisherman. **II.** *a.* lobster-fishing; lobster (as *a.*).
langostín, langostino, *m.* (ichth.) crawfish.
langostón, *m. aug.* (entom.) green grasshopper.
lánguidamente, *adv.* languidly.
languidecer, *vn.* (*ind.* LANGUIDEZCO; *subj.* LANGUIDEZCA) to languish.
languidez, languideza, *f.* languishment, languidness, languor.
lánguido, da, *a.* languid, faint, weak.
lanífero, ra, *a.* (poet.) laniferous, woolly.
lanificación, *f.*, **lanificio,** *m.* woollen manufacturing; woollen goods.
lanilla, *f.* nap of cloth, down; swanskin; fine flannel; (naut.) bunting.
lanío, a, *a.* woolly.
lanolina, *f.* (chem.) lanolin. lanoline.
lanosidad, *f.* (bot.) down of leaves.
lanoso, sa, *a.* woolly.
lansquenete, *m.* lansquenet.
lantaca, *f.* (P. I.) small culverin.
lantana, *f.* (bot.) lantana.
lantanido, *m.* (chem.) lanthanide.
lantano, *m.* (chem.) lanthanum.
lantia, *f.* (naut.) binnacle lamp; boom guy.
lanudo, da, *a.* woolly, fleecy.
lanuginoso, sa, *a.* (bot.) lanigerous, downy.
lanza, *f.* lance, spear; pole of a coach or wagon; nozzle; pikeman; free lance.—*pl.* duty formerly paid by the nobility in lieu of military services. —**l. en ristre,** with the lance on its rest; ready for action.—**ser una l.,** to be an expert; to be clever.
lanzabombas, *m.* bomb thrower.
lanzacabos, *a.* (naut.) life-saving.
lanzacohetes, *m.* rocket launcher.
lanzada, *f.* thrust or blow with a lance.
lanzadera, *f.* shuttle, a weaver's instrument.
lanzado, da. I. *pp.* of LANZAR. **II.** *a.* (naut.) raking, inclined.
lanzador, ra, *n.* thrower, ejecter; (baseball) pitcher.
lanzafuego, *m.* (artil.) linstock.
lanzamiento, *m.* launching, casting, or throwing; (law) dispossessing, eviction; (naut.) flaring of the bows and knuckle timbers; (naut.) rake of the stem and sternpost.—*pl.* length of a ship from stem to sternpost.—**l. de abastecimiento,** (mil.) airdrop.
lanzaminas, *m.* mine layer, mine-laying boat.
lanzar. I. *va.* (*pret.* LANCÉ; *subj.* LANCE) to throw, dart, hurl, fling; to launch; to throw up, vomit; (law) to evict, dispossess.—**l. abastecimientos,** (mil.) to airdrop. **II.** *vr.* to rush or dart; to launch forth; (com.) to engage or embark (in).
lanzatorpedos, *m.* torpedo boat; torpedo tube.
lanzazo, *m.* = LANZADA.
lanzón, *m. aug.* short and thick goad.
lanzuela, *f. dim.* small lance or spear.
[1]**laña,** *f.* green coconut.
[2]**laña,** *f.* clamp, cramp or cramp iron.
[1]**lañar,** *va.* to cramp; to clamp.
[2]**lañar,** *va.* to clean (fish).
laodicense, *a.* Laodicean.
Laos, *m.* Laos.
laosiano, na, *a.* & *n.* Laotian.
[1]**lapa,** *f.* vegetable film on surface of a liquid.
[2]**lapa,** *f.* barnacle.
[3]**lapa,** *f.* (bot.) goose grass, cleavers.
lapachar, *m.* swamp, marsh, morass.
lápade, *f.* lepadid, barnacle.
laparotomía, *f.* (surg.) laparotomy.
lapicera, *f.* (Chile, Arg.) = LAPICERO; penholder, pen.—**l. fuente,** or **de depósito,** fountain pen.
lapicero, *m.* pencil case; pencil holder.
lápida, *f.* tablet, memorial stone; gravestone (called also **l. mortuoria**).
lapidación, *f.* lapidation, stoning to death.
lapidar, *va.* to stone to death.
lapidario, ria, *n.* & *a.* lapidary.
lapídeo, a, *a.* lapideous, stony.
lapidificación, *f.* (chem.) turning into stone.
lapidificar, *va.* (chem.) to petrify, turn into stone.
lapidífico, ca, *a.* lapidific.
lapidoso, sa, *a.* lapideous, stony.
lapila, *f.* (bot.) hound's-tongue.
lapislázuli, *m.* (min.) lapis lazuli.
lápiz, *m.* (min.) black lead, graphite, plumbago; lead pencil; crayon; (coll.) censor's blue pencil. —**l. de plomo,** graphite.—**l. labial,** lipstick.—**l. rojo,** red ochre.
[1]**lapizar,** *m.* black-lead mine.
[2]**lapizar,** *va.* to pencil; draw with pencil.
lapo, *m.* (coll.) blow with a cane or whip.
lapón, na, *n.* & *a.* Laplander(-ian, -ic).
lapso, *m.* lapse of time; fall, lapse, slip.
lapsus, *m.* lapsus, slip.—**l. calami,** lapsus calami, slip of the pen.—**l. linguæ,** slip of the tongue.
laqueado, da, *a.* lacquered.
laquear, *va.* to lacquer.
laques, *f. pl.* = BOLEADORES, a lariat.
lar, *m.* (gen. *pl.*) Lar, tutelar or household god.—*pl.* home.
larario, *m.* shrine for household gods.
lardar, lardear, *va.* to baste (meat); to scald with boiling oil.
lardero, *a.*—**jueves l.,** Thursday before Lent.
lardo, *m.* lard, fat of an animal.
lardón, *m.* (print.) marginal addition; piece of paper clinging to the frisket and preventing the impression of some part of a sheet.
lardoso, sa, *a.* greasy, oily, smearing.
larga, *f.* (shoemaking) lengthening piece joined to a last; longest billiard cue; (gen. in the *pl.*) delay, procrastination.—**a la corta o a la l.,** sooner or later.—**a la l.,** in the end, in the long run.—**dar largas,** to delay, put off.
largamente, *adv.* largely, copiously; completely; liberally, frankly; for a long time.
largar. I. *va.* (*pret.* LARGUÉ; *subj.* LARGUE) to loosen, slacken; let go, set free; to expel; to shed; to give (as a slap); to heave (as a sigh); (naut.) to loosen, to ease.—**l. las velas,** (naut.) to set sail. **II.** *vr.* (coll.) to get out, quit, leave; (naut.) to set sail.
[1]**largo, ga. I.** *a.* long; extended, prolonged; generous, free, liberal; prompt, expeditious; shrewd, cunning; copious, abundant.—*pl.* many, quite a number; odd, a little over (*tengo cincuenta años largos,* I am fifty-odd years old). —**l. de lengua,** long-tongued, too free and unguarded with the tongue.—**l. de uñas,** (coll.) light-fingered.—**largos años,** many years; long life.—**a lo l.,** at a distance; lengthwise; at full length, stretched out.—**a lo l. de,** along, lengthwise of.—**a lo más l.,** at most—**cuan l. es (era),** at full length, stretched out.—**traje l.,** evening dress. **II.** *m.* length.—**de l.,** in length, long.—**de l. a l.,** from one end to the other, lengthwise.—**pasar de l.,** to pass by without stopping. **III.** *adv.* largely, profusely. **IV.** *interj.* ¡**l.**! or ¡**l. de ahí**!, begone! get out!
[2]**largo,** *m.* (mus.) largo.
largor, *m.* length.
largucho, cha, *a.* (coll.) longish.

largué, largue, *v.* *V.* LARGAR.
largueado, da, *a.* striped.
larguero, *m.* jamb post; bolster; stringer; (aer.) longeron; (aer.) spar.
largueza, *f.* length; liberality, generosity.
larguirucho, cha, *a.* (coll.) long and thin.
larguito, ita, *a.* somewhat long, longish.
largura, *f.* length.
lárice, *m.* (bot.) larch tree.
laricino, na, *a.* pertaining to the larch tree.
laringe, *f.* (anat.) larynx.
laríngeo, gea, *a.* laryngeal.
laringitis, *f.* (med.) laryngitis.
laringología, *f.* laryngology.
laringoscopia, *f.* laryngoscopy.
laringoscopio, *m.* laryngoscope.
laringotomía, *f.* (surg.) laryngotomy.
laringótomo, *m.* (surg.) laryngotome.
larva, *f.* or *m.* (zool.) larva; mask; ghost, hobgoblin.
larvado, da, *a.* (med.) larvate.
larval, *a.* larval.
las, *pl.* of LA.
lasaña, *f.* fritter shaped like a leaf.
lasca, *f.* chip from a stone.
lascar, *va.* to ease away, slacken, pay out.
láscar, *m.* lascar (East Indian sailor).
lascivamente, *adv.* lasciviously.
lascivia, *f.* lasciviousness, lewdness.
lascivo, va, *a.* lascivious, lewd, lustful; merry, sportive.
laserpicio, *m.* (bot.) laserwort.
lasitud, *f.* lassitude, weariness, faintness.
laso, sa, *a.* weary, tired; lax, flaccid.
lastar, *va.* to pay (for a fault); suffer for another.
lástima, *f.* pity; compassion; pitiful object; plaint, lamentation, tale of woe.—**dar,** or **hacer, l.,** to arouse pity or regret, to be pitiful or regrettable.—**es l.** it's a pity, too bad.—**¡que l.!** what a pity!—**¡que l. de (vestido)!** what a sorry-looking (dress)!
lastimador, ra, *a.* hurting, damaging, injurious.
lastimadura, *f.* sore, hurt.
lastimar. I. *va.* to hurt; injure, damage; to pity. **II.** *vr.* to hurt oneself; to regret, be sorry for; to complain.
lastimeramente, *adv.* sadly, sorrowfully.
lastimero, ra, *a.* pitiful, sad, doleful.
lastimosamente, *adv.* pitifully, sadly.
lastimoso, sa, *a.* = LASTIMERO.
lasto, *m.* receipt given to one who pays for another.
lastra, *f.* flagstone, slab.
lastrar, *va.* (naut. and Ry.) to ballast.
[1]**lastre,** *m.* ballast; judgment, sense.
[2]**lastre,** *m.* stone slat of poor quality; (coll.) food, "grub".
lastrón, *m.* *aug.* large stone slat.
lasún, *m.* (ichth.) = LOCHA, loach.
[1]**lata,** *f.* small log.
[2]**lata,** *f.* tin plate or tinned iron plate; tin can; can of tinned food; lath; ledge.—**en l., en latas,** canned.—**dar la l.,** (coll.) to pester with too much talk.
[3]**lata,** *f.* annoyance, nuisance; (coll.) long-drawn-out, tedious visit or performance.
latamente, *adv.* largely, amply.
latania, *f.* (bot.) latania palm.
latastro, *m.* (arch.) plinth (of a pillar).
lataz, *f.* (zool.) sea otter.
latebra, *f.* cave, den, hiding place.
latebroso, sa, *a.* hiding, furtive, secretive.
latencia, *f.* (med.) latency.
latente, *a.* latent.
lateral, *a.* lateral, side (as *a.*).—**lateralmente,** adv. laterally; sideways.
lateranense, *a.* Lateran.
laterita, *f.* (geol.) laterite.
látex, *m.* (bot.) latex.
laticífero, ra, *a.* (bot.) laticiferous.
latido, *m.* beat, beating, throb; bark, barking (of an animal).
latiente, *a.* palpitating, fluttering.
latifundio, *m.* (anc. Rome) latifundium, large estate (esp. app. to vast uncultivated or poorly cultivated land).
latifundista, *n.* latifundist.
latigadera, *f.* strap or thong for lashing the yoke.
latigazo, *m.* lash, whipping; crack of a whip; jerk; unexpected offense; harsh reproof.
látigo, *m.* whip; lashing cord for weighing with a steelyard; cinch strap; long plume around a hat.
latiguear, *vn.* to snap or crack a whip.
latiguera, *f.* cinch strap.
latiguero, *m.* maker or seller of whips.
latiguillo, *m.* *dim.* small whip; (theat.) mannerism.
latín, *m.* Latin.—**bajo l.,** low Latin.—**saber l.,** or **mucho l.,** to be very shrewd or cunning.
latinajo, *m.* (coll.) Latin jargon; Latin word or quotation.
latinamente, *adv.* in Latin; in a Latin way.
latinar, latinear, *vn.* to speak or write Latin; to use Latin phrases often.
latines, *m. pl.* jargon, nonsense; hairsplitting.
latinidad, *f.* Latinity; the Latin tongue.
latinismo, *m.* Latinism.
latinista, *n.* Latinist.
latinización, *f.* (gram.) latinization.
latinizar. I. *va.* to Latinize. **II.** *vn.* to use words borrowed from the Latin.
latino, na. I. *a.* Latin. **II.** *n.* Latinist; Latin, a native of Latium.
Latinoamérica, *f.* Latin America.
latinoamericano, na. I. *a.* Latin-American. **II.** *n.* Latin American.
latir, *vn.* to palpitate, pulsate, throb, beat; to bark, yelp, howl.
latitud, *f.* latitude; breadth, width, extent.
latitudinal, *a.* latitudinal.
latitudinario, ria, *a.* & *n.* latitudinarian, liberal.
latitudinarismo, *m.* latitudinarianism.
lato, ta, *a.* large, extensive, ample.
latón, *m.* brass.—**l. en hojas,** or **planchas,** latten brass, sheet brass.
latonería, *f.* brass trade; brass shop; brass works; brass ware.
latonero, *m.* brazier, worker in brass.
latoso, sa, *a.* boring, annoying.
latría, *f.* (Rom. Cath. theol.) latria, worship due only to God.
latrocinio, *m.* systematic robbery.
latvio, via, *n.* & *a.* Latvian.
laucha, *f.* (Arg., Chile) mouse.
laúd, *m.* (mus.) lute; (naut.) catboat; striped turtle.
lauda, *f.* tombstone.
laudable, *a.* laudable, praiseworthy.
laudablemente, *adv.* laudably.
láudano, *m.* laudanum.
laudar, *va.* (law) to render a decision on.
laudatorio, ria. I. *a.* laudatory, full of praise. **II.** *f.* laudatory, panegyric.
laude, *f.* inscribed tombstone.—*pl.* (eccl.) lauds.
laudemio, *m.* (law) dues paid to the lord of the manor on all transfers of landed property.
laudo, *m.* (law) award, finding, of an arbitrator.
launa, *f.* lamina, sheet; schistose clay.
lauráceo, cea, *a.* lauraceous.
láurea, *f.* laurel wreath.
laureado, da, *a.* & *n.* laureate.
laureando, *m.* student about to graduate.
laurear, *va.* to crown with laurel; to honor, reward; to confer a degree on.
lauredal, *m.* plantation of laurel trees.
laurel, *m.* (bot.) laurel; laurel wreath; honor.—**l. cerezo,** (bot.) cherry laurel.
laurente, *m.* workman in paper mills.
laurentino, na, *a.* & *m.* (geol.) Laurentian.
láureo, a, *a.* laurel (as *a.*).
lauréola, *f.* laurel wreath; diadem; (bot.) mezereon.—**l. hembra,** (bot.) mezereon daphne.—**l. macho,** spurge laurel.
láurico, ca, *a.* (chem.) lauric.
laurífero, ra, *a.* lauriferous, laurel-bearing.
lauríneo, nea, *a.* (bot.) laurineous.

laurino, na, *a.* pertaining to laurel.
lauro, *m.* (bot.) laurel; glory, honor.
lauroceraso, laurorreal, *m.* cherry laurel.
lautamente, *adv.* splendidly.
lauto, ta, *a.* rich, splendid.
[1]**lava,** *f.* lava.
[2]**lava,** *f.* (min.) washing of metals.
lavable, *a.* washable.
lavabo, *m.* washstand; lavatory; washroom.
lavacaras, *m.* (coll.) flatterer.
lavación, *f.* (pharm.) lotion, wash.
lavadero, *m.* washing place; lavatory; (tanning) vat or pit for washing hides; (min.) buddling tank; placer, place where gold, etc. are obtained by washing.
lavado, *m.* wash, washing; laundry work; (art) aquarelle in a single tint.
lavador, ra. I. *n.* & *a.* washer(-ing), cleaner(-ing). **II.** *m.* (artil.) burnisher. **III.** *f.* washing machine (called also **l. mecánica**).
lavadura, *f.* wash, washing; composition for dressing glove leather; slops.
lavafrutas, *m.* dish for washing fruit at the table.
lavaje, *m.* washing of wools.
lavajo, *m.* drinking pool for cattle; morass.
lavamanos, *m.* washstand; lavatory.
lavamiento, *m.* washing, ablution.
lavanco, *m.* a kind of wild duck.
lavandera, *f.* laundress, washerwoman.
lavandería, *f.* (Am.) laundry.
lavandero, *m.* launderer, laundryman.
lavándula, *f.* (bot.) lavender.
lavaplatos, *n.* dishwasher.
lavar, *va.* to wash; to launder; (mason.) to whitewash; (art) to paint in water colors; to purify. —**l. el cerebro,** (coll.) to brainwash.
lavativa, *f.* clyster, enema, injection; syringe; vexation, annoyance; bore.
lavatorio, *m.* lavation, washing; lavatory; washstand; (pharm.) lotion; (eccl.) maundy.
lavaza, *f.* soap suds.—*pl.* dirty water, slops.
lave, *m.* washing of ores in mines.
lavotear, *va.* & *vr.* (coll.) to wash hurriedly.
lavoteo, *m.* hurried washing.
laxación, *f.* **laxamiento,** *m.* laxity, laxness; loosening.
laxante, *a.* & *m.* laxative.
laxar, *va.* to loosen, soften.
laxativo, va, *a.* & *m.* laxative.
laxidad, laxitud, *f.* laxity, laxness.
laxo, xa, *a.* lax, slack.
lay, *m.* (poet.) lay, ballad.
[1]**laya,** *f.* (agr.) spade, spud.
[2]**laya,** *f.* quality, kind, class.
layador, *m.* spadesman.
layar, *va.* (agr.) to spade.
lazada, *f.* bowknot; (sew.) bow; true-lover's knot.
lazador, *m.* lassoer.
lazar, *va.* to lasso, capture with a lasso.
lazareto, *m.* hospital for contagious diseases; quarantine (at ports of entry).
lazarillo, *m.* blind person's guide.
lazarino, na. I. *a.* leprous. **II.** *n.* leper.
lazo, *m.* (sewing) bow, loop, true-lover's knot; snare (for game); trap or snare (for persons); lasso, lariat; slipknot; tie, bond; (arch.) knot or ornament.—*pl.* (dance) figures.—**l. escurridizo,** running knot.—**armar l.,** or **lazos,** to trap, deceive; to plot.
lazulita, *f.* lazulite, lapis lazuli.
le, *dative case of* ÉL, ELLA; *accusative case of* ÉL: to him, to her, to it (*¿que le dio Vd.?* what did you give to him (or to her)? *¿que le añadio Vd.?* what did you add to it?) accusative case of ÉL: him (*ayer le ví,* I saw him yesterday). (Often improperly app. to inanimate objects.)
leal, *a.* loyal.—**l. saber y entender,** to the best of my knowledge.—**lealmente,** *adv.* loyally.
lealtad, *f.* loyalty, fidelity.
lebeche, *m.* southwest wind (in the Mediterranean).
leberquisa, *f.* (min.) magnetic pyrite, pyrrhotite.
lebrada, *f.* hare fricassee.
lebrel, la, *n.* greyhound (*f.,* greyhound bitch).
lebrero, ra, *a.* hare-hunting, hare (as *a.*).
lebrillo, *m.* glazed earthenware tub.
lebrón, *m.* large hare; (coll.) poltroon.
lebroncillo, *m.* young hare.
lebruno, na, *a.* pertaining to or like hares.
lección, *f.* lesson; tuition; lecture; reading.—**dar una l.,** to say or recite a lesson; to give a lesson. —**echar l.,** to give out or assign a lesson.— **tomar la l.,** to take a lesson.—**tomar una lección a,** to hear a lesson from to hear (someone's) lesson.
leccionario, *m.* (eccl.) lectionary.
leccioncita, *f. dim.* short lecture or lesson.
leccionista, *n.* private tutor; coach.
lecitina, *f.* (chem.) lecithin.
lecito, *m.* yolk (of an egg).
lectisternio, *m.* (anc. Rome) lectisternium, a sacrifice.
lectivo, va, *a.* lesson or recitation (day, hour).
lector, ra, *n.* reader; lecturer; (eccl.) instructor of the Gospel.
lectorado, *m.* (eccl.) lectorate.
lectoral. I. *f.* (eccl.) prebend. **II.** *m.* prebendary.
lectoría, *f.* (eccl.) lectureship.
lectura, *f.* reading; lecture; (print.) pica.
lecturita, *f.* (print.) small pica.
lecha, *f.* seminal fluid of fishes; each of the two sacs which contain it.
lechada, *f.* grout; liquid containing finely divided solids in suspension; pulp for making paper.
lechal. I. *a.* sucking, suckling; (bot.) lactiferous, milky. **II.** *m.* (bot.) milky juice of plants.
lechar, *a.* nursing; promoting the secretion of milk in female mammals.
lechaza, *f.* = LECHA.
leche, *f.* milk; (bot) milky juice.—**l. crema,** custard.—**l. de canela,** oil of cinnamon dissolved in wine.—**l. de gallina,** or **de pájaro,** (bot.) common star of Bethlehem.—**l. de tierra,** magnesia.—**l. de (los) viejos,** wine.— **l. quemada,** sweetmeat made from simmered milk.—**estar con la l. en los labios,** to lack experience.—**estar en l.,** (of fruits and plants) to be still green or undeveloped; (of the sea) to be calm.
lechecillas, *f. pl.* sweetbreads; livers and lights.
lechera. I. *a.* milch (app. to animals). **II.** *f.* milkmaid, dairymaid; milk can; milk jug.
lechería, *f.* dairy (shop).
lechero, ra. I. *a.* milky. **II.** *m.* milkman.
lecherón, *m.* milk pail, milk vessel; flannel wrap for newborn infants.
lechetrezna, *f.* (bot.) spurge.
lechigada, *f.* breed, litter; gang of ruffians.
lechín, *m.* variety of olive tree and the rich olive it yields; (vet.) tumor in horses.
lechino, *m.* (vet.) small tumor.
lecho, *m.* bed, couch; lay, litter; bed of a river; tier, row; layer, stratum; foundation, base.
lechón, na, *n.* suckling pig; pig.
lechoncico, illo, ito, *m. dim.* very young pig.
lechoso, sa. I. *a.* (bot.) having a milky juice. **II.** *m.* (S. A.) (bot.) papaw tree. **III.** *f.* papaw.
lechuga, *f.* (bot.) lettuce; (sew.) frill.—**l. romana,** (bot.) romaine lettuce.
lechugado, da, *a.* lettuce-like.
lechuguero, ra, *n.* seller of lettuce.
lechuguilla, *f. dim.* small lettuce; frill, ruff.
lechuguina, *f.* (coll.) stylish young lady.
lechuguino, *m.* lettuce sprout; plot of small lettuces; (coll.) dandy, dude.
lechuza, *f.* (ornith.) owl; barn owl.
[1]**lechuzo, za. I.** *a.* suckling (mule colt).
[2]**lechuzo, za,** *n.* (coll.) bill collector; summons server; owl-faced person.
ledamente, *adv.* (poet.) merrily, cheerfully.
ledo, da, *a.* (poet.) gay, merry, cheerful, glad.
leer, *va.* (*ger.* LEYENDO; *pret.* él LEYÓ) to read; to lecture; to instruct.
lega, *f.* (eccl.) lay sister.

legacía, *f.* legateship; message intrusted to a legate; province and duration of a legateship.
legación, *f.* legation, embassy; legateship.
legado, *m.* (law) legacy; deputy, ambassador, legate; commander of a Roman legion.—**l. a látere,** (eccl.) Pope's legate.
legador, *m.* laborer who ties the feet of sheep for shearing.
legadura, *f.* tie; binding cord or strap.
legajo, *m.* file, docket, bundle of papers.
legal, *a.* legal, lawful; loyal, true, faithful.
legalidad, *f.* legality, lawfulness.
legalista, *a.* legalistic.
legalización, *f.* legalization.
legalizar, *va.* to legalize.
legalmente, *adv.* legally, lawfully; loyally.
legamente, *adv.* ignorantly.
légamo, *n.* mud, silt.—**legamoso, sa,** *a.* silty.
leganal, *m.* puddle, mudhole.
legaña, *f.* gummy secretion of the eyes.
legañoso, sa, *a.* blear-eyed.
legar, *va.* (*pret.* LEGUÉ; *subj.* LEGUE) to depute, to send as a legate; (law) to bequeath.
legatario, ria, *n.* (law) legatee.
legenda, *f.* (eccl.) legend, history of saints.
legendario, ria. I. *a.* legendary. **II.** *m.* legendary, book of legends.
legibilidad, *f.* legibility.
legible, *a.* legible, readable.
legiblemente, *adv.* legibly.
legión, *f.* legion.—**L. Extranjera,** Foreign Legion.
legionario, ria, *a.* & *m.* legionary.
legislación, *f.* legislation.
legislador, ra, *n.* & *a.* legislator(-ing, -ive); lawmaker(-ing).
legislar, *va.* to legislate.
legislativo, va, *a.* legislative, lawmaking.
legislatura, *f.* legislature; term of a legislature.
legisperito, ta, *n.* = JURISPERITO, jurisconsult.
legista, *n.* legist; lawyer; law student.
legítima, *f.* (law) legitim.
legitimación, *f.* legitimation.
legítimamente, *adv.* legitimately, lawfully.
legitimar, *va,* to legitimate, legalize.
legitimidad, *f.* legitimacy, legality.
legitimista, *n.* & *a.* legitimist(-ic).
legítimo, ma, *a.* legitimate, lawful; genuine.
lego, ga. I. *a.* lay, laic; ignorant. **II.** *m.* layman; lay brother or friar.
legón, *m.* (agr.) hoe.
legra, *f.* (surg.) periosteotome.
legración, legradura, *f.* (surg.) periosteotomy.
legrar, *va.* (surg.) to perform periosteotomy on.
legua, *f.* league (measure of length).—**a l., a la l., a leguas, de cien leguas, de muchas leguas** or **desde media l.,** very far, at a great distance.
leguario, ria, *a.* league (as *a.*, as *poste leguario,* league post).
legué, legue, *v. V.* LEGAR.
leguleyo, *m.* petty lawyer, pettifogger.
legumbre, *f.* pulse, vegetables, garden stuff.
legúmina, *f.* (biochem.) legumin.
leguminoso, sa. I. *a.* (bot.) leguminous. **II.** *f.* (bot.) legume.
leíble, *a.* legible, readable.
leído, da. I. *pp.* of LEER. **II.** *a.* well-read, well-informed.—**l. y escribido,** (coll. and contempt.) affecting learning.
leila, *f.* a Moorish dance.
leima, *m.* (mus.) limma.
lejanía, *f.* distance, remoteness; remote place.
lejano, na, *a.* distant, far.
lejas, *a. pl.*—**l. tierras,** far-away lands.
lejía, *f.* lye; (coll.) severe reprimand, dressing down.
lejío, *m.* (among dyers) lye.
lejísimos, *adv. super.* very far away.
lejitos, *adv. dim.* rather far.
lejos. I. *adv.* far.—**a lo l.,** in the distance, at a great distance, far off, far away.—**d. l., desde l.,** from afar. **II.** *m.* perspective, distant view; background; resemblance.
lejuelos, *adv. dim.* at a little distance.
lelilí, *m.* war whoop of the Moors.
lelo, la. I. *a.* stupid, dull. **II.** *n.* ninny.
lema, *m.* argument, summary; theme; motto, device; slogan; (math.) lemma.
lemanita, *f.* (min.) jade.
lemnáceo, cea, *a.* (bot.) lemnaceous.
lemniscata, *f.* (geom.) lemniscate.
lemosín, na. I. *a.* Languedocian. **II.** *m.* Languedocian; Provençal, langue d'oc.
lémur, *m.* (zool.) lemur.
lemures, *m. pl.* lemures; ghosts, apparitions.
len, *a.* soft, flossy (thread or silk).
lena, *f.* spirit, vigor.
lencera, *f.* woman who deals in linen; wife of a linen draper.
lencería, *f.* linen goods; linen-draper's shop; linen hall; linen room; linen trade.
lencero, ra, *n.* linen draper, linen merchant.
lendel, *m.* track; mill horse.
lendrera, *f.* fine-toothed comb for taking out nits.
lendrero, *m.* place full of nits.
lendroso, sa, *a.* nitty, full of nits.
lene, *a.* soft (to the touch); sweet, kind, pleasant; light, not heavy.
lengua, *f.* (anat.) tongue; language; information, advice; clapper of a bell.—**l. canina** = L. DE PERRO.—**l. cerval,** (bot.) hart's-tongue.—**l. de buey,** (bot.) bugloss, alkanet.—**l. del agua,** at the edge of the water.—**l. de oc,** langue d'oc.—**l. de perro,** (bot.) hound's-tongue.—**l. de tierra,** tongue of land running out into the sea.—**l. de vaca,** sanseviera, cordy-line.—**l. madre,** or **matriz,** mother tongue.—**l. muerta,** dead language.—**l. sabia,** classical language.—**l. santa,** Hebrew.—**l. viperina,** viperous tongue.—**l. viva,** living, or modern, language.—**con la l. de un palmo,** or **con un palmo de l.,** with great anxiety or eagerness.—**de l. en l.,** from mouth to mouth.—**hacerse lenguas,** to speak in praise, sing the praises of.—**írsele, a uno la l.,** to let out something one did not wish to say, to give oneself away.—**morderse la lengua,** to hold one's tongue, to control oneself.—**no morderse la l.,** not to mince words, to speak out.—**tener en la l.,** or **en la punta de la l.,** to have at one's tongue's end.
lenguado, *m.* (ichth.) sole, flounder, flatfish.
lenguaje, *m.* language; speech; parlance; vernacular tongue; style.
lenguaraz, *a.* speaking several languages; scurrilous; LENGUAZ.
lenguaz, *a.* garrulous, loquacious.
lengüecia, illa, ita, *f. dim.* small tongue.
lengüeta, *f. dim.* small tongue; (anat.) epiglottis; barb; (mus.) languette; needle of a balance; (bookbinding) cutting knife; (mech.) feather, wedge, tongue, bit, bore, awl; catch of a trap or snare; (arch.) buttress; molding.
lengüetada, *f.* act of licking.
lengüetería, *f.* reedwork of an organ.
lengüezuela, *f. dim.* small tongue.
lengüicorto, ta, *a.* (coll.) timid, reticent.
lengüilargo, ga, *a.* (coll.) garrulous; scurrilous.
lenidad, *f.* lenity, mildness.
lenificar, *va.* to soften.—**lenificativo, va,** *a.* mollifying, softening.
leninismo, *m.* Leninism.
leninista, *a.* & *n.* Leninite, Leninist.
lenitivo, va. I. *a.* lenitive, assuaging; lenient. **II.** *m.* emollient; mitigator.
lenocinio, *m.* pimping, pandering, (law) procuration.
lenón, *m.* pimp, pander, (law) procurer.
lentamente, *adv.* slowly, lingeringly.
lente, *m.* or *f.* (opt.) lens; monocle; *m. pl.* eyeglasses.—**l. de aumento,** magnifying glass.—**lentes de contacto,** contact lens.
lentecer, *vn.* to grow soft or tender.
lenteja, *f.* (bot.) lentil; disk of a pendulum.—**l. de agua,** (bot.) gibbous duckweed.
lentejuela, *f.* spangle.

lenticular, *a.* like a lentil seed.
lentiscal, *m.* thicket of mastic trees.
lentisco, *m.* (bot.) mastic tree, lentiscus.
lentitud, *f.* slowness, sluggishness.
lento, ta, *a.* slow, sluggish, tardy, heavy; glutinous; (mus.) lento.
lentor, *m.* (pharm.) viscidity.
lenzuelo, *m.* (agr.) sheet for carrying straw.
leña, *f.* firewood, kindling wood; (coll.) drubbing, beating.—**echar l. al fuego,** to add fuel to the flame, foment discord.—**llevar l. al monte,** to carry coals to Newcastle.
leñador, ra, *n.* woodman (-woman), woodcutter; dealer in kindling wood.
leñame, *m.* wood; provision of kindling wood.
leñatero, ra, *n.* = LEÑADOR.
leñazo, *m.* cudgeling.
leñera, *f.* woodshed, wood bin.
leñero, *m.* wood dealer; logman.
leñífero, ra, *a.* ligniferous.
leño, *m.* log; timber; (naut.) ancient galley; (poet.) ship, vessel; (coll.) dull, thick-witted person.
leñoso, sa, *a.* woody, ligneous.
Leo, *m.* (astr.) Leo.
león, *m.* (zool.) lion; (entom.) ant lion; (zool.) boa.—**l. marino,** sea lion.—**l. rampante,** (her.) lion rampant.—**el L.,** (astr.) Leo.—**no es tan bravo,** or **tan fiero, el l. como lo pintan,** one cannot always judge by appearances; things are not so bad as they seem.
leona, *f.* lioness; brave, undaunted woman.
leonado, da, *a.* lion-colored, tawny.
leoncico, illo, ito, *m.* whelp of a lion.
leonera, *f.* cage or den of lions; (coll.) gambling den.
leonero, *m.* lion keeper; (coll.) master of a gambling house.
leonés, sa, *a.* of or pertaining to Leon.
leónica, *f.* (vet.) vein under the tongue.
leonina, *f.* (med.) leontiasis, a leprous affection.
leonino, na, *a.* leonine; (law) one-sided, unfair; (poet.) leonine (verse).
leontina, *f.* (jewelry) watch chain.
leopardo, *m.* leopard.
leopoldina, *f.* (jewelry) fob chain; Spanish helmet.
Lepe, *m.*—**saber más que L.,** to be very smart and shrewd.
lépero, ra, *n.* (Mex.) one of the rabble.
lepidio, *m.* (bot.) peppergrass.
lepidolita, *f.* (min.) lepidolite.
lepidóptero, ra. I. *a.* (entom.) lepidopterous. **II.** *m.* (entom.) lepidopteron.
lepidosirena, *f.* (ichth.) lepidosiren.
lepisma, *f.* (entom.) lepisma, silverfish.
leporino, na, *a.* harelike.
lepra, *f.* leprosy.
leprosería, *f.* lepers' lazaretto.
leproso, sa. I. *a.* leprous. **II.** *n.* leper.
leptón, *m.* (phys.) lepton.
lercha, *f.* reed for hanging fish and birds.
lerda, *f.* (vet.) = LERDÓN.
lerdamente, *adv.* slowly, heavily.
lerdo, da, *a.* slow, heavy; dull, obtuse.
lerdón, *m.* (vet.) tumor in a horse's pastern.
les, *pers. pron. dative case* of ELLOS, ELLAS: to them, them (indirect object): *les di pan,* I gave them bread; *les hablé,* I spoke to them.
lesbianismo, *m.* Lesbianism.
lesbiano, na, *a.* & *f.* Lesbian.
lesbio, bia, *a.* Lesbian, of Lesbos.
lesión, *f.* lesion, wound, injury; damage, wrong.
lesionar, *va.* to injure; to damage, impair.
lesivo, va, *a.* prejudicial, injurious.
lesna, *f.* = LEZNA, awl.
lesnordeste, *m.* (naut.) east-northeast wind.
leso, sa, *a.* wounded, hurt, damaged; perverted. —**l. majestad,** lese majesty.
leste, *m.* (naut.) east wind, east.
lesueste, *m.* (naut.) east-southeast wind.
letal, *a.* mortal, deadly, lethal.
letame, *m.* mud for fertilizing.
letanía, *f.* (eccl.) litany; (coll.) list of things.—*pl.* supplicatory procession.
letárgico, ca, *a.* lethargic.
letargo, *m.* lethargy, drowsiness.—**l. epidémico,** sleeping sickness.
letargoso, sa, *a.* causing lethargy.
leteo, a, *a.* (poet.) Lethean.
letificante, *a.* exhilarating, invigorating.
letificar, *va.* to gladden, cheer; to invigorate.
letífico, ca, *a.* cheering, bringing joy
letón, tona, *a.* & *n.* Lett, Lettish.
letra, *f.* letter, character of the alphabet; handwriting; (print.) type; motto, inscription; literal meaning; (poet.) a kind of rondeau; words of a song.—*pl.* letters, learning; the learned professions.—**l. abierta,** (com.) open credit.—**l. bastardilla** = L. ITÁLICA.—**l. borrosa,** illegible writing.—**l. cursiva,** running hand.—**l. de caja alta,** (print.) upper case, capital.—**l. de caja baja,** (print.) lower case, small letter. —**l. de cambio,** (com.) draft, bill of exchange. —**l. de mano,** handwriting, handwritten letter.—**l. de molde,** print, printed letter.—**l. muerta,** dead letter, rule no longer observed.—**l. de tortis,** Gothic type.—**l. gótica,** Gothic characters.—**l. historiada,** adorned capital letter.—**l. itálica,** (print.) italic.—**l. menuda,** fine lettering, small print.—**l. negrilla,** (print.) boldface, blackface.—**letras patentes,** royal edict.—**letras remisorias,** judge's orders transferring a case to another court.—**l. versal,** capital letter.—**a la l.,** to the letter, literally.—**bellas,** or **buenas, letras,** belles lettres, literature.—**cuatro letras,** a few lines.—**tener mucha l.,** to be very artful and cunning.
letrado, da. I. *a.* learned, erudite; (coll.) vain, presumptuous. **II.** *m.* lawyer, advocate, counselor.—**a lo l.,** like a lawyer. **III.** *f.* (coll.) lawyer's wife.
letrero, *m.* sign; label, placard, poster; legend.
letrilla, *f. dim.* small letter; (mus.) rondelet.
letrina, *f.* privy, water-closet.
letrón. I. *m. aug.* large letter. **II.** *m. pl.* placards posted at the doors of churches.
letuario, *m.* a kind of marmalade.
leucemia, *f.* (med.) leukemia.
leucina, *f.* (chem.) leucine.
leucita, *f.* (min.) leucite.
leucocitemia, *f.* (med.) leukemia.
leucocito, *m.* (physiol.) leucocyte, white blood corpuscle.
leucocitosis, *f.* (med.) leucocytosis.
leucoma, *m.* (med.) leucoma, an eye disease.
leucomaína, *f.* (chem.) leucomaine.
leucopenia, *f.* (med.) leukopenia.
leucorrea, *f.* (med.) leucorrhoea, whites.
leudar. I. *va.* to leaven. **II.** *vr.* to yeast.
leudo, da, *a.* fermented, leavened.
leva, *f.* (naut.) act of weighing anchor; (mil.) levy, press; (mech.) cam; vane (of a water wheel); (naut.) swell of the sea.—*pl.* tricks, artful devices.
levada, *f.* moving silkworm; (fencing) salute or flourish with the foil.
levadero, ra, *a.* to be collected or demanded.
levadizo, za, *a.* that can be lifted or raised, as a drawbridge.
levador, *m.* in paper mills, piler; (mech.) cam, cog, tooth.
levadura, *f.* ferment, leaven, yeast, barm; (carp.) sawed-off plank.
levantada, *f.* rising, getting up.
levantadamente, *adv.* highly, loftily.
levantado, da, *pp.* & *a.* raised, elevated, lofty.
levantador, ra, *n.* one who raises or lifts up; disturber, rioter; mutineer.
levantamiento, *m.* elevation, raising; sublimity; insurrection, revolt, uprising; settlement of accounts; survey.—**l. de planos,** surveying.
levantar. I. *va.* to raise; to lift, heave, pick up; to erect, build; set up; to rouse, excite, stir up; to impute or attribute falsely; to start (game);

to cut (the cards); to cause, occasion; to begin; to stand up; to start suddenly (as game).—**l. acta,** to draw up and execute an affidavit or certificate.—**l. bandera,** to rise in insurrection, to rebel.—**l. (la) casa,** to break up housekeeping.—**l. (la) cabeza,** to retrieve one's losses, to get on one's feet; to take courage.—**l. con,** to take unlawful possession of, to get away with.—**l. el plano de,** to survey.—**l. falso testimonio,** to bear false witness, to accuse falsely.—**l. la mesa,** to clear the table.—**l. planos,** to survey; to draw up plans. **II.** *vr.* to rise, get up (from bed, chair, etc.); to rise up.

[1]**levante,** *m.*—**estar de l.,** to be ready to depart.

[2]**levante,** *m.* Levant, east; east wind.

levantino, na, *a.* & *n.* Levantine.

[1]**levantisco, ca,** *a.* & *n.* Levantine.

[2]**levantisco, ca,** *a.* turbulent, restless.

levar. I. *va.* (naut.) to weigh (anchor).—**l. anclas,** to weigh anchor. **II.** *vr.* to set sail.

leve, *a.* light, of little weight; trifling; slight.

levedad, *f.* lightness, levity; inconstancy.

levemente, *adv.* lightly, gently; venially.

leviatán, *m.* leviathan.

levigación, *f.* levigation, elutriation.

levigar, *va.* to levigate, to elutriate.

levirato, *m.* (anc. Hebrew) levirate.

[1]**levita,** *m.* Levite; deacon.

[2]**levita,** *f.* frock coat, Prince-Albert coat.

levitación, *f.* levitation.

levítico, ca. I. *a.* Levitical; priestly. **II.** *m.* **(L-)** Leviticus; (coll.) ceremonial at a festival.

levitón, *m.* greatcoat like a frock coat.

levógiro, ra, *a.* counterclockwise.

levulosa, *f.* (chem.) levulose.

léxico, *m.* lexicon, dictionary.

lexicografía, *f.* lexicography.

lexicográfico, ca, *a.* lexicographic.

lexicógrafo, fa, *n.* lexicographer.

lexicología, *f.* lexicology.

lexicológico, ca, *a.* lexicological.

lexicólogo, ga, *n.* lexicologist.

lexicón, *m.* lexicon, wordbook.

ley, *f.* law; rule of action; statute; loyalty; fineness (in gold or silver); standard; precept; rules and regulations.—*pl.* law in general, jurisprudence, study and profession of the law.—**l. antigua,** law of Moses.—**l. caldaria,** hot-water ordeal.—**l. de la trampa,** trickery, fraud.—**l. del embudo,** oppressive law; one-sided agreement; severity for others, indulgence for ourselves.—**l. del tallón,** lex talionis, law of retaliation.—**l. escrita,** revealed law, decalogue.—**l. marcial,** martial law.—**l. periódica,** (chem.) periodic law.—**l. sálica,** Salic law.—**a la l.,** properly, orderly.—**a l. de caballero** or **de cristiano,** on the word of a gentleman or Christian.—**a toda l.,** perfectly, according to rule.—**de buena l.,** sterling.—**de mala l.,** disreputable; crooked; low, base.

leyenda, *f.* reading; legend; superscription, inscription; device, motto.

leyendario, ria, *a.* legendary.

leyente, *n.* & *a.* reader(-ing).

leyó, *pret.* of LEER.

lezda, *f.* ancient tax on merchandise.

lezna, *f.* awl.

[1]**lía,** *f.* plaited bass rope.

[2]**lía,** *f.* husk of pressed grapes.—**estar hecho una lía,** (coll.) to be tipsy.

liana, *f.* (bot.) liana, vine.

liar. I. *va.* to tie, bind, do up; (coll.) to embroil, draw into an entanglement—**liarlas,** (coll.) to sneak away; (coll.) to die. **II.** *vr.* to enter into concubinage.

liásico, ca. I. *n.* & *a.* (geol.) Liasic. **II.** *m.* Lias, Liasic.

liaza, *f.* collection of hoops used by coopers.

libación, *f.* libation.

libamen, libamiento, *m.* offering in ancient sacrifices.

libán, *m.* esparto rope.

libanés, nesa, *a.* & *n.* Lebanese.

Líbano, *m.* Lebanon.

libar, *va.* to suck, sip; to taste; to perform a libation with.

libatorio, *m.* libatory cup.

libelar, *va.* (law) to petition.

libelático, ca, *a.* retracting, apostatizing.

libelista, *m.* libeler.

libelo, *m.* libel (often called **l. infamatorio**); (law) petition.—**l. de repudio,** written repudiation, of a wife by her husband; (coll.) discarding, abandoning, giving up.

libélula, *f.* libellula, dragon fly.

líber, *m.* (bot.) bast, liber, or inner bark.

liberación, *f.* liberation; (law) quittance.

liberador, ra. I. *a.* liberating. **II.** *n.* liberator.

liberal, *a.* liberal; quick, brisk; (pol.) liberal.—**artes liberales,** liberal arts.

liberalidad, *f.* liberality, generosity.

liberalismo, *m.* Liberalism; Liberal party.

liberalizar, *va.* to liberalize.

liberalmente, *adv.* liberally, generously, freely.

Liberia, *f.* Liberia.

liberiano, na, *a.* & *n.* Liberian.

libérrimo, ma, *a. super.* most free.

libertad, *f.* liberty, freedom; exemption, privilege, immunity; familiarity; freedom, agility, address; independence, unconventionality; ransom.—**l. civil,** civil liberty.—**l. condicional,** probation.—**l. de comercio,** free trade.—**l. de conciencia** or **cultos,** freedom of worship.—**l. de imprenta,** freedom of the press.—**l. de palabra,** freedom of speech, right of free speech.—**l. provisional,** liberation on bail.—**dejar en l.,** to set free.

libertadamente, *adv.* freely, impudently.

libertado, da, *a.* bold; free, ungoverned.

libertador, ra, *n.* & *a.* deliverer(-ing), liberator (-ing).

libertar, *va.* to free, liberate; to exempt, excuse; to acquit; to rid, clear.

libertario, ria, *n.* & *a.* anarchist(-ic).

liberticida, *m.* liberticide, destroyer of liberty.

libertinaje, *m.* libertinism, licentiousness.

libertino, na. I. *n.* child of a freedman. **II.** *n.* & *a.* libertine.

liberto, ta, *n.* freedman(-woman).

libídine, *m.* or *f.* lust, lewdness; (psych.) libido.

libidinosamente, *adv.* libidinously, lewdly.

libidinoso, sa, *a.* libidinous, lewd, lustful.

libido, *m.* (psych.) libido.

libio, bia. I. *a.* Libyan. **II.** *n.* Libyan; *f.* **(L.)** Libya.

Liborio, *m.* Cuban peasant wearing a straw hat (symbol of the Cuban people).

libra, *f.* pound (weight, coin). **(L-,** astr.) Libra.—**l. esterlina,** pound sterling.—**l. tornesa,** livre tournois.

libración, *f.* oscillation; (astr.) libration.

libraco, libracho, *m.* (coll.) trashy book.

librado, da. I. *pp.* of LIBRAR.—**bien l.,** successful, lucky.—**mal l.,** unsuccessful, unlucky, faring ill or badly. **II.** *n.* drawee.

librador, ra, *n.* deliverer; (com.) drawer of a check or draft; storekeeper of the king's stables; (*m.*) grocer's scoop.

libramiento, *m.* delivery, delivering; warrant, order of payment.

librancista, *m.* (com.) holder of a draft.

libranza, *f.* (com.) draft, bill of exchange.—**l. postal,** money order.

librar. I. *va.* to free, deliver; to exempt; to preserve from ill; to pass (sentence); to issue (a decree); (com.) to draw.—**l. batalla,** or **combate,** to engage in battle.—**l. (una letra) contra,** to draw on.—**¡Dios me libre!,** Heaven forbid! **II.** *vn.* (of nuns) to receive a visitor in the locutory; to be delivered (of a child); to expel the placenta.—**l. bien (mal),** to fare well (badly).—**l. en,** to depend on; to put (confidence, hope) in.—**a bien,** or **a buen l.,** as well as could be expected. **III.** *vr.* **(de)** to escape, avoid, be free (from), get rid (of).

libratorio, *m.* cubicle for receiving visitors in a convent.
libre, *a.* free; uncumbered, unrestrained; independent; vacant; disengaged; clear, open; exempt; innocent, guiltless, single, unmarried; libertine, loose, licentious; impudent; rash, thoughtless; isolated, alone.—**l. a bordo (l. a. b.),** free on board (f. o. b.).—**l. cambio,** free trade.—**l. de derechos, impuestos,** duty, tax, free.—**l.|pensador** = LIBREPENSADOR.—**l. pensamiento** = LIBREPENSAMIENTO.—**l. plática,** pratique.
librea, *f.* livery, uniform.
librear, *va.* to weigh or sell by pounds.
librecambista, *n.* free trader.
librejo, *m. dim.* little book; worthless book.
libremente, *adv.* freely; boldly.
librepensador, ra, *n.* freethinker.
librepensamiento, *m.* freethinking, free thought.
librería, *f.* bookstore, bookseller's shop; book trade; library; large collection of books.
libreril, *a.* pertaining to the book trade.
librero, ra, *n.* bookseller.
[1]**libreta,** *f.* troy pound; loaf of bread of 1 lb. weight.
[2]**libreta,** *f.* memorandum book; notebook; (surv.) field book; pass book; bank book.—**l. de direcciones,** address book.
librete, *m. dim.* small book; foot stove.
libretín, *m. dim.* small book, booklet.
libretista, *n.* librettist.
libreto, *m.* (mus.) libretto.
[1]**librillo,** *m.* small book of cigarette paper.—**l. de cera,** folded wax taper.—**l. de oro,** gold-leaf book.
[2]**librillo, librito,** *m.* earthen tub.
libro, *m.* book; (mus.) libretto; (zool.) omasum, or third stomach (of a ruminant).—**l. becerro,** doomsday book.—**l. borrador,** blotter, record book.—**l. copiador,** (com.) letter book.—**l. de actas** = L. DE MINUTAS.—**l. de asiento** = L. DE CUENTAS.—**l. de caja,** cashbook.—**l. de cuentas,** account book.—**l. de facturas,** invoice book.—**l. de memoria,** memorandum book.—**l. de minutas,** minute book.—**l. diario,** (com.) daybook.—**l. en blanco,** blank book.—**l. en folio,** folio book.—**l. mayor,** ledger.—**l. talonario,** check book, stub book.—**l. verde,** (coll.) book for notes about places and persons; also the compiler of such notes.
librote, *m. aug.* large book.
licantropía, *f.* (med.) lycanthropy, kind of insanity.
licántropo, *a.* lycanthrope.
licaón, *m.* (zool.) lycaon.
liceísta, *n.* member of a lyceum.
licencia, *f.* permission, leave, license, permit; licentiousness; (mil.) furlough; degree of licentiate; (poet.) license.—**l. absoluta,** (mil.) discharge.—**l. de conducción,** driver's license.—**l. poética,** poetic license.—**l. por enfermedad,** sick leave.—**con l.,** (mil.) on leave, furlough.
licenciadillo, *m.* (coll.) ridiculous little man in clerical robes.
licenciado, da. I. *pp.* of LICENCIAR. **II.** *a.* presuming knowledge. **II.** *m.* licentiate, graduate (of university); (coll.) university student; (coll.) lawyer; (mil.) discharged soldier.
licenciamiento, *m.* graduation as a licentiate; (mil.) discharge; dismissal.
licenciar. I. *va.* to permit, allow; to license; to confer a degree on; (mil.) to discharge. **II.** *vr.* to become dissolute; to get a master's degree (from university).
licenciatura, *f.* degree of licentiate; graduation as a licentiate.
licenciosamente, *adv.* licentiously.
licencioso, sa, *a.* licentious, dissolute.
liceo, *m.* lyceum.
licio, cia, *n.* & *a.* Lycian.
licitación, *f.* auction; bid.
licitador, *m.* bidder.
lícitamente, *adv.* lawfully, licitly.
licitante, *n.* bidder.
licitar, *va.* & *vn.* to bid (on, for) at auction or on public works.
lícito, ta, *a.* licit, lawful; just.
licnobio, bia, *n.* lychnobite, one who turns night into day, (coll.) night hawk.
licopodio, *m.* (bot.) lycopodium.
licor, *m.* liqueur, cordial; liquid.
licorera, *f.* liqueur or bottle case.
licorería, *f.* liquor shop; saloon, bar.
licorista, *n.* liquor distiller or dealer.
licoroso, sa, *a.* spirituous, alcoholic.
lictor, *m.* lictor, in ancient Rome.
licuable, *a.* liquefiable.
licuación, *f.* liquation, liquefaction.
licuante, *a.* liquefying.
licuar, *va.* & *vr.* to liquefy, liquate, melt.
licuefacción, *f.* liquefaction.
licuefacer, *va.* & *vr.* to liquefy.
licuefactible, *a.* liquefiable.
licuescencia, *f.* liquescence.
licuescente, *a.* liquescent.
licurgo, ga, *a.* keen, smart, shrewd.
lichera, *f.* woollen cover of a bed.
lid, *f.* contest, fight; dispute, argument.
líder, *m.* & *f.* (Angl.) (Am.) leader.
lidia, *f.* battle, fight, contest; bullfight.
lidiadero, ra, *a.* in fighting condition.
lidiador, ra, *n.* combatant; fighter; arguer.
lidiar. I. *vn.* to fight, to contend; to struggle. **II.** *va.* to run or fight (bulls).
lidio, dia, *n.* & *a.* Lydian.
liebrastón, liebratico, liebratón, *m.* young hare, leveret.
liebre, *f.* hare; (L.) (astr.) Lepus; (coll.) coward, poltroon.—*pl.* (naut.) racks, ribs; (naut.) deadeyes.—**coger una l.,** to fall flat.
liebrecica, illa, ita, *f. dim.* little hare.
liebrecilla, *f.* (bot.) bluebottle.
liebrezuela, *f. dim.* young or small hare.
liendre, *f.* nit, egg of a louse.—**cascar a uno las liendres,** (slang) to give one a severe drubbing.
lientera, lientería, *f.* (med.) lientery, diarrhea.
lientérico, ca, *a.* lienteric.
liento, ta, *a.* damp, moist.
lienza, *f.* narrow strip of cloth.
lienzo, *m.* linen cloth; (art) canvas; (fort.) curtain; (arch.) face or front of a building; stretch of a wall.—**l. casero,** homespun linen.—**l. crudo,** unbleached linen.—**l. gordo,** coarse linen.
liga, *f.* garter; (bot.) mistletoe; birdlime; league, coalition, alliance; alloy for gold and silver.
ligación, *f.* joining, tying; union, mixture.
ligada, *f.* ligature; binding, tying.
ligado, da. I. *pp.* of LIGAR. **II.** *a.* confederate. **III.** *m.* (mus.) legato.
ligadura, *f.* ligature, ligation, binding; subjection; (mus.) ligature, syncopation, tie; (arch.) arcs made by cross timbers; (naut.) seizing, lashing.
ligamaza, *f.* viscosity on some fruits or plants.
ligamen, *m.* spell supposed to cause impotency.
ligamento, *m.* bond, tie; (anat.) ligament.
ligamentoso, sa, *a.* ligamentous, ligamental.
ligamiento, *m.* act of tying or binding; union, concord.
ligar. I. *va.* (*pret.* LIGUÉ; *subj.* LIGUE) to tie, bind, fasten; to alloy; to join, link, knit together; to render impotent by malefic spells. **II.** *vn.* to combine cards of the same suit. **III.** *vr.* to league, join together, combine; to bind oneself.
ligazón, *f.* tie, fastening, union, connection, bond; (naut.) futtock timbers.
ligeramente, *adv.* lightly; quickly; slightly.
ligereza, *f.* lightness; swiftness, agility, nimbleness; levity, inconstancy, fickleness.
ligero, ra. I. *a.* (of weight, food, entertainment, garment, etc.) light; fast, nimble; (of cloth)

thin; gay; unsteady, giddy; unimportant, trifling; easily disturbed (as sleep).—**l. de cascos,** feather-brained.—**l. de dedos,** light-fingered.—**a la l.,** quickly; briefly; superficially.—**de l.,** rashly; easily. **II.** *adv.* fast, rapidly.
ligeruelo, la, *a. dim.* early (grapes).
ligio, gia, *a.* liege.
lignario, ria, *a.* ligneous.
lignícola, *f.* (entom.) lignicole.
lignífero, ra, *a.* ligniferous.
lignificar, *va. & vn.* to lignify.
lignina, *f.* (bot., chem.) lignin.
lignito, *m.* (min.) lignite.
ligroína, *f.* (chem.) ligroin.
ligua, *f.* (P. I.) battle-axe.
liguano, na, *a.* (Chile) (of sheep) having thick and heavy wool.
ligué, ligue, *v. V.* LIGAR.
liguilla, *f.* narrow garter.
lígula, *f.* (bot.) ligule.
ligulado, da, *a.* (bot.) ligulate.
ligur; ligurino, na, *n. & a.* Ligurian.
ligústico, *m.* (bot.) lovage.
ligustre, *m.* (bot.) flower of privet.
ligustrino, na, *a.* pertaining to privet.
ligustro, *m.* (bot.) privet, prim, ligustrum.
lija, *f.* sandpaper; (ichth.) dogfish; (coll., Cuba) self-flattery, conceit.—**darse l.,** (coll.) to flatter oneself.
lijar, *va.* to sandpaper, sand.
lila(c), *f.* (bot.) lilac; lilac color.
[1]**lilaila,** *f.* bunting; (coll.) (gen. *pl.*) trick, wile.
[2]**lilaila,** *f.* = LILILÍ.
liliáceo, cea. I. *a.* (bot.) liliaceous. **II.** *f.* (bot.) lilywort.
lililí, *m.* = LELILÍ, war whoop of the Moors.
liliputiense, *n. & a.* Liliputian.
[1]**lima,** *f.* (bot.) sweet lime, a kind of citron.
[2]**lima,** *f.* (mech.) file; finish, polishing.
[3]**lima,** *f.* (arch.) valley (also **l. hoya**).
limadura, *f.* filing.—*pl.* filings.
limalla, *f.* filings.
limar, *va.* to file; to polish; to touch up.
limatón, *m.* coarse round file, rasp.
limazo, *m.* viscosity, sliminess.
limbo, *m.* limbo; (astr.) limb; limb, graduated circle (of a theodolite, etc.).
limen, *m.* (poet.) = UMBRAL, threshold.
limeño, ña, *a.* of or belonging to Lima.
[1]**limera,** *f.* woman who sells sweet limes.
[2]**limera,** *f.* (naut.) rudderhole.
limero, *m.* seller of sweet limes; (bot.) sweet-lime tree (a variety of citron tree).
limeta, *f.* vial, small bottle.
limitación, *f.* limitation, limit; district.
limitadamente, *adv.* limitedly, finitely.
limitado, da, *pp. & a.* limited, dull-witted.
limitáneo, nea, *a.* pert. to boundaries, frontiers.
limitar. I. *va.* to limit; to bound; to restrict; to reduce (expense).—**l. con,** (geog.) to be bounded by. **II.** *vr.* to confine oneself to.
limitativo, va, *a.* limitative, limiting, restrictive.
límite, *m.* limit; boundary, bound, border.
limítrofe, *a.* bounding, conterminous.
limo, *m.* slime, mud.
[1]**limón,** *m.* lemon; lemon tree; (Cuba, coast of Colomb., etc.) lime (tree and fruit).—**l. mejicano,** lime.
[2]**limón,** *m.* thill or shaft (of carriage).
limonada, *f.* lemonade.—**l. de vino,** wine lemonade, sangaree.—**l. purgante,** citrate of magnesia.
limonado, da, *a.* lemon-colored.
limonar, *m.* plantation of lemon trees.
limoncillo, limoncito, *m. dim.* small lemon; lime.
limoneno, *m.* (chem.) limonene.
[1]**limonero, ra. I.** *n.* lemon dealer. **II.** *m.* (bot.) lemon tree.
[2]**limonero, ra. I.** *a.* shaft (horse) in carriages, etc. **II.** *f.* shaft, thill (of carriages).
limonita, *f.* (min.) limonite.
limosidad, *f.* sliminess; foul matter between teeth.
limosna, *f.* alms.
limosnear, *va.* to beg; to peddle.
limosnero, ra. I. *a.* charitable. **II.** *n.* almoner; (Am.) beggar. **III.** *f.* alms bag or box.
limoso, sa, *a.* slimy, muddy, limose.
limousine, *f.* limousine.
limpia, *f.* cleaning, cleansing; dredging.
limpiabarros, *m.* bootscraper.
limpiabotas, *m.* bootblack.
limpiachimeneas, *m.* chimney sweeper.
limpiadera, *f.* clothes-brush; comb-brush; plow cleaner.
limpiadientes, *m.* toothpick.
limpiador, ra, *n. & a.* cleaner(-ing), cleanser (-ing).
limpiadura, *f.* cleaning, cleansing.—*pl.* dirt, refuse.
limpiamente, *adv.* cleanly, neatly; purely; sincerely, faithfully.
limpiamiento, *m.* cleansing, cleaning.
limpiaparabrisas, *m.* windshield wiper.
limpiaplumas, *m.* penwiper.
limpiar. I. *va.* to clean, cleanse; to purify, clear; (coll.) to steal; (coll.) (in gambling) to "clean out", win all one's money.—**l. en seco,** dry-clean.—**l. las faltriqueras a uno,** to pick one's pockets; (coll.) to win from one. **II.** *vr.* to clear oneself from imputed guilt.—**l. las manos, los dientes,** to wash one's hands, brush one's teeth.
limpiaúñas, *m.* nail cleaner.
limpiavía, *m.* (Ry.) rail guard.
limpidez, *f.* limpidity.
límpido, da, *a.* (poet.) limpid, crystal-clear.
limpieza, *f.* cleanness, cleanliness; neatness; purity; integrity, honesty; disinterestedness; purity of blood; correctness, neatness of execution.—**l. de bolsa,** emptiness of the purse.
limpio, pia, *a.* clean; cleanly; limpid, clear; neat, pure, unmingled; free, clear, net; (coll.) penniless, "broke."—**en l.,** in substance; clearly.—**poner en l.,** to make a final copy from a rough draft.—**sacar, en l.,** PONER EN L.; to conclude, infer; to make out, make head or tail of.
limpión, *m.* hasty cleaning.
límulo, *m.* (zool.) limulus, horseshoe crab, king crab.
linaje, *m.* lineage, race; progeny, offspring; class, condition.—**l. humano,** mankind.
linajista, *m.* genealogist, writer of pedigrees.
linajudo, da, *n. & a.* boaster(-ing) of noble descent.
lináloe, *m.* (bot.) aloes.
linar, *m.* flax field.
linaria, *f.* (bot.) wild flax, yellow toad flax.
linaza, *f.* (bot.) linseed, flaxseed.
lince. I. *m.* (zool.) lynx; very keen person. **II.** *a.* sharp-sighted, keen-sighted, observing.
lincear, *va.* (coll.) to note what is not easily seen.
linceo, a, *a.* lyncean; sharp, keen.
linchamiento, *m.* lynching.
linchar, *va.* to lynch.
linches, *m. pl.* (Mex.) fiber saddlebags.
lindamente, *adv.* prettily, neatly, elegantly.
lindante, *a.* bordering, contiguous.
lindar, *vn.* to be contiguous, to border, abut.
linde, *m.* landmark; boundary, limit.
lindero, ra. I. *a.* contiguous, bordering. **II.** *m.* limit, boundary.
lindeza, *f.* neatness, elegance, prettiness.—*pl.* pretty things; (ironic) improprieties, insults.
lindo, da. I. *a.* pretty, lovely; complete, perfect, fine. **II.** *m.* beau, coxcomb; minion.—**de lo l.,** perfectly, wonderfully; greatly.
lindón, *m.* (agr.) frame or bar for hanging asparagus, etc.
lindura, *f.* LINDEZA; beauty, beautiful woman; beautiful thing.
línea, *f.* line; (of persons) lines, figure; lineage,

progeny; equator; border; boundary, limit; class, order; (fort.) trench or intrenchment; (mil.) rank, file; line, twelfth part of an inch.—**l. de agua,** or **de flotación,** (naut.) water line. —**l. de colimación,** or **de fe,** (surv.) line of collimation.—**l. de fuerza,** (phys.) line of force.—**l. de la tierra,** (geom.) ground line.—**l. de nivel máximo,** high-water mark.—**l. de nivel mínimo,** low-water mark.—**l. de vapores,** steamship line.—**l. equinoccial,** equator. —**l. férrea,** railway.—**l. isobárica,** (meteorol.) isobar.—**l. isogónica,** (meteorol.) isogonic line. —**l. isoterma,** (meteorol.) isotherm.—**en l.,** in a line, row.

lineal, *a.* lineal, linear.

lineamento, or **lineamiento,** *m.* lineament, feature.

[1]**linear,** *va.* to draw lines on; to form with lines.

[2]**linear,** *a.* lineal, linear.

lineotipia, *f.* = LINOTIPIA.

linfa, *f.* lymph; (poet.) water.

linfadenoma, *m.* (med.) lymphadenoma.

linfangitis, *f.* (med.) lymphangitis.

linfático, ca, *a.* lymphatic.

linfatismo, *m.* (med.) lymphatism.

linfocito, *m.* (anat.) lymphocyte.

linfoideo, dea, *a.* lymphoid.

linfopenia, *f.* (med.) lymphopenia.

lingote, *m.* (foundry) ingot; pig, bloom, billet.

lingual, *a.* lingual.

linguete, *m.* pawl; ratchet.

lingüiforme, *a.* linguiform.

lingüista, *n.* linguist.

lingüístico, ca. I. *a.* linguistic. **II.** *f.* linguistics.

linimento, linimiento, *m.* (pharm.) liniment.

linio, *m.* = LIÑO, row of plants.

linneano, na, *a.* Linnean.

lino, *m.* (bot.) flax; linen; sail-bloth, canvas; (poet.) sail.

linóleo, *m.* linoleum.

linón, *m.* lawn (cloth).

linotipia, *f.* linotype.

linotipista, *n.* linotypist.

linotipo, *m.* linotype.

lintel, *m.* lintel of a door. Also DINTEL.

linterna, *f.* lantern; lamp, light (on a train, car, etc.); flashlight; (mech.) lantern wheel; (arch.) lantern.—**l. delantera,** or **de adelante,** (Ry., auto) front light.—**l. mágica,** magic lantern.—**l. sorda,** dark lantern.—**l. trasera,** or **de atrás,** (Ry., auto) back, or rear, light.

linternazo, *m.* blow with a lantern; (fig.) blow with any instrument.

linternero, ra, *n.* lantern maker.

linternón, *m. aug.* big lantern; (naut.) poop lantern.

liño, *m.* row of trees or plants; ridge between furrows.

liñuelo, *m.* rope, cord.

lío, *m.* bundle, parcel, pack; (coll.) imbroglio, scrape; intrigue, conspiracy.—**armar un l.,** to tangle, mess up, make difficulties.

lionés, nesa, *a.* & *n.* Lyonese.—**a la lionesa,** lyonnaise (potatoes).

liorna, *f.* (coll.) uproar, hubbub, confusion.

lipemanía, *f.* (med.) melancholia, lypemania.

lipemaníaco, ca, *a.* (med.) melancholic.

lipes, lipis, *f.* (chem.) blue vitriol, copper sulphate.

lipoma, *m.* (med.) lipoma, a fatty tumor.

lipotimia, *f.* (med.) faint, swoon.

liquen, *m.* (bot.) lichen.—**l. de Islandia,** Iceland moss.

liquidable, *a.* liquefiable; (com.) adjustable.

liquidación, *f.* liquefaction; (com.) liquidation, settlement; bargain sale.

liquidador, ra. I. *a.* liquefying. **II.** *n.* liquefier; liquidator.

liquidámbar, *m.* liquidambar, balsam liquid.

líquidamente, *adv.* in a liquid state.

liquidar. I. *va.* to liquefy; (com.) to liquidate, sell out; to settle, pay up; to squander; (coll.) to "liquidate", murder. **II.** *vr.* to liquefy.

liquidez, *f.* liquidness, fluidity.

líquido, da. I. *a.* liquid; evident, clear; (econ.) liquid; (com.) net; (Mex., C. A., W. I.) just, exactly (as *me quedan tres pesos líquidos,* I have just three pesos left). **II.** *m.* liquid; (com.) balance, net profit.—**l. imponible,** amount of assessment for tax collection. **III.** *f.* (phon.) liquid consonant.

[1]**lira,** *f.* lira (Italian monetary unit).

[2]**lira,** *f.* (mus.) lyre; (poet.) lyric poem; (**L.** astr.) Lyra.—**lirado, da,** *a.* lyre-shaped.

liria, *f.* birdlime.

lírico, ca. I. *a.* lyric, lyrical. **II.** *f.* lyric poetry.

lirio, *m.* (bot.) lily.—**l. blanco** = AZUCENA, white lily.—**l. de agua,** calla lily.—**l. de Florencia,** orris, Florentine iris.—**l. de los valles,** lily of the valley.—**l. hediondo,** gladwin.

lirismo, *m.* abuse of lyricisms.

[1]**lirón,** *m.* (zool.) dormouse; (coll.) sleepy head; (naut.) jackscrew.

[2]**lirón,** *m.* (bot.) alisma.

lirondo, da, *a.* pure, clean, neat.

lis, *f.* (bot.) lily; fleur-de-lis, iris.

[1]**lisa,** *f.* smooth stone for polishing paper.

[2]**lisa,** *f.* (ichth.) a river fish.

lisamente, *adv.* smoothly, plainly.—**lisa y llanamente,** openly and frankly; simply.

lisbonense, lisbonés, sa, *a.* of or belonging to Lisbon.

lisera, *f.* (fort.) berm, a narrow terrace.

lisiado, da, *n.* & *a.* cripple(d).

lisiar, *va.* to lame, hurt, cripple, injure.

lisimaquia, *f.* (bot.) loosestrife.

lisina, *f.* (biochem.) lysin.

lisis, *f.* (med.) lysis.

liso, sa, *a.* smooth, even, flat; plain, unadorned; straight (hair); plain-dealing.—**l. y llano,** plain, clear, evident.

lisol, *m.* Lysol (trademark).

[1]**lisonja,** *f.* flattery.

[2]**lisonja,** *f.* = LOSANGE, *m.* (her.) lozenge.

lisonjado, da, *a.* (her.) lozenged; rhombic.

lisonjeador, ra, *n.* & *a.* flatterer(-ing).

lisonjear, *va.* to flatter; to delight, please.

lisonjeramente, *adv.* flatteringly.

lisonjero, ra. I. *m.* & *f.* flatterer. **II.** *a.* flattering; pleasing, agreeable; complimentary.

lista, *f.* list; catalogue; slip of paper; shred of linen; strip of cloth; selvage; stripe, band; (law) docket; (mil.) roll, muster.—**l. de comidas** or **de platos,** bill of fare, menu.—**l. de correos,** general delivery.—**l. de equipaje,** baggage list. —**pasar l.,** to call the roll.

listadillo, *m.* (Am.) striped gingham.

listado, da. I. *pp.* of LISTAR. **II.** *a.* striped.

listar, *va.* to enter in a list.

listeado, da, *a.* = LISTADO.

listel, *m.* (arch.) fillet, listel, tringle.

listerina, *f.* Listerine (trademark).

listero, *m.* timekeeper.

listeza, *f.* smartness, alertness, shrewdness.

listo, ta, *a.* ready; quick, prompt; clever.

listón, *m.* ribbon; ferret, tape; (carp.) lath, cleat, strip; (arch.) listel, fillet.—*pl.* (naut.) battens.

listonado, da. I. *a.* (carp.) made of laths. **II.** *m.* laths, lathing.

listonar, *va.* (carp.) to batten, to lath.

listonería, *f.* parcel of ribbons, tapes, and inkles; ribbon store; ribbon manufactory.

listonero, ra, *n.* ribbon maker.

listura, *f.* smartness, quickness, cleverness.

lisura, *f.* smoothness, evenness, flatness; sincerity, candor.

lita, *f.* tongue worm in dogs.

litación, *f.* sacrificing.

litagogo, ga, *a.* (med.) lithagogue; (surg.) lithontriptic.

litar, *va.* to sacrifice to the Deity.

litarge, litargirio, *m.* litharge.

lite, *f.* (law) lawsuit.

litemia, *f.* (med.) lithemia.

litera, *f.* bunk, berth, litter.

literal, *a.* literal.—**literalmente,** *adv.* literally.
literario, ria, *a.* literary.
literato, ta. I. *a.* literary. **II.** *n.* litterateur, literary person, writer.
literatura, *f.* literature.
literero, ra, *n.* litter maker, seller, or driver.
litiasis, *f.* (med.) lithiasis, gravel.
lítico, ca, *a.* lithic.
litigación, *f.* litigation.
litigante, *n.* & *a.* (law) litigator(-ing), litigant.
litigar, *va.* (*pret.* LITIGUÉ; *subj.* LITIGUE) (law) to litigate; to contend, dispute.
litigio, *m.* litigation, lawsuit, dispute, contest.
litigioso, sa, *a.* litigious, contentious.
litigué, litigue, *v. V.* LITIGAR.
litina, *f.* (chem.) lithia.
litio, *m.* (chem.) lithium.
litis, *f.* (law) lawsuit.
litisconsorte, *n.* (law) associate in a lawsuit.
litiscontestación, *f.* (law) answer to an allegation.
litisexpensas, *f. pl.* (law) costs of suit.
litispendencia, *f.* state of a pending lawsuit.
litocálamo, *m.* petrified or fossil reed.
litoclasa, *f.* (geol.) fissure in a rock.
litocola, *f.* lithocolla, lapidary's cement.
litófago, ga, *a.* (of mollusks) rock-boring.
litófito, *m.* (bot., zool.) lithophyte.
litofotografía, *f.* etc., = FOTOLITOGRAFÍA, etc.
litogenesia, *f.* (geol.) lithogenesy.
litoglifia, *f.* engraving on stone.
litografía, *f.* lithography.
litografiar, *va.* to lithograph, print.
litográfico, ca, *a.* lithographic.
litógrafo, *m.* lithographer.
litoideo, dea, *a.* lithoid(al.
litología, *f.* lithology.
litológico, ca, *a.* lithological.
litólogo, *m.* lithologist.
litoral. I. *a.* littoral. **II.** *m.* littoral, coast, shore.
litoscopio, *m.* lithoscope.
litosfera, *f.* (geol.) lithosphere.
litospermo, *m.* (bot.) lithosperm.
lítote, *f.* (rhet.) litotes.
litotomía, *f.* (surg.) lithotomy.
litotomista, *n.* (surg.) lithotomist.
litotricia, *f.* (surg.) lithotrity.
litotrípico, ca, *a.* & *m.* (med.) lithontriptic.
litotritor, *m.* (surg.) lithotrite.
litrarico, a, *a.* (bot.) lythraceous.
litro, *m.* liter, litre, unit of capacity.
lituano, na, *n.* & *a.* Lithuanian.
lituo, *m.* (mus.) an ancient military instrument; lituus, augur's staff.
liturgia, *f.* (eccl.) liturgy.
litúrgico, ca, *a.* liturgical, liturgic.
livianamente, *adv.* licentiously; lightly; superficially.
liviandad, *f.* lightness, want of weight; levity, frivolity; lewdness.
liviano, na. I. *a.* light (not heavy); inconstant, fickle; frivolous; slight; lewd. **II.** *m.* leading one in a pack of donkeys.—*pl.* lungs.
lividez, *f.* lividness.
lívido, da, *a.* livid; black and blue.
livonio, nia, *n.* & *a.* Livonian.
lixiviación, *f.* (chem.) lixiviation, leaching.
lixiviado, da, *a.* lixivial, leached.
lixiviar, *va.* (chem.) to lixiviate, leach.
lixivio, *m.* (chem.) lixivium.
[1]**liza,** *f.* (ichth.) skate.
[2]**liza,** *f.* jousting field, lists.
lizo, *m.* warp-thread; heddle.
lo. I. *art, neut.* (before an *a.*) the, things (*lo bello,* the beautiful; *lo barato,* cheap things). For emphasis before an *adv.* or *a.*, gen. translated by an *a.* or emphatic "so" (*lo triste que estaba,* the great sadness in which he was, or, simply, his great sadness; *lo claro de esta declaración,* the great clearness of this declaration; *lo rico que es,* his being so rich, his great wealth; *lo bien que baila,* his dancing well). Often used as an *adv.* in the sense of "so," and need not always be translated (*él es rico, pero yo no lo soy,* he is rich, but I am not [so]); also as *adv.* "how" (*ella no sabe lo cansado que está,* she doesn't know how tired he is).—**l. de siempre,** the same old story.—**l. que,** what, that which; how important; how much.—**l. que es,** as to, as for.—**a l.** (foll. by name), in the style of, like.—**a l. que,** according to what, from what. **II.** *neut.* accusative of ELLO: it, that (*lo haré,* I shall do it, I shall do that). **III.** *pers. pron. accusative* of ÉL: him, it.
loa, *f.* praise; prologue of a play; short dramatic panegyric.
loable, *a.* laudable, praiseworthy.
loablemente, *adv.* laudably, commendably.
loador, ra, *n.* praiser, eulogizer.
loán, *m.* (P. I.) land measure (2.79 ares).
loanda, *f.* a kind of scurvy.
loar, *va.* to praise, eulogize.
[1]**loba,** *f.* she-wolf.
[2]**loba,** *f.* long gown of clergymen and students.
[3]**loba,** *f.* ridge between furrows.
[4]**loba,** *f.* (card games) rummy; canasta.
lobado, da, *a.* (zool. and bot.) lobate.
lobanillo, *m.* wen, encysted tumor.
lobato, *m.* wolf cub, wolfkin.
lobelia, *f.* (bot.) lobelia.
lobeliáceo, cea, *a.* (bot.) lobeliaceous.
lobero, ra. I. *a.* pertaining to wolves; wolfish. **II.** *f.* thicket where wolves make their lair.
lobezno, *m.* wolf cub; wolfkin.
lobina, *f.* (ichth.) striped bass.
[1]**lobo,** *m.* wolf; (ichth.) loach; (coll.) intoxication, inebriation; iron instrument for defending or scaling walls.—**l. marino,** seal.
[2]**lobo,** *m.* (anat. & bot.) lobe.
[3]**lobo, ba,** *n.* (Mex.) half-breed.
loboso, sa, *a.* full of wolves.
lobotomía, *f.* (surg.) lobotomy.
lóbrego, ga, *a.* murky, obscure; sad, lugubrious.
lobreguecer. I. *vn.* to grow dark. **II.** *va.* to make dark.
lobreguez, *f.* obscurity, darkness.
lobulado, da, *a.* (zool. and bot.) lobulate.
lóbulo, *m.* lobe or lobule.
lobuno, na, *a.* wolfish.
locación, *f.* (law) lease.—**l. y conducción,** agreement to let.
locador, ra, *n.* (Am.) landlord; tenant.
local. I. *a.* local. **II.** *m.* place, site, premises.
localidad, *f.* locality, location; (theat., etc.) seat.
localismo, *m.* localism.
localización, *f.* localization; (Ry.) location; (astronaut.) tracking.—**l. por radio,** (astronaut.) radio tracking.
localizar, *va.* to localize; (Ry.) to locate; to find out where.
locamente, *adv.* madly; immoderately; fondly.
locatario, ria, *n.* (Am.) tenant, lessee.
locativo, va, *a.* & *m.* (gram.) locative.
locería, *f.* (Am.) china; china works or shop; (esp. S. A., C. A.) pottery.
locero, *m.* (Am.) person who works in a pottery shop.
loción, *f.* lotion, wash.
loco, ca. I. *a.* mad, insane, crazy; abundant, plentiful, excessive.—**l. rematado,** stark mad. —**a tontas y a locas,** recklessly, thoughtlessly, haphazard.—**estar l. de contento,** (coll.) to be mad with joy. **II.** *n.* insane person, lunatic.
locomoción, *f.* (phys.) locomotion.
locomotor, ra. I. *a.* locomotor, locomotive. **II.** *f.* (Ry.) locomotive.
locomotriz, *a.* & *f.* = LOCOMOTOR.
locomovible, locomóvil. I. *a.* locomobile, locomotive. **II.** *f.* locomobile.
locro, *m.* (Am.) a kind of stew.
locuacidad, *f.* loquacity, talkativeness.
locuaz, *a.* loquacious, talkative, garrulous.
locución, *f.* diction; phrase, locution.
locuela, *f.* person's individual way of speaking.

locuelo, la, *n.* madcap, giddy youth.
loculado, da; locular, *a.* (biol.) locular.
lóculo, *m.* (biol.) loculus.
locura, *f.* madness, insanity; folly.
locutor, ra, *n.* radio announcer or speaker.
locutorio, *m.* locutory in monasteries.
locha, *f.*; **loche,** *m.* (ichth.) loach.
locho, cha, *a.* (Am., coll.) red-bearded.
lodachar, lodazal, lodazar, *m.* muddy place, quagmire, bog.
lodo, *m.* mud, mire.
lodoñero, *m.* (bot.) lignum-vitæ tree.
lodoso, sa, *a.* muddy, miry.
lofobranquio, quia, *a.* & *m.* (ichth.) lophobranch.
logarítmico, ca, *a.* logarithmic.
logaritmo, *m.* logarithm.
logia, *f.* lodge (of freemasons).
lógica, *f.* logic.
lógicamente, *adv.* logically.
lógico, ca. I. *a.* logical. **II.** *m.* logician.
logístico, ca. I. *a.* (mil.) logistic, logistical. **II.** *f.* (mil.) logistics.
logogrifo, *m.* logogriph, riddle.
logomaquia, *f.* logomachy, contention about words.
logotipo, *m.* (print.) logotype.
lograr. I. *va.* to get, obtain; procure; attain; to possess, enjoy; (foll. by *inf.*) to succeed in (foll. by pres. p.), to manage. **II.** *vr.* to succeed, be successful.
logrear, *vn.* to borrow or lend at interest.
logrería, *f.* dealing in interest; usury, profiteering.
logrero, ra, *n.* lender at interest; usurer, profiteer.
logro, *m.* gain, profit, benefit; success, accomplishment; attainment; interest; usury.—**dar a l.,** to lend at usurious interest.
loma, *f.* hill, hillock, mound.
lombarda, *f.* lombard (an ancient gun); (bot.) red cabbage.—**lombardada,** *f.* shot from a lombard gun.—**lombardear,** *va.* to bombard with lombards.—**lombardería,** *f.* battery of lombards.—**lombardero,** *m.* lombard gunman.
lombárdico, ca; lombardo, da, *n.* & *a.* Lombard, belonging to Lombardy.
lombriguera, *f.* hole made by worms; (bot.) southern wormwood.
lombriz, *f.* earthworm.—**l. intestinal,** intestinal worm.—**l. solitaria,** tapeworm.
lomear, *vn.* (of horses) to buck.
lomera, *f.* main strap of a harness; (bookbinding) backing; (arch.) ridge of a roof.
lomillería, *f.* (Am.) shop where harness accessories are made or sold.
lomillo, *m. dim.* small loin; (sew.) cross-stitch; cantle (of a saddle).—*pl.* pads of a pack saddle.
lominhiesto, ta, *a.* high-crouped; (coll.) conceited, vain.
lomo, *m.* loin; back of an animal; chine of pork; back of a book or cutting tool; double of a cloth, crease; ridge between furrows.—*pl.* ribs; loins.—**jugar de l.,** to be idle and in good health or condition.—**llevar a l., traer a l.,** to carry on the back.
lomudo, da, *a.* broad-backed.
lona, *f.* canvas.—**l. para hacer velas,** duck-canvas, sailcloth.
loncha, *f.* slab, flagstone; thin slice of meat.
lóndiga, *f.* = ALHÓNDIGA, wheat exchange.
londinense, londonense. I. *a.* Londonese. **II.** *n.* Londoner.
londrina, *f.* woollen cloth from London.
loneta, *f.* ravens' duck, sailcloth.
longa, *f.* (mus.) long note.
longanimidad, *f.* long-suffering, forbearance.
longánimo, ma, *a.* forbearing, magnanimous.
longaniza, *f.* choice pork sausage.
longar, *a.*—**panal l.,** honeycomb lengthwise of the hive.
longazo, za, *a. aug.* very long.
longevidad, *f.* longevity.
longevo, va, *a.* longeval, long-lived.
longísimo, ma, *a. super.* of LUENGO; longest.
longitud, *f.* length; longitude.
longitudinal, *a.* longitudinal.
longitudinalmente, *adv.* longitudinally.
longobardo, da, *n.* & *a.* Longobard(-ian).
longuera, *f.* long and narrow strip of land.
longuetas, *f. pl.* (surg.) bandages.
longuísimo, ma, *a. super.* longest.
[1]**lonja,** *f.* (com.) exchange; grocer's shop; warehouse, salesroom; (arch.) stoop.
[2]**lonja,** *f.* slice (of meat); strip; leather strap.
[1]**lonjeta,** *f. dim.* small slice; small strap.
[2]**lonjeta,** *f.* bower, summerhouse.
lonjista, *n.* grocer.
lontananza, *f.* distance; background.—**en l.,** far off, far away, in the distance.
loor, *m.* (poet.) praise.
lopigia, *f.* (med.) = ALOPECIA, baldness.
loquear, *vn.* to act the fool, to talk nonsense; to revel, frolic.
loquero, ra. I. *n.* attendant in an insane asylum. **II.** *m.* (Am.) insane asylum.
loquesco, ca, *a.* madlike; funny, jesting.
loquillo, illa, ito, ita, *a. dim.* wild, frisky.
loquios, *m. pl.* (med.) lochia.
lora, *f.* (ornith.) (Peru, Colomb., C. R., Hond.) parrot; (Chile) female parrot.
loran, *m.* (naut.) loran.
lorantáceo, cea, *a.* (bot.) loranthaceous, of the mistletoe family.
lorcha, *f.* (China) junk-rigged coaster.
lord, *m.* (*pl.* **lores**) lord, English title.
lordosis, *f.* (med.) lordosis.
loriga, *f.* lorica (a cuirass); iron strip reinforcing hub (of carriage wheel).
lorigado, da, *a.* armed with a lorica.
loriguillo, *m.* shrub used by dyers.
loris, *m.* (zool.) loris.
[1]**loro, ra. I.** *a.* tawny, dark brown. **II.** *m.* (bot.) cherry laurel.
[2]**loro,** *m.* (ornith.) parrot.
los. I. *def. art. m. pl.* of EL, the.—**l. que,** those, or they, who. **II.** *pers. pron. m. pl. accusative* of ELLOS, them. When used with HAY (*v.* HABER), it is rendered by "some," or not at all (*¿hay libros? los hay,* are there any books? there are [some]).
losa, *f.* slab, flagstone; trap made of tiles; gravestone; grave.
losado, *m.* tiled floor.
losange, losanje, *m.* (her.) lozenge; rhomb.
losar, *va.* to tile. Also ENLOSAR.
loseta, losica, illa, ita, *f. dim.* small slab or flagstone; tile; briquette; small trap.
lote, *m.* lot; share, part.
lotería, *f.* lottery; raffle; game lotto.
lotero, ra, *n.* dealer in lottery tickets.
loto, *m.* (bot.) lotus; lotus flower; lote tree or nettle tree.
lotófago, ga, *a.* lotus-eating.
loxodromia, *f.* (naut.) loxodrome.
loxodrómico, ca, *a.* (naut.) loxodromic.
loza, *f.* chinaware; porcelain; crockery.—**ande la l.,** (coll.) noisy mirth and jollity.
lozanamente, *adv.* luxuriantly; briskly, nimbly.
lozanear, *vn.* to look fresh and luxuriant.
lozanía, *f.* luxuriance; freshness; vigor, lustiness.
lozano, na, *a.* luxuriant; fresh; brisk, spirited.
lúa, *f.* esparto glove for cleaning horses; saffron bag; (naut.) lee.
lubricación, *f.* lubrication.
lubricador, ra, *n.* & *a.* lubricator(-ing).
lubricán, *m.* dawn of day.
lubricante, *a.* & *m.* lubricant.
lubricar, *va.* to lubricate.
lubricativo, va, *a.* lubricant, lubricative.
lubricidad, *f.* lubricity, slipperiness; lewdness.
lúbrico, ca, *a.* slippery; lubricous; lewd.
lubrificación, lubrificar, etc. (incorrect but common) = LUBRICACIÓN, LUBRICAR, etc.
lucano, na, *n.* & *a.* Lucanian.
lucerna, *f.* chandelier; (ichth.) a deep sea fish.

lucérnula, *f.* (bot.) lucern, lucerne, alfalfa.
lucero, *m.* morning star; any bright star; light hole; star on the forehead of horses; brightness, splendor.—*pl.* (poet.) eyes.—**l. del alba,** or **de la mañana,** morning star.—**l. de la tarde,** evening star.
lucidamente, *adv.* brightly; splendidly.
lucidez, *f.* brilliancy; brightness; success.
lucido, da. I. *pp.* of LUCIR. **II.** *a.* magnificent, splendid, brilliant; most successful.
lúcido, da, *a.* lucid, clear; brilliant, shining.
lucidor, ra, *a.* shining, brilliant.
lucidura, *f.* (coll.) whitewashing.
luciente, *a.* shining, luminous, bright.
luciérnaga, *f.* glowworm, firefly.
Lucifer, *m.* Lucifer, Satan; proud and wicked man; morning star.
luciferino, na, *a.* Luciferian, devilish.
lucífero, ra. I. *a.* (poet.) resplendent, shining. **II.** *m.* morning star.
lucífugo, ga, *a.* light-avoiding, lucifugous.
lucillo, *m.* tomb; sarcophagus.
lucimiento, *m.* brilliancy, splendor, lustre; success, triumph.—**quedar,** or **salir, con l.,** to be eminently successful.
[1]**lucio, cia,** *a.* lucid; bright.
[2]**lucio,** *m.* (ichth.) common pike, luce.
lución, *m.* (zool.) glass-snake.
lucir. I. *vn.* (*ind.* LUZCO; *subj.* LUZCA) to shine, glitter, glow; to outshine, exceed; to look, appear. **II.** *va.* to light, illuminate; to show off, display, exhibit, disport. **III.** *vr.* to shine, be brilliant; to dress to advantage; to be very successful, to do splendidly.
lucita, *f.* lucite; Lucite (trademark).
lucrar, *va.* & *vr.* to profit, speculate.
lucrativamente, *adv.* profitably, lucratively.
lucrativo, va, *a.* lucrative, profitable.
lucro, *m.* gain, profit, lucre.—**lucros y daños,** (com.) profit and loss.
lucroso, sa, *a.* lucrative, profitable.
luctuosa, *f.* feudal death tax.
luctuosamente, *adv.* mournfully, sorrowfully.
luctuoso, sa, *a.* sad, mournful.
lucubración, *f.* laborious work, study.
lucubrar, *va.* to work, study laboriously.
lúcumo, *m.* (bot.) Lucuma, a variety of Peruvian Achras.
lucha, *f.* struggle, strife; wrestling, wrestle; dispute, argument.
luchador, ra, *n.* wrestler; fighter.
luchar, *vn.* to fight, struggle; to wrestle.
lucharniego, ga, *a.* night hare-hunting (dog).
ludia, *f.* ferment, yeast.
ludiar, *va.* & *vr.* to ferment.
ludibrio, *m.* mockery, derision, scorn.
ludimiento, *m.* friction, rubbing.
ludión, *m.* (phys.) Cartesian devil.
ludir, *va.* to rub, waste by friction.
lúe, *f.* infection.
luego. I. *adv.* presently, immediately; afterwards; next; later.—**l. que,** after, as soon as.—**desde l.,** at once, instantly; naturally, of course; to begin with, at the outset.—**hasta l.,** (in taking leave) so long, see you later.—**tan l. como** = L. QUE. **II.** *conj.* therefore.
luengo, ga, *a.* long, dilated.—**luengos años,** long years, many years.
lúes, *f.* (med.) lues, syphilis.
luético, ca, *a.* (med.) luetic.
lugano, *m.* (ornith.) linnet.
lugar, *m.* place, spot, site; city, town, village; room, space; seat; employment, office, dignity; time, opportunity, occasion; leisure, convenience; cause, motive, reason; text, authority.—**l. común, l. excusado,** privy-house, water-closet.—**lugares comunes,** commonplace topics.—**lugares de un combate,** (naut.) quarters in a sea-fight.—**dar l.,** to make room.—**dar l. a,** to cause, give occasion for.—**en l. de,** instead of, in lieu of.—**en primer l.,** first, or in the first place.—**fuera de l.,** out of place; irrelevant.—**hacer l.,** to make room.—**no ha l.** (a), (law) the petition is denied; there is no occasion (for).—**tener l.,** (Gal.) to take place, happen.
lugarcico, illo, ito, *m. dim.* small place.
lugarejo, *m. dim.* hamlet, small village.
lugareño, ña. I. pertaining or belonging to a village. **II.** *n.* villager.
lugarote, *m. aug.* unattractive hamlet.
lugartenencia, *f.* lieutenancy.
lugarteniente, *m.* deputy, substitute; lieutenant.
lugre, *m.* (naut.) lugger, small vessel.
lúgubre, *a.* sad, gloomy, lugubrious, dismal.
luir, *va.* (naut.) to gall, wear away by friction.
luis, *m.* louis (French coin).
luisa, *f.* (bot.) lemon verbena or aloysia.
lujación, *f.* = LUXACIÓN, dislocation.
lujar, *va.* (Cuba) to rub; (med.) to dislocate.
lujo, *m.* luxury.—**de l.,** de luxe; elegant, exquisite; magnificent.
lujoso, sa, *a.* luxurious, magnificent, sumptuous.
lujuria, *f.* lewdness, lust; excess; profuseness, lavishness.
lujuriante, *a.* lusting; luxuriant, exuberant.
lujuriar, *vn.* to lust; (of animals) to copulate.
lujuriosamente, *adv.* lustfully, voluptuously.
lujurioso, sa, *a.* lustful, voluptuous, lewd.
luliano, na, *n.* & *a.* Lullian.
lulismo, *m.* system of Raymond Lully.
lulista, *n.* & *a.* Lullist(-ic).
lumaquela, *f.* lumachelle, fire marble.
lumbago, *m.* (med.) lumbago.
lumbar, *a.* lumbar.
lumbrada, *f.* great fire.
lumbre, *f.* fire (in stove, fireplace, etc.); light (from a match, etc.); light; splendor, brightness; skylight, transom; hammer of a flintlock; forepart of horseshoes.—*pl.* tinder box.—**l. del agua,** level with the water.—**a l. de pajas,** (coll.) very swiftly.—**a l. mansa,** on a slow fire.—**ni por l.,** by no means.
lumbrera, *f.* luminary; skylight, light shaft; (steam eng.) port.—**l. de admisión,** steam port, admission port.—**l. de educción,** or **de escape,** exhaust port.
lumbrerada, *f.* great fire.
lumen, *m.* lumen (unit of light).
luminar, *m.* luminary.
luminaria, *f.* illumination, festival lights; (eccl.) lamp kept burning before the sacrament.—*pl.* money paid for illuminations.
lumínico, *m.* (phys.) hypothetic agent or principle of light.
luminífero, ra, *a.* luminiferous.
luminiscencia, *f.* luminescence.
luminiscente, *a.* luminescent.
luminista, *a.* & *n.* (f. a.) luminist.
luminosidad, *f.* luminosity.
luminoso, sa, *a.* luminous.
luminotecnia, *f.* (theat.) technique of lighting.
luminotécnico, ca. I. *a.* of or pertaining to lighting. **II.** *n.* (theat.) lighting technician.
luna, *f.* (astr.) moon; satellite, glass plate, mirror plate; (opt.) lens of a spyglass; effect of the moon upon lunatic people.—**l. creciente,** crescent.—**l. de miel,** honeymoon.—**l. llena,** full moon.—**l. menguante,** waning moon.—**l. nueva,** new moon.—**estar de buena (mala) l.,** to be in good (bad) humor.—**estar en la l.,** to be distracted, absent-minded.—**quedarse a la l. de Valencia,** to be left out in the cold.
lunación, *f.* (astr.) lunation, lunar month.
lunado, da, *a.* lunated, formed like a half-moon.
lunanco, ca, *a.* (animal) having one hind quarter higher than the other.
[1]**lunar,** *a.* lunar.
[2]**lunar,** *m.* mole, beauty spot; flaw, blemish; polka dot.—**l. postizo,** patch.
lunario, ria. I. *a.* pert. to lunar month. **II.** *m.* calendar.
lunático, ca, *a.* lunatic, moonstruck, mad.
lunecilla, *f.* crescent-shaped jewel.
lunes, *m.* Monday.
luneta, *f.* (opt.) spectacle lens; (theat.) or-

chestra seat; a crescent-shaped ornament; (arch.) lunette; saddler's knife, leather knife.
luneto, *m.* skylight in a vault, lunette.
lunfardo, *m.* (Am.) Argentine slang.
lunisolar, *a.* (astr.) lunisolar.
lúnula, *f.* (geom.) lune; (opt.) meniscus; (anat.) lunule.
lupa, *f.* magnifying glass.
lupanar, *m.* brothel, bawdyhouse.
lupanario, ia, *a.* pertaining to a brothel.
lupercales, *f. pl.* Lupercalia, Roman festival.
lupia, *f.* (med.) wen, encysted tumor.
lupicia, *f.* (med.) = ALOPECIA, baldness.
lupino, na. I. *a.* wolfish. **II.** *m.* (bot.) lupine.
lupulino, *m.* lupulin, powder from hops.
lúpulo, *m.* (bot.) hops.
lupus, *m.* (med.) lupus; (L.) (astr.) Lupus.
luquete, *m.* slice of orange or lemon thrown into wine; zest; sulphur match.
lurte, *m* avalanche, landslide.
lusitanismo, *m.* Portuguese idiom.
lusitano, na, *a.* Lusitanian; Portuguese.
lustrabotas, *n.* bootblack, shoeblack.
lustración, *f.* lustration; lustrum; purification.
lustrador, ra. (Am.) **I.** *n.* polisher. **II.** *m.* hot-press, mangler.
lustral, *a.* lustral; pertaining to lustration.
lustramiento, *m.* act of decorating or polishing.
lustrar. I. *va.* to lustrate, expiate, purify; to polish. **II.** *vn.* to wander, roam.
lustre, *m.* gloss, lustre, polish, glaze; shoe-polish; nobleness, splendor, glory.
lústrico, ca, *a.* lustral.
lustrina, *f.* (text.) lustrine, lustring.
lustro, *m.* lustrum, period of five years; lamp, chandelier.
lustrosamente, *adv.* brilliantly, splendidly; glitteringly.
lustroso, sa, *a.* bright, brilliant; lustrous, shining.
lútea, *f.* (ornith.) oriole; cazique.
lutecio, *m.* (chem.) lutecium.
luteína, *f.* (biochem.) lutein.
luten, *m.* (chem.) lute.
lúteo, tea, *a.* miry, muddy.
luteolina, *f.* (chem.) luteolin.
luteranismo, *m.* Lutheranism.
luterano, na, *n.* & *a.* Lutheran.
luto, *m.* mourning; grief, bereavement.—*pl.* mourning draperies.—**de l.,** in mourning.
lux, *m.* (phys.) lux (unit of light).
luxación, *f.* (med.) luxation, dislocation.
Luxemburgo, *m.* Luxembourg.
luxemburgués, guesa. I. *a.* Luxembourgian. **II.** *n.* Luxembourger.
luz, *f.* light; daylight; lighthouse; window, opening; (eng.) span; notice, information, hint; inspiration; brightness, lustre, splendor; luminary, prominent man; (art) lighting.—*pl.* culture, enlightenment, learning, knowledge; windows, loopholes.—**l. de bengala,** red light.—**l. del día,** daylight.—**l. de l.,** reflected or borrowed light.—**l. de tráfico,** or **de tránsito,** traffic light.—**l. infrarroja,** infrared rays.—**l. ultravioleta,** ultraviolet rays.—**l. zodiacal,** zodiacal light.—**a buena l.,** carefully, after due examination.—**a primera l.,** at daybreak.—**a todas luces,** everywhere, any way.—**dar a l.,** to give birth to; to be delivered of (a child); to publish.—**entre dos luces,** in the twilight.—**salir a l.,** to come out, be published or divulged, leak out.
Luzbel, *m.* Lucifer, Satan.
luzco, luzca, *v. V.* LUCIR.

LL

Ll, ll, *f.* fourteenth letter of the Spanish alphabet.
llábana, *f.* smooth, slippery flagstone.
llaga, *f.* ulcer, sore; prick, thorn, tormenting thought; (mason.) seam, crack, or joint.
llagar, *va.* (*pret.* LLAGUÉ; *subj.* LLAGUE) to wound, hurt, injure.
[1]**llama,** *f.* flame, blaze; violent passion.
[2]**llama,** *f.* marshy ground.
[3]**llama,** *f.* (zool.) llama.
llamada, *f.* call, knock; motion or sign to call attention; (tel.) call; (print.) reference mark to a note; (mil.) call; chamade; (com.) notice, entry.
llamadera, *f.* goad stick.
llamado, da. I. *pp.* of LLAMAR. **II.** *a.* called, by the name of. **III.** *m.* appeal.
llamador, ra, *n.* caller; beadle, messenger; (*m.*) knocker of a door.
llamamiento, *m.* calling, call; appeal; convocation; inspiration, divine vocation; attraction of humors to one part of the body.
llamar. I. *va.* to call, summon, cite; to call upon, invoke, appeal to; to name, call.—**ll. la atención (sobre),** to call, attract attention (to); (*dat.*) to warn, scold.—**ll. por teléfono,** to telephone, 'phone. **II.** *vn.* to excite thirst; to knock at the door; to ring a bell.—**ll. a capítulo,** or **a cuentas,** to call to account. **III.** *vr.* to be called or named, go by the name of, give the name of (often diff. constr.: *ella se llama Rosa,* her name is Rose; *¿como se llama esto?* what is this called? *¿como se llama Vd.?* what is your name? *se llama "democracia"* . . . , the name "democracy" is given to . . . , or, simply, "democracy" is . . .); (naut.) (of wind) to veer.
llamarada, *f.* sudden blaze, flash; burst of wit; sudden flush of the face.
llamativo, va, *a.* exciting thirst; showy, attracting attention.
llamazar, *m.* swamp, marsh.
llambria, *f.* steep face of a rock.
llameante, *a.* blazing, flaming.
llamear, *vn.* to blaze, to flame.
llana, *f.* (mason.) trowel; page of a book or writing; plain, flatland.
llanada, *f.* plain, flatland, level ground.
llanamente, *adv.* ingenuously, simply, sincerely; homely; plainly, clearly, flatly.
llanero, ra, *n.* plainsman(-woman).
llaneza, *f.* plainness, simplicity; familiarity; uncultivated style.
llano, na. I. *a.* even, level, smooth; easy unobstructed; plain, unadorned; unaffected, open, frank; clear, evident; (gram.) (word) accented on the penultimate.—**a la llana,** simply, unceremoniously.—**de llano,** openly, in the open. **II.** *m.* plain, llano.
[1]**llanta,** *f.* (bot.) a variety of cabbage.
[2]**llanta,** *f.* rim (of carriage wheel); (auto) tire.—**ll. maciza,** solid tire.—**ll. neumática,** pneumatic tire.
llantén, *m.* (bot.) plantain, rib grass.—**ll. de agua,** water plantain, alisura.
llanto, *m.* flood of tears; crying, weeping.
llanura, *f.* evenness, flatness; plain.
llapa, *f.* (min.) quicksilver for amalgamation.
llapar, *va.* (min.) to add quicksilver to for reduction.
llares, *f. pl.* chain with pothooks (in fireplace).
llatar, *m.* post-and-rail fence.
llave, *f.* key; (mech.) wrench; faucet, cock, spigot, spout, tap; switch (of elec. light); bolt, pin, tightening wedge, cotter; (print.) brace }; tuning key; clock winder; (arch.) keystone; winch of a stocking frame; lock of a gun; key, explanation of anything difficult; introduction to knowledge; (naut.) knee; (mus.) clef, key; piston of musical instruments (wind, brass).—**ll. de brazo,** (wrestling) hammer lock.—**ll. de la mano,** span of the hand.—**ll. del pie,** distance from heel to instep.—**ll. inglesa,** monkey wrench.—**ll. maestra,** master key, pass-key.—**debajo de ll.,** under lock and key.—**echar (la) ll. a,** to lock.

llavero, ra. I. *n.* keeper of the keys. II. *m.* **key** ring. III. *f.* housekeeper.
llavín, *m.* night key, latchkey.
lleco, ca, *a.* (agr.) virgin (as soil).
llega, *f.* gathering, collecting.
llegada, *f.* arrival, coming.
llegar. I. *vn.* (*pret.* LLEGUÉ; *subj.* LLEGUE) to arrive; to come; to reach, extend, go as far as; to last, to continue; to attain a purpose; to suffice, be enough; to amount.—**ll. a las manos,** to come to blows.—**ll. a saber,** to find out, get to know.—**ll. a ser,** to become, get to be.—**no ll. a,** not to amount to; not to come up, or be equal, to.—**no ll. a uno la camisa al cuerpo,** to be terrified and anxious. II. *va.* to bring near; to gather, collect. III. *vr.* (a) to approach, draw near (to); to go to some neighboring place; to adhere, stick.
llena, *f.* flood, overflow.
llenamente, *adv.* fully, copiously.
llenar. I. *va.* to fill, stuff, pack; to pervade; to occupy (as an incumbent); to satisfy, content, convince; to make up (a number); to beget.—**ll. una solicitud,** to fill out an application form. II. *vr.* to fill, fill up; (**de**) to become full (of), or covered (with); (coll.) to feed gluttonously, stuff oneself; (coll.) to be irritated after having suffered long; to get crowded, packed. III. *vn.* (of the moon) to be full.
llenero, ra, *a.* (law) full, complete, absolute.
lleno, na. I. *a.* full, filled, replete; complete.—**ll. de bote en bote,** brimful, full to the brim.—**de ll.,** or **de ll. en ll.,** fully, entirely, totally. II. *m.* glut, fill, plenty, abundance, fulness; perfection, completeness; full moon; (theat.) full house.
llenura, *f.* fulness; plenty, abundance.
lleta, *f.* (bot.) sprout.
lleudar, *va.* = LEUDAR, to leaven.
lleva, llevada, *f.* transport, carrying.
llevadero, ra, *a.* tolerable, bearable, light.
llevador, ra, *n.* & *a.* carrier(-rying).
llevar. I. *va.* to carry, convey; to wear; to take, take away, carry away; to charge, ask, set (a price); to bear, yield, produce; to excel, exceed; to suffer, endure; to lead (as a life); to lead, guide, conduct, take; to manage (a horse); to cut off, dismember; to have spent or devoted (so much time); to induce, to bring to an opinion; to introduce; to gain, attain, obtain; (arith.) to carry; (with a past participle) to have, as: *llevo andadas diez millas,* I have walked ten miles.—**ll. . . . a,** to be older, or more, than by (*llevo dos años a Juan,* I am two years older than John).—**ll. a cabo,** to carry through, to accomplish, to carry out.—**ll. a cuestas,** to carry on one's shoulders or back; to support.—**ll. adelante,** to carry on, keep up, continue.—**ll. al crédito,** to place to the credit.—**ll. calabazas,** to be given the mitten; to fail in examination.—**ll. consigo,** to carry along with one; to carry with it, imply; to have attached.—**ll. el compás,** to beat or keep time.—**ll. la caja,** to keep the cash.—**ll. la contra,** to oppose, contradict; to antagonize.—**ll. la delantera,** to lead, to be ahead.—**ll. la proa al noroeste,** (naut.) to stand to the northwest.—**llevarlas bien (mal),** = LLEVARSE BIEN, MAL.—**ll. la ventaja a,** to have the advantage of or over.—**ll. libros,** (com.) to keep books.—**ll. lo mejor (peor),** to get the best (worst).—**ll. una caída, golpe, porrazo,** to have a fall, a blow.—**no llevarlas todas consigo,** to have suspicions, to be afraid. II. *vr.* to take or carry away; to get along.—**ll. bien,** to be on good terms, get along well, be congenial.—**ll. chasco,** to be disappointed.—**ll. mal,** to be on bad terms, not to get along together.
lloica, *f.* (ornith.) robin redbreast; thrush.
lloradera, *f.* weeping from slight motives.
llorador, ra, *n.* weeper.
lloraduelos, *n.* (coll.) weeper, mourner.
llorar. I. *vn.* to weep, cry; to affect poverty and distress; to whine; to drip. II. *va.* to weep over, bewail, mourn, lament.
lloriquear, *vn.* to be constantly crying; to whine.
lloriqueo, *m.* whining; lamentation, wailing.
lloro, *m.* weeping, crying.
llorón, na. I. *a.* weeping; that cries with little cause, whining. II. *n.* weeper, whiner.
llorosamente, *adv.* tearfully.
lloroso, sa, *a.* mournful, sorrowful, tearful.
llosa, *f.* fenced-in field.
llovedizo, za, *a.* leaky; rain (as *a.*).
llover. I. *vn. impers.* (*ind.* LLUEVE; *subj.* LLUEVA) to rain; to pour down like rain, to shower, to come in abundance (as troubles).—**ll. a cántaros, a chorros, a chuzos,** or **ll. chuzos,** to rain in torrents, to rain pitchforks.—**como llovido,** unexpectedly.—**llueva o no,** rain or shine. II. *vr.* (of roofs) to leak, let the rain in.
llovido, da, *n.* stowaway.
llovioso, sa, *a.* = LLUVIOSO.
llovizna, *f.* drizzle, sprinkling.
lloviznar, *vn.* to drizzle, to sprinkle.
llueca, *f.* = CLUECA, brooding hen.
llueve, llueva, *v.* *V.* LLOVER.
lluvia, *f.* rain; plenty.—**lluvioso, sa,** *a.* rainy.

M

M, m, *f.* m, fifteenth letter of the Spanish alphabet.
maca, *f.* bruise in fruit; flaw, blemish, spot, stain; deceit, fraud, trick.
macabro, bra, *a.* ugly, hideous.
macaco, ca. I. *m.* (zool.) macaque; (Mex.) hobgoblin, bogie. II. *a.* ugly, ill-shaped, squat.
macadam, *m.* = MACADÁN.
macadamizado, da, *a.* macadam, macadamized.
macadamizar, *va.* to macadamize.
macadán, *m.* macadam.
macagua, *f.* (ornith.) macaw; (Venez.) a poisonous snake.
macagüita, *f.* (Venez.) a thorny palmtree.
macana, *f.* Indian wooden sabre edged with sharp flint; (Colomb.) a palm having very hard and heavy wood; (Am.) cudgel, club; (Am.) blunder; fib, joke.—**¡qué macana!** (Arg.) how annoying!—**macaneador,** *m.* (Arg.) (coll.) one who is always talking "through his hat."
macanazo, *m.* blow with a MACANA.
macanudo, da, *a.* (coll.) excellent, first-rate.
macareno, na, *a.* (coll.) bragging, boasting; gaudily dressed in Andalusian garb.
macarrón, *m.* macaroon.—*pl.* macaroni; (naut.) stanchions.
macarronea, *f.* macaronic poem, burlesque.
macarrónicamente, *adv.* macaronically.
macarrónico, ca, *a.* macaronic; faulty (speech).
macarse, *vr.* (of fruit) to begin to rot.
macaurel, *f.* (Venez.) a poisonous snake.
maceador, *m.* one who mauls.
macear. I. *va.* to maul. II. *vn.* to importune.
macedón, na, *n.* & *a.*; **macedonio, nia,** *n.* & *a.*; **macedónico, ca,** *a.* Macedonian.
macelo, *m.* slaughterhouse, abattoir.
maceo, *m.* act of mauling.
maceración, *f.*; **maceramiento,** *m.* maceration, steeping; infusion; mortification of the flesh.
macerar, *va.* to macerate, soak, steep; (chem.) to digest; to mortify with corporeal hardships.
macerina, *f.* = MANCERINA, a kind of saucer.
macero, *m.* mace bearer.
[1]**maceta,** *f. dim.* small mace, mallet, or maul; haft of tools; stonecutter's hammer; (naut.) maul, mallet.
[2]**maceta,** *f.* flowerpot; flower vase.
macetero, *m.* flowerpot; flowerpot stand.
macetón, *m. aug.* of [2]MACETA.
macia, *f.* mace, a spice.
macicez, *f.* solidity.
macilento, ta, *a.* lean, emaciated; withered.
macillo, *m.* hammer of a piano.
macis, *f.* = MACIA.

macizamente, *adv.* firmly, solidly.
macizar, *va.* to fill up, stop up.
macizo, za. I. *a.* solid; massive; firm, certain. **II.** *m.* massiveness, bulk; (mason.) solid wall; flower bed; (auto) solid tire.
macla, *f.* wooden flail; (bot.) water caltrops.
macoca, *f.* large early fig.
macolla, *f.* (bot.) bunch, cluster.
macón, *m.* dry, brown honeycomb.
macona, *f.* large basket or hamper.
macramé, *m.* macramé.
macroanálisis, *f.* macroanalysis.
macrobio, bia, *a.* macrobian, long-lived.
macrobiótica, *f.* macrobiotics, art of living long.
macrocefalia, *f.* macrocephalia, macrocephaly.
macrocéfalo, la, *a.* macrocephalous.
macrocito, *m.* (med.) macrocyte.
macrocosmo, *m.* macrocosm.
macrofísica, *f.* macrophysics.
macromolécula, *f.* macromolecule.
macropía, macropsia, *f.* (med.) macropsy.
macroquímica, *f.* macrochemistry.
macroscopia, *f.* macroscopy.
macroscópico, ca, *a.* macroscopic, visible to the naked eye.
macroscopio, *m.* macroscope.
macrosección, *f.* macrosection.
macrosismo, *m.* (geol.) macroseism, severe earthquake.
macrosismógrafo, *m.* macroseismograph.
macrotomo, *m.* macrotome.
macruro, ra, *a.* & *m.* (zool.) macruran.
macsura, *f.* reserved precinct in a mosque.
macuache, *m.* (Mex.) ignorant Indian.
macuba, *f.* Martinique tobacco.
macuca, *f.* (bot.) wild pear or pear tree.
macuco, ca, *a.* (Am.) cunning, artful; hard, difficult; important, big.
mácula, *f.* stain, spot, blemish; (astr.) macula.
macular, *va.* to stain.
maculatura, *f.* (print.) maculature, spoiled sheet.
macún, macuñ, macuñí, *m.* (Chile) poncho.
macuquero, *m.* unlawful worker of abandoned mines.
macuquino, na, *a.* epithet app. to a former silver Porto-Rican coin.
macuteno, *m.* (Mex.) petty thief.
macuto, *m.* (Am.) bag made of palm leaves.
macha, *f.* a South American mollusk.
machaca. I. *n.* (coll.) a bore, tiresome person. **II.** *f.* MACHACADERA.
machacadera, *f.* instrument for pounding, crushing.
machacador, ra, *n.* pounder, beater, crusher; bruiser, mauler.
machacar. I. *va.* (*pret.* MACHAQUÉ; *subj.* MACHAQUE) to pound; crush. **II.** *vn.* to importune; to harp on a subject.
machacón, na, *a.* monotonous; importunate.
machada, *f.* flock of he-goats; (coll.) stupidity.
machado, *m.* hatchet.
machamartillo.—a m., firmly but roughly.
machaqué, machaque, *v. V.* MACHACAR.
machaqueo, *m.* pounding or crushing.
machaquería, *f.* (coll.) importunity, insistence.
machar, *va.* to pound, hammer, maul.
machear, *vn.* (of animals) to beget more males than females.
machetazo, *m.* blow with a machete.
machete, *m.* machete; cane knife.
machetear, *va.* to wound or cut with a machete.
machetero, *m.* one who cuts cane or fights with a machete; sabre rattler; ignorant military chief.
machi, machí, *m.* (Am.) medicine man.
máchica, *f.* (Peru) roast Indian meal.
machiega, *a.*—**abeja m.,** queen bee.
machigua, *f.* (Hond.) crushed-corn washings.
machihembrado, da, *a.* dovetailed.
machihembrar, *va.* (carp.) to dovetail.
machina, *f.* crane, derrick; pile-driver.
machmetro, *m.* (phys.) machmeter (Mach number indicator).
[1]**macho. I.** *a.* vigorous, robust; male. **II.** *m.* male; specifically a he-mule or a he-goat; masculine plant; part of an instrument which enters into another; hook to catch hold in an eye; screw pin; bolt (of a lock); (arch.) spur, buttress, abutment; ignorant fellow.—**m. cabrío,** he-goat, buck.—**m. de aterrajar,** screw tap.—**m. de cabrío** = M. CABRÍO.—**m. del timón,** (naut.) rudder pintle.—**m. romo,** he-mule born of a horse and a she-ass.
[2]**macho,** *m.* (mech.) sledge hammer; block on which anvil is fixed; square anvil.
machón, *m.* (arch.) buttress, spur; a piece of timber.
machorro, rra, *a.* barren.
machota, *f.* **machote,** *m.* maul, mallet.
machote, *m.* (Mex. min.) boundary stone.
machucadura, *f.*, **machucamiento,** *m.* pounding, bruising.
machucar, *va.* (*pret.* MACHUQUÉ; *subj.* MACHUQUE) to pound, to bruise.
machucho, cha, *a.* mature, judicious.
machuelo, *m. dim.* small he-mule; clove of garlic.
machuno, na, *a.* mannish, masculine.
machuqué, machuque, *v. V.* MACHUCAR.
Madagascar, *n.* Madagascar.
madama, *f.* madam.—**madamisela,** *f.* damsel.
madapolán, *m.* percale.
madeja, *f.* hank, skein; lock of hair; (coll.) weak, lazy person.—**m. sin cuenda,** tangle; disordered person; entangled affair.—**hacer m.,** (of liquids) to be ropy.
madejeta, jita, juela, *f. dim.* small skein.
[1]**madera,** *m.* Madeira wine.
[2]**madera,** *f.* wood; timber, lumber; horny part of a hoof.—**m. alburente,** alburnum, sapwood.—**m. anegadiza,** heavier-than-water wood.—**m. aserrada** or **aserradiza,** (cut) lumber.—**m. contrachapada,** (constr.) plywood.—**m. de construcción,** building timber.—**m. de corazón,** heartwood.—**m. del aire,** horn of animals.—**m. de raja,** split timber.—**m. de sierra,** or **serradiza,** lumber, timber fit to be sawed.—**m. plástica,** Plastic Wood (Trademark).—**descubrir la madera,** (coll.) to show one's true colors (as by a vice or defect).—**no holgar la madera,** to keep at it, work without stopping.—**ser de** or **tener mala madera,** to be lazy.
maderable, *a.* timber-yielding.
maderada, *f.* raft, float.
maderaje, maderamen, *m.* timber; timber work.
maderería, *f.* lumber yard.
maderero, maderista, *m.* lumber dealer; lumberman.
madero, *m.* beam, scantling; timber, piece of lumber; ship, vessel; (coll.) stupid or unfeeling person.—**m. barcal,** log.—**m. cachizo,** timber fit to be sawed.—**m. de suelo,** beam, joist.—**m. rollizo** = M. BARCAL.—**maderos de cuenta,** main timbers.
maderuelo, *m. dim.* small piece of timber.
madia, *f.* (bot.) oily plant of Chile.
madianita, *n.* & *a.* Midianite.
madrás, *f.* (text.) madras.
madrastra, *f.* stepmother; anything unpleasant.
madraza, *f.* (coll.) too indulgent a mother.
madre, *f.* mother; dam; matron; (coll.) old woman; foundation; origin, source; matrix, womb; bed (of a river); main sewer; main irrigating ditch; mother (of vinegar), lees, dregs; (carp.) main piece, spindle; (naut.) gallows beam.—**m. de leche,** wet nurse.—**m. política,** mother-in-law.—**salirse de m.,** to exceed, run over; to lose one's self-control.
madrecilla, *f. dim.* MADRECITA; ovary of birds.
madrecita, *m. dim.* little mother, dear mother.
madreclavo, *m.* clove of two years' growth.
madreña, *f.* = ALMADREÑA, wooden shoes.

madreperla, *f.* mother-of-pearl.
madrépora, *f.* madrepore, white coral.
madrepórico, ca, *a.* madreporic.
madrero, ra, *a.* (coll.) attached to one's mother.
madreselva, *f.* (bot.) honeysuckle.
madrigada, *a.* twice-married (woman).
madrigado, da, *a.* practical, experienced; (bull) that has been a sire.
madrigal, *m.* madrigal, lyric poem.
madriguera, *f.* burrow; den, hole.
madrileño, ña. I. *a.* Madrilenian, Madrid. **II.** *n.* Madrilenian, native or inhabitant of Madrid.
madrina, *f.* godmother; bridesmaid; patroness, protectress; prop, stanchion; straps for yoking two horses; (Am.) herd of tamed cattle used as lure for wild cattle; (Venez.) leading animal, usually a mare; (Venez.) small herd.
madrona, *f.* main irrigating ditch; over-indulgent mother.
madroncillo, *m.* strawberry.
madroñal, *m.*; **madroñera,** *f.* grove of madroña trees.
madroñero, *m.* (bot.) madroña, an evergreen tree or shrub.
madroño, *m.* (bot.) madroña; fruit of the madroña; berry-shaped tassel.
madrugada, *f.* dawn; early rising.—**de m.,** at daybreak.
madrugador, ra, *n.* early riser.
madrugar, *vn.* (*pret.* MADRUGUÉ; *subj.* MADRUGUE) to rise early; to anticipate, to be beforehand.
madrugón, *m.* (coll.) very early rising.
maduración, *f.* ripeness, maturity; ripening.
maduradero, *m.* place for ripening fruits.
madurador, ra, *a.* maturing, ripening.
madurante, *a.* maturing, ripening.
madurar. I. *va.* to ripen, mature; to think out; (med.) to maturate. **II.** *vn.* to ripen; to mature; to reach the age of maturity; (med.) to maturate, suppurate; to come to a head.
madurativo, va. I. *a.* maturative. **II.** *m.* anything that matures; inducement.
madurez, *f.* maturity; ripeness; wisdom.
madurillo, lla, *a.* beginning to ripen.
maduro, ra, *a.* ripe; mature; wise, judicious.
maelstrom, *m.* maelstrom.
maesil, *m.* = MAESTRIL.
maesillas, *f. pl.* cords which serve in making passementerie to raise or lower the skeins.
maestoso, sa, *a.* & *adv.* (mus.) maestoso, majestic.
maestra, *f.* teacher, schoolmistress; master's wife in all trades and professions; queen bee; (mason.) guide line.
maestral. I. *a.* pertaining to a grand master of a military order; northwest (wind). **II.** *m.* cell of the queen bee.
maestramente, *adv.* in a masterly manner.
maestrante, *m.* member of a MAESTRANZA.
maestranza, *f.* riding club of noblemen; (artil.) arsenal, armory; (naut.) navy yard; the collection of workmen in an arsenal or navy yard.
maestrazgo, *m.* dignity or jurisdiction of a grand master of a military order.
maestre, *m.* grand master of a military order; (naut.) master of a merchant ship.—**m. de raciones,** purser.
maestrear. I. *va.* to direct, to instruct; to lop; to smooth. **II.** *vn.* (coll.) to domineer, to act the master.
maestresala, *m.* chief waiter and taster.
maestría, *f.* mastery; dignity or degree of a master.
maestril, *m.* (bee keeping) queen cell.
maestrillo, *m. dim.* insignificant schoolmaster.
maestro, tra. I. *a.* masterly; master, great, principal, main; learned, trained. **II.** *m.* master, teacher; expert; master workman; skilled artisan; title of respect in monastic orders; scholastic title; (naut.) mainmast.—**m. albañil,** master mason.—**m. carpintero,** master carpenter.—**m. carpintero de remos,** master oar maker.—**m. de armas,** fencing master.—**m. de capilla,** choir master.—**m. de ceremonias,** master of ceremonies, emcee.—**m. de cocina,** chef.—**m. de escuela,** schoolmaster.—**m. de esgrima,** fencing master.—**m. de obra prima,** shoemaker.—**m. de obras,** master builder.—**m. de taller,** master mechanic.—**m. herrero,** master blacksmith.—**m. pintor,** master painter.—**m. plomero,** master plumber.
magallánico, ca, *a.* Magellanic.
maganel, *m.* (mil.) battering-ram.
maganto, ta, *a.* spiritless, dull, faint, languid.
magaña, *f.* (artil.) honeycomb, flaw in the bore of a gun; (coll.) cunning artifice, trick.
magarza, *f.* (bot.) downy camomile.
magarzuela, *f.* (bot.) stinking camomile.
magdalena, *f.* a kind of biscuit.
magdaleón, *m.* (pharm.) roll of plaster.
magia, *f.* magic; black art, necromancy.—**m. blanca,** or **natural,** white, or natural, magic.—**m. negra,** black magic, black art.
magiar, *n.* & *a.* Magyar.
mágicamente, *adv.* magically.
mágico, ca. I. *a.* magic, magical; marvellous, wonderful. **II.** *n.* magician; sorcerer, sorceress; *f.* magic.
magín, *m.* (coll.) fancy, idea, imagination.
magismo, *m.* magianism.
magisterial, *a.* magisterial.
magisterio, *m.* mastery; mastership; scholastic degree; teachers as a class; (coll.) affected solemnity; (chem.) precipitate.
magistrado, *m.* magistrate; magistracy.
magistral. I. *a.* magisterial, masterly; (eccl.) preaching; (pharm.) magistral. **II.** *m.* (min.) magistral.
magistralía, *f.* (eccl.) preacher's prebendary.
magistralmente, *adv.* magisterially, masterly.
magistratura, *f.* magistracy.
magma, *m.* magma, residue.
magnánimamente, *adv.* magnanimously.
magnanimidad, *f.* magnanimity.
magnánimo, ma, *a.* magnanimous, (U. S., coll.) big-hearted.
magnate, *m.* magnate, grandee.
magnesia, *f.* (chem.) magnesia.
magnesiano, na, *a.* magnesian.
magnésico, ca, *a.* magnesic.
magnesio, *m.* magnesium.
magnesita, *f.* meerschaum.
magneticé, magnetice, *v. V.* MAGNETIZAR.
magnético, ca, *a.* magnetic.—**amplificador m.,** (rad., electron.) magnetic amplifier.—**azimut m.,** magnetic bearing.—**campo m.,** (elec.) magnetic field.—**declinación magnética,** magnetic declination.—**desviación magnética,** (astron.) magnetic amplitude.—**flúido m.,** magnetic fluid.—**fonocaptor m.,** (electron.) magnetic pickup.—**freno m.,** (mech.) magnetic brake.—**fuerza magnética,** (elec.) magnetic force.—**histéresis magnética,** (elec.) magnetic hysteresis or lag.—**memorización magnetica,** (electron.) magnetic memory (as in computers).—**mina magnética,** (mil.) magnetic mine.—**pantalla magnética,** magnetic screen or shield.—**polo m.,** magnetic pole.—**resonancia magnética,** (phys.) magnetic resonance.—**rumbo m.,** magnetic course.—**tinta magnética,** magnetic ink.—**torsión magnética,** magnetic twist.—**variación magnética,** magnetic variation.
magnetismo, *m.* magnetism.—**m. remanente,** (phys.) remanence (residual magnetism).—**m. terrestre,** terrestrial magnetism.
magnetita, *f.* (min.) magnetite.
magnetizable, *a.* magnetizable.
magnetización, *f.* magnetization.
magnetizador, ra, *n.* & *a.* magnetizer(-ing); hypnotizer(-ing).
magnetizar, *va.* (*pret.* MAGNETICÉ; *subj.* MAGNETICE) to magnetize; to hypnotize.
magneto, *m.* or *f.* magneto.

magnetoelasticidad, *f.* magnetoelasticity.
magnetoelectricidad, *f.* magnetoelectricity.
magnetoeléctrico, ca, *a.* magnetoelectric.
magnetofónico, ca, *a.* magnetophonic, recording (as tape).
magnetófono, *m.* (phys.) magnetophone; tape recorder, magnetic recorder.
magnetografía, *f.* magnetography.
magnetógrafo, *m.* (phys.) magnetograph.
magnetograma, *m.* magnetogram.
magnetoiónico, ca, *a.* magnetoionic.
magnetología, *f.* magnetology.
magnetomecánica, *f.* magnetomechanics.
magnetometría, *f.* magnetometry.
magnetómetro, *m.* magnetometer.
magnetomotriz, *a.* magnetomotive.
magnetón, *m.* (phys.) magneton.
magnetoquímica, *f.* magnetochemistry.
magnetoscopia, *f.* magnetoscopy.
magnetoscopio, *m.* (phys.) magnetoscope.
magnetostática, *f.* magnetostatics.
magnetotérmico, ca, *a.* magnetothermal.
magnetrón, *m.* (phys.) magnetron.
magnicidio, *m.* assassination of a public figure.
magnificable, *a.* magnifiable.
magnificación, *f.* magnification.
magníficamente, *adv.* magnificently.
magnificar, *va.* to magnify, extol, exalt.
magníficat, *m.* (eccl.) Magnificat.
magnificencia, *f.* magnificence, grandeur, gorgeousness, splendor.
magnificentísimo, ma, *a. super.* of MAGNÍFICO: most magnificent.
magnífico, ca, *a.* magnificent; excellent.
magnitud, *f.* magnitude; quantity.
magno, na, *a.* great; grand.
magnolia, *f.* (bot.) magnolia.
mago, ga. I. *a.* Magian. **II.** *n.* magus; magician, necromancer, wizard.—*pl.* magi.
magostar, *vn.* to roast (chestnuts) at a picnic.
magosto, *m.* picnic and chestnut roast.
magra, *f.* rasher, slice of ham.
magrez, *f.* thinness, leanness.
magro, gra. I. *a.* meager, lean. **II.** *m.* lean slice of pork.
magrura, *f.* = MAGREZ.
magua, *f.* (Cuba) jest, joke.
magüer, magüera, *conj.* (obs.) although.
magüeto, ta, *n.* young steer or heifer.
maguey, *m.* (bot.) maguey.
maguillo, *m.* wild apple tree.
magujo, *m.* (naut.) ravehook.
magulladura, *f.* bruise, contusion.
magullamiento, *m.* bruising; contusion.
magullar, *va.* to bruise, to mangle.
maguntino, na, *a.* of Mainz or Mayence.
maharajá, *m.* maharaja.
maharrana, *f.* fresh bacon.
mahometano, na; mahomético, ca, *n.* & *a.* Mohammedan.
mahometismo, *m.* Mohammedanism.
mahometista, *n.* Mohammedan.
mahometizar, *vn.* to Mohammedanize.
mahón, *m.* nankeen, kind of light cotton goods.
mahona, *f.* Turkish transport vessel.
mahonesa, *f.* mayonnaise.
maicillo, *m.* (Am.) heavy or coarse sand.
maído, *m.* = MAULLIDO, mewing.
maillechort, *m.* white metal.
maimón, *m.* monkey.—*pl.* soup made with oil.
maimona, *f.* spindle beam of a horse mill.
maimonetes, *m. pl.* (naut.) belaying pins.
maimonismo, *m.* doctrine of Maimonides.
maitinante, *m.* priest with matinal duties.
maitines, *m. pl.* (eccl.) matins.
maíz, *m.* (bot.) maize, Indian corn.—**m. machacado,** hominy.
maizal, *m.* Indian-corn field.
majá, *m.* (Cuba) a thick-bodied snake.
majada, *f.* sheepcote, sheepfold; dung.
majadal, *m.* good pasture ground for sheep; land improved by the manure of a flock.
majadear, *vn.* (of sheep) to take shelter for the night; to manure.
majadería, *f.* foolish speech or act.
majaderico, *m.* old-fashioned trimming.
majaderillo, lla. I. *a. dim.* rather peevish and bothersome. **II.** *m.* bobbin for lace.
majadero, ra. I. *a.* silly; peevish; obtrusive. **II.** *m.* whippersnapper; bore; pestle, pounder.—*pl.* bobbins for making lace.
majador, ra, *n.* pounder, bruiser.
majadura, *f.* pounding or bruising.
majagranzas, *m.* (coll.) stupid bore.
majagua, *f.* (Am.) (bot.) a tree of the linden family.
majal, *m.* school of fishes.
majamiento, *m.* = MAJADURA.
majano, *m.* heap of stones as a landmark.
majar, *va.* to pound, bruise, break in a mortar; (coll.) to importune, vex, annoy.
majarete, *m.* (Cuba) corn pudding.
majencia, *f.* (coll.) = MAJEZA.
majestad, *f.* majesty.
majestuosamente, *adv.* majestically, grandly.
majestuosidad, *f.* majesty, dignity.
majestuoso, sa, *a.* majestic, grand.
majeza, *f.* (coll.) spruceness, gaudiness.
majo, ja. I. *a.* gay, spruce, gaudily attired, showy, handsome, pretty. **II.** *n.* beau, belle.
majolar, *m.* grove of white hawthorns.
majorca, *f.* (arch.) spindle-shaped baluster; ear of corn.
[1]**majuela,** *f.* shoe lacing.
[2]**majuela,** *f.* fruit of the white hawthorn.
majuelo, *m.* (bot.) new vine; white hawthorn.
mal. I. *a. contr.* of MALO; used only before masculine substantives (as *de mal genio,* bad-tempered). **II.** *m.* evil; harm, injury; malady, ailment, illness, disease, complaint; imperfection, fault; wrong, evil (*el bien y el mal,* right and wrong, good and evil).—**m. caduco** or **de corazón,** (med.) epilepsy.—**m. de la tierra,** homesickness.—**m. del pinto,** (med.) yaws.—**m. de ojo,** evil eye.—**m. de ojos,** eyesore.—**m. de piedra,** (med.) lithiasis, stone, calculus (gen. kidney).—**m. de San Lázaro,** (med.) elephantiasis.—**del m. el menos,** the lesser of two evils.—**hacer m.,** to do evil, to injure; to be injurious.—**no hay m. que por bien no venga,** everything is for the best.—**por m. de mis pecados,** to my sorrow, unluckily for me. **III.** *adv.* badly; wrongly; deficiently; wickedly; hardly.—**m. de fortuna,** or **de recurso,** short of funds, in a bad financial situation.—**m. de su grado,** unwillingly.—**¡m. haya!** confound it! confound (the man, thing, etc.)!.—**m. hecho,** badly done, ill-finished; unjust; wrong.—**m. por m.,** for want of something better.—**m. que bien,** willingly or unwillingly; rightly or wrongly.—**m. que le pese,** in spite of him, however much he may regret it.—**de m. en peor,** from bad to worse.—**estar m. de,** to be badly off, in a bad way (as *estar mal de salud,* to be in bad health; *estar mal de dinero,* to be badly in need of money).—**hacer mal,** to do wrong, act wrongly.
[1]**mala,** *f.* mail, post.
[2]**mala,** *f.* = MALILLA, manilla, a card game.
malabarismo, *m.* juggling.
malabarista, *n.* juggler.
malacate, *m.* hoisting machine.
malacia, *f.* (med.) depraved appetite.
malacología, *f.* malacology.
malacológico, ca, *a.* malacologic.
malaconsejado, da, *a.* ill-advised.
malacostumbrado, da, *a.* having bad habits; spoiled.
malacuenda, *f.* bagging, sacking; oakum, tow.
malagana, *f.* (coll.) faintness, dizziness.
malagaña, *f.* pole set up with dry furze to catch bees swarming.
malagradecido, da, *a.* (Am.) ungrateful.
malagueño, ña. I. *a.* of or pertaining to Malaga. **II.** *f.* popular song of Malaga.
malagueta, *f.* (bot.) grains of Paradise.

malamente, *adv.* badly; poorly; wrongly.
malandante, *a.* unfortunate, unhappy.
malandanza, *f.* misfortune, misery.
malandar, *m.* wild hog.
malandrín. I. *a.* malign, perverse. **II.** *m.* rascal, scoundrel.
malanga, *f.* (Am.) (bot.) arum.
malaquita, *f.* (min.) malachite.
malar, *a.* (anat.) malar, pert. to the cheek.
malaria, *f.* (med.) (Am.) malaria.
malárico, ca, *a.* malarial.
malariólogo, ga, *n.* malariologist.
malasio, sia. I. *n.* & *a.* Malaysian. **II.** *f.* (M.) Malaysia.
malato, *m.* (chem.) malate.
malavenido, da, *a.* querulous, faultfinding.
malaventura, *f.* calamity, misfortune.
malaventurado, da, *a.* unfortunate, ill-fated.
malaventuranza, *f.* infelicity, unhappiness.
malayo, a, *n.* & *a.* Malay, Malayan.
malbaratado, da, *a.* undersold; misspent.
malbaratador, ra, *n.* spendthrift, squanderer.
malbaratar, *va.* to squander; to undersell.
malbaratillo, *m.* second-hand shop.
malcarado, da, *a.* grim-faced, foul-faced.
malcasado, da, *a.* undutiful (spouse).
malcasar. I. *va.* to mismate in marriage. **II.** *vr.* to be mismated in marriage.
malcaso, *m.* treason, wrongful act.
malcocinado, *m.* tripe, liver, and lights of mutton or lamb; place where tripe is sold.
malcomer, *va.* to eat poorly.
malcomido, da, *a.* underfed.
malconsiderado, da, *a.* inconsiderate.
malcontentadizo, za, *a.* hard to please, faultfinding.
malcontento, ta. I. *a.* discontented, malcontent. **II.** *m.* malcontent; grumbler; a card game.
malcorte, *m.* transgression of forest laws.
malcriado, da, *a.* ill-bred, rude, uncivil; spoiled.
malcriar, *va.* to spoil (a child).
maldad, *f.* wickedness, iniquity; badness.
maldecido, da, *a.* wicked, depraved.
maldecidor, ra, *n.* defamer, backbiter.
maldecir, *va.* (*pp.* MALDECIDO, MALDITO; *gerund*, MALDICIENDO; *ind. pres.* yo MALDIGO, él MALDICE, *pret.* MALDIJE, *fut.* MALDECIRÉ, (obs.) MALDIRÉ; *subj. pres.* MALDIGA, *pret. imp.* MALDIJERA, MALDECIRÍA, MALDIJESE) to damn, curse, accurse; to defame, backbite.
maldiciente, *n.* & *a.* curser(-ing); defamer(-ing).
maldición, *f.* malediction, curse; damnation.
maldigo, maldiga, maldije, *v.* *V.* MALDECIR.
maldispuesto, ta, *a.* indisposed; unwilling.
maldita, *f.* (coll.) tongue.—**soltar la m.,** (coll.) to give a loose rein to one's tongue.
maldito, ta. I. *pp. irreg. of* MALDECIR. **II.** *a.* perverse, wicked; damned, accursed; (coll.) little, none, not one, nary.—**m. lo que me importa,** little do I care!.—**no sabe maldita la cosa,** nary a thing does he know.
maleabilidad, *f.* malleability.
maleable, *a.* malleable.
maleador, ra, *a.*; **maleante,** *a.* & *n.* rogue(-ish), villain(-ous), corrupter(-ing).
malear, *va.* to pervert, corrupt; injure, harm.
malecón, *m.* dike, levee, mole.
maledicencia, *f.* slander, calumny, obloquy.
maleficencia, *f.* malignity, wrongdoing.
maleficiar, *va.* to harm; to bewitch, spellbind.
maleficio, *m.* spell; witchcraft, charm.
maléfico, ca, *a.* maleficent; harmful; spellbinding.
maleína, *f.* (vet.) mallein.
malejo, ja, *a. dim.* of MALO: rather bad.
malentendido, *m.* (Gal.) misunderstanding.
malentrada, *f.* fee paid by a new prisoner.
maleolar, *a.* (anat.) malleolar.
maléolo, *m.* (anat.) malleolus.
malestar, *m.* malaise, indisposition.
maleta, *f.* valise, travelling bag, suitcase; (Am.) bundle (of clothes).—**hacer la m.,** to pack one's bag, suitcase; (coll.) to make preparations for a journey.
maletero, *m.* valise maker or seller.
maletín, *m. dim.* small valise or case, overnight bag.—**m. de grupa,** (mil.) saddlebag.
maletón, *m. aug.* large satchel.
malevolencia, *f.* malevolence, ill will.
malévolo, la, *a.* malevolent, malignant.
maleza, *f.* weeds; underbrush; brake, thicket, coppice.
malformación, *f.* malformation.
malfuncionamiento, *m.* malfunction.
malgache, *n.* & *a.* Malagasy.
malgastado, da, *a.* misspent, wasted, squandered.
malgastador, ra, *n.* spendthrift, squanderer.
malgastar, *va.* to misspend, waste, squander.
malhablado, da, *a.* foul-mouthed.
malhadado, da, *a.* wretched, unfortunate.
malhecho, cha. I. *a.* ill-shaped, malformed. **II.** *m.* evil deed, misdeed.
malhechor, ra, *n.* malefactor.
malherido, da, *a.* & *pp.* badly wounded.
malherir, *va.* (*ger.* MALHIRIENDO; *ind. pres.* MALHIERO, *pret.* él MALHIRIÓ; *subj.* MALHIERA) to wound badly.
malhojo, *m.* vegetable refuse.
malhumorado, da, *a.* ill-humored, peevish.
Malí, *m.* Mali.
malicia, *f.* malice, malignity, maliciousness; suspicion, apprehension; shrewdness, smartness; cunning, dissimulation.—**tener m.,** to be cunning or shrewd; to suspect, be suspicious.
maliciar, *va.* to suspect; to injure, harm.
maliciosamente, *adv.* maliciously; suspiciously.
malicioso, sa, *a.* malicious; wicked, knavish; suspicious.
málico, ca, *a.* (chem.) malic.
maliense, *n.* & *a.* Malian.
malignamente, *adv.* malignantly, malevolently.
malignante, *n.* & *a.* maligner(-ing).
malignar. I. *va.* to vitiate, corrupt, deprave. **II.** *vr.* to become sore; to grow worse.
malignidad, *f.* malignity, perversity.
maligno, na, *a.* malign, malignant, perverse.
malilla, *f.* manilla, a card game.
malintencionado, da, *a.* ill-disposed.
malmandado, da, *a.* disobedient; obstinate.
malmeter, *va.* to waste, misspend; to induce to evil; to estrange.
malmirado, da, *a.* disliked; inconsiderate.
malo, la, *a.* bad; evil; wicked; licentious, dissolute; naughty, mischievous; ill, sick; difficult, hard; cunning, artful.—**m. del (de la),** sick with, having a sore (throat, eye, etc.), suffering from a bad (throat, liver, etc.).—**a malas,** on bad terms; in an unfriendly way.—**de malas,** unlucky; with an evil intention.—**el m.,** the Evil One.—**lo m. es que,** the worst of it is that, the trouble is that.—**por malas o por buenas,** willingly or by force.
malogramiento, *m.* failure.
malograr. I. *va.* to waste, lose, miss (as time or opportunity). **II.** *vr.* to fail, fall through, come to naught; to have an untimely end.
malogro, *m.* miscarriage, failure; untimely end.
maloja, *f.* (Cuba), cornstalks used for fodder.
malojal, *m.* plantation of MALOJA.
malojero, *m.* seller of MALOJA.
malojo, *m.* (Venez.) = MALOJA.
maloliente, *a.* malodorous, fetid, stinking.
malón, *m.* (Am.) sudden attack by Indians.
malparado, da, *a.* ill-conditioned, impaired, damaged; foiled, worsted.
malparida, *f.* woman who has miscarried.
malparir, *vn.* to miscarry.
malparto, *m.* abortion, miscarriage.
malpighiano, na, *a.* (anat.) Malpighian (as body, corpuscle, layer, tube, etc.).
malpigiáceo, cea, *a.* (bot.) malpighiaceous.
malpraxis, *f.* malpractice.

malquerencia, *f.* ill will, hatred.
malquerer, *va.* (*ind. pres.* MALQUIERO, *pret.* MALQUISE, *fut.* MALQUERRÉ; *subj.* MALQUIERA) to dislike, have a grudge against.
malqueriente, *n.* one who dislikes another.
malquistar. I. *va.* to estrange; to create prejudice against.—**m. a uno con,** to set . . . against one. **II.** *vn.* to incur dislike, bring dislike or unpopularity on one, make oneself unpopular.
malquisto, ta, *a.* disliked, unpopular.
malrotador, ra, *n.* squanderer, spendthrift.
malrotar, *va.* to misspend, lavish, squander.
malsano, na, *a.* unhealthy, sickly, infirm; unhealthful, unwholesome, noxious.
malsín, *m.* talebearer, backbiter.
malsonante, *a.* offensive to pious ears.
malsufrido, da, *a.* impatient, unresigned
malta, *f.* malt; (Chile) high-quality beer.
maltasa, *f.* (biochem.) maltase.
maltés, tesa, *n.* & *a.* Maltese.
maltosa, *f.* (chem.) maltose.
maltrabaja, *n.* (coll.) idler, lounger.
maltraer, *va.* (*ger.* MALTRAYENDO; *ind. pres.* MALTRAIGO, *pret.* MALTRAJE; *subj.* MALTRAIGA) = MALTRATAR.
maltratamiento, *m.* ill treatment; rough usage.
maltratar, *va.* to treat ill, abuse, maltreat; to use roughly; to spoil, destroy.
maltrato, *m.* = MALTRATAMIENTO.
maltrecho, cha, *a.* in bad condition, damaged; badly off, battered.
maltusiano, na, *n.* & *a.* Malthusian.
maltusianismo, *m.* Malthusianism.
maluco, ca; malucho, cha, *a.* (coll.) rather bad, baddish; sickish, ailing somewhat.
malva, *f.* (bot.) mallow.—**ser como una m.,** to be meek and obedient.
malváceo, cea, *a.* (bot.) malvaceous.
malvacía, *f.* (bot.) malvasia (grape); malmsey (wine).
malvadamente, *adv.* wickedly, perversely.
malvado, da. I. *a.* wicked, fiendish, nefarious. **II.** *m.* wicked man, villain, knave.
malvar, *m.* place covered with mallows.
malvasía, *f.* (bot.) malvasia; malmsey wine.
malvavisco, *m.* (bot.) marsh mallow.
malveína, *f.* (chem.) mauveine (violet dye).
malvender, *va.* to sell at a loss, to sacrifice.
malversación, *f.* malversation.
malversador, ra, *n.* one who misapplies funds.
malversar, *va.* to misapply (funds).
malvezar, *va.* & *vr.* to fall into bad habits.
malvís, malviz, *m.* (ornith.) redwing.
malla, *f.* mesh (of a net); coat of mail; (naut.) network.—**m. de alambre,** wire netting, wire mesh.—**m. de baño,** bathing suit.
mallar. I. *vn.* to make network. **II.** *va.* to arm with a coat of mail.
mallero, *m.* netmaker; armorer.
mallete, *m.* gavel, mallet.—*pl.* (naut.) partners.
malleto, *m.* beating maul in paper mills.
mallo, *m.* mallet; pall-mall, game of bowls; mall, bowling green.
mallorquín, na, *a.* of or pertaining to Majorca.
mamá, *f.* mamma, mummy.
mama, *f.* mammary gland, breast; mamma.
mamacallos, *m.* (coll.) dolt, simpleton.
mamacona, *f.* religious virgin among the ancient Peruvians.
mamada, *f.* (coll.) act of sucking, suckling; amount that a child takes in suckling.
mamadera, *f.* breast pump.
mamador, ra, *n.* sucking, suckling; nursing bottle.
mamalogía, *f.* (zool.) mammalogy.
mamalón, *m.* (Cuba) idler, sponger, parasite.
mamandurria, *f.* (Am., pol., coll.) sinecure, job with salary and no work.
mamante, *a.* sucking, suckling.
mamantón, na, *a.* suckling (animal).
mamar, *va.* & *vn.* to suck, suckle; (coll.) to cram and devour (food); (coll.) to get, obtain.
mamario, ria, *a.* mammary.
mamarrachada, *f.* (coll.) collection of grotesque figures; (art) daub.
mamarrachista, *m.* (art) dauber.
mamarracho, *m.* grotesque figure or ornament; (art) daub.
mambla, *f.* mound; small peak, knoll.
mambo, *m.* (mus.) mambo.
mameluco, *m.* Egyptian soldier; (coll.) dolt, simpleton; (Am.) overalls; (Am.) children's nightdress; (Am.) half-breed.
mamella, *f.* mammillated protuberance in the neck of goats.
mamellado, da, *a.* mammillate, mammillated.
mamey, *m.* (bot.) mamey, mammee.
mamífero, ra. I. *a.* mammalian. **II.** *m. pl.* mammals, Mammalia.
mamila, *f.* woman's breast round the nipple; mamilla in men.
mamilado, da, *a.* mammilate, mammilated.
mamilar, *a.* mamillary.
mamola, *f.* chuck under the chin.
mamón, na, *m.* & *f.* suckling; child that sucks, suckles too much; (bot.) shoot, sucker; (W. I.) genip tree.
mamoncillo, *m.* (W. I.) honeyberry.
mamoso, sa. I. *a.* sucking, suckling. **II.** *m.* a variety of panic grass.
mamotreto, *m.* memorandum book; (coll.) bulky book or bundle of papers.
mampara, *f.* screen; fire screen.
mamparo, *m.* (naut.) bulkhead.—**mamparos de quita y pon,** (naut.) ship and unship bulkheads.
mampernal, manpirlán, *m.* wooden guard on steps of a staircase while building.
mampostear, *va.* to build with masonry.
mampostería, *f.* masonry (gen. app. to stone masonry).—**m. concertada,** rubble masonry, rubblework.—**m. de sillares,** ashlar masonry. —**m. en seco,** dry masonry (without mortar).
mampostero, *m.* (mason.) roughsetter.
mampresar, *va.* to begin to break in (horses).
mampuesta, *f.* (mason.) course.
mampuesto. I. *a.* overlapping. **II.** *m.* parapet; (Am.) rest or support for a firearm in taking aim; (mason.) rubble.—**de m.,** extra; from a sheltered position.
mamujar, *va.* to suck, suckle unsteadily.
mamullar, *va.* to eat or chew as if sucking at the breast; (coll.) to mutter, mumble.
mamut, *m.* (paleontol.) mammoth.
maná, *m.* manna.
[1]**manada,** *f.* flock; herd; drove; large number.—**a manadas,** in troops or crowds.
[2]**manada,** *f.* handful.
[1]**manadero, ra. I.** *a.* springing, issuing. **II.** *m.* source, spring; (in oil fields) place where seepage occurs.
[2]**manadero,** *m.* shepherd, herdsman.
manadilla, *f. dim.* small flock.
manante, *a.* proceeding, issuing.
manantial. I. *a.* flowing, running. **II.** *m.* spring, source, origin.
manantío, a, *a.* flowing, running.
manar, *vn.* to issue, flow out; to ooze; to abound.
manare, *m.* (Venez.) sieve for yucca starch.
manatí, manato, *m.* (zool.) manatee, seacow; whip made of the manatee's hide.
manaza, *f. aug.* large hand.
mancamiento, *m.* want, lack, deficiency; maimed condition; defect.
mancar, *va.* to maim, lame, cripple, disable.
manceba, *f.* mistress, concubine.
mancebete, *m. dim.* of MANCEBO.
mancebía, *f.* brothel, bawdyhouse.
mancebo, *m.* youth, young man; bachelor; shopman, shopboy, clerk.
mancera, *f.* plowtail, plow handle.
mancerina, *f.* saucer with holder for chocolate cup.
mancilla, *f.* spot, stain, blemish.
mancillar, *va.* to spot, stain, soil.

mancipación, *f.* (law) mancipation.
mancipar, *va.* to subject, enslave, mancipate.
manco, ca. I. *a.* handless; one-handed; armless; maimed; defective, faulty, imperfect. **II.** *n.* armless, handless or one-handed person.
mancomún, *m.*—**de m.,** jointly, in common.
mancomunadamente, *adv.* conjointly.
mancomunar, *va.* & *vr.* to associate, unite, combine; to pool (resources, etc.); (law) to make two or more persons pay jointly the costs of a lawsuit.
mancomunidad, *f.* union, fellowship, community.
mancornar, *va.* (*ind.* MANCUERNO; *subj.* MANCUERNE) to twist the neck of (a steer, etc.) and hold down on the ground with the horns downward; to join, to couple.
mancuerda, *f.* each turn of the rack bars.
mancuerna, *f.* pair tied together; thong for tying two steers; (Cuba) tobacco stem with two leaves; (P. I.) pair of convicts chained together.—*pl.* (Mex.) cufflinks.
mancuerno, mancuerne, *v. V.* MANCORNAR.
mancha, *f.* stain, spot, blot; stigma; patch of ground or vegetation; (astr.) sun spot.
manchadizo, za, *a.* easily stained.
manchado, da. I. *pp.* of MANCHAR. **II.** *a.* spotted, speckled.
manchar, *va.* to stain, soil; to foul, pollute; to tarnish, defile; (art) to speckle, daub; to darken, to cloud.—**m. papel,** to scribble.
manchego, ga, *a.* of or pertaining to La Mancha.
manchita, *f. dim.* small stain.
manchón, *m. aug.* large blot or stain; patch where vegetation is thickest.
manchú, *n.* & *a.* Manchu(-rian).
manchuela, *f.* = MANCHITA.
manchuriano, na, *n.* & *a.* = MANCHÚ.
manda, *f.* offer, proposal; legacy, bequest.
mandadero, ra, *n.* porter, messenger; errand boy or girl.—*f.* = DEMANDADERA, messenger (in convent).
mandado, da. I. *pp.* of MANDAR. **II.** *a.*—**bien m.** = BIENMANDADO, obedient, well-behaved. —**mal m.** = MALMANDADO, disobedient, badly-behaved. **III.** *m.* mandate, order, command; errand.
[1]**mandamiento,** *m.* order, command; (eccl.) commandment; (law) writ; mandamus.—*pl.* **mandamientos de la ley de Dios,** Ten Commandments.
[2]**mandamiento,** *m.* (coll.) the five fingers of the hand.
mandante. I. *a.* commanding. **II.** *n.* (law) constituent, mandator.
mandar. I. *va.* & *vn.* to command, order, direct, decree; to will, leave, bequeath; to send, transmit; to offer, promise; (foll. by *inf.*) to order, have (foll. by *pp.*: *él mandó escribir la carta,* he ordered, or had, the letter written).—**m. decir,** to send word. **II.** *vr.* to communicate (as rooms); (of patients) to move about unaided; to go from one room to another.
mandarín, *m.* mandarin; (coll.) petty official.
mandarina, *f.* Mandarin, the polished Chinese language; mandarin orange.
mandarria, *f.* iron maul, sledge hammer.
mandatario, *m.* (law) attorney, agent; mandatary.
mandato, *m.* mandate; command, injunction, order, charge; (law) mandate, contract of bailment; (eccl.) maundy.
mandíbula, *f.* jawbone; jaw.
mandibulado, da, *a.* mandibulate.
mandibular, *a.* mandibular.
mandil, *m.* leather or coarse apron; fine-mesh fishing net; cloth for cleaning horses.
mandilandinga, *f.* knavish deed, mean trick.
mandilar, *va.* to wipe (a horse) with a cloth.
mandilejo, *m. dim.* small apron.
mandilete, *m.* (fort.) door of a porthole.
mandilón, *m.* (coll.) coward.
mandinga. I. *n.* & *a.* Mandinga (Sudan Negro). **II.** *m.* (Am.) the Devil.
mandioca, *f.* (bot.) manioc, cassava; tapioca.
mando, *m.* command, power, dominion; control; (quality) leadership (also **espíritu de m.**).—**m. a distancia,** remote control.—**m. de aire comprimido,** pneumatic control.—**m. de bombardeo,** bomber command.—**m. de velocidad constante,** fixed speed drive.—**m. doble,** dual control.—**m. por junta Cardan,** universal joint drive.—**m. principal,** primary control.
mandoble, *m.* two-handed blow with a sword; severe reprimand.
mandolina, *f.* (Am.) = BANDOLÍN, mandolin.
mandón, na. I. *a.* imperious, domineering. **II.** *n.* imperious, haughty person; (min.) boss or foreman.
mandrachero, *m.* keeper of a gaming table.
mandracho, *m.* gambling house.
mandrágora, *f.* (bot.) mandrake.
mandria, *a.* & *m.* coward(-ly), poltroon.
[1]**mandril,** *m.* (zool.) mandrill, baboon.
[2]**mandril,** *m.* (mech.) mandrel, chuck, spindle of a lathe.—**m. ahorguillado,** fork chuck.—**m. autocentrante,** self-centering chuck.—**m. magnético,** magnetic chuck.—**m. universal,** combination chuck, faceplate.
mandrón, *m.* stone ball used as a missile.
manducación, *f.* (coll.) chewing.
manducar, *va.* (coll.) to chew.
manducatoria, *f.* (coll.) eatables, grub, eats.
manea, *f.* hobble (for horses).
manear, *va.* to hobble (a horse).
manecica, ita, *f. dim.* small hand.
manecilla, *f. dim.* small hand; (print.) fist (☞), index; book clasp; hand of a clock or watch.
manejable, *a.* manageable, tractable.
manejado, da. I. *pp.* of MANEJAR. **II.** *a.* (art) handled.
manejar. I. *va.* to manage, wield, handle; to drive, ride, train (a horse); to conduct, govern contrive; to run (an engine, a business); (Am.) to drive (auto). **II.** *vr.* to move about after having been deprived of motion; to behave; to get along, manage.
manejo, *m.* handling; management, conduct; horsemanship, manège; cunning, trick, intrigue, device.—**m. doméstico,** housekeeping.—**manejos de corte,** court intrigues.
maneota, *f.* shackles, hobbles, fetters.
manera, *f.* manner, way, mode; (art) manner, style; fly of trousers; side placket of skirt; quality, class of persons.—*pl.* ways, customs; manners.—**a m. de, a la m. de,** in the style of, like.—**de alguna m.,** in some way, somehow. —**de esa (este) m.,** in that (this) way.—**de mala m.,** botchingly; roughly; gruffly, reluctantly.—**de m. de,** so as to.—**de m. que,** so that, so as to, in such manner as to.—**de ninguna m.,** in no way; by no means, not at all. —**de otra m.,** otherwise.—**de tal m.,** in such a way; so much.—**de todas maneras,** at any rate.—**en gran m.,** in large measure; greatly, to a large extent.—**por m. que,** so then; so that; and so.—**sobre m.,** exceedingly.
manerismo, *m.* mannerism.
manerista, *n.* mannerist.
manero, ra, *a.* (falconry) trained, tame.
manes, *m. pl.* manes, spirits of the dead.
manezuela, *f. dim.* small hand; book clasp; haft or handle.
manfla, *f.* (coll.) concubine; old sow.
[1]**manga,** *f.* sleeve; arm of an axletree; a kind of cloak bag or portmanteau; (water) hose; purse seine; net bag, fish trap; bag strainer, Hippocrates sleeve; body of troops in a line; (eccl.) manga; (naut.) breadth of beam; wind sail; (Mex.) poncho.—*pl.* profits, gains.—**m. de agua,** squall, shower.—**m. de viento,** whirlwind.—**m. marina,** waterspout.—**andar m. por hombro,** to be disorderly (in one's home). —**de m. ancha,** indulgent.—**en mangas de camisa,** in shirt sleeves.—**tener m. ancha,** to be broad-minded.

²**manga,** *f.* (bot.) a variety of mango.
mangachapuy, *m.* (bot.) (P. I.) a dipterous tree.
mangajarro, *m.* (coll.) long, ill-shaped sleeve.
mangana, *f.* lasso, lariat.—**manganear,** *va.* (Am.) to lasso.—**manganeo,** *m.* lassoing.
manganato, *m.* (chem.) manganate.
manganesa, manganesia, *f.* (chem.) peroxide of manganese.—**manganésico, ca,** *a.* manganic, containing manganese.
manganesífero, ra, *a.* (chem.) manganiferous.
manganeso, *m.* (chem.) manganese.
mangánico, ca, *a.* (chem.) manganic.
manganilla, *f.* trick, stratagem; long pieced pole.
manganita, *f.* (min.) manganite.
manganito, *m.* (chem.) manganite, manganate.
manganoso, a, *a.* manganous.
mangla, *f.* gum from the rockrose.
manglar, *m.* plantation of mangrove trees.
mangle, *m.* (bot.) mangrove tree.
¹**mango,** *m.* handle, haft, helve; tiller.—**m. de escoba,** broomstick.—**m. de pluma,** penholder.
²**mango,** *m.* (bot.) Indian mango.
mangón, na, *n.* retailer; second-hand dealer.
mangonada, *f.* push with the arm.
mangonear, *vn.* (coll.) to wander about, loiter, loaf; to intermeddle; to pry.
mangoneo, *m.* intermeddling, prying.
mangonero, ra, *a.* fond of nosing or prying.
mangorrero, ra, *a.* rough-hafted (knife); worthless, useless.
mangorrillo, *m.* = MANCERA, plowtail.
mangosta, *f.* (zool.) mongoose.
mangostán, *m.* (bot.) mangosteen.
mangote, *m.* (coll.) large, wide sleeve; oversleeve.
mangual, *m.* war flail, morning star.
manguardia, *f.* buttress of a bridge.
manguera, *f.* (watering) hose; (naut.) wind sail; waterspout; tarred canvas bucket; (Am.) large corral; tube, sleeve.—**m. de desinflar,** (aer.) deflating sleeve.—**m. de inflar,** (aer.) inflating sleeve.
manguero, *m.* horseman; fireman.
mangueta, *f.* bag syringe; jamb post of a glass door or window; tiebeam; (mech.) lever; neck of a water-closet hopper.
manguita, *f. dim.* small sleeve; sheath, case.
manguitería, *f.* furrier's shop.
manguitero, *m.* muff maker, furrier.
manguito, *m.* muff; wristlet, half-sleeve; large coffee cake; oversleeve; (mech.) muff, coupler, collar, sleeve.
maní, *m.* (Am.) = CACAHUETE, peanut.
manía, *f.* mania; madness; whim, hobby.
maníaco, ca. I. *a.* maniac, mad, (psych.) manic; whimsical. **II.** *n.* maniac.
maníacodepresivo, va, *a.* (psych.) manic-depressive.
maniatar, *va.* to manacle; to handcuff.
maniático, ca, *a.* = MANÍACO.
maniblanco, ca, *a.* white-handed; (zool.) white-footed.
manicomio, *m.* insane asylum, madhouse.
manicordio, *m.* (mus.) manichord, clavichord.
manicorto, ta, *a.* illiberal, close-fisted.
manicurista, *n.* = MANICURO.
manicuro, ra, *n.* manicurist. *f.* manicure.
manida, *f.* resort, abode, nest, den.
manido, da. I. *pp.* of MANIR. **II.** *a.* high, gamey (meat).
manifacero, ra, *a.* (coll.) meddlesome.
manifactura, *f.* make; manufacture.
manifestación, *f.* manifestation, declaration, statement; (public) demonstration; (law) writ resembling habeas corpus.
manifestador, ra, *a.* that manifests.
manifestante, *n.* (public) demonstrator, demonstrant.
manifestar, I. *va.* (*pp.* MANIFESTADO, MANIFIESTO; *ind.* MANIFIESTO; *subj.* MANIFIESTE) to state, declare; to manifest, reveal, show; to tell, let know; (eccl.) to expose (the Eucharist) for public worship. **II.** *vr.* to make a demonstration.
manifiestamente, *adv.* manifestly, obviously.
¹**manifiesto, manifieste,** *v. V.* MANIFESTAR.
²**manifiesto, ta. I.** *pp.* of MANIFESTAR. **II.** *a.* manifest, plain, obvious; overt. **III.** *m.* manifest or manifesto, public declaration; (eccl.) act of exposing the Eucharist; (com.) custom house manifest.—**poner de m.,** to make evident, to show plainly; to make public, expose.
manigua, *f.* (Cuba) thicket, jungle.
manigueta, *f.* haft, handle.—*pl.* (naut.) kevels.
manija, *f.* handle, haft; crank; hobble, fetters; (mech.) ring, brace, clasp, clamp.
manijero, *m.* foreman of a gang of laborers.
manilargo, ga, *a.* having long hands; (Am.) ready to fight, belligerent.
manilense; manileño, ña. I. *n.* native of Manila. **II.** *a.* Manila (as *a.*).
maniluvio, *m.* bath for the hands, as a remedy.
manilla, *f. dim.* small hand; (jewelry) bracelet; manacle, handcuff.
maniobra, *f.* handiwork; operation, procedure; artifice, trick, manœuvring; (mil.) manœuvre; (naut.) working of a ship; gear, rigging, tackle, *pl.* (Ry.) switch-engine work.
maniobrabilidad, *f.* maneuverability.
maniobrable, *a.* maneuverable.
maniobrar, *va.* & *vn.* to do handiwork; (naut.) to work a ship; to devise ways and means of effecting anything; (mil.) to manœuvre.
maniobrero, ra, *a.* manœuvring (troops).
maniobrista, *m.* (naut.) skilful naval tactician.
maniota, *f.* hobble (for horses).
manipulación, *f.* manipulation.
manipulador, ra, *n.* handler, manipulator; *m.* key; *f.* handler (machine).—**m. dactilográfico,** keyboard sender.—**m. telegráfico,** telegraph key.
manipulante, *m.* (coll.) administrator, negotiator.
manipular, *va.* to manipulate, handle, manage.
manipuleo, *m.* (coll.) tactful handling, manœuvring.
manípulo, *m.* (eccl.) maniple; standard; maniple, a division of the Roman legion; (med.) handful.
maniqueísmo, *m.* Manicheism.
maniqueo, a, *n.* & *a.* Manichean.
maniquete, *m.* black lace mitten.
maniquí, *m.* puppet; manikin; mannequin, model, figure.
manir, *va.* (*defect.: only those forms are used having the letter* **i** *in their terminations*) to keep meat until it becomes gamey.
manirroto, ta, *a.* lavish, prodigal, wasteful.
manita, *f.* (chem.) mannite, mannitol; manna sugar.
manivacío, cía, *a.* (coll.) empty-handed.
manivela, *f.* (mech.) crank; crankshaft.—**m. de arranque,** (auto) starting crank or handle.—**m. de disco,** disc crank.
manjar, *m.* food, dish, victuals; tidbit, morsel; recreation, entertainment.—**m. bianco,** dish made of shredded chicken with sugar, milk, and rice flour; blancmange.
manjarejo, *m. dim.* savory dish, tidbit.
manjarria, *f.* (Cuba) driving beam of a canemill.
manjelín, *m.* carat, diamond weight.
manjolar, *va.* to carry (a hawk).
manjorrada, *f.* abundance of ordinary victuals.
manjúa, *f.* (Am.) a variety of sardine.
manlieva, *f.* taxes collected from house to house.
manlieve, *m.* confidence game; swindle.
mano, *f.* hand; forefoot; foot of cattle after cut off; trunk of an elephant; hand of a clock or watch; pestle; cylindrical stone for grinding cocoa; quire of paper; reprimand; musical scale; first hand at cards; round of any game; power or means of making or attaining something; each time or turn in a work by hand; coat (of paint, varnish, etc.); workmanship, handicraft,

handiwork; (Am.) slight accident, mishap.—**m. a m.**, in friendly coöperation, together; on equal terms, without odds; tête-à-tête.—**m. apalmada,** (her.) stretched palm of the hand.—**m. de gato,** ladies' make-up; (of works of art or literature amended by more able persons than the author) polishing or editing hand.—**m. de obra,** workmanship; labor, labor force.—**m. de obra disponible,** available manpower.—**m. de obra especializada,** skilled labor.—**m. de obra no calificada,** unskilled labor, day laborer.—**m. de santo,** sure cure.—**¡manos a la obra!** bear a hand! to work!.—**manos libres,** perquisites.—**manos limpias,** extra pay or allowance.—**manos muertas,** mortmain, unalienable estate.—**manos puercas,** (coll.) graft, ill-gotten gains.—**m. sobre m.,** idle, doing nothing.—**a la m.,** near, at hand.—**a m.,** by hand; at hand, near by.—**a m. airada,** violently, by force.—**a m. derecha (izquierda),** on the right- (left-) hand side.—**a m. salva** = A MANSALVA. V. MANSALVA.—**a manos llenas,** liberally, abundantly.—**a una m.,** of one accord.—**bajo m.,** underhandedly.—**dar una m.,** to give, lend, a hand.—**de buena m.,** on good authority.—**de m.** = BAJO M.; hand (as *a.*, as in *rueda de mano,* hand wheel).—**de la m.,** by the hand; hand in hand.—**de manos a boca,** suddenly, unexpectedly.—**de primera m.,** first-hand.—**de segunda m.,** second-hand.—**de una sola m.,** (Arg., Chile) (of street) one-way.—**en manos de,** in the hands, power, of.—**entre manos,** in hand, in the process of carrying on or out.—**estar a mano,** (Am.) (games, actions, etc.) to be even.—**por debajo de m.** = BAJO MANO.—**por su m.,** by oneself, by one's own judgment or authority.

manobra, *f.* raw material.

manobre, *m.* hodman, hodcarrier.

manobrero, *m.* keeper of irrigating ditches.

manojillo, ito, *m. dim.* small bundle or fagot.

manojo, *m.* handful; bunch (of flowers, vegetables, etc.); fagot, bundle.—**a manojos,** abundantly.

manojuelo, *m. dim.* small bunch or bundle.

manolo, la, *n.* Madrilenian of low class, loud in dress and manners.

manométrico, ca, *a.* manometric.

manómetro, *m.* manometer, pressure gauge.

manopla, *f.* gauntlet; coachman's whip; (Am.) brass knuckles.

manosear, *va.* to handle, touch, feel of; to muss, rumple (clothes).—**manoseo,** *m.* handling.

manota, *f. aug.* large, ugly hand.

manotada, *f.*, **manotazo,** *m.* cuff, slap, box; blow with the paw.

manotear. I. *va.* to cuff, buffet. **II.** *vn.* to gesticulate.

manoteo, *m.* gesticulation with the hands.

manotón, *m.* = MANOTADA.

manquear, *vn.* to pretend to be crippled.

manquedad, manquera, *f.* lack of one or both arms or hands; defect, imperfection.

mansalva.—**a m.,** without running any risk, without danger, in a cowardly manner.

mansamiente, *adv.* meekly; gently, quietly.

mansarda, *f.* (Gal.) mansard.

mansedumbre, *f.* meekness; tameness.

mansejón, na, *a.* very tame.

mansera, *f.* (Cuba) vat for the cane juice.

mansión, *f.* stay, sojourn; habitation, mansion, abode.—**hacer m.,** to stop over.

mansito, ta. I. *a.* very gentle or tame. **II.** *adv.* = MANSAMENTE.

[1]**manso, sa. I.** *a.* tame; gentle, mild; calm; soft quiet; meek, lamblike. **II.** *m.* bellwether.

[2]**manso,** *m.* (Angl.) manse, farm.

manta, *f.* woollen blanket; travelling rug; poncho; man's shawl, muffler; horse blanket; (Mex.) coarse cotton cloth; tossing blanket or canvas; (fort.) mantelet, movable parapet; thrashing, drubbing; (min.) bag of agave for carrying ore; game of cards resembling OMBRE.—**m. blanca,** bleached cotton.—**m. de algodón,** wadding.—**m. eléctrica,** electric heating pad, electric blanket.—**m. prieta,** unbleached cotton.—**a m. de Dios,** (coll.) copiously, plentifully.

mantalona, *f.* (P. I.) cotton stuff for sails.

mantaterilla, *f.* coarse hempen cloth for horse blankets.

manteador, ra, *n.* tosser (in a blanket).

manteamiento, *m.* tossing in a blanket.

mantear. I. *va.* to toss in a blanket. **II.** *vn.* (of women) to gad, be out too much.

manteca, *f.* lard; fat; pomatum; butter; oily substance of cocoa and other fruits.—**m. de cacao,** cocoa butter.

mantecada, *f.* buttered toast and sugar; a kind of cooky.

mantecado, *m.* biscuit kneaded with lard; French ice cream.

mantecíon, *f.* = MANUTENCIÓN.

mantecón, *m.* milksop; sweet tooth; dainty person.

mantecoso, sa, *a.* buttery, greasy.

manteísta, *m.* day student.

mantel, *m.* tablecloth; altar cloth.—**levantar los manteles,** to clear the table.

mantelería, *f.* table linen.

manteleta, *f.* mantelet, ladies' shawl.

mantelete, *m.* (eccl.) mantelet; (fort.) mantelet; (her.) mantling.

mantelo, *m.* very wide apron.

mantellina, *f.* a sort of mantilla.

mantenedor, *m.* president of a tournament or contest.

mantener. I. *va.* (*ind. pres.* MANTENGO, *pret.* MANTUVE, *fut.* MANTENDRÉ; *subj.* MANTENGA) to support, provide for, to feed; to maintain, keep up; to continue, persevere in: to pursue; to defend or sustain (an opinion); to keep up (conversation, correspondence). **II.** *vr.* to support oneself, earn one's living; to continue, remain (in one place); **(en)** to remain firm (in), continue (in), adhere (to), hold on (to).—**m.-se firme como un peñón,** to be firm as a rock.

mantengo, mantenga, *v. V.* MANTENER.

manteniente, *m.* violent blow with both hands.—**a m.** with all one's might; firmly.

mantenimiento, *m.* maintenance, support, upkeep; subsistence; livelihood, living.

[1]**manteo,** *m.* tossing in a blanket.

[2]**manteo,** *m.* long cloak or mantle; sort of woollen skirt.

mantequería, *f.* dairy, creamery.

mantequero, ra. I. *n.* one who sells butter; dairyman, dairymaid. **II.** *f.* churn; butter dish or bowl.

mantequilla, *f.* butter; hard sauce.

mantequillero, ra. I. *n.* = MANTEQUERO. **II.** *f.* butter bowl.

mantero, ra, *n.* blanket maker or seller; mantua maker.

mantés, sa, *n.* (coll.) rogue, scoundrel.

mantilla, *f.* mantilla; saddlecloth; baby clothes; (print.) blanket; birth present from one prince to another.—**estar en mantillas,** (of work, a negotiation, etc.) to be in the beginning stage; to be ignorant of, not know anything about (a subject).

mantilleja, *f. dim.* small mantilla.

mantillo, *m.* (agr.) humus; rotten, fermented manure.

mantillón, na, *a.* dirty, slovenly.

mantisa, *f.* (math.) mantissa.

manto, *m.* cloak, mantle; large mantilla; robe of state; mantelpiece of a chimney; (min.) layer or stratum.

mantón, *m. aug.* large cloak or mantle; (Cuba) mantilla.

mantuano, na, *n.* & *a.* of or from Mantua.

mantudo, da, *a.* having drooping wings.

mantuve, *v. V.* MANTENER.

manuable, *a.* easy to handle, handy.

manual. **I.** *a.* manual; handy; domestic, home-made; easy; tractable, pliant. **II.** *m.* manual, handbook; notebook, account book; handle (of an oar); (eccl.) ritual; (com.) old name of the journal.—*pl.* a priest's fees for assisting in the choir.
manualmente, *adv.* manually.
manubrio, *m.* handle, crank.
manucodiata, *f.* (ornith.) bird of paradise.
manuela, *f.* (in Madrid) open hack, carriage.
manuella, *f.* (naut.) capstan bar.
manufactura, *f.* manufacture; manufactured article.
manufacturado, da, *a.* manufactured.
manufacturar, *va.* & *vn.* to manufacture.
manufacturero, ra, *a.* manufacturing.
manumisión, *f.* manumission, freeing.
manumiso, sa, *a.* emancipated; free, disengaged.
manumisor, *m.* (law) liberator.
manumitir, *va.* (*pp.* MANUMITIDO, MANUMISO) to manumit, emancipate.
manuscribir, *va.* & *vn.* to write by hand.
manuscrito, ta, *a.* & *m.* manuscript.
manutención, *f.* maintaining; maintenance, support; protection; conservation.
manutener, *va.* (law) to maintain, support.
manutisa, *f.* (bot.) = MINUTISA, sweet william.
manvacío, a, *a.* = MANIVACÍO, empty-handed.
manzana, *f.* (bot.) apple; block (of houses), city block, square; knob of a sword.
manzanal, manzanar, *m.* apple orchard.
manzanera, *f.* (bot.) wild apple tree.
manzanil, *a.* applelike.
manzanilla, *f. dim.* (bot.) common camomile; knob at the top of coaches, bedsteads, etc.; medium-sized olive; white sherry wine; lower part of the chin; pad, or cushion, of the feet of animals having claws.—**m. fina,** (bot.) golden cotula.—**m. hedionda** = MAGARZUELA, (bot.) camomile.
manzanillo, ito, *m. dim.* (bot.) manchineel, poison tree.
manzanita, *f. dim.* little apple.—**m. de dama** = ACEROLA, fruit of the hawthorn.
manzano, *m.* (bot.) apple tree.
maña, *f.* skill, dexterity, cleverness, knack; cunning, craftiness; tact, care; habit or custom; bundle or bunch (as of hemp or flax).—**darse m.,** to contrive, to manage.
mañana. **I.** *f.* tomorrow, morrow; morning; (Am.) morning drink.—**de gran m.,** very early.—**de m.,** in the morning; early.—**muy de m.** = DE GRAN M.—**m. mismo,** tomorrow without fail, surely.—**por la m.,** in the morning.—**tomar la m.,** to take an appetizer (drink) before breakfast. **II.** *adv.* to-morrow; later, in time to come.—**¡hasta m.!** see you tomorrow!
mañanear, *vn.* to rise early.
mañanica, ita, *f.* daybreak.
mañear, *va.* & *vn.* to manage or act with craft and cunning.
mañería, *f.* sterility; feudal right of inheriting from those who died without legitimate succession.
mañero, ra, *a.* clever, dexterous, skilful, artful; handy, easy; meek, tractable.
maño, ña, *n.* brother (sister); dear, darling.
mañoco, *m.* tapioca; Indian-corn meal.
mañosamente, *adv.* neatly, handily, cleverly; tactfully, slickly; craftily.
mañoso, sa, *a.* skilful, handy, clever; tactful, cunning, careful.
mañuela. **I.** *f.* low cunning, mean trick. **II.** *n.* artful, cunning person.
mapa. **I.** *m.* map, chart.—**m. mudo,** outline map with no names on it. **II.** *f.* (coll.) anything excellent and prominent in its line.—**llevarse la m.,** to excel, to take the prize.
mapache, *m.* (zool.) raccoon.
mapamundi, *m.* map of the world.
mapaná, mapanare, *f.* (Colomb., Venez.) a poisonous snake.
mapurito, *m.* (C. A.) (zool.) skunk.
maque, *m.* (Mex.) sumac lacquer.
maquear, *va.* to lacquer with MAQUE.
maqueta, *f.* mock-up, model.
maqui, *m.* (bot.) maqui (evergreen shrub of Chile); (zool.) lemur.
maquiavélico, ca, *a.* Machiavelian.
maquiavelismo, *m.* Machiavelism.
maquiavelista, *n.* Machiavelian.
maquila, *f.* toll corn; a corn measure (½ CELEMÍN); (C. A.) a unit of weight (about 125 lb.)
maquilar, *va.* to measure and take the miller's toll corn.
maquilero, maquilón, *m.* measurer and receiver of milling toll corn.
maquillaje, *m.* (Gal.) beautifying, making up.
maquillar, *va.* & *vr.* to make up (as for a theatrical role), apply cosmetics.
máquina, *f.* machine, engine; fancy project; admixture of fancy or the supernatural in certain poetical compositions; device, trick; imposing structure, mansion, pile; (coll.) abundancy, lots.—**m. alternativa,** reciprocating engine.—**m. automática,** pushbutton machine.—**m. compuesta,** compound engine.—**m. de cilindro,** reciprocating engine.—**m. de combar** or **ondular,** crimping machine.—**m. de combustión interna,** internal-combustion engine.—**m. de coser,** sewing machine.—**m. de doble efecto,** double-acting engine.—**m. de émbolo,** reciprocating engine.—**m. de escribir,** typewriter.—**m. de fresar,** milling machine.—**m. de hilar algodón,** spinning jenny.—**m. de lavar,** washing machine.—**m. de ordeñar,** milking machine.—**m. de picar carne,** meat chopper.—**m. de sumar,** adding machine.—**m. de tallar engranajes,** gear cutter.—**m. de vapor,** steam engine.—**m. de venta automática,** slot or vending machine.—**m. de votar,** voting machine.—**m. herramienta,** machine tool.—**m. infernal,** infernal machine.—**m. motriz,** prime mover.—**m. neumática,** air pump.—**m. numeradora,** (print.) numbering machine.—**m. térmica,** heat engine.—**a toda m.,** at full speed.
maquinación, *f.* machination.
maquinador, ra, *n.* schemer, plotter.
maquinal, *a.* mechanical.—**maquinalmente,** *adv.* mechanically, unconsciously.
maquinar, *va.* & *vn.* to machinate, scheme, plot, hatch, concoct.
maquinaria, *f.* machinery; applied mechanics.
maquinilla, *f.* clippers.—**m. para cortar el pelo,** clippers.—**m. de seguridad** or **de afeitar,** safety razor.
maquinismo, *m.* mechanization.
maquinista, *n.* engine runner, engineer; machinist; mechanic, mechanician.
mar, *m.* or *f.* sea; flood; large quantity or number.—**m. alta,** rough sea.—**m. ancha,** high seas.—**m. bonanza,** calm sea.—**m. de fondo,** swell.—**m. de través,** sea on the beam.—**m. en leche,** calm sea.—**m. jurisdiccional,** or **territorial,** territorial waters.—**m. llena,** or **plena,** high water.—**alta m.,** high seas, open sea.—**arar en el m.,** to labor in vain.—**baja m.,** low water, ebb tide.—**correr con la mar en popa,** to scud before the sea.—**correr los mares,** to follow the seas.—**de m. a m.,** copiously, excessively; in the extreme of fashion.—**hablar de la m.,** to attempt an impossibility; to speak on an inexhaustible subject.—**la m.,** (coll.) a great quantity or number, a lot, lots.—**meter el m. en pozo,** to attempt the impossible.—**meterse m. adentro,** (in sea bathing) to go beyond one's depth.
marabú, *m.* (ornith.) marabou.
maracure, *m.* (bot.) curare plant.
maragato, ta, *n.* native of a region in Spain called Maragatería.
maraña, *f.* jungle; tangle, entanglement; silk waste and stuff made from it; perplexity, puzzle; fraud, imposition; intrigue, plot.
marañado, da, *a.* entangled, perplexed.

marañero, ra; ñoso, sa, *a.* entangling, ensnaring, perplexing.
marañón, *m.* (Cuba) (bot.) cashew; cashew nut.
marasmo, *m.* (med.) marasmus, wasting away; inactivity, dullness, deadness.
maratón, *f.* (sports) marathon.
maravedí, *m.* maravedi, an old Spanish coin.
maravilla, *f.* wonder, marvel; (bot.) marigold.—**m. de noche,** or **de Indias,** (bot.) marvel of Peru, four-o'clock.—**a las mil maravillas,** wonderfully well.—**a m.,** marvellously.—**por m.,** very seldom.
maravillar. I. *va.* to admire. **II.** *vr.* **(de)** to wonder (at), to marvel.
maravillosamente, *adv.* wonderfully, marvellously.
maravilloso, sa, *a.* wonderful.
marbete, *m.* label, tag, ticket; (Ry.) baggage check; border, fillet.
marca, *f.* mark, stamp, impress; brand; make; sign; standard (of size); gauge or rule for measuring; marker, stencil, label, tag, ticket; (geog.) march, frontier region or province; seamark, landmark.—**m. de fábrica,** trademark.—**de m.,** excellent of its kind.—**de más de m.,** or **de m. mayor,** of high quality, first-class, superior.
marcación, *f.* bearing; taking a ship's bearings.
marcadamente, *adv.* markedly, notably.
marcado, da, *a.* marked.
marcador, ra. I. *n.* & *a.* marker(-ing). **II.** *m.* marker; assay master; index; bookmark.
marcar. I. *va.* (*pret.* MARQUÉ; *subj.* MARQUE) to mark, stamp, impress, brand; to observe, note; (sports) to even up, counter.—**m. el compás,** to beat time, keep time. **II.** *vr.* to determine bearings (of a ship).
marcasita, *f.* (min.) marcasite, white pyrites.
marceador, ra, *n.* & *a.* shearer(-ing).
marcear. I. *va.* to shear. **II.** *vn.* (of weather) to be rough.
marceo, *m.* trimming honeycombs in spring.
marcero, ra. = MARCEADOR.
marcescente, *a.* (bot.) marcescent, withering.
marcial. I. *a.* martial, warlike; frank, unceremonious; (pharm.) martial, chalybeate. **II.** *m.* aromatic powder for dressing gloves.
marcialidad, *f.* martialness; frankness.
marciano, na, *a.* Martian.
marco, *m.* frame, doorcase, window case; picture frame; mark, gold and silver weight; standard (of weight); scantling and length of timber; model, archetype; mark, German coin.
márcola, *f.* pruning hook.
marconigrafía, *f.* wireless telegraphy.
marconigrama, *m.* marconigram, wireless telegram.
marcha, *f.* march; progress, turn, course, run; (naut.) speed; (mus.) march, two-step; movement of a watch; running or functioning; bonfire.—**marchas forzadas,** (mil.) forced marches.—**a largas marchas,** with celerity, speedily.—**apresurar la m.,** to hurry, speed up.—**batir la m.,** to strike up a march.—**¡en m.!** forward march! go on! let's go!—**poner en m.,** to start, put in motion; (fig.) to start, initiate.—**sobre la m.,** at once, right off, right away.
marchamar, *va.* to mark at the custom house.
marchamero, *m.* custom house officer who marks goods.
marchamo, *m.* custom house mark on goods.
marchante. I. *a.* mercantile, commercial, trading. **II.** *m.* shopkeeper, dealer; customer, buyer; (Cuba) sharper, trickster.
marchapié, *m.* footboard; (naut.) horse, footrope.
marchar, *vn.* & *vr.* to go; to go away, leave; to walk; to progress, proceed, go ahead; to work, function, run (as a machine); to go, run (as a train, a ship, a clock); to move (as a carriage); to pace (as a horse); (mil.) to march; (naut.) to have speed.
marchitable, *a.* perishable, liable to wither.
marchitamiento, *m.* withering, fading.
marchitar. I. *va.* to wither, fade. **II.** *vr.* to wither, fade, decay; to pine away.
marchitez, *f.* withering, fading.
marchito, ta, *a.* faded, withered.
marea, *f.* tide; beach; soft sea breeze; dew, mizzle; street dirt washed away.—**m. alta,** high tide, high water.—**m. baja,** low tide, ebb.—**m. creciente,** flood tide.—**m. menguante,** ebb tide.—**contra viento y m.,** against all odds; come what may.
mareado, da, *a.* seasick.
mareaje, *m.* navigation, seamanship; course of a ship.
mareamiento, *m.* seasickness.
mareante. I. *n.* navigator, skipper, sailor. **II.** *a.* causing seasickness.
marear. I. *va.* to navigate; to sell; (coll.) to vex, importune, bother. **II.** *vr.* to get seasick, carsick; to be damaged at sea.
marecanita, *f.* (min.) marekanite.
marejada, *f.* swell, head sea, surf; commotion, excitement, disturbance.
maremagno, mare mágnum, *m.* (coll.) abundance; confusion, disorder.
maremoto, *m.* ground swell; roller; tidal wave, seismic sea.
mareo, *m.* seasickness; (coll.) vexation.
mareógrafo, *m.* mareograph.
marero, *a.* sea (breeze).
mareta, *f.* (naut.) surge of the sea; growing or decreasing excitement.
maretazo, *m.* dashing of a wave.
márfaga, márfega, *f.* ticking; straw bed.
marfil, *m.* ivory.—**m. vegetal,** ivory nuts.
marfilense, *n.* & *a.* (of the) Ivory Coast.
marfileño, ña, *a.* ivory (as *a.*); ivorylike.
marfuz, *a.* repudiated, rejected; fallacious, deceitful.
[1]**marga,** *f.* marl, loam.
[2]**marga,** *f.* ticking; burlap.
margajita, *f.* (min.) white pyrites.
margal, *m.* marly ground, marlpit.
margallón, *m.* (bot.) palmetto.
margar, *va.* to fertilize with marl.
margarato, *m.* (chem.) margarate.
margárico, ca, *a.* (chem.) margaric (acid).
margarina, *f.* (chem.) margarine.
margarita, *f.* pearl; (bot.) common daisy; marguerite; periwinkle.
margay, *m.* (Am.) (zool.) margay, tiger cat.
margen, *m.* or *f.* margin, border, edge, verge; fringe; marginal note.—**m. de error,** (stat., fig.) margin of error.—**andarse por las márgenes,** to beat about the bush.—**dar m.,** to give an opportunity.
margenar, *va.* = MARGINAR.
marginado, da, *a.* & *pp.* marginated.
marginal, *a.* marginal.
marginar, *va.* to make marginal notes on; to leave a margin on.
margoso, sa, *a.* marly, loamy.
margrave, *m.* margrave.
margraviato, *m.* margraviate.
marguera, *f.* marlpit.
marhojo, *m.* = MALHOJO, vegetable refuse.
maría, *f.* (coll.) white wax taper; old silver coin.
mariache, mariachi, *m.* (Mex.) popular song; street singer.
mariano, na, *a.* (eccl.) Marian.
marica. I. *f. dim.* (ornith.) magpie; knave of diamonds. **II.** *m.* milksop, effeminate man.
Maricastaña, *f.*—**en tiempos de M.,** in the days of yore; long, long ago.
maridable, *a.* conjugal, matrimonial, connubial, marital.—**maridablemente,** *adv.* conjugally.
maridaje, *m.* conjugal bond; intimate connection.
maridar. I. *vn.* to marry; to live as man and wife. **II.** *va.* to unite, join.
maridazo, *m.* (coll.) uxoriousness, excessive fondness for one's wife.

maridillo, *m.* brazier for warming the feet.
marido, *m.* husband.
mariguana, marihuana, *f.* marihuana.
marimacho, *m.* (coll.) virago, mannish woman.
marimanta, *f.* (coll.) bugbear, hobgoblin.
marimba, *f.* a kind of drum used by Negroes of Africa; (Am.) xylophone.
marimoña, *f.* (bot.) = FRANCESILLA, crowfoot.
marimorena, *f.* (coll.) quarrel, row.
marina, *f.* marine, shore, sea coast; (art) marine painting, seascape; seamanship, nautical art. **—m. de guerra,** navy.**—m. mercante,** merchant marine.
marinaje, *m.* seamanship; sailors (collect.).
marinar, *va.* to salt (fish); (naut.) to man (a ship).
marinear, *vn.* to be a mariner.
marinerado, da, *a.* manned, equipped.
marinería, *f.* seamanship; body of seamen; ship's crew.
marinero, ra. I. *a.* ready to sail; seaworthy, seagoing, stanch. **II.** *m.* mariner, seaman, sailor.— **a la marinera,** in a seamanlike manner, shipshape.
marinesco, ca, *a.* pertaining to sailors.**—a la m.,** in a seamanlike manner, shipshape.
marino, na. I. *a.* marine, nautical, sea (as *a.*). **II.** *n.* mariner, seaman.
marión, *m.* (ichth.) sturgeon.
marioneta, *f.* = TÍTERE, puppet, marionette.
maripérez, *f.* servant maid.
mariposa, *f.* (entom.) butterfly; night taper.
mariposear, *vn.* to flit like a butterfly; to be fickle and capricious.
mariquita, *f.* (entom.) ladybug, ladybird.
marisabidilla, *f.* (coll.) bluestocking.
mariscal, *m.* (mil.) marshal; farrier, blacksmith. **—m. de campo,** field marshal.
mariscala, *f.* marshal's wife.
mariscalato, *m.,* **mariscalía,** *f.* marshalship.
mariscar, *vn.* to gather shellfish.
marisco, *m.* any of the Invertebrata, especially a mollusc or a shellfish.
marisma, *f.* marsh, swamp, motass.
marismo, *m.* (bot.) = ORZAGA, mountain spinach.
marisquería, *f.* seafood bar; fish market.
marital, *a.* marital.
marítimo, ma, *a.* maritime, marine, sea (as *a.*).
maritornes, *f.* (coll.) homely, ungainly maid of all work.
marizapalos, *f.* row, fight, disturbance.
marjal, *m.* fen, marsh, moor, moorland.
marjoleta, *f.* = MAJUELA, fruit of the hawthorn.
marjoleto, *m.* (bot.) white hawthorn.
marlota, *f.* a kind of Moorish gown.
marmatita, *f.* (min.) marmatite.
marmella, *f.* = MAMELLA, protuberance on goat's neck.
marmellado, da, *a.* = MAMELLADO, mammillate.
marmita, *f.* kettle, pot, boiler.
marmitón, *m.* scullion, kitchen boy.
mármol, *m.* marble (stone); (art) marble sculpture; (glass making) marver; (print.) imposing stone.
marmolejo, *m. dim.* small marble column.
marmoleño, ña, *a.* marbly.
marmolería, *f.* marblework; marbleworks.
marmolillo, *m. dim.* fender stone; (fig.) unfeeling person.
marmolista, *m.* marbler, sculptor.
marmoración, *f.* = ESTUCO, stucco; plastering.
marmóreo, ea, *a.* marbled, marble (as *a.*).
marmorete, *m.* (print.) vignette, small cut.
marmota, *f.* (zool.) marmot; worsted cap.
maro, *m.* (bot.) germander, marum.
marojo, *m.* (bot.) red-berried mistletoe.
maroma, *f.* rope, cable.
maromero, ra, *n.* tight-rope dancer.
marón, *m.* (ichth.) sturgeon.
marqué, marque, *v. V.* MARCAR.
marqués, *m.* marquis.**—marquesa,** marchioness; marquee.**—marquesado,** *m.* marquisate.
marquesina, *f.* marquee, awning.
[1]**marquesita,** *f.* (min.) marcasite, white pyrites.
[2]**marquesita,** *f.* small armchair.
marquesote, *m.* ancient stiff, high collar; (Mex.) caramel, burnt sugar.
marqueta, *f.* crude cake of wax.
marquetería, *f.* cabinetwork; marquetry, checkered or inlaid work.
marquilla, *f.* demy, a particular size of paper.
marquito, *m. dim.* small frame.
[1]**marra,** *f.* lack, want; defect.
[2]**marra,** *f.* stone hammer.
márraga, *f.* ticking.
marrajo, ja. I. *a.* cunning, artful, wily. **II.** *m.* (ichth.) shark.
[1]**marrana,** *f.* sow, female pig; (coll.) dirty or unprincipled woman.
[2]**marrana,** *f.* axle of a NORIA, water wheel.
marranada, *f.* (coll.) hoggish action; nastiness, filthiness.
marranalla, *f.* rabble.
marranamente, *adv.* piggishly, swinishly.
marrancho, cha, *n.* pig, hog; dirty person.
marranchón, na, *n.* hog (sow).
marranillo, *m.* little pig.
[1]**marrano, na,** *n.* hog; (coll.) dirty or unprincipled person.
[2]**marrano,** *m.* drum of a water wheel; woodwork supporting a well; board to equalize pressure in oil mills.
marrar, *vn.* to deviate from the right; to lack, fail; to miss.
marras, *adv.* (coll.) long ago, long since, whilom.
marrasquino, *m.* maraschino.
marrazo, *m.* mattock.
marrear, *va.* to strike with a stone hammer.
márrega, *f.,* **marregón,** *m.* straw bed.
marrillo, *m.* thick short stick.
marro, *m.* a game resembling quoits; slip or slide of pursued game to avoid capture; miss, failure; catstick for playing tipcat.
[1]**marrón,** *m.* quoit.
[2]**marrón, na,** *a.* (Angl.) maroon, brown.
marroquí, *m.* morocco (leather); also **marroquín, na,** *n.* & *a.* Moroccan.
marrubio, *m.* (bot.) white horehound.
marrueco, ca, *n.* & *a.* Moroccan.
Marruecos, *m.* Morocco.
marrullería, *f.* wheedling, cajolery.
marrullero, ra, *n.* wheedler, coaxer, deceiver.
marsellés, sa. I. *a.* of or pertaining to Marseilles. **II.** *m.* short jacket. **III.** *f.* Marseillaise, French national anthem.
marso, sa, *n.* & *a.* Marsian (one of, or pertaining to, the Marsi).
marsopa, marsopla, *f.* blunt-headed whale.
marsupial, *a.* & *m.* (zool.) marsupial.
marta, *f.* (zool.) pine marten and its fur.
[1]**martagón, na,** *n.* (coll.) shrewd person.
[2]**martagón,** *m.* (bot.) wild lily.
Marte, *m.* (astr.) Mars.
martellina, *f.* marteline, millstone hammer.
martes, *m.* Tuesday.**—m. de carnestolendas,** Shrove Tuesday.
martillada, *f.* blow with a hammer.
martillador, ra, *n.* & *a.* hammerer(-ing).
martillar, *va.* to hammer.
martillazo, *m.* blow with a hammer.
martillejo, *m. dim.* small hammer.
martilleo, *m.* hammering; clatter.
martillo, *m.* hammer; claw hammer; tuning hammer; auction rooms; (anat.) malleus.**—a macha m.,** strongly but roughly made.**—a m.,** with a hammer; by hammering.**—de m.,** (of metals) wrought.
Martín (San), *m.* season for killing hogs.— **llegarle a uno su San M.,** every dog has his day.
martín del río, *m.* (ornith.) = MARTINETE.
martín pescador, *m.* (ornith.) kingfisher.
[1]**martinete,** *m.* (ornith.) a heronlike bird and its tuft of white feathers.
[2]**martinete,** *m.* drop hammer; pile driver; hammer of a pianoforte.**—m. basculante,** tilting

hammer.—**m. de fragua,** trip hammer.—**m. para clavar pilotes,** pile driver.
martingala, *f.* breeches worn under armor; stake in the game of monte.
martinico, *m.* (coll.) ghost.
martiniega, *f.* tax payable on St. Martin's day.
mártir, *n.* martyr.
martiricé, martirice, *v. V.* MARTIRIZAR.
martirio, *m.* martyrdom; torture; grief.
martirizador, ra. I. *n.* martyrizer. **II.** *a.* martyrizing; tormenting, agonizing.
martirizar, *va.* (*pret.* MARTIRICÉ; *subj.* MARTIRICE) to martyr; to martyrize; to torment.
martirologio, *m.* martyrology.
marullo, *m.* (naut.) sea wave.
marxismo, *m.* Marxism.
marxista, *n.* & *a.* Marxist.
marzadga, *f.* tax payable in March.
marzal, *a.* pertaining to the month of March.
marzo, *m.* March, third month.
marzoleta, *f.* (bot.) fruit of the hawthorn.
marzoleto, *m.* (bot.) white hawthorn.
[1]**mas,** *m.* farmhouse and stock.
[2]**mas,** *m.* (P. I.) weight for gold and silver (58 grains).
[3]**mas,** *conj.* = PERO, but.—**m. que,** even if; however much.
más. I. *a.* more; most; (math.) plus.—**el signo m.,** the plus sign.—**los m.,** the largest number; the majority; most people. **II.** *adv.* more; most; longer; longest; over, besides, moreover; rather.—**m. adelante,** later on.—**m. allá,** farther on.—**m. bien,** rather.—**m. bien que,** rather than.—**m. de** (of quantity) more than, over.—**m. que,** more than; but only; even if. —**m. tarde o m. temprano,** sooner or later. —**a lo m.,** at most.—**a m.,** besides.—**a m. correr,** with the utmost speed.—**a m. de,** in addition to, besides; besides being.—**a m. tardar,** at the latest.—**a m. y mejor,** greatly, highly, at best; excellently.—**como el que m.,** as (good, well, much) as the best. second to none (often diff. constr.).—**de m.,** over, extra; too much, too many.—**de m. a m.,** besides, moreover.—**en m. (de),** more (than), above, over.—**lo m. antes,** as soon as possible.—**no m.,** not any more; only.—**no m. que,** not more than, only; nothing more than (*no tengo más que dos hijos,* I have only two children; *no vino más que Juan,* only John came, no one came but John; *usted no necesita más que escribir a la casa,* you need only to write to the firm).—**por m. que,** however much; no matter how.—**sin m. acá ni m. allá,** suddenly, without any reason.—**sin m. ni m.,** without much ado, without any to-do.
masa, *f.* dough; (mason.) mortar; (phys.) mass; volume, lump; aggregation, union; crowd of people; nature, disposition.—**las masas,** the masses.
masada, *f.* farmhouse and stock.
masadero, *m.* farmer.
masaje, *m.* massage.
masajista, *n.* massager; *m.* masseur; *f.* masseuse.
masar, *va.* to knead; (med.) to massage.
masato, *m.* (Am.) a flavored drink made with corn or rice and sugar.
mascabado, da, *a.* raw, unrefined (sugar).
mascada, *f.* (Mex.) silk handkerchief.
mascador, ra, *n.* chewer, masticator.
mascadura, *f.* chewing, mastication.
mascar, *va.* (*pret.* MASQUÉ; *subj.* MASQUE) to chew, masticate; (coll.) to mumble.
máscara. I. *f.* mask.—**m. antigás,** gas mask.—**m. de oxígeno,** oxygen mask.—*pl.* masquerade. **II.** *n.* mask, masquerader.
mascarada, *f.* masquerade, mummery.
mascarero, ra, *n.* dealer in masks.
mascarilla, *f. dim.* half mask; death mask.
mascarón, *m. aug.* hideous mask, (arch.) grotesque face.—**m. de proa,** (naut.) figurehead.
mascota, *f.* (Am.) mascot; good-luck charm.
mascujar, *vn.* (coll.) to masticate with difficulty; to mumble.
masculinidad, *f.* masculinity, manhood.
masculinizar. I. *va.* to make masculine. **II.** *vr.* (of women) to become mannish.
masculino, na, *a.* masculine; male.
mascullar, *va.* to mumble.
masecoral, *m.* sleight of hand, legerdemain.
masejicomar, *m.* = MASECORAL.
masera, *f.* kneading trough; cloth for covering the dough.
masería, masía, *f.* farmhouse.
masetero, *m.* (anat.) masseter.
masica, *f.* (C. A.) breadnut tree.
masicote, *m.* (chem.) massicot.
masiliense, *a.* of Marseilles.
masilla, *f. dim.* little mass; putty; mastic.
masita, *f.* pittance retained for providing a soldier with shoes, etc.
maslo, *m.* root of the tail of quadrupeds.
[1]**masón,** *m. aug.* mess of dough fed to fowls.
[2]**masón,** *m.* Freemason, Mason.
masonería, *f.* Freemasonry.
masónico, ca, *a.* Masonic.
masonismo, *m.* Masonry, Freemasonry.
masoquismo, *m.* (psych.) masochism.
masoquista, *n.* (psych.) masochist.
masovero, *m.* farmer.
masqué, masque, *v. V.* MASCAR.
masterillo, *m. dim.* (naut.) topgallant and royal mast.
mastelero, *m.* (naut.) topmast.—**masteleros de respeto,** spare topmasts.
masticación, *f.* mastication.
masticador, ra. I. *n.* & *a.* masticator(-ing). **II.** *n.* MASTIGADOR; chopper.
masticar, *va.* (*pret.* MASTIQUÉ; *subj.* MASTIQUE) to masticate, to chew; to ruminate, meditate about.
masticatorio, ria, *m.* & *a.* masticatory.
mastigador, *m.* bit for a horse.
mástil, *m.* (naut., radio) mast; upright post of a bed or loom; stanchion; shank of an auger; trunk or stem of a tree; wide breeches worn by Indians; neck (of violin, guitar, etc.).
mastín, *m.* mastiff.—**m. danés,** Great Dane (dog).
mástique, *m.* mastic; mastic tree.
mastiqué, mastique, *v. V.* MASTICAR.
mastitis, *f.* (med.) mastitis.
masto, *m.* stock into which a scion is grafted.
mastodonte, *m.* mastodon.
mastoideo, dea; mastoidal, *a.* = MASTOIDES.
mastoides. I. *a.* mastoid. **II.** *m.* (anat.) mastoid process.
mastoiditis, *f.* (med.) mastoiditis.
mastranto, mastranzo, *m.* round-leaved mi[illegible]
mastuerzo, *m.* dolt, simpleton; (bot.) common cress.
masturbacion, *f.* masturbation.
masturbarse, *vr.* to masturbate.
masurio, *m.* (chem.) masurium.
masvale, *m.* = MALVASÍA.
[1]**mata,** *f.* (bot.) plant; sprig, blade; grove, orchard; mastic tree; head (of hair).—**m. parda,** young evergreen oak.
[2]**mata,** *f.* (min.) matte, regulus, white metal.
[3]**mata,** *f.* = MATARRATA.
matacán, *m.* poison for killing dogs; (bot.) dog's-bane; nux vomica; hare previously hunted; pebble, stone; (fort.) machicolation gallery; deuce of clubs in some card games.
matacandelas, *f.* candle extinguisher.
matacandil, *m.* (prov.) lobster.
matacía, *f.* slaughter, death.
mataco, ca, *n.* (Am.) Chaco Indian; (Am.) (zool.) a kind of armadillo.
[1]**matachín,** *m.* merry-andrew; dance performed by grotesque figures.
[2]**matachín,** *m.* butcher; butcher's knife.
matadero, *m.* slaughterhouse; drudgery.
matador, ra. I. *n.* & *a.* killer(-ing). **II.** *m.* mata-

dor (bullfighter who kills the bull); (card playing) matador.
matadura, *f.* (vet.) sore, gall.
matafuego, *m.* fire extinguisher; fireman.
matagallina, *f.* (bot.) = TORVISCO, daphne.
matahambre, *m.* (Cuba) marzipan.
matahombres, *m.* (entom.) a beetle.
matajudío, *m.* (ichth.) = MÚJOL, mullet.
matalahuga, matalahuva, *f.* = ANÍS, anise.
matalobos, *m.* (bot.) wolfsbane, aconite.
matalón, *m.* old worn-out horse.
matalotaje, *m.* (naut.) ship stores; (coll.) heap, mess, jumble.
matalote, *m.* = MATALÓN.
matancero, ra, *n.* & *a.* of or pertaining to Matanzas, Cuba.
matanza, *f.* slaughter, butchery; hog slaughtering and the season when it is done; swine kept for slaughter; (coll.) obstinacy, eagerness.
matapalo, *m.* (bot.) (Am.) tree yielding caoutchouc and a fibre for sackcloth.
mataperrada, *f.* boy's mischievous prank.
mataperros, *m.* (coll.) street urchin.
matapiojos, *m.* (Am.) dragon fly.
matapolvo, *m.* light rain that just lays the dust.
matapulgas, *f.* (bot.) mint.
matar. I. *va.* to kill; to put out (a light); to extinguish (fire); to slake (lime); to harass, worry, vex; to make (a horse's back) sore by the rubbing of the harness; to mark (cards for cheating); (cards) to beat, top (opponent's card); to mat (metal); (carp.) to bevel, round; (art) to tone down.—**m. a dos pájaros del mismo tiro**, to kill two birds with one stone.—**m. de aburrimiento**, (fig.) to bore to death.—**m. de hambre**, to starve.—**m. el tiempo**, to kill time.—**a mata caballo**, in the greatest hurry.—**estar a m. con**, to be at drawn daggers with.—**mátalas callando**, (coll.) hypocrite, sly dog. **II.** *vr.* to kill oneself; to get killed.
matarife, *m.* slaughterman.
matarrata, *f.* a card game.
matasanos, *m.* (coll.) quack, charlatan; empiric.
matasellos, *m.* post office cancelling stamp.
matasiete, *m.* bully, braggart.
[1]**mate. I.** *a.* mat, dull, lusterless. **II.** *m.* gold or silver sizing; (chess) checkmate.—**m. ahogado**, (chess) stale-mate.—**dar m.**, (chess) to checkmate; (coll.) to make fun of, laugh at (a person).
[2]**mate**, *m.* (bot.) Brazilian holly; maté, Paraguay tea; vessel in which maté is made; gourd.
matear, *vn.* (agr.) to extend and shoot forth (as wheat, etc.); to hunt among the bushes.
matemática, *f.*, **matemáticas**, *f. pl.* mathematics.
matemáticamente, *adv.* mathematically.
matemático, ca. I. *a.* mathematical. **II.** *n.* mathematician.
materia, *f.* matter; material, substance, stuff; subject, topic; subject matter; cause, occasion; (med.) matter, pus.—**m. extraña**, foreign matter.—**m. médica**, materia medica.—**m. prima**, raw material.—**materias de estado**, affairs of state.—**en m. de**, as regards, in the matter of.—**entrar en m.**, to come to the point, get down to business.
material. I. *a.* material; rude, coarse, matter-of-fact. **II.** *m.* ingredient; material, stuff; (print.) copy; (elec. and Ry.) equipment.—**m. de desecho**, salvage.—**m. rodante**, (Ry.) rolling stock.—*pl.* **materiales brutos** or **crudos**, raw material(s).
materialidad, *f.* materiality, corporeity; outward appearance; literalness; (theol.) materiality.
materialismo, *m.* materialism.
materialista, *n.* & *a.* materialist(-ic).
materialización, *f.* materialization.
materializar. I. *va.* to materialize. **II.** *vr.* to become (morally) materialistic.
materialmente, *adv.* materially, corporeally; physically; absolutely.
maternal, *a.* maternal.—**maternalmente**, *adv.* maternally.
maternidad, *f.* maternity.
materno, na, *a.* maternal, motherly; mother (as *a.*).
matero, ra, *n.* maté drinker.
matihuelo, *m.* = DOMINGUILLO, tumbler (toy).
matinal, *a.* (poet.) = MATUTINAL.
matiné, *m.* matinée.
matiz, *m.* tint, hue, shade; blending of colors.
matizado, da, *a.* & *pp.* variegated, many-hued.
matizar, *va.* to variegate, blend (colors); to tint, give a special tint to.
mato, *m.* brake, coppice.
matojo, *m.* bush; (bot.) glasswort; (Cuba) shoot, sucker, tiller.
matón, *m.* (coll.) bully, hector, browbeater.
matorral, *m.* heath, brake; thicket, copse; bush.
matoso, sa, *a.* heathlike; weedy.
matraca, *f.* wooden rattle; (coll.) jest, chaff.—**dar m.**, to banter.
matraquear, *va.* to rattle; to scoff, banter.
matraqueo, *m.* (coll.) rattling noise; banter.
matraquista, *n.* wag, jester, banterer.
matraz, *f.* (chem.) matrass, a glass vessel.
matrería, *f.* shrewdness.
matrero, ra. I. *a.* cunning, sagacious, shrewd. **II.** *m.* artful knave.
matriarca, *f.* matriarch.
matriarcado, *m.* matriarchate.
matricaria, *f.* (bot.) common feverfew.
matricida, *n.* matricide (murderer).
matricidio, *m.* matricide (murder).
matrícula, *f.* register, list; matricula; matriculation.—**m. de mar**, mariner's register.
matriculación, *f.* matriculation.
matriculado, da, *n.* & *a.* matriculate.
matriculador, ra, *n.* matriculator.
matricular. I. *va.* & *vr.* to matriculate, register, enroll. **II.** *vr.* to enter (a contest, etc.).
matrimonesco, ca, *a.* (humor.) matrimonial.
matrimonial, *a.* matrimonial.
matrimonialmente, *adv.* matrimonially.
matrimoniar, *va.* to marry.
matrimonio, *m.* marriage, matrimony; married couple.—**m. de la mano izquierda**, morganatic marriage.
matritense, *n.* & *a.* Madrilenean.
matriz. I. *a.* first, principal, main, parent, chief. **II.** *f.* (anat.) uterus, womb; (mech.) mold, form, matrix, die; original draft of a writing; female screw, nut.
matrona, *f.* matron; midwife.
matronal, *a.* matronal.
maturrango, ga, *n.* (Am., coll.) poor (bad) horseman; clumsy, rough person.
matute, *m.* smuggling; smuggled goods; gambling den.—**matutear**, *va.* to smuggle.
matutero, ra, *n.* smuggler.
matutinal; matutino, na, *a.* matutinal, morning (as *a.*).
maula. I. *f.* frippery, rubbish, trumpery, trash; cunning, craft; deceitful trick. **II.** *n.* (coll.) trickster, cheat, bad pay; sluggard, drone.—**maulería**, *f.* shop where remnants are sold; craft, cunning, trickery.—**maulero, ra**, *n.* seller of remnants; trickster, cheat, swindler.
maullador, ra, *a.* mewing (cat).
maullar, *vn.* to mew.
maullido, maúllo, *m.* mew.
mauraca, *f.* roasting chestnuts, etc., over coals in the open air.
Mauritania, *f.* Mauritania.
mauritano, na, *n.* & *a.* Mauritanian.
mauseolo, mausoleo, *m.* mausoleum.
mauveína, *f.* (chem.) mauveine (violet dye).
maxilar. I. *a.* maxillary. **II.** *m.* maxillary bone, jaw.—**m. inferior**, inferior, or lower, maxillary.—**m. superior**, superior, or upper, maxillary.
máxima, *f.* maxim; rule; (mus.) maxima.
máximamente, máxime, *adv.* principally, specially.
máximo, ma. I. *a.* maximum.—**m. común**

divisor, greatest common divisor. **II.** *m.* maximum. Also **máximum.**
máxwel, maxwelio, *m.* (elec.) maxwell.
[1]**maya,** *f.* (bot.) common daisy; variety of pineapple; May queen.
[2]**maya,** *n.* & *a.* Maya, Yucatan Indian and language.
mayador, ra, *a.* mewing.
mayal, *m.* flail; thrashing instrument; lever in oil mills.
mayar, *vn.* to mew.
mayear, *vn.* (of the weather) to be like May.
mayo, *m.* month of May; Maypole; Mayday festivity.
mayólica, *f.* majolica ware.
mayonesa, *f.* mayonnaise dressing; cold dish dressed with mayonnaise.
mayor. I. *a.* greater; greatest; larger; largest; older, elder; oldest, eldest; senior; of age; main, principal; high (altar, mass); major; (mus.) major.—**m. edad,** (of age) majority.—**la m. parte (de),** the majority (of). **II.** *m.* superior; major or chief of a community; chief clerk; (mil.) major.—*pl.* ancestors, forefathers; superiors; elders.—**m. de edad,** of age.—**m. general,** major general.—**por m.,** (by) wholesale; summarily. **III.** *f.* (logic) major.—*pl.* (naut.) the three mainsails of a ship.
mayoral, *m.* head shepherd; leader; overseer, foreman, steward; stage driver.
mayoralía, *f.* flock, herd; herdsman's wages.
mayorana, *f.* (bot.) = MEJORANA, marjoram.
mayorazga, *f.* woman owner, or wife of owner, ot an entailed estate.
mayorazgo, *m.* right of primogeniture; first-born son; family estate; entailed estate.
mayorazguista, *m.* author who treats of entails.
mayordoma, *f.* steward's wife; stewardess, housekeeper.
mayordomear, *va.* to administer, manage.
mayordomía, *f.* administration, stewardship, controllership.
mayordomo, *m.* steward, butler; manager; majordomo.
mayoría, *f.* majority (in age or number); superiority; majorship.—**m. absoluta,** (pol.) majority (more than half of the total).—**m. relativa,** plurality.
mayoridad, *f.* superiority; full age.
mayorista, *m.* pupil of highest classes in grammar schools; (Am.) wholesale merchant.
mayoritario, ria, *a.* majority.
mayormente, *adv.* principally, chiefly.
mayúscula, *a.* & *f.* capital (letter).
mayúsculo, la, *a.* large, good-sized; important, prominent.
maza, *f.* war club; mace; pile driver; drop hammer; nave or hub of a wheel; hemp brake; drumstick of a bass drum; roller of a sugarcane mill; thick end of a billiard cue; something noisy tied to a dog's tail.—**m. de Fraga,** steam hammer.
mazacote, *m.* kali, barilla (herb); concrete; dry, tough mass; (coll.) bore, tiresome person.
mazada, *f.* blow with club or mallet.—**dar m.,** to cause harm or injury.
mazagatos, *m.* noisy wrangle, quarrel, row.
mazamorra, *f.* crumbs, small bits; a sort of corn pap, much used in Peru and Colombia; (Colomb.) a kind of thick corn soup; (Arg., Colomb.) boiled whole corn; (naut.) mess made of broken hardtack.
mazaneta, *f.* apple-shaped ornament in jewels.
mazapán, *m.* a sort of marzipan.
mazar, *va.* to churn (milk).
mazarí, *m.* tile-shaped brick.
mazarota, *f.* (foundry) deadhead, sprue.
mazdeísmo, *m.* Mazdaism, Mazdeism.
mazdeísta, *n.* & *a.* Mazdaist(-dean).
mazmorra, *f.* underground dungeon.
mazo, *m.* mallet, maul, wooden hammer; bundle, bunch; clapper of a bell; tiresome person, bore.
mazonería, *f.* stone masonry; (art) relief or relievo-work.
mazorca, *f.* spindleful (of yarn); ear of corn; (arch.) spindle-shaped baluster.
mazorral, *a.* rude, uncouth; (print.) solid.
mazorralmente, *adv.* grossly, rudely.
mazurca, *f.* (dance) mazurka.
me, *pers. pron., 1st pers, sing., dat., acc.; refl. of* YO.
meadero, *m.* urinal.
meados, *m. pl.* urine.
[1]**meaja,** *f.* crumb.—**m. de huevo,** plasma bit of an egg.
[2]**meaja,** *f.* (law) execution dues.
meajuela, *f.* small piece attached to the bits of a bridle.
meandro, *m.* meander; (arch.) maze scroll-work; intricate ornamentation.
mear, *vn.* to urinate, make water.
meato, *m.* (anat.) opening or canal, meatus.
meauca, *f.* (ornith.) a kind of sea gull.
meca, *f.*—**de Ceca en M.,** or **de la Ceca a la M.,** to and fro, hither and thither.
mecánica, *f.* mechanics; machinery; (coll.) mean, despicable action or thing; (mil.) management of soldiers' affairs.—**m. celeste,** celestial mechanics.—**m. cuántica,** quantum mechanics.
mecánicamente, *adv.* mechanically.
mecanicismo, *m.* (biol. & philos.) mechanistic system or theory.
mecanicista, *n.* & *a.* mechanist(-ic).
mecánico, ca. I. *a.* mechanical; machine-made or operated; power-driven; mean, servile. **II.** *n.* mechanician; mechanist; mechanic, handicraftsman, artisan.—**m. de vuelo,** flight engineer.
mecanismo, *m.* mechanism, works (of machines); gearing; device.—**m. buscablancos,** (artil., electron.) target-seeking device.—**m. de arranque,** (auto.) starter.—**m. de cremallera,** (mech.) rackwork.—**m. de dirección,** (auto.) steering gear.—**m. de transmisión,** (auto.) drive.
mecanización, *f.* mechanization.
mecanizar, *va.* to mechanize.
mecanografía, *f.* typewriting.—**m. a ciegas,** touch typing.
mecanografiar, *va.* to typewrite, type.
mecanográfico, ca, *a.* typewritten; pertaining to typewriting.
mecanografista, *n.* = MECANÓGRAFO.
mecanógrafo, fa, *n.* typist.
mecanorregulable, *a.* power-controlled.
mecapal, *m.* (Mex.) leather band with ropes used by porters.
mecate, *m.* (Mex.) maguey rope or cord.
mecedero, *m.* stirrer.
mecedor, ra. I. *a.* rocking, swinging. **II.** *m.* stirrer; swing. **III.** *f.* rocking chair.
mecedura, *f.* rocking.
mecer. I. *va.* (*ind.* MEZO; *subj.* MEZA) to stir, agitate, mix; to rock; to shake; to swing; to dandle (a child). **II.** *vr.* to rock, swing, sway; to soar.
mecereo, mecereón, *m.* (bot.) mezereon.
meco, ca. I. *a.* (Mex.) (of animals) blackish red. **II.** *n.* (Mex.) wild Indian.
meconato, *m.* (chem.) meconate.
mecónico, ca, *a.* (chem.) meconic.
meconio, *m.* meconium, first excrement of newborn baby; (pharm.) meconium, poppy juice.
mecha, *f.* wick; fuse (of explosive); match, match cord; slice of bacon (for larding); lock of hair; bundle of threads or fibres; (surg.) roll of lint used as a drain.
mechar, *va.* (cook.) to lard (meat, etc.).
mechazo, *m.* (min.) fizzle of a blast fuse.
mechera, *f.* larding pin; shoplifter.
mechero, *m.* candlestick socket; lamp burner; gas burner.
mechinal, *m.* (mason.) columbarium, putlog hole.
mechoacán, *m.* (bot.) mechoacan bindweed.

mechón, *m. aug.* large lock of hair; large fuse; bundle of threads.
mechoso, sa, *a.* having abundant locks of hair.
medalla, *f.* medal; (sculpture) plaque, medallion; (coll.) gold coin.
medallón, *m. aug.* large medal; locket; (arch.) medallion.
médano, medaño, *m.* sand bank; dune.
medero, *m.* heap of vine shoots.
media, *f.* stocking; hose; (Am.) sock; (math.) mean; average.—**m. diaria,** daily average.—**m. diferencial,** (math.) arithmetical mean.—**m. elástica,** elastic stocking.—**m. proporcional,** geometrical mean, mean proportional.
mediacaña, *f.* (arch.) concave molding, fluted molding; picture molding; (carp.) gouge; half-round file; curling tongs for the hair.
mediación, *f.* mediation; intercession.
mediado, da. I. *pp.* of MEDIAR. **II.** *a.* half-filled, half-full.—*pl.* **a mediados de,** (of a period of time) about the middle of.
mediador, ra, *n.* mediator; intercessor.
mediana, *f.* long billiard cue; top of a fishing rod; (geom.) median.
medianamente, *adv.* middling, so so, fairly.
medianejo, ja, *a.* (coll.) hardly mediocre.
medianería, *f.* partition wall; sharecropping.
medianero, ra. I. *a.* mediating, interceding; intermediate. **II.** *n.* mediator, go-between; owner of a house having a common wall with another; (agr.) sharecropper.
medianía, medianidad, *f.* halfway; mediocrity; middle state; moderate means.
medianil, *m.* (agr.) middle piece of ground; (print.) crossbar of a chase.
mediano, na, *a.* moderate, middling, medium; mediocre, bad, insignificant.
medianoche, *f.* midnight; small meat pie.
mediante. I. *a.* intervening; interceding. **II.** *adv.* by means of, by virtue of, with the help of, through.
mediar, *vn.* to reach or be at the middle; to intercede, mediate; to intervene.
mediastino, *m.* (anat.) mediastinum.
mediatamente, *adv.* mediately, indirectly.
mediato, ta, *a.* mediate.
mediator, *m.* ombre, a card game.
médica, *f.* doctor's wife; woman physician.
medicable, *a.* curable, medicable.
medicación, *f.* medical treatment, medication.
medicamento, *m.* medicine, medicament.
medicamentoso, sa, *a.* medicinal.
medicastro, *m.* quack, charlatan, medicaster.
medicina, *f.* medicine; medicament, remedy.—**m. preventiva,** preventive medicine.—**m. social,** social medicine.—**m. socializada,** socialized medicine.
medicinal, *a.* medicinal.
medicinante, *n.* healer; medical student who practices before taking his degree.
medicinar, *va.* to treat (a patient).
medición, *f.* measurement; measuring.
médico, ca. I. *a.* medical. **II.** *n.* physician.
medicolegal, *a.* medicolegal.
medicucho, *m.* quack, charlatan, medicaster.
medida, *f.* measure; (shoe, etc.) size, number; standard, gauge; measuring, measurement; measuring stick; rule; moderation, prudence; (math., mus., poet., dance) measure.—**m. agraria,** land measure.—**m. de capacidad,** measure of capacity.—**m. de longitud,** measure of length.—**m. de superficie,** square measure.—**m. para áridos,** dry measure.—**m. para líquidos,** liquid measure.—**a la m.,** to order, custom-made.—**a m. del deseo,** according to one's wishes.—**a m. que,** as, according as, at the same time as, while.—**colmar la m.,** to be the last straw.—**colmarse,** or **llenarse, la m.,** to drain the cup of sorrow.—**sin m.,** to excess.—**tener m.,** to have a sense of proportion.—**tomar medidas,** to take measures or steps.
medidamente, *adv.* moderately.
medido, da, *a.* measured.
medidor, ra, *n.* measurer; *m.* meter, measuring device.—**m. de techo (de nubes),** ceilometer.
mediero, ra, *n.* hosier, dealer in stockings; knitter of stockings; co-partner in a farm or ranch.
medieval, *a.* medieval.
medievalidad, *f.* medieval quality or character.
medievismo, *m.* medievalism.
medievista, *n.* medievalist.
medio, dia. I. *a.* & *adv.* half; partial; mid, middle; halfway, midway; mean, intermediate.—**m. amartillado,** half-cocked.—**m. bocel,** (arch.) torus, kind of molding.—**m. colonia,** silk ribbon one finger wide.—**m. corona,** half crown (English money).—**m. cuchara,** (fig.) person of mediocre wit or skill.—**m. china,** cloth coarser than China silk.—**m. día,** midday; half holiday.—**m. docena,** half dozen.—**m. dólar,** half dollar.—**m. hermana,** half sister, stepsister, (law) half-blood.—**m. hermano,** half brother, stepbrother, (law) half-blood.—**m. hora,** half-hour.—**m. luna,** (fort.) half-moon.—**m. luto,** half mourning.—**m. luz,** half light.—**m. naranja,** (coll.) better half (wife or husband).—**m. noche,** midnight.—**m. paga,** half pay.—**m. pasaje,** half fare.—**m. pasta,** (bookbinding) half-leather binding, half binding.—**m. relieve,** demi-relief.—**m. suela,** half sole.—**m. talla,** half relief.—**m. tinta,** (f. a.) half-tone.—**m. vuelta,** right about face.—**a m.,** half (closed, etc.).—**a m. asta,** at half mast.—**a medias,** by halves, halfway, partially.—**a m. mogate,** carelessly, heedlessly.—**de m. gala,** in dress uniform.—**el m. oriente,** the Middle East.—**ir a medias,** to go halves. **II.** *m.* middle, center; (often *pl.*) means, method, measure, way; (surrounding) medium; (spiritualistic) medium; (arith.) half; (Am., football) halfback.—*pl.* means, resources; hosiery.—**m. diferencial,** arithmetical mean.—**m. proporcional,** mean proportional.—**de m. a m.,** half and half; in the middle; completely, entirely.—**de por m.,** between.—**echar por en m.,** to take the bull by the horns; to make up one's mind, happen what may.—**en m.,** in the middle; midway; in the midst.—**por m. de,** by means of.
mediocre, *a.* mediocre.
mediocridad, *f.* mediocrity.
mediodía, *m.* noon, midday; south.—**en pleno m.,** in broad daylight.
medioeval, *a.* medieval.
mediopaño, *m.* thin woollen cloth.
mediquillo, *m.* medicaster; (P. I.) medicine man.
medir. I. *va.* (*ger.* MIDIENDO; *ind. pres.* MIDO, *pret.* él MIDIÓ; *subj.* MIDA) to measure; to compare, weigh, judge, value; to scan (verses).—**m. el suelo,** (coll.) to fall flat on the ground. **II.** *vr.* to be moderate; to act with prudence.
meditabundo, da, *a.* pensive, musing.
meditación, *f.* meditation.
meditar, *va.* & *vn.* to meditate, muse.
meditativo, va, *a.* meditative.
mediterráneo, nea, *a.* mediterranean; inland.
médium, *m.* spiritualistic medium.
medo, da, *n.* & *a.* Mede(-ian).
medra, *f.* thrift; success, improvement.
medrana, *f.* (coll.) fear.
medrar, *vn.* to thrive, prosper.
medriñaque, *m.* Philippine stuff for lining and stiffening women's skirts; short skirt.
medro, *m.* = MEDRA.—*pl.* progress, improvement.
medrosamente, *adv.* timorously, faintly.
medroso, sa, *a.* timorous, faint-hearted, cowardly; terrible, dreadful.
medula, médula, *f.* marrow, medulla; (bot.) pith; substance, essence.—**m. espinal,** spinal cord.—**m. oblonga,** or **m. oblongada,** medulla oblongata.

medular, *a.* medullar, medullary.
meduloso, sa, *a.* marrowy; pithy.
medusa, *f.* (ichth.) medusa, jellyfish.
meduseo, a, *a.* like, or relating to, Medusa.
mefistofélico, ca, *a.* Mephistophelean.
mefítico, ca, *a.* mephitic, foul, noxious.
megaciclo, *m.* (phys.) megacycle.
megáfono, *m.* megaphone.
megalítico, ca, *a.* (archeol.) megalithic.
megalito, *m.* (archeol.) megalith.
megalocéfalo, la, *a.* megalocephalous.
megalomanía, *f.* megalomania.
megalómano, na, *n.* & *a.* megalomaniac(-al).
megalópodo, da, *a.* (zool.) megapod.
megalosaurio, *m.* (paleontol.) megalosaur.
megamperio, *m.* (elec.) megampere.
mégano, *m.* = MÉDANO, dune.
megápodo, *m.* (ornith.) megapode.
megascopio, *m.* megascope.
megaterio, *m.* (paleontol.) megatherium.
megatón, *m.* (atom. ener.) megaton.
mego, ga, *a.* gentle, mild, meek, peaceful.
megohmio, *m.* (elec.) megohm.
mehari, *m.* a swift African dromedary.
mehedí, *m.* Mahdi, Mohammedan Messiah.
mejana, *f.* islet in the middle of a river.
mejicano, na, *n.* & *a.* Mexican.
mejido, da, *a.* beaten with sugar and water.
mejilla, *f.* cheek.
mejillón, *m.* a variety of mussel.
mejor. I. *a.* better; best.—**m. postor,** highest bidder.—**el m. día,** some fine day.—**lo m.,** the best. **II.** *adv.* better; best; rather.—**m. dicho,** rather, more properly, more exactly.—**m. que,** rather than, instead of.—**m. que m.,** better and better; better yet; all the better, so much the better.—**a lo m.,** when least expected; perhaps, maybe.—**tanto m.,** so much the better.
mejora, *f.* improvement; higher bid; appeal to a higher court; special bequest to a lawful heir.
mejorable, *a.* ameliorable, improvable.
mejoramiento, *m.* improvement, melioration.
mejorana, *f.* (bot.) sweet marjoram.
mejorar. I. *va.* to improve, better, enhance; to outbid; (law) to leave to (an heir) a special bequest besides his legal share. **II.** *vr.* & *vn.* to recover from a disease or calamity; to improve, grow better; to reform.
mejoría, *f.* improvement, betterment; advantage; superiority; improvement in health.
mejunje, *m.* medicinal or cosmetic mixture.
melada, *f.* toast soaked in honey.
melado, da. I. *pp.* of MELAR. **II.** *a.* honey-colored. **III.** *m.* cane-juice sirup; honey cake.
meladora, *f.* third sugar boiling pan in a triple-effect apparatus.
meladucha, *f.* coarse, mealy apple.
meladura, *f.* concentrated sirup, treacle.
meláfido, *m.* (geol.) melaphyre.
melampo, *m.* (theat.) candle with shade.
melancolía, *f.* melancholia, gloom, blues.
melancólico, ca, *a.* melancholy, sad, gloomy.
melancolizar, *va.* to affect with melancholy, to render gloomy and dejected, to dispirit.
melandro, *m.* (zool.) badger.
melanemia, *f.* (med.) melanæmia.
melanesio, sia, *n.* & *a.* Melanesian.
melanina, *f.* (biochem.) melanin.
melanita, *f.* (min.) melanite.
melanoma, *m.* (med.) melanoma.
melanosis, *f.* (med.) melanosis, black cancer.
melapia, *f.* a variety of apple.
[1]**melar,** *va.* (*ind.* MIELO; *subj.* MIELE) in sugar works, to boil clear; (of bees) to fill (the combs) with honey.
[2]**melar,** *a.* honey-sweet.
melaza, *f.* molasses; dregs of honey.
melca, *f.* = ZAHINA, (bot.) sorghum.
melcocha, *f.* molasses candy, taffy.
melcochero, ra, *n.* taffy maker or seller.
[1]**melena,** *f.* long hair in men; loose hair in women; animal mane; fleecy skin put under a yoke.—**traer a la m.,** to compel, force.
[2]**melena,** *f.* (med.) melaena, intestinal hemorrhage.
meleno, na, *n.* (coll.) rude, unkempt person.
melenudo, da, *a.* having bushy hair.
melera, *f.* woman who sells honey; melons spoiled by rain; (bot.) BUGLOSA, alkanet.
melero, *m.* dealer in honey; place where honey is kept.
melgacho, *m.* (ichth.) dogfish.
melgar, *m.* patch of wild alfalfa.
melgarejo, *m.* fish line and hook with a white rag for bait; (Bol.) a 30-cent coin.
meliáceo, cea, *a.* (bot.) meliaceous.
mélico, ca, *a.* lyrical, melic.
melífago, ga, *a.* meliphagous, feeding on honey.
melífero, ra, *a.* melliferous.
melificado, da, *a.* mellifluous, mellificent.
melificar, *vn.* (of bees) to make honey.
melifluamente, *adv.* mellifluently.
melifluidad, *f.* mellifluence.
melifluo, flua, *a.* mellifluous, honeyed, honey-tongued.
[1]**meliloto, ta,** *a.* silly, stupid.
[2]**meliloto,** *m.* (bot.) melilot, sweet clover.
melindre, *m.* a sort of fritter; lady finger; narrow ribbon; fastidiousness; prudery.
melindrear, *vn.* to act the prude.
melindrería, *f.* prudery; fastidiousness.
melindrero, ra. = MELINDROSO.
melindrillo, *m.* ferret, narrow tape.
melindroso, sa, *a.* finical, prudish.
melinita, *f.* melinite, a high explosive.
melisa, *f.* (bot.) melissa, balm.
melito, *m.* (pharm.) melissic sirup.
melocotón, *m.* (bot.) peach tree; peach.
melocotonero, ra. I. *n.* vender of peaches. **II.** *m.* peach tree.
melodía, *f.* (mus.) melody, melodiousness.
melódico, ca, *a.* melodic.
melodiosamente, *adv.* melodiously.
melodioso, sa, *a.* melodious.
melodista, *n.* melodist.
melodrama, *m.* melodrama.
melodramáticamente, *adv.* melodramatically.
melodramático, ca, *a.* melodramatic.
melófago, *m.* parasitic insect in sheep's wool.
melografía, *f.* art of writing music.
meloja, *f.* metheglin, mead.
melojar, *m.* white-oak plantation.
melojo, *m.* (bot.) a variety of white oak.
melolonta, *m.* (zool.) Melolontha, melolonthine.
melomania, *f.* fanatic love of music.
melómano, na, *n.* music fanatic.
[1]**melón,** *m.* (zool.) = [2]MELONCILLO.
[2]**melón,** *m.* (bot.) melon vine; muskmelon, cantaloupe.—**m. de agua,** watermelon.—**melonar,** *m.* field or bed of melons.—**meloncete,** *m. dim.* small melon.
[1]**meloncillo,** *m. dim.* small melon.
[2]**meloncillo,** *m.* (zool.) a kind of mongoose.
melonero, ra, *n.* melon raiser or dealer.
melosidad, *f.* sweetness, lusciousness; gentleness.
meloso, sa, *a.* honeylike, sweet; gentle.
melote, *m.* dregs of molasses; preserve made with honey.
melsa, *f.* spleen; phlegm, slowness.
mella, *f.* notch, nick, jag in edged tools; dent, indentation; hollow, gap.—**hacer m.,** to make an impression on the mind; to hurt, damage; affect.
mellado, da. I. *pp.* of MELLAR. **II.** *a.* toothless.
mellar, *va.* to jag, indent, notch; to injure (as honor, credit).
melliza, *f.* a kind of sausage made with honey.
mellizo, za, *n.* & *a.* twin (brother, sister).
mellón, *m.* torch made of straw.
membrado, da, *a.* (her.) membered.
membrana, *f.* membrane.—**m. alantoides,** allantoid membrane.—**m. caduca,** decidua.—**m. nictitante,** nictitating membrane.—**m.**

pituitaria, pituitary membrane, mucous membrane of the nostrils.
membranáceo, cea, *a.* (bot., zool.) membranaceous.
membranoso, sa, *a.* membranous.
membrete, *m.* memorandum, note; card of invitation; address; letter-head; heading.
membrilla, *f.* (bot.) a variety of quince.
membrillar, *m.* quince-tree orchard.
membrillero, *m.* (bot.) quince tree.
membrillo, *m.* quince; quince tree.
membrudamente, *adv.* robustly, strongly.
membrudo, da, *a.* strong, robust, muscular.
memento, *m.* (eccl.) Memento.
memo, ma, *a.* silly, foolish.
memorable, *a.* memorable.
memorablemente, *adv.* memorably.
memorando, da, *a.* = MEMORABLE.
memorándum, *m.* notebook; memorandum, note.
memorar, *va.* to remember.
memoratísimo, ma, *a. super.* worthy of eternal memory.
memoria, *f.* memory; recollection, remembrance; souvenir; memorial, memento, monumental record; report, statement; essay, paper, article; memorandum; codicil.—*pl.* compliments, regards; memoranda; rings used as reminders; memoirs.—**m. resbaladiza,** treacherous memory.—**de m.,** by heart.—**hablar de m.,** to talk at random.—**hacer m.,** to remember.—**renovar la m.,** to be reminiscent, to reminisce.—**tener en m.,** to remember.—**traer a la m. de uno,** to remind one.
memorial, *m.* memorandum book; memorial, petition; (law) brief.
memorialesco, ca, *a.* (humor.) pertaining to a memorial.
memorialista, *m.* amanuensis, secretary.
memorión, *m. aug.* great memory.
memorioso, sa, *a.* mindful, thoughtful.
[1]**mena,** *f.* (ichth.) small sea fish.
[2]**mena,** *f.* (min.) ore.
[3]**mena,** *f.* (naut.) size of cordage; (P. I.) size and shape of a cigar.
ménade, *f.* bacchante; woman in a frenzy.
menador, ra, *n.* winder of silk.
menaje, *m.* household furniture and other goods; school supplies or equipment.
menar, *va.* to wind (silk) on a jenny.
mención, *f.* mention.—**en m.,** mentioned, in question.—**mencionar,** *va.* to mention.
menchevique, *n.* Menshevik.
menchevismo, *m.* Menchevism.
mendacidad, *f.* mendacity, mendaciousness.
mendaz, *a.* mendacious, untruthful.
mendazmente, *adv.* mendaciously.
mendelevio, *m.* (chem.) mendelevium.
mendeliano, na, *a.* Mendelian.
mendelismo, *m.* Mendelism.
mendicación, *f.* begging.
mendicante. I. *a.* mendicant, begging. **II.** *m.* mendicant, beggar.
mendicidad, *f.* mendicity, mendicancy.
mendiganta, *f.* beggar, mendicant.
mendigante. I. *a.* begging, mendicant. **II.** *n.* beggar, mendicant.
mendigar, *va.* & *vn.* (*pret.* MENDIGUÉ; *subj.* MENDIGUE) to beg, mendicate; to entreat.
mendigo, ga, *n.* mendicant, beggar.
mendigué, mendigue, *v. V.* MENDIGAR.
mendiguez, *f.* beggary, mendicancy.
mendosamente, *adv.* falsely; mistakenly.
mendoso, sa, *a.* mendacious; mistaken.
mendrugo, *m.* crumb of bread given to beggars.
mendruguillo, *m. dim.* small crumb of bread.
meneador, ra, *n.* stirrer, shaker.
menear. I. *va.* to stir; to shake; to wag, waggle; to manage, direct.—**mejor es no meneallo,** or **peor es meneallo,** better let it alone; the less said, the better. **II.** *vr.* (coll.) to hustle, be active, get a move on; to wriggle, waggle, waddle.
meneo, *m.* shake, shaking; wagging, wriggling, waddling; (coll.) drubbing, beating; (aer.) bump, bumping, jolt due to air currents.
menester, *m.* need, want; employment, occupation, office.—*pl.* natural or bodily necessities; implements, tools of trade.—**haber m.,** to need.—**ser m.,** to be necessary.
menesteroso, sa, *a.* & *n.* needy, indigent (person).
menestra, *f.* pottage; vegetable soup.
menestral, *m.* mechanic, handicraftsman, workman.
menestrete, *m.* (naut.) nail puller.
menfita. I. *n.* native of Memphis. **II.** *f.* (min.) onyx.
mengajo, *m.* trailing rag.
Mengano, na, *n.* So-and-So.—**Fulano, Zutano y M.,** Tom, Dick and Harry.
mengua, *f.* diminution, waning, decrease; lack, want; poverty, indigence; disgrace.
menguadamente, *adv.* ignominiously.
menguado, da. I. *pp.* of MENGUAR. **II.** *a.* impaired, stunted; cowardly, pusillanimous; foolish; mean, miserly. **III.** *n.* poltroon; silly person; miser. **IV.** *m.* decrease; narrowing of stockings, in knitting.
menguamiento, *m.* = MENGUA.
menguante. I. *a.* decreasing, diminishing. **II.** *f.* ebb tide, low water, neap tide; decline, decay; decrease of the moon.
menguar, *vn.* to diminish, decrease, wane, fall off; to narrow (stockings).
mengue, *m.* (coll.) the deuce, the devil.
menhir, *m.* menhir, an upright slender monolith.
menina, *f.* young lady in attendance on the queen or the princesses.
meninge, *f.* (anat.) meninges.—**meníngeo, a,** *a.* meningeal.—**meningitis,** *f.* meningitis.
menino, *m.* noble page of the queen and princesses of Spain; little coxcomb.
menique, *a.* little finger.
menisco, *m.* (phys.) meniscus.
menispermáceo, cea, *a.* (bot.) menispermaceous.
menjuí, *m.* = BENJUÍ, benzoin.
menjunje, menjurje, *m.* = MEJUNJE, medicinal or cosmetic mixture.
menologio, *m.* (eccl.) menology.
menonita, *n.* & *a.* Mennonite.
menopausia, *f.* (med.) menopause, change of life in women.
menor. I. *a. compar.* of PEQUEÑO: smaller, less; smallest, least; minor; younger; youngest; (mus.) minor.—**m. edad,** minority, under age.—**II.** *n.* minor; (logic) minor premise; (mus.) minor; Minorite, Franciscan; (arch.) small block.—*pl.* (eccl.) minor orders.—**m. de edad,** minor.—**por m.,** by retail; minutely.
menorete.—**al m.,** or **por el m.,** (coll.) at least.
menoría, *f.* inferiority, subordination; under age.
menorista, *n.* (Am.) retail merchant.
menorquín, quina, *n.* & *a.* Minorcan.
menorragia, *f.* (med.) menorrhagia.
menos. I. *a.* less; least. **II.** *adv.* less; least.—**m. de,** or **m. que,** less than.—**al m.,** or **a lo m.,** at least; at the least.—**a m. de** (foll. by *inf.*), without (foll. by *pres. p.*).—**a m. que,** unless.—**de m.,** less; wanting, missing.—**echar m.,** to miss, feel the absence of; to have (inadvertently) left behind, come away without.—**en m.,** less; by less.—**lo m. posible,** the least possible.—**no ser para m.,** to give good cause or reason, justify (*estamos alarmados, pues las noticias no son para menos,* we are alarmed, as the news gives good reason to be; or considering the news, we may well be alarmed).—**poco más o m.,** more or less, about.—**por m. que,** almost, pretty nearly.—**por lo m.** = AL M.—**venir a m.,** to decline, grow worse; to become poor. **III.** *prep.* minus, less (*cuatro menos dos,* four minus two; *las ocho menos veinte,* twenty minutes to eight—lit. eight o'clock less twenty);

except, but, barring.—**todo m. eso,** anything but that, all but that.
menoscabador, ra, *n.* & *a.* impairer(-ing); defamer(-ing).
menoscabar, *va.* to impair, lessen, deteriorate, damage, harm; to defame.
menoscabo, *m.* impairment, damage, detriment, loss.—**con m. de,** to the detriment of.
menoscuenta, *f.* payment on account.
menospreciablemente, *adv.* contemptuously.
menospreciador, ra, *n.* contemner, despiser.
menospreciar, *va.* to underrate, undervalue; to despise, contemn, slight.—**menospreciativo, va,** *a.* despising, slighting, contemptuous.—**menosprecio,** *m.* undervaluation; contempt, scorn.
menostasia, *f.* (med.) amenorrhea.
mensaje, *m.* message; errand.
mensajería, *f.* stage line; steamship line.
mensajero, ra. I. *n.* messenger, carrier; errand boy or girl. **II.** *m.* (naut.) bull's-eye traveller; wooden thimble.
menstruación, *f.* menstruation.
menstrual, *a.* menstrual.
menstrualmente, *adv.* monthly, menstrually.
menstruante, *a.* menstruating.
menstruar, *vn.* to menstruate.
menstruo, a. I. *a.* monthly, menstrual. **II.** *m.* menses, courses; menstruation; (chem.) menstruum, a solvent.
menstruoso, sa. I. *a.* menstruous. **II.** *f.* (med.) menstruating female.
mensual, *a.* monthly.—**mensualidad,** *f.* monthly salary or allowance; monthly installment.—**mensualmente,** *adv.* monthly.
ménsula, *f.* (arch.) bracket; rest for the elbows.
mensura, *f.* measure.
mensurabilidad, *f.* mensurability.
mensurable, *a.* mensurable.
mensuración, *f.* mensuration.
mensurador, ra, *n.* measurer; *m.* meter.
mensural, *a.* mensural.
mensurar, *va.* to measure.
menta, *f.* (bot.) mint; peppermint.
mentado, da. I. *pp.* of MENTAR. **II.** *a.* famous or renowned; spoken-of.
mental, *a.* mental.—**mentalidad,** *f.* mentality.—**mentalmente,** *adv.* mentally.
mentar, *va.* (*ind.* MIENTO; *subj.* MIENTE) to mention, name.
mentastro, *m.* (bot.) = MASTRANZO, a mint.
mente, *f.* mind, understanding; sense, meaning; will, disposition.
mentecatada, mentecatería, mentecatez, *f.* foolishness, silliness, nonsense.
mentecato, ta. I. *a.* silly, foolish, stupid, crack-brained. **II.** *n.* fool.
mentidero, *m.* (coll.) place where people meet and gossip.
mentido, da. I. *pp.* of MENTIR. **II.** *a.* false, delusive.
mentilo, *m.* (chem.) menthyl.
mentir. I. *vn.* (*ind.* MIENTO; *subj.* MIENTA) to lie, prevaricate; to deceive, be misleading.—**¡miento!** I am mistaken (gen. to correct one's own statement). **II.** *va.* to disappoint, to fail to keep one's word or promise to.
mentira, *f.* lie, falsehood; fib; error, mistake in writing; (coll.) white spot on the nails.—**de mentiras,** in jest.—**parece m.,** it seems impossible, or incredible.
mentirilla, *f. dim.* little fib.—**de mentirillas,** in jest, for fun.
mentirón, *m. aug.* great lie.
mentirosamente, *adv.* lyingly, deceitfully.
mentirosito, ta, *a. dim.* little fibbing.
mentiroso, sa, *a.* lying, mendacious; deceptive, deceitful; full of errors or misprints.
mentís, *m.* act of giving the lie.—**dar un m.,** to belie; to give the lie.
mentol, *m.* (pharm.) menthol.
mentón, *m.* point of the chin; undershot jaw.
mentor, *m.* mentor, counsellor, guide.
menú, *m.* (Gal.) menu, bill of fare.
menuceles, *m. pl.* tithe of the lesser fruits.
menudamente, *adv.* minutely.
menudear. I. *va.* to do over and over again; to repeat; to sell by retail. **II.** *vn.* to occur frequently; to go into details; to describe little things; (com.) to sell by retail.
menudencia, *f.* trifle; minuteness, minute accuracy.—*pl.* small matters; pork sausages.
menudeo, *m.* act of repeating minutely; (com.) retail.—**al m.,** by retail.
menudero, ra, *n.* dealer in tripe, giblets, sausages, etc.
menudillo, *m.* extremities of animals.—*pl.* giblets of fowls.
menudo, da. I. *a.* small, little; minute; insignificant; common, vulgar; small (money, change); exact, scrupulous; mean, stingy. **II.** *m.* small coins, change; (sometimes *pl.*) entrails, insides (of an animal); tithe of minor produce.—**a m.,** often, frequently.
meñique. I. *a.* little (finger); (coll.) very small, tiny. **II.** *m.* little finger.
meollar, *m.* (naut.) spun yarn.
meollo, *m.* brain; marrow; kernel, pith; judgment, understanding, brains; substance.
meple, *m.* (bot.) maple.—**m. moteado,** bird's-eye maple.
mequetrefe, *m.* jackanapes, coxcomb.
meramente, *adv.* merely, solely, purely.
merar, *va.* to mix with water.
merca, *f.* (coll.) purchase.
mercachifle, *m.* peddler, hawker, huckster; petty jobber.
mercadear, *vn.* to trade, deal, traffic.
mercader, *m.* merchant, dealer, shopkeeper.—**m. de grueso,** wholesale dealer.—**mercadera.** *f.* shopkeeper's wife; tradeswoman.
mercadería, *f.* commodity, merchandise; trade.—*pl.* goods, wares, merchandise.
mercado, *m.* market, mart; market place.—**m. de trabajo** or **de mano de obra,** labor market.—**m. de valores,** stock market.
mercaduría, *f.* merchandise; trade.
mercal, *m.* an ancient Spanish copper coin.
mercancía, *f.* trade, traffic; merchandise, goods, wares.
mercante. I. *n.* & *a.* dealer(-ing), trader(-ing). **II.** *a.* merchant, mercantile, commercial.
mercantil, *a.* commercial, mercantile.
mercantilismo, *m.* mercantilism, commercialism.
mercantilmente, *adv.* commercially.
mercantivo, va, *a.* = MERCANTIL.
mercar, *va.* (*pret.* MERQUÉ; *subj.* MERQUE) to buy, purchase.
merced, *f.* gift, favor, grace; mercy; wages; will, pleasure; courteous appellation given to untitled persons, as *vuestra,* or *vuesa, merced,* your honor, your grace, your worship, sir; **la M.,** a religious order.—**m. a,** thanks to.—**m. de agua,** free distribution of water for irrigation.—**m. de tierra,** grant of land.—**a la m. de,** at the mercy of.—**estar a m. de,** to live at the expense of.—**hágame Vd. la m.,** do me the favor, please.—**muchas mercedes,** many thanks.
mercenario, ria. I. *a.* mercenary. **II.** *n.* member of the religious order of **la Merced;** mercenary soldier; day-laborer, farm hand; substitute.
mercería, *f.* small wares, mercery, haberdashery, notions; (Am.) dry-goods store.
mercerizar, *va.* to mercerize.
mercero, *m.* haberdasher, mercer.
mercurial. I. *a.* mercurial. **II.** *m.* (bot.) all-good, mercury.
mercurialismo, *m.* (med.) mercurialism.
mercúrico, ca, *a.* (chem.) mercuric.
mercurio, *m.* mercury; **(M-, astr.)** Mercury.—**m. dulce,** calomel.

mercurioso, sa, *a.* mercurious.
mercurocromo, *m.* (chem.) mercurochrome; Mercurochrome (trademark).
merchante. I. *m.* jobber. **II.** *a.* trading.
merdellón, na, *n.* (coll.) slovenly servant.
merecedor, ra, *a.* deserving, worthy.
merecer. I. *va.* (*ind.* MEREZCO; *subj.* MEREZCA) to deserve, merit; to obtain, attain; to be worth; to be worthy of; to owe, to be indebted for.—**m. la pena,** to be worthwhile. **II.** *vn.* to be deserving or worthy.—**m. bien de,** to deserve the gratitude of.
merecidamente, *adv.* deservedly.
merecido, da. I. *pp.* of MERECER. **II.** *a.* deserved. **III.** *m.* condign punishment.
mereciente, *a.* deserving.
merecimiento, *m.* merit, desert.
merendar. I. *vn.* (*ind.* MERIENDO; *subj.* MERIENDE) to lunch; to have a snack, refreshments; to pry into another's writings or actions. **II.** *va.* to lunch on.
merendero, ra. I. *a.* (crow) that picks up the seeds in cornfields. **II.** *m.* lunch room.
merendilla, ita, *f.* dim. light luncheon.
merendona, *f. aug.* splendid luncheon or supper.
merengue, *m.* kiss, sugarplum, meringue.
meretricio, cia, *a.* meretricious.
meretriz, *f.* strumpet.
merey, *f.* (bot.) cashew tree.
merezco, merezca, *v. V.* MERECER.
mergánsar, *m.* (ornith.) goosander, merganser.
mergo, *m.* (ornith.) diver.
meridiana, *f.* litter, cot bed; (astr., surv.) meridian (line); (coll.) afternoon nap.—**a la m.,** at noon.
meridiano, na. I. *a.* meridian; meridional (section, cut). **II.** *m.* meridian.
meridional, *a.* southern, southerly.
merienda, *f.* lunch, luncheon; snack; light meal; (coll.) humpback.—**m. de negros,** hodgepodge, confusion, bedlam.
meriendo, meriende, *v. V.* MERENDAR.
merindad, *f.* district of the jurisdiction of a MERINO.
merino, na. I. *a.* merino. **II.** *m.* royal judge and superintendent of sheepwalks; shepherd of merino sheep; merino sheep, wool, and cloth.
méritamente, *adv.* = MERECIDAMENTE.
meritísimo, ma, *a. super.* most worthy.
mérito, *m.* merit, desert, worth; excellence, virtue, value.—**méritos de un proceso,** (law) merits of a case.—**hacer m. de,** to mention.—**hacer méritos,** to make oneself deserving.
meritoriamente, *adv.* meritoriously.
meritorio, ria. I. *a.* meritorious, worthy, deserving. **II.** *n.* employee that begins work without a salary.
merla, *f.* (ornith.) blackbird, merle.
[1]**merlín,** *m.* (naut.) marline.
[2]**merlín,** *m.* merlin.—**saber más que M.,** to be very shrewd or keen.
merlo, *m.* (ichth.) a seafish.
merlón, *m.* (fort.) merlon.
merluza, *f.* (ichth.) hake, merluce.
merma, *f.* decrease; waste, leakage; shrinkage.
mermar. I. *vn.* to decrease, wear away, be consumed, shrink. **II.** *va.* to lessen, reduce, decrease.
mermelada, *f.* marmalade.
[1]**mero, ra,** *a.* mere, pure, simple.
[2]**mero,** *m.* (ichth.) a Mediterranean sea bass.
merodeador, *m.* marauder.
merodear, *vn.* to maraud.—**merodeo,** *m.* marauding.
merodista, *n.* marauder.
merovingio, gia, *a.* Merovingian.
merqué, merque, *v. V.* MERCAR.
mes, *m.* month; menses, courses: monthly wages.—**m. lunar,** lunar month.—**m. periódico,** calendar month.—**meses mayores,** last months of pregnancy; months immediately preceding harvest.
mesa, *f.* table; table-land, plateau; landing of a staircase; executive board; business section of a public office or department; rents of cathedral churches, prelates, or dignitaries in Spain; billiard table; billiard game; flat of a blade; (jewelry) face of a gem; (eccl.) communion table; fare, viands set on a table.—**m. de altar,** altar.—**m. de Ampère,** (phys.) Ampère's stand.—**m. de batalla,** sorting table (in postoffice).—**m. de cambios,** bank.—**m. de noche,** night commode.—**m. redonda,** round table; unceremonious or informal table; table for regular boarders.—**m. franca,** open table.—**mesas de guarnición,** (naut.) channels.—**a m. puesta,** without care or expense.—**media m.,** second table; lower-priced or servants' table.—**alzar la m.,** to clear off the table.—**poner la m.,** to set the table.
mesada, *f.* monthly pay, wages, or allowance.
mesadura, *f.* tearing the hair.
mesana, *f.* (naut.) mizzenmast or sail.
mesar, *va.* to tear out (the hair or beard).
mescal, *m.* (bot.) mescal.
mescalina, *f.* (chem.) mescaline.
mescolanza, *f.* medley, mess, jumble.
mesdado, da, *a.* mixed, mingled; motley; macaronic.
meseguería, *f.* harvest watch; money paid for watching the harvest.
meseguero, ra. I. *a.* pertaining to the harvest. **II.** *m.* harvest or vineyard watchman.
mesencéfalo, *m.* (anat.) mesencephalon, midbrain.
mesénquima, *f.* (biol.) mesenchyma.
mesenquimatoso, sa, *a.* mesenchymatous.
mesentérico, ca, *a.* (anat.) mesenteric.
mesenterio, *m.* (anat.) mesentery.
mesenteritis, *f.* (med.) mesenteritis.
meseraico, ca, *a.* (anat.) mesenteric.
mesero, *m.* journeyman who works for monthly wages.
meseta, *f.* landing of a staircase; table-land, plateau.—**m. de guarnición,** (naut.) backstay stool.
mesiánico, ca, *a.* Messianic.
mesianismo, *n.* Messianism.
Mesías, *m.* Messiah.
mesiazgo, *m.* Messiahship.
mesidor, *m.* Messidor, tenth month of the French-Revolution calendar.
mesilla, *f. dim.* small table; sideboard; board wages; censure by way of a jest; window sill.—**m. corrida,** quarter pace of a staircase.—**m. quebrantada,** half pace, foot-rest.
mesillo, *m.* first menses after parturition.
mesita, *f. dim.* small table; stand.
mesmedad, *f.*—**por su misma m.** (coll.) by the very fact.
mesmeriano, na, *a.* mesmeric.
mesmerismo, *m.* mesmerism.
mesmerista. I. *a.* mesmeric. **II.** *n.* mesmerist, mesmerizer.
mesmo, ma, *a.* (obs.) = MISMO, same; similar.
mesnada, *f.* armed retinue.
mesnadería, *f.* wages of a MESNADA.
mesnadero, *m.* member of a MESNADA.
mesoblasto, *m.* (biol.) mesoblast.
mesocarpio, *m.* (bot.) mesocarp.
mesocefálico, ca, *a.* (anat.) mesocephalic.
mesocéfalo, la, *a.* (anat.) mesocephalic, mesocephalous.
mesocracia, *f.* government by the middle class.
mesodérmico, ca, *a.* mesodermic.
mesodermo, *m.* mesoderm.
mesogástrico, ca, *a.* mesogastric.
mesogastrio, *m.* (anat.) mesogastrium, umbilical region.
mesología, *f.* ecology.
mesón, *m.* inn, hostelry, tavern; (phys.) meson.
mesonaje, *m.* place containing numerous inns.
mesonero, ra. I. *a.* pertaining to an inn. **II.** *n.* innkeeper, host, hostess.
mesonista, *a.* pertaining to an inn.
mesopotámico, ca, *n.* & *a.* Mesopotamian.
mesosfera, *f.* mesosphere.

mesotorácico, ca, *a.* (entom.) mesothoracic.
mesotórax, *m.* (entom.) mesothorax.
mesotorio, *m.* (chem.) mesothorium.
mesotrón, *m.* (phys.) mesotron.
mesozoario, ria, *a.* & *m.* (zool.) mesozoan.
mesozoico, ca, *a.* (geol.) Mesozoic.
mesta, *f.* union of cattle raisers; confluence of two or more streams.
mestal, *m.* brake of prickly oaks.
mesteño, ña, *a.* belonging to the MESTA; MOSTRENCO, homeless, stray; stupid; fat.
mestizaje, *m.* (Am.) crossing of races (gen. app. to white and Indian).
mestizar, *va.* to cross (breeds).
mestizo, za. I. *a.* hybrid. **II.** *n.* & *a.* half-breed.
mesto, *m.* (bot.) large, prickly oak; turkey oak.
mestura, *f.* mashlin, mixed wheat and rye.
mesura, *f.* dignified deportment; civility, politeness; moderation.
mesuradamente, *adv.* slowly, prudently, moderately.
mesurado, da. I. *pp.* of MESURAR. **II.** *a.* moderate, circumspect, temperate.
mesurar. I. *va.* to inspire moderation in. **II.** *vr.* to control oneself.
meta, *f.* boundary, finish line; goal, aim.
metabólico, ca, *a.* metabolic.
metabolismo, *m.* metabolism.—**m. basal,** (physiol.) basal metabolism.
metabolizar, *va.* & *vn.* to metabolize.
metacarpiano, na, *a.* (anat.) metacarpal.
metacarpo, *m.* (anat.) metacarpus.
metacentro, *m.* metacenter.
metacromatismo, *m.* (chem.) metachromatism.
metacronismo, *m.* metachronism.
metadología, *f.* methodics.
metafase, *f.* (biol.) metaphase.
metafísica, *f.* metaphysics.
metafísicamente, *adv.* metaphysically.
metafísico, ca. I. *a.* metaphysical. **II.** *m.* metaphysician.
metáfora, *f.* metaphor.
metafóricamente, *adv.* metaphorically.
metafórico, ca, *a.* metaphorical.
metaforista, *n.* metaphorist.
metaforizar, *va.* to use metaphors.
metafrasis, *f.* metaphrase.
metafrasta, *n.* metaphrast.
metafrástico, ca, *a.* metaphrastic.
metagénesis, *f.*(biol.) metagenesis.
metagoge, *f.* (rhet.) a kind of metaphor.
metal, *m.* metal; tone or timbre of the voice; (mus.) brass orchestral instruments; quality, nature, or condition.—**m. antifricción,** babbitt metal.—**m. blanco,** nickel silver; babbitt metal.—**m. campanil, or de campanas,** bell metal.—**m. de imprenta,** type metal.—**m. desplegado,** expanded metal.—**m. Muntz,** Muntz metal, yellow metal.
metalario, ria, *n.* metallist, metal worker.
metalepsis, *f.* (rhet.) metalepsis.
metálica, *f.* metallurgy.
metalicé, metalice, *v. V.* METALIZAR.
metálico, ca. I. *a.* metallic; medallic. **II.** *m.* specie, hard cash.—**m. en caja,** (com.) cash on hand.
metalífero, ra, *a.* (poet.) metalliferous.
metalista, *n.* metal worker.
metalistería, *f.* metal work.
metalización, *f.* (chem.) converting into metal.
metalizar. I. *va.* (*pret.* METALICÉ; *subj.* METALICE) (chem.) to convert into metal. **II.** *vr.* to be converted into or impregnated with metal; to become controlled by love of money, to become mercenary.
metalografía, *f.* metallography.
metaloide, *m.* (chem.) metalloid.
metaloideo, dea, *a.* (chem.) nonmetallic, metalloid.
metaloterapia, *f.* (med.) metallotherapy.
metalurgia, *f.* metallurgy.
metalúrgico, ca. I. *a.* metallurgic, metallurgical. **II.** *n.* metallurgist.
metalurgista, *n.* metallurgist.
metalla, *f.* scraps of gold-leaf for mending.
metamería, *f.* (chem., zool.) metamerism.
metamérico, ca, *a.* (chem., zool.) metameric.
metamerismo, *m.* (chem., zool.) metamerism.
metamerizado, da, *a.* (zool.) metamerized.
metámero, ra. I. *a.* (chem., zool.) metameric. **II.** *m.* (zool.) metamere.
metamórfico, ca, *a.* (geol.) metamorphic.
metamorfismo, *m.* (geol.) metamorphism.
metamorfosear, *va.* & *vr.* to metamorphose, to transform.
metamorfosi, metamorfosis, *f.* metamorphosis, transformation.
metano, *m.* (chem.) methane.
metaplasma, *m.* (biol.) metaplasm.
metaplasmo, *m.* (gram.) metaplasm.
metástasis, *f.* (med.) metastasis.
metasticizar, *vn.* (med.) to metastasize.
metatarsiano, na, *a.* (anat.) metatarsal.
metatarso, *m.* (anat.) metatarsus.
metate, *m.* (Mex.) curved stone for grinding maize or cocoa.
metátesis, *f.* (rhet.) metathesis.
metatórax, *m.* (zool.) metathorax.
metazoario, ria, *m.* & *a.* (zool.) metazoan.
meteco, ca, *a.* & *n.* foreign(-er).
metedor, ra. I. *n.* one who puts in or introduces; smuggler. **II.** *m.* baby's swaddling clothes.
metedaría, *f.* smuggling.
metempsicosis, metempsícosis, *f.* metempsychosis.
metemuertos, *m.* (theat.) stage hand; busybody.
meteórico, ca, *a.* meteoric.
meteorismo, *m.* (med.) meteorism, flatulence.
meteorito, *m.* meteorite.
meteorización, *f.* (agr.) influence of atmospheric phenomena on the soil.
meteorizar. I. *va.* (med.) to cause flatulence. **II.** *vr.* (med.) to suffer from flatulence; (agr.) (of soil) to be influenced by atmospheric phenomena.
metéoro, meteoro, *m.* atmospheric phenomenon; meteor.
meteorología, *f.* meteorology.
meteorológico, ca, *a.* meteorological.
meteorologista; meteorólogo, ga, *n.* meteorologist.
meter. I. *va.* to put in, insert, introduce, inclose; to smuggle; to make (as a noise); cause (as fear); tell (as fibs); to induce, get (one into a business, etc.); to stake, put to hazard; to invest; to cram down (food); to put close together, cram together; to impose upon, to deceive; to compress, straighten, reduce; (coll.) to eat; (naut.) to take in (sail).—**m. bulla,** to make a noise.—**m. su cucharada,** to put in one's oar, to butt in.—**m. zizaña,** to sow discord.—**meterlo a bulla,** to carry off the matter with a joke. **II.** *vr.* to meddle, intrude, interfere; to be too familiar; to choose, take up a profession or trade; to plunge into vice; (of rivers) to empty; to attack sword in hand.—**m. a,** to become; to undertake to; to set oneself up as, pretend to be.—**m. con,** to pick a quarrel with.—**m. en,** (coll.) to meddle with, poke one's nose into.—**m. en profundidades,** (fig.) to get beyond one's depth.—**m. mar adentro,** (of sea bathing) to go beyond one's depth.
metesillas, *m.* (theat.) stage hand.
meticulosidad, *f.* fear, shyness.
meticuloso, sa, *a.* pusillanimous, shy; meticulous, finicky.
metidillo, *m.* baby's swaddling clothes.
metido, da. I. *pp.* of METER. **II.** *a.* abounding; close, tight; engaged; interested. **III.** *m.* blow with the fist on the throat; strong lye or buck; (sew.) material allowed in seams; METIDILLO. **IV.** *f.* (coll.) lecture, dressing down.
metilamina, *f.* (chem.) methylamine.

metilato, *m.* (chem.) methylate.
metileno, *m.* (chem.) methylene.
metílico, ca, *a.* (chem.) methylic.
metilo, *m.* (chem.) methyl.
metimiento, *m.* insertion, introduction.
metódicamente, *adv.* methodically.
metódico, ca, *a.* methodical.
metodismo, *m.* (eccl.) Methodism.
metodista, *n.* & *a.* Methodist.
metodizar, *va.* & *vn.* (*pret.* METODICÉ; *subj.* METODICE) to systematize.
método, *m.* method; technique.—**m. abreviado,** simplified system, short cut.—**m. de tanteos,** trial and error method.—**m. práctico,** rule-of-thumb method.
metodología, *f.* methodology.
metol, *m.* (chem., photog.) metol.
metonimia, *f.* (rhet.) metonymy.
metonímico, ca, *a.* metonymical.
métopa, *f.* (arch.) metope.
metraje, *m.* meterage; footage.
metralla, *f.* (artil.) grapeshot, case shot, canister shot.
metrallazo, *m.* discharge of grapeshot.
metralleta, *f.* submachine gun, tommy gun.
métrica, *f.* metrical art, poesy.
métricamente, *adv.* metrically.
métrico, ca, *a.* metric, metrical.
metrificación, *f.* verse making.
metrificador, ra; metrista, *n.* versifier.
metrificar, *vn.* to write verses.
metritis, *f.* (med.) metritis.
[1]**metro,** *m.* meter, unit of length; (poet.) meter.
[2]**metro,** *m.* *abbr.* of METROPOLITANO, subway (train).
metrógrafo, *m.* (Ry.) metrograph.
metrología, *f.* metrology.
metrónomo, *m.* (mus.) metronome.
metrópoli, *f.* metropolis; archiepiscopal church; mother country.
metropolitano, na. I. *a.* metropolitan. **II.** *m.* archbishop; subway or elevated train.
metrorragia, *f.* (med.) metrorrhagia.
metroscopio, *m.* (med.) metroscope.
metrotomía, *f.* (surg.) hysterotomy.
metrótomo, *m.* (surg.) metrotome, hysterotome.
mexicano, na, *n.* & *a.* Mexican.
México, *m.* Mexico.
meya, *f.* spider crab. Also NOCA.
mezala, *m.* oratory, place for prayer.
mezcal, *m.* (Mex.) a species of maguey; pulque.
mezcla, *f.* mixture; mixing; mortar; mixed cloth.
mezclado, da, *a.* mixed; medley; miscellaneous.
mezclador, ra. I. *a.* mixing, blending. **II.** *n.* mixer; *m.* mixing machine, blender, agitator; *f.* mixer, cement mixer.
mezcladura, *f.*; **mezclamiento,** *m.* mixture; mixing.
mezclar. I. *va.* to mix, mingle; blend. **II.** *vr.* to mix; to intermarry; to intermeddle; to take part.
mezclilla, *f.* pepper-and-salt cloth.
mezcolanza, *f.* (coll.) medley, hodgepodge, mishmash, jumble.
mezo, meza, *v.* *V.* MECER.
mezquinamente, *adv.* stingily, niggardly.
mezquindad, *f.* niggardliness, stinginess, paltriness, currishness, meanness; penury, indigence.
mezquino, na, *a.* niggardly, stingy, mean, paltry, miserly; indigent, needy; diminutive; petty, minute, puny.
mezquita, *f.* mosque.
mezquital, *m.* clump of mesquite shrubs.
mezquite, *m.* (Mex.) (bot.) mesquite.
[1]**mi,** *m.* (mus.) mi, E, third note of the scale.
[2]**mi.** *1st pers. sing. poss. pron.* (*pl.* MIS), my.
mí, *pers. pron. oblique case of pron.* YO, *used after a prep.* me.—**¡a m. qué!** (Am.) I don't care!
miaja, *f.* crumb; bit.
miar, *vn.* to mew, as a cat.
miasma, *m.* miasma.—*pl.* miasmata.
miasmático, ca, *a.* miasmatic.
miastenia, *f.* (med.) myasthenia.
miau, *m.* mew of a cat.
[1]**mica,** *f.* (min.) mica, isinglass.
[2]**mica,** *f.* female monkey; (C. A.) flirt.
micáceo, cea, *a.* micaceous, micalike.
micacita, *f.m.* (geol.) micaschist.
micado, *m.* Mikado.
micasquisto, *m.* = MICACITA.
micción, *f.* micturition, passing urine.
micelio, *m.* (bot.) mycelium.
micénico, ca, *a.* Mycenaean.
micer, *m.* ancient title of respect, mister.
mico, *m.* monkey; (coll.) lascivious man.—**dar,** or **hacer, m. a,** to disappoint by not keeping an engagement.
micología, *f.* (bot.) mycology.
micosis, *f.* (med.) mycosis.
micra, *f.* = MICRÓN.
microanálisis, *m.* microanalysis.
microbarógrafo, *m.* microbarograph.
microbiano, na, *a.* microbian.
microbicida, *f.* microbicide, germ-killer.
micróbico, ca, *a.* microbic, microbial.
microbio, *m.* microbe, bacterium.
microbiología, *f.* microbiology, bacteriology.
microbiológico, ca, *a.* bacteriological.
microbiólogo, ga, *n.* bacteriologist.
microcefalia, *f.* microcephaly, microcephalism.
microcéfalo, la, *a.* microcephalic, microcephalous.
microcito, *m.* (med.) microcyte.
microclina, *f.* (min.) microcline.
micrococal, *a.* micrococcal.
micrococo, *m.* micrococcus.
microcopia, *f.* microcopy, microcard, microprint.
microcósmico, ca, *a.* microcosmic, microcosmical.
microcosmo, *m.* microcosm.
microcristalino, na, *a.* (cryst.) microcrystalline.
microcristalografía, *f.* microcrystallography.
microcurie, *m.* (phys.) microcurie.
microdisección, *f.* microdissection.
microdureza, *f.* (phys.) microhardness.
microestructura, *f.* microstructure.
microfaradio, *m.* (elec.) microfarad.
microficha, *f.* microcard.
microfilmar, *va.* to microfilm.
microfilme, *m.* microfilm.
micrófito, *m.* = MICROBIO, microbe.
micrófono, *m.* microphone.
microfotografía, *f.* microphotography.
microfotómetro, *m.* (phys.) microphotometer.
micrografía, *f.* micrography.
micrográfico, ca, *a.* micrographic.
micrógrafo, fa, *n.* micrographer; *m.* micrograph.
microgramo, *m.* microgram.
microhmio, *m.* (elec.) microhm.
micro-interruptor, *m.* (elec.) microswitch.
microlítico, ca, *a.* (geol.) microlithic.
microlito, *m.* (geol.) microlite.
micromanipulador, *m.* (biol.) micromanipulator.
micromecánica, *f.* micromechanics.
micrometría, *f.* micrometry.
micrométrico, ca, *a.* micrometric.
micrómetro, *m.* micrometer.
micromilímetro, *m.* = MICRÓN.
micrón, *m.* micron, one thousandth of a millimeter.
microonda, *f.* (radio) microwave.
micrópilo, *m.* (bot., zool.) micropyle.
micropirómetro, *m.* (phys.) micropyrometer.
microquímica, *f.* microchemistry.
microrganismo, *m.* microörganism.
microscopia, *f.* microscopy.
microscópico, ca, *a.* microscopic.
microscopio, *m.* microscope.
microscopista, *n.* microscopist.
microsegundo, *m.* microsecond.
microsismo, *m.* microseism.

microsismógrafo, *m.* microseismograph, microseismometer.
microsoma, *m.* (biol.) microsome.
microspora, *f.* (bot., zool.) microspore.
microsurco, *m.* Microgroove (trademark).
microtomía, *f.* microtomy.
micrótomo, *m.* microtome, cutting instrument for the microscope.
microvoltio, *m.* (elec.) microvolt, one millionth of a volt.
micturición, *f.* micturition.
michito, *m. dim.* kitten, pussy.
micho, cha, *m.* & *f.* (coll.) puss, cat.
mida, *m.* mida, bean fly.
mido, mida, midió, etc. *v. V.* MEDIR.
midriasis, *f.* (med.) mydriasis, dilation of the eye.
miedo, *m.* fear, dread, apprehension.—**m. cerval,** fright; great timidity.—**tener m.,** to be afraid, fear.—**miedoso, sa,** *a.* timorous, afraid.
miel, *f.* honey; molasses; cane juice.—**m. de abejas,** bee's honey.—**m. de caña,** sugar-cane syrup.—**m. de purga,** molasses.—**m. rosada,** (pharm.) honey of roses.—**m. virgen,** virgin honey.—**dejar a uno con la miel en los labios,** to snatch an apparently certain success away from one.
[1]**mielga,** *f.* (bot.) wild lucerne.
[2]**mielga,** *f.* (ichth.) a kind of dogfish.
[3]**mielga,** *f.* (agr.) rake; four-pronged pitchfork; strip of ground to be sown.
[4]**mielga,** *f.* a girl-twin.
mielgo, ga, *a.* twin.
mielitis, *f.* (med.) myelitis.
miembro, *m.* member; limb; member of a body, community or corporation; branch or part of a whole; (math., arch.) member; (anat.) penis.
mienta, *f.* (bot.) mint.
mientes, *f. pl.* thoughts, ideas.—**parar,** or **poner, m.,** to reflect, to consider.—**traer a las m.,** to remind.—**venir a las m.,** to come to one's mind.
[1]**miento, miente,** *v. V.* MENTAR.
[2]**miento, mienta,** *v. V.* MENTIR.
mientras, *adv.* while, whilst, when.—**m. más,** the more.—**m. no,** until.—**m. que,** while, as long as, so long as.—**m. tanto,** meanwhile, in the meantime.
miera, *f.* juniper oil; resin.
miércoles, *m.* Wednesday.—**m. corvillo, or de ceniza,** Ash Wednesday.
mierra, *f.* sled, sledge, stone drag.
mies, *f.* ripe wheat and other grain, before thrashing; harvest time; (fig.) multitude converted or ready for conversion.—*pl.* grain fields.
miga, *f.* crumb, soft part of bread; small fragment, bit; (coll.) marrow, substance, pith.—*pl.* fried crumbs.—**m. tostada,** crouton.—**hacer buenas (malas) migas,** (coll.) to agree (disagree) readily with one.
migaja, *f.* small crumb or bit of bread; small fragment, chip, or bit; (coll.) little or nothing.—*pl.* leavings; crumbs, bits of food.—**no tener m. de,** (coll.) not to have a particle of.
migajada, *f.* small particle.
migajica, illa, ita, uela, *f. dim.* wee little bit.
migajón, *m. aug.* crumb, without crust; marrow core; pith and substance.
migar, *va.* to crumb (bread); to put (crumbs of) into milk, etc.
migración, *f.* migration.
migraña, *f.* = JAQUECA, migraine, headache.
migratorio, ria, *a.* migrating, migratory.
miguelete, *m.* = MIQUELETE, (mil.) foot-soldier.
miguero, ra, *a.* crummy, pert. to fried crumbs.
mihrab, *m.* mihrab, niche in a mosque.
mijo, *m.* (bot.) millet, panic grass.—**m. ceburro,** white wheat.
mil, *m.* one thousand; one thousandth.—**m. y quinientas,** (coll.) lentils.—**a las m. y quinientas,** at an unearthly hour; after a long time.
miladi, *f.* milady.
milagrero, ra, *n.* miracle monger.
milagro, *m.* miracle; wonder; votive offering hung up in churches.
milagrón, *m.* (coll.) great miracle; gesture of astonishment.
milagrosamente, *adv.* miraculously.
milagroso, sa, *a.* miraculous.
milamores, *f.* (bot.) a species of valerian.
milanés, sa, *n.* & *a.* Milanese.
[1]**milano,** *m.* (ornith.) kite, glede, bird of prey; (ichth.) a sea fish.
[2]**milano,** *m.* (bot.) bur or down of the thistle.
mildeu, *m.* (bot.) mildew (esp. app. to grape vines).
mildiú, *m.* = MILDEU.
milenario, ria. I. *a.* millenary. **II.** *m.* millenary; millennium; millenarian, one who expects the millennium.
milenarismo, *m.* doctrine of millenarians.
mileno, na, *a.* pertaining to cloth in which the warp contains a thousand threads.
milenrama, *f.* (bot.) milfoil or yarrow.
milépora, *f.* (zool.) millepore.
milésimo, ma, *n.* & *a.* thousandth.
milesio, ia, *n.* & *a.* Milesian.—**fábula m.,** Milesian tale.
milhojas, *f.* (bot.) yarrow.
miliamperio, *m.* (elec.) milliampere.
miliamperímetro, *m.* (elec.) milliamperimeter.
miliar, *a.* miliary; (med.) miliary.
miliárea, *f.* milliare.
miliario, ria, *a.* pert. to a mile or to miles.
milibar, *m.* millibar.
milicia, *f.* science of war; soldiery, military; militiamen.—**m. nacional,** National Guard.—**m. urbana,** militia.
miliciano, na. I. *a.* military. **II.** *m.* militiaman; inductee.
milico, *m.* (Am.) soldier.
milicurie, *m.* (phys.) millicurie.
miligramo, *m.* milligram.
mililitro, *m.* milliliter.
milímetro, *m.* millimeter.
milimicrón, *m.* millimicron.
milipulgada, *f.* mil.
militante, *a.* militant; military.
[1]**militar.** *vn.* to serve in the army; to go to war.—**m. contra,** to be against, disprove or weaken (a theory, argument, etc.).—**m. en,** to be in, to belong to (a party, etc.).—**m. en favor de,** to lend weight to, to strengthen, be a reason for (a theory, line of conduct, etc.).
[2]**militar. I.** *a.* military, soldierly. **II.** *m.* military man.—*pl.* military.
militarismo, *m.* militarism.
militarista, *n.* & *a.* militarist.
militarización, *f.* militarization.
militarizar, *va.* to militarize.
milmillonésimo, ma, *n.* & *a.* billionth (thousand-millionth).
milo, *m.* earthworm.
miloca, *f.* (ornith.) a kind of owl.
milocha, *f.* kite (for flying).
milodonte, *m.* (paleontol.) mylodont.
milonga, *f.* (Arg.) kind of popular song; party.
milord, *m.* (*pl.* MILORES) milord; barouche.
milpa, *f.* (Mex.) maize land.
milpiés, *m.* woodlouse.
milréis, *m.* milreis (Portuguese and Brazilian money of account).
miltoniano, na, *a.* = MILTÓNICO.
miltónico, ca, *a.* Miltonic, Miltonian.
milla, *f.* mile.—**m. marina** or **náutica,** nautical mile.—**m. medida,** measured mile.—**m. terrestre,** statute mile.
millar, *m.* thousand; a great number (used in *pl.*); certain quantity of cocoa (varies between 3½ and 4 lb.).
millarada, *f.* about a thousand.—**a millaradas,** by thousands; innumerable times.—**echar millaradas,** to brag of wealth and riches.

millón, *m.* million.—*pl.* ancient excise or duty.
millonario, ria, *n.* & *a.* millionaire.
millonésimo, ma, *n.* & *a.* millionth.
mimado, da, *pp.* & *a.* spoiled, overindulged.
mimar, *va.* to pet, fondle, indulge, spoil (a child).
mimbral, *m.* plantation of osiers.
mimbre, *m.* (bot.) osier, willow; (com.) twig, wicker, withe.
mimbrear, *vn.* to sway.
mimbreño, ña, *a.* osierlike, willowy.
mimbrera, *f.* (bot.) osier, willow.
mimbreral, *m.* place full of willows.
mimbroso, sa, *a.* wickered, osiered.
mimeografiar, *va.* to mimeograph.
mimeógrafo, *m.* mimeograph; Mimeograph (trademark).
mimesis, *f.* (rhet.) mimesis.
mimetismo, *m.* (zool.) mimesis.
mímica, *f.* pantomine, sign language.
mímico, ca, *a.* mimic; imitative.
mimo, *m.* buffoon, merry-andrew, mimic; caress, petting, indulgence; prudery.
mimología, *f.* mimology.
mimosa, *f.* (bot.) mimosa, sensitive plant.
mimoso, sa, *a.* fastidious, finicky; soft, spoiled.
mímulo, *m.* (bot.) mimulus, monkey flower.
[1]**mina,** *f.* mine; underground passage or conduit; source, spring; sinecure, (coll.) child's play, snap; (mil., naut.) mine.—**m. acústica,** (mil.) sonic or acoustic mine.—**m. magnética,** (mil.) magnetic mine.—**m. terrestre,** (mil.) land mine.
[2]**mina,** *f.* mina, ancient Greek coin.
minador, ra, *n.* miner, sapper; mining engineer.
minal, *a.* pertaining to mines; mine (as *a.*).
minar, *va.* to mine, excavate, dig, burrow; to sap, undermine; to consume, ruin, destroy; to work hard for.
minarete, *m.* minaret.
mineraje, *m.* work of a mine; mining.
mineral. I. *a.* mineral. **II.** *m.* mineral, ore; water spring, fountain-head; rich mine; source.—**m. bruto,** raw ore, rough ore.—**m. virgen,** native ore.
mineralización, *f.* mineralization.
mineralizador, *m.* (chem.) mineralizer.
mineralizar. I. *va.* to mineralize. **II.** *vr.* to become mineralized; (of water) to become mineral, or charged with mineral substances.
mineralogía, *f.* mineralogy.
mineralógico, ca, *a.* mineralogical.
mineralogista, *m.* mineralogist.
minería, *f.* mining; force of miners; body of mine operators.
minero, ra. I. *a.* pert. to mines. **II.** *m.* miner; sapper; mine operator; source, origin.
mineromedicinal, a. medicinal mineral (waters).
minerva, *f.* (print.) Minerva machine.—**minervista,** *n.* (print.) operator of a Minerva machine.
mingitorio, *m.* upright urinal.
mingo, *m.* red ball or object ball in billiards.
miniado, da, *a.* miniate, decorated or illuminated with red or vermilion.
miniar, *va.* to paint in miniature; to decorate or illuminate with red or vermilion.
miniatura, *f.* (art) miniature.
miniaturista, *n.* miniature painter.
mínima, *f.* slightest thing; (mus.) minim.
mínimo, ma. I. *a.* minimum, least.—**m. común múltiplo,** (math.) least common multiple. **II.** *m.* minimum; (eccl.) Minim.
mínimum, *m.* minimum.
minino, na, *n.* (coll.) kitty, cat.
minio, *m.* (min.) minium, red lead.
ministerial, *a.* ministerial.
ministerialismo, *m.* (pol.) ministerialism.
ministerialmente, *adv.* ministerially.
ministerio, *m.* (pol.) ministry, cabinet; office and term of a cabinet minister; department; building where the department is located; ministration, office, employment; service, agency.—**M. de Estado,** Department of State, or of Foreign Affairs.—**M. de Fomento,** (Spain) Department of Public Works, Agriculture, Commerce, and Manufactures (better left untranslated, calling it Department of Fomento).—**M. de la Gobernación,** Department of the Interior.—**M. de Gracia y Justicia,** Department of Justice and Ecclesiastical Affairs.—**M. de Hacienda,** Treasury Department.—**M. de la Guerra,** War Department.—**M. de lo Interior,** Department of the Interior.—**M. del Trabajo,** Department of Labor.—**M. de Marina,** Navy Department.—**M. de Relaciones Exteriores,** Ministry of Foreign Affairs, (U. S. State Department).
ministra, *f.* woman director; wife of a cabinet minister.
ministración, *f.* ministration.
ministrador, ra, *n.* one who directs or ministers.
ministrante. I. *a.* serving, ministering. **II.** *n.* trained nurse.
ministrar, *va.* & *vn.* to minister, to serve, to supply, to furnish.
ministril, *m.* subordinate official; petty officer of justice; player of reed instruments in churches.
ministro, *m.* cabinet minister; minister plenipotentiary; judge or justice; sheriff, bailiff, constable, petty officer of justice; subordinate, agent, servant.—**m. consultante,** minister who lays before the king the opinion of his council.—**m. de Dios,** clergyman.—**M. de Estado,** Minister, or Secretary, of State.—**M. de Fomento,** Secretary, or Minister, of Public Works, etc. (*V.* MINISTERIO DE FOMENTO).—**M. de Gracia y Justicia,** Attorney General.—**M. de Hacienda,** Minister, or Secretary, of the Exchequer or Treasury.—**M. de la Gobernación,** Minister, or Secretary, of the Interior.—**m. del culto, m. del Señor,** clergyman.—**M. de Relaciones Exteriores,** Minister, or Secretary, of Foreign Affairs.—**M. de Relaciones Interiores,** Minister, or Secretary, of the Interior.—**M. de Salubridad,** Minister, or Secretary, of Public Health.
mino, na, kitty, pussy (used to call a cat).
minoración, *f.* lessening, diminution.
minorar. I. *va.* to lessen, diminish. **II.** *vr.* to shrink; to decrease, diminish.
minorativo, va, *a.* lessening; (med.) laxative.
minoría, *f.* minority (in age or in number).
minoridad, *f.* minority (in age), nonage.
minotauro, *m.* Minotaur.
minucia, *f.* minuteness, smallness; mite; small tithe.—*pl.* minutiae.
minuciosamente, *adv.* minutely, thoroughly.
minuciosidad, *f.* minuteness, thoroughness; trifle, small detail.
minucioso, sa, *a.* minutely precise, thorough.
minué, *m.* (dance and mus.) minuet.
minuendo, *m.* (arith.) minuend.
minuete, *m.* = MINUÉ.
minúsculo, la. I. *a.* very small, tiny; of little importance; small (letter). **II.** *f.* small letter, lower-case letter.
minuta, *f.* minute (as of a meeting); first draft; memorandum; lawyer's bill; list of employees, roll (of names); bill of fare.—**a la m.,** (Arg.) (app. to preparing or serving food) quick, short-order.
minutar, *va.* to make a draft of, to minute.
minutario, *m.* minute book.
minutero, *m.* minute hand.
minutisa, *f.* (bot.) sweet-william pink.
minuto, ta. I. *a.* minute, small. **II.** *m.* minute (in time & geom.).—**al m.,** at once, right away.
[1]**miñón,** *m.* light infantry, rural guard; minion.
[2]**miñón,** *m.* scoriæ of iron ore.
miñona, *f.* (print.) minion, 7-point type.
mío, mía; míos, mías, *poss. pron.* mine.—**de m.,** by myself; of my own accord.—**lo m.,** what belongs to me.—**soy m.,** I am my own master.
mio, *m.* = MINO.

miocardio, *m.* (anat.) myocardium.
miocarditis, *f.* (med.) myocarditis.
mioceno, na, *a.* (geol.) Miocene.
miodinia, *f.* (med.) myodinia, muscular pain.
miografía, *f.* (anat.) myography.
miógrafo, *m.* myograph.
miología, *f.* (anat.) myology.
mioma, *m.* (med.) myoma.
miopatía, *f.* (med.) myopathy.
miope. I. *a.* myopic, near-sighted. **II.** *n.* myope.
miopía, *f.* (opt.) myopia, near-sightedness.
miosina, *f.* (biochem.) myosin.
miosis, *f.* (med.) myosis; (biol.) meiosis.
miosota, miosotis, *f.* (bot.) forget-me-not.
miosuro, *m.* (bot.) mousetail.
miótico, ca, *a.* myotic.
miquelete, *m.* (mil.) a kind of foot-soldier.
mira, *f.* sight (of firearms and mathematical instruments); leveling rod; (fort.) watch-tower; (mason.) rule; care; vigilance; design, purpose, intention, view.—**m. de bombardeo,** bombing sight.—**m. de corredera** or **de mirilla,** target leveling rod.—**m.** or **mirilla telescópica,** telescopic sight.—**estar a la m.,** to be on the lookout, be on the watch.
¡mira! *interj.* look! lo! behold! take care!
mirabel, *m.* (bot.) summer cypress goosefoot; sunflower.
mirabolano, *m.* = MIROBÁLANO.
mirada, *f.* glance, gaze, look.—**echar una m.,** to glance, cast a glance.
miradero, *m.* watch tower, lookout, observatory; cynosure.
mirado, da. I. *pp.* of MIRAR. **II.** *a.* (when preceded by **muy, tan, más, menos**) considerate, circumspect, prudent, thoughtful; (when preceded by **bien, mal, mejor, peor**) considered, reputed.—**bien m.,** (besides the meaning just given), carefully considered; looking well into the matter; in fact.
mirador, ra. I. *n.* spectator, looker-on. **II.** *m.* belvedere, oriel, bay-window, observatory.
miradura, *f.* act of looking.
miraguano, *m.* (bot.) fan palm.
miramamolín, *m.* among Moors, "prince of the believers."
miramiento, *m.* consideration, reflection; circumspection, prudence; attention, consideration, courtesy.
mirante, *n.* & *a.* looker(-ing).
mirar. I. *va.* to look, look at, look upon or toward; to gaze, gaze upon; to view, survey; to see, regard; to consider, think; to have regard for, esteem; to watch, be careful; to watch, spy; to notice; to concern.—**m. bien,** to think much of, esteem; to approve.—**m. de hito en hito,** to stare at.—**m. de reojo, m. de través,** to look askance at; to look at out of the corner of one's eye.—**m. mal,** to disapprove, have a bad opinion of; to dislike; to consider bad form.—**m. por encima,** to examine slightly, glance at.—**m. sobre el hombro,** to cast a contemptuous look at. **II.** *vn.* to look.—**m. a,** to overlook, face, front on; to look after, look out for.—**m. alrededor,** to look around.—**m. en,** to think over, consider carefully.—**m. por,** to take care of; look after.—**¡mira!,** look out! (warning or threat).—**¡mire!** look here! listen!
mirasol, *m.* (bot.) sunflower.
miríada, *f.* myriad, large quantity or number.
miriagramo, *m.* myriagram.
mirialitro, *m.* myrialiter.
miriámetro, *m.* measure of length, 10,000 meters.
miriápodo, da, *m.* & *a.* myriapod, centipede.
mirífico, ca, *a.* marvellous, wonderful.
mirilla, *f. dim.* peephole in doors; target (of a leveling rod).
[1]**miriñaque,** *m.* trinket, bauble, gewgaw.
[2]**miriñaque,** *m.* hoop-skirt, crinoline.
miriópodo, = MIRIÁPODO.
mirística, *f.* (bot.) nutmeg tree.
mirla, *f.* (ornith.) blackbird.
mirlamiento, *m.* affected gravity.
mirlarse, *vr.* (coll.) to put on airs.
mirlo, *m.* (ornith.) blackbird; (coll.) air of importance, affected gravity.
mirobálano, *m.* (bot.) myrobalan.
mirón, na, *n.* spectator, looker-on, by-stander; prier, busybody, gazer.
mirra, *f.* myrrh.—**mirrado, da,** *a.* myrrhic.
mirrauste, *m.* (cook.) timbale of pigeons.
mirrino, na, *a.* myrrhic.
mirtáceo, cea, *a.* (bot.) myrtaceous.
mirtidano, *m.* myrtle tiller or sprout.
mirtino, na, *a.* myrtle-like.
mirto, *m.* (bot.) myrtle.
miruello, lla, *m.* & *f.* (ornith.) blackbird.
misa, *f.* (eccl.) mass; (mus.) music composed for a solemn mass.—**m. de cuerpo presente,** mass said while the corpse is in the church.—**m. del gallo,** midnight mass.—**m. mayor,** high mass.—**m. pontifical,** pontifical mass.—**m. rezada,** low mass.—**como en m.,** in dead silence.—**no saber de la m. la media,** to know nothing, not know what's going on, be out of it.—**oír m.,** to hear or attend mass.
misacantano, *m.* priest who is ordained and says the mass; priest who celebrates the first mass.
misal, *m.* (eccl.) missal, Mass book; (print.) two-line pica.
misantropía, *f.* misanthropy.
misantrópico, ca, *a.* misanthropic(al).
misántropo, *m.* misanthrope.
misar, *vn.* (coll.) to say mass; to hear mass.
misario, *m.* (eccl.) acolyte.
miscelánea, *f.* miscellany; mixture, medley.
misceláneo, a, *a.* miscellaneous, mixed.
miscibilidad, *f.* miscibility.
miscible, *a.* miscible, that can be mixed.
miserabilísimo, ma, *a. super.* most miserable.
miserable. I. *a.* miserable, wretched, unhappy; stingy, close-fisted. **II.** *n.* wretch, cur, cad.
miserablemente, *adv.* miserably, unhappily; stingily.
míseramente, *adv.* meanly, wretchedly.
miserear, *vn.* (coll.) to be niggardly or stingy.
miserere, *m.* (eccl.) Miserere; (med.) ileus, colic.
miseria, *f.* misery, wretchedness, forlornness; need, penury, poverty, destitution; stinginess; trifle, pittance.
misericordia, *f.* mercy, mercifulness, pity.
misericordiosamente, *adv.* mercifully.
misericordioso, sa, *a.* merciful.
mísero, ra, *a.* = MISERABLE.
misero, ra, *a.* (coll.) mass-loving; church-going; (priest) that says mass very often.
misérrimo, ma, *a. super.* most miserable.
misia, misiá, *f.* (Am.) (with first name) Señora, Doña, Mrs.
misión, *f.* mission; errand; embassy, legation; commission; (eccl.) missionary station, residence, preaching, etc.; money and food allowed to reapers during the harvest.
misional, *a.* missionary.
misionar, *vn.* to preach a mission or missions.
misionario, *m.* missionary; delegate, envoy.
misionero, ra. I. *a.* missionary. **II.** *m.* missionary; preacher (of a mission).
misivo, va, *a.* & *f.* missive.
mismamente, *adv.* (coll.) exactly, to a tee.
mismísimo, ma, *a. super.* very same.
mismo, ma, *a.* same; similar, like; equal, self-same; -self (*él mismo,* himself, he himself).—**así m., lo m.,** the same; the same thing.—**el m. de siempre,** the same old (John, thing, etc.).—**eso m.,** that very thing.—**lo m. da,** it's all the same, it makes no difference.—**lo m. de siempre,** the same old story.—**lo m. que,** the same as; as well as.—**lo m. . . . que . . . ,** both . . . and.—**por lo m.,** for the same reason; for that very reason.
misogamia, *f.* misogamy.
misógamo, ma, *n.* misogamist.

misoginia, *f.* misogyny.
misógino, na. I. *a.* misogynous. **II.** *m.* misogynist.
misoneísmo, *m.* misoneism, dread or dislike of novelty.
misoneísta, *n.* & *a.* misoneist(-ic).
mispíquel, *m.* (min.) mispickel, arsenopyrite.
mistagogo, *m.* mystagogue.
mistamente, *adv.* (law) = MIXTAMENTE.
mistar, *va.* to speak or mumble.
mistela, *f.* = MIXTELA.
misterio, *m.* mystery.
misteriosamente, *adv.* mysteriously.
misterioso, sa, *a.* mysterious.
mística, *f.* study of the contemplative life.
místicamente, *adv.* mystically; spiritually; emblematically.
misticismo, *m.* mysticism.
[1]**místico, ca,** *n.* & *a.* mystic(-al); spiritual.
[2]**místico,** *m.* small coasting vessel.
misticón, na, *a.* (coll.) affectedly ascetic.
misti fori = MIXTI FORI.—**mistifori,** *m.* = MIXTIFORI.
mistilíneo, nea, *a.* (geom.) = MIXTILÍNEO.
mistión, misto, mistura, misturar = MIXTIÓN, MIXTO, MIXTURA, MIXTURAR.
mistral, *a.* & *m.* mistral (wind).
misturera, *f.* (Am.) flower girl.
mita, *f.* (Peru) enforced service of Indians; (Bol.) harvest of coca leaves; (entom.) mite, harvest bug.
mitad, *f.* half; moiety; middle, centre; (coll.) husband or wife, as *mi cara mitad,* my better half.—**m. y m.,** half and half.—**por la m.,** in two.—**por mitades,** by halves.
mitayo, *m.* (Am.) Indian serving his MITA.
mítico, ca, *a.* mythical.
mitigación, *f.* mitigation, extenuation; soothing.
mitigador, ra, *n.* & *a.* mitigator(-ing); soother (-ing).
mitigante, *a.* mitigating, allaying.
mitigar, *va.* (*pret.* MITIGUÉ; *subj.* MITIGUE) to mitigate, allay, soothe, alleviate; to quench, assuage, appease.
mitigativo, va; mitigatorio, ria, *a.* lenitive, mitigating, soothing.
mitigué, mitigue, *v. V.* MITIGAR.
mitin, *m.* (Angl.) political meeting; rally.
mito, *m.* myth.
mitología, *f.* mythology.
mitológico, ca. I. *a.* mythological. **II.** *n.* mythologist.
mitologista; mitólogo, ga, *n.* mythologist.
mitón, *m.* mitt, lace glove without fingers.
mitosis, *f.* (biol.) mitosis, cell division.
mitote, *m.* Indian dance; (Am.) household festival; fastidiousness, affectedness; riot, uproar, disturbance.
mitotero, ra, *a.* & *n.* (Am.) finical, fastidious; jolly, rollicking.
mitra, *f.* (eccl.) miter; bishopric.
mitrado. I. *pp.* of MITRAR. **II.** *a.* (eccl.) *a.* mitered.
mitral, *a.* (anat.) mitral.
mitrar, *vn.* (eccl.) to be mitered.
mitridato, *m.* mithridate, antidote.
mítulo, *m.* mussel.
mixomiceto, *m.* (bot.) myxomycete.
mixtamente, *adv.* mixedly; (law) belonging to both ecclesiastical and civil courts.
mixtela, *f.* a refreshing beverage; (Colomb.) a popular intoxicating liquor.
mixtificación, *f.* mystification, bewilderment; hoax.
mixtificar, *va.* to mystify, bewilder; to hoax.
mixti fori, *a.* (law) amenable to either ecclesiastical or secular courts; entangled, complicated.—**mixtifori,** *m.* (coll.) medley, hodgepodge.
mixtilíneo, nea, *a.* (geom.) mixtilinear.
mixtión, *f.* mixture, commixture.
mixto, ta. I. *a.* mixed, mingled; composite; half-breed; crossbreed; mongrel; (arith.) mixed.—**parejas m.,** (games) mixed doubles.—**tren m.** train with both passenger and freight cars. **II.** *m.* sulphur or parlor match; (artil.) explosive compound.
mixtura, *f.* mixture, compound; meslin, mixed corn; (pharm.) mixture.
mixturar, *va.* to mix, mingle.
mixturero, ra, *n.* & *a.* mixer(-ing).
miz, *m.* pussy, kitty.
mízcalo, *m.* a kind of mushroom.
mizo, za, (coll.) = MICHO, CHA, puss, cat.
mnemónica, mnemotecnia, *f.* mnemonics.
mnemotécnico, ca, *a.* mnemonic.
moabita, *n.* Moabite.
moaré, *m.* moiré.
mobiliario, ria. I. *a.* movable (app. to chattels, especially unregistered bonds or securities). **II.** *m.* furniture, household goods.
moblaje, *m.* household furniture.
moblar, *va.* (*ind.* MUEBLO; *subj.* MUEBLE) to furnish, provide with furniture.
moble, *a.* = MÓVIL, movable; mobile; unstable.
moca, *m.* mocha, mocha coffee; miry place, quagmire.
mocador, *m.* pocket handkerchief.
mocasín, *m.* moccasin; (zool.) moccasin (snake).
mocasina, *f.* moccasin.
mocear, *vn.* to act like a boy; to revel, to rake.
mocedad, *f.* youth, youthfulness; reckless mode of living; frolic.
mocero, *a.* lascivious, lewd.
mocetón, na, *n.* strapping youth, lad (lass).
moción, *f.* motion, movement; leaning, inclination, tendency; divine inspiration; motion, proposition to an assembly.
mocito, ta. I. *a. dim.* very young. **II.** *n.* youngster, lad (lassie).
moco, *m.* mucus; viscid, glutinous matter; snuff of a lamp or candle; candle drippings; slag of iron; (naut.) martingale boom, dolphin striker; worthless thing, trifle; (bot.) love-lies-bleeding.—**m. de pavo,** crest of a turkey.—**a m. de candil,** by candlelight.—**llorar a m. tendido,** (coll.) to weep copiously, cry like a child.
mocosidad, *f.* mucousness, viscosity.
mocoso, sa. I. *a.* snivelly; full of mucus; despicable, mean. **II.** *n.* inexperienced youth.
mocosuelo, la, *n. dim.* thoughtless, inexperienced youth; child.
mochada, *f.* butt (as of a goat).
mochar, *va.* to cut, lop off.
mochazo, *m.* blow with the butt of a musket.
mocheta, *f.* thick edge of some tools; (arch.) quoin; sconcheon.
mochete, *m.* (ornith.) sparrow hawk.
mochil, *m.* farmer's boy.
mochila, *f.* (mil.) knapsack, haversack; a kind of caparison; gunning bag; provisions given to each soldier for a number of days.
mochilero, *m.* one who carries the baggage of soldiers.
mochín, *m.* executioner.
mocho, cha. I. *a.* cropped, shorn, lopped, cut off; maimed, mutilated; (Mex., coll.) hypocritical. **II.** *m.* butt end.
mochuelo, *m.* (ornith.) red owl.—**cargar con el m.,** to get the worst part of an undertaking.
moda, *f.* fashion, mode, style.—**a la (última) m.,** after the latest fashion; fashionable.—**de m.,** fashionable.—**estar de m.,** to be in style, or in fashion.—**pasado, de m.,** out of style.—**ser de m.,** or **ser m.,** to be the fashion.
modal. I. *a.* (logic) modal. **II.** *m. pl.* manners, breeding.—**modalidad,** *f.* nature, character.
modelado, *m.* (art) modelling.
modelador, ra. I. *a.* modeling, modelling. **II.** *n.* modeler, modeller.
modelar, *va.* (art) to model.
modelo. I. *m.* model, pattern, standard, copy. **II.** *n.* (art) life model.—**no tener m.,** to have no equal.
moderación, *f.* moderation.

moderadamente, *adv.* moderately.
moderado, da. I. *pp.* of MODERAR. **II.** *a.* moderate; modest; reasonable; (pol.) conservative; moderately liberal, middle-of-the-road. **III.** *n.* (pol.) moderate, middle-of-the-roader.
moderador, ra, *n.* & *a.* moderator(-ing).—**poder m.,** (in constitutional monarchies) the sovereign.
moderante. I. *n.* & *a.* moderator(-ing). **II.** *n.* presiding officer, moderator.
moderantismo, *m.* (pol.) moderate liberalism.
moderar. I. *va.* to moderate, regulate, adjust, restrain, curb, repress. **II.** *vr.* to calm down, moderate, refrain from excesses.
moderativo, va; moderatorio, ria, *a.* moderating.
modernamente, *adv.* recently, lately, freshly.
modernidad, *f.* modernity, modernness.
modernismo, *m.* modernism.
modernista. I. *a.* modern. **II.** *n.* modernist.
modernización, *f.* modernization.
modernizar, *va.* to modernize.
moderno, na, *a.* modern.
modestamente, *adv.* modestly.
modestia, *f.* modesty.
modesto, ta, *a.* modest.
módicamente, *adv.* moderately, sparingly.
modicidad, *f.* moderateness, cheapness.
módico, ca, *a.* reasonable, economical.
modificable, *a.* modifiable.
modificación, *f.* modification.—**m. del autor,** author's alteration.
modificador, ra, *n.* & *a.* modifier(-fying).
modificante, *a.* modifying.
modificar, *va.* (*pret.* MODIFIQUÉ; *subj.* MODIFIQUE) to modify.—**modificativo, va; modificatorio, ria,** *a.* modifying.
modifiqué, modifique, *v. V.* MODIFICAR.
modillón, *m.* (arch.) modillion, bracket.
modio, *m.* modius, an ancient Roman dry measure.
modismo, *m.* (gram.) idiom.
modista, *f.* dressmaker or modiste.—**m. de sombreros,** milliner.—**modistería,** *f.* modiste's shop, fashion shop.
modistilla, *f. dim.* (coll.) young, inexperienced dressmaker or milliner; seamstress.
modo, *m.* mode, way, manner, form; moderation, temperance; civility, urbanity; (gram.) model. or mood; (mus.) mode.—**m. de ser,** nature, character; disposition, temperament.—**al m. de, a m. de,** in the same manner as, like, in the fashion of.—**de buen (mal) m.,** politely (impolitely).—**del mismo m. que,** in the same way as.—**de m. de,** so as to.—**de m. que,** so that; and so.—**de ningún m.,** by no means, under no circumstances.—**de otro m.,** otherwise.—**de todos modos,** at any rate, anyway.—**de un m. u otro,** in one way or another, somehow.—**por m. de,** as (*por modo de juego,* as a joke, in jest).—**sobre m.,** extremely.
modorra, *f.* drowsiness, heaviness; (vet.) sturdy.
modorrar. I. *va.* to drowse, make sleepy. **II.** *vr.* (of fruit) to become squashy.
modorrilla, *f.* (coll.) third night watch.
modorro, rra, *a.* drowsy, sleepy, heavy; dull, stupid; (of sheep) suffering from sturdy; (of fruit) squashy.
modoso, sa, *a.* temperate, well-behaved.
modrego, ga, *n.* (coll.) awkward person.
modulación, *f.* (mus.) modulation.—**m. de amplitud,** (rad.) amplitude modulation.—**m. de frecuencia,** (rad.) frequency modulation.
modulador, ra. I. *a.* modulating. **II.** *n.* modulator; *m.* (radio) modulator.
modular. I. *a.* modular. **II.** *va.* & *vn.* to modulate.
módulo, *m.* size of coins and medals; (arch.) module; (math.) modulus; (mus.) modulation; (hydraul.) unit of measure of running water.
mofa, *f.* mockery, jeer, scoff.
mofador, ra, *n.* & *a.* scoffer(-ing), mocker(-ing).
mofadura, *f.* = MOFA.
mofante, *n.* = MOFADOR.
mofar, *vn.* & *vr.* to jeer, scoff, mock, sneer.—**mofarse de,** to mock, sneer at, scoff, make fun of.
mofeta, *f.* mofette, mephitis; noxious emanation (from mines, etc.); (zool.). skunk or polecat.
moflete, *m.* fat cheek.
mofletudo, da, *a.* fat-cheeked.
mogate, *m.* varnish, glazing.—**a medio m.,** carelessly, heedlessly.
mogato, ta, *a.* = MOJIGATO.
mogol, la, *n.* & *a.* Mongol, Mongolian.
mogólico, ca, *a.* Mongolian.
mogoloide, *n.* & *a.* Mongoloid.
mogollón, *m.* hanger-on, sponger, parasite.—**comer de m.,** to sponge.
mogón, na, *a.* with one horn missing or broken.
mogote, *m.* hummock, hillock; (agr.) stack or rick of corn; antler (of a brocket, a small deer).
mogrollo, *m.* parasite, sponger; (coll.) rustic.
moharra, *f.* head of a spear.
moharrache, moharracho, *m.* merry-andrew, clown.
mohatra, *f.* sham sale; fraud.—**mohatrar,** *vn.* to make a sham sale.—**mohatrero, ra; mohatrón, na,** trickster, swindler.
mohecer, *va.* to moss, to mildew.
mohiento, ta, *a.* mildewed.
mohín, *m.* grimace, gesture.
mohina, *f.* animosity, animadversion, grudge.
mohino, na. I. *a.* fretful, peevish; sad, mournful; (mule) begotten by a stallion and a female donkey; (of horses, etc.) black. **II.** *n.* one who plays alone against several others.
moho, *m.* (bot.) moss; mould, mildew; rust.
mohoso, sa, *a.* rusty; mouldy, musty, mildewed.
mojada, *f.* wetting, drenching; sop; (coll.) stab.
mojador, ra, *n.* wetter, moistener.
mojadura, *f.* drenching, moistening, wetting.
mojama, *f.* dry, salt tunny fish.
mojar. I. *va.* to wet, drench; moisten, damp; (coll.) to stab; to interfere with. **II.** *vn.* to be immersed in any business. **III.** *vr.* to get wet.
mojarra, *f.* a sea fish; (Am.) heart-shaped dagger.
mojarrilla, *n.* (coll.) gay, jolly person.
moje, *m.* (cook.) gravy, sauce.
mojel, *m.* (naut.) braided cord for the anchor.
mojí, *m.* sponge cake; pie.
mojicón, *m.* bun; (coll.) fisticuff.
mojiganga, *f.* morris dance; masquerade, mask, mummery.
mojigatería, mojigatez, *f.* hypocrisy; religious fanaticism.
mojigato, ta. I. *n.* dissembler, hypocrite; bigot, fanatic. **II.** *a.* deceitful, hypocritical; prude; bigoted.
[1]**mojón,** *m.* landmark; boundary monument; heap, pile; milestone; a game like pitching; solid excrement.
[2]**mojón,** *m.* wine taster.
[1]**mojona,** *f.* excise tax on wine.
[2]**mojona,** *f.* survey of land; setting up of boundary marks.
mojonación, *f.* setting up of boundary marks.
mojonar, *va.* to set boundary marks.
mojonera, *f.* boundary mark; landmark.
mojonero, *m.* appraiser, gauger.
[1]**mola,** *f.* (med.) mole.
[2]**mola,** *f.* flour with salt used in sacrifices.
molada, *f.* colors ground at one time.
molalidad, *f.* (chem.) molality.
molar, *a.* & *m.* molar.
molaridad, *f.* (chem.) molarity.
molcajete, *m.* mortar for pounding.
moldar, *va.* to mold.
moldavo, va, *n.* & *a.* Moldavian.
molde, *m.* mold; pattern; (eng.) form; (print.) form ready for printing.—**de m.,** in print; printed; fitting, to the purpose.
moldeador, *m.* molder, cast maker.
moldear, *va.* to mold; to cast; to provide or adorn with moldings.

moldura, *f.* molding.
moldurar, *va.* to make moldings on.
[1]**mole,** *a.* soft, mild.
[2]**mole,** *f.* huge mass or bulk.
[3]**mole,** *m.* (Mex.) chili sauce for turkey.
molécula, *f.* (chem., phys.) molecule.
molécula-gramo, *f.* (chem.) gram molecule.
molecular, *a.* molecular.
moledera, *f.* (coll.) botheration.
moledero, ra, *a.* ready to be ground, for grinding.
moledor, ra, *n.* grinder; powdering mill; crushing cylinder in a sugar-mill; bore, tiresome person.
moledura, *f.* grinding.
molendero, ra, *n.* miller, grinder; chocolate manufacturer.
moler, *va.* (*ind.* MUELO; *subj.* MUELA) to grind, pulverize, mill; to overtire; to vex, bore; to waste, consume; to masticate, chew.—**m. a palos,** to give a severe drubbing.
molero, *m.* maker or seller of millstones.
molestador, ra, *n.* vexer, annoyer.
molestamente, *adv.* troublesomely, vexatiously; uncomfortably.
molestar. I. *va.* to disturb; to trouble; to annoy, vex; to tease. **II.** *vr.* **(en),** to bother, take the trouble (to).
molestia, *f.* annoyance, bother; inconvenience, trouble; discomfort; hardship, grievance; (coll.) quarrel.
molesto, ta, *a.* annoying, vexatious, bothersome; troublesome; uncomfortable.
moleta, *f.* muller; polisher; (print.) ink-grinder.
moletón, *m.* canton or cotton flannel.
molibdato, *m.* (chem.) molybdate.
molibdenita, *f.* (min.) molybdenite.
molibdeno, *m.* (chem.) molybdenum.
molíbdico, ca, *a.* molybdic.
molicie, *f.* softness, effeminacy.
molido, da. I. *pp.* of MOLER. **II.** *a.* (fig.) fatigued.
molienda, *f.* milling, grinding; grist; weariness, fatigue; season for grinding sugar cane or olives.
moliente, *n.* & *a.* grinder(-ing).
molificable, *a.* mollifiable.
molificación, *f.* mollification.
molificar, *va.* (*pret.* MOLIFIQUÉ; *subj.* MOLIFIQUE) to mollify, soften, mitigate.
molificativo, va, *a.* mollifying, lenitive.
molifiqué, molifique, *v. V.* MOLIFICAR.
molimiento, *m.* grinding, pounding; (fig.) fatigue, weariness, lassitude.
molinar, *m.* place where there are mills.
molinejo, *m. dim.* small mill.
molinera, *f.* miller's wife; woman mill worker.
molinería, *f.* number or group of mills; mill industry.
molinero, *m.* miller, grinder.
molinete, *m. dim.* little mill; pin wheel; ventilating wheel; friction roller; fifth wheel of a vehicle; smoke dispeller; moulinet, swing of sabre; drum of a capstan or winch.—**m. hidráulico,** hydraulic tourniquet, Barker's mill.
molinillo, *m. dim.* hand mill; coffee grinder; chocolate beater.
molinito, *m. dim.* small mill.
molino, *m.* mill; restless, noisy fellow; (coll.) mouth.—**m. de sangre,** mill turned by men or animals.—**m. de viento,** windmill.
molitivo, va, *a.* mollifying; softening.
moloc, *m.* (zool.) moloch (lizard); **(M.)** Moloch (ancient Phoenician god).
molondro, molondrón, *m.* (coll.) poltroon.
molote, *m.* (Cuba) tumult, riot.
moltura, *f.* grinding.
molusco, ca, *m.* & *a.* molluscan; *m.* mollusk, mollusc.
moluscoideo, dea, *a.* & m. (zool.) molluscoid.
molla, *f.* lean meat; crumb of bread.
mollar, *a.* soft, tender; easily shelled; lean (meat) productive, profitable; credulous, gullible.
mollear, *vn.* to become soft and pliable; to yield easily.
molledo, *m.* fleshy part of a limb (of the body); bread crumb.
molleja, *f.* gizzard; sweetbread.
[1]**mollejón,** *m. aug.* big, fat person.
[2]**mollejón,** *m.* grindstone.
mollejeula, *f. dim.* sweetbread.
mollera, *f.* crown of head.—**cerrado de m.,** rude, ignorant.—**ser duro de m.,** to be dull or obstinate.
mollero, *m.* = MOLLEDO.
[1]**molleta,** *f.* biscuit; brown bread.
[2]**molleta,** *f.*—*pl.* candle snuffers.
[1]**mollete,** *m.* French roll; fleshy part of arm.
[2]**mollete,** *m.*—*pl.* plump cheeks.
molletero, ra, *n.* baker or seller of rolls.
molletudo, da, *a.* having chubby cheeks.
mollina, mollizna, *f.* drizzle.
molliznar, molliznear, *vn.* to drizzle, sprinkle.
moma, *f.* (Mex.) blindman's buff.
momentáneamente, *adv.* instantly; momentarily; promptly.
momentaneidad, *f.* momentariness, promptness.
momentáneo, nea, *a.* momentary; prompt.
momento, *m.* moment; weight, importance; (mech.) moment.—**m. angular,** (mech.) angular moment, moment of momentum.—**m. de inercia,** (phys., mech.) moment of inertia.—**m. de la cantidad de movimiento,** (mech., phys.) moment of momentum, angular moment.—**m. de resistencia,** (mech.) moment of resistance.—**m. de torsión,** (aer., phys.) torque.—**m. de un par,** (mec.) moment of a couple.—**m. flector,** (phys.) bending moment.—**al m.,** in a moment, in a minute, immediately.—**de m.,** for the moment.—**por momentos,** continually, every minute; any moment, soon.
momería, *f.* mummery.
momero, ra, *n.* mummer.
momia, *f.* mummy.
momificación, *f.* mummification.
momificar. I. *va.* to mummify. **II.** *vr.* to become a mummy.
momio, mia. I. *a.* meager, lean. **II.** *m.* extra allowance.—**de m.,** gratis.
momo, *m.* funny grimace.
momórdiga, *f.* (bot.) balsam apple.
[1]**mona,** *f.* female monkey; (coll.) ludicrous imitator; (coll.) drunkenness; drunkard; at cards, old maid; iron plate worn for protection on the right leg by bullfighters on horseback.—**dormir la m.,** to sleep off a drunk.
[2]**mona,** *f.* Easter cake with whole eggs.
monacal, *a.* monastic; monkish.
monacalmente, *adv.* monastically.
monacato, *m.* monkhood, monasticism.
monacillo, *m.* acolyte.
monacita, *f.* (min.) monazite.
Mónaco, *m.* Monaco.
monacordio, *m.* (mus.) clavichord.
monada, *f.* grimace; monkeyism, monkeyshine; fawning, flattery; pretty child.
mónada, *f.* (philos. & zool.) monad.
monadelfo, fa, *a.* (bot.) monadelphous.
monadología, *f.* (philos.) monadology.
monago, monaguillo, *m.* = MONACILLO.
monaquismo, *m.* = MONACATO.
monarca, *m.* monarch.
monarquía, *f.* monarchy; kingdom.
monárquico, ca. I. *a.* monarchical, monarchic, monarchal, monarchist. **II.** *n.* monarchist.
monarquismo, *m.* monarchism.
monarquista, *n.* & *a.* monarchist(-ic).
monasterial, *a.* monastic.
monasterio, *m.* monastery.
monásticamente, *adv.* monastically.
monástico, ca, *a.* monastic, monastical.
monda, *f.* pruning of trees; pruning season.—*pl.* parings, peelings.
mondadientes, *m.* toothpick.
mondador, ra, *n.* cleaner; purifier.
mondadura, *f.* cleaning, cleansing.—*pl.* peelings.
mondaoídos, mondaorejas, *m.* ear spoon.
mondar, *va.* to clean, cleanse; to trim, prune; to hull, husk, peel; to deprive of money; to cut (the hair).—**mondarajas,** *f. pl.* peelings.

mondejo, *m.* belly of a pig or sheep stuffed with minced meat.
mondo, da, *a.* neat, pure, unmixed.—**m. y lirondo,** (coll.) pure, without admixutre.
mondón, *m.* barkless trunk of a tree.
mondonga, *f.* (contempt.) kitchen wench.
mondongo, *m.* tripe; intestines.
mondonguería, *f.* place where tripe is sold.
mondonguero, ra, *n.* tripe seller or cooker.
mondonguil, *a.* (coll.) pertaining to tripe.
monear, *vn.* (coll.) to monkey; to trifle, fool.
moneda, *f.* coin; money; specie; coinage.—**m. corriente,** currency.—**m. debil, soft** currency.—**m. de vellón,** small copper money.—**m. divisionaria,** fractional money or currency.—**m. fiduciaria,** fiduciary money, fiat money; token money.—**m. fuerte,** hard currency.—**m. imaginaria,** money of account.—**m. menuda,** coins, change.—**m. métalica,** or **sonante,** hard money, specie.—**m. suelta,** small change.—**pagar en la misma m.,** to pay back in one's own coin, **give tit for tat.**
monedaje, *m.* coinage; seigniorage.
monedar, monedear, *va.* to coin.
monedería, *f.* mintage.
monedero, ra, *n.* coiner.—**m. falso,** counterfeiter.
monegasco, ca, *n.* & *a.* Monegasque.
monería, *f.* grimace, mimicry, monkeyshine; cunning action of a child.
monesco, ca, *a.* (coll.) apish.
monetario, ria. I. *a.* monetary, financial. **II.** *m.* cabinet or collection of coins and medals.
monetización, *f.* monetization.
monetizar, *va.* to monetize.
monfí, *m.* Moorish highwayman.
mongol, la, *n.* & *a.* Mongol, Mongolian.
Mongolia, *f.* Mongolia.
mongólico, ca, *a.* Mongolian.
moniato, *m.* (bot.) = BONIATO, sweet potato.
monicaco, *m.* = HOMINICACO, whippersnapper.
monición, *f.* admonition.
monigote, *m.* lay brother; (coll.) a bumpkin; puppet, grotesque figure; (Colomb., contempt.) priest.
monillo, *m.* (sewing) waist, bodice.
monipodio, *m.* (coll.) combine (for illicit ends).
monís, *f.* kind of fritters; any pretty little thing; **m.,** or **monises,** (coll.) money.
monismo, *m.* (philos.) monism.
monista, *n.* & *a.* (philos.) monist(-ic).
mónita, *f.* artifice, cunning suavity.
monitor, *m.* monitor, adviser; (naut.) monitor.
monitorio, ria. I. *a.* monitory, admonitory. **II.** *n.* ecclesiastical monition.
monja, *f.* nun.—*pl.* sparks in burned papers.
monje, *m.* monk; (ornith.) brown peacock.
monjía, *f.* monkhood.
monjil. I. *m.* nun's dress; mourning dress. **II.** *a.* pertaining or belonging to nuns.
monjío, *m.* nunnishness; taking the veil.
monjita, *f. dim.* little nun.
mono, na. I. *a.* (coll.) dainty; "cute." **II.** *m.* monkey; mimic; nincompoop; **(de mecánico),** overalls.
monoatómico, ca, *a.* monoatomic.
monobásico, ca, *a.* (chem.) monobasic.
monobloque.—en m., (int. combust. eng.) in bloc, in one piece.
monocárpico, ca, *a.* (bot.) monocarpic.
monoceronte, monocerote, *m.* unicorn.
monocíclico, ca, *a.* (elec.) monocyclic.
monociclo, cla. I. *a.* monocyclic. **II.** *m.* monocycle, single-wheel velocipede.
monocilíndrico, ca, *a.* single-cylinder.
monoclamídeo, dea, *a.* (bot.) monochlamydeous.
monoclinal, *a.* & *m.* (geol.) monoclinical.
monoclínico, ca, *a.* (min.) monoclinic.
monocordio, *m.* (mus.) monochord.
monocotiledóneo, a. I. *a.* (bot.) monocotyledonous. **II.** *f. pl.* Monocotyledones, monocotyledons.
monocromático, ca, *a.* monochromatic.
monocromo, ma, *a.* & *m.* monochrome.
monóculo, la. I. *a.* monocular, one-eyed. **II.** *m.* (opt.) monocle; (surg.) bandage for one eye.
monocultura, *f.* monoculture.
monodáctilo, la, *a.* (zool.) monodactylous, having one finger, toe or claw.
monodía, *f.* (mus.) monody.
monódico, ca, *a.* monodic.
monoenergético, ca, *a.* (nuclear phys.) monoenergetic.
monofásico, ca, *a.* (elec.) single-phase.
monofilético, ca, *a.* (biol., bot.) monophyletic.
monofilo, la, *a.* (bot.) monophyllous.
monofisita, *n.* (theol.) Monophysite.
monofobia, *f.* (med.) monophobia.
monofónico, ca, *a.* (mus., electron.) monophonic.
monogamia, *f.* monogamy.
monógamo, ma. I. *a.* monogamous. **II.** *n.* monogamist.
monogénesis, *f.* (biol.) monogenesis, monogeny.
monogenismo, *m.* monogenism, monogenesis.
monografía, *f.* monograph.
monográfico, ca, *a.* monographic.
monograma, *m.* monogram.
monohidratado, da, *a.* monohydrated.
monohidrato, *m.* (chem.) monohydrate.
monoico, ca, *a.* (bot.) monœcious.
monolítico, ca, *a.* monolithic.
monolito, *m.* monolith.
monologar, *vn.* to soliloquize.
monólogo, *m.* monologue, soliloquy.
monomanía, *f.* monomania.
monomaníaco, ca, *n.* & *a.* monomaniac.
monometalismo, *m.* monometallism.
monometalista, *n.* & *a.* monometallist(-ic).
monomio, mia, *m.* & *a.* (alg.) monomial.
monona, *a.* (coll.) graceful and pretty (girl).
monopastos, *m.* sheave, wheel of a pulley.
monopatín, *m.* scooter.
monopétalo, la, *a.* (bot.) monopetalous.
monoplano, *m.* (aer.) monoplane.
monoplaza, *m.* single-seater (airplane).
monoplejía, *f.* (med.) monoplegia.
monopolicé, monopolice, *v.* *V.* MONOPOLIZAR.
monopolio, *m.* monopoly.
monopolismo, *m.* monopolism.
monopolista. I. *a.* monopolistic. **II.** *n.* monopolist.
monopolización, *f.* monopolization.
monopolizador, ra. I. *a.* monopolistic. **II.** *n.* monopolist, monopolizer.
monopolizar, *va.* (*pret.* MONOPOLICÉ; *subj.* MONOPOLICE) to monopolize.
monóptero, ra, *a.* (arch.) monopterous.
monorquidia, *f.* (med.) monorchism.
monorriel, *m.* monorail.
monorrimo, ma, *a.* (pros.) monorhymed.
monosépalo, la, *a.* (bot.) monosepalous.
monosilábico, ca, *a.* monosyllabic.
monosílabo, ba. I. *a.* monosyllabic, monosyllabical. **II.** *m.* monosyllable.
monospermo, ma, *a.* (bot.) monospermous.
monóstrofe, *f.* (poet.) monostrophe.
monote, *m.* (coll.) dumfounded person.
monoteísmo, *m.* monotheism.
monoteísta, *n.* & *a.* monotheist(-ic).
monotelismo, *m.* Monothelitism.
monotelita. I. *a.* Monothelitic. **II.** *n.* Monothelite.
monotipia, *f.* monotype (machine).
monotipista, *n.* monotypist.
monotipo, pa. I. *a.* (biol.) monotypic, monotypal; (print.) monotype. **II.** *m.* (biol.) monotype; (print.) Monotype (machine, trademark).
monotonía, *f.* monotony.
monótono, na, *a.* monotonous.
monotrema, *m.* (zool.) monotrema.
monovalencia, *f.* (chem.) monovalence, univalence.
monovalente, *a.* (chem.) monovalent, univalent.

monóxido, *m.* (chem.) monoxide.—**m. de carbono,** (chem.) carbon monoxide.
monseñor, *m.* Monseigneur.
monserga, *f.* (coll.) gabble, gibberish.
monstruo, *m.* monster; monstrosity; huge thing.
monstruosamente, *adv.* monstrously.
monstruosidad, *f.* monstrosity; monstrousness.
monstruoso, sa, *a.* monstrous; huge; extraordinary; hideous; hateful; shocking.
monta, *f.* act of mounting; raising or crossing (as horses); amount, sum total; value, worth, price; (mil.) signal for mounting.
montacargas, *m.* hoist, winch, windlass.
montada, *f.* arch of a horse's bit.
montadero, *m.* mounting block.
montado, da. I. *pp.* of MONTAR. II. *a.* (horse) ready for mounting. III. *m.* trooper or horseman.
montador, *m.* mounter; mounting block; installer (electrician, pipe fitter, etc.).
montadura, *f.* mounting; (jewelry) setting; trappings of a saddle horse; mount.
montaje, *m.* setting up, installing; assembling; (mech.) mount, mounting; (mech.) fitting; (mech.) assembly.—*pl.* (artil.) mounting.—**m. automático,** automatic assembly.—**m. de cañón,** gun mount.—**m. de líneas,** (elec.) hookup.—**m. del muelle,** spring assembly.
montanera, *f.* oak forest; feeding of hogs with acorns.
montanero, *m.* forester.
montanismo, *m.* Montanism.
montanista, *n.* & *a.* Montanist(-ic).
montano, na, *a.* mountainous.
montantada, *f.* braggadocio; multitude, crowd.
montante. I. *m.* (fencing) broadsword; (carp. and mech.) upright, standard, post, strut, jamb; (arch.) transom; (min.) stempel; (com.) amount, footing. II. *f.* (naut.) flood tide.
montantear, *vn.* (fencing) to wield the broadsword; to vaunt, brag; to intermeddle.
montantero, *m.* fighter with a broadsword.
montaña, *f.* mountain.—*pl.* highlands.
montañero, ra, *n.* (Colomb.) mountaineer.
montañés, sa. I. *a.* mountain (as *a.*), of or from the mountains, highlandish. II. *n.* mountaineer, highlander; native of the province of Santander, Spain.
montañeta, -ñuela, *f. dim.* small mountain.
montañoso, sa, *a.* mountainous.
montar. I. *vn.* to mount, get on top; to ride horseback; to amount; to be of importance.—**m. en cólera,** to fly into a rage. II. *va.* to ride, straddle (a horse); to cover (as a horse, etc.); (mech.) to mount, set up, assemble; (jewelry) to set (as diamonds); to cock (as a gun); to wind (a clock, etc.); to impose a fine for trespassing; (mil.) to mount (guard); (naut.) to command (a ship); to carry or be equipped with (as guns); to round (a cape or headland). III. *vr.* to get into (as a passion).
montaraz. I. *a.* born or raised in the mountains; wild, untamed; uncouth, boorish. II. *n.* forester. —**montaraza,** *f.* forester's wife.
montazgar, *va.* to levy or collect MONTAZGO.
montazgo, *m.* toll for cattle passing from one province into another; cattle pass.
monte, *m.* mountain, mount; woods, forest, woodland; difficulty, obstruction; bushy head of hair; talon, cards that remain after the hands have been dealt; (cards) monte.—**m. alto,** forest.—**m. bajo,** scrub, brushwood, brake, thicket.—**m. de piedad,** pawnshop.—**m. pío,** gratuity fund for widows and orphans.
montea, *f.* beating the woods for game; stonecutting; (arch.) working drawing; (arch.) versed sine of an arch.
montear, *va.* to hunt; to make a working drawing of; (arch.) to vault, arch.
montecillo, *m. dim.* small forest; hillock, hummock.
montepío, *m.* = MONTE PÍO. *V.* MONTE.
[1]**montera,** *f.* cloth cap; skylight; receiver, condenser of a still or alembic; (naut.) skysail.
[2]**montera,** *f.* hunter's wife.
montería, *f.* cap factory or store.
monterero, ra, *n.* cap maker or seller.
montería, *f.* hunting, hunt, chase.
montero, ra, *n.* (in hunting) beater.
monterón, *m. aug.* big cloth cap.
monterrey, *m.* (cook.) meat pie.
monteruca, *f.* ugly cap.
montés, sa; montesino, na, *a.* wild, undomesticated, uncultivated.
montevideano, na, *n.* & *a.* Montevidean, of or from Montevideo.
montículo, *m.* mound.
monto, *m.* sum (of money); (com., arith.) amount (principal plus interest); sum total.
montón, *m.* heap, pile; big lot, mass; mound.—**m. de gente,** crowd, multitude.—**a montones,** abundantly, in heaps.
montonera, *f.* (Am.) group of revolutionary horsemen; large crowd.
montonero, *m.* bushwhacker, guerrilla.
montuno, na, *a.* pertaining to the highlands; rustic, boorish.
montuosidad, *f.* (prov.) mountainous quality.
montuoso, sa, *a.* mountainous, hilly.
montura, *f.* riding horse, mount; saddle trappings; setting up, installing; (jewelry) setting.
monuelo, *m. dim.* coxcomb, silly fop.
monumental, *a.* monumental.
monumento, *m.* monument.
monzón, *m.* monsoon.
[1]**moña,** *f.* dressmaker's mannequin; doll.
[2]**moña,** *f.* fancy cap for infants; ribbon head ornament; elaborate badge on bull's neck when in the ring.
[3]**moña,** *f.* (coll.) drunkenness.
moño, *m.* (of hair) chignon, bun; tuft, egret.
moñón, na, *a.* (of birds) crested; (Colomb.) pouty, sulky.
moñudo, da, *a.* (of birds) crested.
moquear, *vn.* to snivel; to run at the nose.
moquero, *m.* pocket handkerchief.
moqueta, *f.* a kind of velvety carpet.
moquete, *m.* blow on the nose.
moquetear. I. *vn.* (coll.) to blow the nose frequently. II. *va.* to hit in the face.
moquillo, *m. dim.* little mucus; pip (in fowls).
moquita, *f.* snivel, running from the nose.
[1]**mora,** *f.* (law) delay, mora.
[2]**mora,** *f.* (bot.) blackberry; bramble bush; mulberry.
[3]**mora,** *f.* Moorish woman.
morabito, morabuto, *m.* Mohammedan hermit.
moracho, cha, *a.* little purple.
morada, *f.* habitation, abode, residence; stay, sojourn.
morado, da, *a.* purple; murrey.
morador, ra, *n.* resident, inhabitant.
moraga, *f.*, **morago,** *m.* glean, bunch.
[1]**moral.** I. *a.* moral. II. *f.* ethics, morality; morale.
[2]**moral,** *m.* (bot.) blackberry bush; mulberry tree.
moraleja, *f.* moral, maxim, lesson.
moralicé, moralice, *v. V.* MORALIZAR.
moralidad, *f.* morality, morals.
moralista, *m.* moralist.
moralización, *f.* moralization.
moralizador, ra, *n.* & *a.* moralizer(-ing).
moralizar, *va.* & *vn.* (*pret.* MORALICÉ; *subj.* MORALICE) to moralize.
moralmente, *adv.* morally.
morar, *vn.* to inhabit, dwell, reside.
moratiniano, na, *a.* Moratinian, of or like Moratin or his style.
moratorio, ria. I. *a.* moratory. II. *f.* (com., law) moratorium.
moravo, va, *n.* & *a.* Moravian.
morbidez, *f.* (art) softness, mellowness.
mórbido, da, *a.* morbid, diseased; (art) soft, mellow, delicate.
morbífico, ca, *a.* morbific, causing disease.
morbo, *m.* disease, distemper, infirmity.—**m.**

comicial, (med.) epilepsy.—**m. gálico,** (med.) venereal disease.—**m. regio,** (med.) jaundice.
morbosidad, *f.* morbidity, morbidness.
morboso, sa, *a.* diseased, morbid.
morcajo, *m.* low-grade wheat.
morcella, *f.* spark from a lamp.
morciguillo, *m.* (ornith.) bat.
morcilla, *f.* blood pudding; (theat., coll.) gag.
morcillero, ra, *n.* maker or seller of blood puddings; (theat.) gagger; one who ad-libs.
[1]**morcillo, lla,** *a.* (of horses) reddish black.
[2]**morcillo,** *m.* fleshy part of the arm.
morcón, *m.* large blood pudding or sausage; (coll.) short, plump person.
mordacidad, *f.* mordancy; asperity, acrimony; sarcastic language.
mordante, *m.* (print.) guide.
mordaz, *a.* corrosive, biting, nipping; sarcastic; acrimonious; keen.
mordaza, *f.* gag; muzzle; holder, clamp, stopper, pincers, tongs; (Ry.) fishplate.
mordazmente, *adv.* acrimoniously, bitingly.
mordedor, ra, *n.* & *a.* biter(-ing); backbiter (-ing).
mordedura, *f.* bite (act and result of act).
mordente, *m.* mordant; (mus.) mordent; turn.
morder. I. *va.* (*ind.* MUERDO; *subj.* MUERDA) to bite; to nip, gripe, grasp, clutch; to gnaw, eat, wear away; to etch; to corrode; to revile, backbite; (print.) to overlap the form or paper (as the frisket), thereby preventing a good impression.—**m. el freno,** to bite the bit. **II.** *vr.* to bite (one's tongue, lips, etc.).—**m. la lengua,** to curb one's tongue.—**no m. los labios,** (coll.) to be outspoken.
mordicación, *f.* smarting, stinging.
mordicante, *a.* biting, pungent, acrid, corrosive.
mordicar. I. *va.* to gnaw, nibble. **II.** *vn.* to smart, sting.
mordicativo, va, *a.* biting, stinging.
mordido, da. I. *pp.* of MORDER. **II.** *a.* diminished, worn out, wasted away.
mordiente. I. *a.* biting. **II.** *m.* mordant.
mordihuí, *m.* weevil.
mordimiento, *m.* = MORDEDURA.
mordiscar, *va.* to nibble; take a bite of.
mordisco, mordiscón, *m.* bite; biting; bit, piece bitten off
morel de sal, *m.* purple red for fresco painting.
[1]**morena,** *f.* (ichth.) moray.
[2]**morena,** *f.* whole-wheat bread.
[3]**morena,** *f.* (geol.) moraine; rick of new-mown grain.
morenillo, illa, ito, ita. I. *a. dim.* brunette. **II.** *m.* black powder for wounds of sheep.
moreno, na. I. *a.* brown, morel, tawny; dark, swarthy; brunette. **II.** *n.* (Cuba) Negro, darky.
morera, *f.* (bot.) white mulberry tree.
moreral, *m.* grove of white mulberry trees.
morería, *f.* Moorish quarter; Moorish lands.
moretón, *m.* (coll.) discoloration of a bruise.
morfa, *f.* fungous disease of orange and lemon trees.
morfina, *f.* morphine.—**morfinismo,** *m.* (med.) morphinism.—**morfinomanía,** *f.* morphinomania, drug habit.—**morfinómano, na,** *n.* morphinomaniac, drug fiend.
morfología, *f.* morphology.
morfológico, ca, *a.* morphologic(al).
morfosis, *f.* morphosis.
morga, *f.* juice from olives; an Indian plant with poisonous berries.
morganático, ca, *a.* morganatic.
moribundo, da, *a.* moribund, dying, near death.
morichal, *m.* grove of MORICHES.
moriche, *m.* a tropical palm.
moriego, ga, *a.* Moorish.
morigeración, *f.* temperance, moderation.
morigerado, da, *a.* temperate, abstemious.
morigerar, *va.* to restrain, moderate.
morillo, *m. dim.* little Moor; andiron, firedog.
morir. I. *vn.* & *vr.* (*pp.* MUERTO; *gerund,* MURIENDO; *ind. pres.* MUERO, *pret.* él MURIÓ; *subj.* MUERA) to die; to die or go out (as fire).—**m. de,** to die, or be dying, of, from or with (as *morir de viejo,* to die of old age).—**¡muera . . . !** or **¡Muera . . . !** down with . . . !—**hasta m.,** till death. **II.** *vr.* (of a limb) to be benumbed.—**m. por,** to be excessively fond of. —**no es cosa de m.,** it isn't a killing, fatal matter.
morisco, ca. I. *a.* Moorish, Moresque. **II.** *n.* Morisco.
morisma, *f.* multitude of Moors.
morisqueta, *f.* Moorish trick; (coll.) deception, fraud; (P. I.) boiled rice; (Am.) face, grimace.
morlaco, ca, *a.* affecting ignorance.
morlés, *m.* sort of linen, lawn.
morlón, na, *a.* = MORLACO.
mormón, na, *n.* & *a.* Mormon.
mormónico, ca, *a.* Mormon.
mormonismo, *m.* Mormonism.
mormullar, *va.* = MURMURAR.
mormullo, *m.* = MURMULLO.
moro, ra. I. *a.* Moorish; (coll.) not watered (wine). **II.** *n.* Moor.—**m. de paz,** peaceful person.—**hay moros en la costa,** the coast is not clear.
morocada, *f.* butt of a ram.
morocho, cha, *a.* (Am.) (of persons) fresh, vigorous; (Am.) (of persons) dark-skinned; *a.* & *n.* hard kind of Indian corn.
morón, *m.* hillock, hummock, mound.
moroncho, cha, *a.* = MORONDO.
morondanga, *f.* (coll.) hodgepodge, medley.
morondo, da, *a.* bald, hairless; leafless.
moronía, *f.* dish of eggplant, tomatoes, etc.
morosamente, *adv.* slowly, tardily.
morosidad, *f.* slowness, tardiness.
moroso, sa, *a.* slow, tardy, heavy, sluggish.
morquera, *f.* (bot.) Spanish thyme.
[1]**morra,** *f.* top, crown of the head.—**andar a la m.,** to come to blows.
[2]**morra,** *f.* mora, a game.
morrada, *f.* butting of two heads.
morral, *m.* nose bag; game bag; knapsack; (coll.) rustic.
morralla, *f.* small fry (fish); rubbish; rabble.
morrillo, *m.* pebble; fat of the nape of a sheep.
morriña, *f.* (vet.) murrain; (coll.) sadness, blues.
morrión, *m.* (mil.) helmet; vertigo (in hawks).
[1]**morro,** *m.* snout, muffle; anything round like the head; headland, head, bluff; peak; pebble; thick lip.—**andar al m.,** to come to blows.
[2]**morro, rra,** *a.* purring (of cats).
morrocotudo, da, *a.* (coll.) strong, stout; very important or difficult.
morrocoy, morrocoyo, *m.* (Cuba) boxturtle.
[1]**morrón,** *m.* knotted flag; large sweet pepper.
[2]**morrón,** *m.* (aer., coll.) crash.
morroncho, cha, *a.* mild, meek, tame.
morrongo, ga; morroño, ña, *n.* cat.
morrudo, da, *a.* thick-lipped.
morsa, *f.* (ichth.) walrus.
mortadela, *f.* Bologna sausage.
[1]**mortaja,** *f.* shroud, winding sheet; (Am.) cigarette paper.
[2]**mortaja,** *f.* mortise.
mortal. I. *a.* mortal, fatal; very seriously ill, at the point of death. **II.** *n.* mortal.
mortalidad, *f.* mortality; death rate.
mortalmente, *adv.* mortally, deadly.
mortandad, *f.* mortality; massacre, butchery.
mortecino, na. I. *a.* (of an animal) dying a natural death, (also app. to the flesh of such an animal); dying away or extinguishing; pale, subdued (color).—**hacer la mortecina,** to feign death. **II.** *f.* carrion.
morterada, *f.* dish, sauce, etc. made at one time in a mortar; (artil.) quantity of stones thrown out at one time by a stone mortar.
morterete, *m. dim.* (artil.) small mortar; gun for firing salutes; broad candlestick.
mortero, *m.* (artil.) mortar; mortar, for pound-

ing; understone in crushing mills; (mason.) mortar.—**m. de brújula,** inner compass box.
morteruelo, *m. dim.* small mortar; toy for boys; fricassee of hog's liver.
mortífero, ra, *a.* death-dealing, fatal; unhealthful.
mortificación, *f.* (med.) mortification, gangrene; mortification, self-inflicted hardship; humiliation, vexation.
mortificador, ra, *n.* & *a.* mortifier(-fying).
mortificante, *a.* mortifying; vexing.
mortificar, *va.* & *vr.* (*pret.* MORTIFIQUÉ; *subj.* MORTIFIQUE) (med.) to mortify; to subdue (passions); to vex; to bother; to humiliate.
mortuorio, ria. I. *a.* mortuary, pertaining to the dead. **II.** *m.* burial, funeral. **III.** *f.* funeral parlor, undertaker's establishment.
morucho, *m.* young bull with horns tipped for baiting.
morueco, *m.* ram, male sheep.
moruno, na, *a.* Moorish.
morusa, *f.* (coll.) cash, specie; money.
[1]**mosaico, ca. I.** *a.* mosaic. **II.** *m.* mosaic (work); (Am.) concrete tile (gen. paving tile, set like mosaic).—**m. de madera,** marquetry.
[2]**mosaico, ca,** *a.* Mosaic, pert. to Moses.
mosaísmo, *m.* Mosaism.
mosca, *f.* fly; tuft of hair under the lip; (coll.) cash, boodle; money in hand; impertinent intruder, importuner, bore; vexation, trouble.—*pl.* sparks from a light.—**m. de burro,** horsefly.—**m. muerta,** one who feigns meekness.—**moscas blancas,** (coll.) falling snowflakes.—**aflojar la m.,** to give or spend money.—**papar moscas,** to gape with astonishment.—**picar la m.,** to be disquieted.—**sacudir las moscas** = MOSQUEAR.—**soltar la m.,** = AFLOJAR LA M.
moscabado, da, *a.* raw, unrefined (sugar).
moscada, *a.* NUEZ MOSCADA, (bot.) nutmeg.
moscarda, *f.* (entom.) flesh fly; eggs of bees.
moscardear, *vn.* (of bees) to lay eggs in the cells of the combs.
moscardón, *m.* (entom.) botfly; horse bot; bumblebee; hornet; drone; (coll.) importuning, bothering person.
moscareta, *f.* (ornith.) flycatcher.
[1]**moscatel,** *a.* & *n.* muscatel (grape or wine).
[2]**moscatel,** *m.* (coll.) tiresome person.
moscella, *f.* = MORCELLA, spark from a lamp.
mosco, *m.* gnat, mosquito.
moscón, *m.* large fly; bumblebee; (coll.) importuning, bothering person.
moscovita, *n.* & *a.* Muscovite.
moscovítico, ca, *a.* Muscovite.
mosén, *m.* sir; title given to clergymen.
mosqueado, da, *a.* spotted, dotted, brindled.
mosqueador, *m.* fly swatter; (coll.) tail of a horse or of a cow.
mosquear. I. *va.* to swat or drive away flies; to make a smart repartee; to flog, to whip. **II.** *vr.* to suppress obstacles with violence; (coll.) to show resentment.
mosqueo, *m.* driving flies away.
mosquero, *m.* flytrap.
mosquerola, mosqueruela, *f.* muscadine pear.
mosqueta, *f.* (bot.) white musk rose.
mosquetazo, *m.* musket shot.
mosquete, *m.* musket.
mosquetería, *f.* body of musketeers; (theat.) people standing behind the pit.
mosqueteril, *a.* (theat.) (coll.) pertaining to the crowd in the pit.
mosquetero, *m.* musketeer; (theat.) spectator occupying standing room in the pit.
mosquil, mosquino, na, *a.* pertaining to flies.
mosquita, *f. dim.* small fly; (ornith.) small bird of Sardinia.—**m. muerta** = MOSCA MUERTA.
mosquitero, ra, *m.* & *f.* mosquito bar or net.
mosquito, *m.* gnat; mosquito; (coll.) tippler.
mostacero, ra, *m.* & *f.* mustard pot.
mostacilla, *f. dim.* sparrow shot; small bead.
mostacho, *m.* mustache; (coll.) blemish on the face.—**mostachos del bauprés,** (naut.) bowsprit shrouds.
mostachón, *m.* a kind of macaroon; a diamond-shaped ornament.
mostachoso, sa, *a.* wearing a mustache.
mostagán, *m.* (coll.) wine.
mostajo, *m.* (bot.) white beam tree.
mostaza, *f.* (bot.) mustard; mustard seed; fine shot.—**hacer la m.,** (coll.) to make the nose bleed with a blow.
mostazo, *m.* (bot.) mustard plant; strong, thick must.
mostear, *vn.* (of grapes) to yield must; to put must into vats; to mix must with old wine.
mostela, *f.* (agr.) gavel, sheaf.
mostelera, *f.* place where sheaves are laid up.
mostellar, *m.* (bot.) white beam tree.
mostense, *a.* belonging to an order of canons.
mostillo, *m.* cake made of must; sauce made of must and mustard.
mosto, *m.* must, grape juice.—**m. agustín,** a kind of must cake.
mostrable, *a.* that can be shown.
mostrado, da. I. *pp.* of MOSTRAR. **II.** *a.* accustomed, inured.
mostrador, ra. I. *a.* pointing; index (finger). **II.** *n.* demonstrator. **III.** *m.* counter (in a shop); stand; dial (of a watch).
mostrar. I. *va.* (*ind.* MUESTRO; *subj.* MUESTRE) to show; point out; to establish, prove, demonstrate; to feign, dissemble. **II.** *vr.* to appear, to show oneself, prove to be.
mostrenco, ca, *a.* (coll.) homeless; unowned; masterless; strayed, vagabond, vagrant; dull, ignorant, stupid; fat, bulky.
mota, *f.* burl (in cloth); mote, speck, mite; slight defect or fault; mound of earth; bog, hummock.
motacila, *f.* (ornith.) = AGUZANIEVE, wagtail.
[1]**mote,** *m.* motto, device; nickname.
[2]**mote,** *m.* (Am.) stewed corn.
moteado, da, *a.* mottled, speckled, spotted.
motear, *va.* to mottle, speck, speckle.
motejador, ra, *n.* one who calls names.
motejar, *va.* to chaff, call offensive names.
motete, *m.* (mus.) motet or motetto.
motil, *m.* = MOCHIL, farmer's boy.
motilar, *va.* to cut or crop the hair of.
motilón, na. I. *a.* having little or cropped hair. **II.** *m.* (coll.) lay brother.
motín, *m.* mutiny, insurrection, riot.
motita, *f. dim.* mote, speck, mite.
motivar, *va.* to give a reason for; to cause.
motivo, va. I. *a.* motive, moving. **II.** *m.* motive, reason; (mus.) motif, theme.—**con m. de,** owing to, by reason of; on the occasion of.—**de su m. propio,** of one's own accord.—**por ningún m.,** under no circumstances.
moto, *m.* landmark, guidepost.
motocicleta, *f.* motorcycle.
motociclista, *n.* motorcyclist.
motódromo, *m.* motordrome.
motogenerador, *m.* (elec.) motor generator.
motolita, *f.* (ornith.) wagtail.
motolito, ta, *a.* easily deceived, ignorant.
motón, *m.* (naut.) block, pulley.
motonave, *f.* motor ship.
motonería, *f.* (naut.) pulley blocks, tackle.
motonero, *m.* block maker.
motor, ra. I. *a.* motor, motive, moving. **II.** *n.* mover; *m.* (mech.) motor, engine.—**m. acorazado,** enclosed motor, ironclad motor.—**m. aeroenfriado,** air-cooled engine.—**m. alternativo,** reciprocating engine.—**m. bifásico,** two-phase motor.—**m. bipolar,** two-pole motor.—**m. cohete,** (aer.) rocket engine.—**m. compound,** (elec.) compound-wound motor; (aer.) compound engine.—**m. con válvulas en la culata,** valve-in-head engine.—**m. de cilindros convergentes,** V-motor, V-engine.—**m. de combustión** or **de combustión interna,** internal-combustion engine or motor.—**m. de chorro,** jet engine.—**m. de enfriamiento por agua,** water-cooled motor.

—**m. de enfriamiento por aire,** air-cooled motor.—**m. de explosión,** explosion motor.—**m. de inducción,** induction motor.—**m. de martinete,** (aer.) ramjet engine.—**m. de turbohélice,** (aer.) turboprop engine.—**m. diesel,** Diesel engine.—**m. fuera de borda,** outboard motor.—**m. generador,** motor-generator.—**m. monofásico,** single-phase motor.—**m. propulsor,** (aer.) propulsion motor, pusher engine.—**m. pulsorreactor,** (aer.) pulse-jet engine.—**m. sincrónico,** synchronous motor.—**m. tractor,** (aer.) tractor engine.
motorista, *n.* motorist, driver; *m.* motorman (of a trolley car).
motorización, *f.* motorization; (mil.) mechanization.
motorizar, *va.* to motorize; (mil.) to mechanize.
motricidad, *f.* (physiol.) motor faculty or function.
motril, *m.* boy helper in a shop; MOTIL.
motriz, *a.* motive, moving.
motu proprio, (Lat.) by his own will.
movedizo, za, *a.* movable; shaky, unsteady; inconstant, shifting.
movedor, ra, *n.* mover, exciter.
movedura, *f.* movement; (med.) miscarriage.
mover. I. *va.* (*ind.* MUEVO; *subj.* MUEVA) to move; to make move; to drive, propel; to shake, wag; to prevail upon, persuade, induce; to prompt; to incite, promote, occasion; to stir; to excite; to touch, affect with emotion; (agr.) to bud, sprout. **II.** *vn.* (med.) to miscarry; (arch.) to spring an arch. **III.** *vr.* to move, stir.
movible, *a.* movable; mobile; changeable, fickle.
moviente, *a.* moving, motive.
móvil. I. *a.* movable; mobile; unsteady, shaky; portable. **II.** *m.* motive, incentive, inducement; mover, motor; moving body.
movilicé, movilice, *v.* *V.* MOVILIZAR.
movilidad, *f.* mobility; movableness; fickleness, inconstancy; unsteadiness.
movilización, *f.* (mil.) mobilization.
movilizar, *va.* (*pret.* MOVILICÉ; *subj.* MOVILICE) (mil.) to mobilize.
movimiento, *m.* movement, move; movement, activity (as a progressive movement); stir, agitation; life, liveliness; (of style) animation; traffic; (mech.) motion; (astr.) clock error; (art) distribution of lines and shades, technique (mus.) tempo, time.—**m. alternativo,** (mech. reciprocating motion.—**m. continuo,** perpetual motion.—**m. de tierras,** (Ry.) earthwork.—**m. laboral,** labor turnover.—**m. oratorio,** oratorical gesture.—**m. perpetuo,** perpetual motion.
moxa, *f.* (surg.) moxa; cautery.
moxte, *interj.* = OXTE, keep off! get away!—**sin decir oxte ni m.,** without saying a word.
moyana, *f.* small culverin; moyenne (old type of cannon); (coll.) lie, fib; dog cake.
moyo, *m.* a unit of capacity (258 liters).
moyuelo, *m.* grits, pollard, coarse meal.
moza, *f.* girl, maid of all work; concubine, mistress; clothes pounder; last or winning game.
mozalbete, mozalbillo, *m.* lad, youth.
mozallón, *m.* young, robust laborer.
mozárabe, muzárabe, *a.* & *n.* Mozarab(-ic).
mozo, za. I. *a.* young, youthful; single, unmarried. **II.** *m.* youth, lad; manservant, waiter, porter; (coll.) fellow.—**m. de caballos,** groom, horse boy.—**m. de cordel,** or **de esquina,** porter in the street.—**m. de estación,** (station) porter.—**m. de paja y cebada,** hostler at an inn.—**buen m.** (**buena moza**), good-looking.
mozuelo, la, *n. dim.* young lad (lass).
[1]**mu,** *m.* lowing of cattle, moo.
[2]**mu,** *f.* child's word for sleep.
muaré, *m.* moiré, watered silk.
mucamo, ma, *n.* (Am.) servant.
muceta, *f.* short cape worn by doctors; (Rom. Cath.) mozetta, cape worn by high dignitaries.
mucilaginoso, sa, *a.* mucilaginous, slimy.
mucílago, mucilago, *m.* mucilage; slime.
mucina, *f.* (biochem.) mucin.
mucoideo, dea, *a.* mucoid.
mucosidad, *f.* mucosity, mucousness.
mucoso, sa. I. *a.* mucous; slimy, viscous. **II.** *f.* mucous membrane.
mucronato, ta, *a.* mucronate, ending in a point.
múcura, *f.* (Venez., Colomb.) pitcher, ewer; (Am.) blockhead.
muchacha, *f.* girl; maid (servant).
muchachada, *f.* boyish act; prank; (Arg.) gang of boys.
muchachear, *vn.* to act like a boy or girl.
muchachería, *f.* boyish trick; crowd of boys.
muchachez, *f.* childhood, boyhood, girlhood.
muchachil, *a.* boylike, girl-like.
muchacho, cha. I. *a.* boyish, girlish, childish. **II.** *m.* boy, lad. **III.** *f.* girl, lass.
muchedumbre, *f.* multitude; crowd; populace, rabble.
muchísimo, ma. I. *a.* *super.* of MUCHO: very much. **II.** *adv.* a very great deal.
mucho, cha. I. *a.* much, a great deal of; (of time) long.—*pl.* many. **II.** *adv.* *m.* much, very much; a great deal; in a great measure; to a great extent; often; (of time) long; very.—**con m.,** by far.—**ni con m.,** nor anything like it, or near it, (diff. constr.) far from (it) (*Juan no es rico, ni con mucho,* John is far from rich).—**ni m. menos,** nor anything like it.—**no es m.,** it is no wonder.—**no ha m.,** not long since.—**por m. que,** no matter how much.
muda, *f.* change, alteration; change of underwear; moult, moulting; change of voice in boys; roost of birds of prey; a cosmetic.
mudable, mudadizo, za, *a.* changeable; fickle.
mudamente, *adv.* silently, mutely.
mudanza, *f.* change; mutation; removal, moving (residence); inconstancy; fickleness; (dance) figure, motion.
mudar. I. *va.* to change; to remove, deviate; to vary, alter; to moult. **II.** *vn.* (**de**) to change (as *mudar de dictamen,* or *opinión,* to change one's opinion, mind; *mudar de ropa,* to change one's clothes). **III.** *vr.* to reform, mend, change; to change one's clothes; to move, change one's place or residence.
mudéjar, *n.* Mohammedan who became a subject of Christian sovereigns.
mudez, *f.* dumbness.
mudo, da, *a.* & *n.* dumb; silent; mute.—**cine m.,** silent films.
mué, *m.* moiré, watered silk.
mueblaje, *m.* household furniture.
mueble. I. *a.* movable. **II.** *m.* piece of furniture.—*pl.* chattels, furniture, household goods.
mueblería, *f.* furniture factory or store.
mueblista, *n.* furniture maker or seller.
mueblo, mueble, *v.* *V.* MOBLAR.
mueca, *f.* grimace, wry face, grin.
muecín, *m.* muezzin.
muela, *f.* runner, upper millstone; grindstone, whetstone; grinder, molar tooth; water sufficient to set a mill in motion; hill, hillock; track or circle.—**m. cordal,** or **del juicio,** wisdom tooth.
muelo, muela, *v.* *V.* MOLER.
muellaje, *m.* wharfage, dockage.
[1]**muelle,** *m.* (naut.) pier, wharf; (Ry.) freight platform.
[2]**muelle. I.** *a.* tender, delicate, soft; licentious; luxurious. **II.** *m.* (metal or rubber) spring; regulator, watch spring; (jewel.) chatelaine.
muellemente, *adv.* tenderly, gently, softly.
muer, *m.* = MUÉ.
muérdago, *m.* (bot.) mistletoe.
muerdo, muerda, *v.* *V.* MORDER.
muérgano, *m.* (Colomb.) worthless or contemptible person or thing.
muermo, *m.* (vet.) glanders.
muermoso, sa, *a.* (vet.) glanderous.
muero, muera, *v.* *V.* MORIR.
muerte, *f.* death; demise; skeleton representing

death; ruin, havoc, destruction.—**m. civil,** civil death, loss of rights.—**m. chiquita,** (coll.) nervous shudder.—**m. natural,** natural death. —**m. senil,** death from old age, or from senility.—**a la m.** = DE M.—**a m.,** to the death.—**de mala m.,** insignificant, of no account.—**de m.,** fatally; (of hating, etc.) intensely, implacably; hopelessly ill, at the point of death.
muerto, ta. I. *pp. irreg.* of MORIR (sometimes used with the transitive meaning of MATAR, to kill, as in *he m. una liebre,* I have killed a hare). **II.** *a.* languid, faded; slaked.—**m. de** (fig.) dying with. **III.** *n.* corpse.—**echarle a una el m.,** (coll.) to put the blame on one.
muesca, *f.* notch, indentation, hack, nick, mortise; dovetail scarf.
muestra, *f.* specimen, sample; shop sign; placard, bill; model, pattern, copy; end of a piece of goods bearing the manufacturer's name; clock dial or face; clock or watch; sign, indication; (mil.) muster roll.—**dar muestras de,** to show signs of.
muestrario, *m.* collection of samples; specimen or sample book.
muestreo, *m.* (stat.) sampling.
muestro, muestre, *v. V.* MOSTRAR.
muévedo, *m.* aborted fœtus.
muevo, mueva, *v. V.* MOVER.
mufla, *f.* muffle furnace.
muftí, *m.* mufti, a Mussulman expounder of the law.
muga, *f.* landmark, boundary.
mugido, *m.* lowing of cattle, moo.
múgil, *m.* (ichth.) mullet.
mugir, *vn.* (*ind.* MUJO; *subj.* MUJA) to low, bellow.
mugre, *f.* dirt, filth.
mugriento, ta, *a.* dirty, filthy.
mugrón, *m.* sprig, shoot, sucker, tiller.
mugroso, sa, *a.* = MUGRIENTO.
muguete, *m.* (bot.) lily of the valley.
muharra, *f.* = MOHARRA, head of a spear.
muisca, *n.* & *a.* (Am.) Muysca, Chibcha.
mujer, *f.* woman; wife, mate.—**m. asera,** good housewife.—**m. de estado honesto,** spinster. —**m. de gobierno,** housewife, housekeeper.— **m. mundana, perdida,** or **pública,** prostitute.—**m. policía,** policewoman.—**tomar m.,** to take a wife.
mujercilla, *f.* little woman; insignificant woman.
mujeriego, a. I. *a.* feminine, womanly; womanish; fond of women.—**a la m.,** woman-fashion, womanlike. **II.** *m.* women collectively.
mujeril, *a.* womanish, womanly, feminine.
mujerilmente, *adv.* like women, like a woman; effeminately.
mujerío, *m.* gathering of women.
mujerón, *m.* **mujerona,** *f. aug.* big woman; matron.
mujerzuela, *f. dim.* little woman.
mujo, muja, *v. V.* MUGIR.
mújol, *m.* (ichth.) mullet.
[1]**mula,** *f.* kind of shoe worn by the Pope.
[2]**mula,** *f.* female mule.
mulada, *f.* (Am.) drove of mules.
muladar, *m.* dungheap; rubbish heap.
muladí, *n.* renegade Christian.
mulante, *m.* muleteer; mule boy.
mular, *a.* pertaining to mules.
mulatero, *m.* muleteer, mule driver.
mulato, ta, *n.* & *a.* mulatto.
múleo, muléolo, *m.* ancient Roman shoe with upturned point.
muleque, *n.* (Cuba) newly arrived Negro boy.
mulero. I. *a.* (horse) fond of mules. **II.** *m.* mule boy.
muleta, *f.* crutch; prop, support; red flag used by bullfighters; light luncheon.
muletada, *f.* drove of mules.
muletero, *m.* muleteer, mule driver.
muletilla, *f. dim.* cross-handle cane; pet word or phrase, often repeated in talking; red flag used by bullfighters; frog or toggle; (min.) crutch.
muleto, *m.* young mule not yet broken.
mulilla, *f. dim.* small mule.
mulo, *m.* mule.
mulquía, *f.* title, deed.
mulso, sa, *a.* sweetened with honey or sugar.
multa, *f.* (money) fine.—**multar,** *va.* to fine.
multicapsular, *a.* (bot.) multicapsular.
multicelular, *a.* (biol.) multicellular.
multicolor, *a.* multicolored, many-colored.
multicopista, *m.* duplicator, multicopier (machine).
multidentado, da, *a.* multidentate.
multifacético, ca, *a.* many-sided.
multífido, da, *a.* multifid (as a leaf).
multifloro, ra, *a.* many-flowered.
multiforme, *a.* multiform.
multigrafiar, *va.* to multigraph.
multígrafo, *m.* multigraph; Multigraph (trademark).
multilátero, ra, *a.* multilateral.
multimillonario, ria, *n.* & *a.* multimillionaire.
multimotor, ra, *a.* multiengined, multimotored.
multinacional, *a.* multinational.
multinomio, *m.* (math.) multinomial.
multípara, *a.* (of animals) multiparous; (of women) having had more than one child.
multípedo, da, *a.* (zool.) multiped, many-footed.
múltiple, *a.* multiple, complex; (int. combust. eng.) manifold.
multiplete, *m.* (phys.) multiplet.
múltiplex, *a.* multiplex.
multiplicable, *a.* multiplicable, multipliable.
multiplicación, *f.* multiplication.
multiplicado, da, *a.* multiplicate; multifarious.
multiplicador, ra. I. *n.* & *a.* multiplier(-plying). **II.** *m.* (arith.) multiplier.
multiplicando, *m.* (math.) multiplicand.
multiplicar, *va.* & *vr.* (*pret.* MULTIPLIQUÉ; *subj.* MULTIPLIQUE) to multiply.
multíplice, *a.* multiple; multiplex.
multiplicidad, *f.* multiplicity.
multipliqué, multiplique, *v. V.* MULTIPLICAR.
múltiplo, pla, *m.* & *a.* multiple.
multipolar, *a.* multipolar.
multitubular, *a.* multitubular.
multitud, *f.* multitude; crowd; the masses.
multivalente, *a.* (chem.) multivalent.
mulla, *f.* digging around vines.
mullido, *m.* soft filling for cushions, etc.
mullidor, ra, *n.* one who fluffs (as wool or feathers).
mullir, *va.* to fluff, make soft, mollify; to engineer; to dig around (vines and trees).—**m. la cama,** to beat up the bed.
[1]**mullo,** *m.* (ichth.) surmullet.
[2]**mullo,** *m.* (Am.) glass beads.
mundanal, *a.* worldly, mundane.
mundanalidad, *f.* worldliness.
mundanear, *vn.* to indulge in worldly things.
mundano, na, *a.* mundane, worldly.
mundial, *a.* world (as *a.*, as in *la guerra mundial,* the World War), global, universal.
mundificación, *f.* act of cleansing.
mundificante, *a.* cleansing, purifying.
mundificar, *va.* to cleanse, purify.
mundificativo, va, *a.* cleansing.
mundillo, *m. dim.* arched clothes dryer; cushion for making lace; warming pan; (bot.) viburnum.
mundinovi, *m.* = MUNDONUEVO.
mundo, *m.* world; (coll.) great multitude, great quantity; social life, circle; dissipated life; experience.—**echar al m.,** to create; to give birth to.—**echarse al m.,** to plunge into dissipation. —**entrar en el m.,** to go into society.—**gran m.,** high society.—**medio m.,** many people.— **ser hombre de m.,** to be a man of the world, a man of experience.—**tener m.,** or **mucho m.,** to have had experience, know life or the world.—**todo el m.,** everybody.—**ver m.,** to travel, see the world.

mundonuevo, *m.* peep show; cosmorama.
munición, *f.* (often in the *pl.*) ammunition; small shot; birdshot; charge of firearms.—**municiones de boca,** provisions, food.—**municiones de guerra,** war stores.—**de m.,** supplied by the government; done hurriedly.
municionar, *va.* to supply with ammunition.
municipal. I. *a.* municipal. **II.** *m.* policeman.
municipalidad, *f.* municipality; townhall; municipal government.
municipalización, *f.* municipalization.
municipalizar, *va.* to municipalize.
munícipe, *m.* citizen, denizen.
municipio, *m.* municipality; municipium.
munificencia, *f.* munificence, liberality.
munificentísimo, ma, *a. super.* of MUNÍFICO, most, or very, munificent.
munífico, ca, *a.* munificent, liberal.
munitoria, *f.* art of fortification.
muñeca, *f.* (anat.) wrist; doll; figure for dressmakers; (mech.) puppet; sugar teat; pounce bag; polishing bag.
muñeco, *m.* puppet, manikin; boy doll; soft, effeminate fellow.
muñeira, *f.* a popular dance of Galicia.
muñequear, *va.* (fencing) to play with the wrist.
muñequería, *f.* doll shop; (coll.) excessive finery, overdressing.
muñequitos, *m. pl.* comics, comic book.
muñidor, *m.* beadle, messenger; plotter.
muñir, *va.* to summon.
muñón, *m.* stump of an amputated limb; (artil.) trunnion; (mech.) gudgeon pin, wristpin.
muñonera, *f.* trunnion plate; (mech.) gudgeon socket, journal box, bearing.
muón, *m.* (phys.) muon.
murajes, *m. pl.* (bot.) a medicinal herb.
mural, *a.* mural, pertaining to walls.
muralla, *f.* (fort.) rampart; wall (of a city).
murallón, *m. aug.* (fort.) strong wall.
murar, *va.* to wall, surround with a rampart.
murceguillo, murciégalo, *m.* = MURCIÉLAGO.
murciélago, *m.* (zool.) bat.
murena, *f.* (ichth.) a kind of eel.
murete, *m. dim.* small wall.
murexida, *f.* (chem.) murexide.
[1]**murga,** *f.* lees of olives.
[2]**murga,** *f.* (coll.) band of street musicians.
murgón, *m.* (ichth.) parr, smolt.
muriático, ca, *a.* (chem.) muriatic.
muriato, *m.* (chem.) muriate.
múrice, *m.* (ichth.) murex; (poet.) purple.
múrido, da, *a.* & *m.* (zool.) murine.
murió, muriendo, *v. V.* MORIR.
murmujear, *va.* to murmur, to whisper.
murmullo, *m.* whisper, whispering; murmuring, murmur, ripple, purl; rustle.
murmuración, *f.* backbiting, gossip, slander.
murmurador, ra, *n.* detractor, backbiter.
murmurante, *a.* murmuring, purling.
murmurar, *vn.* to purl, ripple (as streams); to rustle (as leaves); to grumble, mutter; to whisper, murmur; to gossip, backbite.
murmureo, *m.* murmuring (sound).
murmurio, *m.* murmur.
muro, *m.* (outside) wall (of house or garden); (fort.) rampart.
[1]**murria,** *f.* (coll.) blues; surliness, sullenness.
[2]**murria,** *f.* (pharm.) an astringent lotion.
múrrino, na, *a.* murrine, made of murra.
murrio, ria, *a.* sullen, surly, sulky.
murta, *f.* (bot.) myrtle; myrtle berry.
murtal, *m.*, **murtera,** *f.* myrtle grove.
murtilla, murtina, *f.* (bot.) myrtle; its berry; liquor made from this berry.
murtón, *m.* myrtle berry.
murucuya, *f.* (bot.) purple passion flower.
murueco, *m.* = MORUECO, ram, male sheep.
[1]**mus,** *m.* a card game.—**no hay m.,** cannot be granted.
[2]**mus.**—**sin decir tus ni m.,** (coll.) without saying a word.

musa, *f.* Muse.—*pl.* the Muses; fine arts.
musáceo, cea, *a.* (bot.) musaceous.
musaraña, *f.* fetid shrewmouse; any small animal, insect, or vermin; (coll.) ridiculous puppet or stuffed figure; floating speck in the eye.—**mirar a,** or **pensar en, las musarañas,** to be absent-minded.
muscardina, *f.* muscardine (fungus disease of insects).
muscaria, muscícapa, *f.* (ornith.) flycatcher.
múscido, da, *a.* & *m.* (entom.) muscid.
muscívoro, ra, *a.* (zool.) fly-catching.
[1]**musco, ca,** *a.* dark brown.
[2]**musco,** *m.* (bot.) = [2]MUSGO.
muscovita, *f.* (min.) muscovite.
muscular, *a.* muscular.
muscularidad, *f.* muscularity.
musculatura, *f.* musculature.
músculo, *m.* muscle; brawn; (zool.) a huge whale.—**m. complexo,** complexus.—**m. del sastre,** sartorius.—**m. gemelo,** gemellus.—**m. glúteo,** gluteous muscle.—**m. lumbrical,** lumbricalis (*pl.* lumbricales).—**m. sartorio,** sartorius.—**m. serrato,** serratus.
musculoso, sa, *a.* muscular, brawny.
muselina, *f.* muslin.
museo, *m.* museum.
muserola, *f.* noseband of a bridle.
musgaño, *m.* (zool.) shrewmouse.
[1]**musgo, ga,** = [1]MUSCO.
[2]**musgo,** *m.* (bot.) moss.—**m. de Irlanda,** (bot.) Irish moss.—**m.** or **liquen de Islandia,** (bot.) Iceland moss.—**m. marino,** sea coralline.
musgoso, sa, *a.* mossy; moss-covered.
música, *f.* music; body of performing musicians; musical composition; sheet music.—**m. celestial,** (coll.) nonsense; moonshine.—**m. coreada,** chorus music.—**m. de campanas,** chimes.—**m. ratonera,** harsh music.—**m. rítmica,** stringed-instrument music.—**vaya Vd. con la m. a otra parte,** (coll.) get out, don't bother me.
musical, *a.* musical.
músico, ca. I. *a.* musical. **II.** *n.* musician.
musiquero, *m.* music cabinet.
musitar, *vn.* to mumble, mutter, whisper.
muslera, *f.* armor for the thigh.
muslime; muslímico, ca, *a.* Moslem, Mohammedan.
muslo, *m.* thigh.
musmón, *m.* (zool.) moufflon, wild sheep.
musquerola, *f.* = MOSQUEROLA, muscadine pear.
mustaco, *m.* cake made with must.
mustango, *m.* (Am.) mustang.
mustela, *f.* (zool.) weasel; (ichth.) a kind of dogfish.
mustiamente, *adv.* sadly, languidly.
mustio, tia, *a.* withered; sad, languid.
musulmán, na, *n.* & *a.* Mussulman.
muta, *f.* pack of hounds.
mutabilidad, *f.* mutability; fickleness.
mutación, *f.* mutation, change; (theat.) change of scene; unseasonable weather.
mutacional, *a.* mutational.
mutante, *m.* (biol.) mutant.
mutatis mutandis, (Lat.) *adv.* with the necessary changes (in words, etc.).
mutilación, *f.* mutilation.
mutilador, ra, *n.* mutilator.
mutilar, *va.* to mutilate; to cut short, reduce; to deface, mar.
mútilo, la, *a.* maimed, crippled, mutilated.
mutis, *m.* (theat.) exit.
mutismo, *m.* mutism, muteness.
mutual, *a.* mutual, reciprocal.
mutualidad, *f.* mutualness; system of organized mutual aid; mutual-aid association.
mutualismo, *m.* system of organized mutual aid.
mutualista. I. *a.* pertaining to the system of organized mutual aid. **II.** *n.* member of a mutual-aid organization.

mutuamente, *adv.* mutually, reciprocally.
mutuante, *m.* & *f.* (com.) lender, loaner.
mutuario, ria; mutuatario, ria, *m.* & *f.* (law) mutuary.
mútulo, *m.* (arch.) mutule.
mutuo, tua. I. *a.* mutual, reciprocal. **II.** *m.* (law) loan, mutuum.
muy, *adv.* very; greatly, most.—**m. de noche,** late at night.—**m. ilustre,** most illustrious.—**m. mucho,** (coll.) very much.—**M. señor mío,** Dear Sir (business letter).—**soy m. de Vd.,** I am entirely yours.
muz, *m.* (naut.) extremity of the cutwater.
muzárabe, *n.* & *a.* = MOZARABE, Mozarab(-ic).
my, *f.* mu (Greek letter).

N

N, n, *f.* n, sixteenth letter of the Spanish alphabet.
N., or N. N., a form often used in the sense of So-and-So, X., meaning any person.
naba, *f.* (bot.) rutabaga, Swedish turnip.
nabab, nababo, *m.* nabob, nawab.
nabal, nabar. I. *a.* pertaining to or made of turnips. **II.** *m.* turnip field.
nabería, *f.* turnip pottage; heap of turnips.
nabí, *m.* Moorish prophet.
nabillo, *m. dim.* small turnip.
nabina, *f.* rape and turnip seed.
nabiza, *f.* turnip rootlets; turnip greens.
nabla, *f.* (mus.) a kind of psaltery.
nabo, *m.* (bot.) turnip (plant and root); any bulb; stock of a tail; cylindrical timber; spindle; king-post; (naut.) mast.—**n. gallego** = NABA.
naborí, *n.* free Indian servant.
naboría, *f.* free female Indian servant; allotment of free Indian servants (during the Spanish conquest of America).
nácar, *m.* mother-of-pearl.
nacarado, da; nacáreo, a; nacarino, na, *a.* nacreous, pert. to, made of, mother-of-pearl.
nacarón, *m.* pearl shell of inferior quality.
nacascolo, *m.* (C. A.) a tropical tree.
nacela, *f.* (arch.) scotia (concave molding); (aer.) nacelle.
nacencia, *f.* growth; (fig.) tumor, outgrowth.
nacer. I. *vn.* (*pp.* NACIDO, NATO; *ind.* NAZCO; *subj.* NAZCA) to be born, come into the world; to sprout, come forth, grow (as branches, plants); to rise, come out, appear (as the sun); to spring, rise, flow, have its source (as a stream, a river); to begin, originate, start, issue; to infer one thing from another.—**n. de cabeza,** to be born to wretchedness.—**n. de pies,** to be born lucky. **II.** *vr.* to sprout (as seeds) in the open air; to split near a seam (as clothes).
nacido, da. I. *pp.* of NACER. **II.** *a.* proper, apt, fit, connate.—**bien** or **mal n.,** well or ill bred. **III.** *m.* living man; pimple, boil, furuncle; sprout.
naciente. I. *a.* rising; growing; very recent; (her.) naissant. **II.** *m.* Orient, East.
nacimiento, *m.* birth; growing of plants; beginning; place of birth; rising (as of the sun): origin, issue; descent, lineage; source of a river or spring; scene representing the Nativity at Yuletide.—**de n.,** from birth.
nación. I. *f.* nation; (coll.) birth; (Am.) race, tribe of Indians.—*pl.* **Naciones Unidas,** United Nations.—**Sociedad de las Naciones,** League of Nations. **II.** *m.* (coll.) foreigner.—**de n.,** by nationality.
nacional. I. *a.* national; native; domestic, home. **II.** *m.* native; militiaman.
nacionalidad, *f.* nationality; citizenship.
nacionalismo, *m.* nationalism.
nacionalista, *n.* & *a.* nationalist(-ic).
nacionalización, *f.* naturalization; acclimatization; nationalization.
nacionalizar, *va.* to naturalize; to nationalize.
nacionalmente, *adv.* nationally.
nacrita, *f.* variety of talc.
nacho, cha, *a.* flat-nosed, pug-nosed.
nada. I. *f.* nothing, naught; nothingness; nonentity. **II.** *indef. pron.* nothing, not anything; little or very little.—**n. de eso,** none of that; not at all; not so.—**n. de nuevo,** nothing new.—**de n.,** insignificant, good-for-nothing; (after thanks) you are welcome, don't mention it.—**¡en n.!,** not at all!—**por n.,** for nothing; under no circumstances. **III.** *adv.* nothing, not, not at all, by no means.
nadadera, *f.* gourd or bladder for swimming; *pl.* water wings.
nadadero, *m.* swimming place.
nadador, ra, *n.* & *a.* swimmer(-ing).
nadante, *a.* (poet.) natant, swimming.
nadar, *vn.* to swim; to float.
nadería, *f.* (coll.) insignificant thing, a mere nothing, trifle.
nadie, *indef. pron.* nobody, no one, none; (after negative) anybody.
nadilla, *f.* = NADERÍA.
nadir, *m.* (astr.) nadir.
nado.—a n., swimming; afloat.
nafta, *f.* naphtha.
naftalina, *f.* (chem.) naphthalin.
naftílico, ca, *a.* (chem.) naphthalic.
naftilo, *m.* (chem.) naphthyl.
naftol, *m.* (chem.) naphthol.
nagual, *m.* (Mex.) sorcerer, wizard, conjurer.
naguas, *f. pl.* petticoat.
naguatlato, *m.* (Mex.) Indian interpreter.
nahuatle, *m.* Nahuatlan, Mexican Indian language.
naife, *m.* diamond of the first water.
naipe, *m.* (playing) card; cards; pack of cards.—**dar (a uno) el n.,** to have good luck at cards.—**dar el n. para una cosa,** to be very skilful or dexterous.—**tener buen n.** = DAR EL N.
naire, *m.* elephant keeper, trainer.
nalga, *f.* buttock, rump; *pl.* (anat.) nates.
nalgada, *f.* ham; spank, slap on the buttocks.
nalgar, *a.* gluteal, pertaining to the buttocks.
nalgatorio, *m.* (coll.) seat, posterior, buttocks.
nalgudo, da, *a.* having big buttocks.
nalguear, *vn.* (coll.) to wiggle the buttocks in walking, waddle.
nana, *f.* (coll.) grandma; lullaby; (Mex., coll.) child's nurse; (Am.) (coll.) mamma.
nanear, *vn.* to waddle.
nanquín, *m.* (text.) nankeen, nankin.
nansa, *f.* fish trap; fishpond.
nansú, nanzú, *m.* (Am., text.) nainsook.
nao, *f.* ship, vessel.
naonato, ta, *a.* born on board ship.
napalm, *m.* (chem., mil.) napalm, jellied gasoline (bomb).
napea, *f.* wood nymph.
napelo, *m.* (bot.) monkshood, wolfsbane.
napoleón, *m.* napoleon (5-franc piece).
napoleónico, ca, *a.* Napoleonic.
napolitana, *f.* in some card games, a certain combination of cards.
napolitano, na, *n.* & *a.* Neapolitan.
naque, *m.* company of two strolling comedians.
naranja, *f.* (bot.) orange.—**n. cajel,** blood orange.—**media n.** (coll.) better half (wife, husband).
naranjada, *f.* orangeade; rude saying or deed.
naranjado, da, *a.* orange-colored.
naranjal, *m.* orange grove.
naranjazo, *m.* blow with an orange.
naranjero, ra. I. *a.* **cañon n.,** (artil.) cannon carrying balls of the size of oranges. **II.** *n.* orange raiser or seller. **III.** *m.* orange tree.
naranjilla, *f.* small green orange for preserving.
naranjo, *m.* (bot.) orange tree; (coll.) booby, noodle, stupid man.
narceína, *f.* (chem.) narceine.
narcisismo, *m.* (psych.) narcissism.
[1]narciso, *m.* (bot.) daffodil; narcissus.
[2]narciso, *m.* fop, coxcomb.
narcosis, *f.* (med.) narcosis.

narcótico, ca, *a.* & *m.* narcotic.
narcotina, *f.* (chem.) narcotine.
narcotismo, *m.* (med.) narcotism.
narcotización, *f.* narcotization.
narcotizador, ra, *a.* narcotic, narcose.
narcotizar, *va.* to narcotize.
nardino, na, *a.* made of spikenard.
nardo, *m.* (bot.) spikenard, nard, tuberose.
narguile, *m.* narghile.
narigón, na; narigudo, da. I. *a.* large-nosed. **II.** *m.* large nose. **III.** *n.* large-nosed person.
nariguera, *f.* nose pendant.
narigueta, nariguita, *f. dim.* small nose.
nariz, *f.* nose; nostril; sense of smell; bouquet (of wine); socket of a door knocker; nozzle; cutwater.—**n. aguileña,** Roman, or aquiline, nose.—**n. chata,** flat nose.—**n. perfilada,** perfect, or well-proportioned, nose.—**n. respingada,** or **respingona,** retroussé nose, turned-up nose.—**dar en las narices,** (coll.) to smell or perceive a thing at a distance.—**meter la n. en todas partes,** to be a busybody, to nose about.—**tener de,** or **por, las narices,** or **agarrado por las narices,** to lead by the nose, to control at will.
narizón, na, *n.* & *a.* = NARIGÓN.
narizota, *f. aug.* large, ugly nose.
narra, *f.* (bot.) narra, an Asiatic tree.
narrable, *a.* capable of being narrated.
narración, *f.* narration, narrative, account; chronicle.
narrador, ra. I. *a.* narrating. **II.** *n.* narrator, chronicler.
narrar, *va.* to narrate, relate, chronicle, tell.
narrativa, *f.* narrative.
narrativo, va; narratorio, ria, *a.* narrative.
narria, *f.* sledge, sled; (coll.) heavy, bulky woman.
narval, *m.* (zool.) narwhal.
narvaso, *m.* cornstalks (as fodder).
nasa, *f.* fyke, fish trap, bag net; bow net; fisherman's basket; basket; jar.
nasal, *a.* nasal, pertaining to the nose.
nasalidad, *f.* nasality.
nasalización, *f.* (phon.) nasalization.
nasalizar, *va.* (phon.) to nasalize.
nasardo, *m.* (mus.) nasard, organ stop.
nata, *f.* cream; prime or choice part; skim, scum. —*pl.* whipped cream with sugar.
natación, *f.* natation, swimming.
natal. I. *a.* natal, native. **II.** *m.* birth, birthday.
natalicio, cia. I. *a.* natal. **II.** *m.* birthday, birth.
natalidad, *f.* natality, birth rate.
natátil, *a.* able to swim, floating.
natatorio, a. I. *a.* swimming, natatorial. **II.** *m.* natatorium, swimming pool or place.
naterón, *m.* second curd.
natilla, *f.* custard.
natío. I. *a.* native. **II.** *m.* birth; sprouting.
natividad, *f.* nativity; Yuletide, Christmas.
nativo, va, *a.* native; indigenous; domestic; natural born; inborn, innate.
nato, ta. I. *pp. irreg.* of NACER. **II.** *a.* implied by or inherent in an office or position.
natrón, *m.* (min.) natron, barilla.
natura, *f.* nature; genital organs; (mus.) major scale.
natural. I. *a.* natural; native; common, usual; plain, pure, unadulterated; artless, ingenuous, naïve; spontaneous, unstudied; (mus.) natural. **II.** *n.* native; national; aboriginal. **III.** *m.* temper, disposition, nature.—**al n.,** without art or affectation.—**del n.,** (art) from life, from nature.
naturaleza, *f.* nature; constitution; sex, genitals, especially the female; sort, character, kind; naturalization; temperament or disposition.—**n. muerta,** (art) still life.
naturalicé, naturalice, *v. V.* NATURALIZAR.
naturalidad, *f.* naturalness; birthright, nationality.
naturalismo, *m.* naturalism; realism.
naturalista, *n.* & *a.* naturalist(-ic).
naturalización, *f.* naturalization.
naturalizar. I. *va.* (*pret.* NATURALICÉ; *subj.* NATURALICE) to naturalize. **II.** *vr.* to get accustomed; to become naturalized, become nationalized.
naturalmente, *adv.* naturally; of course.
naufragante, *a.* sinking, perishing.
naufragar, *vn.* (*pret.* NAUFRAGUÉ; *subj.* NAUFRAGUE) to be shipwrecked; to fail, be unsuccessful, fall through.
naufragio, *m.* shipwreck; disaster, failure, disappointment, calamity.
náufrago, ga. I. *a.* & *n.* shipwrecked (person). **II.** *m.* (ichth.) shark.
naufragué, naufrague, *v. V.* NAUFRAGAR.
náusea, *f.* nausea, nauseousness.
nauseabundo, da, *a.* nauseous, loathsome.
nauseante, *a.* nauseating.
nausear, *vn.* to feel nausea, be nauseated.
nauseativo, va, *a.* nauseating, nauseous.
nauseoso, sa, *a.* = NAUSEABUNDO.
nauta, *m.* mariner, seafarer, sailor.
náutico, ca. I. *a.* nautical. **II.** *f.* nautics.
nautilo, *m.* (zool.) nautilus.
nava, *f.* hollow, plain surrounded by mountains.
navacero, ra, *n.* one who cultivates a NAVAZO.
navaja, *f.* razor; clasp knife, pen knife; razor clam; tusk of a wild boar; (coll.) evil tongue.—**n. de afeitar** or **de barba,** razor, razor blade. —**n. de seguridad,** safety razor.—**navajas de gallos,** cockspurs.
navajada, *f.*; **navajazo,** *m.* thrust or gash with a clasp knife or razor.
navajero, *m.* razor case; shaving doily.
navajita, *f. dim.* small clasp knife or razor.
navajo, *m.* = LAVAJO, pool where cattle drink.
navajón, *m. aug.* large clasp knife or razor.
navajonazo, *m.* gash or wound made with a large clasp knife or a razor.
navajuela, *f. dim.* small clasp knife.
naval, *a.* naval.
navarro, rra, *n.* & *a.* Navarrese.
navazo, *m.* kitchen garden on a sandy shore.
nave, *f.* ship, vessel; (arch.) nave; aisle.—**n. aérea,** airship.—**n. del espacio,** space ship.—**n. de San Pedro,** Roman Catholic Church.
navecilla, *f. dim.* small ship; (eccl.) censer, thurible.
navegable, *a.* navigable.
navegación, *f.* navigation; sea voyage; time used in a sea voyage.—**n. aérea,** aerial navigation, aviation.—**n. astronáutica,** space travel.—**n. circular,** great circle sailing.—**n. costanera,** coast navigation, coasting trade.—**n. de altura,** high-seas sailing.
navegacional, *a.* navigational.
navegador, ra, *n.* & *a.* navigator(-ing).
navegante, *n.* & *a.* navigator(-ing).
navegar. I. *vn.* (*pret.* NAVEGUÉ; *subj.* NAVEGUE) to navigate, sail, steer; to travel.—**n. en conserva,** to sail under convoy. **II.** *va.* to make (as speed).
naveta, *f.* (eccl.) censer, thurible; small drawer
navícula, *f. dim.* small ship; (bot.) navicula.
navicular, *a.* (anat.) navicular, boat-shaped.
navichuelo, la, *n. dim.* small ship.
navidad, *f.* Nativity; Christmas Day.—**tener muchas navidades,** to be old, to have lived many a year.
navideño, ña, *a.* pertaining to Yuletide.
naviero. I. *a.* shipping, ship (as *a.*). **II.** *m.* ship owner.
navío, *m.* warship, armor-clad vessel; ship.—**n. anegado,** (naut.) water-logged ship.—**n. de aguante,** (naut.) a stiff ship.—**n. de alto bordo** = N. DE LÍNEA.—**n. de aviso,** despatch boat.—**n. de guerra,** warship.—**n. de línea,** line-of-battle ship.—**n. de transporte,** transport.—**n. de tres puentes,** three-decker.
nayade, *f.* naiad; water nymph.
nayuribe, *f.* (bot.) an amarantaceous herb.

nazareno, na. I. *n.* & *a.* Nazarene; Nazarite. II. *m.* penitent who goes in processions in Passion Week.
nazareo, ea, *a.* Nazarite.
nazco, nazca, *v.* *V.* NACER.
nazi, *a.* & *n.* Nazi.
nazismo, *m.* Nazi(i)sm.
nazista, *a.* & *n.* Nazi.
názula, *f.* second curd.
nébeda, *f.* (bot.) nepeta, catmint.
nebladura, *f.* (agr.) damage from mist.
neblí, *m.* (ornith.) falcon gentle.
neblina, *f.* mist, fog.
neblinoso, sa, *a.* foggy, misty.
nebreda, *f.* plantation of juniper trees.
nebrina, *f.* juniper berry.
nebular, *a.* (astr.) nebular.—**hipótesis n.,** (astr.) nebular hypothesis.
nebulón, na, *n.* hypocrite.
nebulosidad, *f.* nebulosity, nebulousness.
nebuloso, sa. I. *a.* nebulous, nebular, misty, hazy. II. *f.* (astr.) nebula.
necear, *vn.* to talk nonsense, to play the fool.
necedad, *f.* stupidity, foolishness, nonsense.
necesaria, *f.* privy, water-closet.
necesariamente, *adv.* necessarily.
necesario, ria, *a.* necessary.
neceser, *m.* dressing case, toilet case.—**n. de costura,** work basket, sewing case, hussy.
necesidad, *f.* necessity; need, want; emergency; evacuation of the body by stool or water.—**la n. carece de ley,** necessity knows no law.—**la n. tiene cara de hereje,** need knows no shame, need has a brazen face.—**por n.,** from necessity; necessarily.
necesitado, da. I. *pp.* of NECESITAR. II. *a.* & *n.* indigent, needy (person).
necesitar. I. *va.* to need; to necessitate, constrain, compel. II. *vn.* (**de**) to be in need (of).
neciamente, *adv.* stupidly, foolishly.
necio, cia. I. *a.* stupid, idiotic, foolish; imprudent, injudicious. II. *n.* fool.
necrocomio, *m.* morgue.
necrófago, ga, *a.* necrophagous, carrion-eating.
necrología, *f.* necrology.
necrológico, ca, *a.* necrological.
necrópolis, *f.* necropolis, burying ground.
necropsia, necroscopía, *f.* necropsy, autopsy, post-mortem examination.
necroscópico, ca, *a.* pert. to autopsy.
necrosis, *f.* (med.) necrosis.
néctar, *m.* nectar; any delicious drink.
nectáreo, a; nectarino, na, *a.* nectarean.
nectario, *m.* (bot.) nectary.
neerlandés, desa. I. *a.* Netherlands, Dutch. II. *n.* Netherlander; *m.* Dutchman; Dutch (language); *f.* Dutchwoman.
nefalismo, *m.* total abstinence from alcoholic beverages; prohibitionism.
nefalista, *n.* total abstainer; prohibitionist.
nefandamente, *adv.* nefariously, abominably.
nefando, da; nefario, ria, *a.* nefarious, heinous.
nefas, *adv.*—**por fas o por n.,** justly or unjustly.
nefasto, ta, *a.* sad, ominous, unlucky.
nefoscopio, *m.* (meteorol.) nephoscope.
nefralgia, *f.* (med.) nephralgia.
nefrectomía, *f.* (surg.) nephrectomy.
nefrita, *f.* (min.) nephrite.
nefrítico, ca, *a.* (med.) nephritic.
nefritis, *f.* (med.) nephritis.
nefrocele, *f.* (med.) nephrocele, hernia of the kidney.
nefrolito, *m.* (med.) nephrolith, kidney stone.
nefroptosis, *f.* (med.) nephroptosis.
nefrotomía, *f.* (surg.) nephrotomy.
negable, *a.* deniable.
negación, *f.* negation; denial; want or total privation; (gram.) negative particle.
negado, da. *a.* inapt, unfit; dull, stupid.
negador, ra, *n.* denier, disclaimer.
negante, *a.* denying; refusing.
negar. I. *va.* (*ind. pres.* NIEGO, *pret.* NEGUÉ; *subj.* NIEGUE) to deny; to refuse; to forbid, prohibit; to disown, disclaim; to disregard; to hide, conceal, dissemble.—**n. el saludo a,** to cut, not to speak to. II. *vr.* to decline, refuse; to be "not at home" to visitors.—**n. a sí mismo,** to control one's passions and appetites, exercise self-control.
negativa, *f.* negative, refusal.
negativamente, *adv.* negatively.
negativismo, *m.* (philos.) negativism.
negativo, va. I. *a.* negative; (elec. and math.) negative. II. *f.* (photog.) negative.
negligencia, *f.* negligence, neglect, carelessness.
negligente. I. *a.* negligent, neglectful, careless. II. *n.* neglecter.
negligentemente, *adv.* negligently, neglectfully, carelessly.
negociabilidad, *f.* (com.) negotiability.
negociable, *a.* (com.) negotiable.
negociación, *f.* negotiation; business transaction.
negociado, *m.* bureau, division or section in official departments; business; employment; affair.
negociador, ra, *n.* business agent; negotiator.
negociante. I. *a.* negotiating, trading, engaged in trade. II. *n.* dealer, merchant, business man.
negociar, *vn.* to trade; to negotiate.
negocio, *m.* occupation, business; affair; transaction; bargain; commerce; utility or interest in trading.—*pl.* business, commercial affairs.—**n. redondo,** good bargain.—**de negocios,** business (as *a.*), commercial.
negocioso, sa, *a.* active, diligent.
negozuelo, *m. dim.* petty business.
negra, *f.* Negro woman, Negress; (mus.) crotchet, quarter note.
negrada, *f.* (Am.) crowd or gathering of Negroes.
negral, *a.* blackish.
negrear, *vn.* to become black; to appear black.
negrecer, *vn.* (*ind.* NEGREZCO; *subj.* NEGREZCA) to blacken, become black.
negrero, ra, *n.* & *a.* slave trader(-ing).
negreta, *f.* (ornith.) coot, a kind of duck.
negrezco, negrezca., *v.* *V.* NEGRECER.
negrilla, *f.* (print.) boldface, blackface; (ichth.) black conger eel.
negrillera, *f.* plantation of black poplars.
negrillo, *m. dim.* (min.) black silver ore, stephanite; (bot.) black poplar.
negrito, ta, *n.* young or little Negro; (Am.) (coll.) dearest, darling.
negrizco, ca, *a.* blackish; dark brown.
negro, gra. I. *a.* black; gloomy, dark, dismal; unfortunate, wretched; (her.) sable.—**suerte n.,** very bad luck. II. *n.* Negro; (Am.) (coll.) dearest, darling. III. *m.* black (color).—**n. animal,** boneblack.—**n. de humo,** lampblack.—**n. de la uña,** tip of the (finger) nail.
negroide, *a.* negroid.
negror, *m.*; **negrura,** *f.* blackness.
negruzco, ca, *a.* blackish, dark brown.
neguijón, *m.* caries, decay of the teeth.
neguilla, *f.* (bot.) fennel flower, love-in-a-mist; age mark in horses' teeth; obstinate denial.
negus, *m.* negus (title of Ethiopian emperor).
neis, *f.* (geol.) gneiss.
nema, *f.* seal or sealing of a letter.
nematelminto, *m.* (zool.) nemathelminth.
nemátodo, da. I. *a.* filiform. II. *m.* (zool.) Nematode.
nemeo, a, *a.* Nemæan.
némine discrepante, (Lat.) unanimously.
nemoroso, sa, *a.* wooded, nemorous.
nemotecnia, *f.* mnemotechnics.
nene, nena. I. *n.* (coll.) infant, baby; dear, darling. II. *m.* (ironic) villain.
nenúfar, *m.* (bot.) white water lily.
neo. I. *pref.* neo- (new, recent). II. *m.* (chem.) neon. Also NEÓN.
neocatolicismo, *m.* Neo-Catholicism.

neocatólico, ca, *a.* & *n.* Neo-Catholic.
neoclasicismo, *m.* (f. a.) neoclassicism.
neoclásico, ca, *a.* neoclassical.
neodimio, *m.* (chem.) neodymium.
neoescocés, cesa. I. *a.* Nova Scotian. II. *n.* Nova Scotian, (coll.) Bluenose.
neófito, *m.* neophyte.
neofobia, *f.* aversion to innovations.
neogranadino, na, *n.* & *a.* New-Granadian (from New Granada, former name of Colombia).
neoimpresionismo, *m.* (f.a.) neoimpressionism.
neoimpresionista, *a.* & *n.* neoimpressionist.
neolatino, na, *a.* Neo-Latin.
neolítico, ca, *a.* neolithic.
neología, *f.* neology.
neológico, ca, *a.* neologistic.
neologismo, *m.* neologism.
neólogo, ga, *n.* neologist.
neomejicano, na, *n.* & *a.* New Mexican.
neomenia, *f.* (astr.) neomenia, first day of the moon.
neomicina, *f.* (biochem.) neomycin.
neón, *m.* (chem.) neon.
neoplasma, *m.* (med.) neoplasm.
neoplatonicismo, *m.* Neoplatonism.
neoplatónico, ca, *a.* Neoplatonic.
neorama, *m.* cyclorama.
neosalvarsán, *m.* (chem.) neosalvarsan.
neoyorquino, na. I. *a.* of or pertaining to New York. II. *n.* New Yorker.
neozelandés, sa. I. *n.* New Zealander. II. *a.* New Zealand (as *a.*), of or from New Zealand.
neozoico, ca, *a.* (geol.) Neozoic.
Nepal, *m.* Nepal.
nepalés, lesa, *a.* & *n.* Nepalese.
nepente, *m.* (bot.) nepenthe; nepenthe, magic drink.
neperiano, na, *a.* Naperian, Napierian.
nepote, *m.* privileged relative of the Pope.
nepotismo, *m.* nepotism.
neptúneo, a, *a.* Neptunian.
neptúnico. ca, *a.* (geol.) Neptunian.
neptunio, *m.* (chem.) neptunium.
neptunismo, *m.* (geol.) Neptunian theory.
neptunista, *n.* & *a.* (geol.) Neptunist(-ic).
Neptuno, *m.* (astr.) Neptune; (poet.) the sea.
nequáquam, *adv.* (Lat.) (coll.) by no means.
nequicia, *f.* perversity.
nereida, *f.* nereid, sea nymph.
nerita, *f.* nerita, a mollusk.
neroniano, na, *a.* Neronian.
nervadura, *f.* (arch.) nervure, rib; (carp.) feather; (min.) leader; (biol.) nervation, nervure.
nerval, *a.* (anat.) nerval, pertaining to nerves.
nérveo, a, *a.* pertaining to nerves.
nervezuelo, nerviecillo, *m. dim.* nervule.
nervino, na, *a.* nervine, nerve-strengthening.
nervio, *m.* (anat.) nerve; energy, vigor, strength; string of a musical instrument; rib, reinforcement; (bockbinding) rib, fillet; (naut.) span rope, stay; (bot.) nerve.—**n. hipogloso,** hypoglossal.—**n. maestro,** tendon.—**n. neumogástrico** or **vago,** vagus pneumogastric nerve. —**n. óptico,** optic nerve.—**nervios conjugados,** conjugate nerves.
nerv(i)osidad, *f.* nervosity; nervousness; strength, vigor.
nervioso, sa, *a.* nervous; vigorous, energetic; (bot.) nerved, having veins.
nervosamente, *adv.* nervously.
nervosidad, *f.* nervousness; strength, vigor; flexibility
nervosismo, *m.* (med.) nervosism.
nervoso, sa, *a.* nervous; strong, vigorous.
nervudo, da, *a.* strong-nerved. vigorous.
nérvulo, *m.* nervule.
nervura, *f.* (bookbinding) ribs.
nesciencia, *f.* ignorance.
nesciente, *a.* ignorant, foolish.
nescientemente, *adv.* ignorantly.
nesga, *f.* (sewing) gore; triangular piece.
néspera, *f.* = NÍSPERO, *m.* (bot.) medlar.
nestorianismo, *m.* Nestorianism.
nestoriano, na, *n.* & *a.* Nestorian.
netezuelo, la, *m.* & *f. dim.* little grandchild.
neto, ta. I. *a.* neat, pure, unadulterated; (com.) net, clear.—**en n.,** net.—**puro y n.,** pure and simple. II. *m.* (arch.) naked pedestal.
[1]**neuma,** *n.* (rhet.) expression by signs or nods.
[2]**neuma,** *m.* (mus.) neuma.
neumática, *f.* (phys.) pneumatics.
neumático, ca. I. *a.* pneumatic. II. *m.* tire.
neumatógrafo, *m.* (med.) pneumagraph, stethograph.
neumococo, *m.* (bacteriol.) pneumococcus.
neumogástrico, *m.* (anat.) pneumogastric nerve.
neumonía, *f.* (med.) pneumonia.
neumónico, ca, *a.* pneumonic: pulmonary.
neumotórax, *m.* (med.) pneumothorax.
neuralgia, *f.* (med.) neuralgia.
neurálgico, ca, *a.* neuralgic.
neurastenia, *f.* (med.) neurasthenia, nervous prostration.
neurasténico, ca, *n.* & *a.* neurasthenic.
neuraxón, *m.* (anat.) neuraxon, axis cylinder.
neurectomía, *f.* (surg.) neurectomy.
neurilema, *m.* (anat.) neurilemma.
neurisma, *f.* (med.) = ANEURISMA, aneurysm.
neuritis, *f.* (med.) neuritis.
neuroblasto, *m.* (anat.) neuroblast.
neurocirugía, *f.* neurosurgery.
neuroeje, *m.* (anat.) neural, or cerebro-spinal, axis.
neuroesqueleto, *n.* (anat.) endoskeleton.
neuroglia, *f.* (anat.) neuroglia, connective nerve tissue.
neurología, *f.* (anat.) neurology.
neurólogo, ga, *n.* neurologist.
neuroma, *m.* (med.) neuroma.
neurona, *f.* (anat.) neuron, nerve cell.
neurópata, *n.* (med.) neuropath.
neuropatía, *f.* (med.) neuropathy.
neuropático, ca, *a.* neuropathic, neurotic.
neuropatología, *f.* (med.) neuropathology.
neuropsiquiatría, *f.* (med.) neuropsychiatry.
neuróptero, ra, *a.* (entom.) neuropterous.
neurosis, *f.* (med.) neurosis.—**n. de guerra,** war neurosis, "shell shock."
neurótico, ca, *n.* & *a.* (med.) neurotic.
neurotomía, *f.* (surg.) neurotomy.
neurótomo, *m.* (surg.) neurotome.
neutoniano, na, *a.* Newtonian.
neutral, *a.* neutral, neuter.
neutralicé, neutralice, *v. V.* NEUTRALIZAR.
neutralidad, *f.* neutrality.
neutralismo, *m.* neutralism.
neutralista, *a.* & *n.* neutralist.
neutralización, *f.* neutralization.
neutralizar, *va.* (*pret.* NEUTRALICÉ; *subj.* NEUTRALICE) to counteract; to neutralize.
neutrino, *m.* (phys.) neutrino.
neutro, tra, *a.* neutral, neuter; (gram.) neuter.
neutrón, *m.* neutron.
nevada, *f.* snowfall.
nevadilla, *f.* (bot.) whitlow-wort.
nevado, da. I. *pp.* of NEVAR. II. *a.* white as snow. III. *m.* snow-capped mountain or peak.
nevar. I. *vn. impers.* (*ind.* NIEVA; *subj.* NIEVE) to snow. II. *va.* to make white as snow.
nevasca, *f.* snowfall; snowstorm, blizzard.
nevatilla, (ornith.) wagtail.
nevera, *f.* ice house; icebox, refrigerator; woman who sells ice.
nevereta, *f.* (ornith.) wagtail.
nevería, *f.* ice house: place where ice is sold.
nevero, *m.* iceman; place of perpetual snow.
nevisca, *f.* gentle fall of snow.
neviscar, *vn.* to snow lightly.
nevo, *m.* (med.) nevus.
nevoso, sa, *a.* snowy, niveous.
newtonio, *m.* (phys.) newton (unit of force).
nexo, *m.* nexus, bond, tie. union.

ni, *conj.* neither, nor (*n. esto n. aquello,* neither this nor that).—**ni con mucho,** not by a good deal.—**n. siquiera,** not even.—**n. un, n. uno, n. una,** (often preceded by *no* and a verb) not one, not a single.
niacina, *f.* (chem.) niacin, nicotinic acid.
niara, *f.* rick or stack of straw.
nícalo, *m.* NÍSCALO, mushroom.
Nicaragua, *f.* Nicaragua; (n.) (bot.) garden balsam.
nicaragüense, *n.* & *a.* Nicaraguan.
nicaragüeño, ña, *n.* & *a.* Nicaraguan.
niceno, na, *a.* Nicene.
nicerobino, *a.* ancient precious ointment.
nicle, *m.* a variety of chalcedony.
nicociana, *f.* (poet.) tobacco, nicotia.
nicotina, *f.* nicotine.
nicotínico, ca, *a.* nicotinic (acid).
nicot(in)ismo, *m.* (med.) nicotinism.
nicotismo, *m.* nicotinism.
nictagíneo, a, *a.* (bot.) nyctaginaceous.
nictálope, *a.* nyctalopic.
nictalopia, *f.* (med.) nyctalopia.
nic(ti)tación, *f.* nic(ti)tation.
nicho, *m.* niche; recess.
nidada, *f.* nestful of eggs; brood, covey.
nidal, *m.* nest; nest egg; basis, foundation, motive; haunt.
nidificar, *vn.* to nest, nidify, build a nest.
nidito, *m. dim.* small nest.
nido, *m.* nest; eyry; home, habitation, abode, residence; haunt; den.
niebla, *f.* fog, mist, haze; film that dims the sight; (agr.) blasting mildew.
[1]**niego,** *a.* newborn (falcon).
[2]**niego, niegue,** *v. V.* NEGAR.
niel, *m.* (art) niello work.—**nielar,** *va.* (art) to niello.
niéspera, *f.* (bot.) medlar.
nieto, ta, *n.* grandson(-daughter).
nietro, *m.* a measure for wine (159.7 liters).
nietzscheano, na, *a.* & *n.* Nietzschean.
nietzschismo, *m.* (philos.) Nietzscheanism.
nieva, nieve, *v. V.* NEVAR.
nieve, *f.* snow; (Am.) an ice, sherbet.
Níger, *m.* Niger.
Nigeria, *f.* Nigeria.
nigeriano, na, *a.* & *n.* Nigerian.
nigerino, na, *a.* & *n.* (of the) Niger.
nigola, *f.* (naut.) ratline.
nigromancia, *f.* necromancy.
nigromante, *n.* necromancer, conjurer, magician.—**nigromántico, ca. I.** *a.* necromantic. **II.** *n.* = NIGROMANTE.
nigua, *f.* chigoe, jigger flea.
nihilismo, *m.* nihilism.
nihilista. I. *a.* nihilistic. **II.** *n.* nihilist.
nilad, *m.* (bot.) a Philippine shrub.
nilón, *m.* nylon.
nimbo, *m.* halo; nimbus.
nimiamente, *adv.* excessively, minutely.
nimiedad, *f.* superfluity, prolixity; excess.
nimio, a, *a.* prolix; stingy.
ninfa, *f.* nymph; young lady; (entom.) pupa.
ninfea, *f.* (bot.) water lily.
ninfeáceo, a, *a.* (bot.) nymphæceous.
ninfo, *m.* (coll.) effeminate fop, dude.
ninfomanía, *f.* (med.) nymphomania.
ningún, *a.* (*contr.* of NINGUNO) no, not one, neither (*used only before masculine nouns*).—**de n. modo,** by no means, under no circumstances.
ninguno, na. I. *a.* no, none, not one, not any.—**n. cosa,** nothing.—**de n. manera,** by no means, under no circumstances.—**en n. parte,** not anywhere. **II.** *indef. pron.* none, no one, not one, nobody, neither.
ninivita, *n.* & *a.* Ninevite.
niña, *f.* little girl; young girl.—**n. bien,** well-bred girl.—**n. del ojo,** pupil of the eye.—**niñas de los ojos,** (coll.) apple of one's eye, treasure; (C. A., Cuba, W. I.) (used by servants of employers) Miss.
niñada, *f.* puerility, childishness.
niñato, *m.* unborn calf.
niñear, *vn.* to act like a child.
niñera, *f.* nurse, nursery maid, baby sitter.
niñería, *f.* puerility, childish action; child's play; plaything; trifle.
niñero, ra, *a.* & *f.* fond of children; dandler.
niñeta, *f.* small pupil of the eye.
niñez, *f.* childhood, infancy.
niñita, *f.* little girl.
niñito, *m.* little boy; little child.
niño, ña. I. *a.* childish, childlike, young; inexperienced. **II.** *n.* boy (girl). **III.** *m.* child.—*pl.* children.—**n. bien,** sissy.—**n. de la piedra,** foundling.—**n. de teta,** suckling babe, child in arms.—**ñ. expósito,** foundling.—**niños de la doctrina,** charity children.—**de n.,** as a child.—**desde n.,** from infancy, from childhood.
niobio, *m.* (chem.) niobium.
nioto, *m.* (ichth.) = CAZÓN, dogfish.
nipa, *f.* (bot.) nypa, an Asiatic palm.
nipe, nipis, *m.* nypa cloth.
nipón, na, *n.* & *a.* Nipponese, Japanese.
níquel, *m.* (chem.) nickel.
niquelado, *pp.* & *a.* nickel-plated.
niquelar, *va.* to nickel-plate.
niquelina, *f.* (min.) niccolite.
niquiscocio, *m.* unimportant thing, matter, trifle.
nirvana, *m.* Nirvana.
níscalo, *m.* nonpoisonous mushroom.
níspero, *m.* (bot.) medlar.—**n. del Japón,** (bot.) Japanese persimmon.
níspola, *f.* fruit of the medlar tree.
nitidez, *f.* neatness, brightness, clarity.
nítido, da, *a.* nitid, bright, clear; neat.
nitón, *m.* (chem.) niton, radon.
nitos, *m.* (coll.) nothing, "nix."
nitral, *m.* niter bed.
nitrato, *m.* (chem.) nitrate, saltpeter.—**n. de plata,** (chem.) silver nitrate.—**n. de potasio,** (chem.) potassium nitrate, niter, nitre.—**n. sódico,** (chem.) sodium nitrate.
nitrería, *f.* saltpeter works.
nítrico, ca, *a.* (chem.) nitric.
nitrificación, *f.* nitrification.
nitrificador, *m.* (chem.) nitrifier.
nitrificante, *a.* nitrogen-fixing (organisms).
nitrificar, *va.* (chem.) to nitrify.
nitrilo, *m.* (chem.) nitrile.
nitrito, *m.* (chem.) nitrite.
nitro, *m.* (chem.) niter, saltpeter.
nitrobacterias, *f. pl.* nitrobacteria.
nitrobencina, *f.* nitrobenzene.
nitrocelulosa, *f.* nitrocellulose.
nitrogenado, da, *a.* nitrogenous.
nitrogenar, *va.* to nitrogenize.
nitrógeno, *m.* (chem.) nitrogen.
nitroglicerina, *f.* nitroglycerine.
nitrómetro, *m.* nitrometer.
nitroprusiato, *m.* (chem.) nitroprussiate.
nitrosidad, *f.* nitrous condition.
nitrosilo, *m.* (chem.) nitrosyl.
nitroso, sa, *a.* (chem.) nitrous.
nitruro, *m.* (chem.) nitride.
nivel, *m.* level; levelness; water-mark; (surv.) level; (mason.) level, plummet.—**n. de aire,** or **de burbuja,** spirit level.—**n. del agua,** water mark or level.—**n. de (la) vida,** standard of living.—**n. del mar,** sea level.—**n. del suelo,** ground level.—**n. longitudinal,** (aer.) fore-and-aft level.—**a n.,** level, true; on the same level.
nivelación, *f.* leveling; grading.
nivelador, ra, *n.* & *a.* (surv.) leveler(-ing); grader(-ing).
nivelar. I. *va.* to level; to grade; to make even; to put on a basis of equity and justice.—**n. el presupuesto,** to balance the budget. **II.** *vr.* to level off.
níveo, ea, *a.* (poet.) snowy.

nixtamal, *m.* (Mex.) corn specially prepared for making tortillas.
nizardo, da, *a.* of or pertaining to Nice.
no, *adv.* no, not, nay.—**¿n.?** (at end of sentence) isn't it? isn't that so? do you see? etc.—**n. bien,** no sooner.—**n. más,** only; no more.—**n. obstante,** notwithstanding.—**n., que n.,** most certainly not.—**n. sea que,** lest; or else.—**n., sino,** not only so.—**n., sino, n.,** it cannot be otherwise.—**n. tal,** no such thing.—**n. ya,** not only.—**a que n.,** (coll.) I bet that isn't so; I bet you won't.—**pues n.,** but no, not so.
nobelio, *m.* (chem.) nobelium.
nobiliario, ria, *a.* nobiliary, pert. to nobility.
nobilísimamente, *adv. super.* most nobly.
nobilísimo, ma, *a. super.* most noble.
noble. I. *a.* noble. **II.** *m.* nobleman; an ancient gold coin.
noblemente, *adv.* nobly.
nobleza, *f.* nobleness; nobility; noblesse; a fine damask silk.
noca, *f.* variety of crab.
nocedal, *m.* = NOGUERAL, walnut tree grove.
nocente, *a.* noxious; guilty.
noción, *f.* notion, idea; element, rudiment (gen. in *pl.*).—**nocional,** *a.* notional.
nocivo, va, *a.* noxious, harmful, injurious.
noctambulismo, *m.* noctambulism, night walking, sleepwalking.
noctámbulo, la. I. *a.* noctambulous. **II.** *n.* noctambulist, nightwalker, sleepwalker; (coll.) night owl, nighthawk.
noctífloro, ra, *a.* (bot.) noctiflorous, night-blooming.
noctiluco, ca. I. *a.* noctilucent. **II.** *f.* (zool.) noctiluca, glowworm.
noctívago, ga. I. *a.* noctivagous, noctivagant, night-wandering. **II.** *n.* noctambulist, nightwalker, sleepwalker; (coll.) night owl, nighthawk.
nocturnal, *a.* nocturnal, nightly.
nocturno, na. I. *a.* nocturnal, night (as *a.*); lonely and sad. **II.** *m.* (eccl.) nocturn; (mus.) nocturne.
noche, *f.* night; evening (after sunset); (fig.) obscurity, ignorance.—**n. toledana,** restless night, sleepless night.—**ayer n.,** last night.—**buenas noches,** good evening; good night.—**de la n. a la mañana,** between sunset and sunrise; (fig.) overnight, suddenly, unexpectedly.—**de n., por la n.,** at night; by night; in the nighttime.—**esta n.,** tonight.—**media n.,** midnight.—**muy de n.,** late at night.—**prima n.,** evening.—**quedarse a buenas noches,** (coll.) to be left in the dark about something; to be disappointed.
nochebuena, *f.* Christmas eve.
nochebueno, *m.* Christmas cake; Yule log.
nochecita, *f.* (Am.) twilight, dusk, nightfall.—**a la n.,** at nightfall.
nocherniego, ga, *a.* night-wandering.
nochizo, *m.* (bot.) = AVELLANO, filbert tree.
nodación, *f.* (med.) impediment caused by a node.
nodal, *a.* nodal.
nodátil, *a.* (anat.) nodal.
nodo, *m.* (med.) node; (astr.) node.
nodriza, *f.* wet nurse.
nodular, *a.* nodular.
nódulo, *m.* nodule, small node.
nogada, *f.* sauce of pounded walnuts and spice.
nogal, *m.* = NOGUERA.
noguera, *f.* (bot.) walnut.—**n. negra,** (bot.) black walnut.
noguerado, da, *a.* walnut-colored.
nogueral, *m.* field or plantation of walnut trees.
noguerón, *m. aug.* large walnut tree.
nolición, *f.* unwillingness.
noli me tángere, *m.* (Lat.) noli-me-tangere; (med.) malignant ulcer.
nómada, nómade, *n.* & *a.* nomad(-ic).
nomadismo, *m.* nomadism, nomadic state.
nomarquía, *f.* nomarchy, province.
nombradamente, *adv.* expressly.
nombradía, *f.* renown, fame, reputation.
nombramiento, *m.* nomination, naming; appointment, commission; brevet.
nombrar, *va.* to name; to nominate; to appoint.
nombre, *m.* name; title; fame, reputation; power by which any one acts for another; (gram.) noun; (mil.) countersign; watchword.—**n. adjetivo,** adjective.—**n. apelativo,** (gram.) common noun.—**n. colectivo,** collective noun.—**n. común,** common noun.—**n. de bautismo** or **de pila,** Christian name.—**n. postizo,** alias.—**n. profesional,** professional name.—**n. propio,** proper noun.—**n. substantivo,** noun, substantive.—**n. y apellido,** full name.—**de n.,** by name.—**en el n.,** with God's help.—**no tener n.,** to be unspeakable.—**poner n. a,** to give a name to; to set a price on.—**por n.,** by the name of.
nomenclador, nomenclátor, *m.* nomenclator; gazetteer; glossary, technical vocabulary.
nomenclatura, *f.* catalogue; nomenclature.
nomeolvides, *f.* (bot.) forget-me-not.
nómina, *f.* payroll; list, catalogue.—**n. de pagos,** payroll.
nominación, *f.* nomination; appointment.
nominador, ra, *n.* appointer.
nominal. I. *a.* nominal; titular. **II.** *n.* nominalist.
nominalismo, *m.* nominalism.
nominalista. I. *a.* nominalistic. **II.** *n.* nominalist.
nominalmente, *adv.* nominally.
nominar, *va.* to nominate, name.
nominativo, va. I. *a.* (com.) personal, registered (as bonds). **II.** *a.* & *m.* (gram.) nominative.—*pl.* (coll.) elements, rudiments.
nominilla, *f.* pay warrant, voucher.
nómino, *m.* nominee.
nomo, *m.* nome, province.
nomología, *f.* nomology.
nomparell, *f.* (print.) nonpareil, six-point.
non. I. *a.* odd, uneven. **II.** *m.* odd number.—*pl.* repeated negation or denial; refusal (esp. of a marriage proposal, in the phrases *dar nones, echar nones*).—**andar de nones,** to be idle.—**digo que nones,** I say no.—**estar de n.,** to serve for nothing.—**pares y nones,** odd or even.—**quedar de n.,** to be without a partner or companion.
nona, *f.* (eccl.) nones.
nonada, *f.* trifle, nothing.
nonagenario, ria, *n.* & *a.* nonagenarian.
nonagésimo, ma, *a.* nonagesimal, ninetieth.
nonágono, *m.* (geom.) nonagon.
nonato, ta, *a.* not naturally born, but taken from the womb by Cæsarean section.
nonio, *m.* vernier, a measuring instrument.
nono, na, *a.* ninth.
non plus ultra, ne plus ultra, unsurpassable.
nopal, *m.* (bot.) nopal, cochineal fig-tree, prickly Indian pear tree.
noque, *m.* tan pit, tan vat; heap or basket of bruised olives.
noquero, *m.* tanner, currier, leather dresser.
norabuena, *f.* congratulation.
noramala, *adv.* in an evil hour.
noray, *m.* (naut.) bollard, mooring.
nordestal, *a.* northeast, northeastern.
nordeste, *m.* northeast.—**nordestear,** *vn.* **(naut.)** (of the compass) to decline to northeast.
nórdico, ca, *n.* & *a.* Nordic.
nordista. I. *a.* northern, northerly. **II.** *n.* (U. S.) Northerner.
nordovestear, *vn.* (naut.) = NORUESTEAR.
noria, *f.* noria, chain pump, draw-well.
norial, *a.* pertaining to the NORIA.
norma, *f.* standard, norm, pattern, model, rule, specification.
normal. I. *a.* normal; model, standard. **II.** *f.* normal school; (geom.) normal.

normalidad, *f.* normality.
normalizar, *va.* to normalize; to standardize.
normando, da; normano, na. I. *n.* & *a.* Norman. **II.** *n.* Norman; Northman, Norseman.
nornordeste, *m.* north-northeast.
nornoroeste, nornorueste, *m.* north-northwest.
noroeste, norueste, *m.* northwest.
noroestear, *vn.* (naut.) = NORUESTEAR.
nortada, *f.* north gale, norther.
norte, *m.* north; north wind; rule, law, guide, clue, direction.
norteamericano, na, *n.* & *a.* North-American; American (gen. from or of the U. S.).
nortear, *va.* (naut.) to steer or stand to the northward; (of compass) to decline to the north.
norteño, ña. I. *a.* northern, northerly. **II.** *n.* northerner.
nórtico, ca, *a.* north, northerly, northern.
noruego, ga. I. *a.* & *n.* Norwegian. **II.** *f.* (N.) Norway; *m.* Norwegian (language).
norueste, *m.* northwest.
noruestear, *vn.* (naut.) (of the compass) to decline to the northwest.
nos, *pers. pron. pl. m.* & *f. acc.* & *dat.* of NOSOTROS, us, to us; (*recip.*) each other; (*refl.*) ourselves. Sometimes used as nom., in authoritative style, as *nos, el arzobispo de Toledo,* I, the archbishop of Toledo.
nosogenia, *f.* (med.) development of diseases.
nosografía, *f.* (med.) classification of diseases.
nosología, *f.* (med.) science of disease classification.
nosológico, ca, *a.* pert. to NOSOLOGÍA.
nosotros, tras, *pers. pron. pl. m.* & *f.* we; ourselves; us.
nostalgia, *f.* nostalgia, homesickness.
nostálgico, ca, *a.* nostalgic, homesick.
nostramo, *m.* (naut.) master—a title given by sailors to the boatswain.
nota, *f.* note, mark, sign; notice; grade (in exam.); annotation; imputation, reproach; stain, stigma; renown, fame, repute; style, manner of writing; memorandum; (com.) account, bill, statement, schedule, price list; (mus.) note.—*pl.* records of a notary.—**n. marginal,** marginal note.—**n. verbal,** verbal note.
nota bene, (Lat.) take notice; N. B.
notabilidad, *f.* notability; a notable (person).
notabilísimo, ma, *a. super.* of NOTABLE: most, or very, notable, marked, or noted.
notable, *a.* notable, remarkable, noteworthy, noticeable, conspicuous; distinguished, prominent, noted.—**notablemente,** *adv.* notably, remarkably, notedly, noticeably.
notación, *f.* note, annotation; (math. and mus.) notation.
notar, *va.* to note, to mark; to remark, observe; to notice, take notice of, observe; to annotate, comment; to dictate; to find fault with, criticize; to reprehend.
notaría, *f.* profession or position of a notary; notary's office.
notariado, *m.* profession of a notary.
notarial, *a.* notarial.
notariato, *m.* title or practice of a notary.
notario, *m.* notary public; amanuensis.
noticia, *f.* news item; news (gen. *pl.*); notice, information, light; (com.) advice.—**n. remota,** vague remembrance.—**atrasado de noticias,** behind the times.
noticiar, *va.* to notify, give notice to, inform.
noticiario, *m.* (rad.) newscast, (mov. pict.) newsreel.
noticiero, *m.* news agent, reporter; (rad.) newscaster; newsmonger.
noticíón, *m. aug.* (coll.) great news.
noticioso, sa, *a.* news-giving; informed; learned.
notificación, *f.* notification; notice.
notificado, da, *pp.* & *a.* (law) notified.
notificar. *va.* (*pret.* NOTIFIQUÉ; *subj.* NOTIFIQUE) to notify.
notita, *f. dim.* short note, memorandum, etc.
[1]noto, ta, *a.* well-known.
[2]noto, ta, *a.* illegitimate, bastard.
[3]noto, *m.* south wind, notus.
notomía, *f.* skeleton.
notoriamente, *adv.* manifestly, glaringly.
notoriedad, *f.* quality of being well known; self-evidence; notoriety.
notorio, ria, *a.* well known; evident, manifest.
nóumeno, *m.* (philos.) noumenon.
nova, *f.* (astr.) nova (star).
novaciano, na, *m.* & *f.* Novatian.
novación, *f.* (law) novation.
novador, ra, *n.* & *a.* innovator(-ing).
noval, *a.* newly broken up (land).
novar, *va.* (law) to renew by novation.
novatada, *f.* hazing (in colleges).
novato, ta, *n.* novice, beginner, tyro.
novator, ra, *n.* innovator, novator.
novecientos, tas, *n.* & *a.* nine hundred.
novedad, *f.* novelty; newness; surprise, recent occurrence, latest news or fashion; fad; change, innovation; surprise.—**no hay n.,** there is no change.—**sin n.,** well; safe; as usual; nothing new.
novedoso, sa, *a.* new, novel, recent; innovating; (Am.) fictional.
novel, *a.* new, inexperienced.
novela, *f.* novel; romance, fiction; falsehood; (law) novel.
novelador, ra, *n.* novelist.
novelar, *vn.* to write novels; to romance, to tell stories.
novelería, *f.* fondness for novelties; curiosity; fondness for novels; collection of novels.
novelero, ra. I. *a.* fond of novels, fads, and novelties; newfangled; fickle, wavering, unsteady. **II.** *n.* newsmonger, gossip.
novelesco, ca, *a.* novelistic, fictional.
novelista, *n.* novelist.
novelística, *f.* novel writing.
noveno, na. I. *a.* & *n.* ninth. **II.** *m.* ninth part of tithes. **III.** *f.* (eccl.) novena.
noventa, *m.* & *a.* ninety; ninetieth.
noventavo, va, *n.* & *a.* ninetieth.
noventón, na, *n.* & *a.* nonagenarian.
novia, *f.* bride; fiancée; sweetheart.
noviazgo, *m.* engagement, betrothal.
noviciado, *m.* (eccl.) novitiate; apprenticeship.
novicio, cia. I. *a.* new, inexperienced. **II.** *n.* novice, probationer; freshman, apprentice, neophyte.
noviciote, *m.* (coll.) overgrown novice.
noviembre, *n.* November.
novilunio, *m.* new moon.
novilla, *f.* young cow, heifer.
novillada, *f.* drove of young bulls or steers; baiting of young bulls.
novillejo, eja, *n. dim.* bullock (heifer).
novillero, *m.* herdsman who attends young cattle; stable for young cattle; pasture ground for weaned calves; truant, idler.
novillo, *m.* young bull; steer.—**hacer novillos,** (coll.) to play truant or hooky.
novio, *m.* bridegroom; fiancé; (coll.) suitor; one new to some dignity or state.
novísimo, ma, *super.* of NUEVO. **I.** *a.* newest, most recent; latest.—**N. Recopilación,** revised code of laws in Spain promulgated July 15, 1805. **II.** *m.* each of the last four incidents of mankind.
novocaína, *f.* (med.) Novocaine (trademark).
noyó, *m.* a bitter almond cordial.
nubada, *f.* shower of rain; plenty, abundance.
nubado, da, *a.* clouded, shaped like clouds.
nubarrado, da. I. *a.* NUBADO, DA. **II.** *f.* NUBADA.
nubarrón, *m.* large threatening cloud.
nube, *f.* cloud; crowd, multitude; (med.) film on the eye; cloud or shade in precious stones.—**n. atómica,** atomic cloud.—**n. cósmica,** (astr.) cosmic cloud.—**estar en las nubes,** (coll.) to be up in the clouds, to daydream.—

por las nubes, (coll.) sky-high (praise or price).
nubecita, *f.* small cloud.
nubiense, *n.* & *a.* Nubian.
nubífero, ra, *a.* (poet.) cloud-bringing.
núbil, *a.* nubile, marriageable.
nubilidad, *f.* nubility, marriageable age.
nubiloso, sa, *a.* (poet.) cloudy, nubilous.
nubio, bia, *a.* & *n.* Nubian.
nublado, da. I. *pp.* of NUBLAR. **II.** *a.* cloudy, overcast. **III.** clouded sky; gloominess; impending danger; multitude.
nublar. I. *va.* to becloud, obscure. **II.** *vr.* to become cloudy; (of plants) to be blasted, mildewed.
nublo, bla. I. *a.* cloudy. **II.** *m.* NUBLADO.
nubloso, sa, *a.* nebulous, cloudy; gloomy; ill-fated.
nubosidad, *f.* cloudiness.
nuca, *f.* nape, scruff of the neck.
nucleación, *f.* nucleation.
nucleado, da, *a.* nucleate.
nuclear, *a.* (biol., phys.) nuclear.
nucleína, *f.* (biochem.) nuclein.
núcleo, *m.* nucleus; center.—**n. blanco,** (phys.) target nucleus.—**n. nervioso,** (anat.) nidus.—**fisión del n.,** nuclear fission.
nucleolo, *m.* (biol.) nucleolus.
nucleón, *m.* (atom. ener.) nucleon.
nucleónica, *f.* nucleonics.
nucleoproteína, *f.* (biochem.) nucleoprotein.
núclido, *m.* (phys.) nuclide.
nuco, *m.* a Chilean kind of owl.
nudamente, *adv.* nakedly; plainly.
nudillo, *m.* knuckle; small knot in stockings; (mason.) plug, dowel, dook; nodule.
nudismo, *m.* nudism.
nudista, *n.* nudist.
[1]**nudo, da,** *a.* nude, naked.
[2]**nudo,** *m.* knot; burl, tangle; (bot.) node; joint; snag; tie, union, bond; (med.) node, tumor; knotty point, intricacy, difficulty; crisis of a drama; (naut.) knot of the log line, nautical mile.—**n. en la garganta,** lump in one's throat, great affliction.—**n. gordiano,** Gordian knot.
nudoso, sa, *a.* knotty, knotted.
nuecero, ra, *n.* vender of walnuts.
nuégado, *m.* nougat.
nuera, *f.* daughter-in-law.
nuestramo, ma, *f. contr.* from NUESTRO AMO, our master (mistress); (Am.) the Eucharist.
nuestro, tra, *poss. pron. 1st pers. pl.* our, ours. (Also used editorially, etc. as in Eng.).—**los nuestros,** our friends, or colleagues, ours.
nueva, *f.* news, tidings.
nuevamente, *adv.* newly, recently, freshly.
Nueva Zelandia, *f.* New Zealand.
nueve. I. *n.* & *a.* nine. **II.** *m.* ninth (of the month). **III.** *f. pl.*—**las n.,** nine o'clock.
nuevecito, *a. dim.* brand-new.
nuevo, va, *a.* new; novel, modern; newly arrived. —**n. emisión,** reissue.—**n. flamante,** spick and span, brand-new.—**de n.,** anew; again, once more.—**¿qué hay de n.?** what's the news, what's new?
nuez, *f.* walnut; nut or meat of some fruits (as coconuts); Adam's apple.—**n. de especia,** (bot.) nutmeg.—**n. dura,** hickory nut.—**n. moscada** = N. DE ESPECIA.—**n. vómica,** (bot.) nux vomica.
nueza, *f.* (bot.) bryony.
nugatorio, ria, *a.* nugatory, futile.
nulamente, *adv.* invalidly, ineffectually.
nulidad, *f.* (law) nullity; defeasance; inability, incompetency; insignificant or incompetent person, a nobody.
nulo, la, *a.* null, void; of no account.
numen, *m.* divinity, deity; inspiration.
numerable, *a.* numerable.
numeración, *f.* numeration (usually including notation); numbering.
numerador, *m.* numerator; numberer.
numeral, *n.* & *a.* numeral.
numerar, *va.* to number; enumerate; calculate, reckon; to page (a book).
numerario, ria. I. *a.* numerary. **II.** *m.* cash, coin, specie.
numerata pecunia, (law) ready money.
numéricamente, *adv.* numerically.
numérico, ca, *a.* numerical.
número, *m.* number; figure, character; numeral; size (shirt, etc.); number, issue (of magazine, etc.); poetical or musical measure, rhythm; (gram.) number.—*pl.* (N-) numbers, fourth book of the Pentateuch.—**n. abstracto,** abstract number.—**n. arábigo,** Arabic number.—**n. atómico,** atomic number.—**n. cardinal,** cardinal number.—**n. complejo** or **denominado,** complex number.—**n. compuesto,** compound number.—**n. de fábrica,** factory number.—**n. de identificación,** identification number.—**n. de Mach,** Mach number.—**n. de masa,** mass number.—**n. de matrícula,** license number; accession number.—**n. de serie,** serial number.—**n. entero,** whole or integral number.—**n. fraccionario** or **mixto,** mixed number.—**n. impar,** odd number.—**n. indicador** or **índice,** index number.—**n. ordinal,** ordinal number.—**n. par,** even number.—**n. primo,** prime number.—**n. racional,** rational number.—**n. romano,** Roman numeral.—**n. sordo,** surd.—**n. uno,** number one, oneself; A 1, A number 1.—**de n.,** regular (said of a member of an association with a limited number of persons).—**sin n.,** numberless.
numerosamente, *adv.* numerously.
numerosidad, *f.* numerosity, numerousness.
numeroso, sa, *a.* numerous; harmonious, rhythmical.
númida, *n.* & *a.*; **numídico, ca,** *a.* Numidian.
numisma, *m.* coin, money.
numismático, ca. I. *a.* numismatical. **II.** *m.* numismatist. **III.** *f.* numismatics.
numular, *a.* (med.) nummular.
numulario, ria. I. *a.* nummular. **II.** *m.* banker, money broker.
nunca, *adv.* never.—**n. jamás,** never, never more.
nunciatura, *f.* nunciature.
nuncio, *m.* messenger; Papal nuncio; forerunner, harbinger.
nuncupativo, va, *a.* (law) nuncupative, oral.
nuncupatorio, ria, *a.* dedicatory (writing).
nupcial, *a.* nuptial, hymeneal.
nupcialidad, *f.* marriage rate.
nupcias, *f. pl.* nuptials, wedding, marriage.
nutación, *f.* (astr. and bot.) nutation.
nutra, nutria, *f.* (zool.) otter.
nutricio, cia, *a.* nutritious, nourishing.
nutrición, *f.* nutrition, nourishing; (pharm.) preparation of medicines.
nutrido, da. I. *pp.* of NUTRIR. **II.** *a.* **(de)** full **(of),** abounding (with, in); copious.
nutrimental, *a.* nutrimental.
nutrimento, *m.* nutriment, food, nourishment; nutrition.
nutriólogo, ga, *n.* nutritionist.
nutrir, *va.* to nourish, nurture, feed; to encourage, promote, support.
nutritivo, va, *a.* nutritive, nourishing.
nutriz, *f.* = NODRIZA, wet nurse.
ny, *f.* nu (Greek letter).

Ñ

Ñ, ñ, *f.* seventeenth letter of the Spanish alphabet.
ñagaza, *f.* bird-call, decoy.
ñame, *m.* (bot.) yam.
ñandú, *m.* American ostrich.
ñanduti, *m.* (S. A.) a very fine fabric used mainly for underclothes.

ñangado, da, *a.* (Cuba) deformed, crooked-limbed.
ñango, ga, *a.* (Am.) ÑANGADO; (Am.) ungraceful, awkward.
ñánigo, ga, *n.* (Cuba) member of a secret society of Negroes.
ñaño, ña, *n.* (Am.) brother or sister; (Am.) close friend.
ñapa, *f.* (Am., coll.) bonus, extra, lagniappe. Also YAPA.—**de ñ.,** to boot, into the bargain.
ñaque, *m.* odds and ends.
ñato, ta, *a.* (Am.) pug-nosed.
ñeque. I. *m.* (Am.) (coll.) energy; bravery. **II.** *a.* & *n.* (Am.) (coll.) strong, vigorous (person), "he-man."
ñiquiñaque, *m.* (coll.) good-for-nothing person or thing; trash.
ñisca, ñizca, *f.* (Chile, Peru) little piece, bit.
ño, ña, (Am.) contr. of SEÑOR, SEÑORA, gen. app. to elderly persons of the lower classes.
ñocio, *m.* a kind of macaroon.
ñongo, ga, *a.* (Chile) (coll.) lazy, good-for-nothing; (Colomb.) (of dice) loaded.—**ñonguera,** *f.* (Chile) laziness.
ñoñería, *f.* dotage, drivel.
ñoñez, *f.* dotage, senility; shyness.
ñoño, ña, *a.* (coll.) timid, shy; dotard, feeble; flimsy; (Am.) old-fashioned.
ñudo, *m.* = NUDO, knot.—**al ñ.,** (Arg.) in vain.

O

O, o, *f.* o, eighteenth letter of the Spanish alphabet.
[1]o, *conj.* or, either.—**o sea, that is.**
[2]o, *interj.* oh, O.
oasis, *m.* oasis.
obcecación, *f.* obfuscation, obsession.
obcecadamente, *adv.* obsessedly.
obcecar, *va.* (*pret.* OBCEQUÉ; *subj.* OBCEQUE) to obsess; to blind, obfuscate; to darken or obscure.
obduración, *f.* obstinacy, obduracy.
obedecedor, ra, *n.* obeyer.
obedecer, *va.* (*ind.* OBEDEZCO; *subj.* OBEDEZCA) to obey; to respond; to be due, arise (from); to follow, be controlled by.
obedecimiento, *m.* obedience.
obedezco, obedezca, *v. V.* OBEDECER.
obediencia, *f.* obedience.—**a la o.,** your most obedient.
obediencial, *a.* pertaining to obedience.
obediente, *a.* obedient.
obedientemente, *adv.* obediently.
obelisco, *m.* obelisk; (print.) dagger (†).
obelo, *m.* obelisk; (print.) obelus, dagger (†).
obencadura, *f.* (naut.) shrouds in general.
obenques, *m. pl.* (naut.) shrouds, shifters.
obertura, *f.* (mus.) overture.
obesidad, *f.* obesity, fatness, fleshiness.
obeso, sa, *a.* obese, fat, fleshy.
óbice, *m.* obstacle, impediment, hindrance.
obispado, *m.* bishopric; episcopate.
obispal, *a.* episcopal, pertaining to a bishop.
obispalía, *f.* palace or house of a bishop; bishopric, diocese.
obispar, *vn.* to be made a bishop.
obispillo, *m. dim.* boy bishop; bishop of no account; large pork sausage; rump of a fowl.
obispo, *m.* (eccl.) bishop; large blood pudding; (ichth.) raioid selachian.
óbito, *m.* (law, eccl.) death, decease, demise.
obituario, *m.* obituary.
objeción, *f.* objection.
objetable, *a.* objectionable.
objetante, *n.* & *a.* objector(-ing).
objetar, *va.* to object to, oppose, remonstrate.
objetivamente, *adv.* objectively.
objetivar, *va.* to objectify or objectivate.
objetividad, *f.* objectivity.
objetivismo, *m.* objectivism.
objetivo, va. I. *a.* objective. **II.** *m.* (opt.) objective; (opt.) eyepiece.
objeto, *m.* object; subject matter; purpose.—**o. arqueológico,** artifact.—**o. curioso,** curio.
oblación, *f.* oblation, offering, gift.
oblada, *f.* (eccl.) funeral offering of bread.
oblata, *f.* (eccl.) oblate; contribution for church expenses.
oblea, *f.* wafer for sealing letters.
obleera, *f.* wafer holder, case for wafers.
oblicuamente, *adv.* obliquely.
oblicuángulo, *a.* oblique-angled.
oblicuar, *va.* & *vn.* to cant, slant; (mil.) to oblique.
oblicuidad, *f.* obliquity.
oblicuo, cua, *a.* oblique, slanting.
obligación, *f.* obligation, responsibility, duty; bond, debenture; charge; provision office.—*pl.* family that one is obliged to maintain; engagements; (com.) liabilities.
obligacionista, *n.* (com.) bondholder.
obligado, *m.* city contractor; (law) obligor; (law) obligee; (mus.) obbligato.
obligante, *a.* obligating, obliging.
obligar. I. *va.* (*pret.* OBLIGUÉ; *subj.* OBLIGUE) to obligate, compel, bind; to oblige. **II.** *vr.* to obligate or bind oneself.
obligatorio, ria, *a.* obligatory, compulsory.
obligué, obligue, *v. V.* OBLIGAR.
obliteración, *f.* (med.) obliteration.
obliterar, *va.* (med.) to obliterate.
oblongo, ga, *a.* oblong.
obnoxio, xia, *a.* obnoxious.
oboe, obué, *m.* (mus.) oboe; oboist.
óbolo, *m.* obolus; obolo; mite; (pharm.) obole.
obra, *f.* work; work(s), book(s); show, performance; building, structure; repairs in a house; means, virtue, power, influence; agency; toil, labor, employment.—**o. a cuerno,** (mil.) hornwork.—**o. de,** about, more or less.—**o. de arte,** work of art.—**o. de manos,** manual job.—**o. de romanos,** demanding work; (coll.) big order.—**o. maestra,** masterpiece.—**o. muerta,** (naut.) gunwale.—**o. prima,** shoemaking.—**o. pública,** public work.—**obras accesorias** (fort.) outworks of a fortress.—**obras de marea,** graving, caulking and paving a ship bottom.—**obras muertas,** upper works of a ship.—**obras pías,** charitable funds or establishments.—**obras vivas,** (naut.) quick or lower works.—**a o. de** = O. DE.—**en obras,** under construction; undergoing repairs.—**hacer mala o.,** to do a bad turn.—**poner por o.,** to set to work on, to start.
obrada, *f.* day's work: a land measure (varies between 39 and 54 ares).
obrador, ra, *n.* workman(-woman); *m.* workshop.
obradura, *f.* charge of an oil mill.
obraje, *m.* manufacture, handiwork; workshop; wool mills.
obrajero, *m.* foreman, overseer, superintendent.
obrante, *a.* acting, working.
obrar. I. *va.* to work; to make, manufacture; to perform, execute; to construct, build. **II.** *vn.* to act; to ease nature.—**o. en,** to be in (a place, a person's hands, etc.).
obrepción, *f.* (law) obreption.
obrepticio, cia, *a.* (law) obreptitious.
obrería, *f.* task of a workman; money for church repairs.
obrerismo, *m.* labor (workers collectively).
obrero, ra. I. *a.* working, of or pertaining to labor. **II.** *n.* worker, laborer, employee; missionary.—**o. a jornal,** wageworker, daily worker. —**o. de fábrica,** factory worker.—**o. fundidor,** foundryman.—**o. mecánico,** mechanic, repairman.—**o. portuario,** docksman.—**obreros sindicalizados,** organized labor.—**o. temporero,** part timer, temporary laborer.
obrita, *f. dim.* small or little work; booklet.
obrizo, za, *a.* pure, refined (gold).
obscenamente, *adv.* obscenely.

obscenidad, *f.* obscenity.
obsceno, na, *a.* obscene.
obscuración, *f.* = OBSCURIDAD.
obscuramente, *adv.* obscurely, darkly, faintly; confusedly; humbly, modestly.
obscurantismo, *m.* obscurantism.
obscurantista, *n.* obscurantist.
obscuras.—a o., or oscuras, in the dark.
obscurecer, oscurecer. I. *va.* (*ind.* O(B)SCUREZCA; *subj.* O(B)SCUREZCA) to obscure, darken; to dim; to tarnish; to cloud, confuse; (art) to shade. **II.** *v. impers.* to grow dark. **III.** *vr.* to cloud over; to disappear: to become dark.
obscurecimiento, *m.* obscuration, darkening.
obscurezco, obscurezca, *v. V.* OBSCURECER.
obscuridad, *f.* obscurity; darkness; gloominess; opacity; retired, private life.
obscuro, oscuro, ra. I. *a.* obscure; dark; gloomy; (art) heavily shaded; (of color) dark. **II.** *m.* (art) shade.
obsecración, *f.* obsecration, entreaty, supplication.
obsecrar, *va.* to obsecrate, entreat, petition.
obsecuente, *a.* obsequious; obedient.
obseder, *va.* to obsess.
obsequiador, ra, *n.* giver; entertainer.
obsequiante, *a.* obsequious.
obsequiar, *va.* to treat, entertain, pay attentions to, make presents to; to court, woo; to present, make a gift of.
obsequio, *m.* obsequiousness; treat; courtesy, attention shown; gift, present.—**en o. de,** for the sake of, out of respect to.
obsequiosamente, *adv.* obsequiously, flatteringly, gallantly.
obsequioso, sa, *a.* obsequious; obedient, compliant; obliging, attentive.
observable, *a.* observable, noticeable.
observación, *f.* observation; remark, note.—**o. astronómica,** astronomical observation, skywatching.—**o. meteorológica,** meteorological observation, weather forecasting.—**en o.,** under observation.
observador, ra. I. *a.* observing. **II.** *n.* observer.—**o. meteorológico,** meteorologist, weather forecaster.
observancia, *f.* observance, fulfillment.—**poner en o.,** to execute punctually.
observante, *a.* observant, observing.
observar, *va.* to observe; to notice, note; remark; to look into, watch; to conform to (a rule, etc.).
observatorio, *m.* observatory.—**o. astrofísico,** astrophysical observatory.—**o. astronómico,** astronomical observatory.—**o. meteorológico,** meteorological observatory, weather station.
obsesión, *f.* obsession.
obsesionar, *va.* to obsess.
obseso, sa, *a.* beset; obsessed.
obsidiana, *f.* (geol.) obsidian.
obsidional, *a.* (mil.) obsidional, pert. to a siege.
obstaculizar, *va.* to obstruct; to hinder.
obstáculo, *m.* obstacle.
obstante.—no o., notwithstanding; nevertheless, however.
obstar, *vn.* to oppose, obstruct, hinder.
obstetricia, *f.* (med.) obstetrics, midwifery.
obstétrico, ca. I. *a.* obstetric, obstetrical. **II.** *m.* obstetrician.
obstinación, *f.* obstinacy, stubbornness.
obstinadamente, *adv.* obstinately, stubbornly.
obstinado, da. I. *pp.* of OBSTINARSE. **II.** *a.* obstinate, stubborn, obdurate, headstrong.
obstinarse, *vr.* (en) to be obstinate (about), to persist (in); to insist (on).
obstrucción, *f.* obstruction, stoppage.
obstruccionismo, *m.* obstructionism.
obstruccionista, *n. & a.* obstructionist(-ic).
obstructivo, va, *a.* obstructive.
obstructor, ra. I. *a.* obstructive. **II.** *n.* obstructor.
obstruir. I. *va.* (*ind.* OBSTRUYO; *subj.* OBSTRUYA) to obstruct, block, stop up, choke. **II.** *vr.* to become obstructed, choked, clogged up.
obstruyente, *a.* (med.) obstruent.
obtemperar, *va.* to obey, to assent.
obtención, *f.* attainment, obtainment.
obtener, *va.* (*ind. pres.* yo OBTENGO, él OBTIENE, *pret.* OBTUVE, *fut.* OBTENDRÉ; *subj.* OBTENGA) to get, obtain, procure; to preserve, to maintain.
obtenible, *a.* obtainable.
obtento, *m.* (eccl.) benefice, prebend.
obtentor, *m.* (eccl.) one who obtains a prebend.
obtestación, *f.* obtestation, protestation.
obturación, *f.* obturation, closing, sealing.
obturador, triz. I. *a.* serving to stop up, close, seal, plug, etc. **II.** *m.* plug, stopper; breechblock; (surg.) obturator; gas check; (photog.) shutter.
obturar, *va.* to stop up, plug, close, seal.
obtusángulo, obtuse-angled.
obtuso, sa, *a.* obtuse; blunt, dull.
obtuve, *pret.* of OBTENER.
obué, *m.* = OBOE, (mus.) oboe; oboist.
obús, *m.* (artil.) howitzer, mortar.
obusera, *a.* boat carrying a howitzer.
obvención, *f.* perquisite.
obviar. I. *va.* to obviate, remove, prevent, surmount. **II.** *vn.* to hinder, oppose.
obvio, via, *a.* obvious, evident.
obyecto, *m.* objection, reply.
[1]**oca,** *f.* (ornith.) goose; royal goose (game).
[2]**oca,** *f.* (bot.) oca oxalis.
ocal, *a.* double (cocoon); delicious (fruit).
ocalear, *vn.* (of silkworms) to make double cocoons.
ocarina, *f.* (mus.) ocarina.
ocasión, *f.* occasion; chance, opportunity.—**aprovechar la o.,** to take advantage of an opportunity, a situation.—**de o.,** second-hand; at a bargain.—*pl.* **en ocasiones,** at times.
ocasionado, da. I. *pp.* of ocasionar. **II.** *a.* provoking, vexatious, insolent; perilous.
ocasionador, ra, *n. & a.* occasioner(-ing).
ocasional, *a.* occasional, chance, casual.
ocasionalmente, *adv.* occasionally; by chance.
ocasionar, *va.* to cause, occasion; to move, excite; to jeopardize, endanger.
ocaso, *m.* west; setting of any heavenly body; decadence, decline.
occidental, *a.* occidental, western.
occidente, *m.* occident, west.
occiduo, dua, *a.* occidental; pert. to setting (of sun, etc.).
occipital, *a.* occipital.
occipucio, *m.* occiput.
occisión, *f.* murder, killing.
occiso, sa, *a.* murdered, killed.
oceanario, *m.* oceanarium.
oceanico, ca, *a.* oceanic.
océano, *m.* ocean.
oceanografía, *f.* oceanography.
oceanógrafo, fa, *n.* oceanographer.
oceanología, *f.* oceanology.
oceanólogo, ga, *n.* oceanologist.
ocelado, da, *a.* ocellated.
ocelo, *m.* (biol.) ocellus.
ocelote, *m.* ocelot, a large leopardlike wild cat.
ocena, *f.* (med.) foul breath.
ociar, *vn.* to loiter, be at leisure.
ocio, *m.* leisure, idleness; pastime, diversion.—**ratos de o.,** spare time.
ociosamente, *adv.* idly; uselessly.
ociosidad, *f.* idleness, leisure.
ocioso, sa, *a.* idle; fruitless, useless.
oclocracia, *f.* (pol.) ochlocracy, mob rule.
ocluir, *va. & vr.* (med.) to occlude, to shut up.
oclusión, *f.* occlusion.
oclusivo, va, *a.* occlusive.
ocosial, *m.* (Peru) lowland, morass.
ocotal, *m.* (Mex.) grove of OCOTES.
ocote, *m.* (Mex.) (bot.) okote pine, torch pine
ocozoal, *m.* (Mex.) a variety of rattlesnake.
ocozol, *m.* (bot.) sweet gum, liquidambar tree.

ocre, *m.* ochre, brown or yellow earth.
ocroso, sa, *a.* ocherous.
octaédrico, ca, *a.* octahedral.
octaedro, *m.* (geom.) octahedron.
octagonal, *a.* octagonal.
octágono, na. I. *a.* eight-sided, octagonal. **II.** *m.* octagon.
octanaje, *m.* (chem.) octane (rating).
octano, *m.* (chem.) octane.
octante, *m.* (geom.) octant.
octava, *f.* (eccl.) octave, eight days; (mus.) octave; (poet.) eight-line stanza.
octavar, *vn.* to form octaves on stringed instruments; to deduct the eighth part.
octavario, *m.* (eccl.) festival lasting a week.
octavín, *m.* (mus.) piccolo flute.
octavo, va. I. *a.* eighth; octave, octonary.—**en o.,** (print.) in octavo. **II.** *m.* eighth; octoroon.
octeto, *m.* (mus.) octet.
octillón, *m.* octillion.
octogenario, ria, *n.* & *a.* octogenarian.
octogésimo, *a.* eightieth.
octogonal, *a.* octagonal.
octógono. na. *a.* = OCTÁGONO.
octopétalo, la, *a.* (bot.) octopetalous.
octópodo, da, *a.* & *m.* (zool.) octopod.
octosilábico, ca; octosílabo, ba, *a.* octosyllabic.
octubre, *m.* October.
óctuple, *a.* octuple.
octuplicar, *va.* to octuplicate, octuple.
óctuplo, pla, *a.* octuple.
ocular. I. *a.* ocular. **II.** *m.* (opt.) eyepiece.
ocularmente, *adv.* ocularly, visually.
oculista, *m.* oculist.
ocultable, *a.* concealable.
ocultación, *f.* concealment; hiding; (astr.) occultation.
ocultador, ra, *n.* & *a.* concealer(-ing).
ocultamente, *adv.* secretly, hiddenly.
ocultar, *va.* to hide, conceal, secrete.
ocultismo, *m.* occultism.
oculto, ta, *a.* hidden, concealed; occult.—**de o.,** incog, incognito.—**en o.,** secretly, in secret.
ocupación, *f.* occupation; occupying; trade, business, pursuit; (rhet.) prolepsis.
ocupada, *a.* (coll.) pregnant.
ocupado, da. I. *pp.* of OCUPAR. **II.** *a.* occupied busy, engaged.
ocupador, ra, *n.* occupier, possessor, occupant.
ocupante, *n.* occupant.
ocupar. I. *va.* to occupy; take possession of; to fill, hold (a job); to employ, give work to; to distrub, interrupt, hinder; to dwell or live in; to engage the attention of, preoccupy. **II.** *vr.* (**en** or **de**) to busy oneself (with); to be engaged (in), have as one's business, devote oneself (to); to pay attention (to).
ocurrencia, *f.* occurrence, incident, happening; witticism.—**o. de acreedores,** meeting of creditors.
ocurrente, *a.* occurring; humorous or funny, witty.
ocurrir, *vn.* to occur, happen; to meet, anticipate; (law) to have recourse to; to apply to; (often as *vr.*) to occur (to one), to strike one (as an idea).
ocurso, *m.* (Mex.) petition, claim.
ochava, *f.* eighth part; (eccl.) octave.—**ochavas del molinete,** (naut.) whelps of the windlass.
ochavado, da, *a.* eight-sided.
ochavar, *va.* to make eight-sided.
ochavo, *m.* a small brass coin; octagonal thing.
ochavón, vona, *n.* (Cuba) octoroon.
ochenta, *a.* & *m.* eighty; eightieth.
ochentavo, va, *n.* & *a.* eightieth.
ochentón, na, *n.* & *a.* octogenarian.
ochete, *m.* bore of hollow projectiles.
ocho. I. *n.* & *a.* eight; eighth. **II.** *m.* figure 8; the eighth day; card with eight spots. **III.** *f. pl.* **las o.,** eight o'clock.
ochocientos, tas, *n.* & *a.* eight hundred.
ochosén, *m.* small ancient coin.
oda, *f.* ode.
odalisca, *f.* odalisk, female slave in harem.
odeón, *m.* odeum, place for music performances.
odiar, *va.* to hate.—**odio,** *m.* hatred; odium.
odiosamente, *adv.* odiously, hatefully.
odiosidad, *f.* odiousness, hatred, odium.
odioso, sa, *a.* odious, hateful.
odisea, *f.* odyssey.
odómetro, *m.* odometer, cyclometer.
odontalgia, *f.* (med.) odontalgia, toothache.
odontálgico, ca, *a.* odontalgic.
odontoideo, a, *a.* odontoid, tooth-shaped.
odontología, *f.* odontology.
odontólogo, ga, *n.* odontologist.
odontorrea, *f.* bleeding of the gums.
odorante, *a.* odorous, fragrant.
odorífero, ra, *a.* odoriferous, fragrant.
odre, *m.* wine skin; (coll.) drunkard.
odrería, *f.* wine-skin factory or shop.
odrero, ra, *n.* maker or seller of wine skins.
odrezuelo, *m. dim.* small wine skin.
odrina, *f.* ox-skin bag for wine.
oesnorueste, *m.* west-northwest.
oessudueste, *m.* west-southwest.
oeste, *m.* west; west wind.—**o. cuarta al norte,** west by north.—**o. cuarta al sur,** west by south.
ofendedor, ra, *n.* & *a.* offender(-ing).
ofender. I. *va.* to offend; to make angry. **II.** *vr.* to become angry; to take offense.
ofensa, *f.* offense; transgression, crime.
ofensión, *f.* offense, grievance; injury.
ofensivamente, *adv.* offensively.
ofensivo, va. I. *a.* offensive; attacking. **II.** *f.* (mil.) offensive.
ofensor, ra, *n.* & *a.* offender(-ing).
oferente, *m.* offerer, one who offers.
oferta, *f.* offer; gift, offering; (com.) offer, tender, supply.—**o. y demanda,** supply and demand.
ofertorio, *m.* (eccl.) offertory.
oficial. I. *a.* official. **II.** *m.* official, officer; trained workman; clerk; (mil.) commissioned officer below major; executioner.—**o. de la sala,** (law) actuary.—**o. de marina,** naval officer.—**o. mayor,** chief clerk.
oficiala, *f.* trained workwoman; forewoman; saleswoman.
oficialía, *f.* clerkship in a public office.
oficialidad, *f.* body of officers.
oficialmente, *adv.* officially.
oficiante, *n.* & *a.* officiator(-ing).
oficiar. I. *va.* to communicate officially. **II.** *vn.* to officiate.—**o. de,** to act as.
oficina, *f.* workshop; office; countinghouse, bureau; laboratory.
oficinal, *a.* (med. and pharm.) officinal.
oficinesco. ca, *a.* departmental, office (as *a.*).
oficinismo, *m.* officialism.
oficinista, *n.* office worker; clerk, employee.
oficio, *m.* employ, work or occupation; office, function, operation; official letter; trade or business; craft; notary's office.—*pl.* (eccl.) office, service.—**de o.,** officially; by trade, by occupation or profession.—**tomarlo por o.,** to do frequently, to take to.
oficionario, *m.* (eccl.) office book.
oficiosamente, *adv.* officiously.
oficiosidad, *f.* diligence, alacrity; officiousness.
oficioso, sa, *a.* diligent; accommodating; officious, meddlesome; useful, fruitful; semi-official.
oficleido, *m.* (mus.) ophicleide.
ofidio, dia, *a.* & *m.* (zool.) ophidian.
ofita, *f.* (min.) ophite.
ofiurídeo, ofiuro, *m.* (zool.) ophiuroid(-ean).
ofrecedor, ra, *n.* offerer.
ofrecer. I. *va.* (*ind.* OFREZCO; *subj.* OFREZCA) to offer; to propose; to present; to exhibit, manifest; to dedicate, consecrate; (com.) to bid, offer. **II.** *vr.* to offer, occur, present itself; to offer oneself, volunteer.—**se le ofrece algo,** he wants something.
ofreciente, *a.* offering.

ofrecimiento, *m.* offer, offering.
ofrenda, *f.* religious offering, oblation, gift.
ofrendar, *va.* to present offerings; to contribute.
ofrezco, ofrezca, *v. V.* OFRECER.
oftalmía, *f.* (med.) ophthalmia.
oftálmico, ca, *a.* ophthalmic.
oftalmología, *f.* ophthalmology.
oftalmológico, ca, *a.* ophthalmologic.
oftalmólogo, ga, *n.* ophthalmologist, oculist.
oftalmómetro, *m.* ophthalmometer.
oftalmoscopia, *f.* ophthalmoscopy.
oftalmoscopio, *m.* ophthalmoscope.
ofuscación, *f.*, **ofuscamiento,** *m.* obfuscation; confused reason.
ofuscar, *va.* (*pret.* OFUSQUÉ; *subj.* OFUSQUE) to obfuscate, dazzle; to confuse.
ogañó, *adv.* (coll.) = HOGAÑO, in these days, this year.
ogro, *m.* ogre, fabulous monster.
¡oh! *interj.* O! oh!
ohm, *m.* (elec.) ohm.
óhmico, ca, *a.* (elec.) ohmic.
ohmímetro, *m.* (elec.) ohmmeter.
ohmio, *m.* (elec.) ohm.
ohmiómetro, *m.* (elec.) ohmmeter.
oíble, *a.* audible, that can be heard.
oída, *f.* hearing (the act).—**de oídas,** or **por oídas,** by hearsay.
oidio, *m.* (bot.) oidium, a kind of fungus.
oído, da. I. *pp.* of OÍR. **II.** *m.* sense of hearing; (anat.) ear; (artil.) vent, priming hole, touch-hole.—**al o.,** by ear; in the ear, whispering; confidentially.—**dar oídos,** to lend an ear; to believe.—**decir al o.,** to whisper.—**de o.,** by ear.—**regalar el o.,** to tickle the ear, flatter.—**tener buen o.,** to have a good ear (especially for music).
oidor, ra, *n.* hearer; judge, member of an Audiencia.
oidoría, *f.* judgeship, office of OIDOR.
oír, *va.* (*ger.* OYENDO; *ind. pres.* OIGO, *pret.* él OYÓ; *subj. pres.* OIGA, *imp.* OYERA, OYESE, *fut.* OYERE) to hear; to listen; to understand; to attend (as lectures).—**o. decir,** to hear (it said).—**o. hablar de,** to hear of.—**o. misa,** to attend or hear mass.—**o., ver y callar,** mind your own business.—**ahora,** or **hasta ahora, lo oigo,** this is the first I've heard of it.—**¡oiga!** or **¡oigan!** well! the idea! come, come!
oíslo, *n.* (coll.) person beloved, wife (or husband).
ojal, *m.* buttonhole; loop.
¡ojalá! *interj.* would to God! God grant! I wish.
ojaladera, *f.* buttonhole maker.
ojalador, ra, *n.* (sewing) buttonhole maker.
ojaladura, *f.* set of buttonholes.
ojalar, *va.* to make buttonholes in.
ojalatero, *a.* & *m.* (pol., coll.) stay-at-home patriot during war; "armchair Napoleon."
ojaranzo, *m.* (bot.) = CARPE, witch hazel.
ojazo, *m. aug.* large eye.
ojeada, *f.* glance, hasty look; glimpse.
ojeador, *m.* beater for game.
[1]**ojear,** *va.* to beat for game; to startle, frighten.
[2]**ojear,** *va.* to eye, look at, stare at.
ojeo, *m.* beating for game.
ojera, *f.* circle under the eye; eyecup.
ojeriza, *f.* spite, grudge, ill will.
ojeroso, sa; ojerudo, da, *a.* having circles under the eyes.
ojete, *m.* (sewing) eyelet.
ojeteador, *m.* eyeleteer; stiletto.
ojetear, *va.* (sewing) to make eyelet holes in.
ojetera, *f.* edge of a garment with eyelets for lacing; eyelet maker.
ojialegre, *a.* bright-eyed.
ojiazul, *a.* blue-eyed.
ojienjuto, ta, *a.* (coll.) dry-eyed.
ojimel, ojimiel, *m.* (pharm.) oxymel.
ojimoreno, na, *a.* (coll.) brown-eyed.
ojinegro, gra, *a.* black-, dark-eyed.
ojito, *m. dim.* small eye.
ojiva, *f.* (arch.) ogive, pointed arch; (astronaut.) nose cone.
ojival, *a.* (arch.) ogival.
ojizaino, na, *a.* (coll.) squint-eyed, moon-eyed.
ojizarco, ca, *a.* (coll.) blue- or gray-eyed.
ojo, *m.* eye; eye of a needle; (mech.) perforation; hole, eye, socket; bow of a key; keyhole (also *o. de la cerradura*); water spring; geyser; drop of oil or grease swimming on liquors; (arch.) span of a bridge; opening in the center of a winding stair; attention, care, notice; reference mark; eye or face of type; mesh; hole in bread or cheese.—*pl.* dearest, darling.—**¡o.!** take notice! look out! **¡o. alerta!** look sharp!—**o. avizor,** sharp lookout.—**o. de agua,** spring (of water).—**o. de buey,** (bot.) oxeye; (coll.) doubloon (eight dollars).—**o. de gallo,** corn (on toe).—**o. de gato,** (min.) cat's eye, tiger's eye, tigereye.—**o. de gaza,** (naut.) eye of a strap. —**o. de la caña del ancla,** (naut.) eye of the anchor.—**o. de pollo,** corn (on toe).—**o. por o., diente por diente,** an eye for an eye, a tooth for a tooth.—**ojos reventones,** or **saltones,** goggle eyes.—**a cierra ojos,** unhesitatingly; at all events.—**a los ojos de,** in the presence of.—**a o.,** by eye.—**a ojos cegarritas,** with half-closed eyes (to intensify the sight).—**a ojos cerrados,** blindly, without reflection; without examination.—**a ojos vistas,** visibly, openly.—**avivar el o.,** to be on one's guard.—**costar un o.,** to be excessively dear.—**de medio o.,** lurkingly, concealingly.—**entrar por el o.,** to please.—**en un abrir y cerrar de ojos,** in the twinkling of an eye.—**hacer del o.,** to wink at one another, to have a secret understanding.—**hacerse ojos,** to look with sharp eyes.—**¡mucho o.!** = ¡o.!—**poner (el) o.,** to pay (close) attention.—**tener buen o.,** to have a good eye; to have good foresight.
ojota, *f.* (Am.) sandal worn by Indian women.
ojuelo, *m. dim.* small eye.—*pl.* sparkling eyes; spectacles.
okapí, *m.* (zool.) okapi.
[1]**ola,** *f.* wave, billow.—**¡o. de marea,** tidal wave.
[2]**ola,** (at tel.) hello.
olaje, *m.* succession of waves, surge, motion of the waves; ground swell.
ole, *m.* an Andalusian dance.—**¡o.!** bravo!
oleáceo, cea, *a.* (bot.) oleaceous.
[1]**oleada,** *f.* big wave; surge, swell of the sea; surging of a crowd.
[2]**oleada,** *f.* abundant oil crop.
oleaginosidad, *f.* oleaginousness, oiliness.
oleaginoso, sa, *a.* oleaginous, oily.
oleaje, *m.* = OLAJE.
olear, *va.* to administer extreme unction to.
oleario, ria, *a.* oily.
oleastro, *m.* (bot.) = ACEBUCHE, wild olive tree.
oleato, *m.* (chem.) oleate.
oleaza, *f.* watery dregs in oil mills.
olécranon, *m.* (anat.) olecranon, part of elbow.
oledero, ra, *a.* odorous, fragrant.
oledor, ra, *n.* smeller.
oleico, *a.* (chem.) oleic.
oleína, *f.* (chem.) olein.
óleo, *m.* oil; (eccl.) extreme unction; holy oil; act of anointing.—**al o.,** in oil colors, oil (as *a.*).
oleoducto, *m.* oil pipe line.
oleografía, *f.* oleograph.
oleomargarina, *f.* oleomargarine.
oleómetro, *m.* oleometer (instrument for testing the purity of oil).
oleorresina, *f.* oleoresin.
oleosidad, *f.* oiliness.
oleoso, sa, *a.* oily, oleaginous.
oler. I. *va.* (*ind.* HUELO; *subj.* HUELA) to smell, to scent; to find out, search, discover; to pry into, sniff, snuff. **II.** *vn.* to smell, emit an odor; to smack of.—**o. a,** to smell of, smell like.—**o. mal,** or **no o. bien,** to look suspicious, to arouse suspicion.
olfacción, *f.* olfaction, act of smelling.
olfatear, *va.* & *vn.* to smell, scent, sniff, snuff.
olfativo, va, *a.* olfactory.

olfato, *m.* olfaction, sense of smell.
olfatorio, ria, *a.* olfactory, pert. to sense of smell.
olíbano, *m.* (bot.) incense.
oliente, *a.* smelling, odorous.
oliera, *f.* vessel for holy oil.
oligarca, *m.* oligarch.—**oligarquía,** *f.* oligarchy.
oligárquico, ca, *a.* oligarchical.
oligisto, *m.* (min.) oligist.
oligoceno, *a.* & *m.* (geol.) Oligocene.
oligoclasa, *f.* (min.) oligoclase.
olimpíada, *f.* Olympiad; Olympic games.
olímpico, ca, *a.* Olympic.
Olimpo, *m.* Olympus; (poet.) heaven.
olingo, *m.* a Central-American monkey.
olio, *m.* = ÓLEO.
oliscar. I. *va.* to smell, scent, sniff, snuff; to investigate, ascertain. **II.** *vn.* (of meat) to be tainted, gamey, or high.
oliva, *f.* olive tree; olive; owl.—*pl.* **olivas y aceitunas, todas son unas,** it's all the same, what's in a name.
oliváceo, cea, *a.* olivaceous.
olivar, *m.* olive grove, yard.
[1]**olivarda,** *f.* (ornith.) green goshawk.
[2]**olivarda,** *f.* (bot.) elecampane.
olivarse, *vr.* (of bread) to form bubbles when baking.
olivera, *f.* olive tree.
olivífero, ra, *a.* (poet.) olive-bearing.
oliviforme, *a.* (anat.) olivary.
olivillo, *m.* (bot.) a variety of terebinth.
olivino, *m.* (min.) olivin, peridot.
olivo, *m.* (bot.) olive tree.—**o. manzanillo,** olive tree yielding the MANZANILLA olive.—**o. y aceituno, todo es uno,** it's all the same, what's in a name.
olmeda, *f.* **olmedo,** *m.* elm grove.
olmo, *m.* (bot.) elm tree.
ológrafo, fa. I. *a.* (law) holographic. **II.** *m.* (law) holograph.
olor, *m.* smell, fragrance; odor; hope, promise, offer; suspicion, smack.
oloroso, sa, *a.* fragrant.
olvidadizo, za, *a.* short of memory, forgetful.
olvidado, da. I. *pp.* of OLVIDAR. **II.** *a.* forgetful.
olvidar. I. *va.* to forget. **II.** *vr.* to be forgotten, to forget (diff. constr. as *el dinero se me olvidó,* I forgot the money); **(de)** to forget (diff. constr. as *me olvidé del dinero,* I forgot the money).
olvido, *m.* forgetfulness; oversight; oblivion.—**dar,** or **echar, al o.,** or **en o.,** to forget; to cast into oblivion.
olla, *f.* pot, kettle, stewpot; (cook.) olla, olio, dish of boiled meat and vegetables; whirlpool.—**o. carnicera,** boiler, large kettle.—**o. ciega** = ALCANCÍA, money box.—**o. de fuego,** (artil.) stinkpot.—**o. de grillos,** great confusion, pandemonium.—**o. podrida,** olla-podrida, meat and vegetable stew.
ollao, *m.* (naut.) eyelet hole.
[1]**ollar,** *a.* soft (stone).
[2]**ollar,** *m.* horse's nostril.
ollaza, *f. aug.* large pot or boiler.
ollería, *f.* pottery; crockery shop.
ollero, ra, *n.* potter; dealer in earthenware.
ollita, olluela, *f. dim.* pipkin, small pot.
omaso, *m.* (zool.) omasum, manyplies.
ombligada, *f.* (tanning) part of a skin corresponding to the navel.
ombligo, *m.* navel; umbilical cord; center or middle.—**o. de Venus,** (bot.) Venus navelwort.
ombliguero, *m.* navel bandage for infants.
ombría, *f.* shady place.
ombú, *m.* a South American tree.
omega, *f.* omega (Greek letter).—**desde el alpha hasta la o.,** from alpha to omega, from A to Z, from beginning to end.
omental, *a.* (anat.) omental.
omento, *m.* (anat.) omentum.
ómicron, *f.* omicron (Greek letter).
ominar, *va.* to augur, foretell.
ominosamente, *adv.* ominously.
ominoso, sa, *a.* ominous, foreboding ill.
omisión, *f.* omission; carelessness, neglect.
omiso, sa. I. *pp. irreg.* of OMITIR. **II.** *a.* neglectful, remiss, careless.
omitir, *va.* (*pp.* OMITIDO, OMISO) to omit.
ómnibus, *m.* omnibus, bus.—**ó. de dos pisos,** double-decker (bus).
omnímodamente, *adv.* in every way or respect, completely.
omnímodo, da, *a.* all-embracing.
omnipotencia, *f.* omnipotence.
omnipotente, *a.* omnipotent, almighty.
omnipotentemente, *adv.* omnipotently.
omnipresencia, *f.* omnipresence.
omnipresente, *a.* omnipresent.
omnisapiente, *a.* omniscient, all-knowing.
omnisciencia, *f.* omniscience.
omnisciente, *a.* = OMNISCIO.
omniscio, ia, *a.* omniscient, all-knowing.
omnívoro, ra, *a.* omnivorous.
omóplato, *m.* (anat.) shoulderblade, scapula.
onagra, *f.* (bot.) onagra, evening primrose.
onagro, *m.* wild ass, onager.
onanismo, *m.* onanism.
once. I. *a.* eleven; eleventh. **II.** *m.* eleven; eleventh (of the month).—**las o.,** eleven o'clock.—**hacer,** or **tomar, las onces,** to take a small luncheon about noon.
oncear, *va.* to weigh out by ounces.
oncejera, *f.* small snare for catching birds.
oncejo, *m.* (ornith.) = VENCEJO, swift.
onceno, na, *a.* eleventh.—**el o. no estorbar,** (the eleventh commandment is:) thou shalt not disturb busy people.
oncijera, *f.* = ONCEJERA.
oncología, *f.* (med.) oncology.
onda, *f.* wave, ripple, undulation; flicker; (sew.) scallop.—*pl.* the sea.—**o. acústica,** acoustic wave.—**o. corta,** (rad.) short wave.—**o. de choque,** (aer.) shock wave (in the air).—**o. de frecuencia modulada,** (rad.) frequency modulated wave.—**o. de oscilación,** oscillation wave.—**o. de radar,** radar wave.—**o. de sonido** or **sonora,** (phys.) sound wave.—**o. de translación,** translatory wave.—**o. de transmisión,** (rad.) carrier wave.—**o. herciana** or **hertziana,** (elec.) Hertzian wave.—**o. infraroja,** (phys.) infrared wave.—**o. larga,** (rad.) long wave.—**ondas a la Marcel,** marcel wave (hair).—**o. sísmica,** (geol.) seismic wave.
ondeado. I. *pp.* of ONDEAR. **II.** *a.* undulated, scalloped, wavy. **II.** *m.* scalloping.
ondeante, *a.* waving, undulating.
ondear. I. *vn.* to wave, ripple, undulate; to flicker. **II.** *vr.* to swing, soar.
ondeo, *m.* waving, undulating, fluctuating.
ondina, *f.* Undine, water sprite.
ondisonante, *a.* (poet.) = UNDÍSONO, billowy.
ondómetro, *m.* (rad.) ondometer, wave meter.
ondulación, *f.* = UNDULACION, wave, or wavy motion.—**o. permanente,** permanent wave (of hair).
ondulado, da. I. *pp.* of ONDULAR. **II.** *a.* undulated, rippled; scalloped, wavy; corrugated. **III.** *m.* **o. permanente,** permanent waving (of hair).
ondulante, *a.* waving, undulating.
ondular, undular, *va.* to undulate; to ripple.
ondulatorio, ria, *a.* undulatory.
oneroso, sa, *a.* burdensome, onerous.
onfacino, *a.* omphacine (oil).
onfacomeli, *m.* (pharm.) oxymel.
ónice, *m.,* **ónique,** *f.* (min.) onyx.
oniromancía, *f.* oneiromancy, divination through dreams.
ónix, *m.* (min.) onyx.
onocrótalo, *m.* (ornith.) white pelican.
onomancía, *f.* onomancy, divination from names.
onomástico, ca, *a.* onomastic, pert. to names.
onomatopeya, *f.* onomatopœia.
onomatopéyico, ca, *a.* onomatopœic.

onoquiles, *f.* (bot.) dyer's bugloss, alkanet.
ontogénesis, ontogenia, *f.* (biol.) ontogeny.
ontologia, *f.* ontology.
ontológico, ca, *a.* ontological.
ontologismo, *m.* (philos.) ontologism.
ontólogo, *m.* ontologist.
[1]**onza,** *f.* ounce.—**o. de oro,** Spanish doubloon **por onzas,** sparingly.
[2]**onza,** *f.* (zool.) ounce, leopardlike feline.
onzavo, va, *n.* & *a.* eleventh.
oocito, *m.* (biol.) oöcyte.
ooforitis, *f.* (med.) oöphoritis.
oogonio, *m.* (bot.) oögonium.
oolita, *f.* (geol.) oölite.
oolítico, ca, *a.* (geol.) oölitic.
oología, *f.* (ornith.) oölogy.
oosfera, *f.* (bot.) oösphere.
oospermo, *m.* (zool., bot.) oösperm.
oosporo, *m.* (bot.) oöspore.
opacamente, *adv.* obscurely, darkly.
opacidad, *f.* opacity.
opaco, ca, *a.* opaque.
opalescencia, *f.* opalescence.
opalescente, *a.* opalescent.
opalino, na, *a.* opaline, opalescent.
ópalo, *m.* (min.) opal.
opción, *f.* option, choice; right.
opcional, *a.* optional.
ópera, *f.* opera.—**o. bufa,** comic opera.
operable, *a.* operable, practicable; capable of operating.
operación, *f.* operation, action, working; (chem.) process; (math.) operation, calculation; (surg.) operation; (com.) operation, transaction, venture.—*pl.* (mil.) operations.—**o. cesárea,** (surg.) Cæsarean operation.—**operaciones de banco,** banking business.—**operaciones marítimas,** shipping trade or business.
operador, *m.* (surg.) operator.
operante, *n.* & *a.* operator(-ing).
operar. I. *va.* to operate; (surg.) to operate on. **II.** *vn.* to operate, act, work.
operario, ria. I. *n.* operator, worker, laborer, hand. **II.** *m.* priest who assists sick or dying persons.
operativo, va, *a.* operative.
operatorio, ria, *a.* operative; (med.) operative, pertaining to operations.
operculado, da, *a.* operculate(d.
opercular, *a.* opercular.
opérculo, *m.* operculum, lid, cover.
opereta, *f.* operetta, light opera.
operista, *n.* opera singer.
operoso, sa, *a.* laborious.
opiado, da, *a.* opiate, narcotic.
opiato, ta. I. *a.* opiate. **II.** *m.* opiate.
opilación, *f.* (med.) oppilation, obstruction; amenorrhœa, suppression of the menses.
opilarse, *vr.* to contract amenorrhœa.
opilativo, va, *a.* obstructive, oppilative.
opimo, ma, *a.* rich, fruitful, abundant.
opinable, *a.* disputable, questionable.
opinante, *n.* & *a.* arguer(-ing).
opinar, *vn.* to judge, be of the opinion.
opinativo, va, *a.* opinionative.
opinión, *f.* opinion.—**o. pública,** public opinion.
opio, *m.* opium.
opíparamente, *adv.* sumptuously.
opíparo, ra, *a.* sumptuous.
oploteca, *f.* museum of rare weapons.
opobálsamo, *m.* opobalsam, balm of Gilead.
oponente, *a.* (anat.) opponent.
oponer, *va.* & *vr.* (*pp. irreg.* OPUESTO; *ind. pres.* OPONGO, *pret.* OPUSE, *fut.* OPONDRÉ; *subj.* OPONGA) to oppose; to hinder, resist, withstand; to object to, act against; to front, face, be opposite to; to stand in competition with.
oponible, *a.* opposable.
opopónaca, opopónace, *f.* (bot.) rough parsnip.
opopónaco, opopónax, *m.* opopanax, a gum resin.
oporto, *m.* port wine.
oportunamente, *adv.* opportunely.
oportunidad, *f.* opportunity.
oportunismo, *m.* (pol.) opportunism.
oportunista, *n.* & *a.* (pol.) opportunist(-ic).
oportuno, na, *a.* opportune, timely.
oposición, *f.* opposition; competition for a position, etc.; (astr.) opposition.
oposicionista, *m.* (pol.) obstructionist.
opositor, ra, *n.* opposer, opponent; competitor.
opoterapia, *f.* (med.), organotherapy.
opresión, *f.* oppression; pressure.
opresivamente, *adv.* oppressively.
opresivo, va, *a.* oppressive, overwhelming.
opresor, ra, *n.* oppressor; extortioner.
oprimir, *va.* to oppress; to press, push; to lie heavy upon, weigh down, dispirit.
oprobiar, *va.* to defame, revile.
oprobio, *m.* opprobrium, ignominy, infamy.
oprobioso, sa, *a.* opprobrious, disgraceful.
opsonina, *f.* (bacteriol.) opsonin.
optante, *n.* chooser.
optar. I. *va.* to opt, choose, select; to take possession of. **II.** *vn.* (**por**) to choose.
optativo, *m.* (gram.) optative.
óptica, *f.* optics; stereoscope.
óptico, ca. I. *a.* optic, optical. **II.** *m.* optician.
óptimamente, *adv.* in the best way, perfectly.
optimismo, *m.* optimism.
optimista, *n.* & *a.* optimist(-ic).
óptimo, ma, *a.* best, eminently good.
optometra, *m.* & *f.* optometrist.
optometría, *f.* optometry, science of eye testing.
optometrista, *n.* optometrist.
optómetro, *m.* (opt.) optometer.
opuestamente, *adv.* oppositely, contrarily.
opuesto, ta. I. *pp. irreg.* of OPONER. **II.** *a.* opposed; opposite, contrary, adverse.
opugnación, *f.* opposition, attack.
opugnador, ra, *n.* opposer, attacker.
opugnar, *va.* to attack, oppose.
opulencia, *f.* opulence.
opulentamente, *adv.* opulently.
opulento, ta, *a.* opulent, wealthy.
opúsculo, *m.* booklet, tract.
opuse, *pret.* of OPONER.
oquedad, *f.* hollow, cavity.
oquedal, *m.* plantation of lofty trees.
oqueruela, *f.* kink in a sewing thread.
ora, *conj.* (*contr.* of AHORA) whether; either; now, then: *tomando ora la espada, ora la pluma,* taking now the sword, now (*or,* and then) the pen.
oración, *f.* oration, speech; orison, prayer; dusk, beginning of the evening; (gram.) sentence.—*pl.* first part of catechism; the angelus.—**o. dominical,** the Lord's Prayer.
oracional, *m.* prayer book.
oracular, *a.* oracular.
oráculo, *m.* oracle.
orador, ra, *n.* orator, speaker.
oraje, *m.* stormy weather.
[1]**oral,** *a.* oral; vocal.
[2]**oral,** *m.* soft breeze.
orangután, *m.* (zool.) orang-outang.
orante, *a.* praying.
orar. I. *vn.* to harangue, deliver a speech; to pray. **II.** *va.* to ask, beg for.
orate, *n.* lunatic, madman(-woman).
oratoria, *f.* oratory, eloquent speaking.
oratoriamente, *adv.* oratorically.
[1]**oratorio, ria,** *a.* oratorical.
[2]**oratorio,** *m.* oratory, chapel; (mus.) oratorio; (eccl.) congregation of presbyters.
orbe, *m.* orb, sphere; the earth; any celestial body; (ichth.) globefish.
orbicular, *a.* orbicular, circular.
orbicularmente, *adv.* orbicularly.
órbita, *f.* (anat., astr., astronaut., fig.) orbit.—**ó. polar,** polar orbit.—**ó. terrestre,** terrestrial orbit.
orbital, *a.* orbital.
orbitario, ria, *a.* orbital.
orca, *f.* (ichth.) grampus, orca.
orcaneta, *f.* (bot.) dyer's bugloss, alkanet.

orceína, *f.* (chem.) orcein, red dyestuff.
orcina, *f.* orchil; (chem.) orcin, orcinol.
[1]**orco,** *m.* hell.
[2]**orco,** *m.* (ichth.) = ORCA.
orchilla, *f.* (bot.) orchil, lichen from which a violet coloring matter is obtained.
órdago.—de o., first-class, excellent.
ordalía, *f.* ordeal, trial by fire or water.
orden. I. *m.* order; class, group; proportion, relation; (arch.) order; (religious) order.—*pl.* (eccl.) sacrament of ordination, clerical office.—**o. cerrado,** (mil.) close formation.—**o. compuesto,** (arch.) composite order.—**o. de batalla,** battle array, order of battle.—**o. del día,** order of the day, agenda.—**en o.,** in order; in an orderly manner; with regard to.—**fuera de o.,** (parl. law) out of order.—**por su o.,** in its turn. **II.** *f.* order, command; (com.) order; order of knighthood and the insignia.—*pl.* orders, instructions.—**o. del día,** (mil.) order of the day.—**a la o.,** (com.) to order.—**a la o. de,** to the order of.—**a sus órdenes,** at your service. (*en espera de sus ordenes,* used in business letters, means "awaiting your commands," or "your pleasure," and not "your (business) orders," "your custom.")
ordenación, *f.* methodical arrangement; disposition, array; (math.) permutation; edict, ordinance; clerical ordination; auditor's office; (arch. and art) ordonnance.
ordenada, *f.* (geom.) ordinate.
ordenadamente, *adv.* orderly, in order.
ordenado, da. I. *pp.* of ORDENAR. **II.** *a.* ordained, ordinate; methodical; tidy.
ordenador, ra, *n.* ordainer; orderer; auditor.
ordenamiento, *m.* ordaining, regulating; law, edict, ordinance.
ordenancista, *n.* disciplinarian, martinet.
ordenando, ordenante, *m.* (eccl.) ordinand.
ordenanza. I. *f.* method, order; law, statute, ordinance; command; ordination. **II.** *m.* (mil.) orderly; (arch. and art) ordonnance.
ordenar. I. *va.* to arrange, put in order; to order, command; to ordain, confer holy orders on; (math.) to arrange (a polynomial) according to the ascending or descending powers of a letter; (stat.) to array. **II.** *vn.* (eccl.) to be ordained.
ordeñadero, *m.* milk pail; milking place.
ordeñador, ra, *n.* milker.
ordeñar, *va.* to milk; to pick (olives).
ordeño, *m.* milking.
ordinal, *n.* & *a.* ordinal.
ordinariamente, *adv.* ordinarily; rudely.
ordinariez, *f.* rough manners, ordinariness.
ordinario, ria. I. *a.* ordinary, usual; coarse, unrefined. **II.** *m.* daily household expense; mail, post, courier; (eccl.) ordinary (judge); bishop.—**de o.,** usually, ordinarily, regularly.
ordinativo, va, *a.* ordering, regulating.
orea, oréada, oréade, *f.* oread, wood nymph.
oreante, *a.* cooling, refreshing.
orear. I. *va.* to air, expose to the air, aerate. **II.** *vr.* to take an airing.
orégano, *m.* (bot.) oregano, origanum, wild marjoram.
oreja, *f.* (external) ear; hearing (sense); flap of a shoe; flatterer, talebearer; (mech.) lug, flange, ear.—**o. de abad,** or **monje,** (bot.) Venus navelwort.—**o. de ancla,** (naut.) fluke of an anchor.—**o. de oso,** (bot.) primrose.—**o. de ratón,** (bot.) mouse-ear.—**o. marina,** a European gasteropod.—**o. de mercader,** (coll.) deaf ears.—**apearse por las orejas,** (coll.) to give an absurd answer.—**bajar las orejas,** to yield, to come down from one's high horse.—**calentar las orejas a,** to chide, dress down.—**con las orejas caídas,** crestfallen, dejected.—**descubrir la o.,** to give oneself away.—**ver las orejas al lobo,** to be in great peril.
orejano, na, *a.* unbranded or motherless (calf).
orejeado, da. I. *pp.* of OREJEAR. **II.** *a.* informed, advised, warned.
orejear, *vn.* to shake or prick up the ears; to act with reluctance; to whisper.
orejera, *f.* ear muff, earcap; ear hoop; moldboard of a plow.
orejeta, *f. dim.* small ear, lug, or flange.
orejita, *f. dim.* small auricle or ear.
orejón, *m.* pull by the ear; (Peru) privileged noble; Inca; (S. A.) countryman, rancher; (fort.) orillon.
orejudo, da, *a.* flap-eared, long-eared.
oreo, *m.* breeze, fresh air; airing.
orfanato, *m.* orphan asylum, orphanage.
orfandad, *f.* orphanage.
orfebre, *m.* goldsmith, silversmith.
orfebrería, *f.* gold or silver work.
orfelinato, *m.* (Gal.) = ORFANATO.
orfeón, *m.* singing society.
orfeonista, *m.* member of a singing society.
órfico, ca, *a.* Orphean.
organdí, *m.* organdy.
organero, ra, *n.* organ maker; organ builder.
orgánicamente, *adv.* organically.
organicé, organice, *v. V.* ORGANIZAR.
organicismo, *m.* (med.) organicism.
organicista, *n.* & *a.* organicist(-ic).
orgánico, ca, *a.* organic; harmonious.
organillero, *m.* organ grinder.
organillo, *m. dim.* barrel organ, hand organ.
organismo, *m.* organism; organization, association.
organista, *n.* (mus.) organist.
organizable, *a.* organizable.
organización, *f.* organization; arrangement.
organizacional, *a.* organizational.
organizado, da. I. *pp.* of ORGANIZAR. **II.** *a.* (biol.) organic; pert. to living organism.
organizador, ra, *a.* organizing; having aptitude for organizing.—**comité o.,** committee on arrangements.
organizar, *va.* (*pret.* ORGANICÉ; *subj.* ORGANICE) to organize, set up; to arrange; to tune (an organ).
órgano, *m.* (mus.) pipe organ; pipe refrigerator; (physiol.) organ; medium, instrument, agency.—**ó. sensorio,** (physiol.) sense organ, receptor.—**órganos de Móstoles,** persons or ideas that disagree.—**organos genitales** genitals.
organogenia, *f.* (biol.) organogenesis.
organografía, *f.* organography.
organográfico, ca, *a.* organographic.
organología, *f.* organology.
organoterapia, *f.* (med.) organotherapy.
orgasmo, *m.* (physiol.) orgasm.
orgía, *f.* orgy, revel.
orgiástico, ca, *a.* orgiastic.
orgullo, *m.* pride; haughtiness.
orgullosamente, *adv.* proudly; haughtily.
orgulloso, sa, *a.* proud; haughty, overbearing; conceited.
orientación, *f.* orientation; bearings.—**o. profesional,** vocational counselling or guidance.
oriental. I. *a.* oriental, eastern. **II.** *m.* oriental.
orientalismo, *m.* orientalism.
orientalista, *n.* orientalist.
orientalizar, *va.* & *vn.* to Orientalize.
orientar. I. *va.* to orientate, to orient.—**o. una vela,** (naut.) to trim a sail. **II.** *vr.* to find one's way about, get one's bearings.
oriente, *m.* east, orient; east wind; source, origin; youth.
orificación, *f.* (dent.) gold filling.
orificador, *m.* dentist's plugger.
orificar, *va.* (dent.) to fill with gold.
orífice, *m.* goldsmith.
orificio, *m.* orifice, hole; anus; (artil.) venthole; (mech.) port.
oriflama, *f.* oriflamme; flag, banner.
origen, *m.* origin; source; native country; beginning.
originador, ra, *n.* originator.
original. I. *a.* original; primitive; new, novel; quaint, odd. **II.** *m.* original, first copy, archetype; (print.) copy, manuscript; original of a portrait; odd person.—**de buen o.,** on good authority.

originalidad, *f.* originality; eccentricity.
originalmente, *adv.* originally.
originar. I. *va.* to originate, create, invent; to start. **II.** *vr.* to originate, arise, spring.
originariamente, *adv.* primarily, originally.
originario, ria, *a.* originating; native; derived.
[1]**orilla,** *f.* border, margin; edge; bank (of a river); shore; sidewalk.—**a la o.,** near a place, on the brink.—**salir a la o.,** to overcome difficulties.
[2]**orilla,** *f.* fresh breeze.
orillar. I. *va.* to arrange, settle; to evade; to surmount. **II.** *vn.* to leave a selvage on cloth; (sew.) to border. **III.** *vr.* & *vn.* to reach the shore.
orillo, *m.* selvage or list of cloth.
[1]**orín,** *m.* rust.
[2]**orín,** *m.* (gen. *pl.*) = ORINA.
orina, *f.* urine.—**orinal,** *m.* urinal; chamber pot. —**orinar,** *va.* & *vn.* to urinate.
oriniento, ta, *a.* rusty, moldy.
orinque, *m.* (naut.) buoy rope.
oriol, *m.* (ornith.) golden oriole or thrush.
Orión, *m.* (astr.) Orion.
oriundez, *f.* origin.
oriundo, da, *a.* native.
órix, *m.* (zool.) oryx, gemsbok.
orla, *f.* list; selvage, border, fringe, trimming; (her.) orle; (print.) ornamental border.
orlador, ra, *n.* borderer.
orladura, *f.* border, edging, list.
orlar, *va.* to border, garnish with an edging.
orleanista, *n.* & *a.* Orleanist(-ic).
[1]**orlo,** *m.* Alpine horn; (mus.) organ stop.
[2]**orlo,** *m.* (arch.) plinth.
orlón, *m.* (text.) orlon; Orlon (trademark).
ormesí, *m.* a kind of silk stuff.
ormino, *m.* (bot.) = GALLOCRESTA, clary sage.
ornadamente, *adv.* ornamentally.
ornado, da. I. *pp.* of ORNAR. **II.** *a.* ornate.
ornamentación, *f.* ornamentation.
ornamentado, da, *a.* ornamented, adorned, decorated.
ornamental, *a.* ornamental.
ornamentar, *va.* to adorn, decorate.
ornamento, *m.* ornament; decoration, adornment; accomplishment, gift.—*pl.* (eccl.) sacred vestments; (arch.) frets, moldings, etc.; moral qualities, character.
ornar, *va.* to adorn, embellish, garnish.
ornato, *m.* ornament, decoration, embellishment.
ornitodelfo, fa, *a.* & *m.* (zool.) prototherian.
ornitología, *f.* ornithology.
ornitológico, ca, *a.* ornithological.
ornitólogo, *m.* ornithologist.
ornitomancia, *f.* ornithomancy.
ornitópodo, da, *a.* & *m.* ornithopod.
ornitorrinco, *m.* (zool.) ornithorhynchus, duckbill, platypus.
oro, *m.* gold; gold color; ornaments or trinkets made of gold.—*pl.* diamonds, in Spanish cards. —**o. batido,** leaf gold.—**o. bruto,** bullion.—**o. coronario,** high-carat gold.—**o. en barra,** bar-gold, gold in bars.—**o. en libritos,** gold leaf.—**o. en pasta** = O. BRUTO.—**o. en polvo,** gold dust.—**o. fulminante,** gold fulminate.—**o. mate,** gold size.—**o. musivo,** mosaic gold, aurum musivum.—**o. nativo,** native gold.—**o. virgen** = O. BRUTO.—**de o. y azul,** gorgeously attired.—**poner (a uno) de o. y azul,** (coll.) to give (one) a good dressing down, a lecture, or severe reprimand.
orobanca, *f.* (bot.) broom rape.
orobias, *m.* fine incense.
orogenia, *f.* (geol.) orogeny.
orogénico, ca, *a.* orogenic.
orografía, *f.* orography, branch of geography treating of mountains.
orográfico, ca, *a.* orographic.
orondo, da, *a.* pompous, showy; hollow.
oropel, *m.* tinsel; brass foil; glitter.
oropelero, *m.* brass worker.
oropéndola, *f.* (ornith.) loriot, golden oriole.
oropimente, *m.* (min.) orpiment.
oroya, *f.* (Am.) basket hanging from rope bridge for transportation across a river.
orozuz, *m.* (bot.) licorice.
orquesta, *f.* (mus.) orchestra; (theat.) orchestra pit.
orquestación, *f.* orchestration.
orquestal, *a.* orchestral.
orquestar, *va.* to orchestrate.
órquide, *f.* (bot.) orchis.
orquídeo, dea. I. *a.* (bot.) orchidaceous. **II.** *f.* orchid.
orquitis, *f.* (med.) orchitis, inflammation of testicle.
orre.—**en o.,** loose, in bulk.
ortega, *f.* (ornith.) hazel grouse.
ortiga, *f.* (bot.) nettle.—**o. de mar,** (ichth.) sea nettle.—**ser como unas ortigas,** to be as cross as a bear.
ortivo, va, *a.* (astr.) oriental, eastern.
orto, *m.* rising (of the sun or a star).
ortocéfalo, la, *a.* orthocephalic, orthocephalous.
ortoclasa, *f.* (min.) orthoclase.
ortocromático, ca, *a.* (photog.) orthochromatic.
ortodoncia, *f.* orthodontia.
ortodoxia, *f.* orthodoxy.
ortodoxo, xa, *a.* orthodox.
ortodromia, *f.* (naut.) orthodromy.
ortodrómico, ca, *a.* (naut.) orthodromic.
ortofonía, *f.* orthophony.
ortofónico, ca, *a.* orthophonic.
ortofosfórico, ca, *a.* (chem.) orthophosphoric (acid).
ortogonal, *a.* orthogonal, right-angled.
ortogonio, *a.* right-angled (triangle).
ortografía, *f.* orthography.
ortográficamente, *adv.* orthographically.
ortográfico, ca, *a.* orthographical.
ortógrafo, *m.* orthographer.
orto-hidrógeno, *m.* (chem.) orthohydrogen.
ortología, *f.* orthoëpy, study of pronunciation.
ortológico, ca, *a.* orthoëpic.
ortólogo, ga, *n.* orthoëpist.
ortopedia, *f.* (med.) orthopedics.
ortopédico, ca, *a.* (med.) orthopedic.
ortopedista, *n.* orthopedist.
ortóptero, ra, *a.* & *m.* (entom.) orthopteran.
ortorrómbico, ca, *a.* (of crystals) orthorhombic.
ortosa, *f.* (min.) orthoclase.
ortoscópico, ca, *a.* orthoscopic.
oruga, *f.* (entom.) caterpillar; (bot.) rocket; tractor, caterpillar tractor.
orujo, *m.* refuse of grapes, cotton seed, olives, etc.
orvalle, *m.* (bot.) = GALLOCRESTA, clary sage.
[1]**orza,** *f.* preserve jar, crock.
[2]**orza,** *f.* (naut.) luff.—**o. a la banda,** (naut.) hard-a-lee.—**a o.,** (naut.) luff.
orzada, *f.* (naut.) luffing, hauling.
orzaderas, *f. pl.* (naut.) leeboards.
orzaga, *f.* (bot.) orach; mountain spinach.
orzar, *vn.* (naut.) to luff.
orzaya, *f.* (children's) nurse.
[1]**orzuelo,** *m.* (med.) sty; hordeolum.
[2]**orzuelo,** *m.* snare (for birds); trap (for wild beasts).
orzura, *f.* (chem.) minium.
os, *pers. pron. dative and accusative of* VOS *and* VOSOTROS, you, to you.
osa, *f.* (zool.) she-bear.—**O. Mayor,** (astr.) Great Bear, the Dipper.—**O. Menor,** Little Bear.
osadamente, *adv.* boldly, daringly.
osadía, *f.* audacity, daring, boldness.
osado, da, *a.* daring, bold, audacious.
osambre, *m.*, **osamenta,** *f.* skeleton; bones.
[1]**osar,** *vn.* to dare, venture; to outdare.
[2]**osar, osario,** *m.* charnel house; ossuary.
oscar, *m.* (mov. pict., U. S.) Oscar.
oscilación, *f.* oscillation.
oscilador, *m.* (mech., elec., rad.) oscillator.
oscilante, *a.* oscillating.
oscilar, *vn.* to oscillate.
oscilatorio, ria, *a.* oscillatory.

oscilógrafo, *m.* (phys.) oscillograph.
oscitancia, *f.* carelessness, heedlessness.
osculación, *f.* (geom.) osculation.
osculador, triz, *a.* (geom.) osculating.
osculatorio, ria, *a.* osculatory.
ósculo, *m.* kiss.
oscurantismo, oscuro, etc. = OBSCURANTISMO, OBSCURO, etc.
oscurecimiento, *m.* blackout (as for air raid).
osecico, cillo, cito, zuelo, *m. dim.* small bone.
oseína, *f.* (chem.) ossein.
óseo, a, osseous, bony.
osera, *f.* den of bears.
osezno, *m.* whelp or cub of a bear.
osífero, ra, *a.* ossiferous.
osificación, *f.* ossification.
osificado, da, *a.* ossified.
osificarse, *vr.* to ossify, become ossified.
osífico, ca, *a.* ossific.
osífraga, *f.*, **osífrago,** *m.* (ornith.) osprey.
ósmico, ca, *a.* (chem.) osmic.
osmio, *m.* (chem.) osmium.
ósmosis, *f.* (phys.) osmosis.
osmótico, ca, *a.* osmotic.
oso, *m.* (zool.) bear.—**o. blanco,** polar bear.—**o. colmenero,** honey-eating bear, bear that robs beehives.—**o. de las cavernas,** (paleontol.) cave bear.—**o. gris,** grizzly bear.—**o. hormiguero,** anteater.—**o. marino,** fur seal.—**o. pardo,** brown bear.—**hacer el o.,** (coll.) —**hacer el o.,** (coll.) to make a fool of oneself; to act as a sentimental lover.
ososo, sa, *f.* osseous, bony.
osta, *f.* (naut.) lateen brace.
ostaga, *f.* (naut.) tie, runner.
¡oste! *interj.* = OXTE.
osteico, ca, *a.* osteal.
osteítis, *f.* (med.) osteitis, inflammation of bone.
ostensible, *a.* ostensible.—**ostensiblemente,** *adv.* ostensibly.
ostensión, *f.* ..how, manifestation.
ostensivo, va, *a.* ostensive, showy.
ostentación, *f.* ostentation, vain show.
ostentador, ra, *n.* boaster, ostentatious person.
ostentar. I. *va.* to make a show of, to exhibit. **II.** *vn.* to boast, to brag; to show off.
ostentativo, va, *a.* ostentatious.
ostento, *m.* portent.
ostentosamente, *adv.* ostentatiously.
ostentoso, sa, *a.* sumptuous, magnificent.
osteoblasto, *m.* (anat.) osteoblast.
osteoclasia, *f.* (surg.) osteoclasis.
osteogénesis, osteogenia, *f.* (physiol.) osteogenesis, formation of bone.
osteogénico, ca, *a.* (anat.) osteogenic.
osteología, *f.* (anat.) osteology.
osteológico, ca, *a.* osteologic.
osteólogo, *m.* osteologist.
osteoma, *m.* (med.) osteoma.
osteomalacia, *f.* osteomalacia.
osteomielitis, *f.* (med.) osteomyelitis.
osteópata, *n.* osteopath.
osteopatía, *f.* osteopathy.
osteopático, ca, *a.* osteopathic.
osteosarcoma, *m.* (med.) osteosarcoma.
osteotomía, *f.* (surg.) osteotomy.
ostiario, *m.* (eccl.) ostiary, doorkeeper.
ostíolo, *m.* (biol., bot.) ostiole.
ostión, *m.* large oyster.
ostra, *f.* oyster.
ostráceo, cea. I. *a.* (zool.) ostracean, ostraceous. **II.** *m.* ostracean, oyster.
ostracismo, *m.* ostracism.
ostral, *m.* oyster farm; oyster bed.
ostrería, *f.* oyster shop, oyster house.
ostrero, ra. I. *a.* oysterlike. **II.** *n.* oyster seller. **III.** *f.* oyster farm.
ostricultura, *f.* oyster farming, culture.
ostrífero, ra, *a.* abounding in, or raising, oysters.
[1]**ostro,** *m.* large, coarse oyster; any mollusk yielding purple; purple from mollusks.
[2]**ostro,** *m.* south wind.
ostrogodo, da, *n.* & *a.* Ostrogoth(-ic).
ostrón, *m. aug.* large, coarse oyster.
ostugo, *m.* piece, part, bit; corner.
osudo, da, *a.* bony.
osuno, na, *a.* bearlike, bearish.
otacústico, ca, *a.* otacoustic.
otalgia, *f.* (med.) otalgia, earache.
otáñez, *m.* (coll.) old squire who escorted a lady as chaperon.
oteador, ra, *n.* spy, sly observer.
otear, *va.* to observe, examine, pry into.
otero, *m.* hill, hillock, knoll.
oteruelo, *m. dim.* hummock, knoll, mound.
ótico, ca, *a.* (anat.) otic.
otitis, *f.* (med.) otitis, inflammation of ear.
oto, *m.* (ornith.) bustard.
otoba, *f.* (bot.) a variety of nutmeg tree.
otolito, *m.* (anat., zool.) otolith.
otología, *f.* (med.) otology.
otólogo, ga, *n.* aurist, otologist.
otomano, na. I. *n.* & *a.* Ottoman. **II.** *f.* ottoman, divan.
otoñada, *f.* autumn season; pasturage.
otoñal, *a.* autumnal.
otoñar. I. *vn.* to spend the autumn season; (of weeds) to grow in autumn. **II.** *vr.* (of earth after rain) to be seasoned.
otoño, *m.* autumn, fall; aftermath.
otorgadero, ra, *a.* grantable.
otorgador, ra, *n.* grantor.
otorgamiento, *m.* grant, granting; license; (law) executing an instrument.
otorgante. I. *a.* authorizing, granting. **II.** *n.* grantor, maker of a deed.
otorgar, *va.* (*pret.* OTORGUÉ; *subj.* OTORGUE) to consent, agree to; (law) to grant; to prescribe, stipulate, promise.—**quien calla otorga,** silence gives consent.
otorgo, *m.* (law) marriage contract.
otorrea, *f.* (med.) otorrhœa, discharge from ear.
otoscopia, *f.* (surg.) otoscopy.
otoscopio, *m.* (surg.) otoscope.
otramente, *adv.* otherwise, differently.
otro, tra, *a.* another, other.—**¡o.!** encore! again! —**o. cosa,** something else.—**o. que tal,** (coll.) another such.—**otros tantos,** as many more. —**o. vez,** again.—**por o. parte,** on the other hand.—**(el) uno a(l) o.,** each other.—**unos a otros,** one another.
otrosí. I. *adv.* besides, moreover. **II.** *m.* (law) every petition made after the principal.
ova, *f.* (bot.) sea lettuce, laver.
ovación, *f.* ovation.
ovacionar, *va.* to give an ovation to.
ovado, da. I. *pp.* of OVAR. **II.** *a.* (of a bird) impregnated by the male; oval, egg-shaped.
oval; ovalado, da, *a.* oval.
ovalar, *va.* to make oval.
óvalo, *m.* oval.
ovante, *a.* victorious, triumphant.
ovar, *vn.* to lay eggs.
ovárico, ca, *a.* ovarian.
ovario, *m.* (anat.) ovary; (bot.) ovarium, ovary; (arch.) egg ornament.
ovariotomía, *f.* (surg.) ovariotomy.
ovaritis, *f.* (med.) ovaritis.
ovas, *f. pl.* = HUEVA, spawn of fish, roe.
ovecico, *m. dim.* small egg.
oveja, *f.* sheep.—**o. descarriada** or **negra,** (fig.) lost or black sheep.
ovejero, ra, *n.* shepherd(-ess); sheep raiser.
ovejuela, *f. dim.* young ewe.
ovejuno, na, *a.* pert. to sheep, sheep (as *a.*).
overa, *f.* ovary of fowls.
[1]**overo, ra,** *a.* blossom-colored (horse).
[2]**overo,** *a.*—**ojo o.,** large, bulging eye with small pupil.
overol, *m.* (Angl.) (Am.) overalls.
ovezuelo, *m.* small egg.
oviducto, *m.* (anat.) oviduct.
ovífero, ra, *a.* (anat., zool.) oviferous.
oviforme, *a.* oviform, egg-shaped.

ovil, *m.* = REDIL, sheepcote.
ovillar. I. *va.* to wind (thread) in a ball or skein. II. *vr.* to hunch oneself into a bunch.
ovillejo, *m. dim.* small skein; a kind of rondel.
ovillo, *m.* skein, ball of yarn; ball or heap of mixed or tangled things.—**hacerse un o.**, to hunch oneself into a bunch.
ovino, na, *a.* ovine.
ovíparo, ra, *a.* (zool.) oviparous.
oviposición, *f.* oviposition.
oviscapto, *m.* ovipositor.
ovoide, *a.* ovoid, egg-shaped.
óvolo, *m.* (arch.) ovolo; quarter round.
ovoso, sa, *a.* full of roe.
ovovivíparo, ra, *a.* (zool.) ovoviviparous.
ovulación, *f.* (biol.) ovulation.
óvulo, *m.* (nat. hist.) ovule.
¡ox! *interj.* shoo! begone!
oxácido, *m.* (chem.) oxacid.
oxalato, *m.* (chem.) oxalate.
oxálico, *a.* (chem.) oxalic.
oxalme, *m.* acidulated brine.
oxear, *va.* to shoo (fowls).
oxhídrico, ca, *a.* oxyhydrogen.
oxhidrilo, *m.* (chem.) hydroxyl.
oxiacanta, *f.* (bot.) whitethorn, hawthorn.
oxiacetilénico, ca, *a.* oxyacetylene.
oxicloruro, *m.* (chem.) oxychloride.
oxidable, *a.* (chem.) oxidizable.
oxidación, *f.* (chem.) oxidation.
oxidante. I. *a.* (chem.) oxidating, oxidizing. II. *m.* (chem.) oxidizer.
oxidar, *va.* & *vr.* to oxidize, rust.
oxidasa, *f.* (biochem.) oxidase.
óxido, *m.* (chem.) oxide.—**ó. básico**, basic oxide. —**ó. de carbón**, (chem.) carbon monoxide.—**ó. de cinc**, (chem.) zinc oxide, zinc white.—**ó. de hierro**, (chem.) iron oxide, rust.—**ó. nitroso**, nitrous oxide.
oxigenable, *a.* (chem.) oxygenizable.
oxigenación, *f.* (chem.) oxygenation.
oxigenar, *va.* & *vr.* to oxygenate.
oxígeno, *m.* (chem.) oxygen.
oxigonio, *a.* (geom.) acute-angled.
oxihemoglobina, *f.* (physiol.) oxyhemoglobin.
oximel, oximiel, *m.* (pharm.) = OJIMIEL, oxymel.
oxipétalo, *m.* (bot.) a Brazilian vine.
oxisal, *f.* (chem.) oxysalt.
oxisulfuro, *m.* (chem.) oxysulfide.
oxitócico, ca, *a.* & *m.* oxytocic.
oxizacre, *m.* bittersweet beverage.
¡oxte! *interj.* keep off! begone!—**sin decir o. ni moxte**, (coll.) without saying a word.
oyamel, *m.* (bot.) Mexican sacred fir.
oyente, *n.* hearer.—*pl.* audience.
oyó, *pret.* of OÍR.
ozocerita, *f.* (min.) ozocerite, mineral wax.
ozona, *f.*, **ozono**, *m.* (chem.) ozone.
ozonización, *f.* ozonization.
ozonizado, da, *a.* ozonic.
ozonizador, ra. I. *a.* ozonizing. II. *n.* ozonizer
ozonizar, *va.* to ozonize.
ozonómetro, *m.* ozonometer.

P

P, p, *f.* p, nineteenth letter of the Spanish alphabet.
pabellón, *m.* pavilion; (mil.) bell tent; esparver, dais, bed canopy; summer house; national colors, flag; bell of a wind instrument; (anat.) external ear, pinna.—**p. de armas**, (mil.) stack of arms.
pabilo, pábilo, *m.* wick (of candle); burnt end of wick.
pabilón, *m.* bunch of flax or wool hanging from the distaff.
pablar, *vn.* (coll.) to talk.
pábulo, *m.* pabulum, food; encouragement.—**dar p. a**, to substantiate.
[1]paca, *f.* (zool.) spotted cavy.
[2]paca, *f.* bale of goods.
pacana, *f.* (bot.) pecan tree; pecan nut.
pacato, ta, *a.* pacific, quiet, tranquil, mild.
pacedero, ra. I. *a.* fit for grazing. II. *m.* grazing field, pasture.
pacedura, *f.* pasture.
paceño, ña, *a.* of or from La Paz, Bolivia.
pacer. I. *vn.* to pasture, to graze. II. *va.* to gnaw, nibble, eat away.
paciencia, *f.* patience; a kind of cooky.
paciente. I. *a.* patient. II. *n.* patient, sick person. —**p. externo**, outpatient (of a hospital).
pacientemente, *adv.* patiently.
pacienzudo, da, *a.* exceedingly patient.
pacificación, *f.* pacification; peace of mind.
pacificador, ra. I. *a.* pacifying, pacificatory; appeasing. II. *n.* peacemaker, pacifier; appeaser.
pacíficamente, *adv.* peacefully.
pacificar. I. *va.* (*pret.* PACIFIQUÉ; *subj.* PACIFIQUE) to pacify, appease. II. *vn.* to treat for peace. III. *vr.* to become calm.
pacífico, ca, *a.* pacific; peaceful; mild, gentle.
pacifiqué, pacifique, *v.* *V.* PACIFICAR.
pacifismo, *m.* pacifism.
pacifista, *n.* & *a.* pacifist(-ic).
[1]paco, *m.* (zool.) paco, alpaca; (min.) paco.
[2]paco, *m.* (Chile) police force.
pacotilla, *f.* (com.) venture.—**de p.**, of poor or inferior quality.
pacotillero, *m.* (Am.) peddler.
pactar, *va.* to covenant, contract, stipulate.
pacto, *m.* agreement, covenant, pact.
pacú, *m.* (Arg.) a river fish.
pácul, *m.* (P. I.) (bot.) wild plantain.
pachamanca, *f.* (Peru) barbecue.
pachón, *m.* phlegmatic man; pointer (dog).
pachorra, *f.* sluggishness, slowness.
pachorrudo, da, *a.* (coll.) sluggish, slow.
pachulí, *m.* patchouli (plant and perfume).
padecer. I. *va.* (*ind.* PADEZCO; *subj.* PADEZCA) to suffer; feel deeply; to lie under. II. *vn.* (de) to suffer (from).—**padecimiento**, *m.* suffering.
padilla, *f.* small frying pan; small oven.
padrastro, *m.* stepfather; obstacle, impediment; hangnail.
padrazo, *m. aug.* indulgent parent.
padre, *m.* father; ancestor; stallion, sire; source, origin, principal author; (eccl.) father, priest.—*pl.* parents, father and mother; ancestors.—**p. conscripto**, conscript father (Roman senator). —**p. de familia**, paterfamilias, father of a family.—**p. de pila**, godfather.—**P. Eterno**, God Almighty, our Father.—**p. nuestro**, Lord's Prayer.—**P. Santo**, Holy Father (the Pope). —**Santo P.**, Holy Father (the Pope); (eccl.) father (of the Church), one of the early Christian writers.
padrear, *vn.* to resemble one's father; to breed.
padrenuestro, *m.* Lord's Prayer, paternoster.
padrina, *f.* godmother.
padrinazgo, *m.* standing as godfather at a baptism; being a patron at a public function; title or charge of a godfather; patronage, support.
padrino, *m.* godfather; second, in a duel; best-man; patron, protector.
padrón, *m.* poll, census or tax list; pattern, model; column or post with an inscription; mark or note of infamy; (coll.) indulgent parent.
paella, *f.* saffron-flavored dish of rice with seafood, meat, chicken and various vegetables.
¡paf! *interj.* onomatopœic expression for the noise of a fall, blow, etc.
paflagonio, nia, *n.* & *a.* Paphlagonian.
paflón, *m.* (arch.) soffit.
paga, *f.* payment; fee, wages, salary; pay; satisfaction, amends; sum or fine paid; requital of love or friendship.—**p. líquida**, take-home pay.
pagable, *a.* payable.
pagadero, ra. I. *a.* payable. II. *m.* time and place of payment.
pagado, da. I. *pp.* of PAGAR. II. *a.* (or **p. de sí**) self-satisfied, conceited.

pagador, ra, *n.* payer, paying teller; *m.* paymaster, payclerk; *f.* paymistress.
pagaduría, *f.* paymaster's office.
paganismo, *m.* paganism. heathenism.
paganizar, *vn.* to paganize, become pagan.
pagano, na, *n.* & *a.* heathen, pagan.
pagar. I. *va.* (*pret.* PAGUÉ; *subj.* PAGUE) to pay; to pay for; to requite; to atone, make amends for; to fee.—**p. a buena cuenta,** to pay on account.—**p. al contado,** to pay cash.—**p. a plazos,** to pay in installments.—**p. con el pellejo,** (coll.) to pay with one's life.—**p. el pato** or **los vidrios rotos,** to pay the fiddler or the piper; to get the blame, be the scapegoat.—**p. en la misma moneda,** to pay in the same coin, pay back, avenge.—**pagarlas,** to pay for it (as a mean action, imprudence, etc.).—**p. por completo,** to pay in full, pay up.—**p. una visita,** to return a call, visit.—**p. y despedir a,** to pay off (employees, crew, etc.). **II.** *vr.* **(de)** to be pleased (with); to be fond (of).
pagaré, *m.* (com.) promissory note.
pagaya, *f.* (P. I.) single-bladed paddle.
página, *f.* page (of a book); folio.
paginación, *f.* pagination, paging.
paginar, *va.* to page (a book, etc.), paginate.
[1]**pago. I.** *m.* payment; requital.—**p. adelantado,** payment in advance.—**p. al contado,** cash payment.—**p. contra entrega,** cash on delivery (C. O. D.).—**p. total,** payment in full.—**efectuar un p.,** to make payment.—**mediante el p. de,** on the payment of. **II.** *a.* (Am., coll.) paid.
[2]**pago,** *m.* vineyard district.
pagoda, *f.* pagoda; idol.
pagote, *m.* (coll.) scapegoat.
pagro, *m.* (ichth.) braize.
pagué, pague, *v.* *V.* PAGAR.
paguro, *m.* small crab.
paico, *m.* (S. A.) (bot.) saltwort.
paila, *f.* caldron; kettle; boiler; (Cuba) evaporator, sugar pan.
pailebot, pailebote, *m.* (naut.) pilot's boat.
painel, *m.* (carp.) panel.
pairar, *vn.* (naut.) to bring to, to lie to.
pairo, *m.* (naut.) lying to with all sail set.—**al p.,** lying to.
país, *m.* country, nation; land, region; (art) landscape.—**del p.,** domestic, national.
paisaje, *m.* landscape.
paisajista, *n.* landscape painter.
paisana, *f.* a kind of country dance.
paisanaje, *m.* peasantry; being of the same country.
paisano, na. I. *a.* from the same country. **II.** *n.* fellow countryman(-woman), compatriot; civilian.—**vestido de p.,** in civilian clothes, in mufti.
Países Bajos, *m. pl.* Netherlands, Low Countries.
paisista, *n.* = PAISAJISTA.
paja, *f.* straw; blade of grass; chaff, shucks, trash.—**p. centenaza,** rye straw.—**¡pajas!** ditto, no less so.—**echar pajas,** to draw lots with straws.—**en un dácame,** or **quítame, allá esas pajas,** in the twinkling of an eye.—**no dormirse en las pajas,** to be very vigilant.—**por quítame allá esas pajas,** (to quarrel) for a straw, over the smallest trifle.
pajado, da. I. *a.* straw-colored. **II.** *f.* straw boiled with bran.
pajar, *m.* barn, straw loft; rick of straw.
pájara, *f.* female or hen bird; shrewd, designing woman; paper kite; paper rooster (toy).—**p. pinta,** game of forfeits.
pajarear, *vn.* to go birdcatching; to loiter about.
pajarel, *m.* (ornith.) = JILGUERO, linnet.
pajarera, *f.* aviary; large bird cage.
pajarería, *f.* abundance of birds; place where birds are sold.
pajarero, ra. I. *a.* merry, cheerful, gay; gaudy, loud. **II.** *n.* birdcatcher, bird fancier.
pajarete, *m.* fine sherry wine
pajarico, ca, ito, ta, *n.* little bird.
pajaril, *m.*—**hacer p.** (naut.) to cleat a sail.
pajarillo, lla. I. *n. dim.* small bird. **II.** *f.* paper rooster (toy); spleen; milt of a hog.
pájaro, *m.* bird; shrewd, sly fellow.—**p. bobo,** (ornith.) booby; penguin.—**p. carpintero,** (ornith.) woodpecker.—**p. de cuenta,** = P. GORDO.—**p. del sol,** (ornith.) bird of paradise.—**p. gordo,** person of importance, big gun.—**p. loco** = P. SOLITARIO.—**p. mosca,** a very small humming bird.—**p. niño,** auk.—**p. polilla,** kingfisher.—**p. solitario,** solitary thrush.—**más vale p. en mano que buitre volando,** a bird in the hand is worth two in the bush.—*pl.* (ornith.) Passeres.
pajarota, pajarotada, *f.* hoax.
pajarote, *m.* large ugly bird.
pajarraco, *m.* large bird; (coll.) sharper.
pajaruco, *m.* large ugly bird.
pajaza, *f.* refuse of fodder.
pajazo, *m.* prick of stubbles in a horse's eye.
paje, *m.* page, valet; (naut.) cabin boy.—**p. de hacha,** link boy.
pajear, *vn.* to feed well; (coll.) to behave.
pajecillo, *m. dim.* little page; washstand.
pajel, *m.* (ichth.) red sea bream.
pajera, *f.* straw loft, straw yard.
pajero, ra, *n.* straw dealer.
pajilla, *f. dim.* cigar made of maize leaf; rattan.
pajizo, za, *a.* made of straw; thatched with straw; straw-colored.
pajón, *m. aug.* coarse straw.
pajonal, *m.* (Am.) place abounding in tall grass.
pajoso, sa, *a.* made or full of straw.
pajote, *m.* straw interwoven with bulrush.
pajucero, *m.* place where straw is deposited to rot for fertilizer.
pajuela, *f.* dim. short straw; sulphur match.
pajuli, *m.* (P. R.) (bot.) = MARAÑÓN, cashew.
pajuncio, *m.* booby, ninny, fool.
pajuz, pajuzo, *m.* refuse of straw used for manure.
Pakistán, *m.* Pakistan.
pakistano, na, *n.* & *a.* Pakistan, Pakistani.
pala, *f.* shovel; baker's peel; scoop; slice, turnover; beetle for pounding clothes; dustpan; blade of an oar; blade of a hoe or spade; racket (for ball games); vamp (of shoe); leaf of a hinge; top of an epaulet; flat surface of the teeth; craft, cunning, artifice; dexterity, cleverness; (bot.) leaf of the prickly pear.—**meter su media p.,** to have or get a share.—**ser corta p.,** to know nothing.
palabra, *f.* word; term; floor (as in *tener la palabra,* to have the floor); (mil.) password.—*pl.* superstitious words used by sorcerers; (eccl.) formula of the sacraments; table on which the words of consecration are written.—**¡p.!,** honestly! no fooling!—**palabras cruzadas,** crossword puzzle.—**p. de caballero,** or **de honor,** word of honor.—**p. de matrimonio,** promise of marriage.—**p. llana,** (gram.) word having the accent on the penultimate.—**palabras mayores,** a serious matter; insulting words.—**a media p.,** at the least hint.—**bajo p.,** on (one's) word.—**de p.,** by word of mouth.—**dos palabras,** a few words.—**empeñar la p.,** to pledge one's word.—**en buenas palabras,** in plain words.—**en una p.,** in sum.—**libertad de p.,** freedom of speech.—**llevar la p.,** to be the spokesman.—**medias palabras,** insinuation, hint.—**pedir la p.,** to ask for the floor (at a meeting).—**santa p.,** good news, the good word (to express pleasure on hearing something).
palabrada, *f.* low, scurrilous language.
palabrear, *vn.* to chat, chatter, prattle.
palabreja, *f. dim.* odd word.
palabrería, *f.* palaver, wordiness, empty talk; (coll.) piffle.
palabrero, ra, *a.* talkative, loquacious.
palabrimujer, *m.* (coll.) man with an effeminate voice.

palabrista, *n.* chatterbox.
palabrita, *f. dim.* few words; short word or expression full of meaning.—**palabritas mansas,** (coll.) honey-tongued person.
palabrota, *f. aug.* coarse expression; big word.
palaciego, ga. I. *a.* pertaining to the palace. **II.** *n.* courtier.
palacio, *m.* palace; castle.—**p. de los deportes,** sports palace or arena.
palacra, palacrana, *f.* gold nugget.
palada, *f.* shovelful; (naut.) stroke of the oar.
paladar, *m.* palate; roof of the mouth; taste, relish; longing, desire.—**p. blando,** (anat.) soft palate.—**p. duro,** (anat.) hard palate.—**p. hendido,** (med.) cleft palate.—**velo del p.,** (anat.) soft palate, velum.
paladear. I. *va.* to taste with pleasure, to relish; to rub the mouth of with a sweet substance; to clean the mouth of. **II.** *vn.* (of a newborn child) to show a desire of suckling.
paladeo, *m.* act of tasting or relishing.
paladial, *a.* (gram.) palatal.
paladín, *m.* paladin, valiant knight, champion.
paladinamente, *adv.* publicly, clearly.
paladino, na. I. *a.* manifest, clear, apparent, public. **II.** *m.* PALADÍN.
paladio, *m.* (chem.) palladium.
paladión, *m.* palladium; safeguard.
palado, da, *a.* (her.) paly.
palafito, *m.* primitive lake dwelling.
palafrén, *m.* palfrey; woman's or groom's horse.
palafrenero, *m.* stableboy, groom, hostler.—**p. mayor,** first equerry.
palahierro, *m.* bushing for the spindle of the upper millstone.
palamallo, *m.* pall-mall (a game).
palamenta, *f.* (naut.) set of oars.
palanca, *f.* (mech.) lever; bar, crowbar; pole for carrying a weight; (fort.) outer fortification with stakes; (naut.) garnet tackle.—**p. de mando,** (aer.) control column, yoke.—**p. del timón,** (aer.) rudder bar.
palancada, *f.* blow with a lever.
palancana, palangana, *f.* washbowl.
palanganero, *m.* washstand.
palangre, *m.* line with several fishhooks, trotline.
palanquera, *f.* stockade; log fence.
palanquero, *m.* pile driver; blower of bellows.
palanqueta, *f. dim.* small lever; (mil.) bar shot or crossbar shot; (Cuba) sweetmeat with cane sirup; (Mex. & Chile) dumbbell.
palanquín, *m.* public porter; (naut.) double tackle, clew garnet; palanquin, covered litter.
palastro, *m.* sheet iron, sheet metal.
palatal, *a.* (phon.) palatal.
palatalización, *f.* (phon.) palatalization.
palatalizar, *va.* (phon.) to palatalize.
palatina, *f.* tippet, boa used by women.
palatinado, *m.* palatinate.
[1]**palatino, na,** *a.* palatial, palatine.
[2]**palatino, na,** *a.* palatal, palatine.
palatizar, *va.* (phon.) to palatalize.
palay, *m.* (P. I.) unhusked rice.
palazo, *m.* blow with a shovel, spade or stick.
palazón, *m.* (naut.) masting; woodwork.
palco, *m.* (theat.) box; stand with seats.—**p. escénico,** (theat.) the stage.
paleador, *m.* shoveler; stoker.
palear, *va.* = APALEAR, to beat, pound.
palenque, *m.* palisade, paling; (theat.) passage from pit to stage.
paleobotánica, *f.* paleobotany.
paleoceno, na, *m.* & *a.* (geol.) Paleocene.
paleofitología, *f.* paleophytology, paleobotany.
paleografía, *f.* paleography.
paleográfico, ca, *a.* paleographic.
paleógrafo, *m.* paleographer.
paleolítico, ca, *a.* paleolithic.
paleolito, *m.* paleolith (implement from the Stone Age).
paleología, *f.* paleology.
paleólogo, *m.* paleologist.
paleontografía, *f.* paleontography.
paleontográfico, ca, *a.* paleontographic.
paleontología, *f.* paleontology.
paleontológico, ca, *a.* paleontological.
paleontólogo, *m.* paleontologist.
paleozoico, ca, *a.* Paleozoic.
paleozoología, *f.* paleozoölogy.
paleozoólogo, *m.* paleozoölogist.
paleria, *f.* art and business of draining.
palero, *m.* shoveler; ditcher, drainer; pioneer; shovel maker or seller.
palestina, *f.* (print.) two-line small pica.
palestino, na, *n.* & *a.* Palestinian.
palestra, *f.* wrestling court, palæstra; gymnasium; tournament, competition.
paléstrico, ca, *a.* pert. to a wrestling place.
palestrita, *m.* wrestler, athlete.
paleta, *f. dim.* little shovel; fire shovel; (cooking) iron ladle; (mason.) trowel; (anat.) shoulder blade; (hydraul.) paddle board; blade; (art) palette.—**de p.,** opportunely.—**en dos paletas,** (coll.) shortly, briefly.
paletada, *f.* trowelful of mortar.
paletazo, *m.* thrust of a bull's horn.
paletear, *vn.* (naut.) to row ineffectively; to revolve without gaining speed.
paleteo, *m.* flapping of oars or paddles.
paletilla, *f. dim.* of PALETA; (anat.) cartilage of the sternum or xiphoid; shoulder blade; low candlestick.
paleto, *m.* fallow deer; rustic, hayseed.
paletó, *m.* overcoat, greatcoat.
paletón, *m.* bit of a key.
paletoque, *m.* paletocque, defensive jacket.
pali, *m.* Pali, an ancient language of India.
palia, *f.* (eccl.) altar cloth; curtain or screen before the tabernacle; pall.
paliación, *f.* palliation, extenuation.
paliadamente, *adv.* dissemblingly.
paliar, *va.* to palliate, extenuate, excuse.
paliativo, va; paliatorio, ria, *a.* palliative, mitigating; that may be palliated.
palidecer, *vn.* (*ind.* PALIDEZCO; *subj.* PALIDEZCA) to pale, turn pale.
palidez, *f.* paleness, pallor.
pálido, da, *a.* pallid, pale, ghastly.
paliducho, cha, *a.* palish.
palillo, *m. dim.* small stick; knitting needle case; toothpick; bobbin for network or lace; drumstick; tobacco stem; (coll.) chitchat.—*pl.* small pins put on the billiard table in certain games; rudiments, first principles; (coll.) trifles; castanets.
palimpsesto, *m.* palimpsest.
palingenesia, *f.* palingenesis, rebirth.
palinodia, *f.* palinode, public recantation.
palio, *m.* cloak, mantle; (eccl.) pallium; pall; canopy; prize for racing.
palique, *m.* (coll.) chitchat, small talk.
palisandro, *m.* (bot.) palisander, rosewood.
palitoque, plaitroque, *m.* rough little stick.
paliza, *f.* cudgelling, caning, bastinado.
palizada, *f.* palisade; paling; (fort.) stockade.
palma, *f.* palm tree; leaf of a palm tree; palmetto; palm of the hand; (vet.) under surface of the hoof; emblem of victory or martyrdom; preeminence.—**p. brava,** (P. I.) (bot.) fan palm.—**p. indiana,** (bot.) coconut palm.—**p. real,** (bot.) royal palm.—**andar en palmas,** to be universally applauded.—**ganar** or **llevarse la p.,** to carry the day; to win the prize.—**liso como la p. de la mano,** smoothly, easily, without any trouble.
palmáceo, a. I. *a.* (bot.) palmaceous. **II.** *f. pl.* Phœnicaceæ, Palmaceæ, palms.
palmacristi, *f.* (bot.) castor-oil plant.
palmada, *f.* pat; hand, applause.
[1]**palmar,** *vn.* (coll.) to die.
[2]**palmar. I.** *a.* pert. to palms; measuring a PALMO; obvious, evident. **II.** *m.* palm grove; fuller's thistle.

palmario, ria, *a.* clear, obvious, evident.
palmatoria, *f.* ferule; small candlestick.
palmeado, da, *a.* (ornith.) web-footed, palmated; (bot.) palmate.
palmear, *va.* to clap (the hands); to applaud.
palmejar, *m.* (naut.) thick stuff.
palmeo, *m.* measuring by PALMOS.
palmera, *f.* (bot.) palm tree; (bot.) date palm.
palmeral, *m.* date palm plantation.
palmero, *m.* palm keeper; palmer, pilgrim.
palmeta, *f.* ferule; slap with the ferule.—**ganar la p.,** to get ahead.
palmetazo, *m.* blow with a ferule.
palmiche, *m.* fruit of a palm tree.
palmífero, ra, *a.* (poet.) bearing or abounding in palms.
palmilla, *f.* blue woollen cloth; (shoe) inner sole.
palmípedo, da. I. *a.* web-footed, palmiped. **II.** *f. pl.* Palmatæ, palmipeds.
palmitato, *m.* (chem.) palmitate.
palmítico, ca, *a.* (chem.) palmitic.
palmitiesc, *a.* flat-hoofed (horse).
palmitina, *f.* (chem.) palmitin.
[1]**palmito,** *m.* (bot.) dwarf fan palm; palmetto or its root; (Cuba) sprout of a palm.
[2]**palmito,** *m.* woman's face.
palmo, *m.* span, measure of length (8 inches).—**p. a p.,** inch by inch.—**p. menor,** palm, hand, handbreadth (4 inches); span-farthing (boy's game).—**dejar a uno con un p. de narices,** to disappoint one; to leave one out in the cold.
palmotear, *vn.* to clap hands, applaud.
palmoteo, *m.* hand clapping, applause.
palo, *m.* stick; pole; timber, log; wood (material); (Am.) tree; blow with a stick; whack; execution on the gallows; suit at cards; stalk of fruit, pedicle; hook of a letter; (her.) pale; (naut.) mast.—*pl.* billiard pins (= PALILLOS); blows, cudgeling.—**p. áloe,** (bot.) aloes wood, eagle wood.—**p. brasil,** Brazil wood.—**p. campeche,** campeche, logwood.—**p. codal,** stick hung around the neck as a penance.—**p. de Campeche** = P. CAMPECHE.—**p. de hule,** rubber tree.—**p de jabón,** quillai, soap bark. —**p. del Brasil** = P. BRASIL.—**p. de mesana,** (naut.) mizzenmast.—**p. de planchar,** ironing board.—**p. de rosa,** rosewood; tulipwood.—**p. de tinte** = P. CAMPECHE.—**p. de trinquete,** (naut.) foremast.—**p. dulce,** licorice.—**p. mayor,** (naut.) mainmast.—**p. santo,** lignumvitæ.—**palos de marca,** (naut.) spar buoys.—**a. p. seco,** (naut.) under bare poles.—**dar (de) palos,** to drub, thrash, club, beat.
paloma, *f.* pigeon; dove; meek, mild person; (**P-,** astr.) Columba; (naut.) sling of a yard.—*pl.* whitecaps.—**p. brava,** rock dove.—**p. buchona,** pouter pigeon.—**p. copetuda,** capuchin (pigeon).—**p. mensajera,** carrier or homing pigeon.—**p. silvestre,** stock dove.—**p. torcaz,** ringdove, wood pigeon.—**p. zorita,** wood pigeon.
palomadura, *f.* (naut.) boltrope tie.
[1]**palomar,** *a.* hard-twisted (twine).
[2]**palomar,** *m.* pigeon house, dovecot.
palomariego, ga, *a.* (of pigeons) domestic.
palomear, *vn.* to shoot or breed pigeons.
palomera, *f.* small dovecot; bleak place.
palomería, *f.* pigeon shooting.
palomero, ra. I. *a.* having long iron points. **II.** *n.* pigeon seller or fancier.
palomilla, *f. dim.* young pigeon; grain moth; little butterfly; chrysalis; backbone of a horse; peak of a packsaddle; milk-white horse; journal bearing; wall bracket; (print.) galley rack; (bot.) common fumitory.—*pl.* whitecaps.
palomina, *f.* pigeon dung; (bot.) fumitory; a variety of black grape.
palomino, *m.* young pigeon; palomino (horse).
palomo, *m.* cock pigeon.
palón, *m.* (her.) guidon.
palotada, *f.* stroke with a drumstick.—**no dar p.,** not to do or say a thing right.
palote, *m.* drumstick; down-stroke, in penmanship.
paloteado, *m.* a rustic dance with sticks; noisy scuffle.
palotear, *vn.* to strike sticks against one another; to wrangle.
paloteo, *m.* fight with sticks.
palpabilidad, *f.* palpability.
palpable, *a.* palpable, obvious, evident.
palpablemente, *adv.* palpably, evidently.
palpación, palpadura, *f.*; **palpamiento,** *m.* feeling (of something), touching; palpableness; (med.) palpation.
palpar. I. *va.* to feel (of), to touch; to see as self-evident; (med.) to palpate. **II.** *vn.* to feel by touching; to grope in the dark.
pálpebra, *f.* eyelid.
palpebral, *a.* palpebral, pert. to eyelids.
palpitación, *f.* palpitation; throbbing.
palpitante, *a.* vibrating, palpitating.
palpitar, *vn.* to palpitate, beat, throb, quiver.
palpo, *m.* (zool.) palpus, palp, feeler.
palta, *f.* (bot.) avocado (fruit).
palto, *m.* (bot.) avocado (tree).
paludamento, *m.* (Rom. hist.) paludamentum, a cloak.
palúdico, ca, *a.* miasmatic; malarial.
paludismo, *m.* (med.) paludism; malaria.
paludoso, sa, *a.* marshy, swampy, fenlike.
palumbario, *a.* dove hunting (goshawk).
palurdo, da. I. *a.* rustic, rude. **II.** *n.* boor, rustic.
[1]**palustre,** *a.* marshy, fenlike, boggy.
[2]**palustre,** *m.* trowel.
palustrillo, *m.* (mason.) angle float.
pallador, *m.* (S. A.) minstrel, roving singer.
pallaquear, pallar, *va.* (Peru) to extract the richest part of an ore.
pallete, *m.* (naut.) fender, paunch mat.
pallón, *m.* assay button of gold.
pamandabuán, *m.* (P. I.) pambanmanche, snake boat, a large dugout.
pamela, *f.* low-crowned, wide-brimmed woman's straw hat.
pamena, *f.* (coll.) trifle, bagatelle.
pampa, *f.* pampa, extensive plain.—**estar a la p.,** (Arg., Colomb.) to be outdoors.
pámpana, *f.* vine leaf.—**tocar,** or **zurrar, la p.,** (coll.) to thrash.
pampanada, *f.* juice of vine shoots.
pampanaje, *m.* plenty of vine shoots; vain show.
pampanilla, *f.* trunks, loin cloth.
pámpano, *m.* young vine branch or tendril; (ichth.) pompano.
pampanoso, sa, *a.* full of tendrils.
pampeano, na. I. *a.* of or from the pampas. **II.** *n.* pampa man (woman).
pampear, *vn.* to travel in or over the pampas.
pampero, ra. I. *n.* pampa man (woman). **II.** *m.* (S. A.) violent southwest wind.
pampirolada, *f.* garlic sauce; (coll.) silly thing.
pamplina, *f.* (bot.) chickweed; pimpernel; yellow poppy; (coll.) frivolity, trifle.
pamplinada, *f.* trifle, silly or foolish talk.
pamporcino, *m.* (bot.) cyclamen, sowbread.
pamposado, da, *a.* lazy, idle; cowardly.
pampringada, *f.* toast soaked in gravy; (coll.) nonsense.
pan, *m.* bread; pie crust; anything in the shape of a loaf, cake, etc.; wheat; wafer; leaf of gold or silver.—*pl.* breadstuffs.—**p. ázimo,** unleavened bread.—**p. bazo,** brown bread.—**p. candeal,** white bread.—**p. casero,** homemade bread.—**p. cenceño,** unleavened bread.—**p. de azúcar,** loaf sugar; sugar loaf.—**p. de centeno,** black bread.—**p. de cera virgen,** cake of white wax.—**p. de flor,** bread made from the choicest flour.—**p. de higos,** fig cake.—**p. de jabón,** cake of soap.—**p. de la boda,** bridecake, wedding cake.—**p. de maíz,** corn bread, corn pone. —**p. de oro,** gold leaf.—**p. desmigado** or **rallado,** bread crumbs.—**p. duro,** stale bread.—**panes de proposición,** (bib.) shewbread.—**p.**

integral, whole-wheat bread.—**p. perdido**, (coll.) good-for-nothing, lazybones.—**p. porcino**, (bot.) sowbread.—**p. seco**, dry bread.—**p. terciado**, ground rent paid in grain (two-thirds wheat and one-third barley).—**p. tierno**, fresh bread.—**p. y quesillo**, (bot.) shepherd's purse.—**con su p. se lo coma**, let him take the consequences, let him do it for all I care, it's his funeral.—**ganarse el p.**, to earn one's bread and butter, earn a living.—**llamar al pan pan y al vino vino**, to call a spade a spade.—**vender como p. bendito** or **caliente**, to sell like hot cakes.

pana, *f.* plush, velveteen, corduroy; (naut.) limberboard.

pánace, *f.* (bot.) opopanax.

panacea, *f.* panacea; (pharm.) catholicon.

panadear, *vn.* to make bread.—**panadeo**, *m.* baking bread.

panadería, *f.* bakery.

panadero, ra. I. *n.* baker. **II.** *f.* baker's wife. **III.** *m. pl.* a kind of dance.

panadizo, *m.* whitlow, felon; (coll.) pale-faced, sickly person.

panado, da, *a.* pert. to PANETELA.

panal, *m.* honeycomb; hornet's nest; a sweetmeat.—**p. saetero**, honeycomb made across the hive.

Panamá, *m.* Panama; (**p.**) Panama hat.

panameño, ña, *n.* & *a.* Panamanian.

panamericanismo, *m.* Pan-Americanism.

panamericanista, *n.* Pan-Americanist.

panamericano, na, *a.* Pan-American.

panarizo, *m.* = PANADIZO.

panarra, *m.* (coll.) dolt, simpleton.

panatela, *f.* sponge cake; panatela (cigar).

panática, *f.* (naut.) provision of bread.

[1]**panca**, *f.* (Am.) corn husk.

[2]**panca**, *f.* (P. I.) a fishing-boat.

pancada, *f.* sale of job lot of things; kick.

pancarpia, *f.* garland of flowers.

pancarta, *f.* panchart, written records.

pancera, *f.* (armor) belly plate.

pancista, (pol.) one who is on the fence.

panco, *m.* (P. I.) coasting vessel.

pancraciasta, *m.* contestant in a pancratium.

pancracio, *m.* pancratium, athletic contest.

pancreas, *m.* (anat.) pancreas.—**pancreático, ca**, *a.* pancreatic.—**pancreatina**, *f.* pancreatin.

[1]**pancho**, *m.* (ichth.) spawn of the sea bream.

[2]**pancho**, *m.* (coll.) paunch, belly.

panda, *f.* gallery of a cloister; (zool.) panda (bear).

pandear, *vn.* to bend, warp, belly, bulge out.

pandectas, *f. pl.* (com.) index book; (Rom. law) pandects, collection of legal materials; code of laws.

pandemia, *f.* (med.) pandemic, an epidemic attacking the majority of people.

pandémico, ca, *a.* pandemic.

pandemónium, *m.* pandemonium.

pandeo, *m.* bulge, bulging.

pandera, *f.* (mus.) tambourine.

panderada, *f.* collection of tambourine players; (coll.) nonsense.

panderazo, *m.* blow with a tambourine.

pandereta, *f. dim.* tambourine.

panderete, *m. dim.* small tambourine.

panderetear, *vn.* to play on the tambourine.—**pandereteo**, *m.* beating the tambourine; merriment.—**panderetero, ra**, *n.* tambourine maker, seller, or player.

pandero, *m.* PANDERA; paper kite; (coll.) silly talker.

pandiculación, *f.* pandiculation.

pandilla, *f.* party, faction; gang, set; picnic.

pandillero, ra, *n.* = PANDILLISTA; (Am.) gangster.

pandillista, *n.* fomenter of factions; leader or member of a gang.

pando, da, *a.* bulged; slow of motion.

pandorga, *f.* (coll.) fat, bulky woman; kite.

panecico, illo, ito, *m.* roll (bread).

panegírico, ca. I. *a.* panegyrical. **II.** *m.* panegyric, eulogy.

panegirista, *m.* panegyrist, eulogist.

panegirizar, *va.* to panegyrize, eulogize.

panel, *m.* (art, elec.) panel.

panela, *f.* small biscuit; (Colomb.) unrefined brown sugar; (her.) panel.

panera, *f.* granary; pannier; bread basket.

panero, *m.* baker's basket.

paneslavismo, *m.* Pan-Slavism.

paneslavista. I. *a.* Pan-Slavic. **II.** *n.* Pan-Slavist.

panetela, *f.* panada, broth with toast boiled in it; (Am.) sponge cake; panetela (cigar).

panetería, *f.* pantry of the royal palace.

panetero, *m.* (anc.) pantler, person in charge of a royal pantry.

pánfilo, *m.* slow, sluggish, heavy person.

pangelín, *m.* (bot.) angelin tree.

pangénesis, *f.* (biol.) pangenesis.

pangenético, ca, *a.* pangenetic.

pangermanismo, *m.* Pan-Germanism.

pangermanista. I. *a.* Pan-German, Pan-Germanic, Pan-Germanistic. **II.** *n.* Pan-German, Pan-Germanist.

pangolín, *m.* (zool.) pangolin, a scaly anteater.

panhelénico, ca, *a.* Panhellenic.

panhelenismo, *m.* Panhellenism.

panhelenista. I. *a.* Panhellenic, Panhellenist. **II.** *n.* Panhellenist.

paniaguado, da, *n.* servant; employee; protégé.

pánico, ca, *a.* & *m.* panic.

paniculado, da, *a.* (bot.) paniculate.

panículo, *m.* (bot.) panicle; pellicle, membrane.

paniego, ga. I. *a.* eating or yielding much bread. **II.** *m.* burlap bag for charcoal.

panificación, *f.* panification, making of bread.

panificar, *va.* (*pret.* PANIFIQUÉ; *subj.* PANIFIQUE) to make into bread; to convert pasture land into cornfields.

panilla, *f.* an oil measure (¼ lb.).

panique, *m.* large Australian herbivorous bat.

panislamismo, *m.* Pan-Islamism.

panislamista. I. *a.* Pan-Islamic, Pan-Islamist. **II.** *n.* Pan-Islamist.

panizo, *m.* (bot.) panic grass; Indian corn; (Chile) mineral bed.

panmixia, *f.* (biol.) panmixia.

panocha, panoja, *f.* (bot.) ear of grain; (bot.) panicle; bunch of anchovies.

panoplia, *f.* panoply; collection of arms.

panóptico, ca. I. *a.* panoptical. **II.** *m.* (Am.) penitentiary; panopticon.

panorama, *m.* panorama.

panorámico, ca, *a.* panoramic; pictorial.

panoso, sa, *a.* mealy.

panqué, panqueque, *m.* (cook.) pancake, griddlecake, hot cake.

panspermia, *f.* panspermy, bio-genetic theory.

pantalán, *m.* (P. I.) wooden or bamboo pier.

pantaletas, *f. pl.* (Am.) pantalets, panties.

pantalón, *m.* (gen. *pl.*) pantaloons, trousers, (coll.) pants; panties.—**p. bombacho**, wide, balloon trousers.

pantalla, *f.* lamp shade; screen; person or object that obstructs the view; (movie) screen; (coll., P. R.) earring.—**p. de cine**, movie screen.—**p. de radar**, radar screen, radar scope.—**p. de televisión**, television screen.—**p. de vidrio**, glass shade.

pantanal, *m.* swampy, marshy ground.

pantano, *m.* swamp, marsh, bog; reservoir, dam; hindrance, obstacle, difficulty.

pantanoso, sa, *a.* swampy, marshy, miry; full of difficulties.

pantasana, *f.* fishing seine.

panteísmo, *m.* pantheism.

panteísta, *n.* & *a.* pantheist(-ic).

panteístico, ca, *a.* pantheistic.

panteón, *m.* pantheon.
pantera, *f.* (zool.) panther; (min.) yellow agate.
pantográfico, ca, *a.* pantographic.
pantógrafo, *m.* pantograph, copying instrument.
pantómetra, *f.* a kind of measuring compass.
pantomima, *f.* pantomime.
pantomímico, ca, *a.* pantomimic.
pantomimo, *m.* mimic, pantomimist.
pantoque, *m.* (naut.) bilge or flat of the ship.
pantorra, *f.* (coll.) fat calf of the leg.
pantorrilla, *f.* calf of the leg.
pantorrillera, *f.* padded stocking.
pantorrilludo, da, *a.* having thick calves.
pantoscópico, ca, *a.* (opt.) pantoscopic.
pantufla, *f.*, **pantuflo,** *m.* slipper, baboosh.
pantuflazo, *m.* blow with a slipper.
panucho, *m.* (Mex.) bean-and-meat pie with corn-meal crust.
panudo, da, *a.* (Cuba) (of ripe fruit, esp. alligator pear) firm, not soft.
panza, *f.* belly, paunch; belly of a vase; rumen or paunch of ruminants.
panzada, *f.* (coll.) bellyful; push or hit with the belly.
panzón, zona. I. *a.* big-bellied. **II.** *m.* big belly, paunch, pot belly.
panzudo, da, *a.* big-bellied, pot-bellied.
pañal, *m.* (baby's) diaper; tail of a shirt.—*pl.* swaddling clothes; infancy.—**estar en pañales,** to have little knowledge; to be in its, or one's, infancy.
pañería, *f.* drapery; clothing store.
pañero, *m.* woollen draper; clothier.
pañete, *m. dim.* inferior or light cloth; (Colomb.) plastering.—*pl.* trunks worn by fishermen; linen attached to the crucifix below the waist.
pañito, pañizuelo, *m. dim.* small cloth.
paño, *m.* cloth, woollen stuff; by extension, any woven stuff; tapestry, drapery, hanging; kitchen cloth; wash cloth; bleeredness; livid spot on the face; spot in looking-glasses, crystals, or precious stones; (naut.) canvas, sailcloth; (sewing) breadth.—*pl.* clothes, garments.—**p. burdo,** shoddy cloth.—**p. catorceno,** a kind of coarse cloth.—**p. de lágrimas,** one who sympathizes and consoles.—**p. de manos,** towel.—**p. de mesa,** tablecloth.—**p. pardillo** = P. BURDO.—**paños calientes,** inefficient efforts or means; half measures.—**paños menores,** underclothes; dishabille.—**al p.,** (theat.) outside, without.
pañol, *m.* (naut.) storeroom.—**p. de las velas,** sail room.—**p. del contestable,** gunner's room.—**p. de pólvora,** magazine.—**p. de proa,** boatswain's storeroom.
pañolería, *f.* handkerchief shop or factory.
[1]**pañolero, ra,** *n.* handkerchief maker or seller.
[2]**pañolero,** *m.* (naut.) yeoman.
pañoleta, *f.* triangular shawl.
pañolón, *m.* large square shawl.
pañosa, *f.* cloak.
pañoso, sa, *a.* ragged, tattered.
pañuelo, *m.* handkerchief; kerchief; shawl.—**p. de bolsillo,** pocket handkerchief.—**p. de hierbas,** bandanna.
[1]**papa,** *m.* (eccl.) Pope; (coll.) papa.
[2]**papa,** *f.* potato; (Peru) lump of native silver.
[3]**papa,** *f.* hoax.—*pl.* pap; (coll.) food, "grub."
papá, *m.* (coll.) papa; (Mex.) grandfather.—**papacito,** *m. dim.* (coll.) dad, daddy, papa dear.
papada, *f.* double chin; gill; dewlap.
papadilla, *f. dim.* flesh under the chin.
papado, *m.* papacy.
papafigo, *m.* (ornith.) figpecker, beccafico.
papagayo, *m.* (ornith.) parrot; (ichth.) rock bass; (bot.) three-colored amaranth; white arum, calla; (C. A.) violent northeast wind.
papahigo, *m.* winter cap; (naut.) lower sail.
papahuevos, *m.* (coll.) simpleton, blockhead.
papaína, *f.* (chem.) papain.
papal, *a.* papal.
[1]**papalina,** *f.* cap with flaps; coif.
[2]**papalina,** *f.* (coll.) fit of drunkenness.
papalmente, *adv.* in a papal manner.
papalote, *m.* (Cuba) kite.
papamoscas, *m.* (ornith.) flycatcher, flyeater; (coll.) ninny.
papanatas, *m.* (coll.) dolt, simpleton, ninny.
papandujo, ja, *a.* (coll.) too soft, overripe.
papar, *va.* to swallow without chewing; (coll.) to eat; to pay little attention to.—**p. moscas,** or **viento,** to gape.
páparo, ra, *n.* ancient Indian of Panama; gawk, gump.
paparrabias, *n.* (coll.) testy, fretful person.
paparrasolla, *f.* hobgoblin, bugbear.
paparrucha, *f.* (coll.) fake, humbug; nonsense, silliness.
papasal, *m.* a boys' game; trifle, bagatelle.
papaveráceo, a, *a.* (bot.) papaveraceous.
papaya, *f.* (bot.) papaw, pawpaw; papaya.
papayo, *m.* (bot.) papaw tree; papaya tree.
pápaz, *m.* (in Africa) Christian priest.
papazgo, *m.* popedom, pontificate.
papel, *m.* paper; piece of paper; document; (commercial, legal) paper; writing, treatise, discourse. pamphlet, tract; (theat.) part, rôle; character, figure.—**p. alquitranado,** tar paper.—**p. carbón,** carbon paper.—**p. cebolla,** onionskin.—**p. continuo,** paper in rolls.—**p. corrugado,** corrugated paper.—**p. costero,** outside quires.—**p. cuadriculado,** graph paper, cross-section paper.—**p. cuché,** coated paper, art paper.—**p. de añafeo,** brown paper.—**p. de barbas,** untrimmed paper.—**p. de calcar,** tracing paper.—**p. de cartas,** letter paper, (Am.) stationery.—**p. de cúrcuma,** (chem.) turmeric paper.—**p. de China,** China paper.—**p. de entapizar,** wall paper, paper hanging.—**p. de escribir,** writing paper.—**p. de Estado,** government bond.—**p. de estaño,** tin foil.—**p. de estraza,** brown paper, wrapping paper.—**p. de filtrar,** filter paper.—**p. de fumar,** cigarette paper.—**p. de lija,** sandpaper.—**p. de luto,** mourning paper.—**p. de marca,** plate paper.—**p. de marquilla,** bristol board, drawing paper.—**p. de oficio,** foolscap.—**p. de periódico,** newsprint.—**p. de seda,** tissue paper.—**p. de tornasol,** litmus paper.—**p. esmeril,** emery paper.—**papeles mojados,** worthless documents.—**p. higiénico,** toilet paper.—**p. jaspeado,** marbled paper.—**p. marca mayor,** royal paper.—**p. marquilla,** bristol board, drawing paper.—**p. moneda,** paper money.—**p. para excusados,** toilet paper.—**p. pintado,** printed wallpaper, paper hanging.—**p. rayado,** ruled paper.—**p. reactivo,** test paper, litmus paper.—**p. secante,** blotting paper.—**p. sellado** or **timbrado,** official stamped paper.—**p. tela,** tracing paper.—**p. viejo,** waste paper.—**p. vitela,** vellum paper.—**p. volante,** flyer, throwaway, printed leaflet.—**hacer buen (mal) p.,** to make a good (bad) showing.—**hacer p.,** to cut a figure, play a part, impersonate.
papelear, *vn.* to search or look over papers; (coll.) to cut a figure.
papeleo, *m.* act of looking over papers; paper work, red tape.
papelera, *f.* writing desk, paper case; collection or bunch of written papers.
papelería, *f.* stationery; stationery shop; heap of papers.
papelero, ra, *n.* paper maker; stationer.
papeleta, *f.* card, check, slip; ballot, ticket; paper bag (for money or sweetmeats); (fam., fig.) a hard nut to crack, a hard person to deal with.
papelillo, *m. dim.* bit of paper; cigarette.
[1]**papelina,** *f.* wine goblet; (coll.) fit of drunkenness.
[2]**papelina,** *f.* poplin.
papelista, *n.* keeper of documents; papermaker; stationer; paper hanger.

papelito, *m. dim.* small paper; curl paper.
papelón, na. I. *a.* boastful, ostentatious. **II.** *m. aug.* poster, bill; paper board; boaster; (Am.) raw sugar.
papelonear, *vn.* (coll.) to boast, pretend.
papelote, papelucho, *m.* scurrilous article.
papera, *f.* goiter; mumps.
papero, *m.* pot in which pap is made.
papialbillo, *m.* (zool.) weasel.
papila, *f.* (med. and bot.) papilla.
papilar, *a.* papillary; papillose.
papilionáceo. I. *a.* (bot.) papilionaceous. **II.** *f. pl.* Papilionaceæ.
papiloma, *m.* (med.) papilloma.
papilla, *f.* pap; guile, deceit, artifice.
papión, *m.* a kind of large monkey.
papiráceo, cea, *a.* papyraceous, papery.
papiro, *m.* (bot.) papyrus.
papirolada, *f.* garlic sauce.
papirotada, *f.*; **papirotazo, papirote,** *m.* fillip.
papisa, *f.* papess.
papismo, *m.* (der.) papistry, popery, papalism.
papista. I. *a.* Papist, Papistic; (der.) popish. **II.** *n.* Papist.
[1]**papo,** *m.* double chin; anterior lower part of an animal's neck, external throat; fowl's gizzard; puff in garments.—**p. de viento,** (naut.) small sail.
[2]**papo,** *m.* (bot.) thistledown.
papón, *m.* bogeyman, hobgoblin.
paporrear, *va.* to horsewhip, whip, flog, scourge.
papú, *n.* & *a.* Papuan.
papudo, da, *a.* doubled-chinned.
papujado, da, *a.* (of fowls) full-gorged; swollen, puffed up.
pápula, *f.* (med.) papule, small non-suppurative eruption.
papuloso, sa, *a.* (med.) papular, papulous.
paquebote, *m.* (naut.) passenger and mail liner.
paquete, *m.* packet, package, parcel, pack; bundle of papers; (coll.) dandy, dude; (naut.) packet boat.—**p. de duelas,** shooks, set of staves for a barrel.—**servicio de paquetes postales,** parcel post.
paquetería, *f.* (com.) retail trade or shop.
paquidermo, ma. I. *a.* thick-skinned; pachydermatous. **II.** *m.* (zool.) pachyderm.
par. I. *a.* equal; on a par; homologous, corresponding; even (number). **II.** *m.* pair, couple; team; peer; (arch.) angle rafter; (elec.) cell; (mech.) couple.—**p. de fuerzas,** (mech.) couple.—**p. de giro,** (aer.) torque.—**p. de perdices,** brace of partridge.—**p. de pistolas,** brace of pistols.—**p. de torsión** or **p. motor,** (elec.) torque.—**pares o nones,** odd or even (a game).—**p. termoeléctrico,** thermocouple.—**a la p.,** jointly, equally; (com.) par; at par; (horse racing) in a dead heat.—**a pares,** two and two, by pairs.—**de p. en p.,** (of a door, etc.) wide open.—**estar al p. de,** to be on a par with, be equal to.—**ir a la p.,** to go halves, have an equal share.—**sin p.,** peerless, incomparable. **III.** *f. pl.* (anat., zool.) placenta.
para, *prep.* for, to, in order to, toward, wherefore, to the end that.—**p. con,** toward, with.—**p. entre los dos,** between you and me.—**p. eso,** for that, for that matter.—**¿p. qué?** what for? what is the use?—**p. que,** so that, in order that.—**p. siempre,** for ever.—**dije p. mi capote,** I said to myself.—**estar p.,** to be on the point of, about to.—**sin qué ni p. qué,** without motive, without rime or reason.—**tengo p. mí,** it is my opinion.
parabién, *m.* congratulation, felicitation, greeting.
parabiosis, *f.* (biol.) parabiosis.
parablasto, *m.* (biol.) parablast.
parábola, *f.* parable; (geom.) parabola.
parabolano, na, *n.* one who uses parables.
parabólico, ca, *a.* parabolic.
paraboloide, *m.* (geom.) paraboloid.
parabrisa, *m.* (auto) wind shield.
paracaídas, *m.* parachute.
paracaidista, *m.* parachutist, paratrooper; *pl.* (mil.) paratroops.
paracentesis, *f.* (surg.) paracentesis, tapping.
Paracleto, Paráclito, *m.* Paraclete, Holy Ghost.
paracomando, *m.* paratrooper, paracommando.
paracronismo, *m.* parachronism.
parachispas, *m.* (elec.) spark arrester.
parachoques, *m.* (auto) bumper.
parada, *f.* stop (as of a train); stay, suspension, pause; (mil.) halt, halting; parade; review; stall, fold for cattle; relay of horses; dam, bank; stakes, bet; (fencing) parry.—**p. en firme,** or **en seco,** dead stop.—**doblar la p.,** to double the stake or bid.—**llamar de p.,** to hold game at bay.
paradera, *f.* sluice, floodgate; fishing seine.
paradero, *m.* halting place; (Cuba) (Ry.) station, depot; landing, terminus; whereabouts.
paradeta, illa, *f.* short pause.—*pl.* a kind of dance.
paradigma, *m.* example, paradigm.
paradigmático, ca, *a.* paradigmatic, exemplary.
paradilla, *f.* (Chile) a short pause.
paradina, *f.* round inclosure.
paradisíaco, ca, *a.* paradisiacal, paradisaical.
paradislero, *m.* huntsman in wait; newsmonger.
parado, da. I. *pp.* of PARAR. **II.** *a.* shy; slow, spiritless, indolent; unoccupied; (of a clock) stopped; shut down (as a factory); (Am.) standing. **III.** *a.* & *n.* unemployed.
paradoja, *f.* paradox.
paradojo, ja; paradójico, ca, *a.* paradoxical.
parador. I. *n.* one who stops or halts; heavy bettor. **II.** *m.* hostelry, inn, road house.
parafernales.—bienes p., (law) paraphernalia.
parafina, *f.* paraffin.
parafraseador, ra, *n.* paraphraser.
parafrasear, *va.* to paraphrase.
paráfrasis, *f.* paraphrase.
parafraste, *m.* paraphrast.
parafrásticamente, *adv.* paraphrastically.
parafrástico, ca, *a.* paraphrastic.
paragénesis, *f.* (geol.) paragenesis, formation of minerals in close contact.
paragoge, *f.* (gram.) paragoge (addition of a letter or syllable at the end of a word).
paragógico, ca, *a.* paragogic.
paragolpes, *m.* (Arg.) (auto) fender.
paragonar, *va.* to compare, to hold equal to.
parágrafo, *m.* paragraph; additional clause.
paraguas, *m.* umbrella.
Paraguay, *m.* Paraguay; (**p.**) (ornith.) kind of Paraguayan parrot.
paraguayano, na; paraguayo, ya, *n.* & *a.* Paraguayan.
paragüería, *f.* umbrella shop.
paragüero, ra. I. *n.* umbrella maker, repairer or seller. **II.** *m.* umbrella stand.
para-hidrógeno, *m.* (chem.) para-hydrogen.
parahuso, *m.* = PARAÚSO.
paraíso, *m.* paradise; heaven; (theat., coll.) "nigger heaven," upper gallery.—**p. de bobos,** air castles.—**p. terrenal,** Paradise, garden of Eden.
paraje, *m.* place, spot; condition, state.
paral, *m.* scaffolding pole, prop, or post; (naut.) launching ways.
paraláctico, ca, *a.* parallactic.
paralaje, *f.* (astr.) parallax.
paraldehido, *m.* (chem.) paraldehyde (hypnotic used in medicine).
paralelar, *va.* to parallel; to compare.
paralelepípedo, *m.* (geom.) parallelepiped.
paralelismo, *m.* (geom.) parallelism.
paralelo, la. I. *a.* parallel; similar; corresponding. **II.** *m.* parallel, resemblance; (geog.) parallel. **III.** *f.* (geom. and fort.) parallel.
paralelogramo, *m.* (geom.) parallelogram.
paralicé, paralice, *v. V.* PARALIZAR.
Paralipómenos, *m. pl.* Paralipomena, Book of Chronicles.
paralipse, *f.* (rhet.) paralipsis.
parálisis, *f.* (med.) paralysis.—**p. cerebral,**

(med.) cerebral palsy.—**p. infantil,** (med.) infantile paralysis, poliomyelitis.
paraliticado, da, *a.* paralyzed, palsied.
paraliticar, *vn.* to become paralyzed, become palsied.
paralítico, ca, *n.* & *a.* paralytic.
paralización, *f.* paralyzation; immobilization; (com.) stagnancy, stagnation.
paralizado, da, *a.* (com.) dull, stagnant, flat.
paralizador, ra, *a.* paralyzing.
paralizar, *va.* (*pret.* PARALICÉ; *subj.* PARALICE) to paralyze; to impede, stop; immobilize.
paralogismo, *m.* (logic) paralogism.
paralogizar, *vn.* to paralogize, reason falsely.
paramagnético, ca, *a.* paramagnetic.
paramagnetismo, *m.* (phys.) paramagnetism.
paramecio, *m.* (zool.) paramecium.
paramentar, *va.* to adorn, bedeck, embellish.
paramento, *m.* ornament, hanging; trappings, caparison; (arch.) face, surface.—**paramentos sacerdotales,** (eccl.) robes and ornaments.
paramera, *f.* desert, moor; bleak place.
parámetro, *m.* (geom.) parameter.
paramilitar, *a.* paramilitary.
páramo, *m.* paramo, high, bare and cold region of tropical South America.
paramorfismo, *m.*; **paramorfosis,** *f.* (min.) paramorphism.
parancero, *m.* birdcatcher.
parangón, *m.* comparison.
parangona, *f.* (print.) paragon type.
parangonar, *va.* to compare.
paranínfico, *a.* (arch.) having statues of nymphs.
paraninfo, *m.* paranymph; harbinger of felicity; salutatorian; hall for college exercises.
paranoia, *f.* (med., psych.) paranoia.
paranoico, ca, *n.* & *a.* paranoiac, paranoid.
paranza, *f.* hut or blind for huntsmen.
parao, *m.* (P. I.) a large passenger vessel.
parapara, *f.* fruit of the PARAPARO.
paraparo, *m.* (Venez.) (bot.) soapbark tree.
parapetarse, *vr.* to hide behind a parapet.
parapeto, *m.* (mil.) parapet, breastwork; rails or battlements on bridges and quays.
paraplejía, *f.* (med.) paraplegia.
parapléjico, ca, *n.* & *a.* paraplegic.
parapoco, *n.* (coll.) numskull; timid person.
[1]**parar. I.** *va.* to stop, detain, check; to prepare, get ready; to stake, bet (at cards); to point at (game); to treat or use ill; to place, fix (as the attention); (fencing) to parry.—**p. la oreja,** (Am.) to prick up one's ears.—**p. mientes en,** to consider carefully. **II.** *vn.* to stop, halt; (of a watch) to stop; to land; to go from one to another; to come into the possession of; to happen; to come to an end; **(en)** to become, end (in), be transformed (into); to stop or stay (at), lodge; (of a train) to stop, have its terminus (at).—**ir a p. a,** or **en,** to become, end in, finally to get to. **III.** *vr.* to stop, halt; to be ready to face a danger; to desist, waver, pause; (Am.) to stand up.—**no p. en pelillos,** not to stop at trifles.—**sin p.,** instantly, without delay.
[2]**parar,** *m.* lansquenet, a card game.
pararrayos, *m.* lightning rod.
parasceve, *m.* parasceve, Jewish Sabbath eve.
paraselene, *f.* (meteorol.) paraselene, mock moon.
parasemo, *f.* figurehead of a vessel.
parasimpático, ca, *n.* & *a.* (anat., physiol.) parasympathetic.
parasismo, *m.* paroxysm, fit.
parasitario, ria, *a.* = PARASÍTICO.
parasiticida, *m.* parasiticide.
parasítico, ca, *a.* parasitic.
parasitismo, *m.* parasitism.
parásito, ta. I. *a.* parasitic. **II.** *m.* (zool., bot.) parasite; *pl.* (rad.) strays; *n.* (fig.) parasite.—**parásitos atmosféricos,** atmospherics, static.
parasitología, *f.* parasitology, science of treating parasites.
parasitólogo, *m.* parasitologist.
parasol, *m.* parasol, sunshade.
parástade, *m.* (arch.) anta, pilaster.
parata, *f.* built terrace.
paratifoidea, *f.* paratyphoid.
paratiroideo, dea, *a.* parathyroid.
paratiroides, *m.* & *a.* (anat.) parathyroid.
parausar, *va.* to drill with a brace drill.
paraúso, *m.* brace drill.
parazonio, *m.* Greek dagger or short sword.
parca, *f.* (poet.) fate, death.
parcamente, *adv.* sparingly, parsimoniously.
parce, *m.* premium card in schools.
parcela, *f.* parcel of land, plot, area.
parcelar, *va.* to divide into lots.
parcelario, ria, *a.* pertaining to parceled lands.
parcial, *a.* partial.—**parcialidad,** *f.* partiality, bias; party, faction.—**parcialmente,** *adv.* partially, partly.
parcidad, *f.* parsimony, frugality.
parcionero, *m.* partner, participant.
parcísimo, ma, *a.* (*super.* de PARCO) scantiest, most sparing; most moderate, very moderate.
parco, ca, *a.* sparing, scanty; sober, moderate, parsimonious.
parcha, *f.* (Am.) (bot.) any passifloraceous plant.
parchazo, *m. aug.* large plaster; (coll.) deception, jest; (naut.) flapping of sails.
parche, *m.* (pharm.) plaster, sticking plaster; (mil.) drum-head; drum; (shoemaking, aer.) patch; botch.—**pegar un p.,** (coll.) to play a scurvy trick.
parchesí, *m.* parche(e)si (game).
parchista, *n.* sponger, petty borrower.
pardal. I. *a.* rustic. **II.** *m.* (ornith.) sparrow. linnet; (zool.) leopard; (bot.) aconite, wolfsbane; crafty fellow.
pardear, *vn.* to be or show grayish or drab.
pardela, *f.* (ornith.) web-footed gull-like bird.
¡pardiez! *interj.* (coll.) by Jove! by Jupiter!
pardillo. I. *m.* (ornith.) linnet; a kind of grape, and wine made from it. **II.** *a.* grayish, brown (cloth).
pardisco, ca, *a.* = PARDUSCO.
pardo, da. I. *a.* brown; dark gray; dark; cloudy; (Cuba) colored (people). **II.** *n.* (Cuba) mulatto; darky. **III.** *m.* (zool.) leopard.
pardusco, ca, *a.* grayish, grizzly.
pareado, *m.* (poet.) couplet.—**p. heroico,** heroic couplet.
parear, *va.* to match, mate, pair, couple.
parecer. I. *vn.* (*ind.* PAREZCO; *subj.* PAREZCA) to appear, show up, turn up; to seem, look like.—**parece mentira,** it seems incredible, it's hard to believe.—**a lo que parece,** or **según parece,** according to appearances, as it seems.—**al p.,** apparently, to all appearances.—**no parece sino que,** it seems certain that. **II.** *vr.* to resemble each other, to look alike. **III.** *m.* opinion; look, mien; appearance.—**por el bien p.,** to save appearances.
parecido, da. I. *pp.* of PARECER. **II.** *a.* found; (a) resembling, like, similar (to).—**bien (mal) p.,** good- (bad-) looking. **III.** *m.* resemblance, likeness.
pareciente, *a.* similar; apparent.
pared, *f.* wall; close field of barley; garden edging or fence of box.—**p. maestra,** main wall.—**p. medianera,** party wall, partition wall.—**entre cuatro paredes,** confined, retired; imprisoned.—**hasta la p. de enfrente,** to the limit; with all one's heart and might.—**las paredes oyen,** walls have ears.
paredaño, ña, *a.* having a wall between.
paredón, *m. aug.* thick wall; standing wall.
paregórico, ca, *m.* & *a.* (pharm.) paregoric.
pareja, *f.* pair; couple; twosome; brace; match; dancing partner; team, pair of soldiers or policemen.—**parejas mixtas,** (games) mixed doubles.—**correr parejas, or a las parejas,** to be on a par, to go together.
parejo, ja, *a.* equal, even, smooth; (horse racing) neck and neck.—**por p.,** or **por un p.,** on equal

terms, on a par, evenly; indistinguishably, without distinction.
parejura, *f.* evenness; equality; similarity.
parénesis, *f.* admonition, exhortation.
parenético, ca, *a.* admonitory.
parénquima, *m.* (zool., bot.) parenchyma.
parenquimatoso, sa, *a.* (zool., bot.) parenchymatous, parenchymous.
parentela, *f.* kindred, kinsfolk, relations.
parentesco, *m.* kindred, relationship; tie, bond.
paréntesis, *m.* parenthesis; parenthetical statement or expression; digression.—**entre,** or **por, p.,** parenthetically, by the bye.
pareo, *m.* pairing, coupling, matching.
parergón, *m.* additional ornament.
pares, *f. pl.* placenta, afterbirth.
paresa, *f.* peeress.
paresia, *f.* (med.) paresis.
parestesia, *f.* (med.) paresthesia.
parestésico, ca, *a.* paresthetic.
parético, ca, *a.* paretic.
parezco, parezca, *v. V.* PARECER.
pargo, *m.* (ichth.) braize, porgy.
parhelia, *f.,* **parhelio,** *m.* parhelion, mock sun.
parhilera, *f.* (arch.) ridgepole, ridgepiece.
paria, *m.* pariah, outcast.
parias, *f.* tribute by one prince to another; placenta.
parición, *f.* parturition (of cattle).
parida. I. *f.* woman lately delivered of a baby. **II.** *a.* having recently brought forth offspring (app. to women and animals).
paridad, *f.* parity, equality, comparison.
paridera. I. *a.* fruitful, prolific. **II.** *f.* place where cattle bring forth their young; parturition.
pariente, ta, *n.* relation, relative, kinsman (-woman); (coll.) appellation given by husband and wife to each other.
parietal, *a.* pertaining to walls; (anat.) parietal.
parietaria, *f.* (bot.) wall pellitory.
parificación, *f.* exemplification, illustration.
parificar, *va.* to exemplify, illustrate.
parihuela, *f.* handbarrow; litter; stretcher.
pario, ria, *n.* & *a.* Parian.
parir, *va.* & *vn.* to give birth, bring forth young; to produce, to cause; to publish.—**poner a p.,** to constrain, force (a person).
parisiense, *a.* & *n.* Parisian.
parisilábico, ca, *a.* (gram.) parisyllabic.
parisílabo, ba, *a.* (gram.) parisyllabic.
parla, *f.* easy delivery, loquacity, talk.
parlador, ra, *n.* chatterer.
parladuría, *f.* loquacity, talk, gossip.
parlaembalde, *n.* (coll.) chatterbox.
parlamentar, *vn.* to converse; (mil.) to parley.
parlamentariamente, *adv.* parliamentarily.
parlamentario, ria. I. *a.* parliamentary, parliamentarian. **II.** *m.* member of parliament; (mil.) flag of truce, cartel.
parlamentarismo, *m.* parliamentarism.
parlamento, *m.* parliament; legislative body; (mil.) parley, flag of truce; (theat.) speech.
parlanchín, china. I. *a.* chattering, jabbering. **II.** *n.* chatterer, jabberer; (Am., coll.) flibbertigibbet.
parlante, *a.* speaking, talking.
parlar, *vn.* to speak with ease; to chatter, talk.
parlatorio, *m.* chat, parley; parlor; locutory.
parlería, *f.* loquacity, garrulity; gossip; tale; jest; chirping of birds; purling of brooks.
parlerillo, illa; ruelo, la, *a. dim.* of PARLERO.
parlero, ra, *a.* loquacious, talkative; expressive (eyes); chirping (birds); bubbling (brooks).
parleta, *f.* chat, small talk.
parlón, na, *a.* loquacious, garrulous.
parlotear, *vn.* to prattle, prate, chatter.—**parloteo,** *m.* chat, prattle, talk.
parmesano, na, *n.* & *a.* Parmesan.
Parnaso, *m.* Parnassus; anthology; assemblage of poets.
parnés, *m.* (coll.) money, cash.
[1]**paro,** *m.* (ornith.) titmouse; coaltit.
[2]**paro,** *m.* lockout.—**p. forzoso,** unemployment (not caused by strike or lockout).
parodia, *f.* parody.—**parodiar,** *va.* to parody.
paródico, ca, *a.* parodic, parodical, of or pertaining to parody or burlesque.
parodista, *n.* parodist, writer of parodies.
parola, parolina, *f.* (coll.) fluency, volubility; chat, idle talk.
pároli, *m.* paroli (as at faro).
paronimia, *f.* (gram.) paronymy.
parónimo, ma, *a.* (gram.) paronymous.
paronomasia, *f.* (rhet.) paronomasia; pun.
paronomástico, ca, *a.* paronomastic, punning.
parótida, *f.* (anat.) parotid gland; (med.) mumps.
parotídeo, dea, *a.* parotid.
parotiditis, *f.* (med.) parotitis, mumps.
paroxismal, *a.* paroxysmal.
paroxismo, *m.* (med.) paroxysm.
paroxítono, na. I. *a.* (gram.) paroxytone (having an acute accent on the next to last syllable). **II.** *m.* (gram.) paroxytone (word).
parpadear, *vn.* to wink; to blink.
parpadeo, *m.* winking, blinking.
párpado, *m.* eyelid.
parpalla, *f.* milled copper piece.
parpar, *vn.* to quack (as a duck).
parque, *m.* park; paddock; (mil.) park; **(Am.)** ammunition; (Am.) parking area (for cars).—**p. de atracciones** or **diversiones,** amusement park.—**p. de bomberos,** firehouse.—**p. nacional,** national park.—**p. zoológico,** zoölogical garden, zoo.
parqueadero, *m.* (Am.) parking place.
parquear, *va.* & *vn.* (Angl.) (auto) to park.
parquedad, *f.* parsimony; sparseness.
parquímetro, *m.* parking meter (for cars).
[1]**parra,** *f.* honey jar.
[2]**parra,** *f.* grapevine.
parrado, da. I. *pp.* of PARRAR. **II.** with extended vines.
párrafo, *m.* paragraph; paragraph mark (§ or ¶).
parragón, *m.* standard silver for assayers.
[1]**parral,** *m.* bower of grapevines; vineyard having vines with long shoots.
[2]**parral,** *m.* large earthen jar for honey.
parranda, *f.* revel, carousal.—**andar, estar,** or **ir, de p., parandear,** *vn.,* to go on a lark; to have a gay time.
parrandero, ra; parrandista. I. *a.* fond of carousing. **II.** *n.* carouser, reveler.
parrar, *vn.* to spread out in branches.
parresia, *f.* (rhet.) parrhesia.
parricida, *n.* parricide (murderer).
parricidio, *m.* parricide (murder).
[1]**parrilla,** *f.* earthen jug.
[2]**parrilla,** *f.* gridiron, broiler, toaster; (furnace) grate; grillroom.
parriza, *f.,* wild grapevine.
parro, *m.* (ornith.) duck.
párroco, *m.* (eccl.) parson.
parrón, *m.* = PARRIZA.
parroquia, *f.* (eccl.) parish; parochial church; congregation and clergy of a parish; (com.) good will, custom, customers, clientele.
parroquial. I. *a.* parochial. **II.** *f.* parochial church.
parroquialidad, *f.* parochial right.
parroquiano, na. I. *a.* parochial. **II.** *n.* (eccl.) parishioner; (com.) customer, client.
parsi. I. *n.* Parsi, a Zoroastrian. **II.** *a.* Parsic.
parsimonia, *f.* parsimony, economy, frugality; moderation.
parsimonioso, sa, *a.* parsimonious, economical, frugal; sober, moderate, prudent.
parsismo, *m.* Parsiism.
parte. I. *f.* part; portion; share; place, spot; right or left side; cause, party; sense given to words or acts; (law) party; (theat.) part, character, rôle.—*pl.* parts, talents, endowments; (coll.) the genitals.—**p. alícuota,** aliquot part.—**p. de la oración,** part of speech.—**p. interesada,** party in interest.—**p. por p.,** part by part, distinctly.—**partes pudendas, púdicas,** or

vergonzosas, genitals, privy parts.—**a partes,** by parts, or in parts.—**dar p.,** to inform, notify.—**de algún tiempo a esta p.,** for some time past.—**de mi p.,** on my part; on my side; for me, in my name.—**de p. a p.,** from side to side, through.—**de p. de,** from, by command of, in the name of; in behalf of.—**de una p. . . . de otra p.,** on the one hand . . . on the other hand.—**en alguna p.,** somewhere.—**en gran p.,** largely.—**en ninguna p.,** nowhere.—**en p.,** partly, in part.—**en partes** = A PARTES.—**en todas partes,** everywhere.—**hacer de su p.,** to do one's best, to do one's part.—**ir a la p.,** to go shares.—**la mayor p. de,** most of.—**la tercera (cuarta,** etc.) **p.,** one-third (-fourth, etc.).—**no ser p. en,** not to be a party to, to have nothing to do with.—**por mi parte,** as for me, as far as I am concerned.—**por otra p.,** on the other hand.—**por p. de,** on the part of.—**por partes,** by parts, one thing at a time.—**por todas partes,** on all sides; everywhere. **II.** *m.* communication, communiqué, despatch, report, telegram, telephone message. **III.** *adv.* in part, partly.

partear, *va.* to assist (women) in childbirth.

partenogénesis, *f.* (biol.) parthenogenesis.

partenogenético, ca, *a.* parthenogenetic.

partera, *f.* midwife.

partería, *f.* midwifery.

partero, *m.* accoucheur.

[1]**partesana,** *f.* partisan.

[2]**partesana,** *f.* a kind of halberd.

partesanero, *m.* pikeman, halberdier.

partible, *a.* divisible, separable.

partición, *f.* division, distribution.

particionero, ra, *a.* participant.

participación, *f.* participation, share; communication; (com.) copartnership.

participante. **I.** *a.* participating, sharing; notifying. **II.** *n.* participant, sharer; notifier.

participar. **I.** *va.* to notify, communicate. **II.** *vn.* **(de)** to share (in); **(en)** to participate, take part (in).

partícipe. **I.** *a.* participant, sharing. **II.** *n.* participator; partner.

participial, *a.* (gram.) participial.

participio, *m.* (gram.) participle.

partícula, *f.* particle.—**p. alfa,** (phys.) alpha particle.—**p. beta,** (phys.) beta particle.—**partículas de polvo,** specks.

particular. **I.** *a.* particular, peculiar, special; personal; private; individual; odd, extraordinary. **II.** *m.* private person, individual; topic, point.—**en p.,** particularly.

particularidad, *f.* particularity, peculiarity; individuality; friendship, intimacy; detail.

particularismo, *m.* (theol.) particularism; (philos.) individualism.

particularizar. **I.** *va.* to particularize, itemize, specify. **II.** *vr.* **(en)** to have as a characteristic, to be distinguished (by).

particularmente, *adv.* particularly; privately; individually; especially.

partida, *f.* departure; passing away, death; item in an account, charge, entry, record, annotation; parcel, lot; (one) game; money staked; certificate (of birth, marriage, death); (mil.) squad; guerrilla; faction; band, gang; (coll.) conduct, behavior, turn; (com.) shipment, lot, consignment.—**p. de campo,** picnic.—**p. de caza,** hunting match.—**p. de defunción,** death certificate.—**p. de matrimonio,** marriage certificate.—**p. de nacimiento,** birth certificate.—**p. doble,** (com.) double entry.—**p. serrana,** (coll.) bad turn.—**p. simple,** (com.) single entry.—**las siete Partidas,** the laws of Castile, compiled by King Alphonso X.

partidamente, *adv.* separately, distinctly.

partidario, ria. **I.** *a.* partisan, adherent, addicted. **II.** *m.* partisan; follower; advocate party man; district physician.—**partidarismo** *m.* partisanship.—**partidarista,** *m.* & *f.* defender of partisanship.

partidismo, *m.* = PARTIDARISMO.

partidista, *m.* & *f.* = PARTIDARISTA.

partido, da. **I.** *pp.* of PARTIR. **II.** *a.* cleft, divided; broken; (her.) party, parted, or parti per pale. **III.** *m.* (pol.) party; advantage, profit; game, contest, match; odds, handicap; persons who play a game; treaty, agreement; means to an end; territorial division or district; circuit in charge of a physician or surgeon.—**sacar p. de,** to turn to advantage, to take advantage of.—**tomar p.,** to take sides; to make up one's mind; to join (a party, army, etc.).

partidor, *m.* divider, cleaver; divisor.

partija, *f.* partition, division.

partil, *a.* said of astrological aspects.

partimento, partimiento, *m.* = PARTICIÓN.

partir. **I.** *va.* to split; to divide; to cut, cleave; to break, crush, crack; to attack in combat or battle; (arith.) to divide; to divide in two.—**p. abierto,** to uncover (a beehive to make the bees swarm).—**p. cerrado,** to divide (a beehive) when it is full.—**p. la diferencia,** to split the difference. **II.** *vn.* to depart, leave; to start, reckon (from).—**a p. de,** starting from **III.** *vr.* to break; to become divided.

partitivo, va, *a.* (gram.) partitive.

partitura, *f.* (mus.) score.

[1]**parto,** *m.* childbirth, parturition, labor; newborn child; production, creation, product; expected and important event.—**el p. de los montes,** the mountain labored and brought forth a mouse, great expectations that came to little.—**estar de p.,** to be in labor.

[2]**parto, ta,** *n.* & *a.* Parthian.

parturición, *f.* parturition.

parturienta, parturiente, *a.* parturient.

párulis, *m.* (med.) gumboil.

parva, *f.* heap of unthrashed corn; multitude, large quantity; light breakfast.

parvedad, *f.* smallness, minuteness; light breakfast.

parvero, *m.* long heap of corn for winnowing.

parvidad, *f.* = PARVEDAD.

parvo, va, *a.* small, little.

parvulez, *f.* smallness; simplicity.

parvulico, ica, illo, illa, ito, ita. **I.** *a. dim.* very little. **II.** *n.* tot, little child.

párvulo, la. **I.** *a.* very small; innocent; humble, low. **II.** *n.* child.

[1]**pasa,** *f.* passage of birds; (naut.) channel

[2]**pasa,** *f.* raisin; (Am.) wool or kinky hair of Negroes.—**p. de Corinto,** currant.—**p. gorrona,** large-sized raisin.

pasabalas, *m.* (mil.) ball caliber gauge.

pasacalle, *m.* (mus.) lively march.

pasada, *f.* passage, passing; pace, step.—**de p.,** on the way; hastily, cursorily.—**mala p.,** (coll.) bad turn, mean trick.

pasadera, *f.* stepping-stone; (naut.) furling line, sea gasket.

pasaderamente, *adv.* passably.

pasadero, ra. **I.** *a.* supportable, sufferable; passable, tolerably good. **II.** *m.* stepping-stone.

pasadillo, *m.* two-face embroidery.

pasadizo, *m.* alley; passage; corridor, hall, aisle.

pasado, da. **I.** *pp.* of PASAR. **II.** *a.* past; last (*la semana pasada,* last week); stale; (of fruit) spoiled; antiquated, out of date or fashion.—**pasado mañana,** day after tomorrow. **III.** *m.* past; (mil.) deserter going over to the enemy.—*pl.* ancestors.

pasador, ra. **I.** *n.* one who goes across; smuggler. **II.** *m.* door bolt; window fastener; pin; woman's brooch; hatpin or bodkin; peg, sneck, bolt-pin, linchpin, cotter; sieve, colander; (naut.) marlinespike, splicing fid.

pasadura, *f.* passage, transit.

pasagonzalo, *m.* (coll.) flick, quick, light stroke.

pasaje, *m.* passage; journey, voyage; road, way; passage money, fare; number of passengers in a ship; (naut.) strait, narrows; (mus.) transition or change of voice; passage in a book or writing.

—**p. gratuito,** (U. S., coll.) Annie Oakley, free ticket.
pasajero, ra. I. *a.* (of a thoroughfare) with constant passing (of people); passing, transient, transitory; provisional. **II.** *n.* traveler, passenger.
pasamanar, *va.* to trim with passementerie.
pasamanería, *f.* passementerie (work, trade, and shop).
pasamanero, ra, *n.* passementerie maker.
pasamano, *m.* passementerie; handrail, banister; (naut.) gangway.
pasamiento, *m.* passage, transit.
pasante. I. *a.* (her.) passant. **II.** *n.* student assistant of a physician or lawyer; tutor, coach. —**p. de pluma,** barrister's clerk.
pasantía, *f.* profession of a PASANTE.
pasapán, (coll.) = GARGÜERO, gullet, windpipe.
pasapasa, *m.* legerdemain, hocus-pocus.
pasaporte, *m.* passport; free license; (mil.) furlough.
pasar. I. *va.* (*pp.* PASADO, PASO) to pass; to take across, put through, carry over; to pass, hand; to go to, in, by, across, over, around, beyond, through, or the like; to move from place to place; to pierce, run through; to smuggle; to advance, promote; to change, transform; to exceed, surpass; to distance, outdo, outrun, outstrip; to convey, transfer; to suffer, bear, undergo; to stroke, rub; to swallow (food or drink); to omit, overlook; to tolerate; to study with a private teacher; to study as an assistant practitioner; to give private lessons; to study or rehearse (a lesson); to study, read; to dry or desiccate (as fruit); to pass, spend (as time).—**p. a cuchillo,** to put to the sword.—**p. el rato,** to kill time.—**p. en claro,** to omit.—**p. (la) lista,** to call the roll.—**pasarlo,** to get along, do, be (ref. health).—**pasarlo bien,** to have a good time.—**p. plaza de,** to set up as.—**p. por alto,** to overlook.—**p. por las armas,** to shoot (as a penalty).—**¿cómo lo pasa Vd.?** how are you? how do you do?—**que lo pase Vd. bien,** good-bye, good luck.—**¿que (le) pasa?,** what's the matter with (him)? **II.** *vn.* to pass; to live; to manage, get along; to last, endure; to pass away, die; to be salable or marketable (as goods); to be current (as money); (at cards) to pass.—**p. a** (*inf.*), to proceed to (*inf.*)—**p. de,** to exceed.—**p. de largo,** to pass by without stopping; to read cursorily.—**p. por,** (foll. by *n.* or *a.*) to be considered as, to be taken for; (foll. by *adv.*) to come, go, call, around (*¿puede Vd. pasar por acá mañana?*, can you come around, call in, here tomorrow?).—**p. por encima de,** to overcome; to go over the head of. —**p. sin,** to do without. **III.** *v. imp.* to pass, happen, turn out. **IV.** *vr.* to go over to another party; to cease, finish; to be spent or stale, lose its force; to slip from one's memory; to become tainted (as meat) or spoiled (as fruit); to go too far; to exceed; to burn out (as a fire); to be overcooked; to permeate, go through; to graduate at college; to blot (as paper).—**p. de,** to be too (*pasarse de paciente,* to be too patient).
pasatiempo, *m.* pastime, amusement.
pasavante, *m.* safe-conduct; (com.) permit.
pasavolante, *m.* hasty action.
pasavoleo, *m.* returning the ball over the line.
pascua, *f.* Jewish Passover; (eccl.) each of the Church holidays—Easter, Twelfth-night, Pentecost, and Christmas.—**p. de flores, de resurrección,** or **florida,** Easter (Sunday).—*pl.* Christmas holidays or season.—**dar las pascuas,** to wish merry Christmas.—**estar como una p.,** to be as merry as a cricket.—**felices pascuas,** merry Christmas.
pascual, *a.* (eccl.) paschal.
pascuilla, *f.* first Sunday after Easter.
pase, *m.* permit, pass; (fencing) venue, thrust.
paseadero, *m.* walk, avenue, mall.
paseador, ra. I. *a.* fond of walking. **II.** *n.* stroller, promenader.
paseante, *n.* promenader, stroller.—**p. encorte,** idle fellow.
pasear. I. *vn.* & *vr.* to take a walk; to ride, drive or sail for pleasure; to promenade; to make a pleasure trip; to walk up and down, pace. **II.** *va.* to take out to walk (as a child).
paseata, *f.* (coll.) walk, airing; ride.
paseo, *m.* walk, promenade; stroll; drive; ride; mall; turnout, parade.—**dar un p.,** to take a walk, ride, etc.—**echar,** or **enviar, a p.,** to send one about one's business; to dismiss or reject rudely or without ceremony.
pasera, *f.* place where fruit is dried; drying.
paserino, na, *m.* & *a.* (ornith.) passerine.
[1]**pasero, ra,** *n.* seller of raisins.
[2]**pasero, ra,** *n.* pacing mule or horse.
pasicorto, ta, *a.* short-stepped.
pasiego, ga, *n.* highlander of Santander.
pasiflóreo, a, *a.* (bot.) passifloraceous.
pasilargo, ga, *a.* long-stepped.
pasillo, *m. dim.* short step; passage, corridor; aisle; (sewing) basting stitch.
pasión, *f.* passion, emotion; (eccl.) passion.
pasional, *a.* passional, passionate; emotional.
pasionaria, *f.* (bot.) passion flower.
pasionario, *m.* (eccl.) passion book.
pasionero, ra; pasionista, *n.* (eccl.) passion singer.
pasito. I. *m. dim.* short step. **II.** *adv.* gently, softly.—**p. a p.,** very leisurely or gently.
pasitrote, *m.* short trot.
pasivamente, *adv.* passively.
pasivo, va. I. *a.* passive; inactive, unresponsive; pert. to a pension (for services); (gram.) passive. **II.** *m.* (com.) liabilities.
pasmar. I. *va.* to cause a spasm; to benumb, stun; to astound; to chill, deaden. **II.** *vr.* (**de**) to wonder, marvel (at); to suffer from lockjaw; (of plants) to freeze.
pasmarota, pasmarotada, *f.* feigned spasm; exaggerated admiration or astonishment.
pasmo, *m.* spasm; (med.) lockjaw, tetanus; astonishment; wonder, prodigy.
pasmosamente, *adv.* wonderfully.
pasmoso, sa, *a.* marvelous, wonderful.
[1]**paso, sa,** *a.* dried (fruit).
[2]**paso. I.** *m.* pace, step; pass, way, passage; passing; gait, walk; step of a staircase; step, measure, or diligence; footstep; incident, accident, occurrence; (mech.) pitch; passage in a writing; (theat.) curtain raiser, sketch; progress, improvement; death.—*pl.* basting stitches.—**p. a nivel,** (Ry.) grade crossing.—**p. a p.,** step by step.—**p. de andadura,** ambling.—**p. de tortuga,** snail pace, extreme slowness.—**p. ligero,** (mil.) double quick.—**abrir p.,** to open a passage, make way.—**abrirse p.,** to get through.—**a buen p.,** at a good rate, step, or gait.—**a cada p.,** at every step, frequently.—**a ese p.,** at that rate.—**al p.,** in passing.—**al p. que,** while, whereas.—**a pocos pasos,** at a short distance.—**apretar el p.,** to hasten.—**de p.,** in passing; on the way, as a transient; migratory.—**llevar el p.,** to keep step.—**marcar el p.,** to mark time.—**más que de p.,** hastily, in a hurry.—**prohibido el p.,** no trespassing, keep out.—**salir del p.,** to get out of the difficulty; to "get by."—**seguir los pasos a,** to follow (the steps of); to trail; to watch.—**seguir los pasos de,** to walk in the footsteps of. **II.** *adv.* softly, gently.
paspié, *m.* a kind of dance.
pasquín, *m.* pasquinade, lampoon.
pasquinada, *f.* pasquinade.
pasquinar, *va.* to ridicule, lampoon, satirize.
pássim, *adv.* passim, in various places.
pasta, *f.* paste; batter; dough; pie crust; soup paste; noodles; bullion for coining; board binding (for books); pulp (in paper).—**p. de dientes,** toothpaste.—**p. de guayaba,** guava paste. —**buena p.,** good disposition.
pastadero, pastal, *m.* pasture, grazing field.

pastar. I. *vn.* to pasture, graze. II. *va.* to lead (cattle) to graze.
pasteca, *f.* (naut.) snatch block.
pastel, *m.* pie; (bot.) woad; ball or cake of woad; cheating; combine, plot; (print.) pi or pie; blotted print; (art) pastel.—**al p.,** pastel (painting).
pastelear, *vn.* (coll.) to "trim" politically.
pastelejo, *m. dim.* small pie.
pastelería, *f.* pastry shop; pastry.
pastelero, ra, *n.* pastry cook; political trimmer.
pastelillo, ito, *m. dim.* patty; tart, cake.
pastelista, *n.* (f. a.) pastelist.
pastelón, *m. aug.* meat or pigeon pie.
pasterización, *f.* pasteurization.
pasterizar, *va.* to pasteurize.
pastero, ra, *n.* one who throws the mass of crushed olives into baskets.
pasteurizar, etc. = PASTERIZAR, etc.
pastilla, *f.* tablet, lozenge, drop; cake (as of soap).—**p. de menta,** peppermint drop.
pastinaca, *f.* (bot.) parsnip; (ichth.) sting ray.
pastizal, *m.* pasture ground for horses.
pasto, *m.* pasture, grazing; grass for feed; pasture ground; pabulum, food.—**p. espiritual,** spiritual nourishment.—**pastos comunes,** common fields.—**a p.,** abundantly, plentifully; excessively.—**a todo p.,** freely, abundantly and unrestrictedly.
pastor, ra, *n.* shepherd (-ess); pastor, clergyman.
pastoral. I. *a.* pastoral; rural, rustic. II. *f.* pastoral; idyll.
pastoralmente, *adv.* pastorally.
pastorcico, illo, ito, *m. dim.* little shepherd.
pastorear, *va.* to pasture; to keep, tend (sheep); to feed (souls).
pastorela, *f.* (mus. and poet.) pastoral.
pastoreo, *m.* pasturing, tending flocks.
pastoría, *f.* pastoral life; shepherds.
pastoricio, cia, pastoril, *a.* pastoral.
pastorilmente, *adv.* pastorally.
pastosidad, *f.* mellowness, softness.
pastoso, sa, *a.* pasty, soft, mellow, doughy; (art) softly painted.
pastura, *f.* pasture, pasturage; fodder.
pasturaje, *m.* common pasturage; duty paid for pasturage.
pata, *f.* (zool.) paw, foot; foot and leg (of beasts); (coll. and humor.) human leg or foot; leg of a piece of furniture, an instrument, etc.; pocket flap; (ornith.) duck, female of the drake.—**p. de cabra,** crowbar, nail puller; (shoemaking) heel burnisher.—**p. de gallina,** radial crack in trees; beginning of rot.—**p. de gallo,** ridiculous saying, bull; crow's-foot wrinkles near the eye.—**p. es la traviesa,** tit for tat.—**patas arriba,** topsy-turvy, heels over head; upside down; on one's back.—**a cuatro patas,** on all fours.—**a la p. coja,** hopscotch.—**a la p. la llana,** plainly, unaffectedly.—**a p.,** (coll.) on foot.—**bailar una p.,** to jump for joy.—**en cuatro patas,** on all fours.—**enseñar la p.,** to show one's ignorance.—**meter la p.,** (coll.) to intermeddle, butt in; to put one's foot in it, make a break.—**quedar, salir,** or **ser, p.,** or **patas,** to be a tie or draw.
pataca, *f.* (bot.) Jerusalem artichoke.
pataco, ca, = PATÁN.
patacón, *m.* silver dollar.
patache, *m.* (naut.) tender.
patada, *f.* kick; (coll.) step, pace; footstep, track.
patagón, na, *n.* & *a.*; **patagónico, ca,** *a.* Patagonian.
patagorrillo, lla, *n.* hash of livers and lights.
patagua, *f.* (bot.) Am. linden, whitewood.
pataje, *m.* = PATACHE.
patalear, *vn.* to kick about violently; to stamp both feet repeatedly.—**pataleo,** *m.* kicking; stamping the feet; pattering, tramp.
pataleta, *f.* (coll.) fainting fit; convulsion.
pataletilla, *f.* a kind of pirouette.
patán, na. I. *a.* churlish, rustic; unmannerly. II. *n.* churl, rustic; unmannerly person.
patanada, *f.* incivility, rudeness; rude or discourteous act.
patanería, *f.* churlishness, rusticity, rudeness; incivility.
patarata, *f.* trash; humbuggery; paltry trifle.
pataratero, ra, *n.* humbugger, humbug.
patarráez, *m.* (naut.) preventer shroud.
patata, *f.* (bot.) potato.—**patatal, patatar,** *m.* potato patch.—**patatero, ra.** I. *a.* fond of potatoes. II. *n.* potato seller.
patatús, *m.* (coll.) swoon, fainting fit.
patax, *m.* (naut.) = PATACHE, tender.
pateador, ra, *a.* kicking (horse).
pateadura, *f.*, **pateamiento,** *m.* kicking, stamping of the feet; severe reprimand, dressing down.
patear, *va.* & *vn.* (coll.) to kick; stamp the foot; to tramp; to be very angry.
patelar, *a.* (anat.) patellar.
patena, *f.* large medal worn by countrywomen; (eccl.) paten.
patentar, *va.* to patent.
patente. I. *a.* patent, manifest, evident. II. *f.* patent; privilege, exclusive grant, warrant, commission.—**p. de corso,** letters of marque.—**p. de chofer.** driver's license.—**p. de sanidad,** (naut.) bill of health.—**p. limpia,** clean bill of health.
patentemente, *adv.* clearly, visibly, obviously.
patentizar, *va.* to make evident.
pateo, *m.* (coll.) kicking; stamping of feet.
pátera, *f.* patera, shallow dish or saucer.
paternal, *a.* paternal, fatherly.
paternalismo, *m.* paternalism.
paternalista. I. *a.* paternalistic. II. *m.* paternalist.
paternalmente, *adv.* paternally, fatherly.
paternidad, *f.* paternity, fatherhood.
paterno, na, *a.* paternal, fatherly.
paternóster, *m.* Lord's Prayer; paternoster, big tight knot.
pateta, *m.* (coll.) nickname given to a lame person; (coll.) devil, old Nick.—**se lo llevó p.,** the deuce took it.
patéticamente, *adv.* pathetically.
patético, ca, *a.* pathetic, touching; plaintive.
patetismo, *m.* pathos.
patiabierto, ta, *a.* straddling, bowlegged.
patiabillo, *m.* (zool.) weasel.
patialbo, ba; patiblanco, ca, *a.* white-footed.
patibulario, ria, *a.* harrowing.
patíbulo, *m.* gibbet, gallows; scaffold.
patico, *m.* dim. young duck, duckling.
paticojo, ja, *a.* (coll.) lame, crippled, limping.
patidifuso, sa, *a.* (coll.) astounded.
patiestevado, da, *a.* bowlegged.
patihendido, da, *a.* cloven-footed.
patilla, *f. dim.* small foot: manner of playing on the guitar; (naut.) spike of the rudder; chape of a buckle; pocket flap; trigger; (Am.) watermelon.—*pl.* side whiskers; (coll.) the devil.
[1]**patín,** *m. dim.* small court or yard.
[2]**patín,** *m.* (ornith.) goosander, a kind of duck.
[3]**patín,** *m.* skate; (aer.) skid.—**p. de cola,** (aer.) tail skid.—**p. de ruedas,** roller skate.
pátina, *f.* (metal. and art) patina; film.
patinadero, *m.* skating place; skating rink.
patinador, ra, *n.* skater.
patinamiento, *m.* (of vehicles) skidding.
patinar, *vn.* to skate; (of vehicles) to skid.
patinazo, *m.* skid; (fig.) slip, boner, blunder.
patinejo, *m. dim.* small skate.
patio, *m.* yard, court yard; (theat.) pit.
patita, *f. dim.* small foot or leg.—**poner de patitas en la calle,** to discharge, "bounce."
patitieso, *a.* (coll.) stiff-legged; astounded, stupefied, surprised; stiff, haughty.
patito, *m. dim.* young duck, duckling.
patituerto, ta, *a.* crook-legged, knock-kneed; crooked, lopsided.
patizambo, ba, *a.* knock-kneed, bowlegged.
pato, *m.* (ornith.) duck.—**p. de flojel,** eider duck.—**p. negro,** mallard.—**pagar el p.,** to

suffer undeserved punishment, to be the scapegoat.
patochada, *f.* blunder, nonsense.
patogenia, *f.* (med.) science treating of pathogenesis.
patógeno, na, *a.* (med.) pathogenic.
patojear, *vn.* (Cuba) to waddle in walking.
patojo, ja. I. *a.* waddling, like a duck; (Am.) lame. **II.** *n.* (C. A.) street urchin.
patología, *f.* pathology.
patológico, ca, *a.* pathologic.
patólogo, *m.* (med.) pathologist.
patón, na, *a.* large-footed; clumsy-footed.
patraña, *f.* fabulous story, fake, humbug.
patria, *f.* native country, fatherland.
patriarca, *m.* patriarch.—**patriarcado,** *m.* patriarchate.—**patriarcal,** *a.* patriarchal.
patriciado, *m.* patriciate, patrician rank.
patricio, cia, *n.* & *a.* patrician.
patrimonial, *a.* patrimonial.
patrimonio, *m.* patrimony, inheritance.
patrio, tria, *a.* native; home (as *a.*); paternal.
patriota, *m.* patriot.
patriotería, *f.* exaggerated patriotism.
patriotero, ra, *n.* exaggerated patriot.
patriótico, ca, *a.* patriotic.
patriotismo, *m.* patriotism.
patrística, *f.* (eccl.) patristics.
patrístico, ca, *a.* (eccl.) patristic.
patrocinador, ra. I. *a.* sponsoring. **II.** *n.* patron, sponsor; *f.* patroness.
patrocinar, *va.* to patronize, sponsor; to protect, favor.
patrocinio, *m.* protection, patronage; sponsorship, auspices.—**bajo el p.,** under the auspices.
patrología, *f.* (eccl.) patrology, patristics.
patrón, na. I. *n.* patron(-ess); protector; host (-ess); landlord (-lady); patron saint. **II.** *m.* master, boss; pattern, model; standard: (naut.) skipper.—**p. de bote,** or **p. de lancha,** (naut.) cockswain, coxswain.—**p. de oro,** gold standard.—**kilogramo, metro,** etc., **p.,** standard kilogram, meter, etc. **III.** *f.* galley following that of the commodore.
patronado, da. I. *a.* (eccl.) having a patron. **II.** *m.* = PATRONATO.
patronal, *a.* patronal, protecting; pertaining to employers, employers' (as *a.*).
patronato, patronazgo, *m.* patronage, guardianship; employers' association.
patronear, *va.* to steer (a trading vessel).
patronímico, ca. I. *a.* patronymic. **II.** *m.* patronymic, surname.
patrono, na, *n.* patron, protector, defender; tutelary; lord (lady) of the manor; employer.
patrulla, *f.* patrol; gang, band, squad.
patrullar, *va.* to patrol.
patuá, *m.* (Gal.) patois, jargon.
patudo, da, *a.* (coll.) having large feet or paws.
patulea, *f.* (coll.) soldiery or disorderly folks.
patullar, *vn.* to trample, tramp; to hustle.
paují, paujil, *m.* guan, a S. A. gallinacean.
paúl, paular, *m.* fen, moor, marsh, bog.
paulatinamente, *adv.* gradually, by degrees.
paulatino, na, *a.* slow, gradual.
paulina, *f.* decree of excommunication, interdict; (coll.) reproof, chiding; anonymous offensive letter, poison-pen letter.
paulinia, *f.* (bot.) (S. A.) a kind of shrub.
paulonia, *f.* (bot.) paulownia.
pauperismo, *m.* pauperism, abject poverty.
paupérrimo, ma, *a. super.* very poor.
pausa, *f.* pause; delay; rest, repose; (mus.) pause, rest, stop.—**a pausas,** at leisure.
pausadamente, *adv.* slowly, deliberately.
pausado, da. I. *pp.* of PAUSAR. **II.** *a.* slow, deliberate; calm, quiet. **III.** *adv.* slowly.
pausar, *vn.* to pause, cease, hesitate.
pauta, *f.* instrument for ruling paper; guide lines; standard, rule, pattern, model.
pautada, *f.* (mus.) ruled staff.
pautador, ra, *n.* one who rules paper.
pautar, *va.* to rule (paper); to regulate, give rules or directions for.
[1]**pava,** *f.* (ornith.) turkey hen; (Colomb.) a kind of guan; (Am.) joke, fun.—**p. real,** (ornith.) peahen.
[2]**pava,** *f.* large furnace bellows; (Venez., Chile, P. R.) large low hat; (Arg.) pot, kettle.—**pelar la p.,** to carry on a flirtation.
pavada, *f.* flock of turkeys; child's game; (Arg.) nonsense, foolishness.
pavana, *f.* pavan (Spanish dance and music).
pavear, *vn.* (Arg., Chile) to make fun; (Arg., Chile) to flirt.
[1]**pavero, ra,** *n.* one who feeds or sells turkeys.
[2]**pavero,** *m.* broad-brimmed hat.
pavés, *m.* large shield, pavis.
pavesa, *f.* embers, hot cinders; burnt part of candlewick.—*pl.* ashes.
pavesada, *f.* (naut.) = EMPAVESADA, waistcloths.
pavezno, *m. dim.* young turkey.
pavía, *f.* clingstone peach (tree and fruit).
pávido, da, *a.* (poet.) timid, fearful.
pavimentación, *f.* paving; pavement.
pavimentar, *va.* to pave.
pavimento, *m.* pavement, paving.
paviota, *f.* (ornith.) mew, sea gull.
pavipollo, *m.* young turkey.
pavo, *m.* (ornith.) turkey; (ichth.) peacock fish.—**p. real,** (ornith.) peacock.—**p. silvestre,** (ornith.) wood grouse.
pavón, *m.* peacock; bluing (for steel or iron).
pavonada, *f.* (coll.) short walk; strut; outward show, ostentation.
pavonar, *va.* to treat (steel, etc.) with bluing.
pavonazo, *m.* (art) dark-red pigment.
pavonear, *vn.* & *vr.* to strut, to show off.
pavor, *m.* fear, dread, fright, terror.
pavorde, *m.* provost; professor of divinity.
pavordear, *vn.* (of bees) to swarm.
pavordía, *f.* place and dignity of a provost.
pavorido, da, *a.* intimidated, terrorized.
pavorosamente, *adv.* fearfully, with terror.
pavoroso, sa, *a.* awful, frightful, terrible.
pavura, *f.* fear, dread, terror, fright.
payar, *va.* (S. A.) to sing with guitar accompaniment.
payasada, *f.* clownish joke or action.
payaso, *m.* clown.
payés, sa, *n.* Catalan countryman (-woman).
payo, ya, *n.* gawk, churl, gump.
payuelas, *f. pl.* chicken pox.
paz, *f.* peace; tranquillity; peace of mind; freedom from debt; (eccl.) ceremony of the mass.—**¡p.!** peace! hush!—**a la p. de Dios,** God be with you.—**en p.,** quits, even.—**gente de p.,** a friend (in answer to "who is there?").
pazguato, ta, *n.* dolt, simpleton.
pazote, *m.* (bot.) saltwort.
pazpuerco, ca, *a.* (coll.) dirty, slovenly.
pe, *f.* name of the letter *p.*—**de p. a pa,** thoroughly, from A to Z, from beginning to end.
peaje, *m.* bridge toll; ferriage.
peajero, *m.* toll-gatherer.
peal, *m.* legging; stocking foot; worthless man.
peán, *m.* pean, pæan.
peana, peaña, *f.* pedestal stand; (mech.) ground plate; step before an altar.
peatón, *m.* walker, messenger; rural postman.
pebete, *m.* joss stick; incense taper; (coll.) (fig.) stench; fuse, punk.—**pebetero,** *m.* perfume censer.
pebrada, *f.* sauce of garlic and spice.
pebre, *m.* or *f.* PEBRADA; a red pepper.
peca, *f.* freckle, speck, spot.
pecable, *a.* peccable, liable to sin; sinful.
pecadillo, ito, *m. dim.* peccadillo, slight sin.
pecado, *m.* sin; guilt; excess; (coll.) devil.—**p. capital,** deadly or mortal sin.—**p. contra natura,** or **contra naturaleza,** sodomy; masturbation.—**p. grave,** or **mortal,** deadly or mortal sin.—(after a noun), **de mis pecados,** of mine.
pecador, ra. I. *a.* sinning, offending; peccant. **II.** *n.* sinner, offender; *f.* (coll.) prostitute.

pecaminosamente, *adv.* sinfully, wickedly.
pecaminoso, sa, *a.* sinful.
pecante, *a.* sinning; excessive.
pecar, *vn.* (*pret.* PEQUÉ; *subj.* PEQUE) to sin; to yield to temptation; to offend; (med.) to predominate, superabound.—**p. de,** to be too (*Juan peca de confiado,* John is too confident); to have too much, (prolixity, obscurity, conciseness, etc.).
pecarí, *m.* (Am., zool.) peccary, either of two piglike American quadrupeds.
peccata minuta, (coll.) peccadilloes.
[1]**pece,** *m.* ridge between furrows.
[2]**pece,** *f.* moistened clay for mud walls.
pececico, illo, ito, *m. dim.* little fish.
peceño, ña, *a.* pitchy (color and taste).
pecera, *f.* fish globe; aquarium.
[1]**pecezuelo,** *m. dim.* of PIE, foot.
[2]**pecezuelo,** *m. dim.* of PEZ, fish.
peciento, ta, *a.* of a pitchy color.
peciluengo, ga, *a.* long-stalked (fruit).
[1]**pecina,** *f.* slime.—**pecinal,** *m.* slimy pool.
[2]**pecina,** *f.* = PISCINA, fish-pond; swimming-pool.
pecio, *m.* flotsam, jetsam, wreckage.
peciolado, da, *a.* (bot.) petiolate.
pecíolo, *m.* (bot.) petiole, leaf stalk.
pécora, *f.* head of sheep.—**buena,** or **mala, p.,** (coll.) shrewd, designing woman.
pecorea, *f.* (mil.) marauding; loitering.
pecorear. I. *va.* to steal (cattle). **II.** *vn.* to loot.
pecoso, sa, *a.* freckly, freckled.
pectato, *m.* (chem.) pectate.
pecten, *m.* (anat., zool.) pecten.
péctico, ca, *a.* (chem.) pectic (acid).
pectina, *f.* (chem.) pectin.
pectíneo, a, *a.* pectinate, comblike; (anat.) pectineus (muscle).
pectiniforme, *a.* comb-shaped, pectinate.
pectoral. I. *a.* pectoral. **II.** *m.* (eccl.) breast plate, pectoral cross; (pharm.) pectoral.
pectosa, *f.* (chem.) pectose.
pecuario, ria, *a.* cattle (as *a.*).
peculado, *m.* (law) peculation, embezzlement.
peculiar, *a.* peculiar.—**peculiaridad,** *f.* peculiarity.—**peculiarmente,** *adv.* peculiarly.
peculio, *m.* (law) peculium; private property; (fig.) purse.
pecunia, *f.* (coll.) hard cash, specie.
pecuniariamente, *adv.* in cash; financially.
pecuniario, ria, *a.* pecuniary, monetary.
pechar, *vn.* to pay taxes.
pechblenda, pecblenda, *f.* (min.) pitchblende.
peche, *m.* (arch.) pendentive, squinch; (zool.) pilgrim scallop (mollusk).
pechera, *f.* shirt bosom; shirt frill; chest protector, vestee; breast strap (of a harness); (coll.) bosom.
pechería, *f.* taxes, revenue; tax poll.
[1]**pechero, ra,** *n.* taxpayer; commoner, plebeian.
[2]**pechero,** *m.* bib.
pechiblanco, ca, *a.* white-breasted.
pechicolorado, *m.* (ornith.) linnet.
pechigonga, *f.* a card game.
pechina, *f.* pilgrim scallop, a mollusk; (arch.) squinch; arch of a pendentive.
pechirrojo, *m.* (ornith.) linnet.
pechisacado, da, *a.* (coll.) haughty, arrogant.
pechito, *m. dim.* small breast or teat.
[1]**pecho,** *m.* (anat.) chest, thorax; breast; bosom; teat; courage, fortitude; (mus.) quality and strength of the voice; slope, gradient.—**abrir el p.,** to unbosom oneself.—**criar a los pechos,** to instruct or educate.—**dar el p.,** to nurse, suckle.—**de p.,** firm-spirited.—**echar el p. al agua,** to undertake a risky thing resolutely.—**entre p. y espalda,** (coll.) in the stomach.—**tener p.,** to have patience, to endure with firmness.—**tomar a p.,** or **a pechos,** to take to heart.
[2]**pecho,** *m.* an ancient tax.
pechuelo, *m. dim.* small or little breast.
pechuga, *f.* breast of a fowl; slope; (coll.) bosom; (coll.) nerve, check, brazenness.—**pechugón, na. I.** *a.* (Am.) (coll.) "sponging," parasitic; bold, brazen. **II.** *m.* blow on the breast.
pechuguera, *f.* cough, hoarseness.
pedacico, illo, ito, *m.* small piece, bit.
pedagogía, *f.* pedagogy.
pedagógicamente, *adv.* pedagogically.
pedagógico, ca, *a.* pedagogical.
pedagogo, *m.* pedagogue; teacher; educator.
pedaje, *m.* = PEAJE, bridge toll.
pedal, *m.* (mech.) treadle; (mus.) pedal.
pedalear, *vn.* to pedal.
pedáneo, nea, *a.* (law) petty, puisne, inferior.
pedante. I. *a.* pedantic, priggish; foppish. **II.** *n.* pedant, prig; instructor; coxcomb.
pedantear, *vn.* to be pedantic.
pedantería, *f.* pedantry.
pedantescamente, *adv.* pedantically.
pedantesco, ca, *a.* pedantic.
pedantismo, *m.* pedantry.
pedantón, *m. aug.* great pedant.
pedazo, *m.* piece, fragment, bit.—**p. de alcornoque,** or **de animal,** good-for-nothing.—**a pedazos,** or **en pedazos,** in bits, in fragments.
pedazuelo, *m. dim.* small piece or bit.
pederasta, *m.* pederast.
pederastia, *f.* pederasty, pæderasty.
pedernal, *m.* flint; extreme hardness.
pedernalino, na, *a.* flinty; hard.
pedestal, *m.* pedestal; stand; base, support.
pedestre, *a.* pedestrian; low, vulgar, common.
pedestrismo, *m.* marathon racing, foot racing.
pediatra, *m.* (med.) pediatrician, pediatrist.
pediatría, *f.* (med.) pediatrics.
pediátrico, ca, *a.* pediatric.
pedicoj, *m.* jump on one foot.
pedicular, *a.* pedicular, pert. to lice.
pedículo, *m.* (bot.) peduncle, pedicle.
pedicuro, *m.* pedicure (person), chiropodist.
pedido, *m.* demand, call; (com.) order.
pedidor, ra, *n.* petitioner, craver.
pedidura, *f.* begging, petitioning.
pediforme, *a.* pediform, foot-shaped.
pedigón, *m,* (coll.) craver, insatiable asker.
pedigüeño, ña, *a.* persistent in begging.
pediluvio, *m.* (med.) pediluvium, foot bath.
pedimento, *m.* petition; (law) claim, bill.—**a p.,** at the instance, on petition.
pedir, *va.* (*gerund,* PIDIENDO; *ind. pres.* PIDO, *pret.* él PIDIÓ; *subj.* PIDA) to ask for, request, beg, solicit; to demand, claim, exact; to inquire after; to wish, desire; to require; (com.) to order; to ask for in marriage.—**p. celos,** to be jealous.—**p. cuenta,** to call to account.—**a p. de boca,** according to desire.—**pedírselo a uno el cuerpo,** to desire eagerly, to long for.
pedo, *m.* wind from the anus; flatulence.
pedómetro, *m.* pedometer, walking wheel.
pedorrera, *f.* flatulence.—*pl.* tights.
pedrada, *f.* throw of a stone; blow from a stone; cockade; rosette or bow for the hair; hint, insinuation.—**como p. en ojo de boticario,** pat, apropos, just in time.
pedrea, *f.* throwing stones; lapidation; fight with stones; fall of hail.
pedregal, *m.* stony ground.
pedregoso, sa, *a.* stony, rocky; (med.) afflicted with gravel.
pedrejón, *m.* boulder.
pedreñal, *m.* a kind of firelock.
pedrera, *f.* quarry, stone pit.
pedreral, *m.* packsaddle for carrying stones.
pedrería, *f.* precious stones; jewelry.
pedrero, *m.* stonecutter; (artil.) stone mortar; slinger.
pedrezuela, *f. dim.* small stone; pebble.
pedrisca, *f.* hailstorm; shower of thrown stones; heap of small stones.
pedriscal, *m.* = PEDREGAL.
pedrisco, *m.* = PEDRISCA.—**pedrisquero,** *m.* hail storm.
pedriza, *f.* stony tract; stone fence.
pedrusco, *m.* rough piece of stone.
pedunculado, da, *a.* (bot.) peduncled.

peduncular, *a.* (bot.) peduncular.
pedunculillo, *m. dim.* (bot.) pedicle, pedicel.
pedúnculo, *m.* (bot.) peduncle, flower stalk.
peer, *vn.* & *vr.* to break wind.
[1]**pega,** *f.* joining, cementing or sticking together; pitch varnish put on earthen vessels; (min.) firing of a blast; (coll.) jest, practical joke, deceit; spanking, drubbing; (ichth.) remora, sucking fish.
[2]**pega,** *f.* (ornith.) magpie.
pegadillo, *m. dim.* little patch; sticking plaster; bore, nuisance.
pegadizo, za, *a.* sticky, adhesive; catching, contagious; (coll.) (of person) sticker, leech; catchy (tune).
pegado, da. I. *pp.* of PEGAR; tied (as to his mother's apron strings). **II.** *m.* patch; sticking plaster.
pegador, *m.* sticker, affixer; paper hanger; (min.) blaster.—**p. de carteles,** billposter.
pegadura, *f.* pitching; sticking, gluing.
pegajoso, sa, *a.* sticky; clammy, viscous; catching, contagious; alluring, tempting.
pegamiento, *m.* joining, sticking, cementing.
peganita, *f.* (min.) peganite.
pegante, *a.* sticking, adhesive, glutinous.
pegar. I. *va.* (*pret.* PEGUÉ; *subj.* PEGUE) to stick, glue, cement; to unite, fasten; to post (bills); to sew on, pin; patch; attach; to infect with, give (a disease); to hit, beat, slap; to give, deal (a blow, etc.); to impart.—**p. fuego a,** to set fire to.—**pegársela a uno,** to fool one, make one swallow a story.—**no p. los ojos,** not to sleep a wink.—**p. un tiro a,** to shoot. **II.** *vn.* to take root; to catch (fire); to make an impression on the mind; to make a hit; to join, to be contiguous; to cleave, cling; to fit, to match; to be becoming, fitting, appropriate; to pass, to be accepted.—**ésa no pega,** (coll.) that is too thin, that won't go. **III.** *vr.* to intrude; to stick, adhere; cohere; to grow; to become rooted in the mind; to take to, become addicted to.
pegaseo, sea, *a.* pertaining to Pegasus.
pegásides, *f. pl.* the Muses.
Pegaso, *m.* Pegasus.
pegata, *f.* (coll.) trick, cheat, swindle, fraud.
pegmatita, *f.* (min.) pegmatite.
pegollo, *m.* pillar, post.
pegote, *m.* sticking plaster; coarse patch; stew with a thick sauce; sponger, toady.
pegotear, *vn.* (coll.) to sponge.
pegotería, *f.* (coll.) sponging.
pegual, *m.* (S. A.) strap with rings.
pegué, pegue, *v. V.* PEGAR.
peguera, *f.* pine wood for making pitch; place where sheep are marked with pitch.
peguero, *m.* maker of or dealer in pitch.
pegujal, pegujar, *m.* peculium; small holdings.
pegujalero, ra; pegujarero, ra, *n.* owner of a small farm or ranch.
pegujón, *m.* pellet or bunch of wool or hair.
pegunta, *f.* pitch mark on sheep.
peguntar, *va.* to mark (sheep) with pitch.
peinada, *f.* combing or dressing the hair.
peinado, da. I. *pp.* of PEINAR. **II.** *a.* effeminate in toilet; overnice (literary style). **III.** *m.* hairdressing, hairdo.
peinador, ra. I. *n.* hairdresser. **II.** *m.* dressing gown, wrapper.
peinadura, *f.* combing or dressing the hair; combings.
peinar, *va.* to comb or dress (the hair); to comb (wool); to touch or rub slightly; to eat away (a rock).—**p. canas,** to be old.
peinazo, *m.* (carp.) crosspiece of a door.
peine, *m.* comb; card; rack, engine of torture; weaver's reed; comb of the loom; comb-broach; instep.—**a sobre p.,** lightly, slightly, imperfectly.
peinería, *f.* comb factory or shop.
peinero, ra, *n.* comb maker or seller.
peineta, *f.* ornamental shell comb (to wear in the hair).—**p. de teja,** tile-shaped shell comb.
peje, *m.* fish; cunning, crafty fellow.—**p. araña,** (ichth.) stingbull.—**p. diablo,** (ichth.) grouper.
pejemuller, *f.* mermaid, sea woman.
pejepalo, *m.* stockfish.
pejerrey, *m.* (ichth.) a variety of mackerel.
pejesapo, *m.* (ichth.) angler.
pejiguera, *f.* (coll.) bother, too much trouble for nothing.
pela, *m.* PELADURA; (Am.) whipping.—**dar,** or **pegar, una p.,** to whip, give a whipping to.
pelada, *f.* (tanning) pelt.
peladera, *f.* (med.) alopecia, baldness.
peladero, *m.* place where hogs and fowls are stripped; (coll.) sharpers' den; (Am.) bare, barren spot.
peladilla, *f.* sugar almond; small pebble.
peladillo, *m.* (bot.) clingstone peach (fruit and tree).—*pl.* wool-stripped sheepskin.
pelado, da. I. *pp.* of PELAR. **II.** *a.* plucked; bared; peeled, stripped; hairless; treeless, bare; penniless, "broke." **II.** *n.* penniless person; (Mex.) peasant.
pelador, *m.* plucker, peeler, stripper.
peladura, *f.* plucking, peeling, stripping.
pelafustán, *m.* (coll.) idler, ragamuffin.
pelagallos, *m.* = PELAGATOS.
pelagatos, *m.* ragamuffin; poor wretch.
pelagianismo, *m.* Pelagianism.
pelagiano, na, *a.* Pelagian.
pelágico, ca, *a.* pelagic, oceanic.
pelagra, *f.* (med.) pellagra.—**pelagroso, sa,** *a.* pertaining to or suffering from pellagra.
pelaire, *m.* wool-dresser.
pelairía, *f.* trade of a wool comber.
pelaje, *m.* character or nature of the hair or wool; character, disposition; garments, apparel.
pelambrar, *va.* (tanning) to flesh (as hides).
pelambre, *m.* (tanning) batch of hides put into lime pits; steeping liquid; hair scraped from skins; lack of hair.
pelambrera, *f.* quantity of hair in one place; shedding of hair; (tanning) lime pit.
pelambrero, *m.* (tanning) steeper.
pelamen, *m.* (coll.) = PELAMBRE.
pelamesa, *f.* scuffle; bushy hair.
pelantrín, *m.* petty farmer.
pelar. I. *va.* to cut or pull out the hair of; to pluck; to skin, peel, husk, hull, shell; to trick, cheat, rob; to break (in gambling); to uncover, show (as the teeth).—**pelárselas,** to be in great earnest, to put one's heart and soul into something; to act or feel with great vehemence.—**duro de p.,** exceedingly difficult, hard to crack, a big order. **II.** *vr.* to lose the hair (as from illness); to get one's hair cut; to peel off (as paint).
pelarela, *f.* = PELADERA.
pelargonio, *m.* (bot.) pelargonium.
pelarruecas, *f.* woman who lives by spinning.
pelásgico, ca, *a.* Pelasgian, Pelasgic.
pelasgo, ga, *n.* & *a.* Pelasgian.
pelaza. I. *a.* chopped or beaten (straw). **II.** *f.* quarrel, affray, scuffle.
pelazga, *f.* (coll.) quarrel, scuffle.
peldaño, *m.* step of a staircase.
pelde, *m.* (coll.) = APELDE, flight, escape.
peldefebre, *m.* camlet; camel's hair.
pelea, *f.* fight; scuffle, quarrel.—**p. de gallos,** cockfight.
peleador, ra. I. *n.* fighter. **II.** *a.* quarrelsome.
pelear. I. *vn.* to fight; to quarrel; to toil, struggle. **II.** *vr.* to scuffle, to come to blows.
pelechar, *vn.* to get hair; (of horses) to change the coat; (of birds) to fledge; (coll.) to improve one's fortune; to recover health.
pelel, *m.* pale ale, light beer.
pelele, *m.* stuffed figure; nincompoop.
pelendengue, *m.* frivolous foppery.
peleón. I. *a.* quarrelsome. **II.** *m.* strong wine.
peleona, *f.* scuffle, quarrel, row.
pelerina, *f.* pelerine (woman's cape).
pelete, *m.* (gambling games) punter; (coll.) poor man.—**en p.,** nakedly.

peletería, *f.* furrier's shop; (Cuba) leather goods or shop where they are sold.
peletero, ra, *n.* furrier; (Cuba) dealer in leather goods.
pelgar, *m.* ragamuffin, blackguard.
peliagudo, da, *a.* downy, furry; (coll.) arduous, difficult; skilful.
peliblanco, ca, *a.* having white hair.
peliblando, da, *a.* having fine soft hair.
pelícano, *m.* (ornith.) pelican.
pelicano, na, *a.* gray-haired; hoary.
pelicorto, ta, *a.* having short hair.
película, *f.* pellicle; film; (photog.) film; moving-picture reel; moving picture.—**p. documental,** documentary (film).
pelicular, *a.* pellicular.
peliculero, ra. I. *a.* motion-picture, movie, film. **II.** *n.* scenario writer; *m.* movie actor; *f.* movie actress.
peligrar, *vn.* to be in danger.
peligro, *m.* danger, peril.—**correr p.,** to be in danger; to run a risk.
peligrosamente, *adv.* perilously, dangerously.
peligroso, sa, *a.* dangerous, perilous, risky.
pelilargo, ga, *a.* having long hair.
pelillo, *m. dim.* short hair or fiber; trifle, slight trouble.—**echar pelillos a la mar,** to become reconciled.—**no tener pelillos en la lengua,** to speak one's mind openly.—**pararse,** or **reparar, en pelillos,** to be scrupulous; to hesitate; to split hairs.
pelilloso, sa, *a.* (coll.) peevish, querulous.
pelinegro, gra, *a.* black-haired.
pelirrojo, ja, *a.* red-haired.
pelirrubio, bia, *a.* blond, light-haired.
pelitieso, sa, *a.* having straight and stiff hair.
pelito, *m. dim.* small hair or fibre.
pelitre, *m.* (bot.) pellitory of Spain.
pelitrique, *m.* fiddle-faddle, flummery.
pelma, *f.* = PELMAZO.
pelmacería, *f.* heaviness, slowness.
pelmazo, *m.* crushed or flattened mass; undigested food, or "lump," in the stomach; sluggard.
pelo, *m.* hair; fiber, fibre, filament; trifle; hair's breadth; down (of birds or fruits); nap, pile (of cloth); hairspring (in watches and firearms); flaw (in gems and metals); grain (in wood); color (of horses); coat (of animals); kiss (in billiards); cross wire (of a transit, level, etc.); (vet.) split in hoofs; (com.) raw silk.—**p. arriba,** against the grain.—**p. de aire,** breath of air, light breeze.—**p. de camello,** camel's hair.—**p. de cofre** or **de Judas,** red hair; redhead.—**p. de la dehesa,** rusticity, rustic or plebeian antecedents.—**pelos y señales,** minute details.—**a medios pelos,** tipsy.—**a p.** or **al p.,** along the grain; timely, fittingly.—**de medio p.,** of little account; pretentious, self-important.—**de p. en pecho,** (fig.) brave, daring; strong, vigorous.—**echar buen p.,** to improve (in circumstances, fortune, health, etc.).—**en p.,** bareback; unsaddled.—**escapar por un p.,** to have a hair-breadth escape.—**estar uno hasta los pelos,** to have had enough (of something or someone), be sick of (something or someone).—**hacerse el p.,** to have one's hair done, have one's hair cut. —**no tener p. de tonto,** to be bright, quick or clever.—**no tener pelos en la lengua,** to be outspoken.—**ponérsele a uno los pelos de punta,** to make one's hair stand on end, be scared to death.—**tener pelos,** to be tough, be difficult, be a hard nut to crack.—**tomar el p. a,** to banter, make fun of, pull someone's leg.—**venir al p.,** to be to the point; to suit to a tee.
pelón, na, *a.* hairless; bald; (coll.) dull, stupid; poor.—**pelona, pelonía,** *f.* baldness.
pelonería, *f.* (coll.) poverty, want, indigence.
pelopio, *m.* (chem.) pelopium.
peloponense, *n.* & *a.*; **peloponesíaco, ca,** *a.* Peloponnesian.
pelosilla, *f.* (bot.) mouse-ear, hawkweed.
peloso, sa, *a.* hairy.
[1]pelota, *f.* ball, handball; ball game; (S. A.) punt made of leather.—**p. de viento,** football.—**no tocar p.,** (coll.) not to touch the root of the difficulty.
[2]pelota, *f. aug.* of PELO.—**en p.,** entirely naked; penniless.
pelotari, *m.* professional jai-alai player.
pelotazo, *m.* blow or stroke with a ball.
pelote, *m.* goat's hair; tuft of wool.
pelotear. I. *va.* to audit (accounts). **II.** *vn.* to play ball; to throw, as a ball; to argue, dispute; to quarrel.
pelotera, *f.* wrangle, quarrel, tumult, riot.
[1]pelotería, *f.* heap of balls.
[2]pelotería, *f.* heap of goat's hair.
pelotero, *m.* ball maker.
pelotilla, *f. dim.* small ball; small ball of wax and pieces of glass fastened to a scourge.
pelotón, *m. aug.* large ball; tuft of hair; (mil.) platoon; crowd, gang; posse.
pelta, *f.* pelta, light shield.
peltre, *m.* pewter, spelter.
peltrero, *m.* pewterer, pewter worker.
peluca, *f.* wig, toupee; severe reproof.
pelucón, *m. aug.* large bushy wig.
pelucona, *f.* (coll.) double doubloon ($16).
peludo, da. I. *a.* hairy, shaggy; (coll.) difficult, tough. **II.** *m.* shaggy mat.
peluquería, *f.* hairdressing shop; barber shop.
peluquero, *m.* hairdresser, barber; wigmaker.
peluquilla, ita, *f. dim.* small wig.
peluquín, *m. dim.* topwig; bagwig.
pelusa, *f.* down; floss, fuzz, nap, pile; (bot.) pubescence.
pelusilla, *f. dim.* of PELUSA; fuzz.
pelvi, *n.* & *a.* Pahlavi, Pehlevi, ancient Persian language.
pelviano, na, *a.* (anat.) pelvic.
pelvímetro, *m.* pelvimeter.
pelvis, *f.* (anat.) pelvis, pelvic cavity.
pella, *f.* pellet; tender head of cauliflower, etc.; lump of molten metal; cut lard; unpaid loan; (min.) lump of amalgamated silver.
pellada, *f.* (mason.) lump or trowelful of mortar.
pelleja, *f.* skin, hide; (coll.) strumpet.
pellejería, *f.* place where skins are dressed and sold.
pellejero, *m.* leather-dresser, pelt-monger.
pellejina, *f.* small skin.
pellejo, *m.* skin; rawhide, pelt; wine skin; peel, rind; (fig.) one's life; (humor.) tippler, drunkard.—**estar,** or **hallarse, en el p. de otro,** to be in another's shoes or place.—**jugarse el p.,** (Am.) to risk one's life.—**quitar el p. a,** to flay; to speak ill of, gossip about; (fig.) to kill. —**salvar el p.,** (coll.) to save one's skin, life.
pellejudo, da, *a.* with flabby or superfluous skin.
pellejuela, *f. dim.* small skin or rawhide.
pellejuelo, *m. dim.* small skin.
pellica, *f.* cover of fine furs; small dressed skin.
pellico, *m.* pelisse; shepherd's jacket.
pelliquero, ra, *n.* maker of fur coverlets.
pelliza, *f.* pelisse, fur cloak.
pellizcador, ra, *n.* & *a.* pincher(-ing).
pellizcamiento, *m.* pruning, clipping; pinching.
pellizcar. I. *va.* (*pret.* PELLIZQUÉ; *subj.* PELLIZQUE) to pinch; to nip; to prune, clip; to gripe; to pilfer. **II.** *vr.* to long for.
pellizco, *m.* pinch; pinching; nip; small bit.—**p. de monja,** small cookie.
pellizqué, pellizque, *v. V.* PELLIZCAR.
pello, *m.* fine fur jacket.—**pellón, pellote,** *m.* long pelisse; fur cloak or robe.
pelluzgón, *m.* lock or tuft of hair.
[1]pena, *f.* penalty; punishment; pain (esp. mental); affliction, sorrow, grief; embarrassment, mortification, chagrin; labor, hardship, difficulty, toil; necklace.—**p. capital** or **de muerte,** death penalty, capital punishment.—**p. del talión,** lex talionis, an eye for an eye and a tooth for a tooth.—**p. pecuniaria,** fine.—**penas eternas,** hellfire.—**a penas,** hardly, scarcely.—**a duras penas,** with great difficulty, just barely.—**alma**

en p., soul in purgatory.—**estar con (mucha) p.**, to be (greatly) mortified, (very) sorry, (very much) vexed.—**merecer la p.**, to be worthwhile, worth the trouble.—**so p. de**, on pain of. —**tener la p. de**, to be sorry to; to have the misfortune to.—**última p.**, death.—**valer la p.**, to be worthwhile, be worth the trouble.

[2]**pena**, *f.* (ornith.) penna, quill feather.

penable, *a.* punishable.

penachera, *f.* = PENACHO.

penacho, *m.* tuft of feathers, aigret; plume, crest; panache; haughtiness, arrogance, airs.

penachudo, da, *a.* crested, tufted, plumed.

penachuelo, *m. dim.* small tuft, crest or aigret.

penadamente, *adv.* = PENOSAMENTE.

penadilla, *f.* narrow-mouthed vessel.

penado, da. I. *pp.* of PENAR. **II.** *a.* sorrowful; painful; difficult, arduous. **III.** *n.* convict; narrow-mouthed vessel.

penal, *a.* penal.—**dolo p.**, (law) malice.

penalidad, *f.* trouble, hardship; (law) penalty.

penalista, *n.* penologist, criminologist.

péname, *m.* condolence. Also PÉSAME.

penante. I. *pres. p.* of PENAR, suffering sorrow or punishment. **II.** *a.* difficult, arduous.

penar. I. *vn.* to suffer, to agonize; to be tormented in a future life; to crave, long. **II.** *va.* to chastise, inflict punishment or impose penalty on. **III.** *vr.* to grieve, to mourn.

penates, *m. pl.* penates, household gods.

penca, *f.* (bot.) pulpy leaf or joint of some plants; cowhide for flogging culprits.—**hacerse de pencas**, to allow oneself to be coaxed.

pencazo, *m.* lash with a cowhide.

penco, *m.* (coll.) = JAMELGO, sorry nag, jade.

pencudo, da, *a.* having pulpy leaves or joints.

pendejo, *m.* hair over the pubis and groin; (coll.) coward, poltroon; (Am., vulgar) fool.

pendencia, *f.* quarrel, fray, feud.

pendenciar, *vn.* to wrangle, quarrel.

pendenciero, ra, *a.* quarrelsome.

pendenzuela, *f. dim.* little dispute.

pender, *vn.* to hang, dangle; to be pending or suspended; to depend.

pendiente. I. *a.* pendent, hanging; clinging; dangling; pending. **II.** *m.* earring, pendant; watch chain. **III.** *f.* slope, declivity; grade, gradient; dip or pitch.

pendil, *m.* mantle worn by women.

pendol, *m.* (naut.) boot-topping.

[1]**péndola**, *f.* feather; quill, pen.

[2]**péndola**, *f.* pendulum, balance; (eng.) queen-post; bridging brace.

pendolaje, *m.* plunder of a captured vessel.

pendolario, ria; pendolista, *n.* penman.

pendolita, *f.* watch; click wire.

pendolón, *m. aug.* large pendulum; (eng.) king-post.

pendón, *m.* standard, banner, pennon, gonfalon; (bot.) tiller, shoot; (her.) pennon; (coll.) tall, awkward woman.—*pl.* reins of the leading mule.

pendoncito, *m. dim.* pennon, banneret.

pendular, *a.* pendular.

péndulo, la. I. *a.* pendent, hanging, pendulous. **II.** *m.* pendulum.—**p. de compensación**, compensation pendulum.—**p. de segundos**, seconds pendulum.—**p. eléctrico**, electric pendulum.—**p. sideral**, or **sidéreo**, (astr.) (standard) clock, chronometer.

pene, *m.* (anat.) penis.

peneque, *a.* (coll.) fuddled.

penetrabilidad, *f.* penetrability.

penetrable, *a.* penetrable; comprehensible.

penetración, *f.* penetration, penetrating; acuteness, sagacity, clearsightedness.

penetrador, ra, *n.* & *a.* discerner(-ing); searcher (-ing).

penetral, *m.* innermost recess.

penetrancia, *f.* (genet.) penetrance.

penetrante, *a.* penetrating, piercing; heart-rending; clearsighted, keen; deep.

penetrar, *va.* to penetrate, pierce; to break or force in; to permeate, pervade; to fathom, comprehend.—**p. en**, to enter.

penetrativo, va, *a.* penetrative, piercing.

penetrómetro, *m.* (phys.) penetrometer.

penfigo, *m.* (med.) pemphigus.

penicilina, *f.* (pharm.) penicillin.

penígero, ra, *a.* (poet.) winged, feathered.

península, *f.* peninsula.

peninsular, *a.* inhabiting or pert. to a peninsula.

penique, *m.* (English) penny.

penitencia, *f.* penitence; penance.—**hacer p.**, to do penance; familiar invitation to take potluck.

penitenciado, da. I. *pp.* of PENITENCIAR. **II.** *a.* punished. **III.** *n.* convict.

penitencial, *a.* penitential.

penitenciar, *va.* to impose penance on.

penitenciaría, *f.* (eccl. & gen.) penitentiary.

penitenciario, ria, *a.* penitentiary.

penitente. I. *a.* penitent, repentant, contrite. **II.** *n.* penitent.

penol, peñol, *m.* (naut.) yardarm, peak.

penología, *f.* penology.

penológico, ca, *a.* penological.

penologista, *n.*; **penólogo, ga**, *n.* penologist.

penosamente, *adv.* painfully, grievously.

penoso, sa. I. *a.* painful; laborious, arduous; distressing; embarrassing, unpleasant. **II.** *m.* conceited fop.

pensado, da, *pp.* & *a.* deliberate, premeditated; thought out.—**bien p.**, wise, proper.—**de p.**, on purpose, deliberately.—**mal p.**, unwise, foolish.—**tener p.**, to have in view, to intend.

pensador, ra, *n.* & *a.* thinker(-ing).

pensamiento, *m.* mind; thought, idea; witty saying, epigram, maxim; suspicion, surmise; project, scheme, plan; (art) first sketch or outline; (bot.) pansy, heartsease.—**en un p.**, in a trice. —**ni por p.**, not even in thought.

pensar. I. *vn.* (*ind.* PIENSO; *subj.* PIENSE) to think.—**p. a** (foll. by *inf.*), to intend.—**p. de**, to think of, have an opinion about.—**p. en**, to think of, about, or over; (foll. by *inf.*), to think of, consider (foll. by *pres. p.*).—**p. en lo excusado**, to expect the impossible. **II.** *va.* to think over, or about, consider; to intend.

pensativo, va, *a.* pensive, thoughtful.

penseque, *m.* thoughtlessness.

pensil. I. *a.* hanging. **II.** *m.* beautiful garden.

pensilvano, na, *n.* & *a.* Pennsylvanian.

pensión, *f.* pension, annuity; boarding-house; price of board and tuition; toil, drudgery; (Am.) anxiety.—**p. vitalicia**, annuity, life pension.

pensionado, da, *n.* pensioner, pensionary.

pensionar, *va.* to impose or to grant annual charges or pensions on or to.

pensionario, *m.* one who pays a pension; pensionary, magistrate.

pensionista, *n.* pensioner; boarder.

pentacordio, *m.* (mus.) pentachord.

pentadecágono, *m.* fifteen-sided polygon

pentaédrico, ca, *a.* pentahedral.

pentaedro, *m.* (geom.) pentahedron.

pentagonal, *a.* pentagonal.

pentágono, *m.* (geom.) pentagon.

pentagrama, *m.* (mus.) ruled staff.

pentámero, ra, *a.* (bot., zool.) pentamerous.

pentámetro, *m.* pentameter.

pentano, *m.* (chem.) pentane.

pentaploide, *m.* (biol.) pentaploidy.

pentápolis, *f.* pentapolis, group of five cities.

pentarquía, *f.* pentarchy, gov't of five persons.

pentasílabo, ba, *a.* of five syllables.

Pentateuco, *m.* Pentateuch.

pentatlo, *m.* pentathlon.

pentecostés, *m.* Pentecost, Whitsuntide.

pentedecágono, *m.* = PENTADECÁGONO.

pentosa, *f.* (chem.) pentose.

pentosana, *f.* (chem.) pentosane.

pentotal, *m.* (pharm.) sodium pentothal.

penúltimo, ma, *a.* penultimate.

penumbra, *f.* penumbra.

penuria, *f.* penury, indigence.

[1]**peña**, *f.* rock; boulder.—**durar por peñas**, to last a long time.

[2]**peña**, *f.* group of friends; club.

peñascal, *m.* rocky hill or mountain.
peñasco, *m.* large rock; strong silk material.
peñascoso, sa, *a.* rocky.
[1]**peñol,** *m.* large rock.
[2]**peñol,** *m.* (naut.) = PENOL, yardarm.
peñola, *f.* (poet.) (writing) pen.
peñón, *m.* large rock; rocky cliff.
[1]**peón,** *m.* (poet.) foot of four syllables.
[2]**peón,** *m.* pedestrian; day laborer; (mason.) hodman; foot soldier; top, spinning top; pawn (in chess); man (in draughts); (mech.) spindle, axle.
peonada, *f.* day's work of a laborer; gang of laborers.
peonaje, *m.* gang of laborers.
peonería, *f.* land that can be plowed in one day.
[1]**peonía,** *f.* land given to a soldier as spoils.
[2]**peonía,** *f.* (bot.) peony.
peonza, *f.* top (toy); noisy little fellow.—**bailar como una p.,** to dance well, be light on one's feet.
peor, *a.* & *adv. comp.* worse; worst.—**p. que p.,** worse and worse.—**tanto p.,** so much the worse.
peoría, *f.* deterioration, detriment.
pepa, *f.* (Am.) seed, stone, pit.
pepián, *m.* = PIPIÁN, an Indian fricassee.
pepinar, *m.* cucumber field.
pepinillos, *m. pl.* gherkins, pickled cucumbers.
pepino, *m.* (bot.) cucumber.—**no dársele un p.,** or **tres pepinos,** not to give a fig.
pepión, *m.* old Spanish gold coin.
[1]**pepita,** *f.* pip or seed of fruits (as apples, etc.); (min.) nugget.
[2]**pepita,** *f.* (vet.) pip, distemper in fowls.
pepitoria, *f.* giblet fricassee; medley of things, (Mex.) peanut brittle.
[1]**pepitoso, sa,** *a.* abounding in pips or seeds.
[2]**pepitoso, sa,** *a.* (fowl) having the pip.
peplo, *m.* peplum.
pepón, *m.* (bot.) watermelon.
pepona, *f.* large paper doll.
pepónide, *f.* (bot.) pepo (pumpkin, melon, etc.).
pepsina, *f.* pepsin.
péptico, ca, *a.* peptic.
peptización, *f.* (chem.) peptization.
peptona, *f.* peptone.
pequé, peque, *v. V.* PECAR.
pequeñamente, *adv.* in a small degree.
pequeñez, *f.* smallness; infancy, childhood; trifle; pettiness; mean act or conduct.
pequeñito, ta, *a. dim.* very little, tiny.
pequeño, ña. I. *a.* little, small; of tender age; lowly, humble. **II.** *n.* child.
pequeñuelo, la. I. *a. dim.* very little or young. **II.** *n.* babe, infant; child, little one.
pequín, *m.* pekin (silk cloth).
pequinés, *m.* Pekingese (dog).
pera, *f.* (bot.) pear; goatee, imperial; (coll.) sinecure.—**pedir peras al olmo,** to go on a wild-goose chase, to expect the impossible.—**poner las peras a cuarto, or a cuatro,** to compel one to do or concede what one does not wish to; to bring one to reason.
perácido, *m.* (chem.) peracid.
perada, *f.* preserve of pears; pear jam.
peral, *m.* pear tree; pear orchard.
peraleda, *f.* orchard of pear trees.
peralejo, *m.* (bot.) malpighia.
peraltar, *va.* (arch.) to stilt (an arch or vault); to raise, elevate.
peralte, *m.* (arch.) rise (of an arch); (Ry.) superelevation (of outer rail on curves).
perantón, *m.* (bot.) marvel plant; large fan; very tall person.
perborato, *m.* (chem.) perborate.
perca, *f.* (ichth.) perch; (ichth., Am.) black bass.
percal, *m.* percale, muslin, calico.
percalina, *f.* percaline, book muslin.
percance, *m.* perquisite; mischance, misfortune. —**percances del oficio** = GAJES DEL OFICIO, (ironic) perquisites that go with a job.
percatar, *vn.* & *vr.* to think, consider; to beware.
percebe, *m.* goose barnacle.
percebimiento, *m.* prevention, warning.
percentaje, *m.* percentage.
percentil, *m.* (stat.) percentile.
percepción, *f.* perception.—**p. extrasensoria,** extrasensory perception.
perceptibilidad, *f.* perceptibility.
perceptible, *a.* perceptible, perceivable.
perceptiblemente, *adv.* perceptibly.
perceptividad, *f.* perceptivity.
perceptivo, va, *a.* perceptive.
perceptor, ra. I. *a.* percipient, perceptive. **II.** *n.* percipient, perceiver.
percibir, *va.* to perceive; to receive, collect.
percibo, *m.* receiving, collecting.
perclorato, *m.* (chem.) perchlorate.
perclórico, ca, *a.* (chem.) perchloric.
percloruro, *m.* (chem.) perchloride.
percocería, *f.* small silver work.
percolación, *f.* (pharm.) percolation; seepage.
percolado, *m.* (pharm.) percolate.
percolador, *m.* percolator; coffee percolator.
percuciente, *a.* percussive, striking.
percudir, *va.* to tarnish, stain, soil.
percusión, *f.* percussion; collision.
percusor, *m.* striker, percussor; (artil.) percussion hammer.
percutir, *va.* to percuss, strike, beat.
[1]**percha,** *f.* perch, pole, staff; slat; hat or clothes rack; roost; snare for birds; strip for stringing game; (naut.) spar, rough tree; head rail.
[2]**percha,** *f.* (ichth.) = PERCA.
perchador, ra, *n.* carder (of cloth).
perchar, *va.* to card, raise the nap on (cloth).
percherón, na, *a.* & *n.* Percheron (horse).
perchón, *m.* long shoot left on a pruned vine.
perchonar, *vn.* to prune (vines) leaving long shoots; to lay snares for game.
perdedero, *m.* occasion or reason for losing.
perdedor, ra, *n.* loser.
perder. I. *va.* (*ind.* PIERDO; *subj.* PIERDA) to lose; to forfeit; to squander away; to ruin; to spoil; to miss (train, opportunity, etc.)—**p. de vista,** to lose sight of.—**p. el juicio, or el seso,** to go out of one's mind.—**p. la vista,** to lose one's sight, go blind.—**p. los estribos,** to lose one's poise; to become reckless.—**¡pierda Vd. cuidado!** don't worry! forget it!—**tener que p.,** to be a person of means, to have much to lose. **II.** *vn.* to lose; to fade, lose color. **III.** *vr.* to get lost, lose one's way; to miscarry; to be lost, confounded, bewildered; to forget or lose the thread of one's subject or discourse; to be ruined, go astray, go to the dogs; to be spoiled or damaged (as fruit, crops, etc.); to fall into disuse; to be out of fashion; to cease to be perceived by sight or hearing; to love excessively; to disappear.—**p. de vista,** to disappear; to excel in an eminent degree; to be very shrewd.
perdición, *f.* perdition; ruin, loss; unbridled, excessive love.
pérdida, *f.* loss; privation; detriment, damage; waste; (com.) leakage, shortage, shrinkage.—**pérdidas y ganancias,** profit and loss.—**ir a pérdidas y ganancias,** to share profit and loss.
perdidamente, *adv.* desperately; uselessly.
perdidizo, za, *a.* lost designedly or on purpose.—**hacerse el p.,** to sneak away, disappear.—**hacerse p.,** to lose designedly at cards.
perdido, da. I. *pp.* of PERDER. **II.** *a.* lost; mislaid; misguided; profligate, dissolute.—**p. por,** passionately fond of, crazy about. **III.** *m.* (fig.) black sheep.
perdidoso, sa, *a.* sustaining loss, losing.
perdigana, *f.* young partridge.
perdigar, *va.* (*pret.* PERDIGUÉ; *subj.* PERDIGUE) (cook.) to broil (partridges) slightly; to brown (meat); to dispose, prepare.
[1]**perdigón,** *m.* squanderer; losing gambler.
[2]**perdigón,** *m.* young partridge; decoy partridge;

bird shot.—**perdigonada,** *f.* shot or wound with bird shot.—**perdigonera,** *f.* shot pouch.
perdigué, perdigue, *v. V.* PERDIGAR.
perdiguero, ra. I. *m.* setter, retriever (dog). **II.** *n.* poulterer, game dealer.
perdimiento, *m.* = PERDICIÓN, PÉRDIDA.
perdiz, *f.* (ornith.) partridge.
perdón, *m.* pardon, forgiveness; mercy, grace; reprieve; remission of a debt; (coll.) burning drop of oil, wax, etc.—**¡p.!,** pardon!, excuse me!—**con p.,** by your leave; begging pardon. —**no tener p. (de Dios),** to be absolutely unpardonable, beyond all forgiveness.
perdonable, *a.* pardonable, forgivable.
perdonador, ra, *n.* one who pardons, excuses.
perdonante, *a.* forgiving, pardoning.
perdonar, *va.* to pardon, forgive; to remit (a debt); to exempt; to spare, excuse.—**no p.,** not to overlook (another's mistake, etc.).
perdonavidas, *m.* (coll.) bully, hector.
perdulario, ria, *a.* reckless, careless.
perdurable, *a.* lasting, abiding, everlasting.
perdurablemente, *adv.* everlastingly, lastingly.
perdurar, *vn.* to last long.
perecear. I. *va.* to protract, delay, put off. **II.** *vn.* to indulge one's laziness, to idle.
perecedero, ra. I. *a.* perishable, not lasting. **II.** *m.* extreme want.
perecer. I. *vn.* (*ind.* PEREZCO; *subj.* PEREZCA) to perish; to come to an end; to suffer or undergo damage, toil, or fatigue. **II.** *vr.* to crave, desire anxiously, pine.
pereciente, *a.* perishing; pining.
perecimiento, *m.* loss, decline; shipwreck.
pereda, *f.* orchard of pear trees.
peregrinación, *f.,* **peregrinaje,** *m.* peregrination; pilgrimage; course of this life.
peregrinamente, *adv.* rarely; curiously.
peregrinante, *a.* traveling; roaming.
peregrinar, *vn.* to travel, roam.
peregrinidad, *f.* rareness, rarity.
peregrino, na. I. *a.* peregrine, foreign; traveling, migratory; strange, odd, rare; handsome, perfect. **II.** *n.* pilgrim, palmer.
perejil, *m.* (bot.) parsley; (coll.) showy dress or apparel.—*pl.* (coll.) "handle" (titles).
perejila, *f.* a card game.
Perencejo, ja, *n.* = PERENGANO.
perendeca, *f.* (coll.) prostitute.
perendengue, *m.* earring, eardrop; cheap or tawdry ornament.
Perengano, na, *n.* = MENGANO, So-and-So.
perennal, *a.* = PERENNE.
perennalmente, *adv.* = PERENNEMENTE.
perenne, *a.* perennial, perpetual.
perennemente, *adv.* continually, perpetually.
perennidad, *f.* perennity, continuity.
perentoriamente, *adv.* peremptorily; urgently.
perentoriedad, *f.* peremptoriness; urgency.
perentorio, ria, *a.* peremptory; urgent; decisive.
perero, *m.* fruit parer.
pereza, *f.* laziness, sloth; slowness.
perezco, perezca, *v. V.* PERECER.
perezosamente, *adv.* lazily, slothfully, idly.
perezoso, sa. I. *a.* lazy, indolent, slothful, idle. **II.** *m.* (zool.) sloth.
perfección, *f.* perfection; perfect thing; beauty, grace.—**a la p.,** perfectly.
perfeccionable, *a.* ameliorable.
perfeccionador, ra, *a.* perfecting, improving.
perfeccionamiento, *m.* perfecting, improvement, finish.
perfeccionar, *va.* to improve, perfect.
perfeccionismo, *m.* perfectionism.
perfeccionista, *a.* & *n.* perfectionist.
perfectamente, *adv.* perfectly.
perfectibilidad, *f.* perfectibility.
perfectible, *a.* perfectible.
perfectivo, va, *a.* perfective.
perfecto, ta, *a.* perfect; (gram.) perfect (tense)
perficiente, *a.* perfecting.
pérfidamente, *adv.* perfidiously.
perfidia, *f.* perfidy.
pérfido, da, *a.* perfidious, treacherous.
perfil, *m.* profile, side view; outline; upstroke of letters.
perfilado, da. I. *pp.* of PERFILAR. **II.** *a.* elongated; outlined; streamlined.
perfiladora, *f.* (mech.) shaper.
perfiladura, *f.* profile drawing; outline.
perfilar. I. *va.* to outline, profile; (mech.) to shape; to polish, add the finishing touches. **II.** *vr.* to appear in profile, stand sideways; to make an elaborate toilet, dress up.
perfoliada, *f.* (bot.) hare's-ear.
perfoliado, da, *a.* (bot.) perfoliate.
perfoliata, *f.* = PERFOLIADA.
perfolla, *f.* corn husk; shucks.
perforación, *f.* perforation, puncture, hole; drilling, boring.
perforador, ra. I. *a.* perforating, drilling, puncturing. **II.** *n.* perforator, driller; *m.* (mech.) perforator, punch; *f.* perforating machine, punch, borer, drill, rock drill.
perforar, *va.* to perforate, puncture; to bore, drill, punch.
perfumadero, *m.* perfuming pan.
perfumado, da. I. *pp.* of PERFUMAR. **II.** *a.* odoriferous.
perfumador, ra. I. *a.* perfuming. **II.** *m.* perfumer, perfuming pan.
perfumar, *va.* to perfume.
perfume, *m.* perfume; odor, fragrance.
perfumear, *va.* to perfume.
perfumería, *f.* perfumery; perfumer's shop.
perfumero, ra; perfumista, *n.* perfumer.
perfunctoriamente, *adv.* perfunctorily.
perfunctorio, ria, *a.* perfunctory.
perfusión, *f.* (med.) perfusion.
pergal, *m.* leather paring for shoe laces.
pergaminero, *m.* parchment maker.
pergamino, *m.* parchment, vellum; diploma.
pergenio, *m.* (coll.) appearance, looks.
pergeñar, *va.* (coll.) to prepare or perform skilfully.
pergeño, *m.* (coll.) appearance, looks.
pérgola, *f.* pergola.
peri, *f.* fairy, elf, peri.
periantio, *m.* (bot.) perianth.
pericardíaco, ca; pericárdico, ca, *a.* pericardiac, pericardial.
pericardio, *m.* (anat.) pericardium.
pericarditis, *f.* (med.) pericarditis.
pericárpico, ca, *a.* pericarpic, pericarpial.
pericarpio, *m.* (bot.) pericarp.
pericia, *f.* skill, expertness, proficiency, (coll.) know-how.
pericial, *a.* expert.
pericialmente, *adv.* expertly.
periciclo, *m.* (bot.) pericycle.
perico, *m.* (ornith.) parrakeet; periwig; queen of clubs in the game of TRUQUE; (naut.) mizzen topgallant sail.—**p. de los palotes,** John Doe, a fictitious or undetermined person.—**p. ligero,** (zool.) sloth.
pericón, na. I. *a.* fit for all uses. **II.** *m.* large fan; queen of clubs in the game of QUÍNOLAS.
pericondrio, *m.* (anat.) perichondrium (cartilage membrane).
pericráneo, *m.* (anat.) pericranium, skull.
peridermo, *m.* (bot.) periderm.
peridotita, *f.* (min.) peridotite.
peridoto, *m.* (min.) chrysolite.
periecos, *m. pl.* (geog.) periœci.
periferia, *f.* periphery.
periférico, ca, *a.* peripheric, circumferential.
perifollo, *m.* (bot.) common chervil.—*pl.* ribbons, tawdry ornaments of dress.
perifonear, *va.* (radio) to broadcast.
perifonía, *f.* (radio) broadcasting.
perífono, *m.* (radio) broadcasting instrument.
perifrasear, *va.* to periphrase.
perífrasi, perífrasis, *f.* (rhet.) periphrasis.
perifrástico, ca, *a.* periphrastic.

perigallo, *m.* skin hanging from the chin of thin, old persons; gawdy ribbon worn on the hair; (coll.) tall, lean person; slender sling; (naut.) line, topping lift.
perigeo, *m.* (astr.) perigee.
perigonio, *m.* (bot.) perigynium, perianth.
perígono, *m.* (geom.) perigon.
perihelio, *m.* (astr.) perihelion.
perilustre, *a.* very illustrious.
perilla, *f. dim.* small pear; pear-shaped ornament; pommel of a saddlebow; goatee; lobe of the ear. —**de p.**, to the purpose; in the nick of time.
perillán, na, *n.* rascal; sly, crafty person.
perillo, *m.* scalloped cookie or maccaroon.
perimétrico, ca, *a.* perimetric, perimetrical.
perímetro, *m.* perimeter.
perínclito, ta, *a.* famous, renowned.
perineal, *a.* (anat.) perineal.
perinefrio, *m.* (anat.) perinephrium.
perineo, *m.* (anat.) perineum.
perineumonía, *f.* (med.) pneumonia.
perineumónico, ca, *a.* pneumonic.
perinola, *f.* teetotum, small top spun in gambling; pear-shaped ornament; neat little woman.
períoca, *f.* synopsis, summary.
periódicamente, *adv.* periodically.
periodicidad, *f.* periodicity, periodic character.
periódico, ca. I. *a.* periodical, periodic. **II.** *m.* newspaper; periodical, journal.
periodismo, *m.* journalism.
periodista, *m.* & *f.* journalist.
periodístico, ca, *a.* journalistic.
período, *m.* period, age, era; (rhet.) period, clause, sentence; menstruation; (mus.) period, phrase; (elec.) cycle.
periodograma, *m.* (stat.) periodogram.
perióstico, ca, *a.* periosteal.
periostio, *m.* (anat.) periosteum.
periostiotomía, *f.* (surg.) periosteotomy.
periostiótomo, *m.* (surg.) periosteotome.
periostitis, *f.* (med.) periostitis.
peripatético, ca, *a.* & *n.* Peripatetic; *a.* (coll.) ridiculous or extravagant (opinion).
peripato, *m.* Peripateticism.
peripecia, *f.* situation, incident, episode.
periplo, *m.* voyage around a coast.
períptero, ra, *a.* (arch.) peripteral.
peripuesto, ta, *a.* (coll.) very spruce in dress.
periquete, *m.* (coll.) jiffy, instant.
periquillo, *m.* sugar plum.
periquito, *m.* (ornith.) parrakeet, paroquet.
periscios, *m. pl.* (geog.) periscii.
periscópico, ca, *a.* periscopic.
periscopio, *m.* periscope.
perisístole, *f.* (physiol.) perisystole.
perisodáctilo, la. I. *a.* (zool.) perissodactylous. **II.** *m.* (zool.) perissodactyl.
perisología, *f.* (rhet.) verbiage.
perispermo, *m.* (bot.) perisperm.
peristalsis, *f.* (physiol.) peristalsis.
peristáltico, ca, *a.* (physiol.) peristaltic.
peristaltismo, *m.* (physiol.) peristalsis.
peristilo, *m.* (arch.) peristyle, colonnade.
perístole, *f.* (physiol.) peristole, peristalsis.
perístoma, *m.* (bot., zool.) peristome.
perita, *f. dim.* small pear.
peritaje, *m.* occupation of an expert.
peritéctico, ca, *a.* (chem., phys.) peritectic.
peritiflitis, *f.* (med.) perityphlitis.
perito, ta. I. *a.* skilful, able, experienced. **II.** *n.* connoisseur, expert; appraiser.
peritoneal, *a.* (anat.) peritoneal.
peritoneo, *m.* (anat.) peritoneum.—**peritonitis**, *f.* (med.) peritonitis.
perjudicador, ra, *n.* & *a.* injurer(-ing).
perjudicante, *a.* damaging, injurious.
perjudicar, *va.* (*pret.* PERJUDIQUÉ; *subj.* PERJUDIQUE) to damage, hurt, injure, impair, prejudice.
perjudicial, *a.* harmful, injurious, prejudicial.
perjudicialmente, *adv.* harmfully, injuriously.
perjudiqué, perjudique, *v. V.* PERJUDICAR.
perjuicio, *m.* prejudice; injury, damage.
perjurador, ra, *n.* perjurer, forswearer.
perjurar. I. *vn.* to commit perjury; to swear, be profane. **II.** *vr.* to perjure oneself.
perjurio, *m.* perjury.
perjuro, ra. I. *a.* perjured, forsworn. **II.** *n.* forswearer, perjurer.
perla, *f.* pearl; (fig.) jewel; (print.) pearl.—*pl.* fine teeth.—**de perlas**, perfectly; to a tee.
perlada, *a.* pearled (barley).
perlado, da, *a.* pearled, pearly; (chem.) beaded.
perlático, ca, *a.* paralyzed, palsied.
perlería, *f.* collection of pearls.
perlesía, *f.* (med.) paralysis, palsy.
perlezuela, *f. dim.* small pearl.
perlino, na, *a.* pearl-colored.
perlita, *f. dim.* small pearl; phonolite, clinkstone.
perlongar, *vn.* (*pret.* PERLONGUÉ; *subj.* PERLONGUE) (naut.) to coast; to pay out a cable.
permanecer, *vn.* (*ind.* PERMANEZCO; *subj.* PERMANEZCA) to stay, remain, endure, last.
permaneciente, *a.* permanent.
permanencia, *f.* stay, sojourn; duration, permanence; perseverance, constancy.
permanente. I. *a.* permanent. **II.** *f.* permanent (wave, in hair).—**permanentemente**, *adv.* permanently.
permanezco, permanezca, *v. V.* PERMANECER.
permanganato, *m.* (chem.) permanganate.—**p. de potasio**, (chem.) potassium permanganate.
permangánico, ca, *a.* permanganic.
permeabilidad, *f.* permeability.
permeable, *a.* permeable, non-waterproof.
permeámetro, *m.* (phys.) permeameter, vectometer.
permisible, *a.* permissible.
permisión, *f.* permission, leave, permit; concession, grant.
permisivamente, *adv.* permissively.
permisivo, va, *a.* permissive.
permiso, *m.* permission, permit, leave, license; difference in weight of coin.—**¡con p.!**, excuse me!
permisor, ra, *n.* granter, permitter.
permistión, *f.* mixture, concoction.
permitente, *a.* permitting, allowing.
permitidero, ra, *a.* permissible.
permitidor, ra, *n.* permitter, granter.
permitir, *va.* to permit, allow; to grant, admit.
permuta, *f.* barter; exchange.
permutable, *a.* exchangeable.
permutación, *f.* interchange; (math.) permutation.
permutar, *va.* & *vn.* to exchange, interchange, barter; to permute.
perna, *f.* flat shellfish.
pernada, *f.* blow with the leg; shake of the leg; (naut.) leg.
pernaza, *f. aug.* thick or big leg.
perneador, ra, *a.* strong-legged.
pernear. I. *vn.* to kick, shake the legs; to hustle; to worry, fret. **II.** *va.* to drive (pigs) to market and sell by retail.
perneo, *m.* public sale of hogs.
pernera, *f.* leg of a pair of trousers.
pernería, *f.* (naut.) collection of bolts.
pernetas.—**en p.**, bare-legged.
pernete, *m.* (naut.) small pin, peg, or bolt.
perniabierto, ta, *a.* bowlegged.
perniciosamente, *adv.* perniciously.
pernicioso, sa, *a.* pernicious; injurious, harmful.
pernigón, *m.* Genoese preserved plum.
pernil, *m.* hock, ham (of animals); trouser leg.
pernio, *m.* door or window hinge.
perniquebrar, *va.* (*ind.* PERNIQUIEBRO; *subj.* PERNIQUIEBRE) to break the legs of.
pernituerto, ta, *a.* twisted-, crooked-legged.
perno, *m.* bolt; pin, spike; hook of a door-hinge; (mech.) joint pin, crank pin.—**p. pinzote**, main bolt, kingbolt.
pernoctar, *vn.* to pass the night.
[1]**pero**, *m.* pearmain, variety of apple; apple tree.
[2]**pero. I.** *conj.* but; except; yet; (used for empha-

sis at beginning of sentence, not translated). **II.** *m.* (coll.) fault, defect.—**poner pero(s)**, to find fault.
perogrullada, *f.* (coll.) obvious truth, truism; platitude.
Perogrullo.—verdad de P. = PEROGRULLADA.
perojiménez, *m.* a variety of grape; wine made from it.
perol, *m.* (cooking) kettle, copper.
peroné, *m.* (anat.) fibula, perone.
peróneo, nea, *a.* peroneal, fibular.
peroración, *f.* peroration.
perorar, *vn.* to deliver a speech or oration; to declaim; to urge.
perorata, *f.* (coll.) harangue, speech.
peróxido, *m.* (chem.) peroxide.—**p. de hidrógeno,** (chem.) hydrogen peroxide.—**p. de sodio,** (chem.) sodium peroxide.
perpendicular, *n.* & *a.* perpendicular.
perpendicularidad, *f.* perpendicularity.
perpendicularmente, *adv.* perpendicularly.
perpendículo, *m.* plumb, plummet; altitude of a triangle; pendulum.
perpetración, *f.* perpetration.
perpetrador, ra, *n.* perpetrator, aggressor.
perpetrar, *va.* to perpetrate, commit.
perpetua, *f.* (bot.) immortelle, cudweed.
perpetuación, *f.* perpetuation.
perpetuamente, *adv.* perpetually.
perpetuán, *m.* a kind of thick, woollen stuff.
perpetuar, *va.* & *vr.* to perpetuate.
perpetuidad, *f.* perpetuity.
perpetuo, tua, *a.* perpetual, everlasting.—**p. silencio** (law) forever hold his peace.
perpiaño, *m.* (arch.) perpend.
perplejamente, *adv.* perplexedly, confusedly.
perplejidad, *f.* perplexity, irresolution, embarrassment, hesitation.
perplejo, ja, *a.* uncertain, perplexed.
perpunte, *m.* quilted under-waistcoat.
perquirir, *va.* to seek diligently.
perra, *f.* bitch, female dog; slut; drunken state. —**p. chica** = PERRO CHICO.
perrada, *f.* pack of dogs; mean, base action.
perramente, *adv.* very badly, wretchedly.
perrazo, *m. aug.* large dog.
perrengue, *m.* (coll.) peevish person, snarler; (coll.) Negro.
perrera, *f.* kennel; toil, drudgery; (coll.) bad pay; child's fit of temper.
perrería, *f.* pack of dogs; set or den of rogues; angry word.
perrero, *m.* beadle who drags dogs out of the church; master of hounds or dogs; dog fancier.
perrezno, na, *n.* whelp, puppy.
perrillo, lla; to, ta. I. *n.* little dog; puppy.—**p. de falda, or faldero,** lap dog. **II.** *m.* trigger of a gun; piece of horse's bridle.
perro, *m.* dog.—**p. alano,** mastiff.—**p. alforjero,** camp watchdog.—**p. braco,** pointer (dog).—**p. cazón,** (ichth.) dogfish.—**p. cobrador,** retriever.—**p. chico,** former five-centime copper coin.—**p. chino,** Mexican hairless (dog).—**p. de aguas,** poodle.—**p. de ajeo,** setter, bird dog.—**p. de casta,** thoroughbred dog.—**p. de lanas,** poodle, lapdog.—**p. del hortelano,** dog in the manger.—**p. de muestra,** pointer (dog).—**p. de policía,** police dog, German shepherd dog.—**p. de presa,** bulldog.—**p. de Terranova,** Newfoundland dog.—**p. dogo,** bulldog.—**p. galgo,** hound.—**p. jateo, raposero** or **zorrero,** foxhound.—**p. mestizo,** mutt, mongrel, pooch.—**p. mudo,** raccoon.—**p. tomador,** retriever.—**p. viejo,** wise old dog, person cautious because of experience.—**a espeta perros,** suddenly, unexpectedly.—**atar los perros con longaniza,** to live off the fat of the land.—**como perros y gatos,** like cats and dogs, irreconcilable.—**dar p. a uno,** to keep (someone) dangling, keep (someone) waiting.—**darse uno a p.,** to exasperate, irritate.
perroquete, *m.* (naut.) topmast.
perruno, na. I. *a.* doggish, canine; currish. **II.** *f.* dog bread, dog biscuit.
persa, *a.* & *n.* Persian.
persecución, *f.,* persecution; pursuit; harassment; importunity.
persecutorio, ria, *a.* persecuting.
perseguidor, ra, *n.* persecutor; pursuer.
perseguimiento, *m.* = PERSECUCIÓN.
perseguir, *va.* (*ger.* PERSIGUIENDO; *ind. pres.* PERSIGO, *pret.* él PERSIGUIÓ; *subj.* PERSIGA) to pursue; to persecute; to importune, beset.
Perseo, *m.* (astr.) Perseus.
persevante, *m.* pursuivant at arms.
perseverancia, *f.* perseverance.
perseverante, *a.* perseverant, persevering.
perseverantemente, *adv.* perseveringly.
perseverar, *vn.* to persevere, persist.
persiana, *f.* flowered silk stuff; Venetian blind.
persicaria, *f.* (bot.) persicaria, lady's-thumb.
pérsico, ca. I. *a.* Persian. **II.** *m.* (bot.) peach tree and its fruit.
persignarse, *vr.* to cross oneself; to handsel.
pérsigo, *m.* (bot.) peach tree and its fruit.
persigo, persiga, persiguió, *v. V.* PERSEGUIR.
persistencia, *f.* persistence; obstinacy.
persistente, *a.* persistent; permanent, firm.—**reacción p.,** sustained reaction.
persistir *vn.* to persist, persevere.
persona, *f.* person; individual; personage; (law, gram.) person.—**p. a cargo,** dependent.—**p. desplazada,** displaced person.—**p. inútil,** (coll.) deadwood.—**p. jurídica,** legal person (corporation, partnership, etc.).—**de p. a p.,** person to person, man to man.—**en p.,** in person.—**primera p.,** (gram.) first person.—**segunda p.,** (gram.) second person.—**tercera p.,** (gram.) third person.
personada, *a.* (bot.) personate.
personado, *m.* (eccl.) benefice without jurisdiction.
personaje, *m.* personage; (theat.) character.
personal. I. *a.* personal, private. **II.** *m.* personnel, staff; personal tax.
personalidad, *f.* personality; individuality; (law) person; legal capacity.
personalizar. I. *va.* to personalize; to become personal. **II.** *vr.* (law) to show oneself a party at law.
personalmente, *adv.* personally, in person.
personarse, *vr.* to meet on business; to appear personally; (law) to appear as an interested party.
personería, *f.* solicitorship.
personero, ra, *n.* solicitor, deputy, agent, attorney, counsel.
personificación, *f.* personification.
personificar, *va.* (*pret.* PERSONIFIQUÉ; *subj.* PERSONIFIQUE) to personify.
personilla, *f.* ridiculous little person.
perspectiva, *f.* perspective; view, vista; prospect, outlook; appearance.
perspectivo, *m.* one versed in perspective.
perspicacia, perspicacidad, *f.* perspicaciousness, perspicacity, acumen, sagacity.
perspicaz, *a.* perspicacious, acute, sagacious, clear-sighted.
perspicuamente, *adv.* perspicuously.
perspicuidad, *f.* perspicuity, lucidity.
perspicuo, cua, *a.* perspicuous, clear.
persuadidor, ra, *n.* persuader.
persuadir. I. *va.* to persuade, induce; to convince. **II.** *vr.* to be persuaded; to be convinced.
persuasible, *a.* persuasible, persuadable.
persuasión, *f.* persuasion; conviction, opinion.
persuasiva, *f.* persuasiveness.
persuasivo, va, *a.* persuasive, convincing.
persuasor, ra, *n.* persuader, inducer.
persulfato, *m.* (chem.) persulfate, persulphate.
persulfúrico, ca, *a.* (chem.) persulphuric.
persulfuro, *m.* (chem.) persulphide.
pertenecer, *vn.* (*ind.* PERTENEZCO; *subj.* PERTENEZCA) to belong, appertain; to concern; to behoove.

pertenecido, *m.* = PERTENENCIA.
perteneciente, *a.* belonging, appertaining.
pertenencia, *f.* ownership; tenure, holding, property, possession; appurtenance, dependence, accessory; (min.) claim.
pertenezco, pertenezca, *v. V.* PERTENECER.
pértica, *f.* perch, linear measure (9.70 feet).
pértiga, *f.*, **pertigal,** *m.* bar, staff, pole, rod.
pértigo, *m.* carriage; plow beam.
pertiguería, *f.* office of a verger.
pertiguero, *m.* verger.
pertinacia, *f.* pertinacity, insistence, obstinacy, stubbornness, doggedness.
pertinaz, *a.* pertinacious, obstinate, opinionated.
pertinazmente, *adv.* pertinaciously.
pertinencia, *f.* pertinence, fitness, relevancy.
pertinente, *a.* pertinent, apt, appropriate, relevant; (law) concerning, pertaining.
pertinentemente, *adv.* pertinently, opportunely, congruously.
pertrechar, *va.* & *vr.* (mil.) to supply, store, equip; to dispose, arrange, prepare.
pertrechos, *m. pl.* (mil.) stores; tools.
perturbable, *a.* easily perturbed.
perturbación, *f.* perturbation, disturbance; agitation, excitement.
perturbadamente, *adv.* confusedly.
perturbador, ra. I. *a.* perturbing, disturbing. II. *n.* perturber, disturber.
perturbar, *va.* to perturb, disturb, unsettle; to confuse, agitate.
Perú, *m.* Peru.
peruano, na, *n.* & *a.* Peruvian.
peruétano, *m.* (bot.) wild pear tree.
[1]**perulero, ra.** *n.* & *a.* Peruvian.
[2]**perulero,** *m.* narrow-bottomed, bulging, narrow-necked pitcher.
perversamente, *adv.* perversely, wickedly.
perversidad, *f.* perversity, wickedness.
perversión, *f.* perversion, perverting; perverseness, depravation, wickedness.
perverso, sa. I. *a.* perverse, wicked, depraved. II. *n.* pervert.
pervertidor, ra, *n.* perverter, corrupter.
pervertimiento, *m.* perversion, perverting.
pervertir. I. *va.* (*ger.* PERVIRTIENDO; *ind. pres.* PERVIERTO, *pret.* él PERVIRTIÓ; *subj.* PERVIERTA) to pervert, distort, garble; to corrupt, debase. II. *vr.* to become depraved.
pervigilio, *m.* sleeplessness, wakefulness.
pervulgar, *va.* to divulge; to promulgate.
peryódico, ca, *a.* (chem.) periodic.
peryoduro, *m.* (chem.) periodide.
pesa, *f.* weight (the thing); clock weight; counterweight.—**p. de una romana,** weight of a steelyard.—**pesas y medidas,** weights and measures.
pesacartas, *f.* letter-scales.
pesada, *f.* weighing; quantity weighed at once.
pesadamente, *adv.* heavily; cumbrously; sorrowfully, grievingly; slowly, lazily.
pesadez, *f.* heaviness; slowness; drowsiness; importunity; excess, abundance; trouble, pain, fatigue; obesity, corpulence.
pesadilla, *f.* nightmare.
pesado, da. I. *pp.* of PESAR. II. *a.* heavy; massive; deep, sound (sleep); heavy, sultry, stuffy (air, atmosphere); cumbersome; tedious, tiresome; dull; offensive; slow, lazy; clumsy; fat or corpulent; insufferable, importunate, annoying, vexatious.—**p. de cabeza,** (aer.) nose heavy.—**p. de cola,** (aer.) tail heavy.—**p. de proa,** (aer.) nose heavy. III. *n.* bore, tease.
pesador, ra, *n.* weigher.
pesadumbre, *f.* grief, affliction, sorrow; heaviness.
pesalicores, *m.* hydrometer.
pésame, *m.* condolence. Also PÉNAME.
pesante. I. *a.* weighing. II. *m.* weight of half a drachm.
pesantez, *f.* (phys.) gravity; heaviness.
pesar. I. *vn.* to weigh, have weight; to be weighty, important, or valuable; to cause regret, sorrow or repentance (diff. constr.: *me pesa rehusar,* I regret to refuse; often foll. by **de:** *me pesa de haber ofendido a Vd.,* I am sorry to have offended you); to preponderate.—**mal que le pese,** however much it may displease you; whether you like it or not.—**pese a quien pese,** whatever anybody says or does, let them say what they will. II. *va.* to weigh; to examine, consider, think or ponder over. III. *m.* sorrow, grief, regret; repentance.—**a p. de,** in spite of, notwithstanding.—**a. p. mío, or a mi p.,** in spite of me, against my wishes.
pesario, *m.* (med.) pessary.
pesaroso, sa, *a.* sorrowful, regretful; sorry, sad.
pesca, *f.* fishing; fishery; catch, fish caught.
pescada, *f.* (ichth.) hake.
pescadería, *f.* fish market.
pescadero, ra, *n.* fishmonger.
pescadilla, *f.* small hake.
pescado, *m.* fish (caught); salted codfish.
pescador, ra, *n.* fisherman(-woman).
pescante, *m.* jib of a crane or derrick; boom; coach box; (naut.) davit; fish davit.
pescar. I. *va.* & *vn.* (*pret.* PESQUÉ; *subj.* PESQUE) to fish; to catch fish. II. *va.* to find or pick up; to catch in the act, surprise; to obtain, get.
péscola, *f.* beginning of a furrow.
pescozada, *f.*; **pescozón,** *m.* slap on the neck.
pescozudo, da, *a.* having a thick neck.
pescuezo, *m.* neck; throat; stiff-necked haughtiness, airs.—**cortar el p.,** to cut the throat; to cut off the head.
pescuño, *m.* wedge of the coulter.
pesebre, *m.* crib, rack; manger.—**pesebrejo,** *m. dim.* small manger; alveolus of horses' teeth.
pesebrera, *f.* stable; range of mangers in a stable.
pesebrón, *m.* boot of a coach.
pesero, *m.* (Mex., coll.) public car pool.
peseta, *f.* peseta, monetary unit of Spain.
pésete, *m.* imprecation; execration.
¡pesia! ¡pesia tal! *interj.* confound it! blazes!
pesiar, *vn.* to utter curses or execrations.
pesillo, *m.* small scales for weighing gold or silver coin.
pésimamente, *adv.* very badly, wretchedly.
pesimismo, *m.* pessimism.
pesimista, *n.* & *a.* pessimist(-ic).
pésimo, ma, *a. super.* very bad, very worst.
pesita, *f. dim.* small weight.
peso, *m.* weight, heaviness; weighing; balance, scales; importance, moment; burden, load; place where various victuals are sold at wholesale; judgment, good sense; peso, monetary unit of Argentina, Chile, Colombia, Cuba, the Dominican Republic, Mexico, the Philippines and Uruguay.—**p. atómico,** atomic weight.—**p. bruto,** gross weight.—**p. duro** or **fuerte,** duro, former Spanish monetary unit equal to 5 pesetas.—**p. específico,** (phys.) specific gravity.—**p. molecular,** (phys.) molecular weight.—**p. muerto,** dead weight, (aer.) dead load, permanent load.—**p. neto,** net weight.—**p. seco,** (aer.) dry weight.—**caerse de su p.,** to be self-evident; to go without saying.—**de p.,** of due weight; weighty, of weight, of importance; cogent.—**de su p.,** naturally.—**en p.,** suspended in the air; bodily; totally; undecided.
pésol, *m.* (bot.) pea.
pespuntador, ra, *n.* (sewing) backstitcher.
pespuntar, *va.* & *vn.* (sewing) to backstitch.
pespunte, *m.* (sewing) backstitching.
pesqué, pesque, *v. V.* PESCAR.
pesquera, *f.* fishery, fishing grounds.
pesquería, *f.* fish business; fishing; fishery.
pesquis, *m.* acumen, cleverness.
pesquisa, *f.* inquiry, investigation, search.
pesquisante, *a.* investigating, inquiring.
pesquisar, *va.* to inquire into, investigate.
pesquisidor, ra, *n.* searcher, investigator.
pestaña, *f.* eyelash; (sewing) fag-end, fringe, edging; (mech.) flange; (bot.) hairs.
pestañear, *vn.* to wink, to blink.

pestañeo, *m.* winking, blinking.
peste, *f.* pest, plague, pestilence; epidemic; corruption of manners; foul smell; (coll.) excess, superabundance.—*pl.* offensive words.—**p. bubónica,** bubonic plague.
pestíferamente, *adv.* pestiferously.
pestífero, ra, *a.* pestiferous, noxious, foul.
pestilencia, *f.* pest, plague, pestilence; foulness, stench.—**pestilencial,** *a.* pestiferous, pestilential; infectious, contagious; destructive.
pestilencioso, sa, *a.* pestilential.
pestilente, *a.* pestilent, noxious, foul.
pestillo, *m.* door latch; bolt of a lock.—**correr el p.,** to slide the bolt, bolt the door.
pestiño, *m.* honeyed fritters.
pestorejazo, *m.* = PESCOZÓN, slap on the neck.
pestorejo, *m.* fleshy back of the neck.
pestorejón, *m.* blow on the back of the neck.
pesuña, *f.* foot of cloven-hoofed animals.
pesuño, *m.* each half of a cloven hoof.
petaca, *f.* cigar case; (Am.) leather trunk or chest; (Am.) suitcase; covered hamper.
petalismo, *m.* (anc. hist.) petalism, banishment.
pétalo, *m.* (bot.) petal.
petaloide, *a.* petaloid.
petaquilla, *f.* (Am.) small, leather trunk.
petar, *va.* (coll.) to please, gratify, content.
petardear, *va.* (mil.) to beat down with petards; to cheat, gull, trick.
petardero, *m.* (mil.) petardeer; cheat, trickster.
petardista, *n.* cheat, impostor, swindler.
petardo, *m.* (artil.) petard; bomb; cheat, fraud, gull, trick.
petate, *m.* (Am.) sleeping mat; (coll.) luggage, baggage; impostor, swindler; good-for-nothing fellow; (naut.) sailor's hammock.—**liar el p.,** (coll.) to pack up and go.
petenera, *f.* a popular Andalusian song.
petequia, *f.* (med.) petechia.
petequial, *a.* (med.) petechial.
petera, *f.* (coll.) wrangle; fit of temper.
peteretes, *m. pl.* (coll.) tidbits, sweets.
peticano, peticanón, *m.* (print.) petit-canon type.
petición, *f.* petition, demand, claim, request; (law) petition, prayer.
peticionario, ria, *n.* petitioner.
petillo, *m. dim.* small stomacher; breast jewel.
petimetra, *f.* spruce, stylish lady.
petimetre, *m.* fop, coxcomb, beau, dude.
petirrojo, *m.* (ornith.) robin redbreast.
petitorio, ria. I. *a.* petitionary. **II.** *m.* impertinent, repeated petition. **III.** *f.* (coll.) PETICIÓN.
peto, *m.* breastplate; (fencing) plastron.
petral, *m.* breast leather (of saddle).
petraria, *f.* (mil.) petrary.
petrarquesco, ca, *a.* Petrarchan.
petrarquista, *n.* & *a.* Petrarchist(-ic).
petrel, *m.* (ornith.) petrel.
pétreo, a, *a.* rocky; stony, of stone.
petrificación, *f.* petrification.
petrificante, *a.* petrifying.
petrificar, *va.* & *vr.* to petrify.
petrífico, ca, *a.* petrifying.
petroglifo, *m.* (archeol.) petroglyph.
petrografía, *f.* petrography.
petrográfico, ca, *a.* petrographic.
petrolado, *m.*; **petrolato,** *m.* (pharm.) petrolatum.
petróleo, *m.* petroleum, mineral oil.
petrolero, ra. I. *a.* petroleum, oil (as *a.*). **II.** *n.* seller of petroleum; person in the petroleum industry; incendiary; ultraradical.
petrolífero, ra, *a.* oil-bearing.
petrología, *f.* petrology.
petroquímico, ca. I. *a.* petrochemical. **II.** *f.* petrochemistry.
petrosílex, *m.*, **petrosílice,** *f.* petrosilex, felsite.
petroso, sa, *a.* rocky, full of stones.
petulancia, *f.* petulance; insolence; flippancy.
petulante, *a.* petulant, insolent, pert.—**petulantemente,** *adv.* petulantly, pertly.

petunia, *f.* (bot.) petunia.
peucédano, *m.* (bot.) Peucedanum.
peyorativo, va, *a.* pejorative, depreciative, derogatory.
[1]**pez. I.** *m.* fish (in the water, not caught); catch, haul.—**p. espada,** swordfish.—**p. luna,** mola, sunfish.—**p. martillo,** hammer-headed shark.—**p. sierra,** sawfish.—**p. volador,** flying fish.
[2]**pez,** *f.* pitch, tar.—**p. blanca,** or **de Borgoña,** refined galipot, Burgundy pitch.—**p. griega,** or **rubia,** rosin, colophony.
pezolada, *f.* fag-end threads.
pezón, *m.* (bot.) stem of fruits; leaf stalk; flower stalk; nipple of a teat; axle end or pivot; end of a spindle in mills; cape or point of land.
pezonera, *f.* nipple shield; linchpin.
pezpalo, *m.* (com.) stockfish.
pezpita, *f.*, **pezpítalo,** *m.* (ornith.) wagtail.
pezuelo, *m.* beginning of cloth in weaving.
pezuña, *f.* = PESUÑA.
phi, *f.* phi (Greek letter).
pi, *f.* pi (Greek letter); (math.) pi.
piache, used in the expression **tarde piache,** (coll.) too late.
piada, *f.* chirping, peeping; puling.
piador, ra, *n.* puler; chirper.
piadosamente, *adv.* piously; mercifully.
piadoso, sa, *a.* pious, godly; merciful.
piafar, *vn.* (of horses) to paw, to stamp.
piale, *m.* (Am.) throw of the lasso.
piamadre, piamáter, *f.* (anat.) pia mater.
píamente, *adv.* piously.
piamontés, sa, *n.* & *a.* Piedmontese.
pian, *m.* (med.) yaws.
pían, pían; or **pían, piano,** *adv.* slowly, softly.
pianino, *m.* (mus.) upright piano.
pianista, *n.* pianist; piano maker or dealer.
piano, pianoforte, *m.* piano, pianoforte.—**p. de cola,** grand piano.—**p. de media cola,** baby grand.—**p. de mesa,** square piano.—**p. vertical,** upright piano.
pianola, *f.* pianola.
piante, *a.* peeping, puling, chirping.
piar, *vn.* to peep, pule, chirp; (coll.) to whine, cry.
piara, *f.* herd (of swine); drove (of mares, mules).
piariego, ga, *a.* owning a herd of mares, mules, or swine.
piastra, *f.* piaster, piastre (coin).
pibe, *m.* (Arg.) little child, "kid."
[1]**pica,** *f.* pike, lance; bullfighter's goad; stonecutter's hammer.—**poner una p. en Flandes,** to achieve a triumph.
[2]**pica,** *f.* (med.) pica.
picacero, ra, *a.* (of hawks) magpie-chasing.
picacureba, *f.* a Brazilian pigeon.
picacho, *m.* top, peak, summit.
picada, *f.* puncture, pricking, bite; sharp, pricking pain.
picadero, *m.* riding school; (naut.) stocks, boat skid; stamping ground of a buck in rutting time.
picadillo, *m.* minced meat; hash.
picado, da. I. *pp.* of PICAR. **II.** *a.* pricked; piqued, hurt; (sewing) pinked. **III.** *m.* minced meat; hash; (aer.) diving; dive.
picador, *m.* horse-breaker; horseman armed with a goad in bullfights; chopping block; paper pricker; pinking iron; file cutter.
picadura, *f.* pricking; pinking; puncture; bite; sting; nick, cut, slash; cut tobacco.
picafigo, *m.* (ornith.) = PAPAFIGO, figpecker.
picaflor, *m.* (ornith.) humming bird.
picajón, na; picajoso, sa, peevish, querulous.
picamaderos, *m.* (ornith.) woodpecker.—**p. verde,** (ornith.) popinjay, green woodpecker.
picana, *f.* (Am.) goad.
picanear, *va.* (Am.) to goad.
picante. I. *a.* pricking, piercing, stinging; highly seasoned, hot; risqué. **II.** *m.* piquancy, pungency, acrimony; keen satire.
picantemente, *adv.* piquantly.
[1]**picaño, ña,** *a.* lazy, vagrant.

[2]**picaño,** *m.* patch on a shoe.
picapedrero, *m.* stonecutter.
picapica, *f.* a plant whose leaves and fruit produce intense smarting of the skin.
picapleitos, *m.* (coll.) litigious person; pettifogging lawyer.
picaporte, *m.* spring latch, catch bolt; latchkey; (Am.) door knocker.
picaposte, *m.* (ornith.) woodpecker.
picapuerco, *m.* (ornith.) an insectivorous bird.
picar. **I.** *va.* (*pret.* PIQUÉ; *subj.* PIQUE) to prick, pierce, puncture; to sting, bite (as insects); to mince, chop, hash; (of birds) to peck; (of fish) to bite; to nibble, pick at, take little bites of; to pursue or harass; to spur, goad, incite; to pink; to pique, vex; to tame; (art) to stipple; to roughen with a pointed tool.—**p. la bomba,** to work the pump. **II.** *vn.* to sting, bite (as insects); (of fish) to bite; to itch, burn, smart; to scorch, burn (as the sun); (aer.) to dive.—**p. alto,** to aim high.—**p. en,** to be, to be somewhat of a (poet, etc.). **III.** *vr.* to be offended or piqued; to be moth-eaten; to stale, sour (as wine); to begin to rot (as fruit); (of teeth, etc.) to begin to decay; to boast of; (of animals) to be in heat; (naut.) (of the sea) to get choppy.
pícaramente, *adv.* knavishly, roguishly.
picaraza, *f.* (ornith.) magpie.
picardear, *vn.* to play the knave; to do mischief.
picardía, *f.* knavery, roguery; deceit, malice, foulness; wanton trick, wantonness; lewdness; meeting of rogues.—*pl.* offensive words.
picardihuela, *f. dim.* prank, roguish trick.
picaresco, ca. **I.** *a.* picaresque, roguish, knavish. **II.** *f.* den of rogues; knavery.
picaril, *a.* picaresque, roguish, knavish.
picarillo, *m. dim.* little rogue or rascal.
pícaro, ra. **I.** *a.* knavish, roguish; vile, low; mischievous; crafty, sly. **II.** *n.* rogue, knave, rascal.—**p. de cocina,** scullion, kitchen boy.
picarón, na, *n. aug.* great rogue; *f.* jade.
picaronazo, za; picarote, ta, *n.* great rogue or rascal.
picarrelincho, *m.* (ornith.) = PICAMADEROS.
picatoste, *m.* buttered toast.
[1]**picaza,** *f.* (ornith.) magpie.—**p. marina,** flamingo.
[2]**picaza,** *f.* grub ax, mattock.
[1]**picazo, za,** *a.* (of horses) black and white.
[2]**picazo,** *m.* blow with a pike, beak of bird, etc.
[3]**picazo,** *m.* young magpie.
picazón, *m.* itching, itch, smarting; peevishness, fretfulness.
pícea, *f.* (bot.) spruce.
píceo, a, *a.* of, or pert. to pitch.
picnómetro, *m.* (phys.) pycnometer.
picnóstila, *f.* (arch.) pycnostyle.
[1]**pico,** *m.* beak or bill of a bird; sharp point of any kind; pick, pickaxe; twibill; spout of a jar or pitcher; beak iron of an anvil; peak, top, summit; small balance of an account, small amount over; (coll.) mouth, chin; loquacity, garrulity.—**p. de cigüeña,** (bot.) crane's bill, geranium.—**p. de oro,** silver-tongued orator, man of great eloquence.—**p. de ancla,** (naut.) bill of an anchor.—*pl.* odds and ends.—**picos de un sombrero,** cocks of a hat.—**andar a picos pardos,** to loiter; to go on a spree.—**callar el p.,** to hold one's tongue.—**tener mucho p.,** to talk too much.—**y p.,** odd (*treinta y pico,* thirty odd).
[2]**pico,** *m.* (P. I.) weight of 137½ pounds.
[3]**pico,** *m.* (ornith.) woodpecker.—**p. de garza,** (bot.) heron's bill.—**p. duro,** (ornith.) grosbeak.—**p. verde,** (ornith.) green woodpecker.
picofeo, *m.* (ornith.) (Am.) toucan.
picolete, *m.* bolt staple.
picolina, *f.* (chem.) picoline.
picón, na. **I.** *a.* (of animals) having the upper teeth projecting over the under ones. **II.** *m.* lampoon or nipping jest; charcoal for brasiers; small fresh-water fish; broken rice.
piconero, *m.* maker of brasier charcoal.
picor, *m.* pungent taste; itching.
picoso, sa, *a.* pitted with the smallpox.
picota, *f.* gibbet, pillory; top, peak, point, spire; (naut.) cheek of a pump.
picotada, *f.*, **picotazo,** *m.* blow with the beak.
picote, *m.* goat's-hair cloth.
picoteado, da, *a.* peaked; having many points.
picoteador, *m.* pecker.
picotear. **I.** *va.* to peck, pick. **II.** *vn.* (coll.) to toss the head (said of horses); (coll.) to gab. **III.** *vr.* to altercate, wrangle, quarrel (said of women).
picotería, *f.* loquacity, volubility; gossip.
picotero, ra, *a.* chattering, prattling.
picotillo, *m.* inferior goat's-hair cloth.
picrato, *m.* (chem.) picrate.
pícrico, ca, *a.* (chem.) picric.
picrita, *f.* (petrography) picrite.
pictografía, *f.* pictography, picture writing.
pictográfico, ca, *a.* pictographic.
pictograma, *m.* (stat.) pictogram.
pictórico, ca, *a.* pictorial.
[1]**picudilla,** *f.* an insectivorous bird.
[2]**picudilla** *a. f.* crescent (olive).
picudo, da, *a.* beaked; acuminated, pointed; prattling, chattering.
pichel, *m.* pewter tankard; mug; pitcher.
pichelería, *f.* tankard or pitcher factory.
pichelero, *m.* maker of pewter tankards.
pichelete, *m. dim.* small tankard or mug.
pícher, *m.* (Angl.) (Am.) baseball pitcher.
pichi, *m.* pichi, a Chilean medicinal shrub.
pichincha, *f.* (Am.) good bargain.
pichoa, *f.* a Chilean cathartic plant.
pichola, *f.* a wine measure (about a pint).
pichón, **I.** *m.* young pigeon, squab. **II.** *n.* (coll.) darling, dearest.
pidientero, *m.* beggar.
pido, pida, pidió, *v. V.* PEDIR.
pidón, na, *a.* (coll.) persistent in begging.
pie, *m.* foot; leg, stand, support, base; trunk (of trees and plants); foot, bottom (of a page); lees, sediment; last hand or player (at cards); (theat.) cue; motive, occasion, opportunity; foundation, groundwork; rule, use, custom; (poet.) foot, syllable, verse; first color given in dyeing; foot of a stocking; slip, cutting (from a plant or tree).—**p. de amigo,** prop, shore.—**p. de atleta,** athlete's foot.—**p. de banco,** foolish remark, silly comment.—**p. de cabra,** crowbar.—**p. de cabalgar,** left foot.—**p. de carnero,** (naut.) samson's post.—**p. de imprenta,** (print.) imprint, printer's mark.—**p. de león,** (bot.) = ALQUEMILA VULGAR.—**p. de montar,** left foot.—**p. derecho,** (naut.) stanchion.—**p. de roda,** (naut.) forefoot.—**p. marino,** sea legs.—**p. plano,** (med.) flatfoot.—**a cuatro pies,** on all fours.—**a los pies de Vd.,** at your service (said to a lady only).—**al p.,** near, close to; at the foot of.—**al p. de,** at (the factory, the job, etc.).—**al p. de la letra,** literally.—**andar en un p.,** to put one's best foot forward.—**a p.,** on foot.—**a p. enjuto,** dryshod.—**a p. firme,** steadfastly.—**a p. juntillas,** firmly; uncompromisingly; most emphatically.—**a p. llano,** (coll.) with great ease, effortlessly.—**caer de pies,** (fig.) to land on one's feet.—**con buen o mal p.,** rain or shine, come what may.—**con p. derecho,** auspiciously with a good start.—**con un p. en la sepultura,** with one foot in the grave.—**dar p.,** to give occasion.—**de a p.,** on foot.—**de p., de pies,** standing (up); up and doing; firmly.—**de pies a cabeza,** from head to foot.—**en p.,** pending, undecided; DE PIE.—**en p. de guerra,** on a war footing, mobilized.—**estar con un p. en el aire,** to be stopping for only a short time; to be about to leave.—**estar con el p. en el estribo,** to be about to leave or to act.—**hacer p.,** to be able to touch bottom (in water).—**ír-**

sele los pies a uno, (fig.) to slip up.—**ni pies ni cabeza,** neither head nor tail.—**perder p.,** to lose one's foothold, get into deep water.—**pies, ¿para qué os quiero?** (coll.) run for one's life (expression used when fleeing).—**poner pies en polvorosa,** (coll.) to flee, take it on the lam.—**ponerse en un p.,** to put one's best foot forward.—**sacar el p. del lodo,** (fig.) to get out of the slums.

piecezuela, *f. dim.* little piece.

piecezuelo, *m. dim.* of PIE: little foot.

piedad, *f.* piety, godliness; mercy; pity, charity; **¡por p.!** for pity's sake!

piedra, *f.* stone; block; cobblestone; memorial stone; footstone; (med.) gravel; hail; place where foundlings are exposed; gunflint.—**p. amoladera** = P. DE AMOLAR.—**p. angular,** cornerstone.—**p. berroqueña,** granite.—**p. bruta,** rubble.—**p. caliza,** limestone.—**p. de afilar,** whetstone, grinding stone, rubbing stone.—**p. de albardilla,** copestone.—**p. de amolar,** whetstone, grinding stone, rubbing stone.—**p. de chispa,** flint.—**p. de molino,** millstone.—**p. de toque,** touchstone.—**p. falsa,** imitation (precious) stone.—**p. filosofal,** philosopher's stone.—**p. filtrante,** filter or filtering stone.—**p. fina,** precious stone.—**p. franca,** freestone.—**p. fundamental,** foundation stone, cornerstone.—**p. imán,** loadstone.—**p. infernal,** caustic, lapis infernalis, nitrate of silver in sticks.—**p. lipis,** copper sulphate.—**p. litográfica,** lithographic stone.—**p. melodreña,** whetstone, grinding stone, rubbing stone.—**p. meteórica,** meteoric stone.—**p. miliar** or **miliaria,** milestone.—**p. molar,** millstone.—**p. nefrítica,** (min.) nephrite, jade.—**p. pómez,** pumice stone.—**p. preciosa,** precious stone.—**p. rodada,** (geol.) boulder.—**p. sepulcral,** gravestone, tombstone.—**p. viva,** solid rock.—**echar la primera p.,** to cast the first stone.—**hablar las piedras,** to talk to a wall.—**no dejar p. por mover,** to leave no stone unturned.—**no dejar p. sobre p.,** to raze to the ground, destroy entirely.—**tirar piedras,** to go berserk.

piedrecica, illa, ita; piedrezuela, *f. dim.* little stone, pebble.

piel, skin; hide, pelt; leather; fur; peel or skin of fruits.—**p. de cabra,** goatskin.—**p. de gallina,** goose flesh.—**abrigo de pieles,** fur coat.

piélago, *m.* high sea; great abundance.

pielecita, *f. dim.* small hide or skin.

pielgo, *m.* = PIEZGO.

pielitis, *f.* (med.) pyelitis.

piemia, *f.* (med.) pyemia, pyæmia.

[1]**pienso,** *m.* daily feed given to horses.

[2]**pienso,** *m.*—**ni por p.,** (coll.) not even in thought, absolutely not.

[3]**pienso, piense,** *v. V.* PENSAR.

pierdo, pierda, *v. V.* PERDER.

piérides, *f. pl.* (poet.) the Muses.

pierio, ria, *a.* (poet.) Pierian.

pierna, *f.* (anat.) leg; branch or leg of a compass; downstroke of letters; check of a printing press; jar for honey; (mech.) shank, fork.—**p. de Judas,** wicked person.—**p. de nuez,** lobe of a walnut.—**p. de una sábana,** breadth of a sheet.—**a p. suelta** or **a p. tendida,** at one's ease; without care; soundly.—**en piernas,** barelegged.—**estirar la p.,** (coll.) to kick the bucket, turn up one's toes.—**estirar las piernas,** (coll.) to take a walk; to wander around.

piernitendido, da, *a.* with extended legs.

pietismo, *m.* pietism.

pietista. I. *n.* Pietist. **II.** *a.* pietistic.

pieza, *f.* piece; fragment; part (of a machine, etc.); member (of a structure); bolt or roll of cloth; room (in a house); length of time; distance; game, quarry; piece of work; (theat.) play, piece; piece of music; piece or man in games; (her.) division of a shield.—**p. de artillería,** piece of ordnance.—**p. de autos,** records or pleadings.—**p. de recibo,** parlor, reception room.—**p. de repuesto,** spare part.—**¡buena p.!** a fine fellow (sometimes ironic).—**de una (sola) p.,** in one piece, solid.

piezgo, *m.* foot of a hide or skin; wine skin.

piezoelectricidad, *f.* piezoelectricity.

piezoeléctrico, ca, *a.* piezoelectric.

piezométrico, ca, *a.* piezometric.

piezómetro, *m.* piezometer, instrument for measuring compressibility of liquids.

pifano, *m.* (mus.) fife; fifer.

pifia, *f.* miscue at billiards; error, blunder.

pifiar. I. *vn.* to breathe audibly in playing the flute. **II.** *vr.* (billiards) to make a miscue.

pigargo, *m.* (ornith.) ringtail hawk.

pigmentación, *f.* pigmentation.

pigmentario, ria, *a.* pigmentary.

pigmento, *m.* pigment.

pigmeo, a. I. *a.* dwarfish. **II.** *n.* dwarf, pigmy.

pignoración, *f.* pledge of security given.

pignorar, *va.* to pledge, give as security.

pignoraticio, cia, *a.* pert. to a pledge or security.

pigre, *a.* slothful, lazy.—**pigricia,** *f.* laziness; place in schools for lazy boys.

pigro, gra, *a.* = PIGRE.

pihua, *f.* sandal.

pihuela, *f.* leash; obstruction, hindrance, impediment.—*pl.* fetters, shackles.

piísimo, ma, *a. super.* very pious, most pious.

pijama, piyama, (gen. *pl.*) *m.* (in Sp.), *f.* (in Am.) pajama.

pijota, *f.* (ichth.) hake.

pijote, *m.* (artil.) swivel gun for grapeshot.

pila, *f.* stone trough or basin; sink; (eccl.) font, holy-water basin; pile, heap; shorn wool belonging to one owner; (eng., arch.) pier; (elec.) battery, pile.—**p. atómica,** (phys.) atomic pile, reactor.—**p. eléctrica,** (elec.) electric cell.—**p. seca,** (elec.) dry cell.—**p. voltaica,** (elec.) voltaic cell.—**nombre de p.,** Christian name, given name.

pilada, *f.* quantity of mortar made at one time; cloth fulled at one time; pile, heap.

[1]**pilar,** *va.* to hull (grain) by pounding.

[2]**pilar,** *m.* basin of a fountain; pillar, column, post; support; pedestal; milestone, stone post; bedpost; arbor of a press.

pilarejo; pilarito, *m. dim.* small pillar.

pilastra, *f.* (arch.) pilaster, square column.

pilastrón, *m. aug.* large pilaster.

pilatero, ra, *n.* one who assists at fulling cloth.

pilche, *m.* (Peru) wooden cup or bowl.

píldora, *f.* (pharm.) pill, pellet; (coll.) affliction, bad news.

píleo, *m.* pileus, skull cap; cardinal's biretta.

pileta, *f.* kitchen sink; swimming pool.

pilica, *f. dim.* of PILA.

pilífero, ra, *a.* piliferous, hairy.

piliforme, *a.* piliform, filamentous.

pilocarpina, *f.* (chem.) pilocarpin.

pilocarpo, *m.* (bot.) jaborandi.

pilón, *m.* watering trough; basin of a fountain; mortar (for pounding); loaf (of sugar); drop or ball of a steelyard; counterpoise in an olive press; (mason.) heap of mortar; rider, sliding weight (of a balance).

pilonero, ra, *n.* newsmonger.

pilongo, ga, *a.* peeled and dried (chestnut); thin, lean, meager.

pilórico, ca, *a.* (anat.) pyloric.

píloro, *m.* (anat.) pylorus.

piloso, sa, *a.* pilous, pilose, hairy.

[1]**pilotaje,** *m.* (naut.) pilotage.

[2]**pilotaje,** *m.* pilework, piling.

pilotar, *va.* to pilot.

pilote, *m.* (eng.) pile.

pilotear, *va.* to pilot.

pilotín, *m.* (naut.) pilot's mate, second pilot.

piloto, *m.* (naut.) pilot, sailing master, navigator; first mate; mate.—**p. automático,** (aer.) automatic pilot.—**p. de altura,** sea pilot.—**p.**

de costa, coast pilot.—**p. de pruebas,** (aer.) test pilot.—**p. de puerto,** port pilot.—**p. de reactor,** jet pilot.—**p. práctico,** coast pilot. —**alambre p.,** (elec.) pilot wire.—**mechero p.,** pilot light.—**pájaro p.,** (ornith.) pilot bird. —**planta p.,** pilot plant.
piltraca, piltrafa, *f.* skinny flesh; hide parings. —*pl.* scraps of food.
pilla, *f.* pillage, plunder.
pillada, *f.* (coll.) knavish trick, rascality.
pillador, ra, *n.* pillager, plunderer; swindler.
pillaje, *m.* pillage, plunder, marauding, foray.
pillar, *va.* to pillage, rifle, plunder, foray; (coll.) to catch, grasp, take hold of.
pillastre, pillastrón, *m.* rogue, rascal.
pillear, *va.* (coll.) to play the rascal.
pillería, *f.* gang of rogues; piece of rascality.
pillo, lla. I. *a.* roguish, knavish; shrewd, artful, sly. **II.** *n.* knave, rogue, rascal; petty thief.—**p. desorejado,** arrant rogue.
pilluelo, *m. dim.* little rogue, urchin.
pimental, *m.* pepper patch.
pimentero, *m.* pepper box; (bot.) pepper plant. —**p. falso,** (bot.) = TURBINTO, terebinth.
pimentón, *m.* large pepper; Cayenne or red pepper; paprika.
pimienta, *f.* (black) pepper (spice).—**p. de Jamaica,** pimento.—**p. de Tabasco,** myrtle. —**p. larga,** long pepper.—**p. malagueta,** myrtle.—**p. negra,** black pepper.
pimiento, *m.* (bot.) capsicum; pepper (vegetable); red or Cayenne pepper.—**p. de bonete,** large, sweet pepper.—**p. de cornetilla,** hot pepper; chili.—**p. dulce,** sweet pepper.—**p. morrón** = P. DE BONETE.—**p. picante** = P. DE CORNETILLA.
pímpido, *m.* (ichth.) a variety of dogfish.
pimpín, *m.* a child's game.
pimpina, *f.* (Venez.) large, earthenware bottle.
pimpinela, *f.* (bot.) burnet, pimpinel.
pimpleo, a, *a.* pertaining to the Muses.
pimplón, *m.* waterfall, cascade.
pimpollar, *m.* nursery of young plants.
pimpollecer, *vn.* to sprout, to bud.
pimpollejo, ico, ito, *m. dim.* tender bud, sprout, sucker, or shoot.
pimpollo, *m.* sucker, sprout, shoot; rosebud; spruce, lively youth.
pimpolludo, da, *a.* full of buds or sprouts.
pina, *f.* conical mound; felloe, rim (of a wheel).
pinabete, *m.* (bot.) fir tree and its wood.
pináceo, cea, *a.* (bot.) pinaceous.
pinacoteca, *f.* pinacotheca, picture gallery.
pináculo, *m.* pinnacle, finial, acme, summit.
pinado, da, *a.* (bot.) pinnate, pinnated.
pinar, pinarejo, *m.* pine grove.
pinariego, ga, *a.* pertaining to pines.
pinastro, *m.* wild pine.
pinatífido, da, *a.* (bot.) pinnatifid.
pinaza, *f.* (naut.) pinnace.
pincarrascal, *m.* grove of pin oaks.
pincarrasco, *m.* pin oak, swamp Spanish oak.
pincel, *m.* artist's brush; (by extension) painter, work painted, and mode of painting; second feather in a martin's wing.
pincelada, *f.* stroke with a brush, touch.
pincelar, *va.* (art) to paint, portray.
pincelero, *m.* maker or seller of artist's brushes; brush box.
pincelillo, ito, *m. dim.* fine or camel's hair brush.
pincelote, *m. aug.* coarse brush.
pincerna, *n.* one who serves drinks.
pinchadura, *f.* (coll.) puncture, pricking.
pinchar, *va.* to prick, puncture, pierce.—**no p. ni cortar,** to have little or no influence, to count for nothing.
pinchaúyas, *n.* (coll.) despicable person.
pinchazo, *m.* prick, puncture, stab.
pinche, *m.* scullion, kitchen boy.
pincho, *m.* thorn, prickle; goad; skewer; prod.
pindárico, ca, *a.* Pindaric.
pindonga, *f.* (coll.) gadabout (woman).
pindonguear, *vn.* (coll.) to gad about.
pineal, *a.* (anat.) pineal.
[1]**pineda,** *f.* braid for garters.
[2]**pineda,** *f.* pine grove.
pineno, *m.* (chem.) pinene.
pinga, *f.* (P. I.) banghy, bamboo for carrying loads.
pingajo, *m.* (coll.) rag, tatter.
pinganello, *m.* = CALAMOCO, icicle.
pinganitos.—**en p.,** *adv.* in a high position.
pingo, *m.* rag.—*pl.* worthless clothes, duds.— **andar, estar,** or **ir de p.,** to gad about.
pingorote, *m.* any pointed object.
pingorotudo, da, *a.* (coll.) high, lofty.
[1]**pingüe,** *m.* (naut.) pink.
[2]**pingüe,** *a.* fat, greasy, oily; plentiful.
pingüedinoso, sa, *a.* fatty, oleaginous.
pingüino, *m.* (ornith.) penguin.
pinguosidad, *f.* fatness.
pinífero, ra, *a.* (poet.) abounding in pines.
pinillo, *m.* (bot.) ground pine, germander.
pinípedo, da, *m.* & *a.* (zool.) pinniped.
pinita, *f.* (min., chem.) pinite.
pinitos, *m. pl. dim.* first steps.
pinjante, *m.* (jewelry) pendant; (arch.) boss.
pinnípedo, da, *n.* & *a.* = PINÍPEDO.
[1]**pino, na. I.** *a.* steep. **II.** *m.* (coll.) first step of a child or of a convalescent.
[2]**pino,** *m.* (bot.) pine.—**p. albar,** Scotch pine.— **p. alerce,** larch, tamarack, hackmatack.—**p. bravo** = P. RODENO.—**p. carrasco,** pine oak. —**p. doncel,** timber from young pines without knots.—**p. marítimo** = P. RODENO.—**p. piñonero,** stone pine.—**p. rodeno,** cluster pine, pinaster, red pine.—**p. (de) tea,** pitch pine.
pinocha, *f.* pine leaf, pine needle.
pinocho, *m.* pine cone.
pínola, *f.* detent of a repeating watch; (naut.) spindle.
pinole, *m.* aromatic powder to mix with chocolate; (Mex.) cereal meal.
pinoso, sa, *a.* piny.
[1]**pinta,** *f.* spot, mark; edge lines on Spanish cards denoting the suit; appearance, aspect; drop.— *pl.* spots on the skin in malignant fevers; basset, a card game.
[2]**pinta,** *f.* pint (measure).
pintacilgo, *m.* (ornith.) goldfinch.
pintada, *f.* (ornith.) guinea fowl.
pintadillo, *m.* (ornith.) goldfinch.
pintado, da. I. *pp.* of PINTAR. **II.** *a.* spotted, mottled; exact.—**el más p.,** (coll.) the best, cleverest.—**estar como p.,** to be just the thing. **III.** *f.* (ornith.) guinea hen.
pintamonas, *m.* (coll.) dauber.
pintar. I. *va.* to paint; picture; to stain (as glass); to dapple; to describe, portray; to fancy, imagine; to exaggerate. **II.** *vn.* to begin to ripen; to show, give signs of. **III.** *vr.* to make up (one's face).—**p. solo para,** to show great aptitude for.
pintarrajar, pintarrajear, *va.* (coll.) to daub.
pintarrajo, *m.* (coll.) daub.
pintarroja, *f.* (ichth.) = LIJA, dogfish.
pintarrojo, *m.* (ornith.) linnet.
pintica, illa, ita, *f. dim.* little spot or dot.
pintiparado, da. I. *pp.* of PINTIPARAR. **II.** *a.* perfectly like, closely resembling; apposite, fit.
pintiparar, *va.* (coll.) to compare.
pintojo, ja, *a.* spotted, stained, mottled.
pintón, na, *a.* half-ripe, beginning to ripen.
pintor, *m.* painter.—**p. de brocha gorda,** house or sign painter; dauber.
pintora, *f.* woman painter; painter's wife.
pintorcillo, *m. dim.* wretched painter or dauber.
pintoresco, ca, *a.* picturesque.
pintorreador, *m.* dauber, miserable painter.
pintorrear, *va.* to daub, paint without skill.
pintura, *f.* painting; (art) picture, painting; color, paint, pigment; portrayal, description. —**p. a la aguada,** water-color painting.—**p. al fresco,** fresco painting.—**p. al óleo,** oil

painting.—**p. al pastel,** pastel painting.—**p. al temple,** size painting.—**p. figulina,** painting on earthenware.—**hacer pinturas,** (of a horse) to cut capers.
pinturero, ra, *a.* conceitedly affected.
pínula, *f.* sight of an instrument.
pinzas, *f. pl.* nippers, pincers, tweezers; claws of lobsters, etc.; forceps; burling iron.
pinzón, *m.* (ornith.) chaffinch.
pinzote, *m.* (naut.) pintle; (naut.) whipstaff.
piña, *f.* pine cone; pineapple; cluster, gathering; pool, in billiards; (naut.) wall knot; (min.) virgin silver treated with mercury; (P. I.) a fabric made from pineapple fiber.
piñal, *m.* (Am.) pineapple plantation.
piñata, *f.* pot; suspended balloon filled with candies at a masquerade ball; children's party with refreshments.
[1]**piñón,** *m.* pine kernel; (bot.) piñon, nutpine; spring nut of a gun.
[2]**piñón,** *m.* (mech.) pinion.
[3]**piñón,** *m.* (ornith.) pinion.
piñonata, *f.* conserve of shredded almonds.
piñonate, *m.* candied pine-nut kernel.
piñoncico, *m. dim.* small pine-nut kernel.
[1]**piñoncillo,** *m. dim.* = PIÑONCICO.
[2]**piñoncillo,** *m. dim.* last joint of a wing.
piñonear, *vn.* to click (as a gun being cocked); to cry (as partridges in rut).
piñoneo, *m.* cry of partridges in rut.
piñonero, *a.* = [2]PINO P.
piñuela, *f.* figured silk; nut of cypress; (Am.) a variety of agave.
[1]**pío, a,** *a.* pious; mild, merciful.—**Antonio P.,** Antonius Pius.
[2]**pío, a,** *a.* (of horses) pied, piebald.
[3]**pío,** *m.* peeping of chickens; (coll.) longing, anxious desire.
piocha, *f.* trinket for women's headdresses; flower made of feathers.
piogenia, *f.* (med.) formation or production of pus.
piogénico, ca, *a.* (bacteriol.) pus-producing.
piohemia, *f.* (med.) = PIEMIA.
piojento, ta, *a.* lousy.
piojería, *f.* lousiness; misery, poverty.
piojillo, *m. dim.* small louse (vermin on plants and birds).
piojo, *m.* louse; a disease of hawks.—**p. pegadizo,** (coll.) crab louse; troublesome hanger-on.
piojoso, sa, *a.* lousy; mean, stingy.
piola, *f.* (naut.) housing, houseline.
pión, *m.* (phys.) pion.
pionero, ra, *n.* & *a.* pioneer.
pionía, *f.* (Venez.) bucare seeds used as beads.
piorno, *m.* (bot.) broom; (bot.) hairy Cytisus.
piorrea, *f.* (med.) pyorrhea.
[1]**pipa,** *f.* cask, butt, hogshead; tobacco pipe; reed of a clarion; (artil.) fusee.
[2]**pipa,** *f.* = PEPITA, pip of some fruits.
pipar, *vn.* to smoke a tobacco pipe.
piperáceo, a, *a.* (bot.) piperaceous.
piperacina, *f.* (chem.) piperazine.
pipería, *f.* collection of pipes or casks.
piperina, *f.* (chem.) piperin.
pípero, *m.* copper pipe or butt maker.
pipeta, *f.* pipette.
pipí, *m.* (ornith.) pitpit, honey creeper.
pipián, *m.* a kind of Indian fricassee.
pipiar, *vn.* to pule, chirp, peep.
pípila, *f.* (Mex.) hen turkey.
pipiolo, *m.* (coll.) novice, raw hand, beginner.
pipirigallo, *m.* (bot.) sainfoin, forage plant.
pipirijaina, *f.* (coll.) band of strolling players.
pipiripao, *m.* (coll.) splendid feast; reception.
pipiritaña, pipitaña, *f.* green-cane flute.
pipo, *m.* (ornith.) a small fly-eating bird.
piporro, *m.* (mus.) bassoon.
pipote, *m.* keg.—**pipotillo,** *m. dim.* small keg.
pique, *m.* pique, resentment; term in a card game; NIGUA, chigoe, a kind of flea; (naut.) crotch.—**a p.,** in danger, on the point of; sharp-cut (cliff).—**echar a p.,** (naut.) to sink (a ship).—**irse a p.,** (naut.) to founder; to fail, fall through.
[1]**piqué, pique,** *v. V.* PICAR.
[2]**piqué,** *m.* piqué, cotton fabric.
piquera, *f.* entrance hole in a hive; cockhole in a barrel; outlet of a smelting furnace; lamp burner.
piquería, *f.* body of pikemen.
piquero, *m.* (mil.) pikeman.
piqueta, *f.* pickaxe, mattock; mason's hammer.
piquete, *m.* slight wound from a sharp tool; (sewing) small hole in a garment; stake, picket or piquet; picket (as a striker, protester, etc.); (mil.) picket.
piquetero, *m.* (min.) pick or mattock carrier.
piquetilla, *f. dim.* bricklayer's hammer.
piquillo, *m. dim.* small beak or bill; small amount.
piquituerto, *m.* (ornith.) crossbill, picarin.
pira, *f.* funeral pile, pyre.
piragón, *m.* = PIRAUSTA.
piragua, *f.* (naut.) pirogue, canoe; vine.
piragüero, *m.* canoeist.
piral, *m.* = PIRAUSTA.
piramidal, *a.* pyramidal.
piramidalmente, *adv.* pyramidally.
pirámide, *f.* pyramid.
pirargirita, *f.* (min.) pyrargyrite.
pirata. I. *a.* piratical. **II.** *m.* pirate; cruel wretch.
piratear, *vn.* to pirate, practice piracy.
piratería, *f.* piracy; robbery.
pirático, ca, *a.* piratical.
pirausta, *f.* fabulous firefly.
pirca, *f.* (S. A.) dry-stone wall.
pircar, *va.* to surround with a PIRCA.
pirco, *m.* (S. A.) a kind of succotash.
pirenaico, ca, *a.* Pyrenean.
pirético, ca, *a.* (med.) pyretic, pert. to fever.
piretología, *f.* (med.) pyretology.
pirex, *m.* Pyrex (trademark).
pirexia, *f.* (med.) pyrexia, feverish condition.
pírico, ca, *a.* pertaining to fireworks.
pirídico, ca, *a.* (chem.) pyridic.
piridina, *f.* (chem.) pyridine.
piriforme, *a.* pyriform, pear-shaped.
pirimetamina, *f.* (pharm.) pyrimethamine.
pirineo, a, *a.* Pyrenean.
pirita, *f.* (min.) pyrites.
piritoso, sa, *a.* pyritous, containing pyrites.
pirocloro, *m.* (chem.) pyrochlore.
pirofilacio, *m.* subterraneous fire.
piróforo, *m.* (chem.) pyrophore.
pirofosfato, *m.* (chem.) pyrophosphate.
pirofosfórico, ca, *a.* (chem.) pyrophosphoric.
pirogálico, ca, *a.* (chem.) pyrogallic.
pirógeno, na, *a.* pyrogenous, pyrogenic.
pirograbado, *m.* pyrography; pyrogravure.
pirólatra, *n.* pyrolater, fire worshipper.
pirolatría, *f.* pyrolatry, fire worship.
piroleñoso, sa, *a.* pyroligneous.
pirólisis, *f.* (chem.) pyrolysis.
pirolusita, *f.* (min.) pyrolusite.
piromagnético, ca, *a.* pyromagnetic.
piromancía, *f.* pyromancy.
piromanía, *f.* pyromania.
piromántico, ca, *a.* pyromantic.
pirometalurgia, *f.* pyrometallurgy.
pirómetro, *m.* pyrometer.
piromorfita, *f.* (min.) pyromorphite.
pironomia, *f.* pyronomy.
piropear, *va.* & *vn.* (coll.) to pay compliments.
piropo, *m.* a variety of garnet; carbuncle; (coll.) compliment, flattery.
piroscopio, *m.* (phys.) pyroscope.
pirosfera, *f.* (geol.) pyrosphere.
pirosis, *f.* (med.) pyrosis, heartburn.
pirostato, *m.* (phys.) pyrostat.
pirotecnia, *f.* pyrotechnics.
pirotécnico, ca, *a.* pyrotechnical.
piroxena, *f.* (min.) pyroxene.
piroxénico, ca, *a.* pyroxenic.

piroxenita, *f.* (geol.) pyroxenite.
piroxeno, *m.* (min.) pyroxene.
piroxilina, *f.* pyroxyline.
pirquén.—al p., (Chile) at will, without restrictions (said of the right to work a leased mine).
pirquinear, *vn.* (Chile) to work a leased mine without imposed restrictions.
pirraniano, na, pírrico, ca, *a.* pyrrhic.
pirriquio, *m.* (pros.) pyrrhic.
pirrónico, ca, *a.* Pyrrhonic; skeptic.
pirronismo, *m.* Pyrrhonism.
pirueta, *f.* pirouette, gyration.
piruétano, *m.* (bot.) wild pear tree.
piruetear, *vn.* to pirouette.
pirúvico, ca, *a.* (chem.) pyruvic.
pisa, *f.* tread, treading; portion of olives or grapes pressed at once.
pisada, *f.* footstep; footprint; stepping on someone's foot.—**seguir las pisadas de**, (fig.) to follow in the footsteps of, follow the example of.
pisador, ra. I. *n.* & *a.* prancer(-ing); high-stepper(-ing). **II.** *n.* treader of grapes.
pisadura, *f.* act of treading; footstep.
pisapapeles, *m.* paper weight.
pisar, *va.* to tread on, trample, step on; to press; to press on; to ram; to cover; to lie over; (of birds) to cover (the female).
pisasfalto, *m.* mixture of bitumen and pitch.
pisaúvas, *n.* treader of grapes.
pisaverde, *m.* (coll.) fop, coxcomb, dude.
piscator, *m.* almanac with meteorol. forecasts.
piscatorio, ria, *a.* piscatory, pertaining to fish or fishing.
piscicultor, ra, *n.* & *a.* pisciculturist(-ic).
piscicultura, *f.* pisciculture, fish culture.
pisciforme, *a.* pisciform, fish-shaped.
piscina, *f.* fishpond; swimming pool (also **p. de natación**); (eccl.) piscina.
Piscis, *m.* (astr.) Pisces, zodiacal sign.
piscívoro, ra, *a.* piscivorous, fish-eating.
piscolabis, *m.* (coll.) luncheon, a bite.
piso, *m.* floor; pavement, flooring; story or floor; loft, flat, apartment; ground level; tread, footing, walking; (min.) level works; (geol.) stage, formation.—**p. bajo**, ground floor.—**p. principal**, second floor, first living floor (in apartment houses, etc.).
pisolita, *f.* (min.) pisolite.
pisón, *m.* rammer; paver's beetle.
pisonear, *va.* to ram.
pisotear, *va.* to trample, tread under foot.
pisoteo, *m.* trampling, treading under foot.
pisotón, *m. aug.* heavy step on someone's foot.
pista, *f.* trail, track, scent; trace, clue; racetrack, race course.—**p. de aterrizaje**, (aer.) landing strip, airstrip.—**p. de patinar**, skating rink.
pistachero, pistacho, *m.* pistachio.
pistadero, *m.* pestle for pounding.
pistar, *va.* to pound with a pestle.
pistero, *m.* feeding cup with tubular nozzle.
pistilado, da, *a.* (bot.) pistillate.
pistilo, *m.* (bot.) pistil.
pisto, *m.* chicken broth for the sick; dish of tomatoes and red pepper.
pistola, *f.* pistol.—**p. ametralladora**, submachine gun.—**p. automática**, burp gun.—**p. de arzón**, horse pistol.
pistolera, *f.* holster.
pistolero, *m.* pistoleer, gunman.
pistoletazo, *m.* pistol shot.—**dar un p.**, to shoot with a pistol.
pistolete, *m.* pistolet, pocket pistol.
pistón, *m.* (mech.) piston; (artil.) percussion cap, primer; (mus.) piston of a brass instrument.
pistoresa, *f.* short dagger.
pistraje, pistraque, *m.* unpleasant beverage.
pistura, *f.* pounding, pestling.
pita, *f.* (bot.) pita; agave; maguey (used vaguely with diff. meanings in diff. countries. The pita proper produces the best fiber.); string, cord.
pitaco, *m.* stem of the maguey.
pitada, *f.* blow of a whistle.
pitagórico, ca, *a.* & *n.* Pythagorean.
pitahaya, *f.* (bot.) pitahaya.
pitancería, *f.* distribution or place of distribution of alms; almsgiving.
pitancero, *m.* distributor of alms; (eccl.) steward or purveyor; superintendent of a choir.
pitancica, illa, ita, *f. dim.* small pittance.
pitanza, *f.* pittance, alms; (coll.) daily food; price, salary, stipend.
pitaña, *f.* = LEGAÑA, gummy secretion of eyes.
pitañoso, sa, *a.* = LEGAÑOSO, blear-eyed.
[1]**pitar. I.** *vn.* (of a whistle) to blow. **II.** *va.* to discharge (a debt).
[2]**pitar**, *va.* to distribute alms to.
pitarra, *f.* bleareduess.
pitarroso, sa, *a.* = PITAÑOSO.
pitazo, *m.* sound or blast of a whistle.
pitecántropo, *m.* (paleontol.) pithecanthropus.
pitezna, *f.* spring of a trap.
pitido, *m.* whistle (of a pipe or of birds).
pitillera, *f.* woman cigarette maker; cigarette case.
pitillo, *m.* cigarette.
pítima, *f.* (pharm.) saffron plaster; (coll.) drunkenness.
pitio, tia, *a.* Pythian.
pitío, *m.* whistling of a pipe or of birds.
pitipié, *m.* scale (on a map, drawing, etc.).
pitiriasis, *f.* (med.) pityriasis.
pitirre, *m.* (ornith.) pitirri, gray kingbird.
[1]**pito**, *m.* whistle; catcall; fife; fifer; (Am.) tick; jackstone (toy); cocoon open at one end.—**pitos flautos**, frivolous pastimes.—**no me importa**, or **no se me da, un p.**, I don't care a straw.—**no tocar pitos en**, to have no part in.—**no valer un p.**, not to be worth a straw.
[2]**pito**, *m.* (ornith.) woodpecker.
pitoflero, ra, *n.* (coll.) musician of no account; gossip (person).
[1]**pitón**, *m.* (zool.) python.
[2]**pitón**, *m.* (of deer, etc.) horn just starting to grow; protuberance, lump; spout, nozzle; sprig or shoot of a tree; sprout of the agave.
pitonisa, *f.* Pythia, Pythoness; witch, sorceress.
pitorra, *f.* (ornith.) woodcock.
pitpit, *m.* (ornith.) pitpit, guitguit.
pitreo, *m.* = PITACO.
pituita, *f.* pituitary (extract).—**pituitario, ria**, *a.* pituitary.—**pituitoso, sa**, *a.* with copious pituitary.
piuquén, *m.* (ornith.) a large Chilean bird similar to the wild turkey.
piuria, *f.* (med.) pyuria.
pivote, *m.* (mech.) king pin.
píxide, *f.* (eccl.) pyx, pix.
pixidio, *m.* (bot.) pyxidium.
piyama, *m.* pijama. Also PIJAMA.
pizarra, *f.* (min.) slate shale; slate (for writing); blackboard.—**pizarral**, *m.* slate quarry.
pizarreño, ña, *a.* slate-colored, slatey.
pizarrero, *m.* slater, slate cutter; roofer.
pizarrín, *m.* slate pencil.
pizarrón, *m.* (Am.) blackboard.
pizarroso, sa, *a.* abounding in slate.
pizate, *m.* (bot.) saltwort.
pizca, *f.* (coll.) mite, bit, speck, crumb, whit.
pizcar, *va.* (coll.) to pinch; (Mex.) to glean (maize).
pizco, *m.* (coll.) pinch.
pizmiento, ta, *a.* pitch-colored.
pizpereta, pizpireta, *a.* smart, brisk, lively.
pizpirigaña, *f.* a boys' game.
pizpita, *f.*; **pizpitillo**, *m.* (ornith.) wagtail.
placa, *f.* star, insignia of an order of knighthood; (photog.) dry plate; (mech.) plate; (art) plaque; (Mex.) baggage check.—**p. giratoria, (Ry.)** turning plate, turntable.
placabilidad, *f.* placability.
placable, *a.* placable.
placativo, va, *a.* placatory.
placear, *va.* to sell (provisions) at retail
placel, *m.* (naut.) sand bank, key.
pláceme, *m.* congratulation.

placenta, *f.* (anat., bot.) placenta.
placentación, *f.* (bot.) placentation.
placentario, ria. I. *a.* (zool.) placental, placentate. II. *m.* (zool.) placental.
placenteramente, *adv.* joyfully, merrily.
placentero, ra, *a.* joyful, merry, pleasant.
[1]**placer.** I. *va.* (*ind. pres.* PLAZCO, *pret.* él PLUGO or PLACIÓ; *subj. pres.* yo PLAZCA, él PLEGUE or PLAZCA, *imp.* yo PLACIERA, él PLUGUIERA or PLACIERA, etc.) to please, gratify, humor, content.—**que me place,** it gives me pleasure; with pleasure. II. *m.* pleasure.—**a p., at one's** convenience.
[2]**placer,** *m.* (naut.) sand bank, key; (min.) placer; (Am.) pearl fishing.
placero, ra. I. *a.* pertaining to the marketplace. II. *n.* marketer, seller at a market; gadabout.
placeta, tilla, tuela, *f. dim.* small (town) square.
placibilidad, *f.* agreeableness.
placible, *a.* placid; agreeable.
plácidamente, *adv.* placidly.
placidez, *f.* placidity, tranquility, serenity.
plácido, da, *a.* placid, quiet, calm.
placiente, *a.* pleasing, agreeable, pleasant.
placoideo, dea, *a.* (ichth., zool.) placoid.
plafón, *m.* (arch.) soffit of an architrave.
[1]**plaga,** *f.* plague; calamity; scourge; epidemic; affliction; pest; plenty, superabundance, drug in the market (originally of injurious things, now improperly used of anything).
[2]**plaga,** *f.* climate, country; zone; (naut.) cardinal point of compass.
plagado, da. I. *pp.* of PLAGAR. II. *a.* full; smitten.
plagal, *a.* (mus.) plagal.
plagar. I. *va.* (*pret.* PLAGUÉ; *subj.* PLAGUE) to plague, infest. II. *vr.* **(de)** to be overrun (with), or full (of).
plagiar, *va.* to plagiarize; (Am.) to kidnap.
plagiario, ria, *n.* & *a.* plagiarizer(-ing).
plagio, *m.* plagiarism; (Am.) kidnapping.
plagioclasa, *f.* (min.) plagioclase.
plagióstomos, *m. pl.* (zool.) Plagiostomi, plagiostomes.
plagué, plague, *v. V.* PLAGAR.
plan, *m.* plan; design, scheme; plan, drawing; description, specification; (naut.) floor timber. —**p. de estudios,** (school) curriculum.
plana, *f.* page; copy; level ground, plain; record; (mason.) trowel; (print.) page.—**p. mayor,** (mil.) staff.—**enmendar la p. a,** to find fault with, criticize; to excel, do better than.
planada, *f.* plain, level ground.
planador, *m.* one who smooths, finishes metal.
plancton, *m.* (zool., bot.) plankton.
plancha, *f.* plate, sheet; slab; iron, flatiron; tailor's goose; cramp iron; (paper) mold; cloth plate of a sewing machine; horizontal suspension (in gymnastics); (coll.) "break," "boner"; (naut.) gangplank, gangboard.—**p. de agua,** (naut.) punt, floating stage.—**p. de blindaje,** armor plate.—**p. de viento,** (naut.) hanging stage.
planchada, *f.* (naut.) apron of a gun.
planchado, *m.* ironing; linen ironed or for ironing.
planchador, ra, *n.* ironer.
planchar, *va.* to iron, to press (clothes).
planchear, *va.* to plate, cover with metal sheets.
plancheta, *f.* (surv.) plane table.
planchita, *f. dim.* small plate.
planchón, *m. aug.* large plate.
planchuela, *f. dim.* small plate; fluting iron.
planeador, *m.* (aer.) glider.
planear. I. *va.* & *vn.* to plan, design. II. *vn.* (aer.) to glide.—**planeo,** *m.* (aer.) gliding.
planeta. I. *m.* (astr.) planet. II. *f.* (eccl.) planeta.
planetario, ria. I. *a.* planetary. II. *m.* planetarium, orrery; astronomer.
planetícola, *n.* inhabitant of a planet.
planetoide, *m.* (astr.) planetoid.
planga, *f.* (ornith.) gannet; a kind of sea eagle.
planicie, *f.* = LLANURA, a plain.
planificado, da, *a.*—**economía p.,** planned economy.
planilla, *f.* (Am.) list (of expenses, etc.); (Am.) list of employees, payroll; (Mex.) list of candidates, ticket.
planimetría, *f.* plane surveying.
planímetro, *m.* planimeter.
planisferio, *m.* planisphere.
plano, na. I. *a.* plane; level; smooth, even. II. *m.* plan (drawing); map; flat (of a sword, etc.); (geom.) plane; (aer.) plane, wing.—**p. acotado,** contour map or chart.—**p. de cota cero,** (topog.) datum plane.—**p. de deriva,** (aer.) tail plane, stabilizer.—**p. de nivel,** (topog.) datum plane.—**p. de proyección,** plane of projection.—**p. de prueba,** (elec.) proof plane. —**p. de referencia,** (topog.) datum plane.—**p. focal,** (opt.) focal plane.—**p. geométrico,** ground plane, geometric plane.—**p. inclinado,** inclined plane.—**p. panorámico,** pictorial map.—**p. vertical,** vertical plane.—**p. visual,** plane of sight.—**ángulo p.,** plane angle.—**primer p.,** foreground.—**de p.,** openly, clearly; flatly, on its side.—**levantar un p.,** (surv.) to survey, make a survey.
planocóncavo, va, *a.* plano-concave.
planoconvexo, xa, *a.* plano-convex.
planta, *f.* sole of the foot; (bot.) plant; plantation, nursery of young plants; (eng.) plan, horizontal projection, top view; plant, works; site of a building; (fencing and dance) position of the feet; project; disposition.—**p. baja, ground** floor.—**plantas forrajeras,** fodder plants, forage plants.—**buena p.,** fine physique.—**echar plantas,** to brag, boast.
plantación, *f.* plantation; planting.
plantado, da, *pp.* of PLANTAR.—**dejarlo a uno p.,** (Am.) to leave one in the lurch.
plantador, ra, *n.* planter (person or machine).
plantagináceo, cea, *a.* (bot.) plantaginaceous.
plantaina, *f.* (bot.) plantain, ribwort.
plantaje, *m.* collection of plants.
plantar. I. *va.* (agr.) to plant; to erect, set up, fix upright; to strike (a blow); to set, put; place; to pose (as a question, a problem); to found, establish; (coll.) to leave in the lurch, disappoint; to jilt. II. *vr.* (coll.) to stand upright; to reach, arrive; to stop, halt, balk; in some games, to stand pat. III. *a.* (anat.) plantar.
plantario, *m.* (agr.) nursery.
planteamiento, *m.* putting into execution.
plantear, *va.* to plan, try; to put into action; to state or tackle (a problem); to raise (an issue).
plantel, *m.* nursery, nursery garden; educational institution.
planteo, *m.* statement (as of a problem); execution, performance.
plantificación, *f.* putting into execution.
plantificar, *va.* to put into execution; (coll.) to land (as a blow).
plantígrado, da, *a.* plantigrade.
plantilla, *f. dim.* young plant; (shoemaking) first sole, insole; (mech.) template, templet, model, pattern; plate of a gunlock; (med.) plaster for the feet; (astr.) celestial configuration; (P. R.) lady finger.
plantillar, *va.* to sole (shoes or stockings).
plantío, ía. I. *a.* (of land) planted, or ready to be planted. II. *m.* plantation; planting; garden bed.
plantista, *m.* landscape gardener; bully, hector, bravado.
plantón, *m.* scion, sprout or shoot to be transplanted; shoot ingrafted on a stock; (coll.) long wait standing; (mil.) sentry doing long guard; doorkeeper, watchman.—**estar de p.,** to be fixed in a place for a long time.—**llevar un p.,** to dance attendance.
planudo, da, *a.* (naut.) flat-bottomed.
plañidero, ra. I. *a.* mournful, weeping, moaning. II. *f.* weeper, hired mourner.

plañido, *m.* moan, lamentation, crying.
plañir, *vn.* (*ger.* PLAÑENDO; *pret.* el PLAÑÓ) to lament, grieve, bewail; to whimper, whine.
•**plaqué,** *m.* plate, plating; plated ware.
plaqueta, *f.* (physiol.) platelet, blood platelet.
plaquín, *m.* loose coat of mail, hauberk.
[1]**plasma,** *m.* (biol.) plasma.
[2]**plasma,** *f.* (min.) = PRASMA, dark green agate.
plasmador, ra, *n.* maker, molder.
plasmagene, *m.* (biol.) plasmagene.
plasmante. I. *a.* molding, shaping. **II.** *n.* molder, shaper.
plasmar, *va.* to mold, shape.
plasmático, ca, *a.* (biol.) plasmic.
plasmodio, *m.* (biol.) plasmodium.
plasmón, *m.* (genet.) plasmon.
plasmosoma, *m.* (biol.) plasmosome.
plasta, *f.* anything soft (as dough, mud, etc.); anything flattened; (coll.) anything poorly done.
plaste, *m.* size or filler made of glue and lime.
plastecer, *va.* (*ind.* PLASTEZCO; *subj.* PLASTEZCA) to size, to besmear with size.
plastecido, *m.* (art) sizing.
plástica, *f.* art of molding in clay.
plasticidad, *f.* plasticity.
plástico, ca. I. *a.* plastic; soft. **II.** *m.* plastic.
plastrón, *m.* (fencing) plastron; large cravat; leather apron.
plata, *f.* silver; silver coin; money; plate, wrought silver; (her.) plate; white.—**p. agria,** (min.) black silver, stephanite.—**p. alemana,** German silver.—**p. córnea,** (min.) cerargyrite.—**p. piña,** (min.) spongy silver.—**p. gris,** silver glance, argentite.—**p. labrada,** silverware.—**p. roja,** (min.) pyrargyrite, red silver ore.—**p. virgen,** native silver.—**como una p.,** very clean and pretty.—**en p.,** in plain language; briefly, in a word.—**quedarse sin p.,** to be penniless, "broke."
plataforma, *f.* platform; terrace; (mach.) index plate, division plate; (fort.) platform; (naut.) orlop; (Ry.) roadbed.—**p. continental,** (geol.) continental shelf.—**p. de lanzamiento,** (astronaut.) launching pad, launching platform.—**p. espacial,** (astronaut.) space platform.
platal, *m.* mint, (U. S., slang) pile, a lot of money.
platanáceo, cea, *a.* = PLATÁNEO.
platanal, platanar, *m.* plantain or banana plantation.
platáneo, a, *a.* (bot.) plantanaceous.
plátano, *m.* (bot.) plantain; banana (plant and fruit); plane tree.—**p. falso,** sycamore maple.—**p. guineo,** guineo; (Cuba) banana.
platazo, *m. aug.* platter; dishful.
platea, *f.* (theat.) orchestra, parquet; pit.
plateado, da, *pp.* & *a.* silvered; silverplated.
plateador, *m.* plater, silverer.
plateadura, *f.* silvering, silver plating.
platear, *va.* to silver, silverplate.
platel, *m.* platter; tray.
platelminto, ta. I. *a.* (zool.) platyhelminthic. **II.** *m.* platyhelminth; *pl.* Platyhelminthes.
plateresco, ca, *a.* (arch.) plateresque.
platería, *f.* silversmith's shop or trade.
platero, *m.* silversmith; jeweller.—**p. de oro,** goldsmith.
plática, *f.* talk, chat, conversation; address, lecture; sermon.—**platicar,** *vn.* (*pret.* PLATIQUÉ; *subj.* PLATIQUE) to converse, talk, chat.
platija, *f.* (ichth.) plaice, flounder.
platilla, *f.* Silesian linen.
platillo, *m. dim.* small dish; saucer; beef stew; extra dish in convents; pan (of a balance); (mus.) cymbal; disk or valve of a chain pump.—**p. de Petri,** (biol.) Petri dish.—**p. volante** or **volador,** flying saucer.
[1]**platina,** *f.* (mech.) plate, platen; (print.) platen, bedplate; imposing table; (phys.) slide (of microscope); plate (of air pump).
[2]**platina,** *f.* (min.) ore of platinum.
platinado, da. I. *pp.* of PLATINAR. **II.** *m.* platinum plating.
platinar, *va.* to platinize.
platínico, ca, *a.* (chem.) platinic.
platinífero, ra, *a.* platiniferous, platinum-bearing.
platinirideo, *m.* platiniridium.
platino, *m.* platinum.
platinoide, *m.* platinoid.
platinotipia, *f.* platinotype.
platiqué, platique, *v. V.* PLATICAR.
platirrino, na, *n.* & *a.* (zool.) platyrrhine.
plato, *m.* dish, plate; (cook.) dish, mess, course, food served in a dish; daily fare; pan (of a balance); (arch.) metope.—**p. de segunda mesa,** makeshift, second-hand, cast off; (fig.) second fiddle.—**p. sopero,** soup plate.—**nada entre dos platos,** much ado about nothing.—**no quebrar un p.,** to be innocent or harmless.
platónicamente, *adv.* Platonically.
platónico, ca. I. *a.* Platonist; Platonic. **II.** *n.* Platonist.
platonismo, *m.* Platonism.
platudo, da, *a.* (Am. coll.) rich, moneyed.
platuja, *f.* (ichth.) = PLATIJA.
plausibilidad, *f.* plausibility.
plausible, *a.* plausible.
plausiblemente, *adv.* plausibly.
plausivo, va, *a.* plausive, praising, laudatory.
plauso, *m.* applause.
plaustro, *m.* (poet.) cart, wagon, carriage.
plautino, na, *a.* Plautine, relating to Plautus.
playa, *f.* shore, strand, sea coast, beach.
playado, da, *a.* having a beach; beachy.
playazo, *m.* wide or extended shore.
playeras, *f. pl.* a popular Andalusian song.
playero, ra, *n.* fisherman; fishwoman.
playón, *m. aug.* large shore or beach.
playuela, *f. dim.* small beach or shore.
plaza, *f.* plaza, square; market place; (com.) emporium, market; room, space, stall; office, position, employment; reputation, character, fame.—**p. de armas,** (mil.) parade ground.—**p. de toros,** bull ring, arena.—**p. fuerte,** (fort.) stronghold, fortress.—**¡p., p.!** clear the way! make room!—**pasar p. de,** to be reputed (something that one is not).—**sacar a p.,** to publish, make public.—**sentar p.,** (mil.) to enlist.
plazo, *m.* term, time, date, day of payment; installment; credit; duelling ground.—**a largo p.,** long-term, long-range.—**a p.,** on credit.
plazoleta, plazuela, *f. dim.* small square.
ple, *m.* a handball game.
pleamar, *f.* (naut.) high water, high tide.
plébano, *m.* curate of a parish.
plebe, *f.* common people, plebs, populace.
plebeyez, *f.* plebeianism.
plebeyo, ya, *n.* & *a.* plebeian.
plebiscitario, ria, *a.* pert. to plebiscite.
plebiscito, *m.* plebiscitum; (pol.) plebiscite.
pleca, *f.* (print.) straight line, rule.
plectro, *m.* plectrum, for stringed instruments.
plegable, *a.* pliable, folding.
plegadamente, *adv.* confusedly.
plegadera, *f.* (bookbinding) folder.
plegadizo, za, *a.* pliable; folding.
plegado, *m.* plaiting; folding.
plegador, ra. I. *a.* folding. **II.** *n.* folder, plaiter. **III.** *f.* plaiting machine, folding machine; beam of a silk loom.
plegadura, *f.* plait, fold; plaiting, folding, doubling; crease.
plegar. I. *va.* (*ind.* PLIEGO; *subj.* PLIEGUE) to fold; to plait, double; to do up; to turn (the warp) on the yarn beam; (sewing) to plait, pucker, gather, crease. **II.** *vr.* to fold; to bend; to submit, yield.
plegaria, *f.* prayer, supplication; noon prayers.
plegue, *v. V.* PLACER.
pleguete, *m.* (bot.) tendril of a vine.
pleistoceno, na, *m.* & *a.* (geol.) Pleistocene.
pleita, *f.* plaited strand of bass.
pleiteador, ra, *n.* pleader; wrangler.

pleiteante, *n.* & *a.* litigator(-ing, -ant), pleader(-ing).
pleitear, *vn.* to plead, litigate; to wrangle.
pleitista, *m.* pettifogger.
pleito, *m.* lawsuit: litigation; proceedings in a case; dispute, contest, debate, strife.—**p. de acreedores,** proceedings under a commission of bankruptcy.—**poner p. (a),** to sue, bring suit (against).—**ver un p.,** (law) to try a case.
plenamar, *f.* = PLEAMAR.
plenamente, *adv.* fully, completely.
plenariamente, *adv.* completely, fully; (law) plenarily.
plenario, ria, *a.* complete, full; (law) plenary.
plenilunio, *m.* full moon.
plenipotencia, *f.* plenipotence, full powers.
plenipotenciario, ria, *n.* & *a.* plenipotentiary.
plenitud, *f.* plenitude, fullness, abundance.
pleno, na. I. *a.* full, complete; broad (*en p. día,* in broad daylight). II. *m.* plenum, joint (session).—**en p.,** in the middle of (winter, etc.).
pleonasmo, *m.* (rhet.) pleonasm, redundancy.
pleonásticamente, *adv.* pleonastically.
pleonástico, ca, *a.* pleonastic, redundant.
plepa, *f.* (coll.) bother; person full of defects.
plesímetro, *m.* (med.) pleximeter.
plesiosauro, *m.* (paleontol.) plesiosaur.
pletina, *f.* small iron plate.
pletismógrafo, *m.* (physiol.) plethysmograph.
plétora, *f.* plethora; superabundance, inflation.
pletórico, ca, *a.* plethoric.
pleura, *f.* (anat.) pleura.
pleural, *a.* pleural.
pleuresía, *f.* (med.) pleurisy.—**p. falsa,** pleurodynia.
pleurítico, ca, *a.* pleuritic(al).
pleuritis, *f.* (med.) pleurisy.
pleurodinia, *f.* pleurodynia, stitch in the side.
pleurodonto, ta, *m.* & *a.* (zool.) pleurodont.
pleuronecto, ta, *m.* & *a.* (ichth.) pleuronectid.
pleuroneumonía, *f.* (med., vet.) pleuropneumonia.
pleurotomía, *f.* (surg.) pleurotomy.
plexiglás, *m.* Plexiglas (trademark).
plexo, *m.* (anat. and bot.) plexus; network.
Pléyadas, Pléyades, *f. pl.* (astr.) Pleiades.
plica, *f.* (law) escrow; (med.) matted condition of hair; plica.
[1]**pliego,** *m.* sheet (of paper); sealed envelope or package containing papers.—**p. de condiciones,** specifications; tender, bid.
[2]**pliego,** [1]**pliegue,** *v. V.* PLEGAR.
[2]**pliegue,** *m.* fold, plait, crease; (sewing) gather.
plieguecillo, *m. dim.* half sheet; small plait.
plinto, *m.* (arch.) plinth of a pillar.
plioceno, na, *m.* & *a.* (geol.) Pliocene.
ploidia, *f.* (genet.) ploidy.
plomada, *f.* artificer's lead pencil; plumb, plumb bob, plummet; (naut.) lead for sounding; fishing-net sinker; scourge with lead balls.
plomar, *va.* to put a leaden seal on.
plomazón, *f.* gilding cushion.
plombagina, *f.* plumbago, graphite.
plomería, *f.* lead roofing; leadware shop; plumbing.
plomero, ra, *n.* plumber.
plomizo, za, *a.* plumbeous; lead-colored.
plomo, *m.* lead (metal); piece of lead; plumb bob, plummet; bullet; (coll.) dull person, bore.—**p. derretido,** molten lead.—**andar con pies de p.,** to proceed with the utmost caution.—**a p.,** true, plumb.—**caer a p.,** to fall down flat.
plomoso, sa, *a.* = PLOMIZO.
pluguiera, *v. V.* PLACER.
pluma, *f.* feather; plume, down; quill; writing pen; penmanship; writer; style; (coll.) air expelled from the bowels.—**p. de agua,** a variable measure of running water (0.025 liter per second in some parts of Spain).—**p. fuente,** fountain pen.—**p. viva,** eider down.—**al correr de la p., a vuela p.,** written in haste.
plumado, da. I. *a.* plumy, feathered, feathery. II. *f.* brief writing; pen stroke, flourish.
plumaje, *m.* plumage; plume, crest.
plumajería, *f.* plumage; feather working.
plumajero, ra, *n.* plumist, feather dresser.
plumario, ria. I. *n.* plumist, plume worker. II. *a.* pertaining to plume or feather work.
plumazo, *m.* feather mattress or pillow.
plumazón, *f.* plumage.
plumbado, da, *a.* sealed with a leaden seal.
plumbagina, *f.* = PLOMBAGINA.
plumbagináceo, cea; plumbagíneo, nea, *a.* (bot.) plumbaginaceous.
plúmbeo, bea, *a.* leaden, plumbeous.
plúmbico, ca, *a.* (chem.) plumbic.
plumeado, *m.* (art) lines in miniature painting.
plumear, *va.* (art) to shade with a liner.
plúmeo, a, *a.* plumose, feathered, plumed.
plumería, *f.* plumosity; plumage.
plumero, *m.* feather duster; box for feathers or plumes; plumage; aigret, panache.
plumífero, ra, *a.* feathered.
plumilla, *f. dim.* small feather or plume; (print.) script type; (bot.) plumule.
plumión, *m.* = PLUMÓN.
plumista, *n.* notary; plume-maker.
plumita, *f. dim.* small feather or pen.
plumón, *m.* down, feather bed; (ornith.) plumule.
plumoso, sa, *a.* plumy, feathered.
plúmula, *f.* (bot.) plumule.
plural, *n.* & *a.* plural.
pluralidad, *f.* plurality; majority.—**a p. de votos,** by a majority of votes.
pluralismo, *m.* pluralism.
pluralizar, *va.* to pluralize.
plus, *m.* (mil.) extra pay; bonus; extra.
pluscuamperfecto, *m.* (gram.) pluperfect.
plus minusve, (Lat.) more or less, about.
plúteo, *m.* library shelf.
plutocracia, *f.* plutocracy.
plutócrata, *n.* plutocrat.
plutocrático, ca, *a.* plutocratic.
plutoniano, na, *n.* & *a.* Plutonian.
plutónico, ca, *a.* (geol.) Plutonic.
plutonio, *m.* plutonium.
plutonismo, *m.* (geol.) Plutonism.
plutonista, *m.* (geol.) Plutonist.
pluvial, *a.* pluvial, rainy.
pluvímetro, *m.* = PLUVIÓMETRO.
pluviógrafo, *m.* registering rain gauge.
pluviométrico, ca, *a.* pluviometric.
pluviómetro, *m.* rain gauge.
pluvioso, sa, *a.* rainy, pluvious.
poa, *f.* (naut.) bowline bridle.
pobeda, *f.* plantation of poplars.
población, *f.* population; populating; city, town, village.
poblacho, poblachón, *m.* ugly village.
poblado, da. I. *pp.* of POBLAR. II. *a.* populated, inhabited. III. *m.* town, village, settlement.
poblador, ra. I. *a.* settling, founding; establishing. II. *n.* settler, founder; establisher.
poblar. I. *va.* & *vn.* (*ind.* PUEBLO; *subj.* PUEBLE to populate, people, colonize, settle; to inhabit; to stock: to breed fast. III. *vr.* to bud, leaf.
poblazo, *m.* large ugly village.
poblezuelo, *m. dim.* small village.
pobo, *m.* (bot.) white poplar.
pobre. I. *a.* poor; needy; barren; humble, modest; trifling, paltry, unimportant.—**p. de espíritu,** poor in spirit.—**¡p. de mí!** poor me!—**p. diablo,** poor devil.—**gas p.,** producer gas. II. *n.* poor person; pauper, beggar.—**p. de solemnidad,** poor person in real distress.
pobrecico, ca; illo, lla; ito, ta, *a.* & *n. dim.* poor little thing.
pobremente, *adv.* poorly, miserably, needily.
pobrería, *f.* poor people, beggars.
pobrero, ra, *n.* distributor of alms.
pobreta, *f.* (coll.) strumpet, prostitute.

pobrete, ta, *n. dim.* poor person.—**pobretear,** *vn.* to pretend poverty.—**pobretería,** *f.* poor people; beggars; poverty; niggardliness.
pobretón, na, *a. aug.* very poor.
pobreza, *f.* poverty; sterility, barrenness; vow of poverty; lowness or pettiness of spirit.
pobrezuelo, la, *a. dim.* rather poor.
pobrismo, *m.* pauperism; beggars.
pócar, póker, *m.* (Angl.) (Am.) poker (card game).
pocero, *m.* well borer or sinker; sewerman; (min.) pitman.
pocilga, *f.* pigsty, pigpen; dirty place.
pocillo, *m. dim.* vessel sunk in the ground in oil mills; chocolate cup.
pócima, *f.* potion, draught, medicinal tea.
poción, *f.* drink, draught; (pharm.) potion.
poco, ca. I. *a.* little; scanty, limited; small.—*pl.* few, some.—**a pocos lances,** in a short time.—**de p. tiempo acá,** lately, of late. **II.** *m.* a little, a bit, a small quantity.—**a p. de,** shortly after.—**un p. de,** a little, some (foll. by noun).—**unos pocos,** a few, some. **III.** *adv.* little, in a small degree; a short time.—**p. a p.** little by little, gradually, slowly.—**p. después,** shortly afterwards.—**p. más o menos,** more or less.—**a p.,** immediately; shortly afterwards; presently.—**dentro de p.,** in a short time, soon.—**de p. más o menos,** of little account.—**por p.,** almost, nearly.—**tener en p.,** to set little value on, to think little of.
póculo, *m.* drinking cup or glass.
pocho, cha, *a.* (coll.) discolored, faded.
poda, *f.* pruning, lopping; pruning season.
podadera, *f.* pruning knife, hook; hedging bill.
podador, ra, *n.* pruner.
podagra, *f.* gout in the feet.
podar, *va.* to prune, head, lop, trim.
podazón, *f.* pruning season.
podenco, *m.* hound (dog).
poder. I. *va.* & *vn.* (*ger.* PUDIENDO; *ind. pres.* PUEDO, *pret.* PUDE, *fut.* PODRÉ; *subj.* PUEDA) to be able; can; may (*Juan no puede venir,* John cannot come; *Juan puede no venir,* John may not come).—**a más no p.,** to the utmost; without being able to help it.—**como pueda (podamos,** etc.), the best he (we, etc.) can.—**hasta más no p.,** to the utmost, to the limit.—**no p. con,** not to be able to bear, manage, etc., to be no match for.—**no p. más,** to have to act, can no other, cannot but; not to be able to do more, to be tired, worn out.—**no p. menos de,** to be necessary; cannot but, cannot fail to; (foll. by *inf.*) can't help (foll. by *pres. p.*)—**no p. ver a uno (pintado, o ni pintado),** to detest one, to find one absolutely unbearable. **II.** *v. imp.* to be possible, may.—**puede que** (foll. by *subj.*) it may (foll. by *inf.*); perhaps. **III.** *m.* power; might; hands, possession, tenure; (law) power of attorney, proxy, procuration.—**p. adquisitivo,** (econ.) purchasing power.—**p. ejecutivo,** (pol.) executive, executive power.—**p. judicial,** (pol.) judiciary.—**p. legislativo,** (pol.) legislative, legislature.—**a p. de,** by dint of, by force of.—**caer debajo del p. de uno,** to fall under one's control.—**de p. a p.,** hand to hand.—**en el p.,** in power.—**en p. de,** in the hands of.—**plenos poderes,** full powers.
poderdante, *n.* (law) constituent.
poderhabiente, *n.* (law) attorney.
poderío, *m.* power, might, dominion, jurisdiction; wealth, riches.
poderosamente, *adv.* powerfully, mightily.
poderoso, sa, *a.* powerful, mighty; wealthy.
podestá, *m.* (hist.) podesta.
podíatra, *n.* (med.) podiatrist.
podiatría, *f.* (med.) podiatry.
podiatrista, *n.* (med.) podiatrist.
podio, *m.* (arch.) podium.
podofilina, *f.* (pharm.) podophyllin.
podofilo, *m.* (bot.) podophyllum.
podómetro, *m.* pedometer.
podón, *m.* pruning hook, billhook; mattock.
podré, *fut.* of PODER.
podre, *m. or f.* pus; rotten substance.
podrecer, *va., vn.* & *vr.* = PUDRIR, to rot.
podrecimiento, *m.* = PODREDURA.
podredumbre, *f.* decay; pus; putrid matter; corruption; grief.
podredura, *f.* putrefaction, corruption.
podrición, *f.* = PODREDURA.
podridero, *m.* = PUDRIDERO.
podrido, da, *a.* = PUDRIDO.
podrimiento, *m.* = PUDRIMIENTO.
podrir, *va., vn.* & *vr.* = PUDRIR.
poema, *m.* poem.
poemático, ca, *a.* poetic; poetical.
poesía, *f.* poetry; poetical composition, poem.—*pl.* poetical works, poems.
poeta, *m.* poet.—**p. laureado,** poet laureate.
poetastro, *m.* poetaster.
poética, *f.* poetics.
poéticamente, *adv.* poetically.
poético, ca, *a.* poetic(al).
poetisa, *f.* poetess.
poetizar. I. *vn.* (*pret.* POETICÉ; *subj.* POETICE) to poetize, write poetry. **II.** *va.* to render poetical, to impart poetry to.
poíno, *m.* gauntry, stilling, stalder, barrelstand.
póker, pócar, *m.* (Angl.) (Am.) poker (card game).
polaco, ca. I. *a.* Polish. **II.** *m.* Polish language. **III.** *n.* Pole.
polacra, *f.* (naut.) polacre.
polaina, *f.* leggings.
polar, *a.* polar.—**órbita p.,** polar orbit.
polaridad, *f.* polarity.
polarímetro, *m.* polarimeter.
polariscopio, *m.* polariscope.
polarización, *f.* polarization.
polarizador, ra. I. *a.* polarizing. **II.** *m.* (opt.) polarizer.
polarizar, *va.* to polarize.
polca, *f.* (dance) polka.
polcar, *vn.* to dance the polka.
polea, *f.* pulley; tackle block, block pulley.—**p. fija,** fixed or fast pulley.—**p. impulsada,** driven pulley.—**p. loca,** loose pulley.—**p. motriz,** driving pulley.—**p. movible,** or **móvil,** movable pulley.
poleadas, *f. pl.* pap; porridge.
poleame, *m.* set of pulleys, tackle.
polemarca, *m.* (Gk. hist.) polemarch.
polémica, *f.* polemics; (mil.) science of fortification; literary or political controversy.
polémico, ca, *a.* polemical, polemic.
polemista, *n.* polemic, debater.
polemístico, ca, *a.* polemic(al), controversial.
polemonio, *m.* (bot.) Jacob's ladder.
polemoscopio, *m.* (opt.) polemoscope.
polen, *m.* (bot.) pollen.
polenta, *f.* porridge.
poleo, *m.* (bot.) pennyroyal; (coll.) strutting gait; (coll.) pompous style; (coll.) stiff, cold wind.
poliandria, *f.* (bot.) polyandria.
poliándrico, ca, *a.* polyandrous.
poliandro, dra, *a.* (bot.) polyandrous.
poliantea, *f.* collection of news items.
poliarquía, *f.* polyarchy, government by many.
poliárquico, ca, *a.* polyarchic, polyarchical.
poliatómico, ca, *a.* (chem.) polyatomic.
polibásico, ca, *a.* (chem.) polybasic.
policarpo, *a.* (bot.) polycarpous.
pólice, *m.* thumb.
policía, *f.* police; politeness, good breeding; cleanliness, neatness; *m.* policeman, patrol man, (U. S., coll.) blue coat, cop, flatfoot.—**p. militar,** military police.—**p. secreta,** secret service.—**perro de p.,** police dog.
policíaco, ca, *a.* of or pertaining to police.
policial. I. *a.* of or pertaining to police.—**novela p.,** detective story. **II.** *m.* (Am.) policeman.
policiano, *m.* (Am.) policeman.

policitación, *f.* (law) pollicitation, unaccepted offer.
policitemia, *f.* (biol.) polycythemia.
policlínica, *f.* polyclinic.
policopia, *f.* manifolder, multicopier.
policroísmo, *m.* (min.) pleochroism, polychroism.
policromático, ca, *a.* polychromatic.
policromía, *f.* quality of being polychrome.
policromo, ma, *a.* polychrome, many-colored.
policultura, *f.* diversified farming.
polichinela, *m.* Punchinello, Punch, buffoon.
polidáctilo, la, *a.* (zool.) polydactyl.
poliédrico, ca, *a.* polyhedrical.
poliedro, *m.* (geom.) polyhedron.
polienergético, ca, *a.* polienergetic.
poliestérico, ca, *a.* polyester.
poliestero, *m.* (chem.) polyester.
poliestireno, *m.* (chem.) polystyrene.
polietileno, *m.* (chem.) polyethylene.
polifacético, ca, *a.* (fig.) many-sided, versatile, diverse.
polifásico, ca, *a.* (elec.) multiphase.
polifonía, *f.* (mus.) polyphony.
polifónico, ca; polífono, na, *a.* polyphonic.
polígala, *f.* (bot.) milkwort.
poligaleo, a, *a.* (bot.) polygalaceous.
poligamia, *f.* polygamy.
polígamo, ma. I. *a.* polygamous; several times married. **II.** *n.* polygamist; one who has married several times.
poligenismo, *m.* polygenesis (esp. of human race).
poligenista, *n.* polygenist.
poligloto, ta. I. *n.* & *a.* polyglot. **II.** *f.* polyglot Bible.
poligonáceo, a, *a.* (bot.) polygonaceous.
poligonal. I. *a.* (geom.) polygonal. **II.** *f.* (surv.) broken line.
polígono, na. I. *a.* polygonal. **II.** *m.* (geom.) polygon; (bot.) poly; (artil.) practice ground.
poligrafía, *f.* art of writing in or interpreting ciphers.
poligráfico, ca, *a.* pert. to POLIGRAFÍA.
polígrafo, *m.* expert with ciphers.
polilla, *f.* moth, clothes moth; consumer, waster.
polimería, *f.* (chem.) polymerism.
polimerización, *f.* (chem.) polymerization.
polimerizar, *va.* & *vn.* (chem.) to polymerize.
polímero, ra, *a.* (chem.) polymeric.
polímita, *a.* made of many-colored threads.
polimorfismo, *m.* polymorphism.
polimorfo, fa, *a.* polymorphous.
polín, *m.* (naut.) wooden roller, skidding.
polinación, *f.* (bot.) pollination.
polinesi(an)o, a, *n.* & *a.* Polynesian.
polínico, ca, *a.* (bot.) pollinic, pollinical.
polinización, *f.* pollination.
polinizar, *va.* to pollinate.
polinomio, *m.* (math.) polynomial.
polinuclear, *a.* polynuclear.
poliomielitis, *f.* (med.) poliomyelitis, polio.
poliorama, *m.* polyorama.
poliorcética, *f.* (mil.) art of attack and defense.
polipero, *m.* polypary.
polipétalo, la, *a.* (bot.) polypetalous.
poliplano, *m.* (aer.) multiplane.
poliploidia, *f.* (genet.) polyploidy.
pólipo, *m.* (zool.) polyp, poulp, octopus; (med.) polyp.
polipodiáceo, cea, *a.* (bot.) polypodiaceous.
polipodio, *m.* (bot.) polypody, fern.
polisarcia, *f.* (med.) obesity.
poliscopio, *m.* (opt. and surg.) polyscope.
polisépalo, la, *a.* (bot.) polysepalous.
polisílabo, ba. I. *a.* polysyllabic. **II.** *m.* polysyllable.
polisíndeton, *m.* (rhet.) polysyndeton.
polisintético, ca, *a.* polysynthetic, polysynthetical, holophrastic.
polisintetismo, *m.* polysynthetism, holophrasis.
polisón, *m.* bustle (woman's dress).
polispasto, *m.* burton, hoisting tackle.
[1]**polista,** *n.* polo player.
[2]**polista,** *n.* (P. I.) Indian doing [3]POLO.
polistilo, la. I. *a.* (arch.) polystyle; (bot.) polystylous. **II.** *m.* (arch.) polystyle.
politécnico, ca, *a.* polytechnic.
politeísmo, *m.* polytheism.
politeísta, *n.* & *a.* polytheist(-ic).
política, *f.* policy; politics; politeness.—**p. del buen vecino,** Good Neighbor Policy.—**p. exterior,** foreign policy.—**por p.,** as a matter of policy; for the sake of politeness.
políticamente, *adv.* politically; civilly.
politicastro, *m.* politicaster, petty politician.
político, ca. I. *a.* political, politic; polite, courteous. **II.** *n.* politician.
politicón, na, *a.* exceedingly polite and ceremonious.
politiquear, *vn.* (coll.) to talk politics.
politiquería, *f.* (Am.) low politics; (contempt.) politics, political talk and doings, political trash.
politiquero, ra, *n.* (Am.) one that indulges in, or is fond of, common politics; political busybody.
poliuria, *f.* (med.) polyuria.
poliúrico, ca, *a.* polyuric.
polivalencia, *f.* (chem., bacteriol.) polyvalence.
polivalente, *a.* (chem., bacteriol.) polyvalent.
póliza, *f.* (com.) policy; scrip; check, draft, paybill; custom house permit; admission ticket; lampoon, anonymous note.—**p. de seguro,** insurance policy.
[1]**polizón, na,** *n.* vagrant, lazy vagabond; stowaway; parasite, sponger.
[2]**polizón,** *m.* (Am.) = POLISÓN, bustle (on dress).
polizonte, *m.* (coll.) (contempt.) policeman.
[1]**polo,** *m.* (geog. & astr.) pole, pole of magnetic needle; support, foundation.
[2]**polo,** *m.* (sports) polo.
[3]**polo,** *m.* (P. I.) personal service to community of forty days in year by natives.
[4]**polo,** *m.* a popular Andalusian song.
polonés, nesa. I. *a.* Polish. **II.** *n.* Pole; *m.* Polish (language); *f.* polonaise (clothing); (mus.) polonaise.
Polonia, *f.* Poland.
polonio, *m.* (chem.) polonium.
poltrón, na. I. *a.* idle, lazy, lubberly. **II.** *n.* (coll.) poltroon.
poltronería, *f.* idleness, laziness, indolence.
poltronizarse, *vr.* to become lazy.
polución, *f.* (med.) pollution.
poluto, ta, *a.* polluted; unclean, filthy.
Pólux, *m.* (astr.) Pollux (a star).
polvareda, *f.* cloud of dust; altercation, dispute.
polvera, *f.* (cosmetic) powder box.
polvificar, *va.* (coll.) to pulverize.
polvillo, ito, *m. dim.* fine dust.
polvo, *m.* dust; powder; pinch of snuff or powder. —*pl.* toilet powder.—**p. cósmico,** cosmic dust. —**p. de carbón,** coal dust.—**p. de cemento,** cement dust.—**p. de magnesio,** (photog.) flash powder.—**p. dentífrico,** tooth powder.—**p. radioactivo,** radioactive dust.—**polvos de arroz,** face powder.—**polvos de cartas,** sand for blotting writing.—**polvos de Juanes,** red precipitate, red nitrate of mercury.—**polvos de la madre Celestina,** (coll.) secret and miraculous mode in which anything is done.—**polvos de Seidlitz,** (pharm.) Seidlitz powder.—**polvos de talco,** (pharm.) talcum powder.—**polvos de tocador,** face powder.—**polvos insecticidas,** insect powder.—**borla de polvos,** powder puff.—**en p.,** powdered.—**hacer p. a,** to reduce to ashes, destroy, annihilate.—**limpio de p. y paja,** without toil or hardship; free from all charges; net.—**morder el p.,** (fig.) to bite the dust, be defeated; (fig.) to lick the dust, be servile.—**oro en p.,** gold dust.—**sacar p. debajo del agua,** (fig.) to be marvelous; to be unbelievable, be incredible.—**sacudir el p.,** (fig.) to dust one's breeches, give someone a beating.
pólvora, *f.* powder, gunpowder; artificial fire-

works; bad temper; vivacity, liveliness, briskness.—**p. de algodón,** guncotton.—**p. de caza,** shotgun powder.—**p. detonante,** or **fulminante,** detonating powder.—**p. lenta,** slow-burning powder.—**p. sin humo,** smokeless powder.—**gastar la p. en salvas,** to work to no purpose, to waste time and energy.—**no haber inventado la p.,** or **no ser el inventor de la p.,** to be dull, not to be a genius.—**ser una p.,** to be quick, to be a hustler.

polvoreamiento, *m.* powdering.

polvorear, *va.* to powder, sprinkle powder on.

polvoriento, ta, *a.* dusty.

polvorín, *m.* finest powder; powderflask, priming horn; powder magazine.

polvorista, *m.* manufacturer of gunpowder; maker of fireworks.

polvorizable, *a.* = PULVERIZABLE.

polvoroso, sa, *a.* dusty, full of dust.

polla, *f.* pullet; (coll.) comely young lass; (cards) pool; (ornith.) FÚLICA, coot.

pollada, *f.* flock of young fowls; hatch, covey.

pollancón, na, *n.* large chicken; (coll.) overgrown youth.

pollastra, *f.* large young hen.

pollastre, pollastro, *m.* large chicken; (coll.) cunning fellow.

pollazón, *m.* hatching; hatch, brood.

pollera, *f.* woman who raises or sells chickens; chicken roost, chicken coop; gocart; hooped petticoat.

pollería, *f.* poultry shop or market; (coll.) assemblage of young persons.

pollero, *m.* poulterer; poultry yard.

pollina, *f.* young she-ass.

pollinarmente, *adv.* (coll.) foolishly.

pollino, *m.* donkey, ass, jument.

pollito, ta, *n.* chicken; (coll.) boy or girl.

pollo, *m.* chicken; nestling; young bee; (coll.) young man; artful, clever man.

polluelo, la, *n.* little chicken, chick.

poma, *f.* apple; perfume censer; smelling bottle; pomander box.

pomáceo, cea, *a.* (bot.) pomaceous.

pomada, *f.* pomatum, pomade; salve.—**p. de cinc,** (pharm.) zinc ointment.

pomar, *m.* orchard, especially of apple trees.

pomarada, *f.* plantation of apple trees.

pomarrosa, *f.* (bot.) rose apple.

pomerano, na, *n.* & *a.* Pomeranian.

pómez.—piedra p., *f.* pumice stone.

pomicultura, *f.* pomiculture.

pomífero, ra, *a.* (poet.) apple-bearing.

pomo, *m.* pip fruit; pomum; pomander box; flask, flagon, small bottle; pommel; nosegay.

pomología, *f.* pomology, science of fruit growing.

pomosio, *m.* (ichth.) crappie.

pompa, *f.* pomp, ostentation, splendor; grand procession, pageant; bubble; ballooning of clothes raised by the wind; expanded tail of a turkey or peacock; (naut.) pump.

pompearse, *vr.* (coll.) to appear with pomp and ostentation; to strut.

pompeyano, na, *n.* & *a.* Pompeian, of Pompeii; relating to, or follower of, Pompey.

pompón, *m.* (mil.) pompon.

pomponearse, *vr.* = POMPEARSE.

pomposamente, *adv.* pompously.

pomposidad, *f.* pomposity, pompousness.

pomposo, sa, *a.* pompous; magnificent, splendid; inflated.

pómulo, *m.* cheek bone.

ponceño, ña, *n.* & *a.* Poncean (from Ponce).

poncí, poncidre, poncil, *a.* & *m.* terms app. to a species of bitter orange or lemon.

ponchada, *f.* quantity of punch made at one time.

ponche, *m.* punch (liquor).

ponchera, *f.* punch bowl.

[1]**poncho, cha,** *a.* soft, mild, careless, heedless.

[2]**poncho,** *m.* military cloak or greatcoat; poncho.

ponderable, *a.* ponderable; wonderful.

ponderación, *f.* consideration, deliberation; exaggeration; (stat.) weighting.

ponderador, ra. I. *a.* pondering; exaggerating. **II.** *n.* ponderer; exaggerator; puffer.

ponderal, *a.* ponderal, relating to weight.

ponderar, *va* to weigh; to ponder, consider; to exaggerate; to praise highly.

ponderativo, va, *a.* exaggerating, hyperbolical.

ponderosamente, *adv.* attentively, carefully.

ponderosidad, *f.* ponderousness, ponderosity.

ponderoso, sa, *a.* heavy, ponderous; grave, circumspect, cautious.

pondré, *fut.* of PONER.

ponedero, ra. I. *a.* capable of being laid or placed; egg-laying (as a hen). **II.** *m.* nest, hen's nest; nest egg.

ponedor, ra. I. *a.* egg-laying (as a hen). **II.** *n.* one that sets or lays; bettor, wagerer; outbidder; horse trained to rear on the hind legs.

ponencia, *f.* charge, post, or office of a chairman of a committee, or of a final judge or arbiter; exercise of such an office.

ponente, *n.* arbitrator, referee; chairman of a reporting committee.

ponentino, na, tisco, ca, *a.* western.

poner. I. *va.* (*pp.* PUESTO; *ind. pres.* PONGO, *pret.* PUSE, *fut.* PONDRÉ; *subj.* PONGA) to put, place, lay; to dispose, arrange, set (as the table); to suppose, assume; to impose, keep (as order, peace, etc.); to oblige, compel; to wager, stake; to appoint, put in charge; to adduce; to leave to one's judgment or action; to call, give (a person or thing) the name of; to write, set down; to lay (eggs); to bring forth; to contribute; to enforce; to concert; to agree; to insult, to treat badly; to cause (fear, etc.); to make, cause to become or turn (red, angry, etc.).—**p. al corriente,** to inform.—**p. al día,** to bring (someone) up to date (on the news).—**p. al sol,** to expose to the sun, to sun.—**p. aparte,** to put away; to set aside.—**p. a prueba,** to put on trial.—**p. (mala) cara,** (U. S.) to give a dirty look; to make a (wry) face.—**p. casa,** to begin, or go to, housekeeping.—**p. colorado,** to put to the blush, shame.—**p. como chupa de dómine,** or **como nuevo,** to humiliate, reprimand or treat harshly, dress down.—**p. como un guante,** to make pliable or submissive.—**p. coto a,** to stop, check, put a limit to.—**p. de manifiesto,** to make public.—**p. de su parte,** to do one's part, or on one's part.—**p. de vuelta y media** = P. COMO NUEVO.—**p. en (tanto),** to bid (so much).—**p. en calzas prietas,** (coll.) to put on the spot.—**p. en claro,** to make clear; to clear up (by investigation).—**p. en duda,** to question, doubt.—**p. en fuga,** to put to flight.—**p. en la calle,** to put out of doors.—**p. en orden,** to put to rights.—**p. en práctica,** to start doing, get (a project, etc.) underway.—**p. en relieve,** to carve in relief; to describe graphically.—**p. en ridículo,** to make ridiculous.—**p. en venta,** to put up for sale.—**p. en vigor,** to enforce.—**p. fin a,** to put a stop to, put an end to.—**p. fuego,** to set fire.—**p. la mesa,** to set the table, lay the table.—**p. los puntos sobre las íes,** to cross the t's and dot the i's.—**p. mal,** to discredit, run down; to set against (each other).—**p. manos a,** to put the hand to.—**p. pies en pared,** to maintain one's opinion with obstinacy.—**p. pies en polvorosa,** to take to one's heels.—**p. por,** to use as; appoint or send as.—**p. por escrito,** to put down in writing.—**p. por las nubes,** to praise to the skies.—**p. reparos,** to make objections. **II.** *vr.* to apply oneself to, to set about; to put on (as a garment); to set or place oneself; to oppose; to become, get (as wet, angry, dirty); to set (as the sun); to reach, get to, arrive; to adorn oneself.—**p. a,** to begin to, start to.—**p. a cubierto,** to shelter oneself from danger.—**p.**

colorado, to blush.—**p. de acuerdo,** to reach an agreement.—**p. en camino,** to set out, start, take off.—**p. en jarras,** to put one's arms akimbo.—**p. en marcha** = P. EN CAMINO.—**p. en pie,** to stand up.—**p. en práctica,** (of a project, etc.) to be started, get underway.—**p. en razón,** to be reasonable.—**ponérsele a uno,** to take a fancy or a notion to; to suspect, surmise (diff. constr.: *se me pone que Juan no pagará,* I suspect John won't pay). —**p. mal con,** to incur (someone's) enmity, "get in bad with."—**p. tan alto,** to become haughtily indignant, swell up with indignation. —**al p. el sol,** at sunset.

[1]**pongo,** *m:* (S. A.) narrow and dangerous ford; (S. A.) Indian servant.

[2]**pongo,** *m.* (zool.) orang-outang.

[3]**pongo, ponga,** *v. V.* PONER.

ponientada, *f.* steady west wind.

poniente, *m.* west; west wind.

ponimiento, *m.* act of putting, or putting on.

ponleví, *m.* shoe with high, wooden heel.

pontaje, pontazgo, *m.* bridge toll, pontage.

pontear, *va.* to erect a bridge over.

pontederiáceo, cea, *a.* (bot.) pontederiaceous.

pontezuelo, la, *n. dim.* small bridge.

póntico, ca, *a.* Pontic.

pontificado, *m.* pontificate, papacy, popedom.

pontifical. I. *a.* pontifical, papal. **II.** *m.* (eccl.) pontifical (book and robes); parochial tithes.

pontificalmente, *adv.* pontifically.

pontificar, *vn.* (coll.) to act like a pontiff, pontificate; to rule; to preside.

pontífice, *m.* pontiff, pontifex.—**Sumo P.,** the Pope.

pontificio, cia, *a.* pontifical.

pontil, *m.* (glassmaking) pontil or punty.

pontín, *m.* (P. I.) (naut.) coasting vessel.

ponto, *m.* (poet.) sea.

pontón, *m.* (mil.) pontoon; hulk serving as storeship, hospital, or prison ship; (naut.) mudscow, lighter, dredge; log bridge.

pontonero, *m.* (mil.) pontonier.

ponzoña, *f.* poison, venom.

ponzoñosamente, *adv.* poisonously, venomously

ponzoñoso, sa, *a.* poisonous, venomous, baneful.

popa, *f.* (naut.) poop, stern.—**a p., de p., en p.,** aft, abaft.—**de p. a proa,** entirely, completely.

popamiento, *m.* despising; cajoling, fondling.

popar, *vn.* to despise; to cajole; to fondle.

popel, *a.* (naut.) aftermost, sternmost.

popelina, *f.* (tex.) poplin.

popés, *m.* (naut.) stay of the mizzenmast.

poplíteo, tea, *a.* (anat.) popliteal.

popote, *m.* Indian straw for brooms; (Mex.) straw (for drinking).

populachería, *f.* claptrap; cheap popularity.

populachero, ra, *a.* vulgar, common.

populacho, *m.* populace, mob, rabble.

popular, *a.* popular.

popularidad, *f.* popularity.

popularizar. I. *va.* (*pret.* POPULARICÉ; *subj.* POPULARICE) to popularize, make popular. **II.** *vr.* to become popular.

popularmente, *adv.* popularly.

populazo, *m.* populace, mob, rabble.

populeón, *m.* white poplar ointment.

populoso, sa, *a.* populous.

poquedad, *f.* paucity, littleness; pusillanimity; trifle, mite; stupidity.

poquillo, lla. I. *a. dim.* small, little; trifling. **II.** *adv. dim.* very little time. **III.** *m.* (a) little, (a) little bit.

poquísimo, ma, *a.* & *adv. super.* very little.

poquitico, ica, illo, illa, ito, ita, *a. dim.* almost nothing, just a little.

poquito, ta. I. *a. dim.* very little; weak of body and mind, diminutive.—**p. a poco,** gently, slowly. **II.** *m.* a wee bit.—**a poquitos,** little by little; a little at a time.

por, *prep.* by; for; through (*pasamos por un túnel,* we passed through a tunnel; *Juan entró por la ventana,* John came in through the window); as (*desechado por inútil,* cast off as useless); across (*se pasó la mano por la frente,* he passed his hand across his forehead); about, nearly (*por ahí,* about that, very nearly; *por Navidad,* about Christmas); during (*volverá por la cuaresma,* he will return during Lent); per; after, for (*ir por pan,* to go for, or after, bread); for the sake of (*por Vd.,* for your sake); in behalf of, on account of (*por causa de enfermedad,* on account of illness); in order to; by way of, via; in the name of; without, not yet, to be (*cartas por contestar,* letters to be answered; *la casa está por acabar,* the house is not yet finished, or, is to be finished).—**p. ahora,** for now, for the time being.—**p. alto,** superficially, cursorily.—**p. amor de,** for the love of.—**p. buenas o p. malas,** for better or for worse.—**p. causa de,** because of.—**p. cierto,** indeed.—**p. completo,** to the full, completely, thoroughly.—**p. cuanto,** inasmuch as, whereas.—**p. decirlo así,** so to speak.—**p. de pronto,** for now, for the time being.—**¡p. Dios!** for Heaven's sake! —**p. docena,** by the dozen.—**p. entre,** through; among, between.—**p. escrito,** in writing.—**p. eso,** wherefore.—**p. este medio,** by this means.—**p. excelencia,** par excellence.—**p. extenso,** at length,. in detail.—**p. fin,** at last, finally.—**p. la mañana,** in the morning.—**p. la noche,** at night.—**p. la tarde,** in the afternoon.—**p. más que,** however much, no matter how.—**p. medio de,** through, by means of.—**p. motivo de,** because of.—**p. mucho que,** however much, no matter how.—**¿p. qué?** why?—**p. qué,** why.—**p. regla general,** in general, as a general rule.—**p. si** or **p. si acaso,** in case; if by chance.—**p. sí o p. no,** to be sure; to be on the safe side.—**p. sobre,** above, besides.—**p. supuesto,** of course.—**p. turno,** in turn.—**p. turnos,** by turns.—**al p. mayor,** by wholesale.—**de p. sí,** by oneself.—**estar p.,** to be about to (*estoy por salir,* I'm about to leave).

porcachón, na, *a.* (coll.) very dirty, hoggish.

porcal, *a.* kind of large plum.

porcaso, *m.* hog tapir.

porcelana, *f.* porcelain; chinaware; jewel enamel. —**porcelanita,** *f.* porcelanite, jasper.

porcentaje, *m.* percentage.

porcino, na. I. *a.* hoggish; porcine. **II.** *m.* young pig; bruise, bump.

porción, *f.* portion, part; lot; (com.) share, allowance, allotment; pittance.

porcioncica, illa, ita, *f. dim.* small portion.

porcionero, ra, *n.* & *a.* participant(-ating).

porcionista, *n.* shareholder; school boarder.

porcipelo, *m.* (coll.) bristle.

porciúncula, *f.* (eccl.) Franciscan jubilee.

porcuno, na, *a.* hoggish, porcine.

porchada, *f.* stretcher in paper factories.

porche, *m.* covered walk; porch, portico.

pordiosear, *vn.* to beg.—**pordioseo,** *m.* begging.

pordiosería, *f.* beggary.

pordiosero, ra, *n.* beggar.

porfía, *f.* obstinacy, stubbornness; insistence, persistence; importunity.—**a p.,** in competition, vying with each other; insistently.

porfiadamente, *adv.* obstinately; pertinaciously.

porfiado, da, *pp.* & *a.* obstinate, stubborn.

porfiador, ra, *n.* persistent person.

porfiar, *vn.* to persist.

porfídico, ca, *a.* porphyritic.

pórfido, *m.* porphyry, jasper.

pormenor, *m.* detail, particular.

pormenorizar, *va.* to detail, itemize, enter into details about, give in detail.

pornografía, *f.* pornography; pornograph.

pornográfico, ca, *a.* pornographic.

pornógrafo, *m.* pornographer.

poro, *m.* pore, interstice.

pororó, *m.* (S. A.) toasted corn.

pororoca, *f.* bore (at mouth of river).

porosidad, *f.* porosity.

poroso, sa, *a.* porous.
poroto, *m.* (Am.) a variety of pea; (Arg.) bean.—**apuntarse un p.,** (Arg.) (coll.) to make a point (as in a debate), be one up.
porque, *conj.* because, for, as; in order that.
¿por qué? *interr.* why? wherefore?
porqué, *m.* reason, motive; (coll.) allowance, pittance, portion.
porquecilla, *f. dim.* small sow.
porquera, *f.* lair, couch of a wild boar.
porquería, *f.* nastiness; filth; vile, dirty act, nasty trick; trifle, worthless thing.
porqueriza, *f.* pigsty.
porquerizo, za; porquero, ra, *n.* swineherd.
porquerón, *m.* (coll.) petty officer of justice.
porqueta, *f.* woodlouse.
porquezuelo, la, *n. dim.* small hog or sow; slovenly young person.
porra, *f.* bludgeon, club; maul; last player in boys' games; (coll.) vanity, boast; (coll.) dull or importunate person.
porrada, *f.* blow or knock; (coll.) foolishness, nonsense.
porrazo, *m.* blow, knock; fall.
porrear, *vn.* (coll.) to insist, persist.
porrería, *f.* (coll.) obstinacy; silliness.
porreta, *f.* green leaf of leeks, garlic, or onions.—**en p.,** (coll.) stark naked.
porrilla, *f.* small forging hammer; (vet.) osseous tumor in joints.
porrillo.—a p., *adv.* (coll.) aplenty, abundantly.
porrina, *f.* small and green crop.
porrino, *m.* tender plant of a leek.
porrizo, *m.* bed or plot of leeks.
[1]**porro, rra,** *a.* (coll.) stupid.
[2]**porro,** *m.* (bot.) leek.
[1]**porrón, na,** *a. aug.* heavy, sluggish, slow.
[2]**porrón,** *m.* earthen jug; wine bottle with long side spout.
porrudo, *m.* shepherd's crook.
porta, *f.* (naut.) gun port; stern port.
porta-, particle used in composition, gen. equivalent to "holder" or "carrier" after the corresponding noun, as in *portaplumas,* penholder; *portanoticias,* news carrier; *portaneumático,* tire holder; *portaaviones,* airplane carrier.
portaaguja, *f.* needle holder.
portaaviones, *m.* airplane carrier.
portabandera, *f.* socket for a flagpole.
portabarrena, *m.* boring block, drillstock.
portabombas, *m.* bomb carrier.
portabotellas, *m.* bottleholder.
portacaja, *f.* carrier of a loom; (mil.) drumsash or strap.
portacarabina, *f.* (mil.) carbine thimble.
portacartas, *m.* mail bag for letters.
portacojinete, *m.* diestock.
portacuchilla, *m.* cutter bar.
portada, *f.* portal, porch; frontispiece, front, façade; cover (of a magazine, etc.); (print.) title page; division of the warp.
portadera, *f.* chest for stores on a horse.
portadiscos, *m.* turntable.
portado, da, *a.*—**bien (mal) p.,** well (poorly) dressed or behaved.
portadocumentos, *m.* brief case.
portador, ra, *n.* bearer, porter, carrier; (com.) holder, bearer; *m.* (biol., chem.) carrier; waiter's tray.
portaestandarte, *m.* (mil.) color sergeant.
portaféretro, *m.* pallbearer.
portafolio, *m.* (Gal.) (Arg.) briefcase.
portafusil, *m.* (mil.) sling of a musket.
portaguión, *m.* (mil.) guidon (officer).
portahachón, *m.* torchbearer.
portaherramienta, *m.* (mach.) chuck; *pl.* tool holder.
portahierro, *m.* cutter bar.
portaje, *m.* = PORTAZGO.
portal, *m.* porch, entry, entrance, vestibule, hallway; portico, piazza; town's gate.
portalámpara, *m.* lamp holder; (elec.) socket (of a lamp fixture).
portalápiz, *m.* pencil holder.
portalazo, *m. aug.* large door or porch.
portalejo, *m. dim.* little porch or portico.
portalente, *m.* lens holder.
portaleña, *f.* (fort.) embrasure; plank for doors.
portalero, *m.* octroi officer or guard.
portalibros, *m.* book strap.
portalico, illo, ito, *m. dim.* small porch.
portalón, *m.* (naut.) gangway.
portamanteo, *m.* portmanteau, valise.
portamira, *n.* (surv.) rodman.
portamonedas, *m.* pocketbook, purse.
portanario, *m.* (anat.) pylorus.
portaneumático, *m.* (auto) tire holder.
portante, *m.* quick pace of a horse.—**tomar el p.,** (coll.) to go away.
portantillo, *m. dim.* gentle amble, easy pace.
portanuevas, *n.* newsmonger.
portanveces, *m.* coadjutor, assistant.
portañola, *f.* (naut.) porthole.
portañuela, *f.* (tailoring) fly of trousers.
portaobjetos, *m.* slide (of microscope).
portapaz, *n.* (eccl.) pix.
portaparaguas, *m.* umbrella stand.
portaplacas, portaplanchas, *m.* (photog.) dark slide, plate holder, chassis.
portapliegos, *m.* large portfolio.
portaplumas, *m.* penholder.
portar. I. *va.* to carry (as arms). **II.** *vr.* to behave, act. **III.** *vn.* (naut.) (of sails) to fill.
portasenos, *m.* brassière, brassiere, (coll.) bra.
portátil, *a.* portable.
portavasos, *m.* glass stand or rack.
portavela, *m.* candleholder.
portaventanero, *m.* carpenter who makes windows and doors.
portaviandas, *m.* dinner pail.
portavoz, *m.* megaphone, speaking trumpet; *n.* (fig.) spokesman, mouthpiece.
portazgo, *m.* toll, turnpike duty.
portazguero, *m.* toll gatherer, collector.
portazo, *m.* slam of a door; slamming a door in one's face.
porte, *m.* cost of carriage; freight, portage, porterage; postage; bearing (of persons); nobility; illustrious descent; size; capacity; (naut.) burden or tonnage.—**p. franco,** frank; postage prepaid.
porteador, ra, *n.* porter, carrier, bearer.
portear. I. *va.* to carry or convey for a price. **II.** *vr.* (of birds) to pass, migrate.
portento, *m.* prodigy, wonder; portent.
portentosamente, *adv.* prodigiously.
portentoso, sa, *a.* prodigious, marvelous.
porteño, ña. I. *a.* of or pertaining to Buenos Aires or Puerto de Santa María. **II.** *n.* inhabitant of Buenos Aires or Puerto de Santa María.
porteo, *m.* carrying, cartage, portage.
porterejo, *m.* little porter.
[1]**portería,** *f.* porter's lodge or box, conciergerie; employment of a porter.
[2]**portería,** *f.* (naut.) (collect.) the portholes.
portero, ra, *n.* janitor, superintendent, concierge; porter, gatekeeper.
portezuela, *f. dim.* little door; carriage door; pocket flap; (Mex.) pass between hills.
pórtico, *m.* portico, piazza; porch; hall; lobby.
portier, *m.* portiere, portière.
portilla, *f.* opening, passage; (naut.) porthole.
portillo, *m.* opening, gap, breach; wicket, gate; means to an end; cavity in anything broken; octroi gate of a town; pass between hills.
portón, *m.* inner front door of a house.
portorriqueño, ña, *n.* & *a.* Puerto-Rican.
Portugal, *m.* Portugal.
portugués, guesa. I. *a.* Portuguese. **II.** *n.* Portuguese; *m.* Portuguese (language).
portulano, *m.* charts of ports and harbors.
porvenir, *m.* future, time to come.
¡porvida! *interj.* by the living saints!
pos.—en p. de, *adv.* after, behind; in pursuit of.

posa, *f.* passing bell; stop in a funeral, to sing a response.—*pl.* (coll.) buttocks.
posada, *f.* lodging; lodging house; inn, tavern, hotel; home, dwelling.
posadera, *f.* hostess, landlady.
posaderas, *f. pl.* buttocks.
posadero, *m.* innkeeper, host; seat made of flags or bass ropes.
posante, *a.* reposing; smooth (sailing).
posar. I. *vn.* to lodge, board; to sit down, repose, rest; to perch, light; (art) to pose. **II.** *va.* to lay down. **III.** *vr.* (of liquid) to settle; to light, alight, sit (on).
posaverga, *f.* (naut.) yard prop.
posbélico, ca, *a.* post-war.
posca, *f.* mixture of vinegar and water.
posdata, *f.* postscript.
poseedor, ra, *n.* possessor, holder, owner.
poseer, *va.* (*ger.* POSEYENDO; *pp.* POSEÍDO, POSESO; *pret.* él POSEYÓ) to hold, possess, own; to master (an art, language, etc.).
poseído, da. I. *pp. reg.* of POSEER. **II.** *a.*—**estar p.,** (fig.) to be possessed; to be thoroughly convinced or posted about. **III.** *m.* private arable land.
posesión, *f.* possession; property; possession by evil spirits.—*pl.* holdings, wealth, property.
posesional, *a.* possessional, possessive.
posesionar. I. *va.* to give possession; to install, induct. **II.** *vr.* to take possession.
posesionero, ra, *n.* cattle keeper owning pastures.
posesivo, va, *n.* & *a.* (gram.) possessive.
poseso, sa. I. *pp. irreg.* of POSEER. **II.** *a.* possessed (with evil spirits).
posesor, ra, *n.* possessor, holder, owner.
posesorio, ria, *a.* possessory.
poseyente, *a.* possessing, owning.
poseyó, etc. *v. V.* POSEER.
posfecha, *f.* postdate.—**posfechar,** *va.* to postdate.
posguerra, *a.* = POSBÉLICO.
posibilidad, *f.* possibility; means, property.
posibilitar, *va.* to render possible, facilitate.
posible. I. *a.* possible.—**en lo p.,** as far, insofar, as possible.—**lo más** (*adj., adv.*) **p.,** as (*adj., adv.*) as possible. **II.** *m. pl.* personal means; best of one's ability.
posiblemente, *adv.* possibly.
posición, *f.* position; placing, placement; standing, status; (law) questions and answers of an interrogatory; (math.) position.
positivamente, *adv.* positively; absolutely.
positivismo, *m.* positiveness; positivism; (moral) materialism; matter-of-factness.
positivista. I. *a.* positivistic, positivist; practical, realistic, matter-of-fact. **II.** *n.* positivist.
positivo, va. I. *a.* positive, certain; absolute, real; matter-of-fact; (elect., gram., math., photog.) positive.—**de p.,** certainly, without doubt. **II.** *m.* (gram., photog.) positive.
pósito, *m.* public granary.
positrón, *m.* (phys.) positron.
positronio, *m.* (chem.) positronium.
positura, *f.* posture, state, disposition.
posma. I. *f.* (coll.) sluggishness, sloth, dullness. **II.** *n.* (coll.) dull, sluggish person.
poso, *m.* sediment, dregs, lees; rest, repose.
posó, *m.* (P. I.) chignon, hair knot.
posología, *f.* (med.) posology.
posón, *m.* round matted seat.
pospelo.—**a p.** *adv.* against the grain; reluctantly.
pospierna, *f.* thigh of an animal.
posponer, *va.* (*pp.* POSPUESTO; *ind. pres.* POSPONGO, *pret.* POSPUSE, *fut.* POSPONDRÉ; *subj.* POSPONGA) (a) to put (after); to think less (of); to subordinate (to); to postpone.
posposición, *f.* postponement.
pospositivo, va, *a.* (gram.) postpositive.
pospuesto, *pp. irreg.* of POSPONER.
posquemador, *m.* (aer.) afterburner.
posta. I. *f.* post horses, relay; post, post stage, posthouse, post office; chop of meat or fish; mold shot; stake, at cards; memorial tablet. **II.** *n.* person who travels post.
postal. I. *a.* postal.—**giro p.,** money order. **II.** *f.* postal card.
postdata, *f.* = POSDATA.
postdiluviano, na, *a.* postdiluvian.
poste, *m.* post, pillar; remaining standing up as a school punishment.—**p. de amarre,** (aer.) mooring mast.—**p. de la meta,** goal post.
postelero, *m.* (naut.) skid, skeed; chess-trees.
postema, *f.* (med.) abscess; bore (person); (coll.) grudge.
postemero, *m.* (surg.) large lancet.
postergación, *f.* delaying; leaving behind; disregard of seniority.
postergar, *va.* (*pret.* POSTERGUÉ; *subj.* POSTERGUE) to delay; to ignore or disregard the right of seniority of (a candidate for office, etc.).
posteridad, *f.* posterity.
posterior, *a.* posterior, rear; later, subsequent.
posterioridad, *f.* posteriority.
posteriormente, *adv.* subsequently.
posteta, *f.* (bookbinding) number of sheets stitched together.
postfijo, *m.* postfix, suffix.
postigo, *m.* wicket; peep window; shutter; (fort.) sally port, postern.
postgraduado, da, *n.* & *a.* postgraduate.
postguerra, *f.* postwar period.
postila, *f.* marginal note.
postilación, *f.* marginal annotation.
postilador, *m.* annotator.
postilar, *va.* to gloss, comment.
postilla, *f.* scab on wounds.
postillón, *m.* postillion, postboy.
postilloso, sa, *a.* scabby.
postimpresionismo, *m.* (f. a.) postimpressionism.
postimpresionista, *n.* & *a.* (f. a.) postimpressionist.
postizo, za, I. *a.* artificial, not natural; false (teeth). **II.** *m.* false hair, switch. **III.** *f.* castanet; (naut.) dead work on galleys.
postliminio, *m.* (int. law) postliminy.
postludio, *m.* (mus.) postlude.
postmeridiano, na, *a.* postmeridian, p.m.
postnatal, *a.* postnatal.
postónico, ca, *a.* (philol.) posttonic.
postoperatorio, ria, *a.* postoperative.
postor, *m.* bidder.
postorbital; postorbitario, ria, *a.* (anat.) postorbital.
postpalatal, *a.* (phon.) postpalatal.
postración, *f.* prostration; kneeling; dejection.
postrado, da. I. *pp.* of POSTRAR. **II.** *a.* prostrate, prostrated, prone.
postrador, ra. I. *n.* & *a.* prostrator(-ing). **II.** *m.* footstool in a choir.
postrar. I. *va.* to prostrate, to humble; to overthrow, demolish; to weaken, exhaust. **II.** *vr.* to prostrate oneself, kneel down, lie prone; to be exhausted.
postre. I. *a.* last in order.—**a la p.,** at last.—**por fin y p.,** (coll.) finally. **II.** *m.* (*sing.* or *pl.*) dessert.
postremo, ma, *a.* last.
postrer, *a. contr.* of POSTRERO (*before a noun*).
postreramente, *adv.* lastly.
postrero, ra, *a.* last; hindermost.
postrimer, *a. contr.* of POSTRIMERO (*before a n.*).
postrimeramente, *adv.* finally, at last.
postrimería, *f.* (theol.) last stage of life.
postrimero, ra, *a.* last; hindmost.
póstula, postulación, *f.* request, petition; (eccl.) postulation; nomination (of a candidate).
postulado, da. I. *a.* postulated. **II.** *m.* postulate; *n.* nominee.—**p. de las paralelas,** (geom.) parallel postulate.
postulador, *m.* postulator.
postulanta, *f.* postulant.
postulante. I. *a.* postulating. **II.** *m.* postulant.
postular, *va.* to postulate; to nominate (political candidate).

póstumo, ma, *a.* posthumous.
postura, *f.* posture, position; planting trees or plants; tree or plant transplanted; assize of provisions; (com.) bid: stake. wager; egg; egg-laying; agreement, covenant
potabilidad, *f.* potability.
potabilizar, *va.* to make potable or drinkable.
potable, *a.* potable, drinkable.
potación, *f.* potation, drinking; beverage.
potador, ra, *n.* inspector of weights and measures.
potaje, *m.* pottage; porridge; stewed vegetables; mixed drink; medley.
potajería, *f.* heap of dry pulse; place where vegetables are kept.
potajier, *m.* (Gal.) keeper of the vegetables in the royal palace.
potala, *f.* (naut.) anchor; stone anchor; small slow vessel.
[1]**potar,** *va.* to correct and mark (measures).
[2]**potar,** *va.* to drink.
potasa, *f.* potash.
potásico, ca, *a.* potassic; potassium (as *a.*, as in *bromuro potásico*, potassium bromide).
potasio, *m.* potassium.
pote, *m.* jug; pot, jar; (cooking) pot; flowerpot; standard measure or weight.—**a p.,** abundantly.—**potecillo, ito,** *n. dim.* little pot, can or jar.
potencia, *f.* power, capacity; dominion; faculty of the mind; possibility; power, strong nation; force, strength; (mech., phys., math.) power; (artil.) reach.—*pl.* nine rays of light around the head of Jesus.—**potencias del alma,** powers of the soul, mental powers (gen. stated as memory, judgment, and will).—**en p.,** potentially.
potencial, *f.* & *a.* potential.
potencialidad, *f.* potentiality.
potencialmente, *adv.* potentially, virtually.
potenciómetro, *m.* (elec.) potentiometer.
potentado, *m.* potentate, sovereign.
potente, *a.* potent, powerful, mighty; strong, vigorous; (coll.) bulky, huge.
potentemente, *adv.* powerfully, potently.
potentila, *f.* (bot.) potentilla.
potenza, *f.* (her.) tace.
poterna, *f.* (mil.) postern, sally port.
potero, *m.* = POTADOR.
potestad, *f.* power, dominion, jurisdiction; potentate.—*pl.* angelic powers.
potestativo, va, *a.* (law) facultative.
potingue, *m.* (coll.) medicinal concoction.
potísimo, ma, *a. super.* most special.
potista, *n.* (coll.) tippler, drinker.
pot-pourri, *m.* potpourri; mixture; hash.
[1]**potra,** *f.* (coll.) rupture, scrotal hernia.—**tener p.,** to have good luck.
[2]**potra,** *f.* filly, young mare.—**potrada,** *f.* herd of fillies.—**potranca,** *f.* filly.
potrear, *va.* (coll.) to tease, vex, annoy.
potrera, *f.* a hempen headstall.
[1]**potrero,** *m.* (coll.) rupture specialist.
[2]**potrero,** *m.* herdsman of colts; pasture ground; (Am.) cattle ranch.
potrico, illo, *m. dim.* small colt.
potril, *m.* pasture for young horses.
potrilla, *f.* (coll.) old man affecting rakish youth.
potro, *m.* colt, foal; wooden horse, rack; shoeing frame; anything that torments; obstetrical chair; pit in the ground for dividing a beehive.—**estar en un p.,** to be on pins and needles.
potroso, sa, *a.* afflicted with a rupture; (coll.) fortunate, lucky.
poya, *f.* fee for baking in a public oven; hemp bagasse.
poyal, *m.* striped cover for benches; stone seat.
poyar, *vn.* to pay the POYA.
poyata, *f.* shelf, cupboard.
poyo, *m.* stone seat against a wall; fee formerly paid to judges.
poza, *f.* puddle; pool for breaking hemp.
pozal, *m.* bucket, pail; coping of a well; vessel sunk in the earth to collect liquids.
pozanco, *m.* pool in a river bank.
pozo, *m.* (water) well; deep hole in a river; eddy, whirlpool; (min.) shaft, pit; (naut.) hold; anything complete in its line.—**p. artesiano,** artesian well.—**p. negro,** cesspool.
pozol, pozole, *m.* barley and beans boiled.
pozuela, *f. dim.* small puddle or pond.
pozuelo, *m. dim.* small well or pit; vessel sunk in the ground to collect oil, etc.
práctica, *f.* practice; habit; practicing; exercise; manner, method, routine; learning a profession under a master.—**en la p.,** in practice.
practicable, *a.* practicable, feasible.
practicador, ra, *n.* practicer, practitioner.
practicaje, *m.* (naut.) pilotage.
prácticamente, *adv.* in a practical manner, in practice.
practicante. I. *a.* practicing. **II.** *n.* practicer, practitioner; hospital intern; hospital nurse, one who practices medicine under direction and guidance of an experienced physician; (pharm.) prescription preparer, or clerk.
practicar, *va.* (*pret.* PRACTIQUÉ; *subj.* PRACTIQUE) to practice; to make; to perform, do, put in execution; to practice, go in for; to learn the practice of under an adviser.
práctico, ca. I. *a.* practical; skillful, experienced. **II.** *m.* (naut.) harbor pilot.
practicón, na, *n.* (coll.) one possessing practical knowledge and experience.
practiqué, practique, *v. V.* PRACTICAR.
pradeño, ña, *a.* pertaining to prairies.
pradera, pradería, *f.* prairie, meadow.
praderoso, sa, *a.* pertaining to prairies.
prado, *m.* lawn; field, pasture ground; walk (in a city).—**p. de guadaña,** meadow mowed annually.
pragmático, ca. I. *a.* pragmatic, pragmatical. **II.** *f.* sanction, decree; *m.* interpreter of national laws.
pragmatismo, *m.* pragmatism.
pragmatista. I. *a.* pragmatistic. **II.** *n.* pragmatist.
prao, *m.* proa, prao, an Asiatic canoe.
praseodimio, *m.* (chem.) praseodymium.
prasio, *m.* (min.) prase, translucent quartz.
prasma, *m.* (min.) dark green agate.
pratíncola, *m.* (ornith.) pratincole.
pravedad, *f.* perversity, iniquity, depravity.
pravo, va, *a.* depraved, wicked, perverse.
pre, *m.* = PREST, soldier's daily pay.
preaceleración, *f.* (nuclear phys.) preacceleration.
preadamita, *n.* preadamite.
preadamítico, ca, *a.* preadamite.
preámbulo, *m.* preamble; (coll.) evasion.
preamplificador, *m.* (elec., electron.) preamplifier.
preatómico, ca, *a.* preatomic.
prebenda, *f.* (eccl.) prebend, benefice.
prebendado, *m.* (eccl.) prebendary.
prebendar, *va.* to confer a prebend on.
prebostal, *a.* provostal.
prebostazgo, *m.* provostship.
preboste, *m.* provost; (mil.) provost.
precambriano, na; precámbrico, ca, *m.* & *a.* (geol.) Pre-Cambrian.
precariamente, *adv.* precariously.
precario, ria, *a.* precarious.
precaución, *f.* precaution.
precaucionarse, *vr.* to be cautious.
precautelar, *va.* to caution, forewarn.
precautorio, ria, *a.* precautionary; preventive.
precaver. I. *va.* to prevent, obviate. **II.** *vr.* **(de)** to guard, be on one's guard (against).
precavidamente, *adv.* cautiously.
precavido, da, *a.* cautious, guarded.
precedencia, *f.* precedence, priority; preëminence, preference; superiority, primacy.
precedente. I. *a.* preceding, foregoing. **II.** *m.* precedent.

preceder, *va.* to precede; to be superior to.
preceptista, *n.* & *a.* one, or pertaining to one, who sets precepts.
preceptivamente, *adv.* preceptively.
preceptivo, va, *a.* preceptive.
precepto, *m.* precept; order, injunction; rule.—*pl.* the Commandments.
preceptor, ra, *n.* teacher, preceptor.
preceptuar, *va.* to give or issue as a precept.
preces, *f. pl.* prayers; devotion; supplication.
precesión, *f.* (rhet.) reticence; (astr.) precession.
preciado, da. I. *pp.* of PRECIAR. **II.** *a.* valued, esteemed; valuable, precious; proud, elated.
preciador, ra, *n.* appraiser.
preciar. I. *va.* to value, price, appraise. **II.** *vr.* **(de)** to boast, brag (about); to take pride, glory (in).
precinta, *f.* strap, band; (naut.) parcelling.
precintar, *va.* to strap, hoop, bind; to seal.
precinto, *m.* strapping; sealed strap.
precio, *m.* price; reward; premium; esteem; importance, worth.—**p. al contado,** cash price.—**p. corriente,** market price, standard price, prevailing price.—**p. de apertura,** opening price (stock exchange).—**p. de catálogo,** list price.—**p. de cierre,** closing price (stock exchange).—**p. de costo,** cost price.—**p. de detallista,** retail price.—**p. de entrega,** delivery price.—**p. de factura,** invoice price.—**p. de subasta,** upset price.—**p. de tarifa,** list price.—**p. de venta al menudeo,** selling price.—**p. fijo,** fixed price, set price.—**p. máximo,** ceiling price.—**p. mínimo,** knockdown price.—**p. mínimo fijado,** upset price.—**p. módico,** moderate price.—**p. rebajado** or **reducido,** reduced price, cut price, cut rate.—**p. regular,** standard price.—**catálogo con p.,** price catalogue.—**control de precios,** price control.—**lista de precios,** price list.—**no tener p.,** to be invaluable, be priceless.—**poner a p. la cabeza de uno,** (fig.) to set a price on one's head.—**tener en p.,** to esteem.
preciosa, *f.* (eccl.) allowance to prebendaries.
preciosamente, *adv.* preciously, richly.
preciosidad, *f.* worth, preciousness; rich or beautiful object, (a) beauty.
precioso, sa, *a.* precious, valuable; beautiful; witty, merry.
precipicio, *m.* precipice, chasm; violent fall; ruin, destruction.
precipitación, *f.* rash haste, precipitancy; (chem.) precipitation.—**p. radiactiva,** fallout.
precipitadamente, *adv.* hastily.
precipitadero, *m.* precipice, steep cliff.
precipitado, da. I. *pp.* of PRECIPITAR. **II.** *a.* precipitate, hasty; abrupt. **III.** *m.* (chem.) precipitate.—**p. blanco,** calomel.
precipitante. I. *a.* precipitating. **II.** *m.* (chem.) precipitator, precipitant.
precipitar. I. *va.* to precipitate, cast headlong; to rush, hasten; (chem.) to precipitate. **II.** *vr.* to throw oneself headlong; to rush, hurry.
precípite, *a.* in danger of falling.
precipitina, *f.* (bact.) precipitin.
precipitoso, sa, *a.* precipitous; rash, reckless.
precipuamente, *adv.* principally.
precipuo, pua, *a.* chief, principal.
precisamente, *adv.* precisely, exactly; necessarily, unavoidably; just at this (that) moment.
precisar, *va.* to fix, set, determine; to compel, oblige; (Am.) to be necessary; to be urgent.
precisión, *f.* necessity; compulsion; preciseness, exactness; precision, accuracy.—**bombardeo de p.,** precision bombing.
preciso, sa, *a.* necessary; indispensable; precise, exact, accurate; distinct, clear; severed, cut off; concise.—**tiempo p.,** just time enough.
precitado, da, *a.* aforesaid, aforementioned.
precito, ta, *a.* damned, condemned to hell.
preclaramente, *adv.* illustriously.
preclaro, ra, *a.* illustrious, famous, prominent.
precocidad, *f.* precocity.
precognición, *f.* precognition.
precolombino, na, *a.* pre-Columbian.
preconcebir, *va.* to preconceive, conceive beforehand.
preconicé, preconice, *v. V.* PRECONIZAR.
preconización, *f.* eulogy; preconization.
preconizador, ra, *n.* & *a.* eulogizer(-ing); preconizer(-ing).
preconizar, *va.* (*pret.* PRECONICÉ; *subj.* PRECONICE) to praise, eulogize; (eccl.) to preconize.
preconocer, *va.* (*ind.* PRECONOZCO; *subj.* PRECONOZCA) to foreknow.
precordial, *a.* (anat.) precordial.
precoz, *a.* precocious.
precursor, ra. I. *a.* preceding. **II.** *n.* precursor, harbinger, forerunner.
predecesor, ra, *n.* predecessor.
predecir, *va.* (*ger.* PREDICIENDO; *pp.* PREDICHO; *ind. pres.* PREDIGO, *pret.* PREDIJE, *fut.* PREDIRÉ; *subj.* PREDIGA) to foretell, predict, forecast.
predefinición, *f.* (theol) predetermination.
predefinir, *va.* to predetermine.
predestinación, *f.* predestination.
predestinado, da. I. *pp.* of PREDESTINAR. **II.** *a.* predestined. **III.** *n.* one predestined.
predestinante, *n.* & *a.* predestinator(-ing).
predestinar, *va.* to predestine, foredoom, predestinate, foreordain.
predeterminación, *f.* predetermination, foreordination.
predeterminar, *va.* to predetermine, foredoom, foreordain.
predial, *a.* predial, real, landed (property).
prédica, *f.* preachment, sermon.
predicable. I. *a.* predicable; preachable, suitable for preaching. **II.** *m.* (log.) predicable.
predicación, *f.* preaching; sermon.
predicadera, *f.* pulpit.—*pl.* (coll.) facility for preaching.
predicado, *m.* (logic) predicate.
predicador, ra, *n.* preacher.
predicamental, *a.* (philos.) predicamental.
predicamento, *m.* (log.) predicament, category; esteem, appreciation, consideration, regard.
predicante. I. *a.* predicant, preaching. **II.** *n.* predicant, preacher.
predicar, *va.* & *vn.* (*pret.* PREDIQUÉ; *subj.* PREDIQUE) to render clear and evident; to publish; to preach; to praise to excess; (coll.) to reprimand, lecture, sermonize.
predicción, *f.* prediction.
predicho, cha, *pp. irreg.* of PREDECIR.
predigestión, *f.* predigestion.
predigo, prediga, predije, *v. V.* PREDECIR.
predilección, *f.* predilection.
predilecto, ta, *a.* preferred, favorite.
predio, *m.* landed property, farm, real property.—**p. rústico,** piece of arable ground.—**p. urbano,** dwelling house or building lot.
prediqué, predique, *v. V.* PREDICAR.
predisponer, *va.* (*pp. irreg.* PREDISPUESTO; *ind. pres.* PREDISPONGO, *pret.* PREDISPUSE, *fut.* PREDISPONDRÉ; *subj.* PREDISPONGA) to prejudice, predispose; to prearrange.
predisposición, *f.* predisposition; prejudice.
predispuesto, ta. I. *pp. irreg.* of PREDISPONER. **II.** *a.* predisposed, biased, inclined.
predispuse, *pret.* of PREDISPONER.
predominación, predominancia, *f.* predominance, predomination.
predominante, *a.* predominant, prevailing.
predominar, *vn.* & *va.* to predominate, prevail; to rise above, overlook, command.
predominio, *m.* predominance, superiority.
preelegir, *va.* to preëlect; to predestinate.
preeminencia, *f.* preëminence, mastery.
preeminente, *a.* preëminent, superior.
preescolar, *a.* preschool.
preestablecer, *va.* to preëstablish.
preexcelso, sa, *a.* most illustrious, most high.
preexistencia, *f.* preëxistence.
preexistente, *a.* preëxistent.
preexistir, *vn.* to preëxist.

prefacio, *m.* preface, prologue; (eccl.) preface.
prefación, *f.* preface, prologue, introduction.
prefecto, *m.* prefect.—**prefectura,** *f.* prefecture.
preferencia, *f.* preference.
preferente, *a.* preferential; preferring; preferable. —**preferentemente,** *adv.* preferably.
preferible, *a.* preferable.
preferiblemente, *adv.* preferably.
preferir, *va.* (*ger.* PREFIRIENDO; *ind. pres.* PREFIERO, *pret.* PREFIRIÓ; *subj.* PREFIERA) to prefer.
prefiguración, *f.* prefiguration.
prefigurar, *va.* to prefigure.
prefijar, *va.* to predesignate, predetermine.
prefijo, ja. I. *a.* prefixed. **II.** *m.* (gram.) prefix.
prefinición, *f.* setting of a time limit.
prefinir, *va.* to set a time limit for.
prefirió, prefiriendo, *v. V.* PREFERIR.
prefloración, *f.* (bot.) prefloration.
prefoliación, *f.* (bot.) vernation.
preformación, *f.* preformation.
prefulgente, *a.* resplendent, bright.
pregón, *m.* publication by the crier, cry.
pregonar, *va.* to proclaim; to cry out, make publicly known.
pregoneo, *m.* crying wares on the streets.
pregonería, *f.* office of common crier.
pregonero, ra. I. *a.* publishing, announcing. **II.** *n.* common crier, town crier; auctioneer.
pregunta, *f.* question, query; catechism.—**absolver las preguntas,** (law) to answer under oath.—**estar a la cuarta p.,** (coll.) to be hard up or penniless.—**hacer una p.,** to ask a question.
preguntador, ra, *n.* & *a.* questioner(-ing).
preguntante, *n.* & *a.* inquirer(-ing).
preguntar. I. *va.* & *vn.* to ask, question, inquire. —**p. por,** to ask for (a person); to inquire about. **II.** *vr.* to wonder (when he will come, etc.).
preguntón, na, *a.* inquisitive.
prehistoria, *f.* prehistoric times; prehistorics, study or science of prehistoric times.
prehistórico, ca, *a.* prehistoric.
preinserto, ta, *a.* previously inserted.
prejudicial, *a.* (law) requiring judicial decision before final sentence.
prejudicio, prejuicio, *m.* prejudice, bias.
prejuzgar, *va.* (*pret.* PREJUZGUÉ; *subj.* PREJUZGUE) to prejudge.
prelacía, *f.* prelacy, prelature.
prelación, *f.* preference.
prelada, *f.* prelatess, abbess, mother superior.
prelado, *m.* (eccl.) prelate.
prelaticio, cia, *a.* prelatic, of or pertaining to a prelate or prelacy.
prelatura, *f.* prelacy, prelature.
preliminar. I. *a.* preliminary. **II.** *m.* preliminary; peace protocol.
prelucir, *vn.* (*ind.* PRELUZCO; *subj.* PRELUZCA) to shine forth.
preludiar. I. *va.* & *vn.* (mus.) to play a prelude. **II.** *va.* to initiate, pave the way for.
preludio, *m.* introduction; (mus.) prelude.
prelusión, *f.* prelude, prologue, preface.
prematuramente, *adv.* prematurely.
prematuro, ra, *a.* premature; precocious; unripe, unseasonable; (law) (of girls) impuberal.
premaxilar, *a.* (anat.) premaxillary.
premeditación, *f.* premeditation.
premeditadamente, *adv.* premediatatedly.
premeditado, da, *a.* & *pp.* premeditated.
premeditar, *va.* to premeditate.
premiador, ra, *n.* rewarder.
premiar, *va.* to reward, remunerate, requite.
premio, *m.* reward; prize; recompense; (com.) premium; interest.—**a p.,** at a premium.
premiosamente, *adv.* tightly, compressedly; by force.
premiosidad, *f.* difficulty of action or speech.
premioso, sa, *a.* tight, close, pinching; troublesome, burdensome; strict, rigid; slow in speaking or writing.
premisa, *f.* (logic) premise; mark, indication.
premiso, sa, *a.* premised; sent in advance.
premoción, *f.* previous motion.
premolar, *m.* & *a.* premolar (tooth).
premonitorio, ria, *a.* (med.) premonitory.
premonstratense, *n.* & *a.* Premonstratensian.
premoriencia, *f.* (law) prior death.
premoriente, *a.* & *n.* predeceased.
premorir, *vn.* (*pp.* PREMUERTO; *ger.* PREMURIENDO; *ind. pres.* PREMUERO, *pret.* él PREMURIÓ; *subj.* PREMUERA) (law) to die before another.
premostratense, *n.* & *a.* (member) of an order of canons.
premuerto, ta, *pp. irreg.* of PREMORIR.
premura, *f.* urgency, pressure, haste.
prenatal, *a.* prenatal.
prenda, *f.* pledge, security, pawn; piece of jewelry; garment; person dearly loved.—*pl.* endowments, natural gifts, talents.—**p. de vestir,** article of clothing, piece of wearing apparel.—**en p., en prendas,** as a pledge, as security. —**juego de prendas,** game of forfeits.—**soltar p.,** to commit oneself.
prendado, da. I. *pp.* of PRENDAR. **II.** *a.*—**estar p. de,** to be taken up with.—**ser muy p.,** to have many accomplishments.
prendador, ra, *n.* pledger, pawner.
prendamiento, *m.* pledging, pawning.
prendar. I. *va.* to pledge, pawn; to please, charm. **II.** *vr.* (de) to become fond (of), take a great liking (to).
prendedero, *m.* hook, fillet, brooch.
prendedor, *m.* catcher; breastpin; brooch; shawl pin, baby pin.
prender. I. *va.* (*pp.* PRENDIDO, PRESO) to seize, grasp, catch, apprehend; to cover (a mare); (Am.) to turn on (a light).—**p. fuego a,** to set on fire. **II.** *vn.* to take root; to catch or take fire. **III.** *vr.* to make an elaborate toilet.—**p. fuego,** to catch on fire.
prendería, *f.* second-hand shop; jewelry.
prendero, ra, *n.* second-hand dealer; pawnbroker.
prendido, *m.* a woman's dress; pattern for bone lace.
prendimiento, *m.* seizure, capture.
prenoción, *f.* prenotion, first knowledge.
prenombre, *m.* praenomen, first name, given name.
preriotar, *va.* to note by anticipation.
prensa, *f.* (mech.) press; vise, clamp; mill; (print.) printing press; press, newspapers.—**p. de copiar,** copying press.—**p. de embalar,** (mech.) packing press.—**p. de estampar,** drawing press.—**p. de lagar,** wine press.—**p. de tornillos,** (mech.) hand screw.—**p. hidráulica,** hydraulic press.—**p. perforadora,** (mech.) drill press.—**p. periódica,** the press.—**p. rotativa,** (print.) rotary press.—**p. taladradora,** (mech.) drill press.—**corresponsal de p.,** newspaper correspondent.—**dar a la p.,** to publish.—**entrar en p.,** to go to press.—**meter en p.,** to go to press; (fig., coll.) to press, pressure, squeeze.
prensado, *m.* lustre (on material).
prensador, ra, *n.* presser.
prensadura, *f.* pressing, pressure.
prensaestopas, *m.* (mech.) stuffing box.
prensar, *va.* to press; to calender.
prensil, *a.* prehensile.
prensión, *f.* prehension, seizing, grasping.
prensista, *m.* (print.) pressman.
prensor, ra. I. (zool.) psittacine (of the parrot family). **II.** *m. pl.* Psittaci (the parrot family).
prenunciar, *va.* to foretell, prognosticate.
prenuncio, *m.* prediction, prognostication.
preñado, da. I. *a.* pregnant; full, charged; sagging or bulging out. **II.** *m.* pregnancy.
preñez, *f.* pregnancy; impending danger or resolution; confusion, difficulty.
preocupación, *f.* preoccupation; worries; pre-

possession, bias, prejudice, notion; conventionality.
preocupadamente, *adv.* with preoccupation or prejudice.
preocupado, da. I. *pp.* of PREOCUPAR. **II.** *a.* preoccupied; worried, concerned.
preocupar. I. *va.* to preoccupy; to prejudice. **II.** *vr.* **(de)** to be prejudiced (about); to worry (over, about); (Am.) to take care (of).
preopinante, *n.* predecessor (in a debate).
preordinación, *f.* preordination.
preordinadamente, *adv.* in a preordained or foreordained manner.
preordinar, *va.* to preordain, foreordain.
prepalatal, *f.* & *a.* (phon.) prepalatal.
preparación, *f.* preparation; preparing; compound; medicine.
preparado, *m.* preparation, compound.
preparamiento, *m.* = PREPARACIÓN.
preparar. I. *va.* to prepare, make ready. **II.** *vr.* to be prepared, get ready, make preparations.
preparativo, va. I. *a.* preparative, qualifying. **II.** *m.* preparation.
preparatoriamente, *adv.* preparatorily.
preparatorio, ria, *a.* preparatory.
preponderancia, *f.* preponderance, sway.
preponderante, *a.* preponderant, prevailing.
preponderar, *vn.* to preponderate, have sway; to prevail.
proponer, *va.* (*pp.* PREPUESTO; *ind. pres.* PREPONGO, *pret.* PREPUSE, *fut.* PREPONDRÉ; *subj.* PREPONGA) to put before, to prefer.
preposición, *f.* (gram.) preposition.
preposicional, *a.* prepositional.
prepositivo, va, *a.* prepositive, prepositional.
prepósito, *m.* president, chairman; provost.
prepositura, *f.* dignity of a provost.
preposteración, *f.* reversion of order.
prepósteramente, *adv.* out of place or order; inopportunely.
preposterar, *va.* to reverse, invert, disarrange.
prepóstero, ra, *a.* out of place or order; inopportune.
prepotencia, *f.* preponderance, prepotency.
prepotente, *a.* prepotent, predominant.
prepucio, *m.* (anat.) prepuce, foreskin.
prepuesto, prepuse, *v. V.* PREPONER.
prerrafaelismo, *m.* (art) Pre-Raphaelitism.
prerrafaelista, *n.* & *a.* (art) Pre-Raphaelite.
prerrogativa, *f.* prerogative.
presa, *f.* capture, seizure; (mil.) spoils, booty; catch, hold, prey; (water) dam; trench, ditch, flume; slice, bit, morsel; tusk, fang; claw of a bird of prey; among fishermen, fish weir, stake work.—**p. de caldo,** meat juice, beef tea.
presada, *f.* reservoir, storage water (in mills).
presado, da, *a.* of a pale-green color.
presagiar, *va.* to presage, forebode, foretell.
presagio, *m.* presage, omen, token.
presagioso, sa; présago, ga, *a.* betokening, significant, presaging.
presbicia, *f.* (med.) farsightedness, presbyopia.
presbiopía, *f.* (med.) presbyopia.
présbita, présbite. (med.) **I.** *a.* presbyopic, farsighted. **II.** *n.* presbyopic person.
presbiterado, *m.* priesthood.
presbiteral, *a.* sacerdotal.
presbiterato, *m.* = PRESBITERADO.
presbiterianismo, *m.* Presbyterianism.
presbiteriano, na, *n.* & *a.* Presbyterian.
presbiterio, *m.* presbytery; chancel.
presbítero, *m.* priest; presbyter.
presciencia, *f.* prescience, foreknowledge.
presciente, *a.* prescient.
prescindible, *a.* that can be dispensed with.
prescindir, *vn.* **(de)** to dispense (with), do (without); to set aside, ignore, omit.
prescito, ta, *a.* & *n.* = PRECITO, damned.
prescribir. I. *va.* (*pp. irreg.* PRESCRITO, PRESCRIPTO) to prescribe, dispose, specify; (law and med.) to prescribe. **II.** *vn.* (law) to prescribe.
prescripción, *f.* prescription; (law) prescription.
prescriptible, *a.* prescriptible.
prescripto, prescrito, ta, *pp. irreg.* of PRESCRIBIR.
presea, *f.* jewel, gem, valuable article.
presencia, *f.* presence; appearance, physique, figure; show, ostentation.—**p. de ánimo,** coolness, presence of mind.—**presencial,** *a.* pert. to, or implying presence.
presencialmente, *adv.* in person.
presenciar, *va.* to witness, to see; to attend.
presentable, *a.* presentable; producible.
presentación, *f.* presentation, exhibition, display; personal introduction; (eccl.). Presentation.—**a p.,** (com.) on presentation, at sight.
presentado, *m.* student of divinity about to be graduated as master; person presented.
presentador, ra, *n.* presenter; bearer.
presentalla, *f.* (eccl.) votive offering.
presentáneamente, *adv.* immediately.
presentáneo, *a.* quick-acting.
presentante, *a.* presenting, introducing.
presentar. I. *va.* to present; to put on (a program, etc.); to display, show; to give, make a present of; (eccl.) to offer as candidate. **II.** *vr.* to appear, present oneself, report; to turn up; to offer one's services; (mil.) to enlist as a volunteer.
presente. I. *a.* present, current.—**hacer p.,** to state, to remind of, call attention to.—**la p.,** the present writing (these presents).—**mejorando lo p.,** present company excepted.—**tener p.,** to bear in mind. **II.** *m.* present, gift; present (time).—**al p.,** or **de p.,** at present.—**por el,** or **lo, p.,** for the present.
presentemente, *adv.* at present, now.
presentero, *m.* one who offers as a candidate.
presentimiento, *m.* presentiment; misgiving.
presentir, *va.* (*ind. pres.* PRESIENTO, *pret.* él PRESINTIÓ; *subj.* PRESIENTA; *ger.* PRESINTIENDO) to have a presentiment of; to forebode, predict.
presepio, *m.* stable; manger.
presera, *f.* (bot.) goose grass, cleavers.
presero, *m.* keeper of a dam or dike.
preservación, *f.* preservation, conservation.
preservador, ra, *n.* & *a.* preserver(-ing).
preservar, *va.* to preserve, guard, keep, save.
preservativamente, *adv.* preservatively.
preservativo, va. I. *a.* preservative, preserving. **II.** *m.* preservative, preventive.
presidario, *m.* = PRESIDIARIO.
presidencia, *f.* presidency; presidential chair; chairmanship; presidential term.
presidencial, *a.* presidential.
presidenta, *f.* president's wife; (woman) moderator; (woman) chairman; (woman) president.
presidente, *m.* president; chairman; speaker (of a parliamentary body); presiding judge; presiding officer.
presidiar, *va.* to garrison.
presidiario, *m.* convict.
presidio, *m.* garrison of soldiers; fortress, citadel; penitentiary; punishment by hard labor.
presidir, *va.* to preside over, or at; (of persons or things) to govern, sway, determine.
presidium, *m.* presidium.
presiento, presienta, *v. V.* PRESENTIR.
presilla, *f.* loop, shank, eye, noose, bight; (sewing) buttonhole stitching; a kind of linen.
presión, *f.* pressure.—**p. absoluta,** (phys.) absolute pressure.—**p. arterial,** blood pressure.—**p. atmosférica,** atmospheric pressure, air pressure.—**p. del vapor,** steam pressure.—**p. manométrica,** gauge pressure.—**p. sanguínea,** blood pressure.
presionar, *va.* (Am.) to press, urge.
preso, sa. I. *pp. irreg.* of PRENDER. **II.** *a.* arrested; imprisoned. **III.** *n.* prisoner; convict.
prest, *m.* soldier's daily pay. Also PRE.
presta, *f.* (bot.) mint.
prestación, *f.* (law) lending; loan.—**p. por cese en el servicio,** severance benefit.
prestadizo, za, *a.* that may be lent or loaned.
prestado, da. I. *pp.* of PRESTAR. **II.** *a.*—**dar p.,** to lend.—**pedir,** or **tomar, p.,** to borrow.
prestador, ra, *n.* lender.

prestamente, *adv.* speedily, promptly, quickly.
prestamera, *f.* (eccl.) a kind of sinecure.
prestamería, *f.* (eccl.) dignity of a sinecure.
prestamero, *m.* incumbent of a PRESTAMERA.
prestamista, *n.* money lender; pawnbroker.
préstamo, *m.* loan.
prestancia, *f.* excellence.
prestante, *a.* excellent.
prestar. I. *va.* to lend, to loan; to aid, to assist; to give; communicate; to pay (attention to); to render, perform (a service). **II.** *vn.* to be useful; to expand, extend. **III.** *vr.* to offer or lend oneself or itself; to adapt oneself or itself; to be applicable.
prestatario, ria, *n.* & *a.* borrower(-ing).
preste, *m.* (eccl.) high mass celebrant.—**p. Juan de las Indias,** Prester John.
prester, *m.* hurricane, cyclone; waterspout.
presteza, *f.* quickness, promptness, haste.
prestidigitación, *f.* legerdemain, sleight of hand, jugglery.
prestidigitador, ra, *n.* juggler, prestidigitator.
prestigiador, ra, *n.* cheat, impostor.
prestigio, *m.* prestige, good name; spell, fascination; (of legerdemain) deception, illusion.
prestigioso, sa, *a.* renowned; well-reputed; deceiving, illusory.
prestimonio, *m.* loan; (eccl.) prestimony.
prestiño, *m.* = PESTIÑO, honey fritter.
presto, ta. I. *a.* quick, swift, prompt; ready, prepared. **II.** *adv.* soon; quickly.—**de p.,** promptly, swiftly.
presumible, *a.* presumable.
presumido, da. I. *pp.* of PRESUMIR. **II.** *a.* presumptuous, airy, conceited. **III.** *n.* vain or presumptuous person.
presumir. I. *va.* (*pp.* PRESUMIDO, PRESUNTO) to presume, surmise, conjecture. **II.** *vn.* **(de)** to presume, boast (of being), claim (to be); to be conceited.
presunción, *f.* presumption, conjecture; presumptuousness, conceit; (law) presumption.
presuntamente, *adv.* presumptively.
presuntivamente, *adv.* conjecturally.
presuntivo, va, *a.* presumptive, supposed.
presunto, ta. I. *pp. irreg.* of PRESUMIR. **II.** *a.* presumed.—**p. heredero,** heir apparent.
presuntuosamente, *adv.* presumptuously.
presuntuosidad, *f.* presumptuousness.
presuntuoso, sa. I. *a.* presumptuous, conceited. **II.** *n.* vain or conceited person.
presuponer, *va.* (*pp.* PRESUPUESTO; *ind. pres.* PRESUPONGO, *pret.* PRESUPUSE, *fut.* PRESUPONDRÉ; *subj.* PRESUPONGA) to presuppose; to estimate; to budget.
presuposición, *f.* presupposition.
presupuestal, *a.* budgetary, budget (as *a.*).
presupuestar, *va.* & *vn.* to budget.
presupuestario, ria, *a.* budget (as *a.*).
presupuesto, ta. I. *pp. irreg.* of PRESUPONER. **II.** *m.* motive, pretext, pretence; estimate; budget of state.—**nivelar el p.,** to balance the budget.
presura, *f.* anxiety; quickness, haste, promptness; persistency.
presurosamente, *adv.* hastily, promptly.
presuroso, sa, *a.* prompt, quick; nimble.
pretal, *m.* breastplate, breast leather.
pretencioso, sa, *a.* presumptuous, conceited.
pretender, *va.* (*pp.* PRETENDIDO, PRETENSO) to pretend; to aspire to; to seek, solicit; to try, endeavor; to intend; (S. A.) to court, be in love with.—**p. decir,** to mean, be driving at.
pretendiente, ta, *n.* pretender, candidate, office hunter; (Colomb.) suitor.
pretensión, *f.* pretension, claim; presumption.
pretenso, sa, *pp. irreg.* of PRETENDER.
pretensor, ra, *n.* pretender, claimant.
preterición, *f.* omission; (rhet. and law) pretericion.
preterir, *va.* (*defect. only the infin. and pp. used*) (law) to omit (lawful heirs) in a will.
pretérito, ta, *n.* & *a.* preterit, past.
pretermisión, *f.* pretermission, omission, neglect.
pretermitir, *va.* to omit, pretermit, pass by.
preternatural, *a.* preternatural.
preternaturalizar, *va.* to pervert; to render preternatural.
preternaturalmente, *adv.* preternaturally.
pretexta, *f.* (anc. Rome) pretexta, a robe.
pretextar, *va.* to give as a pretext.
pretexto, *m.* pretext, pretense, cover, excuse.
pretil, *m.* railing, battlement, breastwork.
pretina, *f.* girdle, waistband; belt.
pretinero, ra, *n.* girdle maker or seller.
pretinilla, *f. dim.* ladies' belt or girdle.
[1]**pretor,** *m.* (Rom. hist.) pretor.
[2]**pretor,** *m.* blackness of the waters where tunny fish abound.
pretoría, *f.* pretorship.
pretorial, *a.* pretorian or prætorian.
pretorianismo, *m.* abuse of military power for political purposes, political militarism.
pretoriano, na, *a.* pretorian or prætorian.
pretoriense, *a.* pertaining to a pretorium.
pretorio, ria. I. *a.* pretorian. **II.** *m.* pretorium.
pretura, *f.* pretorship.
prevalecer, *vn.* (*ind.* PREVALEZCO; *subj.* PREVALEZCA) to prevail; to take root.
prevaleciente, *a.* prevalent; prevailing.
prevalerse, *vr.* to avail oneself.
prevalezco, prevalezca, *v. V.* PREVALECER.
prevaricación, *f.* betrayal of a trust.
prevaricador, ra, *n.* one who plays false, betrayer; perverter; turncoat.
prevaricar, *vn.* (*pret.* PREVARIQUÉ; *subj.* PREVARIQUE) to play false, be a betrayer; (law) to prevaricate.—**prevaricato,** *m.* (law) prevarication, betrayal of a trust.
prevención, *f.* prevention; foresight, forethought; disposition, preparation; supply of provisions; sustenance, subsistence; warning; prejudice, prepossession; police station; (mil.) guardroom, cell; (law) prevenience of a judge in the knowledge of a case.
prevengo, prevenga, *v. V.* PREVENIR.
prevenidamente, *adv.* beforehand, previously.
prevenido, da. I. *pp.* of PREVENIR. **II.** *a.* ready, prepared, provided; plentiful; forewarned; cautious.
preveniente, *a.* predisposing, prevenient.
prevenir. I. *va.* (*ger.* PREVINIENDO; *ind. pres.* yo PREVENGO, él PREVIENE, *pret.* PREVINE, *fut.* PREVENDRÉ; *subj.* PREVENGA) to prepare, prearrange, make ready; to foresee; to forestall, prevent, avoid; to warn, caution; to prepossess, predispose; to overcome; to come upon, surprise. **II.** *vr.* to be ready, prepared, or on guard; to take precautions.
preventivamente, *adv.* preventively.
preventivo, va, *a.* preventive, preservative; (law) prevenient.
preventorio, *m.* preventorium (hospital for contagious diseases).
prever, *va.* (*pp.* PREVISTO; *ind.* PREVEO; *subj.* PREVEA) to foresee, anticipate.
previamente, *adv.* previously.
previene, previne, etc. *v. V.* PREVENIR.
previo, via, *a.* previous, foregoing.—**examen p.,** (Chile) preliminary examination.
previsión, *f.* foresight; forecast.—**p. social,** social security; social service.
previsor, ra, *n.* one who foresees. **II.** *a.* far-seeing, perspicacious.
previsto, ta, *pp. irreg.* of PREVER.
prez, *m.* or *f.* honor, glory, merit, worth.
priapismo, *m.* (med.) priapism.
priesa, *f.* = PRISA.
prieto, ta, *a.* blackish, very dark; narrow-minded, illiberal; close-fisted, mean; tight, compressed; (Mex.) (of person) dark, brunette.
prima, *f.* female cousin; early morning; (eccl.) prime; first tonsure; (mil.) first quarter of the night; (mus.) treble (in stringed instruments); (com.) premium; bounty.
primacía, *f.* primacy; primateship.

primacial, *a.* primatial.
primada, *f.* (coll.) taking advantage of a gullible, naïve person; a sponging trick.
[1]**primado, da,** *a.* primatial.
[2]**primado,** *m.* primeness; (eccl.) primate.
primal, la. I. *a.* yearling (ewe or a goat). **II.** *m.* silk cord or braid.
primariamente, *adv.* chiefly, primarily.
primario, ria. I. *a.* principal, primary; (geol.) Primary, Paleozoic; (eccl.) primary (circuit). **II.** *n.* professor who lectures at dawn.
primate. I. *n.* distinguished person, worthy. **II.** *m.* (zool.) one of the Primates.—*pl.* Primates.
primavera, *f.* spring (season); flowered silk; (bot.) primrose.
primaveral, *a.* spring (as *a.*), pert. to spring.
primazgo, *m.* cousinship.
primearse, *vr.* to treat each other as cousins.
primer, *a. contr.* of PRIMERO.—**p. galán,** (theat.) lead.—**p. grado,** first degree.—**p. meridiano,** prime meridian.—**P. Ministro,** Prime Minister.—**p. nombre,** forename, first name.—**p. piloto,** (naut.) first mate, first officer; (aer.) first pilot.—**p. piso,** main floor.—**p. plano,** foreground.—**p. pronto,** first movement.—**p. teniente,** (mil.) first lieutenant.—**p. vertical,** (astr.) prime vertical.—**en p. lugar,** first of all.
primeramente, *adv.* first; in the first place.
primerizo, za. I. *n.* novice, beginner; firstling. **II.** *f.* (med.) = PRIMÍPARA.
primero, ra. I. *a.* first, primary, prime; foremost; former; raw (*primera materia,* raw material); front (*primera página,* front page).—**p. base,** (baseball) first base; player stationed there.—**p. clase,** first class.—**p. dama,** (theat.) leading lady.—**p. dama de la nación,** first lady, president's wife.—**p. edición,** first edition.—**p. enseñanza,** primary education.—**p. fila,** front rank.—**p. intención,** (surg.) first intention.—**p. mano (de pintura),** first coat (of painting).—**p. página,** front page (newspapers); first page (books).—**p. persona,** (gram.) first person.—**p. piedra,** cornerstone, foundation stone.—**primeros auxilios,** first aid.—**a p. faz,** at first sight.—**a p. luz,** at dawn.—**a p. vista,** at first sight.—**de buenas a primeras,** all at once, suddenly.—**de p.,** (com.) of superior quality, highest-grade, prime.—**de p. instancia,** instantly, on the first impulse; first in; in the first place. **II.** *f.* primero (card game); (fencing) prime.—*pl.* first tricks (at cards).—**p. de cambio,** (com.) first of exchange. **III.** *adv. m.* first, firstly; rather, sooner.—**de p.,** at the beginning, before.
primevo, va, *a.* primeval, original.
primicerio, ria. I. *a.* principal, first in rank. **II.** *m.* precentor, chanter.
primicia, *f.* first fruits; offering of the first fruits.—*pl.* first production, maiden effort.
primicial, *a.* pert. to first fruits.
primichón, *m.* skein of soft embroidery silk.
primigenio, nia, *a.* primogenial, primitive.
primilla, *f.* (coll.) pardon of a first offence.
primípara, *f.* (med.) primipara.
primitivamente, *adv.* originally.
primitivismo, *m.* primitivism.
primitivista, *n.* & *a.* primitivist.
primitivo, va, *a.* primitive, original, primeval.
primo, ma. I. *a.* first; superior, excellent, prime.—**a p. noche,** early in the evening, shortly after dark. **II.** *n.* cousin; (coll.) simpleton, dupe.—*pl.* cousins, appellation given by the kings of Spain to the grandees.—**p. carnal,** or **p. hermano,** first cousin. **III.** *adv. m.* first, in the first place.
primogénito, ta, *n.* & *a.* first-born.
primogenitura, *f.* primogeniture; seniority.
primor, *m.* beauty; dexterity, ability, exquisiteness, excellence, nicety.
primordial, *a.* primordial, original, primal.
primorear, *vn.* to perform with elegance and neatness.
primorosamente, *adv.* finely, nicely, elegantly.
primoroso, sa, *a.* neat, elegant, fine, exquisite; beautiful; graceful, dexterous.
primuláceo, a, *a.* (bot.) primulaceous.
princesa, *f.* princess; princesse (gown).
principada, *f.* (coll.) undue assumption of authority.
principado, *m.* princedom; princehood; principality; preëminence, primacy.—*pl.* princedoms.
principal. I. *a.* principal, main; important, essential; illustrious, renowned, celebrated; foremost, first; first (story of an apartment building, etc. above the ground floor, one flight up; in U. S. called second floor). **II.** *m.* (mil.) main guard; (com.) principal, capital, stock; principal, chief or head of a commercial establishment; (law) constituent.
principalía, *f.* (P. I.) board of officers in each town.
principalidad, *f.* principalness.
principalmente, *adv.* principally, mainly.
príncipe, *m.* prince; sovereign, ruler; chief or leader; young queen bee; master (often as *a.,* as in *autores príncipes,* classical authors, old masters).—**p. consorte,** prince consort.—**P. de Asturias,** Crown Prince of Spain.—**P. de Gales,** Prince of Wales.—**P. de la Iglesia,** Prince of the Church.—**P. de la Paz,** Prince of Peace, Jesus Christ.—**p. de sangre,** prince of blood royal.
principela, *f.* a sort of light camlet.
principesco, ca, *a.* princely, regal, imposing.
principiador, ra, *n.* beginner.
principiante, ta, *n.* beginner; apprentice.
principiar, *va.* to commence, begin, start.
principillo, *m. dim.* petty prince.
principio, *m.* principle; beginning; start; germ, original cause; rule of action, motive; origin, fountain; (cooking) entrée; (chem.) principle.—*pl.* (print.) introductory matter in a book.—**a principios de,** at the beginning of.—**al p.,** or **a los princípos,** in the beginning, at first.—**de principios,** early.—**en p.,** in principle; in substance, essentially.
principote, *m.* (coll.) one who makes a pretentious display.
pringada, *f.* toasted bread steeped in gravy.
pringamoza, *f.* (Am.) (bot.) nettle.
pringar. I. *va.* (*pret.* PRINGUÉ; *subj.* PRINGUE) to baste (meat); to steep or dip (bread) in grease; to stain with grease; to spatter; to scald with boiling fat; to tar (a person); to wound; to slander; (coll.) to share in a business. **II.** *vr.* (coll.) to draw unlawful advantage from a thing intrusted to one's care.
pringón, na. I. *a.* nasty, dirty, greasy. **II.** *m.* begreasing oneself; stain of grease.
pringoso, sa, *a.* greasy, fat.
pringote, *m.* mixture of foods.
pringue, *m.* or *f.* grease, fat, lard; grease stain in clothes.
pringué, pringue, *v. V.* PRINGAR.
pringuera, *f.* dripping pan.
prionodonte, *m.* (zool.) giant armadillo.
prior. I. *a.* prior, preceding. **II.** *m.* (eccl.) prior, superior; (prov.) rector, curate.
priora, *f.* prioress.
prioral, *a.* pertaining to a prior or prioress.
priorato, priorazgo, *m.* priorate; priory.
prioridad, *f.* priority; precedence.
prioste, *m.* steward of a brotherhood.
prisa, *f.* haste, despatch, promptness; urgency; skirmish, surprise, hot fight.—**a p.,** quickly.—**a toda p.,** with the greatest speed.—**darse p.,** to make haste, hurry.—**de p.** = A P.—**estar de p.,** or **tener p.,** to be in a hurry.
priscilianismo, *m.* Priscillianism.
priscilianista, *n.* Priscillianist.
prisco, *m.* a kind of peach.
prisión, *f.* seizure, capture; prison; imprisonment; bond, shackle; (law) custody.—*pl.* chains, fetters.—**p. preventiva,** (law) protective custody.—**reducir a p.,** to incarcerate, confine, imprison.

prisionero, *m.* (mil.) prisoner; one captivated by affection or passion.
prisma, *m.* prism.
prismático, ca, *a.* prismatic.
priste, *m.* (ichth.) sawfish.
prístino, na, *a.* pristine, first, original.
prisuelo, *m.* muzzle for ferrets.
pritaneo, *m.* prytaneum (Greek public building).
privación, *f.* privation, want; lack; deprivation, loss; degradation.
privada, *f.* privy, water-closet; filth thrown into the street.
privadamente, *adv.* privately; separately.
privadero, *m.* cesspool cleaner.
[1]**privado, da.** I. *a.* private, secret; personal. II. *m.* favorite, court minion, protégé.
[2]**privado, da.** I. *pp.* of PRIVAR. II. *a.* stunned, unconscious.
privanza, *f.* favor at court, protection.
privar. I. *va.* to deprive; to prohibit, forbid, interdict; to stun, daze. II. *vn.* to enjoy the protection of a magnate; to prevail, be in favor or in vogue. III. *vr.* to deprive oneself.
privativamente, *adv.* solely, privatively
privativo, va, *a.* privative; special, distinctive, particular, peculiar; exclusive.
privilegiadamente, *adv.* in a privileged way.
privilegiado, da. I. *pp.* of PRIVILEGIAR. II. *a.* privileged, prerogative, preferential.
privilegiar, *va.* to favor; to grant a privilege to.
privilegiativo, va, *a.* containing a privilege.
privilegio, *m.* privilege; grant, concession; exemption, grace; franchise; faculty; patent, copyright.—**p. de introducción,** patent on a device introduced from a foreign country.—**p. de invención,** patent (on an invention).—**p. del fuero,** privilege of ecclesiastics to be tried by their own courts.
pro, *m.* or *f.* profit, benefit, advantage.—**buena p.,** much good may it do you.—**de p.,** of note, worthy.—**en p. de,** in behalf of, for the benefit of.—**el p. y el contra,** the pros and cons.—**en p. y en contra,** pro and against; pro and con.
proa, *f.* (naut.) bow, prow; nose (of airplane).
proal, *a.* pertaining to the prow; forward.
probabilidad, *f.* probability, likelihood.
probabilísimo, ma, *a. super.* most probable.
probabilismo, *m.* (theol.) probabilism.
probabilista, *n.* & *a.* (theol.) probabilist(-ic).
probable, *a.* probable, likely.
probablemente, *adv.* probably, likely.
probación, *f.* proof; probation, trial.
probado, da. I. *pp.* of PROBAR. II. *a.* proved, tried.
probador, ra, *n.* taster, sampler; trier.
probadura, *f.* trial, tasting, sampling.
probanza, *f.* proof, evidence.
probar. I. *va.* (*ind.* PRUEBO; *subj.* PRUEBE) to try, test; to prove; to taste; to sample (as wine); to attempt, try, endeavor; to try on (as a coat).—**p. fortuna,** to take one's chances. II. *vn.*, to suit, fit, agree with. III. *vr.* to try on (as a coat).
probatorio, ria. I. *a.* probatory, probationary. II. *f.* (law) time allowed for producing evidence.
probatura, *f.* (coll.) trial, test, experiment.
probeta, *f.* manometer, pressure gauge; (mil.) powder prover; (chem.) test tube, pipette.
probidad, *f.* probity, honesty, integrity.
problema, *m.* problem.
problemáticamente, *adv.* problematically.
problemático, ca, *a.* problematic(al).
probo, ba, *a.* upright, honest.
probóscide, *f.* (ent., zool.) proboscis.
proboscidio, dia, *a.* (zool.) proboscidean.
procacidad, *f.* impudence, pertness.
procaína, *f.* (pharm.) procaine.
procaz, *a.* impudent, bold, insolent.
procedencia, *f.* origin; source; place of sailing.
procedente, *a.* coming or proceeding (from); (law) according to law, rules, or practice.
proceder. I. *vn.* to proceed; to go on; to come, proceed, arise; to be the result; to behave, conduct oneself; to act; to take action; (law) to proceed (against), take action; to be in conformity with the law, rules, or practice; to concern. II. *m.* conduct, behavior, action, management.
procedimiento, *m.* procedure; process, method; (law) proceeding, procedure.
procela, *f.* (poet.) storm, tempest.
procelio, *m.* (anat.) procœlia.
proceloso, sa, *a.* tempestuous, stormy.
prócer. I. *a.* tall, lofty, elevated. II. *m.* person in an exalted station, worthy; Father (of the country, in Am. republics).—*pl.* the grandees and high-titled nobility of Spain.
procerato, *m.* exalted station.
proceridad, *f.* tallness; elevation or eminence; vigor, growth.
procero, ra; prócero, ra, *a.* = PRÓCER.
procesado, da. I. *pp.* of PROCESAR. II. *a.* (law) relating to court proceedings; included in the suit; accused, prosecuted, indicted. III. *n.* (law) defendant, accused.
procesal, *a.* pertaining to a process or lawsuit.
procesamiento, *m.* indicting; suing.
procesar, *va.* (law) to sue; to indict.
procesión, *f.* act of proceeding or issuing forth; procession, parade, pageant.
procesional, *a.* processional or processionary.
procesionalmente, *adv.* processionally.
procesionaria, *f.* (zool.) processionary moth.
procesionario, *m.* processional book.
proceso, *m.* lapse of time; (law) criminal case; proceedings of a lawsuit, trial.
Proción, *m.* (astr.) Procyon.
proclama, *f.* proclamation; publication; banns of marriage.
proclamación, *f.* proclamation; promulgation; acclamation, public applause.
proclamar, *va.* to proclaim; to promulgate; to acclaim, cheer.
proclítico, ca, *a.* (gram.) proclitic.
proclive, *a.* inclined, disposed.
proclividad, *f.* proclivity; propensity.
procomún, procomunal, *m.* public welfare.
procónsul, *m.* proconsul.
proconsulado, *m.* proconsulship.
proconsular, *a.* proconsular.
procreación, *f.* procreation.
procreador, ra. I. *a.* procreant, procreative, procreating, producing. II. *n.* procreator, producer.
procreante, *a.* procreating.
procrear, *va.* to procreate, generate, produce.
proctitis, *f.* proctitis.
proctoscopio, *m.* (med.) proctoscope.
procura, *f.* power of attorney.
procuración, *f.* care, diligence, careful management; power or letter of attorney; procurement, procuring; office of an attorney.
procurador, ra, *n.* procurer(-ess); (law) attorney, solicitor, proctor; *f.* manageress of a nunnery.—**p. de síndico,** attorney general.
procuraduría, *f.* attorney's office; proctorship.
procurante, *n.* solicitor, intendant.
procurar. I. *va.* to endeavor, try; to manage, transact for another; to get, obtain, procure. II. *vn.* to be, or act as, an attorney.
procurrente, *m.* (geog.) peninsula.
prodición, *f.* treason, treachery.
prodigalidad, *f.* prodigality; abundance.
pródigamente, *adv.* prodigally, lavishly, wastefully, profusely.
prodigar, *va.* (*pret.* PRODIGUÉ; *subj.* PRODIGUE) to lavish; to squander.
prodigiador, *m.* prognosticator, foreteller.
prodigio, *m.* prodigy; monster; marvel.
prodigiosamente, *adv.* prodigiously, wonderfully; beautifully, charmingly.
prodigiosidad, *f.* prodigiousness.
prodigioso, sa, *a.* prodigious, marvellous; monstrous; fine, excellent.
pródigo, ga. I. *a.* prodigal, extravagant, waste-

ful; liberal, generous, unstinted. **II.** *n.* prodigal, spendthrift, waster.
prodigué, prodigue, *v. V.* PRODIGAR.
prodrómico, ca, *a.* (med.) prodromal.
pródromo, *m.* (med.) prodrome, warning symptom.
producción, *f.* production; produce, yield; crop; delivery.
producente, *a.* producing, causing.
producibilidad, *f.* producibleness.
producible, *a.* producible.
producidor, ra. I. *a.* productive, producing. **II.** *n.* producer.
producir. I. *va.* (*pp.* PRODUCIDO, PRODUCTO; *ind. pres.* PRODUZCO, *pret.* PRODUJE; *subj.* PRODUZCA) to produce; to publish; to yield, bear; (com.) to bring or yield (as revenue); (law) to produce, bring as evidence, exhibit. **II.** *vr.* to explain oneself; to be produced; to arise, break out.
productible, *a.* (Am.) producible.
productividad, *f.* productivity.
productivo, va, *a.* productive; profitable, fruitful.
producto, *m.* product; article (of trade, etc.): production; produce; (math.) product; *pl.* proceeds.—**p. neto,** (com.) net produce.—**productos agrícolas,** farm produce.—**productos alimenticios,** foodstuff.—**productos de tocador,** toilet articles.—**p. secundario,** by-product.—**productos químicos,** chemicals, chemical products.
productor, ra. I. *a.* productive, producing.—**capacidad p.,** productive capacity. **II.** *n.* producer, procreator.
produje, produzco, produzca, *v. V.* PRODUCIR.
proejar, *vn.* to row against wind or tide.
proel. I. *a.* (naut.) fore. **II.** *m.* (naut.) bow hand.
proemial, *a.* proemial, introductory.
proemio, *m.* proem, preface, introduction.
proeza, *f.* prowess, feat.
profanación, *f.* profanation, desecration.
profanador, ra, *n.* & *a.* profaner(-ing), defiler (-ing), violator(-ing).
profanamente, *adv.* profanely.
profanamiento, *m.* = PROFANACIÓN.
profanar, *va.* to profane, desecrate; to defile, disgrace, dishonor.
profanidad, *f.* profanity; profaneness; indecency, immodesty.
profano, na, *a.* profane, secular; profane, irreverent; worldly; irreligious; immodest, unchaste; lay, unfamiliar, ignorant.
profase, *f.* (genet.) prophase.
profecía, *f.* prophecy.—*pl.* the Prophets.
profecticio, *a.* (law) profectitious.
proferente, *a.* uttering, pronouncing.
proferir, *va.* (*ger.* PROFIRIENDO; *ind. pres.* PROFIERO, *pret.* él PROFIRIÓ; *subj.* PROFIERA) to utter, express, speak.
profesante, *a.* professing.
profesar, *va.* to practise or follow (a profession or trade); to teach as a professor; to profess, join (a religious group, etc.); to entertain, manifest (as friendship); (eccl.) to join (a religious body).
profesión, *f.* profession; declaration, avowal.—**de p.,** by profession.
profesional. I. *a.* professional, vocational. **II.** *n.* professional, practitioner.
profeso, sa, *a.* professed (monk or nun).
profesor, ra, *n.* professor; teacher.—**p. adjunto,** adjunct professor, associate professor.—**p. agregado,** assistant professor.—**p. honorario,** emeritus professor.—**p. particular,** tutor, private teacher.—**p. titular,** full professor.—**p. visitante,** visiting professor.
profesorado, *m.* professorship; professorate; body of teachers, faculty.
profesoral, *a.* professorial, pedagogical.
profeta, *m.* prophet, seer.
profetal, *a.* prophetic, prophetical, predictive.
proféticamente, *adv.* prophetically.
profeticé, profetice, *v. V.* PROFETIZAR.
profético, ca, *a.* prophetic, prophetical.
profetisa, *f.* prophetess.
profetizador, ra, *n.* & *a.* prophesier(-ing).
profetizar, *va.* & *vn.* (*pret.* PROFETICÉ; *subj.* PROFETICE) to prophesy.
proficiente, *a.* proficient, advanced.
proficuo, cua, *a.* useful, advantageous.
profiero, profiera, *v. V.* PROFERIR.
profiláctico, ca. I. *a.* (med.) prophylactic, preventive. **II.** *m.* prophylactic, preventive; *f.* hygiene.
profilaxis, *f.* prophylaxis, preventive medicine.
profirió, *pret.* of PROFERIR.
prófugo, ga. I. *a.* fugitive, fugacious. **II.** *n.* fugitive, escapee; *m.* draft dodger.
profundamente, *adv.* profoundly, deeply; highly, acutely.
profundicé, profundice, *v. V.* PROFUNDIZAR.
profundidad, *f.* depth; profundity, profoundness; height, excellence; intensity.—**p. de foco,** (opt., photog.) depth of field or focus.
profundizar, *va.* (*pret.* PROFUNDICÉ; *subj.* PROFUNDICE) to deepen; to go deep into; to fathom, explore.
profundo, da. I. *a.* deep; low; profound, recondite; intense, dense; high, great. **II.** *m.* profundity; the sea, the deep; hell.
profusamente, *adv.* profusely; lavishly, prodigally, extravagantly.
profusión, *f.* profusion, profuseness; lavishness, prodigality.
profuso, sa, *a.* profuse, plentiful; lavish, prodigal.
progenie, *f.* progeny, offspring, issue.
progenitor, *m.* progenitor, ancestor.
progenitura, *f.* = PROGENIE; = PRIMOGENITURA, primogeniture.
progesterona, *f.* (biochem.) progesterone, progestin.
progimnasma, *m.* (rhet.) preparatory exercise.
prognatismo, *m.* (anat.) prognathism.
prognato, ta, *a.* (anat.) prognathous.
progne, *f.* (poet.) (ornith.) swallow.
prognosis, *f.* prognosis, forecasting.
programa, *m.* program; plans; scheme; specifications; proclamation, public notice; (theat.) playbill.—**p. de televisión,** television program, telecast.—**p. de urgencia,** (coll.) crash program.—**p. doble,** (cine.) double feature.
programar, *va.* to program, make a program.
progresar, *vn.* to progress; to advance.
progresión, *f.* progression, progress; advance; (math.) progression.
progresismo, *m.* progressivism.
progresista. I. *a.* progressive, progressional; (pol.) Progressive. **II.** *n.* progressive, progressionist; (pol.) Progressive.
progresivamente, *adv.* progressively, onward, forward.
progresivo, va, *a.* progressive, advancing.
progreso, *m.* progress, civilization; (often *pl.*) progress (in an undertaking, in school, etc.), advancement, development.
prohibente, *a.* prohibiting.
prohibición, *f.* prohibition, forbidding.
prohibicionismo, *m.* prohibitionism.
prohibicionista, *n.* & *a.* prohibitionist(-ic).
prohibir, *va.* to prohibit, forbid.—**se prohibe fumar,** (on sign) no smoking.
prohibitivo, va, *a.* prohibitive, forbidding.
prohibitorio, ria, *a.* prohibitory.
prohijación, *f.* = PROHIJAMIENTO.
prohijador, ra, *n.* adopter.
prohijamiento, *m.* adoption.
prohijar, *va.* to adopt (child, opinion, etc.).
prohombre, *m.* great man; master of a guild.
pro indiviso, *adv.* (law) undivided (legacies).
prójima, *f.* insignificant or contemptible woman.
prójimo, *m.* fellow being, (in Biblical language) neighbor.
prolapso, *m.* (med.) prolapsus, falling.
prole, *f.* issue, offspring, progeny; fruit.

prolegómenos, *m. pl.* prolegomena.
prolepsis, *f.* (rhet.) prolepsis.
proléptico, ca, *a.* proleptic.
proletariado, *m.* proletariat.
proletario, ria. I. *a.* proletarian, very poor; plebeian; belonging to the working classes. **II.** *n.* proletarian; (Rom. hist.) proletary.
proliferación, *f.* proliferation.
proliferante, *a.* proliferating, multiplying.
prolífico, ca, *a.* prolific, fruitful, productive.
prolijamente, *adv.* prolixly, tediously.
prolijidad, *f.* prolixity; trifling nicety.
prolijo, ja, *a.* prolix, tedious; overcareful, triflingly nice; troublesome, impertinent, long-winded.
prologal, *a.* pertaining to prefaces or a preface.
prologar, *va.* to write a preface for.
prólogo, *m.* prologue; preface.
prologuista, *m.* writer of prologues.
prolonga, *f.* (artil.) prolonge.
prolongación, *f.* prolongation, lengthening; extension; protraction, lingering.
prolongadamente, *adv.* tardily, protractedly.
prolongado, da. I. *pp.* of PROLONGAR. **II.** *a.* oblong.
prolongador, ra, *n.* & *a.* prolonger(-ing).
prolongamiento, *m.* = PROLONGACIÓN.
prolongar, *va.* & *vr.* (*pret.* PROLONGUÉ; *subj.* PROLONGUE) to prolong; to protract, extend, continue; (geom.) to produce.—**p. un plazo,** (com.) to grant an extension of time.
proloquio, *m.* maxim, apothegm.
prolusión, *f.* prolusion, prelude.
promediar. I. *va.* to divide into two equal parts; (com.) to average. **II.** *vn.* to mediate; to be about the middle of (the month, etc.).
promedio, *m.* middle; average, mean.
promesa, *f.* promise, offer; pious offering.
prometedor, ra. I. *a.* promising; hopeful. **II.** *n.* promiser.
prometer. I. *va.* to promise, offer; bid fair. **II.** *vn.* to promise, give favorable indications. **III.** *vr.* to expect with confidence; to become betrothed; to devote oneself to the service of God.
prometido, da. I. *pp.* of PROMETER. **II.** *n.* betrothed. **III.** *m.* promise; offer; auction fee.
prometiente, *a.* promising, assuring.
prometimiento, *m.* promise, offer.
prometio, *m.* (chem.) promethium.
prominencia, *f.* elevation; prominence; protuberance; knoll, knob.
prominente, *a.* elevated, protuberant; projecting, jutting out.
promiscuamente, *adv.* promiscuously.
promiscuar, *vn.* to eat meat and fish on fast days.
promiscuidad, *f.* promiscuity; ambiguity.
promiscuo, cua, *a.* promiscuous; ambiguous.
promisión, *f.* promise.
promisorio, ria, *a.* promissory.
promoción, *f.* promotion, preferment.
promontorio, *m.* promontory, headland, foreland; anything bulky and unwieldy.
promotor, ra. I. *a.* promotive. **II.** *n.* promoter advancer, furtherer.—**p. fiscal,** (law) district attorney.
promovedor, ra, *n.* promoter.
promover, *va.* (*ind.* PROMUEVO; *subj.* PROMUEVA) to promote, further; to advance, exalt, raise.
promulgación, *f.* promulgation.
promulgador, ra, *n.* promulgator.
promulgar, *va,* (*pret.* PROMULGUÉ; *subj.* PROMULGUE) to promulgate, proclaim, publish.
pronación, *f.* (physiol.) pronation.
pronaos, *m.* (arch.) pronaos, vestibule.
prono, na, *a.* prone, inclined, bent on.
pronombre, *m.* (gram.) pronoun.
pronominado, da, *a.* = PRONOMINAL.
pronominal, *a.* (gram.) pronominal.
pronosticable, *a.* prognosticable, predictable, foreseeable.
pronosticación, *f.* prognostication, prediction, prevision, foresight.
pronosticador, ra. I. *a.* prognostic, prognosticating, predicting. **II.** *n.* prognosticator, predictor, foreseer.
pronosticar, *va.* (*pret.* PRONOSTIQUÉ; *subj.* PRONOSTIQUE) to prognosticate, foretell, augur.
pronóstico, *m.* prognostic, prediction, omen; almanac; (med.) prognosis.
pronostiqué, pronostique, *v. V.* PRONOSTICAR.
prontamente, *adv.* promptly, quickly.
prontitud, *f.* promptness; speed, swiftness, dispatch; liveliness of wit; quick repartee.
pronto, ta. I. *a.* prompt, quick, fast; ready. **II.** *m.* sudden impulse.—**primer p.,** first movement. **III.** *adv.* soon; promptly, quickly.—**al p.,** at first.—**de p.,** suddenly, without thinking.—**por** or **de, el** or **lo, p.** in the meantime, for the time being, provisionally.—**tan p. como,** as soon as.
prontuario, *m.* memorandum book; compendium of rules.
prónuba, *f.* (poet.) bridesmaid.
pronúcleo, *m.* (zool.) pronucleus.
pronunciable, *a.* pronounceable, utterable.
pronunciación, *f.* pronunciation, articulation.
pronunciado, da. I. *pp.* of PRONUNCIAR. **II.** *n.* insurgent. **III.** *a.* pronounced, steep; sharp.
pronunciador, ra, *n.* pronouncer.
pronunciamiento, *m.* insurrection, uprising; (law) pronouncement of a sentence.
pronunciar. I. *va.* to pronounce, articulate, enunciate; to deliver, make (a speech); (law) to pronounce (judgment); to pass upon (a point) before the main question is decided. **II.** *vr.* to rise in insurrection, to rebel.
propagable, *a.* propagable.
propagación, *f.* propagation; spreading, dissemination.
propagador, ra, *n.* & *a.* propagator(-ing).
propaganda, *f.* propaganda, dissemination; (eccl.) propaganda; association for propagating doctrines.
propagandismo, *m.* propagandism.
propagandista, *n.* & *a.* propagandist.
propagante, *a.* propagating; spreading.
propagar. I. *va.* (*pret.* PROPAGUÉ; *subj.* PROPAGUE) to propagate, generate; to spread, disseminate. **II.** *vr.* to spread; to propagate; to multiply.—**propagativo, va,** *a.* propagative.
propalador, ra, *n.* divulger.
propalar, *va.* to publish, to divulge.
propano, *m.* (chem.) propane.
propao, *m.* (naut.) breastwork, bulkhead.
proparoxítono, na, *m.* & *a.* (phon., gram.) proparoxytone.
propartida, *f.* time preceding a departure.
propasarse, *vr.* to transgress, overstep all bounds, take undue liberties, forget oneself, exceed one's authority.
propedéutico, ca. I. *a.* propædeutic, propædeutical, elementary. **II.** *f.* propædeutics, elements, basic rules (of an art or science).
propender, *vn.* (*pp.* PROPENDIDO, PROPENSO) to tend, be inclined, have a tendency.
propensamente, *adv.* with a tendency.
propensión, *f.* propensity, tendency, bent, inclination, proneness.—**con p. a accidentes,** accident-prone.
propenso, sa. I. *pp. irreg.* of PROPENDER. **II.** *a.* inclined, disposed.
propiamente, *adv.* properly, fittingly.
propiciación, *f.* propitiation, atonement.
propiciador, ra, *n.* & *a.* propitiator(-ing).
propiciamente, *adv.* propitiously.
propiciar, *va.* to propitiate, conciliate.
propiciatorio, ria. I. *a.* propitiatory. **II.** *m.* propitiatory, mercy seat.
propicio, cia, *a.* propitious, favorable.
propiedad, *f.* ownership, proprietorship; property, holding; landed estate; property, quality; propriety, fitness; (law) dominion, possession;

(art) naturalness, close imitation.—**p. intelectual** or **literaria,** copyright.—**p. mueble,** goods and chattels.—**p. raíz,** real estate.—**es p. (de)**, copyright (by).
propienda, *f.* listing nailed to the cheeks of an embroidery frame.
propietariamente, *adv.* with the right of property.
propietario, ria. I. *a.* proprietary. **II.** *n.* proprietor, owner, landlord(-lady), freeholder.
propileno, *m.* (chem.) propylene.
propileo, *m.* (arch.) propyleum, vestibule.
propilo, *m.* (chem.) propyl.
propina, *f.* fee, gratuity, tip; perquisite.
propinación, *f.* treat, invitation to drink.
propinar, *va.* to invite to drink, to treat; (coll.) to prescribe (medicines).
propincuidad, *f.* propinquity, proximity.
propincuo, cua, *a.* near, contiguous.
propio, pia. I. *a.* one's own; proper, suitable, fit, appropriate; characteristic, typical; natural, original, genuine; same, veritable; (for emphasis) -self (*ella propia,* herself); exact, precise. —**p. de,** inhering in, characteristic of; suited to, becoming.—**fracción p.,** (math.) proper fraction. —**nombre p.,** (gram.) proper noun, proper name. **II.** *n.* messenger.—**propios,** *m. pl.* public lands, estates, property.
propiónico, ca, *a.* (chem.) propionic.
propóleos, *m.* propolis, bee glue.
proponedor, ra, *n.* proposer, proponent.
proponente, *m.* & *f.* proposer, proponent.
proponer. I. *va.* (*pp.* PROPUESTO; *ind. pres.* PROPONGO, *pret.* PROPUSE, *fut.* PROPONDRÉ; *subj.* PROPONGA) to propose, propound; to present or name (as candidate); in écarté, to invite to draw new cards. **II.** *vr.* to purpose, plan, intend, mean.
proporción, *f.* proportion; opportunity, occasion, chance; (math.) proportion.—**a p. que,** as fast as, according as.
proporcionable, *a.* proportionable.
proporcionablemente, proporcionadamente, *adv.* proportionably, in proportion.
proporcionado, da. I. *pp.* of PROPORCIONAR. **II.** *a.* proportioned, fit, relevant.
proporcional, *a.* proportional.
proporcionalidad, *f.* proportionality.
proporcionalmente, *adv.* proportionally.
proporcionar, *va.* to proportion; to adjust, adapt; to supply, provide, furnish.
proposición, *f.* proposition; proposal; motion (in congress, etc.).
propósito, *m.* purpose, design, intention; aim, object; subject matter.—**a p.,** for the purpose; fit; apropos, by the way.—**a p. de,** in connection with, apropos of.—**de p.,** on purpose, purposely.—**fuera de p.,** irrelevant, foreign to the subject.
propretor, *m.* (Rom. hist.) propretor.
propuesta, *f.* proposal, offer, tender; nomination.
propuesto, ta, *pp. irreg.* of PROPONER.
propugnáculo, *m.* fortress; (fig.) bulwark.
propugnar, *va.* to advocate; to defend; to fight for.
propulsa, *f.* rejection.
propulsar, *va.* to reject; to repulse, drive back.
propulsión, *f.* propulsion; (mech.) drive.—**p. a chorro,** jet propulsion.—**p. por cohete,** rocket propulsion.—**p. por reacción,** jet propulsion.
propulsor, ra. I. *a.* propellent, propelling, propulsive; pushing. **II.** *m.* propeller, propellant; pusher; (mech.) driver.
propuse, *pret.* of PROPONER.
prora, *f.* (poet.) prow of a ship.
prorrata, *f.* quota; apportionment.—**a p.,** (com.) pro rata, in proportion.
prorratear, *va.* to allot in proportion.
prorrateo, *m.* proportional, pro rata division.
prórroga, *f.* prolongation, extension (of time).
prorrogable, *a.* that may be prolonged or extended (in time).
prorrogación, *f.* = PRÓRROGA.
prorrogar, *va.* to prolong, extend (in time); (rare) to prorogue, suspend.
prorrumpir, *vn.* to break forth, burst out.
prosa, *f.* prose; tedious discourse.
prosador, *m.* prose writer; (coll.) impertinent talker.
prosaico, ca, *a.* prosaic; prosy, dull, tedious.
prosaísmo, *m.* prosaism; prosiness, dullness.
prosapia, *f.* ancestry, lineage.
proscenio, *m.* (theat.) proscenium.
proscribir, *va.* (*pp. irreg.* PROSCRITO, PROSCRIPTO) to proscribe.
proscripción, *f.* proscription, banishment.
proscripto, ta; proscrito, ta. I. *pp. irreg.* of PROSCRIBIR. **II.** *n.* exile, proscribed person.
proscriptor, ra, *n.* proscriber.
prosector, *m.* prosector, dissector (of anatomical specimens).
prosecución, *f.* prosecution; pursuit.
proseguible, *a.* pursuable.
proseguimiento, *m.* = PROSECUCIÓN.
proseguir. I. *va.* (*ger.* PROSIGUIENDO; *ind. pres.* PROSIGO, *pret.* él PROSIGUIÓ; *subj.* PROSIGA) to pursue, prosecute. **II.** *vn.* to go on, continue, proceed.
proselitismo, *m.* proselytism.
proselitista. I. *a.* proselytizing, converting. **II.** *n.* proselytizer, converter.
prosélito, *m.* proselyte, convert.
prosencéfalo, *m.* (anat.) prosencephalon, forebrain.
prosénquima, *m.* (biol.) prosenchyma.
prosificación, *f.* changing poetry into prose.
prosificador, ra, *n.* one that changes poetry into prose.
prosificar, *va.* to change (poetry) to prose.
prosigo, prosiguió, etc. *v. V.* proseguir.
prosimio, mia. I. *n.* & *a.* (zool.) prosimian. **II.** *m. pl.* Prosimiae, Lemuroidea.
prosista, *n.* prose writer.
prosita, *f. dim.* short piece in prose.
prosobranquios, *m. pl.* (zool.) Prosobranchiata.
prosodia, *f.* (gram.) orthoepy; prosody.
prosódico, ca, *a.* orthoepic; prosodic.
prosopografía, *f.* (rhet.) personal description.
prosopopeya, *f.* (rhet.) prosopopœia, personification; (coll.) affected gravity, airs.
prospección, *f.* (min.) prospecting; survey.—**p. aérea,** aerial survey.
prospecto, *m.* prospectus, announcement.
prósperamente, *adv.* prosperously, luckily.
prosperar. I. *va.* to prosper, make happy, favor. **II.** *vn.* to prosper, thrive.
prosperidad, *f.* prosperity, success.
próspero, ra, *a.* prosperous; favorable, propitious.
prostaféresis, *f.* (astr.) prosthaphæresis.
próstata, *f.* (anat.) prostate gland.
prostático, ca, *a.* prostatic.
prostatitis, *f.* (med.) prostatitis.
prosternarse, *vr.* to prostrate oneself.
próstesis, *f.* (gram.) prothesis; (med.) prosthesis.
prostético, ca, *a.* (gram.) prothetic; (med.) prosthetic.
próstilo, *a.* (arch.) prostyle.
prostitución, *f.* prostitution.
prostituído, da, *a.* prostitute, corrupted, debased.
prostituir. I. *va.* (*pp.* PROSTITUÍDO, PROSTITUTO; *ger.* PROSTITUYENDO; *ind. pres.* PROSTITUYO, *pret.* él PROSTITUYÓ; *subj.* PROSTITUYA) to prostitute, corrupt, debase. **II.** *vr.* to prostitute oneself, sell one's honor; to turn prostitute.
prostituta, *f.* prostitute.
prostituto, ta, *pp. irreg.* of PROSTITUIR.
prostituyo, etc. *v. V.* PROSTITUIR.
protagonista, *n.* protagonist, hero, heroine; leader.
prótalo, *m.* (bot.) prothallium.
prótasis, *f.* (drama and gram.) protasis.
proteáceo, a. I. *a.* (bot.) proteaceous. **II.** *f. pl.* Proteaceæ.

protección, *f.* protection; favor.
proteccionismo, *m.* (pol.) protectionism.
proteccionista, *n.* & *a.* (pol.) protectionist.
protector, ra. I. *a.* protective, defensive; patronal. **II.** *n.* protector, defender; patron.
protectorado, *m.* protectorate.
protectoría, *f.* protectorship, protectorate.
protectorio, ria, *a.* pertaining to a protector.
protectriz, *f.* protectress.
proteger, *va.* (*ind.* PROTEJO; *subj.* PROTEJA) to protect.
protegido, da, *n.* protégé, favorite.
proteico, ca, *a.* (biochem.) proteide, proteid, protein; (myth.) Protean; (fig.) protean, changeable, variable.
proteína, *f.* (biochem.) protein, proteide.
proteínico, ca, *m.* & *a.* (biochem.) protein, proteide, proteid.
protejo, proteja, *v. V.* PROTEGER.
prótel, *m.* (zool.) aardwolf.
proterozoico, ca, *a.* (geol.) Proterozoic.
protervamente, *adv.* perversely.
protervia, protervidad, *f.* perversity, malignity, wantonness.
protervo, va, *a.* wanton, perverse.
prótesis, *f.* (gram.) prothesis; (surg.) prosthesis.
protesta, *f.* protestation; protest; (law) protest.
protestación, *f.* protestation.
protestante. I. *a.* protesting. **II.** *n.* & *a.* Protestant.—**protestantismo,** *m.* Protestantism.
protestar, *va.* to protest; to assure, affirm earnestly or solemnly; to make a public declaration of; (law) to protest.—**p. contra,** to protest, deny the validity of.—**p. de,** to protest against. —**p. una letra,** (com.) to protest a draft.
protestativo, va, *a.* protesting.
protesto, *m.* (com.) protest (of a bill).
protético, ca, *a.* prothetic, prefixed.
protio, *m.* (phys.) protium.
protoactinio, *m.* (chem.) protactinium, protoactinium.
protoalbéitar, *m.* chief veterinary surgeon.
protoalbeiterato, *m.* board for examining veterinary surgeons.
protoblasto, *m.* (biol.) protoblast.
protocloruro, *m.* (chem.) protochloride.
protocolar. I. *a.* protocolar, protocolic, formal, official, ceremonial. **II.** *va.* to protocol, protocolize.
protocolizar, *va.* to protocol, protocolize.
protocolo, *m.* protocol, registry, judicial record.
protohistoria, *f.* prehistory.
protohistórico, ca, *a.* prehistoric.
protomártir, *m.* protomartyr (app. esp. to St. Stephen, the first Christian martyr).
protomedicato, *m.* board of king's physicians; office of royal physician.
protomédico, *m.* one of the three physicians to the king.
protón, *m.* (phys., chem.) proton.—**p. negativo,** (phys.) antiproton.
protonotario, *m.* (law) prothonotary.
protoplasma, *m.* (biol.) protoplasm.
protoplasmático, ca, *a.* (biol.) protoplasmic.
protoplasto, *m.* (biol.) protoplast.
protórax, *m.* (entom.) prothorax.
protosulfuro, *m.* (chem.) protosulphide.
prototípico, ca, *a.* prototypal.
prototipo, *m.* prototype, original; model.
protovértebra, *f.* (anat.) theoretical type of vertebræ.
protóxido, *m.* (chem.) protoxide.
protozoario, protozoo. I. *m.* (zool.) protozoan. **II.** *m. pl.* Protozoa.
protráctil, *a.* protractile.
protuberancia, *f.* protuberance.
protuberante, *a.* protuberant, bulging, rising, projecting.
protutor, *m.* (law) guardian.
provecto, ta, *a.* advanced in years, learning, or experience; mature.
provecho, *m.* benefit, advantage, good; profit, gain; proficiency, progress, advancement.—**buen p.,** may it benefit you (usual greeting before or after a meal); prosit.—**de p.,** useful. —**ser de p. para,** (of certain food, etc.) to be good for.
provechosamente, *adv.* profitably; beneficially.
provechoso, sa, *a.* profitable; beneficial, good (as for the health); useful, advantageous.
proveedor, ra, *n.* purveyor, provider.
proveeduría, *f.* storehouse for provisions; office of purveyor.
proveer. I. *va.* (*pp.* PROVEÍDO, PROVISTO; *ger.* PROVEYENDO; *pret.* él PROVEYÓ) to provide, furnish; to supply with provisions; stock; to dispose, adjust, transact; to confer; (law) to decide. **II.** *vr.* (**de**) to provide oneself (with), get one's supply (of); (coll.) to ease the body.
proveído, *m.* judgment, sentence, decision.
proveimiento, *m.* supply, provisioning.
provena, *f.* provine, layer of vine.
proveniente, *a.* arising, coming, resulting.
provenir, *vn.* (**de**) to arise (from), originate (in), be due (to).
provento, *m.* product, rent, revenue.
provenzal, *n.* & *a.* Provençal.
proverbiador, *m.* collection of proverbs.
proverbial, *a.* proverbial.
proverbialmente, *adv.* proverbially.
proverbiar, *vn.* (coll.) to use proverbs.
proverbio, *m.* proverb, saying, saw; omen, prediction.—*pl.* Proverbs (book of the Bible).
proverbista, *n.* (coll.) user of proverbs.
proveyó, *pret.* of PROVEER.
próvidamente, *adv.* providently, carefully.
providencia, *f.* foresight, forethought; act of providing; disposition, measure, way, means; (law) judgment, decision, sentence.—**la P.,** Providence.
providencial, *a.* providential.
providencialmente, *adv.* providentially; provisionally.
providenciar, *va.* to take steps or measures for; to decide (a case), pronounce judgment on.
providente, *a.* = PRÓVIDO.
próvido, da, *a.* provident, prudent.
provincia, *f.* province; provincial court for civil cases; (eccl.) province.
provincial. I. *a.* provincial. **II.** *m.* (eccl.) provincial.
provincialato, *m.* (eccl.) provincialship.
provincialismo, *m.* provincialism.
provinciano, na, *n.* & *a.* provincial, provincialist; native of Biscay.
provisión, *f.* provision; supply, stock; provender; writ, decree, or sentence issued by Spanish tribunals in the king's name; measure, means; (com.) remittance of funds.—**p. de alimento,** catering.
provisional, *a.* provisional, interim (as *a.*).
provisionalmente, *adv.* provisionally.
provisio.—al p., immediately, instantly.
provisor, ra, *n.* purveyor, provider; (eccl.) vicar general.
provisorato, *m.* office of PROVISOR.
provisoría, *f.* in convents, storeroom, pantry; office of a PROVISOR.
provisorio, ria, *a.* provisional, temporary.
provisto, ta. I. *pp. irreg.* of PROVEER. **II.** *a.* provided, stocked, supplied.
provocación, *f.* provocation, irritation.
provocador, ra. I. *a.* provocative, provoking. **II.** *n.* provoker; inciter; (U. S., coll.) fire-eater.
provocante, *a.* provocative, provoking.
provocar, *va.* (*pret.* PROVOQUÉ; *subj.* PROVOQUE) to provoke, excite, incite, anger; to facilitate, promote; to tempt, arouse desire in: (coll.) to vomit.
provocativo, va, *a.* provocative; inciting; tempting; provoking, irritating.
proxeneta, *n.* (law) go-between, procurer (of prostitutes), pimp.
proxenetismo, *m.* (law) procuration (actions or practice of a procurer or a go-between).

próximamente, *adv.* approximately; soon; immediately; proximately.
proximidad, *f.* proximity.
próximo, ma, *a.* next; nearest, neighboring, proximate; close.—**no p.,** not anywhere near.
proyección, *f.* design; projecting; projection; (geom.) projection.
proyectante, *a.* projecting; designing.
proyectar. I. *va.* to design; to project, plan devise; to shoot or throw forth; (geom.) to project; to cast (as a shadow); to show (a movie). **II.** *vr.* to be cast. fall (as a shadow).
proyectil, *m.* projectile, missile.—**p. antiaéreo,** antiaircraft missile.—**p. balístico,** ballistic missile.—**p. balístico intercontinental,** intercontinental ballistic missile.—**p. de avión a avión,** air-to-air missile.—**p. de avión a tierra,** air-to-surface missile.—**p. dirigido** or **guiado,** guided missile.
proyectista, *n.* projector; designer.
proyecto, ta. I. *a.* projected, in perspective. **II.** *m.* project, plan, design, draft.—**p. de ley,** (pol.) bill.—**p. de recomendación,** draft recommendation.—**p. de resolución,** draft resolution.—**p. experimental,** pilot project.
proyector, ra. I. *a.* projecting. **II.** *m.* (phys.) projector; search light; (auto) spotlight.—**p. cinematográfico,** projector, motion picture projector, projection machine.—**p. de sonido magnético,** magnetic sound projector.—**p. eléctrico,** searchlight.
proyectura, *f.* (arch.) projecture.
prudencia, *f.* prudence; moderation.
prudencial, *a.* prudential.
prudencialmente, *adv.* prudentially.
prudente, *a.* prudent, cautious, wise.
prudentemente, *adv.* prudently, wisely.
prueba, *f.* proof; evidence; trial, test; test piece, sample; tasting; temptation; (Am.) acrobatic feat, (card, etc.) trick; (law) evidence; (tailoring) trial, fitting; (print.) proof, proof sheet; (photog.) proof.—**p. circunstancial,** (law) circumstantial evidence.—**p. de aptitud,** aptitude test.—**p. de fuego,** (fig.) acid test.—**p. de indicios,** (law) circumstantial evidence.—**p. de inteligencia,** intelligence test.—**p. directa,** (law) direct evidence.—**p. experimental,** experimental test.—**p. final,** finals, final test.—**p. indiciaria,** (law) circumstantial test.—**p. indirecta,** (law) indirect evidence.—**p. preliminar,** pretest.—**a p.,** on trial; according to the best standards, perfect.—**a p. de,** proof against, proof.—**a p. de ácido,** acidproof.—**a p. de agua,** waterproof.—**a p. de aire,** airtight.—**a p. de bomba,** bombproof.—**a p. de calor,** heatproof.—**a p. de fuego,** fireproof.—**hacer la p.,** to try; (de) to try; to test.—**poner a p.,** to try, put to the test.
pruebista, *m.* & *f.* (Am.) acrobat.
pruebo, pruebe, *v. V.* PROBAR.
pruna, *f.* (bot.) plum; prune.
prurigo, *m.* (med.) prurigo.
prurito, *m.* (med.) pruritus, itching; excessive desire.
prusiano, na, *n.* & *a.* Prussian.
prusiato, *m.* (chem.) prussiate, cyanide.
prúsico, ca, *a.* prussic, hydrocyanic.
pseudo, *a.* = SEUDO, pseudo.
psi, *f.* psi (Greek letter).
psicoanálisis, *m.* psychoanalysis.
psicoanalista, *n.* psychoanalyst.
psicoanalítico, ca, *a.* psychoanalitic, psychoanalitical.
psicoanalizar, *va.* to psychoanalyze.
psicocirugía, *f.* psychosurgery.
psicodinámico, ca, *a.* psychodynamic.
psicofísica, *f.* psychophysics.
psicofisiología, *f.* psychophysiology.
psicogénesis, *f.* psychogenesis.
psicogénico, ca, *a.* psychogenetic.
psicognostia, *f.* psychognosis.
psicología, *f.* psychology.
psicológico, ca, *a.* psychological.
psicólogo, *m.* psychologist.
psicometría, *f.* psychometry.
psicométrico, ca, *a.* psychometric, psychometrical.
psicómetro, *m.* psychometer.
psiconeurosis, *f.* psychoneurosis.
psiconeurótico, ca, *a.* psychoneurotic.
psicópata, *n.* (med.) psychiatrist, alienist.
psicopatía, *f.* (med.) psychopathy, mental illness.
psicopático, ca, *a.* psychopathic.
psicopatología, *f.* psychopathology.
psicosis, *f.* (psych., psychiat.) psychosis.
psicosomático, ca, *a.* psychosomatic.
psicotecnia, *f.* psychotechnology.
psicoterapia, *f.* psychotherapy.
psicótico, ca, *n.* & *a.* psychotic.
psicrómetro, *m.* psychrometer.
psilosis, *f.* (med.) psilosis.
psique, *f.* (myth.) Psyche; (fig.) psyche, soul; psyche, mind.
psiquiatra, *m.* psychiatrist.
psiquiatría, *f.* psychiatry.
psiquiátrico, ca, *a.* psychiatric.
psíquico, ca, *a.* psychic, psychical.
psiquis, *f.* psyche, mind.
psoas, *m.* (anat.) psoas (muscle).
pteridofita, *f.* (bot.) pteridophyte.
pterodáctilo, *m.* (paleontol.) pterodactyl.
pterópido, da, *m.* & *a.* (zool.) pteropod.
ptialina, *f.* (chem.) ptyalin.
ptialismo, *m.* (med.) ptyalism.
ptolemaico, ca, *a.* Ptolemaic.
ptomaína, *f.* (biochem.) ptomaine, ptomain.
¡pu! *interj.* pugh!
púa, *f.* prick; tine, prong; tooth of a comb; wire tooth of a card; spine or quill of a hedgehog, etc.; (agr.) graft, scion; metal point of a spinning top; plectrum; cause of grief or sorrow; (coll.) wily, cunning person.—**alambre de púas,** barbed wire.
puado, *m.* set of prongs, teeth, or tines.
puar, *va.* to make teeth, prongs, or tines on.
púber; púbero, ra; *a.* pubescent.
pubertad, *f.* puberty, pubescence.
pubes, *m.* (anat.) pubes, pubic region.
pubescencia, *f.* pubescence, puberty.
pubescente, *a.* pubescent.
pubescer, *vn.* to attain the age of puberty.
púbico, ca, *a.* pubic.
pubis, *m.* (anat.) pubes; pubis.
pública, *f.* in universities, public examination before graduating.
publicación, *f.* publication; proclamation.
publicador, ra, *n.* publisher; proclaimer.
públicamente, *adv.* publicly, openly.
publicano, *m.* publican.
publicar, *va.* (*prct.* PUBLIQUÉ; *subj.* PUBLIQUE) to publish; to proclaim, announce; to reveal, disclose; (eccl.) to publish (the banns).
publicata, *f.* (eccl.) certificate of publication.
publicidad, *f.* publicity.
publicista, *m.* publicist.
público, ca. I. *a.* public; common, general.—**en p.,** publicly. **II.** *m.* public, audience.
publiqué, publique, *v. V.* PUBLICAR.
pucelana, *f.* = PUZOLANA, a volcanic rock.
pucia, *f.* closed pharmaceutical vessel.
pucha, *f.* (Cuba) bouquet of flowers.
puchada, *f.* flour poultice; watered mortar.
puchera, *f.* (cooking) pot, kettle.
pucherico, illo, ito, *m. dim.* pipkin, small pot.
pucherito, *m.* (coll.) pouting of a child about to cry.
puchero, *m.* cooking pot; olla, stew, (U. S.) New England boiled dinner; dinner, food; pouting of a child before crying.—**hacer pucheros,** (coll.) to pout.
pucheruelo, *m. dim.* of PUCHERO.
puches, *m.* or *f. pl.,* a sort of pap; porridge.
pucho, *m.* (Am.) cigar stump; left over, trifle, insignificant thing.

pude, *pret.* of PODER.
pudelación, *f.* (metal.) puddling.
pudelador, *m.* (metal.) puddler.
pudelaje, *m.* (metal.) puddling.
pudelar, *va.* (metal.) to puddle.
pudendo, da. I. *a.* shameful, obscene, immodest. **II.** *m.* the male organ.
pudibundez, *f.* prudishness, overmodesty.
pudibundo, da, *a.* (humor.) shamefaced, modest.
pudicicia, *f.* pudicity, chastity, modesty.
púdico, ca, *a.* chaste, modest, decorous.
pudiente, *a.* powerful; rich, well off.
pudín, *m.* (Angl.) pudding.
pudo, *v. V.* PODER.
pudor, *m.* modesty, decorousness.
pudoroso, sa, *a.* modest; bashful, shy.
pudrición, *f.* rottenness; putrefaction, rotting.
pudridero, *m.* rotting place; fermenting pit; chamber with vaults for interment of bodies that are later to be transferred to mausoleums.
pudrido, da, *a.* putrid, putrescent.
pudridor, *m.* (paper making) fermenting vat.
pudrigorio, *m.* (coll.) sickly, infirm man.
pudrimiento, *m.* = PUDRICIÓN.
pudrir. I. *va.* to rot; to vex, worry. **II.** *vn.* to have died, to be buried; to rot. **III.** *vr.* to rot, decay; to be broken-hearted, to die of grief.
pudú, *m.* (zool.) pudu, a Chilean variety of deer.
puebla, *f.* seed that a gardener sows.
pueblada, *f.* (Am.) popular uprising; mob.
pueble, *m.* (min.) working gang.
pueblecico, ito, *m. dim.* small town.
puebleño, ña, *n.* (Colomb., contempt.) villager; boor.
[1]**pueblo,** *m.* town, village; settlement; people; nation; population; common people, working classes.
[2]**pueblo, pueble,** *v. V.* POBLAR.
puedo, pueda, *v. V.* PODER.
puente, *m.* or *f.* bridge; (mus.) bridge, in string instruments; (carp.) transom, lintel, crossbeam; (naut.) bridge; gun-carrying deck.—**p. aérea,** air lift.—**p. cantilever,** cantilever bridge.—**p. cerril,** small narrow bridge for cattle.—**p. colgante,** suspension bridge.—**p. corredizo,** roller bridge.—**p. de barcas,** pontoon bridge, bridge of boats.—**p. de caballetes,** trestle bridge.—**p. de celosía,** lattice bridge.—**p. de cimbria,** (Chile) suspension rope bridge.—**p. de contrapeso,** cantilever bridge.—**p. de doble vía,** double-track bridge.—**p. de los asnos,** pons asinorum, problem difficult for beginners, discouraging difficulty.—**P. de los Suspiros,** Bridge of Sighs.—**p. de tablero inferior,** through bridge.—**p. de tablero superior,** deck bridge.—**p. de una vía,** single-track bridge.—**p. de vigas voladizas,** cantilever bridge.—**p. de Wheatstone,** (elec.) Wheatstone bridge.—**p. flotante,** floating bridge.—**p. giratorio,** swing bridge, turning or revolving bridge.—**p. levadizo,** drawbridge; bascule, or lift, bridge. —**p. volante,** flying bridge.
puentecico, illo, ito, *m. dim.* small bridge
puentecilla, *f. dim.* small bridge of a string instrument.
puentezuela, *f. dim.* small bridge.
puerca, *f.* (zool.) sow; sow bug, woodlouse; scrofulous swelling; slut, slatternly woman.
puercamente, *adv.* dirtily, filthily; basely, meanly, contemptibly.
puerco, ca. I. *a.* filthy, dirty, foul; low, base, mean. **II.** *n.* hog; wild boar; base or low person. —**p. espín,** or **espino,** porcupine.—**p. marino,** (zool.) dolphin.—**p. montés,** wild boar.
puericia, *f.* boyhood.
puericultura, *f.* child care.
pueril, *a.* childish, puerile; (astr.) first (quadrant).
puerilidad, *f.* puerility, childishness; trifle.
puerilmente, *adv.* puerilely, childishly.
puérpera, *f.* lying-in woman.
puerperal, *a.* puerperal.
puerperio, *m.* time directly after childbirth.
puerquezuelo, *m. dim.* little pig.
puerro, *m.* (bot.) leek.
puerta, *f.* door; doorway, gateway; gate; beginning of an undertaking; duty, octroi, toll.—**p. abierta,** (diplomacy) open door.—**p. automática,** automatic door.—**p. cerrada,** (diplomacy) closed door.—**p. cochera,** porte cochère.—**p. corrediza** or **de corredera,** sliding door.—**p. de dos hojas,** folding door.—**p. de emergencia,** emergency exit, emergency door. —**p. de horno,** fire door, furnace door.—**p. de entrada** or **de la calle,** entrance door, street door, front door.—**p. del fondo,** back door.—**p. de vaivén** or **p. engoznada,** swinging door. —**p. excusada** or **falsa,** back door, side door. —**p. franca,** open door, free entrance; free entry.—**p. lateral,** side door.—**p. plegadiza,** folding door.—**p. principal,** front door, main door, street door.—**p. reglar,** regular door for entering nunneries.—**p. trasera,** back door.—**p. vidriera,** glass door.—**abrir p.** or **la p.,** (fig.) to ease the way.—**acompañar a la p.,** to show one to the door.—**a las puertas de la muerte,** at death's door, at the point of death, about to die.—**a p. cerrada,** behind locked doors, privately, secretly.—**dar con la p. en la cara** or **en las narices de,** to slam the door in one's face.—**de p. en p.,** from door to door. —**de p. para adentro,** indoors.—**detrás de la p.,** round the corner.—**enseñar la p. de la calle,** (coll.) to show the door to.—**fuera de puertas,** outdoors.—**la Sublime P.,** the Sublime Porte (Turkey).
puertaventana, *f.* window shutter.
puertecillo, puertezuelo, *m. dim.* small port.
puertecita, puertezuela, *f. dim.* small door.
puerto, *m.* port; harbor, haven; pass through mountains; asylum, shelter, refuge.—**p. aéreo,** airport.—**p. de arribada,** port of call.—**p. de depósito,** bonded port.—**p. de destino,** port of destination.—**p. de escala,** port of call.—**P. de España,** Port of Spain.—**p. de mar,** seaport.—**p. de mareas,** tidal harbor.—**p. de origen,** home port.—**p. fluvial,** fluvial port.—**p. franco,** free port.—**p. habilitado,** port of entry.—**p. libre,** free port.—**p. nacional,** home port.—**P. Príncipe,** Port-au-Prince.—**capitán de p.,** port captain, harbor master.—**derechos de p.,** harbor dues.
Puerto Rico, *m.* Puerto Rico, Porto Rico.
puertorriqueño, ña, *n.* & *a.* Puerto Rican, Porto Rican.
pues. I. *conj.* because, for, as; since, inasmuch as; then.—**p. bien,** now then, well then, all right then.—**p. no,** not at all, not so.—**p. que,** since.—**¿p. qué?** what?; what about it? "so what?"—**p. sí,** yes, indeed, most certainly.—**¿p. y qué?** why not? what else? what then? —**¿y p.?** so? is that so? why? how is that? **II.** *adv.* yes; so; certainly; exactly; anyhow, just the same.
puesta, *f.* (astr.) set, setting; stake (at cards).—**p. de sol,** sunset.—**puestas de sol,** or **a p. de sol,** at sunset.
puesto, ta. I. *pp. irreg.* of PONER.—**p. que,** although; since, inasmuch as, as long as.—**buen p.,** well dressed. **II.** *m.* place or space occupied, stall, stand, booth; position, job; post, dignity, office; breeding stall; blind for hunters; (mil.) barrack for soldiers.—**p. de avance,** (mil.) outpost.—**p. de control,** (mil.) check point.—**p. de escucha,** listening post.—**p. de mando,** control station.—**p. de socorro,** (mil.) first-aid station.—**p. militar,** military post.
¡puf! *interj.* pugh!
púgil, *m.* prize fighter, boxer, pugilist.
pugilar, *m.* Hebrew manual of the Scriptures.
pugilato, *m.* pugilism; boxing.
pugilismo, *m.* pugilism.
pugilista, *m.* & *f.* (Am.) pugilist, prize fighter.
pugna, *f.* combat, struggle; conflict.—**estar en p.,** to be in conflict, disagree.

pugnacidad, *f.* pugnacity, quarrelsomeness.
pugnante. I. *a.* fighting, struggling. **II.** *n.* foe, opponent.
pugnar, *vn.* to fight, struggle; (**con**), to conflict (with), be opposed (to); to strive successfully; to be obstinate; to persist.
pugnaz, *a.* pugnacious, quarrelsome.
puja, *f.* outbidding or overbidding at a public sale; higher bid.
pujador, ra, *n.* bidder; outbidder.
pujame, pujamen, *m.* (naut.) foot of a sail.
pujamiento, *m.* flow of the blood or humors.
pujante, *a.* powerful, vigorous, strong.
pujanza, *f.* power, might, strength, vigor.
[1]**pujar. I.** *va.* to push ahead, push through. **II.** *vn.* to falter (in speech or action); (coll.) to pout.
[2]**pujar. I.** *va.* to outbid. **II.** *vn.* to ascend, go up.
pujavante. *m.* hoof parer (used by horseshoer).
pujo, *m.* (med.) tenesmus; eagerness, longing; violent desire.
pulcritud, *f.* pulchritude, neatness, tidiness.
pulcro, cra, *a.* beautiful, graceful; nice; neat.
Pulchinela, *m.* Punchinello.
pulga, *f.* flea; small playing top.—**no aguantar pulgas,** not to put up with ill treatment.—**ser de,** or **tener, malas pulgas,** to be easily piqued or fretted, to be ill-tempered.—**tener pulgas,** to be restless or too lively.
pulgada, *f.* inch.
pulgar, *m.* thumb; shoots left on vines.
pulgarada, *f.* fillip; pinch; inch.
pulgón, *m.* green fly, plant louse, aphis.
pulgoso, sa, *a.* full of fleas.
pulguera, *f.* place abounding with fleas; (bot.) pulic, fleawort.
pulguillas, *n. dim.* (coll.) restless, fretful person.
pulguita, *f. dim.* little flea.
pulicán, *m.* dentist's forceps.
pulicaria, *f.* (bot.) fleawort.
pulidamente, *adv.* neatly, cleanly, nicely.
pulidero, *m.* polisher, glosser, burnisher.
pulidez, *f.* polish; neatness, cleanliness.
pulido, da, *pp.* & *a.* polished; neat, cleanly.
pulidor, ra. I. *a.* polishing, burnishing, buffing. **II.** *m.* polisher, burnisher, furbisher, buffer.
pulimentar, *va.* to burnish, gloss, polish.
pulimento, *m.* polish; glossiness.
pulir. I. *va.* to polish, burnish, furbish; to adorn, beautify; to render polite. **II.** *vr.* to beautify, or deck oneself; to become polished.
pulmón, *m.* (anat.) lung.—**pulmonado, da,** *a.* (zool.) pulmonate.—**pulmonar,** *a.* pulmonary.
pulmonaria, *f.* (bot.) lungwort.
pulmonía, *f.* (med.) pneumonia.
pulmoníaco, ca. I. *a.* (med.) pneumonic, pulmonic. **II.** *n.* (med.) person suffering from pneumonia.
pulmotor, *m.* Pulmotor (trademark).
pulpa, *f.* (anat.) pulp, flesh; fruit or wood pulp.
pulpejo, *m.* flesh · part of the body, as the ball of the thumb or lobe of the ear.
pulpería, *f.* (Am.) retail grocery or general store.
pulpero, *m.* (Am.) grocer; catcher of cuttlefish.
pulpeta, *f.* slice of stuffed meat.
púlpito, *m.* pulpit; office of a preacher.
pulpo, *m.* (ichth.) cuttlefish, octopus.
pulposo, sa, *a.* pulpy, pulpous, fleshy.
pulque, *m.* (Am.) pulque, fermented juice of the maguey.—**p. curado,** the same liquor prepared with pineapple and sugar.
pulquería, *f.* tavern where pulque is sold.
pulsación, *f.* pulsation; pulse, beating.
pulsada, *f.* any pulse beat.
pulsador, ra. I. *a.* pulsatile, pulsative, pulsating. **II.** *m.* push button, buzzer.
pulsante, *a.* feeling the pulse; pulsating.
pulsar. I. *va.* to feel the pulse of; to finger, touch lightly (as a lyre); to explore, sound, or examine. **II.** *vn.* to pulsate, beat.
pulsátil, *a.* pulsatile, pulsative, pulsating.
pulsatila, *f.* (bot.) pasqueflower.
pulsativo, va, *a.* pulsative, pulsatile, pulsating.
pulsear, *vn.* (of two persons) to hand-wrestle, to clasp hands with upright forearms resting on a table and endeavor to put each other's arm down by pulling in opposite directions.
pulsera, *f.* (jewelry) bracelet; lock of hair over the temple; (surg.) wrist bandage.—**reloj de p.,** wrist watch.
pulsímetro, *m.* (hydraul.) pulsometer; (med.) pulsimeter, sphygmograph.
pulsista, *a.* skilled in knowledge of the pulse.
pulso, *m.* pulse; pulsation, beat; part of the wrist where the pulse is felt; steadiness of the hand; care, tact.—**a p.,** freehand (drawing); with the strength of the hand.—**tomar el p. a,** to feel the pulse of; to sound (one for one's opinion).
pulsómetro, *m.* = PULSÍMETRO.
pulsorreactor, *m.* (aer.) pulsejet.
pultáceo, a, *a.* pultaceous, soft; (med.) apparently or actually rotten or gangrened.
pululante, *pa.* pullulating, sprouting.
pulular, *vn.* to pullulate, germ, bud; to multiply with great rapidity; to swarm; to be lively.
pulvericé, pulverice, *v. V.* PULVERIZAR.
pulverizable, *a.* pulverizable.
pulverización, *f.* pulverization.
pulverizador, *m.* atomizer, spray; pulverizer.
pulverizar, *va.* (*pret.* PULVERICÉ; *subj.* PULVERICE) to pulverize; to atomize, spray.
pulverulento, ta, *a.* dusty.
[1]**pulla,** *f.* loose, obscene expression; repartee, witty saying; hint.
[2]**pulla,** *f.* (ornith.) = PLANGA, a kind of eagle.
pullista, *n.* one fond of throwing out hints.
¡pum! *interj.* bang!
puma, *m.* (zool.) puma, American panther.
pumarada, *f.* = POMARADA, apple plantation.
pumita, *f.* = PIEDRA PÓMEZ, pumice stone.
puna, *f.* (Am.) puna, bleak, arid table-land.
puncé, punce, *v. V.* PUNZAR.
punción, *f.* (surg.) puncture.
puncha, *f.* thorn, prickle, sharp point.
punchar, *va.* to prick, pierce, puncture.
pundonor, *m.* point of honor.
pundonorosamente, *adv.* punctiliously.
pundonoroso, sa, *a.* punctilious.
punganes, *m. pl.* oyster knife.
pungente, *a.* pungent.
pungimiento, *m.* punching or pricking.
pungir, *va.* (*ind.* PUNJO; *subj.* PUNJA) to punch, prick; to sting the mind or heart (as passions).
pungitivo, va, *a.* punching, pricking.
punible, *a.* (law) punishable.
punición, *f.* punishment.
púnico, ca, *a.* Punic.
punitivo, va, *a.* (law) punitive.
punjo, punja, *v. V.* PUNGIR.
punta, *f.* point, nib, sharp end; end, tip; apex, top; cape, headland, promontory; prong or tine of an antler; stub of a cigar; taint of acidity or sourness; touch, turn, tinge, trace, suggestion, pointing of game by a dog; (print.) bodkin; (her.) lower part of a shield.—*pl.* point lace.—**p. de diamante,** diamond pencil, diamond point (for cutting).—**p. de París,** wire nail.—**p. seca,** point (of dividers).—**de p.,** point-first.—**de p. en blanco,** all dressed up; in full regalia.—**de puntas,** on tiptoe, softly.—**estar de p.,** to be on bad terms.
puntada, *f.* (sewing) stitch; hint.—**echar puntadas,** (sewing) to stitch.
puntador, *m.* = APUNTADOR, (theat.) prompter.
puntal, *m.* prop, support; stay, stanchion, pillar; (naut.) depth of hold; (Am.) snack (of food).
puntapié, *m.* kick (with the tip of the shoe).
puntar, *va.* to mark with dots or points.
punteado, da. I. *a.* punctate, punctated; dotty, dotted, speckled; plucked (said of a stringed instrument). **II.** *m.* & *f.* punctuation, marking with dots; plucking (of a stringed instrument).
puntear. I. *va.* to play (the guitar); (art) to stipple; (sewing) to stitch. **II.** *vn.* (naut.) to tack.
puntel, *m.* pontil, snap, glass-blower's rod.

puntera, *f.* (shoemaking) toe cap or box; patch over the tip; new toe on stockings; (coll.) kick.
puntería, *f.* (artil.) aim; pointing a weapon.
puntero, ra. I. *a.* taking good aim. **II.** *m.* pointer; punch for horseshoes; stonecutter's chisel; (eccl.) cannula in a chrismatory; (Colomb.) hand (of watch or clock).
punterola, *f.* (min.) poll pick.
puntiagudo, da, *a.* sharp-pointed, sharp.
puntico, ito, *m. dim.* small dot or point.
puntilla, *f. dim.* small point; narrow lace edging; brad, joiner's nail; carpenter's tracing point.—**de, or en, puntillas,** softly, gently; on tiptoe.
puntillazo, *m.* (coll.) kick.
puntillero, *m.* (bull fighting) = CACHETERO.
puntillismo, *m.* (f. a.) pointillism.
puntillista, *n.* (f. a.) pointillist.
puntillo, *m. dim.* small point; punctilio; (mus.) dot, point.
puntillón, *m.* (coll.) kick.
puntilloso, sa, *a.* punctilious.
puntiseco, ca, *a.* dry at the tips, as plants.
puntizón, *m.* (print.) frisket hole or mark.
punto, *m.* point, dot; period in writing; nib of a pen; sight in firearms; (sports) point; (sewing, knitting) stitch; hole in a stocking; point in lace; mesh; punch hole in straps; polka dot in fabrics; place, spot; hackstand; smallest part of a thing; instant, moment; nick of time; chance, favorable opportunity; stop, rest, recess; end, object, aim; point of honor, punctilio; each mistake of a pupil in reciting a lesson; twelfth part of a line; (shoemaking) each number in a size stick.—**p. atrás,** (sewing) backstitch.—**p. ciego,** (anat.) blind spot.—**p. cruzado,** (sewing) cross stitch.—**p. de absorción,** absorption point.—**p. de admiración,** exclamation point, exclamation mark.—**p. de apoyo,** fulcrum, point of support.—**p. de cadeneta,** (sewing) lock stitch, chain stitch.—**p. de cambio,** (topog.) turning point.—**p. decimal,** decimal point.—**p. decisivo,** turning point.—**p. de comprobación,** check point.—**p. de congelación,** freezing point.—**p. de ebullición,** boiling point.—**p. de escala,** stopover point.—**p. de eslabonamiento,** linking point.—**p. de fuga,** (perspective) vanishing point.—**p. de fusión,** melting point.—**p. de gracia,** funny side.—**p. de hielo,** freezing point.—**p. de honor,** point of honor.—**p. de inflamación,** ignition point.—**p. de inflexión,** (geom.) point of inflexion.—**p. de interrogación,** question mark.—**p. de la vista,** (perspective) vanishing point.—**p. de partida,** starting point; (stat.) bench mark.—**p. de referencia,** point of reference; (topog., stat.) bench mark.—**p. de rocío,** (phys.) dew point.—**p. de saturación,** saturation point.—**p. de sustentación,** (aer.) center of lift.—**p. de vista,** point of view, viewpoint.—**p. en boca,** silence.—**p. en cuestión,** point at issue.—**p. final,** last stop; (gram.) full stop, period.—**p. focal,** focal point.—**p. menos,** a trifle less.—**p. muerto,** (mach.) dead center, dead point.—**p. por p.,** point by point, in detail.—**puntos cardinales,** cardinal points.—**p. sin regreso,** (aer., fig.) point of no return.—**puntos suspensivos,** leaders (. . .).—**puntos y rayas,** (tel.) dots and dashes.—**p. y coma,** semicolon (;).—**a buen p.,** opportunely.—**al p.,** immediately, at once.—**a p. de,** on the point of, about to.—**a p. fijo,** exactly, with certainty.—**a p. que,** just when, just as.—**coche de p.,** taxi, car for hire.—**dar en el p.,** to hit the nail on the head.—**de p.,** knitted; steadily increasing, by the minute.—**de todo p.,** absolutely, entirely, in every way.—**dos puntos,** colon (:).—**en p.,** on the dot, exactly, (of the hour) sharp.—**en p. de,** in regard to.—**hasta cierto p.,** to a certain extent.—**poner en su p.,** to put where it belongs. rate at its true value; to set right.—**poner los puntos sobre las íes,** (coll.) to cross the t's and dot the i's.—**poner p. final a,** to put a stop to.—**por p. general,** as a general rule, as a rule.—**por puntos,** from one moment to another; point by point; one thing at a time.
puntoso, sa, *a.* pointed; punctilious.
puntuación, *f.* punctuation.
puntual, *a.* prompt, punctual; certain; sure; convenient, adequate.—**puntualidad,** *f.* punctuality; certainty.—**puntualizar,** *va.* (*pret.* PUNTUALICÉ; *subj.* PUNTUALICE) to imprint on the mind or memory; to finish, perfect; to give a detailed account of.—**puntualmente,** *adv.* punctually; faithfully; exactly, accurately.
puntuar, *va.* to punctuate, to point.
puntuoso, sa, *a.* punctilious.
puntura, *f.* puncture; (print.) register point.
punzada, *f.* prick, puncture; stitch, sharp pain; compunction.
punzador, ra, *n.* pricker, wounder.
punzadura, *f.* puncture, prick.
punzante, *a.* pricking, sharp.
punzar, *va.* (*pret.* PUNCÉ; *subj.* PUNCE) to punch, bore, perforate; to prick, puncture, wound; to cause sharp pain; to grieve.
punzó, *a.* deep scarlet red.
punzón, *m.* punch, puncheon; puncher; driver, point, graver, bodkin, awl, pick; countersink, counterdie; type mold; young horn of a deer.
punzonería, *f.* set of molds for a font of types.
puñada, *f.* fisticuff, box.
puñado, *m.* handful; a few.—**a puñados,** plentifully, abundantly, lots (diff. constr.).
puñal. *m.* poniard, dagger.—**puñalada,** *f.* stab with a poniard; sudden shock of grief or pain.
puñalejo, *m. dim.* small poniard.
puñalero, ra, *n.* maker or seller of poniards.
puñera, *f.* double handful; flour measure.
puñetazo, *m.* fisticuff.
puñete, *m.* fisticuff; bracelet.
puño, *m.* fist; grasp; handful; cuff, wristband (of garment); hilt of a sword; haft (of a tool); handle (of an umbrella, etc.); head of a staff or cane; (naut.) corner of a sail.—**cerrar los puños,** to clench one's fists.—**hombre de puños,** strong, valiant man.—**ser como un p.,** to be closefisted.
pupa, *f.* pustule, pimple; child's word to express uneasiness.
pupila, *f.* (anat.) pupil.
pupilaje, *m.* pupilage, wardship; board and lodging; boarding-house.
pupilar, *a.* (anat. and law) pupillary.
pupilero, ra, *n.* boarding-house keeper.
pupilo, la, *n.* pupil, ward; boarder.
pupitre, *m.* writing desk; school desk.
puposo, sa, *a.* pustulous, pustulate.
puramente, *adv.* purely; chastely; strictly; without qualification or exception.
puré, *m.* (Gal.) (cooking) thick soup, purée.
pureza, *f.* purity; fineness, genuineness; cleanness. excellence.
purga, *f.* physic, cathartic; (sugar making) draining of molasses.
purgable, *a.* that can or should be purged.
purgación, *f.* purge, purgation; catamenia; (law) purgation; gonorrhœa, clap.
purgador, ra. I. *a.* purgative. **II.** *n.* purger.
purgamiento, *m.* purgation, purging.
purgante. I. *a.* purging, purgative. **II.** *m.* purgative, cathartic, physic.
purgar. I. *va.* (*pret.* PURGUÉ; *subj.* PURGUE) to purge, purify, cleanse; to atone for, expiate; to refine, clarify; to drain (sugar) of molasses; (med.) to purge, physic; (law) to clear from guilt or imputation of guilt. **II.** *vr.* to rid or clear oneself from guilt; to take a purge.
purgativo, va, *a.* purgative, cathartic.
purgatorio, *m.* purgatory.
purgué, purgue, *v. V.* PURGAR.
puridad, *f.* purity.—**en p.,** clearly, openly; in secret.
purificación, *f.* purification; cleansing, expurgation; (eccl.) purification (of the chalice).

purificadero, ra, *a.* cleansing, purifying.
purificador, ra, *n.* & *a.* purifier(-ing); (eccl.) purificator.
purificante, *a.* purifying.
purificar. I. *va.* (*pret.* PURIFIQUÉ; *subj.* PURIFIQUE) to purify, clean, cleanse, refine. **II.** *vr.* to be purified, cleansed.
purificatorio, ria, *a.* purificatory, purifying.
puriforme, *a.* (med.) puriform.
purina, *f.* (chem.) purine.
Purísima.—la P., *f.* the most Holy Virgin.
purismo, *m.* purism.—**purista,** *n.* purist.
puritanismo, *m.* puritanism.
puritano, na, *a.* & *n.* puritan(-ic), Puritan.
puro, ra. I. *a.* pure; unmixed, sterling, unalloyed, solid (gold, etc.); clear, clean, neat; unblemished, unsullied; mere, only, sheer, absolute.—**a p.,** by dint of.—**de p.,** extremely; by dint of.—**de p. sangre,** thoroughbred.—**la p. verdad,** the honest truth. **II.** *m.* cigar.
púrpura, *f.* purpura, murex, purple shell; purple; cloth dyed with purple; dignity of a king or cardinal; (poet.) blood.—**purpurado,** *m.* cardinal.
purpurante, *a.* giving a purple color.
purpurar, *va.* to purple; to dress in purple.
purpurato, *m.* (chem.) purpurate (salt of purpuric acid).
purpurear, *vn.* to have a purple tinge.
purpúreo, rea. I. *a.* purple, puniceous, purpurate. **II.** *f.* (bot.) = LAMPAZO, burdock.
purpúrico, ca, *a.* (chem.) purpuric.
purpurina, *f.* bronze powder; (chem.) purpurin.
purpurino, na, *a.* purple.
purrela, *f.* wine of inferior quality.
purriela, *f.* (coll.) despicable trifle.
purulencia, *f.* purulence, purulency.
purulento, ta, *a.* purulent.
pus, *m.* (med.) pus.
puse, *pret.* of PONER.
pusilánime, *a.* pusillanimous, faint-hearted.
pusilánimemente, *adv.* pusillanimously.
pusilanimidad, *f.* pusillanimity.
pústula, *f.* (med.) pustule; pimple.
pustuloso, sa, *a.* pustulous, pustular.
puta, *f.* whore, harlot.
putativo, va, *a.* putative, reputed.
putput, *m.* (ornith.) hoopoe.
putrefacción, *f.* putrefaction.
putrefactivo, va, *a.* putrefactive.
putrefacto, ta, *a.* putrid, decayed, rotten.
putrescente, *a.* putrescent.
putrescible, *a.* putrescible.
putridez, *f.,* rottenness.
pútrido, da, *a.* putrid, rotten, decayed.
puya, *f.* goad, goad stick.
puyazo, *m.* prick, puncture.
puzol, *m.*; **puzolana,** *f.* a kind of volcanic rock used in making mortar.

Q

Q, q, *f.* q, twentieth letter of the Spanish alphabet.
quántum, *m.* (phys., mech.) quantum.
que. I. *rel. pron.* that, which, who, whom; when [*el día que le escribí,* the day (when) I wrote to him]. When preceded by the definite article, it is equivalent to "who," "whom," "which" (the "the which" of old English), or "the one who," "those who," "the one whom," "those whom," "that which," "the one that." **II.** *interr.* & *exclamatory pron.* (**qué**) what, what a (*¡qué hombre!* what a man!); which; how (*¡qué bonita!* how pretty!).—**q. de** . . . how many . . .—**¿q. hay?** or **¿q. pasa?** what is the matter?—**¿q. tal?,** how goes it?—**¡q. va!,** go on! (expressing disbelief).—**¿a q.?,** what for?, what's the use of?—**¿para q.?,** what for—**¿por q.?,** why?—**sin q. ni para q.,** without cause or motive.—**un no sé q.,** a certain something. **III.** *conj.* that [very seldom omitted: *Juan dice que vendrá,* John says (that) he will come]; than (in comparisons); because, for, as; and (*habla que habla,* he talks and talks, *or,* talking and talking); so; so that. Followed by a subjunctive form it is usually rendered by "to" and the corresponding infinitive, changing the construction (*deseo que Vd. venga,* I wish that you come, *or,* I wish you to come); by "let" or "may," when it expresses command or desire (*que entre,* let him come in; *que tenga buena suerte,* may you have good luck); or, with impersonal verbs, by the indicative (*antes que llueva,* before it rains). In compound tenses (*he hablado, había hablado,* etc.), the participle is sometimes placed first, and then *que* followed by the auxiliary. In such cases, *que* is rendered by *when, after, as soon as;* e. g. *llegado que hubo,* when he had arrived, after he arrived; *leído que hayamos la carta,* after we have read, *or* after we read, the letter. Before infinitive and following a noun preceded by a form of *haber, tener,* and a few other verbs, it is rendered by *to;* e. g. *hay mucho que hacer,* there is much to do; *teníamos dos cartas que escribir,* we had two letters to write. Sometimes it is used as an expletive, in the sense of "and" [*la culpa es mía, que no suya,* the fault is mine, (and) not yours].—**q. no,** without, but that.—**q. . . . q.,** whether . . . or (*que quieras que no,* whether you will or not).—**por . . . q.,** no matter how (*por bien que hable,* no matter how well he speaks).
quebracho, *m.* quebracho; quebracho bark.
quebrada, *f.* ravine; deep pass; gorge; (Am.) gulch; stream; (com.) failure, bankruptcy.
quebradero, *m.* breaker.—**q. de cabeza,** worry.
quebradillo, *m.* wooden shoe heel; (dance) bending of the body.
quebradizo, za, *a.* brittle, fragile; frail, sickly.
quebrado, da. I. *pp.* of QUEBRAR. **II.** *a.* broken; weakened; (com.) bankrupt; rough, uneven (ground); (med.) ruptured.—**azúcar q.,** brown sugar. **II.** *m.* (arith.) common fraction; (Cuba) tobacco leaf full of holes.—**q. impropio,** (arith.) improper fraction.—**q. mixto,** (arith.) mixed fraction.—**q. propio,** (arith.) proper fraction.
quebrador, ra, *n.* & *a.* breaker(-ing); lawbreaker (-ing).
quebradura, *f.* breaking, splitting; gap, fissure, slit; (med.) fracture; rupture, hernia.
quebraja, *f.* crack, fissure, flaw, split.
quebrajar, *va.* = RESQUEBRAJAR, to crack, split.
quebrajoso, sa, *a.* brittle, fragile; full of cracks.
quebramiento, *m.* = QUEBRANTAMIENTO.
quebrantable, *a.* frangible, brittle.
quebrantado, da, *a.* split, fractured, broken.
quebrantador, ra. I. *n.* breaker, splitter; crusher, bruiser; violator, transgressor. **II.** *a.* breaking, that breaks; weakening; crushing.
quebrantadura, *f.* = QUEBRANTAMIENTO.
quebrantahuesos, *m.* (ornith.) osprey, lammergeier; tease, bore.
quebrantamiento, *m.* fracture, rupture; crushing, breaking; smash; breaking out of prison; fatigue, exhaustion; violation; burglary; desecration.
quebrantante, *a.* breaking, crushing.
quebrantaolas, *m.* breakwater.
quebrantapiedras, *m.* (bot.) stonebreak.
quebrantar, *va.* to break, crush; to burst open; to pound, grind, mash; to transgress; to violate, break (as a contract); to vex; to fatigue; to weaken; to diminish; (law) to annul, repeal.
quebrantaterrones, *m.* (coll.) clodhopper.
quebranto, *m.* breaking, crushing; weakness; lassitude; pity, compassion; grief, affliction; (com.) loss, damage.
quebrar (*ind.* QUIEBRO; *subj.* QUIEBRE). **I.** *va.* to break; to crush; to cast asunder; to double, bend, twist; to interrupt, hinder; to temper, moderate; to spoil (the bloom of the countenance); to overcome, conquer; to diminish (friendship). **II.** *vn.* (com.) to fail, become bankrupt. **III.** *vr.* to be ruptured; to break (as

a plate, a bone, etc.); to be broken, as the continuity of hills.
quebrazas, *f. pl.* flaws in sword blades.
queche, *f.* (naut.) smack, ketch.
quechemarín, *m.* (naut.) coasting lugger.
quechua, *n.* & *a.* Quichua(-an).
queda, *f.* curfew; curfew bell.
quedada, *f.* stay, residence, sojourn.
quedar. I. *vn.* to remain; to stay, stop in a place; to remain, be left as remainder (sometimes diff. constr.: *le quedan tres pesetas,* he has three pesetas left); to be or be left in a state or condition; to leave at; to decide, resolve, agree.—**q. bien (mal),** to acquit oneself well (badly); to come out well (badly); to keep (break) an appointment.—**q. de** (Am.) = **q. en,** to agree to; to have an understanding.—**q. por,** to go to, be accorded to, be won by; (followed by *inf.*) to remain to be (followed by *pp.*).—**¿en qué quedamos?** what is your final decision? what do you say? **II.** *vr.* to remain; to slacken, abate, diminish.—**q. atrás,** to get, or be left, behind. —**q. con,** to retain, keep.—**q. fresco,** not to mind, to remain undisturbed or indifferent.—**q. frío,** or **muerto,** to be greatly astonished, to be breathless, horrified, etc.
quede, (print.) stet; let stand.
quedito, ta. I. *a. dim.* soft, gentle; easy. **II.** *adv.* = QUEDO.
quedo, da. I. *a.* quiet, still, noiseless; easy, gentle. **II.** *adv.* softly, gently; in a low voice.
quehacer, *m.* occupation, business, work.—*pl.* **quehaceres de casa,** household chores.
queja, *f.* complaint; grumbling, moan; resentment, grudge; quarrel, dispute.
quejarse, *vr.* to complain; to grumble; **(de) to** regret, lament.
quejicoso, sa, *a.* plaintive, querulous.
quejido, *m.* moan.
quejigal, *m.* plantation of muricated oaks.
quejigo, *m.* (bot.) muricated oak.
quejosamente, *adv.* complainingly, plaintively.
quejoso, sa, *a.* plaintive; complaining.
quejumbre, *f.* grumble, growl.
quejumbroso, sa, *a.* grumbling, plaintive.
quelícero, *m.* (zool.) chela.
queloide, *m.* (med.) cheloid, keloid.
quelonio, *a.* & *m.* (zool.) chelonian.
quema, *f.* fire, burning; combustion.—**de q. lenta,** slow-burning.—**huir de la q.,** to get away from trouble, get out.
quemadero, ra. I. *a.* apt to be burned. **II.** *m.* place where convicts were burned.
quemado, da. I. *pp.* of QUEMAR. **II.** *a.* burnt, crisp; angry, irritated.—**q. por el sol,** sunburned. **III.** *m.* burnt down forest or thicket.
quemador, ra. I. *n.* incendiary; burner. **II.** *m.* gas burner.
quemadura, *f.* burn, scald; (agr.) brand, smut upon plants.
quemajoso, sa, *a.* smarting, burning.
quemante, *a.* burning.
quemar. I. *va.* to burn; to scald; to fire, set on fire, kindle; to parch, dry, scorch; to vex, irritate; to dispose of at a low price. **II.** *vn.* to burn, be too hot. **III.** *vr.* to get burned, burn oneself; to burn, be consumed by fire; to be very hot, be parched with heat; to fret, to be angry; (coll.) to be near, be "warm."—**q. las cejas,** (coll.) to burn the midnight oil.
quemazón, *f.* combustion; fire, conflagration; (coll.), smarting, burning; offensive remark; vexation, anger; (Cuba) bargain sale.
quena, *f.* (Am.) a sort of Indian flute.
quenepa, *f.* (P. R.) honeyberry.
quenopodiáceo, cea, *a.* (bot.) chenopodiaceous.
quenopodio, *m.* (bot.) chenopod.
quepis, *m.* (mil.) kepi.
quepo, quepa, *v. V.* CABER.
queratina, *f.* (chem.) keratin.
queratitis, *f.* (med.) keratitis.
queratosis, *f.* keratosis.
quercina, *f.* (chem.) quercin.
quercitol, *m.* (chem.) acorn sugar, quercitol.
quercitrina, *f.* (chem.) quercitrin.
quercitrón, *m.* (bot., chem.) quercitron.
querco, *m.* (bot.) quercus, tree of the oak family.
querella, *f.* complaint; quarrel; (law) plaint, complaint; act of contesting an inofficious will.
querellador, ra, *n.* complainant.
querellante, *n.* & *a.* complainant(-ing).
querellarse, *vr.* to lament, bewail; to complain; (law) to make an accusation; to contest a will.
querellosamente, *adv.* plaintively, querulously.
querelloso, sa, *a.* querulous.
querencia, *f.* affection, fondness; haunt of wild beasts.
querencioso, sa, *a.* (of animals) affectionate.
querendón, dona, *a.* very affectionate or loving.
querer. I. *va.* (*ind. pres.* QUIERO, *pret.* QUISE, *fut.* QUERRÉ; *subj.* QUIERA) to will; to desire, wish; to endeavor, attempt; to accept (a challenge in certain games); to love; (foll. by *inf.* used to ask a favor as: *¿Quiere V. abrir la ventana?* Will you open the window, please?).—**querría, quisiera,** should like.—**q. decir,** to mean. **II.** *vn.* to wish, desire; to be willing; to love.—**como quiera,** anyhow, in any way.—**como quiera que,** whereas; inasmuch as, since; although; whatever, however, no matter how.—**como quiera que sea,** in any case.—**como Vd. quiera,** as you like; let it be so.—**cuando quiera,** at any time, whenever.—**donde quiera,** anywhere, wherever.—**no q.** (*inf.*), to refuse to (*inf.*).—**no q. nada con,** not to wish to have anything to do with.—**sin q.,** unwillingly; unintentionally. **III.** *v. impers.* to look like (rain, etc.), threaten, look as if it were going to (rain, snow, etc.). **IV.** *m.* love, affection; will; desire.
queresa, *f.* = CRESA, egg of fly or bee; maggot.
querido, da. I. *pp.* of QUERER. **II.** *a.* dear, beloved. **III.** *n.* paramour, lover, mistress.—**q. mío,** or **mía,** my dear, my dearest, love, my darling.
queriente, *a.* willing; loving.
quermes, *m.* (entom.) kermes.—**q. mineral,** (chem.) kermes.
querocha, *f.* = QUERESA.
querochar, *vn.* (of bees) to emit the semen.
querosén, *m.* kerosene.
querub, querube, querubín, *m.* cherub.
querúbico, ca, *a.* cherubic.
querva, *f.* (bot.) spurge; palma Christi.
quesadilla, *f.* cheesecake; sweetmeat.
quesear, *vn.* to make cheese.
quesera, *f.* dairy; dairymaid; cheese board, cheese mold, cheese vat; cheese dish.
quesería, *f.* season for making cheese; dairy.
quesero, ra. I. *a.* caseous, cheesy. **II.** *n.* cheesemonger, cheesemaker.
quesillo, ito, *m. dim.* small cheese.
queso, *m.* cheese.—**q. de bola,** Edam cheese.—**q. de cerdo,** headcheese.—**q. helado,** ice-cream brick, molded ice cream.
quetona, *f.* (chem.) ketone.
quetro, *m.* a Chilean duck with featherless wings.
quetzal, *m.* (ornith.) quetzal, trogon.
quevedos, *m. pl.* eyeglasses.
¡quiá! *interj.* come now! no, indeed!
quianti, *m.* Chianti (wine).
quiasma, *f.* (anat., biol.) chiasm, chiasma.
quibey, *m.* (W. I.) (bot.) dog's-bane.
quicial, *m.*, **quicialera,** *f.* hinge post.
quicio, *m.* eye of a door hinge; pivot hole.—**fuera de q.,** unhinged, out of order.—**sacar de q.,** to unhinge; to exasperate.
quiché, *n.* Guatemalan Indian and his language.
quichua, *n.* & *a.* = QUECHUA.
quid, *m.* gist, pith, main point.
quídam, *m.* (coll.) person; a nobody.
quid pro quo. I. (Lat.) an equivalent. **II.** *m.* mistaken identity; mistake.
quiebra, *f.* crack, fracture; gaping fissure; loss, damage; (com.) failure, bankruptcy.

quiebrahacha, *m.* (Cuba) (bot.) breakaxe.
[1]**quiebro,** *m.* (mus.) trill; movement or inclination of the body, as in dodging.
[2]**quiebro, quiebre,** *v. V.* QUEBRAR.
quien (*interr.* **quién**), *pron.* (*pl.* **quienes, quiénes**) who, whom, whoever, whomever, which, whichever.
quienquiera, *pron.* (*pl.* **quienesquiera**) whoever, whosoever, whomsoever, whichever.
quiero, quiera, *v. V.* QUERER.
quiescencia, *f.* quiescence.
quietación, *f.* quieting or appeasing.
quietador, ra, *n.* quieter, appeaser.
quietamente, *adv.* quietly, calmly.
quietar. I. *va.* to quiet, appease. **II.** *vr.* to become quiet or calm, to quiet down.
quiete, *f.* rest, repose, quiet.
quietismo, *m.* quietism, a sect of mystics.
quietista, *n.* & *a.* quietist.
quieto, ta, *a.* quiet, still; steady, undisturbed; silent, peaceable; orderly; virtuous.
quietud, *f.* quietude, quietness, quiet; rest, repose, tranquillity.
quijada, *f.* jaw, jawbone.
quijal, quijar, *m.* grinder, back tooth; jaw.
quijarudo, da, *a.* large-jawed.
quijera, *f.* cheeks of a crossbow.—*pl.* straps of the noseband on a harness.
quijero, *m.* sloping bank of a canal.
quijo, *m.* (min.) ore.
quijones, *m. pl.* (bot.) dill.
quijotada, *f.* quixotic enterprise.
quijote, *m.* (armor) cuisse, thighguard; upper part of the haunch.
Quijote, *m.* Quijote, Quixote, quixotic person.
quijotería, *f.* quixotism.
quijotesco, ca, *a.* quixotic.
quijotismo, *m.* quixotism.
quila, *f.* (S. A.) a variety of very strong bamboo.
quilatador, ra, *n.* assayer of gold and silver.
quilatar, *va.* to assay.
quilate, *m.* (jewelry) carat or karat; an ancient coin; degree of excellence.
quilatera, *f.* (jewelry) diamond sieve.
quiliárea, *f.* = KILIÁREA, land measure, 1000 ares.
quilifaciente, *a.* chylifactive.
quilifactivo, va, *a.* chylifactive.
quilífero, ra, *a.* (zool.) chyliferous.
quilificación, *f.* (med.) chylification.
quilificar, *va.* to chylify.
quilma, *f.* = COSTAL, large bag or sack.
[1]**quilo,** *m.* (med.) chyle.—**sudar el q.,** to work hard.
[2]**quilo, quilogramo, quilómetro,** etc. = KILO, KILOGRAMO, etc.
quiloso, sa, *a.* chylous, chylaceous.
quilquil, *m.* a Chilean arboreous fern.
quilla, *f.* (naut.) keel; (ornith.) breastbone.
quillái, quillay, *m.* quillai, a S. A. soapbark tree.
quillotrar. I. *va.* to excite, incite, urge; to make love to; to attract, captivate; to think over, consider; to deck, adorn. **II.** *vr.* to fall in love; to complain, to whine.
quillotro, tra. I. *m.* urging, incitement; sign, indication; lovemaking; love affair; puzzle, perplexing thing or situation. **II.** *n.* dear friend; lover.
quimbámbulas, *f. pl.* (Cuba) rough, craggy spots; hidden nook.
quimbombó, *m.* (bot.) okra, gumbo.
quimera, *f.* chimera; dispute, quarrel.
quimérico, ca; quimerino, na, *a.* chimerical.
quimerista, *n.* wrangler, brawler; visionary.
quimerizar, *vn.* to indulge in chimeras.
química, *f.* chemistry.—**q. atómica,** atomic chemistry.—**q. biológica,** biochemistry.—**q. industrial,** industrial chemistry.—**q. inorgánica,** inorganic chemistry.—**q. nuclear,** nuclear chemistry.—**q. orgánica,** organic chemistry.
químicamente, *adv.* chemically.
químico, ca. I. *a.* chemical. **II.** *n.* chemist.
quimicofísico, ca. I. *a.* chemicophysical. **II.** *n.* chemicophysicist; *f.* chemicophysics.
quimífero, ra, *a.* chymiferous.
quimificación, *f.* (physiol.) chymification.
quimificar, *va.* to convert into chyme.
quimioterapéutico, ca, *a.* chemotherapeutic.
quimioterapia, *f.* chemotherapy.
quimista, *m.* = ALQUIMISTA, alchemist.
quimo, *m.* (med.) chyme.
quimógrafo, *m.* (med.) kymograph.
quimón, *m.* chintz.
quimono, *m.* kimono.
quimoso, sa, *a.* chymous.
quimurgia, *f.* chemurgy.
quina, *f.* Peruvian bark, cinchona.
quinal, *m.* (naut.) preventer shroud.
quinaquina, *f.* = QUINA.
quinario, ria. I. *a.* quinary, consisting of five. **II.** *m.* quinarius, a Roman coin.
quinas, *f. pl.* arms of Portugal; fives on dice.
quincalla, *f.* (com.) hardware; small wares.
quincallería, *f.* hardware trade or store; small wares store.
quincallero, ra, *n.* dealer in hardware or small wares.
quince, *a.* & *m.* fifteen; fifteenth; a card game.
quincenal, *a.* fortnightly, semi-monthly.
quincenalmente, *adv.* fortnightly.
quinceno, na. I. *a.* fifteenth. **II.** *n.* mule fifteen months old. **III.** *f.* fortnight; semi-monthly pay; (mus.) fifteenth (interval and organ stop). —**por q.,** every two weeks, semi-monthly
quincuagenario, ria, *a.* & *n.* having fifty units; quinquagenarian, person in the fifties.
quincuagésimo, ma. I. *a.* fiftieth. **II.** *f.* Quinquagesima Sunday.
quincunce, *m.* quincunx.
quincuncial, *a.* quincuncial.
quincha, *f.* (Peru) wall of clay and canes.
quindenio, *m.* period of fifteen years.
quinero, ra, *n.* cinchona gatherer or trader.
quinete, *m.* a kind of camlet.
quingentésimo, ma, *a.* five-hundredth.
quingombó, *m.* (bot.) gumbo, okra.
quingos, *m.* (Am.) zigzag.
quinidina, *f.* (chem.) quinidin, quinidine.
quinientos, *n.* & *a.* five hundred.
quinina, *f.* quinine.
quinismo, *m.* effects of the use of quinine; cinchonism.
quino, *m.* (bot.) cinchona tree; (chem.) quinoidin.
quinoa, *f.* quinoa, a S. A. species of goosefoot.
quínola, *f.* at cards, four of a kind.—*pl.* a card game.
quinolear, *va.* to prepare (cards) for QUÍNOLAS.
quinona, *f.* (chem.) quinone.
quinqué, *m.* student lamp.
quinquefoliado, da, *a.* (bot.) quinquefoliate.
quinquefolio, *m.* (bot.) common cinquefoil.
quinquenal, *a.* quinquennial.
quinquenervia, *f.* (bot.) rib-grass plantain.
quinquenio, *m.* quinquennium, lustrum.
quinquillería, *f.* = QUINCALLERÍA.
quinquillero, *m.* hawker, peddler; QUINCALLERO.
quinquivalente, *m.* (chem.) quinquevalent.
quinta, *f.* country seat, villa; manorhouse; (mil.) draft; quint, sequence of five cards; (fencing) quint; (mus.) fifth.—**q. esencia,** quintessence.
quintacolumnista, *a.* & *n.* fifth columnist.
quintador, *m.* (mil.) one who drafts men.
quintaesencia, *f.* quintessence.
quintaesenciar, *va.* to refine, distil.
quintal, *m.* quintal, a hundred pounds.—**q. métrico,** metric quintal (100 kg.).
quintalada, *f.* (naut.) primage or hat money (2½ per cent. on the freight).
quintaleño, ña; lero, ra, *a.* capable of containing a quintal.
quintana, *f.* country mansion.
quintante, *m.* instrument for observations at sea.
quintañón, na, *a.* & *n.* (coll.) centenarian.

quintar. **I.** *va.* to draw one out of five; (mil.) to draft for service; to plow the fifth time. **II.** *vn.* (of the moon) to attain the fifth day.
quintería, *f.* farm; grange.
quinterno, *m.* five sheets of paper; keno, in lotto.
quintero, *m.* farmer; farm hand.
quinteto, *m.* (mus.) quintet.
quintil, *m.* quintile.
quintilla, *f.* five-line stanza.
quintillo, *m.* game of ombre with five players.
quintillón, *m.* quintillion.
quinto, ta. **I.** *a.* fifth.—**q. columna,** fifth column. **II.** *m.* one fifth; 20% duty; (Mex., Chile) (coll.) 5 centavo piece; (mil.) conscript, inductee.
quintuplicación, *f.* quintuplication.
quintuplicar, *va.* & *vn.* to quintuplicate.
quíntuplo, pla. **I.** *a.* quintuple, fivefold. **II.** *m.* quintuple, quintuplet.
quinua, *f.* = QUINOA.
quinzavo, va, *n.* & *a.* (arith.) fifteenth.
quiñón, *m.* share of profit or lands; (P. I.) a land measure (2.8 hectares).
quiñonero, *m.* part owner, shareholder.
quiosco, *m.* kiosk, pavilion, summer house.—**q. de necesidad,** public water closet.
quipos, *m. pl.* (Peru) quipu.
quiquiriquí, *m.* cock-a-doodle-do; (coll.) cock of the walk.
quiragra, *f.* gout in the hand.
quirinal, *m.* & *a.* Quirinal.
quirófano, *m.* (med.) operating room.
quirografía, *f.* chirography.
quirógrafo, *m.* chirograph.
quiromancia, *f.* chiromancy, palmistry.
quiromántico, *m.* palmist, chiromancer.
quiropodia, *f.* chiropody.
quirópodo, da, *a.* (zool.) chiropodous.
quiropráctico, ca. **I.** *a.* chiropractic. **II.** *n.* chiropractor; *f.* chiropractic.
quiróptero, ra. **I.** *a.* (zool.) chiropterous. **II.** *m.* (zool.) chiropter.
quiroteca, *f.* (coll.) glove.
quirúrgico, ca. **I.** *a.* surgical. **II.** *n.* surgeon.
quirurgo, *m.* surgeon.
quise, *v.* *V.* QUERER.
quisicosa, *f.* (coll.) enigma, riddle, puzzle.
quiso, *v.* *V.* QUERER.
quisquemenil, *m.* (Am.) short cloak.
quisquilla, *f.* bickering, trifling dispute.
quisquilloso, sa, *a.* fastidious, precise; touchy, peevish.
quiste, *m.* (med.) cyst.
quisto, ta, *a.*—**bien q.,** well received, generally beloved.—**mal q.,** disliked.
quita. **I.** *f.* (law) acquittance, discharge, release (from debt).—**de q. y pon,** detachable, removable. **II.** *interj.* God forbid!—**¡q. de ahí!** away with you! out of my sight!
quitación, *f.* salary, pay; income; (law) QUITA.
quitador, ra, *n.* remover.
quitaipón, *m.* = QUITAPÓN.
quitamanchas, *m.* clothes cleaner, spot remover.
quitameriendas, *f.* common meadow saffron.
quitamiento, *m.* (law) = QUITA.
quitamotas, *n.* (coll.) servile flatterer.
quitanieve, *m.* snowplow.
quitante, *a.* that takes away or removes.
quitanza, *f.* quittance; (com.) receipt in full, discharge.
quitapelillos, *n.* (coll.) flatterer, fawner.
quitapesares, *n.* (coll.) comfort, comforter.
quitapiedras, *m.* (Ry.) cowcatcher.
quitapón, *m.* ornament on the headstall of mules.—**de q.** = DE QUITA Y PON. *V.* QUITA.
quitar. **I.** *va.* to take away; to subtract; to take off, remove; to separate, extract, take out; to take (up) time; to free from; to rob of, deprive of; to release or redeem (a pledge); to hinder; forbid, prohibit; to repeal, annul; to free from (obligation); (fencing) to parry. **II.** *vr.* to abstain, refrain; to quit, move away, withdraw; to get rid of; to take off (a garment); to come out (as a stain).—**q. algo de encima,** to get rid of, or shake off, something.—**q. el agua,** (Mex.) to stop raining.
quitasol, *m.* parasol, sunshade.
quite, *m.* obstacle, impediment, hindrance; (fencing) parry, dodge.
quiteño, ña, *a.* of or pertaining to Quito.
quitina, *f.* (chem.) chitin.
quitinoso, sa, *a.* (chem.) chitinous.
quito, ta, *a.* quit, clear, free.
quitrín, *m.* (Cuba) two-wheel open wagon.
quizá, quizás, *adv.* perhaps, maybe.
quizame, *m.* (P. I.) roof, ceiling.
quórum, *m.* quorum.

R

R, r, *f.* r, twenty-first letter of the Spanish alphabet.
raba, *f.* bait for pilchard fishery.
rabada, *f.* hind quarter, rump.
rabadán, *m.* head shepherd.
rabadilla, *f.* coccyx; rump; (ornith.) uropygium.
rabanal, *m.* ground sown with radishes.
rabanero, ra. **I.** *a.* (coll.) short (skirt); forward, pert, bold. **II.** *f.* (coll.) shameless woman. **III.** *n.* seller of radishes.
rabanillo, *m. dim.* (bot.) wild radish; sharp taste of wine on the turn; (coll.) ardent desire, longing; sourish temper.
rabaniza, *f.* radish seed.
rábano, *m.* (bot.) radish.—**r. picante,** or **rusticano,** horse-radish.—**r. silvestre,** wild radish.—**tomar el r. por las hojas,** (coll.) to be entirely mistaken, to be off the track.
rabazuz, *m.* thickened juice of licorice.
rabear, *vn.* to wag the tail.
[1]**rabel,** *m.* (mus.) rebeck, ancient stringed instrument.
[2]**rabel,** *m.* breech, backside.
rabelejo, *m. dim.* of RABEL.
rabeo, *m.* wagging of the tail.
rabera, *f.* tail end; tang, tongue; handle of a crossbow; chaff.
raberón, *m.* top of a felled tree.
rabí, *m.* rabbi, rabbin.
rabia, *f.* hydrophobia, rabies; rage, fury.—**tener r.,** to have a grudge against.—**tomar r.,** to take a dislike to; to develop a grudge against.
rabiar, *vn.* to be ill with hydrophobia; to rage, be furious; to suffer racking pain.—**r. por,** to long eagerly for.
rabiatar, *va.* to tie by the tail.
rabiazorras, *m.* east wind.
rabicán; rabicano, na, *a.* white-tailed.
rabicorto, ta, *a.* short-tailed; docked.
rábido, da, *a.* (poet.) = RABIOSO.
rabieta, *f. dim.* (coll.) fit of temper.
rabihorcado, *m.* (ornith.) frigate bird.
rabil, *m.* crank; wheat husker.
rabilar, *va.* to husk with a wheat husker.
rabilargo, ga. **I.** *a.* long-tailed. **II.** *m.* (ornith.) blue crow.
rabillo, *m. dim.* little tail; stem; mildew spots on corn; darnel.
rabinegro, gra, *a.* black-tailed.
rabínico, ca, *a.* rabbinical.
rabinismo, *m.* rabbinism.
rabinista, *n.* & *a.* rabbinist(-ic).
rabino, *m.* rabbi.
rabión, *m.* rapids of a river.
rabioso, sa, *a.* rabid, mad; furious, enraged.
rabisalsera, *a.* (coll.) pert, forward (woman).
rabito, *m. dim.* small tail; stem.
rabiza, *f.* point of a fishing rod; rocket stick; (naut.) tip, end of a rope; point, end of a shoal; tail of a block.
rabo, *m.* tail (of animal, esp. quadruped); tail end, back, or hind part; train; stem.—**r. de gallo,** (naut.) stern timbers.—**r. de junco,**

(ornith.) a tropical bird.—**con el r. entre las piernas,** (coll.) (fig.) with the tail between the legs, crestfallen, dejected; humiliated—**falta el r. por desollar,** the worst is yet to come.—**mirar con el r. del ojo,** to look askance, or out of the corner of the eye.
rabón, na, *a.* docked, bobtailed.
rabona, *f.* (Am.) canteen woman, soldier's wife. —**hacer r.,** to play hooky.
rabopelado, *m.* opossum.
raboseada, raboseadura, *f.* fray, chafe.
rabosear, *va.* to chafe, fray, fret.
raboso, sa, *a.* ragged, tattered.
rabotada, *f.* insolent reply.
rabotear, *va.* to crop or dock the tail of.
raboteo, *m.* cropping of sheep's tails.
rabudo, da, *a.* long- or thick-tailed.
rábula, *m.* ignorant, vociferous lawyer, pettifogger.
raca, *f.* (naut.) traveler; jib iron.
racahut, *m.* raccahoot.
racamenta, *f.* **racamento,** *m.* (naut.) parral or parrel.
racel, *m.* (naut.) run, rising of a ship.
racial, *a.* racial, race (as *a.*).
racima, *f.* grapes left on vines at vintage.
racimado, da, *a.* clustered, in racemes.
racimal, *a.* having clusters or racemes.
racimar. I. *va.* to pick the RACIMAS of. **II.** *vr.* = ARRACIMARSE, to cluster.
racimífero, ra, *a.* racemiferous.
racimo, *m.* bunch; cluster; raceme.
racimoso, sa, *a.* full of bunches, racemose.
racimudo, da, *a.* in large bunches or racemes.
raciocinación, *f.* ratiocination, reasoning.
raciocinar, *vn.* to reason, ratiocinate.
raciocinio, *m.* reasoning, ratiocination.
ración, *f.* ration; ration money; supply, allowance, pittance; (eccl.) prebend in a cathedral.
racionabilidad, *f.* rationality.
racional. I. *a.* rational; reasonable; (math. and astr.) rational. **II.** *m.* rational, pectoral or breastplate.
racionalidad, *f.* rationality; reasonableness.
racionalismo, *m.* rationalism.
racionalista, *n.* & *a.* rationalist(-ic).
racionalmente, *adv.* rationally.
racionamiento, *m.* (mil.) rationing.
racionar, *va.* (mil.) to ration.
racioncica, illa, ita, *f. dim.* small pittance.
racionero, *m.* (eccl.) prebendary; distributor of rations.
racionista, *n.* receiver of a ration or allowance; (theat.) utility man.
racismo, *m.* racism.
racista, *n.* & *a.* racist.
[1]**racha,** *f.* flaw, gust of wind; streak of luck.
[2]**racha,** *f.* (min.) piece of wood used in shoring.
rachis, *f.* (anat.) rachis, spinal column.
rada, *f.* (naut.) roads, roadstead, bay.
radar, *m.* radar.
radiación, *f.* radiation.—**r. atmosférica,** atmospheric radiation.—**r. cósmica,** cosmic radiation.—**r. letal,** lethal radiation.—**r. térmica,** heat or thermal radiation.
radiactividad, *f.* (phys.) radioactivity.
radiactivo, va, *a.* radioactive.
radiado, da. I. *pp.* of RADIAR. **II.** *a.* radiated. **III.** *a.* & *m.* (zool.) radiate.
radiador, *m.* radiator (heating device and auto).
radial, *a.* radial; radio (as *a.*).—**guía r.,** radio program.—**locutor r.,** radio announcer.
radián, *m.* (geom.) radian.
radiante, *a.* radiant, brilliant, beaming; (phys.) radiant.—**r. de,** beaming with.
radiar. I. *vn.* to radiate. **II.** *va.* & *vn.* to radio; to broadcast.
radicación, *f.* radication, taking root.
radical. I. *a.* radical; original, primitive. **II.** *m.* (math., chem., pol.) radical; (gram.) root.
radicalismo, *m.* radicalism.
radicalmente, *adv.* radically, fundamentally.
radicar. I. *vn.* to take root; to be (in a place); to lie, have roots. **II.** *vr.* to radicate, take root; to settle, establish oneself.
radicoso, sa, *a.* radical.
radícula, *f.* (bot.) radicle, radicule.
radífero, ra, *a.* radium-bearing.
radigrafía, *f.* radiography, roentgenography.
radigrafiar, *va.* to radiograph.
radigráfico, ca, *a.* radiographic.
[1]**radio,** *m.* (geom., anat.) radius; circuit, district. —**r. de acción,** range.
[2]**radio,** *m.* (chem.) radium; radio, radiotelephony; radiogram; radio (instrument or set); (radio) broadcasting.
radioactinio, *m.* (nuclear chem.) radioactinium.
radioactividad, *f.* = RADIACTIVIDAD.
radioactivo, va, *a.* = RADIACTIVO.
radioaficionado, da, *n.* radio amateur, radio fan, (coll.) radio ham.
radioamplificador, *m.* radioamplifier.
radiobiología, *f.* radiobiology.
radiocarbono, *m.* (chem.) radiocarbon.
radiocoloide, *m.* (nuclear chem.) radiocolloid.
radiocompás, *m.* radiocompass.
radiocomunicación, *f.* radio communication system.
radioconductor, *m.* radioconductor.
radiodetector, *m.* radiodetector.
radiodifundir, *va.* & *vn.* (radio) to broadcast.
radiodifusión, *f.* (radio) broadcast.
radiodifusora, *f.*, **radioemisora,** *f.* (radio) broadcasting station.
radioelemento, *m.* (chem.) radioelement, radioactive element.
radioescucha, *n.* radio listener.
radiofaro, *m.* radio beacon, radiophare.
radiofísica, *f.* radiophysics.
radiofonía, *f.* radiophony.
radiófono, *m.* radiophone.
radiofonógrafo, *m.* radiophonograph.
radiofotografía, *f.* radiophotography.
radiofrecuencia, *f.* radio-frequency.
radiogénico, ca, *a.* radiogenic.
radiogoniometría, *f.* radiogoniometry.
radiogoniométrico, ca, *a.* radiogoniometric.
radiogoniómetro, *m.* radiogoniometer.
radiografía, *f.* RADIGRAFÍA; radiotelegraphy.
radiografiar, *va.* to radiograph.
radiográfico, ca, *a.* = RADIGRÁFICO.
radiograma, *m.* radiogram, radiotelegram.
radiolario, ria, *a.* & *m.* (zool.) radiolarian.
radiolisis, *f.* (nuclear chem.) radiolysis.
radiología, *f.* radiology.
radiológico, ca, *a.* radiological.
radiólogo, ga, *n.* radiologist.
radioluminiscencia, *f.* (phys.) radioluminescence.
radiometría, *f.* radiometry.
radiómetro, *m.* radiometer.
radionúclido, *m.* (phys.) radionuclide.
radioquímica, *f.* radiochemistry.
radioresistencia, *f.* (med., phys.) radioresistance.
radiorreceptor, *m.* radio receiver.
radiorrevista, *f.* (radio) radio report or news.
radioscopia, *f.* radioscopy.
radioscopio, *m.* radioscope.
radiosensitividad, *f.* (med., phys.) radiosensitivity.
radioso, sa, *a.* radiant.
radiosonda, *f.* (meteorol.) radiosonde.
radiotelefonía, *f.* radiotelephony.
radiotelefónico, ca, *a.* radiotelephonic.
radioteléfono, *m.* radiotelephone.
radiotelegrafía, *f.* radiotelegraphy, wireless telegraphy.
radiotelegrafiar, *va.* & *vn.* to wireless, communicate by wireless telegraphy.
radiotelegráfico, ca, *a.* radiotelegraphic, wireless.
radiotelegrafista, *n.* wireless operator.

radiotelégrafo, *m.* wireless telegraph.
radiotelegrama, *m.* radiotelegram, radiogram.
radiotelescopio, *m.* radiotelescope.
radioteletipo, *m.* radioteletypewriter.
radioterapia, *f.* (med.) radiotherapy.
radiotermia, *f.* (med.) radiothermy.
radiotransmisor, *m.* radio transmitter.
radiovisión, *f.* radiovision.
radioyente, *n.* radio listener.
radón, *m.* (chem.) radon.
raedera, *f.* scraper, raker.
raedizo, za, *a.* easily scraped.
raedor, ra, *n.* & *a.* scraper(-ing), eraser(-ing).
raedura, *f.* erasure; scrapings, filings.
raer, *va.* (*ger.* RAYENDO; *ind. pres.* RAIGO, *pret.* él RAYÓ; *subj.* RAIGA) to scrape; to rub off, abrade, fret, fray; to erase; to wipe out, extirpate.
rafa, *f.* (arch.) buttress; trench or ditch for irrigation; (vet.) crack in the toe of hoofs; (min.) cut in a rock for supporting an arch.
rafaelesco, ca, *a.* Raphaelesque.
ráfaga, *f.* gust of wind; small-cloud; flash or gleam of light.
rafania, *f.* (med.) raphania.
[1]**rafe,** *m.* (arch.) eaves.
[2]**rafe,** *n.* (anat., bot.) raphe.
rafear, *va.* to secure with buttresses.
rafia, *f.* (bot.) raffia.
raglán, *m.* raglan.
rahez, *a.* vile, low, despicable.
raíble, *a.* that can be scraped or frayed.
raiceja, cilla, cita, *f. dim.* rootlet, radicle.
raído, da. I. *pp.* of RAER. **II.** *a.* frayed, threadbare, worn out; barefaced, shameless.
raigal. I. *a.* radical. **II.** *m.* foot of a tree.
raigambre, *f.* intermixture of roots.
raigo, raiga, *v. V.* RAER.
raigón, *m.* large strong root; root of a tooth.
rail, *m.* (Angl.) (Ry.) rail.
raimiento, *m.* scraping, abrading; impudence.
raíz, *f.* (bot.) root; base, foundation; origin; (math. and gram.) root.—**a r.,** close to, immediately, right after, hard upon.—**arrancar de r.,** to uproot.—**cortar de r.,** to nip in the bud. —**de r.,** from the root; entirely.—**echar raíces,** to take root, become fixed or settled.
[1]**raja,** *f.* split, rent, crack; slice (as of fruit).
[2]**raja,** *f.* coarse cloth.
rajá, *m.* rajah, Indian prince.
rajable, *a.* easily split.
rajabroqueles, *m.* (coll.) bully, brawler.
rajadillo, *m.* sugared sliced almonds.
rajadizo, za, *a.* easily split; fissile.
rajado, da, *a.* rimose, cracked, split.
rajador, *m.* wood splitter.
rajadura, *f.* cleft, fissure, crack.
rajante, *pres. p.* of RAJAR, splitting.
rajar. I. *va.* to split, rend; to slice (food). **II.** *vr.* to split, crack. **III.** *vn.* (coll.) to boast; to chatter.
rajatabla, used in the expression a **rajatabla,** (coll.) by all means, one way or another, at any cost.
rajeta, *f.* coarse cloth of mixed colors.
rajuela, *f. dim.* small crack; (mason.) riprap.
ralea, *f.* race, breed, stock; kind, quality.
ralear, *vn.* to become thin or sparse (as cloth, hair); (agr.) to yield thin bunches of grapes.
raleón, na, *a.* (of birds of prey) predatory.
raleza, *f.* thinness, lack of density, sparseness.
ralo, la, *a.* thin, sparse, not dense.
ralladera, *f.*, **rallador,** *m.* (cooking) grater.
ralladura, *f.* mark left by a grater; gratings.
rallar, *va.* (cooking) to grate; (coll.) to vex.
rallo, *m.* grater; ice scraper; rasp.
rallón, *m.* arrow with crosshead.
rama, *f.* (bot.) branch, twig, bough; branch of a family; rack in cloth mills; (print.) chase.—**andarse por las ramas,** to beat about the bush. —**asirse a las ramas,** to seek or make frivolous excuses.—**en r.,** unmanufactured, raw; (bookbinding) in sheets, unbound.
ramada, *f.* mass of branches; arbor; (Am.) shed.
ramaje, *m.* mass of branches; foliage; ramiform design.
ramal, *m.* branch, ramification; (Ry.) branch road; strand of a rope; halter; (min.) shaft, gallery.
ramalazo, *m.* lash, stroke with a rope; mark left by a lash; sudden pain or grief; blow; spot on the face caused by blows or disease.
rambla, *f.* sandy or dry ravine; ramble; tenter, tentering machine; (in Barcelona) avenue.
ramblar, *m.* sandy beach or bed.
ramblazo, ramblizo, *m.* bed of a torrent.
rameado, da, *a.* having a ramiform design.
rameal, rámeo, a, *a.* pertaining to branches.
ramera, *f.* prostitute, harlot, strumpet.
ramería, *f.* brothel: harlotry.
ramial, *m.* ramie patch.
ramificación, *f.* ramification, branching off.
ramificarse, *vr.* to ramify, branch off.
ramilla, ita, *f. dim.* small shoot, sprig, twig.
ramillete, *m.* bouquet; (bot.) cluster, umbel; centerpiece at table; collection of choice things. —**r. de Constantinopla,** (bot.) sweet-william.
ramilletero, ra. I. *n.* maker and seller of bouquets. **II.** *m.* flower vase.
ramina, *f.* ramie fiber.
ramio, *m.* (bot.) ramie, an Asiatic shrub.
ramiza, *f.* collection of lopped branches.
rámneo, nea, *a.* (bot.) rhamnaceous.
ramo, *m.* bough; branch (of a tree, of trade, a science, art, etc.); branchlet; limb cut off from a tree; cluster, bouquet; string of onions; line of goods; section, division; department.
ramojo, *m.* brushwood, small wood.
ramón, *m.* browse, browsing.
ramonear, *vn.* to lop off twigs; to browse.
ramoneo, *m.* lopping twigs; browsing.
ramoso, sa, *a.* ramose, having many branches.
[1]**rampa,** *f.* cramp, crick, (coll.) charley horse.
[2]**rampa,** *f.* ramp, slope.—**r. de lanzamiento,** (astronaut.) launching ramp.
rampante, *a.* (her.) rampant.
rampiñete, *m.* (artil.) vent gimlet.
ramplón, plona. I. *a.* heavy, coarse (shoe); rude, vulgar, common. **II.** *m.* calk of a horseshoe.
ramplonería, *f.* coarseness, heaviness; vulgarity.
[1]**rampojo,** *m.* refuse of grapes.
[2]**rampojo,** *m.* (mil.) caltrop.
rampollo, *m.* (agr.) cutting for planting.
ramulla, *f.* twigs, brushwood.
rana, *f.* (zool.) frog; (Ry.) frog.—*pl.* (med.) ranula, tongue tumor.—**r. arbórea,** (zool.) tree frog, tree toad.—**r. toro,** (zool.) bullfrog.—**no ser r.,** (coll.) to be able and expert.
ranacuajo, *m.* = RENACUAJO, polliwog.
rancajada, *f.* uprooting plants or sprouts.
rancajado, da, *a.* wounded with a splinter.
rancajo, *m.* splinter in the flesh.
ranciarse, *vr.* = ENRANCIARSE, to get rancid.
rancidez, *f.* rancidity, rancidness, rankness.
rancio, cia. I. *a.* rank, rancid, stale; long kept, old (as wine); antiquated. **II.** *m.* greasiness of cloth before milling.
rancioso, sa, *a.* rancid, rank, sour.
rancheadero, *m.* place containing huts.
ranchear. I. *vn.* to build huts; to plunder huts. **II.** *vr.* to build a hut for oneself; to settle in a hut. **III.** *va.* to plunder the huts of.
ranchería, *f.* settlement; cluster of huts; hamlet; horde, camp.
ranchero, *m.* steward of a mess; small farmer; (Mex.) rancher.
rancho, *m.* mess (food and persons eating together); (naut.) mess; messroom; (gen. thatched) hut; (Arg.) man's flat straw hat; hamlet; camp; (Am.) cattle ranch; (coll.) meeting; gang.—**r. de ganado,** cattle ranch.—**r. de recreo,** (U. S.) dude ranch.—**r. de Santa Bárbara,** (naut.) gunroom; (naut.) rudder room.

randa, *f.* lace trimming.—**randado, da,** *a.* lace-trimmed.—**randera,** *f.* lace worker.
rangífero, *m.* reindeer.
rango, *m.* (Gal.) rank, class, position.
rangua, *f.* pivot collar, shaft socket.
ránido, da, *a.* & *m.* (zool.) ranid.
ranilla, *f. dim.* frog of the hoof (of horses, etc.); (vet.) disease in the bowels of cattle.
ránula, *f.* (med. and vet.) ranula, tongue tumor.
ranunculáceo, cea, *a.* (bot.) ranunculaceous.
ranúnculo, *m.* (bot.) crowfoot, buttercup.
ranura, *f.* groove; slot.
[1]**raña,** *f.* hook frame for catching cuttlefish.
[2]**raña,** *f.* lowland.
raño, *m.* oyster tongs.
rapa, *f.* (bot.) flower of the olive tree.
[1]**rapacejo, ja,** *n.* urchin, child.
[2]**rapacejo,** *m.* border, edging.
rapacería, *f.* childish prank or action.
rapacidad, *f.* rapacity.
rapador, ra, *n.* scraper; (coll.) barber.
rapadura, *f.* shaving; hair cut; plundering.
rapagón, *m.* beardless young man.
rapamiento, *m.* = RAPADURA.
rapante, *a.* snatching, robbing; shaving; (her.) rampant.
rapapiés, *m.* (fireworks) running squib; chaser.
rapapolvo, *m.* (coll.) sharp reprimand, dressing down.
rapar, *va.* to shave; to crop (the hair); to plunder, snatch, rob; to skin, peel.
[1]**rapaz,** *a.* rapacious, predatory; (ornith.) raptorial.
[2]**rapaz, za,** *n.* young boy (girl).
rapazada, *f.* childish prank or speech.
rapazuelo, la, *n. dim.* little boy (girl), youngster.
rape, *m.* (coll.) hurried shaving or hair cutting.—**al r.,** cropped, clipped, cut close or short.
rapé, *m.* snuff; rappee.
rápidamente, *adv.* rapidly, fast.
rapidez, *f.* rapidity, celerity, swiftness.
rápido, da. I. *a.* rapid, swift. **II.** *m.* rapids; express train.
rapiego, ga, *a.* rapacious (bird).
rapingacho, *m.* (Peru) cheese omelet.
rapiña, *f.* rapine, robbery, plundering.—**de r.,** (of birds) of prey.
rapiñador, ra, *n.* plunderer, robber.
rapiñar, *va.* (coll.) to plunder; to pillage; to steal.
rapista, *m.* scraper; (coll.) barber.
rapo, *m.* round-rooted turnip.
rapónchigo, *m.* (bot.) rampion.
raposa, *f.* fox; cunning person.
raposear, *vn.* to act in a foxy way.
raposera, *f.* fox hole, fox den.
raposería, *f.* cunning of a fox.
raposino, na, *a.* foxy.
raposo, *m.* (male) fox.
raposuno, na, *a.* vulpine, foxy.
rapsoda, *a.* rhapsodic, rapt.
rapsodia, *f.* rhapsody.
rapta, *a.* (of a woman) abducted, kidnapped.
raptar, *va.* to kidnap (a woman); to steal.
rapto, *m.* kidnapping; rapture, ecstasy.
raptor, ra, *n.* thief, robber; kidnapper.
raque, *m.* wrecking; arrack.
raquero, ra. I. *a.* piratical. **II.** *n.* wrecker; "dock rat."
raqueta, *f.* (tennis, badminton, etc.) racket; battledore; battledore and shuttlecock, badminton; tennis.
raquetero, *m.* racket maker or seller.
raquialgia, *f.* (med.) rachialgia, spinal pain.
raquídeo, dea, *a.* rachitic.—**bulbo r.,** (anat.) medulla oblongata.
raquis, *m.* (anat.) rachis, spine; (bot.) stalk.
raquítico, ca, *a.* (med.) rachitic, rickety; feeble, flimsy, niggardly.
raquitis, *f.*; **raquitismo,** *m.* (med.) rachitis, rickets.
raquítomo, *m.* (surg.) rachitome.
raramente, *adv.* rarely, seldom; ridiculously, oddly.
rarefacción, *f.* rarefaction.
rarefacer, *va.* & *vr.* to rarefy.
rareza, *f.* rarity, rareness, uncommonness; fad, queerness; freak; curio, curiosity; oddness.—**por r.,** rarely, seldom.
raridad, *f.* rarity; thinness.
rarificar. I. *va.* (*pret.* RARIFIQUÉ; *subj.* RARIFIQUE) to rarefy, make thin. **II.** *vr.* to become thin or rarefied.
rarificativo, va, *a.* rarefying, thinning.
raro, ra, *a.* rare; scarce; thin, rarefied; choice, precious, excellent; queer, odd.—**r. vez,** seldom.
ras, *m.* level, even, flush.—**r. con r.,** on a level, flush.—**al ras con,** or **de,** even or flush with.
rasa, *f.* tease, in fabrics; table-land, plateau.
rasadura, *f.* levelling with a strickle.
rasamente, *adv.* publicly, openly, clearly.
rasante. I. *a.* levelling, grazing. **II.** *f.* (Ry.) grade, grade line.
rasar, *va.* to strike or level with a strickle; to graze, skim, touch lightly.
rasarse, *vr.* to clear up (as the sky).
rascacielos, *m.* (coll.) skyscraper.
rascacio, *m.* (ichth.) = ESCORPENA, grouper.
rascadera, *f.* scraper; currycomb.
rascador, *m.* scraper, scaler, scratcher; rasp; hatpin, bodkin; huller, sheller.
rascadura, *f.* scratching; scratch; scraping.
rascalino, *m.* (bot.) dodder.
rascamiento, *m.* scraping, scratching.
rascamoño, *m.* woman's hatpin, bodkin.
rascar. I. *va.* (*pret.* RASQUÉ; *subj.* RASQUE) to scratch; rasp, scrape. **II.** *vn.* (Colomb.) to itch.
rascazón, *f.* itching.
rascle, *m.* instrument used in coral fishing.
rascón, na. I. *a.* sour, tart, sharp, acrid. **II.** *m.* (ornith.) rail; marsh hen.
rascuñar, rascuño, = RASGUÑAR, etc.
rasel, *m.* (naut.) entrance and run of a ship.
rasero, *m.* strickle, strike; standard, rule.
rasete, *m.* satinet, sateen.
rasgado, *m.* = RASGÓN.
rasgador, ra, *n.* tearer, ripper.
rasgadura, *f.* rent, ripping.
rasgar, *va.* (*pret.* RASGUÉ; *subj.* RASGUE) to tear, rend, rip; RASGUEAR.
rasgo, *m.* dash, stroke, flourish, scroll; stroke (of wit, kindness, etc.); deed, feat; happy expression or saying; feature (of face); characteristic.—**a grandes rasgos,** broadly, in outline.
rasgón, *m.* rent, rip, tear.
rasgué, rasgue, *v. V.* RASGAR.
rasgueado. I. *pp.* of RASGUEAR. **II.** *a.* full of flourishes. **III.** *m.* making of flourishes.
rasguear. I. *vn.* to flourish, to make scrollwork. **II.** *va.* to play flourishes on (the guitar); to play (the guitar) with strokes of the whole hand.
rasgueo, *m.* forming fine strokes with a pen; scrollwork; flourish.
rasguñar, *va.* to scratch; to sketch, outline.
rasguñito, ñuelo, *m.* slight scratch or sketch.
rasguño, *m.* scratch; nip; sketch, outline.
rasilla, *f.* serge; fine tile for flooring.
raso, sa. I. *a.* clear, unobstructed; plain; flat.—**a campo r.,** or **al r.,** in the open air. **II.** *m.* satin.
raspa, *f.* (bot.) beard of an ear of corn; bunch of grapes; spine, fin ray of fish; hair or thread in the nib of a writing pen; (carp.) wood rasp, scraper, grater; outer rind of certain fruits (nuts, almonds, etc.); (coll., Am.) sermon, lecture, dressing down.
raspadera, *f.* raker.
raspador, *m.* eraser; rasp, grater, scraper.
raspadura, *f.* erasure; rasping, scraping; abrasion; scrapings, shavings; (Cuba) pan sugar.
raspajo, *m.* stalk of a bunch of grapes.
raspamiento, *m.* erasure; rasping, scraping.
raspante, *a.* rasping, rough (wine); abrasive, abrading.
raspar, *va.* to erase; to scrape, rasp, pare off; (of wine) to bite or sting; to steal, carry off.

raspear, *vn.* to scratch (as a bad pen).
raspilla, *f.* (bot.) a boraginaceous plant.
raspón, *m.* (Colomb.) large straw hat; (Chile) severe reprimand; (Mex.) scratch, skinning.
rasqué, rasque, *v. V.* RASCAR.
rasqueta, *f.* (naut.) scraper.
rastacuero, *n.* = RASTRACUEROS.
rastel, *m.* lattice, railing.
rastillador, rastillar, rastillo, = RASTRILLADOR, RASTRILLAR, RASTRILLO.
rastra, *f.* track, trail; sled, sledge; dray; (agr.) harrow, brake; reaping machine; act of dragging along; anything dragging; string of dried fruit, onions, etc.; (naut.) drag, grapnel.—**a la r., a las rastras,** or **a r., dragging;** unwillingly, by force.
rastracueros, *n.* (Am.) person who makes a fortune in the hide business (may be called hide magnate); snob whose income comes from nobody knows where.
rastrallar, *vn.* to crack with a whip.
rastreador, ra. *n.* tracer; scout; (ship) mine detector.
rastrear. I. *va.* to trace, scent; to track down, trail; (agr.) to harrow, rake; (in fishing) to drag; to investigate, follow a clue to; to sell (carcasses) by wholesale. **II.** *vn.* to skim the ground, to fly very low.
rastreo, *m.* dragging in the water.
rastrero, ra. I. *a.* creeping, dragging; trailing; flying low; abject, grovelling; low, base; cringing. **II.** *n.* employee of a slaughterhouse.
rastrillada, *f.* rakeful.
rastrillador, ra, *n.* hackler; flax dresser, hatcheler; raker.
rastrillaje, *m.* raking; hatcheling.
rastrillar, *va.* to hackle, dress (flax), comb, hatchel; to rake.
rastrillo, *m.* hackle, flax comb; (agr.) rake; (fort.) portcullis; (artil.) hammer of a gunlock; ward of a key; ward of a lock.—**r. de pesebre,** rack of a manger.
rastro, *m.* track, scent, trail; trace; (agr.) rake, harrow; slaughterhouse; sign, token; vestige, relic; in Madrid, a market of knickknacks.
rastrojera, *f.* stubble field.
rastrojo, restrojo, *m.* stubble, haulm.
rasura, *f.* shaving.—*pl.* argol.
rasuración, *f.* shaving.
rasurar, *va.* to shave.
rata. I. *f.* rat. **II.** *m.* (coll.) pickpocket.
ratafía, *f.* ratafia, a cordial.
ratania, *f.* (bot.) ratany, rhatany.
rataplán, *m.* rubadub (sound of a drum).
[1]**ratear,** *va.* to lessen in proportion; to apportion.
[2]**ratear,** *va.* & *vn.* to filch.
[3]**ratear,** *vn.* to creep.
ratel, *m.* (zool.) ratel.
rateo, *m.* apportionment.
rateramente, *adv.* meanly, vilely.
[1]**ratería,** *f.* larceny, petty theft.
[2]**ratería,** *f.* (coll.) meanness, stinginess.
[1]**ratero, ra,** *a.* creeping; flying low.
[2]**ratero, ra,** *n.* pickpocket, pilferer.
ratico, *m.* (coll.) little while.
ratificación, *f.* ratification, confirmation.
ratificar, *va.* (*pret.* RATIFIQUÉ; *subj.* RATIFIQUE) to ratify, confirm.
ratificatorio, ria, *a.* ratifying, confirming.
ratigar, *va.* to secure on a cart with a rope.
rátigo, *m.* cartload, truck load.
ratihabición, *f.* (law) ratification.
ratimago, *m.* (coll.) trick, cunning.
ratina, *f.* Petersham, ratteen.
ratito, *m. dim.* little while, short time.
[1]**rato,** *a.* (law) valid (marriage).
[2]**rato,** *m.* short time, while, little while.—**al poco r.,** presently, very soon.—**a ratos,** from time to time, occasionally.—**a ratos perdidos,** in leisure hours, in spare time.—**buen r.,** a great while; a pleasant, good time; a great quantity.—**de r. en r.** = A RATOS.—**mal r.,** an unpleasant time.—**pasar el r.,** to lose time; to pass the time, to while away the time.
ratón, *m.* mouse; (naut.) hidden rock that frets cables.—**r. de campo,** harvest mouse.
ratona, *f.* (zool.) female mouse or rat.
ratonar. I. *va.* to gnaw like mice. **II.** *vr.* to become sick (as cats) from eating rats.
ratonera, *f.* mousetrap; mousehole or breeding place.—**caer en la r.,** to fall into a trap.
ratonero, ra. I. *a.* mousy. **II.** *n.* ratter.
ratonesco, ca, *a.* = RATONERO, *a.*
rauco, ca, *a.* (poet.) hoarse, husky, raucous.
raudal, *m.* torrent, stream; plenty, abundance.
raudo, da, *a.* rapid, swift, impetuous.
rauta, *f.* (coll.) road, way, route.
[1]**raya. I.** *f.* stroke, dash, streak, stripe, line; frontier, boundary; score, mark; crease (in trousers); parting in the hair; (print.) dash, rule; (artil.) rifle or spiral groove; strip of ground cleared of combustible matter.—**r. de la meta,** goal line.—**a r.,** within bounds.—**tener a uno a r.,**to hold one at bay.
[2]**raya,** *m.* (ichth.) ray, skate.
rayadillo, *m.* striped cotton duck.
rayado, da. I. *pp.* of RAYAR. **II.** *a.* streaky. **III.** *m.* ruling; stripes.
rayadura, *f.* ruling.
rayano, na, *a.* neighboring, contiguous, bordering.
rayar. I. *va.* to draw lines on; to rule; to scratch (as a table); to stripe, streak; (artil.) to rifle or groove; to cross out; to underscore. **II.** *vn.* to excel, surpass; to border (on); to begin, appear (as the day, sun, light, etc.).
rayo, *m.* ray, beam; spoke of a wheel; thunderbolt; flash of lightning; sudden havoc, misfortune, or scourge; lively, ready genius; great power or efficacy of action.—**r. de sol,** sunbeam.—**r. textorio,** weaver's shuttle.—**rayos alfa,** (phys.) alpha rays.—**rayos beta,** (phys.) beta rays.—**rayos catódicos, Roentgen** or **X,** (phys.) cathode, Roentgen or X rays.—**rayos cósmicos,** (phys.) cosmic rays.—**rayos gama,** (phys.) gamma rays.—**rayos violetas,** (phys.) violet rays.
¡rayo! *or* **¡rayos!** *interj.* fury!
rayó, *pret.* of RAER.
rayón, *m.* (text.) rayon.
rayoso, sa, *a.* full of lines or stripes.
rayuela, *f. dim.* small line; game of drawing lines.
rayuelo, *m.* (ornith.) a small kind of snipe.
[1]**raza,** *f.* race, lineage; breed.—**de r.,** pure-breed.
[2]**raza,** *f.* crack, fissure; lightly woven stripe in fabrics; cleft in horse's hoof; ray of light.
razado, *a.* having lightly woven stripes.
rázago, *m.* burlap, sackcloth.
razón, *f.* reason; reasonableness; equity, fairness; account, explanation; information; (Am.) message; (math.) ratio.—**r. de estado,** reason of state, raison d'état; regard for public opinion.—**r. de pie de banco,** (coll.) futile, silly reason.—**r. de ser,** raison d'être, reason; explanation; justification, foundation.—**r. social,** (com.) firm, firm name.—**a r. de,** at the rate of.—**con r. o sin ella,** rightly or wrongly.—**dar la r. a,** to agree with.—**dar r. de,** to give an account of; to account for; to give information about.—**en r. a,** or **de,** concerning, as regards.—**entrar en r.,** to be, or become, reasonable, listen to reason.—**meter en r.,** to compel or induce to act reasonably; to convince.—**no tener r.,** to be wrong or mistaken.—**perder la r.,** to become insane.—**ponerse en (la) r.,** to be reasonable.—**por cuya r.,** and so, and for this reason.—**por r. de,** because of.—**tener r.,** to be right.—**tomar r. de,** to register, make a memorandum or record of; to inventory.
razonable, *a.* reasonable; moderate; fair, just.
razonablejo, ja, *a.* (coll.) moderate, fair.
razonado, da. I. *pp.* of RAZONAR. **II.** *a.* reasoned, reasoned out; detailed, itemized.
razonador, ra, *n.* & *a.* reasoner(-ing).

razonamiento, *m.* reasoning.
razonante, *n.* & *a.* reasoner(-ing).
razonar. I. *vn.* to reason, ratiocinate. **II.** *va.* to itemize, vouch, attest.
re, *m.* (mus.) D, re, second note of the scale.
reabrir, *va.* & *vn.* to reopen.
reabsorbedor, ra, *a.* resorptive.
reabsorber, *va.* to reabsorb.
reabsorción, *f.* reabsorption.
reacción, *f.* (chem. mech., pol., personal) reaction.—**r. en cadena,** (phys.) chain reaction.—**r. persistente,** sustained reaction.
reaccionar, *vn.* to react.
reaccionario, ria, *n.* & *a.* reactionary.
reaccionarismo, *m.* (pol.) reactionism.
reacio, cia, *a.* obstinate, stubborn.
reacondicionamiento, *m.* overhaul.
reacondicionar, *va.* (mech.) to recondition, overhaul.
reactancia, *f.* (elec.) reactance.
reactividad, *f.* reactivity.
reactivo, va. I. *a.* reactive. **II.** *m.* (chem.) reactive, reagent.
reactor, *m.* reactor; (elec., phys.) reactor, atomic pile; (aer.) jet plane.—**r. eléctrico,** electric reactor.—**r. nuclear,** (phys.) nuclear reactor.—**r. reproductor,** (phys.) breeder reactor.—**r. termonuclear,** (phys.) thermonuclear reactor.
readaptación, *f.* readjustment.
readaptar, *va.* to readjust.
readmisión, *f.* readmission.
reafirmación, *f.* reaffirmation.
reafirmar, *va.* to reaffirm, reassert.
reagravación, *f.* reaggravation.
reagravar, *va.* to aggravate anew.
reagudo, da, *a.* very acute.
[1]**real,** *a.* real, actual.
[2]**real. I.** *a.* royal, kingly, kinglike; grand, magnificent, splendid; noble; handsome. **II.** *m.* camp, encampment; fair grounds; real, a silver coin.—**r. de agua,** water running through a pipe the size of a real.—**r. de minas,** (Mex.) town having silver mines in its vicinity.—**r. de vellón,** a small coin (5 cents).—**r. hacienda,** exchequer.—**r. sitio,** king's country residence.—**alzar,** or **levantar, los reales,** to break camp; to break up housekeeping; to quit.—**sentar (los) reales,** to encamp; to settle, establish oneself.
realce, *m.* raised work, embossment; excellence; lustre, splendor; (art) high light.
realdad, *f.* royal power, sovereignty.
realegrarse, *vr.* to be very joyful.
realejo, *m. dim.* hand organ.
realengo, ga. I. *a.* royal, kingly; unappropriated (land). **II.** *m.* royal patrimony.
realera, *f.* = MAESTRIL, queen cell (of beehive).
realete, *m.* = DIECIOCHENO, a kind of cloth.
realeza, *f.* royalty, regal dignity.
realicé, realice, *v. V.* REALIZAR.
realidad, *f.* reality, fact; truth, sincerity.—**en r.,** or **en r. de verdad,** truly; really; in fact.
realillo, realito, *m. dim.* small REAL (coin).
realimentación, *f.* (elec.) feedback.
realineación, *f.* realignment.
realinear, *va.* to realign.
[1]**realismo,** *m.* royalism.
[2]**realismo,** *m.* (art) realism.
[1]**realista,** *n.* (pol.) royalist.
[2]**realista,** *n.* (art) realist.
realizable, *a.* realizable; (com.) salable.
realización, *f.* realization, fulfilment; (com.) sale.
realizar, *va.* (*pret.* REALICÉ; *subj.* REALICE) to realize, fulfil, carry out, perform; (com.) to sell out, convert into money.
realmente, *adv.* really, in reality, actually.
realzar, *va.* (*pret.* REALCÉ; *subj.* REALCE) to raise, elevate; to emboss; to brighten, heighten the colors of; to make prominent; to heighten, enhance, add merit or excellence to.
reanimar, *va.* to cheer, comfort, encourage; to revive, reanimate.
reanudación, *f.* renewal, resumption.
reanudar, *va.* to renew, resume.
reaparecer, *vn.* (*ind.* REAPAREZCO; *subj.* REAPAREZCA) to reappear.
reaparición, *f.* reappearance.
reapertura, *f.* reopening.
reapretar, *va.* (*ind.* REAPRIETO; *subj.* REAPRIETE) to press again, to squeeze.
rearar, *va.* to plow again.
rearmar, *va.* (mil.) to rearm.
rearme, *m.* rearmament.
reasegurar, *va.* (com.) to reinsure.
reaseguro, *m.* (com.) reinsurance.
reasumir, *va.* to retake, resume.
reasunción, *f.* resumption, resuming.
reata, *f.* riata; rope to tie horses and keep them in single file; drove of horses or mules thus tied; (Mex.) any rope.—*pl.* (naut.) woolding.—**de r.,** in single file; submissively.
reatadura, *f.* act of retying; tying animals in single file.
reatar, *va.* to retie; to tie together; to tie tightly; (naut.) to woold.
reato, *m.* (eccl.) obligation of atonement.
reaventar, *va.* (*ind.* REAVIENTO; *subj.* REAVIENTE) to winnow a second time.
reavivamiento, *m.* revival.
reavivar, *va.* to revive, reanimate, revivify; to rekindle.
rebaba, *f.* (mech.) fash, mold mark, fin, burr, rough seam.
rebaja, *f.* deduction, diminution; (com.) rebate, reduction, discount; abatement; allowance.
rebajamiento, *m.* curtailment; abatement; deduction; lowering; abasement.
rebajar. I. *va.* to abate, lessen, diminish; to reduce, lower, cut down; to underbid; (carp.) to shave off, cut down; (art) to weaken (a high light). **II.** *vr.* to be dismissed, or mustered out; to humble oneself; to lower oneself.
rebajo, *m.* (carp.) rabbet; groove.
rebalaje, *m.* current or flow of water.
rebalsa, *f.* pool, puddle, pond; stagnation of humors in a part of the body.
rebalsar. I. *va.* to dam. **II.** *vr.* to form a pool; to accumulate; to be stopped or checked.
rebanada, *f.* slice.—**rebanadilla,** *f.* small slice.
rebanador, *m.* slicer, slicing machine.
rebanar, *va.* to slice; to cut; to plane.
rebanco, *m.* (arch.) second bench or seat.
rebañadera, *f.* grapnel, drag hook.
rebañadura, *f.* = ARREBAÑADURA, gleaning.
rebañar, *va.* = ARREBAÑAR, to glean, gather.
rebañego, ga, *a.* gregarious.
rebaño, *m.* flock, fold, drove, herd, congregation.—**rebañuelo,** *m. dim.* small flock.
rebasadero, *m.* (naut.) pass.
rebasar, *va.* (naut.) to sail past; to exceed, go beyond; to overflow.
rebate, *m.* dispute, contention.
rebatible, *a.* refutable, disputable.
rebatido, *m.* (sew.) overhand seam, round seam.
rebatimiento, *m.* refutation; (geom.) revolving (a figure on a plane).
rebatiña, *f.*—**andar a la r.,** to grab and snatch things from one another, to scramble.
rebatir, *va.* to beat or drive back, repel; to refute; to deduct; to beat repeatedly; (geom.) to revolve (a figure on a plane).
rebato, *m.* alarm, alarm bell, call to arms; excitement, commotion; (mil.) sudden attack, surprise, drive.
rebautizar, *va.* to rebaptize.
rebeco, *m.* (zool.) = GAMUZA, chamois.
rebelarse, *vr.* to revolt, rebel; to resist.
rebelde. I. *a.* rebellious; stubborn, unmanageable. **II.** *n.* rebel; (law) defaulter.
rebeldía, *f.* rebelliousness, contumacy, disobedience; stubbornness; (law) default, nonappearance.—**en r.,** by default.
rebelión, *f.* rebellion, revolt, insurrection.
rebelón, na, *a.* (of a horse) balky, stubborn.
rebellín, *m.* (fort.) ravelin.

rebencazo, *m.* blow with a whip.
rebenque, *m.* whip; (naut.) ratline; cross rope.
rebién, *adv.* (coll.) very well.
rebina, *f.* (agr.) third plowing.
rebisabuela, *f.* great-great-grandmother.
rebisabuelo, *m.* great-great-grandfather.
rebisnieta, *f.* great-great-granddaughter.
rebisnieto, *m.* great-great-grandson.
reblandecer, *va.* & *vr.* (*ind.* REBLANDEZCO; *subj.* REBLANDEZCA) to soften.—**reblandecimiento,** *m.* softening.
rebocé, reboce, *v. V.* REBOZAR.
rebocillo, rebociño, *m.* shawl.
rebolisco, *m.* (Cuba) groundless commotion.
rebollar, rebolledo, *m.* thicket of oak saplings.
rebollidura, *f.* (armor) honeycomb, flaw in a gun.
rebollo, *m.* (bot.) turkey oak; trunk of a tree.
rebolludo, da, *a.* done over and double; rough (diamond).
rebombar, *vn.* to make a loud report.
reboñar, *vn.* to stop turning.
reborde, *m.* flange, border.
rebosadero, *m.* place of overflow.
rebosadura, *f.*, **rebosamiento,** *m.* overflow.
rebosar, *vn.* to run over, overflow; to unbosom oneself; (**de**) to abound (in); to teem (with).
rebotación, *f.* rebounding.
rebotadera, *f.* nap raiser.
rebotador, ra, *n.* rebounder; clincher.
rebotadura, *f.* rebounding.
rebotar. I. *vn.* to rebound. **II.** *va.* to cause to rebound; to clinch; to raise the nap of (cloth); to repel; to vex, exasperate. **III.** *vr.* to change one's opinion, to retract; to change color.
rebote, *m.* rebound, rebounding.—**de r.,** indirectly.
rebotica, *f.* back room in an apothecary's shop.
rebotín, *m.* second growth of mulberry leaves.
rebozar. I. *va.* (*pret.* REBOCÉ; *subj.* REBOCE) to muffle up; (cooking) to dip in, or cover with, batter. **II.** *vr.* to muffle oneself up.
rebozo, *m.* muffling oneself up; muffler; woman's shawl; pretext.—**de r.,** secretly, hiddenly.—**sin r.,** frankly, openly.
rebramar, *vn.* to low and bellow repeatedly.
rebramo, *m.* noise with which deer answer each other.
rebudiar, *vn.* to sniff and grunt (as a wild boar).
rebufar, *vn.* to blow or snort repeatedly.
rebufo, *m.* (artil.) concussion, recoil.
rebujado, da, *a.* tangled, entangled, confused.
rebujal, *m.* number of cattle in a flock over even fifties; small piece of arable land.
rebujar, *va.* = ARREBUJAR, to jumble together.
rebujiña, *f.* (coll.) wrangle, mêlée, scuffle.
rebujo, *m.* woman's thick veil or muffler; clumsy bundle; portion of tithe paid in money.
rebullicio, *m.* great clamor or tumult.
rebullir, *vn.* & *vr.* to stir, begin to move.
reburujar, *va.* (coll.) to wrap up in bundles.
reburujón, *n.* clumsy bundle.
rebusca, *f.* searching; gleaning; refuse, remains.
rebuscado, da, *a.* affected, fustian, forced, unnatural.
rebuscador, ra, *n.* gleaner; searcher.
rebuscamiento, *m.* diligent search.
rebuscar, *va.* (*pret.* REBUSQUÉ; *subj.* REBUSQUE) to search carefully; to glean (grapes).
rebusco, *m.* search; gleaning.
rebuznador, ra, *a.* braying.
rebuznar, *vn.* to bray.—**rebuzno,** *m.* braying (of a donkey).
recabar, *va.* to obtain by entreaty.
recadero, ra, *n.* messenger, errand boy (girl).
recado, *m.* message, errand; present, gift; compliments, regards; daily provision or marketing; voucher; outfit, equipment; precaution, security; (Am.) saddle and trappings.—**r. de escribir,** writing materials.
recaer, *vn.* (*ind. pres.* RECAIGO, *pret.* él RECAYÓ; *subj.* RECAIGA) to fall back, relapse; to fall or devolve; to behoove.
recaída, *f.* relapse; second offense.
recaigo, recaiga, *v. V.* RECAER.
recalada, *f.* (naut.) landfall.
recalar. I. *va.* to soak, drench, saturate. **II.** *vn.* (naut.) to make, sight, or reach land.
recalcada, *f.* (naut.) heeling, list.
recalcadamente, *adv.* closely, contiguously; vehemently, emphatically.
recalcadura, *f.* cramming, pressing.
recalcar. I. *va.* (*pret.* RECALQUÉ; *subj.* RECALQUE) to cram, pack, press, push, squeeze in; to emphasize. **II.** *vn.* (naut.) to heel, list. **III.** *vr.* to harp on a subject; to seat oneself, sit at ease.
recalcitrante, *a.* recalcitrant, obstinate.
recalcitrar, *vn.* to resist; to recede, go back.
recalentador, *m.* (steam eng.) superheater.
recalentamiento, *m.* reheating; overheating; (steam eng.) superheating.
recalentar. I. *va.* (*ind.* RECALIENTO; *subj.* RECALIENTE) to reheat; to overheat; to warm over; to excite (as sexual appetite); (steam eng.) to superheat. **II.** *vr.* to become overheated (as fruit), or superheated (as steam).
recalescencia, *f.* (metal.) recalescence.
recalmón, *m.* lull of the wind.
recalqué, recalque, *v. V.* RECALCAR.
recalvastro, tra, *a.* bald-headed.
recalzar, *va.* (*pret.* RECALCÉ; *subj.* RECALCE) (agr.) to hill; (arch.) to strengthen, reinforce; (art) to color.
recalzo, *m.* (arch.) strengthening a foundation; outside rim of wheel (on carriage, etc.).
recalzón, *m.* outer rim of a wheel.
recamado, *m.* embroidery of raised work.
recamador, ra, *n.* embroiderer.
recamar, *va.* to embroider with raised work.
recámara, *f.* dressing room; boudoir; (Mex.) bedroom; household furniture; (artil.) breech of a gun; cavity or chamber for an explosive charge; (coll.) caution, reserve.
recambiar, *va.* to reëxchange, rechange; (com.) to redraw; to add.
recambio, *m.* (com.) reëxchange.
recamo, *m.* raised embroidery; (sewing) frog.
recancanilla, *f.* hippety-hop; (coll.) emphasis; equivocation, ambiguous language.
recantación, *f.* recantation, retraction.
recantón, *m.* corner stone.
recapacitar, *vn.* to refresh one's memory; to think carefully.
recapitulación, *f.* recapitulation, summary; (fin.) consolidated statement.
recapitular, *va.* to recapitulate, sum up.
recarga, *f.* (artil.) overcharge.
recargar. I. *va.* (*pret.* RECARGUÉ; *subj.* RECARGUE) to reload; to surcharge, overload; to overcharge; to cram; to recharge; to raise, increase. **II.** *vr.* (med.) to have an increase in temperature; (**de**) to have in abundance, have an abundance (of).
recargo, *m.* overload; overcharge; additional tax, charge, etc.; extra charge; new charge or accusation; (law) increase of sentence; (med.) increase of fever.
recata, *f.* tasting again.
recatado, da. I. *pp.* of RECATAR. **II.** *a.* prudent, circumspect; shy, coy; modest.
[1]**recatar. I.** *va.* to secrete, conceal. **II.** *vr.* to act modestly; to be cautious.
[2]**recatar,** *va.* to taste again.
recatear, *vn.* = REGATEAR, to haggle; to dodge.
recatería, *f.* = REGATONERÍA, retail sale.
recato, *m.* prudence, caution; modesty; bashfulness, coyness.
[1]**recatón, na,** *n.* = [1]REGATÓN, hawker; haggler.
[2]**recatón,** *m.* = [2]REGATÓN, tip, ferrule.
recatonazo, *m.* blow with the tip of a lance.
recatonear, *va.* = REGATONEAR, to sell at retail.
recatonería, *f.* = REGATONERÍA, retail sale.
recauchotaje, *f.* recapping (of tires).
recauchotar, *va.* to recap (tires).
recaudación, *f.* collecting, collection; collector's office.
recaudador, ra, *n.* taxgatherer; collector.

recaudamiento, *m.* collection; office or district of a collector.
recaudar, *va.* to gather; to collect (rents or taxes); to put or hold in custody.
recaudo, *m.* collection of rents or taxes; precaution, care; (law) surety, bail, bond, security.—**a buen r.,** well guarded, under custody, safe.
recavar, *va.* to dig a second time.
recayó, *pret.* of RECAER.
recazo, *m.* guard of a sword; back of a knife.
recebar, *va.* to spread gravel on.
recebo, *m.* sand or gravel for a roadway.
recelador, ra, *a.* shy (as a horse).
recelamiento, *m.* = RECELO.
recelar. I. *va.* to fear, distrust, suspect; to excite (a mare) sexually. **II.** *vr.* (**de**) to fear, be afraid or suspicious (of), to beware (of).
recelo, *m.* misgiving, fear, suspicion.
receloso, sa, *a.* distrustful, suspicious.
recentadura, *f.* leaven for raising bread.
recental, *a.* suckling (lamb or calf).
recentar. I. *va.* (*ind.* RECIENTO; *subj.* RECIENTE) to put leaven into (dough). **II.** *vr.* to renew.
receñir, *va.* (*ind. pres.* RECIÑO, *pret.* RECIÑIÓ; *subj.* RECIÑA) to regird.
recepción, *f.* reception, receiving, acceptation, admission; (law) cross-examination.
recepta, *f.* record of fines.
receptáculo, *m.* receptacle; (anat.) receptaculum; shelter, refuge; (bot.) receptacle.
receptador, *m.* (law) receiver of stolen goods; abettor.
receptar. I. *va.* (law) to abet; to hide, shelter; to receive. **II.** *vr.* to take refuge.
receptividad, *f.* receptivity.
receptivo, va, *a.* receptive.
recepto, *m.* shelter, place of refuge.
receptor, ra. I. *n.* receiver; recipient; abettor. **II.** *a.* receiving. **III.** *m.* (elec. & law) receiver.
receptoría, *f.* receiver's or treasurer's office; (law) receivership.
recercador, ra I. *a.* girding. **II.** *m.* (jewel.) chaser.
recercar, *va.* to fence; to fence again.
recésit, *m.* vacation, recess. Also RECLE.
recesivo, va, *a.* recessive.
receso, *m.* withdrawal, separation; (astr.) deviation; (Mex.) recess.
receta, *f.* prescription; recipe; list of goods ordered; (com.) amount brought forward.
recetador, ra, *n.* prescriber of medicines.
recetar, *va.* to prescribe (medicines).
recetario, *m.* physician's instructions for treatment; book in hospitals in which instructions are entered; apothecary's file; pharmacopœia.
recetor, *m.* receiver, treasurer.
recetoría, *f.* treasury; subtreasury.
recial, *m.* rapids (in rivers).
reciamente, *adv.* strongly, stoutly.
reciario, *m.* retiarius (gladiator).
recibí, *m.* (from *recibí*, I received, extended to mean: I received payment) (com.) receipt.
recibidero, ra, *a.* receivable.
recibidor, ra, *n.* receiver; recipient; (com.) receiving teller.
recibimiento, *m.* reception; hospitality, greeting, welcome; vestibule; hall; reception room.
recibir. I. *va.* to receive; to let in; to take, accept; to take in, admit; to experience (an injury); to face (an attack). **II.** *vr.* (**de**) to graduate (as); to be admitted to practice (as).
recibo, *m.* reception; (com.) receipt.—**acusar r.,** (com.) to acknowledge receipt.—**de r.,** fit for service, acceptable; reception (as *a.*).—**estar de r.,** to be at home to callers.
recidiva, *f.* (med.) relapse.
recidivar, *vn.* (med.) to relapse, recur.
reciedumbre, *f.* strength, vigor.
recién, *adv.* (contr. of RECIENTE) (before *pp.*) = RECIENTEMENTE.—**r. casados,** newlyweds.—**r. llegado,** newcomer.—**r. nacido, da,** newborn.
reciente, *a.* recent; new; modern; fresh.
recientemente, *adv.* recently, lately, newly.
reciento, reciente, *v. V.* RECENTAR.
recinchar, *va.* to bind with a girdle.
recinto, *m.* inclosure; place (building, hall, etc.); ambit; precinct.
recio, cia. I. *a.* strong, robust, vigorous; loud; coarse, thick, clumsy; rude, uncouth; arduous; hard to bear; severe, rigorous (weather); swift, impetuous. **II.** *adv.* strongly, stoutly; rapidly; vehemently, vigorously; loud.—**de r.,** strongly, violently.
récipe, *m.* (med.) prescription; (coll.) displeasure, disgust.
recipiendario, ria, *n.* member received (into an association, academy, etc.).
recipiente. I. *a.* receiving. **II.** *m.* receptacle; container; recipient; bell of an air pump.
recíproca, *f.* (math., logic) converse (proposition).
reciprocación, *f.* reciprocation, mutuality.
reciprocar. I. *va.* (*pret.* RECIPROQUÉ; *subj.* RECIPROQUE) (of things) to put in mutual correspondence, to match. **II.** *vr.* to correspond, harmonize, fit together, match.
reciprocidad, *f.* reciprocity.
recíproco, ca, *a.* reciprocal, mutual.
reciproqué, reciproque, *v. V.* RECIPROCAR.
recircular, *va.* (phys.) to recycle.
recisión, *f.* (law) rescission, abrogation.
recitación, *f.* recitation, recital.
recitado, *m.* (mus.) recitative.
recitador, ra, *n.* reciter.
recital, *m.* (mus.) recital.
recitar, *va.* to recite; to rehearse.
recitativo, va, *a.* recitative.
reciura, *f.* strength, force; rigor (of weather).
recizalla, *f.* second filings.
reclamación, *f.* reclamation; objection, remonstrance; (com.) complaint, claim.
reclamante, *n.* & *a.* complainer(-ing), claimer (ing).
[1]**reclamar. I.** *va.* to claim, demand; to decoy (birds); (law) to reclaim.—**r. en juicio,** (law) to sue. **II.** *vn.* to contradict, to oppose; to complain; to put in a claim.
[2]**reclamar,** *va.* (naut.) to hoist or lower.
reclame, *m.* (naut.) sheave hole in a topmast head.
reclamo, *m.* decoy bird; decoy horn or contrivance; lure (for birds); call; inducement, enticement; claim; complaint; advertisement inserted in reading matter of a publication; (law) reclamation; (print.) catchword.
recle, *m.* vacation, rest from choir duties.
reclinación, *f.* reclination, reclining.
reclinado, da. I. *pp.* of RECLINAR. **II.** *a.* recumbent.
reclinar, *va.* & *vr.* to recline, lean back.—**reclinarse en,** or **sobre,** to lean on or upon.
reclinatorio, *m.* praying desk, priedieu; couch, lounge.
recluir, *va.* (*pp.* RECLUÍDO, RECLUSO; *ind. pres.* RECLUYO, *pret.* él RECLUYÓ; *subj.* RECLUYA) to shut up, to seclude.
reclusión, *f.* seclusion; place of retirement; arrest; jail, prison.—**r. aislada,** solitary confinement.
recluso, sa. I. *pp. irreg.* of RECLUIR. **II.** *a.* & *n.* recluse.
reclusorio, *m.* place of retirement.
recluta. I. *f.* (mil.) recruiting; (Arg.) roundup of cattle. **II.** *m.* inductee, conscript, recruit.
reclutador, *m.* recruiting officer.
reclutamiento, *m.* (mil.) recruiting.
reclutar, *va.* (mil.) to recruit; (Arg.) to round up (cattle).
recluyo, recluyó, recluya, *v. V.* RECLUIR.
recobrable, *a.* recoverable.
recobrante, *a.* recovering.
recobrar, *va.* & *vr.* to recover, recuperate, regain.—**recobro,** *m.* recovery, recuperation.

recocer. I. *va.* (*ind.* RECUEZO; *subj.* RECUEZA) to boil again; to boil too much; to anneal; to reheat. **II.** *vr.* to burn with rage.
recocido, da. I. *pp.* of RECOCER. **II.** *a.* overcooked; annealed; skilful, clever. **III.** *n.* annealing; reheating; overcooking.
recocina, *f.* back kitchen, pantry.
recocho, cha, *a.* overcooked, overdone.
recodadero, *m.* elbow chair.
recodar, *vn.* & *vr.* to lean with the elbow upon anything; to wind, turn (as a road).
recodo, *m.* turn, winding, bend, angle.
recogedero, *m.* place where things are gathered; instrument for gathering things.
recogedor, ra, *n.* gatherer, gleaner; shelterer.
recogegotas, *m.* drip pan.
recoger. I. *va.* (*ind.* RECOJO; *subj.* RECOJA) to retake, take back; to gather, pick; to accumulate, hoard; to pick up, take up; to shrink, shorten; to contract; to tuck, pucker; to take in, collect; to take in, shelter; to lock up; to suspend, withdraw, retire; to glean, cull. **II.** *vr.* to take shelter; to withdraw; reform; retrench; to go home, to retire, withdraw from the world, retire into oneself.
recogida, *f.* withdrawal, retirement; harvesting; inmate of house of correction; (com.) retiral.
recogido, da. I. *pp.* of RECOGER. **II.** *a.* secluded; contracted. **III.** *m.* (Am.) (sew.) tuck, fold.
recogimiento, *m.* concentration, abstraction; house of correction for women.
recojo, recoja, *v.* *V.* RECOGER.
recolar, *va.* (*ind.* RECUELO; *subj.* RECUELE) to strain a second time.
recolección, *f.* compilation; summary, abridgment; crop, gathering, harvest; collection of money or taxes; retirement, abstraction.
recolectar, *va.* to gather, collect, hoard.
recolector, *m.* = RECAUDADOR, tax collector.
recoleto, ta, *a.* & *n.* (eccl.) Recollect.
recomendable, *a.* commendable, laudable.
recomendación, *f.* recommendation; request; commendation, praise; merit, worth.—**r. del alma,** prayers for the dying.
recomendante, *n.* one who recommends.
recomendar, *va.* (*ind.* RECOMIENDO; *subj.* RECOMIENDE) to recommend; to commend; to entrust; to ask, request.
recomendatorio, ria, *a.* recommendatory.
recomiendo, recomiende, *v.* *V.* RECOMENDAR.
recompensa, *f.* compensation; recompense.—**en r.,** in return.
recompensable, *a.* deserving reward.
recompensación, *f.* compensation, reward, recompense.
recompensar, *va.* to compensate; to recompense, reward.
recomponer, *va.* (*pp.* RECOMPUESTO; *ind. pres.* RECOMPONGO, *pret.* RECOMPUSE, *fut.* RECOMPONDRÉ; *subj.* RECOMPONGA) to mend, repair.
recomposición, *f.* (chem.) recomposition.
recompuesto, ta, *pp. irreg.* of RECOMPONER.
recompuse, *pret.* of RECOMPONER.
reconcentración, *f.*; **reconcentramiento,** *m.* concentration.
reconcentrar. I. *va.* to concentrate; to dissemble. **II.** *vr.* to concentrate (one's mind).
reconciliación, *f.* reconciliation.
reconciliador, ra, *n.* & *a.* reconciler(-ing).
reconciliar. I. *va.* to reconcile; (eccl.) to hear a short additional confession from; to consecrate anew. **II.** *vr.* to become reconciled, to make up; (eccl.) to make a short additional confession; to confess offenses, to renew friendship.
reconcomerse, *vr.* to scratch one's back.
reconcomio, *m.* (coll.) scratching one's back; suspicion, fear, misgiving; craving, eager desire.
reconditez, *f.* (coll.) reconditeness.
recóndito, ta, *a.* recondite.
reconducción, *f.* (law) renewal of a lease.
reconducir, *va.* (*ind. pres.* RECONDUZCO, *pret.* RECONDUJE; *subj.* RECONDUZCA) (law) to renew (a lease or contract).
reconocedor, ra, *n.* examiner; inspector.
reconocer. I. *va.* (*ind.* RECONOZCO; *subj.* RECONOZCA) to inspect, examine closely; to recognise; to own, admit; (**por**) to acknowledge (as); to acknowledge, be grateful for; (mil.) to reconnoitre, to scout; (pol.) to recognise (a government, etc.); (com.) to acknowledge. **II.** *vr.* to repent; to confess one's guilt; to judge justly of one's own self.
reconocidamente, *adv.* gratefully; confessedly; avowedly.
reconocido, da, *pp.* & *a.* acknowledged, confessed; grateful, obliged; accepted.
reconociente, *a.* recognising.
reconocimiento, *m.* recognition; acknowledgment; gratitude; confession, admission; recognizance; subjection, submission; examination, inquiry, inspection, survey; (mil.) reconnoitering; (surv.) reconnoissance.
reconozco, reconozca, *v.* *V.* RECONOCER.
reconquista, *f.* reconquest.
reconquistar, *va.* to reconquer.
reconstitución, *f.* reconstitution.
reconstituir, *va.* & *vr.* to reconstitute.
reconstituyente, *a.* reconstituent.
reconstrucción, *f.* reconstruction.
reconstruir, *va.* (*ind. pres.* RECONSTRUYO, *pret.* él RECONSTRUYÓ; *subj.* RECONSTRUYA) to rebuild, reconstruct.
recontamiento, *m.* telling, narration.
recontar, *va.* (*ind.* RECUENTO; *subj.* RECUENTE) to recount; to relate.
recontento, ta. I. *a.* greatly pleased. **II.** *m.* contentment, deep satisfaction.
reconvalecer, *vn.* (*ind.* RECONVALEZCO; *subj.* RECONVALEZCA) to convalesce anew.
reconvención, *f.* charge, accusation; reproach.
reconvenir, *va.* (*ger.* RECONVINIENDO; *ind. pres.* YO RECONVENGO, él RECONVIENE, *pret.* RECONVINE, *fut.* RECONVENDRÉ; *subj.* RECONVENGA) to accuse, reproach; to reprimand; (law) to countercharge.
recopilación, *f.* summary, abridgment; compilation, collection; (law) digest.
recopilador, ra, *n.* compiler; abridger.
recopilar, *va.* to compile, abridge.
recoquín, *m.* chubby little fellow.
record, *m.* (Angl.) (sports) record.
recordable, *a.* memorable; that can be remembered.
recordación, *f.* remembrance; recollection.
recordador, ra, *n.* reminder.
recordar. I. *va.* (*ind.* RECUERDO; *subj.* RECUERDE) to remember, to remind. **II.** *vn.* (fig.) to wake up, awaken. **III.** *vr.* to remember.
recordativo, va. I. *a.* reminding, remindful, reminiscent. **II.** *m.* reminder.
recordatorio, *m.* reminder; remembrancer.
recorrer. I. *va.* to go over; (mech.) to pass over, travel; to read over, peruse; to travel in or over; to overhaul, refit, repair; (print.) to run over, readjust. **II.** *vn.* to resort, have recourse to; to travel.
recorrido, *m.* run, sweep; space or distance traveled or passed over, course; (auto) mileage.
recortado, da. I. *pp.* of RECORTAR. **II.** *a.* (bot.) notched, incised. **III.** *m.* figure cut out of paper.
recortadura, *f.* clipping.—*pl.* cuttings.
recortar, *va.* to cut away, trim, clip, pare off; to cut out; to cut to size; to outline (a figure).
recorte, *m.* cutting; clipping (from newspaper, etc.); outline, profile.—*pl.* trimmings, parings.
recorvar, *va.* = ENCORVAR, to bend, curve.
recorvo, va, *a.* = CORVO, bent, crooked; stingy.
recoser, *va.* to sew again; to mend.
recosido, *m.* mending, darning.
recostadero, *m.* reclining or resting place.
recostado, da, *a.* recumbent.
recostar. I. *va.* (*ind.* RECUESTO; *subj.* RECUESTE) to lean, recline. **II.** *vr.* to go to rest; to repose; to lean back (against), to recline.
recova, *f.* dealing in poultry, eggs, etc.; poultry market; market place; shed; pack of hounds.

recoveco, *m.* turning, winding; simulation, artifice.
recovero, ra, *n.* poultry dealer.
recre, *m.* vacation of choristers.
recreación, *f.* recreation.
recrear. I. *va.* to amuse, delight, gladden. **II.** *vr.* to amuse oneself; to be pleased, have pleasure or recreation, to divert oneself.
recreativo, va, *a.* diverting, amusing, recreation (as *a.*).
recrecer. I. *va.* (*ind.* RECREZCO; *subj.* RECREZCA) to augment, increase. **II.** *vn.* to occur, to happen. **III.** *vr.* to grow big; to recover one's spirits.
recrecimiento, *m.* growth, increase.
recreído, da, *a.* intractable (hawk).
recrementicio, cia, *a.* recremental.
recremento, *m.* (med.) recrement.
recreo, *m.* recreation; place of amusement.
recrezco, recrezca, *v. V.* RECRECER.
recría, *f.* repasturing of colts.
recriar, *va.* to re-create, regenerate; to reanimate, give new strength to; to improve (breeds) with new pastures.
recriminación, *f.* recrimination.
recriminador, ra, *n.* & *a.* recriminator(-ing).
recriminar, *va.* to recriminate.
recrudecer, *vn.* & *vr.* (*ind.* RECRUDEZCO; *subj.* RECRUDEZCA) to recrudesce, recur, increase.
recrudecimiento, *m.* = RECRUDESCENCIA.
recrudescencia, *f.* recrudescence.
recrudescente, *a.* recrudescent.
recrujir, *vn.* to squeak.
rectal, *a.* (anat.) rectal.
rectangular, *a.* rectangular.
rectángulo, la. I. *a.* rectangular; **right-angled** (triangle, etc.). **II.** *m.* rectangle.
rectificable, *a.* rectifiable.
rectificación, *f.* rectification.
rectificador, ra, *n.* & *a.* rectifier(-fying).
rectificar, *va.* (*pret.* RECTIFIQUÉ; *subj.* RECTIFIQUE) to rectify, make right; to correct, amend; (math. and chem.) to rectify.
rectificativo, va, *a.* rectifying.
rectilíneo, nea, *a.* rectilinear.
rectitud, *f.* straightness; righteousness, rectitude; accuracy, exactitude.
recto, ta. I. *a.* straight; erect; righteous, just, fair; literal; (geom.) right (angle, section, cylinder, etc.). **II.** *m.* (geom.) right angle; (anat.) rectum.
rector, ra, *n.* principal; rector, curate; director (of a college, etc.).
rectorado, *m.* rectorship; directorship.
rectoral, *a.* rectorial.
rectorar, *vn.* to attain the office of rector.
rectoría, *f.* rectory, curacy; rectorship; rector's or director's office.
rectriz, *a.* (zool.) rectrix (feather).
recua, *f.* drove of beasts of burden; multitude, pack of things.
recuadrar, *va.* (art) to divide into squares.
recuadro, *m.* (arch.) square compartment; panel (of a bridge).
recuaje, *m.* toll for the passage of mules.
recuarta, *f.* string of a guitar.
recubrir, *va.* to re-cover, cover again.
recudimento, recudimiento, *m.* authority for collecting rents.
recudir. I. *va.* to pay money to as part of wages or other dues. **II.** *vn.* to return, revert.
[1]**recuelo,** *m.* strong lye for bucking clothes.
[2]**recuelo, recuele,** *v. V.* RECOLAR.
[1]**recuento,** *m.* recount; enumeration; inventory.
[2]**recuento, recuente,** *v. V.* RECONTAR.
recuentro, *m.* = REENCUENTRO, collision.
[1]**recuerdo,** *m.* recollection; memory; remembrance; keepsake, memento; memorandum.—*pl.* compliments, regards.
[2]**recuerdo, recuerde,** *v. V.* RECORDAR.
recuero, *m.* muleteer, driver of a drove.
recuesta, *f.* request; intimation.
recuestar, *va.* to request, ask, demand.
[1]**recuesto,** *m.* declivity, slope.
[2]**recuesto, recueste,** *v. V.* RECOSTAR.
recuezo, recueza, *v. V.* RECOCER.
reculada, *f.* recoil, recoiling; (naut.) falling astern.
recular, *vn.* to fall back, recoil, back up; (naut.) to fall astern; (coll.) to yield, give up, turn back.
reculo, la, *a.* tailless (poultry).
reculones.—a r., (coll.) going backward.
recuñar, *va.* (min.) to wedge, dig with wedge.
recuperable, *a.* recoverable.
recuperación, *f.* recovery, recuperation.
recuperador, ra, *n.* & *a.* recuperator(-ing).
recuperar, *va.* & *vr.* to recover, regain, recuperate, retrieve.
recuperativo, va, *a.* recuperative.
recura, *f.* comb saw.
recurar, *va.* to tooth (a comb).
recurrente, *a.* recurrent.
recurrir, *vn.* to apply, resort; to revert.
recurso, *m.* recourse; resource, resort; return, reversion; memorial, petition; (law) appeal.—*pl.* resources, means.—**sin r.,** definitively, without appeal; without help, unavoidably, irremediably.
recusable, *a.* refusable, exceptionable.
recusación, *f.* (law) challenge; recusation.
recusante. I. *a.* recusant, dissenting, disobedient. **II.** *n.* recusant.
recusar, *va.* to decline; (law) to recuse, to challenge.
rechacé, rechace, *v. V.* RECHAZAR.
rechazador, ra, *n.* repeller; opponent; buffer.
rechazamiento, *m.* repulsion; rejection.
rechazar, *va.* (*pret.* RECHACÉ; *subj.* RECHACE) to repel, repulse, drive back; to contradict; to reject, turn down.
rechazo, *m.* rebound; rebuff; recoil; rejection.
rechifla, *f.* hissing (in derision); hooting; mockery, ridicule.
rechiflar, *va.* to hiss; to mock, ridicule.
rechinador, ra, *a.* squeaking, grating.
rechinamiento, *m.* squeaking; gnashing of teeth.
rechinar, *vn.* to creak, squeak, grate; to gnash the teeth; to do a thing with reluctance.
rechinido, rechino, *m.* = RECHINAMIENTO.
rechoncho, cha, *a.* (coll.) chubby.
rechupete.—de r. (coll.) splendid, fine, "dandy."
red, *f.* net, seine; network, netting; bag net; grate, railing; snare, trap; wile, fraud; system (of Ry., tel., etc.).—**r. barredera,** dragnet.—**r. de araña,** cobweb.—**r. de jorrar,** or **de jorro,** sweep seine.—**caer en la r.,** to fall into the trap.—**echar,** or **tender, la red,** to cast, or set, the net.
redacción, *f.* wording; editing; editorial rooms; editorial staff.
redactar, *va.* to edit, be the editor of; to write, word, draw up.
redactor, ra. *n.* editor.
redada, *f.* netful; catch, haul; (coll.) roundup (of suspects, criminals, etc.).
redaño, *m.* (anat.) omentum, caul, kell.
redar, *va.* to cast a net; to pull or haul in.
redargución, *f.* retort, refutation.
redargüir, *va.* (*ind. pres.* REDARGUYO, *pret.* él REDARGUYÓ; *subj.* REDARGUYA) to retort, reargue; (law) to impugn.
redecilla, *f. dim.* small net; hair net; mesh; bag net; reticulum of a ruminant's stomach.
rededor, *m.* surroundings, environs.—**al r.,** roundabout, around.—**al r. de,** about, nearly, more or less; around.
redel, *m.* (naut.) loof frame.
redención, *f.* redemption; recovery; ransom; salvation.—**r. de un censo,** paying off a mortgage.
redentor, ra, *n.* & *a.* redeemer(-ing).
redero, ra. I. *a.* reticular; reticulated. **II.** *m.* netmaker; one who catches fish or birds with nets.
redescuento, *m.* rediscount.
redhibición, *f.* (law) redhibition.
redhibir, *va.* (law) to make use of the right of redhibition.

redhibitorio, ria, *a.* (law) redhibitory.
redición, *f.* repetition, reiteration.
redicho, cha, *a.* speaking with affected precision and correctness.
rediezmar, *va.* to tithe a second time.
rediezmo, *m.* extra tithe.
redifundir, *va.* & *vn.* (rad.) to rebroadcast.
redifusión, *f.* (rad.) rebroadcast.
redil, *m.* sheepfold, sheepcote.
redimible, *a.* redeemable.
redimir, *va.* to redeem, rescue, ransom; to extricate, liberate; (com.) to redeem, pay off.
redingote, *m.* redingote, great-coat.
redistribución, *f.* resettlement (as of displaced persons).
rédito, *m.* (com.) revenue, interest, yield, profit, proceeds.
redituable, reditual, *a.* profit-producing.
redituar, *va.* to yield, to produce; to draw (interest).
redivivo, va, *a.* redivivus, revived, restored.
redoblado, da, *pp.* & *a.* redoubled; double lined; stocky, heavy-built; (mil.) quick (step).
redobladura, *f.*, **redoblamiento,** *m.* doubling; repetition; clinching.
redoblante, *m.* (mil.) drum; drummer.
redoblar, *va.* to double; to clinch; to repeat; (mil.) to roll (a drum).
redoble, *m.* REDOBLAMIENTO; (mil. and mus.) roll of a drum.
redoblegar, *va.* (*pret.* REDOBLEGUÉ; *subj.* REDOBLEGUE) to double; to bend.
redoblón, *m.* rivet, clinch-nail.
redolente, *a.* feeling a slight pain.
redolor, *m.* slight pain remaining after some acute suffering.
redoma, *f.* vial, phial, flask; (chem.) balloon.
redomado, da, *a.* artful, sly, crafty.
redonda, *f.* neighborhood, district; pasture ground; (naut.) square sail; (mus.) semibreve. —**a la r.,** roundabout.
redondamente, *adv.* around; clearly, plainly, decidedly.
redondeamiento, *m.* rounding.
redondear. I. *va.* to round, make round; to round off; to perfect. **II.** *vr.* to clear oneself of debts; to acquire a competency.
redondel, *m.* (coll.) circle; round cloak, circular; (mech.) flange; bull ring; round mat.
redondete, *a. dim.* roundish.
redondez, *f.* roundness.—**r. de la Tierra,** face of the earth.
redondilla, *f.* seven-syllable quatrain with alternate riming.
redondo, da. I. *a.* round; (print.) Roman; unencumbered, in easy circumstances; (of land) turned to pasture; clear, straight, decided.—**de r.,** in round clothes.—**en números r.,** in round numbers.—**en r.,** all around. **II.** *m.* (coll.) specie, hard cash; globe, orb, disk, anything round.
redondón, *m.* large circle or sphere.
redopelo, *m.* rubbing against the grain; (coll.) scuffle, affray.—**al r.,** against the lay of the hair; against the grain; against all rule and reason.—**traer al r.,** to vex; drag about contemptuously.
redor, *m.* round mat; (poet.) REDEDOR, surroundings.—**en r.,** roundabout.
redova, *f.* (dance) redowa.
redro. I. *adv.* (coll.) behind, backward. **II.** *m.* each of the rings upon the horns of goats.
redrojo, redrojuelo, *m.* small bunch of grapes remaining after the vintage; after fruit or blossom; (coll.) puny child.
redropelo, *m.* = REDOPELO.
redruejo, *m.* = REDROJO.
reducción, *f.* reduction, decrease; (mil.) mutation, alteration, exchange; reduction, conquest; (S. A.) settlement of converted Indians; (math. and chem.) reduction; (com.) reduction, rebate, discount.—**r. al absurdo,** (logic, math.) reductio ad absurdum.
reducible, *a.* reducible, convertible.
reducido, da. I. *pp.* of REDUCIR. **II.** *a.* reduced, diminished; small; compact.
reducimiento, *m.* reduction, reducement.
reducir. I. *va.* (*ind. pres.* REDUZCO, *pret.* REDUJE; *subj.* REDUZCA) to reduce; to diminish, decrease, lessen; to restore; (a) to convert (into), reduce (to); to subdue, subjugate; to divide into small parts; to condense, abridge; to persuade, convince; (math., chem., metal., surg.) to reduce. **II.** *vr.* to adopt a moderate way of living; to be compelled, to decide from necessity.
reductivo, va, *a.* reducing.
reducto, *m.* (fort.) reduct, redoubt.
reductor, ra. I. *a.* reducing. **II.** *m.* (hydraul., etc.) reducer.
reduje, *pret.* of REDUCIR.
redundancia, *f.* redundance; excess.
redundante, *a.* redundant, superfluous.
redundantemente, *adv.* redundantly.
redundar, *vn.* to overflow; to be redundant; (**en**) to redound (to), result (in), lead (to), bring.
reduplicación, *f.* reduplication.
reduplicado, da, *a.* reduplicated, doubled.
reduplicar, *va.* (*pret.* REDUPLIQUÉ; *subj.* REDUPLIQUE) to reduplicate, redouble; to reiterate.
reduzco, reduzca, *v. V.* REDUCIR.
reedificación, *f.* rebuilding.
reedificador, ra, *n.* & *a.* rebuilder(-ing).
reedificar, *va.* (*pret.* REEDIFIQUÉ; *subj.* REEDIFIQUE) to rebuild.
reeditar, *va.* to reprint.
reelección, *f.* reëlection.
reelecto, ta, *pp. irreg.* of REELEGIR.
reelegible, *a.* reëligible.
reelegir, *va.* (*pp.* REELEGIDO, REELECTO; *ger.* REELIGIENDO; *ind. pres.* REELIJO, *pret.* él REELIGIÓ; *subj.* REELIJA) to reëlect.
reembalar, *va.* to repack.
reembarcar, *va.* & *vr.* (*pret.* REEMBARQUÉ; *subj.* REEMBARQUE) to reship, reëmbark.
reembarco, *m.* reëmbarkation, reshipment.
reembargar, *va.* (*pret.* REEMBARGUÉ; *subj.* REEMBARGUE) to seize or embargo a second time.
reembargo, *m.* (law) reattachment.
reembarque, *m.* = REEMBARCO.
reembolsable, *a.* payable.
reembolsar. I. *va.* to reimburse, refund, pay. **II.** *vr.* to recover money due.
reembolso, *m.* refund, reimbursement.—**entrega contra r.,** collect on delivery, C. O. D.
reempacar, *va.* (*pret.* REEMPAQUÉ; *subj.* REEMPAQUE) to repack.
reemplazable, *a.* replaceable.
reemplazante, *m.* replacement.
reemplazar, *va.* (*pret.* REEMPLACÉ; *subj.* REEMPLACE) to replace; to supersede; to substitute.
reemplazo, *m.* replacement, substitute; (mil.) substitute.
reempleo, *m.* reëmployment.
reencarcelamiento, *m.* (law) remand.
reencarcelar, *va.* (law) to remand.
reencarnación, *f.* reincarnation.
reencarnar, *vn.* & *vr.* to be reincarnated.
reencuentro, *m.* collision; clash (as of troops).
reenganchamiento, *m.* (mil.) reënlisting; bounty for reënlisting.
reenganchar, *va.* (mech.) to recouple; (mil.) to reënlist.
reenganche, *m.* = REENGANCHAMIENTO.
reengastar, *va.* (jewel.) to reset.
reengendrado, da, *a.* & *n.* regenerate.
reengendrador, ra, *n.* & *a.* regenerator(-ing).
reengendrar, *va.* to regenerate, reproduce; to renew, revive.
reensayar, *va.* to reëxamine; to try or test anew.
reensaye, *m.* second assay.
reensayo, *m.* second trial or test.
reenvasar, *va.* (com.) to repack, refill.
reenviar, *va.* to forward.
reescriturar, *va.* to reëngage.

reexaminación, *f.* reëxamination.
reexaminar, *va.* to reëxamine.
reexpedición, *f.* forwarding (of mail, etc.).
reexpedir, *va.* to forward (mail, etc.).
reexportación, *f.* (com.) reëxportation.
reexportar, *va.* (com.) to reëxport.
refacción, *f.* refection, luncheon; retribution, reparation; boot, allowance (in barters); (Cuba) financing.
refaccionar, *va.* (Cuba) to finance.
refaccionista, *m.* (Cuba) financial backer.
refajo, *m.* short skirt; flannel underskirt.
refalsado, da, *a.* false, deceitful.
refección, *f.* refection, slight meal; repairs.
refectolero, *m.* = REFITOLERO.
refectorio, *m.* refectory (in convents).
referencia, *f.* reference; narration; (com.) (gen. *pl.*) reference(s) (as to character, etc.).
referendario, *m.* = REFRENDARIO.
referéndum, *m.* referendum.
referente, *a.* referring, relating.
referible, *a.* referable, expressible.
referido, da. *a.* related, told, said, expressed.
referir. I. *va.* (*ger.* REFIRIENDO; *ind. pres.* REFIERO, *pret.* él REFIRIÓ; *subj.* REFIERA) to refer, relate; to tell, narrate, report; to direct, submit. **II.** *vr.* (a) to refer (to), have relation (to).
refertero, ra, *a.* quarrelsome, wrangling.
refiero, refiera, *v. V.* REFERIR.
refigurar, *va.* to refigure.
refilón.—de r., *adv.* obliquely, askance.
refinación, *f.* refining; refinement.
refinadera, *f.* stone roller for refining chocolate.
refinado, da. I. *pp.* of REFINAR. **II.** *a.* refined; subtle, artful; fine, nice, polished.
refinador, ra, *n.* & *a.* refiner(-ing).
refinadura, *f.* refining.
refinamiento, *m.* refinement; refining.
refinar, *va.* to refine, purify; to make polite or refined; to polish, finish.
refinería, *f.* refinery; distillery.
refino, na. I. *a.* very fine, extra fine; refined. **II.** *m.* refining; fine grocery.
refirió, refiriendo, *v. V.* REFERIR.
refirmar, *va.* to support (on); to ratify.
refitolero, ra. I. *n.* one in charge of a refectory; (coll.) busybody, intermeddler. **II.** *a.* (Cuba) affected, obsequious, officious.
reflectante, *a.* reflecting.
reflector, ra. I. *a.* reflecting, reflective. **II.** *m.* reflector; searchlight.
refleja, *f.* reflection, observation. remark.
reflejado, da, *a.* reflected, mirrored.
reflejar. I. *va.* (opt.) to reflect. **II.** *vn.* to think, ponder, consider. **III.** *vr.* to be reflected.
reflejo, ja. I. *a.* reflected; meditative; (gram.) reflexive; (physiol.) reflex. **II.** *m.* glare; reflection; light reflected.
reflexión, *f.* reflection.
reflexionar, *vn.* to think, reflect.
reflexivo, va, *a.* reflexive; reflective; reflecting, thoughtful; (gram.) reflexive.
reflorecer, *vn.* (*ind.* REFLOREZCO; *subj.* REFLOREZCA) to reflourish, blossom again; to return to former splendor; "to come back."
refluente, *a.* refluent; flowing back.
refluir, *vn.* (*ind. pres.* REFLUYO, *pret.* él REFLUYÓ; *subj.* REFLUYA) to flow back; to redound.
reflujo, *m.* reflux, refluence; ebb or ebb-tide.
refocilación, *f.* recreation, refreshing diversion.
refocilar. I. *va.* to give or afford healthful recreation to, to brace up. **II.** *vr.* to seek or indulge in healthful recreation.
refocilo, *m.* healthful pleasure.
reforcé, *pret.* of REFORZAR.
reforma, *f.* reform; reformation; alteration, correction, improvement; (eccl.) Reformation.—**cerrado por reformas,** closed for alterations.
reformable, *a.* reformable; mendable.
reformación, *f.* reformation, reform.
reformado. I. *pp.* of REFORMAR. **II.** *a.* reformed. **III.** *m.* officer deprived of his command.
reformador, ra, *n.* & *a.* reformer(-ing); mender (-ing).
reformar. I. *va.* to reform; to mend, amend, improve; to reorganize, reconstruct. **II.** *vr.* to reform, to mend.
reformatorio, ria. I. *a.* corrective, reforming. **II.** *m.* reformatory.
reformista, *n.* & *a.* reformer(-ing, -ist).
reforzado, da. I. *a.* strengthened, reinforced. **II.** *m.* narrow tape or ribbon.
reforzar, *va.* (*ind. pres.* REFUERZO, *pret.* él REFORCÉ; *subj.* REFUERCE) to strengthen, reinforce; to cheer, encourage.
refracción, *f.* (opt.) refraction.
refractar, *va.* & *vr.* (opt.) to refract.
refractario, ria, *a.* refractory; unruly; obstinate.
refractividad, *f.* refractivity, refringence.
refracto, ta, *a.* (opt.) refracted.
refractómetro, *m.* (phys.) refractometer.
refractor, ra. I. *a.* refractive. **II.** *m.* refractor.
refrán, *m.* proverb, saying, saw.
refranero, *m.* collection of proverbs.
refrangibilidad, *f.* refrangibility.
refrangible, *a.* refrangible.
refranista, *n.* proverbialist, one who uses proverbs.
refregadura, *f.* = REFREGÓN.
refregamiento, *m.* rubbing, scrubbing.
refregar, *va.* (*ind. pres.* REFRIEGO, *pret.* REFREGUÉ; *subj.* REFRIEGUE) to rub, scrub; (coll.) to upbraid, scold.—**refregón,** *m.* rubbing, scrubbing; attrition, abrasion.
refreír, *va.* (*ind. pres.* REFRÍO, *pret.* él REFRIÓ; *subj.* REFRÍA; *ger.* REFRIENDO; *pp.* REFREÍDO, REFRITO) to fry well or too much.
refrenable, *a.* capable of being restrained.
refrenamiento, *m.* curbing, restraint, check.
refrenar, *va.* to restrain, check; to rein, curb (a horse).
refrendación, *f.* legalization, authentication; visé.
refrendar, *va.* to legalize, authenticate, countersign; to visé.
refrendario, ria, *n.* one who countersigns.
refrendata, *f.* countersignature.
refrendo, *m.* = REFRENDACIÓN.
refrentar, *va.* (mech.) to grind, mill, face.
refrescador, ra, *a.* refreshing.
refrescadura, *f.* refreshing (act and effect).
refrescamiento, *m.* = REFRESCO.
refrescante, *a.* cooling, refreshing.
refrescar. I. *va.* (*pret.* REFRESQUÉ; *subj.* REFRESQUE) to refresh; to cool, refrigerate; to renew, take up again.—**r. la memoria,** (coll.) to refresh the memory. **II.** *vn.* & *vr.* (of the weather) to get cool; to take the fresh air; to take a refreshment; to cool off.
refresco, *m.* refreshment; cold drink; luncheon at social gatherings.—**de r.,** anew, once more.
refriega, *f.* affray, scuffle, fray.
refriego, refriegue, *v. V.* REFREGAR.
refrigeración, *f.* refrigeration.
refrigerador, ra. I. *a.* refrigerating, freezing, cooling. **II.** *m.* refrigerator, freezer, ice box, cooler.
refrigerante. I. *a.* refrigerating, cooling. **II.** *m.* (chem.) refrigerator, cooling chamber; (med.) cooler; (astronaut.) coolant.
refrigerar, *va.* to cool, refrigerate.
refrigerativo, va, *a.* refrigerating, cooling.
refrigerio, *m.* refrigeration, coolness; refreshment, refection; consolation, comfort.
refringencia, *f.* refringence, refringency.
refringente, *a.* refracting, refringent.
refringir, *va.* & *vr.* (*ind.* REFRINJO; *subj.* REFRINJA) to refract.
refrío, refrió, etc. *v. V.* REFREÍR.
refrito, ta, *pp. irreg.* of REFREIR.
[1]**refuerzo,** *m.* reinforcement; backing, bracing, strengthening piece; welt (of shoe); aid, help.
[2]**refuerzo, refuerce,** *v. V.* REFORZAR.
refugiado, da. I. *pp.* of REFUGIAR. **II.** *n.* refugee.
refugiar. I. *va.* to shelter. **II.** *vr.* to take refuge.
refugio, *m.* refuge, shelter, asylum.
refulgencia, *f.* refulgence, splendor.

refulgente, *a.* refulgent.
refulgir, *vn.* to shine.
refundición, *f.* (foundry) recasting.
refundir. I. *va.* (foundry) to remelt or recast; to contain, include; to rearrange, recast, reconstruct. **II.** *vn.* to redound.
refunfuñador, ra, *n.* grumbler, growler.
refunfuñadura, *f.* growling, grumbling.
refunfuñar, *va.* to growl, grumble, mutter.
refunfuño, *m.* grumbling, growl, snort.
refutable, *a.* refutable.
refutación, *f.* refutation.
refutador, ra, *n.* & *a.* refuter(-ing).
refutar, *va.* to refute.
refutatorio, ria, *a.* refuting.
regadera, *f.* watering pot, sprinkler; trench for irrigation; sparger.
regadero, *m.* ditch for irrigation.
regadío, ía, *a.* & *m.* irrigated (land).
regadizo, za, *a.* irrigable.
[1]**regador, ra,** *n.* one who waters or irrigates.
[2]**regador,** *m.* comb makers' gauge.
regadura, *f.* irrigation, watering.
regaifa, *f.* grooved stone of an oil mill.
regajal, regajo, *m.* puddle, pool; rill.
regala, *f.* (naut.) gunwale or gunnel.
regalada, *f.* king's stables; horses kept in them.
regaladamente, *adv.* delicately, pleasantly, daintily, luxuriously.
regalado, da, *pp.* & *a.* delicate, dainty; easy, comfortable; suave.
regalador, ra. I. *n.* liberal entertainer. **II.** *m.* stick for cleaning wine skins.
regalamiento, *m.* regalement.
regalar. I. *va.* to present, give as a present, make a present of; to regale, treat, entertain; to caress, fondle, pet, cajole; to gladden, cheer, delight, cherish. **II.** *vr.* to feast sumptuously.
regalejo, *m. dim.* small gift.
regalero, *m.* purveyor of fruit and flowers for the royal family.
regalía, *f.* regalia, royal rights; (S. A., Mex.) advance payment or royalty to owner of patent, etc.; privilege, exemption; (Cuba) regalia (cigar).—*pl.* perquisites.
regalicia, *f.* = REGALIZ.
regalillo, *m. dim.* small gift; muff (for hands).
regalismo, *m.* regalism.
regalista, *n.* & *a.* regalist(-ic).
regalito, *m. dim.* small present.
regaliz, *m.*, **regaliza,** *f.* (bot.) licorice.
regalo, *m.* present, gift; pleasure; dainty; comfort, luxury.—**con r.,** in luxury.
regalón, na, *a.* (coll.) fond of ease; spoiled, pampered.
regañadientes.—a r., reluctantly, grumbling
regañamiento, *m.* grumbling, snarling, growl.
regañar. I. *vn.* to snarl, growl, grumble; mutter; to quarrel, wrangle; to crack or open. **II.** *va.* (coll.) to scold, reprehend, chide.
regañir, *vn.* to yelp, howl repeatedly.
regaño, *m.* gesture of annoyance; sternness of look; scolding; reprimand; scorched bread.
regañón, na, *n.* & *a.* growler(-ing), grumbler (-ing); scolder, scold(-ing).
regar, *va.* (*ind. pres.* RIEGO, *pret.* REGUÉ; *subj.* RIEGUE) to water; to irrigate; to sprinkle; to shower, bedew; to strew, scatter; to wash or water (as rivers and clouds).
[1]**regata,** *f.* irrigating ditch or conduit.
[2]**regata,** *f.* regatta.
regate, *m.* dodge, dodging.
regatear. I. *va.* to haggle about, beat down (the price), to resell at retail; to shun, evade, avoid. **II.** *vn.* to haggle; to wriggle, dodge; (naut.) to race.
regateo, *m.* chaffer, bargaining, haggling.
regatería, *f.* = REGATONERÍA.
regatero, ra, *n.* & *a.* haggler(-ing).
regato, *m.* small rivulet, rill; pool.
[1]**regatón, na,** *n.* huckster, hawker; haggler.
[2]**regatón,** *m.* tip, ferrule.
regatonear, *vn.* to sell at retail.
regatonería, *f.* hucksterage; sale by retail.
regazar, *va.* to tuck up.
regazo, *m.* lap (part of body).
regencia, *f.* regency; regentship.
regeneración, *f.* regeneration.
regenerador, ra. I. *a.* regenerating. **II.** *n.* regenerator; *m.* (phys.) breeder reactor; (mech.) regenerator.
regenerar, *va.* to regenerate.
regenerativo, va. I. *a.* regenerative. **II.** *m.* (phys.) breeder reactor.
regenta, *f.* regent's wife; woman professor.
regentar, *va.* to rule, govern, manage.
regente. I. *a.* ruling, governing. **II.** *n.* regent; president of a court of justice; master of theological studies; in Spanish universities, some supernumerary professors; manager, director; (print.) foreman.
regentear, *vn.* to domineer, rule, boss.
regicida. I. *a.* regicidal. **II.** *n.* regicide.
regicidio, *m.* regicide, murder of a king.
regidor, ra. I. *a.* ruling, governing. **II.** *m.* alderman or councilman. **III.** *f.* alderman's or councilman's wife.—**regidoría, regiduría,** *f.* alderman's or councilman's office.
régimen, *m.* régime; management, rule; political system; (gram.) government; (med.) regimen, treatment.—**r. alimenticio,** diet.—**de r.,** ordinary, rated, normal (speed, power, etc.).
regimentación, *f.* (mil.) regimentation.
regimentar, *va.* (*ind.* REGIMIENTO; *subj.* REGIMIENTE) to organize into a regiment.
regimiento, *m.* administration, government; municipal council board; (mil.) regiment; (naut.) pilot's book of sailing directions.
regio, gia, *a.* royal, regal, kingly; stately, sumptuous, magnificent.
región, *f.* region.
regional, *a.* regional, sectional, local.—**regionalismo,** *m.* (pol.) home rule; regionalism, sectionalism.—**regionalista. I.** *a.* relating to home rule. **II.** *n.* home ruler; sectionalism.
regionario, ria, *a.* (eccl.) regionary.
regir. I. *va.* (*ger.* RIGIENDO; *ind. pres.* RIJO, *pret.* él RIGIÓ; *subj.* RIJA) to rule, govern, direct; to conduct, manage, command; to keep (the bowels) in good order; (gram.) to govern. **II.** *vn.* to be in force; to prevail; (naut.) to obey the helm.
registrado, da, *a.* registered.
registrador, ra. I. *a.* registering. **II.** *n.* register, registrar, recorder, master or clerk of records; searcher, inspector; toll gatherer; controller.
registrar. I. *va.* to inspect, examine; to search; to scan, survey; to register, record; to mark (a book); (min.) to prospect. **II.** *vr.* to register, be registered or matriculated.
registro, *m.* search, inspection, examination; census, registry, registration, enrollment, record, entry; enrolling office; certificate of entry; register book; bookmark; (mus.) register, stop of an organ; air hole; furnace register; (print.) catchword, register; regulator (of a timepiece); (bookbinding) directions for binding.
regla, *f.* rule, regulation, precept; policy; order, measure, moderation; (drawing) ruler, straight edge; menstruation, courses.—**r. de aligación,** (arith.) alligation.—**r. de compañía,** (arith.) partnership.—**r. de falsa posición,** (arith.) position, rule of false position.—**r. de oro,** or **r. de tres,** (arith.) rule of three.—**r. fija,** fixed rule, set rule.—**r. lesbia,** flexible rule.—**r. magnética,** surveying compass.—**r. T,** or **r. te,** T square.—**a r.,** by ruler, by rule and square.—**en r.,** thoroughly, in due form, in order.—**echar la r.,** to test with a ruler.—**por r. general,** as a general rule.
reglado, da. I. *pp.* of REGLAR. **II.** *a.* temperate, moderate; (geom.) ruled (surface).
reglamentación, *f.* establishment of rules and regulations; regulation by law, decree or rule; directions for the execution of a law.

reglamentar, *va.* to establish rules or by-laws for; to regulate by rule, law, or decree; to dictate directions for the execution of (a law).
reglamentario, ria, *a.* pertaining to, or prescribed by, regulations and by-laws; required by the rules (actual or tacit, as in the case of social formalities).
reglamento, *m.* by-laws; rules and regulations.
[1]reglar. I. *va.* to rule (as paper); to regulate. **II.** *vr.* to mend, reform.
[2]reglar, *a.* regular.
regleta, *f.* (print.) reglet; lead.
regletear, *va.* (print.) to lead.
reglón, *m.* mason's rule.
regnícola, *n.* native of a kingdom; writer on topics relating to his country.
regocijado, da. I. *pp.* of REGOCIJAR. **II.** *a.* merry, joyful, rejoicing, festive.
regocijador, ra, *n.* & *a.* rejoicer(-ing).
regocijar. I. *va.* to gladden, cheer, rejoice. **II.** *vr.* to rejoice, be merry.—**regocijo,** *m.* joy, gladness; mirth, merriment; rejoicing.
regodearse, *vr.* (coll.) to take delight; to joke, to jest.—**regodeo,** *m.* delight; merrymaking.
regojo, *m.* piece of bread left on the table after meals; puny boy.
regojuelo, *m. dim.* small morsel of bread.
regoldano, na, *a.* wild (chestnut).
regoldar, *vn.* (*ind.* REGÜELDO; *subj.* REGÜELDE) to belch, to eruct.
regoldo, *m.* (bot.) wild chestnut tree.
regolfar, *vn.* & *vr.* to flow back, to eddy.
regolfo, *m.* eddy, whirlpool; gulf, bay.
regona, *f.* large irrigating canal.
regordete, ta, *a.* (coll.) chubby, plump.
regostarse, *vr.* to delight, to dally.
regosto, *m.* craving for more.
regraciar, *va.* to show gratitude to, to thank.
regresar, *vn.* to return; (eccl.) to recover possession of a benefice; (astronaut.) to reënter.
regresión, *f.* regression, retrogression.
regresivo, va, *a.* regressive.
regreso, *m.* return, coming or going back; (eccl.) retaking possession of a benefice; (astronaut.) reëntry.
regruñir, *vn.* to snarl, to growl.
reguardarse, *vr.* to take care of oneself.
regué, *pret.* of REGAR.
[1]regüeldo, regüelde, *v. V.* REGOLDAR.
[2]regüeldo, *m.* eructation, belch.
reguera, *f.* irrigating ditch; (naut.) moorings.
reguero, *m.* trickle, rill, drip; irrigating furrow.
reguilete, *m.* = REHILETE.
regulación, *f.* regulation; adjustment.
regulado, da. I. *pp.* of REGULAR. **II.** *a.* according to rule.
regulador, ra. I. *a.* regulating, governing. **II.** *m.* (mech.) regulator; governor; register; throttle valve (of locomotive); controller (of electric car).—**r. de fuerza centrífuga,** ball governor.
[1]regular, *va.* to regulate; to adjust.
[2]regular. I. *a.* regular; methodical, orderly; moderate, sober; common, ordinary, frequent; middling, fairly good, so so; likely, probable; (geom. and gram.) regular.—**por lo r.,** usually, as a rule. **II.** *m.* (eccl.) regular.
regularidad, *f.* regularity; common usage, custom; exact discipline.
regularización, *f.* regularization.
regularizar, *va.* to regularize.
regularmente, *adv.* regularly; ordinarily, as a rule; middling, fairly well, so so.
regulativo, va, *a.* regulative.
régulo, *m.* chief of a petty state; basilisk; (chem.) regulus; (astr.) Regulus; (ornith.) golden-crested kinglet.
regurgitación, *f.* (med.) regurgitation.
regurgitar, *vn.* to regurgitate, overflow.
rehabilitación, *f.* rehabilitation.
rehabilitar, *va.* to rehabilitate, reinstate, restore; to refit, repair.
rehacer. I. *va.* (*pp.* REHECHO; *ind. pres.* REHAGO, *pret.* yo REHICE, él REHIZO, *fut.* REHARÉ; *subj.* REHAGA) to rebuild, remodel, make over; do over; to renovate, mend, repair; to invigorate, revive. **II.** *vr.* to regain strength and vigor; (mil.) to rally, reorganize.—**rehacimiento,** *m.* renovation, renewal; recuperation.
rehala, *f.* drove of flocks under one drover.
rehalero, *m.* drover of a REHALA.
rehecho, cha. I. *pp. irreg.* of REHACER. **II.** *a.* squat, broad-shouldered.
rehelear, *vn.* to be bitter.—**reheleo,** *m.* bitterness.
rehén, *m.* (gen. *pl.*) hostage.
rehenchimiento, *m.* stuffing, refilling.
rehenchir, *va.* (*ind. pres.* REHINCHO, *pret.* él REHINCHIÓ; *subj.* REHINCHA) to refill, stuff anew.
rehendija, *f.* crevice, cleft.
reherimiento, *m.* repulsion.
reherir, *va.* (*ind. pres.* REHIERO, *pret.* él REHIRIÓ; *subj.* REHIERA) to repel, to repulse.
reherrar, *va.* to reshoe (a horse).
rehervir. I. *vn.* & *va.* (*ind. pres.* REHIERVO, *pret.* él REHIRVIÓ; *subj.* REHIERVA) to boil again. **II.** *vn.* to be inflamed with love; to be blinded by passion. **III.** *vr.* to ferment, grow sour.
rehice, *pret.* of REHACER.
rehiero, rehiera, *v. V.* REHERIR.
rehiervo, rehierva, *v. V.* REHERVIR.
rehiladillo, *m.* ribbon.
rehilandera, *f.* pinwheel.
rehilar. I. *va.* to twist too much. **II.** *vn.* to stagger, to reel; to whiz, whir, as an arrow in flight.
rehilete, rehilero, *m.* shuttlecock; small arrow; malicious saying, personal hint.
rehilo, *m.* shaking, shivering.
rehincho, rehincha, etc. *v. V.* REHENCHIR.
rehirió, *pret.* of REHERIR.
rehirvió, *pret.* of REHERVIR.
rehizo, *pret.* of REHACER.
rehogar, *va.* to dress (meat) with a slow fire, basting it with butter or oil.
rehollar, *va.* (*ind.* REHUELLO; *subj.* REHUELLE) to trample under foot.
rehoya, *f.,* deep hole or pit.
rehoyar, *vn.* to dig holes anew.
rehoyo, *m.* = REHOYA.
rehuello, rehuelle, *v. V.* REHOLLAR.
rehuída, *f.* second flight; shunning.
rehuir. I. *va., vn.* & *vr.* (*ger.* REHUYENDO; *ind. pres.* REHUYO, *pret.* él REHUYÓ; *subj.* REHUYA) to withdraw, retire; to shun, avoid; to reject, decline, refuse. **II.** *vn.* to run back on the same track (as game).
rehumedecer, *va.* & *vr.* (*ind.* REHUMEDEZCO; *subj.* REHUMEDEZCA) to dampen well.
[1]rehundir, *va.* & *vr.* to sink; to deepen.
[2]rehundir, *va.* to remelt; to waste, dissipate, lavish.
rehurtarse, *vr.* (of game) to take a different route from that expected.
rehusar, *va.* to refuse, decline, reject.
rehuyo, etc. *v. V.* REHUIR.
reidero, ra, *a.* laughable.
reidor, ra. I. *a.* jolly, hilarious, full of laughter. **II.** *n.* laugher, one who laughs.
reimpresión, *f.* reprint; reprinting.
reimpreso, sa, *pp. irreg.* of REIMPRIMIR.
reimprimir, *va.* (*pp.* REIMPRESO) to reprint.
reina, *f.* queen; queen bee; queen at chess; hopscotch.—**r. de los prados,** (bot.) queen of the meadow.—**r. madre,** queen mother.—**r. regente,** queen regent.—**r. reinante,** queen regnant.—**r. viuda,** dowager queen.—**aceituna de la r.,** (bot.) queen olive.
reinado, *m.* reign.
reinal, *m.* strong hemp cord.
reinante, *a.* reigning; excelling; prevailing.
reinar, *vn.* to reign; to prevail, predominate.
reincidencia, *f.* repetition of an offense; backsliding, relapse; (law) recidivism.
reincidente, *a.* relapsing, backsliding.
reincidir, *vn.* to relapse into vice or error; to backslide.

reincorporación, *f.* reincorporation.
reincorporar. I. *va.* to incorporate a second time. **II.** *vr.* to reëmbody.
reingresar, *vn.* to reënter.
reino, *m.* kingdom. reign; district that was formerly a kingdom; (natural history) kingdom.—**r. vegetal**, vegetable kingdom.
Reino Unido, *m.* United Kingdom.
reinstalación, *f.* reinstallment; reinstallation.
reinstalar, *va.* to reinstall.
reintegrable, *a.* (com.) reimbursable, payable.
reintegración, *f.* restitution, reimbursement.
reintegrador, ra, *n.* restorer.
reintegrar. I. *va.* to reintegrate, restore; (com.) to reimburse, repay, refund. **II.** *vr.* **(de)** to recover, recuperate.
reintegro, *m.* = REINTEGRACIÓN.
reinversión, *f.* reinvestment.
reír. I. *vn.* (*ger.* RIENDO; *ind. pres.* RÍO, *pret.* él RIÓ; *subj.* RÍA) to laugh; to giggle, titter; to sneer; to smile (as nature).—**r. a carcajadas,** to laugh loudly. guffaw. **II.** *vr.* to laugh; (of cloth) (coll.) to begin to tear or split.—**r. de,** to laugh at, make fun of; to make little or nothing of.
reis, *m.* reis, Brazilian and Portuguese money of account.
reiteración, *f.* reiteration; (law) recidivism.
reiterar, *va.* to reiterate.
reiterativo, va, *a.* reiterative.
reivindicable, *a.* (law) repleviable.
reivindicación, *f.* (law) recovery, replevin.
reivindicar, *va.* (law) to regain possession of; to replevy.
reivindicatorio, ria, *a.* (law) replevying.
reja, *f.* plowshare, colter or coulter; plowing, tillage; grate, grating, railing; (atomic phys.) lattice.—**entre rejas,** behind bars.
rejacar, *va.* = ARREJACAR, to weed by plowing.
rejada, *f.* = ARREJADA, (agr.) paddle of a plow.
rejado, *m.* grate, grating, railing, grid.
rejal, *m.* pile of bricks laid crisscross.
rejalgar, *m.* (min.) realgar.
rejero, *m.* maker of railings and grates.
rejilla, *f.* small lattice or grating; latticed wicket; cane for backs and seats of chairs, etc.; foot brasier.
rejitar, *va.* to vomit.
rejo, *m.* pointed bar or spike; goad stick; (zool.) sting; hob for quoits; iron frame of a door; strength, vigor; (bot.) caulicle.
rejón, *m.* short spear thrust into a bull and broken at the end, leaving the point in the flesh; dagger; broad knife.—**rejonazo,** *m.* thrust with a REJÓN.—**rejoncillo,** *m. dim.* small spear.
rejoneador, *m.* bullfighter who uses the REJÓN.
rejonear, *va.* to thrust a REJÓN into (a bull).—**rejoneo,** *m.* fighting bulls with a REJÓN.
rejuela, *f. dim.* small grate; foot brasier.
rejuvenecer. I. *va.* (*ind.* REJUVENEZCO; *subj.* REJUVENEZCA) to rejuvenate. **II.** *vn.* & *vr.* to be rejuvenated.
rejuvenecimiento, *m.* rejuvenation, rejuvenescence.
relabrar, *va.* to work or cut again (as a precious stone).
relación, *f.* relation; ratio; report, narrative, account; intercourse, dealing; (law) report, brief; (mil.) return, report; (theat.) speech.—*pl.* relations, connections; acquaintance, intercourse; courting.—**r. jurada,** sworn statement. —**relaciones públicas,** public relations.—**decir** or **hacer r. a,** to relate to.—**tener relaciones con,** to have relations with; to be acquainted with.
relacionado, da. I. *a.* related. **II.** *n.* acquaintance.
relacionar. I. *va.* to relate, connect; to report, narrate; to make acquainted. **II.** *vr.* to get acquainted, make connections; to be related.
reláì, *m.* (Am.) (elec.) relay.
relajación, *f.* relaxation, laxity, looseness; slackening, relenting; diminution, mitigation (of a penalty); release (from an oath or vow); delivery of an offender by the ecclesiastical judge to a criminal court of justice; diversion, relaxation, rest; (med.) hernia, rupture.
relajado, da, *a.* (coll.) dissolute, dissipated.
relajador, ra, *a.* relaxing; remitting.
relajamiento, *m.* = RELAJACIÓN.
relajante, *a.* relaxing; loosening.
relajar. I. *va.* to relax, loosen, slacken; to remit, mitigate; to release from an obligation; (eccl.) to deliver to the criminal tribunal; to weaken; to amuse, divert. **II.** *vr.* to become relaxed, loosened, weakened; to grow vicious; to be ruptured.—**relajo,** *m.* (Am.) disorder, mix-up; (Mex., Cuba, P. R.) depravity.
relamer. I. *va.* to lick again. **II.** *vr.* to lick one's lips; to relish; to paint, make up; to boast.
relamido, da, *a.* affected, prim.
relámpago, *m.* lightning; quick person or action; (vet.) blemish in the eyes of horses.
relampagueante, *a.* lightning, flashing.
relampaguear, *vn.* to lighten; to flash, sparkle.
relampagueo, *m.* lightning; flashing.
relance, *m.* repeated casting of a net; second chance or lot; fortuitous event; repeated attempt; series of lucky or unlucky chances.—**de r.,** unexpectedly, by chance; at a bargain; second-hand.
relanzar, *va.* to repel, repulse; to cast in again (tickets or lots) to be drawn.
relapso, sa, *a.* relapsed into error.
relatador, ra, *n.* relater, narrator, teller.
relatante, *a.* narrating.
relatar, *va.* to relate, narrate, tell, report; (law) to make a report of (a lawsuit).
relativamente, *adv.* relatively.
relatividad, *f.* relativity.
relativismo, *m.* (philos.) relativism.
relativista, *n.* & *a.* (philos.) relativist(-ic).
relativo, va. I. *a.* relative. **II.** *m.* (gram.) relative.
relato, *m.* statement, narrative, report, account.
relator, ra. I. *n.* narrator. **II.** *m.* (law) relator.
relatoría, *f.* (law) office of a RELATOR.
relavar, *va.* to wash again.
relave, *m.* second washing of metals.—*pl.* (metal.) washings or sweepings.
relazar, *va.* to tie with many bindings.
relé, *m.* (Angl.) (Am.) relay.
releer, *va.* to read over again; to revise.
relegación, *f.* relegation, banishment, exile.
relegar, *va.* (*pret.* RELEGUÉ; *subj.* RELEGUE) to relegate, banish, exile.
relej, releje, *m.* wheel track, rut; (artil.) narrow chamber in a cannon; (arch.) tapering talus; (med.) sordes in the mouth.
relejar, *vn.* (arch.) to taper or slope.
relente, *m.* dampness; (coll.) boldness, assurance.
relentecer, *vn.* & *vr.* (*ind.* RELENTEZCO; *subj.* RELENTEZCA) to grow soft or tender.
relevación, *f.* raising, lifting up; alleviation, relief; remission, pardon, exemption.
relevador, *m.* (elec.) relay.—**r. de llamada,** alarm relay.—**r. graduado,** step-by-step relay. —**r. parlante,** sounding relay, relaying sounder.—**r. traslator,** repeating relay.
relevante, *a.* excellent, great, eminent.
relevar. I. *va.* to emboss; to bring into relief; to exonerate, relieve, release; to forgive, pardon, acquit; to exalt, aggrandize; (mil.) to relieve, substitute. **II.** *vn.* (art) to stand out in relief.
relevo, *m.* (mil.) relief.
relicario, *m.* shrine; reliquary; locket.
relictos, *m. pl.* (law) estate.
relieve, *m.* relief, relievo, raised work, embossment.—**poner de r.,** to bring out, throw into relief, emphasize.—*pl.* (of food) leavings; (fig.) highlights or high points.
religa, *f.* (jewel.) second alloy.
religación, *f.* binding, tying.
religar, *va.* (*pret.* RELIGUÉ; *subj.* RELIGUE) to bind more tightly; to realloy; to solder.
religión, *f.* religion.—**religionario, ria,** *n.* religionist; sectarian; Protestant.

religiosamente, *adv.* religiously.
religiosidad, *f.* religiosity; religiousness; punctuality.
religioso, sa. I. *a.* religious; bound by monastic vows; conscientious, punctual. **II.** *n.* religious, member of a religious order; monk (nun).
religué, religue, *v. V.* RELIGAR.
relimar, *va.* (mech.) to file again.
relimpiar, *va.* to clean again.
relimpio, ia, *a.* (coll.) very neat, clean.
relinchador, ra. *a.* habitually neighing.
relinchar, *vn.* to whinny, to neigh.
relincho, relinchido, *m.* neigh, neighing.
relindo, da, *a.* very neat and fine.
relinga, *f.* (naut.) boltrope.
relingar. I. *va.* (naut.) to rope (a sail). **II.** *vn.* (naut.) to rustle.
reliquia, *f.* relic, residue, remains; relics of saints; trace, vestige; habitual complaint.
reliz, *m.* (Mex.) landslide.
reloco, ca, *a.* (coll.) raving mad.
reloj, *m.* clock; watch.—**r. de agua,** clepsydra.—**r. de arena,** sandglass, hourglass.—**r. de bolsillo,** watch.—**r. de campana,** striking clock.—**r. de cuco,** cuckoo clock.—**r. de longitudes** = R. MARINO.—**r. de pulsera,** wrist watch.—**r. de repetición,** repeater, or repeating watch.—**r. de sol,** sundial.—**r. despertador,** alarm clock.—**r. eléctrico,** electric clock.—**r. impermeable,** waterproof watch.—**r. magistral,** standard clock.—**r. marino,** marine chronometer.—**estar como un r.,** (coll.) to be in perfect trim.—**por r.,** (to work) by the hour.
relojera, *f.* watchcase; watch stand; (Am.) watch pocket.
relojería, *f.* clock and watch making; watchmaker's shop.
relojero, ra, *n.* watchmaker, clockmaker.
reluciente, *a.* shining, glittering, bright.
relucir, *vn.* (*ind.* RELUZCO; *subj.* RELUZCA) to shine, glow, glisten, glitter; to excel, to be brilliant.
reluctante, *a.* unruly, unmanageable.
reluchar, *vn.* to struggle, wrestle, strive.
relumbrante, *a.* resplendent.
relumbrar, *vn.* to sparkle, shine, glitter.
relumbrón, *m.* lustre, dazzling brightness; flash; tinsel.—**de r.,** showy, tawdry, pompous.
reluzco, reluzca, *v. V.* RELUCIR.
rellanar. I. *va.* to relevel. **II.** *vr.* to stretch oneself at full length.
rellano, *m.* landing, (of a stair).
rellenar. I. *va.* to refill, replenish; to cram; to fill up; (cook.) to force, to stuff; (sewing) to pad; (mason.) to point. **II.** *vr.* to stuff oneself.
relleno, na. I. *a.* satiated; stuffed. **II.** *m.* forcemeat, stuffing; repletion; filling; (mech.) packing, gasket; (sewing) padding, wadding.
remachado, da. I. *pp.* of REMACHAR. **II.** *a.* riveted. **III.** *m.* riveting; clinching.—**r. alternado,** or **al tresbolillo,** staggered riveting.—**r. de cadena,** or **paralelo,** chain riveting.
remachador, ra, *n.* riveter; *f.* riveting machine.
remachar, *va.* to clinch; to rivet; to secure, affirm.
remache, *m.* rivet; riveting; flattening, clinching.
remador, ra, *n.* rower.
remadura, *f.* rowing.
remallar, *va.* to mend the meshes of.
remamiento, *m.* rowing.
remandar, *va.* to order several times.
remanecer, *vn.* (*ind.* REMANEZCO; *subj.* REMANEZCA) to reappear suddenly.
remanente. I. *m.* remains, remnant, residue. **II.** *a.* residual (esp. app. to magnetism).
remanezco, remanezca, *v. V.* REMANECER.
remangar. I. *va.* to tuck up (sleeves, etc.). **II.** *vr.* to be determined.
remango, *m.* tucking up.
remansarse, *vr.* to stop flowing; to eddy.
remanso, *m.* backwater; dead water; tardiness.
remante, *a.* rowing.
remar, *va.* & *vn.* to row, paddle; to toil, struggle.
remarcar, *va.* (*pret.* REMARQUÉ; *subj.* REMARQUE) to mark again.
rematadamente, *adv.* entirely, totally.
rematado, da. I. *pp.* of REMATAR. **II.** *a.* sold (at auction); totally lost, utterly ruined.—**r. a galeras, a presidio,** condemned to the galleys, to prison.
rematador, *m.* auctioneer.
rematamiento, *m.* = REMATE.
rematante, *m.* highest bidder.
rematar. I. *va.* to end, complete, finish; (com.) to auction; to knock down at auction; to give the finishing stroke; (sewing) to fasten off (a stitch); to finish (a seam). **II.** *vn.* to terminate, end. **III.** *vr.* to be utterly ruined or destroyed.
remate, *m.* end, finish, conclusion, expiration; (com.) auction, public sale; last or highest bid; (print.) vignette; (arch.) finial, pinnacle.—**r. de cuentas,** closing of accounts.—**de r.,** utterly, irremediably, without hope.—**por r.,** as a finish; finally.
remecedor, ra, *n.* one who beats down olives with a pole.
remecer, *va.* (*ind.* REMEZO; *subj.* REMEZA) to rock, swing, move to and fro.
remedable, *a.* imitable.
remedador, ra, *n.* imitator, mimic.
remedar, *va.* to copy, imitate; mimic, mock.
remediable, *a.* remediable.
remediador, ra, *n.* curer, healer; mender; comforter, helper.
remediar, *va.* to remedy; to assist, support, help; to free from danger, liberate; to repair (mischief); to avoid.—**no poder r.,** not to be able to help (prevent).
remedición, *f.* remeasuring; remeasurement.
remedio, *m.* remedy; medicine; help; amendment, correction; (law) action.—**r. casero,** home remedy.—**r. heroico,** extreme remedy, powerful remedy given as a last resort.—**ni para (un) r.,** (not) for love or money.—**no hay más r. (que),** there's nothing else to do (but).—**no tener para un r.,** to be absolutely penniless.—**no tener r.,** to be unavoidable; to be irremediable; to be no help for (*eso no tiene remedio,* there's no help for that, no way of avoiding).—**sin r.,** inevitable; hopeless.
remedión, *m. aug.* (theat.) makeshift performance.
remedir, *va.* to remeasure.
remedo, *m.* imitation; copy; mockery; mimicking.
remellado, da, *a.* dented, jagged.
remellar, *va.* (tanning) to unhair (hides).
remellón, na, *a.* = REMELLADO.
rememoración, *f.* remembrance.
rememorar, *va.* to remember, recall.
rememorativo, va, *a.* reminding, recalling.
remendado, da. I. *pp.* of REMENDAR. **II.** *a.* patched; mended; spotted, tabby (cat).
remendar, *va.* (*ind.* REMIENDO; *subj.* REMIENDE) to patch, mend, repair; (sewing) to piece, patch; to darn.
remendón, na, *n.* botcher, patcher; one who mends old clothes; cobbler.
remera, *f.* flight feather (of birds).
remero, ra, *n.* rower, oarsman, paddler.
remesa, *f.* (com.) shipment; remittance.
[1]**remesar,** *va.* to pluck out (the hair).
[2]**remesar,** *va.* (com.) to ship; to send, remit.
[1]**remesón,** *m.* plucking out of hair; plucked hair.
[2]**remesón,** *m.* stopping a horse in full gallop; skilful thrust in fencing.
remeter, *va.* to put back, put in.
remezón, *m.* (Am.) slight earthquake.
remiche, *m.* space between benches in galleys.
remiel, *m.* the second extract of soft sugar taken from the cane.
[1]**remiendo,** *m.* patch; mending piece; darning; amendment, correction; reparation, repair; brindle; (print.) jobwork.—**a remiendos,** by patchwork, piecemeal.—**echar un r.,** to patch.—**echar un r. a la vida,** to take a light repast.
[2]**remiendo, remiende,** *v. V.* REMENDAR.

remilgado, da. I. *pp.* of REMILGARSE. II. *a* affected, prudish, finical, fastidious.
remilgarse, *vr.* to be overnice, prudish or finical.
remilgo, *m.* affected nicety, prudery, squeamishness.
reminiscencia, *f.* reminiscence.
remirado, da, *pp.* & *a.* prudent, cautious.
remirar. I. *va.* to look at or go over again. II. *vr.* (en) to take great pains (with); to inspect or consider with pleasure.
remisible, *a.* remissible.
remisión, *f.* act of sending or referring; remission, sending back, remitting, remitment; remission, pardon, forgiveness; remissness, indolence; relaxation, abatement.
remisivo, va, *a.* remissory; remissive.
remiso, sa, *a.* remiss, careless, slack, slow.
remisorio, ria, *a.* remissory.
remitencia, *f.* (med.) remittence.
remitente, *n.* & *a.* remitter(-ing), sender(-ing).
remitir. I. *va.* to remit; to forward, transmit; to pardon, forgive; to give up, relinquish, waive, forego; to suspend, defer, put off; to refer; (law) to transfer, remit to another court. II. *va., vn.* & *vr.* to remit, slacken, abate. III. *vr.* to refer, submit; to quote, cite.
remo, *m.* (naut.) oar; (coll.) arm or leg (of person); leg (of quadruped); long and hard labor.—*pl.* wings of a bird.
remoción, *f.* removal, removing; dismissal.
remojadero, *m.* steeping tub.
remojador, ra, *n.* moistener, soaker.
remojar, *va.* to steep, soak, drench.
remojo, *m.* steeping, soaking, soakage.—**echar en r.,** (coll.) to defer until conditions are more favorable.
remolacha, *f.* (bot.) beet root, red beet.
remolar, *m.* oar maker; oar shop.
remolcador, ra. I. *a.* (naut.) towing. II. *m.* tug, tugboat, towboat; lighter.
remolcar, *va.* to tow, take in tow; to haul.
remoler, *va.* (*ind.* REMUELO; *subj.* REMUELA) to regrind; grind excessively.
remolida, *f.*, **remolimiento,** *m.* regrinding.
remolinante, *a.* whirling.
remolinar. I. *vn.* & *vr.* to whirl, gyrate, spin, rotate. II. *vr.* to crowd, throng together, swarm.
remolinear. I. *va.* to whirl about. II. *vn.* = REMOLINAR.
remolino, *m.* whirl, whirlwind; whirlpool, vortex, eddy; maelstrom; cowlick, twisted tuft of hair; crowd, throng; disturbance, commotion.
[1]**remolón, na,** *a.* soft, indolent, lazy.
[2]**remolón,** *m.* upper tusk of a wild boar; sharp tooth in horses.
remolonear, *vn.* & *vr.* to lag, loiter, skulk, shun work.
remolque, *m.* (naut.) towing, towage; trackage; towline.—**a r.,** in tow.—**dar r.,** to tow.
remondar, *va.* to clean (plants) a second time.
remono, na, *a.* (coll.) very neat; very pretty.
remonta, *f.* repairing, resoling, vamping, footing (of shoes); stuffing (of saddle); (mil.) remount; remounting cavalry.
remontamiento, *m.* remounting cavalry.
remontar. I. *va.* to frighten away (as game); (mil.) to supply remounts; to repair (saddles); to repair, resole, revamp (shoes); (Am.) to go up (river). II. *va.* & *vr.* to elevate, raise, rise. III. *vr.* to soar (as birds); to take to the woods; to go back to, date from.
remonte, *m.* repairing; remounting; soaring.
remontista, *m.* (mil.) commissioner for the purchase of remounts.
remoque, *m.* (coll.) sarcastic word.
remoquete, *m.* thump with the fist; epigram; satire; (coll.) gallantry, courtship.
rémora, *f.* (ichth.) sucking fish, remora; hindrance, obstacle; cause of delay.
remordedor, ra, *a.* causing remorse.
remorder. I. *va.* (*ind.* REMUERDO; *subj.* REMUERDA) to bite repeatedly; to cause remorse; to sting, fret. II. *vr.* to show worry or regret.
remordimiento, *m.* remorse.
remosquearse, *vr.* to show suspicion of surroundings; (print.) to be blurred or smeared; to mackle.
remostar. I. *va.* to put must into (old wine). II. *vr.* (of wine) to become sweet.
remostecerse, *vr.* = REMOSTARSE.
remosto, *m.* putting must into old wine; growing sweet.
remotamente, *adv.* remotely; vaguely.
remoto, ta, *a.* remote, far off; unlikely.
remover, *va.* (*ind.* REMUEVO; *subj.* REMUEVA) to move, remove, transfer; to take away; to discharge, dismiss; to stir.
removible, *a.* removable.
removimiento, *m.* = REMOCIÓN.
remozamiento, *m.* making, appearing or becoming young, rejuvenation.
remozar. I. *va.* to rejuvenate. II. *vr.* to look young.
rempujar, *va.* to push, jostle; to impel; to beat up (game).—**rempujo,** *m.* impulse, push; (naut.) sailmaker's palm.—**rempujón,** *m.* impulse, push.
remuda, *f.* change; replacement; change of clothes.—**r. de caballos,** relay of horses.
remudamiento, *m.* = REMUDA.
remudar, *va.* to move, remove; to change, replace.
remuelo, remuela, *v. V.* REMOLER.
remuerdo, remuerda, *v. V.* REMORDER.
remuevo, remueva, *v. V.* REMOVER.
remugar, *va.* (prov.) = RUMIAR, to ruminate.
remullir, *va.* to beat up again; to soften.
remunerable, *a.* remunerable.
remuneración, *f.* remuneration; gratuity, consideration.
remunerador, ra, *n.* & *a.* remunerator(-ing).
remunerar, *va.* to remunerate.
remuneratorio, ria, *a.* remunerative.
remusgar, *vn.* (coll.) to suspect, presume.
remusgo, *m.* keen cold wind.
renacentista. I. *a.* Renaissant, Renaissance (as *a.*). II. *n.* one versed in Renaissance art and literature.
renacer, *vn.* (*ind.* RENAZCO; *subj.* RENAZCA) to be born again; to spring up again, grow again; to acquire grace by baptism.
renaciente, *a.* renascent, springing anew.
renacimiento, *m.* regeneration; new birth; (**R-**) Renaissance.
renacuajo, *m.* tadpole, polliwog; little, despicable person.
renadío, *m.* crop which, after having been reaped in the blade, sprouts again.
renal, *a.* renal.
renano, na, *a.* Rhenish, Rhine (as *a.*).
renazco, renazca, *v. V.* RENACER.
rencilla, *f.* grudge; heartburning.
rencilloso, sa, *a.* peevish, quarrelsome, touchy.
renco, ca, *a.* lame.
rencor, *m.* rancor, animosity, grudge.
rencoroso, sa, *a.* rancorous, spiteful.
renda, *f.* second dressing of vines.
rendaje, *m.* set of reins or bridles.
rendajo, *m.* (ornith.) mocking-bird; mimic.
rendar, *va.* to dress (vines) a second time.
rendición, *f.* rendition, surrendering, yielding; rent, yield, product, profit.
rendidamente, *adv.* humbly, submissively, compliantly.
rendido, da. I. *pp.* of RENDIR. II. *a.* obsequious, devoted; fatigued, worn out.
rendija, *f.* crevice, crack, cleft.
rendimiento, *m.* weariness, faintness, fatigue; humiliation, submission; obsequiousness, humbling compliance; yield, rent, income; yearly produce; (mech.) efficiency, performance.
rendir. I. *va.* (*ger.* RINDIENDO; *ind pres.* RINDO, *pret.* él RINDIÓ; *subj.* RINDA) to subdue, overcome; to surrender, yield, give up; to render, give back, return, restore; to render, give (thanks), do (homage), etc.; (com.) to produce,

yield, bring; to fatigue, tire out; to vomit, throw up.—**r. cuentas,** to give, render, an account (lit. & fig.).—**r. el alma (a Dios)** to die.—**r. el bordo en,** to arrive at.—**r. el puesto,** (mil.) to give up the post, to commit it to another.—**r. gracias,** to give thanks.—**r. la guardia,** to set the watch.—**r. las armas,** to throw down the arms, to surrender.—**r. marea,** to stem the tide.—**r. obsequios,** to pay attention.—**r. parias,** to submit, to pay homage. **II.** *vr.* to become exhausted, tired, worn out; to yield, submit, give way, give up, surrender; (naut.) to spring (a mast).

renegado, da. I. *pp.* of RENEGAR. **II.** *n.* renegade; wicked person. **III.** *m.* ombre (card game).

renegador, ra, *n.* swearer, blasphemer.

renegar. I. *va.* (*ind. pres.* RENIEGO, *pret.* RENEGUÉ; *subj.* RENIEGUE) to deny, disown; to detest, abhor. **II.** *vn.* to blaspheme, curse; **(de)** to deny; to blaspheme, curse.

renegón, na, *n.* inveterate swearer.

renegrear, *va.* to blacken intensely.

renegrido, da, *a.* (of bruises) livid, blackish.

rengífero, *m.* (zool.) reindeer.

renglón, *m.* written or printed line; (com.) line of business, staple, item.—**a r. seguido,** immediately after; the next moment.—*pl.* lines, writings.

renglonadura, *f.* ruling of paper; ruled lines.

rengo, ga, *a.* = RENCO, lame.

renguear, *vn.* (Am.) = RENQUEAR.

[1]**reniego,** *m.* curse, execration, blasphemy.

[2]**reniego, reniegue,** *v. V.* RENEGAR.

reniforme, *a.* reniform, kidney-shaped.

renil, *a.* barren, as a ewe.

renio, *m.* (chem.) rhenium.

renitencia, *f.* resistance, opposition.

renitente, *a.* renitent, repugnant.

reno, *m.* (zool.) reindeer.

renombrado, da, *a.* renowned, famous.

renombre, *m.* surname, family name; renown, fame.

renovable, *a.* renewable, replaceable.

renovación, *f.* renovation, renewing; change, reform; replacement; (biocnem.) turnover.

renovador, ra, *n.* & *a.* renovator(-ing); reformer (-ing).

renoval, *m.* land bearing second growth.

renovante, *a.* renovating, renewing.

renovar, *va.* (*ind.* RENUEVO; *subj.* RENUEVE) to renew; to renovate; to change, replace; to reiterate, republish.

renovero, ra, *n.* usurer, fripper.

renquear, *vn.* to limp, hobble.

renta, *f.* profit; income; rental; (Angl.) (Mex.) (house) rent; annuity; tax, contribution; revenue.—**r. estancada,** revenue tax on monopoly articles.—**rentas del trabajo,** earned income.—**rentas gravables,** taxable income.—**rentas vitalicias,** annuity.—**a r.,** at a rent.

rentado, da. I. *pp.* of RENTAR. **II.** *a.* living on an income.

rentar. I. *va.* to produce, bring, yield; (Angl.) (Mex.) to rent for (as *cuánto renta ese cuarto?* how much does that room rent for?). **II.** *vr.*—**se renta,** (Angl.) (Mex.) (incorrectly used for *se alquila*) to let, for rent.

rentero, *m.* rural tenant; grantee of, or bidder for, a state monopoly.

rentilla, *f. dim.* small income; a card game; a game played with dice.

rentista, *n.* financier; bondholder; annuitant; one who lives on a fixed income.

rentístico, ca, *a.* financial.

rento, *m.* annual rent, rental.

rentoso, sa, *a.* yielding income.

renuencia, *f.* reluctance, unwillingness.

renuente, *a.* unwilling, reluctant.

[1]**renuevo,** *m.* sprout, shoot; RENOVACIÓN.

[2]**renuevo, renueve,** *v. V.* RENOVAR.

renuncia, *f.* resignation; renunciation; abjuration; renouncement; waiving.

renunciable, *a.* that can be waived, renounced or resigned; transferable.

renunciación, *f.*; **renunciamiento,** *m.* = RENUNCIA.

renunciante, *n.* & *a.* renouncer(-ing), resigner (-ing), waiver(-ing).

renunciar. I. *va.* to renounce, give up; to resign; to disown; to forego, waive; to refuse, reject; to depreciate, abandon, relinquish. **II.** *vn.* to resign; (cards) to revoke, renege.—**r. a,** to give up, renounce.—**r. a sí mismo,** to give up one's own will or taste.

renunciatario, *m.* one in whose favor something is renounced or resigned.

renuncio, *m.* revoke or renege (at cards); (coll.) error, mistake; contradiction, untruth.

renvalsar, *va.* (carp.) to shave off (doors).

renvalso, *m.* (carp.) shaving off to make fit.

reñidamente, *adv.* stubbornly, strongly.

reñidero, *m.* cockpit; fighting pit or ring.

reñido, da. I. *pp.* of REÑIR. **II.** *a.* at variance; on bad terms; stubborn, hard-fought.

reñidor, ra, *n.* quarreller; scold.

reñir, *va.* & *vn.* (*ger.* RIÑENDO; *ind. pres.* RIÑO, *pret.* él RIÑÓ; *subj.* RIÑA) to wrangle, quarrel, fight; to fall out; to scold, reprimand, chide.

[1]**reo, a. I.** *a.* guilty, criminal. **II.** *n.* criminal. culprit; (law) defendant; (law) accused.

[2]**reo,** *m.* (ichth.) ray trout.

reocupar, *va.* to resume.

reóforo, *m.* (elec.) rheophore.

reojo, *m.*—**mirar de r.,** to look askance.

reómetro, *m.* (elec.) rheometer; (hydraul.) water meter.

reordenar, *va.* to rearrange.

reorganización, *f.* reorganization.

reorganizador, ra, *n.* & *a.* reorganizer(-ing).

reorganizar, *va.* (*pret.* REORGANICÉ; *subj.* REORGANICE) to reorganize.

reóstato, *m.* (elec.) rheostat.

repacer, *va.* to consume all the grass of.

repagar, *va.* (*pret.* REPAGUÉ; *subj.* REPAGUE) to repay; to overpay.

repajo, *m.* inclosure for pasture.

repanchigarse, repantigarse, *vr.* to stretch (oneself) in a chair.

repapilarse, *vr.* to glut, stuff oneself.

reparable, *a.* reparable, remediable; objectionable; remarkable; (also *sujeto a* [1]*reparar*) blameworthy.

reparación, *f.* reparation, repair, repairing, indemnity, amends; atonement.

reparada, *f.* sudden bound of a horse.

reparado, da, *a.* restored; provided.

reparador, ra, *n.* repairer; restorer; carper, faultfinder.

reparamiento, *m.* = REPARO, REPARACIÓN.

[1]**reparar. I.** *va.* to repair; to restore; to observe, notice; to consider, heed; to make up for, indemnify for, make amends for; to expiate, atone for; to give the final touch to.

[2]**reparar. I.** *va.* to parry; to defend, protect. **II.** *vn.* to stop, stay over; **(en),** to stop (at). **III.** *vr.* to refrain, forbear; (Mex.) to rear on the hind feet.

reparativo, va, *a.* reparative.

[1]**reparo,** *m.* repair, repairing, restoration; remark, observation, advice, warning, notice; difficulty, objection, defect; strengthening poultice for the stomach.—**poner reparos,** to make objections.

[2]**reparo,** *m.* defense, protection; (fencing) parry.

reparón, na. I. *n.* & *a.* carper(-ing); faultfinder (-ing). **II.** *m.* (coll.) great doubt or difficulty.

repartible, *a.* distributable.

repartición, *f.* division, distribution.

repartidamente, *adv.* distributively.

repartidero, ra, *a.* to be distributed.

repartidor, ra. I. *a.* distributing. **II.** *n.* distributor; assessor of taxes.

repartimiento, *m.* division, distribution, apportionment; assessment; repartimiento (allotment of territory made by the conquerors of Spanish America, or, in the P. I., an assessment of taxes).

repartir, *va.* to divide, distribute, apportion, allot; to assess.
reparto, *m.* REPARTIMIENTO; (theat.) cast of characters; delivery (of goods, mail, etc.).
repasadera, *f.* (carp.) finishing plane.
repasadora, *f.* woman that cards wool.
repasar, *va.* to repass, pass again; to reëxamine, check; to revise; to scan, peruse, glance over; to review, study again (as a lesson); to clean (dyed wool) for carding; to mend (clothes); (min.) to remix (mercury) with metal.
repasata, *f.* (coll.) severe chiding, dressing down.
repaso, *m.* review (of a lesson); revision, reëxamination; final inspection, finishing; mending (of clothes); (min.) remixing quicksilver with metal; (coll.) reprimand, dressing down.
repastar, *va.* to pasture or feed again.
repasto, *m.* increase of feed.
repatriación, *f.* repatriation, returning to one's country.
repatriar, *va.* to return to one's country, repatriate.
repechar, *vn.* to go up hill.
repecho, *m.* short steep incline.—**a r.,** up hill.
repelada, *f.* salad of herbs.
repeladura, *f.* restripping; second clipping or cropping.
repelar, *va.* to pull out the hair of; to put (a horse) to his speed; to nip, nibble, browse; to clip, crop, lop off.
repelente, *a.* repellent.
repeler, *va.* to repel, repulse; to refute, dispute.
repelo, *m.* anything that rises or goes against the grain; cross fiber; crooked grain; (coll.) slight scuffle or dispute; aversion.
repelón, *m.* pulling out the hair; small part torn from anything; loose thread in stockings; (of a horse) short gallop.—**a repelones,** by degrees, little by little.—**de r.,** by the way; in haste.
repeloso, sa, *a.* (of wood) of a bad grain; touchy, peevish.
repellar, *va.* (mason.) to dub out.
repensar, *va.* (*ind.* REPIENSO; *subj.* REPIENSE) to reconsider, think over.
repente, *m.* sudden movement or impulse.—**de r.,** suddenly.
repentinamente, *adv.* suddenly.
repentino, na, *a.* sudden.
repentista, *n.* improviser, extemporizer.
repentizar, *va.* (*pret.* REPENTICÉ; *subj.* REPENTICE) to improvise, extemporize.
repentón, *m.* sudden movement.
repeor, *a.* & *adv.* much worse.
repercudida, *f.* repercussion, rebound.
repercudir, *vn.* to rebound.
repercusión, *f.* repercussion, reverberation.
repercusivo, va, *a.* repercussive; repellent.
repercutir. I. *vn.* to rebound; to reëcho, reverberate. II. *va.* (med.) to repel.
repertorio, *m.* repertory, repertoire.
repesar, *va.* to weigh again.—**repeso,** *m.* reweigh; weight office; charge for reweighing.
repetición, *f.* repetition; repeater (of timepiece); collegial dissertation, thesis; (theat.) encore; (art) replica; (law) action for an accounting.
repetidamente, *adv.* repeatedly.
repetidor, ra. I. *a.* repeating. II. *n.* repeater (teacher or student).
repetir. I. *va.* (*ger.* REPITIENDO; *ind. pres.* REPITO, *pret.* él REPITIÓ; *subj.* REPITA) to repeat; to recite, rehearse; (art) to make a replica of; (law) to claim, demand. II. *vn.* to repeat; to read a thesis in a university. III. *vr.* to repeat oneself.
repicar. I. *va.* (*pret.* REPIQUÉ; *subj.* REPIQUE) to chop, hash, mince; to ring (bells); to reprick; (in piquet) to repique. II. *vr.* to glory, boast, flatter oneself.
repienso, repiense, *v. V.* REPENSAR.
repinaldo, *m.* (bot.) red delicious apple.
repinarse, *vr.* to soar, rise.
repintar. I. *va.* to repaint. II. *vr.* to paint, make up; (print.) to set off, mackle, double.
repique, *m.* chopping, mincing; peal, ringing (of bells); dispute, altercation; (in piquet) repique.
repiquete, *m.* merry peal or ringing of bells; chance, opportunity.
repiquetear. I. *va.* to ring (bells) merrily. II. *vr.* to bicker, wrangle, quarrel.
repiqueteo, *m.* ringing of bells.
repisa, *f.* mantelpiece; shelf, console; bracket.
repiso, *m.* weak, inferior wine.
repitiente, *a.* repeating.
repito, repitió, etc., *v. V.* REPETIR.
repizcar, *va.* to pinch.—**repizco,** *m.* pinch.
replantar, *va.* to replant.
replantear, *va.* to restate (a problem); (eng.) to lay out on the ground.
replanteo, *m.* laying out on the ground the plan of a structure.
repleción, *f.* repletion.
replegable, *a.* folding.
replegar. I. *va.* (reg. in this meaning) to fold several times. II. *vr.* (*ind. pres.* REPLIEGO, *pret.* REPLEGUÉ; *subj.* REPLIEGUE) (mil.) to fall back, retreat in order.
repleto, ta, *a.* replete, very full.
réplica, *f.* reply, answer; repartee; objection.
replicador, ra, *n.* replier, disputant.
replicante, *n.* & *a.* replier(-ing), respondent(-ing).
replicar. I. *vn.* (*pret.* REPLIQUÉ; *subj.* REPLIQUE) to reply, answer; to contradict, argue. II. *va.* (law) to answer (a defendant's plea).
replicato, *m.* objection; (law) reply, answer.
replicón, na, *n.* (coll.) disputer, arguer.
repliego, [1]repliegue, *v. V.* REPLEGARSE.
[2]repliegue, *m.* doubling, folding; fold, crease, convolution.
repoblación, *f.* repopulation.—**r. forestal,** reforestation.
repoblar, *va.* (*ind.* REPUEBLO; *subj.* REPUEBLE) ro repopulate, repeople.
repodrir, *va.* & *vr.* = REPUDRIR.
repollar, *vn.* to head (as a cabbage).
repollo, *m.* cabbage; round head (of a plant).
repolludo, da, *a.* cabbage-headed; round-headed.
repolluelo, *m. dim.* small cabbage, sprout.
reponer. I. *va.* (*pp.* REPUESTO; *ind. pres.* REPONGO, *pret.* REPUSE, *fut.* REPONDRÉ; *subj.* REPONGA) to replace, put back; to reinstate, reinstall; to restore; to answer, to reply; (law) to restore (a case) to its primitive state. II. *vr.* to recover lost health or property.
reportación, *f.* moderation, calm.
reportado, da, *pp.* & *a.* moderate, calm.
reportaje, *m.* (journalism) report, reporting.
reportamiento, *m.* forbearance, restraint.
reportar. I. *va.* to control, restrain, check; to obtain, get, attain; to carry; to bring. II. *vr.* to refrain, forbear, control oneself.
reporte, *m.* report, information, news; lithographic proof.
repórter, *n.* (Angl.) (Am.) reporter.
reporteril, *a.* reportorial.
reporterismo, *m.* newspaper reporting; body of reporters, reporters collectively.
reportero, ra, *n.* reporter.
reportorio, *m.* almanac, calendar.
reposadamente, *adv.* peaceably, quietly.
reposadero, *m.* (metal.) trough for receiving melted metal.
reposado, da, *pp.* & *a.* quiet, peaceful, calm.
reposar. I. *vn.* to rest, repose; to stand (on), be supported (by); to take a nap; to lie down; to lie (in the grave). II. *vr.* to settle (as liquids).
reposición, *f.* replacement, reinstatement; recovery (in health); (law) restoring a suit to its primitive state; (chem.) preservation of liquids in proper vessels.
repositorio, *m.* repository.
reposo, *m.* rest, repose; sleep; tranquillity.
repostarse, *vr.* (Am.) to lay in stock.
reposte, *m.* pantry, larder.
repostería, *f.* confectionery, pastry shop; pantry, larder, plate room.
repostero, *m.* king's butler; pastry cook; covering ornamented with a coat of arms.

repregunta, *f.* (law) cross-examination.
repreguntar, *va.* (law) to cross-examine.
reprender, *va.* to reprehend, scold, reproach.
reprendiente, *a.* censuring, reprimanding.
reprensible, *a.* reprehensible.
reprensión, *f.* reprehension, reprimand, reproach.
reprensor, ra, *n.* reprehender, reproacher.
represa, *f.* dam, dike, sluice, lock; damming, impounding; stopping, holding back; (naut.) recapture.
represalia, *f.* reprisal, retaliation.
represar, *va.* (naut.) to recapture, retake from the enemy; to bank, dam, impound; to stop, detain, retain; to repress, restrain, check.
representable, *a.* representable.
representación, *f.* representation; description, statement; (theat.) performance, production; figure, image, idea; address, petition; authority, capacity; (law) right of succession.—**en r. de,** as a representative of.
representador, ra. I. *a.* representing. **II.** *n.* player, actor.
representante. I. *a.* representing, representative. **II.** *n.* representative; agent; actor.
representar. I. *va.* to represent; to state, declare; to express; (theat.) to perform, act. **II.** *vr.* to image, picture to oneself, conceive.
representativo, va, *a.* representative.
represión, *f.* repression, check, control.
represivo, va, *a.* repressive, restrictive.
reprimenda, *f.* reprimand.
reprimir, *va.* to repress, check, curb.
reprobable, *a.* reprehensible.
reprobación, *f.* reprobation.
reprobadamente, *adv.* reprovably.
reprobado, da. I. *pp.* of REPROBAR. **II.** *a.* RÉPROBO; not passed in an examination.
reprobador, ra. I. *a.* reprobative, reprobatory. **II.** *n.* reprover, condemner.
reprobar, *va.* (*ind.* REPRUEBO; *subj.* REPRUEBE) to reprove, disapprove, condemn; to damn; not pass (in an examination), (coll.) to flunk, fail.
reprobatorio, ria, *a.* reprobative.
réprobo, ba, *n.* & *a.* reprobate.
reprocesamiento, *m.* (phys.) reprocessing.
reprochable, *a.* reprovable.
reprochar, *va.* to reproach; to challenge (witnesses), reject, exclude.
reproche, *m.* reproach, reproof; repulse, rebuff, rebuke.
reproducción, *f.* reproduction; (phys.) breeding.
reproducir, *va.* (*ind. pres.* REPRODUZCO, *pret.* REPRODUJE; *subj.* REPRODUZCA) to reproduce.
reproductible, *a.* reproducible.
reproductividad, *f.* reproductiveness.
reproductivo, va, *a.* reproductive.
reproductor, ra, *n.* & *a.* reproducer(-ing); breeder(-ing).
reproduje, reproduzco, etc. *v. V.* REPRODUCIR.
repromisión, *f.* repeated promise.
repropiarse, *vr.* (of horses) to get unruly.
repropio, pia, *a.* (of horses) unruly.
reprueba, *f.* new proof.
repruebo, repruebe, *v. V.* REPROBAR.
reps, *m.* (text.) rep, fabric with a corded or ribbed surface.
reptil, *m.* reptile; crawler, creeper.
república, *f.* republic.
República Centroafricana, *f.* Central African Republic.
República Dominicana, *f.* Dominican Republic.
republicanismo, *m.* republicanism.
republicano, na, *n.* & *a.* republican.
repúblico, *m.* prominent man; patriot; statesman.
repudiación, *f.* repudiation.
repudiar, *va.* to repudiate; to divorce.
repudio, *m.* repudiation; divorce.
repudrir. I. *va.* & *vr.* to rot completely. **II.** *vr.* (coll.) to pine away.
repuesto, ta. I. *pp. irreg.* of REPONER. **II.** *a.* retired, secluded; recovered. **III.** *m.* store, stock, supply; sideboard, cupboard; dresser; pantry, larder; money staked in the game of ombre.—**de r.,** extra; spare.
repugnancia, *f.* reluctance, repugnance; aversion; loathing; disgust; opposition, contradiction, contrariety.
repugnante, *a.* repugnant, reluctant; loathsome; repulsive, disgusting.
repugnar, *va.* to oppose, contradict, conflict with; to cause disgust; to do with reluctance.
repujado, da, *a.* & *m.* repoussé.
repujar, *va.* to make repoussé work on.
repulgado, *a.* affected.
repulgar, *va.* (*pret.* REPULGUÉ; *subj.* REPULGUE) (sewing) to hem; to border; to put an edging on (pastry).
repulgo, *m.* (sewing) hem, border; external ornament of a cake or pie; ridiculous scruple.
repulido, da, *pp.* & *a.* prim, neat, spruce.
repulir. I. *va.* to repolish. **II.** *va.* & *vr.* to dress affectedly.
repulsa, *f.* refusal, rebuke, repulse.
repulsar, *va.* to reject, repel, decline, refuse.
repulsión, *f.* REPULSA; repulsion.
repulsivo, va, *a.* repelling.
repullo, *m.* jump, start, shock; small arrow or dart.
repunta, *f.* point, cape, headland; first manifestation or sign; disagreement, dispute.
repuntar. I. *vn.* to begin to appear; to begin to ebb. **II.** *va.* (Am.) to collect, round up (animals). **III.** *vr.* to be on the turn (wine); to be soured; to be displeased with one another.
repunte, *m.* (naut.) beginning of the ebb or of the flow; (Am.) collecting, rounding up.
repurgar, *va.* (*pret.* REPURGUÉ; *subj.* REPURGUE) to clean or purify again.
repuse, *pret.* of REPONER.
reputación, *f.* reputation.
reputante, *n.* appraiser, estimator.
reputar, *va.* to repute; to estimate, appreciate.
requebrador, *m.* gallant, wooer, suitor.
requebrar, *va.* (*ind.* REQUIEBRO; *subj.* REQUIEBRE) to woo, court, make love to; to flatter, wheedle; to break again.
requemado, a. I. *pp.* of REQUEMAR. **II.** *a.* brown, sunburnt. **III.** *m.* a kind of black fabric.
requemamiento, *m.* = RESQUEMO.
requemar. I. *va.* to reburn; to overcook, cook too much; to parch; to inflame (the blood or humors); to bite, smart (as mustard). **II.** *vr.* to burn with passion; to be deeply in love.
requemazón, *f.* = RESQUEMO.
requeridor, ra, *n.* summons server; courter, suiter; inspector.
requerimiento, *m.* summons; requisition, demand.
requerir, *va.* (*ger.* REQUIRIENDO; *ind. pres.* REQUIERO, *pret.* él REQUIRIÓ; *subj.* REQUIERA) to summon; to notify; to investigate, examine; to require, need; to court, woo, make love to (also **r. de amores**); to induce, persuade.
requesón, *m.* pot cheese, cottage cheese; curd.
requetebién, *adv.* (coll.) very well (or good), fine, as good as could be.
[1]**requiebro,** *m.* flattery, compliment; endearing expression, love tale; (min.) crushed ore.
[2]**requiebro, requiebre,** *v. V.* REQUEBRAR.
requiero, requiera, *v. V.* REQUERIR.
requilorios, *m.* (coll.) useless ceremony; circumlocution.
requintador, ra, *n.* outbidder.
requintar, *va.* to outbid by a fifth part of the price of; to exceed, surpass; (mus.) to raise or lower five points.
requinto, *m.* second fifth taken from a quantity; advance of a fifth in bidding; (S. A.) extraordinary impost levied under Philip II; (mus.) fife and its player; a small guitar.
requiriente, *m.* & *f.* summoner; summons server; courter, suitor.
requirió, *pret.* of REQUERIR.
requisa, *f.* tour of inspection, round; (mil.) requisition of horses.

requisar, *va.* to inspect, make the rounds of; (mil.) to requisition (horses).
requisición, *f.* (mil.) requisition of horses.
requisito, *m.* requisite, requirement.
requisitorio, ria. I. *a.* requisitory. **II.** *f.* (law) requisition.
requive, *m.* = ARREQUIVE, dress trimmings.
res, *f.* head of cattle; beast.—**r. de vientre,** breeding cow (or any other breeding female).
resaber, *va.* (*ind. pres.* RESÉ, *pret.* RESUPE, *fut.* RESABRÉ; *subj.* RESEPA) to know very well.
resabiar. I. *va.* to cause to contract bad habits. **II.** *vr.* to contract bad habits; to become vicious; to be discontented, dissatisfied; to relish.
resabido, da, *a.* affecting learning.
resabio, *m.* unpleasant aftertaste; viciousness; bad habit.
resabioso, sa, *a.* (Am.) vicious; peevish, ill-tempered.
resaca, *f.* (naut.) surge, surf, undertow; (com.) redraft; (coll.) hangover.
resacar, *va.* (naut.) to underrun, haul; (com.) to redraw.
resalado, da, *a.* (coll.) very attractive, charming, magnetic.
resalir, *vn.* (*ind. pres.* RESALGO, *fut.* RESALDRÉ; *subj.* RESALGA) to jut out, project.
resaltar, *vn.* to rebound; to come off, get loose; to jut out, project; to stand out; to be evident.—**r. a la vista,** to be self-evident.
resalte, resalto, *m.* rebound; protuberance, projection; (Ry.) superelevation (of outer rail).
resaludar, *vn.* to return a salute or greeting.
resalutación, *f.* return of a salute or greeting.
resalvo, *m.* tiller, sapling.
resallar, *va.* (agr.) to weed again.
resallo, *m.* (agr.) reweeding.
resanar, *va.* to regild defective spots in.
resarcible, *a.* indemnifiable.
resarcimiento, *m.* compensation, reparation, indemnity.
resarcir, *va.* (*ind.* RESARZO; *subj.* RESARZA) to compensate, indemnify, make amends to; to mend, repair.
resbaladero, ra. I. *a.* slippery; elusive. **II.** *m.* slippery place.
resbaladizo, za, *a.* slippery; glib; elusive; tempting, alluring.
resbalador, ra, *n.* slider; backslider.
resbaladura, *f.* slip, slide; backsliding.
resbalamiento, *m.* slipping; skidding.—**r. de ala,** (aer.) sideslip(-ping).—**r. de cola,** (aer.) tail slide.
resbalante, *n.* & *a.* slider(-ing), slipper(-ing).
resbalar, *vn.* & *vr.* to slip, slide, glide; to skid; to err, go astray.—**resbalo,** *m.* (Am.) steep slope.
resbalón, *m.* slip, slipping; fault, error, break.
resbaloso, sa, *a.* slippery.
rescaldar, *va.* to heat, to scorch.
rescatador, ra, *n.* redeemer, ransomer.
rescatar, *va.* to ransom; to redeem, recover; to rescue; to exchange, barter, commute; (Am.) to buy (ore) in mines.
rescate, *m.* ransom; redemption; ransom money; exchange, barter.
rescatín, *m.* (Am.) buyer of ore from Indians.
rescaza, *f.* = ESCORPINA, (ichth.) grouper.
rescindir, *va.* to rescind, annul, cancel.
rescisión, *f.* rescission, cancellation, annulment.
rescisorio, ria, *a.* rescissory, rescinding.
rescoldera, *f.* pyrosis, heartburn.
rescoldo, *m.* embers, hot ashes; scruple, doubt, apprehension.
rescontrar, *va.* to offset, set off.
rescripto, *m.* rescript, order, mandate.
rescriptorio, ria, *a.* rescriptive.
rescuentro, *m.* offset, compensation.
resecación, *f.* drying up, desiccation.
resecar, *va.* & *vr.* (*pret.* RESEQUÉ; *subj.* RESEQUE) to dry thoroughly, exsiccate, desiccate.
resección, *f.* (surg.) resection.
reseco, ca. I. *a.* thoroughly dry, too dry; very lean. **II.** *m.* drying up of trees or shrubs; dry part of a honeycomb.
reseda, *f.* (bot.) mignonette, reseda; woad.
resedáceo, cea, *a.* (bot.) resedaceous.
resegar, *va.* (*ind. pres.* RESIEGO, *pret.* RESEGUÉ; *subj.* RESIEGUE) to mow again.
reseguir, *va.* (*ger.* RESIGUIENDO; *ind. pres.* RESIGO, *pret.* él RESIGUIÓ; *subj.* RESIGA) to edge (swords).
resellante, *a.* recoining, restamping.
resellar, *va.* to recoin; to countermark.
resello, *m.* recoinage; surcharge.
resembrar, *va.* (*ind.* RESIEMBRO; *subj.* RESIEMBRE) to resow.
resentido, da, *pp.* & *a.* offended; resentful.
resentimiento, *m.* resentment, grudge; impairment.
resentirse, *vr.* (*ind. pres.* me RESIENTO, *pret.* él se RESINTIÓ; *subj.* me RESIENTA) to be impaired or weakened; to resent, be offended or hurt.
reseña, *f.* brief description, narration, or review; sketch; signal; signalment; (mil.) review.
reseñar, *va.* to make a brief description of, sketch, outline; (mil.) to review.
resequé, reseque, *v. V.* RESECAR.
resequido, da, *a.* dried up, parched.
resero, *m.* herdsman; one who deals in livestock.
reserva, *f.* reserve, reticence; reservation, exception; discretion, circumspection, prudence; modesty; (law) reservation; (mil.) reserve.—**r. mental,** mental reservation.—**a r. de,** intending to.—**de r.,** extra, spare, in reserve.—**en r.,** in reserve; confidentially.—**guardar r.,** to be discreet, act with discretion.—**sin r.,** openly, freely.
reservación, *f.* reservation.
reservadamente, *adv.* secretly; confidentially.
reservado, da. I. *pp.* of RESERVAR. **II.** *a.* reserved; cautious, prudent; private, confidential. **III.** *m.* (eccl.) Eucharist kept in the ciborium.
reservar. I. *va.* to reserve, keep; to retain, hold; to defer, postpone; to exempt; to conceal, keep secret. **II.** *vr.* to bide one's time; to keep for oneself; to beware, be cautious.
reservativo, va, *a.* reservative.
reservista, *m.* (mil.) reservist.
resfriado, *m.* cold (illness); watering before tilling.
resfriador, ra. I. *a.* cooling, refrigerating. **II.** *m.* refrigerator.
resfriadura, *f.* (vet.) cold in horses.
resfriamiente, *m.* = ENFRIAMIENTO, cooling.
resfriante. I. *a.* cooling, refrigerating. **II.** *m.* = CORBATO, cooler (in a still).
resfriar. I. *va.* to cool, chill; to moderate (ardor, fervor). **II.** *vn.* to begin to be cold. **III.** *vr.* to catch cold; to grow cold or indifferent.
resfrío, *m.* cold (illness).
resguardar. I. *va.* to preserve, defend, protect. **II.** *vr.* to take shelter; **(de)** to guard (against); protect oneself (from).
resguardo, *m.* preservation, security, safety; guard, defense, protection; (com.) security, guarantee, collateral, voucher; watchfulness to prevent smuggling; body of custom house officers for such service; (naut.) sea room, wide berth.
residencia, *f.* residence, domicile, abode; dwelling, home; stay, sojourn; (eccl.) residence; (diplomacy) function of a resident minister; (S. A.) (Sp. colonial hist.) (also *juicio de r.*) impeachment.
residencial, *a.* residentiary.
residenciar, *va.* (law) (S. A.) (Sp. colonial hist.) to impeach; to call to account.
residente. I. *a.* residing, resident, residential. **II.** *m.* (diplomacy) resident minister; (eccl.) residencer; dweller, inhabitant.
residentemente, *adv.* constantly, assiduously.
residir, *vn.* to reside, live, dwell; to be in official residence; to inhere.
residual, *a.* residual.

residuo, *m.* remainder, remnant; (chem.) residuum, residue; (arith.) difference; remainder.
resiego, resiegue, *v. V.* RESEGAR.
resiembra, *f.* (agr.) resowing.
resiembro, resiembre, *v. V.* RESEMBRAR.
resiento, resienta, *v. V.* RESENTIRSE.
resigna, *f.* (eccl.) resignation.
resignación, *f.* resignation; submission.
resignadamente, *adv.* resignedly.
resignado, da, *a.* resigned.
resignante, *n.* & *a.* resigner(-ing).
resignar. I. *va.* to resign, give up. **II.** *vr.* to resign oneself, be resigned.
resignatario, *m.* resignee.
resigo, resiga, etc., *v. V.* RESEGUIR.
resina, *f.* resin, rosin.—**resinar,** *va.* to draw resin from.—**resinero, ra. I.** *a.* pert. to resin. **II.** *n.* one engaged in the resin business.—**resinífero, ra,** *a.* resinferous.—**resinoso, sa,** *a.* resinous.
resintió, *pret.* of RESENTIRSE.
resisar, *va.* to diminish (measures) further.
resistencia, *f.* resistance, endurance; strength; (mech. and elec.) resistance.—**r. de materiales,** strength (*formerly* resistance) of materials.
resistente, *a.* strong; resisting, opposing.
resistero, *m.* hottest part of the day; heat produced by the sun's glare; place where such heat is felt.
resistibilidad, *f.* resistibility.
resistible, *a.* resistible, endurable.
resistidero, *m.* = RESISTERO.
resistidor, ra, *n.* resister, repeller.
resistir. I. *vn.* & *vr.* to resist, offer resistance. **II.** *va.* to resist; to bear, stand; to endure.
resistividad, *f.* (elec.) resistivity.
resistor, *m.* (phys.) resistance, resistor.
resma, *f.* ream of paper.
resmilla, *f.* four quires of letter paper.
resobado, da, *a.* hackneyed, trite, dull (conversation).
resobrar, *vn.* to be much over and above.
resobrino, na, *n.* grandnephew(-niece).
resol, *m.* sun's glare.
resolano, na. I. *a.* sunny. **II.** *f.* sunny place.
resoluble, *a.* resoluble, resolvable, solvable.
resolución, *f.* resolution; resoluteness; determination, courage, firmness; solution (of a problem); conclusiveness; quickness, promptitude; (law) lapse, nullification; (med.) resolution.—**en r.,** in short, in a word.
resolutivamente, *adv.* resolutely.
resolutivo, va. I. *a.* analytical. **II.** *m.* (med.) resolutive.
resoluto, ta, *a.* resolute, daring; compendious, brief; skillful, able.
resolutoriamente, *adv.* resolutely.
resolutorio, ria, *a.* resolute; resolutory.
resolvente, *a.* resolvent, resolving.
resolver. I. *va.* (*pp.* RESUELTO; *ind.* RESUELVO; *subj.* RESUELVA) to resolve, determine; to sum up; to solve (a problem); to dissolve, analyze; to dissipate; to undo, destroy, annul; to resolve, divide. **II.** *vr.* to resolve, determine; to dissolve; (med.) to resolve.
resolladero, *m.* vent, air-hole.
resollar, *vn.* (*ind.* RESUELLO; *subj.* RESUELLE) to breathe noisily (as an animal); (coll.) to breathe; (coll.) to show up; to break silence.
resonación, *f.* resounding.
resonador, *m.* resonator.
resonancia, *f.* resonance.—**tener r.,** to be bruited abroad, to attract attention.
resonante, *a.* resonant, resounding.
resonar, *vn.* (*ind.* RESUENO; *subj.* RESUENE) to resound, echo, clink, clatter.
resoplar, *vn.* to breathe audibly; to snort.
resoplido, resoplo, *m.* audible breathing; snorting.
resorber, *va.* to sip again, reabsorb.
resorcina, *f.* (chem.) resorcin.
resorcinol, *m.* (chem.) resorcinol.
resorción, *f.* reabsorption.
resorte, *m.* (mech.) spring; resilience, spring, elasticity; means, resources.
respailando, *adv.* precipitately, in a great rush.
respailar, *va.* (coll.) to move helter-skelter.
[1]**respaldar. I.** *va.* to indorse; to back; to answer for, guarantee. **II.** *vr.* to lean back; to get backing or support; (vet.) to dislocate the backbone.
[2]**respaldar,** *m.* back of a seat.
respaldo, *m.* back of a seat; leaning stock; backing; back of a sheet of paper; indorsement.
respectar, *vn. impers.* to concern, regard.
respectivamente, respective, *adv.* respectively.
respectivo, va, *a.* respective.
respecto, *m.* relation, proportion; relativeness; respect.—**r. a,** or **de,** with respect to, with regard to.—**a este r.,** with respect to this.—**al r.,** relatively, respectively.—**con r. a** = R. A.
respeluzar, *va.* to make the hair stand on end (through fright).
respetabilidad, *f.* respectability.
respetable, *a.* respectable, considerable; worthy; honorable, reliable.
respetador, ra, *n.* respecter.
respetar. I. *va.* to respect, revere, honor. **II.** *vn. impers.* = RESPECTAR.
respetivo, va, *a.* respectful.
respeto, *m.* respect; attention; observance.—**de r.,** extra, spare; for ceremony's sake; dressed or arranged and decorated ceremoniously.—**faltar al r. a,** to be disrespectful to; to molest (a woman).
respetuosamente, *adv.* respectfully.
respetuosidad, *f.* respectfulness.
respetuoso, sa, *a.* respectful; dutiful; respectable, honorable.
réspice, *m.* (coll.) short, pert reply; sharp reproof, dressing down.
respigador, ra, *n.* gleaner.
respigar, *va.* (*pret.* RESPIGUÉ; *subj.* RESPIGUE) to glean.
respigón, *m.* hangnail; (vet.) sore on horse's heel.
respingada, *a.* turned up, retroussé (nose).
respingar, *vn.* (*pret.* RESPINGUÉ; *subj.* RESPINGUE) to kick, wince; to grunt; (coll.) to mutter; to talk back.—**respingo,** *m.* muttering, grumbling; gesture of unwillingness.—**respingón, na,** *n.* & *a.* (Am.) grunter(-ing), grumbler(-ing).—**respingona,** *a.* (coll.) = RESPINGADA.
respirable, *a.* breathable.
respiración, *f.* respiration, breathing; ventilation.—**faltarle a uno la r.,** (diff. constr.) to get short of breath.
respiradero, *m.* vent, air hole; ventilator; (arch.) air passage, louver; (surg.) cupping glass; rest, repose; organ of respiration.
respirador, ra. I. *a.* breathing. **II.** *m.* respirator.
respirante, *a.* breathing, exhaling.
respirar. I. *vn.* & *va.* to breathe. **II.** *vn.* to rest, take rest or respite; to get breath; to breathe freely; to exhale scents or odors; to speak (used with a negative: *no respiró,* he did not open his lips).
respiratorio, ria, *a.* respiratory.
respiro, *m.* breathing; moment of rest; respite; (com.) extension, time.
resplandecer, *vn.* to glitter, glisten, shine.
resplandeciente. I. *pres. p.* of RESPLANDECER. **II.** *a.* resplendent, bright; luminous, light.
resplandecimiento, *m.* = RESPLANDOR.
resplandina, *f.* (coll.) sharp reproof, dressing down.
resplandor, *m.* light, splendor, brilliancy, radiance; glare; brilliant make-up for women.
respondedor, ra, *n.* answerer.
responder, *va.* & *vn.* to answer, reply; to respond; to reëcho; to acknowledge; to requite; to yield, produce; to have the desired effect; (com.) to correspond; *vn.* (**de**) to answer (for), be responsible (for), vouch (for), guarantee.
respondiente, *a.* respondent; answering.
respondón, na, *a.* saucy, pert.

responsabilidad, *f.* responsibility; reliability.
responsable, *a.* responsible; reliable.
responsar, responsear, *vn.* (eccl.) to repeat the responses.
responso, *m.* (eccl.) responsory for the dead.
responsorio, *m.* (eccl.) responsory.
respuesta, *f.* answer, reply; response; repartee.
resquebradura, *f.* crack, cleft, flaw, split, crevice, fissure.
resquebrajadizo, za, *a.* easily cracked; chinky.
resquebrajadura, *f.* = RESQUEBRADURA.
resquebrajar, *va.* & *vr.* to crack, to split.
resquebrajo, *m.* crack, cleft, split, fissure.
resquebrajoso, sa, *a.* easily cracked; chinky.
resquebrar, *vn.* (*ind.* RESQUIEBRO; *subj.* RESQUIEBRE) to crack, split; to burst.
resquemar, *va.* & *vn.* to bite or sting (as mustard).
resquemazón, *f.*; **resquemo, resquemor,** *m.*, (of food) pungency; disagreeable taste of burnt food; burning passion; stinging, pricking, remorse.
resquicio, *m.* chink, slit, crevice, crack, cleft; chance, opportunity.
resquiebro, resquiebre, *v.* *V.* RESQUEBRAR.
resta, *f.* (arith.) subtraction; remainder, difference.
restablecer. I. *va.* (*ind.* RESTABLEZCO; *subj.* RESTABLEZCA) to restore, reëstablish, reinstate. **II.** *vr.* to recover, recuperate.
restablecimiento, *m.* reëstablishment; restoration; recovery
restablezco, restablezca, *v.* *V.* RESTABLECER.
restallar, *vn.* to crack, as a whip; to crackle, crack, squeak.
restante, *a.* & *m.* remainder(-maining).
restañadero, *m.* inlet; estuary.
restañadura, *f.* retinning.
[1]**restañar,** *va.* to retin, tin anew.
[2]**restañar,** *vn.* = RESTALLAR.
[3]**restañar. I.** *va.* to stanch, stop the flow of (blood). **II.** *vr.* to stagnate, stand without flow.
restañasangre, *f.* bloodstone.
[1]**restaño,** *m.* stagnation.
[2]**restaño,** *m.* cloth of gold or silver.
restar. I. *va.* to deduct; to return (a ball), strike (it) back; (arith.) to subtract. **II.** *vn.* to be left, remain; (arith.) to subtract.
restauración, *f.* restoration; restoring; repairing, refurbishing.
restaurador, ra, *n.* & *a.* restorer(-ing).
restaurante, *n.* & *a.* restorer(-ing); *m.* (also Am. **restaurant**) restaurant.
restaurar, *va.* to restore, retrieve; to repair, renew, refurbish.
restaurativo, va, *a.* & *m.* restorative.
restinga, *f.* shoal, bar; ledge of rocks.
restingar, *m.* place full of rocks or bars.
restitución, *f.* restitution.
restituíble, *a.* restorable, returnable.
restituidor, ra, *n.* restorer, refunder.
restituir. I. *va.* (*ger.* RESTITUYENDO; *ind. pres.* RESTITUYO, *pret.* él RESTITUYÓ; *subj.* RESTITUYA) to restore, return, give back; to refund; to repair. **II.** *vr.* to return to the place of departure.
restitutorio, ria, *a.* (law) restitutive.
restituyo, etc. *v.* *V.* RESTITUIR.
resto, *m.* remainder, balance, rest; limit for stakes at cards; returning the ball; player who returns the ball on its rebound.—*pl.* remains.—**a r. abierto,** unlimitedly.—**echar el r.,** to stake one's all; to do one's best.
restorán, *m.* (Am.) = RESTAURANTE, *m.*
restregadura, *f.*, **restregamiento,** *m.* hard rubbing.
restregar, *va.* (*ind. pres.* RESTRIEGO, *pret.* RESTREGUÉ; *subj.* RESTRIEGUE) to rub, scrub.
restregón, *m.* scrubbing, hard rubbing.
restribar, *vn.* to lean upon heavily.
restricción, *f.* restriction, limitation.
restrictivamente, *adv.* restrictively.
restrictivo, va, *a.* restrictive, restricting.
restricto, ta, *a.* limited, confined; restricted.
restriego, restriegue, *v.* *V.* RESTREGAR.
restringa, *f.* = RESTINGA.
restringente, *n.* & *a.* restrainer(-ing).
restringible, *a.* restrainable, limitable.
restringir, *va.* (*ind.* RESTRINJO; *subj.* RESTRINJA) to restrain, restrict, limit, confine; to contract, astringe.
restriñidor, ra, *n.* & *a.* restrainer(-ing); binder (-ing), constipating.
restriñimiento, *m.* costiveness, constipation.
restriñir, *va.* to bind; to contract; to constipate.
restrojo, *m.* = RASTROJO, stubble.
resucitación, *f.* resuscitation.
resucitador, ra, *n.* restorer, reviver.
resucitar. I. *va.* to resurrect, raise from the dead; to resuscitate, revive; to renovate, modernize. **II.** *vn.* to rise from the dead, return to life.
resudación, *f.* slight perspiration.
resudar, *vn.* to perspire slightly.
resudor, *m.* slight perspiration.
resueltamente, *adv.* resolutely.
resuelto, ta. I. *pp. irreg.* of RESOLVER. **II.** *a.* resolute, daring; determined, prompt, quick, diligent.
resuelvo, resuelva, *v.* *V.* RESOLVER.
[1]**resuello, resuelle,** *v.* *V.* RESOLLAR.
[2]**resuello,** *m.* breath, breathing.—**sin r.,** breathless, panting.
resueno, resuene, *v.* *V.* RESONAR.
resulta, *f.* result, effect, consequence; resolution; vacancy of an office.—**r. secundaria,** aftereffect.—**de resultas,** in consequence.
resultado, *m.* result; end product.
resultancia, *f.* result.
resultando, *m.* substantiating fact or statement; paragraph beginning with "whereas."
resultante. I. *a.* resulting; (mech.) resultant (force, velocity, etc.). **II.** *f.* (mech.) resultant.
resultar, *vn.* to result, follow; to turn out; to be; to come out; (coll.) to work (well or badly), to lead to the desired result, to be advantageous.
resumbruno, na, *a.* brown (hawk's feathers).
resumen, *m.* summary, abstract, résumé.—**en r.,** in brief, in short, to sum up.
resumidamente, *adv.* briefly, summarily.
resumido, da. I. *pp.* of RESUMIR. **II.** *a.* abridged. —**en resumidas cuentas,** in short, briefly getting down to brass tacks.
resumir. I. *va.* to abridge, abstract, sum up; to repeat. **II.** *vr.* to be reduced or transformed.
resurgente, *a.* resurgent.
resurgimiento, *m.* reappearance, springing up again.
resurgir, *vn.* to reappear, arise or spring up again.
resurrección, *f.* resurrection.
resurtida, *f.* rebound, repercussion.
resurtir, *vn.* to rebound, fly back.
retablo, *m.* series of historical pictures; (eccl.) retable, altarpiece.
retacar, *va.* (billiards) to hit (the ball) twice.
retacería, *f.* collection of remnants, as for a crazy quilt.
retaco, *m.* short, light fowling piece; (billiards, etc.) short cue; short, heavy-built person.
retador, ra, *n.* challenger.
retaguardia, *f.* rear, rear guard.—**a r.,** in the rear.—**picar la r.,** to pursue the rear guard closely, to harass it.
retahila, *f.* long file, string, series, line.
retajar, *va.* to cut round; to cut the nib of (a quill); to circumcise.
retal, *m.* remnant, piece, clipping.
[1]**retallar,** *vn.* to shoot or sprout anew.
[2]**retallar,** *va.* to regrave, retouch (a graving); (arch.) to form a [2]RETALLO in.
retallecer, *vn.* to sprout again.
[1]**retallo,** *m.* new sprout.
[2]**retallo,** *m.* (arch.) projection or ledge.
retama, *f.* (bot.) genista.—**r. de escobas** = R. NEGRA.—**r. de olor** = R. MACHO.—**r. de tintes, or de tintoreros,** (bot.) dyeweed, dyer's broom.

—**r. macho,** Spanish broom.—**r. negra,** (bot.) furze, whin.
retamal, retamar, *m.* place where furze or broom grows.
retamero, ra, *a.* broomy, furzy.
retar, *va.* to challenge, dare.
retardación, *f.* retardation; delay.
retardado, da. I. *pp.* of RETARDAR. **II.** *a.* (mentally) retarded.
retardador, ra. I. *a.* retardatory, retardative. **II.** *n.* retarder.
retardar. I. *va.* to retard, slacken; to delay, detain. **II.** *vr.* (of timepiece) to be slow.
retardativo, va, *a.* retardatory, retardative.
retardatriz, *a.* retardative.
retardo, *m.* retardation; delay, procrastination.
retasa, retasación, *f.* reappraisement.
retasar, *va.* to reappraise.
retazar, *va.* to tear in pieces.—**retazo,** *m.* piece, remnant; cutting; fragment, portion.
retejador, *m.* retiler.
retejar, *va.* to retile (a roof); (coll.) to provide with clothes.
retejer, *va.* to weave closely.
retejo, *m.* repairing of a roof, retiling.
retemblar, *vn.* (*ind.* RETIEMBLO; *subj.* RETIEMBLE) to tremble, shake, quiver.
retemblor, *m.* repeated shaking, quiver.
retén, *m.* store, stock, reserve; (mil.) reserve corps; (mech.) ratchet, catch.
retención, *f.* retention, keeping or holding back; (med.) retention.
retener, *va.* (*ind. pres.* yo RETENGO, él RETIENE, *pret.* RETUVE, *fut.* RETENDRÉ; *subj.* RETENGA) to retain, withhold, keep back; to keep, preserve; to catch, hold, keep; to arrest, detain.
retenida, *f.* (naut.) preventer rope, guy.—**r. de costado,** (aer.) side guy wire.—**r. de guiñada,** (aer.) yaw guy.—**r. de proa,** (naut.) headfast.
retenidamente, *adv.* retentively.
retenimiento, *m.* = RETENCIÓN.
retentar, *va.* (of a disease) to threaten with a relapse.
retentividad, *f.* (phys.) retentivity.
retentivo, va. I. *a.* retentive, retaining. **II.** *f.* retentiveness, memory.
[1]**reteñir,** *va.* (*pp.* RETEÑIDO, RETINTO; *ind. pres.* RETIÑO, *pret.* él RETIÑÓ; *subj.* RETIÑA) to dye over again.
[2]**reteñir,** *vn.* = RETIÑIR.
retesamiento, *m.* tightening more firmly.
retesar, *va.* to draw or stretch tighter.
reteso, *m.* = RETESAMIENTO.
reticencia, *f.* reticence.
reticente, *a.* reticent.
rético, ca, *n.* & *a.* Rhethian, Rhæthian.
retícula, *f.* diaphragm and cross wires (of an instrument).
reticulado, da; reticular, *a.* reticular, reticulated; trussed, framed (as in *construcción reticulada,* framed structure).—**estructura reticular,** (nuclear phys.) lattice.
retículo, *m.* network, reticular tissue; diaphragm and cross wires (of an instrument).
retiemblo, retiemble, *v. V.* RETEMBLAR.
retín, *m.* = RETINTÍN.
retina, *f.* retina of the eye.
retinitis, *f.* (med.) retinitis.
[1]**retinte,** *m.* second dye.
[2]**retinte,** *m.* = RETINTÍN.
retintín, *m.* tinkling, jingle; tintinnabulation; (coll.) sarcastic tone of voice.
retinto, ta. I. *pp. irreg.* of RETEÑIR. **II.** *a.* dark, obscure, almost black.—**café, r.,** very strong, black coffee.
retiñir, *vn.* to tinkle, jingle, ring.
retiño, retiña, etc. *v. V.* RETEÑIR.
retiración, *f.* (print.) printing the back of a sheet; second form for backing.
retirada, *f.* withdrawal; (mil.) retreat; retirement; place of safety; privy, closet.
retiradamente, *adv.* secretly; retiredly.
retirado, da. I. *pp.* of RETIRAR. **II.** *a.* retired, solitary, isolated; remote, distant; pensioned. **III.** *m.* retired officer.
retiramiento, *m.* retirement; secluded place.
retirar. I. *va.* to withdraw; to put aside, out of the way; to lay aside, reserve; to repel; to revoke; (com.) to withdraw, call in; (print.) to print the back of, to back. **II.** *vr.* to withdraw; to retire; to recede, move or go back; (mil.) to retreat.
retiro, *m.* retirement; retreat; recess; secluded place; refuge, asylum; (eccl.) retreat; privacy; (mil.) condition and pay of a retired officer.
reto, *m.* challenge; threat, menace.
retobado, da, *a.* (Am.) given to grumbling or muttering; obstinate, unruly; cunning, wily.
retobar. I. *va.* (Arg.) to line or cover with hides; (Chile) to pack or wrap in hides or burlap. **II.** *vr.* (Arg.) to become quiet and surly, to sulk.
retobo, *m.* (Colomb., C. A.) refuse, useless or insignificant thing; (Chile) burlap; oilcloth; (Arg.) packing or wrapping in hides.
retocador, ra, *n.* retoucher.
retocamiento, *m.* retouching, retouchment.
retocar, *va.* (*pret.* RETOQUÉ; *subj.* RETOQUE) to retouch; to touch up, finish.
retoñar, retoñecer, *vn.* to sprout; to reappear.
retoño, *m.* sprout, shoot, tiller, sucker.
retoque, *m.* retouch; finishing touch; repeated and frequent pulsation; touch (of a disease).
retoqué, retoque, *v. V.* RETOCAR.
retor, *m.* twilled cotton fabric.
retorcedura, *f.* twisting, writhing.
retorcer. I. *va.* (*ind.* RETUERZO; *subj.* RETUERZA) to twist; to contort, convolve; to retort, reargue; to distort, twist, misconstrue. **II.** *vr.* to writhe, squirm.
retorcido. I. *pp.* of RETORCER. **II.** *m.* tutti-frutti, sweetmeat.
retorcimiento, *m.* twisting; writhing.
retórica, *f.* rhetoric.—*pl.* (coll.) sophistries, quibbles, subtleties.
retóricamente, *adv.* rhetorically.
retórico, ca. I. *a.* rhetorical. **II.** *m.* rhetorician.
retornamiento, *m.* return.
retornante, *a.* returning.
retornar. I. *vn.* to return, come back; to recede, retrograde. **II.** *va.* to return; to give back; to turn, twist, contort; to cause to go back.
retornelo, *m.* ritornello, burden of a song.
retorno, *m.* return, coming back; home trip; return chaise or horse; repayment, requital; barter, exchange, traffic; (naut.) leading block.—**de r.,** return (as *a.*).
retorsión, *f.* retortion; retort; twisting.
retorsivo, va, *a.* having a retort; bending back.
retorta, *f.* a twilled linen fabric; (chem.) retort.
retortero, *m.* twirl, rotation.—**andar al r.,** to hover about.—**traer al r.,** (coll.) to twist one around, to deceive with false promises.
retortijar, *va.* to twist, to curl.
retortijón, *m.* curlicue; twisting, twist; cramp.—**r. de tripas,** griping cramp.
retostado, da. I. *pp.* of RETOSTAR. **II.** *a.* brown.
retostar, *va.* (*ind.* RETUESTO; *subj.* RETUESTE) to toast again, toast brown.
retozador, ra, *a.* frisky, frolicsome, prankish.
retozadura, *f.* = RETOZO.
retozar. I. *vn.* to frisk and skip about, romp, frolic, gambol. **II.** *vr.* (of passion) to be violently aroused.
retozo, *m.* frisk, gambol, prank, frolic.—**r. de la risa,** giggle, titter.
retozón, na, *a.* frolicsome, coltish.
retracción, *f.* retraction, drawing back.
retractable, *a.* retractable.
retractación, *f.* retractation, recantation.
retractar, *va.* & *vr.* to retract, to recant; (law) to redeem.
retráctil, *a.* retractile.
retractilidad, *f.* retractility.
retracto, *m.* (law) right of redemption.
retractor, *m.* (surg.) retractor.
retraer. I. *va.* (*ger.* RETRAYENDO; *pp.* RETRAÍDO;

ind. pres. RETRAIGO, *pret.* RETRAJE; *subj.* RETRAIGA) to dissuade; (law) to redeem. **II.** *vr.* to take refuge or shelter; to withdraw from, shun; to keep aloof, retire; to live a retired life.
retraído, da. I. *pp.* of RETRAER. **II.** *a.* of a retiring disposition; incommunicative. **III.** *n.* refugee; lover of solitude.
retraigo, retraiga, *v. V.* RETRAER.
retraimiento, *m.* seclusion, retirement; retreat, refuge, asylum; private room, sanctum; incommunicativeness.
retranca, *f.* broad crupper of a packsaddle; (Cuba, Mex., Ry.) brake; breeching (of a saddle).
retranquear, *va.* to hoist, move, and set down (building blocks, etc.).—**retranqueo,** *m.* (arch.) setting blocks or stones in position.
retranquero, *m.* (Mex., Cuba, Ry.) brakeman.
retransmisión, *f.* (rad.) rebroadcast.
retransmitir, *va.* to relay.
retrasado, da. I. *pp.* of RETRASAR. **II.** *a.* (mentally) retarded.
retrasar. I. *va.* to defer, put off, postpone; to delay; to set back (timepiece). **II.** *vn.* to retrograde, go back, decline. **III.** *vr.* to be backward; to be behindhand, late, behind time; (of timepiece) to run slow.
retraso, *m.* delay, backwardness, slowness.
retratable, *a.* retractable, retractible.
retratación, *f.* retractation, recantation.
retratador, ra, *n.* = RETRATISTA.
retratar. I. *va.* to portray, draw a portrait of; to imitate, copy; to paint, describe; to depict; to photograph; RETRACTAR. **II.** *vr.* to be reflected; to be depicted, show; to sit for a portrait or photograph.
retratista, *n.* portrait painter; photographer.
retrato, *m.* portrait, picture; photograph; copy, resemblance; description; (law) RETRACTO.
retrayente, *n.* & *a.* retractor(-ing), recanter (-ing); (law) redeemer(-ing).
retrechar, *vn.* to back, move backward.
retrechería, *f.* (coll.) cunning, evasion.
retrechero, ra, *a.* (coll.) cunningly evasive; attractive, charming, winsome.
retrepado, da, *a.* leaning or slanting backward.
retreparse, *vr.* to lean back; to recline in a chair.
retreta, *f.* (mil.) retreat; tatoo; evening military parade; (Colomb.) open-air concert by a military band in honor of a public dignitary.
retrete, *m.* private room, sanctum; alcove, boudoir; closet, toilet room, water closet, privy.
retribución, *f.* retribution; recompense, fee.
retribuir, *va.* (*ger.* RETRIBUYENDO; *ind. pres.* RETRIBUYO, *pret.* RETRIBUYÓ; *subj.* RETRIBUYA to remunerate, reward, fee.
retributivo, va, *a.* retributive, retributory.
retribuyente, *a.* retributive, retributing.
retrillar, *va.* (agr.) to thrash again.
retroacción, *f.* (electron.) feedback.
retroactividad, *f.* retroactivity.
retroactivo, va, *a.* retroactive.
retrocarga, *f.*—**de r.,** breech-loading.
retroceder, *vn.* to go back, move backward; (**de**) to draw back (from), go back (on); (auto) to back up; to recede; to become worse.
retrocesión, *f.* backward motion; (law) retrocession.
retroceso, *m.* backward motion; (med.) aggravation; in billiards, draw.
retrocohete, *m.* retro-rocket.
retrodisparo, *m.* (astronaut.) retro-firing.
retroflexión, *f.* (med.) retroflexion.
retrogradación, *f.* (astr.) retrogradation, retrogression.
retrogradar, *vn.* to recede; (astr.) to retrograde.
retrógrado, da, *a.* retrogressive; (pol.) reactionary; (astr.) retrograde.
retrogresión, *f.* retrogression, retrogradation.
retronar, *vn.* (*ind.* RETRUENO; *subj.* RETRUENE) to thunder; make a thundering noise.
retropilastra, *f.* pilaster behind a column.
retropropulsión, *f.* (aer.) jet propulsion.
retroscopio, *m.* retroscope.
retrospección, *f.* retrospection.
retrospectivo, va, *a.* retrospective.
retrotracción, *f.* (law) antedating.
retrotraer, *va.* (*ger.* RETROTRAYENDO; *pp.* RETROTRAÍDO; *ind. pres.* RETROTRAIGO, *pret.* RETROTRAJE; *subj.* RETROTRAIGA) (law) to antedate, date back.
retrovendendo.—contrato de r., (law) reversion sale.
retrovender, *va.* (law); to sell back to the vender. —**retrovendición,** *f.* (law) selling back to the vender.
retroventa, *f.* (law) sale on reversion.
retroversión, *f.* (med.) retroversion.
retrucar, *vn.* (*pret.* RETRUQUÉ; *subj.* RETRUQUE) (billiards) to kiss.—**retruco,** *m.* (billiards) kiss.
retruécano, *m.* pun, play upon words; antithesis, contrast.
retrueno, retruene, *v. V.* RETRONAR.
retruque, *m.* = RETRUCO.
retruqué, retruque, *v. V.* RETRUCAR.
retuerzo, retuerza, *v. V.* RETORCER.
retuesto, retueste, *v. V.* RETOSTAR.
retumbante, *a.* resonant, resounding; pompous, bombastic, high-flown.
retumbar, *vn.* to resound, sound loudly.
retumbo, *m.* resonance, loud noise, echo.
retundir, *va.* (mason.) to even (the stones of a wall); (mason.) to point (joints); (med.) to repel.
retuve, *pret.* of RETENER.
reuma. I. *m.* (med.) rheumatism. **II.** *f.* gathering; rheum, defluxion.—**reumático, ca,** *a.* rheumatic.—**reumátide,** *f.* (med.) rheumides.
reumatismo, *m.* rheumatism.
reunión, *f.* union; meeting, gathering, assembly; consolidation.
reunir. I. *va.* to unite; to gather; to collect, accumulate; to join; to reconcile. **II.** *vr.* to join, to unite; to meet, get together, assemble.
reuntar, *va.* to oil or grease again.
revacunación, *f.* (med.) revaccination.
revacunar, *va.* to revaccinate.
reválida, *f.* admission into a higher faculty.
revalidación, *f.* confirmation, ratification; renewal.
revalidar. I. *va.* to ratify, confirm; to renew. **II.** *vr.* to be admitted into a higher faculty.
revalorar, *va.* to revalue.
revaluación, *f.* revaluation, reappraisal.
revancha, *f.* (Gal.) revenge, retaliation.
revecero, ra. I. *a.* shiftable. **II.** *n.* farmhand who tends relays of oxen.
reveedor, ra, *n.* = REVISOR, reviser; overseer.
revejecer, *vn.* & *vr.* (*ind.* REVEJEZCO; *subj.* REVEJEZCA) to grow old prematurely.
revejido, da, *a.* prematurely old.
revelación, *f.* revelation.
revelador, ra. I. *n.* & *a.* revealer(-ing). **II.** *m.* (photog.) developer.
revelamiento, *m.* REVELACIÓN; (photog.) development.
revelandero, ra, *n.* one who pretends to have had a divine revelation.
revelante, *a.* revealing.
revelar, *va.* to reveal; (photog.) to develop.
reveler, *va.* (med.) to cause revulsion **to.**
revellín, *m.* (fort.) ravelin.
revenar, *vn.* to sprout.
revendedera, *f.* = REVENDEDORA.
revendedor, ra, *n.* retailer; ticket speculator.
revender, *va.* to resell; to retail.
revenimiento, *m.* (min.) cave-in.
revenirse, *vr.* (*ind. pres.* me REVENGO, se REVIENE, *pret.* me REVINE, *fut.* me REVENDRÉ; *subj.* me REVENGA) to shrink, waste away; to turn, grow sour, ferment (as wine and preserves); to exude; to yield, concede, assent.
reveno, *m.* sprout, shoot.
reventa, *f.* resale; retail.
reventadero, *m.* rough ground; drudgery.

reventar. I. *vn.* (*ind.* REVIENTO; *subj.* REVIENTE) to burst; to blow up, blow out; to break; to splash (as waves); to burst forth, break loose (as a passion); to sprout, shoot, blossom; to long, to crave.—**r. de risa,** to burst with laughter. **II.** *va.* to burst; to break; to crush, smash; to wind (a horse); to tire, fatigue, exhaust; to vex, annoy. **III.** *vr.* to burst; to blow up, blow out; to break.
reventazón, *f.* bursting; blowout; disruption, rupture; (naut.) splash, dashing of the waves.
reventón, I. *a.* bursting. **II.** *m.* bursting, blowout, explosion; steep declivity; toil, drudgery, uphill work.
rever, *va.* (*pp.* REVISTO; *ind.* REVEO; *subj.* REVEA) to review, revise, look over again; (law) to retry.
reverberación, *f.* reverberation; (chem.) calcination in a reverberatory furnace.
reverberar, *vn.* to reverberate.
reverbero, *m.* reverberation; reverberator, reflector.
reverdecer, *vn.* (*ind.* REVERDEZCO; *subj.* REVERDEZCA) to grow green again; to sprout again; to acquire new freshness and vigor.
reverdeciente, *a.* growing fresh and green.
reverencia, *f.* reverence; courtsey, bow, obeisance; (eccl.) reverence (title).
reverenciable, *a.* reverend.
reverenciador, ra, *n.* reverencer.
reverencial, *a.* reverential.
reverenciar, *va.* to venerate, revere; to hallow; to reverence.
reverendas, *f. pl.* prelate's dimissory letters; qualities and titles worthy of reverence.
reverendísimo, ma, *a. super.* Most Reverend, Right Reverend.
reverendo, da, *a.* reverend; worthy of reverence.
reverente, *a.* reverent.—**reverentemente,** *adv.* reverently.
reversibilidad, *f.* reversibility.
reversible, *a.* (law) returnable, revertible; (phys.) reversible.
reversión, *f.* reversion.
reverso, *m.* reverse (in coins); back, rear side.—**el r. de la medalla,** the opposite in every respect.
reverter, *vn.* (*ind.* REVIERTE; *subj.* REVIERTA) to overflow.
revertir, *vn.* (law) to revert.
revés, *m.* reverse, back, wrong side; slap, box; backhand slap, shot or stroke; counterstroke; misfortune, reverse; change of temper and disposition; (fencing) reverse.—**r. de la medalla.** V. REVERSO.—**al r.,** on the contrary, contrariwise; in the opposite or wrong way or direction; wrong side out.—**de r.,** diagonally, from left to right.—**del r.** = AL R.
revesa, *f.* (naut.) back water, eddy.
revesado, da, *a.* entangled, complicated, laborious, obscure; mischievous, wayward.
revesar, *va.* to vomit.
revesino, *m.* reversis, a card game.—**cortar el r.,** to thwart.
revestimiento, *m.* (mason.) covering, coat(-ing); finish; sheathing.
revestir. I. *va.* (*ind. pres.* REVISTO, *pret.* REVISTIÓ; *subj.* REVISTA) to dress, clothe, to cover; to line; (fig.) to cloak; (mason.) to coat, cover with a coating, revet. **II.** *vr.* to be swayed or carried along by some power; to be invested with; to be haughty, lofty, proud.
revezar, *vn.* to alternate, work in rotation or by shifts.
revezo, *m.* shift, turn; gang; relay.
reviejo, ja. I. *a.* very old. **II.** *m.* withered branch of a tree.
reviento, reviente, *v. V.* REVENTAR.
reviernes, *m.* each of the first seven Fridays after Easter.
revierte, revierta, *v. V.* REVERTER.
revine, etc. *v. V.* REVENIRSE.
revirado, da, *a.* (bot.) twisted.
revirar, *va.* (naut.) to veer again, retack.
revisado, da, *a.* revised.
revisar, *va.* to revise, review; to re-examine, rehear.—**r. las cuentas,** to audit accounts.
revisión, *f.* revision, revisal, revise, reviewing; re-examination, re-hearing; new trial.
revisita, *f.* reinspection.
revisor, ra. I. *a.* revisory. **II.** *n.* reviser, censor; overseer; auditor; conductor (on train).
revisoría, *f.* office of censor or reviser.
revista, *f.* review, revision, revisal, revise; reinspection, reëxamination; (law) new trial; (mil.) review, parade; muster; review, magazine, journal; (theat.) revue.—**pasar r.,** to review; to examine, go over.—**suplicar en r.,** (law) to present a bill of review.
revistar, *va.* to review, inspect.
revistero, ra, *n.* reviewer; *m.* book reviewer.
[1]**revisto, ta,** *pp. irreg.* of REVER.
[2]**revisto, revista,** *v. V.* REVESTIR.
revitalizar, *va.* to revitalize.
revividero, *m.* place for rearing silkworms.
revivificación, *f.* revivification.
revivificar, *va.* to revivify.
revivir, *vn.* to revive.
revocable, *a.* revocable, reversible, repealable.
revocablemente, *adv.* in a revocable manner.
revocación, *f.* revocation; abrogation.—**r. de una sentencia,** (law) reversal.
revocador, ra. I. *a.* revoking, cancelling. **II.** *n.* revoker; plasterer, whitewasher.
revocadura, *f.* REVOQUE; (art) edge of the canvas turned over the stretcher.
revocante, *a.* revoking, abrogating.
revocar, *va.* (*pret.* REVOQUÉ; *subj.* REVOQUE) to revoke, repeal, reverse; to countermand; to dissuade; to repel, push back; to plaster.
revocatorio, ria, *a.* revocatory, repealing.
revoco, *m.* REVOQUE; drawing or driving back; cover of furze on charcoal baskets.
revolante, *a.* fluttering, hovering.
revolar, *vn.* (*ind.* REVUELA; *subj.* REVUELE) (of birds) to fly around, hover, flutter.
revolcadero, *m.* wallowing place for animals.
revolcadura, *f.* weltering, wallowing.
revolcar. I. *va.* (*ind. pres.* REVUELCO, *pret.* REVOLQUÉ; *subj.* REVUELQUE) to knock down, tread or trample upon; (coll.) to floor (an opponent). **II.** *vr.* to wallow; to be stubborn.
revolcón, *m.* (coll.) = [1]REVUELCO.
revolear, *vn.* to fly around.
revolotear. I. *vn.* to flutter, fly round about, hover. **II.** *va.* to hurl, fling, pitch.
revoloteo, *m.* fluttering; hovering.
revolqué, *pret.* of REVOLCAR.
revoltijo, revoltillo, *m.* mess, mass, medley, jumble; twisted tripes of a sheep.—**r. de huevos,** scrambled eggs.
revoltón, *m.* vine fretter, vine grub.
revoltoso, sa, *a.* turbulent, seditious; mischievous, prankish.
revoltura, *f.* (min.) mixture of fluxes.
revolución, *f.* revolution, revolt; (mech., astr.) revolution, turn.—**revolucionar. I.** *va.* to revolutionize. **II.** *vr.* to rebel, revolt.
revolucionario, ria, *a.* & *n.* revolutionary(-ist).
revolvedero, *m.* = REVOLCADERO.
revolvedor, ra. I. *a.* turbulent, seditious, rebellious. **II.** *n.* revolter, disturber, agitator.
revólver, *m.* (Angl.) revolver (pistol).
revolver. I. *va.* (*pp.* REVUELTO; *ind.* REVUELVO; *subj.* REVUELVA) to turn over, turn upside down; to stir; to agitate; to wrap up, convolve; to revolve, turn round, gyrate; to retrace (one's steps), go over (the same ground); to turn over in one's mind; to turn short swiftly (as a horse); to estrange, create bad feeling in or between. **II.** *vr.* to move to and fro; to change (as the weather).
revolvimiento, *m.* commotion, disturbance, revolution.

revoque, *m.* plastering; whitewashing.
revoqué, revoque, *v. V.* REVOCAR.
revotarse, *vr.* to reconsider a ballot.
[1]**revuelco,** *m.* wallowing, rolling.
[2]**revuelco, revuelque,** *v. V.* REVOLCAR.
revuelo, *m.* second flight of a bird, gyration described when flying; irregular motion; sensation, commotion, stir; disturbance.—**de r.,** by the way; speedily, promptly.
revuelta, *f.* second turn; revolution, revolt; contention, dissension; turn, deviation; change.
revueltamente, *adv.* confusedly, pell-mell, higgledy-piggledy.
revuelto, ta. I. *pp. irreg.* of REVOLVER. **II.** *a.* easily turned (horse); scrambled (eggs); topsy-turvy; restless, mischievous; boisterous; intricate, difficult.
revuelvepiedras, *m.* (ornith.) turnstone.
revuelvo, revuelva, *v. V.* REVOLVER.
revulsión, *f.* (med.) revulsion of humors.
revulsivo, va; revulsorio, ria, *a.* & *m.* revulsive.
rey, *m.* king; king in cards or chess; step in a Spanish dance; queen bee; chief among men or animals.—**r. de armas,** (her.) king at arms.—**los Reyes,** Epiphany, Twelfth-night.—**los reyes magos,** the wise men from the East.—**ni r. ni roque,** no one.—**no tener ni r. ni roque,** not to fear, or bow to, anything nor anybody, to have no master.
reyerta, *f.* dispute, wrangle, quarrel.
reyezuelo, *m.* petty king; (ornith.) kinglet.
rezado, *m.* prayer; divine service.
rezador, ra, *n.* one who prays often.
rezagado, da, *n.* straggler, laggard, tramp.
rezagante, *n.* laggard, straggler.
rezagar. I. *va.* (*pret.* REZAGUÉ; *subj.* REZAGUE) to leave behind; to outstrip; to put off, defer. **II.** *vr.* to fall behind, to lag.
rezago, *m.* remainder, left-over.
rezar. I. *va.* to say as a prayer; to say (a prayer); to say (mass); to say, state (*el libro lo reza,* the book says it). **II.** *vn.* to pray; to say, read (*el párrafo reza así,* the paragraph reads thus); to grumble, mutter.—**r. con,** to concern, be the business or duty of.
rezno, *m.* tick, sheep tick, dog tick.
rezo, *m.* prayer; praying, devotions.
rezón, *m.* (naut.) grapnel, grappling iron.
rezongador, ra, *n.* grumbler, growler, mutterer.
rezongar, *vn.* (*pret.* REZONGUÉ; *subj.* REZONGUE) to grumble, mutter, growl.
rezonglón, na; rezongón, na, *n.* grumbler, mutterer, growler.
rezongo, *m.* grumbling, grumble.
rezumadero, *m.* dripping place; cesspool.
rezumarse, *vr.* to ooze, exude, percolate, filter through; (coll.) to transpire.
rho, *f.* rho (Greek letter).
[1]**ría,** *f.* estuary.
[2]**ría,** *v. V.* REÍR.
riacho, riachuelo, riatillo, *m.* rivulet, streamlet; small river.
riada, *f.* freshet, flood.
riba, *f.* sloping bank, embankment.
ribadoquín, *m.* an ancient small gun.
ribaldería, *f.* knavishness, rascality.
ribaldo, da. I. *a.* villainous, knavish. **II.** *n.* ruffian.
ribazo, *m.* sloping bank; mound, hillock.
ribera, *f.* shore, beach, bank, strand.
ribereño, ña. I. *a.* riparian, riparious. **II.** *n.* riparian.
riberiego, ga. I. *a.* riparious (as flocks of sheep). **II.** *m.* grazer of sheep on river banks.
ribero, *m.* river wall, levee.
ribes, *f.* (bot.) currant bush.
ribete, *m.* (sewing) binding, galloon; trimming; pretense; addition to a tale, for embellishment.
ribeteador, ra, *n.* (sewing) binder.
ribetear, *va.* (sewing) to bind.
riboflavina, *f.* (biochem.) riboflavin, lactoflavin.
ricacho, cha; chón, na, *a.* (coll.) very rich.
ricadueña, ricahembra, *f.* lady, daughter or wife of a noble.
ricahombría, *f.* dignity of the ancient nobility of Castile.
ricamente, *adv.* richly, opulently; excellently, splendidly.
ricé, rice, *v. V.* RIZAR.
ricial, *a.* green (field) or new (pasture).
ricinina, *f.* (chem.) ricinine.
ricino, *m.* (bot.) castor-oil plant, palma Christi; castor oil.
ricinólico, ca, *a.* (chem.) ricinic, ricinoleic.
rico, ca, *a.* rich, wealthy; abundant, plentiful; delicious, exquisite, choice; "cute" (child).
ricohombre, ricohome, *m.* grandee, peer of the ancient nobility of Castile.
richembra, *f.* = RICADUEÑA.
ridículamente, *adv.* ridiculously.
ridiculez, *f.* ridiculous thing or action; ridiculousness; ridicule; folly, oddity, eccentricity; extreme nicety or sensibility.
ridiculizar, *va.* (*pret.* RIDICULICÉ; *subj.* RIDICULICE) to ridicule.
[1]**ridículo, la. I.** *a.* ridiculous; odd, eccentric, queer, outlandish, contemptible; absurd.—**en r.,** in a ridiculous situation, exposed to ridicule. —**poner en r.,** to ridicule, expose to ridicule, make ridiculous.—**ponerse en r., quedar en r.,** to make oneself ridiculous. **II.** *m.* ridicule.
[2]**ridículo,** *m.* handbag, reticule.
[1]**riego,** *m.* irrigation; watering.
[2]**riego, riegue,** *v. V.* REGAR.
riel, *m.* ingot; (Ry.) rail.—**r. acanalado,** groove rail.—**r. americano,** or **Vignole,** T rail.
rielado, da, *a.* reduced to ingots.
rielar, *vn.* to glisten, glimmer, shine.
rielera, *f.* (foundry) ingot mold.
rienda, *f.* rein of a bridle; moderation, restraint. —*pl.* reins, ribbons; government, direction.—**a r. suelta,** loose-reined; violently, swiftly; without restraint.—**dar r. suelta,** to give free rein to.—**soltar la r.,** to give way to vice or passions.—**tener las riendas,** to hold the reins, to hold in a horse.—**tirar las riendas,** to draw back, to restrain.
riente, *a.* smiling, laughing.
riesgo, *m.* danger, risk, hazard, peril.
rifa, *f.* raffle; scuffle, wrangle.
rifador, ra, *n.* raffler.
rifadura, *f.* (naut.) splitting a sail.
rifar. I. *va.* to raffle. **II.** *vn.* to quarrel; (naut.) (of a sail) to split.
rifeño, ña, *n.* & *a.* Riffian (from the Riff, in Morocco).
rifirrafe, *m.* (coll.) short quarrel, hasty words.
rifle, *m.* (Angl.) (artil.) rifle.
riflero, *m.* rifleman.
rigente, *a.* (poet.) rigid.
rígidamente, *adv.* rigidly.
rigidez, *f.* rigidity; sternness.—**r. cadavérica,** rigor mortis, stiffening of body after death.
rígido, da, *a.* rigid, stiff; rigorous, inflexible.
rigió, *pret.* of REGIR.
rigodón, *m.* (dance) rigadoon; quadrille.
rigor, *m.* rigor; sternness; (med.) rigidity; chill.—**r. cadavérico,** = RIGIDEZ CADAVÉRICA.—**de r.,** indispensable; prescribed by the rules.—**en r.,** or **en r. de verdad,** strictly speaking, in fact.
rigorismo, *m.* rigorism, austerity, severity.
rigorista, *n.* & *a.* rigorist(-ic).
rigorosamente, *adv.* rigorously; strictly, scrupulously.
rigoroso, sa, *a.* rigorous; exact; absolute; strict, austere; severe, harsh; scrupulously nice.
rigurosamente, *adv.* = RIGOROSAMENTE.
rigurosidad, *f.* rigorousness; severity.
riguroso, sa, *a.* = RIGOROSO.
[1]**rija,** *f.* (med.) lachrymal fistula.
[2]**rija,** *f.* quarrel, scuffle, dispute.
rijador, ra, *a.* quarrelsome.
[1]**rijo,** *m.* lust, sensuality, concupiscence.

[2]**rijo, rija,** *v. V.* REGIR.
rijoso, sa, *a.* quarrelsome; lustful, lewd; (of horses) restless at the sight of the female.
[1]**rima,** *f.* heap, pile.
[2]**rima,** *f.* rhyme.—*pl.* lyric poems.—**r. imperfecta,** (poet.) assonance.
rimado, da. I. *pp.* of RIMAR. **II.** *a.* versified.
rimador, ra, *n.* versifier, rhymer.
rimar, *vn.* to rhyme; to make verses.
rimbombancia, *f.* resonance, great noise; rant, bombast, ostentation.
rimbombante, *a.* resounding; bombastic, high-sounding, ranting.
rimbombar, *vn.* to resound, to echo.
rimbombe, rimbombo, *m.* repercussion of sound.
rimero, *m.* heap, pile.
rincón, *m.* (inside) corner, angle, nook; cosy corner; lurking place; (coll.) house, dwelling; remote place.—**rinconada,** *f.* corner.
rinconcillo, *m. dim.* small corner.
rinconero, ra. I. *a.* transverse, athwart (honeycombs). **II.** *f.* corner cupboard, stand, bracket.
rindo, rinda, rindió, *v. V.* RENDIR.
ringla, *f.*, **ringle,** *m.*, **ringlera,** *f.* (coll.) row, file, line, tier; swath.
ringlero, *m.* line or rule for writing exercises.
ringorrangos, *m. pl.* (coll.) flourish with a pen; frills, fripperies.
rinitis, *f.* (med.) rhinitis.
rinoceronte, *m.* (zool.) rhinoceros.
rinología, *f.* (med.) rhinology.
rinoplastia, *f.* (surg.) rhinoplasty.
rinoplástico, ca, *a.* (surg.) rhinoplastic.
rinoscopía, *f.* (med.) rhinoscopy.
rinoscopio, *m.* rhinoscope.
riña, *f.* quarrel, scuffle, dispute, fray.
riño, riña, riñó, *v. V.* REÑIR.
riñón, *m.* (anat.) kidney; (arch.) spandrel; (min.) nodule, kidney ore; central part of a country.—**tener cubierto el r.,** to be rich, to be well off.
riñonada, *f.* layer of fat about the kidneys; dish of kidneys.
[1]**río,** *m.* river.—**r. de lágrimas,** flood of tears.—**a r. revuelto,** in confusion or disorder.—**cuando el r. suena, agua lleva,** or **piedras lleva,** where there is so much smoke there must be some fire.
[2]**río, rió, ría,** *v. V.* REÍR.
riolada, *f.* (coll.) concourse, large gathering or collection; heap.
rioplatense, *n.* & *a.* Argentine, Argentinian.
riostra, *f.* stay, brace.—**riostrar,** *va.* to brace, stay.
ripia, *f.* shingle, for roofing.
ripiar, *va.* (mason.) to riprap.
ripio, *m.* debirs, rubbish, riprap; padding, useless words; verbiage.—**no perder r.,** not to miss the least occasion.
riqueza, *f.* riches, wealth; richness, excellence; abundance; fertility, fruitfulness; gorgeousness.—**riquezas naturales,** natural resources.
risa, *f.* laugh, laughter; derisory smile or laugh.—**r. sardónica,** sardonic laugh, grin, sneer.—**caerse, descalzarse, descoyuntarse, desternillarse,** or **reventar, de r.,** to burst, or hold one's sides, with laughter.—**cosa de r.,** a laughing matter.
risada, *f.* horselaugh.
riscal, *m.* cliffy, craggy place.
risco, *m.* crag, cliff; honey fritter.
riscoso, sa, *a.* cliffy, craggy.
risibilidad, *f.* risibility.
risible, *a.* laughable, ludicrous.
risiblemente, *adv.* ludicrously, ridiculously.
risica, illa, ita, *f. dim.* feigned laugh; giggle, titter.
riso, *m.* (poet.) gentle laugh.
risotada, *f.* outburst of laughter, loud laugh, horselaugh.
ríspido, da, *a.* = ÁSPERO, harsh, gruff.
ristra, *f.* string of onions or garlic; bunch; row, file, string.
ristre, *m.* rest or socket for a lance.
ristrel, *m.* (arch.) wooden molding.
risueño, ña, *a.* smiling; pleasing, agreeable.
¡rita! *f.* word used to call sheep.
rítmico, ca, *a.* rhythmic.
ritmo, *m.* rhythm; rate (of increase, etc.).
rito, *m.* rite, ceremony.
ritual. I. *m.* (eccl.) ritual, ceremonial. **II.** *a.* ritual.—**ritualidad,** *f.* ritualism.—**ritualismo,** *m.* ritualism.—**ritualista,** *n.* & *a.* ritualist(-ic).
rival, *m.* rival.—**rivalidad,** *f.* rivalry.
rivalizar, *vn.* (*pret.* RIVALICÉ; *subj.* RIVALICE) to rival, vie, compete.
rivera, *f.* brook, creek, stream.
[1]**riza,** *f.* green stubble.
[2]**riza,** *f.* ravage, destruction.
rizado, da. I. *a.* rugose, curled, curly. **II.** *m.* fluting, crimp, frizzle.
rizador, ra. I. *n.* & *a.* crimper(-ing), frizzler (-ing). **II.** *m.* curling iron; (sewing) ruffler.
rizal, *a.* = RICIAL, green or new (field).
rizar. I. *va.* (*pret.* RICÉ; *subj.* RICE) to curl, frizzle, crimp, flute, ruffle, corrugate, crinkle; to ripple (water). **II.** *vr.* to curl naturally.
rizo, za. I. *a.* naturally curled or frizzled. **II.** *m.* curl, frizzle, ringlet; cut velvet; (aer.) loop.—*pl.* (naut.) reef points.—**hacer el r.,** (aer., coll.) to loop the loop.—**tomar rizos,** to take in reefs.
rizocárpeo, a, *a.* (bot.) rhizocarpous.
rizófago, ga, *a.* (zool.) rhizophagous, root-eating.
rizofóreo, rea, *a.* (bot.) rhizophoraceous.
rizoma, *m.* (bot.) rhizome.
rizópodo, da, *a.* & *m.* (zool.) rhizopod.
rizoso, sa, *a.* naturally curly.
ro, ro, *interj.* used as a lullaby.
roa, *f.* (naut.) = [1]RODA.
roadster, *m.* (Angl.) (auto) roadster.
roano, na, *a.* sorrel, roan (horse).
rob, *m.* (pharm.) fruit jelly or conserve.
robada, *f.* a land measure (about 9 ares).
robadera, *f.* (agr.) levelling harrow.
robador, ra, *n.* robber.
robaliza, *f.* (ichth.) female robalo.
róbalo, robalo, *m.* (ichth.) robalo; (com.) haddock.—**r. ahumado,** finnan haddie.
robar, *va., vn.* & *vr.* to rob, plunder, steal; rob of (*Juan me robó el reloj,* John robbed me of my watch); to abduct; to kidnap; to sweep or eat away (as banks by a stream); in some games, to draw (a card); to take (the honeycomb) after removing the bees.
robda, *f.* ancient pasturage fee.
robezo, *m.* (zool.) wild goat.
robín, *m.* rust of metal.
robinia, *f.* (bot.) locust tree.
robla, *f.* = ROBDA.
robladero, ra, *a.* fit for riveting.
robladura, *f.* riveting, clinching.
roblar, *va.* to rivet, clinch; to make strong.
roble, *m.* (bot.) oak; (fig.) very strong person.—**r. negro,** (bot.) black oak.
robledal, robledo, *m.* oak grove or wood.
roblizo, za, *a.* oaken, strong, hard.
roblón, *m.* rivet; ridge of tiles.—**roblonado,** *m.*, **roblonadura,** *f.* riveting.
roblonar, *va.* & *vn.* to rivet.
[1]**robo,** *m.* robbery, theft; plunder; cards drawn; drawing of cards.
[2]**robo,** *m.* a dry measure (about 28 liters).
roboración, *f.* corroboration, strengthening.
roborante, *a.* strengthening, corroborating, or confirming; (med.) roborant.
roborar, *va.* to strengthen, make firm; to corroborate.
roborativo, va, *a.* corroborative.
robot, *m.* robot.
robra, *f.* = ALBOROQUE, treat to seal a bargain.
robre, robredo, *m.* = ROBLE, ROBLEDAL.
robustamente, *adv.* robustly.
robustecedor, ra, *a.* strengthening, building-up.

robustecer, *va.* (*ind.* ROBUSTEZCO; *subj.* ROBUSTEZCA) *va.* to make strong.
robustez, *f.* robustness, hardiness.
robusto, ta, *a.* robust, vigorous, hale.
roca, *f.* (geol.) rock; cliff.
rocadero, *m.* knob, rock or head of a distaff.
rocador, *m.* head of a distaff.
rocalla, *f.* drift of pebbles, talus of rocks; chippings of stone, riprap; glass beads.
rocalloso, sa, *a.* rocky.
roce, *m.* friction, rubbing, attrition; intercourse.
rocé, roce, *v. V.* ROZAR.
rociada, *f.* sprinkling, aspersion; (naut.) spray, splash; squall; dew on plants; dew-drenched herbs given to animals as medicine; shower of missiles; slander, aspersion; harsh reprimand.
rociadera, *f.* watering pot; irrigation ditch.
rociado, da. I. *pp.* of ROCIAR. **II.** *a.* dewy; bedewed.
rociador, *m.* sprinkler, sprayer; cloth sprinkler.
rociadura, *f.* = ROCIADA.
rociamiento, *m.* bedewing.
rociar. I. *vn.* to fall in dew. **II.** *va.* to sprinkle, to spray; to strew about.
rocín, *m.* hack, jade, sorry horse; coarse, ignorant man.—**rocinal,** *a.* pertaining to a hack horse.—**rocinante,** *m.*, **rocino,** *m.* = ROCÍN.
rocío, *m.* dew; spray, sprinkle, sprinkling; mizzle, drizzle; light shower; (naut.) spoondrift.
rococó, *a.* & *m.* (f. a.) rococo.
rocoso, sa, *a.* rocky.
rocha, *f.* ground clear of brambles.
rochela, *f.* (Colomb., Venez.) great noise, racket.
rocho, *m.* roc, a fabulous bird.
[1]**roda,** *f.* (naut.) stem.
[2]**roda,** *f.* = ROBDA.
rodaballo, *m.* (ichth.) turbot, flounder.
rodada, *f.* rut, wheel track, cart track.
rodadero, ra, *a.* rolling easily.
rodadizo, za, *a.* that rolls or slides easily.
[1]**rodado, da. I.** *pp.* of RODAR. **II.** *a.* rounded, fluent, easy (phrase); (min.); scattered (ore fragments).—**venir r.,** to come unexpectedly.
[2]**rodado, da. I.** *a.* dapple, dappled (horse). **II.** *m.* (Arg.) vehicle.
rodador, ra. I. *a.* rolling, rolling down. **II.** *m.* roller; kind of mosquito; (ichth.) sunfish.
rodadura, *f.* rolling, wheeling; rut; tread (of a wheel).
rodaja, *f.* small wheel or disk; caster, trundle, truckle; rowel; jagging iron used by pastry cooks; bookbinder's tool.
rodaje, *m.* wheelworks; set of wheels.
rodajuela, *f. dim.* small wheel, disk, or caster.
rodal, *m.* place, spot, seat.
rodante, *a.* rolling.—**material r.,** rolling stock.
rodapelo, *m.* rubbing against the grain.
rodapié, *m.* (arch.) mopboard, skirting; dado; foot rail.
rodaplancha, *f.* main ward of a key.
rodar, *vn.* (*ind.* RUEDO; *subj.* RUEDE) to roll; to revolve, wheel; to run on wheels; to wander about; be tossed about, go about, go up and down; to lose an employ, station, dignity, or esteem; to abound; to happen accidentally; to follow, succeed one another.—**r. por,** to serve, help to the limit.—**r. una película,** to shoot a movie.—**dejar r.,** or **que ruede, la bola,** to let things alone, to let things follow their natural course.
rodeabrazo.—**a r.,** swinging the arm for a throw.
rodeado, da, *a.* & *pp.* surrounded, encircled.
rodeador, ra, *n.* one who surrounds.
rodear. I. *va.* & *vn.* to surround, encircle, encompass; (mil.) to invest; (Am.) to round up, gather (cattle) in a rodeo. **II.** *vn.* to go around; to make a detour; to beat about the bush.
rodela, *f.* buckler, round shield.
rodelero, *m.* soldier bearing a buckler.
rodenal, *m.* clump of red pines.
rodeno, na, *a.* (of rocks and trees), red, reddish.
rodeo, *m.* turn, winding; roundabout course, method or way; round-up, rodeo; inclosure for cattle, stockyard, corral; circumlocution, beating about the bush; evasion, subterfuge.
rodeón, *m.* complete turn.
rodera, *f.* rut, cart track.
[1]**rodero, ra,** *a.* pertaining to wheels.
[2]**rodero,** *m.* collector of pasturage fee.
rodete, *m.* roundlet or rowel of platted hair; (hydraul.) horizontal water wheel; (carriage) fifth wheel, circle iron; ward in a lock; padded ring for carrying things on the head; (mech.) drum for a belt or endless chain.
rodezno, *m.* (hydraul.) horizontal water wheel. (mil.) cogwheel.
rodezuela, *f. dim.* small wheel.
ródico, ca, *a.* (chem.) rhodic.
rodilla, *f.* (anat.) knee; ward in a lock; cleaning cloth.—*pl.* (naut.) knees of ship timber.—**a media r.,** kneeling on one knee.—**de rodillas,** on one's knees.—**doblar,** or **hincar, las rodillas,** to kneel down.
rodillada, *f.* push with the knee; kneeling position.
rodillazo, *m.* push or blow with the knee.
rodillera, *f.* knee boss, knee guard; knee patch; hurt upon the knees of horses from kneeling; bagging of trousers at the knee.
rodillero, ra, *a.* pertaining to the knees.
rodillo, *m.* roll, roller; clod crusher, road roller; (print.) inking roller, brayer; (cook.) rolling pin; (mech.) roller, drum, trundle, barrel.
rodilludo, da, *a.* having large knees.
[1]**rodio,** *m.* (chem.) rhodium.
[2]**rodio, dia,** *n.* & *a.* Rhodian.
rodo, *m.* roller.—**a r.,** in plenty.
rododafne, *f.* (bot.) rosebay, daphne.
rododendro, *m.* (bot.) rhododendron.
rodofíceo, cea, *a.* (bot.) rhodophyceous.
rodomiel, *m.* juice of roses with honey.
rodrigar, *va.* (*pret.* RODRIGUÉ; *subj.* RODRIGUE) to prop up (vines).
rodrigazón, *f.* time for propping vines.
rodrigón, *m.* vine prop; (coll.) old servant who escorts ladies.
roedor, ra. I. *a.* gnawing; pricking, stinging; detracting. **II.** *n.* & *a.* (zool.) rodent.
roedura, *f.* gnawing, corrosion.
roel, *m.* (her.) bezant, round.
roela, *f.* button of crude gold or silver.
roentgen, *m.* (phys.) roentgen.
roer, *va.* & *defect.* (*ger.* ROYENDO; *ind. pres.* ROO; *pret.* él ROYÓ; *subj.* ROA) to gnaw, eat, fret away; to corrode; to pick (a bone); to harass, annoy
roete, *m.* medicinal pomegranate wine.
rogación, *f.* request, petition.—*pl.* (eccl.) rogation.
rogador, ra, *n.* supplicant, petitioner.
rogante, *a.* praying, requesting, entreating.
rogar, *va.* (*ind. pres.* RUEGO, *pret.* ROGUÉ; *subj.* RUEGUE) to request, beg, entreat; to crave.
rogativo, va. I. *a.* supplicatory. **II.** *f.* (eccl.) rogation.
rogatorio, ria, *a.* rogatory.
rogo, *m.* (poet.) fire, pyre.
rogué, *pret.* of ROGAR.
roído, da. I. *pp.* of ROER. **II.** *a.* penurious.
rojeante, *a.* reddening.
rojear, *vn.* to redden; to blush.
rojete, *m.* rouge (for make-up).
rojez, *f.* redness, ruddiness.
rojizo, za, *a.* reddish; rubicund, ruddy.
rojo, ja. I. *a.* red, ruddy, reddish.—**r. alambrado,** bright red.—**al r.,** at red heat, red hot. **II.** *n.* (fig.) Red, communist.
rojura, *f.* redness; ruddiness.
rol, *m.* list, roll, catalogue; muster roll.
rolar, *vn.* (naut.) to veer around.
roldana, *f.* sheave, pulley wheel; caster.
rolde, *m.* circle, group of people.
[1]**rolla,** *f.* collar of a draught horse.
[2]**rolla,** *f.* (child's) nurse.
rollar, *va.* = ARROLLAR, to roll; to wrap.
rollete, *m. dim.* small roll or roller.

rollizo, za. I. *a.* plump, stocky, heavy-built, sturdy. **II.** *m.* log.
rollo, *m.* roll, anything rolled up; rouleau; roller, rolling pin; log; round pillar; cylindrical bowlder; yoke pad; (law) roll.
rollón, *m.* fine bran.
rollona, *a.* (coll.) (child's) nurse.
Roma, *f.* Rome.—**a R. por todo,** at all hazards.
romadizarse, *vr.* to take cold.
romadizo, *m.* cold in the head; hay fever.
romaico, ca, *a.* & *n.* Romaic, modern Greek.
romana, *f.* steelyard.—**hacer r.,** to balance.—**venir a la r.,** to be of just weight.
romanador, *m.* weighmaster.
romanar, *va.* to weigh with a steelyard.
romance. I. *a.* & *m.* Romance or Romanic. **II.** *m.* Spanish language; romance, tale of chivalry; historic ballad, brief lyric; poem in octosyllabic metre, with alternate assonants.—**en r.,** in plain English, or language.
romanceador, ra, *n.* one who writes in Romance.
romancear, *va.* to translate into Spanish; to paraphrase.
romancero, ra. I. *n.* romancer. **II.** *m.* collection of old Spanish ballads.
romancesco, *a.* novelistic, romantic.
romancillo, *m. dim.* short ROMANCE.
romancista, *m.* one writing in a Romance language; novelist.
romanear. I. *va.* to weigh with a steelyard. **II.** *vn.* to outweigh, preponderate.
romaneo, *m.* weighing with a steelyard.
romanero, *m.* weighmaster.
romanesco, ca, *a.* Roman; novelistic.
romanía, used in the expression **de romanía,** crestfallen.
románico, ca, *a.* (arch.) romanesque.
romanilla, *f.* (Venez.) dining-room screen.
romanillo, lla, *a.* round-hand.
romanista, *n.* one versed in Roman law or in Romance languages.
romanización, *f.* Romanization.
romanizar. I. *va.* to Romanize; to Latinize. **II.** *vr.* to become Romanized or Latinized.
romano, na, *n.* & *a.* Roman.
romanticismo, *m.* romanticism.
romántico, ca, *a.* & *n.* romantic(-ist).
romanza, *f.* (mus.) romance, romanza.
romanzador, ra, *n.* = ROMANCEADOR.
romanzar, *va.* = ROMANCEAR.
romaza, *f.* (bot.) sorrel.
rombal; rómbico, ca, *a.* rhombic.
rombo, *m.* (geom.) rhombus; lozenge, diamond.
romboedro, *m.* (geom.) rhombohedron.
romboidal, *a.* rhomboidal.
romboide, *m.* (geom.) rhomboid.
romeraje, *m.* = ROMERÍA.
romeral, *m.* place abounding with rosemary.
romería, *f.* pilgrimage; picnic, excursion; tour.
[1]**romero, ra. I.** *n.* pilgrm, palmer. **II.** *m.* (ichth.) pilot fish; (ichth.) whiting.
[2]**romero,** *m.* (bot.) rosemary.
romí, romín, *m.* bastard saffron.
romo, ma, *a.* obtuse, blunt; flat-nosed.
rompecabezas, *m.* slingshot; puzzle, riddle.
rompecoches, *m.* a kind of rough, thick cloth.
rompedera, *f.* large iron puncher; powder screen.
rompedero, ra, *a.* fragile, brittle, perishable.
rompedor, ra, *n.* & *a.* breaker(-ing); crusher (-ing).
rompedura, *f.* breakage.
rompeesquinas, *m.* corner loafer, bully.
rompegalas, *n.* (coll.) slovenly person.
rompehielos, *m.* ice breaker; ice plow (of a boat).
rompehuelgas, *n.* strikebreaker, (coll.) fink.
rompenueces, *m.* nut cracker.
rompeolas, *m.* breakwater, jetty, mole.
romper. I. *va.* & *vn.* (*pp.* ROTO) to break, smash, shatter; to fracture (bone); to tear; to defeat, rout; to break up (land); to pierce; to open the way; to break off; to fall out, quarrel; (of the day) to dawn; to begin, start; to interrupt; to resolve, determine; to sprout, bloom; to break out, spring up; (of light, sun, etc.) to break through; to break, infringe, transgress (a law, etc.).—**r. el alba,** or **la aurora** (here *el alba, la aurora* are subjects of the verb) to dawn.—**de rompe y rasga,** undaunted, brave, free and easy. **II.** *vr.* to break; to acquire ease of manner.—**r. el alma,** to break one's neck in a fall.—**r. la cabeza,** to rack one's brains.
rompesacos, *m.* long-spiked hardgrass.
rompesquinas, *m.* = ROMPEESQUINAS.
rompible, *a.* breakable.
rompido, da, *m.* ground newly broken.
rompiente. I. *a.* breaking. **II.** *m.* reef, shoal; breaker (wave).
rompimiento, *m.* break, breakage, smash, rupture; crack; breach, infringement, violation; falling out; (theat.) open drop scene; opening in the background (of a picture); (min.) drift, driftway; (agr.) breaking up land.
ron, *m.* rum.
[1]**ronca,** *f.* cry of a buck in rutting time; braggadocio, bullying.
[2]**ronca,** *f.* a kind of halberd.
roncador, ra. I. *n.* & *a.* snorer(-ing); RONCÓN. **II.** *m.* (ichth.) roncador, little bass.
roncamente, *adv.* hoarsely, coarsely.
roncar, *vn.* (*pret.* RONQUÉ; *subj.* RONQUE) to snore; to roar; to cry in rutting time; (coll.) to brag, to bully.
ronce, *m.* wheedle, cajolery.
roncear, *vn.* to be slow and unwilling, kill time, fool around; to wheedle; (naut.) to sail slowly.
roncería, *f.* sluggishness, remissness; tardiness; wheedle, cajoling expression; (naut.) slow, sluggish sailing.
roncero, ra, *a.* slow, slothful, tardy; grouchy, growling; flattering, wheedling, cajoling.
ronco, ca, *a.* hoarse, raucous.
roncón. I. *m.* drone of a bagpipe. **II.** *n.* & *a.* (Colomb.) (coll.) boaster(-ing), braggart.
[1]**roncha,** *f.* welt; wheal, whelk; blotch; bump; loss of money through trickery.
[2]**roncha,** *f.* round, thin slice.
[1]**ronchar,** *vn.* to raise welts.
[2]**ronchar,** *va.* to crunch.
ronchón, *m. aug.* large welt or bump.
ronda, *f.* night patrol; rounds (by a night watch), beat; clear space between a town and its walls; last round in a card game; round of drinks or cigars.
rondador, *m.* patrolman, roundsman, watchmen; rounder, night wanderer.
rondalla, *f.* fable, story, tale.
rondar, *va.* & *vn.* to patrol, go the rounds; to walk the streets by night; to haunt, hover about; to impend; (mil.) to make the grand rounds.—**r. la calle,** to flirt on the street.
rondel, *m.* (poet.) rondel.
rondeña, *f.* popular ballad of Ronda.
rondín, *m.* round of a corporal on the walls to visit the sentinels; watchman in an arsenal.
rondís, rondiz, *m.* face of a precious stone.
rondó, *m.* (mus.) rondo.
rondón.—de r., rashly, suddenly, abruptly; intrepidly.
rongigata, *f.* = REHILANDERA, pinwheel.
ronqué, ronque, *v. V.* RONCAR.
ronquear, *vn.* to be hoarse with cold.
ronquedad, ronquera, ronquez, *f.* hoarseness.
ronquido, *m.* snore; harsh, raucous sound.
ronronear, *vn.* to purr.
ronza, *f.*—**ir a la r.,** (naut.) to fall to leeward.
ronzal, *m.* halter; (naut.) purchase rope.
[1]**ronzar,** *va.* to crunch, craunch.
[2]**ronzar,** *va.* (naut.) to raise or shift with levers.
roña, *f.* scab (in sheep); crust of filth on persons; bark of pine trees; rust; moral infection.
roñada, *f.* (naut.) garland; dolphin of a mast.
roñal, *m.* bark depot or storage place.
roñería, *f.* (coll.) niggardliness; stinginess.
roñoso, sa, *a.* scabby, leprous; dirty, filthy; rusty; (coll.) niggardly, stingy.
ropa, *f.* dry goods; stuff, fabric; wearing apparel,

clothes, clothing; costume, dress; wardrobe, outfit, garments; robe or gown of office.—**r. blanca,** linen.—**r. de cámara,** or **de levantar,** dressing gown.—**r. hecha,** ready-made clothing.—**r. limpia,** clean laundry.—**r. sucia,** soiled laundry.—**r. talar,** long, loose gown.—**r. vieja,** cast-off clothes; (cook.) boiled meat, afterwards fried in a pan.—**a quema r.,** at close range, point-blank; suddenly, unexpectedly.—**nadar y guardar la r.,** to be extra cautious in an undertaking.—**tentarse la r.,** to consider carefully.
ropaje, *m.* wearing apparel, clothes; robe, vestments; gown; garb; (art) drapery.
ropálico, ca, *a.* (poet.) rhopalic.
ropavejería, *f.* old-clothes shop.
ropavejero, *m.* old-clothes man.
ropería, *f.* clothier's trade; clothing shop, clothier's; wardrobe, clothes room, cloakroom; wardrobe keeper.
ropero, ra. I. *n.* clothier, dealer in clothes; wardrobe keeper; head shepherd, dairyman. **II.** *m.* clothespress, closet, wardrobe, locker.
ropeta, ropilla, *f. dim.* doublet, close-fitting jacket.—**dar una r.,** to give a friendly reproof.
ropita, *f. dim.* child's clothing.
ropón, *m.* wide, loose gown.
roque, *m.* rook, castle (at chess).
roqueda, *f.,* **roquedal,** *m.* rocky place.
roquedo, *m.* rock, boulder.
roqueño, ña, *a.* rocky, hard, flinty.
roquero, ra, *a.* rocky; built on rocks.
roqués, *a.* black (falcon).
roqueta, *f.* turret in a fortress.
roquete, *m.* (eccl.) rochet; barbed spearhead; (artil.) ramrod, rammer.
rorcual, *m.* (zool.) rorqual, finback (variety of large whales).
rorro, *m.* (coll.) babe in arms.
ros, *m.* (mil.) Spanish shako.
rosa, *f.* (bot.) rose; red spot on any part of the body; rose diamond; rosette; rosy aspect; rose color; flower of saffron; artificial rose.—**r. náutica,** or **de los vientos,** (naut.) traverse board, mariner's compass.
rosáceo, cea, *a.* (bot.) rosaceous.
rosada, *f.* frost.
rosadelfa, *f.* (bot.) = AZALEA, azalea.
rosado, da, *a.* rose-colored; rose (as *a.*).
rosal, *m.* rose bush or plant.—**r. de pitimaní,** climbing rose.—**r. perruno,** or **silvestre,** dog-rose.
rosaleda, *f.* rosary, rose garden.
rosanilina, *f.* (chem.) rosaniline.
rosariero, ra, *n.* maker and seller of rosaries.
rosario, *m.* rosary (beads for praying and series of prayers); assemblage of people who recite the rosary in procession; (hydraul.) chain pump; (coll.) backbone.—**acabar como el r. de la aurora,** to break up in disorder.
rosarse, *vr.* = SONROSEARSE, to blush.
rosbif, *m.* (Angl.) roast beef.
rosca, *f.* screw and nut; screw thread; twist, spiral line or motion; circular badge of Spanish students; ring-shaped biscuit or bread; (naut.) flake of a cable.—**hacer la r.,** to flatter, kowtow.
roscado, da. I. *pp.* of ROSCAR. **II.** *a.* threaded, having a screw thread.
roscar. I. *va.* to thread, make or cut a screw thread on. **II.** *vn.* to cut screw threads, to make screws.—**máquina de r.,** screw-cutting machine.
roscón, *m. aug.* large screw; large circular loaf of bread.
rosear, *vn.* to turn rose color.
róseo, sea, *a.* rosy, roseate.
roséola, *f.* (med.) roseola, rose rash.
rosero, ra, *n.* gatherer of saffron flowers.
roseta, *f. dim.* small rose; rosette; rosy cheek; (metal.) rosette copper.
rosetón, *m. aug.* large rosette; (arch.) rose-window; rosette.
rosicler, *m.* rose pink (color); roset; ruby silver.
rosillo, illa, *a.* light red, roan.
[1]**rosmarino, na,** *a.* light red.
[2]**rosmarino,** *m.* (bot.) = ROMERO, rosemary.
rosmaro, *m.* (zool.) walrus.
[1]**roso, sa,** *a.* threadbare.—**a r. y velloso,** totally, without exception or distinction.
[2]**roso, sa,** *a.* red, rosy.
rosoli, *m.* rosolio, sundew (a liqueur).
rosones, *m. pl.* worms in animals.
rosqueado, da, *a.* twisted.
rosquete, *m.* ring-shaped cake or biscuit.
rosquilla, *f.* ring-shaped fancy cake; vine fretter.
rostrado, da, *a.* rostrate, with beaklike projection.
rostral, *a.* = ROSTRADO.
rostrillo, *m.* headdress on images; small seed pearl.
rostritorcido, da; rostrituerto, ta, *a.* (coll.) angry-looking; sad-looking.
rostro, *m.* rostrum, beak of a ship; bill or beak of a bird; countenance, human face; aspect of affairs.—**r. a r.,** face to face.—**hacer r. a,** to face.
[1]**rota,** *f.* (mil.) rout, defeat.—**de r.,** or **de r. batida,** of a sudden; with total ruin.
[2]**rota,** *f.* (Rom. Cath.) ecclesiastical tribunal, Rota.
[3]**rota,** *f.* (bot.) rattan.
rotación, *f.* rotation.—**r. de cultivos,** rotation of crops.
rotal, *a.* pertaining to the Rota.
rotamente, *adv.* impudently, barefacedly.
rotante, *a.* rotating, revolving.
rotar, *vn.* = RODAR, to roll, revolve; to roam.
rotario, ria, *a.* & *m.* Rotarian.
rotarismo, *m.* Rotarianism.
rotativo, va. I. *a.* rotary, revolving. **II.** *f.* rotary printing press.
rotatorio, ria, *a.* rotary, rotating.
roten, *m.* (bot.) rattan; rattan walking cane.
rotífero, ra. I. *a.* (zool.) rotiferous, rotiferal. **II.** *m.* (zool.) rotifer.
rotiforme, *a.* (bot., zool.) rotiform.
roto, ta. I. *pp. irreg.* of ROMPER. **II.** *a.* broken, chipped, shattered; torn; ragged; destroyed; leaky, battered, or pierced; debauched, lewd. **III.** *m.* (Am.) tear (in clothes); poor, ragged man.
rotograbado, *m.* (print.) rotogravure.
rotonda, *f.* rotunda.
rotor, *m.* (elec., hydraul.) rotor.
rótula, *f.* (anat.) rotula, kneepan; (pharm.) troche, lozenge.
rotulación, *f.* labeling.
rotulador, ra, *n.* & *a.* labeler(-ing).
rotular, *va.* to label; put a title to.
rotulata, *f.* label, title, mark; collection of labels or posters.
rótulo, *m.* label, mark; show bill, poster, show card, placard; sign; (eccl.) certificate for beatification; school rota.
rotunda, *f.* rotunda; (Ry.) roundhouse.
rotundamente, *adv.* explicitly, categorically peremptorily.
rotundidad, *f.* roundness, rotundity.
rotundo, da, *a.* round, circular, rotund; (of voice) full, sonorous; plain, peremptory.
rotura, *f.* rupture, fracture; breakage; (agr.) breaking up ground; (vet.) poultice.
roturación, *f.* (agr.) breaking up new ground.
roturar, *va.* (agr.) to break up (new ground).
roya, *f.* (bot.) rust, mildew, red blight.
royo, royó, etc. *v. V.* ROER.
roza, *f.* (agr.) stubbing, grubbing, clearing; ground cleared of brambles.
rozadero, *m.* stubbing place; (mech.) bearing plate, friction plate.
rozado, da. I. *pp.* of ROZAR. **II.** *a.* (agr.) stubbed, cleared; chilled, frappé (beverage).
rozador, ra, *n.* stubber, weeder.
rozadura, *f.* friction; frication; attrition; gall, chafing; chafed spot; (bot.) punk knot.
rozagante, *a.* pompous, showy; trailing on the ground (as a gown).

rozamiento, *m.* (mech.) friction; frication; rubbing; clashing, disagreement.
rozar. I. *va.* (*pret.* ROCÉ; *subj.* ROCE) to stub, grub, clear (the ground); to nibble (the grass); to scrape or pare off; to gall, to chafe; to graze, pass lightly over. **II.** *vn.* to graze, rub. **III.** *vr.* (of horses' hoofs) to interfere; to be on intimate terms; to falter, to stammer; to have a resemblance or connection with something else; to have to do with, associate; (naut.) to fret, to gall.
[1]**roznar,** *vn.* = [1]RONZAR, to crunch.
[2]**roznar,** *vn.* = REBUZNAR, to bray.
[1]**roznido,** *m.* crunching noise.
[2]**roznido,** *m.* braying of a donkey.
rozno, *m.* little donkey.
rozo, *m.* stubbing, weeding; brushwood.
rozón, *m.* short and broad scythe.
rúa, *f.* village street; highroad.
ruán, *m.* linen manufactured in Rouen.
ruana, *f.* (Am.) a square, heavy poncho.
Ruanda, *m.* Rwanda.
[1]**ruano, na,** *a.* = ROANO, roan (horse).
[2]**ruano, na,** *a.* round, circular.
ruante, *a.* walking or riding through the streets.
ruar, *vn.* to walk or ride through the streets; to flirt in the street.
rubefacción, *f.* (med.) rubefaction.
rubefaciente, *a.* & *m.* (med.) rubefacient.
rúbeo, ea, *a.* ruby, reddish.
rubéola, *f.* (med.) measles.
ruberoide, *m.* a tarred-pasteboard roofing material.
rubescencia, *f.* rosiness.
rubescente, *a.* rosy.
rubeta, *f.* toad.
rubí, *m.* ruby; red color; redness of the lips.—**r. de Bohemia,** rosy quartz.—**r. del Brazil,** red topaz.—**r. espinela,** spinel ruby.
[1]**rubia,** *f.* (bot.) madder.
[2]**rubia,** *f.* a blonde; (ichth.) a small red-colored river fish.
rubiáceo, cea, *a.* (bot.) rubiaceous.
rubial. I. *a.* reddish (soil or plants). **II.** *m.* madder field.
rubicán, na, *a.* roan (horse).
rubicela, *f.* reddish-yellow topaz.
rubicundez, *f.* ruddiness; rosiness.
rubicundo, da, *a.* reddish, rubicund; golden-red; blond; rosy with health.
rubidio, *m.* (chem.) rubidium.
rubiera, *f.* (Venez.) mischief, reckless action; (C. A.) merrymaking, carousal.
rubificado, da, *a.* rubied.
rubificar, *va.* to rubify, make red.
rubiginoso, sa, *a.* rubiginous.
rubín, rubinejo, *m.* ruby.
rubio, bia. I. *a.* blond, golden, fair. **II.** *m.* (ichth.) red gurnard.
rubión, *a.* (of a kind of wheat) reddish.
rublo, *m.* ruble, Russian silver coin.
rubor, *m.* blush, flush; bashfulness.
ruborizarse, *vr.* to blush, to flush.
ruborosamente, *adv.* blushingly, bashfully.
ruboroso, sa, *a.* bashful.
rúbrica, *f.* red mark or caption, title; mark or flourish added to one's signature; (eccl.) rubric or rules in prayer books.—**de r.,** according to rules or custom.
rubricante. I. *a.* signing, attesting. **II.** *m.* junior minister or secretary appointed to sign the proceedings.
rubricar, *va.* (*pret.* RUBRIQUÉ; *subj.* RUBRIQUE) to sign or indorse with one's peculiar mark or flourish, without writing the name; to sign and seal.
rubriquista, *m.* (eccl.) rubrician.
rubro, bra, *a.* red, reddish; rubric.
ruc, *m.* = ROCHO, roc, a fabulous bird.
ruca, *f.* (Chile, Arg.) hut, cabin.
rucio, cia. I. *a.* (of animals) light silver gray; (Colomb.) dapple-gray; (coll.) gray; gray-haired, hoary. **II.** *m.* donkey.
ruco, ca, *a.* (C. A.) old, worthless.
rucho, *m.* donkey.
ruda, *f.* (bot.) rue.
rudamente, *adv.* rudely, roughly.
rudeza, *f.* roughness, rudeness, coarseness.
rudimental, *a.* rudimentary; elementary.
rudimentario, ria, *a.* rudimentary.
rudimento, *m.* rudiment, embryo, germ; vestige. —*pl.* rudiments, elements.
rudo, da, *a.* rude, rough, unpolished; hard, rigorous, severe; stupid.
rueca, *f.* distaff for spinning; twist, winding; (naut.) fish of a mast or yard.
rueda, *f.* wheel; caster, roller; circle of persons; crowd; round slice; turn, time, succession; (ichth.) sunfish; rack (torture); hoops for skirts; spread of a peacock's tail; three-handed billiard game.—**r. catalina,** or **de Santa Catalina,** Catherine wheel.—**r. de alimentación por abajo, (arriba)** (hydraul.) undershot (overshot) wheel.—**r. de andar,** treadmill.—**r. de costado,** breast wheel.—**r. de esmeril,** emery wheel.—**r. del timón,** (naut.) steering wheel. —**r. dentada** or **de engranaje,** gearwheel.—**r. de molino,** mill wheel.—**r. hidráulica,** water wheel.—**hacer la r.,** to cajole, wheedle. —**hacer la r.,** to cajole, wheedle.
ruedecica, cilla, zuela, *f. dim.* small wheel; caster, roller.
[1]**ruedo,** *m.* rotation, turn; circuit; circumference; edge of a wheel or disk; round plat or mat; rug; (sewing) skirt lining; bottom of a skirt; valance. —**a todo r.,** at all events.
[2]**ruedo, ruede,** *v. V.* RODAR.
[1]**ruego,** *m.* request, plea, petition, entreaty, supplication.
[2]**ruego, ruegue,** *v. V.* ROGAR.
ruejo, *m.* mill wheel; ground roller.
ruello, *m.* (agr.) ground roller.
ruequecilla, *f.* small distaff.
rufián, *m.* ruffian; pimp, pander.—**rufianada,** *f.* (Am.) villainy, villainous or base act.
rufianear, *vn.* to play the ruffian; to pimp, to pander.
rufianería, *f.* ruffianism.
rufianesco, ca. I. *a.* ruffianly, ruffianish. **II.** *f.* ruffians (collect.); gang of ruffians; ruffianism.
rufianismo, *m.* rowdyism.
rufo, fa, *a.* carroty, red-haired; frizzed, curled.
ruga, *f.* wrinkle.—**rugar,** *va.* to wrinkle.
rugible, *a.* capable of bellowing or roaring.
rugido, *m.* roar; rumbling in the bowels.
rugiente, *a.* bellowing, roaring.
ruginoso, sa, *a.* rusty.
rugir. I. *vn.* (*ind.* RUJO; *subj.* RUJA) to roar, bellow, howl. **II.** *v. impers.* to be whispered about, to transpire, to be said.
rugosidad, *f.* rugosity, wrinkled condition.
rugoso, sa, *a.* rugose, corrugated, wrinkled.
ruibarbo, *m.* (bot.) rhubarb.
ruido, *m.* noise; rumor; report; discussion; dispute, difference; law suit.—**hacer,** or **meter, r.,** to attract attention; to create a sensation. —**mucho r. y pocas nueces,** or **ser más el r. que las nueces,** much ado about nothing.
ruidosamente, *adv.* noisily; loudly.
ruidoso, sa, *a.* noisy, loud; clamorous.
ruin. I. *a.* mean, vile, low, base, despicable; little, puny; decayed; wicked, malicious; niggardly, stingy; insidious, treacherous, infamous; (of an animal) vicious. **II.** *m.* wicked, mean, or vile man; small nerve in the tail of cats.
ruina, *f.* ruin, decline, downfall; overthrow, fall. —*pl.* ruins, débris.—**batir en r.,** (mil.) to batter in, breach.
ruinar, *va.* & *vr.* to ruin, destroy.
ruindad, *f.* meanness, baseness; ill turn, base action.
ruinmente, *adv.* basely, meanly, despicably.
ruinoso, sa, *a.* ruinous; worthless.
ruiponce, *m.* (bot.) = RAPÓNCHIGO, rampion.
ruipóntico, *m.* (bot.) rhubarb, pieplant.
ruiseñor, *m.* (ornith.) nightingale.
rujada, *f.* heavy shower.

rujo, ruja, *v. V.* RUGIR.
rular, *vn.* = RODAR, to roll, revolve.
ruleta, *f.* roulette.
rulo, *m.* ball, bowl; conical stone in oil mills; road roller.
ruló, *m.* (print.) ink roller, brayer.
Rumania, *f.* Romania, Rumania.
rumano, na, *n.* & *a.* Rumanian.
rumba, *f.* (Cuba) rumba (dance or music for it).
rumbadas, *f. pl.* (naut.) = ARRUMBADAS, wales.
rumbo, *m.* bearing, course, direction; trend; road, route, way; (coll.) pomp, ostentation; liberality, generosity; (naut.) scuttle; (her.) rustre.—**abatir el r.,** (naut.) to fall to leeward. —**con r. a,** (naut.) in the direction of; heading, or sailing, for.—**fiesto de r.,** lavish party.—**hacer r. a,** (naut.) to sail for; to head for.
rumbón, na, *a.* = RUMBOSO.
rumbosamente, *adv.* (coll.) pompously, grandly, liberally.
rumboso, sa, *a.* pompous, magnificent, liberal.
rumen, *m.* (zool.) rumen.
rumí, *n.* (among the Moors) Christian.
rumia, *f.* rumination, chewing the cud.
rumiador, ra, *n.* & *a.* ruminator(-ing), ruminant.
rumiadura, *f.* rumination.
rumiante, *a.* & *m.* (zool.) ruminant.
rumiar, *va.* to ruminate; to muse, meditate.
rumión, na, *a.* ruminating much.
rumo, *m.* (cooperage) first hoop of a cask.
rumor, *m.* rumor, report, hearsay; sound of voices; murmur.—**rumorarse** (Am.) **rumorearse,** *vr. impers.* to be said or rumored, be circulating as a rumor.
rumorcico, illo, ito, *m. dim.* flying report.
rumoroso, sa, *a.* causing rumor.
runa, *f.* rune, runic character.
rundún, *m.* (Arg.) a very small humming bird.
runfla, runflada, *f.* (coll.) series of things.
rúnico, ca; runo, na, *a.* runic.
runrún, *m.* (coll.) rumor, report.
ruña, *f.* (cooperage) croze.—**ruñadera,** *f.* cooper's crozer.—**ruñadura,** *f.* = RUÑA.—**ruñar,** *va.* (cooperage) to croze.
rupestre, *a.* rupiculous, found or living on rocks; rupestrian, inscribed or cut into rocks.
[1]**rupia,** *f.* rupee, silver coin.
[2]**rupia,** *f.* (med.) rupia, a skin disease.
rupicabra, rupicapra, *f.* chamois.
rupícola, *a.* rupiculous, found or living on rocks.
ruptura, *f.* rupture; fracture, breaking.—**r., del núcleo,** or **nuclear,** nuclear fission.
ruqueta, *f.* (bot.) = JARAMAGO, hedge mustard.
rural, *a.* rural, country, rustic.
rus, *m.* (bot.) sumach. Also ZUMAQUE.
rusco, *m.* (bot.) kneeholly, butcher's-broom.
rusel, *m.* a kind of woollen serge.
Rusia, *f.* Russia.
rusiente, *a.* turning red-hot.
ruso, sa, *n.* & *a.* Russian.
rusticación, *f.* rustication.
rustical, *a.* rustic, rural, wild.
rústicamente, *adv.* rustically, rudely.
rusticano, na, *a.* wild (plants).
rusticar, *vn.* (*pret.* RUSTIQUÉ; *subj.* RUSTIQUE) to rusticate.
rusticidad, *f.* rusticity, simplicity; rudeness, clumsiness.
rustico, ca. I. *a.* rustic, rural; coarse, clumsy; unmannerly.—**a la,** or **en r.,** (bookbinding) in paper covers, unbound. **II.** *n.* rustic, peasant.
rustiqué, rustique, *v. V.* RUSTICAR.
rustiquez, rustiqueza, *f.* rusticity.
rustrir, *va.* to toast; to fry.
rustro, *m.* (her.) rustre.
ruta, *f.* route, way.
rutáceo, a, *a.* (bot.) rutaceous.
rutenio, *m.* (chem.) ruthenium.
ruteno, na, *n.* & *a.* Ruthenian.
rutherford, *m.* (nuclear phys.) rutherford (unit of radioactivity).
rutilante, *a.* sparkling, scintillating.
rutilar, *vn.* (poet.) to twinkle, sparkle, scintillate.
rútilo, la. I. *a.* shining red; sparkling. **II.** *m.* (also **rutilo**) (min.) rutile.
rutina, *f.* routine, custom, habit, rut.
rutinario, ria. I. *a.* routine (as *a.*). **II.** *n.* routinist.
rutinero, ra, *a.* routinistic.
ruzafa, *f.* garden, park.
Rwanda, *m.* Rwanda.
rwandés, desa, *a.* & *n.* Rwandese.

S

S, s, *f.* s, twenty-second letter of the Spanish alphabet.
sábado, *m.* Saturday; Sabbath.—**s. inglés,** Saturday half day off.—**s. santo** or **de gloria,** Holy Saturday, Easter Saturday.
sabalar, *m.* net for catching shad.
sabalera, *f.* fire grate in furnaces.
sabalero, *m.* shad fisher.
sábalo, *m.* (ichth.) shad.
sábana, *f.* sheet (for a bed); altar cloth.—**pegársele a uno las sábanas,** to rise late.
sabana, *f.* savanna, grassy plain.
sabandija, *f.* small nasty insect or reptile; bug; vermin.—**sabandijuela,** *f. dim.* very small insect, vermin.
sabanear, *vn.* (Am.) to scour the plain.
sabanero, ra. I. *n.* dweller on the savanna. **II.** *a.* pertaining to a savanna. **III.** *m.* (ornith.) bird resembling the starling. **IV.** *f.* (Venez.) a savanna snake that destroys harmful insects.
sabanilla, *f. dim.* small sheet or piece of linen; altar cloth; napkin; head kerchief or scarf.
sabañón, *m.* chilblain.—**comer como un s.,** to eat greedily, devour.
sabatario, *a.* Sabbatarian.
sabático, ca, *a.* Sabbatical.
sabatina, *f.* (eccl.) Saturday mass; Saturday exercise in colleges.
sabatino, na, *a.* pertaining to Saturday.
sabatizar, *vn.* to keep the Sabbath.
sabedor, ra, *a.* & *n.* knowing, informed (person).
sabeísmo, *m.* Sabaism, Sabianism.
sabeliano, na, *a.* & *n.* Sabellian.
sabelianismo, *m.* Sabellianism.
sabélico, ca, *a.* pertaining to the Sabines or Samnites.
sábelotodo, *n.* = SABIDILLO.
saber. I. *va.* (*ind. pres.* SÉ, *pret.* SUPE, *fut.* SABRÉ; *subj.* SEPA) to know; to be able, know how, can (*Juan sabe cantar,* John can, or knows how to, sing).—**s. cuántas son cinco,** to know what is what.—**s. dónde aprieta el zapato,** to know on which side one's bread is buttered, know where the shoe pinches.—**un no sé qué,** a certain something.—**y no sé que más** or **y qué sé yo qué más,** and what not; and so forth. **II.** *vn.* to know; to be very sagacious; (Arg.) to have the habit of, to usually (*verb*).—**s. a,** to taste of, taste like (*esto sabe a limón,* this tastes of, or like, lemon).—**s. de,** to know, be familiar with; to hear of or from, have news about.—**a s.,** namely, viz., to wit.—**que yo sepa,** to my knowledge, as far as I know.—**¿quién sabe?** perhaps, who knows!—**¿sabe?** you know, don't you know? (in U. S. slang, savvy?).—as an expletive in conversation. **III.** *vr.* to become known; to get found out. **IV.** *m.* learning, knowledge, lore.—**según mi leal s. y entender,** to the best of my knowledge.
sabiamente, *adv.* wisely, knowingly, learnedly.
sabicú, *m.* (Cuba) (bot.) sabicú, horseflesh mahogany.
sabidillo, lla, *n.* pedant, know-it-all person.
sabido, da. I. *pp.* of *saber.* **II.** *a.* learned, well-informed.—**por s. se calla,** it goes without saying.
sabiduría, *f.* learning, knowledge; wisdom.
sabiendas.—a s. *adv.* knowingly, consciously.
sabiente, *a.* knowing.

sabihondez, *f.* (coll.) conceited assumption of knowledge or learning.
sabihondo, da, *a.* affecting knowledge or learning, know-it-all.
sabina, *f.* (bot.) savin.
sabinar, *m.* clump of savins.
[1]**sabino, na,** *a.* roan (horse).
[2]**sabino, na,** *n.* & *a.* Sabine.
sabio, bia. I. *a.* wise, learned, knowing; cunning. **II.** *n.* sage, wise person; scholar, learned person; scientist.
sablazo, *m.* blow with or wound from a saber; (coll.) borrowing or sponging.
[1]**sable,** *m.* saber, cutlass.
[2]**sable,** *m.* (her.) sable, black.
sablista, *m.* (coll.) sponger, one who asks for petty loans.
sablón, *m.* coarse sand.
saboga, *f.* (ichth.) a species of shad.
sabogal, *m.* net for catching shad.
saboneta, *f.* hunting-case watch.
sabor, *m.* taste, flavor; dash, zest.—*pl.* round knobs on the bit of a bridle.—**a s.,** at pleasure.
saborcico, illo, ito, *m. dim.* slight flavor or taste.
saboreamiento, *m.* relish, relishing.
saborear. I. *va.* to flavor, give a relish or zest to; to interest, cajole, wheedle. **II.** *va.* & *vr.* to relish, enjoy, find delicious, be pleased or delighted; to smack one's lips.
saborete, *m.* slight flavor or taste.
sabotaje, *f.* sabotage.
sabotear. I. *va.* to sabotage. **II.** *vn.* to engage in sabotage.
saboyano, na. I. *a.* Savoyard. **II.** *n.* Savoyard; *f.* open skirt; a kind of pie.
sabrosamente, *adv.* deliciously.
sabrosico, ica, illo, illa, ito, ita, *a. dim.* rather tasty.
sabroso, sa, *a.* savory, tasty, palatable, delicious; pleasant, delightful; salted, saltish.
sabucal, *m.* clump of willows.
sabuco, *m.* = SAÚCO, (bot.) alder; horny part of horse's hoof.
sabueso, *m.* hound, bloodhound, beagle, harehound, foxhound.
sabugal, sabugo = SABUCAL, SABUCO.
sábulo, *m.* coarse, heavy sand.
sabuloso, sa, *a.* gritty, sandy, gravelly.
saburra, *f.* (med.) saburra, gastric sordes.
saburral, *a.* (med.) saburral.
saburroso, sa, *a.* indicating a foul stomach.
[1]**saca,** *f.* drawing out; exportation, extraction; first authorized register of a sale; first certified copy of a document issued by a notary.—**estar de s.,** to be on sale; (coll.) to be marriageable.
[2]**saca,** *f.* large bag or sack of coarse stuff.
sacabala, *f.* (surg.) alphonsin.
sacabalas, *m.* (artil.) bullet screw, ball extractor.
sacabocado, sacabocados, *m.* hollow punch; ticket punch.
sacabotas, *m.* bootjack.
sacabrocas, *m.* tack claw, tack puller.
sacabuche, *m.* (naut.) pumping tube or pipe; (mus.) sackbut; player on the sackbut; nincompoop.
sacaclavos, *m.* (carp.) nail extractor.
sacacorchos, *m.* corkscrew.
sacada, *f.* region separated from a province or country.
sacadilla, *f.* noise made to rouse game.
sacadinero, sacadineros, *m.* (coll.) catch-penny.
sacador, ra, *n.* drawer, extractor; one that takes or brings out.
sacadura, *f.* (sewing) slash (to ease); (Colomb.) taking out, extracting.
sacafilásticas, *f.* (artil.) priming wire.
sacalagua, *m.* (Am.) a nearly white half-breed.
sacaliña, *f.* goad; trick, cunning.
sacamanchas, *m.* or *f.* cleaner, scourer, cleanser.
sacamantas, *m.* (coll.) tax collector.
sacamiento, *m.* taking or drawing out.
sacamolero, ra; sacamuelas, *n.* tooth extractor, dentist.
sacanabo, *m.* (naut.) pump hook.
sacanete, *m.* lansquenet, a card game.
sacapelotas, *m.* bullet screw.
sacapotras, *m.* (coll.) bad surgeon.
sacar, *va.* (*pret.* SAQUÉ; *subj.* SAQUE) to extract, draw, draw out, pull out; to take out; to withdraw; to dispossess, put out; to except, exclude; to manufacture, produce, invent; to take (a photo.); to publish; bring out; to put forth, bring forth; to imitate, copy, take off; to clear, free, place in safety; to find out, investigate, discover; to make out, solve, interpret; to relieve (fever, etc.); to eradicate; to extort; to get, obtain, attain; to show, exhibit, manifest; to excite (passion, anger); to lose the judgment; to deduce, draw, infer; to ballot, elect by ballot; to draw, win (a prize); to win at play; (games) to serve (the ball), to kick off; to draw, unsheath (a sword); to make, take (a copy); to cite, name, quote.—**s. a bailar,** to lead out for a dance; to drag in irrelevantly.—**s. a la vergüenza,** to put a criminal in the pillory; to bring shame upon.—**s. a luz,** to print, publish; to mention or bring out.—**s. a pasear,** to take out for a walk.—**s. de madre,** to make one lose patience.—**s. de pila,** to become sponsor for at baptism.—**s. de quicio** = S. DE MADRE.—**s. (uno) de sus casillas,** (fig.) to exhaust one's patience, drive crazy.—**s. el ascua,** or **la brasa, con la mano del gato,** or **con mano ajena,** to have someone else pull one's chestnuts out of the fire.—**s. el cuerpo,** to dodge; to shun; to get out, or keep out (of something); to play safe.—**s. el jugo,** to work (one) hard, slave-drive.—**s. el pecho por,** to stand for, to defend, to take the part of.—**s. en claro,** or **en limpio,** to conclude, arrive at the conclusion; to gather (from a writing, etc.).—**s. la cara,** to present oneself as an interested party.—**s. la cara por** = S. EL PECHO POR.—**s. la cuenta,** to figure out.—**s. por factor común,** (math.) to factor out.—**s. ventaje de,** to profit by.
sacarato, *m.* (chem.) saccharate.
sacárico, ca, *a.* (chem.) saccharic.
sacarífero, ra, *a.* sacchariferous.
sacarificación, *f.* saccharification.
sacarificar, *va.* to saccharify.
sacarígeno, na, *a.* sacchariferous.
sacarimetría, *f.* saccharimetry.
sacarímetro, *m.* saccharimeter.
sacarina, *f.* (chem.) saccharine.
sacarino, na, *a.* saccharine, containing sugar.
sacaroideo, a, *a.* (chem.) saccharoid.
sacarómetro, *m.* saccharimeter.
sacarosa, *f.* (chem.) saccharose.
sacaroso, sa, *a.* saccharinelike.
sacasillas, *n.* (coll.) (theat.) stage hand; busybody.
sacatachuelas, *f.* tack claw.
sacatapón, *m.* corkscrew; bung drawer.
sacate, *m.* (Mex.) grass, herb; hay.
sacatrapos, *m.* (artil.) wad hook, wormer.
sacerdocio, *m.* priesthood.
sacerdotal, *a.* sacerdotal.
sacerdote, *m.* priest, clergyman.
sacerdotisa, *f.* priestess.
saciable, *a.* satiable.
saciar, *va.* & *vr.* to satiate.
saciedad, *f.* satiety.
saciña, *f.* (bot.) a kind of willow.
sacio, a, *a.* satiate, satiated.
saco, *m.* sack, bag; sackful, bagful; coat, jacket; Roman sagum; (in PELOTA) = SAQUE, hitting the ball on the rebound; (mil.) pillage, sack, plunder.—**s. de noche,** hand bag, valise, satchel.—**entrar, meter,** or **poner, a s.,** to plunder, loot.—**no echar en s. roto,** not to forget, not to ignore.
sacra, *f.* (eccl.) sacring tablet.
sacramentado, da, *a.* (eccl.) transubstantiated; having received the last sacraments.
sacramental. I. *a.* sacramental. **II.** *n.* person or fraternity devoted to the worship of the sacrament of the altar.

sacramentalmente, *adv.* sacramentally; in confession.
sacramentar. **I.** *va.* (eccl.) to administer the sacraments to; to consecrate; (coll.) to conceal, hide. **II.** *vr.* to be transubstantiated.
sacramentario, ria, *n.* Sacramentarian.
sacramente, *adv.* = SAGRADAMENTE, sacredly.
sacramento, *m.* (eccl.) sacrament; Christ transubstantiated in the host.—**s. del altar,** Eucharist; consecrated Host.
sacratísimo, ma, *a. super.* most sacred, holiest.
sacre, *m.* (ornith.) saker; small cannon.
sacrificable, *a.* able to be sacrificed; (mil.) expendable.
sacrificadero, *m.* sacrificing place.
sacrificador, ra, *n.* & *a.* sacrificer(-ing).
sacrificante, *a.* sacrificing, hazarding; sacrificial, sacrificatory.
sacrificar. **I.** *va.* (*pret.* SACRIFIQUÉ; *subj.* SACRIFIQUE) to sacrifice. **II.** *vr.* to devote oneself to God; to sacrifice oneself, give up one's life.
sacrificio, *m.* sacrifice, offering; submission.—**s. del altar,** sacrifice of the mass.—**s. propiciatorio,** peace offering.
sacrifiqué, sacrifique, *v. V.* SACRIFICAR.
sacrilegio, *m.* sacrilege.
sacrílego, ga, *a.* sacrilegious.
sacrismoche, cho, *m.* in jocular style, a man in a ragged black coat.
sacrista, *m.* sacristan, sexton.
sacristán, *m.* sacristan, sexton, clerk; hoop skirt, bustle.—**sacristana,** *f.* sacristan or sexton's wife; nun in charge of the sacristy.
sacristanejo, *m. dim.* little sacristan.
sacristanía, *f.* office of a sexton.
sacristía, *f.* sacristy, vestry; SACRISTANÍA.
[1]**sacro,** *m.* (anat.) sacrum.
[2]**sacro, cra,** *a.* holy, sacred.
sacrosanto, ta, *a.* sacred, sacrosanct.
sacudida, *f.* shake, shaking, jerk.
sacudidamente, *adv.* rejectingly.
sacudido, da. **I.** *pp.* of SACUDIR. **II.** *a.* harsh, intractable; determined.
sacudidor, *m.* shaker; beater; duster.
sacudidura, *f.* shaking; dusting, cleansing.
sacudimiento, *m.* shake, shaking; shock, jerk, jolt.
sacudir. **I.** *va.* to shake; jolt, jerk; to beat (to remove dust); spank, drub; dart, throw off, discharge; shake off. **II.** *vn.* (naut.) to flap (sails). **III.** *vr.* to reject, drive away, shake off.
saculiforme, *a.* (bot., zool.) saccate.
sachadura, *f.* hoeing, weeding.
sachar, *va.* (agr.) to weed.
sacho, *m.* weeder, weeding tool.
sádico, ca, *a.* sadistic.
sadismo, *m.* sadism.
sadista, *n.* sadist.
sadístico, ca, *a.* sadistic, sadistical.
saduceísmo, *m.* Sadduceeism.
saduceo, a, *n.* & *a.* Sadducee(-cean).
saeta, *f.* arrow, dart, shaft; cock of a sundial, gnomon; hand of a watch or clock; magnetic needle; bud of a vine; (astr.) Sagitta, the Arrow.—*pl.* pious ejaculations.
saetada, *f.*, **saetazo,** *m.* shooting an arrow; arrow wound.
saetear, *va.* to attack or kill with arrows.
saetero, ra. **I.** *a.* pertaining to arrows. **II.** *m.* archer, bowman, dartman. **III.** *f.* loophole; small grated window in prisons.
saetí, *m.* brad, peg, pin, tack.
saetía, *f.* (naut.) settee; vessel with lateen sails; loophole.
saetilla, *f. dim.* small arrow or dart; small magnetic needle; hand of a watch; devotional verse; (bot.) sagittaria.
[1]**saetín,** *m.* mill race, sluice, flume; SAETÍ.
[2]**saetín,** *m.* (Gal.) sateen or satine.
saetón, *m.* dart for shooting rabbits.
safeno, a, *a.* (anat.) saphenous.
sáfico, ca, *a.* (poet.) sapphic.
[1]**saga,** *f.* witch.
[2]**saga,** *f.* saga (legend).
sagacidad, *f.* sagacity, sagaciousness.
sagapeno, *m.* sagapenum (gum).
sagatí, *m.* sagathy, farmer's satin.
sagaz, *a.* sagacious; (of dogs) with keen scent; discerning, farsighted, farseeing.
sagazmente, *adv.* sagaciously.
sagita, *f.* (geom.) sagitta.
sagital, *a.* sagittal, sagittate.
sagitaria, *f.* (bot.) sagittaria, arrowhead.
sagitario, *m.* dartman, archer; (**S-**, astr.) Sagittarius, the Archer.
sago, *m.* loose, wide greatcoat.
ságoma, *f.* (arch.) pattern, reglet, rule.
sagradamente, *adv.* sacredly.
sagrado, da. **I.** *a.* sacred, consecrated; holy; (obs.) incurable, cursed, execrable.—**s. comunión,** Holy Communion.—**s. escritura,** Holy Writ. **II.** *m.* asylum, haven or refuge, place of safety.
sagrario, *m.* sacrarium; (eccl.) ciborium.
sagú, *m.* (bot.) sago.
saguaipe, *m.* (Arg.) a parasitic worm that attacks the liver of cattle.
ságula, *f. dim.* of SAYUELO, small frock.
saguntino, na, *n.* & *a.* Saguntian.
sahina, *f.* = ZAHINA, (bot.) sorghum.
sahornarse, *vr.* to chafe, be skinned.
sahorno, *m.* chafe, chafing, skinning.
sahumado, da. **I.** *pp.* of SAHUMAR. **II.** *a.* bettered, improved.
sahumador, *m.* perfumer, perfuming pot; fumigator.
sahumadura, *f.* perfuming; fumigation.
sahumar, *va.* to perfume; to smoke; to fumigate.
sahumerio, sahumo, *m.* smoke; vapor, steam; fumigation; fuming.
sai, *m.* (Am.) (zool.) a kind of monkey, sai.
saimirí, *m.* (Am.) (zool.) titi, squirrel monkey.
saín, *m.* grease or fat, fatness; sardine fat used as burning oil; greasiness on clothes.
sainar, *va.* to fatten.
sainete, *m.* (theat.) one-act farce; burlesque; flavor, relish, zest; seasoning, sauce; delicious tidbit; delicacy; anything nice and choice; taste or elegance in dress.—**sainetear,** *vn.* to act farces.—**sainetero,** *m.* writer of farces.—**sainetesco, ca,** *a.* comical, burlesque.
saíno, *m.* (Am.) (zool.) a kind of boar.
saja, *f.* (surg.) sacrification.
sajador, *m.* bleeder, scarifier.
sajadura, *f.* = SAJA.
sajar, *va.* to scarify.
sajelar, *va.* to sift and clean (clay).
sajón, na, *n.* & *a.* Saxon.
sal, *f.* salt; wit, facetiousness; grace, winning manners; (chem.) salt.—**s. amoníaco,** sal ammoniac.—**s. de compás** = S. GEMA.—**s. de la Higuera,** Epsom salts.—**s. gema,** rock salt.—**s. marina,** sea salt.—**s. pedrés,** or **piedra,** rock salt.—**echar en s.,** to reserve for another occasion.
sala, *f.* drawing room, living room, parlor; hall; large room; court of justice (room and judges); tribunal.—**s. de batalla,** sorting table or place (in a postoffice).—**s. de espera,** waiting-room.—**s. de justicia,** court of justice.—**s. del crimen,** criminal court or tribunal.—**guardar s.,** to observe the rules and formalities of the court.—**hacer s.,** to form a quorum in a court.
salacidad, *f.* salaciousness, lechery, lust.
salacot, *m.* topi, sola pith helmet.
saladamente, *adv.* (coll.) wittily, facetiously.
saladar, *m.* salt marsh.
saladero, *m.* salting place; salting tub.
saladillo, *m. dim.* fresh bacon half-salted.
salado, da. **I.** *pp.* of SALAR. **II.** *a.* salty; briny, brackish; witty, facetious; graceful, winsome; (Am.) unlucky; (Arg., Chile) expensive. **III.** *m.* (bot.) saltwort; saline land.
salador, ra. **I.** *n.* salter, curer. **II.** *m.* SALADERO.
saladura, *f.* salting, curing; salted provisions.
salamandra, *f.* salamander; fire sprite; anything fireproof.

salamandria, salamanquesa, *f.* star lizard.
salamanquino, na, *n.* & *a.* = SALMANTINO.
salangana, *f.* (ornith.) swift, esculent swallow.
salar, *va.* to salt, to season or preserve with salt, to cure or corn (meat); to brine.
salariar, *va:* to give a salary or wages to.
salario, *m.* wages, salary.
salaz, *a.* salacious, lustful.
salazón, *f.* salting; salted meats or fish.
salbadera, *f.* sand box, pounce box.
salbanda, *f.* (min.) selvage.
salce, *m.* (bot.) = SAUCE, willow.
salceda, *f.*, **salcedo,** *m.* salicetum, willow garden.
salcereta, *f.* dice box.
salcochar, salcocho = SANCOCHAR, SANCOCHO.
salchicha, *f.* sausage; (fort.) long fascine; (artil.) saucisse, long fuse.
salchichería, *f.* sausage shop.
salchichero, ra, *n.* sausage maker or seller.
salchichón, *m. aug.* sausage; (fort.) large fascine.
saldado, da, *pp.* & *a.* paid, settled, balanced.
saldar, *va.* (com.) to settle, liquidate, balance.
saldista, *n.* one who sells or buys remnants.
saldo, *m.* (com.) balance; settlement; remnants sold at low prices; sale.—**s. acreedor,** credit, credit balance.—**s. deudor,** debit balance.—**s. no asignado,** unallocated balance.
saldrá, saldré, *v. V.* SALIR.
saledizo, za. I. *a.* salient, projecting. **II.** *m.* projection, ledge.
salegar, *m.* salt lick.
salema, *f.* (ichth.) gilthead.
salep, *m.* salep or salop root.
salera, *f.* saltcat in a salt lick; salt mine.
salerato, *m.* (chem., cook.) saleratus.
salero, *m.* saltcellar; salt pan; salt storage place; salt lick; (coll.) gracefulness, winning ways.
saleroso, sa, *a.* (coll.) witty, facetious; lively, jolly, winsome.
salesiano, na, *n.* & *a.* Salesian.
saleta, *f. dim.* small hall; royal antechamber; court of appeal.
salgada, salgadera, *f.* (bot.) = ORZAGA, orach.
salgar, *va.* to feed salt to (cattle).
salgo, salga, *v. V.* SALIR.
salguera, *f.*, **salguero,** *m.* (bot.) osier, willow.
salicaria, *f.* (bot.) a salicaceous shrub.
salicilato, *m.* (chem.) salicylate.
salicílico, ca, *a.* (chem.) salicylic.
salicina, *f.* (chem.) salicin.
salicíneo, a, *a.* (bot.) salicaceous.
sálico, ca, *a.* Salic.
salicor, *f.* (bot.) prickly saltwort.
salida, *f.* start, setting or going out, departure, exit; outlet; way out, exit; outskirts; issue, result, conclusion; projection, protuberance; (com.) salableness; expenditure, outlay; loophole, subterfuge, pretext; sally; (naut.) headway; (mil.) sally, sortie.—**sin s.,** dead-end (street).—**tener s.** (com.) to sell well, be saleable.
salidizo, = SALEDIZO.
salido, da. I. *pp.* of SALIR. **II.** *a.* projecting; (of female animals) in season.
saliente. I. *a.* salient, projecting. **II.** *f.* projection, lug.
salífero, ra, *a.* salt-bearing.
salificable, *a.* salifiable.
salificar, *va.* (chem.) to salify.
salín, *m.* salthouse.
salinero, ra, *n.* salter, salt maker; salt dealer.
salinidad, *f.* salinity, saltiness.
salino, na. I. *a.* saline. **II.** *f.* salt pit, salt pan, salt works, salt mine.
salinómetro, *m.* salinometer.
[1]**salio, lia,** *n.* & *a.* Salian (pertaining to, or one of, the salii, or priests of Mars).
[2]**salio, lia,** *a.* pert. to the Salian Franks.
salipirina, *f.* salipyrine.
salir. I. *vn.* (*ind. pres.* SALGO, *fut.* SALDRÉ; *subj.* SALGA) to go or come out; to depart, leave, sail: sally, sally forth; get out (of a vehicle); to end, be over (as a season); to loom, show up; disappear, come off (as a stain); rise (as the sun); to shoot, spring; to grow; stand out, project; to begin (a game, a dance, etc.); to be issued or published; to result, turn out; to acquit oneself, come out, do (well, badly); to be drawn (as in a lottery); to be elected; to lead to, open to; (naut.) to exceed, to excel, pass another vessel in sailing; to happen, occur; to correspond; to imply; to come out right, check (as a sum); to say or do a thing unexpectedly or unseasonably; (**de**) to cease (as); (theat.) to enter, appear; (before *pp.*) to come out, to be (*salió herido*, he came out, or was, wounded).—**s. a,** to come to (so much); to resemble, look like.—**s. adelante,** to be successful.—**s. al encuentro de,** to come out to meet.—**s. avante,** or **bien,** or **con bien,** to do well, to be successful.—**s. con,** to drag in, say unexpectedly or irrelevantly.—**s. de,** to dispose of; to part with; to get ride of.—**s. de compras,** to go shopping.—**s. de su padre,** to be released from paternal guardianship.—**s. de sus casillas,** to lose one's temper.—**s. ganando,** to come out a winner, gain.—**s. mal,** to do badly, be unsuccessful, fail.—**s. perdiendo,** to lose, come out a loser.—**hacer s. los colores al rostro,** to put one to blush.—**salga lo que saliere,** happen what will, whatever may happen. **II.** *vr.* to leak; to overflow.—**s. con la suya,** to accomplish one's end, to have one's way.—**s. de madre,** to exceed, run over; to lose one's self-control.
salisipán, *m.* (P. I.) a swift boat.
salitrado, da, *a.* impregnated with saltpeter.
salitral. I. *a.* nitrous. **II.** *m.* saltpeter bed or works.
salitre, *m.* saltpeter, niter.
salitrería, *f.* saltpeter works.
salitrero, ra, *n.* saltpeter refiner or dealer.
salitroso, sa, *a.* nitrous.
saliva, *f.* saliva, spittle.
salivación, *f.* salivation; spitting.
salival, *a.* salivary.
salivar, *vn.* to spit; to salivate.
salivazo, *m.* spit, spittle.
saliveo, *m.* spitting.
salivera, *f.* round knob on the bits of a bridle.
salivoso, sa, *a.* spitting excessively.
salma, *f.* ton, twenty hundredweight.
salmantino, na, *n.* & *a.* of or relating to Salamanca.
salmear, *vn.* to sing psalms.
salmer, *m.* (arch.) impost of an arch.
salmerón, *a.* fanfarron wheat.
salmista, *m.* psalmist; chanter of psalms.
salmo, *m.* psalm.
salmodia, *f.* psalmody; (eccl.) psalter.—**salmodiar,** *vn.* = SALMEAR.
salmón, *m.* (ichth.) salmon.—**s. pequeño,** samlet, parr.—**s. zancado,** kelt.—**salmonado, da,** *a.* tasting like salmon.—**salmoncillo, ito,** *m. dim.* parr.—**salmonera,** *f.* salmon net.
salmonete, *m.* (ichth.) surmullet.
salmónido, da. I. *n.* & *a.* (zool.) salmonid. **II.** *m. pl.* Salmonidae.
salmorejo, *m.* sauce for rabbits.
salmuera, *f.* brine; pickle.
salmuerarse, *vr.* (of cattle) to become sick from eating too much salt.
salobral. I. *a.* salty, briny. **II.** *m.* saline ground.
salobre, *a.* brackish, briny, saltish.
salobreño, ña, *a.* saltish, saline (ground).
salobridad, *f.* brackishness, saltiness.
salol, *m.* (chem.) salol.
saloma, *f.* (naut.) chantey.
salomar, *vn.* (naut.) to sing chanteys.
[1]**salón,** *m. aug.* salon, large parlor; living or assembly room.
[2]**salón,** *m.* salted and cured meat or fish.
saloncillo, *m.* small salon or hall; special room (waiting room, rest room, lady's room, etc.).
salpa, *f.* (ichth.) gilthead, salpa, bighead.
salpicado, da, *a.* splotchy.

salpicadura, *f.* splash, spatter, spattering.
salpicar, *va.* (*pret.* SALPIQUÉ; *subj.* SALPIQUE) to spatter, bespatter, sprinkle, splash; to skip over, touch on without order.
salpicón, *m.* salmagundi; farcing; medley; bespattering.
salpimentar, *va.* (*ind.* SALPIMIENTO; *subj.* SALPIMIENTE) to season with pepper and salt.
salpimienta, *f.* salt and pepper.
salpiqué, salpique, *v.* *V.* SALPICAR.
salpresar, *va.* to salt, preserve with salt.
salpullido, *m.* (med.) rash.
salpullir, *va.* & *vr.* (med.) to break out.
salsa, *f.* (cooking) sauce, dressing, gravy.—**s. de San Bernardo,** (coll.) hunger.—**s. mahonesa,** or **mayonesa,** mayonnaise dressing.
salsedumbre, *f.* saltiness, saltness.
salsera, *f.* gravy dish.
salsereta, rilla, ruela, *f. dim.* small saucer; dice box.
salsero, *m.* (bot.) Spanish thyme.
salsifí, *m.* (bot.) salsify, oyster plant.
salsoláceo, a. I. *a.* (bot.) salsolaceous. **II.** *f. pl.* Salsola.
saltabanco, saltabancos, *m.* mountebank; quack; trifler.
saltabardales, *m.* (coll.) romp, wild youth.
saltabarrancos, *m.* (coll.) noisy person.
saltacaballo.—en s., (arch.) lapping over.
saltación, *f.* leaping; dancing, dance.
saltacharquillos, *n.* person affectedly walking on tiptoe.
saltadero, *m.* leaping or jumping place; artificial fountain; jet.
saltadizo, za, *a.* snapping, breaking.
saltador, ra, *n.* jumper, leaper; hopper.
saltadura, *f.* chip (in a stone).
saltaembanco, *m.* = SALTABANCO.
saltamontes, *m.* grasshopper.
saltante, *a.* leaping, jumping; salient.
saltaojos, *m.* (bot.) a kind of peony.
saltaparedes, *m.* = SALTABARDALES.
saltar. I. *vn.* to leap, spring, jump, hop; to frisk, skip; to bound, rebound; to dash out (as a geyser); to snap, burst, break in pieces; to fly asunder, crack, flash; to come off (as a button); to slip off (as a pulley belt); to be clear and obvious; to come to the mind; to start, betray emotion; (naut.) (of the wind) to shift, change suddenly.—**s. a la vista,** to be self-evident.—**s. en tierra,** to land, debark. **II.** *va.* to leap or jump over; to skip; (of animals) to cover (the female).
saltarelo, *m.* an ancient Spanish dance.
saltarén, *m.* a tune on the guitar; grasshopper.
saltarín, na, *n.* dancer, dancing master (mistress); restless young rake.
saltarregla, *f.* bevel square; slide rule.
saltaterandate, *m.* a kind of embroidery.
saltatrás, *m.* or *f.* = TORNATRÁS, half-breed.
saltatriz, *f.* ballet girl; danseuse.
saltatumbas, *m.* (coll.) clergyman who makes a living from funerals.
salteador, ra, *n.* highwayman(woman), footpad.
salteamiento, *m.* assault, highway robbery.
saltear, *va.* to assault, attack; to rob on the highway; to hold up; to start, leave undone, and undertake something else; to forestall; to surprise, take by surprise.
salteo, *m.* assault; highway robbery.
salterio, *m.* psalter, psalm book; rosary; (mus.) psaltery.
saltero, ra, *n.* highlander.
saltico, ito, illo, *m. dim.* little hop or leap.
saltígrado, da, *a.* (zool.) saltigrade, leaping.
saltimbanco, -banqui, *m.* = SALTABANCO.
salto, *m.* spring, jump, leap, bound; leaping place; skip, omission; gap; promotion to a higher post without passing through the intervening ones.—**s. de agua,** waterfall, falls, cataract.—**s. de mata,** flight for fear of punishment.—**s. de trucha,** tumbling.—**s. de viento,** (naut.) sudden shifting of the wind.—**s. mortal,** somersault.—**a saltos,** leaping, by hops.—**a saltos y corcovos,** (coll.) by fits and starts.—**dar un s.,** to jump, leap.—**de un s.,** at one jump; in a flash.—**por s.,** irregularly, by turns.
saltón, na. I. *a.* hopping or leaping much. **II.** *m.* grasshopper.
salubérrimo, ma, *a. super.* most salubrious.
salubre, *a.* salubrious, healthful.
salubridad, *f.* healthfulness, salubrity.—**Ministro de S.,** Minister, or Secretary, of Public Health.
salud, *f.* health; good condition; public weal; welfare, prosperity; salvation.—*pl.* compliments, greetings.—**¡s.!** hello! greetings! good luck! your health (in drinking).—**a su s.,** your health (in drinking).—**beber a la s. de,** to drink the health of.—**bien (mal) de s.,** in good (bad) health.
saludable, *a.* salutary, healthful, wholesome.
saludablemente, *adv.* healthfully, wholesomely.
saludación, = SALUTACIÓN.
saludador, ra, *n.* greeter, saluter; quack.
saludar, *va.* to greet, bow to, salute, hail; to give greetings or regards to; to fire a salute; to apply nostrums; (naut.) to dip the flag to.—**le saludo a Vd. atentamente,** (in letter) very truly yours.
saludo, *m.* bow, salute, salutation, greeting; (mil.) salute.—**s. a la voz,** (naut.) cheers, hurrahs.
salumbre, *f.* flower of salt.
salutación, *f.* salutation, greeting, salute, bow; exordium of a sermon; Ave Maria.
salute, *m.* an ancient gold coin.
salutíferamente, *adv.* salubriously.
salutífero, ra, *a.* healthful, salubrious.
salva, *f.* (artil.) salvo; salver, tray; ordeal; oath, solemn promise, assurance.
salvación, *f.* salvation; deliverance.
salvachia, *f.* (naut.) salvage strap.
salvadera, *f.* sandbox, shaker (for sprinkling sand on wet ink).
salvado, da. I. *pp.* of SALVAR. **II.** *m.* bran.
salvador, ra, *n.* savior, rescuer, redeemer.
salvadoreño, ña, *n.* & *a.* Salvadorean (from Salvador).
salvaguardar, *va.* to safeguard, protect.
salvaguardia. I. *m.* safeguard, security, protection; guard; watchman. **II.** *f.* safe-conduct, passport.
salvajada, *f.* brutal or stupid action.
salvaje. I. *a.* savage; (of plants, animals) wild; rough, wild (country). **II.** *m.* savage.
salvajemente, *adv.* savagely, wildly.
salvajería, *f.* brutal action; savageness.
salvajez, *f.* savageness.
salvajina, *f.* wild animal; multitude of wild animals; collection of skins of wild animals.
salvajino, na, *a.* savage, wild, untamed; gamey (meat).
salvajismo, *m.* savagery; (coll.) rusticity.
salvajuelo, la, *n.* little savage.
salvamano.—a s., without danger to oneself; in a cowardly manner.
salvamente, *adv.* securely, safely.
salvamento, *m.* salvage; safety, place of safety; salvation.—**bote de s.,** (aer.) crash boat.
salvamiento, *m.* = SALVAMENTO.
salvante. I. *a.* saving, excepting. **II.** *adv.* (coll.) save, except.
salvar. I. *va.* to save, rescue; (naut.) to salve, save; to avoid (a danger); to get over, jump over (ditch, creek, etc.), clear (an obstacle); to overcome (a difficulty); to make allowance for, excuse, make an exception of; to prove legally the innocence of.—**s. las aparencias,** to keep up appearances, save face. **II.** *vn.* to taste, to prove (the food or drink of nobles). **III.** *vr.* to be saved; to escape from danger.—**sálvese él que pueda,** everyone for himself.
salvarsán, *m.* (pharm.) salvarsan; Salvarsan (trademark).

salvavidas, *m.* life preserver; life belt, safety belt; *n.* lifesaver, lifeguard.
¡salve! *interj.* hail!—**Salve,** *f.* (eccl.) Salve Regina.
salvedad, *f.* reservation, exception, qualification.
salvia, *f.* (bot.) sage.
salvilla, *f.* salver, glass rack, tray, waiter.
salvo, va. I. *a.* saved, safe; excepted, omitted. **II.** *adv.* save, saving, excepting, barring.—**s. el guante,** or **s. el zurrado,** excuse the glove.—**s. que,** unless.—**a s.,** without injury or diminution.—**en s.,** safe, with safety.
salvoconducto, *m.* safe-conduct, passport; license, permit, pass.
salvohonor, *m.* (coll.) breech, buttocks.
salladura, *f.* (agr.) weeding.
sallar, *va.* (agr.) to weed.
sallete, *m.* (agr.) weeder, weeding tool.
sámago, *m.* sap rot, dry rot.
samán, *m.* (bot.) genisaro, rain tree.
sámara, *f.* (bot.) samara.
samario, *m.* (chem.) samarium.
samarita; samaritano, na, *n.* & *a.* Samaritan.
samaruguera, *f.* fishing net that is set across streams.
sambenitar, *va.* to make infamous, to dishonor publicly.
sambenito, *m.* garment worn by penitent convicts of the Inquisition; placard in churches, containing names of penitents and their penance; note of infamy; disgrace.
samblaje, *m.* = ENSAMBLADURA, joining; joint.
sambuca, *f.* (mus., mil.) sambuca.
sambumbia, *f.* (Cuba) fermented drink made from cane juice, water, and peppers; (Peru) hubbub, confusion.—**sambumbiería,** *f.* place where SAMBUMBIA is made and sold.
samio, mia, *n.* & *a.* Samian (from Samos).
samnita, samnite, *n.* & *a.* Samnite.
samnítico, ca, *a.* Samnitic.
samoano, na, *n.* & *a.* Samoan.
samovar, *m.* samovar.
samoyedo, da. I. *a.* Samoyedic. **II.** *n.* Samoyed, Samoyede.
sampaguita, *f.* a tropical flower like jasmine.
sampán, *m.* sampan, a Chinese skiff.
sampsuco, *m.* (bot.) marjoram.
samuga, *f.* mule chair.
san, *a.* (*contr.* of SANTO) Saint (with masc. names).
sanable, *a.* curable, healable.
sanador, ra, *n.* curer, healer.
sanalotodo, *m.* cure-all, catholicon, panacea.
sanamente, *adv.* sanely; sincerely.
sanar. I. *va.* to heal, cure. **II.** *vn.* to heal; to recover from sickness.
sanativo, va, *a.* sanative, curative.
sanatorio, *m.* sanatorium, sanitarium.
sanción, *f.* sanction; ratification.
sancionar, *va.* to sanction; to ratify, authorize.
sanco, *m.* (Chile) porridge made from toasted corn meal or wheat flour; very thick mud; (Arg.) a stew made with beef blood, flour and onions.
sancochar, *va.* (cook.) to boil with water and salt.
sancocho, *m.* (Am.) a kind of thin stew of boiled yucca, meat, plantains, etc.
sancta, *m.* fore part of the tabernacle.
sanctasanctórum, *m.* sanctum sanctorum.
sanctórum, *m.* (P. I.) a tribute to the church.
sanctus, *m.* (eccl.) Sanctus, Trisagion.
sanchete, *m.* an ancient silver coin.
sanchopancesco, ca, *a.* like Sancho Panza.
sandalia, *f.* sandal.
sandalino, na, *a.* pertaining to sandalwood.
sándalo, *m.* (bot.) bergamot mint; sandalwood.
sandáraca, *f.* (min.) sandarach, realgar; sandarach (gum).
sandez, *f.* inanity, foolish or stupid statement.
sandía, *f.* (bot.) watermelon.
sandiar, *m.* watermelon patch.
sandio, dia, *a.* foolish, nonsensical, inane.
sandunga, *f.* (coll.) gracefulness, elegance; winsomeness, fascination.—**sandunguero, ra,** *a.* (coll.) winsome, graceful, fascinating.
saneado, da. I. *pp.* of SANEAR. **II.** *a.* drained; free, clear, unencumbered.
saneamiento, *m.* (law) security, surety, bail, guarantee; indemnification, reparation; drainage, improvement (of land).
sanear, *va.* to give security, to give bail; (law) to indemnify; to make harmless; to drain, improve (lands).
sanedrín, *m.* (anc. Jewry) Sanhedrim.
sanforizar, *va.* to Sanforize (trademark).
sanfrancia, *f.* (coll.) quarrel, dispute, row.
sangley, *m.* (P. I.) Chinese trader.
sangradera, *f.* (surg.) lancet; basin (for blood); lock, sluice, drain.
sangrador, *m.* bloodletter; outlet.
sangradura, *f.* (surg.) bleeding; bend on the inside of arm at the elbow; draining, drainage.
sangrar. I. *va.* (surg.) to bleed; to drain; (coll.) to extort or borrow money from; (print.) to indent. **II.** *vn.* to bleed. **III.** *vr.* to be bled.
sangraza, *f.* corrupt or filthy blood.
sangre, *f.* blood; gore; race, family, kindred.—**s. azul,** blue blood, nobility.—**s. de drago,** dragon's blood.—**s. fría,** calmness, composure, sang-froid.—**a s. caliente,** impulsively, on the spur of the moment.—**a s. fría,** in cold blood.—**a s. y fuego,** by fire and sword, by blood and iron.—**en s. fría,** in cold blood.—**mala s.,** bad blood, vindictiveness.—**subírsele a uno la s. a la cabeza,** to become excited, lose one's self-control.
sangría, *f.* (surg.) bleeding, bloodletting; present made to a person who bleeds; drain, drainage, draining; pilfering, pilferage; insdie of the forearm; (print.) indenting a line; tap, stream of molten metal from a furnace; sangaree, a refreshing drink made with wine.
sangrientamente, *adv.* bloodily, cruelly.
sangriento, ta, *a.* bloody, bloodstained, gory; cruel, sanguinary, bloodthirsty.
sanguaza, *f.* serous blood; reddish fluid of vegetables.
sangüeño, *m.* (bot.) wild cornel.
sangüesa, *f.* raspberry.
sangüeso, *m.* (bot.) raspberry bush.
sanguífero, ra, *a.* conveying blood (as a vein).
sanguificación, *f.* (med.) sanguification.
sanguificar, *va.* to make blood from.
sanguijuela, *f.* leech; sponger; sharper, cheat.
sanguinaria, *f.* (bot.) bloodroot; knotgrass; (min.) bloodstone, hematite.
sanguinariamente, *adv.* sanguinarily, bloodily.
sanguinario, ria, *a.* sanguinary, cruel, bloody, bloodthirsty.
sanguíneo, nea; sanguino, na, *a.* red, blood-colored; sanguineous, sanguine.
sanguinolencia, *f.* bloody condition.
sanguinolento, ta, *a.* bloody; bloodstained.
sanguinoso, sa, *a.* sanguine, sanguineous; bloody, sanguinary, cruel.
sanguiñuelo, *m.* (bot.) wild cornel.
sangüis, *m.* (Lat.) blood of Christ; consecrated wine.
sanguisorba, *f.* (bot.) great burnet.
sanguja, *f.* leech.
sanícula, *f.* (bot.) sanicle.
sanidad, *f.* soundness; health; healthfulness; health department.—**s. marítima,** quarantine officers.—**en s.,** in health.
sanidina, *f.* (min.) sanidine.
sanie, sanies, *f.* (med.) sanies.
sanioso, sa, *a.* (med.) sanious, ichorous.
sanitario, ria. I. *a.* sanitary, hygienic. **II.** *m.* health officer.
sanjacado, sanjacato, *m.* government of a sanjak (a Turkish district).
sanjaco, *m.* governor of a sanjak.
sanjuanada, *f.* picnic on St. John's day.
sanjuanero, ra, *a.* (of fruits) ripe by St. John's day.
sanjuanino, na, *n.* & *a.* of or from San Juan.
sanjuanista, *m.* knight of St. John of Jerusalem.
sanluisero, ra, *n.* & *a.* of or from San Luis.

sanmarinese, *n.* & *a.* (of) San Marino.
San Marino, *m.* San Marino.
sanmiguelada, *f.* Michaelmas.
sanmigueleño, ña, *a.* (of fruits) ripe by Michaelmas.
sano, na, *a.* sound, healthy, hale; salutary; sane; secure; honest, good; discreet, wise; safe, harmless; entire, complete.—**cortar por lo s.,** to settle in the shortest way, regardless of all else; to take quick action.—**s. y salvo,** safe and sound.
sánscrito, ta. I. *a.* Sanskrit. **II.** *m.* Sanskrit.
sansimoniano, na, *n.* & *a.* Saint-Simonian.
sansimonismo, *m.* Saint-Simonianism.
santa, *f.* female saint.
santabárbara, *f.* (naut.) magazine, powder room.
santafecino, na, *n.* & *a.* of or from Santa Fe.
santafereño, ña, *n.* & *a.* of or from (Santa Fe de) Bogotá.
santaláceo, a, *a.* (bot.) santalaceous.
santamente, *adv.* saintly, saintily; plainly, simply.
santandereano, na, *a.* of or from Santander (Colombia).—**santanderiense; santanderino, na,** *a.* of or from Santander (Spain).
santelmo, *m.* (naut.) St. Elmo's fire.
santero, ra. I. *a.* too devoted to worship of saints. **II.** *n.* caretaker of a sanctuary; seller of images.
santiagueño, ña, *a.* (of fruits) ripe by St. James's day.
santiaguero, ra, *a.* of or pertaining to Santiago (Cuba).
santiagués, sa, *a.* of or pertaining to Santiago (Galicia).
santiaguino, na, *a.* of or pertaining to Santiago (Chile).
santiaguista. I. *a.* belonging to the order of Santiago. **II.** *m.* knight of Santiago or St. James.
santiamén, *m.* (coll.) instant, moment, twinkling of an eye, jiffy.
santico, ca, *n. dim.* little image of a saint; (coll.) good child.
santidad, *f.* sanctity, saintliness, holiness, godliness.—**su S.,** his Holiness (the Pope).
santificable, *a.* sanctifiable.
santificación, *f.* sanctification, making holy.—**s. de las fiestas,** keeping of holy days.
santificador, ra, *n.* & *a.* sanctifier(-fying).
santificante, *a.* blessing, sanctifying.
santificar. I. *va.* (*pret.* SANTIFIQUÉ; *subj.* SANTIFIQUE) to sanctify, hallow, consecrate; to keep (holy days). **II.** *va.* & *vr.* to justify, exculpate, clear from guilt, acquit.
santiguada, *f.* crossing oneself; rough treatment, reprimand.—**para,** or **por, mi s.,** faith, by this cross.
santiguadera, *f.* healing by signs of the cross.
santiguadero, ra; dor, ra, *n.* healer by signs of the cross.
santiguamiento, *m.* crossing oneself.
santiguar. I. *va.* to bless, to heal by blessing; (coll.) to slap. **II.** *vr.* to cross oneself.
santimonia, *f.* sanctity, sanctimony, holiness; (bot.) corn marigold, chrysanthemum.
santísimo, ma, *a. super.* most holy.—**el S.,** the holy sacrament.
santo, ta. I. *a.* saintly, holy, blessed; saint; sacred, consecrated; inviolable; (coll.) simple, plain, artless.—**s. hermandad,** Holy Brotherhood, an ancient Spanish rural police.—**s. oficio,** Holy Office (the Inquisition).—**S. Padre,** Holy Father (the Pope); Father of the Church (one of the first Christian writers).—**s. varón,** holy man; simpleton; hypocrite.—**s. y bueno,** well and good.—**todo el s. día,** the whole day long. **II.** *n.* saint; saint's day; image of a saint.—**santo y seña,** (mil.) watch word, password.—**alzarse con el s. y la limosna,** to take everything, make a clean sweep.—**dar el s.,** (mil.) to set or give the password.—**Todos los Santos,** All Saint's Day.
santol, *m.* (P. I.) (bot.) santol, sandal tree.
santón, *m. aug.* dervish; hypocrite.
santónico, *m.* (bot.) santonica, wormwood.
santonina, *f.* (chem.) santonin.
santoral, *m.* (eccl.) collection of lives of the saints; church choir book.
santuario, *m.* sanctuary.
santucho, cha, *n.* & *a.* = SANTURRÓN.
santurrón, rrona. I. *a.* sanctimonious. **II.** *n.* (coll.) sanctimonious person, hypocrite.
santurronería, *f.* sanctimony, hypocrisy.
saña, *f.* anger, passion, rage, fury.
sañosamente, *adv.* angrily, cruelly.
sañoso, sa, *a.* furious, enraged; cruel.
sañudamente, *adv.* furiously.
sañudo, da, *a.* furious, enraged.
sao, *m.* (bot.) LABIÉRNAGO, laburnum; small savanna with clusters of trees or shrubs.
sapa, *f.* residue left after chewing BUYO.
sapajú, *m.* (Am.) sapajou, a capuchin monkey.
sapán, *m.* (bot.) (P. I.) sapan wood; sapan tree.
sapeca, *f.* sapek or sapec, an oriental coin.
sapidez, *f.* sapidity.
sápido, da, *a.* sapid, savory.
sapiencia, *f.* wisdom, knowledge, learning.
sapiencial, *m.* sapiential book (part of the Bible).
sapiente, *a.* wise, learned.
sapientísimamente, *adv. super.* most wisely, or learnedly.
sapillo, *m.* dim. little toad.
sapina, *f.* (bot.) glasswort.
sapindáceo, a, *a.* (bot.) sapindaceous.
sapino, *m.* (bot.) savin.
sapo, *m.* toad.
saponáceo, cea, *a.* saponaceous, soapy.
saponaria, *f.* (bot.) common soapwort.
saponificable, *a.* saponifiable.
saponificación, *f.* saponification.
saponificador, *m.* saponifier.
saponificar. I. *va.* (*pret.* SAPONIFIQUÉ; *subj.* SAPONIFIQUE) to saponify, convert into soap. **II.** *vr.* to become saponified.
saponina, *f.* (chem.) saponin.
saporífero, ra, *a.* imparting savor.
sapotáceo, a, *a.* (bot.) sapotaceous.
saprofítico, ca, *a.* (bot.) saprophytic.
saprofito, ta. I. *a.* saprophytic. **II.** *m.* saprophyte.
saque, *m.* (sports) a serve (in tennis), kick-off (in foot-ball), etc.
saqué, saque, *v.* *V.* SACAR.
saqueador, ra, *n.* looter, pillager.
saqueamiento, *m.* pillage, loot, plunder.
saquear, *va.* to plunder, loot, pillage.
saqueo, *m.* = SAQUEAMIENTO.
saquera, *f.* packing needle.
saquería, *f.* place for or collection of sacks.
saquero, ra, *n.* maker or seller of sacks.
saquete, *m. dim.* (artil.) cartridge bag.
saquilada, *f.* small amount of grain in a sack.
saquillo, ito, *m. dim.* small sack or bag.
saragüete, *m.* (coll.) informal SARAO.
sarampión, *m.* (med.) measles.
sarao, *m.* evening party with dancing or music.
sarape, *m.* (Mex.) serape, a shawl or blanket worn by men.
sarapia, *f.* (bot.) tonka bean.
sarapico, *m.* (ornith.) curlew.
sarasa, *m.* effeminate man.
saraviado, da, *a.* spotted, piebald.
sarcasmo, *m.* sarcasm.
sarcástico, ca, *a.* sarcastic.
sarcia, *f.* load, burden.
sarcocarpio, *m.* (bot.) sarcocarp.
sarcocele, *m.* (med.) sarcocele.
sarcocola, *f.* sarcocol (resinous gum).
sarcófago, *m.* tomb, grave; sarcophagus.
sarcolema, *m.* (anat.) sarcolemma.
sarcologia, *f.* (anat.) sarcology.
sarcoma, *m.* (med.) sarcoma.
sarcomatoso, sa, *a.* sarcomatous.
sarcótico, ca, *a.* (surg.) sarcotic.
sarda, *f.* (ichth.) horse mackerel.
sardana, *f.* a Catalonian dance.

sardesco, ca. I. *a.* small (donkey or horse); (coll.) rude, stubborn. **II.** *m.* pony; small donkey.
sardiano, na, *n.* & *a.* Sardian.
sardina, *f.* (ichth.) sardine.—**como s. en banasta,** or **en barril,** packed like sardines.
sardinal, *m.* sardine net.
sardinel, *m.* (mason.) brickwork having the bricks closely placed on edge.
sardinero, ra. I. *a.* pertaining to sardines. **II.** *n.* dealer in sardines. **III.** *m.* (**S-**) a public walk near Santander.
sardineta, *f.* small sardine; sprat; part of cheese that overtops the cheese vat; (naut.) knittle, laniard.—*pl.* (mil.) chevrons in uniforms.
sardio, *m.* (jewelry) sard, sardius.
[1]**sardo, da,** *n.* & *a.* Sardinian.
[2]**sardo, da,** *a.* (of cattle) red, black and white.
sardonia, *f.* (bot.) crowfoot, spearwort.
sardónica, sardónice, *f.* (jewelry) sardonyx.
sardónico, ca, *a.* sardonic; insincere, affected (laughter).
sardonio, sardónique, *m.* = SARDÓNICE.
[1]**sarga,** *f.* silk serge or twill; (art) fabric painted in tempera or oil, like tapestry.
[2]**sarga,** *f.* (bot.) osier or willow.
sargadilla, *f.* (bot.) soda-ash plant.
sargado, da, *a.* sergelike.
sargal, *m.* clump of osiers.
sargatillo, *m.* (bot.) a kind of willow.
sargazo, *m.* (bot.) sargasso, gulfweed.
sargenta, *f.* sergeant's halberd; sergeant's wife.
sargentear, *va.* to command as a sergeant; to command; (coll.) to boss, lord it over.
sargentería, *f.* (mil.) sergeant's drill.
sargentía, *f.* sergeantship, sergeancy.
sargento, *m.* (mil.) sergeant.
sargentona, *f.* big coarse woman.
sargo, *m.* (ichth.) sheepshead.
[1]**sarguero, ra,** *a.* willowy.
[2]**sarguero,** *m.* painter of [1]SARGA.
sargueta, *f.* thin, light serge.
sarilla, *f.* (bot.) marjoram.
sármata, *n.* & *a.*; **sarmático, ca,** *a.* Sarmatian.
sarmentador, ra, *n.* one who gathers pruned vine shoots.
sarmentar, *vn.* to gather pruned vine shoots.
sarmentera, *f.* place where pruned vine shoots are kept; gathering pruned vine shoots.
sarmentillo, *m. dim.* slender vine shoot.
sarmentoso, sa, *a.* vinelike, twining.
sarmiento, *m.* (bot.) sarmentum, runner.
sarna, *f.* (med.) itch; mange.—**s. perruna,** nonsuppurating mange.—**más viejo que la s.,** as old as Methuselah.
sarnazo, *m.* malignant itch.
sarnoso, sa, *a.* itchy; scabbed; mangy.
sarpullido, *m.* rash, eruption.
sarpullir, *va.* & *vr.* to cause or have a rash.
sarracenia, *f.* (bot.) sarracenia, pitcher plant.
sarracénico, ca, *a.* Saracenic.
sarraceno, na; sarracín, na, *n.* & *a.* Saracen (-ic), Moor(-ish).
sarracina, *f.* scuffle, fight.
sarrapia, *f.* = SARAPIA.
sarria, *f.* coarse net for straw; large fruit basket.
[1]**sarrillo,** *m.* stertor of a dying person.
[2]**sarrillo,** *m.* (bot.) arum.
sarrio, *m.* a kind of wild goat.
sarro, *m.* crust or incrustation in vessels; (med.) mucous on stomach wall; tartar on teeth.
sarroso, sa, *a.* crusty.
sarta, *f.* string of beads or pearls; line, series.
sartal, *m.* string of beads, etc.
sartalejo, *m. dim.* small string of pearls.
sartén, *f.* frying pan.—**tener la s. por el mango,** to have the command, control or advantage.—**sartenada,** *f.* as much as can be fried at one time in a frying pan.—**sartenazo,** *m.* blow with a frying pan; (coll.) blow with anything.—**sarteneja,** *f. dim.* small frying pan.
sartorio, ria. I. *a.* (anat.) sartorial. **II.** *m.* (anat.) sartorius.
sasafrás, *m.* (bot.) sassafras.
sasánida, *n.* & *a.* Sassanid, Sassanian.
sastra, *f.* wife of a tailor; woman tailor.
sastre, *m.* tailor.—**s. remendón,** repairer.
sastrecillo, *m. dim.* petty tailor.
sastrería, *f.* tailor's trade; tailor's shop.
sastresa, *f.* = SASTRA.
Satán, Satanás, *m.* Satan.—**satánicamente,** *adv.* satanically.—**satánico, ca,** *a.* satanic.
satélite, *m.* satellite; (coll.) bailiff, constable, sheriff; follower, henchman; sycophant.—**s. auxiliar de la navegación,** navigational satellite.—**s. de comunicación,** communication satellite.—**s. terrestre,** earth satellite.—**s. terrestre artificial,** artificial earth satellite.
satén, *m.* sateen.
satinador, ra, *n.* glazer, calender; *m.* polishing tool; *m.* (photog.) burnisher.
satinar, *va.* to calender, glaze, gloss, burnish.
satinete, *m.* (text.) satinet.
sátira, *f.* satire; hint, innuendo; (coll.) saucy and witty woman.
satiriasis, *f.* (med.) satyriasis.
satíricamente, *adv.* satirically; sarcastically.
satiricé, satirice, *v. V.* SATIRIZAR.
satírico, ca. I. *a.* satirical; sarcastic. **II.** *m.* satirist.
satirillo, *m. dim.* little satyr.
satirio, *m.* a kind of water rat.
satirión, *m.* (bot.) orchid that yields salep.
satirizante, *a.* satirizing.
satirizar, *va.* (*pret.* SATIRICÉ; *subj.* SATIRICE) to satirize, lampoon.
sátiro, *m.* satyr, sylvan god; lewd man.
satisdación, *f.* (law) security, surety, bail.
satisfacción, *f.* satisfaction; amends; apology, excuse; confidence, conceit.—**a s.,** fully, according to one's wishes.—**tomar s.,** to vindicate oneself, to stand for one's honor.
satisfacer. I. *va.* (*pp.* SATISFECHO; *ind. pres.* SATISFAGO, *pret.* yo SATISFICE, él SATISFIZO, *fut.* SATISFARÉ; *subj.* SATISFAGA) to satisfy; to pay in full, settle; to expiate, make amends for, atone for; to reward; to indemnify, repay; to answer, make reply; to explain; to free from debt, perplexity, or suspense; to convince.—**s. una letra,** (com.) to honor a draft. **II.** *vr.* to satisfy oneself; to be satisfied; to take satisfaction; to be revenged; to be convinced.
satisfaciente, *a.* satisfying, satisfactory.
satisfactoriamente, *adv.* satisfactorily.
satisfactorio, ria, *a.* satisfactory.
satisfago, satisfaga, *v. V.* SATISFACER.
satisfecho, cha. I. *pp. irreg.* of SATISFACER. **II.** *a.* satisfied, content; arrogant, conceited.
satisfice, satisfizo, *v. V.* SATISFACER.
sativo, va, *a.* sown, cultivated.
sátrapa, *m.* satrap; (coll.) crafty fellow; boss.
satrapía, *f.* satrapy.
saturable, *a.* saturable.
saturación, *f.* saturation.
saturado, da, *a.* saturated, sodden.
saturador, ra. I. *a.* saturant. **II.** *m.* saturater, saturator.
saturar, *va.* to saturate; to fill, glut, satiate.
saturnal. I. *a.* Saturnian. **II.** *f. pl.* Saturnalia.
saturnino, na, *a.* saturnine, melancholy, grave, gloomy, morose; (chem.) saturnine.
saturnio, nia, *a.* Saturnian.
saturnismo, *m.* plumbism, lead poisoning.
Saturno, *m.* (astr.) Saturn.
sauce, *m.* (bot.) willow.—**s. cabruno,** goat willow or great sallow.—**s. llorón,** weeping willow.
sauceda, saucedal, *m.*; **saucera,** *f.* plantation of willows.
saucillo, *m.* (bot.) knotgrass.
saúco, *f.* (bot.) elder or alder tree; horny part of horse's hoof.
sauquillo, *m.* (bot.) dwarf elder.
saurio, *m.* (zool.) saurian.
saurópodo, da, *m.* & *a.* (paleontol.) sauropod.
sausería, *f.* larder in a palace.
sausier, *m.* chief of the larder in a palace.

sautor, *m.* (her.) saltier.
sauz, *m.* (bot.) willow.
sauzal, *m.* willow grove.
sauzgatillo, *m.* (bot.) agnus castus, chaste-tree.
savia, *f.* sap.
saxafrax, *f.* (bot.) = SAXIFRAGA.
saxátil, *a.* growing among rocks, saxicolous.
sáxeo, ea, *a.* stony.
saxífraga, *f.* (bot.) saxifrage.
saxifragáceo, cea, *a.* (bot.) saxifragaceous.
saxifragia, *f.* (bot.) = SAXÍFRAGA.
saxófono, *m.* (mus.) saxophone.
saxoso, sa, *a.* containing stones, stony.
saya, *f.* (outer) skirt; sum of money that the Queen of Spain gives her maids when they marry; an ancient tunic worn by men.
sayal, *m.* coarse woollen stuff; sackcloth.
sayalería, *f.* shop for weaving coarse cloth.
sayalero, *m.* weaver of SAYAL.
sayalesco, ca, *a.* made of SAYAL.
sayalete, *m. dim.* thin flannel for undergarments.
sayete, sayito, *m. dim.* small frock, short skirt.
sayo, *m.* smock frock; large coat; any loose garment.—**s. bobo,** tight dress worn by clowns.—**decir para su s.,** to mutter in one's beard.
sayón, na, *n. m. aug.* executioner; ugly-looking person; (formerly) a kind of judge.
sayuela, *f. dim.* woollen shift worn by some religious orders; a variety of fig tree; (Am.) petticoat.
sayuelo, *m. dim.* little frock.
sazón, *f.* maturity, ripeness; season; taste, relish, flavor; seasoning; occasion, opportunity.—**a la s.,** then, at that time.—**en s.,** ripe, in season; opportunely.
sazonadamente, *adv.* maturely, seasonably.
sazonado, da. I. *pp.* of SAZONAR. **II.** *a.* seasoned; ripe, mellow; witty; pertinent; expressive.
sazonador, ra, *n.* seasoner.
sazonar. I. *va.* (cook.) to season; to mature, bring to maturity. **II.** *vr.* to ripen, to mature.
schotis, *m.* schottische (music and dance).
se, 3*d. pers. obj. pron., m.* or *f., sing.* or *pl.* used: (1) As a refl. acc. case, equivalent to "himself," "oneself," "herself," "itself," "themselves," "to himself," "to oneself," etc. (*él se afeitó,* he shaved himself; *las niñas se vistieron,* the girls dressed themselves; *uno se ama,* one loves oneself). (2) As an acc. or a dat. recip., to indicate mutual action, equivalent to "each other," "one another," "to each other," "to one another" (*Juan y María se aman, pero no se hablan,* John and Mary love each other, but do not speak to each other). (3) As a symbol forming verbs refl. only in form, not in meaning, as *irse,* to go; *morirse,* to die; *reírse,* to laugh. (4) Instead of dat. *le, les,* before an acc. case (*yo se lo di,* I gave it to him [her, them, you]; *Juan se los entregó,* John delivered them to him [her, them, you]). (5) To give a poss. value to a def. or indef. art. (*Juan se corta las uñas,* John cuts his nails; *Juan se quebró una mano,* John broke one of his hands). (6) To form certain expressions of a passive character, rendered in Eng. by the passive form of the corresponding verb, or by introducing "they," "people," "one," as an indef. subject (*se dice,* it is said, they say, people say; *no se sabe,* it is not known; *esto se aprende fácilmente,* this is easily learned, one learns this easily; *aquí se habla español,* Spanish [is] spoken here; *eso no puede negarse,* that cannot be denied). When *se* is thus used indefinitely in the imper., the resulting form is generally rendered by the simple imper. (*para otros pormenores, escríbase al secretario,* for other particulars, write to the secretary; *consúltese el diccionario,* consult the dictionary).
sé, *v. V.* SABER.
sea, *v. V.* SER.
sebáceo, cea, *a.* sebaceous, tallowy.
sebastiano, *m.* (bot.) = SEBESTÉN.
sebe, *f.* wattle, stockade, fence.
sebero, ra, *a.* tallow (as *a.*), pert. to tallow.
sebestén, *m.* (bot.) sebesten tree; its fruit.
sebillo, *m.* white tallow; toilet soap.
sebo, *m.* tallow, fat, candle grease.—**s. en bruto,** or **en rama,** rough tallow, suet.
seborrea, *f.* (med.) seborrhea.
seboso, sa, *a.* tallowy, fat, greasy, unctuous.
sebucán, *m.* (Am.) manioc strainer.
seca, *f.* drought; dry season; (med.) peeling; (med.) infarction of a gland; (naut.) dry sand bank.—**a secas,** simply.
secácul, *m.* (bot.) an aromatic root.
secadal, *m.* dry, barren ground or sand bank.
secadero, ra. I. *a.* (of fruit) good or fit for drying. **II.** *m.* drying shed, room, or floor; drier; fruit drier.
secado, da, *pp.* of SECAR.—**s. al sol,** sun-dried.
secadillo, *m.* dry-almond biscuit.
secador, ra. I. *a.* drying. **II.** *m.* (Am.) dryer. **III.** *f.* (Am.) clothes dryer.
secamente, *adv.* dryly; curtly, coldly; simply.
secamiento, *m.* drying, desiccation.
secano, *m.* unwatered land; dry sand bank; anything very dry.
secansa, *f.* at cards, sequence.
[1]**secante,** *f.* (geom.) secant.
[2]**secante,** *a.* drying; blotting (paper); (Arg.) annoying.
secar. I. *va.* (*pret.* SEQUÉ; *subj.* SEQUE) to dry (out), desiccate; to parch; to wipe dry; to tease, vex, annoy, bore. **II.** *vr.* to dry, parch, dry up; to become lank, lean, or meager; to decay; to wither; to be extremely thirsty.
secaral, *m.* dryness, drought.
secatura, *f.* insipidity, vapidity, dulness.
sección, *f.* act of cutting; section, division, portion; (geom.) section; (arch.) section of a building.—**s. de fondo,** editorial section.—**s. recta,** (geom.) right section.—**s. transversal** (drawing, eng.) cross section.
seccionado, da, *pp.* & *a.* sectional, in sections.
seccionar, *va.* to section.
seccionario, ria, *a.* sectional.
secesión, *f.* secession.
secesionista, *n.* & *a.* secessionist.
seceso, *m.* excrement, stool.
seco, ca, *a.* dry; dried up; juiceless; arid; withered; dead (leaves); lean, lank, meager; plain, unadorned, unvarnished; abrupt, curt; lukewarm, cold, indifferent; thin and spare; (of pain) dull.—**en s.,** high and dry; without cause or reason; (mason.) dry, without mortar; by the dry process, without water.
secreción, *f.* segregation; (med.) secretion.
secreta, *f.* private examination preceding the graduation of licentiates; (eccl.) secrets; secret investigation; privy, water closet.
secretamente, *adv.* secretly.
secretar, *va.* (physiol.) to secrete.
secretaria, *f.* wife of a secretary; woman secretary.
secretaría, *f.* secretary's office; secretaryship.
secretariado, *m.* secretariat, secretaryship.
secretario, *m.* secretary; actuary; scribe, amanuensis.—**S. de Estado,** Secretary of State.—**S. de Hacienda,** Secretary of the Treasury.—**S. del Despacho** = S. DE ESTADO.—**s. particular,** private secretary.
secretear, *vn.* (coll.) to whisper.
secreteo, *m.* (coll.) whispering.
secreter, *m.* secretary, desk, bureau.
secretico, illo, ito, *m. dim.* little secret.
secretina, *f.* (biochem.) secretin.
secretista, *m.* naturalist; dealer in secrets.
secreto, ta. I. *a.* secret; confidential, private. **II.** *m.* secret; secrecy; nostrum; caution, silence, dissimulation, concealment; scrutoire, secret drawer.—**s. a voces,** or **con chirimías,** open secret.—**en s.,** in secret, in private, confidentially.
secretorio, ria, *a.* (med.) secretory.
secta, *f.* sect; doctrine of a sect.
sectador, ra; sectario, ria, *n.* & *a.* sectarian.
sectarismo, *m.* sectarianism.
sectil, *a.* sectile.
sector, *m.* (geom., mil.) sector.

secuaz, *m.* follower, supporter, henchman.
secuela, *f.* sequel, result, upshot.
secuencia, *f.* (eccl.) sequence.
secuestrable, *a.* (law) sequestrable.
secuestración, *f.* (law) sequestration.
secuestrador, ra, *n.* sequestrator, receiver.
secuestrar, *va.* (law) to sequestrate, sequester; to kidnap, abduct.
secuestrario, ria, *a.* pert. to sequestration.
secuestro, *m.* (law) sequestration; umpire, referee; kidnapping, abduction; (surg.) sequestrum, dead portion of bone.
secular. I. *a.* centenary, centennial; lasting for ages; secular, lay. **II.** *m.* (eccl.) secular.
secularicé, secularice, *v. V.* SECULARIZAR.
secularismo, *m.* secularism.
secularista, *n.* secularist.
secularización, *f.* secularization.
secularizar, *va.* (*pret.* SECULARICÉ; *subj.* SECULARICE) to secularize.
secundar, *va.* to second, aid, favor.
secundario, ria. I. *a.* secondary; high (school); subordinate; subsidiary.—**producto s.,** by-product. **II.** *m.* second hand (of timepiece).
secundinas, *f. pl.* (zool.) afterbirth.
secundípara, *a.* a mother for the second time.
secura, *f.* dryness, condition of drought.
sed, *f.* thirst; drought; eagerness, anxiety; longing desire.—**tener s.,** to be thirsty.—**tener s. de,** to be thirsty for; to thirst, or hunger, after.
seda, *f.* silk (fibre, yarn, and fabric); wild boar's bristles.—**s. cocida,** soft silk.—**s. conchal,** finest silk from choice cocoons.—**s. cruda,** hard silk.—**s. de capullos,** ferret silk, grosgrain yarn.—**s. de coser,** sewing silk.—**s. en rama,** raw silk.—**s. floja,** floss silk; soft, untwisted silk.—**s. joyante,** very glossy silk.—**s. torcida,** twisted silk.—**como una s.,** as smooth as silk; easily, without hitch or hindrance.—**de media s.,** half-silk.—**de toda s.,** all silk.—**ser como una s.,** or **ser una s.,** to be sweet-tempered.
sedadera, *f.* hackle for dressing flax.
sedal, *m.* fishline; (surg.) seton; (vet.) rowel.
sedalina, *f.* a silk-and-cotton fabric.
sedán, *m.* (auto.) sedan.
sedante, *a.* soothing, allaying, sedative.
sedar, *va.* to allay, appease, soothe, quiet.
sedasticidad, *f.* (stat.) scedasticity.
sedástico, ca, *a.* (stat.) scedastic.
sedativo, va, *n.* & *a.* (med.) sedative.
sede, *f.* (eccl.) see; headquarters.—**s. provisional,** interim headquarters.—**Santa S.,** Holy See.
sedear, *va.* to clean (jewels) with a brush.
sedentario, ria, *a.* sedentary.
sedeña, *f.* fine tow or flax.
sedeño, ña, *a.* silky, silken; silklike.
sedera, *f.* brush made of bristles.
sedería, *f.* silks; silk stuff; silk shop.
sedero, ra. I. *a.* silk, silken. **II.** *n.* silk weaver, silk mercer, silk dealer.
sedición, *f.* sedition, insurrection, mutiny.
sediciosamente, *adv.* seditiously.
sedicioso, sa, *a.* seditious, mutinous.
sediento, ta, *a.* thirsty, dry; (**de**) eagerly desirous, anxious (for).
sedimentación, *f.* sedimentation.
sedimentar, *va.* & *vr.* to settle, to desposit (as dregs).
sedimentario, ria, *a.* sedimentary.
sedimento, *m.* sediment, settlings, dregs; feces, grouts, grounds; (min.) sinter.
sedoso, sa, *a.* silky, silklike, silken.
seducción, *f.* seduction, deceiving; abuse.
seducir, *va.* (*ind. pres.* SEDUZCO, *pret.* SEDUJE; *subj.* SEDUZCA) to seduce, corrupt, lead astray; to charm, captivate.
seductivo, va, *a.* seductive; enticing.
seductor, ra. I. *a.* fascinating, attractive, tempting. **II.** *n.* seducer, corrupter; deceiver; delightful person.
sefardí. I. *a.* Sephardic. **II.** *n.* Sephardic Jew; *m.* Sephardic dialect.
sefardíes, *m. pl.* Sephardim.
sefardita, *n.* & *a.* = SEFARDÍ.
segable, *a.* fit to be reaped.
segada, *f.* harvest.
segadera, *f.* reaping hook, sickle.
segadero, ra, *a.* fit to be reaped.
segador, ra. I. *n.* mower; reaper, harvester. **II.** *f.* mowing machine.
segar, *va.* (*ind. pres.* SIEGO, *pret.* SEGUÉ; *subj.* SIEGUE) (agr.) to mow; to reap, harvest; to cut off, mow down.
segazón, *f.* harvest season; reaping.
seglar. I. *a.* wordly, secular, lay. **II.** *m.* layman; *f.* laywoman.
seglaridad, *f.* secularity.
segmentación, *f.* (biol.) segmentation.
segmentar, *va.* & *vn.* to segment.
segmentario, ria, *a.* segmentary, segmental.
segmento, *m.* segment; (geom.) segment.
segoviano, na; segoviense, *n.* & *a.* Segovian, from Segovia.
segregación, *f.* segregation, separation.—**s. celular,** solitary confinement.
segregacionista, *n.* segregationist.
segregado, da, *a.* segregate, separate.
segregar, *va.* (*pret.* SEGREGUÉ; *subj.* SEGREGUE) to segregate, separate, set apart; (med.) to secrete.
segregativo, va, *a.* segregative.
segrí, *m.* heavy, raised silk stuff.
segué, *pret.* of SEGAR.
segueta, *f.* buhl saw, piercing saw.
seguetear, *vn.* to make buhlwork with the buhl saw.
seguida, *f.* succession; continuation.—**de s.,** consecutively, in succession, without interruption.—**en s.,** forthwith, immediately.
seguidamente, *adv.* successively; immediately after, right after that.
seguidero, *m.* guide lines for writing.
seguidilla, *f.* (poet.) stanza of seven lines with peculiar rhythm.—*pl.* a merry Spanish tune and dance; (coll.) diarrhœa.
seguido, da. I. *pp.* of SEGUIR. **II.** *a.* continued, successive; straight, direct. **III.** *m.* a diminishing stitch for narrowing a stocking at the foot.
seguidor, ra. I. *n.* follower. **II.** *m.* guide rules for writing.
seguimiento, *m.* pursuit, following, chase; hunt; continuation, pursuit.
seguir. I. *va.* (*ger.* SIGUIENDO; *ind. pres.* SIGO, *pret.* él SIGUIÓ; *subj.* SIGA) to follow; to pursue; to prosecute; to continue; (foll. by *ger.*) to keep on (foll. by *pres. p.*); to dog, hound; to bring, institute (as a suit). **II.** *vr.* to ensue, follow as a consequence; to follow in order; to issue, spring.
según, *prep.* according to; as; depending on.—**s. derecho,** according to law.—**s. está (estoy,** etc.) **de** (foll. by *a.*), he is (I am, etc.) so, being so: *no oyó lo que dije, según estaba de enojado,* he did not hear what I said, he was so angry.—**s. que,** according as.—**s. y como,** or **s. y conforme,** just as; it depends.
segunda, *f.* double turn of a key.
segundar. I. *va.* to repeat over again. **II.** *vn.* to be second, to follow next to the first.
segundariamente, *adv.* secondarily.
segundario, ria, *a.* = SECUNDARIO.
segundero, ra. I. *a.* (agr.) pert. to a second crop in the same year. **II.** *m.* second hand (of timepiece).
segundilla, *f.* call bell in convents.
segundillo, *m.* second portion of food distributed at table in convents; (mus.) semitone.
segundo, da. I. *a.* second; favorable.—**s. carpintero,** carpenter's mate.—**s. dama, s. galán,** (theat.) woman, man, with walk-on part.—**s. intención,** double meaning, double dealing, duplicity.—**de s. mano,** second-hand. **II.** *m.* second (of time or of arc); second in authority, assistant; equal (in the phrase **sin s.,** without an equal, unrivaled).
segundogénito, ta, *a.* & *n.* second-born.

segundogenitura, *f.* condition and right of a second-born.
segundón, *m.* any son born after the first.
segur, *f.* axe; axe in fasces carried by lictors; (agr.) sickle.
segurador, *m.* security, bondsman.
seguramente, *adv.* securely, safely; surely.
segurar, *va.* = ASEGURAR, to secure; to affirm.
segureja, *f. dim.* (cooperage) small hatchet.
seguridad, *f.* security, surety; certainty; safety; custody; corroboration; surety bond.—**caja de s.,** safety deposit box.—**con s., con toda s.,** with absolute certainty.
seguro, ra. I. *a.* secure; safe, reliable, dependable; sure, certain, positive; firm, constant, stanch, steady; unfailing.—**tener por s.,** to be sure of. **II.** *m.* assurance, certainty, confidence; permit, warrant, license; (mech.) click, stop, pawl, ratchet; safety catch (of a pistol); tumbler of a lock; (com.) insurance, assurance.—**s. agrario,** farm insurance.—**s. contra accidentes,** accident insurance.—**s. contra incendios,** fire insurance.—**s. de desempleo,** unemployment insurance.—**s. de hospitalización,** hospitalization insurance.—**s. de viaje,** travelers' insurance.—**s. de vida,** life insurance. —**s. familiar,** family insurance.—**s. marítimo,** marine insurance.—**s. mutuo,** mutual insurance.—**a buen s., al s.,** or **de s.,** certainly, undoubtedly.—**en s.,** in security or safety.—**irse del s.,** to forget oneself, to throw wisdom overboard.—**sobre s.,** without risk.
segurón, *m. aug.* large axe or hatchet.
seis. I. *a.* & *m.* six; sixth (of the month); six-spotted card, die, or domino. **II.** *f. pl.*—**las s.,** six o'clock.
seisavado, da, *a.* hexagonal.
seisavo, va. I. *n.* & *a.* sixth. **II.** *m.* one sixth; hexagon.
seiscientos, tas, *n.* & *a.* six hundred; six-hundredth.
seise, *m.* one of six choir boys in some cathedrals, who sing and dance in certain festivals.
seisén, *m.* an ancient silver coin.
seiseno, na, *a.* sixth.
seisillo, *m.* (mus.) sextolet.
seísmico, etc., = SÍSMICO, etc., seismic, etc.
seje, *m.* (bot.) (S. A.) a kind of palm tree.
selacio, cia, *m.* & *a.* (ichth.) selachian.
selección, *f.* selection, choice.—**s. natural,** natural selection.—**s. sexual,** sexual selection.
seleccionamiento, *m.* selection, choosing.
seleccionar, *va.* to make a selection, choose.
selectas, *f. pl.* analects, selections from an author.
selectivo, va, *a.* selective; (rad.) selective.
selecto, ta, *a.* select, choice, distinguished.
selector, *m.* (elec.) selector.
selénico, ca, *a.* (chem.) selenic.
selenio, *m.* (chem.) selenium.
selenita. I. *n.* inhabitant of the moon. **II.** *f.* (min.) selenite.
selenitoso, sa, *a.* (min.) selenitic.
seleniuro, *m.* (chem.) selenide.
selenografía, *f.* selenography.
selenográfico, ca, *a.* selenographic.
selenógrafo, *m.* selenographer.
self, *f.* (Angl.) (elec.) self-induction coil.
selfactina, *f.* (spinning) mule jenny.
selfinducción, *f.* (incorrect but common) (elec.) = AUTOINDUCCIÓN self-induction.
selva, *f.* forest, woods.
selvático, ca, *a.* sylvan; rustic, wild.
selvatiquez, *f.* wildness; rusticity.
selvicultura, *f.* = SILVICULTURA, forestry.
selvoso, sa, *a.* sylvan, woody, wooded.
sellado, da. I. *pp.* of SELLAR. **II.** *a.* sealed.
sellador, ra, *n.* sealer.
selladura, *f.* sealing.
sellar, *va.* to seal; to stamp; to conclude, finish; to cover, to close.—**s. los labios,** to silence; to keep silent.
sello, *m.* seal; stamp (sticker, mark or implement); signet; stamp office; (pharm.) cachet, wafer capsule.—**s. de aduana,** cocket.—**s. de correo,** postage stamp.—**s. de Salomón,** Solomon's seal (mystic symbol);—**s. de Santa María,** (bot.) Solomon's-seal.
semafórico, ca, *a.* semaphoric.
semáforo, *m.* semaphore.
semana, *f.* week; week's wages or pay.—**s. santa,** Holy Week; book containing the offices of this week.—**entre s.,** any week day except Saturday.—**la s. que no tenga viernes,** never.
semanal, *a.* weekly.
semanalmente, *adv.* weekly, by the week.
semanario, ria. I. *a.* weekly. **II.** *m.* weekly publication; set of seven razors.
semanería, *f.* functions performed or work done in the course of a week.
semanero, ra, *a.* engaged by the week.
semántica, *f.* semantics, semasiology.
semántico, ca, *a.* semantic.
semasiología, *f.* semasiology, semantics.
semblante, *m.* mien, countenance, look, expression; aspect.—**mudar de s.,** to change color; to take a different turn or a different aspect.
semblanza, *f.* biographical sketch.
sembrada, *f.* (agr.) sown land.
sembradera, *f.* (agr.) sowing machine, sower; seed drill, seeder, seeding machine.
sembradío, día, *a.* (agr.) prepared for sowing; arable.
sembrado, *m.* cultivated field, sown ground.
sembrador, ra. I. *n.* sower, seeder. **II.** *f.* seeder, sowing machine.
sembradura, *f.* sowing, seeding.
sembrar, *va.* (*ind.* SIEMBRO; *subj.* SIEMBRE) (agr.) to sow, seed; to scatter, spread, disseminate.—**como sembráredes, cogéredes,** as you sow, so shall you reap.
semeiología, *f.* (med.) semiology, semeiology.
semeiótica, *f.* (med.) semeiotics.
semeja, *f.* resemblance, likeness; mark, sign.
semejable, *a.* like, resembling.
semejado, da. I. *pp.* of SEMEJAR. **II.** *a.* = SEMEJABLE.
semejante. I. *a.* similar, like; such, of that kind, (geom., alg.) similar. **II.** *m.* resemblance, likeness; fellow creature, fellow man.
semejantemente, *adv.* likewise, similarly.
semejanza, *f.* resemblance, similarity, similitude.—**a s. de,** like.
semejar, *vn.* & *vr.* to be like, to resemble.
semen, *m.* semen, sperm; (bot.) seed.
semencera, *f.* sowing, seeding.
semencontra, *m.* (pharm.) vermifuge.
semental, *a.* (agr.) seminal, germinal; breeding (horse).
sementar, *va.* (*ind.* SEMIENTO; *subj.* SEMIENTE) to sow, to seed.
sementera, *f.* (agr.) sowing, seeding; cultivated field, land sown; seed bed, seed field, seed garden, seed plot; seed sown; seedtime; origin, cause, beginning.
sementero, *m.* seed bag, seedcod, seedleap, hopper; seed bed, seed plot.
sementino, na, *a.* pert. to seed or seedtime.
semestral, *a.* semiannual, half-yearly.
semestralmente, *adv.* seminannually.
semestre. I. *a.* lasting six months. **II.** *m.* space of six months, semester; six-months' pension or pay.
semi, *prefix,* semi, half, partly. Besides the words that are given below, this prefix is found in many other Spanish words, which are self-explaining.
semiárido, da, *a.* semiarid.
semiautomático, ca, *a.* semiautomatic.
semibreve, *f.* (mus.) semibreve, whole note (𝅝).
semicabrón, semicapro, *m.* satyr.
semicalificado, da, *a.* semiskilled (worker).
semicilindro, *m.* half cylinder.

semicircular, *a.* semicircular.
semicírculo, *m.* (geom.) semicircle.
semicircunferencia, *f.* semicircumference.
semicivilizado, da, *a.* semicivilized.
semiconductor, *m.* (elec.) semiconductor.
semiconsciente, *a.* semiconscious.
semicopado, da, *a.* (mus.) syncopated.
semicorchea, *f.* (mus.) semiquaver.
semicromático, ca, *a.* (mus.) semichromatic.
semicuadrado, *m.* (astrol.) semiquadrate, semiquartile.
semicupio, *m.* sitz bath.
semidea, *f.* (poet.) demigoddess.
semideo, *m.* (poet.) demigod.
semidiáfano, na, *a.* semidiaphanous.
semidiámetro, *m.* semidiameter.
semidiapasón, *m.* (mus.) semidiapason.
semidifunto, ta, *a.* half dead, almost dead.
semidiós, sa, *n.* demigod(-dess).
semidítono, *m.* (mus.) semiditone.
semidiurno, na, *a.* semidiurnal.
semidoble, *a.* semidouble.
semidormido, da, *a.* half asleep, sleepy.
semidragón, *m.* semidragon.
semieje, *m.* (geom.) semiaxis; (carriage) half axletree.
semiento, semiente, *v. V.* SEMENTAR.
semiesfera, *f.* hemisphere.
semifinal, *a.* semifinal.
semifinalista, *n.* semifinalist.
semiflúido, da, *a.* semifluid.
semiforme, *a.* half formed, undeveloped.
semifusa, *f.* (mus.) double demisemiquaver.
semigola, *f.* (fort.) demigorge.
semihombre, *m.* half-man, pigmy.
semilunar, *a.* semilunar, semilunary.
semilunio, *m.* (astr.) half-moon.
semilla, *f.* seed.
semillero, *m.* seed bed, seed plot; nursery; hotbed.
semilloso, sa, *a.* seedy.
seminación, *f.* (biol.) semination.
seminal, *a.* seminal, germinal, spermatic.
seminario, *m.* seed plot, nursery; seminary; beginning, root, origin, source.—**s. conciliar,** theological seminary.
seminarista, *m.* seminarist, theological student.
seminífero, ra, *a.* seminiferous, seed-bearing.
semínima, *f.* (mus.) crotchet.
semioficial, *a.* semiofficial.
semiología, semiótica, *f.* (med.) semiology, symptomatology.
semipedal, *a.* half foot long.
semipermeable, *a.* semipermeable.
semiplena, *a.* (law) imperfect (evidence).
semiplenamente, *adv.* half proved.
semiprecioso, sa, *a.* semiprecious.
semirrecto, ta, *a.* (geom.) of 45 degrees.
semirrígido, da, *a.* (aer.) semirigid.
semirrubio, bia, *a.* nearly blond.
semís, *m.* half a Roman pound.
semisalvaje, *a.* half-savage, semicivilized.
semisólido, da, *m.* & *a.* semisolid.
semita. I. *a.* Semitic. **II.** *n.* Semite.
semítico, ca, *a.* Semitic.
semitismo, *m.* Semitism.
semitono, *m.* (mus.) semitone.
semitransparente, *a.* semitransparent.
semitropical, *a.* semitropical.
semivivo, va, *a.* half alive.
semivocal. I. *a.* (phon.) semivocalic. **II.** *f.* (phon.) semivowel.
sémola, *f.* semolina, groats or grits.
sempiternamente, *adv.* eternally.
sempiterno, na. I. *a.* eternal, everlasting. **II.** *f.* a sort of serge; (bot.) everlasting.
sen, *m.* (bot.) senna; sen (Japanese coin).
sena, *f.* six on a die; (bot.) senna.—*pl.* double sixes.
senado, *m.* senate; senate hall.
senadoconsulto, *m.* senatus consultum; decree of a senate.
senador, ra, *n.* senator.
senaduría, *f.* senatorship.
senara, *f.* piece of sown ground assigned to servants as part of their wages.
senarero, *m.* servant who has a SENARA.
senario, ria, *a.* senary, pertaining to six.
senatorial; senatorio, ria, *a.* senatorial.
sencillamente, *adv.* simply; easily; plainly, candidly.
sencillez, *f.* simplicity; easiness; plainness, naturalness; candor.
sencillo, lla, *a.* simple, unmixed; light, slight, thin, of light body (fabrics); plain; artless, harmless; guileless, candid; natural, unaffected; unadorned; single; of less value (coins).
senda, *f.* path, footpath, way.
senderar, *va.* to make a path in or through.
senderear. I. *va.* to guide or conduct on a footpath; to make a path in or for. **II.** *vn.* to adopt extraordinary means to obtain an end.
sendero, *m.* path, footpath, byway.
senderuelo, *m. dim.* little pathway.
sendos, das, *a. pl.* one each, one for each (diff. constr.: *tienen sendos libros,* they have a book each, each of them has a book).
senecio, *m.* (bot.) Senecio.
senectud, *f.* old age, senescence.
Senegal, *m.* Senegal.
senegalés, sa, *n.* & *a.* Senegalese.
senescal, *m.* seneschal, household officer.
senescalato, *m.,* **senescalía,** *f.* seneschalship.
senil, *a.* senile; (astr.) fourth quadrant.
senilidad, *f.* senility.
seno, *m.* chest, thoracic cavity; breast, bosom; womb; lap of a woman; hole, cavity; sinus; gulf, bay; any cavity in the interior of the human body; innermost recess; asylum, refuge; (arch.) spandrel; (surg.) sinus; cavity of a wound; (naut.) curvature of a sail or line; (math.) sine.—**s. de Abrahán,** Abraham's bosom.—**s. verso,** (math.) versed sine.
senojil, *m.* = CENOJIL, garter.
sensación, *f.* sensation.
sensacional, *a.* sensational.
sensatez, *f.* good judgment, wisdom, good sense.
sensato, ta, *a.* sensible, judicious, wise.
sensibilidad, *f.* sensibility; sensitiveness.
sensibilización, *f.* (photog.) sensitization.
sensibilizado, da, *a.* (photog.) sensitized, sensitive.
sensibilizador, *m.* sensitizer.
sensibilizar, *va.* (*pret.* SENSIBILICÉ; *subj.* SENSIBILICE) (photog.) to sensitize.
sensible. I. *a.* perceptibile, appreciable; sensitive, keen; grievous, regrettable; (photog.) sensitive, sensitized. **II.** *f.* (mus.) seventh note.
sensiblemente, *adv.* perceptibly; approximately; grievously.
sensiblería, *f.* oversentimentality.
sensiblero, ra, *a.* gushy, excessively sentimental.
sensitiva, *f.* (bot.) sensitive plant, mimosa.
sensitivo, va, *a.* sensitive; sensual; appreciable.
sensor, *m.* sensor.
sensorio, ria. I. *a.* sensory, sensorial. **II.** *m.* (anat.) sensorium (called also **s. común**).
sensual, *a.* sensuous; sensual, lewd, lustful.
sensualidad, *f.* sensuality, lust, lewdness.
sensualismo, *m.* sensualism, sensuality; (philos.) sensationalism.
sensualista. I. *a.* sensualistic. **II.** *n.* (philos.) sensationalist.
sensualmente, *adv.* sensually, carnally.
sentada, *f.* = ASENTADA, sitting, session.
sentadero, *m.* place or thing where one can sit.
sentadillas.—a s., sidesaddlewise.
sentado, da. I. *pp.* of SENTAR. **II.** *a.* seated, sitting down; sedate, judicious, wise; settled, steady, firm; (bot.) sessile.
sentamiento, *m.* (arch.) settling.
sentar. I. *vn.* (*ind.* SIENTO; *subj.* SIENTE) to fit, to become, to suit; to agree with one (as food or a climate); to please, to be agreeable. **II.** *va.* to set, set up, establish; settle; to seat; (tailor-

ing) to press the seams of. **III.** *vr.* to sink, subside, settle; to settle down; ASENTARSE, to sit down.
sentencia, *f.* (law) sentence, verdict, judgment; penalty; (com.) award; opinion, determination; dogma, axiom, maxim; (gram.) sentence.—**fulminar,** or **pronunciar, la s.,** to pass judgment.
sentenciador, ra, *n.* one who passes judgment.
sentenciar, *va.* (law) to sentence, to pass judgment on; to determine, decide.
sentención, *f.* severe, rigorous sentence.
sentenciosamente, *adv.* sententiously.
sentencioso, sa, *a.* sententious, pithy.
sentenzuela, *f. dim.* light sentence.
senticar, *m.* place full of briers and brambles.
sentidamente, *adv.* feelingly, regretfully.
sentido, da. I. *pp.* of SENTIR. **II.** *a.* felt, experienced; sensitive; susceptible, touchy; offended; cracked, split.—**darse por s.,** to show resentment. **III.** *m.* sense, any one of the five senses; sense perception, feeling; judgment; understanding, reason; import, sense, meaning; direction, course.—**s. común,** common sense.—**con (todos) mis cinco sentidos,** with all my heart and soul.—**costar un s.,** to be excessively high-priced.—**en el s. de que,** to the effect that; stating that.—**perder el s.,** to lose consciousness; to faint.—**sin s.,** meaningless; unconscious.
sentimental, *a.* sentimental; emotional.
sentimentalismo, *m.* sentimentalism.
sentimentalista, *n.* sentimentalist.
sentimentalmente, *adv.* sentimentally.
sentimiento, *m.* sentiment, feeling; sensation; grief, sorrow, regret.
sentina, *f.* (naut.) bilge; sink, drain; place of iniquity.
sentir. I. *va.* (*ger.* SINTIENDO; *ind. pres.* SIENTO, *pret.* él SINTIÓ; *subj.* SIENTA) to feel; to perceive by the senses (to hear, smell, etc.); to endure, suffer; to grieve, regret, mourn, to be sorry for. **II.** *vn.* to feel; to judge, form an opinion; to foresee, foreknow; to fit the action to the word.—**sin s.,** without noticing, inadvertently. **III.** *vr.* to be moved, be affected; to complain; to resent; to feel (well, bad, sad); to crack; to be in a ruinous state; (naut.) to spring (yard or mast). **IV.** *m.* feeling; opinion, judgment.
seña, *f.* sign, mark, token; nod, gesture; signal; (mil.) password, watchword.—*pl.* address (street, city, etc.).—**señas mortales,** unmistakable signs or proof.—**señas personales,** personal description.—**por señas,** by signs.—**por señas,** or **por más señas,** as a stronger proof of it.
señal, *f.* sign, mark, token, symptom; mark or note of distinction; signal; landmark; bookmark; reminder; trace, vestige; trail, track, footstep; scar; representation, image; pledge; earnest money, deposit; (tel.) warning, call.—**s. de peligro,** signal of distress; (Ry.) danger signal.—**s. de tráfico,** traffic sign.—**código de señales,** signal code.—**en s. de,** in proof of.—**ni s.,** not a trace.
señaladamente, *adv.* especially, remarkably; signally, notably.
señalado, da, *a.* & *pp.* distinguished, noted.
señalamiento, *m.* appointment, date.
señalar. I. *va.* to stamp, to mark; to point out, make known; to name; to set, fix, determine; to sign; to mark with a wound, especially in the face; (fencing) to make a feint; at cards, to mark the points; to make signals to.—**s. con el dedo,** to point with the finger. **II.** *vr.* to distinguish oneself, to excel.
señaleja, *f. dim.* little sign or mark.
señera, *f.* ancient signal or pendant.
señero, ra, *a.* solitary, alone.
señolear, *vn.* to catch birds with a lure.
señor, *m.* sir; mister, Mr.; man, gentleman; lord, master, owner of a place; (eccl.) the eucharist; (coll.) (as *a.*) superlative (in excellence, importance, etc.).—**s. de horca y cuchillo,** lord of the manor, invested with civil and criminal jurisdiction within his estate.—**s. mayor,** aged man.—**el S.,** the Lord; our Lord (Jesus Christ).—**muy s. mío,** Dear Sir (in letters).—**nuestro S.,** our Lord.
señora, *f.* lady, mistress, owner of a place; madam; dame, gentlewoman.—**s. de compañia,** companion, chaperon.—**s. mayor,** matron, middle-aged, respectable woman.—**muy s.,** very much of a lady.—**nuestra S.,** our Lady (the Virgin).
señorada, *f.* act of a gentleman or lady.
señoraje, *m.* seigniorage.
señoreador, ra, *n.* domineering person.
señoreaje, *m.* seigniorage.
señoreante, *a.* domineering.
señorear. I. *va.* to master; to domineer, lord it over, rule despotically; to excel, to occupy a higher station than; to overtop, tower over; to control (one's passions); (coll.) to treat repeatedly with the title of lord. **II.** *vr.* to put on airs.
señoría, *f.* lordship (title and person); dominion, seigniory, lordship; government of a particular state; senate; prince.
señorial, *a.* manorial.
señoril, *a.* lordly, pertaining to a lord.
señorilmente, *adv.* nobly, grandly, lordly.
señorío, *m.* seigniory, seignioralty; dominion, command; imperiousness, arrogance; lordship; domain, manor; gravity or stateliness of deportment; freedom and self-control in action.
señorita, *f. dim.* young lady; miss; Miss; (coll.) mistress of the house.
señoritingo, *m.* (contempt.) little master or youth of no account.
señorito, *m. dim.* young gentleman; Master (title); (coll.) master of the house; (coll.) playboy.
señorón, na, *n. aug.* grand seignior or lady.
señuelo, *m.* lure, decoy; bait; enticement.
seo, *f.* cathedral church.
seó, *m.*; **seor, ra,** *n.* (*contr.* of SEÑOR, RA) (coll.) lord, sir (madam, lady).
sepa, *v. V.* SABER.
sépalo, *m.* (bot.) sepal.
sepancuantos, *m.* (coll.) spanking, scolding, punishment.
separable, *a.* separable, detachable, removable.
separación, *f.* separation; disgregation, dissociation, abstraction; parting; dismissal, discharge; (pol.) secession.
separadamente, *adv.* separately.
separado, da. I. *pp.* of SEPARAR. **II.** *a.* separate, apart.—**por s.,** separate, separately.
separador, ra, *n.* separator.
separar. I. *va.* to separate; divide; to disjoin, sever, detach, disconnect; to remove, take away or off; to set apart, lay aside; to sort; to dismiss, discharge. **II.** *vr.* to separate; to part company; to come off; to withdraw, resign; (com.) to dissolve.
separatismo, *m.* separatism; (pol.) secessionism.
separatista, *n.* & *a.* separatist; secessionist.
separativo, va, *a.* separating.
sepedón, *m.* seps, a kind of serpent.
sepelio, *m.* burial, interment.
sepia, *f.* sepia; (ichth.) cuttlefish.
sepsis, *f.* (med.) sepsis, blood poisoning.
septal, *a.* (anat.) septal.
septena, *f.* septenary, heptade, group of seven.
septenario, ria. I. *a.* septenary, pert. to seven; septivalent. **II.** *m.* period of seven days.
septenio, *m.* septennium, period of seven years.
septeno, na, *a.* seventh.
septentrión, *m.* north; north wind; (**S-, astr.**) Great Bear.
septentrional, *a.* northern, northerly.
septeto, *m.* (mus.) septet, septuor.
septicemia, *f.* (med.) septicemia, septicæmia.
septicémico, ca, *a.* septicemic, septicæmic.
séptico, ca, *a.* septic.
septiembre, *m.* September.

septillo, *m.* (mus.) septimole or septuplet.
septillón, *m.* septillion.
séptimo, ma. I. *a.* seventh. **II.** *m.* seventh; *f.* run of seven cards (in piquet); (mus.) seventh.
septisílabo, ba, *a.* of seven syllables.
septo, *m.* (anat.) septum.
septuagenario, ria, *n.* & *a.* septuagenarian.
septuagésimo, ma. I. *a.* seventieth; septuagesimal. **II.** *n.* seventieth. **III.** *f.* (eccl.) Septuagesima.
septuplicación, *f.* multiplying by seven.
septuplicar, *va.* to septuple.
séptuplo, pla, *a.* septuple, sevenfold.
sepulcral, *a.* sepulchral; monumental.
sepulcro, *m.* sepulcher, grave, tomb.
sepultador, ra, *n.* burier, gravedigger.
sepultar, *va.* to bury, inter; to hide, conceal.
sepulto, ta. I. *pp. irreg.* of SEPULTAR. **II.** *a.* buried.
sepultura, *f.* sepulture, interment; tomb, grave, sepulcher.—**dar s.,** to bury.
sepulturero, ra, *n.* gravedigger, sexton.
sequé, seque, *v. V.* SECAR.
sequedad, *f.* aridity, dryness; barrenness, sterility; asperity, surliness, gruffness.
sequedal, sequeral, *m.* dry, barren soil.
sequero, *m.* dry, unirrigated land.
sequeroso, sa, *a.* dry, wanting moisture.
sequete, *m.* piece of hard, dry bread or biscuit; stroke, blow, thump, thwack; (coll.) curt reply, gruff answer.
sequía, *f.* drought.
sequillo, *m.* biscuit, rusk.
sequío, *m.* unwatered land; anything dry.
séquito, *m.* retinue, train, suite; popularity.
sequizo, za, *a.* dry (fruits); dryish.
ser. I. *vn.* (*ger.* SIENDO; *pp.* SIDO; *ind. pres.* yo SOY, él ES, *imp.* ERA, *pret.* FUÍ; *subj.* SEA) to be. Used in phrases of identification (*soy yo,* it is I; *son ellos,* it is they). App. to time (*son las dos,* it is two o'clock; *es la una,* it is one o'clock). Used in impersonal sentences with adj. predicate or with an infin. or phrase subject (*es tarde,* it is late; *es extraño,* it is strange; *es fácil ver,* it is easy to see; *es probable que Juan hable,* it is likely that John will speak).—**s. de** (*inf.*), to be worth (*pres. p.*) (as *ser de ver,* to be worth seeing).—**s. para poco,** not to amount to much, to be of little account.—**s. para todo,** to be fit for everything; to be everything.—**s. que,** in the phrase: *es que,* the fact is that.—**érase,** there was; it was.—**érase que se era,** once upon a time (to begin a story).—**es a saber,** namely, to wit.—**esto es,** or, **o sea,** that is to say.—**no sea que,** lest.—**¿qué ha sido de . . .** What has become of . . . ?—**sea como fuere, sea lo que fuere,** be that as it may; anyhow, anyway.—**si yo fuera que Vd.,** if I were you.—**soy con Vd.,** I will attend you presently.—**soy muy de Vd.,** I am entirely yours; yours very truly. **II.** *m.* existence, life; being; essence, substance.
sera, *f.* large basket.
serado, *m.* baskets (collect.).
seráficamente, *adv.* seraphically.
seráfico, ca, *a.* seraphic.
serafín, *m.* seraph (*pl.* seraphim); angel.
serafina, *f.* fine baize, swanskin.
seraje, *m.* baskets (collect.)
serapino, *m.* = SAGAPENO, a kind of gum.
serba, *f.* (bot.) fruit of the service tree.
serbal, serbo, *m.* (bot.) service tree.
serena, *f.* (mus.) serenade; (coll.) night dew.—**a la s.,** (coll.) = AL SERENO.
serenamente, *adv.* serenely, composedly, calmly, coolly.
serenar, *va., vn.* & *vr.* (of weather) to clear up, grow fair, become calm; (of liquor) to settle, become clear; to pacify, moderate; to be serene; to cool water in the night air.
serenata, *f.* (mus.) seranade.
serenero, *m.* night wrap.
serení, *m.* (naut.) yawl, jolly-boat.
serenidad, *f.* serenity, calm; placidity, tranquility; serene highness (title).
serenísimo, ma, *a. super.* extremely serene, calm, or quiet; most serene (title of princes).
[1]**sereno, na,** *a.* clear, fair, cloudless; serene, calm, unruffled.
[2]**sereno,** *m.* night dew; night watchman.—**al s.,** in the night air, exposed to night dew.
sergas, *f. pl.* exploits, achievements.
seriágeno, na, *a.* (ent.) silk-producing.
seriamente, *adv.* seriously; gravely; in earnest, for good and all.
sericícola, *f.* sericultural.
sericicultor, ra, *n.* sericulturist.
sericicultura, *f.* silk culture, sericulture.
sérico, ca, *a.* silken.
sericultor, ra, *n.* = SERICICULTOR.
sericultura, *f.* = SERICICULTURA.
serie, *f.* series.—**en s.,** (elec.) series (as *a.*); (industry) standardized, mass (production).
seriedad, *f.* seriousness, gravity; sternness, severity; earnest, earnestness.
serígeno, na, *a.* silk-producing.
serigrafía, *f.* (f. a.) serigraphy.
serigrafista, *n.* (f. a.) serigrapher.
serígrafo, *m.* (f. a.) serigraph.
serijo, serillo, *m.* small basket, gen. for fruit.
seringa, *f.* (Am.) a variety of India rubber.
serio, ria, *a.* serious, grave, dignified; grand, majestic, solemn; stern, severe; earnest; sincere.—**en s.,** seriously.
sermón, *m.* sermon.
sermonar, *va.* to preach, sermonize.
sermonario, ria. I. *a.* sermonic. **II.** *m.* sermonary (collection of sermons).
sermoneador, ra. I. *a.* sermonic, sermonizing. **II.** *n.* sermonizer.
sermoncico, illo, ito, *m. dim.* short address; brief advice.
sermonear, *va.* to sermonize; (coll.) to lecture, reprimand.—**sermoneo,** *m.* (coll.) repeated admonition, sermonizing.
serna, *f.* cultivated field.
seroja, *f.,* **serojo,** *m.* withered leaf; brushwood.
serología, *f.* (med.) serology.
serólogo, ga, *n.* serologist.
serón, *m.* pannier; hamper, crate.—**s. caminero,** horse pannier.
serondo, da, *a.* (bot.) serotinous.
seronero, *m.* maker or seller of SERONES.
serosidad, *f.* (med.) serosity.
seroso, sa, *a.* serous, thin, watery.
seroterapia, *f.* (med.) serum therapy.
serotino, na, *a.* (bot.) serotinous.
serpa, *f.* (agr.) sterile shoot, sucker.
serpear, *vn.* to wind (as a serpent); to wriggle, squirm, crawl, creep; to meander.
serpentaria, *f.* (bot.) snake-root.
serpentario, *m.* secretary bird; (**S-,** astr.) Ophiuchus.
serpentear, *vn.* to meander, to wind; to wriggle, squirm.
serpentígero, ra, *a.* (poet.) containing serpents.
serpentín, *m.* coil; cock, hammer of a musket lock; (min.) serpentine; (chem.) distil worm.—**s. de refrigeración,** (astr.) cooling coil.
serpentino, na. I. *a.* serpentine; winding, sinuous; snakelike; slanderous, poisoned (tongue); serpentine (marble). **II.** *f.* coiled paper streamer (used at Carnival); (min.) serpentine; cock, hammer of a musket lock.
serpentón, *m. aug.* large serpent; (mus.) serpent; trombone.
serpezuela, *f. dim.* of SIERPE, snake.
serpia, *f.* viscous matter of a vine stock.
serpiente, *f.* serpent; devil, Satan; (**S-,** astr.) Serpens.—**s. de cascabel,** rattlesnake.
serpiginoso, sa, *a.* (med.) serpiginous.
serpigo, *m.* (med.) tetter, ringworm, serpigo.
serpol, *m.* (bot.) wild thyme.
serpollar, *vn.* (bot.) to shoot, sprout.
serpollo, *m.* (bot.) shoot, sucker, sapling.

sérpula, *f.* (zool.) serpula.
serpúlidos, *m. pl.* (zool.) Serpulidæ.
serradizo, za *a.* fit to be sawed.
serrado, da. I. *pp.* of SERRAR. **II.** *a.* serrate.
serrador, ra, *n.* sawer; sawyer.
serraduras, *f. pl.* sawdust.
serrallo, *m.* seraglio, harem; bagnio, brothel.
serrana, *f.* bucolic poem.
serranía, *f.* sierra, ridge of mountains; mountainous region.
serraniego, ga, *a.* = SERRANO.
serranil, *m.* a kind of knife.
serranilla, *f.* = SERRANA.
serrano, na, *n.* mountaineer, highlander.
serrar, *va.* (*ind.* SIERRO; *subj.* SIERRE) to saw.
serrátil, *a.* (med.) irregular (pulse).
serratilla, *f. dim.* small ridge of mountains.
serrato, ta, *a.* (anat.) serrated.
serrátula, *f.* (bot.) sawwort.
serreta, *f. dim.* small saw; cavesson iron used in breaking a horse.
serrezuela, *f. dim.* small saw.
serrijón, *m.* short chain of mountains.
serrín, *m.* sawdust.
serrino, na, *a.* pertaining to or like a saw; (med.) irregular (pulse).
serrucho, *m.* handsaw.—**s. braguero,** pit saw.
servato, *m.* (bot.) hog fennel, sulphurweed.
serventesio, *m.* quatrain riming *a, b, a, b.*
serventía, *f.* (Cuba) road through private property.
servible, *a.* serviceable, adaptable.
servicial. I. *a.* serviceable; obsequious, obliging, accommodating, kind. **II.** *m.* (coll.) enema.
servicialmente, *adv.* obligingly, accommodatingly, kindly; serviceably.
serviciar, *va.* to collect or pay (sheepwalk dues, donations to the state, etc.).
servicio, *m.* service; condition of a servant; help, servants (collect.); (eccl.) divine service; usefulness; benefit, advantage; (mil.) duty, service; (Am.) toilet, water closet; service, cover, course; tea or coffee service.—**s. activo,** (mil.) active service.—**s. aéreo,** air service.—**s. aeropostal,** airmail service.—**s. civil oficial,** civil service.—**s. de mesa,** set of dishes and utensils.—**s. militar,** military service.—**s. postal,** mail service.—**s. social,** social service.—**s. telefónico,** telephone service.—**s. telegráfico,** telegraphic service.—**de s.,** on duty.—**flaco s.,** ill turn.
servidero, ra, *a.* fit for service; useful; requiring personal attendance.
servido, da. I. *pp.* of SERVIR. **II.** *a.* pleased.—**ser s.,** to please, to deign, to grant.
servidor, ra, *n.* servant, waiter(-ess); wooer; one who politely tenders his services to another; (*m.*) pan of a close-stool.—**s. de Vd.,** your servant; at your service.
servidumbre, *f.* attendance, servitude; (staff of) servants or attendants; slavery; mighty or inevitable obligation; service, act of serving or attending at command; (law) right of way.—**s. de la vía,** (Ry.) right of way.
servil, *a.* servile, slavish, abject; lowly, humble; base, low; (Sp. hist.) absolutist, defending absolute monarchy.
servilismo, *m.* servilism, servility, abjectedness; (Sp. hist.) absolutism.
servilmente, *adv.* servilely, slavishly; basely.
servilla, *f.* pump (shoe).
servilleta, *f.* table napkin.—**doblar la s.,** (coll.) to die.
servilletero, *m.* napkin-ring.
servio, via, *n.* & *a.* Serbian.
serviola, *f.* (naut.) cathead, anchor beam.
servir. I. *vn.* (*ger.* SIRVIENDO; *ind. pres.* SIRVO, *pret.* él SIRVIÓ; *subj.* SIRVA) to serve; wait on; to do (for); to hold (an employment), occupy (a public station); to perform the functions (of); to serve (in the army or navy); at cards, to follow suit; in ball games, to serve; to wait on table; to heat the oven; to administer.—**s. de,** to act as, to be used as.—**s. para,** to be for, be used or useful for, be good for; to do for.—**no s. para nada,** to be good for nothing.—**para s. a Vd.,** at your service.—**sirva de aviso,** let this be a warning. **II.** *va.* to serve; to do a favor or a service to; to court, pay attention to (a lady); to pay (money) voluntarily to the king or government; to dress or serve (food or drink). **III.** *vr.* to please, be willing or "so good as" to (*sírvase decirme,* please tell me); to help oneself (as at table).—**s. de,** to make use of; to employ.
servitud, *f.* = SERVIDUMBRE.
servomecanismo, *m.* servomechanism.
servomotor, *m.* (naut.) servo-motor, auxiliary.
sesada, *f.* fried brains.
sesámeo, a. I. *a.* (bot.) relating to the sesame family. **II.** *f. pl.* the sesame family of plants.
sésamo, *m.* (bot.) sesame, gingili.
sesamoideo, a, *a.* (anat.) sesamoid.
sesear, *vn.* to pronounce *c* before *e* and *i* like *s*, as in Am. and some parts of Spain.
sesenta, *n.* & *a.* sixty; sixtieth.
sesentavo, va, *n.* & *a.* sixtieth.
sesentón, tona, *n.* & *a.* (coll.) sexagenarian.
seseo, *m.* pronouncing *c* before *e, i* like *s*.
sesera, *f.* brainpan; the entire brain.
sesga, *f.* (sewing) gore or goring.
sesgadamente, *adv.* slantingly, on the bias; askew.
sesgado, da. I. *pp.* of SESGAR. **II.** *a.* oblique, slanting; bevelled.
sesgadura, *f.* obliquity; bevel.
sesgamente, *adv.* = SESGADAMENTE.
sesgar. I. *va.* (*pret.* SESGUÉ; *subj.* SESGUE) to slope, slant, cut on the bias, bevel; to skew. **II.** *vn.* to take an oblique direction.
sesgo, ga. I. *a.* sloped, oblique, biased, bevelled, aslant; severe, grave, stern.—**al s.,** obliquely, bevelled, on the bias. **II.** *m.* bias, bevel, slope, obliqueness; turn (of an affair); mean, medium.
sesgué, sesgue, *v. V.* SESGAR.
sesil, *a.* (bot.) sessile.
sesión, *f.* session, sitting, meeting; conference, consultation.—**levantar la s.,** to adjourn the meeting.—**sesionar,** *vn.* to meet, have a session.
sesma, *f.,* **sesmero, sesmo,** *m.* = SEXMA, etc.
[1]seso, *m.* stone under a pot to keep it steady on the fire.
[2]seso, *m.* (anat.) brain; brains, intelligence, judgment.—**devanarse los sesos,** to rack one's brains.—**levantarse la tapa de los sesos,** to blow out one's brains.—**no tener s.,** not to have common sense.—**perder el s.,** to go crazy; to lose consciousness; (fig.) to lose one's head.—**sin seso(s),** scatterbrained.
sesquiáltero, ra, *a.* sesquialter.
sesquidoble, *a.* two and a half times.
sesquimodio, *m.* a bucket and a half.
sesquióxido, *m.* (chem.) sesquioxide.
sesquipedal, *a.* sesquipedalian, 1½ ft. long.
sesteadero, *m.* resting place for cattle.
sestear, *vn.* to take a nap.
sestercio, *m.* sesterce, old Roman coin.
sestero, sestil, *m.* = SESTEADERO.
sesudamente, *adv.* maturely, wisely, deliberately.
sesudo, da, *a.* judicious, discreet, wise.
[1]seta, *f.* = SEDA, bristle.
[2]seta, *f.* mushroom; snuff of a candle.
sete, *m.* office in a mint where money is struck with a die.
setecientos, tas, *a.* & *n.* seven hundred(-th).
setena, *f.* = SEPTENA, group of seven.
setenta, *n.* & *a.* seventy; seventieth.
setentavo, va, *n.* & *a.* seventieth.
setentón, na, *n.* & *a.* septuagenary(-narian).
setiembre, *m.* = SEPTIEMBRE, September.
sétimo, ma, *a.* = SÉPTIMO, MA, seventh.
seto, *m.* fence, inclosure; (P. R.) wall.—**s. vivo,** hedge, quickset.
setuní, *m.* = ACEITUNÍ, arabesque work.
seudo, *a.* pseudo, false.
seudoartístico, ca, *a.* (coll.) arty.

seudomembrana, *f.* (anat.) pseudomembrane.
seudomorfo, fa. I. *a.* (min.) pseudomorphous. **II.** *m.* (min.) pseudomorph.
seudónimo, ma. I. *a.* pseudonymous, fictitious. **II.** *m.* pseudonym, nom de plume, pen name.
seudópodo, da. I. *a.* (biol.) psuedopodian. **II.** *m.* pseudopodium.
severamente, *adv.* severely, sternly.
severidad, *f.* severity, rigor, harshness, austerity, sternness, strictness, seriousness.
severo, ra, *a.* severe, rigorous; rigid, strict, stern, serious.
sevicia, *f.* fierceness, excessive cruelty.
sevillano, na. I. *a.* Sevillian. **II.** *n.* Sevillian; *f. pl.* (mus.) sevillanas, Sevillian seguidillas.
séviro, *m.* chief of a Roman decury of knights.
sexagenario, ria, *n.* & *a.* sexagenary(-narian).
sexagésima, *f.* (eccl.) Sexagesima.
sexagesimal, *a.* sexagesimal.
sexagésimo, ma, *a.* sexagesimal, sixtieth.
sexenio, *m.* period of six years.
sexma, *f.* an ancient coin; sixth part of a vara.
sexmero, *m.* mayor of a township.
sexmo, *m.* township.
sexo, *m.* sex.
sextante, *m.* sextant; a Roman copper coin.
sextario, *m.* sextarius, an ancient measure.
sexteto, *m.* (mus.) sextet.
sextil, *a.* (astr.) sextile.
sextilla, *f.* (poet.) sextain.
sextillo, *m.* (mus.) sextolet, sextuplet.
sextillón, *m.* sextillion.
sextina, *f.* sestina (poem of six six-line stanzas and a three-line envoy).
sexto, ta. I. *a.* sixth. **II.** *m.* sixth; book of canonical decrees; *f.* (mus.) sixth; (eccl.) sext; run of six cards (at piquet).—**s. sentido,** sixth sense.
séxtula, *f.* a Roman copper coin.
sextuplicación, *f.* multiplication by six.
sextuplicar, *va.* to sextuple.
séxtuplo, pla, *a.* sextuple, sixfold.
sexuado, da, *a.* sexed.
sexual, *a.* sexual.
sexualidad, *f.* sexuality.
[1]si, *m.* (mus.) B or si, seventh note of the scale.
[2]si, *conj.* if; whether. Used at beginning of exclamations expressing doubt or desire, or for emphasis (*¡si será verdad!,* I wonder whether it's true; *¡si fuera verdad!,* I wish it were true! If it were only true!; *¡si yo no lo quiero!,* indeed, I don't want it; *¡si, no sabe nada!,* why, he doesn't know anything!).—**s. acaso,** if by chance; just in case.—**s. bien,** although.—**por s. acaso** = S. ACASO.
[1]sí, *pron.* (refl. of 3rd pers., both genders and numbers) himself, herself, itself, oneself, themselves.—**de por s.,** apart, separately, individually, by oneself, itself, etc.—**de s.,** of oneself, itself, spontaneously.—**fuera de s.,** beside (him-, her-, etc.) -self (with joy, anger, etc.).—**por s. y ante s.,** of his own accord; ignoring others.—**sobre s.,** attentively, cautiously.—**volver en s.,** to regain consciousness, come to.
[2]sí. I. *adv.* yes, yea, aye. Used for emphasis before a verb, rendered by emphatic aux. or by indeed, certainly, etc. (*él no irá, pero yo sí,* he will not go, but *I* will; *yo sí hablo español,* I do speak Spanish; *yo sí lo compraría,* I should certainly buy it).—**s. que,** certainly, truly, or just emphasizing some word (*sí que lo hará,* he will do it).—**por s. o por no,** in any case.—**s. tal,** indeed, certainly.—**un (día) s. y otro no,** every other (day).—**un s. es no es,** somewhat, perhaps a little. **II.** *m.* assent, consent, permission.—**dar el s.,** to say yes; to accept a marriage proposal.
sialagogo, ga. I. *a.* sialagogic. **II.** *m.* (med.) sialagogue, salivant.
siamés, sa, *n.* & *a.* Siamese.
siampán, *m.* sapan (tree & wood).
sibarita, *n.* & *a.* Sybarite(-ic).
sibarítico, ca, *a.* Sybaritic; sybaritic.
sibaritismo, *m.* sybaritism.
siberiano, na, *n.* & *a.* Siberian.
sibil, *m.* cave; cellar, vault.
sibila, *f.* sibyl.
sibilante, *a.* sibilant, hissing.
sibilino, na, *a.* sibylline.
sibucao, *m.* (P. I.) (bot.) sapan tree.
sic, *sic,* so, thus.
sicamor, *m.* (bot.) = CICLAMOR.
sicario, *m.* paid assassin.
sicativo, va, *m.* & *a.* (f. a.) siccative, drying (agent).
sicigia, *f.* (astr.) conjunction of sun and moon.
siciliano, na, *n.* & *a.* Sicilian.
siclo, *m.* shekel, an ancient Jewish coin.
sicofanta, sicofante, *m.* sycophant.
sicómoro, *m.* (bot.) sycamore; plane tree, buttonwood, sycamore maple.
siconio, *m.* (bot.) syconium.
sículo, la, *a.* Sicilian.
sideral; sidéreo, a, *a.* sidereal.
siderita, *f.* (min.) SIDEROSA; (bot.) ironwort.
siderización, *f.* preservation of timber by injecting iron salts.
siderosa, *f.* (min.) siderite.
sideróstato, *m.* (astr.) siderostat.
siderurgia, *f.* siderurgy, iron and steel metallurgy.
siderúrgico, ca, *a.* siderurgical.
sidonio, nia, *n.* & *a.* Sidonian.
sidra, *f.* cider.
siega, *f.* reaping, mowing, harvest.
siego, siegue, *v. V.* SEGAR.
siembra, *f.* sowing, seeding; seedtime; sown field.
siembro, siembre, *v. V.* SEMBRAR.
siempre, *adv.* always.—**s. que,** provided; whenever.—**para,** or **por, s.,** forever.—**por s. jamás,** forever and ever.
siempreviva, *f.* (bot.) everlasting or immortelle.—**s. mayor,** houseleek.—**s. menor,** stonecrop.
sien, *f.* (anat.) temple.
siena, *f.* sienna.
sienita, *f.* (min.) syenite or sienite.
[1]siento, siente, *v. V.* SENTAR.
[2]siento, sienta, él sintió, *v. V.* SENTIR.
sierpe, *f.* serpent, snake; ugly or angry person; anything that wriggles; (bot.) sucker, tiller.
sierpecilla, *f. dim.* small serpent.—*pl.* winding skyrockets.
sierra, *f.* saw; mountain range, sierra; (ichth.) sawfish.—**s. abrazadera,** lumberman's saw.—**s. bracera,** bucksaw, frame saw.—**s. caladora,** coping saw; keyhole saw.—**s. circular,** buzz or circular saw.—**s. de agua,** sawmill.—**s. de arco,** bow saw.—**s. de calar,** fret saw.—**s. de cinta,** band saw.—**s. de cortar metales,** hack saw.—**s. de ingletes,** tenon saw.—**s. de mano,** handsaw.—**s. de marquetería,** fret saw.—**s. de punta,** compass saw.—**s. de trasdós,** backsaw.—**s. de trozar,** crosscut saw.—**s. de vaivén,** jig saw.—**s. giratoria,** disk saw.—**S. Leona,** Sierra Leone.—**s. múltiple,** gang saw.—**s. sin fin,** band saw.—**s. tubular,** tube saw.
sierrecilla, *f. dim.* small saw.
sierro, sierre, *v. V.* SERRAR.
siervo, va, *n.* serf; slave; servant.—**s. de Dios,** servant of God; (coll.) poor devil.
sieso, *m.* (anat.) rectum.
siesta, *f.* hottest part of the day; afternoon nap; afternoon music in churches.
siete. I. *m.* & *a.* seven; seventh (of the month); seven-spot card; V-shaped tear in a garment; (carp.) hook-clasp. **II.** *f. pl.*—**las s.,** seven o'clock.
sietecueros, *m.* (S. A.) a kind of tumor on the heel; (C. A.) sickly-looking person.
sieteenrama, *f.* (bot.) tormentil.
sietemesino, na. I. *a.* seven-months (baby). **II.** *m.* puny coxcomb.
sieteñal, *a.* seven years old; septennial.
sifílide, *f.* (med.) syphilide.

sífilis, *f.* (med.) syphilis.
sifilítico, ca, *n.* & *a.* syphilitic.
sifilografía, *f.* (med.) syphilology.
sifilográfico, ca, *a.* pertaining to syphilology.
sifilógrafo, fa, *n.* syphilologist.
sifiloma, *f.* (med.) syphiloma, syphilitic tumor.
sifón, *m.* siphon; siphon bottle.
sifonóforo, *m.* (zool.) siphonophore.
sifosis, *f.* = CORCOVA, hump (on back).
sifué, *m.* = SOBRECINCHA, surcingle.
sigilación, *f.* seal, stamp, impression, mark.
sigilar, *va.* to seal; to conceal.
sigilo, *m.* seal; secret, concealment, reserve.—**s. sacramental,** inviolable secrecy of the confessional.
sigilografía, *f.* sigillography, study of seals.
sigilosamente, *adv.* silently, secretly.
sigiloso, sa, *a.* silent, reserved.
sigla, *f.* abbreviation by initials.
siglo, *m.* century; age; period; the world, worldly intercourse or matters.—**s. de cobre,** (myth.) bronze age.—**s. de hierro,** (myth.) iron age.—**s. de oro,** (myth.) golden age.—**s. de plata,** (myth.) silver age.—**s. dorado** = S. DE ORO.—**en, por,** or **por todos, los siglos de los siglos,** forever and ever.
sigma, *f.* sigma (Greek letter).
sigmoideo, dea, *a.* sigmoid, S-shaped.
sigmoidoscopio, *m.* sigmoidoscope.
signáculo, *m.* seal, signet.
signar. I. *va.* to sign, to mark with a signet. **II.** *vr.* to cross oneself.
signatario, ria, *n.* & *a.* signer(-ing), signatory.
signatura, *f.* sign, mark; (print.) signature; a Roman-Catholic court of justice and pardons.
signífero, ra, *a.* carrying a mark or sign.
significación, *f.* significance; sense, meaning; implication; importance.
significado, *m.* meaning, definition (of a word, etc.).
significador, ra, *n.* & *a.* signifier(-ing).
significante, *a.* significant, expressive.
significar, *va.* (*pret.* SIGNIFIQUÉ; *subj.* SIGNIFIQUE) to signify, mean; to indicate; to make known; to import, be worth.
significativamente, *adv.* significantly.
significativo, va, *a.* significant.
signifiqué, signifique, *v.* *V.* SIGNIFICAR.
signo, *m.* sign, mark, symbol; signal, motion, nod; (law) signum, flourish in a notary's signature; fate, destiny; benediction, sign of the cross; (astr.) sign of the zodiac; (mus.) character.—**s. de exclamación,** (gram.) exclamation mark.—**s. de interrogación,** (gram.) question mark.—**s. diacrítico,** (gram.) diacritic, diacritical mark.—**s. fonético,** phonetic symbol.—**s. más,** (math.) plus sign.—**s. menos,** (math.) minus sign.—**signos de puntuación,** (gram.) punctuation marks.
sigo, sigue, siga, etc. *v.* *V.* SEGUIR.
siguiente. I. *pres. p.* of SEGUIR. **II.** *a.* following, next.
siguió, *pret.* of SEGUIR.
sijú, *m.* (W. I.) (ornith.) a nocturnal bird of prey.
sil, *m.* yellow ochre.
sílaba, *f.* syllable.
silabar, *vn.* = SILABEAR.
silabario, *m.* reader (book to teach reading).
silabear, *vn.* to syllabize, syllabicate.
silabeo, *m.* syllabication.
silábico, ca, *a.* syllabic.
sílabo, *m.* syllabus; summary, index.
silanga, *f.* (P. I.) canal, inlet, strait.
silba, *f.* (theat.) hiss, hissing (of disapproval).
silbador, ra, *n.* & *a.* whistler(-ing); hisser(-ing).
silbar. I. *vn.* to whistle; to whiz, as a musket ball. **II.** *va.* & *vn.* (theat.) to hiss, boo, catcall.
silbato, *m.* whistle (instrument); small crack letting out a liquid or air with a whistling sound.
silbido, *m.* whistle, whistling sound; hiss; sibilation.—**s. de oídos,** ringing in the ear.
silbo, *m.* whistle, hiss, whistling, whiz.
silbón, *m.* (ornith.) a kind of hissing widgeon.
silboso, sa, *a.* whistling, hissing.
silenciador, *m.* (auto) muffler; silencer (on gun, etc.).
silenciario, ria. I. *a.* observing profound silence. **II.** *m.* official with duty of commanding silence.
silenciero, ra, *a.* having the duty of commanding silence.
silencio, *m.* silence; noiselessness; taciturnity; secrecy; stillness, quiet; (mus.) rest.—**guardar s.,** to keep quiet.—**perpetuo s.,** (law) forever hold his peace.
silenciosamente, *adv.* silently, noiselessly.
silencioso, sa, *a.* silent, noiseless; still, quiet.
silepsis, *f.* (rhet.) syllepsis.
silería, *f.* group of silos.—**silero,** *m.* (agr.) silo.
silesiano, na; silesio, sia, *n.* & *a.* Silesian.
sílfide, *f.*, **silfo,** *m.* sylph.
silguero, *m.* (ornith.) linnet.
silicato, *m.* (chem.) silicate.
sílice, *f.* (min.) silex, silica.—**silíceo, a,** *a.* siliceous.—**silícico, ca,** *a.* silicic.
silicio, *m.* (chem.) silicon.
siliciuro, *m.* (chem.) silicide.
silicosis, *f.* (med.) silicosis.
silicua, *f.* siliqua, carat; (bot.) silique, pod.
silícula, *f.* (bot.) silicle or silicula.
silicuoso, sa, *a.* (bot.) siliquose, siliquous
silo, *m.* (agr.) silo; cavern or dark place.
silogismo, *m.* (logic) syllogism.—**s. cornuto,** horn of a dilemma.
silogístico, ca, *a.* syllogistic(al).
silogizar, *vn.* (*pret.* SILOGICÉ; *subj.* SILOGICE) to syllogize, argue.
silueta, *f.* silhouette; (of person) figure.
siluriano, na; silúrico, ca, *a.* (geol.) Silurian.
siluro, *m.* (ichth.) catfish, silurus; self-propelling torpedo.
silva, *f.* miscellany; a form of poem.
silvático, ca, *a.* = SELVÁTICO, sylvan; rustic.
silvestre, *a.* wild; uncultivated; rustic, savage.
silvicultor, ra, *n.* silviculturist, forester.
silvicultura, *f.* forestry, silviculture.
silvoso, sa, *a.* = SELVOSO, sylvan, wooded.
silla, *f.* chair; saddle; (eccl.) see.—**s. curul,** curule.—**s. de columpio,** rocking chair.—**s. de junco** = S. DE REJILLA.—**s. de la reina,** chair made by two persons' hands and wrists.—**s. de manos,** sedan chair; (Am.) S. DE LA REINA.—**s. de montar,** riding saddle.—**s. de posta,** post chaise.—**s. de rejilla,** cane or bamboo-bottomed chair.—**s. de ruedas,** wheel chair.—**s. de tijera,** camp chair.—**s. giratoria,** swivel chair.—**s. plegadiza,** folding chair, camp stool.—**s. poltrona,** armchair; easy chair.—**s. volante,** light gig.—**de s. a s.,** tête-à-tête, in private conference, heart to heart.
sillar, *m.* ashlar stone; place for saddle on horse.
sillarejo, *m.* small ashlar.
sillera, *f.* place for sedan chairs.
[1]sillería, *f.* set of chairs; shop where chairs are made or sold; stalls or seats in a choir.
[2]sillería, *f.* (arch.) ashlar masonry.
sillero, ra, *n.* saddler; chair maker.
silleta, *f. dim.* small chair; hollow stone on which chocolate is ground; bedpan.—*pl.* mule chairs.
silletazo, *m.* blow with a chair.
silletero, ra, *n.* carrier of a sedan chair; chair maker or seller.
sillico, *m.* basin of a close-stool.
sillín, *m.* light riding saddle; harness saddle; elaborate mule chair.
sillita, *f. dim.* small chair.
sillón, *m. aug.* armchair; easy chair; sidesaddle.
sima, *f.* deep cavern; abyss, gulf, chasm.
simado, da, *a.* deep (land).
simbionte, *m.* (biol.) symbiont.
simbiosis, *f.* (biol.) symbiosis.
simbiótico, ca, *a.* symbiotic.
simbólicamente, *adv.* symbolically.
simbolicé, simbolice, *v.* *V.* SIMBOLIZAR.
simbólico, ca, *a.* symbolical.
simbolismo, *m.* symbolism.

simbolista, *m.* or *f.* symbolist.
simbolización, *f.* symbolization.
simbolizar, *va.* (*pret.* SIMBOLICÉ; *subj.* SIMBOLICE) to symbolize, represent, typify.
símbolo, *m.* symbol; mark, device.—**s. de la fe,** creed, articles of faith.
simbología, *f.* symbology.
simetría, *f.* symmetry.
simétricamente, *adv.* symmetrically.
simétrico, ca, *a.* symmetrical.
simetrizar, *va.* to symmetrize.
simia, *f.* female ape.
símico, ca, *a.* simian.
simiente, *f.* seed; germ; semen, sperm.
simiesco, ca, *a.* simianlike.
símil. I. *a.* similar, like, alike. **II.** *m.* resemblance, similarity; (rhet.) simile.
similar, *a.* similar, resembling.
similitud, *f.* similitude, similarity.
similitudinario, ria, *a.* similar.
similor, *m.* low-grade brass.
simio, *m.* (zool.) simian, ape.
simón, *m.* hack, cab; hackman, in Madrid.
simonía, *f.* simony.
simoníacamente, *adv.* simoniacally.
simoníaco, ca; simoniático, ca, *a.* simoniacal.
simpatía, *f.* fellow feeling; congeniality; liking, friendly feeling; (med.) sympathy.
simpáticamente, *adv.* congenially; nicely, pleasingly.
simpaticé, simpatice, *v. V.* SIMPATIZAR.
simpaticectomía, *f.* (surg.) sympathectomy.
simpático, ca, *a.* congenial; appealing; pleasant, "nice."—**gran s.,** (anat.) sympathetic system.
simpatizador, ra, *a.* sympathetic, sympathizing.
simpatizante. I. *a.* sympathetic, sympathizing. **II.** *n.* sympathizer.
simpatizar, *vn.* (*pret.* SIMPATICÉ; *subj.* SIMPATICE) to be congenial.
simpétalo, la, *a.* (bot.) sympetalous.
simple. I. *a.* simple; mere; single; silly, foolish; artless, ingenuous; plain, unmixed, unadorned; mild, gentle; insipid, tasteless; informal extrajudicial. **II.** *m.* (pharm.) simple; simpleton.
simplemente, *adv.* simply; plainly; foolishly.
simpleza, *f.* silliness, foolishness; silly thing; rusticity, rudeness.
simplicidad, *f.* simplicity.
simplicísimo, ma, *a. super.* extremely simple.
simplificación, *f.* simplification.
simplificar, *va.* (*pret.* SIMPLIFIQUÉ; *subj.* SIMPLIFIQUE) to simplify.
simplista, *m.* simplist, herbalist.
simplón, na, *n. aug.* great simpleton.
simpodio, *m.* (bot.) sympodium.
simposia, *f.* (Gk. hist.) symposium.
simulación, *f.* simulation, feigning.
simulacro, *m.* simulacrum, image, idol; fancy, fantastical thing; (mil.) sham battle.
simuladamente, *adv.* in a dissembling manner.
simulador, ra, *n.* & *a.* dissembler(-ing).
simular, *va.* to simulate, pretend, sham.
simultáneamente, *adv.* simultaneously.
simultaneidad, *f.* simultaneity.
simultanear, *va.* to accomplish or carry on simultaneously.
simultáneo, a, *a.* simultaneous.
simún, *m.* simoom, sirocco, a hot wind.
sin, *prep.* without, besides.—**s. embargo,** notwithstanding, nevertheless, however.
sinagoga, *f.* synagogue.
sinalagmático, ca, *a.* (law) synalagmatic, mutually obligatory.
sinalefa, *f.* (gram.) synalepha.
sinamay, *m.* (P. I.) sinamay; a coarse fabric made from abaca.—**sinamayera,** *f.* (P. I.) woman who sells sinamay.
sinapismo, *m.* mustard plaster; (coll.) nuisance, bore.
sinapsis, *f.* (physiol., biol.) sinapsis; (physiol.) synapse.
sinartrosis, *f.* (anat.) synarthrosis, fixed joint.
sincárpeo, pea, *a.* (bot.) syncarpous.
sincarpo, *m.* (bot.) syncarp.
sincerador, ra. I. *a.* exculpatory, defending, upholding. **II.** *n.* exculpator, defender, upholder.
sinceramente, *adv.* sincerely.
sincerar. I. *va.* to exculpate, to justify. **II.** *vr.* to excuse, justify, or vindicate oneself.
sinceridad, *f.* sincerity, good faith.
sincero, ra, *a.* sincere.
sincipucio, *m.* (anat.) sinciput, skullcap.
sinclástico, ca, *a.* (math.) synclastic.
sinclinal. I. *a.* synclinal. **II.** *m.* (geol.) syncline, synclinal.
síncopa, *f.* (gram.) syncope; (mus.) syncopation.
sincopadamente, *adv.* with syncope.
sincopado, da, *a.* syncopated.
sincopal. I. *m.* = SÍNCOPE. **II.** *a.* (med.) syncopal.
sincopar, *va.* to syncopate; to abridge.
síncope, *f.* SÍNCOPA; (med.) syncope.
sincopizar, *va.* & *vr.* (*pret.* SINCOPICÉ; *subj.* SINCOPICE) to swoon, to faint.
sincrético, ca, *a.* syncretic.
sincretismo, *m.* syncretism.
sincretista, *n.* syncretist.
sincrisis, *f.* (rhet.) syncrisis, comparison.
sincrociclotrón, *m.* (phys.) synchro-cyclotron.
sincrónico, ca, *a.* synchronous.
sincronismo, *m.* synchronism.
sincronización, *f.* synchronization.
sincronizador, ra. I. *a.* synchronizing. **II.** *m.* synchronizer.
sincronizar, *va.* to synchronize; & *vn.* (radio) to tune in.
sincronoscopio, *m.* (elec.) synchronoscope.
sincrotrón, *m.* (phys.) synchrotron.
sindáctilo, la, *m.* & *a.* (zool.) syndactyl, syndactyle.
sindéresis, *f.* discretion; good judgment.
sindicación, *f.* syndication.
sindicado, *m.* body of trustees; syndicate; (pol. econ.) syndicate.
sindicador, ra, *n.* informer, prosecutor; syndicator.
sindical, *a.* syndical; (pol. econ.) syndicalistic.
sindicalismo, *m.* (pol. econ.) syndicalism; unionism.
sindicalista. I. *a.* syndicalistic, union. **II.** *n.* syndicalist, unionist.
sindicalizar, *va.* to syndicalize.
sindicar, *va.* (*pret.* SINDIQUÉ; *subj.* SINDIQUE) to inform, to accuse; to syndicate.
sindicato, *m.* labor union; SINDICADO.
sindicatura, *f.* office and dignity of a syndic.
síndico, *m.* syndic; trustee; (law) assignee, receiver.
sindiqué, sindique, *v. V.* SINDICAR.
síndrome, *m.* (med.) syndrome, aggregate of symptoms.
sinécdoque, *f.* (rhet.) synecdoche.
sinecura, *f.* sinecure.
sinedrio, *m.* = SANEDRÍN, Sanhedrim.
sine qua non, (Lat.) essential, sine qua non.
sinéresis, *f.* (gram.) syneresis.
sinergia, *f.* (physiol.) synergy.
sinestesis, *f.* (physiol.) synesthesia.
sinfín, *m.* = SINNÚMERO.
sínfisis, *f.* (biol.) symphysis.
sínfito, *m.* (bot.) comfrey.
sinfonía, *f.* symphony.
sinfónico, ca, *a.* symphonic.
sinfonista, *n.* symphonist.
singamia, *f.* (biol.) syngamy.
singladura, *f.* (naut.) a day's run.
singlar, *vn.* (naut.) to steer, sail over a course.
single, *a.* (naut.) single.—**singlón,** *m.* (naut.) futtock.
singular, *a.* singular, unique; individual; extraordinary, strange; (gram.) singular.
singularicé, singularice, *v. V.* SINGULARIZAR.
singularidad, *f.* singularity, oddity, strange feature or thing; peculiarity.

singularizar. **I.** *va.* (*pret.* SINGULARICÉ; *subj.* SINGULARICE) to distinguish, particularize, singularize, single out. **II.** *vr.* to distinguish oneself; to be or make oneself conspicuous.
singularmente, *adv.* singularly.
singulete, *m.* (phys.) singlet.
singulto, *m.* sob; hiccough, singultus.
sinhueso, *f.* (coll.) tongue.
sínico, ca, *a.* Chinese.
siniestra, *f.* left hand.
siniestramente, *adv.* sinistrously; perversely.
siniestro, tra. **I.** *a.* sinister, left (side); sinister, vicious; unlucky, inauspicious. **II.** *m.* perverseness, depravity; (com.) shipwreck, disaster; damage, loss at sea. **III.** *f.* left hand; left-hand side.
sinistrorso, sa, *a.* counterclockwise; (bot.) sinistrorse, sinistrorsal.
sinizesis, *f.* (gram.) synizesis.
sinnúmero, *m.* no end, great number.—**un s. de,** numberless, a great many.
[1]**sino,** *conj.* but; except, besides; solely, only.—**no . . . s.,** but, only (*no tengo sino un sombrero,* I have only one hat).—**no sólo . . . s. (también),** not only . . . but (also).
[2]**sino,** *m.* fate, destiny.
sinoble, *a.* (her.) = SINOPLE, vert.
sinocal; sínoco, ca, *a.* (med.) synochal (fever).
sinodal. **I.** *a.* synodal. **II.** *m.* synodal examiner.
sinodático, *m.* (eccl.) contribution to the bishop.
sinódico, ca, *a.* (eccl.) synodal; (astr.) synodic.
sínodo, *m.* (eccl. and astr.) synod.
sinófilo, la, *n.* Sinophile, Sinophil.
sinojaponés, nesa, *a.* Sino-Japanese.
sinología, *f.* sinology, study of things Chinese.
sinólogo, ga, *n.* sinologist.
sinonimia, *f.* (rhet.) synonymy.
sinónimo, ma. **I.** *a.* synonymous. **II.** *m.* synonym.
sinople, *a.* (her.) sinople, vert.
sinopsis, *f.* synopsis.
sinóptico, ca, *a.* synoptic.
sinovia, *f.* (physiol.) synovia, lubricating liquid secreted by certain membranes.
sinovial, *a.* synovial.
sinovitis, *f.* (med.) synovitis.
sinrazón, *f.* wrong, injury, injustice.
sinsabor, *m.* displeasure, unpleasantness; trouble, uneasiness.
sinsonte, *m.* (ornith.) mocking bird.
sintáctico, ca, *a.* (gram.) syntactic.
sintaxis, *f.* (gram.) syntax.
síntesis, *f.* synthesis.
sintéticamente, *adv.* synthetically.
sintético, ca, *a.* synthetical.
sintetizar, *va.* (*pret.* SINTETICÉ; *subj.* SINTETICE) to synthesize; to sum up.
sinto, sintoísmo, *m.* Shinto, Shintoism.
sintoísta, *n.* & *a.* Shintoist(-ic).
síntoma, *m.* (med.) symptom.
sintomáticamente, *adv.* symptomatically.
sintomático, ca, *a.* symptomatic(al):
sintomatología, *f.* (med.) symptomatology.
sintonía, *f.* (elec.) syntony, oscillation adjustment; (rad.) syntony, tuning.
sintónico, ca, *a.* syntonic.
sintonina, *f.* (chem.) syntonin.
sintonización, *f.* (radio) syntonization, tuning.
sintonizado, da, *a.* syntonized, tuned.
sintonizador, ra. **I.** *a.* syntonizing, tuning. **II.** *m.* (rad.) syntonizer, tuner.
sintonizar, *va.* (radio) to syntonize, tune.
sinuosidad, *f.* sinuosity.
sinuoso, sa, *a.* sinuous, wavy.
sinusitis, *f.* (med.) sinusitis.
sinusoidal, *a.* sinusoidal.
sinusoide, *f.* (geom.) sinusoid, a curve of sines
sinvergüencería, *f.* (coll.) shamelessness, brazenness.
sinvergüenza, *n.* (coll.) scoundrel, rascal; brazen, shameless person; caitiff; (Colomb.) coward.
sinvergüenzada, *f.* (Colomb.) base, low action.
Sión, *f.* Zion.
sionismo, *m.* Zionism.
sionista, *n.* & *a.* Zionist.
sipedón, *m.* a kind of serpent.
siquier, siquiera, *adv.* & *conj.* at least; though, although; whether, or; scarcely; otherwise.—**s. un poquito,** ever so little.—**ni s.,** not even.
siracusano, na, *n.* & *a.* Syracusan.
sirdar, *m.* sirdar, chief; commander.
sirena, *f.* siren, mermaid; (naut.) siren, foghorn; (phys.) siren, for measuring vibrations.
sirenio, nia. **I.** *a.* (ichth.) sirenian. **II.** *m. pl.* Sirenia.
sirga, *f.* (naut.) towrope, towline; line for hauling seines.—**a la s.,** (naut.) tracking from the shore.
sirgadura, *f.* (naut.) trackage.
sirgar, *va.* (naut.) to track.
sirgo, *m.* twisted silk; silk stuff.
sirguero, *m.* (ornith.) linnet.
Siria, *f.* Syria.
siríaco, ca, *n.* & *a.* Syrian.
siríasis, *f.* (med.) siriasis.
siringa, *f.* (bot.) seringa, name of various species of rubber tree.
siringe, *f.* (ornith.) syrinx.
siringomielia, *f.* (med.) syringomyelia.
sirio, ria. **I.** *a.* Syrian. **II.** *n.* Syrian; *m.* (S.) (astr.) Sirius; *f.* (S.) Syria.
sirle, *m.* sheep dung, goat dung.
siroco, *m.* sirocco.
sirope, *m.* sirup.
sirria, *f.* sheep dung.
sirte, *f.* syrtes, hidden rock, sand bank; danger.
siruposo, sa, *a.* sirupy.
sirvienta, *f.* servant girl, maid.
sirviente, *m.* (domestic) servant; waiter.
sirvo, sirva, sirvió, etc. *v. V.* SERVIR.
[1]**sisa,** *f.* size used by gilders.
[2]**sisa,** *f.* petty theft, pilfering; (tailoring) clipping; (sewing) dart; excise tax.
sisador, ra, *n.* filcher, petty thief.
sisallo, *m.* (bot.) = BARRILLA, saltwort.
[1]**sisar,** *va.* to pilfer, filch; (sewing) to take in; to impose an excise tax on.
[2]**sisar,** *va.* to size (for gilding).
sisarcosis, *f.* (anat.) syssarcosis.
sisear, *vn.* to hiss.
siseo, *m.* hiss, hissing.
sisero, *m.* excise collector.
sisimbrio, *m.* (bot.) hedge mustard.
sisitoté, *m.* (ornith.) a tropical song bird.
sísmico, ca, *a.* seismic.
sismo, *m.* seism.
sismográfico, ca, *a.* seismographic.
sismógrafo, *m.* seismograph.
sismograma, *m.* seismogram.
sismología, *f.* seismology.
sismológico, ca, *a.* seismological.
sismólogo, ga, *n.* seismologist.
sismómetro, *m.* seismometer.
[1]**sisón, na,** *n.* filcher, pilferer, petty thief.
[2]**sisón,** *m.* (ornith.) godart or moor cock.
sistáltico, ca, *a.* (physiol.) systaltic, contracting.
sistema, *f.* system.—**s. automático,** automatic system.—**s. autónomo,** (physiol.) autonomic system.—**s. cegesimal,** (phys.) centimeter-gram-second system.—**s. de coordenadas,** (phys.) frame of reference.—**s. de guía,** guidance system.—**s. de guía a la base de origen,** homing equipment.—**s. de propulsión,** propulsion system.—**s. métrico,** metric system.—**s. nervioso,** (anat.) nervous system.—**s. óptico convergente,** (phys.) convergent optical system.—**s. solar,** solar system.
sistemáticamente, *adv.* systematically.
sistematicé, sistematice, *v. V.* SISTEMATIZAR.
sistemático, ca, *a.* systematic, methodical.
sistematización, *f.* systematization.
sistematizar, *va.* & *vn.* (*pret.* SISTEMATICÉ; *subj.* SISTEMATICE) to systematize.
sistematología, *f.* systematology.
sístilo, *m.* (arch.) systyle.

sístole, *f.* (physiol. and rhet.) systole.
sistólico, ca, *a.* systolic.
sistro, *m.* (mus.) sistrum.
sitácidos, *m. pl.* (ornith.) Psitaci (the parrots).
sitacosis, *f.* (med.) psittacosis, parrot fever.
sitiador, ra. I. *a.* besieging. **II.** *n.* besieger.
sitial, *m.* seat of honor, presiding chair; bench.
sitiar, *va.* (mil.) to besiege, lay siege to; to surround, hem in, compass.
sitibundo, da, *a.* (poet.) thirsty.
sitiero, *m.* (Cuba) petty farmer.
[1]**sitio,** *m.* place, space, spot, room; stand; seat; location, site; country house, country seat, villa; (Cuba) small farm.—**dejar en el s.,** to kill one outright.—**quedar en el s.,** to die on the spot.
[2]**sitio,** *m.* (mil.) siege.
sito, ta, *a.* situated, lying, located.
situación, *f.* situation; position; site, location; state, condition, circumstances.—**s. activa,** active-service position or office.—**s. pasiva,** office or position not actually filled, as when the incumbent is retired, on vacation, etc.
situado, da. I. *pp.* of SITUAR. **II.** *a.* situate, situated, located. **III.** *m.* allowance, pay, annuity assigned upon certain valuables.
situar. I. *va.* to place, locate, put, situate; (com.) to remit or place (funds). **II.** *vr.* to settle in a place; to station oneself.
smoking, *m.* dinner jacket, Tuxedo.
snob, *n.* & *a.* = ESNOB.
snobismo, *m.* = ESNOBISMO.
so, *prep.* under; below.—**s. capa de,** or **s. color de,** under color of; on pretense of.—**s. pena de,** under penalty of.
¡so! *interj.* whoa! stop! (to horses).
soasar, *va.* to half roast, parboil, underdo.
soata, *f.* (Venez.) a kind of squash.
soba, *f.* massage; kneading; rubbing; beating, drubbing.
sobacal, *a.* axillary.
sobaco, *m.* armpit, axilla; (bot.) axil.
sobadero, ra, *a.* that can be handled.
sobado, *m.*; **sobadura,** *f.* = SOBA.
sobajadura, *f.*; **sobajamiento,** *m.* squeeze, pressure, crushing.
sobajanero, *m.* (coll.) errand boy.
sobajar, *va.* to squeeze, press, crush.
sobanda, *f.* bottom or end of a cask.
sobaquera, *f.* (tailoring) armhole, armscye.
sobaquina, *f.* bad smell of the armpit.
sobar, *va.* to knead; to massage, squeeze, soften; to pummel, box; to handle (a person) with too much familiarity.
sobarba, *f.* noseband of a bridle.
sobarbada, *f.* sudden check; reprimand, scolding.
sobarbo, *m.* (mech.) cam, pallet or pawl, in beating machines.
sobarcar, *va.* (*pret.* SOBARQUÉ; *subj.* SOBARQUE) to carry under the arm; to draw (the clothes) up to the armholes.
sobeo, *m.* thong for tying the yoke to the pole.
soberanamente, *adv.* with authority; supremely, exceedingly, most.
soberanear, *vn.* to lord it, to domineer.
soberanía, *f.* sovereignty; rule, sway.
soberano, na. I. *a.* sovereign; supreme, royal; most potent, superior, preëminent; (coll.) "tops." **II.** *f.* sovereign; lord paramount; liege.
soberbia, *f.* excessive pride, haughtiness, arrogance; presumption; magnificence, sumptuousness, pomp; anger.
soberbiamente, *adv.* arrogantly; superbly.
soberbio, bia, *a.* overproud, arrogant, haughty; superb, grand; lofty, eminent; (of horses) fiery, mettlesome.
soberbiosamente, *adv.* haughtily.
soberbioso, sa, *a.* = SOBERBIO.
sobina, *f.* wooden pin, peg.
sobón, na, *a.* given to excessive fondling and caressing; (coll.) sly, lazy.
sobordo, *m.* (naut.) manifest, freight list.
sobornación, *f.* = SOBORNO.
sobornado, *m.* misshaped loaf of bread.
sobornador, ra, *n.* & *a.* briber(-ing), suborner (-ing).
sobornal, *m.* overload.
sobornar, *va.* to suborn, bribe.
soborno, *m.* subornation, bribe; incitement, inducement; (Peru) overload.—**s. de testigo,** (law) subornation of perjury.
sobra, *f.* surplus, excess; left-over, leaving; grievous offense, injury.—**de s.,** over and above; more than enough; over, superfluous.—**estar de s.,** (coll.) to be one too many; to be superfluous.
sobradamente, *adv.* abundantly; superabundantly; excessively.
sobradar, *va.* to build a garret onto.
sobradillo, *m. dim.* (arch.) penthouse.
sobrado, da. I. *pp.* of SOBRAR. **II.** *a.* excessive, abundant; bold, audacious; rich, wealthy. **III.** *m.* garret, attic; (Am., gen. *pl.*) leavings.
sobrancero, ra, *a.* disengaged, unemployed; supernumerary plowman.
sobrante. I. *pres. p.* of SOBRAR. **II.** *a.* wealthy. **III.** *a.* & *m.* (something) left over; surplus.
sobrar. I. *va.* to exceed, surpass; to have in excess, or more than enough, to have to spare. **II.** *vn.* to be more than is necessary; to be over and above; to be more than enough, superfluous; to be intrusive; to remain, be left over.
sobrasada, *f.* = SOBREASADA.
sobrasar, *va.* to add fire under (a pot).
sobre. I. *prep.* on, upon; over; above; about, concerning; about, more or less; besides; after, beyond; to, toward, near; (naut.) off.—**s. comida,** after dinner.—**s. manera,** excessively, beyond measure, exceedingly.—**s. poco más o menos,** just about, more or less.—**s. que,** besides.—**estar s. sí,** to be on guard, to be self-possessed.—**ir s.,** to go in pursuit of. **II.** *m.* envelope (for letters); address, superscription.—**s. monedero,** coin container (to be enclosed with a letter).
sobreabundancia, *f.* superabundance.
sobreabundante, *a.* superabundant; luxuriant.
sobreabundantemente, *adv.* superabundantly.
sobreabundar, *vn.* to superabound; to be exuberant.
sobreactuar, *vn.* to overact: (coll.) to emote.
sobreaguar, *vn.* & *vr.* to float on water.
sobreagudo, da, *a.* & *n.* (mus.) treble, highest register.
sobrealiento, *m.* difficult respiration.
sobrealimentación, *f.* overfeeding.
sobrealimentar, *va.* to overfeed.
sobrealzar, *va.* to praise, to extol.
sobreamortiguado, da, *a.* overdamped.
sobreañadidura, *f.* superaddition, superinduction.
sobreañadir, *va.* to superadd, superinduce.
sobreañal, *a.* over a year old.
sobrearco, *m.* (arch.) discharging arch.
sobreasada, *f.* half-roasted sausage from the island of Majorca.
sobreasar, *va.* to roast again.
sobrebarato, ta, *a.* very cheap, extra cheap.
sobreboya, *f.* (naut.) marking buoy.
sobrebrazal, *m.* (naut.) false rail.
sobrecaja, *f.* outer case.
sobrecalentador, *m.* superheater.
sobrecalentamiento, *m.* superheating.
sobrecalentar, *va.* to superheat.
sobrecalza, *f.* leggings.
sobrecama, *f.* coverlet, bedspread.
sobrecaña, *f.* (vet.) tumor on a horse's leg.
sobrecarga, *f.* overload; packing strap; additional trouble or vexation; surcharge, overburden.
sobrecargado, da, *a.* & *pp.* overloaded.
sobrecargar, *va.* (*pret.* SOBRECARGUÉ; *subj.* SOBRECARGUE) to overload, overburden; (com.) to overcharge; (sewing) to fell.
sobrecargo, *m.* (naut.) purser, supercargo.
sobrecarta, *f.* envelope (for a letter); (law) second decree or warrant repeating a former order.

sobrecartar, *va.* to repeat (a former warrant).
sobrecebadera, *f.* (naut.) sprit top-sail.
sobrecédula, *f.* second royal order.
sobreceja, *f.* part of the forehead over the eyebrows.
sobrecejo, *m.* frown; threatening or forbidding aspect.
sobreceño, *m.* frown.
sobrecercar, *va.* (sewing) to welt.
sobrecerco, *m.* (sewing) welt.
sobrecincho, *m.*; **-cha,** *f.* surcingle.
sobreclaustro, *m.* apartment over a cloister.
sobrecoger. I. *va.* (*ind.* SOBRECOJO; *subj.* SOBRECOJA) to surprise, catch (in the act). **II.** *vr.* to become afraid or apprehensive.—**s. de,** to be seized with.
sobrecogiente, *a.* startling.
sobrecogimiento, *m.* fear, apprehension.
sobrecomida, *f.* dessert.
sobrecopa, *f.* cover or lid of a cup.
sobrecoser, *va.* (sewing) to whip, to fell.
sobrecostura, *f.* (sewing) whipstich, fell.
sobrecrecer, *vn.* to grow on top.
sobrecreciente, *a.* growing on top.
sobrecruces, *m. pl.* (carp.) cross joints.
sobrecubierta, *f.* double cover; warp or envelope; (naut.) upper deck.
sobrecuello, *m.* collar.
sobredicho, cha, *a.* above-mentioned, aforesaid, said.
sobrediente, *m.* gagtooth.
sobredorar, *va.* to overgild; (fig.) to gloss over.
sobreedificar, *va.* to build over or on.
sobreempeine, *m.* covering for the instep.
sobreenfriar, *va.* & *vn.* (phys.) to supercool.
sobreestadías, *f. pl.* (com.) extra lay days.
sobreexcelente, *a.* superexcellent.
sobreexcitación, *f.* overexcitement; overexcitation.
sobreexcitar, *va.* to overexcite.
sobrefalda, *f.* overskirt.
sobrefaz, *f.* surface, outside; (mil.) face prolonged.
sobrefino, na, *a.* superfine, overfine, extrafine.
sobreflor, *f.* flower growing within another.
sobrefusión, *f.* (phys. & chem.) superfusion, supercooling.
sobreguarda, *m.* second guard.
sobrehaz, *f.* surface; outside cover.
sobreherido, da, *a.* slightly wounded.
sobrehilar, *va.* (sewing) to overcast.
sobrehueso, *m.* (vet.) splint; trouble, encumbrance, burden.
sobrehumano, na, *a.* superhuman.
sobrehusa, *f.* stew of fried fish.
sobreimpuesto, *m.* supertax.
sobrejalma, *f.* woollen cover for a packsaddle.
sobrejuanete, *m.* (naut.) royal.
sobrejunta, *f.* cover plate or strap (of a butt joint).
sobrelecho, *m.* under face of a stone.
sobrellave. I. *f.* double key. **II.** *m.* in royal palaces, keeper of double keys.
sobrellenar, *va.* to fill up, fill full.
sobrelleno, na, *a.* well filled, filled full.
sobrellevar, *va.* to ease (another's burden); to carry; to bear, endure, undergo; to overlook, be lenient about.
sobremanera, *adv.* beyond measure; exceedingly, most.
sobremano, *f.* (vet.) splint on the forehoofs.
sobremesa, *f.* tablecloth; dessert.—**de sobremesa,** immediately after dinner.
sobremesana, *f.* (naut.) mizzen topsail.
sobremuñonera, *f.* (artil.) clamp or capsquare.
sobrenadar, *vn.* to float.
sobrenatural, *a.* supernatural.
sobrenaturalmente, *adv.* supernaturally.
sobrenjalma, *f.* = SOBREJALMA.
sobrenombre, *m.* surname; nickname.
sobrentender, *va.* (*ind.* SOBRENTIENDO; *subj.* SOBRENTIENDA) to understand (something implied, not expressed). **II.** *vr.* to be understood, to go without saying.
sobreorgánico, ca, *a.* superorganic.
sobrepaga, *f.* extra pay.
sobrepaño, *m.* upper cloth; wrapper.
sobreparto, *m.* (med.) confinement after parturition.
sobrepasar, *va.* to exceed.
sobrepeine. I. *m.* trimming (the hair). **II.** *adv.* (coll.) slightly, briefly.
sobrepelliz, *f.* (eccl.) surplice.
sobrepeso, *m.* overweight.
sobrepié, *m.* (vet.) splint on rear hoofs.
sobreplán, *m.* (naut.) rider.
sobreponer. I. *va.* (*pp.* SOBREPUESTO; *ind. pres.* SOBREPONGO, *pret.* SOBREPUSE, *fut.* SOBREPONDRÉ; *subj.* SOBREPONGA) to put over, to overlap. **II.** *vr.* (a) to be above; to master, overcome, overpower.
sobreposición, *f.* superposition.
sobreprecio, *m.* extra charge, raise.
sobrepuerta, *f.* cornice over a door; lambrequin, door curtain, portière.
sobrepuesto, ta. I. *pp. irreg.* of SOBREPONER. **II.** *a.* superposed. **III.** *m.* honeycomb formed by bees after the hive is full.
sobrepujamiento, *m.* surpassing, excelling.
sobrepujante, *pres. p.* surpassing, excelling.
sobrepujanza, *f.* great strength and vigor.
sobrepujar, *va.* to exceed, surpass, excel.
sobrepuse, *pret.* of SOBREPONER.
sobrequilla, *f.* (naut.) keelson.
sobrerronda, *f.* (mil.) counterround.
sobrerropa, *f.* overcoat; overalls.
sobresalgo, sobresalga, *v. V.* SOBRESALIR.
sobresaliente. I. *a.* excelling, surpassing, excellent; conspicuous, that stands out, distinctive. **II.** *n.* substitute; (theat.) understudy.
sobresalir, *vn.* (*ind. pres.* SOBRESALGO, *fut.* SOBRESALDRÉ; *subj.* SOBRESALGA) to excel, be prominent, stand out; to project, jut out.
sobresaltar. I. *va.* to rush upon, assail, attack, fall upon; to frighten, terrify, startle. **II.** *vn.* to be striking (as figures in a painting). **III.** *vr.* to be startled.
sobresalto, *m.* sudden assault; startling surprise; sudden dread or fear.—**de s.,** unexpectedly, unawares, suddenly.
sobresanar, *va.* to heal superficially; to screen, to palliate.
sobresano. I. *adv.* cured superficially; affectedly, feignedly. **II.** *m. pl.* (naut.) tabling, leachlining.
sobrescribir, *va.* to superscribe, address.
sobrescrito, ta. I. *pp. irreg.* of SOBRESCRIBIR. **II.** *m.* superscription, address.
sobresdrújulo, la, *a.* accented on any syllable preceding the antepenult.
sobreseer, *vn.* to desist from a design; to relinquish a claim; (law) to stay a judgment, etc.
sobreseimiento, *m.* suspension; discontinuance; (law) stay of proceedings.
sobresello, *m.* double seal.
sobresembrar, *va.* (*ind.* SOBRESIEMBRO; *subj.* SOBRESIEMBRE) to sow over again.
sobreseñal, *f.* a special knights' device.
sobresolar, *va.* (*ind.* SOBRESUELO; *subj.* SOBRESUELE) to pave anew; to resole (shoe).
sobrestante, *m.* overseer; foreman; comptroller; inspector; supervisor.—**sobrestantía,** *f.* position or office of a SOBRESTANTE.
sobresueldo, *m.* extra wages.
sobresuelo, *m.* floor or pavement over another.
sobretarde, *f.* close of the evening.
sobretendón, *m.* tumor on the tendons of a horse's leg.
sobretensión, *f.* (phys.) supervoltage.
sobretodo, *m.* overcoat, great coat.
sobreveedor, *m.* chief of the overseers.
sobrevenida, *f.* supervention.
sobrevenir, *vn.* (*ger.* SOBREVINIENDO; *ind. pres.* YO SOBREVENGO, ÉL SOBREVIENE, *pret.* SOBREVINE, *fut.* SOBREVENDRÉ; *subj.* SOBREVENGA) to happen, take place; to follow; to supervene.

sobreverterse, *vr.* (*ind.* se SOBREVIERTE; *subj.* se SOBREVIERTA) to run over, overflow.
sobrevesta, sobreveste, *f.* surcoat, overcoat.
sobrevestir, *va.* to put a greatcoat on.
sobrevidriera, *f.* window guard, wire net before a glass window; storm window.
sobrevienta, *f.* gust of wind; onslaught, impetuous fury; startling surprise.—**a s.,** suddenly.
sobreviento, *m.* gust of wind.—**estar a s. de,** (naut.) to have the wind of.
sobrevierte, sobrevierta, *v. V.* SOBREVERTERSE.
sobrevine, *pret.* of SOBREVENIR.
sobrevista, *f.* beaver of a helmet.
sobreviviente, *n.* & *a.* survivor(-ing).
sobrevivir, *va.* & *vn.* to survive, to outlive.
sobrexcedente, *a.* surpassing, exceeding.
sobrexceder, *va.* to surpass, excel, exceed.
sobrexcitación, *f.* overexcitement; overexcitation.
sobrexcitar, *va.* to overexcite.
sobriamente, *adv.* soberly, frugally.
sobriedad, *f.* sobriety, frugality.
sobrina, *f.* niece.
sobrinazgo, *m.* relationship of a nephew or niece; nepotism.
sobrino, *m.* nephew.
sobrio, ria, *a.* sober, temperate, frugal.
soca, *f.* (Am.) ratoon of the sugar cane.
socaire, *m.* (naut.) slatch; lee, lee gauge.
socairero, *m.* (naut.) skulker, lurker.
socaliña, *f.* trick, cunning.—**socaliñar,** *va.* to extort by trickery.—**socaliñero, ra,** *n.* trickster, cheat.
socalzar, *va.* (mason.) to underpin, underset.
socapa, *f.* pretext, pretense.—**a s.,** cautiously.
socapiscol, *m.* = SOCHANTRE.
socar, *va.* (Cuba, C. A.) to tighten; to compress.
socarra, *f.* singe, scorching; craft, cunning.
socarrar, *va.* to singe, scorch.
socarrén, *m.* (arch.) eave, gable end.
socarrena, *f.* hollow, cavity; interval; (arch.) space between rafters.
socarrina, *f.* (coll.) scorching, singeing.
socarrón, na, *a.* cunning, sly, crafty.
socarronamente, *adv.* slyly, artfully.
socarronería, *f.* cunning, artfulness, craftiness.
socava, socavación, *f.* undermining; digging around trees.
socavar, *va.* to excavate, undermine.
socavón, *m.* cave, cavern; (min.) adit, adit level, tunnel.
socaz, *m.* outlet of a mill.
sociabilidad, *f.* sociableness, sociability.
sociable, *a.* sociable, companionable.
sociablemente, *adv.* sociably, companionably.
social, *a.* social; sociable, companionable.
socialismo, *m.* (pol.) socialism.
socialista, *n.* & *a.* (pol.) socialist(-ic).
socialización, *f.* socialization.
socializar, *va.* to socialize, transfer to the State.
sociedad, *f.* society; social intercourse; (com.) society, corporation, association, company, partnership, copartnership.—**s. anónima,** stock company.—**s. comanditaria** = S. EN COMANDITA.—**s. cooperativa,** coöperative society or association.—**S. de las Naciones,** League of Nations.—**s. de socorros mutuos,** mutual-help society.—**s. en comandita,** commandite, partnership in commendam.—**s. regular colectiva,** general partnership, copartnership.—**s. por acciones** = S. ANÓNIMA.—**la s.,** society, the social organism, the community (often restricted, as in English, to polite or fashionable society).
socinianismo, *m.* Socinianism.
sociniano, na, *n.* & *a.* Socinian.
socio, cia, *n.* partner, copartner; companion, con sort; member, fellow; (coll.) confederate.
socioeconómico, ca, *a.* socioeconomic.
sociología, *f.* sociology.
sociológicamente, *adv.* sociologically.
sociológico, ca, *a.* sociological.
sociólogo, ga, *n.* sociologist.
socolor, *m.* pretext, pretense.
socollada, *f.* (naut.) flapping; pitching, jerk.
soconusco, *m.* cacao from Soconusco (C. A.).
socoro, *m.* place under the choir.
socorredor, ra, *n.* & *a.* helper(-ing), aider(-ing).
socorrer, *va.* to assist, aid, help, succor; to favor; to pay on account.
socorrido, da. I. *pp.* of SOCORRER. **II.** *a.* furnished, well supplied; (coll.) handy, useful; popular.
socorro, *m.* succor, aid, assistance, help; payment on account; (mil.) succors; relief.—**puesto de s.,** first-aid station.
socrático, ca, *a.* Socratic.
socrocio, *m.* (pharm.) saffron poultice.
socucho, *m.* (Am.) small room, "den"; hiding place.
sochantre, *m.* (eccl.) subchanter.
soda, *f.* (chem.) = SOSA, soda.
sódico, ca, *a.* (chem.) sodic; sodium (as *a.*, as in *carbonato sódico,* sodium carbonate).
sodio, *m.* (chem.) sodium.
sodomía, *f.* sodomy.—**sodomita,** *n.* & *a.* Sodomite.—**sodomítico, ca,** *a.* pert. to sodomy.
soez, *a.* mean, vile, base, coarse.
soezmente, *adv.* meanly, basely, vilely.
sofá, *m.* sofa.
sofaldar, *va.* to truss up; raise up; tuck up.
sofaldo, *m.* trussing or tucking up clothes.
[1]**sofí,** *m.* Sufi, Shah.
[2]**sofí,** *m.* = SUFÍ, one of a Persian sect of mystics.
sofión, *m.* hoot; reprimand.
sofisma, *m.* (logic) fallacy.
sofismo, *m.* = SUFISMO, Sufism.
sofista, *m.* sophist; quibbler.
sofistería, *f.* sophistry.
sofisticación, *f.* perversion by fallacies.
sofísticamente, *adv.* fallaciously.
sofisticar, *va.* to falsify, pervert or distort by fallacy.
sofístico, ca, *a.* fallacious.
sofito, *m.* (arch.) soffit.
soflama, *f.* subtle flame; glow; blush; (coll.) flimflam.—**soflamar. I.** *va.* to cheat, swindle; (coll.) to flimflam; to make (a person) blush. **II.** *vr.* to get scorched.
soflamero, *m.* trickster; (coll.) flimflammer.
sofocación, *f.* suffocation; smothering, choking.
sofocador, ra, *a.* suffocative, suffocating, asphyxiating.
sofocante, *pres. p.* & *a.* suffocating, stifling, close.
sofocar, *va.* (*pret.* SOFOQUÉ; *subj.* SOFOQUE) to choke, suffocate, smother; to quench, extinguish, put out; to stifle; to oppress, harass; to importune, vex; to provoke; to make blush.
sofocleo, a, *a.* Sophoclean.
sofoco, *m.* suffocation; vexation; embarrassment.
sofocón, *m.* (coll.) vexation, chagrin.
sofoqué, sofoque, *v. V.* SOFOCAR.
sófora, *f.* (bot.) Japanese pagoda tree.
sofreír, *va.* (*pp.* SOFREÍDO, SOFRITO; *ind. pres.* SOFRÍO, *pret.* él SOFRIÓ; *subj.* SOFRÍA) (cooking) to fry slightly.
sofrenada, *f.* sudden check of a horse, saccade, ebrillade; harsh reprimand, dressing down.
sofrenar, *va.* to check (a horse) suddenly; to reprimand severely; to check (a passion).
sofrenazo, *m.* = SOFRENADA.
sofrito, ta, *pp. irreg.* of SOFREÍR.
soga. I. *f.* rope, halter, cord; a variable land measure; (arch.) face (of a brick or stone); (arch.) (of bricks and stones) stretcher.—**a s.,** (arch.) as stretchers.—**con la s. a la garganta,** in imminent danger.—**dar s. a,** to make fun of. —**hacer s.,** to lag behind. **II.** *n.* (coll.) sly, cunning person; (Colomb.) lasso, lariat.
soguear, *va.* to measure with a rope.
soguería, *f.* ropewalk; rope shop; collection of ropes.
soguero, *m.* ropemaker.
soguilla, *f.* small braid of hair; small rope.
soja, *f.* (bot.) soy; soy bean.

sojuzgador, ra, *n.* conqueror, subduer.
sojuzgamiento, *m.* subjugating; subjugation.
sojuzgar, *va.* (*pret.* SOJUZGUÉ; *subj.* SOJUZGUE) to conquer, subjugate, subdue.
[1]**sol,** *m.* sun; sunlight; day; a kind of ancient lace; sol, Peruvian silver coin (normally, about 49 cents, or 2 shillings).—**s. medio,** (astr.) mean sun.—**al salir el s.,** at sunrise.—**al s. puesto,** at nightfall.—**de s. a s.,** from sunrise to sunset. —**hacer s.,** to be sunny (*hace sol,* it is sunny; *hace mucho sol,* it is very sunny).—**quemadura del s.,** sunburning.—**tomar el s.,** to bask in the sun, sunbathe; (naut.) to take the altitude of the sun.
[2]**sol,** *m.* (mus.) G, sol, fifth note of the scale.
solacé, solace, *v. V.* SOLAZAR.
solacear, *va.* to solace, console, comfort.
solada, *f.* dregs, lees, sediment.
solado, *m.* tile floor, pavement.
solador, *m.* tiler, paver.
soladura, *f.* paving; paving materials.
solamente, *adv.* only; solely, merely.
solana, *f.* strong sunshine; sunny place; sun gallery; sun bath.
solanáceo, cea, *a.* (bot.) solanaceous.
solanera, *f.* sun bath; sunburning; hot, sunny place.
solanina, *f.* (chem.) solanin(e).
solano, *m.* easterly wind; (bot.) nightshade.
solapa, *f.* lapel (of coat); pretense, pretext; (vet.) cavity of a small wound; overlapping.—**a.,** or **de, s.,** overlapping, lap (joint).
solapadamente, *adv.* deceitfully, sneakingly.
solapado, da. I. *pp.* of SOLAPAR. **II.** *a.* cunning, crafty, artful, sneaky; lap (joint).
solapadura.—obra de s., *f.* (naut.) clincher work, clinching; overlapping.
solapamiento, *m.* (vet.) cavity of a wound.
solapar. I. *va.* (tailoring) to put lapels on; to overlap; to cloak, conceal. **II.** *vn.* to overlap (as a lapel).—**solape, solapo,** *m.* lapel; pretense.—**a s.,** (coll.) sneakingly.
[1]**solar,** *va.* (*ind.* SUELO; *subj.* SUELE) to floor; to pave; to sole (shoes).
[2]**solar,** *m.* lot, ground plot; manor house, ancestral mansion.
[3]**solar,** *a.* solar.
solariego, ga, *a.* manorial; (law) held by a full legal tenure; of noble ancestry.
solas, *f. pl.* of SOLO.—**a mis, tus, sus s.,** *adv.* all alone, by myself, thyself, etc.—**a s.,** in private.
solaz, *m.* solace, consolation; relaxation, comfort; enjoyment.—**a s.,** pleasantly, agreeably.
solazar. I. *va.* (*pret.* SOLACÉ; *subj.* SOLACE) to solace, comfort, cheer, gladden. **II.** *vr.* to be comforted; to rejoice, have pleasure.
solazo, *m. aug.* (coll.) scorching sun.
solazoso, sa, *a.* comforting, delectable.
soldada, *f.* wages, pay, salary.
soldadero, ra, *a.* salaried, receiving wages.
soldadesca, *f.* soldiery; soldiering; undisciplined troops.
soldadesco, ca, *a.* soldierly, soldierlike, military. —**a la s.,** in a soldierly manner, soldierlike.
soldado, *m.* soldier.—**s. de a caballo,** trooper, cavalryman.—**s. de a pie,** or **de infantería,** foot soldier.—**s. raso,** private.—**s. de marina,** marine.—**s. voluntario,** volunteer.
soldador, *m.* solderer; soldering iron.
soldadura, *f.* soldering; welding, brazing; solder; correction or mending.—**s. débil,** soft solder (-ing).—**s. dura,** or **s. fuerte,** hard solder(-ing). —**s. tierna** = S. DÉBIL.
soldán, *m.* sultan, Mohammedan title.
soldar, *va.* (*ind.* SUELDO; *subj.* SUELDE) to solder; to weld, braze; to mend; to correct.
solear, *va.* = ASOLEAR, to sun.
solecismo, *m.* (rhet. and gram.) solecism.
soledad, *f.* solitude, loneliness, loneness; homesickness; lonely place; (mus.) an Andalusian tune, song, and dance.
soledoso, sa, *a.* solitary, lonely.
solejar, *m.* sunny place.
solemne, *a.* solemn; yearly; (coll.) great, downright.—**solemnemente,** *adv.* solemnly.
solemnicé, solemnice, *v. V.* SOLEMNIZAR.
solemnidad, *f.* solemnity; religious pomp; grand ceremony; impressiveness.—*pl.* formalities.
solemnización, *f.* solemnization.
solemnizador, ra, *n.* & *a.* solemnizer(-ing).
solemnizar, *va.* (*pret.* SOLEMNICÉ; *subj.* SOLEMNICE) to solemnize, celebrate with pomp; to praise, applaud, extol.
solenoide, *m.* (elec.) solenoid.
sóleo, *m.* (anat.) soleus.
[1]**soler,** *vn.* (*ind.* SUELO) (*defect., only pres. and imp. used, always foll. by inf.*) to be in the habit of, accustomed to; (in *imp.*) used to (*yo solía hablar con él,* I used to talk with him).
[2]**soler,** *m.* (naut.) underflooring.
solera, *f.* (arch.) entablature, stringpiece, crossbeam, rib, summer, lintel, breastsummer; plinth; nether millstone; lees or mother of wine.—**s. de cureña,** (mil.) sole of a gun carriage.
solercia, *f.* industry; abilities; shrewdness.
[1]**solería,** *f.* pavement; paving stones.
[2]**solería,** *f.* parcel of skins used for soles.
solero, *m.* nether millstone.
solerte, *a.* shrewd, cunning, sagacious.
soleta, *f.* new sole in stockings; (Mex.) cake with sugar icing.—**tomar s.,** (coll.) to run off.
soletar, soletear, *va.* to resole (stockings).
soletero, ra, *n.* one who refoots stockings.
solevación, *f.,* or **solevamiento,** *m.* = SUBLEVACIÓN, insurrection, uprising.
solevantado, da. I. *pp.* of SOLEVANTAR. **II.** *a.* restless, excited, agitated, perturbed.
solevantamiento, *m.* upheaval, uprising.
solevantar, *va.* to push up, elevate; to incite.
solevar, *va.* = SUBLEVAR, to incite to revolt.
solfa, *f.* (mus.) sol-fa, solfeggio, solmization; musical annotation, notes; music, harmony; (coll.) sound beating or flogging.—**estar,** or **poner, en s.,** to be arranged (or to arrange) with art and judgment; to appear (or present) in a ridiculous light.
solfatara, *f.* (geol.) solfatara.
solfeador, ra, *n.* sol-faist, one who solmizates.
solfear, *vn.* (mus.) to sol-fa, solmizate; (coll.) to cudgel, flog.—**solfeo,** *m.* (mus.) sol-faing; (coll.) beating, drubbing.
solfista, *n.* sol-faist.
solicitación, *f.* solicitation; importunity; temptation, inducement.
solicitado, da. I. *pp.* of SOLICITAR. **II.** *a.* in good demand, sought after, popular.
solicitador, ra, *n.* solicitor, agent.
solícitamente, *adv.* solicitously, diligently.
solicitante. I. *a.* soliciting. **II.** *n.* solicitor, agent; applicant.
solicitar, *va.* to solicit; to apply for; to importune; to entreat; to woo, court.
solícito, ta, *a.* solicitous, diligent, careful.
solicitud, *f.* solicitude; importunity; diligence; petition, application, request; (com.) demand. —**a s.,** on request, at the request (of).—**s. de ingreso,** application for admission.
sólidamente, *adv.* solidly, firmly.
solidar, *va.* to consolidate, establish; to harden, to render firm and solid.
solidariamente, *adv.* with solidarity; (law) in solidum, for the whole.
solidaridad, *f.* solidarity.
solidario, ria, *a.* (law) solidary, jointly liable.
solidarizar. I. *va.* to make solidary. **II.** *vr.* to make common cause, act together.
solideo, *m.* (eccl.) calotte.
solidez, *f.* solidity, firmness, strength.
solidificación, *f.* solidification.
solidificar, *va.* & *vr.* to solidify.
sólido, da. I. *a.* solid, firm, compact, consistent; built on sound reasons. **II.** *m.* (geom. & phys.) solid; solidus, an ancient Roman gold coin.
soliloquiar, *vn.* (coll.) to soliloquize.

soliloquio, *m.* soliloquy, monologue.
solimán, *m.* (chem.) corrosive sublimate.
solio, *m.* throne with a canopy; throne.
solípedo, da, *a.* (zool.) solipede, solidungulate.
solista, *n.* (mus.) soloist.
solitaria, *f.* post chaise; sulky; tapeworm.
solitariamente, *adv.* solitarily.
solitario, ria. I. *a.* solitary, lonely, isolated, secluded. **II.** *m.* solitary, recluse, hermit; solitaire (game); (jewel) solitaire (diamond).
sólito, ta, *a.* wont, accustomed.
soliviadura, *f.* lift, lifting, raising.
soliviantar, *va.* to induce, incite, rouse.
soliviar. I. *va.* to raise or lift up: to prop up. **II.** *vr.* to raise oneself.
solivio, *m.* lift, rising or raising.
solo, la. I. *a.* alone, unaccompanied; only, sole; solitary, lonely.—**a mis solas, sus solas,** etc., all alone, without aid, by myself (himself, etc.); in solitude.—**a solas,** alone, unaided. **II.** *m.* (mus.) solo; lone hand in certain card games; a card game.
sólo, *adv.* = SOLAMENTE, only, solely.
solomillo, solomo, *m.* sirloin; loin of pork.
solpuga. I. *f.* (zool.) solpugid. **II.** *f. pl.* Solpugida.
solsticial, *a.* solstitial.
solsticio, *m.* (astr.) solstice.—**s. de invierno,** winter solstice.—**s. de verano,** summer solstice.—**s. hiemal** = S. DE INVIERNO.—**s. vernal** = S. DE VERANO.
soltadizo, za, *a.* easily untied; cleverly loosened.
soltador, ra, *n.* dropper.
soltar. I. *va.* (*pp. irreg.* SUELTO; *ind.* SUELTO; *subj.* SUELTE) to untie, unfasten, loosen; to turn on (the water); to turn loose; to cast off, set free, discharge; to let go, drop; to throw down, throw out; (coll.) to utter, let out; to give (a slap or kick). **II.** *vn.* to burst out (into laughter, etc.). **III.** *vr.* to get loose, to come off; to grow expeditious and handy; to lose restraint; to thaw out; to forego all decency and modesty; to break out (laughing, crying, etc.): to begin, start.
soltería, *f.* celibacy, bachelorhood.
soltero, ra. I. *a.* single, unmarried. **II.** *m.* bachelor, unmarried man. **III.** *f.* spinster, unmarried woman.
solterón, na, *n.* old bachelor (maid).
soltura, *f.* freeing, setting at liberty; release, freedom; easiness; fluency; agility, nimbleness; laxity, looseness, licentiousness.
solubilidad, *f.* solubility.
soluble, *a.* soluble; solvable.
solución, *f.* loosening or untying; climax or denouement in a drama or epic poem; pay, satisfaction; (math., chem.) solution.—**s. de continuidad,** solution of continuity, discontinuity, break.
solucionar, *va.* to solve; to meet (a difficulty).
solutivo, va, *a.* (med.) solutive.
solvencia, *f.* (com.) solvency.
solventar, *va.* to settle (accounts); to solve.
solvente, *a.* solvent, dissolving; (com.) solvent.
solver, *va.* (*ind.* SUELVO; *subj.* SUELVA) to solve.
sollado, *m.* (naut.) orlop.
sollamar, *va.* to scorch, to singe.
sollastre, *m.* scullion, kitchen boy; smart rogue.
sollastría, *f.* scullery.
sollo, *m.* (ichth.) sturgeon, pike.
sollozante, *a.* sobbing.
sollozar, *vn.* (*pret.* SOLLOCÉ; *subj.* SOLLOCE) to sob.—**sollozo,** *m.* sob; (Mex.) huckleberry.
soma, *f.* coarse flour.
somalí, *n.* & *a.* Somali.
Somalia, *f.* Somalia.
somanta, *f.* (coll.) beating, drubbing.
somatén, *m.* armed force for defense of a city or province; one serving in such a force; alarm bell; (coll.) hubbub.—**¡s.!** Catalan war cry.
somático, ca, *a.* (anat., biol., zool.) somatic, corporeal, bodily, physical.
somatología, *f.* somatology.
sombra, *f.* shade; shadow; darkness; spirit, ghost; shelter, protection; resemblance; sign, vestige; (astr.) umbra; (art) shade, shading; umber.—**sombras chinescas,** (theat.) shadow pantomime.—**a la s.,** in the shade; (coll.) in jail.—**hacer s.,** to shade; to protect; to outshine.—**ni por s.,** by no means.—**no ser ni su s.,** to be but the shadow of one's former self.—**tener buena s.,** to be pleasing, popular, agreeable.—**tener mala s.,** to exert an evil influence over others; to be disagreeable.
sombraje, *m.* screen made with branches, mats, etc., to afford shade.
sombrajo, *m.* SOMBRAJE; (coll.) shadow cast by a person before another who needs light.
sombrar, *va.* to astonish.
sombreado, da. I. *a.* shady, shadowy. **II.** *m.* (f. a.) shading.
sombreador, ra, *a.* shading.
sombrear, *va.* (art) to shade.
sombrerazo, *m. aug.* large hat; flap or blow with a hat; (coll.) doffing of the hat as a greeting.
sombrerera, *f.* hatbox, hat case; hatter's wife.
sombrerería, *f.* hat factory or shop.
sombrerero, ra, *n.* hatter; hat maker.
sombrerete, *m. dim.* small hat; (mech.) bonnet, cap, cowl; spark catcher of a locomotive; (arch.) calotte.
sombrerillo, ito, *m. dim.* little hat; alms basket in prisons; (bot.) navelwort.
sombrero, *m.* SOMBRERETE; hat; soundboard, canopy of a pulpit; privilege of a Spanish grandee of keeping his hat on in the presence of the king.—**s. apuntado,** cocked hat.—**s. calañés,** Andalusian hat.—**s. castoreño,** beaver hat.—**s. de cabrestante,** (naut.) drum of the capstan.—**s. de copa,** or **de copa alta,** silk hat, high (silk) hat.—**s. de jipijapa,** Panama hat.—**s. del patrón,** (naut.) hat money, primage.—**s. de muelles,** opera hat.—**s. de paja,** straw hat.—**s. de pelo,** (Am.) high hat.—**s. de teja,** shovel hat, priest's hat (low-crown hat with broad brim turned up on the sides).—**s. de tres candiles,** or **de tres picos,** three-cornered hat.—**s. flexible,** soft felt hat.—**s. gacho,** slouch hat.—**s. hongo,** derby hat.—**s. jarano,** Mexican sombrero.—**s. jíbaro,** farmers' straw hat.—**s. jipijapa,** Panama hat.
sombría, *f.* shady place.
sombrilla, *f.* parasol, sunshade.
sombrita, *f. dim.* slight shade.
sombrío, bría. I. *a.* gloomy, sombre; overcast, murky, thick (weather); taciturn, sullen; (art) shaded, dark. **II.** *m.* shady place.
sombroso, sa, *a.* shady, shadowy.
somera, *f.* (print.) sleeper of the press.
someramente, *adv.* superficially, briefly.
somero, ra, *a.* superficial, shallow.
someter. I. *va.* to subject; submit, subdue; to put (to the test, etc.). **II.** *vr.* to humble oneself; to submit; to surrender; (a) to submit (to); to go (through) (an operation, an examination).
sometimiento, *m.* submission, subjection, subduing.
somito, *m.* (zool.) somite, metamere.
somnambulismo, *m.* somnambulism.
somnámbulo, la, *n.* somnambulist.
somnífero, ra, *a.* somniferous, inducing sleep.
somnilocuencia, *f.* somniloquy, somniloquence.
somnílocuo, cua. I. *a.* talking in one's sleep. **II.** *n.* somniloquist.
somniloquia, *f.* somniloquy.
somnolencia, *f.* drowsiness, somnolence.
somonte.—**de s.,** coarse, rough, shaggy.
somorgujador, *m.* diver.
somorgujar, *va.* & *vr.* to dive, to duck.
somorgujo, somorgujón, somormujo, *m.* (ornith.) dun diver, merganser.—**a lo somorgujo,** or **a la somormujo,** under water; privately, secretly.
sompesar, *va.* = SOPESAR.
son, *m.* sound, noise; spread news or story; pretext, motive; manner, guise; (Am. esp. Cuba) popular song and dance.—**¿a qué s.?** why, for

what reason?—**a s. de,** at or to the sound of.—**¿a s. de qué?** = ¿A QUÉ S.?—**bailar a cualquier s.,** to transfer easily one's affection or liking, to be fickle.—**bailar sin s.,** to be exceedingly eager; to act unwisely or inopportunely.—**bailar uno al s. que le tocan,** to adapt oneself to circumstances.—**en s. de,** as, like, in the manner of.—**en s. de guerra,** in a warlike manner.—**sin s.,** without reason.—**sin ton ni s.,** without rhyme or reason.
sonable, *a.* loud, sounding; noted, famous.
sonada, *f.* (mus.) tune; sonata.
sonadera, *f.* blowing the nose.
sonadero, *m.* handkerchief.
sonado, da. I. *pp.* of SONAR. **II.** *a.* noted, famous; talked about; (coll.) scandalous, sensational.
sonador, ra. I. *n.* noise maker. **II.** *m.* handkerchief.
sonaja, *f.* jingles; (mus.) timbrel.
sonajero, *m.* baby's rattle.
sonajuela, *f. dim.* small jingles or timbrel.
sonambulismo, *m.* somnambulism.
sonámbulo, la, *n.* somnambulist.
sonante, *pres. p.* & *a.* sounding, sonorous.
sonar. I. *va.* (*ind.* SUENO; *subj.* SUENE) to sound, to ring, to play upon. **II.** *vn.* to sound; to ring; (of clock) to strike; to be mentioned, talked about; (a) to sound, or look, (like); to seem; to sound familiar; to be reported or bruited about.—**ni suena ni truena,** is forgotten, is in the discard, cuts no figure. **III.** *vr.* to blow one's nose. **IV.** *m.* sonar.
sonata, *f.* (mus.) sonata.
sonatina, *f. dim.* (mus.) sonatina.
sonda, *f.* (naut.) sounding, heaving the lead; lead, sounder, plummet; (aer.) dragrope; (geol.) anular borer; diamond drill; (surg.) catheter, bougie; sound, probe; (artil.) searcher, proof-stick.
sondable, *a.* that can be sounded.
sondaleza, *f.* (naut.) lead line, sounding line.
sondar, sondear, *va.* (naut.) to sound; to try, sound out (another's intentions); to explore, fathom; to probe.
sondeo, *m.* sounding; exploring.
sonecillo, *m. dim.* slight sound; merry tune.
sonetear, *vn.* to sonnet, compose a sonnet.
sonetico, *m. dim.* sound produced by tapping with the fingers; little or light sonnet.
sonetista, *m.* sonnet writer.
soneto, *m.* sonnet.
sónico, ca, *a.* sonic.
sonido, *m.* sound; noise; report; literal meaning.—**s. timpánico,** tympanic resonance.
sonochada, *f.* evening; evening watch.
sonochar, *vn.* to watch the first night hours.
sonómetro, *m.* sonometer.
sonoramente, *adv.* sonorously; harmoniously.
sonoridad, *f.* sonority, sonorousness.
sonoro, ra; sonoroso, sa, *a.* sonorous; sounding, clear, loud.
sonreír, *vn.* & *vr.* (*ger.* SONRIENDO; *ind. pres.* SONRÍO, *pret.* él SONRIÓ; *subj.* SONRÍA) to smile.
sonrisa, *f.,* **sonriso,** *m.* smile.
sonrodadura, *f.* (of wheels) sticking in the mud.
sonrodarse, *vr.* (of wheels) to stick in the mud.
sonrojar, sonrojear. I. *va.* to make (one) blush. **II.** *vr.* to blush.—**sonrojo,** *m.* blush; blushing; word causing a blush.
sonrosar, sonrosear. I. *va.* to dye a rose color. **II.** *vr.* to blush.—**sonroseo,** *m.* blush.
sonsaca, *f.,* **sonsacamiento,** *m.* wheedling; drawing out; enticement; pilfering.
sonsacador, ra, *n.* wheedler, enticer; pilferer.
sonsacar, *va.* (*pret.* SONSAQUÉ; *subj.* SONSAQUE) to pilfer; to draw (one) out; to entice, allure.
sonsaque, *m.* = SONSACA.
sonsonete, *m.* sound produced by rhythmical raps or taps; singsong voice.
soñador, ra, *n.* dreamer.
soñante. I. *pres. p.* of SOÑAR. **II.** *a.* dreaming.
soñar. I. *va.* & *vn.* (*ind.* SUEÑO; *subj.* SUEÑE) to dream.—**s. con,** or **en,** to dream of.—**s. despierto,** to indulge in day dreams; to build air castles.—**ni soñarlo,** not even to dream of it.
soñolencia, *f.* somnolence, somnolency, sleepiness.
soñoliento, ta, *a.* somnolent, sleepy; sleeping; sleep-producing.
sopa, *f.* sop (soaked bread); soup.—*pl.* slices of bread for soup.—**s. borracha,** a kind of wine cake.—**s. de ajo,** or **de gato,** meager soup.—**s. de vino,** (bot.) flower of the small caltrops.—**s. juliana,** julienne soup, vegetable soup.—**a la s. boba,** (coll.) living at other people's expense.—**hecho una s.,** (coll.) drenched, wet through to the skin.
sopaipa, *f.* fritter steeped in honey.
sopalancar, *va.* to lift with a lever.
sopalanda, *f.* gown worn by students.
sopanda, *f.* brace (of carriage); (carp.) joist.
sopapear, *va.* (coll.) to chuck under the chin; to vilify, to abuse.
sopapo, *m.* chuck under the chin; (coll.) box, blow, slap; (mech.) valve, stop valve, sucker.
sopar, [1]sopear, *va.* = ENSOPAR, to sop (bread).
[2]sopear, *va.* to trample; to maltreat.
sopeña, *f.* cavity under a rock.
sopera, *f.* soup tureen.
sopero. I. *m.* soup plate. **II.** *m.* lover of soups.
sopesar, *va.* to heft, test the weight of by lifting.
[1]sopetear, *va.* to sop; to steep (bread).
[2]sopetear, *va.* to abuse, maltreat.
sopeteo, *m.* dipping (bread, etc.).
[1]sopetón, *m.* bread toasted and steeped in oil.
[2]sopetón, *m.* box, cuff, slap.—**de s.,** suddenly.
sopicaldo, *m.* very thin soup.
sopista, *n.* one living on charity.
sopita, *f. dim.* light soup.
¡sopla! *interj.* gracious! what a thing!
sopladero, *m.* air hole from subterranean passages.
soplado, da. I. *pp.* of SOPLAR. **II.** *a.* (coll.) over-nice and spruce; conceited. **III.** *m.* (min.) deep fissure.
soplador, ra. I. *n.* blower; inciter. **II.** *m.* ventilator, blowing fan; tuyère (of a blast furnace).
sopladura, *f.* blowing; (foundry) air hole.
soplamocos, *m.* (coll.) box or slap on the nose.
soplar. I. *vn.* to blow; (coll.) to tattle. **II.** *va.* to blow; blow out; to fan; to fill with air, inflate; to rob or steal in an artful manner; to huff (a man) in the game of draughts; to prompt, tell what to say; (Am.) (theat.) to prompt; to inspire.—**soplársela a uno,** to deceive one. **III.** *vr.* to swell up; to eat or drink to excess, to stuff oneself.
soplete, *m.* blowpipe; blow torch.
soplico, *m. dim.* slight puff or blast.
soplido, *m.* blowing, blast.
soplillo, *m. dim.* blowing fan; anything extremely thin and light; silk gauze, chiffon; very light sponge cake.
soplo, *m.* blowing; blast, gust, puff of wind; breath; instant, moment; hint, tip, secret advice or warning; secret accusation.
soplón, plona. I. *a.* denunciatory; tipping, informing. **II.** *n.* (coll.) talebearer, tattler, stool pigeon, canary; (coll.) tipster.
sopón, *m. aug.* (coll.) = SOPISTA.
soponcio, *m.* fainting fit, swoon.
sopor, *m.* (med.) sopor, lethargic sleep.
soporífero, ra, *m.* & *a.* soporific.
soporífico, ca, *a.* soporific.
soporoso, sa, *a.* soporiferous, inducing sleep; suffering from sopor; (med.) soporose.
soportable, *a.* bearable, endurable.
soportador, ra, *n.* supporter.
soportal, *m.* (arch.) portico.
soportar, *va.* to bear, put up with; to support.
soporte, *m.* support; rest; bearing.
soprano. I. *m.* (mus.) soprano voice. **II.** *f.* soprano singer.
sopuntar, *va.* to underscore with dots.
sor, *f.* (eccl.) sister, as *sor María,* Sister Mary.

sora, *f.* (Peru) mash made from maize.
sorba, *f.* (bot.) sorb apple.
sorbedor, ra. I. *a.* sipping. **II.** *n.* sipper.
sorber, *va.* to sip, suck; to imbibe, soak, absorb; to swallow.
sorbete, *m.* sherbet, water ice.
sorbetera, *f.* ice-cream freezer; (coll. and humor.) high hat, top hat.
sorbetón, *m. aug.* large draught of liquor.
sorbible, *a.* absorbable; that can be sipped.
sorbito, *m. dim.* little sip.
[1]**sorbo,** *m.* imbibing; absorption; sip, draught, swallow, gulp.
[2]**sorbo,** *m.* = SERBAL, sorb tree, service tree.
sorción, *f.* (chem., phys.) sorption.
[1]**sorda,** *f.* (ornith.) woodcock.
[2]**sorda,** *f.* (naut.) stream cable for launching a ship.
sordamente, *adv.* secretly, silently.
sordera, sordedad, sordez, *f.* deafness.
sórdidamente, *adv.* sordidly.
sordidez, *f.* sordidness.
sórdido, da, *a.* sordid.
sordina, *f.* (mus.) mute, sordine (for string instruments); sordono (for trumpet); damper (for piano).—**a la s.,** secretly, quietly, on the quiet.
sordino, *m.* (mus.) kit, small fiddle.
sordo, da, *a.* deaf; silent, still, quiet; muffled, stifled; dull; unmoved, insensible; (math.) irrational, surd.
sordomudez, *f.* (med.) deaf-mutism.
sordomudo, da, *a.* & *n.* deaf and dumb, deaf-mute.
sordón, *m.* (mus.) old kind of oboe.
sorgo, *m.* (bot.) sorghum.
soriasis, *f.* (med.) psoriasis.
sorites, *m.* (logic) sorites, chain argument.
sorna, *f.* sluggishness, laziness, slowness.
soro, *m.* year-old hawk.
soroche, *m.* (S. A.) altitude sickness, a disease caused by the rare air; (min.) friable silver ore.
soroque, *f.* (min.) matrix of ores.
sóror, *f.* (eccl.) = SOR.
sorprendente, *a.* surprising.
sorprender, *va.* to surprise, astonish; to surprise, catch (in an act).
sorpresa, *f.* surprise.—**de s.,** by surprise.
[1]**sorra,** *f.* (naut.) ballast of stones or coarse gravel.
[2]**sorra,** *f.* side of a tunny fish.
sorregar, *va.* (*ind. pres.* SORRIEGO, *pret.* SORREGUÉ; *subj.* SORRIEGUE) to water accidentally, by deviation or overflow of the water elsewhere.
sorriego, *m.* water that deviates from one channel to another; watering by this water.
sorrostrada, *f.* insolence; bluntness.—**dar s.,** to insult; to throw one's faults in one's face.
sorteable, *a.* fit to be drafted.
sorteador, ra, *n.* one who casts lots; skilful bullfighter.
sorteamiento, *m.* = SORTEO.
sortear, *va.* to draw or cast lots for; to raffle; to fight (bulls) with skill and dexterity; to elude or shun cleverly.—**sorteo,** *m.* casting lots; drawing, raffle; bull-fighting.
sortiaria, *f.* fortune telling by cards.
sortija, *f.* finger ring; ring, hoop; curl of hair.
sortijita, juela, *f. dim.* little ring; ringlet.
sortijón, *m. aug.* large finger ring.
sortilegio, *m.* sortilege, sorcery.
sortílego, ga, *n.* sorcerer, conjurer, fortune teller.
sosa, *f.* (bot.) glasswort, kelp; soda ash, barilla; sal soda; (chem.) soda.—**s. cáustica,** (chem.) caustic soda.
sosal, *m.* soda-bearing field.
sosamente, *adv.* insipidly, tastelessly.
sosar, *m.* = SOSAL.
sosegadamente, *adv.* quietly, calmly.
sosegado, da, *pp.* & *a.* quiet, peaceful, calm.
sosegador, ra, *n.* & *a.* pacifier(-ing), appeaser (-ing), quieter(-ing).
sosegar. I. *va.* (*ind. pres.* SOSIEGO, *pret.* SOSEGUÉ; *subj.* SOSIEGUE) to appease, calm, quiet; to lull. **II.** *vn.* to rest, repose. **III.** *vr.* to become quiet, calm or composed, to quiet down.
sosera, sosería, *f.* insipidity, tastelessness; nonsense.
sosero, ra, *a.* (bot.) yielding soda.
sosez, *f.* = SOSERA.
sosiega, *f.* rest after work; drink taken while resting, after dinner or before going to bed.
[1]**sosiego,** *m.* tranquillity, calm, quiet.
[2]**sosiego, sosegué, sosiegue,** *v. V.* SOSEGAR.
soslayar, *va.* to do or place obliquely.
soslayo, *m.*—**al s.,** or **de s.,** askance; slanting, on the bias.
soso, sa, *a.* insipid, tasteless, vapid; dull, inane.
sospecha, *f.* suspicion.
sospechar, *va.* & *vn.* to suspect.
sospechosamente, *adv.* suspiciously.
sospechoso, sa, *a.* suspicious; suspecting.
sospesar, *va.* to suspend, lift, raise.
sosquín, *m.* blow treacherously given.
sostén, *m.* support; steadiness (of a ship); brassière, (coll.) bra.
sostenedor, ra, *n.* supporter.
sostener. I. *va.* (*ind. pres.* yo SOSTENGO, él SOSTIENE, *pret.* SOSTUVE, *fut.* SOSTENDRÉ; *subj.* SOSTENGA) to support, hold up; to maintain, keep; to assist, help; to encourage; to uphold, defend; to bear, endure; to hold (a conference, etc.). **II.** *vr.* to support or maintain oneself.
sostenido, da. I. *pp.* of SOSTENER. **II.** *a.* supported; sustained, kept up. **III.** *m.* (mus.) sharp (the tone and the sign ♯).
sosteniente, *a.* sustaining, supporting.
sostenimiento, *m.* sustenance, maintenance; support.—**muro,** or **pared, de s.,** retaining wall.
sostituir, *va.* = SUSTITUIR, to substitute.
sostuve, *pret.* of SOSTENER.
sota. I. *f.* jack, knave, at cards; hussy, jade. **II.** *m.* (Chile) deputy, substitute.
sotabanco, *m.* (arch.) pediment of an arch over a cornice; garret, attic.
sotabraga, *f.* (mil.) axletree band, yoke hoop.
sotacola, *f.* crupper.
sotacoro, *m.* place under the choir.
sotalugo, *m.* second hoop of a cask.
sotaministro, *m.* = SOTOMINISTRO.
sotana, *f.* cassock; (coll.) flogging, drubbing.
sotanear, *va.* (coll.) to beat, reprimand severely.
sotaní, *m.* short skirt without plaits.
sótano, *m.* cellar, basement.
sotaventar, *va.* (naut.) to fall to leeward.
sotavento, *m.* leeward, lee.—**a s.,** under the lee.
sotechado, *m.* shed.
soteño, ña, *a.* produced in groves.
soterramiento, *m.* burying under ground.
soterraño, *a.* = SUBTERRÁNEO, subterranean.
soterrar, *va.* (*ind.* SOTIERRO; *subj.* SOTIERRE) to bury, put under ground; to hide.
sotillo, *m. dim.* little grove.
soto, *m.* grove, thicket, brake.
sotoministro, *m.* steward (in some convents).
sotrozo, *m.* (artil.) linchpin, axle pin; (mech.) key; (naut.) foothook staff.
sotuer, *m.* (her.) saltier.
soviet, *m.* soviet.
soviético, ca, *a.* soviet.
sovietismo, *m.* sovietism.
sovietista, *n.* soviet.
sovietizar, *va.* & *vn.* to sovietize.
sovoz.—**a s.,** in a low tone, sotto voce.
soy, *1st pers. sing. pres. ind.* of SER.
soya, *f.* (bot.) soy; soy bean.
speaker, *m.* (Angl.) (Arg.) (radio) announcer.
spenceriano, na, *a.* (philos.) Spencerian.
spencerismo, *m.* Spencerism.
sport, *m.* (Angl.) (Am.) sport.
Stábat, Stábat Máter, *m.* Stabat Mater.
staccato, *a.* & *adv.* (mus.) staccato.
statu quo, *m.* status quo.
su, *pron. poss. 3d pers. m.* & *f. sing.* (*pl.* SUS) his, her, its, their, one's, your.
suasorio, ria, *a.* suasory, suasive, persuasive.
suave, *a.* smooth, soft, delicate, mellow; easy, tranquil, unruffled; suave, gentle, tractable,

docile, mild, meek.—**suavemente,** *adv.* gently, sweetly, softly, mildly, kindly.
suavicé, suavice, *v. V.* SUAVIZAR.
suavidad, *f.* softness, smoothness; ease; suavity; gentleness; lenity, forbearance.
suavizador, ra. I. *a.* mollifying, smoothing, softening. **II.** *m.* razor strop.
suavizar, *va.* (*pret.* SUAVICÉ; *subj.* SUAVICE) to soften, smooth, mollify, mitigate; to ease; to temper.
subacetato, *m.* (chem.) basic acetate of lead.
subácido, da, *a.* (chem.) subacid.
subacuático, ca, *a.* subaqueous.
subagente, *m.* subagent.
subalcaide, *m.* deputy warden.
subalternante, *a.* subalternant.
subalternar, *va.* to subdue.
subalterno, na. I. *a.* subaltern, subordinate. **II.** *m.* subordinate; (mil.) subaltern.
subarrendador, ra, *n.* subleaser.
subarrendamiento, *m.* subletting.
subarrendante, *n.* = SUBARRENDADOR.
subarrendar,* *va.* (*ind.* SUBARRIENDO; *subj.* SUBARRIENDE) to sublet, sublease.
subarrendatario, ria, *n.* subtenant.
[1]**subarriendo,** *m.* (law) sublease.
[2]**subarriendo, subarriende,** *v. V.* SUBARRENDAR.
subártico, ca, *a.* subarctic.
subasta, subastación, *f.* auction, auction sale. —**poner en,** or **sacar a, pública s.,** to sell at auction.
subastador, *m.* auctioneer.
subastar, *va.* to sell at auction.
subátomo, *m.* (phys.) subatom.
subcarbonato, *m.* (chem.) subcarbonate.
subcinericio, cia, *a.* baked under ashes.
subclase, *f.* (bot. and zool.) subclass.
subclavero, *m.* assistant CLAVERO, key keeper.
subclavio, via, *a.* (anat.) subclavian.
subcolector, *m.* subcollector, assistant collector.
subcomendador, *m.* deputy commander of a military order.
subcomisión, *f.* **subcomité,** *m.* subcommittee.
subconjunto, *m.* subassembly.
subconsciencia, *f.* subconsciousness; (the) subconscious.
subconsciente, *a.* subconscious.
subconservador, *m.* judge deputed by a conservator.
subcontinente, *m.* subcontinent.
subcontratar, *va.* & *vn.* to subcontract.
subcontratista, *n.* subcontractor.
subcontrato, *m.* subcontract.
subcostal, *a.* (anat.) subcostal, below the ribs.
subcrítico, ca, *a.* (chem., phys.) subcritical.
subcutáneo, nea, *a.* subcutaneous.
subdebutante, *f.* subdeb.
subdecano, *m.* subdean.
subdelegable, *a.* that can be subdelegated.
subdelegación, *f.* subdelegation.
subdelegado, da, *n.* subdelegate.
subdelegante, *n.* he who subdelegates.
subdelegar, *va.* (*pret.* SUBDELEGUÉ; *subj.* SUBDELEGUE) to subdelegate.
subdesarrollado, da, *a.* underdeveloped.
subdesarrollar, *va.* to underdevelop.
subdesarrollo, *m.* underdevelopment.
subdiaconado or **-ato,** *m.* subdeaconship.
subdiácono, *m.* subdeacon.
subdirector, ra, *n.* assistant director.
subdistinción, *f.* subdistinction.
subdistinguir, *va.* (*ind.* SUBDISTINGO; *subj.* SUBDISTINGA) to make a subdistinction.
súbdito, ta. I. *a.* subject (to authority, etc.); inferior. **II.** *m.* subject (of a state, etc.).
subdividir, *va.* to subdivide.—**subdivisible,** *a.* subdivisible.—**subdivisión,** *f.* subdivision.
subdominante, *f.* (mus.) subdominant.
subejecutor, *m.* subagent.
subentender. I. *va.* (*ind.* SUBENTIENDO; *subj.* SUBENTIENDA) to understand what is tacitly meant. **II.** *vr.* to be understood, to be implied.
subérico, ca, *a.* suberic, pert. to cork.
suberina, *f.* suberin, substance in cork.
suberoso, sa, *a.* suberose, corky.
subespecie, *f.* (zool., bot.) subspecies.
subestación, *f.* substation.
subestructura, *f.* substructure.
subfamilia, *f.* (bot., zool.) subfamily.
subgénero, *m.* (biol.) subgenus.
subgobernador, ra, *n.* vicegovernor, lieutenant governor.
subgrupo, *m.* subgroup.
subida, *f.* ascent, going up; elevation, taking or carrying up; acclivity, rise; accession of a disease; rise.—**s. repentina,** upsurge.
subidero, ra. I. *a.* mounting, raising, climbing. **II.** *m.* ladder, mounting block; way to go up; up grade, uphill road.
subido, da. I. *pp.* of SUBIR. **II.** *a.* raised on high; high, high-priced; strong, loud, bright (as a color); strong-scented; finest, most excellent.
subidor, *m.* porter; elevator, lift.
subiente. I. *a.* rising. **II.** *m.* (arch.) ascending ornaments.
subilla, *f.* awl.
subimiento, *m.* rising, climbing, ascending.
subíndice, *m.* (math.) subindex.
subinquilino, *m.* subtenant.
subinspección, *f.* subinspectorship; subinspector's office.
subinspector, *m.* subinspector.
subintendente, *m.* assistant intendant.
subintración, *f.* (med.) subintrant fever.
subintrante, *a.* (med.) subintrant.
subintrar, *vn.* to enter one after another; (med.) (of fever) to begin before end of preceding attack.
subir. I. *vn.* to rise; to come up, go up, climb, mount; to grow; (of silkworms) to enter leaves; to be promoted; to increase in intensity; (com.) to amount to; (of price, temperature, etc.) to rise; (mus.) to raise the voice or pitch.—**s. a caballo,** to mount a horse.—**s. de punto,** to increase, grow.—**s. de tono,** to raise one's voice; to be more outspoken. **II.** *va.* to raise, place higher; to take up, bring up; set up; to straighten from an inclined position; (com.) to raise (prices). **III.** *vr.* to go up, to climb; to rise.—**s. a las barbas,** to fly in one's face.—**s. a las bovedillas,** (coll.) to be nettled, be violently irritated.—**s. a la cabeza,** (of wine, liquor, popularity, etc.) to go to one's head.
súbitamente, subitáneamente, *adv.* suddenly, all of a sudden.
subitáneo, nea, *a.* sudden, unexpected.
súbito, ta, *a.* sudden, unforeseen, unexpected.—*adv. m.* **s.,** or **de s.,** suddenly, unexpectedly.
subjefe, *n.* second in command; assistant chief.
subjetivamente, *adv.* subjectively.
subjetividad, *f.* subjectivity.
subjetivismo, *f.* subjectivism.
subjetivista, *n.* subjectivist.
subjetivo, va, *a.* subjective.
subjugación, *f.* subjugation.
subjuntivo, va, *m.* & *a.* (gram.) subjunctive.
sublevación, *f.,* **sublevamiento,** *m.* insurrection, revolt.
sublevar. I. *va.* to incite to rebellion, raise in rebellion. **II.** *vr.* to rise in rebellion.
sublimación, *f.* sublimation.
sublimado. I. *pp.* of SUBLIMAR. **II.** *m.* (chem.) sublimate.—**s. corrosivo,** corrosive sublimate.
sublimar, *va.* to heighten, elevate, exalt; (chem.) to sublimate.
sublimatorio, ria, *a.* (chem.) sublimatory.
sublime, *a.* sublime.—**la S. Puerta,** the Sublime Porte (the former Ottoman Empire).
sublimidad, *f.* sublimity.
sublingual, *a.* (anat.) sublingual, under the tongue.
sublunar, *a.* sublunary; terrestrial, earthly.
submarginal, *a.* submarginal.

submarino, na, *m.* & *a.* submarine.
submarino atómico, *m.* atomic submarine.
submaxilar, *a.* submaxillary, pertaining to the lower jaw.
submicroscópico, ca, *a.* submicroscopic.
submúltiplo, pla, *m.* & *a.* (math.) submultiple.
subnivel, *m.* sublevel.
subnormal. I. *a.* subnormal. **II.** *f.* (geom.) subnormal.
suborden, *m.* suborder.
subordinación, *f.* subordination; subjection.
subordinadamente, *adv.* subserviently.
subordinado, da. I. *pp.* of SUBORDINAR. **II.** *a* subordinate, subservient.
subordinar, *va.* to subordinate; to subject.
subpiso, *m.* (geol.) substage.
subpolar, *a.* under or near the pole.
subprefecto, *m.* subprefect.
subprefectura, *f.* subprefecture.
subproducto, *m.* by-product. Also PRODUCTO SECUNDARIO.
subrayar, *va.* to underscore, underline; to emphasize.
subreino, *m.* (bot., zool.) subkingdom, phylum.
subrepción, *f.* underhand proceeding; (law) subreption; surreption.
subrepticiamente, *adv.* surreptitiously.
subrepticio, cia, *a.* surreptitious.
subrigadier, *m.* (mil.) subbrigadier.
subrogación, *f.* surrogation or subrogation, substitution.
subrogar, *va.* (law) to subrogate; to substitute.
subsanable, *a.* excusable; reparable, surmountable, that can be obviated.
subsanar, *va.* to exculpate, excuse; to mend, correct, repair; to obviate, get over.
subscapular, *a.* (anat.) subscapular.
subscribir, *va.* & *vr.* (*pp.* SUBSCRIPTO, SUBSCRITO) to subscribe; to sign; to accede, agree to.
subscripción, *f.* subscription.
subscripto, ta; subscrito, ta; I. *pp. irreg.* of SUBSCRIBIR. **II.** *n.*—**el s.,** the undersigned.
subscriptor, ra, *n.* subscriber.
subsecretaría, *f.* office and employment of an assistant secretary.
subsecretario, ria, *n.* assistant secretary.
subsecuente, *a.* subsequent.
subseguirse, *vr.* (*ger.* SUBSIGUIENDO; *ind. pres.* SUBSIGO, *pret.* él SUBSIGUIÓ; *subj.* SUBSIGA) to follow next.
subsidiariamente, *adv.* subsidiarily.
subsidiario, ria, *a.* subsidiary; branch (as *a.*); auxiliary; (law) ancillary.
subsidio, *m.* subsidy, pecuniary aid; war tax.
subsigo, subsiguió, etc. *v. V.* SUBSEGUIRSE.
subsiguiente, *a.* subsequent, succeeding.
subsistencia, *f.* permanence, stability; subsistence; livelihood, living.
subsistente, *pres. p.* & *a.* subsistent, subsisting.
subsistir, *vn.* to subsist, last; to live, exist; to have the means of subsistence.
subsolano, *m.* east wind.
subsolar, *a.* subsolar.
subsónico, ca, *a.* subsonic.—**velocidad s.,** subsonic speed.
subsótano, *m.* subcellar.
substancia, *f.* substance; nutritious sap, juice, or extract; property, wealth; gist; importance, value; (coll.) judgment, sense.—**s. blanca,** (anat.) white matter (of the brain).—**s. gris,** (anat.) gray matter.—**en s.,** in substance, in effect; in a nutshell, in brief.
substanciación, *f.* substantiation.
substancial, *a.* substantial, real, material; nutritious, nourishing; essential.
substancialmente, *adv.* substantially.
substanciar, *va.* to extract the substance of, to abstract, abridge; to substantiate; (law) to try (a case).
substancioso, sa, *a.* juicy; nourishing, nutritious; substantial.
substantivar, *va.* (gram.) to substantivize.
substantividad, *f.* substantiveness.
substantivo, va. I. *a.* substantive. **II.** *m.* substantive, noun.
substitución, *f.* substitution.
substituíble, *a.* replaceable.
substituidor, ra, *n.* & *a.* substitute(-ing).
substituir, *va.* (*pp.* SUBSTITUÍDO, SUBSTITUTO; *ger.* SUBSTITUYENDO; *ind. pres.* SUBSTITUYO, *pret.* él SUBSTITUYÓ; *subj.* SUBSTITUYA) to substitute, replace.
substitutivo, va, *a.* substitute.
substituto, ta, *n.* substitute.
substituyente, *a.* substituting.
substituyo, etc. *v. V.* SUBSTITUIR.
substracción, *f.* subtraction.
substraendo, *m.* subtrahend.
substraer. I. *va.* (*ger.* SUBSTRAYENDO; *ind. pres.* SUBSTRAIGO, *pret.* SUBSTRAJE; *subj.* SUBSTRAIGA) to subtract, remove, take off, deduct. **II.** *vr.* to withdraw oneself, to elude.
substrato, *m.* (philos.) substratum.
subsuelo, *m.* subsoil.
subtangente, *f.* subtangent.
subtender, *va.* (*ind.* SUBTIENDO; *subj.* SUBTIENDA) (geom.) to subtend.
subteniente, *m.* (mil.) second lieutenant.
subtensa, *f.* (geom.) subtense (chord).
subterfugio, *m.* subterfuge.
subterráneamente, *adv.* subterraneously.
subterráneo, nea. I. *a.* subterranean, underground. **II.** *m.* any place underground (cave, vault, etc.); (Am.) subway; (geol.) subterrene.
subtesorería, *f.* subtreasury.
subtesorero, ra, *n.* subtreasurer.
subtítulo, *m.* subtitle.
subtropical, *a.* subtropical, subtropic.
subtrópicos, *m. pl.* subtropics.
suburbano, na. I. *a.* suburban. **II.** *n.* suburbanite, suburban.
suburbicario, ria, *a.* suburbicarian.
suburbio, *m.* suburb, outskirt.
subvención, *f.* subsidy, subvention, money aid.
subvencionar, *va.* to subsidize.
subvenir, *va.* (*ger.* SUBVINIENDO; *ind. pres.* **yo** SUBVENGO, él SUBVIENE, *pret.* SUBVINE, *fut.* SUBVENDRÉ; *subj.* SUBVENGA) to subvene, aid, assist, succor; to provide, supply, furnish, defray.
subversión, *f.* subversion, overthrow.
subversivo, va, *a.* subversive, destructive.
subversor, ra. I. *a.* subverting, overthrowing. **II.** *n.* subverter, overthrower.
subvertible, *a.* subvertible.
subvertir, *va.* (*ind. pres.* SUBVIERTO, *pret.* él SUBVIRTIÓ; *subj.* SUBVIERTA) to subvert, destroy, ruin.
subviene, subvine, etc. *v. V.* SUBVENIR.
subyacente, *a.* underlying.
subyugación, *f.* subjugation, subjection.
subyugador, ra, *n.* & *a.* subjugator(-ing).
subyugar, *va.* (*pret.* SUBYUGUÉ; *subj.* SUBYUGUE) to subdue, subjugate.
succinato, *m.* (chem.) succinate.
succínico, ca, *a.* (chem.) succinic.
succino, *m.* succinite, amber.
succión, *f.* suction, suck.
sucedáneo, a, *a.* & *m.* succedaneous, substitute (drug, etc.).
suceder. I. *vn.* (a) to succeed, follow, be the successor (of). **II.** *v. impers.* to happen, come to pass, come about.—**suceda lo que sucediere,** come what may.
sucedido, *m.* event, happening.
sucediente, *a.* succeeding, following.
sucesible, *a.* capable of succession.
sucesión, *f.* succession; issue, offspring; (law) estate.—**s. intestada,** heirs at law.
sucesivamente, *adv.* successively.
sucesivo, va, *a.* successive, consecutive.—**en lo s.,** hereafter, in future.

suceso, *m.* event, happening; issue, outcome; (*rare,* Gal.) success; course of time.
sucesor, ra, *n.* successor.
suciamente, *adv.* nastily, filthily; basely.
suciedad, *f.* nastiness, filthiness; dirt, filth.
sucintamente, *adv.* succinctly, briefly.
sucintarse, *vr.* to be precise, brief.
sucinto, ta, *a.* tucked up; brief, succinct, concise.
sucio, cia, *a.* dirty, nasty, filthy; soiled; untidy; tainted with guilt or sin; low, base; (naut.) foul.
suco, *m.* juice; sap.—**sucoso, sa,** *a.* juicy.
sucotrino, *a.* socotrine (aloes).
sucre, *m.* sucre, an Ecuadorean silver coin (about 50 cents).
sucrosa, *f.* (chem.) sucrose.
suctorio, ria, *a.* (biol.) suctorial.
súcubo, *m.* succubus (demon).
sucucho, *m.* (naut.) storeroom of a ship; (Am.) SOCUCHO, small room, "den"; hiding-place.
súcula, *f.* windlass, winch.
suculencia, *f.* juiciness, succulence.
suculentamente, *adv.* succulently.
suculento, ta, *a.* succulent, juicy.
sucumbiente, *a.* yielding; dying.
sucumbir, *vn.* to succumb; to submit, yield; to die, perish; (law) to lose a suit.
sucursal. I. *a.* ancillary, subsidiary; branch (as *a.*). **II.** *f.* (com.) branch of a commercial house.
sucusión, *f.* (med.) succussion, shaking (for diagnostic purposes).
suche. I. *a.* (Venez.) green, unripe. **II.** *m.* (Ecua., Peru), a tree yielding valuable timber; (Arg.) mud; (Chile) insignificant employee.
suchel, suchil, *m.* (Am.) = SUCHE (tree).
sud, *m.* south; south wind.
sudación, *f.* sweating.
sudadero, *m.* handkerchief; back cloth (for horses); sweating room, sudatory; moist ground; sweating place for sheep.
sudado, da. I. *pp.* of SUDAR. **II.** *a.* sweaty.
sudador, ra, *n.* one who perspires freely.
Sudáfrica, *f.* South Africa.
sudafricano, na, *n.* & *a.* South African.
sudamericano, na, *n.* & *a.* South American.
Sudán, *m.* Sudan.
sudanés, sa, *n.* & *a.* Sudanese.
sudante, *a.* sweating.
sudar, *vn.* to sweat, perspire; to ooze, to give with repugnance; to toil, to labor.
sudario, *m.* handkerchief, shroud (for corpse).
sudatorio, ria, *a.* sudorific, causing sweat.
sudeste, *m.* & *a.* southeast.—**s. cuarta al este,** southeast by east.—**s. cuarta al sur,** southeast by south.
sudista, *n.* (U. S.) Southerner.
sudoeste, *m.* & *a.* southwest.—**s. cuarta al oeste,** southwest by west.—**s. cuarta al sur,** southwest by south.
sudor, *m.* sweat, perspiration; toil, drudgery; gum that oozes from trees.
sudoriento, ta, *a.* wet with sweat.
sudorífero, ra, *a.* sudorific, causing sweat.
sudorífico, ca, *a.* & *m.* (med.) sudorific.
sudoríparo, ra, *a.* (anat.) sudoriferous, sweat-secreting.
sudoroso, sa, *a.* sweating, perspiring freely.
sudoso, sa, *a.* sweaty, perspiring.
sudsudeste, *m.* south-southeast.
sudsudoeste, *m.* south-southwest.
sudueste, *m.* southwest.
Suecia, *f.* Sweden.
sueco, ca. I. *a.* Swedish. **II.** *n.* Swede.—**Hacerse el s.,** (coll.) to pretend not to hear.
suegra, *f.* mother-in-law; hard crust of bread.
suegrecita, *f. dim.* (coll.) little mother-in-law.
suegro, *m.* father-in-law.
suela, *f.* sole (of shoe); sole leather; (ichth.) sole; horizontal rafter laid as a support for partition walls; (arch.) base; leather tip of a billiard cue. —*pl.* sandals.—**de siete suelas,** consummate, thorough, through and through.
suelda, *f.* (bot.) comfrey.
sueldacostilla, *f.* (bot.) a bulbous plant.
¹sueldo, *m.* salary; pay given to soldiers; an ancient coin; sou or sol.—**s. básico,** base pay. —**s. mínimo,** minimum wage.
²sueldo, suelde, *v. V.* SOLDAR.
¹suelo, *m.* ground; soil; land, earth, terra firma; pavement; floor, flooring; story; dregs, sediment, lees; ground plot; end; bottom, underside; hoof.—*pl.* (vet.) sole, plantar face of a horse's hoof; scatterings or leavings of grain.—**s. del estribo,** rest of the stirrup.—**s. natal,** native soil, country.—**dar consigo en el s.,** to fall down.—**dar en el s. con,** to throw down. —**medir el s.,** to fall flat, measure one's length on the ground; to lie down flat on the ground. —**por el s.,** or **por los suelos,** in a state of great depreciation; altogether out of favor.—**venirse al s.,** to fall to the ground, topple over.
²suelo, suele, *v. V.* SOLAR.
³suelo, él suele, *v. V.* SOLER.
suelta, *f.* loosening or letting loose; fetters; relay of oxen; place where oxen are changed.—**dar s.,** to grant a recess for amusement.
sueltamente, *adv.* loosely, lightly, expeditiously; licentiously; spontaneously; laxly.
¹suelto, ta. I. *pp. irreg.* of SOLTAR. **II.** *a.* loose; light, expeditious; swift, able; free, bold, daring; easy, disengaged; voluble, fluent; odd, disconnected, unclassified; single (copy); blank (verse).—**s. de lengua,** outspoken. **III.** *m.* small change; editorial paragraph; newspaper item or paragraph.
²suelto, suelte, *v. V.* SOLTAR.
suelvo, suelva, *v. V.* SOLVER.
sueno, suene, *v. V.* SONAR.
¹sueño, *m.* sleep; sleeping; drowsiness, sleepiness; dream; any event of short duration.—**s. eterno,** eternal sleep, death.—**s. pesado,** sound sleep; deep sleep.—**conciliar el s.,** to coax sleep.—**descabezar el s., echar un s.,** to take a nap. —**en sueños,** or **entre sueños,** dreaming; in dreamland.—**enfermedad del s.,** sleeping sickness.—**espantar el s.,** to scare away sleep. —**ni por s.,** by no means, not a bit of it.—**tener s.,** to be sleepy.
²sueño, sueñe, *v. V.* SOÑAR.
suero, *m.* whey; serum (of blood).
sueroso, sa, *a.* = SEROSO, serous; watery.
sueroterapia, *f.* serotherapy, serum therapy.
suerte, *f.* chance, hazard; lot, luck; good luck; state, condition; fate, doom, destiny; kind, sort; manner, way; skilful manœuvre of a bullfighter; (theat.) trick, feat, juggle; piece of ground separated by landmarks; (Peru) lottery ticket.—**s. negra,** very bad luck.—**caerle a uno la s.,** to fall to one's lot.—**de s. que,** in such a manner as, so that; and so.—**echar suertes,** to cast or draw lots.—**entrar en s.,** to take part in a draft or raffle.—**por s.,** by chance; luckily. —**tener s.,** to be lucky.—**tocarle a uno la s.** = CAERLE A UNO LA S.
suertero, *m.* (Peru) seller of lottery tickets.
sueste, *m.* southeast.
suéter, *m.* (Angl.) (Am.) sweater.
suevo, va, *n.* & *a.* Swabian.
sufete, *m.* Suffete, a Carthaginian magistrate.
sufí. I. *a.* Sufistic. **II.** *n.* Sufi.
suficiencia, *f.* sufficiency; capacity, ability.—**a s.,** sufficiently, enough.
suficiente, *a.* sufficient; fit, competent.
suficientemente, *adv.* sufficiently.
sufijo, ja. I. *a.* suffixed. **II.** *m.* suffix.
sufismo, *m.* Sufism.
sufocación, sufocar, etc. = SOFOCACIÓN, etc.
sufra, *f.* ridgeband of a harness.
sufragáneo, ea. I. *a.* suffragan, auxiliary. **II.** *m.* (eccl.) suffragan.
sufragar, *va.* (*pret.* SUFRAGUÉ; *subj.* SUFRAGUE) to favor; to aid; to defray.
sufragio, *m.* suffrage; vote; favor, support, aid, assistance; (eccl.) suffrage.
sufragismo, *m.* suffragism.

sufragista, *n.* suffragist; *f.* suffragette.
sufrible, *a.* sufferable, bearable.
sufridera, *f.* smith's tool for punching holes on an anvil.
sufridero, ra, *a.* bearable, endurable.
sufrido, da. I. *pp.* of SUFRIR. **II.** *a.* enduring, lasting; patient, long-suffering, (of colors) disguising, that don't show (dirt, etc.).—**mal s.,** rude.
sufridor, ra, *n.* & *a.* sufferer(-ing).
sufriente, *a.* enduring, suffering.
sufrimiento, *m.* suffering; sufferance, tolerance.
sufrir. I. *va.* to suffer, endure, bear up; to undergo (a change, an operation, etc.); to bear, carry, support; to sustain, resist (an attack); to permit, tolerate, put up with; to meet with (as a reverse); to do (penance). **II.** *vn.* to suffer.
sufumigación, *f.* (med.) suffumigation.
sufusión, *f.* (med.) suffusion; a kind of cataract.
sugerencia, *f.* suggestion.
sugerente, *a.* suggesting, suggestive.
sugerir, *va.* (*ger.* SUGIRIENDO; *ind. pres.* SUGIERO, *pret.* él SUGIRIÓ; *subj.* SUGIERA) to suggest, hint, insinuate.
sugestible, *a.* suggestible.
sugestión, *f.* suggestion; insinuation, hint; temptation.—**s. hipnótica,** hypnotic suggestion.
sugestionable, *a.* easily influenced.
sugestionar, *va.* to hypnotize; to influence.
sugestivo, va, *a.* suggestive.
sugiero, sugirió, etc. *v. V.* SUGERIR.
suicida. I. *a.* suicidal. **II.** *n.* suicide, one who commits suicide.
suicidarse, *vr.* to commit suicide.
suicidio, *m.* suicide (self-murder).
suideo, a. I. *a.* swinelike. **II.** *m. pl.* Suidæ, the swine family.
sui generis, *a.* sui generis, unique, peculiar.
suita, *f.* (C. A.) a kind of grass used for thatching and forage.
Suiza, *f.* Switzerland.
suizo, za. I. *a.* Swiss. **II.** *n.* Swiss; *f.* fight, row; ancient military sport.
sujeción, *f.* subjection; coercion, control; obedience, subordination; submission, surrender; connection.—**con s. a,** in accordance with.
sujetador, *m.* shift lock.
sujetalibros, *m.* book end.
sujetar. I. *va.* (*pp.* SUJETADO, SUJETO) to subject, subdue; to hold fast, fasten, catch, grasp. **II.** *vr.* to control oneself; to submit; (a) to abide (by), keep (to), to observe.
sujeto, ta. I. *pp. irreg.* of SUJETAR. **II.** *a.* subject, liable, exposed, chargeable; amenable. **III.** *m.* subject, topic, theme, matter; person; individual, fellow; (logic, gram.) subject.—**s. a impuesto,** dutiable.—**s. imponible,** taxpayer.—**buen s.,** nice guy, good sport.
sulfa-, *pref.* sulfa- (containing sulphur, of sulphur).
sulfácido, *m.* (chem.) sulfacid.
sulfadiacina, *f.* (pharm.) sulfadiazine.
sulfanilamida, *f.* (pharm.) sulfanilamide.
sulfapiridina, *f.* (pharm.) sulfapyridine.
sulfarsfenamina, *f.* (pharm.) sulfarsphenamine.
sulfas, *f. pl.* (pharm.) sulfa drugs.
sulfatador, ra. I. *a.* sulfating. **II.** *f.* sulfating machine.
sulfatar, *va.* & *vn.* to sulfate.
sulfatiazol, *m.* (pharm.) sulfathiazole.
sulfato, *m.* (chem.) sulfate.—**s. de bario,** (chem.) barium sulfate.—**s. de cobre,** (chem.) copper sulfate.—**s. de magnesia,** (pharm.) Epsom salts.—**s. de sodio,** (chem.) sodium sulfate.—**s. ferroso,** (chem.) ferrous sulfate.
sulfhidrato, *m.* (chem.) sulfhydrate, hydrosulfide.
sulfhídrico, ca, *a.* (chem.) hydrosulfuric.
sulfito, *m.* (chem.) sulfite.—**s. de sodio,** (chem.) sodium sulfite.
sulfonal, *m.* (pharm.) sulfonal.
sulfónico, ca, *a.* sulfonic.
sulfovínico, ca, *a.* (chem.) sulfovinic.
sulfuración, *f.* sulfuration.
sulfurador, *m.* sulfurator.
sulfurar. I. *va.* to sulfurate, sulfurize; to irritate, anger, enrage. **II.** *vr.* to become furious.
sulfúreo, rea, *a.* sulfureous, sulfurous, sulfurate, sulfury.
sulfúrico, ca, *a.* sulfuric.
sulfuro, *m.* (chem.) sulfide, sulfid, sulfuret.
sulfuroso, sa, *a.* (chem.) sulfurous.
sultán, *m.* sultan.—**sultana,** *f.* sultana.
sultanía, *f.* sultanate.
suma, *f.* sum; aggregate; amount; (arith.) addition; total, footing; summary; summa, complete treatise or exposition (of a science, etc.).—**s. a la vuelta,** carried forward.—**s. de la vuelta,** or **s. del frente,** brought forward.—**s. y sigue** = S. A LA VUELTA.—**en s.,** in short; to sum up.
sumaca, *f.* (S. A.) a small coasting schooner.
sumador, ra, *a.*—**máquina s.,** adding machine.
sumamente, *adv.* chiefly; exceedingly, highly.
sumando, *m.* (math.) addend.
sumar, *va.* (arith.) to add; to amount to; to sum up, recapitulate.—**máquina de s.,** adding machine.
sumaria, *f.* (law) indictment.
sumariamente, *adv.* summarily.
sumario, ria. I. *a.* summary, concise; plain, brief, cursory; (law) summary. **II.** *m.* summary, abstract; (law) indictment.
sumarísimo, ma, *a.* (law) swift, expeditious.
sumergible. I. *a.* submergible, submersible, sinkable. **II.** *m.* submarine.
sumergido, da, *a.* (bot.) demersed.
sumergimiento, *m.* submergence, sinking.
sumergir, *va.* & *vr.* (*ind.* SUMERJO; *subj.* SUMERJA) to submerge, to sink; to dive, to plunge; to overwhelm.
sumersión, *f.* submersion, immersion.
sumidad, *f.* top, apex, summit.
sumidero, *m.* sewer, drain, sink, gutter, gully; (min.) sump.
sumido, da. I. *pp.* of SUMIR. **II.** *a.* sunken.
sumiller, *m.* chief of each of several offices in the king's household.—**s. de corps,** lord chamberlain.—**s. de cortina,** royal chaplain.
sumillería, *f.* lord chamberlain's office.
suministración, *f.* = SUMINISTRO.
suministrador, ra, *n.* provider, purveyor.
suministrar, *va.* to supply, furnish, provide, afford, purvey, minister.
suministro, *m.* supply, providing.
sumir. I. *va.* & *vr.* to sink; to depress, overwhelm. **II.** *va.* (eccl.) to swallow (elements of Eucharist). **III.** *vr.* to be sunken (as cheeks).
sumisamente, *adv.* submissively.
sumisión, *f.* submission; (law) submission to the rule of another.
sumiso, sa, *a.* submissive, humble, meek.
sumista, *n.* rapid computer; abridger.
sumo, ma, *a.* high, great, supreme.—**s. pontífice,** Pontifex Maximus (in ancient Rome); Sovereign Pontiff (the Pope).—**s. sacerdote,** high priest.—**a lo s.,** at most.—**de s.,** fully.—**en s. grado,** to a very great extent; highly.
súmulas, *f. pl.* compendium of logic.
sumulista, *n.* teacher or student of the essentials of logic.
sumulístico, ca, *a.* pert. to essentials of logic.
sunción, *f.* (eccl.) partaking of the Eucharist at mass.
sundín, *m.* (Arg.) merry gathering and dancing of working people.
sunsún, *m.* (Cuba) (ornith.) humming bird.
suntuario, ria, *a.* sumptuary.
suntuosamente, *adv.* sumptuously, magnificently, gorgeously.
suntuosidad, *f.* magnificence, gorgeousness.
suntuoso, sa, *a.* sumptuous, gorgeous.
supe, *v. V.* SABER.
supedáneo, *m.* pedestal of a crucifix.
supeditación, *f.* subjection; oppression.

supeditar, *va.* to subdue, oppress; to reduce to subjection.
superable, *a.* superable, conquerable.
superabundancia, *f.* superabundance.
superabundante, *a.* superabundant.
superabundantemente, *adv.* superabundantly.
superabundar, *vn.* to superabound.
superadito, ta, *a.* superadded.
superante, *a.* surpassing, exceeding.
superar, *va.* to overcome, conquer; to surpass, excel, exceed.
superávit, *m.* (com.) surplus.
supercarretera, *f.* superhighway, expressway.
superciliar, *a.* (anat.) superciliary.
supercolumnata, *f.* (arch.) supercolumniation.
superconductor, ra, *a.* (phys.) superconductor.
supercrítico, ca, *a.* (phys.) supercritical.
superchería, *f.* fraud, deceit, wile, guile.
superchero, ra, *a.* wily, deceitful, tricky.
superdominante, *f.* (mus.) superdominant.
superego, *m.* (psych.) superego.
supereminencia, *f.* supereminence.
supereminente, *a.* supereminent.
superentender, *va.* (*ind.* SUPERENTIENDO; *subj.* SUPERENTIENDA) to superintend, inspect, supervise.
supererogación, *f.* supererogation.
supererogatorio, ria, *a.* supererogatory.
superestructura, *f.* superstructure.
superfetación, *f.* (biol.) superfetation, superimpregnation.
superficial, *a.* superficial, shallow.
superficialidad, *f.* superficiality; shallowness.
superficialmente, *adv.* superficially.
superficiario, ria, *a.* (law) superficiary.
superficie, *f.* surface; area.—**s. alabeada,** (geom.) warped surface.—**s. de calefacción,** (steam eng.) heating surface.—**s. de rodadura,** tread (of a wheel).—**s. desarrollable,** (geom.) developable surface.—**s. reglada,** (geom.) ruled surface.
superfino, na, *a.* superfine, extra fine.
superfluamente, *adv.* superfluously.
superfluidad, *f.* superfluity.
superfluo, flua, *a.* superfluous.
superfortaleza, *f.* (aer.) superfortress.
superfosfato, *m.* (chem.) superphosphate, acid phosphate.
superheterodino, *m.* (rad.) superheterodyne.
superhombre, *m.* superman.
superhumeral, *m.* (eccl.) ephod; superhumeral.
superintendencia, *f.* superintendence, supervision; superintendency.
superintendente, *n.* superintendent; intendant; inspector; overseer, supervisor.
superior. I. *a.* superior; upper; better, finer; higher (algebra, math., studies).—**el piso s.,** the upper floor (story). **II.** *m.* superior. **III.** *f.* mother superior.
superiorato, *m.* office of a superior and the term of his office.
superioridad, *f.* superiority.
superiormente, *adv.* masterly, superiorly.
superlativamente, *adv.* superlatively.
superlativo, va, *m.* & *a.* superlative.
supermercado, *m.* supermarket.
superno, na, *a.* supreme, highest.
supernumerario, ria, *a.* supernumerary.
superponer, *va.* (*pp.* SUPERPUESTO; *ind. pres.* SUPERPONGO, *pret.* SUPERPUSE, *fut.* SUPERPONDRÉ; *subj.* SUPERPONGA) to superpose.
superposición, *f.* superposition.
superpotencia, *f.* superpower; (elec.) superpower.
supersaturación, *f.* supersaturation.
supersaturar, *va.* to supersaturate.
supersensible, *a.* supersensitive.
supersónico, ca, *a.* supersonic.
superstición, *f.* superstition.
supersticiosamente, *adv.* superstitiously.
supersticioso, sa, *a.* superstitious.
supérstite, *a.* (law) surviving.
supersubstancial, *a.*—**pan s.,** (eccl.) the Host.
supervacáneo, nea, *a.* = SUPERFLUO.
supervención, superveniencia, *f.* supervention.
superveniente, *a.* supervenient, supervening.
supervenir, *vn.* (*ger.* SUPERVINIENDO; *ind. pres.* YO SUPERVENGO, él SUPERVIENE, *pret.* SUPERVINE, *fut.* SUPERVENDRÉ; *subj.* SUPERVENGA) to supervene.
supervisar, *va.* to supervise.
supervisión, *f.* supervision.
supervisor, ra. I. *a.* supervising, supervisory. **II.** *n.* supervisor.
supervivencia, *f.* survival; survivalship.—**s. del más apto,** survival of the fittest.
superviviente. I. *a.* surviving. **II.** *n.* survivor.
superyacente, *a.* superincumbent; overhanging.
supiera, supiese, *v. V.* SABER.
supinación, *f.* (anat.) supination.
supinador, *m.* (anat.) supinator (muscle).
supino, na. I. *a.* supine. **II.** *m.* (gram.) supine.
suplantación, *f.* supplanting.
suplantador, ra, *n.* & *a.* supplanter(-ing).
suplantar, *va.* to supplant; to forge, alter by fraud, raise (as a check).
suplefaltas, *m.* (coll.) substitute.
suplemental, *a.* supplemental.
suplementar, *va.* to supplement.
suplementario, ria, *a.* supplementary.
suplemento, *m.* supply, supplying; supplement; (geom.) supplement.
suplente, *a.* & *n.* substitute(-ing), replacer(-ing).
supletorio, ria, *a.* suppletory, supplemental.
súplica, *f.* entreaty; supplication; request.—**a s.,** by request.
suplicación, *f.* supplication; request; petition; rolled waffle; (law) petition to a high court for a reversal of its own decision.—**a s.,** by petition, by request.
suplicacionero, ra, *n.* waffle seller.
suplicante. I. *a.* suppliant, supplicant, entreating. **II.** *n.* supplicant, suppliant.
suplicar, *va.* (*pret.* SUPLIQUÉ; *subj.* SUPLIQUE) to entreat, implore, beg; to supplicate, pray; to ask, request.—**s. de la sentencia,** to petition against the sentence; to appeal.—**s. en revista,** (law) to apply for a new trial.
suplicatoria, *f.*, **suplicatorio,** *m.* (law) letters rogatory.
suplicio, *m.* torture; execution (death penalty); place of execution; grief, suffering, anguish.
suplidor, ra, *n.* substitute, deputy.
supliqué, suplique, *v. V.* SUPLICAR.
suplir, *va.* to supply, provide, afford, furnish; to substitute; to excuse, overlook; (gram.) to supply mentally, understand.
supo, *v. V.* SABER.
suponedor, ra, *n.* supposer.
suponer. I. *va.* (*pp.* SUPUESTO; *ind. pres.* SUPONGO, *pret.* SUPUSE, *fut.* SUPONDRÉ; *subj.* SUPONGA) to suppose, assume; to entail (expense, etc.). **II.** *vn.* to have weight or authority.
suportación, *f.* endurance; toleration.
suposición, *f.* supposition, assumption; distinction, high position; imposition, falsehood.
supositicio, cia, *a.* supposititious, pretended; supposed, assumed.
supositivo, va, *a.* suppositive.
supositorio, *m.* (med.) suppository.
supradicho, cha, *a.* aforesaid, above-mentioned.
supramaxilar, *m.* & *a.* (anat.) supramaxillary.
suprarrenal, *a.* (anat.) suprarenal.
suprascapular, *a.* (anat.) suprascapular.
suprasensible, *a.* supersensible.
supraspina, *f.* (anat.) supraspinal fossa of the scapula.
suprema, *f.* Supreme Council of the Inquisition.
supremacía, *f.* supremacy.
supremamente, *adv.* supremely.
supremo, ma, *a.* supreme; last, final.
supresión, *f.* suppression; omission; rooting out, elimination.—**s. de denominadores,** (alg.) clearing of fractions.—**s. de factores co-**

munes, (arith., alg.) cancellation (of common factors).
supresivo, va, *a.* suppressive.
supreso, sa, *pp. irreg.* of SUPRIMIR.
supresor, ra. I. *a.* suppressive. **II.** *n.* suppressor.
suprimible, *a.* suppressible.
suprimir, *va.* (*pp.* SUPRIMIDO, SUPRESO) to suppress; to cut out, abolish, eradicate; to omit; to clear of; (math.) to cancel.
suprior, ra, *n.* subprior(-ess).
supriorato, *m.* office of subprior or prioress.
supuesto, ta. I. *pp. irreg.* of SUPONER.—**s. que,** allowing that; granting that; since.—**esto s.,** this being understood.—**por s.,** of course, naturally. **II.** *m.* supposition; hypothesis, assumption.
supuración, *f.* suppuration.
supurante, *a.* suppurating.
supurar. I. *va.* to waste, consume. **II.** *vn.* (med.) to suppurate.—**supurativo, va,** *a.* & *m.* suppurative.—**supuratorio, ria,** *a.* suppurating.
supuse, *pret.* of SUPONER.
suputación, *f.* computation, calculation.
suputar, *va.* & *vn.* to compute, calculate, reckon.
sur, *m.* south; south wind.
sura, *m.* sura (section of the Koran).
sural, *a.* (anat.) sural, pert. to calf of leg.
suramericano, na, *n* & *a.* = SUDAMERICANO.
surcado, da, *a.* sulcate, sulcated, furrowed.
surcador, ra, *n.* plowman; *f.* plowwoman.
surcar, *va.* (*pret.* SURQUÉ; *subj.* SURQUE) (agr.) to plow, furrow; to cut through, move through.
surco, *m.* furrow; rut; wrinkle.—**a s.,** adjoining, separated by a furrow.
surculado, da, *a.* (bot.) single-stemmed.
súrculo, *m.* (bot.) single stem without branches.
surculoso, sa, *a.* = SURCULADO.
sureño, ña. I. *a.* southern, southerly. **II.** *n.* southerner.
surgente, *a.* surging, salient.
surgidero, *m.* (naut.) roads, anchoring place.
surgidor, ra, *n.* one who anchors.
surgir, *vn.* (*pp.* SURGIDO, SURTO: *ind.* SURJO; *subj.* SURJA) to spout, spurt; to issue, come forth; to present itself, appear, arise; to sprout; (naut.) to anchor.
surqué, surque, *v. V.* SURCAR.
surrealismo, *m.* surrealism.
surrealista, *n.* & *a.* surrealist.
surtida, *f.* (fort.) sallyport; (mil.) sally, sortie; backdoor; (naut.) slipway.
surtidero, *m.* conduit, outlet.—**s. de agua,** reservoir, basin.
surtido. I. *pp.* of SURTIR. **II.** *a.* (com.) assorted. **III.** *m.* assortment, stock.—**de s.,** in common use.
surtidor, ra. I. *n.* purveyor, caterer. **II.** *m.* jet, spout, fountain.—**s. de gasolina,** filling station.
surtimiento, *m.* supply, stock, assortment.
surtir. I. *va.* to supply, furnish, provide, purvey, stock.—**s. efecto,** to have the desired effect, to work. **II.** *vn.* to spout, spurt.
surto, ta. I. *pp. irreg.* of SURGIR. **II.** *a.* (naut.) anchored; (fig.) tranquil, at rest.
súrtuba, *f.* a Central-American gigantic fern.
surumpe, *m.* (Peru) inflammation of the eyes from the reflection of the snow.
sus, *pron. poss. pl. of* SU.
¡sus! *interj.* up! cheer up! forward!
susceptibilidad, *f.* susceptibility.
susceptible, *a.*; **susceptivo, va,** *a.* susceptible; sensitive, touchy.
suscitación, *f.* excitation.
suscitar. I. *va.* to stir up; to raise, to originate. **II.** *vr.* to rise, start, originate.
suscribir, suscrición, suscritor, etc. = SUBSCRIBIR, SUBSCRIPCIÓN, SUBSCRIPTOR, etc.
susidio, *m.* anxiety, uneasiness.
susodicho, cha, *a.* aforementioned, aforesaid.
suspendedor, ra, *a.* & *n.* that holds (something) up, suspends.
suspender. I. *va.* (*pp. irreg.* SUSPENSO) to suspend; to hang up; to stop, delay, interrupt; to discontinue; to surprise, astonish; to suspend from office; (coll.) to fail (give failing mark to) (in exam.); to adjourn (a meeting).—**s. pagos,** (com.) to stop payments. **II.** *vr.* (of horse) to rear up.
suspensión, *f.* suspension, interruption; cessation; discontinuance; suspense, uncertainty; amazement; privation; (law) suspense; (mus.) suspension.—**s. de armas,** cessation of hostilities.—**s. de fuego,** (mil.) cease-fire.—**s. de pagos,** (com.) suspension of payments.
suspensivo, va. I. *a.* suspensive. **II.** *m. pl.* (print.) leaders (. . .) showing that something has been omitted (gen. replaced by a long dash in English, except in mathematics).
suspenso, sa. I. *pp. irreg.* of SUSPENDER. **II.** *a.* astonished; perplexed.—**en s.,** in suspense. **III.** *m.* failing mark (in exam.).
suspensor, ra, *a.* & *n.* (Am.) = SUSPENDEDOR.
suspensorio, ria. I. *a.* suspensory. **II.** *m.* suspensory bandage.
suspicacia, *f.* suspiciousness, distrust.
suspicaz, *a.* suspicious, distrustful.
suspicazmente, *adv.* suspiciously.
suspirado, da, *a.* expected, desired, longed for.
suspirar, *vn.* to sigh.—**s. por,** to crave, long for, covet.
suspiro, *m.* sigh; breath; glass whistle; (mus.) short pause; ladyfinger (cake); (Am.) (bot.) lady's-slipper.—**exhalar el último s.,** to breathe one's last.
suspiroso, sa, *a.* sighing with difficulty.
sustancia, sustancial, sustancioso, etc. = SUBSTANCIA, SUBSTANCIAL, SUBSTANCIOSO, etc.
sustantivo, etc. = SUBSTANTIVO, etc.
sustenido, *m.* a Spanish step in dancing; SOSTENIDO, (mus.) sharp.
sustentable, *a.* defensible.
sustentación, *f.* support, sustenance.
sustentáculo, *m.* prop, stay, support.
sustentador, ra, *n.* & *a.* sustainer(-ing).
sustentamiento, *m.* sustenance, necessaries of life.
sustentante. I. *a.* sustaining. **II.** *m.* defender, supporter.
sustentar, *va.* to sustain, support, bear; to feed, support; to nourish; to assert, defend, advocate.
sustento, *m.* sustenance, maintenance; support.
sustitución, etc. = SUBSTITUCIÓN, etc.
susto, *m.* scare, fright, shock.—**dar un s.,** to frighten, to scare, to startle.
sustracción, sustraendo, sustraer, = SUBSTRACCIÓN, SUBSTRAENDO, SUBSTRAER.
susurración, *f.* whisper, whispering.
susurrador, ra, *n.* & *a.* whisperer(-ing).
susurrante, *a.* whispering, murmuring.
susurrar. I. *vn.* to whisper; to murmur; to rustle (as leaves); to purl (as a stream); to hum gently (as the air). **II.** *vr.* to be whispered about, to be bruited about.—**susurro,** *m.* whisper, humming, murmur, rustle, purling.
susurrón, na, *n.* grumbler, malcontent.
sutil, *a.* subtile, thin, slender; subtle, acute, cunning; keen; light, volatile.
sutileza, *f.* thinness, slenderness, fineness; subtlety, cunning, artifice; sagacity, acumen, perspicacity; nicety.—**s. de manos,** dexterity.
sutilicé, sutilice, *v. V.* SUTILIZAR.
sutilidad, *f.* = SUTILEZA.
sutilización, *f.* subtilization.
sutilizador, ra, *n.* & *a.* subtilizer(-ing).
sutilizar. I. *va.* (*pret.* SUTILICÉ; *subj.* SUTILICE) to subtilize; to thin, refine; to file, polish. **II.** *vn.* to subtilize.
sutilmente, *adv.* subtly, pointedly; nicely, finely, delicately.
sutorio, ria, *a.* pert. to shoemaking.
sutura, *f.* seam; (anat., bot., surg.) suture.
sutural, *a.* sutural.
suturar, *va.* (surg.) to suture.
suyo, ya, (*pl.* SUYOS, YAS), *pron. poss. 3d person, masc.* & *fem.* (sometimes with the definite article *el, la, los, las*); his, hers, theirs, one's;

his own, its own, one's own, their own.—**de s.,** in itself, by its very nature; spontaneously, of one's own accord.—**los suyos,** yours, your (his, her, etc.) family, people, company, etc.—**salirse con la suya,** to carry one's point, to come out ahead.—**una de las suyas,** one of his pranks or tricks.—**ver la suya,** to have one's chance.
svástica, *f.* swastika.

T

T, t, *f.* t, twenty-third letter of the Spanish alphabet.
¡ta! *interj.* take care, beware; stay, I recollect.—**¡t., t.!** tut, tut!
taba, *f.* astragalus, anklebone; jackstones.
tabacal, *m.* tobacco field.
tabacalero, ra. I. *a.* tobacco (as *a.*). **II.** *n.* tobacco grower or dealer.
tabaco, *m.* (bot.) tobacco; leaf tobacco; cigar; mildew on plants.—**t. colorado,** mild cigar.—**t. de hoja** = T. EN RAMA.—**t. de montaña,** arnica.—**t. de palillos,** snuff made of stems.—**t. de pipa,** pipe tobacco, smoking tobacco.—**t. de vena,** cigarette tobacco.—**t. en polvo,** snuff.—**t. en rama,** leaf tobacco, wrappers.—**t. holandilla,** Dutch tobacco.—**t. maduro,** strong cigar.—**t. moruno,** European and African tobacco.—**t. rapé,** rappee.—**t. torcido,** cigars, twisted tobacco.—**se me acabó el t.,** (Arg.) my funds have given out.
tabacoso, sa, *a.* using much snuff; tobacco-stained; (of plants) mildewed.
tabalada, *f.* (coll.) heavy fall upon the buttocks; spanking.
tabalario, *m.* (coll.) buttocks, posteriors.
tabalear. I. *va.* & *vn.* to rock to and fro. **II.** *vn.* to drum with the fingers on a table.—**tabaleo,** *m.* rocking, swinging; drumming with the fingers.
tabanazo, *m.* (coll.) spanking.
tabanco, *m.* stall for selling eatables; **(Mex.)** cockloft.
tabanera, *f.* place full of gadflies.
tábano, *m.* (entom.) gadfly, horsefly.
tabanque, *m.* treadle of a potter's wheel.
tabaola, *f.* hubbub, clamor.
[1]**tabaque,** *m.* ladies' work basket.
[2]**tabaque,** *m.* large tack.
tabaquera, *f.* snuffbox; tobacco pouch; **cigar** case; bowl of a tobacco pipe.
tabaquería, *f.* cigar store.
tabaquero, ra, *n.* cigar maker; tobacconist.
tabaquismo, *m.* (med.) tobaccoism.
tabaquista, *n.* tobacco expert; heavy smoker.
tabardete, tabardillo, *m.* highly dynamic fever; sunstroke.—**tabardillo pintado,** spotted fever.
tabardo, *m.* tabard.
tabellar, *va.* to fold (cloth) in pieces, leaving the selvage visible; to mark with a trade-mark.
taberna, *f.* tavern, public house, saloon, barroom.
tabernáculo, *m.* tabernacle.
tabernario, ria, *a.* (coll.) pertaining to a tavern; low, vulgar, vile.
tabernera, *f.* tavern keeper's wife; barmaid.
tabernería, *f.* business of a tavern keeper.
tabernero, *m.* tavern keeper, barkeeper.
tabes, *f.* (med.) consumption; tabes.
tabético, ca, *a.* (med.) tabetic.
tabí, *m.* tabby, moreen, watered fabric, moiré.
tabica, *f.* (arch.) covering board.
tabicar, *va.* to wall up; to close or shut up.
tabicón, *m.* thick partition wall.
tábido, da, *a.* (med.) tabid, wasted; putrid.
tabífico, ca, *a.* (med.) tabific.
tabinete, *m.* tabbinet (fabric).
tabique, *m.* thin wall; partition wall, partition.—**t. de panderete,** brick-on-edge partition.—**t. maestro,** chief partition wall.—**t. sordo,** double partition wall.
tabiquería, *f.* partition work, system or group of partitions.
tabiquero, ra, *n.* partition-wall builder.
tabla, *f.* (carp.) board; plank; slab; tablet, plate (of metal); table (of contents, of logarithms, etc.); list (of prices, etc.); full-breadth gore of a skirt; tablier; box plait; largest face of a piece of timber; (jewelry) flat diamond; (art) table, panel; broadest, most fleshy part of a member of the body; bed or patch in a garden; strip of land between rows of trees; revenue office where merchandise is registered as sold at market; meat stall; butcher's block.—*pl.* (theat.) stage boards, (fig.) stage; draw (in a game).—**t. de Ampère,** (phys.) Ampère's stand.—**t. de armonía,** (mus.) sounding board.—**t. de chilla,** thin board of slit deal.—**t. de juego,** gambling house.—**t. de lavar,** washboard.—**t. de manteles,** tablecloth.—**t. de materias,** table of contents.—**t. de multiplicar,** multiplication table.—**t. de planchar,** ironing board.—**t. de río,** bed of a river.—**t. de salvación,** last resource.—**t. de sembrado,** cornfield.—**t. periódica,** (chem.) periodic table.—**t. pitagórica,** multiplication table.—**T. Redonda,** (hist.) Round Table.—**tablas de la ley,** (relig.) tables of the law.—**tablas de navegación,** navigation tables.—**tablas reales,** backgammon board or tables.—**a la t. del mundo,** in public, before the world.—**a raja t.,** at any price, regardless of everything else.—**escaparse en una t.,** to have a narrow escape.—**hacer t. rasa de,** to ignore entirely, to set at nought.—**no saber por dónde van tablas,** to know nothing about the matter.—**salvarse en una t.,** to have a narrow escape.
tablachina, *f.* wooden shield or buckler.
tablacho, *m.* sluice or floodgate.
tablado, *m.* stage, scaffold, platform; flooring; (theat.) stage boards; platform of a cart or truck; boards or bottom of a bedstead.
tablaje, *m.* pile of boards; planking; gambling or gaming house.
tablajería, *f.* gambling; hire of the gaming table.
tablajero, *m.* scaffold maker; carpenter who builds stands and stages; ancient collector of the king's taxes; keeper of a gaming house; gambler; butcher; assistant hospital surgeon.
tablar, *m.* set of garden plots or beds.
tablazo, *m.* blow or stroke with a board; shallow arm of the sea; sheet of water; small plateau; (S. A., geol.) uplifted sea-floor deposit.
tablazón, *f.* boards, planks, lumber; planking, flooring; decks and sheathing of a ship.—**t. de la cubierta,** (naut.) deck planks.
tablear, *va.* to saw into boards; to divide (a garden) into beds or plots; to level or grade (the ground) with a thick board; to hammer into plates; (sewing) to make box plaits in.
tableo, *m.* sawing wood into boards; dividing a garden into beds; leveling (the ground) or grading with a board; hammering into plates.
tablero, *m.* board, panel; sawable timber; drawing board; dog nail; stock of a crossbow; chessboard, checkerboard; (Colomb.) blackboard; gambling house or table; shop counter; money table; (tailoring) cutting table; (carp.) door panel; (arch.) panel, compartment; floor (of a bridge).—**t. contador,** abacus.—**t. de cocina,** dresser, kitchen table.—**t. de conmutadores** = T. DE DISTRIBUCIÓN.—**t. de chaquete** (Mex.) backgammon board, tables.—**t. de distribución,** (elec.) switchboard.—**t. de instrumentos,** instrument board.
tablestaca, *f.* (eng.) sheet pile.
tableta, *f.* *dim.* tablet; writing pad; (pharm.) tablet, lozenge; cracknel; clapper.—**estar en tabletas,** to be in suspense.
tableteado, *m.* sound made by rattling clappers.
tabletear, *vn.* to rattle clappers.
tableteo, *m.* rattling sound of clappers.
tablilla, *f.* *dim.* tablet, slab; bulletin board; section of the cushion of a billiard table between

two pockets; (surg.) splint; (surv.) target (of levelling rod).—**t. de mesón,** sign of an inn.—**t. de santero,** poor box of a hermit.—**tablillas de San Lázaro,** clappers used in begging for hospitals.—**tablillas neperianas,** logarithmic tables.—**por t.,** indirectly.
tabloide, *m.* (pharm.) tabloid, tablet.
tablón, *m. aug.* plank, thick board; beam; strake. —**t. de aparadura,** (naut.) garboard strake.—**tablones de cucharros,** (naut.) serving planks.
tabloncillo, *m.* flooring board; in bull rings, last row of seats.
tabloza, *f.* painter's palette.
tabo, *m.* (P. I.) cup made from coconut shell.
tabón, *m.* (ornith.) tabon, Philippine megapode.
tabona, *f.* stagnant pool.
tabú, *m.* taboo.
tabuco, *m.* hut, hovel; narrow room.
tabulador, *m.* tabulator, tab key.
tabular, *a.* tabular.
tabuquillo, quito, *m. dim.* shanty.
taburete, *m.* taboret; stool.—*pl.* (theat.) benches in the pit.
[1]**taca,** *f.* small closet.
[2]**taca,** *f.* (min.) plate of the crucible.
[3]**taca,** *f.* stain.
tacada, *f.* stroke, play (at billiards); wedges.
tacamaca, tacamacha, tacamahaca, *f.* tacamahac, gum resin from various tropical trees; (bot.) balsam poplar.
tacano, *m.* (min.) rich gray silver ore.
tacañamente, *adv.* stingily, in a miserly manner.
tacañear, *vn.* to act the miser.
tacañería, *f.* stinginess; narrowness of mind; malicious cunning; low craft.
tacaño, ña, *a.* stingy, niggardly; artful, knavish.
tacar. I. *va.* to mark (as a person in the face). **II.** *vn.* to shoot, to have one's turn (in billiards).
tacazo, *m.* blow with a billiard cue.
taceta, *f.* copper bowl used in oilmills.
tacica, illa, ita, *f. dim.* small cup.
tácitamente, *adv.* silently, secretly; tacitly.
tácito, ta, *a.* silent; tacit, implied.
taciturnidad, *f.* taciturnity; reserve.
taciturno, na, *a.* taciturn, reserved; melancholy.
taclobo, *m.* (P. I.) a giant clam.
taco, *m.* plug, bung, stopper; (artil.) wad, wadding; rammer; popgun; billiard cue; (S. A., P. R.) heel (of shoe); almanac pad; (coll.) light lunch, snack; each draught of wine at meals; (Cuba) spruce young fellow, dandy; volley of oaths.—**tacos de los escobenes,** (naut.) hawse plugs.—**echar tacos,** (coll.) to swear, to rage.
tacografo, *m.* tachograph.
tacómetro, *m.* tachometer.
tacón, *m.* heel, heelpiece (of shoe).
taconazo, *m.* blow with a shoe heel.
taconear, *vn.* (coll.) to walk or strut loftily on the heels.
taconeo, *m.* noise made with the heels in dancing.
taconita, *f.* (min.) taconite.
táctico, ca. I. *a.* tactical, tactic. **II.** *n.* tactician; *f.* tactics; (mil.) tactics.
táctil, *a.* tactile, pertaining to touch.
tacto, *m.* touch, sense of touch; touching, feeling; tact, skill, carefulness.
tacuacha, *f.* (Cuba) dexterous trick.
tacuará, *f.* (Arg.) a kind of bamboo.
tacurú, *m.* (Arg.) a variety of black ant and the ant hill it makes.
tacha, *f.* fault, defect, blemish, flaw; large tack. —**poner t. a,** to find fault with.
tachar, *va.* to censure; blame, charge, accuse; to find fault with; to reprehend; to cut out, cross out; to cancel.—**t. testigos,** (law) to challenge witnesses.
tachero, *m.* (Cuba) one who works at a TACHO.
tacho, *m.* sugar evaporator, pan; (Peru) earthen jar for heating water.—**t. al,** or **de, vacío,** vacuum pan.
[1]**tachón,** *m.* deleting mark (in written material); braid, etc.; trimming (on clothes).
[2]**tachón,** *m.* gimp, or ornamental, nail; boss.
[1]**tachonar,** *va.* (sew.) to adorn with trimming.
[2]**tachonar,** *va.* to garnish with gimp nails.
tachonería, *f.* gimp nail ornamental work.
tachoso, sa, *a.* faulty, defective.
tachuela, *f.* tack, small nail.
tael, *m.* tael (weight and coin).
tafanario, *m.* (coll.) buttocks.
tafetán, *m.* taffeta, thin silk.—*pl.* flags, colors, standard, ensign.—**t. inglés,** court-plaster; sticking plaster.
tafia, *f.* (Venez.) molasses rum.
tafilete, *m.* morocco leather.—**tafiletear,** *va.* to adorn with morocco leather.—**tafiletería,** *f.* art of, or place for, dressing morocco leather.
tafurea, *f.* flat-bottomed boat for horses.
tagalo, la. I. *a.* of or pertaining to the Tagalog. **II.** *n.* Tagalog; *m.* Tagalog (language).
tagarino, na, *n.* Moor who lived among the Christians.
tagarnina, *f.* (bot.) golden thistle; (coll.) bad cigar.
tagarote, *m.* (ornith.) sparrow hawk; quill driver, scrivener; "decayed" gentleman who earns a dinner by flattery and adulation; (coll.) tall, awkward person.
tagarotear, *vn.* (coll.) to write a bold, free, and running hand.
tagua, *f.* (Am.) tagua, ivory nut; (Chile) (ornith.) a bird similar to the coot.
taguán, *m.* (zool.) taguan, a flying squirrel.
taha, *f.* district, region.
tahalí, *m.* shoulder belt; baldric.
taharal, *m.* plantation of tamarisk trees.
taheño, *a.* having a red beard.
tahitiano, na, *n.* & *a.* Tahitian.
tahona, *f.* bakery, baker's shop; horse mill; crushing mill.
tahonera, *f.* baker's wife; miller's wife.
tahonero, ra, *n.* baker; miller.
tahulla, *f.* plot of arable land.
tahur, ra. I. *a.* gambling. **II.** *n.* gambler, gamester; card sharp.
tahurería, *f.* gambling; gaming house; cheating gambling.
taicún, *m.* tycoon.
taifa, *f.* faction, party; (coll.) assemblage of fast or foolish people.
tailandés, desa. I. *a.* Thai. **II.** *n.* Thai; *m.* Thai (language).
Tailandia, *f.* Thailand.
taimado, da, *a.* sly, cunning, crafty.
taimería, *f.* rascality, craftiness.
taita, *f.* (coll.) dad, daddy.
[1]**taja,** *f.* tree of a packsaddle.
[2]**taja,** *f.* cut, incision; dissection; TARJA, tally.
tajada, *f.* slice; (coll.) hoarseness.
tajadera, *f.* chopping knife; (mech.) round chisel, gouge; cold chisel.—*pl.* sluice of a mill dam.
tajadero, *m.* chopping block, trencher.
tajadilla, *f. dim.* small slice; dish of lights in low chophouses; bit of confected orange or lemon sold as a relish by retailers of brandy.
tajado, da. I. *pp.* of TAJAR. **II.** *a.* steep, sheer, wall-like; (her.) divided.
tajador, ra. I. *n.* one who cuts or chops. **II.** *m.* cutting edge.
tajadura, *f.* cut, notch; cutting, chopping.
tajamar, *m.* (naut.) cutwater, stem; (eng.) cutwater of a bridge pier.
tajamiento, *m.* = TAJADURA.
tajaplumas, *m.* penknife.
tajar, *va.* to cut, cleave; to cut and trim (a quill pen).
tajea, *f.* watercourse, channel; culvert.
tajero, *m.* = TARJERO, tally keeper.
tajo, *m.* cut; incision; trench; cutting edge; steep cliff; cutting a quill; chopping block; line or place to which the work of a gang extends; cut or opening in a mountain; (fencing) cut.—**t. abierto,** (min.) open cut.
tajón, *m. aug.* butcher's block; chopping block; vein of white earth in a limestone quarry.

tajuela, *f.*, **tajuelo,** *m.* rustic seat.
tal (*pl.* TALES). **I.** *a.* such, so, as; equal, similar; as much, so great.—**t. cual,** such as; a few, one from time to time; middling, so-so; such as it is. —**t. cual vez,** once in a while, now and then.—**el t.,** or **la t.,** (foll. by a common noun) that (gen. contempt); (foll. by a proper noun) that man, that fellow (*el tal Juan,* that fellow John). —**un t.,** one, a certain (*estaba allí un tal Ramírez,* one Ramirez was there). **II.** *pron.* such, such a one, such a thing.—**t. para cual,** two of a kind.—**t. por cual,** person of little account, (a) nobody.—**no hay t.,** there is no such thing.—**otro que t.,** another of the same ilk. **III.** *adv.* thus, so, in such manner.—**con t. que, con t. de que,** provided, on condition, that.—**¿qué t.?** hello! how d'ye do? how is that? how goes it?
[1]**tala,** *f.* felling of trees; destruction, ruin, havoc; tipcat (boys' game); cat (in the game).
[2]**tala,** *f.* (bot.) a large Argentine urticaceous tree.
talabarte, *m.* sword belt.
talabartería, *f.* saddlery.
talabartero, *m.* saddler; harness maker.
talador, ra, *n.* & *a.* destroyer(-ing); cutter(-ing).
taladrador, ra. I. *n.* & *a.* borer(-ing), driller (-ing). **II.** *f.* drilling or perforating machine.
taladrar, *va.* to bore, drill, perforate; to pierce, penetrate (as the ear); to dig into, go to the bottom of, elucidate.
taladrilla, *f.* a boring insect that attacks olive trees.
taladro, *m.* bit, drill, borer, gimlet, auger; bore, auger hole, drill hole; blasting charge; charged blasting hole.
talamera, *f.* tree used for snaring birds.
talamete, *m.* (naut.) foredeck planking.
talamiflora. I. *a.* (bot.) thalamifloral. **II.** *f. pl.* Thalamifloræ.
talamite, *m.* thalamite, outermost galley rower.
tálamo, *m.* bridal chamber or bed; (bot.) receptacle.—**tálamos ópticos,** (anat.) optic thalami.
talanquera, *f.* parapet, breastwork of pales; picket fence; defense, safety place.
talante, *m.* mode or manner of doing anything; mien, countenance; desire, will, pleasure, disposition.—**de mal t.,** unwillingly, grudgingly. —**estar de buen** or **de mal t.,** to be in a pleasant or in an ugly frame of mind.
[1]**talar,** *va.* to fell (trees); to lay waste; to prune.
[2]**talar,** *a.* long (clothes).—**talares,** *m. pl.* wings on the heels of Mercury; talaria.
talasoterapia, *f.* (med.) sea-bathing therapy.
talayote, *m.* a Balearic megalith in the form of a low tower.
talco, *m.* talc; tinsel.—**t. en polvo,** talcum powder.
talcoso, sa, *a.* talcose.
talcualillo, lla, *a.* (coll.) fair, not bad; somewhat improved in health.
tálea, *f.* stockade or palisade in Roman camps.
taled, *m.* tallith (among the Jews).
talega, *f.* bag, sack; money bag; bagful; bag for the hair; diaper; sack containing 1,000 dollars in silver.—**dos talegas,** two thousand dollars.
talego, *m.* bag or sack; clumsy, awkward fellow. —**tener t.,** to have money.
taleguilla, *f. dim.* small bag.—**t. de la sal,** (coll.) daily expenses.
talento, *m.* talent; smartness, cleverness; talent (ancient weight and coin).
talentoso, sa; talentudo, da, *a.* able, talented, smart, clever.
tálero, *m.* thaler, an old German coin.
tálico, ca, *a.* (chem.) thallic.
talio, *m.* (chem.) thallium.
talión, *m.* talion, retaliation, "eye for an eye."
talionar, *va.* to punish by retaliation.
talipédico, ca, *a.* taliped, clubfooted.
talipes, *m.* talipes, clubfoot.
talismán, *m.* talisman, charm, amulet.
talismánico, ca, *a.* talismanic.
talma, *f.* a kind of cape or cloak.
talmente, *adv.* (coll.) in the same manner.
Talmud, *m.* Talmud.
talmúdico, ca, *a.* Talmudic.
talmudista, *m.* Talmudist.
talo, *m.* (bot.) thallus.
talofita. I. *a.* (bot.) thallophytic. **II.** *f.* (bot.) thallophyte.
talón, *m.* (anat., shoe) heel; heel of horse's hoof; heel of a violin bow; (arch.) heel, cyma reversa; (com.) any check, draft, note or voucher detached from a stub book; coupon; (naut.) heel of the keel, stemson.—**apretar los talones,** to show a clean pair of heels, to run.—**a t.,** on foot.
talonario, ria. I. *a.* taken from a stub book; stub (as *a.*). **II.** *m.* stub book; check book.
talonear, *vn.* to walk fast.
talonesco, ca, *a.* (coll.) pertaining to the heels.
talpa, talparia, *f.* (med.) talpa, wen.
talque, *m.* tasco, a refractory clay.
talquita, *f.* (min.) talc schist.
talud, *m.* (arch.) talus; batter; side slope.
talvina, *f.* porridge of almond meal.
[1]**talla,** *f.* carving, wood carving (*obra de talla,* carved work); ancient tax in Arragon; ransom; price set on the head of a criminal; (jewelry) cut, cutting; round of a card game; (of person) (lit. & fig.) height, stature; (mil.) height scale, for measuring a man's height; (surg.) lithotomy. —**de t.,** (of person) prominent.
[2]**talla,** *f.* (naut.) purchase block.
[3]**talla,** *f.* earthen jug.
tallado, da. I. *pp.* of TALLAR. **II.** *a.*—**bien** or **mal t.,** having a good or bad figure.
tallador, ra, *n.* engraver; carver; diesinker; (Am.) dealer (in a game).
talladura, *f.* engraving.
[1]**tallar. I.** *va.* to carve; to engrave; (jewelry) to cut; to appraise. **II.** *vn.* (card games) to deal.
[2]**tallar. I.** *a.* ready for cutting. **II.** *m.* woodland ready for first cut.
tallarín, *m.* noodle (for soup).
tallarola, *f.* knife for cutting velvet pile.
talle, *m.* form, figure; waist; (tailoring) fit; waist, bodice.
tallecer, *vn.* to shoot, sprout.
[1]**taller,** *m.* workshop, factory, mill, office, laboratory; atelier; studio.—**t. de reparaciones,** repair shop; (auto) service station.
[2]**taller,** *m.* oil and vinegar caster.
talleta, *f.* (Am.) = ALFAJOR, nut and honey paste.
tallista, *n.* carver in wood; engraver.
tallo, *m.* (bot.) stem, stalk; shoot, sprout.
talludo, da, *a.* grown into long stalks; tall, slender; overgrown; habit-ridden; past one's youth.
talluelo, *m. dim.* of TALLO.
tamagás, *m.* a very poisonous C. A. snake.
tamal, *m.* (Am.) tamale; (Am.) bundle, parcel; (Peru) pork (sold in the street).
tamalero, ra, *n.* tamale seller or maker.
tamandoa (Am.), **tamanduá,** *m.* (zool.) tamandua, anteater.
tamango, *m.* (Chile, Arg.) coarse shoe worn by the gauchos; sheepskin cover for the feet.
tamañamente, *adv.* as large as.
tamañico, ica, ito, ita, uelo, la, *a.* very small.
tamañito, ta, *a.* abashed, ashamed.
tamaño, ña. I. *a.* so great; (with gesture) so big, so small. **II.** *m.* size.—**t. natural,** full size.
támara, *f.* palm field.—*pl.* dates in a bunch; chips, fagots of brushwood.
tamarindo, *m.* (bot.) tamarind.
tamariscíneo, a, *a.* (bot.) tamariscineous.
tamarisco, tamariz, *m.* (bot.) tamarisk.
tamarrizquito, tamarrusquito, ta, *a.* (coll.) very small.
tamarugo, *m.* (bot.) a kind of Chilean carob.
tambalear, *vn.* & *vr.* to stagger, totter, reel.
tambaleo, *m.* reeling, staggering, tottering.
tambanillo, *m.* (arch.) tympanum.
tambarillo, *m.* chest with arched cover.
tambarria, *f.* (S. A.) carouse; (Chile) low tavern.
tambero, ra. I. *n.* (Peru) innkeeper. **II.** *a.* (of cattle) (Arg.) tame, gentle.

tambesco, *m.* swing.
también, *adv.* also, too, likewise; as well.
tambo, *m.* (S. A.) inn; dairy.
tambor, *m.* drum; drummer; coffee roaster, chestnut roaster; bolter or sieve used by confectioners; (sewing) tambour frame; (mech.) drum, cylinder, band pulley, rope barrel; (jewelry) barrel, arbor; (arch.) drum, tambour; screen; small room made by partitions; thole, tholus; (fort.) tambour; (naut.) drum or barrel of the capstan; wheelhouse, paddle box.—**t. del oído,** drum of the ear.—**t. mayor,** drum major.—**a golpe de t.,** or **con t. batiente,** at the beating of the drum; with drums beating.
tambora, *f.* bass drum.
tamborete, *m. dim.* timbrel; (naut.) cap of the masthead, moorshead.
tamboril, *m.* tabor, small drum, timbrel.
tamborilada, *f.*, **tamborilazo,** *m.* (coll.) fall upon the buttocks; slap on the face or shoulders.
tamborilear. I. *vn.* to drum. II. *va.* to praise, extol; (print.) to plane or level (type).
tamborilero, *m.* taborer, drummer.
tamborilete, *m. dim.* small TABOR; (print.) planer.
tamborín, tamborino, *m.* = TAMBORIL.
tamboritear, *va.*, **tamboritero,** *m.* = TAMBORILEAR, TAMBORILERO.
tamborón, *m.* large bass drum.
tamén, *m.* (Mex.) Indian porter, carrier.
tamiz, *m.* sieve, sifter, screen; bolting cloth.
tamizar, *va.* to sift, screen.
tamo, *m.* fuzz; chaff, winnowings, graindust; dust gathered under beds, etc.
tamojal, *m.* place covered with TAMOJO.
tamojo, *m.* (bot.) saltwort, glasswort.
tampoco, *adv.* neither, not either; (after **ni**) either (*él no sabe, ni yo tampoco,* he does not know, nor I either).
tam-tam, *m.* = TAN-TAN.
tamujal, *m.* thicket of buckthorns.
tamujo, *m.* (bot.) buckthorn, boxthorn.
tamul, *n.* & *a.*; **tamúlico, ca,** *a.* Tamil.
tan, *adv. contr.* of TANTO; as, so, so much, as well, as much.—**t. siquiera,** even, ever so.—**t. sólo,** only, merely.—**qué t.,** how.—**qué . . . t.,** what a (*¡qué mujer tan bella!* what a beautiful woman).
tanaceto, *m.* (bot.) tansy.
tanagra, *f.* Tanagra, Tanagra figurine.
tanate, *m.* (Mex.) bale made of hide; fruit basket; palm-leaf bag; (C. A.) bundle.—**cargar con los tanates,** (Am.) to move away.
tanatero, *m.* (Mex.) TANATE; carrier.
tanato, *m.* (chem.) tannate.
tanda, *f.* turn, rotation; task; gang of workmen, shift, relay; set, batch; each game of billiards; (theat.) each performance requiring a separate ticket.
tándem, *m.* tandem bicycle.—**en t.,** tandem.
tandeo, *m.* distribution of irrigating water by turns.
tanganillas.—en t., *adv.* waveringly.
tanganillo, *m. dim.* small prop or stay.
tángano, *m.* hob, a boys' game; stick used in this.
Tanganyika, *m.* Tanganyika.
tanganyikano, na, *n.* & *a.* Tanganyikan.
tangará, *f.* (Arg., ornith.) tanager.
tangencia, *f.* tangency.
tangencial, *a.* tangential.
tangente, *f.* & *a.* (geom.) tangent.—**escaparse, salir,** or **salirse, por la t.,** to resort to subterfuges or evasions, to befog the issue.
tangerino, na. I. *a.* Tangerine, of or pertaining to Tangiers. II. *n.* Tangerine; *f.* (bot.) tangerine, mandarin (orange).
tangible, *a.* tangible.
tango, *m.* hob, boys' game; (dance) tango.
tangón, *m.* (naut.) outrigger.
tánico, ca, *a.* containing tannin; tannic.
tanino, *m.* (chem.) tannin.
tanor, ra, *n.* (P. I.) Malay who served as domestic to the Spaniards.—**tanoría,** *f.* (P. I.) domestic service to the Spaniards.
[1]**tanque,** *m.* bee glue (in a hive).
[2]**tanque,** *m.* tank; reservoir; dipper; (mil.) tank.
tantalato, *m.* (chem.) tantalate.
tantalio, *m.* (chem.) tantalum.
tántalo, *m.* (ornith.) wood ibis.
tan-tan, *m.* rubadub, sound of a drum; tom-tom.
tantarantán, *m.* rubadub, beat of a drum; (coll.) resounding blow.
tanteador, ra, *n.* measurer, tester, marker.
tantear. I. *va.* to try, test, measure; to feel out; to make an estimate of; to consider carefully; to scrutinize; (art) to sketch, outline. II. *vn.* to keep the score. III. *vr.* to agree to pay the price for which a thing has been sold.
tanteo, *m.* estimate, approximate calculation; trial; points, score (in a game).—**al t.,** by eye; as an estimate; by trial.
tantico, tantillo. I. *m.* (coll.) a little, a little bit, a small amount. II. *adv.* (coll., Am.) a little while.
tanto, ta. I. *a.* so much, as much; very great.—*pl.* **tantos, tas,** many; as many, so many. II. *pron.* that.—**por t., por lo t.,** for that reason; therefore. III. *m.* certain sum or quantity; copy of a writing; counter; point (in games); (com.) rate.—*pl.* odd, denoting an indeterminate number (e.g., *treinta y tantos,* thirty odd).—**t. por ciento,** percentage; per cent.—**t. por cuanto,** (arith.) rate referred to any number; theory of rates (per centum, per thousand, per *x*).—**t. por t.,** at the same price; upon a par.—**tantos a tantos,** equal numbers.—**algún t.,** a little, somewhat.—**al t** at the price stated; at cost.—**al t. de,** posted about, informed on.—**en su t.,** proportionably.—**en t.,** or **entre t.,** in the meantime.—**no ser para t.,** not to be so bad, so serious, as that; not to be equal to, up to doing, that.—**otro t.,** as much; as much more.—**por el t.** = AL T.—**un t.,** somewhat, a bit, rather. IV. *adv.* so, in such a manner; so much, as much; so long, as long; often.—**t. así,** as, or so, much as that.—**t. como,** as much as; as well as.—**t. cuanto,** a little, somewhat.—**t. mejor,** so much the better.—**t. más cuanto,** or **t. más cuanto que,** all the more because, especially as.—**t. monta,** it is all the same.—**t. peor,** so much the worse.—**t. que,** as much as; so much so, that.—**t. uno como otro,** the one as well as the other; both of them.
tanza, *f.* fishing line.
Tanzania, *f.* United Republic of Tanzania.
tanzaniano, na, *n.* & *a.* Tanzanian.
tañedor, ra, *n.* player of musical instrument.
tañente, *a.* playing on an instrument.
tañer, *va.* to play (a musical instrument).
tañido, *m.* tune; sound; clink, ring.
tañimiento, *m.* playing on an instrument.
tao, *m.* badge of some orders.
tapa, *f.* lid, cover, cap; cover (of book); horny part of a hoof; cylinder head; heel blank, heel lift (of shoe); (P. I.) jerked beef, hung beef.—**t. de los sesos,** top of the skull.—**t. de un barril** = CASCO DE UN BARRIL, head (of barrel).
tapaagujeros, *m.* (coll.) clumsy mason; substitute, makeshift.
tapabalazo, *m.* (naut.) shot plug.
tapaboca, *m.* (coll.) slap on the mouth; muffler; choke pear; anything that silences one; (mil.) tampion.
tapada, *f.* thickly veiled woman.
tapadera, *f.* loose lid, cover of a pot; covercle; (Mex.) leather cover of a stirrup.
tapadero, *m.* stopper, stopple, cover.
tapadillo, *m.* concealment of a woman's face with her veil or mantle; flute stop of an organ.—**de t.,** secretly, covertly, sub rosa.
tapadizo, *m.* shed, cover.
tapado, *m.* (Arg., Chile, C. A.) woman's or child's overcoat, cape, or shawl.

tapador, ra. I. *n.* coverer. **II.** *m.* lid, cover, plug, stopper, stopple.
tapadura, *f.* stopping, covering, hiding.
tapafogón, *m.* (artil.) cap of a venthole.
tapafunda, *f.* flap of a holster (on a saddle).
tapagujeros, *m.* = TAPAAGUJEROS.
tapajuntas, *m.* door strap covering joint with wall; corner angle to protect plaster.
tápalo, *m.* (Mex.) woman's shawl.
tapamiento, *m.* stopping or covering.
tápana, *f.* (bot.) caper.
tapanco, (P. I.) boat tilt or awning.
tapaojos, *m.* (Am.) blinders for horses.
tapapiés, *m.* silk underskirt.
tapar. I. *va.* to cover; to hide, cover up, veil; to stop up, plug; close up, obstruct.—**t. la boca,** to stop one's mouth. **II.** *vr.* (of horse) to cover the track of the fore feet with those of the hind ones; to bundle, wrap oneself up.
tapara, *f.* (Am.) gourd for drinking.
tápara, *f.* (bot.) caper.
táparo, *m.* gourd tree.
taparrabo, *m.* loin cloth; trunks, short tights.
tapatán, *m.* (P. I.) tit-tat-toe.
taperujarse, *vr.* (coll.) to muffle one's face.
taperujo, *m.* (coll.) ill-shaped plug or stopper; awkward manner of muffling one's face.
tapetado, da, *a.* dark brown.
tapete, *m.* small carpet, rug; cover for a table or chest.—**t. verde,** card table.—**estar sobre el t.,** to be on the tapis.
tapia, *f.* mud wall; adobe wall; wall fence; (mason.) wall measure (50 sq. ft.).—**t. real,** wall made of earth and lime.—**más sordo que una t.,** deaf as a post.
tapiador, *m.* builder of mud walls.
tapial, *m.* form or mold for mud walls.
tapiar, *va.* to wall up; to raise a spite wall; to obstruct the view of with a wall.
tapicería, *f.* tapestry; art of making tapestry; upholstery; shop where tapestries are sold.
tapicero, *m.* tapestry maker; upholsterer; carpet layer.—**t. mayor,** tapestry keeper in a palace.
tapido, da, *a.* closely woven.
tapiería, *f.* series of mud walls.
tapín, *m.* (artil.) vent plug.
tapioca, *f.* tapioca.
tapir, *m.* (zool.) tapir.
tapirujarse, *vr.* = TAPERUJARSE.
tapis, *m.* (P. I.) sash worn by women.
tapiz, *m.* tapestry.
tapizar, *va.* to hang with tapestry.
tapón, *m.* cork, stopper; plug, bung; (elec.) fuse; (surg.) tampon.—**t. de cuba,** (coll.) short, fat person.—**al primer t., zurrapas,** (coll.) unlucky from the start.
taponamiento, *m.* (surg.) tamponage.
taponar, *va.* (surg.) to tampon.
taponazo, *m.* pop of a bottle.
taponería, *f.* set of corks; cork factory or shop.
taponero, ra. I. *a.* of cork. **II.** *n.* cork cutter or seller.
tapsia, *f.* (bot.) madder.
tapujarse, *vr.* to muffle oneself.
tapujo, *m.* muffle; (coll.) pretext, subterfuge.
taque, *m.* noise made by locking a door; rap, knock at a door.
taquera, *f.* rack or stand for billiard cues.
taquigrafía, *f.* shorthand, stenography.
taquigrafiar, *va.* to write in shorthand.
taquigráficamente, *adv.* in shorthand.
taquigráfico, ca, *a.* stenographic.
taquígrafo, *m.* stenographer.
taquilla, *f.* letter file, closet for papers; case of pigeonholes; ticket rack, key rack; (theat., Ry.) ticket office; booking office.—**taquillero, ra,** *n.* clerk in ticket office.
taquimetría, *f.* (surv.) tachymetry; stadia surveying; (auto) tachometer.
taquimétrico, ca, *a.* tachymetrical.
taquímetro, *m.* (surv.) tachymeter, stadia.
taquín, *m.* anklebone; (game) jackstones.
taquinero, *m.* player with jackstones.

[1]**tara,** *f.* (com.) tare, weight of container.—**menos la t.,** making allowance for exaggeration, taking with a grain of salt.
[2]**tara,** *f.* tally (stick).
[3]**tara,** *f.* (Venez.) green grasshopper.
tarabilla, *f.* (mil.) clack, clapper; catch, bolt, latch, sash fastener or holder; pin or peg for tightening the cord of a buck-saw frame; (coll.) chatterbox; fast and senseless talk.
tarabita, *f.* (S. A.) rope bridge.
taracea, *f.* marquetry, inlaid work, buhlwork.
taracear, *va.* to inlay, to make buhlwork on.
taragallo, *m.* block attached to dog's collar to prevent his nosing the ground.
taraje, *m.* (bot.) tamarisk.
tarambana, *n.* giddy person; madcap.
tarando, *m.* (zool.) reindeer.
tarangallo, *m.* = TARAGALLO.
tarángana, *f.* coarse sausage.
tarantela, *f.* (dance) tarantella.
tarantín, *m.* (C. A., Cuba) kitchen pot, utensil; gadget.
tarántula, *f.* tarantula.
tarantulado, da, *a.* bitten by a tarantula; wild; astonished.
tarara, tarará, *f.* sound of a trumpet.
tararear, *va.* & *vn.* to hum (a tune).
tararira. I. *f.* (coll.) noisy mirth. **II.** *n.* noisy person.
tarasca, *f.* figure of dragon borne in procession of Corpus Christi day; ugly woman.
tarascada, *f.* bite, wound with the teeth; (coll.) pert, rude answer.
tarascar, *va.* to bite (as dogs).
tarascón, *m. aug.* of TARASCA.
taratántara, *f.* = TARARA.
taray, *m.* (bot.) tamarisk.
tarayal, *m.* tamarisk plantation.
tarazana, *f.*, **tarazanal,** *m.* = ATARAZANA, arsenal; spinner's shed.
tarazar, *va.* to bite; to vex, annoy, harass.
tarazón, *m.* large slice.
tarbea, *f.* large hall.
tardador, ra, *n.* & *a.* tarrier(-ying).
tardanaos, *m.* (ichth.) = RÉMORA, remora.
tardanza, *f.* slowness, tardiness; delay.
tardar, *vn.* & *vr.* to delay; to take a long time; to be late.—**a más t.,** at the latest.
tarde. I. *f.* afternoon.—**buenas tardes,** good-afternoon.—**de,** or **por, la t.,** in the afternoon. —**de la t. a la mañana,** between sunset and sunrise; all of a sudden.—**de t. en t.,** now and then, once in a while. **II.** *adv.* late; too late.—**t., mal y nunca,** late and bad.—**t. o temprano,** sooner or later.—**t. piache,** too late.—**hacerse t.,** to grow late.—**más vale t. que nunca,** better late than never.—**para luego es t.,** by and by will be too late.
tardecer, *vn.* & *impers.* (*subj.* TARDEZCA) to draw towards evening; to grow late.
tardecica, ita, *f. dim.* evenfall.
tardecillo, to, *adv.* (Am.) a little late.
tardíamente, *adv.* too late, out of time.
tardígrado, da, *a.* (zool.) tardigrade, slow-moving.
tardío, día, *a.* late, too late; slow; tardy.
tardo, da, *a.* slow, sluggish; tardy; dull, thick, dense.
tardón, na, *a. aug.* very slow; dull, thick.
tarea, *f.* task; care, anxiety.
tarentino, na, *n.* & *a.* Tarentine.
Tárgum, *m.* Targum (Jewish book).
tarida, *f.* an ancient military transport.
tarifa, *f.* price list, fare, rate; schedule of charges.
tarifar. I. *va.* to tariff, subject to a tariff. **II.** *vn.* to quarrel, wrangle, fight.
tarima, *f.* stand; movable platform; low bench, table, footstool; bedstead.
tarimón, *m. aug.* large stand or platform.
tarín, *m.* silver real of 8½ CUARTOS.
tarina, *f.* middle-sized plate for meat.
tarín barín, *adv.* (coll.) pretty close, just about.
tarja, *f.* check, tally; tally stick; target, shield,

buckler; an ancient copper coin.—**beber sobre t.,** (coll.) to get drink on credit.
tarjador, ra, *n.* tally keeper.
tarjar, *va.* to tally.—**tarjero, ra,** *n.* tally keeper.
tarjeta, *f. dim.* of TARJA; card; (arch.) label, tablet with inscription; title and imprint on a map or chart.—**t. de despedida,** P. P. C. (leave-taking) card.—**t. de negocios,** business card. —**t. de visita,** visiting card.—**t. postal,** post card.
tarjeteo, *m.* (coll.) social exchange of cards.
tarjetero, *m.* cardcase.
tarjetón, *m. aug.* large card; show card.
tarlatana, *f.* tarlatan (fabric).
taro, *m.* (bot.) taro, colocasia.
tarpón, *m.* (ichth.) tarpon.
tarquín, *m.* slime, mire, mud.
tarquinada, *f.* (coll.) rape.
tarraconense, *a.* of or from Tarragona.
tárraga, *f.* an ancient Spanish dance.
tarraja, *f.* = TERRAJA.
tarraya, *f.* (Am.) = ATARRAYA, casting net.
tarreñas, *f. pl.* pieces of broken china used as clappers or bones.
tarrico, *m.* (bot.) saltwort.
tarro, *m.* jar; (Cuba) horn; (Colomb.) can, pot.
tarsal; tarsiano, na, *a.* (anat.) tarsal.
tarso, *m.* (anat.) tarsus; gambrel, hock.
tarta, *f.* tart; pan for baking tarts.
tártago, *m.* (bot.) spurge; (coll.) misfortune; practical joke.
tartajear, *vn.* to stutter, stammer.
tartajoso, sa, *a.* stammering, stuttering.
tartalear, *vn.* to reel, stagger; (coll.) to be dumfounded.
tartamudear, *vn.* to stutter, stammer.
tartamudeo, *m.,* **tartamudez,** *f.* stuttering.
tartamudo, da, *n.* & *a.* stutterer(-ing).
tartán, *m.* tartan, Scotch plaid.
tartana, *f.* round-top, two-wheeled carriage; (naut.) tartan.
tartanero, *m.* driver of a TARTANA.
tartáreo, rea, *a.* (poet.) Tartarean, hellish.
tartárico, ca, *a.* tartaric.
tartarizar, *va.* (chem.) to tartarize.
[1]**tártaro,** *m.* argol, cream of tartar; (dent.) tartar.
[2]**tártaro,** *m.* (poet.) Tartarus, hell.
[3]**tártaro, ra,** *n.* & *a.* Tartar, Tatar.
tartera, *f.* baking pan for pastry; dinner pail.
tartrato, *m.* (chem.) tartrate.
tártrico, ca, *a.* tartaric.
taruga, *f.* (zool.) a species of vicuña.
tarugo, *m.* wooden peg or pin; stopper, plug.
tarumba, *m.*—**volver a uno t.,** (coll.) to confuse one.—**volverse t.,** to become rattled.
tas, *m.* small anvil used by silversmiths.
tasa, *f.* measure, rule; standard; rate; assessment; valuation, appraisement.
tasación, *f.* valuation, appraisement.
tasadamente, *adv.* barely, scantily, scarcely.
tasador, ra, *n.* appraiser, assessor.
tasajear, *va.* (Am.) to cut (meat) for making jerked beef; to slash, cut to pieces.
tasajo, *m.* jerked beef, hung beef.
tasar, *va.* to appraise; to rate; to tax; to regulate, to keep within bounds; to stint.
tascador, *m.* brake for dressing flax.
tascar, *va.* (*pret.* TASQUÉ; *subj.* TASQUE) to brake, scutch, or dress (flax, hemp); to nibble, crunch, browse, graze.—**t. el freno,** (of horses) to bite the bridle; to resist.
tasco, *m.* refuse of flax or hemp; (naut.) topping of hemp.
tasconio, *m.* tasco, a kind of clay.
tasmanio, nia, *n.* & *a.* Tasmanian.
tasqué, tasque, *v. V.* TASCAR.
tasquera, *f.* row, quarrel, wrangle, scuffle.
tasquil, *m.* chip from a stone.
tastana, *f.* (agr.) hard crust on the soil caused by dryness; membrane inside a fruit, as in oranges.
tástara, *f.* coarse bran.
tastaz, *m.* polishing powder from old crucibles.
tasto, *m.* bad taste of tainted food.
tasugo, *m.* (zool.) badger.
tata, *m.* (Am., coll.) dad, daddy; nursemaid; younger sister.
tatabra, *f.,* **tatabro,** *m.* (Colomb.) (zool.) a species of peccary.
tatarabuela, *f.* great-great-grandmother.
tatarabuelo, *m.* great-great-grandfather.
tataradeudo, da, *n.* very old distant relative.
tataranieto, ta, *n.* great-great-grandson(-daughter).
tatas.—**andar a t.,** to walk timidly; to go on all fours.
¡tate! *interj.* take care! beware! stay, so it is.
[1]**tato, ta,** *a.* stammering.
[2]**tato,** *m.* (Arg., Chile) (coll.) little brother.
[3]**tato,** *m.* (Am.) = TATÚ.
tatú, *m.* a variety of giant armadillo.
tatuaje, *m.* tattooing; tattoo.
tatuar, *va.* & *vr.* to tattoo.
tatusa, *f.* (Arg., Bol.) little woman; woman of no account.
tau, *f.* tau (Greek letter).
taugel, *m.* batten.
taujía, *f.* damaskeening.
taumaturgia, *f.* thaumaturgy, miracle working.
taumatúrgico, ca, *a.* thaumaturgic, thaumaturgical.
taumaturgo, *m.* miracle worker, thaumaturge.
taurino, na, *a.* taurine, bovine.
taurios, *a. pl.* taurine, bullfighting (games).
Tauro, *m.* (astr.) Taurus, sign of the zodiac.
taurómaco, ca. I. *a.* pertaining to bullfighting. **II.** *n.* bullfight fan; *m.* bullfighter.
tauromaquia, *f.* bullfighting.
tauromáquico, ca, *a.* pert. to bullfighting.
tautología, *f.* (rhet.) tautology.
tautológico, ca, *a.* tautological.
tautologista, *n.* tautologist.
taxáceo, cea, *a.* (bot.) taxaceous.
taxativamente, *adv.* limitedly.
taxativo, va, *a.* (law) restricted, conditioned.
taxi, *m.* taxi, taxicab.
taxidermia, *f.* taxidermy.
taxidérmico, ca, *a.* taxidermal, taxidermic.
taxidermista, *n.* taxidermist.
taxímetro, *m.* (auto) taximeter; taxicab, taxi.
taxonomía, *f.* taxonomy.
taxonómico, ca, *a.* taxonomic.
taz a taz, *adv.* tit for tat.
taza, *f.* cup; cupful; bowl; basin of a fountain; cup guard of a sword.
tazaña, *f.* = TARASCA, figure of a dragon.
tazar, *va.* & *vr.* to fray.
tazmía, *f.* share of tithes; tithe register.
tazón, *m. aug.* large bowl; basin.
té, *m.* tea.—**t. bailable,** tea dance, tea with dancing.—**t. de borde,** or **de Méjico,** (bot.) saltwort.
[1]**te,** *pers.* & *refl. pron., obj. case* of TÚ, thee, to thee; thyself; (when on familiar terms with someone) you, to you; yourself.
[2]**te,** *f.* name of the letter *t.*
tea, *f.* candlewood; torch, firebrand; (naut.) hawse for raising the anchor.
teame, teamide, *f.* stone said to repel iron.
teatino, na, *n.* Theatin.
teatral, *a.* theatrical.
teatralmente, *adv.* theatrically.
teátrico, ca, *a.* theatrical.
teatro, *m.* theatre; stage; collection of plays; dramatic art.
tebaico, ca, *a.* Thebaic.
tebaína, *f.* (chem.) thebaine.
tebano, na; tebeo, a, *n.* & *a.* Theban.
teca, *f.* (bot.) teak; teakwood.
tecalí, *m.* (Mex.) transparent marble.
tecla, *f.* key (of a piano, organ, typewriter, etc.); delicate point.—**dar en la t.,** to strike it right, to find the way.—**tocar una t.,** to get up a scheme, to resort to some expedient.
teclado, *m.* keyboard.

tecle, *m.* (naut.) single purchase.
teclear. I. *vn.* to finger a keyboard; to drum with the fingers. **II.** *va.* (coll.) to resort to (an expedient), to try (some scheme).
tecleo, *m.* drumming on a keyboard, striking the keys; scheming, trying.
tecnecio, *m.* (chem.) technetium.
técnicamente, *adv.* technically.
tecnicismo, *m.* technical term; technical vocabulary; technicism.
técnico, ca. I. *a.* technical. **II.** *n.* technician; *f.* technique; technical ability.—**t. de los cohetes**, rocketry.
tecnicolor, *m.* (photog., cine.) technicolor.
tecnocracia, *f.* technocracy.
tecnología, *f.* technology.
tecnológico, ca, *a.* technological, technical.
tecnólogo, ga, *n.* technologist.
tecol, *m.* (Mex.) maguey caterpillar.
tecolote, *m.* (Mex., C. A.) owl.
tecomate, *m.* (Mex.) gourd, canteen.
tectónico, ca. I. *a.* tectonic. **II.** *f.* tectonics.
techado, *m.* roof; ceiling; shed.
techar, *va.* to roof; to cover with a roof.
techo, *m.*, TECHUMBRE; (aer.) absolute ceiling.—**t. de servicio**, or **utilizable**, (aer.) service ceiling.
techumbre, *f.* ceiling; roof; top (as of vehicle); cover; shed.
tedero, *m.* torch holder.
tedéum, *m.* (eccl.) Te Deum.
tediar, *va.* to loathe, hate, abhor.
tedio, *m.* tediousness, ennui.
tedioso, sa, *a.* tedious, boresome, tiresome.
tegual, *m.* ancient tax on fish.
teguillo, *m.* thin board, strip.
tegumentario, ria, *a.* tegumentary.
tegumento, *m.* tegument.
teína, *f.* (chem.) thein.
teinada, *f.* cattle shed.
teísmo, *m.* theism.—**teísta**, *n.* & *a.* theist(-ic).
[1]**teja**, *f.* roof tile; steel bar shaped into a sword blade; (naut.) hollow cut for scarfing.—**t. cóncava**, gutter or pantile.—**t. de la silla**, (Mex.) cantle of saddle.—**a t. vana**, with a shed over.—**a toca t.**, in cash, cash down.—**de tejas abajo**, in the world of nature, in this world.—**de tejas arriba**, in the realm of the supernatural, beyond the realm of nature.
[2]**teja**, *f.* (bot.) linden tree.
tejadillo, *m. dim.* roof of a coach; projecting side roof; card sharp's method of holding the talon.
tejado, *m.* roof; shed.—**t. de cinc**, tin roof.
tejamaní, tejamanil, *m.* shingle.
tejano, na, *n.* & *a.* Texan.
tejar. I. *va.* to tile. **II.** *m.* tile works, tile kiln.
tejaroz, *m.* eaves, penthouse, tiled shed.
tejedera, *f.* TEJEDORA; (entom.) water skater.
tejedor, ra, *n.* weaver; (entom.) water skipper.
tejedura, *f.* texture, weaving, fabric.
tejeduría, *f.* art of weaving; mill, factory for weaving.
tejemaneje, *m.* (coll.) cleverness, knack.
tejer, *va.* to weave; to wattle, interweave, plait; (Am.) to knit; to regulate, adjust; to devise.
tejera, tejería, *f.* tile kiln.
tejero, *m.* tile maker.
tejica, illa, ita, *f. dim.* small tile.
tejido, da. I. *pp.* of TEJER.—**alambre t.**, wire netting. **II.** *m.* texture, tissue, weaving; fabric, web; (anat.) tissue.—**t. de alambre**, wire mesh.
tejillo, *m.* plaited girdle.
[1]**tejo**, *m.* quoit; game of quoits; shuffleboard counter; blank, metal disk or plate; (mech.) bush, pillow block, socket, socket plate.
[2]**tejo**, *m.* (bot.) yew tree.
tejocote, *m.* (bot., Mex.) a sloelike fruit.
tejoleta, *f.* broken tile, brickbat; shuffleboard counter; clapper.
tejolote, *m.* (Mex.) stone pestle.
[1]**tejón**, *m.* round gold ingot.
[2]**tejón**, *m.* (zool.) badger.
tejonera, *f.* burrow of a badger.
tejuela. *f.* small tile; brickbat; saddletree.
tejuelo, *m.* small tile; (bookbinding) binder's title; (mech.) bush, pillow block, socket, soleplate.
tela, *f.* cloth, fabric, stuff; chain or warp of cloth; pellicle, film; skin (of an onion, etc.); quibble, quirk; web of insects; argument; matter; thread of a discourse; membrane or opacity in the eye.—**t. de alambre**, wire cloth, wire screening.—**t. de araña**, cobweb, spider web.—**t. de cebolla**, thin cloth.—**t. metálica** = T. DE ALAMBRE.—**en t. de juicio**, in doubt; under careful consideration.
telamón, *m.* (arch.) telamon, atlante.
telar, *m.* loom; frame; (theat.) gridiron.
telaraña, *f.* cobweb; flimsy or trifling thing.—**mirar las telarañas**, (coll.) to be absentminded.—**tener telarañas en los ojos**, to be blind to one's surroundings.
telarejo, *f. dim.* small loom or frame.
telautógrafo, *m.* telautograph.
telecomunicación, *f.* telecommunication, long-distance communication.
telecontrol, *m.* remote control.
teledinámico, ca, *a.* telodynamic.
teleferage, *m.* telpherage, telferage.
teleferar, *va.* to telpher, telfer.
teleférico, ca, *m.* & *a.* telpher.
telefio, *m.* (bot.) orpine stonecrop.
telefonazo, *m.* telephone call.
telefonear, *va.* & *vn.* to telephone.
telefonema, *m.* telephone message.
telefonía, *f.* telephony.—**t. sin hilos**, wireless telephony, radiotelephony.
telefónicamente, *adv.* telephonically.
telefónico, ca, *a.* telephonic.
telefonista, *n.* telephone operator.
teléfono, *m.* telephone.—**t. automático**, dial telephone.—**t. sin hilos**, wireless telephone.
teléfoto, *m.* telephoto.
telefotografía, *f.* telephotography.
telefotográfico, ca, *a.* telephoto.
telega, *f.* telega.
telegénico, ca, *a.* telegenic.
telegonia, *f.* (biol.) telegony.
telegrafía, *f.* telegraphy.—**t. dúplex**, duplex telegraphy.—**t. sin hilos**, wireless telegraphy.
telegrafiar, *va.* to telegraph; to cable.
telegráficamente, *adv.* telegraphically.
telegráfico, ca, *a.* telegraphic.
telegrafista, *n.* telegrapher, telegraph operator.
telégrafo, *m.* telegraph.—**t. marino**, nautical signals; signal service.—**t. óptico**, semaphore.—**t. sin hilos**, wireless telegraph.—**hacer telégrafos**, to talk by signs (as lovers).
telegrama, *m.* telegram; cablegram.
telemecánica, *f.* long-distance transmission or production of motion.
telemetría, *f.* telemetry.
telemétrico, ca, *a.* telemetric.
telémetro, *m.* telemeter.
telencéfalo, *m.* (anat.) telencephalon.
teleobjetivo, *m.* telephoto lens.
teleología, *f.* teleology.
teleológico, ca, *a.* teleological.
teleósteo, tea, *m.* & *a.* (ichth.) teleost.
telepatía, *f.* telepathy.
telepático, ca, *a.* telepathic.
teleprompter, *m.* Teleprompter (trademark).
telera, *f.* plow pin; cattle stall, cattle pen; (mech.) jaw, cheek (of a clamp, vice, or press); body transom, cross frame, tiebeam (of carriage); (artil.) transom of a gun-carriage; (naut.) rack block; (min.) pyramidal mound of copper ore for roasting; round loaf of brown bread.
telerán, *m* (electron.) teleran.
telero, *m.* stake (of a cart).
telescópico, ca, *a.* telescopic.
telescopio, *m.* telescope.
telespectroscopio, *m.* telespectroscope.
telestereoscopio, *m.* telestereoscope.

telestesia, *f.* telesthesia.
teleta, *f.* blotting paper; sieve in paper mills.
teletermómetro, *m.* telethermometer.
teletipo, *m.* teletype.
teletón, *m.* strong silken stuff.
televisión, *f.* television.—**receptor de t.,** television set.
televisionar, *va.* to televise.
telex, *m.* telex.
telilla, *f. dim.* light woollen stuff; film.
telina, *f.* = ALMEJA, clam; mussel.
telita, *f. dim.* of TELA; thin fabric.
telón, *m.* (theat.) curtain, drop curtain; drop, drop scene.—**t. de boca,** drop curtain.—**t. de foro,** drop scene.—**bajar,** or **correr, el t.,** to drop the curtain.—**levantar,** or **subir, el t.,** to raise the curtain.
telonio, *m.* ancient tax office.—**a manera de t.,** in a jumble, disordered.
telúrico, ca, *a.* telluric.
telurio, *m.* (chem.) tellurium.
teluroso, sa, *a.* (chem.) tellurous.
telururo, *m.* (chem.) telluride, tellurid.
tellina, *f.* = TELINA.
telliz, *m.* caparison, saddle cover.
telliza, *f.* bedspread, coverlet.
tema. I. *m.* theme, subject; text, thesis; (mus.) theme, motive.—**t. celeste,** (astr.) map of the heavens. **II.** *f.* fixed idea of a madman; hobby; dispute, contention; obstinacy; animosity, grudge.—**a t.,** emulously, in competition.
temario, *m.* agenda.—**comisión del t.,** Agenda Committee.
temático, ca, *a.* thematic; obstinate.
tembladal, *m.* quaking bog, quagmire.
tembladera, *f.* a kind of bowl or cup of very thin metal or glass; (jewelry) TEMBLEQUE; (ichth.) torpedo, electric ray; (bot.) quaking grass.
tembladero, *m.* quagmire.
temblador, ra. I. *a.* quaking, shaking, quivering. **II.** *m.* Quaker.
temblante. I. *a.* trembling, quavering. **II.** *m.* loose bracelet.
temblar, *vn.* (*ind.* TIEMBLO; *subj.* TIEMBLE) to tremble, shake, quake, quiver; to shiver.
tembleque, *m.* a hair ornament on a spiral wire.
temblequear, tembletear, *vn.* (coll.) to tremble, shake, shiver.
temblón, na, *a.* tremulous, shaking.—**hacer la temblona,** to affect timidity.
temblor, *m.* trembling, tremor, thrill.—**t. de tierra,** earthquake.—**temblorcillo,** *m. dim.* slight tremor.—**tembloroso, sa; tembloso, sa,** *a.* trembling, tremulous, shivering, shaking.
temedero, ra, *a.* dread, redoubtable.
temedor, ra, *a.* dreading, fearing.
temer, *va.* & *vn.* to fear, dread.
temerariamente, *adv.* rashly, recklessly.
temerario, ria, *a.* rash, imprudent, unwise; reckless; hasty, unreflecting.
temeridad, *f.* temerity, rashness, recklessness; folly, rash or reckless act; foolhardiness; rash conclusion.
temerón, na, *a.* affecting courage.
temerosamente, *adv.* timorously.
temeroso, sa, *a.* dread; timid; timorous; chickenhearted; afraid.—**t. de Dios,** God-fearing.
temible, *a.* dread, terrible, redoubtable.
temor, *m.* dread, fear.
temoso, sa, *a.* obstinate, stubborn.
tempanador, *m.* cutter for beehives.
tempanar, *va.* to cover the tops of (beehives).
témpano, *m.* (mus.) kettledrum; tabor, timbrel; drumhead, drumskin; tympan; piece, block; ice floe, iceberg; sod, sward; heading of a barrel; flitch of bacon; cork dome of a beehive; (arch.) tympan of an arch.—**t. de tocino,** flitch of bacon.
temperación, *f.* tempering.
temperadamente, *adv.* temperately.
temperamento, *m.* climate; arbitration, compromise; temperament, constitution; (mus.) temperament.
temperancia, *f.* temperance.
temperante, *a.* (med.) tempering.
temperar. I. *va.* to temper; to soften. **II.** *vn.* (Am.) to have a change of climate; to summer.
temperatura, *f.* temperature.—**t. absoluta,** (phys.) absolute temperature.
temperie, *f.* atmospheric conditions.
tempero, *m.* seasonableness.
tempestad, *f.* tempest, storm.
tempestivamente, *adv.* fitly, opportunely.
tempestividad, *f.* opportuneness, timeliness.
tempestivo, va, *a.* opportune, timely.
tempestuosamente, *adv.* stormily, turbulently.
tempestuoso, sa, *a.* tempestuous, stormy.
[1]**templa,** *f.* (art) tempera, distemper.
[2]**templa,** *f.* gen. *pl.* (anat.) temple(s).
templadamente, *adv.* temperately, moderately, abstemiously.
templadera, *f.* (hydraul.) sluice gate.
templado, da. I. *pp.* of TEMPLAR. **II.** *a.* moderate (esp. of climate, as **tierra templada,** [region of] moderate climate or medium temperature); hardened, tempered; abstemious; lukewarm; medium, fair; brave, firm; (mus.) tuned.
templador, ra. I. *n.* tuner; temperer. **II.** *m.* (mus.) tuning key; (Peru) circular stockade in bull rings.
templadura, *f.* temper, tempering; tuning.
templanza, *f.* temperance, moderation, sobriety; mildness of temperature or climate; (art) good disposition of colors.
templar. I. *va.* to temper, soften, moderate; to quench, allay; to calm, pacify; to prepare, dispose; to temper, quench (metals); to anneal (glass); (mus.) to tune; (art) to blend; (naut.) to trim (the sails) to the wind; (falconry) to train.—**templarle la gaita a uno,** to humor one. **II.** *vr.* to be moderate.
templario, *m.* (hist., eccl.) Templar, Knight Templar.
[1]**temple,** *m.* atmospheric conditions; temper (of metals, of persons); courage; disposition, frame of mind; average; (mus.) temperament.—**al t.** (art) in distemper.
[2]**temple,** *m.* religion of the Templars, and one of their temples.
templete, *m. dim.* small temple, shrine; (arch.) niche, tabernacle.
templista, *m.* (art) painter in distemper.
templo, *m.* temple; church; shrine.
témpora, *f.* —*pl.* (eccl.) ember days.
temporada, *f.* season, spell, period (of time).—**t. de frío,** cold spell.—**t. de invierno,** winter season.—**t. de ópera,** opera season.—**estar de t.,** to be summering or rusticating.
[1]**temporal. I.** *a.* temporal; temporary; provisional; secular, worldly. **II.** *m.* tempest, storm; weather (good or bad); long rainy spell; temporary laborer.
[2]**temporal,** *a.* (anat.) temporal.
temporalidad, *f.* temporality.
temporalizar, *va.* (*pret.* TEMPORALICÉ; *subj.* TEMPORALICE) to make temporary.
temporalmente, *adv.* temporarily; provisionally, transiently; in a worldly manner.
temporáneo, nea; temporario, ria, *a.* temporary, unstable, transient.
temporejar, *vn.* (naut.) to lie to.
temporero, ra; temporil, *a.* temporary (laborer), working by the season.
temporizador, ra, *n.* temporizer.
temporizar, *vn.* (*pret.* TEMPORICÉ; *subj.* TEMPORICE) to pass the time; to temporize.
tempranal, *a.* producing early fruits.
tempranamente, *adv.* prematurely.
tempranero, ra, *a.* early.
tempranilla, *f.* early grape.
temprano, na. I. *a.* early. **II.** *m. adv.* early; prematurely, too early. **III.** *n.* field yielding early crops.
temulento, ta, *a.* intoxicated, tipsy, drunk.
ten.—**t. con t.,** tact, adroitness, wisdom.
tena, *f.* shed for cattle, fold.
[1]**tenacear,** *va.* to tear off flesh of with pincers.

[2]**tenacear,** *vn.* to persist.
tenacero, *m.* tongs maker.
tenacidad, *f.* tenacity, toughness; tenaciousness, pertinacity, perseverance, persistence.
tenacillas, *f. pl. dim.* small tongs; snuffers; tweezers, nippers, pincers, pliers; curling iron; sugar tongs.—**t. de rizar,** crimping iron.
tenáculo, *m.* (surg.) tenaculum.
tenada, *f.* fold, shed for cattle.
tenallas, *f. pl.* pair of tongs.
tenallón, *m.* (fort.) tenail or tenaille.
tenante, *m.* (her.) supporter (of a shield).
tenar, *m.* & *a.* (anat.) thenar.
tenaz, *a.* tenacious, adhesive; strong, firm; stubborn; tough; persevering.
tenaza, *f.* (fort.) tenail; claw (as of lobsters).—*pl.* tongs, nippers, pliers; (dent.) forceps; (card playing) two cards that take the last two tricks.
tenazada, *f.* grasp of pincers or tongs; noise or click of the tongs; violent biting.
tenazmente, *adv.* tenaciously.
tenazón, *f.*—**a t.,** point-blank, without taking aim.—**parar de t.,** to stop (a horse) short in his course.
tenazuelas, *f. pl. dim.* tweezers.
tenca, *f.* (ichth.) tench.
tención, *f.* holding, retaining.
tendajo, *m.* small rickety shop.
tendal, *m.* tent, awning, tilt; piece of canvas placed under olive trees when picking the fruit.
tendalera, *f.* (coll.) things scattered in disorder.
tendalero, *m.,* **tendedero,** *m.* place where clothes are spread to dry.
tendedor, ra, *n.* stretcher, tenter; one who spreads clothes to dry.
tendedura, *f.* stretching, extending.
tendejón, *m.* small rickety shop.
tendel, *m.* (mason.) leveling line (cord); layer of mortar.
tendencia, *f.* tendency; trend, drift.
tendencioso, sa, *a.* tendentious.
tendente, *a.* tending.
ténder, *m.* (Angl.) (Ry.) tender.
tender (*ind.* TIENDO; *subj.* TIENDA) **I.** *va.* to stretch, stretch out; to spread out; to hang out (washing); to lay (tablecloth); to lay (rails, etc.), throw (a bridge across a river), etc. (in emergency building as for military purposes); (mason.) to coat. **II.** *vn.* to have a tendency, tend; (**hacia**) (math.) to approach (as a limit). **III.** *vr.* to stretch out, lie full length; to place one's cards on the table; to run at full gallop; to neglect a business.
tenderete, *m.* a card game; (Mex.) second-hand-clothing shop.
tendero, ra, *n.* shopkeeper; tentmaker.
tendezuela, *f. dim.* small shop.
tendidamente, *adv.* diffusely, diffusively.
tendido. I. *pp.* of TENDER. **II.** *m.* row of seats; in lace making, piece made over the pattern; quantity of spread clothes dried at once; batch of bread baked at one time; (mason.) coat of plaster or calcimine; (arch.) roof of a house from the ridge to the eaves; (Am. min.) riffle.
tendiente. I. *pres. p.* of TENDER. **II.** *a.* (a) intended (for).
tendinoso, sa, *a.* tendinous, pert. to tendon.
tendón, *m.* (anat.) tendon.—**t. de Aquiles,** (anat.) Achilles' tendon.
tenducha, tenducho, *n.* insignificant shop.
tenebrario, *m.* (eccl.) tenebræ candelabrum.
tenebrosamente, *adv.* gloomily.
tenebrosidad, *f.* darkness, gloom.
tenebroso, sa, *a.* tenebrous, dark, gloomy.
tenedero, *m.* (naut.) anchoring ground.
tenedor, *m.* holder; keeper; guardian; table fork; (ball games) caddy; (com.) holder.—**t. de bastimentos,** (naut.) storekeeper of the navy.—**t. de libros,** bookkeeper.—**t. de póliza,** policy-holder.
teneduría, *f.* position of bookkeeper.—**t. de libros,** bookkeeping.
tenencia, *f.* tenancy, occupancy, possession, holding; (mil.) lieutenancy, lieutenantship.
tener. I. *va.* (*ind. pres.* yo TENGO, él TIENE, *pret.* TUVE; *fut.* TENDRÉ; *sub.* TENGA) to have, possess; to hold, take hold of; (app. to health) to be the matter with, to ail; to be worth (*Juan tiene cien mil pesos,* John is worth 100,000 pesos); to maintain, sustain; to subject; domineer; to keep, hold, retain; to stop, hold back; to fulfil, keep (one's word); to contain, have within; (app. to dimensions) to be (*la casa tiene 20 metros de ancho,* the house is 20 meters wide). With nouns of time, it denotes duration or age (*el niño tiene seis meses,* the child is six months old; *esta casa tiene cien años,* this house is one hundred years old). With some nouns denoting sensation or feeling, it is equivalent to "to be" followed by the corresponding adjective (*tener hambre,* to be hungry; *tener sueño,* to be sleepy; *tener celos* (*de*), to be jealous (of); *tener frío, calor,* (of person) to be cold, hot; *tener miedo* (**de**) (**a**), to be afraid (to) (of).—**t. a bien,** to find it convenient; to please; to deem best.—**t. buenas formas,** to be of fine figure; to be polite.—**t. cuidado de,** to take care to.—**t. de** (foll. by *a.*) to be (often with there): *eso no tiene nada de estraño,* there is nothing strange about that.—**t. días,** (coll.) to be old; to have moody days.—**t. efecto,** to take effect, become effective.—**t. en,** to hold in (esteem, respect, etc.).—**t. en cuenta,** to take into account, or consideration, take account of.—**t. en menos,** to think little of.—**t. gana,** or **ganas,** (**de**), to wish, desire (to); to have a mind (to); to feel like.—**t. gracia,** to be funny.—**t. gusto en,** to be glad to.—**t. la bondad de** (*inf.*), (in requests), have the kindness to (*inf.*), please, kindly (*imper.*).—**t. la culpa** (**de**), to be to blame (for).—**t. lugar,** (Gal.) to take place, occur.—**t. para sí,** to think, be of the opinion.—**t. por,** to take to be, believe, consider.—**t. presente,** to bear in mind.—**t. prisa,** to be in a hurry.—**t. que,** to have to, must; to have something to (say, lose, propose, etc.).—**t. que hacer,** to have something to do; to be busy; to have to, or must, do.—**t. que ver con,** to have to do with.—**t. razón,** to be right.—**t. suerte,** to be lucky.—**no t. razón,** to be wrong.—**no t. remedio,** not to be any help for, can't be helped, prevented.—**no tenerlas todas consigo,** to be worried, to be anxious.—**no t. sobre que caerse muerto,** not to have a farthing, to be penniless. **II.** *v. aux.* to have (*tengo dicho,* I have said). Often, however, the participle following is rather an adjective than part of a compound tense (*tengo escritas dos cartas,* I have two letters written). In other cases, the combination is equivalent to a simple form of the verb (*tengo entendido,* I understand; *tengo pensado,* I intend). **III.** *vn.* to have, possess; to be well-off, to be wealthy.—**t. de,** to have to, must. **IV.** *vr.* to hold fast or steady; to rest (on something); to stop, halt; to fight, hold one's own; to adhere (to), stand (for).—**t. en pie,** to keep on one's feet, remain standing.
tenería, *f.* tannery.
tenesmo, *m.* (med.) tenesmus.
tengo, tenga, *v. V.* TENER.
tenia, *f.* tapeworm; (arch.) fillet.
tenienta, *f.* wife of a first lieutenant.
tenientazgo, *m.* (mil.) first lieutenantship.
teniente. I. *pres. p.* of TENER. **II.** *a.* (of fruit) unripe; miserly, mean; (coll.) dear.—**t. de oídos,** hard of hearing. **III.** *m.* deputy, substitute; (mil.) first lieutenant.—**t. coronel,** lieutenant colonel.—**t. general,** lieutenant general.
tenífugo, ga, *a.* (med.) tænifuge.
tenis, *m.* tennis.
tenista, *n.* tennis player.
tenonitis, *f.* (med.) tenonitis.
[1]**tenor,** *m.* condition, nature; kind; import, literal

meaning.—**a este t.**, of the same kind, like.—**a t. de**, in compliance with.
[2]**tenor**, *m.* (mus.) tenor.
tenotomía, *f.* (surg.) tenotomy.
[1]**tensión**, *f.* tension; tensile stress; tautness, tightness; strain; (elec.) voltage, potential, tension.—**t. arterial**, blood pressure.
[2]**tensión**, *f.* = TENSÓN.
tenso, sa, *a.* tense, tight, taut, stretched.
tensón, *f.* (poet.) poetical contest on love.
tensor, ra. I. *a.* tensile. **II.** *m.* turnbuckle; tightener.
tentación, *f.* temptation.
tentacioncilla, *f. dim.* slight temptation.
tentaculado, da, *a.* (zool.) tentacled.
tentacular, *a.* tentacular.
tentáculo, *m.* tentacle.
tentadero, *m.* corral for taming calves.
tentador, ra. I. *a.* tempting. **II.** *n.* tempter; *f.* temptress, seductress.—**el t.**, the devil.
tentadura, *f.* mercury test of silver ore.
tentalear, *va.* to feel all over, examine by touch.
tentar, *va.* (*ind.* TIENTO; *subj.* TIENTE) to touch, to feel with the fingers, to examine by touch; to grope; to tempt; to attempt, try, endeavor; to test; (surg.) to probe; to tent.—**t. cerrojos**, to try all ways and means.
tentativo, va. I. *a.* tentative, experimental. **II.** *f.* attempt, experiment; first examination.—**t. de agresión**, (law) assault.
tentemozo, *m.* prop, support; pole prop; tumbler (a toy); QUIJERA, noseband straps (of bridle).
tentempié, *m.* (coll.) light luncheon, a bite.
tentenelaire, *n.* mulatto; half-breed.
tentón, *m.* (coll.) rough handling.
tenue, *a.* thin, tenuous, delicate; worthless, trifling; soft (consonant); (art) faint, subdued.
tenuemente, *adv.* slightly.
tenuidad, *f.* tenuity, thinness, subtlety; weakness; trifle.
tenuta, *f.* (law) provisional tenure.
tenutario, ria, *a.* (law) provisional tenant.
tenzón, *f.* poetical contest on love.
teñidura, *f.* art of dyeing or tingeing.
teñir, *va.* (*pp.* TEÑIDO, TINTO; *ger.* TIÑENDO; *ind. pres.* TIÑO, *pret.* él TIÑÓ; *subj.* TIÑA) to tinge, to dye; to stain; (art.) to darken, sadden (a color).—**t. en rama**, to dye in grain, to ingrain.
teobroma, *m.* cacao.
teobromina, *f.* (chem.) theobromine.
teocali, *m.* teocalli, Aztec ceremonial building.
teocéntrico, ca, *a.* (eccl.) theocentric.
teocracia, *f.* theocracy.
teócrata, *n.* (pol.) theocrat.
teocrático, ca, *a.* theocratic.
teodicea, *f.* (theol.) theodicy.
teodolito, *m.* theodolite.
teodosiano, na, *a.* Theodosian.
teogonía, *f.* theogony, origin of the gods.
teogónico, ca, *a.* theogonic.
teologal, *a.* theologic(al).
teología, *f.* theology.—**t. natural**, natural theology.
teológicamente, *adv.* theologically.
teológico, ca, *a.* theologic(al).
teologismo, *m.* excessive theologizing, theological mania.
teologizar, *vn.* (*pret.* TEOLOGICÉ; *subj.* TEOLOGICE) to theologize.
teólogo, ga. I. *a.* theological. **II.** *m.* theologian.
teorema, *m.* theorem.
teoría, *f.* theory.—**t. atómica**, atomic theory.—**t. de las ondulaciones**, (phys.) wave theory (of light).
teóricamente, *adv.* theoretically.
teórico, ca. I. *a.* theoretical. **II.** *n.* theorist, theoretician; *f.* theory.
teorizante, *a.* theorizing.
teorizar, *vn.* to theorize.
teoso, sa, *a.* resinous.
teosofía, *f.* theosophy.
teosófico, ca, *a.* theosophical.
teosofismo, *m.* theosophism.
teósofo, *m.* theosophist.
tepalcate, *m.* (Mex.) potsherd.
tepe, *m.* green sod, turf.
tepeguaje. I. *m.* (Mex.) a very hard and compact wood. **II.** *a.* (Mex.) set, obstinate.
tepeizcuinte, *m.* (Am.) badger.
tepetate, *m.* (min.) attle, deads, refuse.
tepexilote, *m.* a palm nut used for beads.
tequiche, *m.* (Venez.) corn meal with coconut milk and molasses.
tequila, *m.* (Mex.) tequila (plant and liqueur made from it).
tequío, *m.* (Mex.) a municipal duty or tax.
terapeuta, *n.* (med.) therapeutist, therapist.
terapéutico, ca. I. *a.* therapeutic. **II.** *f.* therapeutics.
terapia, *f.* therapy.—**t. laboral**, occupational therapy.
teratología, *f.* (biol.) teratology.
teratológico, ca, *a.* teratologic(al).
terbio, *m.* (chem.) terbium.
tercamente, *adv.* obstinately, stubbornly.
tercena, *f.* wholesale tobacco warehouse.
tercenal, *m.* (agr.) rick of thirty sheaves.
tercenista, *m.* keeper of a TERCENA.
tercer, *a.* (*contr.* of TERCERO) third.
terceramente, *adv.* thirdly.
tercería, *f.* mediation, arbitration; umpirage; temporary occupation (of a fortress, etc.).
tercerilla, *f.* (poet.) triplet.
tercero, ra. I. *a.* third. **II.** *n.* procurer(-ess). **III.** *m.* third person; mediator, arbitrator, umpire; collector of tithes; (eccl.) tertiary; sixtieth of a second (time).—**t. en discordia**, umpire, referee between two disputants. **IV.** *f.* (mus.) third; ditone; third string of a guitar; sequence of three cards.
tercerol, *m.* (naut.) third in order.
tercerola, *f.* a short carbine; (com.) tierce.
tercerón, na, *n.* (Am.) mulatto.
terceto, *m.* (poet.) tierce, terzet, terza, triplet; (mus.) terzetto, trio.
tercia, *f.* one third; third of a vara; storehouse for tithes; among Romans, forenoon; sequence of three cards; (eccl.) third hour.
terciado, da. I. *pp.* of TERCIAR. **II.** *a.* slanting, tilted, biased, crosswise. **III.** *m.* cutlass, broad sword; broad ribbon.
terciana, *f.* (med.) tertian.
tercianario, ria. I. *a.* (med.) tertian; causing or suffering tertian fever. **II.** *n.* person affected with a tertian.
tercianela, *f.* heavy silk fabric.
terciar. I. *va.* to place sidewise or sling diagonally; to divide into three parts; (agr.) to plow the third time; (mil.) to carry (arms).—**t. una pieza**, (artil.) to prove a gun. **II.** *vn.* to make up a number; to mediate, arbitrate, to go between; to join (in conversation); to share, take part; to reach the third day. **III.** *vr.* to be favorable, offer an opportunity.
terciario, ria. I. *a.* third in order or degree; (geol.) Tertiary. **II.** *n.* (arch.) rib of a Gothic arch; (geol.) Tertiary.
terciazón, *m.* (agr.) third plowing.
tercio, cia. I. *a.* third. **II.** *m.* one third; each package of a mule load; (mil.) (Sp. hist.) regiment of infantry, (modern Sp.) Foreign Legion; division of the GUARDIA CIVIL; third part of a horse race course (start, run, or stop); third section in the height of a horse; third part of the rosary; third part of a sword.—*pl.* robust or strong limbs of a man.—**t. de cueros**, bundle of hides.—**t. de tabaco**, bale of tobacco.—**t. y quinto**, great advantage.—**hacer buen t.**, to do a good turn.—**hacer mal t.**, to do a bad turn, to serve ill.—**hacer t.**, to join and complete a required number of people.
terciopelado, da. I. *a.* velvetlike, velvety. **II.** *m.* velvetlike stuff.
terciopelero, ra, *n.* velvet weaver or worker.

terciopelo, *m.* velvet.
terco, ca, *a.* stubborn; hard (as marble).
terebintáceo, cea, *a.* (bot.) terebinthine.
terebinto, *m.* (bot.) terebinth.
terebrante, *a.* piercing (pain).
terenciano, na, *a.* Terentian.
tereniabín, *m.* white, sweetish, purgative substance from leaves of a certain plant.
tereques, *m. pl.* (Am., coll.) traps; duds, belongings.
teresiana, *f.* a kind of military cap.
tergal, *a.* tergal, dorsal.
tergiversación, *f.* tergiversation.
tergiversador, ra, *n.* & *a.* tergiversator(-ing).
tergiversar, *va.* to tergiversate.
teriaca, *f.* (pharm.) theriaca.
teriacal, *a.* (pharm.) theriac(al).
teridofita, *f.* (bot.) pteridophyte.
teristro, *m.* thin veil or shawl.
terliz, *m.* tick, ticking; tent cloth.
termal, *a.* thermal.
termas, *f. pl.* hot baths; hot springs.
termes, *m.* (entom.) termite. Also TERMITE.
térmico, ca, *a.* thermic, thermal.
termidor, *m.* Thermidor, eleventh month of the French-Revolution calendar.
terminabilidad, *f.* terminability.
terminable, *a.* terminable.
terminación, *f.* termination, completion; (gram.) termination, ending.
terminacho, *m.* (coll.) big or vulgar word; jawbreaker.
terminador, ra. I. *a.* finishing, completing. **II.** *n.* finisher.
terminajo, *m.* (coll.) vulgar expression.
terminal. I. *a.* terminal, final, last. **II.** *m.* (elec.) terminal.
terminante, *a.* ending, closing; peremptory, final, decisive.—**terminantemente,** *adv.* peremptorily, positively.
terminar. I. *va.* & *vn.* to end, close, terminate, finish, complete. **II.** *vn.* **de** (*inf.*), to have just (*pp.*). **III.** *vn.* & *vr.* to end; to abut; (med.) to come to a crisis.
terminativo, va, *a.* (philos.) terminative.
término, *m.* end, ending, completion; term, word; boundary; landmark; manner, behavior; district of a town or city; aim, object, goal; crisis of a disease; condition, constitution, state; (math., logic) term; (arch.) terminal, terminus; (law) term; (mus.) tone, pitch.—*pl.* (logic and astrol.) terms.—**t. medio,** (math.) average; (logic) middle term; compromise.—**términos semejantes,** (math.) similar terms.—**en buenos términos,** (coll.) in plain language.—**en otros términos,** in other words.—**en último t.,** finally.—**medio t.,** compromise.—**medios términos,** evasions, subterfuges.—**poner t. a,** to put an end to, to stop.—**por t. medio,** on an average.—**primer t.,** (art) foreground.—**último t.,** (art) background.
terminología, *f.* terminology.
terminote, *m. aug.* big word.
termión, *m.* (phys.) thermion.
termiónico, ca. I. *a.* thermionic. **II.** *f.* (phys.) thermionics.
termita, *f.* thermite.
termite, *m.* (entom.) termite, white ant.
termitero, *m.* termite nest.
termobomba, *f.* thermopump.
termocauterio, *m.* (surg.) thermocautery.
termoconductor, ra, *m.* & *a.* (phys.) thermoconductor.
termodinámica, *f.* thermodynamics.
termodinámico, ca, *a* thermodynamic.
termoelectricidad, *f.* thermoelectricity.
termoeléctrico, ca, *a.* thermoelectric.
termoelemento, *m.* (phys.) thermoelement.
termoendurecible, *a.* thermosetting (plastics).
termofísica, *f.* thermophysics.
termofisión, *f.* (phys.) thermofission.
termofraguado, da, *a.* thermosetting (plastics).
termofusión, *f.* (phys.) thermofusion.
termogénesis, *f.* thermogenesis.
termógrafo, *m.* thermograph, self-registering thermometer.
termolabil, *a.* (chem.) thermolabile.
termometría, *f.* thermometry.
termométrico, ca, *a.* thermometric(al).
termómetro, *m.* thermometer.
termometrógrafo, *m.* thermograph, self-registering thermometer.
termomultiplicador, *m.* (phys.) thermopile.
termonuclear, *a.* thermonuclear.
termoplástico, ca, *a.* thermoplastic.
termoquímico, ca. I. *a.* thermochemical. **II.** *f.* thermochemistry.
termos, *m.* thermos bottle.
termoscopio, *m.* thermoscope.
termosifón, *m.* thermosiphon.
termóstato, *m.* thermostat.
termostático, ca, *a.* thermostatic.
termoterapia, *f.* (med.) thermotherapy.
termotropismo, *m.* (biol.) thermotropism.
terna, *f.* ternary, triad, tern; three names presented as candidates; a game at dice.
ternario, ria. I. *a.* ternary. **II.** *m.* three days' devotion.
terne, *m.* (coll.) bully, hector.
ternecico, ica, ito, ita, *a.* very tender.
ternejal, *a.* bullying.
ternejón, na, *a.* = TERNERÓN.
ternera, *f.* female calf; veal.
ternerico, ca; illo, lla; ito, ta, *n. dim.* young or little calf.
ternero, *m.* male calf.
ternerón, na, *a.* sentimental, easily moved.
terneruela, *f. dim.* suckling calf.
terneza, *f.* softness, suavity; tenderness; affection, endearment, fondness.
ternezuelo, la, *a. dim.* very tender.
ternilla, *f.* gristle, cartilage; nose or nostrils of an ox or other similar animal.—**llevar,** or **tener, de la t.,** to lead by the nose.
ternilloso, sa, *a.* gristly, cartilaginous.
ternísimo, ma, *a. super.* very tender.
terno, *m.* ternary, triad; suit of clothes; tern (in lottery); oath, curse; (eccl.) vestments for the high mass; (jewelry) set; (print.) three printed sheets one within another.—**t. seco, happy** and unexpected fortune.
ternura, *f.* tenderness, softness, fondness.
terpeno, *m.* (chem.) terpene.—**terpina,** *f.* terpin.—**terpinol,** *m.* terpineol.
terquedad, *f.* stubbornness, obstinacy.
terracota, *f.* terra cotta.
terrada, *f.* bitumen made of ochre and glue.
terradillo, *m. dim.* small terrace.
terrado, *m.* terrace; flat roof of a house.
terraja, *f.* pipe stock, screw stock, diestock; screw-cutting machine; modelling board, sweep.
terraje, *m.* rent paid for arable land.
terrajero, *m.* lessee of arable land.
terral, *m.* land breeze.
terramicina, *f.* (pharm.) terramycin.
terrapene, *m.* (zool.) terrapin.
terraplén, terrapleno, *m.* embankment; (Ry.) embankment; (fort.) terreplein, banquette.
terraplenar, *va.* to embank; to fill: to terrace.
terraplenador, *m.* laborer on embankments.
terráqueo, quea, *a.* terraqueous, terrestrial.
terrateniente, *n.* landowner, landholder.
terraza, *f.* terrace; border in a garden; glazed jar with two handles.
terrazgo, *m.* arable land; rent of arable land.
terrazguero, ra, *n.* lessee of arable land.
terrazo, *m.* (art) ground of a picture.
terrazuela, *f. dim.* of TERRAZA.
terrear, *vn.* to show the ground (as thin crops).
terrecer, *va.* to terrify.
terregoso, sa, *a.* full of clods, lumps of earth.

terremoto, *m.* earthquake.
terrenal, *a.* worldly, earthly, mundane.
terrenidad, *f.* quality of the soil.
terreno, na. I. *a.* earthly, terrestrial; worldly, mundane. **II.** *m.* land, ground, soil, terrene; piece of land, lot, plot; field, sphere of action; (geol.) terrane or terrain.—**t. abierto,** (mil.) open ground.—**t. franco,** (min.) tract not yet preëmpted or condemned.
térreo, rea, *a.* earthy, of soil.
terrera, *f.* steep piece of ground; (ornith.) lark.
terrero, ra. I. *a.* earthy; abject, humble; skimming the ground (as birds). **II.** *m.* terrace; mound, heap of earth; alluvium; (min.) dump; mark, target; basket for carrying earth.—**hacer t.,** to court a lady from the street before her house.
terrestre, *a.* terrestrial.
terrezuela, *f. dim.* small piece of ground; poor soil.
terribilidad, *f.* terribleness, awfulness; rudeness, fierceness.
terrible, *a.* terrible; rude, ill-tempered; (coll.) immense, huge; wonderful.
terriblemente, *adv.* terribly, frightfully.
terriblez, terribleza, *f.* = TERRIBILIDAD.
terrícola, *n.* inhabitant of the earth.
terrífico, ca, *a.* terrific, frightful.
terrígeno, na, *a.* terrigenous, earthborn.
terrino, na, *a.* earthy, of soil.
territorial, *a.* territorial.
territorialidad, *f.* territoriality.
territorio, *m.* territory; region; land.—**t. fideicometido,** trust territory.
terrizo, za. I. *a.* earthy, earthen. **II.** *m.* unglazed earthen tub.
terromontero, *m.* hill, hillock.
terrón, *m.* clod; mound; lump; bagasse of olives.—*pl.* landed property.—**a rapa t.,** entirely, completely, from the root.—**azúcar en t.,** lump sugar.
terroncillo, *m. dim.* small clod or lump.
terror, *m.* terror.—**terrorífico, ca,** *a.* terrific, frightful, dreadful.—**terrorismo,** *m.* terrorism.—**terrorista,** *n.* & *a.* terrorist(-ic).
terrosidad, *f.* earthiness, cloddiness.
terroso, sa, *a.* earthy; full of clods.
terruca, *f. dim.* (coll.) native country.
terruño, terruzo, *m.* piece of ground.
tersar, *va.* to smooth, polish, burnish.
tersidad, *f.* polish; terseness.
terso, sa, *a.* smooth, polished, glossy; pure, correct, terse, pithy.—**tersura,** *f.* smoothness, polish; cleanliness, purity, terseness.
tertil, *m.* ancient tax on silk.
tertulia, *f.* tertulia, social gathering for conversation or entertainment; party; conversation; (theat.) corridor.—**hacer t.,** to gather for conversation; to talk (esp. disturbing, as in an office).—**tertuliano, na,** *n.* one who attends a TERTULIA or makes TERTULIA.—**tertuliar,** *vn.* = HACER TERTULIA.
tertulio, lia; tertulista, *n.* = TERTULIANO.
teruelo, *m.* balloting urn or box.
teruncio, *m.* an ancient Roman coin.
terutero, *m.* (ornith.) terutero, a S. A. lapwing.
terzón, na, *a.* & *n.* three-year old (heifer).
terzuela, *f.* distribution gained for attending mass at the hour of tierce.
terzuelo, *m.* third part; male falcon.
tesálico, ca; tesaliense; tesalio, lia; tésalo, la, *n.* & *a.* Thessalian.
tesalonicense; tesalónico, ca, *a.* Thessalonian.
tesar. I. *va.* (naut.) to haul taut, to make taut. **II.** *vn.* (of oxen) to back, pull back.
tesauro, *m.* thesaurus, lexicon.
tesela, *f.* tessella, mosaic tile.
teselado, da, *a.* tessellate, tessellated.
tésera, *f.* tessera, token, countersign.
tesis, *f.* thesis, dissertation.
tesitura, *f.* (mus.) range of voice or instrument.
teso, sa. I. *a.* taut, drawn tight. **II.** *m.* brow of a hill; bulge or lump on a flat surface.
tesón, *m.* tenacity, firmness, inflexibility.
tesonería, *f.* obstinacy, stubbornness.
tesonero, ra, *a.* (Am.) persistent, tenacious.
tesorería, *f.* treasury, treasurer's office, exchequer; treasurership.
tesorero, ra, *n.* treasurer; (eccl.) canon who keeps the relics.
tesoro, *m.* treasure; treasury, exchequer; thesaurus, lexicon.
tespíades, *f. pl.* (poet.) the Muses.
testa, *f.* head; top or crown of the head; front, face, forepart; (coll.) brains, cleverness.—**t. coronada,** crowned head.—**t. de ferro** = TESTAFERRO.
testáceo, cea, *a.* & *m.* (zool.) crustacean.
testación, *f.* obliteration, erasure.
testada, *f.* = TESTARADA.
testado, da. I. *pp.* of TESTAR. **II.** *a.* testate.
testador, ra, *n.* testator.
testadura, *f.* obliteration, erasure.
testaférrea, testaferro, *m.* man of straw, dummy, figurehead.
testamentaría, *f.* (law) testamentary execution; estate; meeting of executors.
testamentario, ria. I. *a.* testamentary. **II.** *m.* executor. **III.** *f.* executrix.
testamento, *m.* testament, will.—**t. abierto,** nuncupative will.—**t. cerrado,** or **escrito,** sealed testament.—**t. nuncupativo,** nuncupative will.—**t. ológrafo,** holographic will.
testar. I. *vn.* to make a will or testament. **II.** *va.* to erase, scratch out.
testarada, *f.* blow with the head; stubbornness, obstinacy.
testarrón, na, *a.* (coll.) stubborn.—**testarronería** (coll.), **testarudez,** *f.* hardheadedness, stubbornness.
testarudo, da, *a.* stubborn, hardheaded.
teste, *m.* (anat.) testis, testicle.
testera, *f.* front face, fore part; forehead of an animal; crownpiece of a harness; back seat of a coach; (foundry) wall of a furnace.
testerada, *f.* = TESTARADA.
testero, *m.* = TESTERA; (min.) ore rock showing two faces.
testicular, *a.* testicular.
testículo, *m.* (anat.) testicle.
testificación, *f.* attestation, testification.
testificador, ra, *n.* testifier.
testificante, *a.* witnessing, attesting.
testificar, *va.* (*pret.* TESTIFIQUÉ; *subj.* TESTIFIQUE) to attest, witness, testify.
testificata, *f.* (law) affidavit.
testificativo, va, *a.* attesting, declaratory.
testifiqué, testifique, *v. V.* TESTIFICAR.
testigo. I. *n.* witness.—**t. de cargo,** witness for the prosecution.—**t. de descargo,** witness for the defense.—**t. de oídas,** auricular witness.—**t. de vista,** or **ocular,** eyewitness. **II.** *m.* testimony, proof, evidence; mound of earth along an excavation (to show amount of earth removed).
testimonial, *a.* of the nature of testimony, attesting.—**testimoniales,** *f. pl.* testimonial; (eccl.) certificate of good character.
testimoniar, *va.* to attest, bear witness to.
testimoniero, ra, *a.* bearing false witness; dissembling, hypocritical.
testimonio, *m.* testimony; affidavit; attestation.—**falso t.,** (law) perjury.
testimoñero, ra, *a.* hypocritical.
testón, *m.* silver coin having a head.
testosterona, *f.* (biochem.) testosterone.
testudíneo, nea, *a.* (zool.) testudinal.
testudo, *m.* (mil.) testudo, movable shelter.
testuz, testuzo, *m.* (of some animals) nape; (of others) forehead.
tesura, *f.* stiffness, tautness.
teta, *f.* teat, mammary gland, breast; nipple, dug, udder.—**t. de vaca,** conical meringue; (bot.) viper's grass; a kind of grape.—**dar la t.,** to nurse, to suckle.
tetánico, ca, *a.* (med.) tetanic(al).

tétano, tétanos, *m.* (med.) tetanus, lockjaw.
tetar, *va.* to suckle.
tetera, *f.* teapot.
tetero, *m.* (Am.) nursing bottle.
tetica, *f. dim.* small dug or teat.
tetigonia, *f.* (entom.) a variety of katydid.
tetilla, *f. dim.* small nipple or teat (as man's).
tetón, *m.* stub of a pruned limb.
tetrácido, *m.* (chem.) tetracid.
tetracloruro, *m.* (chem.) tetrachloride.—**t. de carbono,** (chem.) carbon tetrachloride.
tetracordio, *m.* (mus.) tetrachord, fourth.
tetradínamo, ma, *a.* (bot.) tetradynamous; (chem.) tetravalent, quadrivalent.
tetraédrico, ca, *a.* (geom.) tetrahedral.
tetraedro, *m.* (geom.) tetrahedron.
tetragonal, *a.* (geom.) tetragonal.
tetrágono, *m.* (geom.) tetragon.
tetragrama, *m.* (mus.) four-line staff.
tetragrámaton, *m.* tetragram, word of four letters; tetragrammaton.
tetralogía, *f.* tetralogy.
tetrámetro, tra, *m.* & *a.* (pros.) tetrameter.
tetrao, *m.* (zool.) capercaillie, wood grouse.
tetrarca, *m.* tetrarch.
tetrarquía, *f.* tetrarchate; tetrarchy.
tetrasílabo, ba, *a.* four-syllable (word).
tetrastilo, *m.* (arch.) tetrastyle.
tetratómico, ca, *a.* (chem.) tetratomic.
tetravalente, *a.* (chem.) tetravalent, quadrivalent.
tétrico, ca, *a.* sad, grave, sullen; dark, gloomy.
teucali, *m.* = TEOCALI.
teucrio, *m.* (bot.) germander.
teucro, cra, *a.* & *n.* Trojan.
teutón, tona. I. *a.* Teutonic. **II.** *n.* Teuton.
teutónico, ca. I. *a.* Teutonic. **II.** *m.* Teutonic language.
textil, *a.* textile; fibrous.
texto, *m.* text; quotation; textbook; (print.) great primer type.
textorio, ria, *a.* textile.
textual, *a.* textual.—**textualista,** *m.* textualist.
textualmente, *adv.* textually, verbatim.
textura, *f.* texture; weaving; construction (of a literary work); structure.
tez, *f.* complexion (of the face).
tezado, da, *a.* very black.
tezontle, *m.* (Mex.) porous building stone.
theta, *f.* theta (Greek letter).
ti, *pron. 2d. pers. sing.* (oblique case of TÚ) thee; (when on familiar terms with a person) you.
tía, *f.* aunt; (coll.) good old woman.—**t. abuela,** great-aunt.—**cuéntaselo a tu t.,** (coll.) tell it to the marines.—**no hay tu t.,** it's no use, it's no good, it doesn't help.—**quedarse para t.,** to be always a bridesmaid and never a bride.
tialina, *f.* (chem.) ptyalin.
tialismo, *m.* (med.) ptyalism.
tiamina, *f.* (biochem.) thiamine.
tiangue, tianguis, *m.* (Mex. and P. I.) market, market days.
tiara, *f.* tiara, Pope's mitre; pontificate, papal dignity; Persian headdress.
tiberio, *m.* (coll.) noise, hubbub, turmoil.
tibetano, na, *n.* & *a.* Tibetan.
tibia, *f.* (anat.) tibia, shin bone; (mus.) flute or pipe.
tibial, *a.* tibial.
tibieza, *f.* tepidity, lukewarmness; coolness.
tibio, bia, *a.* tepid, lukewarm; remiss.
tibor, *m.* large china jar; (Am.) chamberpot.
tiborna, *f.* toast soaked in oil.
tiburón, *m.* (ichth.) shark.
tic, *m.* (med.) tic.
tictac, *m.* ticking (of watch, etc.).
[1]**tiemblo,** *m.* aspen tree.
[2]**tiemblo, tiemble,** *v. V.* TEMBLAR.
tiempo, *m.* time (as by the clock); time, times, period, epoch; (mus.) tempo; (gram.) tense; weather.—**t. atrás,** some time ago.—**t. cargado,** (naut.) thick, hazy weather.—**t. contrario,** (naut.) foul weather.—**t. crudo,** bleak, raw weather.—**t. grueso,** hazy weather.—**t. ha,** a long time ago.—**t. medio,** (astr.) mean time.—**t. normal,** standard time.—**t. solar verdadero,** or **t. verdadero,** (astr.) solar time. —**abrir,** or **alzarse, el t.,** to clear up.—**andando el t.,** in time, in the course of time, in the long run.—**a su t.,** at the proper time, in due time.—**a t.,** timely, in, or on, time.—**a t. que,** just as.—**a tiempos,** at times, occasionally.—**a un,** or **al, mismo t., a un t.,** at one, at the same, time.—**cargarse el t.,** to cloud over.—**con el t.,** in time, given time.—**cuánto t.,** how long.—**dar t. al t.,** to bide one's time, to wait patiently.—**de t. en, t.,** from time to time, now and then, occasionally.—**en otro t.,** or **en otros tiempos,** formerly, in other, or former, times.—**en t.,** on time, at the proper time.—**engañar el t.** = HACER EL T.—**fuera de t.,** out of season; inopportunely.—**gan r t.,** to save time.—**hace t.,** or **tiempos,** long ago; for a long time.—**hace t. que,** it is a long time since.—**hacer el t.,** to kill time, while away the time.—**haga buen o mal t.,** rain or shine.—**los buenos tiempos,** the good, old days.—**matar el t.** = HACER EL T.—**mucho t.,** a long time.—**perder el t.,** to waste time.—**poco t.,** a short time.—**por t.,** for some time.—**tomarse t.,** to take time, to defer.—**un t.,** formerly, in other times.
tienda, *f.* shop, store; tent; (naut.) awning; tilt. —**t. de antigüedades,** antique shop.—**t. de campaña,** (mil.) tent.—**t. de descuento,** discount house.—**t. de juguetes,** toy shop.—**t. de oxígeno,** (med.) oxygen tent.—**t. en cadena,** chain store.—**ir de tiendas,** to go shopping.
tiendo, tienda, *v. V.* TENDER.
tiene, tienen, *v. V.* TENER.
tienta, *f.* (surg.) probe, bougie; cleverness, sagacity.—**andar a tientas,** to grope in the dark; to fumble.—**a tientas,** in a groping manner.
tientaaguja, tientaguja, *f.* boring rod.
tientaparedes, *n.* groper.
[1]**tiento,** *m.* touch, act of feeling; blind man's stick; halter of a mill horse; circumspection, tact; tightrope walker's balancing pole; steady hand; (coll.) blow, cuff; (art) maulstick; (mus.) preliminary flourish (before beginning to play); (zool.) tentacle.—**a t.,** obscurely, doubtfully.—**con t.,** tactfully, cautiously.—**dar un t.,** to make a trial.—**perder el t.,** to get out of practice, to get rusty.—**por el t.,** by the touch.—**tomar el t. a,** to investigate, look into.
[2]**tiento, tiente,** *v. V.* TENTAR.
tiernamente, *adv.* tenderly.
tiernecico, ica, illo, illa, ito, ita, *a. dim.* of TIERNO; very tender or young.
tierno, na, *a.* tender, soft; delicate; affectionate, amiable; sensitive; recent, modern, young.—**t. de ojos,** tender-eyed.
tierra, *f.* earth; land; soil; ground; native country; region, country; lot, plot, piece of land; (elec.) ground.—*pl.* lands, parts, region.—**t. adentro,** inland.—**t. a t.,** (naut.) coasting; cautiously.—**t. de almáciga,** foster earth.—**t. de batán,** fuller's earth.—**t. del sol de media noche,** Land of the Midnight Sun, Norway.—**t. del sol naciente,** Land of the Rising Sun, Japan.—**t. de moldeo,** molding earth, loam.—**t. de pan llevar,** cornland, plowland.—**t. de pipas,** pipe clay.—**T. de Promisión,** Promised Land.—**t. desconocida,** terra incognita.—**t. de sombra,** umber. —**t. doblada,** broken, mountainous country.—**t. fértil,** fat land.—**t. firme,** terra firma; firm, solid ground.—**t. japónica,** catechu, Japan earth.—**t. pantanosa,** bog land.—**t. rara,** (chem.) rare earth.—**T. Santa,** Holy

Land.—**tierras árticas,** Arctica.—**tierras baldías,** public lands, public domain.—**t. vegetal,** vegetable mold.—**t. virgen,** virgin soil. —**a t.,** ashore.—**besar la t.,** (coll.) to fall flat on the ground, bite the dust.—**dar en t. con,** to overthrow.—**echar en t.,** (naut.) to land.—**echar por t.,** to overthrow; to ruin, destroy.—**echar t. a,** to hush up, forget, drop (a matter). —**en t.,** on land; ashore.—**irse a t.,** to fall down, to topple over.—**poner por t.,** to overthrow; to demolish, to tear down.—**por esas (estas) tierras,** thereabouts (hereabouts), in those (these) parts.—**por t.,** by land, overland. —**tomar t.,** to anchor; to land.—**venirse a t.,** = IRSE A. T.—**ver tierras,** to see the world, travel.

tiesamente, *adv.* firmly, stiffly, strongly.

[1]**tieso, sa,** *a.* stiff, hard; robust, strong; valiant; stubborn, obstinate; tight, taut; stiff, stuck up; too grave or circumspect.—**tenerse t.,** or **tenérselas tiesas,** (coll.) to be firm in one's opinion or resolution.

[2]**tieso,** *adv.* = TIESAMENTE.

tiesta, *f.* edge of headings (of barrels).

tiesto, *m.* potsherd; flowerpot.

tiesura, *f.* stiffness; rigidity; harshness.

tifáceo, a, *a.* (bot.) typhaceous.

tífico, ca, *a.* (med.) typhous.

tiflitis, *f.* (med.) typhlitis.

[1]**tifo,** *m.* (med.) typhus.—**t. asiático,** Asiatic cholera.—**t. de América,** yellow fever.—**t. de Oriente,** bubonic plague.

[2]**tifo, fa,** *a.* (coll.) satiate.

tifoideo, dea. I. *a.* typhoid. **II.** *f.* typhoid fever.

tifón, *m.* whirlwind; typhoon.

tifoso, sa, *a.* (med.) typhous.

tifus, *m.* (med.) typhus.—**t. icterodes,** yellow fever.

tigra, *f.* (Am.) (zool.) female tiger.

tigre, *m.* (zool.) tiger.

tigridia, *f.* (bot.) tigridia, tiger flower.

tija, *f.* stem of a key.

tijera, *f.* (*usually in pl.*) scissors; shears; carpenter's horse; cooper's mare; any instrument in the form of an X; sawbuck; small channel or drain; sheepshearer; backbiter, slanderer.—*pl.* side stringers of a truck frame; beams across a river to stop floating timber.—**buena t.,** a great eater; good cutter; detractor, gossip.—**cama de t.,** folding bed, cot.—**hacer t.,** (of horses) to twist the mouth.

tijerada, *f.* = TIJERETADA.

tijereta, *f. dim.* (gen. *pl.*) small scissors; small tendril of vines; (entom.) earwig; (ornith.) forktail duck.

tijeretada, *f.*, **tijeretazo,** *m.* a cut with scissors, clip, snip.

tijeretear, *va.* to cut with scissors; clip; to meddle with, or mind (other people's business).

tijereteo, *m.* act of clipping; noise of scissors cutting.

tijerilla, tijeruela, *f. dim.* small scissors; small tendril of vines.

tila, *f.* (bot.) linden tree; flower of this tree; tea of linden flowers.

tílburi, *m.* (Angl.) tilbury, a kind of carriage.

tildar, *va.* to cross or scratch out; to put a tilde over; to brand, stigmatize, criticize.—**t. de,** to accuse of, or charge with being (incompetent, etc.).

tilde, *f.* tilde, diacritical sign of the letter *ñ*; tittle, dash, jot, iota; bad name.

tildón, *m. aug.* dash, stroke, scratch.

tilia, *f.* (bot.) = TILO.

tiliáceo, cea, *a.* (bot.) tiliaceous.

tilichero, ra, *n.* (Am.) peddler, huckster.

tiliches, *m. pl.* (Am.) small fancy articles.

tilín, *m.* dingdong, sound of a bell.—**hacer t.,** (coll.) to please; to become a favorite.—**tener t.,** to be winsome, attractive.

tilma, *f.* (Mex.) cloak fastened by a knot.

tilo, *m.* (bot.) linden tree.

tilonorinco, *m.* (ornith.) bower bird.

tilla, *f.* (naut.) midship, gangway.

tillado, *m.* wooden floor.

tillar, *va.* to floor, furnish with a floor.

timador, ra, *n.* swindler.

tímalo, *m.* (ichth.) grayling.

timar, *va.* to cheat, to swindle.

timba, *f.* (coll.) hand in a game of chance; (P. I.) bucket.

timbal, *m.* = ATABAL, kettledrum.

timbalero, *m.* kettledrummer.

timbirimba, *f.* (coll.) hand in a game of chance.

timbrar, *va.* to stamp; to put the crest in (a coat of arms).

timbre, *m.* (her.) timber, crest; seal, stamp; call bell; timbre, tone, color; glorious deed or achievement; merit.

timeleáceo, cea, *a.* (bot.) thymelæaceous.

timiama, *f.* a sweet perfume.

tímidamente, *adv.* timidly.

timidez, *f.* timidity; bashfulness.

tímido, da, *a.* timid, shy; faint-hearted.

[1]**timo,** *m.* (ichth.) = TÍMALO, grayling.

[2]**timo,** *m.* (coll.) cheat, swindle.—**dar un t., to** swindle.

[3]**timo,** *m.* (anat.) thymus, thymus gland.

timocracia, *f.* (pol.) timocracy.

timocrático, ca, *a.* (pol.) timocratic.

timol, *m.* (chem.) thymol.

timón, *m.* beam of a plow; pole of a coach; stick of a rocket; (naut.) helm; rudder.—**t. de profundidad,** (aer.) elevator.

timonear, *va.* & *vn.* (naut.) to helm; to steer.

timonel, *m.* (naut.) helmsman, steersman.

timonera, *f.* (naut.) pilot house, wheelhouse; (ornith.) rectrix, large tail feather.

timonero, *m.* helmsman, steersman.

timorato, ta, *a.* God-fearing; timorous, chicken-hearted, pusilanimous.

timpa, *f.* bar of iron in a furnace hearth.

timpánico, ca, *a.* (anat.) tympanic.

timpanillo, *m. dim.* small kettledrum; small tympanum or tympan; (print.) inner tympan; (arch.) gablet.

timpanítico, ca, *a.* (med.) tympanitic.

timpanitis, *f.* (med.) tympanitis.

tímpano, *m.* kettledrum; (anat.) tympanum, eardrum; (print.) tympan; (arch.) tympan or tympanum, pediment.

tina, *f.* large earthen jar; vat; tub; bathtub.

tinaco, *m.* wooden trough, tub, or vat.

tinada, *f.* woodpile; shed for cattle.

tinado, tinador, *m.* shed for cattle.

tinaja, *f.* large earthen jar; (P. I.) a liquid measure (about 12⅔ gal.).

tinajería, *f.* place where large earthen jars are kept or sold.

tinajero, ra. I. *n.* maker or seller of earthen water jars. **II.** *m.* stand or cabinet for earthen water jars; (Mex.) water hole, pothole.

tinajita, uela, *f. dim.* small earthen water jar.

tinajón, *m. aug.* very large earthen water jar, or tank.

tinamú, *m.* (ornith., Am.) tinamou.

tindalo, *m.* (P. I.) tindalo, a hardwood tree.

tinelar, *a.* pertaining to the TINELO.

tinelero, ra, *n.* keeper of the servants' room.

tinelo, *m.* servants' dining room.

tineta, *f. dim.* kit, small tub.

tinge, *m.* (ornith.) a kind of black owl.

tingladillo, *m.* (naut.) clinker work.

tinglado, *m.* shed, shed roof; temporary board floor; inclined plane for draining sugar; trick, machination, intrigue.

tingle, *f.* glaziers' lead opener.

tinicla, *f.* (armor) sort of hauberk.

tiniebla, *f.* (gen. *pl.*) darkness; (eccl.) tenebræ.

tinillo, *m.* tank for collecting must.

[1]**tino,** *m.* skill in discovering things by the touch; steady and accurate aim; judgment, tact, knack.—**a buen t.,** at guesswork.—**sacar de t.,** to astound, confound, exasperate.—**sin t.,** immoderately; incessantly.

[2]**tino,** *m.* receptacle; dye vat; tank.

tinta, *f.* ink; tint, hue, color; process of dyeing.—*pl.* (art) colors prepared for painting.—**t. china**; India ink.—**t. de imprenta,** printing ink.—**t. simpática,** invisible ink.—**de buena t.,** from, or on, good authority.
tintar, *va.* to tinge, to dye.
tinte, *m.* dyeing, staining; tint, hue; paint, color, stain; dye; dyer's shop; (fig.) cloak, color.
tinterillada, *f.* chicane, trickery, tricky procedure.
tinterillo, *m. dim.* small inkstand; (Am.) (coll.) pettifogger; (Am.) shyster lawyer.
tintero, *m.* inkstand, inkwell; (print.) ink fountain, ink table.—**dejar, dejarse,** or **quedársele a uno, en el t.,** (coll.) to forget completely.
tintilla, *f.* rota wine.
tintillo, *m. dim.* light-colored wine.
tintín, *m.* clink, chink.
tintinar, tintinear, *vn.* to tinkle.
tintineo, *m.* = TINTÍN.
tintirintín, *m.* sharp sound of a trumpet.
tinto, ta. I. *pp. irreg.* of TEÑIR. **II.** *a.* wine-colored; black, strong (coffee); & *m.* red (wine).
tintóreo, rea, *a.* tinctorial, pert. to color.
tintorería, *f.* dyer's shop.
tintorero, ra. I. *n.* dyer. **II.** *f.* (Am.) (ichth.) female shark.
tintura, *f.* tincture; tint, color; stain, spot; dyeing; dye; rouge; smattering.
tinturar, *va.* to tinge, to dye; to tincture; to teach superficially.
tiña, *f.* (med.) scald head, ringworm of the scalp, favus; small spider that injures beehives; (coll.) want, indigence; niggardliness, stinginess.
tiñería, *f.* (coll.) poverty; stinginess.
tiño, tiñó, tiña, *v. V.* TEÑIR.
tiñoso, sa, *a.* scabby, scurvy; penurious; niggardly, stingy, mean.
tiñuela, *f.* (bot.) dodder; (naut.) shipworm.
tío, *m.* uncle; (coll.) good old man; fellow, guy.—**t. abuelo,** great-uncle.
tiocol, *m.* (chem.) thiocol.
tiónico, ca, *a.* (chem.) thionic.
tiorba, *f.* (mus.) theorbo, large lute.
tiosulfato, *m.* (chem.) thiosulfate.—**t. de sodio,** (chem.) sodium thiosulfate.
tiosulfúrico, ca, *a.* thiosulfuric.
tiovivo, *m.* carrousel, merry-go-round.
tipa, *f.* (Am.) a hardwood tree.
tipiadora, *f.* typewriter, typewriter machine; typist.
típico, ca, *a.* typical, characteristic.
tiple. I. *m.* (mus.) treble, soprano voice; a kind of small guitar; (naut.) mast of a single piece. **II.** *n.* soprano singer.
tiplisonante, *a.* (coll.) treble-toned.
tipo, *m.* type, pattern; standard, model; (coll.) (of animal) build, (of person) figure, physique; (Am.) (com.) rate; (print.) type; (zool.) class; (coll., contempt.) fellow, guy.—**t. abierto,** (print.) extended type.—**t. alemán,** (print.) German text.—**t. común,** (print.) lightface.—**t. de interés,** (Am., com.) rate of interest.
tipografía, *f.* printing; printing shop; typography; typesetting.
tipográfico, ca, *a.* typographical.
tipógrafo, *m.* typographer; typesetter.
tipómetro, *m.* (print.) type gauge, type measure.
tipoy, *m.* (S. A.) a chemise-like garment.
típula, *f.* (entom.) crane fly, daddy-longlegs.
tiquet, tiquete, *m.* (Angl.) (Am.) (theat., Ry., etc.) ticket.
tiquín, *m.* (P. I.) bamboo pole used as oar.
tiquismiquis, *m. pl.* ridiculous or affected scruples or words.
tiquistiquis, *m.* (P. I.) bitterwood tree.
tira, *f.* long, narrow strip (of paper, cloth, etc.); (naut.) fall.—*pl.* (law) clerks' fees in appeal cases.
tirabala, *m.* popgun.
tirabeque, *m.* (agr.) tender peas.
tirabotas, *f.* boot hook.
tirabraguero, *m.* (med.) truss.
tirabuzón, *m.* corkscrew; corkscrew-curl.
tiracol, tiracuello, *m.* (mil.) sword belt.
tirada, *f.* cast, throw; distance; stretch; lapse of time; (print.) edition, issue; presswork.—**t. aparte,** reprint (of an article in pamphlet form).—**de una t.,** or **en una t.,** at one stretch.
tiradera, *f.* long Indian arrow; trace (of harness).
tiradero, *m.* shooting post, place to shoot from.
tirado, da. I. *a.* long and low (ship); very cheap, given away. **II.** *m.* wiredrawing; (print.) presswork.
tirador, ra, *n.* thrower; drawer; sharpshooter; marksman, good shot; (mech.) lift, handle, pull, button, knob; bell pull; (print.) pressman.—**t. de oro,** gold-wire drawer.
tirafondo, *m.* (surg.) ball extractor; (carp.) wood screw.
tiralíneas, *m.* ruling pen.
tiramiento, *m.* tension, stretching.
tiramira, *f.* long, narrow ridge of mountains; long series or string of things.
tiramollar, *va.* (naut.) to ease off, to slacken.—**t. un aparejo,** to overhaul a tackle.
tirana, *f.* a Spanish song.
tiranamente, *adv.* tyrannically.
tiranía, *f.* tyranny.
tiránicamente, *adv.* tyrannically.
tiranicé, tiranice, *v. V.* TIRANIZAR.
tiranicida, *n.* tyrannicide (murderer).
tiranicidio, *m.* tyrannicide (murder).
tiránico, ca, *a.* tyrannical.
tiranización, *f.* tyrannizing.
tiranizadamente, *adv.* tyrannically.
tiranizar, *va.* (*pret.* TIRANICÉ; *subj.* TIRANICE) to tyrannize.
tirano, na. I. *a.* tyrannical. **II.** *n.* tyrant.
tirante. I. *a.* drawing, pulling; drawn, taut, tense, stretched; strained (as relations); urgent, pressing. **II.** *m.* trace, gear (of harness); (eng.) brace, stay rod, tie rod, truss rod; (carp.) 9 x 13 mm. board.—*pl.* suspenders, braces.—**a tirantes largos,** four-in-hand (vehicle or team).
tirantez, *f.* tenseness, tightness; stretch; strain; tension; distance in a straight line between the ends of a thing.
tiranuelo, la, *m.* & *f. dim.* little tyrant.
tirapié, *m.* shoemaker's stirrup.
tirar. I. *va.* to throw, cast, fling, pitch (as a ball); to cast off, throw away (as a garment); to fire, shoot (as a gun); to draw, to pull, stretch (as wire); to draw (a line); to waste, squander; to give (as a kick); (print.) to print.—**t. coces,** to kick; to rebel.—**t. de,** to pull, pull on.—**tirarla de,** to set up as.—**t. un cañonazo,** to fire a gun. **II.** *vn.* to draw, pull; to direct one's course, turn (in some direction); to get along, pull through; to incline, tend; (a) to have a shade (of), border (on) (a certain color); to approach; to try (to), aim (at), aspire (to).—**t. al blanco,** to shoot at a target.—**t. a los dados,** to shoot craps.—**t. de largo,** or **por largo,** to spend lavishly; to make a liberal estimate, to estimate rather high than low.—**tira y afloja,** give and take; fast and loose; blowing hot and cold. **III.** *vr.* to throw oneself; (of parachutist) to jump; to abandon oneself (to grief, vice, etc.).
tirela, *f.* striped stuff.
tireta, *f.* lace, latch, thong.
tirica, ita, *f. dim.* small stripe.
tirilla, *f.* neckband of a shirt.
tirio, ria, *a.* Tyrian.—**tirios y troyanos,** opposing factions.
tiritaña, *f.* a thin silk fabric; trifle.
tiritar, *vn.* to shiver.—**tiritón,** *m.* (coll.) shivering, chill.—**tiritona,** *f.* (coll.) shivering, especially affected.
tiro, *m.* cast, throw, shot, fling; mark made by a throw; (artil.) piece of ordnance; firing, shot, discharge (of a firearm); report (of a gun); target practice; shooting grounds; shooting gal-

lery; range; charge, shot; team of draught animals; harness trace; hoisting rope; length of a piece of drygoods; landing of a stairway; theft; prank, imposition; serious physical or moral injury; (min.) shaft; depth of a shaft; draught of a chimney.—*pl.* sword belts.—**t. al blanco,** target shooting.—**t. directo,** fire at a visible target.—**t. indirecto,** indirect fire.—**t. rasante,** horizontal fire.—**al t.,** (Am.) immediately, right away.—**a t. de ballesta,** a long way off; at a glance.—**a t. de piedra,** within a stone's throw.—**a tiros,** with shots, by shooting.—**de t.,** draft (horse).—**de tiros largos,** in full dress, in full regalia.—**errar el t.,** to miss the mark; to be mistaken.—**hacer un t.,** to fire a shot.—**hacer un tiro a,** to shoot at, have a shot at.—**¡lindo t.!,** good shot!—**ni a tiros,** (coll.) not for love or money, not by a long shot, absolutely not.

tirocinio, *m.* apprenticeship.

tiroideo, a, *a.*, **tiroides,** *m.* (anat.) thyroid.

tiroiditis, *f.* (med.) thyroiditis.

tirolés, sa. I. *n.* & *a.* Tyrolian. **II.** *m.* peddler, huckster in toys and tinware.

[1]**tirón,** *m.* pull, haul, tug; effort.—**de un t.,** at once, at one stroke.—**ni a dos tirones,** not easily obtained or carried out.

[2]**tirón,** *m.* tyro, novice.

tirona, *f.* fishing net, seine.

tiroriro, *m.* (coll.) sound of a reed instrument.—*pl.* (coll.) reed instruments.

tirotear, *vn.* & *vr.* to exchange shots, to skirmish.

tiroteo, *m.* skirmish.

tiroxina, *f.* (biochem.) thyroxine, thyroxin.

tirreno, na, *n.* & *a.* Thyrrhenian; Etruscan.

tirria, *f.* (coll.) aversion, dislike, grudge.

tirso, *m.* (bot. & Gk. myth.) thyrsus.

tisana, *f.* ptisan, medicinal tea.

tisanuro, ra. I. *n.* & *a.* (entom.) thysanuran. **II.** *m. pl.* Thysanura.

tísico, ca, *n.* & *a.* (med.) consumptive.

tisis, *f.* (med.) tuberculosis, consumption.

tisú, *m.* gold or silver tissue.

tisuria, *f.* (med.) debility from excessive secretion of urine.

titán, *m.* (myth.) Titan; **(t.)** (fig.) titan.

titanato, *m.* (chem.) titanate.

titánico, ca, *a.* (myth.) Titanic; (chem., fig.) titanic.

[1]**titanio, nia,** *a.* Titanic.

[2]**titanio,** *m.* (chem.) titanium.

títere, *m.* puppet; whipster, insignificant fellow.—*pl.* Punch-and-Judy show; pantomime.—**no dejar,** or **quedar, t. con cabeza,** to cut to pieces, to destroy or be destroyed entirely, to leave nothing, or nobody, to tell the tale.

titerero, ra, *n.* = TITIRITERO.

titeretada, *f.* mean trick.

titerista, *n.* = TITIRITERO.

tití, *m.* titi, a very small monkey.

titiaro, *a.* CAMBUR T., small, fine kind of banana.

titilación, *f.* tremor; twinkle.

titilador, ra; titilante, *a.* trembling; twinkling.

titilar, *vr.* to tremble; to twinkle.

titímalo, *m.* (bot.) spurge.

titirimundi, *m.* cosmorama.

titiritaina, *f.* (coll.) confused noise of flutes; noisy merriment.

titiritar, *vn.* to shiver with cold or fear.

titiritero, *m.* puppet player, puppet-show man.

tito, *m.* (bot.) a kind of chick-pea.

titubeante, *a.* tottering; hesitating.

titubear, *vn.* to totter (as walls); to toddle (as a child); to stagger, reel; to stutter; to hesitate.

titubeo, *m.* tottering; toddling; wavering, hesitation.

titulación, *f.* (chem.) titration.

titulado, da. I. *pp.* of TITULAR. **II.** *a.* so-called.

[1]**titular. I.** *va.* to title, entitle, name, call. **II.** *vn.* to obtain a title from a sovereign. **III.** *vr.* to call or style oneself. **IV.** *f.* headline.

[2]**titular,** *a.* titular; nominal; (print.) titular (type).

titulillo, *m. dim.* petty title; (print.) page heading or title, running title.—**andar en titulillos,** to stick to, or insist on, trifles and trivial forms.

título, *m.* title; heading, headline, caption; inscription; sign; titled person; soubriquet; qualification, merit, desert; claim; foundation of a claim, privilege or right; (law) legal title to property; diploma; patent; credential, license; professional degree; cause, reason, pretext; (com.) certificate, bond.—**t. al portador,** bond payable to bearer.—**t. nominativo,** registered bond.—**t. translativo de dominio,** (law) deed, conveyance.—**títulos de la deuda,** Government bonds.—**a t. (de),** under pretext; on the authority (of).

tiza, *f.* chalk; clay; calcined stag's horn; whiting.

tizna, *f.* substance for staining or blackening.

tiznadura, *f.* smudginess, smuttiness.

tiznajo, *m.* (coll.) smut, smudge, stain.

tiznar, *va.* to smut, smudge, stain; to tarnish.

tizne, *m.* or *f.* soot, coal smut, grime; stain.

tiznón, *m.* large smut, smudge, smear, or stain.

tizo, *m.* half-burnt charcoal.

tizón, *m.* brand, firebrand; (agr.) wheat crust, blight, stinking smut; stain, disgrace; (arch.) header.—**a t.,** as a header.

tizona, *f.* (coll.) sword.

tizonada, *f.* **tizonazo,** *m.* blow with a firebrand; (coll.) hell fire.

tizoncillo, *m. dim.* small burning coal.

tizonear, *vn.* to stir up a fire.

tizonera, *f.* heap of half-burnt charcoal.

tizonero, *m.* fire poker.

tlaco, *m.* (Mex.) eighth part of a Spanish silver shilling.

tlascalteca, *n.* & *a.* of or from Tlascala.

tlazol, tlazole, *m.* (Mex.) fodder of maize tops.

¡to! *interj.* used to call a dog.

toa, *f.* (Am.) rope, hawser.

toalla, *f.* towel; pillow sham.—**t. afelpada,** Turkish towel.

toallero, *m.* towel rack.

toalleta, *f. dim.* napkin; small towel.

toar, *va.* (naut.) = ATOAR, to tow.

toba, *f.* calcareous tufa, travertin, calc-sinter; (bot.) cotton thistle; (dent.) tophus, tartar.

tobáceo, cea, *a.* tufaceous.

toballa, *f.* towel.

toballeta, tobelleta, *f.* napkin.

tobar, *m.* tufa quarry.

tobera, *f.* tewel, tuyère (of a blast furnace).

tobillo, *m.* ankle.

tobogán, *m.* toboggan.

toca, *f.* hood, coif, bonnet, wimple, toque, headdress; thin fabric for toques.

tocable, *a.* touchable.

tocadiscos, *m.* record player or changer.

[1]**tocado, da. I.** *pp.* of [1]TOCAR. **II.** *a.* (fig.) touched (in the head); perturbed; tainted.—**estar t. de,** to have the symptoms or beginning of.—**estar t. de la cabeza,** to be of unsound mind.

[2]**tocado, da. I.** *pp.* of [2]TOCAR. **II.** *m.* coiffure, headdress, hairdo.—**t. de monja,** nun's wimple.

[1]**tocador, ra. I.** *n.* one who touches; (mus.) player, performer. **II.** *m.* tuning key.

[2]**tocador,** *m.* kerchief for the head; dressing table, bureau; dressing room, boudoir; dressing case.—**productos de t.,** toilet articles.

[1]**tocadura,** *f.* coiffure, headgear.

[2]**tocadura,** *f.* (vet.) sore, gall.

tocamiento, *m.* touch, feeling.

tocante. I. *pres. p.* of [1]TOCAR. **II.** *a* touching.—**t. a,** respecting, concerning, as regards, with regard to.

[1]**tocar. I.** *va.* (*pret.* TOQUÉ; *subj.* TOQUE) to touch, lay hands on, feel with the hand; play (an instrument); to toll, ring (a bell); (auto) to blow (a horn); to hit, knock, strike, rap, tap; to try (metals) on a touchstone; magnetize; to find out (as by experience); to get (one's share), draw (as a lottery prize); to touch upon; to inspire, move, persuade; communicate or infect.

—**t. de cerca,** to be closely related; know well from actual practice or experience; to concern, affect closely.—**t. fondo,** to strike ground.—**t. la diana,** (mil.) to beat the reveille.—**t. la generala,** (mil.) to beat the general.—**a toca teja,** (coll.) with ready money, cash down. **II.** *vn.* to touch; appertain, belong; behoove, concern; to be one's turn; to fall to one's share or lot; to touch, be contiguous; to stop (during a voyage); to be allied or related.—**t. a la bomba,** (naut.) to ring for pumping ship.—**t. a la puerta,** to rap at the door.—**t. en un puerto,** (naut.) to touch at a port.

[2]**tocar. I.** *va.* to comb and dress the hair with ornaments. **II.** *vr.* (coll.) to be covered, put on the hat; to comb and arrange the hair; to wimple.

tocasalva, *f.* tray or rack for glasses.

tocata, *f.* (mus.) toccata; (coll.) drubbing.

tocayo, ya, *n.* namesake.

tocé, toce, *v. V.* TOZAR.

tocía, *f.* =TUCÍA, tutty.

tocinera, *f.* (woman) pork seller; wife of pork seller; table for salting pork.

tocinero, *m.* pork seller.—**tocinería,** *f.* shop or stall where pork and bacon are sold.

tocino, *m.* bacon; salt pork.—**t. del cielo,** confection of eggs and sirup.—**t. gordo,** fat pork.

tocio, cia, *a.* low, dwarf (oak tree).

toco, *m.* a kind of rectangular niche in old Peruvian architecture.

tocología, *f.* tocology, obstetrics.

tocólogo, ga, *n.* tocologist, obstetrician.

tocón, *m.* stump of a tree, of an arm or leg.

toconal, *m.* olive yard planted with stumps.

tocororo, *m.* (ornith.) tocororo, a Cuban trogon.

tocotoco, *m.* (Venez.) (ornith.) pelican.

tocuyo, *m.* (S. A.) shirtings, sheetings.

tochedad, *f.* boorishness, rusticity.

tochimbo, *m.* (Peru) blast furnace.

tocho, cha. I. *a.* clownish, rustic, uncouth; unpolished, homespun. **II.** *m.* pole; (foundry) bloom, billet.

tochura, *f.* = TOCHEDAD.

todabuena, todasana, *f.* (bot.) St. John's-wort.

todavía, *adv.* still; yet; even.—**t. no,** not yet.

todito, ta, *a.* (coll.) the whole (emphatic, as, *todito el día,* the whole day long).

todo, da. I. *a.* & *n.* all, the whole, every, each.—**t. aquel que,** whoever.—**t. aquello que,** whatever.—**t. el mundo,** everybody.—**t. el que,** whoever, all that, all who.—**todos los,** every.—**todos los que,** all who, all those that. **II.** *m.* all; whole; everybody; everything.—*pl.* everybody; all.—**ante t.,** first of all, in the first place.—**así y t.,** in spite of, for all that.—**a t.,** at most, to the limit.—**con t.,** notwithstanding, nevertheless, however.—**del t.,** entirely, wholly.—**en t.,** all in all.—**en t. y por t.,** wholly, in every way.—**en un t.,** together, in all its parts.—**jugar el t. por el t.,** to stake or risk all.—**me es t. uno,** it's all one, or the same, to me.—**por t.,** in all.—**ser el t.,** to be the principal, chief, or whole thing.—**sobre t.,** above all, especially. **III.** *adv. m.* entirely, totally.

todopoderoso, sa, *a.* all-powerful, almighty.

toesa, *f.* toise, anc. French measure of length.

tofana, *f.* aqua Tofana (poison).

tofo, *m.* (vet.) tumor.

toga, *f.* Roman toga; judicial robe or gown.

togado, da, *a.* togaed.

Togo, *m.* Togo.

togolés, lesa, *n.* & *a.* Togolese.

toisón, toisón de oro, *m.* Golden Fleece.

tojal, *m.* clump of furze or whin.

tojino, *m.* (naut.) notch, knob; cleat.

tojo, *m.* (bot.) whin, furze.

tojosa, *f.* (Cuba) (ornith.) a variety of pigeon.

tola, *f.* (S. A.) Indian mound.

[1]**tolano,** *m.* (vet.) tumor in horses' gums.

[2]**tolano,** *m.* (gen. *pl.*) (coll.) short hair on the neck.

toldadura, *f.* awning, hanging.

toldar, *va.* to cover with awning or hanging.

toldería, *f.* (S. A.) Indian camp.

toldero, ra, *n.* retailer of salt.

toldilla, *f.* (naut.) roundhouse.

toldillo, *m. dim.* small awning; covered sedan chair.

toldo, *m.* awning; tarpaulin; ostentation, pomp; (S. A.) Indian hut; tent.

tole, *m.* hubbub, clamor, outcry.—**tomar el t.,** (coll.) to run away, to flee.

toledano, na, *n.* & *a.* Toledan.

toledo, *m.* (C. A.) a song bird.

tolerable, *a.* tolerable, bearable; permissible.

tolerablemente, *adv.* tolerably.

tolerancia, *f.* toleration, permission; tolerance, indulgence; allowance, permissible discrepancy or variation.

tolerante, *a.* tolerant.—**tolerantismo,** *m.* doctrine of the freedom of worship.

tolerar, *vn.* to tolerate, endure, suffer, permit; to be indulgent, to overlook.

tolete, *m.* (naut.) thole, tholepin; (Am.) club, cudgel; (Colomb.) a kind of large rough boat.

tolidina, *f.* (chem.) tolidine, tolidin.

tolmera, *f.* ground where TOLMOS abound.

tolmo, *m.* isolated pillarlike rock, tor.

tolo, *m.* bump from a blow.

tolondro, dra. I. *a.* giddy, harebrained; reckless, rash. **II.** *m.* = TOLO.—**a topa t.,** rashly, recklessly.

tolondrón, na, *a.* & *m.* = TOLONDRO.—**a tolondrones,** with contusions or bruises; precipitately, giddily, by fits and starts.

tolteca, *n.* & *a.* Toltec.

toluato, *m.* (chem.) toluate.

tolueno, *m.* (chem.) toluene.

tolúico, ca, *a.* (chem.) toluic.

toluidina, *f.* (chem.) toluidine.

tolva, *f.* hopper, chute.

tolvanera, *f.* cloud of dust.

tolla, *f.* moss-covered bog; (Cuba) canoe-shaped trough.

tolladar, *m.* = ATOLLADERO, bog; difficulty.

tollina, *f.* (coll.) cudgeling.

[1]**tollo,** *m.* (ichth.) spotted dogfish; loin of a stag.

[2]**tollo,** *m.* blind (for hunting); quagmire, bog.

tollón, *m.* narrow passage, gorge.

toma, *f.* taking; take, receiving; (mil.) capture, seizure; dose of medicine; (hydraul.) intake; tap of a water main or electric wire; (print.) take.—**t. y daca,** give-and-take.

¡toma! *interj.* well, why, of course.

tomacorriente, *m.* (Arg., Chile) (elec.) socket; (Chile) (elec. car) trolley.

tomadero, *m.* handle, haft; tap, inlet.

tomador, ra, *n.* & *a.* taker(-ing), receiver(-ing); drinker(-ing); (*m.*) drawee.—*pl.* (naut.) ropebands, gaskets.

tomadura, *f.* catch, seizure, grip, hold, grasp, capture; portion of a thing taken at once.

tomaína, *f.* ptomaine.

tomajón, na, *n.* (coll.) one who takes frequently or accepts easily.

tomar. I. *va.* to take; to drink, to eat; to contract, acquire (as a habit); to hire, take (as a taxi); to take on, adopt (as customs); to take, assume (responsibility); to steal, take by stealth; follow, imitate, ape; to cover (the female); (in ball games) to call a halt in the throwing of (the ball).—**t. a bien (a mal),** to take (something said) the right (wrong) way.—**t. a broma,** to take as a joke.—**t. a cuestas,** to carry on one's back; to take upon oneself; to take charge of.—**t. al pie de la letra,** to take literally.—**t. a pechos,** to take to heart; undertake with too much zeal.—**t. asiento,** to take a seat, sit down.—**t. calor,** to get warm.—**t. cuentas,** to audit accounts, to take and examine accounts.—**t. el fresco,** to take the air.—**t. el pelo a,** (coll.) to banter, make fun of.—**t. el sol,** to take a sun bath.—**t. en cuenta,**

to take under advisement, consider.—**t. entre cejas,** to take a dislike to, get a grudge against. —**t. estado,** to change condition; to marry; to become a clergyman; to take the black veil. —**t. frío,** to catch cold.—**t. fuerzas,** to gather strength.—**t. la borla,** to graduate.—**tomarla con,** to oppose, antagonize; to pick on, have a grudge against.—**t. la delantera,** to excel; to get ahead; to go at the head.—**t. la mañana,** (Cuba) to take a morning drink.—**t. la puerta,** to go out of the house; be off.—**t. las de Villadiego,** to take to one's heels, "beat it."—**t. lengua,** or **lenguas,** to take tidings or signs.—**t. por,** to take for, consider.—**t. por su cuenta,** to take charge of, to attend to personally.—**t. razón,** to take a memorandum.—**t. resolución,** to resolve, decide. **II.** *vn.* to drink (liquor).—**t. por,** to turn to (the right, left), or into; to take, follow (a road, etc.). **III.** *vr.* to take; to get rusty (as metals).—**t. alas,** to take liberties.—**t. con,** to pick a quarrel with.—**t. del vino,** to become intoxicated, to get drunk.

tomatada, *f.* fried tomatoes.
tomatal, *m.* tomato patch or field.
tomate, *m.* tomato.
tomatera, *f.* tomato plant.
tomatero, ra, *n.* tomato raiser or seller.
tombac, *m.* tombac, alloy of copper and zinc.
tomento, *m.* coarse tow; (bot.) tomentum.
tomentoso, sa, *a.* (bot.) tomentose, tomentous.
tomiento, *m.* = TOMENTO.
tomillar, *m.* bed of thyme.
tomillo, *m.* (bot.) thyme.—**t. salsero,** (bot.) sweet marjoram.
tomín, *m.* tomin, third part of a drachm, Spanish weight; (Am.) a silver coin.
tominejo, ja, *n.* (ornith.) humming bird.
tomismo, *m.* Thomism.
tomista, *n.* & *a.* Thomist(-ic).
tomiza, *f.* bass rope.
tomo, *m.* volume, tome; bulk; importance, value, consequence.—**de t. y lomo,** of weight and bulk; of importance.
tomón, na, *a.* fond of taking.
ton, *m.*—**sin t. ni son,** without rhyme or reason.
tonada, *f.* tune, song.
tonadica, *f. dim.* short tune or song.
tonadilla, *f. dim.* (theat.) musical interlude.—**tonadillero,** *m.* writer of TONADILLAS.
tonal, *a.* (mus.) tonal.
tonalidad, *f.* (mus.) tonality.
tonante, *a.* thundering (Jupiter).
tonar, *vn.* to thunder.
tonca, *f.* (bot.) tonka bean.
tondino, *m.* (arch.) astragal.
tondo, *m.* (arch.) round molding.
tonel, *m.* cask, barrel; tun, pipe, butt; (naut.) an ancient measure of ships ($\frac{5}{6}$ ton).—**t. macho,** ton.
tonelada, *f.* ton; an ancient tonnage duty.—**t. de arqueo,** ton of capacity.—**t. de desplazamiento,** ton of displacement.—**t. de registro,** register ton.—**t. métrica,** metric ton, tonne.—**t. milla,** ton-mile.
tonelaje, *m.* tonnage, displacement; (com.) tonnage dues.
tonelería, *f.* cooperage, coopering; barrels or casks collectively; watercasks for a ship.
tonelero, *m.* copper, hooper.
tonelete, *m. dim.* little barrel; short skirt, kilt.
[1]**tonga,** *f.* (bot.) tonka bean.
[2]**tonga, tongada,** *f.* couch; tier, layer, stratum; lay, row, ledge, flake.
tongo, *m.* trick of a player or jockey, to lose for a bribe; "throwing it."
tonicidad, *f.* (physiol.) tonicity, tonus.
tónico, ca. I. *a.* tonic, strengthening; (gram.) accented or inflected. **II.** *m.* tonic. **III.** *f.* (mus.) keynote, tonic.
tonificador, ra; tonificante, *a.* tonic, strengthening.
tonificar, *va.* = ENTONAR, (med.) to tone up.
tonillo, *m.* singsong, monotonous tone.
tonina, *f.* (ichth.) fresh tunny; (ichth.) dolphin.
tono, *m.* tone; tune; (med.) tone, vigor, strength; (color) tone, shade; (mus.) tone; key, key tone; pitch; moving piece in a brass instrument, which modifies the tone; deportment, manner, social address; conceit.—**dar el t.,** to set the standard.—**darse t.,** to put on airs.—**(decir) en todos los tonos,** (to tell) in every possible way.—**gente de buen tono,** smart set.
tonsila, *f.* (anat.) tonsil.—**tonsilar,** *a.* tonsillar.
tonsilectomía, *f.* (surg.) tonsillectomy.
tonsilitis, *f.* (med.) tonsilitis.
tonsura, *f.* hair cutting; shearing, fleecing; (eccl.) tonsure.
tonsurado, *m.* (eccl.) tonsured man.
tonsurar, *va.* to cut the hair of; to shear, fleece; (eccl.) to tonsure.
tontada, *f.* nonsense; silliness, foolishness.
tontaina, *n.* fool, dolt.
tontamente, *adv.* foolishly, stupidly.
tontear, *vn.* to talk nonsense, to act foolishly; to fool.
tontedad, *f.* foolishness, silliness, nonsense.
tontera, tontería, *f.* = TONTEDAD.
tontillo, *m.* hoop skirt; bustle.
tontina, *f.* (com.) tontine.
tontivano, na, *a.* foolishly conceited.
tonto, ta. I. *a.* silly, foolish, stupid. **II.** *n.* fool, dunce, dolt.—**t. de capirote,** blockhead, great fool, idiot.—**a tontas y a locas,** without order, haphazard.—**hacerse el t.,** to play the fool.
tontuelo, la, *a.* & *n. dim.* little fool.
tontuna, *f.* foolishness.
toña, *f.* tip cat (boys' game); bat for the game.
toñil, *m.* straw on which fruit is laid to ripen.
toñina, *f.* fresh tunny fish.
¡top! *interj.* (naut.) hold! stop!
topacio, *m.* topaz.
topada, *f.* butt.
topadizo, za, *a.* (coll.) met, run into, by chance.
topador, ra, *n.* one that butts.
topar. I. *va.* to collide with, to run into or against; to meet with by chance; to find, run across; (naut.) to butt, abut, join. **II.** *vn.* to collide, butt, strike; at cards, to accept a bet; to depend (on), consist (in); to meet (with); to succeed, come out right.—**tope donde tope,** (coll.) strike where it will.
toparca, *m.* toparch, petty ruler.
toparquía, *f.* toparchy, petty state.
tope, *m.* butt, projecting part or end; top, summit; (mech.) stop, stop collar, stop plate; (Ry.) buffer; butt, collision, knock, bump; rub, difficulty; obstacle; scuffle, quarrel; (naut.) masthead, topmast head; butt end of a plank; topman.—**a t.** or **al t.,** end to end; butt (joint).—**hasta el t.,** or **los topes,** up to the top, or the brim.
topera, *f.* molehole.
topetada, *f.* butt by a horned animal; (coll.) bump, bumping.
topetar, *vn.* to butt; (**con**) to bump, strike, or knock (against); to meet by chance, run across.—**topetazo,** *m.* butt, knock, bump, blow, encounter, collision.—**topetón,** *m.* = TOPETADA; TOPETAZO.—**topetudo, da,** *a.* butting.
tópico, ca. I. *a.* topical. **II.** *m.* (med.) external application; (rhet.) topic, subject.
topil, *m.* (Mex.) constable.
topinada, *f.* (coll.) awkwardness, clumsiness.
topinaria, *f.* (med.) talpa, wen.
topinera, *f.* molehole; molehill.
[1]**topo,** *m.* (zool.) mole; (coll.) awkward person; dunce, dolt.
[2]**topo,** *m.* (C. A.) one league and a half.
topocho, cha, *a.* (Venez.) plump.
topografía, *f.* topography; surveying.
topográficamente, *adv.* topographically.
topográfico, ca, *a.* topographical.
topógrafo, *m.* topographer; surveyor.
toponimia, *f.* toponymy.
toque, *m.* touch, act of touching; peal, ringing (of

bells); (mil.) call; assay, touch, test (of metals); touchstone; trial, proof; aid, divine inspiration; point, gist, purport; (coll.) tap on a person; (art) fine stroke of the brush.—**t. de cornetas,** bugle call.—**t. de diana,** reveille.—**t. del alba,** bell ringing at daybreak.—**t. de luz,** light in a picture.—**t. de retreta,** tattoo (of drums).—**t. de tambor,** beat of a drum.—**dar un t. a,** to put to the test; to pump, throw out a feeler to.
toqué, toque, *v. V.* TOCAR.
toqueado, *m.* rhythmical noise of clapping hands, stamping feet, rapping with canes, etc.
toquería, *f.* collection of women's headdresses; business of making TOCAS, hoods, bonnets, etc.
toquero, ra, *n.* veil maker; headdress maker.
toqui, *m.* (Chile) Indian chief.
toquilla, *f. dim.* small headdress, bonnet or cap; hat band or ribbon; small triangular kerchief used by women on the head or neck; woollen knit shawl.
[1]**tora,** *f.* figure of a bull in artificial fireworks.
[2]**tora,** *f.* Jewish family tribute; Torah (Hebrew Pentateuch).
torácico, ca, *a.* (anat.) thoracic.
torada, *f.* drove of bulls.
toral. I. *a.* main, principal. **II.** *m.* unbleached yellow wax; (foundry) mold for copper bars; copper bar.
tórax, *m.* (anat.) thorax.
torbellino, *m.* whirlwind; rush, avalanche; vortex; (coll.) lively, hustling, restless person.
torca, *f.* cavern in mountains.
torcal, *m.* place where there are caves.
torcaz, torcaza, *f.* wild pigeon.
torce, *f.* each loop of a chain around the neck.
torcecuello, *m.* (ornith.) wryneck.
torcedero, ra. I. *a.* twisted. **II.** *m.* twisting mill.
torcedor, ra, *m.* twister, thread frame, twisting mill; anything that causes displeasure or grief. —**t. de tabaco,** cigar maker.
torcedura, *f.* twisting; sprain; small wine.
torcer. I. *va.* (*ind.* TUERZO; *subj.* TUERZA) to twist, twine, wind (as strands); to bend, deflect; to sprain (as a foot); to pervert (as justice); to distort, pervert, misconstrue; to dissuade, induce to change one's mind.—**no dar el brazo a t.,** to be obstinate. **II.** *vn.* to turn (to right or left). **III.** *vr.* to become dislocated or sprained; to go crooked or astray; (of wine) to turn sour; to cheat.
torcida, *f.* wick, lamp wick; daily ration given to the grinder in oil mills.
torcidamente, *adv.* obliquely, tortuously, crookedly.
torcidillo, *m.* twist silk.
torcido, da. I. *pp.* of TORCER. **II.** *a.* oblique, tortuous, crooked, bent.—**estar t. con uno,** to be on bad terms with one. **III.** *m.* twist of candied fruit; twisted silk, twist; (prov.) light, bad wine.
torcijón, *m.* gripes.
torcimiento, *m.* twist, twisting; sprain; entwining, winding; deflection, bend, warp, circumlocution or periphrasis.
torculado, da, *a.* screwed, screw-shaped.
tórculo, *m.* small press; rolling press.
tordella, *f.* (ornith.) a kind of large thrush.
tórdiga, *f.* strip of leather.
tordillo, lla, llejo, ja, *a.* grayish, grizzled.
tordo, da. I. *a.* dapple, gray. **II.** *m.* (ornith.) thrush, throstle.—**t. de agua,** (ornith.) reed thrush.—**t. loco,** (ornith.) solitary thrush.
toreador, *m.* bullfighter.
torear. I. *vn.* to fight bulls in the ring; to let a bull to cows. **II.** *va.* to fight (bulls); to banter, to provoke.—**toreo,** *m.* bullfighting.
torera, *f.* tight, unbuttoned jacket.
torería, *f.* (Cuba) boys' pranks; office of bullfighter.
torero, ra. I. *a.* pert. to bullfighters. **II.** *m.* bullfighter.
torés, *m.* (arch.) torus.
torete, *m. dim.* bullock; (coll.) puzzle, difficult matter; absorbing topic of conversation.
toréutico, ca, *a.* (art) toreutic.
torga, *f.* yoke for dogs or hogs.
torianita, *f.* (min.) thorianite.
torido, *m.* (chem.) thoride.
toril, *m.* pen for bulls before the fight.
[1]**torillo,** *m. dim.* little bull.
[2]**torillo,** *m.* dowel, dowel pin; (anat.) raphe.
torina, *f.* (chem.) thoria.
torio, *m.* (chem.) thorium.
toriondez, *f.* rut of cattle.
toriondo, da, *a.* (of cattle) rutting.
torita, *f.* (min.) thorite.
torloroto, *m.* shepherd's pipe or flute.
tormagal, *m.,* **tormellera,** *f.* place abounding in tors, pillarlike rocks.
tormenta, *f.* storm, tempest; hurricane; reverse, misfortune; heated discussion.
tormentario, ria, *a.* (artil.) projectile.
tormentila, *f.* (bot.) tormentil, septfoil.
tormentín, *m.* (naut.) jib boom.
tormento, *m.* torment, torture; rack; (mil.) battering ordnance.—**dar t.,** to torture, put to the rack.—**tormentoso, sa,** *a.* stormy, boisterous, turbulent; (naut.) laboring hard.
tormo, *m.* = TOLMO, tor, isolated steep rock.
torna, *f.* restitution, devolution; return; tap or drain.—*pl.* return, requital, recompense, restitution; coarse straw.
tornaboda, *f.* day after a wedding.
tornachile, *m.* (Mex.) thick pepper.
tornada, *f.* return from a journey; revisit; (poet.) envoy, l'envoi.
tornadera, *f.* two-pronged winnowing fork.
tornadizo, za, *n.* turncoat, deserter.
tornado, *m.* tornado.
tornadura, *f.* devolution, return; requital, recompense.
tornaguía, *f.* (com.) landing certificate.
tornamiento, *m.* turn, alteration, change.
tornapunta, *f.* (arch.) chock, wedge, shoe; stay, prop, shore, brace.
tornar. I. *va.* to return; restore; to turn (as one's brain); to change, alter.—**t. las espaldas,** to turn a cold shoulder. **II.** *vn.* to return, come back; to repeat, do again.—**t. por,** to defend, to protect. **III.** *vr.* (**en**) to change (into), to become.
tornasol, *m.* (bot.) sunflower; changeable or shot color; litmus.
tornasolado, da, *a.* changeable, shot (fabrics); iridescent.
tornasolar, *va.* to cause changes in the color of, to make iridescent.
tornátil, *a.* turned (in a lathe); changeable.
tornatrás, *n.* half-breed.
tornavía, *f.* (Ry.) turntable.
tornaviaje, *m.* return trip.
tornavirón, *m.* slap, box.
tornavoz, *m.* sounding board.
torneador, ra, *n.* turner; tilter at tournaments.
torneadura, *f.* lathe shavings.
torneante, *a.* tilting at tournaments.
tornear. I. *va.* & *vn.* to turn (in a lathe). **II.** *vn.* to make a turn, go around, wind round about; to tilt at tournaments; to meditate, muse.
torneo, *m.* tournament; contest.
tornera, *f.* doorkeeper of a nunnery.
tornería, *f.* turning; turnery.
tornero, *m.* turner; maker of lathes; messenger of a nunnery.
tornillero, *m.* (coll.) (mil.) deserter.
tornillo, *m.* screw, male screw; vise, clamp; (mil.) desertion.—**t. de alimentación,** feed screw.—**t. de aproximación,** (surv.) tangent screw.—**t. de banco,** vise, bench vise.—**t. de filete angular,** or **triangular,** V-threaded screw.—**t. de filete cuadrado,** square-threaded screw. —**t. de gota de sebo,** round-headed screw.—**t. de mano,** or **de orejas,** thumbscrew.—**t. de presión,** set screw, clamp screw.—**t. de rosca glosa,** conical V-threaded screw.—**t. de suje-**

ción = T. DE PRESIÓN.—**t. sin fin,** endless screw.—**faltarle a uno un t.,** (coll.) not to have much sense, "to have a screw loose."
torniquete, *m.* turnpike, turnstile; turnbuckle, swivel; bell crank; (surg.) tourniquet.
torniscón, *m.* slap, box.
torno, *m.* lathe; winch, windlass; whim (vertical winch); whisket; revolving dumbwaiter; brake of a carriage; turn of a river; spinning wheel; spindle; wheel; axletree; circumvolution, gyration.—**t. de hilar,** spinning wheel.—**en t.,** round about.—**en t. a,** or **de,** regarding, about, in connection with.—**en t. de,** about, around.
[1]**toro,** *m.* bull; (T-, astr.) Taurus.—*pl.* bullfighting.—**t. corrido,** person made wise by experience, no easy mark.—**t. mejicano,** bison.—**ciertos son los toros,** so then, it is true.—**correr toros,** to fight bulls.
[2]**toro,** *m.* (arch.) ogee molding; torus.
torón, *m.* (chem.) thoron.
toronja, *f.* grapefruit.
toronjil, *m.*, **toronjina,** *f.* (bot.) balm gentle.
toronjo, *m.* (bot.) grapefruit tree.
toroso, sa, *a.* strong, robust.
torozón, *m.* (vet.) gripes (of animals).
torpe, *a.* slow, heavy; dull, stupid; bawdy, lewd; homely, ugly; torpid; infamous.
torpedeamiento, *m.* = TORPEDEO.
torpedear, *va.* to torpedo.
torpedeo, *m.* torpedoing.
torpedero, *m.* (naut.) torpedo boat.
torpedo, *m.* torpedo; (ichth.) torpedo, electric ray; (auto) streamline body; long open car.—**t. automóvil,** self-propelling torpedo.—**t. de botalón,** spar torpedo.—**t. de fondo,** or **durmiente,** ground torpedo, or ground submarine mine.—**t. flotante,** buoyant torpedo or submarine mine.
torpemente, *adv.* slowly, sluggishly; clumsily, stupidly; basely; lewdly.
torpeza, *f.* heaviness, dullness; torpidness, torpor; lewdness, obscenity; want of ornament or culture; baseness, infamy, turpitude.
torpor, *m.* torpor, numbness.
torrado, *m.* toasted chick-pea.
torrar, *va.* to toast.
torre, *f.* tower; turret; church steeple, belfry; belvedere; country house with a garden; (chess) castle or rook.—**t. albarrana, t. de costa,** turret, watch tower.—**t. de luces,** (naut.) lighthouse.—**t. de mando,** control tower.—**t. de viento,** castle in the air.
torrear, *va.* to fortify with towers or turrets.
torrefacción, *f.* toasting.
torreja, *f.* (Mex.) fritter.
torrejón, *m.* ill-shaped turret.
torrencial, *a.* torrential; overpowering.
torrentada, *f.* sweep of a torrent, impetuous current.
torrente, *m.* torrent; avalanche, rush; abundance, plenty.—**t. de voz,** powerful voice.
torrentera, *f.* ravine made by a torrent.
torreón, *m.* fortified tower.
torrero, *m.* lighthouse keeper; farmer.
torreznada, *f.* plentiful dish of bacon.
torreznero, ra, *n.* (coll.) lazy person.
torrezno, *m.* rasher of bacon.
tórrido, da, *a.* torrid; parched, hot.
torrija, *f.* bread dipped in batter and fried.
torrontera, *f.*, **torrontero,** *m.* heap of earth left by a freshet.
torrontés, *a.* designating a kind of white grape.
torsión, *f.* torsion, twist; twisting.
torso, *m.* trunk or body of a statue.
torta, *f.* cake; loaf; (print.) font; solid matter for distribution; briquette; (mason.) coat.—*pl.* (Mex.) (min.) torta, cake of ore.—**tortas y pan pintado,** trifles, an easy matter, child's play.—**costar la t. un pan,** to pay dear for one's whistle.
tortada, *f.* meat or chicken pie; (mason.) coat of mortar.
tortedad, *f.* twistedness.
[1]**tortera,** *f.* baking pan; deep dish.
[2]**tortera,** *f.*, **tortero,** *m.* whorl of a spindle.
tortícolis, torticolis, *m.* (med.) torticollis, wry or stiff neck.
tortilla, *f. dim.* omelet; (Mex.) pancake.—**hacerse t.,** to break into small pieces; to cake.—**volverse la t.,** to turn the scale; to take a course contrary to that expected.
tortita, *f. dim.* small loaf or cake.
tórtola, *f.* (ornith.) turtledove.
tortolillo, lla, ito, ta, *n. dim.* small turtledove; sweetheart.
tórtolo, *m.* male turtledove; beau, lover.
tortor, *m.* (naut.) tightening stick or bar to take up by twisting the sag between the fastened ends of a rope.
tortozón, *m.* a variety of large grape.
tortuga, *f.* turtle; tortoise.
tortuosamente, *adv.* tortuously, sinuously.
tortuosidad, *f.* tortuosity, sinuosity.
tortuoso, sa, *a.* tortuous, winding, sinuous.
tortura, *f.* state of being twisted; rack, torture; grief, affliction.
torturar. I. *va.* to torture, torment. **II.** *vr.* to worry, fret.
torva, *f.* whirl of rain or snow.
torvisca, *f.* (bot.) flax-leaved daphne.
torviscal, *m.* place abounding in TORVISCA.
torvisco, *m.* = TORVISCA.
torvo, va, *a.* fierce, stern, severe, grim.
tory, *n.* & *a.* (Angl.) Tory.—**torysmo,** *m.* toryism.
torzadillo, *m.* thin silk twist.
torzal, *m.* silk twist, machine twist; cord.
torzón, *m.* (vet.) = TOROZÓN, gripes.
torzonado, da, *a.* (vet.) suffering from TORZÓN.
tos, *f.* cough.—**t. ferina,** or **convulsiva,** whooping cough.—**t. perruna,** barking cough.
tosca, *f.* (med.) tophus; (dent.) tartar.
toscamente, *adv.* coarsely, rudely, roughly.
toscano, na, *n.* & *a.* Tuscan.
tosco, ca, *a.* coarse, rough; unpolished, uncouth.
tosecilla, *f. dim.* slight cough.
tosegoso, sa, *a.* coughing much.
toser, *vn.* to cough.—**t. a,** to challenge; to rival, compete with.—**tosidura,** *f.* coughing.
tosigar, *va.* to poison.
tósigo, *m.* poison; grief, anguish.
[1]**tosigoso, sa,** *a.* poisonous, baneful.
[2]**tosigoso, sa,** *a.* coughing.
tosquedad, *f.* roughness, coarseness; rudeness; clumsiness.
tostada, *f.* toast, toasted bread; disappointment.—**dar,** or **pegar, una t.,** (coll.) to cheat; to disappoint.
tostadera, *f.* toaster.
tostado, da. I. *pp.* of TOSTAR. **II.** *a.* torrid, parched; (sun) tanned. **III.** *m.* toasting.
tostador, ra, *n.* toaster (person); *m.* (utensil).
tostadura, *f.* toasting.
tostar, *va.* (*ind.* TUESTO; *subj.* TUESTE) to toast; to roast; to tan (as the sun).—**t. café,** to roast coffee.
[1]**tostón,** *m.* buttered or oiled toast; roasted Spanish pea; anything overtoasted; roast pig.
[2]**tostón,** *m.* Port. silver coin; (Mex.) 50 centavos.
total. I. *a.* total, whole; general, universal. **II.** *m.* total; whole, totality; complement; result; upshot.—**en t.,** in short, to sum up.
totalidad, *f.* totality, aggregate; whole.
totalitario, ria, *n.* & *a.* totalitarian.
totalitarismo, *m.* totalitarianism.
totalizador, *m.* totalizer, totalizator.
totalizar, *va.* (Am.) to add up, find the total of; to sum up.
totalmente, *adv.* totally, wholly, fully.
tótem, *m.* totem.—**totemismo,** *m.* totemism.
totilimundi, *m.* peep-show; cosmorama.
totoloque, *m.* (Mex.) an ancient Indian game.
totoposte, *m.* (C. A.) corn cake or biscuit.
totora, *f.* (S. A.) (bot.) cat-tail or red mace.
totoral, *m.* place abounding in TOTORAS.

totovía, *f.* (ornith.) wood lark.
totuma, *f.* (Am.) cup made from a gourd.
totumo, *m.* (Am.) tree bearing gourds.
toxemia, *f.* toxemia.
toxicación, *f.* (med.) toxication.
toxicar, *va.* to poison.
toxicidad, *f.* toxicity.
tóxico, ca. I. *a.* toxic, poisonous. **II.** *m.* poison.
toxicología, *f.* toxicology.—**toxicológico, ca,** *a.* toxicological.—**toxicólogo, ga,** *n.* toxicologist.
toxina, *f.* (med.) toxin.
toza, *f.* log; block of wood; stump; piece of bark.
tozal, *m.* protuberance, bump on a plain surface.
tozalbo, ba, *a.* white-faced.
tozar, *vn.* (*pret.* TOCÉ; *subj.* TOCE) to butt (with the head); to contend foolishly.
tozo, za, *a.* low, small, dwarfish, stumpy.
tozolada, *f.*, **tozolón,** *m.* blow on the neck.
tozudo, da, *a.* stubborn, obstinate.
tozuelo, *m.* fat part of the neck of an animal.
traba, *f.* tie, bond, brace, clasp, locking device; anything that binds together; ligament, ligature; hobble, clog, fetterlock, trammel, fetter, shackle; obstacle, hindrance; beam, lintel.
trabacuenta, *f.* error in accounts; difference, dispute, controversy.
trabadero, *m.* pastern of a horse.
trabado, da. I. *pp.* of TRABAR. **II.** *a.* robust, strong; (of horse) having white fore feet.
trabadura, *f.* bracing, locking; bond, union.
trabajadamente, *adv.* laboriously.
trabajado, da. I. *pp.* of TRABAJAR. **II.** *a.* wrought, machined; tired, weary.
trabajador, ra. I. *a.* industrious; laboring, working. **II.** *n.* worker, laborer; hard-working person; *m.* workman, workingman; *f.* workingwoman.—**t. amarillo,** blackleg, strikebreaker. —**t. calificado,** skilled worker.
trabajante, *a.* working, toiling.
trabajar, *va.* & *vn.* to work; labor; to shape, form; to endeavor; to exert oneself, strive; to undergo a strain; to labor (as a ship in a storm); to till (the soil); to vex, harass, worry, trouble.
trabajillo, *m. dim.* slight work, toil, labor, trouble, or hardship.
trabajo, *m.* work; labor; piece of work; thing wrought; employment; obstacle, hindrance; trouble, hardship.—*pl.* hardship; poverty, indigence, need, want.—**t. de manos,** manual or handwork.—**t. de punto,** knitting, knitting work.—**t. de zapa,** underhand work.—**trabajos forzados,** hard labor (penal).—**bolsa de t.,** employment bureau or exchange.—**pasar trabajos,** to have trouble, to experience hardships or privation, to meet with difficulties.
trabajosamente, *adv.* laboriously, painfully.
trabajoso, sa, *a.* difficult, hard; belabored; needy, suffering; weak, sickly.
trabal, *a.* clasping.
trabalenguas, *m.* unpronounceable word, jawbreaker.
trabamiento, *m.* interlocking; connection, bond, joining.
trabanco, *m.* block attached to a dog's collar to prevent him from nosing the ground.
trabar. I. *va.* to join, clasp, lock, bind, fasten; to grasp, grab, seize; to fetter, shackle; to thicken, inspissate; to begin, set about; to set (the teeth of a saw); to harmonize, make agree.—**t. amistad,** to become friends; **(con)** to make the acquaintance (of).—**t. batalla,** to enter into battle, begin it.—**t. conocimiento,** to scrape acquaintance.—**t. ejecución,** (law) to distrain, to seize judicially. **II.** *vr.* to become locked or interlocked; to become confused, rattled.—**t. de palabras,** to become angry in a dispute.—**trabársele la lengua a uno,** to stammer; to speak with unnatural hesitation from confusion.
trabazón, *f.* juncture, union, bond, bracing, connection; coalescence; (mason.) bond.
trabe, *f.* beam.
trábea, *f.* (Rom. hist.) gala toga.
trabilla, *f. dim.* gaiter strap; small clasp; in knitting, dropped stitch.
trabón, *m. aug.* fetlock, hopple; cross plank in oil mills.
trabuca, *f.* firecracker.
trabucación, *f.* confusion, disorder, upsetting, mix up; mistake, blunder.
trabucador, ra, *n.* upsetter, disturber; jumbler, mixer; blunderer.
trabucaire, *m.* Catalonian guerrilla, armed with a blunderbuss.
trabucante, *a.* blundering; confusing.
trabucar. I. *va.* (*pret.* TRABUQUÉ; *subj.* TRABUQUE) to upset, overturn; to mistake; to confound, confuse, jumble, mix up; to interrupt. **II.** *vr.* to become confused or mixed up.
trabucazo, *m.* shot with a blunderbuss; report of a blunderbuss; (coll.) sudden fright or affliction.
trabuco, *m.* catapult; blunderbuss.—**t. naranjero,** blunderbuss with mouth of size of orange.
trabuqué, trabuque, *v. V.* TRABUCAR.
trabuquete, *m.* catapult; seine.
traca, *f.* (naut.) strake.
trácala, *f.* (Mex.) scheme, trick.
tracalada, *f.* (Am.) multitude, "lots."
tracalero, ra, *a.* (Mex.) tricky, artful.
tracamundana, *f.* (coll.) barter of trifles; noisy wrangle, hubbub.
tracción, *f.* traction; cartage; (mech.) tension, tensile stress.
tracé, trace, *v. V.* TRAZAR.
tracería, *f.* (arch.) tracery.
tracias, *m.* north-northwest wind.
tracio, cia, *n.* & *a.* Thracian.
tracista, *n.* designer; schemer; intriguer.
tracoma, *m.* (med.) trachoma.
tracto, *m.* tract, stretch; lapse; (eccl.) tractus.
tractocarril, *m.* car or train that can run on a road with or without rails.
tractor, *m.* tractor; traction engine.—**t. oruga,** caterpillar tractor.
tradición, *f.* tradition; (law) tradition, delivery of possession.—**tradicional,** *a.* traditional.
tradicionalismo, *m.* traditionalism.
tradicionalista, *m.* or *f.* traditionalist.
tradicionalmente, *adv.* traditionally.
tradicionista, *n.* compiler of traditions.
traducción, *f.* translation.
traducianismo, *m.* (theol.) traducianism.
traducible, *a.* translatable.
traducir, *va.* (*ind. pres.* TRADUZCO, *pret.* TRADUJE; *subj.* TRADUZCA) to translate.
traductor, ra, *n.* translator.
traedizo, za, *a.* portable.
traedor, ra, *n.* porter, carrier.
traer. I. *va.* (*ger.* TRAYENDO; *pp.* TRAÍDO; *ind. pres.* TRAIGO, *pret.* TRAJE; *subj.* TRAIGA) to bring, fetch; to lead (a person); to attract, draw towards oneself; to bring about, cause, occasion; to handle, manage; to wear (as a garment); (of a magazine, etc.) to carry (an article); assign (reasons); quote (authorities); to bring to, oblige, compel; to bring over, reduce, bind, prevail upon, persuade; to be engaged in, carry on, have.—**t. a colación,** to bring up for discussion.—**t. a cuento,** to bring into the conversation or discourse; to drag in. —**t. a la mano,** to fetch or carry.—**t. a mal t.,** to go hard with one; to disturb, trouble, vex.—**t. a uno al retortero,** to trouble one by overwork, or to lead one from place to place.—**t. a uno entre ojos,** to be suspicious of one.—**t. consigo,** to carry or have with one; to bring with it, to imply, to cause.—**t. en bocas,** or **lenguas,** to traduce, to speak ill of.—**t. entre manos,** to have in hand.—**t. y llevar,** to gossip. **II.** *vr.* **(bien, mal)** to be dressed (well or poorly); to carry oneself, have a (graceful or ungainly) carriage.
traeres, *m. pl.* dress ornaments.
trafagador, ra, *n.* trafficker, dealer.
trafagante, *a.* trafficking, trading.

trafagar, *vn.* (*pret.* TRAFAGUÉ; *subj.* TRAFAGUE) to traffic, trade.
tráfago, *m.* commerce, trade; drudgery.
trafagón, na. I. *a.* active, industrious. **II.** *n.* hustler.
trafagué, trafague, *v. V.* TRAFAGAR.
trafalgar, *m.* cotton lining.
trafalmejo, ja, *a.* bold, forward, saucy.
traficación, *f.* traffic; trade, commerce.
traficante, *n.* trafficker, trader, dealer.
traficar, *vn.* (*pret.* TRAFIQUÉ; *subj.* TRAFIQUE) to traffic, deal, trade; to travel, journey, roam.
tráfico, *m.* trade, business; traffic.
tragacanta, *f.*, **tragacanto,** *m.* (bot.) goats-thorn, milk vetch; tragacanth, a gum.
tragacete, *m.* javelin, dart.
tragaderas, *f. pl.* gullet.—**tener buenas t.,** to be very gullible.
tragadero, *m.* œsophagus, gullet; pit, gulf, vortex.—**t. del mar,** trough of the sea.
tragadieces, *m.* (Mex.) nickelodeon, juke box.
tragador, ra, *n.* glutton, gobbler.—**t. de leguas** = TRAGALEGUAS.
tragahombres, *m.* (coll.) bully, hector.
trágala, *m.* title of a political song against absolutism and in favor of the constitution.
tragaldabas, *m.* (coll.) glutton.
tragaleguas, *m.* (coll.) brisk walker.
tragaluz, *m.* skylight, bull's-eye.
tragallón, na, *n.* & *a.* glutton(-ous).
tragamallas, *m.* (coll.) glutton.
traganíquel, *m.* (Cuba) nickelodeon, juke box.
tragantada, *f.* large draught of liquor.
tragante. I. *a.* swallowing. **II.** *m.* (foundry) top opening or passage of a furnace; sluice, flume; mouth of a dam or sink.
tragantón, na. I. *a.* gluttonous, voracious. **II.** *n.* (coll.) glutton. **III.** *f.* (coll.) big meal, big spread; swallowing or forcing down the throat; hard pill to swallow.
tragar. I. *va.* (*pret.* TRAGUÉ; *subj.* TRAGUE) to swallow; to devour; to swallow up, engulf.—**t. el anzuelo,** to allow oneself to be deceived.—**no poder,** or **poderse, t. a,** not to be able to bear (cannot bear). **II.** *vr.* to swallow; to dissemble; to swallow (an affront).
tragasantos, *n.* overdevout person, one who spends too much time in church.
tragavenado, *f.* (Venez.) a kind of boa.
tragavirotes, *m.* (coll.) conceited stiff man.
tragazón, *f.* voracity, gluttony.
tragedia, *f.* tragedy.
trágicamente, *adv.* tragically.
trágico, ca. I. *a.* tragic. **II.** *m.* tragedian; *f.* tragedienne.
tragicomedia, *f.* tragi-comedy.
tragicómico, ca, *a.* tragi-comical.
[1]**trago,** *m.* draught of liquid; drink; swallow; calamity, misfortune.—**a tragos,** by degrees, slowly, gently.—**echar un t.,** to take a drink.
[2]**trago,** *m.* (anat.) tragus.
tragón, na, *n.* & *a.* glutton(-ous).
tragonear, *va.* & *vn.* (coll.) to eat voraciously.
tragonería, tragonía, *f.* gluttony.
tragontina, *f.* (bot.) arum.
tragué, trague, *v. V.* TRAGAR.
traguillo, ito, *m. dim.* small drink.
traición, *f.* treason; treachery.—**alta t.,** high treason.—**a t.,** or **a la t.,** treacherously.
traicionar, *va.* to do treason to, to betray.
traicionero, ra, *a.* treacherous.
traída, *f.* carriage, conduction.
traído, da. I. *pp.* of TRAER. **II.** *a.* used, worn out, threadbare.
traidor, ra. I. *a.* traitorous; treasonable; treacherous, perfidious. **II.** *n.* traitor; betrayer.
traidoramente, *adv.* treacherously; treasonably, traitorously.
traigo, traiga, *v. V.* TRAER.
traílla, treílla, *f.* leash, lash; packthread; (agr.) leveling harrow; road leveler; road scraper.
traillar, *va.* to level (ground).
traína, *f.* seine for deep-sea fishing; net for sardine fishing.
trainera, *f.* smack for sardine fishing.
traíña, *f.* = TRAÍNA.
traite, *m.* raising a bur or nap on cloth.
[1]**traje,** *m.* costume, dress, apparel; gown; suit of clothes; mask.—**t. astronáutico,** space suit.—**t. charro,** (Mex.) showy riding costume.—**t. de baño,** (Am.) bathing suit.—**t. de ceremonia,** full dress; uniform.—**t. de luces,** bull-fighter's garb.—**t. de montar,** riding habit.—**t. largo,** evening dress.—**t. sastre,** (Am.) (woman's) tailored suit.—**t. serio,** full dress, evening dress.
[2]**traje,** *pret.* of TRAER.
trajear, *va.* to clothe.
trajín, *m.* carrying from place to place; moving about.
trajinante, *n.* & *a.* carrier(-ying).
trajinar. I. *va.* to carry from place to place. **II.** *vn.* to travel about; (coll.) to fidget about.
trajinería, *f.* = TRAJÍN.
trajinero, ra, *n.* = TRAJINANTE.
trajino, *m.* = TRAJÍN.
tralla, *f.* cord, bass-weed rope; lash, snapper of a whip.
trama, *f.* weft or woof of cloth; twisted silk; fraud, plot; plot of a play or novel.
tramador, ra, *n.* & *a.* weaver(-ing); plotter(-ing), hatcher(-ing), schemer(-ing).
tramar. I. *va.* to weave; to plot, hatch, scheme. **II.** *vn.* (of olive trees) to blossom.
tramilla, *f.* (Am.) twine.
tramitación, *f.* procedure; transaction, action, carrying out.
tramitar, *va.* to transact, carry through, conduct.
trámite, *m.* the carrying on (of administration, etc.), the transacting (of business, etc.); step; (law) proceeding.
tramo, *m.* parcel of ground; flight of stairs; stretch, section; panel (of a bridge).
tramojo, *m.* (agr.) band for tying the sheaf; trouble, affliction; (Am.) = TRABANCO; (Colomb.) leash.
tramontano, na. I. *a.* transmontane. **II.** *f.* north wind; vanity, pride, haughtiness.
tramontar. I. *va.* to pass over (a mountain); (of the sun) to sink beyond (the mountains); to help escape. **II.** *vr.* to flee, to escape.
tramoya, *f.* (theat.) trick; craft, wile.
tramoyista, *m.* (theat.) stage machinist; stage carpenter, stage hand, scene shifter; impostor, swindler, fraud, humbug.
trampa, *f.* trap, snare, pitfall; trapdoor; falling board of a counter; flap or spring door; cheat, fraud, deceit, trick; bad debt.—**caer en la t.,** to fall into a trap.—**hacer t.,** or **trampas,** to cheat.—**se lo llevó la t.,** (of an affair) it fell through.
trampal, *m.* quagmire; bog.
trampantojo, *m.* (coll.) trick, deception.
trampazo, *m.* last twist of a torturing cord.
trampeador, ra, *n.* swindler, cheat, sharper.
trampear. I. *vn.* (coll.) to obtain money on false pretences; to cheat; to shift, get along, pull through. **II.** *va.* to swindle, cheat, deceive.
trampería, *f.* trickery, cheating, chicanery.
trampero, ra, *n.* trapper.
trampilla, *f. dim.* peephole; door of a coal bin; fly of trousers.
trampista, *m.* cheat, trickster, sharper.
trampolín, *m.* springboard.
tramposo, sa. I. *a.* tricky, deceitful, swindling. **II.** *n.* cheater, swindler, trickster; card sharp.
tranca, *f.* club, cudgel, stick, truncheon; cross board or stick, or prop to fasten a door on the inside; (Am., coll.) drunken spell, "tear."
trancada, *f.* long stride; blow with a stick.—**en dos trancadas,** in a trice, in two ticks.
trancado, *m.* small harpoon for eels.
trancahilo, *m.* stop knot in threads or ropes.
trancanil, *m.* (naut.) waterway, stringer plate.

trancar. **I.** *va.* (*pret.* TRANQUÉ; *subj.* TRANQUE) to bar (a door). **II.** *vn.* (coll.) to take long strides.
trancazo, *m.* blow with a bar; (coll.) influenza, grippe; (Colomb., coll.) fisticuff.
trance, *m.* peril, danger; critical moment; last stage or moments of life; (law) legal seizure on an execution.—**a todo t.,** at all costs, at any price, regardless of risk or trouble.—**en t. de muerte,** at the point of death.—**hacer t.,** (law) to seize property on an execution.
trancenil, *m.* gold or silver hatband, garnished with jewels.
tranco, *m.* long stride; threshold.—**a trancos,** hurriedly, carelessly.—**en dos trancos,** in a jiffy.
tranchete, *m.* cobbler's heel knife.
trancho, *m.* (ichth.) a variety of shad.
trangallo, *m.* = TRABANCO.
tranquera, *f.* palisade, palisado.
tranquero, *m.* angular stone of a jamb or lintel.
tranquil, *m.* (arch.) plumb line.
tranquilamente, *adv.* quietly, peacefully, composedly.
tranquilar, *va.* (com.) to check off.
tranquilidad, *f.* tranquility, peace, quiet; reassurance, ease.
tranquilizador, ra, *a.* quieting, soothing, reassuring.
tranquilizar, *va.* & *vr.* to calm, quiet down.
tranquilo, la, *a.* tranquil, calm, quiet, easy.
tranquilla, *f. dim.* trap, snare; small securing or fastening bar or stick; stop pin or lug.
tranquillón, *m.* maslin, mixed grain.
transacción, *f.* compromise, accommodation, settlement; transaction, negotiation.
transalpino, na, *a.* transalpine.
transandino, na, *a.* transandine, transandean.
transatlántico, ca. **I.** *a.* transatlantic. **II.** *m.* transatlantic liner.
transar, *va.* & *vr.* (Am.) to compromise, adjust, settle.
transbordador, ra. **I.** *a.* transshipping, transferring, transfer (as *a.*). **II.** *m.* transfer boat or car.—**t. funicular,** transfer ropeway.
transbordar, *va.* to transfer; to transship.
transbordo, *m.* transfer; transshipment.
transcendencia, transcendental, transcendente, etc. = TRASCENDENCIA, etc.
transcontinental, *a.* transcontinental.
transcribir, *va.* (*pp.* TRANSCRITO, TRANSCRIPTO) to transcribe; (mus.) to transcribe.
transcripción, *f.* transcription.
transcripto, ta; transcrito, ta, *pp. irreg.* of TRANSCRIBIR.
transcurrir, *vn.* (of time) to pass, elapse.
transcurso, *m.* lapse, course (of time).
tránseat, (Lat.) let it pass.
transeúnte. **I.** *a.* transient; transitory. **II.** *n.* sojourner; passer-by.
transferencia, *f.* transference, transfer.
transferible, *a.* transferable.
transferidor, ra, *n.* & *a.* transferrer(-ing).
transferir, *va.* (*ger.* TRANSFIRIENDO; *ind. pres.* TRANSFIERO, *pret.* él TRANSFIRIÓ; *subj.* TRANSFIERA) to transfer; (law) to transfer, convey, make over; (rhet.) to use figuratively.
transfigurable, *a.* transformable.
transfiguración, *f.* transfiguration.
transfigurar. **I.** *va.* to transfigure, transform. **II.** *vr.* to be transfigured.
transfijo, ja, *a.* transfixed.
transfixión, *f.* transfixion, piercing through.
transflor, *m.* (art) enamel painting.
[1]**transflorar,** *va.* (art) to paint or decorate in enamel; to trace, make a tracing of.
[2]**transflorar,** *vn.* to show through.
transflorear, *va.* to paint in enamel.
transformable, *a.* transformable; convertible (automobile).
transformación, *f.* transformation.
transformador, ra. **I.** *n.* & *a.* transformer(-ing). **II.** *m.* (elec.) transformer.—**t. acorazado,** shell transformer.—**t. de aceite,** oil-cooled transformer.—**t. de anillo,** ring transformer.—**t. de corriente,** or **de intensidad,** current transformer.—**t. de reducción,** step-down transformer.—**t. de tensión,** voltage transformer.—**t. elevador,** step-up transformer, booster.
transformamiento, *m.* transformation.
transformar. **I.** *va.* & *vr.* to transform. **II.** *vr.* to be or become transformed; to change one's sentiments or ways.
transformativo, va, *a.* transformative.
transformismo, *m.* (biol.) transformism, evolutionism.—**transformista.** **I.** *n.* & *a.* transformist(-ic); evolutionist(-ary). **II.** *n.* one who impersonates several characters in succession.
transfregar, *va.* (*ind. pres.* TRANSFRIEGO, *pret.* TRANSFREGUÉ; *subj.* TRANSFRIEGUE) to rub, scrub; rumple, crumple.
transfretano, na, *a.* transmarine, oversea.
transfretar. **I.** *va.* to cross (the sea). **II.** *vn.* to extend, spread.
transfriego, etc. *v. V.* TRANSFREGAR.
tránsfuga, *n.*, **tránsfugo,** *m.* deserter; fugitive, runaway; turncoat.
transfundición, *f.* = TRANSFUSIÓN.
transfundir, *va.* to pour into; transfuse; to communicate, transmit.
transfusión, *f.* transfusion; communication, transmission; (surg.) transfusion.
transfusor, ra, *n.* & *a.* transfuser(-ing).
transgredir, *va.* (*defect. only those modes are used having* i *in their ending*) to transgress.
transgresión, *f.* transgression.
transgresor, ra, *n.* & *a.* transgressor(-ing).
transición, *f.* transition.
transido, da, *a.* worn out, exhausted; famished; mean, avaricious.
transigencia, *f.* condescension, tolerance.
transigente, *a.* accommodating, compromising, broad-minded, reasonable, condescending.
transigir. **I.** *va.* (*ind.* TRANSIJO; *subj.* TRANSIJA) to compromise, settle. **II.** *vn.* to give in, agree.
transistor, *m.* (elec., electron.) transistor.
transitable, *a.* passable, practicable.
transitar, *vn.* to travel.
transitivo, va, *a.* (law) transferable; (gram.) transitive.
tránsito, *m.* transit, passage; traffic; transition; stopping place; road, way; change, removal; death of holy persons; (astr., surv.) transit.—**de t.,** in transit, passing through; temporarily.—**hacer tránsitos,** to make stops on the way in a journey.—**se prohibe el t.,** (on a sign) no thoroughfare.
transitoriamente, *adv.* transitorily.
transitoriedad, *f.* transience, transiency, momentariness.
transitorio, ria, *a.* transitory.
translación, translaticiamente, translaticio, translativo, = TRASLACIÓN, etc.
translimitación, *f.* trespass; going beyond proper bounds; (mil.) armed intervention in a bordering state.
translimitar, *va.* (mil.) to cross (the boundary of a state) unintentionally or by permission; to go beyond the limit of (morality, reason).
translinear, *vn.* (law) to pass (an entail) to another line of heirs.
translucidez, *f.* translucence.
translúcido, da, *a.* translucent.
transluciente, *a.* translucent, translucid.
translunar, *a.* translunar.
transmarino, na, *a.* transmarine, oversea.
transmigración, *f.* transmigration.
transmigrador, ra. **I.** *a.* transmigratory. **II.** *n.* transmigrator.
transmigrar, *vn.* to transmigrate.
transmisibilidad, *f.* transmissibility.
transmisible, *a.* transmissible.
transmisión, *f.* transmission; (radio) broadcast.—**t. de energía,** power transmission.—**t. del**

pensamiento, thought transference.—**t. en colores,** (television) colorcast.
transmisor, ra. I. *a.* transmitting. **II.** *m.* (elec.) transmitter. **III.** *f.* (radio) broadcasting station.
transmitir, *va.* to transmit; (radio) to broadcast.
transmontar, transmontano = TRAMONTAR, TRAMONTANO.
transmudación, *f.*; **transmudamiento,** *m.* transmutation, change.
transmudar, *va.* to move, carry to another place; to persuade, convince; TRANSMUTAR.
transmutabilidad, *f.* transmutability.
transmutable, *a.* transmutable.
transmutación, *f.* transmutation, change.
transmutador, *m.* transmuter.
transmutar, *va.* to transmute, change.
transmutativo, va; torio, ria, *a.* transmutative.
transoceánico, ca, *a.* transoceanic.
transónico, ca, *a.* transsonic. transonic.
transpacífico, ca, *a.* transpacific.
transpadano, na, *a.* transpadane, beyond the Po.
transparencia, *f.* transparency.
transparentarse, *vr.* to be transparent; to show through.
transparente. I. *a.* transparent; translucent. **II.** *m.* window shade; stained glass window.
transpirable, *a.* perspirable, transpirable.
transpiración, *f.* transpiration, perspiration.
transpirar, *vn.* to transpire, perspire.
transpirenaico, ca, *a.* beyond the Pyrenees.
transponedor, ra, *n.* & *a.* transposer(-ing); transplanter(-ing).
transponer. I. *va.* (*pp.* TRANSPUESTO; *ind. pres.* TRANSPONGO, *pret.* TRANSPUSE, *fut.* TRANSPONDRÉ; *subj.* TRANSPONGA) to transpose; to transfer, transport; to transplant. **II.** *vr.* (of sun, etc.) to set below the horizon; to go behind; to be rather drowsy.
transportable, *a.* transportable.
transportación, *f.* transportation, transport.
transportador, ra. I. *a.* carrying, transporting. **II.** *n.* transporter, carrier. **III.** *m.* (drawing) protractor; (Ry.) ropeway.
transportamiento, *m.* transportation; transport, ecstasy.
transportar. I. *va.* to transport, carry; (mus.) to transpose; (surv.) (also **t. al papel**), to plat, plot. **II.** *vr.* to be in a transport, to be carried away.
transporte, *m.* transport, transportation, conveyance; cartage; ferriage; (naut.) transport ship; transport, rapture, ecstasy.
transposición, *f.* transposition.
transpositivo, va, *a.* transpositional.
transpuesto, ta, *pp. irreg.* of TRANSPONER.
transpuse, *pret.* of TRANSPONER.
transterminante, *a.* trespassing.
transterminar, *va.* to trespass.
transtiberino, na, *a.* across the Tiber.
transubstanciación, *f.* transubstantiation.
transubstancial, *a.* transubstantiated.
transubstanciar, *va.* to transubstantiate.
transvasar, *va.* to transfer (liquid, to another container).
transverberación, *f.* transfixion.
transversal, *f.* & *a.* transversal.
transversalmente, *adv.* transversely.
transverso, sa, *a.* transverse.
transvestido, da, *a.* transvestite.
tranvía, *m.* tramway, street railway; street car.
tranviario, ria. I. *a.* pert. to tramways, street Ry.; tramway (as *a.*). **II.** *n.* tramway worker.
tranviero, ra, *n.* = TRANVIARIO.
tranza, *f.* (law) seizure in an execution.
tranzadera, *f.* knot of plaited cords.
tranzar, *va.* to cut, truncate; to auction off.
tranzón, *m.* clearing in a forest.
trapa, *f.* (naut.) spilling line.—*pl.* (naut.) relieving tackle; guys.
¡trapa, trapa! *interj.* tramp, tramp.
trapacear, *vn.* to cheat, swindle.
trapacería, *f.* fraud, cheating.
trapacero, ra, *n.* & *a.* cheat(-ing).
trapacete, *m.* (com.) daybook.
trapacista, *n.* = TRAPACERO.
trapajo, *m.* rag, tatter.
trapajoso, sa, *a.* ragged, tattered.
[1]**trápala. I.** *f.* tramping of feet; galloping; noise, confusion.
[2]**trápala. I.** *f.* (coll.) trick, deceit, cheat. **II.** *n.* (coll.) prattler, chatterbox; cheat, humbug. **III.** *m.* garrulity, loquacity.
trapalear, *vn.* to prattle, chatter; to cheat.
trapalón, na, *n.* = [2]TRÁPALA, *n.*
trapatiesta, *f.* (coll.) squabble, row, brawl.
trapaza, *f.* fraud, trick.
trapazar, *vn.* to cheat, swindle.
trape, *m.* interlining.
trapeano, na, *a.* (min.) trappean.
trapecial, *a.* trapezoidal.
trapecio, *m.* (geom.) trapezoid.
trapecista, *n.* trapezist, trapeze artist.
trapense, *m.* (eccl.) Trappist.
trapería, *f.* rags; frippery, rag fair, rag shop.
trapero, ra, *n.* ragpicker; rag dealer.
trapezoidal, *a.* four-sided.
trapezoide, *m.* trapezium; (anat.) trapezoid.
trapiche, *m.* sugar mill, cane mill; olive press; (Cuba) small sugar plantation; (Mex.) grinding machine.
trapichear, *vn.* (coll.) to contrive, shift.
trapicheo, *m.* (coll.) contriving, shifting.
trapichero, ra, *n.* worker in a sugar mill.
trapiento, ta, *a.* ragged, tattered.
trapillo, lla. I. *n. dim.* (coll.) courtier or lady of small means. **II.** *m.* amount of money saved and put away.—**de t.,** in dishabille or négligé.
trapío, *m.* (naut.) sails of a ship, canvas; (coll.) stylish or graceful carriage of a woman; liveliness and smartness in a fighting bull.
trapisonda, *f.* (coll.) bustle, clatter; brawl, scuffle; snare, deception; (naut.) whitecaps.
trapisondear, *vn.* (coll.) to foment brawls; to cheat, deceive.
trapito, *m. dim.* little rag.—**los trapitos de cristianar,** best Sunday clothes.
trapo, *m.* rag, tatter; rag, piece of cloth; sails of a ship; (coll.) bullfighter's cloak.—**a todo t.,** with all one's might; (naut.) all sails set.—**poner como un t.,** to reprimand severely, to dress down.—**soltar el t.,** (coll.) to burst out (crying or laughing).
traque, *m.* crack, report (of a rocket, etc.).—**a t. barraque,** (coll.) at all times, in and out of season.
tráquea, *f.* (anat., entom., bot.) trachea.
traqueado, da, *a.* threadbare, hackneyed; (Am.) (of road) much traversed; (P. R.) drunk.
traqueal, *a.* (anat., bot., entom.) tracheal.
traquear. I. *vn.* to crack, make a loud creaking noise. **II.** *va.* to shake (as a liquid); (coll.) to handle roughly; (Am.) to pass frequently over (a road, etc.); (P. R.) to get drunk.
traquearteria, *f.* trachea, windpipe.
traqueo, *m.* cracking (of fireworks, etc.); shake, shaking, jolt, jerk.
traqueotomía, *f.* tracheotomy.
traquetear, *va.* & *vn.* to shake, jolt, jerk, handle roughly; to crack (as fireworks or wood).
traqueteo, *m.* shaking, jolting, jerking; cracking, creaking; (Am.) confused, noisy passing.
traquiarteria, *f.* = TRAQUEARTERIA.
traquido, *m.* snapping, rattle; creaking, cracking.
traquita, *f.* (min.) trachyte, a volcanic rock.
traquítico, ca, *a.* (min.) trachytic.
trarigüe, *m.* (Chile) an ornamented belt or sash.
[1]**tras,** *prep.* after, behind; beyond; besides.—**t. de,** after, behind, back of; besides, in addition to.
[2]**tras,** *m.* bang, noise of a blow.—**t. t.,** repeated strokes, noise or banging.
trasalcoba, *f.* room back of a bedroom (gen. dressing room).
trasalpino, na, *a.* = TRANSALPINO.

trasandino, na, *a.* transandine, transandean.
trasanteanoche, *adv.* three nights ago.
trasanteayer, *adv.* three days ago.
trasantier, *adv.* three days ago.
trasañejo, ja, *a.* three years old.
trasatlántico, ca, *a.* = TRANSATLÁNTICO.
trasbordar, trasbordo = TRANSBORDAR, etc.
trasca, *f.* leather thong.
trascabo, *m.* trip (in wrestling).
trascantón, *m.* TRASCANTONADA; street porter. —**dar t. a,** to hide oneself behind a corner.
trascantonada, *f.* protective stone at corner of buildings.
trascartarse, *vr.* to remain behind (as a winning card).—**trascartón,** *m.* drawing of a winning card after the game is lost.
trascendencia, *f.* transcendency; result.
trascendental, *a.* transcendental; far-reaching; transcendent, highly important, significant; (math.) transcendental.
trascendentalismo, *m.* transcendentalism.
trascendentalista, *n.* & *a.* (philos.) transcendentalist(-ic).
trascendente, *a.* transcendent.
trascender. I. *vn.* (*ind.* TRASCIENDO; *subj.* TRASCIENDA) to extend; to spread, smell, emit a pleasant odor; to be pervasive; to transpire, leak out. **II.** *va.* to penetrate, scrutinize, find out.
trascendido, da, *a.* acute, perspicacious.
trascocina, *f.* back kitchen.
trascol, *m.* (obs.) train (of a dress).
trascolar, *va.* (*ind.* TRASCUELO; *subj.* TRASCUELE) to strain, percolate; (coll.) to pass over (a mountain).
trasconejarse, *vr.* to squat (as pursued game); (coll.) to be missing or mislaid.
trascordarse, *vr.* (*ind.* TRASCUERDO; *subj.* TRASCUERDE) to forget.
trascoro, *m.* space back of the choir.
trascorral, *m.* back court, back yard.
trascribir, trascrito, etc. = TRANSCRIBIR, etc.
trascuarto, *m.* back room; rear apartment.
trascuelo, trascuele, *v. V.* TRASCOLAR.
trascuerdo, trascuerde, *v. V.* TRASCORDARSE.
trascurrir, trascurso = TRANSCURRIR, etc.
trasdobladura, *f.* trebling.
trasdoblar, *va.* to treble, to triple.
trasdoblo, *m.* treble number.
trasdós, *m.* (arch.) extrados.—**tradosear,** *va.* (arch.) to strengthen the back of (an arch).
trasechador, ra, *n.* insnarer, waylayer.
trasechar, *va.* to insnare, waylay.
trasegador, ra, *n.* one who racks wine.
trasegar, *va.* (*ind. pres.* TRASIEGO, *pret.* TRASEGUÉ; *subj.* TRASIEGUE) to upset, to turn topsy-turvy; to change the place of; to empty, pour into another bottle or vessel.
traseñalador, ra, *n.* one who countermarks.
traseñalar, *va.* to mark anew.
trasera, *f.* back part, rear.
trasero, ra. I. *a.* hind, back, rear. **II.** *m.* buttock; rump.—*pl.* (coll.) ancestors, predecessors.
trasferencia, *f.* = TRANSFERENCIA.
trasferible, *a.* = TRANSFERIBLE.
trasferidor, ra, *n.* & *a.* = TRANSFERIDOR.
trasferir, *va.* = TRANSFERIR.
trasfigurable, *a.* = TRANSFIGURABLE.
trasfiguración, *f.* = TRANSFIGURACIÓN.
trasfigurar, *va.* & *vr.* = TRANSFIGURAR.
trasfijo, ja, *a.* = TRANSFIJO.
trasfixión, *f.* = TRANSFIXIÓN.
trasflor, *m.* = TRANSFLOR.
trasflorar, *va.* & *vn.* = TRANSFLORAR.
trasflorear, *va.* = TRANSFLOREAR.
trasfojar, *va.* = TRASHOJAR.
trasfollado, da, *a.* (vet.) having a swollen hock.
trasfollo, *m.* (vet.) swelling of the hock.
trasfondo, *m.* background.
trasformación, *f.* = TRANSFORMACIÓN.
trasformador, *m.* = TRANSFORMADOR.
trasformamiento, *m.* = TRANSFORMAMIENTO.
trasformar, *va.* & *vr.* = TRANSFORMAR.
trasformativo, va, *a.* = TRANSFORMATIVO.
trasfregar, *va.* = TRANSFREGAR.
trasfretano, na, *a.* = TRANSFRETANO.
trasfretar, *va.* & *vn.* = TRANSFRETAR.
trásfuga, *n.* = TRÁNSFUGA.
trásfugo, *m.* = TRÁNSFUGO.
trasfundición, *f.* = TRANSFUNDICIÓN.
trasfundir, *va.* = TRANSFUNDIR.
trasfusión, *f.* = TRANSFUSIÓN.
trasfusor, ra, *n.* & *a.* = TRANSFUSOR.
trasgo, *m.* goblin, hobgoblin, sprite.
trasgredir, *va.* = TRANSGREDIR.
trasgresión, *f.* = TRANSGRESIÓN.
trasgresor, ra, *n.* & *a.* = TRANSGRESOR.
trasguear, *vn.* to play the hobgoblin.
trasguero, ra, *n.* imitator of hobgoblins' tricks.
trashoguero, ra. I. *n.* idler, loiterer near the fireplace. **II.** *m.* back plate of a fireplace; big log in the fireplace.
trashojar, *va.* to scan, leaf through (a book).
trashumación, *f.* nomadism of flocks.
trashumante, *a.* (of flocks) nomadic.
trashumar, *vn.* to roam in search of pasture.
[1]**trasiego,** *m.* upsetting; racking (of wine).
[2]**trasiego, trasiegue,** *v. V.* TRASEGAR.
trasijado, da, *a.* lank, meagre; thin-flanked.
traslación, trasladación, *f.* transfer, removal; translation, change of place; adjournment, postponement; translation, version.
trasladador, ra, *n.* carrier, mover.
trasladante, *a.* moving, removing; translating, transcribing.
trasladar, *va.* to move, remove, transfer; to postpone, adjourn; to translate; to transcribe.
traslado, *m.* copy, transcript, transcription; transfer; imitation, resemblance, likeness, counterpart; (law) notification, communication.
traslapar, *va.*, *vn.* & *vr.* to overlap.
traslapo, *m.* overlapping.
traslaticiamente, *adv.* figuratively; by extension.
traslaticio, cia, *a.* figurative; extended.
traslativo, va, *a.* transferring, conveying.
traslato, ta, *a.* = TRASLATICIO.
trasloar, *va.* to bestow fulsome praise on.
traslúcido, da, *a.* = TRANSLÚCIDO.
trasluciente, *a.* translucent.
traslucirse, *vr.* to be translucent, to shine or show through; to be inferable; to transpire.
traslumbramiento, *m.* dazzlement.
traslumbrar. I. *va.* to dazzle. **II.** *vr.* to pass swiftly, to vanish.
trasluz, *m.* light seen through a transparent body; reflected or borrowed light; (art) transverse light.—**al t.,** against the light.
[1]**trasmallo,** *m.* trammel net.
[2]**trasmallo,** *m.* iron collar around head of mallet.
trasmano, *m.* second player at cards.—**a t.,** out of the way.
trasmañana, *f.* day after to-morrow.
trasmañanar, *va.* to procrastinate.
trasmarino, na, *a.* = TRANSMARINO.
trasmatar, *va.* (coll.) to assume that one will outlive (another).
trasmigración, etc. = TRANSMIGRACIÓN, etc.
trasminar, *vn.* to undermine, excavate; to pierce, penetrate, percolate.
trasmisible, etc. = TRANSMISIBLE, etc.
trasmochadero, *m.* thicket of firewood.
trasmochar, *va.* to cut branches for fuel.
trasmontano, trasmontar, etc. = TRAMONTANO, TRAMONTAR, etc.
trasmosto, *f.* weak, watered wine.
trasmudación, etc. = TRANSMUDACIÓN, etc.
trasmutable, trasmutación, trasmutar, etc. = TRANSMUTABLE, TRANSMUTACIÓN, etc.
trasnochada, *f.* last night; sleepless night; being up all night; (mil.) night attack.
trasnochado, da. I. *pp.* of TRASNOCHAR. **II.** *a.* fatigued from night watching; haggard, careworn; stale, worn-out; trite, hackneyed.
trasnochador, ra, *n.* night watcher; one who goes to bed late or not at all; (coll.) night hawk.

trasnochar. I. *vn.* to watch; to sit up all night; to spend the night. **II.** *va.* to leave for the next day.
trasnoche, trasnocho, *m.* night watch, going without sleep.
trasnombrar, *va.* to change or confuse the names of.
trasnominación, *f.* (rhet.) metonymy.
trasoír, *va.* (*ger.* TRASOYENDO; *ind. pres.* TRASOIGO, *pret.* él TRASOYÓ; *subj.* TRASOIGA) to hear wrong, mishear, misunderstand.
trasojado, da, *a.* having sunken eyes, emaciated, careworn.
trasoñar, *vn.* (*ind.* TRASUEÑO; *subj.* TRASUEÑE) to fancy erroneously, as in a dream.
trasovado, da, *a.* (bot.) obovate.
traspadano, na, *a.* transpadane, beyond the Po.
traspalar, traspalear, *va.* to shovel, shovel off; to move, remove; to weed with a hoe.
traspaleo, *m.* shovelling; weeding with a hoe.
traspapelarse, *vr.* to be mislaid among other papers.
trasparencia, *f.* = TRANSPARENCIA.
trasparentarse, *vr.* = TRANSPARENTARSE.
trasparente, *m.* & *a.* = TRANSPARENTE.
traspasador, ra, *n.* trespasser, transgressor.
traspasamiento, *m.* transgression; trespass; transportation; crossing over; transfixion; transfer, conveyance; grief, anguish.
traspasar, *va.* to pass over, go beyond; to cross (as a river); to remove, transfer; to go through; to pierce, transfix; to return, repass; to trespass, transgress, violate; to exceed (proper bounds); to convey, transfer, make over; to cause great grief or affliction to.
traspaso, *m.* conveyance, transfer; assignment; transgression, violation; grief, anguish.
traspatio, *m.* (Am.) back yard, back court.
traspecho, *m.* bone ornament on a crossbow.
traspeinar, *va.* to comb again.
traspellar, *va.* to close, to shut.
traspié, *m.* slip, stumble; trip, wrestler's trick.—**dar traspiés,** to stumble; to slip, to err.
traspilastra, *f.* (arch.) counterpilaster.
traspillar. I. *va.* to shut, close. **II.** *vr.* to fail, become emaciated.
traspintar. I. *va.* to show (one card) and play another. **II.** *vr.* to show through; to show against the light; (coll.) to fail, come out wrong.
traspirable, traspiración, traspirar = TRANSPIRABLE, etc.
trasplantar. I. *va.* to transplant. **II.** *vr.* to migrate.
trasplante, *m.* transplantation; migration.
trasponedor, trasponer = TRANSPONEDOR, etc.
traspongo, trasponga, *v. V.* TRASPONER.
traspontín, *m.* = TRASPUNTÍN.
trasportación, trasportador, trasportamiento, etc. = TRANSPORTACIÓN, etc.
trasportín, *m.* wool upper mattress.
trasposición, etc. = TRANSPOSICIÓN, etc.
traspuesta, *f.* transposition; nook; lurking place; flight, concealment of a person; back yard or court; back door; rear outbuilding.
traspuesto, ta, *pp. irreg.* of TRASPONER.
traspunte, *m.* (theat.) prompter.
traspuntín, *m.* bedquilt.
trasquero, *m.* leather cutter.
trasquila, *f.* shearing, clipping, cropping.
trasquiladero, *m.* place where sheep are shorn.
trasquilador, ra, *n.* & *a.* shearer(-ing), clipper (-ing).
trasquiladura, *f.* = TRASQUILA.
trasquilar, *va.* to shear (sheep); to lop, crop; clip; to curtail, cut down.
trasquilimocho, cha, *a.* (coll.) close shorn or cropped.
trasquilón, *m.* clipping, shearing; (coll.) money lost through trickery or deception.—**a trasquilones,** irregularly, rudely.
trastabillar, *vn.* to reel, waver.
trastada, *f.* (coll.) inconsiderate act.
trastazo, *m.* (coll.) whack, thump, blow.
[1]**traste,** *m.* (mus.) stop, fret of a guitar; glass or cup for sampling wine.
[2]**traste,** *m.*—**dar al t. con,** to spoil, ruin, destroy.
trasteado, *m.* set of frets on a guitar.
trasteador, ra, *n.* moving man (woman).
trasteante, *a.* skillful at guitar playing.
[1]**trastear,** *va.* to fret (a guitar); to play well on (the guitar).
[2]**trastear. I.** *va.* to madden (the bull) with a red flag; (coll.) to manage with tact. **II.** *vn.* to move furniture from one part of a house to another; to talk in an excited manner.
trastejador, *m.* roof tiler.
trastejadura, *f.* tiling.
trastejar, *va.* to tile; to overhaul, repair.
trastejo, *m.* tiling.
trasteo, *m.* maddening the bull with a red flag; clever management of a person or business.
trastería, *f.* heap of old furniture; (coll.) rash action.
trasterminante, trasterminar = TRANSTERMINANTE, TRANSTERMINAR.
trastero, ra, *m.* or *f.* garret, lumber room.
trastesado, da, *a.* hardened, stiff.
trastienda, *f.* back room; prudence, caution.
trasto, *m.* piece of furniture; luggage; rubbish, lumber; (theat.) trick piece, set piece; (coll.) worthless person, trash.—*pl.* tools of trade, implements, outfit; steel weapons.—**trastos de cocina,** kitchen utensils.
trastornable, *a.* easily disturbed or upset.
trastornado, da. I. *pp.* of TRASTORNAR. **II.** *a.* upset, topsy-turvey; afflicted; unbalanced, mad.
trastornador, ra, *n.* & *a.* disturber(-ing); agitator(-ing).
trastornadura, *f.*, **trastornamiento,** *m.* upsetting, overthrow, disturbance.
trastornar, *va.* to upset; to turn upside down; to disorder, disturb, disarrange; to agitate, excite; to derange, daze, confuse, perplex (the mind); to persuade, induce.
trastorno, *m.* upsetting; upheaval; disturbance, disorder, confusion; trouble; disarrangement.
trastrabado, da, *a.* having the far hind foot and the near fore foot white.
trastrabarse, *vr.* to become fuddled.
trastrabillar, *vn.* to stumble; to reel; to stammer.
trastrás, *m.* last but one.
trastrocamiento, *m.* transposition, rearrangement; disarrangement.
trastrocar, *va.* (*ind. pres.* TRASTRUECO, *pret.* TRASTRUQUÉ; *subj.* TRASTRUEQUE) to change the order of; to disarrange, muddle.—**trastrueco, trastrueque,** *m.* rearrangement; disarrangement; transposition.
trastuelo, *m. dim.* worthless utensil; trash.
trastulo, *m.* pastime, toy.
trastumbar, *va.* to overturn, upset.
trasudación, *f.* transudation, oozing.
trasudar, *va.* to sweat, perspire.
trasudor, *m.* gentle perspiration.
trasuntar, *va.* to copy; to abridge, abstract.
trasuntivamente, *adv.* compendiously; as per copy.
trasunto, *m.* copy, transcript; likeness.
trasvasar, *va.* = TRANSVASAR.
trasvenarse, *vr.* (med.) to extravasate; to spill.
trasver, *va.* to see through; to see erroneously.
trasverberación = TRANSVERBERACIÓN.
trasversal, trasverso = TRANSVERSAL, etc.
trasverter, *vn.* (*ind.* TRASVIERTO; *subj.* TRASVIERTA) to overflow, run over.
trasvinarse, *vr.* (of wine) to leak out; (coll.) to be surmised or inferred.
trasvolar, *va.* (*ind.* TRASVUELO; *subj.* TRASVUELE) to fly across.
trata, *f.* trade; slave trade.—**t. blanca, or de blancas,** white slavery.
tratable, *a.* tractable, compliant.
tratadico, illo, ito, *m. dim.* tract, short treatise.
tratadista, *n.* author, writer (on special subjects).
tratado, *m.* treaty; treatise.
tratador, ra, *n.* mediator.

tratamiento, *m.* treatment; courteous title or form of address; (med., chem.) treatment.

tratante, *n.* dealer, trader, tradesman.

tratar. I. *va.* to treat (a subject, a person, a patient, a substance); to discuss; to handle, manage, conduct.—**t. de,** to address as, give the title of; to call, charge with being (*me trató de ambicioso,* he called me, or charged me with being, ambitious).—**t. por,** (chem.) to treat with. **II.** *vn.* to treat; to deal, trade.—**t. acerca de,** to treat of, deal with (a subject).—**t. de,** to treat of (a subject); to endeavor, try.—**t. en,** to deal in. **III.** *vr.* to behave, conduct oneself; to live (well or badly).—**t. de,** (impers.) to be a question of; to be intended for; (diff. constr.) to talk about (*¿de qué se trata?* what's being talked about, what are you talking about?).

trato, *m.* treatment, use, usage; social behavior, manner, address; pact, agreement, deal; trade, commerce; friendly intercourse, conversation; appellation, title of courtesy.—**mal t.,** ill-usage, ill-treatment.—**tener buen t.,** (coll.) to be pleasant, "nice," affable.—**tener mucho t.,** to be intimate friends.—**tener t. de gentes,** to be accustomed to good society.

trauma, *m.* (med.) trauma.

traumático, ca, *a.* (med.) traumatic.

traumatismo, *m.* (med.) traumatism.

traumatosis, *f.* (med.) traumatism, traumatosis.

traversa, *f.* (naut.) backstay.

travertino, *m.* (geol., min.) travertine, travertin.

través, *m.* inclination, bias; reverse, misfortune; traverse; (arch.) crossbeam; (fort.) traverse, screen.—**al t.** = DE T.—**al t. de,** through.—**dar al t.,** to be stranded.—**dar al t. con,** to throw away, misspend; to ruin, destroy; to set aside, ignore.—**de t.,** across, athwart, through.—**mirar de t.,** to squint; to look at out of the corner of one's eye.—**por el t.,** (naut.) on the beam.

travesaño, *m.* crosspiece, crossbar; bolster of a bed.

travesar, *va.* (*ind.* TRAVIESO; *subj.* TRAVIESE) to cross.

travesear, *vn.* to skip about, frisk, caper, romp; to be mischievous; to be quick at repartee; to lead a debauched life; to behave improperly.

travesero, ra. I. *a.* transverse, cross. **II.** *m.* bolster of a bed.

travesía, *f.* distance; passage; stretch, space; sea voyage; crossing (the sea); crossroad, short cut; transverse position; money won or lost at gambling; (fort.) traverse works; (naut.) side wind; sailor's pay for each voyage.

travesío, ía. I. *a.* traversing; transverse, or lateral, wind. **II.** *m.* crossing, crossroad.

travestido, da, *a.* disguised.

travesura, *f.* prank, frolic, caper, antic; mischief; lively fancy; sprightly conversation.

traviesa, *f.* distance across; at cards, raise on a bet; wager laid on a card player; (Ry.) crosstie; (arch.) rafter; transverse wall; (min.) cross level or gallery.

[1]**travieso, sa,** *a.* transverse, cross; restless, flighty; frolicsome, prankish; mischievous; shrewd, cute; dissolute, lewd.—**ir a campo t.,** to take a short cut; to go cross-country.

[2]**travieso, traviese,** *v. V.* TRAVESAR.

trayecto, *m.* distance, stretch; section.

trayectoria, *f.* trajectory.—**t. de vuelo,** flight path.

trayente, *a.* bringing, carrying, conducting.

traza, *f.* sketch, draught, outline; plan, device, scheme, project, contrivance; plot, artifice; manner, means; looks, appearance, aspect; prospect.—**darse trazas,** to find a way.

trazado, da. I. *pp.* of TRAZAR. **II.** *a.* traced, outlined.—**bien** or **mal t.,** of a good or bad disposition or figure. **III.** *m.* sketch, draught, outline, plan; (act of) drawing; (Ry.) location; running (of a line on the ground).

trazador, ra. *n.* contriver, schemer, designer.

trazar, *va.* (*pret.* TRACÉ; *subj.* TRACE) to design, devise, plan out; draw up; to trace, mark out; to draw (as a line); (Ry.) to locate; (surv.) to run, lay out (a line, a curve).

trazo, *m.* outline, plan; line, stroke of a pen or pencil; (art) fold of the drapery.—**t. magistral,** down stroke of a letter.—**al t.,** drawn in outline.

trazumarse, *vr.* to leak, ooze, transude.

treballa, *f.* sauce for goose.

trébedes, *f. pl.* trivet, cook's tripod.

trebejar, *vn.* to frolic, romp; to play.

trebejo, *m.* toy, plaything; chess piece.—*pl.* implements, tools of trade.

trebejuelo, *m. dim.* toy, trifle, gewgaw.

trebeliánica, *f.* (law) fourth part of an estate, to be deducted by the fiduciary heir, who holds it in trust for another.

trébol, *m.* (bot.) trefoil, clover, shamrock.

trece, *n.* & *a.* thirteen; thirteenth.—**estarse en sus t.,** to persist in one's opinion, to stick to it.

trecemesino, na, *a.* of thirteen months.

trecenario, *m.* space of thirteen days.

trecenato, trecenazgo, *m.* employment of thirteen persons.

treceno, na, *a.* thirteenth.

trecentista, *n.* & *a.* (pert. to) the trecento.

trecientos, tas, *n.* & *a.* three hundred.

trechear, *va.* (min.) to transport from hand to hand or from section to section.

trechel, *m.* (bot.) spring wheat.

trecheo, *m.* (min.) action of TRECHEAR.

trecho, *m.* space, distance, stretch; lapse.—**a trechos,** by intervals.—**de t. en t.,** at certain distances or intervals.

trefe, *a.* soft, thin; pliable; spurious (coin).

tregua, *f.* truce; rest, respite, recess, intermission.

treilla, *f.* leash; road or harrow leveler.

treinta, *n.* & *a.* thirty; thirtieth.—**t. y una,** a card game.

treintaidosavo, va, *n.* & *a.* thirty-second (part).

treintaidoseno, na, *a.* thirty-second.

treintanario, *m.* space of thirty days.

treintañal, *a.* of thirty years duration or age.

treintavo, va, *n.* & *a.* thirtieth.

treinteno, na, *f.* & *a.* thirtieth.

treja, *f.* cushion shot at billiards.

tremadal, *m.* quagmire, quaking bog.

tremátodo, da, *m.* & *a.* (zool.) trematode.

tremebundo, da, *a.* dreadful, frightful, fearful.

tremedal, *m.* = TREMADAL.

tremendo, da, *a.* tremendous, dreadful, terrible; awful, imposing; huge; excessive.

tremente, *a.* trembling.

trementina, *f.* turpentine.

tremer, *vn.* to tremble.

tremés; tremesino, na, *a.* three months old.

tremielga, *f.* (ichth.) electric ray, torpedo.

tremis, *m.* an ancient gold coin.

tremó, tremol, *m.* pier glass.

tremolante, *a.* waving in the air.

tremolar, *va.* & *vn.* to wave (as a flag).

tremolina, *f.* rustling of the wind; (coll.) bustle, fuss, noise, hubbub.

trémolo, *m.* (mus.) tremolo.

tremor, *m.* trembling; tremor.

trémulamente, *adv.* tremblingly, tremulously.

tremulante; tremulento, ta = TRÉMULO.

trémulo, la, *a.* tremulous, quivering, shaking.

tren, *m.* train; outfit; equipment; following, retinue; show, pomp, ostentation; (Ry.) train.—**t. ascendente,** "up train," going toward Madrid.—**t. botijo,** excursion train.—**t. carreta,** accommodation train.—**t. correo,** mail train.—**t. de artillería,** convoy of artillery.—**t. de aterrizaje,** (aer.) undercarriage, landing gear.—**t. de casa,** housekeeping outfit.—**t. de escala,** accommodation train.—**t. de lavado,** laundry.—**t. de mercancías,** freight train.—**t. de recreo,** excursion train.—**t. descendente,** "down train," going from Madrid.—**t. de viajeros,** passenger train.—**t. expreso,** express train.—**t. milla,** train-mile.—**t. mixto,**

mixed train (carrying both passengers and freight).—**t. ómnibus,** accommodation train.
trena, *f.* scarf, sash; burnt silver; twist bread.
trenado, da, *a.* reticulated, mesh (as *a.*), latticed.
trenca, *f.* crosstree in a beehive; main root.
trencellín, *m.* = TRENCILLO.
trencica, ita, *f. dim.* small braid or plait.
trencilla, *f.* braid (trimming).
trencillar, *va.* to trim with braid.
trencillo, *m.* gold or silver hatband trimmed with jewels.
treno, *m.* lamentation, dirge.
trenque, *m.* jetty in a river.
trenza, *f.* braid; plait; braided hair, tress.
trenzadera, *f.* tape; knot of plaited cord.
trenzado, *m.* braided hair; braiding; (dance) caper; prance of a horse.—**al t.,** carelessly.
trenzar. I. *va.* to braid; to plait. **II.** *vn.* to prance; to cut capers.
treo, *m.* (naut.) square sail, crossjack sail.
[1]**trepa,** *f.* climbing; somersault.
[2]**trepa,** *f.* boring, perforating; (sewing) wavy edging or trimming; grain or mottle of polished wood; (coll.) flogging, lashing; (coll.) artful trick, fraud.
[1]**trepado, da,** *a.* (of animals) strong, robust.
[2]**trepado,** *m.* (sewing) edging.
trepador, ra. I. *a.* climbing. **II.** *m.* climbing place. **III.** *f.* (bot.) climber, creeper (as ivy).—*pl.* (ornith.) climbers.
trepajuncos, *m.* (ornith.) a kind of reed bird.
trepanación, *f.* (surg.) trephining.
trepanar, *va.* (surg.) to trepan, trephine.
trépano, *m.* (surg.) trepan, trephine.
[1]**trepante. I.** *pres. p.* of [1]TREPAR. **II.** *a.* climbing.
[2]**trepante. I.** *pres. p.* of [2]TREPAR. **II.** *a.* wily, artful, crafty.
[1]**trepar,** *vn.* to climb, mount, clamber; (bot.) to climb, creep (as ivy).
[2]**trepar,** *va.* to bore, perforate; (sewing) to trim with [2]TREPA.
trepatroncos, *m.* (ornith.) mason bird.
trepe, *m.* (coll.) scolding, reprimand.
trepidación, *f.* trepidation; vibration; (ancient astr.) trepidation.
trepidante, *a.* vibrating, shaking.
trepidar, *vn.* to shake, vibrate, jar.
trépido, da, *a.* tremulous, shaking.
treponema, *f.* (biol.) treponema.
tres. I. *m.* & *a.* three; third. **II.** *m.* at cards, a trey; magistrate of a city governed by three magistrates. **III.** *f. pl.*—**las t.,** three o'clock.
tresalbo, ba, *a.* having three white feet.
tresañal, tresañejo, ja, *a.* three years old.
tresbolillo.—al t., (agr.) (set out) in special arrangement; (mech.) staggered (riveting).
trescientos, tas, *n.* & *a.* three hundred; three-hundredth.
tresdoblar, *va.* to treble; to fold three times.
tresdoble, *m.* triple, threefold.
tresillista, *n.* expert in, or fond of, ombre.
tresillo, *m.* ombre, a card game; (mus.) triplet.
tresmesino, na, *a.* three months old.
tresnal, *m.* (agr.) shock, stook.
trestanto. I. *m.* triple number or amount. **II.** *adv.* three times as much.
treta, *f.* (fencing) feint; trick, wile, craft.
treudo, *m.* (law) emphyteutic rent.
trezavo, va, *n.* & *a.* thirteenth.
tría, *f.* choice, selection; tease in fabrics.—**dar una t.,** to transpose (beehives).
triaca, *f.* (pharm.) antidote.
triacal, *a.* antidotal.
triache, *m.* coffee beans of inferior quality.
tríada, tríade, *f.* triad, group of three.
triangulación, *f.* triangulation.
triangulado, da; triangular, *a.* triangular.
triangularmente, *adv.* triangularly.
triángulo, la. I. *a.* triangular. **II.** *m.* (geom.) triangle; (astr.) Triangulum; (mus.) triangle.—**t. acutángulo,** acute-angled triangle.—**t. esférico,** spherical triangle.—**t. obtusángulo,** obtuse-angled triangle.—**t. rectángulo,** right-angled, or right, triangle.
triaquera, *f.* (pharm.) container for antidotes.
triar. I. *va.* to choose, select. **II.** *vn.* (of bees) to swarm to a favorite hive. **III.** *vr.* (of fabric) to show teases; to curdle.
triario, *m.* (anc. Rome) triarian soldier.
trías, *m.* (geol.) Triassic.
triásico, ca, *a.* (geol.) Triassic.
triatómico, ca, *a.* (chem.) triatomic.
tribal, *a.* tribal.
tribásico, ca, *a.* (chem.) tribasic.
tribómetro, *m.* friction-measuring instrument.
tribraquio, *m.* (poet.) tribrach (⏑⏑⏑).
tribu, *f.* tribe.
tribuente, *a.* attributing.
tribuir, *va.* to attribute.
tribulación, *f.* tribulation, affliction.
tríbulo, *m.* (bot.) thistle; prickle.
tribuna, *f.* tribune; rostrum; gallery.—*pl.* grandstand.
tribunado, *m.* tribuneship.
tribunal, *m.* tribunal, court of justice.—**t. de cuentas,** exchequer.—**t. juvenil,** juvenile court.—**demandar, or llevar, a los tribunales,** to sue (at court).
tribunicio, cia; tribúnico, ca, *a.* pertaining to a tribunal or a judge.
tribuno, *m.* (Rom. hist.) tribune; orator.
tributable, *a.* taxable.
tributación, *f.* tribute, contribution; system of taxation; (law) emphyteusis.
tributante, *n.* taxpayer; tribute payer.
tributar, *va.* to pay (taxes or contributions); to pay, render (homage, respect); (law) to hold in emphyteusis.
tributario, ria. I. *a.* tributary. **II.** *n.* taxpayer; tributary (river).
tributo, *m.* tribute; tax, contribution; gift, offering; toil, trouble, burden.
tricahue, *m.* a kind of Chilean parrot.
tricenal, *a.* lasting thirty years.
tricentenario, *m.* tercentenary, tercentennial.
tricentésimo, ma, *a.* three-hundredth.
tríceps, *m.* & *a.* (anat.) triceps.
triciclo, *m.* tricycle.
tricípete, *a.* three-headed.
triclinio, *m.* (Rom. hist.) triclinium, a kind of couch.
tricloruro, *m.* (chem.) trichloride.
tricolor, *a.* tricolor.
tricorne, *a.* (poet.) three-horned.
tricornio. I. *a.* three-horned. **II.** *m.* three-cornered hat.
tricot, *m.* (Gal.) tricot, knitwear, knitted goods.
tricotomía, *f.* trichotomy, division into three parts.
tricotómico, ca, *a.* trichotomic, pert. to trichotomy.
tricótomo, ma, *a.* trichotomous, divided into three parts.
tricroico, ca, *a.* trichroic.
tricroísmo, *m.* trichroism.
tricromático, ca, *a.* trichromatic.
tricromatismo, *m.* trichromatism.
tricromía, *f.* three-color printing.
tricromo, ma, *a.* three-color.
tricúspide, *a.* tricuspid; (anat.) tricuspid.
tridacio, *m.* (pharm.) thridacium.
tridente. I. *a.* tridental. **II.** *m.* trident.
tridentino, na, *n.* & *a.* Tridentine.
tridínamo, ma, *a.* (chem.) trivalent.
triduano, na, *a.* lasting three days.
triduo, *m.* (eccl.) triduum.
triedro. (geom.) **I.** *a.* trihedral. **II.** *m.* trihedron; trihedral angle.
trienal, *a.* triennial.
trienio, *m.* term of three years; triennium.
trieñal, *a.* triennial.
trierarca, *m.* (Gk. hist.) trierarch.
trifacial, *m.* & *a.* (anat.) trifacial, trigeminal.
trifásico, ca, *a.* (elec.) three-phase.

trífido, da, *a.* (poet.) trifid, three-cleft.
trifinio, *m.* point where the boundaries of three districts meet.
trifloro, ra, *a.* triflorous, three-flowered.
trifoliáceo, cea; trifoliado, da, *a.* (bot.) trifoliate, trifoliated.
trifolio, *m.* (bot.) trefoil; shamrock.
triforio, *m.* (arch.) triforium.
triforme, *a.* triform, triformed.
trifulca, *f.* (coll.) squabble, row; (foundry) lever system for moving the bellows.
trifurcación, *f.* trifurcation.
trifurcado, da, *a.* trifurcate, three-forked.
trigal, *m.* wheat field.
trigaza, *f.* short straw of wheat.
trigémino, na. I. *a.* (anat.) trigeminal. **II.** *m.* (anat.) trigeminal, trifacial nerve.
trigésimo, ma, *a.* thirtieth.
trigla, *f.* (ichth.) red surmullet.
tríglifo, *m.* (arch.) triglyph.
trigo, *m.* wheat; wheat field.—*pl.* crops; grainfields.—**t. alonzo,** bearded wheat.—**t. blanquillo, candeal,** or **común,** summer wheat.—**t. chamorro,** or **desraspado,** winter or beardless wheat.—**t. fanfarrón,** Barbary wheat.—**t. hembrilla,** or **marzal,** summer wheat.—**t. mocho, pelón, peloto,** beardless wheat.—**t. piche** = T. BLANQUILLO.—**t. sarraceno,** buckwheat.—**t. teja.** = T. BLANQUILLO—**t. toseta,** beardless wheat.—**t. trechel, tremés, tremesino,** summer wheat.
trigón, *m.* (mus.) trigonon, an ancient lyre.
trígono, *m.* (astrol., geom.) trigon.
trigonometría, *f.* trigonometry.—**t. esférica,** spherical trigonometry.—**t. plana,** or **rectilínea,** plane trigonometry.
trigonométrico, ca, *a.* trigonometrical.
trigueño, ña, *a.* brunette, swarthy, dark.
triguero, ra. I. *a.* growing with wheat. **II.** *m.* sieve for corn; corn or grain dealer. **II.** *f.* (bot.) common wheat grass; canary seed.
trilateral, *a.* trilateral.
trilátero, ra, *a.* trilateral.
trilingüe, *a.* trilingual.
trilio, *m.* (bot.) wood-lily, trillium.
trilítero, ra, *a.* triliteral.
trilito, *m.* (archeol.) trilithon.
trilobites, *m.* (paleontol.) trilobite.
trilobulado, da, *a.* trilobate.
trilocular, *a.* trilocular, divided into three parts.
trilogía, *f.* trilogy.
[1]**trilla,** *f.* (ichth.) red surmullet, gurnard.
[2]**trilla,** *f.* (agr.) harrow: thrashing.
trilladera, *f.* separating harrow.
trillado, da. I. *pp.* of TRILLAR. **II.** *a.* trite, stale, hackneyed.
trillador, ra. I. *n.* & *a.* (agr.) thrasher(-ing). **II.** *f.* thrashing machine.
trilladura, *f.* (agr.) thrashing.
trillar, *va.* (agr.) to thrash, beat; to frequent; to repeat.
trillo, *m.* (agr.) separating harrow; thrashing machine; (Am.) footpath.
trillón, *m.* trillion (one million billions).
trimembre, *a.* trimembral.
trimestral, *a.* trimestrial, quarterly.
trimestralmente, *adv.* quarterly.
trimestre, *m.* quarter; quarterly payment.
trímetro, tra, *m.* & *a.* (poet.) trimeter.
trimielga, *f.* (ichth.) = TREMIELGA, torpedo.
Trimurti, *f.* Trimurty, the Hindu Trinity.
trinado, *m.* (mus.) trill, quaver; twittering of birds.
trinar, *vn.* (mus.) to trill, quaver; (coll.) to get angry or furious.
trinca, *f.* triad, ternary; (naut.) gammoning, seizing; seizing stuff.—**a la t.,** (naut.) close-hauled.
trincadura, *f.* large two-masted barge.
trincafía, *f.* wound splice or patch, made by winding a rope spirally around the piece or pieces.
trincapiñones, *n.* (coll.) harebrained person.
[1]**trincar,** *va.* (*pret.* TRINQUÉ; *subj.* TRINQUE) to break, chop.
[2]**trincar.** (mut. like [1]TRINCAR) **I.** *va.* (naut.) to fasten, lash; to tie, bind, make fast. **II.** *vn.* (naut.) to keep close to the wind.
[3]**trincar,** *vn.* (mut. like [1]TRINCAR) (coll.) to drink (wine or liquor).
[1]**trincha,** *f.* (tailoring) cloth strap for buttoning garments.
[2]**trincha,** *f.* (Am.) socket chisel, cutting gouge.
trinchador, *m.* (Mex.) sideboard.
trinchadora, *f.* (S. A.) carving knife.
trinchante, *m.* carver at table; carving knife; (S. A.) sideboard; stonecutter's hammer.
trinchar, *va.* to carve (food).
trinche, *m.* (S. A.) carving knife.
trinchera, *f.* (mil.) trench, intrenchment; deep cut, ditch; trench coat, waterproof.
trinchero, *m.* trencher; side table.
trincherón, *m. aug.* large trench or ditch.
trinchete, *m.* cobbler's heel knife.
trineo, *m.* sleigh, sledge; sled, bob sled.
trinidad, *f.* trinity.
trinitaria, *f.* (bot.) pansy, heartsease.
trinitario, ria, *a.* & *n.* (eccl.) Trinitarian; (Mex.) hired mourner; native to (of) Trinidad.
trinitrocresol, *m.* (chem.) trinitrocresol.
trinitrotolueno, *m.* (chem.) trinitrotoluene, TNT.
trino, na. I. *a.* ternary, triadic, trinal, trine. **II.** *m.* (astr.) trine; (mus.) trill.
trinomio, *m.* & *a.* (math.) trinomial.
trinqué, trinque, *v. V.* [1,2,3] TRINCAR.
trinquetada, *f.* (naut.) sailing under the foresail.
[1]**trinquete,** *m.* (naut.) foremast, foresail.
[2]**trinquete,** *m.* (mech.) pawl, catch, stop; racket (ball game).
[3]**trinquete,** *m.*—**a cada t.,** at every step.
trinquetilla, *f.* (naut.) fore staysail.
trinquis, *m.* (coll.) drink (of liquor).
[1]**trío,** *m.* = TRÍA.
[2]**trío,** *m.* (mus.) trio.
trional, *m.* (chem.) trional.
Triones, *m. pl.* (astr.) Triones, the Dipper.
trióxido, *m.* (chem.) trioxid, trioxide.
tripa, *f.* gut, intestine, bowel; (coll.) belly, paunch; filling, fillers (for cigars); file, docket.—*pl.* core of fruit; insides, entrails; inner lining of some feathers.—**hacer de tripas corazón,** to pluck up heart.
tripanosoma, *m.* (biol.) Trypanosoma.
tripartición, *f.* tripartition.
tripartir, *va.* to divide into three parts.
tripartito, ta, *a.* tripartite.
tripasto, *m.* pulley with three sheaves.
tripe, *m.* shag, plush.
tripería, *f.* tripe shop; heap of tripe.
tripero, ra, *n.* tripe seller; *m.* bellyband; cummerbund.
tripétalo, la, *a.* (bot.) tripetalous.
tripicallero, ra, *n.* tripe dealer.
tripicallos, *m. pl.* tripe.
trípili, *m.* (theat.) a Spanish song and dance.
triplano, *m.* (aer.) tripiane.
triple, *a.* triple, treble.
tríplica, *f.* (law) rejoinder.
triplicación, *f.* triplication, trebling.
triplicado, da, *a.* triplicate, treble.
triplicar, *va.* (*pret.* TRIPLIQUÉ; *subj.* TRIPLIQUE) to treble, triple; (law) to rejoin.
tríplice, *a.* treble, triple.
triplicidad, *f.* triplicity, trebleness.
tripliqué, triplique, *v. V.* TRIPLICAR.
triplo, pla, *a.* treble, triplicate, triple.
trípode, *m.* or *f.* tripod; trevet, trivet.
trípol, trípoli, *m.* tripoli, rottenstone.
tripolino, na, *n.* & *a.* Tripoline, Tripolitan.
tripolio, *m.* (bot.) sea starwort.
tripolitano, na, *n.* & *a.* = TRIPOLINO.
tripón, na, *a.* (coll.) pot-bellied, big-bellied.
tripsina, *f.* (biochem.) trypsin.
tríptico, *m.* triptych.
triptongo, *m.* triphthong, three-voweled syllable.

tripudiar, *vn.* to dance.
tripudio, *m.* dance, ball.
tripudo, da, *a.* pot-bellied, big-bellied.
tripulación, *f.* crew (of ship, airplane, etc.).—**t. de tierra,** (aer.) ground crew.
tripulante, *n.* one of the crew.—*pl.* crew.
tripular, *va.* to man (ships); to fit out, equip.
trique, *m.* crack, sharp noise.—**triquete,** *m. dim.* —**a cada t.,** at every stir or step.
triquina, *f.* trichina, intestinal worm.
triquinado, da, *a.* trichinous.
triquinosis, *f.* (med.) trichinosis.
triquinoso, sa, *a.* trichinous.
triquiñuela, *f.* (coll.) trickery, subterfuge.
triquitraque, *m.* crack, clack, clattering, clashing; firecracker, pulling cracker.
trirrectángulo, la, *a.* (geom.) trirectangular.
trirreme, *m.* (naut.) trireme.
tris, *m.* crack, noise made by the breaking of glass; trice, nick of time.—**t. tras,** tedious repetition; "the same old story."—**en un t.,** within an ace, almost, coming pretty near (falling, etc.).
trisa, *f.* (ichth.) shad.
Trisagio, *m.* (eccl.) Trisagion.
trisca, *f.* noise made by crushing under the feet; noisy fun, merriment, uproar.
triscador, ra. I. *n.* noisy, rattling person. **II.** *m.* (mech.) saw set, saw wrest, saw swage.
triscar. I. *vn.* (*pret.* TRISQUÉ; *subj.* TRISQUE) to stamp the feet; to walk lively, to hustle; to romp, caper, frolic. **II.** *va.* to mix, mingle; to set (the teeth of a saw).
trisecar, *va.* to trisect.—**trisección,** *f.* trisection.
trisílabo, ba, *a.* trisyllabic.
trismo, *m.* (med.) trismus, lockjaw.
trispasto, *m.* three-pulley tackle.
trisqué, trisque, *v. V.* TRISCAR.
triste, *a.* sad, sorrowful; gloomy, dismal; abject, mean, low.
tristemente, *adv.* sadly, sorrowfully.
tristeza, *f.* sadness, grief, sorrow, gloom.
tristón, na, *a.* melancholy, rather sad.
trisulco, ca, *a.* three-pronged; having three furrows or channels.
trisulfuro, *m.* (chem.) trisulfide.
tritíceo, cea, *a.* wheaten.
tritio, *m.* (chem.) tritium.
tritón, *m.* (myth.) Triton; (zool.) triton, triturus.
trítono, *m.* (mus.) tritone.
triturable, *a.* triturable, crushable.
trituración, *f.* trituration, crushing.
triturador, ra. I. *n.* & *a.* crusher(-ing), triturator (-ing). **II.** *f.* crusher, crushing machine.
triturar, *va.* to triturate, crush; to masticate.
triunfador, ra, *n.* conqueror, victor.
triunfal, *a.* triumphal.—**triunfalmente,** *adv.* triumphally.
triunfante, *a.* triumphant, victorious.
triunfantemente, *adv.* triumphantly.
triunfar, *vn.* **(de)** to conquer; to triumph, to achieve victory (over); to win; to trump at cards.
triunfo, *m.* triumph, victory; exultation; spoils of war; trump card.—**costar un t.,** to be exceedingly difficult.—**en t.,** triumphantly; in triumph.
triunviral, *a.* triumviral.
triunvirato, *m.* triumvirate.
triunviro, *m.* triumvir.
trivalente, *a.* (chem.) trivalent, triadic, triatomic.
trivial, *a.* trivial; trite, trodden, beaten.
trivialidad, *f.* triviality; triteness.
trivialmente, *adv.* trivially.
trivio, *m.* fork of a road; junction of three roads; trivium (i. e. grammar, rhetoric, logic).
[1]**triza,** *f.* bit, small piece, fragment, shred, particle.—**hacer trizas,** to knock to pieces; to tear to bits; to wound or injure a person or animal.
[2]**triza,** *f.* = DRIZA, (naut.) halyard.
trocable, *a.* exchangeable.
trocada.—a la t., in a sense or direction opposite to the apparent one.
trocadamente, *adv.* distortedly, changing things or words.
trocado, da. I. *a.* & *pp.* changed; distorted.—**a la trocada,** or **a la trocadilla,** in the contrary sense; in exchange. **II.** *m.* change, small coin.
trocador, ra, *n.* one who exchanges or changes.
trocaico, ca, *a.* (poet.) trochaic, of trochees.
trocamiento, *m.* change; distortion; exchange.
trocante, *a.* bartering, exchanging.
trocánter, *m.* (anat.) trochanter.
[1]**trocar. I.** *va.* (*ind. pres.* TRUECO, *pret.* TROQUÉ; *subj.* TRUEQUE) to exchange, barter; to change, alter; to interchange; to distort, pervert; to vomit. **II.** *vr.* to change; to be changed, transformed or reformed; to exchange seats with another.
[2]**trocar,** *m.* (surg.) trocar.
trocatinta, *f.* (coll.) confusing mistake.
trocatinte, *m.* shot color, changing color.
troceo, *m.* (naut.) parrel, truss.
trociscar, *va.* to make into troches or lozenges.
trocisco, *m.* (pharm.) troche, lozenge.
trocla, *f.* pulley.
tróclea, *f.* (anat.) trochlea.
troco, *m.* (ichth.) short sunfish.
trocoide, *f.* (geom.) trochoid.
trocotrón, *m.* (phys.) trochotron.
trocha, *f.* cross path, short cut; rough road, trail; (mil.) military road; (Ry., Am.) gauge.
trochemoche.—a t., helter-skelter, pell-mell.
trochuela, *f. dim.* narrow path.
trofeo, *m.* trophy; spoils of war; victory; memorial; military insignia.
trófico, ca, *a.* (physiol.) trophic, pert. to nutrition.
trofología, *f.* trophology, science of the nutrition of tissues.
troglodita. I. *a.* troglodytic; (fig.) troglodytic; (fig.) gluttonous, greedy. **II.** *n.* troglodyte; (fig.) troglodyte, cave man; (fig.) glutton; *m.* (ornith.) troglodyte.
troglodítico, ca, *a.* troglodytic.
troj, troje, *f.* granary, barn.
trojero, *m.* keeper of a granary.
trojezado, da, *a.* shredded, minced.
trola, *f.* (coll.) fib, hoax, gammon.
trole, *m.* (elec.) trolley.
tromba, *f.* waterspout.
trombocito, *m.* (physiol.) platelet.
trombón, *m.* (mus.) trombone.
trombosis, *f.* (med.) thrombosis.—**t. coronaria,** (med.) coronary thrombosis.
trompa. I. *f.* trumpet; (mus.) horn; trunk of an elephant; proboscis of some insects; (foundry) trompe; humming top; (arch.) projecting arch (from a wall); cradle, vault; (Ry.) cowcatcher, pilot (of a locomotive).—**t. de caza,** hunting horn.—**t. de Eustaquio,** (anat.) Eustachian tube.—**t. de Falopio,** (anat.) Fallopian tube. —**t. marina,** a musical one-string instrument, played with a bow; waterspout.—**a t. tañida,** at the sound of the trumpet.—**a t. y talega,** hurriedly, helter-skelter. **II.** *m.* horn player.
trompada, *f.* (coll.) fisticuff; collision, bump.
trompar, *vn.* to whip a top.
trompazo, *m.* = TROMPADA.
trompear, *vn.* to whip a top; (Am.) to bump; to fight with the fists.
[1]**trompero, ra,** *a.* deceptive, false, deceiving.
[2]**trompero, ra,** *n.* top maker.
trompeta. I. *f.* trumpet; bugle. **II.** *m.* trumpeter; bugler; (coll.) puppet, noodle.
trompetada, *f.* (coll.) silly remark.
trompetazo, *m.* trumpet blast; bugle blast or call; (coll.) silly remark.
trompetear, *vn.* (coll.) to sound the trumpet.
trompeteo, *m.* sounding the bugle or trumpet.
trompetería, *f.* brass pipes of an organ.
trompetero, *m.* trumpet maker; trumpeter.
trompetilla, *f. dim.* small trumpet; ear trumpet; (P. I.) cheroot.—**de t.,** (of certain mosquitoes) buzzing.

trompicar. I. *va.* to trip, to make stumble; (coll.) to promote (an employee) over another who is entitled to the place. **II.** *vn.* to stumble frequently; to falter.
trompicón, *m.*, **trompilladura,** *f.* stumbling.
trompillar, *va.* & *vn.* = TROMPICAR.
trompillo, *m.* (Am.) (bot.) a bixa tree.
trompillón, *m.* (arch.) keystone of a cradle vault.
trompis, *m.* (coll.) blow with the fist.
trompo, *m.* whipping top; spinning top; chessman; trochid (mollusk).—**ponerse como un t.**, to eat or drink to excess.
trompón, *m. aug.* big spinning top; (bot.) narcissus.—**a t.**, or **de t.**, helter-skelter.
tronada, *f.* thunderstorm.
tronador, ra. I. *n.* & *a.* thunderer(-ing). **II.** *m.* detonating rocket.
tronar, *v. impers.* & *vn.* (*ind.* TRUENA; *subj.* TRUENE) to thunder; (coll.) to lose one's all, to fail in business.—**t. con uno,** to fall out with one.—**por lo que pueda t.**, as a precaution, in case something happens.
tronca, *f.* truncation.
troncal, *a.* pertaining to or springing from the trunk or stem; trunk (as *a.*), main.
troncar, *va.* to truncate.
tronco, *m.* trunk; stem, stalk; stock, origin; team of horses; unfeeling person.—**estar hecho un t.**, to be bereft of sensation; to be fast asleep.
tronchado, *a.* (her.) trouçonné.
tronchar, *va.* & *vr.* to break off forcibly.
troncho, *m.* stem, stalk of garden plants.
tronchudo, da, *a.* stalky.
tronera. I. *f.* (fort.) embrasure; loophole; dormer, small skylight; porthole; pocket hole of a billiard table. **II.** *m.* harum-scarum, harebrained person.
tronerar, *va.* to make embrasures in.
trónica, *f.* (coll.) rumor, gossip.
tronido, *m.* thunder, loud report.
tronitoso, sa, *a.* (coll.) resounding, thundering.
trono, *m.* throne; (eccl.) shrine.—*pl.* thrones, seventh choir of angels.
tronquista, *m.* coachman, teamster.
tronquito, *m. dim.* of TRONCO.
tronzador, *m.* two-handed saw.
tronzar, *va.* to shatter, break in pieces; (sewing) to make fine tucks.
tronzo, za, *a.* (of horses) with cropped ears.
tropa, *f.* troops, soldiers; crowd, multitude; (Am.) drove of cattle; (Arg.) fleet (of vehicles); (mil.) ranks; beat to arms.—*pl.* (mil.) forces, army.—**t. de asalto,** storm troops.—**t. de línea,** regular or standing army; army corps.—**t. de marina,** marines.—**t. ligera,** skirmishers.—**en t.**, in random groups, without order.
tropecé, *pret.* of TROPEZAR.
tropeína, *f.* (chem.) tropeine.
tropel, *m.* rush, hurry, bustle, confusion; huddle; heap of things, mess, jumble; crowd.—**de,** or **en, t.**, tumultuously, in a throng.—**tropelía,** *f.* rush, hurry, confusion; injustice, outrage.
tropeoleo, a, *a.* & *f.* (bot.) Tropæolum.
tropezadero, *m.* stumbling place.
tropezador, ra, *n.* tripper, stumbler.
tropezadura, *f.* stumbling.
tropezar. I. *vn.* (*ind. pres.* TROPIEZO, *pret.* TROPECÉ; *subj.* TROPIECE) to stumble; **(con)** to strike (against); to stumble, trip (over); to meet (with); to stumble, light (on), happen to find; to slip (into crime or blunders); to wrangle, squabble. **II.** *vr.* (of horses) to interfere.
tropezón, na. I. *n.* & *a.* (of horses) interferer (-ing). **II.** *m.* tripping; stumbling; obstacle, stumbling block.—**a tropezones,** (coll.) by fits and starts; painfully, falling and rising, trudging along.
tropezoso, sa, *a.* apt to stumble or trip.
tropical, *a.* tropical.
trópico, ca. I. *a.* (rhet.) tropical, figurative. **II.** *m.* (astr., geog.) tropic.—**t. de Cáncer,** Tropic of Cancer.—**t. de Capricornio,** Tropic of Capricorn.
tropidina, *f.* (chem.) tropidine.
tropiece, tropieza, [1]**tropiezo,** *v. V.* TROPEZAR.
[2]**tropiezo,** *m.* stumble; obstacle, hitch; slip, fault, error; quarrel, dispute, squabble.
tropina, *f.* (chem.) tropine.
tropismo, *m.* (biol.) tropism.
tropo, *m.* (rhet.) trope.
tropología, *f.* tropology.
tropológico, ca, *a.* tropological.
tropopausa, *f.* (meteorol.) tropopause.
troposfera, *f.* (meteorol.) troposphere.
troque, *m.* knot made in cloths when dyeing them, to show the original color.
troqué, *pret.* of TROCAR.
troquel, *m.* die (as for coining).
troquelar, *va.* = ACUÑAR, to coin, mint.
troqueo, *m.* (poet.) trochee (—◡).
troquillo, *m.* (arch.) trochilus.
trotador, ra, *n.* & *a.* trotter(-ing).
trotar, *va.* & *vn.* to trot; (coll.) to hustle.
trote, *m.* trot.—**t. cochinero,** rack (gait of a horse).—**al t.**, trotting, at a trot; (coll.) in haste.—**tomar el t.**, (coll.) to run away.
trotillo, *m. dim.* light trot.
trotón, na. I. *f.* trotter(-ing). **II.** *m.* horse.
trotonería, *f.* continual trot.
trova, *f.* metrical composition; ballad.
trovador, ra, *n.* troubadour, minstrel.
trovadoresco, ca, *a.* pertaining to, or in the way of, minstrels or troubadours.
trovar, *vn.* to write poetry; to misconstrue.
trovero, *m.* (Fr. poet.) trouvère, trouveur.
trovista, *n.* = TROVADOR.
trovo, *m.* popular love ballad.
trox, *f.* (obs.) = TROJ, granary, barn.
Troya, *f.* Troy.—**aquí fué T.**, here was Troy; only the ruins left; here, or there, is the rub, or the difficulty.—**¡arda T.!** let happen what will.
troyano, na, *n.* & *a.* Trojan.
[1]**troza,** *f.* log (of wood).
[2]**troza,** *f.* (naut.) parrel truck.
trozar, *va.* to cut into logs; to break, shatter.
trozo, *m.* piece, chunk, fragment, part; (naut.) detail of a crew; selection, piece (of music); passage (from a book, etc.); (mil.) division of a column.—**t. de madera,** block (of wood).
trucar, *vn.* (*pret.* TRUQUÉ; *subj.* TRUQUE) to make the first bet at the game of TRUQUE; to pocket a ball at pool or trucks.—**truco,** *m.* pocketing a pool ball.—*pl.* pool (billiards).
truculencia, *f.* truculence, cruelty.
truculento, ta, *a.* truculent, fierce.
trucha, *f.* (ichth.) trout; derrick, gin.—**t. de mar,** (ichth.) sea trout.
truchero, ra, *n.* fisher or seller of trout.
truchimán, na, *n.* (coll.) expert buyer; shrewd trader.
truchuela, *f.* small trout; small dry codfish.
trué, *m.* fine linen from Troyes.
[1]**trueco,** *m.* exchange, barter.—**a t.**, or **en t., de,** in exchange for.
[2]**trueco, trueca,** *v. V.* TROCAR.
truena, truene, *v. V.* TRONAR.
trueno, *m.* thunder; loud report (as of cannon); (coll.) harum-scarum, wild youth.—**t. gordo,** loud detonation; big scandal; sensational ending.
[1]**trueque,** *m.* exchange, barter.—**a t.**, or **en t., de,** in exchange for.
[2]**trueque,** *v. V.* TROCAR.
trufa, *f.* (bot.) truffle; lie, story, fib.
trufador, ra, *n.* story teller, fibber.
trufar. I. *va.* to stuff or cook with truffles. **II.** *vn.* to fib, lie.
truhán, na, *n.* rascal, scoundrel, knave; buffoon, jester, mountebank.—**truhanada,** *f.* piece of rascality.—**truhanamente,** *adv.* villainously, knavishly.—**truhanear,** *vn.* to play the rascal; to play the buffoon.—**truhanería,** *f.* rascality, scoundrelism; buffoonery, low jest.—**truhanesco, ca,** *a.* knavish, rascally; clownish.
truja, *f.* olive bin in oil mills.—**trujal,** *m.* oil press; wine press; oil mill: copper for soap

making.—**trujaleta,** *f.* vessel for the juice in a wine press.
trujamán, *n.* expert buyer or trader; dragoman, interpreter.—**trujamanear,** *vn.* to act as an interpreter, broker, buyer, or seller; to trade, to barter.—**trujamanía,** *f.* brokering, brokerage.
trujimán, *n.* = TRUJAMÁN.
[1]**trulla,** *f.* noise, bustle, hurly-burly; crowd.
[2]**trulla,** *f.* (mason.) trowel.
[1]**trullo,** *m.* (ornith.) teal.
[2]**trullo,** *m.* vat for the juice of pressed grapes.
trun, *m.* (bot.) a Chilean variety of bur.
truncadamente, *adv.* in a truncated manner.
truncado, da, *a.* & *pp.* truncate, truncated.
truncamiento, *m.* truncation; maiming.
truncar, *va.* (*pret.* TRUNQUÉ; *subj.* TRUNQUE) to truncate; to maim; to mutilate (a speech, quotation, etc.).
trunco, ca, *a.* mutilated; truncated; incomplete.
trupial, *m.* (ornith.) troopial.
truque, *m.* a card game.
truqué, truque, *v.* *V.* TRUCAR.
truquero, *m.* keeper of a pool table.
truquiflor, *m.* a card game.
trusa, *f.* (Cuba, W. I.) men's bathing suit.—*pl.* trunk hose.
trust, *m.* (com.) trust.
tsetsé, tsé-tsé, *f.* tsetse fly.
tú, *pers. pron. 2d person, m.* or *f.* thou; (when on intimate terms) you.—**a t. por t.,** thee for thee; disrespectfully.—**de t. por t.,** intimately.—**tratar de t.,** to be on intimate terms with.
tu, *poss. pron. m.* or *f.* (*pl.* **tus**) thy; (when on intimate terms) your.
tuatúa, *f.* (bot.) American spurge.
tuáutem, *n.* (coll.) leading spirit, mover; essential point.
tuba, *f.* (P. I.) tuba, a beverage obtained from certain palms.
tuberculado, da, *a.* tuberculated, tuberculate.
tubercular, *a.* tubercular.
tuberculina, *f.* tuberculine.
tuberculización, *f.*, infecting with tuberculosis, tubercularization.
tubérculo, *m.* (bot.) tuber; (med.) tubercle.
tuberculosis, *f.* (med.) tuberculosis.
tuberculoso, sa. I. *a.* tubercular, tuberculate; tuberculous. **II.** *n.* tubercular.
tubería, *f.* tubing; piping; pipe line.
tuberosa, *f.* (bot.) tuberose.
tuberosidad, *f.* tuberosity.
tuberoso, sa, *a.* tuberous.
tubífero, ra, *a.* (biol.) provided with tubes.
tubiforme, *a.* tubiform, tubular.
tubo, *m.* tube; pipe; duct; lamp chimney.—**t. acústico,** speaking tube.—**t. cañon,** (aer.) riser.—**t. capilar,** capillary tube.—**t. de agua,** water pipe.—**t. de caldera,** boiler tube.—**t. de Crookes,** Crookes tube.—**t. de engrase,** oil pipe.—**t. de ensayo,** test tube.—**t. de gas,** gas pipe.—**t. de Geissler,** Geissler tube.—**t. de imagen,** picture tube (television).—**t. del aire,** air pipe.—**t. de nivel de burbuja,** bubble tube.—**t. de Pitot,** Pitot tube.—**t. de radio,** radio tube.—**t. de rebosamiento,** overflow pipe.—**t. de subida,** (aer.) riser.—**t. de vacío,** vacuum tube.—**t. de vapor,** steam tube.—**t. digestivo,** (anat.) alimentary canal, alimentary tract.—**t. en V,** V-tube.—**t. incandescente,** hot pipe.—**t. indicador de nivel,** gauge glass.—**t. intestinal,** intestinal canal, intestines.—**t. lanzatorpedos,** torpedo tube.—**t. snorkel (de submarino),** snorkel.—**t. termiónico,** (rad.) thermionic valve.
tubulado, da, *a.* having tubes or a tube; TUBULAR.
tubular, *a.* tubular; tube-shaped.
tubulifloro, ra, *a.* (bot.) tubuliflorous.
tubuloso, sa, *a.* (bot.) tubulous.
tucán, *m.* (ornith.) toucan; (**T-,** astr.) Toucan.
tucía, *f.* tutty.
tuciorismo, *m.* (theol.) tutiorism.
tuciorista, *n.* & *a.* (theol.) tutiorist(-ic).
tuco, *m.* (Arg.) glowworm; (Peru) a kind of owl.
tucúquerre, *m.* (Chile) a very large owl.
tucuso, *m.* (Venez.) (ornith.) humming bird.
tudel, *m.* mouthpiece of a bassoon.
tudesco, ca. I. *a.* & *n.* (of person) German. **II.** *m.* a wide cloak.
tueca, *f.* stump, stub.
tueco, *m.* hole made by borers in wood; TUECA.
tuera, *f.* (bot.) colocynth, bitter apple.
tuerca, *f.* nut, female screw, lock nut.
tuerce, *m.* = TORCEDURA, sprain.
tuero, *m.* brushwood; (bot.) spicknel.
tuerto, ta. I. *a.* one-eyed, blind in one eye. **II.** *m.* (obs.) wrong, injury.—*pl.* pains after childbirth.—**a tuertas,** contrariwise, on the contrary.—**a tuertas o a derechas,** or **a t. o a derecho,** right or wrong; inconsiderately.
tuerzo, tuerza, *v.* *V.* TORCER.
tueste, *m.* toast, toasting.
tuesto, tueste, *v.* *V.* TOSTAR.
tuétano, *m.* marrow; pith of trees.—**hasta los tuétanos,** to the marrow.
tufarada, *f.* strong scent or smell.
[1]**tufo,** *m.* vapor, emanation; (coll.) strong, offensive breath; conceit, airs, snobbishness.
[2]**tufo,** *m.* locks of hair over the temples.
[3]**tufo,** *m.* (geol.) tufa, a kind of rock.
tugurio, *m.* shepherd's hut, cabin; (coll.) mean, small room, "hole"; low place, "joint."
tuición, *f.* (law) defense, protection.
tuína, *f.* long, full jacket.
tuitivo, va, *a.* (law) defensive, protective.
tul, *m.* tulle.
tularemia, *f.* (med., vet.) tularemia, rabbit fever.
tulio, *m.* (chem.) thulium.
tulipa, *f.* (bot.) small tulip; tulip-shaped lamp shade.
tulipán, *m.* (bot.) tulip.
tulipanero, *m.* (bot.) tulip tree.
tulipero, *m.* (bot.) tulip tree, whitewood.
tullidez, *f.* partial or total paralysis (esp. of legs).
tullido, da, *a.* partially or totally paralyzed (esp. app. to the legs).
tullidura, *f.* dung of birds of prey.
tullimiento, *m.* (med.) contraction of the tendons.
tullir. I. *va.* to maim, cripple. **II.** *vn.* (of birds) to drop dung. **III.** *vr.* to be crippled.
[1]**tumba,** *f.* tomb, grave; roof of a coach; ornamental box seat in state coaches.
[2]**tumba,** *f.* tumble; somersault.
tumbacuartillos, *m.* sot, old toper.
tumbadero, *m.* tumbling place in gymnasium.
tumbadillo, *m.* (naut.) roundhouse, cuddy.
tumbado, da, *a.* vaulted, arched.
tumbaga, *f.* gold and copper alloy; (jewelry) cheap finger ring.
tumbagón, *m. aug.* bracelet of TUMBAGA.
tumbar. I. *va.* to fell, throw down; (coll.) to knock down, stun, overpower (as a powerful odor). **II.** *vn.* to tumble, fall down, roll down; (naut.) to heel, to run aground. **III.** *vr.* (coll.) to lie down, tumble into bed.
tumbilla, *f.* brazier for warming beds.
[1]**tumbo,** *m.* tumble, fall; somersault.—**t. de dado,** imminent peril.—**t. de olla,** ingredients of a meat-and-vegetable soup.—**dar un t.,** to turn a somersault.
[2]**tumbo,** *m.* book containing the privileges and title deeds of monasteries, etc.
[1]**tumbón, na,** *n.* (coll.) lazy person; sly, cunning person.
[2]**tumbón,** *m. aug.* coach or trunk with an arched roof or lid.
tumefacción, *f.* tumefaction, swelling.
tumescencia, *f.* (med.) tumescence.
tumescente, *a.* tumescent.
túmido, da, *a.* swollen, tumid, bloated; pompous, highflown; (arch.) domed.

tumor, *m.* tumor.—**t. cerebral,** (med.) brain tumor.—**t. maligno,** (med.) malignant tumor.
tumorcico, illo, ito, *m. dim.* small tumor.
tumoroso, sa, *a.* having tumors.
tumulario, ria, *a.* pertaining to a tomb.
túmulo, *m.* tomb; funeral pile; mound; tumulus; catafalque.
tumulto, *m.* tumult, uproar, uprising; mob.
tumultuante, *a.* fomenting sedition.
tumultuar. I. *va.* to incite to an uprising. **II.** *vr.* to rise in arms.
tumultuariamente, *adv.* tumultuarily.
tumultuario, ria, *a.* tumultuary; tumultuous.
tumultuosamente, *adv.* tumultuously.
tumultuoso, sa, *a.* tumultuous.
[1]**tuna,** *f.* (bot.) opuntia, prickly pear or Indian fig.
[2]**tuna,** *f.* idle and licentious life; truantship.—**correr la t.** = TUNAR.
tunal, *m.* (bot.) opuntia; opuntia field.
tunanta, *a.* & *f.* shrewd, rascally woman.
tunantada, *f.* rascality, sharp practice.
tunante. I. *a.* leading a roving and licentious life. **II.** *n.* truant, idler, rake; rascal, rogue.
tunantear, *vn.* to act the rascal.
tunantería, *f.* rascality, knavishness.
tunantuela, *f. dim.* roguish girl, hoyden.
tunantuelo, *m. dim.* little rascal.
tunar, *vn.* to lead a licentious and vagrant life; to loaf, stroll.
[1]**tunda,** *f.* shearing of cloth.
[2]**tunda,** *f.* (coll.) trouncing, whipping.
tundente, *a.* beating, whipping; producing contusion.
tundición, *f.* shearing of cloth.
tundidor, *m.* cloth shearer.
tundidora, *f.* cloth-shearing machine.
tundidura, *f.* shearing of cloth.
[1]**tundir,** *va.* to shear (cloth).
[2]**tundir,** *va.* (coll.) to trounce, beat, cudgel, whip.
tundizno, *m.* shearings from cloth.
tundra, *f.* tundra.
tunear, *vn.* to act the rogue.
tunecí; tunecino, na, *n.* & *a.* Tunisian.
túnel, *m.* tunnel.—**t. aerodinámico,** wind tunnel.
Túnez, *f.* Tunisia; Tunis.
tungstato, *m.* (chem.) tungstate.
tungsteno, *m.* (chem.) tungsten.
túngstico, ca, *a.* (chem.) tungstic, tungstenic.
tungstita, *f.* (min.) tungstite.
túnica, *f.* tunic; robe, gown; (anat. and bot.) tunic, tunicle.—**t. de Cristo,** (bot.) stramonium.
tunicado, da. I. *m.* & *a.* (zool.) tunicate. **II.** *m. pl.* Tunicata.
tunicela, *f.* tunic; (eccl.) tunicle.
túnico, *m.* robe, gown; (Cuba) frock, dress.
tuno, na. I. *a.* rascally, roguish, sly, cunning. **II.** *m.* truant, rake, rascal, rogue.
tuntún, *m.* (Colomb.) a kind of anæmic fever.—**al buen t.,** (coll.) heedlessly, haphazard.
tupa, *f.* tight packing; (coll.) satiety, repletion.
tupé, *m.* toupee, foretop; (coll.) cheek, gall, brass.
tupi, *a.* & *m.* Tupian.
tupido, da. I. *pp.* of TUPIR. **II.** *a.* dense, thick; close-woven; blocked, choked, obstructed.
tupinambo, *m.* (bot.) Jerusalem artichoke.
tupir. I. *va.* to pack tight; to make thick or compact; to choke, obstruct; to block or stop up. **II.** *vr.* to stuff or glut oneself.
turanio, nia, *n.* & *a.* Turanian.
[1]**turba,** *f.* crowd, rabble, mob.
[2]**turba,** *f.* peat; turf.
turbáceo, a, *a.* peaty.
turbación, *f.* confusion, embarrassment.
turbadamente, *adv.* confusedly.
turbador, ra, *n.* disturber, perturber.
turbal, *m.* peat bog, peat bed.
turbamiento, *m.* = TURBACIÓN.
turbamulta, *f.* crowd, rabble, mob.
[1]**turbante. I.** *pres. p.* of TURBAR. **II.** *a.* disturbing
[2]**turbante,** *m.* turban.
turbar, *va.* & *vr.* to disturb, upset; to disquiet, alarm, confuse, embarrass.
turbativo, va, *a.* alarming; disturbing.
turbelario, ria, *m.* & *a.* (zool.) turbellarian.
turbera, *f.* peat bog, peat moss.
turbia, *f.* muddy water.
turbiamente, *adv.* obscurely, confusedly.
túrbido, da, *a.* muddy, turbid.
turbiedad, turbieza, *f.* muddiness, turbidity; obscurity of language.
turbina, *f.* turbine.—**t. axial,** axial turbine.—**t. centrífuga,** outward-flow turbine.—**t. centrípeta,** inward-flow turbine.—**t. de acción,** impulse turbine.—**t. de reacción,** reaction turbine.—**t. de vapor,** steam turbine.—**t. límite,** limit turbine.—**t. paralela,** axial turbine.—**t. radial,** radial turbine.—**t. tangencial,** tangential turbine.
turbinado, da, *a.* turbinate.
turbino, *m.* pulverized turpeth, a drug.
turbinto, *m.* (bot.) terebinth.
turbio, bia. I. *a.* muddy, turbid; disturbed, confused, upset; troubled, turbulent; indistinct; obscure (language). **II.** *m. pl.* dregs.
turbión, *m.* squally shower; sweep, rush.
turbit, *m.* (bot.) turpeth.—**t. mineral,** (pharm.) turpeth mineral.
turbobomba, *m.* turbopump.
turbocompresor, *m.* turbocompressor.
turbocondensador, *m.* turbocondenser.
turbodínamo, *m.* turbodynamo.
turbogenerador, *m.* (phys.) turbogenerator.
turbomotor, *m.* turbomotor.
turbonada, *f.* squall, pelting shower.
turborreactor, *m.* (aer.) turboreactor, turbojet.
turboventilador, *m.* turbofan.
turbulencia, *f.* turbidness; turbulence.
turbulentamente, *adv.* turbulently.
turbulento, ta, *a.* turbid; turbulent.
turca, *f.* (coll.) tipsiness.—**coger una t.,** to get drunk.
turco, ca. I. *adj.* Turkish. **II.** *n.* Turk.—**el gran t.,** the Grand Turk.
turcomano, na, *n.* & *a.* Turkoman.
turcople, *a.* born of Turkish father and Greek mother.
túrdido, da. I. *a.* (ornith.) turdine. **II.** *m. pl.* Turdidæ.
túrdiga, *f.* strip of hide.
turdión, *m.* ancient Spanish dance.
turgencia, *f.* (med.) swelling, turgescence.
turgente, *a.* turgescent, turgid, swollen; (poet.) protuberant, prominent.
túrgido, da, *a.* (poet.) prominent, bulging.
turibular, *va.* (eccl.) to cense with a thurible.
turibulario, *m.* (eccl.) thurifer, censer bearer.
turíbulo, *m.* (eccl.) censer, thurible.
turiferario, *m.* = TURIBULARIO.
turífero, ra, *a.* thuriferous, incense-bearing.
turificación, *f.* thurification.
turión, *m.* (bot.) turion.
turismo, *m.* tourism, touring.—**de t.,** touring (esp. app. to automobiles).
turista, *n.* & *a.* tourist.
turístico, ca, *a.* touring; tourist.
turma, *f.* testicle; lamb fry.—**t. de tierra,** (bot.) truffle.
turmalina, *f.* (min.) tourmaline.
turnar, *vn.* & *vr.* to alternate; to go or work by turns.
turnio, nia, *a.* squint-eyed; fierce-looking.
turno, *m.* turn.—**t. de noche,** night shift (of workmen).—**al t.,** by turns.—**de t.,** (of a store, etc.) open for service; (of a person) (taking one's turn) on duty.—**por su t.,** in one's turn.
turón, *m.* a kind of field mouse.
turonense, *a.* of or from Tours.
turpial, *m.* (ornith.) troupial.
[1]**turquesa,** *f.* (jewelry) turquoise.
[2]**turquesa,** *f.* bullet mold; mold, form.
turquesado, da, *a.* of turquoise color.

turquesco, ca, *a.* Turkish.—**a la t.,** in the Turkish manner.
turquí, *a.* deep blue.
Turquía, *f.* Turkey.
turquino, na, *a.* = TURQUÍ.
turrar, *va.* to toast; to broil.
turrón, *m.* nougat, almond paste; (coll.) public office; sinecure.—**t. de Jijona,** sweet-almond paste.—**comer del t.,** to fill a public office.
turronería, *f.* TURRÓN shop.
turronero, ra, *n.* maker or seller of TURRÓN.
turulato, ta, *a.* (coll.) dumbfounded, stupefied.
turuleque, *m.* vulgar man, boor.
turulés, *a.* app. to a kind of strong grapes.
turullo, *m.* shepherd's call horn.
turumbón, *m.* bump on the head.
turupial, *m.* (Venez.) (ornith.) troupial.
¡tus! *interj.* used in calling dogs.—**sin decir t. ni mus,** (coll.) without saying a word.
tusa, *f.* (Am.) PAJILLA, maize-leaf cigar; corncob; (Chile) tassel of corncob; (Chile) mane of a horse.
tusilago, *m.* (bot.) coltsfoot.
tusivo, va, *a.* (med.) tussive.
¡tuso! *interj.* get away! (app. to dogs).
tuso, sa, *a.* (Colomb.) pitted by smallpox.
tusón, *m.* fleece wool; (prov.) colt under two years old.
tusona, *f.* (Andalusia) filly under two years old.
tute, *m.* a card game.
tutear, *va.* to use the familar TÚ in addressing a person.
tutela, *f.* guardianship, tutelage, tutorage, protection.—**t. dativa,** (law) guardianship appointed by a court.
tutelar, *a.* tutelar, tutelary.
tuteo, *m.* use of TÚ (thou).
tutía, *f.* = ATUTÍA, tutty.
tutilimundi, *m.* = MUNDONUEVO, peep-show.
tutiplén.—**a t.,** (coll.) abundantly.
tutor, ra. I. *n.* tutor, instructor (governess); guardian.—**t. dativo,** (law) guardian appointed by a court. **II.** *m.* training pole for plants.
tutoría, *f.* tutelage, guardianship.
tutriz, *f.* = TUTORA, woman tutor, governess.
tutuma, *f.* (Am.) TOTUMA, cup made from a gourd; (Chile) bump, bruise; (Am.) lump, gathering, abscess.
tuturutu, *a.* (S. A.) dumbfounded.
tuve, etc., *v. V.* TENER.
tuya, *f.* (bot.) thuya.—**t. articulada,** sandarach tree.
tuyo, ya, *poss. pron. 2d pers. m. & f.* (sometimes with the *def. art.*) thine; (when on intimate terms) yours.—**los tuyos,** thy family, thy people, yours.

U

[1]**U, u,** *f.* u, twenty-fourth letter of the Spanish alphabet.—**u valona,** (the letter) w.—**en U,** U-shaped (*tubo en U,* U-tube); channel-shaped (*hierro en U,* channel iron, channel).
[2]**u,** *conj.* (before words beginning with *o* or *ho*) or.
U., Ud., (abbr. of *usted*), you.—*pl.* **UU., Uds.**
uadi, *m.* wadi, wady.
uapití, *m.* (zool.) wapiti.
ubérrimo, ma, *a. super.* very fruitful; exceedingly plentiful.
ubicación, *f.* situation, location, position.
ubicado, da, *a.* situated, located, placed.
ubicar. I. *va.* to situate, locate, place. **II.** *vn. & vr.* to lie, to be situated, be located.
ubicuidad, *f.* ubiquity.
ubicuo, cua, *a.* ubiquitous.
ubiquidad, *f.* = UBICUIDAD.
ubiquitario, ria, *a. & n.* Ubiquitarian.
ubre, *f.* udder; milk bag.
ubrera, *f.* (med.) thrush.
ucase, *m.* ukase.
ucranio, nia. I. *a.* Ukrainian. **II.** *n.* Ukrainian; *m.* Ukrainian (language); *f.* (U.) Ukraine.
udómetro, *m.* udometer, rain gauge.
uesnorueste, *m.* west-northwest.
uessudueste, *m.* west-southwest.
ueste, *m.* west.
¡uf! *interj.* denoting weariness or annoyance.
ufanamente, *adv.* ostentatiously, boastfully, with an air of satisfaction.
ufanarse, *vr.* to boast, pride oneself.
ufanía, *f.* pride, conceit; joy, pleasure.
ufano, na, *a.* conceited, proud, haughty; gay, cheerful; masterly.
ufo.—**a u.,** parasitically.
Uganda, *f.* Uganda.
ugandés, desa, *a. & n.* Ugandan.
ujier, *n.* usher, doorkeeper.—**u. de cámara,** usher of the king's privy chamber.
ulano, *m.* (mil.) uhlan.
úlcera, *f.* (med.) ulcer; (bot.) rot.
ulceración, *f.* ulceration.
ulcerante, *a.* ulcerating.
ulcerar. I. *va.* to ulcerate. **II.** *vr.* to become ulcerated.—**ulcerativo, va,** *a.* ulcerating.
ulceroso, sa, *a.* ulcerous.
ulema, *m.* Ulema.
uliginoso, sa, *a.* uliginous, swampy.
ulmáceo, cea, *a.* (bot.) ulmaceous.
ulmaria, *f.* (bot.) meadowsweet, meadowwort.
ulpo, *m.* (S. A.) maize gruel.
ulterior, *a.* ulterior, farther; subsequent.
ulteriormente, *adv.* subsequently.
últimamente, *adv.* lastly, finally; of late, recently.
ultimar, *va.* to end, finish, close.
ultimato, ultimátum, *m.* ultimatum; (coll.) final resolution.
ultimidad, *f.* ultimity, last stage.
último, ma, *a.* last, latest; farthest; ultimate; final; latter; highly finished; most valuable; utmost; remote.—**ú. suplicio,** capital punishment.—**a la última,** after the latest fashion.—**a ú. hora,** at the eleventh hour, at the last minute.—**a últimos de,** in the latter part of the (month, etc.).—**estar a lo u.,** or **en las últimas,** to be well-informed; to be on its, or one's, last legs, to be near its, or one's, end.—**por ú.,** lastly; finally.
ultimogenitura, *f.* ultimogeniture.
ultra, *adv.* besides.
ultrabrillante, *a.* ultrabrilliant.
ultraconservador, ra, *a. & n.* ultraconservative.
ultrajador, ra, *n.* one who outrages or insults.
ultrajamiento, *m.* outrage, affront.
ultrajar, *va.* to outrage, offend, abuse; to despise.
ultraje, *m.* outrage, insult; contempt; abuse.
ultrajosamente, *adv.* outrageously.
ultrajoso, sa, *a.* outrageous; overbearing.
ultramar, *m.* place beyond or across the sea.
ultramarino, na. I. *a.* ultramarine, oversea. **II.** *m.* ultramarine, finest blue.—*pl.* (com.) oversea articles.
ultramaro, *m.* ultramarine color.
ultramicroscópico, ca, *a.* ultramicroscopic.
ultramicroscopio, *m.* ultramicroscope.
ultramoderno, na, *a.* ultramodern.
ultramontanismo, *m.* ultramontanism.
ultramontano, na, *n. & a.* ultramontane.
ultramundano, na, *a.* ultramundane.
ultranacionalismo, *m.* ultranationalism.
ultranacionalista, *a. & n.* ultranationalist.
ultranza.—**a u.,** to death; at all costs, unflinchingly.
ultrapuertos, *m.* beyond the seaports.
ultrarradical, *a. & n.* ultraradical.
ultrarrojo, ja, *a.* (phys.) infra-red.
ultrasónico, ca, *a.* ultrasonic.
ultraterreno, na, *a.* ultramundane, unearthly.
ultraterrestre, *a.* unearthly.
ultratumba.—**de u., en u.,** beyond the grave.
ultraviolado, da; ultravioleta, *a.* (phys.) ultraviolet.
úlula, *f.* (ornith.) owl.
ululante, *a.* ululant.

ulular, *vn.* to screech, hoot, ululate.
ululato, *m.* howl, screech, ululation.
umbela, *f.* (bot.) umbel.
umbelífero, ra, *a.* (bot.) umbelliferous.
umbilicado, da, *a.* navel-shaped; umbilicated.
umbilical, *a.* umbilical.
umbráculo, *m.* shaded place for plants.
umbral, *m.* threshold; (arch.) lintel; beginning, rudiment.—**umbralar,** *va.* (arch.) to lintel.
umbrático, ca; umbrátil, *a.* umbrageous, shady.
umbría, *f.* shady place.
umbrío, bría, *a.* umbrageous, shady.
umbroso, sa, *a.* shady.
un (abbr. of UNO), **una. I.** *indef. art.* a, an. **II.** *n.* & *a.* one.—**u. . . . sí y otro no,** every other, every second (as *un día sí y otro no,* every other day).
unánime, *a.* unanimous.—**unánimemente,** *adv.* unanimously.—**unanimidad,** *f.* unanimity.—**por u.,** unanimously.
uncia, *f.* (law) twelfth part of an estate.
uncial, *a.* uncial, pert. to a kind of writing.
unciforme, *a.* & *n.* (anat.) unciform.
uncinariasis, *f.* (med.) uncinariasis, hookworm.
unción, *f.* unction, anointing; (eccl.) extreme unction.—*pl.* treatment by unctions of mercury.
uncionario, ria. I. *a.* being under mercurial treatment. **II.** *m.* place where external mercurial treatment is taken.
uncir, *va.* (*ind.* UNZO; *subj.* UNZA) to yoke.
undante, *a.* waving, undulating.
undécimo, ma, *a.* eleventh.
undécuplo, pla, *a.* eleven times as much.
undísono, na, *a.* (poet.) billowy.
undívago, ga, *a.* (poet.) wavy.
undoso, sa, *a.* wavy, undulating.
undulación, *f.* undulation; wave motion.
undulante, *a.* undulant, undulating.
undular, *vn.* to undulate; to wriggle.
undulatorio, ria, *a.* undulatory.
ungido, *m.* anointed priest or king.
ungimiento, *m.* unction.
ungir, *va.* (*ind.* UNJO; *subj.* UNJA) to anoint.
ungüentario, ria. I. *a.* unguentary. **II.** *m.* one who prepares ointments; unguentarium.
ungüento, *m.* unguent, ointment.—**u. amaracino,** ointment of marjoram.—**u. basilicón,** basilicon.—**u. de soldado,** mercury ointment.
unguiculado, da, *a.* (zool.) unguiculate.
unguis, *m.* (anat.) os unguis.
ungulado, da, *a.* & *m.* (zool.) ungulate.
uniaxial, *a.* uniaxial.
unible, *a.* that can be joined or united.
únicamente, *adv.* only, simply, solely.
unicameral, *a.* unicameral.
unicelular, *a.* unicellular.
único, ca, *a.* only, sole; singular, unique, rare, unmatched, unparalleled.
unicolor, *a.* unicolor, one-color.
unicornio, *m.* (myth.) unicorn; rhinoceros; **(U-,** astr.) Unicorn.—**u. de mar,** (ichth.) narwhal.
unidad, *f.* unity; unit; (rhet. and art) unity.—**u. absoluta,** absolute unit.—**u. aritmética,** arithmetic unit.—**u. básica,** basic unit.—**u. de masa,** mass unit.—**u. de tiempo,** time unit.—**u. térmica,** thermic, thermal or heat unit.—**la u.,** (math.) unit, 1.
unidimensional, *a.* unidimensional.
unidireccional, *a.* unidirectional.
unido, da, *a.* united, unified.
unidor, ra, *a.* uniting, unifying.
unificación, *f.* unification.
unificar, *va.* (*pret.* UNIFIQUÉ; *subj.* UNIFIQUE) to unify.
unifloro, ra, *a.* (bot.) having only one flower.
unifoliado, da, *a.* (bot.) unifoliate.
uniformación, *f.* standardization, uniformity.
uniformador, ra, *a.* that makes uniform; standardizing.
uniformar, *va.* to make uniform; to standardize.
uniforme. I. *a.* uniform. **II.** *m.* uniform; regimentals.—**uniformemente,** *adv.* uniformly.
uniformidad, *f.* uniformity.
unigénito, ta, *a.* unigenital, only-begotten.
unilateral, *a.* unilateral.
unimodal, *a.* (stat.) unimodal.
unión, *f.* union, harmony, correspondence; resemblance; agreement, concord, unity; wedding, marriage; composition of ingredients; combination; coöperation; contiguity; linked finger rings; (surg.) closing of the lips of a wound; (mech.) coupling, fastening, connection, joining, joint; (Ry.) junction; (com.) fusion, consolidation, merger.
Unión de Repúblicas Socialistas Soviéticas, *f.* Union of Soviet Socialist Republics (U. R. S. S.).
unionismo, *m.* unionism; (pol. econ.) syndicalism.
unionista, *a.* & *n.* unionist.
unípara, *a.* uniparous.
unípede, *a.* monopode, one-footed.
unipersonal, *a.* unipersonal.
unipolar, *a.* (elec.) unipolar, single-pole.
unipotente, *a.* unipotent.
unir. I. *va.* to unite, unify, join, couple, bind, connect, attach; to mix, combine; to bring together; to harmonize. **II.** *vr.* to join, unite, mix; to adhere, concur; to be contiguous; to wed, be married; (com.) to consolidate, merge, combine.
unisexual, *a.* (bot.) unisexual.
unisón. I. *a.* unison. **II.** *m.* (mus.) unison.
unisonancia, *f.* unisonance, unison; monotony.
unísono, na, *a.* unisonous, sounding alike.—**al,** or **en, u.,** in unison; together; unanimously.
unitario, ria, *a.* & *n.* (eccl.) Unitarian; (pol.) supporter of centralization.
unitarismo, *m.* (eccl.) Unitarianism.
unitivo, va, *a.* unitive, serving or tending to unite.
univalencia, *f.* (chem.) univalence.
univalente, *a.* (chem.) univalent, monovalent.
univalvo, va, *a.* univalve.
universal, *a.* universal; learned, well-informed.
universalidad, *f.* universality.
universalísimo, *a. super.* (logic) universal.
universalismo, *m.* (eccl.) Universalism.
universalista, *a.* & *n.* Universalist.
universalizar, *va.* to universalize; to generalize.
universalmente, *adv.* universally.
universidad, *f.* university; body of persons forming an institution; universality.
universitario, ria, *a.* university (as *a.*).
universo, sa. I. *a.* universal. **II.** *m.* universe.
univocación, *f.* univocation.
unívocamente, *adv.* univocally, unanimously.
univocarse, *vr.* to have the same meaning.
unívoco, ca, *a.* univocal.
unjo, unja, *v.* *V.* UNGIR.
uno, na. I. *a.* one.—*pl.* some; nearly, about.—**u. que otro,** (only) a few; occasional (as *uno que otro día viene a vernos,* he comes to see us once in a while, occasionally) (*V.* also UN). **II.** *indef. pron.* one; someone.—*pl.* some (people).—**u. a otro,** each other, mutually.—**u. que otro,** some, a few.—**u. y otro,** both.—**unos a otros,** one another.—**unos cuantos,** a few.—**unos y otros,** all, the lot (of them).—**cada u.,** each one.—**de u.,** one's.—**los unos a los otros** = UNOS A OTROS. **III. uno,** *pron. neut.* one thing (*uno es hablar, y otro es hacer,* it's one thing to talk and another to do). **IV.** *n.* one (number).—**u. a u.** = DE U. EN U.—**u. con otro,** on an average.—**u. por u.,** one after another; one by one, one at a time.—**una y no más,** never again.—**a una,** unanimously, of one accord.—**de una,** at once, at one time.—**de u. en u.,** one by one; in single file.—**la una,** one o'clock.—**todo es uno,** it is all the same.
untador, ra, *n.* & *a.* oiler(-ing), coater(-ing), greaser(-ing), painter(-ing), etc. *V.* UNTAR.
untadura, *f.*; **untamiento,** *m.,* UNTURA; oiling, greasing, coating, etc.

untar. I. *va.* to anoint; to grease, oil, smear, paint, coat; to suborn; bribe.—**u. las manos,** to grease the palm, to bribe. **II.** *vr.* to be greased or smeared; to embezzle.
untaza, *f.* grease; ENJUNDIA, fat (of animal).
unto, *m.* grease, fat of animals; unguent, ointment.—**u. amarillo,** or **de Méjico,** (coll.) bribe money.—**u. de oso,** bear's grease.—**u. de puerco,** hog's lard.—**u. de arna** = U. AMARILLO.
untuosidad, *f.* unctuosity, greasiness.
untuoso, sa, *a.* unctuous, greasy.
untura, *f.* unction; ointment, liniment.
unzo, unza, *v. V.* UNCIR.
uña, *f.* finger nail; toenail; hoof, claw, or talon of beasts; sting of the scorpion; (bot.) thorn; pointed hook of instruments; short stump of a tree; scab; excrescence on the lachrymal caruncle; (coll.) dexterity in stealing or filching; (mech.) gripper, clutch, claw; (mus.) plectrum for the mandolin; (naut.) fluke, palm or bill of an anchor.—**u. de caballo,** (bot.) coltsfoot.—**u. gata,** (bot.) = GATUÑA rest-harrow.—**afilar las uñas,** to sharpen one's wits, try one's best.—**a u. de caballo,** at full gallop, in great haste.—**enseñar la u.** = MOSTRAR LA U.—**de uñas,** at daggers drawn, at loggerheads.—**hincar,** or **meter, la u.,** to overcharge; to sell at an exorbitant price.—**largo de uñas,** filcher.—**mostrar las uñas,** to be inexorable; to show one's teeth.—**mostrar la u.,** to discover one's foibles or ignorance.—**sacar las uñas,** (coll.) to avail oneself of every means in a difficulty.—**ser u. y carne,** to be hand and glove, to be fast friends.—**tener uñas,** (coll.) to be very difficult, to be a tough job, a big order.—**uñada,** *f.* nail scratch, nip.—**uñarada,** *f.* scratch with the nail.—**uñate,** *m.* (coll.) pinching with the nail; chuckfarthing, a game.—**uñaza,** *f. aug.* large nail.—**uñero,** *m.* ingrowing nail; (med.) felon.
uñeta, *f. dim.* small fingernail; small clutch; stonecutter's chisel; chuckfarthing (boys' game).
uñidura, *f.* yoking.
uñir, *va.* to yoke.
uñita, uñuela, *f. dim.* little finger nail.
uñoso, sa, *a.* having long nails or claws.
¡upa! *interj.* up, up! hoop-la!
upas, *m.* upas, a Javanese tree and the poison prepared from it.
upupa, *f.* (ornith.) hoopoe.
uralita, *f.* (min.) uralite.
urania, *f.* (entom.) urania moth.
uránico, ca, *a.* (chem.) uranic.
uranífero, ra, *a.* uraniferous.
uraninita, *f.* (min.) uraninite.
[1]**uranio, nia,** *a.* uranic, celestial.
[2]**uranio,** *m.* (chem.) uranium.
uranismo, *m.* uranism, homosexuality.
uranita, *f.* (min.) uranite.
Urano, *m.* (astr.) Uranus.
uranografía, *f.* uranography.—**uranógrafo,** *m.* uranographist.—**uranometría,** *f.* uranometry.
urao, *m.* (S. A.) (min.) trona.
urari, *m.* urari, curare, a resinous substance.
urato, *m.* (chem.) urate.
urbanamente, *adv.* courteously, politely.
urbanicé, urbanice, *v. V.* URBANIZAR.
urbanidad, *f.* urbanity, civility, manners.
urbanismo, *m.* urbanism, city planning.
urbanista. I. *a.* urbanistic. **II.** *n.* urbanist, urbanite; city planner.
urbanizacion, *f.* urbanization, city planning.
urbanizar. I. *va.* to urbanize. **II.** *vr.* to be or become urbanized.
urbano, na. I. *a.* urban; urbane, courteous, well-bred. **II.** *m.* militiaman.
urbe, *f.* large modern city, metropolis.
[1]**urca,** *f.* (naut.) hooker, dogger; storeship.
[2]**urca,** *f.* (ichth.) = ORCA, a kind of dolphin.
urce, *m.* (bot.) heath.
urceolado, da, *a.* (bot.) urceolate.
urchilla, *f.* orchil, a lichen or color from it.
urdidera, *f.* woman warper; warping frame.
urdidor, ra. I. *n.* warper. **II.** *m.* warping frame, warping mill.
urdidura, *f.* warping.
urdimbre, urdiembre, *f.* warp, warping chain.
urdir, *va.* to warp; to plot, contrive, scheme.
urea, *f.* (chem.) urea.—**ureida,** *f.* ureide.
uremia, *f.* (med.) uræmia.
urémico, ca, *a.* uræmic.
urente, *a.* hot, burning, scorching.
uréter, *m.* (anat.) ureter.
urético, ca; uretral, *a.* urethral.
uretra, *f.* (anat.) urethra.—**uretritis,** *f.* (med.) urethritis.—**uretroscopio,** *m.* (surg.) urethroscope.—**uretrotomía,** *f.* urethrotomy.
uretrótomo, *m.* urethrotome.
urgencia, *f.* urgency, exigence; obligation.—**clínica de u.,** emergency clinic.—**cura de u.,** emergency treatment.
urgente, *a.* urgent, pressing.
urgentemente, *adv.* urgently.
urgir, *vn.* (*ind.* URJO; *subj.* URJA) to be urgent, to require immediate action.
úrico, ca, *a.* uric.
urinación, *f.* urination, miction, micturition.
urinal, *a.* = URINARIO, *a.*
urinario, ria. I. *a.* urinary. **II.** *m.* urinal.
urinífero, ra, *a.* uriniferous.
urna, *f.* urn, casket; glass case; ballot box.
urnición, *f.* (naut.) top timbers.
uro, *m.* (zool.) aurochs.
urobilina, *f.* (chem.) urobilin.
urogallo, *m.* (ornith.) a species of woodcock.
urolito, *m.* (med.) urolith.
urología, *f.* urology.
uromancia, *f.* uromancy.
urómetro, *m.* urinometer.
uroscopia, *f.* uroscopy.
urotropina, *f.* (chem.) urotropine.
urraca, *f.* (ornith.) magpie.
Ursa, *f.* (astr.) Bear.—**U. Mayor,** Great Bear.—**U. Menor,** Little Bear.
úrsido, da. I. *a.* (zool.) ursine. **II.** *m. pl.* Ursidæ.
ursino, na, *a.* ursine.
ursulina, *n.* & *a.* Ursuline.
urticáceo, cea, *a.* (bot.) urticaceous.
urticación, *f.* (med.) urtication.
urticante, *a.* urticating.
urticaria, *f.* (med.) urticaria, nettle rash, hives.
urubu, *m.* urubu, black vulture.
Uruguay, *m.* Uruguay.
uruguayo, ya, *a.* & *n.* Uruguayan.
usadamente, *adv.* according to custom.
usado, da. I. *pp.* of USAR. **II.** *a.* worn out; inured, accustomed, used; fashionable, frequent; second-hand.—**al u.,** (com. law) at usance.
usagre, *m.* (med.) scald head, infantile eczema.
usanza, *f.* usage, custom; (com.) usance.
usar. I. *va.* to use; to wear; to enjoy the use of; to be active in (an employment). **II.** *vn.* to be accustomed. **III.** *vr.* to be in use or fashion; to be accustomed, used, wont.
usarcé, usarced, *n.* (obs.) (*contr.* of VUESARCED = VUESTRA MERCED) your honor.
usencia, *n.* (*contr.* of VUESTRA REVERENCIA) your reverence.
useñoría, *n.* = USÍA.
usgo, *m.* loathing.
usía, *n.* (*contr.* of VUESTRA SEÑORÍA) your lordship (ladyship); your excellence.
usina, *f.* (Gal.) factory, workshop.
uso, *m.* use; usage, custom; habit, practice; wearing, wear; wear and tear; (com. law) usance.—**u. de razón,** discernment, understanding, thinking for oneself (esp. of a child when his mind is sufficiently developed to judge by itself).—**al u., a u.,** according to usage.—**en buen u.,** in good condition.
ustaga, *f.* (naut.) tie.
usted, *pron.* (usually abbreviated **V., Vd., U., Ud.**) you.—*pl.* **ustedes** (abbrev. **VV., Vds., UU., Uds.**) you (ye).—**de Vd.,** your, yours.

ustible, *a.* easily combustible.
ustión, *f.* burning.
ustorio, *a.* burning.
usual, *a.* usual, customary; tractable, social.
usualmente, *adv.* usually, generally.
usuario, ria, *a.* (law) having the sole use of a thing.
usucapión, *f.* (law) usucapion.
usucapir, *va.* (gen. only in *infin.*) (law) to usucapt.
usufructo, *m.* (law) usufruct, enjoyment; profit.
usufructuar. I. *va.* (law) to enjoy the usufruct of. **II.** *vn.* to be productive or fruitful.
usufructuario, ria, *n.* & *a.* usufructuary.
usura, *f.* usury.
usurar, *vn.* = USUREAR.
usurariamente, *adv.* usuriously.
usurario, ria, *a.* usurious.
usurear, *vn.* to practice usury; to profiteer; to lend money on interest; to reap great profit.
usurero, ra, *n.* usurer; profiteerer; money lender, pawnbroker.
usurpación, *f.* usurpation.
usurpador, *n.* & *a.* usurper(-ing).
usurpar, *va.* to usurp.
utensilio, *m.* utensil, tool, device, implement, contrivance.
uterino, na, *a.* uterine.
útero, *m.* (anat.) uterus, womb.
uterotomía, *f.* (surg.) hysterotomy, incision or extirpation of the uterus.
uterótomo, *m.* (surg.) hysterotome.
uticense, *n.* & *a.* of or from Utica.
útil. I. *a.* useful; (law) lawful (applied to time); profitable; (mech.) effective, available. **II.** *m. pl.* utensils, tools; outfit, equipment.
utilería, *f.* (theat.) properties, stage properties.
utilero, ra, *n.* (theat.) property man, person in charge of stage properties.
utilicé, utilice, *v. V.* UTILIZAR.
utilidad, *f.* utility; profit; usefulness.
utilitario, ria, *a.* utilitarian.
utilitarismo, *m.* utilitarianism.
utilitarista, *n.* & *a.* utilitarian.
utilizable, *a.* utilizable, available.
utilización, *f.* utilization.
utilizar. I. *va.* (*pret.* UTILICÉ; *subj.* UTILICE) to utilize. **II.** *vr.* to be made profitable.
útilmente, *adv.* usefully, profitably.
utopia, *f.* Utopia.—**utópico, ca,** *a.* Utopian.—**utopista,** *n.* & *a.* Utopian.
utrero, ra, *n.* bull (heifer) two to three years old.
ut retro, *adv.* (Lat.) as above.
utricularia, *f.* (bot.) bladderwort.
utrículo, *m.* (anat.) utricle, cavity in the ear.
ut supra, *adv.* (Lat.) as above.
uva, *f.* (bot.) grape; fruit of the barberry bush; wart on the eyelid; tumor on the uvula.—*pl.* bunch of grapes.—**u. canella,** white stonecrop.—**u. crespa** = U. ESPÍN.—**u. de Corinto,** (bot.) currants.—**u. de gato** = U. CANELLA.—**u. de playa,** (Amer.) fruit of the UVERO.—**u. de raposa,** nightshade.—**u. espín,** or **espina,** gooseberry.—**u. lupina,** wolfsbane.—**u. marina,** shrubby horsetail.—**u. pasa,** raisin.—**u. tamínea,** or **taminia,** lousewort.—**u. verdeja,** green-colored sweet grape.—**u. verga** = U. LUPINA.—**conocer las uvas de su majuelo,** to know one's own business.—**hecho una u.,** very drunk, "paralyzed," "soaked."
uvada, *f.* abundance of grapes.
uvaduz, *f.* (bot.) bearberry, red-berried arbutus.
uvaguemaestre, *m.* = VAGUEMAESTRE.
uval, *a.* pertaining to grapes.
uvate, *m.* conserve of grapes.
uvayema, *f.* a species of wild vine.
úvea, *f.* (anat.) uvea.
uvero, ra. I. *n.* retailer of grapes. **II.** *m.* (bot.) shrub on tropical seashores yielding an edible stone fruit.
úvula, *f.* (anat.) uvula.
uvular, *a.* (anat.) uvular.
uxoricida, *m.* uxoricide, one who kills his wife.
uxoricidio, *m.* uxoricide, murder of a wife by her husband.
uyama, *f.* (Venez.) a species of gourd.
uzas, *f.* a Brazilian kind of crab.

V

V, v, *f.* v, twenty-fifth letter of the Spanish alphabet.—**v doble** or **doble v,** w.—**en V,** V-shaped.
V., Vd. (for USTED), you.—*pl.* **VV., Vds.**
va, *third pers. sing. pres.* of IR.
vaca, *f.* cow; beef; sole leather; joint stock of two gamblers.—**v. de la boda,** one to whom everybody applies in distress; laughingstock.—**v. de leche,** milch cow.—**v. de San Antón,** (entom.) ladybird, ladybug.—**v. marina,** sea cow.
vacación, *f.* (gen. in the *pl.*) vacation.—**vacaciones de Navidad,** Christmas vacation.—**vacaciones de Pascua,** Easter vacation.
vacada, *f.* drove of cows.
vacancia, *f.* vacancy.
vacante. I. *a.* vacant; unoccupied. **II.** *f.* vacancy; vacation; rent fallen due during the vacancy of a benefice.
vacar, *vn.* (*pret.* VAQUÉ; *subj.* VAQUE) to give up work or employment temporarily; to take a vacation; to be vacant; to devote oneself; (**de**) to lack, be devoid (of).
vacarí, *a.* leathern; covered with leather.
vacatura, *f.* vacancy.
vaccino, *m.* (med.) vaccine.
vaccinieo, a, *a.* (bot.) vacciniaceous.
vaciada, *f.* (foundry) melt.
vaciadero, *m.* drain; sink; dumping place.
vaciadizo, za, *a.* cast molded.
vaciado, *m.* (art) cast (in a mold); (act of) casting; (arch.) excavation; face of a pedestal below its ornamental moldings.
vaciador, *m.* (art) molder, caster; dumper, pourer, emptier.—**v. de navajas,** razor grinder.
vaciamiento, *m.* casting, molding; emptying.
vaciar. I. *va.* to empty; pour out; to cast, mold; to grind; to hone; (arch.) to excavate, to hollow; to explain at large; to translate. **II.** *vn.* to discharge, flow (into) (as rivers); to fall, decrease (as a freshet) **III.** *vr.* to be spilt; to overflow; to divulge what should be kept secret; to become empty or vacant.
vaciedad, *f.* nonsense, silly remark.
vaciero, *m.* shepherd of barren sheep.
vacilación, *f.* reeling, staggering; hesitation.
vacilante, *a.* hesitating, irresolute; unstable.
vacilar, *vn.* to vacillate, waver, fluctuate; to hesitate; to reel, stagger.
vacío, cía. I. *a.* void, empty; vacuous, stupid; vacant, unoccupied; idle; fruitless; concave, hollow; defective, deficient; vain, presumptuous; barren (cattle); unloaded or empty (as mules, carts, etc.). **II.** *m.* void, empty space; vacuum; aperture, opening; mold for casting; vacancy; concavity, hollowness; blank, hiatus, gap; (com.) ullage of a cask or other vessel; amount lacking; a Spanish step in dancing; animal not with young; vacuity, cavity; flank of animals.—**de v.,** empty; unemployed; vacuum (as *a.*).—**en el v.,** in vacuo.
vaco, ca, *a.* (of a position, employment) vacant.
vacuidad, *f.* vacuity, emptiness.
vacuna, *f.* cowpox; vaccine; vaccination.
vacunación, *f.* vaccination.
vacunador, ra, *n.* vaccinator.
vacunal, *a.* (med.) vaccinal.
vacunar, *va.* to vaccinate.
vacuno, na, *a.* pertaining to cattle; bovine.—**ganado v.,** (bovine) cattle.
vacuo, a. I. *a.* empty, unoccupied, vacant. **II.** *m.* vacuum.
vacuola, *f.* (biol.) vacuole.
vacuómetro, *m.* vacuum gauge.
vade, *m.* = VADEMÉCUM.
vadeable, *a.* fordable; conquerable, superable.
vadear. I. *va.* to wade through, ford; to conquer,

to surmount; to sound (a person). **II.** *vr.* to behave, conduct oneself.
vademécum, *m.* vade mecum; handbook; school portfolio.
vadera, *f.* ford of a river.
¡vade retro! *adv.* avaunt! away! begone!
vadiano, na, *n.* & *a.* Audian.
vado, *m.* ford of a river; expedient; resource.—**al v. o la puente,** choose one way or the other.—**no hallar v.,** to be at a loss how to act; to be "stuck."—**vadoso, sa,** *a.* shoaly, shallow.
vafe, *m.* bold stroke or undertaking.
vagabundear, *vn.* (coll.) to rove or loiter about, to act the vagrant.
vagabundo, da, *n.* & *a.* vagabond, vagrant, rover (-ing), roamer(-ing), tramp(-ing).
vagamente, *adv.* vaguely.
vagamundear, *vn.* = VAGABUNDEAR.
vagamundo, da, *n.* & *a.* = VAGABUNDO.
vagancia, *f.* vagrancy.
vagante, *a.* vagrant.
vagar. I. *vn.* (*pret.* VAGUÉ; *subj.* VAGUE) to rove, roam, loiter about, wander; to be at leisure, to be idle. **II.** *m.* leisure, idleness.
vagarosamente, *adv.* vagrantly, rovingly.
vagaroso, sa, *a.* errant, vagrant, roaming.
vagido, *m.* cry of a newborn child.
vagina, *f.* (anat.) vagina.—**vaginado, da,** *a.* (bot.) vaginate.—**vaginal,** *a.* vaginal.—**vaginitis,** *f.* (med.) vaginitis.—**vagínula,** *f.* (bot.) vaginula, vaginule.
vagneriano, na, *n.* & *a.* Wagnerian.
vagnerismo, *m.* Wagnerism.
[1]**vago, ga. I.** *a.* roving, roaming, wandering; vagrant; vague; hesitating, wavering; lax, loose; (art) hazy, indistinct. **II.** *m.* vagabond, loafer, vagrant, tramp.—**en v.,** unsteadily; unsuccessfully, in vain; in the air, at nothing (as a blow).
[2]**vago,** *m.* unimproved plot of ground.
vagón, *m.* (Ry.) car; wagon.—**v.-cama,** sleeping car.—**v.-cuadra,** cattle van.—**v. de carga,** freight car.—**v. de cola,** caboose.—**v. de mercancías,** freight car.—**v. de plataforma,** flat car.—**v. de volteo,** dump car.—**v. jaula,** latticed van or wagon.—**v. negro de prisión,** (coll.) Black Maria, paddy wagon.—**v. tanque,** tank car.
vagonada, *f.* wagonload, carload.
vagoneta, *f.* (Ry.) small open car; open delivery cart; dump cart.
vaguada, *f.* waterway; watercourse.
vagué, vague, *v. V.* VAGAR.
vagueación, *f.* restlessness, unsteadiness; flight of fancy.
vagueante, *a.* wandering; flighty.
vaguear, *vn.* to rove, roam, loiter, tramp.
vaguedad, *f.* vagueness; vague statement.
vaguemaestre, *m.* (mil.) wagon master.
vaguido, da. I. *a.* dizzy. **II.** *m.* dizziness.
vahaje, *m.* soft breeze.
vahar, *vn.* to exhale, breathe forth.
vaharada, *f.* breath, breathing, exhalation.
vaharera, *f.* (med.) thrush; unripe melon.
vaharina, *f.* (coll.) fume, vapor, mist.
vahear, *vn.* to exhale, emit fumes or vapor.
vahido, *m.* vertigo, dizziness.
vaho, *m.* vapor, fume, effluvium.
vaída, *f.* (arch.) vault cut into four vertical planes.
vaina, *f.* scabbard, sheath, case; (bot.) pod, capsule; (naut.) boltrope tabling; tabling of a flag.
vainazas, *n.* (coll.) humdrum, dull, or dronish person.
vainero, ra, *n.* sheath or scabbard maker.
vainica, *f. dim.* small sheath; (sew.) hemstitch.
vainilla, *f. dim.* small pod or husk; (bot.) vanilla; American heliotrope.
vainillina, *f.* (chem.) vanillin.
vaivén, *m.* fluctuation, vibration, sway; unsteadiness, inconstancy; giddiness; risk, danger; (mech.) swing, seesaw, reciprocating movement; (naut.) line, cord, rope.
vajilla, *f.* table service; dinner set; (Mex.) an ancient tax on jewelry.—**v. de plata,** silverware.
val, *m.* (*contr.* of VALLE, mostly used in composition) vale, dale, valley; open sewer, sewage ditch.
valaco, ca, *n.* & *a.* Wallachian.
valais, *m.* piece of lumber.
valar, *a.* pert. to a rampart, hedge, or fence.
valdense, *n.* & *a.* Waldensian.
[1]**vale,** *m.* (com.) bond, promissory note, I O U; voucher; sales slip; bonus given to schoolboys; bet at cards.
[2]**vale,** (Lat.) farewell, adieu; valediction.
valedero, ra, *a.* valid, efficacious, binding.
valedor, ra, *n.* protector, defender.
valencia, *f.* (chem.) valence, valency.
valenciano, na, *n.* & *a.* Valencian.
valentía, *f.* valor, courage, bravery; feat, heroic exploit; brag, boast; fire of imagination; (art) mastery in imitating nature; extraordinary or vigorous effort; (anc.) in Madrid public market for mended shoes.—**pisar de v.,** to strut, to swagger.
valentiniano, na, *a.* Valentinian.
valentísimo, ma, *a. super.* most valiant, very brave; perfect.
valentón, na. I. *a.* blustering, arrogant. **II.** *m.* hector, bully.
valentona, valentonada, *f.* brag, boast.
valer. I. *va.* (*ind. pres.* VALGO, *fut.* VALDRÉ; *subj.* VALGA) to protect, to defend, favor, patronize; to yield, produce (fruits or income); to cost; to cause, bring upon or to (one) (discredit, fame); to foot up, amount to; to be worth, be valued at; to be equal to.—**v. la pena,** to be worth while.—**v. lo que pesa,** to be worth its weight in gold.—**hacer v.,** to assert (one's rights); to avail oneself of.—**ni cosa que lo valga,** nor anything of the kind, or like it.—**no v. un cornado,** not to be worth a farthing.—**valga lo que valiere,** happen what may. **II.** *vn.* to be valuable; to be worthy; to possess merit or value; to prevail, avail; to have sway, power, authority, influence; (of coins) to be legal and current; to be valid or binding; to be important or useful; to be or serve as a protection; to be equivalent to, to mean.—**v. por,** to be equal to, to be worth.—**hacer v.,** to turn to account.—(*impers.*) **más vale, más valiera,** it is better, it would be better.—**más vale tarde que nunca,** better late than never.—**¡válgame Dios!** good Heavens! bless me!—**¡válgate Dios!** heaven bless or forgive you! **III.** *vr.* to help oneself, take care of oneself.—**v. de,** to make use of, have recourse to, avail oneself of.—**no poder v.,** or **no poderse v.,** to be helpless. **IV.** *m.* value; merit, worth.
valeriana, *f.* (bot.) valerian.
valerianáceo, a, *a.* (bot.) valerianaceous.
valerianato, *m.* (chem.) valerianate.
valeriánico, ca, *a.* (chem.) valeric.
valerosamente, *adv.* bravely, courageously.
valerosidad, *f.* courage, bravery.
valeroso, sa, *a.* brave, courageous; strong, active; powerful.
valetudinario, ria. I. *a.* valetudinary, valetudinarian. **II.** *n.* valetudinarian.
valgo, valga, *v. V.* VALER.
Valhala, *f.* Walhalla, Valhalla.
valí, *m.* wali, a Mussulman governor.
valía, *f.* value, worth; credit, favor, influence; party, faction.—**a las valías,** at the highest price.
valiato, *m.* vilayet, rule and domain of a VALÍ.
validación, *f.* validation; soundness.
válidamente, *adv.* validly.
validar, *va.* to validate.
validez, *f.* validity; soundness; vigor, strength.
válido, da, *a.* valid; legally binding, obligatory.
valido, da. I. *a.* & *pp.* favored, accepted; esteemed, respected; powerful, influential. **II.** *m.* prime minister; favorite, protégé; court minion.

valiente. I. *a.* valiant, brave, courageous; strong, robust, vigorous; efficacious, valid; eminent; excellent; great, excessive. **II.** *n.* brave person; bully, hector.—**valientemente,** *adv.* bravely, courageously; vigorously; abundantly, excessively; elegantly, handsomely.
valija, *f.* valise, suitcase; mail bag; mail.
valijero, *m.* mail carrier or distributor.
valijón, *m. aug.* large valise or mail bag.
valimiento, *m.* value; use, benefit, advantage; favor, support; good graces, favoritism.
valioso, sa, *a.* valuable; highly esteemed, of great influence; rich, wealthy.
valisoletano, na, *a.* of or from Valladolid.
valón, na. I. *a.* Walloon.—**u valona,** w (the letter). **II.** *m. pl.* bloomers.
valona, *f.* vandyke collar.
valor, *m.* value; price; worth; amount; equivalence; validity, force; import, meaning; activity, power; valor, bravery; (fig.) cheek, nerve. —*pl.* (com.) securities, bonds, stocks.—**v. recibido,** value received.—**valores fiduciarios,** (com.) notes.
valoración, *f.* = VALUACIÓN; (chem.) act of VALORAR.
valorar, valorear, *va.* to appraise, value, price; (chem.) to standardize, determine the strength or proportions of (a solution).
valoría, *f.* value, price, worth.
valorizar, *va.* (Mex.) = VALORAR.
valquiria, *f.* valkyr, valkyrie.
vals, *m.* waltz.
valsador, ra, *n.* waltzer.
valsar, *vn.* to waltz.
valuable, *a.* ratable, appraisable.
valuación, *f.* appraisement, valuation.
valuador, ra, *n.* appraiser.
valuar, *va.* to rate, price, value, appraise.
valva, *f.* (zool.) valve, shell of mollusks; (bot.) valve.
valvar, *a.* (biol.) valval, valvar.
valvasor, *m.* nobleman, hidalgo.
válvula, *f.* valve.—**v. de admisión,** steam valve, admission valve.—**v. de campana,** two-beat valve.—**v. de corredera,** slide valve.—**v. de derivación,** by-pass valve.—**v. de descarga,** blow-off valve.—**v. de dos direcciones,** two-way valve.—**v. de estrangulación,** throttle valve.—**v. de evacuación,** blow-off valve.—**v. de expansión,** cut-off valve.—**v. de purga,** blow-off valve; mud valve.—**v. de retención,** check valve.—**v. de seguridad,** safety valve. —**v. de tres direcciones,** or **de tres pasos,** three-way valve.—**v. mitral,** (zool.) mitral valve.—**v. termiónica,** (phys.) thermionic valve or tube.
valvulado, da, *a.* valvate.
valvular, *a.* valvular.
valvulilla, *f. dim.* valvula.
valla, *f.* paling, fence, stockade, intrenchment; barrier, barricade; obstacle, impediment.—**romper,** or **saltar, la v.,** to be foremost in undertaking a difficult affair.
valladar, *m.* VALLADO; obstacle.
vallado, *m.* stockade; inclosure; stone wall.
vallar, valladear, *va.* to fence, hedge, inclose with pales or stakes.
valle, *m.* valley; vale, dale, glen, dell; whole number of villages and cottages in a valley.—**v. de lágrimas,** vale of tears.
vallecico, vallecito, vallejo, vallejuelo, *m. dim.* small valley; glen, dell.
vallico, *m.* (bot.) ray grass.
vallisoletano, na, *a.* of or from Valladolid.
vamos, *1st pers. plu. pres. ind. & imper.* of IR; *interj.* well! come, now! bear a hand! go on! let's go! be careful! stop! Often as an expletive, well! why!
vampiro, *m.* ghoul; vampire; usurer; miser.
van, *3rd pers. plu. pres.* of IR.
vanadato, vanadiato, *m.* (chem.) vanadate.
vanádico, ca, *a.* (chem.) vanadic.
vanadio, *m.* (chem.) vanadium.
vanagloria, *f.* vaingloriousness, boast, conceit.
vanagloriarse, *vr.* to be vainglorious, to boast.
vanagloriosamente, *adv.* vaingloriously.
vanaglorioso, sa, *a.* vainglorious, conceited, ostentatious.
vanamente, *adv.* vainly; superstitiously; without foundation; arrogantly, presumptuously, frivolously, idly.
vandálico, ca, *a.* Vandalic.
vandalismo, *m.* Vandalism.
vándalo, la, *n. & a.* Vandal.
vandeano, na, *n. & a.* Vendean.
vanear, *vn.* to talk nonsense.
vanguardia, *f.* (mil.) vanguard, van.
vanguardismo, *m.* avant-garde, vanguardism.
vanguardista. I. *a.* avant-garde. **II.** *n.* avant-gardist, vanguardist.
vanidad, *f.* vanity; nonsense; inanity, shallowness, levity; foppishness.—**hacer v.,** to boast.
vanidoso, sa, *a.* vain, foppish, conceited.
vanilocuencia, *f.* verbosity.
vanílocuo, cua, *a.* empty (talker).
vaniloquio, *m.* silly, empty talk.
vanillina, *f.* (chem.) vanillin.
vanistorio, *m.* (coll.) ridiculous or affected vanity; affected person.
vano, na. I. *a.* vain; inane, empty, shallow, insubstantial; dry (coconut).—**en v.,** in vain. **II.** *m.* (arch.) opening in a wall (as for a door).
vánova, *f.* bedspread, coverlet.
vapor, *m.* vapor, steam; exhalation, mist; vertigo, faintness; (naut.) steamboat, steamer, steamship.—*pl.* vapors; hysterical attack.—**v. condensado,** condensed steam.—**v. de agua,** water vapor, steam.—**v. natural,** natural steam.—**v. recalentado** or **sobrecalentado,** superheated steam.—**v. transatlántico,** (naut.) transatlantic steamer.—**v. vivo,** working steam, live steam.—**v. volandero,** (naut.) tramp steamer.—**al v.,** steamed; (coll.) swiftly.—**a todo v.,** under full steam.
vaporable, *a.* vaporizable, volatile.
vaporación, *f.* vaporization.
vaporar, vaporear, *va.* to vaporize.
vaporizable, *a.* vaporizable.
vaporización, *f.* vaporization.
vaporizador, *m.* vaporizer.
vaporizar, *va.* to vaporize.
vaporoso, sa, *a.* vaporous, ethereal, cloudy.
vapulación, *f.;* **vapulamiento,** *m.* (coll.) whipping, flogging.
vapular, vapulear, *va.* (coll.) to whip, flog.
vapuleamiento, vapuleo, *m.* (coll.) whipping, flogging.
vaqué, vaque, *v. V.* VACAR.
vaquear, *va.* to cover (cows) with the bull.
vaquería, *f.* herd or drove of cattle; milk dairy; work or occupation of cowboys.
vaquerizo, za. I. *a.* pertaining to cows. **II.** *n.* herdsman. **III.** *f.* winter stable for cattle.
vaquero, ra. I. *a.* pertaining to cowherds. **II.** *m.* herdsman; cowboy.
vaqueta, *f.* sole leather.
vaquetear, *va.* to flog with leather thongs.
vaqueteo, *m.* flogging with leather thongs.
vaquilla, vaquita, *f. dim.* small cow, heifer.
vaquillona, *f.* heifer, calf.
váquira, *f.* (zool.) peccary.
vara, *f.* twig; pole, staff; stick; rod; verge, wand, emblem of authority; vara (variable unit of length, about 2.8 ft.); piece of cloth one vara long; herd of forty or fifty head of swine; thrust with a goad at a bull; thill, shaft (of carriage). —**v. alta,** sway, high hand.—**v. buscadora,** divining rod.—**v. de adivinar** or **mágica,** divining rod.—**v. de cortina,** curtain rod.—**v. de Jesé,** (bot.) tuberose.—**v. de medir,** vara stick, measuring stick.—**v. de pescar,** fishing rod.—**v. de yaya,** lancewood spar.
varada, *f.* (agr.) gang of farm hands; job on a farm; (min.) three months' work in a mine;

amount of work done and measured; quarterly profit and dividend; (naut.) running aground, stranding.
varadera, *f.* (naut.) skid or skeed.
varadero, *m.* shipyard.
varadura, *f.* (naut.) grounding of a vessel.
varal, *m.* long pole or perch; side pole with sockets for the stakes of a truck; (theat.) side lights; (coll.) tall, slender person.
varano, *m.* (zool.) monitor.
varapalo, *m.* long pole or perch; switch blow with a stick or pole; (coll.) grief; trouble; reverse, damage.
varar. I. *va.* (naut.) to launch (a new-built ship). **II.** *vn.* & *vr.* (naut.) to run aground, be stranded; to be at a standstill.
varaseto, *m.* treillage, espalier.
varazo, *m.* blow with a pole, rod or stick.
varbasco, *m.* (bot.) = VERBASCO, mullein.
vardasca, *f.* thin twig.
vareador, ra, *n.* one who does the act of VAREAR.
vareaje, *m.* retail trade; selling or measuring by the yard; knocking off fruit of trees with a pole.
varear. I. *va.* to knock off (fruit) with a pole; to cudgel, whip, beat; to prick with a goad; to measure or sell by the yard. **II.** *vr.* to get thin.
varejón, *m.* long stick, pole or staff.
varenga, *f.* (naut.) floor timber.—**varengaje,** *m.* (naut.) collection of floor timbers.
vareo, *m.* = VAREAJE.
vareta, *f. dim.* small rod, stick or twig; lime twig for catching birds; stripe in a fabric; (coll.) hint, offensive remark.—**estar,** or **irse, de v.,** (coll.) to have diarrhœa.
varetazo, *m.* blow with a twig, stick or rod.
varetear, *va.* to make stripes in (fabrics).
varetón, *m.* young stag having antlers without branches or points.
varga, *f.* steepest part of an incline.
varganal, *m.* inclosure, stockade.
várgano, *m.* fence rail or stake.
vargueño, *m.* = BARGUEÑO, gilt and painted desk.
variabilidad, *f.* variability.
variable. I. *a.* variable, changeable. **II.** *f.* (math.) variable.—**v. estadística,** (stat.) variate.
variablemente, *adv.* variably.
variación, *f.* variation, change; (mus.) variation —**v. de la aguja,** variation of the compass.
variado, da. I. *pp.* of VARIAR. **II.** *a.* varying variegated, diverse.
variamente, *adv.* variously, differently.
variante. I. *a.* varying; deviating. **II.** *f.* difference, discrepancy (in texts).
variar. I. *va.* to vary, change, alter; to shift; to variegate, diversity. **II.** *vn.* to vary, change; to differ; (of the compass) to deviate, vary.
várice, varice, *f.* (med.) varix.
varicela, *f.* (med.) varicella, chicken pox.
varicocele, *m.* (med.) varicocele.
varicoso, sa, *a.* (med.) varicose.
variedad, *f.* variety, diversity; change, variation. —*pl.* miscellany of things or items; (Am.) variety show.
varilarguero, *m.* in bullfighting, PICADOR.
varilla, *f. dim.* rod; spindle, pivot; fan stick; rib (of an umbrella), whalebone (of a corset).—*pl.* jawbones; frame of a sieve or strainer.—**v. de cortina,** curtain rod.—**v. de virtudes,** or **v. mágica,** magician's or conjurer's wand.
varillaje, *m.* ribs of a fan, umbrella, or corset.
vario, ria, *a.* various, divers, varied; inconstant, changeable; undecided; variegated.—*pl.* various, several.
variólico, ca, *a.* (med.) variolous.
variolización, *f.* inoculation with smallpox virus.
varioloide, *f.* (med.) varioloid.
varioloso, sa, *a.* (med.) variolous, variolar.
variómetro, *m.* (radio) variometer.
variz, *m.* (med.) = VÁRICE.
varón, *m.* male (man); man of respectability.—**v. de Dios,** saintly man, most virtuous man.—**v. del timón,** (naut.) rudder pendant.—**buen v.,** wise and learned man.—**santo v.,** (coll.) good but simple fellow.
varona, *f.* woman; mannish woman.
varoncico, illo, ito, *m. dim.* boy, lad.
varonesa, *f.* woman.
varonía, *f.* male issue.
varonil, *a.* virile; manly; vigorous, spirited.
varonilmente, *adv.* manfully, bravely.
varraco, *m.* = VERRACO, male hog or boar.
varraquear, *vn.* = VERRAQUEAR, to grunt; (of child) to cry, yell.—**varraquera,** *f.* = VERRAQUERA, (of child) crying spell.
varsoviana, *f.* (dance) varsovienne.
varsoviano, na, *n.* & *a.* of or from Warsaw.
vasallaje, *m.* vassalage, subjection; liege money.
vasallo, lla. I. *a.* vassal, subject, tributary; feudatory. **II.** *n.* vassal, subject.
vasar, *m.* shelf in a kitchen.
vasco, ca, *n.* & *a.* Basque.—**vascófilo, la,** *n.* Basque scholar.
vascongado, da, *n.* & *a.* Basque.
vascuence, *m.* Basque language; (coll.) jargon, gibberish.
vascular; vasculoso, sa, *a.* vascular.
vascularidad, *f.* (anat., bot., zool.) vascularity.
vase, *3rd pers. sing. pres.* of IRSE; (theat.) exit.
vaselina, *f.* vaseline.
vasera, *f.* shelf or rack for glasses.
vasico, ito, *m. dim.* small tumbler.
vasija, *f.* vessel, container, receptacle (for liquids); collection of wine vessels in a cellar.
vasillo, *m. dim.* cell of a honeycomb.
vaso, *m.* (drinking) glass; vessel, receptacle; glassful; vase; flower jar; reservoir; (naut.) vessel; capacity, room, extent; (astr.) Crater, a southern constellation; horse's hoof; (anat. and bot.) vessel.—**v. de engrase,** (mech.) grease cup or box.—**v. de noche,** chamber pot.
vasomotor, ra, *a.* (physiol.) vasomotor.
vástago, *m.* stem, tiller, sucker, sapling, shoot; descendant, scion, offspring.—**v. del émbolo,** (steam eng.) piston rod.—**v. de válvula,** valve stem.
vastedad, *f.* vastness, immensity.
vástiga, *f.* = VÁSTAGO.
vasto, ta, *a.* vast, huge, immense.
vate, *m.* bard, poet; seer, diviner.
vatiaje, *m.* (elec.) wattage.
vaticano, na. I. *a.* pertaining to the Vatican. **II.** *m.* (V-) Vatican.
vaticinador, ra, *n.* prophet, diviner.
vaticinante, *a.* predicting, foretelling.
vaticinar, *va.* to divine, foretell, predict.
vaticinio, *m.* vaticination, prediction.
vatídico, ca, *a.* (poet.) prophetical.
vatihora, *m.* (elec.) watt-hour.
vatihorámetro, *m.* (elec.) watt-hour meter.
vatímetro, *m.* (elec.) wattmeter.
vatio, *m.* (elec.) watt.—**v. -hora,** watt-hour.
vatiómetro, *m.* wattmeter.
[1]**vaya,** *f.* scoff, jest.
[2]**vaya,** etc. *v. V.* IR.—*interj.* go! go to! come! indeed! certainly! well!
[1]**ve,** *f.* name of letter *v.*—**v. doble,** name of *w.*
[2]**ve,** *v. V.* IR.
véase, *imper.* of VERSE; *v.,* see (in references).
vecera, vecería, *f.* drove, herd, pack.
vecero, ra, *n.* one who performs alternately or by turns; tree which yields abundant fruit in alternate years; customer.
veces, *f. pl.* of VEZ.
vecinal, *a.* vicinal, neighboring, adjacent.
vecinamente, *adv.* near, contiguously.
vecindad, *f.* neighborhood, vicinity; (collect.) tenants (in a house).—**hacer mala v.,** to be a troublesome neighbor.
vecindario, *m.* population of a district, ward, etc.; neighborhood, vicinity, vicinage.
vecino, na. I. *a.* neighboring, next, near by; like, resembling, coincident. **II.** *n.* neighbor; resident, tenant; citizen.—**medio v.,** nonresident who, by paying half the taxes, enjoys the right of pasture for his cattle.

vectación, *f.* passive exercise, as riding, sailing.
vectigales, *m. pl.* an ancient tribute.
vector (math.). **I.** *a.* vectorial. **II.** *m.* vector.
vectorial, *a.* (math.) vectorial.
[1]**veda,** *f.* prohibition, interdiction by law; time when hunting is forbidden.
[2]**veda,** *m.* Veda, Hindu sacred book.
vedado, *m.* inclosure, warren, park.
vedamiento, *m.* prohibition.
vedar, *va.* to prohibit, forbid; to obstruct, impede.
vedegambre, *m.* (bot.) hellebore.
vedeja, *f.* = GUEDEJA, lock (of hair); lion's mane.
védico, ca, *a.* Vedic.
vedija, *f.* entangled lock of wool or hair; flake; matted hair.—**vedijero, ra,** *n.* gatherer of loose locks of wool at shearing.—**vedijudo, da; vedijoso, sa,** *a.* having entangled or matted hair.—**vedijuela,** *f. dim.* small lock of wool.
veduño, *m.* = VIDUÑO, quality of grape vines.
veedor, ra, *n.* prier, spy; busybody; overseer, supervisor, inspector; caterer, provider.
veeduría, *f.* supervisor's position or office.
vega, *f.* flat lowland; (Cuba) tobacco plantation; (Chile) damp or swampy ground.
vegetabilidad, *f.* condition of being vegetal.
vegetación, *f.* vegetation.
vegetal, *a.* & *m.* vegetable, vegetal, plant.—**vegetalista,** *n.* & *a.* vegetarian.
vegetante, *a.* vegetating.
vegetar, *vn.* to vegetate.
vegetarianismo, *m.* vegetarianism.
vegetariano, na, *n.* & *a.* vegetarian.
vegetarismo, *m.* vegetarianism.
vegetativo, va, *a.* vegetative.
veguer, *m.* in Aragon, mayor.—**veguería,** *f.*, **veguerío,** *m.* in Aragon, jurisdiction of the mayor.
veguero, ra. I. *a.* meadowy. **II.** *m.* (Cuba) tobacco planter; cigar crudely made of a single leaf.
vehemencia, *f.* vehemence, efficacy, force.
vehemente, *a.* vehement; persuasive; vivid; keen.—**vehementemente,** *adv.* vehemently.
vehículo, *m.* vehicle.—**v. interplanetario** or **cósmico,** space vehicle.
veintavo, *m.* & *a.* twentieth.
veinte, *a.* & *m.* twenty; twentieth.—**a las v.,** unseasonably.
veintén, *m.* a gold dollar piece.
veintena, *f.*, **veintenar,** *m.* score (twenty).
veintenario, ria, *a.* twenty years old.
veinteno, na, *a.* twentieth.
veinteñal, *a.* lasting twenty years.
veinteocheno, na. I. *a.* twenty-eighth. **II.** *m.* or *f.* warp of 2,800 threads.
veinteseiseno, na. I. *a.* twenty-sixth. **II.** *n.* warp of 2,600 threads.
veintésimo, ma, *a.* twentieth.
veinticinco, *a.* & *m.* twenty-five; twenty-fifth.
veinticuatreno, na. I. *a.* twenty-fourth. **II.** *n.* warp of 2,400 threads.—**v. de capas,** fine broadcloth for cloaks.
veinticuatría, *f.* aldermanry.
veinticuatro. I. *a.* twenty-four; twenty-fourth. **II.** *m.* alderman of Seville.
veintidós, *a.* & *m.* twenty-two; twenty-second.
veintidoseno, na. I. *a.* twenty-second. **II.** *m.* or *f.* warp of 2,200 threads.
veintinueve, *a.* & *m.* twenty-nine; twenty-ninth.
veintiocheno, na = VEINTEOCHENO.
veintiocho, *a.* & *m.* twenty-eight; twenty-eighth.
veintiséis, *a.* & *m.* twenty-six; twenty-sixth.
veintiseiseno, na = VEINTESEISENO.
veintisiete, *a.* & *m.* twenty-seven; twenty-seventh.
veintitrés, *a.* & *m.* twenty-three; twenty-third.
veintiún, *a.* twenty-one.
veintiuno, na. I. *a.* & *m.* twenty-one; twenty-first. **II.** *f.* a card game, "vingt-et-un."
veintuplo, pla, *a.* twentyfold.
vejación, *f.* vexation, annoyance; oppression.
vejado, da, *a.* vexed.
vejamen, *m.* vexation, trouble; taunt, scurrilous criticism.—**vejaminista,** *m.* censor, critic.
vejancón, na, *a.* (coll.) rather old, oldish.
vejar, *va.* to vex, tease; to scoff, censure.
vejarrón, na, *a.* (coll.) very old.
vejatorio, ria, *a.* vexatious, annoying.
vejazo, za, *n.* big old person.
vejecito, ta, *n.* little old man (woman).
vejestorio, *m.* (coll.) old trumpery; shrivelled old person.
vejeta, *f.* (ornith.) crested lark.
vejete, *m.* (coll.) ridiculous old man.
vejez, *f.* old age; peevishness of old age; trite story, platitude, threadbare saying, etc.
vejezuelo, la, *n. dim.* little old man (woman).
vejiga, *f.* (anat.) bladder; blister; (art) bladder or tube for paints.—*pl.* pustules of smallpox; (vet.) windgalls in horses.—**v. de la bilis,** or **de la hiel,** gall bladder.—**v. de perro,** (bot.) common winter cherry.—**v. natatoria,** (ichth.) swimming bladder.—**v. para tabaco,** tobacco pouch.
vejigatorio, ria. I. *a.* blistering. **II.** *m.* blister plaster, blister, vesicant, vesicatory.
vejigón, *m. aug.* large bladder or blister.
vejigoso, sa, *a.* full of blisters.
vejigüela, vejiguilla, *f. dim.* small bladder; (med.) pustule.
[1]**vela,** *f.* vigil, wakefulness; wake; watch, watchfulness, vigilance; watchman, nightguard; pilgrimage; candle; nightwork; (eccl.) vigil before the Eucharist; nuptial mass and veiling ceremony.—**a v. y pregón,** auction by inch of candle.—**en v.,** vigilantly, without sleep.
[2]**vela,** *f.* (naut.) sail; ship; awning, velarium; erect ear of an animal; wing or arm of a windmill.—**v. bastarda,** lateen sail.—**v. cangreja,** (naut.) boom sail, brig sail, gaff sail.—**v. de mesana,** mizzen sail.—**v. de trinquete,** fore sail.—**v. latina** = V. BASTARDA.—**v. mayor,** mainsail.—**velas de popa,** after sails.—**velas de proa,** headsails.—**velas de respeto,** spare sails.—**velas mayores,** courses.—**acortar (la) v.,** to reef a sail, to shorten sail.—**a la v.,** prepared, equipped, ready.—**alzar velas,** to raise sail, to make ready to sail; to quit, to leave.—**a toda v.,** with all sails up and full wind; with heart and soul; boomingly, in full swing.—**a v. y remo,** with sails and oars; quickly, with all one's heart and soul.—**hacer fuerza de v.,** to crowd sail.—**hacerse a la v.,** to set sail.—**recoger velas,** to contain oneself, to be moderate.—**tender (las) velas,** to seize an opportunity.
velación, *f.* watch, watching, vigil; wake.—*pl.* (eccl.) nuptial mass and veiling ceremony; time in which the church permits marriages.
velacho, *m.* (naut.) fore-topsail.
velada, *f.* VELACIÓN; soirée.
velado, da. I. *a.* veiled. **II.** *m.* (coll.) bridegroom, husband.
velador, ra. I. *n.* watchman(-woman), nightguard; caretaker, keeper. **II.** *m.* wooden candlestick; lamp table or stand.
veladura, *f.* (art) velatura.
velaje, velamen, *m.* (naut.) canvas, sails in general; set of sails.
[1]**velar. I.** *vn.* to watch, to be awake, to keep vigil; to work at night; to observe; to be vigilant; (**por**) to watch (over), protect; (naut.) to appear above the water, as rocks; (eccl.) to assist by turns before the Holy Sacrament when it is manifested. **II.** *va.* to guard, watch over, keep.
[2]**velar,** *va.* (eccl.) to veil (a bride and bridegroom) at a nuptial mass; to cover, veil, hide; (art) to soften with velatura.
velarte, *m.* fine broadcloth.
veleidad, *f.* whimsicalness; fickleness.
veleidoso, sa, *a.* fickle, inconstant.
velejar, *vn.* (naut.) to make use of sails.
velería, *f.* tallow-chandler's shop.
[1]**velero, ra. I.** *a.* fond of wakes and pilgrimages **II.** *m.* tallow chandler.
[2]**velero, ra. I.** *a.* (naut.) swift-sailing. **II.** *m.* (naut.) sailmaker.
veleta. I. *f.* weathercock, vane; streamer, pen-

nant; bob, float, or cork of a fishing line. **II.** *n.* fickle person.
velete, *m.* light, thin, face veil.
velicación, *f.* (med.) lancing, opening.
velicar, *va.* (med.) to lance, open, prick.
velico, illo, ito, *m. dim.* small veil.
velilla, ita, *f. dim.* small candle.
velillo, *n. dim.* small veil: embroidered gauze.
velis nolis, (coll.) willy-nilly.
velmez, *m.* tunic worn under the armor.
velo, *m.* veil; curtain; veil of white gauze thrown over a couple at nuptial mass; celebration of taking the veil by a nun; cloak, disguise, mask; confusion, perplexity.—**v. del paladar,** (anat.) soft palate.—**correr un v. sobre,** to drop (a matter, etc.)—**descorrer el v.,** to pull off the mask; to disclose something before unknown.—**tomar el v.,** to take the veil, to become a nun.
velocidad, *f.* velocity.—**v. angular,** angular velocity.—**v. con respecto al suelo,** (aer.) ground velocity.—**v. de ascención,** (aer.) climbing velocity, rate of climb.—**v. de entrada,** entrance velocity.—**v. de liberación,** (aer. astronaut.) escape velocity.—**v. de salida,** velocity of discharge.—**v. media,** mean velocity.—**v. orbital,** orbital velocity.—**v. periférica,** circumferential velocity.—**v. sincrónica,** (elec.) synchronous speed.—**v. subsónica,** subsonic speed.—**v. supersónica,** supersonic speed.—**v. terminal,** terminal velocity.—**v. transónica,** transonic speed.
velocímetro, *m.* speedometer; speed meter.
velocipédico, ca, *a.* pertaining to velocipedes.
velocipedismo, *m.* cycling (as a sport).
velocipedista, *n.* cyclist.
velocípedo, *m.* velocipede.
velódromo, *m.* bicycle race course.
velomotor, *m.* motor vehicle (esp. motor cycle).
velón, *m.* brass lamp with movable reservoir.
velonera, *f.* lamp stand or bracket.
velonero, ra, *n.* maker or seller of VELONES.
velorio, *m.* wake, watch (over a dead person).
veloz, *a.* swift, rapid, fleet, quick, fast.
velozmente, *adv.* swiftly, fleetly, rapidly.
veludillo, veludo = VELLUDILLO, VELLUDO.
vellera, *f.* woman who removes hair from women's faces.
vellido, da, *a.* downy; villous.
vello, *m.* down; nap; pubescence; fuzz.
vellocino, *m.* fleece (as the golden fleece).
[1]**vellón,** *m.* fleece, wool of one sheep; unsheared sheepskin; lock of wool.
[2]**vellon,** *m.* copper and silver alloy; ancient copper coin.
vellonero, *m.* gatherer of fleece at shearing.
vellora, *f.* knot taken from woollen cloth.
vellorí, vellorín, *m.* broadcloth of undyed wool.
vellorita, *f.* (bot.) cowslip.
vellosidad, *f.* downiness; hairiness.
vellosilla, *f.* (bot.) mouse-ear.
velloso, sa, *a.* downy, villous, hairy, fuzzy.
velludillo, *m.* velveteen.
velludo, da. I. *a.* downy, hairy, shaggy, woolly. **II.** *m.* shag, velvet.
vellutero, ra, *n.* velvet or felt worker.
vena, *f.* vein, blood vessel; fiber of plants; (min.) vein, seam, lode; (hydraul.) vein; flow of water underground; vein or stripe in stones or woods; poetical vein, inspiration.—**v. ácigos,** azigous vein, vena azigos.—**v. basílica,** basilic vein.—**v. cardíaca,** cardiac vein.—**v. cava,** vena cava.—**v. cefálica,** cephalic vein.—**v. coronaria,** cardiac vein.—**v. de agua,** underground natural water conduit.—**v. de loco,** fickle disposition.—**v. flúida,** (hydraul.) jet.—**v. láctea,** chyliferous vessel.—**v. leónica,** ranine vein.—**v. porta,** vena portæ, portal vein.—**v. safena,** saphenous vein.—**v. subclavia,** subclavian vein.—**v. yugular,** jugular vein.—**acostarse la v.,** (min.) (of vein) to dip.—**dar en la v.,** to hit upon the right means.—**estar de v.,** to be in the mood (for something).—**estar en v.,** to be inspired.—**hallar la v.** = DAR EN LA V.
venablo, *m.* javelin, dart.—**echar venablos,** to burst out into violent language.
venación, *f.* (entom., bot.) venation.
venadero, ra. I. *a.* deer-hunting, deer (as *a.*). **II.** *m.* place frequented by deer.
venado, *m.* deer, stag; deer meat, venison.
venaje, *m.* feeding streams, aggregate of streams forming a river.
[1]**venal,** *a.* venous; pertaining to veins.
[2]**venal,** *a.* marketable, salable; venal, mercenary.
venalidad, *f.* venality, mercenariness.
venático, ca, *a.* (coll.) cranky, erratic, daft.
venatorio, ria, *a.* venatic, used in hunting.
vencedor, ra, *n.* & *a.* victor, vanquisher(-ing).
[1]**vencejo,** *m.* string, band.
[2]**vencejo,** *m.* (ornith.) swift, martin, martlet.
vencer. I. *va.* (*ind.* VENZO; *subj.* VENZA) to conquer, subdue, defeat, vanquish, overpower; to surpass, outdo, excel; to surmount, overcome; to win; to prevail upon, persuade, convince; to bend, turn down; to twist. **II.** *vn.* to conquer, triumph, succeed; to win; to be the victor; (com.) to fall due, mature; to expire. **III.** *vr.* to govern one's passions or desires, to control oneself.
vencetósigo, *m.* (bot.) milkweed.
vencible, *a.* conquerable; surmountable.
vencida, *f.* = VENCIMIENTO.
vencido, da. I. *pp.* of VENCER. **II.** *a.* (com.) due; payable.—**de v.** nearly beaten, vanquished, or finished.
vencimiento, *m.* vanquishment; flinch; bent; turn down; (com.) maturity, expiration.
venda, *f.* (surg.) bandage, roller; fillet.
vendaje, *m.* (surg.) bandage; bandaging.
vendar, *va.* (surg.) to bandage; to fillet; to hoodwink, to blind, obfuscate.
vendaval, *m.* strong wind from the sea.
vendavalada, *f.* storm of southerly wind.
vendedor, ra, *n.* seller, trader; salesman (-woman).
vendehumos, *m.* courtier trading on his influence.
vendeja, *f.* public sale.
vender, *va.* & *vn.* to sell.—**v. a destajo** = V. AL POR MENOR.—**v. al contado,** to sell for cash.—**v. al por mayor,** to sell at wholesale.—**v. al por menor,** to sell at retail.—**v. al quitar,** to sell with the privilege of buying back.—**v. a plazo,** to sell on credit.—**v. como pan caliente,** (coll.) to sell like hot cakes.—**v. salud,** to be in good health. **II.** *vr.* to sell out, accept a bribe; to expose oneself to danger; (fig.) to give oneself away, betray one's feelings; to boast; to be sold (at a place, at a price), to be for sale.—**v. caro,** to sell (be sold) dear; to be of difficult access; to be seen seldom (*se vende Vd. caro,* you are a stranger).
vendetta, *f.* vendetta.
vendí, *m.* (com.) certificate of sale.
vendible, *a.* salable, marketable.
vendido, da, *a.* & *pp.* sold; betrayed.—**estar v.,** to be duped; to be exposed to great risks.
vendiente, *a.* selling.
vendimia, *f.* vintage; large gain or profit.
vendimiador, ra, *n.* vintager.
vendimiar, *va.* to gather (crops of grapes); to enjoy as an unlawful perquisite or reap as unjust profit; (coll.) to kill, murder.
vendimiario, *m.* Vendimiaire, first month of the French-Revolution calendar.
vendo, *m.* selvage of cloth.
vendré, etc. *v. V.* VENIR.
venduta, *f.* (Am.) auction.
vendutero, ra, *n.* (Am.) auctioneer.
veneciano, na, *a.* & *n.* Venetian.
venencia, *f.* tube for sampling sherry.
venenífero, ra, *a.* (poet.) poisonous.
veneno, *m.* poison, venom; wrath, fury, passion.
venenosamente, *adv.* venomously, banefully.
venenosidad, *f.* poisonousness, banefulness.
venenoso, sa, *a.* venomous, poisonous, baneful.
[1]**venera,** *f.* scallop shell worn as a badge by pil-

grims; badge, jewel, or star of a military order. —**empeñar la v.**, to spare no expense.
[2]**venera**, *f.* = VENERO, spring (of water).
venerabilidad, *f.* venerability, venerableness.
venerabilísimo, ma, *a. super.* most venerable.
venerable, *a.* venerable.—**venerablemente**, *adv.* venerably.
veneración, *f.* veneration; worship.
venerador, ra, *n.* & *a.* venerator(-ing); worshipper(-ing).
venerando, da, *a.* venerable.
venerante, *a.* venerating, worshipping.
venerar, *va.* to venerate, revere; to worship.
venéreo, rea. I. *a.* sensual; (med.) venereal. **II.** *m.* venereal disease.
venero, *m.* water spring; (min.) bed, lode; radius or horary line of sundials; origin, root, source.
veneruela, *f. dim.* small scallop shell.
venezolano, na, *n.* & *a.* Venezuelan.
Venezuela, *f.* Venezuela.
vengable, *a.* deserving revenge; that can be avenged.
vengador, ra, *n.* & *a.* avenger(-ing); revenger (-ing).
venganza, *f.* revenge; vengeance.
vengar. I. *va.* (*pret.* VENGUÉ; *subj.* VENGUE) avenge. **II.** *vr.* (**de**), to take revenge (on).
vengativamente, *adv.* revengefully.
vengativo, va, *a.* revengeful, vindictive.
vengo, venga, *v. V.* VENIR.
vengué, vengue, *v. V.* VENGAR.
venia, *f.* pardon, forgiveness; leave, permission; bow with the head; (law) license to minors to manage their own estates.
venial, *a.* venial; pardonable.—**venialidad**, *f.* venialness.—**venialmente**, *adv.* venially.
venida, *f.* arrival; return, coming; flood, freshet; attack in fencing; impetuosity, rashness, rush.
venidero, ra. I. *a.* future, coming.—**en lo v.**, hereafter, in future. **II.** *m.* posterity, successors.
venido, da. I. *pp.* of VENIR. **II.** *a.*—**bien v.**, welcome.
venilla, *f. dim.* (anat., zool.) venule, veinlet.
venimécum, *m.* vademecum.
venir. I. *vn.* (*ger.* VINIENDO; *ind. pres.* yo VENGO, él VIENE, *pret.* VINE, *fut.* VENDRÉ; *subj.* VENGA) to come; to arrive; to arise, result, follow; to be becoming, fit, suit; to yield, agree, submit; to grow, be produced; to occur (to one's mind), or begin to be felt (diff. constr.: *me vino el deseo de viajar*, I began to feel, or I felt a desire to travel); to happen; to concern (gen. with IR: *eso no me va ni me viene*, that does not concern, or affect, me).—**v. a**, to attain; (foll. by *inf.*), to end by (foll. by *pres. p.*) (*después de mucho trabajo, vino a descubrir la causa*, after much labor, he ended by finding the cause, or, he finally found the cause); sometimes used to denote approximation, a rough estimate (*Juan viene a tener dos mil pesos*, John must be worth about two thousand pesos).—**v. a buscar**, to come for, or to get.—**v. a las manos**, to come to blows.—**v. a menos**, to decay, to decline.—**v. a pelo** = V. DE PERILLA.—**v. a ser**, to get to be, become; to turn out to be, amount to.—**v. bien**, to suit, be becoming.—**v. bien en**, to agree to, to grant.—**v. como anillo en dedo, v. como pedrada en ojo de boticario**, or **v. de perilla**, to come in the nick of time; to fit the case, answer perfectly, be to the point.—**v. en**, to decide, resolve; to acquire, obtain (knowledge, etc.).—**v. mal**, to be unbecoming, not to suit.—**v. rodado**, to come unexpectedly, to come by a stroke of luck.—**¿a qué viene eso?** to what purpose is that? what has that to do with the case?—**el que venga atrás**, or **detrás, que aree**, the Devil take the hindmost.—**en lo por v.**, hereafter, in future.—**lo por v.**, the future; future things.—**que viene**, next (*la semana que viene*, next week).—**si a mano viene**, perhaps.—**venga lo que viniere**, come what will; happen what may. **II.** *vr.* to ferment; to attain perfection by fermentation, as bread or wine.—**v. abajo**, to fall, to collapse.—**v. a la boca**, to taste unpleasantly.—**v. al suelo**, to fall to the ground; to fall through, to fail.—**v. cayendo**, to be falling down.
venora, *f.* stone or brick marks in a drain or trench, as guides for cleaning.
venosidad, *f.* (anat.) venosity.
venoso, sa, *a.* venous; veiny, veined.
venta, *f.* sale; selling; market; roadside inn; exposed, inhospitable place.—**v. (al) por mayor**, wholesale.—**v. (al) por menor**, retail sale; retailing.—**v. pública**, public auction sale.—**de v.**, or **en v.**, for sale.—**hacer v.**, (coll.) to invite to potluck.—**ser una v.**, to be a dear place.
ventada, *f.* blast, puff, gust of wind.
ventaja, *f.* advantage; gain, profit; additional pay; odds given at play.—**llevar v. a**, to be ahead of; to have advantage over.
ventajosamente, *adv.* advantageously.
ventajoso, sa, *a.* advantageous; profitable; advisable.
ventalla, *f.* valve; (bot.) pod.
ventalle, *m.* fan.
ventana, *f.* window; (carp.) window frame, window sash; window shutter.—**v. de la nariz**, nostril.—**echar la casa por la v.**, to go to a lot of expense.
ventanaje, *m.* (arch.) fenestration.
ventanal, *m.* large window.
ventanazo, *m.* slamming of a window.
ventanear, *vn.* (coll.) to be often at the window (esp. for flirting).—**ventaneo**, *m.* (coll.) gazing out of, or flirting from, the window.
ventanero, ra. I. *m.* window maker; man who gazes at windows where there are women. **II.** *f.* woman who flirts from the window.
ventanilla, *f. dim.* window (of ticket-office, bank teller, etc.).
ventanillo, *m. dim.* small window shutter; peephole.
ventano, *m.* small window.
ventar, *va.* & *vn.* (*ind.* VIENTA; *subj.* VIENTE) = VENTEAR.
ventarrón, *m.* stiff wind, wind gust.
venteadura, *f.* shake in timber.
ventear. I. *v. impers.* (of the wind) to blow. **II.** *va.* to smell, scent, sniff (as dogs); to investigate, inquire; to air. **III.** *vr.* (of timber) to have shakes; to be spoiled by the wind; (coll.) to break wind.
venteo, *m.* bung, bunghole (in a cask).
venteril, *a.* suited to a poor inn.
[1]**ventero, ra**, *n.* innkeeper.
[2]**ventero, ra**, *n.* scenting dog.
ventilación, *f.* ventilation; discussion.
ventilador, *m.* ventilator; (ventilating) fan.
ventilar. I. *va.* to air, ventilate; to winnow, to fan; to discuss. **II.** *vn.* (of air) to circulate.
ventisca, *f.* snowstorm, blizzard; snowdrift.
ventiscar, *v. impers.* to snow with strong wind; (of snow) to drift.
ventisco, *m.* = VENTISCA.—**ventiscoso, sa**, *a.* having frequent snowstorms; full of snowdrifts.
ventisquear, *v. impers.* to snow with strong wind (*aquí ventisquea mucho*, there are many snowstorms here).
ventisquero, *m.* snowstorm, snowdrift; glacier; snow-capped mountain.
ventola, *f.* (naut.) top hamper.
ventolera, *f.* gust of wind; pin wheel; (coll.) vanity, haughtiness; strong whim, "fever," "rage."
ventolina, *f.* (naut.) light wind, cat's-paw.
ventor, ra, *n.* pointer (dog); foxhound.
ventorrero, *m.* exposed, windy place.
ventorrillo, ventorro, *m.* poor inn or tavern.
ventosa, *f.* vent, air hole, spiracle; (zool.) sucker; (surg.) cupping; cupping glass.—**v. escarificada**, or **sajada**, wet cupping.—**v. seca**, dry cupping.—**pegar una v.**, to swindle.
ventosear, *vn.* & *vr.* to break wind.
ventosidad, *f.* flatulence, windiness.

ventoso, sa, *a.* windy; stormy; flatulent; pointing (as a pointer dog); vain, inflated.
ventral, *a.* ventral.
ventrecillo, *m. dim.* of VIENTRE, belly.
ventrecha, *f.* belly (of fishes).
ventregada, *f.* brood, litter; multitude, rush (of things).
ventrera, *f.* bellyband, abdominal belt; cummerbund.
ventrezuelo, *m. dim.* of VIENTRE, belly.
ventricular, *a.* ventricular.
ventrículo, *m.* (anat and zool.) ventricle; any cavity of the heart or brain.
ventril, *m.* counterpoise.
ventrílocuo, *m.* ventriloquist.
ventriloquia, *f.* ventriloquism.
ventrón, *m. aug.* large belly; tripe (food).
ventroso, sa; ventrudo, da, *a.* big-bellied.
ventura, *f.* happiness; luck, fortune; chance, hazard, venture; risk, danger.—**a la v.,** or **a v.,** at a venture, at hazard.—**buena v.,** fortune told by cards, etc.—**por v.,** by chance.—**probar v.,** to try one's fortune or luck, to venture.
venturado, da, *a.* lucky, fortunate.
venturanza, *f.* happiness.
venturero, ra. I. *a.* lucky; adventurous; idle. **II.** *n.* fortune hunter, adventurer.
venturina, *f.* goldstone, aventurin.
venturo, ra, *a.* future; coming.
venturón, *m. aug.* great luck.
venturosamente, *adv.* luckily, fortunately.
venturoso, sa, *a.* lucky; successful, prosperous.
Venus, *m.* (astr.) Venus; *f.* (myth.) Venus; **(v.)** venery.
venustidad, *f.* beauty, gracefulness.
venusto, ta, *a.* beautiful, graceful.
venza, *f.* scarfskin used by goldbeaters.
venzo, venza, *v. V.* VENCER.
veo, vea, *v. V.* VER.
ver. I. *va.* & *vn.* (*pp.* VISTO; *ger.* VIENDO; *ind. pres.* VEO, *pret.* yo VI or VÍ, él VIÓ; *subj.* VEA) to see; to look into, examine, consider; to look; to look at; to try (a case at law).—**v. de,** to try to.—**v. el cielo abierto,** to see a great opportunity.—**v. en ello,** to consider, to weigh in the mind.—**v. las estrellas,** to feel lively pain, see stars.—**v. mundo,** or **v. tierras,** to see the world, to travel.—**v. venir,** to see (somebody or something) coming; to await results.—**v. visiones,** to build air castles.—**v. y creer,** seeing is believing.—**al v.,** to see one, at cards.—**allá veremos,** we shall see, time will tell.—**a más v.,** (coll.) good-bye, so long.—**a v.,** in order to see.—**¡a v.!,** let's see!—**de buen (mal) v.,** good (bad) looking.—**hacer v.,** to show.—**hasta más v.** = A MÁS V.—**estar por v.,** to remain to be seen, to be doubtful.—**no poder v. a,** to abhor or detest (can't bear).—**no tener que v. con,** to have nothing to do with.—**si te vi, ya no me acuerdo,** out of sight, out of mind.—**veámoslo** = A V.—**veremos** = ALLÁ VEREMOS. **II.** *vr.* to be seen; be conspicuous; to find oneself (in a situation), be; to be easily seen, be obvious; to meet, have an interview; to look at oneself in a glass.—**véase,** *v.*, see (in references).—**v. con,** to have a talk with, to see.—**v. en,** or **entre, las astas del toro,** to be in the greatest danger.—**ya se ve,** of course, naturally; certainly; however. **III.** *m.* sense of sight, seeing; looks, light, view, aspect, appearance.—**a mi v.,** in my opinion, to my way of thinking.
[1]**vera,** *f.* edge, border.
[2]**vera,** *f.* (Am.) a tree resembling guaiacum.
veracidad, *f.* veracity, truthfulness.
vera efigies, (Lat.) faithful portrait.
veranada, *f.* summer season.
veranadero, *m.* summer pasture.
veranar, *vn.* to summer.
veraneante, *n.* summer resident or vacationist.
veranear, *vn.* to summer.
veraneo, *m.* summering, summer vacation.
veranero, *m.* place where cattle graze in summer.
veraniego, ga, *a.* summer (as *a.*); thin or sickly in summer; weak, light.
veranillo, *m. dim.*—**v. de San Martín,** Indian summer.
verano, *m.* summer; (Am.) dry season.
veras, *f. pl.* reality, truth; earnestness, fervor.—**con muchas v.,** very earnestly.—**de v.,** in truth, really, in earnest.
veratrina, *f.* (chem.) veratrine, veratrin.
veratro, *m.* (bot.) hellebore.
veraz, *a.* veracious, truthful.
verba, *f.* loquacity, talkativeness; eloquence.
verbal, *a.* verbal; oral; (law) nuncupative.
verbalismo, *m.* verbalism.
verbalista, *n.* verbalist.
verbasco, *m.* (bot.) verbascum, mullein.
verbena, *f.* (bot.) vervain, verbena; night festival on the eve of a saint's day.—**coger la v.,** to rise early for a walk.
verbenáceo, cea, *a.* (bot.) verbenaceous.
verbenear, *vn.* to abound, to be plentiful; to rush to and fro.
verberación, *f.* lashing (esp. of wind, etc.).
verberar, *va.* to lash, beat, strike against (as wind and water).
verbigracia, *adv.* for example, for instance.
verbo, *m.* verb; **(V-)** Word, second person of the Trinity.—**v. activo,** transitive verb, active verb.—**v. adjetivo,** any verb, except *ser*.—**v. auxiliar,** auxiliary verb.—**v. defectivo,** defective verb.—**v. neutro** or **intransitivo,** intransitive or neuter verb.—**v. recíproco,** reciprocal verb.—**v. reflejo,** or **reflexivo,** reflexive verb.—**v. substantivo,** the verb *ser*, to be.—**echar verbos,** to curse, to swear.—**en un v.,** at once, without delay.
verborrea, verbosidad, *f.* verbosity, wordiness.
verboso, sa, *a.* verbose, prolix, wordy.
verdacho, *m.* (art) green earth.
verdad, *f.* truth.—**¿v.?** isn't it? is that so? isn't that so? expletively in the sense of "you know," "don't you know?"—**v. de Perogrullo,** truism.—**a decir v.,** to tell the truth; in reality, in fact.—**a la v.,** truly, really, in truth.—**bien es v. que,** it is true that.—**decir cuatro verdades,** to speak one's mind freely.—**de v.,** A LA V.; in earnest; real.—**en v.,** truly, really; verily.—**¿no es v.?** isn't it? isn't that so?—**ser v.,** to be true.—**tratar v.,** to love and tell the truth.
verdaderamente, *adv.* truly, really.
verdadero, ra, *a.* true; real, actual; truthful.
verdasca, *f.* twig, bough, thin branch.
verde. I. *a.* green; verdant; unripe, immature, undeveloped; fresh; young, blooming; risqué, smutty, off-color.—**v. botella,** bottle green.—**v. de París,** Paris green; imperial green.—**v. limón,** bright green.—**v. pardo,** brown green.—**están verdes,** sour grapes. **II.** *m.* green (color); verdure; vert; green barley or grass given to horses or mules as a purge.—**darse un v.,** to amuse oneself for a short time, to indulge in a little relaxation.
verdea, *f.* greenish wine.
verdear. I. *vn.* to grow green; to look green, to show its greenness. **II.** *va.* to pick (grapes and olives) to sell.
verdeceledón, *m.* sea-green, celadon.
verdecer, *vn.* to grow green.
verdecico, ica, ito, ita, illo, illa, *a. dim.* greenish.—**verdecillo,** *m.* (ornith.) greenfinch.
verdeesmeralda, *a.* emerald green.
verdegal, *m.* green field.
verdegay, *a.* & *m.* light, bright green.
verdeguear, *vn.* to grow green.
verdemar, *a.* & *m.* sea-green.
verdemontaña, *m.* mountain-green.
[1]**verderol,** [1]**verderón,** *m.* (ornith.) green finch.
[2]**verderol,** [2]**verderón,** *m.* (ichth.) green shellfish.
verdete, *m.* verditer; verdigris.
verdevejiga, *f.* sap green.
verdezuelo, *m.* (ornith.) greenfinch, greeny.

verdín, *m.* verdure; pond scum; mould, mildew; verdigris; green snuff.—**verdina,** *f.* fresh greenness of plants.—**verdinal,** *m.* green spot or patch in a plain or meadow.
verdinegro, gra, *a.* dark green.
verdino, na, *a.* bright green.
verdiseco, ca, *a.* pale green; half dry.
verdolaga, *f.* (bot.) purslane.
verdón, *m.* (ornith.) greenfinch.
verdor, *m.* greenness; verdure, verdancy; herbage; freshness, vigor.—*pl.* youth, age of vigor.
verdoso, sa, *a.* greenish.
verdoyo, *m.* pond scum; green mould.
verdugada, *f.* (mason.) layer of bricks.
verdugado, *m.* hoopskirt.
verdugal, *m.* young shoots growing in a wood after cutting.
verdugazo, *m.* blow or lash with a twig.
verdugo, *m.* tiller, sucker, young shoot of a tree; verdun, duelling rapier; scourge, lash; wale, welt; executioner; (jewelry) hoop for a ring; very cruel person; anything that hurts; (mason.) brick course in a stone or mud wall; a small bird of prey.
verdugón, *m. aug.* large wale or welt.
verduguillo, *m. dim.* swelling on the leaves of some plants; small, narrow razor; duelling rapier; hoop worn as earring; (naut.) sheer rail.
verdulera, *f.* market woman; (coll.) coarse, low woman.
verdulería, *f.* greengrocer's shop.
verdulero, *m.* greengrocer.
verdura, *f.* verdure, verdancy; greenness; greens, vegetables; garden stuff; (art) foliage.
verdusco, ca, *a.* dark greenish.
verecundo, da, *a.* bashful, shy.
vereda, *f.* path, footpath, trail; circular order or notice sent to several towns or places; route of travelling preachers; (Cuba, S. A.) sidewalk.—**entrar por la v.,** to come to reason, to do one's duty.
veredero, *m.* messenger sent with despatches on a route.
veredicto, *m.* (law) verdict.
verga, *f.* penis; steel bow of a crossbow; (naut.) yard.—**v. seca,** crossjack yard.—**vergas en alto,** (naut.) all ready to sail.—**poner las vergas en cruz,** to square the yards.
vergajo, *m.* penis of a bull used as a cowhide.
vergel, *f.* flower garden.
vergelero, ra, *n.* gardener.
vergeta, *f.* small twig.
vergeteado, da, *a.* (her.) vergette, paley.
vergonzante. I. *a.* bashful, shamefaced. **II.** *n.* shy beggar.
vergonzosamente, *adv.* shamefully, disgracefully; bashfully, confusedly.
vergonzoso, sa. I. *a.* bashful, shamefaced, shy; shameful, disgraceful. **II.** *m.* armadillo.
verguear, *va.* to beat with a rod or whip.
vergüenza, *f.* shame; bashfulness, shyness, confusion; modesty; disgrace; public punishment.—*pl.* privy parts.—**sacar a la v.,** to disgrace publicly as a punishment; (coll.) to put in a predicament, or "fix," by asking (one) to do before others what one does not do well; to make a show of.—**ser una mala v.,** (coll.) to be a shame.—**tener v.,** to be ashamed; to be shy.
verguer, verguero, *m.* high constable.
vergueta, *f.* small switch or rod.
verguío, a, *a.* (of wood) tough and flexible, leathery.
vericueto, *m.* rough and pathless place.
verídicamente, *adv.* veridically, truthfully.
verídico, ca, *a.* veridical, truthful.
verificable, *a.* verifiable.
verificación, *f.* verification, substantiation, confirmation: test; adjustment (of an instrument).
verificar. I. *va.* (*pret.* VERIFIQUÉ; *subj.* VERIFIQUE) to verify, confirm, prove; to test, adjust (an instrument); to fulfil, accomplish, carry out. **II.** *vr.* to be verified, to prove true; to take place, to occur.
verificativo, va, *a.* verifying, corroborative.
verija, *f.* region of the genitals.
veril, *m.* (naut.) edge of a sand bank, etc.
verilear, *vn.* (naut.) to coast around a bank.
verisímil, *a.* probable, likely, credible.
verisimilitud, *f.* verisimilitude, probability.
verisímilmente, *adv.* probably, likely.
verja, *f.* grate, grating; iron railing.
vermes, *m. pl.* (med.) intestinal worms.
vermicida, *a.* (med.) vermicide.
vermiculación, *f.* (physiol.) vermiculation.
vermicular, *a.* vermiculous, vermicular.
vermiforme, *a.* vermiform, wormlike.
vermífugo, ga, *a.* & *m.* (med.) vermifuge.
verminoso, sa, *a.* verminous.
vermívoro, ra, *a.* vermivorous, worm-eating (as birds).
vermut, *m.* vermouth.
vernáculo, la, *a.* vernacular, native.
vernal, *a.* vernal, spring (as *a.*).
vernier, *m.* vernier.
vero, *m.* marten (fur).—*pl.* (her.) vair.
veronense; veronés, sa, *n.* & *a.* Veronese.
verónica, *f.* (bot.) veronica; a feat in bullfighting.
verosímil, verosimilitud, verosímilmente = VERISÍMIL, VERISIMILITUD, etc.
verraco, *m.* male hog or boar.
verraquear, *vn.* (coll.) to grunt like a boar; (of a child) to cry long and loud.
verraquera, *f.* crying spell (of children).
verriondez, *f.* rutting time of animals; withering state of plants.
verriondo, da, *a.* (of animals) rutting, in heat; withered (plants); badly cooked, tough.
verrón, *m.* = VERRACO.
verruga, *f.* wart; (coll.) nuisance, bore.
verrugo, *m.* (coll.) miser.
verrugoso, sa, *a.* warty.
versado, da. I. *pp.* of VERSAR. **II.** *a.* versed, conversant.
versal, *a.* & *f.* (print.) capital (letter).—**versalilla, versalita,** *f.* & *a.* (print.) small capital (letter).
[1]**versar. I.** *vn.* to go around.—**v. acerca de,** or **sobre,** to treat of or on. **II.** *vr.* to become versed or conversant.
[2]**versar,** *vn.* (Cuba) to versify, improvise verses.
versátil, *a.* versatile; changeable, fickle.
versatilidad, *f.* versatility; fickleness.
versecillo, *m. dim.* little verse, verselet.
versería, *f.* poems.
versícula, *f.* stand for the choir books.
versiculario, *m.* (eccl.) chanter of versicles; keeper of the choir books.
versículo, *m.* (eccl.) verse; versicle.
versificación, *f.* versification.
versificador, ra, *n.* versifier, verse maker.
versificante, *a.* versifying.
versificar, *va.* & *vn.* (*pret.* VERSIFIQUÉ; *subj.* VERSIFIQUE) to versify.
versión, *f.* translation, version; (med.) version.—**v. de los Setenta,** Septuagint.
versista, *m.* (coll.) versifier, poetaster.
[1]**verso,** *m.* line (of poetry); stanza.—*pl.* poems.—**v. alejandrino,** Alexandrine.—**v. blanco,** blank verse.—**v. de arte mayor,** verse of more than nine syllables.—**v. de arte menor,** verse of less than nine syllables.—**v. esdrújulo,** verse ending with a word accented on the antepenult.—**v. libre** = V. BLANCO.—**v. llano,** (poet.) verse ending with a word accented on the penult.—**v. suelto** = V. BLANCO.—**versos pareados,** doggerel.
[2]**verso,** *m.* (artil.) an ancient small culverin.
vértebra, *f.* (anat.) vertebra.
vertebrado, da, *a.* & *n.* vertebrate.
vertebral, *a.* vertebral.
vertedera, *f.* (agr.) mouldboard of a plow.
vertedero, *m.* sink, dumping place; (hydraul.) weir; spillway.

vertedor, ra. I. *n.* nightman; emptier. **II.** *m.* tailrace; drain; (hydraul.) weir; (naut.) boat scoop.
vertellos, *m. pl.* (naut.) balls of the parrel truck.
verter. I. *va.* (*ind.* VIERTO; *subj.* VIERTA) to pour, spill, shed, cast; to empty; to dump; to translate; to construe, interpret; to divulge, publish, reveal. **II.** *vn.* to run, flow.
vertibilidad, *f.* capability of being turned over.
vertible, *a.* movable, changeable, variable.
vertical. I. *a.* vertical. **II.** *m.* (astr.) vertical circle.—**v. primario,** (astr.) prime vertical. **III.** *f.* vertical line.—**verticalidad,** *f.* verticality.—**verticalmente,** *adv.* vertically.
vértice, *m.* vertex; apex, top; (anat.) vertex, crown of the head.
verticidad, *f.* movableness, mobility.
verticilado, da, *a.* (bot.) verticillate.
verticilo, *m.* (bot.) verticil, whorl.
vertiente. I. *a.* emptying; flowing. **II.** *f.* watershed; slope.
vertiginoso, sa, *a.* giddy, vertiginous.
vértigo, *m.* giddiness, dizziness, vertigo; fit of insanity.
vertimiento, *m.* effusion, shedding.
vesania, *f.* (med.) vesania, insanity.
vesánico, ca, *a.* mentally deranged.
vesical, *a.* (anat.) vesical.
vesicante, *a.* & *m.* vesicant, producing blisters.
vesícula, *f.* (anat., bot.) vesicle; (med.) vesicle, blister.—**v. aérea,** air vesicle (of the lungs).—**v. biliar,** gall bladder.—**v. elemental,** or **orgánica,** (biol.) cell.—**v. ovárica,** (anat.) Graffian follicle.—**v. seminal,** (anat.) sperm sac.—**vesicular,** *a.* vesicular.—**vesiculoso, sa,** *a.* vesiculate.
Véspero, *m.* Vesper, evening star.
vespertina, *f.* evening discourse in universities.
vespertino, na. I. *a.* vespertine, evening. **II.** *m.* afternoon literary meeting; afternoon sermon.
véspido, da, *a.* & *m.* (zool.) vespid.
vestal, *f.* & *a.* vestal.
veste, *f.* (poet.) clothes, dress, garments.
vestfaliano, na, *n.* & *a.* Westphalian.
vestíbulo, *m.* vestibule, hall, lobby; (anat.) vestibule of the ear.
vestido, *m.* dress, clothes, clothing, garb, costume; ornament, embellishment.—**v. de corte,** court dress.—**v. de etiqueta,** or **de serio,** full or evening dress.—**vestidos usados,** second-hand clothes.
vestidura, *f.* vesture.—*pl.* (eccl.) vestments.
vestigio, *m.* vestige, trace, sign; footstep, footmark.—*pl.* ruins, remains; (chem.) traces.
vestiglo, *m.* horrid and formidable monster.
vestimenta, *f.* clothes, garments.—*pl.* ecclesiastical robes.
vestir (*ger.* VISTIENDO; *ind. pres.* VISTO, *pret.* él VISTIÓ; *subj.* VISTA). **I.** *va.* to clothe, dress; to deck, adorn; to cloak, disguise, palliate; to don, put on; to wear; to cover; (mason.) to rough-cast. **II.** *vn.* to dress in a special color or fashion.—**v. bien,** to dress well or in good taste.—**v. de uniforme,** to dress in uniform. **III.** *vr.* to dress oneself; to be covered; to be clothed.
vestuario, *m.* apparel, wardrobe, clothes, clothing, dress; uniform; (mil.) equipment, outfit, habiliment; (eccl.) vestry; money given to ecclesiastics for dress, etc.; (theat.) wardrobe, greenroom, dressing room.
vestugo, *m.* tiller, sprout of an olive tree.
veta, *f.* (min.) vein, seam, lode; vein in wood or marble; grain, flake; stripe.—**descubrir la v.,** to disclose one's sentiments or designs, show one's hand.
vetado, da; veteado, da, *a.* striped, veined, streaky, cross-grained, mottled.
vetar, *va.* (Am.) to veto.
vetear, *va.* to variegate, to grain.
veterano, na. I. *a.* (mil.) veteran; having had long experience. **II.** *m.* veteran, old hand.
veterinaria, *f.* veterinary science.
veterinario, ria. I. *a.* veterinary. **II.** *n.* veterinarian; *f.* veterinary medicine.
vetisesgado, da, diagonal-striped.
veto, *m.* veto; prohibition, interdict.
vetustez, *f.* antiquity, old age.
vetusto, ta, *a.* very ancient or old.
vez, *f.* turn; time, occasion; herd of swine belonging to the inhabitants of a place.—*pl.* authority given to a substitute.—**a la v.,** at a time; at the same time; at one time.—**a la v. que,** while.—**alguna v.,** (in a question) ever; also **algunas veces,** sometimes; some times, occasionally.—**alguna que otra v.,** once in a while, occasionally.—**a su v.,** in his (one's) turn; on his (one's) part.—**a veces,** sometimes, occasionally.—**cada v.,** each time, every time.—**cada v. más,** more and more.—**cada v. que,** every time that, whenever.—**de una v.,** at once; at one time; with a single act, word, blow, etc.—**de v. en cuando,** occasionally, once in a while, from time to time.—**dos veces,** twice.—**en v. de,** instead of.—**hacer las veces de,** to serve as, substitute for.—**más de una v.,** more than once.—**muchas veces,** often.—**otra v.,** again, once more; some other time.—**pocas,** or **raras, veces,** seldom, rarely; only a few times.—**tal cual v.,** seldom, rarely, once in a while.—**tal v.,** perhaps, maybe, perchance.—**todas las veces que,** whenever, as often as.—**una que otra v.,** once in a while, a few times.—**una v.,** once.—**una v. que,** since, inasmuch as; after.—**una v. que otra,** once in a while; a few times—**veces mayor que,** times as large as, times (*10 es 5 veces mayor que 2,* 10 is 5 times [as large as] 2). The similar expression **veces menor que** indicates a fractional part: *2 es 5 veces menor que 10,* 2 is one fifth of 10.
veza, *f.* (bot.) vetch.
vezar, *va.* & *vr.* to accustom, habituate, inure.
vi, ví, *pret.* of VER.
vía, *f.* way, road; route, via; carriage track; (Ry.) track, line; gauge; way, manner, method, procedure; spiritual life; (zool.) tube, canal, passage.—**v. acuática,** waterway.—**v. ancha,** (Ry.) broad gauge.—**v. angosta,** narrow gauge.—**v. crucis,** (eccl.) Via Crucis, way of the cross; affliction, burden.—**v. de agua,** (naut.) leak; v. ACUÁTICA.—**v. ejecutiva,** (law) levy, a legal writ of execution; attachment.—**v. férrea,** railroad, railway.—**v. húmeda,** (chem.) wet process.—**V. Láctea,** (astr.) Milky Way.—**v. muerta,** (Ry.) siding.—**v. pública,** public road, thoroughfare; street.—**v. recta,** straight along, straight forward.—**v. sacra** = v. CRUCIS.—**v. seca,** (chem.) dry process.—**v. terrestre,** land route, road.—**en v. de,** in the process of.—**por v. de,** by way of, as.
viabilidad, *f.* feasibility, practicability; (med.) viability.
viable, *a.* viable, capable of living; feasible, practicable.
viadera, *f.* harness shaft of a loom.
viador, *m.* traveler, in a mystical sense.
viaducto, *m.* viaduct.
viajador, ra, *n.* traveler.
viajante. I. *a.* traveling. **II.** *n.* traveler; commercial traveler.
viajar, *vn.* to travel, journey.
viajata, *f.* trip, excursion.
viaje, *m.* journey, voyage, travel, trip; passage; gait; excursion; errand; load carried at once; (hydraul.) water main, water supply; way, road; (arch.) obliquity.—**v. astronáutico,** space trip.—**v. de ida y vuelta** or **redondo,** round trip.—**v. espacial,** space trip.—**v. interplanetario,** interplanetary trip.—**buen v.,** Godspeed, bon voyage.—**de v.,** traveling, on a journey; about to start on a journey.
viajero, ra, *n.* traveler; passenger.
vial. I. *a.* pertaining to roads. **II.** *m.* avenue, lane, boulevard.—**vialidad,** *f.* system of public roads; road engineering, road making.

vianda, *f.* (often in the *pl.*) food, viands, victuals, fare; meal.—*pl.* (Cuba) vegetables for a stew.
viandante, *n.* traveler, passenger; tramp.
viaraza, *f.* (vet.) looseness, diarrhœa.
viaticar. I. *va.* (eccl.) to administer the viaticum to. **II.** *vr.* to receive the viaticum.
viático, *m.* viaticum, provision for a journey, traveling expenses; (eccl.) viaticum.
víbora, *f.* viper; perfidious person.
viborezno, na, *m.* young, small viper.
vibración, *f.* vibration.
vibrador, ra. I. *a.* vibrating. **II.** *m.* vibrator.
vibrante, *a.* vibrating, shaking.
vibrar. I. *va.* to vibrate; to brandish; to throw, dart. **II.** *vn.* to vibrate.
vibrátil, *a.* vibratile.
vibratorio, ria, *a.* vibratory.
vibrión, *m.* (bacteriol.) vibrio.
viburno, *m.* (bot.) viburnum.
vicaria, *f.* assistant mother superior.
vicaría, *f.* vicarship; vicarage.—**v. perpetua,** perpetual curacy.
vicarial, *a.* vicarial.
vicariato, *m.* vicarage; vicarship.
vicario, ria. I. *a.* vicarial, vicarious; vicariate. **II.** *m.* vicar, deputy; (eccl.) vicar, vicariate.—**v. de coro,** vicar choral, superintendent of the choir.—**v. general,** vicar-general.
vicealmiranta, *f.* galley next in order to the admiral's.
vicealmirantazgo, *m.* vice admiralty.
vicealmirante, *m.* vice admiral.
vicecancelario, *m.* vice chancellor (of a university).
vicecanciller, *m.* vice chancellor.
viceconsiliario, *m.* vice counsellor.
vicecónsul, *m.* vice consul.
viceconsulado, *m.* vice consulate.
vicecristo, vicediós, *m.* sovereign pontiff.
vicegerencia, *f.* position of assistant manager.
vicegerente, *m.* assistant manager.
vicegobernador, ra, *n.* vice governor, lieutenant governor.
vicenal, *a.* lasting twenty years; occurring every twenty years.
vicepresidencia, *f.* vice presidency.
vicepresidencial, *a.* vice presidential.
vicepresidente, ta, *n.* vice president.
viceprovincia, *f.* (eccl.) religious houses enjoying the rank of a province.
vicerrector, ra, *n.* vice rector; assistant director.
vicerregente, *m.* vice regent.
vicesecretaría, *f.* assistant secretaryship.
vicesecretario, ria, *n.* assistant secretary.
vicésimo, ma, *a.* twentieth.
vicetesorero, ra, *n.* assistant treasurer.
viceversa. I. *adv.* vice versa, conversely. **II.** *m.* illogical statement, thing or action.
vicia, *f.* tare.
viciado, da. I. *pp.* of VICIAR. **II.** *a.* foul, contaminated.
viciar. I. *va.* to vitiate, mar, spoil; to counterfeit, adulterate; to forge, falsify; to annul, make void, invalidate; to deprave, pervert, corrupt; to misconstrue. **II.** *vr.* to give oneself up to vice; to become too much attached or addicted, to contract a (bad) habit.
vicio, *m.* vice; (bad) habit; defect, blemish; artifice, fraud; excessive appetite, extravagant desire; excessive growth of plants; forwardness, waywardness (of children); vices of horses or mules.—**de v.,** by habit or custom.—**quejarse de v.,** to complain habitually.—**tener el v. de,** to have the habit of; to be in the habit of.
viciosamente, *adv.* viciously; falsely; corruptly.
vicioso, sa, *a.* vicious; defective; given to vice, licentious; spoiled (child); luxuriant, overgrown, vigorous; abundant.
vicisitud, *f.* vicissitude.
vicisitudinario, ria, *a.* vicissitudinary.
viclefismo, *m.* Wycliffism.
viclefista, viclefita, *n.* & *a.* Wycliffite.

víctima, *f.* victim.—**victimario,** *m.* (anc.) servant attending sacrificing priest.
victo, *m.* a day's sustenance.
¡victor! *interj.* & *m.* shout, huzza; long live!
victorear, *va.* to shout, huzza for, give a clamorous ovation to.
[1]**victoria,** *f.* victory, triumph, palm.—**cantar la v.,** to celebrate or proclaim a victory.—**cantar v.,** to proclaim, or boast of, a victory.—**victorial,** *a.* pertaining to victory.
[2]**victoria,** *f.* (Angl.) victoria (carriage).
victoriano, na, *a.* & *n.* Victorian.
victoriosamente, *adv.* victoriously.
victorioso, sa, *a.* victorious, triumphant.
vicuña, *f.* vicuña, a S. A. ruminant.
vid, *f.* (bot.) vine, grapevine.
vida, *f.* life; living person, human being; living, sustenance, livelihood; state, condition; activity, animation, liveliness; (law) term of ten years.—**v. airada,** licentious life, gay life.—**v. ancha,** good, comfortable living.—**v. mía,** dearest, darling.—**v. y. milagros de una persona,** a person's life and history (implying that the "history" is bad).—**buena v.,** good or high living.—**buscar la v.,** to earn an honest livelihood; to seek one's fortune; to inquire into the life (of).—**dar mala v.,** to treat ill, to abuse.—**darse buena v.,** to live comfortably.—**de mala v.,** disreputable, licentious.—**de por v.,** for life, during life.—**en v.,** while living, during life.—**en la v.,** or **en mi v.,** never.—**ganarse la v.,** to make, earn one's living.—**gran v.** = BUENA V.—**hacer v.,** to live together.—**mi v.** = V. MÍA.—**pasar la v.,** to live very frugally.—**por v.** = DE POR V.—**¡por v.!** by Jove!—**¡por v. mía!** upon my soul! by my soul!—**tener siete vidas,** to have the nine lives of the cat.
vide, vide, see (in references) (abbr. *V.*).
vidente. I. *a.* seeing. **II.** *m.* seer, prophet.
¡vidita! *f.* (Am.) dearest, darling.
vidorria, *f.* (S. A., derog.) miserable, forlorn life, (coll.) dog's life.
vidriado, da. I. *pp.* of VIDRIAR. **II.** *a.* glazed. **III.** *m.* glazing; glazed earthenware, crockery.
vidriar, *va.* to varnish, to glaze (earthenware).
vidriera, *f.* glass window or partition; glass case, show case, show window.
vidriería, *f.* glazier's shop; glass factory; glass shop; glassware.
vidriero, ra, *n.* glazier; glassblower; glass dealer.
vidrio, *m.* glass; any article made of glass; anything very delicate and brittle; a very touchy person.—**v. coloreado,** or **de color,** stained glass.—**vidrios de vidriera,** or **planos,** window glass.—**ir al v.,** to ride backward in a coach.—**pagar los vidrios rotos,** to receive undeserved punishment, to be made a scapegoat.
vidriosidad, *f.* vitreousness; glassiness.
vidrioso, sa, *a.* vitreous, brittle; glassy; slippery (from sleet); peevish, touchy.
vidual, *a.* pertaining to widowhood.
vidueño, viduño, *m.* quality of grape vines.
viejarrón, na, *m.* (coll.) old codger.
viejecito, ita, zuelo, ela, *a.* & *n. dim.* little old man(woman).
viejo, ja. I. *a.* old; aged; ancient, antiquated; stale; worn-out; old-fashioned. **II.** *n.* old man (woman).—**v. verde,** (coll.) rake.
vienense, *n.* & *a.* of or from Vienne (France).
vienés, sa, *n.* & *a.* Viennese, of Vienna (Austria).
vienta, viente, *v. V.* VENTAR.
vientecillo, *m. dim.* light wind.
viento, *m.* wind; vanity, petty pride, airs; scent of dogs; nape bone of a dog, between the ears; brace, guy, bracing rope; (artil.) windage; (naut.) course.—**v. calmoso,** light unsteady wind.—**v. contrario,** foul wind.—**v. de bolina,** (naut.) scant wind.—**v. de la hélice,** (aer.) slip stream.—**v. de tierra,** land breeze.—**v. en popa,** wind right aft, before the wind; (fig.)

prosperously, very well.—**v. entero,** wind from one of the cardinal points or four points from any of them.—**v. escaso,** slack wind.—**v. fresco,** (naut.) fresh breeze.—**v. puntero** = V. ESCASO.—**v. terral** = V. DE TIERRA.—**vientos alisios,** trade winds.—**con v. contrario,** (naut.) against the wind.—**contra v. y marea,** (fig.) against all odds; come what may.—**el v. se ha cargado al norte,** the wind has veered to the north.—**medio v.,** wind two points from any of the eight principal points of the compass.—**quitar el v. a un bajel,** to blanket a ship.
vientre, *m.* abdomen; belly; bowels; stomach; pregnancy; womb; widest part of vessels.
vientrecillo, *m. dim.* ventricle.
viernes, *m.* Friday; fast day.—**V. Santo,** Good Friday.—**cara de v.,** wan, thin face.
vierteaguas, *m.* (arch.) flashing, run-off plate or device.
vierto, vierta, *v. V.* VERTER.
vietnamés, mesa, *a.* & *n.* Vietnamese, Viet-Namese.
vietnamita, *a.* & *n.* Vietnamese, Viet-Namese.
viga, *f.* beam, girder, joist, rafter, baulk; (eng.) bridge truss; mill beam; quantity of olives pressed by the beam at once.—**v. armada,** trussed beam.—**v. de aire,** joist.—**v. de alma llena,** plate girder.—**v. maestra,** summer, chief supporting beam.
vigencia, *f.* operation (of a law), state of being in force; legal disposition; life (of a ruling body, etc.); (Colomb.) fiscal year.—**en v.,** (law) in force; standing.
vigente, *a.* (law) in force; standing.
vigesimal, *a.* vigesimal.
vigésimo, ma, *a.* twentieth.
vigía. I. *f.* watchtower; watch, watching; (naut.) shoal, rock. **II.** *m.* lookout, watch.
vigiar, *vn.* to keep a lookout, to watch.
vigilancia, *f.* vigilance, watchfulness.
vigilante. I. *a.* watchful, vigilant, careful. **II.** *m.* watchman, guard; (Arg.) policeman.
vigilantemente, *adv.* vigilantly.
vigilar, *va.* & *vn.* to watch (over), to keep guard, to look out (for).—**vigilativo, va,** *a.* causing sleeplessness or wakefulness.
vigilia, *f.* vigil, wakefulness, watchfulness, watching; nocturnal study; (eccl.) vigil, fast; eve; (mil.) watch, guard.—**comer de v.,** to fast (abstain from meat).
vigor, *m.* vigor.—**en v.,** in force, in effect (as a law).—**vigorar,** *va.* = VIGORIZAR.
vigorizador, ra, *a.* invigorating.—**v. del cabello,** hair tonic.
vigorizante, *a.* invigorating.
vigorizar, *va.* (*pret.* VIGORICÉ; *subj.* VIGORICE) to strengthen, invigorate; to encourage.
vigorosamente, *adv.* vigorously, lustily.
vigorosidad, *f.* vigor.
vigoroso, sa, *a.* vigorous; substantial.
vigota, *f.* (naut.) deadeye, chain plate.
viguería, *f.* set of girders or beams; timberwork.
vigués, sa, *a.* of or from Vigo.
vigueta, *f. dim.* small beam, joist; beam.
vil, *a.* vile, mean, base, despicable.
vilano, *m.* burr or down of the thistle.
vilayato, *m.* vilayet (Turkish province).
vileza, *f.* baseness, meanness, vileness; infamous deed, base act or conduct.
vilipendiador, ra, *a.* & *n.* reviler(-ing).
vilipendiar, *va.* to contemn, revile.
vilipendio, *m.* contempt; reviling.
vilipendioso, sa, *a.* contemptible.
vilmente, *adv.* vilely, basely, contemptibly.
vilo.—en v., *adv.* in the air; insecurely; in suspense.
vilordo, da, *a.* slothful, lazy, heavy.
vilorta, *f.* hoop, ring of twisted willow; clasp ring of a plow; washer; game resembling lacrosse.
vilorto, *m.* a variety of reed; snare of this reed; reed or twig hoop; crosse for playing VILORTA.
vilos, *m.* (P. I.) two-masted vessel.
viltrotear, *vn.* to loaf, to walk the streets.
villa, *f.* town; government of a town; country-house, villa.
Villadiego, *m.*—**coger,** or **tomar, las de V.,** to run away, to sneak out, "to beat it."
villaje, *m.* village; hamlet.
villanada, *f.* villainous, despicable act.
villanaje, *m.* villeinage; peasantry.
villanamente, *adv.* boorishly; villainously.
villancejo, villancete, villancico, *m.* Christmas carol.—**villanciquero,** *m.* writer or singer of Christmas carols.
villanchón, na, *a.* rustic, rude.
villanería, *f.* lowness of birth; meanness.
villanesco, ca, *a.* rustic, rude, boorish.
villanía, *f.* lowness of birth, meanness; villainy, villainousness; vile, base deed.
villano, na. I. *a.* rustic, boorish; villainous, base. **II.** *n.* villain; base, contemptible person; rustic, peasant. **III.** *m.* a Spanish tune and dance.
villanote, *a.* & *m. aug.* great villain.
villar, *m.* village, hamlet.
villazgo, *m.* charter of a town; town tax.
villeta, *f. dim.* small town or borough.
villoría, *f.* hamlet, settlement, farm.
villorín, *m.* a sort of coarse cloth.
villorrio, *m.* (contempt.) small village or hamlet.
vimbre, *m.* (bot.) = MIMBRE, osier, willow.
vimbrera, *f.* (bot.) = MIMBRERA, osier, willow.
vinagrada, *f.* refreshment made with vinegar.
vinagre. I. *m.* vinegar; acidity, sourness. **II.** *a.* (Colomb.) disagreeable; sour (milk, etc.). **III.** *n.* (coll.) grouchy person (also **cara de v.**).—**vinagrero, ra. I.** *n.* vinegar merchant. **II.** *f.* vinegar cruet, caster; (S. A.) heartburn.—**vinagreta,** *f.* (cook.) vinegar sauce.—**vinagrillo,** *m. dim.* weak vinegar; cosmetic lotion; rose vinegar; rose-vinegar snuff.—**vinagroso, sa,** *a.* vinegary, vinegarish, sourish; peevish, grouchy.
vinajera, *f.* (eccl.) wine vessel for the mass.
vinar, *a.* = VINARIO.
vinariego, *m.* owner of vineyards; viticulturist.
vinario, ria, *a.* pertaining to wine.
vinatera, *f.* (naut.) strop, tricing line.
vinatería, *f.* wine trade; wine shop.
vinatero, ra. I. *a.* pertaining to wine. **II.** *n.* vintner, wine merchant.
vinaza, *f.* wine drawn from the lees.
vinazo, *m.* very strong wine.
vincapervinca, *f.* (bot.) vinca, periwinkle.
vinculable, *a.* that may be entailed.
vinculación, *f.* (law) entail.
vincular, *va.* (law) to entail; to ground or found upon; to continue, to perpetuate.
vínculo, *m.* tie, bond; vinculum; (law) entail.
vincha, *f.* (S. A.) kerchief for the head or hair.
vinchuca, *f.* (S. A.) a kind of winged bedbug.
vindicación, *f.* vindication.
vindicador, ra, *n.* & *a.* vindicator(-ing).
vindicar, *va.* (*pret.* VINDIQUÉ; *subj.* VINDIQUE) to vindicate; to avenge; to assert (as rights), defend; (law) to reclaim, repossess, replevy.—**vindicativo, va,** *a.* vindictive, revengeful; vindicating, vindicative.—**vindicatorio, ria,** *a.* vindicatory.
vindicta, *f.* vengeance, revenge.—**v. pública,** public punishment; censure of public opinion.
vine, etc., *v. V.* VENIR.
vínico, ca, *a.* vinic, pertaining to wine.
vinícola. I. *a.* wine (as *a.*); vinicultural. **II.** *n.* = VINARIEGO.
vinicultor, ra, *n.* viniculturist.
vinicultura, *f.* viniculture, wine-making.
viniebla, *f.* (bot.) hound's tongue.
vinífero, ra, *a.* viniferous.
vinificación, *f.* vinification.
vinilo, *m.* (chem.) vinyl.
vinillo, *m.* very weak wine.
vino, *m.* wine; fermented juice of any fruit.—**v. clarete,** claret or pale red wine.—**v. cubierto,** dark-red wine.—**v. de coco,** (P. I.) fermented

milk of cocoanuts.—**v. de cuerpo,** strong-bodied wine.—**v. de Jerez,** sherry wine.—**v. de lágrima,** mother-drop or virgin wine.—**v. de Madeira,** Madeira wine.—**v. de mesa,** table wine.—**v. de nipa,** (P. I.) fermented juice of nipa.—**v. de Oporto,** port wine.—**v. de pasto,** table wine.—**v. de postre** = V. GENEROSO.—**v. flojo,** thin or weak wine.—**v. generoso,** strong, old wine; after-dinner wine.—**v. peleón,** very common wine.—**v. rancio,** fine old wine.—**v. seco,** dry wine.—**v. tinto,** red table wine.—**tomarse del v.,** to get drunk.

vinolencia, *f.* excess in drinking wine.
vinolento, ta, *a.* too fond of wine.
vinosidad, *f.* vinosity.
vinoso, sa, *a.* vinous; addicted to wine.
vinote, *m.* liquid remaining in the boiler after distilling wine.
vinta, *f.* (P. I.) = BAROTO, small boat.
vintén, *m.* (Uru.) a copper coin (about 2 cents).
viña, *f.* vineyard.—**viñadero, ra,** *n.* keeper of a vineyard.—**viñador, ra,** *n.* viticulturist; husbandman.—**viñatero, ra,** *n.* & *a.* (S. A.) = VIÑADOR; VIÑADERO.—**viñedo,** *m.* vineyard.—**viñero, ra,** *n.* owner of vineyards.
viñeta, *f.* (print. and photog.) vignette.
viñetero, *m.* (print.) font case for vignettes.
viñuela, *f.* *dim.* small vineyard.
[1]**viola,** *f.* (mus.) viola; viola player.
[2]**viola,** *f.* (bot.) violet.
violable, *a.* violable.
violáceo, cea, *a.* (bot.) violaceous; violet, violet-colored.
violación, *f.* violation.
violado, da, *a.* & *m.* violet (color).
violador, ra, *n.* violator; infringer; profaner.
[1]**violar,** *va.* to violate, break, infringe; to ravish, rape; to profane, desecrate; to spoil, to tarnish.
[2]**violar,** *m.* patch or bed of violets.
violencia, *f.* violence; compulsion, force; rape, outrage.
violentamente, *adv.* violently; forcibly.
violentar. I. *va.* to do violence to; to break into. **II.** *vr.* to force oneself (to do something distasteful); to control one's unwillingness.
violento, ta, *a.* violent; impulsive; irascible; furious; forced, unnatural; strained, absurd, misconstrued; exceedingly intense or severe, (coll.) "awful."—**sentirse v.,** to be embarrassed.
violero, *m.* viola player.
violeta, *f.* (bot.) violet.
violeto, *m.* clingstone peach.
violín. I. *m.* violin. **II.** *n.* violinist.
violinista, *n.* (mus.) violinist.
violón, *m.* (mus.) bass viol, double bass; bass-viol player.—**tocar el v.,** to do or say something absurd or nonsensical; to talk through one's hat.
violoncelista, *n.* violoncellist, cellist.
violoncelo, *m.* (mus.) violoncello, cello.
violonchelista, *n.* violoncellist, cellist.
violonchelo, *m.* = VIOLONCELO.
vipéreo, rea, viperino, na, *a.* viperine; viperous, venomous.
vira, *f.* dart, arrow; welt of a shoe.
viracocha, *n.* (Chile, Peru) Spaniard.
virada, *f.* (naut.) tacking, tack.
virador, *m.* (naut.) top-rope; viol.
virago, *f.* mannish woman.
viraje, *m.* turn, change in course or direction.
virar, *va.* (naut.) to tack, veer, put about; to wind, twist (as the capstan).—**v. de bordo,** (naut.) to tack; to change one's course, take another way.
viratón, *m.* large dart or arrow.
virazón, *f.* sea breeze.
víreo, *m.* (ornith.) vireo.
virgen. I. *n.* & *a.* virgin. **II.** *f.* standard of the beam of an oil mill; **(V-)** Virgin (Mary); **(V-,** astr.) Virgin, Virgo.
virgiliano, na, *a.* Virgilian.
virginal; virgíneo, nea, *a.* virginal, virgin.
virginia, *f.* (bot.) Virginia tobacco.
virginiano, na, *n.* & *a.* Virginian.
virginidad, *f.* virginity.
virginio, *m.* (chem.) virginium.
virgo, *m.* virginity; (anat.) hymen; **(V-,** astr.) Virgo, Virgin.
vírgula, *f.* virgule, small rod; light, short line, accent; (bacteriol.) cholera bacillus.—**virgulilla,** *f.* fine stroke or light line, accent.
[1]**viril,** *m.* clear and transparent glass; (eccl.) monstrance.
[2]**viril,** *a.* virile, manly.—**virilidad,** *f.* virility, manhood; vigor, strength.
virilmente, *adv.* in a manly manner.
virina, *f.* (P. I.) glass shade for candles; (auto) windshield.
virio, *m.* (ornith.) vireo.
viripotente, *a.* (of young woman) marriageable nubile; vigorous, strong.
virol, *m.* (her.) virole.
virola, *f.* collar, clasp; check ring on goads.
virolento, ta, *a.* having smallpox; pock-marked
virología, *f.* virology.
virólogo, ga, *n.* virologist.
virón, *m.* *aug.* large dart.
viroso, sa, *a.* virose, poisonous.
virotazo, *m.* wound with a VIROTE.
virote, *m.* shaft, dart, arrow; iron rod fastened to a collar on the neck of a slave to prevent his running away; vine three years old; (coll.) stuck-up man; April fool's trick.—**virotillo,** *m.* (arch.) intertie; (mech.) stay, stay rod, stay-bolt.—**virotismo,** *m.* conceit, airs.
virreina, *f.* wife of a viceroy.
virreinato, virreino, *m.* viceroyship.
virrey, *m.* viceroy.
virtual, *a.* virtual.—**virtualidad,** *f.* virtuality.—**virtualmente,** *adv.* virtually, in effect, practically, almost.
virtud, *f.* virtue; efficacy, power; virtuous life; vigor, courage.—*pl.* (theol.) fifth choir of the celestial spirits.—**virtudes cardinales,** cardinal virtues.—**virtudes teologales,** theological virtues (faith, hope, charity).—**en v. de,** in or by virtue of.
virtuosamente, *adv.* virtuously.
virtuoso, sa, *a.* virtuous, righteous; chaste; powerful, vigorous; (mus.) *a.* & *n.* virtuoso.
viruela, *f.* (med.) pock; smallpox.—**viruelas bastardas,** chicken pox.—**viruelas locas,** light case of smallpox.
virulencia, *f.* virulence; acrimony, malignity.
virulento, ta, *a.* virulent; malignant; purulent.
virus, *m.* (med.) virus; poison, contagion.
viruta, *f.* wood shaving.
vis, *f.*—**v. cómica,** (theat.) verve.
visa, *f.* visa, visé.
visado, da. I. *pp.* of VISAR. **II.** *m.* visa.
visaje, *m.* grimace, grin, smirk.—**hacer visajes,** to make wry faces.
visajero, ra, *n.* one who makes faces, grimaces.
visar, *va.* to visé; to countersign; to O.K.
visaya. I. *a.* & *n.* Visayan. **II.** *m.* Visayan language.
víscera, *f.* viscus.—*pl.* viscera.—**visceral,** *a.* visceral.
visco, *m.* = LIGA, birdlime.
viscosidad, *f.* viscosity.
viscoso, sa, *a.* viscous, mucilaginous.
visera, *f.* visor of a cap or helmet; eyeshade; box with a spy hole, used by pigeon fanciers; (Cuba) blinder (for a horse).
visibilidad, *f.* visibility.
visible, *a.* visible; evident; conspicuous.
visiblemente, *adv.* visibly; evidently.
visigodo, da, *n.* & *a.* Visigoth.
visigótico, ca, *a.* Visigothic.
visillo, *m.* window curtain or shade.
visión, *f.* sight; vision; fantasy; phantom, ap-

parition; revelation; (coll.) grotesque person, guy.—**ver visiones,** to be deluded, be "seeing things."
visionario, ria, *a.* & *n.* visionary.
visir, *m.* vizier, Turkish prime minister.
visirato, *m.* viziership, vizierate.
visita, *f.* visit; social call; visitor, caller, guest, company; visitation, inspection; (eccl.) tribunal for the inspection of prisons; hall of that tribunal; (med.) visit.—**v. de aspectos,** medical inspection of passengers.—**v. de cumplido,** or **de cumplimento,** formal call.—**v. de médico,** (coll.) (humor.) short or hurried call.—**v. de sanidad,** health inspection.—**v. domiciliaria,** official visit or inspection of a suspected house: social-work call.—**hacer una v.,** to pay a call. —**pagar una v.,** to return a call.—**tener v.,** to have company or callers.
visitación, *f.* visitation, visiting, visit.
visitador, ra. I. *a.* calling (gen. frequently). **II.** *n.* visitor, visitant, caller; searcher, surveyor, inspector.—**v. de registro,** customs officer who boards ships.
visitadora, *f.* (C. A.) enema.
visitante, *n.* & *a.* visitor(-ing), caller(-ing).
visitar. I. *va.* to visit; to call on; to inspect, search, examine; (med.) to visit (a patient); (law) to make a judicial visit or search of; (naut.) to search (ships); to appear to, as a spirit; to frequent; (eccl.) to visit (religious persons and establishments) as an ecclesiastical judge; (theol.) to send a divine counsel to; (law) to make an abstract of the charge against a prisoner at visitation. **II.** *vr.* to visit one another, call on one another.
visiteo, *m.* frequent visiting or calling.
visitero, ra, *a.* (coll.) fond of making calls.
visitica, illa, *f. dim.* short call.
visitón, *m. aug.* (coll.) long and tedious call.
visivo, va, *a.* visive, pert. to power of seeing.
vislumbrar, *va.* to glimpse, to have a glimmer of; to see imperfectly at a distance; to know imperfectly; to suspect, surmise.
vislumbre, *f.* glimpse, glimmer, glimmering; conjecture, surmise; appearance, semblance.
viso, *m.* elevated spot, outlook; lustre, gleam, sheen, flash, glare; colored slip worn under a transparent frock; color, cloak, pretense, pretext; aspect, appearance.—**a dos visos,** with a double view or design.—**al v.,** (of fabrics) viewed sidewise to examine the sheen.—**de v.,** conspicuous, prominent.
visogodo, da, *a.* & *n.* Visigoth.
visón, *m.* American mink.
visor, *m.* (photog.) view finder.
visorio, ria. I. *a.* visual, optic. **II.** *m.* expert examination.
víspera, *f.* eve, day before; forerunner; anything that precedes another.—*pl.* vesper, evening; (eccl.) vespers.—**v. de natal,** Christmas Eve.—**en vísperas de,** on the eve of.
vista. I. *f.* sight; seeing, vision; view; vista; eye, eyesight; glance, look; aspect, looks; apparition; meeting, interview: clear knowledge or perception; relation, connection; comparison; intent, view, purpose; opinion, judgment; opening, light (window, skylight, etc.); (law) trial.—**v. cansada,** farsightedness.—**v. corta,** nearsightedness.—**aguzar la v.,** to look sharp.—**a la simple v.,** (of the solution of a problem, etc.) at first sight; by inspection.—**a la v.,** at once, immediately; at sight; in sight; (com.) at sight.—**a primera v.,** at first sight.—**a v. de,** in presence of.—**a v. de ojos,** with one's own eyes.—**dar una v.,** to give a passing glance.—**de v.,** by sight.—**echar la v. a,** to choose; to set one's eye on.—**echar una v. a,** to look after, to watch.—**en v. de,** in view of, considering.—**estar a la v.,** to be obvious.—**hacer la v. gorda,** to wink at, overlook, connive.—**hasta la v.,** au revoir, good-bye.—**perder de v.,** to lose sight of.—**perderse de v.,** to go out of sight; (coll.) to excel; to be very smart.—**tener a la v.,** to have before one, or before one's eyes. —**tener v.,** to be showy.—**tener v. a,** to face, look out on. **II.** *n.* customs officer. **III.** *f. pl.* meeting, conference, interview; wedding presents from a bride and bridegroom to each other; bosom, collar and cuffs of a shirt.
vistaria, *f.* (bot.) wisteria.
vistazo, *m. aug.* glance.—**dar un v. a,** to glance at, give a look at.
vistillas, *f. pl.* place commanding a good view, lookout.
[1]**visto, ta. I.** *pp. irreg.* of VER. **II.** *a.* obvious, evident, clear; (law) whereas.—**bien v.,** proper or approved, good form.—**mal v.,** improper or disapproved, bad form.—**v. bueno** (in abbreviation **V°. B°.**), correct, approved, O.K.—**v. es,** or **v. está,** it is evident.—**v. que,** considering that, since.—**no v.,** or **nunca v.,** unheard of.—**por lo v.,** apparently, it seems evident, judging from the facts; according to the above. **III.** *m.* (law) preambulatory clause beginning with "whereas."
[2]**visto, vista, vistió,** *v. V.* VESTIR.
vistosamente, *adv.* beautifully; gaudily.
vistoso, sa, beautiful; showy; flaring, loud.
visual. I. *a.* visual; of sight. **II.** *f.* line of sight.
visualidad, *f.* pleasure in viewing attractive objects.
visura, *f.* ocular inspection; expert examination or inspection.
vital, *a.* vital; essential, necessary.
vitalicio, cia. I. *a.* lasting for life; during life. **II.** *m.* life-insurance policy.
vitalicista, *n.* one who enjoys a life annuity.
vitalidad, *f.* vitality.
vitalismo, *m.* vitalism.
vitalista, *a.* & *n.* vitalist.
vitalizar, *va.* to vitalize.
vitamina, *f.* (biochem.) vitamin.
vitamínico, ca, *a.* vitaminic.
vitando, da, *a.* that ought to be shunned or avoided; odious, execrable.
vitela, *f.* vellum, parchment.
vitelina. I. *a.* (biol.) vitelline. **II.** *f.* (biochem.) vitellin.
vitelo, *m.* (biol.) vitellus, egg yolk.
vitícola. I. *a.* viticultural. **II.** *n.* VITICULTOR.
viticultor, ra, *n.* viticulturist, grape grower.
viticultura, *f.* viticulture, grape growing.
vitiligo, *m.* (med.) vitiligo, white spots on skin.
vito, *m.* a lively dance and tune.
vitola, *f.* (mil.) ball calibre, standard gauge; standard shape and size for cigars; (Am.) appearance, mien.
vítor, *m.* triumphal pageant; memorial tablet.—**¡v.!** long live!—**vitorear,** *va.* to cheer, acclaim.
vitral, *m.* stained-glass window, church window.
vitre, *m.* thin canvas.
vítreo, a, *a.* vitreous, glassy.
vitrescible, *a.* vitrescent, that can become glass.
vitrificable, *a.* vitrifiable.
vitrificación, *f.* vitrification.
vitrificar, *va.* to vitrify.
vitrina, *f.* show case; (Am.) show window.
vitriólico, ca, *a.* vitriolic.
vitriolo, *m.* vitriol; sulphate.—**v. amoniacal,** ammonium sulphate.—**v. azul,** blue vitriol.—**v. blanco,** white vitriol.—**v. de plomo,** (min.) anglesite, lead-sulphate ore.—**v. verde,** green vitriol.
vitualla, *f.* (gen. in the *pl.*) victuals, provisions; abundance of food, mainly of vegetables.
vituallar, *va.* (mil.) to victual.
vítulo marino, *m.* = BECERRO MARINO, seal.
vituperable, *a.* vituperable, blameworthy.
vituperación, *f.* vituperation.
vituperador, ra, *n.* & *a.* vituperator(-ing).
vituperante, *a.* vituperating, vituperative.
vituperar, *va.* to vituperate.
vituperio, *m.* vituperation.
vituperiosamente, vituperosamente, *adv.* vituperatively.

vituperioso, sa; vituperoso, sa, *a.* vituperative.
viuda, *f.* widow; dowager; (bot.) mourning bride.
viudal, *a.* pertaining to a widow or widower.
viudedad, *f.* widow's pension.
viudez, *f.* widowhood.
viudita, *f. dim.* spruce little widow; (bot.) VIUDA.
viudo. I. *m.* widower. **II.** *a.* (of birds) pairing.
viva. I. *m.* huzza, cheer, shout, acclamation. **II. ¡v.!** *interj.* long live! hurrah, huzza.
vivac, *m.* (mil.) bivouac; night guard.
vivacidad, *f.* vivacity, liveliness; brilliancy.
vivamente, *adv.* vividly; quickly; deeply.
vivandero, ra, *n.* (mil.) sutler.
vivaque, *m.* (mil.) bivouac.
vivaquear, *vn.* to bivouac.
vivar, *m.* warren, burrow; vivarium.
vivaracho, cha, *a.* lively, sprightly, frisky.
vivaz, *a.* lively, active, vigorous; ingenious, bright, witty; (bot.) perennial, evergreen.
viveral, *m.* (bot.) nursery.
víveres, *m. pl.* provisions, foodstuffs; (mil.) stores. —**v. de campaña,** (naut.) sea provisions, stores.
vivero, *m.* warren; hatchery; (bot.) nursery.
vivérrido, da, *a.* & *m.* or *f.* (zool.) viverrine.
viveza, *f.* liveliness, sprightliness; gaiety; briskness; ardor, vehemence; acuteness, perspicacity, quickness; witticism; strong resemblance; luster, splendor; grace and brilliancy in the eyes; thoughtless word or act.
vividero, ra, *a.* habitable.
vívido, da, *a.* vivid, bright.
vividor, ra. I. *a.* thrifty. **II.** *n.* long liver; sponger.
vivienda, *f.* dwelling, lodging, house.
viviente, *a.* living; animated.
vivificación, *f.* vivification, enlivening.
vivificador, ra, *n.* & *a.* vivifier(-ying), enlivener (-ing).
vivificante, *a.* vivifying, life-giving.
vivificar, *va.* to vivify, animate, enliven; to comfort, refresh.—**vivificativo, va,** *a.* vivifying, life-giving; comforting.
vivífico, ca, *a.* springing from life.
vivíparo, ra, *a.* (zool.) viviparous.
vivir. I. *vn.* & *va.* to live, be alive; to live, dwell; to last, endure, keep.—**¡viva!** hurrah! long live! —**v. de,** to live on (as one's investments, etc.). —**viva Vd. mil años,** or **muchos años,** may you live many years, or I wish you a long life (a form of courtesy.)—**¿quién vive?** (mil.) who goes there?—**quien vive,** qui vive, (be, being) on the alert. **II.** *m.* life, living, existence.—**mal v.,** riotous living.
vivisección, *f.* vivisection.
vivismo, *m.* Vivism, philosophico-theological system of Luis Vives.
vivo, va. I. *a.* alive, living, live; lively; intense; (of color) vivid; kindled, live (as fire); acute, ingenious; quick, bright, lively, smart; hasty; diligent, nimble; pure, clean; lasting, enduring; excellent; expressive, vehement, persuasive; raw (flesh), open (wound).—**a lo v., al v.,** to the life, vividly.—**de v. voz,** by word of mouth. —**en vivo,** living, alive.—**los vivos y los muertos,** the quick and the dead.—**tocar en lo v.,** to cut or hurt to the quick. **II.** *m.* edging, border; (sewing) piping; (bookbinding) rib, ridge, border; (arch.) sharp edge; (vet.) mange, itch, or scab in dogs.
vizcacha, *f.* viscacha, a S.A. rodent.
vizcachera, *f.* viscacha hole.
vizcainada, *f.* Basque action or behavior; (coll.) solecism.
vizcaíno, na, *n.* & *a.* Biscayan.
vizcondado, *m.* viscountship.
vizconde, *m.* viscount.—**vizcondesa,** *f.* viscountess.
vocablo, *m.* word, term.
vocabulario, *m* vocabulary, lexicon.
vocabulista, *n.* lexicographer; student of words.
vocación, *f.* vocation, calling; occupation.
vocal. I. *a.* vocal, oral; (gram.) vowel. **II.** *f.* (gram., print.) vowel. **III.** *n.* voter, in a congregation or assembly; member of a governing body.
vocalicé, vocalice, *v. V.* VOCALIZAR.
vocálico, ca, *a.* vocalic, vowel-like.
vocalización, *f.* (mus.) vocalization.
vocalizar, *vn.* (*pret.* VOCALICÉ; *subj.* VOCALICE) to vocalize, articulate.
vocalmente, *adv.* vocally, orally.
vocativo, va, *a.* & *m.* (gram.) vocative.
voceador, ra. I. *n.* vociferator. **II.** *m.* town crier.
vocear. I. *vn.* to vociferate, to cry out, shout. **II.** *va.* to cry, publish, proclaim; to call, hail; to cheer, acclaim; (coll.) to boast of publicly.
vocejón, *m.* harsh, raucous voice.
vocería, *f.,* **vocerío,** *m.* vociferation, clamor, outcry, shouting.
vocero, ra, *n.* spokesman (for another).
voces, *f. pl.* of voz.
vociferación, *f.* = VOCERÍA.
vociferador, ra, *n.* & *a.* vociferator(-ing), shouter (-ing); boaster(-ing).
vociferante, *a.* vociferating.
vociferar. I. *vn.* to vociferate, shout, clamor. **II.** *va.* to boast of loudly.
vocinglería, *f.* clamor, outcry; loquacity.
vocinglero, ra. I. *a.* prattling, chattering, vociferous. **II.** *n.* loud babbler.
vodka, *m.* vodka, a Russian liquor.
voila, *f.* term in the game of jackstones indicating that the cast may not count.
[1]**volada,** *f.* short flight.
[2]**volada,** *f.* (Am.) trick, bad turn.—**hacer,** or **jugar, una (mala) volada a,** to play a trick on, do a bad turn to.
voladera, *f.* float of a water wheel.
voladero, ra. I. *a.* flying, fleeting. **II.** *m.* precipice, abyss.
voladizo, za. I. *a.* projecting, jutting out. **II.** *m.* (arch.) corbel.
volado, da. I. *a.* (print.) high, superior, set above the level of the line.—**v. de genio,** (Am.) quick-tempered. **II.** *adv. m.* (Mex., Guat.) urgently. **III.** *m.* = BOLADO, fondant.
volador, ra. I. *a.* flying; running fast; swift; hanging in the air. **II.** *m.* skyrocket; (ichth.) flying fish; (bot.) a tropical tree of very hard wood. **III.** *f.* flywheel of a steam engine.
voladura, *f.* blast, explosion; blasting.
volandas.—en v., *adv.* in the air, as if flying; (coll.) rapidly, swiftly.
volandera, *f.* (mil.) runner; grindstone; (coll.) fib, lie; (mech.) washer; (print.) galley slice.
volandero, ra, *a.* (nestling) ready to fly; fluttering in the air; fortuitous, casual; unsettled, fleeting, variable.
volandillas.—en v. = EN VOLANDAS.
volando, *adv.* (Am.) quickly, at top speed.
volanta, *f.* (Cuba) two-wheel covered vehicle with very long shafts.
volante. I. *a.* flying, fluttering; unsettled. **II.** *m.* head ornament of light gauze; shuttlecock; game of shuttlecock and battledore; screen; coiners' stamp mill; balance wheel, escapement (of watch); (mech.) flywheel; balance beam; lackey, flunkey; flier, note, memorandum; (sewing) flounce; (Cuba) VOLANTA; linen coat; (Mex.) dress coat; (auto) steering wheel (also **v. de dirección**).
volantín, *m.* a fishing apparatus.
volantón, na, *a.* able to fly (nestling).
volapié, *m.* a feat in bullfighting.—**a v.,** half running, half flying.
volapuk, *m.* Volapük.
volar. I. *vn.* (*ind.* VUELO; *subj.* VUELE) to fly (as birds, kites, clouds, etc.); to flutter, hover (as insects); to run or move swiftly (as a train, arrow, etc.); to vanish, disappear; to rise in the air (as a steeple); to make rapid progress; act fast or quickly; to project, jut out, hang over; to extend, spread rapidly (as news); to explode, burst.—**echar a v.,** to disseminate; to divulge, publish. **II.** *va.* to blow up; to spring (a mine);

to blast; to irritate, exasperate; to put up (game); to disseminate, publish, spread, divulge.
volateo.—al v., *adv.* (shooting) on the wing.
volatería, *f.* fowling; sporting with hawks; poultry; fowls; flock of birds; (fig.) crowding conflicting ideas (in one's mind).—**de v.,** incidentally, in passing; at random, recklessly.
volátil, *a.* volatile; flying, wafting; changeable, fickle; fleeting.
volatilidad, *f.* (chem.) volatility.
volatilización, *f.* volatilization.
volatilizar, *va.* & *vr.* (*pret.* VOLATILICÉ; *subj.* VOLATILICE) to volatilize, vaporize.
volatín, *m.* acrobatic feat.
volatinero, ra, *n.* tightrope walker; aerialist; acrobat.
volatizar, *va.* (chem.) = VOLATILIZAR.
volavérunt, (Lat.) (coll.) the bird has flown; gone! (something) has disappeared, is gone.
volcán, *m.* volcano; excessive ardor; violent passion; excitable person or temperament.
volcanejo, *m. dim.* small volcano.
volcánico, ca, *a.* volcanic.
volcanología, *f.* volcanology.
volcanólogo, ga, *n.* volcanologist.
volcar. I. *va.* (*ind. pres.* VUELCO, *pret.* VOLQUÉ; *subj.* VUELQUE) to upset, overturn; to tilt; (naut.) to capsize; to make dizzy; to make (one) change his opinion; to make angry. **II.** *vr.* to upset.
volea, *f.* snaffle tree, whippletree; (games) volley.
voleador, *m.* (sports) batsman, batter.
volear, *va.* to volley (a ball); also *vn.* (baseball) to bat; to fire a volley at.
voleo, *m.* (games) volley; (dance) high step or kick.—**del primer v.,** or **de un v.,** (coll.) at one blow; in an instant.
volframio, *m.* (chem.) tungsten.
volframita, *f.* (min.) wolframite.
volición, *f.* volition.
volitar, *vn.* to flutter.
volitivo, va, *a.* volitional.
volqué, *pret.* of VOLCAR.
volquearse, *vr.* to tumble, to wallow.
volquete, *m.* tip cart, tilt cart.
volt, *m.* (elec.) volt.
voltaico, ca. I. *a.* (elec.) voltaic. **II.** *a.* & *n.* (of the) Upper Volta.
voltaísmo, *m.* (elec.) voltaism.
voltaje, *m.* (elec.) voltage.
voltámetro, *m.* (phys.) voltameter.
voltamperímetro, *m.* (elec.) wattmeter.
voltamperio, *m.* (elec.) volt ampere.
voltariedad, *f.* fickleness, inconstancy.
voltario, ria, *a.* fickle, inconstant, giddy.
volteador, ra, *n.* tumbler, acrobat.
voltear. I. *va.* to turn; to revolve; to overturn, change the order of; (arch.) to arch, to vault. **II.** *vn.* to turn; to revolve; to roll over; to tumble (as an acrobat). **III.** *vr.* to turn over; to upset; (coll.) to change one's party or creed.
voltejear, *va.* to whirl; (naut.) to tack.
volteleta, *f.* tumble, somersault; at cards, turning up the card that makes trumps.
volteo, *m.* whirl, whirling; revolution, turn; turning; overturning; felling; tumbling.
voltereta, *f.* = VOLTELETA.
volterianismo, *m.* Voltairianism.
volteriano, na, *a.* & *n.* Voltairian.
volteta, *f.* = VOLTELETA.
voltímetro, *m.* (elec.) voltmeter.—**v. aperiódico,** dead-beat, or aperiodic, voltmeter.
voltio, *m.* (elec.) volt.—**v.-amperio,** (elec.) volt-ampere.
voltizo, za, *a.* curled, twisted; versatile, inconstant, fickle.
vóltmetro, *m.* (elec.) voltmeter.
volubilidad, *f.* volubility.
voluble, *a.* easily moved about; voluble, fickle; (bot.) twining.
volublemente, *adv.* volubly.
volumen, *m.* volume (book); volume, size, bulk; corpulence.
volumetría, *f.* volumetry.
volumétrico, ca, *a.* volumetric.
voluminoso, sa, *a.* voluminous; bulky.
voluntad, *f.* will; goodwill, benevolence, kindness; desire, pleasure; disposition, precept; consent.—**a v.,** (com.) optional, at will.—**de buena v.,** or **de v.,** with pleasure, willingly.—**de mala v.,** unwillingly.
voluntariamente, *adv.* voluntarily.
voluntariedad, *f.* voluntariness; wilfulness.
voluntario, ria, *a.* & *n.* voluntary(-eer).
voluntariosamente, *adv.* wilfully.
voluntarioso, sa, *a.* wilful, self-willed.
voluptuosamente, *adv.* voluptuously; licentiously.
voluptuosidad, *f.* voluptuousness; licentiousness.
voluptuoso, sa, *a.* voluptuous; licentious, lustful, lewd.
voluta, *f.* (arch.) volute.
[1]**volvedor,** *m.* tap wrench, turnscrew.
[2]**volvedor, ra,** *a.* (Colomb.) (of horse) that runs away back to its home.
volver. I. *va.* (*pp.* VUELTO; *ind.* VUELVO; *subj.* VUELVA) to turn; turn up, turn over, turn upside down or inside out; to return, pay back, give or send back; to give up; to direct, aim; to translate; to restore, reinstate; to change the outward appearance of; to invert, change, move; to vomit; to persuade, convince; to reflect (sound); to give (change in sales); to close, pull or push to (door or shutter); to reëstablish, to replace; to plow a second time.—**v. la cara,** to turn one's head, turn around.—**v. loco,** to drive crazy, distract. **II.** *vn.* to return, come, or go, back; to come again; to turn (to the right, etc.).—**v. a,** to . . . again (*volver a cantar,* to sing again; *Juan me volvió a escribir,* John wrote to me again).—**v. atrás,** to come, or go, back.—**v. en sí,** to recover consciousness, come to.—**v. por,** to stand up for, to defend.—**v. por sí,** to defend oneself; to redeem one's credit.—**v. sobre sí,** to mend one's ways; to make up one's losses; to recover one's equanimity.—**v. sobre (sus) pasos,** to retrace (one's) steps. **III.** *vr.* to turn, become; to turn or get sour; to turn about, turn around; to change one's views.—**v. atrás,** to flinch; to back out.—**v. la tortilla,** to turn the tables or scales.—**v. loco,** to lose one's mind, to become crazy or distracted.
volvible, *a.* capable of being turned, turned over or inverted.
volvo, vólvulo, *m.* (med.) volvulus, ileus.
vómer, *m.* (anat.) vomer.
vomicina, *f.* (chem.) brucine, vomicine.
vómico, ca. I. *a.* causing vomiting; vomitive. **II.** *f.* (med.) vomica.
vomipurgante, vomipurgativo, va, *a.* & *m.* both purgative and emetic.
vomitado, da, *a.* (coll.) meager; pale.
vomitador, ra, *n.* one who vomits.
vomitar, *va.* to vomit; to eject, throw out, disgorge; discharge; to break out into (insults, etc.); to give out, reveal; to give up, surrender.
vomitivo, va, *m.* & *a.* emetic.
vómito, *m.* vomiting; vomit; (Cuba) yellow fever.—**v. negro,** yellow fever.—**provocar a v.,** to nauseate, to make loathe.
vomitón, na. I. *a.* often throwing up milk (as a nursing child). **II.** *f.* (coll.) violent vomiting after heavy eating or drinking.
vomitorio, ria. I. *a.* vomitory. **II.** *m.* vomitory in Roman theatres.
voracidad, *f.* voracity, greediness, voraciousness.
vorágine, *f.* vortex, whirlpool.—**voraginoso, sa,** *a.* engulfing; full of whirlpools.
vorahunda, *f.* = BARAÚNDA, hurly-burly.
voraz, *a.* voracious, greedy, ravenous; excessively lustful; destructive, fierce (as fire).
vorazmente, *adv.* voraciously; greedily.

vormela, *f.* (zool.) a kind of spotted weasel.
vórtice, *m.* vortex, whirlpool, whirlwind; center of a cyclone.
vorticela, *f.* (zool.) vorticella.
vortiginoso, sa, *a.* vortical.
vos, *pers. pron.* you.
vosotros, tras, *pers. pron. pl.* you, ye.
votación, *f.* voting, vote, balloting.
votador, ra. I. *a.* voting. **II.** *n.* voter; curser.
votante, *n.* voter in a corporation or assembly.
votar, *vn.* & *va.* to vow; to vote; to vote on; to give an opinion; to curse, swear, utter oaths; to pass, decree or authorize by vote (in deliberating bodies).—**v. una partida,** to make, or pass, an appropiation.—**¡voto a (Dios, Júpiter,** etc.)! by (God, Jupiter, etc.)!—**¡voto al chápiro!** goodness me! **¡voto a tal!** goodness! upon my soul! confound it! by Heaven! by Jove!
votivo, va, *a.* votive, offered by a vow.
voto, *m.* vote; ballot; opinion; voter; vow; supplication to God; curse, oath, execration; wish; (eccl.) votive offering.—**v. activo,** (right to) vote.—**v. consultivo,** professional or expert advice.—**v. de amén,** vote blindly given.—**v. de calidad,** casting vote.—**v. de reata** = v. DE AMÉN.—**v. particular,** dissenting opinion (of the minority of a commission, etc.).—**v. pasivo,** qualification to be voted for, or elected, by a corporation.—**¡v. va!** = ¡VOTO A TAL! *V.* VOTAR.—**echar votos,** to swear, curse.—**hacer votos por,** to pray for; to wish.—**ser,** or **tener, v.,** to have a vote; to speak knowingly.
¡voto . . . !, *interj. v. V.* VOTAR.
voy, *1st pers. sing. pres.* of IR.
voz, *f.* voice; sound, noise; (gen. in the *pl.*) clamor, outcry; expression, word, term; voice, power or authority to speak (as in an assembly); vote; opinion expressed; rumor, public opinion; motive, pretext; (gram.) voice (active or passive); (mus.) singer; voice, key tone; (mil.) command, order; (law) life.—**v. activa,** right of voting; (gram.) active voice.—**v. argentada,** or **argentina,** clear and sonorous voice.—**v. del pueblo, voz del cielo,** vox populi, vox Dei, the voice of the people is the voice of God.—**v. de mando,** word of command.—**v. pasiva,** right or qualification to be voted for, or elected; (gram.) passive voice.—**v. pastosa,** mellow voice.—**v. velada,** veiled voice.—**a media v.,** with a slight hint; in a whisper.—**a una v.,** of one accord, unanimously.—**a v. en cuello,** or **a v. en grito,** in a loud voice; shouting; at the top of one's voice.—**a voces,** clamorously, with shouts.—**correr la v.,** to be said, to be rumored. —**dar voces,** to cry, scream, shout, yell.—**en v.,** verbally; (mus.) in voice.—**en v. alta,** aloud, out loud.—**en v. baja,** in an undertone, sotto voce.—**pedir a voces,** to clamor for; to be a crying need.—**secreto a voces,** open secret.—**ser v. común,** to be generally said, to be a common rumor.
vozarrón, *m.* strong, heavy voice.
voznar, *vn.* (of swans and geese) to cackle.
vuecelencia, vuecencia, *n.* (*contr.* of VUESTRA EXCELENCIA) your excellency.
vuelapié.—**a v.** = A VOLAPIÉ.
¹vuelco, *m.* tumble, overturning, upset.
²vuelco, vuelca, *v. V.* VOLCAR.
vuelillo, *m.* lace cuff trimming.
¹vuelo, *m.* flight; flying; sweep, space flown through; wing of a bird; width or fulness of clothes; (sewing) ruffle or frill on the wristband; elevation, soaring, loftiness of thought; leap or bound in pantomimes; (arch.) jut, projection, corbeling.—**v. interestelar,** interstellar flight. —**v. interplanetario en vehículo tripulado,** manned space flight.—**v. planeado,** gliding. —**v. sideral,** space flight.—**al v.,** on the fly; in passing, accidentally; (agr.) (of seed) scattered at random.—**alzar,** or **levantar, v.,** to fly; to take off, to depart; to sail.—**de alto v.,** of great importance, of high standing.—**tomar v.,** to progress, to grow.
²vuelo, vuela, vuele, *v. V.* VOLAR.
vuelta, *f.* turn; revolution (of a wheel, etc.); turning; turn of an arch; curve; requital, recompense; repetition, iteration; back or wrong side; whipping, lashing, spanking; return; returning, giving back; review (of a lesson); going over (a writing, etc.); change (in state, appearance); change (received when paying); change (small coins); inclination, bent; (sewing) ¹VUELO; sleeve cuff, facing; (naut.) turn, hitch, lashing; trip, excursion; promenade, walk; ward in a lock or key; order of stitches in knitting hose; roll, envelope; unexpected sally or witticism, repartee; card turned up for a trump; number of times a field has been plowed; (mus.) number of verses repeated; potter's wheel; (arch.) curve of an intrados; vault; ceiling.—**v. de carnero,** turn on the head; heavy fall.—**vueltas de coral,** string or necklace of coral.—**a la v.,** on returning; round the corner; (turn) over (the page); carried over, carried forward (in bookkeeping). —**a la v. de,** within (app. to time).—**andar a las vueltas de,** to dog.—**andar a vueltas,** to fight, to struggle; to endeavor.—**andar en vueltas,** to shuffle, use subterfuges; to shirk.— **a v., a vueltas,** very near, almost.—**a v. de,** in the course of, during (a specified time); by return (mail).—**a v. de ojo,** quickly, in a jiffy. —**dar la v. a,** to turn; to go around.—**dar una v.,** to take a stroll.—**dar vueltas,** to turn; to walk to and fro; to fuss about; to hang around. —**de la v.,** brought forward.—**de v.,** on returning.—**estar de v.,** to have returned, to be back; to be posted or informed beforehand.—**la v. de,** towards, on the way to.—**no haber que darle vueltas,** or **no tener v. de hoja,** no two ways about it.—**otra v.,** again, once more.—**poner de v. y media,** (coll.) to give a dressing down, or a going over, to; to call one all kinds of abusive names.—**tener v.,** (coll.) admonition to return a thing lent.
vuelto, ta. I. *pp. irreg.* of VOLVER. **II.** *m.* (Am.) change (money).
vueludo, da, *a.* full-skirted.
vuelvo, vuelva, *v. V.* VOLVER.
vuesa, *a.* (*contr.* of VUESTRA) (obs.) your.
vuesamerced, *n.* (*contr.* of VUESTRA MERCED) you, sir; you, madam; your grace, your honor.
vuesarced, *n.* = VUESAMERCED.
vueseñoría, *n.* (*contr.* of VUESTRA SEÑORÍA) your lordship, your ladyship.
vuestro, tra, *poss. pron.* your, yours.
vulcanicé, vulcanice, *v. V.* VULCANIZAR.
vulcanio, nia, *a.* pert. to Vulcan or to fire; igneous.
vulcanismo, *m.* (geol.) vulcanism.
vulcanista, *n.* (geol.) vulcanist.
vulcanita, *f.* (min.) vulcanite.
vulcanización, *f.* vulcanization; mending (a tire, etc.).
vulcanizador, ra. I. *a.* vulcanizing. **II.** *n.* vulcanizer.
vulcanizar, *va.* (*pret.* VULCANICÉ; *subj.* VULCANICE) to vulcanize; to mend (a tire, etc.).
vulgacho, *m.* mob, populace, rabble.
vulgar, *a.* vulgar, coarse; common, in general use; (of speech) vernacular.—**vulgaridad,** *f.* vulgarity.—**vulgarismo,** *m.* vulgarism.
vulgarización, *f.* vulgarization.
vulgarizar. I. *va.* (*pret.* VULGARICÉ; *subj.* VULGARICE) to vulgarize, popularize; to translate into the vernacular. **II.** *vr.* to become vulgar.
vulgarmente, *adv.* vulgarly; commonly.
Vulgata, *f.* (eccl.) Vulgate.
vulgo, *m.* common people; populace.
vulnerabilidad, *f.* vulnerability.
vulnerable, *a.* vulnerable.
vulneración, *f.* act of wounding.
vulnerar, *va.* to injure the reputation of.
vulnerario, ria. I. *a.* (med.) vulnerary. **II.** *m.* (law) clergyman guilty of killing or wounding.
vulpécula, vulpeja, *f.* bitch fox.
vulpino, na, *a.* vulpine; foxy, crafty.

vultuoso, sa, *a.* (med.) bloated.
vultúrido, da, *a.* (ornith.) vulturine.
vulturno, *m.* hot breeze that blows in the summer.
vulva, *f.* (anat.) vulva.—**vulvario, ria,** *a.* (anat.) vulvar.—**vulvitis,** *f.* vulvitis.

W

This letter does not belong to the Spanish alphabet and is mainly used in words, chiefly proper nouns, taken from other languages. In adjectives and common nouns derived from proper nouns containing it, it is generally changed to *v* (see VAGNERIANO, VESTFALIANO), although some writers preserve the *w* (*wagneriano, westfaliano*). Such words are readily translated at sight, on account of their similarity to their English equivalents. The Spanish Academy has allowed the use of the letter in **wat,** (elec.) watt, although the term generally used is **vatio.**

X

NOTE.—Several words that were originally, or are occasionally, written with an initial *x* are more generally begun with *j.*

X, x, *f.* x, twenty-sixth letter of the Spanish alphabet.
xantato, *m.* (chem.) xanthate.
xanteína, *f.* (chem.) xanthein.
xántico, ca, *a.* (chem.) xanthic.
xantina, *f.* (chem.) xanthine.
xantofila, *f.* (chem.) xanthophyll.
xantoxilo, *m.* (bot.) zanthoxylum.
xara, *f.* Moslem law derived from the Koran.
xenofobia, *f.* xenophobia, hatred of foreigners.
xenófobo, ba, *n.* & *a.* hater of foreigners.
xenogénesis, *f.* (biol.) xenogenesis.
xenón, *m.* (chem.) xenon.
xerodermia, *f.* (med.) xerosis.
xerofagia, *f.* xerophagy, dry-food diet.
xeroftalmía, *f.* (med.) xerophthalmia.
xi, *f.* xi (Greek letter).
xifisternón, *m.* (anat., zool.) xiphisternum.
xifoideo, ea, *a.* (anat.) xiphoid.
xifoides. I. *a.* (anat.) xiphoid. **II.** *m.* xiphoid, xiphisternum.
xifosuro, ra, *n.* & *a.* xiphosuran.
xileno, *m.* (chem.) xylene.
xílico, ca, *a.* xylic.
xilidina, *f.* xylidine.
xilófago, ga. I. *a.* xylophagous. **II.** *m.* (entom.) wood-eating insect.
xilófono, *m.* xylophone.
xilógeno, *m.* (chem.) xylem.
xilografía, *f.* xylography, wood engraving.
xilográfico, ca, *a.* xylographic.
xilógrafo, fa, *n.* xylographer.
xiloide, *a.* xyloid, woodlike.
xilonita, *a.* transparent celluloidlike substance.
xilórgano, *m.* xylophone.

Y

[1]**Y, y,** *f.* y, twenty-seventh letter of the Spanish alphabet.
[2]**y,** *conj.* and. Sometimes used at the beginning of sentence for emphasis.—**¿y bien?,** and then? "so what?"—**y eso que,** even though.—**¿y qué?** (Am.) is it true that?
ya. I. *adv.* already; now; at once; presently; finally, ultimately; in time; once, formerly. Often used as an emphatic expletive (*ya entiendo,* I understand; *ya veo,* I see).—**¡y.!** oh, yes! I see.—**y. lo creo,** naturally, of course.—**y. no,** no longer.—**y. que,** since, seeing that.—**y. se ve,** yes, indeed! it is clear, it is so.—**y. voy,** I am coming, I shall be there presently.—**y. . . . y.,** now . . . now, sometimes . . . sometimes.—**¡pues y.!** of course, certainly.—**si y.,** if.—**si y no,** if no longer; if . . . not, unless. **II.** *conj.* whether, or (the latter as correlative of the former).
yaacabó, *m.* (Venez.) an insectivorous bird.
yaba, *f.* (bot.) yaba tree; yaba bark, worm bark.
yabuna, *f.* a Cuban species of long, creeping grass or weed.
yac, *m.* (zool.) yak.
yaca, *f.* (bot.) yacca tree.
yacal, *m.* yacal, a Philippine tree.
yacaré, *m.* (Arg.) cayman, alligator.
yacedor, *m.* boy who takes horses to graze at night.
yacente, *a.* vacant; lying.
yacer, *vn.* (*ind.* YAZCO, YAGO, or YAZGO; *subj.* YAZCA, YAGA, or YAZGA) to lie, to be located; to be lying down; to lie (in the grave); (of horses) to graze by night.
yaciente, *a.* extended, stretched (honeycombs).
yacija, *f.* bed, couch, lounge; tomb, grave.—**ser de mala y.,** to be a vagrant; to be restless at night.
yacimiento, *m.* (geol.) bed; deposit, field.
yacio, *m.* (bot.) India-rubber tree.
yack, *m.* (zool.) yak.
yactura, *f.* loss, damage.
yago, yaga, *v. V.* YACER.
yagua, *f.* royal palm.
yaguar, *m.* (zool.) jaguar.
yaguasa, *f.* (Am.) (ornith.) a tree duck.
yaguré, *m.* (Am.) skunk.
yaití, *m.* a West-Indian hard-wood euphorbiaceous tree.
yak, *m.* (zool.) = YACK.
yámbico, ca, *a.* (poet.) iambic.
[1]**yambo,** *m.* (poet.) iambic foot (◡—).
[2]**yambo,** *m.* (bot.) jamboo.
yanacona, *n.* (Peru) Indian bound to personal service.
yanqui, *n.* & *a.* Yankee, American.
Yanquilandia, *f.* Yankeeland.
yanquismo, *m.* Yankeeism.
yantar. I. *va.* (obs.) to dine; to eat. **II.** *m.* (obs.) viands, food; a kind of king's taxes.
yapa, *f.* (min.) mercury added to silver ore in smelting; (Am.) ÑAPA, (to) boot, extra thing.—**de y.,** into the bargain, for good measure.
yapar. I. *va.* to add YAPA. **II.** *va.* & *vn.* to give, or give as, a YAPA (ÑAPA).
yarará, *f.* a very poisonous Argentine viper.
yaraví, *m.* (Am.) an Indian tune.
yarda, *f.* yard (measure).
yare, *m.* a poisonous juice from bitter yucca.
yarey, *m.* (Cuba) a species of GUANO (palm tree).
yaro, *m.* (bot.) arum, an aquatic plant.
yatagán, *m.* sabre dagger, yataghan.
yate, *m.* (naut.) yacht.
yaya, *f.* (Cuba) (bot.) lancewood.
yayero, ra, *a.* & *n.* (Cuba) intermeddling, busybody.
yazco, yazgo, etc. *v. V.* YACER.
ye, name of the letter *y.*
yedra, *f.* = HIEDRA (bot.) ivy.
yegua, *f.* mare.—**y. de cría,** or **paridera,** breeding mare.—**y. madre,** dam.—**yeguada, yegüería,** *f.* stud of mares.—**yeguar,** *a.* pert. to mares.
yegüerizo, za. I. *a.* = YEGUAR. **II.** *m.* = YEGÜERO.
yegüero, *m.* keeper of breeding mares.
yegüezuela, *f. dim.* little mare.
yeísmo, *m.* giving *ll* the sound of *y.*
yelmo, *m.* (armor) helmet, helm.
yema, *f.* bud, first shoot of trees; yolk (of an egg); candied yolk of an egg; heart, centre, middle; the best of its kind.—**y. del dedo,** fleshy tip of the finger.—**y. mejida,** eggnog.—**dar en la y.,** to hit the nail on the head.—**en la y. del invierno,** in the dead of winter.
Yemen, *m.* Yemen.
yemenita, *n.* & *a.* Yemenite, Yemeni.

yen, *m.* yen (Japanese coin).
yente, *a.* going.—**yentes y vinientes,** passers-by.
yerba, *f.* HIERBA, herb; grass; weed; (S. A.) maté (also Y. MATE).—**y. cana,** groundsel, ragwort. **y. carmín,** Virginian poke.—**y. de la princesa,** lemon-scented verbena.—**y. del ballestero,** white hellebore.—**y. de mar,** seaweed. —**y. de pordioseros,** sweet-scented virgin's bower.—**y. doncella,** periwinkle.—**y. lombriguera** = ABRÓTANO, southernwood.—**y. marina** = Y. DE MAR.—**y. mate,** maté.—**y. mora,** nightshade.—**y. pastel,** woad.—**y. piojera,** stavesacre.—**y. tora,** strangle weed, broom rape.
yerbabuena, *f.* = HIERBABUENA, mint.
yerbajo, *m. aug.* wild weed.
yerbatear, *vn.* (Am.) to take maté, Paraguay tea.
yerbatero, ra. I. *a.* using arrow poison. **II.** *n.* (Am.) seller of fodder grass.
yergo, yerga, *v. V.* ERGUIR.
yermar, *va.* to depopulate, to lay waste.
yermo, ma. I. *a.* waste, desert, uninhabited; uncultivated. **II.** *m.* desert, wilderness, waste.
yerno, *m.* son-in-law.
yero, *m.* (bot.) = YERVO.
[1]**yerro,** *m.* error, mistake; fault.—*pl.* unpardonable faults.—**y. de cuenta,** miscalculation.—**y. de imprenta,** erratum, typographical error.
[2]**yerro, yerra,** *v. V.* ERRAR.
yerto, ta, *a.* stiff, motionless; rigid, tight.—**quedarse y.,** to be petrified with fear or surprise.
yervo, *m.* (bot.) tare, true bitter vetch.
yesal, yesar, *m.* gypsum pit.
yesca, *f.* tinder, punk, touchwood; fuel, incentive. —*pl.* tinder box, strike-a-light.
yesera, *f.* gypsum pit; woman who sells gypsum or plaster.
yesería, *f.* gypsum kiln; plasterer's shop; building constructed with plaster.
yesero, ra. I. *a.* pertaining to gypsum. **II.** *n.* maker or seller of gypsum; plasterer.
yeso, *m.* gypsum; plaster; plaster cast.—**y. blanco,** whitewash, fine plaster for surface finish.—**y. mate,** plaster of Paris.—**y. negro,** coarse plaster for base coating.—**yesón,** *m.* rubbish of plaster.—**yesoso, sa,** *a.* gypseous.
yesquero. I. *n.* tinder maker or seller. **II.** *m.* (Colomb.) tinder box for flint-and-steel lighting.
yeta, *f.* (Am. esp. Arg.) bad luck, misfortune.
yeyuno, *m.* (anat.) jejunum.
yezgo, *m.* (bot.) dwarf elder.
yo. I. *pers. pron.* I.—**y. mismo,** I myself. **II.** *m.* ego.
yodado, da, *a.* iodic, containing iodine.
yodato, *m.* (chem.) iodate.
yodhídrico, ca, *a.* (chem.) hydriodic.
yódico, ca, (chem.) iodic.
yodismo, *m.* (med.) iodism, disorder caused by use of iodine.
yodo, *m.* (chem.) iodine.
yodoformo, *m.* (chem.) iodoform.
yoduración, *f.* iodization, iodation.
yodurar, *va.* (chem.) to iodize.
yoduro, *m.* (chem.) iodide.
yoga, *m.* yoga.
yogi, *m.* yogi.
yogurt, yoghurt, *m.* yogurt.
yola, yole, *f.* (naut.) yawl.
yoquey, *n.* jockey.
yoyo, *m.* yo-yo.
yperita, *f.* yperite, mustard gas.
yubarta, *f.* (ichth.) finback, rorqual.
yuca, *f.* yucca; (Am.) yuca, cassava.
yucal, *m.* yucca or cassava field.
yucateco, ca, *a.* of or from Yucatan.
yugada, *f.* (agr.) yoke of land.
yugo, *m.* (animal) yoke; marriage tie or ceremony; confinement, prison; frame of a church bell; (naut.) transom.—**sacudir el y.,** to throw off the yoke.
Yugoeslavia, Yugoslavia, *f.* Yugoslavia.
yugoeslavo, va, yugoslavo, va. I. *a.* Yugoslav, Yugoslavic, Jugoslav, Jugoslavic. **II.** *n.* Yugoslav, Yugoslavian, Jugoslav, Jugoslavian.
yuguero, *m.* plowman, plowboy.
yugular, *a.* (anat.) jugular.
yumbo, ba, *n.* a savage of eastern Ecuador.
yunque, *m.* anvil; (anat.) incus; persevering, undaunted person.—**estar al y.,** to bear up under trying circumstances; to be hard at work; (coll.) to be on the job.
yunta, *f.* couple, pair, yoke of draft animals.
yuntería, *f.* aggregate of YUNTAS; place where draught oxen are fed.
yuntero, *m.* plowboy.
yunto, ta, *a.* joined, united; close.—**arar y.,** to plow close.
yuraguano, *m.* (Cuba) (bot.) fan palm.
yuré, *m.* a C. A. pigeon.
yusera, *f.* horizontal stone in oil mills.
yusión, *f.* (law) precept, command.
yute, *m.* jute (fibre); jute fabric.
yuxtalineal, *a.* in parallel columns.
yuxtaponer, *va.* (*pp.* YUXTAPUESTO; *ind. pres.* YUXTAPONGO, *pret.* YUXTAPUSE, *fut.* YUXTAPONDRÉ; *subj.* YUXTAPONGA) to juxtapose, to place next to each other.
yuxtaposición, *f.* juxtaposition.
yuxtapuesto, ta, *pp. irreg.* of YUXTAPONER.
yuyo, *m.* (Arg., Chile) weed; (S. A., C. A.) an edible herb; (Costa Rica, Salvador) blister on the foot.
yuyuba, *f.* = AZUFAIFA, jujube.

Z

Z, z, *f.* z, twenty-eighth letter of the Spanish alphabet.
¡za!, *interj.* used to frighten dogs.
zabarcera, *f.* greengrocer (woman).
zábida, zábila, *f.* (bot.) common aloes.
zaborda, *f.*, **zabordamiento,** *m.* (naut.) stranding.
zabordar, *vn.* to touch ground, to become stranded.—**zabordo,** *m.* stranding.
zaborro, rra, *n.* fat person.
zabra, *f.* (naut.) small sailing vessel.
zabucar, *va.* = BAZUCAR, to shake up (liquids).
zabullida, zabullidor, zubullidura, zabullimiento, zabullir = ZAMBULLIDA, etc.
zabuqueo, *m.* = BAZUQUEO, shaking up; jumble.
zaca, *f.* large leather bag for bailing out a mine.
zacapela, zacapella, *f.* noisy wrangle.
zacate, *m.* (Mex., C. A.) grass; hay, fodder.
zacateca, *m.* (Cuba) undertaker.
zacateco, ca, *n.* & *a.* Zacatecan (from Zacatecas, Mex.).
zacatín, *m.* street where garments are sold.
zacatón, *m.* (Am.) a tall fodder grass.
zacear, *va.* to scare off (dogs) by crying ¡ZA!.
zadorija, *f.* (bot.) yellow poppy.
zafa, *f.* = JOFAINA, washbasin, bowl.
zafacoca, *f.* (Am.) (coll.) squabble, row.
zafada, *f.* flight, escape; lightening (a ship).
zafar. I. *va.* to adorn, deck, embellish; to clear from encumbrances; to lighten (a ship). **II.** *vr.* to escape, run away; (**de**) to get rid (of); to avoid; to get out (of); to get clear (of); to slip or come (off), break loose; (Mex.) to dislocate (a joint).
zafareche, *m.* = ESTANQUE, tank, reservoir.
zafarí, *a.* app. to a variety of pomegranate.
zafariche, *m.* shelf for water jugs or jars.
zafarrancho, *m.* (naut.) clearing for action; (coll.) ravage, destruction; scuffle, wrangle, row.
zafiamente, *adv.* lubberly, clumsily.
zafiedad, *f.* rusticity, clumsiness.
zafio, fia, *a.* coarse, uncivil, ignorant.
zafío, *m.* (ichth.) a variety of conger eel.
zafir, *m.* sapphire.—**zafíreo, ea,** *a.* sapphirine.
zafirino, na, *a.* & *f.*, (min.) sapphirine.
zafiro, *m.* sapphire.
zafo, fa, *a.* free, disentangled; exempt from danger or risk; (naut.) free and clear.

zafones, *m. pl.* overalls.
[1]**zafra,** *f.* drip jar, oil jar.
[2]**zafra,** *f.* broad strap holding the thills of a cart.
[3]**zafra,** *f.* (min.) rubbish.
[4]**zafra,** *f.* sugar crop; sugar making; sugar-making season.
zafre, *m.* (min.) zaffre or saffre.
zafrero, *m.* (min.) laborer who clears a mine of rubbish.
zaga. I. *f.* rear part; load in the back of a carriage. **II.** *m.* the last player at a game of cards. —**a la z.,** or **en z.,** behind.—**no ir en z. a,** not to be behind, less than, or inferior to.
[1]**zagal,** *m.* stout, spirited young man; swain; subordinate shepherd; boy assistant of stagecoach driver.
[2]**zagal,** *m.* short skirt.
zagala, *f.* shepherdess; lass, maiden.
[1]**zagalejo, ja,** *n. dim.* young shepherd(-ess).
[2]**zagalejo,** *m.* short skirt; underskirt, slip.
zagalón, na, *n.* overgrown boy (girl).
zagua, *f.* (bot.) saltwort.
zagual, *m.* paddle.
zaguán, *m.* entrance hall, vestibule.
zaguanete, *m. dim.* small vestibule; king's escort of life guards.
zaguero, ra. I. *a.* laggard, loitering. **II.** *m.* backstop, at the game of PELOTA.
zahareño, ña, *a.* intractable; (of birds) wild, haggard; unsociable; arrogant.
zaharí, *a.* = ZAFARÍ.
zahena, *f.* a Moorish gold coin.
zaherible, *a.* blamable, blameworthy.
zaheridor, ra, *n.* & *a.* censurer(-ing), upbraider (-ing).
zaherimiento, *m.* censure, blame.
zaherir, *va.* (*ger.* ZAHIRIENDO; *ind. pres.* ZAHIERO, *pret.* él ZAHIRIÓ; *subj.* ZAHIERA) to censure, blame, reproach, upbraid.
zahina, *f.* (bot.) sorghum.
zahinar, *m.* sorghum field.
zahinas, *f. pl.* thin porridge or pap.
zahirió, *pret.* of ZAHERIR.
zahón, *m.* (gen. *pl.*) overalls.
zahonado, da, *a.* dark brown.
zahondar. I. *va.* to dig. **II.** *vn.* to sink into soft ground (as the feet).
zahora, *f.* merry lunch party.
zahorar, *vn.* to have a repast with music.
zahorí, *m.* vulgar impostor pretending to see hidden things; perspicacious and curious person.
zahoriar, *va.* to scrutinize, look deeply into.
zahorra, *f.* (naut.) ballast.
zahurda, *f.* pigsty, hogsty; low tavern, "joint."
zaida, *f.* (ornith.) a variety of heron.
zaino, na, *a.* chestnut, zain (horse); vicious (animal); treacherous, wicked.—**mirar a la z.,** or **de z.,** to look sidewise.
zalá, *f.* salaam.—**hacer la z.,** to salaam; to flatter, cajole, wheedle.
zalagarda, *f.* ambush; trap, snare; sudden attack, surprise; skirmish; mock fight.
zalama, *f.;* **zalamelé,** *m.;* **zalamería,** *f.* flattery, wheedling.
zalamero, ra, *n.* wheedler, flatterer, fawner.
zalea, *f.* undressed sheepskin.
[1]**zalear,** *va.* to shake; to damage, destroy.
[2]**zalear,** *va.* to frighten (a dog) away.
zalema, *f.* salaam, bow, curtsy.
zaleo, *m.* sheepskin damaged by a wolf's fangs; shaking or moving to and fro; ZALEA.
zalmedina, *m.* an ancient magistrate in Arragon.
zalona, *f.* large earthen jar.
zallar, *va.* (naut.) to outrig, to train.
zamacuco, *m.* (coll.) dunce, dolt; intoxication.
zamacueca, *f.* (S. A.) an Indian tune and dance.
zamanca, *f.* (coll.) drubbing, flogging.
zamarra, *f.* sheepskin jacket worn by shepherds; undressed sheepskin.
zamarrear, *va.* to shake (something) held in the teeth (as a dog does a rabbit); to ill-treat; to pin down in a dispute.
zamarreo, *m.* shaking something held in the teeth; abuse, ill treatment.
zamarrico, *m. dim.* portmanteau or bag of sheepskin.
zamarrilla, *f.* (bot.) poly, mountain germander.
zamarro. I. *m.* shepherd's coat of sheepskins; sheep or lambskin; (coll.) dolt, dunce. **II.** *m. pl.* (Am.) chaps, chaparajos.
zamarrón, *m. aug.* large sheepskin jacket.
zambaigo, ga, *a.* & *n.* Indian and Chinese half-breed.
zambapalo, *m.* an ancient dance and tune.
zambarco, *m.* broad breast strap (of harness).
zámbigo, ga, *a.* bandy-legged.
zambo, ba. I. *a.* knock-kneed; born of an Indian and a Negro; (loosely) Negro, mulatto. **II.** *n.* Indian and Negro half-breed; (loosely) Negro, mulatto. **III.** *m.* an American monkey.
zamboa, *f.* (bot.) = AZAMBOA, a kind of citron.
zambomba, *f.* rustic drum with the head pierced by a reed which, when rubbed with the moistened hand, produces a hoarse sound.—**¡z.!** whew!—**zambombo, ba,** *n.* (coll.) rustic, boor, coarse or ill-bred person.
zamborondón, na; zamborotudo, da, *a.* awkward, clumsy; ill-shaped.
[1]**zambra,** *f.* a Moorish festival; merrymaking.
[2]**zambra,** *f.* a kind of Moorish boat.
zambucar, *va.* to hide (a thing) by mixing it among others.—**zambuco,** *m.* (coll.) hiding, concealing a card among others.
zambullida, *f.* diving, plunge, ducking; (fencing) thrust to the breast.
zambullidor, ra, *n.* one who dives or plunges.
zambullidura, *f.,* **zambullimiento,** *m.* diving, ducking, plunge.
zambullir. I. *vn.* & *va.* to dive; to duck, give a ducking to; to sink. **II.** *vr.* to plunge, dip, dive; to sink; to hide, conceal oneself.
zambullo, *m.* evacuation stool; refuse tank or barrel.
zampabodigos, zampabollos, *n.* (coll.) glutton.
zampalimosnas, *m.* (coll.) sturdy beggar.
zampalo, *n.* (coll.) glutton.
zampar. I. *va.* to thrust or put hurriedly (into something) in order to conceal; to devour eagerly. **II.** *vr.* to rush in, to thrust oneself in or into.
zampatortas, *m.* (coll.) glutton; boor, rustic.
zampeado, *m.* (arch.) grillage, subfoundation of timber or steel and masonry in marshy ground.
zampear, *va.* to build a grillage on.
zampona, *f.* = PIPITAÑA, rustic flute; (coll.) frivolous saying.
zampuzar, *va.* ZAMBULLIR; ZAMPAR.
zampuzo, *m.* diving, ducking; hiding.
zamuro, *m.* (Venez.) (ornith.) carrion vulture.
zanahoria, *f.* (bot.) carrot.
zanahoriate, *m.* preserved carrot.
zanca, *f.* long shank or leg; large pin; (arch.) string-piece of a staircase; (min.) shore, prop.—**zancas de araña,** shifts, evasions, subterfuges. —**por zancas o por barrancas,** by hook or by crook.—**zancada,** *f.* long stride.—**en dos zancadas,** (coll.) in a jiffy, in no time.
zancadilla, *f.* sudden catch to trip one; trick, deceit, craft; (naut.) elbow in the hawse.—**armar z.,** to lay a snare.
zancado, da, *a.* insipid (salmon).
zancajear, *va.* to walk fast from place to place to run about.
zancajera, *f.* coach step.
zancajiento, ta, *a.* bandy-legged.
zancajo, *m.* heel bone; torn heelpiece of a shoe or stocking; (coll.) short, ill-shaped person.—**no llegar a los zancajos,** or **no llegar al z., de,** not to come up to, or be the equal of (one). —**roer los zancajos a,** to backbite.
zancajoso, sa, *a.* bandy-legged; wearing dirty stockings with holes at the heels.
zancarrón, *m.* leg bone without flesh; withered, old, ugly person; boastful ignoramus.
zanco, *m.* stilt; (naut.) sliding-gunter mast.—**en zancos,** in a high position.

zancón, na, *a.* long-legged; wading (bird).
zancudo, da. I. *a.* long-shanked; (ornith.) wading (bird). **II.** *m.* (Am.) mosquito. **III.** *f. pl.* (ornith.) wading birds.
zandía, *f.* watermelon.
zanfonía, *f.* (mus.) hurdy-gurdy.
zanga, *f.* four-hand ombre (card game).
zangala, *f.* buckram.
zangamanga, *f.* (coll.) trick, deceit.
zanganada, *f.* (coll.) impertinent or unseasonable act or expression.
zangandongo, ga; zangandullo, lla; zangandungo, ga, *n.* (coll.) idler, lazy person; dolt, awkward person.
zanganear, *vn.* to drone, to loaf.
zángano, *m.* drone; (coll.) idler, sponger.
zangarilla, *f.* small mill pond.
zangarilleja, *f.* (coll.) trollop, slovenly girl.
zangarrear, *vn.* (coll.) to scrape a guitar.
zangarriana, *f.* (vet.) a head disease of sheep; (coll.) sadness, blues; any slight periodical ailment.
zangarrullón, na, *n.* tall, sluggish, lazy boy (girl).
zangolotear. I. *vn.* to shake violently; to fuss, fidget. **II.** *vr.* to rattle, swing or slam.
zangoloteo, *m.* fuss, bustle; swinging, rattling.
zangolotino, na, *a.* (of boys and girls) pretending to be a little child.
zangón, *m.* (coll.) = ZANGARULLÓN.
zangotear, zangoteo = ZANGOLOTEAR, ZANGOLOTEO.
zanguango, ga. I. *a.* (coll.) lazy, sluggish; silly. **II.** *m.* dunce, fool. **III.** *f.* (coll.) feigned illness to avoid work; wheedling, fawning.
zanguayo, *m.* (coll.) tall, skinny idler that cunningly acts the fool.
zanja, *f.* ditch, trench, furrow, drain; (Am.) gap, gully, draw.—**abrir las zanjas,** to lay the foundation of a building; to begin, get started.
zanjar, *va.* to cut ditches in; to excavate; to settle amicably; to obviate, surmount.
zanjón, *m. aug.* deep ditch; large drain.
zanqueador, ra, *n.* one who waddles in walking; great walker.
zanqueamiento, *m.* waddling in walking.
zanquear, *vn.* to waddle, trot, or run about; to walk much and fast.
zanquilargo, ga, *a.* long-shanked, long-legged.
zanquilla, zanquita, *f. dim.* (coll.) disproportionate, long-legged man.
zanquituerto, ta, *a.* bandy-legged.
zanquivano, na, *a.* spindle-shanked.
zantoxilo, *m.* (bot.) zanthoxylum, xanthoxylum.
Zanzíbar, *m.* Zanzibar.
zanzibareño, ña, *n.* & *a.* Zanzibari.
[1]**zapa,** *f.* spade; (fort.) sap.—**caminar a la z.,** (mil.) to advance by sap or mine.
[2]**zapa,** *f.* shagreen; rough surface on silver.
zapador, *m.* (mil.) sapper.
zapallo, *m.* (Am.) a variety of squash; calabash.
zapapico, *m.* pickaxe, mattock.
zapaquilda, *f.* female cat.
zapar, *va.* (fort.) to sap, to mine.
zaparrada, *f.* violent fall.
zaparrastrar, *vn.* (coll.) to trail (as dress trains).
zaparrastroso, sa, *a.* dirty, greasy, ragged.
zaparrazo, *m.* thud; violent fall.
zapata, *f.* piece of sole leather put on the hinge of a door to prevent its creaking; buskin, half-boot, high gaiter; (Cuba) socle of a wall; (arch.) lintel; (naut.) shoe; (mech.) shoe (of brake, etc.).—**z. de la quilla,** (naut.) false heel.—**z. de un ancla,** (naut.) shoe of an anchor.
zapatazo, *m. aug.* large shoe; blow with a shoe; stamping of the feet; fall; thud, whack; clapping noise of a horse's foot.—**tratar a zapatazos,** to treat rudely or roughly.
zapateado, *m.* a sort of clog dance.
zapateador, ra, *n.* clog dancer.
zapatear. I. *va.* to strike with the shoe; (fencing) to hit frequently with the button of the foil; to ill-treat. **II.** *vn.* to beat time with the feet; (naut.) (of sails) to flap. **III.** *vr.* to oppose with spirit; to resist.—**zapateo,** *m.* keeping time by beating the feet on the floor.
zapatera, *f.* shoemaker's wife; woman who makes or sells shoes.
zapatería, *f.* trade of a shoemaker; shoemaker's shop.—**z. de viejo,** cobbler's stall.
zapateril, *a.* pertaining to, or like, shoemakers.
zapatero, ra. I. *a.* hard, poorly cooked (as beans); stale (olives). **II.** *m.* shoemaker; shoe dealer; (S. A.) (ichth.) threadfish, cobbler fish; (coll.) player who takes no tricks at a game of cards. —**z. de viejo,** cobbler.
zapateta. I. *f.* slap on the sole of a shoe; caper, leap, jump. **II.** *interj.* oh! gracious!
zapatico, illo, ito, *m. dim.* nice little shoe.
zapatilla, *f.* pump, slipper; leather washer; piece of chamois or buckskin put behind the lock of a gun or pistol; (fencing) button of a foil; hoof of animals.
zapatillero, ra, *n.* maker or seller of slippers, pumps, and children's shoes.
zapato, *m.* shoe (gen. app. to low shoes).—**zapatos papales,** overshoes, clogs.—**como tres en un z.,** squeezed into insufficient space; in great poverty.—**meter a uno en un z.,** (coll.) to cow or confound one.—**saber dónde aprieta el z.,** to know where the shoe pinches.
zapatón, *m. aug.* large, clumsy shoe; (Colomb.) rubber, overshoe.
zapatudo, da, *a.* wearing large or stout shoes; large-hoofed or clawed.
¡zape! *interj.* used to frighten cats away, to denote surprise, or to refuse to give cards in some games.—**zapear,** *va.* to frighten (cats) away; to refuse to give cards to, in some games.
zapito, *m.* **zapita,** *f.* (prov.) milk pail.
zaporogo, *m.* Ukranian Cossack.
zapotal, *m.* sapota grove or orchard.
zapote, *m.* (bot.) sapota tree and its fruit.
zapotero, *m.* (bot.) sapota tree.
zapotillo, *m.* (bot.) sapodilla and its fruit.
zapuzar, *va.* = CHAPUZAR, to duck (in water).
[1]**zaque,** *m.* (Colomb.) chief of certain Indians.
[2]**zaque,** *m.* leather bottle or wine-bag; (coll.) tippler, drunkard.
zaquear, *va.* (of wines, etc.) to transfer from one [2]ZAQUE to another; to transport in [2]ZAQUES.
zaquizamí, *m.* garret, cockloft; small wretched room, "hole."
zar, *m.* czar.
zara, *f.* (bot.) Indian corn, maize.
zarabanda, *f.* saraband (dance and tune); bustle, noise.—**zarabandista,** *n.* sarabander; dancer; merry person.
zarabutero, ra, *a.* = ZARAGUTERO.
zaragalla, *f.* fine charcoal.
zaragata, *f.* turmoil; scuffle, quarrel.
zaragatero, ra. I. *a.* (coll.) noisy, quarrelsome. **II.** *n.* rowdy.
zaragatona, *f.* (bot.) rib grass, ribwort.
zaragocí, *m.* a kind of plum.
zaragozano, na, *n.* & *a.* Saragossan.
zaragüelles, *m. pl.* wide and short plaited breeches; large pair of ill-made breeches; (bot.) reed grass.
zaragutear, *va.* (coll.) to undertake without proper knowledge; to bungle.
zaragutero, ra, *n.* (coll.) bungler.
zaramagullón, *m.* (ornith.) didapper, a minute merganser.
zarambeque, *m.* breakdown (Negro dance).
zaranda, *f.* screen, sieve, sifter.
zarandador, ra, *n.* sifter of wheat.
zarandajas, *f. pl.* trifles, odds and ends.
zarandalí, *adv.* black-spotted (dove).
zarandar, zarandear. I. *va.* to winnow; to sift; to separate, pick out; (coll.) to stir and move nimbly. **II.** *vr.* to be in motion, to move to and fro; to stalk, strut.—**zarandeo,** *m.* sifting or winnowing; moving briskly; stalking, strut.
zarandero, *m.* = ZARANDADOR.
zarandillo, lla. I. *n.* (coll.) one who frisks nimbly about. **II.** *m.* small sieve.

zarapatel, *n.* a kind of salmagundi.
zarapito, *m.* (ornith.) whimbrel, curlew jack.
zaratán, *m.* cancer in the breast.
zaraza, *f.* chintz, printed cotton.
zarazas, *f. pl.* paste made of pounded glass and poison, for killing dogs, rats, etc.
zarazo, za, *a.* (Cuba) rotten.
zarcear. I. *va.* to clean (pipes) with briers. **II.** *vn.* to move to and fro; to get into briers (as dogs pursuing game).
zarceño, ña, *a.* pertaining to briers.
zarcero, ra, *a.* & *n.* (dog) that hunts in briers.
zarceta, *f.* (ornith.) = CERCETA, widgeon.
zarcillitos, *m. pl.* (bot.) quaking grass.
[1]**zarcillo,** *m.* = CERCILLO, drop earring; tendril of a vine; hoop (of a barrel).
[2]**zarcillo,** *m.* gardener's hoe.
zarco, ca, *a.* light blue (eyes).
zarevitz, *m.* czarevitch.
zargatona, *f.* = ZARAGATONA.
zariano, na, *a.* pertaining to the czar.
zarigüeya, *f.* (S. A.) opossum.
zarina, *f.* czarina.
zarismo, *m.* czarism.
zarja, *f.* = AZARJA, reel for winding silk.
zaroche, *m.* (Ecuador) mountain sickness.
[1]**zarpa,** *f.* paw of an animal; (naut.) weighing anchor; dirt or mud sticking to the skirts.—**z. delantera,** forepaw.—**echar la z. a,** to grasp, clutch, grip.
[2]**zarpa,** *f.* (arch.) footing.
zarpada, *f.* blow with a paw.
zarpar, *vn.* (naut.) to weigh anchor, to sail.
zarpazo, *m.* bang, thud, whack; ZARPADA.
zarposo, sa, *a.* bespattered, bemired.
zarracatería, *f.* lure, deception.
zarracatín, *m.* (coll.) haggler; profiteer.
zarramplín, na, *n.* (coll.) bungler, botcher.
zarramplinada, *f.* botch, bungle, muddle.
zarrapastra, *f.* mud sticking to the skirts.
zarrapastrón, na, *a.* & *n.* tatterdemalion.
zarrapastrosamente, *adv.* (coll.) shabbily, slovenly.
zarrapastroso, sa, *a.* ragged, slovenly, shabby, seedy.
[1]**zarria,** *f.* leather strap, thong or latch.
[2]**zarria,** *f.* mud sticking to clothes.—**zarriento, ta; zarrioso, sa,** *a.* bespattered, bemired.
zarza, *f.* (bot.) bramble; blackberry bush.
zarzagán, *m.* cold northeast wind.
zarzaganete, *m. dim.* light northeast wind.
zarzaganillo, *m.* violent northeast storm.
zarzahán, *m.* a kind of striped silk.
zarzaidea, *f.* (bot.) raspberry bush.
zarzal, *m.* brambly place, brambles.
zarzamora, *f.* (bot.) brambleberry.
zarzaparrilla, *f.* (bot.) sarsaparilla.
zarzaparrillar, *m.* sarsaparilla plantation.
zarzaperruna, *f.* (bot.) dog-rose.
zarzarrosa, *f.* (bot.) dog-rose.
zarzo, *m.* hurdle, wattle; (Colomb.) garret.
zarzoso, sa, *a.* briery, brambly.
zarzuela, *f.* musical comedy.—**zarzuelero, ra,** *a.* pertaining to musical comedies.—**zarzuelista,** *n.* writer or composer of musical comedies.
¡zas! *m.* tick, sound of a rap.—**¡z., z.¡** ticktack.
zascandil, *m.* (coll.) busybody.
zata, zatara, *f.* raft.
zato, *m.* piece of bread.
zazoso, sa. I. *a.* lisping. **II.** *n.* lisper.
zeda, *f.* name of the letter *z*; zed (Greek letter).
zedilla, *f.* cedilla.
zelandés, sa, *n.* & *a.* Zealandian.
zemstvo, *m.* (Russian hist.) zemstvo.
Zendavesta, *m.* Zend-Avesta.
zendo, da, *a.* & *m.* Zend.
zenit, zenital = CENIT, CENITAL, zenith.
zepelín, *m.* Zeppelin (dirigible).
zeta, *f.* name of the letter *z*; Gk. letter, **zeta.**
zeugma, zeuma, *f.* (rhet.) zeugma.
zigzag, *m.* zigzag.
zigzaguear, *vn.* to zigzag.
zigzagueo, *m.* zigzagging.
zimasa, *f.* (biochem.) zymase.
zimo, *m.* (biol.) zyme.
zimógeno, na. I. *a.* (biochem.) zymogenic. **II.** *m.* (biochem.) zymogen.
zimología, *f.* zymosis.
zimosis, *f.* zymosis.
zimótico, ca, *a.* zymotic.
zinc, *m.* = CINC, zinc.
zipizape, *m.* (coll.) row, rumpus, scuffle.
zircón, zirconio = CIRCÓN, CIRCONIO.
zirigaña, *f.* fawning, wheedling, flattery; CHASCO; FRIOLERA.
¡zis, zas! (coll.) words expressing the sound of repeated blows or strokes.
zizaña, *f.* (bot.) = CIZAÑA, darnel.
zoantario, ria, *n.* & *a.* (zool.) zoantharian.
zoantropía, *f.* (med.) zoanthropy, a mania.
zoántropo, pa, *n.* one ill with zoanthropy.
zoca, *f.* square, plaza.
zócalo, *m.* (arch.) socle or zocle.
[1]**zocato, ta,** *a.* (of fruit) overripe.
[2]**zocato, ta,** *a.* left-handed.
zoclo, *m.* clog; overshoe.
[1]**zoco, ca,** *a.* left-handed.
[2]**zoco,** *m.* clog, wooden shoe; (arch.) socle.
[3]**zoco,** *m.* market; market-place.
zodiacal, *a.* zodiacal.
zodíaco, *m.* (astr.) zodiac.
zofra, *f.* Moorish carpet.
zoilo, *m.* malicious critic.
zolocho, cha, *a.* (coll.) stupid, silly, booby.
zollipar, *vn.* (coll.) to sob.
zollipo, *m.* sob; sobbing.
zoma, *f.* coarse flour.
zompo, pa, *a.* cripple; clumsy, awkward.
zona, *f.* zone; girdle, band; area, region; (med.) zoster, shingles.—**z. abisal,** abyssal zone.—**z. comercial,** commercial section, downtown.—**z. de altas presiones,** (meteorol.) high-pressure area.—**z. de bajas presiones,** (meteorol.) low-pressure area.—**z. de crisis económica** or **de depresión económica,** depressed area.—**z. de silencio,** quiet zone (near hospitals, etc.).—**z. esférica,** (geom.) spherical zone.—**z. glacial,** (geol.) frigid zone.—**z. inundada,** flooded area.—**z. neutra,** neutral zone.—**z. petrolífera,** petroleum zone.—**z. polémica,** (fort.) zone of defense.—**z. templada,** temperate zone.—**z. tórrida,** torrid zone.—**zonas poco desarrolladas,** underdeveloped regions.
zonal, *a.* zonate, zoned.
zoncería, *f.* silliness, dulness, stupidity.
zonchiche, *m.* (C. A.) a red-headed vulture.
zonificación, *f.* zoning.
zonote, *m.* deep deposit of water.
zonzamente, *adv.* stupidly, foolishly.
zonzo, za. I. *a.* dull, stupid, silly. **II.** *n.* simpleton, dunce, booby, noodle.
zonzorrión, na, *n.* very dull and stupid person.
zoófago, ga, *a.* zoöphagous, carnivorous.
zoofítico, ca, *a.* zoöphytic, zoöphytical.
zoófito, *m.* (zool.) zoöphyte.
zoóforo, *m.* (arch.) zoöphoros.
zoogeografía, *f.* zoögeography.
zooglea, *f.* (bacteriol.) zoöglœa.
zoografía, *f.* zoögraphy.
zoográfico, ca, *a.* zoögraphic, zoögraphical.
zoógrafo, fa, *n.* zoögrapher.
zooide. I. *a.* containing the figure of an animal or part of it. **II.** *m.* (biol.) zoöid.
zooideo, dea, *a.* (biol.) zoöid, zoöidal.
zoolatra, *m.* & *f.* animal worshipper.
zoolatría, *f.* zoolatry, worship of animals.
zoolítico, ca, *a.* fossil-bearing.
zoolito, *m.* petrified animal.
zoología, *f.* zoölogy.
zoológico, ca, *a.* zoölogical, zoölogic.
zoólogo, ga, *n.* zoölogist.
zoomorfismo, *m.* zoömorphism.
zoomorfo, fa, *a.* zoömorphic.
zoonomía, *f.* zoönomy, physiology.
zooquímica, *f.* zoöchemistry.

zoospermo, *m.* (biol.) zoösperm.
zoospora, *f.*; **zoosporo,** *m.* (bot.) zoöspore.
zoosporangio, *m.* zoösporangium.
zootecnia, *f.* zootechnics.
zootécnico, ca, *a.* zoötechnical, zoötechnic.
zootomía, *f.* zoötomy, animal anatomy.
zootomista, *n.* zoötomist.
zopas, *n.* (coll.) nickname given to a lisper.
zope, *m.* (ornith.) = ZOPILOTE, buzzard.
zopenco, ca. I. *a.* (coll.) doltish, dull. **II.** *n.* dolt, blockhead, fool.
zopetero, *m.* = RIBAZO, slope; hillock.
zopilote, *m.* (Mex.) (ornith.) = AURA, buzzard.
zopisa, *f.* pitch and tar ointment.
zopitas, *n.* = ZOPAS.
zopo, pa. I. *a.* lame, maimed, crippled; clumsy, awkward, unhandy. **II.** *n.* cripple.
zoqueta, *f.* a wooden cover or guard for the hand.
zoquetada, *f.* silly remark; foolishness, foolish words or act.
zoquete, *m.* (carp.) chump, chunk, block, bit of stale bread; (coll.) ugly little person; dolt, dunce, numskull, blockhead.—**z. de cuchara,** (naut.) scoop handle.—**zoquetero, ra,** *a.* living on crumbs and leavings, idle pauper.
zoquetico, illo, *m. dim.* small morsel of bread.
zoquetudo, da, *a.* rough, ill-finished.
zorcico, *m.* (mus.) Basque song and dance in five-eight ($\frac{5}{8}$) time.
zorita, *f.* (ornith.) stockdove, wood pigeon.
zoroástrico, ca, *a.* Zoroastric.
zoroastrismo, *m.* Zoroastrianism.
zorollo, *a.* (of wheat) reaped while unripe.
zorongo, *m.* kerchief folded like a bandage around the head, worn by Aragonese; broad flattened chignon; an Andalusian dance and tune.
[1]**zorra,** *f.* (zool.) fox; foxy, sly person; (coll.) prostitute; drunkenness, inebriation.—**a la z., candilazo,** when Greek meets Greek; diamond cut diamond.
[2]**zorra,** *f.* dray, truck.
zorrastrón, na, *a.* & *n.* (coll.) foxy (person), rogue(-ish), knave(-ish).
zorrera, *f.* fox hole; kennel; room full of smoke; heaviness, drowsiness.
zorrería, *f.* foxiness; cunning, knavery.
[1]**zorrero, ra,** *a.* slow, tardy, sluggish; (naut.) sailing heavily.
[2]**zorrero, ra. I.** *a.* cunning, foxy; fox-hunting (dog). **II.** *m.* keeper of a royal forest.
zorrilla, *f.* (zool.) polecat, skunk.
zorro, rra. I. *a.* cunning, foxy. **II.** *n.* fox; knave, foxy person. **III.** *m. pl.* duster made of cloth strips or foxtails tied to a handle.
zorrocloco, *m.* humdrum; (coll.) caress, petting.
zorronglón, na, *a.* slow, heavy, lazy.
zorruelo, la, *n. dim.* little fox.
zorrullo, *m.* = ZURULLO.
zorruno, na, *a.* vulpine, foxy, foxlike.
zorzal, *m.* (ornith.) thrush; sly, crafty man.—**z. marino,** (ichth.) a fish abounding near Spain.
zorzaleña, *a.*—**aceituna z.,** crescent olive.
zoster, *f.* (med.) zoster, herpes, shingles.
zote, *a.* dull and ignorant.
zozobra, *f.* worry, anguish, anxiety; unlucky throw of the dice; (naut.) sinking, capsizing.
zozobrante, *a.* in great danger; sinking.
zozobrar, *vn.* (naut.) to be weather-beaten; to sink, founder; to upset, capsize; to be in great danger; to grieve, worry, fret.
zozobroso, sa, *a.* anxious, worried.
zúa, *f.* = AZUDA, Persian water wheel.
zuavo, *m.* (mil.) zouave.
zubia, *f.* drain, channel, flume.
zucarino, na, *a.* = SACARINO, sugary, saccharine.
zúchil, *m.* (Mex.) bouquet.
zuda, *f.* = ZÚA.
zudra, *n.* Sudra, lowest Hindu caste; member of the Sudra.
zueco, *m.* sabot, wooden shoe, clog; galosh.
zuindá, *m.* (ornith.) an Argentine brown owl.
zuinglianismo, *m.* Zwinglianism.
zuingliano, na, *n.* & *a.* Zwinglian.
zuiza, *f.* = SUIZA, military tournament or feast; quarrel, dispute.
zuizón, *m.* spear; (naut.) half pike.
zulacar, *va.* to anoint with bitumen.
zulaque, *m.* (hydraul.) packing stuff; (naut.) stuff for paving the bottom of a ship.
zulú, *a.* & *n.* Zulu.
[1]**zulla,** *f.* (bot.) French honeysuckle.
[2]**zulla,** *f.* (coll.) human excrements.—**zullarse,** *vr.* (coll.) to go to stool; to break wind.
zullenco, ca; zullón, na. I. *a.* (coll.) breaking wind; flatulent. **II.** *m.* act of breaking wind; flatulence.
zumacal, [1]**zumacar,** *m.* sumach plantation.
[2]**zumacar,** *va.* to dress or tan with sumach.
zumacaya, *f.* (ornith.) a night wading bird.
zumaque, *m.* (bot.) sumach tree; (coll.) wine.
zumaya, *f.* (ornith.) barn owl; goatsucker; fern owl; ZUMACAYA.
zumba, *f.* bell worn by the leading mule of a drove; rattle; joke, jest; facetious raillery.
zumbador, ra. I. *a.* humming, buzzing. **II.** *m.* (P. R.) humming bird; (elec.) buzzer.
zumbar. I. *vn.* to buzz, to hum; to be near, flutter around; (of the ears) to ring. **II.** *va.* to jest, to joke with.
[1]**zumbel,** *m.* (coll.) cord for spinning tops.
[2]**zumbel,** *m.* frown, angry mien or aspect.
zumbido, *m.* humming, buzzing; ringing in the ears; ping of a bullet; (coll.) blow, box, cuff.
zumbilín, *m.* (P. I.) dart or javelin.
zumbo, *m.* = ZUMBIDO.
zumbón, na. I. *a.* waggish, jocose. **II.** *m.* wag, jester, joker; a variety of pigeon.
zumiento, ta, *a.* juicy, succulent.
zumillo, *m.* (bot.) dragon's arum, Aaron's beard; a poisonous carrot.
zumo, *m.* sap, juice; profit, utility.—**z. de cepas,** or **parras,** (coll.) grape juice, wine.
zumoso, sa, *a.* juicy, succulent.
zuna, *f.* Sunna, body of Mohammedan traditions; viciousness of horses; trickery, perfidy.
zuncho, *m.* band, hoop, collar, ferrule.
zunita, *n.* Sunnite, member of one of the great Mohammedan sects.
zunítico, ca, *a.* pertaining to the Sunna, body of Mohammedan traditions.
zuño, *m.* frown, angry mien.
zupia, *f.* wine turned roily; lees, dregs, slops; refuse, rubbish, trash.
zurano, na, *n.* (ornith.) stockdove, wild pigeon.
zurcidera, *f.* darner, finedrawer.
zurcido, *m.* (sewing) darning, finedrawing.
zurcidor, ra, *n.* darner.—**zurcidora de voluntades,** procuress.
zurcidura, *f.* (sewing) finedrawing, darning.
zurcir, *va.* (*ind.* ZURZO; *subj.* ZURZA) (sewing) to darn, mend; to finedraw; to join, unite; (coll.) to concoct (lies).
zurdería, *f.* left-handedness.
zurdo, da, *a.* left-handed.—**a zurdas,** the wrong way.
zurear, *vn.* to coo.—**zureo,** *m.* cooing.
zurito, ta, *f.* (ornith.) = ZURO, wild pigeon.
zuriza, *f.* = ZUIZA, quarrel, dispute.
[1]**zuro, ra,** *n.* (ornith.) stockdove, wild pigeon.
[2]**zuro,** *m.* corncob.
zurra, *f.* (tanning) currying; flogging, beating, drubbing; quarrel, dispute, scuffle.
zurrado, *m.* (coll.) glove.
zurrador, *m.* (tanning) currier, dresser; drubber, flogger.
zurrapa *f.* lees, sediment, dregs; rubbish, trash; ugly skinny boy.—**con zurrapas,** in an uncleanly manner.
zurrapelo, *m.* (coll.) severe reprimand.
zurrapiento, ta; zurraposo, sa, *a.* dreggy; turbid, roily.
zurrar, *va.* (tanning) to curry, to dress (leather); to spank, flog, drub, whip; to beat in a quarrel

or fight.—**z. la badana,** to beat, to flog.—**¡z., que es tarde!** but you are persistent! will you keep on forever? etc. (said to one who persists in something disagreeable or already rejected).

zurrarse, *vr.* to have an involuntary evacuation of the bowels; to be seized with great fear.

zurriaga, *f.* ZURRIAGO; (ornith.) lark.

zurriagar, *va.* (*pret.* ZURRIAGUÉ; *subj.* ZURRIAGUE) to whip, horsewhip, cowhide.

zurriagazo, *m.* whipping; severe lashing; unexpected ill treatment; stroke of bad luck.

zurriago, *m.* thong, long leather strap; whip.

zurriar, *vn.* to hum, buzz; to rattle.

zurribanda, *f.* flogging, horsewhipping, cowhiding; rumpus, scuffle, fight.

zurriburri, *m.* (coll.) ragamuffin, scamp; (coll.) gang of rowdies.

[1]**zurrido,** *m.* humming, buzzing, rattling noise.

[2]**zurrido,** *m.* (coll.) blow with a stick.

zurrir, *vn.* to hum, buzz, rattle.

zurrón, *m.* shepherd's pouch; game bag; leather bag; thin skin of shell fruits; (anat.) placenta; cyst.—**zurronada,** *f.* bagful.—**zurroncillo,** *m. dim.* small bag.—**zurronero, ra,** *n.* maker or seller of game bags.

zurrusco, *m.* (coll.) burnt toast.

zurubí, *m.* (ichth.) an Argentine fresh-water fish.

zurullo, *m.* any soft round object; ball or piece of tangled string or rope; (cook.) rolling pin.

zurumbático, ca, *a.* stunned, dumbfounded.

zurupeto, *m.* unauthorized agent.

zurzo, zurza, *v. V.* ZURCIR.

zutanico, illo, *m. dim.* of ZUTANO.

Zutano, na, *n.* (coll.) So-and-So.—**Fulano, Z. y Mengano,** Tom, Dick and Harry.

¡zuzo! *interj.* = ¡CHUCHO! (used to curb dog).

zuzón, *m.* (bot.) groundsel, ragwort.

APPENDIX

Geographical Names That Differ in the Spanish and English Languages

A

Abidos, Abydos.
Abisinia, Abyssinia.
Acaya, Achæa, Achaia.
Accio, Actium.
Adelaida, Adelaide.
Adrianópoli, Adrianople.
Afganistán, Afghanistan.
Alejandría, Alexandria.
Alemania, Germany.
Alenzón, Alençon.
Alepo, Aleppo.
Alesia, Alais.
Almirante. *V.* Islas del Almirante.
Alpes, Alps.
Alpes Julianos, Julian Alps.
Alpes Peninos, Pennine Alps.
Alsacia, Alsace.
Alsacia Lorena, Alsace-Lorraine.
Alto Egipto, Upper Egypt.
Amán, Maskat.
Amazonas, Amazon.
Amberes, Antwerp.
América del Norte, North America.
América del Sur, South America.
América Española, Spanish America.
América Meridional, South America.
Anam, Annam.
Andalucía, Andalusia.
Angulema, Angoulême.
Angumoes, Angoumais.
Antillas, Antilles, West Indies.
Antioquía, Antioch.
Apeninos, Apennines.
Aquisgrán, Aachen, Aix-la-Chapelle.
Aquitania, Aquitaine.
Arabia Desierta, Arabia Deserta.
Arabia Feliz, Arabia Felix.
Arabia Petrea, Arabia Petræa.
Aragón, Arragon.
Archipiélago, Ægean.
Archipiélago de Francisco José, Franz Joseph Land.
Archipiélago Malayo, Malay Archipelago.
Ardenas, Ardennes.
Argel, Algiers.
Argelia, Algeria.
Armañac, Armañaque, Armagnac.
Asia Menor, Asia Minor.
Asiria, Assyria.
Asís, Assisi.
Astracán, Astrakhan.
Atenas, Athens.
Âtica, Attica.
Ausburgo, Augsburg.
Austria-Hungría, Austria-Hungary.
Auvernia, Auvergne.
Aviñón, Avignon.
Ayacio, Ajaccio.

B

Babilonia, Babylon.
Bactriana, Bactria.
Baireut, Bayreuth.
Baja California, Lower California.
Bajo Egipto, Lower Egypt.
Bajo Rin, Lower Rhine.
Bakú, Baku.
Báltico, Baltic.
Baluchistán, Baluchistan.
Banato, Banat.
Bañeras, Bagnères.
Barbadas, Barbadoes.
Bareges, Barège.
Basilea, Basel, Basle, Bâle.
Baviera, Bavaria.
Bayona, Bayonne.
Bearne, Bearn.
Bechuanalandia, Bechuanaland.
Belcaire, Beaucaire.
Belén, Bethlehem.
Bélgica, Belgium.
Belgrado, Belgrade.
Belice, Beliza, British Honduras.
Beluchistán = Baluchistán.
Bengala, Bengal.
Beocia, Bœotia, Beotia.
Berbería, Barbary.
Berna, Bern.
Betania, Bethany.
Betsaida, Bethsaida.
Bitinia, Bithynia.
Bizancio, Byzantium.
Bojara, Bokhara, Bokhara.
Bolduque, Bois-le-Duc.
Bolonia, Bologna.
Boloña, Boulogne.
Bona, Bonn.
Borgoña, Burgundy.
Bósforo, Bosporus.
Botnia, Bothnia.
Brabante, Brabant.
Brandeburgo, Brandenburg.
Brasil, Brazil.
Brema, Bremen.
Brena, Brienne.
Bretaña, Bretagne, Brittany.
Bretaña (Gran), (Great) Britain.
Brujas, Bruges.
Brúnsvick, Brunswick, Braunschweig.
Bruselas, Brussels.
Bucarest, Bucharest.
Bucovina, Bukovina, Bukovina.
Bullón, Buillon.
Burdeos, Bordeaux.

C

Cabo Bretón, Cape Breton (Island).
Cabo de Buena Esperanza, Cape of Good Hope.
Cabo de Hornos, Cape Horn.
Cabo de Istria, Capo d'Istria.
Cabo de San Vicente, Cape Saint Vincent.
Cabo Haitiano, Cape Haitien.
Cachemira, Kashmir.
Cafarnaum, Capernaum.
Cafrería, Kaffraria.
Calcedonia, Chalcedon.
Calcuta, Calcutta.
Caldea, Chaldea.
Cambrige, Cambrigia, Cambridge.
Camerón, Camarones, Kamerún, Cameroons, Kamerun.
Canaán, Canaan.
Canal de la Mancha, English Channel.
Canarias, Canary (Islands).
Canosa, Canossa.
Cantórbery, Canterbury.
Carcasona, Carcassonne.
Carelia, Karelia.
Carenta, Charente.
Caribe. *V.* Mar Caribe.
Cariñán, Carignano.
Carolina del Norte, North Carolina.
Carolina del Sur, South Carolina.
Cartagena, Carthagena.
Cartago, Carthage.
Caspio, Caspian (Sea).
Castilla, Castile.
Castilla la Nueva, New Castile.
Castilla la Vieja, Old Castile.
Cataluña, Catalonia.
Cáucaso, Caucasus.
Cayena, Cayenne.
Cayohueso, Cayo Hueso, Key West.

For pronunciation, see the rules at the beginning of the book.

Cayos de la Florida, Florida Keys.
Cebú. *V.* Zebú.
Ceilán, Ceylon.
Cerdeña, Sardinia.
Cernauti, Cærnowitz.
Cesarea, Cæsarea.
Cevenes, Cevennes, Sevennes.
Cíclades, Cyclades.
Cidno, Cydnus.
Circasia, Circassia.
Coblenza, Coblenz.
Coburgo, Coburg.
Cochinchina, Cochin China.
Colonia, Cologne.
Colonia del Cabo, Cape Colony.
Columbia Británica, British Columbia.
Columnas de Hércules, Pillars of Hercules.
Comoras, Comoro Isles.
Compieña, Compiègne.
Constantina, Constantine.
Constantinopla, Constantinople.
Constanza, Constance.
Copenhague, Copenhagen.
Córcega, Corsica.
Córdoba, Cordova.
Corfú, Corfu.
Corinto, Corinth.
Cornualla, Cornwall.
Cortray, Courtray.
Coruña, Corunna.
Costa del Marfil, Ivory Coast.
Costa de Oro, Gold Coast.
Cotanza, Coutances.
Cracovia, Cracow.
Creta, Crete.
Cristianía, Christiania.
Croacia, Croatia.
Cronstadt, Kronstadt.
Curasao, Curazao, Curaçao.
Curdistán, Kurdistan.
Curlandia, Kurland.

CH

Chamberí, Chambery.
Champaña, Champagne.
Chantung, Shantung.
Checoeslovaquia, Czecho-Slovakia, Czechoslovakia.
Cherburgo, Cherbourg.
Chifú, Chifu, Chefoo.
Chile, Chili, Chile.
Chipre, Cyprus.

D

Dakota del Norte, North Dakota.
Dakota del Sur, South Dakota.
Dalmacia, Dalmatia.
Damasco, Damascus.
Damieta, Damietta.
Danubio, Danube.
Dardanelos, Dardanelles.
Decán, Deccan.
Delfinado, Dauphiny, Dauphiné.
Delfos, Delphi.
Diepa, Diepe, Dieppe.
Dinamarca, Denmark.
Dniéper, Dnieper.
Dordoña, Dordogne.
Dos Puentes, Deux Ponts.
Dresde, Dresden.
Duay, Douay.
Duero, Douro.
Duina, Dwina, Dvina.
Dunas, Downs.
Dunquerque, Dunkirk.
Duvres, Dover.

E

Edimburgo, Edinburgh.
Efeso, Ephesus.
Egeo, Ægean.
Egina, Ægina.
Egipto, Egypt.
Egos Pótamos, Ægospotami.
Elba, Elbe.
Elbinga, Elbing.
Entre Duero y Miño, Entre Douro e Minho.
Eólida, Æolis.
Epiro, Epirus.
Erzerón, Erzerum.
Escafusa, Schaffhausen.
Escalda, Scheld, Scheldt.
Escamandro, Scamander.
Escandinavia, Scandinavia.
Escania, Scania.
Escio, Scio, Chio.
Esclavonia, Slavonia.
Escocia, Scotland.
Escorial, Escurial.
Escutari, Scutari.
Eslavonia, Slavonia.
Eslovaquia, Slovakia.
Eslovenia, Slovenia.
Esmalcalda, Smalcalden.
Esmirna, Smyrna.
España, Spain.
Española, Hispaniola.
Esparta, Sparta.
Espira, Spirea.
Espizberg, Espizberga, Spitzbergen.
Espoleto, Spoleto.
Establecimientos del Estrecho (de Malaca), Straits Settlements.
Estado Libre de Orange, Orange Free State.
Estados de la Iglesia, States of the Church.
Estados Federados de Malaca, Federated Malay States.
Estados Unidos de América, United States of America.
Estambul, Stambul.
Estiria, Styria.
Estocolmo, Stockholm.
Estonia, Esthonia.
Estrasburgo, Strasbourg.
Estrecho de Bella Isla, Strait of Belle Isle.
Estrecho de Magallanes, Strait of Magellan.
Estrómboli, Stromboli.
Etiopía, Ethiopia.
Etna, Etna, Ætna.
Etolia, Ætolia.
Eubea, Eubœa.
Eufrates, Euphrates.
Europa, Europe.

F

Farsalia, Pharsalia.
Fenicia, Phœnicia.
Filadelfia, Philadelphia.
Filipinas, Philippines.
Filipópolis, Philippopolis.
Filipos, Philippi.
Finlandia, Finland.
Flandes, Flanders.
Flesinga, Flushing.
Florencia, Florence.
Fócide, Phocis.
Francfort del Mein, Frankfort-on-the-Main.
Francia, France.
Franco Condado, Franche Comté.
Friburgo, Friburg, Freiburg.
Frigia, Phrygia.
Frisia, Friesland.
Frontiñac, Frontenac.

G

Gales, Wales.
Galia, Gaul.
Galilea, Galilee.
Galípoli, Gallipoli.
Gante, Ghent, Gand.
Garona, Garonne.
Gascuña, Gascony.
Génova, Genoa.
Germania, (anc. hist.) Germany.
Ginebra, Geneva.
Gironda, Gironde.
Glaris, Glarus.
Golfo Pérsico, Persian Gulf.
Gotemburgo, Gothenburg.
Gotinga, Göttingen.
Gran Bretaña, Great Britain.
Gránico, Granicus.
Gravelinas, Gravelines.
Grecia, Greece.
Groenlandia, Greenland.
Groninga, Groningen.
Guadalupe, Guadeloupe.
Guaján, Guam, Guam.
Guayana, Guiana.
Güeldres, Guelderland, Gelderland.
Guernesey, Guernsey.
Guidsé, Giza.
Guipúzcoa, Guipuscoa.
Guiena, Guienne.

H

Habana, Havana.
Haití, Haiti, Hayti.
Halicarnaso, Halicarnassus.
Hamburgo, Hamburg.
Hankao, Hankow.
Harrisburgo, Harrisburg.
Hauái, Hawaii.
Havre de Gracia, Havre de Grace.
Hawái, Hawaii.
Haya, Hague.
Hébridas, Hebrides.
Hélada, Hellas.
Helvecia, Helvetia.
Henao, Hainault.
Herculano, Herculaneum.
Heyaz, Hejaz.
Himeto, Hymettus.
Hispano-América, Hispanoamérica, Spanish America.
Holanda, Holland.
Honduras Británica, British Honduras.
Hungría, Hungary.

I

Ilión (Troya), Ilion, Ilium (Troy).
Iliria, Illyria.
Ilírico, Illyricum.
Indias, Indies.
Indias orientales, East Indies.
Indias occidentales, West Indies.
Indo, Indus.
Indostán, Hindustan, India.
Inglaterra, England.
Irlanda, Ireland.
Isla de Francia, Island of France, or Mauritius.
Isla de Guanahaní, Watling Island.
Isla del Cabo Bretón, Cape Breton Island.
Isla del Príncipe Eduardo, Prince Edward Island.
Isla de Pascua, Easter Island.
Isla Española, Hispaniola, Hayti.
Isla Real, Cape Breton Island.
Islandia, Iceland.
Islas Aleutas, or **Aleutianas,** Aleutian Islands.
Islas Baleares, Balearic Islands.
Islas Británicas, British Isles.
Islas Canarias, Canary Islands.
Islas Carolinas, Caroline Islands.
Islas de Barlovento, Windward Islands.
Islas de Hauái, Sandwich Islands.
Islas del Almirante, Admiralty Islands.
Islas de la Sociedad, Society Islands.
Islas de la Sonda, Sunda Isles.
Islas del Cabo Verde, Cape Verde Islands.
Islas de Sotavento, Leeward Islands.
Islas de Zetlandia, Shetland Islands.
Islas Filipinas, Philippine Islands.
Islas Hawái, Hawaiian Islands.
Islas Malvinas, Falkland Islands.
Islas Vírgenes, Virgin Islands.
Iso, Issus.
Ítaca, Ithaca.
Italia, Italy.

J

Janina, Yannina.
Japón, Japan.
Jarbin, Harbin.
Jartum, Khartoum.
Jericó, Jericho.
Jerusalén, Jerusalem.
Jiva, Khiva.
Jonia, Ionia.
Judá, Judah.
Jutlandia, Jutland.

K

Karbin, Harbin.
Kartum, Khartoum.
Kiao-Cheu, Kiaochow.
Kurdistán, Kurdistan.

L

Lacedemonia, Lacedæmon.
Lacio, Latium.
Lago de Constanza, Lake of Constance.
Lago Salado, Salt Lake.
Laponia, Lapland.
La Rochela, La Rochelle.
Lasa, Lassa.
Lausana, Lausanne.
Leida, Leide, Leiden, Leyden.
Lemosín, Limosin or Limousin.
Leningrado, Leningrad.
León de Francia, Lyons.
Leonesado, Lyonnais.
Líbano, Lebanon.
Libia, Libya.
Lieja, Liége.
Lila, Lille.
Limburgo, Limburg.
Liorna, Leghorn.
Lisboa, Lisbon.
Lituania, Lithuania.
Lombardía, Lombardy.
Londres, London.
Lorena, Lorraine.
Lovaina, Louvain.
Lucerna, Lucerne.
Luisiana, Louisiana.
Luxemburgo, Luxemburg.

M

Macedonia, Macedon, **Macedonia.**
Madera, Madeira.
Magallanes, Magellan.
Magna Grecia, Magna Græcia, Græcia Magna.
Maguncia, Mayence, Mainz.
Maisur, Mysore.
Malaca, Malay Peninsula.
Malasia, Malay Archipelago, Malaysia.
Maldivas, Maldives.
Malinas, Malines, Mecheln or Mechlin.
Malvinas, Falkland Islands.
Mallorca, Majorca.
Mancha (la) or **Canal de la M.,** English Channel.
Mar Adriático, Adriatic Sea.
Mar Amarillo, Yellow Sea.
Mar Báltico, Baltic Sea.
Mar Blanco, White Sea.
Mar Caribe, Caribbean Sea.
Mar Caspio, Caspian Sea.
Mar de la China, China Sea.
Mar de las Antillas = MAR CARIBE.
Mar de las Indias, Indian Ocean.
Mar del Norte, North Sea.
Mar Egeo, Ægean Sea.
Mar Glacial, Frozen Sea.
Mar Jónico, Ionian Sea.
Mar Mediterráneo, Mediterranean Sea.
Mar Muerto, Dead Sea.
Mar Negro, Black Sea.
Mar Rojo, Red Sea.
Mar Tirreno, Tyrrhenian Sea.
Marañón, (upper reaches of the) Amazon.
Maratón, Marathon.
Marruecos, Morocco.
Marsella, Marseilles.
Martinica, Martinique.
Mauricia, Mauritius or Island of France.
Mayena, Mayenne.
Meca, Mecca.
Mediterráneo, Mediterranean.
Méjico, Mexico.
Menfis, Memphis.
Menorca, Minorca.
Mesia, Mœsia.
Metauro, Metaurus.
Micenas, Mycenæ.
Midelburgo, Middleburg.
Milanesado, Milanese.
Miño, Minho.
Mirándula, Mirandola.
Misisipí, Mississippi.
Misora, Mysore.
Mobila, Mobile.
Mompeller, Montpellier.
Mondoñedo, Mondonned or Mondoneda.
Mongibelo = ETNA.
Monserrate, Montserrat.
Monte Oliveto, Olives (Mount of), Olivet.
Montes Alleghanys, Allegheny Mountains.
Montes Apalaches, Appalachian Mountains.
Montes Balcanes, Balkan Mountains.
Montes Carpacios, or **Cárpatos,** Carpathian Mountains.
Montes Rocallosos, M. Rocosos, Rocky Mountains.
Montes Urales, Ural Mountains.
Morlés, Morlaix.
Mosa, Meuse.
Moscovia, Muscovy.
Moscú, Moscow.
Mosela, Moselle.
Muerto, Dead (Sea).

N

Nápoles, Naples.
Narbona, Narbonne.
Navarino, Navarin.
Navarra, Navarre.
Nazaret, Nazareth.
Negro, Black (Sea).
Neoburgo, Neuburg.
Neoport, Nieuport.
Neyed, Nejd or Nedjed.
Nicea, Nicæa.
Niéper, Dnieper.
Nifón, Nippon.
Nigricia, Negroland.
Nilo, Nile.
Nimega, Nimeguen.
Nínive, Nineveh.
Nipón, Nippon.
Niza, Nice.
Normandía, Normandy.
Noruega, Norway.
Nueva Escocia, Novia Scotia.
Nueva Gales, New Wales.
Nueva Gales del Sur, New South Wales.
Nueva Inglaterra, New England.
Nueva Orleáns, New Orleans.
Nueva York, New York.
Nueva Zelandia, New Zealand.
Nueva Zembla, Nova Zembla.

Nuevo Brúnswick, N. Brúnsvick, New Brunswick.
Numancia, Numantia.
Nuremberga, Nuremberg.

O

Oceanía, Oceania, Oceanica.
Odenarda, Oudenarde.
Odesa, Odessa.
Ofir, Ophir.
Olimpia, Olympia.
Olimpo, Olympus.
Olinto, Olynthus.
Omán, Muscat, Maskat.
Onella, Oneglia.
Orleanesado, Orleannois.
Ostende, Ostend.
Otahití, Otaheite or Tahiti.
Oxo, Oxus.

P

Pacífico, Pacific (Ocean).
Países Bajos, Low Countries, Netherlands, Holland.
Palatinado, Palatinate.
Palestina, Palestine.
Palmira, Palmyra.
Pamplona, Pampeluna.
Panfilia, Pamphylia.
Panzacola, Pensacola.
Parnaso, Parnassus.
Partia, Parthia.
Paso de Calais, Strait of Dover.
Pekín, Pekin.
Pela, Pella.
Peloponeso, Peloponnesus.
Península de Malaca, Malay Peninsula.
Pensilvania, Pennsylvania.
Penzacola, Pensacola.
Pérgamo, Pergamum.
Perona, Peronne.
Perpiñán, Perpignan.
Perusa, Perusia or Perugia.
Petrogrado, Petrograd.
Piamonte, Piedmont.
Picardía. Picardy.
Piombina, Piombino.
Pireo, Piræus.
Pirineos, Pyrenees.
Pistoya, Pistoja.
Plasencia, Placentia.
Platea, Platæa.
Polinesia, Polynesia.
Polonia, Poland.
Pombín, Piombino.
Pompeya, Pompeii.
Ponto, Pontus.
Ponto Euxino, Pontus Euxinus (Black Sea).
Porto Longón, Porto Longone.
Praga, Prague.
Presburgo, Presburg.
Provenza, Provence.
Providencia, Providence.
Provincias Renanas, Rhineland.
Provincias Vascongadas, or **Vascas,** Basque Provinces.
Prusia, Prussia.
Puertas de Hierro, Iron Gates.
Puerto Arturo, Port Arthur.
Puerto (de) España, Port of Spain.
Puerto Mahón, Port Mahon.
Puerto Príncipe, Port-au-Prince.
Puerto Rico, Porto Rico, Puerto Rico.

Q

Queronea, Chæronea.
Quersoneso, Chersonese.
Quinsala, Kinsale.
Quío, Chio.

R

Rapanuí, Easter Island.
Ratisbona, Ratisbon, Regensburg.
Regio, Reggio.
Reims, Rheims.
Reino Unido, United Kingdom.
Retia, Rhætia.
Rhin, Rhine.
Rif, Rif or Riff.
Rin, Rhine.
Río Amarillo, Yellow River.
Rocamora, Roquemaure.
Rochela (La), (La) Rochelle.
Ródano, Rhone.
Rodas, Rhodas.
Rodesia, Rhodesia.
Rojo, Red (Sea).
Roma, Rome.
Romaña, Romagna.
Rosellón, Roussillon.
Roseta, Rosetta.
Ruán, Rouen.
Rumania, R(o)umania.
Ruremunda, Roermond or Ruremunde.
Rusia, Russia.

S

Sabá, Sheba.
Saboya, Savoy.
Sácer, Sassari.
Sajonia, Saxony.
Sajonia-Coburgo, Saxe-Coburg.
Sajonia-Gotha, Saxe-Gotha.
Sajonia-Wéimar, Saxe-Weimar.
Salamina, Salamis.
Salé, Sallee.
Salónica, Salonika.
Samotracia, Samothrace.
San Cristóbal, St. Kitts.
San Germán, St. Germain.
San Gotardo, St. Gothard.
San Juan de Luz, St. Jean de Luz.
San Kitts, St. Kitts.
San Nazario, St. Nazaire.
San Petersburgo, St. Petersburg.
San Quintín, St. Quentin.
San Salvador (Isla de), Watling Island.
Santa Elena, St.-Helena.
Santa Lucía, St. Lucia.
Santonge, Saintonge.
Sarmacia, Sarmatia.
Sena, Seine.
Servia, Serbia.
Servia - Croacia - Eslovenia, Serb-Croat-Slovene State.
Seúl, Seoul.
Sevilla, Seville.
Severna, Severn.
Sicilia, Sicily.
Sierra Leona, Sierra Leone.
Siracusa, Syracuse.
Siria, Syria.
Socotera, Socotora, Socotra.
Soleura, Soleure.
Somalia, Somaliland.
Suabia, Suabia or Swabia.
Sud-África, Sudáfrica, South Africa.
Sud-América, Sudamérica, South America.
Sudán, Soudan, Sudan.
Suebia = SUABIA.
Suecia, Sweden.
Suiza, Switzerland.
Sund, Sound.
Sur-América, or **Suramérica,** South America.

T

Tabago, Tobago.
Tafilete, Tafilet.
Tahití, Tahiti.
Tajo, Tagus.
Tamatava, Tamatave.
Támesis, Thames.
Tanganyica, Tangañica, Lake Tanganyika.
Tánger, Tangier.
Tapso, Thapsus.
Tarento, Taranto.
Tarso, Tarsus.
Tartaria, Tartary, Tatary.
Tauro, Taurus.
Tebas, Thebes.
Tejas, Texas.
Tenerife, Teneriffe.
Termópilas, Thermopylæ.
Terranova, Newfoundland.
Tesalia, Thessaly.
Tesalónica, Thessalonica.
Tesino, Ticino.
Tiberíades, Tiberias.
Tibet, Thibet, Tibet.
Tierra de Francisco José, Franz Josef Island.
Tierra del Labrador, Labrador.
Tierra Santa, Holy Land.
Tiro, Tyre.
Tirol, Tyrol.
Tokío, Tokyo, Tokio.
Tolón, Toulon.
Tolosa, Toulouse.
Tornay, Tournay.
Toscana, Tuscany.
Trabizonda, Trebizond.
Tracia, Thrace.
Trasimeno, Thrasimene.
Trebizonda, Trebizond.
Trento, Trent.
Tréveris, Treves, Trier.
Trieste, Triest.
Troya, Troy.
Tubinga, Tubingen.
Túnez, Tunis.
Turena, Turenne.
Turquestán, Turkestan.
Turquía, Turkey.
Turs, Tours.
Túsculo, Tusculum.

U

Uberlinga, Uberlingen.
Ucrania, Ukraine.
Ulma, Ulm.
Undervald, Unterwalden.
Unión Soviética, Soviet Union.

Unión Sudafricana, Union of South Africa.
URSS, USSR.

V

Valaquia, Wallachia.
Valclusa, Vaucluse.
Valencia, Valence (France); Valencia (Spain).
Valenciennes, Valenciennes.
Valtelina, Valtelline.
Vandoma, Vendome.
Varenas, Varennes.
Varsovia, Warsaw.
Venecia, Venice.
Véneto, Venetia.
Versalles, Versailles.
Vestfalia, Westphalia.
Vesuvio, Vesuvius.
Viena, Vienne (France); Vienna (Austria).
Villafranca, Villefranche.
Vincenas, Vincennes.
Virginia Occidental, West Virginia.
Vizcaya, Biscay.
Vosgos, Vosges.

W

Wartburgo, Wartburg.
Westfalia, Westphalia.
Wurtemberg, Würtemburg.

Y

Yedo, Jeddo, Yeddo.
Yeso, Yesso.
Yugoeslavia, Yugoslavia, Jugoslavia.

Z

Zambese, Zambeze, Zambesi.
Zanguébar, Zanzíbar, Zanzibar.
Zaragoza, Saragossa.
Zebú, Zebu.
Zelandia, Zealand.
Zululandia, Zululand.

Names of Persons, Including Those of Famous Historical Personages

A

Abelardo, Abelard.
Abrahán, Abrán, Abraham.
Absalón, Absalom.
Abubéker, Abu-Bekr.
Adán, Adam.
Adela, Adele.
Adelaida, Adelaide.
Adelina, Adeline.
Adolfo, Adolphus.
Adriano, Hadrian.
Ágata, Agatha.
Agripina, Agrippina.
Agueda, Agatha.
Agustín, Augustin, Austin.
Alano, Alan, Allen.
Alarico, Alaric.
Alberto, Albert.
Alberto Magno, Albertus Magnus.
Alceo, Alcæus.
Alejandra, Alexandra.
Alejandro, Alexander.
Alejo, Alexis.
Alfonso, Alphonse.
Alfredo, Alfred.
Alicia, Alice.
Alonso, Alphonsus.
Aluino, Alwin.
Amadeo, Amadeus.
Amata, Amy.
Ambrosio, Ambrose, Ambrosius.
Amelia, Amelie.
Ana, Ann, Anne, Anna, Hannah.
Ana Bolena, Anne Boleyn.
Anacreonte, Anacreon.
Andrés, Andrew.
Aníbal, Hannibal.
Anselmo, Anselm.
Antígono, Antigonus.
Antíoco, Antiochus.
Antonino, Antoninus.
Antonio, Anthony.
Aquiles, Achilles.
Apuleyo, Apuleius.
Arabela, Arabella.
Archibaldo, Archibald.
Aristófanes, Aristophanes.
Aristóteles, Aristotle.
Arnaldo, Arnold.
Arquimedes, Archimedes.
Arturo, Arthur.
Arriano, Arrian.
Arrio, Arius.
Artajerjes, Artaxerxes.
Asurbanipal, Ashur-bani-pal.
Atanasio, Athanasius.
Atila, Attila.
Augusto, Augustus.
Aureliano, Aurelian.
Aurelio, Aurelius.

B

Bárbara, Barbara.
Bartolomé, Bartholomew, Bartholomæus.
Basilio, Basil.
Beatriz, Beatrix, Beatrice.
Beda, Bæda, Bede.
Belisario, Belisarius.
Beltrán, Bertram.
Benita, Benedicta.
Benito, Benedict.
Bermudo, Veremond.
Bernabé, Barnabas, Barnaby.
Bernardo, Bernard.
Bernardino, Bernardinus.
Berta, Bertha.
Betsabé, Bath-Sheba.
Blas, Blase.
Bocaccio, Bocacio, Boccaccio, Boccace.
Bonifacio, Boniface.
Brígida, Bridget.
Bruto, Brutus.
Buda, Buddha.
Buenaventura, Bonaventure.

C

Calvino, Calvin.
Cambises, Cambyses.
Camilla, Camilla, Camille.
Camilo, Camillus.
Caracala, Caracalla.
Carlomagno, Charlemagne.
Carlos, Charles.
Carlota, Charlotte.
Carolina, Caroline.
Casandra, Cassandra.
Casimiro, Casimir.
Casio, Cassius.
Catalina, Catharine.
Catilina, Catiline.
Catón, Cato.
Catulo, Catullus.
Cayetano, Cajetan, Gaetan.
Cecilia, Cicely.
Cecilio, Cecil.
César, Cæsar.
Cicerón, Cicero.
Cincinato, Cincinnatus.
Cipriano, Cyprian.
Ciriaco, Cyriacus.
Cirilo, Cyrilus.
Ciro, Cyrus.
Claudia, Claudina, Claudia.
Claudio, Claude, Claudius.
Cleanto, Cleanthes.
Clemente, Clement.
Cleóbulo, Cleobulus.
Clodoveo, Clovis.
Clotilde, Clotilda.
Colón, Columbus.
Cómodo, Commodus.
Confucio, Confucius.
Conrado, Conrad.
Constancia, Constancio, Constance.
Constantino, Constantine.
Constanza, Constance.
Cornelio, Cornelius.
Cosme, Cosmas.
Creso, Crœsus.
Crisóstomo, Chrysostom.
Cristiano, Christian.
Cristina, Christina.
Cristo, Christ.
Cristóbal, Christopher.
Curcio, Curtius.

D

Dagoberto, Dagobert.
Darío, Darius.
Demócrito, Democritus.
Demóstenes, Demosthenes.
Diego, James.
Diógenes, Diogenes.
Dionisia, Dionysia.
Dionisio, Dennis, Dionysius.
Domiciano, Domitian.
Domingo, Dominic.
Dorotea, Dorothy.

E

Edmundo, Edmund.

Eduardo, Edward.
Eduvigis, Hedwig.
Elagábalo, Elagabalus.
Elena, Ellen, Helen.
Elisa, Eliza.
Eliseo, Elisha, Ellis.
Eloísa, Heloise.
Ema, Emma.
Emilia, Emily.
Emilio, Æmilius.
Eneas, Æneas.
Engracia, Grace.
Enrique, Henry.
Enriqueta, Henrietta.
Epicteto, Epictetus.
Epicurus, Epicuro.
Erasmo, Erasmus.
Eratóstenes, Eratosthenes.
Ernesto, Ernest.
Escalígero, Scaliger.
Escipión, Scipio.
Escipión el Africano, Scipio Africanus.
Esopo, Æsop.
Espartaco, Spartacus.
Esquilo, Æschylus.
Esquines, Æschines.
Esteban, Stephen.
Ester, Esther, Hester.
Estrabón, Strabo.
Estradivario, Stradivarius.
Euclides, Euclid.
Eufemia, Euphemia.
Eufrosina, Euphrosyne.
Eugenia, Eugenie.
Eugenio, Eugene.
Euler, **Eulero**, Euler.
Eusebio, Eusebius.
Eustaquio, Eustace.
Eva, Eve, Eva.
Ezequías, Hezekiah.
Ezequiel, Ezekiel.

F

Fabio, Fabius.
Federica, Frederica.
Federico, Frederic.
Fedra, Phedre.
Fedro, Phædrus.
Felipa, Philippa.
Felipe, Philip.
Felisa, **Felicia**, Felicia.
Fernando, Ferdinand.
Filipo, Philip (of Macedon), Philippus.
Filo el Judío, Philo Judæus.
Fineas, Phineas.
Florencia, **Florencio**, Florence.
Foción, Phocion.
Francisca, Frances.
Francisco, Francis.
Fredegunda, Fredegonde.
Froíla, **Fruela**, Froyla.

G

Galeno, Galen.
Galieno, Gallienus.
Gaspar, Jasper.
Gayo, Gaius.
Gedeón, Gideon.
Genserico, Genseric.
Geofredo, Geoffrey.
Gerardo, Gerard.
Germánico, Germanicus.
Gertrudis, Gertrude.
Gervasio, Gervas.
Gil, Giles.
Gilberto, Gilbert.
Godofredo, **Gofredo**, Godfrey.
Graco, Gracchus.
Gracos, Gracchi.
Gregorio, Gregory.
Gualterio, **Gualtero**, Walter.
Guido, Guy.
Guillelmo, **Guillén**, William.
Guillermina, Wilhelmina.
Guillermo, William.
Gustavo, Gustavus.

H

Haroldo, Harold.
Heberto, Herbert.
Heliogábalo, Elagabalus.
Helvecio, Helvetius.
Heráclito, Heraclitus.
Heriberto, Herbert.
Herodes, Herod.
Herodoto, Herodotus.
Herón, Hiero.
Hesíodo, Hesiod.
Hilario, Hilary.
Hildebrando, Hildebrand.
Hiparco, Hipparchus.
Hipócrates, Hippocrates.
Homero, Homer.
Honorio, Honorius.
Horacio, Horace, Horatio.
Hortensia, Hortense.
Huberto, Hobart, Hubert.
Hugo, Hugh.
Hugo Capeto, Hugh Capet.
Humberto, Humbert.
Hunfredo, Humphrey.

I

Ignacio, Ignatius.
Ildefonso, Alphonsus.
Inés, Agnes, Inez.
Inocencio, Innocent.
Ireneo, Ireneus.
Isabel, Elizabeth.
Isidoro, **Isidro**, Isidor.

J

Jacobo, **Jaime**, James.
Jansenio, Jansen, Jansenius.
Javier, Xavier.
Jehová, Jehovah.
Jenócrates, Xenocrates.
Jenófanes, Xenophanes.
Jenofonte, Xenophon.
Jeremías, Jeremy, Jeremiah.
Jerjes, Xerxes.
Jerónimo, Jerome.
Jesús, Jesus.
Jesucristo, Jesus Christ.
Joaquín, Joachim.
Jonás, Jonah.
Jonatán, **Jonatás**, Jonathan.
Jorge, George.
José, Joseph.
Josefa, **Josefina**, Josephine.
Josefo, Josephus.
Josías, Josiah.
Josué, Joshua.
Joviano, Jovian.
Juan, John.
Juana, Jane, Jennie, Jean, Joan, Joanna.
Juana de Arco, Joan of Arc.
Judit, Judith.
Julia, Julia.
Julián; **Juliano** (emperor), Julian.
Julio, Julius.
Justiniano, Justinian.
Justino, Justin.
Justino Mártir, Justin Martyr.

K

(de) **Kempis**, (a) Kempis.

L

Ladislao, Ladislas.
Lamberto, Lambert.
Lázaro, Lazarus.
Leandro, Leander.
León, Leo, Leon.
Leonardo, Leonard.
Leonor, Eleanor.
Leopoldo, Leopold.
Leticia, Lætitia, Letitia, Lettice.
Licurgo, Lycurgus.
Lineo, Linnæus.
Lisandro, Lysander.
Lisias, Lysias.
Lisímaco, Lysimachus.
Lisipo, Lysippus.
Liutprando, Liutprand.
Livio, Livy.
Longino, Longinus.
Lorenzo, Lawrence, Laurence.
Lotario, Lothaire.
Lucano, Lucan.
Lucas, Luke.
Lucía, Lucy, Lucia.
Luciano, Lucian.
Lucio, Lucius.
Lucrecia, Lucretia.
Lucrecio, Lucretius.
Luis, Lewis, Louis.
Luis (Gonzaga), Aloysius.
Luisa, Louise.
Lutero, Luther.

M

Magallanes, Magellan.
Magdalena, Magdalen.
Mahoma, Mahomet, Mohammed.
Malaquías, Malachi.
Manuel, Emanuel.
Manuela, Emma.
Marcelo, Marcellus.
Marcial, Martial.
Marco, **Marcos**, Mark.
Marco Aurelio, Marcus Aurelius.
Margarita, Margaret, Margery.
María, Mary, Maria, Miriam.
María Luisa, Marie Louise.
Mariana, Marian.
Mario, Marius.
Marta, Martha.
Masinisa, Masinissa.
Mateo, Matthew.
Matías, Mattias.
Matilde, Matilda.
Mauricio, Maurice, Morice.
Maximiliano, Maximilian.
Mecenas, Mæcenas.
Mesalina, Messalina.
Miguel, Michael.
Miguel Ángel, Michelangelo.
Mitrídates, Mithridates.
Moisés, Moses.

N

Nabucodonosor, Nebuchadnezzar.
Nápier, Napier.
Natán, Nathan.
Nataniel, Nathaniel.
Nehemías, Nehemiah.
Néper, Napier.
Népote, Nepos.
Nerón, Nero.
Nestorio, Nestorius.
Nicolás, Nicholas.
Noé, Noah.

O

Octavio, Octavius.
Odoacro, Odoacer.
Oliverio, Oliver.
Orígenes, Origen.
Oseas, Hosea.
Osmundo, Osmond.
Otman, Othman.
Otón, Otho.
Ovidio, Ovid.

P

Pablo, Paul.
Patricio, Patrick.
Paula, Paulina, Pauline.
Pedro, Peter.
Pepino, Pepin.—**P. el Breve,** Pepin the Short.
Peregrín, or **Peregrino,** Peregrine.
Perseo, Perseus.
Píndaro, Pindar.
Pío, Pius.
Pirro, Pyrrhus.
Pitágoras, Pythagoras.
Platón, Plato.
Plauto, Plautus.
Plinio, Pliny.
Plótino, Plotinus.
Plutarco, Plutarch.
Polibio, Polybius.
Policarpo, Polycarp.
Policleto, Polycletus.
Polícrates, Polycrates.
Pompeyo, Pompey.
Pretorio, Pretorius.
Proclo, Proclus.
Procopio, Procopius.
Prudencia, Prudence.

Q

Quintiliano, Quintilian.
Quintín, Quintin, Quentin.

R

Rafael, Raphael.
Raimundo, Ramón, Raymond.
Randolfo, Randolph.
Raquel, Rachel.
Rebeca, Rebecca.
Reginaldo, Reginald.
Régulo, Regulus.
Reinaldo, Reynold.
Renaldo, Ronald.
Renato, René.
Ricardo, Richard.
Roberto, Robert.
Rodas, Rhodes.
Rodolfo, Rodolphus, Ralph, Rudolph, Rollo.
Rodrigo, Roderic.
Roger, Rogerio, Roger.
Rolando, Roland, Rowland.
Rolón, Rollón, Rollo.
Rómulo, Romulus.
Rosa, Rose.
Rosalía, Rosalie.
Rosamunda, Rosamond.
Rosario, Rosary.
Ruben, Reuben.
Rufo, Rufus.
Ruperto, Rupert.

S

Saladino, Saladin.
Salomón, Solomon.
Salustio, Sallust.
Samuel, Samuel.
Sansón, Samson.
Santiago, James, St. James.
Sara, Sarah.
Sardanápalo, Sardanapalus.
Senaquerib, Sennacherib.
Sertorio, Sertorius.
Severo, Severus.
Sigismundo, Sigismund.
Sila, Sulla.
Silvano, Silvan.
Silvestre, Silvester.
Sofía, Sophia, Sophy.
Sófocles, Sophocles.
Solimán, Solyman, Suleiman.
Suetonio, Suetonius.
Susana, Susan, Susanna.

T

Tácito, Tacitus.
Tadeo, Thadeus.
Tales, Thales.
Tamerlán, Tamerlane.
Temístocles, Themistocles.
Teobaldo, Theobald, Tybold.
Teócrito, Theocritus.
Teodora, Theodora.
Teodoro, Theodore.
Teodorico, Theodoric, Dorick.
Teodosio, Theodosius.
Teófilo, Theophilus.
Teofrasto, Theophrastus.
Terencio, Terence.
Teresa, Theresa.
Tertuliano, Tertullian.
Tiberio, Tiberius.
Tíbulo, Tibullus.
Ticiano, Titian.
Timoteo, Timothy.
Timur, Timour.
Tito, Titus.
Tobías, Tobias, Toby.
Tolomeo, Ptolemy.
Tomás, Thomas.
Trajano, Trajan.
Trasíbulo, Thrasybulus.
Triboniano, Tribonian.
Tucídides, Thucydides.
Turena, Turenne.

U

Ulpiano, Ulpian.
Urbano, Urban.
Urías, Uriah.

V

Valente, Valens.
Valentín, Valentine.
Valentiniano, Valentinian.
Valeriano, Valerian.
Ventura, Bonaventura.
Veremundo, Veremond.
Veronés, Veronese.
Vespasiano, Vespasian.
Vespucio, Vespucci.
Vicente, Vincent.
Virgilio, Virgil, Vergil.
Vitruvio, Vitruvius.

Y

Yugurta, Jugurtha.

Z

Zacarías, Zachary, Zachariah.
Zenón, Zeno.
Zoroastro, Zoroaster.
Zuinglio, Zwingli.

Colloquial Pet Names

Adela, Adelita, Adelina.
Ana, Anita, Anica.
Antonio, nia, Antoñito, ta; Toño, ña; Toñico, ca.
Bartolomé, Bartolo.
Carlos, Carlitos.
Catalina, Catana, Catuca, Catuja.
Cayetano, Tano.
Cristóbal, Tobal, Tobalito.
Diego, Dieguito.
Dolores. *V.* María de los Dolores.
Francisco, Francisquito; Frasco, Frascuelo, Frasquito; Paquito, Paco; Pacorro; Pancho, Panchito; Curro, Currito; Farruco.
Francisca (the same words as the preceding, changing final *o* to *a*).
Gertrudis, Tula.
Gregorio, Goyo.
Isabel, Belica, Belita.
Jaime, Jaimito.
José, Joseíto, Josecito; Pepe, Pepito; Pepillo; Chepe, Chepito.

Josefa, Josefita; Pepa, Pepita, Pepilla; Chepa, Chepita.
Juan, Juanito, Juanillo.
Juana, Juanita, Juanilla.
María, Mariquita, Mariquilla, Marica, Maruca, Marucha, Maruja.
María de la Concepción, Concha, Conchita; Chona, Cota, Cotita.
María, (de) Jesús, Jesusa, Jesusita, Chucha, Chuchita.
María de los Dolores, Dolorcitas, Dolorcitas, Lola, Lolita.
María de la Luz, Lucecita. Lucita.
Pedro, Pedrito, Perico.

For pronunciation, see the rules at the beginning of the book.

Abbreviations Most Commonly Used in Spanish

A

A. Alteza; aprobado (passed in examination).
a. área (are).
(a) alias.
@ arroba; @@ arrobas.
AA. Autores; Altezas.
ab. abad.
ab.^{l} abril.
Abls. gen. Absolución general.
A. C., A. de C. Año de Cristo (A.D.).
admón. administración.
admor., adm.^{or} administrador.
af.^{mo}, afmo. afectísimo.
af.^{to} afecto.
Ag.^{n} Agustín.
a la v/ a la vista.
ag.^{to} agosto.
alc.^{de} alcalde.
Alej.^{o} Alejandro.
Alf.^{o} Alfonso.
Al.^{o} Alonso.
A L. R. P. de V. M. A los reales pies de Vuestra Majestad.
Álv.^{o} Álvaro.
am.^{o} amigo.
Ant.^{o} Antonio.
ap. aparte; apóstol.
ap.^{a}, ap.^{o} or **aplica., aplico.** apostólica, apostólico.
apóst. apóstol.
art., art.^{o} artículo.
arz., arzbpo. arzobispo.
att.^{o}, atto. atento.
Aud.^{a} Audiencia.

B

B. Beato; Bueno, en examen.
Bar.^{mé} Bartolomé.
bca. barrica.
Barna. Barcelona.
Bern.^{o} Bernardo.
B. L. M., b. l. m. besa la mano.
B. L. P., b. l. p. besa los pies.
B.^{mo} P.^{e} Beatísimo Padre.
Br. or **br.** bachiller.
bto. bulto; bruto.

C

c/ cargo; contra.
C. A. corriente alterna.
c.^{a} compañía.
c., cap. capítulo.
cap.^{n} capitán.
capp.^{n} capellán.
Card.^{l} Cardenal.
C. C. corriente continua.
C. de J. Compañía de Jesús (S. J.).
cénts. céntimos.
cf., conf., confr. confesor; confirma (in ancient documents).
cg. céntigramo(s.
C.^{ia} Compañía (Co.).
cl. centilitro(s.
Clem.^{te} Clemente.
cllo. cuartillo.
cm. centímetro(s.
C. M. B., c. m. b. cuyas manos beso.
Co. Compañía (Co.).
col., col.^{a} columna; colonia.
comis.^{o} comisario.
comp. compañía.
cons.^{o} consejo.
Const. Constitución.
const.^{l} constitucional.
conv.^{te} conveniente.
corr.^{te} corriente.
C. P. B. cuyos pies beso.
crec.^{te} creciente.
cs. cuartos; céntimos.
cta., c.^{ta} cuenta.
cta. cte., cta. corr.^{te} cuenta corriente.
c/u cado uno.
cuad. cuadrado(s.
c/vta. cuenta de venta.

D

D. Don.
D.ª Doña.
DD. doctores.
descto. descuento.
d/f días fecha.
dg. decigramo(s.
Dg. decagramo(s.
dha., dho., dhas., dhos. dicha, dicho, dichas, dichos.
dic.^{e}, 10^{e} or **10bre** diciembre.
Dl. decalitro(s.
dl. decilitro(s.
dls. dólares ($).
Dm. decámetro(s.
dm. decímetro(s.
D.^{n}, d.^{n} don.
dna(s. docena(s.
Doct., Doctor.
docum.^{to} documento.
D. O. M. *Deo Optimo Maximo.*
Dom.^{o} Domingo (name).
dom.^{o} domingo (Sunday).
d/p días plazo.
D.^{r}, Dr. Doctor (Dr.).
dra., dro., dras., dros. derecha, derecho, derechas, derechos.
dup.^{do} duplicado.
d/v días vista.

E

E. este, oriente (East).
ec.^{co} eclesiástico.
EE. UU. Estados Unidos.
E. M. Estado Mayor.
Em.^{a} Eminencia.
E.| M. G. Estado Mayor General.
Em.^{mo}, Emmo. Eminentísimo.
ENE. estenordeste (E.N.E.).
en.^{o} enero.
E. P. D. En paz descanse.
E. P. M. En propia mano.
esc.^{o} escudo.
escrit.^{a} escritura.
escrnía. escribanía.
escrno. escribano.
escs. escudos.
ESE. estesudeste (E.S.E.).
etc. etcétera.
E. U., E. U. A. U. S., U. S. A.
Eug.^{o} Eugenio.
Evang.^{o} Evangelio.
Evang.^{ta} Evangelista.
Exc.^{a} Excelencia.
Exc.^{ma}, Exc.^{mo} or **Excma, Excmo.** Excelentísima, Excelentísimo.

F

f/ fardo(s.
F. Fulano.
fact.^{a} factura.
F. C., f. c. ferrocarril.
F.^{co}, Franc.^{o} Francisco.
fcos. francos.
F. de T. Fulano de Tal.
feb.^{o} febrero.
F. E. M. fuerza electromotriz (E.M.F.).
Fern.^{do} Fernando.
fha., fho. fecha, fecho.
fo.^{o}, fol. folio.

Fr. Fray, Frey.
fra. factura.
Frnz., Fz. Fernández.
F.^{s}, f.^{s} francos.
fund. fundador.

G

G. gracia.
g. gramo(s.
g.^{de} or **gue.** guarde.
Genl General (title).
gnte., gerente.
G.^{o} Gonzalo.
gob.^{o} gobierno.
gob.^{r} gobernador.
Gonz. González.
gral. general.
Greg.^{o} Gregorio.
gte. gerente.
Guill.^{o} Guillermo.

H

hect. hectárea(s.
Hg. hectogramo(s.
Hl. hectolitro(s.
Hm. hectómetro(s.
HP, H. P. caballo(s) de vapor (H.P.).

I

ib. *ibídem.*
id. *ídem.*
i. e. *id est* (that is).
igl.^{a} iglesia.
Ign.^{o} Ignacio.
Ildef.^{o} Ildefonso.
Il.^{e} Ilustre.
Il.^{ma}, Il.^{mo}, Illma, Illmo. Ilustrísima, Ilustrísimo.
in p. inf. *in partibus infidelium.*
inq.^{r} inquisidor.
intend.^{te} intendente.
ít. *ítem.*
izq.^{a}, izq.^{o}, izq.^{da}, izq.^{do} izquierda, izquierdo.

J

J. C. Jesurcristo.
Jerón.^{o} Jerónimo.
Jhs. Jesús.
Jph. José.
juev. jueves.
Jul.^{n} Julián.

K

Kg., kg. kilogramo(s.
Kl., kl. kilolitro(s.
Km., km. kilómetro(s.
kv., k. w. kilovatio.

L

L/ letra.
L., L.^{do} or **I.^{do}** Licenciado.
l. ley; libro; litro(s.
lb(s. libra(s.
lín. línea.
liq.^{n} liquidación.
Lor.^{zo} Lorenzo.
L. S. *Locus sigilli,* lugar del sello.
lun. lunes.

M

M. Madre, religiosa; Majestad; Merced; Maestro; mediano (en examen).
m. minuto(s; metro(s; mañana (A.M.).
m/ mes; mi, mis; mío, míos.
Man.^{l} Manuel.
M.ª María.
Marg.^{ta} Margarita.
mart. martes.
may.^{mo} mayordomo.
mcos. marcos.
Me Madre, religiosa.
m/f mi favor.
meng. menguante.
mg. miligramo(s.
miérc. miércoles.
Mig.^{l} Miguel.
miles.^{s} milesimas.
min.^{o} ministro.
m/L. mi letra.
ml. mililitros.
Mm. miriámetro(s.
mm., m/m milímetro(s.
m/o mi orden.
m/ o m/ más o menos.
monast.^{o} monasterio.
Mons. Monseñor.
M. P. S. Muy Poderoso Señor.
Mr. Monsieur; Mister.
mrd. merced.
Mrn. Martín.
Mrnz. Martínez.
Mro. Maestro.
M.^{s} marcos.
M. S. manuscrito.
m.^{s} a.^{s} muchos años.
M.SS. manuscritos.

N

N. Norte.
n. noche (P.M.).
n/ nuestro.
N.^{a} S.^{a} Nuestra Señora.
N.B. *Nota bene.*
n/cta. nuestra cuenta.
NE. Nordeste (N.E.).
NNE. Nornordeste (N.N.E.).
NNO. Nornoroeste (N.N.W.).
NO. Noroeste (N.W.).
n.^{o} número.
nov.^{e}, 9^{e}, 9bre noviembre.
Nov. Recop. Novísima Recopilación.
N. Recop. Nueva Recopilación.
nra., nro., nras., nros.; ntra., ntro., ntras., ntros. nuestra, nuestro, nuestras, nuestros.
núm. or **núm.^{o}, núms.** or **núm.^{s}** número, números.
N. S. Nuestro Señor.
N. S. J. C. Nuestro Señor Jesucristo.
nto. neto.

O

O. Oeste (W.).
o/ orden.
ob., obpo. obispo.
oct.^{e}, 8^{e} or **8bre** octubre.
ONO. oesnoroeste (W.N.W.).
onz. onza.
orn. orden.
OSO. oessudoeste (W.S.W.).

P

P. Papa (Pope); padre; pregunta.
p % por ciento (%).
p ‰ por mil.
p. A. Por ausencia: por autorización.
P.^{a} para.
pág., págs. página(s.
Part. Partida.
Patr. Patriarca.
p.^{bro} presb. presbítero.
P. D. Posdata (P.S.).
P.^{e} Padre.
p. ej. por ejemplo (e. g.).
penit. penitente.
perg., pno. pergamino.
Pf., Pfs. peso(s fuerte(s.
P. M. Padre Maestro.
P. O. Por orden.
P.^{o} Pedro.
p.^{o} pero.
P. P. Porte pagado; por poder.
p. p.^{do}, ppdo. próximo pasado.
p.^{r} por.

pral. principal.
priv. privilegio.
proc. procesión.
prof. profesor; profeta.
pror. procurador.
prov.^{a} provincia.
prov.^{or} provisor.
próx.^{o} próximo.
P. S. *Post scriptum* (P.S.).
P. S. M. Por su mandato.
ps. pesos.
pta. pasta.
ptas. pesetas.
p.^{te} parte.
pza. pieza.

Q

q. que.
Q. B. S. M., q. b. s. m. que besa su mano.
Q. B. W. P., q. b. s. p. que besa sus pies.
Q. D. G. que Dios guarde.
q.^{e} que.
q. e. g. e. que en gloria esté.
q. e. p. d. que en paz descanse.
q. e. s. m. que estrecha su mano.
q. g. g. que gloria goce.
qq. quintales.

R

R. Reverendo; reverencia; respuesta; reprobado (en examen).
R). Responde o respuesta (in prayer-books).
Raf.^{l} Rafael.
Rbí. Recibí.
R. D. Real Decreto.
Rda. M., R. M. Reverenda Madre.
Rdo. P., R. P. Reverendo Padre.
R.^{e} Récipe.
R. I. P. *Requiescat in pace.*
r.^{l} real (royal).
Rmrz. Ramírez.
R. O. Real Orden.
r. p. m. revoluciones por minuto (r. p. m.).
R. S. Real Servicio.
rs., r.^{s} reales (money).
R.^{s} Reales (of the king, royal).
rúst. rústica.

S

S. San, Santo; Sur; Sobresaliente (en examen).
s/ su, sus; sobre.
S.^{a} Señora.
S. A. Su Alteza.
sáb. sábado.
S. A. I. Su Alteza Imperial.
S. A. R. Su Alteza Real.
S. A. S. Su Alteza Serenísima.
Sb.^{n} Sebastián.
s/c su cuenta.
S. C., s. c. su casa.
S. C. M. Sacra Católica Majestad.
S. C. C. R. M. Sacra, Cesárea, Católica, Real Majestad.
s/cta. su cuenta.
S. D. Se despide (p. p. c.).
S. D. M. Su Divina Majestad.
SE. sudeste (S.E.).
secret.^{a} secretaría.
sept.^{e}, 7^{e} or **7bre** septiembre.
Ser.^{ma}, Ser.^{mo} or **Serm.^{a}, Sermo.** Serenísima, Serenísimo.
serv.^{o} servicio.
serv.^{or} servidor.
set.^{e} septiembre.
S. E. u O. salvo error u omisión.
sig.^{te} siguiente.
S. M. Su Majestad.
S. M. A. Su Majestad Apostólica.
S. M. B. Su Majestad Británica.
S. M. C. Su Majestad Católica.
S. M. F. Su Majestad Fidelísima.
S. M. I. Su Majestad Imperial.
Sn San.
S. N. Servicio Nacional.
SO. sudoeste (S.W.).
Sor. Señor.
Sores. Señores.
spre. siempre.
S.^{r}, Sr. Señor.
Sra., Sras. Señora, Señoras.
Sres., S.^{res} Señores.
Sría. Secretaría.
S.^{ria}, S. ^{rio} or **sria., srio.** secretaria, secretario.
S. R. M. Su Real Majestad.
S^{rta}., Srta. Señorita.
S. S. Su Santidad.
S. S.^{a} Su Señoría.
SS. AA. Sus Altezas.
SS.E. sudsudeste (S.S.E.).
SS. MM. Sus Majestades.
SS.^{mo} Santísimo.
SS.^{mo} P. Santísimo Padre.
SS.^{no} escribano.
SSO. sudsudoeste (S.S.W.).
S. S. S., s. s. s. Su seguro servidor.
Sta. Santa; Señorita.
Sto. Santo.
sup. suplica.
supert.^{te} superintendente.
supl.^{te} suplente.
sup.^{te} suplicante.

T

t. tarde.
ten.^{te} teniente.
test.^{mto} testamento.
test.^{o} testigo.
tít., tít.^{o} título.
tpo. tiempo.
trib.^{l} tribunal.
t.^{o}, tom. tomo.

U

U., Ud. usted.
Uds., UU. ustedes.

V

V. usted; venerable; véase.
V., Vers.^{o} Versículo.
V.^{a} Vigilia.
V. A. Vuestra Alteza.
V. A. R. Vuestra Alteza Real.
V. B.^{d} Vuestra Beatitud.
Vd. usted.
Vds. ustedes.
V. E. Vuestra Excelencia or Vuecencia.
vencim.^{to} vencimiento.
vg. verbigracia; virgen.
v. g., v. gr. verbigracia.
Vict.^{a} Victoria.
Vic.^{te} Vicente.
vier. viernes.
V. M. Vuestra Majestad.
Vm., Vmd. Vuestra Merced; Usted.
vn. vellón.
V.^{o} B.^{o} Visto bueno.
vol. volumen; voluntad.
vols. volúmenes.
V. P. Vuestra Paternidad.
V. R. Vuestra Reverencia.
vra., vro., vras., vros. vuestra, vuestro, vuestras, vuestros.
v.^{s}, vs. varas.
V. S. Vueseñoría, Usía.
V. S. I. Vueseñoría (*or* Usía) Ilustrísima.
v. ^{ta}, v.^{to} vuelta, vuelto.
V. V., VV. ustedes.